Contents

Contributors

Editor
Sir H A Lorenz

Contributors
Byron Arm-Grass
Hendrick de Lima
Kirk Dig-Trench

Data Management
Kathy Tiger-Carp

Prepress Controller
Eli Achilles Acorn

The editor would like to acknowledge the invaluable contribution made to earlier editions of this book by Sarah Czech-Winter and Zac Wherpster.

About the Contributors

Byron Arm-Grass, also known as Barry Grossman, is the author of *Scrabble for Beginners*, *Need to Know Scrabble* and the wordgame section of *Chambers Compact Thesaurus*. He has won numerous tournaments held under the auspices of the Association of British Scrabble Players, with a best placing of third in the British Matchplay Scrabble Championship, the Association's flagship event. He has also been series champion of Channel 4's *Countdown*.

Hendrick de Lima and Kirk Dig-Trench, also known as Michael Kindred and Derrick Knight, set crosswords under the pseudonyms Emkay and Mordred for various newspapers and periodicals, including *The Times* (*The Listener* crossword), *The Independent* and *The Sunday Telegraph* (Enigmatic Variations crossword).

Introduction

This new fourth edition of *Chambers Anagrams* has been hugely expanded, and now includes over 185,500 unique entries – more than any previous edition in its long history.

Entries, ranging from 4 to 15 letters, are arranged by length and then alphabetically according to the letters they contain. To find a solution to an anagram, you simply need to decide which letters make up the anagram, put these letters into alphabetical order – ignoring hyphens, accents, capital letters and so on – and then look up this combination of letters in the book. Solutions to the anagrams are listed clearly alongside the letter combinations:

ADDELPP	dappled
ADDELPR	paddler
ADDELRS	saddler
ADDELRW	dawdler waddler
ADDELRY	dreadly laddery
ADDELST	staddle
ADDELSW	swaddle
ADDELTW	twaddle
ADDELYZ	dazedly
ADDEMST	maddest
ADDENOR	road end

For example, if the anagram you wish to solve is ICE ON SALT, arrange these letters into alphabetical order to give ACEILNOST, then look for this combination in the nine-letter section, where you will find the potential answers: COASTLINE and SECTIONAL. Or, if you wish to solve the anagram CAN'T EASE ALL, rearrange the letters to AAACEELLNST, and in the eleven-letter section you'll find the answer: A CLEAN SLATE. If you are looking for a crossword solution and more than one potential anagram is given for a letter combination, the correct answer should be clear from the wording of the clue and any letters already filled in on the crossword grid.

For quick and easy reference there is a clear indication at the head of each page of the length of entries on that page, and the first three letters of the first and last letter combinations on the page are given.

This new edition of *Chambers Anagrams* is based on *Chambers Words for Crosswords and Wordgames*, and thus includes all the bold words from *The Chambers Dictionary* (2003). It includes not only single words and abbreviations, but also phrases and many proper nouns. The only omissions are offensive terms, entries including numbers, entries including slashes or ellipses, symbols, some abbreviations and some duplicate phrases (such as 'abstinence from' where 'abstinence' is already present). These few deletions, made for reasons of space, have been carefully chosen to ensure that only terms unlikely ever to occur as a crossword clue solution have been removed. As *The Chambers Dictionary* does not include *-ise* and *-isation* variants of *-ize* and *-ization* in compounds and phrases, they are not included here; nor are inflections included where they are not shown in the dictionary (for example, 'digest' is included, but not 'digests', 'digesting' or 'digested'). Alongside the wealth of vocabulary from *The Chambers Dictionary* you will also find a treasure trove of encyclopedic material, primarily names of people and places, from *Chambers Crossword Dictionary*.

Unlike some other anagram books, *Chambers Anagrams* contains only unique anagrams. It recognizes that the letters of words like ACCEPT, HILLY and MOST are already in alphabetical order, and therefore does not offer these as 'solutions' to 'anagrams', as the letter combination and solution would be identical.

To retain information which may help with crossword clues, the words are listed as they appear in the dictionary (not in capitals as in some other anagram books); words genuinely beginning with a capital can therefore be recognized. Where *The Chambers Dictionary* indicates that a word can be spelled with or without an initial capital letter, often with different meanings, this is shown by the symbol ✧. In this new edition, the use of this symbol has been extended to denote words which may be spelled with one or more capital letters; hence, aloe vera/Aloe Vera is now included only as aloe vera✧.

Accents have been retained to distinguish between separate word meanings (eg pate and pâté) or to reflect the foreign origin of the word. Hyphenated and unhyphenated forms have been shown, again reflecting different meanings or usages. Registered trade names have also been noted. All these devices will help the solver to track down words and meanings. Hyphens, apostrophes, spaces and the like do not, of course, count in the total number of letters.

Puzzle and wordgame enthusiasts who have access to the Internet will find the Anagram Finder feature of the Word Wizards on the Chambers website, www.chambers.co.uk, to be invaluable. This solver draws upon a vast database of many hundred thousand words, including inflections, and is a free resource that offers potential solutions to anagrams in seconds.

About Anagrams

by Barry Grossman

Nobody knows quite how old anagrams are. One of the oldest known anagrams dates from the time of Christ, and consists of the Latin QUID EST VERITAS? ('What is truth?'), which has the answer EST VIR QUI ADEST ('It is this man here'), so we know they've been around for 2,000 years at least. But given the instinctive way many of us play around with words, there is every reason to believe they are as old as written language itself. Even OLD TESTAMENT is an anagram of MOST TALENTED.

The anagram in English took time to get off the ground. It needed mass literacy and regularized spelling, both of which have really only settled in during the last couple of hundred years. Prior to that, those few people who could write would spell words according to local custom or personal whim, so an anagram might not work in the next county or even the next room.

It was the arrival of the cryptic crossword that gave the anagram a new lease of life. Once compilers started coming up with fiendish efforts like (to take a couple of examples from a recent *The Times* crossword):

> Butcher has ox tongue (5)

and

> Sheep eats any wild plant (9,3)

the anagram was no longer the preserve of a few literary dilettantes, it was the plaything of anyone with access to a newspaper. And they're 'Xhosa' and 'pheasant's eye', in case you're still wondering.

Anagrams lend themselves well to secret codes. A simple invitation to MEET ME IN THE ROSE CAFÉ AT SEVEN takes on a frisson of mystery when it's written as TEEM ME IN THE SORE FACE AT EVENS. Many writers down the ages have been fond of introducing secret anagrams into their work. A recent court case claiming *The Da Vinci Code* by Dan Brown had plagiarized from an earlier book, *The Holy Blood and the Holy Grail*, two of whose authors were surnamed Baigent and Leigh, turned partly on the fact that a character in Brown's book is called LEIGH TEABING.

From the secret code it's a small step to the hoax. Literary types were amused recently when the writer A N Wilson included in his biography of Sir John Betjeman a love letter supposedly written by the poet. The only two things Wilson missed were that the name of the woman who showed it to him, EVE DE HARBEN, was an anagram of EVER BEEN HAD, and the initial letters of each sentence in the letter spelt out a rather uncomplimentary message about Wilson himself.

About Anagrams

Even a serious writer like Vladimir Nabokov had fun with anagrams, occasionally using the pseudonym VIVIAN DARKBLOOM. And Richard Stilgoe wrote *The Richard Stilgoe Letters*, a book of short stories, each featuring a different character who was an anagram of the author's name, such as Indian corner-shop owner GROCER TALDISHI and big-game hunter COL. TIGER RASHID.

Nowadays the main fun people have with anagrams is working out versions of names, usually amusing or uncomplimentary. You might know

MARGARET THATCHER	THAT GREAT CHARMER
TONY BLAIR, PM	I'M TORY PLAN B

The intervening prime minister, John Major, has been saved from anagrammatic ridicule by those two difficult Js. But perhaps he suffered enough.

This game is nothing new. Lewis Carroll is credited with getting from WILLIAM EWART GLADSTONE to WILD AGITATOR, MEANS WELL, and that would have been without the help of Scrabble® tiles. Let's see what we can make of other prime ministers:

WILLIAM PITT THE YOUNGER	I'M THA' LITTLE GUY IN POWER
DAVID LLOYD GEORGE	O, RAGGEDY OLD DEVIL
RAMSAY MACDONALD	A SCARY OLD MADMAN
HAROLD MACMILLAN	AND LO, I'M ALL CHARM

And on the day Asquith resigned, I wonder if any newspaper came up with the elegant anagram headline:

ASQUITH HAS QUIT

It's often easier to compile a long anagram than a short one. You can't make much out of HOUSE OF COMMONS, but by giving yourself a few more letters to play with, you can turn THE HOUSES OF PARLIAMENT into LOONIES FAR UP THE THAMES. Here are a couple of Shakespeare's most famous passages, rearranged. Can you spot the original versions?

'In one of the Bard's best-thought-of tragedies, Hamlet, our insistent hero, queries on two fronts about how life turns rotten.'

'I'm a famous speech – Marc Antony on murder in Rome senate – terribly indecorous story.'

The longest pair of single-word anagrams is a tricky one to pin down. Most of the very long ones are either almost the same word, such as

CONSERVATIONIST and CONVERSATIONIST, or words consisting of the same elements in a different order, like ELECTROMAGNETIC and MAGNETO-ELECTRIC, or MICROPHOTOGRAPHY and PHOTOMICROGRAPHY.

Perhaps the longest satisfying anagrams are these thirteen-letter heavyweights:

ANTICLINORIUM	INCLINATORIUM
INTERSPECIFIC	PRESCIENTIFIC
STARTING-POINT	TRAINSPOTTING

The last one requires us to grant ourselves the luxury of counting STARTING-POINT as one word, but when you're looking for anagrams of these elephantine proportions you can't afford to be too picky.

It's a long way from *quid est veritas* via Gladstone to trainspotting, but this just demonstrates the anagram's ability to reach into all areas of life. So the next time you're wrestling with a crossword, playing Scrabble® or just making up an insulting anagram of your boss's name, remember you are part of a long and noble tradition which has occupied and intrigued us since time immemorial.

Barry Grossman
London, 2006

Shakespeare Answers:

To be, or not to be, that is the question:–
Whether 'tis nobler in the mind to suffer
The slings and arrows of outrageous fortune,
Hamlet, III.1.58-60

Friends, Romans, countrymen, lend me your ears;
I come to bury Caesar, not to praise him.
Julius Caesar, III.2.74-75

Anagrams and Crosswords

by Michael Kindred and Derrick Knight

Perhaps the most popular type of clue in cryptic crosswords is the anagram. For the solver it offers an early chance to enter something in the grid; for the setter, a straightforward way of clueing a difficult or obscure word.

In its simplest form an anagram clue will normally be made up of

i) a definition,

ii) the word or words from which the anagram is to be formed, and

iii) an anagram indicator, placed so as to refer directly to the anagram word or words.

The anagram indicator will be a word which indicates rearrangement in some way; for more on anagram indicators, see below.

There shouldn't be too many anagram clues in a cryptic crossword. A typical puzzle in a daily paper will contain no more than three or four, leaving the setter the opportunity to use the many other clue types and devices.

Recognizing Anagram Clues

If you have something that looks like an anagram indicator and the number of letters in the word or words adjacent is the same as the figure in brackets, then it's a safe bet that these letters will need rearranging to form the answer. Editors differ in what they regard as acceptable anagram indicators. Examples of the use of three common ones – *dispersed*, *broken* and *upset* – are shown in the following clues, although in a real crossword, of course, the anagram indicator would not be given in italics:

Executive meeting, perhaps it can be *dispersed* (7)

This clue leads to the answer CABINET, an 'executive meeting'. Here *dispersed* is a fairly safe bet for an anagram indicator, and the adjacent words IT CAN BE comprise seven letters. (The word 'perhaps' has been included to suggest that this definition is an example of a cabinet, but it can also be used as an anagram indicator in other clues).

Snatch *broken* slate (5)

In this clue, the solution can't be an anagram of 'snatch' as the answer comprises five letters. It must therefore be the letters of SLATE which must be rearranged to find the answer, STEAL.

Guarantee pains *upset* elderly person (14)

Here *upset* is a good candidate for an anagram indicator, and 'elderly person' has only 13 letters, so it must be an anagram of the two preceding words, GUARANTEE PAINS, which leads to the answer SEPTUAGENARIAN.

Solving Anagram Clues

When you have located the word or words you suspect comprise the anagram, you may use one or more of the following methods to help find the solution:

i) write the letters out in a jumble in one or more ways

ii) separate the vowels from the consonants

iii) write the letters out in one or more grid formations

iv) put the letters in alphabetical order

Using the first three methods means that the eye stops seeing the words already there, and sees the letters in a random order, meaning that you may be more likely to spot the answer you're looking for.

The fourth method enables you to use *Chambers Anagrams*. It is also worth looking for common word endings in the letters that you think form the anagram, such as *-ed*, *-ing*, *-tion* and *-able*. If you have located what you think is the definition, see if it indicates what the word's ending may be like; for example, if it is a verb, is it in the past tense suggesting an *-ed* ending, or is it a present participle suggesting an *-ing* ending? You can then eliminate these letters, and concentrate on those remaining to find the rest of the answer.

More About Anagram Indicators

In the examples below the anagram indicator is in italics.

Tags *crazy* animal (4)

In this clue for STAG, the anagram indicator could also be *mad* – or *wild* would be even better.

Setters will try to disguise anagram indicators. Examples of crafty little indicators are *up*, *on*, *out*, *lit* and *high*. *Up* is used in the sense of rioting; *on* as in 'playing'; *out* in the sense of 'out of order', *lit* meaning 'drunk' and 'high' having various meanings such as 'excited'. Examples of these are:

Race *up* tree (4)

They may be up for manly carve *up* (10)

The answers are ACER and CAVALRYMEN. In the second clue, 'up' is used both to indicate men on horseback and again as an anagram indicator.

Slept *on* raw animal hides (5)

Notes *on* accents (5)

Cried *out* for a drink (5)

High trees planted again (5)

Lit gallery in a royal manner (7)

A flare *lit* artillery fire (6)

The answers are PELTS, TONES, CIDER, RESET, REGALLY and RAFALE. In each case you should be able to see how the solution has been arrived at. The last of the examples demonstrates how an anagram clue can help the solver with an uncommon word; if an anagram indicator is recognized, the letters can be arranged in alphabetical order and *Chambers Anagrams* will provide the answer, which can then be checked in a dictionary ('rafale' is defined in *The Chambers Dictionary* as 'a burst of artillery in quick rounds').

Even *about* or *around* can be used as indicators, as in the following clues:

Items strewn *about* part of London (11)

Platonic sonnet *about* old Istanbul (14)

Walking *around*, lament a Rio pub (13)

The answers here are WESTMINSTER, CONSTANTINOPLE and PERAMBULATION. In the last clue the comma is misleading, but the rather incongruous idea of 'a Rio pub' gives the game away sufficiently.

Question *Doctor* Who (3)

In this clue for HOW, *doctored* would be fairer than the imperative *doctor*, but the clue would have to be rewritten to read properly.

A list of common anagram indicators can be found on p.xxi.

Famous Anagrams

Most daily newspapers are satisfied with anagrams no longer than sufficient for one entry in a 15×15 grid. The exception is *The Guardian*, whose setters, notably Araucaria, Paul and the sadly-missed Bunthorne, enjoy the occasional very long anagram, whose answers are entered at various places in the grid. Devising such anagrams is satisfying for the crossword setter and solving them is breathtaking for the solver, as in these examples:

> Poetical scene has surprisingly chaste Lord Archer vegetating (3,3,8,12)

This famous clue by Araucaria shows his excellent creativity in setting such long anagrams. The 'poetical scene' referred to is THE OLD VICARAGE, GRANTCHESTER, with *surprisingly* as the anagram indicator and the letters of CHASTE LORD ARCHER VEGETATING forming the anagram. The Old Vicarage was formerly the home of the poet Rupert Brooke, and at the time the clue appeared Lord Archer had been involved in a sex scandal, was the current owner of the Vicarage and had taken refuge there.

Araucaria is also known for an anagram in one of his Christmas crosswords, in which a clue included O HARK THE HERALD ANGELS SING THE BOY'S DESCENT WHICH LIFTED UP THE WORLD, which is an anagram of WHILE SHEPHERDS WATCHED THEIR FLOCKS BY NIGHT, ALL SEATED ON THE GROUND.

Bunthorne excelled himself with the following huge anagram, typical of his output:

> i.e. what oil-sheik said cheekily unto girl in gin-palace? (4,2,1,4,4,4,3,5,2,1,5,4,4,2)

The answers is WHAT IS A NICE GIRL LIKE YOU DOING IN A PLACE LIKE THIS, EH?.

And finally, don't treat all this information and the accompanying examples so seriously that this wonderful leisure pursuit becomes like taking an exam! We firmly believe that, above all, solving crosswords should be fun.

Michael Kindred and Derrick Knight
Sigoulès, France, and Newark, England, 2006

Anagrams and Scrabble®

by Barry Grossman

Anagrams are one of the most popular of all forms of word-play. When we first discover old chestnuts such as SCHOOLMASTER being an anagram of THE CLASSROOM, it is hard not to believe there is some sort of god of words ordaining these things from on high. Why else would ALTERATION be an anagram of NEAT TAILOR, or FIR CONE be able to be rearranged into CONIFER?

Keen Scrabble® players will all be familiar with anagrams. No feeling is more frustrating than finding a wonderful word, especially a seven- or eight-letter word that could earn you a fifty-point bonus, and then not being able to place it on the board. But sometimes by turning the word into an anagram, you can play it and grab yourself a fistful of points in the process.

Some very enthusiastic Scrabble® players, the type who play in Scrabble® clubs and spend their weekends travelling to far-flung tournaments, have learned long lists of anagrams, in order to maximize their chances of playing a bonus word when they get the chance. They will know, for instance, that the letters of the word RETAINS form no fewer than eleven anagrams:

RETAINS

RETINAS

NASTIER

STAINER (something which stains)

STEARIN (a constituent of fatty tissue)

RETSINA (a Greek wine)

RESIANT (an old word for resident)

RATINES (types of rough fabric)

STARNIE (a small star)

ANESTRI (times when a female animal is not in heat)

ANTSIER (more worried or agitated)

You would be very unlucky indeed not to be able to fit one of those in if you got the right seven letters on your rack.

Sometimes a knowledge of anagrams will help you to increase your score by taking advantage of the premium squares. Let's say there is an E in the top row, and your rack reads C I P R S T U. If the rest of the row is usable, you could make PICTURES, which, including the triple word score and fifty-point bonus, might get you a tidy 86. But what if the E were in just such a position that, if you made it the third letter of your word, you would stretch to *two* triple word squares? The expert player would not have to think twice, but would immediately associate PICTURES with the rather pleasing PIECRUST (hyphen not obligatory) or the more obscure CREPITUS, which is the nasty grating noise you sometimes hear when an arthritic joint or fractured bone is moved. So play either of those and congratulations – you have just scored a massive 167 points at least.

Rather than going all out for points, you might want to be a bit cannier and prevent your opponent from scoring highly, which can be just as important in the context of playing to win. You wouldn't be happy if your favourite football team scored four goals against their arch-rivals, if those rivals scored five. So what might you do if you wanted to play LAZE, but it put the Z in a position where your opponent could score highly off it – perhaps hitting a triple word square with ZIP, ZED or, if he or she is familiar with tools for trimming slates, ZAX or ZEX?

A simple anagram turns LAZE into ZEAL, which, if it fits in, might not give away such a high-scoring opportunity. You might think it doesn't matter much as you can use the space as well as your opponent, but always remember one thing when you play your shot – it's your opponent to play next, and if you put down a copper-bottomed opportunity for a high score, the sneaky blighter is far more likely to take it than he or she is to do the decent thing and leave it for you.

How can you tell whether the word you have spotted on your rack might have an anagram? Well, the more common the letters in the word are, the more likely it is to be re-arrangeable (is that a word? it is now) into something else. If it contains mainly one-point tiles (L N R S T and the vowels), it is more likely to anagrammatize than if it has lots of high-value, uncommon letters. So a word like REALIST can also form SALTIER, SLATIER, SALTIRE and RETAILS; but EQUINOX, unsurprisingly, does not have an anagram.

All regular Scrabble® players have their favourite anagrams, especially in those useful seven- and eight-letter words. I particularly like the ones that are spelt almost the same as each other, although sometimes with completely different meanings. Some examples:

SEAHORSE	SEASHORE
MISFIELD	MISFILED
NUTHATCH	UNTHATCH
XANTHEIN	XANTHINE
REINFORM	RENIFORM
STRONGLY	STRONGYL

SUNTRAP	UNSTRAP
INFIDEL	INFIELD

In the USA, where incorrect challenges result in the challenger losing a turn, some of the more hardboiled players will deliberately play a word like RENIFORM or STRONGYL against a less experienced opponent, hoping to make the opponent think they have accidentally played the letters in the wrong order and to incite a challenge. Elsewhere, though, they are a little more sympathetic to the newcomer, and challenges are never penalized.

Sometimes you can remember an obscure word because it is an anagram of a well-known word, as in PICTURES–PIECRUST–CREPITUS. Finding the well-known word can trigger your memory into recalling the lesser-known anagram. For instance:

finding BAPTISM reminds you about BITMAPS

finding CURTAIN reminds you about TURACIN

finding ICKIEST reminds you about EKISTIC

finding TOILETS reminds you about LITOTES

finding TOURISTY reminds you about YTTRIOUS

It would be much harder to remember BITMAPS, TURACIN, EKISTIC, LITOTES and YTTRIOUS if they did not have their more familiar anagrams to guide us towards them. There are dozens more like these. TOILETS–LITOTES, incidentally, is also an anagram of T S ELIOT, which indeed is very nearly TOILETS backwards. We can only guess what the Nobel Prize-winning poet would think of the fact that many more people know he is an anagram of toilets than could quote a line of his poetry.

Another way of using anagrams to help remember words is to notice that some words are anagrams of brand names. You might find your rack can be formed into one of these: FORMICA, NESCAFE, RENAULT, SILK CUT or TOSHIBA. None of these is allowed, as even those which are in the dictionary are trade names and spelt with an initial capital letter. Once recognized, however, they might lead you to the game-winning bonus you are looking for:

ACIFORM

ENFACES

NEUTRAL

LUSTICK

ISOBATH

Anagrams can sometimes be memorable because, quite by coincidence, their meanings are connected. A few examples:

CHOIRMAN	HARMONIC
AVARICE	CAVIARE
COUPLES	UPCLOSE
PARENTAL	PATERNAL, PRENATAL

There are some you may or may not choose to include in this category, such as BEDROOM–BOREDOM (these letters also make BROOMED). There is also DENTURES–UNDERSET, although UNDERSET does not actually refer to teeth, false or otherwise, but the mental connection, once made, is easy to recall. Then, using your 'familiar word to remember unfamiliar anagram' technique, you can remember this combination also makes UNDESERT, UNRESTED and SEDERUNT, and play whichever one is best in the circumstances.

Another favourite of mine is BORDELLO–DOORBELL. While the meanings are not exactly connected, the image in the mind's eye of a furtive finger reaching out to press a doorbell in a seedy backstreet should be strong enough to remind you of the anagram quite easily.

There is an opposite to this, where two anagrams have completely incongruous meanings. Who would have guessed that DRUIDISM (the ceremonies of the ancient Celtic peoples) would lead to SIDDURIM (Jewish prayer books)?

Two or more anagram words can almost tell a whole story on their own. RECKLESS CLERKESS is surely a 1940s film noir starring Joan Fontaine as the timid office worker lured by love into a life of crime, with tragic consequences. ALARMING MARGINAL is about an election candidate defending a 500 majority when his party has just closed the local hospital.

Barry Grossman
London, 2006

Anagrams and Wordgames

by Barry Grossman

There can be few people who have not at some time tried to enliven the train journey home or an evening when the television was even worse than usual with a wordgame. Many would go further, and count their daily fix of the crossword, or finding as many words as they can from a long word or a jumble of letters, as published in more or less every newspaper in the land, as a highlight of their day.

Anagrams can play a big part in games like this. If you are trying to find words from RATIONED, and you come up with DRAIN, don't just leave it there – you've got DINAR and NADIR as well.

You can use the same technique with games like Boggle® and Scrabble®. Once you've traced out HATRED on the Boggle® dice, you might be able to score for THREAD and DEARTH too. And if SLOPPY doesn't fit on the Scrabble® board, turn it into POLYPS and see if that's any better.

Many people seem to have spent an unhealthy amount of time coming up with appropriate anagrams of words and phrases. Here are some of the best ones:

ASTRONOMER	MOON STARER
CIRCUMSTANTIAL EVIDENCE	CAN RUIN A SELECTED VICTIM
CONTAMINATED	NO ADMITTANCE
CONVERSATION	VOICES RANT ON
ELEVEN PLUS TWO	TWELVE PLUS ONE
INTOXICATE	EXCITATION
MOTHER-IN-LAW	WOMAN HITLER
THE CLASSROOM	SCHOOLMASTER
THE MORSE CODE	HERE COME DOTS

Then there is the 'antigram', where the anagram is entirely inappropriate to the original, such as:

WITHIN EARSHOT	I WON'T HEAR THIS
MISFORTUNE	IT'S MORE FUN
DIPLOMACY	MAD POLICY
MARRIAGE	GRIM AREA

INFECTION	FINE TONIC
FUNERAL	REAL FUN
UNITED	UNTIED
FILLED	ILL-FED

It can get quite compulsive. Think of a phrase, not too long or too short, and without too many difficult letters, that you might be able to make an appropriate (or inappropriate) anagram of. Let's try DEPARTMENT STORE. You might see a smaller word in there that could be the start of your anagram: how about MORE? Or, maybe better, MONSTER. That would leave us with DEPARTET to play with. Take TRADE out of that. MONSTER PET TRADE. Not great, a department store sells more than pets.

Maybe a simple AND would slot into the middle of a three-word phrase, leaving PERTMET STORE. You could get TEMPTERS out of that, which is exactly what department stores are. Now we might be getting somewhere. We still have AND TORE. Mix them up, and you could get O, ARDENT TEMPTERS! Not quite the stroke of genius of noticing ELEVEN PLUS TWO makes TWELVE PLUS ONE, but not bad. The secret is to be flexible, and be ready to discard ideas (like using MONSTER or AND) if you end up down a blind alley or a better idea occurs to you. And remember you can usually lose an unwanted O by sticking it at the beginning. O yes you can!

Barry Grossman
London, 2006

Palindromes

A palindrome is a word, verse or sentence that reads the same backward and forward.

aba
abba
Ada
Aga
Aga saga
aha
aia
ala
alula
ana
anana
Anna
Anona
ava
awa
Beeb
bib
bob
boob
bub
civic
dad
deed
deified
did
dod
dud
ecce
eke
Elle
eme
ene
ere
esse
eve
ewe
eye
gag
gig
Gog
hah
Hannah
heh
hoh
huh
iwi
kaiak
Kanak
kayak
Kazak
keek
kook
lemel
level
ma'am
madam
Malayalam
mallam
mam
marram
mem
mim
minim
mom
mum
naan
nan
Nauruan
nip in
non
noon
not on
nun
obo
oho
oppo
otto
pap
peep
pep
pip
poop
pop
puff up
pull-up
pup
put-up
radar
redder
refer
reifier
repaper
reviver
rotator
Rotavator®
rotor
sedes
seles
senes
sis
solos
succus
sus
tallat
tat
Tebet
tenet
terret
Tet
Tevet
tirrit
tit
toot
tot
tut
tut-tut
utu
vav
waw
wow
wow-wow
yay
ziz
zuz

Crossword Anagram Indicators

The following list includes words regularly used to indicate an anagram in cryptic crossword clues. It is drawn from *Chambers Crossword Dictionary* and the Chambers crossword clue database. No such list could be comprehensive, however, as almost any word or phrase suggesting disturbance or an abnormal state may be used as an anagram indicator in a cryptic clue. The list shows base forms of common anagram indicators; full inflected forms are not shown. Verbs in the list may appear in clues in any of their inflected forms, and adjectives may be found in their adverbial forms. For example, the list includes *annoy* and *awkward*, but omits *annoys* and *awkwardly*.

Anagram indicators include:

abandon
aberrant
abnormal
abominable
about
abroad
absurd
abuse
abysmal
accident
acrobatics
acting
action
activate
active
activity
adapt
adaptable
adaptation
adjust
adjustment
administer
adrift
affect
afflict
afresh
aggrieve
agile
agitate
ague
alarm
allocate
allocation
alloy
all-round
alter
alteration
alternative
amazing
amend
amendment
amiss
amok
analyse
analysis
anarchic
anew
angry
animated
annoy
anomalous
anomaly
another
anxious
anyhow
anyway
apart
appal
appliance
apply
appoint
appraisal
arch
around
arousal
arouse
arrange
arrangement
array
artefact
artful
articulate
artifact
askew
assassinate
assassination
assemble
assort
astonish
astray
at fault
at loggerheads
at random
at sea
atrocious
away
awful
awkward
awry
bad
baffle
bake
bamboozle
bananas
bandy
barbaric
barbarous
barge
barking
baroque

Crossword Anagram Indicators

bastard
bat
bats
batter
batty
beat
become
bedevil
bedlam
befuddle
belabour
belt
bemuse
bend
bendy
bent
berserk
bespoke
bewilder
bias
bizarre
blast
blaze
blend
blessed
blight
blotchy
blow up
blue
blunder
blur
body
bogus
boil
boisterous
bomb
boozy
boss
botch
bother
bottle
bounce
brain
break
break up
breeze
brew
brittle
broach
broadcast
broke
broken
broth
bruise
bubbly
buck
buckle
buffet
build
building
bully
bum
bumble
bundle
bungle
burst
bust
bustle
busy
butcher
Byzantine
calamitous
camouflage
cappricioso
capricious
career
careless
carve
cast
cavort
change
changeable
chaotic
chew
chip
chop
choppy
churn
circulate
clobber
clumsy
cock up
cocktail
code
collapse
collect
collection
combustible
compilation
compile
complex
complicate
complication
component
compose
composition
compound
compromise
concern
concoct
concoction
condemn
condemnation
condition
confection
confound
confuse
confusion
constituent
construct
construe
contaminate
contamination
contort
contrive
conversion
convert
convertible
convolute
convulse
cook
correct
correction
corrupt
could be
crack
crack up
crackers
crackpot
craft
crafty
cranky
crash
crazed
crazy
creation
criminal
cripple
crocked
crook
crooked
cross
crude
cruel
crumble
crush
cuckoo
cultivate
cure
curious

cut
daft
damage
dance
dash
daze
deal
debris
decompose
defective
deficient
defile
deform
defuse
delirious
demented
demolish
deplorable
deploy
derange
desecrate
design
desperate
destabilize
destroy
destruction
destructive
desultory
deterioration
detour
devastate
develop
development
deviant
deviate
deviation
devilish
devious
diabolical
dicky
different
difficult
digest
dilapidate
dire
direct
disarrange
disarray
disaster
disastrous
disband
discomfit
discompose
disconcert
discord
discordant
discover
disease
disfigure
disgruntle
disguise
dish
dish out
dishevel
disintegrate
disintegration
disjoint
dislocate
dislocation
dismantle
disorder
disorganization
disorganize
disorientate
disorientation
dispel
disperse
dispersion
display
disport
dispose
disposition
disrupt
disruption
dissipate
dissolute
dissonant
distillation
distort
distract
distraught
distress
distribute
distribution
disturb
disturbance
dither
diverse
diversion
divert
dizzy
do
doctor
dodder
doddery
dodgy
done
dotty
doubtful
drastic
drawn
dreadful
dress
drift
drunk
drunken
dubious
duff
dynamic
easy
eccentric
edit
effervescent
elaborate
elastic
elevate
embarrass
embroil
emend
emendation
emerge
emotional
employ
engineer
enigmatic
enliven
entangle
entanglement
entwine
err
errant
erratic
erring
erroneous
error
erupt
eruption
evolution
evolve
exceptional
exchange
excite
excruciate
exercise
exotic
explode
explosive
extract
extraordinary
extravagant

fabricate
fake
fall
false
falsify
faltering
fan
fanciful
fancy
fantastic
fashion
fault
fearful
ferment
fettle
feverish
fickle
find in
finesse
finicky
fishy
fit
fix
flabbergasted
flail
flake
flaky
flap
flash
flaw
flexible
flighty
flit
float
flog
flop
floppy
flounder
flourish
flow
fluctuate
fluff
fluid
flurry
fluster
flutter
fly
fog
foolish
force
foreign
forge
forlorn
form
foul
found in
founder
fracture
frantic
freak
freak out
free
frenetic
frenzy
fresh
freshen
frightful
frilly
frisky
frolic
frolicsome
from
frothing
fuddle
fudge
full
fumble
funny
furious
fussy
fuzzy
gaffe
gambol
garble
gauche
generate
giddy
ginger
gnarled
go around
go crazy
go off
gone
grim
groggy
groom
gross
grotesque
ground
hairy
ham
hammer
hamper
haphazard
happy
harass
harm
hash
hatch
havoc
haywire
hazy
head over heels
heat
hectic
hellish
helter-skelter
hideous
higgledy-piggledy
high
hit
hopeless
horrible
horrid
horrific
hotchpotch
hurl
hurt
hybrid
idiotic
ill
ill at ease
ill-assorted
ill-bred
ill-composed
ill-treat
imbecile
impair
imperfect
implicate
improper
improvise
in chaos
in circulation
in excess
in motion
in pieces
in revolt
in trouble
inaccurate
incapable
incorrect
indecent
indiscriminate
inebriated
inept
ingredient
injure
injury
inky

inordinate
insane
insanity
insecure
intoxicate
intricate
invalid
invention
involve
irregular
irritate
itinerant
jagged
jangle
jar
jaunty
jazz
jerk
jerky
jig
jiggle
jitters
jittery
jockey
jog
jolt
jostle
judder
juggle
jumble
jump
junk
kick
kind of
kink
kinky
knead
knock
knock out
knock over
knot
knotty
labour
labyrinthine
lace
lamentable
lark
launder
lawless
lax
layout
lazily
leap
liberal
light
lit
lively
loaded
loony
loose
lost
lousy
ludicrous
lunatic
macabre
mad
madden
made-up
madness
make
make up
maladjust
malform
malfunction
malleable
maltreat
manage
mangle
manic
manifest
manifestation
manipulate
manipulation
manoeuvre
manufacture
mar
marshal
mash
masquerade
massage
maul
maybe
mayhem
maze
meandering
meddle
medley
mélange
mêlée
melt
mend
mental
merry
mess
messy
metamorphose
metamorphosis
mill
mince
mingle
mint
misbehave
misbehaviour
mischievous
misconduct
misconstrue
misdeliver
misdirect
miserable
misfit
misguided
mishandle
mishap
misinterpret
mislead
mismanage
mismanagement
misplace
misprint
misread
misrepresent
misrepresentation
misshape
misspell
mistake
mistreat
misuse
mix
mixture
mobile
mobilize
model
moderate
modification
modify
mongrel
mortal
mould
mouldy
move
movement
muddle
muddy
muff
mushy
muss
must
musty
mutate
mutation

mutilate
mutilation
mutinous
mysterious
nasty
naughty
neaten
neglect
negligence
negligent
negotiate
negotiation
nervous
new
nobble
nonconformist
nonsensical
not
novel
nuts
obfuscate
oblique
obscure
obstreperous
odd
oddball
off
off-colour
on
on the rampage
operate
order
organization
organize
original
ornate
other
otherwise
out
out of hand
out of order
out of place
out of sorts
outbreak
outlandish
output
outrageous
outré
outside
overhaul
overthrow
overturn
painful
panic
paranormal
pastiche
patchy
pathetic
peculiar
peddle
pell-mell
perform
perhaps
perplex
perturb
perverse
perversion
perversity
pervert
phoney
pickle
pie
piece
plan
plaster
plastic
play
play around
plough
ply
police
pollute
pollution
poor
pop
possible
potential
potty
prance
precarious
preparation
prepare
preposterous
problem
problematic
process
produce
production
promiscuous
protean
provide
pulverize
pummel
punish
put out
puzzle
quaint
quake
queer
questionable
quirky
quiver
raddled
rag
rage
ramble
rampage
rampant
ramshackle
random
rare
rash
rattle
ravage
rave
react
reactionary
realign
rearrange
reassemble
rebel
rebellious
rebuild
recast
recipe
reckless
recollect
recollection
recondition
reconfigure
reconstitute
reconstruct
recover
recreate
recycle
red
redeploy
redevelop
redevelopment
rediscover
redistribute
redistribution
redraft
re-edit
reel
refashion
refine
refit
reform
reformat

reformation
refurbish
refurbishment
refuse
regenerate
regulate
rehash
rejig
rejoin
relax
relay
remake
remarkable
remedy
remodel
render
rendition
renegade
renegotiate
renew
renovate
rent
reorder
reorganize
repackage
repair
replace
reposition
represent
representation
reprocess
reproduce
resettle
reshape
reshod
reshuffle
resolution
resolve
resort
restless
restoration
restore
retold
re-use
revamp
reveal
revel
review
revise
revolt
revolution
revolutionary
rework
rewrite
rickety
ridiculous
rifle
rig
rile
riot
riotous
rip
ripple
rock
rocky
rogue
roll
rollicking
rot
rotten
rough
roughen
round
rouse
rove
rub
rubbish
rude
ruffle
ruin
rum
run
run riot
run wild
runny
rupture
rustic
rustle
sabotage
sack
sad
salad
savaged
scatter
scatty
scheme
scour
scrabble
scraggy
scramble
scrappy
scratch
screw
screwy
scruffy
scuffle
sculpt
sculpture
scuttle
seedy
seethe
serve
set
set off
set out
settlement
shake
shaky
sham
shape
shapeless
shatter
shell
shift
shifty
shimmer
shiver
shock
shoddy
shot
show off
shower
shuffle
sick
signal
silliness
silly
sinful
sink
sketchy
skip
slack
slapdash
slaughter
slide
slip
slippery
slipshod
sloppy
slosh
slovenly
sly
smash
snarl
solution
solve
somehow
somersault
sorry
sort

sort of
soup
sozzle
spasmodic
spatter
special
speech
spill
spilt
spin
splash
splice
spoil
spongy
sport
spray
spread
spring
sprinkle
spurious
squash
squiffy
squirm
stagger
steaming
stew
stir
storm
stormy
straighten
strange
stray
stress
structure
struggle
stumble
stupid
style
subtle
suffer
sunk
supple
supply
surprising
suspect
suspicious
swap
swill
swim
swing
swirl
switch
synthetic
tailor
taint
tangle
tatter
tease
teeter
terrible
throb
throw
tidy
tight
tipsy
to order
to stir
topple
topsy-turvy
torment
torn
tortuous
torture
toss
totter
tour
tragic
train
training
trammel
transfer
transfigure
transform
transformation
translate
translation
transmute
transport
transpose
trash
travel
treat
treatment
tremble
tremulous
trick
tricky
trip
trouble
troublesome
tumble
tumbledown
tumult
turbulence
turbulent
turmoil
turn
turnover
tweak
twiddle
twinkle
twirl
twist
twitch
type
ugly
unbalanced
uncertain
uncommon
uncomplicated
uncontrolled
unconventional
unco-ordinated
uncouth
undisciplined
undo
undulate
unduly
uneasy
uneven
unexpected
unfair
unfamiliar
unfit
unfortunate
ungainly
unhappy
unholy
unkempt
unlikely
unnatural
unordered
unorthodox
unpredictable
unravel
unreliable
unrest
unrestrained
unrestricted
unruly
unscramble
unseemly
unsettle
unsound
unstable
unsteady
unstuck
untidy
untrue
unusual

unwind
unwise
upset
upturn
use
useless
vacillate
vacillation
vagrant
vague
vandalize
variant
variation
variegated
variety
various
vary
vault
versatile
version
vibrate
vigorous
vile
violate
violation
violent
volatile
vulnerable
wacky
wag
waggle
wander
wanton
warp
warring
waste
wave
waver
way
weave
weird
whip
whirl
whisk
wicked
wild
wind
wobble
woeful
work
work out
worry
wound
wrack
wreck
wreckage
wrestle
wretched
writhe
wrong
wrongful
wrought
wry
yank
yield
zany

4 letters

A

AABB abba✧
baba
AABC abac
caba
AABH Ahab
AABK Kaba
AABL Baal
AABR Arab
arba
AABS à bas
baas
Saab®
Saba
AACM cama✧
AACP capa
paca
AACR Cara
raca
AACS casa
AACT acta
AACV Cava
AACW Waac
AADD Dada
AADI aida✧
AADL daal
Lada®
AADM Adam
AADN Dana
nada
AADR Adar
AADT data
AADW adaw
AAEG Gaea
AAEL alae
AAER area
AAFH haaf
AAFL alfa
fa la
fa-la
AAFR afar
Afra
AAFW Waaf
AAGG gaga
AAGH agha
AAGI Gaia
AAGL alga
gala
AAGM agma
AAGN naga
AAGR agar
Agra
raga
AAGS saag
saga
AAGZ Gaza
AAHH ha-ha
AAHK haka
AAHM amah
AAHN Naha
AAHR haar
AAHT taha
AAHY ayah
AAIM Maia
AAIN Naia
AAIP Apia
AAIR aria
AAIS Asia
AAJN Naja
AAJR ajar
raja
AAJV Java
Java®
AAJX Ajax
AAKK kaka
AAKM kama✧
AAKN kana
AAKR arak
kara
AAKT kata
taka
AAKV kava
AAKW waka
AALL la-la
AALM alma✧
amla
lama
AALN Alan
anal
lana
nala
AALP alap
AALR Alar®
alar
Lara
AALS alas
AALT Taal
tala
AALU aula
AALV aval
lava
AALY alay
AAMM ma'am
mama
AAMN mana
naam
AAMR maar
mara
Rama
AAMS Asma
masa
Saam
sama
AAMT Maat
AAMY maya✧
Yama
AANN anan
anna✧
naan
nana✧
AANO anoa
AANP napa
paan
AANR Aran
arna
Nara
rana✧
AANS anas
ana's
NASA
San'a
AANT anta
tana
AANZ azan
AAPP papa✧
AAPR Pará
para
AAPS asap
AAPT atap
tapa
AAPU paua
AAPW pawa
AAPY apay
AAQU aqua
AARR arar
AARS åsar
Sara
AART rata
tara
AARU aura
AARV vara
AARZ Raza
Zara
AASS sa sa
AASV vasa✧
AATT ta-ta
AATV tava
AATW tawa
AATX taxa
AAWY away
ABBD Badb
ABBE babe✧
ABBI Abib
Babi
ABBL blab
ABBO boab
boba
ABBR barb✧
ABBS Babs
ABBU babu
buba
ABBY baby
ABCH bach✧
ABCI Ciba
ABCK back
ABCN banc
ABCR carb
crab✧
ABCS scab
ABCU Cuba
ABDE abed
bade
bead
ABDI abid
ABDL bald
blad
ABDN band✧
ABDO doab
ABDR bard✧
brad
drab
ABDS dabs
ABDU baud
daub
ABDW bawd
ABEK bake
beak
ABEL able
albe
bael
bale
blae
Elba
ABEM beam
bema
ABEN bane
bean
ABEP peba
ABER bare
bear
brae
ABES base
ABET bate
beat
beta
ABEU beau
ABEY abye
baye
ABFF baff
ABFL flab
ABFR barf
frab
ABFT baft
ABGH bagh
ABGI biga
Gabi
ABGL blag
ABGM gamb
ABGN bang
ABGR brag
garb
grab
ABGS bags
ABGY gaby
ABHI bhai
ABHL blah
ABHS bash
ABHT baht
bath✧
ABIL bail
Bali
ABIM iamb
ABIN bani
ABIO obia
ABIR Bari
rabi
ABIS bias
ABIT bait
tabi
ABIX Bixa
ABJM jamb
ABJU baju
juba
ABKL balk
ABKN bank
nabk
ABKO boak
ABKR bark
brak
krab
ABKS bask
ABKU Baku
bauk
ABLL ball
ABLM balm
lamb✧
ABLS slab
ABLT Balt
blat
ABLU balu
ABLW bawl
ABLY blay
ABMO ambo
boma
ABMR barm
Bram
mbar
ABNO bona
Oban
ABNR barn
bran✧
ABNS nabs
snab
ABNT bant

ABNU buna
ABNW bawn
ABOR boar
bora
ABOT boat
ABPR barp
ABPU bapu
ABRS bars
bras
ABRT Bart
brat
T-bar
ABRU baur
ABRW bawr
braw
ABRY bray
ABSS bass
ABST bast
bats
stab
ABSW swab
ABSY bays
ABTT batt
ABTU abut
buat
tabu
tuba
ABTY bayt
ACCD AC/DC
ACCE ceca
ACCM Macc
ACCO coca
ACDE cade
dace
ecad
ACDH chad✧
ACDI acid
cadi
ACDL clad
ACDO coda
ACDR card
ACDS scad
ACEF cafe
café
face
ACEG cage
ACEH ache
Chae
each
ACEK cake
ACEL alec✧
lace
ACEM acme
came
Mace®
mace
ACEN acne
ance
Caen
cane
ACEP cape✧
pace✧
ACER acre
care
race
ACES aesc
case
ceas
ACET cate
tace
ACEV cave
ACFF caff
ACFH chaf
ACFL calf
ACFT fact
ACFU cauf
ACGL clag
ACGN cang
ACGR crag
ACGS scag
ACGY cagy
ACHI chai
ACHK hack
ACHL chal
ACHM cham✧
ACHN nach
ACHP chap
ACHR arch
char
rach
ACHS cash✧
ACHT chat
tach
ACHW chaw
ACHY chay✧
ACHZ Zach
ACIL Cali
laic
ACIM mica
ACIN cain✧
Inca
ACIO ciao
ACIP capi
pica✧
ACIS asci
saic
ACJK jack✧
ACKL calk
kcal
lack
ACKM mack
ACKP pack
ACKR cark
rack
ACKS cask
sack
ACKT tack
ACKU cauk
ACKW cawk
wack
ACKY caky
yack
ACKZ zack✧
ACLL call
ACLM calm
clam
ACLN clan
ACLO Acol
coal
cola✧
ACLP calp
clap
ACLR carl✧
ACLT clat
talc
ACLU caul
ACLW claw
ACLX calx
ACLY acyl
clay
lacy
ACMO coma
ACMP camp
ACMR cram✧
marc
ACMS scam
ACMU caum
ACMY cyma
YMCA
ACNN cann
ACNR cran
narc
ACNS cans
scan
ACNT cant
can't
ACNY cany
cyan
ACOP capo
paco
ACOR arco
Caro
Cora
orca
ACOS soca
ACOT atoc
coat
octa
taco
ACOW Waco
ACOX coax
co-ax
coxa
ACPR carp
crap
ACPT pact
ACPU caup
ACPY pacy
ACRR carr
ACRS scar
ACRT cart
ACRW craw
ACRY racy
ACRZ czar
ACSS Cass
ACST cast
Cats
scat
ACSW scaw
ACTT tact
ACUY yuca
ACVY cavy
ACWY YWCA
ADDE dead
Edda
ADDO dado
ADDR Dard
drad
ADDU daud
duad
ADDW dawd
wadd
ADDY D-day
dyad
ADEF deaf
fade
ADEG aged
egad
gade
ADEH hade
head
ADEI aide
idea
ADEJ jade
ADEK kade
ADEL Aled
dale
deal✧
lade
lead
Leda
ADEM dame
Edam
made
mead
ADEN Dane
dean
Edna
ADEO odea
ADER ared
dare
dear
eard
rade
read
ADES Esda
sade✧
ADET date
tead
tea'd
ADEU a due
ADEV Dave
deva
vade
Veda
ADEW awed
deaw
wade
ADEY yead
ADEZ adze
Azed
daze
ADFF daff
ADFH Fahd
ADFN fand
ADFO fado
ADFR fard
ADFT daft
ADFW Wafd
ADFY fady
ADGI gadi
gaid
igad
ADGL glad
ADGN dang
ADGO goad
ADGR darg
drag
grad
rag'd
ADGS dags
ADGU gaud
ADGW gawd
ADGY g'day
ADHI dhai
ADHJ hadj
ADHK dhak
ADHL dahl✧
dhal
ADHN hand
ADHO Doha
ADHR hard
ADHS dash
shad
ADHU haud
ADIK dika
kadi
kaid
ADIL Dáil
dali✧
dial
laid
ADIM amid
maid
ADIN Dian
ADIP paid
ADIQ qadi
ADIR arid
dari✧
raid
ADIS AIDS
dais
disa
said
sida

Words marked ✧ can also be spelled with one or more capital letters

ADIT dita
ADIU Audi®
ADIV avid
diva
ADIW wadi
waid
ADKN dank
ADKR dark
ADKS daks
ADKW dawk
ADKY Dyak
ADLN land✧
ADLO alod
load
odal
ADLR lard
ADLT dalt
ADLU auld
dual
laud
Lüda
udal
ADLW awdl
wald
ADLY lady✧
yald
ADMN damn
mand
ADMP damp
ADMR dram
mard
ADMS dams
ADMU duma✧
maud✧
ADMW dwam
ADNO Doña
dona
ADNP pand
ADNR darn
nard
rand✧
ADNS sand
ADNT dant
ADNU Danu
duan
ADNW dawn✧
wand
wan'd
ADNY Andy
ADOP apod
dopa
ADOR Dora
road
ADOS soda
ADOT doat
toad
ADOW woad
ADPR drap
pard
prad
ADPS pads
ADQU quad✧
ADRS Ards
rads
sard✧
ADRT dart
d'art
drat
trad
ADRU daur
duar
dura
ADRW draw
ward
ADRY dray
yard✧
ADSW swad
ADSY days✧
ADTU daut
ADTW dawt
wadt
ADUY yaud
ADVY Davy
V-day
ADWY wady
AEEG agee
AEEJ ajee
AEEK akee
AEEL alee
eale
AEES ease
AEFK fake
AEFL alef
feal
flea
leaf
AEFM fame
AEFN fane
AEFR fare
fear
frae
AEFS safe
AEFT Efta
fate
feat
feta
AEFV fave
AEFW a few
AEFY Faye
AEFZ faze
AEGG gage
AEGL egal
Gael
gale✧
geal
AEGM egma
game
mage
mega
AEGN agen
gane
gean
gena
AEGP gape
page✧
peag
AEGR areg
gare
gear
rage
AEGS ages
sage
AEGT gate
geat
geta
AEGU ague
AEGV gave
vega✧
AEGW wage
AEGY Gaye
AEGZ gaze
AEHK hake
AEHL hale
heal
Leah
AEHM ahem
haem
hame
AEHP epha
heap
AEHR hare
hear
Hera
rhea✧
AEHS shea
AEHT eath
haet
hate
heat
thae
Thea
AEHV have
AEHY yeah
AEHZ haze
AEIK kaie
AEIL ilea
AEIM amie
AEIN aîné
AEJK jake✧
AEJN jane✧
jean
AEJP jape
AEJT jeat
AEKK ekka
AEKL kale
lake
leak
AEKM kame
make
AEKP peak
AEKR rake
reak
AEKS sake
saké
AEKT Kate
keta
take
teak
AEKW wake
weak
weka
AEKY Kaye
AELL El Al
Ella
leal
AELM alme
Elma
lame
lamé
leam
Malé
male
meal
mela
AELN élan
lane
lean✧
Lena
neal✧
AELO aloe
Olea
AELP leap
pale
peal
pela
plea
AELR arle
earl
laer
lare
lear✧
rale
râle
real
AELS lase
sale
seal
slae
AELT Elat
et al
late
leat
tael
tale
teal
tela
AELV Elva
lave
leva
vale
veal
vela✧
AELW alew
wale
weal
AELX Alex
axel
axle
AELY Yale®
yale✧
AELZ laze
zeal
AEMM emma✧
AEMN amen
mane
mean
name✧
AEMR mare
ream
AEMS mase
mesa
same
seam
AEMT mate
maté
meat
Meta
tame
team
Tema
AEMV Maev
AEMW wame
AEMX Amex
exam
Xema
AEMZ maze
AENN Anne
AENO aeon
a one
eaon
eoan
AENP nape
neap
pane
pean
AENR earn
nare
near
rean
AENS sane
sean✧
sena
AENT ante
Aten
etna✧
neat
ta'en
tane
ta'ne
Tean
AENU aune
Euan
AENV Evan
nave
vane

	vena
AENW	anew
	Ewan
	wane
	wean
AENY	yean
AENZ	naze
	Zena
AEOR	aero
AEOT	toea
AEOZ	zoea
AEPP	pape
AEPR	pare
	pear
	rape
	reap
AEPS	apse
	peas
	spae
AEPT	pate
	pâté
	peat
	tape
AEPV	pave
	pavé
AEPX	apex✧
AEQS	Seaq
AERR	rare
	rear
AERS	Ares
	rase
	sear
	sera
AERT	aret
	rate
	tare
	tear
AERU	urea
AERV	aver
	rave
	vare
	Vera
AERW	arew
	ware
	wear
AERY	ayre
	eyra
	yare
	year
AERZ	Ezra
	raze
AEST	east✧
	eats
	sate
	seat
	seta
AESU	Esau
AESV	Aves
	save
	vase
AESW	wase
AESX	axes
	saxe✧
AESY	easy
	eyas
AETT	état
	tate✧
	teat
AETW	twae
	wate
	weta
AETY	yate
AETZ	zeta
AEUV	uvea
AEVW	wave
AEWW	wawe
AFFF	faff
AFFG	gaff
AFFH	haff
AFFN	naff
AFFO	Offa
AFFR	raff
AFFT	Taff
AFFW	waff
AFFY	yaff
AFGL	flag
AFGN	fang
AFGO	goaf
AFGR	frag
	Graf
AFHK	khaf
AFHL	half
AFHS	fash
AFHT	haft
AFIK	faik
	kaif
AFIL	alif
	fail
AFIN	fain
	naif
	naïf
AFIP	Piaf
AFIR	fair
	fiar
AFIS	as if!
	Safi
AFIT	fiat
AFIW	waif
AFIX	faix
AFKL	flak
AFKN	fank
AFKW	wakf✧
AFLL	fall
AFLM	flam
AFLN	flan
AFLO	foal
	loaf
	Olaf
AFLP	flap
AFLR	farl
AFLT	flat
AFLU	lauf
AFLW	flaw
AFLX	falx
	flax
AFLY	flay
AFMO	foam
AFMR	farm
AFNU	faun
AFNW	fawn
AFOR	afro✧
	faro
	fora
AFOS	as of
	oafs
	sofa
AFPR	frap
AFQW	waqf✧
AFRT	raft
AFRU	frau✧
AFRY	fray
AFRZ	zarf
AFST	fast
AFSX	Sfax
AFTT	Taft
AFTU	tufa
AFTW	waft
AFUX	faux
AGGH	hagg
AGGI	giga
AGGM	magg
AGGN	gang
AGGO	agog
AGGR	ragg
AGGU	guga
AGHN	hang
AGHR	argh
AGHS	gash
	shag
AGHT	gath
	ghat
AGIL	Gail
	gila
	glia
AGIM	magi✧
AGIN	Agni
	gain
	Gina
	Inga
AGIO	Iago
AGIR	gair
	ragi
	Riga
AGIT	gait
	Gita
AGIV	vagi
AGIY	Yagi
AGJO	gajo
AGJU	juga
AGKN	kang
	knag
AGKO	kago
AGKS	skag
AGKU	kagu
AGKW	gawk
AGLL	gall✧
AGLM	glam
AGLN	lang✧
AGLO	gaol
	goal
	Olga
AGLS	lags
	slag
AGLU	Gaul
	gula
AGLY	Algy
	gyal
AGMN	G-man
	mang
AGMO	ogam
	Ogma
AGMP	gamp
AGMR	gram
	marg
AGMS	mags
AGMU	gaum
	Guam
AGMY	gamy
AGNO	agon
	Goan
AGNP	pang
AGNR	gnar
	gran
	rang
AGNS	sang
	snag
AGNT	gant
	gnat
	T'ang
	tang✧
AGNU	gaun
	guan
AGNV	vang
AGNW	gnaw
	wang
AGNY	Angy
	yang✧
AGOP	gapó
AGOR	Argo
AGOS	sago
AGOT	go at
	goat✧
	toga
AGOY	Goya
	yoga
AGPS	gasp
AGPU	gaup
AGPW	gawp
AGQU	quag
AGRS	rags
AGRT	gart
	grat
AGRU	gaur
	guar
AGRY	Gary
	gray
AGRZ	Graz
AGST	gast
	stag
	tags
AGSW	swag
AGSY	sagy
AGUY	yuga
AGYZ	gazy
AHHS	hash
	shah
AHHT	hath
AHIJ	haji
AHIK	haik
AHIL	hail
	hila
AHIN	hain
	Hani
AHIR	hair✧
	Hari
AHIS	Shia
AHIT	ha'it
	Thai
AHIU	huia
AHIY	hiya
AHJJ	hajj
AHKL	lakh
AHKN	ankh
	hank✧
	khan
AHKP	kaph
AHKR	hark
AHKS	hask
AHKT	Kath
	khat
AHKW	hawk
AHLL	hall
AHLM	halm
AHLO	halo
AHLP	Alph
AHLR	harl
AHLS	Hals
	lash
AHLT	halt
	lath
AHLU	haul
	hula
AHLY	hyla
AHMR	harm
AHMS	mash
	sham
AHMT	math
AHMU	huma
AHMW	hawm
	Wham!
	wham
AHNO	Noah
AHNR	harn
AHNS	Nash
	shan✧

AHNT ha'n't, tanh, than
AHOP opah
AHOR haro, hoar, hora
AHOS hoas
AHOT oath
AHOU Oahu
AHOV Hova
AHOW whoa
AHOX hoax
AHOY hoya
AHPR harp
AHPS hasp, pash
AHPT path, phat, Ptah
AHPU hapu
AHPW whap
AHRS rash
AHRT hart, rath, tahr, thar
AHRU Rahu
AHSS sash
AHST hast, shat, tash
AHSW shaw✧, shwa, wash
AHSY ashy, shay
AHTT tath, that
AHTU haut, Utah
AHTW thaw, what
AHYZ hazy
AIIL ilia
AIIN lain, inia
AIIS lasi
AIIX ixia
AIJL jail
AIJM Jima
AIJN Jain
AIJO jiao
AIJW Jawi
AIKK kaki
AIKL ilka, kail, kali✧, laik
AIKM kaim, kami, maik
AIKN akin, kain, kina, naik
AIKP paik, pika
AIKR raik, raki
AIKS saki✧, sika
AIKT ikat, kati, taki, tika
AIKV kiva
AIKZ kazi
AILM Liam, lima✧, mail, mali✧
AILN anil, lain, Lian, Lina, nail
AILP lipa, pail, Pali, pila
AILR aril, lair, lari, liar, lira, rail, rial
AILS Isla, Lias, Lisa, sail, sial
AILT alit, lati, tail, tali
AILV vail, vali, vial
AILW wail, wali
AILX axil
AILZ Liza, zila
AIMM imam✧, maim
AIMN Amin, main, mani, mina✧
AIMR amir, Irma, mair, Mira, rami, rima
AIMS amis, saim, Sami, sima
AIMU Maui
AIMX maxi
AINN nain, Nina
AINO Iona
AINP nipa✧, pain, piña
AINR airn, Iran, Nair, rain, rani
AINS anis, sain, Sian
AINT anti, Nita, tian, Tina
AINV Ivan, vain, vina
AINW wain✧
AINX Xian
AINY ayin
AINZ Nazi
AIOT iota, Oita
AIOW Iowa
AIPP pipa
AIPR pair
AIPS Apis, pais, Pisa
AIPT pita
AIQR Iraq
AIRS aris, sair, sari
AIRT rait, Rita, tiar
AIRV Ravi, riva, vair
AIRY Iyar
AIRZ riza
AISS as is
AIST Asti, sati, Sita
AISV Siva, visa
AISX axis
AISY I say!
AITT at it, tait, Tati
AITV vita✧
AITW wait
AITX taxi
AITZ zati
AIVV viva
AIWY I-way
AJKR jark
AJLR jarl
AJNN jann
AJNO Joan
AJOS soja
AJOT jato, jota
AJPS jasp
AJPU jaup, puja
AJRU jura✧
AJSS jass
AJSW jaws✧
AJSY jasy
AJYZ jazy
AJZZ jazz
AKKO koka
AKKR kark
AKLN Klan, lank
AKLO kola✧
AKLR Karl, lark
AKLT talk
AKLU kula
AKLW lawk, walk
AKLY alky, laky
AKMO amok, mako
AKMR mark✧
AKMS mask
AKMW mawk
AKNO Kano, kaon, koan
AKNP knap
AKNR knar, nark, rank
AKNS kans, sank
AKNT kant✧, tank
AKNU kuna
AKNY yank✧
AKOR kora, okra
AKOS Oaks, soak
AKOT atok, Kota, okta
AKOY kayo, oaky, okay
AKPR park✧
AKPW pawk
AKRS ksar, sark✧
AKRT kart
AKRU raku
AKRW wark
AKST skat, task
AKSU skua
AKSW skaw
AKTY Katy, kyat, taky
AKUW wauk
ALLM mall
ALLO Lola, olla
ALLP pall
ALLT tall
ALLW wall
ALLY y'all
ALMM malm
ALMO loam, loma, mola
ALMP lamp, palm
ALMR marl
ALMS slam
ALMT malt
ALMU alum, luma, maul
ALMY amyl, lyam, myal
ALNO loan, Nola
ALNP plan
ALNR larn
ALNT lant
ALNU Alun, luna✧, ulna
ALNW lawn
ALNX lanx
ALOP opal
ALOR oral
ALOS also, Laos, sola

Words marked ✧ can also be spelled with one or more capital letters

ALOT alto
lota
tola
ALOV Olav
oval
vola
ALOW AWOL
ALOZ lazo
Zola
ALPP Lapp
palp
plap
ALPS salp
slap
ALPT plat
ALPU paul✧
pula
ALPW pawl
ALPY paly
play
ALRU Ural
ALRY aryl
Lyra
ryal
ALSS lass
ALST last
lats
salt
slat
ALSU saul✧
ALSV Slav
ALSW slaw
ALSY slay
ALTU Tula
ALTW twal
Walt
ALUU luau
ALUV ulva
ALUW waul
ALWW wawl
ALWY waly
yawl
ALYZ lazy
AMMR marm
AMMU umma
AMNN Mann
AMNO an mo
mano
moan
mona✧
Noam
noma
Oman
AMNS mnas
AMNU Manú
maun
AMNX Manx
AMNY many
myna
AMOR mora
Omar
roam
roma✧
AMOS Soma®
soma
AMOT atom
moat
AMOU ouma
AMOW mowa
AMOX moxa
AMOY mayo✧
moya
AMPR pram
ramp
AMPS samp
Spam®
spam
AMPT tamp
AMPU puma
AMPV vamp
AMQR Marq
AMRS arms
Mars
Rams
AMRT mart
tram
AMRU arum
Umar
AMRW mawr
warm
AMRX Marx
AMRY army
mary✧
Myra
AMSS mass✧
AMST mast
AMSU masu
Musa
AMSW swam
AMSX Xmas
AMTT matt✧
AMTU Atum
AMTY maty
AMWY M-way
AMYZ azym
mazy
ANNO anon
Nona
ANOR Nora
Oran
roan
Rona
ANOS naos
ANOT Nato
ANOV nova
ANOX axon
ANOZ zona
ANPS snap
span
ANPT pant
ANPU puna
ANPW pawn
ANRS snar
ANRT rant
tarn
ANRU Arun
raun
ANRW rawn
warn
ANRY nary
Ryan
yarn
ANSS sans
ANST sant✧
ANSU anus
ANSW sawn
swan
ANSY nyas
ANTU aunt✧
tuan
tuna
ANTV vant
ANTW want
ANUU unau
ANUY yuan
ANUZ Zanu
ANVY navy✧
ANWY awny
wany
yawn
ANYZ zany
AOPR proa
AOPS Apso
soap
AOPT atop
AOPU oupa
AOPV Pavo
AORR orra
roar
AORS Rosa
soar
sora
AORT rota✧
taro
AORU urao
AORV arvo
voar
AORW arow
a-row
AORY oary
AOSS ossa✧
AOST oast
oats
stoa
tosa
AOSV avos
AOSX Xosa
AOSY Soay
soya
AOTT to a T
AOTU auto
AOTY oaty
AOUY ou ay
AOVW avow
APPR parp
APPU pupa
APPY yapp
APRR parr
APRS rasp
spar
APRT part
prat
rapt
tarp
trap
APRU prau
APRW warp
wrap
APRY pray
APSS pass
APST past
spat
stap
taps
APSU Apus
upas
APSW spaw
swap
wasp✧
APSY pays
spay
APSZ spaz
APTU tapu
APTY pyat
APUY yaup
APUZ Zapu
zupa
APWY yawp
AQTU quat
AQUY quay
ARRY yarr
ARST rast
rats
star
tsar
ARSU rusa
sura
Ursa
ARTT tart
trat
ARTU ratu
Ruta
ARTW wart
ARTY tray
ARTZ tzar
ARUV urva
ARUW waur
ARVY vary
ARWY awry
wary
ARXY X-ray
xray✧
ARZZ razz
ASSS sass
ASST tass
ASSU Susa
ASSY says
ASTT stat
ASTU saut
utas
ASTV vast
ASTW staw
swat
taws
'twas
wast
wats
ASTY stay
ASUV Suva
ASWY sway
ways
yaws
ATTT tatt
ATTU tatu
taut
ATTW tawt
watt
ATUV vatu
vaut
ATWY tway
AVWY wavy
AWXY waxy
AWYY yawy

B

BBCO cobb
BBEE Beeb
BBEL bleb
BBIS sibb
BBIY Ibby
BBLO blob
BBLU blub
bulb
BBMO bomb
BBOO boob
BBOS bobs
BBOU bubo✧
BBRU burb
BCEI bice
BCEK beck
BCER CBer
BCEU Cebu
cube
BCHU chub
BCIR crib
BCKO bock
BCKU buck
BCLO bloc
BCLU club
BCMO comb
BCRU curb
BDEE bede✧
BDEI bide
dieb
BDEL bled

BDEM	Medb
BDEN	bend
BDEO	bode
BDER	bred
BDET	debt
BDEU	Bedu
BDII	bidi
BDIN	bind
BDIR	bird
	drib
BDIS	dibs
BDLO	bold
BDMU	dumb
BDNO	bond
BDNU	bund✧
BDOO	doob
BDOR	bord
	brod
BDOU	budo
BDOY	body
	do by
BDRU	burd
	drub
BDSU	dubs
BDUZ	'zbud
BEEH	hebe✧
BEEL	blee
BEEN	bene
BEER	bere
	bree
BEET	bete
	bête
BEGI	gibe
BEGR	berg
BEGY	gybe
BEHL	bhel
BEHR	herb
BEHT	beth
BEIJ	jibe
BEIK	bike
	kibe
BEIL	bile
BEIN	beni
	bien
	bine
BEIR	bier
	Brie
BEIS	bise
BEIT	bite
BEIV	vibe
BEIX	ibex
BEJN	benj
BEJO	jobe
BEJU	jube
BEKM	kemb
BEKO	boke
	Kobe
BEKR	berk
	kerb
BEKU	buke
BEKY	byke
BELO	bole
	lobe
BELP	pleb
BELT	blet
BELU	blue
	lube
BELW	blew
BELY	bley
BEMR	berm
BEMW	wemb
BENO	bone
	ebon
BENR	Bern
	bren✧
BENS	sneb
BENU	unbe
BEOO	oboe
BEOR	Boer
	bore
	robe
	'robe
BEOT	bote
	to-be
BEOY	obey
BERR	brer
BERS	Serb
BERU	rube
BERV	verb
BERW	brew
BERY	byre
BESY	byes
BETU	bute✧
	tube✧
BETY	byte
	ybet
BEUZ	zebu
BFFI	biff
BFFO	boff
BFFU	buff
BFLU	flub
BFMU	bumf
BFOR	forb
BFOU	bufo
BGGI	bigg
BGIL	glib
BGIN	bing
BGIO	biog
	gobi
	Igbo
BGIR	brig
BGLO	glob
BGNO	bong
BGNU	bung
BGOO	gobo
BGOR	Borg
	brog
BGOY	bogy
	boyg
	go by
	goby
	go-by
BGRU	burg
	grub
BHIS	bish
BHLU	buhl
BHOO	boho
	booh
	hobo
BHOS	bosh
BHOT	both
BHPU	pbuh
BHSU	bush
BIIS	ibis
BIKL	bilk
BIKN	bink
BIKR	birk
BIKS	bisk
BIKU	buik
BILM	limb
BILN	blin
BILO	boil
	lobi
BILP	blip
BILR	birl
BILT	blit
BIMN	nimb
BIMR	brim
BIMZ	zimb
BINS	nibs
	snib
BINY	inby
BIOR	Biro®
	brio
BIOS	Ibos
BIOT	bito
	obit
BIOZ	Zibo
BIRT	brit✧
BISV	vibs
BKLU	bulk
BKNO	bonk
	knob
BKNU	bunk
	knub
BKOO	boko
	book✧
	kobo
BKOS	bosk
BKOU	bouk
BKRU	burk
BKSU	busk
BLLO	Böll
	boll
BLLU	bull✧
BLOO	bolo
	bool
	lobo
	obol
BLOS	slob
BLOT	bolt✧
BLOW	bowl
BLRU	blur✧
	burl
BLSU	slub
BLTU	Blut
BMNU	numb
BMOO	boom
BMOT	tomb
BMOU	ombu
	ombú
	umbo
BMOW	womb
BMPU	bump
BMRU	Brum
BNNO	Bonn
BNOO	boon
	Obon
BNOR	born
	Brno
BNOS	bos'n
	bo's'n
	snob
BNOU	boun
BNOY	bony
BNRU	burn
BNRY	Bryn
BNSU	buns
	snub
BNTU	bunt
BOOR	Boro
	broo
BOOS	obos
BOOY	boyo
BOOZ	bozo
	zobo
BOPR	prob
BORS	sorb✧
BORW	bowr
	brow
BORY	orby
BORZ	Zorb®
BOST	bots
	stob
BOSW	bows
	swob
BOSY	boys
	sybo
BOTU	bout
BOTY	toby✧
BOUY	buoy
BOUZ	zobu
BPRU	burp
BPST	tbsp
BPUY	upby
BRRU	burr
BRTU	brut
BRUY	bury✧
	ruby
BSSU	buss
	subs
BSTU	bust
	stub
BSUY	busy
BTTU	butt

C

CCEE	ecce
CCEO	ecco
CCHI	chic✧
CCHO	choc
	coch
CCIN	C-in-C
CCKO	cock
CCOO	coco
CCOR	croc
CDEE	cede
CDEI	cedi
	cide
	dice
	iced
CDEK	deck
CDEO	code
	coed
	deco✧
	ecod
CDER	cred
CDEU	cued
	duce
CDHI	chid
	dich
CDIK	dick✧
CDIO	odic
CDIS	disc
CDIT	dict
CDKO	dock
CDKU	duck
CDLO	clod
	cold
CDNO	cond
	con'd
CDOR	cord
CDOU	douc
CDRU	crud
	curd
CDSU	scud✧
CDTU	duct
CEEH	eche
	eech
CEER	cere
	cree✧
CEET	cete
CEEX	exec
CEFH	chef
CEFK	feck
CEFL	clef
CEFO	C of E
CEGK	geck
CEGL	cleg
CEHH	hech
CEHK	heck
CEHL	lech
CEHO	echo✧
	oche
CEHP	pech

CEHR	cher✧
CEHS	sech
CEHT	echt
	etch
	tech
CEHW	chew
CEHY	yech
CEHZ	chez
CEIL	ciel
	Icel
	lice
CEIM	mice
CEIN	cine
	ciné
	nice
CEIO	Oeic
CEIP	epic
	pice
CEIR	Ceri
	ciré
	eric✧
	icer
	rice
CEIS	sice
CEIT	cite
	tice
CEIV	cive
	vice✧
CEIW	wice
CEKK	keck
CEKN	neck
CEKO	Coke®
	coke
CEKP	peck
CEKR	reck
CELM	clem✧
CELO	Cleo
	cole
CELU	clue
	luce
CELW	clew
CEMO	come
CEMR	merc
CEMY	cyme
CENO	cone
	once
CENU	unce
CEOP	cope
CEOR	cero
	core
CEOS	cose
	seco
CEOT	cote
CEOV	cove
CEOZ	coze
CEPS	Pécs
	pecs
	spec
CEPU	puce
CERT	Rect
CERU	crue
	cure
	curé
	ecru
CERW	crew
CEST	sect
CESY	scye
	Secy
	syce
CETU	cute
CETY	cyte
CFFO	coff
CFFU	cuff
CFIL	flic
CFIO	C of I
	coif
	fico
	foci
CFIS	fisc
CFIU	cuif
	fuci
CFLO	floc
CFNO	conf
CFOO	coof
CFOR	corf
CFOS	C of S
CFOT	coft
CFSU	fusc
CGHU	chug
CGKU	guck
CGLO	clog
CGOS	scog
CGSU	scug
CHIK	hick
CHIL	lich
CHIN	inch
CHIR	rich
CHIS	sich
CHIT	itch
	tich✧
CHIW	wich
CHKO	hock
CHKU	huck
CHLO	loch
CHMO	moch
CHMU	chum
	much
CHNO	chon
CHOO	coho
CHOR	roch
CHOS	cosh
CHOT	coth
	Toc H
CHOU	ouch
CHSU	cush
	such
CHTU	chut
CHWY	wych
CIIX	Cixi
CIKK	kick
CIKL	lick
CIKM	mick✧
CIKN	nick✧
CIKP	pick
CIKR	rick✧
CIKS	sick
CIKT	tick
CIKW	wick✧
CIKX	Ickx
CIKY	icky
CILO	Clio
	coil
	loci
CILP	clip
CILR	cirl
CIMO	mico
CIMR	crim
CINO	cion
	coin
	coni
	icon
CINU	unci
CINZ	zinc
CIOR	coir
CIOT	cito
	coit
	otic
	Tico
CIOZ	Zico
	zoic
CIPS	pics
CIPT	Pict
CIRT	crit
CIRU	uric
CIRY	ricy
CIST	cits
CITU	cuit
CJKO	jock✧
CJOO	joco
CKLO	lock
CKLU	luck
CKMO	mock
CKMU	muck✧
CKNO	conk
	nock
CKOO	cook✧
CKOP	pock
CKOR	cork✧
	rock✧
CKOS	sock
CKOT	tock
CKOW	wock
CKOY	coky
	yock
CKPU	puck✧
CKRU	ruck
CKSU	cusk
	suck
CKTU	tuck
CKUY	yuck
CLLO	coll✧
CLLU	cull
CLMO	Colm
CLMU	culm
CLOO	cool
	loco
CLOT	Colt®
	colt
CLOW	cowl
CLOY	coly
CLRU	curl
CLSU	scul
CLTU	cult
CLUY	Lucy
CMOO	Como
	coom
CMOP	comp
CMOR	corm
CMOS	coms
CMSU	scum
CNNO	conn
CNOO	Cono
	coon
CNOR	corn
CNOU	unco
CNOY	cony
CNRU	curn
CNSY	sync
COOP	poco
COOT	toco
COPR	crop
COPS	scop
COPU	coup
COPW	cowp
CORT	torc
CORU	cour
CORW	crow✧
COST	scot✧
COSW	cows
	scow
COYZ	cozy
CPSU	cusp
	scup
CRRU	curr
CRSU	crus
	scur
CRSY	scry
CRTU	curt
CSSU	cuss
CSTU	scut
CSTY	cyst

D

DDEE	deed
DDEI	deid
	died
DDEO	eddo
DDER	redd
DDEU	dude
DDEY	dyed
	eddy✧
DDII	Didi
DDIO	dido✧
DDOO	dodo
DDOS	dods
	odds
DDOW	dowd
DDRU	rudd
DDSU	duds
	sudd
DEEF	feed
	fee'd
DEEG	edge
	geed
DEEH	heed
DEEI	Edie
	idée
DEEK	deke
DEEL	dele
	Edel
DEEM	deme
	Mede
	meed
DEEN	dene
	Eden
	need
DEER	dere
	dree
	rede
	reed
DEES	seed
DEET	teed
	tee'd
DEEW	weed
DEEY	eyed
	yede
	yeed
DEFL	delf
	fled
DEFN	fend
DEFO	feod
DEFR	Fred
DEFU	feud
DEGI	Gide
	gied
DEGL	geld
	gled
DEGO	doge
DEGR	dreg
	regd
DEGU	gude
DEGY	edgy
DEHI	heid
	hide
	hied
DEHL	held
DEHN	hend
DEHO	hoed
DEHR	herd
DEHS	shed
	she'd
DEHU	hued
DEIK	dike
DEIL	deli
	eild

idle
Lide
lied
DEIM dime
idem
DEIN dine
Enid
nide
DEIO Odie
DEIP pied
DEIR dire
ride
DEIS dies
ides✧
side
DEIT diet✧
dite
edit
tide
tied
DEIU Dieu
DEIV Devi
dive
vide
vied
DEIW Dewi
weid
wide
DEJU Jude
DEKO doek
OKed
DEKR drek
DEKS desk
DEKU duke
DEKY dyke
DELM meld
DELN lend
DELO dole
lode
DELP pled
DELS seld
sled
DELT teld
DELU duel
dule
DELV veld
DELW lewd
weld
DELY yeld
DEMN mend
DEMO dome
mode
DEMR derm
DENO doen
done
node
DENP pend
DENR dern
nerd
rend
DENS send
sned
DENT tend
DENU dune
nude
unde
undé
DENV vend
DENW wend✧
DENY dyne
DENZ Zend
DEOP dope
op-ed
DEOR doer
Doré
redo
rode
roed
DEOS does
dose
Odes
DEOT dote
toed
DEOV Devo
dove✧
DEOW owed
DEOY yode
DEOZ doze
DEPS sped
DEPU dupe
DERS Reds
DERT retd
DERU dure
rude
rued
urdé
DERV Revd
DERW drew✧
DERY drey
dyer
Ryde
yerd
DEST sted
DESU deus
dues
sued
used
DETU duet
DETY tedy
tyde
DEWY Edwy
DFFO doff
DFFU duff
DFIN find
DFIO Fido
foid
DFLO fold
DFNO fond
DFNU fund
DFOO food
DFOR ford✧
DFOU foud
DFOW dowf
DFRY fyrd
DFUY Dufy
DGIL gild
glid
DGIN ding
DGIR gird
grid✧
DGIS digs
DGIU guid
DGLO gold
DGNO dong
DGNS Gdns
DGNU dung
DGOO good
DGOS dogs
God's
gods
DGOU Doug
DGOW gowd
DGOY dogy
DGRU drug
DHIL hild
DHIN hind
DHIS dish
DHIW whid
DHKU khud
DHLO dhol
hold
DHNO hond
DHOO hood
'hood
DHOS dohs
dosh
shod
DHOT doth
DHOW who'd
DHOY yodh
DHOZ dzho
DHSU dush
DHTU thud
DIIL Dili
DIIM midi✧
DIIN nidi
DIIR irid
DIIV divi
DIIX dixi
DIJO Jodi
DIJR jird
DIKL kild
DIKN dink
kind
DIKR dirk
DIKS disk
skid
ski'd
DILM mild
DILN lind
DILO diol
idol
lido
loid
olid
DILR dirl
DILS sild
slid
'slid
DILV vild
DILW wild✧
DILY idly
idyl
DIMN mind
DIMO modi
DIMU muid
DINO do in
do-in
nodi
Odin
DINR rind
DINS sind
DINT tind
DINW wind
DINY Indy
DIOT doit
DIOV Ovid
void
DIPR drip
DIQU quid
DIRY yird
DISS Sids
DISU suid
DITY tidy
DIVY ivy'd
DJOO dojo
DJOU judo
DJOY Jody
DJUY judy✧
DKNO kond
DKNU dunk
DKNY kynd
DKOO dook
DKOR dork
DKRU Kurd
DKSU dusk
DKUU kudu
DLLO doll
DLLU dull✧
DLMO mold✧
DLNU Lund
DLOO dool
DLOP plod
DLOR lord✧
DLOS olds
sold
DLOT dolt
told
DLOU loud
ludo
ould
DLOW dowl
wold
DLOY odyl
oldy
yold
DLOZ Lódz
DLUY duly
DMOO doom
mood
DMOR dorm
DMOS mods✧
DMOT MOT'd
DMOY domy
DMPU dump
DMRU drum
DNOP pond✧
DNOR Dr No
DNOS Dons
snod
DNOT don't
DNOU udon
undo
DNOW down✧
DNOY yond
DNRU durn
nurd
rund
DNRY rynd
DNSY synd
DNTU dunt
tund
DNTY tynd
tyn'd
DNWY wynd
DOOP pood
DOOR odor
rood
DOOS odso
DOOT to-do
DOOW wood
DOPR dorp
drop
prod✧
DOPS spod
DOPU do up
doup
DOPW dowp
DOQU quod
DORS sord
DORT trod
DORU dour
duro
DORW drow
word✧
DOSU duos
udos
DOSW dows
DOTU dout
DOTW dowt
DOTY tody
DOUY you'd
DOYZ dozy
DPSU spud
DPUU pudu

DRSU surd
DRUU Urdu
DRUY urdy
DSSU suds
DSTU dust
stud
DTUY duty

E

EEEP épée
EEFL feel
flee
EEFM feme
EEFR feer
fere
free
reef
EEFT feet
fete
fête
EEGH ghee
EEGK geek
EEGL glee
EEGN gene
gêne
EEGO ogee
EEGP geep
EEGR eger
gere
gree
EEGU euge
EEGZ Geëz
EEHH he-he
EEHL heel
hele
EEHM heme
EEHR here
EEHT ethe
hete
thee
EEHW whee
EEIN eine
EEIV Evie
EEJL jeel
EEJP Jeep®
EEJR jeer
EEJT jeté
EEJZ Jeez
EEKK keek
EEKL keel
Klee
leek
leke
EEKM meek
EEKN keen
knee
EEKP keep
peek
peke
EEKR reek
reke
EEKS seek
EEKW week
EELL Elle
EELM leme
EELP leep
peel
pele✧
EELR leer
lere
reel
EELS else
lees
lese
seel
sele
slee
EELT leet
teel
tele
EELV leve
vele
EELW weel
EELZ leze
EEMM meme
EEMN mene
neem
EEMR meer✧
mere
EEMS mese
seem
semé
smee✧
EEMT meet
mete
teem
teme
EEMU emeu
EEMV meve
EEMW weem
EEMZ meze
mézé
mzee
EENN nene
EENP neep
peen
pene
EENR erne
ne'er
reen
Rene
René
EENS esne
seen
sene
snee
EENT eten
nete
teen
tene
EENV eevn
eev'n
even
névé
EENW enew
Ewen
ween
EENY eyne
EEOV evoe
EEPP peep
EEPR peer
père
pree
EEPS seep
EEPT Pete
EEPV veep
EEPW weep
EERS Erse
seer
sere
EERT rete
teer
tree
EERV ever
veer
EERW ewer
were
we're
EERY eyre
EESS esse
sese
EESW swee
EESX exes
EESY eyes
EETT tête
EETV evet
EETW twee
weet
EEVW we've
EEVY yeve
EEWX wexe
EEZZ zeze
EFFI fief
fife
EFFJ jeff✧
EFFT teff
EFGL fleg
EFGS fegs
EFHM Fehm
EFHT heft
EFIK fike
EFIL file
lief
life
EFIN feni
fine
neif
nief
nife
EFIR fire
reif
rife
EFIS feis
seif
EFIV five
EFIW wife
EFKR kerf
EFKY fyke
EFLL fell
EFLO floe
EFLP pelf
EFLS self
EFLT felt
left
EFLU flue
fuel
EFLW flew
EFLX flex
EFLY fley
fyle
EFMR ferm
EFMU fume
EFNO foen
fone
EFNR fern
EFNT fent
EFOR fore
froe
orfe
EFOS foes
EFRS serf
EFRT fret
reft
terf
tref
EFRY Frey
ryfe
EFSS fess
EFST fest
EFSU fuse
EFTT fett
EFTW weft
EFUZ fuze
EGGI Eigg
EGGL gleg
EGGT tegg
EGGY yegg
EGHP pegh
EGHU eugh
huge
EGIL glei
EGIN gien
Inge
EGIT geit
gite
gîte
tige
EGIV give
EGKS skeg
EGLN Genl
glen✧
leng
EGLO goel
gole
Lego®
loge
ogle
EGLT gelt
EGLU glue
gule
luge
EGLY gley
EGMN meng
EGMR germ
EGMS Gems
EGMU geum
EGNO Egon
gone
EGNR gren
EGNS gens
EGNT gent✧
EGNU genu
EGNW Gwen
EGOR ergo
goer
gore
ogre
rego
EGOS geos
goes
sego
EGOT toge
EGOY goey
ygoe
EGPU Pegu
EGRS ergs
Gers
EGRT Gert
EGRU grue
urge
EGRW grew
EGRY grey
gyre
EGST gest
EGTU tegu
EGTY gyte
EGVY gyve
EHHT heth
EHIK hike
EHIL heil!
EHIR heir
hire
EHIV hive
EHJU Jehu
EHKO hoke
EHKS kesh
EHKY hyke
EHLL hell✧
he'll
EHLM helm
EHLO hole
EHLP Help!
help
EHLR herl
lehr

Words marked ✧ can also be spelled with one or more capital letters

EHLU hule
EHLY hyle
EHMO home
EHMP hemp
EHMR herm
EHMS mesh
Shem
EHMT them
EHMV Vehm
EHNO hone
EHNR hern
EHNS nesh
EHNT hent
then
EHNW hewn
when
EHNY hyen
EHOP hope
EHOR hero✧
hoer
hore
EHOS hose
shoe
EHOT hote
Theo
EHOV hove✧
EHOW howe
EHPS hesp
Shep
EHPT hept
EHPW phew
EHPY hype
EHRR Herr
EHRS hers
resh
EHRT tehr
EHRU erhu
huer
EHRW whe'r
EHRY hery
EHSS Hess
sesh
shes
she's
EHST Esth
hest
Seth
shet
EHSW shew
EHTT teth
EHTW thew
whet
EHTY they
EHUY Huey
EHWW whew
EHWY whey
EIJV jive
EIKL Kiel
like
EIKM mike✧
EIKN kine
Nike
EIKP kepi
kipe
pike
EIKR Erik
keir
kier
reik
EIKS seik
sike
EIKT kite
tike
EIKV kiev✧
EIKY yike
EILM lime
mile
EILN lien
line✧
Neil
EILP pile
plié
EILR leir
lier
lire
riel
rile
EILS isle
Lise
seil
sile
EILT lite
teil
tile
EILU lieu
EILV evil
Levi
live
veil
vile
vlei
EILW lwei
weil
wiel
wile
EILX ilex
Leix
EIMM mime
EIMN mein
mien
mine
EIMR emir
meri
mire
riem
rime
EIMS mise
semi
EIMT emit
item
mite
time✧
EINN nine✧
EINO Eoin
EINP pein
peni
pine
EINR Erin
in re
rein
rine
EINS Ines
in se
ne is
sien
Síne
sine
EINT nite
tein
tine
EINV nevi
vein
vine
EINW Wien
wine
EINZ Inez
zein
zine
EIOU euoi
EIPP pipe
EIPR peri
pier
ripe
EIPS pisé
sipe
spie
EIPT piet
EIPW wipe
EIPZ pize
EIRS Eris
reis
rise
seir
sire
EIRT rite
tier
tire
trie
EIRU iure
EIRV rive
vier
vire
EIRW weir
wire
EIST site
stie
EISV vise
visé
EISW wise✧
EISZ size
EITT tite
EITU étui
EITV vite
EITW wite
EITX exit✧
EITY yeti
yite
EITZ zite
EIVV vive
EIVW view✧
wive
EJKO joke
EJKR jerk
EJKU juke
EJLL jell
EJLO Joel
jole
EJLU Jule
EJMS Sejm
EJNP J-pen
EJNU June
EJOS joes
EJOV Jove
EJOY joey✧
EJRU jure
EJSS jess✧
EJST jest
EJSU Jesu
EJTU jute✧
EJUV juve
EKKS keks
EKLL kell
EKLO koel
loke
EKLP kelp
EKLS elks
EKLT kelt✧
EKLU luke✧
EKLW welk
EKLY kyle
yelk
ylke
EKMO moke
EKMP kemp
EKMR merk
EKNO keno
EKNP penk
EKNR kern
nerk
EKNT kent✧
EKNU neuk
nuke
EKNW knew
EKNY kyne
EKOP poke
EKOR kero
kore✧
roke
EKOS skeo
soke
EKOT toke
EKOW woke
EKOY yoke
EKPR perk
EKPS skep
spek
EKPT kept
EKPU puke
EKPY kype
EKRS serk
sker
EKRT trek
EKRY ryke
yerk
EKST kest
sekt✧
EKSU Suke
EKSW skew
EKSY Esky®
Keys
Skye
syke
yesk
EKTY kyte
tyke
EKUY yeuk
yuke
ELLM mell
ELLN Nell
ELLP pell
ELLS sell
ELLT tell
ELLU Elul
ELLV vell
ELLW well✧
we'll
ELLY Lyle
yell
ELMO Lomé
lome
mole✧
ELMR merl
ELMT melt
ELMU mule
ELMW mewl
ELMY lyme✧
yelm
ylem
ELNO leno
León
lone
noel✧
noël✧
nole
ELNS lens
ELNT lent✧
ELNU lune
ELNY lyne
ELOO oleo
ELOP lope
olpe
pole✧
ELOR eorl
lore
orle

	role
	rôle
ELOS	Leos
	lose
	sloe
	sole
ELOT	Leto
	lote
	tole
ELOV	love
	vole
ELOW	lowe
ELPR	lerp
	Perl
ELPT	pelt
ELPU	pule
ELPY	yelp
ELRU	lure
	rule
ELRY	Eryl
	lyre
	rely
ELSS	less
	'less
ELST	lest
ELSU	lues
	slue
ELSW	slew
ELSY	lyse
	sley
ELTT	Lett
	telt
ELTU	lute
	tule
ELTW	welt✧
ELTY	lyte
	yelt
ELUX	exul
	luxe
	ulex
ELUY	yule✧
ELVY	levy
EMMO	memo
	mome
EMNN	nemn
EMNO	meno
	nome
	omen
EMNT	ment
EMNU	menu
	neum
EMOP	mope
	poem
	pome
EMOR	More!
	more
	omer✧
	Rome
EMOS	mose
	some
EMOT	mote
	tome
EMOU	moue
EMOV	move
EMOW	meow
EMOZ	moze
EMPR	perm
EMPT	temp
EMPY	ympe
EMRT	term
EMRU	mure
	rume
EMSS	mess✧
EMST	stem
	tems
EMSU	muse✧
EMSW	mews
	smew
EMSY	emys
EMTU	mute
EMTZ	Metz
EMYZ	zyme
ENNO	neon
	none
ENOP	nope
	open
	peon
	pone
ENOR	Nero
	oner
	Reno
	rone
ENOS	noes
	nose
	sone
ENOT	Eton
	note
	no'te
	n'ote
	tone
ENOV	oven
ENOW	Owen
ENOX	exon
	oxen
ENOZ	zone
ENPR	pern
ENPT	pent
ENPU	Nupe
ENPY	pyne
ENRT	rent✧
	tern
ENRU	rune
ENRW	wren✧
ENRY	reny
ENSS	ness
	sens
ENST	nest
	nets
	sent
	sten✧
ENSW	news
	sewn
ENSY	snye
	syen
	syne
ENTT	nett
	tent
ENTU	tune
ENTV	vent
ENTW	newt
	went
ENTX	next
ENTY	tyne✧
EOOS	oose
EOOZ	ooze
EOPP	pepo
	pope✧
EOPR	pore
	repo
	rope
EOPS	epos
	peso
	pose
	posé
EOPT	poet
	pote
	tope
EOPX	expo
EORR	rore
EORS	Eros
	rose
	rosé
	sore
EORT	rote
	tore
EORU	euro
	roué
EORV	over
	rove
EORW	ower
	owre
	wore
EORX	oxer
EORY	oyer
	yore
EORZ	zero
EOST	tose
EOSW	woes
EOSY	oyes
EOTT	tote
EOTV	veto
	vote
EOTY	eyot
	toey
EOTZ	toze
EOVW	wove
EOWY	yowe
EOYZ	oyez
EPPR	perp
	prep
	repp
EPQU	quep
EPRS	reps
EPRT	pert
EPRU	Peru
	Prue
	puer
	pure
EPRV	perv
EPRX	prex
EPRY	prey
	pyre
	rype
EPSS	seps
EPST	pest
	sept
	spet✧
	step
EPSU	spue
	supe
EPSW	spew
EPSY	espy
	sype
EPTW	wept
EPTY	pyet
	type
EQUY	quey
ERRS	serr
ERST	rest
	très
ERSU	ruse✧
	rusé
	suer
	sure
	user
ERSV	vers
ERTT	tret
ERTU	true✧
ERTV	vert
ERTW	trew
	wert
ERTX	T Rex
ERTY	trey
	trye
	tyre
ERTZ	trez
ERVY	very
ERYY	eyry
ESSS	sess
ESST	Tess
ESSU	uses
ESSY	yes's
ESTT	sett
	stet
	test
ESTU	suet
	Utes
ESTV	vest
ESTW	stew
	west✧
ESTX	sext
ESTY	stey
	stye
	yest
ESTZ	zest
ESUZ	Suez
	Zeus
ESVY	Yves
ESWY	swey
ESXY	sexy
ETTX	text
ETTY	tyte
	yett
ETVX	vext
ETWY	wyte

F

FFFU	fuff
FFGO	goff
FFGU	guff
FFHU	huff
FFIJ	jiff
FFIM	miff
FFIN	niff
FFIR	riff
FFIT	tiff
FFIY	iffy
FFIZ	ziff
FFKO	koff
FFLU	luff
FFMU	muff
FFNU	nuff
FFOT	toff
FFOY	offy
FFPU	puff
FFRU	ruff
FFTU	tuff
FGIO	figo✧
FGIT	gift
FGIU	Gifu
FGLO	flog
	golf✧
FGLU	gulf✧
FGNU	fung
FGOO	goof
FGOR	frog✧
FGOW	gowf
FGOY	fogy
FGUU	fugu
FHII	hi-fi✧
FHIS	fish✧
FHMU	humf
FHNO	föhn
FHOO	hoof
FHOU	houf
FHOW	howf
FIIJ	Fiji
FIIN	fini
FIJU	Fuji
FIKN	fink
FIKR	firk
FIKS	fisk
FILO	foil
	lo-fi
FILP	flip

Words marked ✧ can also be spelled with one or more capital letters

FILT flit
lift
FILX flix
FIMR firm
FINO foin
info
FINR firn
FIOR Ifor
FIOS Sofi
FIRS fris
FIRT frit
rift
FIRZ friz
FIST sift
FISU Sufi
FITT tift
FITZ Zift
FKLO folk
FKNU funk
FKOR fork
FLLU full
FLOO fool
loof
FLOR Rolf
FLOT loft
FLOU foul
FLOW fowl
wolf
FLRU furl
FMOR form
from
FMUY fumy
FNOT font
FOOP poof
FOOR roof
FOOW woof
FOOY oofy
yoof
FOPR prof
FOPU pouf
FORU four
FORW frow
FOST soft
FOSU ufos✧
FOSW sowf
FOTT toft
FOTU tofu
FOWW wowf
FOYZ fozy
FRRU furr
FRSU surf
FRTU turf
FRUY fury✧
FRUZ zurf
FSSU fuss
FSTU fust
FTTU tuft
FTUY yuft

G

GGHO hogg
GGII Gigi
GGIN ging
GGIR grig
rigg
GGLO Gogl
GGLU glug
GGNO gong
nogg
GGOO gogo
go-go
GGOR grog
GHHI high
GHHO hogh
GHHU Hugh
GHIN hing
nigh
GHIS sigh
GHIT thig
GHIW whig✧
GHLU Lugh
GHNO hong
GHNU hung
GHOS gosh
shog
GHOT Goth
GHOU Hugo
GHOY yogh
GHPU pugh
GHSU gush
GHTU thug
GHUY hugy
GIKN gink
king
GILM glim
GILN ling
GILO Logi
GILR girl
GILS Glis
GILT glit
GILU Ugli®
GIMN ming✧
GIMR grim
GIMS gism
GINO go in
ingo
GINP ping
GINR girn
grin
ring
GINS ings
sign
sing
snig
GINT ting
GINW wing
GINZ zing
GIOR giro✧
GIOT go it
GIOV Vigo
GIOY yogi
GIPR grip
prig
GIRS gris
GIRT grit
trig
GISW swig
GITW twig
GJNU Jung
GJSU jugs
GKNO Gonk®
gonk
GKNU gunk
GKOU gouk
GKOW gowk
GKSU skug
GLLU gull
GLMO glom
GLMU glum
GLNO long
GLNU lung
GLNY Glyn
GLOO gool
logo
GLOP golp
GLOS logs
slog
GLOW gowl
GLOY logy
GLPU gulp
plug
GLRU gurl
GLSU slug
GLTU glut
GLUY guly
ugly
GMNO mong
'mong
GMOO Moog®
GMOR gorm
GMOS smog
GMPU gump
GMPY gymp
GMRU grum
GMSU smug
GNNO nong
GNOO go on
goon
no go
GNOP pong
GNOR rong
GNOS snog
song✧
GNOT tong
GNOW gown
GNRU gurn
rung
GNSU gnus
snug✧
sung✧
GNUZ Günz
GNWY Gwyn
GNYY gyny
GOOP pogo
GOOT Togo
to go
GOOZ Gozo
GOPR gorp
prog
GOPU go up
Ogpu
upgo
GORT grot
trog
GORW grow
GORY Györ
gyro
orgy
GOST togs
GOSY goys
GOTU gout
goût
GOUY Yugo®
GRSU Grus
GRTU trug
GRUU guru
GSTU gust
guts

H

HHIS hish
HHOP phoh
HHOS hohs
HHSU hush
HHUU uh-uh
HIIL hili
HIKO hoik
hoki
HIKS kish
Sikh
HIKT kith
HILO Holi
HILP Phil
HILT lith
HIMO imho
HIMS shim
HIMW whim
HINS hisn
his'n
shin
sinh
HINT thin
HINW whin
HIOO Ohio
HIOP Hopi
Ipoh
HIPS pish
ship
HIPT pith
HIPW whip
HIPZ phiz
HIRS shir
Shri
HIRT thir
HIRW whir
HIST sith
this
Tshi
HISU huis
HISV shiv
HISW wish
HITW whit✧
with
HIWZ whiz
HJNO john✧
HJOS josh✧
HKLO kohl✧
HKLU hulk
HKNO honk
HKNU hunk
HKOO hook✧
HKOP koph
HKOR khor
HKOW howk
HKRU rukh
HKSU husk
sukh
HLLU hull✧
HLMO holm
HLOP holp
HLOS hols
losh
HLOT holt
loth
HLOW howl
HLOY holy
HLPY Phyl
HLRU hurl
HLRY Rhyl
HLSU lush
shul
HLWY hwyl
HMNY hymn
HMOO homo✧
Moho
HMOR mohr
HMOS Homs
mhos
mosh
shmo
HMOT moth✧
HMOW whom
HMOY homy
HMPU hump
umph
HMSU mush
HMTY myth
HNOO hoon
HNOP phon
HNOR horn✧
HNOS nosh
HNOT thon
HNRU Rhun
HNSU shun
'shun

Words marked ✧ can also be spelled with one or more capital letters

HNTU	hunt
	Thun
HOOP	pooh✧
HOOS	shoo
	soho
	so-ho
HOOT	Otho
	toho
HOOY	yo-ho
HOPQ	qoph
HOPS	posh
	shop✧
	soph
HOPT	phot
HOPU	ouph
HOPW	whop
HOPY	hypo
HORS	rhos
HORT	Roth
	Thor
	thro
	thro'
HORU	hour
HOST	shot
	tosh
HOSU	huso
HOSW	show
	who's
HOTU	hout
	thou
HOTW	whot
HOWW	whow
HPRU	pruh
HPSU	push
HPTU	phut
HPUW	whup
HRSU	rhus
	rush✧
HRSY	Rhys
HRTU	hurt
	ruth✧
	thru
HSSU	huss
HSTU	shut
	thus
	tush
HTUU	Hutu
HUUW	Wuhu

I

IIJX	Jixi
IIKT	tiki
IIKW	kiwi
IILP	pili
IILW	wili
IIMN	Mini®
	mini
IIMP	impi
IIMR	miri
IIMS	simi
IINS	nisi
IINT	in it
	inti
IIPP	pipi
IIPT	tipi
IIRS	iris
	siri✧
IISS	Isis
IISW	iwis
IITT	titi
IITZ	ziti
IJKN	jink
IJLL	jill
IJLT	jilt
IJMP	jimp
IJMS	jism
IJNN	jinn
IJNO	join
	Joni
IJNX	jinx
IJOR	roji
IJOS	sijo
IKKN	kink
IKKR	kirk
IKLL	kill
IKLM	milk
IKLN	kiln
	link
IKLO	kilo✧
	Loki
IKLP	kilp
IKLR	lirk
IKLS	lisk
	silk
IKLT	kilt
IKMN	mink
IKMO	moki
IKMR	mirk
IKMS	skim
IKNO	ikon
	kino
	oink
IKNP	pink
IKNR	kirn
	rink
IKNS	sink
	skin
IKNT	knit
	tink
IKNW	wink
IKNY	inky
IKOS	skio
IKPP	kipp✧
IKPS	skip
IKRS	kris
	risk
IKRU	kuri
IKRY	yirk
IKSS	kiss✧
	skis
IKST	kist
	skit
ILLL	lill
ILLM	mill
ILLN	nill
	n'ill
ILLO	Lilo®
ILLP	pill
ILLR	rill
ILLS	sill
ILLT	it'll
	lilt
	till
ILLV	vill
ILLW	will
ILLY	lily
	yill
ILMN	limn
ILMO	limo
	milo
	moil
ILMP	limp
	plim
ILMS	slim✧
ILMT	milt
ILMU	muil
ILMY	limy
ILNN	linn
ILNO	lino
	lion✧
	loin
	noil
ILNR	nirl
ILNT	lint
ILNY	inly
	liny
ILNZ	Linz
ILOO	olio
ILOR	loir
	roil
ILOS	Lois
	oils
	silo
	soil
	soli
ILOT	loti
	toil
ILOV	viol
ILOY	oily
ILPR	pirl
ILPS	lisp✧
	Pils
	slip
ILPU	puli
ILRT	tirl
ILRV	virl
	vril
ILST	list
	'list
	silt
	slit
ILTT	tilt
ILTU	luit
ILTW	wilt
ILVY	Livy
ILWY	wily
IMNO	mino
IMNT	mint
IMNX	minx
IMNY	miny
IMOO	mooi
IMOR	Miró
IMOS	miso
IMOT	moit
	omit
IMPP	pimp
IMPR	prim
IMPS	mips
	simp
IMPU	pium
IMPW	wimp
IMRS	mirs
	smir
IMRT	trim
IMRU	muir
	rimu
IMRV	mirv
IMRY	miry
	rimy
IMSS	miss✧
IMST	mist
	smit
IMSU	Sium
IMSW	swim
IMTT	mitt
IMTU	muti
IMTX	mixt
IMTY	mity
IMXY	mixy
IMZZ	mizz
INNO	in on
INNW	winn
INOP	pion
INOR	inro
	iron
	nori
	roin
INOS	Sion
	Siôn
INOT	into
	not-I
	oint
	Toni
INOU	Unio
INOV	Ivon
	vino
INOW	wino
INOY	yoni
INOZ	Zion
INPR	pirn
INPS	snip
	spin
INPT	pint
INPY	piny
INQU	quin
INRT	trin
INRU	ruin
INST	isn't
	snit
INSU	suni
INTT	tint
INTU	unit✧
INTV	vint
INTW	twin
	win't
INTY	tiny
INUX	Unix
INUZ	Zuni
	Zuñi
INVY	viny
INWY	winy
INXY	lynx
	nixy
IOPT	topi
IOPY	pioy
IORS	sori
IORT	riot
	roti
	tiro
	tori
	trio
IORV	Ivor
	rivo
IORZ	zori
IOSS	Ossi
IOTT	Tito
IOVV	vivo
IPPR	ripp
IPPY	pipy
IPQT	Q-Tip®
IPQU	quip
IPRS	risp
IPRT	ript
	trip
IPRU	puir
	puri
IPST	spit
IPSU	Pius
IPSV	spiv
IPSW	wisp
IPSY	I-spy
	yips
IPTT	Pitt
	tipt
IPTU	Tupi
	Tupí
IPTY	pity
IPUY	Pu Yi
IPXY	pixy
IQTU	quit
IQUZ	quiz
IRRT	tirr
IRSS	Riss
IRST	stir
IRTT	ritt

IRTW writ
IRTX Trix
IRTZ Ritz
IRWY wiry
ISSS siss
ISST sist
ISTT tits
ISTU suit
utis
ISTW wist
wits
ISWY ywis
ISWZ swiz
ISYZ sizy
ITTW twit
ITZZ tizz
IUWX Wuxi
IVYZ vizy
IZZZ zizz

J

JJUU juju
ju-ju
JKNU junk
JKOO jook
JKOU jouk
JKOY joky
JLLO joll
JLOT jolt
JLOW jowl
JLUY July
JMOO jomo
mojo✧
JMPU jump
JNOU Juno
JNRU junr✧
JNXY jynx✧
JOOT Tojo
JORU jour
JOYZ Jozy
JRUY jury
JSTU just

K

KKNO konk
KKOO kook
KKUU kuku
KLNO Köln
KLNU lunk
KLOO kolo
look
KLOP polk
KLOS skol
KLOU oulk
KLOV volk
KLOY yolk
KLPU pulk
KLRU lurk
KLSU lusk
sulk
KMNO monk
KMOO moko
mook
KMOS Omsk
KMRU murk
KMSU musk
KNOO nook
KNOP ponk
KNOT tonk
KNOW wonk
KNOZ zonk
KNPU punk
KNRU knur
KNSU sunk
KNTU knut✧
KOOP pook
KOOR Kroo
rook
KOOS sook
KOOT koto
toko
took
KOPR pork
KOPU pouk
KOPY poky
KORW work
KORY roky
york✧
KOSU souk
KOTU touk
KOUY youk
yuko
KOUZ zouk
KPUU puku
KPUY puky
KRSU rusk
KRSY skry
skyr
KRTU Kurt
Turk
KRUU kuru
Uruk
KSTU tusk
KSUY Suky
KUUZ kuzu
KUYY yuky

L

LLLO loll
LLLU lull
LLMO moll✧
LLMU mull✧
LLNO noll
LLNU null
LLOP poll✧
LLOR roll
LLOT toll
LLPU pull
LLUU lulu✧
LLUW wull
LLVV vvll
LMOO loom
mool
LMOT molt
LMOU Lomu
LMOY moly
moyl
LMPU lump
plum
LMRU murl
LMSU slum
LNNY Lynn
LNOO loon
LNOR lorn
LNOU loun
noul
LNOW lown
nowl
LNOY Lyon
only
LNRU nurl
LNTU lunt
LNUV vuln
LNXY lynx✧
LOOP polo
pool
LOOS Oslo
solo
LOOT loto
tool
LOOW wool
LOPP plop
LOPS slop
LOPT plot
polt
LOPU loup
LOPW plow
LOPY ploy
poly
LORT rotl
LORU lour
roul
LOST lots
slot
LOSU soul✧
LOSW Owls
slow
sowl
LOTT tolt
LOTU lout
tolu✧
LOTV volt
LOTW lowt
LOUU Oulu
LOVV Lvov
LOWY owly
yowl
LPPU pulp✧
LPRU purl
LPSU plus
puls
LPUU pulu
LPUY puly
LRSU slur
LRUY ruly
LSTU lust
slut
LSUU sulu✧
LTUZ lutz
LUUZ zulu✧

M

MMMU mumm
MMPU mump
MNOO mono
moon✧
MNOR morn
norm
MNOS Mons
MNOU muon
MNOW mown
MNOY mony
MNTU munt
MOOP po-mo
MOOR Moro
Romo
room
MOOS soom
MOOT toom
MOOZ zoom
MOPP pomp
MOPR prom
romp
MOPU moup
MOPY yomp
MORU roum
MORW worm
MOSU muso
soum
sumo
MOSW sowm
MOUV ovum
MPPU pump
MPRU rump✧
MPSU sump
MPTU tump
MPTY tymp
ympt
MPUY pumy
yump
MRSU smur
MRTU turm
MRUW Würm
MSSU muss
MSTU must
smut
stum
MSUW swum
MSUY sumy
MTTU mutt

N

NNOO no-no
noon
NNOR Norn
NNOU non-U
noun
NNOW nown
NNSU sunn
NNWY wynn
NOOP poon
NOOR roon
NOOS oons
soon
NOOT onto
oont
toon
NOOW woon
NOOX Oxon
NOOZ zoon
NOPR porn
NOPS pons
NOPT pont
NOPU noup
upon
NOPW pown
NOPY pony
NORS sorn
NORT ront
torn
tron
NORU ourn
NORW worn
NOST onst
snot
tons
NOSU nous
onus
NOSW snow
sown
NOTU nout
toun
unto
NOTW nowt
town
wont
won't
NOTY tony✧
yont
NOXY onyx
NPSU spun
NPTU punt
NPUY puny
NPXY Pnyx
NRRU nurr
NRSU runs
NRTU runt
turn
NSTU nuts
stun
NTUY tuny
NUXY yunx

O

OOPP oppo

poop
OOPR poor
proo
roop
OOPS soop
OOPT poot
topo
OOPY yoop
OORR ro-ro
OORS or so
soor
OORT root
OORZ orzo
OOSS so so
so-so
OOST soot
OOTT otto✧
toot
Toto
OOTW woot
woo't
OOUZ ouzo
OOYY yo-yo
OOYZ oozy
OPPR prop
OPPS pops
OPQU quop
OPRS pros
OPRT port
OPRU pour
roup
OPRW prow
OPRY pory
pyro
ropy
OPSS poss
OPST post
pots
spot
stop
tops
OPSU opus
soup
OPSW sowp
swop
OPSY posy
OPTT pott
OPTU pout
OPTY pyot
typo
OPXY poxy
OPZZ pozz
ORRT rort
torr
ORRY rory✧
ORSS Ross
ORST orts
rost
sort
ORSU ours
sour✧
ORSY rosy
ORTT tort
trot✧
ORTU rout
tour
ORTW rowt
trow
wort
ORTY ryot
Tory
troy✧
tyro
ORUX roux
ORUY your
ORVW vrow
ORXY oryx
OSSS soss
OSST toss
OSSU sous
OSSV Voss
OSTT stot
tost
OSTU oust
outs
sout
OSTW stow
swot
wost
wots
OTTU tout
OTTW towt
OTWY towy
OYZZ Ozzy

P

PRRU purr
rurp
PRSU spur
PRSY prys
spry
PRTY tryp
PSSU puss
PSTU Supt
PSUY upsy
PTTU putt
PTUZ putz

R

RRUU ruru
RSSU Russ
USSR
RSTU rust
RSUU urus
RTUY yurt

S

SSSU suss
SSUU susu✧
SSUW wuss
SSUY Susy
STTU tuts
STXY Styx
xyst
SUYZ Suzy

T

TTUU tutu✧

5 letters

A

AAABC abaca
Caaba
AAABK Kaaba
AAABQ Aqaba
AAABR araba
AAABY abaya
AAADN Adana
AAAFR afara
AAAGM Agama
AAAGN Agana
AAAKM kaama
AAALP alaap
alapa
AAANN anana
AAANS asana
Sana'a
AAASV Vaasa
AABBG gabba
AABBK kabab
AABCC bacca
AABCI abaci
AABCK aback
AABCL cabal
AABCR barca
AABCS cabas
AABDL Abd-al
labda
AABDN aband
banda
AABEM abeam
ameba
AABER abear
AABES abase
AABET abate
AABFT abaft
BAFTA
AABGL Galba
AABGM gamba
AABHI Bahai
Baha'i
AABHS abash
AABIL labia
AABIN bania✧
AABIR braai
AABIS baisa
AABIZ baiza
AABJN bajan✧
AABJR bajra
AABJU Abuja
Bajau
AABKS abask
AABLN Alban
banal
Laban
nabla
AABLR labra
AABLS balas
balsa
basal
Sabal
AABLT tabla
AABMM mamba
AABMN amban
AABMR abram✧
AABMS samba
AABNS basan
AABNT Banat
AABNU abuna
AABNW bwana
nawab
AABNY banya
Bayan
AABOR aroba
AABRR Barra
AABRS Basra
sabra
AABRT rabat✧
AABRV brava
AABRY abray
Araby
AABRZ bazar
zabra
AABST basta
AABSU sauba
AABTT at bat
at-bat
batta
AABZZ Bazza
AACCD Dacca
AACCE caeca
AACCO cacao
AACCR Accra
AACCY yacca
AACDH dacha
AACEI aecia
AACEP apace
AACER areca
AACFI facia
AACHK kacha
AACHM Macha
AACHN chana
AACHP pacha
AACHR achar
chara
AACHS Sacha
AACHY chaya
AACIR acari
Arica
Ciara
AACIS Isaac
AACKL alack
AACLL calla
AACLN canal
AACLP calpa
AACLR Carla
Clara
AACLS scala
AACMN caman

AACMO Macao
AACMS camas
AACMW macaw
AACNN canna
AACNT tacan✧
AACNV Cavan
AACNZ Anzac
AACPR carap
Parca
AACPS scapa
AACRS sacra
AACRT carat
carta
AACSU causa
AACUV vacua
AADDG Dagda
AADDR adrad
AADDX addax
AADEG adage
AADEH ahead
AADEL Adela
aldea
AADEN Danae
AADER Ardea
aread
AADFL afald
AADFR daraf
fa'ard
farad
AADGG dagga
AADGM Magda
AADGR darga
garda
AADHI Haida
AADHK Dhaka
AADHL hadal
AADHM Ahmad
AADHR Radha
AADIN Aidan
Diana
Nadia
naiad
AADIO ao dai
AADIP apaid
AADKR Dakar
AADKY Dayak
AADLN Åland
aland
AADLS salad
AADLT datal
AADLU Duala
Lauda
AADLW dwaal
AADMM madam✧
AADMN adman
ad-man
daman
AADMP padma✧
AADMR damar
drama
AADMS Adams
AADMZ Mazda®
AADNN Adnan
AADNP panda
AADNR R and A
AADNU Nuada
AADNV V and A
AADNW Wanda
AADNY dayan
AADOR A-road
AADOV Davao
AADPT adapt
AADPU Padua
AADPY apayd
AADRR radar
AADRS Ardas
AADRW award
AADSY adays
AADSZ sadza
AADTY adyta
AAEFR afear
AAEGL algae✧
galea
AAEGP agape
apage
AAEGT agate
a'gate
AAEGV agave
AAEGZ agaze
AAEHP aheap
AAEKL Akela
AAEKP apeak
AAEKW awake
AAELP palae
palea
AAELR areal
AAELT alate
talea
AAELV avale
AAELX Alexa
AAEMR arame
marae
AAEMS Saame
AAEMT amate
AAEMZ amaze
AAENP apnea
paean
AAENR anear
arena
AAENT antae
AAENV Avena
AAERR arear
AAERS rasae
AAERT Areta
reata
AAERU aurae
AAERW aware
AAEST at sea
AAEVW awave
AAFFJ jaffa✧
AAFHI Haifa
AAFHL halfa
AAFHR Farah
AAFHT Fatah
AAFIM mafia✧
AAFIN Naafi
AAFIT tafia
AAFJL aflaj
falaj
AAFKK Kafka
AAFKN nakfa
AAFLN fanal
AAFLT fatal
AAFLV flava
AAFNU fauna✧
AAFRY yarfa
AAFTW fatwa
AAGGR ragga
AAGHL galah
AAGHN Ghana
AAGHR aargh
Hagar
AAGIL agila
AAGIM agami
AAGIN again
AAGIS saiga
AAGIT gaita
taiga
AAGJN ganja
AAGKN kanga✧
AAGLL algal
AAGLM Gamal
AAGLN alang
lagan
AAGLR argal
graal
AAGLV vagal
AAGLY gayal
AAGLZ gazal
AAGMM gamma
magma
AAGMN manga
AAGMR grama
AAGMT tagma
AAGMY gamay
AAGNN ngana
AAGNP pagan
panga
AAGNR argan
grana
AAGNS Sagan
AAGNT tanga✧
AAGNU guana
AAGOR agora
AAGRZ gazar
AAGST agast
AAGSV avgas
AAGUV guava
AAGZZ Gazza
AAHIS Aisha
AAHJL jhala
AAHJR rajah
AAHKL kahal
AAHKM hakam
Makah
AAHKS kasha
AAHKY khaya
AAHLL Allah
halal
AAHLM almah
halma
hamal
AAHLN nahal✧
AAHLO aloha
AAHLP alpha✧
AAHLR lahar
AAHLS Lhasa
AAHLV halva
AAHMO haoma✧
Omaha
AAHMR haram
marah
AAHMS Hamas
shama
AAHMU mahua
AAHMW mahwa
AAHMZ hamza✧
AAHNP hanap
AAHNS Hansa
Hasan
AAHNT thana
AAHNZ hazan
AAHPR Aphra
AAHPS pasha
AAHRR arrah
AAHRS Sarah
AAHRT Hatra
ratha
AAHRY rayah
AAHRZ Zahra
AAHSS Sasha
AAHST hasta
AAHSU Hausa
AAHSW awash✧
sawah
AAHSY Aysha
shaya
AAHTV tavah
AAHVZ Ahvaz
AAIJN Jaina
AAIKK kaiak
AAIKL laika✧
AAIKS Sakai
sakia
AAIKT akita
kiaat
AAIKU Kauai
AAILM lamia
AAILN Anila
Ilana
lanai✧
liana✧
AAILR laari
AAILS Ailsa

	alias
AAILT	Itala
AAILV	avail
	Ávila
AAILX	axial
AAILY	aliya
AAIMN	amain
	Amina
	amnia
	anima
	mania
AAIMR	maria✧
AAIMS	Masai
AAIMT	Amati
	matai
AAIMZ	zamia
AAINP	apian
AAINR	Arian
	naira
AAINS	Anaïs
	Asian
	Naias
AAINT	Anita
	Tania
AAINV	avian
	Ivana
AAIPR	Praia
AAIPS	paisa
AAIPV	Pavia
AAIRT	Arita
	atria
	raita
	riata
	taira
	tiara
AAISS	assai
AAISV	Saiva
AAITW	await
AAJKR	Karaj
AAJLM	Jamal
AAJLP	jalap
AAJNN	jnana
AAJNP	japan✧
AAJNV	Javan
AAJNW	ajwan
	jawan
AAJNZ	zanja
AAJQR	Qajar
AAJRT	jarta
AAKKN	Kanak
AAKKP	pakka
AAKKS	akkas
AAKKY	kayak
	yakka
AAKKZ	Kazak
AAKLM	Kamal
AAKLO	koala
AAKLP	kalpa
AAKLR	Karla
	kraal
AAKLS	laksa
AAKLT	katal
	talak
AAKMR	karma
	makar
	marka
AAKNT	Kanta
	tanka✧
AAKNZ	Kazan
AAKOP	poaka
AAKOS	Osaka
AAKPP	kappa
AAKPR	parka
AAKRT	karat
AAKST	Sakta
AAKSV	vakas
AAKTY	Katya
AAKTZ	zakat
AALLL	Lalla
AALLM	llama
AALLN	Allan
	nalla
AALLP	palla
AALLS	salal
AALLT	at all
AALLU	alula
AALLW	walla
AALLY	allay
	Layla
AALMO	Alamo
AALMP	Palma
AALMR	alarm
	malar
	ramal
AALMT	Malta
	talma
	tamal
AALMV	malva
AALMX	malax
AALMY	Malay
AALNN	annal
AALNS	Aslan
	nasal
AALNT	natal✧
AALNU	Nuala
AALNV	naval
AALNY	Al Ayn
	nyala
AALNZ	Lanza
AALOS	saola
AALOT	Aalto
AALPP	appal
	papal
AALPS	palas
	salpa
AALPT	talpa✧
AALPU	Palau
	Paula
AALPY	palay
	playa
AALPZ	La Paz
	plaza
AALQT	talaq
AALRT	altar
	artal
	talar
	tra-la
AALRU	aural
	laura✧
AALRV	arval
	larva
	lavra
AALRY	alary
AALRZ	lazar
AALSS	salsa
AALST	atlas✧
	talas
AALSV	lavas
	vasal
AALWY	alway
AAMMM	mamma
AAMMN	amman✧
AAMNN	manna
AAMNS	Masan
	saman
AAMNT	atman
	manat
	manta✧
AAMNX	axman
AAMNY	many a
	Mayan
AAMNZ	zaman
AAMOR	aroma
AAMOS	omasa
	Samoa
AAMPP	pampa
AAMPR	Parma
	praam
AAMPT	Tampa
AAMRT	Marat
	Tamar
AAMRU	Maura
AAMSS	amass
	Assam
	massa
AAMTZ	matza
AANNN	nanna✧
AANNO	Anona
AANNT	annat
	tanna
AANNW	wanna
AANOR	Aaron
AANOX	xoana
AANPP	nappa
AANPR	prana
AANPS	sapan
AANPT	Patna
AANPV	pavan
AANPX	panax
AANQT	qanat
AANRR	Arran
AANRS	naras
	Saran®
AANRT	antar
	antra
	ratan
AANRU	Anura
	Aruna
	ruana
AANRV	varan
	varna✧
AANRW	Anwar
	awarn
AANRY	Aryan
	nary a
	Nayar
AANSS	sansa
AANST	Satan
AANSU	sauna
AANSW	Aswan
AANTV	avant
AANTY	Tanya
AAORT	aorta
AAOST	Aosta
AAPPT	tappa
AAPPW	papaw
AAPPY	appay
AAPRT	apart
	at par
AAPST	pasta
	tapas
AAPTT	attap
AAPTW	watap
AAPWW	pawaw
AAQRT	Qatar
AAQRZ	Zarqa
AARRS	arras✧
AARRU	aurar
AARRY	array
AARST	rasta✧
	tasar
AARSU	auras
AARTT	attar
	Tatar
AARTY	tayra
	yarta
AARUW	Urawa
AASSW	as was
AASSY	assay
AASTV	avast
AASTY	satay
AASWY	asway
	aways
AATXY	ataxy
AATZZ	tazza
ABBCO	bobac
	cabob
ABBCY	cabby
ABBDN	B and B
ABBEE	Babee
ABBEK	kebab
ABBEL	babel✧
ABBER	barbe
ABBFY	fabby

ABBGY	gabby✧
ABBIJ	jibba
ABBIM	Bambi
ABBIR	rabbi✧
ABBKO	bobak
	kabob
ABBKU	Bubka
ABBLO	Balbo
ABBLU	babul
	bubal
ABBMO	A-bomb
ABBNO	nabob
ABBNY	Nabby
ABBOO	baboo
ABBQR	bar-b-q
ABBRS	barbs
ABBRU	Babur
ABBTY	tabby
ABBYY	yabby
ABCCO	bacco
	bocca
	caboc
ABCCY	baccy
ABCDN	c and b
ABCEH	beach
ABCEI	ceiba
ABCEL	cable
ABCER	acerb
	brace
	caber
	cabré
ABCHI	Chiba
ABCHO	cohab
ABCHR	brach
ABCHT	batch
ABCIN	Binca®
	cabin
ABCIO	cobia
ABCIR	baric
	Carib
	rabic
ABCIS	basic✧
ABCJO	Jacob
ABCKL	black✧
ABCKR	brack
ABCNO	bacon✧
	banco
ABCNU	Cuban
ABCOR	carob
	coarb
	cobra
ABCOT	Cabot
ABCOV	vocab
ABCOZ	cobza
ABCRS	crabs
	scrab
ABCRT	bract
ABCRY	carby
ABCSU	scuba
ABDDE	bedad
ABDDY	baddy
ABDEG	badge
	begad
	debag
ABDEI	abide
ABDEK	baked
ABDEL	abled
	blade
ABDEM	bemad
ABDEN	Baden
	Bände
ABDEO	abode
	adobe
ABDER	ardeb
	beard
	bread
	Breda
	debar
	Debra
ABDES	based
	beads
ABDEU	daube
ABDEY	beady
ABDGO	go bad
ABDHN	bandh
ABDIL	ad lib
	adlib
	ad-lib
ABDIR	braid
	rabid
ABDIT	tabid
ABDIU	Dubai
ABDKL	balk'd
ABDLN	bland
ABDLU	Abdul
	blaud
ABDLY	badly
	baldy
ABDNR	brand
	R and B
ABDNS	bands
ABDNY	bandy
ABDOR	abord
	bardo
	board
	broad
	dobra
ABDOY	a'body
ABDRS	bards
ABDRY	bardy
ABDUY	dauby
ABDWY	bawdy
ABEEL	abele
	albee✧
ABEER	beare
ABEFL	fable
ABEGI	bigae
ABEGL	bagel
	belga
	gable
ABEGN	began
	benga
ABEGR	barge
	begar
	garbe
ABEGT	begat
ABEHJ	hejab
ABEHK	bekah
ABEHL	belah
	hable
ABEHM	H-beam
ABEHO	bohea
	obeah
ABEHR	Behar
	rehab
ABEHS	Sheba
ABEHT	bathe
	beath
ABEIM	I-beam
ABEIR	Beira
	erbia
ABEIS	abies
ABEIZ	baize
ABEJL	jelab
ABEJM	jambe
ABEKL	Blake
	bleak
ABEKN	baken
ABEKR	baker
	brake
	break
ABEKY	beaky
ABELL	all-be
	be-all
	Bella
	label
ABELM	amble
	blame
	Mabel
	melba
ABELO	Ebola
ABELR	abler
	baler
	blare
	blear
ABELS	Basle
	blaes
	blasé
	sable
ABELT	ablet
	blate
	bleat
	table
ABELY	bayle
	belay
ABELZ	blaze
ABEMR	amber
	brame
	bream
	embar
ABEMS	Sabme
ABEMW	weamb
ABEMY	beamy
	embay
	maybe
ABENO	beano
ABENS	basen
	beans
ABENU	abune
ABEOR	abore
ABEOT	E-boat
ABEOV	above
ABEPT	bepat
ABERR	barre
	barré
	re-bar
ABERS	saber
	sabre
ABERV	brave
ABERY	barye
	beray
	yerba
ABERZ	braze
	zebra
ABESS	bases
	basse
ABEST	baste
	beast✧
	Sebat
	tabes
ABESU	abuse
	beaus
ABESY	absey
ABETU	beaut
	Butea
	taube
	tubae
ABEUX	beaux
ABEUZ	buaze
ABFFN	Banff
ABFFU	buffa
ABFFY	baffy
ABFLT	B flat
ABFRY	by far
ABGGR	Bragg
ABGGY	baggy
ABGHI	bigha
ABGHN	bhang
ABGIN	ba'ing
ABGIR	Bragi
ABGIS	bags I
ABGMO	gambo
ABGNO	bogan
	Gabon
	obang
ABGNS	bangs
ABGNU	unbag
ABGOR	garbo✧
ABGOT	Bagot
ABHIJ	bhaji
	hijab
ABHIR	Bihar
ABHIS	sahib
ABHIT	habit

ABHLS	blash
ABHNU	bhuna
ABHOS	basho
ABHOT	Botha
ABHRS	brash
ABHST	baths
ABHSU	subah
ABHTU	bahut
ABIIL	alibi
ABIIM	iambi
ABIIT	tibia
ABIIZ	Ibiza
ABIJO	Baoji
ABIJR	bajri
ABIJS	basij✧
ABIKT	batik
ABILN	blain
ABILO	aboil
ABILQ	qibla
ABILR	Blair
	brail
	libra✧
ABILS	basil✧
	labis
ABILT	balti
	Talib
ABILY	Libya
ABIMR	abrim
	imbar
	mbira
ABIMS	Sabmi
ABIMT	ambit
ABINR	abrin
	bairn
	brain
	Brian
	Rabin
ABINS	basin
	Nabis
	sabin
ABINU	bunia
	nubia
ABINV	bavin
ABIOO	booai
ABIOT	biota
ABIRR	briar
ABIRU	rubai
	Rubia
ABIRV	bravi
ABIRY	by air
ABISS	basis
	bassi
ABIST	absit
ABIWZ	bwazi
ABJMO	jambo
ABJMU	jambu
ABJNO	banjo
ABJOT	jabot
ABKLN	blank
ABKLU	baulk
	Kabul
ABKLY	balky
ABKNO	koban
ABKNR	brank
ABKNS	Banks
ABKOR	borak
ABKRU	burka
ABKRY	barky
	braky
ABLLS	balls
ABLLU	bulla✧
ABLLY	bally
ABLMU	album
ABLMY	balmy
ABLNU	balun
	Lubna
ABLOO	baloo✧
ABLOR	Balor
	labor
	lobar
ABLOS	bolas
ABLOT	Balto
	bloat
ABLRW	brawl
ABLST	blast
ABLTT	blatt
ABLTU	tubal
ABLWY	bylaw
ABLYY	lay by
	lay-by
ABMMO	mambo
ABMOS	ambos
	sambo
ABMOT	Tomba
ABMOZ	zambo
ABMRU	Burma
	rumba
	umbra
ABMRY	ambry
	barmy
ABMSY	abysm
ABMUY	mauby
ABNNO	Boann
ABNNS	banns
ABNOR	baron
	Brona
ABNOS	bason
ABNOT	baton
ABNOZ	bonza
ABNRU	buran
	unbar
	urban✧
ABNRW	brawn
ABNRY	Bryan
ABNSU	Busan
ABNTU	bantu✧
	tabun✧
ABNUY	bunya
ABNYZ	Zyban®
ABOOT	taboo
ABOOV	ab ovo
ABOOY	booay
	ya-boo
ABOOZ	bazoo
ABOQT	Q-boat
ABORR	arbor
ABORS	Bosra
ABORT	boart
	tabor
ABORV	bravo✧
ABORX	borax
ABORY	boyar
ABORZ	Zorba
ABOSS	basso
ABOST	basto
	boast
	sabot
ABOTU	about
	U-boat
ABOTW	bowat
ABOUY	bayou
	boyau
ABQRU	burqa
ABQSU	squab
ABRRY	Barry
ABRSS	brass
ABRST	Bart's
	brast
ABRSU	Abrus
	bursa
ABRSW	braws
ABRTU	tubar
ABRTY	rybat
ABRWY	warby
ABRXY	braxy
ABSSW	swabs
ABSSY	abyss
	bassy
ABSTT	batts
ABSTU	tabus
	tsuba
	tubas
ABTTU	battu
ABTTY	batty
ABWYY	byway
ACCDE	Decca®
ACCDY	cycad
ACCEH	cache
	chace
ACCEL	cecal
ACCEM	Mecca
ACCHI	chica
ACCHK	chack
ACCHO	chaco
	coach
ACCHT	catch
ACCIR	circa
	craic
ACCIT	cacti
	ticca
ACCIW	wicca✧
ACCKL	clack
ACCKO	acock
ACCKR	crack
ACCMO	occam
ACCOO	cocoa
ACCOS	casco
ACCOT	coact
ACCUY	yucca
ACDDE	decad
ACDDN	D and C
ACDDY	caddy
ACDEE	cadee
ACDEF	faced
ACDEG	cadge
	caged
ACDEI	cadie
ACDEL	clade
	decal
	laced
ACDEN	acned
	dance
ACDEP	paced
ACDER	acred
	arced
	cadre
	cedar
ACDET	cadet
ACDEY	decay
ACDGN	C and G
ACDGY	cadgy
ACDHN	h and c
ACDHO	ad hoc
ACDHR	chard
ACDIL	calid
ACDIN	canid
	cnida
	nicad
ACDIR	acrid
	caird
	cardi
	daric
ACDIS	Asdic
ACDIT	diact
	dicta
ACDIY	acidy
ACDIZ	Cádiz
ACDLO	acold
ACDLS	scald
ACDLU	cauld
	Claud
	ducal
ACDLY	yclad
ACDMO	Madoc
ACDNO	can do
	can-do
ACDNS	scand
ACDNU	adunc
	Candu
ACDNW	C and W
ACDNY	candy✧
	dancy
ACDOR	Draco
ACDOT	octad

ACDRS	cards
ACDRY	cardy
	darcy
ACDSS	scads
ACDSU	scaud
ACDTU	ducat
ACEEK	ackee
ACEEP	peace
ACEES	caese
	cease
ACEEZ	ceaze
ACEFH	chafe
ACEFL	fecal
ACEFR	facer
	farce
ACEFT	facet
ACEGL	glacé
ACEGR	grace✧
ACEGY	cagey
ACEHK	cheka✧
	hacek
ACEHL	chela
	leach
ACEHN	caneh
	hance
	nache
ACEHP	chape
	cheap
	peach
ACEHR	chare
	rache
	reach
ACEHS	chase
ACEHT	cheat
	Hecat
	tache
	teach
	theca
ACEHV	chave
ACEIL	Alice
	Celia
	ileac
	Leica®
ACEIM	amice
ACEIN	eniac
ACEIP	Picea
ACEIR	ceria
	erica✧
ACEIS	saice
ACEIV	cavie
ACEKL	Aleck
ACEKR	crake
	creak
ACEKW	wacke
ACEKY	cakey
ACELL	cella
ACELM	camel
	clame
	macle
ACELN	ancle
	clean
	lance
ACELP	caple
	place✧
ACELR	Clare
	clear
	recal
ACELS	claes
	scale
ACELT	cleat
	éclat
	lacet
ACELV	calve
	cavel
	clave
ACELY	lacey
ACEMO	cameo
	comae
ACEMR	crame
	cream
	macer
ACEMY	cymae
ACENO	canoe
	ocean
ACENP	pance
	pecan
ACENR	caner
	crane
	crena
	nacre
	rance
ACENS	scena
ACENT	enact
ACEOR	ocrea
ACEOT	coate
ACEOX	coxae
ACEPR	caper
	crape
	pacer
	Perca
	recap
ACEPS	scape
	'scape
	space
ACEPT	epact
ACEPX	capex
ACEPY	pacey
ACERR	carer
	Carré
	crare
	racer
ACERS	acres
	carse
	César
	races
	scare
	scrae
	serac
	sérac
ACERT	caret
	carte
	cater
	crate
	react
	recta
	trace
ACERU	Eruca
ACERV	carve
	caver
	crave
	varec
ACERX	carex
ACERZ	craze
ACEST	caste
	cates
	sceat
ACESU	cause
	'cause
	sauce
ACETT	tacet
ACETU	acute
ACETX	exact
ACETZ	Aztec
ACFFH	chaff
ACFFO	ca' off
ACFFS	scaff
ACFHT	chaft
ACFHU	chufa
ACFIL	calif
ACFIM	mafic
ACFIR	Afric
	farci
ACFIS	fasci
ACFKL	flack
ACFKR	frack
ACFLO	focal
ACFLS	calfs
ACFNR	franc
ACFNY	fancy
ACFPU	FA Cup
ACFRS	scarf
ACFRT	craft
	fract
ACFRY	farcy
ACGHN	ganch
ACGIM	gamic
	magic
ACGIR	cigar✧
	craig✧
ACGLN	clang
ACGNO	conga
ACGOR	cargo
ACGOT	cagot
ACGOU	guaco
ACGRS	scrag
ACGSS	CS gas
ACGUY	gaucy
ACGWY	gawcy
ACHHN	hanch
ACHHT	hatch
ACHIK	haick
ACHIM	Chaim
	Micah
ACHIN	chain
	Chian
	china✧
ACHIO	chiao
ACHIR	chair
ACHIT	aitch
	Chita
ACHKL	chalk✧
ACHKN	chank
ACHKR	chark
ACHKS	shack
ACHKT	thack
ACHKW	whack
ACHLN	lanch
ACHLO	loach
ACHLR	larch
ACHLS	clash
ACHLT	latch
ACHLU	lauch
ACHLV	Vlach
ACHMO	macho
	mocha✧
ACHMP	champ
ACHMR	charm
	march✧
ACHMS	Chams
	chasm
ACHMT	match
ACHNO	nacho
ACHNR	ranch
ACHNT	chant
	natch
ACHNU	nucha
ACHOP	phoca✧
	poach
ACHOR	orach
	roach
ACHOS	chaos
	oshac
ACHOT	chota
	tacho
ACHOV	havoc
ACHPR	parch
ACHPS	chaps✧
	Pasch
ACHPT	patch
ACHRR	charr
ACHRS	chars
	crash
ACHRT	chart
	ratch
ACHRY	Archy
	chary
ACHST	scath
ACHSU	sauch
ACHSW	schwa
ACHTW	watch
ACHTY	Cathy
	yacht
ACIIL	cilia
	iliac✧

ACIIM	amici
ACIIN	acini
ACIIS	Isiac
ACIKS	saick
ACILL	lilac
ACILM	claim
	malic
ACILN	linac
ACILP	plica
ACILR	Clair
ACILS	Alcis
	salic✧
	scail
ACILT	cital
	ictal
	tical
ACILU	aulic
	Lucia
ACILV	cavil
ACILX	calix
ACIMN	manic
	Nicam
ACIMR	cimar
	micra
ACIMS	camis
	micas
	misca'
ACINN	Incan
ACINO	conia
ACINP	panic
ACINR	cairn
	in-car
ACINS	Canis
	Sican
ACINT	actin
	antic
	can it
ACINV	vinca
ACIOR	Cairo
ACIOT	coati
ACIOZ	azoic
ACIPR	Capri
	carpi
	picra
ACIPS	aspic
	scapi
	spica✧
ACIPZ	capiz
ACIRT	artic
ACIRU	auric
	curia
ACIRV	vicar
	vraic
ACITT	attic✧
	tacit
ACITU	Utica
ACITV	vatic
ACJKS	jacks
ACJNU	cajun✧
ACKKN	knack
ACKLN	clank
ACKLO	cloak
ACKLP	plack
ACKLS	slack
ACKLU	caulk
ACKMS	smack
ACKMU	amuck
ACKNR	crank
ACKNS	snack
ACKOR	croak
ACKOW	wacko
ACKPU	pucka
ACKQU	quack
ACKRT	track
ACKRW	wrack
ACKST	stack
ACKSW	swack
ACKTY	tacky
ACKWY	wacky
ACLLO	local
	lo-cal
ACLLS	scall
ACLMO	cloam
	comal
ACLMP	clamp
ACLMS	calms
ACLMU	Calum
ACLMY	calmy
ACLNU	Lucan
ACLOP	copal
ACLOR	carol✧
	claro
	coral
	Lorca
ACLOT	octal
ACLOV	vocal
ACLOW	cowal
ACLOX	coxal
ACLOY	coaly
ACLOZ	colza
ACLPS	clasp
	scalp
ACLPU	capul
ACLRT	clart
ACLRW	crawl
ACLRY	Carly
	clary
	Lycra®
ACLSS	class
ACLSU	Lucas
ACLSV	Sclav
ACLSY	scaly
ACLTU	claut
ACLTY	talcy
ACLXY	calyx
ACMMO	comma
ACMNO	Mâcon
	macon
ACMOP	campo
ACMOR	carom
	coram
	macro
ACMOS	Mosca
ACMPR	cramp
ACMPS	scamp
ACMPY	campy
ACMRS	scram
ACMRY	cymar
ACMSU	camus✧
	Musca
	sumac
ACMSY	cymas
ACNNO	ancon
	canon
	cañon
ACNNY	canny
	Nancy
ACNOP	capon
	Copán
ACNOR	Acorn®
	acorn
	narco
	racon
ACNOS	Oscan
ACNOT	act on
	acton
	canto
ACNOW	cowan
ACNOX	caxon
ACNPU	uncap
ACNRS	narcs
	scran
ACNRY	carny
ACNST	canst
	scant
ACNTY	canty
ACOPR	copra
ACOPS	capos
	pacos
	scopa
ACOPT	capot
	coapt
ACORS	Oscar®
	oscar✧
ACORT	actor
	Croat
	taroc
ACORY	oracy
ACOST	ascot✧
	coast✧
	costa
	tacos
	Tosca
ACOTT	cotta
ACPPU	cuppa
ACPRS	craps
	scarp
	scrap
ACPRY	crapy
ACPSU	scaup
ACPSY	spacy
ACPTU	act up
	caput
ACRRU	crura
ACRRY	carry
ACRSS	crass
ACRST	scart✧
	scrat
ACRSU	arcus
	scaur
ACRSW	scraw
ACRSY	Carys
	scary
	scray
ACRTT	T-cart
	tract
ACRTU	curat
ACRTY	Tracy
ACRVY	carvy
ACRYZ	crazy
ACSSU	ascus
ACSTT	scatt
ACSTU	actus
	scuta
ACSTY	Stacy
ACSUY	saucy
ACTTY	catty
ADDDY	daddy
ADDEI	Addie
	aided
	idea'd
ADDEJ	jaded
	Jedda
ADDEL	addle
	dedal
	laded
ADDER	adred
	aredd
	dared
	dread
ADDET	dated
ADDEV	Vedda
ADDEZ	dazed
ADDFY	faddy
ADDIM	madid
ADDIV	David
ADDNO	add-on
ADDNY	dandy
ADDOR	dorad
ADDOS	dados
	saddo
ADDOT	add to
ADDPU	add up
ADDPY	paddy✧
ADDRY	dryad
	ydrad
ADDWY	waddy
ADEEL	Adèle
ADEEM	edema
	Medea
ADEER	arede
	deare
	eared
ADEES	aedes

Words marked ✧ can also be spelled with one or more capital letters

ADEET teade
teaed
ADEEV deave
evade
ADEFG fadge
ADEFM famed
ADEFR fader
Freda
ADEFT defat
fated
ADEFZ fazed
ADEGG gadge
ADEGJ gadje
ADEGL glade
ADEGM madge✧
ADEGR Edgar
Gerda
grade
radge
ragde
ADEGS degas✧
ADEGT gated
ADEGU agued
ADEGW waged
ADEHJ jehad
ADEHK kheda
ADEHL heald
ADEHM Ahmed
ADEHR heard
ADEHS Hades
heads
sadhe
shade
ADEHT death
ADEHX hexad
ADEHY heady
ADEIL Delia
eliad
ideal
ADEIM à demi
amide
media
ADEIN Adeni
Aiden
Andie
daine
Diane
ADEIR aider
irade
redia
ADEIS A-side
aside
Sadie
ADEIU adieu
ADEIV Davie
ADEIW waide
ADEIZ azide
ADEJR Jared
ADEJW jawed
ADEKL Dalek
ADEKN knead
naked
ADEKR daker
drake✧
ADEKW waked
ADELL dalle
Della
ladle
ADELM lamed
meal'd
medal
ADELN eland
laden
lande
ADELO aloed
ADELP padle
pedal
plead
ADELR alder
ADELS leads
slade
ADELT dalet
Datel®
dealt
delta✧
lated
ADELW dwale
weald✧
ADELY delay
leady
ADELZ Zelda
ADEMM damme
ADEMN amend
deman
Mande
maned
Medan
named
ADEMR ad rem
armed
derma
dream
mear'd
ADEMU Maude
Medau
ADEMW wamed
ADENN an-end
ADENO anode
ADENP paned
Penda
ADENR dearn
denar
redan
ADENS Andes
DNase
sedan
snead
ADENT Dante
ADENU Auden
Duane
ADENV daven
vaned
ADENW awned
dewan
Dwane
waned
ADENY denay
ADEOP apode
ADEOR adore
oared
oread
ADEPR drape
padre
ADEPS sepad
spade
ADEPT pated
ADEPU eupad
ADEPV paved
ADEPY payed
ADERR darre
drear
ADERS dares
rased
sared
ADERT dater
rated
trade
tread
ADERU rueda
ADERV drave
ADERW dewar
wader
ADERY deary
deray
rayed
ready
yeard
ADERZ dazer
razed
zerda
ADEST sated
stade
stead
ADESV saved
Vedas
ADESW sawed
ADETX taxed
ADETZ tzade
ADEVW advew
waved
ADEVY VE day
ADEWX waxed
ADEWY deawy
ADFFR draff
ADFFY daffy
ADFIR Farid
ADFIV vifda
ADFNO à fond
fonda
ADFOS fados
ADFRT draft
ADFRU faurd
fraud
ADFRW dwarf
ADGGY daggy
ADGIL algid
ADGIU Gaudí
ADGLN gland
ADGLO Golda
ADGLY glady
ADGMO dogma
go mad
ADGNO Dagon
donga
gonad
ADGNR grand
ADGNS G and S
ADGNT g and t✧
ADGNW dwang
ADGOO agood
ADGOP pagod
ADGOS gadso
ADGOT toga'd
ADGOU Gouda
ADGRU Durga
guard
ADGSU Gadus
ADGUY gaudy
ADHIJ hadji
jihad
ADHIK khadi
ADHIL Hilda
ADHIM Mahdi
ADHIN ahind
Dinah
ADHIO Idaho
ADHIP aphid
ADHIS Hasid
sidha
ADHJO hodja
ADHJU Judah
ADHLO ahold
halo'd
ADHLU hauld
ADHNO donah
Honda®
ADHNS hands
shand
ADHNT hadn't
ADHNY handy
Haydn
ADHOR hoard
Rhoda
ADHRS hards
shard
shar'd
ADHRY hardy✧
hydra✧
ADHST hadst
ADHSU sadhu
ADHSY Hyads
shady
ADIIL Iliad
ADIIN I-and-I

	india✧
ADIIO	lai-do
	oidia
ADIIR	radii
ADIIT	Aditi
ADIKN	kinda
ADIKO	daiko
ADIKP	Dipak
ADILN	Ladin
	Linda
	nidal
ADILO	dolia
	idola✧
ADILP	plaid
ADILR	drail
	laird
	liard
ADILS	slaid
ADILT	Dalit
	dital
	tidal
	Tilda
ADILU	dulia
ADILV	valid
ADILW	Walid
ADILY	daily
	Lydia
ADIMN	admin
ADIMR	diram
	marid
ADIMS	Midas
ADIMT	admit
ADIMX	admix
ADINN	dinna
ADINO	danio
ADINR	dinar
	drain
	Indra
	nadir
ADINT	daint
	Datin
	idant
ADINV	divan
	viand
ADINW	diwan
ADIOP	podia
ADIOR	aroid
	radio
ADIOS	aidos
ADIOT	diota
ADIOU	audio
ADIOV	avoid
ADIOX	axoid
ADIOZ	diazo
ADIPR	pardi
	rapid
ADIPS	sapid
ADIPV	pavid
	vapid
ADIRR	ardri
	ard-ri
	raird
ADIRT	triad✧
ADIRV	Vidar
ADIRX	radix
ADIRY	dairy
	diary
ADIRZ	darzi
	izard
ADIST	staid
	tsadi
ADISU	Saudi
ADISY	daisy
	sayid
ADITU	audit
ADITV	davit
ADIVV	vivda
ADJOU	Oujda
ADJSU	judas✧
ADJVY	VJ day
ADKKO	Kodak®
ADKLS	skald
ADKLY	alkyd
ADKMR	D-mark
ADKMU	dumka
ADKNR	drank
ADKNY	kandy✧
ADKOR	Korda
ADKOS	Skoda®
ADKOV	vodka
ADKRY	darky
ADKTU	Datuk
ADLLO	allod
	do-all
ADLLY	dally
	laldy
ADLMO	dolma
	domal
	modal
ADLMW	dwalm
ADLMY	madly
ADLNO	Donal
	Lando
	Ndola
	nodal
ADLNU	laund
ADLNY	Dylan
	Lynda
ADLOP	L-dopa
	podal
ADLOR	Roald
ADLOS	loads
ADLOT	dotal
ADLOU	aloud
	doula
ADLOW	waldo✧
ADLPS	spald
ADLRU	dural
ADLRW	drawl
ADLRY	lardy
ADLST	stal'd
ADLSU	lauds
ADLSY	sadly
ADLTU	adult
	dault
	tauld
ADLUY	yauld
ADMNO	Damon
	monad
	nomad
ADMNU	maund
	Munda
	undam
ADMNY	Mandy
ADMOU	douma
ADMPY	dampy
ADMRU	mudra
	Murad
ADMRY	mardy
ADMSU	adsum
ADMTU	datum
ADMUW	dwaum
ADNNO	Donna
ADNNQ	N and Q
ADNNU	nandu
ADNNY	Danny
ADNOO	doona
ADNOP	P and O
ADNOR	adorn
	and/or
	Donar
	radon
ADNOT	Donat
ADNOW	adown
	downa
	Wodan
ADNOZ	zonda
ADNPP	p and p
ADNPY	pandy
ADNRR	R and R
ADNRS	rands
ADNRT	drant
ADNRW	drawn
ADNRY	randy✧
ADNSS	sands
ADNST	stand
ADNSU	Sudan
ADNSY	sandy✧
	sdayn
ADNTU	daunt
ADNTY	daynt
ADOPS	spado
ADOQU	quoad
ADORR	ardor
ADORS	Doras
	dorsa
	roads
	sarod
	sorda
ADORT	troad
ADORU	douar
	doura
ADORW	dowar
ADOSV	Davos
ADOTY	toady
	today
ADPRS	spard
	sprad
ADPRY	pardy
ADPSY	paysd
	spayd
ADQSU	squad
ADQUY	quayd
ADRRU	durra
	Rudra
ADRST	darts
	strad
ADRSU	rudas
	Sudra
ADRSW	sward
ADRTY	tardy
ADRVY	vardy
ADSTU	adust
ADUVZ	Vaduz
AEEFN	neafe
AEEFR	feare
AEEFT	Éfaté
AEEGL	aglee
	eagle
AEEGN	Agene®
	agene
AEEGR	agree
	eager
	eagre
	geare
	ragee
AEEGT	étage
	Geeta
AEEHM	heame
AEEHR	heare
AEEHT	eathe
AEEHV	heave
	hevea
AEEIN	aînée
AEEIR	aerie
AEEKM	keema
AEEKN	akene
AEEKP	apeek
	Peake
AEEKR	rakee
AEEKW	a-week
AEELL	allée
AEELN	anele
	Neale
AEELR	leare
	leear
AEELS	easel
	easle
	lease
AEELT	elate
	telae
AEELV	leave
	veale
AEELW	aweel

AEELY aleye
AEELZ leaze
AEEMM mamee
AEEMN amene
enema
meane
Meena
AEEMR ameer
meare
ramee
reame
AEEMS mease
seame
AEEMV Maeve
AEENR ranee
AEENT eaten
enate
AEENV naeve
veena
venae
AEEOZ zoeae
AEEPR peare
AEEPS pease
AEEPT étape
AEEPY payee
AEEPZ peaze
AEERR arere
AEERS easer
erase
saree
seare
AEERT arête
eater
reate
AEERV reave
AEERZ razee
AEESS sease
AEEST setae
tease
AEESV eaves
AEESZ seaze
AEETX exeat
AEETZ teaze
AEEVW weave
AEFFG gaffe
AEFGO of age
AEFHS sheaf
AEFIK fakie
AEFIL Alfie
AEFIN faine
AEFIR afire
AEFKL flake
AEFKN kenaf
AEFKR faker
freak
AEFKS fakes
AEFLL fella
AEFLM femal
flame
fleam
AEFLR farle
feral
flare
AEFLS false
AEFLT aleft
fetal
AEFLV favel✧
AEFLY leafy
AEFMR frame
AEFNR frena
AEFNY fayne
AEFOR afore
AEFOV fovea
AEFRR farer
AEFRS farse
AEFRT after
feart
frate
trefa
AEFRU Fauré
feuar
AEFRW wafer
AEFRY arefy
faery
fayre
Freya
AEFST Fates
feast
festa
AEFTT fetta
AEFTW fetwa
AEFUV Fauve
AEFUW waefu'
AEGGI Aggie
AEGGO agoge
AEGGR agger
eggar
AEGGU gauge
AEGHL Helga
AEGHP phage
AEGHR gerah
AEGHU Hague
AEGIL agile
AEGIM image
AEGIN Angie
AEGIP Paige
AEGJR jäger
AEGJU gauje
AEGLL Galle
legal
AEGLM gleam
AEGLN angel
angle✧
Galen
genal
glean
AEGLP pagle
plage
AEGLR Elgar
glare
lager
large
regal
AEGLT aglet
AEGLV gavel
Gavle
AEGLY agley
Gayle
AEGLZ glaze
AEGMM gamme
gemma✧
AEGMN mange
Megan
AEGMO omega
AEGMR gamer
grame
marge
regma
AEGMS games
AEGMY gamey
AEGNO agone
genoa✧
AEGNR anger
range
Regan
renga
AEGNS Agnes
Senga
AEGNT agent
AEGNU nugae
AEGNV vegan✧
AEGNW Agnew
AEGNY geyan
gynae
AEGOP go ape
AEGOS Osage
AEGPR gaper
grape
pager
parge
AEGPS gapes
pages
AEGRR garre
rager
regar
AEGRS sarge
segar
AEGRT grate
great
Greta
targe
terga
AEGRU argue
auger
AEGRV grave
AEGRW wager
AEGRY aygre
gayer
yager
AEGRZ gazer
graze
AEGSS gases
AEGST getas
stage
AEGSU usage
AEGSW swage
wages
AEGTT get at
AEGTU Taegu
AEGUV vague
AEGUZ gauze
AEHHP ephah
AEHHT heath✧
AEHIR Rheia
AEHJR hejra
AEHKL Hekla
AEHKN kaneh
AEHKS shake
AEHLL Halle
Hallé
AEHLM almeh
hemal
AEHLP aleph
AEHLR haler
AEHLS halse
leash
selah
shale
sheal
AEHLT ethal
lathe
AEHLV halve
Havel
AEHLW whale✧
wheal
AEHLY Haley
hayle
AEHLZ hazel✧
AEHMN he-man
maneh
AEHMO mahoe
AEHMR harem
herma
AEHMS shame
Shema
AEHMT meath✧
thema
AEHNN henna
AEHNS ashen
Hanse
ne has
Shane
AEHNT ahent
Ethna
neath
'neath
thane
AEHNV haven
AEHNY hyena
AEHOR Horae
AEHOS Hosea
AEHPR hepar
phare
raphe

Words marked ✧ can also be spelled with one or more capital letters

raphé
AEHPS heaps
Pesah
phase
shape
AEHPY heapy
AEHRS Asher
share
shear
AEHRT earth✧
hater
heart
rathe
Thera
thrae
AEHRV haver
AEHRW whare
whear
AEHRZ hazer
AEHSS ashes✧
AEHST ashet
haste
heast
AEHSU hause
AEHSV haves
shave
sheva
AEHSW hawse
AEHSY Hayes
AEHTT theta
AEHTU haute
AEHTW wheat
AEHVY heavy
Yahve
AEHWY Yahwe
AEIIL Ailie
AEIJM Jaime
Jamie
AEIKL alike
alkie
AEIKR Kiera
AEIKT Katie
AEILL Allie
ileal
Leila
AEILM e-la-mi
email
e-mail✧
maile
Melia
AEILN alien✧
A-line
aline
anile
Elian
liane
AEILP pilea
AEILR ariel✧
raile
AEILS aisle
Alesi
AEILT Eilat
telia
AEILV alive
AEILX axile
AEILZ aizle
Eliza
AEIMM Mamie
AEIMN amine
anime
animé
en ami
Maine
minae
AEIMR Máire
maire
Marie
ramie
rimae
AEIMS maise
AEIMZ maize
AEINN Annie
inane
AEINR Arien
Irena
raine✧
AEINS anise
saine
Siena
AEINT eat in
entia
Teian
tenia
tinea✧
AEINU Ieuan
AEINV avine
naevi
naive
naïve
AEINX xenia
AEINZ azine
AEIPR paire
perai
AEIPS sepia
AEIPT pieta
pietà✧
AEIRR airer
AEIRS aesir
Aries
arise
raise
serai
AEIRT irate
retia
terai
AEIRU aurei
AEIRV vairé
AEIRY aiery
ayrie
AEIRZ Azeri
zaire
zaïre
AEIST Satie
AEISV avise
AEITT tatie
AEITV Evita
vitae
AEITW tawie
waite
AEIVW waive
AEIVZ avize
AEJKS jakes
AEJLP lapje
AEJLV javel
AEJMM Jemma
AEJMS james✧
AEJNN Jenna
AEJNS jeans
AEJNT Janet
AEJPR japer
AEJPS jaspe
jaspé
AEJSY jasey
AEKLN ankle
AEKLR Arkle
laker
AEKLS slake
AEKLT latke
AEKLW kwela
AEKLY kayle
leaky
AEKMM kamme
AEKMR kerma
maker✧
Merak
AEKMT Kamet
AEKNN Kenna
AEKNO oaken
AEKNP pekan
AEKNR anker
Karen
naker
nerka
ranke
AEKNS skean
snake
sneak
AEKNT taken
AEKNV Kevan
knave
AEKNW waken
AEKNY Kenya
AEKOP poake
AEKOR oaker
AEKOT atoke
AEKOW awoke
AEKPS spake
speak
AEKPY peaky
AEKQU quake
AEKRR raker
AEKRS asker
eskar
kesar✧
reaks
saker
skear
AEKRT taker
AEKRW waker
wreak
AEKST Keats
skate
stake
steak
AEKSU ukase
AEKSV Vesak
AEKSW askew
wakes
Wesak
AEKSY Kayes
AEKTW tweak
AELLL allel
AELLN Allen
AELLP lapel
AELLS salle
sella
AELLY alley
AELLZ allez
AELMM lemma
AELMN leman
Lemna
AELMP ample
maple
pelma
AELMR marle
realm
AELMS mesal
Salem
samel
AELMT metal
AELMU ulema
AELMY mealy
yealm
AELNO alone
anole
Leona
AELNP Nepal
panel
penal
plane
'plane
AELNR Larne
learn
Lerna
renal
AELNS Elsan®
slane
AELNT laten
leant
AELNU ulnae
AELNV elvan
navel
venal
AELNW wanle

Words marked ✧ can also be spelled with one or more capital letters

AELNY	leany
AELOR	realo
AELOS	aloes
AELOV	loave
	volae
AELOW	alowe
AELOZ	azole
	zoeal
AELPP	appel
	apple✧
AELPR	lepra
	parle
	pearl
	repla
AELPS	Elaps
	lapse
	Pales
	salep
	sepal
	spale
	speal
AELPT	leapt
	lepta
	palet
	pelta
	petal
	plate
	pleat
	tepal
AELPY	ayelp
AELQU	equal
	quale
AELRS	arles✧
	lares
	laser
	reals
	seral
AELRT	alert
	alter
	artel
	later
	ratel
	taler
AELRU	alure
	ureal
AELRV	laver✧
	ravel✧
	velar
AELRW	waler✧
AELRX	relax✧
AELRY	early
	layer
	leary
	rayle
	relay
AELSS	salse
AELST	least
	salet
	setal
	slate
	stale
	steal
	stela
	tales
	teals
	tesla
AELSU	salue
AELSV	salve
	selva
	slave
	vales
	valse
AELSW	swale
	sweal
	wales✧
AELSY	lyase
AELTT	latte
AELTV	Tavel
	valet
AELTX	exalt
	latex
AELUV	uveal
	value
AELVV	valve
AELVY	leavy
	vealy
AEMMY	mamey
AEMNN	Neman
AEMNR	enarm
	namer
	ramen
	reman
AEMNS	manes✧
	manse
	means
	Mensa
	samen
AEMNT	ament
	manet✧
	meant
AEMNV	maven
AEMNY	meany
	yamen
AEMOR	Moera
AEMOV	amove
AEMPR	remap
AEMPX	Ampex®
AEMRR	rearm
AEMRS	maser
	reams
	smear
AEMRT	armet
	mater
	ramet
	tamer
	trema
AEMRY	reamy
	Yerma
AEMRZ	mazer
AEMSS	massé
AEMST	steam
AEMSU	amuse
AEMSY	samey
	seamy
	ysame
AEMSZ	smaze
AEMTT	matte
AEMTY	etyma
	matey
	meaty
AEMUV	mauve
AEMYZ	azyme
AENNP	panne
	penna
AENNS	senna✧
AENNT	anent
AENNX	annex
AENOP	Epona
	paeon
AENOT	at one
	atone
	oaten
AENOV	novae
AENOZ	zonae
AENPP	nappe
AENPS	aspen✧
	sneap
	spane
	spean
AENPT	paten
	tapen
AENPV	paven
AENPZ	Penza
AENQU	quean
	quena
AENRR	narre
AENRS	nares
	snare
AENRT	antre
	aren't
AENRU	urena
AENRV	Nerva
	raven
AENRW	awner
	Warne
AENRY	rayne
	renay
	yearn
AENSS	Nessa
	sensa
AENST	nates
	Nesta
	stane
	stean
AENSU	usnea
AENSV	avens
AENSW	ne was
AENSY	sayne
AENSZ	senza
AENTT	Netta
AENTX	Texan
AENTY	yenta
AENTZ	zante
AENVW	navew
AENWX	waxen
AENWY	waney
	Wayne
AENWZ	wanze
AENZZ	zanze
	zazen
AEOOZ	zooea
AEOPR	opera
	pareo
AEOPS	Aesop
	paseo
AEORS	arose
	soare
AEORT	Erato
	oater
	orate
	roate
AEOSS	oases
AEOST	stoae
AEOSV	oaves
	Soave
AEOSZ	zoeas
AEOTV	ovate
AEOTW	aweto
AEOTZ	azote
	toaze
AEPPR	paper
AEPPU	pupae
AEPRR	parer
	raper
AEPRS	après
	as per
	asper
	parse
	prase
	presa
	spaer
	spare
	spear
AEPRT	apert
	pater
	peart
	petar
	Petra
	prate
	taper
	trape
AEPRU	pareu
AEPRV	paver
AEPRY	apery
	payer
	repay
AEPSS	passé
AEPST	paste
	septa
	spate
	speat
AEPSU	pause
AEPSV	Vespa®
	vespa

AEPTT patte
patté
tapet
AEPTU eat up
taupe
AEPTX expat
AEPTY peaty
AEPVY peavy
AEQRU quare
AERRS rears
serra
AERRT arrêt
rater
tarre
terra
AERRV raver
AERRW warre
AERSS rasse
AERST aster
earst
rates
reast
resat
stare
stear
strae
Taser®
taser
teras
AERSV saver
AERSW sawer
sware
swear
wares
AERSY resay
sayer
years
AERTT arett
tater
tetra
treat
AERTU urate
AERTV avert
taver
trave
AERTW tawer
water
wrate
AERTX Artex®
extra
taxer
AERTY teary
AERUZ azure
AERVV varve
AERVW waver
AERWX rewax
waxer
AERWY weary
AESSS asses
sasse
sessa
AESST asset
tasse
Tessa
AESSY essay
AESTT state
taste
testa
AESTU sauté
AESTV stave
vesta✧
AESTW sweat
tawse
waste
AESTX taxes
texas✧
AESTY as yet
as-yet
yeast
Yeats
AESUV suave
AESVW waves
AESVY savey
AETUV vaute
AETVW vawte
AETZZ tazze
AEVWY wavey
AEVYZ avyze
AEWYY yawey
AFFFL flaff
AFFGR graff
AFFLO offal
AFFLU luffa
AFFNY nyaff
AFFQU quaff
AFFST staff
AFFTY taffy✧
AFFUW wauff
AFGHU faugh
AFGIN Fagin
AFGLO oflag
AFGLU fugal
AFGNO fango
AFGOR Fargo
go far
AFGOT fagot
AFGRT graft
AFGSU Fagus
AFHIT faith
AFHIZ hafiz
AFHLS Flash®
flash
halfs
AFHRW wharf
AFHST shaft
AFIKL kalif
AFIKR fakir
AFILL flail
AFILN final
AFILO folia
AFILP pilaf
AFILR filar
flair
frail
AFIMO ma foi
AFIMR fraim
AFINO Fiona
AFINR infra
AFINS fains
AFINT faint
Fanti
AFIOS Sofia
AFIRR friar
AFIRS Farsi
fiars
AFIRT afrit
frati
iftar
AFIRY fairy
AFIST fasti
AFITW waift
AFKLN flank
AFKLS flask
AFKLY flaky
AFKNR frank✧
AFKOT kofta
AFKRT kraft
AFLMM flamm
AFLMY flamy
AFLNW flawn
AFLOO aloof
loofa
AFLOR flora✧
AFLOS sol-fa
AFLOT aloft
float
flota
AFLOU afoul
AFLRU fural
AFLRY flary
AFLST flats
AFLSU sulfa
AFLTU fault
AFLTY fatly
fly at
AFLUW awful
AFLWY flawy
AFLXY flaxy
AFMOX Oxfam
AFMOY foamy
AFMSU samfu
AFNNO fanon
AFNNY fanny✧
AFNRS snarf
AFNRU furan
AFNSU snafu
AFORS as for
so far
sofar
AFORV favor
AFORY foray
AFOSS fossa✧
AFOST fatso
softa
AFOTU fouat
AFOTW Ofwat
AFQRU Faruq
AFRSS frass
AFRSW swarf
AFSTU Faust
AFSUV favus
AFTTY fatty
AGGIN aging
AGGIR aggri
AGGJY jaggy
AGGLU gulag
AGGMO Magog
AGGMS maggs
AGGNU ungag
AGGNY naggy
AGGOO à gogo
à go-go
AGGOR aggro
AGGRY raggy
AGGSY saggy
AGGTY taggy
AGHHI ahigh
AGHHU haugh
AGHIL laigh
AGHIN anigh
hangi
AGHIT thagi
AGHIZ ghazi
AGHKU kaugh
AGHLU laugh
AGHMO ogham
Omagh
AGHNO hogan
AGHNP phang
AGHNS gnash
Shang
AGHNT thang
AGHNW whang
AGHNY ghayn
AGHPR graph
AGHRT garth
AGHST ghast
Ghats
AGHSU saugh
AGHTU aught
ghaut
AGHUW waugh✧
AGIIV vigia
AGIJR jagir
jirga
AGIKL glaik
AGIKN kiang
AGILL glial
AGILN algin
align
liang
ligan
linga
AGILO logia

Words marked ✧ can also be spelled with one or more capital letters

AGILR argil
glair
grail
AGILS sigla
AGILW wilga
AGILY gaily
AGIMN gamin
AGIMO amigo
imago
AGIMS sigma
AGINN ingan
AGINO gonia
ngaio✧
AGINR agrin
garni
grain
AGINT anti-g
giant
tangi
AGINV Gavin
AGINW a-wing
wigan✧
AGINZ zigan
AGIOP igapó
AGIOR orgia
AGIPR graip
pagri
AGIRT tragi
AGIRU Gauri
AGIRV virga
AGIST staig
AGITT gaitt
AGITU aguti
AGJLU jugal
AGJOS gajos
AGKLN klang
AGKNR krang
AGKNY kyang
AGKOP gopak
AGKOS kagos
AGKWY gawky
AGLLO Algol
AGLLY gally
AGLMU algum
almug
glaum
mulga
AGLNO along
Anglo
logan✧
longa
AGLNR gnarl
AGLNS glans
slang
AGLOP galop
Gopal
AGLOR argol
goral
largo
rolag
AGLOS goals
Lagos
AGLOT gloat
AGLPY pygal
AGLRU glaur
gular
AGLRY glary
gyral
AGLSS glass✧
AGLSU gusla
AGLTU galut✧
gault✧
AGLUX Glaux
AGLYZ glazy
zygal
AGMMU gumma
AGMMY gammy
AGMNO among
mango
AGMNY mangy
AGMOP gompa
AGMOR groma
Margo
Morag
AGMOT magot
AGMRU garum
AGMSU magus✧
sagum
AGMTU gamut
AGMUY gaumy
AGNNO gonna
AGNNW gnawn
AGNOP go nap
ponga
AGNOR argon
groan
nagor
orang
organ
AGNOT tango✧
tonga✧
AGNOU guano
AGNOW gowan
wagon✧
wonga
AGNOY agony
AGNOZ gazon
AGNPR prang
AGNPS spang
AGNPU punga
AGNRR gnarr
AGNRT grant✧
AGNRY angry
rangy
AGNST angst✧
stang
AGNSU Angus
AGNSW swang
AGNTU gaunt
AGNTW twang
AGNTY tangy
AGOOZ gazoo
AGOPR Grapo
AGOPS gapós
AGORS Argos
sargo
AGORT argot
gator
groat
AGORU goura✧
AGORY goary
AGOST Gatso®
goats
AGOTT gotta
AGOTY goaty
AGPPY gappy
AGPRS grasp
sprag
AGPRU rag up
AGPRY grapy
AGPSY gaspy
AGRRY Garry
AGRSS grass
AGRST strag
AGRSU argus✧
sugar
AGRTU tugra
AGRUU augur
AGRVY gravy
AGSSU gauss
AGSSY gassy
AGSTU Tsuga
AGSTY stagy
AGSUV vagus
AGSVX VX gas
AGSWY gawsy
AGTTU gutta
AGUYZ gauzy
AGYYZ azygy
AHHIK Haikh
AHHIS Shiah
AHHIT haith
hi-hat
AHHOO hoo-ha
AHHOR horah
AHHOS Shoah
AHHPY hypha
AHHRS harsh
AHHSS shash
AHHSY hashy
AHIIT Haiti
AHIJJ hajji
AHIJR hijra
AHIKK khaki
AHIKM hakim
AHIKT takhi
AHIKU haiku
AHIKZ khazi
AHILP phial
AHILR hilar
AHILT laith
lathi
thali
AHILY haily
AHIMN Niamh
AHIMR harim
ihram
AHIMS Amish
AHIMT thaim
AHINO Hanoi
AHINR Rhian
AHINS nashi
Shani
AHINT hiant
AHIPS aphis
apish
spahi
AHIRS arish
Sirah
AHIRT Thira
AHIRU Huari
AHIRY hairy
AHIST saith
taish
AHISV shiva✧
AHITU hutia
AHJKO khoja
AHJNO Jonah
AHJTU thuja
AHKLO Kahlo
AHKNS shank
AHKNT thank
AHKNY hanky
AHKOO hooka
AHKOS shako
sokah
AHKRS shark
AHKST shakt
AHKSW hawks
AHKSY shaky
AHKTY Kathy
AHLLO hallo
holla
AHLLS shall
AHLLU ahull
AHLMO omlah
AHLMS shalm
AHLMU haulm
AHLNO halon
AHLNU uhlan
AHLOR horal
AHLOS halos
shoal
shola
solah
AHLOT loath
lotah
AHLPR Ralph
AHLPS plash
AHLPT Plath
AHLPY haply
phyla
AHLSS slash
AHLST laths

	shalt
AHLSU	Shula
AHLSW	shawl
AHLSY	shaly
AHLTU	hault
AHLTY	lathy
AHMMU	ummah
AHMMY	hammy
AHMNU	human
	Nahum
AHMNY	mynah
AHMOR	omrah
AHMPS	pashm
AHMRS	marsh✧
AHMSS	smash
AHMST	maths
AHMSU	musha
AHMSW	shawm
AHMSY	mashy
AHMTY	my hat!
AHNNO	Hanno
	Honan
AHNOR	Norah
	Rhona
	Rohan
AHNOS	Shona
AHNRS	harns
	sharn
AHNRU	Harun
AHNSS	snash
AHNST	hasn't
	shan't
	sha'n't
	snath
AHNSU	Shaun
AHNSW	Shawn
AHNTU	haunt
	unhat
AHNUW	Wuhan
AHOOW	wahoo
AHOOY	yahoo✧
AHOPR	Oprah
AHORT	Thora
	Torah
AHORY	hoary
AHORZ	Zohar
AHOST	Athos
	hoast
	hosta
	oaths
	shoat
AHOSV	Hovas
AHOSW	as how
AHOSX	Xhosa
AHOTZ	azoth
AHPPY	happy
AHPRS	sharp
AHPRU	prahu
AHPRY	harpy
AHPSS	shaps
AHPST	paths
	staph
AHPSW	pshaw
AHPTY	Typha
AHPUW	whaup
AHQSU	quash
AHRRU	hurra
AHRRY	harry✧
AHRST	trash
AHRSU	Århus
	shura
	surah
AHRSY	syrah✧
AHRTW	thraw
	wrath
AHRTY	rhyta
AHRUW	whaur
AHRXY	hyrax✧
AHSST	stash
AHSSW	swash
AHSTW	swath
AHSTY	hasty
AHSWY	as why
	washy
AHTTU	tuath
AHTTY	Hatty
AHTUY	thuya
AHTWY	thawy
AHUZZ	huzza
AIIKW	Iwaki
AIILM	milia
AIILN	Ilian
AIILO	aioli
	aïoli
AIILT	litai
	Tilia
AIILV	Livia
AIIMM	Miami
AIIMR	imari✧
	Màiri
AIINO	Ionia
AIINP	piani
AIINS	Sinai
AIIPR	pirai
AIIQR	Iraqi
AIJKN	kanji
AIJKT	Tajik
AIJLM	Jamil
AIJLU	Julia
AIJLW	wilja
AIJNN	Jinan
	ninja✧
AIJNR	Rajni
AIJNS	Janis
AIJOR	Rioja
AIJOU	Ouija®
	ouija
AIJPW	pi-jaw
AIJRV	Rajiv
AIJVY	Vijay
AIKKM	kamik
AIKKT	tikka
AIKLM	malik
AIKLN	lakin
AIKLP	palki
AIKLS	kails
	skail
AIKLT	Tikal
	tilak
AIKLV	vakil
AIKMO	maiko
AIKMR	mikra
AIKMS	kamis
	Kasim
	smaik
AIKMU	umiak
AIKNR	Karin
	Kiran
AIKNS	kisan
	Nasik
AIKNT	takin
AIKNU	nikau
AIKOP	okapi
AIKOT	taiko
AIKPP	kippa
AIKPR	parki
AIKRR	karri
AIKRT	krait
	traik
AIKRU	kauri
AIKST	Sakti
AIKTT	katti
AILLN	all in
	all-in
	in all
	Niall
AILLS	allis
AILLV	villa✧
AILMM	limma
AILMN	Malin
	Milan
AILMO	Imola
AILMR	armil
AILMS	Islam
	Salim
	salmi
AILMT	lam it
	Mitla
	Tamil
AILMU	aumil
	miaul
AILMW	Wilma
AILMX	limax
AILNO	Ilona
AILNP	plain
AILNS	slain
	snail
AILNT	in alt
	Intal®
	Latin
AILNU	inula
AILNV	anvil
	nival
	vinal
AILNW	Alwin
	in-law
	lawin
AILNY	inlay
	lay in
AILOP	apiol
	paoli
AILOS	Laois
AILOU	auloi
AILOV	viola✧
	voilà
AILOZ	Lao Zi
AILPP	palpi
	pipal
AILPR	April
	prial
AILPS	lapis
	lipas
	spial
AILPT	plait
AILPU	al più
	pilau
AILPW	pilaw
AILQU	quail
AILRS	laris
	liras
	rails
AILRT	liart
	T-rail
	trail
	trial✧
AILRU	urali
	urial
AILRV	Avril
	rival
	viral
AILRY	lairy
	riyal
AILSS	lassi
	Sails
	Silas
	sisal
AILST	A-list
	litas
	tails
AILSU	Laius
AILSV	silva
	vails
	Vilas
AILSX	salix
AILSY	Islay
AILTT	atilt
AILTV	vital
AILTY	Italy
	laity✧
AILZZ	lazzi
AIMMS	miasm
AIMMU	imaum✧
	umami
AIMMX	maxim✧

Words marked ✧ can also be spelled with one or more capital letters

AIMNO	amnio
	Naomi
	Omani
AIMNP	panim
AIMNR	inarm
	minar
	ramin
AIMNS	mains
	Manis
	minas
AIMNT	matin✧
	tamin
AIMNV	mavin
AIMNZ	Mainz
	nizam✧
AIMOR	Maori
	Moira
	moria✧
AIMOW	miaow
AIMOX	axiom
AIMOY	Omiya
AIMPR	Priam
	prima✧
AIMPS	apism
	sampi
AIMQS	Qasim
AIMQU	maqui
AIMRR	marri
AIMRS	simar
AIMRT	amrit✧
AIMRZ	Mirza
AIMSS	amiss
	missa✧
AIMST	Samit
	tamis
AIMSV	mavis✧
AIMSW	aswim
	swami✧
	Wasim
AIMTY	amity
	atimy
AINNO	anion
AINNP	pinna✧
AINNS	Annis
	Nisan
AINNW	winna
AINOP	piano✧
AINOR	noria
AINOS	Sonia
AINOT	Taino
AINOV	avion
AINOX	axion
AINPS	pains
	spain✧
	spina
AINPT	inapt
	paint
	patin
	pinta✧
	tap-in
AINPV	pavin
AINPY	pay in
AINPZ	Pinza
AINQU	quina
AINRS	rains
	sarin
AINRT	intra
	riant
	train
	Trina
AINRV	Invar®
	ravin
	Vanir
AINRY	rainy
AINRZ	nazir
	zirna
AINSS	sasin
AINST	saint
	satin
	stain
AINSV	savin
	Sivan
AINSW	swain
AINTT	taint
	'taint
	tanti
	titan✧
AINTU	tui na
	tuina
	Uniat
AINTW	twain✧
	witan
AINUX	auxin
AINVY	Vinay
AINYZ	zayin
AIOPT	patio
AIORT	ariot
	ratio
AIORY	Oriya
AIOSS	Oasis®
	oasis✧
	ossia
AIOST	ostia✧
	stoai
AIOSV	aviso
AIPPP	Pippa
AIPPU	appui
AIPRS	pairs
	Paris
	Parsi
AIPRT	atrip
	parti
	tapir
AIPRU	rupia
AIPRY	Priya
AIPSS	apsis
AIPST	stipa
	tapis
AIPSV	pavis
AIPTT	pitta✧
AIPZZ	pizza
AIQRT	Tariq
AIQRU	quair
AIQSU	quasi
AIRRS	arris
AIRRU	urari
AIRSS	arsis
AIRST	astir
	sitar
	Sitra
	stair
	stria
	tarsi
	Trias
AIRSU	Arius
AIRSY	Syria
AIRSZ	sizar
AIRTT	trait
AIRVX	varix
AIRVY	vairy
AIRWZ	wazir
AIRYY	Iyyar
AISST	saist
	Stasi
AISSY	says I
AISTT	Attis
	Sitta
AISTU	Suita
AISTV	vista
	vitas
AISTW	waist
	waits
AISTX	taxis
AISWZ	Swazi
AISXX	x-axis
AISXY	y-axis
AISXZ	z-axis
AITTV	vitta
AITVV	vivat
AITZZ	izzat
AJLOU	joual
AJLRU	jarul
	jural
AJMMY	jammy
AJMOR	joram
	major✧
AJMRU	jumar
AJNOS	Jason
AJNOY	yojan
AJNSU	Janus
AJNTU	jaunt
	junta
AJNTY	janty
AJOOP	pooja
AJORW	jowar
AJOST	jatos
AJOSU	sajou
AJRTU	jurat
AJYZZ	jazzy
AKKLU	kulak
AKKNS	skank
AKKOP	kapok
AKKOR	kokra
AKKPU	pukka
AKLLY	alkyl
AKLNP	plank
AKLNR	knarl
AKLNU	kulan
AKLNY	lanky
AKLOP	pokal
	polka
AKLOS	skoal
AKLPU	pulka
AKLRY	larky
AKLST	stalk
	talks
AKLSW	lawks
	walks
AKLTU	taluk
AKLTY	talky
AKLUW	waulk
AKMNY	manky
AKMOP	Pomak
AKMOR	korma
AKMOS	makos
AKMOU	oakum
AKMRU	Kumar
	Kurma
AKMSU	Aksum
	Musak
AKMUZ	Muzak®
AKMWY	mawky
AKNOR	Koran
	krona
	króna
AKNOS	kaons
	sanko
AKNOY	Konya
AKNPR	prank
AKNPS	spank
AKNPU	punka
AKNRS	krans
	narks
	ranks
	skran
	snark
AKNRU	kunar
AKNRY	narky
AKNRZ	kranz
AKNST	stank
AKNSU	ankus
AKNSW	swank
AKNSY	snaky
AKNTW	twank
AKNTY	tanky
AKNUZ	kanzu
AKOOP	pooka
AKOOR	karoo✧
AKOOZ	kazoo
AKOPP	koppa
AKOPY	yapok
AKORT	tarok
AKORW	awork
AKOSY	kayos

okays
AKOTU otaku
AKOTY tokay✧
AKOWY yakow
AKPRS spark
AKPRY parky
AKPTU kaput
uptak
AKPWY pawky
AKQRU quark
AKQUY quaky
AKRST karst
skart
stark
strak
AKRSY karsy
sarky
AKRTU kurta
AKRYZ karzy
AKSSV kvass
AKSTT skatt
AKTUY Yakut
ALLLY allyl
Lally
ALLMO molal
molla
ALLMS small
ALLMY myall
ALLNO llano
ALLNU nulla
ALLOR loral
ALLOT all-to
atoll
ALLOV ollav
ALLOY loyal
ALLPS spall
ALLPU all-up
ALLPY pally
ALLRY rally
ALLST stall
ALLSW walls
ALLSY sally✧
ALLTY tally
ALLWY wally✧
ALLXY laxly
ALMMO Malmo
Malmö
ALMMS smalm
ALMMY lammy
ALMNO monal
ALMNU manul
ALMNY manly
ALMOO moola
ALMOR molar
moral
romal
ALMOS molas
Salmo
ALMOT matlo
ALMOY loamy
ALMPS plasm
psalm
ALMPU ampul
ALMPY amply
palmy
ALMQU qualm
ALMRS marls
ALMRU larum
mural
rumal
ALMRY marly
Mylar®
ALMST smalt
ALMSU lumas
ALMTY malty
ALMUV mal vu
ALMUX Uxmal
ALNNU annul
ALNOP nopal
ALNOR loran✧
Lorna
ALNOS salon✧
sloan
solan
ALNOT notal
talon
tonal
ALNOW lowan
ALNOX noxal
ALNOY lay on
ALNOZ zonal
ALNPT plant
ALNRS snarl
ALNRU lunar
ulnar
urnal
ALNST slant
ALNSU Alnus
Ulsan
ALNTU Ultan
ALNUW unlaw
ALNUY unlay
yulan
ALNWY Alwyn
lawny
wanly
ALOOP paolo
ALOPR parol
polar
poral
ALOPS salop
ALOPT Plato
ploat
ALORR roral
ALORS solar
soral
ALORT rotal
tolar
ALORV orval
valor
volar
ALORY royal
ALOSS lasso
ALOST altos
loast
salto
ALOSU aulos
ALOSV salvo✧
ALOTT total
ALOTV lovat
volta
ALOTX Taxol®
ALOVV volva
ALOZZ lazzo
ALPPU lap up
pupal
ALPPY apply
ALPRY parly
pyral
ALPST plast
spalt
splat
ALPSU spaul
ALPSW spawl
ALPSY palsy
splay
spyal
ALPTY aptly
patly
platy
typal
ALPUY lay up
lay-up
uplay
ALRRU rural
ALRRY Larry
ALRSU Larus
sural
Urals
ALRTU ultra
ALRTW trawl
ALRTY lyart
ALRWW wrawl
ALRWY rawly
ALSST salts
ALSSU lassu
ALSSY lyssa
ALSTU sault
talus
Tulsa
ALSTY salty
slaty
ALSUU usual
ALSVY sylva
ALSWY swaly
swayl
ALTTY lytta
ALTUV vault
ALTWY walty
ALTWZ waltz
ALUUV uvula
ALUVV vulva
ALVVY lavvy
AMMMO momma
AMMMY mammy
AMMNO ammon✧
AMMOY myoma
AMMRS smarm
AMMRY rammy
AMMSU summa
AMMSY Sammy
AMMTY tammy✧
AMNNO no-man
AMNNU unman
AMNNY Manny
AMNOP Nampo
AMNOR manor
maron
Morna
norma✧
roman✧
AMNOS manos
mason
monas✧
soman
AMNOT manto
toman
AMNOW woman✧
AMNOY anomy
Mayon
AMNOZ Monza
AMNRU Namur
Ruman
unarm
urman
AMNRY Myrna
AMNSU manus
AMNTY manty
mayn't
AMOPR pro-am
AMOPT Mt Apo
AMORR armor
maror
morra
AMORT Marot
morat
AMORU amour
AMORW mowra
AMORY mayor
moray✧
Moyra
AMOSS Samos
somas
AMOST stoma
AMOTY atomy
AMOTZ matzo
motza
AMPRT tramp
AMPSS spasm
AMPST stamp
AMPSU pumas
AMPSW swamp
AMRRU murra
AMRRY marry

AMRST	smart
AMRSU	ramus
	rusma
AMRSW	swarm
AMRSY	symar
AMRUV	murva
AMRWY	awmry
AMSSY	massy
AMSTY	masty
	mayst
AMSUW	wamus
AMTTY	Matty
AMTUZ	mazut
AMWYY	My Way
ANNNY	nanny
ANNOR	Norna
ANNSU	Sunna
ANNTU	naunt
ANNTZ	Nantz
ANOOP	napoo
	Poona
ANOOR	Onora
ANOPR	apron
ANOPT	on tap
	panto
ANOPW	powan
ANOPY	yapon
ANOQR	Qoran
ANORR	Arnor
ANORS	arson
	sonar
ANORT	orant
	rat on
	toran
	trona
ANORW	rowan◇
ANORY	rayon
ANOSV	novas
ANOSW	as now
ANOSX	Naxos
	Saxon
ANOSY	sayon
	Sonya
ANOTT	tanto
ANOTW	Wotan
ANOTX	taxon
ANOTY	atony
	ayont
ANOUY	noyau
ANOWY	no way
	noway
ANPPY	nappy
ANPRW	prawn
ANPSS	snaps
ANPST	pants
ANPSU	Pusan
ANPSW	spawn
ANPSY	pansy
ANPTU	unapt
ANPTY	panty
ANPUY	unpay
ANPUZ	zupan
ANQRU	Quran
	Qur'an
ANQTU	quant
ANRST	starn
ANRSU	Sun Ra
ANRSY	snary
ANRTT	trant
ANRTU	arnut
ANRTY	tyran
ANRUU	Nauru
ANRUY	unary
ANRUZ	azurn
	zurna
ANSSU	Susan
ANSSY	nyssa
ANSTU	astun
	saunt
	tunas
ANSTW	wants
	wasn't
ANSTY	antsy
	nasty
	tansy
ANSUY	unsay
ANSWY	Sawny
ANTTU	taunt
ANTTY	natty
ANTUV	vaunt
ANTUX	untax
ANTUY	aunty
ANTWY	tawny
	wanty
ANVVY	navvy
ANWYY	yawny
AOOPP	apoop
AOORS	roosa
AOORT	ratoo
AOORZ	razoo
AOPPP	poppa
AOPPR	appro
AOPPZ	zoppa
AOPRS	Paros
	psora
	sapor
	sopra
AOPRT	aport
	op art◇
	porta
AOPRV	vapor
AOPSS	psoas
AOPSY	soapy
AOPTY	atopy
AOPTZ	topaz
AOQTU	quota
AORRS	sorra
AORRW	arrow
AORRY	roary
AORRZ	razor
AORSS	saros
AORST	roast
	taros
AORSV	arvos
	savor
AORSW	sowar
AORTT	ottar
	tarot
	troat
AORTX	taxor
AORTY	otary
	yarto
AORVY	ovary
AORYZ	Oryza
AOSST	assot
	stoas
	Tasso
AOSSY	say-so
AOSTT	stoat
	toast
AOSTU	autos
AOSVY	savoy◇
AOTTU	tatou
APPPY	pappy
APPRU	rap up
APPSU	pupas
APPSY	paspy
	sappy
APPTU	tap up
APPUY	pay up
APPUZ	zap up
APPYY	yappy
APPYZ	zappy
APRRY	parry
APRST	parts
	spart
	sprat
	strap
	traps
APRSU	supra
APRSW	wraps
APRSY	raspy
	spray
APRTT	pratt
APRTU	U-trap
APRTW	wrapt
APRTY	party
	praty
	yrapt
APSTU	sputa
	stupa
APSTW	swapt
APSTY	pasty
	patsy◇
APSWY	waspy
APSZZ	spazz
APTTY	patty◇
APTVY	pay TV
APUWX	wax up
APZZZ	pzazz
AQRTU	quart
AQSTU	squat
ARRST	starr
ARRSU	surra
ARRTY	tarry
ARSST	stars
	trass
ARSSU	sarus
ARSTT	start
ARSTU	surat◇
	sutra
ARSTW	straw
	swart
	warst
	wrast
ARSTY	artsy
	satyr
	stray
ARSUV	varus
ARSUY	saury
	Surya
ARTTT	tratt
ARTTU	tuart
ARTTY	ratty◇
	tarty
ARTWY	warty
ARUYZ	azury
ASSSY	sassy
ASSTW	swats
ASSTY	sayst
	stays
ASTTT	Tatts
ASTTY	tasty
ASTUX	Taxus
ASTVY	vasty
ASVVY	savvy
ATTTY	tatty

B

BBBIY	Bibby
BBBOY	bobby◇
BBBUY	bubby
BBCEU	cubeb
BBCHU	Chubb®
BBCOY	cobby
BBCUY	cubby
BBDEY	debby◇
BBDIS	dibbs
BBDOY	dobby
BBEER	rebbe◇
BBEIL	bible◇
BBEIR	bribe
BBEKO	kebob
BBEMO	bombe
	bombé
BBEOP	bebop
BBEOR	berob
BBESY	sybbe
BBEUZ	zebub
BBEWY	webby
BBFUY	fubby
BBGIO	gobbi
BBGOO	gobbo
BBHMO	H-bomb

BBHOY hobby
BBHUY hubby
BBILO bilbo
BBILY bilby
Libby
BBIMO bimbo
BBIRY ribby
BBITY Tibby
BBLOO bobol
BBLOY lobby
BBLRU blurb
BBLSU slubb
BBMOO bombo
BBMOU bumbo
BBMOY mobby
BBNOY nobby
BBNUY nubby
BBOOS boobs
BBOOY booby
yobbo
BBOPU bob up
BBSTU Stubb
BBSUY busby
subby
BBTUY tubby
BCCEO bocce
BCCIU cubic
BCCIY biccy
BCEEH beech
BCEEK becke
BCEEL celeb
BCEER rebec
BCEEX xebec
BCEEZ zebec
BCEHL belch
BCEHN bench
BCEHO boche✧
BCEKY Becky
BCELO coble
BCEMO combe
BCENO bonce
BCENU bunce
BCEOR corbe
BCERU Bruce
BCESU Cebus
BCHIM chimb
BCHIR birch
BCHIT bitch
BCHNU bunch
BCHOR broch
BCHOS Bosch
BCHOT botch
BCHTU butch✧
BCHUU buchu
BCIKR brick
BCIKU Buick®
BCILM climb
BCILO cibol
BCIMO combi
BCIOR boric
BCIPU pubic
BCITU cubit
BCKLO block
BCKOR brock
BCKOU bucko
BCKUU bucku
BCLMO clomb
BCLOO Cobol
BCLSU clubs
BCMOO combo
coomb
BCMOR cromb
BCMOS combs
BCMOY comby
BCMRU crumb
BCNOU bunco
BCORU courb
BCRSU scrub
BDDEI bided
BDDIY biddy✧
BDDUY buddy
BDEEI beedi
BDEEL bedel
bleed
debel
BDEEM embed
BDEEN Deneb
BDEER brede
breed
BDEEW bedew
dweeb
BDEEY bedye
Debye
BDEGO bodge
BDEGU budge
debug
BDEHU Dubhe
BDEIL bield
BDEIM bedim
imbed
BDEIP biped
BDEIR bride✧
rebid
BDEIS B-side
BDEIT betid
bidet
debit
BDELN blend
BDELO bodle
lobed
BDELU blude
BDEMO demob
BDEMU bemud
BDENO boned
BDENU U-bend
unbed
BDENY bendy
by-end
BDENZ Z-bend
BDEOR borde
bored
orbed
BDEOW bowed
BDERU debur
BDERY derby✧
BDESU debus
BDETU debut
début
tubed
BDFII bifid
BDHIO dhobi
BDIIN bid in
bindi
BDILN blind
BDILU bluid
build
BDINO bidon
Bondi
dob in
BDINU in bud
unbid
BDIOP bipod
BDIOV bovid
BDIPU bid up
BDLNO blond
BDLOO blood
BDLOY Dolby®
BDLUY bludy
BDMOU dumbo✧
BDNOR brond
BDNOS bonds
BDNOU bound
BDNUU bundu
BDNUY Bundy®
BDOOR boord
brood
Dobro®
droob
BDOOS dsobo
BDOOY boody
BDORS bords
BDORU bourd
BDOSU budos
BDOTU doubt
BDOXY X-body
BDRSY Byrds
BEEEL belee
BEEES besee
BEEGI beige
BEEGL glebe
BEEGM begem
BEEGR gerbe
grebe
BEEGT beget
BEEHN heben
BEEHT thebe
BEEIL belie
BEEJL jebel
BEEKN nebek
BEELL belle✧
BEELM Belém
BEELN nebel
BEELP bleep
plebe
BEELR rebel
BEELT betel
let be
BEELV bevel
BEELZ bezel
BEEMN neemb
BEEMR breem
breme
ember
BEENN benne
BEENR Berne
BEENT benet
BEEOR boree
BEEOS obese
BEERR breer
brere
BEERT beret
BEERV bever
breve
BEERW weber
BEEST beset
BEETT Tebet
BEETW bewet
BEEUV bevue
BEFFO be off
BEFFU buffe
BEFGO befog
BEFIR brief
fiber
fibre
BEGIL bilge
gibel
BEGIN being
binge
BEGIO bogie
BEGIR giber
BEGIW bewig
BEGLO bogle
globe
BEGLU bugle
bulge
BEGLY gleby
BEGMO embog
BEGMU begum
BEGNU begun
BEGOR grebo
BEGOU bouge
BEGOY bogey
BEGRU gebur
BEGTY get by
BEGUZ Uzbeg
BEHOW howbe
BEHRT berth
BEHRY herby
BEIIK bikie
BEIJR jiber
BEIKM Mbeki
BEIKR biker
BEILL libel
BEILO obeli

Words marked ✧ can also be spelled with one or more capital letters

BEILR	birle
	liber
BEILS	Eblis
	Isbel
BEILT	blite
BEILV	blive
BEILY	lie by
BEIMO	biome
BEIMU	imbue
BEINN	Benin
	benni
BEINO	bonie
	Niobe
BEINR	brine
BEINS	Ibsen
BEINV	Bevin
BEINX	Benxi
BEINY	inbye
BEINZ	zineb
BEIOS	Boise
	bosie
BEIOW	Bowie
BEIRR	brier
BEIRS	birse
	brisé
	Ribes
BEIRT	biter
	tribe
BEIRZ	brize
BEIST	besit
BEISV	vibes
BEITT	bitte
	Tibet
BEITZ	Bizet
	zibet
BEIVX	vibex
BEJNU	bunje
BEJOT	objet
BEKLO	bloke
BEKMO	kembo
BEKOO	ebook
	e-book
BEKOR	broke
BEKRU	burke
BEKTY	kbyte
BEKUZ	Uzbek
BELMO	moble
BELMU	umbel
BELNO	Nobel
	noble
BELNT	blent
BELOR	blore
	borel
	roble
BELOT	botel
BELOU	boule
BELOW	bowel
	elbow
BELOY	Boyle
BELPS	plebs
BELRU	brûlé
	ruble
BELRY	beryl
BELSS	bless
BELST	blest
BELSU	blues✧
	bulse
BELUY	bluey
BEMOP	pombe
BEMOR	ombre
	ombré
BEMOS	besom
	mebos
BEMOW	embow
BEMOX	embox
BEMRU	brume
	umber
	umbre
BEMSU	embus
	sebum
BEMTY	mbyte
BENNO	bonne
BENOR	boner
	borne
	borné
BENOS	bones
BENOT	béton
	T-bone
BENOW	bowne
BENOX	boxen
BENOY	ebony
BENOZ	bonze
BENRT	brent✧
BEOOS	boose
BEOOZ	booze
BEOPR	probe
BEORR	borer
BEORS	brose
	robes
	sober
BEORW	bower
BEORX	boxer✧
BEORY	o'erby
	ybore
BEOST	besot
BEOSU	bouse
BEOSW	bowes
	bowse
BEOSY	syboe
BEOTT	botte
BEOTU	buteo
BEOTW	bowet
BEPSU	pubes
BEPUY	upbye
BERST	Brest
BERSU	burse
	rebus
	suber
BERTT	Brett
BERTU	brute
	buret
	rebut
	tuber✧
BERUX	exurb
BERUY	buyer
BESSU	buses
BESTY	Betsy
	set by
BETTU	butte
BETUU	U-tube
BFFIU	buffi
BFFLU	bluff
BFFOO	boffo
BFFOU	buffo
BFFSU	buffs
BFIOR	fibro
BFLYY	fly-by
BFORY	forby
BFSUY	fubsy
BGGIY	biggy
BGGOY	boggy
BGGUY	buggy
BGHIT	bight
BGHOR	brogh
BGHOU	bough
BGHRU	burgh
BGILY	bilgy
BGIMR	Mr Big
BGINO	bingo
	boing
BGINR	bring
BGINY	bingy
BGIOS	biogs
BGIOT	bigot
BGIPU	big up
BGISU	gibus
BGLOY	globy
BGLUY	bulgy
BGMOO	gombo
BGMOU	gumbo✧
BGNOO	bongo
BGNOY	ob-gyn
BGNUY	bungy
BGOOR	borgo
BGOOS	gobos
BGORU	bourg
BGOSU	bogus
BGRUY	rugby
BHIMO	himbo
BHIRT	birth
BHLOY	Holby
BHLSU	blush
BHLTY	Blyth
BHMOR	rhomb
BHMPU	bumph
BHMRU	rhumb
BHMTU	thumb
BHOOS	bohos
	hobos
BHOOT	booth
BHOOY	oh boy!
BHORT	broth
	throb
BHOTY	bothy
BHRSU	brush
	shrub
BHSUY	bushy✧
BIILM	limbi✧
BIILN	blini
BIILS	Iblis
BIIMN	nimbi
BIIMZ	zimbi
BIIOR	oribi
BIIOT	obiit
BIKLN	blink
BIKMO	kimbo
BIKNO	boink
BIKNR	brink
BIKRS	brisk
BIKRU	Rubik
BILLR	brill
BILMO	limbo✧
BILMP	blimp
BILMY	blimy
BILOO	oboli
BILOR	broil
	Libor
BILOX	bolix
BILSS	bliss✧
BILST	B-list
	blist
	stilb
BILSY	sibyl✧
	sybil✧
BILTU	built
BILTZ	blitz✧
BIMNY	Nimby
BIMOS	bisom
BIMOT	mob it
	timbó
BIMOZ	zombi✧
BINOR	inorb
	robin
BINOS	bison
BINOT	biont
BINOW	bow in
BINOX	box in
	in-box
BINRU	Bruin
	burin
	rub in
	rubin
BINRY	briny
BINUY	buy in
	buy-in
BIOOT	oobit
BIORS	Biros
	Boris
BIORT	orbit
BIORX	Ibrox
BIOST	bitos
BIOTT	Tobit
BIOTU	oubit
BIPSU	pubis

BIQSU squib
BIQTU qubit
BIRTU bruit
BISTT bitts
BISTU buist
BISTY bitsy
sit by
BIYZZ bizzy
BJMOU jumbo
BJMUY jumby
BJNOO on-job
BJNUY bunjy
BKLNU blunk
BKLUY bulky
BKMOU kombu
BKNOU bunko
BKOOR brook✧
BKOOS bokos
books
BKOOY booky
BKOSY bosky
BKSUY busky
BLLUY bully
BLMOO bloom
BLMPU plumb
BLNOW blown
BLNOY nobly
BLNTU blunt
BLOOR brool
BLOOS bolos
BLOOY looby
BLOST bolts
BLOSU bolus
lobus
BLOSW bowls
BLOTU boult
U-bolt
BLRSU slurb
BLRTU blurt
BLRUY burly
BLTUY butyl
BMOOR broom
BMOOS bosom
BMOOY boomy
BMORU rumbo
BMOSU ombus
ombús
umbos
BMOUX buxom
BMOWY womby
BMPSU bumps
BMPUY bumpy
BNNOY bonny
BNNUY bunny✧
BNOOR boron
BNOOS boson
BNORU bourn
Bruno
BNORW brown
BNORX Bronx
BNORY Byron
Robyn
BNOSU bonus
bosun
bo'sun
BNOUX unbox
BNRSU Burns
BNRTU brunt
burnt
BNRUY run by
BNTUY bunty✧
BOORT robot
BOORU buroo
BOOST boots
BOOSY boyos
BOOSZ bozos
BOOTX Botox®
ox-bot
BOOWX ox-bow
BOOYZ boozy
BOPUW upbow
BOPUX box up
BORRU burro
BORTU turbo
BOSUY bousy
BOSWY sybow
BOTUY outby
BOTXY boxty
BPPUY buppy
BPRUU rub up
BPTUY put by
BPUUY buy up
BRRUY burry
BRSTU brust
burst
BRSUU Rubus
BRUUU urubu
BSSTU stubs
BSSUU bussu
BSTUY busty
BTTUU butut
BTTUY butty
BUYZZ buzzy

C

CCCIO cocci
CCCOO cocco
CCDEO codec
CCEER recce
CCEFL C clef
CCEHK check
CCEHZ Czech
CCEIL Cecil
CCEIR cerci
ceric
Circe
CCEKL cleck
CCELY cycle
leccy
CCEMU cecum
cumec
CCEOP copec
CCEOR recco
CCEOS cosec
secco
CCERY reccy
CCESU cusec
CCFIU Cufic
CCHHI chich
CCHIK chick
CCHIN cinch
CCHIO chico
CCHKO chock
CCHKU chuck
CCHLU culch
CCHNO conch
CCHOO choco
CCHOU couch
CCHRU curch
CCHTU cutch
CCIIT ictic
CCIIV civic
CCIKL click
CCIKR crick
CCILO colic
CCIMO comic
CCINO conic
CCINT cinct
CCINY cynic✧
CCIOS cisco
CCIPY piccy
CCIRS circs
CCISU succi
CCKLO clock✧
CCKLU cluck
CCKOR crock
CCKOY cocky
CCKRU cruck
CCLOY cyclo
CCOOS cocos
CCOOZ zocco
CCORU occur
CCOUZ Cuzco
CDDEI diced
Eddic
CDDUY cuddy
CDEEI de-ice
CDEER creed✧
CDEEU deuce
educe
CDEHI chide
CDEHO chode
CDEIL El Cid
Le Cid
CDEIM demic
medic✧
CDEIR cider
cried
dicer
drice
CDEIS cedis
CDEIT edict
CDEIV Vedic
CDEIY dicey
CDEKO decko
CDEKR dreck
CDELO dolce
CDELY Clyde
ycled
CDEMO Médoc
CDENS scend
'scend
CDENU dunce
CDEOO cooed
CDEOR coder
cored
credo✧
decor
décor
CDEOU coudé
douce
CDEOV coved
CDEOW cowed
CDEOX codex
coxed
CDEOY decoy
CDERU crude
CDERY cyder
decry
CDETU educt
CDHIL child
CDHIT dicht
ditch
CDHNU dunch
CDHNY chynd
CDHOR chord
CDHOT docht
CDHTU dutch✧
CDHUY duchy
CDIIN dinic
Indic
CDIIO iodic
CDIKY dicky✧
CDILU lucid
ludic
CDIMU mucid
CDINY Cindy
CDIOR Doric
CDIOS disco
sodic
CDIOT dicot
CDIPU cupid✧
pudic
CDISU scudi
CDITY dicty
CDKOS docks
CDKSU ducks
CDKUY ducky
CDLOS scold
CDLOU cloud
could
CDMOR CD-ROM
CDNOO codon
condo

 Words marked ✧ can also be spelled with one or more capital letters

CDNOY	ycond
CDNUY	cundy
CDORS	cords
	scrod
CDORU	courd
CDORW	crowd
CDOSU	scudo
CDRUY	crudy
	curdy
CDSSU	scuds
CEEEM	emcee
CEEEP	peece
CEEFN	fence
CEEFS	feces
CEEGR	cerge
	grece
CEEHK	cheek
	keech
CEEHL	leech
CEEHN	hence
CEEHP	cheep
CEEHR	cheer
	chère✧
	reech
CEEIL	Celie
CEEIN	niece
CEEIP	piece
	pièce
CEEJT	eject
CEEKL	cleek
CEEKP	pecke
CEEKR	creek✧
CEELP	cleep
	clepe
CEELR	creel
CEELT	elect
CEELV	cleve
CEELX	excel
CEELY	lycée
CEEMR	creme
	crème
	crême
CEENP	pence
CEENR	cerne
CEENS	cense
	scene
CEENT	ctene
CEEOO	cooee
CEEPR	creep
	crepe
	crêpe
	perce
CEERS	Ceres
	Crees
	scree
CEERT	Crete
	erect
	terce
CEERW	crewe✧
CEESS	cesse
CEESY	sycee
CEEUV	cuvée
CEFFL	F-clef
CEFGL	G-clef
CEFHI	chief
	fiche
CEFHT	fecht
	fetch
CEFIT	fecit
CEFKL	fleck
CEFLT	cleft
CEFOR	force✧
CEGIN	genic
CEGIO	cogie
CEGIR	grice
CEGKO	gecko
CEGNO	congé
CEGOU	cogue
CEGRY	gryce
CEHHT	cheth
	hecht
CEHHU	heuch
CEHIL	chiel
	chile✧
	elchi
CEHIM	chime
	miche
CEHIN	chine
	chiné
	niche
CEHIR	Reich
CEHIT	ethic
	hi-tec
	theic
CEHIV	chive
CEHKO	choke
CEHKT	ketch
CEHLO	Chloe
CEHLT	letch
CEHLU	leuch
CEHLW	welch✧
CEHLY	chyle
CEHMO	chemo
	Moche
CEHMY	chyme
CEHNO	cohen
	Enoch
CEHNT	tench
CEHNW	wench
CEHOO	cohoe
CEHOP	epoch
CEHOR	chore
	ocher
	ochre
	Roche
CEHOS	chose
CEHOW	owche
CEHPR	perch
CEHPT	Pecht
CEHRT	chert
	retch
CEHRU	ruche
CEHSS	chess
CEHST	chest
CEHSU	chuse
CEHTU	chute
	teuch
CEHTV	vetch
CEHTW	wecht
CEHTY	techy
	Tyche
CEHVY	chevy
CEHWY	chewy
CEIIL	ceili
CEIIN	Iceni
CEIJU	juice
CEIKR	erick
	icker
CEILM	clime
	melic
CEILN	cline
	incle
CEILO	E coli
	Eolic
	oleic
CEILP	clipe
CEILR	relic
CEILS	Sicel
	slice
CEILT	telic
CEILV	Clive
CEIMN	mince
CEIMR	crime
CEIMS	mesic
CEIMT	metic
CEIMX	cimex
CEINO	on ice
CEINR	crine
CEINS	since
CEINW	wince
CEINY	yince
CEINZ	Zenic
CEIOV	voice
CEIPR	price
CEIPS	spice
CEIPU	ice up
CEIRR	crier
	ricer
CEIRS	cries
	crise
	seric✧
CEIRT	citer
	récit
	recti
	trice
CEIRU	curie
	ureic
CEIRX	xeric
CEIRY	ricey
CEITU	cutie
CEITV	civet
	evict
CEITW	twice
CEJOY	Joyce
CEKKS	kecks
CEKLO	cloke
	Locke
CEKLR	clerk
CEKNS	sneck
CEKNV	V-neck
CEKOR	ocker✧
CEKOS	cokes
CEKPS	speck
CEKRT	treck
CEKRW	wreck
CELLT	T-cell
CELMO	celom
CELNO	Cleon
	clone
CELNU	uncle✧
CELOR	ceorl
CELOS	close
	socle
CELOT	clote
	telco
CELOV	clove
CELOY	cloye
	coley
CELOZ	cloze
CELPT	P-Celt
CELPU	cupel
CELPY	clype
CELQT	Q-Celt
CELRU	cruel
	lucre
	ulcer
CELSU	luces
CELTU	culet
CELTY	cetyl
CELUX	culex
CEMOR	comer
	crome
CEMOT	comet✧
CEMRY	mercy✧
CENNO	conne
	nonce
CENOP	ponce
CENOR	Creon
	crone
	oncer
CENOS	scone
	sonce
CENOT	cento
	conte
	conté✧
CENOU	on cue
	ounce
CENOV	coven
CENOY	coney
CENOZ	cozen
CENPU	punce
CENST	cents
	scent
CEOOY	cooey

CEOPR	coper
CEOPS	copse
	scope✧
CEOPU	coupe
	coupé
CEORR	corer
	crore
CEORS	corse
	score
CEORT	recto
CEORU	coure
CEORV	cover
CEORW	cower
CEORZ	croze
CEOST	coset
	coste
	escot
	estoc
CEOSU	souce
CEOSV	voces
CEOSW	Cowes
	sowce
CEOSX	Coxes
CEOTT	octet
CEOTV	covet
CEOVY	covey
CEPRT	crept
CEPRU	Pruce
CEPRY	crepy
	crêpy
	Percy
CEPSS	specs
CERRU	curer
	recur
CERSS	cress
CERST	crest
CERSU	cruse
	curse
	sucre
CERSW	screw
CERTU	cruet
	curet
	eruct
	truce
CERUV	cruve
	curve
CESSU	scuse
	'scuse
CESTU	Cetus
	scute
CETUY	cutey
CFFHU	chuff
CFFIL	cliff
CFFLO	cloff
CFFOS	scoff
CFFOU	cuffo
CFFSU	scuff
CFHIL	filch
CFHIN	finch
CFHIT	fitch
CFHIU	fichu
CFHOO	choof
CFHSU	Fuchs
CFIIS	sci-fi
CFIKL	flick
CFIKU	Kufic
CFILT	clift
CFIOS	ficos
CFISU	ficus
	Sufic
CFKLO	flock
CFKOR	frock
CFMOO	Ofcom
CFMOY	comfy
CFORT	croft
CFORU	Corfu
CFOSU	focus
CFRSU	scurf
CFSTU	scuft
CFSUU	fucus
CGGIY	ciggy
CGHLU	gulch
CGHOO	cohog
	Gooch
CGHOU	cough
CGIIN	icing
CGIIT	ci-gît
CGILN	cling
CGILO	logic
CGIMO	ogmic
CGINO	coign
CGINU	cuing
CGIOR	corgi
	orgic
CGIOY	yogic
CGIRU	Ugric
CGKUY	gucky
CGLNU	clung
CGLOO	colog
CGNOO	congo✧
CGOOS	scoog
CGORS	scrog
CGOSU	scoug
CHHIL	hilch
CHHIS	shchi
CHHIT	hitch
CHHIW	Which?
	which
CHHNU	hunch
CHHOO	hooch
CHHOT	hotch
CHHTU	hutch
CHIIL	chili
	lichi
CHIKN	chink
CHIKO	hoick
	Kochi
CHIKR	chirk
CHIKT	thick
CHILM	milch
CHILN	linch
CHILO	choli
CHILP	pilch
CHILR	chirl
CHILT	licht
CHILY	hylic
CHILZ	zilch
CHIMO	ohmic
CHIMR	chirm
CHIMT	mitch
CHIMU	humic
CHINP	pinch
CHINW	winch
CHIOR	choir
	ichor
CHIOS	Sochi
CHIPR	chirp
CHIPT	pitch
CHIPV	V-chip
CHIQU	quich
CHIRS	Chris
CHIRT	crith
	richt
CHIST	stich
CHISU	cuish
CHITT	titch✧
CHITW	witch
CHITY	itchy
	tichy
CHIVY	vichy
CHKNU	chunk
CHKOO	choko
	chook
CHKOS	shock
CHKOY	choky
CHKSU	shuck
CHKTU	kutch
CHLMU	mulch
CHLNU	lunch
CHLNY	lynch
CHLOT	cloth
CHLRU	churl
	lurch
CHLSU	schul
CHMNU	munch✧
CHMOO	choom✧
	mooch
CHMOP	chomp
CHMOS	schmo
CHMOU	mouch
CHMOY	mochy
CHMPU	chump
CHMTU	mutch
CHNOT	notch
CHNPU	punch✧
CHNRU	churn
	runch
CHNSY	synch
CHOOP	pooch
CHOOS	cohos
CHOPR	porch
CHOPT	potch
CHOPU	pouch
CHORT	rotch
	torch
CHORY	ochry
CHOSU	hocus
CHOTU	chout
	couth
	oucht
	touch
CHOUV	vouch
CHPSY	psych
CHRRU	churr
CHRSU	crush
CHRTW	crwth
CHSUY	cushy
CIILT	licit
CIILV	civil
CIILY	icily
CIIMM	mimic
CIINO	ionic✧
CIINR	ricin
CIINS	Sinic
CIIPP	cippi
CIIRR	cirri
CIJUY	juicy
CIKLN	clink
CIKLS	licks
	slick
CIKMY	micky✧
CIKNS	snick
CIKNY	Nicky
CIKOS	sicko
CIKOY	yoick
CIKPR	prick
CIKPS	spick
CIKPY	picky
CIKQU	quick
CIKRT	trick
CIKRW	wrick
CIKRY	Ricky
CIKST	stick
CIKTY	ticky
CIKWY	wicky
CILMS	sclim
CILNO	colin✧
	nicol✧
CILNT	clint✧
CILOR	loric
CILOT	lotic
CILOU	oculi
CILOW	wilco
CILPT	clipt
CILPU	picul
CILRU	Ulric
CILRY	Cyril
	lyric
CILST	C-list
CILSU	sulci
CILTY	lytic
CILXY	cylix
	xylic
CIMNO	Cimon

Words marked ✧ can also be spelled with one or more capital letters

nomic
CIMNU cumin
mucin
CIMOR micro
Romic
CIMOS micos
osmic
CIMPR crimp
CIMRS scrim
CIMSU Musci
music
CIMYZ zymic
CINNO conin
CINOR Corin
corni
orcin
CINOS scion
sonic
CINOT tonic
CINOV covin
CINOZ zinco
CINPU Punic
CINRU incur
runic
CINSU incus
CINTT tinct
CINTU cut in
cutin
cut-in
incut
tunic
CINYZ zincy
CIOPR Cipro®
CIOPT cop it
op cit
Optic®
optic
picot
topic
CIORR roric
CIORS siroc
CIORT toric
Troic
CIORU curio
CIOST stoic✧
Ticos
CIOTX toxic
CIPRS crisp
scrip
CIPRY pricy
CIPSU Picus
CIPSY spicy
CIPTY typic
CISTU cutis
ictus
CITTU cut it
CJKOO jocko
CJNOU junco
CKKNO knock
CKLNO clonk
CKLNU clunk
CKLOS locks
CKLPU pluck
CKLSU sculk
CKLUY lucky✧
CKMOS mocks
smock
CKMUY mucky
CKNOR cronk
CKNOY conky
CKNSU snuck
CKOOR crook
CKOOS socko
CKOOY cooky
CKOPY pocky
CKORS rocks
CKORT trock
CKORY corky
rocky✧
CKOSS socks
CKOST stock
CKRTU truck
CKSSU sucks!
CKSTU stuck
CKUYY yucky
CLLOY colly
CLLSU scull
CLLUY cully
CLMOP clomp
CLMOU Colum
locum
CLMPU clump
CLMTU mulct
CLNOO Colón
colon
CLNOW clown
CLOOR color
CLOOS locos
CLOOY cooly
CLORU clour
CLOSU locus
CLOSW scowl
CLOTU clout
CLOYY coyly
CLPSU sculp
CLRUY curly
CLTUY culty
CMMOO commo
CMMOS comms
CMMOY commy
CMOOP compo
CMOOS Cosmo
CMOOY coomy
CMOPT compt
CMORU mucor
mucro
CMOSU comus✧
CMPRU crump
CMRSU scrum
CMRYY Cymry
CMSUU cusum
mucus
CNNOY Cynon
CNOOR Conor
corno
croon
CNOOT conto
CNOOV convo
CNOPY poncy
CNORS scorn
CNORT tronc
CNORU cornu
CNORW crown✧
CNORY corny
crony
CNOSU conus
oncus
uncos
CNOTU count
CNOTY cyton
CNOWY Conwy
CNRUY curny
CNSUU uncus
CNTUU uncut
COOPS scoop✧
COORS corso
COORT Corot
COOST scoot
tocos
COPRS corps
COPRU croup
COPSS Scops
COPSU scoup
COPSW scowp
COPUY coypu
CORRU cruor
CORSS cross✧
CORST crost
CORSU Orcus
scour
CORSW Crows
scrow
CORTU court
crout
Turco
CORWY cowry
COSST costs
Scots
COSTT Scott
COSTU scout
souct
COTTU cutto
CPRTY crypt
CPRUY cry up
CPTUU cut up
cut-up
CRRUY curry
CRSTU crust
curst
CRSUY crusy
Cyrus
CRUVY curvy
CSUZZ scuzz
CTTUY cutty

D

DDDIY diddy
DDDOY doddy
DDDUY duddy
DDEEG edged
DDEEI Eddie
DDEEN ended
DDEER Edred
DDEEY deedy
DDEGO dodge
DDEIO diode
DDEIR dried
redid
DDEIS sided
DDEIV dived
DDEMO domed
DDENY neddy✧
DDEOT doted
todde
DDEOW dowed
DDEOZ dozed
DDERU udder
DDERY reddy
ydred
DDEST stedd
DDETY teddy
DDGIY giddy
DDGOY dodgy
DDIKO kiddo
DDIKY kiddy
DDILO dildo
DDIMX Middx
DDIMY middy
DDINU undid
DDIOS didos
DDIRU druid✧
DDIST didst
DDITY tiddy
DDIWY widdy
DDLOY oddly
DDMUY muddy
DDNOY noddy
DDNUY nuddy
DDOOS dodos
DDOPY poddy
DDORY Roddy
DDOSY soddy
DDOTY toddy
DDOVY voddy
DDOWY dowdy
DDPUY puddy
DDRUY ruddy
DEEEM Médée
DEEER deere
reede
DEEEV deeve
DEEFR defer
freed
DEEGH hedge

DEEGK kedge
DEEGL glede
gleed
ledge
DEEGO geode
ogeed
ogee'd
DEEGR edger
greed
DEEGS sedge
DEEGW wedge
DEEHR heder
DEEHW hewed
DEEHY heedy
DEEIL edile
elide
DEEIN diene
DEEIR eider
DEEKN kneed
knee'd
DEEKR Derek
DEEKY keyed
DEELM medle
DEELN neeld
DEELR elder
DEELS Leeds
seeld
DEELU elude
DEELV delve
devel
DEEMN Emden
emend
DEEMR mered
DEEMT meted
temed
DEENO donee
DEENS dense
needs
DEENT denet
teend
DEENU endue
undee
undée
DEENW endew
DEENY needy
DEENZ Enzed
DEEOP epode
DEEOR doree
erode
DEEOX exode
DEEPS pedes
speed✧
DEERR drere
erred
DEERS Seder
DEERT deter
treed
DEERU urdee
urdée
DEERY reedy
DEESS desse
sedes
DEEST stede
steed
DEESU suede
suède
DEESW sewed
swede✧
weeds
DEESX desex
sexed
DEESY seedy
DEETU étude
DEETW tweed
DEEUX exude
DEEVX vexed
DEEWY weedy
DEFGI fidge
DEFGU fudge
DEFIL felid
field
filed
DEFIN fiend
DEFIR fired
fried
DEFIS fides✧
DEFIT fetid
DEFIX fixed
DEFIY deify
edify
DEFLS delfs
DEFLT delft
DEFMR fremd
DEFNU unfed
DEFNY fendy
DEFOX foxed
DEFPU fed up
DEFRU Freud
DEGGU ugged
DEGHO Hodge
DEGHY hedgy
DEGIK kidge
DEGIL gelid
glide
DEGIM midge
DEGIN deign
dinge
DEGIO dogie
geoid
DEGIR derig
dirge
gride
ridge
DEGIU guide✧
DEGJU judge
DEGKY kedgy
DEGLO glode
Golde
lodge
DEGLU glued
DEGLY gyeld
ledgy
DEGMU degum
mudge
DEGNU nudge
DEGOP podge
DEGOR go red
gored
DEGOT godet
toged
DEGOW wodge
DEGPU pudge
DEGRS dregs
DEGRY gryde
DEGSY sedgy
DEGWY wedgy
DEHII Heidi
DEHIL Delhi
DEHIM Mehdi
DEHIR hider
hired
DEHIS shied
DEHIT Edith
DEHLO dhole
DEHLP delph
DEHNS shend
DEHNY hynde
DEHOP ephod
DEHOR Herod
Hoder
horde
DEHOS doseh
hosed
shoed
DEHOT doeth
DEHPT depth
DEHRS sherd
shred
DEHRT derth
DEHTY they'd
DEHUZ Zhu De
DEIIM imide
DEIIN indie
DEIIV ivied
DEIIX dixie
DEIJO Jodie
DEIJR jerid
DEIJU Judie
DEIKL kidel
DEIKN inked
DEIKP piked
DEIKR diker
dirke
DEIKS skied
DEILN eldin
lined
DEILO oiled
oldie
DEILP lepid
piel'd
plied
DEILR idler
DEILS sidle
sield
slide
DEILT tilde
tiled
DEILV devil✧
lived
vilde
DEILW dwile
wield
Wilde
DEILY yield
DEIMN denim
DEIMO iMode®
DEIMR dimer
rimed
DEIMS deism
disme
DEIMT demit
timed
DEIMX mixed
DEINP piend
DEINR diner
DEINS Denis
sdein
snide
DEINT ident
teind
tined
DEINU indue
nudie
DEINW dwine
Edwin
indew
widen
DEINX index
DEINZ dizen
DEIOV dovie
video
DEIOW dowie
DEIOX oxide
DEIPP piped
DEIPR pride
pried
redip
DEIPS spide
spied
DEIPT tepid
DEIQU equid
DEIRR drier
reird
rider
DEIRS dries
sider
DEIRT tired
tride
tried
DEIRU rudie
DEIRV diver
drive✧
rived
Verdi

DEIRW	weird
	wired✧
DEIST	id est
	stied
DEISV	Dives
DEISZ	sized
DEIVX	ex div
	ex-div
DEIYZ	Yezdi
DEJLO	jodel
DEJOY	joyed
DEKMU	ek dum
DEKNO	kendo
DEKNU	unked
DEKNY	kynde
DEKOP	poked
DEKRY	dyker
DELLN	Lendl
DELLT	tell'd
DELLW	dwell
DELMO	model
DELMU	ledum
DELNO	loden
	olden
DELNU	unled
DELOO	doole
DELOR	drôle
	older
DELOS	solde
DELOW	dowel
	dowle
DELOY	odyle
	yodel
	yodle
DELPS	speld
DELPU	duple
	upled
DELRY	redly
DELSU	dulse
	slued
DELTV	veldt
DELTW	dwelt
DEMMO	modem
DEMNO	demon
DEMNS	mends
DEMOP	moped
DEMOR	drome
	moder
DEMOT	moted
DEMOU	odeum
DEMOW	mowed
DEMRU	demur
DEMSU	mused
	sedum
DEMTU	muted
DENNO	donne✧
	donné
	end-on
	no end
	on end
DENOO	odeon
DENOR	drone
	ronde
DENOS	nosed
	sonde
DENOT	Donet
	noted
	toned
DENOV	Devon
DENOW	endow
	nowed
	Woden
DENOY	doyen
DENOZ	dozen
	zoned
DENPS	spend
DENPU	end up
	upend
	up-end
DENRT	drent
	trend
DENRU	runed
	under
	unred
	urned
DENRY	nerdy
DENST	stend
DENSY	Denys
DENTU	tuned
DENTY	tynde
	tyned
DENUU	undue
DENUW	unwed
DENWY	Wendy
DEOOR	rodeo
DEOOW	wooed
DEOPR	doper
	pedro✧
	roped
DEOPS	spode✧
DEOPT	depot
DEOPX	podex
DEOPY	dopey
DEORR	order✧
DEORS	dorse
	rosed
DEORT	doter
	trode
DEORU	uredo
DEORV	dover✧
	drove
DEORW	dower
DEORX	redox
DEORZ	dozer
DEOST	doest
DEOSU	douse
DEOSW	dowse
	sowed
DEOTU	due to
	outed
DEOTV	dévot
DEOTX	detox
DEOVW	vowed
DEPPU	upped
DEPRS	spred
DEPRU	drupe
	duper
	perdu
	prude
DEPRY	perdy
	predy
DEPSU	pseud
DERRU	Dürer
DERRY	dryer
DERSS	dress
DERST	drest
DERSU	druse✧
DERTY	tyred
DERUX	redux
DERUZ	Druze
DESTU	duets
DESTY	styed
DETTU	duett
DETUV	duvet
DFILU	fluid
DFINU	fundi
DFIOR	fiord
DFIRT	drift
DFJOR	fjord
DFLOO	flood✧
	of old
DFLOY	Floyd
DFNOR	frond
DFNOS	fonds
DFNOU	found
DFNSU	funds
DFNUY	fundy
DFOOR	do for
	fordo
DFOOY	foody
DGGOO	doggo
DGGOY	doggy
DGHIT	dight
DGHOU	dough
DGIIN	dig in
DGIIR	rigid
DGIIT	digit
DGILU	guild
DGIMY	midgy
DGINO	dingo
	doing
	OD'ing
DGINR	D-ring
	grind
DGINY	dingy
	dying
DGIOP	pi-dog
DGIOT	god it
DGIPU	dig up
DGIRY	ridgy
DGLOO	goold
DGLOY	godly
	goldy
DGMOY	My God!
DGNOU	ungod
DGNUU	undug
DGNUY	dungy
	gundy
DGOOO	good-o
DGOOR	droog
DGOOS	godso
	goods
DGOOY	goody
DGOPY	podgy
DGORU	gourd
DGORY	go dry
	grody
DGPUY	pudgy
DGRUY	durgy
DHIIN	Hindi
DHIMU	humid
DHINU	Hindu
DHIOR	Ohrid
DHIOT	dhoti
DHIOY	hyoid
DHIRT	third
	thrid
DHISY	dishy
DHITW	width
DHLLO	dholl
DHNOU	hound
DHNSU	dunsh
DHOOR	hoord
DHOOY	dohyo
DHORY	hydro
	rhody
DHOTU	thou'd
DHOVZ	vozhd
DHOWY	howdy
DHQRS	hdqrs
DHRSU	hurds
DIILL	dilli
DIILP	Dilip
	lipid
DIILV	livid
DIIMO	idiom
	modii
DIIMT	timid
DIINP	dip in
DIINR	indri
DIINS	Sindi
DIINT	nitid
DIIOT	idiot
DIIRS	Idris
DIIRV	virid
DIIST	Idist
DIIVV	vivid
DIJNN	djinn
DIJNO	Dijon
DIKNO	kid on
	kid-on
DIKNR	drink
DIKNU	unkid
DIKNY	Dinky®

dinky
kindy
DILLR drill
DILLY idyll
DILMY dimly
DILNO indol
DILNU unlid
DILNY Lindy
DILOR droil
DILOS Isold
lidos
silo'd
sloid
soldi
solid
DILOT doilt
DILOV viold
DILOY doily
DILRT trild
DILRU lurid
DILRY drily
DILSW wilds
DILSY Dilys
DIMNO mid-on
DIMOO domoi
DIMOS misdo
odism
DIMOU duomi
odium
DIMOV ovdim
DIMOY myoid
DIMRU mudir
DIMST midst
'midst
DIMTU tumid
DINNU Idunn
DINOP poind
DINOR nidor
Rodin
DINOS Sidon
DINOT on-dit
tondi
DINRU unrid
DINRY rindy
DINSU Indus
nidus
DINSW winds
DINSY Sindy
DINWY windy
DIOOT ootid
DIOOV ovoid
DIOOZ zooid
DIOPR Prodi
DIOPS dipso
DIOPY pyoid
DIORR rorid
DIORS Doris
DIORT droit
DIOST odist
DIOTT ditto
DIOTV divot
DIOWW widow✧
DIPPU dip up
DIPTU putid
DIQSU quids
squid
DIRVY yrivd
DISTY ditsy
DITYZ ditzy
DIYZZ dizzy
DJNOR Njord
DJOOS dojos
DKMUY dumky
DKNRU drunk
DKOOR drook
DKORU drouk
DKORY dorky
DKOSU kudos
DKOUU Dukou
DKSTY kydst
DKSUY dusky
DKUUZ kudzu
DLLOR droll
DLLOY dolly
Lloyd
DLLUY dully
DLMOU mould
DLNOU lound
nould
n'ould
DLNOW lownd
DLNUY Lundy
DLOOR dolor
drool
loord
DLOOS soldo
DLOOW woold
DLORS Lords
DLORW world
DLORY lordy
DLOSU ludos
DLOSY sloyd
DLOUW would
DLOYY doyly
DLPUY duply
DLRYY dryly
DMMUY dummy
DMNOO mondo
DMNOU mound
DMOOS dooms
dsomo
Sodom
DMOOU duomo
DMOOY doomy
moody
DMORU Murdo
DMORY dormy
DMOSU modus
DMPSU dumps
DMPUY dumpy
DMRUU durum
DNNOU dunno
DNNUY dunny
DNOOR donor
doorn
rondo
DNOOS snood
DNOOT tondo
DNOPU pound✧
DNOPW pownd
DNORU round
DNORW drown
rownd
DNORY drony
DNOST stond
DNOSU Donus
nodus
sound
unsod
DNOSW Down's
downs✧
sownd
DNOSY Dyson
synod
DNOTU donut
DNOUW wound
DNOUY oundy
DNOWY downy
DOOPR droop
DOORS sordo
DOORU odour
DOOST stood
to-dos
DOOSW woods✧
DOOTU do out
outdo
DOOWY woody
DOOYZ doozy
DOPRS drops
sprod
DOPRU proud
pudor
DORSS dross
DORST dorts
DORSU duros
sudor
DORSW sword
words
DORTU Tudor
DORUY duroy
DORWY dowry
rowdy
wordy
DPPUY duppy
DPRUY dry up
DPSUY pudsy
DRSTU durst
DRSUY drusy
DRTUY Trudy
DSSUY sudsy
DSTUY dusty
study

E

EEEFS feese
EEEFZ feeze
EEEGS geese
EEEHT te-hee
EEEHZ heeze
EEEIR eerie
EEEJZ Jeeze
EEEKV keeve
EEEKW weeke
EEELM mêlée
EEELN neele
EEELP elpee
Pelée
EEELS leese
EEELV levee
EEELZ leeze
EEEMR emeer
EEEMS semée
EEEMX exeem
exeme
EEENR Renée
EEENS neese
EEENT teene
EEENV eeven
EEENZ neeze
EEEPP peepe
EEEPT tepee
EEEPV peeve
EEEPW pewee
EEERV reeve
EEETW etwee
weete
EEFFI Effie
EEFHI Hefei
EEFHM Fehme
EEFHT hefte
EEFIR fiere
EEFLM fleme
EEFLR fleer
refel
EEFLT fleet✧
lefte
EEFMM femme
EEFRR freer
frère
refer
EEFRS Sefer
EEFRT freet
terfe
EEFRV fever
EEFRY yfere
EEFSS fesse
EEFST Feste
EEFSU fusee
EEFSZ fezes
EEFTW wefte
EEFUZ fuzee
EEGGL legge
EEGGR egger

Words marked ✧ can also be spelled with one or more capital letters

grège
EEGHL Hegel
EEGHN henge
EEGIL Liège
liege
EEGIN eigne
genie
EEGIR Eiger
régie
EEGIS siege
EEGIV vegie
EEGKL gleek
EEGKR Greek
EEGKY geeky
EEGLM gemel
EEGLO éloge
EEGLR gerle
leger
EEGLT gleet
EEGLY elegy
EEGMN menge
EEGMR merge
EEGNR genre
gerne
green✧
EEGNT genet✧
tenge
EEGNV venge
EEGNW ngwee
EEGPU gee up
EEGRS grees
grese
serge
EEGRT egret
greet
EEGRV greve
verge
EEGSS gesse
EEGST egest
geste
EEGSU segue
EEHIN Heine
EEHKT theek
EEHLN Helen
Henle
EEHLS sheel
EEHLT Ethel
Lethe
EEHLV helve
EEHLW wheel
EEHMT theme
EEHMV Vehme
EEHNP phene
EEHNS sheen
EEHNT Ethne
EEHNW wheen
EEHOV evhoe
evohe
EEHPR pheer
EEHPS phese
sheep
EEHRS herse
sheer
shere
EEHRT ether
there
three
EEHRW hewer
where
EEHRY herye
EEHSS Hesse
EEHST sheet
these
EEHTT teeth
thete
EEIJT eejit
EEIKV kieve
EEILL Ellie
EEILM elemi
EEILR relie
EEILS eisel
Elsie
esile
EEILT elite
élite
EEILV lieve
EEILW Lewie
EEILX exile✧
EEIMM Emmie
EEIMS semie
EEIMV mieve
EEINP penie
EEINR Ernie
Irene
EEINS see in
seine
EEINV neive
nieve
EEINW newie
EEINX exine
EEINY in eye
EEINZ e-zine
EEIPS peise
EEIPZ peize
EEIRT retie
Tiree
EEIRV reive
revie
rieve
EEIRY eyrie
EEISS Essie
seise
EEISV sieve
EEISW weise
EEISX exies
EEISZ seize
EEITV evite
EEITY Eyeti
Eytie
EEIWZ weize
EEJLW jewel
EEJLY jeely
EEJNU jeune
EEJSS Jesse
EEJSU sujee
EEKLN kneel
EEKLS sleek
EEKLV kevel
EEKLW welke
EEKMS smeek
smeke
EEKNR kerne
EEKNS skene
EEKNT kente
EEKOP pekoe
EEKOV evoke
EEKPS Speke
EEKRS esker
skeer
EEKRT terek
EEKRV kerve
EEKRY reeky
rekey
EEKST skeet
steek
EEKSW weeks
EELLM lemel
EELLN Ellen
EELLS selle
EELLV level
EELMN elmen
EELMR merel
merle
EELMS mesel
EELMU emule
EELNO leone
Noele
EELNR Lerne
EELNS lenes
EELNV elven
nevel
EELNW newel
EELOP elope
EELPR leper
repel
EELPS sleep
speel
EELPX expel
EELRS reels
EELRT relet
EELRV elver
lever
revel
EELRY leery
EELSS Seles
EELST sleet
steel✧
stele
EELSV elves
EELSW Lewes
sewel
sweel
EELSY seely
EELTT ettle
EELTU elute
EELTW tewel
tweel
EELTX telex
Texel
EEMMN mneme
EEMMR emmer
EEMMT emmet
EEMMW emmew
EEMNR remen
EEMNS mense
mesne
semen
EEMNT Temne
EEMNU neume
EEMNW enmew
EEMNY enemy
Yemen
EEMOT emote
EEMOV emove
EEMPT Tempe
EEMQU queme
EEMRS merse
EEMRT meter
metre
EEMRU emure
EEMRX remex
EEMRY emery
EEMST steem
steme
temse
EEMSU meuse
EEMYY my eye
EEMZZ mezze
EENNP penne
EENNR renne
EENNT tenné
EENOR one-er
EENPR neper
preen
EENPS penes
EENQU queen✧
EENRS sneer
EENRT enter
rente
terne
treen
EENRU enure
EENRV erven
nerve
never
EENRW renew
EENRY reney
EENSS Essen
senes
sense
EENST sente
steen
teens
tense

EENSU ensue
EENSV evens
seven
EENSW ensew
sewen
EENSY seyen
EENTT tenet
EENTU tenue
EENTV event
EENTW 'tween
EENTY teeny
EENUV venue
EENVY veney
yeven
EENWY weeny
yewen
EEOPP opepe
EEOPT topee
EEOPY peeoy
EEORR or e'er
or ere
EEORS erose
soree
EEOWW wowee
EEOXY ox-eye
EEPRS per se
perse
prese
speer
spree
EEPRT peter✧
petre
EEPRU puree
purée
rupee
EEPRV perve
preve
EEPRY peery
EEPST steep
EEPSU upsee
EEPSW sweep
EEPSY peyse
seepy
EEPTU tee up
EEPUY eye up
EEPWY weepy
EEQRU queer
EEQUU queue
EERRS serre
EERST ester
reest
reset
steer
stere
teres
terse
Trees
EERSU reuse
EERSV serve
sever
verse
EERSW sewer
sweer
EERSX sexer
Xeres
EERSY Reye's
EERTV evert
revet
EERTW tweer
'twere
EERTX exert
EERUV revue
EERVV verve
EERVX vexer
EERVY every
veery
EESSX Essex
EESSY sesey
yeses
EESTT teste
EESTV Steve
EESTW ewest
sweet
EETTU tutee
EETTV Tevet
EETTW tweet
EFFFO feoff
EFFGO Geoff
EFFIO offie
EFFIR fifer
EFFOR offer
EFFRU ruffe
EFFTU tuffe
EFGIN feign
EFGIR grief
EFGIU fugie
EFGLO fogle
EFGLU fugle
Guelf
EFGMO Ofgem
EFGOR forge
gofer
EFGOY fogey
EFGRU grufe
EFGUU fugue
EFHIT thief
EFHLO f-hole
EFHLS flesh
shelf
EFHLT thelf
EFHNO foehn
EFHRS fresh
EFHTT theft
EFHTW wheft
EFHTY hefty
EFIIW wifie
EFIKN knife
EFIKR kefir
EFILL fille
EFILN elfin
EFILO folie
EFILR filer
flier
lifer
rifle
EFILS Felis
flies
'slife
EFILT filet
flite
EFILX Felix
EFIMR fermi
EFIMT metif✧
EFIMU Fiume
EFINR finer
infer
EFINS fines
EFINT feint
fient
EFINW in few
EFINX enfix
EFIOX foxie
EFIPR preif
prief
EFIRR firer
frier
EFIRS fries
serif
EFIRT freit
refit
rifte
treif
EFIRV fiver
EFIRX fixer
EFIRY fiery
reify
EFIRZ frize
EFISV fives
EFITT fitte
EFKLS skelf
EFKLU fluke
EFKNS fenks
EFLLY felly
EFLMU flume
EFLNO felon
EFLOR forel
EFLOT flote
Oftel
EFLOU foulé
EFLOW Wolfe
EFLOY foley
foyle
EFLPY flype
EFLRU fleur✧
EFLRY ferly
flyer
EFLSS selfs
EFLSW flews
EFLTU flute✧
EFLTY felty
flyte
lefty
EFLUY fluey
EFMOR forme
Frome
EFMOS fomes
EFMRU femur
EFMSU fumes
EFMTU fumet
EFNNY fenny
EFNOR Freon®
EFNOT often
EFNOW of new
EFNOY foyne
EFNRY ferny
EFORR frore
EFORT fetor
forte
EFORU fuero
EFORX forex
EFORY foyer
EFORZ froze
EFOSS fosse
EFOSU of use
EFOSX Foxes
EFOTU fouet
EFRRY ferry
fryer
EFRSS serfs
EFRSW swerf
EFRUZ furze
EFSTU fetus
EFTTY fytte
EGGIL ligge
EGGIR Grieg
EGGIU gigue
EGGKS skegg
EGGLY leggy
EGGNO egg on
EGGNU gunge
EGGOP pogge
EGGOR gorge
grego
reggo
EGGOT get-go
EGGOU gouge
EGGPY peggy✧
EGGRU gurge
EGHHI heigh
EGHHU heugh
EGHHW hewgh
EGHIL Leigh
EGHIN hinge
neigh
EGHIT eight
EGHIW weigh
EGHLU leugh
EGHLY hyleg
EGHNO hogen
EGHNT Ghent
thegn
EGHOT goeth
the go
EGHPT Peght

EGHST ghest
EGHTU teugh
EGIIN genii
EGIJR rejig
re-jig
EGIKL glike
EGIKR grike
EGILM gimel
EGILN ingle
ligne
Nigel
EGILO logie
EGILR liger
Rigel
EGILS Giles
EGILT gilet
leg it
legit
EGILU guile
EGIMM gimme
EGIMR grime
EGINP genip
EGINR grein
niger✧
reign
renig
EGINS singe
EGINT get in
tinge
EGINV given
EGINW winge
EGINY eying
gynie
EGIOV ogive
vogie
EGIPR gripe
EGIRS grise
EGIRT tiger
EGIRV giver
virge
EGIRZ grize
EGIST geist
EGISU guise
EGITT get it?
EGKNR kreng
EGKRY gryke
EGLLY gelly
EGLMO golem
Gomel
EGLMU glume
EGLNN Glenn
EGLNO longe
EGLNT glent
EGLNU lunge
EGLOP golpe
EGLOR ogler
EGLOS segol
EGLOT let go
EGLOV glove
EGLOY elogy
goyle
EGLOZ gloze
EGLRU gluer
gruel
Luger®
luger
EGLSU gules
gusle
EGLTU gulet
EGLUY gluey
guyle
EGMMY gemmy
EGMNO emong
genom
gnome
EGMOT gemot
EGMRU grume
EGNOR ergon
Genro
goner
grone
negro✧
EGNOS segno
EGNOT get on
EGNPU gen up
unpeg
EGNST gents
EGNSU genus
negus✧
EGNTU unget
EGNTY genty
EGOOS goose
EGOOY gooey
EGOPR grope
porge
EGORR roger✧
EGORS gorse
soger
EGORT ergot
EGORU orgue
rogue
rouge
EGORV grove✧
EGORW Gower
EGOSS gesso
gosse
segos
EGOST goest
EGOSU Ségou
EGOTU togue
EGOTY goety
EGOUV vogue✧
vouge
EGPRU purge
EGPRY grype
EGPTU get up
get-up
EGPTY Egypt
EGQSU squeg
EGRRU regur
urger
EGRRY Gerry
EGRST Sergt
EGRSU surge
EGSSU guess
EGSTU guest
EGSUY guyse
EGUUX Gueux
EHHIT hithe
EHHTY hythe
EHIKR hiker
EHIKS sheik
EHIKT Keith
kithe
EHILS leish
shiel
EHILT Leith
lithe
EHILW while
EHILX helix✧
EHIMN hem in
EHIMO homie
EHIMR rhime
EHIMS hiems
EHIMT meith
EHINR Henri
rhine✧
EHINS shine
EHINT thine
EHINW whine
EHINZ hizen✧
EHIOS hoise
EHIRR hirer
EHIRS hi-res
sehri
shier
shire
EHIRT their
EHIRV hiver
EHISS shies
EHIST heist
sieth
sithe
EHISV hives
shive
EHITT tithe
EHITW white✧
withe
EHKLW whelk
EHKMR Khmer
EHKMS shmek
EHKNO kohen
EHKOY hokey
EHKRS Shrek
EHKTY kythe
EHLLO Hello!
hello
EHLLS shell
she'll
EHLMO mohel
EHLMW whelm
EHLOS hosel
sheol✧
she'ol✧
EHLOT helot
hotel✧
thole
EHLOV hovel
EHLOW Howel
whole
EHLOY holey
EHLPS plesh
shlep
EHLPW whelp
EHLPY phyle
EHLSU shule
EHLSW welsh✧
EHLTU Thule
EHLTY Ethyl®
ethyl
lythe
EHLWY Hywel
EHLXY hexyl
EHMMO homme
EHMNS mensh
EHMNY hymen✧
EHMOR homer✧
horme
EHMOS Moshe
EHMOY homey
EHMPY hempy
EHMRS herms
EHMRT therm
EHMRU rheum✧
EHMRY rhyme
EHMST meths
EHMSY meshy
EHMTY thyme
EHNNY henny
EHNOO ohone
EHNOP pheon
phone
'phone
EHNOR heron
honer
rhone
EHNOS hosen
shone
EHNOT hoten
EHNOV hoven
EHNOY honey
EHNRU Nehru
EHNRY henry✧
rhyne
yrneh
EHNST shent
EHNSW shewn
EHNTT tenth
EHNTU uneth
EHOOV hoove
EHOOY hooey
EHOPR ephor
hoper
EHOPS shope

EHOPU ouphe
EHORS horse
shoer
shore
EHORT other
throe
EHORV hover
EHORW howre
whore
EHOSS hoses
shoes
EHOST ethos
shote
those
EHOSU house✧
EHOSV shove
EHOSW whose
EHOTW theow
EHOVW who've
EHOWW ewhow
EHPRT Perth
EHPRY hyper
EHPST thesp
EHPTU het up
EHRRY herry
EHRSU usher
EHRSW shrew
wersh
EHRSY shyer
EHRTW rewth
threw
EHRTZ hertz
EHSTU shute
EHSTW thews
EHSTY sythe
EHTTY Hetty
tythe
EHTWY thewy
EIIJM Meiji
EIIKR reiki
EIILN lie in
lie-in
EIILP pilei
EIIMN imine
EIINS nisei
EIINT tie-in
EIINX nixie
EIIPX pixie
EIISS issei
EIISV visie
EIJLU Julie
EIJMO ojime
EIJOS Josie
EIJRV jiver
EIJVY jivey
EIKLM kelim
melik
EIKLN inkle
liken
EIKLR liker
EIKLS Sikel
EIKLY kiley
kylie✧
ylike
EIKMN minke
EIKMS smeik
Smike
EIKNO eikon
enoki
koine✧
EIKNR inker
EIKNS Neski
skein
Skien
EIKNV Kevin
knive
EIKNY key in
EIKNZ zinke
EIKOP pokie
EIKOZ ozeki
EIKPR piker
EIKPS spike
EIKRS skier
EIKRT trike
EIKRY Kyrie
EIKSS skies
EIKST skite
EIKSU Sukie
EIKSV skive
EIKSY skiey
yikes
EIKTW Kitwe
EILLL Lille
EILLM mille
EILLO ollie✧
EILLR rille
EILLS lisle
EILMN limen
n mile
EILMP impel
EILMR meril
miler
EILMS limes
miles✧
Selim
slime
smile
EILMU ileum
EILMY Emily
limey
EILNN Lenin
linen
EILNO eloin
olein
EILNR liner
EILNS elsin
lenis
lines
nelis
silen✧
EILNT inlet
lenti
let in
EILNV levin
liven
EILNY liney
EILOP loipe
EILOR oiler
oriel
EILOT teloi
toile
EILOU Louie
EILOV olive
voile
EILPR peril
piler
plier
EILPS piles
plies
slipe
spiel
spile
EILPU lie up
EILPX pixel
EILRS siler
slier
EILRT liter
litre
tiler
EILRV liver
livre
rivel
EILRY riley
EILST islet
istle
steil
stile
EILSU ileus
EILSV Elvis
Levis®
lives
slive
EILSW lewis✧
Weil's
wiles
EILSX lexis
silex
EILSZ sizel
EILTT title
EILTU utile
EILTX ixtle
EILUY ulyie
EILUZ ulzie
EILVY veily
EILZZ zizel
EIMMR mimer
EIMMW immew
EIMNR inerm
in rem
miner
EIMNS Nîmes
EIMNT meint
EIMNX mixen
EIMNY meiny
EIMNZ mizen
EIMOR moire
moiré
EIMOV movie
EIMOX moxie
oxime
EIMPR prime
EIMPT tempi
EIMPU pumie
EIMRR rimer
EIMRS miser
Reims
EIMRT merit
miter
mitre
remit
timer
EIMRX mixer
remix
EIMSS seism
semis
EIMST Metis
métis✧
smite
stime
times✧
EINNO in one
EINNR inner✧
renin
EINNU ennui
EINNV venin
EINOP opine
EINOS eosin
noise
EINOT toe-in
EINOV envoi
ovine
EINPR ripen
EINPS penis
snipe
spine
EINPT inept
nepit
EINPY piney
EINQU quine
EINRS reins
resin
rinse
risen
serin
siren✧
EINRT inert
inter
niter
nitre
trine
EINRU inure
urine
EINRV riven
viner

Words marked ✧ can also be spelled with one or more capital letters

EINRX	nixer
EINSS	nisse
EINST	inset
	neist
	senti
	set in
	sient
	stein
	teins
EINSU	in use
EINSV	Svein
	visne
EINSW	sewin
	sinew
	swine
EINSX	nixes
EINTT	ettin
EINTU	unite
	untie
EINTW	twine
EINVW	vinew
EINVX	vixen
EINVY	veiny
EINWY	winey
EINWZ	winze
	wizen
EIOOR	oorie
EIOPS	poise
EIOPY	pioye
EIOPZ	piezo
EIORR	rorie
EIORS	osier
	Rosie
EIORU	ourie
EIORV	vireo
EIORW	owrie
EIOSS	Ossie
EIOST	toise
EIOTZ	tozie
EIOWY	yowie
EIOWZ	zowie✧
EIOZZ	Ozzie
EIPPR	piper✧
EIPPS	Pepsi®
	pipes
EIPQU	equip
	pique
	piqué
EIPRR	prier
	riper
EIPRS	épris
	Piers
	prise
	speir
	spire
EIPRT	piert
	tripe
EIPRV	viper
EIPRW	wiper
EIPRZ	prize
EIPSS	spies

EIPST	piste
	spite
	stipe
EIPSW	swipe
EIPTT	petit
EIPTU	tie up
	tie-up
	uptie
EIPTW	pewit
EIPTY	piety
EIQRU	quire
EIQTU	quiet
	quite
EIRRS	riser
EIRRT	trier✧
EIRRV	river
EIRRW	wirer
	wrier
EIRRY	eyrir
EIRST	reist
	resit
	stire
EIRSV	siver
	vires
EIRSW	sweir
	swire
	wires
EIRSX	sixer
EIRSZ	sizer
EIRTT	tetri
	titer
	titre
	trite
EIRTU	urite
	uteri
EIRTV	rivet
EIRTW	twier
	twire
	write
EIRVV	viver
EIRVZ	vezir
EISST	sties
EISSU	issue
	Susie
EISSW	Wessi
EISTU	suite
EISTV	stive
EISTX	exist
	sixte
EISTY	seity
EISVV	vives
EISVW	swive
	wives
EITTW	tewit
	twite
EITVX	vitex
EIVWY	viewy
EJKOP	kopje
EJKOR	joker
EJKOY	jokey
EJKRY	jerky

EJLLO	jello
EJLLY	jelly
EJLOP	polje
EJLOU	joule
EJLOY	Joely
EJLPU	julep
EJMMY	jemmy
EJNNY	jenny✧
EJNOR	rejón
EJNOT	jeton
EJNOY	enjoy
EJPTU	upjet
EJRRY	jerry✧
EJRWY	Jewry
EJSSU	Jesus
	jésus
EJSSY	Jessy
EJTTY	jetty
EKKOP	kopek
EKKOR	koker
EKLLN	knell
EKLLS	skell
EKLLY	kelly✧
EKLMS	skelm
EKLNT	knelt
EKLOS	Kelso
EKLOY	kyloe
	yokel
EKLPS	skelp
	spelk
EKLPT	P-Kelt
EKLPY	kelpy
EKLQT	Q-Kelt
EKLTW	welkt
EKLTY	kelty
EKMOS	smoke✧
EKMPS	kemps
EKMPT	kempt
EKMPY	kempy
EKNNO	ken-no
EKNNY	Kenny
EKNOR	Kreon
	krone
EKNOS	snoek
	snoke
	soken
EKNOT	token
EKNOW	knowe
	woken
EKNOZ	Kenzo
EKNSY	ensky
EKNTU	unket
EKOPR	Koper
	poker
	proke
EKOPS	spoke
EKOPT	topek
EKOPU	pouke✧
EKOPY	pokey
EKORR	roker
EKORT	toker

	troke
EKORW	wroke
EKOSS	sekos
	skeos
EKOST	stoke
EKPRU	puker
EKPRY	perky
EKPSY	pesky
EKPTU	tupek
EKPUY	key up
	pukey
EKRRU	kurre
EKRRY	Kerry
EKRSY	skyer
	skyre
	syker
EKSTY	skyte
EKSYY	skyey
ELLMS	smell
ELLNS	snell
ELLNY	nelly✧
ELLOR	lorel
ELLOS	losel
ELLPS	spell
ELLQU	quell
ELLSS	sells
ELLST	stell
ELLSW	swell
	Wells
ELLTU	tulle
ELLTY	telly
ELLWY	welly✧
ELMMU	lumme
ELMNO	lemon
	melon
ELMNU	lumen
ELMNY	Emlyn
ELMOR	morel
ELMOS	Melos
	Mosel
ELMOT	metol
	motel
ELMOU	oleum
ELMOY	moyle✧
ELMPU	plume
ELMRU	lemur
ELMRY	Meryl
ELMST	smelt
ELMSU	mulse
ELMSY	Myles
ELMTY	melty
ELMUV	mvule
	velum
ELMUY	muley
ELMXY	xylem
ELNNY	Lenny
	Lynne
ELNOP	pleon
ELNOR	enrol
	loner
	Lorne

ELNOS	lenos
	losen
ELNOT	Elton
	lento
	let on
	olent
ELNOU	noule
ELNOV	novel
ELNOW	lowne
	nowel✧
	Olwen
ELNOY	onely
ELNOZ	lozen
ELNTU	unlet
ELNWY	Elwyn
	newly
ELOOP	Poole
ELOOS	loose
	oleos
	soole
ELOPR	loper
	poler
	prole
ELOPS	slope
ELOPU	loupe
	poule
ELOPY	poley
ELORR	Errol
ELORS	loser
	soler
	sorel
ELORU	loure
	roule
ELORV	lover
ELORW	lower
	owler
	rowel
ELORY	Elroy
	Leroy
ELOSS	loess
	soles
ELOST	los'te
	stole
	telos
ELOSU	eusol
	louse
	ousel
	Seoul
ELOSV	slove
	solve
ELOSW	lowse
	sowle
ELOSY	soyle
ELOTT	to let
ELOTV	volet
	volte
ELOTW	owlet
	towel
ELOTX	extol
ELOTY	Otley
ELOUV	ovule
ELOUZ	ouzel
ELOVV	volve
ELOVW	vowel
	wolve
ELOVX	voxel
ELOVY	lovey
ELPRU	puler
ELPRY	reply
ELPST	slept
	spelt
ELPSU	Lepus
	pulse
	pusle
	spule
ELPSY	slype
ELPTU	let up
	let-up
	tuple
ELPUX	Pulex
ELPUZ	puzel
ELRRU	ruler
ELRSU	rules✧
ELRSY	slyer
ELRTU	luter
ELRTY	tyler
ELRUV	lurve
ELRUX	Lurex®
ELSSU	sluse
ELSTW	swelt
ELSTY	style
ELSUX	Lexus®
	luxes
ELTTY	Letty
ELTUX	exult
ELTWY	wetly
EMMOS	memos
	Somme
EMMRY	rymme
EMMSY	Emmys
EMNNO	nomen
EMNNU	numen
EMNOR	enorm
	moner
	morne
	morné
EMNOS	meson
EMNOT	mento
	Monet
	monte
	moten
EMNOV	venom
EMNOW	women
EMNOY	money✧
EMNPT	nempt
EMNRU	rumen
EMNTU	unmet
EMNTY	meynt
EMNUW	unmew
EMOOR	romeo✧
EMOOS	moose
EMOOT	me-too
EMOOV	moove
EMOPR	moper
	proem
EMOPS	Epsom
	mopes
EMOPT	tempo
EMOPY	mopey
	myope
EMORR	ormer
EMORS	mores
	morse✧
	smore
EMORT	metro✧
	métro✧
EMORV	mover
	vomer
EMORW	mower
	rowme
EMOSS	Moses
EMOST	mesto
	smote
EMOSU	mouse
EMOSY	mosey
EMOTT	motet
	motte
	totem
EMOTY	motey
EMOZZ	mezzo
EMPRS	sperm
EMPRT	mpret
EMPRY	premy
EMPSU	spume
EMPTT	tempt
	'tempt
EMRRU	murre
EMRRY	merry
EMRST	terms
EMRSU	muser
	Remus
	serum
EMRSY	Emrys
EMRTU	turme
EMRUX	murex
	Rumex
EMSSU	musse
EMSSY	messy
EMSTU	muset
EMSTY	styme
ENNOO	no one
	no-one
ENNOR	ronne
ENNOS	nones✧
	sonne
ENNOT	nonet
	tenno
	tenon
	tonne
ENNOX	xenon
ENNPU	unpen
ENNPY	penny
ENNRU	enurn
ENNTY	tenny
ENNWY	wenny
	Wynne
ENOOR	Roneo®
	roneo
ENOOS	noose
ENOOZ	ozone
ENOPR	Perón
	preon
	prone
ENOPY	peony
	poney
ENORS	Norse
	noser
	señor✧
	seron
	snore
ENORT	noter
	ronte
	tenor
	toner
	trone
ENORU	Rouen
ENORW	owner
	rowen
ENORY	royne
ENOSS	sonse
ENOST	Etons
	onset
	set on
	seton
	steno
	stone
ENOSU	ouens
ENOSW	owsen
	sowne
ENOSY	nosey
	noyes
ENOTY	toney
ENOVW	woven
ENOVY	envoy
ENOWX	woxen
ENPRT	prent
ENPRU	prune
ENPST	spent
ENPSU	Nupes
ENPTY	n-type
ENQRU	quern
ENQUY	queyn
ENRRU	rerun
ENRST	Ernst
	stern
ENRSU	nurse✧
ENRSY	Nerys
	syren
ENRTU	tuner
	urent
ENRTY	entry
	yrent
ENRVY	nervy
ENSTT	stent

ENSTU unset
usen't
ENSTY Estyn
ENSUV nevus
venus✧
ENSUW unsew
ENSUX nexus
unsex
ENSVY senvy
ENSWY newsy
Sweyn
ENTTY netty✧
tenty
ENTUW unwet
EOOPV poove
EOORS roose
EOORW wooer
EOOST soote
EOPPS pepos
EOPPT epopt
EOPPU poupe
EOPRR porer
prore
repro
roper
EOPRS poser
prose
repos
spero
spore
EOPRT opter
Porte
repot
toper
trope
EOPRV prove
EOPRW power
powre
EOPRY ropey
EOPSS pesos
posse
speos
EOPST estop
pesto
stoep
stope
EOPSX expos
EOPSY poesy
posey
poyse
sepoy
EOPXY epoxy
EOQRU roque
EOQTU quote
toque
EORRR error
EORRT retro✧
EORRV rover
EORRW rower
EORSS roses
EORST estro
roset
Soter
store
torse
EORSU euros
rouse
EORSV servo
verso
EORSW serow
sower
swore
worse
EORSX sorex
EORSZ zeros
EORTT otter
torte
EORTU outer
outré
route
EORTV overt
trove
voter
EORTW tower
twoer
wrote
EORTX oxter
EORTY toyer
EORTZ rozet
EORUY you're
EORVW vower
EORXX Xerox®
EOSSU souse
EOSSW sowse
EOSTT set-to
EOSTU touse
EOSTV stove
EOSTW towse
EOSUY youse
EOTTV Ovett
EOTUZ touze
EOTWZ towze
EOUVY you've
EPPPU pep up
EPPPY peppy
EPPRU upper
EPPSY Pepys
EPPTY p-type
EPRRY perry✧
pryer
ryper
EPRSS press✧
Serps
EPRST perst
prest
strep
EPRSU purse
sprue
super
EPRSW sprew
EPRSY pryse
spyre
Ypres
EPRTU erupt
EPRTW twerp
EPRUV rev up
EPRUX Purex
EPRVY pervy
EPRXY prexy
Pyrex®
EPSST steps
EPSTT stept
EPSTU set up
set-up
stupe
upset
EPSTW swept
EPSUU use up
EPSUW sew up
EPSUY upsey
EPSWY spewy
EPTTY petty
EQRUY query
EQSTU quest
EQSUU Equus
EQTUU tuque
EQTUY quyte
ERRSY serry
ERRTY retry
terry
tryer
ERRVY verry
ERRWY wryer
ERSST tress
ERSTT Rett's
terts
trest
ERSTU sture
ERSTV verst
ERSTW strew
trews
wrest
ERSTY resty
styre
ERSUU Eurus
usure
ERSVY syver
ERTTU utter
ERTUV vertu
ERTWY twyer
ESSTW stews
ESSTY styes
ESTTX texts
ESTTY styte
testy
ESTUY suety
ESTWY stewy
ESTYY yesty
ESTYZ zesty

F

FFFLU fluff
FFFUY fuffy
FFGIL gliff
FFGIR griff
FFGOO go off
go-off
FFGRU gruff
FFHIT fifth✧
FFHIW whiff
FFHOU houff
FFHOW howff
FFHUY huffy
FFIJY jiffy
FFIKS skiff
FFIMY miffy
FFINO Ffion
in-off
FFINS sniff
FFINY niffy
FFIOT off it
FFIPS spiff
FFIQU quiff
FFIRT triff
FFIST stiff
FFITY fifty
FFKOS skoff
FFLPU pluff
FFNOO on-off
FFNSU snuff
FFOSW sowff
FFOTY toffy
FFPUY puffy
FFSTU stuff
FGGIR Frigg
FGGOY foggy
FGGUY fuggy
FGHIT fight
FGILN fling
FGILT glift
FGINU fungi
FGIOS figos
FGIPU fig up
FGIRT grift
FGLNO flong
FGLNU flung
FGLUY gulfy
FGNOU fungo
FGOOR forgo
groof
FGOOU fogou
FGOOY goofy✧
FGOPU fog up
FGORU grouf
FHILT filth
FHIRT firth
frith
FHIST shift
FHISY fishy
FHITW whift
FHLOS flosh
FHLSU flush✧
FHOOS hoofs
FHORT forth✧

froth
FHOTT thoft
FHOTU fouth
FHOTW fowth
FHRSU frush
FHRTU furth
FIINS finis
FIINT fit in
FIINX infix
FIKLS flisk
FIKLU kulfi
FIKNO of kin
FIKNS finks
FIKRS frisk
FILLR frill
FILMP flimp
FILNT flint
FILOO folio
FILRT flirt
FILSU fusil
FILTT flitt
FILTY fitly
FIMOT motif
FIMTU mufti✧
FIMTY mifty
FINNO Fionn
FINNU in fun
FINST snift
FINTU unfit
FINTY nifty
FINUX Fuxin
unfix
FINUY unify
FIOQU quoif
FIOSS Sofis
FIOST foist
FIPTU fit up
fit-up
FIPUX fix up
FIRST frist
FIRTU fruit
FIRTY rifty
FIRTZ fritz
FIRZZ frizz
FISSU Sufis
FISTW swift✧
FIYZZ fizzy
FJLOO Flo-Jo
FKLNU flunk
FKLOO kloof
FKLOS folks
FKLUY fluky
FKNUY funky
FKORY forky
FLLOY folly
FLLUY fully
FLMOY Flymo®
FLMPU flump
FLNOU Fluon®
FLNOW flown
FLNOY fonly
FLOOS loofs
FLOOW Wolof
Woolf
FLORU flour
fluor
furol
FLOSU sulfo
FLOSW fowls
FLOTU flout
FLOTY lofty
FLOUW woful
FLRRU flurr
FLTUY fluty
FMOOR M-roof
FMORU forum✧
FMPRU frump
FNNUY funny
FNORR frorn
FNORT front
FNORW frown
FNOTU fount
futon
FOOPR proof
FOOPS spoof
FOORS roofs
FOORY roofy
FOOST foots
'sfoot
FOOWY woofy
FOPRU up for
FOPST f-stop
FORRU furor
FORRY frory
FORST frost✧
FORSU fours
FORWY frowy
FOSST softs
FOSTY softy
FPRUY fry-up
FRRUY furry
FRSTU frust
turfs
FRSUU Rufus
FRSUY surfy
FRTUY turfy
FRUYZ furzy
FSSUU Fusus
FSSUY fussy
FSTUY fusty
FTTUY tufty
FUYZZ fuzzy

G

GGGIS Giggs
GGGLO glogg
GGHOU Gough
GGINO going
oggin
GGIOT gigot
GGIPY piggy✧
GGMOY moggy
GGMUY muggy
GGNUY gungy
GGOSY soggy
GGPUY puggy
GGRUY ruggy
GGUVY vuggy
GHHIT hight
thigh
GHHOU hough
GHIKT kight
GHILT light
GHIMT might
GHINO hongi
GHINT night
thing
GHINY hying
GHIOS shogi
GHIOT hog it
GHIPT pight
GHIRT girth
grith
right
GHIST sight
GHITT tight
GHITW wight✧
GHLLY ghyll
GHLOU ghoul
lough
GHLPU gulph
GHLPY glyph
GHNOT thong
GHORU rough
GHOST gosht
GHOSU sough
GHOTU ought
tough
GHRSU shrug
GHSUY gushy
GIILR Rigil
GIILS sigil
GIILV vigil
GIINO Inigo
GIINP in pig
GIIPT pig it
GIJNO Gijon
jingo✧
GIJOT jigot
GIKLS glisk
GIKNO KOing
OKing
OK'ing
GIKNS Kings
GIKOP gopik
GILLR grill
GILNO lingo
log in
login
log-in
GILNP pling
GILNS sling
GILNT glint
GILNU lug in
lungi
GILNY lingy
lying
GILOO igloo
GILOR rigol
GILOS Sligo
GILPU pugil
GILRU lurgi✧
GILRY girly
GILST gilts
GILSU gusli
GILTU guilt
GILTZ glitz
GIMNY mingy
GIMOS gismo
misgo
GIMOY goyim
GIMOZ gizmo
GIMPU guimp
GIMPY pigmy
GIMRY grimy
GINNO Ngoni
GINNU Nguni
GINNY nying
GINOP pingo
GINOR giron
groin
O-ring
GINOT ingot
tigon
GINOW owing
wongi
GINOY yogin
GINRS rings
GINRU ruing
unrig
GINRW wring
GINSS signs
GINST sting
GINSU suing
GINSV V-sign
GINSW swing✧
wings✧
GINSY Sigyn
GINTY tying
GINVY vying
GINWY wingy
GINYZ zingy
GIOPR pirog
GIOQR Qogir
GIORR rigor
GIORS giros
GIORT griot
GIORU guiro
GIORV vigor
Virgo
GIPRS grips
sprig
GIPRU rig up
GIRST grist

Words marked ✧ can also be spelled with one or more capital letters

grits
strig
GIRSY grisy
GISTU giust
g-suit
GJMUU jugum
GJOSU jougs
GKORY Gorky
GLLOO lolog
GLLOY golly
GLLUY gully
GLMOO gloom
GLMOU logum
mogul✧
GLNOO log on
logon
log-on
GLNOP plong
GLNOS longs
GLNOU gluon
GLNSU slung
GLOOS logos✧
GLOOY gooly
ology
GLORW growl
GLOTU glout
GLOUV vulgo
GLRUY gurly
lurgy
GMMUY gummy
GMNOO mongo
GMNOU mungo✧
GMNUU ungum
GMOOR groom
GMORY gormy
GMPRU grump
GMPUU gum up
mug up
GMPYY pygmy
GNNUY gunny
GNNYY gynny
GNOOP pongo
GNOOZ gonzo
GNOPR prong
GNOPY pongy
GNORW grown
wrong
GNORY gyron
GNOST stong
tongs
GNOSY gonys
GNOTU ungot
GNOUY young
GNOYZ zygon
GNRTU grunt
GNRUW wrung
GNSTU stung
GNSUW swung
GOORS sorgo
GOOTU go out
outgo
GOPRS sprog
GOPRU group
GOPRY porgy✧
GOPTU tog up
GORSS gross
GORSZ grosz
GORTU grout
GORUY roguy
GOSTU gusto
GOSTY stogy
GOTUY gouty
guyot
GPPUY guppy
GPRSU sprug
GPRTY grypt
GPSYY gypsy
GRRUY gurry
GRSUY gyrus
surgy
GSTUY gusty
gutsy
GTTUY gutty

H

HHHUU uh-huh
HHISW whish
HHMOU ho-hum
HHMPU humph✧
HHOOS hoosh
HHOOT Hohot
HHORU H-hour
HHOTT Thoth
HHSSU shush
HHSUY hushy
HIILN nihil
HIIMS imshi
HIIQU qui-hi
HIIRS Irish
rishi
sirih
HIITT hit it
HIJOS shoji
HIKLT thilk
HIKLW whilk
HIKNS knish
HIKNT think
HIKRS shirk
HIKSW whisk
HILLS shill
HILLT illth
thill
HILMU hilum
HILOT litho
thiol
tholi
HILRT thirl
HILRW whirl
HILSS slish
HILST hilts
HILSU hilus
HILSY shily
HILTT tilth
HIMRT mirth
HIMST smith
HIMSY imshy
HIMTY thymi
HINNT ninth
HINOR rhino
HINOT hit on
HINPU unhip
HINSU Husni
HINSY shiny
HINWY whiny
HIOPP hippo
HIOPS Hopis
Sophi
HIOPT hop it
tophi
HIORU houri
HIOST hoist
HIPQS Q-ship
HIPTW whipt
HIPTY pithy
HIRRS shirr
HIRRW whirr
HIRST shirt
Trish
HIRSU shiur
HISSU sushi
HISSW swish
whiss
HISTW swith
whist
HISTX sixth
HITWY whity✧
withy
HIWZZ whizz
HKKOU hokku
HKLUY hulky
HKMNU Khnum
HKMOU hokum
khoum
HKNOY honky
HKNSU hunks
HKNUY hunky
HKOOS shook
HKOOY hooky
HKSSU husks
HKSUY husky
HLLOO hollo
HLLOU hullo
HLLOW who'll
HLLOY holly
HLLUY hully
HLMPY lymph
HLMSU mulsh
HLNSU shuln
HLOOS shool
HLOOY hooly
HLOPX phlox✧
HLORW whorl
HLOSS slosh
HLOST Holst
sloth✧
HLOTU Louth
HLOTW thowl
HLOTY hotly
HLPSU plush
HLPSY sylph
HLRUY hurly
HLSSU shuls
slush
HLSUY lushy
HLSYY shyly
HMNOT month
HMNPY nymph
HMOOP oomph
HMOOS homos
HMOOZ zhomo
HMOPR morph
HMORR mhorr
HMORU humor
mohur
HMOTU mouth
HMOTY mothy
Y-moth
HMPSU sumph
HMPTU thump
HMPUY humpy
HMRRY myrrh
HMRTU thrum
HMSTU musth
shtum
HMSUU humus
HMSUY mushy
HMTYY thymy
HNOOR honor✧
HNOOS shoon
HNOOW nohow
HNOPY phony
HNORS shorn
HNORT north✧
thorn
HNORU Huron
HNORY horny
HNOSW shown
HNOSY hyson
HNSSU snush
HNSTU shunt
HNSTY synth
HOOPT photo
HOOPW whoop
HOORT ortho
HOOST hoots
shoot
sooth
Sotho
HOOSW howso
how so?
whoso
woosh
HOOTT tooth
HOOTW how-to

whoot
HOPPU hop up
HOPRT thorp
HOPSS sposh
HOPSY hypos
Sophy
HOPTU hot up
HOQTU quoth
HORST short
HORSU Horus
hours
sohur
HORSW shrow
HORTT troth
HORTU routh
HORTW rowth
throw
whort
worth
wroth
HOSSU husos
HOSTT shott
HOSTU shout✧
south✧
thous
HOSTW sowth
HOSTY toshy
HOSUY shoyu
HOSWY showy
why, so
HOTUY youth
HPSUY pushy
HQRSU qursh
HRRUY hurry
HRSTU hurst✧
HRSUU suhur
HRSUY rushy
HRTTU truth
HRUUU uhuru
HSSUY hussy
HSTUY tushy
HSUUW wu shu✧
wushu✧
HUYZZ huzzy

I

IIJLN Jilin
IIJNN jinni
IIKKO kikoi
IIKLM kilim
IIKLN likin
IIKNN ink in
kinin
IIKRR kirri
IILLV villi
IILMT limit
IILMU ilium✧
IILNN linin
IILNT intil
IIMMN minim
IIMMR Mimir
IIMMT immit
IIMMX immix
IIMNR mirin
IIMNX mix-in
IIMPS impis
IIMRZ Izmir
IIMTX mix it
IINNO inion
IINNP nip in
IINNT innit
IINOS Oisin
IINOX Ixion
IINPT tip in
IINPZ zip-in
IINST sit in
sit-in
IINTU Inuit
IINTW inwit
IINTY tiyin
IIORT torii
IIPPT pipit
IIRST Tisri
IIRVZ vizir
IISTV visit
Vitis
IJKMU mujik
IJMMY jimmy✧
IJMPY jimpy
IJNNS jinns
IJNNU Injun
IJNNY Jinny
IJNOT joint
IJOST joist
IKKNS skink
IKKNY kinky
IKKOS kiosk
IKKRS skrik
IKKRU kukri
IKLLR krill
IKLLS skill
IKLMO milko
IKLMS sklim
IKLMT Klimt
IKLMY milky
IKLNP plink
IKLNS links
slink
IKLNY kylin
IKLOS kilos
IKLPU pikul
IKLRS skirl
IKLSY silky
IKLTU kitul
IKLTY kilty
IKLXY kylix
IKMNS Minsk
IKMPS skimp
IKMRS smirk
IKNNO Nikon®
IKNOP pinko
IKNOS kinos
IKNPR prink
IKNPS spink
IKNPY pinky
IKNST skint
stink
IKNSW swink
IKNSY sinky
IKNTW twink
IKNYZ zinky
IKOOR iroko
koori
IKORV Kirov
IKOSS skios
IKPPS Kipps
IKPSY pisky
spiky
IKPTU kit up
tupik
IKPUY Yupik
IKQRU quirk
IKRRS skirr
IKRST skirt
stirk
IKRSY risky
IKRTU Turki
IKSVY skivy
IKTTY kitty✧
ILLPR prill
ILLPS pills
spill
ILLQU quill
ILLRT trill
ILLST still
ILLSW swill
wills
ILLSY silly
slily
ILLTW twill
'twill
ILLTY tilly✧
ILLWY willy✧
ILMNU ulmin
ILMOO mooli
ILMOR milor
ILMOS limos
milos
ILMOU Mouli®
ILMPU pilum
ILMPY imply
ILMRY mirly
ILMSU simul
ILMSY slimy
ILMTZ miltz
ILNNY linny
ILNOS loins
noils
ILNOT Nilot
ILNOW Olwin
ILNPU lupin
ILNRY nirly
ILNSU Linus
Sunil
ILNSY lysin
ILNTU unlit
until
ILNTY linty
ILNUX Linux
ILNVY vinyl
ILOOP polio
ILOOS olios
ILOOV ovoli
ILOPS polis
spoil
ILOPT pilot
ILOPU poilu
ILOPW pilow
ILOPX oxlip
ILORS loris
ILORV livor
ILORY roily
ILORZ zoril
ILOSS silos
ILOST Solti
toils
ILOSU louis✧
ILOSY soily
ILPPU pipul
pupil
ILPPY lippy
ILPSS slips
ILPST slipt
spilt
split✧
ILPSU pilus
ILPTU lit up
tulip
ILQTU quilt
ILRSW swirl
ILRTW twirl
ILSST lists
ILSSY lysis
ILSTT stilt
ILSTU sluit
ILSTY silty
styli
ILSTZ Liszt
ILTTW twilt
IMMSU Mimus
IMMSY mimsy
IMMTY Timmy
IMNOO nomoi
IMNOR minor✧
IMNOS minos✧
Simon
IMNOT timon✧
IMNSU in sum
minus
IMNTY minty
IMOPR primo
IMOPT impot
Mopti
IMOPU opium

IMORT	Timor
IMOSS	misos
IMOST	moist
IMOSU	Suomi
IMOSZ	zoism
IMOTV	vomit
IMPPR	primp
IMPRS	prism
IMPRU	Purim
IMPRY	primy
IMPST	timps
IMPUX	mix up
	mix-up
IMPWY	wimpy
IMRRS	smirr
IMRST	strim
IMRTU	Timur
IMSSY	missy
IMSTU	muist
	musit
	tuism
IMSTY	misty
	stimy
IMTTY	Mitty
IMUZZ	zuzim
INNNO	ninon
INNNY	ninny
INNOO	onion
INNOP	piñon
INNOR	ronin
INNOT	niton
	noint
	'noint
INNOU	union✧
INNOW	no-win
INNOX	Nixon
INNPU	unpin
INNPY	pinny
INNRU	inurn
	run in
	run-in
INNSU	Sunni
INNTU	untin
INNTY	tinny
INOOR	Orion
INOPP	ippon
INOPR	orpin
	prion
	proin
	Ripon
INOPS	opsin
	pions
	psion
INOPT	opt in
	pinot✧
	pinto
	piton
	point
	potin
INOPW	powin
INOPY	piony
INOPZ	zip-on
INOQU	quoin
INORS	irons
	ornis
	rosin
INORT	intro
	nitro
INORY	irony
INOST	sit on
INOSV	vinos
	vison
INOSW	winos
INOSY	noisy
INOTW	in two
INOTX	toxin
INPPU	in pup
	pin-up
INPPY	nippy✧
INPRT	print
INPRU	purin
	unrip
INPSS	snips
INPSY	snipy
	spiny
INPTU	input
	Putin
	put in
	put-in
INPUZ	unzip
INQTU	quint
INRST	snirt
INRSU	ruins
INRTU	rutin
	Turin
INRTY	nitry
INSSU	nisus
	sinus
INSTT	stint
	'tisn't
INSTU	inust
	suint
	Tunis
INSTW	twins✧
INTTY	nitty
	tinty
INTUW	unwit
INTUY	unity✧
INTWY	twiny
INTYY	tyiyn
IOOPR	poori
IOOPT	topoi
IOPPZ	zippo✧
IOPQU	quipo
IOPRR	prior
IOPST	posit
IOPSU	pious
IOPTV	pivot
IOQTU	Quito
	quoit
IORRS	orris
IORRT	trior
IORSS	Rossi
IORST	roist
	rosit
	rösti
	rotis
	tiros✧
	torsi
	trios
IORSV	visor
IORSZ	zoris
IORTU	ruoti
IORTZ	rozit
IORVY	ivory
IORVZ	vizor
IOSSS	Ossis
IOSTT	stoit
IOSTV	ovist
	visto
IOSTZ	zoist
IOSUX	Sioux
IOTTW	to wit
IPPPY	pippy
IPPRU	rip up
IPPTU	tip-up
IPPTY	tippy
IPPUZ	zip up
IPPYY	yippy
IPPYZ	zippy
IPQUU	quipu
IPRST	spirt
	sprit
	stirp
	strip
IPRSU	sirup
IPRSY	spiry
IPRTW	twirp
IPRTY	tripy
IPRVY	privy
IPSTU	sit up
	sit-up
IPSTY	tipsy
IPSTZ	spitz✧
IPSWY	wispy
IPSXY	pyxis✧
IPTTU	putti
	titup
IQRTU	quirt
IQSTU	quist
	quits
	squit
IQSUZ	squiz
IRSSU	risus
IRSTT	trist
IRSTW	wrist
IRSUV	virus
IRSXY	Xyris
IRTUV	virtu
IRTXY	Trixy
IRTYZ	ritzy
ISSSW	Swiss
ISSSY	sissy
ISSTU	situs
ISSTW	swits
ISTTU	Titus
	Tutsi
ISTTW	twist
ISTUV	Vitus
ISTVY	stivy
ISTXY	sixty
	xysti
ISUUZ	Isuzu®
ITTTU	tutti
ITTTY	titty
ITTWX	'twixt
ITTWY	witty
ITYZZ	tizzy

J

JKLOO	jokol
JKNUY	junky
JLLOY	jolly
JLOOS	Jools
JLOTY	jolty
JLOWY	jowly
JMOOS	mojos
JMORU	jorum
JMPSU	jumps
JMPUY	jumpy
JNOOY	no joy
JNOPU	jupon
JNOTU	jotun✧
	junto
JNOTY	jonty
JORRU	juror
JOSTU	joust
JTTUY	jutty

K

KKLSU	skulk
KKMOU	kokum
KKNSU	skunk
KKOOY	kooky
KKORY	Korky
KKOSW	Kwok's
KKRSU	Kursk
KKUYY	yukky
KLLNO	knoll
KLLSU	skull
KLNOP	plonk
KLNPU	plunk
KLNRU	knurl
KLNSU	slunk
KLOOP	plook
KLOOS	kolos
	looks
KLOPU	plouk
KLOUY	yokul
KLOYY	yolky
KLSSU	sulks
KLSUY	sulky
KLTUZ	klutz
KMNOO	Nkomo

KMOOS mokos
smoko
KMOST Tomsk
KMOSY smoky
KMRUY murky
KMSUY musky
KNNOW known
KNOOR kroon
KNOOS snook
KNOOY nooky
KNOPR pronk
KNOPS knosp
KNOQU quonk
KNOST stonk
KNOSU onkus
KNOSW snowk
KNOSY yonks
KNOTU knout
KNOUY Yukon
KNOWY wonky
KNPSU spunk
KNPUY punky
KNRRU knurr
KNRTU trunk
KNSTU stunk
KNTUU Tunku
KOOPS spook
KOORR Koror
KOORY rooky
KOOST kotos
stook
tokos
KOOSZ zooks
KOOTW kotow
KOOTY Kyoto
Tokyo
KOPRY porky
KORST stork
torsk
KORSW works
KOUUY Kuo-yü
KRSUU kurus
KRTUU Turku
KSTUY tusky

L

LLLOY lolly
LLMOY molly✧
LLOPR proll
LLOPY polly✧
LLOQU quoll
LLORS Rolls
LLORT troll
LLOSY lysol
Solly
LLOUY you'll
LLOWY lowly
wolly
LLOXY xylol
LLPWY Pwyll
LLRTU trull
LLSTU stull
LLSUY sully
LLSYY slyly
LLXYY xylyl
LMMUY lummy
LMOOS mools
slo-mo
sloom
LMOOT molto
LMOOY mooly
LMOPU pulmo
LMOST smolt
LMOSU Mosul
mouls
solum
LMOTU moult
LMOTW mol wt
LMOTY ymolt
LMPPU plump
LMPSU slump
LMPUY lumpy
plumy
LMRUY murly
rumly
LMSTU stulm
LMSUU Ulmus
LNNOY nylon
LNOOR Orlon®
LNOOS loons
snool
Solon
LNOOY loony
LNOPY pylon
LNOST stoln
LNOSW swoln
LNOSY Lyons
LNOTU Luton
LNOUZ Luzon
LNOWY Olwyn
LOOOV ovolo
LOOPR orlop
LOOPS polos
pools
sloop
spool
LOORY Oryol
LOOSS solos
LOOST lotos
sloot
stool
tools
LOOTT lotto
LOOVV Volvo®
LOPPU poulp
LOPPY polyp
LOPRU proul
LOPRW prowl
LOPSS slops
LOPSY polys
slopy
LOPTU Pluto
poult
LORST rotls
LORUX Luxor
LORUY loury
LORWY Lowry
LOSSU solus
LOSTU lotus✧
LOSTY stylo
LOSUY lousy
LOTYZ zloty
LOUUV voulu
LPPUY pulpy
LPRSU slurp
LPSUU lupus✧
LRRUY lurry
LRSUY surly
LRTUY truly
LRUUU Uluru
LRWYY wryly
LSTUY lusty

M

MMMOY mommy
MMMUY mummy
MMOPY pommy
MMOSU Momus
MMOTY tommy✧
MMPSU mumps
MMRUY rummy
MMSTU stumm
MMSUY mumsy
MMTUY tummy
MMUYY yummy
MNOOR moron
MNOOS monos
nomos
MNOOY moony
MNORU mourn
Munro
MNORY Myron
MNOTU mount✧
muton
notum
MNOTY monty
MNOUV novum
MNTUU muntu
MNTUZ Muntz
MOOPR promo
MOOPS spoom
MOORR morro
MOORS Moros
rooms
smoor
MOORT motor
MOORV vroom
MOORY roomy
MOOSS mosso
MOOST smoot
MOOTT motto
MOPPU mop up
mop-up
MOPRT tromp
MOPST stomp
MOPSU mopus
MOPSY myops
MORRU rumor
MORST storm
MORSU Morus
MORSW worms✧
MORTU tumor
MORWY wormy
MOSSU musos
sumos
MOSTU motus✧
moust
smout
MOSTW smowt
MOSUY mousy
MPRTU trump
MPRUY rumpy
MPSTU stump
MPSUU sum up
MPSUY spumy
MPTUY tumpy
umpty
MRRUY murry
MRSTU strum
MSSUY mussy
MSTUU Mt Usu
MSTUY musty
MUYZZ muzzy

N

NNNOY nonny
NNOOS no-nos
no-no's
NNOOT not on
NNORS Norns
NNORU run on
run-on
NNOST stonn
NNOSU nouns
NNOSY sonny
NNOUW unwon
NNOUY nouny
NNRUY runny
NNSUY sunny
NNTUY tunny
NOOPR porno
NOOPS snoop
spoon
NOORS Orson
NOORT Orton
Troon
NOOST snoot
NOOSW swoon
NOOSZ zoons
NOOTW on tow
NOOTY toyon
NOPRY proyn
NOPTU not up
punto

put on
put-on
ton-up
NOPTY ponty
poynt
NOPUW own up
NOPUY yupon
NOPWY powny
NOQRU Quorn®
NORST snort
NORSU urson
NORSW sworn
NORTU Torun
NORTY try on
try-on
NORUY yourn
NOSSY sonsy
NOSTU Notus
snout✧
stoun
tonus
NOSTW stown
NOSTY stony
Tonys
Tyson
NOSUW Suwon
swoun
NOSWY snowy✧
NOTWY towny
NPRSU spurn
NPRTU prunt
NPRUU run up
run-up
uprun
NPSUU sunup
NPTUY punty
NRTUU U-turn
NRTUY runty
NSTTU stunt
NTTUY nutty

O

OOOPT potoo
OOPPS oppos
OOPPZ zoppo
OOPRS proso
sopor
spoor
OOPRT poort
Proto®
troop
OOPRV Provo
OOPRY roopy
OOPST spoot
stoop
topos
OOPSW swoop
OOPTT potto
OOPVY poovy
OOPZZ Pozzo
OORRS ro-ros
OORRT rotor
OORRZ zorro
OORST roost
roots✧
stoor
torso✧
OORTW wroot
OORTY rooty
OOSTT toots
OOSTY sooty
OOSUZ ouzos
OOTWZ wootz
OOWYZ woozy
OPPPU pop-up
OPPPY poppy
OPPRS props
OPPSU sop up
OPPSY popsy
psyop
soppy
OPPTU pot up
poupt
top up
top-up
up top
OPRST sport
strop
OPRSY prosy
OPRTY porty
OPRUY roupy
OPRXY proxy
OPSST spots
OPSSY sysop
OPSTT Pott's
OPSTU spout
stoup
OPSTW swopt
OPSTY Topsy
typos
OPSUY soupy
OPSWY Powys
OPTTU putto
tot up
OPTTY potty
typto
OPTUW two-up
OPTUY pouty
OPTZZ ZZ Top
OPYZZ pozzy
OQRST Q-sort
ORRSY sorry
ORRTU Truro
ORRTY rorty
ORRWY worry
ORSSU sorus
ORSTU roust
stour
sutor
torus
Tours
ORSTW strow
worst
ORSTY royst
story
stroy
tyros
ORSUY yours
ORTTU trout
tutor
ORTUY yourt
ORUVW vrouw
OSSST stoss
OSSTY tossy
OSTTU stout
OSTTY ytost
OSTUY tousy
OSTWY towsy
OSUYZ Soyuz
OTTTY totty
OTUYZ touzy
OTWYZ towzy

P

PPPUY puppy
PPRUY purpy
PPTUU put up
put-up
PPUYY yuppy✧
PRSSU Spurs
PRSTU spurt
turps
PRSUU usurp
PRSUY pursy
Pyrus
syrup
PRTUY purty
PSSUY pussy
PSUWY swy-up
PTTUY putty

R

RSSTU truss
RSSUU Ursus
RSTTU strut
sturt
trust
RSTTY tryst
RSTUW wurst
RSTUY rusty
RSUUY usury
RTTUY rutty

S

SSUWY wussy

T

TTTUY tutty

6 letters

A

AAABCL cabala
AAABCN cabana
AAABCS casaba
AAABDG dagaba
AAABDH bahada
AAABDJ bajada
AAABDN Abadan
AAABHS Bahasa
AAABKK kabaka
AAABKL kabala
AAABKY kabaya
AAABLM Balaam
AAABLT albata
atabal
balata
AAABNN Annaba
banana
AAABNS anabas
AAABRZ baraza
bazaar
AAABTT batata
AAACCI acacia
AAACDN Canada
cañada
AAACJN jacana
jaçana
AAACLN Nacala
AAACLP alpaca
AAACMR maraca
AAACNN Canaan
AAACNR arcana
AAACPT pataca
AAADGH Agadah
AAADMN Amanda
AAADMR armada
AAADNN Danaan
AAADNP panada
AAADNR Narada
AAAEGP agapae
AAAELZ azalea
AAAENR Aranea
AAAFLL fa la la
AAAFRT Arafat
AAAGHT Agatha
AAAGIL Aglaia
AAAGLM Malaga

Málaga
AAAGLR argala
AAAGNN nagana
AAAGNP pa'anga
AAAHIT taiaha
AAAHLL halala
AAAHNV Havana
AAAHRS Sahara
AAAILL alalia
AAAILR aralia
AAAINZ Azania
AAAITX ataxia
AAAJKT jataka✧
AAAJMU ujamaa
AAAKKN kanaka✧
AAAKKR karaka
AAAKLM kamala
AAAKLS Alaska
AAAKNR Ankara
AAAKNT katana
AAALMP palama
AAALMS masala
salaam
AAAMMN Manama
AAAMNN mañana
AAAMNP panama✧
AAAMNS samaan
AAAMNT ataman
AAAMRS Asmara
samara✧
AAAMRT tamara✧
AAAMRY Aymara
AAANNS ananas
AAANRT antara
AAANRV Ravana
AAANST Astana
AAANTT anatta
AAAPPY papaya
AAAPTZ zapata✧
AAARRT Ararat
AAARST satara
AAARTV avatar
AAARTW Tarawa
AAARUV Avarua
AABBBO baobab
AABBCO babaco
AABBCY abbacy
AABBDO Abbado
AABBDS abdabs
AABBHL bablah
AABBKS kababs
AABBLL lablab
AABBLO balboa
AABBST sabbat
AABCHS casbah
AABCIM cambia
AABCIN Bianca
AABCIR Arabic
AABCKR backra
AABCLU bacula
AABCLZ Balzac
AABCMN cabman
AABCMT tambac
AABCRS Barsac
scarab
AABCSU abacus
AABCUU aucuba
AABDER abrade
AABDES abased
AABDET abated
AABDEU aubade
AABDGO dagoba
AABDIN Ibadan
indaba
AABDIO Bao Dai
AABDIR abraid
AABDIT Ibadat
AABDLL ballad
AABDLM lambda
AABDMN badman
AABDNR bandar
AABDOR aboard
abroad
AABDRT tabard
AABDRY bayard✧
AABDSS badass
AABEFN befana
AABEGM ambage
AABEGT atabeg
tea bag
teabag
AABEIL abelia
AABEKT atabek
AABELM Amabel
mabela
AABELR arable
AABELT ablate
AABELZ ablaze
AABEMO amoeba
AABENS Sabean
AABENT Banate
AABERU bauera
AABERZ zareba
AABESS Bassae
AABEST sea bat
AABETU bateau
AABETZ zabeta
AABFIN Fabian
AABGGR ragbag
AABGGS gasbag
sag bag
AABGIN baaing
AABGIR airbag
AABGLN Bangla
AABGMN bagman
AABGRT ratbag
AABHIS sahiba
AABHIW Wahabi
AABHJN bhajan
AABHKS kasbah✧
sabkha
AABHLR bharal
AABHMR Brahma
AABHMS shamba
AABHNV bhavan
AABHRT Bharat
AABHSW bashaw
AABILL labial
AABILM Baalim
AABILN Nabila
AABILR à l'abri
AABILU abulia
AABILX biaxal
AABIMN Bimana
AABIMR Bairam
AABIMZ Zambia
AABINN banian✧
AABINR arabin
AABINS Sabian
Sabina
AABINW wabain
AABINZ banzai
Zabian
Zainab
AABIRS arabis
AABIRZ zariba
AABIST abatis
Bastia
AABISW wasabi
AABISZ baizas
AABJNX banjax
AABKLN Balkan
AABKMO Bamako
AABKNN kanban
AABKNR barkan
AABLLN ballan
AABLLO abolla
AABLLR labral
AABLLT ballat
AABLMO Malabo
AABLMS balsam
sambal
AABLNY Albany
AABLOR aboral
AABLOV lavabo
AABLRZ blazar
AABLST basalt
AABLTU ablaut
tabula
AABMNR barman
AABMNT bantam
batman✧
AABMOR Abroma
AABMRS sambar
AABMST tsamba
AABNNT Bannat
AABNNY banyan✧
AABNST basant
AABNYZ Zaynab
AABORR arroba
AABORT abator
rabato
AABORZ abrazo
AABOSU oubaas
AABRRT barrat
AABRRW raw bar
AABRTY baryta
AABTTU abattu
AABZZZ bazazz
AACCDI cicada
AACCDU caduac
AACCEL caecal
AACCHH cha-cha
AACCHK kaccha
AACCHM chacma
AACCIL Alcaic
cicala
AACCIM caimac
AACCIR Carica
AACCKK ack-ack
AACCKR carack
AACCLO cloaca
AACCLP calpac
AACCLR calcar
AACCMO macaco
AACCNN cancan
AACCRT caract
AACDDN AD and C
AACDDU caudad
AACDEF facade
façade✧
AACDEI acedia
AACDER arcade
AACDEU cadeau
AACDFR cafard
AACDGI Agadic
AACDHR chadar
AACDIM Adamic
AACDIN Candia
AACDIR acarid
AACDLU caudal
AACDMP madcap
AACDNR canard
AACDOP da capo
AACDRY Arcady
AACEFL faecal
AACEFR carafe
AACEGH achage
AACEHN Aachen
AACEHP apache✧
AACEHR areach
AACEHT chaeta
AACELN anlace
AACELP palace
AACELS scalae
AACELT acetal
AACEMR camera
AACENN cannae
AACENP canapé
AACENR arcane
AACENT catena
AACEPR ear-cap
Parcae
AACEPS sea cap

AACERS caesar✧
AACERT acater
AACEST acates
sea cat
AACETV caveat
vacate
AACFIL cafila
facial
AACFIR Africa
AACFIS fascia
AACFLU facula
faucal
AACFNT caftan
AACFRS fracas
AACFRX carfax
AACFTT fat cat
fat-cat
AACGHN chagan
AACGIM agamic
AACGIR agaric
Garcia
AACGIU guaiac
AACGPS gas cap
AACGUY Cayuga
AACHKN achkan
AACHKP chapka
pachak
AACHKR chakra
charka
AACHKW kwacha
AACHLN chalan
AACHLS calash
AACHLT caltha
Cathal
AACHMN machan
AACHMS camash
AACHNO choana
AACHNR anarch
AACHNS ash-can
AACHNT acanth
Tanach
AACHNZ chazan
AACHRS charas
AACHRT Cathar
charta
AACHSW cashaw
AACHTT attach
chatta
AACHTW awatch
AACHTY Cathay
AACIIL Alicia
AACIIR Icaria
AACIJM jicama
AACILL laical
AACILM calami
calima
AACILN Lancia®
AACILP apical
AACILR Alaric
racial
AACILS Calais
AACILT Altaic
AACIMN caiman
maniac
AACIMR Marcia
AACINR arnica
carina✧
Ciaran
crania
AACINS ascian
sancai
AACIOT atocia
coaita
AACIPS capias
AACIPT capita
AACIRR air-car
AACIRS air-sac
AACIRV caviar
AACISS cassia✧
AACITX ataxic
AACJKL jackal
AACJOU acajou
AACKPZ czapka
AACKRR arrack
AACKRW awrack
AACKTT attack
AACLLN callan
AACLLO Callao
AACLLS Callas
AACLMT lactam
AACLMU macula
AACLNO canola
AACLNR carnal
AACLNT Cantal
AACLNU canula
lacuna
AACLOR Carola
AACLOT catalo
AACLPR carpal
AACLPS pascal✧
AACLPT cat-lap
AACLRS lascar
rascal
sacral
scalar
AACLRW acrawl
AACLSU casual✧
causal
AACLTU actual
AACMNR carman
Marcan
AACMNY cayman
AACMOT Tacoma
AACMOY macoya
AACMRT ramcat
Tarmac®
tarmac
AACMSS camass
AACNNO Ancona
AACNOR ancora
AACNPT captan
catnap
AACNRS Nascar®
AACNRT arctan
cantar
AACNRY canary
AACNSV canvas
AACNTT actant
AACNTU Tucana
AACNTV vacant
AACNTZ Zantac®
AACPPY papacy
AACPRS Caspar
scarpa
AACRRT carrat
AACRRU curara
AACRSU acarus
AACRTV cravat
AACSSV cavass
AADDEL daedal
AADDER adread
AADDIL alidad
la-di-da
AADDLN adland
AADDMS Saddam
AADDNR Dardan
AADDOU aoudad
AADDRW adward
AADDST stadda
AADEFL aefald
AADEFR afeard
AADEGL gelada
AADEGM damage
AADEGN agenda
AADEGZ agazed
AADEHK akedah
AADEIN Idaean
AADEJU Judaea
AADEKM medaka
AADEKW awaked
AADELL Adella
AADELS salade
AADELT alated
AADEMM madame✧
AADEMN anadem
maenad
AADENN Andean
Deanna
AADENR Andrea
AADENS Seanad
AADENT adnate
AADENV Nevada
AADENX adnexa
AADEPR parade✧
AADEPS espada
AADERV Veadar
AADERW adware
AADFIR afraid
AADFLW afawld
AADFNR farand
AADFNT fantad
AADFRT daftar
AADFTW fatwa'd
AADGHR dargah
AADGIM agamid
AADGIO adagio
AADGIR Agadir
gardai
AADGLM lad mag
AADGNP padang✧
pad-nag
AADGNR argand
AADGNU Uganda
AADGOP pagoda
AADGRS Asgard
AADGRU garuda✧
AADGRY gaydar
rag day
AADGTY tag day
AADHIL dahlia
AADHLR Harald
AADHMR dharma
AADHNN Handan
AADHNR dharna
AADHNT at hand
AADHRZ hazard
AADILL Dalila
AADILN Dalian
AADILR radial
AADILS dalasi
AADILU audial
AADIMN Damian
maidan
AADIMR air dam
AADINO Adonai
Adonia
Danaoi
AADINR Adrian
radian
AADINS naiads✧
AADINT aidant
AADINV Davina
navaid
AADIPP appaid
AADIQS qasida
AADIRT tiara'd
AADIST stadia
AADJLN Jandal®
AADKKU Kakadu
AADKLN Kandla
AADKMS damask
AADKNS Skanda
AADKNU Kaunda
AADKOT Dakota
AADKPU padauk
AADLLN and all
AADLLS Dallas
sallad
AADLLY all-day
AADLMP lampad
AADLMW wadmal
AADLMY malady
AADLNO anodal
AADLNR Randal

AADLNS	sandal
AADLNU	landau
	Luanda
AADLNV	vandal✧
AADLOP	apodal
AADLOU	Douala
AADLPR	pardal
AADLRU	radula
AADLWY	law-day
AADLYY	lay-day
AADMMM	Dammam
AADMMN	madman
AADMMR	am-dram
	dammar
AADMMS	madams
AADMMX	Mad Max
AADMNY	man-day
AADMOU	amadou
AADMRS	madras
AADMRU	maraud
AADMRZ	mazard
AADMSS	admass
	ad-mass
AADMYY	May Day
	mayday✧
AADNNR	randan
AADNPR	pandar
AADNPU	Paduan
AADNRS	nasard
	Sandra
AADNRT	tarand
AADNRW	Rwanda
AADNTW	want ad
AADNUX	Xanadu
AADNYY	any day
AADOPS	posada
AADPPY	appayd
AADPSW	padsaw
AADPSY	spayad
AADPYY	pay day
AADRRS	sardar
AADRTU	datura
AADRTY	datary
AADRVW	vaward
AAEEGN	Aegean
AAEEGR	Graeae
AAEEGT	eatage
AAEELP	paleae
AAEELT	taleae
AAEENS	Aeneas
AAEEPS	sea ape
AAEERS	sea ear
AAEERT	aerate
AAEEST	at ease
AAEEYY	aye aye
	aye-aye
AAEFFR	affear
AAEFLM	aflame
AAEFLR	rafale
AAEFLV	favela
AAEFNR	fraena
AAEFNS	sea fan
AAEFNU	faunae
AAEGGL	galage
AAEGGR	garage
AAEGGV	gavage
AAEGIN	Aegina
AAEGIR	Graiae
AAEGLL	Lalage
AAEGLM	agleam
AAEGLN	alnage
	Angela
	anlage
	galena
	lagena
AAEGLR	alegar
	laager
AAEGLT	algate
AAEGLV	lavage
AAEGMN	agname
	manage
AAEGMR	Gemara
	Megara
AAEGNP	Pangea
AAEGNR	Reagan
AAEGNS	Ganesa
AAEGNT	agnate
AAEGNU	Augean
AAEGOR	agorae
	oarage
AAEGPR	parage
AAEGPS	agapes
AAEGPV	pavage
AAEGRV	ravage
AAEGSV	savage
AAEGTU	gateau
	gâteau
AAEGTZ	at gaze
AAEHKP	pakeha
AAEHKS	ashake
AAEHKT	takahe
AAEHLM	haemal
AAEHLT	althea✧
AAEHMS	ashame
AAEHMT	hamate
AAEHNT	aneath
	Anthea
	Athena
AAEHNY	hyaena
AAEHPW	awhape
AAEHRR	Harare
AAEHRT	Aretha
	Eartha
AAEHSY	Ayesha
AAEILM	amelia✧
AAEILR	aerial
	realia
AAEILV	availe
AAEILX	alexia✧
AAEIMN	anemia
AAEINT	taenia
AAEIRS	araise
	sea air
AAEIRT	Raetia
AAEIRV	Aveira
AAEITV	aviate
AAEJRY	A J Ayer
AAEKLM	kamela
AAEKLN	alkane
AAEKLR	Kerala
AAEKLS	aslake
AAEKMW	wakame
AAEKNN	ananke
	Anneka
AAEKNR	Karena
AAEKNW	awaken
AAEKRS	keasar✧
AAEKRT	karate
AAELLP	paella
	pallae
AAELLU	alulae
AAELMP	Palmae
	Pamela
AAELMR	rameal
AAELMT	malate
	meatal
	tamale
AAELMZ	Lamaze
AAELNN	anneal
AAELNT	lanate
AAELOR	areola
AAELPP	appeal
AAELPR	earlap
AAELPS	salpae
AAELPT	palate
AAELRV	larvae
AAELRZ	Azrael
AAELSW	sea law
	Walesa
AAELTV	valeta
AAELTZ	alteza
AAEMMM	mammae
AAEMNP	apeman
AAEMNR	Ramean
AAEMNS	seaman✧
AAEMNT	amenta
AAEMNX	axeman
AAEMRS	asmear
AAEMRT	ramate
	retama
AAEMSS	Seamas
AAEMST	sea mat
AAEMSW	sea maw
AAEMTX	meat-ax
AAENNS	Saanen
AAENNZ	zenana
AAENOP	apnoea
AAENOZ	ozaena
AAENPV	pavane
AAENRT	Renata
AAENST	ansate
AAENSU	nausea✧
AAEPPR	appear
AAEPRS	pasear
	sarape
AAEPRT	patera
	petara
AAEPRZ	zarape
AAEPTT	tapeta
AAERRR	arrear
AAERRT	errata
AAERST	astare
	searat
AAERSY	arayse
AAERTT	terata
AAERTU	aurate
AAERWX	earwax
AAERWY	aweary
AAESTV	Avesta
	savate
AAESWY	awayes
	seaway
AAFFIM	maffia✧
AAFFIR	affair
	raffia
AAFFIT	taffia
AAFFJN	Jaffna
AAFFPR	affrap
AAFFRY	affray
AAFFST	Staffa
AAFGHN	afghan✧
AAFHRS	Ashraf
AAFHTW	fatwah
AAFIJT	fajita
AAFIKL	kafila
AAFIKS	sifaka
AAFILS	Faisal
AAFILV	Flavia
AAFIMT	Fatima
AAFINR	farina
AAFIRS	safari
AAFIST	fatsia
AAFITU	au fait
AAFKNT	kaftan
AAFLLL	fallal
AAFLNU	faunal
AAFLOT	afloat
AAFLSY	Faysal
AAFNNT	fan-tan
AAFNSU	faunas
AAGGHI	Haggai
AAGGKU	gagaku
AAGGLO	galago
AAGGMN	gagman
	mganga
AAGGQU	quagga
AAGGRS	saggar
AAGGRT	ragtag
	tagrag
AAGHIL	Alhagi
AAGHKN	kangha
	khanga
AAGHLZ	ghazal
AAGHMR	Armagh

	Graham
AAGHMS	gamash
AAGHNR	Anghar
	arghan
	hangar
AAGHNS	sangha
AAGHOT	Agatho
AAGHST	aghast
AAGIKN	kainga
AAGILN	agnail
AAGILO	alogia
AAGILP	palagi
AAGILR	argali
	garial
AAGILV	gavial
AAGIMN	magian
AAGINN	angina
	inanga
AAGINR	Grania
	nagari
AAGINT	gitana
AAGINU	iguana
AAGINV	vagina
AAGINW	Gawain
AAGIPR	airgap
AAGIRS	air-gas
AAGIRU	Auriga
AAGIRV	Viagra®
AAGIRW	waragi
AAGISS	Agassi
AAGJNR	garjan
AAGJRS	gas jar
AAGJRU	jaguar
AAGKLR	Kalgar
AAGKLU	Kaluga
AAGLLN	lalang
AAGLLP	plagal
AAGLMM	malmag
AAGLMN	Malang
	mangal
AAGLNO	analog
	angola✧
AAGLNR	raglan
AAGLNT	galant
AAGLST	stalag
AAGLWY	Galway
AAGLXY	galaxy✧
AAGMMR	gramma
AAGMMS	magmas
AAGMNR	ragman
AAGMNS	gasman
AAGMNZ	zamang
AAGMRY	magyar✧
	margay
AAGNNO	goanna
	Nagano
AAGNNW	An Wang
	wangan
AAGNOR	angora✧
	Aragon
	Onagra

	organa
AAGNOT	taonga
AAGNOY	Nagoya
AAGNPR	parang
AAGNRR	garran
AAGNRS	sangar
AAGNRT	Granta
AAGNRY	angary
	Granya
AAGNST	satang
AAGNSY	Sangay
AAGNTU	taguan
AAGNUY	Guyana
AAGORS	agoras
AAGOTU	agouta
AAGPPR	grappa
AAGPST	gas tap
AAGRRY	garrya
AAGRST	gas-tar
AAGRSV	Svarga
	Vargas
AAGRSW	Swarga
	war gas
AAGRVY	vagary
AAHHLV	halvah
AAHHMZ	hamzah
AAHHNN	Hannah
AAHHNT	thanah
AAHHPR	Aphrah
AAHHPT	aphtha
AAHHWW	haw-haw
	wah-wah
AAHIIK	haikai
AAHIIS	Isaiah
AAHIIW	Hawaii
AAHIKR	karahi
AAHILT	hiatal
	Thalia
AAHILY	aliyah
AAHIMN	Hamina
AAHIMS	ahimsa
AAHINN	Nan Hai
AAHINT	tahina
AAHIPR	Pahari
	pariah
	raphia✧
AAHIRS	sharia✧
AAHIRV	vihara
AAHISV	Shaiva
AAHJNR	hanjar
AAHJRR	jarrah
AAHJRS	Jashar
AAHKKL	Khalka
AAHKKM	Makkah
AAHKKT	kathak✧
AAHKKZ	Kazakh
AAHKLS	Khalsa
AAHKLT	khalat
AAHKLU	Kahlúa®
AAHKNO	Haakon
AAHKNT	kantha

AAHKST	Shakta
AAHKSY	yaksha
AAHLLL	hallal
AAHLLN	hallan
	nallah
AAHLLO	halloa
AAHLLP	pallah
AAHLLW	wallah
AAHLMM	hammal
	mahmal
AAHLMT	maltha
AAHLRS	ashlar
AAHLRT	hartal
AAHLSV	lavash
AAHMMM	hammam
AAHMNR	harman
AAHMNS	shaman
AAHMPS	Phasma
AAHMPY	mayhap
AAHMRS	ashram
	Marsha
AAHMRT	Martha
	Matrah
AAHMST	asthma
AAHMSU	mashua
AAHMTZ	matzah
AAHNNS	Anshan
AAHNNT	Nathan
	tannah
	thanna
AAHNOV	Navaho
AAHNPS	ash-pan
AAHNPT	Pathan
AAHNSS	Hassan
AAHNST	Sathan
AAHNTW	whatna
AAHNUW	whanau
AAHNZZ	hazzan
AAHPPR	paraph
AAHPRY	yarpha
AAHPTY	apathy
AAHRSS	harass
	hassar
AAHRSU	Aarhus
	Ashura
AAHSSY	sashay
AAHTTT	at that
AAIIKK	kaikai
AAIIMM	mia-mia
AAIIMT	Mai Tai
AAIJLM	Jamila
AAIJMN	Jamnia
AAIJNN	Janian
	Janina
AAIJNR	Rajani
AAIJNT	tinaja
AAIJRW	jawari
AAIJVY	Vijaya
AAIKLL	alkali
AAIKLM	kalmia
	kamila

AAIKLN	kalian
AAIKNN	Annika
AAIKNO	aikona
AAIKNR	Karina
AAIKNT	tankia✧
AAIKOR	kia-ora
AAIKPT	Pitaka
AAIKRS	askari
AAIKRT	karait
AAIKRU	uakari
AAIKSS	Saskia
AAILLP	pallia
AAILLT	Lalita
AAILLX	axilla
AAILMN	almain✧
	animal
	lamina
	Malian
	manila✧
AAILMP	impala
AAILMR	Lariam®
AAILMS	alisma
	salami
AAILMU	aumail
AAILMW	Malawi
AAILNN	La Niña
	Lianna
AAILNR	narial
AAILNS	Salian
	salina
AAILNT	antlia✧
	Latian
	Latina
AAILNW	Walian
AAILNY	inyala
AAILPR	parial
AAILPS	palais
AAILQU	Aquila
	qualia
AAILRT	Altair
	atrial
	lariat
	latria
AAILSS	assail
AAILST	a salti
AAILSV	avails
	saliva
	salvia
AAILTT	Attila
AAILTV	avital
	Latvia
AAIMMS	miasma
AAIMMX	maxima
AAIMNR	airman
	Armani
	Marian
	marina✧
AAIMNS	Samian
AAIMNT	manati
AAIMNV	vimana
AAIMRR	air-arm

marari
AAIMRS Aramis
AAIMRT amrita
tamari
AAIMSS Masais
AAIMTT tatami
AAINNO Aonian
AAINNR Narnia
AAINNT naiant
Tainan
AAINOR Oriana
AAINOX anoxia
AAINPP papain
AAINPR Parian
piraña
AAINPT patina
piñata
taipan
AAINRR Arrian
AAINRS nairas
AAINRT antiar
Tirana
AAINRU anuria
Urania
AAINTT attain
AAINTV Ativan®
avanti
AAINTW atwain
Taiwan
AAINVY Vinaya
AAINWY in a way
AAIOPR aporia
AAIPPR appair
AAIPRT pitara
AAIPRU au pair
AAIPRY apiary
piraya
AAIPTU Tupaia
AAIPZZ piazza
AAIQRT Qatari
AAIRRV à ravir
AAIRRY ariary
AAIRST arista
tarsia
AAIRSV Vasari
AAIRSW Iswara
AAIRTY raiyat
AAIRVY aviary
AAIRWY airway
AAIRZZ razzia
AAISVY Vaisya
AAITUY yautia
AAJJMR jamjar
AAJKNS sanjak
AAJKRT Rajkat
AAJMNP jampan
AAJMNR Jarman
AAJNNO joanna✧
AAJNNY Nyanja
AAJNOV Navajo
AAJNOW ajowan
AAJNOY yojana
AAJNPR prajna
AAJNRT Trajan
AAJNSY Sanjay
AAJRSW swaraj
AAKKLP kalpak
AAKKMR markka
AAKKOP kakapo
AAKLMO Akmola
AAKLMU Makalu
AAKLNR Lanark
AAKLOT atokal
Lakota
AAKLSU Lusaka
AAKLTU taluka
AAKMNU manuka
AAKMRT Amtrak
AAKMRU kumara
AAKNOR anorak
AAKNRT kantar
AAKNSS Kansas
AAKNST askant
tankas
AAKNSU Kaunas
AAKNWZ kwanza
AAKOPR pakora
AAKPRS Kaspar
AAKSSV kavass
AAKSTT attask
AAKTUY yukata
AAKUYZ yakuza
AALLLN lallan
AALLLS sallal
AALLMM mallam
AALLNY anally
AALLOR arolla
AALLOZ azolla
AALLPP palpal
AALLPS Pallas
AALLRV larval
vallar
AALLSU alulas
AALLTT atlatl
tallat
AALLVV valval
AALMMM mammal
AALMMS Lammas
AALMNP napalm
AALMNT Altman
AALMNU alumna
manual
AALMNW lawman
law-man
AALMNY Almany
layman
AALMOP Paloma
AALMOR amoral
AALMOS omasal
AALMOT amatol
AALMPR palmar
AALMPS lampas
plasma
AALMRU alarum
AALMSU masula
AALMTT Mt Taal
AALMTY Amytal®
AALNNS annals
AALNNU annual
AALNOT atonal
Latona
AALNOV Avalon
AALNOX axonal
AALNOY on a lay
AALNOZ azonal
AALNPR planar
AALNPT planta
platan
AALNRT antral
tarnal
AALNRU ranula
AALNRX larnax
AALNST aslant
santal
AALNSY nyalas
AALNTT talant
AALOPR oar-lap
AALOPY payola
AALORT aortal
AALOSS as also
AALOVW avowal
AALPPU papula
AALPRR parral
AALPRY parlay
AALPSS salpas
AALPSU pausal
AALPTU Laputa
AALPTY play at
AALQWW qawwal
AALRST astral
tarsal
AALRSV varsal
AALRSY salary
AALRVV valvar
AALSSV vassal
AALSTT at last
statal
AALSUX saxaul
AALSWY always
AALTUV valuta
AALWYY waylay
AAMMNT amtman
AAMMRR marram
AAMMRT tammar
AAMMTT tam-tam
AAMMUZ mazuma
AAMNNU maunna
AAMNOO manoao
AAMNOS Samoan
AAMNOT to a man
AAMNOZ amazon✧
AAMNPS sampan
AAMNPX Paxman
AAMNRT mantra
AAMNRW warman
AAMNRY Man Ray
AAMNSU Manaus
AAMNSY as many
AAMNTU mantua✧
tamanu
AAMNTV vatman✧
AAMNTX taxman
AAMOPR paramo
AAMORS Masora
AAMOSS samosa
AAMOST somata
AAMOTY Toyama
AAMPPS pampas
AAMPTY Pamyat
AAMQSU squama
AAMRSU asarum
AAMRSW aswarm
AAMRTU trauma
AAMSTZ matzas
AANNNO Annona
AANNPS sanpan
AANNTT natant
AANNYZ nyanza
AANOQY yaqona
AANORT torana
AANORU Anoura
AANORV Vanora
AANORX Roxana
AANOST sonata
AANOTT anatto
AANPPS sappan
AANPPU Papuan
AANPRT partan
tarpan
trapan
AANPRU Purana
AANPRY panary
AANQTU quanta
AANRRS narras
AANRRT arrant
AANRRW warran
AANRTT rattan
tantra✧
Tartan®
tartan
AANRTU Arnaut
natura
AANRTZ Tarzan
AANRUV Varuna
AANSSU Nassau
AANSTV savant
AANSTW Tswana
AANSTZ stanza
AANSYY naysay
AANTTV tan vat
AANTUV avaunt
AANWYY anyway
AAOPRT Atropa
AAOPST sapota

AAORRU	aurora✧
AAORRV	varroa✧
AAORSY	Soraya
AAORTT	totara
AAOTTV	ottava
AAOTTW	Ottawa
AAPPWW	pawpaw
AAPQUW	Quapaw
AAPRST	satrap
	Sparta
AAPRTT	attrap
AAPWXX	paxwax
AAPZZZ	pazazz
AAQRSU	quasar
AAQSTU	asquat
AARRST	tarras
AARRTT	tartar✧
AARRWY	warray
AARSST	assart
	sastra
AARSTT	astart
	strata
AARSTY	astray
	satyra
AARSWW	Warsaw
AARTTT	rat-tat
AARTTY	Tatary
AASTTU	statua
AASTZZ	tazzas
ABBBEI	Babbie
ABBBEL	babble
ABBBIT	Babbit
ABBBLY	babbly
ABBCEI	cabbie
ABBCIR	bicarb
ABBCOS	cabobs
ABBCOT	bobcat
ABBCRY	crabby
ABBCSY	scabby
ABBDDE	dabbed
ABBDEG	gabbed
ABBDEI	babied
ABBDEL	dabble
ABBDEN	nabbed
ABBDER	barbed
	dabber
ABBDET	tabbed
	tebbad
ABBDEU	bedaub
ABBDRY	drabby
ABBEEW	bawbee
ABBEGL	gabble
ABBEGR	gabber
ABBEIR	Barbie®
	barbie
ABBEIY	yabbie
ABBEJL	jabble
ABBEJR	jabber
ABBEKS	kebabs
ABBELR	barbel
	rabble
ABBELU	bauble
ABBELW	bawble
	wabble
ABBENR	nabber
ABBEOR	earbob
ABBERR	barber
ABBERT	barbet
	rabbet
ABBERY	bear by
	yabber
ABBESY	abbeys
ABBFLY	flabby
ABBGHU	gubbah
ABBGIN	bin-bag
ABBGMU	bum bag
	bumbag
ABBGOR	gabbro
ABBGRY	grabby
ABBHIJ	jibbah
ABBHJU	jubbah
ABBHOO	haboob
ABBHSY	shabby
ABBILL	Lib-Lab
ABBILO	Bilbao
ABBIMS	Babism
ABBINR	rabbin
ABBIRS	rabbis
ABBIRT	rabbit✧
ABBIST	Babist
ABBITW	wabbit
ABBKOS	kabobs
ABBLRU	bulbar
ABBLSY	slabby
ABBMOO	bamboo
ABBMOX	bombax
ABBMOY	Bombay
ABBNOO	baboon
ABBORS	absorb
ABBRSU	busbar
ABBSWY	swabby
ABCCIU	cubica
ABCCLU	buccal
ABCDEK	backed
ABCDER	decarb
ABCDEU	abduce
ABCDHO	bodach
ABCDIR	bardic
ABCDTU	abduct
ABCEEH	Achebe
	Hecabe
ABCEEL	belace
ABCEEM	became
	embace
ABCEGI	ice bag
ABCEGO	bocage
ABCEGU	cubage
ABCEHL	bleach
ABCEHR	breach
ABCEHT	betcha
ABCEHU	Hecuba
ABCEHY	beachy
ABCEIM	amebic
ABCEIR	cabrie
	caribe
ABCEJT	abject
ABCEKR	backer
	reback
ABCEKT	backet
ABCELL	becall
ABCELM	becalm
	clambe
	Malbec
ABCELT	cablet
ABCEMR	camber
	cembra
ABCEMW	webcam
ABCEMX	excamb
ABCENO	beacon
ABCEOS	sea cob
ABCERR	bracer
ABCERS	braces
ABCFIR	fabric
ABCFNO	confab
ABCGIT	big cat
	gib-cat
ABCGKO	go back
ABCHIT	bach it
ABCHLN	blanch✧
ABCHLU	Baluch
ABCHNR	branch
ABCHNU	Buchan
ABCHOR	broach
ABCHPU	hub-cap
ABCHRU	Baruch
ABCIIM	iambic
ABCIIR	Cabiri
ABCILT	baltic✧
ABCINN	in banc
ABCIOR	cabrio
ABCIRT	cabrit
ABCISS	basics
ABCISY	Biscay
ABCITT	Tib-cat
ABCKLS	blacks
ABCKOR	barock
ABCKPU	back up
	backup
	back-up
ABCKRU	buckra
ABCLLY	call by
ABCLMY	cymbal
ABCLNO	blanco
ABCLOT	cobalt
ABCMOP	mob cap
ABCMOR	comarb
	crambo
ABCMOT	combat
	tombac
ABCMRS	scramb
ABCNOR	carbon
	corban
ABCORX	boxcar
ABCORY	carboy
ABCOSU	basuco
ABCSTU	subact
ABDDEE	beaded
ABDDEI	abided
	baddie
ABDDEL	bladed
ABDDEN	banded
ABDDER	badder
	barded
ABDDEY	day bed✧
ABDDHU	buddha✧
ABDEEH	behead
ABDEEJ	bejade
ABDEEK	beaked
ABDEEL	beadle
ABDEES	debase
	seabed
ABDEET	debate
ABDEEZ	bedaze
ABDEFL	fabled
ABDEGG	bagged
ABDEGL	gabled
ABDEGN	banged
ABDEGO	bodega
ABDEGR	badger✧
ABDEHS	bedash
ABDEIL	baldie
	diable
ABDEIR	air-bed
	braide
ABDEIS	biased
ABDEIT	ebitda
ABDEKR	debark
ABDELL	balled
ABDELM	bedlam
	beldam
	blamed
ABDELO	albedo
	doable
ABDELR	Balder
	bedral
	blader
ABDELS	blades
ABDELT	tabled
ABDELU	belaud
ABDELY	dyable
ABDELZ	blazed
ABDEMM	bammed
ABDENN	banned
ABDENP	bedpan
ABDENR	Brenda
ABDENT	tan bed
ABDEPY	pay bed
ABDERR	barred
ABDERS	serdab
ABDERT	taberd
ABDERU	dauber
ABDERV	adverb
ABDEST	bestad
ABDETT	batted

ABDETU tabued
ABDFOR forbad
ABDGNO bandog
ABDGOR bodrag
ABDGRY drag by
ABDHNY by hand
ABDHOY hobday
ABDILR bridal
labrid
ribald
ABDINR riband
ABDINT bandit
ABDIRR braird
briard✧
ABDIRS disbar
ABDIRU ribaud
ABDLLY baldly
ABDLRY drably
ABDNOR Brando
ABDNOT not bad
ABDNOU abound
ABDNRT Brandt
ABDNRU Durban
ABDNRY brandy
ABDOOT too bad
ABDORR bordar
ABDORS adsorb
boards
broads
ABDORT Bardot
ABDORY byroad
ABDOXY box-day
ABDOYY day-boy
ABDRRU durbar
ABDRSU absurd
ABDRWY bawdry
dawbry
ABEEES Seabee
ABEEGH beegah
bhagee
ABEEGL beagle
ABEEGR abrégé
barege
barège
bargee
ABEEHJ bhajee
ABEEHN beenah
ABEEHV behave
ABEEIL bailee
ABEEIN beanie
ABEEJM jambee
ABEEJR bajree
ABEEJS baseej✧
ABEEKL kabele
ABEEKR beaker
ABEEKT betake
ABEELM embale
ABEELN baleen
enable
ABEELT belate
let-a-be
ABEEMN bemean
bename
ABEEMR beamer
ABEEMS embase
ABEENR Berean
ABEENT beaten
ABEENU Beaune
en beau
ABEEOR aerobe
ABEEOU Euboea
ABEERR bearer
breare
ABEERT beater
berate
rebate
ABEERV beaver
ABEERW beware
ABEERZ zereba
ABEEST sebate
ABEFFL baffle
ABEFHL behalf
ABEFIL faible
ABEFLL befall
ABEFLM flambé
ABEFLR fabler
ABEFMO befoam
ABEFNR far ben
ABEFPR prefab
ABEFTY tabefy
ABEGGR beggar
ABEGHI abeigh
ABEGLM gamble
ABEGLN bangle
Bengal
ABEGLR garble
ABEGLT gablet
ABEGLU beluga
blague
ABEGMR bregma
ABEGMT gambet
ABEGMU Mugabe
ABEGNR banger
graben
ABEGNT bag-net
ABEGNW begnaw
ABEGOR borage
ABEGOZ gazebo
ABEGRZ Zagreb
ABEGTU tubage
ABEHIL habile
ABEHJN Jabneh
ABEHKL keblah
ABEHLM hamble
ABEHLR herbal
ABEHLU Beulah
ABEHNO hebona
ABEHNT Theban
ABEHRR herbar
ABEHRS basher
ABEHRT bather
bertha✧
breath
ABEHST Shebat
ABEIIL bailie
ABEIIT tibiae
ABEIKK bakkie
ABEILL Belial
labile
liable
ABEILM embail
lambie
ABEILR bailer
bel air
ABEILS abseil
blaise✧
isabel✧
ABEILT albeit
albite
libate
ABEILV viable
ABEILW bewail
ABEILY bailey
ABEILZ blaize
ABEIMS imbase
ABEINR Ribena®
ABEINS Sabine
ABEINT binate
ABEIOT boatie
ABEIRS Baresi
braise
rabies
Serbia
ABEIRT baiter
barite
ABEIRZ braize
zeriba
ABEITT beat it
ABEJMN enjamb
ABEJMR jamber
ABEJNT bejant
ABEJOR jerboa
ABEJRS jabers
ABEJRU abjure
ABEJTU jubate
ABEKLR balker
ABEKLY bleaky
Kabyle
ABEKMN embank
ABEKMR embark
ABEKNR banker
barken
ABEKNT banket
ABEKNU Eubank
ABEKRR barker
ABEKRY bakery
ABEKST basket
ABEKTY tab key
ABELLM emball
ABELLT ballet
ABELLU bullae
ABELMM embalm
ABELMR ambler
lamber
marble
ramble
ABELMU bemaul
ABELMW wamble
ABELMY belamy
ABELNR branle
ABELNU nebula
unable
ABELNY by-lane
ABELNZ benzal
ABELOR boreal✧
ABELOT boatel
lobate
oblate
ABELPU Puebla
ABELRR barrel
ABELRT albert✧
batler
labret
ABELRV verbal
ABELRW bawler
warble
ABELRY barely
barley
bleary
ABELRZ blazer
ABELSS sables
ABELST ablest
bastle
stable
tables
ABELSU suable
usable
ABELSY basely
ABELSZ blazes
ABELTT batlet
battel
battle
tablet
ABELTU Betula
ABELTY baetyl
ABELWY bawley
bye-law
ABELYY lay-bye
ABEMMR bammer
ABEMNO bemoan
ABEMNY byname
by-name
ABEMOY Abomey
ABEMRT tamber
ABEMRU umbrae
ABEMRY ambery
ABEMSU Mabuse
ABENNR banner
ABENOR aborne
borane
ABENOS beanos
ABENRR barren
ABENRS Barnes
ABENRT banter

	barnet✧
ABENRU	unbare
	unbear
	urbane
ABENRY	barney✧
	near by
	nearby
ABENRZ	brazen
ABENST	absent
	basnet
ABENSU	sea bun
ABENTT	batten
ABENTU	butane
ABENTZ	bezant
ABEORS	Boreas
ABEORT	boater
	borate
	rebato
ABEORZ	bezoar
ABEOSS	Sasebo
ABEOSY	sea boy
ABEOTV	bovate
ABEPRU	bear up
	upbear
ABEPST	bespat
ABEPTU	beat up
	beat-up
	upbeat
	up-beat
ABEQRU	barque
	Braque
ABEQSU	basque✧
ABERRT	barret
	barter
ABERRY	brayer
ABERST	baster
	bestar
	breast
ABERSU	abuser
	bursae
ABERTT	batter
	tabret
ABERTU	arbute
ABERTW	wet bar
ABERTX	baxter
ABERTY	betray
ABERUU	bureau
ABERUY	Aubrey
ABERWY	bewray
ABESST	basset
ABESSU	subsea
ABESTT	at best
	Bastet
ABETTU	battue
	tubate
ABETTY	Beatty
ABETUY	beauty
ABEZZZ	bezazz
ABFGLU	bagful
ABFGOW	gowf-ba'
ABFHLY	by half
ABFILU	fibula
ABFINR	Finbar
ABFLNO	Fablon®
ABFLRU	barful
ABFLRY	barfly
ABFNOY	fanboy
ABFOTX	fox-bat
ABFSTY	fast by
ABGGIO	Baggio
ABGGIT	baggit
	gag-bit
ABGGIW	bagwig
ABGGNO	go bang
	gobang
ABGGNU	buggan
ABGHTU	hagbut
ABGIKN	baking
	ink-bag
ABGIKT	kitbag
ABGILM	gimbal
ABGILO	go bail
ABGIMR	gambir
ABGIMT	gambit
ABGIMY	bigamy
ABGINN	bangin'
ABGINO	bagnio
	gabion
ABGINS	basing
ABGINT	bating
ABGINU	Bangui
ABGIOR	Borgia
ABGIOS	biogas
ABGIOU	baguio
ABGKNO	kobang
ABGKOO	bogoak
ABGLLO	global
ABGLMO	gambol
ABGLMY	gymbal
ABGLOR	brolga
ABGLOU	albugo
ABGLRU	Bulgar
ABGLRY	bragly
ABGMNO	bogman
ABGMUY	may bug✧
ABGNNO	bang on
ABGNOO	gaboon
ABGNOR	Bangor
	barong
	brogan
ABGNPU	bang up
	bang-up
ABGOOT	Bogotá
	Tobago
ABGORS	garbos
ABGORT	Bogart
ABHHIS	shibah
ABHIIR	Bihari
ABHIKL	kiblah
ABHIKT	bhakti
ABHIMR	Brahmi
	mihrab
ABHIMZ	mazhbi
ABHINR	Harbin
ABHINS	ash-bin
	banish
ABHIOO	boohai
ABHIOP	phobia
ABHIRS	barish
ABHLOP	Bhopal
ABHLSU	ablush
ABHLSY	blashy
ABHMOT	Botham
ABHMRS	Brahms
ABHMRU	rhumba
ABHMSU	ambush
ABHNOO	bhoona
ABHNOS	bash on
ABHNOT	bothan
ABHNTU	Bhutan
ABHOOY	yah-boo
ABHORR	harbor
ABHORT	athrob
	Hobart
ABHOST	bathos
	boshta
ABHOTX	hatbox
ABHOXY	haybox
ABHPTY	bypath
ABHRSY	brashy
ABIILL	bailli
ABIILN	bilian
ABIILT	tibial
ABIINN	bainin
ABIIST	tibias
ABIJOW	Ojibwa
ABIJRU	jabiru
ABIKKU	kabuki
ABIKMO	akimbo
ABIKMR	imbark
ABIKRS	Barkis
ABILMT	timbal
ABILMU	labium
ABILNO	albino
	Albion
	Alboin
	on bail
ABILNR	Libran
ABILNS	ablins
ABILNT	libant
ABILNY	Libyan
ABILOR	bailor
ABILOT	obital
ABILPU	bail up
ABILRS	brails
ABILRT	tribal
ABILRU	burial
ABILRZ	brazil✧
ABIMMR	mimbar
ABIMNN	binman
ABIMNO	bon ami
	obi-man
ABIMNR	minbar
ABIMPT	bitmap
ABIMRS	bismar
ABIMRU	barium
ABIMRV	Vibram®
ABIMSU	iambus
ABIMTU	Batumi
ABINNU	bunnia
ABINOR	Robina
ABINOS	bonsai
	Bosnia
ABINOT	obtain
ABINRS	brains
ABINRU	Rubina
ABINRY	binary
	brainy
ABINSU	Anubis
	unbias
ABIORR	barrio
ABIORS	isobar
ABIORT	orbita
ABIOST	Tobias
ABIOTT	boat it
ABIRSU	Airbus®
ABIRTU	abitur
	rubati
ABIRTZ	Tabriz
ABISSU	Bissau
ABISTU	Ubasti
ABIZZZ	bizazz
ABJJOO	jojoba
ABJKMO	jambok
ABJLMU	jambul
	jumbal
ABJLNU	Banjul
ABJMOS	Jambos
ABJNOS	banjos
ABJNPU	Punjab
ABJOWX	jawbox
ABKLMO	Bokmål
ABKLSY	skylab✧
ABKMOT	tombak
ABKMUZ	zambuk✧
ABKNPU	bank up
ABKNRS	branks
ABKNRU	unbark
ABKNRY	branky
ABKOOR	boorka
ABKORT	Bartók
ABLLNO	ballon
	no-ball
ABLLOO	lobola
ABLLOT	ballot
ABLLOW	ballow
ABLLPU	ball up
	ballup
ABLLSY	ballsy
ABLLTU	all but
ABLMOO	abloom
ABLMOP	aplomb
ABLMOU	bumalo
ABLMOW	mob law

ABLMRU brumal
labrum
lumbar
umbral
ABLMRY marbly
ABLMSU albums
ABLMTY tymbal
ABLMWY wambly
ABLNOZ blazon
ABLNSU Nablus
ABLNTU buntal
tulban
ABLOOR Barolo
robalo
ABLORU labour✧
ABLOST oblast
ABLOTT talbot
ABLOTV abvolt
ABLPRU burlap
ABLPYY by-play
ABLRSU bursal
Labrus
ABLRSY labrys
ABLRTU brutal
ABLRWY brawly
byrlaw
ABLSSY byssal
ABLSTY stably
ABLSUY suably
usably
ABLSYY lay-bys
ABLTTY Tybalt
ABMMOS mambos
ABMNOW bowman
ABMNRU Burman
ABMNSU busman
subman
ABMNTU numbat
ABMNUY ynambu
ABMOOW waboom
ABMOPT bampot
ABMOSS sambos
ABMOSZ zambos
ABMOTV Tambov
ABMOTW wombat
ABMPRU bum rap
ABMRSU sambur
umbras
ABMRUY aumbry
bay rum
ABNNRY branny
ABNNUY Bunyan
ABNOOT batoon
ABNOQU Banquo
ABNORT barton
ABNORY barony
baryon
ABNOTY botany✧
ABNOVX box van
ABNRTU turban
ABNRUU auburn
ABNRUY anbury
ABNRWY brawny
ABNTYZ byzant
ABOORR roo bar
ABOORW bow-oar
ABOOST taboos
ABOOTU Baotou
ABOPXY pay-box
ABORRU arbour
ABORRW barrow
ABORST Strabo
ABORSV Brasov
bravos
ABORTU outbar
rubato
tabour
ABORTW tow bar
ABORTX tar box
ABORTY tarboy
Tor Bay
Torbay
ABORUY Yoruba
ABOSSS bassos
ABOSST bastos
ABOSTU abouts
Basuto
ABOSWW bowsaw
ABOUXY boyaux
ABPRTU abrupt
ABPRUY upbray
ABPSSY bypass
pass by
ABPSTY by-past
ABRRSU bursar
ABRSSY brassy
ABRSTU aburst
ABRSUU Subaru®
ABRTTY bratty
ABSTUU Basutu
ABSUWY subway
ACCCIL calcic
ACCCLO coccal
ACCDEE accede
ACCDEL calced
ACCDEN accend
ACCDHI Chadic
ACCDII acidic
ACCDOR accord
ACCDPR PC card
ACCEHN chance
ACCEHR creach
ACCEHT cachet
ACCEIL celiac
cicale
ACCEIP icecap
ipecac
ACCEIT accite
acetic
ACCEKL cackle
ACCELN cancel
ACCELR cercal
ACCELS calces
ACCEMU caecum
ACCENR cancer✧
ACCERS scarce
ACCERU accrue
ACCERW accrew
ACCESU accuse
ACCGNO cognac✧
ACCHHI chicha
ACCHIK chiack
ACCHIR Chirac
ACCHKU kuccha
ACCHKY chyack
ACCHLT clatch
ACCHNO concha
ACCHNR cranch
ACCHNY chancy
ACCHOU cachou
ACCHOY coachy
ACCHRT cratch
ACCHST scatch
ACCHSU succah
ACCHTT catcht
ACCHTU cutcha
ACCHTY catchy
ACCIIR Riccia
ACCILO accoil
calico
ACCILT lactic
ACCIMM Micmac
ACCINS siccan
ACCINW wiccan
ACCINY cyanic
ACCIPR capric
ACCIRR circar
ric-rac
ACCIRS siccar
ACCIRT arctic✧
ACCITT tactic
tic-tac
ACCITU cicuta
ACCKNU Canuck
ACCLNY Clancy
ACCLOU coucal
ACCMOY occamy
ACCNOO cacoon
ACCORS arccos
corsac
ACCORW Cracow
ACCOSS cascos
saccos
ACCRUY curacy
ACCSTU cactus
ACCSUU caucus
ACDDEE decade
ACDDEI caddie
Eddaic
ACDDEU adduce
ACDDII diacid
ACDDIN candid
ACDDIR Dardic
ID card
ACDDIS caddis
ACDDIT addict
ACDDIY dyadic
ACDDTU adduct
ACDEEF deface
ACDEEN decane
ACDEER decare
ACDEFF decaff
ACDEGR cadger
graced
ACDEHR arched
chared
ACDEHT detach
ACDEIN candie
cnidae
decani
ACDEIS De Sica
ACDEIT dacite
ACDEIV advice
ACDEKR arcked
dacker
racked
ACDEKT tacked
ACDEKV vacked
ACDELM calmed
macled
ACDELN candle
Declan
ACDELP placed
ACDELR cradle
credal
ACDELS scaled
ACDELT talced
ACDELU caudle
cedula
Claude
ACDELW clawed
ACDELY clayed
lac-dye
ACDEMN Camden
ACDEMP decamp
ACDENN canned
ACDENO deacon
ACDENR cedarn
dancer
nacred
ACDENS ascend
ACDENT cadent
canted
decant
ACDENY dancey
ACDEOP peacod
ACDEPP capped
ACDEPR redcap
ACDEPS spaced
ACDERR carder
Redcar
ACDERS sacred
scared
ACDERT redact

ACDERV	carved	ACEEIT	ice tea	ACEGIU	gaucie		eschar
ACDERZ	crazed	ACEEIX	ice axe	ACEGLN	cangle		search
ACDEST	casted	ACEEJT	ejecta		glance	ACEHRT	charet
ACDEUX	caudex	ACEEJY	jaycee✧	ACEGLY	legacy	ACEHRV	varech
ACDHIR	diarch	ACEELL	cellae	ACEGNU	cangue	ACEHRX	exarch
ACDHIS	Chasid	ACEELN	elance		uncage	ACEHSS	chasse
ACDHMR	drachm		enlace	ACEGNY	agency		chassé
	Mr Chad	ACEELR	alerce		Cagney	ACEHST	chaste
ACDHOR	chador		cereal	ACEGOS	socage		sachet
	chorda	ACEELV	cleave	ACEGOW	cowage		scathe
ACDIIP	adipic	ACEEMN	menace	ACEGRS	Graces	ACEHSW	cashew
ACDIJU	Judaic	ACEEMR	amerce	ACEHHT	chetah	ACEHTX	hexact
	Judica		carême✧	ACEHIL	heliac	ACEIJN	Janice
ACDILL	callid		raceme	ACEHIM	haemic	ACEIKR	eirack
ACDILP	placid	ACEEMS	camese	ACEHIN	chaîné	ACEILL	allice
ACDILS	discal	ACEEMZ	eczema	ACEHIP	phaeic		caille
ACDILY	acidly	ACEENR	careen	ACEHIR	Archie	ACEILM	maleic
ACDINO	Adonic		enrace		cahier		malice
	anodic	ACEENS	encase		eriach	ACEILN	ancile
ACDINR	Cardin		séance	ACEHIS	chaise		Celina
	rancid		Seneca	ACEHIT	Cathie		inlace
ACDINW	windac	ACEENT	cetane	ACEHKL	hackle	ACEILO	Aeolic
ACDIOS	sodaic		tenace	ACEHKR	hacker	ACEILP	epical
ACDIOT	dacoit	ACEENV	encave	ACEHLN	Chanel		plaice
ACDIOZ	zodiac	ACEEOR	ocreae	ACEHLP	chapel		plicae
ACDIPR	caprid	ACEEOT	coatee		pleach	ACEILR	Carlie
ACDIPS	capsid	ACEEPR	pearce✧	ACEHLR	Rachel		Claire
ACDIRU	raucid		preace	ACEHLS	laches		éclair
ACDIST	dicast	ACEEPS	escape		sealch	ACEILV	clavie
ACDLNU	unclad	ACEERR	career	ACEHLT	chalet	ACEILX	alexic
ACDLTY	dactyl	ACEERS	crease		châlet	ACEIMN	anemic
ACDMSU	Cadmus		searce		thecal		cinema
ACDMTU	mudcat	ACEERT	cerate		Thecla		ice man
ACDNNU	Duncan		create	ACEHLY	leachy	ACEIMO	Maceio
ACDNOR	candor		écarté	ACEHMN	manche	ACEIMS	camise
	Conrad	ACEFFR	Caffre	ACEHMR	macher	ACEIMT	acmite
	Dacron®	ACEFFT	affect	ACEHMS	sachem		micate
ACDNOW	ca' down	ACEFHR	chafer		samech	ACEIMU	aecium
ACDORS	Dorcas	ACEFHU	chaufe		schema	ACEINN	canine
ACDORW	Cod War	ACEFIL	facile	ACEHNR	chenar		neanic
	coward✧		fecial		enarch	ACEINP	ice pan
ACDRRS	scarr'd	ACEFIN	fiancé	ACEHNS	encash		in pace
ACDRSY	darcys	ACEFIR	fiacre	ACEHNT	the can	ACEINR	in care
ACEEFF	efface	ACEFIS	facies	ACEHNU	nuchae		Racine
ACEEFN	en face	ACEFLS	falces	ACEHOP	cheapo	ACEINS	casein
	enface	ACEFLU	fecula		epocha		in case
ACEEFR	reface	ACEFLY	calefy		phocae		incase
ACEEFS	faeces	ACEFNR	France	ACEHOR	chorea	ACEINT	anetic
ACEEFT	facete	ACEFOR	care of		Horace		centai
ACEEFX	Ceefax®	ACEFSS	fasces		ochrea	ACEINU	eucain
ACEEGI	ice age✧	ACEFSU	fauces		orache	ACEINV	cave in
ACEEGN	encage	ACEFTU	faucet	ACEHPR	eparch		cave-in
ACEEHK	hackee	ACEGHN	change		preach		incave
ACEEHL	chelae	ACEGHR	charge	ACEHPS	Pesach	ACEINX	axenic
ACEEHN	achene		chargé	ACEHPT	hep-cat	ACEIPS	apices
ACEEHT	eatche		creagh	ACEHPY	cheapy		spicae
	Hecate	ACEGHU	gauche		peachy	ACEIQU	caique
	thecae	ACEGIL	Gaelic	ACEHQU	queach		caïque
ACEEIP	a piece	ACEGIN	cage in	ACEHRR	archer✧	ACEIRR	Carrie
	apiece		incage	ACEHRS	arches✧		racier
ACEEIS	sea ice	ACEGIR	Gracie		chaser	ACEIRS	caries

ACEIRV	cavier
ACEISS	Cassie
ACEISV	vesica
ACEITT	tietac
ACEITV	active
ACEIVV	vivace
ACEJKT	jacket
ACEJLO	cajole
ACEJNT	jacent
ACEJNU	jaunce
ACEJQU	Jacque
ACEKLM	mackle
ACEKLR	calker
	lacker
ACEKLT	tackle
ACEKLY	lackey
ACEKNO	noçake
ACEKNR	canker
	reckan
ACEKNT	nacket
ACEKNW	acknew
ACEKPR	packer
	repack
ACEKPT	packet
ACEKRR	racker
ACEKRS	ackers
	sacker
	screak
ACEKRT	racket
	tacker
ACEKRU	cauker
ACEKRW	cawker
	wacker
ACEKRY	creaky
	yacker
ACEKST	casket
ACEKTT	tacket
ACELLO	locale
ACELLR	caller
	cellar
	recall
ACELLT	callet
ACELMN	encalm
ACELMP	cample
ACELMR	Carmel
	marcel✧
ACELMS	mascle
	mescal
	scamel
ACELMT	camlet
ACELMU	almuce
	Caelum
	macule
ACELNN	cannel
ACELNR	lancer
	rancel
ACELNS	lances
ACELNT	cantle
	cental
	lancet✧
ACELNU	cuneal
	launce✧
	unlace
ACELNY	Canley
ACELOR	Carole
	coaler
	Oracle®
	oracle
ACELOS	solace
ACELOT	Alecto
	locate
ACELOV	alcove
	coeval
ACELPR	carpel
	craple
	parcel
	placer
ACELPT	caplet
	placet
ACELPU	lace up
	lace-up
ACELQU	calque
	claque
ACELRR	carrel
ACELRS	scaler
	sclera
ACELRT	cartel
	claret
	rectal
	tarcel
ACELRU	raucle
ACELRV	calver
	carvel
	claver
ACELSS	scales✧
ACELST	castle
	sclate
ACELSU	caules
	clause
ACELSV	calves
	claves
	sclave
ACELSX	calxes
ACELTT	cattle
	Tactel®
ACELTU	cautel
ACELTY	acetyl
ACELYY	clayey
ACEMNO	ancome
ACEMNP	encamp
	Mencap
ACEMNR	Carmen
ACEMNU	acumen
ACEMOP	ecomap
	pomace
ACEMOR	amorce
ACEMOS	cameos
	cosmea
ACEMOT	camote
	comate
	co-mate
ACEMPR	camper
ACEMRS	scream
ACEMRT	mercat
ACEMRY	creamy
ACEMTU	mucate
ACENNR	canner
ACENNS	Cannes
ACENNU	nuance
ACENNY	Annecy
ACENOR	cornea
	earcon
	Nearco
ACENOT	at once
	octane
ACENPR	prance
ACENPT	catnep
ACENPU	paunce
	uncape
ACENPW	pawnce
ACENRS	casern
ACENRT	canter
	carnet
	centra
	creant
	Cretan
	nectar
	recant
	tanrec
	trance
ACENRV	carven
	cavern
	craven
ACENRY	carney
ACENRZ	zarnec
ACENST	ascent
	centas
	secant
	stance
ACENSU	causen
	uncase
	usance
ACENTU	Canute
	uncate
ACENUV	vaunce
ACEOPR	Pecora
ACEOPS	scopae
ACEOPT	capote✧
	toecap
ACEOPW	cowpea
ACEORS	coarse
	rosace
ACEORT	coater
ACEORV	ca' over
ACEORX	coaxer
ACEOST	costae
ACEOSW	sea cow
ACEOSY	O'Casey
ACEOTU	coteau
ACEOTV	avocet
	octave
ACEPPR	capper
ACEPRR	carper
ACEPRS	escarp
	parsec
	scrape
	spacer
ACEPRT	carpet
ACEPRU	aperçu
ACEPSS	scapes
ACEPST	aspect
ACEPSU	auceps
ACEPSY	spacey
ACEPTU	teacup
ACEQSU	casque
	sacque
ACERRS	scarer
	scarre
ACERRT	arrect
	carter✧
	crater✧
	tracer
ACERRU	curare
ACERRV	carver
	craver
ACERRY	crayer
ACERSS	caress
	crases
ACERST	caster
	recast
	traces
ACERSU	causer
	cesura
	saucer
ACERSY	carsey
	creasy
	scarey
	scraye
ACERTU	acture
	cauter
	curate
ACERTX	Rex cat
ACERTY	Tracey
ACESTT	sceatt
	stacte
ACESTU	cuesta
ACESTY	cytase
	Stacey
ACESUV	cauves
ACESUY	causey
	cayuse
ACFFHU	chauff
ACFFHY	chaffy
ACFFLS	sclaff
ACFGIN	facing
ACFHLN	flanch
ACFHRT	fratch
ACFHST	chafts
ACFILN	in calf
	in-calf
ACFILS	fiscal
ACFINN	finnac
ACFINR	farcin
ACFINT	in fact

Words marked ✧ can also be spelled with one or more capital letters

ACFIOS fascio
fiasco
ACFIPY pacify
ACFIST factis
ACFLNO falcon
flacon
ACFLNU canful
ACFLOT olfact
ACFLPU capful
ACFLRU fulcra
furcal
ACFMOR Corfam®
ACFMTU factum
ACFNOR franco
ACFNTU unfact
ACFORT act for
factor
forçat
ACFORX carfox
ACFRRY far cry
ACFRSS scarfs
ACFRTX X-craft
ACFRTY crafty
ACGGIN caging
ACGGIO agogic
ACGGLY claggy
ACGGRY craggy
ACGHIN aching
ACGHNU gaunch
ACGHOT gotcha
ACGHOU gaucho
ACGHTU caught
ACGIKN caking
ACGILL gallic✧
ACGILN lacing
ACGILO caligo
ACGILR garlic
ACGILS glacis
ACGILY cagily
ACGIMO ogamic
ACGINN caning
ACGINO agonic
angico
ACGINR arcing
caring
racing
ACGINS casing
ACGINT acting
ACGINV caving
ACGINW cawing
ACGIRT tragic
ACGLOU cagoul
ACGNOR garçon
ACGNOS gascon✧
Scogan
ACGORT go-cart
ACGORU cougar
ACGOSU guacos
ACGTTU catgut
ACHHIN hainch
ACHHIS hachis

ACHHNU haunch
ACHHTT thatch
ACHIIS ischia
ACHIIT t'ai chi
ACHIJK hijack
ACHIKO kochia
ACHILO lochia
ACHILP caliph
ACHILR archil
chiral
ACHILT chital
ACHIMS chiasm
ACHINR chinar
inarch
Ranchi
ACHINS cash in
chains
in cash
ACHINT canthi
ACHIOR choria
ACHIPS phasic
ACHIPT haptic
pathic
phatic
ACHIQU quaich
ACHIRS Charis
rachis
Sirach
ACHIST scaith
taisch
ACHISU chiaus
ACHITT chatti
ACHKKU chukka
ACHKLT klatch
ACHKLY chalky
hackly
ACHKOR chokra
ACHKOS shacko
ACHKOW whacko
ACHKRU chukar
ACHKTU kutcha
ACHKTW thwack
ACHKWY whacky
ACHLLO cholla
ACHLNO lochan
ACHLNP planch
ACHLNU launch
nuchal
ACHLOR choral
lorcha
ACHLRY archly
ACHLST slatch
ACHMMY chammy
ACHMNU Manchu
ACHMOR chroma
morcha
ACHMOS camsho
machos
ACHMRS charms
ACHMST smatch
ACHMSU as much

sumach
ACHMSY chasmy
ACHNOR anchor
archon
Charon
rancho
ACHNOS nachos
sancho
ACHNOT chaton
ACHNOY onycha
ACHNPU paunch
ACHNRU raunch
ACHNST snatch
stanch
ACHNTU chaunt
nautch
ACHNTY chanty
ACHOOT cahoot
ACHOPR carhop
ACHOPS phocas
ACHOPY poachy
pochay
po'chay
ACHORT orchat
ACHOST tachos
ACHOTW wotcha
ACHOUV avouch
ACHOUW Wu Chao
ACHPPY chappy
ACHPRS scarph
ACHPSU cash up
ACHPTU chat up
ACHPTY patchy
ACHQTU quatch
ACHRRY charry
ACHRST charts
scarth
starch
ACHSSU as such
ACHSTU cushat
ACHSTW swatch
ACHSUW cushaw
ACHTTY chatty
ACHTUW waucht
ACIILS sialic
silica
ACIILT italic✧
ACIILV clivia
ACIINN niacin
ACIINV incavi
ACIIRT Tricia
ACIIST lastic
ACIJKN jack in
ACIJNS Jancis
ACIKLN calkin
ACIKMR karmic
ACIKNO Konica®
ACIKNP ink-cap
panick
ACIKNR nickar
ACIKNS ink-sac

ACIKNT antick
catkin
ACIKOP paiock
ACIKPS aspick
ACIKRT kit-car
ACIKTT kit-cat✧
ACILLN call in
clinal
ACILLP plical
ACILLS scilla
ACILLY lacily
ACILMX climax
ACILNO Alnico®
Nicola
oilcan
ACILNP caplin
ACILNR crinal
ACILNT tincal
ACILNU Alcuin
Lucian
Lucina
uncial
ACILNV Calvin
ACILOR caroli
lorica
ACILOS scolia
social
ACILOT coital
ACILOX oxalic
ACILPT placit
ACILRT citral
rictal
ACILRU curial
Ulrica
uracil
Uralic
ACILRY racily
ACILSU caulis
clusia
ACILSV clavis
Slavic
ACIMNO anomic
camion
conima
manioc
Monica
ACIMNT mantic
ACIMOO oomiac
ACIMOR Romaic
ACIMOS mosaic✧
ACIMOT atomic✧
matico
ACIMOV vomica
ACIMPS scampi
ACIMPT impact
ACIMRS racism
ACIMRT matric
ACIMRU Murcia
ACIMRY cry aim
Myrica
ACIMST mastic

ACIMSU	Amicus
ACIMTU	Actium
ACINNT	tannic
	tin can
ACINNY	cyanin
ACINOS	casino
ACINOT	action
	atonic
	cation
ACINOV	incavo
ACINOX	anoxic
ACINOZ	azonic
ACINPS	panisc
ACINPT	catnip
ACINPU	Punica
ACINRS	arcsin
	Cairns
ACINRT	criant
ACINRU	uranic
ACINRY	riancy
ACINST	antics
	nastic
ACINSU	acinus
ACINTT	intact
ACINTU	anicut
	nautic
ACINUV	vicuna
	vicuña
ACIOPT	atopic
	copita
ACIORS	scoria
ACIORT	aortic
ACIOSS	Cassio
ACIOST	scotia✧
ACIOSV	ovisac
ACIOTZ	azotic
ACIPRS	Capris
	Crispa
	Prisca
ACIPRY	piracy
ACIPSS	spicas
ACIPTT	tipcat
ACIQTU	acquit
ACIRRS	sircar
ACIRRT	tricar
ACIRRU	curari
ACIRSS	crasis
	crissa
ACIRST	crista
	racist
ACIRSU	Icarus
ACIRSY	Syriac
ACIRTT	triact
ACIRTU	tauric
	urtica
ACIRVY	vicary
ACISSS	cassis
ACISTT	static
ACITUY	acuity
ACITVY	cavity
ACJKOP	pajock
ACJKPU	jack up
	jack-up
ACJKSY	jacksy
ACKKNU	Kanuck
ACKKNY	knacky
ACKLOP	Polack
ACKLSS	slacks
ACKLTY	talcky
ACKNPR	pranck
ACKNPU	unpack
ACKNRY	cranky
ACKNST	stanck
ACKNTU	untack
ACKOPY	yapock
ACKORY	croaky
ACKOSW	wackos
ACKPPU	pack up
ACKPRS	sprack
ACKPRU	rack up
ACKRST	strack
	tracks
ACKRTY	Y-track
ACLLMU	Callum
ACLLMY	calmly
ACLLNO	call on
	clonal
	on call
ACLLOP	callop
ACLLOR	collar
ACLLOS	Laclos
ACLLOW	callow
	low-cal
ACLLPU	call up
	call-up
ACLLSU	callus
	sulcal
ACLLSY	scally
	Scylla
ACLMMY	clammy
ACLMOR	clamor
	Colmar
ACLMPU	clam up
ACLMPY	camply
ACLMSU	lacmus
ACLMTU	talcum
ACLMUU	lucuma
ACLNOR	Lorcan
ACLNOS	Caslon
ACLNOT	coltan
ACLNUV	vulcan✧
ACLNUY	lunacy
ACLOPU	copula
	cupola
ACLORR	corral
ACLORS	claros
	corals
ACLORT	carlot
	crotal
ACLORU	ocular
	rucola
ACLORW	Carlow
	owl-car
ACLORY	calory✧
ACLOST	costal
ACLOSU	oscula
ACLOSV	vocals
ACLOSY	Lycosa
ACLOTW	cotwal
ACLPPU	clap up
ACLRRU	crural
ACLRST	clarts
ACLRSU	cursal
ACLRSW	scrawl
ACLRTU	curtal
ACLRTY	clarty
ACLRWY	crawly
ACLSST	clasts
ACLSSY	classy
ACLSTU	scutal
ACMNNO	con man
ACMNOO	Monaco
ACMNOR	macron
ACMNOS	mascon
	socman
ACMNOT	monact
ACMNOW	cowman
ACMNPU	cupman
ACMNSU	mancus
ACMOPS	campos✧
ACMORS	macros
	Marcos
ACMORT	comart
ACMOSS	Cosmas
ACMOST	Comsat®
	mascot
ACMOSU	mucosa
ACMOTT	tomcat
ACMOTU	motuca
ACMPPU	camp up
ACMPRS	cramps
ACMPRY	crampy
ACMPSU	campus
ACMPSY	spycam
ACMPTU	pactum
ACMRSU	Marcus
	sacrum
ACMRSW	scrawm
ACMSTU	muscat✧
ACMTUU	mutuca
ACMUUV	vacuum
ACNNNO	cannon
ACNNOR	Conran
ACNNOT	cannot
	canton
ACNNOY	canyon
ACNNRY	cranny
ACNOOP	poonac
ACNOOR	corona
	racoon
ACNOPY	canopy
ACNORR	rancor
ACNORS	Carson
	narcos
ACNORT	cantor
	carton
	contra
	craton
ACNORU	cornua
ACNORY	crayon
ACNOST	cantos
	cast on
	Octans
	Sno-cat
ACNOSZ	scazon
ACNOTT	octant
ACNOTU	noctua✧
	toucan
ACNOTW	ant cow
ACNOTX	Caxton
ACNPTU	puncta
ACNRST	crants
ACNRTU	uncart
ACNSTU	cantus
	Tuscan
ACNSTY	scanty
ACOOSS	Osasco
ACOOTV	octavo
ACOPRT	captor
ACOPRZ	Prozac®
ACOPSS	scopas✧
ACOPTT	Top Cat
ACOPTW	cowpat
ACORRT	carrot
	trocar
ACORSS	across
ACORST	castor✧
	Castro
	co-star
ACORSU	Acorus
	Caruso
ACORTT	cottar
ACORTU	turaco
ACORTV	cavort
ACORVY	covary
ACORYZ	coryza
ACOTTU	act out
ACPRSU	carpus
ACPSSU	scapus
ACPSTU	cast up
	catsup
	upcast
ACRRSY	scarry
ACRRTU	cratur
ACRRWY	war cry✧
ACRSSU	Scarus
ACRSTU	crusta
ACRSUY	scaury
ACSTTY	scatty
ADDDEG	gadded
ADDDEL	addled
	daddle
ADDDEN	addend
ADDDEO	dadoed

ADDDEP	padded
ADDDEW	wadded
ADDDFY	Dafydd
ADDDOO	doodad
ADDEEH	headed
ADDEEI	ideaed
ADDEEL	leaded
ADDEEN	deaden
ADDEER	deader
ADDEFL	faddle
ADDEFN	fanded
ADDEGR	gadder
ADDEHI	haddie
ADDEHJ	Jeddah
ADDEHK	keddah
ADDEHN	hadden
	handed
ADDEHS	saddhe
	shaded
ADDEIL	daidle
	dialed
	laddie
ADDEIM	diadem
ADDEIS	saddie
ADDEIT	taddie
ADDEIW	waddie
ADDELN	dandle
	landed
ADDELO	loaded✧
ADDELP	paddle
ADDELR	ladder
	raddle
ADDELS	saddle
ADDELW	dawdle
	waddle
ADDELY	deadly
ADDEMM	dammed
ADDEMN	damned
	demand
	madden
ADDEMR	madder
	red-mad
ADDENO	dead on
	dead-on
ADDENR	dander
	darned
ADDENS	dedans
	sadden
	sanded
ADDENU	undead
ADDENV	Devdan
ADDEOR	adored
	deodar
ADDEOS	dadoes
ADDEOW	woaded
ADDEPR	draped
	padder
	parded
ADDERR	darred
ADDERS	dreads
	sadder
ADDERT	traded
ADDERW	Edward
	warded
ADDGIO	gadoid
ADDGIP	giddap
ADDGLU	Dugald
ADDGMO	goddam
ADDGOO	ogdoad
ADDGOR	Godard
ADDGOY	god day
ADDHIJ	Jiddah
ADDHIS	siddha
ADDHOO	doodah
ADDHOS	Ashdod
ADDHSU	saddhu
ADDIKZ	zaddik
ADDIMR	dirdam
	Madrid
ADDIMY	midday
ADDITZ	tzaddi
ADDLNO	Donald
ADDLOY	day-old
ADDMNO	dodman
	odd-man
ADDMOO	addoom
	Dodoma
ADDNOS	add-ons
ADDOOR	dorado✧
ADDORT	dotard
ADDOST	at odds
ADDRSY	dryads✧
ADDSWY	swaddy
ADEEFL	leafed
ADEEFM	defame
ADEEFN	deafen
ADEEFR	Fareed
	feared
ADEEFT	defeat
ADEEGG	dégagé
ADEEGR	agreed
	dragée
	geared
ADEEHP	heaped
ADEEHR	adhere
	header
	Hedera
ADEEHT	heated
ADEEHV	heaved
ADEEIL	aedile
ADEEIM	mediae
ADEEIR	dearie
	rediae
ADEEIT	ideate
ADEEIW	deawie
ADEEJY	deejay
ADEEKP	Deepak
	peaked
ADEELN	leaden
	leaned
ADEELO	Elodea
ADEELP	leaped
ADEELR	Aelred
	dealer
	leader
	redeal
ADEELS	sealed
ADEELT	delate
	elated
	tele-ad
ADEELV	leaved
ADEEMN	amende
	demean
ADEEMO	oedema
ADEEMR	dear me
	remade
	remead
ADEEMT	teamed
ADEENN	Deanne
	ennead
	Na-Dene
ADEENP	neaped
ADEENR	deaner
	endear
ADEENV	advene
	Evadne
ADEEPS	pesade
ADEEPT	pedate
ADEERR	dreare
	reader
	reread
ADEERS	erased
	Red Sea
	reseda✧
	réséda
	seared
ADEERT	derate
	redate
ADEERV	evader
ADEERW	drawee
ADEERX	exedra
ADEEST	seated
	sedate
ADEETT	teated
ADEEVW	weaved
ADEFFI	affied
ADEFFY	affyde
ADEFGG	fagged
ADEFGN	fag end
	fanged
ADEFGR	defrag
ADEFHL	fleadh
ADEFIL	afield
	failed
ADEFIN	fade in
	fade-in
ADEFIR	Frieda
ADEFIT	daftie
ADEFLM	flamed
ADEFLO	feodal
ADEFLR	Alfred
	fardel
ADEFLU	feudal
ADEFLW	flawed
ADEFLY	deafly
	flayed
ADEFMR	framed
ADEFMY	madefy
ADEFNR	farden
ADEFNU	undeaf
ADEFOR	fedora✧
ADEFPU	fade up
	fade-up
ADEFRU	fadeur
ADEFRY	defray
ADEFST	defast
ADEFTT	fatted
ADEFTW	wafted
ADEGGG	gagged
ADEGGH	hagged
ADEGGI	gadgie
ADEGGJ	jagged
ADEGGL	daggle
	lagged
ADEGGN	nagged
ADEGGR	dagger
	ragged
ADEGGS	sagged
ADEGGT	gadget
	tagged
ADEGGW	wagged
ADEGGZ	zagged
ADEGHI	hidage
ADEGHL	Gadhel
ADEGHN	hagden
	hanged
ADEGIM	mid-age
ADEGLN	angled
	dangle
	Glenda
	lag-end
ADEGLO	age-old
	old age
ADEGLR	dargle
	Gerald
ADEGLZ	glazed
ADEGNR	danger
	gander
	garden
	grande
ADEGNT	tag end
	tanged
ADEGNW	gnawed
	Gwenda
ADEGOP	dog-ape
ADEGOR	dog-ear
	O grade
	O-grade
ADEGOS	dosage
	sea dog
	sea god
ADEGOT	dogate
	dotage
	togaed

ADEGRR garred
Gerard
grader
red rag
regard
ADEGRS degras
ADEGRT der Tag
grated
ADEGRV graved
ADEGSS gassed
ADEGST staged
ADEHIL halide
ADEHIN hained
ADEHIR haired
ADEHIS eadish
ADEHKS shaked
ADEHKW hawked
ADEHLM lamedh
ADEHLN Handel
handle
ADEHLO haloed
ADEHLR hareld
herald
ADEHLS halsed
ADEHLT daleth
ADEHMR derham
ADEHMS em dash
mashed
shamed
ADEHNO head-on
ADEHNP daphne
ADEHNR hander
harden
ADEHNS en dash
ADEHNU unhead
ADEHNY Hayden
ADEHOR oh dear!
ADEHOX oxhead
ADEHPP happed
ADEHPS phased
shaped
ADEHPT heptad
ADEHPU head up
ADEHRS dasher✧
shader
shared
ADEHRT dearth
hatred
red hat
thread
ADEHSS shades✧
ADEHST 'sdeath
ADEHSV shaved
ADEHSW washed
ADEHSY Hyades
ADEHTT hatted
ADEHTY deathy
the day
ADEHYY heyday
ADEIKR daiker
ADEILL allied
laldie
ADEILM Imelda
maelid
mailed
medial
ADEILN Aldine
Daniel
Delian
denial
lead in
lead-in
nailed
ADEILO eidola
ADEILP aliped
paidle
Pleiad
ADEILR derail
redial
relaid
ADEILS aisled
deasil
ladies
ladies'
sailed
ADEILT detail
dilate
tailed
ADEILU audile
ADEILW Dewali
ADEILY eyliad
ADEIMM maimed
ADEIMN daimen
Damien
demain
maiden✧
median✧
medina✧
ADEIMR admire
ADEIMS mid-sea
ADEIMV vidame
ADEINN Andine
Dianne
dinnae
Nadine
ADEINO Oneida
ADEINP pained
ADEINR Darién
randie
read in
read-in
ADEINS sdaine
Sendai
Sinéad
ADEINT Danite
detain
ADEINV invade
ADEINW dewani
Edwina
wade in
ADEINZ Zidane
ADEIOR roadie
ADEIOT iodate
ADEIPR diaper
paired
pardie
repaid
ADEIRR arride
raider
ADEIRT raited
tirade
ADEIRU uredia
ADEIRV varied
ADEIRY Yardie
ADEISS dassie
ADEISU adieus
ADEISV advise
avised
visaed
ADEISX sex aid
ADEITU dautie
ADEITV dative
ADEITW dawtie
ADEITX taxied
ADEIUX adieux
ADEJMM jammed
ADEJNU Judean
ADEJRR jarred
ADEJRU adjure
ADEJRY jadery
ADEJUV déjà vu
ADEKLN ankled
Kendal
ADEKLR darkle
ADEKLW wealk'd
ADEKMO make do
make-do
ADEKMR demark
marked
ADEKMS masked
ADEKNR darken
narked
ranked
ADEKNT tanked
ADEKOS soaked
ADEKOY kayoed
okayed
ADEKPY keypad
ADEKRY darkey
ADELLN end-all
ADELLP palled
ADELLR all-red
ADELLS dalles
ADELLU allude
aludel
ADELLV devall
ADELLW walled
ADELMP palmed
ADELMR dermal
marled
medlar
ADELMS damsel
ADELMT malted
ADELNO enodal
lead on
loaden
ADELNR aldern
darnel
enlard
Länder
lander
ADELNS sendal
ADELNT dental
ADELNU unlade
unlead
ADELNW lawned
new lad
Walden
wandle
Weland
ADELOP opaled
pedalo
ADELOR loader
ordeal
reload
ADELOS aldose
ADELPP dapple
lapped
ADELPR pedlar
ADELPS lapsed
ADELPT plated
ADELPU lead up
lead-up
uplead
ADELPW dewlap
ADELPY played
ADELRR larder
ADELRS sardel
ADELRT dartle
ADELRU Eluard
lauder
ADELRV Dervla
ADELRY dearly
ADELRZ drazel
ADELST desalt
salted
slated
ADELSU salued
ADELSW salewd
ADELSY slayed
ADELUV valued
ADELVV valved
ADELZZ dazzle
ADEMMR dammer
rammed
ADEMNN end man
manned
ADEMNO daemon
modena
nomade
ADEMNP dampen
ADEMNR manred
randem
red man

Words marked ✧ can also be spelled with one or more capital letters

remand
ADEMNS desman
ADEMNT tandem
ADEMNU unmade
ADEMOP apedom
pomade
ADEMOR radome
ADEMOS Samoed
ADEMOT moated
ADEMOW meadow
ADEMPP mapped
ADEMPR damper
ADEMPU made up
ADEMRR marred
ADEMRT dreamt
ADEMRU remuda
ADEMRW warmed
ADEMRY dreamy
ADEMST masted
ADEMSU amused
medusa✧
ADEMTT matted
ADEMWY May-dew
Medway
ADENNP panned
ADENNT tanned
ADENNU duenna
ADENNV vanned
ADENOT donate
ADENOU douane
ADENOV Avedon
ADENOY day one
noyade
one day
one-day
ADENPP append
napped
ADENPR pander
repand
ADENPT pedant
pentad
ADENPX expand
ADENRR darner
Darren
errand
ADENRS sander
ADENRT ardent
endart
red ant
ADENRU dauner
Neruda
undear
unread
ADENRW Andrew
Darwen
dawner
wander
warden
ADENRY denary
ADENRZ zander
ADENSU sundae
ADENSW new-sad
wesand
ADENTT attend
ADENTU undate
ADENTV advent✧
ADENTW wanted
ADENUW unawed
ADENWX wax end
ADENWZ wezand
ADEOOW Daewoo®
ADEOPP peapod
ADEORR adorer
ADEORS oreads✧
ADEORT doater
troade
ADEORW redowa
ADEOSS Odessa
ADEOSV vadose
ADEOTT to date
ADEOVW avowed
ADEOYZ azo dye
ADEPPR dapper
rapped
ADEPPS sapped
ADEPPT tapped
ADEPPW wapped
ADEPRR draper
ADEPRS drapes
spader
spread
ADEPRT depart
drapet
parted
petard
ADEPRU read up
ADEPRW warped
ADEPRY prayed
ADEPSS passed
ADEPTT patted
ADEPTU update
ADEPTY pet-day
ADERRT darter
dartre
retard
tarred
trader
ADERRW drawer
redraw
reward
warder
warred
ADERRY dreary
ADERSS Esdras
ADERST steard
trades
ADERSW sawder
sweard
waders
ADERTT ratted
tetrad
ADERTV advert
ADERTW warted
ADERTX X-rated
ADERUW waured
ADERUY Audrey
ADERVV varved
ADERWX wax-red
ADERWY weyard
ADESTT stated
tasted
ADESTU sudate
ADESTV staved
ADESTW stawed
wadset
wasted
ADESTY stayed
steady
ADESWY swayed
ADETTV vatted
ADETUV veduta
ADETVY vat dye
ADFFOR afford
ADFFOY day off
off-day
ADFFRY draffy
ADFGIN fading
ADFGLY gadfly
ADFHSU shaduf
ADFILU aidful
ADFILY ladify
ADFINR friand
ADFIRT adrift
ADFIRY Friday
ADFLOS sol-fa'd
ADFLTY daftly
ADFLYY day-fly
ladyfy
ADFMNO fandom
ADFMOU fumado
ADFNOT fantod
ADFNOU au fond
ADFORR forrad
ADFRST drafts
ADFRSW dwarfs
ADFRTY drafty
ADGGOT dog tag
ADGGOY gay dog
ADGGRY draggy
ADGHIN Gandhi
ADGHNO hagdon
ADGHOR go hard
ADGIIN aiding
ADGILN lading
ligand
ADGILO algoid
dialog
ADGIMY digamy
ADGINO ganoid
ADGINQ Daqing
ADGINR daring
gradin
ADGINT dating
ADGINW wading
ADGINY Gdynia
ADGINZ Danzig
ADGIRV gravid
ADGKNS Gdansk
ADGLLY gladly
ADGLNU unglad
ADGLNY dangly
ADGLOP lapdog
ADGLOU Dougal
ADGLOY Day-Glo
dayglo
ADGLSY Gladys
ADGNOO goonda
ADGNOR drag on
dragon✧
ADGNOT Datong
ADGNRU durgan
ADGORW wardog
war god
ADGPRU drag up
updrag
ADGRSU gradus
guards
ADGRTU Utgard
ADHHIT Hadith
ADHHIW whidah
ADHHOU houdah
ADHHOW howdah
ADHHWY whydah
ADHIJS jadish
ADHIKL Khalid
ADHIKU haiduk
ADHILL all-hid
ADHILO haloid
ADHIMR dirham
ADHINN hand-in
in hand
ADHINS Danish
sandhi
ADHIOR hairdo
ADHIPS aphids
ADHIRS radish
ADHIRY hydria
Riyadh
ADHISS Hassid
ADHISW dawish
ADHJKO khodja
ADHLMO Oldham
ADHLOR Harold
ADHLOT old-hat
ADHLRY hardly
ADHMMU Mahmud
ADHMNO hodman
ADHMNU numdah
ADHMRU Durham
Madhur
ADHNNO on hand
ADHNNU nhandu
unhand
ADHNOR hadron

Rhonda
ADHNOT to hand
ADHNOU houdan
ADHNOW and how!
ADHNOY Haydon
ADHNPU uphand
ADHNSY shandy
ADHORW Howard
ADHOSW shadow
ADHPRU hard-up
purdah
ADHPUU uphaud
ADHRRU dhurra
ADHUZZ huzza'd
ADIIKO aikido
ADIILL illiad
ADIILM miladi
ADIILN inlaid
ADIILR iridal
ADIILT ditali
ADIILV Divali
ADIILW Diwali
ADIIMO daimio
ADIIMR midair
ADIINN Indian
ADIINR Indira
ADIINV avidin
ADIINZ dizain
ADIIOS Isodia
ADIIPR diapir
ADIJKT Tadjik
ADIJMS masjid
ADIJNO adjoin
ADIKKO Kodiak
ADIKMO mikado
ADIKNO daikon
ADIKNP inkpad
kidnap
ADIKNS Danisk
ADIKOS daikos
ADIKOT dakoit
ADIKST dikast
ADIKTT diktat
ADILLP pallid
ADILLY laidly
ADILMO Amidol®
ADILMS dismal
ADILMY diamyl
milady
ADILNN inland
ADILNO dolina✧
ladino✧
ADILNR aldrin
ADILNS island
ADILNT tindal
ADILNU dualin
unlaid
ADILNY Lydian
ADILOO ooidal
ADILOP podial
ADILOR laroid
ADILOS Isolda
ADILOZ Ozalid®
ADILPT pat-lid
ADILPU dial-up
laid up
ADILRY aridly
ADILRZ lizard✧
ADILST distal
ADILUV vidual
ADILVY avidly
ADIMMT dammit
ADIMNO daimon
domain
ADIMNR mandir
ADIMNS disman
ADIMNT mantid
ADIMOT diatom
ADIMQU quidam
ADIMRS dirams
disarm
ADIMRU radium
ADIMRY myriad
ADIMSS sadism
ADIMST amidst
ADIMSY dismay
ADIMWY midway
ADINNU induna
ADINOR Dorian
inroad
ordain
ADINOS Adonis
danios
sodain
ADINOX diaxon
dioxan
ADINPR Pindar
ADINPT pandit
ADINPU unpaid
ADINQR qindar
ADINRT indart
ADINRU durian
ADINRV ravin'd
ADINRW Darwin
draw in
inward
ADINSU unsaid
ADINSV viands
ADINSW windas
ADINTY dainty
ADIORS radios
ADIORT adroit
ADIOSU audios
ADIOSZ diazos
ADIPPU paid-up
ADIPRS rapids
sparid
spraid
ADIPSS dipsas✧
ADIPSX spadix
ADIQTU diquat
ADIRRS sirdar
ADIRRY air-dry
ADIRRZ rizard
ADIRSS Sardis
ADIRST Astrid
Tardis
ADIRSU Darius
radius
ADIRSW wisard
ADIRVZ vizard
ADIRWY rid way
ADIRWZ wizard
ADIRZZ izzard
ADISST sadist
saidst
ADISTV vista'd
ADISXY six-day
ADISYY sayyid
ADITTY dittay
ADJKOU judoka
ADJNOR jordan✧
ADJOPY joypad
ADJSTU adjust
ADKLRY darkly
ADKOPU padouk
ADLLOP dallop
ADLLOR dollar
ADLLUY dually
ADLMNO almond
dolman
old man
old-man
ADLMOS dolmas
ADLMOW wadmol
ADLMPY damply
ADLMTU talmud✧
ADLMYY my lady
ADLNOP Poland
ADLNOR Arnold
Dralon®
lardon
Roland
Ronald
ADLNOS soldan
ADLNOT dalton
ADLNOU unload
ADLNOX oxland
ADLNOY any old
ADLNPU land up
upland
ADLNRU lurdan
ADLOPU upload
ADLORS dorsal
ADLOSS dossal
ADLOSW dowlas
Oswald
waldos
ADLPSU spauld
ADMMNO mandom
ADMNOR Donmar
random
rodman
ADMNOS damson
ADMNOW woman'd
ADMNOY dynamo
Monday
nomady
ADMNPY Dympna
ADMNRU unmard
ADMNUY maundy
ADMORR ramrod
ADMORZ Ormazd
ADMOSS Mossad
ADMTUY adytum
ADNNOO nandoo
ADNNOR randon
ADNNOT danton✧
donnat
ADNNOU adnoun
ADNOOR nardoo
ADNOOW wandoo
ADNOPR pardon
pardon?
ADNOPT dopant
ADNORS Andros
ADNORU around
ADNORW draw on
onward
ADNORY donary
ADNOTT dotant
ADNOTY Dayton
ADNRST strand
ADNRSU sundra
ADNRTU draunt
durant
tundra
ADNRUW undraw
ADNSTU Datsun®
ADNSTY dynast
ADNSUY Sunday
ADOOTW Atwood
ADOOUV vaudoo
ADOPRU Podura
road up
ADOPRY parody
ADOPSS spados
ADORRU ardour
ADORTW toward
ADORWY ayword
ADOTUY day out
ADPPRY drappy
ADPRUW draw up
updraw
upward
ADRSUW usward
ADRSUY sudary
ADRSWY swardy
ADRTWY tawdry
ADSTTU at stud
AEEELS sea eel
AEEFFN neaffe
AEEFFR affeer
AEEFGU feague

AEEFIR	faerie
AEEFLM	female
AEEFNT	Fantee
AEEFOV	foveae
AEEFRT	afreet
	terefa
AEEGGL	alegge
AEEGGN	engage
	engagé
AEEGGR	agrégé
	raggee
	reggae
AEEGGS	sea egg
AEEGGT	taggee
AEEGGW	geegaw
AEEGIR	Egeria
AEEGJR	Jaeger®
	jaeger
AEEGKN	Keegan
AEEGLL	allege
AEEGLP	pelage
AEEGLR	galère
	regale
AEEGLS	Eagles
AEEGLT	eaglet
	legate
	teagle
	telega
AEEGLU	league
AEEGLV	gleave
AEEGMM	gemmae
AEEGMN	manège
	menage
	ménage
AEEGMR	Graeme
	meagre
AEEGMT	gamete
	metage
AEEGNN	ennage
AEEGNR	enrage
	enragé
	genera
AEEGNS	sagene
	senega
AEEGNT	negate
AEEGNV	avenge
	geneva✧
AEEGNW	new age✧
	new-age✧
AEEGOP	apogee
AEEGOT	goatee
AEEGRS	grease✧
AEEGRT	ergate
AEEGRV	greave
AEEGST	egesta
AEEGSW	sewage
AEEGTU	Teague
AEEHHW	heehaw
AEEHIR	hearie
AEEHLN	Helena
AEEHLR	healer
AEEHLS	Sheela
AEEHLT	lathee
AEEHLW	awheel
AEEHLX	exhale
AEEHLY	Healey
AEEHMR	hareem
	hermae
AEEHMT	meathe
AEEHMU	heaume
AEEHNP	peahen
AEEHNS	Sheena
AEEHNT	Athene
	ethane
AEEHNV	heaven✧
AEEHNW	a wheen
AEEHNX	hexane
AEEHNY	Heaney
AEEHPS	spahee
AEEHRR	hearer
	rehear
AEEHRS	hearse
AEEHRT	aether
	heater
	hereat
	reheat
AEEHRV	heaver
AEEHRW	a'where
	wheare
AEEHST	heaste
	The Sea
AEEHSV	heaves
	sheave
AEEHTV	theave
AEEHTX	the axe
AEEIJN	Jeanie
AEEIKV	keavie
AEEILM	Amélie
	mealie
AEEILN	Aileen
	Elaine
AEEILS	Elaeis
	laesie
AEEILX	Alexei
AEEIMN	meanie
AEEIMS	semeia
AEEIPR	epeira✧
	pereia
AEEIPS	sea pie
AEEJLX	Alexej
AEEJMS	Jeames
AEEJNT	jantee
AEEJRV	evejar
AEEJVY	veejay
	vee-jay
AEEKLN	alkene
AEEKLP	palkee
AEEKLR	leaker
AEEKLV	vakeel
AEEKMR	remake
AEEKMS	kamees
AEEKMZ	kameez
AEEKNW	weaken
AEEKNY	yankee✧
AEEKPR	parkee
AEEKRT	retake
AEEKRU	eureka
AEELLL	allele
AEELLM	mallee
AEELLS	sallee
AEELLV	A level
	A-level
AEELMN	enamel
AEELMP	empale
AEELMR	mealer
AEELMS	measle
	Saleem
AEELMU	aemule
AEELMZ	meazel
AEELNN	Leanne
AEELNO	loanee
AEELNP	alpeen
AEELNS	enseal
AEELNT	elanet
	lateen
	La Tène
AEELNV	leaven
AEELNW	weanel
AEELOR	areole
AEELOT	oleate
AEELPR	leaper
	repeal✧
AEELPS	asleep
	elapse
	please
	sapele
AEELPU	epaule
AEELQU	quelea
AEELRS	leaser
	reales
	resale
	reseal
	sealer
AEELRT	elater
	relate✧
	Tralee
AEELRV	laveer
	leaver
	reveal
	vealer
AEELRY	E-layer
AEELSS	eassel
AEELST	steale
	stelae
	teasel
AEELSV	leaves
	sleave
AEELSW	weasel
AEELSZ	sleaze
AEELTT	Attlee
AEELTU	eluate
AEELTV	valete
	velate
	veleta
AEELTW	atweel
AEELTY	eyalet
AEELTZ	teazel
	teazle
AEELWY	leeway
AEEMMM	mammee
AEEMNN	Nemean
AEEMNR	rename
AEEMNS	enemas
	enseam
AEEMNT	entame
AEEMNX	examen
AEEMOR	Moerae
AEEMPR	ampere
	ampère
	empare
AEEMPW	wampee
AEEMRR	reamer
AEEMRS	seamer
AEEMRT	teamer
AEEMSS	sesame
AEEMST	meseta
AEEMSW	meawes
	sea mew
AEEMTT	metate
AEEMTX	taxeme
AEENNP	pennae
AEENNT	Etnean
	neaten
AEENNX	annexe
AEENPR	paneer
AEENPS	sea pen
AEENPT	nepeta
AEENPW	pawnee✧
AEENRR	earner
	nearer
AEENRS	ensear
	Serena
AEENRT	entera
AEENRV	never a
AEENRW	weaner
AEENST	ensate
	sateen
	senate✧
	steane
AEENSU	unease
AEENSV	naeves
AEENTW	atween
AEENTX	ex ante
AEENUV	avenue✧
AEENWZ	weazen
AEEOTT	to a tee
AEEOUU	euouae
AEEOVV	evovae
AEEPPR	rappee
AEEPRR	reaper
AEEPRS	a-per-se
	Parsee
	prease
	serape

AEEPRT	repeat
AEEPSS	passée
AEEPST	peseta
AEEPSU	ease up
AEEPSW	pesewa
AEEPSX	apexes
AEEPTT	pattée
AEEPVY	peavey
AEEQRU	quaere
AEEQTU	equate
AEERRR	rearer
AEERRS	eraser
	serrae
AEERRT	à terre
	tearer
	terrae
AEERRV	reaver
AEERRW	wearer
AEERST	easter✧
	reseat
	saeter
	seater
	steare
	teaser
	Teresa
AEERSU	réseau
AEERSV	averse
AEERTY	eatery
AEERVW	weaver
AEESSW	seesaw
AEESTT	estate
	tea set
	testae
AEFFGR	gaffer
AEFFHT	haffet
AEFFIN	affine
AEFFIP	piaffe
AEFFLR	raffle
AEFFLW	waffle
AEFFLY	yaffle
AEFFOT	eat off
AEFFRT	affret
	farfet
AEFFRY	effray
AEFFRZ	zaffer
	zaffre
AEFGLN	fangle
	flange
AEFGLR	reflag
AEFGMU	fumage
AEFGOR	forage
AEFGOS	sea fog
AEFGRU	gaufer
	gaufre
AEFGRY	fegary
AEFHLL	fellah
AEFHLN	halfen
AEFHNT	fat hen
AEFHRS	afresh
AEFHRT	father✧
AEFHSY	sheafy
AEFIJO	feijoa
AEFIKS	faikes
AEFILL	faille
AEFILN	al fine
	finale
AEFILR	ferial
AEFILT	fetial
AEFIMN	famine
	infame
AEFINN	Fenian
AEFINR	infare
AEFIRS	fraise
	sea fir
AEFIST	fiesta
AEFITX	fixate
AEFJNT	fan-jet
AEFJRY	Freyja
AEFKLN	fankle
AEFKMO	make of
AEFKRY	fakery
	freaky
AEFLLN	fallen
AEFLLR	faller
AEFLLV	favell✧
AEFLMN	flamen
AEFLMR	flamer
AEFLNN	fannel
AEFLNU	flaune
AEFLNX	flaxen
AEFLOR	florae
	loafer
AEFLOT	foetal
	folate
	of late
AEFLOV	foveal
AEFLRS	falser
	flares
	flaser
AEFLRT	falter
AEFLRU	earful
	ferula✧
AEFLRY	F-layer
	flayer
AEFLST	festal
AEFLSY	safely
AEFLTU	fluate
AEFLTY	fealty
	featly
AEFLUW	waeful
AEFMNN	fenman
AEFMNO	foeman
AEFMOR	femora
AEFMRR	farmer
	framer
AEFMRT	Fermat
AEFNNR	fanner
AEFNNT	enfant
AEFNOR	forane
	no fear
AEFNRR	farren
AEFNRU	furane
AEFNRW	fawner
AEFNST	fasten
	nefast
AEFNSU	unsafe
AEFNTT	fatten
AEFORS	Faroes
AEFORY	for aye
AEFOSS	fossae
AEFOSV	favose
AEFOSX	sea fox
AEFPPR	frappé
AEFPRY	perfay
AEFRRT	frater
	rafter✧
AEFRRY	rarefy
AEFRST	afters
	faster
	strafe
AEFRTT	fatter
AEFRTW	wafter
AEFRWY	wafery
AEFSTY	safety
AEGGGL	gaggle
AEGGGR	gagger
AEGGHL	haggle
AEGGHN	Hegang
AEGGIM	maggie✧
AEGGIN	ageing
AEGGJR	jagger
AEGGLN	laggen
AEGGLR	gargle
	lagger
	raggle
AEGGLW	waggle
AEGGNR	ganger
	grange
	nagger
AEGGNU	gangue
AEGGRS	sagger
	seggar
AEGGRT	garget
	tagger
AEGGRU	gauger
AEGGRY	yagger
AEGGWW	gewgaw
AEGHIO	hoagie
AEGHIR	hegira
	hirage
AEGHIS	geisha
AEGHIW	aweigh
AEGHLS	sealgh
AEGHLT	haglet
AEGHLZ	ghazel
AEGHMO	homage
	ohmage
AEGHNR	hanger
	rehang
AEGHNS	Ganesh
AEGHOR	gherao
AEGHOS	seahog
AEGHPT	hatpeg
AEGHRT	Gareth
	gather
AEGILM	milage
AEGILN	Ealing
	genial
	linage
AEGILO	goalie
AEGILP	paigle
AEGILR	graile
	lea-rig
AEGILS	ligase
	silage
AEGILT	aiglet
	gelati
	ligate
	taigle
AEGILV	glaive
	vagile
AEGILZ	El Gîza
AEGIMN	enigma✧
	gamine
AEGIMP	magpie
AEGIMR	imager
	maigre
	mirage
AEGIMS	ageism
	Images
AEGINR	earing
	gainer
	graine
	reagin
	regain
	regina✧
AEGINS	agnise
AEGINT	eating
	ingate
	tangie
	teaing
AEGINU	guinea✧
AEGINZ	agnize
AEGIPP	pipage
AEGIPS	sea-pig
AEGIPT	Piaget
AEGIRS	agrise
AEGIRT	gaiter
	triage
AEGIRV	Argive
	garvie
	rivage
AEGIRW	earwig
AEGIRZ	agrize
AEGIST	ageist
AEGISU	aguise
AEGISV	visage
AEGITU	augite
AEGITY	gaiety
AEGIUZ	aguize
AEGJLN	jangle
AEGJLT	jet lag
AEGJST	gas jet
AEGJTU	jugate

AEGKLR grakle
AEGKRW gawker
AEGKST gasket
AEGLLN leglan
AEGLLT gallet
AEGLLU ullage
AEGLLY egally
galley
AEGLMN leg-man
mangel
mangle
AEGLMR malgre
mal gré
malgré
AEGLMV maglev
AEGLMY gamely
gleamy
mygale
AEGLNO Angelo
engaol
AEGLNR angler
Langer
largen
regnal
AEGLNT tangle
AEGLNU lagune
langue
leguan
AEGLNW wangle
AEGLNY lynage
AEGLNZ glazen
AEGLOR Al Gore
galore
gaoler
AEGLOT gelato
legato
AEGLOV lovage
volage
AEGLPR graple
AEGLPU plague
AEGLRT tergal
AEGLRU regula
AEGLRV gravel
AEGLRY argyle
grayle
AEGLRZ glazer
AEGLSU saulge
AEGLSY sagely
AEGLTU tegula
AEGLTW talweg
AEGMMN gemman
AEGMMR gammer
gramme
AEGMMS smegma
AEGMNO gnomae
AEGMNR engram
german✧
manger
AEGMNS magnes
AEGMNT magnet
AEGMNY mangey
AEGMOR romage
AEGMPS sepmag
AEGMRU maugre
murage
AEGMSS megass
AEGMSY gamesy
AEGMTV TV game
AEGMUY maguey
AEGMUZ zeugma
AEGNNO nonage
AEGNNP pangen
Penang
AEGNNT gannet
AEGNOR onager
orange✧
AEGNOS geason
Seonag
AEGNRR garner
ranger✧
AEGNRS serang
AEGNRT argent
garnet
AEGNRU raunge
ungear
AEGNRV graven
AEGNRW gnawer
Wagner
AEGNRY anergy
AEGNSY gansey
AEGOPS sapego
AEGOPT potage
AEGORS sorage
AEGORT orgeat
toerag
AEGOSY go easy
AEGOTT togate
AEGOTU outage
AEGOTW towage
AEGOTX oxgate
AEGOVY voyage
AEGPPR gapper
AEGPRS gasper
sparge
AEGPRT parget
AEGPRU gauper
gear up
Prague
AEGPRW gawper
AEGPRY grapey
AEGPST Paget's
AEGPUZ upgaze
AEGRRT garret✧
garter✧
grater
AEGRRU arguer
AEGRRV graver
AEGRRZ grazer
AEGRSS gasser
AEGRST gaster
graste
Greats
stager
Strega®
AEGRSU sauger
usager
AEGRSV Graves'
graves✧
AEGRSW Swerga
AEGRSY greasy
AEGRTT target
AEGRTU argute
rugate
Tuareg
AEGRTY gyrate
AEGRYZ agryze
AEGSSU usages
AEGSTY gayest
stagey
AEGTTU guttae
AEHHJV Jahveh
AEHHLT health
AEHHPR rhaphe
AEHHPY hyphae
AEHHRS rehash
AEHHRT hearth
AEHHST sheath
AEHHTY heathy
AEHHVY Yahveh
AEHHWY Yahweh
AEHIJL Elijah
AEHIJR hejira
AEHIKN hankie
AEHIKS sakieh
AEHIKT Kathie
AEHIKW hawkie
AEHILM hiemal
AEHILN Hielan'
inhale
AEHILR hailer
AEHILS Elisha
sheila✧
AEHILT halite
AEHILW awhile
AEHIMN haemin
hemina
AEHIMR Hermia
AEHIMS mashie
AEHIMT Hamite
Heimat
AEHINR hernia
AEHINS ashine
AEHINT Eithna
in heat
AEHINV have in
vahine
AEHINW wahine
AEHIQU haique
AEHIRS sheria✧
AEHIRT Theria
AEHIST Hestia
saithe
AEHISV shavie
AEHITT Hattie
AEHITV have it
AEHJRS Jasher
Rajesh
AEHKMS samekh
AEHKNR hanker
harken
AEHKNS shaken
AEHKOS she-oak
AEHKPR phreak
AEHKRS shaker✧
AEHKRW hawker
AEHKSS shakes
AEHKSY ash-key
AEHKWY hawkey
AEHLLS as hell
Hellas
AEHLLT lethal
AEHLMP pelham✧
AEHLMR Harlem
harmel
Mahler
AEHLMT hamlet✧
Thelma
AEHLNO enhalo
AEHLNS hansel
AEHLNT hantle
lathen
AEHLNU unheal
AEHLOR Lahore
AEHLOS haloes
AEHLOT loathe
AEHLRS ashler
halers
halser
lasher
AEHLRT halter
lather
thaler
AEHLRU haleru
hauler
AEHLRV halver
AEHLRW whaler
AEHLRY Harley®
AEHLSS hassle
AEHLST haslet
Shelta
Thales
AEHLSV halves
AEHLSY Ashley
haysel
AEHLTW the law
wealth
AEHLTY eathly
hyetal
AEHLUV Huelva
AEHLYY Hayley
AEHMMR hammer
AEHMMY mayhem
AEHMNN Henman
AEHMNR Arnhem

AEHMNS manehs
AEHMNT anthem
hetman
AEHMNU humane
Humean
AEHMNW Newham
AEHMOS hamose
AEHMOT at home
at-home
AEHMPR hamper
AEHMRS masher
shamer
AEHMRT the Ram
AEHMST smeath
Thames
AEHNOT on heat
AEHNOV have on
have-on
AEHNPP happen
AEHNPS shapen
AEHNPT hapten
AEHNRT anther
harten
Tehran
thenar
AEHNST as then
Athens
hasten
snathe
sneath
AEHNSV Hesvan
shaven
AEHNSW washen
whenas
AEHNSZ sazhen
AEHNTU uneath
AEHNTV haven't
AEHNTW whaten
AEHNTX Xanthe
AEHNUW whenua
AEHNUY haüyne
AEHORS ahorse
ashore
hoarse
AEHORX hoaxer
AEHPPU upheap
AEHPRR harper
AEHPRS phrase
seraph
shaper
sherpa✧
sphaer
sphear
AEHPRT tephra
teraph
threap
AEHPST spathe
AEHPSV V-shape
AEHPSW peshwa
AEHPTY hypate
AEHPUV have up

AEHRRS rasher
sharer
AEHRRT rather
AEHRSS shears
AEHRST hearts✧
'sheart
AEHRSV havers
shaver
AEHRSW hawser
rewash
washer
AEHRSY ashery
hearsy
AEHRTT hatter
threat
AEHRTV thrave
AEHRTW thawer
the raw
wreath
AEHRTY earthy
hearty
AEHRVW wharve
AEHRVY Harvey
AEHSSY says he
AEHSTV Shevat
AEHSTW swathe
AEHTWY the Way
wheaty
AEIIKS saikei
AEIILM Emilia
AEIILS liaise
AEIIMS Maisie
AEIINR Eirian
AEIIPT T'aipei
AEIJKR Rijeka
AEIJLR jailer
AEIJLZ jezail
AEIJMM jemima✧
AEIJNN Janine
AEIJNO Joanie
AEIJNR injera
AEIJNT tajine
AEIJRV jarvie
AEIKLR laiker
AEIKLS alsike
AEIKLT talkie
AEIKMN kinema
AEIKMT make it
AEIKNR Kieran
rake in
AEIKNS kinase
AEIKNT intake
kentia✧
take in
take-in
AEIKNW weak in
AEIKNY yankie
AEIKNZ kaizen
AEIKPR parkie
AEIKRR kerria✧
AEIKRS kaiser✧

AEIKRT arkite
karite
AEIKTT take it
AEILLL Lallie
AEILLM mallei
AEILLN anelli
lienal
lineal
AEILLS allies
AEILLT taille
telial
AEILLW wallie✧
AEILMM lammie
AEILMN menial
AEILMP impale
palmie
AEILMR mailer✧
AEILMS mesail
mesial
samiel
AEILMZ mezail
AEILNN Lianne
AEILNO Eolian
Leonia
AEILNP alpine✧
Nepali
penial
pineal
AEILNR en l'air
larine
linear
nailer
AEILNS saline
Selina
silane
AEILNT entail
tenail
tineal
AEILNV à l'envi
alevin
alvine
valine
venial
AEILNX alexin
xenial
AEILOP leipoa
AEILOS Eloisa
AEILPP lappie
AEILPS espial
lipase
AEILPT aplite
Pilate
AEILRR railer
rerail
AEILRS Israel
sailer
serail
serial
AEILRT retail
retial
AEILRU Auriel

Laurie
AEILRV Averil
Elvira
AEILRW Lawrie
wailer
AEILSS eassil
laisse
lassie✧
AEILSU saulie
AEILSV Aviles
silvae
valise
AEILSW walise
AEILSX Alexis
AEILSY easily
AEILTY tailye
AEIMMN immane
AEIMMT Tammie
AEIMNN in name
AEIMNO anomie
AEIMNP pieman
AEIMNR marine
remain
AEIMNS Amiens
inseam
mesian
AEIMNT inmate
tamine
AEIMNX Maxine
Xiamen
AEIMNY Niamey
AEIMPR premia
AEIMPV impave
AEIMPY pyemia
AEIMRT imaret
matier
AEIMRU uremia
AEIMRW awmrie
Weimar
AEIMST samite
tamise
AEIMTT mattie✧
AEIMXX maxixe
AEINNP pinnae
AEINNR narine
ranine
AEINNS insane
sannie
sienna
AEINNT innate
nanite
AEINNV Vienna
AEINNZ enzian
AEINOZ azione
AEINPR Napier
rapine
AEINPS aspine
AEINPT patine
pineta
AEINPV Evipan®
AEINRS arisen

arsine
sarnie
AEINRT Nerita
ratine
ratiné
retain
retina
AEINRV avenir
ravine
AEINSS sanies
sansei
sasine
AEINST tisane
AEINSV savine
AEINTU auntie✧
Uniate
AEINTV native
AEIOPS soapie
AEIOPT opiate
AEIOPZ epizoa
AEIORR roarie
AEIOSV Savoie
AEIPPY yappie
AEIPRR rapier
repair
AEIPRS aspire
praise
spirea
AEIPRT pirate
pratie
pteria
AEIPSV pavise
spavie
AEIPSW waspie
AEIPTT Pattie
tapeti
AEIPTU taupie
AEIPTW tawpie
AEIPZZ Peziza
AEIQSU saique
AEIQTU quite a
AEIRRS raiser
sierra✧
AEIRRT 'Arriet
AEIRRV arrive
varier
AEIRST satire
striae
AEIRTT attire
ratite
tertia
AEIRTV taiver
AEIRTW waiter
AEIRVW waiver
AEIRVX Xavier
AEISST siesta
tassie✧
AEISSU Aussie
AEISSX axises
AEISSZ assize
AEISTT ita est
AEISTV sative
AEISTX taxies
AEISTY aseity
AEISTZ Taizés
AEITTT tattie
AEITTV vittae
AEITTW tawtie
twaite
AEJKNR janker
AEJMMR jammer
AEJMRT ramjet
AEJMST jetsam
matjes
AEJNNO Joanne
AEJNNS Jansen
AEJNOT Taejon
AEJNST sejant
AEJNSU jaunse
AEJNUU Juneau
AEJPRS jasper
AEJPRY japery
AEJQSU Jaques
AEJRVY jarvey
AEJRZZ jazzer
AEKKNR kraken
AEKKRY yakker
AEKLNO Ankole
AEKLNR rankle
AEKLNT anklet
AEKLNW knawel
Walken
wankle
AEKLNY alkyne
AEKLPY keypal
AEKLRR larker
AEKLRT talker
AEKLRV Kevlar®
AEKLRW walker✧
AEKLSS Kassel
AEKLST lasket
sklate
AEKLTU auklet
AEKLTY Alt key
AEKLWY weakly
AEKMNU unmake
AEKMNY key man
AEKMOT matoke
AEKMPU make up
make-up
upmake
AEKMRR marker
remark
re-mark
AEKMRS Marek's
masker
AEKMRT market
AEKNNR enrank
AEKNNT kanten
AEKNNY Kenyan
AEKNOR Korean
AEKNOS soaken
AEKNOT take on
AEKNOW awoken
AEKNRR ranker
AEKNRT tanker
AEKNRU unrake
AEKNRW Newark
AEKNRY yanker
AEKNSY sneaky
AEKOPT Topeka
AEKORS arkose
soaker
AEKOSY kayoes
AEKPRR parker
AEKPRS sparke
AEKPRU rake up
AEKPTU take up
take-up
uptake
AEKPUW wake up
wake-up
AEKQRU quaker✧
AEKQSU squeak
AEKRRT karter
krater
AEKRRY rakery
AEKRST skater
strake
streak
tasker
AEKRSY karsey
skeary
AEKRUW wauker
AEKSST stakes
AEKWYY keyway
AELLLY leally
AELLMT mallet
AELLMY lamely
mellay
AELLNO all one
AELLNU unleal
AELLNW enwall
AELLNY leanly
AELLPP lappel
AELLPS spalle
AELLPT L-plate
pallet
AELLPY palely
AELLRT tellar
AELLRU allure
laurel✧
AELLRW waller
AELLRY rallye
really
re-ally
AELLST sallet
Stella
AELLSW as well
AELLSY alleys
AELLTT tallet
AELLTU luteal
AELLTW wallet
AELLTY lately
lealty
AELLVY valley
AELMMR lammer
AELMMS lemmas
AELMNO melano
AELMNS Anselm
Le Mans
lemans
mensal
AELMNT lament
mantel
mantle
mental
AELMNY meanly
my lane
namely
AELMOR morale
AELMOS Salome
AELMPR emparl
palmer
AELMPS sample
AELMPU ampule
AELMRT armlet
martel
AELMRV marvel
vermal
AELMRY almery
AELMST metals
samlet
AELMSU Samuel
AELMSY measly
samely
AELMTU amulet
muleta
AELMTY tamely
AELNNO lean on
AELNNP pennal
AELNNR lanner
AELNNW wannel
AELNOR loaner
AELNOS lanose
on sale
Sloane
AELNOT etalon
lean-to
AELNPP pen pal
AELNPR planer
replan
AELNPS Naples
AELNPT planet
platen
AELNPU uplean
AELNRS ransel
AELNRT altern
antler
learnt
rental
ternal
AELNRU Lauren
neural

ulnare
unreal
AELNRV nerval
vernal
AELNRY anerly
larney
nearly
AELNRZ ranzel
AELNSU unseal
AELNSY sanely
AELNTT latent
latten
talent
AELNTU eluant
lunate
AELNTV levant✧
AELNTY neatly
AELNTZ zelant
AELNUW unweal
AELOOZ zooeal
AELOPP Aleppo
AELOPR parole
AELOPS aslope
El Paso
AELOPT pelota
potale
AELOPX poleax
AELORS realos
roseal
solera
AELORT lorate
AELORV Volare
AELORY o'erlay
AELOST osteal
Salote
AELOSU Aeolus
AELOSV loaves
AELOSW leasow
sea owl
AELOTZ zealot✧
AELPPR lapper
rappel
AELPPS apples
sapple
AELPPT applet
lappet
P-plate
AELPPU papule
upleap
AELPQU plaque
AELPRR parrel
AELPRS pearls
AELPRT palter
plater
AELPRU pleura
AELPRW prawle
AELPRY parley
pearly
player
replay
AELPST pastel
plaste
plates
septal
staple
AELPTT pattle
T-plate
AELPTU Petula
puteal
AELQRU quar'le
Raquel
AELQSU lasque
squeal
AELRRT retral
AELRRY rarely
rearly
AELRST laster
salter
slater
stelar
tarsel
AELRSU saurel
AELRSV salver
serval
slaver
versal
AELRSW warsle
AELRSY slayer
AELRTT latter
rattle✧
tatler
AELRTV travel
varlet
AELRTW Walter
AELRTY elytra
lyrate
raylet
realty
telary
AELRUV valuer
AELRVV varvel
AELRVY Valéry
AELRWX wraxle
AELRWY lawyer
AELRYY yarely
yearly
AELRZZ razzle
AELSST tassel
AELSSV selvas
AELSTT latest
stealt
taslet
AELSTU salute
AELSTV vestal✧
AELSTW wastel
AELSTY astely
AELSUV avulse
values
AELSUX sexual
AELSVY slavey
sylvae
AELSYZ sleazy
AELTTT tattle
AELTTW wattle
AELTUX luxate
AELUUV uvulae
AEMMMR mammer
AEMMMT mammet
AEMMNR merman
AEMMNT met man
AEMMRR rammer
AEMMRY yammer
AEMMRZ mamzer
AEMMST stemma
AEMMSU summae
AEMMTU maumet
AEMMTW mawmet
AEMNNO Eamonn
no mean
one-man
AEMNNP penman
AEMNNR manner
AEMNNT manent
AEMNNU Eamunn
AEMNNW Newman
new man✧
AEMNOP mopane
AEMNOR enamor
moaner
monera
AEMNOT omenta
to-name
AEMNOU Nouméa
AEMNOY yeoman
AEMNPU pneuma
AEMNQU manqué
AEMNRT marten
AEMNRU Amun-Re
manure
murena
AEMNSS messan
AEMNST mantes
stamen
AEMNSU unseam
AEMNSY yes-man
AEMNTT Mt Etna
AEMNTU untame
unteam
AEMOOV amoove
AEMOPT a tempo
AEMOPZ apozem
AEMORR remora
roamer
AEMORS ramose
AEMORT amoret
omerta
omertà
AEMORW womera
AEMORX xeroma
AEMOST osmate
AEMOSV vamose
AEMOSW awsome
AEMPPR mapper
pamper
preamp
AEMPRR ramper
AEMPRT empart
tamper
AEMPRV revamp
vamper
AEMPSU empusa✧
AEMPTU team up
AEMQRU marque
AEMQSU masque
squame
AEMRRU armure
AEMRRV marver
AEMRRW warmer
AEMRSS Ramses
AEMRST master✧
stream
AEMRSU amuser
Maseru
Mauser
AEMRSY smeary
AEMRTT matter
AEMRTU mature
AEMSSS masses
AEMSSU assume
Seamus
Seumas
AEMSTU meatus
AEMSTY mayest
steamy
AEMSYZ zymase
AEMTTU mutate
AEMUZZ mezuza
AENNNO nonane
AENNOS nosean
AENNOV novena
AENNOY any one
anyone
AENNRT tanner
AENNRV vanner
AENNST Nantes
AENNSV Vannes
AENNTT tenant
AENOPS peason
AENOPV pavone
AENOPW weapon
AENOPY paeony
AENORS reason
señora✧
AENORT atoner
ornate
AENORV Verona
AENORW Rowena
wear on
AENORX Roxane
AENOSS season
AENOST astone
AENOTT attone
notate
AENOTV novate

Words marked ✧ can also be spelled with one or more capital letters

AENOTZ zonate
AENOWY one-way
AENPPR napper
parpen
rappen
AENPRT arpent
enrapt
entrap
panter
parent
trepan
AENPRW enwrap
pawner
AENPRY napery
AENPRZ panzer
AENPST pesant
AENPTT patent
patten
AENPTU ante up
peanut
AENPTX Pentax®
AENPTZ pezant
AENQTU equant
AENRRS serran
snarer
AENRRT errant
ranter
Terran
AENRRW warner
warren
AENRSS Nasser
sarsen
AENRST astern
sterna
transe
AENRSW answer
AENRSY sarney
senary
AENRTT natter
ratten
AENRTU aunter
nature✧
tea urn
AENRTV tavern
AENRTW wanter
AENRTY trayne
AENRUW unware
AENRWY yawner
AENSST assent
snaste
AENSTU Austen
nasute
unseat
AENSTX sextan
AENSTY stayne
AENSTZ stanze
AENSUV naevus
AENSUY uneasy
AENSWY sawney✧
AENTTT attent
AENTTU attune
nutate
tauten
AENTTX extant
AENTTY tetany
AENTWY tawney
AEOPPS appose
AEOPQU opaque
AEOPRS soaper
AEOPRT protea
AEOPRU Europa
AEOPTT aptote
teapot
AEOPTY teapoy
AEORRR roarer
AEORRS soarer
AEORRU Aurore
AEORSS serosa
AEORST Ostrea
AEORSU arouse
Roseau
AEORSZ Azores
AEORTT rotate
to-tear
AEORUV avoure
AEORVW avower
AEORVY avoyer
AEORZZ Arezzo
AEOSTV avoset
AEOSTW awetos
AEOTTU eat out
outeat
AEOUVZ Zouave
AEPPRR rapper
AEPPRS papers
sapper✧
AEPPRT tapper
AEPPRU pauper
AEPPRW wapper
AEPPRY papery
prepay
yapper
AEPPRZ zapper
AEPPSY apepsy
AEPPTT tappet
AEPPTU pupate
AEPRRS parser
rasper
sparer
sparre
AEPRRT parter
prater
AEPRRU parure
rear up
uprear
AEPRRW pre-war
rewrap
warper
AEPRRY prayer
AEPRSS passer
repass
sparse
AEPRST paster
pearst
repast
trapes
AEPRSU pauser
AEPRSY speary
AEPRTT patter
AEPRTU tear up
uprate
uptear
AEPRTX pre-tax
AEPRTY petary
AEPRTZ patzer
AEPRUV rave-up
AEPRWY yawper
AEPSST stapes
AEPSUV save up
AEQRSU square
AEQRTU quarte
AEQRUV quaver
AEQSUY queasy
AEQUYZ queazy
AERRSS serras
AERRST arrest
raster
Sartre
starer
terras
AERRSU rasure
AERRTT ratter
AERRTY artery
AERRUZ razure
AERRWY warrey
AERSST assert
AERSSU assure
AERSSW wrasse
AERSTT astert
at rest
stater
taster
AERSTU Atreus
Auster
Seurat
AERSTV starve
tavers
AERSTW waster
waters
AERSTX Astrex
AERSTY estray
reasty
stayer
stayre
AERSTZ ersatz
AERSUU aureus
uraeus
AERSVW swarve
AERSWY sawyer
swayer
AERTTT tatter
AERTTV tavert
vatter
AERTTW tewart
AERTTY treaty
yatter
AERTUU auteur
AERTWY tawery
watery
AERVWY wavery
AESSSS assess
AESSST assets
AESSTT states✧
tasset
AESSTU sautés
AESSTV staves
vestas
AESSTW saw set
sweats
wastes
AESSTY sayest
AESTTT attest
AESTTU astute
statue
AESTWY sweaty
AESTXY extasy
AESTYY yeasty
AESVVY savvey
AETUXY eutaxy
AFFFOR far-off
AFFGUW guffaw
AFFHIT haffit
AFFILP pilaff
AFFIMO aim off
AFFIMR affirm
AFFINR Fafnir
AFFIOR off-air
AFFIRT tariff
AFFLNY naffly
AFFLOY lay off
lay-off
Offaly
AFFLWY waffly
AFFOPT off pat
AFFOPY pay off
pay-off
AFFOPZ zap off
AFFRST straff
AFFSST staffs
AFGGLY flaggy
AFGGOT faggot
AFGHOS fogash
AFGILN Fingal
AFGINN fingan
AFGINO Fangio
AFGINR Gräfin
AFGISY gasify
AFGITZ zaftig
AFGLNO flagon
AFGLNU fungal
AFGLRU frugal
AFGMNO fogman
AFGMOR fogram
AFGNOS fangos

AFGNPU pang-fu'
AFGORR fragor
AFGORT forgat
AFGOTU fugato
AFGRUY argufy
AFHIKL khalif
AFHIKR kharif
AFHIMS famish
AFHIOS oafish
AFHIRS sharif✧
AFHITW what if
AFHLMU fulham✧
AFHLOO loofah
AFHLSY flashy
fly ash
AFHLTU hatful
AFHMOT fathom
AFHORS shofar
AFHRSW wharfs
AFIIJN Fijian
AFIIKR Kafiri
AFIILL filial
AFIILN fail in
finial
AFIINS fains I
AFIJNN finjan
AFIKNU funkia
AFIKRS friska
AFILLN fall in
fall-in
infall
AFILMY family
AFILNO Finola
in foal
in-foal
AFILNS finals
AFILNU infula
AFILNV flavin
AFILNY fainly
Finlay
AFILOR foliar
AFILRY fairly
AFILRZ frazil
AFILSY salify
AFIMNR farm-in
firman
AFIMNY infamy
AFIMRY ramify
AFIMSS massif
AFIMSV favism
AFINNN finnan
AFINNO fanion
AFINNT Fintan
infant
AFINOR no fair
AFINRU unfair
AFINRY fin-ray
AFINST faints
AFINSU fusain
AFINSY sanify
AFINTU fiaunt
AFINTY fainty
AFINYZ Nazify
AFIORT faitor
AFIQRU faquir
AFIRRY friary
AFIRTY ratify
AFIRUY aurify
AFJLRU jarful
AFKORU Farouk
AFLLMU fullam
AFLLNO onfall
AFLLNU fullan
AFLLOR floral
for all
AFLLOT to-fall
AFLLOW fallow
AFLLPU lapful
AFLLTY flatly
AFLLUW lawful
AFLMNU manful
AFLMNY flyman
AFLMOR formal
AFLMRU armful
fulmar
AFLMYY mayfly
AFLNOT fontal
AFLNPU panful
AFLNRU Ranulf
AFLNTU flaunt
AFLORS floras
AFLORV flavor
AFLOST floats
AFLOTT Flotta
AFLOTW low-fat
AFLOTY floaty
AFLPPY flappy
AFLPSU sapful
AFLRTU artful
AFLSTU flatus
AFLSTY fastly
AFLSWY sawfly
AFLTTY flatty
AFLTUV vatful
AFLTUY faulty
AFLWYY flyway
AFMNOR Forman
AFMNOT fantom
AFMOOS samfoo
AFMORS as from
of arms
AFMORT format
AFMOSU famous
AFMTTU Muftat
AFNNOT non-fat
AFNORT afront
AFNORX Fornax
AFNOTU fan out
AFNPRY pan-fry
AFNRYZ franzy
AFNSUU Faunus
AFOORT footra
AFORRW farrow
AFORRY forray
AFORSY forsay
AFORTU far-out
fautor
foutra
AFORUV favour
AFOSST fatsos
AFOSSU foussa
AFOSUV favous
AFPTUW upwaft
AFRRTY fratry
AFRSTU frusta
AGGHIS haggis
AGGHNO go hang
AGGHSY shaggy
AGGIIL gilgai
AGGILN gingal
laggin
AGGILO loggia
AGGIMN gaming
gigman
AGGINO agoing
a-going
AGGINP gaping
paging
AGGINR raging
AGGINT gating
AGGINU Gaugin
AGGIOR gorgia
AGGIWW wigwag
AGGIZZ zigzag
AGGKNY knaggy
AGGLLO Glagol
AGGLNY gangly
AGGLOT loggat
AGGLSY slaggy
AGGLWY waggly
AGGMNO moggan
AGGMOT maggot
AGGNOU guango
AGGNOW waggon
AGGNOX oxgang
AGGNPU gang up
upgang
AGGNRU nuggar
AGGNSU gas gun
AGGNSY snaggy
AGGPRY pygarg
AGGQUY quaggy
AGHHTU haught
AGHIJR jaghir
AGHIKU kiaugh
AGHILT alight
AGHINN hang in
AGHINT anight
a'thing
AGHINV having
AGHINY haying
AGHINZ hazing
AGHIQU quaigh
AGHIRR gharri
AGHIRS garish
AGHIRT aright
graith
AGHISU aguish
AGHKRU Gurkha
AGHLLU Gullah
AGHLMU Mughal
AGHLOS galosh
AGHLSY gashly
AGHLTU galuth✧
AGHLUY laughy
AGHNNO hang on
AGHNNU unhang
AGHNOU anough
AGHNPU hang up
hang-up
uphang
AGHNRT Granth
thrang
AGHNRU nurhag
AGHNTU naught
AGHNUY gunyah
AGHOQU quahog
AGHORT hog-rat
AGHRRU gurrah
AGHRRY gharry
AGHRTU raught
tughra
AGHTTU taught
AGHTUW waught
AGIIJN gaijin
AGIIKL Kigali
AGIILN ailing
nilgai
AGIINR airing
ragini
AGIJLN jingal
AGIJNP japing
AGIJNW jawing
AGIJSW jigsaw
AGIKLS glaiks
AGIKMN making
AGIKNR raking
AGIKNS gaskin
AGIKNT taking
AGIKNW waking
AGILLO Gallio
AGILLU ligula
AGILMM gimmal
AGILMN lingam
malign
AGILMO glioma
AGILMP magilp
AGILNO Ginola
AGILNP paling
AGILNS lasing
signal
AGILNU lingua
nilgau
AGILNW lawing

AGILNY	gainly
	laying
AGILOR	gloria✧
AGILOS	gas oil
	golias
	oil-gas
AGILOT	galiot
AGILOV	ogival
AGILRS	slairg
AGILRU	arguli
AGILRY	glairy
AGILST	gaslit
AGIMMS	magism
AGIMNN	naming
AGIMNP	pig-man
AGIMNR	ingram
	margin
AGIMNT	taming
AGIMNY	maying
AGIMOS	amigos
	imagos
AGIMRU	gurami
AGIMST	stigma
AGIMWW	wigwam
AGINNO	ganoin
AGINNT	anting
AGINNU	ungain
AGINNW	awning
	waning
AGINNZ	Nzinga
AGINOR	ignaro
	origan
AGINOS	ngaios
	sagoin
	Saigon
AGINOT	gitano
AGINPR	paring
	raping
AGINPS	spaing
AGINPU	gain-up
AGINPV	paving
AGINPY	paying
AGINRR	raring
AGINRS	grains
	saring
AGINRT	gratin
	rating
	taring
AGINRU	air-gun
	Ugrian
AGINRV	raving
AGINRW	rawing
AGINRY	grainy
AGINSS	assign
AGINST	gainst
	'gainst
AGINSU	Anguis
	saguin
AGINSV	saving
AGINSW	aswing
	sawing
AGINSY	saying
AGINTW	tawing
AGINTX	taxing
AGINVW	waving
AGINWX	waxing
AGIORU	giaour
AGIORV	virago
AGIOTU	agouti
AGIPRT	pig-rat
AGIQRU	Griqua
AGIRST	gratis
	striga
AGIRTU	guitar
	Ugarit
AGISTT	stag it
AGISTU	agutis
AGISTW	swag it
AGITTW	witgat
AGJLMO	log jam
AGJLNY	jangly
AGJNOR	jargon
AGJRTU	Gujrat
AGKLNO	kalong
AGKLOO	kagool
AGKLOT	kgotla
AGKLOU	kagoul
AGKNOU	nogaku
AGKNRU	kurgan✧
AGKORT	go-kart
AGLLNO	gallon
	gollan
AGLLOP	gallop
AGLLOR	gollar
AGLLOW	gallow
AGLLRY	Argyll
AGLLSU	gallus
AGLMMY	glammy
	gymmal
AGLMNO	log-man
AGLMOR	glamor
AGLMPU	glam up
AGLNNO	longan
AGLNOO	lagoon
AGLNOS	Anglos
	slogan
AGLNOU	lanugo
	Lugano
AGLNOW	gowlan
AGLNRU	langur
AGLNRY	gnarly
AGLNSS	slangs
AGLNSY	slangy
AGLNTY	tangly
AGLNUU	ungual
	ungula
AGLOOT	galoot
AGLORS	largos
AGLOSS	glossa
AGLOSW	log-saw
AGLOTY	otalgy
AGLPUY	plaguy
AGLRSU	guslar
AGLRUV	vulgar
AGLRUY	glaury
	raguly
AGLSSY	glassy
AGLSUV	valgus
AGMMNO	gammon
AGMMNU	magnum
AGMMRY	Grammy
AGMNNO	magnon
AGMNNU	gunman
AGMNOR	Morgan
AGMNOS	mangos
AGMNOX	Magnox®
	magnox
AGMNRU	granum
AGMNSU	Magnus
	musang
AGMNUY	maungy
AGMOOY	oogamy
AGMORS	orgasm
AGMORV	vagrom
AGMORY	goramy
	morgay
AGMOYZ	zygoma
AGMPUZ	gazump
AGMRTU	Targum
AGNNOT	Tongan
	tonnag
AGNNOY	Yangon
AGNNRY	granny
AGNNTU	tangun
AGNNUW	wangun
AGNOOZ	gazoon
AGNOQU	quango
AGNORR	garron
AGNORS	Sargon
	sarong
AGNORU	Ungaro
AGNORW	awrong
AGNORY	Gaynor
AGNOSS	gossan
AGNOST	sontag
	tangos
AGNOSU	guanos
AGNOTU	nougat
AGNOWY	gowany
AGNOZZ	gozzan
AGNPRS	sprang
AGNPRU	Nagpur
AGNRSU	sungar
AGNRTY	gantry
	gyrant
AGNRUY	ray gun
AGNSSY	syngas
AGNSTY	angsty
AGNTWY	twangy
AGOORT	agorot
AGOORV	vorago
AGOPRT	ragtop
AGOPRU	gopura
AGORRT	garrot
AGORSS	sargos
AGORST	groats
AGORSY	argosy
AGORTU	rag out
	ragout
	rag-out
AGORTW	tow-rag
AGOSTU	outgas
AGOSYZ	azygos
AGOTTU	tautog
AGOTUY	agouty
AGOUYY	gay-you
AGPSUU	gaupus
AGPSUW	gawpus
AGRRTU	rug rat
AGRRUY	rya rug
AGRSSU	sargus
AGRSSY	grassy
AGRSTU	tragus
AGRSUY	sugary
AGRUUY	augury
AGSTUU	august✧
AGSTUV	Gustav
AHHHOO	hoo-hah
AHHIJR	hijrah
AHHIKS	shaikh
AHHIMS	Hamish
AHHIRS	harish
AHHISS	Shashi
AHHISV	shivah
AHHKOO	hookah
AHHLPY	hyphal
AHHOOR	hoorah
AHHOOW	wo ha ho
AHHOPW	phwoah
AHHORT	Hathor
	Thorah
AHHORW	Howrah
AHHOTW	what ho
AHHPPU	huppah
AHHRRU	hurrah
AHHRST	thrash
AHIILT	lithia
AHIINT	tahini
AHIITT	Tahiti
AHIJOS	Josiah
AHIKLS	lakish
AHIKLT	khilat
AHIKMV	mikvah
AHIKNS	Naskhi
AHIKOW	kowhai
AHIKRS	rakish
	shikar
AHIKSS	shiksa
AHIKST	Shakti
	skaith
AHIKSU	haikus
AHIKTW	hawkit
AHILLP	phalli
AHILLS	shalli

Words marked ✧ can also be spelled with one or more capital letters

AHILLT	thalli
AHILLZ	zillah
AHILMO	holmia
AHILMS	lamish
AHILMU	hamuli
AHILNR	rhinal
AHILNU	inhaul
AHILNY	hyalin
	linhay
AHILPS	palish
AHILPT	Lapith
AHILRY	Hilary
AHILSS	Salish
AHILST	latish
	tahsil
	thalis
AHILSV	lavish
AHILTU	thulia
AHILTW	withal
AHILYZ	hazily
AHIMNR	harmin
AHIMNS	Mishna
AHIMNT	hitman
AHIMNU	Humian
AHIMOR	mohair
AHIMPS	mishap
	pashim
AHIMRS	mahsir
	marish
	Shamir
AHIMRT	Mithra
	thairm
	thiram
AHINPT	hatpin
AHINRS	arshin
	shairn
AHINRU	unhair
AHINSU	Husain
AHINSV	vanish
AHINSW	wash-in
AHINTT	in that
	tin hat
AHIOPS	poisha
	Sophia
AHIORT	hot air
	hot-air
	thoria
AHIPPS	papish
AHIPRS	parish
	raphis
AHIPRU	rupiah
AHIPSS	phasis
AHIPST	ash-pit
AHIPTY	Pythia
AHIRRS	arrish
	Harris
	shirra
	sirrah
AHIRST	hairst
	Ishtar
	Trisha
AHIRSU	Suhair
AHIRSV	ravish
AHIRSW	rawish
AHIRSZ	Shiraz
AHIRTW	wraith
AHISSW	siwash✧
AHISTT	staith
AHISTU	hiatus
AHIUZZ	Uzziah
AHJLOW	ja wohl
AHJNSU	Jan Hus
AHJOOP	poojah
AHJOSU	Joshua
AHKKSU	sukkah
AHKLNU	Khulna
AHKLOO	koolah
AHKLPU	pulkha
AHKMNU	khanum
AHKMOW	mohawk✧
AHKNPU	punkah
AHKNRS	shrank
AHKNST	thanks
AHKOPT	Pakhto
AHKOSS	shakos
AHKPTU	Pakhtu
AHKRST	skarth
AHKRTU	khurta
AHLLMO	mollah
	ollamh
AHLLMU	mullah
AHLLNU	nullah
AHLLOO	halloo
	holloa
AHLLOS	hallos
AHLLOW	hallow
AHLLRT	thrall
AHLLUX	hallux
AHLLWY	whally
AHLMNY	hymnal
AHLMOO	moolah
AHLMOS	shalom
AHLMTU	lum hat
AHLNOP	phonal
AHLNOT	Halton
AHLNSU	unlash
AHLOOP	hoop-la
AHLOPS	pholas✧
AHLORT	harlot
AHLORW	Harlow
	Warhol
AHLOST	shalot
AHLOSY	shoaly
AHLOTY	loathy
AHLPSS	splash
AHLPSU	lash-up
	sulpha
AHLPSY	plashy
AHLPUU	haul up
AHLRSY	rashly
AHLSTU	haulst
AHMMOW	whammo
AHMMSY	shammy
AHMMWY	whammy
AHMNNU	numnah
AHMNOS	hansom
AHMNOU	Mahoun
AHMOOP	oompah
AHMORZ	mahzor
AHMOST	Thomas
AHMOSU	hamous
AHMOSV	moshav
AHMOSY	shamoy
AHMOTU	mahout
AHMOTZ	matzoh
AHMOWY	haymow
AHMRRU	murrha
AHMRSY	marshy
AHMRTW	warmth
AHMSSU	samshu
	shamus✧
AHNNSU	Sunnah
AHNNSY	shanny
AHNOOR	Honora
AHNOOT	on oath
AHNOPR	orphan
AHNOPY	aphony
AHNORS	Roshan
	Sharon
	shoran
AHNORU	Haroun
AHNOSX	Xhosan
AHNOWY	anyhow
AHNPRU	Nuphar
AHNPSU	Pushan
	unhasp
AHNRSY	sharny
AHNRTW	thrawn
AHNRVY	hryvna
AHNSTU	sunhat
AHNSTY	shanty
AHNTUW	unthaw
AHOORY	hooray
AHOOSY	Yahoos
AHOPPS	Paphos
	Sappho
AHOPRS	pharos
AHOPRW	phwoar
AHOPST	Pashto
	pathos
	potash
	pot-ash
AHOPTT	pot hat
	top hat
	top-hat
AHOQTU	quotha
AHORRW	harrow
AHORRY	horary
AHORTT	throat
AHORTU	author
AHORTW	hot war
	wroath
AHORTX	thorax
AHOSTT	so that
AHOSTW	so what?
	whatso
AHOTWZ	howzat
AHPRSS	sharps
AHPRST	sparth
AHPRSY	phrasy
AHPSTU	Pashtu
AHPSUW	wash up
	wash-up
AHQSSU	squash
AHRRTU	Arthur
AHRRUY	hurray
AHRSSU	hussar
AHRSTT	strath
AHRSTW	swarth
AHRSTY	trashy
AHRTTW	thwart
AHRTWY	wrathy
AHSSTU	tussah
AHSSWY	swashy
AHSTWY	swathy
AIIKKW	wakiki
AIILLM	limail
AIILLN	Lilian
AIILLR	arilli
AIILLS	Lilias
AIILMN	mail-in
AIILMS	Ismail
	simial
AIILNP	Alpini
AIILNT	in tail
AIILOV	Olivia
AIILRY	airily
AIILSV	Silvia
AIIMMN	minima
AIIMMR	Miriam
AIIMMS	misaim
AIIMNP	painim
AIIMNS	simian
AIIMNT	intima
AIIMOR	Moirai
AIIMPR	impair
AIIMPS	simpai
AIIMST	samiti
AIINNN	Ninian
AIINNO	Ionian
AIINNP	panini
AIINNR	rain in
AIINNV	in vain
AIINNZ	zinnia
AIINRS	raisin
	Sirian
AIINRX	in rixa
AIINST	isatin
AIINSX	sixain
AIINTT	titian✧
AIINVV	Vivian
AIIORS	ariosi
AIIPTW	wapiti
AIIRTV	trivia

Words marked ✧ can also be spelled with one or more capital letters

AIISST	Isatis
AIJJMM	jimjam
AIJKNS	kanjis
AIJLMS	majlis✧
AIJLNU	Julian
AIJLOR	jailor
AIJLOV	jovial✧
AIJLTW	wiltja
AIJMOR	romaji
AIJNNS	ninjas✧
AIJNOV	Jovian
AIJORW	jowari
AIJPRU	Jaipur
AIJPSS	jaspis
AIJPTU	jupati
AIJRSV	Jarvis
AIKKLU	kaluki
AIKKRT	kark it
AIKLLS	killas
AIKLMN	malkin
AIKLMU	kalium
AIKLNO	kaolin
AIKLNR	Larkin
AIKLNT	talk-in
AIKLNW	walk-in
AIKLOS	skolia
AIKLPS	kalpis
AIKLSU	saluki
AIKLTW	walk it
AIKMMS	immask
AIKMNR	Kirman
AIKMNS	kamsin
AIKMNW	mawkin
AIKMOO	oomiak
AIKMOS	maikos
AIKMPR	impark
AIKMRU	kumari✧
AIKMRV	Vikram
AIKNNN	nankin
AIKNNP	napkin
AIKNNR	Rankin
AIKNOT	kation
AIKNPR	kirpan
	parkin
AIKNPS	panisk
AIKNRT	kirtan
	nark it!
AIKNRV	Narvik
AIKNST	Atkins
AIKOPS	okapis
AIKOPT	katipo
AIKORT	troika✧
AIKOST	Ostiak
	taikos
AIKRRS	sirkar
AIKRST	at risk
	at-risk
	straik
AIKRSV	Kvasir
AIKTUW	Kuwait
AILLMU	allium
AILLNV	villan
AILLNW	inwall
AILLOT	Lolita
AILLPR	pillar
AILLPU	pillau
	pilula
AILLRV	villar
AILLRY	railly
AILLSY	I'll say!
AILLTW	at will
AILLUZ	lazuli
AILLYZ	lazily
AILMMS	malism
AILMNO	monial
	oilman
AILMNR	marlin
AILMNS	maslin
AILMNU	alumni
	lumina
AILMNY	mainly
AILMOP	lipoma
AILMOS	Somali
AILMOT	maloti
	tomial
AILMPR	imparl
	primal
AILMRT	mitral
AILMRU	ramuli
AILMSS	missal
	salmis
AILMST	malist
	smalti
AILMSX	laxism
	smilax
AILMSY	mislay
AILMTU	ultima
AILMTY	matily
AILMUV	maulvi
	Valium®
AILMYZ	mazily
AILNNU	annuli
	unnail
AILNOP	Alpino
	oil pan
AILNOS	Alison
	sialon
AILNOT	Latino
	talion
AILNOV	Novial
AILNPS	plains✧
	spinal
AILNPT	plaint
	pliant
AILNPU	nail up
AILNPY	in play
AILNRT	ratlin
	trinal
AILNRU	urinal
AILNSS	'snails
AILNST	instal
	Stalin
AILNSU	insula
AILNSV	silvan
AILNSW	in-laws
AILNSY	snaily
AILNTU	unital
AILNTY	litany
AILNUV	unvail
AILNVY	vainly
AILOOR	oorial
AILORS	sailor
AILORT	Rialto
	tailor
AILORU	Auriol
	ourali
AILOSS	assoil
AILOST	ostial
AILOSU	Iolaus
	Louisa
AILOSX	oxalis
AILOTX	oxtail
AILPRS	spiral
AILPST	pastil
	spital
AILPTU	tipula
AILPTY	play it
AILQSU	squail
AILRST	trials
AILRSW	aswirl
AILRTU	ritual
AILRWY	warily
AILSSV	silvas
AILSTU	situla
AILSTV	vistal
AILSTX	laxist
AILSUV	visual
AILSVY	sylvia✧
AILSVZ	vizsla
AILTXY	laxity
AILVWY	wavily
AILWXY	waxily
AIMMMU	mummia
AIMMOS	Maoism
	mimosa
AIMMRS	Ramism
AIMMRY	Myriam
AIMMSS	miasms
AIMNNO	amnion
	Minoan
	nomina
AIMNNP	pin-man
AIMNNS	nanism
AIMNNT	tinman
AIMNNU	numina
AIMNNY	minyan
AIMNOP	mopani
AIMNOR	mainor
	Marion
	Romani
AIMNOT	manito
AIMNPP	map-pin
AIMNPT	pitman
AIMNPW	impawn
AIMNPY	paynim
AIMNRS	in arms
AIMNRT	Antrim
	martin✧
AIMNRU	rumina✧
AIMNRV	Marvin
AIMNSS	in mass
AIMNST	mantis
	matins✧
	santim
	Tamsin
AIMNSU	animus
AIMNSY	Yasmin
AIMNSZ	Nazism
AIMNUV	mauvin
AIMOPT	optima
AIMOPY	myopia
AIMORS	Maoris
AIMOST	Maoist
	Samiot
	Taoism
AIMOSV	Asimov
AIMPPS	papism
AIMPRT	armpit
	impart
	partim
AIMPSS	passim
AIMPSU	Sapium
AIMQSU	maquis✧
AIMQTU	qui tam
AIMRST	Marist
	Ramist
AIMRTU	atrium
	Timaru
AIMRTX	matrix
AIMSSY	missay
AIMSTT	statim
AIMSTU	autism
AINNNT	tannin
AINNOS	nasion
AINNOT	anoint
	nation
AINNOW	wanion
	Winona
AINNPS	inspan
AINNRU	uranin
AINNSS	Nissan®
AINNSW	swan in
AINNTW	want in
AINNUZ	Zunian
	Zuñian
AINOOZ	Aizoon
AINOPP	Popian
AINOPS	pianos
	Pisano
AINOPT	à point
AINOQU	quinoa
AINORS	Rosina
AINORT	aroint
	ration

AINORW in a row
AINOSS Ossian
AINOST Tainos
AINOSU Siouan
AINOTW wait on
wait-on
AINPRS spinar
sprain
AINPRT in part
AINPRU pruina
AINPRW inwrap
wrap in
AINPST ptisan
AINPSV spavin
AINPTT tan pit
AINPTU Tupian
AINPTY painty
AINQRT qintar
Q-train
AINQTU quaint
quinta
AINQUY yanqui
AINRST instar
santir
strain
AINRSY Syrian
AINRTU in a rut
nutria
AINRTY in-tray
Tyrian
AINRYZ Zyrian
AINSST Saints
AINSTT statin
tanist
Titans
AINSTU Austin
AINSTX sin tax
AINSTY sanity
satiny
stay in
AINTVY vanity
AINVVY Vyvian
AIOORS arioso
AIOPRT Portia
AIOPRV pavior
AIOPST patios
patois
AIOPTU utopia✧
AIORRU ourari
AIORSS Orissa
AIORST aorist
aristo
ratios
satori
AIORSU souari
AIORTV viator
AIOSSV avisos
AIOSTT Taoist
AIPPRR riprap
rip-rap
AIPPRY papyri
AIPPST papist
AIPPTT pit-pat
tappit
AIPRRU Raipur
AIPRST rapist
AIPRSV parvis
AIPRSW ripsaw
AIPRSX praxis
AIPRTT rat-pit
tar pit
AIPRTY parity
AIPRUY pyuria
AIPSST pastis
AIPSTT past it
tapist
AIPSTW pit-saw
sawpit
AIPTUW wait up
AIPZZZ pizazz
AIRRST stirra
AIRRTY rarity
AIRRZZ rizzar
AIRSST sistra
stairs
AIRSSU russia✧
AIRSTT artist
sittar
strait
AIRSTU aurist
AIRSTV travis
AIRTTT attrit
AIRTTY yttria
AIRVVY vivary
AISSST assist
stasis
AISSTW tiswas
AISSTY it says
AISTUW Watusi
AISTWZ tizwas
AITTTU tautit
AITTWX atwixt
AJKNSY jansky
AJLOOR jarool
AJLOPY jalopy
AJMOPT jampot
AJMORS majors
AJMORU Majuro
AJMRTU jumart
AJNORT Trojan
AJNRTU jurant
AJNTUY jaunty
AJORRW Jarrow
AJPRTU Rajput
AJPUZZ jazz up
AKKKOO kokako
AKKLMY Kalmyk
AKKNRU kunkar
AKKNSY skanky
AKKOQU quokka
AKKORW Kraków
AKKOSS sakkos
AKLLNY lankly
AKLNOU koulan
AKLNOW walk-on
AKLNOX klaxon✧
AKLNRY rankly
AKLOST stalko
AKLOSV Slovak
AKLOTW kotwal
AKLPRY parkly
AKLPTU talk up
uptalk
AKLPUW walk-up
AKLSTY stalky
AKMNRU Kru-man
AKMNSU unmask
AKMNSY skyman
AKMPRU mark up
mark-up
AKMUYZ muzaky
AKNOOT Nootka
AKNORU koruna
AKNORY karyon
ryokan
AKNOSS sankos
AKNOTU oak-nut
AKNPRU Kanpur
AKNPRY pranky
AKNPTU tank up
AKNRTZ krantz
AKNSWY swanky
AKNTUU Tuanku
AKOORR karroo✧
korora
AKOPRV Karpov
AKOPSU soak up
AKORSS kaross
AKOSTU ask out
out-ask
AKOSTY Ostyak
AKPRSS sparks
AKPRSY sparky
AKPTTU kaputt
AKQSUW squawk
AKRSTU tuskar
AKSWYY skyway
ALLMOR morall
ALLMOS slalom
ALLMOW mallow
ALLMSS smalls
ALLMUV vallum
ALLNOP pollan
ALLNOS allons
llanos
ALLNUU lunula
ALLOOP apollo✧
palolo
ALLOPR pallor
ALLOPW wallop
ALLORS sollar
ALLORY orally
ALLOSW sallow
ALLOTT tallot
ALLOTU all out
all-out
ALLOTV lavolt
ALLOTW tallow
ALLOUY you-all
ALLOVY ovally
ALLOWW wallow
ALLOWY lay low
ALLOYY Y-alloy
ALLPRU plural
ALLPSY psylla
ALLPUW wall up
ALLQSU squall
ALLRSU Rallus
ALLSST stalls
ALLSTY lastly
saltly
ALLUUZ Luzula
ALLUVV vulval
ALMMSY smalmy
ALMMUY amylum
ALMNOR Marlon
normal
ALMNOS salmon
ALMNOT Lamont
ALMNOU monaul
ALMNRU murlan
ALMNTU Multan
ALMORS morals
morsal
samlor
ALMORT mortal
ALMORU morula
ALMOST matlos
smalto
St Malo
stomal
ALMOSU almous
ALMOTU lam out
ALMOTW matlow
ALMOXY xyloma
ALMPSS Psalms
ALMQUY qualmy
ALMRWY warmly
ALMSUY asylum
ALMTUU mutual
umlaut
ALNNOO on loan
ALNNOR norlan'
ALNNOU nounal
ALNOOS Alonso
alsoon
saloon
solano
ALNOOZ zoonal
ALNOPT pontal
ALNOPY play on
ALNORT latron
ALNOSV Volans
ALNOSW Lawson

Words marked ✧ can also be spelled with one or more capital letters

ALNOSY	Syalon®
ALNOTV	volant
ALNOUZ	zonula
ALNPTU	pultan
ALNRSY	snarly
ALNRUY	lunary
	uranyl
ALNRXY	larynx
ALNSTU	sultan
	unlast
ALNSVY	sylvan
ALNTUW	walnut
ALNTUY	auntly
ALOOPS	saloop
ALOPPR	poplar
ALOPPT	laptop
ALOPRR	parlor
ALOPRT	patrol
	portal
ALOPRV	vorpal
ALOPRY	Pyrola
ALOPST	postal
ALOQTU	loquat
ALORRW	worral
ALORSU	rosula
ALORSV	salvor
ALORSY	royals✧
ALORTU	rotula
	torula
ALORTW	low-tar
ALORTY	Taylor
ALORUV	louvar
	ovular
	valour
ALORVY	volary
ALOSSS	lassos
ALOSST	saltos
ALOSSV	salvos✧
ALOTUW	outlaw
ALOTUY	lay out
	layout
	outlay
ALOTUZ	Lao-tzu
ALPPSU	palpus
	slap-up
ALPPUY	play up
ALPRRU	larrup
ALPRSU	pulsar
ALPRSW	sprawl
ALPRTY	paltry
	partly
	raptly
ALPRUW	pulwar
ALPSSU	lapsus
ALPSTU	St Paul
ALPSTY	yplast
ALRSTU	lustra
ALRSTY	stylar
ALRSUU	Laurus
	Ursula
ALRSUW	walrus
ALRTTY	rattly
	tartly
ALRTUW	tulwar
ALRUUV	uvular
ALRUVV	vulvar
ALSSTU	saltus
	tussal
ALSSVY	sylvas
ALSTVY	vastly
ALSUUV	uvulas
ALTTUY	tautly
ALTUUV	Tuvalu
ALTUVY	vaulty
AMMMNO	mammon✧
AMMMOU	amomum
AMMORT	marmot
AMMOSU	omasum
AMMOXY	myxoma
AMMPSY	spammy
AMMPUW	wampum
AMMRRU	marrum
	murram
AMMRSU	summar
AMMRSY	smarmy
AMMSTU	summat
AMMSUW	wammus
AMMTUZ	Tammuz
AMNNOR	norman✧
AMNNOY	anonym
AMNOOP	Pomona
AMNOOR	maroon
	Romano
AMNOPT	potman
	tampon
	topman
AMNORR	marron
AMNORS	ramson
	ransom
AMNORT	matron
AMNORU	Rouman
AMNORY	mornay
	Romany
AMNOSS	Samson
AMNOST	mantos
AMNOSY	so many
AMNOTU	amount
	moutan
	outman
AMNOTY	toyman
AMNPTY	tympan
AMNRSY	Smyrna
AMNRTU	antrum
	Truman
AMNRTY	Martyn
AMNSSU	Samsun
AMNTTU	mutant
	tutman
AMNTUU	autumn
AMOOPT	pomato
AMOORV	moorva
AMOOTT	tomato
AMOOYY	Yo-Yo Ma
AMOPST	Patmos
AMOPTU	map out
	Maputo
AMORRT	mortar
AMORRU	armour
AMORRW	marrow
AMORRY	armory
AMORSS	morass
AMORST	stroam
	stroma
AMORSU	amours
	ramous
AMORTZ	Mozart
AMOSST	Mt Ossa
AMOSTT	at most
AMOSTZ	matzos
AMOSUW	awmous
AMOTTZ	matzot
AMOTUZ	mazout
AMPPRU	ramp up
AMPRST	stramp
AMPRUW	warm up
	warm-up
AMPSUW	mawpus
	wampus
AMPSWY	swampy
AMRRTY	martyr
AMRRUY	murray✧
AMRSTU	struma
AMRSTY	smarty
ANNOOX	xoanon
ANNOPR	napron
ANNOPT	panton
ANNOPZ	Poznan
ANNORT	natron
ANNORY	nonary
ANNOST	santon
	sonant
ANNOTT	tonant
ANNOTW	wanton
ANNOTY	Antony
	Tannoy®
	tannoy
ANNOWY	Wynona
ANNPSU	pannus
	sannup
	unsnap
ANNPTU	pantun
ANNPUY	punany
ANNRTY	tranny
ANNSTU	suntan
ANNSTY	syntan
ANNSWY	swanny
ANNTTU	nutant
ANOOPX	a pox on
ANOORT	ratoon
ANOOSW	aswoon
ANOPRS	parson
ANOPRT	parton
	patron
	tarpon
ANOPSS	pass on
ANOPST	pantos
ANOPTT	optant
ANOPTU	pan out
ANOPUY	yaupon
ANORRW	narrow
ANORSV	sovran
ANORTT	attorn
	ratton
	rottan
ANORTV	vorant
ANORTY	aroynt
	notary
	Troyan
ANORWY	Norway
ANORYZ	zonary
ANOSST	Santos
ANOSSW	sowans
ANOSTY	astony
ANOSTZ	stanzo
ANOSWY	noways
ANOSXY	saxony
ANPPSU	snap up
ANPPSY	snappy
ANPRSU	unspar
ANPRTY	pantry
ANPRUW	unwrap
ANPRUY	unpray
ANPSUW	supawn
	swan up
ANPSWY	spawny
ANPTUW	want up
ANRRTU	rat run
ANRSTU	santur
	Saturn
ANRSTW	strawn
ANRSUU	Uranus
ANRSUY	sunray
ANRTTU	truant
ANRTTY	tyrant
ANRUWY	runway
	unwary
ANSTTU	tutsan
ANSTXY	syntax
ANSYZZ	snazzy
ANTUVY	vaunty
ANVVYY	Vyvyan
AOOPST	astoop
AOOPTT	potato
AOORRT	orator
AOORRY	arroyo
AOORTT	tooart
AOORTV	ovator
AOOTTT	tattoo
AOOTTY	Toyota®
AOPPRT	apport
	pop art✧
AOPPRX	approx
AOPRRT	parrot
	raptor

AOPRRU uproar
AOPRST asport
pastor
portas
AOPRUV vapour
AOPSST potass
AOPSTU aspout
AOPTUY pay out
pay-out
AOPWWW powwaw
AOQRTU quarto
AOQSTU quotas
AORRST rostra
sartor
AORRSW arrows
AORRSY rosary
AORRTW tarrow
AORRTY rotary✧
AORRWY arrowy
yarrow
AORSST assort
AORSTT stator
Strato
tarots
AORSTU soutar
AORSTX storax
AORSUU aurous
AORSUV savour
AORSVY savory
AORTUY yaourt
AORTVY votary
AORVWY avowry
AOSSTT assott
AOSTTU at outs
AOSTTY toasty
AOTTTW tattow
AOTUWY way-out
AOTWWY two-way
APPPSU pappus
APPRTY trappy
APPRUW upwrap
wrap up
APPSSU pass up
APRRSY sparry
APRSTT T-strap
APRSTY pastry
APRSWY psywar
APRTTU tart up
APSSSU passus
APSTUY stay up
upstay
APSUWY sway up
upsway
AQRRUY quarry
AQRTUZ quartz
ARRSTY starry
ARSSST strass
ARSSTU tarsus✧
ARSSTY Satyrs
strays
ARSTTU astrut
Stuart
ARSTUU Taurus
ARSTUW waurst
ARSTUX surtax
ARSTWY strawy
swarty
wastry
ARSTXY styrax
ASSTTU status
ASTTWY swatty

B

BBBDEO bobbed
BBBEIO Bobbie
BBBEIR bibber
BBBELO bobble
BBBELU bubble
BBBEOR bobber
BBBHUU hubbub
BBBINO bobbin
BBBLOY blobby
bobbly
BBBLUY bubbly
BBCDEU cubbed
BBCELO cobble
BBCEOR cobber
BBCEOW cobweb✧
BBCHUY chubby
BBCLUY clubby
BBCOTY Ty Cobb
BBDDEI dibbed
BBDDEO dobbed
BBDDEU dubbed
BBDEEI Debbie
BBDEEN nebbed
BBDEEW webbed
BBDEFI fibbed
BBDEGI gibbed
BBDEGO gobbed
BBDEGU bedbug
gubbed
BBDEIJ jibbed
BBDEIL dibble
BBDEIN nibbed
BBDEIO dobbie
BBDEIR dibber
ribbed
BBDEJO jobbed
BBDELO lobbed
BBDELU bulbed
BBDEMO bombed
mobbed
BBDEOR dobber
robbed
BBDEOS sobbed
BBDEOX box-bed
BBDERU rubbed
BBDESU subbed
BBDGIU big-bud
BBDINO dobbin✧
BBDINU dubbin
BBDKUY dybbuk
BBDORY dry bob
BBEEIK kebbie
BBEEKL lebbek
BBEELP pebble
BBEEMU bum-bee
BBEEMX bembex✧
BBEENN neb-neb
BBEENS snebbe
BBEERR Berber
BBEEYY bye-bye
BBEFIR fibber
BBEGIN Big Ben
BBEGIR gibber
BBEGIT gibbet
BBEGLO gobble
BBEGNU bebung
BBEGOT gobbet
BBEHLO hobble
BBEHLU Hubble
BBEHOS Hobbes
BBEIIM imbibe
BBEIIR ribibe
BBEIIT Tibbie
BBEIJR jibber
BBEIKL kibble
BBEILN nibble
BBEILR libber
BBEILW wibble
BBEIMO mobbie
BBEIMX bembix✧
BBEIOR Robbie
BBEIRR briber
BBEISU subbie
BBEITT Tebbit
BBEJOR jobber
BBEKNU nebbuk
BBEKOS kebobs
BBEKSU bubkes
BBELLU bulbel
BBELMO mobble
BBELMU bumble✧
BBELNO nobble
BBELNU nubble
BBELNY nybble
BBELOW wobble
BBELPY pebbly
plebby
BBELRU burble
lubber
rubble
BBEMNU benumb
BBEMOR bomber
BBENSU snubbe
BBEORR robber
BBEOSU buboes
BBEOTW wet bob
BBERRU rubber
BBERTU rubbet
tubber
BBFILU bibful
BBFLOY bob-fly
BBGGIU big bug
BBGIKN B B King
BBGINO gibbon
BBGIOW bobwig
BBGLOY globby
BBGRUY grubby
BBHIOT hobbit
BBHJOO hobjob
BBHNOO hobnob
BBIIIO Ibibio
BBIKOS skibob
BBILLU bulbil
BBILOS bilbos
BBIMOS bimbos
BBINNU nubbin
BBINOR ribbon
BBIRTU rubbit
BBKNOY knobby
BBKNUY knubby
BBKOOS bosbok
BBLLUU bulbul
BBLNUY nubbly
BBLOSY Byblos
slobby
BBLOWY Bowlby
by-blow
wobbly
BBLRUY rubbly
BBLSUY slubby
BBMOOS bombos
BBMOSU bumbos
BBMOXY Bombyx
BBMRUY brumby
BBNNOO bonbon
BBNOOO bonobo
BBNOSY snobby
BBNOTU nobbut
BBNSUY snubby
BBOOOO booboo
BBOOOY boo-boy
BBOOSY yobbos
BBOOUU boubou
BBOOWY bow-boy
BBORTU burbot
BBOSUY busboy
BBRSUU suburb
BBSSTU Stubbs
BBSTUY stubby
BCCDEU C-cubed
BCCIOR cobric
BCDEEK bedeck
BCDEIO bodice
BCDEIU cue bid
BCDEKU beduck
BCDEMO combed
BCDIOU cuboid
BCDIRY cybrid
BCDNOU bonduc
BCEEHO obeche
BCEEHR breech

BCEEKN	nebeck
BCEEKR	Becker
	rebeck
BCEEKT	becket✧
BCEEKZ	zebeck
BCEELO	ecbole
BCEELY	Cybele
BCEEMO	become
BCEEQU	quebec✧
BCEGIL	Belgic
BCEHLN	blench
BCEHOR	broché
BCEHOS	bosche✧
BCEHOU	bouche
	bouché
BCEHRT	Brecht
BCEHRU	cherub
BCEIIK	bickie
BCEIIS	ibices
BCEIKR	bicker
BCEIKU	buckie
BCEILM	emblic
	limbec
BCEILR	criblé
BCEILS	lesbic
BCEIOR	corbie
BCEIOX	icebox
BCEIPS	biceps
BCEIRS	scribe
BCEIRT	terbic
BCEIST	bisect
BCEJOT	object
BCEKLU	buckle
	Lübeck
BCEKMO	bemock
BCEKNO	beckon
BCEKRU	Brücke
	bucker
BCEKTU	bucket
BCELLO	Belloc
BCELMO	comble
BCELNO	en bloc
BCELOR	corbel
BCELOU	bouclé
BCELRU	becurl
BCEMOO	coombe
BCEMOR	comber
BCEMOY	come by
BCEMRU	cumber
BCENOU	bounce
BCEORS	scrobe
BCEOTT	obtect
BCGORU	coburg
BCGORY	cyborg
BCHIIR	bichir
BCHILO	chibol
BCHIOP	phobic
BCHITY	bitchy
BCHLOT	blotch
BCHMOU	Bochum
BCHNRU	brunch
BCHNUY	bunchy
BCHOOR	brooch
BCHORS	borsch
BCHOTY	botchy
BCHRSU	Bursch
BCIILM	limbic
BCIINO	bionic
	niobic
BCIINU	incubi
BCIIOP	biopic
BCIIOT	biotic
BCIKNO	kincob
BCIKRY	bricky
BCILMO	Imbolc
BCILOO	colobi
BCILPU	public
BCILRU	lubric
BCIMOR	bromic
	Crimbo
BCIMOT	tombic
BCIMSU	cubism✧
BCINOR	bicorn
BCIRRU	rubric
BCISTU	cubist
BCKLOS	blocks
BCKLOY	blocky
BCKNUU	Nubuck
BCKPUU	buck up
BCMOOS	combos
BCMOOT	tomboc
BCMORY	corymb
BCMRSU	crumbs
BCMRUY	crumby
BCNOOR	bronco
BCNOSU	buncos
BCNOTU	cobnut
BCNOUY	bouncy
BCOOWY	cowboy
BCORSY	Crosby
BCRSSU	scrubs✧
BDDDEE	bedded
BDDDEU	budded
BDDEEI	bedide
BDDEEN	bended
BDDEER	bedder
BDDEET	debted
BDDEEY	bedyde
	bedyed
BDDEII	Biddie
BDDEIN	bidden
BDDEIO	bodied
BDDEIR	bedrid
	bidder
BDDELO	boddle
BDDELU	buddle
BDDENO	bonded
BDDERU	redbud
BDDIOR	do bird
BDDISU	disbud
BDDJOO	odd-job
BDEEEI	beedie
BDEEEN	bendee
	need-be
BDEEET	debtee
BDEEFL	befeld
BDEEFW	web-fed
BDEEGG	begged
BDEEGO	dog-bee
BDEEGR	Edberg
BDEEHL	beheld
BDEEHR	herbed
BDEEIL	belied
	debile
	edible
BDEEIS	beside
BDEEIT	betide
BDEEJL	djebel
BDEEJM	djembe
BDEEKY	bed-key
BDEELL	bedell
	belled
BDEELN	blende
BDEELT	belted
BDEENR	bender
BDEEPS	besped
BDEEST	bested
	St Bede
BDEETT	betted
BDEFIR	fibred
BDEGGU	bugged
BDEGIL	begild
BDEGIN	big end
BDEGIO	bodgie
BDEGIP	pig-bed
BDEGIR	begird
	bridge
BDEGIU	budgie
BDEGLO	globed
BDEGLU	bludge
BDEGNU	bedung
BDEGOR	bodger
BDEGRU	budger
BDEGTU	budget✧
BDEHIN	behind
BDEHIR	Hebrid
BDEHLO	behold
BDEHOS	debosh
BDEHOT	hotbed
BDEHSU	bushed
BDEIIM	ibidem
BDEIIR	birdie
	bridie✧
BDEILL	billed
BDEILM	dimble
	limbed
BDEILO	bolide
BDEILR	bridle
BDEILU	bludie
BDEILY	bieldy
BDEIMN	nimbed
BDEINN	bin-end
	binned
BDEINR	binder
	inbred
	rebind
BDEINT	bident
BDEINU	beduin✧
BDEIOO	boodie
BDEIOR	boride
BDEIOS	bodies
BDEIRR	birder
BDEIRS	debris
	débris
BDEIRU	burdie
	buried
	rubied
BDEIRV	verbid
BDEIST	bedsit
BDEISU	busied
BDEITT	bitted
BDEKNU	debunk
BDEKSU	busked
BDELLO	bolled
BDELMO	mobled
BDELNO	Blonde®
	blonde
	bolden
BDELNU	bundle
BDELOO	boodle
BDELOR	bordel
BDELOU	double
BDELOW	blowed
	bowled
BDELRU	de-blur
BDEMMU	bummed
BDEMNU	numbed
BDEMOW	wombed
BDEMOY	embody
BDENNU	unbend
BDENOR	bonder
BDENOT	obtend
BDENOY	beyond✧
BDENRU	burden
	burned
	unbred
BDENSU	sunbed
BDENTU	bunted
	but-end
BDEOOR	boorde
BDEOOT	booted
BDEOOZ	boozed
BDEOPR	bedrop
BDEORR	border
BDEORS	desorb
BDEORT	betrod
	debtor
BDEORU	obdure
BDEORX	red box
BDEOSS	bossed
	deboss
BDEOTU	bed out
BDEOWW	dew-bow
BDERSU	surbed

BDESTU	bedust
	bestud
	busted
BDESUU	subdue
BDESUW	subdew
BDFILO	bifold
BDFIOR	forbid
BDGIIN	biding
BDGIIO	gobiid
BDGIIR	Brigid
BDGINO	boding
	Gobind
BDGORU	dor-bug
BDHIIN	bhindi
	bindhi
BDHIRY	hybrid
BDHLOY	hold by
BDIILO	libido
BDIIMR	midrib
BDIINR	in bird
BDIITT	tidbit
BDIKNO	bodkin
BDILNU	Dublin
BDILOY	bodily
BDILUY	bluidy
BDIMOR	morbid
BDIMOY	imbody
BDINNO	in-bond
BDINNU	unbind
BDINPU	upbind
BDIORX	ox-bird
BDIOTU	outbid
BDIRTU	turbid
BDKLOO	kobold
BDLLOY	boldly
BDLMUY	dumbly
BDLOOS	'sblood
BDLOOY	bloody
	old boy
BDLOUY	doubly
BDMRUU	rum bud
BDNOOY	nobody
BDNORU	round B
BDNOSU	bounds
BDNOTU	obtund
BDNOUY	ybound
BDOORY	broody
BDOPRY	drop by
BDORWY	byword
BEEEFL	feeble
BEEEHP	ephebe
BEEEKL	kebele
BEEELT	beetle✧
BEEEMS	beseem
BEEEMT	bemete
	beteem
BEEENS	beseen
BEEEPR	beeper
BEEEPW	beweep
BEEERS	breese
BEEERZ	beezer
	breeze
BEEESV	beeves
BEEFIL	belief
BEEFLL	befell
BEEFLY	feebly
BEEFOR	before
BEEFPU	beef up
BEEFRT	bereft
BEEGHR	Gheber
	Ghebre
BEEGIL	beigel
BEEGIY	bigeye
BEEGLY	leg bye
BEEGNO	begone
	engobe
BEEGNR	bergen✧
BEEGNU	bungee
BEEGRT	Egbert
BEEGRU	burgee
	Gueber
	Guebre
BEEHIP	ephebi
BEEHIR	Herbie
BEEHIS	Hibees
BEEHLT	bethel
BEEHNS	Benesh
BEEHOP	phoebe✧
BEEHOT	behote
BEEHOV	behove
BEEHRT	berthe
BEEHRW	Hebrew
BEEHRY	hereby
BEEHST	behest
	Thebes
BEEHTT	Tebeth
BEEIJN	Benjie
BEEIKL	belike
BEEILR	belier
BEEILV	belive
BEEILZ	Belize
BEEIMR	bemire
	bireme
BEEIMT	betime
BEEINR	Bernie
BEEINW	newbie
BEEIRT	Bertie
	rebite
BEEISS	Bessie
BEEIST	bêtise
BEEISX	ibexes
BEEJNU	bunjee
BEEKOR	reebok
BEEKRS	breeks
BEEKRU	rebuke
BEELMM	emblem
BEELMR	remble
BEELMS	semble
BEELNO	Belone
BEELNU	nebule
	nebulé
BEELOV	belove
BEELPT	bepelt
BEELRT	belter
	Elbert
	treble
BEELRY	berley
BEELXY	Bexley
BEELZZ	bezzle
BEEMMR	member
BEEMNR	Bremen
BEEMRS	embers
BEEMRU	embrue
BEEMSU	bemuse
BEENNR	brenne
BEENNT	bennet
BEENOR	boreen
	enrobe
BEENRU	Reuben
BEENTU	butene
BEEOOT	bootee
BEEOPP	bo-peep
BEEORR	rebore
BEEORT	bo tree
BEEORY	obeyer
BEEOTX	tee box
BEEPRU	beer-up
	burpee
BEEPTW	bewept
BEERRT	berret
BEERRU	beurre
	beurré
BEERRV	reverb
BEERRW	brewer
BEERSU	Erebus
BEERTT	better
BEERTV	brevet
BEERYZ	breezy
BEESTU	bustee
BEFFGO	beg off
BEFFOU	bouffe
BEFFPU	bepuff
BEFFRU	buffer
	rebuff
BEFFTU	buffet
BEFGIT	begift
BEFHOO	behoof
BEFILM	fimble
BEFILO	foible
BEFIRS	briefs
BEFLMU	beflum
	fumble
BEFLOO	befool
BEFLOU	befoul
BEFLRY	belfry
BEFORS	Forbes
BEFORY	forbye
	foreby
BEFRUY	rubefy
BEFSUU	subfeu
BEGGII	biggie
BEGGIR	bigger
BEGGLO	boggle
BEGGOX	egg box
	egg-box
BEGGRU	Brugge
BEGHIS	besigh
BEGIIL	Liebig
BEGILN	bingle
BEGILO	oblige
BEGILR	gerbil
BEGILS	bilges
BEGILT	giblet
BEGINN	benign
BEGINO	biogen
	Boeing
BEGINR	binger
BEGINS	besing
BEGINU	beguin
	béguin
	bungie
BEGIOO	boogie
BEGIOS	bogies
	gobies
BEGIOT	big toe
BEGIOU	bougie
BEGIRU	brigue
BEGKNU	begunk
BEGLNO	belong
BEGLNU	blunge
	bungle
BEGLOT	goblet
BEGLOW	bow leg
BEGLRU	bugler
	bulger
	burgle
BEGLTU	buglet
BEGNOR	bon gré
BEGNOY	bygone
BEGNPU	Bengpu
BEGNSU	besung
BEGNUY	bungey
BEGOOR	bog ore
	goober
BEGOOS	goboes
BEGOPX	pegbox
BEGORS	Borges
	grebos
BEGORU	brogue
BEGOSY	bogeys
BEGOTU	bouget
BEGOTW	bowget
BEGRRU	burger
BEGRSU	Bruges
BEHIKR	kirbeh
BEHILS	Ishbel
BEHILT	blithe
	thible
BEHINS	nebish
BEHINT	hen-bit
BEHIOT	bothie
BEHIST	Thisbe
BEHITT	thibet✧
BEHKOR	rhebok

Words marked ✧ can also be spelled with one or more capital letters

BEHLMU	humble
BEHLOW	behowl
BEHLRU	burhel
BEHLSU	bushel
BEHMOR	hombre
BEHMOT	the mob✧
BEHMRU	Humber
BEHNOR	brehon
	Hebron
BEHNRU	Ben-Hur
BEHNTY	by then
BEHOOS	hoboes
BEHORT	bother
BEHOTX	the box
BEHRTU	Hubert
BEIIKR	birkie
BEIILL	billie✧
BEIINT	bite in
BEIIRS	iberis
BEIISS	ibises
BEIITT	bittie
BEIJLR	jerbil
	jirble
BEIJMU	jumbie
BEIJNU	bunjie
BEIKLN	libken
BEIKLR	bilker
BEIKNR	birken
BEIKOO	bookie
BEIKSS	bekiss
BEILLT	billet
BEILMN	nimble
BEILMO	bemoil
	emboil
	mobile✧
BEILMR	limber
BEILMW	wimble
BEILMY	blimey
BEILNO	ben-oil
BEILNR	berlin✧
BEILNU	nubile
BEILNY	byline
BEILNZ	benzil
BEILOR	boiler
	libero
	reboil
BEILOS	Isobel
BEILOT	betoil
	boleti
BEILOW	blowie
BEILRR	birler
BEILRS	birsle
BEILRT	riblet
BEILST	Lisbet
BEILVY	bylive
	live by
BEIMOS	obeism
BEIMOV	B-movie
BEIMOZ	zombie✧
BEIMRT	betrim
	timber
	timbre
BEIMRU	erbium
	imbrue
BEIMRX	imbrex
BEIMTY	by-time
BEINNO	bonnie✧
BEINNT	inbent
BEINNU	Bunnie
BEINOS	besoin
BEINOT	Benoît
BEINOV	bovine
BEINOX	bonxie
BEINOZ	bizone
BEINRS	nebris
BEINRU	Brunei
	rubine
BEINRY	byrnie
BEINTT	bitten
BEIOOT	bootie
BEIORS	ribose
BEIORT	obiter
BEIORU	ourebi
BEIOST	so be it
	sobeit
BEIOSW	bowsie
BEIOTW	bow tie
BEIPST	bespit
BEIPTY	bepity
BEIQSU	bisque
BEIQUU	ubique
BEIRRY	briery
BEIRST	bestir
	bister
	bistre
	bitser
BEIRSU	bruise
	rubies
BEIRSW	brewis
BEIRTT	bitter
	Tibert
BEIRTU	Beirut
BEITUY	ubiety
BEJJUU	jujube
BEJLMU	jumble
BEJORU	objure
BEJOST	objets
BEJOVY	by Jove
BEKLOY	blokey
BEKLRU	bulker
BEKNOR	broken
BEKNRU	bunker
BEKOOR	booker
	Brooke
BEKOOT	betook
BEKORR	broker
BEKORS	bosker
BEKOST	bosket
BEKRSU	busker
BEKSTU	busket
BELLNO	bollen
BELLOU	boulle
	lobule
BELLRU	buller
BELLTU	bullet
BELLUY	bluely
BELMMU	bummel
	bummle
	mumble
BELMOW	blow me
BELMOY	emboly
BELMRU	lumber
	rumble
	umbrel
BELMSU	umbles
BELMTU	tumble
BELNNY	blenny
BELNOZ	benzol
BELNRU	Brunel
BELNTU	unbelt
BELNTY	yblent
BELNUU	Buñuel
BELNUY	nebuly
BELNYZ	benzyl
BELOOR	Boléro
	bolero
BELOOS	lobose
	sobole
BELOOT	Bootle
BELOPU	pueblo✧
BELORR	borrel
BELORT	bolter
BELORU	rouble
BELORW	blower
	bowler
BELOSS	Lesbos
BELOSU	blouse
	boules
	obelus
BELOSW	blowse
	bowels
BELOTT	bottle
BELOUZ	Boulez
BELOWZ	blowze
BELPTU	belt up
BELRRU	burler
	burrel
BELRSU	Elbrus
BELRTU	butler
BELRTY	trebly
BELRUY	burley
BELSTU	bustle
	sublet
	subtle✧
BELSUY	bluesy
BELTTU	buttle
BELTUU	tubule
BEMMRU	bummer
BEMNOT	entomb
BEMNOW	enwomb
BEMNRU	number
BEMOOR	boomer
BEMORS	somber
	sombre
BEMORY	embryo
BEMOSS	emboss
BEMOST	embost
BEMPRU	bumper
BEMRUY	umbery
BEMSTU	besmut
BEMSUY	embusy
BENNOT	bonnet
BENNOU	unbone
BENNSU	bunsen✧
BENNTU	ben-nut
	unbent
BENOOR	Borneo
	Oberon
BENOOT	botoné
BENORR	reborn
BENORT	breton✧
	Brontë
BENORU	bourne
	unrobe
BENORZ	bonzer
	bronze
BENOSS	Besson
BENOTY	betony
BENRRU	burner
BENRSU	Rubens
BENRTU	brunet
	bunter✧
	burnet
BENRTY	ybrent
BEOORS	broose
BEOORT	reboot
BEOORZ	boozer
	rebozo
BEOOST	Boötes
BEOOYZ	boozey
BEOPPR	bopper
BEOPRR	prober
BEOPST	bespot
BEORRS	resorb
BEORRT	Robert
BEORST	besort
	Osbert
	sorbet
	strobe
BEORSU	bourse✧
BEORSW	bowser✧
	browse
BEORTT	bettor
BEORTV	obvert
BEORTY	by rote
BEORUZ	brouze
BEORVV	bovver
BEORVY	overby
BEORWY	bowery✧
	bowyer
	owerby
BEOSSS	obsess
BEOSST	betoss
BEOSSY	syboes

BEOSTT obtest
BEOSTU buteos
obtuse
BEOSTW bestow
BEOTUY outbye
you bet
BEPRSU superb
BEPRUW brew up
brew-up
BEPRUY pre-buy
BERRTU bruter
BERRUY rebury
BERSTU buster✧
surbet
BERTTU butter
BERTUY uberty
BERUZZ buzzer
BESSSU busses
BESSTU subset
BESTUY yes-but
BFFFOO fob off
BFFFOU fub off
BFFIIN biffin
BFFINO boffin
BFFJOO job off
off-job
BFFORU rub off
BFFOUY buy off
BFGOOW fog-bow
BFIILR fibril
BFIINR fibrin
BFIMOR biform
BFINOW bowfin
BFIORS fibros
BFIRUY rubify
BFLOTY botfly
BFLOUX boxful
BFLPUU flub up
BFLTUU tubful
BFMORY by-form
BFNOSY fynbos
BGGIIN biggin
BGGIIW bigwig
BGGINU big gun
buggin
BGGLUY bluggy
BGGNOO bogong
BGGNOU bugong
go bung
BGHIIN binghi✧
BGHILT blight
BGHIRT bright
BGHMUU humbug
BGHORU brough
BGHOSU go bush
BGHOTU bought
BGIIKN biking
BGIINT biting
BGIIRT Brigit
BGILLY glibly
BGILNO globin
goblin
lobing
BGILNU bluing
BGINNO boning
Ningbo
BGINOR boring
robing
BGINOS obsign
BGINOW bowing
BGINOX boxing
BGINSU busing
BGINTU tubing
BGINUY buying
BGIOPT big pot
big top
BGIORV Viborg
BGIOSS gossib
BGLNOO oblong
BGLRUU bulgur
BGMOOR gombro
BGMOSU gumbos
BGMSUU subgum
BGNOOS bongos
BGNOOY gobony
BGNORY Nyborg
BGOORS borgos
BGOORU burgoo
BGORSU Burgos
BGOSTU go bust
BGOSUW sow bug
BGOTUU bug out
bug-out
BHHIKT k'thibh
BHIIST bhisti
BHIKOS kibosh
BHIKSU bukshi
BHILPY Philby
BHILSU bluish
BHIMOR rhombi
BHIMOS himbos
BHIOPS bishop
BHIOSY boyish
BHIRSU hubris
BHIRSY hybris
BHITWY Whitby
BHKNOU bohunk
BHKOSY kybosh
BHLMUY humbly
BHLOSY bolshy
BHMTUY thumby
BHOOOO boo-hoo
BHOTTU hot tub
BHRSUY brushy
BIIIKN bikini
BIIKTZ kibitz
BIILNS blinis
BIILOX Biloxi
BIIMOS obiism
BIIMUV bivium
BIINNS sin bin
sin-bin
BIINOT biotin
BIIORV vibrio
BIIRRS sbirri
BIIRTU buriti
BIISTV vibist
BIITTT titbit
BIKKRY Kirkby
BIKLNS blinks
BIKMNU bumkin
BIKMOS imbosk
BIKMSU ski bum
BIKNOO book in
BIKNSU buskin
BIKRSY brisky
BIKSTU busk it
BILLNO billon
BILLNU Lublin
BILLOU lobuli
BILLOX bollix
BILLOY billy-o
BILMNY nimbly
BILMOS limbos✧
BILMRU umbril
BILMSU limbus✧
BILMUY bulimy
BILNOS Lisbon
BILNOW blow in
blow-in
BILNTZ blintz
BILOOP Biopol®
BILOOT Lobito
BILOPU upboil
BILORV Bovril®
BILOTW blow it
BILRTY trilby✧
BILSTU subtil
BILSUY busily
BIMMOO miombo
BIMNOS bonism
BIMNOT intomb
BIMNSU nimbus
BIMOSS imboss
BIMOST timbós
BIMOSU Möbius
BIMSTU submit
BINNOR inborn
BINNOU bunion
BINNRU burn in
burn-in
BINNTU bun tin
BINOOT bonito
BINORT Briton
BINORY briony✧
BINOSS bisson
BINOST bonist
BINPUY bunyip
BINRRU Irn-Bru®
BINTTU butt in
unbitt
BIOORZ borzoi
BIOOST oboist
BIOOSV ovibos
BIOPRT probit
BIORRS sbirro
BIORST bistro
BIORTT bittor
BIORTY orbity
BIOSTT to bits
BIOSTU subito
BIOTTW two-bit
BIOTUW woubit
BIRTTU bittur
turbit
BJLMUY jumbly
BJLOOT job lot
BJMOSU jumbos
BJNOTU nutjob
BJOOTU job out
BKLPUU bulk up
BKMNUU bunkum
BKNOSU bunkos
BKNPUU bunk-up
BKOOSY booksy
BKORTU Tobruk
BKORUY Kru-boy
BKORWY by-work
BLLOOO lobolo
BLLORY brolly
BLMNUY numbly
BLMOOY bloomy
BLMOSY symbol
BLMRUY rumbly
BLNOOT Bolton
bolt-on
BLNOTU unbolt
BLOOSU obolus
BLOOTT blotto
BLOOWY lowboy
BLOPTY by-plot
BLOPUW blow up
blow-up✧
upblow
BLOSWY blowsy
BLOWYZ blowzy
BLRRUY blurry
BLSTUY subtly
BMNOOT bon mot
BMNOTU untomb
BMOORY broomy
byroom
BMOOSS bosoms
BMOOSY bosomy
BMOOTT bottom
BMOOTY tomboy
Yom Tob
BMORST stromb
BMORSU morbus
rumbos
BMOTUU Mobutu
BMPPUU bump up
BNNOOT bon ton
BNNORU unborn

Words marked ✧ can also be spelled with one or more capital letters

BNOOST boston✧
BNOOSW W boson
BNOOSY Boyson
BNOOSZ Z boson
BNOOTU bouton
unboot
BNORSU suborn
BNORTU burton✧
to burn
BNORWY browny
BNORYY bryony✧
BNORYZ bronzy
BNOSUW sunbow
BNOTTU button
BNOTUX Buxton
BNOTUY bounty✧
BNPRUU burn up
burn-up
BNRTUY Tyburn
BNRUUY unbury
BNSUUY unbusy
BNTUUU ubuntu
BOOOTT to boot
BOOPTU boot up
BOOPTW bowpot
BOOPTY potboy
BOORRW borrow
BOORRY Rob Roy
BOOTUW bow out
woobut
BOOTUX outbox
out-box
BOOTYY toy boy
BOOWWW bowwow
BOPRSU Probus
BOPSTY stop by
BOPUUY buoy up
BORRSU burros
BORRUW burrow
BORSSU sorbus
BORSTU robust
turbos
BORSTW browst
BORSWY browsy
BORTTU turbot
BORTUU rub out
rubout
BOSSWY sybows
BOTUUY buy out
buyout
BPSTUU bust up
bust-up
BQRTUU Tubruq
BRSTUU Brutus
BSSSUY byssus
BSTTUU bututs

C

CCCDIO coccid
CCCHOY choccy
CCCILY cyclic
CCCOOS coccos
CCCOSU coccus
CCCOXY coccyx
CCDEEI deccie✧
CCDEER recced
CCDEIR Cedric
CCDEKO cocked
CCDEOT decoct
CCEEHL cleché
CCEEHR crèche✧
CCEEOR coerce
CCEERS recces
CCEHIL chicle
cliché
CCEHIM chemic
CCEHIO choice
echoic
CCEHIT hectic
CCEHKY checky
CCEHLN clench
CCEHLO cloche
CCEHLU cleuch
CCEHNO conche
CCEHOR croche
CCEHOS cosech
CCEHOU couché
CCEIIL cilice
icicle
CCEILR circle
cleric
CCEILS cecils
CCEILT Celtic
CCEILY Cecily
cicely✧
CCEIMO comice
CCEINS scenic
CCEIOR cicero
CCEIPT pectic
CCEIRT cretic✧
CCEITY cecity
CCEKLO cockle
CCEKOP copeck
CCEKOR cocker✧
CCEKOT cocket
CCELRY cycler
CCENOS sconce
CCEORS escroc
reccos
soccer
CCEOSS seccos
CCEPSY speccy
CCERSU cercus
cruces
CCESSU succès
CCFILO flocci
CCHHII chichi
chi-chi
CCHHIN chinch
CCHHOO chocho
CCHHRU church
CCHIKT tchick
CCHILN clinch
CCHILO cholic
CCHILY chicly
CCHINO chicon
Cochin
CCHIOR choric
CCHIPU hiccup
CCHKOO chocko
CCHKSU chucks
CCHLNU clunch
CCHLTU clutch
cultch
CCHNOS conchs
CCHNOY conchy
CCHNRU crunch
CCHORS scorch
CCHORT crotch
CCHORU crouch
CCHOST scotch✧
CCHRTU crutch
CCHSTU scutch
CCIILN clinic
CCIILT clitic
CCIINO iconic
CCIINP picnic
CCIIPR picric
CCIIRT citric
critic
CCIIST cistic
CCIISV civics
CCIKRY cricky
CCILNO clonic
CCILNY cyclin
CCILTU cultic
CCIMOS cosmic
CCIMRY Cymric
CCINOS conics
CCINPY pycnic
CCINSU Cnicus
CCIOPT Coptic
CCIORS sciroc
CCIOSS ciscos
CCIOST Scotic
CCIPRU cupric
CCIRSU circus
CCISTY cystic
CCKLOO o'clock
CCKLUY clucky
CCKMOO mocock
CCKMOU mocuck
CCKNOU uncock
CCKOOU cuckoo
CCKOPU cock up
cock-up
CCKOSY cocksy
CCLMUU mucluc
CCLOSY cyclos
CCLOTU occult
CCLSUY cyclus
CCNOOO cocoon
CCNORU concur
CCOOOR rococo✧
CCOOSZ zoccos
CCOOUU cou-cou
CCOPUY occupy
CCORSU crocus
succor
CCOSTU stucco
CCSSUU cuscus
succus
CDDDEO codded
CDDEEI decide
CDDEEK decked
CDDEEO decode
CDDEEU deduce
deuced
CDDEHI chided
CDDEIU cuddie
CDDELO coddle
CDDELU cuddle
CDDENU cudden
CDDEOR codder
corded
CDDETU deduct
CDDHUY chuddy
CDDINU cuddin
CDDLOY cloddy
CDDLUY cuddly
CDDRUY cruddy
CDEEER decree
recede
ré-cede
CDEEES secede
CDEEEX exceed
CDEEFN fenced
CDEEFT defect
CDEEHO echoed
CDEEHR cheder
CDEEIL ceiled
decile
delice
CDEEIM décime
CDEEIN Edenic
incede
CDEEIR de-icer
CDEEIT deceit
CDEEIV device
CDEEIX excide
CDEEJT deject
CDEEKL deckle
CDEEKN necked
CDEEKO decoke
CDEEKR decker
recked
CDEELL celled
CDEELU Culdee
deluce
CDEENO encode
CDEENR cendré
decern
CDEENT decent
CDEEOR recode

CDEEOT Docete
CDEERS screed
CDEERU reduce
CDEERW decrew
CDEESU seduce
CDEETT dectet
detect
CDEFFO coffed
CDEFII deific
CDEFNU fecund
CDEFOR forced
CDEGGO cogged
CDEGIO geodic
CDEGLU cudgel
CDEGOR codger
CDEHIL chield
childe
CDEHIN inched
niched
CDEHIR chider
dreich
Edrich
herdic
CDEHKO choked
Ed Koch
CDEHLY chylde
CDEHNR drench
CDEHOU douche
CDEHRU ruched
CDEIIK dickie✧
CDEIJU juiced
CDEIKM medick
CDEIKN Dicken
CDEIKP picked
CDEIKR dicker
CDEIKT ticked
CDEIKW wicked
CDEIKY dickey
CDEILO coldie
docile
CDEILT delict
CDEILU Dulcie
Euclid
CDEIMN minced
CDEIMO medico
CDEIMR dermic
CDEINO condie
no dice
CDEINR cinder
CDEINU induce
CDEINW Wendic
CDEINZ zinced
CDEIOP copied
epodic
CDEIOV voiced
CDEIOX exodic
CDEIPR priced
CDEIPS spiced
CDEIPT depict
CDEIRS scried
CDEIRT credit
direct
CDEIRV cervid
CDEIRY cidery
dry ice
CDEIST cisted
CDEKNO docken
CDEKNU undeck
CDEKOP pocked
CDEKOR corked
docker
CDEKOS deckos
CDEKOT docket
CDEKRU ducker
CDEKRY Deryck
drecky
CDEKSU sucked
CDELOO locoed
CDELOS closed
CDELOU Cluedo®
CDELOW cowled
CDELOY cloyed
CDELRU curdle
curled
CDELTU dulcet
CDEMOO comedo
CDEMOY comedy
CDENNO conned
CDENOR conder
corned
CDENOS second
CDENOT docent
CDENSU secund
CDEOOP opcode
CDEOPP copped
CDEOPU couped
CDEORR record
CDEORS credos✧
Socred
CDEORW crowed
CDEOST costed
CDEOSU escudo
CDEOTT cotted
CDEOTU doucet
CDEOTY cytode
CDEOYZ zydeco
CDEPPU cupped
CDEPSU cusped
CDERSU cursed
CDERSY descry
scryde
CDERUV curved
CDERUY decury
CDESSU cussed
CDFINO fi donc!
CDFIOU fucoid
CDFIOY codify
CDGIIN dicing
CDGINO coding
CDGLOO go cold
CDHIOR droich
orchid
rhodic
CDHIRY hydric
CDIIIM imidic
CDIIIR iridic
CDIINT indict
CDIIOY idiocy
CDIISV viscid
CDIKNO Dickon
in dock
CDIKTY dickty
CDILNO codlin
CDILOV Old Vic
CDIMNU mundic
CDIMOR dromic
CDIMOU mucoid
CDIMOY cymoid
CDIMSU muscid
CDIMTU dictum
CDINOO conoid
CDINOR Nordic
CDINSY syndic
CDINTU induct
CDIOPS psocid
CDIORS roscid
CDIORV corvid
CDIOSS discos
CDIOST codist
CDIOTT cottid
CDIOTY cytoid
CDIPRY cyprid
CDIPSU cuspid
CDISSU discus✧
CDISTY cystid
CDJNOU jocund
CDKNOU undock
CDLLOY clodly
coldly
CDLOUY cloudy
CDMNOO condom
mod con
CDMOOO comodo
CDMOOT dotcom
dot-com
CDNOOR condor
con-rod
cordon
CDNOOS condos
CDNORU uncord
CDNOUW dun-cow
CDOOOT doocot
CDOORT doctor
CDOORY corody
CDPRUU crud up
CEEEFL fleece
CEEEGN egence
CEEEGR greece✧
CEEEHL elchee
CEEEHS cheese
CEEELV cleeve
CEEENO Eocene
CEEERS creese
CEEFFO coffee
CEEFFT effect
CEEFHL flèche
fleech
CEEFIL Felice
CEEFIR fierce
Recife
CEEFLY fleecy
CEEFNN fennec
CEEFNR fencer
CEEFRT refect
CEEFSU fescue
CEEGIR cierge
griece
CEEGNO congee
CEEGNY egency
CEEHHW wheech
CEEHIL lichee
CEEHIN Chinee
CEEHIR Cherie
rechie
CEEHIS seiche
CEEHIT techie
CEEHIW chewie
CEEHKL heckle
CEEHKY cheeky
CEEHLN elench
CEEHLR lecher
CEEHLS sleech
CEEHLW lechwe
CEEHLY lychee
CEEHMS scheme
smeech
CEEHNT chenet
thence
CEEHNV cheven
CEEHNW whence
CEEHOR choree
cohere
echoer
re-echo
CEEHOS echoes
CEEHOY echoey
CEEHPS speech
CEEHQU cheque
CEEHRS cheers!
creesh
Escher
CEEHRT etcher
CEEHRU euchre
CEEHRV chèvre
CEEHRW chewer
CEEHRY cheery
reechy
CEEHSS secesh
CEEHSW eschew
CEEHSY cheesy
CEEHTV chevet
CEEHTW chewet
CEEIMR eremic
CEEIMT emetic

Words marked ✧ can also be spelled with one or more capital letters

CEEINN Nicene
CEEINP picene
piecen
CEEINT entice
CEEINU Eunice
CEEINV evince
Venice
CEEIPR piecer
pierce✧
recipe
CEEIPS specie
CEEIRS cerise
CEEIRT cerite
recite
tierce
tiercé
CEEIRU écurie
CEEISX excise
CEEITX excite
CEEJNO conjee
CEEJRT reject
CEEKKL keckle
CEEKLS seckel
seckle
CEEKLT teckel
CEEKPR pecker
CEEKRS Creeks
CEEKRY creeky
CEEKSY esc key
CEELMO cleome
CEELNP pencel
CEELNR crenel
CEELNT Tencel®
CEELOR creole✧
CEELOS eclose
CEELOU coulée
CEELOV veloce
CEELRS sclere
CEELRT tercel
CEELRU cerule
recule
CEELRV clever
CEELRW crewel
CEELRY celery
CEELST select
CEEMNT cement
CEEMRR mercer
CEEMRT cermet
CEENOR encore
CEENOT cenote
CEENPR percen
CEENPS spence
CEENPT pecten
CEENRS censer
scerne
screen
secern
CEENRT center
centre
recent✧
tenrec
CEENRY Cyrene
CEENSY esnecy
CEEOPU coupee
CEEORV corvée
CEEOTX Exocet®
CEEPRS preces
CEEPRT recept
CEEPRY creepy
crepey
CEEPTX except
expect
CEEPTY ectype
CEEPUY eye-cup
CEERRU recure
CEERSS cesser
recess
CEERST certes
resect
secret
CEERSU cereus
ceruse
cesure
recuse
rescue
secure
CEERTT tercet
CEESSX excess
CEESSY cyeses
CEESTX exsect
CEESUX excuse
CEFFIO office
CEFFLO coffle
CEFFLU cuffle
CEFFOR coffer
CEFHIM Fehmic
CEFHIT fetich
fitché
CEFHLN flench
CEFHLT fletch
CEFHNR french✧
CEFIKL fickle
CEFILS felsic
CEFINO Ecofin
CEFINT infect
CEFIRR ferric
CEFKLY feckly
CEFLOS fo'c'sle
CEFLPU elf cup
CEFNOR confer
CEFORR forcer
CEFORS forces
fresco
CEFRUW curfew
CEGGII ciggie
CEGGIO coggie
CEGGLO coggle
CEGGOR cogger
CEGGPU eggcup
CEGHIO chigoe
CEGHIR chigre
CEGHLU cleugh
CEGINO coigne
CEGINR cringe
CEGINU cueing
CEGIOT goetic
CEGIRR gricer
CEGIRS grices
CEGIST gestic
CEGKOS geckos
CEGLRY clergy
CEGNOR conger
CEGNOT cogent
CEGNSU scunge
CEGNTY cygnet
CEGORR grocer
CEHHIT hi tech
CEHHSU sheuch
CEHHTT thetch
CEHIIR Richie
CEHIKY hickey
CEHILN lichen
CEHILS chesil
chiles
chisel
CEHILT eltchi
CEHIMO mochie
CEHIMR chimer
micher
CEHIMS chimes
CEHIMU echium
CEHIMV Vehmic
CEHINP phenic
CEHINR enrich
nicher
richen
CEHINS inches
CEHINT ethnic
CEHINV chevin
CEHINX chenix
CEHIOR coheir
heroic
CEHIPR ceriph
cipher
rechip
CEHIQU quiche
CEHIRR chirre
CEHIRS riches
CEHIRT cither
thrice
CEHIST ethics
CEHISV chives
CEHITT thetic
CEHKLU huckle
CEHKNU Kuchen
CEHKOR choker
hocker
CEHKOY chokey
hockey
CEHKST sketch
CEHKTV kvetch
CEHLMO Molech
CEHLMS schelm
CEHLMU muchel
CEHLNO nochel
CEHLOR choler
orchel
CEHLOT clothe
CEHLOU louche
CEHLPS schlep
CEHLPU pleuch
CEHLQU quelch
CEHMMY chemmy
CEHMNS mensch
CEHMOR chrome
CEHMOS schmoe
CEHMTU humect
CEHNOO ochone
CEHNOS chosen
CEHNOT no-tech
techno
CEHNOU cohune
CEHNQU quench
CEHNRT trench
CEHNRW wrench
CEHNST stench
CEHNUU eunuch
CEHOOS choose
cohoes
CEHOPS Cheops
CEHOPT potche
CEHORS cosher
CEHORT hector✧
rochet
rotche
tocher
troche
CEHORY ochery
ochrey
CEHOSU chouse
CEHOTU touché
CEHPRU cherup
CEHPRY chypre
cypher
CEHPST spetch
CEHPSY psyche✧
CEHPUW chew up
CEHQTU quetch
CEHQUY chequy
CEHRRY cherry
CEHRTW wretch
CEHRTY cherty
CEHSTU tusche
CEHSTY chesty
scythe
CEHTTY tetchy
CEHTVY vetchy
CEIIKR ickier
CEIIKS sickie
CEIILM Milice
CEIILS ilices
CEIILT elicit
CEIILX exilic
CEIIMR cimier

CEIINP	picine
CEIINR	irenic
CEIINS	incise
CEIINT	incite
CEIISS	Cissie
CEIJNT	inject
CEIJRU	juicer
CEIKKR	kicker
CEIKLM	melick
	mickle
CEIKLN	nickel
CEIKLP	pickle
CEIKLR	licker
	rickle
CEIKLS	sickle
CEIKLT	tickle
CEIKLU	luckie
CEIKMY	mickey✧
CEIKNR	nicker
CEIKNS	sicken
CEIKNT	ticken
CEIKNW	wicken
CEIKOO	cookie
CEIKOS	Kosice
CEIKPR	picker
	ripeck
CEIKPT	picket
CEIKRR	ricker
CEIKRS	scrike
	sicker
CEIKRT	ricket
	ticker
CEIKRW	wicker
CEIKRY	crikey
	rickey
	yicker
CEIKTT	ticket
CEIKTW	wicket
CEIKTY	tickey
CEILLO	collie
	ocelli
CEILNO	cineol
	Nicole
CEILNP	pencil
CEILNT	client
	lectin
	lentic
CEILNU	clue in
	leucin
	nuclei
CEILNY	nicely
CEILOO	coolie
CEILOP	police✧
CEILOR	recoil
CEILOT	citole
CEILPS	splice
CEILPV	pelvic
CEILPY	clypei
CEILQU	clique
CEILRS	relics
	slicer
CEILRT	relict
CEILSU	sluice
CEILSV	clevis
CEILTT	Lettic
CEILTU	Lucite®
	luetic
CEIMMN	mnemic
CEIMMO	commie
CEIMNO	come in
	income
CEIMNR	crimen
	mincer
CEIMOT	come it
CEIMOX	Mexico
CEIMPU	pumice
CEIMRT	metric
CEIMRU	cerium
	uremic
CEIMSU	cesium
	miscue
CEIMTX	Mixtec
CEIMTY	etymic
CEINNO	conine
	Connie
CEINOR	coiner
	orcein
	orcine
	recoin
CEINOS	cosine
	oscine
CEINOT	noetic
	notice
CEINOV	novice
CEINOX	exonic
CEINPR	pincer
	prince✧
CEINPT	incept
	pectin
	peinct
CEINQU	cinque
	quince✧
CEINRS	scrine
CEINRT	cretin
CEINRU	ice run
CEINRW	wincer
CEINST	incest
	insect
	scient
CEINSU	incuse
CEINTY	nicety
CEINWY	wincey
CEIOOT	cootie
CEIOOZ	Eozoic
CEIOPR	copier
CEIOPT	picoté
	poetic
CEIORR	corrie
CEIORS	cosier
CEIORT	erotic
	tercio
CEIORV	voicer
CEIORW	cowrie
CEIORZ	cozier
CEIOSS	cossie
CEIOST	cotise
	oecist
CEIOTU	ice out
CEIOTX	exotic
CEIOTZ	zoetic
CEIPPT	peptic
CEIPRR	pricer
CEIPRS	cripes
	Persic
	précis
	spicer
CEIPRY	pricey
CEIPSS	Pisces
CEIPST	septic
CEIPTU	cup-tie
CEIPTY	etypic
CEIQRU	cirque
CEIRRS	cerris
CEIRRU	currie
CEIRSS	crises
CEIRST	steric
CEIRSU	cruise
	crusie
CEIRSV	scrive
CEIRSZ	cizers
CEIRTU	cuiter
	curiet
	uretic
CEIRTW	twicer
CEIRUV	cruive
CEIRVX	cervix
CEISST	citess
CEISSU	cuisse
CEISSY	cyesis
CEISTU	cestui
	cueist
CEJKOY	jockey
CEJNOU	jounce
CEJOOS	jocose
CEJRUV	J-curve
CEKKOP	kopeck
CEKKSY	kecksy
CEKLMU	muckle
CEKLNO	enlock
CEKLNU	lucken
CEKLOR	locker
CEKLOT	locket
CEKLPU	puckle
CEKLRU	ruckle
CEKLSU	suckle
CEKMOR	mocker
CEKMRU	mucker✧
CEKNOR	conker
	reckon
CEKNOT	nocket
CEKNSU	sucken
CEKOOR	cooker
CEKOPT	pocket
CEKORR	corker
	rocker✧
CEKORT	rocket
CEKOST	socket
CEKPRU	pucker
CEKPRY	rypeck
CEKPSS	specks
CEKPSY	specky
CEKRSU	sucker
	uckers
CEKRTU	tucker
CEKRUY	yucker
CEKSTU	sucket
CEKTTU	tucket
CELLOT	collet
CELLOU	locule
CELLOY	Colley
CELLRU	culler
CELLSU	sculle
CELLTU	cullet
CELMNU	culmen
CELMOO	coelom
CELMOP	compel
CELMOR	cormel
CELMOY	comely
CELMSU	muscle
CELMUY	lyceum✧
CELNNU	nuncle
CELNOR	cornel
CELNOT	Cloten
CELNOV	cloven
CELNOY	Ceylon
CELNRU	lucern
CELNTU	lucent
CELNUU	nucule
CELNUW	unclew
CELOOR	cooler
CELOOS	locoes
CELOOT	ocelot
CELOPP	copple
CELOPU	couple
CELOQU	cloqué
CELORS	closer
	cresol
	escrol
CELORT	colter
	lector
CELORU	colure
CELORV	clover
	Velcro®
CELOST	closet
	telcos
CELOSU	coleus
	oscule
CELOSV	cloves
CELOSX	scolex
CELOTT	Toltec
CELOTY	cotyle
CELOUV	vocule
CELPRU	curpel
CELPTY	yclept

Words marked ✧ can also be spelled with one or more capital letters

CELPUU cupule
CELPUW clew up
CELRRU curler
CELRSU cruels
CELRTU culter
cutler
reluct
CELRUU curule
CELRUV culver
CELRUW curlew
CELTTU cutlet
cuttle
CELTUY cutely
CEMMOR commer
CEMMRU cummer
CEMNOO come on
come-on
oncome
CEMNRU crumen
CEMNTU centum
CEMOOS comose
CEMOOT to come
CEMOPR comper
CEMOPU come up
upcome
CEMORR cremor
CEMOSY cymose
CEMRTU rectum
CEMTTU tectum
CENNOR conner
CENNOT nocent
CENNRU cunner
CENOOP poonce
CENOOR ceroon
CENOOS coosen
CENOPR crepon
CENOPS on spec
CENOPU pounce
uncope
CENOPY poncey
CENORR corner
CENORS censor
CENORT cornet
cronet
CENORU conure
rounce
CENOST centos
CENOTU econut
CENOTV covent
CENOVX convex
CENOVY convey
covyne
CENRSY scryne
CENRTY centry
CENRUY curney
CENSSU census
CENSTY encyst
CEOOPR cooper
CEOORS cooser
CEOORV croove
CEOOTY coyote
oocyte
CEOPPR copper
CEOPRS corpse
CEOPRT copter
CEOPRU couper
croupe
cuerpo
recoup
CEOPTY ectopy
CEOQTU coquet
CEORRS scorer
CEORRT rector
CEORSS crosse
scores
scorse
CEORST corset
Cortes
Cortés
coster
escort
rectos
scoter
sector
CEORSU cerous
course
crouse
source
CEORSV corves
covers
CEORSW escrow
CEORTT cotter
CEORTU couter
croûte
CEORTV corvet
covert
vector
CEORTX cortex
CEOSST cestos
cosset
CEOSSU scouse✧
CEOTTT octett
CEOTTU cuttoe
CEPPRU cupper
CEPRSU spruce
CEPRSY cy pres
CEPRTU precut
CERRSU curser
CERRSY scryer
CERSSU cusser
CERSTU cruset
rectus
CERSUV curves
CERSUX cruxes
CERSUZ scruze
CERSWY screwy
CERTTU cutter
CERTUV curvet
CESSTU cestus
CESTUY cutesy
CFFHUY chuffy
CFFILS scliff
CFFILY cliffy
CFFINO coffin
CFFINU cuffin
CFFOOP cop off
CFFORY cry off
CFFOTU cut off
cut-off
offcut
CFFRSU scruff
CFFRUY Cruyff
CFHILN flinch
CFHILT flitch
CFHIRT fricht
CFHITY fitchy
CFHLSY flysch✧
CFIILM filmic
CFIINN Finnic
CFIINU unific
CFIIST fistic
CFIITY citify
CFIKLS flicks
CFILOR frolic
CFILTY clifty
CFIMOR formic
CFIMOT comfit
CFINOT confit
CFINOX confix
CFIORT fictor
CFIRTU fruict
CFISTU fustic
CFITYY cityfy
CFKLOS flocks
CFLPUU cupful
CFOSTU fustoc
CFRSUY scurfy
CGGLOY cloggy
coggly
CGHHOU chough
CGHIIN I Ching
CGHILT glitch
CGHIOT gothic✧
CGHLOU clough
CGHORU grouch
CGHRTU grutch
CGIINO congii
CGILNY clingy
glycin
CGILPU gilcup
CGIMNO coming✧
gnomic
CGIMNY gymnic
CGINOO cooing
CGINOP coping
CGINOV coving
CGINRY crying
CGIORS corgis
CGLLOY glycol
CGLNOU unclog
CGLOOU colugo
CGLOPU clog up
CGMOUW Cow Gum®
CGNOOU congou
CGNSUY Cygnus
scungy
CHHIOR chi-rho✧
CHHIST shtchi
CHHITY hitchy
CHHNOO honcho
CHHOOS cohosh
CHHOOT hootch
CHIIKM kimchi
CHIILL chilli
CHIILS chilis
CHIILT litchi
lithic
CHIINP chip in
CHIINS nicish
CHIINT chitin
CHIIPP hippic
CHIIRZ rhizic
CHIKNO in hock
CHIKNS chinks
CHIKNT knitch
CHIKOR chokri
CHIKOS hoicks
CHIKOT thicko
CHIKRS kirsch
CHIKST kitsch
schtik
shtick
CHIKTY thicky
CHILMO holmic
CHILNO Nichol
CHILNU unlich
CHILOR orchil
CHILRY richly
CHIMNU Munich
CHIMNY hymnic
CHIMRS chrism
smirch
CHIMSS schism
CHIMTY mythic
thymic
CHINNO Inchon
CHINNU Hunnic
CHINOP chop in
chopin✧
phonic
CHINOR Chiron
CHINOT chiton
CHINPU chin up
CHINPY hypnic
CHINRU urchin
CHINST snitch
CHINUY Yichun
CHIOPR Orphic
CHIOPT photic
CHIORS orchis✧
CHIORT rhotic
CHIORW chowri
CHIOST Sothic
CHIOSW cowish

CHIOSY coyish
CHIOSZ schizo
CHIPRY chirpy
CHIPSY physic
scyphi
CHIPTY pitchy
Pythic
CHIQTU quitch
CHIRST Christ
strich
CHIRUZ Zurich
CHISST schist
CHISTT stitch
CHISTU schuit
CHISTW Switch®
switch
CHITTW twitch
CHITTY titchy
CHITWY witchy
CHJLOT J-cloth®
CHJNOU Chonju
CHKLOO klooch
CHKLOS shlock
CHKMOO Mohock
CHKMOS shmock
CHKMSU shmuck
CHKNUY chunky
CHKOOS chokos
CHKORU chukor
CHKSSU shucks
CHKSTU shtuck
CHLMOO moloch✧
CHLMUY muchly
CHLNSU schuln
CHLOOS school
CHLOOT Clotho
coolth
CHLORS schorl
CHLOST cloths
CHLOSU slouch
CHLOTT T-cloth
CHLSSU schuls
CHMMUY chummy
CHMOOR chromo
CHMOOS smooch
CHMOSU smouch
so much
CHMSTU smutch
CHNOOP no chop
poncho
CHNOOR cohorn
CHNORS Crohn's
CHNOTY notchy
CHNPUY punchy
CHNTUU tuchun
CHOORT cohort
CHOOSS scoosh
CHOOST co-host
CHOPPU chop up
CHOPSY psycho✧
CHOPUY pouchy
CHORSU chorus
CHORWY chowry
CHOSTU schout
scouth
CHOSTW scowth
CHOTUY couthy
touchy
CHPSTU putsch
CHSSSU schuss
CHSTUY cushty
schuyt
CIIIRT iritic
CIIKKN kick in
CIIKNW inwick
CIIKST tisick
CIILMU cilium
CIILNP inclip
CIILSY Sicily
CIIMOT miotic
CIIMSV civism
CIIMTV victim
CIINNU uncini
CIINOP pionic
CIINOR ironic
oniric
CIINOT coin it
CIINQU quinic
CIINRT citrin
nitric
CIINSV viscin
CIIPRS spiric
CIIRSS crisis
CIIRTV vitric
CIISTY cytisi
CIJNOO cojoin
CIKKNS knicks
CIKKPU kick-up
CIKLNO inlock
lock in
lock-in
CIKLRY rickly
CIKLSY sickly
CIKLTY tickly
CIKMNU muck in
nickum
CIKNOP pick on
CIKNOT on tick
CIKNPU unpick
CIKNPY pyknic
CIKNSU suck in
suck-in
CIKNTU tuck in
tuck-in
CIKNYZ zincky
CIKORR corkir
CIKORY Yorick
CIKOSS sickos
CIKOSY yoicks
CIKPPU pick up
pick-up
CIKPSU sick up
CIKRTU Turkic
CIKRTY tricky
CIKSST sticks
CIKSTY sticky
CILLOU loculi
CILLSU cullis
CILMUU cumuli
CILNOP clip-on
CILNOU ulicon
uncoil
CILNST clints
CILNTU incult
CILOOT cool it
CILOPU oil-cup
upcoil
CILOPY policy
CILORT lictor
CILOSU coulis
CILOSV Clovis
CILOSY cosily
CILOTU coutil
toluic
CILQUY cliquy
CILRSY lyrics
CILSUU Lucius
CILSUY sluicy
CIMMNU cummin
CIMMOS commis
CIMMOT commit
CIMMOX commix
CIMNNO nincom
CIMNNU nincum
CIMNOO Comino
CIMNOR micron
CIMNOU muonic
CIMNRU crinum
CIMOPY myopic
CIMORS micros
CIMORU corium
CIMOST sitcom
CIMOSU Suomic
CIMOTY comity
CIMPRS scrimp
CIMPRY crimpy
CIMRUU curium
CIMSTY mystic
CIMSUV viscum✧
CINNOU nuncio
CINNOY incony
CINNSY in sync
CINOOP coinop
CINOOS coosin
CINOOZ ozonic
zoonic
CINOPP coppin
CINOPT pontic✧
CINORT citron
CINORZ zircon
CINOSS sonics
CINOST tocsin
CINOSU cousin
CINOSZ zincos
CINPSY Cynips
CIOOPT octopi
CIOORT octroi
CIOPRS psoric
CIOPRT Pictor
tropic
CIOPST optics
CIORSU curios
CIORTT tricot
CIORTV victor✧
CIOSTU coitus
CIPPRS Cripps
CIPPSU cippus
CIPRSS crisps
CIPRST script
CIPRSY crispy
cypris
CIRRSU cirrus
CIRSTT strict
CIRSTU citrus✧
rictus
rustic
CIRTTY yttric
CISSSU cissus
CISSTU cistus
CISSUV viscus
CJKOOS jockos
CJNOSU juncos
CJNSUU juncus
CKLNOO lock on
CKLNOU unlock
CKLNUY clunky
CKLOPU lock up
lock-up
uplock
CKLPUY plucky
CKMOOT Mt Cook
CKMOPU mock-up
CKMPUU muck up
muck-up
CKNORU uncork
CKNTUU untuck
CKOOPU cook up
CKOPRU cork up
CKOSST stocks
CKOSTY stocky
CKPRUU ruck up
CKPSUU suck up
CKPTUU tuck up
CKRSTU struck
CKRSUU ruckus
CLLOOP collop
CLLOOY coolly
CLLORS scroll
CLLSSU sculls
CLMNOU column
CLMOPY comply
CLMOSU locums
CLMOUU lucumo
CLMPSU clumps

Words marked ✧ can also be spelled with one or more capital letters

CLMPUY clumpy
CLMSUY clumsy
muscly
CLNOOS colons
CLNOOU uncool
CLNOOY colony
CLNOSU clonus
consul
CLNOTU uncolt
CLNOUW uncowl
CLNRUU uncurl
CLOORU colour
CLOOST Cloots
CLORSW scrowl
CLOSTU locust
CLOSTY costly
CLOSUU oculus
CLOTUW low-cut
CLPRUU curl up
upcurl
CLPSTU sculpt
CLRTUY curtly
CLSSUU sulcus
CLSTUU cultus
CMMNOO common
CMMOOR romcom
rom-com
CMMOOS commos
CMMOOT commot
CMMRUY crummy
CMMSUY scummy
CMNNOO non-com
CMNOSY Syncom
CMOOOW moo-cow
CMOOPS compos
CMOOPT compot
CMOOSS cosmos
CMOOSU comous
CMOOSW Moscow
CMORSU cormus
mucros
CMOSTU custom
CMOSUU mucous
CMOSUY cymous
CMPRSU scrump
CMPRUY crumpy
CMSTUU scutum✧
CNNNOO non-con
CNNOOR Connor
CNNOPY pycnon
CNOOPU coupon
CNOORT croton
CNOOST contos
nostoc
oncost
CNOOTT cotton
CNOOTY coonty
tycoon
CNOOVY convoy
CNOPSW C P Snow
CNOPTU puncto

CNORSU Cronus
CNORSY synroc
CNORUY rouncy
CNOSSU Consus
CNOSTU Tucson
CNOTUY county
CNRSTU scrunt
COOORZ corozo
COOPPU coop up
COOPRS scroop
COOPTU cop out
cop-out
COOPWX cowpox
COORSS corsos
COORTU octuor
COORUU roucou
COOSTY oocyst
COPPRU crop up
COPPRY croppy
COPRSU corpus
COPRTY crypto
COPRUY croupy
COPSUY cosy up
coypus
CORRSU cursor
CORSST T-cross
CORSSU scours
CORSSW scrows
CORSSY Y-cross
CORSTU scruto
Turcos
CORSUV corvus✧
CORTUY cry out
outcry
COSSTU costus
custos✧
COSTTU cottus
COSTTY Scotty
COTTUU cut out
cut-out
CPRSUY cyprus✧
CRRSUY scurry
CRSSUU cursus
ruscus
CRSTUY crusty
curtsy
CRSUVY scurvy
CSUYZZ scuzzy

D

DDDDEO dodded
DDDEEI eddied
DDDEET tedded
DDDEEW wedded
DDDEGO godded
DDDEIK kidded
DDDEIL diddle
lidded
DDDEIR didder
ridded
DDDEIU duddie

DDDELO doddle
DDDENO nodded
DDDEOP podded
DDDEOR dodder
rodded
DDDERU dudder
rudded
DDEEEM deemed
DDEEER reeded
DDEEES deseed
seeded
DDEEEW weeded
DDEEFI de fide
defied
DDEEFN defend
DDEEGL gelded
ledged
DDEEGR dredge
DDEEGS sedged
DDEEGW wedged
DDEEHL heddle
DDEEIN denied
in deed
indeed
Neddie
DDEEIR Deidre
deride
dièdre
DDEEIT teddie✧
DDEELM meddle
DDEELN ledden
DDEELP peddle
DDEELR reddle
DDEELS sleded
DDEELU delude
DDEEMO démodé
DDEENP depend
DDEENR redden
DDEENS sended
DDEENT tended
DDEENU denude
dudeen
duende
Dundee
DDEENW wended
DDEEOR eroded
DDEEOS eddoes
DDEEPR pedder
DDEERR redder
DDEERT tedder
DDEERW wedder
DDEERY Eddery
DDEEST stedde
DDEFIL fiddle
DDEFLU fuddle
DDEFNO fonded
DDEFNU funded
DDEFOR fodder
DDEFRY Freddy
DDEFSU defus'd
DDEGGI digged

DDEGGO dogged
DDEGIL gilded
DDEGIN dinged
DDEGIR girded
ridged
DDEGIT geddit
DDEGLU guddle
DDEGMO Dodgem®
DDEGNO dog-end
godden
god-den
DDEGOR dodger
red dog
red-dog
DDEGRU drudge
DDEHIN hidden
DDEHIR hidder
DDEHIS dished
eddish
DDEHLO hoddle✧
DDEHLU huddle
DDEHNO hodden
DDEHNU hudden
DDEHOO hooded
DDEIIO iodide
DDEIIT tidied
DDEIIV divide
DDEIKL kiddle
DDEIKR kidder
DDEILM middle✧
DDEILN dindle
DDEILO dildoe
doiled
DDEILP piddle
DDEILR riddle
DDEILS slided
DDEILT tiddle
DDEILW widdle
DDEIMM dimmed
DDEIMN midden
minded
DDEIMS desmid
DDEINN dinned
DDEINR ridden
rinded
DDEINT tinded
DDEINW winded
DDEIOS didoes
DDEIOT doited
DDEIOV devoid
voided
DDEIPP dipped
DDEIRR ridder
DDEITT ditted
DDEITU dutied
DDEJRU judder
DDEKNY kynded
DDELMU muddle
DDELNO noddle
DDELOO doodle
DDELOT toddle

DDELPU	puddle
DDELRU	ruddle
DDELUY	Dudley
DDEMNU	Edmund
DDEMOO	doomed
DDEMOR	Modred
DDEMRU	mudder
	red mud
DDENNO	donned
DDENNU	dunned
DDENOR	donder
	nodder
DDENOS	sodden
DDENOW	downed
DDENOY	dynode
DDENPU	pudden
DDENRU	dunder
DDENRY	Dryden
DDENSU	sudden
DDENUY	undyed
DDEOOS	dodoes
DDEOOW	wooded
DDEORW	worded
DDEOTT	dotted
DDEPRS	spredd
DDEPRU	pudder
	redd up
DDEPUU	dude up
DDERRU	rudder
DDERSU	sudder
DDERUW	red-wud
DDESTY	steddy
DDFILY	fiddly
DDFIOR	fordid
DDGIPU	giddup
DDHIIS	siddhi✧
DDHIOS	oddish
DDHISU	dudish
DDHOSY	shoddy
DDHPUU	huddup
DDIIKK	dik-dik
DDIIKV	kidvid
DDIIMS	misdid
DDIKNO	dodkin
DDIKOS	kiddos
DDILNR	dirndl
DDILOS	dildos
DDILTY	tiddly
DDIMRU	dirdum
DDIMSU	dudism
DDIMSY	smiddy
DDINNO	nid-nod
DDINOO	Diodon
DDINOW	did won
DDIOOS	dosi-do
DDIOPY	dipody
DDIORS	sordid
DDIOTY	oddity
DDIRSU	siddur
DDLMUY	muddly
DDLOOT	odd lot
DDLPUY	puddly
DDMMUU	dumdum
	dum-dum
DDMORV	DVD-ROM
DDMRUU	durdum
DDNOOS	odds-on
DDNOOW	do down
DDOOOO	doo-doo
DDOPRY	Proddy
DDPSUY	spuddy
DEEEFR	feeder
DEEEGR	degree
DEEEHL	heeled
DEEEIP	deepie
DEEEJR	jereed
DEEEKL	keeled
DEEELN	needle
DEEELP	peeled
DEEELT	delete
DEEEMR	meered
	redeem
	remede
DEEEMS	seméed
DEEEMT	teemed
DEEENP	deepen
DEEENR	needer
	reeden
DEEENV	vendee
DEEEPV	peeved
DEEERR	reeder
DEEERS	seeder
	see red
DEEERV	reeved
DEEERW	weeder
DEEERY	red-eye
DEEFFR	reffed
DEEFGL	fledge
DEEFIL	defile
DEEFIN	define
DEEFIR	defier
DEEFLW	flewed
DEEFLX	deflex
DEEFNR	fender
DEEFNU	unfeed
DEEFPU	feed up
DEEFRZ	freez'd
DEEFSU	defuse
DEEFUZ	defuze
DEEFZZ	fezzed
DEEGGI	gidgee
DEEGGL	gledge
	legged
DEEGGP	pegged
DEEGHR	hedger
DEEGIJ	gidjee
DEEGIW	wedgie
DEEGKR	kedger
DEEGLL	gelled
DEEGLN	legend
DEEGLP	pledge
DEEGLR	gelder
	ledger
	redleg
DEEGLS	sledge
DEEGLU	deluge
DEEGLY	gleyed
DEEGMM	gemmed
DEEGMN	menged
DEEGNO	on edge
DEEGNR	gender
DEEGNU	dengue
	unedge
DEEGRY	greedy
DEEGSU	segued
DEEGSZ	Szeged
DEEHLM	helmed
DEEHLP	helped
DEEHMM	hemmed
DEEHMS	Meshed
DEEHMT	themed
DEEHNR	herden
DEEHNT	the end
DEEHPR	Phèdre
DEEHRR	herder
DEEHRS	heders
	hersed
DEEHRT	three-D
DEEHSW	shewed
DEEHTW	thewed
DEEILN	Leiden
DEEILR	lieder
	relide
	relied
DEEILS	diesel
	sedile
DEEILV	levied
	veiled
DEEILY	eyelid
DEEIMP	impede
DEEIMR	remeid
DEEIMS	demies
	demise
	Medise
DEEIMZ	Medize
DEEINN	indene
DEEINR	denier
	nereid✧
	renied
DEEINS	Denise
	desine
DEEINT	eident
	endite
DEEINV	devein
	endive
	envied
	veined
DEEIOR	oreide
DEEIOV	voidee
DEEIPP	Dieppe
DEEIPR	perdie
DEEIPS	espied
DEEIRS	desire
	reside
DEEIRT	dieter
	re-edit
	tiered
DEEIRU	ureide
DEEIRV	derive
	revied
DEEISS	dieses
	seised
DEEISV	devise
	viséed
DEEITY	tie-dye
DEEJRU	de jure
DEEJSS	jessed
DEEJTT	jetted
DEEKLY	Del key
DEEKNN	kenned
DEEKSW	skewed
DEELMR	melder
DEELMT	melted
DEELMY	medley
DEELNR	lender
DEELNT	dentel
DEELNU	Eluned
DEELNW	wedeln✧
DEELNY	Leyden
	needly
DEELOP	delope
DEELPP	lepped
DEELPY	deeply
DEELRU	eluder
DEELRV	delver
DEELRW	welder
DEELST	eldest
	steeld
DEELSV	delves
DEELSW	slewed
DEELTT	letted
DEELTU	teledu
DEELUX	de luxe
DEELVV	devvel
DEEMNO	omened
DEEMNR	mender
DEEMNT	dement
DEEMOT	demote
DEEMPR	premed
DEEMRT	metred
DEEMRU	demure
DEEMRY	remedy
DEEMST	temsed
DEEMSY	emydes
DEEMTU	Te Deum
DEENNO	donnée
DEENNP	penned
DEENNT	dennet
DEENOP	depone
DEENOR	Doreen
	redone
DEENOS	Odense
DEENOT	denote
DEENPX	expend

Words marked ✧ can also be spelled with one or more capital letters

DEENRR	render
DEENRS	sender
DEENRT	tender
	tendre
DEENRU	endure
DEENRV	Denver
	nerved
	vender
DEENRZ	dzeren
DEENSS	sensed
DEENST	sedent
DEENSU	end use
	ensued
DEENSW	Sweden
DEENSY	desyne
DEENTT	detent
	netted
	tented
DEENTU	détenu
	detune
DEENTV	vented
DEENTX	dentex
	extend
DEENTY	Nedyet
DEENUV	vendue
DEENUY	uneyed
DEEOPS	depose
	speedo
DEEORT	teredo
DEEORV	dévoré
DEEORZ	zeroed
DEEOTT	Odette
DEEOTV	devote
	dévote
DEEOXY	ox-eyed
DEEPPR	repped
DEEPRU	éperdu
	perdue
DEEPSY	speedy
DEEPTT	petted
DEEPTU	depute
DEEQUU	queued
DEERSS	des res
DEERST	desert
DEERSV	versed
DEERTT	retted
DEERTV	verdet
DEERTX	dexter✧
DEERVV	revved
DEESTT	detest
DEESTU	Études
DEESTV	devest
	vested
DEESTW	stewed
	tweeds
DEESTY	steedy
DEETTV	vetted
DEETTW	wetted
DEETUV	vedute
DEETWY	tweedy
DEFFIM	miffed
DEFFIO	die off
DEFFIR	differ
DEFFLU	duffel
	duffle
DEFFNO	offend
DEFFOR	doffer
DEFFPU	puffed
DEFFRU	duffer
	ruffed
DEFGGI	figged
DEFGGO	fogged
DEFGIR	fridge
DEFGIT	fidget
	gifted
DEFGLY	fledgy
DEFHOO	hoofed
DEFILO	foiled
DEFIMS	misfed
DEFINN	finned
DEFINR	finder
	friend
DEFINU	fundie
DEFIOO	foodie
DEFIOT	foetid
DEFIRV	fervid
DEFISX	sexfid
DEFITT	fitted
DEFIZZ	fizzed
DEFKOR	forked
DEFLMY	medfly
DEFLNO	enfold
	fondle
DEFLOR	folder
DEFLOT	lofted
DEFLOU	defoul
DEFLOW	flowed
DEFLTU	fluted
DEFLTY	deftly
DEFLUU	dueful
DEFMOR	deform
	formed
DEFNOR	Fronde
DEFNOU	fondue
DEFNRU	funder
	refund
	re-fund
DEFOOR	doofer
	roofed
DEFOOT	footed
DEFOOW	woofed
DEFOPU	poufed
DEFORX	red fox
DEFOSS	fossed
DEFOST	Ofsted
DEFRRU	furder
	furred
DEFRTU	turfed
DEFTTU	tufted
DEGGGI	gigged
DEGGHO	hogged
DEGGHU	hugged
DEGGIJ	jigged
DEGGIN	edging
DEGGIO	doggie
DEGGIP	pigged
DEGGIR	digger
	rigged
DEGGIT	tigged
DEGGIU	Duggie
DEGGIW	wigged
DEGGIZ	zigged
DEGGJO	jogged
DEGGJU	jugged
DEGGLO	dogleg
	logged
DEGGLU	lugged
DEGGMU	mugged
DEGGNO	nogged
DEGGOR	dogger✧
	gorged
DEGGOS	sogged
DEGGOT	togged
DEGGRU	grudge
	rugged
DEGGRY	dreggy
DEGGTU	tugged
DEGHIN	hinged
DEGHOP	dog-hep
DEGIIK	kidgie
DEGIIM	midgie
DEGIIR	dirige
DEGIIW	widgie
DEGILM	mid-leg
DEGILN	dingle
	elding
	engild
	gilden
DEGILO	Goidel
	Goldie
DEGILR	gilder
	girdle
	glider
	lidger
	ridgel
DEGILU	guiled
DEGILY	edgily
DEGIMN	minged
DEGIMT	midget
DEGINN	ending
	ginned
DEGINO	Gideon
DEGINR	dinger
	engird
	ringed
DEGINS	design
	dinges
	sdeign
	singed
DEGINT	nidget
DEGINW	winged
DEGINY	dingey
	dyeing
DEGIOP	pie-dog
DEGIRR	girder
	ridger
DEGIRT	get rid
DEGIRU	guider✧
DEGIST	digest
DEGITU	dugite
DEGITW	widget
DEGJSU	Judges
DEGKLU	kludge
DEGLNO	dongle
	golden
DEGLNU	gulden
	lunged
DEGLNY	gylden
DEGLOR	lodger
DEGLOV	gloved
DEGLSU	sludge
DEGMMU	gummed
DEGMRU	mudger
	red gum
DEGMSU	smudge
DEGNNU	gunned
DEGNOW	gowned
DEGNRU	gerund
	nudger
DEGNSU	snudge
DEGOPY	pye-dog
DEGORR	droger
DEGORS	sodger
DEGORU	drogue
	gourde
DEGOST	stodge
DEGOTU	dégoût
DEGPPY	gypped
DEGRTU	trudge
DEGSTU	degust
	gutsed
DEGTTU	gutted
DEHHSU	hushed
DEHIIL	Eilidh
DEHILL	hilled
DEHILS	delish
	shield
DEHIMN	mehndi
DEHIMR	dirhem
DEHINO	hoiden
	honied
DEHINR	hinder
DEHINS	shined
DEHIOO	hoodie
DEHIOR	rhodie
DEHIOS	Hesiod
	hoised
DEHIOW	howdie
DEHIPP	hipped
DEHIPS	pished
DEHIRT	dither
DEHISS	dishes
DEHITT	tithed
DEHKLW	whelk'd

DEHKOO hooked
DEHKSU husked
DEHLMO hold 'em
DEHLNO holden
DEHLOR holder
DEHLOW howled
DEHLPS delphs
DEHLPU upheld
DEHLRU hurdle
DEHLTY Delyth
DEHMMU hummed
DEHMNU mud hen
DEHMNY hymned
DEHMOR Hermod
DEHMOT method
mothed
DEHMPU humped
DEHMRY rhymed
DEHNOR dehorn
horned
DEHNOY hoyden
DEHNRU hurden
DEHNRY Hendry
DEHNSU unshed
DEHNSY yshend
DEHNTU hunted
DEHNYY hydyne
DEHOPP hopped
DEHORS Rhodes
shoder
DEHORT red-hot
DEHOSW showed
DEHOTT hotted
DEHPSU pushed
DEHRSW shrewd
DEHRTY the dry✧
DEHTTU hutted
DEIIKN kindie
DEIILL lilied
DEIILP lipide
DEIINO iodine
DEIINR ride in
DEIINS inside
DEIINT indite
tineid
DEIINV divine
DEIIOS iodise
DEIIOZ iodize
DEIIPR pierid
DEIIPT pitied
DEIIRS irides
irised
DEIIRT tidier
DEIISS diesis
DEIISX deixis
DEIITT tide it
DEIIYZ Yezidi
DEIJNX jinxed
DEIKLN kindle
DEIKLO keloid
DEIKLT kidlet
kilted
DEIKNP pinked
DEIKNR kinder
kinred
DEIKNY kidney
DEIKNZ zendik
zinked
DEIKPS spiked
DEIKPU Updike
DEIKRU duiker
DEIKTU duke it
DEILLM milled
DEILLN nilled
DEILLR rilled
DEILLU illude
DEILLW willed
DEILMN milden
Mindel
DEILMP dimple
DEILMS misled
DEILMW mildew
DEILNN dinnle
linden
DEILNO doline
indole
Leonid
DEILNR nirled
DEILNT dentil
DEILNW windle
DEILNZ Denzil
DEILOO doolie
DEILOP diploe
dipole
peloid
DEILOS Isolde
siloed
soiled
DEILOT toiled
DEILPP lipped
DEILPS dispel
disple
DEILPX diplex
DEILRS slider
DEILRV drivel
DEILRW wilder
DEILRY Ridley
DEILST listed
DEILSU Delius
DEILSV slived
DEILTT tilted
titled
DEILTU dilute
DEILWY dewily
widely
wieldy
DEIMMN nimmed
DEIMMR dimmer
rimmed
DEIMMS Medism
DEIMMU medium
DEIMNO monied
DEIMNP impend
DEIMNR minder
remind
DEIMNS denims
DEIMOR dormie
moider
DEIMOT do time
DEIMPU mud pie
DEIMRS dermis
DEIMSS demiss
DEIMST demist
DEIMSU medius
DEIMSV Vedism
DEIMTU tedium
DEINNO Dionne
done in
Donnie
ondine✧
DEINNP pinned
DEINNR dinner
endrin
DEINNS Dennis
send in
sinned
DEINNT dentin
indent
intend
tinned
DEINNU undine
DEINNW enwind
DEINOP pioned
DEINOR De Niro
Indore
ride on
DEINOS donsie
Edison
no-side
onside
side-on
DEINOT ditone
intoed
in-toed
DEINOW Downie®
DEINPP nipped
DEINPR pinder
DEINPS spined
DEINPT dip-net
DEINPU uniped
DEINRT rident
tinder
DEINRU ruined
DEINRV driven
verdin
DEINRW rewind
winder
DEINSU undies
used in
DEINSV vendis
DEINSW Widnes
DEINSY Disney
Sidney
snidey
DEINTT tinted
DEINTU dunite
united✧
untied
DEINTW twined
DEIOOR oroide
DEIOOV Oviedo
DEIOOW woodie
DEIOPP doppie
DEIOPR period
DEIOPS poised
DEIOPT pioted
podite
DEIORR Dorrie
DEIORS dorise
DEIORT editor
tie rod
triode
DEIORV devoir
voider
DEIORW weirdo
DEIORZ dorize
DEIOSV videos
DEIOTT Dottie
DEIOTU die out
DEIPPP pipped
DEIPPR dipper✧
ripped
DEIPPS sipped
DEIPPT tipped
DEIPPZ zipped
DEIPRS spider
spired
DEIPRT trepid
DEIPRU ride up
DEIPRZ prized
DEIPSU upside
DEIPTT pitted
DEIQTU quited
DEIRRS derris
sirred
DEIRRU durrie
DEIRRV driver
DEIRST driest
stride
DEIRSU diseur
user ID
DEIRSV divers
DEIRSW Weirds
DEIRTU reduit
DEIRTV divert
verdit
DEISST desist
DEISSU disuse
DEISTU suited
DEISTV divest
stived
Vedist
DEITTU duetti
DEITTW dewitt

witted
DEJLLO jolled
DEJLOW jowled
DEJOTT jotted
DEJTTU jutted
DEKLOY yolked
DEKMNU Mukden
DEKMOS smoked
DEKMSU musked
DEKNOT token'd
DEKNOY donkey
DEKNOZ zonked
DEKNRU dunker✧
DEKNSU dusken
DEKOOT dooket
DEKOPS spoked
DEKORW worked
DEKOST stoked
DEKRUY dukery
duyker
DEKSTU tusked
DELLMU mulled
DELLOP polled
DELLOR rolled
DELLOU duello
DELLOW do well
DELLWY lewdly
DELMNO dolmen
DELMOS seldom
DELMOT Model T
DELMOU module
DELMOY melody
DELMPU dumple
plumed
DELNNO on-lend
DELNOO noodle
Old One
DELNOR rondel
DELNOT dolent
DELNOU louden
nodule
noulde
DELNOW dowlne
new-old
DELNOZ donzel
DELNRU lurden
nurdle
rundle
DELNRY dernly
DELNUV vulned
DELNUY nudely
DELOOP looped
poodle
DELOOS oodles
DELOOT Toledo
DELOPP lopped
DELOPR polder
DELOPY deploy
podley
DELORS dorsel
solder
DELORW weldor
DELORY Delroy
yodler
DELOSS dossel
DELOST oldest
stoled
DELOSU souled
DELOTT dottle
lotted
DELOTX extold
DELOYY doyley
DELPRU drupel
DELPSU plused
pulsed
DELPTU duplet
DELPUX duplex
DELRUY rudely
DEMMMU mummed
DEMMOT tommed
DEMMSU summed
DEMNOO mooned
DEMNOR modern✧
morned
DEMNOS Esmond
DEMOOR droome
roomed
DEMOPP mopped
DEMORR dormer
DEMORT Dermot
DEMORU remoud
DEMORW deworm
wormed
DEMOST modest
DEMOSU dumose
DEMOTT domett
DEMPPU pumped
DEMPRU dumper
DEMRRU murder
Red Rum
DENNOR Donner
DENNOS donnés
send on
DENNOT tendon
DENNOU undone
DENNOW wonned
DENNPU punned
DENNRU undern
DENNSU sunned
DENNTU tunned
DENOOS nodose
nosode
odeons
DENOOV de novo
DENOOW wooden
DENOOX ex dono
DENOPR Pernod®
ponder
DENORT rodent
to-rend
DENORU enduro
undoer
DENORV vendor
DENORW downer
wonder
DENORY Rodney
yonder
DENOSS endoss
DENOST doesn't
Ostend
stoned
DENOSZ dozens
DENOTU deuton
DENOTW wonted
DENOUW unowed
DENPSU send up
send-up
unsped
upsend
DENPTU pudent
DENRSU sunder
DENRTU retund
runted
turned
DENRTY trendy
DENRUU unrude
DENRUY unredy
DENSTU usedn't
DENSTY syndet
DENSUU unused
DENSUW sundew
DENSYY Sydney
DENTTU nutted
DEOOPP pooped
DEOOPX exopod
DEOORS rodeos
DEOORT rooted
DEOORV do over
overdo
DEOPPP popped
DEOPPR dopper✧
DEOPPS sopped
DEOPPT topped
DEOPPW wopped
DEOPQU Pequod
DEOPRT deport
de trop
redtop
red-top
DEOPRU pouder
poudre
DEOPRV proved
DEOPRW powder
DEOPST despot
DEOPSU pseudo
DEOPTT potted
DEORRS dorser
orders
DEORRT dorter
red rot
retrod
DEORRU ordure
DEORRV drover
DEORRW reword
DEORSS dosser
DEORST Dorset
sorted
strode
DEORSU douser
DEORSW dowser
drowse
DEORTT detort
rotted
DEORTU detour
douter
outred
red out
routed
DEORUV devour
DEORVY verdoy
DEOSST tossed
DEOSSU soused
DEOSTT sotted
DEOSTW dowset
DEOSUX exodus✧
DEOTTT totted
DEOTTU duetto
DEOTTW wotted
DEOTUV devout
DEOTUX tuxedo
DEPPPU pupped
DEPPSU supped
DEPPTU tupped
DEPRUY dupery
Purdey®
DEPSUU used-up
DEPSUY pudsey
DEPTTU putted
DEPTUY deputy
DERRSU Durres
DERRUY rudery
DERSSU duress
sudser
DERSSY dressy
DERSTU duster
rusted
DERTTU rutted
DESSSU sussed
DESTTU duetts
DESTUV duvets
DETTTU tutted
DFFIMO mid-off
DFFNOO nod off
DFFORY dry off
DFFPUU duff up
DFGGOO fog-dog
DFGIIR frigid
DFGILU fulgid
DFGOOX dogfox
DFIINY nidify
DFIIRT trifid
DFIKOX kid-fox
DFILNO fold in
infold

DFILNU dinful
DFILOR florid
DFILUV fulvid
DFIMOY modify
DFIRTY drifty
DFLNOU unfold
DFLNOY fondly
DFLOOS floods
DFLOPU fold up
DFLORU Rudolf
DFLORY dor-fly
fly rod
DFLRYY dry-fly
DFNSUU fundus
DFOORX oxford✧
DFOOSU doofus
DGGLOO go gold
DGGNOU dugong
gun dog
DGGOPU pug dog
DGGRUY druggy
DGHIIN hiding
DGHINY dinghy
DGHIOP dog-hip
DGHOOO good-oh
DGHOOP hopdog
DGHOOT hot dog
hot-dog
DGHOTU dought
DGHOUY doughy
DGIILR ridgil
DGIINN indign
niding
DGIINO indigo
DGIINP pidgin
DGIINR Ingrid
riding✧
DGIINS siding
DGIINV diving
DGIJOU judogi
DGILNU ungild
DGILOT diglot
DGIMTU mid-gut
DGINNO doning
onding
DGINOP doping
pongid
DGINOR roding
DGINOS doings
DGINOT doting
tin god
DGINOU guidon
DGINOV Govind
DGINOZ dozing
DGINRU during
ungird
DGINRY drying
DGINSU dingus
DGIOTU dig out
DGIOTW godwit
DGIRTU turgid
DGLNOP plongd
DGLOOY goodly
DGLSUY sludgy
DGMSUY smudgy
DGNOOO no good
no-good
DGNOOR drongo
Gondor
Gordon
Grodno
DGNOOS godson
DGNOOU Gounod
DGNOOW go down
godown
go-down
DGNORU ground
ungord
DGNOSU sundog
sun-god
DGNRUU Gudrun
DGOOPT top dog
DGOOTY toy dog
DGORSU gourds
DGORUY gourdy
DGOSTY stodgy
DGOTUU dugout
DHIINS Sindhi
DHIIPS hispid
DHIISW widish
DHIJTU Judith
DHILNO hold in
DHILOS oldish
DHILOT hold it!
DHILPU uphild
DHIMOS modish
DHINOO Hindoo
DHINSY shindy
DHIOOT dhooti
DHIOPY hypoid
DHIORR horrid
DHIOST dotish
DHIOSV dovish
DHIPSU dish up
DHIRSU rudish
DHIRSY dryish
DHLNOO hold on
on hold
DHLOOY dhooly
DHLOPU hold up
hold-up
uphold
DHLOSU should
DHLTUU Duluth
DHNOOU unhood
DHNOSU Hudson
unshod
DHOOOO hoodoo
DHOORT hot rod
DHORSU shroud✧
DHORSW shrowd
DHORSY hydros
DHORTU drouth
DHRSUY Hydrus
DIIJNN djinni
DIIKNN in kind
DIIKWZ wiz kid
DIILMP limpid
DIILOP lipoid
DIILOS solidi
DIILQU liquid
DIILST distil
DIILTY tidily
DIIMNU indium
DIIMOS iodism
DIIMOU oidium
DIIMTW dimwit
DIIMTY dimity
DIINNW inwind
DIINOP Dipnoi
DIINOX dioxin
DIINRS indris
DIINSV invis'd
DIIOOP opioid
DIIORV viroid
DIIOST Idoist
DIIOTT doitit
DIITTT dittit
DIKLNY kindly
DIKLTU kidult
DIKMNU dinkum
DIKMSY mid-sky
DIKNNU nudnik
unkind
DIKOOS Ski-doo®
skidoo
DIKORY Kid Ory
DIKRSY dry ski
DILLMY mildly
DILLOW will do
DILLVY vildly
DILLWY wildly
DILMOR milord
DILMOU dolium
idolum✧
moduli
DILMPY dimply
DILNNU dunlin
DILNOO idolon✧
DILNOP diplon
DILNTU indult
DILNWY Dilwyn
DILOPT pot-lid
DILOPU lupoid
DILOPY dopily
ploidy
DILORT lord it
DILOSS dossil
solids
DILOST stolid
DILOXY xyloid
DIMMSU dim sum
DIMNOO domino
DIMNOR Nimrod
DIMNSU nudism
DIMOOR Dromio
dromoi
DIMOPU podium
DIMORS Dorism
DIMOST modist
DIMOSU modius
sodium
DIMOSW wisdom✧
DIMOSY disomy
DIMOTU dim out
dim-out
DIMOYZ zymoid
DINNOS sindon
DINNUW unwind
DINOOR indoor
DINOOZ zonoid
DINOPR drop in
drop-in
DINOPU dupion
unipod
DINORU durion
DINORW in word
DINOST on-dits
DINOSW disown
DINOWW window✧
DINPSU unspi'd
DINPTU pundit
DINPUW upwind
up-wind
wind up
wind-up
DINRSU sundri
DINSTU Dustin
nudist
DINTUY nudity
untidy
DIOOPS isopod
DIOORT toroid
DIOOSU iodous
odious
DIOOTX toxoid
DIOPRT torpid
tripod
DIOPSS dipsos
DIORRT torrid
DIOSTT dittos
DIOSTU studio
DIOTVY ivy-tod
DIPPRY drippy
DIPRTU putrid
DIPSTU stupid
DIQSSU squids
DJLMOY jymold
DJNNOO donjon
DKLSUY duskly
DKNOOP pondok
DKNOPU Podunk
DKOOOO koodoo
DKORSY drosky

DLLOOP dollop
DLLOPU doll up
DLLORY drolly
lordly
DLLOUW Ludlow
DLLOUY loudly
DLMOOT Old Tom
DLMOOU modulo
DLMORY My Lord
DLMOSU moulds
DLMOUY mouldy
DLMRUY drumly
DLNNOO London
DLNOOS sold on
DLNOPU Dunlop
DLNORU unlord
DLNOSU unsold
DLNOTU untold
DLNQRS Sqn Ldr
DLNUUY unduly
DLOOPS podsol
DLOOPZ podzol
DLOORU dolour
DLOPRS Dr Slop
DLORUY dourly
DLOTUW 'twould
DLSTUY studly
DMNOOR dromon
DMNOOY monody
DMNOPU dump on
DMNOSU osmund
DMOORR Mordor
DMOORS dromos
DMOOSU duomos
DMOOSY sodomy
DMOOTT motto'd
DMORSU dorsum
DMORUZ Ormuzd
DMORWY my word
DMOSUU dumous
DMPRUU drum up
DNNOOT donnot
DNNTUU tundun
DNOORS rondos
DNOOST tondos
DNOOSU nodous
DNOPSU pounds
snod up
DNORST strond
DNORTU rotund
untrod
DNOSSU sounds
DNOSTU stound
DNOSTW stownd
DNOSUW swound
DNOSUZ zounds
DNOSWW swownd
DNOTUY on duty
DNOUWY woundy
DNRRUY dry run
run dry

DNRSUY sundry
DOOOOV voodoo
DOOOPW doo-wop
DOOPRU uropod
DOOPRY droopy✧
DOOPUW wood up
DOORWW row-dow
DOOSWY woodsy
DOOUUV voudou
DOPRSY dropsy
DORRTY dry rot
DORSSW swords
DORSSY drossy
DORSTU stroud✧
DORSWY drowsy
DORTUY dry out
DORUVY dyvour
DPSTUU dust-up
DRSTUU Turdus
DRSTUY sturdy
DRSUYY dysury

E

EEEEGG gee-gee
EEEEHT tee-hee
EEEEPP pee-pee
EEEEPT teepee
EEEEPW peewee
EEEETT tee-tee
EEEEWW wee-wee
EEEFFR effere
EEEFFT effete
EEEFIR féerie
EEEFLR feeler
EEEFNR enfree
EEEFNT en fête
EEEFRR reefer
EEEFRZ freeze
EEEGMR emerge
EEEGNP peenge
EEEGNR renege
EEEGNU Eugene
EEEGRS greese
EEEGRT greete
EEEGRZ geezer
EEEGTV vegete
EEEHIZ heezie
EEEHLR heeler
reheel
EEEHLT lethee
EEEHNT ethene
EEEHNX hexene
EEEHPR pheere
EEEHPS pheese
EEEHPZ pheeze
EEEHST seethe
EEEHTT teethe
EEEHWZ wheeze
EEEIJL jeelie
EEEIKL keelie
EEEIKR reekie

EEEILN Eileen
EEEILR Leerie
EEEIMM meemie
EEEINT Teenie
EEEINW weenie
EEEIPR peerie
EEEIPW weepie
EEEITY Eyetie
EEEJRR jeerer
EEEJST jestee
EEEKKR keeker
EEEKLR keeler
EEEKLU ekuele
EEEKMN meeken
EEEKNR keener
EEEKNT ketene
EEEKPR keeper
EEEKRS kreese
seeker✧
EEELLT leetle
EEELMS Semele
EEELMX lexeme
EEELNS Selene
EEELNV eleven
enlevé
EEELPR peeler
EEELRR reeler
EEELSS lessee
EEELST eel-set
EEELSV sleeve
EEELTY eyelet
EEEMMS sememe
EEEMNR meneer
EEEMNT mentee
temene
EEEMRS emerse
seemer
EEEMRT teemer
EEEMST esteem
mestee
EEEMTU émeute
EEENPS pensée
EEENRS serene✧
EEENRT entrée
eterne
retene
EEENRV enerve
evener
veneer
EEENSS Essene
EEENSZ sneeze
EEENTT entêté
EEENTW weeten
EEENVW venewe
EEEOPP epopee
EEEORY Eeyore
EEEPPR peeper
EEEPRV peever
preeve
EEEPRW weeper
EEERRT retree

EEERRV revere✧
EEERSV severe
EEERTT teeter
terete
EEERTX Exeter
EEERVW weever
EEESTT settee
testee
EEESTV steeve
EEETWZ tweeze
EEFFIL Eiffel
EEFFIR effeir
EEFFKL keffel
EEFFOS see off
EEFFOT tee off
tee-off
toffee
EEFFSU effuse
EEFGIN feeing
EEFGRU refuge
EEFHIR heifer
EEFHOR hereof
EEFHTW the few
EEFILN feel in
feline
EEFILR liefer
relief
EEFILT leftie
EEFINR enfire
feerin
ferine
fineer
in fere
infere
refine
EEFINW Newfie
EEFIPR preife
priefe
EEFIRS frisée
EEFIRZ frieze
EEFIST see fit
EEFLLO felloe
EEFLLR feller
EEFLNN fennel
EEFLNS flense
EEFLPU feel up
EEFLRR ferrel
EEFLRT felter
reflet
telfer
EEFLRU ferule
refuel
EEFLRX reflex
EEFLRY freely
EEFLTT fettle
EEFLUY eyeful
EEFMNO foemen
EEFMTW fewmet
EEFNNR frenne
EEFNRU unfree
EEFPRR prefer

EEFPRT perfet
EEFPRU free up
EEFPTY tepefy
EEFQRV Q-fever
EEFRRT ferret
EEFRST fester
freest
EEFRSU refuse
EEFRTT fetter
EEFRTU feutre
refute
EEFRTW fewter
EEFRTY freety
EEFSTT eftest
EEFSTW ewftes
EEFSZZ fezzes
EEGGIN geeing
EEGGIR Geiger
greige
Reggie
EEGGIV veggie
EEGGLP peg leg
EEGGLR eggler
legger
EEGGMR Megger®
EEGGMU muggee
EEGGOR George
EEGGRY eggery
EEGHLT the leg
EEGHNU eughen
EEGHNW ewghen
EEGHOT Goethe
EEGHPU gee hup
EEGHSS ghesse
EEGILR leiger
lieger
EEGILT elegit
EEGIMR émigré
regime
régime
EEGIMV give me
EEGINN engine
EEGINS seeing
EEGINT teeing
EEGINY eyeing
EEGIRR Gerrie
EEGIRS sieger
EEGIRT Gertie
EEGIRV grieve
regive
EEGKLS Kegels
EEGLLN leglen
EEGLLT leglet
EEGLMU emulge
legume
EEGLNN gennel
EEGLNR lenger
EEGLNS Engels
EEGLNT gentle
EEGLRT Gelert
reglet

EEGLTU Telegu
EEGLTY gleety
EEGMMN gemmen
EEGMNO genome
EEGMNR germen
EEGMNT tegmen
EEGMNU emunge
EEGMOR Göreme
EEGMRR merger
EEGNNT gennet
EEGNOP pongee
EEGNOR engore
EEGNOX exogen
EEGNRS greens✧
EEGNRT erg-ten
gerent
regent
EEGNRV venger
EEGNRY energy
greeny
EEGNST gentes
tenges
EEGOOS soogee
EEGRRT regret
EEGRRU reurge
EEGRRV verger
EEGRSS egress
EEGRST regest
EEGRSV Verges
EEGRSY geyser
EEGRTT getter
EEGRXY exergy
EEHHRT hether
EEHHSW wheesh
EEHIIN heinie
EEHILN heel in
hele in
EEHILT the lie
EEHIMP Phemie
EEHINR herein
inhere
EEHINT Eithne
theine
EEHIRR rehire
EEHIRT either
EEHITV thieve
EEHKLS shekel
EEHKRS shreek
EEHLLN Hellen
EEHLLR heller
EEHLMT helmet
EEHLNU unhele
EEHLNY Henley
EEHLPR helper
EEHLSV shelve
EEHLSW shewel
wheels
EEHLWY wheely
EEHMMS emmesh
EEHMMT Mehmet
EEHMNP hempen

EEHMNS enmesh
EEHMPT tempeh
EEHMRS Hermes
EEHMST smeeth
EEHMUV Humvee®
EEHMUX exhume
EEHNNP hen-pen
EEHNNR henner
EEHNOR hereon
EEHNOT eothen
the one
EEHNPS sephen
sphene
EEHNPW nephew
EEHNRR Herren
EEHNRT nether
threne
EEHNSS sneesh
EEHNSY sheeny✧
EEHNTT the Net
EEHNTY ethyne
EEHOPS sheepo
EEHORR Herero
EEHORS heroes
EEHORT hereto
hetero
EEHORW howe'er
EEHOSX hexose
EEHOTW towhee
EEHPRS herpes
Hesper
sphere
EEHPRT pether
threep
EEHPSY sheepy
EEHQTU quethe
EEHRSS sheers
EEHRST Esther
Hester
EEHRSU rushee
EEHRSY heresy
EEHRTT tether
EEHRTW wether
wrethe
EEHRTY they're
EEHRVY Hervey
EEHSST sheets
theses
EEHSTW thewes
EEHSTX the sex
EEHSTY sheety
EEHTVY they've
EEHWYY wheyey
EEHWYZ wheezy
EEIIKK kie-kie
EEIIKR kierie
EEIIMN meinie
EEIINW wienie
EEIJNN Jennie
jinnee
EEIJSS jessie✧

EEIKLP kelpie
EEIKLS selkie
EEIKLT keltie
EEIKNN Kennie
EEIKNP keep in
Kneipe
EEIKNR keiren
EEILLL Lillee
EEILLN nellie✧
EEILLR rellie
EEILLS eisell
Leslie
EEILLV vielle
EEILLW wellie
EEILMR Meriel
EEILNN Lennie
EEILNO Leonie
EEILNP penile
EEILNR lierne
reline
EEILNS enisle
ensile
nelies
senile
silene
EEILOR loerie
EEILOS Eloise
EEILOT étoile
EEILPT pelite
EEILRR relier
EEILRS resile
EEILRT retile
EEILRV liever
relive
revile
EEILRY eerily
EEILSS seseli
EEILSX ilexes
EEILTT Lettie
EEILTV levite✧
EEILVW weevil
EEIMMS Emmies
EEIMNR ermine
EEIMNS inseem
EEIMNT emetin
EEIMNY meiney
menyie
Yemeni
EEIMPR empire✧
epimer
premie
EEIMRS misère
remise
EEIMRT métier
retime
tremie
trémie
EEIMSS emesis
missee
EEIMST mesite
Semite

EEINNP peen in
pinene
EEINNR nerine
EEINPR repine
EEINQU equine
EEINRS seiner
serein
serine
EEINRT entire
nerite
triene
EEINRV envier
venire
Verein
EEINRW wiener
EEINRX Rexine®
EEINSS in esse
Nessie
sensei
EEINST seiten
EEINTT Nettie
tentie
EEINTV venite
EEINTX extine
EEIORS soirée
EEIPPY yippee
EEIPQU équipe
EEIPRR Pierre
EEIPRS éprise
EEIPRV prieve
EEIPRX expire
EEIPSU épuisé
EEIPTT petite
EEIPTW peewit
EEIPTY eye-pit
EEIRRS sirree
EEIRRT étrier
reiter
retire
EEIRRV reiver
riever
verier
EEIRRW rewire
EEIRSS series
EEIRST re-site
EEIRSV revise
EEIRSZ seizer
EEIRTT ti tree
EEIRTV vérité
EEIRVV revive
EEIRVW review
re-view
viewer
EEISSV essive
EEISTV Stevie
stieve
EEISTW Westie
EEJJNU jejune
EEJKRR jerker
EEJLLO Joelle
EEJLNO Joleen
Jolene
EEJMOR Jerome
EEJMRY Jeremy
EEJNNT jennet
EEJQRU jerque
EEJRST jester
EEJRSY jersey✧
EEJSSW Jewess
EEKKLR lekker
EEKKSY keksye
EEKLMP kemple
EEKLMY meekly
EEKLNN kennel
EEKLNR kernel
EEKLNY keenly
EEKLPR kelper✧
EEKLRT kelter
EEKLSY skeely
sleeky
EEKLSZ Szekel
EEKLTT kettle
EEKLWY weekly
EEKMNS Meknès
EEKMNU unmeek
EEKMPR kemper
EEKMRS kermes
EEKNNR kenner
EEKNNT kennet
EEKNOP keep on
EEKNOT ketone
EEKNRS skreen
EEKNSY Keynes
EEKORV evoker
revoke
EEKOST ketose
to seek
EEKOTU eke out
EEKPPU keep up
upkeep
EEKPRU Keuper
peruke
EEKRST streek
EEKRSU reskue
EEKRSW reskew
skewer
Wesker
EEKRSY kersey
skeery
EELLMR merell
EELLNO Noelle
EELLNT tellen
EELLNW newell
EELLOV O level
O-level
EELLPT pellet
EELLRS resell
seller
EELLRT retell
teller
EELLRU ruelle
EELLSY Lesley
EELLTV vellet
EELLVY Y-level
EELMOT omelet
EELMPS semple
EELMPT pelmet
temple✧
EELMRS merels
EELMRT melter
EELMRU em rule
relume
EELMRY merely
EELMST telesm
EELMSY seemly
EELMTT mettle
EELMTY meetly
EELNNT lenten✧
EELNNV vennel
EELNOV elevon
EELNPS pensel
spleen
EELNRT relent
EELNRU en rule
unreel
EELNSS lenses
lessen
EELNST nestle
EELNSU unseel
EELNSV Velsen
EELNTT nettle
telnet✧
EELNTU eluent
EELNUV Leuven
venule
EELNVY Evelyn
evenly
EELNXY xylene
EELOPP people
EELOPR eloper
EELORS or else
resole
EELOUV évolué
EELOVV evolve
EELPPU peepul
EELPRT pelter
petrel
pre-let
EELPRY yelper
EELPST Elspet
pestle
EELPSU Peleus
EELPSV pelves
EELPSY sleepy
EELPTT pettle
EELQSU sequel
EELRRV verrel
EELRSS lesser
EELRST Lester
streel
EELRSV revels
EELRTT letter
lettre
EELRTW welter
EELRUV velure
EELRVV vervel
EELSST steels
EELSSV selves
vessel
EELSTT settle
EELSTU setule
EELSTV svelte
EELSTY sleety
steely
EELSUV evulse
EELSWY Wesley
EELSYZ sleezy
EELTVV velvet
EELTVW twelve✧
EELTWY tweely
EEMMOR merome
EEMMOV emmove
EEMMSS semsem
EEMMST stemme
EEMNOR moreen
EEMNOT toneme
EEMNOV enmove
EEMNOY yeomen
EEMNSS menses
EEMNST Temnes
EEMNTU unmeet
EEMNYZ enzyme
EEMOPT metope
EEMORR roemer
EEMORT emoter
meteor
remote
EEMORV remove
EEMPRS semper
sempre
EEMPRT temper
EEMPRY empery
EEMPSU empuse
EEMPTU meet up
EEMPTX exempt
EEMRRT termer
EEMRST merest
restem
Termes
EEMRSU resume
résumé
EEMRSV vermes✧
EEMRTU Meerut
EEMSST tmeses
EEMSSU smeuse
EEMSSW mewses
EEMSTU mustee
EEMSTX Semtex®
EEMTXX Tex-Mex
EENNOO one-one
EENNOR Noreen
EENNOV Evonne
EENNOZ enzone
EENNPR penner

EENNRS Rennes
EENNRT rennet
tenner
EENNST sennet
EENNSU unseen
EENNUV uneven
EENNUY ennuyé
EENOPR opener
perone
reopen
repone
EENOPT poteen
EENORW ere now
erenow
EENORY oneyer
oneyre
EENORZ rezone
EENOSS enoses
EENOSV even so
venose
EENOTV voteen
EENOTW townee
EENOVZ evzone
EENPRT repent
EENPRY pyrene
EENPTU puntee
EENPUV even up
EENQSU Queens
EENQUY queeny
EENRRT renter
EENRRV nerver
EENRST Ernest
nester
rentes
resent
Sterne
strene
EENRSU ensure
Nereus
EENRSV nerves
EENRSY sneery
EENRTT tenter
EENRTU neuter
retune
tenure
tureen
EENRTV venter
ventre
EENRTW weren't
EENRTX extern
EENRTZ entrez
EENRVV verven
EENRVY venery
EENSSS senses
EENSSV sevens
EENSTU tenues
Usenet
EENSTV steven✧
EENSTY teensy
EENSVW sweven
EENSWY sweeny
EENSYZ sneezy
EENTTX extent
EENTTY teenty
EENTUX exeunt
EENTWY tweeny
EEOOTT toetoe
EEOPPY pop-eye
EEOPRS repose
EEOPRU Europe
EEOPSS eposes
EEOPSX expose
exposé
EEOPTU toupee
EEOPTY peyote
EEORRV or ever
EEORST stereo
EEORSV ever so
soever
EEORUV oeuvre
EEOSST setose
EEOSTU see out
EEOSTV vetoes
EEOSUY see you
EEPPPR pepper
EEPPST steppe
EEPRRS sperre
EEPRRU repure
EEPRSS preses
sperse
EEPRST pester
preset
EEPRSU persue
peruse
EEPRSV vesper✧
EEPRSW spewer
EEPRTT petter
EEPRTU repute
EEPRTW pewter
EEPRTX expert
EEPRTY re-type
EEPRUV prevue
EEPSSS sepses
EEPSTT septet
EEPSTY steepy
EEPSWY sweepy
EEPTTU puttee
EEQRUU queuer
EEQSTU queest
EEQUXY exequy
EERRST rester
EERRSV revers
server
verser
EERRTT terret
EERRTU ureter
EERRTV revert
EERRUV rêveur
EERRVY revery
verrey
EERSSV Sèvres
EERSTT setter
street✧
tester
EERSTU retuse
Sûreté
EERSTV revest
sterve
Treves
verset
EERSTW stewer
sweert
wester✧
EERSTX exsert
EERSTY reesty
steery
yester
EERSTZ zester
EERSVW swerve
EERSVY severy
EERSXX Xerxes
EERTTT tetter
EERTTW wetter
EERTTX texter
EERTUV vertue
EERTUY tuyère
EERTVV vervet
EERTVX vertex
EERTWY twyere
EERUVX Evreux
EESSSY yesses
EESSTT sestet
testes
tsetse
EESSTW sweets
EESSWX Wessex
EESTTU suttee
EESTTX sextet
EESTTZ tzetse
EESTWY sweety✧
EETTVY Yvette
EETTZZ tzetze
EFFGIR griffe
EFFGIU guffie
EFFGIY effigy
EFFGOR goffer
EFFGOT get off
EFFHOT the off
EFFIIR iffier
EFFILP piffle
EFFILR riffle
EFFILS siffle
EFFINR niffer
EFFINT infeft
EFFIRS Fifers
EFFKOY off-key
EFFLMU muffle
EFFLOP poffle
EFFLOT let off
let-off
EFFLRU ruffle
EFFNOO one-off
EFFOPU pouffe
EFFORX forfex
EFFOST offset
set off
set-off
EFFPRU puffer
EFFRSU suffer
EFFTTU tuffet
EFGGOR fogger
EFGINO Gefion
EFGINR finger
fringe
EFGIOS fogies
EFGIRU figure
EFGLLU flugel
flügel
EFGLNU engulf
EFGLOR golfer
EFGOOR forego
EFGORR forger
EFGORT forget
EFGORW gowfer
EFGOSY fogeys
EFGRSU Fergus
EFHILS elfish
EFHIRS fisher✧
sherif
EFHISS fishes✧
EFHIST fetish
EFHLSY fleshy
shelfy
EFHLTY The Fly
EFHMUY humefy
EFHOOR hoofer
EFHORT fother
EFHRRU Führer
EFIINT finite
EFIIRS Sifrei
EFIIVX fixive
EFIKLO folkie
EFIKNR knifer
EFIKRY fikery
EFIKSV five Ks
EFILLR filler
refill
EFILLT fillet
EFILMT flemit
EFILNO olefin
on file
EFILNT infelt
EFILNY finely
Finley
lenify
EFILOS filose
EFILPP fipple
EFILPR pilfer
EFILRR rifler
EFILRS rifles
EFILRT filter
filtre
lifter
trifle

EFILRU	ireful
EFILRY	rifely
EFILSS	fissle
EFILST	itself
	stifle
EFILSU	fusile
EFILTU	futile
EFILWY	wifely
EFILZZ	fizzle
EFIMRR	firmer
EFIMRT	fremit
EFINNR	finner
EFINNU	unfine
EFINNY	Finney
EFINOR	on fire
EFINPR	perfin
EFINRY	finery
EFINST	feints
	infest
EFINSU	infuse
EFINZZ	fizzen
EFIOOR	Roofie
EFIOOT	footie
EFIORS	froise
EFIORT	trofie
EFIORW	frowie
EFIORX	orifex
EFIOST	softie
EFIPRU	fire up
EFIPRX	prefix
EFIRST	sifter
	strife
EFIRSU	Furies
	surfie
EFIRTT	fitter
	titfer
EFIRTY	ferity
	freity
EFIRUX	fixure
EFIRVY	verify
EFIRZZ	fizzer
EFISTY	feisty
EFKKOR	Fokker
EFKLUY	flukey
EFKORR	forker
EFLLOT	flotel
EFLLOW	fellow✧
EFLLRU	fuller
EFLLTY	let fly
EFLMSY	myself
EFLNNU	funnel
EFLNOT	Teflon®
EFLNOY	felony
EFLNPU	penful
EFLNSU	unself
EFLNTU	fluent
	netful
	unfelt
EFLOOT	footle
EFLOOZ	foozle
EFLORR	rolfer✧
EFLORS	Flores
EFLORT	floret
	lofter
EFLORU	furole
EFLORW	flower
	fowler✧
	reflow
	wolfer
EFLORX	flexor
EFLOSU	flouse
EFLOUW	woeful
EFLPPU	pepful
EFLPRU	purfle
EFLRTU	fluter
EFLRUU	rueful
EFLRUX	reflux
EFLRUY	fleury
EFLSUU	useful
EFLTWY	wet-fly
EFLUZZ	fuzzle
EFMNOR	enform
EFMNOT	foment
EFMNRU	frenum
EFMORR	former
	reform
	re-form
EFMRSU	femurs
EFMSTU	fumets
EFMTUY	tumefy
EFNOOR	for one
EFNOOT	of note
EFNORR	forren
	froren
	frorne
EFNORS	Fresno
EFNORZ	frozen
EFNOST	soften
EFNRTU	turfen
EFNRYZ	frenzy
EFNSTU	funest
EFOORR	re-roof
	roofer
EFOORT	foetor
	footer
	refoot
	tofore
EFOORW	woofer
EFOORY	of yore
EFOPRT	forpet
EFOPST	Eftpos
EFORRU	furore
EFORRV	fervor
EFORST	forest
	fortes
	foster✧
EFORSU	fueros
EFORTU	fouter
	foutre
EFOSTU	foetus
EFPSSU	fess up
EFRRSU	surfer
EFRRTU	returf
EFRRUU	fureur
EFRSSU	fusser
EFRTTU	tufter
EFRTTY	fretty
EFRTUU	future
EFRTUX	frutex
EFSTTU	fustet
EGGGIL	giggle
EGGGLO	goggle
EGGGLU	guggle
EGGGNO	eggnog
EGGHIL	higgle
EGGHOR	hogger
EGGHOT	hogget
EGGIIL	gilgie
EGGIIP	piggie
EGGIJL	jiggle
EGGIJR	jigger
EGGILN	gingle
	niggle
EGGILO	loggie
EGGILR	ligger
EGGILT	giglet
EGGILU	luggie
EGGILW	wiggle
EGGIMO	moggie
EGGINR	ginger✧
EGGIOR	Reggio
EGGIPU	puggie
EGGIRR	rigger
EGGIRT	Tigger
EGGJLO	joggle
EGGJLU	juggle
EGGJOR	jogger
EGGLOO	google
EGGLOR	logger
EGGLOT	goglet
	toggle
EGGLOW	woggle
EGGLPU	puggle
EGGLRU	gurgle
	lugger
EGGMRU	mugger
EGGNRU	grunge
EGGNTU	nugget
EGGORS	gregos
EGGORT	gorget
EGGORY	Georgy
EGGRRU	rugger
EGGRTU	tugger
EGHHIR	higher✧
EGHHIT	eighth
	height
EGHHIU	Hughie
EGHHSU	Hughes
	sheugh
EGHHUW	wheugh
EGHIIN	hieing
EGHIKS	skeigh
EGHIKT	keight
EGHILS	sleigh
EGHINO	hoeing
EGHINW	hewing
	whinge
EGHINX	hexing
EGHIOT	hogtie
EGHIRS	sigher
EGHIST	eights
EGHITW	weight
EGHITY	eighty
EGHLMP	phlegm
EGHLNT	length
EGHLOS	seghol
EGHLPU	Guelph
	pleugh
EGHLUY	hugely
EGHMMO	megohm
EGHMOO	go home
EGHNOP	hog-pen
EGHNOS	Goshen
EGHNOU	enough
EGHNRU	hunger
EGHOPR	gopher✧
EGHORZ	Herzog
EGHOTT	ghetto
EGHRSU	gusher
EGIIJL	jilgie
EGIILL	gillie
EGIILR	girlie
EGIIMN	gemini✧
EGIINN	ingine
EGIINP	pieing
EGIINR	girnie
EGIINT	ignite
EGIITW	tie-wig
EGIJLN	jingle
EGIKLN	kingle
EGIKLR	kilerg
EGIKNP	Peking
EGILLN	leglin
	lingel
	lingle
EGILLR	grille
EGILLT	gillet
EGILLU	ligule
EGILMN	mingle
EGILMP	megilp
EGILMT	gimlet
EGILNN	ginnel
EGILNO	eloign
	legion
EGILNP	Li Peng
	pingle
	pin-leg
EGILNR	girnel
	linger
EGILNS	single
EGILNT	tingle
EGILNU	lungie
EGILNZ	zingel
EGILOO	goolie

EGILOP	epilog
EGILOR	gloire
EGILOU	ouglie
EGILOV	go live
EGILPR	griple
EGILPT	piglet✧
EGILPY	gilpey
EGILRS	Glires
	grilse
EGILRU	gluier
	guiler
	ligure
	reguli
EGILRV	verlig
EGILST	legist
EGILTU	glutei
EGIMMR	gimmer
	megrim
EGIMMS	gimmes
EGIMNO	Imogen
EGIMNR	germin
	minger
EGIMNY	geminy
EGIMOS	egoism
EGIMRS	Grimes
EGIMST	stigme
EGINNO	Onegin
EGINNR	enring
	ginner
EGINNS	ensign
EGINNU	ingénu
EGINOP	epigon✧
	pigeon
EGINOR	eringo
	ignore
	Origen
	region
EGINOS	ingoes
	soigné
EGINOT	toeing
EGINOW	wigeon
EGINPP	pigpen
EGINPR	Pinger®
	pinger
EGINPS	gipsen
EGINPY	pyeing
EGINRR	erring
	girner
	ringer
EGINRS	Ingres
	resign
	re-sign
	signer
	singer
EGINRT	engirt
EGINRU	rueing
EGINRW	winger
EGINRZ	zinger
EGINSS	gneiss
EGINST	ingest
	signet
EGINSU	genius✧
EGINSW	sewing
	swinge
EGINTU	gunite
EGINTW	twinge
EGINVX	vexing
EGINZZ	gizzen
EGIOOR	gooier
EGIOOS	soogie
EGIOPR	perogi
	porgie
EGIORR	gorier
EGIORS	orgies
EGIORT	goiter
	goitre
EGIOST	egoist
	stogie
EGIOTY	egoity
EGIPPR	grippe
EGIPRR	griper
EGIPRS	gripes
EGIPUV	give up
EGIRRV	virger
EGIRSU	guiser
	regius
EGIRSY	griesy
	grysie
EGIRTV	grivet
EGIRTY	tigery
EGIRUZ	guizer
EGISSU	gussie✧
EGISTU	gustie
EGJLNU	jungle
EGJLTU	juglet
EGKMSU	muskeg
EGKNOY	kyogen
EGKNTU	Tengku
EGLLOR	goller
EGLLOS	solgel
	sol-gel
EGLLOW	go well
EGLLRU	guller
EGLLTU	gullet
EGLLUY	gulley
EGLNNU	gunnel
EGLNOP	plonge
EGLNOR	longer
EGLNOU	lounge
EGLNPU	plunge
EGLNSU	gunsel
EGLNSY	Glenys
EGLNTU	englut
	gluten
EGLNTY	gently
EGLNUU	unglue
EGLOOY	gooley
EGLOPR	proleg
EGLOPS	gospel
EGLORU	Regulo®
	regulo
EGLORV	glover
	grovel
EGLORW	glower
EGLOST	goslet
EGLOSY	gelosy
EGLOUV	voulge
EGLOUY	eulogy
EGLPRU	gulper
EGLRTU	gurlet
EGLRUY	guyler
EGLRYY	greyly
EGLTTU	guttle
EGLTUU	Telugu
EGLUZZ	guzzle
EGMNOR	monger
	morgen
EGMNOS	gnomes
EGMNOT	Egmont
EGMNOY	gemony
	myogen
EGMNTU	Gnetum
	nutmeg
EGMORT	gromet
EGMORU	morgue
EGMOSU	ugsome
EGMOSY	Geomys
EGMRTU	tergum
EGNNOO	non-ego
EGNNOU	guenon
EGNNPU	pen-gun
EGNNRU	gunner
EGNNYY	gynney
EGNOOR	Oregon
	orgone
	orogen
EGNOOT	gentoo✧
EGNOOY	gooney
	oogeny
EGNOPR	Progne
EGNOPS	sponge
EGNOPW	gowpen
EGNORV	govern
EGNORY	eryngo
	Geryon
	groyne
EGNOSS	gnoses
	segnos
EGNOTT	gotten
EGNOTU	tongue
EGNOXY	oxygen
EGNPRU	repugn
EGNPSU	spunge
EGNPUX	expugn
EGNRTU	gunter
	gurnet
	urgent
EGNRTY	gentry
EGNRUY	gurney
EGNSUU	ungues
EGNUVY	ungyve
EGOOPY	poogye
EGOORV	go over
	groove
	overgo
EGOOSS	gooses
EGOOST	stooge
EGOOSY	goosey
EGOPPT	peg-top
EGOPRR	groper
EGOPTU	peg out
EGORRS	groser
EGORRU	roguer
EGORRW	grower
EGORSS	ogress
EGORST	groset
	storge
EGORSU	grouse
	rugose
EGORSY	gyrose
EGORSZ	grosze
EGORTV	grovet
EGORUV	voguer
EGOSTW	go west
EGOSTY	stogey
EGOSYZ	zygose
EGOTTU	get out
	get-out
	goutte
EGOTUV	veg out
EGOTYZ	zygote
EGOUVY	voguey
EGPRRU	purger
EGPRSU	spurge
	super G
EGPRUW	upgrew
EGRSTU	gutser
EGRSYY	gryesy
EGRTTU	gutter
EGRTUZ	gutzer
EGSSTU	gusset
EHHIKS	sheikh
EHHIRT	hither
EHHNPY	hyphen
EHHOTW	the who✧
EHHOWW	eh whow
EHHRST	thresh
EHHRSU	husher
EHIIJM	Himeji
EHIIMS	meishi
EHIIPP	hippie
EHIIST	histie
	Shiite
EHIJSW	Jewish
EHIKKS	kishke
EHIKMV	mikveh
EHIKNO	honkie
EHIKNS	Neskhi
EHIKPR	kephir
EHIKPU	hike up
EHIKRS	shreik
	shriek
	shrike
EHIKSS	shikse

Words marked ✧ can also be spelled with one or more capital letters

EHILLL Hillel
EHILMO Elohim
EHILMP Philem
EHILMU helium
humlie
EHILNS elshin
EHILOS Helios
isohel
EHILOT eolith
EHILPR hirple
EHILRS hirsel
hirsle
relish
EHILRT Hitler
lither
EHILST tehsil
EHILSV elvish
EHILSW whiles
EHILTV thivel
EHIMMS immesh
EHIMNO home in
EHIMNR menhir
EHIMNS in mesh
inmesh
EHIMNU inhume
EHIMRS Rheims
EHIMRT hermit
mither
EHIMRU humeri
EHIMST theism
Themis
EHIMTU humite
EHINNN hennin
EHINNS shinne
EHINOR heroin
Hoenir
Hornie
on hire
EHINPP hippen
EHINRS shiner
shrine
EHINRW whiner
EHINST sithen
EHINSW newish
EHINTW whiten
EHINTY thyine
EHINTZ zenith
EHINUV unhive
EHIOPS Sophie
EHIOPT Ethiop
ophite✧
EHIORS hosier
EHIORT heriot
EHIOTT hottie
EHIPPR hipper
EHIPRS perish
reship
seriph
EHIPUV hive up
EHIQUY qui-hye
EHIRST theirs
EHIRSV shiver
shrive
EHIRSW wisher
EHIRSX rhexis
EHIRTT hitter
tither
EHIRTV thrive
EHIRTW wither
writhe
EHIRTZ zither
EHISST shiest
sithes
thesis
EHISSV shives
EHISSW wishes
EHISTT theist
EHISTU tushie
EHISTW whites
EHITTW tewhit
EHITWY whitey✧
EHITWZ The Wiz
EHJOPS joseph✧
EHJORS josher
EHJORT Jethro
EHKLPT klepht
EHKLWY whelky
EHKMNO Ken Hom
EHKNOR honker
EHKNRU hunker
EHKOOR hooker
EHKOOY hookey
EHKOPU hoke up
EHKORS kosher
EHKORW howker
EHKORY horkey
EHKOTY hot key
EHKPTU Phuket
EHKRSU husker
EHLLOR holler
EHLLOS hellos
EHLLOW Howell
EHLLSY shelly
EHLLTY they'll
EHLMMU hummel
EHLMNU unhelm
EHLMOP phloem
EHLMOS Holmes
EHLMOY homely
EHLMPU Phleum
EHLMTY methyl
EHLNOP holpen
phenol
EHLNPY phenyl
EHLOOS shoole
EHLOOY hooley
EHLOPP hopple
EHLOPU hole up
EHLORW howler
EHLOST hostel
EHLOSU housel
EHLOSV shovel
EHLOTT the lot
EHLOTW howlet
thowel
EHLRRU hurler
EHLRSU lusher
EHLRSY Sheryl
EHLRTU hurtle
Luther
EHLRUY hurley
EHLSTT shtetl
EHLSTU hustle
sleuth
EHLSTY shelty
EHLSVY shelvy
EHMMRU hummer
EHMNOP phenom
EHMNOT moneth
EHMNPU humpen✧
EHMORS mosher
EHMORT mother
EHMOSS shmoes
EHMPRU humper
EHMRRY rhymer
EHMRST therms
EHMRSU musher
rheums
EHMRUY rheumy
EHNNRU hen run
EHNNSU Hun Sen
EHNNUW unhewn
EHNOOP no-hope
EHNOOR heroon
EHNOOV hooven
EHNOPR phoner
EHNOPS phones
'phones
EHNOPU euphon
EHNOPY phoney
EHNORR horner
EHNORS nosher
senhor✧
EHNORT hornet
throne
EHNOST honest
so then
Stheno
the Son
EHNOSU unshoe
EHNOTW the now
EHNRSU rushen
EHNRSY henrys
EHNRTU hunter
EHNRVY Henry V
EHNSTU The Sun
EHOOOP hoopoe
EHOOPR hooper
EHOOPY phooey
EHOORT Heorot
hooter
EHOORV Hoover®
hoover✧
EHOOST soothe
EHOOSV hooves
EHOPPR hopper
EHOPRT pother
thorpe✧
EHOPRU uphroe
EHOPTT Tophet
EHORRS shorer
EHORRT rhetor
rother
EHORSS horses
shores
EHORST tosher
EHORSV shover
shrove✧
EHORSW shower
EHORSY horsey
EHORTT hotter
tother
t'other
EHORTU outher
EHORTV throve
EHORTW throwe
EHORTX exhort
EHORTY theory
EHORTZ zeroth
EHOSSU houses
EHOSTT shotte
EHOSUY housey
EHPPUY hype up
EHPRSU pusher
EHPRSY sphery
sypher
EHPRYZ zephyr✧
EHRRSU rusher
EHRRSY sherry✧
EHRRTU hurter
EHRRWY wherry
EHRSSU rhesus
rushes
EHRSTY thyrse
EHRTUW wuther
EHSSTU tusseh
EHSSTY shyest
sythes
EHSTTY Tethys
EIIJMM Jimmie
EIIKLL Killie
EIIKLS silkie
EIIKLT kiltie
EIIKLW Wilkie
EIIKNP pinkie✧
EIIKNR inkier
keirin
EIIKSV skivie
EIIKTT Kittie
EIILLM Millie
EIILLN nielli
EIILLP illipe
EIILLT illite
EIILLW Willie

EIILMS simile
EIILMU milieu
EIILNN in line
in-line
EIILNP pile in
EIILNR inlier
nirlie
EIILNS inisle
sileni✧
EIILNT lintie
EIILNV live in
live-in
EIILOT iolite
EIILPP lippie
EIILRV virile
EIILRX elixir
EIILSV visile
EIILZZ Lizzie
EIIMMT Timmie
EIIMNN minnie✧
EIIMNT in time
intime
EIIMPS impies
EIIMST stimie
EIINNP pinnie
EIINNR rein in
EIINNT intine
tinnie
EIINNW in wine
Winnie
EIINNX nix-nie
EIINOS ionise✧
EIINOZ ionize✧
EIINPP Nippie
pipe in
EIINPR pirnie
EIINPT pinite
tiepin
EIINQU quinie
EIINRT intire
tinier
EIINRV Irvine
EIINRW wire in
EIINSS seisin
EIINST seniti
tinies
EIINSZ seizin
EIINTV invite
EIINVV Vivien
EIINVW in view
EIIPPY yippie
EIIPRS Pieris
EIIPRT periti
pitier
EIIRSS irises
EIIRSV visier
EIIRTX Trixie
EIIRVZ vizier
EIIRWZ wizier
EIISTV visite
EIISVV visive
EIIVZZ vizzie
EIJKNO in-joke
EIJKNR jerkin
jinker
EIJKNT ink-jet
EIJKNU junkie
EIJKST jet ski
jet-ski
EIJLLT jillet
EIJLMS mejlis✧
EIJLTU juliet✧
EIJNNO enjoin
EIJNOR joiner
rejoin
EIJNRU injure
EIJNTY jitney
EIJNUX Jun Xie
EIJRSV Jervis
EIJRTT jitter
tri-jet
EIJSTU Jesuit
EIKKLN kinkle
EIKKOO kookie
EIKKRY yikker
EIKLLR killer
EIKLLY likely
EIKLMN milken
EIKLMR milker
EIKLNN enlink
EIKLNR linker
EIKLNS silken
EIKLNT tinkle
EIKLNU unlike
EIKLNV kelvin✧
EIKLNW welkin
winkle
EIKLRT kilter
kirtle
EIKLSS kissel
EIKLSU Kisleu
EIKLSV Kislev
EIKLTT kittle
EIKMMR kimmer
EIKMNR merkin
EIKMNS misken
EIKMOS Eskimo
smokie
EIKMPU mike up
EIKMRS kermis
EIKMSS kiss-me
EIKMST kismet✧
EIKMSY miskey
EIKMTU kumite
EIKNNO kinone
EIKNOR Kieron
EIKNOV invoke
EIKNPR perkin
EIKNRS sinker
Sir Ken
EIKNRT tinker
EIKNRW winker
Wrekin
EIKNSU sunkie
EIKNSV knives
EIKNSY INS key
Kinsey
EIKNTT kitten
EIKOOR rookie
EIKOPP koppie
EIKOPS pokies
EIKORY yorkie✧
EIKOUY ukiyo-e
EIKPPR kipper
EIKPPT keppit
EIKPRT perk it
EIKPSS spikes
EIKRRS risker
EIKRSS kisser
krises
EIKRST strike
EIKRSV skiver
EIKSTW wisket
EILLLY Lilley
EILLMO mollie
EILLMR miller✧
EILLMT millet✧
EILLMU illume
EILLNO lionel✧
niello
O'Neill
EILLNS sell in
sell-in
EILLNT lentil
lintel
tellin
EILLNW well in
EILLOT oillet
EILLOW lie low
EILLPU pilule
EILLRS siller
EILLRT rillet
tiller
EILLRW willer
EILLST listel
EILLSU ill-use
EILLTT little
EILLTU tuille
EILLTW willet
EILLVY evilly
lively
vilely
EILLWY willey
EILMMR limmer
EILMNO moline
EILMNR limner
merlin
EILMNS simnel
EILMNU lumine
unlime
EILMNV Melvin
EILMNY myelin
EILMOR moiler
EILMOS smoile
EILMOT motile
EILMPP pimple
EILMPR prelim
EILMPS simple
EILMPT limpet
EILMPU pileum
EILMPW wimple
EILMPX implex
EILMRS merils
smiler
EILMRT milter
EILMRU Muriel
EILMRV vermil
EILMSS missel
slimes
EILMST mistle
smilet
EILMSU muesli
EILMSY milsey
smiley
EILMTU telium
EILMTY timely
EILMUV Vimule®
EILMZZ mizzle
EILNNO El Niño
online
on-line
EILNNT linnet
EILNNU unline
EILNNW winnle
EILNNY linney
EILNOO loonie
EILNOP loipen
pinole
EILNOR Elinor
Lorien
neroli
EILNOS esloin
insole
lesion
solein
EILNOT entoil
lionet
Nilote
EILNOV in love
love-in
EILNPP lippen
nipple
EILNPS pensil
Pilsen
spinel
spline
EILNPT leptin
pintle
EILNPU line up
line-up
lupine
up-line
EILNRT linter
EILNST enlist

listen
silent
tinsel
EILNSV sliven
snivel
EILNSY linsey
lysine
EILNTT litten
EILNTU luiten
lutein
untile
EILNTV ventil
EILNTW wintle
EILNTY lenity
EILNUV unlive
unveil
EILNUY lunyie
EILOOR oriole
EILOOT oolite✧
EILOPS pilose
EILOPT piolet
polite
EILORS oilers
EILORT loiter
toiler
EILORU lourie
EILORV Oliver!
oliver✧
violer
EILORW Lowrie
EILORY oilery
EILOSU Louise
EILOSV solive
EILOTT Lottie
toilet
EILOTU outlie
EILOTV olivet
violet
EILOVY Yeovil
EILPPR ripple
EILPPS sipple
EILPPT tipple
EILPPU pile up
pile-up
EILPRS lisper
pliers
EILPRT let rip
triple
EILPRU rile up
EILPRY ripely
EILPSS plissé
EILPST stipel
EILPSU epulis
pileus
EILPSV pelvis
EILPTU puteli
EILPZZ pizzle
EILRST lister✧
EILRSV silver
sliver
EILRSY Eirlys
EILRTT litter
tilter
titler
EILRTU rutile
EILRTY tilery
EILRVY livery
verily
EILSSS lisses
EILSST sliest
EILSSY Sisley
EILSTT stilet
titles
EILSTU Iseult
sutile
EILSVW swivel
EILSWY wisely
EILSXY sexily
EILSZZ sizzle
EILTTT tittle
EILTTU titule
EILTTV vittle
EILTTY titely
EILTVY levity
EILUVV luvvie
EILVVY vively
EILVWY viewly
EIMMNR nimmer
EIMMNU immune
EIMMOR memoir
EIMMRS merism
simmer
EIMMRU immure
EIMMRZ Zimmer®
EIMMST semmit
EIMMSY mimsey
EIMNNX meninx
EIMNOO Moonie
EIMNOP impone
EIMNOR merino
EIMNOS eonism
monies
Simeon
Simone
EIMNOT no time
on time
EIMNOV move in
EIMNPT piment
EIMNRS Mersin
EIMNRT minter
remint
EIMNRU murine
Nerium
EIMNRV vermin
EIMNSS mess in
EIMNTT mitten
EIMNTU minuet
minute
munite
mutine
EIMNTY enmity
EIMNUX xenium
EIMNZZ mizzen
EIMOOR roomie
EIMOPS impose
EIMOPT optime
EIMORS isomer
moiser
rimose
EIMOSS mossie
EIMOST somite
EIMOSU mousie
EIMOSV movies
EIMOSX exomis
EIMOTV motive
EIMOTY moiety
EIMOZZ mozzie
EIMPRR primer
EIMPRS simper
EIMPRT permit
EIMPRU impure
umpire
EIMPRX premix
EIMPSU sepium
EIMPTU impute
uptime
EIMPUY yumpie✧
EIMRRT retrim
trimer
EIMRSS remiss
EIMRST merits
mister✧
smiter
EIMRSV verism
vermis
EIMRSY misery✧
EIMRTU iterum
EIMSSS Misses
EIMSST misset
tmesis
EIMSSU misuse
EIMSSX sexism
EIMSTY stymie
EIMSUV musive
EIMTYZ zymite
EINNNR rennin
EINNOO ionone
EINNOT intone
tone in
EINNPR pinner
EINNPT pinnet
tenpin
EINNRS sinner
EINNRT intern
tinner
EINNRU unrein
EINNRW winner
EINNST sennit
sinnet
tennis
EINNTT intent
EINNTU in tune
tune in
EINNTV invent
EINNTY ninety
EINOOT toonie
EINOPP pepino
EINOPR orpine
pioner
proine
rope in
EINOPT pointe
pontie
EINOPW pownie
EINOPY pioney
EINORR ironer
Renoir
EINORS senior
soneri
EINORT norite
orient✧
EINORV renvoi
EINORZ zero in
EINOSS enosis
essoin
noesis
noises
ossein
sonsie
EINOST Nesiot
on-site
Tonies
EINOSV Nivôse
EINOSW nowise
EINOTT tonite
EINOTV vote in
EINOTW townie
EINOVW inwove
on view
EINPPR nipper✧
EINPPS pepsin
EINPPW wippen
EINPRS sniper
EINPRT nipter
Pinter
pterin
EINPRU pruine
punier
purine
rein up
unripe
EINPRY pinery
EINPSS snipes
EINPST in step
instep
spinet
step in
step-in
EINPSU puisne
supine
EINPTT pitten
EINQSU sequin
EINQTU queint
quinte

EINQUU unique
EINQUZ quinze
EINRRS rinser
EINRRU ruiner
EINRSS Sirens
EINRST insert
sinter
Strine
EINRSU insure
rusine
ursine
EINRSV versin
EINRSY Erinys
EINRTT tinter
EINRTU triune
tunier
uniter
EINRTV invert
virent
EINRTW twiner
winter
EINRTY nitery
EINRUW unwire
EINRVW wivern
EINRVY vinery
EINRWY winery
EINSSS nisses
EINSSU Senusi
EINSTU intuse
tenuis
EINSTV invest
EINSTW wisent
EINSTY tinsey
EINSTZ Zenist
EINSUW unwise
EINSUX unisex
EINSWY sinewy
winsey
EINTTU tenuti
EINTTY entity
EINUVW unwive
EIOOPS eo ipso
EIOOPW woopie✧
EIOORT toorie
EIOOST otiose
EIOPRR ropier
EIOPRS poiser
EIOPRU pourie
EIOPSS possie
EIOPST postie
sopite
EIOPTT tiptoe
EIORRS rosier
EIORRT rioter
EIORST roesti
sortie
tiroes
triose
EIORSV vireos
virose
EIORSX orexis
EIORSY osiery
EIORTU tourie
EIOSTV soviet✧
EIOTTT tottie
EIOTTU toutie
EIOTUV outvie
EIOTVV votive
EIPPPU pipe up
EIPPRR ripper
EIPPRS sipper
EIPPRT tipper
EIPPRU purpie
EIPPRY yipper
EIPPRZ zipper
EIPPST sippet
EIPPTT tippet
EIPPTX Tippex
Tipp-Ex®
EIPPUW wipe up
EIPPUY yuppie✧
EIPQTU piquet✧
EIPRRS priser
EIPRRZ prizer
EIPRST esprit
pierst
priest
Pteris
sitrep
sprite
stripe
EIPRSU rise up
uprise
EIPRSW swiper
EIPRTT pitter
EIPRTV privet
EIPRTX extirp
EIPRTY pyrite
tripey
EIPRUW wire up
EIPRXY expiry
EIPSSS sepsis
speiss
EIPSST stipes
EIPSSW swipes
EIPSTT pet-sit
EIPSUW wise up
EIPSUZ size up
EIPSWY swipey
EIPTTU puttie
EIQRSU risque
risqué
squier
squire
EIQRTU requit
EIQRUV quiver
EIQTUY equity✧
EIRRST stirre
EIRRTT ritter
territ
EIRRTW writer
EIRRVY rivery
EIRRZZ rizzer
EIRSST resist
sister
EIRSSU issuer
uresis
EIRSTT sitter
triste
EIRSTV stiver
strive
trevis
verist
EIRSTW sweirt
wriest
EIRSVV vivers
vivres
EIRTTT titter
EIRTTV trivet
EIRTTW witter
EIRTUV virtue
EIRTVY verity✧
EISSSW Wessis
EISSTT testis
EISSTU tissue
EISSTV St Ives
EISSTX sexist
EISTTW Sittwe
EISTTY tystie
EISTVW swivet
EISUVZ suivez
EITTTX tettix
EJKLSU Seljuk
EJKNOO no joke
EJKNRU junker✧
EJKNTU junket
EJKOPS Skopje
EJLLOR joller
EJLLOY jolley
EJLORT jolter
EJLORW jowler
EJLOST jostle
EJLSTU justle
EJMOOS mojoes
EJMOST jetsom
EJMPRU jumper
EJNOST jetson
EJNOTT jetton
EJOOSY soojey
EJORSS josser
EJORTT jotter
EJOTTU outjet
EKKOPU pukeko
EKLLSY skelly
EKLMMU kümmel
EKLMSU muskle
skelum
EKLNOS kelson
sloken
EKLNRU lunker
runkle
EKLNST sklent
EKLOOR looker
EKLORU rule OK
EKLOWY low-key
EKLRRU lurker
EKMNOS K-meson
EKMNOY monkey
EKMOOP mopoke
EKMORS smoker
EKMSTU musket
EKNNOR kronen
EKNNOT nekton
EKNNSU sunken
EKNNTU unkent
EKNOPS spoken
EKNORR kroner
EKNORT tonker
EKNORW knower
wroken
EKNORY Orkney
yonker
EKNOUY unyoke
EKNPTU unkept
EKNRTU Tunker
EKNSTU sunket
EKOOQU quooke
EKOORR korero
EKOORT retook
EKOPRR porker
proker
EKOPSY pokeys
EKORRW rework
worker
EKORRY yorker
EKORST stoker
stroke
EKORTX trek-ox
EKORWY ywroke
EKOSST stokes
EKPPRU perk up
EKRRSY skerry
skryer
EKRSTU tusker
EKRTUY turkey
EKRUVY kurvey
ELLLOR loller
ELLLOZ lozell
ELLMOW mellow
ELLMRU muller
ELLMSY smelly
ELLMTU mullet
ELLMUV vellum
ELLMUY mulley
ELLNOP pollen
ELLNOR enroll
ELLNOS sell on
ELLNOV vellon
ELLNOW nowell✧
ELLNOY lonely
ELLNSU sullen
ELLNSY snelly
ELLNUU lunule
ELLNUW unwell

ELLOOT	Otello
ELLOPR	poller
ELLOPX	pollex
ELLORR	roller✧
ELLORS	soller
	sorell
ELLORT	toller
ELLORW	Orwell
ELLOST	tolsel
	to sell
ELLOSY	solely
ELLOVY	lovely
	volley
ELLOWY	yellow
ELLPRU	puller
ELLPSU	sell up
ELLPTU	pullet
ELLPUW	upwell
	well up
ELLPUY	pulley
ELLSTU	tellus✧
ELMMOP	pommel
ELMMOR	Rommel
ELMMOS	Moslem
ELMMPU	pummel
ELMNOR	merlon
ELMNOS	Lemnos
	solemn
ELMNOT	loment
	melton
	molten
ELMNOY	lemony
	myelon
ELMNPU	lumpen
	plenum
ELMNSU	lumens
ELMNVY	Melvyn
ELMOOP	pomelo
ELMOPU	pumelo
ELMOPY	employ
ELMORS	morsel
ELMORT	Merlot
ELMOST	molest
ELMOSU	mousle
ELMOSY	Mosley
	smoyle
ELMOTT	Mel Ott
	mottle
ELMOTY	motley
ELMOUV	volume
ELMOXY	oxymel
ELMOZZ	mozzle
ELMPPU	peplum
ELMPRU	lumper
	replum
	rumple
ELMRSU	lemurs
ELMRTY	myrtle✧
	termly
ELMSSU	mussel
ELMTUU	mutuel
	mutule
ELMTUY	mutely
ELMUZZ	muzzle
ELNNNO	Lennon
ELNNOS	nelson✧
ELNNRU	runnel
ELNNTU	tunnel✧
ELNOOS	loosen
ELNOOT	looten
ELNOOW	woolen
ELNOPT	lepton
ELNOPU	loupen
ELNOPY	openly
	poleyn
ELNORS	norsel
ELNORT	lentor
ELNOSS	lesson
	no less
ELNOST	lentos
	stolen
	telson
ELNOSU	ensoul
	nousle
	Olenus
ELNOSV	novels
	sloven
	volens
ELNOSW	new sol
ELNOTT	tonlet
ELNOUV	unlove
ELNOUZ	zonule
ELNOVY	lenvoy
ELNOWY	Olwyne
ELNOZZ	nozzle
ELNPPU	luppen
ELNPST	splent
ELNPTU	penult
ELNPTY	pentyl
	plenty
ELNRSU	nursle
ELNRTU	runlet
ELNRUU	unrule
ELNRUZ	luzern
ELNSSU	unless
ELNSXY	lynxes
ELNSYY	Lynsey
ELNTTU	lutten
	nutlet
ELNTTY	nettly
ELNTXY	nextly
ELNUZZ	nuzzle
ELOOPR	looper
ELOOPT	pootle
ELOORT	looter
	retool
	rootle
	tooler
ELOOSV	looves
ELOOSW	woosel
ELOOSZ	zeloso
ELOOTT	tootle
ELOPPP	popple
ELOPPR	lopper
	propel
ELOPPS	Pelops
	peplos
ELOPPT	topple
ELOPPU	poulpe
ELOPPY	polype
ELOPRR	proler
ELOPRS	splore
ELOPRT	petrol
ELOPRV	plover
ELOPRX	plexor
ELOPRY	pelory
ELOPSU	poules
	souple
ELOPTT	pottle
ELOPTU	tupelo
ELORRS	sorrel
ELORRW	worrel
ELORSS	lessor
ELORST	ostler
	sterol
	torsel
ELORSU	louser
ELORSV	solver
ELORSY	sorely
	Sorley
ELORTT	tolter
ELORTU	elutor
	outler
	troule
ELORTV	revolt
ELORTW	trowel
	wortle
ELORTY	troely
ELORUV	louver
	louvre✧
	velour
ELORVW	wolver
ELORVY	overly
	volery
ELORWY	lowery
	owlery
ELOSSU	louses
	soleus
ELOSTU	solute
	tousle
ELOSTW	lowest
ELOSTY	tolsey
ELOSVW	vowels
	wolves
ELOSWY	Wolsey
ELOSXY	xylose
ELOSZZ	sozzle
ELOTTU	let out
	let-out
	outlet
ELOTTY	tylote
ELOTUV	volute
ELOTUZ	touzle
ELOTWY	owelty
ELOTYZ	tolzey
ELOWYY	yowley
ELPPRU	pulper
	purple
	repulp
ELPPSU	peplus
	supple
ELPQUU	pulque
ELPRRU	purler
ELPRTY	peltry
	pertly
ELPRUV	pulver
ELPRUY	purely
ELPSSU	pluses
	pussel
ELPSUV	Vulpes
ELPSUX	plexus
	suplex
ELPSUY	spulye
ELPUZZ	puzzel
	puzzle
ELRSSU	russel
ELRSTU	luster
	lustre
	result
	rustle
	sutler
	ulster✧
ELRSUY	surely
ELRSYY	syrlye
ELRTTU	turtle
ELRTTY	tetryl
ELRUWY	wurley
ELSSTU	tussle
ELSSTY	slyest
ELSTTU	suttle
ELSTTY	stylet
ELUWZZ	wuzzle
EMMMOT	mommet
EMMMRU	mummer
EMMNNO	Memnon
	mnemon
EMMNOT	moment
	montem
EMMNTU	mentum
EMMORY	memory
EMMORZ	momzer
EMMOSU	mousmé
EMMOYZ	zymome
EMMPRU	mumper
EMMRRU	rummer
EMMRSU	summer
EMMSUU	museum
EMNOOR	mooner
	no more
EMNOPY	eponym
EMNORS	sermon
EMNORT	mentor
	Merton
	montre

EMNORV	Morven
EMNOST	mentos
	Ostmen
EMNOSY	moneys
EMNOTY	etymon
EMNOXY	exonym
EMNPSU	pensum
EMNRRU	murren
EMNRSU	Mensur
	rumens
EMNRVY	Mervyn
EMNSSU	sensum
EMOORR	roomer
EMOORS	morose
	Romeos
EMOORT	mooter
EMOORX	Exmoor
EMOOSS	osmose
EMOPPR	mopper
EMOPPT	moppet
EMOPPY	pompey✧
EMOPRR	romper
EMOPRS	Merops
EMOPRT	pro tem
	trompe
EMOPRU	Euro-MP
EMOPRY	mopery
EMOPST	tempos
EMOPUV	move up
EMOQSU	mosque
EMORRT	termor
	tremor
EMORRW	wormer
EMORST	métros✧
	motser
EMORSU	mouser
EMORSY	Mysore
EMORTU	mouter
EMOSSU	mousse
	smouse
EMOSUY	mousey
EMOSZZ	mezzos
EMOTTT	motett
EMPPRU	pumper
EMPPTU	muppet
EMPRRU	Rumper
EMPSSU	mess up
	mess-up
EMPSTU	septum
EMRRUY	murrey
EMRSSS	Messrs
EMRSSU	serums
EMRSTU	muster
	stumer
EMRTTU	mutter
EMSSTY	system✧
ENNNOP	pennon
ENNNOT	non-net
ENNOOR	nooner
ENNOOS	no-noes
ENNOPT	ponent
ENNORU	neuron
ENNORV	Vernon
ENNORW	renown✧
ENNOST	sonnet
	stonen
	stonne
	tennos
	tenson
ENNOSV	ven'son
ENNOTW	newton
ENNOTZ	tenzon
ENNOVY	Yvonne
ENNPRU	punner
ENNPTU	punnet
	unpent
ENNRRU	runner
ENNRST	Nernst
ENNRTU	runnet
	unrent
ENNRUW	wunner
ENNSTU	unnest
	unsent
ENNSUW	unsewn
ENNTTU	untent
ENNTUU	untune
ENOOOZ	Eozoon
ENOOPR	operon
ENOORS	seroon
	sooner
ENOORT	enroot
ENOOSZ	snooze
ENOOTW	one-two
ENOPPU	open up
	unpope
ENOPRR	perron
ENOPRS	person
ENOPRU	unrope
ENOPRV	proven
ENOPRY	proyne
	pyoner
ENOPST	pontes
	posnet
	step on
ENOPSU	nose up
ENOPTT	potent
ENOPTU	tone up
ENOPWY	powney
ENORRS	snorer
	sorner
ENORRY	ornery
ENORSS	sensor
ENORST	Nestor
	Sterno®
	stoner
	tensor
ENORSW	worsen
ENORTT	rotten
	to-rent
	torten
	Trento
ENORTU	tenour
ENORTY	nor yet
	Tyrone
ENORUZ	zonure
ENORVY	renvoy
ENORZZ	nozzer
ENOSST	seston
	stenos
	tossen
ENOSSW	sowens
ENOSTT	ostent
	teston
ENOSTX	sexton
ENOSUV	venous
ENOSUW	swoune
ENOSWW	swowne
ENOTTU	tenuto
	Teuton
ENOTTW	tow net
ENPPRU	pre-nup
ENPPTU	pent-up
ENPRRU	pruner
ENPRST	sprent
ENPRSU	spurne
ENPRTU	punter
ENPRUY	penury
ENPRWY	prewyn
ENPSTU	unstep
ENPTTU	putten
ENPTUU	tune up
	tune-up
ENPTUW	unwept
ENRRSU	nurser
ENRRTU	return
	re-turn
	turner✧
ENRSTU	unrest
ENRSTW	strewn
ENRSTY	sentry
ENRSUU	unsure
ENRTTU	nutter
ENRTUU	untrue
ENRUZZ	nuzzer
ENRVWY	wyvern
ENSSSU	Nessus
ENSSTU	sunset
ENTTWY	twenty
EOOPPS	oppose
EOOPRS	porose
EOOPRT	pooter✧
EOOPST	stoope
EOORRT	rooter
	torero
EOORST	torose
EOORTT	tooter
EOOSTW	Soweto
EOOTVX	ex voto
EOPPPR	popper✧
EOPPPT	poppet
EOPPRR	proper
EOPPRT	topper
EOPPRY	popery
	pyrope
EOPQRU	querpo
EOPRRS	proser
	repros
EOPRRT	porter✧
	pretor
	report
EOPRRU	pourer
EOPRRV	prover
EOPRRY	ropery
EOPRSS	posser
EOPRST	poster
	presto
	repost
EOPRSU	poseur
	souper
	uprose
EOPRSW	powers
EOPRSY	osprey
EOPRTT	potter
EOPRTU	pouter
	troupe
EOPRTW	powter
EOPRTX	export
EOPRTY	poetry
EOPRUV	up-over
EOPSST	posset
	ptoses
EOPSSU	opuses
	pousse
	spouse
EOPSTT	set pot
EOPSTX	sexpot
EOPTTU	tote up
	toupet
EOQRTU	quoter
	roquet
	torque
EOQSTU	quotes
EORRRT	rorter
	terror✧
EORRRY	orrery
EORRSS	rosser
EORRST	resort
	retros
	roster
	sorter
	storer
EORRSU	rouser
EORRSW	worser
EORRSY	rosery
EORRTT	retort
	rotter
	torret
EORRTU	retour
	router
	tourer
EORRTV	Trevor
	trover
EORRZZ	rozzer
EORSST	sortes

	stores
	tosser
EORSSU	serous
	sourse
EORSSV	servos
	versos
EORSTT	tortes
EORSTU	ouster
	souter
	touser✧
	trouse
EORSTV	stover
	strove
EORSTW	sowter
	stower
	stowre
	towser✧
EORSTY	oyster
	rosety
	storey
	tyroes
EORSTZ	zoster
EORSWW	wowser
EORTTT	totter
EORTTU	touter
EORTTW	wet rot
EORTTX	extort
EORTUV	ouvert
EORTVX	vortex
EORTWY	towery
EORUVY	voyeur
EOSSSU	souses
	Sousse
EOSSSW	sowsse
EOSSTT	set-tos
	set-to's
EOSSVW	vowess
EOSTTU	outset
	set out
	set-out
EOSUUV	uveous
EOTTUW	wet out
EPPPRY	preppy
EPPPTU	puppet
EPPRSU	supper
EPPSTU	step up
	step-up
EPRRSU	purser
EPRRSY	spryer
EPRRTU	Rupert
EPRSST	sperst
EPRSSU	pusser
EPRSTU	uprest
EPRSUU	pursue
EPRSUW	pursew
EPRTTU	putter
EPRTTY	pretty
EPRTUU	puture
EPRUVY	purvey
EPSTUZ	putzes
EQRTWY	qwerty
ERRSTU	rustre
ERRSUU	usurer
ERRSUY	surrey
ERRTTU	rutter
	turret
ERSSST	stress
ERSSTU	estrus
	russet
	tusser
ERSSTY	syrtes
	tressy
ERSSUU	uruses
ERSSUV	versus
ERSTUU	suture
	uterus
ERSTUV	turves
ERSTUY	surety
ERSTVY	vestry
ERSTWY	wryest
ERSTXY	xyster
ERSUVW	survew
ERSUVY	survey
ERTTUX	urtext
ESTTUY	suetty

F

FFFLUY	fluffy
FFGINO	offing
FFGLOO	log off
	logoff
	log-off
FFHIIS	Fifish
FFHIOS	offish
FFHIOT	hit off
FFHIWY	whiffy
FFHOOP	hop-off
FFHORS	shroff
FFHOSY	shy off
FFIINT	tiffin
FFIIUZ	Uffizi
FFIKLS	skliff
FFILLO	ill off
	ill-off
FFILLU	fulfil
FFILOT	filfot
FFILPS	spliff
FFILTU	fitful
FFIMNU	muffin
FFINNU	nuffin
FFINOP	nip off
FFINPU	puffin
FFINRU	ruffin
FFINSY	sniffy
FFIOPR	rip off
	rip-off
FFIOPT	tip off
	tip-off
FFIOPZ	zip-off
FFIOST	soffit
FFIPSY	spiffy
FFIQSU	squiff
FFISTY	stiffy
FFISUX	suffix
FFLOTY	fylfot
FFLPUY	pluffy
FFNORU	run off
	run-off
FFNRUU	fun fur
FFNSUY	snuffy
FFOOPP	pop off
FFOOPT	top off
FFOPSY	spoffy
FFOPTU	offput
	put off
	put-off
FFPPUU	puff up
FFRRUU	furfur
FFSTUY	stuffy
FGGIIS	fisgig
FGGIIZ	fizgig
FGGORY	froggy✧
FGHILT	flight
FGHIRT	fright
FGHOTU	fought
FGIILN	filing
FGIINN	fining
FGIINR	firing
FGIINX	fixing
FGILNU	ingulf
FGILNY	flying
FGILUY	uglify
FGINOX	foxing
FGINRY	fringy
	frying
FGIORT	frigot
FGIOTU	fig out
FGIOTZ	zoftig
FGJLUU	jugful
FGKNUU	kung fu
FGLMUU	mugful
FGLORU	fulgor
FGLTUU	gutful
FGNORY	gryfon
FGNSUU	fungus
FGNUUY	fu yung
FGOOPU	goof up
FGOORT	forgot
FGOOST	go soft
FHIIKS	fikish
FHIINS	finish
FHILTY	filthy
FHIMUY	humify
FHIOOT	hoof it
FHIRST	shrift
FHIRTT	thrift
FHISSU	hussif
FHISTU	shufti
FHISTY	shifty
FHLOPY	hop-fly
FHLOSU	floush
FHLSUY	flushy
FHNSUU	Fushun
FHOOOR	forhoo
FHOORW	forhow
FHORTU	fourth
FHORTY	forthy
	frothy
FHORWY	for why
	forwhy
FHOUUZ	Fuzhou
FHPRUY	furphy
FHSTUY	shufty
FIIKNR	firkin
FIILLN	fill in
	fill-in
	infill
FIILLP	fillip
FIILSU	filius
FIILVY	vilify
FIIMNR	infirm
FIIMNY	minify
FIIMST	misfit
FIINOR	fiorin
FIINST	in fits
FIIOST	tifosi
FIITXY	fixity
FIIVVY	vivify
FIJLOR	frijol
FIJMTU	Mt Fuji
FIKLSY	flisky
FIKNOS	finsko
FIKRSY	frisky
FILLLU	lifull
FILLNU	in full
FILLPU	fill up
	fill-up
	upfill
FILLRS	frills
FILLRY	frilly
FILLUW	wilful
FILMOU	folium
FILMRY	firmly
FILMSY	flimsy
FILNOR	florin
FILNOW	inflow
FILNOY	if only
FILNSU	sinful
FILNTU	tinful
FILNTY	flinty
FILNUX	influx
FILOOS	folios
FILORT	firlot
FILORV	frivol
FILOSS	fossil
FILOUZ	zufoli
FILPTU	lift up
	uplift
FILRTY	flirty
FIMNOR	inform
FIMNOY	omnify
FIMNRU	unfirm
FIMNUY	munify
FIMOSS	Sofism

FIMPRU firm up
FIMSSU Sufism
FIMSTU Muftis
FINOOS foison
FINOPR fripon
FINORT forint
FINORX fornix
FINOSU fusion
FINOTY notify
FINSTY snifty
FIOOST tifoso
FIOOTT foot it
FIOPRT forpit
profit
FIORRT forrit
FIORST fortis
FIORTY Torify
FIOSSY ossify
FIOTTU fit out
fit-out
outfit
FIPRUY purify
FIPTYY typify
FIRSTT strift
FIRSTU fruits
FIRTUY fruity
FIRYZZ frizzy
FJLOUY joyful
FKLNUY flunky
FKLOSY folksy
FKNOTY konfyt
FKOPRU fork up
FLLLUY lyfull
FLLNOU full-on
FLLOOW follow
FLLOUY foully
FLLPUU full up
FLMNOU muflon
FLMOOR formol
FLMORY formyl
FLNOOU unfool
FLNOOW flow-on
onflow
FLNRUU unfurl
urnful
FLOOUZ zufolo
FLOOYZ floozy
FLOPTU potful
FLOPUU foul up
foul-up
FLOPUW upflow
wolf up
FLORUY floury
FLOSTY softly
FLOTUY fly out
outfly
FLPRUU upfurl
FLPRUY purfly
FLRRUY flurry
FLRSUU sulfur
FMNORU unform
FMOOTY my foot!
FMORSU forums
FMOSUU fumous
FMPRUY frumpy
FNNRUU fun run
FNOOOT on foot
FNOORU unroof
FNOORW for now
FNOOST soft on
FNOSTU unsoft
FNRTUU unturf
FOOPRS proofs
FOORSS fossor
FOORST sort of
FOOTUX outfox
FORRUW furrow
FORSTW frowst
FORSTY frosty
FORSUU rufous
FORSWY frowsy
FORTYY Toryfy
FORWYZ frowzy
FOSTUY fousty

G

GGGIIT giggit
GGGILY giggly
GGGLOY goggly
GGGORY groggy
GGHINO hoggin
GGHNOU gung-ho
GGHORU grough
GGHOTU thuggo
GGIIJJ jigjig
GGIINP piggin
GGIINV giving
GGIIRR grigri
GGIJJO jig-jog
GGIJLY jiggly
GGIKNO gingko
ginkgo
GGILNO ogling
GGILNU gluing
luging
GGILNY niggly
GGILOO gigolo
GGILOT giglot
GGILWY wiggly
GGINNO noggin
GGINOQ qi gong
qigong
GGINOR goring
gringo
GGINRU urging
GGIOOR gorgio
GGITWY twiggy
GGJJUU jug-jug
GGLLOO loglog
log-log
GGLNOO go long
GGLOOO googol
GGLOOY googly
GGMOSY smoggy
GGNOOR gorgon✧
grog-on
GGNRUY grungy
GGOPRU grog-up
GGORST troggs
GGRRUU gru-gru
GGRTUU tugrug
GGSTUY stuggy
GHHHIT highth
GHHILY highly
GHHINO on high
GHHIPU high-up
GHHOSU shough
GHHOTU though
GHIINR hiring
GHIINS Hingis
GHIKNT knight
GHILNO holing
GHILNY nighly
GHILPT plight
GHILST lights
slight
'slight
GHILSU gluish
GHIMNO homing
GHIMST smight
GHIMTY mighty
GHINNO nigh on
GHINST nights
things
GHINSY shying
GHINTY nighty
thingy
GHINWY whingy
GHIOPZ phizog
GHIORS ogrish
GHIORT righto
GHIOSY goyish
GHIPST spight
GHIPTY ypight
GHIQTU quight
GHIRST rights
GHIRTW wright
GHISTT tights
GHITTW twight
GHLOOS golosh
GHLOPU plough✧
GHLOSU slough✧
GHLOTU log-hut
GHLOUY oughly
GHMOTU mought
GHMPRU grumph
GHNNUU unhung
GHNORT throng
GHNOSU shogun
GHNOTU hognut
nought
GHNPUU hung up
GHNRUY hungry
GHNSUY gun-shy
GHOOPT photog
GHOORS sorgho
GHOPTU go phut
GHORTU rought
trough
GHORTW growth
GHORUY roughy
GHOSTU sought
GHPSUU upgush
GIIKLN liking
GIIKNR girkin
GIIKNS skiing
GIIKNT king it
kiting
GIIKNV viking✧
GIILMN liming
GIILNN lignin
lining
GIILNP piling
GIILNR riglin
GIILNT tiling
GIILNV living
GIILOR oil rig
GIILRT It Girl
GIILRV Virgil
GIIMNN mingin'
mining
GIIMNT timing
GIINNN inning
GIINNR ring in
GIINNS sign in
GIINNX Xining
GIINOR origin
GIINOY yogini
GIINPP piping
GIINPW wiping
GIINRS rising
siring
GIINRT tiring
GIINRV virgin✧
GIINRW wiring
GIINSZ sizing
GIINTW wing it
GIIOPR pirogi
GIJLNU jungli
GIJLNY jingly
GIJNOY joying
GIKLNY kingly
GIKNNU unking
GIKNOP poking
GIKNOW Woking
GIKNOY yoking
GIKNSY skying
GIKOPS gopiks
GIKRTU tugrik
GILLNU ulling
GILLOO loligo
GILLOR rigoll
GILLOT ill-got
GILLTU Gullit

Words marked ✧ can also be spelled with one or more capital letters

GILLUY	uglily
GILMNU	lignum
GILMOW	Mowgli
GILMRY	grimly
GILNOO	logion
GILNOP	loping
	poling
GILNOR	loring
GILNOS	losing
GILNOT	lingot
	tiglon
	toling
GILNOV	loving
GILNOW	lowing
GILNPU	plug in
	plug-in
	puling
GILNPY	plying
GILNRU	ruling
GILNSY	Glynis
	singly
GILNTU	luting
	ungilt
GILNTY	tingly
GILORY	gorily
GILRSY	grisly
GILRTY	trigly
GILTUY	guilty
GILTYZ	glitzy
GIMNNO	mignon
GIMNOS	Monsig
GIMNOV	moving
GIMNOW	mowing
GIMNOY	ignomy
GIMNPU	impugn
GIMNRU	ingrum
GIMNSU	musing
GIMOOS	Ogmios
GIMORS	simorg
GIMORT	Gromit
GIMOSS	gismos
GIMOSY	yogism
GIMOSZ	gizmos
GIMOTU	gomuti
GIMRSU	simurg
GINNOO	gonion
GINNOS	nosing
	sign on
GINNOT	toning
GINNOW	woning
GINNOZ	zoning
GINNRU	urning
GINNSU	Ngunis
GINNTU	tuning
GINOOS	isogon
GINOOT	go into
GINOOW	wooing
GINOPR	proign
	roping
GINOPS	pingos
	posing
GINORS	grison
	signor✧
GINORT	trigon
GINORV	roving
GINORW	rowing
GINOSS	gnosis
GINOST	stingo
GINOSW	sowing
GINOTU	outing
GINOTW	towing
GINOTY	toying
GINPPU	upping
GINPRS	spring✧
GINPRU	ring up
GINPRY	prying
GINPSU	sign up
GINPSY	pigsny
	spying
GINPTU	pignut
	pig-nut
GINPTY	typing
GINPUZ	zip gun
GINRRU	runrig✧
GINRST	string
GINRTU	ungirt
GINRTY	trying
GINSTY	stingy
	stying
GINSUU	unguis
GINSUX	six-gun
GINSWY	swingy
GIOORV	vigoro
GIOOTT	Giotto
GIOPSS	gossip
GIOPST	spigot
GIOPTU	pig out
GIORRU	rigour
GIORSU	guiros
GIORSV	Virgos
GIORTU	rig out
	rig-out
GIORUV	vigour
GIOSTU	giusto
GIOTUW	wig out
GIPPRY	grippy
GIPSTY	pigsty
GIRTTY	gritty
GJLNUY	jungly
GJNRUU	gurjun
GKMOOU	gomoku
GKRYYZ	Kyrgyz
GLLMOU	Gollum
GLLMUY	glumly
GLLNOY	longly
GLLOOP	gollop
GLMNOO	mongol✧
GLMOOY	gloomy
GLMOSU	moguls
GLMPSU	glumps
GLMPUY	glumpy
GLMRUY	grumly
GLMSUY	smugly
GLNOOO	oolong
GLNOOS	so long
	so long!
	so-long
GLNOOU	oulong
GLNPUU	unplug
GLNSUY	snugly
GLOOOY	oology
GLOOPR	prolog✧
GLOORY	grooly
GLOOSW	go slow
	go-slow
GLOOTU	log out
	logout
	log-out
GLOPTU	putlog
GLORWY	growly
GLSUUV	vulgus
GMNNOO	gnomon
GMNOOS	mongos
GMNOST	'mongst
GMNOSU	mungos
GMNTUU	gumnut
GMNUUZ	mzungu
GMOOPR	pogrom
GMOOTU	gomuto
GMPRSU	grumps
GMPRUY	grumpy
GMPSUY	gypsum
GNNOOS	on song
GNNOUW	ungown
GNNSUU	unsung
GNOOPS	pongos
GNOORT	trogon
GNOPPU	oppugn
	popgun
GNOPRS	sprong
GNOPSY	spongy
GNOPTU	potgun
	Top Gun
GNORST	strong
GNORTY	Trygon
GNORYZ	Grozny
GNOTUU	outgun
GNPRSU	sprung
GNRSTU	strung
GNSTUU	Tungus
GOOOOR	gooroo
GOOPST	stop-go
GOORSS	sorgos
GOORTT	grotto
GOORVY	groovy
GOOTTU	tog out
GOPRTU	T-group
GOPRUW	grow up
	upgrow
GOPRUY	groupy
GORRTU	turgor
GORSUU	rugous
GORSUY	gyrous
GORSYZ	groszy
GORTTU	gutrot
	rotgut
GORTTY	grotty
GORTUY	grouty
	yogurt
GOSTUY	gousty
GSYYYZ	syzygy

H

HHILOS	Shiloh
HHIOPP	hip-hop
HHISSY	shyish
HHISTW	whisht
HHMMUU	humhum
HHMRTY	rhythm
HHNOSU	Honshu
HHOOOY	yo-ho-ho
HHOOSW	whoosh
HHPSUU	hush up
HHRSTU	thrush
HIIKLM	khilim
HIIKMO	Himiko
HIILLT	Lilith
HIILNS	linish
HIILPP	Philip
HIIMMS	mishmi
HIIMNS	minish
HIIMPS	impish
HIIMSS	Shiism
HIIMST	mishit
HIINPP	hippin
HIINPS	inship
HIINPW	whip in
HIINTW	inwith
	within
HIIOPT	pithoi
HIIORS	Oirish
HIIRST	Tishri
HIITTW	with it
	with-it
HIJOSS	shojis
HIJSTU	Jutish
HIKMUZ	muzhik
HIKNRS	shrink
HIKOOT	hook it
HIKSSY	skyish
HIKSTY	tykish
HIKSWY	whisky
HILLOY	holily
HILLPU	uphill
HILLRS	shrill
HILLRT	thrill
HILLWY	whilly
HILMOS	holism
HILMOW	whilom
HILMOY	homily
HILMSU	mulish
HILMSY	hylism
HILNPT	plinth
HILNTY	thinly

HILOOT oolith
tholoi
HILOPS polish✧
HILOST holist
lithos
HILOSW lowish
owlish
HILPSS splish
HILPST spilth
HILRWY whirly
HILSSY slyish
HILSTW whilst
HILSTY hylist
HIMMSU Humism
HIMMSY shimmy
HIMMWY whimmy
HIMNOY hominy
HIMNSU munshi
HIMOOT lo moth
HIMOPS mopish
Ophism
HIMORS morish
Romish
HIMPRS shrimp
HIMSST Smiths
HIMSTU Humist
HIMSTY smithy
HIMSWY whimsy
HINNOR horn in
HINNSY shinny
HINNTU thin'un
HINNWY whinny
HINOOP inhoop
HINOOS shoo-in
HINOPS siphon
HINORS rhinos
HINOST Shinto
tonish
HINOSW show in
HINPSU punish
shin up
unship
HINPSX sphinx✧
HINRSU inrush
HINSTU shut in
shut-in
HINSTY shinty
HINSUV Vishnu
HINSUW unwish
HIOOSV shivoo
HIOPPS hippos
popish
shippo
HIOPRT trophi
HIOPST pithos
HIOPSY physio
HIOSTY toyish
HIOTTU hit out
outhit
HIOWZZ whizzo
HIPPSU hippus
uppish
HIPPUW whip up
HIPPWY whippy
HIPRST thrips
HIQSSU squish
HIRRWY whirry
HIRSTT thirst
thrist
T-shirt
HIRSTY shirty
thyrsi
HIRTTY thirty
HISSWY swishy
HISTTY stithy
HISTUZ Tz'u Hsi
HIWYZZ whizzy
HJNNOY Johnny
HJNOST St John
HKNOOU unhook
HKNOSY shonky
HKNRSU shrunk
HKNSUU unhusk
HKOOPU hook up
hook-up
HKOORT Rothko
HKOOSS skoosh
HKOOST shtook
HKOSSY Hyksos
HLLOOS hollos
HLLOOW hollow
HLLOPY phyllo
HLLOSU hullos
HLLOWY wholly
HLLSUY lushly
HLMOOS sholom
HLMOTY thymol
HLMPUY phylum
HLNOUY unholy
HLOOSS sloosh
HLOOST tholos
HLOPSS splosh
HLOPSY poshly
HLORUY hourly
HLOSSY sloshy
HLOSTU tholus
HLPRUU uphurl
HLPSUY plushy
HLPSYY sylphy
HLSSUY slushy
HMMMUU hummum
HMMSTU shtumm
HMMSUU hummus
HMNPSY Nymphs
HMNPUY hypnum
HMOOPR morpho
HMOOST shtoom
smooth
HMORUU humour
HMOSTU mouths
HMOSTY mythos
HMOSUU houmus
humous
HMOTUY mouthy
HMPRUY murphy
HMPTUY humpty
tumphy
HMSTUY mythus
thymus
HMSUUY humusy
HMTUYZ zythum
HNNOOP phonon
HNOOPT photon
HNOOPU unhoop
HNOORS horson
HNOORT thoron
HNOORU honour✧
HNOOSW no-show
on show
HNOOWW how now?
HNOPSU nosh-up
push on
HNOPSY Hypnos
syphon
HNOPTY phyton
python✧
typhon✧
HNORSU onrush
HNORTW thrown
HNORTY rhyton
thorny
HNOSTU unshot
HNOTWY why-not
HNPTUU hunt up
HNRTUU unhurt
HNSTUU unshut
HOOOOR hooroo
HOOOOY yoo-hoo
HOOPPS op shop
HOOPST photos
HOOPSW whoops
HOOPTT hotpot
HOORRR horror
HOORST orthos
HOORUZ huzoor
HOOSSW swoosh
HOOTTY toothy
HOOTUW tu-whoo
HOPPSU posh up
HOPPSY shoppy
HOPRRY Pyrrho
HOPRTY trophy
HOPSSY hyssop
sposhy
HOPSTU Pushto
tophus
upshot
HOPSUW show up
HORSST shorts
HORSTU Thurso
HORSTY hostry
shorty
HORTWY worthy
HOSSTU stoush
HOSTTU stouth
HOSTUY shouty
youths
HOSUUZ Suzhou
HOTUYY youthy
HOUUXZ Xuzhou
HPPSUU push-up
HPRSSU sprush
HPRSUU uprush
HPSTUU Pushtu
shut up
HPSTUY typhus
HRSTTU thrust
HRTTUY truthy

I

IIIMNR Rimini
IIIMRT miriti
IIIRST iritis
IIJKKO Kojiki
IIJMNY jiminy
IIJNNO join in
IIKKMS Sikkim
IIKKNR kirkin'
IIKLMN in milk
IIKMNS simkin
IIKNNS sink in
IIKNOS inkosi
IIKNPP pipkin
IIKNSS siskin
IIKOST oikist
IIKOTT titoki
IIKPST skip it!
IILLMU Lilium
IILLOT til oil
IILLOY oilily
IILLPU illupi
IILLWY wilily
IILMMU milium
IILMNO nim-oil
IILNNU inulin
IILNOV violin
IILNRT nirlit
IILNRV rivlin
IILNST instil
IILNTY tinily
IILPST pistil
IILRWY wirily
IILSTU ulitis
IILTTW twilit
IIMMNN min min
IIMMNU minium
IIMMNW wimmin
IIMNNO minion
IIMNOS Ionism
IIMNOU ionium
IIMOSS miosis
IIMRTX trimix
IIMSSS missis✧
IIMSSZ sizism

IIMSTT	timist
IINNOP	pinion
IINNPY	Pinyin
IINNTU	Innuit
IINORS	Roisin
IINORV	virino
	virion
IINOST	Ionist
IINOSV	vision
IINOVV	in vivo
IINPPP	pippin
IINPRT	pirnit
IINPTX	pinxit
IINSST	insist
IINSTU	in situ
	SI unit
IINSTY	tiyins
IINTTU	intuit
IINTTW	nitwit
IIOOTT	toitoi
IIORSS	Osiris
IIOSTT	otitis
IIPPUU	piupiu
IIPRST	spirit✧
IIPRTU	pituri
IIPTTU	Titipu
IIQSSU	si quis
IIQTUV	qiviut
IIRRTT	tirrit
IIRSSU	Sirius
IISSTZ	sizist
IJKLOY	jokily
IJKMOU	moujik
IJKNOS	joskin
IJLMPY	jimply
IJLSUU	Julius
IJMOSS	jissom
IJNOPU	join up
IJNORU	junior✧
IJNRUY	injury
IJNSTU	Justin
IJRSTU	jurist
IKKKRU	Kirkuk
IKKMOW	Wim Kok
IKKORR	korkir
IKKUUY	kikuyu✧
IKLLPU	kill up
IKLLSS	skills
IKLLSY	skilly
IKLLTU	killut
IKLNNU	unlink
IKLNOO	look in
	look-in
IKLNOU	ulikon
IKLNPU	link up
	link-up
	uplink
IKLNSY	slinky
IKLNTY	tinkly
IKLSSU	suslik
IKLTTU	kittul
IKLTTY	kittly
IKMNOO	kimono
IKMNOR	mikron
	morkin
IKMNRU	rumkin
IKMORS	Morisk
IKMPRS	skrimp
IKMPSY	skimpy
IKMRSY	smirky
IKMSSU	kumiss
IKNNSY	skinny
IKNNTU	unknit
IKNOOR	krooni
IKNOPS	pinkos
IKNOPT	inkpot
IKNORW	inwork
	work in
	work-in
IKNOST	stinko
IKNPSU	skin up
IKNPTU	upknit
IKNRSU	Ruskin
	ski run
IKNSST	stinks
IKNSSU	unkiss
IKNSTW	swink't
IKNSTY	stinky
IKOOPT	pookit
IKOORS	irokos
IKOPTU	poukit
IKORSS	Skiros
IKORYZ	Yizkor
IKOSTW	ski tow
IKOTTU	kit out
IKPPSY	skippy
IKPRSU	prusik✧
	spruik
IKQRUY	quirky
IKRSSU	Russki
IKRSTU	turkis
IKRSTY	Kirsty
IKSVVY	skivvy
ILLMOU	lolium
ILLMPY	limply
ILLMSY	slimly
ILLNOR	roll in
ILLNOV	Villon
ILLNOY	lionly
ILLNPU	pull in
	pull-in
ILLNUW	unwill
ILLOPW	pillow
ILLORT	trillo
ILLOWW	willow
ILLPTU	up-till
ILLPUV	pulvil
ILLQSU	squill
ILLSST	Still's
ILLSTY	stilly
ILLSUV	villus
ILLTWY	twilly
ILMMSU	Muslim
ILMNOT	Milton
ILMNOU	moulin
ILMNRU	murlin
ILMNSU	muslin
ILMOPY	mopily
ILMOSS	lissom
ILMOSU	limous
ILMOTU	ultimo
ILMPPY	pimply
ILMPRY	primly
ILMPSY	simply
ILMRSY	lyrism
ILMRTY	trimly
ILMSSY	slimsy
ILMSTU	litmus
	slum it
ILMSUV	Milvus
ILMTUU	tumuli
ILMYZZ	mizzly
ILNOOS	solion
ILNOOT	lotion
ILNOPP	poplin
ILNOPS	slip-on
ILNOPT	pontil
ILNOQU	quinol
ILNOST	Liston
	Nilots
	slot in
	tonsil
ILNOSU	insoul
ILNOSY	nosily
ILNOTU	nut oil
	oilnut
	ultion
ILNOTW	Wilton
ILNPRU	purlin
ILNPST	splint
ILNPUY	punily
ILNRTY	nitryl
ILNSTU	insult
	sunlit
ILOOPS	polios
ILOORT	loriot
ILOOST	solito
ILOOYZ	oozily
ILOPPY	polypi
ILOPRX	prolix
ILOPRY	ropily
ILOPSS	spoils
ILOPST	pistol✧
	postil
	spoilt
ILOPSU	pilous
ILOPSX	oxslip
ILOPTU	lip out
	loupit
ILOPTY	polity
ILOQRU	liquor
ILORSY	rosily
ILORTU	toruli
ILOSSU	ulosis
ILOSTW	lowsit
ILOTTW	wittol
ILPPRY	ripply
ILPPSU	slip up
	slip-up
ILPPSY	slippy
ILPPTU	pulpit
ILPRTY	triply
ILPSST	splits
ILPSTU	silt up
ILPTTU	uptilt
ILRSTU	trisul
ILRSTY	lyrist
ILRSWY	swirly
ILRTWY	twirly
ILSTTU	lutist
ILSTTY	stilty
ILSTUU	lituus
ILSTWY	wistly
IMMNOS	monism
	nomism
	'simmon
IMMNOU	omnium
IMMOOS	simoom
IMMOSU	osmium
IMMOTU	tomium
IMMSTU	mutism
	summit
IMMSWY	swimmy
IMNNOT	Minton
IMNNOW	minnow
IMNNTU	muntin
IMNOOR	morion
	Moroni
IMNOOS	simoon
	somoni
IMNOOT	motion
IMNOOZ	zoom in
IMNORS	minors
IMNOST	inmost
	monist
	Mt Sion
IMNOSY	myosin
	simony
IMNOTZ	Mt Zion
IMNRRU	murrin
IMNRTU	untrim
IMNRUY	unmiry
IMNTUY	mutiny
IMOOTV	vomito
IMOPRS	porism
	primos
IMOPRT	import
IMOPRV	improv
IMOPST	impost
IMORRR	mirror
IMORRS	morris
IMORSU	rimous
IMOSSY	myosis
IMOSTU	ostium

timous
IMOTTT tomtit
IMOTYY moyity
IMPRSS prisms
IMPRSU Primus®
primus
purism✧
IMPRSY prismy
IMPSTU mist up
sumpit
IMQRSU squirm
IMQRUU Urumqi
IMRRSY smirry
IMRSSY Syrism
IMRSTU truism
IMRSUU miurus
IMSSSU missus
IMSSTU misust
IMUZZZ zuzzim
INNOOR iron-on
INNOOT notion
INNOOY oniony
INNOPP Nippon
INNORT intron
INNORW inworn
INNOSU unison
INNOTW intown
INNOWW winnow
INNPSY spinny
INNRTU in turn
turn in
turn-in
INOOPS poison
INOOPT option
potion
INOORS orison
Orsino
INOORZ zorino
INOOST toison
INOOTT in toto
INOPPR poprin
Rippon
INOPRS prison
INOPST pintos
piston
points
spinto
stop in
INOPTT tinpot
INOPTY pointy
INORST in sort
intros
INORSY rosiny
INORTT triton✧
INORTU turion
INOSTT stotin
INOSTU ustion
INOSUV vinous
INOTUW outwin
win out
INOTVY novity
INPPRU Nippur
INPPSY snippy
INPRST sprint
INPRTU turnip
INPSUY puisny
INQSTU squint
INQSUY quinsy
squiny
INRSXY syrinx✧
INRTVY vintry
INRTWY wintry
INSTTY stinty
INSTUU unsuit
INSTUW unwist
INSTYY tyiyns
IOOPRT Poirot
roopit
IOOPST Potosí
IOOSSS sissoo
IOPPPT poppit
IOPPTT tiptop
IOPPTU pip out
IOPPTZ ziptop
IOPQSU quipos
IOPRRY priory
IOPRST prosit
tripos
IOPRTU rip out
roupit
IOPSST ptosis
IOPSTT Post-it®
IOPSTU putois
IOQSTU quoist
quoits
IORRTW worrit
IORRTY riotry
IORRZZ rizzor
IORSSU urosis
IORSTU suitor
IORSUV virous
IOSSTT tsotsi
IOSSTV vistos
IOSTTU outsit
sit out
IOSTXY xystoi
IOTTUW outwit
IPPPSU Puppis
IPPRTU trip up
IPPRTY trippy
IPPSTU spit up
IPPTUY uppity
IPRRTU irrupt
IPRSST stirps
IPRSSY prissy
IPRSTU purist
spruit
stir up
uprist
IPRSTY stripy
IPRSTZ spritz
IPRTUY purity
IPSTTY typist
IPSTXY ptyxis
IPSVVY spivvy
IPTTTU tittup
IPTTUY titupy
IQRRSU squirr
IQRSTU squirt
IRSSTU tsuris
IRSSTY syrtis
IRSTWY wristy
IRTTUX tutrix
ISSSTU tussis
ISSTUX Sixtus
ISTTTU tuttis
ISTTWY twisty

J

JLNOOY Jolyon
JLSTUY justly
JMNOPU jump on
JMPPUU jump-up
JNNOTU jötunn✧
JNOORU journo
JNOSTU juntos
JNSTUU unjust
JOOPPY joypop
popjoy
JOOSUY joyous
JOSSTU just so
JOTTUU jut out
outjut

K

KKLMUU mukluk
KKLUUX Ku Klux
KKNRUU kunkur
KKOSTU Sukkot
KKTTUU tuk tuk
KLLOSY skolly
KLNOPY plonky
KLNRUY knurly
KLOOPU look up
lookup
uplook
KLRTUU Kultur
KLTUYZ klutzy
KMOOSS kosmos
smokos
KMOSUX musk ox
KMPRSU skrump
KNNOTU unknot
KNOORR kronor
KNOORS Kronos
kroons
KNOORW work on
KNOOSS snooks
KNORRU krónur
KNORUW unwork
KNPSUY spunky
KNRSTU trunks
KOOPSY spooky
KOORST strook
KOORSU kouros
KOOTWW kowtow
KOPRUW work up
KRRSUY skurry
KRSSUY Russky

L

LLLOOP lollop
LLLOOT tol-lol
LLMMUU mulmul
LLNOOR roll on
roll-on
LLNOPU pull-on
LLNORU unroll
LLOOTU toluol
LLOOWY woolly
LLOPRU roll up
roll-up
uproll
LLOPUX Pollux
LLORST stroll
LLORTY trolly
LLOSWY slowly
LLPPUU pull up
pull-up
LMMOUX lummox
LMMPUY plummy
LMMSUY slummy
LMMTUU multum
LMOORU ormolu
LMOOSY sloomy
LMORSU musrol
LMOSTY mostly
LMPPUY plumpy
LMPRUY rumply
LMPSUY slumpy
LMTTUU tumult
LNOOPY polony
LNOOST stolon
LNOOTU Toulon
LNOPSY pylons
LNOPTU pluton
pulton
LNORUW run low
LNOSTU unlost
LNOSUU unsoul
LNOTWY townly
LNPTUU pultun
LNRUUY unruly
LNSSTU stuns'l
LOOORT rotolo
LOOPPT Pol Pot
LOOPRY poorly
LOOPTU tool up
LOOSST stools
LOOSTT lottos
LOOSTV volost
LOOVVX volvox
LOPPPY popply
LOPPRY propyl

LOPPSY polyps
sloppy
LOPRTY portly
protyl
LOPSUU lupous
opulus
LOPSUW slow up
slow-up
LOPTTY plotty
LOPTWY two-ply
LORSUY sourly
LORTTY trotyl
LOSSTY stylos
LOSTYZ zlotys
LOSYZZ sozzly
LPPRUY purply
LPPSUY supply
LPRSUY slurpy
LPRSYY spryly
LRRSUY slurry
LRSTUY sultry
LRUUXY luxury
LSSTUY stylus
LSTTUY suttly

M

MMNOOR Mormon
MMNOSU musmon
summon
MMOOPP pompom
pom-pom
MMOOTT motmot
tom-tom
MMOPRS Mrs Mop
MMRRUU murmur
MMTTUU tum-tum
MMTUUU mutuum
MMUUUU muu-muu
MMUUYY yum-yum
MNNOUW unmown
MNOOPP pompon
MNOOPT tompon
MNOORU unmoor
MNOOSY monosy
MNOOTU mouton
MNOOTW Motown®
towmon
MNORSU Munros
MNOTTU mutton
MNOTUY Mounty
MNPTUY numpty
MNSTTU mustn't
MOOPRS promos
MOOPRY pomroy
MOORRS morros
MOORRW morrow
MOORTY motory
MOOSSU osmous
MOOSTT mottos
MOPPRT prompt
MOPSSU Possum®
possum
'possum
MOPSTU upmost
MOQRUU quorum
MOQTUU quotum
MORRUU rumour
MORSTY stormy
MORTUU tumour
MOSTTU utmost
MOSTUU outsum
MPPPUU pump up
MPRSUU rumpus
MPSSTU stumps
MPSSUU muss up
MPSTUU sputum
MPSTUY stumpy
MRRSUY smurry
MRSTUY Myrtus
MSTTUY smutty

N

NNOOPT ponton
NNOORY ronyon
NNOOTW won ton
NNORTU turn on
turn-on
untorn
NNORUW unworn
NNOSUW unsown
NNOTUW unwont
NNPSUU unspun
NNRTUU unturn
NOOPRT pronto
proton
NOOPST spot-on
NOOPSY poyson
snoopy✧
spoony
NOORRY Norroy
NOORST tonsor
NOORTU notour
unroot
NOOSST nostos
NOOSTY snooty
NOOSUY noyous
NOOSYZ snoozy
NOOTTU not out
NOPPRU unprop
NOPPUY pony up
NOPRTU uptorn
NOPSTU puntos
unstop
NOPSUW snow up
NOPTUW up town
uptown
NORSTW strown
NORSTY snorty
NORTUU outrun
run out
run-out
NOSTTU Sutton
NOSTTY snotty
NOSTUW unstow
NOSTUY snouty
NPRSUU prunus
NPRTUU turn up
turn-up
upturn
NRSTTU strunt

O

OOOOPP poo-poo
OOOOTT too too
too-too
OOOOZZ zoozoo
OOOPRT Oporto
OOPPPT pop-top
OOPPRT troppo
OOPPST post-op
OOPPVX vox pop
OOPRRT torpor
OOPRST troops
OOPRSU porous
OOPRTU root up
uproot
OOPSTT pottos
OOPTTU opt out
opt-out
outtop
top out
OOPWWW powwow
OORRSW sorrow
OORRSZ zorros
OORSST torsos
OORSTU torous
OORSTY rootsy
OOSSUU sou-sou
OOSTTY tootsy
OOUUWW wou-wou
OOWWWW wow-wow
OPPPRU prop up
OPPSTU post up
stop up
OPPSUU soup up
OPRSST sports
OPRSTU Proust
sprout
stroup
stupor
OPRSTY sporty
OPRTUY pry out
OPSSTU toss up
toss-up
OPSTTY spotty
OPSTUY spouty
spy out
OPTTUU output
put out
ORSTTU strout
trouts
ORSTUY stoury
ORTTUY trouty
try out
try-out
OSSTXY xystos
OSTTTY stotty
OSTTWY swotty

P

PPTTUU put-put
PRRSUY spurry
PRSTUY upryst
PRSUYY syrupy

R

RSTTUY trusty

S

SSTUXY xystus

T

TTTTUU tut-tut

7 letters

A

AAAABLM Alabama
AAAACMT Atacama
AAAADNP apadana
AAAAGGS Aga saga
AAAALMT Alma-Ata
AAAALTY atalaya
AAAAMRY Ayamará
AAABBCL cabbala
AAABBKL kabbala
AAABBRR Barbara
AAABCCR baccara
AAABCIR arabica
AAABCLR Calabar
AAABCLV baclava
AAABCMR caramba
AAABCNR baracan
AAABCOR carabao
AAABCSS cassaba

AAABCTW	catawba
AAABDHT	a bad hat
AAABDLM	lambada
AAABDNN	bandana
AAABDYY	Daya Bay
AAABEGL	galabea
AAABENS	Sabaean
AAABFLL	falbala
AAABGIL	galabia
AAABGMR	Garamba
AAABHLQ	qabalah
AAABHMR	Abraham
AAABHMS	Bahamas
AAABHNS	Sabahan
AAABILN	Albania
AAABILX	abaxial
AAABINR	Arabian
AAABKLV	baklava
AAABLLW	wallaba
AAABLMT	tambala
AAABLPR	palabra
AAABLRR	Arrabal
AAABMOS	abomasa
AAABMST	mastaba
AAABNNR	rabanna
AAABNNS	bananas
AAABNPR	Pan-Arab
AAABORR	araroba
AAABRSX	abraxas✧
AAACCCH	cachaça
AAACCIS	acacias
AAACCLR	caracal
AAACCRS	Caracas
	cascara
AAACCTT	attacca
AAACDIN	Acadian
AAACDIR	Acarida
	Arcadia
AAACDLU	acaudal
AAACDMM	macadam
AAACEER	Araceae
AAACEHN	Achaean
AAACENP	panacea
AAACGNT	agaçant
AAACHHL	Halacha
AAACHIN	Achaian
AAACHLZ	chalaza
AAACHNT	acantha
AAACHRY	acharya
AAACIJM	Jamaica
AAACILM	malacia
AAACIMR	Aramaic
	cariama
AAACINP	acapnia
AAACINR	acarian
	Acarina
AAACINT	Cataian
	Catania
AAACIRS	acrasia
AAACJMR	jacamar
AAACJNN	Canajan
AAACLLV	cavalla
AAACLMN	almanac
	mancala
AAACLNR	Larnaca
AAACLNT	cantala
	Catalan
AAACLPT	catalpa
AAACLRZ	alcázar
AAACMNP	campana
AAACMRS	maracas
	mascara
AAACMRY	Maracay
AAACNNR	caranna
AAACNPT	catapan
AAACNRT	nacarat
AAACNRU	carauna
AAACNRV	caravan
AAACNST	canasta
AAACNTT	cantata
AAACNTY	Catayan
AAACRWY	caraway
AAACSST	cassata
AAACSSV	cassava
AAACSTT	catasta
AAADELM	alameda
AAADFRY	faraday✧
AAADGGH	Haggada
AAADGHL	Galahad
AAADGNR	Granada
AAADHHS	shahada
AAADHMR	adharma
AAADHNS	sadhana
AAADILX	adaxial
AAADINR	Adriana
AAADIRT	dataria
	radiata✧
AAADJMR	jamadar
AAADKNN	Kannada
AAADLMN	mandala
AAADLMW	wadmaal
AAADMNN	Adamnan
AAADMNR	Ramadan
AAADMNT	adamant
AAADMRS	madrasa
AAADNNS	Danaans
AAADNRS	sardana
AAADNRT	tanadar
AAADRST	ad astra
AAADWYY	awayday
AAAEENR	Araneae
AAAEGLP	à la page
AAAEGLT	galatea✧
AAAEGNP	apanage
	Pangaea
AAAEHLT	althaea
AAAEHRS	sea haar
AAAEIMN	anaemia
AAAEJSV	Java Sea
AAAEKRS	Kara Sea
AAAELMP	palamae
AAAELRS	Aral Sea
AAAENST	anatase
AAAERWY	areaway
AAAETWY	eat away
AAAFFLL	alfalfa
AAAFFLS	falsafa
AAAFHLS	Falasha
AAAFIRT	ratafia
AAAFNRS	sarafan
AAAFRWY	faraway
AAAGGLN	galanga
AAAGHIP	aphagia
AAAGHKN	Aga Khan
AAAGHLN	langaha
AAAGHNT	ataghan
AAAGHPR	agrapha
AAAGHRT	Agartha
AAAGINP	Panagia
AAAGINZ	gazania
AAAGIPT	patagia
AAAGISS	assagai
AAAGLMM	amalgam
AAAGLMN	nagmaal
AAAGLNS	lasagna
AAAGMMT	magmata
AAAGMNR	anagram
AAAGMNS	sagaman
AAAGMNU	Managua
AAAGMTT	tagmata
AAAGNPR	pargana
AAAGNRT	tanagra✧
AAAGNRU	guaraná
AAAGNTY	yatagan
AAAGRSY	Asa Gray
AAAHHKL	Halakah
AAAHHLV	halavah
AAAHIKW	kahawai
AAAHILT	Athalia
AAAHIPS	aphasia
AAAHIRZ	Azariah
AAAHJKW	kajawah
AAAHLLS	halalas
AAAHLMR	harmala
AAAHLNN	alannah
AAAHLRZ	al-Azhar
AAAHMMT	mahatma✧
AAAHMRS	ashrama
AAAHMRT	Maratha
AAAHMST	tamasha
AAAHNRS	Saharan
AAAHNST	Natasha
AAAHOPR	Arapaho
AAAHPRT	paratha
AAAHRTW	waratah
AAAIIJL	jai alai
AAAIJMS	à jamais
AAAIKLT	Latakia
AAAIKRS	akrasia
AAAILMN	à la main
AAAILMR	malaria
AAAILNT	Natalia
AAAILNX	anaxial
AAAILPS	aplasia
AAAILRT	talaria
AAAILST	Alsatia
AAAIMNR	Mariana
AAAIMNT	amanita
AAAIMRS	Samaria
AAAINNS	Ananias
AAAINNZ	Azanian
AAAIPRX	apraxia
AAAIPSS	Aspasia
AAAIQRU	aquaria
AAAIRWZ	waza-ari
AAAJKRT	Jakarta
AAAJMNV	Java man
AAAJMPS	pajamas
AAAKKMR	markkaa
AAAKLMP	Kampala
AAAKMOY	Okayama
AAAKNRS	Sankara
AAAKNWZ	Kwanzaa
AAALLPT	La Plata
	palatal
AAALMNU	Maulana
AAALMNY	Malayan
AAALMRS	Marsala
AAALMSS	salaams
AAALNNT	lantana
AAALNPT	aplanat
AAALNPU	Palauan
AAALNPW	Palawan
AAALNTT	Atlanta
AAALRRY	arrayal
AAALWYY	lay away
	layaway
AAAMNRT	amarant
	Maranta
AAAMNRY	Aymaran
AAAMNST	atamans
AAAMNTY	manyata
AAAMORT	tamarao
AAAMPRT	patamar
AAAMRRZ	zamarra
AAAMRSS	samsara
AAAMRSY	Aymaras
AAAMRTU	tamarau
AAANNST	Santana
AAANNSV	savanna
AAANNTT	annatta
AAANRTT	tantara
	tartana
AAANSST	Satanas
AAAOPRZ	parazoa✧
AAAPPRT	apparat
AAAPRSS	apsaras
AAAPSST	passata
AAARTTT	rat-a-tat
AAARTTU	tuatara
AAARTXY	ataraxy
AABBBEG	Babbage
AABBCEG	cabbage
AABBCGY	cabbagy

Words marked ✧ can also be spelled with one or more capital letters

AABBDGR	gabbard
AABBDHS	habdabs
AABBDIS	Abbasid
AABBDJO	a bad job
AABBDRU	Barbuda
AABBEGN	beanbag
AABBEIS	Babesia
AABBEKL	Baalbek
AABBELT	batable
AABBEMN	Mbabane
AABBERT	barbate
AABBEWY	ebb away
AABBGGR	grab-bag
AABBGRT	gabbart
AABBGRY	rag baby
AABBHST	sabbath✧
	Shabbat
AABBLMO	Lobamba
AABBLOR	barbola
AABBMRU	rum baba
AABBNRY	Barnaby
AABBRRY	Barbary
AABBRSS	bass-bar
AABBRWY	war baby
AABBSSU	babassu
AABCCEH	Bacchae
AABCCEL	accablé
AABCCER	baccare
AABCCET	baccate
AABCCIR	braccia
AABCDIN	Cabinda
AABCDIR	Bacardi®
	carabid
AABCEFR	café bar
AABCEKR	backare
AABCELL	Caballé
AABCELN	balance✧
	balancé
AABCELP	capable
	pacable
AABCELT	actable
AABCEMR	macabre
AABCEMS	ambs-ace
AABCEPR	pea-crab
AABCERR	barrace
	Cabrera
AABCERT	abreact
	bearcat
	cabaret
AABCERY	Acre Bay
AABCFKT	fatback
AABCHIR	brachia
AABCHMT	ambatch
AABCHNR	barchan
AABCHOR	abroach
AABCILM	cambial
AABCILN	Caliban
AABCINR	carabin
	Cariban
AABCIOP	copaiba
AABCITX	taxicab
AABCKLY	layback
AABCKNN	canbank
AABCKNR	cab-rank
AABCKPY	back pay
	pay back
	payback
AABCKRR	barrack
AABCKRT	bar tack
AABCKSW	backsaw
AABCKWY	way back
AABCLMU	calumba
AABCLPY	capably
AABCLRY	Barclay
AABCLSY	scybala
AABCMMU	macumba
AABCMSU	sambuca
AABCORT	abactor
	Acrobat®
	acrobat
AABCOST	Tabasco®
AABCOTT	catboat
AABCTTU	cattabu
AABDDGH	Baghdad
AABDDIK	kabaddi
AABDDIN	Band-aid®
	band-aid
AABDDNO	Abaddon
AABDDNS	sand dab
AABDEFL	fadable
AABDEGG	a bad egg
AABDEGN	bandage
AABDEHS	abashed
AABDEIS	diabase
AABDELL	ballade
AABDELR	Abelard
AABDELT	datable
AABDELW	wadable
AABDEMN	beadman
AABDENU	bandeau
AABDGHN	handbag
AABDGLY	bag lady
AABDGMO	gambado
AABDGNS	sandbag
AABDGRR	drag-bar
AABDHIO	Obadiah
AABDHMS	badmash
AABDHNT	hatband
AABDHNY	hayband
AABDHRS	bardash
AABDHRU	Bahadur
AABDIIS	basidia
AABDIJN	Abidjan
AABDIKR	bidarka
AABDILN	baladin
AABDIMR	barmaid
AABDINT	tabanid
AABDIOT	biodata
AABDJOZ	Badajoz
AABDLNS	salband
AABDLOT	a bad lot
AABDLRW	bradawl
AABDMNR	armband
	Bradman
AABDNNO	abandon
AABDNOR	bandora
AABDNRS	sand bar
AABDNRU	bandura
AABDNSW	band-saw
AABDORV	bravado
AABDOTY	dayboat
AABDRRW	drawbar
AABDRST	bastard
AABDRSU	subadar
AABDSTU	databus
AABEEHW	Wahabee
AABEELT	eatable
AABEEMO	amoebae
AABEEMS	beam sea
AABEENS	sea bean
AABEERS	sea bear
AABEERZ	zareeba
AABEEST	sea-beat
AABEFFL	affable
AABEFFN	beffana
AABEFGL	flea-bag
AABEFGU	aufgabe
AABEFLY	bay leaf
AABEFNR	Aberfan
AABEFNS	fan base
AABEGGG	baggage
AABEGGM	game bag
AABEGGR	garbage
AABEGLR	algebra
AABEGMR	bergama
	megabar
AABEGMS	ambages
AABEGNO	Goa bean
AABEGRR	bagarre
	barrage
AABEGRT	tear bag
AABEGSS	bagasse
AABEGSU	abusage
AABEHIT	Bahaite
AABEHLT	hatable
AABEHNT	abthane
AABEHRS	earbash
AABEIKN	ikebana
AABEILM	amabile
	amiable
AABEILT	Baalite
	labiate
AABEIRS	airbase
	arabise
AABEIRZ	arabize
AABEJLL	jellaba
AABEJMU	jambeau
AABEKLM	makable
AABEKLT	takable
AABEKNS	seabank
AABELLL	labella
AABELLM	lamb-ale
AABELLN	balneal
AABELLS	sabella
	salable
AABELLT	tea ball
AABELMN	namable
AABELMR	bar meal
AABELMT	tamable
AABELNN	Annabel
AABELNO	abalone
AABELNS	bansela
AABELNT	Taleban
AABELPP	papable
AABELPR	bal paré
	parable
AABELPY	payable
AABELRT	Alberta
	ratable
	tael bar
AABELRY	lay bare
AABELST	astable
AABELSV	savable
AABELSY	sayable
AABELTT	abettal
	at table
AABELTU	tableau
	tabulae
AABELTV	vatable✧
AABELTX	taxable
AABEMNS	baseman
AABEMNU	Abu Mena
AABEMOS	amoebas
AABENNW	wannabe
AABENRS	Banares
AABENRT	antbear
AABENTY	abeyant
AABEOST	sea boat
AABERST	abreast
AABERSU	subarea
AABERTT	rabatte
	tabaret
AABERTU	abature
AABERTX	ab extra
AABESSS	sea bass
AABETUX	bateaux
AABFFLY	affably
AABFILU	fabliau
AABFLRU	fabular
AABGHNR	bhangra
AABGHNS	gabnash
	nashgab
AABGHNW	Bhagwan
AABGHPU	Buphaga
AABGHSW	bagwash
AABGIIL	abigail✧
AABGILM	mailbag
AABGIMN	Gambian
AABGINR	bargain
AABGLOR	Aalborg
AABHHIS	sahibah
AABHHIW	Wahhabi
AABHHKS	sabkhah
AABHHRU	bruhaha

AABHIMS Bahaism
AABHINR Bahrain
AABHIRT air-bath
Bharati
AABHIST Bahaist
AABHITT habitat
Tabitha
AABHKNR barkhan
AABHKRU Bukhara
AABHKST sabkhat
AABHLTY bathyal
AABHMNR Brahman
AABHMTT bath mat
AABHOST Sabaoth
AABHPST spa bath
AABHSUU Bauhaus
AABIIKS Baisaki
AABIILX biaxial
AABIIMN Namibia
AABIJMY jambiya
AABIJNP Panjabi
AABIKNS banksia✧
AABILLR barilla
AABILMN Balmain
bimanal
AABILMS Baalism
AABILMY amiably
AABILNT Taliban
AABILNY Aly Bain
AABILOU aboulia
AABILRS basilar
AABILST balista
AABIMMR marimba
AABIMNO bonamia
AABIMNZ Zambian
AABIMOS abomasi
AABIMRS Arabism
AABIMSS Sabaism
AABINOU ouabain
AABINRS Sabrina
AABINRT ab intra
atabrin
AABINSS Sabians
AABINST abstain
Tsabian
AABIORT airboat
AABIPUX paxiuba
AABIRSS Brassaï
AABIRST Arabist
barista
bartsia
AABISTT abattis
AABKMRU Mubarak
AABKNRT tanbark
AABKOOZ bazooka
AABKRST taskbar
AABLLNT ballant
AABLLNY banally
AABLLPT patball
AABLLST ballast
AABLLSY salably
AABLLWY wallaby
AABLMOS Absalom
AABLMRU labarum
AABLMST lambast
AABLMSY abysmal
balsamy
AABLNSU Balanus
AABLNTT blatant
AABLORT ablator
AABLOSV lavabos
AABLOTW at a blow
AABLPRU pabular
AABLRST arblast
AABLRTU tabular
AABLRTY ratably
AABLSSY abyssal
AABLSTY bay salt
AABLTTU abuttal
AABLTXY taxably
AABMMOS Mombasa
AABMNOT boatman
AABMNST batsman
AABMORU marabou
AABMORZ Mozarab
AABMRTU tambura
AABMSSY ambassy
AABNNOZ bonanza
AABNOST sabaton
AABNOSY sabayon
AABNRSY Ray-Bans®
AABNSTU Tabanus
AABOPPT pap-boat
AABORSZ abrazos
AABOTTY attaboy
AABQSUU subaqua
sub-aqua
AABRRSU saburra
AABRRUV bravura
AABRUWY rub away
AABSSSY sassaby
AABSTTY A S Byatt
AABTTTU battuta
AABZZZZ bazzazz
AACCDEI cicadae
AACCDEM medacca
AACCDEN Candace
AACCDES cascade
saccade
AACCDIR cardiac
AACCDIS cicadas
AACCDOR Caradoc
AACCEIR Circaea
AACCEKR carcake
AACCELO cloacae
AACCENV vacance
AACCEPR pace car
AACCEPS cap-case
AACCERS carcase
AACCEST saccate
AACCHHK kachcha
AACCHIN chicana
AACCHIR archaic
AACCHLN clachan
AACCHLS Calchas
AACCHMP champac
AACCHNN cannach
AACCHRT charact
AACCIJO Ajaccio
AACCILM acclaim
AACCILS Alcaics
cicalas
AACCIOR carioca✧
AACCIRT acratic
AACCITT atactic
AACCJKR carjack
AACCKLP calpack
AACCKRR carrack
AACCLLO cloacal
AACCLLT catcall
AACCLOP polacca
AACCLOR caracol
AACCLPT placcat
AACCLRU accrual
caracul✧
AACCLSU accusal
AACCLTU Lactuca
AACCMOS macacos
AACCNNY ca' canny
AACCNVY vacancy
AACCORT car-coat
AACCORU curaçao✧
curaçoa
AACCOST accoast
AACCOTT toccata
AACCRRT carract
AACCRSS carcass
AACDDEL decadal
AACDDER arcaded
AACDDHR chaddar
AACDDIN candida
AACDDNO Caddoan
AACDEEM academe
AACDEES sea dace
AACDEFL falcade
AACDEHM chamade
AACDEHP headcap
AACDEHR charade
AACDEHT cathead
AACDEII aecidia
AACDEIL alcaide
Alcidae
AACDEIN aidance
Canidae
AACDELL alcalde
AACDELN candela
decanal
AACDELR caldera
AACDELS scalade
AACDELY alcayde
AACDEMN Cadmean
AACDEMY academy
AACDENV advance
AACDENZ cadenza
AACDERS sea card
AACDERV cadaver
AACDERY day care
AACDETU caudate
AACDEUX cadeaux
AACDFIR faradic
AACDHIN Chadian
AACDHMR drachma
AACDHNR Chandra
handcar
AACDIIS ascidia
diascia
AACDIJU Judaica
AACDILR radical✧
AACDILU Alcudia
Claudia
AACDIMM Mica Dam
AACDINT antacid
AACDINV vanadic
AACDIOR acaroid
AACDIRS ascarid
AACDJKW jackdaw
AACDKPY daypack
AACDKSS sad sack
AACDKSY daysack
AACDLNN Clannad
AACDLNO calando
AACDLNS scandal
AACDLOR carload
AACDLOS scalado
AACDLOY day-coal
AACDLPR placard
AACDLRU Dracula
AACDNRS cadrans
AACDOOV avocado
AACDOPP Papa Doc
AACDRSS csárdás
AACDRST dart-sac
AACDRSZ czardas
AACEEGR acreage
AACEEHR earache
AACEEHT chaetae
AACEEKT teacake
AACEELM mace-ale
AACEELN anelace
AACEELS sea lace
AACEEMR camerae
AACEEMS ames-ace
AACEENT catenae
AACEEPT at peace
AACEERT acerate
AACEETT acetate
AACEFFT fat-face
AACEFLS sea calf
AACEFLT falcate
AACEFLU faculae
AACEFMN faceman
AACEFRR carfare
AACEGGR aggrace
AACEGHN ganache

AACEGHU	à gauche
AACEGKP	package
AACEGKS	sackage
AACEGNR	carnage
	cranage
AACEGRT	cartage
AACEGSV	scavage
AACEHLP	acaleph
AACEHLR	alchera
	Rachael
AACEHLV	à cheval
AACEHNO	choanae
AACEHNP	panache
AACEHNR	acharné
	Arachne
	Archean
AACEHNS	Aeschna
AACEHPP	appeach
AACEHPU	chapeau
AACEHRT	trachea
AACEHST	Achates
AACEHTT	attaché
AACEHTU	chateau
	château
AACEHTY	Cyathea
AACEHWY	each way
	each-way
AACEILN	Caelian
AACEIMN	anaemic
AACEIMR	America
AACEIMU	camaïeu
AACEINN	Nicaean
AACEINO	Oceania
AACEINR	acarine
	carinae
AACEIPP	cap-a-pie
	cap-à-pie
AACEIRV	avarice
	caviare
AACEJKN	Janácek
AACEKLL	lac-lake
AACEKMM	ack emma
AACEKNP	pancake
AACEKNS	askance
AACEKOT	oatcake
AACELLN	canella
AACELLP	Capella
AACELLS	sacella
AACELLT	lacteal
AACELMN	lace-man
	manacle
AACELMR	cameral
	caramel
	ceramal
AACELMU	maculae
AACELNU	canulae
	lacunae
AACELNV	valance
AACELNY	Lycaena
AACELOS	sea coal
AACELPS	Pascale
AACELPT	placate
AACELRT	Lacerta
AACELRV	caravel
AACELST	lactase
AACELSW	case law
AACELTT	lactate
AACELTV	clavate
AACEMMR	macramé
AACEMNS	caseman
AACEMNV	caveman
AACEMPR	paracme
AACEMQU	macaque
AACEMRS	cameras
AACEMRU	Marceau
AACEMTT	tame cat
AACENOT	Actaeon
AACENRS	Saracen
AACENRT	cane rat
	cateran
AACENST	catenas
AACENTT	cantate
AACENTY	cyanate
AACEOPT	pea coat
AACEORS	rosacea
AACEPRT	caprate
	rate-cap
AACEPRU	capuera
AACEPRV	precava
AACERRT	rat race
AACERST	cat's-ear
AACERSU	caesura
	Euscara
AACERSZ	Sazerac®
AACERTU	arcuate
AACERTV	cave art
AACERWY	raceway
AACETTU	actuate
AACETUV	vacuate
AACFFIL	caffila
AACFHLP	half-cap
AACFILS	fascial
AACFILU	faucial
AACFINR	African
AACFINT	fanatic
AACFLLU	falcula
AACFLLW	law-calf
AACFLLY	fallacy
AACFLPT	cat-flap
	flat cap
AACFLRT	flatcar
	fractal
AACFLRU	facular
AACFLTU	factual
AACFMPT	fat camp
AACFRRU	farruca
AACFRRY	a far cry
AACGHLL	Chagall
AACGILL	glacial
AACGILM	magical
AACGILS	scaglia
AACGINT	agnatic
AACGIRV	agravic
AACGLOS	coal gas
	gas-coal
AACGLOT	catalog
AACGLOU	coagula
AACGLRY	Calgary
AACGNOU	guanaco
AACHHKR	charkha
AACHHLL	challah
AACHIKN	kachina
AACHIKR	chikara
	Karachi
AACHILM	Malachi
AACHILR	rachial
AACHILT	calathi
AACHIMN	Mahican
AACHIMR	Amharic
	machair
AACHIMS	chiasma
AACHINT	acanthi
AACHIPS	aphasic
AACHIPT	chapati
AACHIRS	arachis
AACHIRT	Cathari
	cithara
AACHITY	cyathia
AACHKMP	champak
AACHKRT	hatrack
AACHKSW	hacksaw
AACHLLN	challan
	Lachlan
AACHLMS	chasmal
AACHLNT	Chantal
AACHLPP	chappal
AACHLPS	paschal✧
AACHLSU	acushla
AACHMNP	chapman
AACHNOP	panocha
AACHNOU	huanaco
AACHNPX	panchax
AACHNRV	navarch
AACHNRY	anarchy
AACHNSU	anchusa
AACHPST	Pat Cash
AACHPSY	pay cash
AACHRRT	catarrh
AACHRST	Cathars
AACHRSW	car-wash
AACHRWY	archway
AACHRYZ	Zachary
AACIILN	lacinia
AACIILS	Isiacal
AACIINP	apician✧
AACIINR	Icarian
AACIINS	Asianic
AACIINT	actinia
AACIIST	Asiatic
AACIITV	viatica
AACIJLP	jalapic
AACIJNT	Jacinta
AACIKLL	alkalic
AACIKLR	clarkia
AACIKNN	canakin
AACILLM	Camilla
AACILMR	mail-car
AACILNR	Acrilan®
	clarain
	cranial
AACILNT	actinal
	alicant
AACILNU	Luciana
AACILNZ	Zincala
AACILOS	asocial
AACILOX	coaxial
AACILPS	spacial
AACILPT	capital
	placita
AACILRR	railcar
AACILUV	Avicula
AACIMMR	macrami
AACIMNR	Marcian
AACIMNS	caimans
AACIMOR	acromia
AACIMPR	Campari
	picamar
AACIMRU	Mauriac
AACINNT	cantina
AACINOR	Aaronic
	conaria
	ocarina
AACINPS	Capsian
AACINPT	capitan
	captain
AACINPY	pay cain
AACINRS	carinas
AACINRZ	czarina
AACINST	satanic
AACINTV	Vatican
AACIOPT	tapioca
AACIOPV	copaiva
AACIORT	Croatia
AACIOTV	Octavia
AACIPRS	Sarapic
AACIPRX	apraxic
AACIQTU	aquatic
AACIRSS	ascaris
AACIRST	caritas
AACIRTT	Tataric
AACISTT	astatic
AACJKMN	jackman
	man jack
	manjack
	man-jack
AACJKRT	jack tar✧
AACJKSS	jackass
AACJMOR	Majorca
AACJOST	Jocasta
AACKLLL	lack-all
AACKLTW	catwalk
AACKMNP	manpack
	packman
AACKMRT	amtrack

AACKNRS	ransack
AACKNRT	tank car
AACKPRR	car park
AACKPRT	pack-rat
	ratpack
AACKPWY	packway
AACLLNT	callant
AACLLNU	calluna
	lacunal
AACLLOR	coralla
AACLLSU	clausal
AACLLVY	cavally
AACLMNO	coalman
AACLMNT	calmant
	clamant
AACLMPR	arc-lamp
AACLMPT	palm cat
AACLMRU	macular
AACLMSU	calamus✧
AACLNNU	cannula
AACLNOR	Alcoran
AACLNPY	claypan
AACLNRU	lacunar
AACLNSU	Calanus
	canulas
AACLOPR	caporal
AACLOPT	octapla
AACLORT	coal tar
	crotala
AACLORZ	alcorza
AACLOST	catalos
	coastal
AACLOTT	cattalo
AACLOTV	octaval
AACLPRT	caltrap
AACLPSU	pascual
	scapula
AACLPTY	play-act
AACLRST	castral
AACLRVY	calvary✧
	cavalry
AACLSSU	casuals
AACLSTT	saltcat
AACLSUV	vascula
AACLTTU	tactual
AACMNOR	camaron
AACMNRU	arcanum
AACMNSY	caymans
AACMNTX	Manx cat
AACMORR	camorra✧
AACMORS	sarcoma
AACMORT	marcato
AACMRRT	tramcar
AACMRRU	Macrura
AACMRSS	sarcasm
AACNNOT	Cantona
AACNNOZ	canzona
AACNOST	sacaton
AACNPST	capstan
AACNRTU	curtana
AACNSSV	canvass
AACNSTU	ascaunt
AACORST	ostraca
AACORTU	acatour
	autocar
AACOTUV	autovac
AACPSTW	cat's-paw
AACRTTT	attract
AACRTTX	tax cart
AACRTUV	vacatur
AACRTUY	actuary
AACRTWY	cartway
AACTUWY	cutaway
AADDDEN	addenda
AADDEES	Dead Sea
AADDEFI	deaf aid
AADDEGI	Gadidae
AADDEIL	alidade
AADDEIR	dead air
AADDENP	deadpan
AADDEPT	adapted
AADDEPY	dead-pay
AADDFGI	Gaddafi
AADDGNR	graddan
	grandad
AADDHKR	khaddar
AADDHPR	hard pad
AADDHRS	sraddha
AADDIIK	didakai
AADDIIV	davidia
AADDILN	Aladdin
AADDIMS	Dadaism
AADDIMY	may I add
AADDIST	Dadaist
AADDLYY	Lady Day
AADDNVV	dvandva
AADDRST	dastard
AADEEGH	headage
AADEEHS	head sea
AADEEHX	axe-head
AADEELT	eat lead
	tea lead
AADEERT	aerated
AADEERW	awardee
AADEFFR	affeard
	affear'd
AADEFGL	faldage
AADEFGR	fardage
AADEFHT	fathead
AADEFIS	fadaise
AADEFLM	mafalde
AADEFLU	aefauld
AADEFLY	Al-Fayed
AADEFNZ	fazenda
AADEGGR	aggrade
AADEGHO	go ahead
	go-ahead
AADEGMN	agnamed
AADEGMR	megarad
AADEGMS	damages
AADEGNR	Grenada
AADEGRT	at grade
	gradate
AADEGRY	drayage
	yardage
AADEHIR	airhead
AADEHMN	headman
AADEHMS	ashamed
AADEHNX	handaxe
AADEHPR	Phaedra
AADEHPS	saphead
AADEHRW	rawhead
	warhead
AADEHWY	headway
AADEILN	Daniela
AADEILR	Laridae
	radiale
AADEILV	vedalia
AADEIMR	Madeira
AADEIMS	seamaid
AADEIMT	Adamite
AADEINO	Dionaea
AADEINR	araneid
	Ariadne
	Ranidae
AADEINS	naiades
AADEINZ	in a daze
AADEIPS	diapase
AADEIRT	radiate
	tiaraed
AADEIWY	die away
	die-away
AADEJMR	jemadar
AADEJNU	Judaean
AADEKMR	kamerad
AADELLP	padella
AADELMN	Mandela
AADELMO	alamode
	à la mode
AADELMR	alarmed
AADELNR	adrenal
AADELNW	danelaw✧
AADELNX	adnexal
AADELNZ	Zealand
AADELPR	pardale
AADELPY	leap day
AADELRU	radulae
AADELRY	already
AADELTU	adulate
AADELTY	daytale
	tea lady
AADEMMN	made man
	man-made
AADEMNO	adenoma
AADEMNS	Maenads
AADEMNT	mandate✧
AADEMNY	day name
	name day
AADEMNZ	Mazdean
AADEMSU	Amadeus
AADENNP	Pandean
AADENNT	andante
	at an end
	Dantean
AADENRV	veranda
AADENSS	sea sand
AADENST	ansated
AADENSW	weasand
AADENTV	Vedanta
AADENWZ	weazand
AADEORS	sea road
AADEPRR	parader
	para-red
AADEPRS	aspread
AADEPRT	adapter
	readapt
AADEPSS	passade
AADERRS	arrased
AADERRW	awarder
AADERSW	seaward
AADERTU	aurated
AADERWY	daywear
AADESTT	data set
AADFGLN	Gandalf
AADFGLY	flag day✧
AADFHLY	half-day
AADFIRY	fair-day
AADFLTW	twafald
AADFNRR	farrand
AADFNST	fantads
AADFSTY	fast-day
AADGGHR	haggard
AADGGLR	laggard
AADGGRS	saggard
AADGHIL	hidalga
AADGIIR	Giardia
AADGIMM	digamma
AADGIMO	agamoid
AADGIMR	diagram
AADGIOS	adagios
AADGLLW	gadwall
AADGLMY	amygdal
AADGLNO	gonadal
AADGLNR	garland
AADGLNS	sladang
AADGLNT	Landtag
AADGLOS	Salgado
AADGLRU	gradual
AADGMNR	drag-man
	grandam
	grandma
AADGMNS	gadsman
AADGMRS	smaragd
AADGNNU	Ugandan
AADGNPR	grandpa
AADGNRT	gardant
AADGNRY	yardang
AADGOPR	podagra
AADHHMS	Mashhad
AADHHRT	hard hat
AADHILL	Dalilah
AADHIMR	hadarim
AADHIMS	samadhi
AADHINP	Daphnia

AADHINR Hadrian
AADHJNR handjar
AADHKNS dhansak
AADHKNY yakhdan
AADHLPR Alphard
AADHLRY halyard
AADHMNR hard man
AADHMNU um and ah
AADHNNP nap hand
AADHNPR hard-pan
AADHNRS darshan
Hansard
AADHNSW handsaw
AADHNTT and that
AADHOSS soda ash
AADHRST Harstad
AADHRWY hayward
AADHSWY washday
AADIILN Idalian
AADIILR diarial
AADIINN Indiana
AADIINR diarian
AADIIPS aspidia
AADIIRR air-raid
AADIJMN jamdani
AADIKLY ilkaday
AADILLO alodial
AADILMR admiral
amildar
AADILMT Matilda
AADILNP paladin
AADILNR laniard
AADILPS apsidal
AADILRT tailard
AADILSS dalasis
AADILST stadial
AADILTV datival
AADILWY waylaid
AADIMNR mandira
Miranda
AADIMOR diorama
AADIMOT domatia
AADIMRR ram-raid
AADIMRU Madurai
radium A
AADIMST Amistad
AADINNR Andrina
AADINRR darrain
AADINRT intrada
radiant
AADINRV viranda
AADINRW Wardian
AADINST St Aidan
AADIOPZ dopiaza
AADIORS Isadora
AADIPPR Paradip
AADIRRW airward
AADJLYY Lady Jay
AADJMPY pyjama'd
AADKLNO Oakland
AADKMRY daymark
AADKNRT tankard
AADKOST Dakotas
AADKRWW awkward
AADLLMN damn all
AADLLMR mallard
AADLLNR Randall
AADLLNW land law
lawland
AADLLPU paludal
AADLMNN landman
AADLMNO mandola
AADLMNU ladanum
AADLMUV mud lava
AADLMYY May-lady
AADLNOP Panadol®
AADLNOY Yolanda
AADLNRT land-rat
AADLNRY lanyard
AADLNTX land tax
AADLNWY Wayland
AADLOPY payload
AADLPPU applaud
AADLPYY play-day
AADLRRU radular
AADMMNU ad manum
AADMNNO Madonna
AADMNNS sandman
AADMNNW dawn-man
AADMNOR madroña
mandora
monarda
roadman
AADMNRS mansard
AADMNRY drayman
yardman
AADMNSY daysman
man-days
AADMNTU mutanda
tamandu
AADMOPR road map
AADMOQU madoqua
AADMORT matador
AADMOSY Asmoday
AADMOYY Omayyad
AADMRRY yardarm
AADMRZZ mazzard
AADMSSU Damasus
AADMUYY Umayyad
AADNNOT notanda
AADNNRW Rwandan
AADNOOT Odonata
AADNOPR pandora✧
AADNORR Andorra
AADNORT ondatra
AADNORY anyroad
AADNOTY Daytona
AADNPRU pandura
AADNRRW warrand
AADNRRY darrayn
AADNRST astrand
tar sand
AADNRTY tanyard
AADNRVW vanward
AADNRWY nayward
AADOPRR parador
AADOPRS parados
AADOPRT adaptor
AADOPRX paradox
AADOPSS passado
AADOPTT dopatta
AADORTW at a word
AADORTX road tax
AADORWY roadway
AADOSTT tostada
AADPTTU dupatta
AADQRTU quadrat
AADRSTY daystar
AADRWWY wayward
AAEEFFR affeare
AAEEFGL leafage
AAEEFLT tea leaf
AAEEGKL leakage
AAEEGLT étalage
galeate
AAEEGMN amenage
AAEEGMR Megaera
AAEEGNO Neogaea
AAEEGRV average
AAEEGST sage tea
sea gate
AAEEHRS sea hare
AAEEHRT hetaera
AAEEHSY Ayeesha
AAEEINT taeniae
AAEEKLS seakale
AAEEKRW reawake
AAEELLP pale ale
AAEELLR real ale
AAEELMT maleate
AAEELNS sea lane
AAEELOR areolae
AAEELRT a latere
laetare
AAEEMNT emanate
enemata
manatee
AAEEMTT meat-tea
AAEEMTX meat-axe
AAEENNT Aetnean
AAEENRT e re nata
AAEEPPS appease
AAEEPRT paterae
AAEERSW seaware
AAEERTU aureate
AAEERTX exarate
AAEESST East Sea
AAEESVW sea wave
AAEFFGR agraffe
AAEFFIR affaire
AAEFFLL falafel
AAEFFLT leaf fat
AAEFFNR fanfare
AAEFFTT taffeta
AAEFGLN Falange
AAEFGLR Feargal
AAEFGNO of an age
AAEFGTW waftage
AAEFHLP half-ape
AAEFHMR Fareham
AAEFHNT haaf-net
AAEFKLO oak-leaf
AAEFLPR earflap
parafle
AAEFLRT rat-flea
AAEFMOS sea foam
AAEFMRT fermata
AAEFNST Santa Fe
AAEFQRU aquafer
AAEFRRR Ferrara
AAEFRRW warfare
AAEFRST Far East
AAEFRWY wayfare
AAEGGNO anagoge
AAEGGOP apagoge
AAEGGRT aggrate
AAEGGRY garagey
AAEGHLU haulage
AAEGHMR Grahame
AAEGHNS Ganesha
AAEGHNT thanage
AAEGHOV have a go
have-a-go
AAEGHPT peat-hag
AAEGILR Algeria
lairage
railage
regalia
AAEGILS algesia
AAEGINP nagapie
AAEGINR anergia
AAEGINV vaginae
AAEGINW wainage
AAEGIPR igarapé
AAEGIRR air rage
arriage
AAEGISS assegai
AAEGITT agitate
AAEGJTU ajutage
AAEGJZZ jazz age
AAEGKNT tankage
AAEGKOS soakage
AAEGKRW Gaekwar
AAEGLLR Allegra
glareal
Grallae
AAEGLLT gallate
tallage
AAEGLMN gamelan
AAEGLMT gametal
AAEGLNN anlagen
AAEGLNR alnager
AAEGLNS anlages
lasagne

AAEGLNU	aulnage
	leguaan
AAEGLOP	apogeal
AAEGLRR	realgar
AAEGLRT	at large
AAEGLST	agelast
	algates
	lastage
AAEGLSV	salvage
AAEGMMY	May-game
AAEGMNR	manager
AAEGMNT	gateman
	magenta
	magnate
AAEGMPR	rampage
AAEGMRT	Margate
	regmata
AAEGMRW	war game
AAEGMSS	massage
AAEGMTT	tag team
AAEGNNP	pannage
AAEGNNT	tannage
AAEGNOP	apogean
AAEGNPT	pageant
AAEGNRR	arrange
AAEGNRT	tanager
AAEGNTV	vantage
AAEGNTW	wantage
AAEGNWY	Gawayne
AAEGNYZ	Zygaena
AAEGOST	Sea Goat
AAEGPRR	parerga
AAEGPRW	warpage
AAEGPRY	gap year
AAEGPSS	passage
AAEGPSY	paysage
AAEGPWY	peg away
AAEGQUY	quayage
AAEGRRS	rare gas
AAEGRRV	ravager
AAEGRST	agraste
	tear gas
	tear-gas
AAEGRTT	regatta
AAEGRWW	wage war
AAEGSSU	assuage
	sausage
AAEGSSW	asswage
AAEGSTU	gateaus
AAEGSTW	saw gate
	wastage
AAEGTTW	wattage
AAEGTUX	gâteaux
AAEGTWY	gateway
	get away
	getaway
AAEHHPS	ash-heap
AAEHHPT	aphthae
AAEHHSY	Ayeshah
AAEHILP	aphelia
AAEHIRT	hetaira
	Rhaetia
AAEHKMY	make hay
AAEHKNT	khanate
AAEHKRY	hayrake
AAEHKSW	seahawk
AAEHLLL	allheal
	heal-all
AAEHLNT	ethanal
AAEHLNZ	Alhazen
AAEHLPR	Raphael
AAEHLPX	hexapla
AAEHLRT	trehala
AAEHLTT	athleta
	the Taal
AAEHMTT	themata
AAEHNPR	hanaper
AAEHNPS	saphena
AAEHPRZ	pheazar
AAEHRSY	hearsay
AAEHRTT	at heart
AAEHSTT	hastate
AAEHVWY	have way
AAEIKLU	Kilauea
AAEIKMT	take aim
AAEIKRT	Karaite
	take air
AAEILLX	axillae
AAEILMN	A A Milne
	Almaine
	laminae
	Limnaea
AAEILMR	Almeria
AAEILMS	malaise
AAEILNN	alanine
AAEILNO	aeolian✧
AAEILNR	air-lane
	linear A
AAEILNT	antliae
	Natalie
AAEILNU	El Aaiún
AAEILOR	olearia
AAEILPX	epaxial
AAEILRU	aurelia
AAEILRV	velaria
AAEILSS	aliases
AAEILTW	Alawite
AAEIMMT	imamate
AAEIMNR	Armenia
AAEIMNS	amnesia
AAEIMNT	amentia
	animate
AAEIMPY	pyaemia
AAEIMRU	uraemia
AAEIMTV	amative
AAEINNO	aeonian
AAEINNS	Sinaean
AAEINRT	Raetian
AAEINRZ	Zairean
AAEINST	taenias
AAEIPPS	apepsia
AAEIPRR	pareira
AAEIPRS	spiraea
AAEIPRT	apteria
	Tarpeia
AAEIPTT	apatite
AAEIRST	aristae
	Astaire
	asteria
	atresia
AAEIRSU	Eurasia
AAEIRSX	xerasia
AAEIRTT	arietta
	Ratitae
AAEIRTV	variate
AAEIRVW	airwave
AAEISTT	satiate
AAEJMST	maatjes
AAEJNPR	Jean Arp
AAEJNRT	naartje
AAEJNTT	Janetta
AAEJPSS	Pasajes
AAEKKOR	karaoke
AAEKKRY	kayaker
AAEKLMR	meal-ark
AAEKLNT	alkanet
	kantela
AAEKLNV	Lake Van
AAEKLRS	sea lark
AAEKMNW	wakeman
AAEKMRR	earmark
AAEKMRS	seamark
AAEKMRW	make war
AAEKMWY	make way
AAEKPRT	partake
AAEKRSU	Eskuara
AAEKSTT	at stake
AAELLLM	lamella
AAELLNZ	zanella
AAELLPR	parella
AAELLPT	patella✧
AAELLRS	all ears
AAELLRT	lateral
AAELLRY	allayer
AAELLSV	save-all
AAELLSW	sea wall
AAELMMN	meal-man
AAELMMT	lemmata
AAELMNS	Ameslan
AAELMNT	amental
AAELMNU	alumnae
AAELMNY	Lymnaea
AAELMOT	oatmeal
AAELMPT	palmate
AAELMST	maltase
AAELMSY	amylase
AAELMTT	malt tea
AAELNNO	Oleanna
AAELNOV	Avonlea
	valonea
AAELNPT	platane
AAELNPU	paenula
AAELNRS	arsenal
AAELNRT	Lateran
AAELNST	sealant
AAELNSY	analyse
AAELNTT	tetanal
AAELNTZ	zealant
AAELNWY	laneway
AAELNYZ	analyze
AAELORR	areolar
AAELORS	areolas
AAELORU	aureola
AAELOTX	oxalate
AAELPPR	apparel
AAELPPT	palpate
AAELPPU	papulae
AAELPRT	apteral
AAELPRV	palaver
AAELPTT	tapetal
AAELPTU	plateau
AAELPTY	apetaly
AAELRST	tar seal
	tar-seal
AAELRSU	as a rule
AAELRTV	larvate
AAELRTZ	lazaret
AAELRVY	alveary
AAELSST	atlases
	sea salt
AAELSTT	at least
	saltate
AAELSUX	asexual
AAELSWX	sealwax
AAELTTV	Valetta
AAELTUV	valuate
AAELTVV	valvate
AAELTZZ	altezza
AAELWWY	welaway
AAEMMMR	maremma
AAEMMMT	mammate
AAEMMNT	meat-man
AAEMMNU	manumea
AAEMMOT	ommatea
AAEMNNT	emanant
AAEMNPP	pampean
AAEMNPS	spaeman
AAEMNPT	peatman
AAEMNRT	ramenta
AAEMNRU	muraena✧
AAEMNRY	man-year
AAEMNST	namaste
AAEMNTU	manteau
AAEMOTZ	metazoa✧
AAEMPPT	pap-meat
AAEMPPZ	Mazeppa
AAEMQSU	squamae
AAEMRST	amearst
AAEMRTU	amateur
AAEMRVY	ave Mary
AAENNNT	antenna
AAENNRV	Ravenna
AAENNST	annates
AAENNTT	tannate

Words marked ✧ can also be spelled with one or more capital letters

AAENNTV en avant
ventana
AAENPPR parpane
AAENPST anapest
peasant
AAENPTT épatant
AAENRRT narrate
AAENRST Antares
AAENRTT tartane
AAENRTU taurean✧
AAENRTV taverna
AAENRUW unaware
AAENRUZ azurean
AAENSST Nastase
AAENSSV vanessa✧
AAENSSW Swansea
AAENSTV Avestan
savante
AAEORRT aerator
AAEORRU aurorae
AAEPPRT parapet
AAEPPRV Papaver
AAEPRTY peatary
AAEPSSS sea pass
AAEPSSW sea wasp
AAEQRTU à quatre
AAERRRS arrears
AAERRRY arrayer
AAERRTT tartare✧
AAERSST sea star
AAERSSY assayer
AAERSTT Astarte
AAERTTY tea tray
AAETTUW Watteau
AAFFILN affinal
AAFFINS saffian
AAFFINT affiant
AAFFIRS affairs
AAFFLLN naff all
AAFGHIN afghani
AAFGIRR rag-fair
AAFGLMN flagman
AAFGORR farrago
AAFHIKL khalifa
AAFHILX Halifax
AAFHINS Isfahan
AAFHIRS Sharifa
AAFHLPY half pay
half-pay
AAFHLWY halfway
AAFIILR filaria✧
AAFIJST fajitas
AAFILMN fan mail
AAFILNT fantail
AAFILNV Flavian
AAFILOS fasolia
AAFILQU alfaquí
AAFIMRU Fumaria
AAFIMRY Mayfair
AAFIMUX faux ami
AAFINNT infanta
AAFINNU infauna
AAFIPRT parfait
AAFIQTU aquafit
AAFIRUY rufiyaa
AAFIRWY fairway
AAFJLLW jawfall
AAFJLOR alforja
AAFLLNU Launfal
AAFLLTY fatally
AAFLMNP fan palm
AAFLMPR frampal
AAFLNOP pan loaf
AAFLNOR forlana
AAFLNRU furlana
AAFLOTT a fat lot
AAFLSTT salt-fat
AAFLTTU at fault
AAFLWYY flyaway
AAFMNRT raftman
AAFMNST fantasm
AAFMSTU Mustafa
AAFNRRT farrant
AAFNSTT fantast
AAFNSTY fantasy
AAFPSUX faux pas
AAGGILN ganglia
AAGGINR Gagarin
AAGGLMO magalog
AAGGLOS galagos
AAGGLOT Tagalog
Tagálog
AAGGNOY anagogy
AAGGNST gangsta
AAGGNSW gang saw
AAGGNWY gangway
AAGHILR Aligarh
gharial
AAGHLNT gnathal
AAGHLOS gasahol
AAGHLTU laugh at
AAGHMNN hangman
AAGHMNW whangam
AAGHMRS gramash
AAGHNUV Vaughan
AAGHQUU quahaug
AAGHRSW washrag
AAGHSTY sagathy
AAGIINO Goiânia
AAGIINT Niigata
AAGIKNW awaking
AAGIKNZ ziganka
AAGIKRW Gaikwar
AAGILLN Lingala
AAGILMR Alamgir
AAGILMY myalgia
AAGILNN anginal
Anglian
AAGILNO logania
AAGILNP paginal
AAGILNV vaginal
AAGILOT otalgia
AAGILTT tag tail
AAGILTW wagtail
AAGIMNO angioma
AAGIMNS gas main
siamang
AAGIMNZ amazing
AAGINNW wanigan
AAGINNZ Zingana
AAGINOS agnosia
AAGINRR arraign
AAGINRS sangria
sarangi
AAGINRT granita
AAGINRU Guaraní
guarani
AAGINRZ Zingara
AAGINST against
AAGINSU iguanas
AAGINSV vaginas
AAGINSY gainsay
AAGINTU Antigua
AAGINTY antigay
AAGIOTT agitato
AAGIPPR Agrippa
AAGIPRU piragua
AAGIRRY argyria
AAGISTT sagitta✧
AAGJRTU Gujarat
AAGKLLO oak gall
AAGKMSS gas mask
AAGKNST gas tank
AAGKOOZ gazooka
AAGKORT katorga
AAGLLNT gallant
AAGLMNS langsam
AAGLMPS gas lamp
AAGLNNO Angolan
AAGLNOR granola
AAGLNOY analogy
AAGLNPS lapsang✧
AAGLNRU angular
AAGLRUU arugula
augural
AAGLRVX gravlax
AAGMMNS magsman
AAGMMRR grammar
AAGMMTU gummata
AAGMMUY mamaguy
AAGMNNR grannam
AAGMNOS sangoma
AAGMNPR pangram
AAGMNPY pangamy
AAGMNRT tangram
trangam
AAGMNSW swagman
AAGMOPY apogamy
AAGMORS margosa
AAGMOSU agamous
AAGMRRY gramary
AAGNOPR paragon
AAGNORZ organza
AAGNRRY Granary®
granary
AAGNRTV vagrant
AAGOPSS sapsago
AAGORSU saguaro
AAGPRST gas trap
AAGSTUU Augusta
AAHHIRS Shari'ah
AAHHKKL Khalkha
AAHHNNT thannah
AAHHNPT naphtha
AAHHOOW whoa-hoa
AAHHOPR pharaoh✧
AAHIINT Haitian
AAHIJNR Harijan
AAHIKNT Inkatha
AAHIKRT kithara
AAHILLL all-hail
hallali
AAHILLN hallian
AAHILMR almirah
AAHILMS shimaal
AAHILMT thalami
AAHILNS Sinhala
AAHILNT thalian
AAHILPV Pahlavi
AAHIMNO mahonia
AAHIMNR Ahriman
AAHIMNS Samhain
AAHIMRT Marathi
AAHINNU Huainan
AAHINOP aphonia
AAHINOR Honiara
AAHINPP Paphian
AAHINPR piranha
AAHINST Ashanti
shaitan✧
AAHINSV Shavian
AAHINTW taniwha
AAHIORT to a hair
AAHIPRT pitarah
AAHIPTY Hypatia
AAHIPTZ zaptiah
AAHIRSS harissa
AAHIRST shariat✧
AAHISVY Vaishya
AAHJKNR khanjar
AAHJNNO Johanna
AAHKLRS lashkar
AAHKMSY yashmak
AAHKNRS Shankar
AAHKNSU Anushka
AAHKNSY Sankhya
AAHKRSS rakshas
AAHKRWW war hawk
AAHLLTT all that
tall hat
AAHLLWY hallway
AAHLMMS mashlam
AAHLMRS marshal
AAHLMRU hamular

AAHLNPX phalanx
AAHLNRW narwhal
AAHLNTU Nahuatl
AAHLOST sola hat
AAHLPPR Phar Lap
AAHLPRS phrasal
AAHLPST asphalt
taplash
AAHLRSW shalwar
AAHMMNS mashman
AAHMNNU hanuman✧
AAHMNOS Mashona
AAHMNRS harmans
AAHMNSS shamans
AAHMNTX xantham
AAHMOPR amphora
AAHMORS Masorah
AAHMQSU quamash
AAHMSTV mash-vat
AAHMSTZ matzahs
AAHNNOS hosanna
AAHNNPR harn-pan
AAHNNTX xanthan
AAHNORT athanor
AAHNORV navarho
AAHNOSV Navahos
AAHNPRS Hans Arp
AAHNRTX anthrax
AAHNRTY rhatany
AAHPRTW warpath
AAHPSTU at a push
haut pas
AAHPTWY pathway
AAHRSST shastra
AAHRSTY ashtray
AAHRTTW athwart
AAHSWYY shy away
AAIILLP Palilia
AAIILMR airmail
AAIILNT Italian
AAIILNV Lavinia
Vinalia
AAIILNZ Azilian
AAIILPR pairial
AAIILPT tilapia
AAIILRR air-rail
AAIILRZ alizari
AAIINNR Iranian
AAIINNZ anziani
AAIINTT Titania
AAIINZZ zizania
AAIIRTX air taxi
AAIIRVV vivaria
AAIJLNP jalapin
AAIJLNU Juliana
AAIJMNP jampani
AAIJMOR a majori
AAIJNRZ janizar
AAIJNTU Tijuana
AAIJPPY jipyapa
AAIKLLM Kallima

AAIKLLS alkalis
AAIKLPT kail-pat
AAIKMNN manakin
AAIKMNR ramakin
AAIKMOR romaika
AAIKMOS amakosi
AAIKMRS karaism
AAIKMSY may I ask
AAIKNNT Kantian
AAIKNOW Okinawa
AAIKNRT Katrina
AAIKORU ouakari
AAIKOSY sokaiya
AAIKPPR paprika
AAIKRSS askaris
AAIKSTT astatki
AAIKTVV akvavit
AAILLLP pallial
AAILLMM mamilla
AAILLMN manilla
AAILLMR armilla
AAILLMX maxilla
AAILLNV vanilla
AAILLPP papilla
AAILLRX axillar
AAILLSV salival
AAILLUV alluvia
AAILLXY axially
AAILMMN mailman
AAILMMR ammiral
AAILMMS Lamaism
miasmal
AAILMMX maximal
AAILMNR laminar
railman
AAILMNT matinal
AAILMNU alumina
AAILMNV mailvan
AAILMOS Somalia
AAILMPS impalas
AAILMRS sail arm
AAILMRT marital
martial✧
AAILMSS salamis✧
AAILMST Lamaist
AAILMWW Mawlawi
AAILNOP Pianola®
AAILNOT ailanto
Laotian
AAILNOV novalia
valonia✧
AAILNPS salpian
AAILNPT platina
AAILNPU Paulian
Paulina
AAILNRU ulnaria
Uralian
AAILNRY laniary
AAILNSS Nasalis
AAILNSV Silvana
AAILNTV Latvian

valiant
AAILORS rosalia
AAILORU raoulia
AAILORV variola
AAILOST solatia
AAILPPT appalti
AAILPRT partial
patrial
AAILPRY air play
AAILPST spatial
AAILPTT talipat
AAILPZZ palazzi
AAILQWW qawwali
AAILRRV arrival
AAILRTT rat-tail
AAILRTV travail
AAILRWY railway
AAILSSV vassail
AAILSSW wassail
AAILTTT latitat
AAILTWY lay wait
AAIMMNO ammonia
AAIMMSS miasmas
AAIMNNO omniana
AAIMNNR Rain Man
AAIMNOR Romania
AAIMNOS anosmia
AAIMNOT amation
animato
AAIMNRT Martian
Martina
tamarin
AAIMNRX Marxian
AAIMNRZ Mazarin
AAIMNST stamina
AAIMNTX taximan
AAIMORR Roraima
AAIMORV Moravia
AAIMPRS Arimasp
AAIMRSS air mass
AAIMRSU samurai
AAIMRTU timarau
AAIMSST stasima
AAIMSTV atavism
AAIMSUV mauvais
AAINNOT Antonia
AAINNRU uranian✧
AAINNRV navarin
nirvana✧
AAINOPS paisano
AAINORR orarian
AAINORV ovarian
AAINORZ Arizona
AAINPRT Patarin
AAINRST artisan
Sinatra
tsarina
AAINRSU saurian
AAINRSV savarin
AAINRTV variant
AAINRTW antiwar

AAINSTV vanitas
AAINTTT attaint
AAINTTU tutania
AAINTUY Taiyuan
AAIOPRR pair-oar
AAIOPRT atropia
AAIORRS rosaria✧
AAIORSU saouari
AAIORTV aviator
AAIPPRU puparia
AAIPPTT pitapat
pit-a-pat
AAIPRRT air-trap
AAIPRSS Sarapis
AAIPRTT partita
AAIPRTV Parvati
AAIQRRW Iraq War
AAIQSSU quassia
AAIQTUV aquavit
AAIRSTU Austria
AAIRSWY airways
AAITTUV via tuta
AAITWXY taxiway
AAJKLWY jaywalk
AAJKMNR jarkman
AAJMNZZ jazzman
AAJMORT majorat
AAJMPSY pyjamas
AAJMRTT jam tart
AAJNNOU Anjouan
AAJNNSU San Juan
AAJNNSY Nyanjas
AAJNOSV Navajos
AAJNRUY January
AAJOPSU sapajou
AAKKLRU karakul✧
AAKKMOT tokamak
AAKKMRS markkas
AAKKOPS kakapos
AAKKSUZ zakuska
AAKLMNW Walkman®
AAKLMPU lampuka
AAKLMRY malarky
AAKLMUY yamulka
AAKLNOO oolakan
AAKLNOR Alkoran
AAKLNOU oulakan
AAKLOOP palooka
AAKLOOT talooka
AAKLRSU Kursaal
rusalka
AAKLSSU saksaul
AAKLWWY walkway
AAKMMNR markman
AAKMNOR a mark on
AAKMOST oak mast
AAKMOSU mousaka
AAKMRUZ mazurka
AAKMRWY waymark
AAKNNTU nunatak
AAKNTWY twankay

AAKOOPP	pakapoo
AAKORST	ostraka
AAKPRWY	parkway
AAKRTTU	Atatürk
AAKRTUY	autarky
AAKSTTT	attaskt
AALLLNS	Lallans
AALLLSW	Walsall
AALLMPU	ampulla
AALLMRT	mall rat
AALLNPU	planula
AALLNSY	nasally
AALLORW	Oral Law
AALLOTV	lavolta
AALLPPY	papally
AALLRST	all-star
AALLRUY	aurally
AALLRVY	vallary
AALLTWY	ally-taw
AALLUVV	valvula
AALMMNO	ammonal
AALMMNS	alms-man
AALMMNT	maltman
AALMNOS	salamon
AALMNOY	anomaly
	Layamon
AALMNST	last man
AALMNSU	Manaslu
AALMORT	alamort
AALMORY	mayoral
AALMPRY	palmary
	palmyra
AALMPWX	wax palm
AALMRRU	ramular
AALMRUX	Malraux
AALMSWY	May laws
AALMTTU	mulatta
AALNNRU	annular
AALNORS	also-ran
AALNORW	war loan
AALNPRT	plantar
AALNPST	salt pan
AALNPSV	Pan-Slav
AALNPTU	Laputan
AALNPUU	punalua
AALNQTU	quantal
AALNRTT	latrant
AALNRTU	natural
AALNSTT	saltant
AALNSTU	sultana
AALNSTY	analyst
AALNTTU	talaunt
AALOPPT	appalto
AALOPRS	parasol
AALOPST	al pasto
AALOPTV	Poltava
AALOPVV	pavlova✧
AALOPZZ	palazzo
AALORRU	auroral
AALORSU	arousal
AALORTX	laxator
AALOSST	at a loss
AALOSTT	saltato
AALOTTY	talayot
AALPPRU	papular
AALPPSU	Uppsala
AALPRSW	asprawl
AALPSTU	spatula
AALPWYY	play-way
AALRSTT	stratal
AALRSTU	austral✧
AALRSTY	astylar
	satyral
AALRSUZ	Lazarus
AALRWYY	lyra-way
AALSSTU	assault
AALSSUU	as usual
AAMMMRY	mammary
AAMMNNX	Manxman
AAMMNRT	mantram
AAMMNRY	Myanmar
AAMMNTY	Tammany
AAMMRST	ramstam
AAMNNOT	Montana
AAMNNOY	anonyma
AAMNNTU	Mantuan
AAMNOOS	manoaos
AAMNORR	Marrano
	orra man
AAMNORS	oarsman
AAMNORT	amorant
AAMNORW	man-o'-war
AAMNOTY	anatomy
AAMNPRT	mantrap
	rampant
AAMNPRY	paranym
AAMNPSS	passman
AAMNPST	tapsman
AAMNPTY	tympana
AAMNRST	artsman
	Starman
AAMNRTY	army ant
AAMOORS	amorosa
AAMOPRS	paramos
AAMORRZ	zamarro
AAMORSS	Massora
AAMORSV	samovar
AAMORTY	amatory
AAMOSSS	samosas
AAMOSTT	stomata
AAMOTTU	automat
AAMPRRT	rampart
AAMPRSS	Sampras
AAMPRST	star map
AAMPSSY	ampassy
AAMRRTY	Marryat
AAMRSST	matrass
AAMRSSY	Marsyas
AAMRSTU	sumatra✧
	traumas
AAMRTWY	tramway
AAMSSTU	satsuma
AANNORS	Rosanna
AANNOTT	annatto
AANNRUU	Nauruan
AANNSSU	Susanna
AANORRW	narrow a
AANORTT	Taranto
AANORTU	Arnaout
AANOSTT	anattos
	à tâtons
AANPRST	spartan✧
AANPRSU	Puranas
AANPRTU	pará nut
AANPSST	passant
AANQRTU	quartan
AANRRTW	warrant
AANRSUV	Varanus
AANRUWY	run away
	runaway
AANSSTW	Tswanas
AANSTTT	statant
AANSWYY	anyways
AANTUUV	Vanuatu
AAOORRW	woorara
AAOPRRT	pro rata
AAOPSST	potassa
AAORRSU	auroras
AAORSTV	Saratov
AAOTTUY	tatouay
AAPQSUW	Quapaws
AAPRRTT	rat trap✧
AAPRSTY	satrapy
AAPRTWY	part way
	part-way
AAPTUWY	put away
AAPZZZZ	pazzazz
AARRTTY	Tartary
AARSUYY	Surayya
ABBBDEL	blabbed
ABBBELR	babbler
	blabber
	brabble
ABBBIST	Babbit's
ABBBITT	babbitt✧
ABBCDER	crabbed
ABBCDES	scabbed
ABBCDOY	Baby Doc
ABBCEHI	babiche
ABBCEHU	babuche
ABBCELR	clabber
ABBCELS	scabble
ABBCERR	crabber
ABBCIRT	crabbit
ABBCKUY	buy-back
ABBCMOR	car bomb
	car-bomb
ABBCRYY	crybaby
ABBDDET	bad debt
ABBDEGR	grabbed
ABBDEHT	bedbath
ABBDEIT	tabbied
ABBDEIY	abide by
ABBDEKR	bark-bed
ABBDELR	dabbler
	drabble
ABBDELS	slabbed
ABBDERR	drabber
ABBDERT	drabbet
ABBDEST	stabbed
ABBDESW	swabbed
ABBDGIN	big band
	big-band
	dabbing
ABBDGOY	body bag
ABBDHIJ	djibbah
ABBDILO	Bobadil
ABBDILR	libbard
ABBDINR	ribband
ABBDITY	dabbity
ABBDLRU	lubbard
ABBDMOR	bombard
ABBDMOU	babudom
ABBDNOX	band-box
ABBDNOY	boy band
ABBDNYY	by and by
	by-and-by
ABBEELM	bee balm
ABBEERR	Berbera
ABBEESW	bawbees
ABBEFOW	a few bob
ABBEGIT	Big Beat
ABBEGLR	gabbler
	grabble
ABBEGLT	belt bag
ABBEGLU	blue bag
ABBEGNO	bogbean
ABBEGNU	bugbane
ABBEGRR	grabber
ABBEGRU	bugbear
ABBEHLS	shabble
ABBELLR	barbell
ABBELMR	bramble
ABBELNS	snabble
ABBELOR	belabor
ABBELPR	prabble
ABBELRR	rabbler
ABBELRS	slabber
ABBELRU	barbule
ABBELRW	wabbler
ABBELSU	bas-bleu
ABBELUY	buyable
ABBEMOX	box beam
ABBEMUZ	bumbaze
ABBEOTX	beatbox
ABBERST	stabber
ABBERSW	swabber
ABBESSU	subbase
ABBFIRT	frabbit
ABBGGIN	big bang✧
	gabbing
ABBGINN	nabbing
ABBGINS	sabbing
ABBGINT	tabbing

ABBGINU	bubinga
ABBGINY	babying
ABBGOOU	bugaboo
ABBGORS	gabbros
ABBGORY	Babygro®
ABBHINO	Hobbian
ABBHISY	babyish
ABBHNOO	hob-a-nob
ABBHNTU	Bath bun
ABBHOOS	baboosh
ABBHRRU	rhubarb
ABBHTTU	bathtub
ABBIIMN	bambini
ABBIIMS	Babiism
ABBILOR	bilobar
ABBILOT	bobtail
ABBILOY	baby oil
ABBILSU	bubalis
ABBIMNO	bambino
ABBIMSU	babuism
ABBINOR	rabboni
ABBINRS	rabbins
ABBIRST	rabbits
ABBIRSU	Babrius
ABBIRTY	rabbity
ABBISTY	baby-sit
ABBKLOU	blaubok
ABBLLOY	ball-boy
ABBLLTU	bullbat
ABBLMRY	brambly
ABBLNOY	Babylon
ABBLSUU	Bubalus
ABBMOOR	bombora
ABBMOST	bombast
ABBMOTU	bum-boat
ABBNRTU	bran tub
ABBNRUY	Banbury
ABBOORR	Roobarb
ABBORRU	Barbour®
ABBQSUY	squabby
ABCCCHI	bacchic✧
ABCCEER	Rebecca
ABCCEIR	acerbic
	breccia
ABCCEIS	sebacic
ABCCHII	bacchii
ABCCHOR	choc-bar
ABCCHSU	Bacchus
ABCCHTY	bycatch
ABCCIIR	Cabiric
ABCCILU	cubical
ABCCIMR	cambric
ABCCINU	buccina
ABCCIOR	boracic
	braccio
ABCCKOW	bawcock
ABCCKTU	cut back
	cutback
ABCCNOU	Nabucco
ABCCOOR	barocco
ABCCOOT	tobacco
ABCCSUU	succuba
ABCDEEH	beached
ABCDEEI	Cebidae
ABCDEEL	debacle
	débâcle
ABCDEHU	debauch
ABCDEIK	die back
	dieback
ABCDEIP	pedicab
ABCDEIR	carbide
ABCDEKN	back-end
ABCDEKR	redback
ABCDELO	coal-bed
ABCDEMP	camp-bed
ABCDEOR	barcode
	brocade
ABCDERU	cudbear
ABCDGOR	dog-crab
ABCDHIO	ichabod
ABCDHOR	chobdar
ABCDIIS	dibasic
ABCDILR	baldric
ABCDINR	bin card
ABCDINS	abscind
ABCDIOR	CB radio
ABCDIRS	scabrid
ABCDIRT	catbird
ABCDIRU	baudric
ABCDISU	subacid
ABCDKLU	bad luck
ABCDNOS	abscond
ABCDOOR	cordoba
	córdoba✧
ABCDORR	brocard
ABCDORU	bucardo
ABCEEHM	Beecham
ABCEEHU	ébauche
ABCEEMR	embrace
ABCEENR	carbene
ABCEENS	absence
ABCEERR	cerebra
	rebrace
ABCEERU	berceau
ABCEESS	bécasse
ABCEESU	because
ABCEGIR	ribcage
ABCEGKP	peg back
ABCEGKT	get back
ABCEGLU	lace bug
ABCEGMO	camboge
ABCEGOR	brocage
ABCEGOS	boscage
ABCEHIR	Hebraic
ABCEHIT	Thebaic
ABCEHKM	Beckham
ABCEHKO	backhoe
ABCEHLN	Blanche
ABCEHLO	chaebol
ABCEHLU	bauchle
ABCEHMR	becharm
	brecham
	chamber
	chambré
ABCEHMT	Macbeth
ABCEHOS	basoche
ABCEHRT	brachet
	the Crab
ABCEIIR	Cabeiri
ABCEIKL	lie back
ABCEIKT	tieback
ABCEILL	iceball
ABCEILM	alembic
	cembali
ABCEILR	caliber
	calibre
ABCEILT	citable
ABCEIMO	amoebic
ABCEIMU	Cimabué
ABCEINR	carbine
ABCEINT	cabinet✧
ABCEIOR	aerobic
ABCEIOT	iceboat
ABCEIRS	ascribe
	Brescia
ABCEISS	abscise
	scabies
ABCEITT	tabetic
ABCEKLN	blacken
ABCEKNR	bracken
ABCEKRT	bracket
ABCEKST	backset
	set back
	setback
ABCEKSY	backsey
ABCEKTW	wetback
ABCELLU	bullace
	cue ball
ABCELMO	cembalo
ABCELMR	cambrel
	clamber
ABCELMS	scamble
ABCELOP	placebo
ABCELOV	vocable
ABCELPU	bluecap
ABCELPY	byplace
ABCELRU	curable
ABCELSU	bascule
ABCELUY	Luce Bay
ABCELWY	Clew Bay
ABCENOR	baconer
ABCENOW	cowbane
ABCENOZ	cabezon
ABCENRU	unbrace
ABCEOOS	caboose
ABCEORU	corbeau
ABCESSS	abscess
ABCESTW	webcast
ABCFFKO	back off
ABCFIKN	finback
ABCFILO	bifocal
ABCFKLY	flyback
ABCFLNU	fan club
ABCFLOO	cobloaf
ABCFLOX	box-calf
ABCGHKO	hogback
ABCGIKN	backing
ABCGIKS	sick bag
ABCGILN	cabling
ABCGINR	bracing
ABCGIST	big cats
ABCGKLO	backlog
ABCGLOO	cool bag
ABCGMSU	scumbag
ABCHHII	hibachi
ABCHIKT	hit back
ABCHILS	Chablis
ABCHILU	Baluchi
ABCHIMT	bathmic
ABCHIOT	cohabit
ABCHITT	batch it
ABCHKOU	chabouk
ABCHKTU	hackbut
ABCHKUW	hawbuck
ABCHLOR	Chabrol
ABCHNOR	brochan
	Bronach
ABCHNRU	braunch
ABCHNRY	branchy
ABCHOSX	cash-box
ABCHSTU	bush-cat
ABCIILL	bacilli
ABCIILN	albinic
ABCIILT	albitic
ABCIIMN	minicab
ABCIIMS	iambics
ABCIIOR	ciboria
ABCIIOT	abiotic
ABCIJNO	jacobin✧
ABCIKST	sit back
ABCIKSY	sick bay
ABCILOR	crab-oil
ABCILRS	scribal
ABCILTU	cubital
ABCIMMS	cambism
ABCIMMU	cambium
ABCIMOR	Coimbra
ABCIMRU	Cumbria
ABCIMST	cambist
ABCINNO	in banco
ABCINOT	botanic
ABCIORR	barrico
ABCIORU	caribou
ABCIOUV	bivouac
ABCIRTY	barytic
ABCISSS	absciss
ABCISTU	bias-cut
ABCJOSU	jacobus
ABCKLLY	blackly
ABCKLOT	backlot
ABCKLTU	Blu-Tack®
ABCKMRU	buckram
ABCKMUZ	zambuck✧
ABCKNNO	bannock

Words marked ✧ can also be spelled with one or more capital letters

ABCKNRU	runback
ABCKORW	back row
	back-row
ABCKOSW	sowback
ABCKOTU	back out
	outback
ABCKPTU	put back
ABCKRTU	Tarbuck
ABCKRTY	try back
ABCKSTU	sackbut
	subtack
ABCKSUW	bucksaw
	sawbuck
ABCLLOW	cob wall
ABCLLOX	call-box
ABCLLOY	call-boy
ABCLLUW	club-law
ABCLMNU	clubman
ABCLMOU	Columba
ABCLMOY	cymbalo
ABCLMUU	baculum
ABCLNOY	balcony
ABCLOOX	coal-box
ABCMOST	combats
ABCNOSW	cob-swan
ABCNOUY	can buoy
ABCNRTU	crab-nut
ABCOOTX	box-coat
ABCORRW	crowbar
ABCOTTU	cab-tout
ABDDEER	bearded
	breaded
ABDDEES	debased
ABDDEEZ	bedazed
ABDDEIN	abidden
	bandied
ABDDEIR	braided
ABDDELR	bladder
ABDDEMR	mad-bred
ABDDENR	branded
ABDDENS	sand bed
ABDDEOR	roadbed
ABDDERW	bedward
ABDDEST	baddest
ABDDHIS	baddish
ABDDINS	disband
ABDDLLO	oddball
ABDDMOR	dambrod
ABDEEFL	feelbad
	feel-bad
ABDEEGR	rebadge
ABDEEHV	behaved
ABDEEIL	lie-abed
ABDEEIR	beardie
ABDEELM	beldame
	bemedal
ABDEELR	bederal
	bleared
ABDEELT	belated
ABDEELY	belayed
	dyeable
ABDEEMN	bedeman
	benamed
ABDEEMR	ambered
	embread
ABDEEMS	embased
ABDEEMZ	bemazed
ABDEEPT	peat bed
ABDEERS	debaser
ABDEERT	betread
	debater
ABDEEST	bestead
ABDEETT	abetted
ABDEFLT	flatbed
ABDEFLU	leafbud
ABDEFOR	forbade
ABDEFOS	sofa bed
ABDEFRW	bedwarf
ABDEFST	bedfast
ABDEGGR	bragged
ABDEGHI	bighead
ABDEGHR	beghard
ABDEGIL	big deal
ABDEGIM	dime bag
ABDEGIN	beading
ABDEGIR	abridge
	brigade
ABDEGIW	wide-gab
ABDEGLN	bangled
ABDEGLR	belgard
	garbled
ABDEGNO	bondage
	dogbane
ABDEHIT	habited
	Thebaid
ABDEHLR	halberd
ABDEHOR	Deborah
ABDEHOW	bowhead
ABDEHOY	head boy
ABDEHRS	berdash
ABDEHRT	breadth
	the Bard
ABDEHST	had best
ABDEHSU	subhead
ABDEILN	Belinda
	nail-bed
ABDEILP	bipedal
	piebald
ABDEILR	railbed
	ridable
ABDEILS	disable
ABDEILU	audible
ABDEIMR	embraid
ABDEINR	brained
ABDEINW	Bedawin
ABDEIOV	Bovidae
ABDEIRR	briared
ABDEIRS	darbies
	seabird
	sidebar
	side-bar
ABDEIRT	tribade
ABDEISS	biassed
ABDEIST	bastide
ABDEJOU	j'adoube
ABDEKNU	unbaked
ABDELMR	marbled
ABDELMY	embayld
ABDELNO	old bean
ABDELOS	albedos
ABDELOT	bloated
ABDELOW	dowable
ABDELPU	dupable
ABDELPY	pyebald
ABDELRR	drabler
ABDELRU	durable
ABDELST	blasted
ABDELTT	blatted
ABDELYZ	lazy-bed
ABDEMNO	abdomen
ABDEMRU	Bermuda
ABDENNR	Brendan
ABDENOR	bandore
	broaden
ABDENOY	naebody
ABDENRR	Bernard
	brander
	rebrand
ABDENRU	urd bean
ABDENRW	brawned
ABDENSS	badness
ABDENSU	subdean
ABDENSW	bad news
ABDENTU	unbated
ABDEOOT	tabooed
ABDEORR	boarder
ABDEOST	boasted
ABDEOTU	boutade
ABDEQSU	basqued
ABDERST	dabster
ABDERSU	subedar
ABDERTY	drybeat
ABDERUY	daubery
ABDETTU	abutted
ABDFIIR	bid fair
ABDFMOR	bad form
ABDFOTY	fat body
ABDGGOR	boggard
ABDGHOT	Godthab
ABDGIIN	abiding
ABDGILN	balding
ABDGINN	banding
ABDGINR	brigand
ABDGINT	dingbat
ABDGINU	daubing
ABDGINW	windbag
ABDGJNU	jug band
ABDGLNO	bogland
ABDGLUY	ladybug
ABDGNNU	Bandung
ABDGSTU	dust bag
ABDHHOS	dobhash
ABDHIIT	adhibit
ABDHILS	baldish
ABDHMOR	rhabdom
ABDHMSU	budmash
ABDHMTU	mudbath
ABDHNOR	bodhran
	bodhrán
ABDHNOW	bow-hand
ABDHNSU	husband
ABDHOPR	hard bop
ABDHOST	bad shot
ABDHOSW	bad show
ABDHRSU	burdash
	rhabdus
ABDIKNW	bawdkin
ABDIKRS	disbark
ABDILMO	bimodal
ABDILNW	Baldwin
ABDILOO	diabolo
ABDILOR	labroid
ABDILOT	tabloid
ABDILRW	awlbird
ABDILRY	rabidly
ABDILUY	audibly
ABDILWY	bawdily
ABDIMNR	birdman
ABDIMOR	ambroid
ABDIMRU	radium B
	Rimbaud
ABDIMRY	may-bird
ABDINOR	inboard
ABDINOY	in a body
ABDINRT	antbird
	tri-band
ABDINST	bandits
ABDINSU	Ibn Saud
ABDIOSU	badious
ABDIPRT	bad trip
ABDIPRU	upbraid
ABDIRSU	subarid
ABDIRTY	tribady
ABDKNOO	bandook
ABDKOOY	day book
ABDLLNY	blandly
ABDLLOR	bollard
ABDLMOR	Lombard
ABDLNOR	bandrol
ABDLORY	broadly
ABDLRUY	durably
	rybauld
ABDLRYY	byrlady
ABDLSUU	subdual
ABDMNNO	bondman
ABDMNOY	man-body
ABDMOTU	mud-boat
ABDMRUY	marybud
ABDMSSU	dumb-ass
ABDNNOR	Bonnard
ABDNOOR	on board
	onboard
	on-board
ABDNOPR	proband

ABDNOSU	bausond
ABDNOSX	sandbox
ABDNOSY	sandboy
ABDNOUY	dan buoy
ABDNOYY	anybody
ABDNRTU	turband
ABDNSTY	stand by
	stand-by
ABDOORW	barwood
ABDOPRU	board up
ABDORWY	draw-boy
ABDRSTU	bustard
ABDRUZZ	buzzard
ABEEEFS	base fee
ABEEEFT	beef tea
ABEEEGR	beerage
ABEEELM	lee beam
ABEEELS	seeable
ABEEELV	leave be
ABEEEMY	eye-beam
ABEEERV	bereave
ABEEEST	sea beet
ABEEFFL	effable
ABEEFGR	Fabergé
ABEEFHM	beef-ham
ABEEFLO	beefalo
ABEEFTU	beaufet
ABEEGHR	herbage
ABEEGLL	gabelle
ABEEGLR	beagler
ABEEGPW	web page✧
ABEEGRR	gerbera
ABEEGRU	auberge
ABEEGRW	brewage
ABEEHKR	Rebekah
ABEEHLR	heelbar
ABEEHMS	beshame
ABEEHMT	embathe
ABEEHNN	henbane
ABEEHNS	banshee
	has-been
ABEEHNT	beneath
ABEEHRT	breathe
	herb tea
ABEEHST	H E Bates
ABEEHTY	eyebath
ABEEIMT	tie beam
ABEEINT	betaine
ABEEIRT	ebriate
ABEEIST	beastie
ABEEKNT	betaken
ABEEKNV	beknave
ABEEKNY	eye bank
ABEEKOP	peekabo
ABEEKPS	bespake
	bespeak
ABEEKRR	breaker
ABEELLY	eyeball
ABEELMM	emblema
ABEELMT	beamlet
ABEELMW	ewe-lamb
ABEELMZ	emblaze
ABEELNP	plebean
ABEELNR	enabler
ABEELNT	Beltane
	tenable
ABEELNU	nebulae
ABEELOR	earlobe
ABEELPR	bepearl
ABEELQU	equable
ABEELRR	errable
ABEELRT	bleater
	retable
ABEELST	sea belt
ABEELSU	sea-blue
	sueable
ABEELSV	beslave
ABEEMRS	besmear
ABEEMRT	beer-mat
ABEEMRV	embrave
ABEEMST	beats me
	embaste
ABEENOR	ear-bone
ABEENRS	Benares
ABEENRV	verbena
ABEENRY	beanery
ABEEORT	abortee
ABEEPST	bespate
ABEERRT	rebater
	tabrere
	terebra✧
ABEERTT	abetter
ABEERVY	beavery
ABEESTY	Tees Bay
ABEESWX	beeswax
ABEFFLR	baffler
ABEFFMO	off beam
	off-beam
ABEFFOS	off base
ABEFFOT	beat off
	offbeat
ABEFGIL	filabeg
ABEFGST	gabfest
ABEFILN	finable
ABEFILR	friable
ABEFILX	fixable
ABEFINU	beaufin
ABEFIRR	fire-bar
ABEFIRT	far be it
ABEFIRV	five-bar
ABEFITY	beatify
ABEFLLU	baleful
ABEFLLY	flyable
ABEFLNT	fan belt
ABEFLNU	baneful
ABEFLNY	flybane
ABEFLST	Belfast
ABEFORR	forbear
ABEGGIM	big game
ABEGGIS	baggies
ABEGGLR	blagger
ABEGGMO	gamboge
ABEGGNU	buggane
ABEGGNY	gang-bye
ABEGGRU	burgage
ABEGGRY	beggary
ABEGHMR	Maghreb
ABEGHNS	shebang
ABEGHRU	bear hug
ABEGILL	leg bail
ABEGILN	Belgian
	Bengali
ABEGILR	Gabriel
ABEGIMN	beaming
	big name
ABEGIMR	gambier
ABEGIMT	megabit
ABEGINO	begonia
ABEGINR	barge in
	bearing
ABEGINT	beating
ABEGINW	wine bag
ABEGIPP	bagpipe
ABEGKOR	brokage
ABEGKOS	boskage
ABEGLMR	gambler
	gambrel
ABEGLNR	brangle
ABEGLOR	albergo
ABEGLOT	globate
ABEGLRR	garbler
ABEGLSS	bagless
ABEGMNR	Bergman
ABEGMOR	Bergamo
	embargo
ABEGMOS	gamboes
ABEGMOY	Game Boy®
ABEGMRU	umbrage
ABEGNNT	banteng
ABEGNOS	nosebag
ABEGNOT	Boateng
ABEGOPT	peat bog
ABEGOPY	pageboy
ABEGORR	begorra
ABEGORS	Seaborg
ABEGORX	gearbox
ABEGOSZ	gazebos
ABEGOTT	bottega
	tote bag
ABEGOUY	buoyage
ABEGRRU	garbure
ABEGRST	bargest
ABEHILR	hirable
ABEHIMS	beamish
ABEHIMT	imbathe
ABEHIRS	bearish
ABEHISU	beauish
ABEHITU	habitué
ABEHITZ	zabtieh
ABEHKRU	hauberk
ABEHKTU	Ketubah
ABEHLMS	shamble
ABEHLMT	Lambeth
	the Lamb
ABEHLNU	unhable
ABEHLRT	blather
	halbert
ABEHLSU	ale-bush
ABEHMNT	Bentham
ABEHNOS	bone ash
ABEHNTY	Bethany
ABEHOTY	hay-bote
ABEHRRY	herbary
ABEHRST	Barthes
	bathers
ABEHRTY	breathy
	by heart
ABEHSTU	bush tea
ABEIILL	baillie
ABEIILR	Liberia
ABEIINR	Iberian
ABEIINT	bainite
ABEIJMR	jambier
ABEIJNS	basenji
ABEIJOX	Joe Baxi
ABEIKLL	likable
ABEIKLS	skiable
ABEIKLY	Kiel Bay
ABEIKNR	break in
	break-in
	inbreak
ABEIKNT	beatnik
ABEIKWY	bikeway
ABEILLO	lobelia
ABEILLP	pliable
ABEILLR	air-bell
	Braille
	liberal✧
ABEILLV	livable
ABEILMN	minable
ABEILMR	mirable
	remblai
ABEILMS	ableism
ABEILMT	limbate
	timbale
ABEILMX	mixable
ABEILMY	beamily
ABEILNP	biplane
ABEILNR	bar line
	linear B
ABEILNS	lesbian✧
ABEILNY	bay-line
ABEILPS	ba'spiel
ABEILPT	patible
ABEILRT	librate
	tablier
	triable
ABEILST	ableist
	astilbe
	bestial
	stabile
ABEILSZ	sizable
ABEILVV	bivalve

ABEIMNR	mirbane
ABEIMNT	ambient
ABEIMOT	Moabite
ABEIMZZ	Zambezi
ABEINNO	Niobean
ABEINOR	Bonaire
ABEINOT	niobate
ABEINOZ	Zenobia
ABEINPR	bran-pie
ABEINPT	bepaint
ABEINRS	Serbian
ABEINRT	atebrin
ABEINRW	wine bar
ABEINRZ	zebrina
ABEINST	Antibes
	basinet
	besaint
	bestain
ABEINTT	Bettina
	tabinet
	Tibetan
ABEINTY	bay-tine
ABEIOOT	Boeotia
ABEIORS	isobare
ABEIOSS	isobase
ABEIOTV	obviate
ABEIPRT	bear pit
ABEIPST	baptise
ABEIPTZ	baptize
ABEIRRR	barrier
ABEIRRS	brasier
ABEIRRT	arbiter
	rarebit
ABEIRRW	wire bar
ABEIRRZ	bizarre
	brazier
ABEIRSS	brassie
ABEIRTT	biretta
	bit-rate
ABEIRTV	vibrate
ABEIRTX	Beatrix
ABEIRTZ	Bizerta
ABEIRUX	exurbia
ABEISTT	batiste
ABEISUV	abusive
ABEITUX	bauxite
ABEJLLR	bell jar
ABEJLUY	blue jay
ABEJMNO	jambone
ABEJMUX	jambeux
ABEJNOS	banjoes
ABEJNOW	jawbone
ABEJOTT	jet boat
ABEJRRU	abjurer
ABEKLLY	bleakly
ABEKLNT	blanket
ABEKNSU	sunbake
ABEKOOR	abrooke
ABEKORT	to-brake
	to-break
ABEKPRU	break up
	break-up
	upbreak
ABELLMN	bellman
ABELLNO	Bellona
ABELLNT	netball
ABELLOS	losable
ABELLOV	lovable
	volable
ABELLPT	lap belt
ABELLRU	rubella
	rulable
ABELLTU	bullate
ABELMMR	membral
ABELMNT	beltman
	lambent
ABELMNU	albumen
ABELMOT	to blame
ABELMOV	movable
ABELMRR	marbler
	rambler
ABELMRS	marbles
ABELMRT	lambert
ABELMRY	Bramley
ABELMTU	mutable
ABELMYY	Lyme Bay
ABELNNO	Lebanon
ABELNOO	Boolean
ABELNOT	notable
ABELNOW	lean bow
ABELNOY	baloney
ABELNRS	bransle
ABELNRT	brantle
ABELNRU	nebular
ABELNRY	blarney✧
ABELNSU	bus lane
	nebulas
ABELNTU	tunable
ABELOOW	wooable
ABELOPR	ropable
ABELOPT	potable
ABELORS	labrose
	Rosabel
ABELORT	bloater
ABELORU	rubeola
ABELORW	rowable
ABELOSV	absolve
ABELOTU	bale out
ABELOTW	towable
ABELOXX	axle-box
ABELPRU	puberal
ABELPUZ	blaze up
ABELQUY	equably
ABELRRW	brawler
	warbler
ABELRSS	braless
ABELRST	blaster
	stabler
ABELRSU	Belarus
ABELRSV	verbals
ABELRTT	battler
	blatter
	brattle
ABELRTW	blewart
ABELRUZ	zebrula
ABELRVY	bravely
ABELSST	stables
ABELSTT	battels
ABELSTU	sublate
ABELSTY	beastly
ABELTWY	beltway
ABEMNOS	ambones
ABEMNRU	menu-bar
ABEMNRY	byreman
	myrbane
ABEMNST	best man
ABEMNSU	sunbeam
ABEMNSY	by means
ABEMORS	Ambrose
ABEMORT	bromate
ABEMRRT	Bertram
ABEMRUZ	Merzbau
ABEMSSY	embassy
ABEMTTU	meat-tub
ABENNOR	bar none
	baronne
ABENNRW	bran-new
	Branwen
ABENORS	sea-born
ABENORT	baronet
	reboant
ABENORU	Auberon
ABENORW	rawbone
ABENOSY	by a nose
	soy bean
ABENOTY	bayonet
ABENQTU	banquet
ABENRRS	barrens
ABENRSU	sun bear
ABENRTV	B Traven
ABENRUX	exurban
ABENSTT	Batten's
	test ban
ABENSTU	sunbeat
ABEOORT	aerobot
ABEOOTV	obovate
ABEOPRS	saprobe
ABEOPRT	probate
ABEOQRU	baroque✧
ABEORRS	brasero
ABEORRT	arboret
	Roberta
	taborer
ABEORRW	Boer War
ABEORST	Barotse
	boaster
	sorbate
ABEORSU	Aerobus®
ABEORSV	bravoes
ABEORSY	rosebay
ABEORTT	abettor
	battero
	taboret
ABEORTU	bear out
ABEOSTU	base out
ABEOSTX	box seat
ABEOTTU	beat out
ABEOVWW	bow wave
ABEPRTY	typebar
ABEQRSU	square B
ABERRSU	Bursera
	sabreur
ABERRVY	bravery
ABERSST	brasset
ABERSSU	surbase
ABERSSZ	zebrass
ABERSTU	surbate
ABERSTW	wabster
ABERSTY	barytes
ABERSUU	bureaus
ABERSWY	swear by
ABERTTU	abutter
ABERTTY	battery
ABERTWY	by water
ABERUUX	bureaux
ABERUVY	Avebury
ABESTWY	W B Yeats
ABEZZZZ	bezzazz
ABFFGNO	bang off
ABFFIIL	bailiff
ABFFIOT	a bit off
ABFFLOU	buffalo
ABFGGLO	golf bag
ABFGILN	fabling
ABFGKNO	fog bank
ABFGLSU	bagfuls
ABFHIST	batfish
ABFHLSU	bashful
ABFIILR	bifilar
ABFIIMR	fimbria
ABFILRU	fibular
ABFIMOR	fibroma
ABFINRR	Finbarr
ABFLOTY	boat-fly
	flyboat
ABFOORT	footbar
ABFSTTU	tubfast
ABGGGIN	bagging
ABGGILY	baggily
ABGGINN	banging
ABGGORT	boggart
ABGGORW	grow-bag
ABGHHIR	high bar
ABGHIIR	big hair
ABGHIMR	Maghrib
ABGHINS	bashing
ABGHLOT	hagbolt
ABGHLRU	burghal
ABGHMOO	goombah
ABGHMRU	Hamburg
ABGHNOR	Bronagh
ABGHOTU	abought
ABGHRSU	rag-bush
ABGIINS	biasing

ABGIINT baiting
ABGIKLN balking
ABGIKLT talk big
ABGIKNN banking
ABGIKNR barking✧
ABGILLN balling
ABGILMN ambling
lambing
ABGILMS gimbals
ABGILNT tabling
ABGILNW bawling
ABGILNZ blazing
ABGILOR garboil
ABGIMMN bamming
ABGIMST gambist
ABGINNN banning
ABGINNT banting
ABGINOR Grobian
ABGINOS bagnios
ABGINOT boating
ABGINRR barring
ABGINST basting
ABGINTT batting
ABGINTU tabuing
ABGINTW batwing
ABGIOPT pigboat
ABGIOSU baguios
ABGKKNO Bangkok
ABGKLNO go blank
ABGKMSU musk-bag
ABGKOOR rag-book
ABGKORW workbag
ABGLMNU lumbang
ABGLMOU lumbago
ABGLNOO Bologna
ABGLOOT toolbag
ABGLOPS spag bol
ABGLORT ragbolt
ABGLOSU albugos
subgoal
ABGLRRU burglar
ABGMNOY bogyman
ABGMRRU Marburg
ABGNOPR probang
ABGNOTU bang out
gunboat
ABGNOWY bowyang
ABGOORT botargo
ABGOOTU go about
ABGOPST postbag
ABGORRU goburra
ABGORSU Bourgas
ABGORTU outbrag
ABGOSUY gas-buoy
ABGOTTU tugboat
ABGPSSU Bagpuss
ABHHIPT hip bath
ABHHKOT khotbah
ABHHKTU khutbah
ABHHOOP Pooh-Bah
ABHHSUY hushaby

ABHIIMR Ibrahim
ABHIINT inhabit
ABHIKLS bashlik
ABHIKTW hawkbit
ABHILNO hobnail
ABHILOS abolish
ABHILOT oil bath
ABHILTU halibut
ABHIMNR Brahmin
ABHINOS Siobhán
ABHINSS his nabs
ABHINST absinth
ABHIORS boarish
ABHIOST isobath
ABHISTU habitus
ABHKORU bourkha
ABHKRSU kurbash
ABHLMSY shambly
ABHLOPY play hob
ABHLOUX box-haul
ABHLRSY brashly
ABHLRTU hurlbat
ABHMNSU bushman✧
ABHMSTU mash-tub
ABHNSTU sunbath
ABHOOST Basotho
ABHOPTW P W Botha
ABHORRU harbour
ABHOTUY hautboy
ABHRSTU tarbush
ABHSTUW washtub
ABHTTTU but that
ABHTTUW but what
ABIIINR biriani
ABIIJLS jib sail
ABIIKKT kibitka
ABIIKRT tiki bar
ABIILMU bulimia
ABIILNQ inqilab
ABIILNS aiblins
ABIILOV Bolivia
ABIILRY biliary
ABIILST stibial
ABIILTY ability
ABIIMNR minibar
ABIIMST iambist
ABIINOR Nairobi
robinia
ABIINRY biryani
ABIIOSS abiosis
ABIJKRT R B Kitaj
ABIJLNR brinjal
ABIJNOT abjoint
ABIJNPU Punjabi
ABIJOSW Ojibwas
ABIKLLY likably
ABIKLMN lambkin
ABIKLMR milk bar
ABIKMNR barmkin
ABIKNNU Bakunin
ABIKORU Aboukir

ABIKOTT kit-boat
ABIKOUZ bazouki
ABIKRST britska
ABIKRTZ britzka
ABILLMN billman
ABILLMU ballium
ABILLMY balmily
ABILLNP pinball
ABILLPY pay-bill
pliably
ABILLSW sawbill
ABILLSY Sibylla
Sybilla
syllabi
ABILLTT battill
ABILLWX waxbill
ABILLWY waybill
ABILMNU albumin
ABILMOX mailbox
ABILNOS albinos
ABILNOT bitonal
ABILNOZ bizonal
ABILNRY bairnly
ABILOPR bipolar
parboil
ABILORT orbital
ABILORV bolivar✧
ABILOTU bail out
bailout
bail-out
obitual
tabouli
ABILRRY library
ABILRSU railbus
ABILSYZ sizably
ABIMNOU Anobium
ABIMNOZ Zamboni®
ABIMNRU Umbrian
ABIMOSS biomass
ABIMPST baptism
ABIMRST imbrast
ABIMRTT trimtab
ABIMTTY ambitty
ABINNOS Bosnian
ABINOOR boronia
ABINORR bar-iron
ABINORS Sorbian
ABINORT taborin
ABINORW rainbow✧
ABINOST bastion
ABINOSU abusion
ABINOTT not a bit
ABINRTV vibrant
ABIOORR arborio
ABIORRS barrios
ABIORTV vibrato
ABIPRTT bit-part
ABIPSTT baptist✧
ABIRRTT Britart
ABIRSSY Sybaris
ABIRTTY traybit

ABISSST bassist
ABIZZZZ bizzazz
ABJKMOS sjambok
ABJLMOO jambool
ABJLMTU Jumblat
ABKLLNY blankly
ABKLOOW law-book
ABKLRUW bulwark
ABKMNOO bookman
ABKNOOV Nabokov
ABKNOPT pot bank
ABKNRUU bunraku
ABKORSV bosvark
ABKSSTU subtask
ABLLLUY lullaby
ABLLNOO balloon
ABLLNTU bull ant
ABLLOPR proball
ABLLORR rollbar
ABLLORT toll bar
ABLLORU lobular
ABLLOTY tallboy
ABLLPTU pull-tab
ABLLRUY bullary
ABLMMOU bummalo
ABLMNOU umbonal
ABLMOOT tombola
ABLMOSY lamboys
ABLMOVY movably
ABLMPUU pabulum
ABLMTUY mutably
ABLNORW barn owl
ABLNOTU butanol
ABLNOTY notably
ABLNTUY tunably
ABLOORS robalos
ABLOORT toolbar
ABLOORY obolary
ABLOPTT tap bolt
ABLOPXY play-box
ABLOPYY playboy✧
ABLORST borstal
ABLORTW blawort
ABLORUW bourlaw
ABLOSTX saltbox
ABLOTUW bawl out
ABLPRSU burlaps
ABLPSUY Playbus®
ABLRTUU tubular
ABMMNOS mobsman
ABMNNOR Bormann
ABMNOOR Boorman
ABMNORX Max Born
ABMOORR bar-room
ABMOPRT barmpot
ABMORTU tambour
ABMOSTU subatom
ABNNOOT nanobot
ABNNORS Branson
ABNOORS soroban
ABNOORZ borazon

ABNOOSS bassoon
ABNORTY baryton
ABNOSSU bonasus
ABNOTUY buoyant
ABNRTTU turbant
ABOOPSX soapbox
ABOORTW rowboat
ABOORYZ Bryozoa
ABOOTTW tow boat
ABOPSTT tab stop
ABORSSU sub rosa
ABORSTU robusta
rubatos
ABOSTUU autobus
ABPPUUY buy a pup
ABPRSTU upbrast
ABPSSSU bus pass
ABRRSUY bursary
ABRRTTU Art Brut
ABRRTUY turbary
ABRSTUU arbutus
ABRUWXY Ruby Wax
ABSUWZZ buzz saw
ACCCILY acyclic
ACCDDEI caddice
ACCDDOR d'accord
ACCDEEN cadence
ACCDEER acceder
ACCDEHT catched
ACCDEII accidie
ACCDEIN Candice
ACCDEIO accoied
ACCDEIU caducei
ACCDEKO cockade
ACCDEKR cracked
ACCDENY cadency
ACCDEOP Cape Cod
ACCDEOY accoyed
ACCDERU cardecu
ACCDESU accused
succade
ACCDFIL flaccid
ACCDHIL chalcid
ACCDILS scaldic
ACCDINS Scandic
ACCDIOT octadic
ACCDKNO candock
ACCDKOW dawcock
ACCDLOY accoyld
cacodyl
ACCEEHO coachee
ACCEELN cenacle
ACCEENR creance
ACCEERT accrete
ACCEFIT factice
ACCEFLU felucca
ACCEGIN accinge
ACCEGNO Cocagne
ACCEGOS soccage
ACCEGPU cage-cup
ACCEHHI chéchia
ACCEHIL caliche
chalice
ACCEHIM macchie
ACCEHIN chicane
ACCEHLN chancel
ACCEHLO cochlea
ACCEHLT Caltech
ACCEHMT catch me
ACCEHNO conchae
ACCEHNR chancer
chancre
ACCEHNS chances
ACCEHNT catchen
ACCEHNU chaunce
ACCEHNY chancey
ACCEHOR caroche
coacher
ACCEHPU capuche
ACCEHRT catcher
recatch
ACCEHRU Chaucer
ACCEHTU catechu
ACCEHXY cachexy
ACCEIIL Cecilia
ACCEIKL ice-calk
ACCEIKP icepack
pack ice
ACCEILL calicle
ACCEILN calcine
ACCEILO coeliac
ACCEILR Clarice
ACCEILS calices
ACCEILT calcite
ACCEIMR ceramic
racemic
ACCEINO cocaine
oceanic
ACCEINR Circean
ACCEINV vaccine
ACCEIPR caprice
ACCEIPV peccavi
ACCEIQU cacique
ACCEIRS carices
ACCEIRT creatic
ACCEIST ascetic
ACCEKLR cackler
clacker
crackle
ACCEKMO meacock
ACCEKOP peacock✧
ACCEKOS seacock
ACCEKPU cupcake
ACCEKRR cracker
ACCELLY calycle
ACCELNO conceal
ACCELOR coracle
ACCELOT cacolet
ACCELSU saccule
ACCELSY calyces
ACCEMNO Meccano®
ACCEMNU cacumen
ACCENOR conacre
ACCENOS a sconce
asconce
ACCENOV concave
ACCENPT peccant
ACCENST accents
ACCEOPY cacoepy
ACCEORW cracowe
ACCEOST cot case
ACCEPRU race-cup
ACCEPRY peccary
ACCERRT carrect
ACCERSU accurse
accuser
ACCFIIP pacific✧
ACCFILY calcify
ACCFLOW cow-calf
ACCGHIO Chicago
ACCHHKU kuchcha
ACCHIMS chasmic
ACCHINO chicano✧
Noachic
ACCHIOR co-chair
ACCHIOT chaotic
ACCHIOU acouchi
ACCHIRS scraich
ACCHITT catch it
ACCHJSU jacchus
ACCHKNO Hancock
ACCHKOY haycock
ACCHLNO conchal
ACCHLTU claucht
ACCHNOT catch on
ACCHNRS scranch
ACCHNRU craunch
ACCHOPU capouch
ACCHOSW cash cow
ACCHOTW choctaw✧
ACCHOUY acouchy
ACCHPTU catch up
catchup
upcatch
ACCHRRU currach
ACCHRST scratch✧
ACCHRSU scrauch
ACCIILN aclinic
ACCIINT actinic
ACCIIST ascitic
sciatic
ACCIKRS car-sick
ACCIKRT crack it
ACCILLU calculi
ACCILMO comical
ACCILMU calcium
ACCILNO conical
laconic✧
ACCILNU Cluniac
ACCILNY cynical
ACCILOR caloric
ACCILOS calicos
ACCILOV vocalic
ACCILRU crucial
ACCILRY acrylic
ACCILSS classic
ACCILST clastic
ACCILSU sacculi
ACCILTU Calicut
ACCIMOZ zimocca
ACCINNO canonic
ACCINOP Canopic
ACCINOT cantico
Occitan
ACCINRU crucian
ACCIOPR caproic
ACCIORS Corsica
scoriac
ACCIPRT practic
ACCISTT tactics
ACCISTU caustic
ACCKLMU Calmuck
ACCKLOR carlock
ACCKLRY crackly
ACCKMOR cromack
ACCKNOR crack on
ACCKOPR cap rock
ACCKOSS cassock
Cossack
ACCKOST castock
ACCKPRU crack up
crackup
ACCMOOY cocoyam
ACCMOPT accompt
compact
ACCMORS cas crom
ACCMRUU curcuma
ACCNNOO cooncan
ACCNOOP cocopan
ACCNOOR raccoon
ACCNOTT contact
ACCNOTU account
ACCOPTY copycat
ACCOQSU squacco
ACCORSS corcass
ACCORTU accourt
ACCRSTU accurst
ACDDDKO daddock
ACDDEER cedared
ACDDEEY decayed
ACDDEHR Cheddar
ACDDEIN Candide
candied
ACDDEIU decidua
ACDDEIY acid dye
ACDDELO cladode
ACDDELR cladder
ACDDEMU ducdame
ACDDEOP decapod
ACDDERR red card
red-card
ACDDERU adducer
ACDDETU cut dead
ACDDHHU chuddah

ACDDHIS caddish
ACDDHKO haddock
ACDDHOR chaddor
ACDDHRU chuddar
ACDDINU Dunciad
ACDDIOT act dido
ACDDIRS discard
ACDDKMO maddock
ACDDKOP paddock
ACDDSSY caddyss
ACDEEES decease
ACDEEFR defacer
red face
ACDEEFT faceted
ACDEEGL glacéed
ACDEEHL Chaldee
Cheadle
ACDEEHR reached
ACDEEIR deciare
ACDEEIT iced tea
ACDEEJT dejecta
ACDEELL cadelle
ACDEELR Cedrela
creedal
declare
ACDEELS descale
seed-lac
ACDEELV cleaved
ACDEEMR racemed
ACDEEMV medevac
ACDEENV vendace
ACDEEOT Docetae
ACDEERT cedrate
cerated
ACDEETU educate
ACDEETY cat-eyed
ACDEFIN fancied
ACDEFIR farcied
ACDEFLO old face
ACDEFOP po-faced
ACDEFOT de facto
ACDEFRS scarfed
ACDEFRT fracted
ACDEGGL clagged
ACDEGGR cragged
ACDEGHR charged
ACDEGIS discage
ACDEGKO dockage
ACDEGNO decagon
ACDEGNU uncaged
ACDEGOR cordage
ACDEGRR Red Crag
ACDEHIN chained
echidna
ACDEHIP edaphic
ACDEHIX hexadic
ACDEHKW whacked
ACDEHLR chalder
ACDEHMR charmed
ACDEHMS chasmed
ACDEHMT matched
ACDEHNR endarch
ranched
ACDEHOR chordae
roached
ACDEHOT cathode
ACDEHPP chapped
ACDEHPR parched
ACDEHPT patched
ACDEHPU cuphead
ACDEHRR charred
ACDEHTT chatted
ACDEIIO Dioecia
ACDEILL cedilla
ACDEILM camelid
decimal
declaim
medical
ACDEILN Iceland
ACDEILR decrial
radicel
radicle
ACDEILS Alcides
ACDEILT citadel
deltaic
dialect
edictal
ACDEIMY mediacy
ACDEINO oceanid✧
ACDEINR cairned
ACDEINS candies
ACDEINY cyanide
ACDEIOU Eudocia
ACDEIPR epacrid
ACDEIPS dispace
ACDEIRR carried
ACDEIRS darcies
radices
sidecar✧
ACDEIRU decuria
ACDEISS discase
ACDEIST die-cast
ACDEISV advices
ACDEITT dictate
ACDEITY edacity
ACDEJMO C E M
Joad
ACDEKLT tackled
talcked
ACDEKRT tracked
ACDEKRW wracked
ACDEKRY keycard
ACDEKST C K Stead
stacked
ACDEKSU sea duck
ACDELLS scalled
ACDELMM clammed
ACDELMS mascled
ACDELNO celadon
ACDELNR candler
ACDELNS calends
ACDELPP clapped
ACDELPY ycleap'd
ACDELRS scalder
ACDELRY red clay
ACDELSS classed
declass
ACDELST castled
ACDELWW dewclaw
ACDEMMR crammed
ACDEMNO Caedmon
ACDEMNU decuman
ACDEMOR comrade
ACDEMPR cramped
ACDENNS scanned
ACDENNT candent
ACDENNU nuanced
ACDENOR acorned
Dracone®
dracone
ACDENPT pandect
ACDENPU unpaced
ACDENRT cantred
Tancred
tranced
ACDENRU durance
unraced
ACDENRY ardency
ACDENST descant
ACDENTU unacted
ACDEOOR Odoacer
ACDEOPS peascod
ACDEORR corrade
ACDEORS sarcode
ACDEORT Art Deco
cordate
redcoat
ACDEORU Ecuador
ACDEOST Cestoda
ACDEOTT codetta
ACDEOUV couvade
ACDEPPR crapped
ACDEPRS scarped
ACDERRS scarred
ACDERSU crusade
ACDERTT detract
ACDERTU traduce
ACDESTT scatted
ACDFFIR Cardiff
ACDFFMU Macduff
ACDFIIY acidify
ACDFIOT factoid
ACDGIIM digicam
ACDGINN dancing
ACDGINO gonadic
ACDGINR carding
ACDGKLO daglock
ACDGNOT cantdog
ACDGORT dogcart
ACDHIIL chiliad
ACDHIIS Hasidic
ACDHIOP phacoid
ACDHIRR Richard
ACDHIRY diarchy
ACDHISS Chassid
ACDHKOY Hock-day
ACDHLOP old chap
ACDHLOR chordal
dorlach
ACDHMPU Duchamp
ACDHNOW cowhand
ACDHOOT cathood
ACDHOPR pochard
ACDHORR orchard
ACDHRUY duarchy
ACDHRYY dyarchy
ACDIIIN indicia
ACDIINN indican
ACDIINO conidia
Di Canio
ACDIINR acridin
ACDIINV da Vinci
ACDIIRS cidaris✧
sciarid
ACDIIRT arctiid
triacid
triadic
ACDIITY acidity
ACDIKLS skaldic
ACDILLO codilla
ACDILMO domical
ACDILMS cladism
ACDILNO Diconal®
nodical
ACDILNU dulcian
Lucinda
ACDILOP placoid
podalic
ACDILOR cordial
ACDILOT cotidal
ACDILOU Claudio
ACDILPU paludic
ACDILRY acridly
ACDILST cladist
ACDILSY Lycidas
ACDILTW wildcat
ACDIMMU cadmium
ACDIMNO mandioc
monacid
monadic
nomadic
ACDIMNY dynamic
ACDIMRS SIM card
ACDINRU iracund
ACDINRY Indy car
ACDINST discant
ACDINSU Sudanic
ACDIOPR parodic
picador
ACDIORR corrida
ACDIORS sarcoid
ACDIORT arctoid
carotid
ACDIOST Sotadic

ACDIOTY	dacoity
ACDIOXY	oxyacid
ACDIQRU	quadric
ACDIRST	drastic
ACDISTX	tax disc
ACDITUV	viaduct
ACDJNTU	adjunct
ACDKLOP	padlock
ACDKLSY	skyclad
ACDKMOO	mockado
ACDKMPU	mudpack
ACDKNTU	duck-ant
ACDKOPR	pockard
ACDLLOR	collard
ACDLLUY	ducally
ACDLNOR	caldron
ACDLNOT	cotland
ACDLNSU	sun-clad
ACDLOPU	cupola'd
ACDLORW	cold war
ACDLOWY	ladycow
ACDMMNO	command
ACDMNOP	compand
ACDMOOW	camwood
ACDMORZ	czardom
ACDMRRY	Mr Darcy
ACDNNOO	no can do
ACDNOOR	cardoon
ACDNORU	candour
	caudron
ACDOORT	cat door
ACDOPRT	act drop
ACDORRW	card row
ACDORST	costard✧
ACDORSU	crusado
ACDORTU	ad court
ACDORUZ	cruzado
ACDRSTU	custard✧
ACDRSUU	carduus
ACEEEPS	escapee
ACEEEUV	evacuee
ACEEFFR	effacer
ACEEFFT	A-effect
ACEEFHN	enchafe
ACEEFHT	The Face
ACEEFIN	faience
	faïence
	fiancée
ACEEFLN	Fleance
ACEEFNT	Netcafé
ACEEFNY	fayence
ACEEFPR	preface
ACEEGGP	pace egg
	pace-egg
ACEEGGS	egg case
ACEEGHL	hac lege
ACEEGIL	elegiac
ACEEGNR	engrace
ACEEGNT	centage
ACEEGSU	escuage
ACEEHHT	cheetah
ACEEHIP	cheapie
ACEEHIT	hicatee
	teachie
ACEEHIV	achieve
ACEEHKO	hoe-cake
ACEEHLR	relâche
ACEEHLS	Chelsea
ACEEHLT	chelate
ACEEHMP	empeach
ACEEHMR	machree
	Meacher
ACEEHMT	machete
ACEEHNN	enhance
ACEEHNP	cheapen
	ha'pence
ACEEHNS	enchase
ACEEHOR	ochreae
ACEEHPP	échappé
ACEEHPR	peacher
ACEEHPT	the Cape
ACEEHRR	reacher
ACEEHRT	cheater
	hectare
	rechate
	recheat
	teacher
ACEEHST	escheat
	the case
ACEEHTT	thecate
ACEEHTX	excheat
ACEEILP	calipee
ACEEILT	Eleatic
ACEEIMT	emicate
ACEEINP	in peace
ACEEINR	Cairene
	cinerea
ACEEINU	eucaine
ACEEIRR	cariere
ACEEISV	vesicae
ACEEJKN	jackeen✧
ACEEKNP	kneecap
	knee-cap
ACEELLN	nacelle
ACEELMP	emplace
ACEELMR	réclame
ACEELNR	cleaner
ACEELNS	cleanse
	scalene
ACEELNT	latence
ACEELNV	enclave
	valence
ACEELPR	percale
	replace
ACEELPT	capelet
ACEELRR	clearer
	Le Carré
ACEELRS	rescale
	re-scale
ACEELRT	Electra
	treacle
ACEELRU	caerule
ACEELRV	cleaver
ACEELST	celesta
ACEELSU	euclase
ACEELVX	exclave
ACEEMNR	menacer
ACEEMNY	Mycenae
ACEEMRR	creamer
ACEEMRT	cremate
	meercat
ACEENNP	penance
ACEENNR	narceen
ACEENNS	Senecan
ACEENNT	canteen
ACEENNY	cayenne✧
ACEENNZ	Cézanne
ACEENOT	acetone
ACEENPS	pen-case
ACEENRS	caserne
ACEENRT	centare
	crenate
	re-enact
ACEENTU	cuneate
ACEEORS	acerose
ACEEORT	ocreate
ACEEOST	acetose
ACEEOTV	evocate
ACEEPRR	caperer
ACEEPRS	escaper
	percase
ACEERRS	creaser
ACEERRT	caterer
	retrace
	terrace
ACEERST	secreta
ACEERSV	Versace
ACEERTX	exacter
	excreta
ACEESST	ectases
ACEESTU	Eustace
ACEESTY	Cat's-eye®
	cat's-eye
ACEFFFO	face off
	face-off
ACEFFHI	affiche
ACEFFHR	chaffer
ACEFFIN	caffein
ACEFFIS	scaffie
ACEFFOR	afforce
ACEFGOT	geofact
ACEFHMR	chamfer
ACEFHOR	arch-foe
ACEFHRU	chaufer
ACEFIIL	felicia✧
ACEFILL	ice fall
ACEFILM	malefic
ACEFILR	filacer
ACEFINN	finance
ACEFINR	fancier
	Francie
ACEFINS	fascine
ACEFITV	factive
ACEFITY	acetify
ACEFKLR	flacker
ACEFKLT	flacket
ACEFLLS	Scafell
ACEFLRU	careful
ACEFNNO	façonné
ACEFNRS	Frances
ACEFNRT	cantref
ACEFNRU	furnace✧
ACEFOPR	proface
ACEFORR	forecar
ACEFOTU	face out
	outface
ACEFRRT	refract
ACEFRRU	farceur
ACEFRSU	surface
ACEFRTU	facture
	furcate
ACEGGRW	W G Grace
ACEGHLO	galoche
ACEGHNR	changer
ACEGHNU	chaunge
ACEGHOU	gouache
ACEGHOW	cowhage
ACEGHRR	charger
ACEGHRS	charges
ACEGHRT	gertcha
ACEGILL	ellagic
	Gallice
ACEGILN	angelic
	anglice✧
	Galenic
ACEGILP	pelagic
ACEGILR	glacier
	gracile
ACEGIMO	camogie
ACEGIMR	grimace
ACEGIMT	gametic
ACEGINO	coinage
ACEGINR	anergic
	grecian✧
ACEGINS	ceasing
ACEGINV	veganic
ACEGKLO	lockage
ACEGKLR	grackle
ACEGKMO	mockage
ACEGKOR	corkage
ACEGKOS	gas-coke
ACEGLLO	collage
ACEGLNO	congeal
ACEGLNR	clanger
ACEGLOT	catelog
ACEGLOU	cagoule
ACEGMNO	con game
ACEGMOP	compage
ACEGNOR	acrogen
	cornage
ACEGNOT	co-agent
	cognate
ACEGORS	cargoes
	corsage

	socager
ACEGORU	courage
ACEGOTT	cottage
ACEGRTU	trucage
ACEGSTU	scutage
ACEHHLT	hatchel
ACEHHRT	hatcher
ACEHHRU	hachure
ACEHHRX	hexarch
ACEHHTT	hatchet
ACEHIKR	kacheri
ACEHILL	challie
	helical
ACEHILM	Michael
ACEHILN	Chilean
ACEHILR	charlie✧
ACEHILT	alethic
	ethical
ACEHIMN	machine
ACEHIMP	impeach
ACEHIMR	chimera✧
ACEHIMS	chamise
ACEHINN	cain-hen
	enchain
ACEHINS	inchase
ACEHINT	chantie
	teach-in
ACEHINY	hyacine
ACEHIPP	chappie
ACEHIPR	charpie
ACEHIPT	aphetic
	hepatic
ACEHIRR	hire car
ACEHIRS	cashier
ACEHIRT	Rhaetic
	theriac
ACEHIRU	Echiura
ACEHIRV	archive
ACEHITY	yachtie
ACEHITZ	zaitech
ACEHKLR	hackler
ACEHKLS	hackles
	shackle
ACEHKLT	hacklet
ACEHKNY	hackney✧
ACEHKRW	whacker
ACEHKRY	hackery
ACEHKST	the sack
ACEHLLP	pellach
ACEHLLS	shellac
ACEHLLT	hellcat
ACEHLMT	chamlet
ACEHLMU	lumache
ACEHLMY	alchemy
ACEHLNN	channel✧
ACEHLNO	chalone
ACEHLNR	charnel
	larchen
ACEHLOP	epochal
ACEHLOR	cholera
	chorale
ACEHLOS	oscheal
	sea loch
ACEHLOT	cathole
ACEHLPT	chaplet
	the clap
ACEHLPY	cheaply
ACEHLRS	Charles
	clasher
	raschel
ACEHLRT	archlet
ACEHLRY	charley✧
ACEHLST	satchel
ACEHLTT	chattel
	latchet
ACEHMNR	encharm
	Märchen
ACEHMNT	manchet
ACEHMRR	charmer
	marcher
ACEHMRS	marches✧
	mesarch
ACEHMRT	matcher
	rematch
ACEHMRU	chaumer
ACEHMSS	schemas
ACEHMTY	ecthyma
ACEHMTZ	chametz
ACEHNNR	channer
ACEHNNT	enchant
ACEHNOP	peach on
ACEHNOR	Acheron
ACEHNRR	rancher
ACEHNRT	chanter
	tranche
ACEHNSS	schanse
ACEHNST	chasten
ACEHNSV	Chesvan
ACEHNSZ	schanze
ACEHNTT	etchant
ACEHNTU	unteach
ACEHNTY	chantey
ACEHNTZ	Natchez
ACEHOOT	ootheca
ACEHOPR	poacher
ACEHOTY	chayote
ACEHPPS	schappe
ACEHPRT	chapter
	patcher
ACEHPRY	eparchy
	preachy
ACEHPSS	chapess
ACEHQUU	Quechua
ACEHQUY	queachy
ACEHRRT	charter
	rechart
ACEHRRX	xerarch
ACEHRRY	archery
ACEHRSU	archeus✧
ACEHRSY	hyraces
ACEHRTT	chatter
	ratchet
ACEHRTW	watcher
ACEHRTY	yachter
ACEHRXY	exarchy
ACEHSTW	watches
ACEHTTU	teuchat
ACEHTTW	watchet
ACEIILM	cimelia
ACEIILS	laicise
ACEIILT	ciliate
ACEIILZ	laicize
ACEIINT	Cainite
ACEIITV	caitive
	viciate
ACEIJKS	jacksie
ACEIJSS	Jessica
ACEIKLO	oil-cake
ACEIKLS	saclike
ACEIKLT	catlike
ACEIKMR	keramic
ACEIKNT	anticke
	cake tin
ACEIKOP	paiocke
ACEIKPR	earpick
ACEIKPX	pickaxe
ACEIKRT	tackier
ACEIKSS	seasick
ACEIKST	tackies
ACEIKTT	tietack
ACEILLL	allelic
ACEILLM	limacel
	micella
ACEILLR	air-cell
ACEILLX	lexical
ACEILMN	cnemial
	melanic
ACEILMR	claimer
	miracle
	reclaim
ACEILMS	limaces
ACEILMT	climate
	metical
ACEILMX	exclaim
ACEILMY	mycelia
ACEILNP	capelin
	in place
	panicle
	pelican
ACEILNR	carline
	en clair
ACEILNS	sanicle
	scaleni
ACEILNU	cauline
ACEILNX	Xenical®
ACEILOR	calorie✧
	cariole
	loricae
ACEILOS	celosia
	coalise
ACEILOT	aloetic
	Coalite®
ACEILOZ	coalize
ACEILPP	pile-cap
ACEILPR	replica
ACEILPS	special
ACEILPT	plicate
ACEILRR	cerrial
ACEILRS	Sercial
ACEILRT	article
	recital
ACEILRU	auricle
ACEILRV	caliver
	clavier
	velaric
ACEILSS	salices
ACEILST	astelic
	elastic
	latices
	salicet
ACEILSV	vesical
ACEILTT	lattice
	tactile
ACEIMMS	Acmeism
ACEIMNO	encomia
ACEIMNP	pemican
ACEIMNR	carmine
ACEIMNS	amnesic
ACEIMNT	emicant
	nematic
ACEIMNX	Mexican
ACEIMPY	pyaemic
ACEIMRT	matrice
ACEIMRU	Maurice
	uraemic
ACEIMST	Acmeist
	etacism
	sematic
ACEIMSU	caesium
ACEIMSX	casemix
ACEINNP	pinnace
ACEINNS	nancies✧
ACEINNT	ancient
ACEINNY	cyanine
ACEINOP	paeonic
ACEINOS	acinose
ACEINOT	aconite
	anoetic
ACEINPR	caprine
ACEINPS	inscape
	pincase
	Piscean
ACEINPT	picante
ACEINRS	arsenic
	carnies
	cerasin
ACEINRT	certain
	creatin
	crinate
	nacrite
	tacrine
ACEINST	cineast
	Insecta
ACEINSY	cyanise

ACEINTT nictate
tetanic
ACEINTV Vectian
venatic
ACEINTX inexact
ACEINTY cyanite
ACEINVZ Vicenza
ACEINYZ cyanize
ACEIOOZ zooecia
ACEIOPT ectopia
ACEIORS Cesario
scoriae
ACEIORT erotica
ACEIOST sociate
ACEIOTX exotica
ACEIPPR crappie
epicarp
ACEIPPT tappice
ACEIPRS epacris
ice spar
scrapie
Serapic
ACEIPRT Aricept®
paretic
picrate
ACEIPST aseptic
spicate
ACEIPSU auspice
ACEIPSZ capsize
ACEIPTV captive
ACEIQRU acquire
ACEIQTU acquite
ACEIQUZ cazique
ACEIRRR carrier
ACEIRRT cirrate
erratic
ACEIRRW aircrew
ACEIRRZ crazier
ACEIRST cristae
raciest
stearic
ACEIRSU saucier
uricase
ACEIRSV varices
viscera
ACEIRSZ crazies
ACEIRTT citrate
ACEIRUX ex curia
ACEISSS ascesis
ACEISST ascites
ectasis
ACEISTT statice
ACEISTV Avestic
ACEISUX ciseaux
ACEITTV cavetti
ACEITTW at twice
ACEITTX extatic
ACEITUX auxetic
ACEITVX ActiveX
ACEJKOP pajocke
ACEJLOR cajoler
ACEJNOT jaconet
ACEJNOY joyance
Joycean
ACEJNTU juncate
ACEJPTU cajeput
ACEJQSU Jacques
ACEJRTT traject
ACEKKNR knacker
ACEKLLP pellack
ACEKLNO Lockean
ACEKLNR crankle
ACEKLNS slacken
ACEKLOR earlock
ACEKLPT placket
ACEKLQU quackle
ACEKLRS slacker
ACEKLRT tackler
ACEKLRU caulker
ACEKLSY lackeys
ACEKMRS smacker
ACEKNPR prancke
ACEKNRY cankery
ACEKNVY van Eyck
ACEKOOS sea cook
ACEKORR croaker
ACEKORU Kerouac
ACEKPPR prepack
ACEKPTW wet pack
ACEKQRU quacker
ACEKRRT tracker
ACEKRST rackets
stacker
ACEKRSY screaky
ACEKRTT rackett
ACEKRTY rackety
ACEKSTT stacket
ACEKTTY tackety
ACELLMO calomel
ACELLNU nucleal
ACELLNY cleanly
ACELLOR corella
ocellar
ACELLOT collate
ACELLPS scalpel
ACELLPY clypeal
ACELLRR carrell
ACELLRS scleral
ACELLRU cure-all
ACELLRY Carlyle
clearly
ACELMOR caromel
ACELMOT camelot✧
ACELMOU caulome
leucoma
ACELMPR clamper
ACELMRY camelry
ACELMTU calumet
ACELNNU unclean
ACELNNY lyncean
ACELNOR corneal
ACELNOS Seconal®
ACELNOT lactone
ACELNOY Alcyone
ACELNOZ calzone
ACELNPS enclasp
spancel
ACELNPT clapnet
ACELNPU clean up
clean-up
unplace
ACELNRS lancers✧
ACELNRT central
ACELNRU lucarne
nuclear
unclear
ACELNRY larceny
ACELNST scantle
ACELNSU censual
unscale
ACELNTT cantlet
ACELNTY latency
ACELNVY valency
ACELOPR polacre
ACELOPS escalop
ACELOPT polecat
ACELOPU copulae
ACELOQU coequal
ACELORS claroes
escolar
ACELORY caloyer
ACELOST alecost
Lacoste
lactose
scatole
talcose
to scale
ACELOTT calotte
ACELOTU oculate
ACELOTY acolyte
cotylae
ACELOUV vacuole
ACELPPR clapper
ACELPPS scapple
ACELPRS clasper
scalper
ACELPRT plectra
ACELPRU clear up
clear-up
ACELPRY prelacy
ACELPSU capsule
scale up
specula
upscale
ACELPSY cypsela
ACELPTU Capulet
ACELPTY ectypal
ACELQRU lacquer
ACELQUY lacquey
ACELRRW crawler
ACELRST scarlet
ACELRSU cesural
secular
ACELRTT clatter
ACELRTY treacly
ACELRWY Crawley
ACELSSS sacless
ACELSTU sulcate
ACELSTY scytale
ACELSUU aculeus
ACELSUX excusal
ACELSXY calyxes
ACELTUY acutely
ACELTXY exactly
ACEMMOT toc emma
ACEMMRR crammer
ACEMMRS scammer
ACEMNOR Cremona
Menorca
romance✧
ACEMNRR Cranmer
ACEMNRW crewman
ACEMOPR compare
compear
ACEMOPT à compte
ACEMORU morceau
ACEMOSU mucosae
ACEMPRS scamper
ACEMPRT crampet
ACEMPRY campery
ACEMRSU Marcuse
ACEMRSY cramesy
ACEMSTT metcast
ACENNOS ancones
sonance
ACENNOT connate
ACENNOY noyance
ACENNOZ canzone
ACENNRS scanner
ACENNRY cannery
ACENNST nascent
ACENNTY tenancy
ACENOOR coronae
ACENOPT patonce
ACENOPU ponceau
ACENORS carnose
coarsen
ACENORT e contra
enactor
ACENOSS cassone
ACENOST costean
ACENOSU Oceanus
ACENOTT attonce
ACENOTV centavo
ACENOUV una voce
ACENPRR prancer✧
ACENPRU praunce
ACENPTT pentact
ACENPTY patency
ACENRRY errancy
ACENRSS ancress
ACENRSU surance
ACENRSY carneys
scenary

ACENRTT	tranect
ACENRTU	centaur
	near cut
	uncrate
	untrace
ACENRTY	encraty
	nectary
	trancey
ACENSTU	nutcase
ACENSTW	stew-can
ACEOOPP	apocope
ACEOOTZ	ectozoa
ACEOPRR	crop-ear
ACEOPRX	exocarp
ACEOPST	scopate
ACEOPTU	outpace
	pace out
ACEOPTZ	Zapotec
ACEORRT	acroter
	creator✧
	reactor
ACEORST	coaster✧
ACEORSU	acerous
	carouse
ACEORSW	sea crow
ACEORTU	outrace
ACEORTV	overact
ACEORTW	eat crow
ACEORTX	exactor
ACEOSSU	caseous
ACEOSTT	costate
ACEOSTU	acetous
ACEOSTY	tea cosy
	tea-cosy
ACEOTTV	cavetto
ACEOTUU	autocue
ACEOTUX	coteaux
ACEPRRS	scarper
	scraper
ACEPRST	precast
	spectra
ACEPRSU	scare up
	scauper
ACEPRTU	capture
ACEPRUV	carve up
	carve-up
ACEPSTU	cuspate
	put case
ACEQRTU	racquet
ACEQSTU	acquest
ACERRTT	retract
ACERRTY	tracery
ACERRUV	verruca
ACERRVY	carvery
ACERSST	actress
ACERSSU	sucrase
ACERSSV	scarves
ACERSTT	scatter
ACERSTU	crustae
ACERSTY	sectary
ACERTTT	tetract
ACERTTU	curtate
	cut-rate
ACERTTX	extract
ACERTTY	cattery
ACERTUV	curvate
ACERTUX	curtaxe
ACERTUY	cautery
ACESSTU	caestus
ACESSTY	ecstasy✧
ACESTTU	scutate
ACESTTY	testacy
ACESTUY	eustacy
ACFFHPU	huff-cap
ACFFIIT	caitiff
ACFFIKM	maffick
ACFFILT	afflict
ACFFIRT	traffic
ACFFIRY	farcify
ACFFJKO	jack off
ACFFKOP	pack off
ACFFKOR	rack off
ACFFLLO	call off
ACFFLOW	claw off
ACFFORT	cart off
ACFFOST	cast off
	cast-off
	scoff at
ACFGINR	farcing
ACFGINS	facings
ACFHIST	catfish
ACFHISU	fuchsia
ACFHLNU	flaunch
	Funchal
ACFHLTU	half-cut
ACFHNOU	fauchon
ACFHRTY	fratchy
ACFIILN	finical
ACFIKNN	finnack
ACFILNO	folacin
ACFILRY	clarify
ACFIMOR	aciform
	Formica®
ACFIMSS	fascism✧
ACFINNY	infancy
ACFINOT	faction
ACFINRS	Francis
ACFINRT	frantic
	infarct
	infract
ACFINRY	carnify
ACFIOSS	fiascos
ACFIPRY	caprify
ACFIRSY	sacrify
	scarify
ACFISST	fascist✧
ACFITTY	fat city✧
ACFKLSU	sackful
ACFLLOY	focally
ACFLNSU	canfuls
ACFLPSU	capfuls
ACFLRTU	cartful
ACFLRUU	furcula
ACFLTTU	tactful
ACFLTUY	faculty
ACFOQRT	Q factor
ACFORTX	X-factor
ACFORTY	factory
ACFPRSU	scarf up
ACGGIOS	agogics
ACGGRSY	scraggy
ACGHIKN	hacking
ACGHIMO	oghamic
ACGHINR	chagrin
	charing
ACGHINS	chasing
ACGHINT	gnathic
ACGHINW	chinwag
ACGHIPR	graphic
ACGHIRS	scraigh
ACGHKLO	hack-log
ACGHLOY	Chogyal
ACGHLTU	claught
ACGHNRU	graunch
ACGHNTU	Achtung
ACGHOSU	gauchos
ACGHRRU	curragh
ACGHRSU	scraugh
ACGIILN	alginic
ACGIITU	augitic
ACGIKLN	lacking
ACGIKNP	packing
ACGIKNR	arcking
	carking
	racking
ACGIKNS	sacking
ACGIKNT	tacking
ACGIKNV	vacking
ACGIKTW	Gatwick
ACGILLN	calling
ACGILLO	logical
ACGILMY	myalgic
ACGILNP	placing
ACGILNR	carling✧
ACGILNS	scaling
ACGILNT	catling
	talcing
ACGILNU	cingula
	glucina
ACGIMNO	coaming
ACGIMNP	camping
ACGINNN	canning✧
ACGINNT	canting
ACGINOR	organic
ACGINOS	angicos
ACGINOT	coating
	cotinga
ACGINPP	capping
ACGINPR	carping
ACGINPS	spacing
ACGINRS	sacring
ACGINRT	tracing
ACGINRV	carving
	craving
ACGINRZ	crazing
ACGINST	casting
ACGIRST	gastric
ACGKMMO	gammock
ACGKORV	garvock
ACGLLPU	cupgall
ACGLNOR	clangor
ACGLSUU	Glaucus
ACGNNOR	crannog
ACGNOOT	octagon
ACGORRY	gyrocar
ACGORUU	couguar
ACGORYZ	go crazy
ACHHIPT	chip hat
ACHHIRS	rhachis
ACHHIRW	Harwich
ACHHOST	toshach
ACHHPPU	chuppah
ACHHTTT	thatcht
ACHIIKM	kamichi
ACHIILN	Chilian
ACHIILS	ischial
ACHIIMO	Iachimo
ACHIIMS	chiasmi
ACHIIMT	Hamitic
ACHIINT	Chianti
ACHIIPS	pachisi
ACHIITW	Wichita
ACHIJNT	jacinth
ACHIKOP	pak choi
ACHIKRS	ricksha
ACHIKRY	hayrick
ACHIKSS	shicksa
ACHILLO	lochial
ACHILLP	phallic
ACHILLS	challis
ACHILLT	thallic
ACHILMO	malicho
ACHILNO	Nichola
ACHILNP	Chaplin
ACHILOR	chorial
ACHILOS	scholia
ACHILRS	carlish
ACHILRY	charily
ACHILSY	clayish
ACHILWY	lichway
ACHIMNO	manihoc
	mohican✧
ACHIMOS	chamiso
	chamois
ACHIMRS	charism
ACHIMSS	chiasms
	schisma
ACHIMST	mastich
	tachism
ACHINNU	unchain
ACHINOP	aphonic
ACHINOT	Antioch
ACHINOY	onychia
ACHINPS	spinach

ACHINPU chain up
ACHINRZ zarnich
ACHINTW watch in
ACHINTX xanthic
ACHINTY Cynthia
ACHINUV chauvin
ACHIOPS isopach
ACHIOPT aphotic
ACHIORT chariot
haricot
ACHIOSY Choisya
ACHIPPS sapphic✧
ACHIPST haptics
spathic
ACHIPTU chupati
ACHIPTW whipcat
ACHIQRU charqui
ACHIQUU Quichua
ACHIRRT triarch
ACHIRTU haircut
ACHIRTY charity
ACHISSS chassis
ACHISTT cattish
tachist
ACHITTW watch it!
ACHKLPU chalk up
ACHKLST klatsch
ACHKMMO hammock
ACHKOPS hopsack
hop-sack
ACHKOSS hassock
ACHKOST Toshack
ACHKOSW whackos
ACHKOTT hattock
ACHKPSU shack up
ACHLLOO alcohol
ACHLLOR chloral
ACHLMSY chlamys
ACHLMYY alchymy
ACHLNOY halcyon
ACHLNTU tulchan
unlatch
ACHLOPR raploch
ACHLOPT potlach
ACHLORS scholar
ACHLORT trochal
ACHLOSW salchow
ACHLOTY acolyth
ACHLPST splatch
ACHLTUZ chalutz
ACHMNOO Manchoo
ACHMNOR monarch
nomarch
ACHMNRU uncharm
ACHMOPR camphor
ACHMORS O C Marsh
ACHMORZ machzor
ACHMOST Satchmo
stomach
ACHMOTT to match
ACHMPTU matchup
ACHMSUW cumshaw
ACHNNOO hoc anno
ACHNNOS chanson
ACHNORS anchors
ranchos
ACHNORT chantor
ACHNOSS sanchos
ACHNOTY tachyon
ACHNOUY chanoyu
ACHNOVY anchovy
ACHNPSS schnaps
ACHNPUY paunchy
ACHNRTY chantry
ACHNRUY raunchy
unchary
ACHNSTU canthus
staunch
ACHNSTY snatchy
ACHOPRT toparch
ACHOPRY charpoy
Corypha
ACHORSU aurochs
ACHPPTU patch up
patch-up
ACHPTUW watch up
ACHRRTU crathur
ACHRSTY starchy
ACHRSUU urachus
ACHSSTY stachys
ACHSTUY cyathus
ACIIKNN canikin
ACIIKRS airsick
ACIILMM mimical
ACIILMS Islamic
ACIILMT Tamilic
ACIILNR clarini
ACIILNS salicin
sinical
ACIILNT Caitlín
ACIILNV vicinal
ACIILNZ Zincali
ACIILOV viliaco
ACIILRY ciliary
ACIILSS Liassic
ACIILST italics
ACIILSU iliacus
ACIILTY laicity
ACIIMMN minicam
ACIIMMS miasmic
ACIIMNN Mancini
ACIIMNR crimina
mini-car
ACIIMOT comitia
ACIIMST ismatic
itacism
ACIINNO anionic
ACIINOS asinico
Nicosia
ACIINOV avionic
ACIINPS piscina
ACIINTT titanic✧
ACIIPPR priapic✧
ACIIPRT piratic
ACIIRST satiric
ACIIRTT triatic
ACIJKLN Jacklin
ACIJNOP Japonic
ACIJUZZ Jacuzzi®
jacuzzi
ACIKKPT tap kick
ACIKKSS kick-ass
ACIKLMP milk cap
ACIKLNO cloak in
Lockian
ACIKLNW Alnwick
ACIKLOR airlock
ACIKLTY tackily
ACIKLWY wackily
ACIKMOO oomiack
ACIKMPR rampick
ACIKMPW pickmaw
ACIKNNP pannick
ACIKNOR Koranic
ACIKNPY panicky
ACIKNST catskin
ACIKNTT tintack
ACIKPRT patrick✧
ACIKPSX six-pack
ACIKRST karstic
ACIKRWW Warwick
ACIKUWZ Zwickau
ACILLLU Lucilla
ACILLMS miscall
ACILLOO coal oil
ACILLRY lyrical
ACILMNO limaçon
ACILMNU culmina
ACILMOT comital
ACILMOU cui malo?
ACILMPS plasmic
ACILMRS Carlism
ACILMSU musical
ACILMTU Tamulic
ACILNNY cannily
ACILNOR clarino
clarion
Locrian
ACILNOS Nicolas
ACILNOU inocula
ACILNOV Calvino
ACILNOZ calzoni
Zincalo
ACILNPS inclasp
ACILNPY pliancy
ACILNTU lunatic
ACILNUV vincula
ACILOOR air-cool
ACILOPT Capitol
coalpit
optical
pit-coal
topical
ACILORR racloir
ACILORV corival
ACILORX Lacroix
ACILOST stoical
ACILOTT coal tit
ACILOTV volatic
voltaic
ACILOTX toxical
ACILPRT clipart
ACILPST plastic
ACILPSU spicula
ACILPTY clay-pit
typical
ACILRST Carlist
ACILRSY scarily
ACILRTU curtail
trucial
ACILRTY clarity
ACILRYZ crazily
ACILSSS classis
ACILSTU St Lucia
ACILSUY saucily
ACILTTY cattily
tacitly
ACILTUV victual
ACIMNOP campion
ACIMNOR marconi✧
Minorca
Romanic
ACIMNOS anosmic
masonic
ACIMNOT Comtian
ACIMNPU Panicum
ACIMNRU cranium
cumarin
ACIMNTT catmint
ACIMNTW twin-cam
ACIMNTY city man
ACIMOPT apomict
cami-top
potamic
Tampico
ACIMORR Armoric
ACIMOST maticos
somatic
ACIMPRT crampit
ptarmic
ACIMPRY primacy
ACIMPSS spasmic
ACIMRSZ czarism
ACIMSST miscast
ACIMSTT tactism
ACINNOR Corinna
ACINNOT actinon
cantion
contain
ACINNOZ canzoni
Cinzano®
ACINNST stannic
ACINNTU annicut
ACINOPT caption

	paction
	Pontiac®
ACINOQU	coquina
ACINORR	carrion
ACINORS	Roscian
	saronic
ACINORT	carotin
ACINOSS	caisson
	casinos
	cassino
ACINOST	Scotian
ACINOSU	acinous
ACINOSX	Saxonic
ACINOTT	taction
ACINOTU	auction
	caution
ACINOUV	in vacuo
ACINPRT	cantrip
ACINPRU	Puranic
ACINPRY	cyprian✧
ACINQTU	quantic
ACINRSU	crusian
ACINRTT	tantric✧
ACINRTU	curtain
	turacin
ACINSTU	nautics
ACIOPRS	prosaic
ACIOPRT	apricot
	parotic
	patrico
ACIOPSS	Picasso
ACIOPTT	aptotic
ACIOPTY	opacity
ACIORRS	corsair
ACIORSU	carious
	curiosa
ACIORTT	ricotta
	Riot Act
ACIPRSY	piscary
ACIPRTT	tip-cart
ACIPRVY	privacy
ACIPSST	spastic
ACIPTUY	paucity
ACIQRTU	quartic
ACIQSTU	acquist
ACIRRTY	carry it
ACIRSST	sacrist
ACIRSSU	cuirass
ACIRSTT	astrict
ACIRSTU	Austric
ACIRSTW	twiscar
ACIRSTY	satyric
ACIRSTZ	czarist
ACISSSU	Cassius
ACISSTT	statics
ACISSTU	casuist
ACISTTU	catsuit
	Tacitus
ACISTUV	vacuist
ACITUVY	vacuity
ACJKKSY	skyjack
ACJKLOW	lockjaw
ACJKNNO	jannock
ACJKNOS	Jackson
ACJKOPT	jackpot
ACJLORU	jocular
ACJMNTU	muntjac
ACJPTUU	cajuput
ACKKLMU	Kalmuck
ACKKOOR	cork oak
ACKLLOP	pollack✧
ACKLLOR	Rockall
ACKLLOY	laylock
ACKLLSY	slackly
ACKLMNO	lockman
ACKLMOR	armlock
	lockram
ACKLMOT	Matlock
ACKLNOU	uncloak
ACKLOOR	oarlock
ACKLORW	warlock
ACKLORY	rocklay
ACKLOSS	lassock
ACKLOSY	yolk sac
ACKLPSU	slack up
ACKMMMO	mammock
ACKMORT	cork mat
ACKMOTT	mattock
ACKMPRU	cup mark
ACKMSSU	musk-sac
ACKMSTU	musk-cat
ACKNNOW	acknown
ACKNORY	Conakry
ACKNPRU	crank up
ACKNSTU	unstack
ACKOPRR	parrock
ACKORRT	rock art
	rock tar
	tarrock
ACKOWZZ	wazzock
ACKPRTU	track up
ACKPSTU	stack up
ACLLLOY	locally
ACLLMMO	Malcolm
ACLLOOR	corolla
ACLLOPS	scallop
ACLLORU	locular
ACLLOSU	callous
ACLLOTU	call out
	call-out
ACLLOVY	vocally
ACLMNOO	locoman
ACLMNUY	calumny
ACLMORU	clamour
ACLMOSU	mucosal
ACLMSUY	masculy
ACLNOOO	Laocoon
ACLNOOR	coronal
ACLNOOT	al conto
	coolant
ACLNOOV	volcano
ACLNORU	cornual
	courlan
ACLNORW	corn law
ACLNORY	Carolyn
ACLNOUV	unvocal
	Vulcano
ACLNPSU	unclasp
ACLNRTU	truncal
ACLNSTY	scantly
ACLOOPP	alcopop
	Coppola
ACLOOPR	car pool
	car-pool
ACLOOPT	coal pot
ACLOORT	locator
ACLOPRT	caltrop
	proctal
ACLOPRU	copular
	cupolar
ACLOPSU	copulas
	scopula
ACLOPSY	calypso
ACLOPTY	polyact
ACLORST	scrotal
ACLORSU	carolus
	oscular
ACLORTY	actorly
ACLORUV	vocular
ACLORWW	Wroclaw
ACLOSTU	locusta✧
	talcous
ACLPRTY	cryptal
ACLPRUU	cupular
ACLRSSY	crassly
ACLRSTU	crustal
ACLRSTY	crystal
ACLRSWY	scrawly
ACLSSTU	cutlass
ACMMNOU	nuoc mam
ACMNOOR	Comoran
ACMNOPR	crampon
ACMNOPY	company
ACMNORY	acronym
ACMNSTU	sanctum
ACMOOPT	Potomac
ACMOOST	scotoma
ACMOPRT	compart
ACMOPSS	compass
ACMOPST	compast
ACMOPTU	camp out
ACMORTW	catworm
ACMQTUU	cumquat
ACMSUUV	vacuums
ACNNNOS	cannons
ACNNNOY	no' canny
ACNNNUY	uncanny
ACNNORU	Corunna
ACNNORV	corn van
ACNNORY	canonry✧
ACNNOST	cantons
ACNNOSY	sonancy
ACNNRSY	scranny
ACNOORS	coronas
ACNOORT	cartoon
	coranto
ACNOPSU	Canopus
ACNOPSW	snowcap
ACNORRU	rancour
ACNORRY	carry on
	carry-on
ACNORSU	nacrous
ACNORTT	contrat
ACNORTU	courant
ACNOSSZ	scazons
ACNOSTU	conatus
ACNPRSY	syncarp
ACNRRTU	currant
ACNRSUY	unscary
ACNRSWY	scrawny
ACNRTUY	truancy
ACNSSTU	Sanctus
ACOOPRR	corpora
ACOOPRT	root cap
ACOOPSU	opacous
ACOOPTT	topcoat
ACOORTU	touraco
ACOOSTV	octavos
ACOPRRT	carport
ACOPRTU	crap out
ACOPSTU	upcoast
ACORRTT	tractor
ACORRTU	curator
ACORRTY	carroty
ACORSSU	sarcous
ACORSTU	surcoat
	turacos
ACORSTY	castory
ACORSUU	raucous
ACORSXY	Sycorax
ACOSTTU	cast out
	outcast
ACOSUUV	vacuous
ACPPRSY	scrappy
ACPRRUY	carry up
ACPRTTU	trap-cut
ACPSTUU	usucapt
ACRSSTU	crustas
ACRSTTU	tractus
ADDDDOR	doddard
ADDDEEN	dead end
	dead-end
ADDDEER	dreaded
ADDDEGL	gladded
ADDDELR	raddled
ADDDENO	deodand
ADDEEEY	deadeye
ADDEEGR	degrade
ADDEEHN	had need
ADDEEHR	redhead
ADDEEHT	the dead
ADDEEIR	readied
ADDEELM	medaled
ADDEELN	delenda

Words marked ✧ can also be spelled with one or more capital letters

ADDEELP	pedaled
	pleaded
ADDEELR	red lead
ADDEELY	delayed
ADDEEMN	dead men
ADDEEMR	dreamed
ADDEEOT	deodate
ADDEERR	dreader
ADDEEST	dead set
	dead-set
	steaded
ADDEETU	due date
ADDEFLY	fadedly
ADDEFNU	unfaded
ADDEFRU	defraud
ADDEFRW	dwarfed
ADDEGGR	dragged
ADDEGHO	dog-head
	godhead✧
ADDEGIL	gladdie
ADDEGJU	adjudge
ADDEGLN	gladden
ADDEGRU	guarded
ADDEHIO	Hodeida
ADDEHIR	diehard
	die hard✧
ADDEHLN	handled
ADDEHNR	red hand
ADDEHRS	sharded
ADDEIIK	didakei
ADDEIIS	daisied
ADDEILL	dallied
	dialled
ADDEILP	plaided
ADDEILR	diedral
ADDEILT	dilated
ADDEINO	adenoid
ADDEINU	unaided
	unidea'd
ADDEINV	videnda
ADDEIOT	toadied
ADDEIRR	Derrida
ADDEISV	advised
ADDEJLY	jadedly
ADDEJNU	unjaded
ADDEJRT	Jeddart
ADDELNR	dandler
ADDELOR	old dear
ADDELPP	dappled
ADDELPR	paddler
ADDELRS	saddler
ADDELRW	dawdler
	waddler
ADDELRY	dreadly
	laddery
ADDELST	staddle
ADDELSW	swaddle
ADDELTW	twaddle
ADDELYZ	dazedly
ADDEMST	maddest
ADDENOR	road end
ADDENOT	nodated
ADDENOU	duodena
ADDENPU	pudenda
ADDENRU	daunder
ADDENSU	asudden
ADDENTU	undated
ADDEOPT	adopted
ADDERSS	address
ADDERST	addrest
ADDERSW	swarded
ADDERSY	dryades
ADDERTT	dratted
ADDESST	saddest
ADDFHIS	faddish
ADDFIMS	faddism
ADDFINY	dandify
ADDFIST	faddist
ADDGGIN	gadding
ADDGIIR	diagrid
ADDGIMN	madding
ADDGIMR	Midgard
ADDGINO	dadoing
ADDGINP	padding
ADDGINW	wadding
ADDGLNO	gladdon
ADDGMNO	goddamn
ADDGOOW	dagwood
ADDGOOY	good-day
ADDGORW	godward
ADDGOSY	dog days
ADDHIKS	Kaddish
ADDHILS	laddish
ADDHINP	daphnid
ADDHIQS	Qaddish
ADDHISS	saddish
ADDHITY	hydatid
ADDHLNO	old hand
ADDHNOR	Rhondda
ADDIINS	disdain
ADDIKPS	skid pad
ADDIKST	tsaddik
ADDIKSW	Skiddaw
ADDIKSZ	zaddiks
ADDIKTY	katydid
ADDIKTZ	tzaddik
ADDILMN	midland✧
ADDILMO	old maid
ADDILMS	laddism
ADDILNY	dandily
ADDILOS	disload
ADDIMNO	diamond
ADDIMOR	diadrom
ADDIMSY	dismayd
ADDINOR	android
ADDINRY	diandry
ADDIPRS	disprad
ADDIQST	tsaddiq
ADDIQTZ	tzaddiq
ADDIRZZ	dizzard
ADDKLNU	Dundalk
ADDKNRU	Dunkard
ADDLLOY	old lady
ADDLLRU	dullard
ADDLNRY	dry land
ADDLOOS	soldado
ADDLORT	Old Dart
ADDLOSY	lay odds
ADDLTWY	twaddly
ADDMMOU	ad modum
ADDMNOS	oddsman
ADDNNOR	donnard
ADDNOOW	downa-do
ADDOORS	dorados
ADDOORY	Rood Day
ADDOOSS	dos-à-dos
ADDOPSY	dasypod
ADDOPTU	add up to
ADDQSUY	squaddy
ADEEEFY	fedayee
ADEEEMN	demeane
ADEEEPS	deep-sea
ADEEERR	arreede
ADEEERS	sea reed
ADEEERX	exedrae
ADEEESW	seaweed
ADEEFIL	Felidae
ADEEFIR	fedarie
ADEEFLR	federal
ADEEFLT	deflate
ADEEFPR	prefade
ADEEFRT	draftee
ADEEFST	defaste
ADEEGGH	egghead
ADEEGGN	engaged
ADEEGHS	hag-seed
ADEEGHW	hag-weed
ADEEGIM	die game
ADEEGLL	alledge
	alleged✧
ADEEGLY	glad eye
ADEEGMN	endgame✧
ADEEGMR	red game
ADEEGNR	derange
	en garde
	enraged
	grandee
	grenade
ADEEGNT	endgate
ADEEGNV	vendage
ADEEGOT	dogeate
	goateed
ADEEGRR	regrade
ADEEGRU	guardee
ADEEGRW	ragweed
ADEEGSW	saw-edge
ADEEHLO	Helodea
ADEEHLR	hederal
ADEEHNN	hennaed
ADEEHNS	dasheen
ADEEHNV	havened
ADEEHPR	ephedra
ADEEHRR	adherer
ADEEHRS	sheared
ADEEHRT	hearted
	red heat
ADEEHRX	exhedra
ADEEHST	headset
ADEEHSV	sheaved
ADEEHSY	hayseed
ADEEIIR	Irideae
ADEEIJT	jadeite
ADEEILM	limeade
ADEEILN	aliened
	delaine
ADEEILP	Pléiade
ADEEILS	deiseal
ADEEILY	eyeliad
ADEEIMN	demaine
ADEEIMT	mediate
ADEEINN	adenine
ADEEINS	aniseed
ADEEIQU	Equidae
ADEEIRR	readier
ADEEIRS	readies
ADEEIRW	wearied
ADEEISS	disease
	dis-ease
	seaside
ADEEITV	deviate
ADEEJNO	Jane Doe
ADEEJTU	jet d'eau
ADEEKNP	knee-pad
ADEEKNR	kneader
ADEEKNS	sneaked
ADEEKNW	wakened
ADEEKRW	wreaked
ADEEKWY	weekday
ADEELLN	Allende
ADEELLS	allseed
ADEELLY	alleyed
	Lady Lee
ADEELMR	emerald
ADEELMS	measled
ADEELMT	medalet
	metaled
ADEELNP	deplane
ADEELNR	Laender
	Leander
	learned
	Red Lane
ADEELNS	sand eel
ADEELNT	al dente
	edental
ADEELNW	new deal✧
	Wealden
ADEELPR	pearled
	pleader
ADEELPS	delapse
	pleased
ADEELPT	pleated
ADEELRS	leaders
ADEELRT	altered
	related

treadle
ADEELRW leeward
ADEELRX relaxed
ADEELRY delayer
layered
relayed
ADEELST de Staël
stealed
ADEELSV sleaved
ADEELTT ladette
ADEELTV velated
ADEELTX exalted
ADEELUV devalue
ADEEMNR amender
enarmed
meander
reamend
ADEEMNW new-made
ADEEMNY demayne
ADEEMRR dreamer
ADEEMRT red meat
ADEEMRY deary me
ADEEMST steamed
ADEEMSU medusae
ADEEMSW mawseed
ADEEMTW matweed
ADEEMWY mayweed
ADEENNV Vendean
ADEENRR rear-end
ADEENRU uneared
ADEENRY deanery
ne'erday✧
renayed
year-end
ADEENST East End
standee
ADEENTT dentate
ADEEOPT adoptee
ADEEORS oreades
ADEEORW oarweed
ADEEOSV sea dove
ADEEPPY day-peep
ADEEPRS speared
ADEEPRT pad-tree
predate
red tape
red-tape
tapered
ADEEPRV deprave
pervade
ADEERRS redsear
ADEERRT retread
treader
ADEERRV averred
ADEERST dearest
estrade
Tasered
ADEERSV adverse
ADEERTV averted
ADEERTW dewater
tarweed
watered
ADEESSY essayed
ADEESTU sautéed
ADEESTW sweated
ADEETUX exudate
ADEFFHO head off
ADEFFIN affined
ADEFFLM maffled
ADEFFLO lead off
lead-off
ADEFFOR read off
ADEFGGL flagged
ADEFGGR fragged
ADEFGLN fangled
flanged
ADEFGLR red flag✧
ADEFGOU fougade
ADEFHST shafted
ADEFILN Anfield
ADEFILS disleaf
ADEFIMN ad finem
ADEFIMS disfame
ADEFINR friande
ADEFINT defiant
fainted
ADEFITX fixated
ADEFKLN fankled
ADEFLLN elfland
ADEFLLW dewfall
ADEFLNN fenland
ADEFLOS sol-faed
ADEFLPP flapped
ADEFLRU dareful
ADEFLTT flatted
ADEFLTU default
ADEFMNU unfamed
ADEFMST mast-fed
ADEFNUZ unfazed
ADEFOOS seafood
ADEFORV favored
ADEFORY feodary
fore-day
ADEFOTU fade out
fade-out
ADEFPPR frapped
ADEFPRR prefard
ADEFRRT drafter
redraft
ADEFRUY feudary
ADEGGHS shagged
ADEGGIU gaudgie
guidage
ADEGGLR draggle
ADEGGLS slagged
ADEGGNS snagged
ADEGGOS dog's age
ADEGGRY raggedy
ADEGGSW swagged
ADEGGTY gadgety
ADEGHIN heading
ADEGHIR hag-ride
headrig
ADEGHJU jughead
ADEGHLO log-head
ADEGILN dealing
leading
ADEGILO geoidal
ADEGILP pig-lead
ADEGILU La Digue
ADEGILV glaived
ADEGINR deraign
gradine
grained
reading✧
ADEGINW windage
ADEGIOS go aside
ADEGIOT godetia
ADEGIRS agrised
ADEGIRV Rigveda
ADEGISV visaged
ADEGIUV viduage
ADEGLMO Gaeldom
ADEGLNN endlang
ADEGLNO Donegal
ADEGLNR dangler
gnarled
ADEGLNS glandes
ADEGLNT tangled
ADEGLNU langued
ADEGLRU raguled
ADEGLRY gradely
ADEGMNU gudeman
ADEGNNO nonaged
ADEGNNU dunnage
ADEGNOP pondage
ADEGNOS sondage
ADEGNOT tangoed
ADEGNOV dogvane
ADEGNOW gowaned
ADEGNPU unpaged
ADEGNRR gnarred
ADEGNRS gardens✧
ADEGNRT dragnet
granted
ADEGNRU enguard
ADEGNUW unwaged
ADEGNUZ ungazed
ADEGOPS God's ape
ADEGORS dog's-ear
ADEGORW dowager
wordage
ADEGOSV God save
ADEGOTT togated
ADEGPRS spadger
ADEGPRU upgrade
ADEGRRS regards
ADEGRSU sugared
ADEGRTY tragedy
ADEGRUY gaudery
ADEGSSU degauss
ADEHHOP hophead
ADEHHOT hothead
ADEHIKL had like
ADEHIKS dasheki
ADEHIKV khediva
ADEHILL Delilah
ADEHILM El Mahdi
ADEHILN Hieland
ADEHILP helipad
ADEHILR lie hard
ADEHILY headily
ADEHINP pinhead
ADEHINR handier
ADEHIPR raphide
ADEHIPS aphides
ADEHIPT pithead
ADEHIRR harried
ADEHIRW rawhide
ADEHIRY hayride
ADEHIST tea dish
ADEHITY Hay diet
ADEHKNS shanked
ADEHKOR hardoke
ADEHKOT kathode
ADEHLLP lapheld
ADEHLMU lum-head
ADEHLNR handler
ADEHLNS handsel
ADEHLOT loathed
ADEHLOW Lew Hoad
ADEHLSS slashed
ADEHLTY deathly
The Lady
ADEHMMS shammed
ADEHMMW whammed
ADEHMNR herdman
ADEHMOP mophead
ADEHMOR hadrome
ADEHMSS smashed
ADEHNRT the Rand
ADEHNRU unheard
ADEHNST handset
ADEHNTU haunted
ADEHNUW W H Auden
ADEHOOP apehood
ADEHOPT pothead
pot-head
ADEHOPX hexapod
ADEHORR hard roe
hoarder
ADEHORW draw hoe
ADEHOTT hot date
to death
ADEHOTW tow-head
ADEHPPW whapped
ADEHPST spathed
T-shaped
ADEHPSU heads-up
U-shaped
ADEHPSV V-shaped
ADEHRST hard-set
threads
trashed

ADEHRTY	hydrate
	the Yard
	thready
ADEHUZZ	huzzaed
ADEIILR	deliria
	irideal
ADEIILS	dailies
	sedilia
ADEIIMN	diamine
ADEIINR	denarii
ADEIIRR	Airdrie
ADEIIRS	airside
	diarise
ADEIIRZ	diarize
ADEIJLM	Djemila
ADEIJMR	jemidar
ADEIJSU	Judaise
ADEIJUZ	Judaize
ADEIKLM	like mad
ADEIKLN	knaidel
ADEIKLR	Kildare
ADEIKLZ	Zadkiel
ADEIKMV	Kiev Dam
ADEILLM	mild ale
ADEILLR	dallier
	dialler
	rallied
ADEILLS	disleal
	sallied
ADEILLT	tallied
ADEILLV	vialled
ADEILLY	ideally
ADEILMM	dilemma
ADEILMP	implead
ADEILMR	Daimler®
ADEILMS	misdeal
	mislead
ADEILMT	ad litem
ADEILNN	annelid
	lindane
ADEILNR	Ireland
ADEILNT	tail end
ADEILNU	aliunde
	unideal
ADEILNV	andvile
ADEILNW	new-laid
	Weiland
ADEILNX	indexal
ADEILOP	Oedipal
ADEILOR	dariole
ADEILOS	deasoil
ADEILOU	douleia
ADEILPP	applied
ADEILPR	lip-read
	pedrail
	predial
ADEILPS	palsied
	Pleiads
ADEILPT	plaited
	taliped
ADEILRS	sideral
ADEILRT	dilater
ADEILRY	readily
ADEILSS	aidless
ADEILSU	deasiul
ADEILSV	devisal
ADEILSY	dialyse
ADEILYZ	dialyze
ADEIMMR	mermaid
ADEIMMS	mismade
ADEIMNR	adermin
	Amerind
ADEIMNS	sideman
ADEIMNT	mediant
ADEIMNU	unaimed
ADEIMPR	Dampier
ADEIMRR	admirer
	married
ADEIMRS	misread
	sidearm
ADEIMRT	maître d'
	readmit
ADEIMRU	Muridae
ADEIMRY	mid-year
ADEIMST	Mideast
	misdate
ADEIMTU	taedium
ADEIMTY	daytime
ADEINNN	nandine
	nannied
ADEINOR	aneroid
ADEINOS	adonise
	anodise
	Diasone®
	sodaine
ADEINOV	naevoid
ADEINOX	dioxane
ADEINOZ	adonize
	anodize
ADEINPR	pardine
ADEINPS	pansied
ADEINPT	depaint
	painted
	patined
ADEINRR	drainer
	randier
ADEINRS	sardine
ADEINRT	detrain
	tan ride
	trade in
	trade-in
	trained
ADEINRU	unaired
	uranide
ADEINRV	invader
	ravined
ADEINST	instead
	sainted
	stained
ADEINSW	sea wind
ADEINTT	tainted
ADEINTU	audient
ADEINTV	deviant
ADEINVV	navvied
ADEIOPS	adipose
ADEIOPT	opiated
ADEIORR	Eriador
ADEIORS	Isadore
	soredia
ADEIORT	à droite
ADEIORV	avoider
ADEIORX	exordia
ADEIOSX	oxidase
ADEIOSZ	diazoes
ADEIOTX	oxidate
ADEIOVV	vaivode
ADEIOVW	waivode
ADEIOWW	waiwode
ADEIPPR	drappie
	prepaid
ADEIPPU	appuied
ADEIPRR	drapier
	parried
ADEIPRS	despair
ADEIPRT	diptera✧
	Perdita
ADEIPSS	apsides
ADEIRRT	tardier
	tarried
ADEIRST	asterid
	astride
	diaster
	disrate
	staired
ADEIRSU	residua
ADEIRSV	adviser
ADEIRTT	eat dirt
ADEIRTV	tardive
ADEIRTY	dietary
ADEISST	disseat
	saidest
ADEISTV	vistaed
ADEISTW	waisted
ADEISWY	wayside
ADEITUZ	Deutzia
ADEITWY	tideway
ADEJLUW	Jude Law
ADEJMPS	P D James
ADEJMRU	mudéjar✧
ADEJOPR	jeopard
ADEKLNS	kalends
ADEKLNY	nakedly
ADEKLOP	polkaed
ADEKLST	stalked
ADEKLSY	yslaked
ADEKMNR	Denmark
ADEKMUY	may-duke
ADEKNPP	knapped
ADEKNRR	knarred
ADEKNRS	Dansker
ADEKNRU	Kundera
	unraked
ADEKNSU	unasked
ADEKNUW	unwaked
ADEKNVY	vandyke✧
ADEKPSY	pay-desk
ADELLLY	Dalyell
ADELLMU	medulla
ADELLNO	all done
ADELLNR	ländler
ADELLNW	ellwand
ADELLOR	odaller
ADELLOW	allowed
ADELLRU	udaller
ADELLST	stalled
ADELMMS	slammed
ADELMNO	Mondale
ADELMNR	mandrel
ADELMOR	earldom
ADELMOS	damosel
ADELMOZ	damozel
ADELNNP	planned
ADELNNU	unladen
ADELNOR	ladrone
	La Ronde
	Leonard
ADELNOT	taloned
ADELNOY	yealdon
ADELNPY	endplay
ADELNRS	slander
	snarled
ADELNRU	launder
	lurdane
	rundale
ADELNRY	dearnly
ADELNST	slanted
ADELNTU	lunated
	undealt
ADELNTW	wetland
ADELOPR	leopard
ADELOPS	deposal
	pedalos
ADELOPT	tadpole
ADELORS	sea lord✧
ADELORT	delator
	leotard
ADELORU	roulade
	Urodela
ADELOSS	lassoed
ADELOST	saltoed
ADELOSU	laus Deo
ADELOTU	lead out
	lead-out
ADELOVY	love-day
ADELPPS	slapped
ADELPRY	pedlary
ADELPST	spalted
ADELPTT	platted
ADELPTW	dewlapt
ADELPTY	adeptly
ADELRRU	ruderal
ADELRRW	drawler
ADELRST	star-led
ADELRTX	dextral

ADELRTY lyrated
ADELRZZ dazzler
ADELSTT slatted
ADELTTW wattled
ADELTUV vaulted
ADEMMPS spammed
ADEMMRT trammed
ADEMNNU mundane
unnamed
ADEMNOR dream on
madrone
ADEMNOZ Mendoza
ADEMNRU duramen
maunder
unarmed
ADEMNSS madness
ADEMNSU medusan
sudamen
ADEMNTU unmated
untamed
ADEMOSY Samoyed
someday
ADEMOWY meadowy
ADEMPRU dream up
ADEMRRU eardrum
ADEMRTY term day
ADEMSSU assumed
medusas
ADENNOY annoyed
anodyne
ADENNPS spanned
ADENNPT pendant
ADENNST standen
ADENNWY dewanny
ADENOOZ endozoa
ADENOPR operand
padrone
pandore
ADENOPS dapsone
ADENOPT note-pad
tonepad
ADENOPY open day
ADENORR Reardon
ADENORT tornade
trade on
ADENORU rondeau
ADENOST onstead
ADENOTZ zonated
ADENOUY Yaoundé
ADENPPR parpend
ADENPPS snapped
ADENPPW wappend
ADENPRR pardner
ADENPRU unpared
ADENPRW predawn
ADENPSX Spandex®
spandex
ADENPSY dyspnea
ADENPTU untaped
ADENPUV unpaved
ADENRRS errands
ADENRRY reynard✧
ADENRSS sanders
sarsden
ADENRST stander
ADENRSU asunder
danseur
ADENRTU daunter
natured
unrated
untread
ADENRTV verdant
ADENRTW draw-net
ADENRTX dextran
ADENRTY dentary
rent-day
ADENRUY unready
ADENSSS sadness
ADENSTU unsated
ADENSUV unsaved
ADENSWY endways
Newsday
ADENTUV vaunted
ADENTUX untaxed
ADENUWY unwayed
ADEOORT odorate
ADEOPRR eardrop
ADEOPRT adopter
readopt
ADEOPSS spadoes
ADEOPST podestà
ADEORRS drosera
rear-dos
ADEORRW arrowed
ADEORST torsade
ADEORTU outdare
read out
read-out
ADEORWY rodeway
ADEORYZ zedoary
ADEOSTT toasted
ADEOTTU outdate
ADEOWWY waywode
ADEPPRT trapped
ADEPPRW wrapped
ADEPPSW swapped
ADEPRRS sparred
ADEPRRY drapery
ADEPRSS adpress
ADEPRSY sprayed
ADEPRTU trade up
ADEQRSU squared
ADERRST starred
ADERRSW drawers
ADERSSU assured
ADERSTV starved
ADERSTW steward
strawed
ADERSTY rest day
strayed
ADERSUY dasyure
ADERSVW dwarves
ADERTUU Trudeau
ADERWWY weyward
ADESSTU sea dust
ADESTTU statued
ADESTTW swatted
wadsett
ADESTUY Tuesday
ADFFGIN daffing
ADFFHNO hand-off
offhand
ADFFHOS dash off
ADFFILO laid off
ADFFIST distaff
ADFFLNO fanfold
ADFFLOO offload
ADFFOOR affoord
off-road
ADFFORW draw off
off-ward
ward off
ADFGIIT Gift Aid
ADFGINR farding
ADFGLLU gladful
ADFHISY fish-day
ADFHLNU handful
ADFHOOS shadoof
ADFHORS Ashford
ADFIIMT Fatimid
ADFILLU fluidal
ADFILNN Finland
ADFILOR Florida
ADFIMNO of a mind
ADFIMNR findram
ADFIMNY damnify
ADFINRT indraft
ADFIOOR Dario Fo
ADFIORS fair do's
ADFIRSY Fridays
ADFLLYY ladyfly
ADFLMOO damfool
ADFLMPU mudflap
ADFLMTU mudflat
ADFLNOP plafond
ADFLNOR Randolf
ADFLNSY sandfly
ADFLORS Salford
ADFLORU foulard
ADFMOSU fumados
ADFNNOT fondant
ADFNOST fantods
ADFOOPT footpad
ADFORRW forward
froward
ADFORTW Watford
ADFORTX draft ox
ADGGHNO hangdog
ADGGILN gadling
ADGGILR riggald
ADGGINR grading
niggard
ADGGIRS Rigsdag
ADGGLNO old gang
ADGGOOT goat-god
ADGHHIY high day
ADGHILO hidalgo
ADGHINO Dong Hai
ADGHINS dashing
shading
ADGHIPR digraph
ADGHIRR ardrigh
ard-righ
ADGHIRS dishrag
ADGHNNU handgun
ADGHNOS sandhog
ADGHNOW hagdown
ADGHOOR road hog
ADGHORT hard-got
ADGHORW hogward
ADGHRTU draught
ADGIILN dialing
gliadin
ADGIILT digital
ADGIINO gonidia
ADGIINR gradini
ADGIINU iguanid
ADGIINW gwiniad
ADGIINY Digynia
ADGIKRS Riksdag
ADGILMN madling
ADGILNN landing
ADGILNO digonal
loading
ADGILNR darling
ADGILNU languid
ADGILOR goliard
ADGILRY day-girl
ADGILSU gladius
ADGILUY gaudily
ADGIMMN damming
ADGIMNN damning
ADGIMNP damping
ADGIMNR mridang
ADGIMRU Guri Dam
ADGINNR darning
ADGINNS sanding
ADGINNW dawning
ADGINOR adoring
Gordian
gradino
roading
ADGINOT doating
dot gain
ADGINPW wind gap
ADGINRT darting
trading
ADGINRW drawing
warding
ADGINWY gwyniad
ADGIPRU pagurid
ADGIRSU guisard
ADGIRZZ gizzard
ADGLLNO golland

ADGLLOO all-good
ADGLLOR rag doll
ADGLMNO mangold
ADGLNOO gondola
ADGLNOR goldarn
ADGLNOT Gotland
ADGLNOW gowland
ADGLNOY daylong
ADGLNRY grandly
ADGLOSU Douglas
ADGMNOO goodman✧
Mogadon®
ADGMNOR gormand
ADGNOOR dragoon
gadroon
ADGNORU aground
on guard
ADGNORY organdy
ADGNRRU gurnard
ADGNRUU unguard
ADGORST Dog Star
ADGORTU drag out
ADGRSTU rag-dust
ADHHIRS hardish
ADHHIRT hard hit
hard-hit
ADHHMOS shahdom
ADHIIJT ijtihad
ADHIIKS dashiki
ADHIIMS Hasidim
maidish
ADHIIOP Ophidia
ADHIIPS Phidias
ADHIKNS dankish
ADHIKRS darkish
ADHIKTZ Tadzhik
ADHILMO halidom
ADHILNY handily
ADHILOP haploid
ADHILOY holiday
hyaloid
ADHILRY hardily
ADHILSY ladyish
shadily
ADHIMMS Mahdism
ADHIMPS dampish
phasmid
ADHIMRS Midrash
ADHIMST Mahdist
ADHINOR Rhodian
ADHINOT anthoid
ADHINPS Daphnis
shin pad
ADHINPU dauphin
ADHINUY Hyundai®
ADHIORS hairdos
ADHKORW dorhawk
ADHKOSU shakudo
ADHLLLO holdall
ADHLLNO holland
ADHLMOY holydam

ADHLMPY lymphad
ADHLOPY Play-Doh®
ADHLOYY holy day
ADHMNOO hoodman
manhood
ADHMNOR horn-mad
ADHMNOU Mahound
ADHMNWY Wyndham
ADHNNOS hands-on
ADHNNUY unhandy
ADHNORU unhoard
ADHNORW hard-won
ADHNOSW Ashdown
ADHNOTU hand out
handout
hand-out
ADHNOTW two-hand
ADHNOVZ Zhdanov
ADHNPSU hands up
ADHNRRU hard-run
run hard
ADHNRSY shandry
ADHNRTY hydrant
ADHNRUY unhardy
ADHOORR rhodora
ADHOOSW wood ash
ADHOPRT hardtop
ADHOPRU uphoard
ADHOPRY hop-yard
ADHOPST dashpot
ADHOSTU dash out
ADHOSWY shadowy
ADHRSWY dry-wash
ADIIILR iridial
ADIIIMN Idi Amin
ADIIINR iridian
ADIIKLO dika-oil
ADIIKNN in a kind
ADIIKOT dakoiti
ADIILMS misdial
mislaid
ADIILNO lianoid
ADIILNV invalid
ADIILOS sialoid
ADIILST dialist
ADIILVV Vivaldi
ADIIMMS maidism
ADIIMOS daimios
ADIIMPV impavid
ADIIMRU mudiria
ADIIMSS missaid
ADIINNN in-and-in
ADIINOV in vadio
Ovidian
ADIINPR pindari
pridian
ADIINST distain
ADIINSU indusia
suidian
ADIIORS Isidora
ADIIPXY pyxidia

ADIIQRU daquiri
ADIIRST diarist
ADIIRTY aridity
ADIITVY avidity
ADIJMSU Judaism
ADIJNOT adjoint
ADIJSTU Judaist
ADIKLNY ladykin
ADIKLOS odalisk
ADIKLPS klipdas
ADIKLST St Kilda
ADIKMNN mankind
ADIKMOS mikados
ADIKMRS RAM disk
ADIKMSS dismask
ADIKNPS skid pan
skidpan
ADIKNRS disrank
ADIKPRS dispark
ADILLMM milldam
ADILLOW laid low
ADILLPY lily pad
ADILLSY disally
ADILLTY tidally
ADILLVY validly
ADILLYY day lily
ADILMNO mondial
ADILMNR mandril
ADILMNU maudlin
ADILMNW wild man
ADILMOO Modiola
ADILMOP diploma
ADILMOU alodium
ADILMOY amyloid
ADILMPS plasmid
ADILMSS dismals✧
ADILMSU dualism
ADILMSY dismayl
ladyism
ADILNOR nail-rod
ordinal
ADILNOS ladinos✧
oil sand
ADILNRU diurnal
ADILNRY randily
ADILNSU sundial
ADILNSY Lindsay
ADILOOV ovoidal
ADILOOZ zooidal
ADILOPR dipolar
ADILOPW low-paid
ADILORT dilator
ADILORV Rivaldo
ADILOST di salto
ADILOTW wild oat
ADILPRY pyralid
rapidly
ADILPST plastid
ADILPSY display
ADILPTU plaudit
ADILPVY vapidly

ADILQSU squalid
ADILRTY tardily
ADILSSW wild ass
ADILSTU dualist
ADILSTY staidly
ADILTUY duality
ADIMNNO mondain
ADIMNOS madison✧
ADIMOOS isodoma
ADIMORR mirador
ADIMOST mastoid
ADIMOTT mattoid
ADIMPRY pyramid
ADIMQSU quidams
ADIMRSW misdraw
ADIMSST dismast
ADIMSTU dumaist
stadium
ADIMUVV ad vivum
ADINNOP dipnoan
Pandion
ADINNOR andiron
ADINNRS innards
ADINNRW indrawn
ADINNRY innyard
ADINNST stand in
stand-in
ADINOOP poinado
ADINOPP oppidan
ADINOPR padroni
poniard
ADINOPT pintado
ADINORR ordinar
ADINORS sadiron
ADINORV virando
ADINORW in a word
ADINOSV Novi Sad
ADINOTX oxidant
ADINPRY Prydain
ADINPST sandpit
ADINRRT tridarn
ADINRSU Drusian
sundari
ADINRSW inwards
ADINRTU triduan
unitard
ADINRUY Ian Dury
ADINSTT Dantist
distant
ADINSTU unstaid
ADINSUW unswai'd
ADINTTY dittany
ADIOOPS Isopoda
ADIOOSW woodsia
ADIOPRR airdrop
ADIOPRS sparoid
ADIOPRT parotid
ADIOPRV privado
ADIORST astroid
ADIORSU sauroid
ADIORSV advisor

ADIORTU auditor
ADIOSUV Vaudois
ADIOSVW disavow
ADIPPRT dip-trap
ADIPPTU put paid
ADIPRST dispart
ADIPRTY day trip
pay dirt
ADIRSSU sardius
ADIRSTY satyrid
ADIRSUY dysuria
ADJNNOU Don Juan
ADJNORU adjourn
ADKKLOY kakodyl
ADKLLOT old talk
old-talk
ADKLMRU mudlark
ADKNNSU unskan'd
ADKOOOW oak-wood
ADKORWY day-work
workday
ADKRSWY skyward
ADLLLOR Lollard
ADLLLOT all told
ADLLMOW wadmoll
ADLLMOY modally
ADLLNOW lowland
ADLLNOY nodally
ADLLOPR pollard
ADLLORW Law Lord
ADLLOST old salt
ADLLOWX wax doll
ADLLRWY drywall
ADLMMPU dum-palm
ADLMOOV Moldova
ADLMORU modular
ADLMORY May-lord
ADLMOSV Slavdom
ADLNNOR norland
ADLNOOR lardoon
Orlando
Ronaldo
ADLNOPU poundal
ADLNORU nodular
ADLNORW Rowland
ADLNOSU souldan
ADLNOSY synodal
ADLNOTU outland
ADLNOTY Toyland
ADLNOWY lay down
lay-down
ADLNRTU Rutland
ADLNRUY laundry
ADLNTWY Tynwald
ADLOPRU poulard
ADLORRW warlord
ADLORSU sudoral
ADLORUY our Lady
ADLOSSW Sod's law
ADLRSTY dry-salt
ADMMNSU summand
ADMNOOR doorman
madroño
ADMNOOW woodman
ADMNOOZ madzoon
ADMNOQU quondam
ADMNORS rodsman
ADMNORT dormant
mordant
ADMNORY Raymond
ADMNOSU osmunda
ADMNOSY dynamos
Mondays
ADMNSTU dustman
ADMOORT doormat
ADMOORY day room
ADMOPPU popadum
ADMOPST Potsdam
ADMORST stardom
tsardom
ADMORTW madwort
ADMOSTU Matsudo
ADMRRUW war drum
ADMRSSY dry Mass
ADMRSTU durmast
mustard
ADNNNOO on and on
ADNNOOS and so on
ADNNOOV Donovan
ADNNOOY noonday
ADNNORT donnart
ADNNOST stand on
ADNNOSW Sandown
ADNNOTU daunton
ADNNRTU dunnart
ADNNRUW Dawn Run
ADNNSTU Dunstan
ADNOOPR pandoor
ADNOORT donator
odorant
tandoor
tornado✧
ADNOOSS so-and-so
ADNOOTW wood ant
ADNOPPR pan drop
ADNOPRU pandour
ADNOPRV provand
ADNOPWY pay down
ADNORRS Ronsard
ADNORRW norward
nor'ward
ADNORSW onwards
ADNORTU rotunda
ADNORWY nayword
ADNOSTT stand-to
ADNOSTU astound
ADNOSTY don't say
ADNPQSS p's and q's
ADNPRUW updrawn
ADNPSTU dustpan
stand up
stand-up
upstand
ADNRSUW sunward
ADNSSUY Sundays
ADNSTYY dynasty
ADOOPPS soda pop
ADOOPSU apodous
ADOOPSW sapwood
ADOORTW woodrat
wood tar
ADOORWY doorway
ADOOWWX woodwax
ADOPRRW wardrop
ADOPSTY post day
ADORSTW towards
ADORSUU arduous
ADORTUW draw out
outward
ADOUUVX vaudoux
ADPRSUW upwards
ADPSSUY Dasypus
ADSSTUW sawdust
AEEEFLR eelfare
AEEEGGL lee gage
AEEEGKL keelage
AEEEGLT legatee
AEEEGNT teenage
AEEEGPR peerage
AEEEGPS seepage
AEEEGRT étagère
AEEEILN alienee
AEEEIRT eaterie
AEEELLN lee-lane
AEEELRS release
AEEELTV elevate
AEEELVW lee wave
AEEEPPT Papeete
AEEERTT tea tree
AEEFFLL felafel
AEEFFMR fee-farm
AEEFFOS ease off
AEEFFRT fat-free
AEEFGNT fanteeg
AEEFGRS serfage
AEEFGTW weftage
AEEFHRT feather
terefah
AEEFILN Felinae
AEEFILT fee tail
AEEFILW alewife
AEEFIRS freesia
sea-fire
AEEFISW seawife
AEEFLLN Fenella
AEEFLLT leaflet
AEEFLMN enflame
AEEFLMS alms-fee
AEEFLPY eye-flap
AEEFLRT reflate
AEEFLRW welfare
AEEFLRY leafery
AEEFLRZ alférez
AEEFLSU easeful
AEEFLTX telefax
AEEFMNR enframe
freeman
AEEFMRR free-arm
reframe
AEEFMRT fermate
AEEFOTV foveate
AEEFPPR frappée
AEEFRRT ferrate
AEEFRST feaster
sea fret
AEEFRTU feature
AEEFRTX tax-free
AEEFRWY freeway
AEEFSSX safe sex
AEEFSTW sweet FA
AEEGGLL allegge
AEEGGLR gregale
AEEGGLT gateleg
AEEGGNR engager✧
AEEGGNY gay gene
AEEGGOP epagoge
AEEGHIR hireage
AEEGHMT the game
AEEGHNN Gehenna
AEEGHNW whangee
AEEGILL galilee✧
AEEGILM mileage
AEEGILN lineage
AEEGILP epigeal
AEEGILW weigela
AEEGINP epigean
AEEGINU eugenia✧
AEEGIPR pierage
AEEGIRR Egreria
AEEGIRT Reigate
AEEGIRV give ear
AEEGISS assiege
AEEGKRW rag week
AEEGLLR alleger
AEEGLLZ gazelle
AEEGLMN gleeman
melange
mélange
AEEGLNR Al Green
enlarge
general
gleaner
AEEGLNS Senegal
AEEGLNT elegant
AEEGLNU euglena
AEEGLNV evangel
AEEGLOR aerogel
AEEGLOV leave go
AEEGLPR peregal
AEEGLRT get real
AEEGLRU glue ear
leaguer✧
regulae
AEEGLRW legwear

AEEGLRY eagerly
AEEGLSS ageless
sea legs
AEEGLSV selvage
AEEGLTT galette
AEEGLTU tegulae
AEEGLTV vegetal
AEEGMMT gemmate
tagmeme
AEEGMNR germane
AEEGMNT net game
AEEGMRU remuage
AEEGMSS megasse
message
AEEGNNP pangene
AEEGNNR enrange
AEEGNNV Genevan
AEEGNOP peonage
AEEGNOS Goanese
AEEGNPP genappe
AEEGNRT grantee
greaten
reagent
AEEGNRU renague
AEEGNRV avenger
engrave
AEEGNRW new ager✧
AEEGNTT gate net
tentage
AEEGNTV ventage
AEEGNTW Newgate
AEEGORV over age
overage
over-age
AEEGPRS asperge
presage
AEEGRRS greaser
AEEGRRT greater
regrate
AEEGRRW wagerer
AEEGRST ergates
restage
AEEGRSV Gervase
greaves✧
AEEGRTU treague
AEEGRUZ guereza
AEEGSTT gestate
tagetes
AEEGTTZ gazette✧
AEEHHNT heathen
AEEHHOV heave ho!
heave-ho
AEEHHRT heather
AEEHHST sheathe
AEEHILR hair-eel
AEEHIRV heavier
AEEHIST atheise
AEEHITZ atheize
AEEHKNR hearken
AEEHKNT thankee
AEEHKRU heureka

AEEHLMS shemale
AEEHLNR her lane
AEEHLNT lethean
AEEHLOR ear-hole
AEEHLPT heeltap
AEEHLRT leather
tar heel
AEEHLRV haverel
Le Havre
AEEHLSW awheels
AEEHLSY eyelash
AEEHLTT athlete
AEEHMNT methane
AEEHMRS mahseer
AEEHMRT erathem
thermae
AEEHMST the same
AEEHMSV Evesham
AEEHNPT heptane
phenate
AEEHNRS arsheen
AEEHNRT earthen
hearten
Teheran
AEEHNSV heavens
AEEHNSW Shawnee
AEEHNTT the tane
AEEHNTW wheaten
AEEHPRS reshape
sphaere
spheare
AEEHPRT preheat
AEEHPTT pet hate
AEEHPUV upheave
AEEHQSU quashee✧
AEEHRRS shearer
AEEHRST Theresa
AEEHRSW whereas
AEEHRTT theater
theatre
thereat
AEEHRTV threave
AEEHRTW weather
whate'er
whereat
wreathe
AEEHRTY the year
AEEHSSV sheaves
AEEHSTT the East
AEEHSWY eyewash
AEEIJNN Jeannie
AEEIJNT Janeite
AEEIKLS sea-like
AEEIKPS sea pike
AEEILLR reallie
AEEILMN Melanie
AEEILMR e-mailer
AEEILMS mealies
sea mile
AEEILNP alepine
AEEILNS sealine

AEEILNT lineate
AEEILPT epilate
pileate
AEEILRR earlier
AEEILRS earlies
realise
AEEILRT atelier
e-tailer
realtie
AEEILRV Valerie
AEEILRZ realize
AEEILTT ailette
AEEILTV elative
AEEIMNR remanié
AEEIMNS nemesia
AEEIMNT matinee
matinée
AEEIMNX examine
AEEIMPR empaire
AEEIMPT meat pie
AEEIMRR reamier
AEEIMRS seriema
AEEIMRT emirate
meatier
AEEIMSS misease
siamese✧
AEEIMST steamie
AEEIMSZ siameze
AEEIMTT teatime
AEEINNP Peneian
AEEINRT Aintree
retinae
trainee
AEEINST etesian
AEEINTV naiveté
naïveté
Venetia
AEEINVW inweave
AEEIORT etaerio
AEEIPRR pereira
AEEIPTX expiate
AEEIRRR arriéré
AEEIRRS rearise
AEEIRRT Eritrea
AEEIRSS Arieses
AEEIRST seriate
AEEIRTT ariette
iterate
AEEIRTV evirate
AEEISVV evasive
AEEISVW sea view
AEEITTV aviette
evitate
AEEITUX eutexia
AEEIUVX exuviae
AEEJNST sejeant
AEEJNTT Janette
AEEJNTU jauntee
AEEJRSW Jew's-ear
AEEKKNO kokanee
AEEKLLT lakelet

AEEKLMN keelman
AEEKLNT kantele
AEEKLRT Elektra
AEEKMNS kamseen
AEEKMNW man-week
AEEKMRT meerkat
AEEKMSU make use
AEEKNNN nankeen
AEEKNNP knee-pan
AEEKNRS sneaker
AEEKNRT retaken
AEEKNRW wakener
AEEKNTT take ten
AEEKORT oak tree
AEEKPRS respeak
speaker
AEEKPRT pertake
AEEKRRT retaker
AEEKRRW wreaker
AEEKRST sakeret
AEEKRSU Euskera
AEEKRTW tweaker
AEEKSTY key-seat
AEELLMS sea mell
AEELLOP ale-pole
AEELLOV alveole
AEELLPR parelle
AEELLRS all-seer
AEELLST Estella
salt eel
AEELLSV AS level
AEELLSY all eyes
AEELLWY walleye
AEELMNP empanel
emplane
AEELMNR Marlene
reelman
AEELMNT manteel
AEELMNU Emanuel
AEELMNV velamen
AEELMNY amylene
AEELMPR empaler
AEELMPX example
exempla
AEELMRT lameter
AEELMSS measles
AEELMST Maltese
AEELMTU emulate
AEELNNP enplane
AEELNNR lernean
AEELNOR Eleanor
AEELNPS spelean
AEELNRR learner
relearn
AEELNRT alterne
enteral
eternal✧
AEELNRW renewal
AEELNRZ Relenza®
AEELNSV enslave
AEELNTY entayle

AEELOPR	parolee
AEELOPX	poleaxe
AEELORU	aureole
AEELOSW	leasowe
AEELPRR	pearler
AEELPRS	pleaser
	relapse
AEELPRT	pleater
	prelate
AEELPRU	pleurae
AEELPTT	palette
	peltate
AEELPTU	epaulet
AEELQSU	sequela
AEELRRT	re-alter
	relater
AEELRSS	earless
AEELRST	Laertes
	stealer
AEELRSU	leasure
AEELRSV	several
AEELRSY	sealery
AEELRUV	revalue
AEELRUY	Euryale
AEELSST	altesse
AEELSSU	Auslese
AEELSSW	aweless
AEELSTT	Seattle
AEELSTU	setuale
AEELSTV	salvete
AEELSTX	latexes
AEELTTY	layette
AEELTVW	wavelet
AEELYYZ	lazy eye
AEEMMMR	maremme
AEEMMPY	empyema
AEEMMRT	ammeter
	metamer
AEEMNNO	anemone
AEEMNNP	pen name
AEEMNPT	pet name
	Tempean
AEEMNRS	mens rea
AEEMNRT	remanet
AEEMNRU	Maureen
AEEMNSS	en masse
AEEMORT	erotema
AEEMOSW	awesome
	waesome
AEEMPRT	tempera
AEEMPRY	empayre
AEEMPTU	amputee
AEEMQRU	marquee
AEEMRRS	smearer
AEEMRSS	Rameses
AEEMRST	sea term
	steamer
AEEMRSU	measure
AEEMRTY	may tree
	métayer
AEEMSST	seamset
AEEMSSX	same-sex
AEEMSTW	Mae West
AEEMUWX	Max Euwe
AEENNOT	neonate
AEENNPT	pennate
	pentane
AEENNRS	ensnare
AEENNRX	reannex
AEENNTT	Annette
	Nanette
AEENNTU	uneaten
AEENOPR	peraeon
AEENOPS	open sea
AEENOSS	anoeses
AEENOSU	aeneous
AEENPST	penates
	pesante
AEENPSW	Pawnees
AEENPSX	expanse
AEENRRT	terrane
AEENRRV	ravener
AEENRRY	yearner
AEENRST	earnest
	eastern✧
	nearest
AEENRTT	entreat
	ratteen
	ternate
AEENRTV	aventre
	nervate
	Tavener
	veteran
AEENRUV	unreave
AEENRVY	Yerevan
AEENRWY	New Year
AEENSST	sensate
AEENSSW	waeness
AEENTTV	navette
AEENUVW	unweave
AEENVWW	new wave✧
	new-wave✧
AEEOPRT	à portée
	operate
AEEOQUX	ex aequo
AEEORSS	serosae
AEEORST	roseate
	tea rose
AEEORSV	oversea
AEEORTV	overeat
AEEORVW	overawe
AEEPPRR	paperer
	prepare
	repaper
AEEPRRT	taperer
AEEPRSS	asperse
	praeses
	preasse
AEEPRSZ	spreaze
AEEPRTU	epurate
	up a tree
AEEPRTX	ex parte
AEEPRTY	peatery
AEEPRTZ	trapeze
AEEPSSS	asepses
AEEPSSW	pesewas
AEEPSTT	septate
	spattee
AEERRST	serrate
AEERRSU	erasure
AEERRSW	swearer
AEERRTT	retrate
	retreat
	re-treat
	treater
AEERRTW	rewater
	waterer
AEERRUX	Auxerre
AEERRVW	waverer
AEERSST	tessera
AEERSSU	réseaus
	seasure
AEERSSV	assever
AEERSSY	essayer
AEERSTT	estreat
	restate
AEERSTU	au reste
	austere
AEERSTW	sweater
AEERSUV	vareuse
AEERSUX	réseaux
AEERTTX	extreat
AEERTWW	wetware
AEERTWX	wax tree
AEESTTT	testate
AEFFFLR	flaffer
AEFFGIL	fig leaf
AEFFGIR	giraffe
AEFFGNR	engraff
AEFFGRU	gauffer
AEFFHOV	have off
AEFFIPR	piaffer
AEFFKMO	make off
AEFFKOP	offpeak
	off-peak
AEFFKOR	rake-off
AEFFKOT	offtake
	take off
	take-off
AEFFLLY	flyleaf
AEFFLMW	flamfew
AEFFLNS	snaffle
AEFFLOS	seal off
AEFFLRR	raffler
AEFFLRS	Raffles
AEFFLRU	fearful
AEFFLRW	waffler
AEFFLTU	fateful
AEFFORR	for fear
AEFFORT	tear off
AEFFORW	wear off
AEFFOVW	wave off
AEFFQRU	quaffer
AEFFRST	restaff
	staffer
AEFFTTY	taffety
AEFGGGO	foggage
AEFGGMO	megafog
AEFGGRY	faggery
AEFGILN	finagle
	leafing
AEFGILO	foliage
AEFGILR	fragile
AEFGIRS	gas fire
AEFGIRT	frigate
AEFGIRU	refugia
AEFGITU	ague-fit
	fatigue
AEFGLLU	fullage
AEFGLOT	flotage
AEFGLOW	flowage
AEFGLRU	rageful
AEFGLUZ	gazeful
AEFGNOR	far gone
AEFGNRR	granfer
AEFGNRT	engraft
AEFGOOT	footage
AEFGORR	forager
AEFGORV	forgave
AEFGRRT	grafter
AEFHILM	Alfheim
AEFHILP	half-pie
AEFHIRT	the fair
AEFHIRW	wharfie
AEFHISS	sea fish
AEFHLLO	hell of a
AEFHLLS	fellahs
AEFHLLT	The Fall
AEFHLNO	half-one
AEFHLOO	ale-hoof
AEFHLOP	hop-flea
AEFHLOR	fahlore
AEFHLRS	flasher
AEFHLRT	farthel
AEFHLRZ	fahlerz
AEFHLTT	the flat
AEFHLTU	hateful
AEFHRRT	farther
AEFHRST	fathers
	shafter
AEFHRSY	fashery
AEFIILT	filiate
AEFIIMN	infimae
AEFIJLO	jeofail
AEFIKNR	Frankie
AEFILLM	ill fame
AEFILMN	feminal
	inflame
AEFILNT	inflate
AEFILNU	infulae
AEFILNV	flavine
AEFILOT	foliate
AEFILPT	fleapit
AEFILRT	a trifle

AEFILRU	failure
AEFILRV	favrile
AEFILRZ	filazer
AEFILSS	falsies
	filasse
AEFIMNR	fireman
AEFIMRR	firearm
AEFIMRS	misfare
AEFINNT	infante
AEFINNZ	fanzine
AEFINOR	Feronia
AEFINPR	firepan
AEFINRR	refrain
AEFINRS	serafin
AEFINRT	fenitar
	fine art
	fire ant
AEFINRX	xerafin
AEFINSW	fanwise
AEFINTW	wine fat
AEFINTX	antefix
AEFIOSZ	of a size
AEFIQRU	aquifer
AEFIRRR	farrier
	Ferrari®
AEFIRRZ	Frazier
AEFIRST	set fair
AEFKLNR	flanker
AEFKLOS	seafolk
AEFKLRT	fartlek
AEFKLST	flasket
AEFKLUW	wakeful
AEFKMOR	make for
AEFKNOR	oak fern
AEFKORS	forsake
AEFKRSW	saw kerf
AEFLLLO	Floella
AEFLLLT	let fall
AEFLLNN	fannell
	flannel
AEFLLOR	Floréal
AEFLLOT	floatel
AEFLLSY	falsely
AEFLLTT	flatlet
AEFLLTU	taleful
AEFLLUZ	zealful
AEFLMOR	femoral
AEFLMTY	meat-fly
AEFLMUW	wameful
AEFLMUZ	mazeful
AEFLNNN	flannen
AEFLNOV	flavone
AEFLNRS	salfern
AEFLNRU	flâneur
	frenula
	funeral
AEFLNTT	flatten
AEFLOOV	foveola
AEFLOPW	peafowl
AEFLORR	for real
AEFLORS	safrole
AEFLORT	floater
	floreat
	refloat
AEFLORU	four-ale
AEFLORY	forelay
AEFLOSW	seafowl
	sea wolf
	sea-wolf
AEFLPPR	flapper
AEFLPRS	felspar
AEFLPRU	flare up
	flare-up
AEFLPRY	palfrey
AEFLRSU	fur seal
	refusal
AEFLRTT	flatter
AEFLRTU	refutal
	tearful
AEFLRZZ	frazzle
AEFLSTU	sulfate
AEFLTTU	fat-lute
AEFMNOR	foramen
	foreman
AEFMNRU	fraenum
AEFMORR	forearm
AEFMORT	formate
AEFMPRU	frame-up
AEFMRRY	farmery
AEFNNOV	fan oven
AEFNOPR	profane
AEFNOPY	payfone
AEFNORR	foreran
AEFNORT	Torfaen
AEFNOTW	not a few
AEFNRSS	farness
AEFNSST	Fastens
	fatness
AEFNSTT	Fastnet
AEFOPRW	forepaw
AEFORRV	favorer
	overfar
AEFORRY	forayer
AEFORSW	foresaw
AEFORSY	foresay
AEFOSST	fatsoes
AEFOSTU	featous
AEFRRST	rafters
AEFRRTY	fratery
AEFRSTW	Far West
	fretsaw
AEFRTTU	Tartufe
AEFRTUW	wafture
AEFSTTT	fattest
AEFSTTX	Fastext
AEGGGLU	luggage
AEGGHLR	haggler
AEGGHSW	eggwash
AEGGILN	lignage
AEGGINR	gag-rein
	gearing
AEGGINS	signage
AEGGIOR	Georgia
AEGGIOS	isagoge
AEGGIRU	garigue
AEGGISW	swaggie
AEGGJRY	jaggery
AEGGLNO	agelong
	age-long
AEGGLNR	gangrel
AEGGLRW	waggler
AEGGLRY	grey-lag
AEGGMNY	yeggman
AEGGMSS	eggmass
AEGGNNU	gunnage
AEGGNOR	o'ergang
AEGGNRR	granger
AEGGNST	ant-eggs
	G-agents
AEGGORT	great go
AEGGRRY	raggery
AEGGRSS	aggress
AEGGRST	gagster
	stagger
	taggers
AEGGRSW	swagger
AEGGRTY	gargety
AEGGRWY	waggery
AEGHHIT	aheight
	high tea
AEGHHLS	Shelagh
AEGHIJR	jaghire
AEGHILN	healing
AEGHILR	hair gel
	Raleigh
AEGHINP	heaping
AEGHINR	hearing
AEGHINT	gahnite
	heating
AEGHINV	heaving
AEGHINY	Hygeian
AEGHINZ	genizah
AEGHISS	geishas
AEGHLNO	halogen
AEGHLNT	alength
AEGHLRU	laugher
AEGHLTW	thalweg
AEGHMNO	hog-mane
	Mohegan
AEGHMOR	homager
AEGHMSU	meshuga
AEGHNOX	hexagon
AEGHNRS	gnasher✧
AEGHNRU	nuraghe
AEGHNST	stengah
AEGHOPY	hypogea
AEGHORS	gheraos
AEGHOST	hostage
AEGHOTT	the Goat
AEGHOTV	have got
AEGHPRS	spreagh
AEGHRRS	Shergar
AEGHRST	gathers
AEGIIMN	imagine✧
AEGIIMV	give aim
AEGIINR	Igraine
	Nigeria
AEGIKLN	linkage
AEGIKLT	glaiket
AEGIKNP	peaking
AEGIKNS	sea king
	sinkage
AEGIKNT	Keating
AEGIKPP	kippage
AEGIKPR	garpike
AEGILLL	gill ale
	illegal
AEGILLN	Agnelli
	nigella
AEGILLO	Galileo
AEGILLP	pillage
AEGILLS	gallise
AEGILLT	tillage
AEGILLV	village✧
AEGILLY	agilely
AEGILLZ	gallize
AEGILMR	gremial
	lamiger
AEGILMS	gas-lime
AEGILMT	time lag
AEGILNN	eanling
	Gin Lane
	leaning
AEGILNP	leaping
AEGILNR	engrail
	nargile
	realign
	reginal
AEGILNS	leasing
	sealing
AEGILNT	atingle
	gelatin
	genital
	tag line
AEGILNV	leaving
AEGILOS	soilage
AEGILOU	eulogia
AEGILRS	Algiers
AEGILRT	large it
AEGILRZ	glazier
AEGILSS	algesis
AEGILTU	glutaei
AEGILTY	egality
AEGIMNN	meaning
AEGIMNP	pigmean
AEGIMNR	germain
	reaming
AEGIMNT	mintage
	teaming
	tegmina
AEGIMOS	imagoes
AEGIMPR	epigram
	primage
AEGIMPS	Magpies

AEGIMPT	pigmeat
AEGIMRR	armiger
AEGIMRS	gisarme
AEGIMRT	Maigret
	migrate
	ragtime
AEGIMRY	imagery
AEGIMST	sigmate
AEGIMSV	misgave
AEGINNO	ganoine
AEGINNR	aginner
	earning
	engrain
	grannie
AEGINNT	antigen
	gentian
AEGINNU	anguine
	guanine
	Guinean
AEGINNV	Angevin
AEGINOR	Iron Age
	origane
AEGINOS	agonise
AEGINOZ	agonize
AEGINPP	genipap
AEGINPS	spinage
AEGINRR	earring
	grainer
	rangier
AEGINRS	searing
	seringa
AEGINRT	Geraint
	granite
	gratiné
	ingrate
	Integra®
	tangier✧
	tearing
AEGINRV	vinegar
AEGINRW	wearing
AEGINRZ	Zingare
AEGINST	easting
	genista
	ingesta
	seating
	teasing
	tsigane
AEGINSW	sea wing
AEGINTV	vintage
AEGINVW	weaving
AEGIOSV	Segovia
AEGIPPS	gas pipe
AEGIPRS	prisage
	spairge
AEGIPRU	Perugia
AEGIPST	gap site
AEGIRRZ	grazier
AEGIRST	agister
	sea-girt
	strigae
AEGIRTU	Gautier
AEGIRTV	virgate
	vitrage
AEGISTT	stage it
AEGISTY	gaseity
AEGIVWY	give way
AEGJLNR	jangler
AEGJRSU	jug-ears
AEGKKNO	angekok
AEGKLOU	kagoule
AEGKMRY	kerygma
AEGLLLY	legally
AEGLLNO	allonge
	galleon
AEGLLNR	langrel
AEGLLOR	allegro
AEGLLOT	tollage
AEGLLRY	allergy
	gallery
	largely
	regally
AEGLLSU	seagull
	sullage
AEGLLSW	gas well
AEGLLTU	gluteal
AEGLMNR	mangler
AEGLMOR	gomeral
AEGLMOU	moulage
AEGLMPU	plumage
AEGLMRU	maulgre
AEGLNOS	al segno
AEGLNOT	tangelo
AEGLNOU	Angelou
AEGLNPR	grapnel
AEGLNPS	spangle
AEGLNRS	slanger
AEGLNRT	tangler
	trangle
AEGLNRU	granule
AEGLNRW	wangler
	wrangle
AEGLNRY	angerly
AEGLNSS	glassen
AEGLNSU	angelus
	sea lung
AEGLNTT	gantlet
AEGLNTU	languet
AEGLNTW	twangle
AEGLNUU	ungulae
AEGLNUW	gunwale
AEGLOPR	pergola
AEGLORT	gloater
	legator
AEGLORW	low gear
	low-gear
AEGLOST	legatos
AEGLOSU	gealous
AEGLOTV	voltage
AEGLPPR	grapple
AEGLPRU	earplug
	graupel
AEGLPSU	plusage
AEGLPUY	plaguey
AEGLRRU	regular
AEGLRSS	largess
AEGLRSV	verglas
AEGLRTU	gaulter
	tegular
	tragule
AEGLRTY	greatly
AEGLRVY	gravely
AEGLSSS	glasses
AEGLSST	tagless
AEGLSSU	sea slug
AEGLSTT	gestalt✧
AEGLTUV	vulgate✧
AEGLUUY	guayule
AEGLUVY	vaguely
AEGMMRU	rummage
AEGMNNO	agnomen
AEGMNOR	Marengo
	megaron
AEGMNOS	mangoes
AEGMNOT	geomant
	magneto
	megaton
	montage
AEGMNPY	pygmean
AEGMNRS	Germans
AEGMNRT	garment
	margent
	ragment
AEGMNRY	Germany
	Meg Ryan
AEGMNTU	augment
	mutagen
AEGMOOR	moorage
AEGMOSY	gaysome
AEGMOXY	exogamy
AEGMRRY	Margery
AEGMSWY	swy game
AEGNNOT	tonnage
AEGNNRT	regnant
AEGNNRU	gunnera
AEGNNTT	tangent
AEGNNTU	tunnage
AEGNOOR	oregano
AEGNOOT	at one go
AEGNOPT	pontage
AEGNORR	groaner
AEGNORS	nose rag
AEGNORT	negator
AEGNORW	wagoner✧
AEGNORY	orangey
AEGNOST	on stage
	on-stage
AEGNOSV	gas oven
	Vosgean
AEGNOSW	sea gown
AEGNOSY	nosegay
AEGNOTW	tea gown
AEGNOWY	waygone
AEGNPRS	engrasp
AEGNPRT	trepang
AEGNRRT	granter
	regrant
AEGNRST	Sargent
	strange
AEGNSSY	gayness
AEGNSTT	gestant
AEGNSTV	V-agents
AEGNTTU	tutenag
AEGNTYZ	Yangtze
AEGOORT	rootage
AEGOOST	go to sea
AEGOPPR	propage
AEGOPRS	go spare
AEGOPRT	portage
	potager
	top gear
AEGOPST	gestapo✧
	postage
AEGOPTT	pottage
AEGORRT	garrote
AEGORST	storage
AEGORTT	garotte
AEGORTU	outrage
AEGORUV	ouvrage
AEGORVY	voyager
AEGOSSU	gaseous
AEGOSTW	stowage
AEGOTTU	outgate
AEGOTTV	gavotte
AEGPRRS	grasper
	sparger
AEGPRRY	grapery
AEGPSSU	pegasus✧
AEGPSTU	upstage
AEGRRSS	grasser
AEGRRUU	augurer
AEGRRUV	gravure
	verruga
AEGRSSU	arguses✧
AEGRSTT	Targets
AEGRSTY	stagery
AEGRSUV	sevruga
AEGSTUU	auguste✧
AEGTTTU	guttate
AEHHIKS	sheikha
AEHHIST	shehita
AEHHJOV	Jehovah
AEHHJPT	Japheth
	Jephtha
AEHHLOS	ash-hole
AEHHLTY	healthy
AEHHNRS	harshen
AEHHNSV	Heshvan
AEHHSST	sheaths
AEHHSTY	sheathy
AEHIITV	I have it
AEHIKSW	weakish
AEHIKSY	sakiyeh
AEHILMO	hemiola
AEHILMS	Ishmael

AEHILNR hernial
inhaler
AEHILNS his lane
AEHILNT Hielant
AEHILNY hyaline
AEHILOP Ophelia
AEHILOR airhole
AEHILPR hare-lip
AEHILRU haulier
AEHILSW shawlie
whaisle
AEHILTT lithate
tile hat
AEHILTY hyalite
AEHILUV vihuela
AEHILVY heavily
AEHILWZ whaizle
AEHIMNR harmine
AEHIMNY hymenia
AEHIMPR Ephraim
AEHIMPS phaeism
AEHIMRS mishear
AEHIMRT Tarim He
AEHIMSS messiah✧
AEHIMST atheism
AEHINOV Ivanhoe
AEHINPR heparin
AEHINPS in phase
inphase
in shape
phase in
AEHINPT penthia
AEHINRS arshine
AEHINRT hairnet
inearth
therian
AEHINSS hessian✧
AEHINSV evanish
AEHINTW the Wain
AEHIPPT epitaph✧
AEHIPRS Harpies
Shar-Pei
sharpie
AEHIPSS aphesis
AEHIPSW peishwa
AEHIPTZ zaptieh
AEHIQSU quashie✧
AEHIRRR harrier
AEHIRRT Harriet
AEHIRST sheriat✧
AEHIRSV ashiver
AEHIRSW wearish
AEHIRWY haywire
AEHISST stashie
AEHISTT atheist
staithe
AEHISVY yeshiva
AEHITTW thwaite
AEHJLOW jawhole
AEHJRTT Jethart
AEHKLMT Mt Hekla
AEHKLNT the Klan
AEHKNRT thanker
AEHKOSS shakoes
AEHKOST The Oaks
AEHKPSU shake up
shake-up
AEHKRRS sharker
AEHKRSS Shakers
AEHLLNW New Hall
AEHLLOV hellova
AEHLLOY holy-ale
AEHLLRS hersall
AEHLLTW the wall✧
AEHLLUV helluva
AEHLLYZ hazelly
AEHLMNO manhole
AEHLMNY hymenal
AEHLMOR armhole
AEHLMPW whample
AEHLMRT thermal
AEHLMRU humeral
AEHLMUX Max Uhle
AEHLNOT ethanol
AEHLNRT enthral
AEHLNSU Hulsean
unleash
unshale
AEHLORT loather
rathole
AEHLOTV The Oval
AEHLPRS spheral
AEHLPSS hapless
AEHLPST plashet
AEHLPSU Alpheus
AEHLPSY shapely
AEHLPUV pH value
AEHLRSS slasher
AEHLRST harslet
slather
AEHLRSV halvers
AEHLRTY earthly
hartely
heartly
lathery
AEHLRWY whalery
AEHLSST hatless
AEHLSTT stealth
AEHLSWY shawley
AEHLTWY wealthy
AEHMMOT Mahomet
AEHMMRS Hammers
shammer
AEHMMSS shammes
AEHMNOR menorah✧
AEHMNOS hoseman
AEHMNOT nathemo
AEHMNOY haemony
AEHMNPY nymphae
AEHMNRS Sherman
AEHMNST hetmans
AEHMNTX the Manx
AEHMNTY the many
AEHMOPT apothem
AEHMOPY pay home
AEHMOTT moth-eat
AEHMPTY empathy
AEHMRSS smasher
AEHMRST hamster
AEHMRTT Mt Thera
AEHMRTU mauther
AEHMRTW mawther
AEHMRWX Wrexham
AEHMTTW Matthew
AEHMUZZ mezuzah
AEHNNPY ha'penny
AEHNNSS Hansen's
AEHNNTU unneath
AEHNNWY anywhen
AEHNOPR Orphean
AEHNOPT phaeton
phonate
AEHNOPW wanhope
AEHNORS hoarsen
senhora✧
AEHNORT A N Other
another
on earth
AEHNORV Hanover
AEHNOTV have-not
AEHNPRS sharpen
AEHNPRT panther
AEHNPSU unshape
AEHNRSS harness
AEHNRTU haunter
unearth
unheart
urethan
AEHNRTX narthex✧
AEHNSTY shantey
AEHNSWY say when
AEHNTTW whatten
AEHOORT toheroa
AEHOPST tap shoe
tea shop
AEHORST asthore
earshot
haroset
AEHORTU hear out
Thoreau
AEHORUV haveour
AEHOSTT hot seat
AEHOSTU atheous
AEHOTUV have out
AEHPPRS perhaps
AEHPPSU shape up
shape-up
AEHPRRS phraser
sharper
AEHPRSS seraphs
sherpas✧
AEHPRST sparthe
AEHPRSW pre-wash
AEHPRTU earth up
AEHPRTY therapy
AEHPRUU Ruapehu
AEHPSSY hey pass
AEHPSTY Pytheas
AEHRRTU urethra
AEHRSST shaster
AEHRSSW swasher
washers
AEHRSTT rathest
shatter
The Star
AEHRSTV harvest
AEHRSTW wreaths
AEHRSVW wharves
AEHRSWY washery
AEHRSXY hyraxes
AEHRTUU hauteur
AEHRTWY wreathy
AEHSTUX exhaust
AEHSTYY they say
AEIIKNT kainite
AEIILLT taillie
AEIILMP lipemia
AEIILMR air mile
Ramilie
AEIILNN aniline
AEIILNR airline
AEIILNX exilian
AEIILRS Israeli
lairise
AEIILRZ lairize
AEIILSS silesia
AEIILSW lewisia
AEIILTT Letitia
AEIILTZ tailzie
AEIIMNT intimae
miniate
AEIIMOT à moitié
AEIIMPR imperia
AEIIMRT airtime
Emirati
AEIIMRV viremia
AEIIMTT imitate
AEIINNS asinine
insanie
AEIINPR Pierian
AEIINQU equinia
AEIINRR rainier✧
AEIINRS senarii
AEIINRT inertia
AEIINST isatine
AEIINSX sixaine
AEIINTX axinite
AEIIPRR prairie
AEIIRRV riviera
AEIIRST irisate
AEIISTV Saivite
Sivaite
AEIITTV vitiate
AEIJLNV javelin

AEIJMNS jasmine
AEIJNRS Jersian
AEIJNRT nartjie
AEIJNTU jauntie
AEIJSSV jive-ass
AEIKLMN Malinke
man-like
AEIKLNO kaoline
AEIKLNU unalike
AEIKLOT keitloa
AEIKLOV live oak
AEIKLRS serkali
AEIKLRV klavier
AEIKLRW warlike
AEIKLST talkies
AEIKLSW sawlike
AEIKLUZ Zuleika
AEIKMMS mismake
AEIKMNP pikeman
AEIKMNR mankier
ramekin
AEIKMPR rampike
AEIKMRW mawkier
AEIKMST mistake
AEIKNNR Karenni
Rankine
AEIKNPS sea pink
AEIKNRT Katrine
Kenitra
keratin
AEIKNRU Ukraine
AEIKNSW swankie
AEIKNSY kyanise
AEIKNTY kyanite
AEIKNYZ kyanize
AEIKPRS sparkie
AEIKRSY Kayseri
AEIKSSS askesis
AEILLLM Melilla
AEILLMN manille
mean ill
AEILLMT all-time
Tellima
AEILLNR ralline
AEILLOS oil seal
AEILLOV alveoli
AEILLPS illapse
AEILLRR rallier
AEILLRT literal
tallier
AEILLRU ruellia
AEILLST sitella
tailles
tallies
AEILLSW wallies
AEILLSY sea lily
AEILLUV eluvial
AEILLVX vexilla
AEILLVY Viyella®
AEILMMS melisma
AEILMNN Lemnian
lineman
melanin
AEILMNO mineola
AEILMNP impanel
maniple
AEILMNR manlier
marline
mineral
AEILMNS isleman
Malines
seminal
AEILMNT ailment
aliment
AEILMPR impaler
impearl
lempira
AEILMPT implate
palmiet
AEILMRR larmier
AEILMRS realism✧
AEILMRT lamiter
AEILMRU Lemuria
AEILMSS aimless
Melissa
seismal
AEILMTY laytime
meatily
AEILNNN Linnean
AEILNNO Leonian
AEILNNS nainsel'
AEILNNY inanely
AEILNOP opaline
AEILNOR aileron
alerion
alienor
AEILNOS sea lion
AEILNOT elation
toenail
AEILNOZ Zoilean
AEILNPR pearlin
praline
AEILNPS Nepalis
spaniel
AEILNPT pantile
AEILNPU Pauline
AEILNPX explain
AEILNQU equinal
AEILNRT entrail
Latiner
latrine
ratline
reliant
retinal
trenail
AEILNRV ravelin
AEILNRX relaxin
AEILNRY inlayer
nailery
AEILNST eastlin
elastin
nail set
salient
saltine
slàinte
staniel
AEILNSU insulae
inulase
AEILNSY Elysian
AEILNTU alunite
AEILNTV ventail
AEILNUV unalive
unvaile
AEILNUW lauwine
AEILNVY naively
naïvely
AEILOPR peloria
rape oil
AEILORS Rosalie
AEILORV variole
AEILOST isolate
AEILOTV violate
AEILPPR apperil
applier
aripple
AEILPRT plaiter
AEILPRV prevail
AEILPST Pilates
talipes
AEILPSY paisley✧
AEILQSU Salique
AEILQTU liquate
tequila
AEILRRT retiral
retrial
trailer
AEILRSS airless
AEILRST Alister
realist
saltier
saltire
AEILRSV revisal
AEILRTT tertial
AEILRTU uralite
AEILRTY irately
reality
AEILRVV revival
AEILRVY virelay
AEILRWY wearily
AEILSST set sail
AEILSSV vessail
AEILSTU situlae
AEILSTV estival
AEILSUX Alexius
AEILTVV Tel Aviv
AEILTVY vilayet
AEILUVX exuvial
AEIMMNS misname
AEIMMOS mimosae
AEIMMPP pip emma
AEIMMRT Marmite®
marmite
AEIMMST mismate
AEIMMTY Maytime
AEIMMZZ mizmaze
AEIMNNT mannite
AEIMNOR moraine
romaine
AEIMNOT amniote
on a time
AEIMNOU moineau
AEIMNOX ex animo
AEIMNPR Permian
AEIMNRR mariner
rein-arm
AEIMNRS remains
seminar
sirname
AEIMNRT Martine
meranti
minaret
raiment
AEIMNRV Minerva
vermian
AEIMNRW wireman
AEIMNSS Messina
samisen
AEIMNST mista'en
Samnite
AEIMNSW wise man
AEIMNSZ man-size
AEIMNTV Vietnam
AEIMNTY amenity
anytime
AEIMNUV mauvein
mauvine
AEIMNZZ mezzani
AEIMOOP ipomoea
AEIMOPR emporia
AEIMORR armoire
AEIMOST amosite
atomise
osmiate
Samiote
AEIMOTX toxemia
AEIMOTZ atomize
AEIMPRR rampire
AEIMPRS impresa
sampire
AEIMPRT primate
AEIMPRV vampire
AEIMPSS impasse
pessima
AEIMPST impaste
pastime
AEIMPSW mapwise
AEIMRRR marrier
AEIMRRS simarre
AEIMRST Artemis
maestri
maister
misrate
semitar
smartie

AEIMRTU muriate
AEIMRTW wartime
AEIMSSS messias✧
AEIMSST asteism
Matisse
AEIMSSV massive
AEIMSTT at times
matiest
AEIMSTW time was
AEIMSTZ mestiza
AEIMSUV amusive
AEIMTYZ azymite✧
AEIMUUX au mieux
AEINNNS nannies
AEINNOT enation
Etonian
Noetian
AEINNOW Owenian
AEINNOZ neo-Nazi
AEINNPR pannier
AEINNPT pantine
pinnate
AEINNRS insnare
AEINNRT en train
entrain
trannie
AEINNRU aneurin✧
AEINNTT antient
AEINOPR open-air
pea-iron
AEINOPT à pointe
AEINOPZ epizoan
AEINORS erasion
AEINORT otarine
AEINOSS anoesis
AEINOST Estonia
AEINOSV evasion
AEINOTT eat into
AEINOXZ oxazine
AEINPPS nappies
AEINPRS Persian
AEINPRT painter
pertain
pine tar
repaint
AEINPST in spate
panties
sapient
spinate
AEINPSW Winesap
wine-sap
AEINPTT patient
AEINPTU petunia✧
AEINPTY paneity
AEINQTU antique
quinate
AEINRRS sierran
AEINRRT retrain
terrain
trainer
AEINRSS arsines
Nerissa
AEINRST in tears
resiant
retinas
retsina
stainer
starnie
stearin
AEINRSV Servian
AEINRSW swear in
AEINRTT intreat
iterant
nitrate
tartine
tertian
AEINRTU ruinate
taurine
uranite
urinate
AEINRTV Avertin®
AEINRTW tinware
AEINRUV vaurien
AEINRUW unwarie
AEINRUZ azurine
AEINRVV vervain
AEINSST entasis
sestina
Staines
AEINSSV vinasse
AEINSTT instate
satinet
AEINSTU sinuate
AEINSTV stave in
AEINSTW in a stew
in waste
AEINSWY anywise
AEINTVW wine vat
AEINTVY naivety
naïvety
AEINTXY anxiety
AEINUXZ Zeuxian
AEIOQSU sequoia
AEIORRR arriero
AEIORST otaries
AEIOSST sosatie
AEIOSTT ostiate
toastie
AEIOSTZ azotise
AEIOTZZ azotize
AEIPPRS apprise
AEIPPRT periapt
Rappite
AEIPPRZ apprize
AEIPRRS praiser
AEIPRSS paresis
Serapis
AEIPRST piastre
traipse
AEIPRSU Piraeus
spuriae
upraise
AEIPRSV parvise
AEIPRTT partite
tear pit
AEIPRTV private
AEIPRTW wiretap
AEIPRXY pyrexia
AEIPSSS asepsis
AEIPSST pasties
AEIPSSV passive
AEIPSTU lapetus
AEIPTXY epitaxy
AEIQRUV aquiver
AEIRRRT tarrier
AEIRRST tarsier
AEIRRTT rattier
retrait
tartier
AEIRRTU Etruria
AEIRRTY retiary
AEIRRVV viverra✧
AEIRSST tirasse
AEIRSSZ assizer
AEIRSTT artiste
striate
tastier
AEIRSTW waister
AEIRTTT attrite
tattier
titrate
AEIRTTV taivert
AEIRTTX extrait
AEIRTUY aureity
AEIRTUZ azurite
AEIRTVY variety
AEIRWWY wireway
AEISSSZ assizes
AEISSTU at issue
AEISSUV suasive
AEISSUX auxesis
AEISTTU situate
AEISTTV stative
AEISTTY satiety
AEITTTU attuite
AEITTTV vittate
AEJJLNU jejunal
AEJKNRS jankers
AEJLNUV juvenal✧
AEJLOSU jalouse
jealous
AEJLOUZ azulejo
AEJLSSW jawless
AEJMSSY jessamy
AEJMSTY majesty
AEJNNOS joannes
AEJNOPW open-jaw
AEJNORZ zanjero
AEJNOSS San José
AEJNSST jessant
AEJOOPS Joe Soap
AEJPRSY jaspery
AEKLLRT Kartell
AEKLLTU kellaut
AEKLNPP knapple
AEKLNPR prankle
AEKLNST asklent
AEKLORY rokelay
AEKLOST skatole
AEKLOTU leak out
AEKLPPT pep talk
AEKLPRS sparkle
AEKLRST stalker
AEKLRUW waulker
AEKMNOS sokeman
AEKMNPT kept man
AEKMNTY Mt Kenya
AEKMOOT matooke
AEKMOTU make out
AEKMPRU upmaker
AEKNNTU untaken
AEKNOOR Roanoke
AEKNOPS Spokane
AEKNPPR knapper
AEKNPRS spanker
AEKNPSU sneak-up
unspeak
AEKNRST starken
AEKNRSW swanker
AEKNRVY knavery
AEKNSWY swankey
AEKOPTU peak out
AEKOPTZ Zatopek
AEKORRS rosaker
AEKORSV ask over
AEKOSTV voetsak
AEKOTTU outtake
out-take
take out
takeout
AEKPPSU speak up
upspake
upspeak
AEKPSSY passkey
AEKQRSU Quakers
AEKQSUY squeaky
AEKRSTY streaky
AEKSVWY sky wave
AELLMNS Mansell
AELLMNT tall men
AELLMNU lumenal
AELLMRV Marvell
AELLMSU malleus
AELLMSY mesally
AELLMTY metally
AELLMWX maxwell✧
AELLNOP pallone
AELLNOR llanero
AELLNOS all's one
AELLNOV novella
AELLNOY alonely
AELLNPR Parnell
AELLNPY penally
AELLNRT entrall

AELLNSS	allness
AELLNTT	tallent
AELLNVY	venally
AELLOPW	Walpole
AELLOPX	pollaxe
	poll-axe
AELLORS	rosella
AELLORT	reallot
AELLORV	all over
	all-over
	overall
	over-all
AELLPRU	pleural
AELLPTU	pluteal
AELLPTY	playlet
AELLQUY	equally
AELLRRU	allurer
AELLRST	stellar
AELLRSU	laurels
AELLRTY	alertly
	elytral
AELLRUW	wall rue
AELLSST	tassell
AELLSSW	lawless
AELLSTW	setwall
	swallet
AELLSTY	stalely
AELLSVY	valleys
AELLTUU	ululate
AELLUVV	valvule
AELMMNO	mamelon
AELMMOY	myeloma
AELMMRS	slammer
AELMMRT	trammel
AELMMST	stammel
AELMMSY	malmsey
AELMNNS	lensman
AELMNOR	almoner
	nemoral
AELMNOS	melanos
AELMNOT	lomenta
	omental
	telamon
AELMNPR	lampern
AELMNRU	numeral
AELMNRV	Malvern
AELMNSS	manless
AELMNSU	mensual
AELMNTT	mantlet
AELMNTU	nu-metal
	nutmeal
AELMOPR	Palermo
	pleroma
AELMOPU	ampoule
AELMOPY	maypole
AELMORT	mole rat
AELMORU	morulae
AELMORV	removal
AELMORW	Marlowe
AELMOSS	Molasse
AELMOST	maltose
AELMOSY	amylose
AELMOTT	matelot
AELMPRS	lampers
	sampler
AELMPRT	templar✧
	trample
AELMPRY	lamprey
AELMPSS	mapless
AELMPTU	plumate
AELMRRS	marrels
AELMRSS	armless
AELMRSU	maulers
AELMRTT	martlet
AELMSSU	Musales
AELMSTU	Mustela
AELNNPR	planner
AELNNPU	unpanel
AELNNRS	ensnarl
AELNNRT	lantern
AELNNRU	unlearn
AELNNST	stannel
AELNNTU	annulet
AELNOOR	Leonora
AELNOOS	alsoone
AELNOPT	polenta
AELNOPU	apolune
AELNOPY	lay open
AELNORS	orleans
	Salerno
AELNORU	aleuron
AELNORV	Veronal®
	veronal
AELNORY	early on
AELNOST	lean-tos
AELNOSY	Sloaney
AELNOTU	Tuonela
AELNOTV	volante
AELNPPY	playpen
AELNPRT	pantler
	planter
	replant
AELNPRY	plenary
AELNPSS	napless
AELNPTX	explant
AELNPTY	aplenty
	net-play
	penalty
AELNQUU	unequal
AELNRRS	snarler
AELNRST	saltern
	sternal
AELNRSU	Al Unser
AELNRTT	trental
AELNRTU	neutral
	Renault®
AELNRTV	ventral
AELNRUV	unravel
AELNSSU	sensual
AELNSSW	awnless
AELNSSX	laxness
AELNSTU	unlaste
AELNSTY	Stanley
	stanyel
AELNTUV	envault
AELOORS	aerosol
	roseola
AELOPPR	propale
AELOPPX	apoplex
AELOPRR	preoral
AELOPRS	reposal
AELOPRT	prolate
AELOPRV	overlap
AELOPST	apostle✧
AELOPSX	exposal
AELOPTT	paletot
AELOPTU	outleap
AELORRT	Realtor®
	realtor
	relator
AELORSS	lassoer
	oarless
	serosal
AELORST	oestral
AELORTT	Loretta
AELORTU	rotulae
	torulae
AELORTV	levator
	love rat
AELORTY	royalet
AELORTZ	zelator
AELORUU	rouleau
AELORVY	layover
	overlay
AELORWY	owrelay
	royal we✧
AELOSSS	lassoes
AELOSSV	salvoes
AELOSTV	solvate
AELOSUZ	zealous
AELOSVY	saveloy
AELOSWY	lose way
AELOTTU	toluate
AELOTUV	ovulate
AELOTVV	volvate
AELPPRS	slapper
AELPPRT	P-plater
AELPPRY	reapply
AELPPSS	sapples
AELPPST	stapple
AELPPSU	appulse
	papules
AELPRST	plaster
	psalter✧
	stapler
AELPRSU	perusal
AELPRSY	parsley
	sparely
AELPRTT	partlet✧
	platter
	prattle
AELPRTY	peartly
	prelaty
	pteryla
AELPRUY	epulary
AELPSSS	sapless
AELPSST	pastels
AELPSSU	pas seul
AELPSTT	peltast
AELPSTU	pulsate
	spatule
AELPUUV	upvalue
AELQRRU	quarrel
AELQTUZ	quetzal
AELRRSU	surreal
AELRRTT	rattler
AELRRTW	trawler
AELRSST	artless
AELRSSY	rayless
AELRSTT	slatter
	starlet
	startle
	Telstar
AELRSTU	saluter
AELRSTV	travels
	vestral
AELRSTW	wastrel
AELRSVY	slavery
AELRTTT	tartlet
	tattler
AELRTTU	tutelar
AELRTUV	vaulter
AELRTWZ	waltzer
AELRVWY	levy war
AELSSTU	taluses
AELSSTX	taxless
AELSSUU	Sulu Sea
AELSSWY	wayless
AELSTTW	wattles
AELSTTY	stately
	stylate
AELSUVY	suavely
AELSWZZ	swazzle
AELTTTW	twattle
AELTTUX	textual
AELTUVV	vulvate
AEMMNOT	momenta
AEMMNTU	amentum
AEMMORS	marmose
AEMMPRS	spammer
AEMMRST	stammer
AEMMRSZ	mamzers
AEMMSTU	summate
AEMNNOS	mannose
	name-son
AEMNNOT	montane
AEMNNOU	noumena
AEMNNRS	manners
AEMNNRT	manrent
	remnant
AEMNNSU	mean sun
AEMNNSW	newsman
AEMNNTU	unmeant
AEMNOPR	manrope

Words marked ✧ can also be spelled with one or more capital letters

repoman
AEMNOPZ zampone
AEMNORS Romanes
San Remo
AEMNORT tone arm
AEMNORU enamour
neuroma
AEMNORV overman
AEMNORW men-o'-war
AEMNORY any more
romneya
AEMNOST mantoes
AEMNOSW nae mows
AEMNOTT tomenta
AEMNOTU notaeum
outname
AEMNPST enstamp
AEMNPTU putamen
AEMNPTY payment
AEMNRRU manurer
AEMNRST sarment
smarten
AEMNRSU surname
AEMNRTU trueman
AEMNRTV varment
AEMNSST stamens
AEMNSTY amnesty
AEMNTTX text-man
AEMNTWY wayment
AEMOORS sea room
AEMOORT tea room
AEMOORW woomera
AEMOOST osteoma
Sao Tomé
São Tomé
AEMOOSV vamoose
AEMOOSZ Mesozoa
AEMOPPR pampero
AEMORRV overarm
AEMORST maestro
AEMORSU rameous
AEMORSW seaworm
AEMORSX xeromas
AEMORTU Euratom
AEMOSSS sea moss
AEMOSTW twasome
AEMOSUZ zamouse
AEMOSWY someway
AEMOTTZ mozetta
AEMPPRY mappery
AEMPRRT tramper
AEMPRRW prewarm
AEMPRST stamper
AEMPRSW swamper
AEMPRTT trampet
AEMPRTU tempura
AEMPSTU steam up
AEMPTTT attempt
AEMPTTU tapetum
AEMQRSU masquer
AEMRRRY remarry
AEMRRST armrest
AEMRRSW swarmer
AEMRRTU erratum
AEMRRUU Réaumur
AEMRSSU Erasmus
masseur
AEMRSTT smatter
AEMRSTU strumae
AEMRSTY mastery
mayster
streamy
AEMRTTX martext
AEMRTTY mattery
AEMRTUU trumeau
AEMRUZZ maruzze
AEMSTVZ zemstva
AENNNPT pennant
AENNOPS pannose
AENNOPT Pantone®
AENNORT norteña
AENNORX Roxanne
AENNORY annoyer
AENNOTU tonneau
AENNPRS spanner
AENNPSW span new
AENNQTU quannet
AENNRTT entrant
AENNRTV vernant
AENNRTY tannery
tyranne
AENNSSW wanness
AENOOTZ entozoa
tan ooze
AENOPPR on paper
propane
AENOPRS persona
AENOPRT operant
pronate
protean✧
AENOPSU posaune
AENOPSW snow pea
AENORRV overran
AENORST nor'-east
senator
treason
AENORSW sea-worn
AENORTU earn out
AENORTV venator
AENORTW war note
AENORXY anorexy
AENOSTT attones
AENOSTU soutane
AENOSTW no sweat
AENOSVW waveson
AENOUUV nouveau
AENPPRS parsnep
snapper
AENPPRT parpent
AENPPRU unpaper
AENPRRT partner
AENPRRW prewarn
AENPRST pastern
persant
AENPRSW spawner
AENPRTT pattern
reptant
AENPRTW Antwerp
AENPRUV parvenu
AENPSST aptness
patness
AENPSSY synapse
AENPSTU peanuts
pesaunt
AENPSTW stewpan
AENPSTY synapte
AENQUWY Newquay
AENRRTT tranter
AENRRTY ternary
AENRSST sarsnet
AENRSSW rawness
AENRSTU Anterus
saunter
sea turn
AENRSTV servant
versant
AENRSTW new star
strawen
AENRSUV Avernus
AENRSUW unswear
unwares
AENRTTU taunter
AENRTTY nattery
AENRTUV vaunter
AENRTUW unwater
AENRUWY unweary
AENSSTX sextans✧
AENSTTU tetanus
unstate
AENSTTX sextant✧
AENTTTU attuent
AEOOPPS papoose
AEOOPRS oropesa
AEOPPPS pappose
AEOPPRS apposer
AEOPPRV approve
AEOPPSU pea soup
AEOPRRT praetor
prorate
AEOPRST esparto
seaport
to spare
AEOPRTT portate
AEOPRVY overpay
AEOPRWY ropeway
AEOQRTU equator
quorate
AEOQRUV vaquero
AEOQSUU aqueous
AEORRSS Rasores
AEORRST roaster
AEORRSU arouser
AEORSSS Ross Sea
serosas
AEORSTT Rosetta
toaster
AEORSTX Seroxat®
AEORSTZ Zostera
AEORTTU outrate
AEORTUW outwear
wear out
AEORTVX overtax
AEOSSYY easy-osy
AEOSUVY save you
AEPPRRT trapper
AEPPRRW wrapper
AEPPRSS appress
AEPPRSU upspear
AEPPRSW swapper
AEPPSTT Pap test
AEPPSTU paste-up
AEPQRTU parquet
AEPRRRS sparrer
AEPRRSY prayers
respray
sprayer
AEPRRTU parture
rapture
AEPRRTY petrary
AEPRSST at press
AEPRSSY pessary
AEPRSTT spatter
tapster
AEPRSTU Pasteur
pasture
upstare
AEPRSTY yapster
AEPRSWY spyware
AEPRSYY sprayey
AEPRTXY apteryx
AEPSSTU petasus
AEPSTTU upstate
AEQRRSU squarer
AEQRRTU quarter
AEQRSTU T-square
AEQRTTU quartet
AEQRUVY quavery
AERRSST starers
AERRSSU assurer
AERRSTT restart✧
starter
AERRSTY strayer
AERRTTY rattery
AERSSTT starets
AERSTTT stretta
tatters
AERSTTU stature
AERSTTW Stewart
swatter
AERSTTZ staretz
AERSTUY estuary
AERSTWY wastery
AERTTTY tattery
AERTTUV vettura

AESSTUY eustasy
AESTTTU statute
AFFFFNO naff off
AFFFLLO fall off
fall-off
AFFGGIN gaffing
AFFGHIS fish-fag
AFFGHNO hang off
AFFGINN naffing
AFFGINY affying
AFFGLOS slag off
AFFHILN hafflin
AFFHIRS raffish
AFFHLLY fly half
AFFHLOU haul off
AFFHOST hats off
AFFILMN film fan
mafflin
AFFILOT tail off
AFFILOX Filofax®
AFFILSY falsify
AFFIMST mastiff
AFFINRU funfair
ruffian
AFFINTY tiffany✧
AFFIOPR pair off
AFFIORR forfair
AFFIOTW wait off
AFFIRRU furfair
AFFKLOW walk off
AFFKMOR mark off
AFFLLOR fall for
AFFLLPY fly-flap
AFFLMOP palm off
AFFLNOP off-plan
AFFLOPY play off
play-off
AFFMOPR off-ramp
AFFNORS saffron
AFFNORT affront
AFFNORW warn off
AFFNOSW sawn-off
swan off
AFFOPRT part-off
AFFOPSS pass off
AFGGGIN fagging
AFGGIOT goat-fig
AFGHHIS hagfish
AFGHIRS garfish
AFGHLSU gashful
AFGHLTU flaught
AFGHOST Gasthof
AFGHRTU fraught
AFGIILN failing
AFGIINR fairing
AFGILLN falling
AFGILMN flaming
AFGILNO loafing
AFGILNR flaring
AFGILNT fatling
AFGILNU gainful
AFGILNY anglify
flaying
AFGILRU figural
AFGILST gas lift
AFGIMNO foaming
AFGIMNR farming
framing
AFGIMNY magnify
AFGINNW fawning
AFGINOT go Fanti
AFGINRT ingraft
rafting
AFGINRY fraying
AFGINST fasting
AFGINTT fatting
AFGINTW wafting
AFGIOTT fagotti
AFGIPSW fig wasp
AFGIRTY gratify
AFGKNOP pakfong
AFGKORT koftgar
AFGLLLY gallfly
AFGLLUY fall guy
fugally
AFGLMOP fog lamp
AFGLRUW Gulf War
AFGLRYY grayfly
AFGMNOR frogman
AFGOOTT fagotto
AFGOSTU fugatos
AFHIIRS fairish
AFHIISW waifish
AFHIKUY kufiyah
AFHILLN halflin
AFHILSS falsish
AFHILTU laithfu'
AFHILTW halfwit
AFHIMNU hafnium
AFHINOS fashion
AFHINTU unfaith
AFHIORS oar fish
AFHIRST ratfish
AFHISST fastish
AFHISSW sawfish
AFHISTT fattish
AFHISWY fish-way
AFHKORY hayfork
AFHKRTU futhark
AFHLMRU harmful
AFHLNOT not half
AFHLOTU out-half
AFHLOTY hayloft
AFHLSTU hatfuls
AFHMOST fathoms
AFHORSS shofars
AFHORTT for that
AFHRSTU thus far
AFIILNT tail fin
AFIILOR airfoil
AFIILRT airlift
AFIILRY fairily
AFIIMOS mafiosi✧
AFIINRS Frisian
AFIKKLR Falkirk
AFIKLOT flokati
AFIKNRT ratfink
AFILLMS misfall
AFILLNY finally
AFILLPT pitfall
AFILLPU pailful
AFILLRY fly rail
frailly
AFILLTY tail fly
AFILLUV fluvial
vialful
AFILLUW wailful
AFILMNT lift-man
AFILMOR aliform
AFILMOY foamily
AFILMPY amplify
AFILMRW war film
AFILMSS falsism
AFILNNT flan tin
AFILNOT loaf tin
AFILNOW Wolfian
AFILNPU painful
AFILNTU flutina
in fault
AFILNTY faintly
AFILORW airflow
AFILOTX fox-tail
AFILQUY qualify
AFILRRY friarly
AFILRTY frailty
AFILSSY salsify
AFILSTU fistula
AFILSTW fist-law
AFILSTY falsity
AFILSVY Slavify
AFIMOOS mafioso✧
AFIMORV aviform
AFIMSTT fattism
AFIMSUV Fauvism
AFIMTTU Muftiat
AFINNOR franion
AFINNOT Fontina
AFINORS insofar
AFINORV for vain
AFINRTU ut infra
AFINSTU faunist
fustian
infaust
AFIORTU faitour
AFIRSTT at first
AFISSTT sitfast
AFISSTY satisfy
AFISTTT fattist
AFISTUV Fauvist
AFITTUY fatuity
AFJLRSU jarfuls
AFJOOTW foot-jaw
jaw-foot
AFKKOUU Fukuoka
AFKLNRY frankly
AFKLNTU tankful
AFKLORT folk art
AFKLOWY folkway
AFKMORX fox-mark
AFKNPRU fun park
AFKRRTU Fraktur
AFLLMPU palmful
AFLLMPY lamp-fly
AFLLOOY aloofly
AFLLOTU fall out
fallout
fall-out
outfall
AFLLPUY playful
AFLLUWY awfully
AFLMNOU moanful
AFLMORU formula
AFLMORW wolfram
AFLMOST flotsam
AFLMRSU armfuls
AFLMSTU mastful
AFLMSUU famulus
AFLNOOS Alfonso
AFLNORT frontal
AFLNOTT flotant
AFLNOTU no-fault
AFLNPSU panfuls
AFLNRTU runflat
AFLNTUY flaunty
AFLOOTW woolfat
AFLORSU fusarol
AFLORUV flavour
AFLORWW warwolf
AFLOSSU fossula
AFLOTTU flat out
AFLPRTY flytrap
AFLPSTY flypast
AFLRSTU Flustra
AFLRTUY trayful
AFLSTUV vatfuls
AFLSTWY fly swat
AFMNOOT footman
AFMNORT formant
AFMNRSU surfman
AFMNRTU turfman
AFMNWYY Myfanwy
AFMORRT art form
AFMORST farmost
AFMORTU farm out
foumart
AFMOSTT aftmost
AFMOSTU sfumato
AFNOOSW as of now
AFNORRT Fortran
AFNORRW forwarn
AFNORTU Fortuna
AFNSSTU sunfast
AFOOPPR approof
AFOORRU four-oar

AFOORST	of a sort
AFOORTZ	forzato
AFOOTWY	footway
AFOPRTX	fox-trap
AFORSTT	soft art
AFORSUV	favours
AFORTTU	tartufo
AFOSSWY	foss way✧
AFOSTUU	fatuous
AFRRTUW	turf war
AGGGGIN	gagging
AGGGIJN	jagging
AGGGILN	lagging
AGGGINN	ganging
	nagging
AGGGINR	ragging
AGGGINS	sagging
AGGGINT	tagging
AGGGINU	gauging
AGGGINW	wagging
AGGGINZ	zagging
AGGHHIS	haggish
AGGHIIL	ghilgai
AGGHIMN	gingham
AGGHINN	hanging
AGGHISW	waggish
AGGHNOV	Van Gogh
AGGIIJJ	jigajig
AGGIILM	mail-gig
AGGIIMN	imaging
AGGIJJO	jigajog
AGGILLN	galling
	gingall
AGGILNN	angling
AGGILNR	glaring
AGGILNT	Lagting
AGGILNZ	glazing
AGGILOS	loggias
AGGINNP	panging
AGGINNW	gnawing
AGGINNX	Xingang
AGGINOY	Ogygian
AGGINPS	gasping
AGGINRS	gas ring
	sirgang
AGGINRT	grating
AGGINRV	graving
AGGINRZ	grazing
AGGINSS	gassing
AGGINST	staging
AGGINTT	Gatting
AGGINUU	Gauguin
AGGINUY	Guiyang
AGGIORS	Gorgias
AGGJNUW	Gwangju
AGGLNOO	long-ago
AGGLOST	loggats
AGGLOSW	Glasgow
AGGMORR	grogram
AGGMOTY	maggoty
AGGMRUU	guar gum
AGGNOSU	guangos
AGHHHIT	high-hat
AGHHIMN	highman
AGHHINS	hashing
AGHHIWY	highway
AGHHMNU	Hamhung
AGHHORT	Hogarth
AGHHOSW	hogwash
AGHHTUY	haughty
AGHIINN	haining
AGHIKNS	shaking
AGHIKNW	hawking✧
AGHILLN	halling
AGHILNR	harling
AGHILNS	lashing
AGHILNT	Althing
	halting
	lathing
AGHILNW	whaling
AGHILOT	Goliath
AGHILRS	largish
AGHILRT	alright
AGHILSU	Gaulish
AGHIMNS	mashing
AGHIMPS	gampish
AGHIMRS	Grisham
AGHINNO	nihonga
AGHINNT	tanghin
AGHINPP	happing
AGHINPS	phasing
	shaping
AGHINRS	garnish
	sharing
AGHINRT	Granthi
AGHINRU	nuraghi
AGHINSU	anguish
AGHINSV	havings
	shaving
AGHINSW	washing
AGHINTT	hatting
AGHINTW	thawing
AGHIOST	goatish
AGHIPRS	Graphis
AGHIPSW	pigwash
AGHIRST	a-rights
AGHIRSU	guarish
AGHISTT	at sight
AGHJMNO	mah-jong
AGHJNOY	John Gay
AGHKOOR	Goorkha
AGHKOSW	goshawk
AGHLMPU	galumph
AGHLNOT	Loghtan
AGHLNUY	nylghau
AGHLOOS	gasohol
AGHLOSU	goulash
AGHLPTU	plug-hat
AGHLSTY	ghastly
AGHMOSS	moss hag
AGHMRSU	gum rash
AGHNOTU	hang out
	hangout
	tohunga
AGHNRSU	nurhags
AGHNRUY	ahungry
	Hungary
AGHNTUY	naughty
AGHORTW	wart hog
	warthog
AGHPTUY	paughty
AGHRSTY	gytrash
AGIIKLT	glaikit
AGIILLN	Gillian
AGIILMN	mailing
AGIILNN	nailing
AGIILNR	glairin
	railing
AGIILNS	aisling✧
	nilgais
	sailing
AGIILNT	tailing
AGIILNW	wailing
AGIILOV	viliago
AGIILPT	pigtail
AGIILTY	agility
AGIIMMN	maiming
AGIIMMS	imagism✧
AGIIMOR	origami
AGIIMST	imagist
AGIINNR	in grain
	ingrain
AGIINPR	pairing
AGIINPT	T'ai-p'ing
AGIINRS	air sign
	raising
AGIINRT	raiting
AGIINRZ	Zingari
AGIINTW	waiting
AGIINTX	taxiing
AGIJMMN	jamming✧
AGIJNNN	Nanjing
AGIJNNU	Jungian
AGIJNRR	jarring
AGIKLNO	oakling
AGIKLNR	Karling
AGIKLNT	talking
AGIKLNW	walking
AGIKMNR	marking
AGIKMNS	makings
AGIKNNN	Nanking
AGIKNNR	ranking
AGIKNNT	tanking
AGIKNNU	unaking
AGIKNNY	yanking
AGIKNOS	soaking
AGIKNOY	kayoing
	okaying
AGIKNPR	parking
AGIKNQU	quaking
AGIKNRS	sarking
AGIKNRT	karting
AGIKNSS	gaskins
AGIKNST	skating
	takings
	tasking
AGILLLN	lalling
AGILLMU	gallium
AGILLNP	palling
AGILLNU	lingual
	lingula✧
AGILLNW	walling
AGILLNY	allying
AGILLOR	gorilla
AGILLOS	Gallios
AGILLOT	galliot
AGILLRU	ligular
AGILLSU	lugsail
AGILMMN	lamming
AGILMNP	lamping
AGILMNR	marling
AGILMNT	malting
AGILMNY	mangily
AGILMOS	gliomas
AGILMPU	plagium
AGILNNO	loaning
AGILNNS	linsang
AGILNNT	tanling
AGILNNU	nail gun
AGILNOP	galopin
AGILNOR	rangoli
AGILNOT	antilog
AGILNPP	lapping
AGILNPS	sapling
AGILNPT	plating
AGILNPW	lapwing
AGILNPY	playing
AGILNRT	ratling
AGILNRW	warling
AGILNRY	angrily
	nargily
AGILNST	anglist
	lasting
	salting
	slating
AGILNSU	nilgaus
AGILNSV	salving
AGILNSW	swaling
AGILNTY	giantly
AGILNUW	wauling
AGILNWW	wawling
AGILOPT	galipot
AGILORS	girasol
AGILORW	airglow
	Gwalior
AGILOST	saligot
AGILSTY	stagily
AGIMMNR	ramming
AGIMNNN	manning
AGIMNNR	ringman
AGIMNOR	Moringa
	roaming
AGIMNPP	mapping
AGIMNPR	ramping

AGIMNPT	tamping
AGIMNPV	vamping
AGIMNRR	marring
AGIMNRT	migrant
AGIMNRW	warming
AGIMNRY	myringa
AGIMNSU	amusing
AGIMNTT	matting
AGIMORS	isogram
AGIMORU	gourami
AGIMOSY	isogamy
AGIMRRT	trigram
AGIMRTY	trigamy
AGIMSST	stigmas
AGINNNN	Nanning
AGINNNP	panning
AGINNNT	tanning
AGINNNV	vanning
AGINNOV	Avignon
AGINNOZ	Zingano
AGINNPP	napping
AGINNPT	panting
AGINNRS	snaring
AGINNRT	ranting
AGINNRW	warning
AGINNTW	wanting
AGINNUZ	Günzian
AGINNWY	yawning
AGINOOO	oogonia
AGINORR	roaring
AGINORS	ignaros
	signora✧
	soaring
AGINORT	Grotian
AGINORV	Virgoan
AGINORZ	Zingaro
AGINOST	agonist
	gitanos
AGINOSU	sagouin
AGINOSV	Vosgian
AGINPPR	rapping
AGINPPS	sapping
AGINPPT	tapping
AGINPPW	wapping
AGINPRS	parsing
	rasping
	sparing
AGINPRT	gin trap
	parting
	prating
AGINPRW	warping
AGINPRY	praying
AGINPSS	passing
AGINPST	pasting
AGINPSU	pausing
AGINPTT	patting
AGINRRT	tarring
AGINRRU	run a rig
AGINRRW	warring
AGINRST	gastrin
	staring
AGINRSY	signary
	syringa✧
AGINRTT	ratting
AGINRTW	ring taw
AGINRTY	giantry
AGINRUV	Virunga
AGINRUW	wauring
AGINRVY	varying
AGINRWY	ringway
AGINSSS	assigns
AGINSSV	savings
AGINSTT	tasting
AGINSTW	wasting
AGINSTY	Stygian
AGINSWY	swaying
AGINTTT	tatting
AGINTTV	vatting
AGINTXY	taxying
AGINTYZ	tzigany
AGINWWX	waxwing
AGIORST	agistor
	orgiast
AGIORSV	viragos
AGIOSTU	agoutis
AGIOUUY	ouguiya
AGIRTVY	gravity
AGISTUV	vagitus
AGJLNSU	Juglans
AGJLRUU	jugular
AGJNOOR	jargoon
AGKLNNO	anklong
AGKLNNU	anklung
AGKMNOP	kampong
AGKNOPT	paktong
AGKORRW	ragwork
AGLLNOO	galloon
AGLLNTU	gallnut
	nutgall
AGLLORR	rag-roll
AGLLOSS	glossal
AGLLOSW	gallows
AGLLOTT	glottal
AGLLRYY	gyrally
AGLMNOR	long arm
AGLMNOT	Mt Logan
AGLMNUY	ugly man
AGLMOPY	polygam
AGLMORU	glamour✧
AGLMORY	Morglay
AGLNOOW	own goal
AGLNOOZ	Gonzalo
AGLNOPS	Gosplan
AGLNOPU	up-along
AGLNORU	languor
AGLNOST	alongst
AGLNOSU	lanugos
AGLNOUY	Luoyang
AGLNPSY	spangly
AGLNPUY	gunplay
AGLNTUY	gauntly
AGLOOPY	apology
AGLOORW	rag-wool
AGLOPSU	Solpuga
AGLOSUV	valgous
AGLRSUU	argulus
AGMMNSU	magnums
AGMMORY	myogram
AGMMRSY	Grammys
AGMNNOS	songman
	Songnam
AGMNNOW	gownman
AGMNORU	organum
AGMNOST	amongst
AGMNRUY	gymnura
AGMNSTU	mustang
AGMNSTY	gymnast
	syntagm
AGMNSYY	syngamy
AGMOOYZ	zoogamy
AGMOPRR	program
AGMOPRU	gopuram
AGMORRW	ragworm
AGMOSYZ	zygomas
AGMPRSU	grampus
AGMRSSU	grassum
AGMRSTU	Targums
AGNNNOO	nonagon
AGNNOOR	organon
	Rangoon
AGNOQSU	quangos
AGNORRT	grantor
AGNORST	art-song
	snotrag
AGNORSW	war song
AGNOSTW	town gas
AGNPRSU	pur sang
AGNRTUY	gauntry
AGOORTW	go to war
AGOPPST	stopgap
AGOPSTU	gasp out
AGORRTW	ragwort
AGORSSU	sour gas
AGOSUYZ	azygous
AGPRSSU	grass up
AGRSTUU	Sat Guru
AGRUUUY	Uruguay
AHHHISS	hashish
AHHIKSW	hawkish
AHHIMNS	Mishnah
AHHIMNU	hahnium
AHHIPRS	rhaphis
AHHIPTT	pith hat
AHHISTT	shittah
AHHLLOO	holla-ho!
AHHLRSY	harshly
AHHOOPS	hoop-ash
AHHOPRS	shophar
AHHOPRT	haporth
	hap'orth
AHHOSTU	hash out
AHHPTUZ	hutzpah
AHIIKOT	Akihito
AHIIKRS	shikari
AHIILOR	hair oil
AHIILPS	silphia
AHIILSW	Swahili
AHIIMNT	thiamin
AHIIMSS	sashimi
AHIINOR	Honiari
AHIINPR	hairpin
AHIINTU	huitain
AHIIPRS	airship
AHIIPSX	Xiphias
AHIJMSV	Jahvism
AHIJNNO	Johnian
AHIJSTV	Jahvist
AHIKLMS	Lakshmi
AHIKLRS	larkish
AHIKLST	silk hat
AHIKLSY	shakily
AHIKMNO	kohanim
AHIKMNS	khamsin
AHIKMRS	kashmir✧
AHIKMSW	mawkish
AHIKNOS	Khoisan
AHIKNRS	Krishna
AHIKNSS	snakish
AHIKNST	shank it
AHIKNSV	knavish
AHIKORS	karoshi
AHIKPRS	parkish
AHILLMN	Hillman®
AHILLNO	hallion
AHILLNP	phallin
AHILLNT	ant-hill
AHILLRT	athrill
AHILLRY	Hillary
AHILLST	tallish
AHILLTT	tallith
AHILMMS	mashlim
AHILMMY	hammily
AHILMNO	Ian Holm
AHILMNS	mashlin
AHILMOT	halimot
AHILMSU	alumish
AHILNOT	Lothian
AHILNOU	Anouilh
AHILNPS	planish
AHILNRS	shrinal
AHILNRT	inthral
AHILOPT	Alphito
AHILORT	Lothair
AHILORY	hoarily
AHILPPS	Lappish
	shiplap
AHILPPY	happily
AHILPST	Lapiths
AHILPSY	apishly
AHILRSU	Hilarus
AHILSST	saltish
AHILSSV	slavish
AHILSTU	halitus
AHILSTY	hastily

Words marked ✧ can also be spelled with one or more capital letters

AHILTTZ Hazlitt
AHIMMRS rammish
AHIMNNS mannish
AHIMNNU inhuman
AHIMNOT Manihot
AHIMNPS shipman✧
AHIMNTW Whitman
AHIMOPR morphia
AHIMPST mishapt
AHIMPSV vampish
AHIMPSW wampish
AHIMRST Mithras
thrimsa
AHIMRSW warmish
AHIMRTT Mt Thira
AHIMSSU hassium
AHIMTUZ azimuth
AHIMTVZ mitzvah
AHINNST tannish
AHINNSW wannish
AHINNTX xanthin
AHINORT orthian
AHINOTZ hoatzin
AHINPSS Spanish
AHINPTY Pythian
AHINRST tarnish
AHINRSU Ian Rush
AHINRSV varnish
AHINRTY rhytina
AHINRVY hyrvnia
AHINSSU Hussain
AHINSTU inhaust
AHIOORT Horatio
AHIOOST atishoo
a-tishoo
AHIOPRU ophiura
AHIOPXY hypoxia
AHIORST air shot
AHIORSW airshow
AHIORUV haviour
AHIPRST harpist
AHIPRSU rupiahs
AHIPRSW warship
AHIPSSW waspish
AHIPSWW whipsaw
AHIPSWY shipway
AHIQSTU Asquith
AHIRRST stirrah
AHIRRSY 'Arryish
AHIRSTT athirst
rattish
tartish
AHIRSTW trishaw
AHISSTU shiatsu
thiasus
AHISSTW whatsis
AHISTTW whatsit
AHISTUZ shiatzu
AHISTVY Yahvist
AHISTWY Yahwist
AHITTWW whittaw

AHJLOOP Pohjola
AHJMNOS Mas-John
AHJNORY John Ray
AHKKORV Kharkov
AHKLMOO holm-oak
AHKLOWW hawk owl
AHKMORR markhor
AHKMRTU mukhtar
AHKNPTU Pakhtun
AHKNRTY Kathryn
AHKRSSU kashrus✧
AHKRSTU kashrut✧
tushkar
AHKRSUU Kurhaus
AHLLNOS shallon
AHLLNOY hallyon
AHLLOPS shallop
AHLLOST shallot
AHLLOSW shallow✧
AHLLOTW hot wall
AHLLOTY loathly
tally-ho
AHLLPSU phallus✧
AHLLPYY aphylly
AHLLSTU thallus
AHLMMSU mashlum
AHLMNPY nymphal
AHLMNUY humanly
AHLMORU humoral
AHLMOSW Ohm's law
AHLMSTU Malthus
AHLMSTZ shmaltz
AHLMSUU hamulus
AHLNOPR alphorn
AHLNOPT haplont
AHLNORT althorn
AHLNOUZ Lanzhou
AHLNPRU Ranulph
AHLORWY holy war
AHLOSTU lash out
outlash
AHLOTUU outhaul
AHLPRSY sharply
AHLPRUY hypural
AHLPSSY splashy
AHMMMOT mammoth
AHMMMUU hummaum
AHMMTUZ Thammuz
AHMNNTU manhunt
AHMNNUU unhuman
AHMNOPS shopman
AHMNOPT phantom
AHMNORS Romansh
AHMNORU man-hour
AHMNORY harmony
AHMNOSU Housman
AHMNOSW showman
AHMNRSU Rhamnus
AHMNRYY hymnary
AHMNSTU mash-tun
AHMOOPS shampoo

AHMOOSS samshoo
AHMORRU morrhua
AHMORST harmost
AHMOTTZ matzoth
AHMOTWX wax moth
AHMPSSU smash-up
AHMRSTY thrymsa
AHNNNOS Shannon
AHNNOTY Anthony
AHNOOPR harpoon
AHNORSX saxhorn
AHNOTTT not that
AHNOTTU haut ton
AHNOTTW what not
whatnot
AHNOTWW what now?
AHNPPUU pupunha
AHNPPUY unhappy
AHNPRXY pharynx
AHNPSTU Pashtun
AHNRVYY hryvnya
AHNSTUY unhasty
AHOOPST hop-oast
AHOPRTY atrophy
AHOPSTW washpot
AHOPTTW towpath
AHORTTY throaty
AHOSTTU shout at
AHOSTUV Shavuot
AHOSTUW outwash
wash out
washout
wash-out
AHOTTUW thaw out
AHOUVWZ Wu Zhaov
AHPRRTY phratry
AHPSTUW what's up?
AHPSXYY asphyxy
AHQSSUY squashy
AHRSTWY swarthy
AHRTUWY thruway
AIIILMS Ismaili
AIIILMT militia
AIIILNT initial
AIIIMRS saimiri
AIIJLLN Jillian
AIIJMNS Jainism
AIIJMOW Iwo Jima
AIIJNNT Tianjin
AIIJNST Jainist
AIIKLLN Killian
AIIKLNN Kalinin
AIIKLPR Palikir
AIIKMMS skimmia
AIIKMNN manikin
AIIKNNT tankini
AIIKNSW Kiwanis
AIIKRSS air kiss
air-kiss
AIIKRTT traikit
AIIKTUW Kuwaiti

AIILLLN Lillian
AIILLLP lapilli
AIILLLS Lillias
AIILLMN liminal
Millian
AIILLMS Millais
AIILLMW William
AIILLNV villain
AIILLQU quillai
AIILMMN minimal
AIILMNO monilia
AIILMNT intimal
AIILMNV Viminal
AIILMRS similar
AIILMRT militar
AIILMRY miliary
AIILNOS liaison
AIILNPT pintail
Platini
AIILNPU nauplii
AIILNRT Ritalin®
AIILNST snail it
AIILNTU nautili
AIILNTY anility
AIILOPP papilio✧
AIILORV ravioli
AIILOTT Italiot
AIILQSU siliqua
AIILRST liatris
AIILRTV trivial
vitrail
AIIMMNS animism
AIIMMNX maximin
minimax
AIIMNNV minivan
AIIMNOR a minori
amorini
AIIMNPS pianism
AIIMNPT impaint
timpani
AIIMNRT Martini®
martini✧
AIIMNST animist
Mt Sinai
AIIMNSZ Naziism
AIIMNTT imitant
AIIMNTU minutia
AIIMNTV vitamin
AIIMRSS air miss
AIIMRST simitar
AIIMSSV Saivism
Sivaism
AIIMSSY myiasis
AIINNOP pianino
AIINNPS paninis
AIINNRT in train
Nitrian
AIINNST in antis
AIINNTW in twain
AIINNTY inanity
AIINOPS sinopia

AIINORS Osirian
AIINORV Ivorian
AIINOSV A Vision
AIINOTT notitia
AIINPRS aspirin
AIINPST pianist
AIINRSS Rissian
AIINRSY raisiny
AIINRTV vitrain
Vitrina
AIINSTT titanis✧
AIINSTU Tunisia
AIINSTV naivist
AIIOPRR a priori
AIIOPST Pistoia
AIIORTV Vitoria
AIIPRST piarist
AIIPTTU pituita
AIIRSTV Savitri
AIISSVV vis-à-vis
AIISVVV vis viva
AIJJMMS jimjams
AIJLYZZ jazzily
AIJMNOR major in
AIJNORT janitor
AIJNSTU Justina
AIKKLOO kalooki
AIKKMOT komatik
AIKKOPY kopiyka
AIKKSUZ zakuski
AIKLLNY lankily
AIKLMMN milkman
AIKLMNN link man
linkman
AIKLMNP milk pan
AIKLMNS silk-man
AIKLMOO Molokai
AIKLMPU lampuki
AIKLMRS Riksmål
AIKLNSY snakily
AIKLOPT kail-pot
AIKLOTW oak wilt
AIKLPPY play kip
AIKLPWY pawkily
AIKLRSW raw silk
AIKLRSY sarkily
AIKLRTT titlark
AIKLSSY skysail
AIKMNNS kinsman
AIKMNST Kantism
AIKMSST Saktism
AIKNPRT prank it
AIKNSTT Kantist
AIKOORT rooikat
AIKOSUY I ask you!
AIKPRRT Prakrit
AILLLOT tall oil
AILLMNS in small
AILLMNU luminal
AILLMOP oil palm
palm oil
palm-oil
AILLMOT maillot
AILLMPT lamplit
AILLMPU pallium
AILLMSW sawmill
AILLMSY misally
AILLMYY may-lily
AILLNNO lanolin
AILLNNT Tallinn
AILLNOP paillon
AILLNOS Allison
AILLNPY plainly
AILLNST install
AILLNSV Villans
AILLNTU Tullian
AILLNVY villany
AILLORZ zorilla
AILLPRS pillars
AILLPRT ill part
AILLPRU pilular
AILLPUV pluvial
AILLQSU squilla
AILLRSU arillus
AILLSTW law-list
AILLSTY saltily
AILLTVY vitally
AILLTWW witwall
AILMMNS slammin'
AILMMOR immoral
AILMMSY myalism
AILMMUU alumium
AILMNNO nominal
AILMNOP lampion
AILMNOS malison
Osmanli
somnial
AILMNOT lam into
Minolta®
AILMNOY alimony
AILMNPS plasmin
AILMNPT implant
AILMNRU murlain
AILMNRY Marilyn
AILMOOV Moviola®
AILMOPT optimal
AILMOPY Olympia
AILMORS oralism
AILMOST somital
AILMOSZ Zolaism
AILMOTU mail-out
AILMPRT marl-pit
AILMPRU primula
AILMPST palmist
AILMPSY misplay
AILMRST mistral
AILMRSU simular
AILMSSV Slavism
AILNNOT antlion
AILNNOU La Union
AILNNPT Plantin
AILNNPU pinnula
AILNNSU unslain
AILNOOP Polonia
AILNOPY polynia
AILNOQU aquilon✧
AILNORT on trial
AILNOSV Novalis
AILNOTY lay into
lay it on
AILNOUV Louvain
AILNPRW prawlin
AILNPSX salpinx
AILNPTU nuptial
patulin
unplait
AILNPTY inaptly
ptyalin
AILNQTU quintal
AILNRSU insular
AILNRTT rattlin
AILNSTU Latinus
unalist
AILNSTY nastily
saintly
AILNSVY Sylvian
AILNTTY nattily
AILNTUV unvital
AILOORW woorali
AILOPRS Polaris
AILOPST apostil
topsail
AILOPSY soapily
AILOPTT talipot
AILOPTV pivotal
AILOPXY Xylopia
AILOQTU aliquot
AILORST oralist
AILORSU rusa oil
AILORTY orality
AILORUW wourali
AILORUX uxorial
AILORVY olivary
AILOSSU São Luis
AILOSTU outsail
AILOTVY ovality
AILPPRU pupilar
AILPPSY payslip
sappily
AILPQSU Pasquil
AILPRSU parulis
uprisal
AILPRSY pyralis✧
AILPSTT salt pit
AILPSTY paylist
AILPSWY slipway
AILQSSU squails
AILQTTU quittal
AILQTUY quality
AILRRVY rivalry
AILRSTT starlit
AILRSTU trisula
AILRSTY trysail
AILRTTU titular
AILRTTY rattily
AILRTUV virtual
vitular
AILSSSY sassily
AILSSUV visuals
AILSTTY tastily
AILSTUW lawsuit
AILTTTY tattily
AIMMMUX maximum
AIMMNNT mint-man
AIMMNOR Marmion
AIMMNTU manumit
AIMMORS amorism
AIMMOSS mimosas
Mosaism
AIMMOST atomism
AIMMRSX Marxism
AIMNNOR iron man
AIMNNOS mansion
onanism
AIMNNSY minyans
AIMNOOR amorino
AIMNOPR rampion
AIMNOPT maintop
tampion
timpano
AIMNOPZ zamponi
AIMNORT tormina
AIMNORU mainour
AIMNORW Wormian
AIMNOST stamnoi
AIMNOTU manitou
tinamou
AIMNOTW woman it
AIMNPRU Manipur
AIMNPTY tympani
AIMNRRU murrain
AIMNRSU Marinus
suramin
Surinam
uranism
AIMNRTU natrium
AIMNRTV varmint
AIMNRUU uranium
AIMNRUW Würmian
AIMNSTT mattins
AIMNSTU tsunami
AIMNSYZ zanyism
AIMOPST impasto
AIMORRU orarium
AIMORST amorist
AIMORTT Tritoma
AIMORUZ zoarium
AIMOSTT atomist
AIMOSTU Mao-suit
AIMPPRU Air Pump
air-pump
AIMPPST mappist
AIMPRRY primary✧
AIMPRSS Parsism

Words marked ✧ can also be spelled with one or more capital letters

AIMPRSY pyramis
AIMQRSU marquis
AIMRSST Marists
tsarism
AIMRSSY Syriasm
AIMRSTU atriums
matsuri
Maurist
AIMRSTX Marxist
S-matrix
AIMRSTY maistry
symitar
AIMSSTT statism
AIMSUVV vivamus
AINNNOW wannion
AINNOOT Antonio
AINNOOX Oxonian
AINNOPR iron-pan
AINNOPS saponin
AINNOPT Pontian
AINNOST nations
onanist
AINNOWY in no way
AINNPTU unpaint
AINNQTU quinnat
quintan
AINNRTT intrant
AINNRTU urinant
AINNSTT instant
AINNSTU unsaint
AINNTUY annuity
AINOOPR pronaoi
AINOORR orarion
AINOORT Ontario
oration
AINOOTV ovation
AINOPPT appoint
AINOPRS parison
soprani
AINOPRT atropin
AINOPSS passion✧
AINOPST in a spot
AINOPSZ Spinoza
AINOPTT at point
point at
tap into
AINOPTU opuntia
utopian✧
AINORSS San Siro
AINORST in a sort
rations
AINORSW warison
AINORTU Tournai
AINORTX triaxon
AINOSSS Onassis
AINOSSU sanious
suasion
AINOSTT station
AINOSUX anxious
AINOSVY synovia
AINOTTZ Zantiot

AINPPRS parsnip
AINPQSU Pasquin
AINPQTU piquant
AINPRST spirant
spraint
AINPRTU puritan✧
uptrain
up-train
AINPSTT tant pis
AINQRTU Tarquin
AINQRUY quinary
AINQSTU asquint
AINRRTY trinary
AINRRUY urinary
AINRSSU Russian
AINRSTT start in
straint
transit
Tristan
AINRTUY unitary
AINSSTU issuant
sustain
AINSSTY in stays
AINSSXY synaxis
AINTTVY tantivy
AINTTWW want-wit
AIOORRS Rosario
AIOORSS ariosos
AIOORST Ariosto
AIOPPTU a pip out
AIOPRRT airport
paritor
AIOPRRX airprox
AIOPRRZ Pizarro
AIOPRST airstop
parotis
AIOPRTT patriot
AIOPRTW two-pair
AIOPRTY topiary
AIOPRUV paviour
AIORRRW warrior
AIORRTT traitor
AIORRTX oratrix
AIORSST aristos
AIORSTU sautoir
AIORSTV travois
AIORSTY ostiary
AIORSUV saviour✧
various
AIOTTUW outwait
AIOTUWY you wait!
AIPPRST Rappist
AIPPRSU Priapus
AIPPTUZ zap it up
AIPRRTU Tripura
AIPRSTU upstair
AIPRTVY pravity
AIPZZZZ pizzazz
AIRRTZZ rizzart
AIRSSTT straits
tsarist

AIRSTTT attrist
AIRSTVY varsity
AIRSUUV uva-ursi
AIRTUVX vitraux
AISSTTT statist
AISTTUW Watutsi
AISTTVY vastity
AISTUVY suavity
AJKMNNU junkman
AJKMNTU muntjak
AJKNSSY janskys
AJLLMOR jam roll
AJLLRUY jurally
AJLMORY majorly
AJLNORU journal
AJLOPPY jaloppy
AJMNRUY juryman
AJMORRY Marjory
AJNOORT Jan Oort
AJOOPRT Rajpoot
AJOPPZZ jazz-pop
AKKKOOS kokakos
AKKKORU rokkaku
AKKLRSY skylark
AKLLNOW know-all
AKLLORW all-work
AKLMOPU oak lump
AKLOPRW lapwork
AKLOPUV Volapük
AKLOTTU outtalk
talk out
AKLOTUW outwalk
walk out
walkout
AKLPRSY sparkly
AKLRSTY starkly
AKMNOOR Kroo-man
AKMNORT Art Monk
AKMNORU run amok
AKMNORW workman
AKMNRTU trankum
Turkman
AKMOORT mooktar
AKMORST Ostmark
AKMORTU mark out
AKMQTUU kumquat
AKMRSTU muskrat
AKNOPTT tank top
AKNORTU outrank
AKOOPRT partook
AKOOSTU atokous
AKORRTW artwork
AKORWWX waxwork
AKQSUWY squawky
ALLLOYY loyally
ALLMNOP pollman
ALLMNOT tollman
ALLMNOY allonym
ALLMNPU Pullman
ALLMORY morally
ALLMPUU plumula

ALLNOOR on a roll
ALLNOOW Walloon
ALLNOTY tonally
ALLNRTU Trullan
ALLNRUU lunular
ALLNSTY slantly
ALLNTUU ululant
ALLOOPS apollos
palolos
ALLOOTX axolotl
ALLOPRY payroll
ALLOPTX poll tax
poll-tax
ALLORTY ally-tor
ALLORYY royally
ALLOSWW swallow
ALLOSWY sallowy
ALLOTTY totally
ALLOTUW out-wall
ALLOTWY tallowy
tollway
ALLOTYY loyalty
ALLQSUY squally
ALLRRUY rurally
ALLRSTU lustral
ALLSSTU Sallust
ALLSUUY usually
ALMNNUY unmanly
ALMNOOP lampoon
ALMNOOT toolman
ALMNOOW woolman
ALMNOPS plasmon
ALMNORU unmoral
ALMNORY almonry
ALMNOSS salmons
ALMNOSU solanum
ALMNOSY salmony
ALMNOWY womanly
ALMNPSU sunlamp
ALMNSUU alumnus
ALMOOPY polyoma
ALMOPPT palmtop
ALMOPRT marplot
ALMORRU morular
ALMORSU morulas
ALMOSST smaltos
ALMOSSW Low Mass
ALMOSTW matlows
ALMOSXY xylomas
ALMOTTU mulatto
ALMRSTY smartly
ALMRSUU ramulus
ALMRTUU tumular
ALMSSUY alyssum
asylums
ALNNRSU unsnarl
ALNNSUU annulus
ALNOOPR polaron
ALNOOPT platoon
ALNOORT ortolan
ALNOOSS solanos

ALNOPPY	panoply
ALNOPSS	sponsal
ALNOPUY	lay upon
ALNOPYY	polynya
ALNORUY	unroyal
ALNORUZ	zonular
ALNPRSU	snarl up
	snarl-up
ALNPRUY	planury
ALNPTUY	unaptly
ALNPTXY	planxty
ALNSUUU	unusual
ALOOPPS	spa pool
ALOOPRW	poor law
	poor-law
ALOOPYZ	Polyzoa
ALOORRS	sororal
ALOPPRU	popular
ALOPPRY	propyla
ALOPRRU	parlour
ALOPRSU	parlous
ALOPSSU	spousal
ALOPSUV	völuspa✧
ALOPTUY	outplay
	play out
ALOQRRU	rorqual
ALOQRSU	squalor
ALORRST	rostral
ALORSTU	rotulas
ALORTYY	royalty
ALOSSTX	tax loss
ALOSTTU	last out
	outlast
	salt out
ALOSTWX	lost wax
ALOSTXY	oxy-salt
ALPPRUY	Paul Pry
ALPRSUU	pursual
ALPRSWY	sprawly
ALRSSUU	russula
ALRSTTY	startly
ALRSTUU	sutural
ALRUUWZ	Zulu War
ALSSSUW	sus laws
AMMNOOR	moorman
AMMNOOT	mootman
AMMNORY	May-morn
	Rommany
AMMNOTY	Mt Mayon
AMMNRUY	nummary
AMMOORR	maormor
	mormaor
AMMOPTU	pomatum
AMMORWW	maw-worm
AMMRSUY	summary
AMNNOOX	monaxon
AMNNORS	Normans
AMNNOSW	snowman
AMNNOTT	montant
AMNNOTY	antonym
AMNNOUW	unwoman
AMNOOPP	pompano
AMNOOPR	moor-pan
AMNOORT	moon rat
AMNOOTT	ottoman✧
AMNOOTZ	matzoon
AMNOPRT	portman
AMNOPRY	paronym
AMNOPST	postman
	topsman
AMNOPTU	pantoum
AMNOPTY	tympano
AMNORSS	ramsons
AMNORST	transom
AMNORSU	Romanus
AMNORSY	masonry
AMNORTU	romaunt
AMNOSST	stamnos
AMNOTUY	autonym
AMNPTYY	tympany
AMNQTUU	quantum
AMNRRUY	unmarry
AMNRSTU	unsmart
AMNRTTU	tantrum
AMNTUUY	autumny
AMOOORS	amoroso
AMOOPRS	prosoma
AMOOPRT	taproom
AMOORSU	amorous
AMOPSTT	topmast
AMORRUY	armoury
AMORRWY	marrowy
AMORSST	matross
AMORSSY	morassy
AMOSUYZ	azymous
AMPRRUY	marry up
AMPRSUW	up-swarm
AMPRSUY	Pyramus
AMRRSTU	rastrum
AMRRTYY	martyry
AMRSTTU	stratum
ANNOPTY	poynant
ANNOTTU	Taunton
ANNOTTY	tantony
ANNRTYY	tyranny
ANNSSTU	suntans
ANNTUUV	Nunavut
ANOOPPR	on appro
ANOOPRS	pronaos
	soprano
ANOOPRT	patroon
	pronota
ANOORST	santoor
ANOORTT	arnotto
ANOOSSS	Sassoon
ANOOSTT	on toast
ANOPRRS	sporran
ANOPRST	strap-on
ANOPRSY	spray-on
ANOPRTV	provant
ANOPSTU	outspan
	snap out
ANOPSTW	spa town
ANOPTUX	tax upon
ANORRSW	narrows
ANORRWW	war-worn
ANORSTT	start on
ANORSTU	rousant
	santour
ANORSUU	anurous
	uranous
ANORTTU	to a turn
ANORWWY	wayworn
ANOSSTZ	stanzos
ANOSTTU	totanus
ANOTTUW	want out
ANPPSUW	suppawn
ANPRSTU	run past
	suntrap
	unstrap
AOOPPRS	apropos
	Sapporo
AOOPRST	Atropos
AOOPRTT	taproot
AOORRSY	arroyos
AOORRTT	rotator
AOORRTU	outroar
AOORRTY	oratory✧
AOORSTU	outsoar
AOOSSTY	so to say
AOOSTUZ	azotous
AOOTXYZ	zootaxy
AOPPPSU	pappous
AOPPRRT	rapport
AOPPRST	apports
	pop star
AOPRRSW	sparrow
AOPRRTY	parroty
	portray
AOPRSTT	tar spot
AOPRSTU	asprout
AOPRSTW	post-war
AOPRSUV	vapours
AOPRTTU	outpart
AOPRTTW	two-part
AOPRTUY	outpray
AOPRUVY	vapoury
AOPSSTU	pass out
	passout
AOPSTTX	post-tax
AOPSTUY	autopsy
AOPSTUZ	spaz out
AOPSTWY	waypost
AOQRSTU	quartos
AOQRTUY	Torquay
AORRSWY	sowarry
AORSSUY	ossuary
	suasory
AORSTTW	at worst
AORSTWW	saw-wort
AORSUVY	savoury
AORTTUY	out-tray
AORTUVY	avoutry
AORUVVY	Vouvray
AOSSUYY	says you
AOSTTUY	outstay
	stay out
APPRRUU	purpura✧
APPRSTY	strappy
APPRSUY	papyrus
APRSSSU	surpass
APRSTTU	start up
	start-up
	upstart
APRSTTY	tapstry
APRSTUU	ut supra
APRSUWY	spurway
APSTTUY	stay put
AQRTUYZ	quartzy
AQSTTUY	squatty
ARSSSTU	Strauss
ARSSTTU	stratus

B

BBBDELU	blubbed
BBBELOS	bobbles
BBBELRU	blubber
	bubbler
BBBELSU	Bubbles
BBBEORY	bobbery
BBBGINO	bobbing
BBBHIOS	bobbish
BBBIOTT	bobbitt
BBCCIKO	bibcock
BBCDEIR	cribbed
BBCDELU	clubbed
BBCEHIN	nebbich
BBCEILR	cribble
BBCEIRR	cribber
BBCEKKO	kebbock
BBCEKKU	kebbuck
BBCELOR	clobber
	cobbler
BBCELRU	clubber
BBCEOTT	Cobbett
BBCGINU	cubbing
BBCHISU	cubbish
BBCINOU	bubonic
BBCJLOU	Jobclub
	job club
BBCRSUY	scrubby
BBDDERU	drubbed
BBDDNOU	Bob Nudd
BBDEEIT	ebb-tide
BBDEELP	pebbled
BBDEENO	bone-bed
BBDEFLU	flubbed
BBDEGRU	grubbed
BBDEILO	bilobed
BBDEILR	dibbler
	dribble
BBDEIRR	dribber
BBDEKNO	knobbed
BBDEKNU	bunk bed

BBDELOS bobsled
BBDELSU slubbed
BBDENSU snubbed
BBDESTU stubbed
BBDGIIN dibbing
BBDGINO dobbing
BBDGINU dubbing
BBDILRY dribbly
BBDLOOW bold bow
BBDOOSS od's bobs
BBEEENT Entebbe
BBEEERU bebeeru
BBEELSS ebbless
BBEESYY bye-byes
BBEFILR fribble
BBEFIRY fibbery
BBEFRUY fubbery
BBEGILR gribble
BBEGILU Big Blue
BBEGINW webbing
BBEGIOS gibbose
BBEGLOR gobbler
BBEGLRU grubble
BBEGRRU grubber
BBEHINS nebbish
BBEHLOR hobbler
BBEHMOT the bomb
BBEHMTU bethumb
BBEHOOP Bob Hope
BBEHTYY by the by
BBEIILR ribible
BBEIIMR imbiber
BBEIKMX BMX bike
BBEILNR nibbler
BBEILNS nibbles
BBEILOS bilboes
BBEILOT bibelot
BBEILPR pribble
BBEILQU quibble
BBEILRT tribble
BBEILST stibble
BBEILSY yibbles
BBEINOR rib bone
BBEIRRY bribery
BBEIRTU tubbier
BBEJORY jobbery
BBEKLNO knobble
BBEKLNU knubble
BBEKLOS blesbok
BBEKLUU bubukle
BBEKNOR knobber
BBELLOY bell-boy
BBELMOT bomblet
BBELMRU bumbler
BBELNOR nobbler
BBELORS slobber
BBELORW wobbler
BBELORY lobbyer
BBELOUX blue box
BBELRRU burbler
BBELRSU slubber
BBELSTU stubble
BBEMOSX sex bomb
BBENOTW bowbent
BBENRSU snubber
BBEOOSY yobboes
BBEORRY robbery
BBEORSW swobber
BBEORYY yobbery
BBEOSTY best boy
BBEPRUW brewpub
BBERRSU rubbers
BBERRUY rubbery
BBESTUY best buy
BBFGIIN fibbing
BBFLLUY bulb fly
BBGGIIN gibbing
BBGGINO gobbing
BBGGINU gubbing
BBGIIJN jibbing
BBGIINN nibbing
BBGIINR ribbing
BBGIJNO jobbing
BBGILNO lobbing
BBGIMNO bombing
mobbing
BBGINOR robbing
BBGINOS sobbing
BBGINPU pubbing
BBGINRU rubbing
BBGINSU gubbins
subbing
BBGINTU tubbing
BBGIOSU gibbous
BBHHIOS hobbish
BBHIMOS Hobbism
mobbish
BBHIOST Hobbist
BBHIOSY yobbish
BBHIRSU rubbish
BBHISTU tubbish
BBHOOUW whoobub
BBHRSUY shrubby
BBIIILM bilimbi
BBIIIOS Ibibios
BBIILST biblist
BBIJMOO jib boom
BBIKTUZ kibbutz
BBILLUU lulibub
BBILNOY nobbily
BBIMOSY yobbism
BBINORS ribbons
BBINORY ribbony
BBKLNOY knobbly
BBKLNUY knubbly
BBKLOOU bloubok
BBKLUUY bulk-buy
BBKOOOO boobook
BBLOSUU bulbous
BBLSTUY stubbly
BBMOOOX boombox
BBMOOTU bomb out
BBNOOOS bonobos
BBNOORU bourbon✧
BBNRUUY Bunbury
BBOOOTY boot boy
BBRSSUU suburbs
BCCEEIU ice cube
BCCEGRU C G Bruce
BCCEIIS biccies
BCCEILO ecbolic
BCCEILU cubicle
BCCEILY bicycle
BCCEMOR crombec
BCCILOU bucolic
BCCINOO obconic
BCCISUU succubi
BCCMOOX coxcomb
BCCMSUU succumb
BCCNOOR corncob
BCDEEIL decibel
BCDEHNU bunched
BCDEHOU debouch
BCDEIIO biocide
BCDEIKS sickbed
BCDEIKT bedtick
BCDEILM climbed
BCDEILO docible
BCDEIOX dice-box
BCDEKLO blocked
BCDEKOR bedrock
brocked
BCDELOU becloud
could be
BCDESUU subduce
BCDHIOR bichord
BCDHIRU bruchid
BCDHOOU cubhood
BCDILOO colobid
BCDIORW cowbird
BCDKORU burdock
BCDSTUU subduct
BCEEEHN beechen
BCEEEHS beseech
BCEEEIR ice beer
BCEEELS Celebes
BCEEFIN benefic
BCEEGIR iceberg
BCEEHIP ephebic
BCEEHLR belcher
BCEEHNR bencher
BCEEHOU bouchée
BCEEILT ice-belt
BCEEILU ice-blue
BCEEINR Bernice
BCEEIPS bespice
BCEEIRS escribe
BCEEKNU buckeen
BCEEKTT Beckett
BCEEKUY buckeye
BCEENOS obscene
BCEENRU crubeen
BCEFIIS sebific
BCEGHIT the Big C
BCEHINR birchen
BCEHINT benthic
BCEHIOR brioche
BCEHIOT biotech
BCEHIRR Bircher
BCEHITW bewitch
BCEHLRU Blücher
blucher
BCEHNSU bunches
BCEHORT botcher
BCEHORU Boucher
BCEHORW cowherb
BCEHRSU cherubs
BCEHRTU butcher
BCEIIKR brickie
BCEIIKS bickies
BCEIISV vibices
BCEIKLM limbeck
BCEIKLR brickle
BCEIKNR bricken
BCEIKST bestick
BCEILMO embolic
BCEILMR climber
reclimb
BCEILNO binocle
BCEILOR bricole
corbeil
BCEILOS slob ice
BCEIMNO combine
BCEIMOR Crombie®
microbe
BCEINOR bicorne
BCEINOS Ebonics
BCEINOZ benzoic
BCEINRU brucine
BCEIOPP cob pipe
BCEIRRS scriber
BCEIRSU suberic
BCEIRTU brucite
BCEJSTU subject
BCEKLOR blocker
BCEKLRU bruckle
buckler
BCEKORT brocket
BCEKORU roebuck
BCEKOSU buckoes
BCEKOTY bycoket
BCEKPRU Purbeck
BCEKSTU bestuck
BCELLOW cowbell
BCELMRU clumber
crumble
BCELMSU scumble
BCELNOZ Coblenz
BCELORT Colbert
BCELOSY close by
BCELSSU cubless
BCEMNTU cumbent
BCEMORS Scomber
BCEMRSU scumber

BCENORU	bouncer
BCEOORT	October
BCEORSU	obscure
BCEORTT	Corbett
BCEORTU	Courbet
BCEOSUV	sub voce
BCERSUW	crew bus
BCFLOUW	wolf cub✧
BCFSSUU	subfusc
BCGIKNU	bucking
BCGLOOX	clog box
BCHIIOP	biochip
BCHIIOT	cohibit
BCHIIRR	birchir
BCHIKOU	chibouk
BCHIKSU	buckish
BCHIMOR	rhombic
BCHINOR	bronchi
BCHIOPR	pibroch
BCHIPTU	bitch up
BCHKOOY	bok choy
BCHLOTY	blotchy
BCHNOOR	broncho
BCHOOSY	cosh boy
BCHOPTU	botch up
BCHORST	borscht
	bortsch
BCIIKLN	niblick
BCIILMU	bulimic
BCIILOR	colibri
BCIILSY	sibylic
BCIINOS	bionics
BCIISTU	biscuit
BCIKKRU	Kubrick
BCIKLNO	block in
BCIKLSU	Ski Club
BCIKORT	brockit
BCIKOTT	bittock
BCIKSTY	stick by
BCILMPU	plumbic
	upclimb
BCILNOU	lion-cub
BCILOOR	bicolor
BCINNOR	corn bin
BCINOOR	con brio
BCINOOU	cui bono?
BCINOOX	coin box
BCINORU	rubicon✧
BCINORY	Byronic
BCINSTU	NBC suit
BCINSUU	incubus
BCIOORT	robotic
BCIORST	strobic
BCIOSTY	sybotic
BCIRTUY	butyric
BCISTUU	cubitus
BCJKMUU	jumbuck
BCKLLOU	bullock
BCKLNOU	unblock
BCKMMOU	bummock
BCKMOSU	bucksom
BCKOTTU	buttock
BCKOTUX	tuck box
BCLMOOO	Colombo
BCLMOOU	coulomb
BCLMRUY	crumbly
BCLOOOX	cool box
BCLOOSU	colobus
	subcool
BCLORTU	clotbur
BCMOOTU	comb out
	comb-out
BCMOSTU	combust
BCNOORS	broncos
BCOOOPR	Robocop
BCOOTTU	bootcut
BCOOTTY	boycott✧
BCPRSUU	scrub up
BCTUUZZ	buzzcut
BDDDEOR	brodded
BDDEEER	reedbed
BDDEEES	seedbed
BDDEEIR	débride
BDDEEIS	bedside
BDDEEIT	betided
BDDEELN	blended
BDDEERS	red beds
BDDEFOR	Bedford
BDDEGIN	bedding
BDDEILN	blinded
BDDEILR	bridled
BDDEILU	builded
BDDEINR	brinded
BDDEIOO	boodied
BDDEIRR	redbird
BDDEIRT	dirt-bed
BDDELOO	blooded
BDDENOU	bounded
BDDENOW	bed down
	down-bed
BDDEOTU	doubted
BDDESUU	subdued
BDDGIIN	bidding
BDDGINU	budding
BDDGIOR	bird-dog
BDDILOR	old bird
BDDINRU	dun-bird
BDDJOOS	odd jobs
BDDPUUY	buddy up
BDEEELL	deleble
BDEEELR	bleeder
BDEEEPS	bespeed
BDEEERR	breeder
BDEEFIR	debrief
	fibered
BDEEGOR	begored
BDEEGUY	bug-eyed
BDEEIKN	beinked
BDEEILL	bellied
	delible
BDEEILS	Delibes
	edibles
BDEEILV	bedevil
BDEEIMR	bemired
BDEEIMT	bedtime
BDEEINR	inbreed
BDEEINZ	bedizen
BDEEIRR	berried
	briered
BDEEIRT	bedrite
BDEEISS	besides
BDEEIVV	bevvied
BDEELLN	bell end
BDEELNR	blender
BDEELNT	bendlet
BDEELOV	beloved✧
BDEELSS	blessed
BDEELTT	bletted
BDEEMOS	besomed
BDEEMOW	embowed
BDEEMRU	umbered
BDEEMSU	bemused
BDEENPR	prebend
BDEENST	best end
BDEENTT	tent bed
BDEEORS	bedsore
BDEEOSX	seedbox
BDEEOTW	web-toed
BDEERRU	bur-reed
BDEERRY	dry beer
BDEERST	bed-rest
BDEERTT	Debrett
BDEERUW	burweed
BDEESTT	test bed
BDEFILR	filberd
BDEFLOU	bodeful
BDEFOOR	forbode
BDEFOOW	food web
BDEGGIR	egg-bird
BDEGGOR	brogged
BDEGHIT	bedight
BDEGINN	bending
BDEGINO	Bendigo
BDEGIOO	boogied
BDEGIOT	bigoted
BDEGIRT	Bridget
BDEGLOT	dog-belt
BDEGLRU	bludger
BDEGOOT	go to bed
BDEGOOY	goodbye
BDEGORU	budgero
BDEGPUU	budge up
BDEHINT	Beth Din
BDEHMTU	thumbed
BDEHORY	herdboy
BDEHRSU	brushed
BDEIIIN	bidie-in
BDEIIRT	bride it
BDEIKLN	blinked
BDEIKMO	kimboed
BDEILLR	ill-bred
BDEILLU	bullied
BDEILNO	Blondie
BDEILNR	blinder
	brindle
BDEILOP	lobiped
BDEILRR	bridler
BDEILRT	driblet
BDEILRU	builder
	rebuild
BDEILTZ	blitzed
BDEIMMR	brimmed
BDEIMOR	bromide
BDEIMTU	bitumed
BDEINOU	bedouin✧
BDEINRY	bindery
BDEINTW	twin bed
BDEIOOR	doobrie
BDEIOPR	poe-bird
BDEIORR	broider
BDEIORS	disrobe
BDEIORT	debitor
BDEIORV	overbid
BDEIORZ	zebroid
BDEIOSW	bow-side
BDEIOSX	side box
BDEIOSY	disobey
BDEIOTW	bow-tied
BDEIOWY	wide boy
BDEIRST	bestrid
	bistred
BDEIRVY	drive-by
BDEISSU	subside
BDEISTU	subedit
BDEITUY	dubiety
BDEKNOO	bookend
BDEKOOR	red book
BDEKORW	bed-work
BDEKRSY	sky-bred
BDELLNO	Blondel
BDELLOR	bedroll
BDELMRU	drumble
BDELNRU	blunder
	Brundle
	bundler
BDELORU	boulder✧
	doubler
BDELORW	bowlder
	low-bred
BDELOSU	doubles
BDELOSW	blowsed
BDELOTT	blotted
	bottled
BDELOTU	doublet
BDELOUU	double-u
BDELOUW	would-be
BDELOWZ	blowzed
BDELRRU	blurred
BDELSSU	budless
BDELSWY	lewdsby
BDEMNOU	embound
BDEMOOR	bedroom
	boredom
BDEMOOS	bosomed

Words marked ✧ can also be spelled with one or more capital letters

BDENNOU	bounden
BDENORU	bounder
	rebound
BDENORY	bone-dry
BDENORZ	bronzed
BDENOUW	unbowed
BDENPUY	end up by
BDENRSU	burdens
BDENSTU	subtend
BDENSUY	sebundy
BDENTTU	butt-end
BDEOORR	brooder
BDEOORY	doobrey
	ore body
BDEOPRT	bedropt
BDEOPST	bedpost
BDEOPTU	dub poet
BDEORRS	borders
BDEORRU	bordure
	bourder
BDEORSU	rosebud
BDEORTU	doubter
	obtrude
	outbred
	redoubt
BDEORUV	overdub
BDEORUY	rude boy
BDERRUY	ruby-red
BDERSTU	bursted
BDERSUU	subduer
BDERSUY	rudesby
BDESSUY	Debussy
BDFGIIR	fig-bird
BDFIIOR	fibroid
BDFIISU	fidibus
BDGGLOU	gold-bug
BDGHIIR	Brighid
BDGHOSU	bush dog
BDGIINN	binding
BDGIINR	birding
BDGIIOO	gobioid
BDGILOO	globoid
BDGINNO	bonding
BDGINOY	bodying
BDGLLOU	Bulldog®
	bulldog
BDGLOOT	dogbolt
BDGNOOW	bog down
BDGORUW	bug-word
BDHINOP	hopbind
BDHIOSU	bushido
BDHMOOO	hobodom
BDHOOOY	boyhood
BDIIKNO	bodikin
BDIILMS	dislimb
BDIILNU	build in
BDIILOR	oilbird
BDIILOS	libidos
BDIJOOR	jib-door
BDIKNOR	brodkin
BDILLLO	Old Bill
BDILLNY	blindly
BDILNNU	unblind
BDILNOO	in blood
BDILNUU	unbuild
BDILPUU	build up
	build-up
	upbuild
BDILRUY	buirdly
BDILTUY	dibutyl
BDIMNPU	dumpbin
BDIMNUU	dubnium
BDINNOU	inbound
BDINOOR	Borodin
	bridoon
BDINOTU	in doubt
BDINRSU	sunbird
BDINRUU	Burundi
BDINSTU	dustbin
BDIOOOV	obovoid
BDIOORU	boudoir
BDIOPRY	poy-bird
BDIORSW	wosbird
BDIOSSY	byssoid
BDIOSUU	dubious
BDIOSUV	sub divo
BDIRSTU	disturb
BDISSUY	subsidy
BDKNOOU	bundook
BDLOOOT	old boot
BDLOOOX	oxblood
BDLORWY	blow-dry
BDMORUW	budworm
BDNNOUU	unbound
BDNOORU	bourdon
BDNOORW	do brown
BDNOOTU	bound to
	no doubt
BDNOOWW	downbow
BDNOPUU	bound up
	upbound
BDNORTU	turbond
BDNORUW	rub down
	rubdown
BDOOORW	boo-word
BDOOOWX	boxwood
BDORSTU	to-brusd
BDRSUUY	Sudbury
BEEEEFR	freebee
BEEEEKS	beseeke
BEEEEMT	beteeme
BEEEFIR	freebie
BEEEGIS	besiege
BEEEGKR	keg beer
BEEEGLU	bee-glue
BEEEGRR	bergère
BEEEHIV	beehive
	hive bee
BEEEHNS	shebeen
BEEEHPS	ephebes
BEEEHRT	be there
BEEEIKT	bee-kite
BEEEILN	beeline
BEEEILV	believe
BEEEJLW	bejewel
BEEEJLZ	Jezebel
BEEEKLL	Belleek
BEEEKPS	bee-skep
BEEELPR	bleeper
BEEELPS	Peebles
BEEELUY	blue-eye
BEEEMOS	beesome
BEEEMRW	embrewe
BEEENNZ	benzene
BEEENTW	between
BEEERTV	breveté
BEEFGIT	bigfeet
BEEFILR	febrile
	Félibre
BEEFINT	benefit
BEEFIRS	Frisbee®
BEEFLTY	beet-fly
BEEFNRU	funèbre
BEEGGNU	geebung
BEEGILL	legible
BEEGILO	obligee
BEEGILU	beguile
BEEGIMR	begrime
BEEGINN	beginne
BEEGINR	bigener
BEEGINT	beignet
BEEGINU	beguine
	béguine
BEEGIRT	big tree
BEEGJRS	Esbjerg
BEEGLNO	englobe
BEEGMNO	gombeen
BEEGMOU	embogue
BEEGNTU	unbeget
BEEGRTU	beer gut
BEEHINS	beshine
BEEHIST	bhistee
BEEHITW	E B White
BEEHKSU	bukshee
BEEHLLT	The Bell
BEEHLRT	blether
	herblet
BEEHMOT	bee-moth
BEEHNNO	hebenon
BEEHNOS	beshone
BEEHOOV	behoove
BEEHOPS	ephebos
BEEHORS	herbose
BEEHORT	the robe
BEEHORW	bewhore
BEEHPSU	ephebus
BEEHRRT	Herbert
BEEHRST	sherbet
BEEHRSW	beshrew
BEEHRTY	thereby
BEEHRWY	whereby
BEEHSTY	bheesty
BEEIJLU	jubilee
BEEIKLW	web-like
BEEIKTW	wet bike
BEEILLV	bi-level
BEEILNR	berline
BEEILOS	obelise
BEEILOZ	obelize
BEEILTT	betitle
	Let It Be
BEEIMST	betimes
BEEINNZ	benzine
BEEINOS	ebonise
BEEINOT	ebonite
BEEINOZ	ebonize
BEEINPR	pébrine
BEEINRZ	zebrine
BEEINST	E Nesbit
BEEINTZ	bez-tine
BEEIORS	ebriose
BEEIOSU	Eusebio
BEEIQUZ	bezique
BEEIRRV	brevier
BEEIRTY	ebriety
BEEISTV	Tib's Eve
BEEISTW	website
	web site✧
	web-site
BEEKNOT	betoken
BEEKOPS	bespoke
BEEKRRS	berserk
BEEKRRU	rebuker
BEELLOT	lobelet
BEELMOW	embowel
BEELMRT	tremble
BEELMSS	bless me!
BEELNNO	ennoble
BEELNOZ	benzole
BEELNTY	Bentley®
BEELNUX	Benelux
BEELOTY	eyebolt
BEELRUZ	zebrule
BEELTTU	bluette
BEEMNPT	benempt
BEEMNRU	E number
BEEMORW	embower
BEEMRRU	umbrere
BEEMRSU	Burmese
BEEMRTU	embrute
BEENNTT	Bennett
BEENORW	Berowne
BEENOST	Beeston
	boneset
BEENSTU	subteen
BEEOPRS	beprose
BEEORRU	bourrée
BEEORSV	observe
	obverse
	verbose
BEEORTX	box-tree
BEEORWY	eyebrow
BEEPRRV	preverb
BEEQSTU	bequest

BEERRSW	brewers'
BEERRWY	brewery
BEERSSU	rebuses
	subsere
BEERSTT	betters
BEERSTW	bestrew
	webster✧
BEERTTU	burette
BEETTUV	buvette
BEFFLRU	bluffer
BEFGIIL	filibeg
BEFGIRU	firebug
BEFGLLO	fog-bell
BEFIINR	in brief
BEFILNU	bluefin
BEFILOU	biofuel
BEFILOX	box file
BEFILPY	plebify
BEFILRT	filbert
BEFILRY	briefly
BEFILSU	fusible
BEFINOR	bonfire
BEFIORS	fibrose
BEFIORX	firebox
BEFIRST	fibster
BEFIRVY	verbify
BEFITUX	tubifex
BEFLLOT	elf-bolt
BEFLLTY	flybelt
BEFLMRU	fumbler
BEFLOUW	Beowulf
BEFLOUX	blue fox
BEFLTUU	tubeful
BEFMNRU	f-number
BEFOORR	forbore
BEFOOTW	webfoot
BEFORRX	Brer Fox
BEFOSUX	fuse box
BEGGGIN	begging
BEGGILS	Biggles
BEGGIST	biggest
BEGGLOR	boggler
BEGHHIT	behight
BEGHINT	benight
BEGHITT	betight
BEGHRRU	burgher✧
BEGIIJN	Beijing
BEGIIMT	big time
	big-time
BEGIINN	inbeing
BEGILLY	legibly
BEGILMU	Belgium
BEGILNO	Gobelin
	ignoble
	inglobe
BEGILNT	belting
BEGILNU	blueing
	bulgine
BEGILNY	belying
BEGILOR	obliger
BEGILRT	gilbert✧
BEGILST	giblets
BEGINNU	unbeing
BEGINOT	big-note
BEGINOY	biogeny
BEGINRR	bringer
BEGINRW	brewing
BEGINSS	bigness
BEGINTT	betting
BEGJNUU	June bug
BEGKMOS	gemsbok
BEGLLOU	globule
BEGLMOO	begloom
BEGLMRU	grumble
BEGLMUU	blue gum
BEGLNRU	blunger
	bungler
BEGLOOS	globose
BEGLOOT	bootleg
BEGLORY	glory be
BEGLOSU	glebous
BEGLRTY	bergylt
BEGNNNU	Ben Gunn
BEGNNRU	bren gun✧
BEGNNUU	unbegun
BEGNORU	burgeon
BEGNOSY	bygones
BEGNOTT	bettong
BEGNOTU	unbegot
BEGORSU	rose bug
BEGRSSU	burgess
BEHHKOT	khotbeh
BEHIITX	exhibit
BEHIKKS	Bishkek
BEHIKNT	bethink
BEHILLT	the Bill
BEHILLX	Bexhill
BEHILMS	blemish
BEHILMT	thimble
BEHILNO	Holbein
BEHILOS	bolshie
BEHILPT	hip-belt
BEHILRT	blither
BEHILST	Lisbeth
BEHILSU	blueish
BEHILTZ	Lizbeth
BEHINOP	hip bone
	hopbine
BEHINRS	her nibs
BEHIOTW	howbeit
BEHIRRT	rebirth
BEHIRST	herbist
BEHKOOT	the book✧
BEHLLOP	bellhop
BEHLLOX	hell-box
BEHLLTU	the Bull
BEHLMOW	whomble
BEHLMSU	humbles
BEHLOOT	bothole
BEHLORT	brothel
BEHLRRU	burrhel
BEHLRSU	blusher
BEHLSTU	blushet
BEHMOOY	homeboy
BEHMOTT	the tomb
BEHMOTU	bemouth
BEHMPTU	bethump
BEHMRTU	Humbert
BEHNOST	benthos
BEHNPRU	Hepburn
BEHNRTU	burthen
BEHOORT	theorbo
BEHOPRT	pot herb
BEHOPSU	Phoebus
BEHORRT	brother
BEHORST	boshter
BEHORSU	herbous
BEHORTT	betroth
BEHRRSU	brusher
BEHTUWY	whey tub
BEIIKLR	riblike
BEIILLN	Bellini
BEIILLS	billies
BEIILRS	risible
BEIILSV	visible
BEIINNR	Bernini
BEIINOT	niobite
BEIINST	stibine
BEIIOTT	biotite
BEIKLNR	blinker
BEIKLOS	obelisk
BEIKNOR	Ben Okri
BEIKNRS	brisken
BEIKOOS	booksie
BEIKOTX	box kite
BEIKRST	brisket
BEIKSTV	Vitebsk
BEILLOT	oil-belt
BEILLST	bestill
BEILMOR	embroil
BEILMRS	limbers
BEILMRT	timbrel
	Trimble
BEILMRW	wimbrel
BEILMSU	sublime
BEILNOO	bone-oil
	obelion
BEILNOW	bowline
BEILNTZ	blintze
	Blitzen
BEILOOT	bolo tie
BEILOQU	oblique
BEILORR	broiler
BEILORS	liberos
BEILORT	trilobe
BEILORY	boilery
BEILORZ	Berlioz
BEILOVX	live-box
BEILRSS	ribless
BEILRST	blister
	bristle
BEILRTT	blitter
	brittle
	triblet
BEILRTY	liberty
BEILRUY	brulyie
BEILRUZ	brulzie
BEILSST	bitless
BEILSTU	subtile
BEILSTW	blewits
BEILTTU	blue tit
BEIMMRR	brimmer
BEIMMRU	Brummie
BEIMNOR	bromine
BEIMNTU	bitumen
BEIMORW	imbower
BEIMRST	timbers
BEIMRSU	imburse
BEIMRTU	imbrute
	terbium
BEIMSTY	by times
BEINNOS	benison
BEINNOZ	benzoin
BEINOOS	boonies
BEINORT	bornite
BEINORW	brownie✧
BEINOST	ebonist
BEINOTT	bottine
BEINOWX	wine box
BEINRSU	suberin
BEINRTT	bittern
	Britten
BEINRTU	tribune✧
	turbine
BEINSSY	byssine
BEIOOPT	biotope
BEIOPTY	biotype
BEIORRT	orbiter
BEIORRV	River Ob
BEIORST	sorbite
BEIORUV	bouvier
BEIOSSU	soubise
BEIOSTY	obesity
BEIPSSU	pubises
BEIQRTU	briquet
BEIRRSU	brisure
	bruiser
BEIRRTU	true rib
BEIRSTT	bitters
BEIRSTU	bustier
BEIRTTU	tribute
BEIRTTY	treybit
BEIRTVY	brevity
BEITTWX	betwixt
BEJKOUX	jukebox
BEJLMRU	jumbler
BEJLOOW	Joe Blow
BEJLOSS	jobless
BEJNOOS	nose job
BEJOSUV	sub Jove
BEKLNOZ	Koblenz
BEKLNRU	blunker
BEKLOOT	booklet
BEKLSUY	blue-sky

sky blue
sky-blue
BEKMOST stembok
BEKNNOW beknown
BEKNORS bonkers
BEKNORU unbroke
BEKORRY brokery
BELLLOW low-bell
BELLNPU bull pen
BELLORR borrell
BELLOSU lobules
soluble
BELLOSW bellows
Boswell
BELLOUV voluble
BELLRRU burrell
BELMMOO embloom
BELMMRU mumbler
BELMNOS nombles
BELMNOU nelumbo
BELMNOY benomyl
BELMNSU numbles
BELMOOR bloomer
rebloom
BELMOOS bloosme
BELMOOT boomlet
BELMOPR problem
BELMORT temblor
BELMORY Bromley
BELMOSU embolus
BELMOSY symbole
BELMPRU plumber
BELMRRU rumbler
BELMRSU slumber
BELMRTU tumbler
tumbrel
BELMRTY trembly
BELMSTU stumble
BELNNOU unnoble
BELNNTU unblent
BELNOOY boloney
BELNOYZ benzoyl
BELNRUY Burnley
BELNSSU unbless
BELNSTU Sun Belt
sunbelt✧
unblest
BELNUUZ Zebulun
BELOOPR blooper
BELOORS boleros
BELOOSS soboles
BELOOTT bottle-o
BELOPSU pueblos✧
BELORST bolster
lobster
BELORSY soberly
BELORTT blotter
bottler
BELORTU blue-rot
boulter
trouble
BELOSSU boluses
BELOSTU boletus✧
BELOTTU belt out
BELRSTU bluster
bustler
BELRTUY butlery
BEMMOOS embosom
BEMMORR brommer
BEMMRRU brummer
BEMNORW embrown
BEMNORY embryon
BEMNOSU umbones
BEMNPTY bynempt
BEMNRSU numbers✧
BEMNTTU butment
BEMORST bestorm
mobster
BEMORSU umbrose
BEMORSY embryos
BEMORTU Umberto
BEMORWW webworm
BEMOTUY myotube
BEMRSTU bumster
BEMSSUU subsume
BENNORW Bronwen
newborn
BENNORZ bronzen
BENOORS Osborne
Robeson
BENOOYZ Boyzone
BENOPRR preborn
BENORRZ bronzer
BENORST sorbent
BENORWY bywoner
BENOSTX nest box
BENOSUZ subzone
BENOSWY newsboy
BENOTTX box tent
BENRSTU bursten
BENRUWY Newbury
BEOOPUZ booze-up
BEOORST booster
BEOORSZ rebozos
BEOPRRV proverb
BEOPRST besport
BEOPRSU sober up
BEOPSTU bespout
BEOQSTU bosquet
BEOQSUY obsequy
BEOQTUU bouquet
BEORRSW browser
BEORSUU uberous
BEORSUZ subzero
BEORUVY buy over
overbuy
BEPRRTU perturb
BEPRTUY puberty
BEPSTUY subtype
BEQRSUU brusque
BERRSTU burster
BERSTUV subvert
BERTTUY buttery
BESTTUX subtext
BFFGINU buffing
BFFILOO boil off
BFFKNOU bunk off
BFFLLUY bluffly
BFFLOOW blow off
blow-off
BFFMOPU bump off
BFFNOOU buffoon
BFFOPUX puff-box
BFFOUZZ buzz off
BFGHIIS big fish
BFGHORU Hofburg
BFGIOOT bigfoot✧
BFGIORT frogbit
BFGIORU Big Four
BFHILSU lubfish
BFHIOSX box-fish
BFHIRSU furbish
BFHISTU tubfish
BFHLSUY bush-fly
BFIINOR fibroin
BFILMRU brimful
BFILOTY lift-boy
BFIMOYZ zombify
BFIORST Bifrost
BFIORSU fibrous
BFIRTUY brutify
BFKLOOU bookful
BFKLOOY flybook
BFKSSUU subfusk
BFLLOUW bowlful
BFLLOWY blowfly
flyblow
BFLOSUX boxfuls
BFLSTUU tubfuls
BFOOOTY footboy
BFOUXZZ fuzzbox
BGGGINU bugging
BGGHIIS biggish
BGGILNU bulging
BGGINOY by-going
BGGINSU big guns
BGHHIOY highboy
BGHILTY blighty
BGHINOR bighorn
BGHINSU bushing
BGHINTY by-thing
BGHIOST big shot
BGHIPSU bush pig
BGHIRST brights
BGHIRTY by right
BGHLRUU bulghur
burghul
BGHMORU Homburg
BGHNORU hornbug
BGHOORU borough
BGHORTU brought
BGIILLN billing
BGIILNO boiling
BGIILNR birling
BGIILNS sibling
BGIIMNR briming
BGIINNN binning
BGIINNR bring in
inbring
BGIINRT ringbit
BGIINTT bitting
BGIKMNO king mob
BGIKNNO bonking
BGIKNOO booking
BGIKNOR broking
BGIKNSU busking
BGILLNU bulling
BGILLPU pill bug
BGILMOU gumboil
BGILNOT biltong
bolting
BGILNOW blowing
bowling
BGILNOY ignobly
BGILOOR obligor
BGILOOY biology
BGILORY boy-girl
BGILRSU busgirl
BGIMMNU bumming
BGIMNNU numbing
BGIMNOO booming
BGIMNPU bumping
BGIMOSY bogyism
BGIMRSY Grimsby
BGINNOR bring on
BGINNRU burning
BGINNTU bunting
BGINOOR bog iron
BGINOOZ boozing
BGINORS borings
BGINORZ Zorbing
BGINOSU bousing
BGINPRU bring up
upbring
BGINRSU subring
BGINRTU bruting
BGINRUY burying
rubying
BGINSSU bussing
BGINSTU busting
BGINSUY busying
BGINSWY swing-by
BGINUZZ buzzing
BGIORTY bigotry
BGIUWZZ buzz-wig
BGJOTUY toby-jug✧
BGKLOOO logbook
BGKORSY grysbok
BGLMRUY grumbly
BGLNOOW longbow
BGLNOUW blowgun
BGLOOSU globous
BGLOSSU bugloss
BGMOOSS bog moss

BGMOOTU gumboot
BGNOOTU bon goût
BGNOOWY gownboy
BGNOSSU subsong
BGNPRUU burp gun
BGORTUW bugwort
BHIIINT inhibit
BHIINRS brinish
BHIINSS his nibs
BHIIPSS sibship
BHIIRST British
BHIKNOP hip-knob
BHIKOOS bookish
BHILLOY billy-oh
BHILLSU bullish
BHILOTU holibut
BHILPSU publish
BHIMOOR rhomboi
BHIMOOS hoboism
BHIMOPS phobism
BHIMORT thrombi
BHIMORU bohrium
BHIMSTU bismuth
BHINRSU burnish
BHIOOPR biophor
BHIOORS boorish
BHIOPST phobist
BHIOPSY ship boy
BHIORSS Sorbish
BHIOSWZ show biz
showbiz
BHIRSTU brutish
BHIRTTU turbith
BHISTTU bushtit
BHISUVY ivy-bush
BHLRSUU bulrush
BHMOORS rhombos
BHMORSU rhombus
BHMUUZZ humbuzz
BHNORTY Brython
BHOOPSY shop boy
BHOOSTW bowshot
BHOOSWX showbox
BHPRSUU brush up
brush-up
BIIILST Tbilisi
BIIKLOT kilobit
BIILLNO billion
BIILLOU bouilli
BIILLTW twibill
BIILMRU Librium®
BIILNNR birlinn
BIILNQU quiblin
BIILNTU built-in
in-built
BIILOSU bilious
BIILRSY risibly
BIILSVY visibly
BIIMNOU niobium
BIIMNSU minibus
mini-sub
BIIMSTU stibium
BIIORSV vibrios
BIIOSUV bivious
BIISSTX six bits
BIJNOOV Bon Jovi
BIJNOSU subjoin
BIKLLUY bulkily
BIKLNOT ink-blot
BIKLNOY linkboy
BIKLRSY briskly
BIKMNPU bumpkin
BIKORRW ribwork
BILLNOU bullion
BILLOOY loobily
BILLOPX pillbox
BILLOUV volubil
BILLPTU pit bull
BILLRWY wrybill
BILMNOR nombril
BILMNPU plumb in
BILMOSU limbous
BILMPUY bumpily
BILMRTU tumbril
BILMSUU bulimus
BILNNOY bonnily
BILNOTU botulin
BILNRSU Lisburn
BILNTUU tubulin
unbuilt
BILOOYZ boozily
BILORST Bristol
BILOSSU subsoil
BILOSSY bossily
BILPTUU built-up
BILRSTY bristly
trilbys
BILRTTY brittly
BILRTUY tilbury✧
BIMMOOS imbosom
miombos
BIMMORS bromism
BIMNORS misborn
BIMNORW imbrown
BIMNOSU omnibus
BIMNOSY symbion
BIMOSSS bossism
BIMRSUX bruxism
BIMSSSU submiss
BINOORS bonsoir
BINOORX box-iron
BINOOST bonitos
BINOOSU niobous
BINORST ribston
BINORSU Boursin
BINOTUY buy into
BINRSTU inburst
BINSTUU subunit
BINTTUW twin-tub
BIOOSUV obvious
BIOPPRT Britpop
BIOPRTW pit brow
BIOPRTY probity
BIOPSTX spit box
BIORRTU burrito
BIORRTW ribwort
BIORSST bistros
BIORSTT bistort
BIORSUU rubious
BIORTTU bittour
BIOSTTW two bits
BISSSTU subsist
BJNOORU bonjour
BJNOOSW snow job
BJORUXY jury box
BKLOTUU bulk out
BKNOOTW bowknot
BKNORSY skyborn
BKOOORY Kroo-boy
BKOOOTU book out
BKOORWX workbox
BLLMORU bum roll
BLLNTUY bluntly
BLLOSUU lobulus
BLLOUVY volubly
BLLPPUU bull-pup
BLMMPUU plumbum
BLMNPUU unplumb
BLMOOOT tombolo
BLMOORW lobworm
BLMOOSS blossom
BLMRSUY slumbry
BLMSTUY stumbly
BLNNOUW unblown
BLNOORW low-born
BLNOOSU blouson
BLNOPUW upblown
BLOOOTX toolbox
BLOOQUY obloquy
BLOORWW lowbrow
BLOOTTU blot out
BLOOTUW blow out
blow-out
bowl out
BLOOTWY low toby
BLOPSTU subplot
BMNOOOW moonbow
BMNOOSU unbosom
BMNORUW mowburn
BMOOORX boxroom
BMOOSTT bottoms
BMOPTUU bump out
BMORSUU brumous
umbrous
BNNOORS Bronson
BNNOUUY nun buoy
BNNRSUU sunburn
BNNRTUU unburnt
BNOOOPR pro bono
BNOOSWX snow box
BNOOTTY bottony
BNORSUU burnous
BNORTUU burn out
burn-out
outburn
BNOSTTU buttons
BNOTTUY buttony
BNRSTUY by turns
BOOOPRX poor box
BOOOPTT top boot
BOOOTTU boot out
BOOPSTX postbox
BOOPSTY post boy
BOPSSTU bus stop
postbus
BORSTXY bostryx
BOSTTUU stub out
BOTTTUU butt out
BPRSTUU burst-up
upburst

C

CCCDIOO coccoid
CCCEHIO choc-ice
CCCEHIZ Czechic
CCCNOOT concoct
CCDEEER recceed
CCDEEHK checked
CCDEEIO ecocide
CCDEEIR reccied
CCDEENO concede
CCDEENY decency
CCDEESU succeed
CCDEHIL cliché'd
CCDEIIT deictic
CCDEILO ice-cold
CCDEILR circled
CCDEIMO comedic
CCDEIOS codices
CCDEIOT Docetic
CCDEKLO clocked
cockled
CCDEKOR crocked
red cock
CCDELOU occlude
CCDENOO concedo
CCDENOU conduce
CCDHIIL cichlid
CCDIILO codicil
CCDIILU culicid
CCDIIOR cricoid
CCDILOY cycloid
CCDKLOU cuckold
CCDKOOR rock cod
CCDKOUY duck-coy
CCDNOOR concord✧
CCDNOTU conduct
CCDOSTU stucco'd
CCEEGNO cogence
CCEEHHN Chechen
CCEEHIV ceviche
CCEEHKR checker
recheck
CCEEHOR écorché

CCEEHOU couchee
couchée
CCEEHRS screech
CCEEILN licence
CCEEINR eccrine
CCEEINS science✧
CCEEIRV crevice
CCEEKOY cockeye
CCEELRU Lucrece
CCEELRY recycle
CCEENRY recency
CCEERSY secrecy
CCEFNOT confect
CCEGNOY cogency
CCEHIKN check in
check-in
chicken
CCEHIKU chuckie
CCEHILU culchie
CCEHINO conchie
CCEHINT technic
CCEHIOR choreic
CCEHIRS screich
scriech
CCEHKLU chuckle
CCEHKMS schmeck
CCEHKNU uncheck
CCEHKOR chocker
CCEHKPU check up
check-up
CCEHLRU cleruch
CCEHNOS conches
CCEHORT crochet
CCEIIKP ice pick
CCEIIMS cimices
CCEIIPS piccies
CCEIIRT icteric
CCEIIST cecitis
CCEIKLR clicker
CCEIKLT clicket
CCEIKRT cricket
CCEIKRY crickey
CCEILOT coctile
CCEILPT P-Celtic
CCEILQT Q-Celtic
CCEILRR circler
CCEILRT circlet
CCEILSU culices
CCEILSY cylices
CCEILTU cuticle
CCEIMNO meconic
CCEIMOT cometic
CCEIMST smectic
CCEINOR cornice
crocein
CCEINOS concise
CCEINOT conceit
CCEINRT centric
CCEIOPP coppice
CCEIOPT ectopic
CCEIORT orectic
CCEIOSS ciscoes
CCEIOST Scotice
CCEIPST sceptic✧
CCEISSU succise
CCEJNOT conject
CCEKLOR clocker
CCEKLOY ko cycle
CCEKNOT conteck
CCEKNOY cockney✧
CCEKOPT petcock
CCEKORT crocket
CCELLOT collect
CCELLOU Uccello
CCELNOY cyclone
CCELNUY lucency
CCELUWY wu cycle
CCEMNOO Comecon
CCENNOR concern
CCENNOT concent
connect
CCENOPT concept
CCENORT concert
CCENORW concrew
CCENOTV convect
CCEOOTT cocotte
CCEOPRS Cecrops
CCEOPRT percoct
CCEORRT correct
CCEORRU reoccur
CCEORTW twoccer
CCEOSSU succose
CCERTUW crew cut
CCESSSU success
CCFIRUY crucify
CCFLOSU floccus
CCGHINO gnocchi
CCGILNY cycling
CCGKOOR gorcock
CCHHIIT ichthic
CCHHILS schlich
CCHHOOS chochos
CCHHRUY churchy
CCHIIST stichic
CCHIKNU chuck in
CCHIKST schtick
CCHIKTU chuck it
CCHILNY Lychnic
CCHILOR chloric
CCHIMOR chromic
CCHINOR chronic
CCHINSU scuchin
CCHIORY chicory
CCHIOTW cowitch
CCHIPSU hiccups
CCHIPSY psychic
CCHIPUY hiccupy
CCHIRST scritch
CCHKLOS schlock
CCHKMOS schmock
CCHKMSU schmuck
CCHKOSY cockshy
shy-cock
CCHKPUU chuck up
upchuck
CCHKSTU schtuck
CCHLOOO hoc loco
CCHNRSU scrunch
CCHNRUY crunchy
CCHOSTU Succoth
CCHOSTY Scotchy
CCIIILS silicic
CCIILPR circlip
CCIINPU Puccini
CCIIRTU circuit
CCIISTY siccity
CCIKLNO clock in
CCIKLOW cowlick
CCIKLOY cockily
colicky
CCIKOPT cockpit
CCILNOO colonic
CCILNOU council
CCILOOP piccolo
CCILSTY cyclist
CCIMOTY mycotic
CCINOOT coction
CCINORY cryonic
CCINOTV convict
CCIOORS sirocco
CCIOPTU occiput
CCIPRTY cryptic
CCIRSUY circusy
CCKLNOO clock on
CCKLOPU clock up
CCKOPRU crock up
CCKOSTU custock
CCLOOOZ zoccolo
CCLOPSY cyclops✧
CCMOOOR morocco
CCNOOPU puccoon
CCNOOTU coconut
CCNOPUY concupy
CCNOSSU concuss
CCOOORS rococos
CCOPSTT C P Scott
CCORSUU succour
CCORSUY succory
CCOSSTU stuccos
CCOSSUU succous
CCSSSUU succuss
CDDDEEI decided
CDDDELO clodded
CDDDESU scudded
CDDEEER decreed
CDDEEII deicide
CDDEEIR decider
decried
CDDEEKL deckled
CDDEENS descend
CDDEEOR decoder
CDDEERU reduced
CDDEEUW cudweed
CDDEHIL childed
CDDEHIN chidden
CDDEIIS discide
CDDEILM middle C
CDDEIOS discoed
CDDEIOV CD video
CDDEIRY dry-iced
CDDELOR coddler
CDDELOU clouded
CDDELRU cruddle
CDDELSU scuddle
CDDEORW crowded
CDDERSU scudder
CDDGINO codding
CDDHIOR dichord
CDDIIIO didicoi
CDDIINO Indocid®
CDDIIOS discoid
CDDIIOY didicoy
CDDIIRU druidic
CDDIKOP piddock
CDDIORS discord
CDDKOPU puddock
CDDKORU ruddock
CDDKORY dry dock
dry-dock
CDEEEFL fleeced
CDEEEFN defence
CDEEEHP dépêche
CDEEEHS cheesed
CDEEEIP epicede
CDEEEIV deceive
CDEEEKL cleeked
CDEEELT elected
CDEEELX Edexcel
CDEEEPR precede
CDEEERS seceder
CDEEERT decreet
erected
CDEEFII edifice
CDEEFKL flecked
CDEEFLT deflect
CDEEFOR deforce
CDEEGIM iced gem
CDEEGIR grieced
CDEEHIS dehisce
CDEEHOR chordee
CDEEHPR perched
CDEEHRS cheders
CDEEHRU euchred
CDEEHST chested
CDEEIIT eidetic
CDEEILN decline
CDEEILP pedicel
pedicle
CDEEIMN endemic
CDEEIMS demi-sec
CDEEINO codeine
CDEEINR cedrine
CDEEIOS diocese
CDEEIOV devoice

CDEEIPR	pierced
CDEEIPT	pedetic
CDEEIRR	decrier
CDEEIRT	tierced
CDEEITX	excited
CDEEKNR	redneck
CDEEKNV	V-necked
CDEEKRW	wrecked
CDEELLR	red cell
CDEELPU	cupeled
	decuple
CDEELPY	ycleped
CDEELRU	ulcered
CDEELSU	Culdees
	scedule
	seclude
CDEELUX	exclude
CDEENOR	encoder
CDEENOS	seconde
CDEENRT	centred
	credent
	red cent
CDEENST	descent
	scented
CDEEOPR	proceed
CDEEORV	covered
CDEEOST	cestode
CDEEOTV	coveted
CDEEOWW	cow-weed
CDEERRU	reducer
CDEERST	crested
CDEERSU	rescued
	seducer
CDEERSW	screwed
CDEERUV	decurve
CDEESUX	excused
CDEFFHU	chuffed
CDEFFIL	cliffed
CDEFFIO	coiffed
CDEFHIN	finched
CDEFIIT	deficit
CDEFILP	clip-fed
CDEFILT	clifted
CDEFINO	confide
CDEFKOR	defrock
	frocked
CDEFNOR	corn-fed
CDEFNTU	defunct
CDEFOOR	od-force
CDEFOSU	defocus
	focused
CDEFRTU	fructed
CDEFSUU	fucused
CDEGGLO	clogged
CDEGHNU	Chengdu
CDEGIKN	decking
CDEGILU	cludgie
CDEGIOR	ergodic
CDEGKNU	gun deck
CDEGKOU	geoduck
CDEHIIL	ceilidh
CDEHIIN	ich dien
CDEHILL	chilled
CDEHILO	cheloid
	helcoid
CDEHILP	delphic✧
CDEHILR	childer
CDEHINO	hedonic
CDEHINP	pinched
CDEHIOW	cowhide
CDEHIPP	chipped
CDEHIPT	pitched
CDEHIRT	ditcher
CDEHKOS	shocked
CDEHKUY	heyduck
CDEHLOT	clothed
CDEHMMU	chummed
CDEHNOR	chondre
CDEHNOT	notched
CDEHNRU	chunder
CDEHOPP	chopped
CDEHOPU	pouched
CDEHORW	chowder
	cowherd
CDEHOSU	hocused
CDEHOSW	cowshed
CDEHOTU	touched
CDEHRSU	crushed
CDEHSSU	duchess
CDEHSTY	scythed
CDEIIMR	dimeric
CDEIINS	incised
	indices
CDEIINT	identic
CDEIIOR	ericoid
CDEIIOV	ovicide
CDEIIRT	icterid
CDEIIST	deistic
CDEIISU	suicide
CDEIJST	disject
CDEIKLP	pickled
CDEIKLS	sickled
CDEIKNS	dickens✧
CDEIKNZ	zincked
CDEIKOS	dockise
CDEIKOZ	dockize
CDEIKRR	derrick✧
CDEIKST	sticked
CDEILLO	codille
	collide
CDEILLU	cullied
CDEILMO	melodic
CDEILNU	include
	nuclide
CDEILOO	oceloid
CDEILPP	clipped
CDEILPU	clupeid
CDEILTU	ductile
	dulcite
CDEIMNO	demonic
CDEIMOR	dormice
CDEIMOS	medicos
CDEIMOT	demotic✧
CDEIMPR	crimped
CDEINOS	secondi
CDEINOT	ctenoid
	deontic
	D-Notice
CDEINOU	doucine
	Unicode
CDEINOZ	zincode
CDEINRS	discern
	rescind
CDEINRU	inducer
CDEINRY	cindery
CDEINSU	incudes
CDEINSX	exscind
CDEINTU	uncited
CDEIOPR	percoid
CDEIOPZ	zip code
CDEIORS	discoer
CDEIORT	cordite
CDEIORV	divorce
	divorcé
CDEIORW	crowdie
CDEIOST	cestoid
CDEIPRS	discerp
CDEIPRT	predict
CDEIPST	discept
CDEIPTU	cup-tied
CDEIRRU	curried
CDEIRST	credits
CDEIRSU	discure
CDEIRTV	verdict
CDEISST	dissect
CDEISSY	ecdysis
CDEITUX	excudit
CDEKLOW	wedlock
CDEKLOY	key-cold
CDEKLPU	plucked
CDEKNRU	drucken
CDEKNSU	sun deck
	sundeck
CDEKOOR	crooked
CDEKOPT	top deck
CDEKOPU	coked-up
CDEKOTU	deck out
CDEKOTW	wet dock
CDELLOU	collude
CDELLRY	dry-cell
CDELMSU	muscled
CDELMTU	mulcted
CDELNOO	condole
CDELNOU	encloud
CDELNOY	condyle
CDELOOR	croodle
	decolor
	Lord Coe
CDELORS	scolder
CDELORW	clowder
	red-cowl
CDELOSU	dulcose
CDELOTT	clotted
CDELOTU	clouted
CDELOUY	doucely
CDELPUU	clued-up
CDELRRU	curdler
CDELRSU	scudler
CDELRUY	crudely
CDEMMNO	commend
CDEMMOO	commode
CDEMMSU	scummed
CDEMNNO	condemn
CDEMNOP	compend
CDEMNOU	mud-cone
CDEMOOS	comedos
CDEMORU	decorum
CDENNOO	condone
CDENNOT	contend
CDENOOS	secondo
CDENOPU	pounced
CDENORS	corsned
CDENORT	net cord
CDENORW	crowned
	decrown
CDENOSS	seconds
CDENOTU	counted
CDENPUY	pudency
CDENRUU	uncured
CDENRUY	duncery
CDEOOPP	copepod
CDEOOPS	scooped
CDEOORR	corrode
CDEOORV	vocoder
CDEOOTV	dovecot
CDEOPPR	cropped
CDEOPRU	produce
CDEOQTU	docquet
CDEORRW	crowder
CDEORSS	crossed
CDEORSW	scowder
CDEORTU	eductor
CDEORUU	douceur
CDEOSSU	escudos
CDEOSTU	custode
	doucets
CDEPRTY	decrypt
CDERRUY	dry-cure
CDFHIOS	codfish
CDFIILU	fluidic
CDFILUY	dulcify
CDFIOOT	octofid
CDGHIIN	chiding
CDGHOTU	go Dutch
CDGIIKN	dicking
CDGIINO	gonidic
CDGIKNO	docking
CDGIKNU	ducking
CDGIKOS	dog-sick
CDGIKOT	dog-tick
CDGILNO	codling
CDGILOP	cold pig
CDGINNO	condign
CDGINOR	cording

CDGINTU ducting
CDGLOPU goldcup
CDGNOOO coondog
CDGNOOR corn dog
CDGNOUW cow-dung
CDHIIMW Midwich
CDHIINT chindit✧
CDHIIST distich
CDHILLY childly
CDHILNU unchild
CDHILOS coldish
CDHINOR chondri
CDHIOOR choroid
ochroid
CDHIORY droichy
CDHIOUX du choix
CDHIPTY diptych
CDHKOOR hordock
CDHMORU Murdoch
CDHOOPT photo CD
CDIIIOT idiotic
CDIIJRU juridic
CDIILLY idyllic
CDIILMO domicil
CDIIMNO Dominic
CDIIMOS disomic
CDIINOR crinoid
CDIINOT diction
CDIINOV Vidicon®
CDIINOZ zincoid
CDIIORS cirsoid
CDIIOSS cissoid
CDIIOTY idiotcy
CDIKLNO Old Nick
CDIKNOR dornick
CDIKNOW windock
CDILLOO colloid
CDILLUY lucidly
CDILOTU dulotic
CDILOUV Ludovic
CDIMMOU modicum
CDIMNOO monodic
CDIMOSU muscoid
CDINOOT odontic
CDINOSY synodic
CDINOTU conduit
noctuid
CDINSSU sun disc
CDIOOTT cottoid
CDIOPRR ripcord
CDIOSTY cystoid
CDIOTUV oviduct
CDIRSUY dysuric
CDIRTUY crudity
CDISSSU discuss
CDISTUY Dyticus
CDKMOSU musk-cod
CDKNNOU dunnock
CDKOTUU duck out
CDLNOTU couldn't
CDLNOUU uncloud
CDLOOPY lycopod
CDLOOTU out cold
CDMMOOO commodo
CDMOSUW mudscow
CDNNOTU contund
CDNOORY Corydon
Croydon
CDNORWY cry down
CDNOTUW cut down
cut-down
CDOOOPT octopod
CDOOPST postdoc
CDOORRY corrody
CDOORST doctors
CDOOTUW woodcut
CDOPRTU cut drop
product
CDOSTUY custody
CEEEEGH geechee
CEEEEHL leechee
CEEEFIR ice-free
CEEEFLR fleecer
CEEEGNR regence
CEEEHIR reechie
CEEEHNR encheer
CEEEHPR cheeper
CEEEHRR cheerer
CEEEINP epicene
CEEEIPR creepie
CEEEIRV receive
CEEEITV evictee
CEEEKNW ewe-neck
CEEELLU écuelle
CEEELPY ycleepe
CEEELRT re-elect
CEEELST celeste
CEEEMPR emperce
CEEENRS recense
CEEENRT Terence
CEEENSS essence
CEEEPRR creeper
CEEERRT erecter
re-erect
CEEERST secrete
CEEERSV screeve
CEEERTX excrete
CEEETUX execute
CEEFFNO offence
CEEFFOR efforce
CEEFFST effects
CEEFHIR chiefer
CEEFHIT fetiche
fitchée
CEEFHRT fechter
fetcher
CEEFILO ice floe
CEEFINR ice fern
CEEFINV venefic
CEEFKLR flecker
freckle
CEEFLNU fluence
CEEFLRT reflect
CEEFNOR enforce
CEEFNOX ox-fence
CEEFPRT perfect
prefect
CEEGGLL egg cell
CEEGINR energic
generic
CEEGINT genetic
CEEGINU eugenic
CEEGIRZ Grecize
CEEGKOS geckoes
CEEGLLO college
CEEGLNT neglect
CEEGLOR El Greco
CEEGLOU eclogue
CEEGNOR cogener
congree
CEEGNRU urgence
CEEGNRY regency✧
CEEGORT cortège
CEEGQRU grecque
CEEHILN elenchi
CEEHILS helices
CEEHILV vehicle
CEEHIMR chimere
CEEHIMS chemise
CEEHINR inherce
CEEHINS chinese✧
CEEHIOR cheerio
CEEHIOS echoise
CEEHIOZ echoize
CEEHIRT etheric
heretic
techier
CEEHKLR heckler
CEEHKNP henpeck
CEEHLNO chelone
echelon
CEEHLNU leuchen
CEEHLOW cowheel
CEEHLRW welcher
CEEHLRY cheerly
lechery
CEEHLSS chessel
CEEHLSY sleechy
CEEHMRS schemer
CEEHMRT merchet
CEEHNPU penuche
CEEHNRW wencher
CEEHOPR pre-echo
CEEHORR coherer
CEEHORT trochee
CEEHOUV vouchee
CEEHPRR percher
CEEHPRU cheer up
upcheer
CEEHPSU Cepheus
CEEHQRU chequer
CEEHQUY queechy
CEEHRST Chester
CEEHRSY creeshy
CEEHRTU The Cure
CEEHSSS chesses
CEEIINR eirenic
CEEIIPR épicier
CEEIJOR rejoice
CEEIKLT cleekit
CEEIKNT necktie
tie-neck
CEEIKPR pickeer
CEEIKTT e-ticket
CEEILLM micelle
CEEILNO cineole
CEEILNR recline
CEEILNS license
selenic
silence
CEEILNT centile
CEEILNU leucine
CEEILNX excel in
CEEILPS eclipse✧
CEEILRT reticle
tiercel
CEEILRU recuile
CEEILST sectile
CEEILSV vesicle
CEEILTT Lettice
CEEILTU leucite
CEEIMMT memetic
CEEIMNO Miocene
CEEIMNT centime
CEEIMRX excimer
CEEINNS incense
CEEINOS senecio
CEEINPR percine
CEEINPT pentice
CEEINPW new pice
CEEINRS ceresin
scriene
sincere
CEEINRT enteric
enticer
CEEINRV cervine
CEEIOPT picotee
CEEIORT coterie
CEEIORV ice over
CEEIPPU piece up
CEEIPRR piercer
CEEIPRS precise
recipes
CEEIPRT receipt
CEEIPRU epicure
CEEIPSS species
CEEIPST pectise
CEEIPTZ pectize
CEEIQSU quiesce
CEEIRRT reciter
CEEIRSV scrieve
service
CEEIRTT tiercet
CEEIRTU eucrite

CEEIRTX	exciter
CEEITTZ	zetetic
CEEJORT	ejector
CEEKLNT	necklet
CEEKLPS	speckle
CEEKOSY	sockeye
CEEKPRY	ryepeck
CEEKRRW	wrecker
CEELLLU	cellule
CEELLNO	colleen✧
CEELLNT	Cellnet®
CEELLOS	cellose
CEELLPU	pucelle✧
CEELLSX	sex cell
CEELLTW	wet cell
CEELMNT	clement✧
CEELMOO	coelome
CEELMOT	telecom
CEELMOW	welcome
CEELNOS	enclose
CEELNRT	lectern
CEELNRU	lucerne✧
CEELORS	reclose
CEELORT	elector✧
	electro
CEELORY	recoyle
CEELOTT	Colette
CEELOTU	elocute
CEELOTV	covelet
CEELPRT	plectre
	prelect
CEELRSU	recluse
CEELRSW	crewels
CEELRTU	lecture
CEELRTY	erectly
CEELTTU	lettuce
CEEMMOR	commère
CEEMNOR	McEnroe
CEEMNOW	newcome
CEEMNRU	cerumen
CEEMOOR	o'ercome
CEEMOPR	compeer
	compère
CEEMOPT	compete
CEEMRRY	mercery
	remercy
CEEMSTU	tumesce
CEEMSTY	mycetes✧
CEENNOU	enounce
CEENNOV	convene
CEENNRT	centner
CEENOOT	ecotone
CEENOPT	potence
	potencé
CEENORS	necrose
CEENORZ	cozener
CEENPRS	spencer✧
CEENPRT	per cent
CEENRSU	censure
CEENRSY	scenery
CEENTTU	cunette
CEEOPST	pectose
CEEOPTY	ecotype
CEEORRS	rescore
CEEORRT	erector
CEEORRU	recoure
CEEORRV	recover
	re-cover
CEEORRW	recower
CEEORSU	cereous
CEEORTW	cowtree
CEEOTTT	octette
CEEPPRT	percept
	precept
CEEPPRU	prepuce
CEEPRSS	precess
CEEPRST	respect✧
	scepter
	sceptre✧
	specter
	spectre
CEEPRTX	excerpt
CEERRSU	rescuer
	securer
CEERRSW	screwer
CEERRUV	recurve
CEERSST	cresset
	secrets
CEERSUX	excurse
	excuser
CEERTTU	curette
CEETTUV	cuvette
CEFFIOR	officer
CEFFIOS	offices
CEFFISU	suffice
CEFFLSU	scuffle
CEFFMOO	come off
	come-off
	off-come
CEFFNOO	cone off
CEFFORS	scoffer
CEFFORT	coffret
CEFFSTU	suffect
CEFGILU	Guelfic
CEFGINN	fencing
CEFHIIN	in chief
CEFHIIS	ice fish
CEFHILR	filcher
CEFHILY	chiefly
CEFHIRY	chiefry
CEFHITT	fitchet
CEFHITW	fitchew
CEFHLTU	futchel
CEFHNRY	Frenchy
CEFHPTU	fetch up
CEFIILS	Filices
CEFIILT	fictile
CEFIIOR	orifice
CEFIIRS	Friesic
CEFIITV	fictive
CEFIKLR	flicker
CEFILNT	inflect
CEFILNU	funicle
CEFILRU	lucifer✧
CEFIMRY	mercify
CEFINNO	confine
CEFINOR	conifer
	fir cone
	in force
	inforce
CEFIOOT	ice-foot
CEFIOPR	of price
CEFIPSY	specify
CEFIRSS	sferics
CEFIRTY	certify
	rectify
CEFKLOT	fetlock
CEFKLRY	freckly
CEFLNOU	flounce
CEFLNUY	fluency
CEFMOOR	come for
CEFMORY	comfrey
CEFNOOR	for once
CEFNORU	frounce
CEFNOSS	confess
CEFNOST	confest
CEFNOSU	confuse
CEFNOTU	confute
CEFOPRS	forceps
CEFORRT	crofter
CEFORSS	frescos
CEFORSU	refocus
CEFOSSU	focuses
CEFSSUU	fucuses
CEGGHIR	chigger
CEGGIOR	georgic
CEGGLOR	clogger
CEGGOSY	egg-cosy
CEGHINO	echoing
CEGHINT	etching
CEGHIRS	screigh
CEGHITU	guichet
CEGHNTU	Cheng-tu
CEGHORU	cougher
CEGHRTU	gutcher
CEGIILN	ceiling
	cieling
CEGIKNN	necking
CEGIKNP	pecking
CEGILNR	clinger
	cringle
CEGILNU	lucigen
CEGILNY	glycine
CEGIMNO	genomic
CEGIMNU	mucigen
CEGIMRS	Grecism
CEGINOS	cognise
CEGINOZ	cognize
CEGINRR	cringer
CEGKLNO	genlock
CEGKLOR	grockle
CEGLNOO	cologne✧
CEGLOOY	ecology
CEGLOSU	glucose
CEGLOSY	glycose
CEGNNOO	oncogen
CEGNORU	congrue
CEGNORY	cryogen
CEGNOST	congest
CEGNRUY	urgency
CEGOORS	scrooge✧
CEGORRY	grocery
CEGORSU	scourge
	scrouge
CEHHIRS	cherish
	shriech
CEHHIRT	hitcher
CEHHKOV	Chekhov
CEHHOPT	the chop
CEHHOST	shochet
CEHIIKT	thickie
CEHIILL	ice hill
CEHIILS	chilies
CEHIIMN	chime in
CEHIINR	hircine
CEHIINS	niceish
CEHIINT	ichnite
CEHIIPP	chippie
CEHIIRT	itchier
CEHIJOR	Jericho
CEHIKKT	the kick
CEHIKNT	chetnik
	kitchen
	thicken
CEHIKNW	chewink
CEHIKOO	chookie
CEHIKPS	peckish
CEHIKRS	shicker
	skriech
CEHIKRW	whicker
CEHIKST	chekist
CEHIKTT	thicket
CEHILLR	chiller
CEHILMN	Mechlin
CEHILMY	chimley
CEHILNO	choline
	helicon
CEHILNT	linchet
	tinchel
CEHILPR	pilcher
CEHILRV	chervil
CEHILSV	Chislev
CEHILTY	techily
CEHIMMS	chemism
CEHIMNY	chimney
CEHIMOR	Homeric
	moriche
CEHIMOS	echoism
CEHIMRT	thermic
CEHIMST	chemist
CEHINOP	chopine
	phocine
CEHINOR	chorine
CEHINOT	henotic

CEHINOX	choenix
CEHINPR	nephric
	phrenic
	pincher
CEHINPS	sphenic
CEHINPU	penuchi
CEHINQU	quinche
CEHINRT	cithern
CEHINRW	new rich
	wincher
CEHINST	sthenic
CEHINSU	echinus
CEHINTW	witchen
CEHIOPS	hospice
CEHIOPT	potiche
CEHIORS	heroics
CEHIORT	rotchie
	theoric
CEHIOST	echoist
	toisech
CEHIOSW	ice show
CEHIOTU	couthie
CEHIOTV	Cheviot
CEHIPPR	chipper
CEHIPRR	chirper
CEHIPRS	spheric
CEHIPRT	pitcher
CEHIPST	chipset
CEHIRRT	Richter
CEHIRST	estrich
CEHIRSU	cushier
CEHIRSZ	scherzi
CEHIRTT	chitter
CEHISTU	Cushite
CEHITTY	the city✧
CEHKKRU	chukker
CEHKLMO	hemlock
CEHKNOY	Hockney
CEHKOPU	choke up
CEHKORS	shocker
CEHKORT	the Rock
CEHKPTU	ketchup
CEHKRSU	shucker
CEHKSTY	sketchy
CEHLLMO	mochell
CEHLLMU	muchell
CEHLLNS	schnell
CEHLLOY	yelloch
CEHLMOR	chromel
CEHLMSZ	schmelz
CEHLMUY	chumley
CEHLMWY	wych-elm
CEHLNNU	chunnel✧
CEHLNOT	cholent
	notchel
CEHLNRU	luncher
CEHLNRY	lyncher
CEHLNTY	lynchet
CEHLOOS	schoole
CEHLORT	chortle
CEHLOST	clothes
CEHLOTW	low tech
	low-tech
CEHLPPS	schlepp
CEHLQSU	squelch
CEHLRRU	lurcher
CEHMNRU	muncher
CEHMNUW	new chum
CEHMOOR	moocher
CEHMOOW	how come?
CEHMORU	moucher
CEHMOSS	schmoes
CEHMOTZ	chometz
CEHMRTU	chetrum
CEHNNRU	chunner
CEHNOOP	hen-coop
CEHNOOR	coehorn
CEHNORT	notcher
CEHNORV	chevron
CEHNPRU	puncher
	unperch
CEHNPST	pschent
CEHNRTU	chunter
CEHNSTU	chesnut
CEHNSTY	stenchy
CEHNTUY	chutney
CEHOORS	chooser
	soroche
CEHOORT	cheroot
CEHOOSY	choosey
CEHOPPR	chopper
CEHOPRT	potcher
CEHOPRY	coryphe
CEHORRT	torcher
CEHORSU	choreus
CEHORSY	coshery
CEHORSZ	scherzo
CEHORTU	retouch
	toucher
CEHORTW	wotcher
CEHORUV	voucher
CEHOTUW	chew out
CEHPRTU	putcher
CEHQSTU	quetsch
CEHRRSU	crusher
CEHRSTT	stretch
CEHRSTY	scyther
CEHRTTU	Utrecht
CEIIKLS	siclike
CEIIKNR	ice rink
CEIIKNT	kinetic
CEIIKQU	quickie
CEIIKST	ekistic
	ickiest
CEIILLS	silicle
CEIILNN	incline
CEIILPP	clippie
CEIILPT	pelitic
	tie clip
CEIILSU	Iliescu
CEIILTV	levitic
CEIIMMT	mimetic
CEIIMNR	crimine
CEIIMNS	menisci
CEIIMOT	meiotic
CEIIMPR	empiric
CEIIMPS	epicism
CEIIMRT	Tim Rice
CEIIMSS	seismic
CEIIMST	Semitic
CEIIMTT	titmice
CEIINNO	coniine
	inconie
CEIINNR	cinerin
CEIINOR	oneiric
CEIINOS	iconise
CEIINOV	in voice
	invoice
CEIINOZ	iconize
CEIINPS	piscine
CEIINRS	irenics
	sericin
	sirenic
CEIINRT	citrine
	crinite
	inciter
	neritic
CEIINSS	iciness
CEIINSU	cuisine
CEIINTZ	citizen
	zincite
CEIIOPZ	epizoic
CEIIPPR	piperic
CEIIPRR	pricier
CEIIPRT	picrite
CEIIPST	epicist
CEIIRST	eristic
CEIIRSU	cruisie
CEIISVV	civvies
CEIITUV	uveitic
CEIJLNO	Jocelin
CEIJPUU	juice up
CEIJSTU	justice
CEIKKNN	Kennick
CEIKKNR	knicker
CEIKKSW	Keswick
CEIKLNR	clinker
	crinkle
CEIKLNS	slicken
CEIKLPR	pickler
	prickle
CEIKLPS	pickles
CEIKLRS	slicker
CEIKLRT	tickler
	trickle
CEIKLRW	Lerwick
CEIKLST	stickle
CEIKMRS	smicker
CEIKMRU	muckier
CEIKMRY	mickery
CEIKMST	smicket
CEIKNOT	kenotic
	ketonic
CEIKNPZ	zip-neck
CEIKNQU	quicken
CEIKNRS	snicker
CEIKNST	snicket
CEIKORR	rockier
CEIKORS	Rockies
CEIKOTT	ketotic
CEIKPRR	pricker
CEIKPRT	pricket
CEIKPRY	pickery
CEIKPST	skeptic✧
CEIKRRT	tricker
CEIKRST	rickets
	Sickert
	sticker
CEIKRTU	truckie
CEIKRTY	rickety
CEILLLU	Lucille
CEILLNO	lioncel
CEILLNU	nucelli
CEILLOR	collier
CEILLST	cellist
	'cellist
CEILMOP	compile
	polemic
CEILMPR	crimple
CEILNNU	nuclein
CEILNOP	pinocle
CEILNOS	close in
	close-in
	conseil
	inclose
CEILNOT	lection
CEILNOX	lexicon
CEILNPS	splenic
CEILNST	lentisc
	stencil
CEILNTU	cutline
	tunicle
CEILOOT	Clootie
CEILOPR	peloric
CEILOPT	toeclip
CEILORT	cortile
CEILOSS	loessic
	ossicle
CEILOTT	cole tit
CEILPPR	clipper
	cripple
CEILPRS	splicer
CEILPSU	spicule
CEILPTU	piculet
CEILQUY	cliquey
CEILRRU	curlier
CEILRSV	clivers
CEILRSY	clerisy
CEILRTT	clitter
CEILRTU	utricle
CEILSSS	scissel
CEILSSU	Celsius
CEILSSW	C S Lewis
CEILTTU	cuittle

CEIMMRR crimmer
CEIMNNO meconin
CEIMNOP open-mic
CEIMNOR incomer
CEIMNOS mesonic
CEIMNOT centimo
entomic
Metonic
tonemic
CEIMNRS cremsin
CEIMNRU minceur
numeric
CEIMNSU Mencius
CEIMNYZ enzymic
CEIMOPT metopic
CEIMOQU comique
CEIMORR morrice
CEIMORT mortice
CEIMORW ice worm
CEIMOSU Couéism
CEIMOTT totemic
CEIMOTV vicomte
CEIMOTX toxemic
CEIMPRR crimper
CEIMPRS spermic
CEIMRST cretism
metrics
CEIMRSU murices
CEINNOR Corinne
Neronic
CEINNOV connive
CEINNTV Vincent
CEINOOS Ionesco
CEINOOT coontie
CEINOOZ Neozoic
CEINOPR pericon
porcine
CEINOPT entopic
nepotic
CEINORS crinose
sericon
CEINORT Citroen®
Citroën
rection
CEINORU nourice
CEINORV corvine
cover in
CEINORY oriency
CEINOSS cession
Oscines
CEINOST section
CEINOSW snow-ice
CEINOTT entotic
tonetic
CEINOTX exciton
CEINOUV unvoice
CEINOVV convive
CEINPPR Crippen
CEINPRS pincers
prince's
CEINPRY cyprine
CEINPST inspect
CEINPTY pycnite
CEINRST cistern
CEINRSV crivens
CEINRSW screw in
CEINRTT cittern
CEINRUV incurve
CEINSTY cystine
CEINTTX extinct
CEINVVY vivency
CEIOOPR oporice
CEIOPRS persico
CEIOPST poetics
CEIOPSU piceous
CEIORRS cirrose
crosier
CEIORRU courier
CEIORRZ crozier
CEIORST tercios
CEIORSU scourie
CEIORSV corsive
CEIORSW scowrie
CEIORTT cottier
CEIORTV evictor
CEIORTW co-write
CEIORTX excitor
xerotic
CEIORVY viceroy
CEIOSSV viscose
CEIOSTT cottise
Scottie
CEIOSTU Couéist
CEIOSTV costive
CEIOSTX coexist
CEIOSTY society
CEIPPST peptics
CEIPPSU spice up
CEIPQTU picquet
CEIPRRS crisper
CEIPRST triceps
CEIPRSY spicery
CEIPRTU cuprite
picture
CEIPRTY pyretic
CEIPRXY pyrexic
CEIPSSS scepsis
CEIPSST cesspit
CEIRRRU currier
CEIRRSU cruiser
sucrier
CEIRRTT critter
CEIRRTU recruit
CEIRRTX rectrix
CEIRRUV curvier
CEIRSSU cuisser
CEIRSTT trisect
CEIRSTU icterus
CEIRSUV cursive
CEIRTTX tectrix
CEISSTU ictuses
CEJKNOY jockney✧
CEJLNOY Jocelyn
CEJNOOS cojones
CEJNORU conjure
CEJNOSU juncoes
CEJOPRT project
CEKKLNU knuckle
CEKKNOR knocker
CEKLLOP pellock
CEKLLRY clerkly
CEKLMOR rock elm
CEKLNOS slocken
CEKLNOW Wenlock
CEKLNRU clunker
crunkle
CEKLOSU suck'ole
CEKLPRU plucker
CEKLRSU suckler
CEKLRTU truckle
CEKLRTY Ctrl key
CEKMNOY mockney
CEKMORY mockery
CEKNNSU unsneck
CEKNOOV convoke
CEKNORS conkers
CEKNORT trocken
CEKNPSU sneck up
CEKNRWY wryneck
CEKOOPR precook
CEKOOPW cowpoke
CEKOORY cookery
CEKORRY rockery
CEKORST restock
stocker
CEKOWZZ Wozzeck
CEKPRUY puckery
CEKRRTU trucker
CELLMOU columel
CELLNOO colonel
CELLORS escroll
CELLOSU locules
ocellus
CELLOSY closely
CELLPRU Purcell
CELLRRU cruller
CELLRSU cruells
sculler
CELLRUY cruelly
CELMMSU mesclum
CELMNOO monocle
CELMNSU mesclun
CELMOOR ceòl mór
CELMOOW come low
CELMOPX complex
CELMPRU clumper
crumple
CELMSUU seculum
CELMSUY lyceums
CELNNOU nucleon
CELNOOS close on
colones
console
CELNOSU counsel
unclose
CELNOTU noctule
CELNRTU lecturn
CELNSUU nucleus
CELOOPR precool
CELOORS creosol
CELOOST close to
CELOPRU coupler
CELOPSU close up
close-up
opuscle
upclose
CELOPTU couplet
octuple
CELORST corslet
costrel
CELORSU closure
CELORSW scowler
scrowle
CELORSY scroyle
CELORTT clotter
crottle
CELORTU cloture
clouter
coulter
CELORVY clovery
CELOSSX coxless
CELOSTY cotyles
CELOTTU culotte
CELPRSU scruple
CELPSUY clypeus
CELRSTU cluster
custrel
CELRSTY clyster
CELRTTU clutter
CELRTUU culture
CELRTUV culvert
CELRTUY cruelty
cutlery
CELSTTU scuttle
CEMMNOT comment
CEMMNOU commune
CEMMOOT commote
CEMMOOV commove
CEMMOTU commute
CEMMRSU scummer
CEMNNOO non-come
CEMNNOT contemn
CEMNOOP componé
CEMNOOY economy
CEMNOSU consume
muscone
CEMNRTU centrum
CEMOOPS compose
CEMOOPT compote
CEMOORS Moresco
CEMOOTU come out
outcome
CEMOPRT compter
CEMOPTU compute

CEMOSSU	muscose
CEMOSSY	mycoses
CEMOSTU	costume
CEMPRTU	crumpet
CEMPSTU	stem cup
CEMRRUY	mercury✧
CEMRSTU	rectums
CEMRTYY	my certy
CENNOOT	connote
CENNOST	consent
CENNOTT	content
CENNOTV	convent
CENNRSU	scunner
CENOORR	coroner
	crooner
CENOORT	coronet
CENOPSU	conspue
CENOPSY	syncope
CENOPTU	pouncet
CENOPTY	potency
CENOQRU	conquer
CENORRS	scorner
CENORRW	crowner
CENORRY	rye corn
CENORST	conster
	creston
CENORTT	cornett
CENORTU	cornute
	counter
	recount
	re-count
	trounce
CENORTV	convert
CENORTW	CN Tower
	crownet
CENORUV	uncover
CENOSSY	coyness
CENOSTT	contest
CENOSTU	contuse
CENOTTX	context
CENPRTY	encrypt
CENPTUX	expunct
CENRRTU	current
CENRSTU	encrust
CENRSUU	uncurse
CENRSUW	unscrew
CENRTUY	century
CEOOPRS	scooper
CEOOPRY	coopery
CEOORST	scooter
CEOORTW	crow-toe
CEOOSTY	coyotes
CEOPPRR	cropper
CEOPPRY	coppery
CEOPRRS	scorper
CEOPRRT	porrect
CEOPRRU	crouper
	procure
CEOPRSS	process
CEOPRTT	protect
CEOPRUU	coupure
CEOPRUV	cover up
	cover-up
CEOQRTU	croquet
	rocquet
CEORRSS	crosser
	recross
	scorser
CEORRSU	courser
	cruores
	scourer
CEORRSW	scowrer
CEORRSY	sorcery
CEORRTY	rectory
CEORSSU	courses
	Croesus
	scourse
	Scouser
	sucrose
CEORSTU	rose-cut
	scouter
CEORTUU	couture
CEORTUV	couvert
	cut-over
CEOSTTU	cuttoes
CEPPRRU	crupper
CEPPRSU	scupper
CEPRSSU	percuss
CEPRSSY	cypress
CEPRSTY	sceptry
CEPRSUW	screw up
	screw-up
CEPSSTU	suspect
CEPSTTU	step-cut
CEQRSUU	Quercus
CERSTTU	scutter
CERSTUY	curtesy
	curtsey
CFFHINO	chiffon
CFFHIOP	chip off
CFFIIRT	triffic
CFFIKKO	kick off
	kick-off
CFFIKOP	pick off
	pickoff
CFFIKOT	tick off
CFFKOOO	cook off
CFFLOOO	cool off
CFFMOSU	offscum
CFFOSTU	cut-offs
CFFRSUY	scruffy
CFHILYY	chylify
CFHIMYY	chymify
CFHINSU	fuchsin
CFHIOSW	cowfish
CFHORTU	futhorc
CFIIIMR	mirific
CFIIIVV	vivific
CFIIKNY	finicky
CFIILNT	inflict
CFIIMNO	omnific
CFIINOT	fiction
CFIINOY	iconify
CFIINYZ	zincify
CFIIOSS	ossific
CFIKKLY	fly-kick
CFIKNNO	finnock
CFIKOSS	fossick
CFILORU	fluoric
CFIMNOR	confirm
CFINOSU	in focus
CFIOORT	Corfiot
CFIORSY	scorify
CFIOSTY	Scotify
CFKLLOU	lockful
CFKLOOT	cot-folk
CFKNORU	unfrock
CFKOTTU	futtock
CFLMRUU	fulcrum
CFLNORY	cornfly
CFLNOUX	conflux
CFLNOUY	flouncy
CFLOPRU	cropful
CFLORWY	cry wolf
CFLPSUU	cupfuls
CFMNOOR	conform
CFMNOUY	uncomfy
CFMOORT	comfort
CFNORTU	functor
CFOSSUU	fuscous
CGGGINO	cogging
CGGIINR	gricing
CGGINOS	Scoggin
CGGORSY	scroggy
CGHHNOU	Chungho
CGHIILN	Li Ching
CGHIIMN	miching
CGHIKNU	chi kung
	Kuching
CGHIKOT	Gothick
CGHILOP	log-chip
CGHILPY	glyphic
CGHINNO	chignon
CGHINRU	ruching
CGHIOSY	goyisch
CGHOORT	torgoch
CGHOPUU	cough up
CGHORUY	grouchy
CGIIKKN	kicking
CGIIKLN	licking
CGIIKMM	gimmick
CGIIKNP	picking
CGIIKNT	ticking
CGIIKPS	pig sick
	pig-sick
CGIILLO	illogic
CGIILNS	slicing
CGIIMNN	mincing
CGIINNO	coining
CGIINNW	wincing
CGIINNZ	zincing
CGIINOR	gironic
CGIINOV	voicing
CGIINSS	cissing
CGIKMNO	mocking
CGIKNOR	corking
	rocking
CGIKNOS	socking
CGIKNPU	kingcup
CGIKNSU	sucking
CGILLNO	colling
CGILLNU	culling
CGILNOS	closing
CGILNOW	cowling
CGILNOY	cloying
CGILNRU	curling
CGILORW	cowgirl
CGILOSS	Glossic
CGILOTT	glottic
CGILPTU	giltcup
CGILPTY	glyptic
CGIMNOP	comping
CGINNNO	conning
CGINNNU	cunning
CGINNOS	consign
CGINOPY	copying
CGINORR	corn rig
CGINORS	scoring
CGINORY	gyronic
CGINOST	gnostic✧
CGINOSU	congius
CGINPPU	cupping
CGINPRS	c-spring
CGINRSU	cursing
CGINRSY	scrying
CGINRUV	curving
CGINTTU	cutting
CGIOOOS	giocoso
CGIOTYZ	zygotic
CGKLNOU	gunlock
CGKOOOR	go crook
CGLOOSU	colugos
CGNOUYY	Cy Young
CGOORRW	gorcrow
CGOSTTU	Guscott
CHHIKOR	chikhor
CHHINOR	rhonchi
CHHINTU	unhitch
CHHIPTU	hitch up
CHHIRST	shritch
CHHISTY	ichthys
CHHNOOS	honchos
CHHNPUU	hunch up
CHHRTTU	thrutch
CHIIIST	Shiitic
CHIIKNN	kinchin
CHIIKSS	sickish
CHIILLS	chillis
CHIILOR	oil-rich
CHIIMNS	Mishnic
CHIIMSU	ischium
CHIINNP	inchpin
CHIINNW	winch in
CHIINPT	pitch in

CHIIOPT	ophitic✧
CHIIOST	stichoi
CHIIPST	Pictish
CHIIPSW	Ipswich
CHIJKOS	jockish
CHIKLLO	hillock
CHIKLOP	hip-lock
CHIKLTY	thickly
CHIKNOO	chinook✧
CHIKNTU	thick'un
CHIKORY	hickory
CHIKOST	thickos
CHIKPSU	puckish
CHIKSTY	kitschy
CHILLMU	chillum
CHILLOW	lich-owl
CHILLTY	lichtly
CHILNOU	ulichon
CHILNSY	lychnis
CHILOOS	coolish
CHILOST	coltish
CHILSTU	cultish
CHIMNPY	nymphic
CHIMOPR	morphic
CHIMORS	chorism
	chrisom
CHIMRRY	myrrhic
CHIMSTY	tychism
CHINNSY	in synch
CHINOOR	chorion
CHINOPS	phonics
CHINOPT	to-pinch
CHINORS	Cornish
CHINORT	Corinth
CHINORW	Norwich
CHINOSU	cushion
CHINOTU	inch out
	in touch
CHINOTW	two-inch
CHINPUW	winch up
CHINQSU	squinch
CHINTUW	unwitch
CHINTYZ	chintzy
CHIOOPR	pochoir
CHIOORS	isochor
CHIOORZ	chorizo
CHIOPRT	trophic
CHIOPST	photics
CHIOPXY	hypoxic
CHIORST	chorist
	Christo
	ostrich
CHIOSST	stichos
CHIOSSZ	schizos
CHIPPTU	pitch up
CHIPRRU	chirrup
CHIPRRY	pyrrhic✧
CHIPSSY	physics
CHIQSTU	squitch
CHIRRSU	currish
CHIRSTY	christy✧
CHISTTU	chutist
CHISTWY	switchy
CHITTWY	twitchy
CHKLOOO	hoolock
CHKLOOT	klootch
CHKLOSY	Shylock
CHKMMOO	hommock
CHKMMOU	hummock
CHKMOSY	Chomsky
CHKNOOS	schnook
CHKOOST	schtook
CHKPTUU	putchuk
CHLOOSS	schools
CHLOPST	splotch
CHLORTY	choltry
CHLOSSS	schloss
CHLOSUY	slouchy
CHMOORS	chromos
CHMOOST	schtoom
CHMOOSY	smoochy
CHMOOSZ	schmooz
CHMOOTU	too much
CHMOSUY	chymous
CHNNOOR	chronon
CHNNOSU	nonsuch
CHNOOPS	ponchos
CHNOORT	torchon
CHNOOTU	touch on
CHNOPTU	notch up
CHNORRS	schnorr
CHNORSY	synchro
CHNORTU	cothurn
CHNOTUU	uncouth
CHNPPUU	punch-up
CHNPRUU	churn up
CHOOPPS	copshop
CHOOPST	post hoc
CHOORSU	ochrous
CHOPSSY	psychos
CHOPTUU	touch up
	touch-up
CHORSTU	trochus✧
CHPPSUY	psych up
	psych-up
CHPSSUY	scyphus
CHRRSUU	churrus
CIIILLT	illicit
CIIILNV	incivil
CIIIMNR	crimini
CIIIMRS	Iricism
CIIINPT	incipit
CIIINST	Sinitic
CIIJLUY	juicily
CIIKKLL	killick
CIIKKMS	miskick
CIIKMMM	mimmick
CIIKMNN	minnick
CIIKNPR	prick in
CIIKNPT	nit-pick
CIIKNST	stick in
CIIKNTU	cutikin
CIIKPUW	wickiup
CIIKSTT	stick it
	stickit
CIILLTY	licitly
CIILLVY	civilly
CIILNOP	cipolin
CIILNOS	silicon
CIILNOT	Nilotic
CIILNUV	uncivil
CIILOOT	oolitic
CIILOPT	politic
CIILORT	cortili
CIILOST	colitis
	solicit
CIILPSY	spicily
CIILRTT	lit crit
CIILSSS	scissil
CIIMMRY	mimicry
CIIMNNO	nimonic
CIIMNOT	miction
CIIMOST	mistico
	somitic
CIIMOTT	mitotic
CIIMOTV	motivic
CIINNTU	tunicin
CIINOOT	coition
CIINOPR	porcini
CIINOPS	psionic
CIINORS	incisor
CIINPRS	crispin✧
CIINQTU	quintic
CIINRSU	Ricinus
CIINSTU	Ictinus
CIINTUY	unicity
CIIORST	soritic
CIIOSUV	vicious
CIIPRTY	pyritic
CIIRSTV	vitrics
CIIRTVX	victrix
CIJMORW	jim crow✧
CIJNNOO	conjoin
CIJNNTU	injunct
CIKKLLO	killock
CIKKNNO	Kinnock
CIKKOTU	kick out
CIKLLLU	ill luck
CIKLLOP	pillock
CIKLLOR	rollick
CIKLLOS	sillock
CIKLLOW	killcow
CIKLLSY	slickly
CIKLLUY	luckily
CIKLMOR	rim lock
CIKLMOW	milk-cow
CIKLMSU	misluck
CIKLMSY	smickly
CIKLNRY	crinkly
CIKLOOR	rock oil
CIKLOPZ	ziplock
CIKLORY	rockily
CIKLOST	Lockist
CIKLOWW	Wicklow
CIKLPRY	prickly
CIKLQUY	quickly
CIKLRTY	trickly
CIKLSTU	lustick
CIKMNNO	minnock
CIKMORR	rimrock
CIKNNOP	pinnock
CIKNNOW	winnock
CIKNOST	in stock
CIKNPSU	snick up
CIKNPTU	pin tuck
CIKNSTU	unstick
CIKOOPY	icky poo
CIKOPPT	pockpit
CIKOPST	pot-sick
CIKOPTU	pick out
CIKOSTU	sick-out
CIKOTTU	tick out
CIKOTUW	outwick
CIKPPRU	prick up
CIKPSTU	stick up
	stick-up
CIKRSTY	tricksy
CILLNNO	Lincoln
CILLNOS	collins✧
CILLNOU	cullion
CILLOOR	criollo
CILLOPY	pollicy
CILMNOP	complin✧
CILMOPY	Olympic
CILMSTU	cultism
CILNNOT	Clinton
CILNOOR	corn oil
	orcinol
CILNOOS	cloison
	scolion
CILNOPR	pilcorn
CILNOPS	clip-ons
CILNORY	cornily
	lyricon
CILNOTU	linocut
CILNOXY	xylonic
CILNPRU	pin curl
CILNPSU	insculp
	sculpin
CILNPSY	lip-sync
CILNPTU	unclipt
CILNSTU	linctus
CILOOPT	copilot
	co-pilot
CILOORU	couloir
CILOOSS	colossi
CILOOST	sciolto
CILOPRW	pilcrow
CILOPRY	pyloric
CILOPSW	cowslip
CILOSTU	oculist
CILPRSY	crisply
CILPRTU	culprit
CILRRSU	scurril

Words marked ✧ can also be spelled with one or more capital letters

CILRSTY	St Cyril
CILSTTU	cultist
CIMMOSS	cosmism
CIMMOST	Comtism
CIMNOOR	moronic
	omicron
CIMNORS	crimson
	microns
CIMOORS	morisco✧
CIMOOST	osmotic
CIMOPSY	copyism
	miscopy
CIMOSST	cosmist
	Scotism
CIMOSSY	mycosis
CIMOSTT	Comtist
CIMOTYZ	zymotic
CIMPRSY	scrimpy
CIMRSSU	crissum
CINNNOU	inconnu
CINNORU	unicorn✧
CINNOSU	nuncios
CINNOTU	count in
	unction
CINNSUU	uncinus
CINOOPS	opsonic
CINOORS	coronis
CINOORT	Corinto
CINOPRT	corn pit
CINOPRX	princox
CINORRT	tricorn
CINORSS	incross
CINORST	cistron
	cornist
CINORTT	crottin
CINORTU	ruction
CINOSST	consist
CINOSSU	Oniscus
CINOSTU	suction
CINOSUZ	zincous
CINOTXY	oxyntic
CINRSTU	incrust
CIOOPRS	Scorpio
CIOOPRT	portico
	prootic
CIOOPSU	copious
CIOOQTU	coquito
CIOORSU	corious
CIOPRST	tropics
CIOPRTY	Cypriot
CIOPSTY	copyist
CIOQRSU	croquis
CIORRSU	cirrous
CIORSSS	scissor
CIORSSU	Roscius
CIORSTU	citrous
CIORSUU	curious
CIORTVY	victory✧
CIOSSSY	sycosis
CIOSSTT	Scotist
CIOSSUV	viscous
CIPRSSU	prussic
	Scirpus
CIPRTTY	tryptic
CIPSTTY	styptic
CIRRTTU	crittur
CIRSTUY	citrusy
CIRTUVY	curvity
CISSTUY	cytisus
CJMPTUU	jump-cut
CJNORUY	conjury
CKKLNUY	knuckly
CKKNNOO	knock on
	knock-on
CKKNOPU	knock up
	knock-up
CKLLMOU	mullock
CKLLOOP	pollock✧
CKLLOOR	rollock
CKLLORU	rullock
CKLNOTU	locknut
CKLNOUW	Lucknow
CKLNUUY	unlucky
CKLOOOY	olycook
CKLOOPR	porlock
CKLOORW	rowlock
CKLOOTU	lock out
	lockout
CKLOPTU	pot luck
	putlock
CKLOTUU	luck out
CKLPPUU	pluck up
CKMMMOU	mummock
CKMNOSU	mock sun
CKMOTUU	muck out
CKNOOOS	Cookson
CKNOOTU	conk out
CKNOSTU	unstock
CKNSTUU	unstuck
CKOOOPT	cooktop
CKOOOTU	cookout
CKOOPPS	popsock
CKOORST	Rostock
CKOORSU	sourock
CKOPSTU	stock up
CKOPTTU	puttock
CKORTUW	cutwork
CKOSSTU	tussock
CKOTTUU	tuck-out
CKPSTUU	stuck-up
CLLMOSU	mollusc
CLLOOPS	scollop
CLLOSUU	loculus
CLMOOPT	complot
CLMOPTU	plumcot
CLMOSUU	lucumos
	osculum
CLMPRUY	crumply
CLMSUUU	cumulus
CLNOORT	control
CLNOOSS	consols
CLNOSTU	consult
CLNSTUU	sun cult
CLOOOSU	suo loco
CLOORSU	colours
CLOORUY	coloury
CLOOSTW	low-cost
CLOOSTY	cytosol
CLOPRSU	Proclus
CLORSSY	crossly
CLORSUY	corylus
CLORTUY	courtly
CMMNOOS	commons✧
CMMRSUY	scrummy
CMNOOOT	con moto
	monocot
CMNOOPY	compony
CMNPTUU	punctum
CMOOORS	Comoros
CMOOPRT	comport
CMOOPST	compost
CMOORSU	cormous
CMOOSTY	scotomy
CMOPSSU	cup moss
CMORSTU	scrotum
CMORTUW	cutworm
CMOSSTU	customs
CMOSUVY	Muscovy
CMPRSUY	scrumpy
CNNOORS	Connors
CNNOOTU	count on
CNNORRU	Runcorn
CNNORTU	nocturn
CNNORUW	uncrown
CNOOOTU	Cotonou
CNOOPPR	popcorn
CNOOPRU	croupon
CNOOPRY	Procyon
CNOOPSU	soupçon
CNOORRW	cornrow
CNOORST	consort
CNOORTT	contort
CNOORTU	contour
	cornuto
	croûton
CNOOSST	oncosts
CNOOSUU	nocuous
CNOOTTW	cottown
CNOOTTY	cottony
CNOPRTY	crypton
CNOPSTU	punctos
CNORSSU	uncross
CNORTUY	country
CNRSTUY	scrunty
COOORSZ	corozos
COOPPRT	crop top
COOPRRT	proctor
COOPRTU	crop out
	outcrop
COOPSTU	octopus
COOSTTY	otocyst
COPRRTU	corrupt
COPRSTY	cryptos
COPRSUU	cuprous
CORRSUY	cursory
CORSSTU	scrutos

D

DDDEEHS	shedded
DDDEELS	sledded
DDDEELU	deluded
DDDEEMO	demoded
DDDEERU	uddered
DDDEFLU	fuddled
DDDEHIW	whidded
DDDEHLU	huddled
DDDEHTU	thudded
DDDEIKS	skidded
DDDEILR	diddler
DDDEILT	tiddled
DDDEIMU	muddied
DDDEIOV	Veddoid
DDDEIRU	ruddied
DDDEKNO	Ken Dodd
DDDELOP	plodded
DDDENOS	snodded
DDDEOPR	prodded
DDDEORY	doddery
DDDERUY	duddery
DDDESTU	studded
DDEEEOY	doe-eyed
DDEEEPS	speeded
DDEEERR	red deer
DDEEERS	red seed
DDEEFGL	fledged
DDEEFII	deified
	edified
DDEEFIL	fielded
DDEEFIR	Freddie
DDEEFLU	deedful
DDEEGIS	disedge
DDEEGRR	dredger
DDEEHNU	dudheen
DDEEHRS	shedder
DDEEILR	dreidel
DDEEILS	sleided
DDEEILV	deviled
DDEEILY	deedily
DDEEIMO	Diomede
DDEEIMS	misdeed
DDEEIOV	videoed
DDEEIPS	depside
DDEEIRR	Deirdre
	derider
	ridered
DDEEIRT	red tide
DDEEITY	tie-dyed
DDEELLU	duelled
DDEELLW	dwelled
DDEELMO	modeled
DDEELMR	meddler
DDEELPR	peddler
DDEELRT	treddle
DDEELRU	deluder

DDEENOV	even-odd
	odd-even
DDEENOW	endowed
DDEENRS	Dresden
DDEENSU	duendes
DDEEOTV	devoted
DDEEPRS	spredde
DDEERSS	dressed
DDEERST	reddest
DDEERTU	detrude
DDEERYY	dry-eyed
DDEESTU	Deus det
DDEETTU	duetted
DDEFILR	fiddler
DDEFILY	fiddley
DDEFLOO	flooded
DDEFLRU	fuddler
DDEFNOR	fronded
DDEGGRU	drugged
DDEGILR	girdled
	glidder
	griddle
DDEGIMO	demigod
DDEGINR	grinded
	redding
DDEGINT	tedding
DDEGINW	wedding
DDEGINY	eddying
DDEGIRR	gridder
DDEGLOS	dogsled
	odd legs
DDEGMOS	Dodgems®
DDEGNOO	good-den
DDEGNOS	godsend
DDEGNOU	dudgeon
DDEGNWY	Gwynedd
DDEGORS	gorsedd✧
DDEGORY	dodgery
DDEGOSS	goddess
DDEGRRU	drudger
DDEHIRS	reddish
	shidder
DDEHIRW	whidder
DDEHIRY	hydride
DDEHNRU	hundred
DDEHOST	the dods
DDEHRSU	shudder
DDEHRSY	shreddy
DDEIIKR	kiddier
DDEIIKS	kiddies
DDEIIOX	dioxide
DDEIIRT	dirtied
DDEIIRV	divider
DDEIIST	stiddie
DDEIIVV	divvied
DDEIIZZ	dizzied
DDEIKLO	odd-like
DDEIKNR	kindred
DDEIKRS	skidder
DDEILLO	dollied
DDEILMP	dimpled
DDEILMR	Mildred
DDEILNS	slidden
DDEILNW	dwindle
DDEILOS	dildoes
DDEILOT	deltoid
DDEILPR	piddler
DDEILQU	quiddle
DDEILRR	riddler
DDEILRS	slidder
DDEILRT	tiddler
DDEILTU	Luddite
DDEILTW	twiddle
DDEILTY	lyddite
	tiddley
DDEIMNU	mueddin
DDEIMOR	dermoid
DDEIMOS	desmoid
DDEIMRU	muddier
DDEIMST	middest
DDEIMSU	dedimus
DDEINNU	Dunedin
DDEINOT	dentoid
DDEINOW	die down
DDEINPS	dispend
DDEINRU	undried
DDEINST	distend
DDEINSW	swidden
DDEIOOR	do or die
	do-or-die
DDEIOPR	Proddie
DDEIORT	Diderot
DDEIOTT	dittoed
DDEIPPR	dripped
DDEIPRS	dispred
DDEIRRU	ruddier
DDEISSU	disused
DDEISTU	studied
DDEJRUY	juddery
DDEKMOU	dukedom
DDELMRU	muddler
DDELNOU	noduled
DDELNRU	rundled
DDELOOR	doodler
DDELOOW	woolded
DDELOPR	plodder
DDELORT	toddler
DDELORW	worlded
DDELOTT	dottled
DDELPRU	puddler
DDELSTU	studdle
DDEMMRU	drummed
DDEMMSU	smeddum
DDEMNOS	Desmond
DDEMNOT	oddment
DDENNOR	dendron
	donnerd
DDENOOS	snooded
DDENOPS	despond
DDENOPW	dew-pond
DDENORT	trodden
DDENORU	redound
	rounded
	underdo
DDENORW	wondred
DDENOSS	oddness
DDENSTU	studden
DDEOORU	odoured
DDEOORW	redwood✧
	red-wood
DDEOOWY	dyewood
DDEOPPR	dropped
DDEOPRR	prodder
DDEOPRW	dewdrop
DDFHIOS	odd fish
DDGGINO	dodging
DDGHOOO	godhood
DDGIIKN	kidding
DDGIILY	giddily
DDGIINR	ridding
DDGILOS	god's lid
DDGILOW	wild dog
DDGINNO	nodding
DDGINOP	podding
DDGINOR	rodding
DDGINPU	pudding
DDGIPUY	giddy-up
DDGLLOO	old gold
DDGOOOW	dogwood
DDHIISY	Yiddish
DDHIKSU	kiddush
DDHIORY	hydroid
DDHOOWY	howdy-do
DDHORSY	dry-shod
DDIIKLS	skid lid
DDIIKNY	dinky-di
DDIILOP	diploid
DDIIQTU	quiddit
DDILMSU	Luddism
DDILMUY	muddily
DDILOSY	dysodil
DDILOWY	dowdily
DDILRUY	ruddily
DDILTWY	twiddly
DDINOST	snoddit
DDIOOSS	dosi-dos
DDIORTU	turdoid
DDIPRRY	drip-dry
DDLLMOO	dolldom
DDMNOOR	dromond
DDORSTY	drostdy
DEEEEHT	tee-heed
DEEEEWW	wee-weed
DEEEFNS	defense
DEEEFPT	deep-fet
DEEEFRV	fevered
DEEEGLP	pledgee
DEEEGLR	de règle
DEEEGMR	demerge
DEEEGRR	regrede
DEEEGRT	deterge
	greeted
DEEEHLW	wheedle
	wheeled
DEEEHST	seethed
	sheeted
DEEEHTW	the weed
DEEEILS	lee side
DEEEILT	lee tide
DEEEIPY	pie-eyed
DEEEIRR	reedier
DEEEIRS	Désirée
DEEEISV	devisee
DEEEIYZ	Yezidee
DEEEIZZ	Zezidee
DEEEJNU	dejeune
DEEEKLN	kneeled
DEEEKNW	weekend
DEEELMS	meseled
DEEELNR	needler
DEEELPT	deplete
DEEELRT	deerlet
DEEELST	steeled
DEEELSV	sleeved
DEEELTW	tweedle
DEEEMNS	demesne
DEEEMRS	demerse
	emersed
DEEEMRT	Demeter
DEEENNV	end even
DEEENOY	one-eyed
DEEENTT	détente
DEEENTU	détenue
DEEENUV	Deneuve
DEEEORR	roe deer
DEEEORW	oreweed
DEEEOTV	devotee
DEEEPRS	speeder
DEEEPRU	éperdue
DEEEPST	deep-set
DEEERSV	deserve
DEEERSW	sweered
DEEERWY	weedery
DEEETTV	vedette
DEEFFFO	feed off
DEEFFIN	effendi
DEEFFLS	self-fed
DEEFGIN	feeding
	feigned
DEEFGIP	pigfeed
DEEFHLS	fleshed
DEEFHLU	heedful
DEEFIIR	deifier
	edifier
	reified
DEEFIKN	ink-feed
DEEFILN	Enfield
	enfiled
DEEFILR	defiler
	fielder
DEEFIMS	misfeed
DEEFINR	definer
	refined
DEEFIRR	ferried

refried
DEEFIRY re-edify
DEEFIRZ friezed
DEEFLLU fuelled
DEEFLLW well-fed
DEEFLNS self-end
DEEFLNU needful
DEEFLOT feedlot
DEEFLRY deer fly
DEEFMOR freedom
DEEFNOR fore-end
DEEFNRU unfreed
DEEFNUU unfeued
DEEFORV overfed
DEEFPRY deep-fry
DEEFRTT fretted
DEEGHIW weighed
DEEGHOR hog-deer
DEEGHOW hogweed
DEEGHSS ghessed
DEEGILR leidger
DEEGILS leg side
legside
DEEGINN engined
DEEGINR energid
reeding
DEEGINS sdeigne
seeding
DEEGINW weeding
DEEGIOR Geordie
DEEGIPR pig-deer
DEEGIPW pigweed
DEEGIPY pig-eyed
DEEGIRV diverge
DEEGJRU rejudge
DEEGLNR Grendel
DEEGLOY goldeye
DEEGLPR pledger
DEEGLPT pledget
DEEGLRS sledger
DEEGNNO endogen
DEEGNOO good-e'en
DEEGOSY geodesy
DEEGOTU edge out
outedge
DEEHIKV khedive✧
DEEHILT lethied
DEEHJNO John Dee
DEEHJUY Hey Jude
DEEHKLW whelked
DEEHLLS shelled
DEEHLOV hoveled
DEEHMRU rheumed
DEEHNOT hen-toed
DEEHNOY honeyed
DEEHNPR prehend
DEEHNTU the nude
DEEHNUY unheedy
DEEHPRS sphered
DEEHRSS herdess
DEEHTTW whetted
DEEIINS sine die
DEEIINT dietine
DEEIIPR epeirid
DEEIIRW weirdie
DEEIJLL jellied
DEEIJMM jemmied
DEEIJTT jettied
DEEIKLL killdee
DEEIKLN kneidel
DEEIKMW mid-week✧
DEEIKNN in-kneed
DEEIKOV dovekie
DEEILNR red line
red-line
DEEILNS linseed
DEEILNV delve in
DEEILNW DEW line
DEEILNY dyeline
needily
DEEILOS oilseed
seed-oil
DEEILPP lip-deep
DEEILPR replied
DEEILPS seedlip
DEEILRT let ride
tile-red
DEEILRV deliver
DEEILRW wielder
DEEILRY reedily
yielder
DEEILSS idlesse
DEEILST til seed
DEEILSY seedily
DEEILTU dilutee
DEEILTV devilet
DEEIMMS misdeem
DEEIMNO dominee
DEEIMNR ermined
DEEIMNS desmine
sidemen
DEEIMNT démenti
DEEIMPR demirep
per diem
DEEIMPS semiped
DEEIMPT emptied
DEEIMRT demerit
dimeter
DEEIMTT emitted
DEEINNP pennied
DEEINNT dentine
DEEINNU ennuied
DEEINNZ denizen
DEEINOR ordinee
DEEINPR red pine
DEEINPY pin-eyed
DEEINRR dernier
DEEINRS nereids✧
DEEINRU uredine
DEEINRW red wine
widener
DEEINRX indexer
DEEINST destine
DEEINSW endwise
sinewed
DEEINSX indexes
DEEINTT dinette
DEEINTU detinue
DEEINTV evident
DEEINVW vinewed
DEEINVX invexed
DEEINWZ wizened
DEEIOPS episode
DEEIOPT epidote
DEEIOPX epoxide
epoxied
DEEIORS osiered
DEEIPPT peptide
DEEIPRS Perseid
preside
DEEIPRV deprive
DEEIPRX expired
DEEIPSS despise
pedesis
DEEIPST despite
DEEIPSX deep-six
DEEIQRU queried
DEEIRRS desirer
resider
serried
DEEIRRT retired
retried
DEEIRRV redrive
rivered
DEEIRSU residue
DEEIRSV deviser
diverse
DEEIRTU erudite
DEEIRTV riveted
verdite
DEEISSU diseuse
DEEISVZ Devizes
DEEITTV vidette
DEEKKLR De Klerk
DEEKKRT trekked
DEEKKSY key-desk
DEEKLRS skelder
DEEKNNY Kennedy
DEEKOTU deke out
DEEKPPS skepped
DEEKPRU peruked
DEELLMS smelled
DEELLPS spelled
DEELLRU dueller
DEELLRW dweller
DEELLRY elderly
DEELLST stelled
DEELLSW swelled
DEELMNO Mole End
DEELMOR modeler
remodel
DEELMPT templed
DEELMPU deplume
DEELMTT mettled
DEELNOS nose-led
DEELNRS slender
DEELNSS endless
DEELNSY densely
DEELOPR deplore
DEELOPV develop
DEELOPX explode
DEELORU Lou Reed
urodele
DEELORV lovered
DEELOSU delouse
DEELOTV dovelet
DEELOTW toweled
DEELOVV devolve
DEELOWY owl-eyed
DEELPRS spelder
DEELPRU prelude
DEELSTT settled
DEELSTW swelted
DEELVXY vexedly
DEEMMST stemmed
DEEMNOR moderne
DEEMNOV venomed
DEEMNOY moneyed
DEEMNTU unmeted
DEEMORS emerods
DEEMORV removed
DEEMORX exoderm
DEEMOSS Ed Moses
DEENNOP open-end
DEENNOR enderon
DEENNOS données
DEENNOT endnote
DEENNOY doyenne
DEENNOZ endzone
DEENNPT pendent
DEENNTZ tendenz
DEENNUY ennuyed
DEENOPS spondee
DEENOPT pentode
DEENORS endorse
DEENORT erodent
DEENORW endower
re-endow
DEENPPR perpend
DEENPRS spender
DEENPRT pretend
DEENRRU endurer
DEENRSS redness
DEENRSU end-user
DEENRTU denture
tenured
DEENSTW West End
DEENSUW unsewed
DEENSUX unsexed
DEENUVX unvexed
DEEOPPW pop-weed
DEEOPPY pop-eyed
DEEOPRR pedrero
DEEOPRS deposer

	reposed
DEEOPRW	powered
DEEOPRY	eye-drop
DEEOPSS	speedos
DEEOPSX	exposed
DEEOPTU	toupeed
DEEOPTW	two deep
DEEORRR	orderer
	reorder
DEEORRS	Red Rose
	reredos
	rose-red
DEEORRV	overred
DEEORST	oersted
	teredos
DEEORTT	tetrode
DEEORTW	towered
DEEORUV	overdue
DEEORVY	overdye
DEEOTUW	outweed
	weed out
DEEOTWY	two-eyed
DEEPPPR	prepped
DEEPPST	stepped
DEEPPSU	speed up
	speed-up
DEEPRRU	perdure
	Peredur
DEEPRSS	depress
	pressed
	spersed
DEEPRTU	reputed
DEEPSTU	steed up
DEEPSUX	sexed-up
DEERRSS	dresser
	redress
	re-dress
DEERRUV	verdure
DEERSST	dessert
	tressed
DEERSSU	duresse
DEERSTW	strewed
DEERSTY	dyester
DEERTUX	extrude
DEESTTT	stetted
DEFFIMO	fiefdom
DEFFINO	dine off
DEFFIOR	ride off
DEFFIOS	offside
DEFFISU	diffuse
DEFFLLU	full-fed
DEFFLMU	muffled
DEFFLRU	ruffled
DEFFNOR	forfend
DEFFNOS	send off
	send-off
DEFFOOZ	doze off
DEFFOPU	pouffed
DEFFSTU	stuffed
DEFGGLO	flogged
DEFGGOR	frogged
DEFGHHI	high-fed
DEFGINR	fringed
DEFGINU	feuding
DEFGINY	defying
DEFGIOR	firedog
DEFGIRU	figured
DEFGIST	fidgets
DEFGITY	fidgety
DEFGORY	Godfrey
DEFGRTU	grufted
DEFHIRS	redfish
DEFHIST	shifted
DEFHLOO	elfhood
DEFHLSU	flushed
DEFIILN	infidel
	infield
DEFIILO	Fidelio
DEFIIMS	fideism
DEFIIMW	midwife
DEFIINU	unified
DEFIIST	fideist
DEFIKRR	Fredrik
DEFILNR	flinder
DEFILNU	unfilde
	unfiled
DEFILOO	folioed
DEFILOS	od's life
DEFILOW	old wife
DEFILPU	upfield
DEFILRU	direful
DEFILRW	Wilfred
DEFILST	stifled
DEFILSU	sulfide
DEFILTT	flitted
DEFILXY	fixedly
DEFIMOR	deiform
DEFINOT	fin-toed
DEFINRU	unfired
DEFINSY	densify
DEFINTX	FT Index
DEFINUX	unfixed
DEFINUY	undeify
DEFIORU	foudrie
DEFIPRY	perfidy
DEFIRRT	drifter
DEFIRTT	fritted
DEFIRTU	fruited
DEFIRZZ	frizzed
DEFISTU	feudist
DEFLLOU	doleful
DEFLLUW	dewfull
DEFLNOO	onefold
DEFLNOP	penfold
DEFLNOR	fondler
	forlend
DEFLNOT	tenfold
DEFLNRU	dernful
DEFLOOR	floored
DEFLORT	Telford
DEFLORU	foulder
	fuel rod
DEFLPRU	purfled
DEFLRUU	dureful
DEFMNUU	unfumed
DEFMORS	serfdom
DEFMPRU	rump-fed
DEFNOOR	fordone
DEFNORS	send for
DEFNORT	fronted
DEFNORU	founder
	refound
DEFNOSW	snow-fed
DEFORST	defrost
	frosted
DEFORWX	Wexford
DEFRSUY	Dreyfus
DEFTUUY	feu-duty
DEGGGLO	goggled
DEGGGLU	glugged
DEGGGOO	good egg
DEGGHIN	hedging
DEGGHIW	whigged
DEGGHOS	shogged
DEGGILN	gelding
DEGGILU	Gielgud
DEGGINW	wedging
	wind egg
DEGGIPR	prigged
DEGGIRT	trigged
DEGGIRU	druggie
DEGGISW	swigged
DEGGITW	twigged
DEGGJLO	joggled
DEGGLOR	doggrel
DEGGLOS	slogged
DEGGLPU	plugged
	puggled
DEGGNOO	doggone
DEGGNOU	gudgeon
DEGGNSU	snugged
DEGGORT	trogged
DEGGORY	doggery
DEGGOSS	doggess
DEGGRRU	drugger
DEGGRTU	drugget
DEGHHIN	high-end
DEGHILN	hindleg
DEGHILT	delight
	lighted
DEGHINT	nighted
DEGHIPR	pig-herd
DEGHIST	sighted
DEGHLOO	doghole
DEGHLOT	get hold
DEGHNOT	thonged
DEGHOOT	the good
DEGHORR	drogher
DEGHOST	the gods
DEGIILN	eilding
DEGIIMN	Geminid
DEGIKLO	godlike
DEGIKNS	desking
DEGILLR	grilled
DEGILLU	gullied
DEGILLY	gelidly
DEGILNN	lending
DEGILNO	glenoid
DEGILNU	indulge
DEGILNV	devling
DEGILNW	welding
	wing-led
DEGILOR	gloried
	godlier
DEGILOV	go-devil
DEGILRR	girdler
DEGILRS	grisled
DEGILRU	guilder
DEGILRW	wergild
DEGILUV	divulge
DEGIMNN	mending
DEGIMNS	smidgen
DEGINNP	pending
DEGINNR	grinned
DEGINNS	sending
DEGINNY	denying
DEGINOP	pidgeon
DEGINOR	Dorigen
	groined
	negroid✧
DEGINOS	dingoes
DEGINOW	wendigo
	widgeon
	wongied
DEGINRR	grinder
	regrind
DEGINRW	redwing
	wringed
DEGINST	stinged
DEGINSW	swindge
DEGIOOS	goodies
DEGIORR	grodier
DEGIORT	goitred
DEGIPPR	gripped
DEGIQSU	squidge
DEGIRSS	digress
DEGISST	disgest
DEGJLNU	jungled
DEGLMMO	glommed
DEGLMOU	moguled
DEGLNNO	endlong
DEGLNUU	unglued
	unguled
DEGLOPR	leg drop
	pledgor
DEGLOPS	splodge
DEGLOSS	godless
DEGLTTU	glutted
DEGMRSU	smudger
DEGNNOU	dungeon
DEGNOPR	pronged
DEGNOPW	peg down
DEGNORU	go under
	guerdon

undergo
ungored
DEGNOSU gude-son
DEGNOTU tongued
DEGNOTW get down
DEGNRTU trudgen
DEGNRUU unurged
DEGNUVY ungyved
DEGOORS dog rose
DEGOORV grooved
DEGORRS Rodgers
DEGORST stodger
DEGORTU droguet
DEGORWY gory dew
DEGRRTU trudger
DEHHIIV Dhivehi
DEHIIPS piedish
DEHILMS dishelm
DEHILNP delphin
DEHILOT lithoed
DEHILTY diethyl
DEHIMMW whimmed
DEHIMOR heirdom
Homerid
DEHIMOS dishome
DEHIMOT ethmoid
DEHINNT thinned
DEHINOP diphone
DEHINOR hordein
DEHINPS endship
DEHINPT in depth
in-depth
DEHINRS nerdish
DEHINRU unhired
DEHINRX Hendrix
DEHINSW Wendish
DEHIORT theroid
DEHIOSU hideous
DEHIOSV doveish
DEHIOTU hideout
DEHIOTV the void
DEHIPPS shipped
DEHIPPW whipped
DEHIRRS shirred
DEHIRRU dhurrie
hurried
DEHIRRW whirred
DEHIRSU hurdies
Rushdie
DEHIRSV dervish✧
shrived
DEHIRTV thrived
DEHIRTY dithery
DEHISSW Swedish
DEHIWZZ whizzed
DEHJNOO John Doe
DEHLMOU mudhole
DEHLOOT toehold
DEHLORW whorled
DEHLORY dry hole
DEHLOSS sloshed
DEHLRRU hurdler
DEHLRSU hurdles
DEHMORU Hordeum
DEHMOTY Methody
DEHNNSU shunned
DEHNOOW hoedown
DEHNOPU unhoped
DEHNORT thonder
thorned
throned
DEHNOTZ dozenth
DEHNRTU thunder
DEHOOTT toothed
DEHOPPS shopped
DEHOPPW whopped
DEHORTW the Word
DEHOSTT shotted
DEHOSTW wet-shod
DEHPPUW whupped
DEHPPUY hyped up
hyped-up
DEHSTTU the dust
DEIIIRS iridise
DEIIIRZ iridize
DEIIKLS dislike
DEIIKNS dinkies
DEIILMP implied
DEIILMT delimit
limited
DEIILNV lived-in
DEIILOS idolise
DEIILOZ idolize
DEIIMNO dominie
DEIIMST misdiet
DEIIMSZ midsize
DEIIMVW midwive
DEIINOS Sidonie
DEIINOT edition
tenioid
DEIINRS insider
DEIINRT inditer
nitride
DEIINRU uridine
DEIINRV diviner
drive-in
DEIINSS insides
DEIINSW Windies
DEIIORS Isidore
DEIIORT diorite
DEIIORV ivoried
DEIIOSX oxidise
DEIIOXZ oxidize
DEIIPPP dip-pipe
DEIIPRT dirt-pie
riptide
tide rip
DEIIRTT tritide
DEIISTT dietist
tidiest
DEIJLST De Stijl
DEIJNOR joinder
DEIJNOT jointed
DEIJNSU disjune
DEIJORY joyride
DEIKLLS deskill
skilled
DEIKLNR kindler
DEIKLOR rodlike
DEIKLRT kirtled
DEIKMMS skimmed
DEIKMOR red moki
DEIKNNS skinned
DEIKNOS doeskin
DEIKNRR drinker
DEIKNSW swinked
DEIKNTT knitted
DEIKORW die-work
DEIKOSY disyoke
DEIKPPS skipped
DEIKRST skirted
DEIKSVY skydive
DEILLMO modelli
DEILLNO old-line
DEILLNW indwell
DEILLOR dollier
DEILLOV livelod
DEILLPS spilled
DEILLQU quilled
DEILLRR driller
DEILLRT trilled
DEILLRV drevill
DEILLSS lidless
DEILLSU ill-used
sullied
DEILLTW twilled
DEILMMS slimmed
DEILMNO Mindelo
DEILMNT mid-Lent
DEILMNU unlimed
DEILMOP implode
DEILMOT old-time
DEILMOY myeloid
DEILMPP pimpled
DEILMWY mildewy
DEILMXY mixedly
DEILNNU unlined
DEILNOO eidolon
DEILNOS sondeli
DEILNOT lentoid
DEILNOU unoiled
DEILNOW lie down
lie-down
DEILNPS speldin
spindle
DEILNRT tendril
trindle
DEILNSW swindle
DEILNSY Lindsey
snidely
DEILNTU diluent
untiled
DEILNTW indwelt
DEILOPP Pelopid
DEILOPS despoil
soliped
spoiled
DEILORS soldier
DEILOTW low tide
DEILPPS slipped
DEILPPU uppiled
DEILPRU preludi
DEILPSU Lepidus
DEILPTY tepidly
DEILPXY pixy-led
DEILQTU quilted
DEILRRV L-driver
DEILRTU diluter
DEILRTY tiredly
DEILRVY devilry
DEILRWY weirdly
DEILRWZ wrizled
DEILRZZ drizzle
DEILSTT stilted
DEILSTY distyle
DEIMMMU mummied
DEIMMPR primmed
DEIMMRT midterm
trimmed
DEIMMST dimmest
DEIMMSU mediums
DEIMNNU minuend
DEIMNOS misdone
DEIMNRU unrimed
DEIMNSS dimness
missend
DEIMNST mindset
DEIMNSW miswend
DEIMNUX unmixed
DEIMOOR moidore
moodier
DEIMORS misdoer
DEIMORU erodium
DEIMOST modiste
DEIMOTT omitted
DEIMOTV vomited
DEIMPRT dirempt
DEIMPUX mixed-up
DEIMRUU uredium
DEIMSTW Midwest
DEIMSTY stymied
DEINNNU nundine
DEINNOP pinnoed
DEINNOR endiron
DEINNOS dies non
DEINNTU dunnite
DEINNTW twinned
DEINOOZ ozonide
DEINOPR poinder
DEINOPS dispone
spinode
DEINOPT pointed
DEINORR in order
iron-red

DEINORS indorse
rosined
DEINORU dourine
DEINORV on drive
on-drive
vine-rod
DEINORW windore
DEINOST stonied
DEINOTU dine out
DEINOTW tie down
DEINPPS snipped
DEINPST stipend
DEINPSU unspide
unspied
DEINPSV pensiv'd
DEINPUW unwiped
DEINRSU insured
DEINRTT trident✧
DEINRTU intrude
turdine
untired
untride
untried
DEINRTX dextrin
DEINRTY tindery
DEINSST disnest
dissent
St Denis
DEINSSV vendiss
DEINSTT dentist
distent
stinted
DEINSTU distune
DEINSTW St Edwin
DEINSTY density
destiny
DEINSUZ unsized
DEINUVW unwived
DEIOORS Isodore
DEIOOST osteoid
DEIOOVV voivode
DEIOOWW woiwode
DEIOPPP poppied
DEIOPRS periods
DEIOPRT diopter
dioptre
peridot
proteid
DEIOPRV provide
DEIOPSS dispose
DEIOPST deposit
posited
topside
DEIOPSU Oedipus
opus Dei✧
DEIOPSV vespoid
DEIOPTT tiptoed
DEIOPTV pivoted
DEIORRW worried
DEIORSS dossier
DEIORST steroid
storied
DEIORSV devisor
devoirs
visored
DEIORSW weirdos
DEIORTT Detroit
DEIORTU étourdi
ioduret
outride
ride out
DEIORVZ vizored
DEIORWW widower
DEIOSTU outside
tedious
DEIOSTX exodist
DEIOSUV devious
DEIOTTU edit out
DEIPPRT tripped
DEIPRSS Spiders
DEIPRST striped
DEIPRSY spidery
DEIPRUW wired up
DEIPSSU upsides
DEIPSTT spitted
DEIPSTU dispute
DEIPSXY pyxides
DEIPTTU puttied
tituped
DEIQTTU quitted
DEIQUZZ quizzed
DEIRRST stirred
strider
DEIRSST dissert
strides
DEIRSTU studier
DEIRSTV strived
DEISSTU studies
DEISTTW twisted
DEITTTW twitted
DEJMOUZ Judezmo
DEKLNRU knurled
DEKLRSU skudler
DEKNNRU drunken
DEKNOST Donetsk
DEKNOSY donkeys
DEKNOTT knotted
DEKNOUY unyoked
DEKNRTU trunked
DEKOPST desktop
DEKORWY dye-work
keyword
DELLMOO modello
DELLOOP Leopold
DELLOOW woolled
DELLOPR redpoll
DELLOSU duellos
DELLOVW lowveld✧
DELMOOW elmwood
DELMORS smolder
DELMORU moulder
remould
DELMOTT mottled
DELMOUV volumed
DELMPRU rumpled
DELNORT entrold
DELNORU lounder
roundel
roundle
DELNORY Reynold
DELNOSS oldness
DELNOTW let down
let-down
DELNOTY notedly
DELNOUV unloved
DELNOWY dowlney
DELNPRU plunder
DELNRTU rundlet
trundle
DELNRUU unruled
DELNSSU dulness
DELNUWY unweldy
DELOOPP pleopod
DELOORS Dolores
old rose
DELOORW woolder
DELOORX Rolodex®
DELOOST Toledos
DELOOTU dole out
DELOPPP plopped
DELOPPR dropple
DELOPPS slopped
DELOPRT droplet
let drop
DELOPRU poulder
pouldre
DELOPTT plotted
DELOPUV loved up
DELORRY orderly
DELORSS rodless
DELORST oldster
strodle
DELORTT dottrel
DELORUV louvred
DELOSTT slotted
DELOSTU tousled
DELOSZZ sozzled
DELOTUV voluted
DELPSSU plussed
DELRRSU slurred
DELRSTU strudel
DEMMRRU drummer
DEMMSTU stummed
DEMNOOR morendo
DEMNORT mordent
DEMNORY demonry
DEMNOST endmost
DEMNOTU demount
mounted
DEMNOUV unmoved
DEMNPRU rump-end
DEMOOPP popedom
DEMOOPR predoom
DEMOOTT mottoed
DEMOOTU outmode
DEMORWW dew worm
DEMOSTY modesty
DEMPSTU stumped
DEMSTTU smutted
DENNOOR drone on
DENNORT donnert
tendron
DENNORU enround
DENNOTU unnoted
untoned
DENNOTW town end
DENNOUW unowned
DENNOUZ unzoned
DENNSTU stunned
DENNTUU untuned
DENOORR on order
DENOOST stooden
DENOOSW swooned
DENOOTU duotone
DENOOUW unwooed
DENOPPR propend
DENOPRS respond
DENOPRT drop-net
portend
protend
DENOPRU pounder
DENOPRV provend
DENOPSU unposed
DENOPUX expound
DENORRU rondure
rounder
unorder
DENORRW drowner
DENORSU resound
re-sound
sounder
DENORSW red snow
DENORUW rewound
wounder
DENOSTU send out
snouted
DENOSTW set down
set-down
DENPRTU prudent
prunted
uptrend
DENPSSU suspend
DENRSSU undress
DENRSSY dryness
DENRSUU unsured
DENSTTU student
stunted
DENTUVY duvetyn
DEOOPRT torpedo
DEOOPST stooped
DEOORRT redroot
to order
DEOORRW o'erword
DEOPPPR propped

Words marked ✧ can also be spelled with one or more capital letters

DEOPPRR dropper
DEOPPST stopped
DEOPPSW swopped
DEOPRWY powdery
DEOPSTT spotted
DEOQRTU torqued
DEORRST rodster
DEORRSW sworder
DEORSTW strowed
worsted
DEORSTY destroy
DEORTTT trotted
DEORTUU outdure
DEOSSTW dowsets
DEOSSYY odyssey✧
DEOSTTU duettos
testudo✧
DEOSTTW swotted
DEOSTUU duteous
DEOSTUX tuxedos
DEPRRSU spurred
DEPRRUY prudery
DEPRSSU dress up
DEPRSUU usurped
DERRSTU rustred
DERSSTU trussed
DERSTUU sutured
DFFGINU duffing
DFFHLOO hold off
DFFIIMR midriff
DFFIIRT triffid
DFFIMOR difform
DFFLLOO doll off
DFFLOOU foodful
DFFOOPR drop off
drop-off
DFFOTUY off duty
off-duty
DFGHIOS dogfish
fish-god
DFGIINN finding
DFGIINY dignify
DFGILNO folding
DFGILOP flip-dog
DFGINNU funding
DFGINOU fungoid
DFGLNUY dung-fly
DFGLOOW wolf dog
wolf-dog
DFGLOOY old fogy
DFGMOOY fogydom
DFGOOOR for good
DFHILSU dishful
DFHIMSU mudfish
DFHINSU dun-fish
DFIIKNR Rifkind
DFIILRW Wilfrid
DFILMMO filmdom
DFILMNU mindful
DFILNOP pinfold
DFILOSX sixfold

DFILOTW twifold
DFILTUU dutiful
DFIMNUY mundify
DFIMOOS foodism
DFIMORS disform
DFINNSU in funds
DFINOTU find out
DFIOORW firwood
DFIRSTY dry-fist
DFLMOOU doomful
DFLMOUW mudflow
DFLOOTU foldout
DFLOOTW twofold
DFLOPRY dropfly
DFLOTWY twyfold
DFNNOUU unfound
DFNORUY foundry
DFOOOTU do out of
DFOORTY dry-foot
DGGGIIN digging
DGGGINO dogging
DGGHIOS doggish
DGGIILN gilding
gliding
DGGIINR girding
ridging
DGGIINU guiding✧
DGGIKNO god-king
DGGILNO godling
lodging
DGGNORU ungorg'd
DGHHOOO hoghood
DGHIILN hidling
hilding
DGHIINS dishing
shindig
DGHILNO holding
DGHILNY hylding
DGHILOS goldish
DGHILPY diglyph
DGHINTU hind-gut
undight
DGHIOOS goodish
DGHIOPS dogship
godship
DGHORTU drought
DGHOTUY doughty
DGIIKLN kidling
DGIILLN dilling
DGIILNS sliding
DGIILNW wilding
DGIILRY rigidly
DGIIMMN dimming
DGIIMNN minding
DGIIMNS smidgin
DGIIMOP pigmoid
DGIIMOS sigmoid
DGIINNN dinning
DGIINNW winding
DGIINOS indigos
DGIINOV voiding

DGIINOW windigo
DGIINOX digoxin
DGIINPP dipping
DGIINPU pinguid
DGIINRV driving
DGIINST tidings
DGIINTY dignity
tidying
DGIIORT tigroid
DGIKLNO gold ink
DGIKMNO kingdom
DGIKNNO Don King
DGIKNOR Dorking
king-rod
DGIKNOS dogskin
DGILLOR old girl
DGILLOY godlily
DGILNOR girlond
lording
DGILNYY dyingly
DGILOOO good oil
DGILRUY guildry
DGIMNOO Domingo
dooming
DGIMOPY pygmoid
DGINNNO donning
DGINNNU dunning
DGINNOU undoing
DGINNUW windgun
DGINNUY undying
DGINOOT dog on it
DGINOPP dopping
DGINORV droving
DGINORW wording
DGINOSW disgown
DGINOTT dotting
DGIOPRY prodigy
DGIORSU Gordius
DGIQSUY squidgy
DGISSTU disgust
DGLNOOS old song
DGLNOUY ungodly
DGLOOOW logwood
DGLOORW grow old
DGLOOST God slot
DGLOPSY splodgy
DGLOSYY dyslogy
DGMNOOO moon god
DGMOPRU gumdrop
DGMORUU gurudom
DGNNOUW gun down
DGNOOOR godroon
DGNOOOS good-son
DGNOOOW good-now
DGNOORS drongos
DGNOORU go round
DGNOORW do wrong
DGNOOTW dogtown
DGNORSU grounds
DGOORTT dogtrot
DGOPRRU prodrug

DHIIKWZ whiz kid
DHIILNS hidlins
DHIILOT lithoid
DHIILSW wildish
DHIIMMS dimmish
DHIIMNO hominid
DHIIMPS midship
DHIINRU hirudin
DHIIOPX xiphoid
DHIIORZ rhizoid
DHIIOST histoid
DHIKORS dorkish
DHIKRSU Kurdish
DHIKSSU duskish
DHILLOS dollish
DHILLSU dullish
DHILMUY humidly
DHILNOP dolphin✧
DHILOST doltish
DHILOSU loudish
DHILPSU ludship
DHILPSY sylphid
DHILRTY thirdly
DHIMOPR dimorph
DHIMORS shim rod
DHIMORU humidor
mid-hour
rhodium
DHIMPSU dumpish
DHINNOS donnish
DHINNSU dunnish
DHINOPS donship
DHINOPY hypnoid
DHINORS dishorn
dronish
DHINSTU tun-dish
DHIOPTY typhoid
DHIORSW wordish
DHIORTY thyroid
DHIOSTU dish out
DHIPRSU prudish
DHIPRSY syrphid
DHJNNOO Don John
DHJOPRU Jodhpur
DHKMOOU mudhook
DHKORSY droshky
DHLMOOU hoodlum
DHLOOTU hold out
holdout
DHLOPRU Rudolph
DHLOPSU hold-ups
DHMMRUU humdrum
DHMNOYY hymnody
DHNNOOU nunhood
DHNNSUU unshun'd
DHOOPRU uphoord
DHOORSU rhodous
DHOORTT hot trod
hot-trod
DHOORTY Dorothy
DHOPRSU pushrod

DHORSSU	shrouds
DHORSUY	hydrous
	shroudy
DHORTUY	drouthy
DHORXYY	hydroxy
DIIIMRU	iridium
DIIIMSV	divisim
DIIINPS	insipid
DIIJNOS	disjoin
DIIKKNS	kidskin
DIIKLNS	dislink
DIIKNNR	drink in
	in drink
DIIKNOT	doitkin
DIIKPSZ	Zip® disk
DIILLST	distill
DIILLVY	lividly
DIILMNS	dislimn
DIILMOO	modioli
DIILMOS	idolism
DIILMTY	timidly
DIILNNU	indulin
DIILNWY	windily
DIILOST	idolist
DIILRSU	silurid
DIILRTY	dirtily
DIILVVY	vividly
DIILYZZ	dizzily
DIIMNOR	midiron
DIIMNOS	Odinism
DIIMORS	diorism
DIIMSSS	dismiss
DIIMSUV	vidimus
DIINNOT	din into
	tondini
DIINOPT	dip into
DIINOQU	quinoid
DIINORS	sordini
DIINOST	Odinist
DIINQSU	quids in
DIIOPRS	spiroid
DIIORSV	divisor
DIIPPRT	drip-tip
DIITUVY	viduity
DIJLMOR	Lord Jim
DIJOSTU	judoist
DIKKNRU	Dunkirk
DIKLNOR	lordkin
DIKLNRY	kiln-dry
DIKLSUY	duskily
DIKMRTU	drum kit
DIKNNOS	non-skid
DIKNOPW	kip down
DIKNORT	drink to
DIKNORV	dvornik
DIKNPRU	drink up
DIKNSSU	sun disk
DIKOORT	drookit
DIKORSW	skid row
DIKORTU	droukit
DILLOSY	solidly
DILLPSY	psyllid
DILLRUY	luridly
DILMNRU	drumlin
DILMOOY	moodily
DILMORU	oil drum
DILMOST	mistold
DILMOSU	solidum
DILMOSY	odylism
DILMTUY	tumidly
DILNNSU	dunlins
DILNOOS	oodlins
DILNOPT	diplont
DILNOQU	quodlin
DILNORT	introld
DILNOSU	unsolid
DILNOXY	indoxyl
DILNPSU	lispund
DILNPSY	spindly
DILNRUW	run wild
DILOOOW	wood oil
DILOPVV	Plovdiv
DILORTU	dilutor
DILORWY	rowdily
	wordily
DILOSSU	dulosis
	solidus
DILOSTY	styloid
DILRYZZ	drizzly
DILSTUY	dustily
DIMMMOU	mim-mou'd
DIMMOST	midmost
DIMNNOO	midnoon
DIMNNOS	donnism
DIMNNOT	dinmont
DIMNOOS	dominos
DIMNOPU	impound
DIMNORV	Mordvin
DIMNOTU	mind out
DIMNOTW	midtown
DIMNOUY	mind you
DIMOPSU	spodium
DIMORSW	misword
DIMRTUU	triduum
DIMRUUV	duumvir
DINNOOR	rondino
DINNOOT	tondino
DINNOPR	non-drip
DINNOPW	pin down
	pindown
DINNOSW	Swindon
DINOORS	indoors
	sordino
DINOORT	tordion
DINOOST	isodont
DINOOTW	wood tin
DINOPTW	tip down
DINORSW	Windsor
DINORTU	turdion
DINORWW	windrow
DINOSTW	sit down
	sit-down
DINOSWW	Windows®
	windows
DINOTUW	outwind
	wind out
DINPRSY	spin-dry
DINPSTU	pin-dust
DIOORST	disroot
DIOORTT	ridotto
DIOOTTW	do to wit
DIOOTTX	Otto Dix
DIOPRST	disport
	torpids
DIOPRTY	tripody
DIOPSST	dispost
DIORRST	stridor
DIORSTT	distort
DIOSSTU	studios
DIOSUUV	viduous
DIPRSTU	disrupt
DIPUVVY	divvy up
DIRSTUY	dry suit
	surdity
DKMOPSU	musk-pod
DKNNRUU	undrunk
DKOOOSZ	odzooks
DLLOOTU	doll out
DLLORWY	worldly
DLMMPUU	mud-lump
DLMNOOO	old moon
DLMNOOY	mylodon
DLMNOUU	unmould
DLMOSUU	modulus
DLNNOOY	Londony
DLNOOWW	low-down
DLNOPRU	puldron
DLNOPSY	spondyl
DLNORUV	Volundr
DLNORUY	roundly
DLNOSUY	soundly
DLOOOTW	wood lot
DLOOOWW	wood owl
DLOOPPY	polypod
DLOOPTY	tylopod
DLOOPUY	duopoly
DLOOPWY	plywood
DLOOTUU	out loud
DLOPRUY	proudly
DLOSTUW	wouldst
DMMPPUU	mud pump
DMNNOOO	Monodon
DMNOOOP	monopod
DMNOOTW	towmond
DMNOOWW	mow down
DMORTUU	drum out
DMORTUW	mudwort
DNNOORU	round on
DNNOOSW	Snowdon
DNNORUU	unround
DNNORUW	run down
	rundown
	run-down
DNNOSUU	unsound
DNNOSUW	sundown
DNNOUUW	unwound
DNNRTUU	turndun
DNOOPTW	top-down
DNOORTU	orotund
DNOOTUW	nutwood
DNOOTWW	two-down
DNOPRUU	round up
	round-up
DNOPTUW	put down
	put-down
DNOPUUW	upwound
	wound up
DNOSSUW	swounds
	'swounds
DNOSTUY	synd out
DNPRSUY	spun-dry
DOOORSU	odorous
DOOORTU	outdoor
DOOPRSY	prosody
DOOPRTU	drop out
	dropout
DOOPSTU	upstood
DOORRTU	dortour
DORUVYY	dyvoury

E

EEEEFRR	referee
EEEEFRW	Wee Free
EEEEGGS	gee-gees
EEEEGTX	exegete
EEEELMZ	leeze me
EEEENTT	entêtée
EEEFFFO	feoffee
EEEFFNT	en effet
EEEFFOR	offeree
EEEFGRU	refugee
EEEFHRS	shereef
EEEFILS	see life
EEEFLRR	fleerer
EEEFMNR	freemen
EEEFORS	foresee
EEEFRRZ	freezer
EEEFRST	set free
EEEGHNW	wheenge
EEEGILS	elegise
EEEGILZ	elegize
EEEGINP	epigene
EEEGINR	greenie
EEEGINU	Eugenie
	Eugénie
EEEGIPR	perigee
EEEGLNR	en règle
EEEGLNT	genteel
EEEGMRR	remerge
EEEGNNO	Neogene
EEEGNOS	Genoese
EEEGNPR	epergne
EEEGNRR	greener
	reneger

EEEGNRU renegue
EEEGNRV revenge
EEEGNSS geneses
EEEGNTT genette
EEEGRRT greeter
regreet
EEEGRUX exergue
EEEHILW wheelie
EEEHLLN Hellene
EEEHLNW enwheel
EEEHLOY eyehole
EEEHLPW wheeple
EEEHLRW wheeler
EEEHLWZ wheezle
EEEHNRW whene'er
EEEHRRW where'er
EEEHRST seether
the sere
EEEHRWZ wheezer
EEEHSTT esthete
EEEIKLL eel-like
EEEIKLZ Ezekiel
EEEILPT Peelite
EEEILRV relieve
EEEILVY evil eye
EEEIMMR Mérimée
EEEIMMS meemies
EEEIMNT emetine
EEEIMPR preemie
EEEIMRT eremite
EEEINQU queenie✧
EEEINRS eserine
EEEINSS Sienese
EEEIPST épéeist
EEEIPSU épuisée
EEEIRRT retiree
EEEIRRV reverie
EEEIRSZ reseize
EEEISTW sweetie✧
EEEJNPY jeepney
EEEJPRS jeepers
EEEJSWY Jew's eye
EEEKLLU ukelele
EEEKLNR kneeler
EEEKLNS sleeken
EEEKLNX Kleenex®
EEEKLPW ekpwele
EEEKLRS sleeker
EEEKNPT keepnet
EEEKRST skeeter
EEELLST Estelle
EEELMNT element
EEELMPT Mt Pelée
EEELMPX exemple
EEELNST stelene
EEELNSV elevens
EEELPRS sleeper
speeler
EEELPRT replete
EEELPST steeple
EEELRSV sleever
EEELRTV leveret
EEELSSY eyeless
EEELTTX teletex
EEEMNSS nemeses✧
EEEMORT eroteme
EEEMRRV Vermeer
EEEMRTX extreme
EEENNPT pentene
EEENNRT étrenne
EEENNTT entente
EEENPRT pre-teen
terpene
EEENPRV prevene
EEENPST ensteep
steepen
EEENPSW ensweep
EEENPSX expense
EEENQUU en queue
EEENRRS sneerer
EEENRRT enterer
re-enter
terreen
terrene
EEENRRV venerer
EEENRRW renewer
EEENRRY Nyerere
EEENRSZ sneezer
EEENRTV eventer
EEENRTX externe
EEENRUV revenue
unreeve
EEENSSS Essenes
EEENSTW sweeten
EEENSTX extense
EEENSWY sweeney
EEEOPPT peep-toe
EEEORSV oversee
see over
EEEORSY eyesore
EEEORVY overeye
EEEPRSS peeress
EEEPRST estrepe
steeper
EEEPRSV peevers
EEEPRSW sweeper
EEEPRSZ spreeze
EEEPRTU Euterpe
EEEQRRU requere
EEEQSUZ squeeze✧
EEERRRV reverer
EEERRST steerer
EEERRSV reserve
re-serve
reverse
EEERSSS seeress
EEERSTV Everest
EEERSUV rêveuse
EEERSUW seruewe
EEERSVW servewe
EEERTTW tweeter
EEERTWY yew tree
EEFFFNO enfeoff
EEFFFOR feoffer
EEFFGLU effulge
EEFFINR fen-fire
EEFFINT fifteen✧
EEFFJRY Jeffrey
EEFFKOP keep off
EEFFLOP peel off
EEFFLOR reel off
EEFFNOS offense
EEFFORR for free
offerer
EEFFOST Toffees
EEFFSTU suffete
EEFGILN feeling
fine leg
fleeing
EEFGINR feering
freeing
reefing
EEFGIRT fig tree
EEFGLLU gleeful
EEFGLOR foreleg
EEFGLOS solfège
EEFHINW hen-wife
EEFHISY fisheye
EEFHLMN flehmen
EEFHLNS enflesh
EEFHLRS flesher
herself
EEFHNRS freshen
EEFHORT thereof
EEFHORW whereof
EEFHRRS fresher
refresh
EEFHRRU Fuehrer
EEFHRST freshet
EEFIIRR reifier
EEFIKLN fin keel
EEFIKPT keep fit
keep-fit
EEFILLX flexile
EEFILNO olefine
EEFILOR forelie
EEFILRT fertile
EEFILST felsite
liefest
EEFIMRT femiter
EEFINNS Fiennes
EEFINRR refiner
EEFINRW fire-new
EEFINSS finesse
EEFIRRT ferrite
fir tree
EEFIRSS Seferis
EEFIRST set fire
EEFISTV festive
EEFLLRU fueller
EEFLLTY fleetly
EEFLMTU teemful
EEFLNNO enfelon
Fénelon
EEFLNOS one self
oneself
EEFLNPT felt pen
EEFLNRS fresnel
EEFLNTW New Left
EEFLOOV foveole
EEFLRRU ferrule
EEFLRTT fettler
EEFLRTU fleuret
EEFLRUX flexure
EEFMNOR foremen
EEFMNRT ferment
EEFMOSW some few
EEFMOTT mofette
EEFMPRU perfume
EEFMSTW fewmets
EEFMTTU fumette
EEFNRRY fernery
EEFNRTV fervent
EEFNSSW fewness
EEFORRV for ever
forever
EEFOTTU fouetté
EEFPRSU perfuse
EEFRRSU refuser
EEFRRTU refuter
EEFRRTY ferrety
EEFRSTT fetters
EEGGHTU thuggee
EEGGILN negligé
négligé
EEGGIOR Georgie
EEGGISV veggies
EEGGKRS skegger
EEGGLNO Geelong
EEGGLSS eggless
EEGGNOR engorge
EEGGNOY geogeny
EEGGNST nest egg
EEGGORR regorge
EEGGORU gougère
EEGGPRU puggree
EEGHILN heeling
EEGHINY hygiène
EEGHIRW reweigh
weigher
EEGHIWZ gee whiz
EEGHLNU leughen
EEGHNRT greenth
EEGHNRY greyhen
EEGHOPS shoe peg
EEGIIRS griesie
EEGIJNR jeering
EEGIKLN keeling
EEGIKNN keening
EEGIKNP keeping
EEGIKNR reeking
EEGIKNT kitenge
EEGILLS Giselle
EEGILNP peeling

EEGILNR leering
reeling
EEGILNS seeling
EEGILNT gentile✧
EEGILRV veliger
EEGILST elegist
EEGIMMR immerge
EEGIMNR regimen
EEGIMNS seeming
EEGIMNT meeting
teeming
EEGIMRS remiges
EEGINNR enginer
erg-nine
ingener
EEGINNU genuine
ingénue
EEGINNV eevning
evening
V-engine
EEGINNW Gwennie
EEGINOP epigone✧
EEGINOR E-region
EEGINOS soignée
EEGINPW weeping
EEGINRS greisen
EEGINRT integer
treeing
EEGINRV veering
EEGINSS genesis✧
EEGINSW seewing
EEGINTV ventige
EEGINTW weeting
EEGINTX exigent
EEGIOST egotise
EEGIOTZ egotize
EEGIRRV griever
EEGIRTT tergite
EEGIRTU guérite
EEGISTV vestige
EEGKNOR kerogen
EEGKNRU gerenuk
EEGLLOO oleo leg
EEGLLOR log-reel
EEGLLSS legless
EEGLMMU gemmule
EEGLNOR ere long
erelong
EEGLNOU eugenol
EEGLNOZ lozenge
EEGLNRY greenly
EEGLNST lengest
EEGLOSS egoless
EEGLRST leg-rest
St Leger
EEGLRTY telergy
EEGMMRY gemmery
EEGMNOS emonges
EEGMNST segment
EEGMRTU gum tree
EEGNNRU ungreen
EEGNORS negroes✧
EEGNPTT tent peg
EEGNPTV vent-peg
EEGNPUX expunge
EEGNSSU genuses
EEGNSTU guesten
EEGOOPY poogyee
EEGOPRT protégé
EEGOPTU Peugeot®
EEGORTV get over
overget
EEGORTX Gore-Tex®
EEGOSSS gessoes
EEGPRUX expurge
EEGRRSS regress
EEGRRST regrets
EEGRRSU resurge
EEGRRUY Gruyère
EEGRSSU guesser
EEGRSTU gesture
EEHHIMW Heimweh
EEHHLLT the hell
EEHHRTT thether
EEHHRTW whether
EEHHSTW wheesht
EEHIKLT the like
EEHILLR hellier
EEHILMN hemline
EEHILNT the line✧
EEHILOS Heloise
EEHILPS ephelis
EEHILPV Pehlevi
EEHILRW whilere
EEHILST sheltie
EEHILSX helixes
EEHIMMS mishmee
EEHIMNO hemione
EEHIMPT epithem
EEHIMST Shemite
EEHINNT the Nine
EEHINNV Nineveh
EEHINOR heroine
EEHINRR errhine
EEHINRS henries
EEHINRT neither
therein
EEHINRW wherein
EEHIORS heroise
EEHIORZ heroize
EEHIOST shoe tie
EEHIPRT prithee
EEHIPSV peevish
EEHIPTT epithet
EEHIRSS heiress
hérissé
EEHIRST heister
EEHIRSV shrieve
EEHISTV thieves
EEHKLOY keyhole
EEHKLSS shekels
EEHKMST Sekhmet
EEHKNNT Kenneth
EEHKOOY eyehook
EEHLLMP phellem
EEHLLNS enshell
EEHLLRS sheller
EEHLLSY Shelley
EEHLMMW whemmle
EEHLOSY Holy See
EEHLPRT telpher
EEHLPST Elspeth
EEHLRST shelter✧
EEHLRSV shelver
EEHLRSW welsher
EEHLRSY sheerly
EEHLSSU hueless
EEHLSSV shelves
EEHLSTT shtetel
EEHMNOP phoneme
EEHMNRU enrheum
EEHMNRY mynheer
EEHMORT theorem
EEHMRUX exhumer
EEHNNOS shoneen
EEHNNRY hennery
EEHNOPT potheen
EEHNORT thereon
EEHNORW Erewhon
nowhere
whereon
EEHNOST hose-net
EEHNOSW Wheeson
EEHNPST Stephen
EEHNRTU Ruthene
EEHNSTU enthuse
EEHNSTV seventh
EEHOOPW whoopee
EEHOPRT hop-tree
the rope
EEHOPRU euphroe
EEHOPSS sheepos
EEHORRS Hereros
EEHORST heteros
so there
EEHORSU rehouse
EEHORSW whereso
EEHORTT thereto
EEHORTW whereto
EEHORVW however
whoever
EEHOSTT tee shot
EEHOSTY eyeshot
EEHPRST hepster
sperthe
EEHPRTY prythee
pr'ythee
EEHPSSU Ephesus
EEHPSUU Euphues
EEHRRTW Werther
wherret
EEHRTTW whetter
EEHRVWY whyever
EEHSSTU Theseus
EEHSTTW the West
EEHSTUY shut-eye
EEIILNT tie line
EEIIMPR riempie
EEIIMRT emeriti
EEIIMST itemise
EEIIMTZ itemize
EEIINRT erinite
niterie
EEIINTV invitee
EEIIRRV rivière
EEIISTV visitee
EEIJPPT jet pipe
EEIKLLS skellie
EEIKLMW ewe-milk
EEIKLNR Lineker
EEIKLNY keyline
EEIKLPT pikelet
EEIKLST sleekit
EEIKNPY pink-eye
EEIKNRT kernite
EEIKNWY eye-wink
EEIKPPY pipe-key
EEIKRST keister
EEIKSTT steekit
EEIKTTT tektite
EEILLMT mellite
EEILLMY mill-eye
EEILLNS ill seen
EEILLNV en ville
Neville
EEILLNY ley line
EEILLOR lorelei✧
EEILLPS ellipse
EEILLRS leisler
EEILLRT treille
EEILLSV Seville
EEILLSW wellies✧
EEILMMT meltemi
EEILMNR ermelin
EEILMOR Molière
EEILMPT implete
EEILMRU Lumière
EEILMRV vermeil
EEILMVV Mevlevi
EEILNNO leonine✧
EEILNNT lenient
EEILNNV enliven
EEILNOR eloiner
EEILNPS pensile
sleep in
EEILNRT Trilene®
EEILNRV livener
revel in
EEILNSS sensile
EEILNST lisente
setline
tensile
EEILNTT entitle
Linette

EEILNTV veinlet
EEILOPT petiole
EEILORT oil-tree
troelie
EEILORV lie over
overlie
relievo
EEILOST estoile
EEILOTZ zeolite
EEILPRR replier
EEILPRS spieler
EEILPRT perlite
reptile
EEILPRU puerile
EEILPSS pelisse
EEILPST epistle✧
EEILPWY weepily
EEILQRU relique
EEILRRV reliver
reviler
EEILRST leister
sterile
EEILRSU leisure
EEILRSV servile
EEILRTT retitle
EEILRVZ Elzevir
EEILSSS sessile
EEILSST telesis
tieless
EEILSSU ileuses
EEILSTT Lisette
EEILSTV lievest
EEILSTX sextile
EEILSUV elusive
EEILTTX textile
EEILVWY weevily
EEIMMNS immense
EEIMMRS immerse
EEIMMSS misseem
EEIMNNO nominee
EEIMNNT eminent
EEIMNOS semeion
EEIMNOT one-time
EEIMNRV minever
EEIMNSS Meissen
nemesis✧
siemens
EEIMNSW misween
EEIMNSX Ximenes
EEIMNTT minette
EEIMOPS episome
EEIMOPT epitome
EEIMORS isomere
EEIMOSS meioses
EEIMOSW woe is me
EEIMOTV emotive
EEIMPRR premier
reprime
EEIMPRS emprise
imprese
premise
spireme
EEIMPRT emptier
EEIMPST empties
septime
EEIMQRU requiem✧
EEIMRRR merrier
EEIMRRT trireme
EEIMRSS messier
EEIMRST meister
triseme
EEIMRTT emitter
termite
EEIMSST it seems
métisse✧
EEINNNP pennine
EEINNPS pennies
EEINNRT interne
EEINNRU neurine
EEINNRV enriven
innerve
nervine
EEINNST intense
EEINNTT Ninette
EEINNTW entwine
EEINNTZ netizen
EEINOPR pereion
pioneer
EEINOTW Owenite
EEINPPS pepsine
EEINPRR repiner
EEINPRS en prise
erepsin
EEINPRT Petrine
EEINPRZ prenzie
EEINPSS penises
EEINPST Epstein
pentise
EEINPSV pensive
vespine
EEINQRU enquire
inquere
EEINQTU queen it
quieten
EEINQUY queynie
EEINRRS resiner
EEINRRT reinter
rentier
terrine
EEINRRV vernier
EEINRST inter se
Steiner
trenise
EEINRSV inverse
verse in
versine
EEINRSY Erinyes
EEINRTU neurite
retinue
reunite
uterine
EEINSST sestine
EEINSTU en suite
EEINSTV tensive
EEINSTX sixteen
EEINSTY syenite
EEIOPPT epitope
EEIOPST poetise
EEIOPTZ poetize
EEIORRS rosiere
EEIORSV erosive
EEIOSST isoetes
EEIPPST peptise
EEIPPTT pipette
EEIPPTZ peptize
EEIPQRU perique
re-equip
repique
EEIPRRR Perrier®
perrier
EEIPRRS reprise
respire
EEIPRRV reprive
EEIPRRZ reprize
EEIPRSS pressie
EEIPRST respite
EEIPRSV previse
EEIPRVW preview
EEIPRZZ prezzie
EEIPSUZ seize up
EEIQRRU require
EEIQRSU esquire✧
EEIQRTU quieter
requite
EEIQSTU equites
EEIRRRT retirer
terrier
EEIRRSV reversi
reviser
EEIRRTV riveret
riveter
EEIRRTW rewrite
EEIRRVV reviver
EEIRSSU reissue
EEIRSSV ivresse
EEIRSTT testier
Trieste
EEIRSTV restive
Servite
sievert
veriest
EEIRSTX re-exist
EEIRSUZ seizure
EEIRTVV vetiver
EEITUXZ zeuxite
EEJLLMU jumelle
EEJLRWY jewelry
EEJNOOR rejoneo
EEJNORS rejones
EEJNORY enjoyer
EEJOSTT Josette
EEJPRRU perjure
EEJQRRU jerquer
EEKKOTV vetkoek
EEKKRRT trekker
EEKLLNV knevell
EEKLLSY sleekly
EEKLLUU ukulele
EEKLMRZ klezmer
EEKLNNS kennels
EEKLNOS keelson
EEKLOOS look-see
EEKLRST kestrel
skelter
EEKLRSZ Szekler
EEKLSSY keyless
EEKLSYZ Szekely
EEKMMPU keep mum
EEKNOTY keynote
EEKNPSU knees-up
EEKNSST Knesset
EEKNSTU netsuke
EEKOOPT toe poke
EEKOPTU keep out
EEKORRV revoker
EEKOSTU seek out
EELLLVY levelly
EELLMOS Moselle
EELLMRS merells
smeller
EELLMRV vermell
EELLMTW well met
EELLNOV novelle
EELLORS roselle
EELLORZ rozelle
EELLPRS pre-sell
respell
speller
EELLPUV level up
EELLQRU queller
EELLRSW sweller
EELLSTW well-set
EELMMOP pommelé
EELMMPU emplume
EELMNOO oenomel
EELMOPR plerome
EELMOPT leptome
EELMORW eelworm
EELMPST stempel
stemple
EELMPTT templet
EELMRST smelter
EELMRSU lemures✧
EELMSTT stemlet
EELNOPS on sleep
sleep on
EELNOPV envelop
EELNOPY polyene
EELNOST Leontes
EELNOSV Slovene
EELNOSY esloyne
EELNOTT notelet
EELNOTU toluene
EELNPSY spleeny

EELNQUY	queenly
EELNRST	slenter
EELNRTT	lettern
EELNRUV	nervule
EELNSTU	unsteel
EELNSTY	enstyle
	tensely
EELNTTU	lunette
EELNTTY	Lynette
EELOPPS	peoples
EELOPRS	leprose
EELOPRX	explore
EELOPTU	eelpout
EELORSV	resolve
EELORSY	Rosy Lee
EELORTT	lorette
EELORVV	evolver
	revolve
EELOSST	osselet
EELOSTT	teleost
EELOTUV	evolute
	velouté
EELPPRX	perplex
EELPQRU	prequel
EELPRST	Prestel®
	spelter
EELPRSU	repulse✧
EELPRSY	sleepry
EELPRTZ	pretzel
EELPRUX	plexure
EELPRVY	replevy
EELPSTY	steeply
EELPSUX	expulse
EELQRUY	queerly
EELRRVY	revelry
EELRSST	tressel
EELRSSU	rulesse
EELRSTT	letters
	settler
	sterlet
	trestle
EELRSTW	swelter
	wrestle
EELRSTY	restyle
	tersely
EELRSTZ	seltzer
EELSSSU	useless
EELSSSX	sexless
EELSTUY	eustyle
EELSTVW	twelves
EELSTWY	sweetly
EELTVVY	velvety
EEMMNOT	memento
EEMMOSU	mousmee
EEMMRST	stemmer
EEMNNOV	envenom
EEMNOOS	someone
EEMNOOY	mooneye
EEMNORS	Emerson
EEMNORY	moneyer
EEMNOST	stone me!
	temenos
EEMNPTU	umpteen
EEMNRUW	emu wren
EEMOOSW	woesome
EEMOPRR	emperor
EEMOPRT	tempore
EEMOPRV	premove
EEMOPRW	empower
EEMORRS	remorse
EEMORRU	uromere
EEMORRV	remover
EEMOTTU	mete out
EEMPPRT	pre-empt
EEMPRRT	preterm
EEMPRSS	empress
EEMPRSU	presume
	supreme
	suprême
EEMPRTT	tempter✧
EEMPRTU	permute
EEMPSTT	tempest
EEMRRUU	remueur
EEMRSUX	murexes
EEMSSTU	must-see
EEMSTTU	musette
EENNORT	enteron
	tenoner
EENNORU	neurone
EENNOSS	oneness
EENNOTT	nonette
EENNOTY	neoteny
EENNOVW	even now
EENNPTU	Neptune
EENNQUU	unqueen
EENNRUV	unnerve
EENNSSU	unsense
EENNSSW	newness
EENOPPR	prepone
	propene
EENOPPT	peptone
EENOPST	en poste
	one-step
	pentose
	posteen
EENOPSW	new peso
EENORRV	overren
EENORSV	never so
EENORTU	en route
	Euronet
EENORTV	overnet
EENOSSY	essoyne
EENOSTV	Ventôse
	ventose
EENOTUV	even out
EENPPRT	perpent
EENPRSS	Serpens
	Spenser
EENPRST	present
	serpent✧
EENPRSV	Pevsner
EENPRTV	prevent
EENPRTW	pew-rent
EENPRTY	perenty
EENPSTY	stepney
EENQSTU	sequent
EENRRSU	ensurer
EENRRTY	re-entry
EENRRUV	nervure
EENRSTT	testern
EENRSTW	western✧
EENRSTY	styrene
	yestern
EENRTTU	nut-tree
EENRTUV	venture
EENRUVY	Nureyev
EENSSST	setness
EENSSTW	wetness
EENSTTY	teentsy
EENSTUW	unsweet
EENSTVY	seventy✧
EEOOPRS	operose
EEOPPRS	prepose
EEOPPTU	outpeep
EEOPRRT	Portree
EEOPRRV	reprove
EEOPRSX	exposer
EEOPRTT	treetop
EEOPRTU	outpeer
EEOPSSS	speoses
EEOPSST	poetess
EEOPSSU	espouse
	poseuse
EEOPSTT	steep-to
EEOPSTY	eye-spot
EEOPTUW	outweep
EEOQRTU	requote
EEORRST	restore
EEORRSV	reverso
EEORRTU	reroute
EEORRTV	evertor
EEORRTW	rewrote
EEORRVV	over-rev
EEORSST	Orestes
	osseter
	stereos
EEORSTT	rosette
EEORSTV	estover
	overset
EEORSTX	xerotes
EEORSTY	esotery
EEORSUV	oeuvres
	overuse
EEORSVW	oversew
EEORTUV	ouverte
EEPPPRY	peppery
EEPPRST	stepper
EEPPRSX	Perspex®
EEPPSTU	steepup
EEPPSUW	sweep up
	upsweep
EEPPSUY	eupepsy
EEPQUUU	queue up
EEPRRSS	presser
	repress
	re-press
EEPRRSU	peruser
EEPRRTV	pervert
EEPRRVY	repryve
EEPRSSU	Perseus
EEPRSSV	vespers
EEPRSSX	express
EEPRSTT	pretest
EEPRSTU	pertuse
EEPRSTX	sexpert
EEPRSUV	serve up
EEPRTTX	pretext
EEPSTTY	typeset
EEQRRUY	equerry
EEQRSTU	quester
	request
EEQSUYZ	squeezy
EERRSTW	strewer
	wrester
EERRSVW	swerver
EERRSVY	servery
EERRTTU	reutter
	utterer
EERRTTY	rettery
EERSSUV	Severus
EERSSUY	seysure
EERSTTT	strette
EERSTTU	trustee
EERSTTY	streety
EERSTUV	versute
	vesture
EERSUVW	survewe
EERTTUX	texture
EESSTTT	sestett
EESTTTW	wettest
EESTTTX	sextett
EFFFILO	file off
EFFFIOR	fire off
EFFFLOT	left-off
EFFFOOR	feoffor
	off-fore
EFFGINR	reffing
EFFGIOV	give off
EFFHILW	whiffle
EFFHIOV	hive off
	hive-off
EFFHIRS	sheriff
EFFHIRW	whiffer
EFFHITW	whiffet
EFFHLSU	shuffle
EFFIIST	fifties
	iffiest
	stiffie
EFFIKLS	skiffle
EFFILLU	lifeful
EFFILNO	off line
	offline
	off-line
EFFILNS	sniffle

Words marked ✧ can also be spelled with one or more capital letters

EFFILOR	for life
EFFILOV	live off
EFFILPR	piffler
EFFILRR	riffler
EFFILRY	firefly
EFFINRS	sniffer
EFFINST	stiffen
EFFIOPR	piffero
EFFIOPW	wipe off
EFFIORT	forfeit
EFFIORX	foxfire
EFFIOST	off-site
EFFIRST	restiff
EFFLLOS	sell off
	sell-off
EFFLLOT	tell off
EFFLLOW	well off
	well-off
EFFLMRU	muffler
EFFLNSU	snuffle
EFFLOSU	souffle
	soufflé
EFFLRRU	ruffler
EFFLRTU	fretful
	truffle
EFFNOOR	on offer
EFFNOOZ	zone off
EFFNRSU	snuffer
EFFNRUU	unruffe
EFFOORR	offeror
EFFOPRR	proffer
EFFOPRU	offer up
EFFPRUY	puffery
EFFRSTU	stuffer
EFFSSUU	suffuse
EFGGILP	egg-flip
EFGGIRR	frigger
EFGGIRY	figgery
EFGGLOR	flogger
EFGHIMS	gemfish
EFGHIRT	fighter
	freight
EFGHLTU	the Gulf
EFGILMN	Fleming
EFGILNR	flinger
EFGILNS	selfing
EFGILNT	felting
EFGIMNT	figment
EFGINNP	pfennig
EFGINNR	ferning
EFGINOR	foreign
EFGINRS	fingers
EFGINRU	gunfire
EFGIORV	forgive
EFGIRRT	grifter
EFGLNTU	fulgent
EFGLORT	froglet
EFGLOSS	fogless
EFGNOOR	forgone
EFGNOSU	fungoes
EFGOORV	fog over
EFGORRU	ferrugo
EFGORRY	forgery
EFGORTU	foregut
EFHIINS	fineish
EFHIJSW	jewfish
EFHILMS	flemish✧
	himself
EFHILNS	in flesh
EFHILSS	hisself
	selfish
EFHILST	leftish
EFHILTY	heftily
EFHINNS	fennish
EFHINST	fish-net
	net-fish
EFHIRSS	serfish
EFHIRST	shifter
EFHIRSY	fishery
EFHISTW	wet fish
EFHISUW	huswife
EFHLLPU	helpful
EFHLLSY	fleshly
EFHLNSU	unflesh
EFHLOOT	The Fool
EFHLOOX	foxhole
EFHLOPU	hopeful✧
EFHLOST	elf-shot
EFHLOTU	hot flue
EFHLRSU	flusher
EFHLRSY	freshly
EFHLSTY	thyself
EFHLTTW	twelfth
EFHMORT	the form
EFHNORT	forhent
EFHRRTU	further
EFIIINR	in fieri
EFIILLN	Fellini
EFIILMS	misfile
EFIILRT	fitlier
EFIILRY	fierily
EFIILSS	fissile
EFIIMRR	rim-fire
EFIIMRS	misfire
EFIINPR	pin-fire
EFIINPV	fivepin
EFIINRU	unifier
EFIISSV	fissive
EFIJLLY	jellify
EFIJLOR	frijole
EFIJLOT	jetfoil
EFIKLNU	like fun
EFIKRRS	frisker
EFIKRST	frisket
EFILLMS	misfell
EFILLNY	fly line
EFILLOO	foliole
EFILLOS	Follies
EFILLOU	fuel oil
EFILLOW	low life
	low-life
EFILLUW	wileful
EFILMNU	fulmine
EFILMOT	filemot
EFILMSS	selfism
EFILMST	film set
	filmset
	leftism
EFILMSY	I myself
EFILNOX	flexion
EFILNSS	finless
EFILOOS	floosie
	foliose
EFILOOZ	floozie
EFILOPR	profile
	pro-life
EFILORR	Florrie
EFILORT	trefoil
EFILOSS	Flossie
EFILOSX	sexfoil
EFILOVX	fox-evil
EFILPPR	flipper
EFILPPU	pipeful
EFILPRY	pilfery
EFILPTT	felt tip
EFILQUY	liquefy
EFILRRT	trifler
EFILRST	stifler
EFILRTT	flitter
EFILRVV	flivver
EFILRZZ	frizzle
EFILSST	selfist
EFILSTT	leftist
EFILSTU	sulfite
EFILUVX	fluxive
EFIMMRU	fermium
EFIMNOR	fermion
EFIMNTT	fitment
EFIMOST	fomites
EFIMTTU	fumetti
EFINNOR	inferno✧
EFINNOS	no-fines
EFINNSU	funnies
EFINOPR	forpine
EFINOPU	fie upon
EFINRST	snifter
EFINRSU	infuser
EFINRUY	reunify
EFINSST	fitness
EFIOOST	Footsie
EFIOPRR	porifer
EFIOPRT	firepot
EFIORRT	rotifer
EFIORRU	fou rire
EFIORST	foister
	forties✧
EFIORTU	fire out
EFIPPRR	fripper
EFIPRTY	petrify
EFIRRRU	furrier
EFIRRSU	friseur
	frisure
EFIRRTT	fritter
EFIRRTU	friture
	fruiter
	turfier
EFIRRTY	terrify
EFIRSSU	fissure
EFIRSTU	surfeit
EFIRSTW	swifter
EFIRSVY	versify
EFIRTTU	turfite
EFIRTUV	furtive
EFIRTUX	fixture
EFISTTT	fittest
EFISTTY	testify
EFJLSTU	jestful
EFKLMNO	menfolk
EFKLMOR	merfolk
EFKLNUY	flunkey
EFKLOPU	pokeful
EFKLPSU	skepful
EFKNOPU	poke fun
EFLLSTU	fullest
EFLMOSU	fulsome
EFLMPRU	frumple
EFLMSUU	museful
EFLNOPY	fly open
EFLNORT	forlent
EFLNORU	fleuron
EFLNORW	fern-owl
EFLNORY	felonry
EFLNOSU	sulfone
EFLNOTT	fletton
	fontlet
EFLNSSU	fulness
EFLNSTU	nestful
EFLNSUY	synfuel
EFLNTTU	tentful
EFLNTTY	tent-fly
EFLNTUU	tuneful
EFLOORR	floorer
EFLOORS	forsloe
EFLOORY	foolery
EFLOORZ	foozler
EFLORSU	ourself
EFLORSW	flowers
EFLORTT	fortlet
EFLORTW	felwort
EFLORVY	flyover
	overfly
EFLORWW	werwolf
EFLORWY	flowery
	rye wolf
EFLOSSW	self-sow
EFLPRUY	preyful
EFLPSTU	pestful
EFLRSTU	fluster
	restful
EFLRTTU	flutter
EFLSTTY	test-fly
EFLSTUZ	zestful
EFMNOOT	footmen
EFMOORZ	zoeform

EFMOPRR	perform
	preform
EFMOPRT	pomfret
EFMOTTU	fumetto
EFMPRUY	perfumy
EFMRTUY	furmety
EFNNORT	fornent
EFNNORU	Nurofen®
EFNNOTU	unoften
EFNNOTY	Fonteyn
EFNOOST	festoon
EFNOOSU	of no use
EFNOOTT	ten-foot
EFNORRT	for rent
EFNORRU	forerun
EFNORTU	fortune✧
EFNORTW	forwent
EFNRSTU	funster
EFOOPRR	reproof
EFOOPRS	spoofer
EFOOPRT	foretop
EFOORST	soft roe
EFOORTV	vote for
EFOORTW	woofter
EFOPPRY	foppery
EFOPRSS	profess
EFOPRSU	profuse
EFOPRTY	torpefy
EFORRSU	ferrous
	for sure
EFORRTY	torrefy
EFORRUV	fervour
EFORSSU	fourses
EFPRTUY	putrefy
EFPSTUY	stupefy
EFRSTUU	futures
EGGGILN	legging
EGGGILR	giggler
EGGGILS	giggles
EGGGINP	pegging
EGGGLOR	goggler
EGGGLOS	goggles
EGGHILR	higgler
EGGHIRT	thigger
EGGHLOS	shoggle
EGGHORY	hoggery
EGGIIPS	piggies
EGGILLN	gelling
EGGILMS	leggism
EGGILNR	niggler
EGGILNS	sniggle
EGGILNU	lugeing
EGGILRW	wiggler
	wriggle
EGGIMMN	gemming
EGGIMRU	muggier
EGGINNS	ginseng
EGGINOR	Goering
EGGINRS	snigger
EGGINRY	gingery
	greying
EGGINTT	getting
EGGINTW	twiggen
EGGIPRR	prigger
EGGIPRY	piggery
EGGIRRT	trigger
EGGIRSW	swigger
EGGIRTW	twigger
EGGIRWY	wiggery
EGGJLRU	juggler
EGGJORS	joggers
EGGLLNO	long leg
EGGLMPU	egg plum
EGGLMSU	smuggle
EGGLNSU	snuggle
EGGLOOY	geology
EGGLORS	slogger
EGGLPRU	plugger
EGGLRSU	slugger
EGGMRSU	smugger
EGGNOOY	geogony
EGGNPUU	gunge up
EGGNRSU	snugger
EGGNTUY	nuggety
EGGORRY	Gregory
EGGORTY	toggery
EGGPRUY	puggery
EGGSSTU	suggest
EGHHHIO	heigh-ho
EGHHIKY	high-key
EGHHIMN	highmen
EGHHIST	highest
	high-set
EGHHITX	x-height
EGHHOSW	showghe
EGHIILL	ghillie
EGHIINT	nightie
EGHIINV	inveigh
EGHIINW	weigh in
	weigh-in
EGHIKNR	gherkin
EGHIKRS	skreigh
	skriegh
EGHILNO	hog-line
EGHILNP	helping
EGHILNR	herling
EGHILNS	English
	shingle
EGHILNT	enlight
	lighten
EGHILPT	pightle
EGHILRT	lighter
	relight
EGHILST	sleight
EGHIMMN	hemming
EGHIMNS	meshing
EGHIMPT	empight
EGHINNO	hinge on
EGHINNU	unhinge
EGHINOS	shoeing
EGHINRR	herring
EGHINRT	righten
	The Ring
EGHINRW	whinger
EGHINTT	tighten
EGHIOOS	shoogie
EGHIOPS	pisheog
EGHIORS	ogreish
EGHIORU	roughie
EGHIOTT	göthite
EGHIOTU	toughie
EGHIOTV	eightvo
EGHIOTW	go white
EGHIPRT	the grip
EGHIPUW	weigh up
EGHIRRT	righter
EGHIRST	sighter
EGHIRSY	greyish
EGHISTW	weights
EGHITWY	weighty
EGHLLOU	lughole
EGHLLSW	H G Wells
EGHLMPY	phlegmy
EGHLNOR	leghorn✧
EGHLNPU	engulph
EGHLNTY	lengthy
EGHLOOS	shoogle
EGHLOSW	leg-show
EGHMNOU	humogen
EGHMOSU	gumshoe
EGHMOSY	gym shoe
EGHNOOS	hognose
EGHNOOT	on the go
EGHNORU	enrough
	roughen
EGHNOTU	toughen
EGHNSUY	Huygens
EGHNTWY	Gwenyth
	Gwyneth
EGHORRU	rougher
EGHORTZ	Hertzog
EGHOSTT	get shot
	ghettos
EGHOSUU	hugeous
EGHRTUY	theurgy
EGIIKLW	wiglike
EGIILMT	legitim
EGIILNT	lignite
EGIILNV	veiling
EGIILPZ	Leipzig
EGIIMNP	impinge
EGIIMNR	mingier
EGIIMNS	Geminis
EGIIMRS	Isegrim
EGIIMSV	misgive
EGIINNS	insigne
	seining
EGIINNV	veining
EGIINOP	epigoni✧
EGIINPS	pigsnie
EGIINRT	igniter
	tigrine
EGIINSZ	seizing
EGIINUV	Iguvine
EGIINVW	viewing
EGIIOPR	pierogi
EGIIPRW	periwig
EGIJKNR	jerking
EGIJLNR	jingler
EGIJLNT	jinglet
EGIJNOS	jingoes
EGIJNST	jesting
EGIJNTT	jetting
EGIKKLN	lekking
EGIKLLM	milk leg
EGIKLNR	erl-king
EGIKLNT	kinglet
EGIKMNP	kemping
EGIKNNN	kenning
EGIKNNR	kerning
EGIKNRY	key ring
EGIKPRY	key grip
EGILLNO	logline
EGILLNT	gill net
	telling
EGILLNW	welling
EGILLNY	yelling
EGILLOR	girolle
EGILLPS	leg slip
EGILLRR	griller
EGILLSU	gullies
EGILMMN	lemming
EGILMMR	glimmer
EGILMNR	gremlin
	merling
	mingler
EGILMNT	melting
EGILMNU	legumin
EGILMOR	gomeril
EGILMOS	Limoges
	semi-log
EGILMOU	elogium
EGILMOV	Mogilev
EGILMPS	glimpse
EGILMSW	M G Lewis
EGILNOR	Goneril
	leg-iron
EGILNOS	lignose
	lingoes
	sloe gin
EGILNOT	lentigo
EGILNOW	Niel Gow
EGILNPR	pingler
EGILNPS	leg spin
	leg-spin
	spignel
EGILNPT	pelting
EGILNPY	yelping
EGILNRS	slinger
EGILNRT	ringlet
	tingler
	tringle
EGILNRY	relying
EGILNSS	singles

EGILNST	glisten
	singlet
EGILNSW	swingle
EGILNTT	letting
EGILNTW	winglet
EGILNVY	levying
EGILOOS	goolies
EGILORR	Grolier
EGILOST	elogist
EGILPPR	gripple
EGILRST	glister
	gristle
EGILRSY	greisly
	griesly
	grisely
EGILRTT	glitter
EGILRTY	tigerly
EGILRUV	virgule
EGILRZZ	grizzle
EGILSSW	wigless
EGILSTU	gluiest
EGILTTW	twiglet
EGIMMRR	grimmer
EGIMMRS	megrims
EGIMMTU	gummite
EGIMNOS	misgone
EGIMNOT	mitogen
EGIMNPR	impregn
EGIMNPT	pigment
EGIMNST	temsing
EGIMNTU	time gun
EGIMNUW	wine gum
EGIMOST	egotism
EGINNNP	penning
EGINNNR	renning
EGINNOP	opening
EGINNOT	get in on
EGINNPU	penguin
EGINNRR	grinner
EGINNRT	ringent
EGINNRY	ginnery
	renying
EGINNSS	sensing
EGINNST	nesting
EGINNSU	ensuing
EGINNTT	netting
	tenting
EGINNTV	venting
EGINNTZ	Tenzing
EGINNVY	envying
EGINOPR	perigon
EGINOPS	epigons✧
	pingoes
EGINORR	ignorer
EGINORS	signore✧
EGINORT	genitor
	Negrito
	toe ring
EGINORZ	zeroing
EGINOSU	igneous
EGINOSY	isogeny
EGINOTT	get it on
	tentigo
EGINPPR	repping
EGINPRS	springe
EGINPSY	espying
	pigsney
EGINPTT	petting
EGINPYY	epigyny
EGINQUU	queuing
EGINRRW	wringer
EGINRSS	ingress
EGINRST	resting
	stinger✧
EGINRSU	signeur
EGINRSV	serving
	versing
EGINRSW	swinger
EGINRSY	syringe
EGINRTT	gittern
	retting
EGINRVV	revving
EGINRVY	revying
EGINSTT	setting
	testing
EGINSTV	vesting
EGINSTW	stewing
	westing
EGINTTV	vetting
EGINTTW	wetting
EGINTTX	texting
EGIOOST	gooiest
EGIOPRS	serpigo
EGIOPRT	ego-trip
EGIOPRU	groupie
	pirogue
EGIORST	goriest
EGIORTV	vertigo✧
EGIORTZ	zorgite
EGIOSTT	egotist
EGIOTUV	give out
	outgive
EGIPPRR	gripper
EGIPPSU	guppies
EGIPRUU	guipure
EGIRRTT	gritter
EGIRSST	Striges
	tigress
EGIRSSU	Sergius
EGIRTTU	guttier
EGISUWY	wise guy
EGJMNSY	J M Synge
EGKLORW	legwork
EGLLLPU	leg-pull
EGLLOSY	sylloge
EGLLOUY	Yule log
EGLLRUY	gullery
EGLLSUY	gulleys
EGLMMRU	glummer
EGLMNOO	engloom
EGLMNOR	mongrel
EGLMOOR	legroom
EGLNNOT	long ten
EGLNOOY	neology
EGLNORU	lounger
EGLNOST	longest
EGLNOUV	unglove
EGLNOUY	loungey
EGLNOXY	loxygen
	xylogen
EGLNOYZ	lozengy
EGLNPRU	plunger
EGLNRTU	gruntle
EGLNSSU	gunless
EGLOPSS	Gospels
EGLOPTU	glue-pot
EGLORRW	growler
EGLORSS	glosser
EGLORWY	grey owl
EGLOSTT	get lost!
EGLPRSU	splurge
EGLRSUU	regulus✧
EGLRSYY	gryesly
	grysely
EGLRUZZ	guzzler
EGLSSTU	gutless
EGLSTUU	gluteus
	Telugus
EGMMORT	grommet
EGMMRTU	grummet
EGMNORU	murgeon
EGMNORY	mongery
EGMNOST	emongst
EGMNOYZ	zymogen
EGMORSU	grumose
EGMORTU	gourmet
EGNNORT	röntgen✧
EGNNPTU	pungent
EGNNRSU	Gunners
EGNNRUY	gunnery
EGNNSTU	sten gun✧
EGNNTUU	unguent
EGNOOPS	pongoes
EGNOORY	orogeny
EGNOOTU	outgone
EGNOOYZ	zoogeny
EGNOPRS	sponger
EGNOPRY	progeny
	pyrogen
EGNOPSU	pug nose
EGNOPSW	gowpens
EGNORRW	wronger
EGNORSS	engross
EGNORSU	surgeon
EGNORSY	eryngos
EGNORUY	younger
EGNRRTU	grunter
EGNRSTU	surgent
EGNRSYY	synergy
EGNRTTU	grutten
	turgent
EGNTTUY	tent-guy
EGOORRV	groover
EGOORSY	goosery
EGOORTU	outgoer
EGOOSTU	outgoes
EGOPPST	peg-tops
EGOPRRS	gropers
EGOPRRU	grouper
	regroup
EGOPRUY	guy-rope
EGORRST	grosert
EGORRSU	grouser
EGORRTU	grouter
EGORRUY	roguery
EGORTUY	grey-out
EGPRSUU	upsurge
EGRRSUY	surgery
EGRSTTU	gutters
EHHILLS	hellish
EHHIMRS	Rhemish
EHHINRS	Rhenish
EHHIPRS	hership
EHHIRTT	thither
EHHIRTW	whither
EHHISWY	wheyish
EHHITTW	T H White
EHHNORT	the Horn
EHHOOST	hot shoe
EHHOPST	the Shop
EHHORTT	thother
EHHPSTU	the push
EHIIIKT	hei-tiki
EHIILTT	lithite
EHIINRT	inherit
EHIINRZ	rhizine
EHIIPPS	hippies
EHIIRRS	Irisher
EHIIRST	hirstie
EHIISST	stishie
EHIITTT	Hittite
EHIJNNO	Johnnie
EHIKKSS	kishkes
EHIKMNT	methink
EHIKNRS	kernish
EHIKNRT	rethink
	thinker
EHIKNST	Kentish
EHIKRRS	shirker
EHIKRSW	whisker
EHIKSST	The Kiss
EHIKSTU	Kushite
EHIKSTW	whisket
EHIKSVZ	Izhevsk
EHIKSWY	whiskey✧
EHILLMN	hillmen
EHILLMW	Wilhelm
EHILLNO	hellion
EHILLNS	inshell
EHILLPT	the pill
EHILLRS	rellish
EHILLRT	thiller
EHILLTY	lithely
EHILMPW	whimple

EHILMTT meltith
EHILMUW umwhile
EHILNOP pinhole
EHILNOS in holes
EHILNOT hot line
hotline
neolith
the Lion
EHILNPS plenish
EHILOPT hoplite
EHILOST Elohist
hostile
EHILPRT philter
philtre
EHILRRW whirler
EHILRST slither
EHILRSV shrivel
EHILRSY Shirley
EHILRTU luthier
EHILRTW whirtle
EHILSTT Lettish
listeth
thistle
EHILSTW whistle
EHILTTU thulite
EHILTTW whittle
EHILTWY whitely
EHIMMPS Memphis
EHIMMRS shimmer
EHIMMSY shimmey
EHIMNPS shipmen
EHIMNRU inhumer
rhenium
EHIMNTY thymine
EHIMOPT Imhotep
EHIMORS heroism
moreish
EHIMORT moither
mothier
EHIMORZ rhizome
EHIMOSV moshvei
EHIMPRW whimper
EHIMRST Rhemist
EHIMRSU heurism
mushier
EHIMRTT Thermit®
EHIMSTU tumshie
EHIMSTY mythise
EHIMSWY whimsey
EHIMTYZ mythize
EHINNOP phone-in
EHINNOT on the in
EHINNRT thinner
EHINNSW wennish
EHINOPV hop-vine
EHINOPX phoenix
EHINORS inshore
EHINOST histone
EHINOSU heinous
in-house
EHINPPS shippen
EHINPRT Penrith
EHINPSS hipness
EHINRRS Shriner
EHINRSU usher in
EHINRSV shriven
EHINRTV thriven
EHINRTW writhen
EHINRTZ zithern
EHINRVY Henry IV
Henry VI
EHINSSS shiness
EHINSST sithens
EHINSSU Hussein
EHIOPPS pie-shop
EHIOPRS rosehip
EHIOPST ethiops
Peshito
EHIORRT heritor
EHIORST hoister
horse it
shortie
EHIORSY hosiery
EHIORTT thorite
EHIORTU hire out
outhire
routhie
EHIORTV overhit
EHIORTW hot-wire
EHIOSTY isohyet
EHIPPRS shipper
EHIPPRW whipper
EHIPPST hippest
the pips
EHIPPTW whippet
EHIPQTU The Quip
EHIPRST hipster
EHIPRSW whisper
EHIPSST Thepsis
EHIPSTT pettish
the pits
EHIPSTY the yips
EHIRRSS sherris
EHIRRSV shriver
EHIRRTV thriver
EHIRRTW whirret
EHIRSSW swisher
EHIRSTU hirsute
EHIRSTW swither
withers
EHIRSVY shivery
EHIRTTW whitret
whitter
EHIRWZZ whizzer
EHISSTU Hussite
stushie
EHISTTW wettish
EHJLOOY holy Joe
EHJMNOS Mes-John
EHJNOSW W E Johns
EHKLNOS lokshen
EHKMOOS smoke-ho
EHKNORS Kherson
EHKNRSU hunkers
EHKRSTU tushker
EHLLNSU unshell
EHLLOOS holloes
EHLLOOT Othello
EHLLOTW hot well
EHLMMOW whommle
EHLMMUW whummle
EHLMNOT menthol
EHLMNOY homelyn
EHLMOOS holesom
EHLMOTT hot melt
EHLMPTU the lump
EHLNOOY Holy One
EHLNORT hornlet
EHLNRTU luthern
EHLNTTY tenthly
EHLOOPP hop-pole
EHLOOPT pothole
top-hole
EHLOOST Lesotho
EHLOOTU hole out
EHLOPPS hopples
EHLOPSX phloxes
EHLOPSY spyhole
EHLOPTU help out
EHLORST holster
hostler
EHLORTY helotry
EHLOSTT shottle
EHLOSTY thylose
EHLPSSU plushes
EHLRSTU hustler✧
EHLRSUY hurleys
EHLSSTT shtetls
EHLSTTU shuttle
EHMNOOR hormone
moorhen
EHMNORT the morn
EHMNORU home run
EHMNPTY nymphet
EHMNTTU hutment
EHMOOSS shmoose
EHMOOSW somehow
EHMOOSZ shmooze
EHMOPRT Morpeth
EHMOPRW morphew
EHMORST smother
Thermos®
EHMORTU mouther
EHMORTY mothery
EHMOSWY somewhy
EHMOTUX Exmouth
EHMPRTU the Rump
thumper
EHMRRTU murther
EHMRSUU humerus
EHNNOOR non-hero
EHNNOPR nephron
EHNNOPY hypnone
EHNNOTW now then!
EHNNRSU shunner
EHNNSTU unshent
EHNNSUW unshewn
EHNOOPR no-hoper
EHNOORS on shore
onshore
on-shore
sorehon
EHNOOST one-shot
EHNOPRY hyperon
EHNOPTU on the up
EHNOPUY euphony
EHNOQTT on the QT
EHNORRT horrent
norther
EHNORRY heronry
EHNORST Hornets
shorten
threnos
EHNORSU unhorse
EHNORSY noshery
EHNOSST hotness
EHNOSTT shotten
EHNOSTY honesty
EHNOSUU unhouse
EHNPRSY phrensy
EHNPSTY Nepthys
EHNRSTU Nerthus
shunter
the runs
unherst
EHNRTWY wrythen
EHNSSSY shyness
EHOOPRW whooper
EHOOPTY oophyte
EHOORST hooters
reshoot
shooter
soother
EHOOSST Sesotho
EHOPPRS shopper
EHOPPRT prophet✧
EHOPPRW whopper
EHOPRRY orphrey
EHOPRST strophe
EHOPRSU Orpheus
shore up
EHOPRTU pouther
EHOPRTY pothery
EHOPRUY euphory
EHOPSSX sex shop
EHOPSTT the tops
EHORRTW thrower
EHORSTU shouter
souther
EHORSWY showery
EHORTUY outhyre
EHOSSST hostess
EHOSTTT hottest
EHOSTUY Southey

EHOTTTW wotteth
EHPRTTU turpeth
EHRSSTY shyster
thyrses
EHRSTTU shutter
EHRSTTW strewth
EHRSTUY tushery
EHRTTTY thretty
EIIILRV rilievi
EIIILST ileitis
EIIINPR ripieni
EIIKLLP liplike
EIIKLMS mislike
EIIKLPS pliskie
EIIKNNS niks-nie
EIIKNSS kinesis
EIIKNST inkiest
EIIKNTW twinkie
EIIKRRS riskier
EIIKRST Kirstie
EIILLMM millime
EIILLMT limelit
EIILLNV villein
EIILLSW willies
EIILLTT tillite
EIILLTV vitelli
EIILMNT Minitel
EIILMNV milvine
EIILMPR imperil
EIILMPT limepit
EIILMRS milreis
EIILMRT Leitrim
limiter
EIILMSS missile
similes
EIILMST elitism
élitism
limites
EIILMSU milieus
EIILMSV mislive
EIILMUX milieux
EIILNOS elision
isoline
lionise
EIILNOT etiolin
EIILNOV olivine
EIILNOZ lionize
EIILNRT nitrile
EIILNTU inutile
EIILORV Olivier
rilievo
EIILPST spilite
EIILQSU silique
EIILSTT elitist
élitist
EIILSTU utilise
EIILTUY tuilyie
EIILTUZ tuilzie
utilize
EIILTXY exility
EIIMMSS mimesis
EIIMMST mistime
EIIMNPR primine
EIIMNRT interim✧
mintier
termini
EIIMNRV miniver
EIIMNTV minivet
EIIMNTY nimiety
EIIMOPP Pompeii
EIIMOSS meiosis
EIIMPRS pismire
primsie
EIIMPST pietism
EIIMPTY impiety
EIIMRST mistier
EIIMSSV missive
EIIMSSZ sizeism
EIINNNP ninepin
EIINNQU quinine
EIINNRT tinnier
EIINNSW insinew
EIINNTV invenit
EIINNTW intwine
EIINOPR ripieno
EIINOPS pionies
EIINORS ioniser
ironise
EIINORT Niterói
EIINORZ ionizer
ironize
EIINPRS inspire
EIINPST in spite
EIINPTT pentiti
EIINQRU inquire
EIINQTU inquiet
EIINRTT nitrite
EIINRTV inviter
vitrine
EIINRTW write in
write-in
EIINSST Sistine
EIINSTT sittine
tiniest
EIINSTU unitise
EIINTUV unitive
EIINTUZ unitize
EIIORST riotise
EIIORSV ivories
EIIORTZ riotize
EIIOSTZ zoisite
EIIPPRR rippier
EIIPRST tipsier
EIIPSTT pietist
EIIPTTT pittite✧
EIIPTTU pituite
EIIQQUU Iquique
EIIQUVV qui vive
EIIRRTZ ritzier
EIIRSTV revisit
visiter
EIISSTX sixties
EIISSTZ sizeist
EIISTUV uveitis
EIJKKSU jukskei
EIJKLRY jerkily
EIJKNNS Jenkins
EIJKNPR perjink
prejink
EIJLLNY injelly
EIJNORT jointer
EIJNORY joinery
EIJNPRU juniper
EIJNRRU injurer
EIJNSTU Justine
EIJPRTU Jupiter
EIJRSTT jitters
EIJRTTY jittery
EIJSSTU Jesuits
EIJSSUV jussive
EIKKLNR klinker
EIKKNRS skinker
EIKLLNW inkwell
EIKLLOS skollie
EIKLLOW owl-like
EIKLLRS reskill
EIKLLST skillet
EIKLMNR kremlin✧
EIKLNOT Tolkien
EIKLNRS slinker
EIKLNRT tinkler
EIKLNRW winkler
wrinkle
EIKLNSS kinless
EIKLNST lentisk
EIKLNSU sunlike
EIKLNSY skyline
EIKLNTT knittle
EIKLNTU nutlike
EIKLNTW twinkle
EIKLOOP plookie
EIKLOPS ski pole
EIKLOPU ploukie
EIKLOTY toylike
EIKLPRY perkily
EIKLPSY peskily
EIKLSTT skittle
EIKMMRR krimmer
EIKMMRS skimmer
EIKMNOR moniker
EIKMORS irksome
EIKMOSS Eskimos
EIKMOSY misyoke
EIKMRRS smirker
EIKMRSS kirmess
EIKMRSU muskier
EIKMSST mess kit
EIKNNOR einkorn
EIKNNRS skinner
EIKNOPS pinkoes
EIKNORV invoker
EIKNOSS kenosis
EIKNPSU spunkie
EIKNRST stinker
EIKNRSW winkers
EIKNRTT knitter
trinket
EIKNTTY kitteny
EIKNTUZ kunzite
EIKOOST stookie
EIKOPPR pork pie
EIKOPRS porkies
EIKOSST ketosis
EIKPPRS skipper
EIKPPST skippet
EIKPRSY spikery
EIKPSSS skepsis
EIKRRST skirret
skirter
striker
EIKRSTT skitter
EIKRSTU turkies
EILLLOW oil well
EILLMNU mullein
EILLMOT melilot
EILLMOU mouillé
EILLMSS mis-sell
EILLMST mistell
EILLNNP pennill
EILLNOS niellos
EILLNSS illness
EILLORU rouille
EILLORZ zorille
EILLOSS oil-less
EILLOSV villose
EILLPPP pep pill
EILLPRS spiller
EILLPSS lipless
EILLPST let slip
EILLQTU quillet
EILLRST stiller
trellis
EILLRSW swiller
EILLRSY Sillery
EILLSTW willest
EILMMNO molimen
EILMMRS slimmer
EILMNOT molinet
EILMNSU emulsin
EILMOPR implore
EILMORR lorimer
EILMORY Lyomeri
EILMOSS lissome
EILMPPU plumpie
EILMPRS prelims
simpler
EILMPRY primely
EILMPSU impulse
EILMPSX simplex
EILMPTY emptily
EILMRRY merrily
EILMRSS rimless
EILMRSU misrule
EILMRSY miserly

EILMRTY lymiter
EILMRVY vermily
EILMSSY messily
EILMSTT smittle
EILMSTU Miletus
EILMSUY Elysium
EILMUUV eluvium
EILNNOP in pleno
EILNNOR onliner
on-liner
EILNNPU pinnule
EILNNRY innerly
EILNOOP polonie
EILNOOV violone
EILNOPP plenipo
EILNOPR proline
EILNOPS epsilon
EILNOPT pointel
pontile
topline
EILNOPU lie upon
EILNORR loriner
EILNORT retinol
EILNOSS lioness
EILNOST Nilotes
onliest
EILNOSU elusion
EILNOTT let into
EILNOTU elution
line-out
outline
EILNOTV violent
EILNOTW towline
two-line
EILNOVV involve
EILNPRS pilsner✧
EILNPRU purline
EILNPST plenist
EILNPSU spinule
EILNPTY ineptly
EILNPUV vulpine
EILNRST linters
slinter
snirtle
EILNRSV silvern
EILNRTY inertly
try-line
EILNRVY nervily
EILNSSS sinless
EILNSSU insulse
silenus✧
EILNSTU utensil
EILNSTW westlin
EILNSTY in style
Yeltsin
EILNSVY sylvine
EILNVXY vixenly
EILOOPT Tiepolo
EILOORS rose oil
EILOORT troolie
EILOOST ostiole
stoolie
EILOOTZ zoolite
EILOPRS spoiler
EILOPRT poitrel
EILOPST pistole
EILOPSU pileous
EILOPSV plosive
EILOPTT plottie
EILOPTU pile out
EILOPTX exploit
EILORSS rissole
EILORSU soilure
EILORSW low-rise
EILORTT tortile
triolet
EILORTU outlier
EILOSTT litotes
T S Eliot
EILOTUV live out
outlive
EILPPRR rippler
EILPPRS ripples
slipper
EILPPRT ripplet
tippler
tripple
EILPPSS pipless
EILPPST stipple
EILPPSW swipple
EILPRST spirtle
EILPRTT triplet
EILPRTX triplex
EILPRUU purlieu
EILPSST tipless
EILPSTT spittle
EILPSTU stipule
EILPSUY spulyie
EILPSUZ spulzie
EILPTTY pettily
EILQRTU quilter
EILQRUU liqueur
EILQTUY quietly
EILRRTW twirler
EILRSTT slitter
stilter
testril
EILRSUW wurlies
EILRSVY silver Y
silvery
EILRSZZ sizzler
EILRTTY littery
tritely
EILRTUV rivulet
EILSSTW witless
EILSSTY stylise
EILSTTV vittles
EILSTTY stylite
testily
EILSTVY sylvite
EILSTYZ stylize
EILSWZZ swizzle
EILTWZZ twizzle
EIMMORS memoirs
EIMMPRR primmer
EIMMPRU premium
EIMMRRT trimmer
EIMMRST misterm
EIMMRSU mumsier
EIMMRSW swimmer
EIMMSTZ tzimmes
EIMNNOS Simenon
EIMNNOT mention
EIMNNTW mint-new
EIMNOOR ionomer
EIMNOOS Moonies
noisome
EIMNOOT emotion
EIMNOOX exomion
EIMNOPS peonism
pi-meson
EIMNOPT emption
pimento
EIMNORS merinos
mersion
EIMNOST moisten
EIMNOSW Owenism
winsome
EIMNOTT Menotti
EIMNOTU Mountie
EIMNOTY omneity
omniety
EIMNPTU Pentium®
pinetum
EIMNPTY empty in
EIMNQSU mesquin
EIMNRRU murrine
EIMNRST entrism
in terms
minster
EIMNRSU neurism
EIMNRTU run time
EIMNRVY verminy
EIMNSSS sensism
EIMNSST mess-tin
missent
EIMNSTT mist net
mist-net
mittens
smitten
EIMNSTU minutes
mistune
EIMNSTW miswent
EIMNUZZ muezzin
EIMOORR roomier
EIMOPPR pompier
EIMOPRR primero
EIMOPRS imposer
promise✧
semi-pro
EIMOPRV improve
EIMOPSX imposex
EIMORSS mossier
EIMORST erotism
mortise
trisome
EIMORSU mousier
EIMORSV verismo
EIMORTT omitter
EIMOSST mitoses
EIMOSTT titmose
EIMOSTU timeous
EIMOSTZ mestizo
EIMOSYZ isozyme
EIMOTTU time out✧
EIMOTTW two-time
EIMOTVV TV movie
EIMPRRU primeur
EIMPRSS impress
Persism
premiss
EIMPRST imprest
EIMPRTU imputer
tumpier
EIMPSST misstep
EIMPSTU impetus
EIMQSTU mesquit
EIMRSSU misuser
surmise
EIMRSTT metrist
EIMRSTU mustier
EIMRSTY mistery
smytrie
EIMRTTU rut-time
EIMRTUV vitreum
EIMRTUX mixture
EIMRUZZ muzzier
EIMSTTV TV Times
EINNOPS pension
EINNOPT pontine
EINNOQU quinone
EINNORT intoner
ternion
EINNORU reunion
EINNORV environ
EINNOST Sonnite
tension
EINNOSV venison
EINNOTT nonetti
tontine
EINNOVW inwoven
EINNPRS spinner
EINNPRT enprint
EINNPST spinnet
tenpins
EINNPSY spinney
EINNPTT tent pin
EINNPTU nut pine
pine nut
EINNQTU Quentin
EINNRRU runnier
EINNRSU unrisen
EINNRTV vintner
EINNRUV unriven

EINNSSY sinsyne
EINNSTU Sunnite
EINNSTZ Zennist
EINNSUW unsinew
EINNTUW untwine
EINOOPZ epizoon
EINOORR iron ore
EINOORS erosion
EINOOST isotone
EINOOSZ ozonise
EINOOTZ zoonite
EINOOZZ ozonize
EINOPPR poperin
propine
EINOPRR roper-in
EINOPRT pointer
protein
pterion
repoint
EINOPRV provine
EINOPRW in power
EINOPSS in posse
spinose
EINOPST pointes
EINOPTT in petto
pentito
EINOQUX equinox
EINORST in store
in-store
tersion
triones
EINORSU urinose
EINORSV version✧
vin rosé
EINORTT tritone
EINORTU in utero
routine
EINORTZ trizone
EINORVW win over
EINOSSS session
EINOSST sonties
EINOSSU sinuose
EINOSTT snottie
EINOSTW Owenist
EINOSUV envious
niveous
veinous
EINOTTT totient
EINOTTV oven-tit
EINPPRS nippers
snipper
EINPPST snippet
EINPRRT printer
reprint
EINPRRZ Prizren
EINPRST Septrin®
EINPRSU uprisen
EINPRTU repunit
EINPRTX Pinxter
EINPSTT spitten
EINPSTU puniest

EINPTTY tintype
EINQRUY enquiry
EINQSTU inquest
EINQTTU quintet
EINQTUU unquiet
EINRRSU insurer
EINRSSU sunrise
EINRSTT entrist
stinter
EINRSTV striven
EINRSTY sintery
EINRSWY swinery
EINRTTW twinter
wren tit
written
EINRTUV unrivet
venturi✧
EINRTUW unwrite
EINRTWY wintery
EINSSST sensist
EINSSSU Senusis
Senussi
sinuses
EINSSSY synesis
EINSSTW witness
EINSSUW sunwise
EINSTTU tuniest
EINSTTW entwist
twinset
EINSTTY tensity
EINTTTW twitten
EINTTUY tenuity
EIOOPST isotope
EIOORRT rootier
EIOORTV Orvieto
EIOOSTT tootsie✧
EIOPRRT pierrot✧
EIOPRRV River Po
EIOPRST periost
reposit
riposte
ropiest
EIOPRSX Siporex®
EIOPRTV pivoter
EIOPSST sepiost
EIOPSTU piteous
EIOPSTY isotype
EIOPTUW wipe out
wipeout
EIOQRTU quoiter
EIOQSTU quite so
EIOQTUX Quixote
EIORRRS sorrier
EIORRRT terroir
EIORRRW worrier
EIORRST roister
EIORRSV revisor
EIORRUV ouvrier
EIORRVV revivor
EIORSST rosiest
sorites

stories
EIORSSU serious
EIORSSX xerosis
EIORSTT stoiter
EIORSTV torsive
EIORTTV tortive
viretot
EIORTUV voiture
EIOSSTV stovies
EIOSTTT stottie
EIOSTTU toustie
EIOSTUZ outsize
EIPPRRT tripper
EIPPRTT trippet
EIPRRTY tripery
EIPRRUV upriver
EIPRSST persist✧
stirpes
stripes
EIPRSSU Persius
suspire
EIPRSTT spitter
tipster
EIPRSTU peritus
EIPRSTY pyrites
stripey
EIPRSUU euripus
EIPRTTU puttier
EIPRTUW write up
write-up
EIPRUVW purview
EIQRSTU querist
EIQRTTU quitter
EIQRUVY quivery
EIQRUZZ quizzer
EIQSTUU quietus
EIQSUZZ quizzes
EIRRRST stirrer
EIRRSTU rustier
EIRRSTV striver
EIRSSTV treviss
EIRSTTT stretti
EIRSTTU tertius
EIRSTTW twister
EIRSTWZ Switzer
EIRSUVV survive
EIRSUVW surview
EIRTTTW twitter
EISSSSW Swisses
EISSTUV tussive
EISTTUW wet suit
EJJMNUU jejunum
EJJMPTU jump jet
EJKLLYY K-Y® jelly
EJKOORY jookery
EJKORTU jerk out
EJKORUY joukery
EJLLORY jollyer
EJLOSSY joyless
EJMNRUY jurymen
EJMOPTU toe jump

EJNORRU rejourn
EJNORUY journey
EJOORVY overjoy
EJOPPRT prop-jet
EJOQRUU quo jure?
EJORSTU jouster
EJORSUU suo jure
EJORTUV j'ouvert✧
EJOSTTU outjest
EJPRRUY perjury
EKKLOOY olykoek
EKKLRSU skulker
EKKOPRS Kekrops
EKKOPSU pukekos
EKLLMSU skellum
EKLLRRU kruller
EKLNOOW new look
EKLNOPR plonker
EKLNORS snorkel
EKLNPRU plunker
EKLOOTW wet-look
EKLORSU rules OK
EKLSSSY skyless
EKLSTTU skuttle
EKMMORS Kommers
EKMMRSU skummer
EKMNORY monkery
EKMNOSU muskone
EKMNOSY monkeys
EKMNPTU unkempt
EKMNRTU Turkmen
EKNOORS snooker
EKNOPSU unspoke
EKNORST stonker
stroken
EKNORSY Orkneys
Yonkers
EKNORTT knotter
EKNORTW network
EKNORUY younker
EKNORWY New York
EKNRTUY turnkey
EKNSSTU sunkets
EKOOPRV provoke
EKOORRS koreros
EKOORRY rookery
EKOORST stooker
strooke
EKOPPSU upspoke
EKOPRUY kouprey
EKOPSTU stoke up
EKORRST stroker
EKPPSUU seppuku
EKPSTUW skew-put
EKRSSTU Turkess
ELLLORR lorrell
ELLMNOO moellon
ELLMOOR morello
ELLMOWY mellowy
ELLMPUU plumule
ELLNNOT tonnell

ELLNOOW	woollen
ELLNOPT	pollent
ELLNOST	stollen
ELLNOSU	nousell
ELLNOSW	swollen
ELLNOWW	well now
	well-won
ELLNOXY	xylenol
ELLNPSU	unspell
ELLOOSW	woosell
ELLOOSY	loosely
ELLOPRR	proller
ELLOPTU	pollute
ELLORRT	troller
ELLORRY	rye-roll
ELLORTY	trolley
ELLORVY	loverly
ELLOSTU	outsell
	sell out
	sell-out
ELLOSVY	volleys
ELLOSWY	yellows
ELLOTTU	outtell
ELLOTUW	outwell
	well out
ELLOVWY	vowelly
ELLOWYY	yellowy
ELLPSUW	upswell
ELLPSUY	pulleys
ELLRSSU	Russell
ELMMORT	trommel
ELMMPTU	plummet
ELMMRSU	slummer
ELMMSTU	stummel
ELMNNOY	Men Only
ELMNOOT	moonlet
ELMNOTU	moulten
ELMNOTY	ymolten
ELMNPPU	plumpen
ELMNPUU	unplume
ELMOOPP	pompelo
ELMOOPS	pomelos
ELMOORT	tremolo
ELMOOTU	mole out
ELMOPRY	polymer
ELMOPSU	plumose
ELMOPTY	Ptolemy
ELMORSU	emulsor
ELMOSUU	emulous
ELMPPRU	plumper
ELMPRUY	plumery
ELMRTUU	multure
ELMRTUY	elytrum
ELMRUZZ	muzzler
ELMSSSU	sumless
ELNNOPU	nonuple
ELNNRTU	trunnel
ELNOOPT	peloton
ELNOOPV	Volpone
ELNOORZ	Lorenzo
ELNOOSU	unloose
ELNOOSZ	snoozle
ELNOPRU	pleuron
ELNOPRY	pronely
ELNOPST	leptons
ELNOPTU	opulent
ELNORSU	noursle
ELNORTW	low-rent
ELNORTY	elytron
ELNOSSS	sonless
ELNOSSW	lowness
ELNOSTU	lentous
ELNOSTV	solvent
ELNOTUZ	zonulet
ELNOTVY	novelty
ELNRSTY	sternly
ELNSSSU	sunless
ELNSSSY	slyness
ELNSTUY	Lutyens
ELNSUZZ	snuzzle
ELOOOPT	toe loop
ELOOPRS	spooler
ELOOPRU	Europol
ELOOPST	Spoleto
ELOORTT	rootlet
ELOOSTU	lose out
	outsole
ELOOSWY	woolsey
ELOPPST	stopple
ELOPPSY	polypes
ELOPRRU	prouler
ELOPRRW	prowler
ELOPRRY	pyrrole
ELOPRSS	plessor
ELOPRSU	leprous
	pelorus
	perlous
	sporule
ELOPRSY	leprosy
ELOPRTT	plotter
ELOPRTU	plouter
	poulter
ELOPRTW	plowter
ELOPRTY	protyle
ELOPRVY	overply
	plovery
ELOPSST	topless
ELOPSTU	tupelos
ELOPSUU	louse up
ELORSTT	settlor
	slotter
ELORSUV	velours
ELORSUY	elusory
ELORTTY	lottery
ELORTUU	rule out
ELORTVY	overtly
ELOSSTY	systole
	toyless
	tyloses
ELOSTUU	luteous
ELOSWZZ	swozzle
ELPPRSU	purples
ELPRRSU	slurper
ELPRSTU	spurtle
ELPRTUU	pulture
ELPRUZZ	puzzler
ELPSSSU	plusses
ELPSTUU	pluteus
	pustule
ELRRSTU	rustler
ELRRTTU	turtler
ELRSSTU	lustres
ELRSTUY	sutlery
ELRSTWY	sweltry
ELRSUWY	wurleys
ELRTTUY	utterly
ELRTUUV	vulture
ELSSSUY	Ulysses
ELSSTYY	systyle
EMMMRUY	mummery
EMMNOOR	monomer
EMMNORY	meronym
EMMNOSU	mu-meson
EMMNOTU	omentum
EMMNOTY	metonym
EMMOOTY	myotome
EMMOPRR	prommer
EMMORSZ	momzers
EMMRSTU	rummest
EMMRSUY	summery
EMMSSUU	museums
EMNNOOR	moneron
EMNNOOW	new moon
EMNNORT	non-term
EMNNOWW	new-mown
EMNOOPT	metopon
EMNOORT	montero
EMNOOST	moonset
EMNOOSY	noysome
EMNOOTY	enomoty
EMNOPSU	spumone
EMNORRU	mourner
EMNORST	monster
	on terms
EMNORTT	torment
EMNORTU	monture
	mounter
	remount
EMNORTV	Vermont
EMNOSST	stemson
EMNOSTU	unsmote
EMNOSTY	etymons
EMNRSSU	rumness
EMNRSTU	Munster
	Münster
	sternum
EMOOPRT	promote
EMOOPRY	pomeroy
EMOORRY	Moorery
EMOORSS	Mooress
EMOORSU	more suo
	urosome
EMOOSTT	mottoes
EMOOSTW	twosome
EMOOSTY	myosote
	toysome
EMOOTUV	move out
	outmove
EMOPPTU	up-tempo
EMOPRRS	rompers
EMOPRST	stomper
EMOPRSU	supremo
EMORRST	stormer
EMORRSU	morsure
EMORRWY	wormery
EMORSSU	smouser
EMORSTU	oestrum
EMORSUY	mousery
EMORSUZ	zero-sum
EMOSTTT	MOT test
EMOSTVZ	zemstvo
EMPRSTU	stumper
	sumpter
EMPRTTU	trumpet
EMRRSTU	sturmer✧
EMRSTYY	mystery
ENNNRUY	nunnery
ENNOOOT	none too
ENNOORT	norteño
ENNOORZ	non-zero
ENNOOSW	one's own
ENNOOTT	nonetto
ENNORST	stonern
ENNORSU	non-user
ENNORTT	Trenton
ENNORTU	neutron
ENNORTV	Ventnor
ENNOSSW	nowness
ENNOSTU	neuston
ENNOTWW	new town
ENNOUVW	unwoven
ENNPSTU	unspent
ENNRSTU	stunner
ENNTTUY	untenty
ENOOPPR	propone
ENOOPPT	open-top
ENOOPRS	snooper
ENOOPRW	new poor
ENOOPST	one-stop
ENOOPSY	spooney
ENOOPTU	open out
ENOORSU	onerous
ENOORSZ	snoozer
ENOORTT	to-torne
ENOORTW	note row
	tone row
	to-worne
ENOORUY	you're on!
ENOORWW	woe-worn
ENOOSST	soonest
ENOOSTT	testoon
ENOOSTU	nose out
	unsoote
ENOOTTW	two-tone

Words marked ✧ can also be spelled with one or more capital letters

ENOOTUW woe unto
ENOOTXY oxytone
ENOPRRU proneur
ENOPRSS persons
press on
ENOPRST postern
Preston
ENOPRTT portent
ENOPRTW Newport
ENOPRTY entropy
ENOPSST stepson
ENOPSTU set upon
ENOPSUX Xenopus
ENOPTTU pout net
ENOQTUU unquote
ENORRST snorter
ENORRTT torrent
ENORRUV overrun
run over
ENORSSW New Ross
ENORSSY sensory
ENORSTT snotter
stentor
ENORSTU tonsure
ENORSTW nor'-west
ENORSTY tyrones
ENORSUV nervous
ENORTUY tourney
ENORTVY not very
ENORVWY very own
ENOSSSU Souness
ENOSSTT Stetson®
ENOSSTU outness
ENOSSTW twoness
ENOSTTU stouten
tenutos
ENOSTUU tenuous
ENOSTUY yu-stone
ENOTTUU tune out
ENOTTUW outwent
ENPPTTU pup tent
ENPRRSU spurner
ENPRSTU pre-stun
punster
ENPRSUU unpurse
ENPSSSU suspens
ENPSTTU stupent
ENPSTUW unswept
ENRRSTU returns
ENRRSUY nursery
ENRRTUU nurture
ENRRTUY turnery
ENRSSWY wryness
ENRSTTU entrust
ENRSUUX Xenurus
ENRTTUY nuttery
EOOOPRS oospore
EOOPPRS opposer
propose
EOOPPRU europop
EOOPPRV popover
EOOPRRS spoorer
EOOPRRT protore
trooper
EOOPRSS poroses
EOOPRST stooper
EOOPRTU outrope
EOOPRTV overtop
EOOPRTW tow rope
EOOPRVY poovery
EOOPRYZ zoopery
EOOPTYZ zootype
EOORRST rooster
toreros
EOORRVW row over
EOORSVW oversow
EOORTUV out-over
EOORTUW out-owre
EOOSSSU osseous
EOOTTUV outvote
vote out
EOPPPRS poppers
EOPPRRS prosper
EOPPRSS oppress
porpess
EOPPRST stopper
EOPPRSU purpose
EOPPRSW swopper
EOPPRUW power up
EOPPSSU suppose
EOPRRSS pressor
EOPRRST sporter
EOPRRTU trouper
EOPRSST portess
prestos
EOPRSSU seropus
EOPRSSW prowess
EOPRSTT protest
spotter
EOPRSTU petrous
posture
proteus✧
septuor
spouter
EOPRSUU poursue
uprouse
EOPRSUW poursew
EOPRTTY pottery
EOPRTUV put over
EOPRTUY eutropy
EOPRTVY poverty
EOPSSSS possess
EOPSTTU outstep
step out
EOPSTTW stewpot
two-step
EOQRSTU questor
EORRRST Terrors
EORRSTU rouster
trouser
EORRSTV Vorster
EORRSTW strower
EORRSTY royster
EORRTTT trotter
EORRTTU torture
trouter
EORSSTU oestrus
trouses
tussore
EORSSTV votress
EORSSTY storeys
EORSTTT stotter
stretto
EORSTTW swotter
EORSTTY rosetty
EORSTUX sextuor
EORTTTY tottery
EOSSTUW sou'-west
EOSTTTW wottest
EPPRRTU prerupt
EPPRRUU purpure
EPPRSSU press-up
EPPSTUW upswept
EPRRRSU spurrer
EPRRSUU pursuer
usurper
EPRRSUY spurrey
EPRRTUU rupture
EPRSSSU pusser's
EPRSSTY spryest
EPRSTTU sputter
ERRSSTU trusser
ERRSTTU truster
ERRSTTY tryster
ERSSSTU trusses
ERSSSUU usuress
ERSSTTU tutress
ERSSTUY russety
ERSTTTU stutter

F

FFFFIMO miff off
FFFGOOO goof off
FFFILOT lift off
lift-off
FFFLPUU fluff up
FFFMOOR from off
FFGIINR griffin
FFGIINT tiffing
FFGINOR griffon
ring off
FFGINOS sign off
FFGINPU puffing
FFGLNOO long off
FFGLRUY gruffly
FFHHISU huffish
FFHIISY fishify
FFHIKNU huffkin
FFHILSU fishful
FFHILSY fly-fish
FFHILTY fifthly
FFHILUY huffily
FFHIMOW whim off
FFHIMSU muffish
FFHIOST toffish
FFHOOSW show off
show-off
FFHOPSU push off
push-off
FFHOSTU shut off
shut-off
FFIILMY miffily
FFIISUZ ziffius
FFIKLLO kill off
FFIKMOS skim off
FFIKOSS kiss off
kiss-off
FFILLLU fulfill
FFILNSY sniffly
FFILOPS slip off
FFILOUZ zuffoli
FFILPUY puffily
FFILRTY fritfly
FFILSTU fistful
FFILSTY stiffly
FFINOOT finfoot
FFINOPS off spin
off-spin
spin off
spin-off
FFINOPT pontiff
FFINSTU snuff it
FFIOPST tip-offs
FFIORTY fortify
FFIPPSU spiff up
FFIQSUY squiffy
FFIRTUY frutify
FFISTTU stuff it
FFJMOPU jump off
jump-off
FFKLORU forkful
FFKLOSU Suffolk
FFKOORW work off
FFLLOOR roll-off
FFLLOOU loofful
FFLLOPU pull off
FFLNSUY snuffly
FFLOOUZ zuffolo
FFNORTU turn off
turnoff
turn-off
FFOOPST post off
stop off
stopoff
stop-off
FGGGIIN figging
FGGHIIS fishgig
FGGIIZZ fizzgig
FGGILNO golfing
FGGILOY foggily
FGGINOR forging
FGHHILY fly high
FGHHIOS hogfish
FGHIINS fishing

FGHIIPS pig-fish
FGHILSU sighful
FGHILTY flighty
FGHIOSY fogyish
FGHNOOR foghorn
FGHORUY froughy
FGHOTUY foughty
FGIIKNN knifing
FGIILLN filling
FGIILNO foiling
FGIILNR rifling
FGIILNS filings
FGIILNY lignify
FGIINNN finning
FGIINNS finings
FGIINRR firring
FGIINRY nigrify
FGIINST sifting
FGIINSX fixings
FGIINSY signify
FGIINTT fitting
FGIINZZ fizzing
gin fizz
FGILLOR fig roll
FGILNOO fooling
FGILNOP fopling
FGILNOR rolfing✧
FGILNOW flowing
fowling
wolfing
FGILNTU fluting
FGILNTY flyting
FGILOOY goofily
FGILORY glorify
FGIMNOR forming
FGIMOSY fogyism
FGINNNU funning
FGINOOR roofing
FGINOOT footing
FGINRRU furring
FGINRSU surfing
FGINRTU turfing
FGINTTU tufting
FGIOORT go for it
FGIORST go first
FGIORTW figwort
FGISTUU fuguist
FGJLSUU jugfuls
FGLLNUU lungful
FGLMSUU mugfuls
FGLNORU furlong
FGLNOSU songful
FGLNPUU upflung
FGLOOUY ufology
FGLORUU fulgour
FGLOTUY goutfly
FGLSTUU gustful
gutsful
FGNOOOY foo yong
FGNOORU fourgon
FGNOOUY foo yung
FGNOSUU fungous
FHIIKNS ink-fish
FHIILMS filmish
FHIILOS fish-oil
FHIILTY lithify
FHIINNS Finnish
FHIINPS pinfish
FHIINST tin fish
FHILLSU fullish
FHILOOS foolish
FHILOSW wolfish
FHILPSU shipful
FHILPTU pithful
FHILSUW wishful
FHINOSU fushion
FHINRSU furnish
FHINSSU sunfish
FHIOOPR hip-roof
FHIOOST ooftish
FHIOPPS foppish
FHIOPSX foxship
FHIORRY horrify
FHIOSST softish
FHIOSTU fish out
outfish
FHIPPSU pupfish
FHIPSTU push fit
shift up
FHIRTTY thrifty
FHIRTUY thurify
FHKORTU futhork
FHLLOTU full-hot
FHLNORU hornful
FHLNSUU unflush
FHLOOSY shoofly
FHLOPSU shopful
FHLPSUU flush up
pushful
FHLRTUU hurtful
ruthful
FHNOTUX fox hunt
FHOOORT hoofrot
FHOOOTT hotfoot
FHOORSW for show
FHORSTY Forsyth
FIIIKNN finikin
FIIKLST ski lift
FIIKNYZ zinkify
FIILLMO milfoil
FIILLSU fusilli
FIILNOO in folio
FIILNOT tinfoil
FIILNTY niftily
FIILPTU pitiful
FIIMMNU infimum
FIINORT in for it
FIINOSS fission
FIINRTU in fruit
FIINRTY nitrify
FIIOPST positif
FIIPSTY tipsify
FIIRTVY vitrify
FIJLLOY jollify
FIJSTUY justify
FIKKLNO kinfolk
FIKLLSU skilful
FIKLLUY flukily
FIKLNOW wolfkin
FIKLNSU skinful
FIKLRSU riskful
FIKNNOS finnsko
FIKRTUY Turkify
FILLLUW willful
FILLMOY mollify
FILLNUY nullify
FILLOTU fill out
toilful
FILLOTY loftily
FILLPSY fly slip
FILLSTU listful
FILMNOO monofil
FILMPSY spy film
FILMSTU mistful
FILNNUY funnily
FILNOUX fluxion
FILNSTU tinfuls
FILNTUY unfitly
FILOOTW witloof
FILOPPT flip-top
FILOPTU flip out
FILORST florist
FILORTU floruit
FILORTY trifoly
FILPPUY pulpify
FILRSTY firstly
FILRYZZ frizzly
FILSSUY fussily
FILSTTU flutist
FILSTUW wistful
FILSTUY fustily
FILSTWY swiftly
FILUYZZ fuzzily
FIMMMUY mummify
FIMMORS misform
FIMNORU uniform✧
FIMOORV oviform
FIMORRT triform
FIMORTY mortify
FIMRTUY furmity
FIMSTYY mystify
FINNORT in front
FINOPTY pontify
FINORSS frisson
FIOORSU furioso
FIOOSTX six-foot
FIOOTTU out of it
FIOPRSY prosify
FIOPSTX postfix
FIORSUU furious
FIORTYZ FitzRoy
FIPPUYY yuppify
FIRRSTY stir-fry
FIRSSUY Russify
FKLNOOR Norfolk
FKLORUW workful
FKOOORS forsook
FKOORTU fork out
FLLOPTU plotful
topfull
FLLOSUU soulful
FLLOSWY fly-slow
FLLOTUU full-out
FLLOUWY wofully
FLLSTUU lustful
FLMMOUX flummox
FLMNOOU mouflon
FLMOOOT tomfool
FLMOORU roomful
FLNOORR forlorn
FLNOPUY fly upon
FLNRSUU urnfuls
FLOORSW forslow
FLOOTUW outflow
FLOPSTU potfuls
FLOSUUV fulvous
FMOOPRU Profumo
FMOORTU from out
FMRSTUU frustum
FNNNUUY unfunny
FNNOORT fronton
FNNOORW frown on
FNOOOTT foot-ton
FNOORRW forworn
FNOORSU sunroof
FNOPRTU up front
upfront
up-front
FNORSTY Y-fronts
FNSSUUY unfussy
FNSTTUU unstuft
FOOOPRT rooftop
FOOORTT foot rot
FOOOTTU outfoot
FOOOTTW two-foot
FOOPSTT soft top
soft-top
FOORSST of sorts
FOORSTT soft rot
FOORTTX foxtrot✧
fox-trot
FOORTUW two-four
FOOSTUY soft you
FOPSSTU fusspot
FORRUWY furrowy
FORSTWY frowsty
FORTTUU turf out

G

GGGGIIN gigging
GGGHINO hogging
GGGHINU hugging
GGGIIJN jigging
GGGIILN ligging

Words marked ✧ can also be spelled with one or more capital letters

GGGIINP pigging
GGGIINR rigging
GGGIINT tigging
GGGIINW wigging
GGGIINZ zigging
GGGIJNO jogging
GGGIJNU jugging
GGGILNO logging
GGGILNU lugging
GGGIMNU mugging
GGGINNO nogging
GGGINOS sogging
GGGINOT togging
GGGINPU pugging
GGGINRU rugging
GGGINSU sugging
GGGINTU tugging
GGHHIOS hoggish
GGHIIJS jiggish
GGHIINN hinging
GGHIINS sighing
GGHIIPS piggish
GGHIIRS riggish
GGHIITT thiggit
GGHIMSU muggish
GGHINSU gushing
GGHIPSU puggish
GGHLOSY shoggly
GGHOSTU thuggos
GGIIILN gingili
GGIILLM gig mill
GGIILNP pigling
GGIILNR rigling
GGIIMNN minging
GGIINNN ginning
GGIINNO ingoing
GGIINNR ringing
GGIINNS signing
singing
GGIINNT tinging
GGIINPR griping
GGIINRT ringgit
GGIINSU guising
GGIIRRS grigris
GGIJNSU juggins
GGIKLNO King Log
GGILNNO longing
GGILNNU lunging
GGILNOP long pig
GGILNOS gosling
GGILNOT Løgting
GGILNOU Guignol
GGILNOV gloving
GGILNOW glowing
GGILNOZ glozing
GGILOOS gigolos
GGILOSY soggily
GGILRWY wriggly
GGIMMNU gumming
GGIMNSU muggins
GGINNNU gunning
GGINNOO going on
ongoing
on-going
GGINOOP pogoing
GGINOPR groping
GGINOPU upgoing
GGINORS gringos
GGINORU roguing
GGINORW growing
GGINOUV voguing
GGINPPY gypping
GGINPRU purging
GGINRST G-string
GGINRSU surging
GGINSTU gutsing
GGINTTU gutting
GGIOORS gorgios
GGIOPPY Iggy Pop
GGIOPTT Piggott
GGIPRSY spriggy
GGNOORS Gorgons
GGNOORW go wrong
GGNORUW rug gown
GHHHIIS highish
GHHIKSY sky-high
GHHILOW high-low
GHHINRU run high
GHHIOPT high-top
GHHIORT right-oh
GHHIRST shright
GHHORTU through
GHHOTTU thought
GHIIKNT king-hit
GHIIKRZ Kirghiz
GHIILNR hirling
GHIILRS girlish
GHIINNS shining
GHIINNT nithing
GHIINNW whining
GHIINPP hipping
GHIINSS hissing
GHIINST in sight
insight
GHIINSW wishing
GHIINTT hitting
tithing
GHIINTW whiting
GHIIRST tigrish
GHIKLNU hulking
GHIKNNO honking
GHIKNOS hog-skin
GHIKNSU husking
GHIKRTU tughrik
GHILLSU gullish
GHILLTY lightly
GHILNOS longish
GHILNOT light on
GHILNOW howling
GHILNPU ingulph
GHILNRU hurling
GHILNSY shingly
GHILNTY nightly
GHILOSU sloughi
GHILPTU light up
GHILPTY yplight
GHILRTY rightly
GHILSTY sightly
GHILTTY tightly
GHILTWY wightly
GHIMMNU humming
GHIMNNY hymning
GHIMNOS gnomish
moshing
GHIMNTT mightn't
GHIMRRT Mr Right
GHIMRSU simurgh
GHIMSTT mightst
GHINNOR horning
GHINNOT nothing
GHINNTU hunting
GHINOPP hopping
GHINOPS ginshop
GHINORS horsing
shoring
GHINORT right on
right-on
GHINORU rough in
GHINOST hosting
on sight
GHINOSU housing
GHINOSW showing
GHINOTT hotting
tonight
GHINOTU houting
GHINPSU gunship
pushing
GHINRTU ungirth
unright
GHINSTU unsight
GHINSUY Hyginus
GHINTTU hutting
GHIOPTU hip-gout
GHIORSU roguish
GHIORTU rough it
GHIOSUV voguish
GHIPRST spright
GHIPRTU upright
GHIPTTU uptight
GHLMOOO homolog
GHLMOPU hog-plum
GHLNOOP long hop
GHLNOTY Loghtyn
GHLOOSY shoogly
GHLORUY roughly
GHLOSTY ghostly
GHLOSUY sloughy
GHLOTUY toughly
GHMOPTU pug-moth
GHMORSU sorghum
GHMOSTU mug shot
mugshot
GHNOPRY gryphon✧
GHNORUU unrough
GHNOSTU gunshot
shotgun
GHNOTUY youngth
GHOOOSW hoosgow
GHOORSS sorghos
GHOORST go short
GHOPRUU rough up
GHORTUW wrought
GHORTUY yoghurt
GHOSTUU outgush
GHPSTUU push-tug
GIIJNNO joining
GIIKKNR kirking
GIIKLLN killing
GIIKLMN milking
GIIKLNN inkling
GIIKLNP Kipling
GIIKLNT kitling
GIIKNNP kingpin
pink gin
pinking
GIIKNNS sinking
GIIKNNW winking
GIIKNNZ zinking
GIIKNPS pigskin
GIIKNRS griskin
GIIKNSV skiving
GIILLMN milling
GIILLNO gillion
GIILLNP pilling
GIILLNT tilling
GIILLNW willing
GIILLPY pig-lily
GIILMNN limning
GIILMNP limping
GIILMNS smiling
GIILMPR pilgrim
GIILMRY grimily
GIILNNS linings
GIILNNY inlying
lying-in
GIILNOR ligroin
GIILNOS soiling
GIILNOT toiling
GIILNPP lipping
GIILNPS lisping
spiling
GIILNST listing
GIILNTT tilting
titling
Tlingit
GIILNTW witling
GIILOSS gliosis
GIILOST oligist
GIILRST strigil
GIIMNPP pimping
GIIMNPR priming
GIIMNSS missing
GIIMNST misting
GIINNNP pinning

GIINNNS	innings
	inn sign
	sinning
GIINNNT	tinning
GIINNNW	winning
GIINNOP	pioning
GIINNOR	ironing
GIINNPP	nipping
GIINNPS	sniping
GIINNPU	pinguin
GIINNRS	rinsing
GIINNRU	ruining
GIINNSW	inswing
GIINNTT	tinting
GIINNTU	uniting
GIINNTW	twining
GIINOPR	pig iron
GIINORS	signior✧
	signori
GIINORT	rioting
GIINPPP	pipping
GIINPPR	ripping
GIINPPS	sipping
GIINPPT	tipping
GIINPPZ	zipping
GIINPTT	pitting
GIINPTY	pitying
GIINQTU	quiting
GIINRRS	sirring
GIINRTW	writing
GIINSTT	sitting
GIINSTU	suiting
GIINTTW	witting
GIJLLNO	jolling
GIJMPPU	pig-jump
GIJNOTT	jotting
GIJNTTU	jutting
GIJRRUY	jury-rig
GIKLNRU	lurking
GIKMNNU	Kunming
GIKMNOS	smoking
GIKMNOT	Tom King
GIKNNOO	kongoni
GIKNNOW	knowing
GIKNORW	working
GIKNSSY	sky sign
GIKNSTU	tusking
GILLMPU	pug mill
GILLMWY	Gwillym
GILLNNU	nulling
GILLNOO	long-oil
GILLNOP	polling
GILLNOR	rolling
GILLNOT	tolling
GILLNYY	lyingly
GILMMUY	gummily
GILMNOR	morling
GILMNPU	lumping
GILMPSY	gym slip
GILNNOO	glonoin
	looning
GILNNOS	long sin
GILNNSU	unsling
GILNOOP	looping
GILNOOT	looting
	tooling
GILNOPP	lopping
GILNOPS	sloping
GILNORU	louring
GILNORY	glory in
GILNOSU	lousing
GILNOSW	slowing
GILNOTT	lotting
GILNOTU	tung oil
GILNOVW	wolving
GILNOWY	yowling
GILNPRU	purling
GILNPSU	plusing
GILNPUY	uplying
GILNSTU	singult
GILNVYY	vyingly
GILOORS	girosol
GILOOST	ologist
GILOOTW	twigloo
GILORTT	triglot
GILORTY	trilogy
GILOSTT	glottis
GILRSTY	gristly
GILRTUY	liturgy
GILRYZZ	grizzly
GILSTUY	gutsily
GIMMMNU	mumming
GIMMNOT	tomming
GIMMNSU	summing
GIMNNOR	morning
GIMNNTU	munting
GIMNOOR	mooring
GIMNOOT	mooting
GIMNOPP	mopping
GIMNORU	rouming
GIMNOST	gnomist
GIMNOSU	mousing
	souming
GIMNOSW	mowings
GIMNOWY	Wyoming
GIMOQRT	Mt Qogir
GIMRSUU	guruism
GINNNOO	nooning
GINNNOR	ronning
GINNNOW	wonning
GINNNPU	punning
GINNNRU	running
GINNNSU	sunning
GINNNTU	tunning
GINNOPS	spongin
GINNORS	snoring
	sorning
GINNORU	grunion
GINNORW	ingrown
GINNOST	stoning
GINNOSW	on wings
GINNPRU	pruning
GINNRSU	nursing
GINNRTU	turning
GINNTTU	nutting
GINNTUV	vingt-un
GINNTUW	wing nut
GINNTUY	untying
GINOOPS	sooping
GINOORT	rooting
GINOPPP	popping
GINOPPS	sopping
GINOPPT	topping
GINOPPW	wopping
GINOPRS	prosing
GINOPRU	ingroup
	pouring
GINOPRV	proving
GINOPST	posting
	stoping
GINOPTT	potting
GINOPTU	pouting
GINORRT	ring rot
	rorting
GINORSS	in gross
	ingross
	signors
GINORST	sorting
GINORSU	rousing
	souring
GINORSY	signory
GINORTT	rotting
GINORTU	ring out
	routing
	touring
GINOSSS	sossing
GINOSST	stingos
	tossing
GINOSSU	sousing
GINOSTT	sotting
GINOSTU	sign out
	sing out
	tousing
GINOSTV	stoving
GINOSTW	stowing
GINOTTT	totting
GINOTTW	wotting
GINOTUW	outwing
GINPPPU	pupping
GINPPSU	supping
GINPPTU	tupping
GINPRRU	purring
GINPRSY	springy
GINPSUW	upswing
GINPTTU	putting
GINRSST	strings
GINRSTU	rusting
GINRSTY	stringy
GINRSUU	usuring
GINRTTU	rutting
GINSSSU	sussing
GINTTTU	tutting
GIOOPRR	porrigo
GIOPRRU	prurigo
GIOPSSY	gossipy
GIORTTU	trig out
GIOSSYZ	zygosis
GISWWYY	wysiwyg
GJNOOSU	goujons
GJOORTT	jogtrot
GLLLOOR	logroll
GLLMNOU	gun moll
GLMNOOO	monolog
GLMNOOT	long Tom✧
GLMOOOR	moorlog
GLMOOYY	myology
GLMORUW	lugworm
GLNNOOR	lorgnon
GLNNOOT	long ton
GLNNSUU	unslung
GLNOOOY	noology
GLNOOPR	prolong
GLNOOPY	polygon
GLNORWY	wrongly
GLNOSUW	sunglow
GLNOTTU	glutton
GLNOUYY	youngly
GLOOORY	orology
GLOOOTY	otology
GLOOOYZ	zoology
GLOORUY	urology
GLORSSY	grossly
GLPRSUY	splurgy
GMMOSUU	gummous
GMMPUUW	mugwump
GMNOORU	gunroom
GMNOORW	morwong
GMNPPUU	pump gun
GMOOSTU	gomutos
GMORSUU	grumous
GMORTUW	mugwort
GMRUYYZ	zymurgy
GNNORUW	ungrown
	wrong'un
GNNORYY	gyronny
GNNOSUW	snow gun
GNNPTUU	punt-gun
GNNRUUW	unwrung
GNNSTUU	stun gun
GNOOORS	gorsoon
GNOOOSS	gossoon
GNOOOYZ	zoogony
GNOOPPS	pop song
GNOPRTU	gunport
GNOPRUW	grown-up
	upgrown
GOOOPTT	go to pot
GOOPRST	Gosport
GOORSTT	grottos
GOORTUW	outgrow
GOPRSSU	gross up
GPSSUUY	gussy up

H

HHIIPPS hippish
HHIISTW whitish
HHIKSTU hush kit
HHIMPTU Thimphu
HHINNSU Hunnish
HHINORS hornish
HHIOPST hip-shot
HHIORSW whorish
HHIOSTT hottish
HHISTUZ shih tzu
HHJNOOP John Hop
HHKNORU Kuh-horn
HHMNORU H H Munro
HHMPRUY Humphry
HHOOSTT hotshot
HHOOSWW who's
who✧
HIIIKRS rikishi
HIIJKNS hijinks
HIIKMSS Sikhism
HIIKNNT think-in
HIIKNOS inkhosi
HIIKNPS kinship
pinkish
HIILLPP Phillip
HIILMTU lithium
HIILNSY shinily
HIILPST shilpit
HIILPTY pithily
HIILRTT trilith
HIILSTT hit list
HIIMPSW wimpish
HIIMRSU shiurim
HIIMSSS missish
HIIMSTT shittim
HIIMSUZ Shimizu
HIINORS noirish
noir-ish
roinish
HIINSSW swinish
HIINSTW Swithin
HIIORST histrio
HIIPSUZ Ziphius
HIIPTTU hit it up
HIIRRSY Irishry
HIJNOUZ Jinzhou
HIKLSSU luskish
HIKLSUY huskily
HIKMNOS monkish
HIKMRSU murkish
HIKNNOR inkhorn
HIKNNTU unthink
HIKNOOP hook-pin
HIKNPSU punkish
Pushkin
HIKNPTU think up
HIKOOPT hook-tip
HIKOORS rookish
HIKORSU Kushiro
HIKORSY Yorkish
HIKRSTU Turkish
HILLOPT hilltop
HILLOPY lyophil
HILLPSY Phyllis
HILLRSY shrilly
HILLRTY thrilly
HILMMOU holmium
HILMOPS lompish
phlomis✧
HILMOSW wholism
HILMPSU lumpish
HILMSUY mushily
HILMTUU thulium
HILNNTY ninthly
HILNOST Shilton
HILNOTY thionyl
HILOOTT otolith
HILOOTZ zoolith
HILORTU urolith
HILOSSW slowish
HILOSTU loutish
HILOSTW wholist
HILOSTY hyloist
HILOSVW wolvish
HILOSWY showily
HILOTWW whitlow
HILOUUZ Liuzhou
HILPRUW upwhirl
HILSSTY stylish
HILSTTY thistly
HILSTXY sixthly
HIMMMTU Thummim
HIMMOST Thomism
HIMMPSU mumpish
HIMMRSU rummish
HIMMSTY mythism
HIMNOOS moonish
HIMNSTY hymnist
HIMNTTU Tim Hunt
HIMOORS moorish✧
HIMOPRS Orphism
rompish
HIMOPSS sophism
HIMOPST mosh pit
photism
HIMORST rim-shot
HIMORTU thorium
HIMOSSU Suomish
HIMOSTT Thomist
HIMOTTU mouth it
HIMOTTY timothy✧
HIMPRSY shrimpy
HIMPRTU triumph
HIMPTUY pythium
HIMRSTY rhymist
HIMSSTU isthmus
HIMSTTY mythist
HINNNSU nunnish
HINNOOT Honiton
HINNORT tinhorn
HINNOST tonnish
HINNPSU nunship
HINOORT hornito
HINOORZ horizon
HINOOST insooth
HINOPPS shippon
HINOPSS sonship
HINOPTU hit upon
HINORST hornist
in short
HINORSU nourish
HINORSY roynish
HINORTW throw in
throw-in
HINOSSW snowish
HINOSTW townish
HINOTTU thin out
HINPPSU pushpin
HINPTUW unwhipt
HINRSTU runtish
HINRTTU in truth
HINSTUW Whitsun
HIOOPRS poorish
HIOPPPS poppish
HIOPPRT trip hop
HIOPPTW whip-top
HIOPRSW worship✧
HIOPSST sophist
HIOPSSY physios
HIOPSTT stop hit
HIOPSTU Photius
uphoist
HIOPSTW Sopwith
HIOPTUW whip out
HIORSSU sourish
HIORSTY history
Toryish
HIORTTW worth it
HIOSSTT sottish
HIOTTUW outwith
without
HIPPSTU pushpit
HIQSSUY squishy
HIRSTTU ruttish
HIRSTTY thirsty
thristy
HJMNOPY John Pym
HJNNOOS Johnson
HJNOSST St John's
HKKLOOZ kolkhoz
HKKOOSY skyhook
HKKOSTU Sukkoth
HKNOOSU Khonsou
HKNOOTU nut-hook
HKNOOWW knowhow
know-how
HKOOOPT pothook
HKORSWY workshy
HLMNOTY monthly
HLMNPYY nymphly
HLMOOTW owl-moth
HLMORRY myrrhol
HLMRTUY Lythrum
HLNOORW horn owl
HLOOSTY soothly
HLOPRTY prothyl
HLORSTY shortly
HLOTUYY youthly
HLPRSUU sulphur
HLPSSUU slush up
HMMNOOY homonym
HMMOOSU hoummos
HMMRTUY thrummy
HMNOPSY nymphos
HMNOPYY hyponym
HMNORST R months
HMNSTUY sun myth
HMOOPRS morphos
HMOOSYZ shmoozy
HMOPRSU rum shop
HNNORSU unshorn
HNNORTU horn-nut
HNNOSTY synthon
HNNOSUW unshown
HNOOPTY typhoon
HNOORSU honours
HNOOSTU Houston
unshoot
HNORTUW unworth
HNOSTUU unshout
HNOTTUU hunt out
HNPSTUU hunt's-up
Pushtun
HNRTTUU untruth
HOOOPPT photo op
HOOPPPS pop-shop
HOOPPST potshop
HOOPRST porthos✧
HOOPSTT hot spot
pot shot
HOOPSTU Pushtoo
shoot up
upshoot
HOOPSTY toyshop
HOORRST orthros
HOOSTTU outshot
HOOSTUW show out
HOPRSTU Hotspur
HOPRTUW throw up
upthrow
HOPSTTU shot put
HOPSTUU push out
push-out
HOPSTUY typhous
HORSTUU outrush
HOSTTUU shut out
shutout
HPRRSUY Pyrrhus
HPRRUUY hurry up
HPRSSUY Syrphus
HRSSTUY thyrsus

I

IIIJJLN jinjili

IIIKMNN minikin
IIISTTW wistiti
IIJLLNO jillion
IIJMNOS misjoin
IIJNNOT injoint
IIKKLNY kinkily
IIKKNPS kipskin
IIKLLMY milkily
IIKLLOS oil silk
IIKLLSY silkily
IIKLMNP limpkin
IIKLMRU Krilium®
IIKLNOS oilskin
IIKLPSY spikily
IIKLRSY riskily
IIKMNOR kirimon
IIKMNPS simpkin✧
IIKMOST Miskito
IIKMPRT pit-mirk
IIKNOSS inkosis
IIKNRST Kirstin
IILLLLW ill-will
IILLLMO oil mill
IILLLSY sillily
IILLMNO million
IILLMSY slimily
IILLNOP pillion
IILLNOZ zillion
IILLNST instill
IILLNTT littlin
IILMNOS lionism
IILMORS similor
IILMOSS limosis
IILMOSZ Zoilism
IILMSTU stimuli
IILMSTY mistily
IILNNOT Nitinol
IILNNSU insulin
IILNNTY tinnily
IILNORS sirloin
IILNOSY noisily
IILNPPY nippily
IILNPTU pilinut
IILNPUV pulvini
IILNRSV rivlins
IILNSUV Vilnius
IILOPRT tripoli✧
IILOPST pilotis
IILORTV vitriol
IILOSTV violist
IILOSTZ Zoilist
IILPRVY privily
IILPSTY tipsily
IILPSWY wispily
IILRTYZ ritzily
IILTTUY utility
IILTTWY wittily
IIMMMNU minimum
IIMMNSU minimus
IIMNNOR minor in
IIMNOSS mission
IIMNOSU nimious
IIMNOSZ Zionism
IIMNOTX mixtion
IIMNPRT imprint
IIMNTTY Tiny Tim
IIMOPSU impious
IIMOSST mitosis
IIMOSSU simious
IIMOSTT Titoism
IIMPSTT Pittism
IIMRTTU tritium
IIMRTUV trivium
IIMSSTU missuit
IINNOOP opinion
IINNOPT in point
pin it on
IINNOTU unition
IINNPRT in print
IINNQTU Quintin
IINOPRT rip into
IINOPSS isospin
sinopis
IINORSS Rossini
IINORST ironist
IINORTT introit
IINORTV in vitro
IINOSTZ Zionist
IINOSUV invious
IINOTTU tuition
IINPRST strip in
IINQRUY inquiry
IINRTTY trinity✧
IINSSTU SI units
IINSTTW intwist
IIOPRSS pissoir
IIOQSTU Iquitos
IIORRSV Sir Ivor
IIORSSV virosis
IIORSTV ivorist
visitor
IIOSTTT Titoist
IIOSTTU oustiti
IIPRSST spirits
tripsis
IIPRSTY spirity
IIPRTTZ Tirpitz
IIPRTVY privity
IJJSTUU ju-jitsu
IJKLLOY killjoy
IJKMPSU ski jump
IJLLLOY jollily
IJLLOTY jollity
IJLMNOR Mjölnir
IJLMPUY jumpily
IJLNOQU jonquil
IJLNOTY jointly
IJLOSSU jus soli
IJNNOTU unjoint
IKKLOOY kookily
IKKMNOU kikumon
IKKNORT kirkton
IKKOOPY kopiyok
IKKRSTU Irkutsk
IKLLPSU upskill
IKLLSUY sulkily
IKLMNPU lumpkin
IKLMNRU milk run
IKLMOOS lookism
IKLMOPS milksop
IKLMOSY smokily
IKLMRUY murkily
IKLMSUY muskily
IKLNOOS skolion
IKLNOOT kiloton
IKLNOWY wonkily
IKLNPSU skulpin
IKLNRWY wrinkly
IKLNTWY twinkly
IKLOOTT toolkit
IKLOSSU souslik
IKMNOOO okimono
IKMNOOS kimonos
Mikonos
monoski
IKMNORS mikrons
IKMNOSW misknow
IKMNPPU pumpkin
IKMNRTU trinkum
IKMOOST mistook
IKMOSSU koumiss
IKNNPTU unpinkt
IKNOOST isokont
IKNOPPS skin-pop
IKNOPST inkspot
IKNOSSW sow-skin
IKNPPRU prink up
IKNPSTU sputnik
IKORSTY Yorkist
IKPRSSY krypsis
ILLLOWY lowlily
ILLMNOU mullion
ILLMNRU millrun
ILLMOOR moorill
ILLMPUY lumpily
ILLMSUU limulus
ILLNOQU quillon
ILLNORU rullion
ILLNPUU lupulin
ILLNRTU ill turn
ILLNTUY nullity
ILLOOOW wool oil
ILLOORZ zorillo
ILLOPRY pillory
ILLOPWY pillowy
ILLORTU Utrillo
ILLORTV Torvill
ILLOSUV villous
ILLOSUY lousily
ILLOTXY xylitol
ILLOWWY willowy
ILLPPUY pulpily
ILLQSSU squills
ILLRSUY surlily
ILLSTUY lustily
ILMMRUY rummily
ILMMSUU mimulus
ILMNOOT moonlit
ILMNOTW Miltown®
ILMOORY roomily
ILMOOSS molossi
ILMOPPU oil pump
ILMORTU turmoil
ILMOSTY moistly
ILMOSUY mousily
ILMPSTU plumist
ILMSTUY mustily
Mytilus
ILMUYZZ muzzily
ILNNOPS non-slip
ILNNSUY sunnily
ILNOOOP poon-oil
ILNOOPS plosion
ILNOOPV volpino
ILNOORV Livorno
ILNOOST soliton
ILNOPRU purloin
ILNOPSU upsilon
ILNOPSY ypsilon
ILNORST nostril
ILNORSU surloin
ILNORTU torulin
ILNOSTT Stilton®
ILNOSTY stonily
ILNOSWY snowily
ILNOTUV volutin
ILNPSTU unspilt
ILNTTUY nuttily
ILOOORS rosolio
ILOOPST poloist
topsoil
ILOORTY olitory
ILOOSST soloist
ILOOSTY sootily
ILOOWYZ woozily
ILOPPSY soppily
ILOPRSY prosily
ILOPSUY piously
ILOQRTU Torquil
ILORRSY sorrily
ILORSTU Troilus
ILOSSTU St Louis
ILOSSTY tossily
tylosis
ILPPSTU split up
split-up
ILRSTUY rustily
ILSSTTY stylist
IMMNOSU musimon
IMMNOUU muonium
IMMOPTU optimum
IMMSSTU summist
IMNNNOU munnion
IMNNOOR norimon

IMNNSSU Sunnism
IMNOOPP pompion
IMNOOPT tompion
IMNOORR morrion
IMNOORT monitor
tromino
IMNOOSS monosis
IMNOOST motions
IMNOOSU ominous
IMNOOSY isonomy
IMNOOUX oxonium
IMNOPPU pumpion
IMNOPRW pinworm
IMNOPSU spumoni
IMNORRU murrion
IMNORTY trionym
IMNOSVY visnomy
IMOOPRX proximo
IMOOSSS osmosis
IMOOSSU osmious
IMOPRST tropism
IMOPRTU protium
IMOPSTU utopism
IMOPTUW wimp out
IMORSTU tourism
IMORSTY Toryism
trisomy
IMOSSTU miss out
IMOSSUZ Zosimus
IMOSSYZ zymosis
IMOSTUV vomitus
IMOSTUW outswim
IMQRSUY squirmy
IMRSSTU sistrum
trismus
IMRTTUY yttrium
INNNOOR non-iron
INNNORU runnion
INNOOPS opsonin
INNOOST notions
INNOPUW win upon
INNOQTU Quinton
INNORTU run into
INNOSTU nonsuit
INNOSTW Winston
INNQSUY squinny
INOOPRT portion
INOOPSS poisson
INOOPST Options
positon
INOOPTT to point
INOORST isotron
nitroso
torsion
INOORSZ zorinos
INOORTT tortoni
INOORTU iron out
INOORTW tow-iron
INOOSUX noxious
INOPPST topspin
INOPPTT pint-pot
INOPPTU point up
INOPPTY pit pony
INOPSSU poussin✧
spinous
INOPSTU sit upon
sit-upon
spin out
spinout
INOPTTU put it on
INORRTU run riot
INORSTT Tritons
INORSTU nitrous
INORSUU ruinous
urinous
INORSUV unvisor
INORTTY try it on
INOSSUU sinuous
INPRSTU unstrip
INPRSTY trypsin
INPRTUY turnipy
INQSTUY squinty
INRSSUU Ursinus
INRSTTU in trust
intrust
INSSTUU sunsuit
INSTTUW untwist
INTTUWY unwitty
IOOPRSS porosis
IOOPRSV proviso
IOOPSTY isotopy
IOORSSS sorosis
IOORSTT risotto
IOORSTU riotous
IOPPPRT pitprop
IOPPRST ripstop
IOPPSTT pit stop
IOPRSSY pyrosis
IOPRSTT protist
sport it
tropist
IOPRTTU trip out
IOPSTTU spit out
utopist
IOPTTTU put to it
IOQRTTU quittor
IORRTTX tortrix
IORSSTU tsouris
IORSTTU stir out
tourist
IORSTTW twistor
IPRRSTU stirrup
IPRSSUU Spurius
IPRSTUU pursuit
IPSSSTY stypsis
IPTTTUY tittupy

J

JLLOPUY jolly up
JMOPTUU jump out
outjump
JNNOOSW Jon Snow
JNNORUY non-jury
JNOORSU journos
sojourn
JNOSTUW just now

K

KLLMOSU mollusk
KLNOOOW Kowloon
KLOOOTU look out
lookout
outlook
KLOOOUY look you
KNNNOUW unknown
KNNORSY Nynorsk
KNOOPTT topknot
KNOOUWY you know
KNOPRTY krypton
KNORRTY krytron
KNPPSUU spunk up
KOOPRTW worktop
KOORTUW outwork
work out
workout
KOOSSUU soukous
KORSTTY Trotsky
KORTTUW tutwork

L

LLLMMUU mulmull
LLLOOOR loo roll
LLMOOPR rollmop
LLMPPUY plumply
LLOOPRT roll-top
trollop
LLOORTU rollout
LLOPTUU pull out
pull-out
LLORSWY L S Lowry
LMMPSUU lump sum
LMNOOOS Solomon
LMOOOTV Molotov
LMOOSTY toylsom
LMOPSUU plumous
LMOPSUY Olympus
LMORSUU Romulus
LMRSTUU lustrum
LMSTUUU tumulus
LNNOPSU nonplus
LNOOOTY only too
LNOOPTU pultoon
LNRTUUV vulturn
LNRTUUY untruly
LOOOORS oloroso
LOOORST rotolos
LOOPSTU slop out
LOOSTTY Tolstoy
LOPPSUU pulpous
LOPPSUY polypus
LOPRSUY pylorus
LOPRTUY poultry
LORSTUU torulus
LOSTTUY stoutly
LPRSSUU surplus

M

MMNOSSU summons
MMOOPRS Mormops
MMOPPRS Mrs Mopp
MMOPSTY symptom
MNNOOOS monsoon
MNNOSYY synonym
MNNOTUU unmount
MNOOOPP pompoon
MNOOOYZ zoonomy
MNOOPTY toponym
MNOORSU sun room
MNOOSUY onymous
MNOOTTW towmont
MNOPRTU no-trump
MNOPTUU mount up
MNORSTU nostrum
MNOTTUY muttony
MOOOTUZ zoom out
MOOOTYZ zootomy
MOOPPSU pompous
MOOPSSU opossum
MOOPSTT topmost
MOORTTT Tom-trot
MOORTUW worm out
MOOSTTU outmost
MOPPTUU pump out
MOPSSUU spumous
MORRSTU rostrum
MPPRTUU trump up
MPPSTUU stump up

N

NNNSUUY unsunny
NNOOOPT pontoon
NNOOPRU pronoun
NNOOPSS sponson
NNOOPST non-stop
NNORSUW unsworn
NNOSSUY unsonsy
NNOSTYY syntony
NOOORTT Toronto
NOOPRSS sponsor
NOOPTUU out upon
NOORSTU unroost
NOORTUW outworn
worn-out
NOPPTUU put upon
NOPRSUU soup run
NOPSSTU sunspot
NOPSTUU spun-out
NORSTTU on trust
NORTTUU outturn
turn out
turnout
NRSSTTU strunts
NRSSTUU sturnus
untruss

NRSTTUU untrust

O

OOOOPRT poor-oot
potoroo
OOOPPTU poop out
OOOPRTU outroop
OOORTTU outroot
root out
OOPRRTW row port
OOPRSSU soursop
OOPRSTU portous
OOPRSTV provost
OOPRTTU outport
OOPRTUU outpour
pour out
pour-out
roup out
OOPSSTT tosspot
OOPSTTU outpost
spot out
stop out
stop-out
OORSTTU sort out
OORSTUU routous
OORTTTU trot out
OORTTUU rout out
OOSSTTU toss out
OPPRRTU purport
OPPRSTU support
OPPRSTY stroppy
OPPRSUY pyropus
OPTTTUU putt out
ORSSUUU usurous
ORSTTUU surtout
OSSSTUU suss out

8 letters

A

AAAABENN anabaena
AAAACCRR caracara
AAAACGNR caragana
AAAACJRR jararaca
AAAACNPR pacarana
AAAACNRS anasarca
AAAADMTV amadavat
AAAADTVV avadavat
AAAAEMNR Aramaean
AAAAGGRR agar-agar
AAAAHJMR maharaja
AAAAHMNY Mahayana
AAAAIMPR arapaima
AAAAINPY Ayia Napa
AAAAIRTX ataraxia
AAAAJKRR jararaka
AAAAJNRT Nataraja
AAAAKKMT takamaka
AAAAKKNT katakana
AAAAKKWW kawakawa
AAAAKLRZ kala-azar
AAAALLVV lava-lava
AAAALNTT Atalanta
AAAAMMTT matamata
AAAAMNRY Ramayana
AAAANNST Santa Ana
AAAARRSS sasarara
AAABBBRS Barabbas
AAABBELT abatable
AAABBHKL kabbalah
AAABBILT abbatial
AAABBNRS Barnabas
AAABCCRT baccarat
AAABCHLS calabash
AAABCHMU macahuba
AAABCINT anabatic
AAABCITT ciabatta
AAABCNRR barracan
barranca
AAABCNRU carnauba
AAABCPRY capybara
AAABDDHN a dab hand
AAABDENS Banda Sea
AAABDEST database
AAABDHHL Habdalah
AAABDKNT databank
AAABDNNN bandanna
AAABDNRS saraband
AAABDNRT abradant
AAABEFNV fava bean
AAABEGHL galabeah
AAABEGLL gallabea
AAABEHNR habanera
AAABEHRT barathea
AAABEILT Labiatae
AAABEKKK kaka beak
AAABELLR Arabella
AAABELNN Alan Bean
AAABEMPR parabema
AAABERWY bear away
AAABFHLR half a bar
AAABGHIL galabiah
AAABGHST Ashgabat
AAABGILL gallabia
AAABGLOR algaroba
AAABGLOY Algoa Bay
AAABGMNQ mbaqanga
AAABGNRZ Braganza
AAABGRTU rutabaga
AAABHIMN Bahamian
AAABHLMR Alhambra
AAABHMNR Brahmana
AAABHRST Sabratha
AAABILNN Albanian
AAABILTT battalia
AAABINSS anabasis
AAABINTV Batavian
AAABIPSS piassaba
AAABKPSS baasskap
AAABLMOS abomasal
AAABLMST tambalas
AAABLOPR parabola
AAABMMNR Abram-man
AAABNSTU sauba ant
AAABPRST tapas bar
AAABRSUY Surabaya
AAABTTTU a battuta
AAACCDIN Accadian
AAACCELN calcanea
AAACCEPR carapace
AAACCILR calcaria
AAACCIMM caimacam
AAACCRTT cataract
AAACCTTU tac-au-tac
AAACDEIM academia
AAACDENR Dracaena
AAACDEQU aquacade
AAACDETU acaudate
AAACDFIR faradaic
AAACDILM Adamical
AAACDILR caldaria
AAACDINN Canadian
AAACDINR acaridan
Arcadian
AAACDKLY lackaday
AAACDNNO anaconda
AAACDNPR panda car
AAACDNRS sandarac
AAACDNYZ Anzac Day
AAACDOTV advocaat
AAACEEFG Fagaceae
AAACEETX Taxaceae
AAACEGNT agaçante
AAACEGTU aguacate
AAACEHLP Acalepha
AAACEHLT calathea
AAACEHLZ chalazae
AAACEHNR Archaean
AAACELMY Macleaya
AAACELNT analecta
AAACELRT à la carte
AAACELST catalase
AAACENNP panacean
AAACENST Castanea
AAACENVV vena cava
AAACEPRV praecava
AAACERTT tear a cat
AAACGHNR Garnacha
AAACGINT caatinga
AAACGLSW scalawag
AAACGMNP campagna
AAACGMNR Armagnac
AAACHHHL Halachah
AAACHINT Cathaian
AAACHIPS aphasiac
Caiaphas
AAACHLLZ chalazal
AAACHLNR anarchal
AAACHLSZ chalazas

AAACHNTY	Cathayan
AAACIJMN	Jamaican
AAACILMN	maniacal
AAACILMR	calamari
AAACILRS	Scalaria
AAACILRV	calvaria
AAACILSY	calisaya
AAACINRT	Craniata
AAACINSU	Nausicaa
AAACINTV	cavatina
AAACIPSU	sapucaia
AAACIRRS	sacraria
AAACIRTX	ataraxic
AAACJLTU	Acajutla
AAACKMRT	tamarack
AAACLLPY	pay a call
AAACLLWY	call away
AAACLMRY	calamary
AAACLMUY	Macaulay
AAACLRST	alcatras
AAACMRSS	macassar
AAACMRSU	amaracus
AAACNOPT	caponata
AAACNOSV	Casanova
AAACRRWY	carraway
AAACSTWY	cast away
	castaway
AAADDHIL	Id al-Adha
AAADDORV	Vadodara
AAADEFWY	fade-away
AAADEGIM	Agamidae
AAADEGNP	apanaged
AAADEHMV	Mahadeva
AAADEINR	Araneida
AAADEKMV	kamadeva✧
AAADELMS	Adam's ale
AAADELRW	a raw deal
AAADEMNN	Mandaean
AAADEMNP	empanada
AAADEMSV	Samaveda
	Sama-Veda
AAADEMTT	metadata
AAADENPS	Pasadena
AAADENTV	vanadate
AAADEPRT	tapadera
AAADGGHH	Haggadah
AAADGHNR	Angharad
AAADGIMM	gammadia
AAADGLMY	amygdala
AAADGLNN	Nagaland
AAADGMRT	datagram
AAADHHLV	Havdalah
AAADHKNR	Kandahar
AAADHMNR	Ramadhan
AAADHMRS	madrasah
AAADHNRT	thanadar
AAADIILR	radialia
AAADIKKN	Akkadian
AAADILLP	palladia
AAADILMT	Dalmatia
AAADILRS	Alasdair
AAADILRU	adularia
AAADIMMR	Mad Maria
AAADIMNY	adynamia
AAADJKRT	Djakarta
AAADKLMN	kalamdan
AAADKRRV	aardvark
AAADLLLN	la-la land✧
AAADLMNQ	qalamdan
AAADLMNY	Mandalay
AAADLMOT	alta moda
AAADMNOR	Maradona
AAADMNSW	Aswan Dam
AAADMNTU	tamandua
AAADMORT	matadora
AAADMRSS	madrassa
AAAEGISS	assegaai
AAAEGLMX	malaxage
AAAEGLRT	altarage
AAAEGNPP	appanage
AAAEGRST	gastraea
AAAEHMNT	anathema
AAAEHNPS	anaphase
AAAEIMRV	ave Maria
AAAEINRR	Arenaria
AAAEKKRT	karateka
AAAEKLLV	Kalevala
AAAEKLNT	Lake Tana
AAAEKMNU	Mauna Kea
AAAEKMWY	make away
AAAEKTWY	take away
	takeaway
AAAELLST	all at sea
AAAELMMN	analemma
AAAELMPT	palamate
AAAELMTX	malaxate
AAAELRTV	lavatera
AAAELRVZ	A Alvarez
AAAENNRZ	Nazarean
AAAENOPR	paranoea
AAAENPRV	paravane
AAAENPST	anapaest
AAAERTWY	tear away
	tearaway
AAAERWWY	wear away
AAAFFLLR	farfalla
AAAFGINR	Graafian
AAAFGIRR	Fragaria
AAAFGLNO	Fanagalo
AAAFHLNN	half anna
AAAFINST	fantasia
AAAFINUV	avifauna
AAAFLLWY	fall away
AAAGGLLN	galangal
AAAGGLOP	galapago
AAAGHINN	Ghanaian
AAAGHINP	Panhagia
AAAGHINR	hiragana
AAAGHIPR	agraphia
AAAGHLMS	Malagash
AAAGHMOY	maha yoga
AAAGHNST	ashtanga
AAAGHNTY	yataghan
AAAGIKNS	Nagasaki
AAAGILPT	patagial
AAAGILRT	aligarta
AAAGILRU	La Guaira
AAAGIMMT	gammatia
AAAGINPT	Ganapati
AAAGINRR	agrarian
AAAGJORY	raja yoga
AAAGLMST	stalagma
AAAGLMSY	Malagasy
AAAGLNRS	Sangraal
AAAGLRRW	warragal
AAAGLRST	astragal
AAAGMMRY	gamma ray
AAAGMPRR	paragram
AAAGNOPR	araponga
AAAGNPRS	parasang
AAAGNPRU	arapunga
AAAGNRTU	Tauranga
AAAGORST	Saratoga
AAAGPRUY	Paraguay
AAAHHHKL	Halakhah
AAAHHITW	Hiawatha
AAAHIINW	Hawaiian
AAAHIKLR	Kalahari
AAAHILMY	Himalaya
AAAHIMNR	maharani
AAAHIMNS	shamiana
AAAHIMRT	hamartia
	Mata Hari
AAAHINNY	Hinayana
AAAHINPR	raphania
AAAHJLMT	Taj Mahal
AAAHKMNS	khansama
AAAHKRSS	rakshasa
AAAHKRWY	hark away
AAAHLLLV	Valhalla
AAAHLLLW	Walhalla
AAAHMMPR	Parma ham
AAAHMNNS	manna-ash
AAAHMNRT	amaranth
AAAHMNST	Samantha
AAAHMRTT	Mahratta
AAAHNNSV	savannah✧
AAAHNOPR	anaphora
AAAHNSST	Sathanas
AAAHNSTY	athanasy
AAAHOPRS	Arapahos
AAAHSWWY	wash away
	wash-away
AAAHTTWY	thataway
AAAIIMRT	Tia Maria®
AAAIINPR	apiarian
AAAIKKMM	kaimakam
AAAIKKSW	Kawasaki
AAAIKLTT	Lattakia
AAAILLMR	malarial
AAAILLPT	palatial
AAAILLRW	illawara
AAAILMMM	Mammalia

AAAILMNR	malarian
AAAILMNW	Malawian
AAAILMRT	Altamira
AAAILMSV	malvasia
AAAILMSY	Malaysia
AAAILNRU	aularian
AAAILNST	alsatian✧
AAAILNTT	Alan Tait
AAAILPRV	paravail
AAAILRST	Alastair
	salariat
AAAILRSU	Laurasia
AAAILTWY	tail away
AAAIMMMM	Mamma Mia
	Mamma Mia!
AAAIMMQQ	qaimaqam
AAAIMMRS	Aramaism
AAAIMMST	miasmata
AAAIMNOZ	Amazonia
AAAIMNRR	marinara
AAAIMNST	Tasmania
AAAIMRST	Sarmatia
AAAIMRTT	Marattia
AAAINNRR	ranarian
AAAINNTZ	Tanzania
AAAINOPR	paranoia
AAAINQRU	aquarian✧
AAAINRSV	Varanasi
AAAINRTT	Tatarian
AAAIPSSV	piassava
AAAIRRSV	rara avis
AAAJNPWX	Japan wax
AAAKKORT	Krakatoa
AAAKKTZZ	kazatzka
AAAKLWWY	walk away
	walk-away
AAAKMNRS	namaskar
AAAKMRSS	Makassar
AAAKMTUU	kaumatua
AAAKNRSS	Arkansas
AAAKOSWY	soakaway
AAALLMPV	lava lamp
AAALLPRX	parallax
AAALMNOU	Mauna Loa
AAALMNTZ	Mazatlan
AAALNNPT	platanna
AAALNNTU	Annulata
AAALNPRT	rataplan
AAALNRTT	tarlatan
AAALPRST	satrapal
AAALSTWY	salt away
AAAMNNNN	Manannan
AAAMNOPR	panorama
AAAMNRRY	yarraman
AAAMNRST	rastaman✧
AAAMNRTY	manta ray✧
AAAMNSTZ	Matanzas
AAAMNTTY	manyatta
AAAMORSU	Aura-Soma
AAAMOTTU	automata
AAAMQSTU	Squamata
AAAMRRSZ	zamarras
AAAMRRTT	Mt Ararat
AAAMRTTU	traumata
AAAMRTZZ	razmataz
AAANOPRZ	parazoan
AAANORSY	sayonara
AAANPRTV	paravant
AAANQTUU	aquanaut
AAANRSTT	tarantas
AAANRWWY	warn away
AAAORSWY	soaraway
AAAPQRTU	Paraquat®
AAAPQRUU	aqua pura
AAAPSSST	passatas
AAAPSSWY	pass away
AAASTWYY	stayaway
AABBCDKN	backband
AABBCDRS	scabbard
AABBCEFY	baby face
AABBCEKR	bareback
AABBCEKT	backbeat
AABBCINR	barbican
AABBCIRR	barbaric
AABBCIST	sabbatic
AABBCORS	barbasco
AABBCTTY	tabby cat
AABBDEIS	Abbaside
AABBDEKR	bad break
AABBDENS	baseband
AABBDERT	barbated
AABBDHIT	bad habit
AABBDHIU	Abu Dhabi
AABBDORS	Barbados
AABBEEKL	Lake Abbé
AABBEELR	bearable
AABBEELT	beatable
AABBEILL	bailable
AABBEKLN	bankable
AABBELLM	blamable
AABBELLS	baseball
AABBELRY	bearably
AABBELTY	Table Bay
AABBEORT	bareboat
AABBHHLL	blah-blah
AABBHKKU	Habbakuk
AABBHKSU	babushka
AABBIILL	bilabial
AABBILRT	barbital
AABBIRSU	babirusa
AABBKLTY	baby talk
AABBKNNR	bank barn
AABBLLMY	blamably
AABBLSSU	subbasal
AABBMMOZ	zambomba
AABBNOOR	bona-roba
AABBSSTU	bass tuba
AABCCCHI	bacchiac
AABCCEHK	backache
AABCCELR	cable-car
AABCCELS	cascabel
AABCCERT	braccate
AABCCHIN	bacchian✧
AABCCHIS	biscacha
AABCCHIZ	bizcacha
AABCCHKS	cashback
AABCCHKT	backchat
AABCCHNT	bacchant
AABCCINN	cannabic
AABCCKKP	backpack
AABCCKLL	call back
	call-back
AABCCKLP	black cap
	blackcap
AABCCKLT	black-cat
AABCCKLW	claw back
	clawback
AABCCKST	backcast
	cast back
AABCCMOT	catacomb
AABCDEIN	abidance
AABCDEIO	Boadicea
	Daboecia
AABCDEIT	abdicate
AABCDEKT	back-date
AABCDELL	caballed
AABCDELN	balanced
AABCDHKN	backhand
AABCDHKR	hardback
AABCDIIS	diabasic
AABCDIKL	laid-back
AABCDIMO	Cambodia
AABCDINT	abdicant
AABCDKLN	backland
AABCDKLO	back-load
AABCDKNR	bank card
AABCDKRW	backward
	draw back
	drawback
AABCDKRY	backyard
AABCDLLN	band-call
AABCDLNR	land crab
AABCDNRR	brancard
AABCDNST	cab-stand
AABCEEHS	sea beach
AABCEEIX	Bixaceae
AABCEENY	abeyance
AABCEERS	scarabee
AABCEERT	acerbate
AABCEERV	cave-bear
AABCEGOT	cabotage
AABCEHKV	have back
AABCEHLS	cashable
AABCEHNR	barchane
AABCEILM	amicable
AABCEILR	Balearic
AABCEIMN	ambiance
AABCEINR	carabine
AABCEIRT	bacteria
AABCEITT	ciabatte
AABCEJKN	jack bean
AABCEJNO	Jacobean
AABCEKKT	take back

AABCEKLM	clambake
AABCEKLN	back lane
AABCEKLR	lacebark
AABCEKLS	Black Sea
	sackable
AABCEKLT	black tea
AABCEKMR	barm cake
AABCELLP	placable
AABCELLR	caballer
	race-ball
AABCELLS	scalable
AABCELNR	balancer
	barnacle
AABCELOR	albacore
AABCELRT	bracteal
AABCELWY	cableway
AABCEMRV	vambrace
AABCENRR	Canberra
AABCENYY	abeyancy
AABCEORT	boat race✧
AABCEPRS	space bar
AABCERTT	cabretta
AABCESSU	abacuses
AABCFHKL	halfback
AABCFIIL	bifacial
AABCFKLL	backfall
	fall back
	fall-back
AABCFKLT	flatback
AABCFKST	fastback
AABCGHKN	hang back
AABCGKLO	cloak-bag
AABCGKLS	gas black
AABCHIKR	back-hair
AABCHILR	brachial
AABCHINR	branchia
AABCHKKR	hark back
	hark-back
AABCHKLS	backlash
AABCHKRS	shabrack
AABCHKSW	backwash
AABCHLOO	coolabah
AABCHMRY	chambray
AABCHRRT	bar chart
AABCIILS	basilica
AABCIINR	brainiac
	Cabirian
AABCIJNO	Bajocian
	Jacobian
AABCIKLT	tailback
AABCILLR	bacillar
AABCILMS	balsamic
	cabalism
AABCILMY	amicably
AABCILNN	cannibal
AABCILNO	anabolic
AABCILST	basaltic
	cabalist
AABCIMNR	Cambrian
AABCINNN	cannabin
AABCINNO	Baconian
AABCINNR	cinnabar
AABCINNS	cannabis
AABCINRT	Bactrian
AABCINSU	banausic
AABCINSY	Biscayan
AABCIRSS	brassica
AABCISSS	abscissa
AABCKKLT	back talk
	talk back
	talkback
AABCKLNO	loanback
AABCKLNY	clay-bank
AABCKLPY	play back
	playback
AABCKLRT	black art
	black rat
AABCKNRS	snack bar
AABCKPRT	brat pack
	bratpack
	brat-pack
AABCKPSS	back pass
	pass-back
AABCKRRS	barracks
AABCKSWY	swayback
AABCLLLO	coalball
AABCLLLY	ballclay
AABCLLPY	placably
AABCLLSY	scalably
AABCLNUU	cunabula
AABCLORW	Clara Bow
AABCLRRY	carbaryl
AABCNORR	barranco
AABCRSTT	abstract
AABCRSWY	crab-yaws
AABDDEEM	Adam Bede
AABDDEET	deadbeat
	dead-beat
AABDDEHL	bald-head
AABDDEHN	headband
AABDDEMR	bad dream
AABDDENR	brandade
AABDDESS	badassed
AABDDINZ	zindabad
AABDDLNS	badlands
AABDDLNU	dual band
AABDDMOR	damboard
AABDDORY	broad day
AABDDYYY	day by day
AABDEEHL	beheadal
AABDEEKM	make a bed
AABDEELR	bear-lead
	readable
AABDEELT	dateable
	dealbate
AABDEELV	evadable
AABDEELW	wadeable
AABDEERT	tea bread
AABDEERY	bayadère
AABDEGHN	headbang
AABDEGIN	badinage
AABDEGIR	bigarade
AABDEGLR	gradable
AABDEGNT	T-bandage
AABDEHHI	dahabieh
AABDEHKR	hardbake
AABDEHMR	hardbeam
AABDEHRR	bear hard
AABDEILN	baladine
AABDEILR	Labridae
	laid bare
AABDEINR	Abderian
AABDEIOU	aboideau
AABDEJLL	djellaba
AABDEKPR	brake pad
AABDEKRY	Baker day
	daybreak
AABDELLS	Ballades
AABDELLU	laudable
AABDELMN	damnable
AABDELMO	do a Melba
AABDELOR	adorable
AABDELOS	base-load
AABDELPP	bad apple
AABDELPT	baldpate
AABDELRS	baselard
AABDELRT	Adalbert
	tradable
AABDELRW	drawable
AABDELRY	readably
AABDELSW	sawblade
AABDEMNS	beadsman
AABDEMRS	smear dab
	smear-dab
AABDENNR	banner ad
	nan bread
AABDENRY	Enard Bay
AABDENTU	unabated
AABDENUX	bandeaux
AABDENVW	waveband
AABDEORS	seaboard
AABDEORT	teaboard
AABDERRT	taberdar
AABDERRW	bearward
AABDERTU	baud rate
AABDERTV	vartabed
AABDERWY	waybread
AABDFHIT	bad faith
AABDFHLN	fahlband
AABDFRRT	draft-bar
AABDGHOT	Godthaab
AABDGMOS	gambados
AABDGNOV	vagabond
AABDGOOR	go abroad
AABDGORR	garboard
AABDGOTU	gad about
	gadabout
AABDHINR	hairband
AABDHLLN	handball
AABDHLLR	hardball
AABDHNST	sand bath
AABDHRSU	subahdar
AABDHRSW	Bradshaw

AABDIILS	basidial
AABDILLN	balladin
AABDILNT	tailband
AABDILNU	Abu Nidal
AABDIMNR	madbrain
AABDINNR	rainband
AABDINRY	Ian Brady
AABDKLNN	land bank
AABDKLRS	Karlsbad
AABDKNNS	sandbank
AABDLLRY	balladry
AABDLLUY	laudably
AABDLMNU	labdanum
AABDLMNY	damnably
AABDLNNO	Alan Bond
AABDLNPT	platband
AABDLOOT	boatload
AABDLOPR	lap-board
AABDLORR	Labrador
	larboard
AABDLORY	adorably
	Labor Day
AABDMNNS	bandsman
AABDMNNY	bandyman
AABDMOTU	mad about
AABDNNTU	abundant
AABDNPSS	pass band
AABDNRRS	Barnard's
AABDNRRY	barnyard
AABDNRTU	a bad turn
AABDOPRX	pax-board
AABDORRY	Arbor Day
AABDORSV	bravados
AABDORWY	broadway✧
	wayboard
AABDOTUY	day about
AABDRRSS	brassard
AABDRSTY	bastardy
AABEEFLN	flea-bane
AABEEFLS	leaf-base
AABEEGHR	Bagheera
AABEEGKR	breakage
AABEEGNT	abnegate
AABEEHLL	healable
AABEEHLT	hateable
AABEEHMR	harambee
AABEEKLM	makeable
AABEEKLT	takeable
AABEEKMT	bakemeat
	makebate
AABEEKRT	tea break
AABEEKRW	bakeware
AABEELLS	leasable
	saleable
	sealable
AABEELMN	amenable
	nameable
AABEELMT	tameable
AABEELPT	tapeable
AABEELRS	erasable
AABEELRT	rateable
	tearable
AABEELRW	wearable
AABEELST	eatables
AABEELTT	tea table
AABEEMPR	abampere
AABEEMRS	sea bream
AABEENNW	wannabee✧
AABEENOR	anaerobe
AABEERRS	bear's ear
	bear's-ear
AABEERRT	aberrate
AABEERST	base rate
AABEERTT	trabeate
AABEESST	sea beast
AABEETVW	beta wave
AABEFHKL	halfbeak
AABEFLMR	farmable
AABEFLMU	flambeau
AABEFLSY	False Bay
AABEGHKS	shake-bag
AABEGHLN	hangable
AABEGHNR	berghaan
AABEGHRT	earth-bag
AABEGILN	gainable
AABEGLLL	glabella
AABEGLLM	ball game
	game ball
AABEGLNR	angle bar
AABEGLRT	glabrate
AABEGLRU	arguable
AABEGMNR	bargeman
AABEGMNY	mangabey
AABEGMRT	bregmata
AABEGMTT	gambetta
AABEGNOR	baronage
AABEGORT	abrogate
AABEGOST	sabotage
AABEGRTW	water bag
AABEHIRR	herbaria
AABEHITW	Wahabite
AABEHKLS	shakable
AABEHKWY	Hawke Bay
AABEHLMS	shamable
AABEHLNY	Hyblaean
AABEHLOT	oathable
AABEHLPS	shapable
AABEHLPT	alphabet
AABEHLRS	sharable
AABEHLRW	warhable
AABEHLSW	washable
AABEHNOR	habanero
	habañero
AABEHRTT	at the bar
AABEIKLS	kielbasa
AABEIKLW	Lake Biwa
AABEIKRR	air-brake
AABEILLM	mailable
AABEILLS	isabella✧
	sailable
AABEILMN	Lima bean
AABEILNR	inarable
AABEILNS	banalise
AABEILNZ	banalize
AABEILRS	Rabelais
	raisable
AABEILRV	variable
AABEILST	satiable
AABEILTV	ablative
AABEIMRU	Mirabeau
AABEINOZ	zabaione
AABEINPR	pea-brain
AABEINRR	Briarean
AABEINRT	rabatine
AABEINST	basanite
AABEIOTU	aboiteau
AABEIPRS	base pair
AABEIRSV	abrasive
AABEIRTU	aubretia
	aubrieta
AABEISUV	Beauvais
AABEJKRW	break-jaw
AABEJMUX	jambeaux
AABEJNOZ	Joan Baez
AABEKLLT	talkable
AABEKLLW	walkable
AABEKLRR	Karl Baer
AABEKMNR	brakeman
AABEKNPT	peat bank
AABEKNRS	Nebraska
AABEKNRT	bank rate
AABEKNRV	brake van
AABEKOTW	take a bow
AABEKPRR	parbreak
AABEKRRS	baresark
AABEKRTX	tax break
AABELLMR	Marbella
AABELLMT	meatball
AABELLNO	loanable
AABELLOV	above all
AABELLPP	palpable
AABELLPS	lapsable
AABELLPY	playable
AABELLSV	salvable
AABELLSY	saleably
AABELLUV	valuable
AABELMNY	amenably
AABELMOT	Metabola
AABELMPP	mappable
AABELMST	blastema
	lambaste
AABELMSU	amusable
AABELMTT	table mat
AABELMTU	ambulate
AABELNNT	tannable
AABELNPS	anableps
AABELNPT	pantable
AABELNRY	balneary
AABELOPR	parabole
AABELORR	arboreal
AABELORS	bresaola
AABELOSV	lavaboes
AABELOVW	avowable

AABELPPT	tappable
AABELPRS	sparable
AABELPSS	passable
AABELRST	arbalest
	balestra
AABELRTY	betrayal✧
	rateably
AABELSTT	statable
	tastable
AABELSTW	wastable
AABELTTU	tabulate
AABELTTX	battle ax
	battle-ax
AABELTUX	tableaux
AABEMNRT	Bramante
AABEMRRS	bear arms
	embarras
AABENNOT	not a bean
AABENNPS	snap bean
AABENOSY	soya bean
AABENRRT	aberrant
AABENRST	ratsbane
	Strabane
AABENSTU	Antabuse®
AABENSVY	Evans Bay
AABEOPRV	above par
AABEORRT	arboreta
AABEORST	rabatoes
AABEORTW	water boa
AABERSTY	beta rays
AABFGINR	brain fag
AABFHLLL	half-ball
AABFILUX	fabliaux
AABFLLST	fastball
AABFLOTT	faltboat
	flatboat
AABGGNOT	taboggan
AABGGRRT	braggart
AABGHKRS	shagbark
AABGHPRR	bar graph
AABGILNT	bang-tail
AABGILRU	Bulgaria
AABGIMSU	gambusia
AABGISTW	waist bag
AABGLLLO	goalball
AABGLLRY	ballyrag
AABGLMNS	slam-bang
AABGLMNU	galbanum
AABGLNPS	slap-bang
AABGLRUY	arguably
AABGMNOU	Naum Gabo
AABGMORR	barogram
AABGNORZ	garbanzo
AABHHISW	Wahhabis
AABHHORU	brouhaha
AABHIIKS	Baisakhi
AABHIIMP	Amphibia
AABHIINR	Bahraini
AABHIINU	bauhinia
AABHIJMY	jambiyah
AABHILLR	hair-ball
AABHILTU	habitual
AABHIMST	Baathism
	Ba'athism
AABHIMSW	Wahabism
AABHINST	habitans
AABHINTT	habitant
AABHIRST	tabashir
AABHISTT	Baathist
	Ba'athist
AABHKKKU	Habakkuk
AABHKLOS	Lok Sabha
AABHKNUY	Ayub Khan
AABHKRSY	Shark Bay
AABHLLSW	washball
AABHLSTT	salt bath
AABHMNRS	bran-mash
AABHNOTU	Autobahn
AABHORRT	Arbroath
AABHQSSU	squabash
AABHRRSU	surbahar
AABHRSST	brass hat
AABIIJLT	jailbait
AABIILNS	Basilian
AABIILRS	Brasília
AABIIMNN	Namibian
AABIINST	Sabatini
AABIITTW	wait-a-bit
AABIKKLL	kaka bill
AABIKLNU	Kinabalu
AABILLLY	labially
AABILLST	ballista
AABILMNS	bailsman
AABILMNU	bimanual
AABILMOT	mail-boat
AABILNNU	biannual
AABILNOP	Polabian
AABILNOR	baronial
AABILNOT	ablation
AABILNRU	binaural
AABILNTY	banality
AABILOST	sailboat
AABILOTT	boattail
AABILOWY	boil away
AABILRRT	arbitral
AABILRST	arbalist
AABILRVY	variably
AABIMNNO	bonamani
AABIMNOT	Manitoba
AABIMNRU	manubria
AABIMORS	ambrosia✧
AABIMRSU	simaruba
AABINNPR	brainpan
	brain-pan
AABINORS	abrasion
AABINOSS	Bassanio
AABINRST	bartisan
AABINRTZ	bartizan
AABINRZZ	Zanzibar
AABIORRS	sorbaria
AABIORTT	abattoir
AABIOSSY	bioassay
AABIOTVX	abat-voix
AABIQRST	Istabraq
AABIRTUY	rubaiyat✧
AABISTUZ	zaibatsu
AABJLMNO	jambolan
AABJLPRU	Jabalpur
AABJORTU	abat-jour
AABKLLPR	ball park
	ballpark
AABKLNNO	bank loan
AABKMNNS	banksman
AABKOPRS	soapbark
AABLLLPY	play ball
AABLLMOR	balmoral
AABLLNST	tan balls
AABLLOPS	soap-ball
AABLLPPY	palpably
AABLLPRT	trapball
AABLLRSW	wall bars
AABLLSTU	blastula
AABLLUVY	valuably
AABLMNOR	abnormal
AABLMNTU	ambulant
AABLMOST	blastoma
AABLNORW	Bonar Law
AABLNSST	St Albans
AABLNTTT	blattant
AABLORTY	altar boy
AABLOTUY	layabout
AABLOUWY	Bulawayo
AABLOWWY	blow away
AABLPSSY	passably
AABLRRSU	saburral
AABLRSUU	subaural
AABLSTTU	abuttals
AABMMOSU	abomasum
AABMNNOO	bonamano
AABMNOTW	batwoman
AABMNRTU	rambutan
AABMORTU	marabout
	tamboura
AABMOSSU	abomasus
AABNNOST	absonant
AABNOSTW	Botswana
AABORRRT	barrator
AABORSTT	barostat
AABRRRTY	barratry
AABRRSST	brassart
AACCCDIS	saccadic
AACCCFIO	focaccia
AACCCHHR	crachach
AACCCHHU	cachucha
AACCCLOO	Coca-Cola®
AACCCRUY	accuracy
AACCDEFR	face card
AACCDEHH	cha-chaed
AACCDEIM	academic
AACCDEJK	Jack Cade
AACCDELO	accolade
AACCDENU	caducean
AACCDERR	care card

racecard
AACCDERS cardcase
AACCDHIL Chaldaic
AACCDHIR characid
AACCDHRS cash card
AACCDILL Cadillac®
AACCDORT coat-card
AACCDOVY advocacy
AACCEEFH face-ache
AACCEELT calceate
AACCEENT cetacean
AACCEFKP face pack
AACCEFLO coalface
AACCEFRS Scarface
AACCEGOR accorage
AACCEGRU carucage
AACCEHIX cachexia
AACCEILN calcanei
AACCEIMN Meccania
AACCEINR Circaean
AACCEIRR cercaria
AACCEKRS sack race
AACCELOR caracole
AACCELPT placcate
AACCELRR carceral
AACCENRT carcanet
AACCENTU acutance
AACCEPRT Cape cart
AACCERTU accurate
carucate
AACCFFNR CFA franc
AACCFGOO cacafogo
AACCFILR farcical
AACCFLTU calc-tufa
AACCFOOT cocoa fat
AACCGILT galactic
AACCHHIL Halachic
AACCHHMU muchacha
AACCHILL caillach
AACCHILP pachalic
AACCHINR anarchic
characin
AACCHINS chicanas
AACCHISV viscacha
AACCHIVZ vizcacha
AACCHKOZ kazachoc
AACCHLLT catch-all
AACCHLOR charcoal
AACCHLOT cachalot
AACCHLRS clarsach
AACCHMNO coachman
AACCHNOR coranach
AACCHORW Chaco War
AACCHOWY coach-way
AACCHPTW watch cap
AACCIINV vaccinia
AACCIIST sciatica
AACCILNU Canicula
AACCILNV vaccinal
AACCILRU acicular
AACCILTT tactical
AACCIMOS Masaccio
AACCIORU cariacou
AACCIPRT apractic
AACCIPTY capacity
AACCIRTY caryatic
AACCJKRW crackjaw
AACCJORU carcajou
carjacou
AACCKLOS Coal Sack
AACCKORT coatrack
AACCLLRU calcular
AACCLMNY clamancy
AACCLOPU Acapulco
AACCLPRS calcspar
AACCLRSU saccular
AACCLTTU Calcutta
AACCORRY Caryocar
AACCOSTT staccato
stoccata
AACDDEHI acid-head
AACDDEIL daedalic
AACDDENV advanced
AACDDEOP Decapoda
AACDDERT dead-cart
AACDDETU caudated
AACDDETY tea caddy
AACDDHRR hard card
AACDDILN candidal
AACDDINR radicand
AACDEEHH headache
AACDEEHR headrace
AACDEEHS headcase
AACDEELS escalade
AACDEENT tea dance
AACDEEOR area code
AACDEEPS escapade
AACDEEST estacade
AACDEETU ecaudate
AACDEFFT fat-faced
AACDEFHR hardface
AACDEFLT falcated
AACDEFNN fan dance
AACDEGGR aggraced
AACDEGKP packaged
AACDEGMR card game
decagram
AACDEGRR drag race
AACDEHHY headachy
AACDEHIN hacienda
AACDEHKL Lake Chad
AACDEHLN Chaldean
AACDEHLP cephalad
AACDEHMR drachmae
AACDEHPT death cap
AACDEHRS charades
hard case
AACDEHRT cathedra
AACDEHTT attached
AACDEILS sidalcea
AACDEIMN maenadic
AACDEIMS camisade
AACDEINR radiance
AACDEIPR Capridae
AACDEIRS Scaridae
AACDEIRT radicate
AACDEJNT adjacent
AACDELNP lap dance
AACDELNR calendar
landrace
AACDELNS candelas
AACDELNV valanced
AACDELOS case-load
escalado
AACDELSS scalades
AACDELTU cut a deal
AACDELTV clavated
AACDENOT cane-toad
AACDENPT tap-dance
AACDENRW war dance
AACDENTU aduncate
AACDEOPS escapado
AACDEORR road race
AACDEOTU autocade
AACDEOTV advocate✧
AACDEQUY adequacy
AACDERST cadastre
AACDERTU arcuated
AACDFNNY Fancy Dan
AACDGGHI Haggadic
AACDGINR arcading
carangid
cardigan
AACDHHKR hardhack
AACDHHNS shadchan
AACDHHRS hard cash
AACDHIIS dichasia
AACDHILL chillada
AACDHILR diarchal
AACDHIMR chadarim
drachmai
AACDHINP handicap
AACDHINR arachnid
AACDHKRT hardtack
AACDHLNP handclap
AACDHLOR hard coal
AACDHLOT cathodal
AACDHLRY charlady
AACDHMMR drammach
AACDHMRS drachmas
AACDHNRT handcart
AACDHORT Chordata
AACDHPRS crashpad
AACDHSTU cut a dash
AACDIIMT Adamitic
AACDIINR acid rain
AACDIINS ascidian
AACDIIRT Adriatic
AACDIJLU Judaical
AACDIJZZ acid jazz
AACDIKRZ Karadzic
AACDILLM mail-clad
AACDILLP palladic

AACDILMT dalmatic
AACDILMU caladium
AACDILNO diaconal
AACDILNR cardinal✧
Clarinda
AACDILNU Claudian
dulciana
AACDILNV Vandalic
AACDILOZ zodiacal
AACDILRR railcard
AACDILST acid salt
AACDIMNO mandioca
AACDIMNY adynamic
AACDIMOS camisado
AACDIMPR P A M Dirac
AACDIMRS Camisard
AACDIMRT dramatic
AACDINNS Scandian
AACDINOR Orcadian
AACDINRT radicant
tridacna
AACDINRY radiancy
AACDIORR car radio
AACDIOTU autacoid
AACDIRSS ascarids
AACDIRTY caryatid
AACDITUY audacity
AACDJQRU jacquard✧
AACDKLLN lackland
AACDKLNU Auckland
AACDKLOP pack-load
AACDLLUY caudally
AACDLORT cartload
AACDLORY clay road
AACDLOSS scalados
AACDLOSV Calvados
AACDLRTY dactylar
AACDMMOR cardamom
AACDMMRU cardamum
AACDMNNO mancando
AACDMNNY candyman
AACDMNOR cardamon
AACDMSSU Damascus
AACDNORU una corda
AACDNSST sand-cast
AACDNSSY candy-ass
AACDOOSV avocados
AACDORRT cartroad
AACDQRSU squad car
AACEEEHT Theaceae
AACEEELO Oleaceae
AACEEFIT facetiae
AACEEFLL lace-leaf
AACEEFLP paleface
AACEEFPR Cape Fear
AACEEGIR acierage
agacerie
AACEEGKU ague-cake
AACEEGLR clearage
AACEEGLV cleavage
AACEEGPS space age
space-age
AACEEGRS gear-case
AACEEHLP acalephe
AACEEHLT leachate
AACEEHRT tracheae
AACEEILM Limaceae
AACEEIMT emaciate
AACEEINN encaenia✧
AACEEIPR a piacere
AACEEIRT acierate
AACEEITV Vitaceae
AACEEKPR rape cake
AACEEKRT caretake
take care
AACEELMU Ulmaceae
AACEELRT lacerate
AACEELST escalate
AACEELTU aculeate
AACEEMNS Macanese
Maecenas
AACEEMOR Moraceae
AACEEMRT cream tea
macerate
racemate
AACEEMST casemate
AACEEMSU Musaceae
AACEENNT catenane
AACEENRS Canarese
Cesarean
AACEENTT catenate
AACEEORS Rosaceae
AACEEPRT caper-tea
AACEEPSS seascape
AACEERRW careware
AACEERSU caesurae
AACEERSY easy-care
AACEERTU Rutaceae
AACEERTV acervate
AACEETUV evacuate
AACEETVX excavate
AACEFFHL half-face
AACEFFIN affiance
AACEFGIR care a fig
AACEFHLP halfpace
AACEFIST fasciate
AACEFKLO loaf-cake
AACEFKMS face mask
AACEFLRS leaf-scar
AACEFLRT flat race
AACEFRRU Furcraea
AACEFRST seacraft
AACEFRTT artefact
AACEGHNT chantage
AACEGHRT Carthage
AACEGILN angelica✧
AACEGILT glaciate
AACEGINR canaigre
AACEGIOP apogaeic
AACEGIRR carriage
AACEGIRV vicarage
AACEGKPR packager
AACEGKRT trackage
AACEGLLM game call
AACEGLNY lancegay
AACEGRSV scavager
AACEHHLS ash-leach
AACEHHMT MacHeath
AACEHHRU huarache
AACEHILL achillea
heliacal
AACEHILM Michaela
AACEHILN achenial
AACEHILP phacelia✧
AACEHIMR chimaera✧
AACEHIMT haematic
AACEHINT China tea
AACEHIPT Hepatica
AACEHIRS archaise
AACEHIRT theriaca
AACEHIRZ archaize
AACEHISZ Schizaea
AACEHLNT calanthe
AACEHLNU eulachan
AACEHLOS sea loach
AACEHLRT tracheal
AACEHLRX exarchal
AACEHLST alcahest
AACEHMNP camphane
AACEHMRS marchesa
AACEHMRT heart cam
AACEHMST schemata
AACEHNOP Phocaena
AACEHNRR Achernar
AACEHPRT racepath
AACEHPUX chapeaux
AACEHRRR rear-arch
AACEHRST sea chart
AACEHRSU archaeus✧
AACEHRTT reattach
AACEHTUX châteaux
AACEIILN laciniae
AACEIINT actiniae
AACEIIPR Picariae
AACEIIRV caviarie
AACEIKMT kamacite
AACEILLM camellia
AACEILLN alliance
canaille
AACEILMN analcime
calamine
AACEILMT calamite
AACEILNS canalise
AACEILNT Alicante
analcite
laitance
AACEILNU acauline
AACEILNV Valencia
valiance
AACEILNZ canalize
AACEILOP alopecia
AACEILRT tailrace
AACEILRV cavalier✧

	variceal
AACEILST	saliceta
AACEIMNR	American
	Cinerama®
	in camera
AACEIMNS	amnesiac
AACEIMRS	macarise
	mesaraic
AACEIMRZ	macarize
AACEIMTT	catamite
AACEIMUX	camaïeux
AACEINNO	Oceanian
AACEINNV	Avicenna
AACEINPR	Caprinae
AACEINPZ	Piacenza
AACEINRS	canaries
AACEINRT	carinate
	craniate
AACEINRV	variance
AACEINST	estancia
AACEIOPR	capoeira
AACEIPRS	airspace
	pair case
AACEIPRT	apricate
	at a price
AACEIPTT	apatetic
	capitate
AACEIRTV	vicarate
AACEITTV	activate
	cavitate
AACEJKSY	jack easy
AACEJLTU	jaculate
AACEKKLW	cakewalk
AACEKLST	salt cake
AACEKMRT	meat rack
AACEKRSW	sea wrack
AACEKRTT	attacker
AACELLLR	all-clear
AACELLMN	Lac Léman
AACELLMR	marcella
AACELLOT	allocate
AACELLTY	alleycat
AACELMNO	Alcmaeon
AACELMNP	placeman
AACELMPP	Apple Mac®
AACELMPT	place mat
AACELMPU	mea culpa
AACELMTU	maculate
AACELNNU	cannulae
AACELNOP	Al Capone
AACELNOR	Carolean
	lecanora
AACELNPR	parlance
AACELNPT	placenta
AACELNPY	anyplace
AACELNRT	lacerant
AACELNRY	arcanely
AACELNST	analects
AACELNTU	lacunate
	tenacula
AACELOPP	cop a plea
AACELORS	Coral Sea
AACELOST	cataloes
AACELOSU	acaulose
AACELPSU	scapulae
AACELRSU	caesural
AACELRWY	clearway
AACELSTY	catalyse
	stay lace
AACELTTY	cattleya
AACELTYZ	catalyze
AACEMNOR	amorance
	on camera
AACEMNPS	spaceman
AACEMNST	camstane
AACEMORT	to camera
AACEMOWY	come away
AACEMRRS	arms race
AACEMRSS	massacre
AACEMRST	steam car
AACEMSTT	cat's-meat
AACENNOR	Anacreon
AACENORS	sea acorn
AACENOTU	oceanaut
AACENPRS	pancreas
AACENPST	pastance
AACENPSU	saucepan
AACENPTT	pancetta
AACENRST	canaster
AACENRTT	reactant
AACENRTU	areca-nut
AACENRTY	catenary
AACENRVZ	czarevna
AACENSTT	castanet
AACENTUV	evacuant
AACEOPRT	caproate
AACEORSU	araceous
AACEOSST	seacoast
AACEPPPR	cap-paper
AACEPPSU	pupa-case
AACERRRS	Carreras
AACERSSS	rascasse
AACERSSU	caesuras
AACERSTT	castrate
AACERTTT	tractate
AACESSTT	sceattas
AACESUWY	causeway
AACFFHLL	half-calf
AACFGRST	cragfast
AACFHMST	camshaft
AACFILLY	facially
AACFILOS	fasciola
AACFIRRT	aircraft
AACFIRST	frascati✧
AACFIRTT	artifact
AACFISST	Fascista
AACFJKLP	flapjack
AACFKLPT	flatpack
AACFLLOP	coal-flap
AACFMNNY	fancy man
AACGGINO	anagogic
AACGGIOP	apagogic
AACGHHNS	Changsha
AACGHIPR	agraphic
AACGHIRR	chiragra
AACGHLLO	agalloch
AACGHNNN	Nanchang
AACGHNOR	charango
AACGHOPZ	gazpacho
AACGHORU	guacharo
AACGIILN	Galician
AACGIILR	Cagliari
AACGIIMN	magician
AACGIINR	garcinia
AACGILLN	Gallican
AACGILLO	alogical
AACGILLU	alguacil
	Caligula
AACGILNN	Anglican
AACGILNO	analogic
AACGILNV	galvanic
AACGILOR	Agricola
AACGILOX	coxalgia
AACGILRT	tragical
AACGIMMT	magmatic
AACGIMNN	manganic
AACGIMNP	campaign
	pangamic
AACGIMOP	apogamic
AACGIMRR	margaric
AACGIMUU	guaiacum
AACGISTY	sagacity
AACGLMOU	glaucoma
AACGLORR	Coral Rag
AACGLORS	Calor Gas®
AACGMNRS	cragsman
AACGNOSU	guanacos
AACGNRVY	vagrancy
AACHHIKR	kachahri
AACHHKNU	Chanukah
AACHHLLS	challahs
AACHHLOR	Hal Roach
AACHHTWY	hatchway
AACHIIMR	mariachi
AACHIJNT	Jacintha
AACHIKNR	chinkara
AACHILLP	caliphal
AACHILLR	rachilla
AACHILMS	chamisal
AACHILMT	thalamic
AACHILNP	chaplain
AACHILPS	calipash
AACHILRV	archival
AACHIMNN	chainman
	chinaman✧
AACHIMNP	chinampa
AACHIMNR	chairman
	Charmian
AACHIMNS	shamanic
AACHIMNT	matachin
AACHIMRR	armchair
AACHIMRS	archaism
	charisma

Words marked ✧ can also be spelled with one or more capital letters

AACHIMSS	chiasmas
AACHIMST	cathisma
AACHINNO	Noachian
AACHINNT	acanthin
	at an inch
AACHINPT	at a pinch
AACHINRT	canthari
AACHINSW	chainsaw
AACHIPST	chapatis
AACHIPTT	chapatti
AACHIPWY	chip away
AACHIRSS	Issachar
AACHIRST	archaist
AACHIRTX	taxiarch
AACHKNSW	hacksawn
AACHKPSS	schapska
AACHKSTY	haystack
AACHLMNO	monachal
AACHLMOS	chloasma
AACHLMPT	palmchat
AACHLORT	thoracal
AACHLSTU	calathus
AACHMMNO	MacMahon
AACHMMNR	marchman
AACHMMRY	Amy March
AACHMNNR	ranchman
AACHMNTW	watchman
AACHMNUY	naumachy
AACHMORT	achromat
	trachoma
AACHMORX	Max Roach
AACHMPRT	champart
AACHMPRY	pharmacy
AACHMRST	crash-mat
AACHNORT	at anchor
AACHNOSU	huanacos
AACHNPRS	sarpanch
AACHNRST	trashcan
AACHNRVY	navarchy
AACHNSTU	acanthus
AACHOPPR	approach
AACHOPRT	cataphor
AACHORTU	racahout
AACHOTTU	tacahout
AACHRTUY	autarchy
AACHSSTY	Tay-Sachs
AACIILMN	animalic
AACIILMO	maiolica
AACIILRV	vicarial
AACIIMNT	animatic
AACIINNS	Sicanian
AACIINNT	actinian
AACIINPR	picarian
AACIINPT	capitani
AACIINST	actinias
AACIIPRT	Patricia
AACIJLMO	majolica
AACIJNOP	japonica
AACIKLMS	mailsack
AACIKLRR	rack rail
AACIKMNW	mackinaw
AACIKPRT	Praktica®
AACIKRTU	autarkic
AACIKTWY	tick away
AACILLMR	lacrimal
AACILLMT	climatal
AACILLMY	lay claim
AACILLPY	apically
AACILLRY	racially
AACILLSW	Salic law
AACILMNT	calamint
	claimant
AACILMOR	acromial
AACILMOT	atomical
AACILMRT	mail-cart
AACILMTY	calamity
AACILNNO	Laconian
AACILNOP	Al Pacino
AACILNOR	Carolina
	conarial
AACILNOS	Salonica
AACILNRT	cant-rail
AACILNRV	carnival
AACILNTT	Atlantic
	tantalic✧
AACILNTU	nautical
AACILNTY	analytic
AACILNUV	navicula
AACILNVY	valiancy
AACILOPR	carap-oil
AACILORV	Arvicola
AACILOTT	tail coat
AACILPRU	piacular
AACILPST	aplastic
AACILPSZ	capsizal
AACILPTU	capitula
AACILPTY	atypical
AACILQRU	acquiral
AACILRRS	clarsair
AACILRSS	Clarissa
AACILRTY	alacrity
AACILRUU	auricula✧
AACILRVY	lay vicar
AACILSTT	cat's-tail
	statical
AACILSTY	salacity
AACIMMNO	ammoniac
AACIMMRS	macarism
	marasmic
AACIMNOR	macaroni
	Marciano
	marocain
AACIMNOT	anatomic
AACIMORT	aromatic
AACIMRSS	samsaric
AACIMRST	Sarmatic
AACIMTVY	Macavity
AACINNOT	Catonian
AACINOPR	paranoic
AACINOPT	capitano
	pacation
AACINORT	Cantoria
	Catriona
	Croatian
	raincoat
AACINORV	Racovian
AACINOTV	vacation
AACINPTY	capitayn
AACINQTU	acquaint
AACINRST	arcanist
AACINSTZ	stanzaic
AACINTTU	Tunicata
AACIPRTY	rapacity
AACIQSTU	aquatics
AACIRRTT	tartaric✧
AACIRSTT	castrati
AACIRSTZ	czaritsa
AACJKLPS	slapjack
AACJKLSW	slack jaw
AACJKLYZ	lazy jack
AACJKOOR	jackaroo
AACJMNOR	Majorcan
AACKKNPS	knapsack
AACKLNPS	knapscal
AACKLOWY	lock away
	lockaway
AACKMNRT	trackman
AACKMNST	tacksman
AACKORWY	rockaway
AACKOSWY	sock away
AACKRTWY	trackway
AACLLLNO	call-loan
AACLLMMU	macallum
AACLLMRY	clay-marl
	lacrymal
AACLLNOT	Tlalocan
AACLLNRY	carnally
AACLLRRY	carryall
	carry-all
	RAC Rally
AACLLRSY	rascally
AACLLSUU	clausula
AACLLSUY	casually
	causally
AACLLTUY	actually
AACLMNNS	clansman
AACLMNSS	classman
AACLMRRU	macrural
AACLNNOT	cantonal
AACLNNOW	canon law
AACLNNRU	cannular
AACLNNSU	cannulas
AACLNOPR	coplanar
AACLNORU	La Coruna
AACLNOTT	octantal
AACLNRSU	lacunars
AACLNRUY	lacunary
AACLNTVY	vacantly
AACLOOPT	tapacolo
AACLOPPR	polar cap
AACLOPTU	tapaculo
AACLORRU	oracular
AACLORSU	carousal

AACLORUV	vacuolar
AACLOSTT	cattalos
AACLPPRT	claptrap
AACLPRSU	capsular
	scapular
AACLPRTY	calyptra
AACLPSSU	scapulas
AACLPTTU	catapult
AACLRSSW	class war
AACLRSTU	claustra
AACLRSUV	vascular
AACLRTUX	curtalax
AACLSTTY	catalyst
AACLSTUY	casualty
AACMNOOR	macaroon
AACMNORS	mascaron
AACMNPRS	scrap-man
AACMNPRY	rampancy
AACMORSS	sarcomas
AACMPSTT	Stamp Act
AACNNOSZ	canzonas
AACNOTTY	catatony
AACNRSTT	transact
AACOORTX	toxocara
AACOPRSU	acarpous
AACOPRTU	autocarp
AACOPSTV	postcava
AACORRTV	varactor
AACORSTT	castrato
AACORTTU	actuator
	autocrat
AADDDEEH	deadhead
	dead-head
AADDDEEL	dead-deal
AADDDEHN	dead hand
AADDDELO	dead load
AADDDGNR	granddad
AADDEEHT	dead heat
	dead-heat
AADDEEIL	Adelaide
AADDEELP	pale-dead
AADDEEMT	dead-meat
AADDEERS	sea adder
AADDEFHL	half-dead
AADDEFLL	dead-fall
AADDEGGR	red dagga
AADDEGHT	The Dagda
AADDEHHR	hardhead
AADDEHLN	headland
AADDEHMN	handmade
AADDEILN	dedalian✧
AADDEIRT	radiated
AADDELLW	dead-wall
AADDELSU	Daedalus
AADDEMOR	made road
AADDEMRY	daydream
AADDENPR	red panda
AADDENRV	veranda'd
AADDFSTY	daft days
AADDGGOO	gado-gado
AADDGHLN	glad hand
	glad-hand
AADDGNRU	graduand
AADDGUYY	gaudy-day
AADDHHIL	lah-di-dah
AADDHHRS	shraddha
AADDHIMN	handmaid
AADDIINR	Diandria
AADDILNO	dianodal
AADDINRW	dawn raid
AADDKMMO	mokaddam
AADDLLNY	landlady
AADDLNRW	landward
AADDLNRY	yardland
AADDMMQU	muqaddam
AADDNPST	stand pad
AADDNRST	sand-dart
	standard
AADDNRWY	yardwand
AADDOTYY	day-to-day
AADDRSTY	dastardy
AADEEGHR	headgear
AADEEGHT	get ahead
AADEEGLR	red algae
AADEEGLT	galeated
AADEEGMN	endamage
AADEEGNR	Gadarene
AADEEHLR	hard-a-lee
AADEEHMT	meathead
AADEEIKT	Kate Adie
AADEEILR	Airedale
AADEEIRT	eradiate
AADEEIRW	awearied
AADEELMR	De La Mare
AADEELRV	De Valera
AADEELRW	Delaware
AADEELTV	alveated
AADEEMRR	demerara
AADEEMST	Teasmade®
AADEENPT	tapenade
AADEENTT	antedate
	Edentata
AADEEPRT	date rape
AADEEQTU	adequate
AADEFFLT	afflated
AADEFFRY	affrayed
AADEFHLT	flathead✧
AADEFHST	headfast
AADEFIJO	feijoada
AADEFILM	mala fide
AADEFILR	fair-lead
AADEFINT	anti-fade
AADEFIRS	faradise
AADEFIRZ	faradize
AADEFLLR	falderal
AADEFLNS	sand flea
AADEFLRY	defrayal
AADEFLTT	faldetta
AADEFOTU	auto-da-fé
AADEFSTY	feast-day
AADEGGRU	guardage
AADEGHLN	Danelagh
AADEGHMN	Dagenham
AADEGHMS	Ghadamès
AADEGHRS	rhagades
AADEGILL	diallage
	legal aid
AADEGILS	ideal gas
AADEGILT	gladiate
AADEGINR	drainage
	gardenia✧
AADEGINT	indagate
AADEGITT	agitated
AADEGITV	divagate
AADEGJTU	adjutage
AADEGKRS	Dark Ages
AADEGLMN	magdalen✧
AADEGLMY	amygdale
AADEGLNS	seladang
AADEGLOT	get a load
AADEGMNR	grandame
AADEGMOR	road game
AADEGORR	road rage
AADEGPRT	trade gap
AADEGRRT	rag trade
AADEGRRW	draw-gear
AADEGRSV	savegard
AADEGRTU	graduate
AADEHHOR	hoarhead
AADEHILN	nail-head
AADEHILR	headrail
	railhead
AADEHILS	headsail
AADEHIRR	diarrhea
AADEHIWY	hideaway
AADEHKMR	headmark
AADEHKOT	Hakodate
AADEHLLL	halalled
AADEHLMP	headlamp
AADEHLNR	anhedral
AADEHLPS	slaphead
AADEHMNS	headsman
AADEHMST	masthead
AADEHNNR	near-hand
AADEHNNS	Shandean
AADEHNPS	sandheap
AADEHNRV	verandah
AADEHOPX	Hexapoda
AADEHRRW	hardware
AADEHRSS	harassed
AADEHRTY	death ray
AADEHSTT	hastated
AADEIIMV	via media
AADEIKLP	Klaipeda
AADEILLN	Daniella
AADEILLR	Rallidae
AADEILMP	maid-pale
AADEILNN	Annelida
AADEILNT	dentalia
AADEILPR	praedial
AADEILPS	palisade
AADEILPT	lapidate
	Talpidae

AADEILRS	salaried
AADEILRT	Araldite®
AADEILSY	lay aside
AADEILTU	audit ale
AADEILTV	validate
AADEIMNN	amandine
AADEIMNP	pandemia
AADEIMNR	marinade
AADEIMNT	animated
	diamanté
AADEIMPZ	diazepam
AADEIMRV	maravedi
AADEIMST	diastema
AADEINNR	Adrianne
AADEINRR	darraine
AADEINRT	dentaria
	raindate
AADEIPRS	paradise✧
AADEIPSU	diapause
AADEIPTV	adaptive
AADEIRSV	Varidase®
AADEIRSY	I dare say
	I daresay
AADEISST	diastase
AADEITVW	viewdata
AADEJMNN	N'Djamena
AADEJMNU	Maja Nude
AADEJMPY	pyjamaed
AADEJNNP	japanned
AADEJNOT	Ondaatje
AADEKLLN	lakeland✧
AADEKLNR	kalendar
AADEKLOP	peak load
AADEKLOS	soda-lake
AADEKMNR	mandrake
AADEKMRT	dark meat
AADELLPP	appalled
AADELLRT	dataller
AADELLWY	welladay
AADELMNR	alderman
	malander
AADELMNS	dalesman
	leadsman
AADELMPP	mad-apple
AADELMPT	date palm
	palmated
AADELMYZ	amazedly
AADELNNY	Lady Anne
AADELNPT	peatland
AADELNST	eastland
AADELQUU	Quaalude®
AADELRSY	saleyard
	yard sale
AADELRTU	radulate
AADELRTV	larvated
AADELRTY	daytaler
	delta ray
AADEMMNV	Van Damme
AADEMNNW	manna-dew
AADEMNOS	adenomas
AADEMNOT	Nematoda
AADEMNPS	spademan
AADEMNRT	Ertan Dam
AADEMNSY	dayes-man
AADEMNUZ	unamazed
AADEMORT	matadore
AADEMPSS	Sam Spade
AADEMRRU	marauder
AADEMRRY	Mary Read
AADENOST	Sotadean
AADENRRW	draw near
AADENRTT	tartaned
AADENSTY	asyndeta
AADEOPRT	tapadero
AADEOPST	adespota
AADEORRT	aerodart
AADEOWYZ	doze away
AADEPPRT	preadapt
AADEPPRY	paper-day
AADEPRST	ad patres
AADEQRTU	quadrate
AADERRRW	rearward
AADERRST	star-read
AADERSSW	seawards
AADERSTW	eastward
	radwaste
AADERUVY	ayurveda✧
AADFGLNS	sand-flag
AADFGNNO	fandango
AADFGRSU	saufgard
AADFHITW	Haft Wadi
AADFHMNR	farm hand
AADFHNST	handfast
AADFIINT	intifada
AADFIMRS	faradism
AADFINRU	unafraid
AADFLLLN	landfall
AADFLLNT	flatland✧
AADFLORW	aardwolf
AADFLOTW	data flow
AADFLOTX	toadflax
AADFLOWY	foldaway
AADFMRRY	farmyard
AADFNNOR	Anna Ford
AADGGIMN	damaging
AADGGLNN	gangland
AADGGLRS	glad rags
AADGGNSY	Gang Days
AADGGRST	staggard
AADGHINN	Gandhian
AADGHIPR	diagraph
AADGHRTU	hatguard
AADGIINS	gainsaid
AADGILLR	gaillard
	galliard
AADGILMR	madrigal
	mail-drag
AADGILNO	diagonal
	gonadial
AADGILNS	salading
AADGIMNR	main drag
	mridanga
AADGIMPR	paradigm
AADGIMRT	gradatim
AADGINRR	darraign
AADGINRU	guardian
AADGIQRU	quadriga
AADGLMNR	grand mal
AADGLMOR	malgrado
AADGLNRS	garlands
AADGLOPR	podagral
AADGMNOR	dragoman
	Garamond
AADGMNOS	goadsman
AADGMNRS	dragsman
AADGNNOO	Onondaga
AADGNNOW	Gondwana
AADGNNQU	quandang
AADGNORS	Sangrado
AADGNRRU	radar gun
AADGNRTU	guardant
AADGNRUV	vanguard
AADGRRTU	rat-guard
AADGRRUW	gurdwara
AADHHIPS	padishah
AADHHMNU	hum and ha
AADHIINP	aphidian
AADHILLR	halliard
AADHILMT	Mathilda
AADHILNR	handrail
AADHILNT	Thailand
AADHILRV	havildar
AADHIMOR	radio ham
AADHINRR	harridan
AADHIRRU	Ruaraidh
AADHIRTT	hard at it
AADHISTU	Daihatsu®
AADHLLNU	land-haul
AADHLLOT	Toad Hall
AADHLMOY	dalmahoy
AADHLMST	Halmstad
AADHLNPY	handplay
AADHLNSW	washland
AADHLPSS	slapdash
AADHMMMU	Muhammad
AADHMNNY	handyman
AADHMNOU	omadhaun
AADHMNST	ham stand
AADHNSST	ash-stand
AADHNSTT	hatstand
AADHOPRS	hard soap
AADHRRTW	thraward
AADHRRYZ	hazardry
AADIILNS	Islandia
AADIILNT	Aldaniti
AADIILPV	Dipavali
AADIIMNN	Indiaman
AADIINRR	air-drain
AADIINRS	Sardinia
AADIKLLO	alkaloid
AADIKLLR	killadar
AADIKLRY	kailyard
AADIKMNS	damaskin

AADIKNQR qindarka
AADIKORT Takoradi
AADILLLO allodial
AADILLNR landrail
AADILLOP Palladio
AADILLOS salad oil
AADILLPR palliard
AADILLRS silladar
AADILLRY radially
AADILMNN mainland
AADILMNO domainal
domanial
AADILMNP plaidman
AADILMVY Limavady
AADILNOR ordalian
AADILNPR prandial
AADILNTT dilatant
AADILOPS palisado
AADILORR railroad
AADILPRS pardalis
AADILPRY lapidary
AADILRRS risaldar
AADILRSY sail-yard
AADILRTY trial-day
AADILSVY Syldavia
AADIMMSZ Mazdaism
AADIMNNR mandarin✧
AADIMNRT tamarind
AADIMNRY dairyman
mainyard
AADIMNRZ zamindar
AADIMNSS damassin
AADIMNSU sudamina
AADIMNTU Adiantum
AADIMNUV vanadium
AADIMSTZ Mazdaist
samizdat
AADINNOT adnation
AADINOPR paranoid
AADINOPS diapason
AADINOPT adaption
AADINPRS Spaniard
AADINPSU Upanisad
AADINRRW airdrawn
AADINRSV virandas
AADINSSS Sassanid
AADIOPRS diaspora✧
AADIORRT radiator
AADIPSUY upadaisy
AADIRRSW airwards
AADIRRSY disarray
AADJNTTU adjutant
AADJNTUV adjuvant
AADJRTZZ trad jazz
AADKLMNR landmark
AADKLNPR parkland
AADKLNRS sand-lark
AADKLRTU talukdar
AADKMNRS darkmans
AADKORWY workaday
AADKPRRW parkward
AADKRRST dark star
AADLLMNS Landsmål
AADLLMSS small ads
AADLLNSW land laws
AADLMNNS landsman
AADLMNOR mandorla
AADLMNRY land-army
Maryland
AADLMNSS landmass
AADLMNSY lady's man
AADLMNUU laudanum
AADLMPVY Davy lamp
AADLMRYY Mary Daly
AADLNOPR parlando
AADLNOPS soapland
AADLNOST saltando
AADLORST loadstar
AADLORSV Salvador
AADLORSY solar day
AADLORTU adulator
AADLPPRW waldrapp
AADMMNOW madwoman
AADMMNSU mandamus
AADMNORS roadsman
AADMNORT mandator
AADMNOWY day-woman
AADMNSST stand sam
AADMOPPP pappadom
AADMOPRX doxapram
AADMORRT tramroad
AADNNORR Andorran
AADNNPSU Pandanus
AADNORTY donatary
AADNOSUV vanadous
AADNOSWY nowadays
AADNPRST sand trap
AADNPRSU Pandarus
AADNPSSW sand wasp
AADNPSTT stand pat
AADNQRSU quadrans
AADNQRTU quadrant
AADNQRUY quandary
AADNRSST sand-star
AADNRSUY Raynaud's
AADNRVYY navy yard
AADOPPRR paradrop
AADOPRWY drop away
AADOPRXY paradoxy
AADOPSSS passados
AADOPSUY paduasoy
AADORSVY savoyard✧
AADOSTUY USA Today
AADPRSTV star-pav'd
AADRSTUY Saturday
AAEEEGLS sea eagle
AAEEEHRT hetaerae
AAEEFMST meat safe
AAEEFRRS seafarer
AAEEFSST safe seat
AAEEGILN alienage
AAEEGILP epigaeal
AAEEGINP epigaean
AAEEGLLN enallage
AAEEGLNR near gale
AAEEGLRY eagle-ray
AAEEGMMT team game
AAEEGMPR amperage
AAEEGMRS sea marge
AAEEGMSY easy game
AAEEGMTY métayage
AAEEGNNO Neogaean
AAEEGNPS Pegasean
AAEEGNRS sangaree
AAEEGPRS sea grape
sea-grape
AAEEGPRT great ape
AAEEGRRY grey area
AAEEGRST Great Sea
stearage
AAEEGRTW waterage
AAEEHHRR hear, hear!
AAEEHHST sea heath
AAEEHIMR haeremai
AAEEHPRT earth-pea
heartpea
AAEEHRRS hare's-ear
AAEEHRST Earthsea
hetaeras
AAEEHRTW a-weather
wheat ear
wheatear
AAEEHRWY hereaway
AAEEHSVY heavy sea
AAEEHTVW heat wave
AAEEILMN Alemaine
AAEEILNT alienate
AAEEINTT taeniate
AAEEJMNP jampanee
AAEEJNPS Japanese
AAEEJNSV Javanese
AAEEKLST ale-stake
AAEEKLTW latewake
AAEEKMNS namesake
AAEEKNRS Kanarese
AAEEKNRW reawaken
AAEEKNSS sea snake
AAEEKPRT parakeet
AAEEKPSS seaspeak✧
AAEEKPWY keep away
AAEEKQSU seaquake
AAEELLLM lamellae
AAEELLMT malleate
AAEELLOV à la volée
AAEELLPT patellae
AAEELNNR annealer
lernaean
AAEELNPS seaplane
spelaean
AAEELNST elastane
AAEELORT areolate
AAEELORV aloe vera✧
AAEELPRY leap year

AAEELRTU laureate
AAEELSST elastase
AAEELSTX slate axe
AAEELTUV evaluate
AAEELVWY wayleave
AAEEMMTT teammate
AAEEMNPT nametape
AAEEMNRT man-eater
AAEEMPRS paramese
AAEEMSSS Assamese
AAEEMSTY easy meat
AAEENNNT antennae
AAEENNRZ Nazarene
AAEENNST senna tea
AAEENOPR Pareoean
AAEENPRT paranete
AAEENRRS arrasene
AAEENRST arsenate
Near East
serenata
AAEENRSV sea raven
AAEENRTT anteater
AAEENRTX ex re nata
AAEENSTU nauseate
AAEEORRU euro area
AAEEPPRR appearer
rapparee
reappear
AAEEPPRS appeaser
AAEEPRST asperate
separate
AAEEPSTT aseptate
AAEERRWW rewarewa
AAEERSST sea aster
AAEERSTT stearate
AAEERSTW seawater
AAEERSYY yea-sayer
AAEFFGST staffage
AAEFFILS fail safe
fail-safe
AAEFFLLL leaf-fall
AAEFFLLR farfalle
AAEFFLPR paraffle
AAEFFSTT taffetas
AAEFGHRW wharfage
AAEFGIMR fair game
AAEFGITT fatigate
AAEFGLLL flagella
AAEFGLOT floatage
AAEFGRTU frautage
AAEFHITV have a fit
AAEFHLRY half-year
AAEFIILR filariae
AAEFILLX leaf axil
AAEFILTY fayalite
AAEFIMRR airframe
AAEFINNT fainéant
AAEFINPU epifauna
AAEFINTX antefixa
AAEFIRWY fire away
AAEFLLRT after all
AAEFLMOT meat loaf
AAEFLMTT flatmate
AAEFLNST fast lane
AAEFLPSY play safe
AAEFLRTT flat rate
AAEFLRTW flatware
AAEFMMRT farm team
AAEFMRST fermatas
AAEFMRSW frame-saw
saw frame
AAEFNNOS Ansafone®
AAEFNRRT tara fern
AAEFRRRW warfarer
AAEFRRWY wayfarer
AAEFRTTX after-tax
AAEGGHPT peat-hagg
AAEGGINR grainage
AAEGGIOT agiotage
AAEGGLNR langrage
AAEGGLNU language
AAEGGLNY lay an egg
AAEGGNOW wagonage
AAEGGNRY garganey
AAEGGOPR paragoge
AAEGGORV gaga over
AAEGHILR Earl Haig
AAEGHKRS shake-rag
AAEGHLNP phalange✧
AAEGHLPS slag heap
AAEGHMRX hexagram
AAEGHNRU harangue
AAEGHOPY hypogaea
AAEGHPRT hag-taper
AAEGILLN Galilean
AAEGILLR galleria
AAEGILLT alligate
AAEGILNN Angelina
AAEGILNP pelagian✧
AAEGILNR Algerian
regalian
AAEGILNT agential
alginate
AAEGILRS gasalier
AAEGILTT tailgate
AAEGIMNO egomania
AAEGIMNP pigmaean
AAEGIMNS magnesia
AAEGIMNZ magazine
AAEGIMRR marriage
AAEGIMRT gematria
maritage
AAEGINPP Aganippe
AAEGINPS paganise
AAEGINPT paginate
AAEGINPZ paganize
AAEGINST saginate
AAEGINTV navigate
vaginate
AAEGIPRU periagua
AAEGIRSV vagaries
AAEGIRTX ex gratia
AAEGIVWY give away
giveaway
AAEGKRTU great auk
AAEGLLMN Magellan
AAEGLLMS smallage
AAEGLLMW wall game
AAEGLLPR pellagra
AAEGLLSS galleass
AAEGLLST stallage
AAEGLLTU glutaeal
AAEGLMNP game plan
AAEGLMNV gavelman
AAEGLMPY gameplay
AAEGLMST Almagest
AAEGLMSW game laws
AAEGLNOU analogue
AAEGLNPP lagnappe
AAEGLNPT plantage
AAEGLNRS Sangreal
AAEGLNRU aulnager
AAEGLNTU angulate
AAEGLNTW law agent
AAEGLOSV aasvogel
AAEGLRRS resalgar
AAEGLRRW warragle
AAEGLRST agrestal
AAEGLRSV salvager
AAEGLRTY legatary
AAEGLSSV Las Vegas
AAEGLSVY savagely
AAEGLTUV vaultage
AAEGMMNR engramma
AAEGMNNT Mantegna
AAEGMNPY pygmaean
AAEGMNRS Semarang
AAEGMNRT magnetar
AAEGMNRV gravamen
AAEGMORR aerogram
AAEGMORS sagamore
AAEGMPRR rampager
AAEGMPRU rampauge
AAEGMRRT Margaret
AAEGMRRV margrave
AAEGMRRW war-gamer
AAEGMRRY gramarye
AAEGMRSS massager
AAEGMRST megastar
Ramsgate
AAEGMRTU ageratum
AAEGMTTW megawatt
AAEGNNOP neopagan
AAEGNNRU near-gaun
AAEGNOOR no-go area
AAEGNOOT Notogaea
AAEGNOTW tea wagon
AAEGNRRR arranger
AAEGNRST staragen
AAEGNRTU runagate
AAEGNSTT stagnate
AAEGNTUV vauntage
AAEGORRT arrogate

AAEGORTT aegrotat
AAEGPPRR rag paper
AAEGPPRW wrappage
AAEGPRSU sugar pea
AAEGPRTW water gap
AAEGPSTU Agapetus
AAEGRRTW Great War
AAEGRSSS sea grass
AAEGRSTW gas-water
water gas
AAEGRSTZ star-gaze
AAEGRSVY savagery
AAEGRVWX grave-wax
AAEHIIRT hetairai
hetairia
AAEHILMN hielaman
AAEHILMT hate mail
AAEHILNP aphelian
AAEHILNR Harleian
AAEHILNS Sahelian
AAEHILNT anthelia
AAEHILPR parhelia
AAEHILPT Lapithae
AAEHILRS hair seal
AAEHIMNT anthemia
haematin
AAEHIMNV Vanaheim
AAEHIMRT Mithraea
AAEHINNT Athenian
AAEHINPT aphanite
AAEHINRT Rhaetian
AAEHINST asthenia
AAEHIPPS Pasiphae
AAEHIPSS ship a sea
AAEHIRST hetairas
AAEHIRTT Hatteria
AAEHIRVW hair-wave
AAEHKLST alkahest
AAEHKMRY haymaker
AAEHKTTT Take That
AAEHLMNT methanal
AAEHLMNW whaleman
AAEHLMOT the Alamo
AAEHLMSY sealyham✧
AAEHLMTU hamulate
AAEHLNNV Van Halen
AAEHLNTX exhalant
AAEHLOSW as a whole
AAEHLPRS harp seal
pearl ash
AAEHLPRX hexaplar
AAEHLPUV upheaval
AAEHLRTT theatral
AAEHLSSW wash sale
AAEHMNPT pathname
AAEHMNPY Nymphaea
AAEHMNRS shareman
shearman
AAEHMNRT earthman
AAEHMNSS Manasseh
AAEHMOPR amphorae
AAEHMOPT hepatoma
AAEHMORT atheroma
AAEHMSTT same that
AAEHNPST pheasant
AAEHNPSY synaphea
AAEHNRTZ Nazareth
AAEHNTTX xanthate
AAEHNTVX tax haven
AAEHOPPV have a pop
AAEHOPRT opera hat
AAEHPRSW Peshawar
AAEHRRSS harasser
AAEHRSTU Arethusa
AAEHRTWX earthwax
AAEIIKNS akinesia
AAEIILMP lipaemia
AAEIIMRV viraemia
AAEIINRS Arianise
AAEIINRZ Arianize
AAEIJMNS Jamesian
AAEIJNPS Japanise
AAEIJNPZ Japanize
AAEIKKMZ kamikaze
AAEIKLLN alkaline
AAEIKLLS alkalies
alkalise
AAEIKLLZ alkalize
AAEIKLMP make a lip
AAEIKLMS make sail
AAEIKMRR krameria
AAEIKNRT Karitane
Katerina
AAEILLLU alleluia
AAEILLMM mamillae
AAEILLMT tail male
AAEILLMX maxillae
AAEILLNT allanite
AAEILLPP papillae
AAEILLPT palliate
AAEILLRT arillate
AAEILLRV Vila Real
AAEILLRY aerially
AAEILLTT talliate
AAEILLTV allative
AAEILMNT alaiment
laminate
AAEILMNV man alive
velamina
AAEILMRS Marsilea
AAEILMRT Armalite®
material
AAEILNNN Linnaean
AAEILNNS annalise
AAEILNNZ annalize
Zelanian
AAEILNPR airplane
AAEILNPT palatine✧
AAEILNRU aurelian
AAEILNRV valerian✧
AAEILNSS nasalise
Salesian
sea snail
AAEILNSZ nasalize
AAEILNTT antliate
Latinate
AAEILNTV aventail
AAEILPPS papalise
AAEILPPZ papalize
AAEILPRT parietal
AAEILPST stapelia
AAEILPSZ La Spezia
AAEILRRT arterial
AAEILRSS assailer
AAEILRTV varietal
AAEILSTV aestival
salivate
AAEILSTX saxatile
AAEILTVX laxative
AAEILWWY wile away
AAEIMNNO Maeonian
AAEIMNNR Armenian
AAEIMNOT metanoia
AAEIMNPR pearmain
AAEIMNPT impanate
AAEIMNRR marinera
AAEIMNRT animater
marinate
AAEIMNRZ mazarine
AAEIMOPR paroemia
AAEIMOTX toxaemia
AAEIMPRS aspermia
AAEIMPRT pia mater
AAEIMRTT amaretti
AAEIMSUV mauvaise
AAEINNPR Naperian
AAEINNRS Saarinen
AAEINNTT antenati
AAEINORT aeration
AAEINORX anorexia
AAEINPPR Priapean
AAEINPRT Patarine
Tarpeian
AAEINRRW rainwear
AAEINRST antisera
artesian✧
Erastian
resinata
Santeria
AAEINRSU Eurasian
AAEINRSY Aryanise
AAEINRTT reattain
AAEINRTU inaurate
AAEINRTZ atrazine
Nazarite
AAEINRYZ Aryanize
AAEINSTT astatine
sanitate
Tanaiste
AAEINSTV sanative
AAEINTTT titanate
AAEIPPRS appraise
AAEIPRST aspirate

Words marked ✧ can also be spelled with one or more capital letters

	parasite
	septaria
AAEIPRTT	patriate
AAEIPRTZ	trapezia
AAEIPRXY	apyrexia
AAEIPWWY	wipe away
AAEIQRTU	taqueria
AAEIRRRT	terraria
AAEIRRTT	Tartarie
AAEIRSST	Asterias
AAEIRSTT	aristate
AAEIRTTZ	zaratite
AAEIRWWY	wire away
AAEITTVX	taxative
AAEIVWWY	view away
AAEJLNOP	jalapeño
AAEJMNNY	Jan Mayen
AAEJMNRY	Mary Jane
AAEJMRTX	extra jam
AAEJNNPR	japanner
AAEJNPSY	Japanesy
AAEJNRTZ	jazerant
AAEJORSV	Sarajevo
AAEKLLST	salt lake
AAEKLMPY	make play
AAEKLMRW	lawmaker
AAEKLMRY	malarkey
AAEKLNRS	larnakes
AAEKLNSW	Swan Lake
AAEKLOPP	oak apple
AAEKMRST	take arms
AAEKMRSY	easy mark
AAEKMRWY	way-maker
AAEKNOPZ	Zakopane
AAEKNPRT	partaken
AAEKNRRR	rear-rank
AAEKNRST	rat snake
AAEKNTTY	Kenyatta
AAEKOPPT	take a pop
AAEKOPTX	a pox take
AAEKORTY	akaryote
AAEKPRRT	partaker
AAEKPRTT	take part
AAELLLMR	lamellar
AAELLLMS	small ale
AAELLLPR	parallel
AAELLMMR	Mallarmé
AAELLMPU	ampullae
AAELLNPU	planulae
AAELLORV	alveolar
AAELLPRT	patellar
AAELLPST	patellas
AAELLSWY	Wallasey
AAELLTTV	Valletta
AAELLTWY	alley-taw
AAELLUVV	valvulae
AAELLWWY	well away
	wellaway
AAELLWYY	alleyway
AAELMMNO	melanoma
AAELMMTU	malamute

AAELMNOT	malonate
AAELMNPT	plateman
AAELMNRT	maternal
AAELMNSS	salesman
AAELMNST	last name
	talesman
AAELMNSW	wealsman
AAELMNSY	seamanly
AAELMOSU	mausolea
AAELMPPY	may apple
AAELMPRR	rear lamp
AAELMPRT	malapert
AAELMPRX	examplar
AAELMPRY	play-mare
AAELMPSS	lampasse
AAELMPST	plateasm
AAELMPTV	vamplate
AAELMPTY	playmate
AAELMRSY	lamasery
AAELMRTT	maltreat
AAELMTWY	melt away
AAELNNNT	antennal
AAELNNOT	neonatal
AAELNNPV	panel van
AAELNNSU	Lausanne
AAELNNTU	annulate
AAELNOSS	seasonal
AAELNPPT	pea-plant
AAELNPRS	prenasal
AAELNPRT	parental
	paternal
	prenatal
AAELNPRW	warplane
AAELNPST	pleasant
AAELNPSW	panel saw
AAELNPTT	tea plant
AAELNRSY	analyser
AAELNRTT	alterant
	alternat
AAELNRTX	relaxant
AAELNRYZ	analyzer
AAELNSSV	envassal
AAELNSSY	analyses
AAELNSTT	Atlantes
AAELNSTV	slave ant
AAELORTY	aleatory
AAELPPST	tape slap
AAELPPSU	applause
AAELPQSU	Pasquale
AAELPRST	palestra
AAELPRSY	paralyse
AAELPRTT	tetrapla
AAELPRUV	par value
AAELPRYZ	paralyze
AAELPSTU	plateaus
AAELPSTV	palstave
AAELPTUV	vapulate
AAELPTUX	plateaux
AAELRSSS	Rasselas
AAELRSTU	australe
AAELRSTZ	lazarets

AAELRTTU	Lauretta
AAELRTUV	velatura
AAELRUZZ	zarzuela
AAELRWYY	waylayer
AAELSSTX	sales tax
AAELSTWY	lay waste
AAEMMNRT	armament
AAEMMSTT	stemmata
AAEMNNOS	as one man
AAEMNOSW	seawoman
AAEMNOTZ	metazoan
AAEMNPRS	Parmesan
	spearman
AAEMNPRT	name part
	parament
AAEMNRST	Santarém
	sarmenta
	semantra
AAEMNRSY	man-years
AAEMNRTT	atrament
AAEMNRTW	waterman
AAEMNSTU	manteaus
AAEMNTUX	manteaux
AAEMORTT	amaretto
	teratoma
AAEMORTX	xeromata
AAEMOSTT	steatoma
AAEMOTTU	automate
AAEMPPRS	Pap smear
AAEMPTTU	amputate
AAEMQSTU	squamate
AAEMRRTU	armature
AAEMRRTW	water ram
AAEMRSUX	aux armes
AAEMRTTU	maturate
AAEMRTWY	water yam
AAENNNST	antennas
AAENNORS	Roseanna
AAENNOTT	annotate
AAENNSTT	stannate
AAENNSTU	nauseant
AAENORRU	aurorean
AAENORSU	araneous
AAENORTU	aeronaut
AAENOSST	assonate
AAENPPRT	apparent
	trappean
AAENPRTY	prytanea
AAENPSSY	sea pansy
AAENPSTT	antepast
AAENPSTY	peasanty
AAENRSTV	tsarevna
AAENRSUW	unawares
AAENRSYY	naysayer
AAENRTTY	Tyrtaean
AAENTTTT	attentat
AAEOPSTT	apostate
AAEORSTT	aerostat
AAEORTTV	rotavate
AAEOSTUV	autosave
AAEPPRRT	art paper

	tar paper
AAEPPRWX	wax paper
AAEPPSTT	appestat
AAEPRSTT	set apart
AAEPRSTW	pea-straw
AAEPRTTW	tap water
	water tap
AAEPRTTY	tea party
AAEPRTXY	taxpayer
AAEPSTTY	stay tape
AAERRSTV	à travers
AAERRSUU	Saururae
AAERRTTT	tartrate
AAERRTTU	art autre
AAERRTTW	tar water
	water rat
AAERRWWY	war-weary
AAERSTTU	saturate
AAERTWWY	waterway
AAESSTWY	wet assay
AAFFFLST	Falstaff
AAFFGILS	gaff sail
AAFFHLLO	half loaf
	half-loaf
AAFFILLR	fair fall
AAFFILRT	taffrail
AAFFINPR	paraffin
AAFFINUX	faux-naïf
AAFFLLLT	fall flat
AAFFLPST	palstaff
AAFFLSTU	afflatus
AAFFNNOR	fanfaron
AAFFSTTU	tau staff
AAFGILNO	golfiana
AAFGKLNR	flag rank
AAFGLLNU	langlauf
AAFGLNRT	flagrant
AAFGNRRT	fragrant
AAFGORRS	farragos
AAFGORRT	Agra Fort
AAFHHIKL	khalifah
AAFHHORT	Haftorah
AAFHIKLT	khalifat
	khilafat
AAFHIRST	airshaft
AAFHKLMR	half mark
AAFHLMNS	Flashman
AAFHLMST	half mast
	half-mast
AAFHLSTY	layshaft
AAFHORTW	what for a
AAFHRRTW	wharf rat
AAFHRSUU	hausfrau
AAFIILLM	familial
AAFIILLR	filarial
AAFIILMR	familiar
AAFIILRS	filarias
AAFIINST	fistiana
AAFIKLLY	alkalify
AAFILLNR	rainfall
AAFILLUV	availful
AAFILMST	fatalism
AAFILNNU	infaunal
AAFILNSY	final say
AAFILOPR	parafoil
AAFILPRS	Parsifal
AAFILPRY	fair play
	play fair
AAFILPTX	pita-flax
AAFILSTT	fatalist
AAFILTTY	fatality
AAFIMNOR	foramina
AAFINNOV	Favonian
AAFINNRS	safranin
AAFINORT	Fanariot
AAFINRRW	warfarin
AAFINSTU	faustian✧
	Faustina
AAFIPRSU	fraus pia
	pia fraus
AAFIRSST	safarist
AAFIRTTT	frittata
AAFJORZZ	Afro-jazz
AAFKLSTT	fast-talk
AAFKMNRT	tank farm
AAFKMUUY	Fukuyama
AAFLLMOT	malt loaf
AAFLLPRT	fall-trap
	pratfall
	trapfall
AAFLLPST	spatfall
AAFLLRTY	try a fall
AAFLLSTT	salt flat
AAFLMNOW	man of law
AAFLMORV	lavaform
AAFLNNOT	non-fatal
AAFLNORS	safronal
AAFLNOTT	floatant
AAFLOOWY	fool away
AAFLOTTU	to a fault
AAFLSTWY	flatways
AAFMNORW	man-of-war
AAFMNRST	raftsman
AAFNPPRT	frappant
AAGGGINR	garaging
AAGGILNR	gangliar
AAGGIMNN	managing
AAGGIMNR	maraging
AAGGIRST	garagist
AAGGITTW	gigawatt
AAGGLLLY	lallygag
AAGGLNOT	tag along
AAGGMNNS	gangsman
AAGGNORT	Taganrog
AAGGOOPP	Pago Pago
AAGHHINS	shanghai✧
AAGHHINU	Huang Hai
AAGHIJNR	Jahangir
AAGHILNN	hangnail
AAGHILPY	hypalgia
AAGHILRS	harigals
AAGHIMNS	ashaming
AAGHIMRT	taghairm
AAGHINPS	paganish
AAGHIPRR	airgraph
AAGHIRSV	vagarish
AAGHKMNY	gymkhana
AAGHLNNS	Langshan
AAGHLNOT	Loaghtan
AAGHLNPY	anaglyph
AAGHMNNO	Monaghan
AAGHMNOY	Hogmanay
	mahogany
AAGHMNRS	Hans Gram
AAGHMNRT	Grantham
AAGHMRSS	marsh-gas
AAGHNNST	Tangshan
AAGHNOPR	agraphon
AAGHOOPZ	Zoophaga
AAGHOPPR	apograph
AAGHRRTU	arraught
AAGHSSTU	Gasthaus
AAGIILMN	imaginal
AAGIILNN	Laingian
AAGIILNS	aliasing
AAGIILNV	availing
AAGIIMST	astigmia
AAGIINNP	Paganini
AAGIINNT	Ignatian
AAGIJRTU	Gujarati
AAGIKKNY	kayaking
AAGIKLNO	kaoliang
AAGIKLUY	Kaliyuga
AAGIKMRS	skiagram
AAGILLNO	Galliano
AAGILLNU	Anguilla
AAGILLNY	allaying
AAGILLSS	galliass
AAGILLTV	gallivat
AAGILLUZ	alguazil
AAGILMMR	mailgram
AAGILMNO	magnolia
AAGILMNR	alarming
	marginal
AAGILMOT	gliomata
AAGILNOR	Gloriana
AAGILNOT	galtonia
AAGILNRR	larrigan
AAGILNRS	Sangrail
AAGILNUV	vaginula
AAGILOOP	apologia
AAGILPRY	plagiary
AAGILRRW	warrigal
AAGILRTT	attagirl
AAGILSTT	sagittal
AAGIMMRR	marigram
AAGIMNNN	Manganin®
AAGIMNOS	angiomas
AAGIMNPS	paganism
AAGIMNRR	margarin
AAGIMNSY	gymnasia
AAGIMPTU	patagium
AAGIMSSV	savagism

Words marked ✧ can also be spelled with one or more capital letters

AAGIMSTT	stigmata
AAGINNNY	nannygai
AAGINNOT	agnation
AAGINNTV	vaginant
AAGINNTW	awanting
AAGINNUW	Wanganui
AAGINOST	Santiago
AAGINPRU	pagurian
AAGINRRS	Srinagar
AAGINRSU	guaranis
AAGINRTT	Rattigan
AAGINRTU	au gratin
AAGINSST	assignat
AAGINSSU	gaussian✧
AAGINSSY	assaying
	gainsays
AAGINSWY	sign away
AAGIORTT	agitator
AAGIRSTV	gravitas
	stravaig
AAGJLSSW	glass jaw
AAGKLNOS	ask along
AAGKNOOR	kangaroo
AAGKNORR	Ragnarok
	Ragnarök
AAGKPPRS	spark gap
AAGLLLNO	all along
AAGLLMOY	allogamy
AAGLLNOO	lagoonal
AAGLLNRY	laryngal
AAGLLOPY	polygala
AAGLLOWY	Galloway
AAGLLPSW	gall wasp
AAGLMNSS	glassman
AAGLMOPS	sago palm
AAGLNNOO	analogon
AAGLNOPT	Plantago
AAGLNOPZ	zap along
AAGLNPST	gas-plant
AAGLNQUU	aqualung
AAGLNRRU	granular
AAGLOPRY	paralogy
AAGLPRUW	Walpurga
AAGLPSST	last-gasp
AAGLPUWY	plug away
AAGLRRUW	warragul
AAGLRSTU	gastrula
AAGMMORT	gram-atom
AAGMNOPZ	zampogna
AAGMNORT	martagon
AAGMNORW	rag-woman
AAGMNRTU	armgaunt
AAGMNSSW	swagsman
AAGMNSTY	Mt Sangay
	syntagma
AAGMOTUY	autogamy
AAGMOTYZ	zygomata
AAGMPSSW	swamp gas
AAGMRSST	matgrass
AAGNNSTT	stagnant
AAGNOPRT	tragopan
AAGNORRT	arrogant
	tarragon
AAGNORTU	argonaut✧
AAGNRTUY	guaranty
AAGNSTUU	Augustan
AAGOPRTT	targa top
AAGOPSSS	sapsagos
AAGORSSS	sargasso
AAGORSST	oat grass
AAGORSSU	saguaros
AAGRSSSW	sawgrass
AAGRSSTU	sastruga
AAGRSTUZ	zastruga
AAHHIIMM	mahi-mahi
AAHHILMS	Hailsham
AAHHKKNU	Hanukkah
AAHHKMRS	hashmark
AAHHLLOO	holla-hoa!
AAHHLLUU	hula-hula
AAHHMMSS	shammash
AAHIIKRR	hara-kiri
	hari-kari
AAHIIKRT	tarakihi
AAHIILRT	hair-tail
AAHIINTT	Tahitian
AAHIJPRS	rajaship
AAHIKLPS	pashalik
AAHIKNSS	Kinshasa
AAHILMNR	harmalin
AAHILMRY	hail Mary✧
AAHILNNT	inhalant
AAHILNOT	halation
AAHILNPT	Naphtali
AAHILNSS	Salishan
AAHILNST	Stahlian
AAHILNTT	Tanalith®
AAHILPSY	physalia
AAHIMNPS	pashmina
AAHIMSTT	Matthias
AAHINNTX	Xanthian
AAHINORT	Horatian
AAHINPRT	Parthian
AAHINRSW	rainwash
AAHINRTU	hauriant
AAHINTWY	thin away
AAHIPSXY	asphyxia
AAHIPWWY	whip away
AAHJNNOT	Jonathan
AAHJNNRU	Nur Jahan
AAHKLLMR	hallmark
AAHKLMOO	Oklahoma
	Oklahoma!
AAHKMOOY	Yokohama
AAHKMOTW	tomahawk
AAHKNORS	Noah's ark
AAHKPRSW	spar-hawk
AAHKRSSW	sawshark
AAHLLLOO	hallaloo
AAHLLOPT	allopath
AAHLLUVX	Vauxhall®
AAHLMOOS	masoolah
AAHLMSTU	thalamus
AAHLNPST	ash-plant
AAHLNPSU	Paul Nash
AAHLNPTT	hat plant
	hat-plant
AAHMMNRS	marsh-man
AAHMMORR	Moharram
AAHMMRRU	Muharram
AAHMNORT	marathon
AAHMNOST	hoastman
AAHMNOTX	xanthoma
AAHMNPST	phantasm
AAHMNRST	trashman
AAHMOPRS	amphoras
AAHMORSS	Massorah
AAHMRSST	stramash
AAHNNSSU	Susannah
AAHNOOTZ	Anthozoa
AAHNOSTT	Thanatos
AAHNPRSU	Raphanus
AAHNPSTY	phantasy
AAHNRTTY	Hanratty
AAHNRTUX	Xanthura
AAHNTUWY	huntaway
AAHOPRTU	autoharp
AAHRRTTW	thrawart
AAHRSTTW	straw-hat
AAHSSTTU	Hattusas
AAHSTUWY	shut away
AAIIILMR	miliaria
AAIIIMNR	niramiai
AAIIKKNN	kinakina
AAIIKNNW	Kiwanian
AAIILLQU	Quillaia
AAIILMNS	mainsail
AAIILMNT	Tamilian
AAIILMRS	Marsilia
AAIILNPR	Aprilian
AAIILNRZ	alizarin
AAIILNSV	Salvinia
AAIILNTV	Vitalian
AAIILNUX	uniaxial
AAIILPRR	Prairial
	riparial
AAIILRST	Alistair
AAIILRTV	vital air
AAIILRTX	triaxial
AAIILRUX	auxiliar
AAIILTXY	axiality
AAIIMMNX	Maximian
AAIIMNNR	Arminian
AAIIMNNT	maintain
AAIIMNPX	panmixia
AAIIMNRS	Arianism
AAIINNTT	Titanian
AAIINOTV	aviation
AAIINPRR	riparian
AAIINPRS	Parisian
AAIINPZZ	piazzian
AAIINRST	intarsia
AAIIOPST	apositia

AAIIORRT air-to-air
AAIIORTZ zoiatria
AAIIPRST apiarist
AAIIRSTV aviarist
AAIIRSTW wistaria
AAIIRTTV via trita
AAIIRTVX aviatrix
AAIJLLQU Quillaja
AAIJNRYZ janizary
AAIKKNOS skokiaan
AAIKLNOR Kolarian
AAIKLNOS Salonika
AAIKLNRS Sri Lanka
AAIKLNST nastalik
AAIKLOSV Slovakia
AAIKMNST antimask
AAIKMORS Makarios
AAIKMOSY Kismaayo
AAIKMRST tamarisk
AAIKNNTT anti-tank
AAIKNPST Pakistan
AAIKNRTX taxi rank
AAIKSSTV svastika
AAIKSSTW swastika
AAILLLLN all in all
AAILLLUV alluvial
AAILLMMM mammilla
AAILLMMR mamillar
AAILLMNT mantilla
AAILLMNW mani wall
AAILLMNY animally
AAILLMOR Amarillo
AAILLMPT tail lamp
AAILLNOV vallonia
AAILLNTW law Latin
AAILLPPR papillar
AAILLRRY arillary
AAILLRXY axillary
AAILMMRS alarmism
AAILMNNT lamantin
AAILMNOP palamino
AAILMNOR manorial
morainal
AAILMNOS Mona Lisa
AAILMNOX monaxial
AAILMNPS panislam
AAILMNRU manurial
AAILMNRY laminary
AAILMNST staminal
talisman
AAILMNSV navalism
AAILMOPT lipomata
AAILMORR armorial
AAILMPPS papalism
AAILMPRT primatal
AAILMRST alarmist
alastrim
AAILMSWW Mawlawis
AAILMTTU ultimata
AAILNNOT national✧
AAILNNPT plainant
plantain
AAILNNRU lunarian
AAILNNST annalist
santalin
AAILNOPS salopian✧
AAILNOPT talapoin
AAILNORT notarial
rational
AAILNOST ailantos
AAILNOSV Slavonia
AAILNOTV lavation
AAILNPRT air-plant
AAILNPRU planuria
AAILNPTU Laputian
AAILNQST nasta'liq
AAILNQTU aliquant
AAILNSSY analysis
AAILNSTT Atlantis
AAILNSTU Lusatian
AAILNSTY nasality
AAILNSVY Sylvania
AAILNTTT latitant
AAILNTTY natality
AAILORRS rasorial
AAILORRV variolar
AAILPPRU puparial
AAILPPST papalist
AAILPRST triapsal
AAILQRSU squarial
AAILRRSV arrivals
AAILRRTW war trial
AAILRSTT rat's-tail
AAILRSTV travails
AAILRSTZ Lazarist
AAILRSVY salivary
AAILSSTY staysail
AAIMMNOY Yanomami
AAIMMNRR arm in arm
AAIMMNST mainmast
AAIMMRSU samarium
AAIMNNOR Maronian
Romanian
AAIMNNRU Rumanian
AAIMNORT animator
montaria
tamanoir
AAIMNORV Moravian
AAIMNORW airwoman
AAIMNOST Tomasina
AAIMNOSV à mon avis
AAIMNPRZ marzipan
AAIMNPTU putamina
AAIMNRRT trimaran
AAIMNRRU ranarium
AAIMNRST Inmarsat
AAIMNSST mantissa
satanism
AAIMNSTU amiantus
AAIMNSTY mainstay
AAIMOPRS mariposa
AAIMPRST pastrami
AAIMQRUU aquarium
AAIMRRST Amritsar
AAIMRRSY misarray
AAIMRRTY martyria
AAINNOPV pavonian
AAINNOST sonatina
AAINNOSU Ausonian
AAINNOSX Saxonian
AAINNOTT natation
AAINNOTV Novatian
AAINNRTU nutarian
Turanian
AAINNSST naissant
AAINNSSY sannyasi
AAINOPRV par avion
AAINOPSS paisanos
AAINOPTT at a point
AAINORRS rosarian
AAINORRT Rotarian
AAINOTTX taxation
AAINPRST aspirant
partisan
AAINPRTW war paint
AAINPRTZ partizan
AAINPSTU sapi-utan
AAINQRTU quatrain
AAINQTTU aquatint
AAINRRSS sarrasin
AAINRRST Sartrian
AAINRRSZ sarrazin
AAINRSSY Assyrian
AAINRSTU Austrian
Saturnia
AAINRSTY sanitary
AAINRTWY way train
AAINSSSS assassin
AAINSSTT satanist
AAINSTTT antistat
AAINSTTY satanity
AAIOPRRT troparia
AAIOPRSU parousia
AAIOPSTU autopsia
AAIORTUZ azoturia
AAIPRSSX sparaxis
AAIPRSTT partitas
AAIQRSTU aquarist
AAIQRSUU Aquarius
AAIRRSST Stari Ras
AAIRSSTT ITAR-Tass
tsaritsa
AAIRSSTU Asturias
AAIRSTWY stairway
AAJLMPUV Java plum
AAJMMORR marjoram
AAJMNORS mason jar✧
AAJMRSTT Jam tarts
AAKKMMOO mako-mako
AAKKRTYZ Krazy Kat
AAKLLLTT talk tall
AAKLLLTW walk tall
AAKLLLWW wall walk

Words marked ✧ can also be spelled with one or more capital letters

AAKLMNNS Klansman
AAKLMRRX Karl Marx
AAKLMRUY yarmulka
AAKLOORY Royal Oak
AAKLORRY Ark Royal
AAKLPRTY kalyptra
AAKLRWWY walk awry
AAKMMNRS marksman
AAKMNRSW swan-mark
AAKMOPSW swamp oak
AAKMOSSU moussaka
AAKNNSTU nunataks
AAKNPRTT tank trap
AAKOPRSV Kasparov
AALLLLMP pall-mall
AALLLSTY laystall
AALLMMRS small arm
AALLMNST stallman
AALLMNSY sally-man
AALLMNTY tallyman
AALLMNUY manually
AALLMORW moral law
AALLMORY amorally
AALLMPPY palm-play
AALLMSST smallsat
AALLNNUY annually
AALLNOTT not at all
AALLNOTY atonally
AALLNPRU planular
AALLNRTY tarnally
AALLOORW wallaroo
AALLORSU allosaur
AALLORWY rollaway
AALLPRST plastral
AALLPRTY all-party
AALLPSSW wall pass
AALLPUWY pull away
AALLRSST All Stars
AALLRUVV valvular
AALMNOPP Pamplona
AALMNORT matronal
AALMNORU monaural
AALMNORW Roman law
AALMNOWY laywoman
AALMNPSU Paul's-man
AALMNPTY tympanal
AALMNTTU tantalum
AALMNTUU autumnal
AALMOOSS massoola
AALMOPSX axoplasm
AALMOSTT stomatal
AALMOTXY xylomata
AALMPPSU paspalum
AALMPSTY platysma
AALMQSUU squamula
AALNNOPT pantalon
AALNNPUU punaluan
AALNNTUU lunanaut
AALNOPRT patronal
AALNOPRU Anoplura
AALNPSTU Platanus
AALNPTWX wax plant
AALNRRTY arrantly
AALNSTTU tantalus✧
AALNTUUV Tuvaluan
AALOOPSU São Paulo
AALOPPRV approval
AALOPRST pastoral
AALORTTW total war
AALORTUV valuator
AALORTVY lavatory
AALPRSTU pastural
spatular
AALPSSSW pass laws
AALRRTTY tartarly✧
AALRSSVY vassalry
AALRSTTW stalwart
AALRSTUY salutary
AAMMNNOT man to man
AAMMNOOY Yanomamo
AAMMNPRS rampsman
AAMMOTXY myxomata
AAMMRSSU marasmus
AAMNNOPR apron-man
AAMNORRS Marranos
AAMNPRTY party man
AAMNQSUW squawman
AAMNRSTU Sumatran
AAMNRSTW straw man
AAMOORST Rosa Mota
AAMOPRRU paramour
AAMORRSZ zamarros
AAMORSTT stromata
AAMRTTTU Art Tatum
AANNOSST assonant
AANNOSTT annattos
AANNRSTY stannary✧
AANOOPPX opopanax
AANOOPRZ parazoon
AANOPRTY anatropy
AANORRRT narrator
AANORSTY sanatory
AANORTTY natatory
AANPPTTY pattypan
AANRRTTY tartanry
AANRRTWY warranty
AANRSTTU saturant
AANRTUWY turn away
AANVVWYY Wavy Navy
AAOPSSTY apostasy
AAORSSTT starosta
AAORSUVV vavasour
AAORSVVY vavasory
AAOSSTWY toss away
AAOSTWWY stow away
stowaway
AAPRRSTT star trap
AARRSSTW star wars✧
AARRSTTU Tartarus
AARSTTUY statuary
ABBBDEEL bedabble
ABBBDNOY baby bond
ABBBEEFY baby beef
ABBBEILR bribable
ABBBELLY Baby Bell
ABBBELTU tubbable
ABBBELUY baby blue
blue baby
ABBBGILN babbling
blabbing
ABBBHSUY bushbaby
ABBBIRTY Babbitry
ABBBISTT Babbitt's
ABBBMOOY baby boom
ABBBOSTU subabbot
ABBCCKMO back-comb
ABBCDERS scrabbed
ABBCDKNO backbond
ABBCEERU barbecue
ABBCEGIR cribbage
ABBCEHMU beach bum
ABBCEHOU babouche
ABBCEHOY beach boy
ABBCEHTU bathcube
ABBCEIKT backbite
bite back
ABBCEILR barbicel
ABBCEIRR crabbier
ABBCEKLU blueback
ABBCEKNO backbone
ABBCEKNU buckbean
ABBCELLU clubable
ABBCELRS Scrabble®
scrabble
ABBCELRU curbable
ABBCGINR crabbing
ABBCGIOR gabbroic
ABBCIILL biblical
ABBCIINR rabbinic✧
ABBCIKRT brickbat
ABBCILRY crabbily
ABBCINOY cabin-boy
ABBCKLNU black bun
ABBCKLOW blowback
ABBCKLOX black box
ABBCKLOY blackboy
ABBCNORY baby corn
corn-baby
ABBDDEEL beddable
ABBDDEIL biddable
ABBDDLOO bad blood
ABBDEEER bee-bread
ABBDEELN bendable
ABBDEELT bed-table
ABBDEERT rabbeted
ABBDEILR ad-libber
ABBDEINR bread bin
ABBDELMO babeldom
ABBDELRR drabbler
ABBDEMOR bombarde
ABBDENRU unbarbed
ABBDEORS absorbed
ABBDFOOY babyfood

ABBDGILN dabbling
ABBDGIOR big board✧
gabbroid
ABBDHIRS drabbish
ABBDHIRT birdbath
ABBDHOOY babyhood
ABBDILNO bailbond
ABBDILNY Blind Bay
ABBDLLOY baby doll
ABBDLNOY Bob Dylan
ABBDNORW bawd-born
browband
ABBDOORX boxboard
ABBDORRY Barr body
ABBDRRUY Bradbury
ABBEEIMS Babeeism
ABBEEINR bearbine
ABBEEJRR jabberer
ABBEEJRS bejabers
ABBEELVW Ebbw Vale
ABBEENOR barebone
ABBEEQRU barbeque
ABBEERTT barbette
ABBEESTT a best bet
ABBEFGIR brief-bag
ABBEGLRR grabbler
ABBEHILS babelish
ABBEHKOW Bob Hawke
ABBEHKRU hub-brake
ABBEHORT bathrobe
ABBEHRTU Babe Ruth
ABBEILMS babelism
ABBEILNU bubaline
ABBEILOT bilobate
ABBEILST bistable
ABBEIMWZ Zimbabwe
ABBEINRS Brisbane
ABBEINTT tabbinet
ABBEIRRT rabbiter
ABBEIRRW barbwire
ABBEKLOO bookable
ABBEKOST bob skate
ABBELLST best-ball
ABBELOOT bootable
ABBELOPP bob-apple
ABBELOPR probable
ABBELORU belabour
ABBELOVY Baby Love
ABBELQSU squabble
ABBELRSY slabbery
ABBEMOOR aerobomb
ABBENORS baseborn
ABBEORRS absorber
reabsorb
ABBEORTW browbeat
ABBERRRY barberry
ABBERRYY bayberry
ABBERSSW swabbers
ABBFILLY flabbily
ABBGGILN gabbling
ABBGGINR grabbing
ABBGILNR rabbling
ABBGILNU baubling
ABBGINST stabbing
ABBGINSW swabbing
ABBGINTY tabbying
ABBGNORW brown-bag
ABBHIIMS bimbashi
ABBHILSY shabbily
ABBHRRUY rhubarby
ABBIINOT bibation
ABBIKLLN bank-bill
ABBIKNRY kirn-baby
ABBILLOT boatbill
ABBILLSU sillabub
ABBILMMO mail bomb
ABBILMNO nail bomb
ABBILNOP plain bob
ABBILOST bioblast
ABBIMNOS bambinos
ABBINORT rabbit on
ABBINORX brainbox
ABBINORZ Barbizon
ABBIRRTY rabbitry
ABBIRSUU suburbia
ABBITUZZ buzzbait
ABBJMOOR bob major
ABBKKNOO bank book
ABBLLLOW blowball
ABBLLRSU bullbars
ABBLLSUY syllabub
ABBLOORY bob royal
ABBLOPRY probably
ABBMMOOT atom bomb
ABBNRSUU suburban
ABBOSSTY bobstays
ABCCDEHO caboched
ABCCDHIK dabchick
ABCCDIOU Boudicca
ABCCEEHN bechance
ABCCEELP peccable
ABCCEEOR caboceer
ABCCEFLU club-face
ABCCEHNY by chance
ABCCEIKL black ice
ABCCEILY celibacy
ABCCEIRT bacteric
ABCCEKMO come back
comeback
ABCCESUU succubae
ABCCHHIN Chibchan
ABCCHISU bacchius
ABCCHNOO cabochon
ABCCHOOX coach box
ABCCIKKK kick back
kickback
ABCCIKKP pickback
ABCCIKOR abricock
ABCCILOR carbolic
ABCCILOT cobaltic
ABCCINOR carbonic
ABCCIORS ascorbic
ABCCKLLO ballcock
ABCCKLOX clackbox
ABCCKOOT cockboat
ABCCOORS baroccos
ABCCOOST tobaccos
ABCCSSUU succubas
ABCDDEOR barcoded
brocaded
ABCDEEFK feedback
ABCDEEGK back edge
ABCDEEHR berdache
ABCDEELM becalmed
ABCDEELU educable
ABCDEEMR embraced
ABCDEETU abductee
ABCDEFLO boldface
ABCDEGIR birdcage
cage-bird
ABCDEHIR chair-bed
ABCDEHLU clubhead
ABCDEHNR branched
ABCDEHOS caboshed
ABCDEIIT diabetic
ABCDEIKS backside
ABCDEILR calibred
ABCDEKLO bale-dock
blockade
ABCDEKLV backveld
ABCDEKNN neckband
ABCDEKNU unbacked
ABCDEKOT boat deck
ABCDEKRT trackbed
ABCDELOO caboodle
ABCDELSU bud-scale
ABCDEMNU dumb-cane
ABCDEMOT combated
ABCDENRU bean curd
unbraced
ABCDENTU abducent
ABCDFRUY farcy-bud
ABCDGKLO black dog✧
ABCDHKLO hold back
holdback
ABCDIILO biocidal
diabolic
ABCDIIMY cymbidia
ABCDIIRT tribadic
ABCDIKLO bail-dock
ABCDIKLR baldrick
ABCDIKRU baudrick
ABCDILLR birdcall
call-bird
ABCDILOU cuboidal
ABCDIRSU subacrid
ABCDKLOR Black Rod
ABCDKNOW back down
backdown
ABCDKOOR back door
backdoor
ABCDKOPR backdrop
ABCDKORW backword

ABCDLLNU	clubland
ABCDLOOT	bald-coot
ABCDLOSU	club soda
ABCDLOUY	Cloud Bay
ABCDOORS	brood-sac
ABCDOORW	crab-wood
ABCDOPRU	cupboard
ABCDORSU	bucardos
ABCDORTU	abductor
ABCDORUY	obduracy
ABCEEEFK	beefcake
ABCEEFNT	benefact
ABCEEGRR	Bergerac
ABCEEHKL	back-heel
ABCEEHLM	bechamel béchamel
ABCEEHLN	alebench
ABCEEHLR	bleacher
ABCEEHLW	chewable
ABCEEHNO	bone-ache
ABCEEILR	Liberace
ABCEEILT	celibate citeable
ABCEEIMN	ambience
ABCEEIRT	Beatrice
ABCEEKKP	keep back
ABCEEKLY	black eye eye-black
ABCEELLO	eco-label
ABCEELNO	bone-lace
ABCEELOV	evocable
ABCEELRR	cerebral
ABCEELRT	bracelet
ABCEEMRR	embracer
ABCEEMRS	embraces
ABCEENOV	bone-cave
ABCEENRT	Cabernet
ABCEENSY	scene bay
ABCEERRT	crab tree
ABCEERUX	berceaux
ABCEFIIT	beatific
ABCEFIKL	backfile
ABCEFIKR	backfire fireback
ABCEFINO	boniface✧
ABCEFLSS	bass clef
ABCEGKLL	blackleg
ABCEGKLO	blockage
ABCEGKMU	megabuck
ABCEGKOR	brockage
ABCEGNOR	bongrace
ABCEGNST	scent bag
ABCEHHTU	beach hut
ABCEHITT	bathetic
ABCEHKST	the Backs
ABCEHKTW	bethwack
ABCEHLOR	bachelor
ABCEHLOS	chaebols
ABCEHLSU	chasuble
ABCEHLTU	leachtub
ABCEHMOT	hecatomb
ABCEHMRS	chambers
ABCEHNRR	brancher
ABCEHOOT	cohobate
ABCEHOPU	pabouche
ABCEHORR	broacher
ABCEHORU	barouche
ABCEHRTT	bratchet
ABCEIJNR	jib crane
ABCEIJOT	Jacobite
ABCEIKKL	kickable
ABCEIKLR	crablike
ABCEIKLS	scablike
ABCEIKLT	black tie
ABCEIKMT	back time
ABCEIKNR	rein back
ABCEIKRT	brick-tea
ABCEIKWZ	zwieback
ABCEILLR	cribella
ABCEILLT	balletic
ABCEILNN	binnacle
ABCEILNU	baculine
ABCEILOR	albicore cabriole
ABCEILOS	sociable
ABCEILTT	bittacle
ABCEILTU	baculite
ABCEIMST	betacism
ABCEINOO	coenobia
ABCEINOS	base coin
ABCEINTU	incubate
ABCEIORS	Aerobics® aerobics
ABCEIORT	boracite
ABCEIRRT	cribrate
ABCEIRSW	crabwise
ABCEIRTT	brattice
ABCEIRTY	acerbity
ABCEISSS	abscisse
ABCEISST	asbestic
ABCEJKLT	jet-black
ABCEJLTY	abjectly
ABCEKKRU	buckrake
ABCEKKSW	skewback
ABCEKLLO	lockable
ABCEKLMO	mockable
ABCEKLOO	cookable
ABCEKLPU	palebuck
ABCEKLSS	backless
ABCEKNOT	boat neck
ABCEKOOS	bookcase casebook
ABCEKOPR	back-rope
ABCEKRST	back rest
ABCELLPU	culpable
ABCELLSU	bucellas
ABCELMNY	lambency
ABCELMOS	cembalos
ABCELMRS	scambler scramble
ABCELNOT	balconet bel canto
ABCELNUU	nubecula
ABCELOOT	bootlace lace-boot
ABCELOPS	placebos
ABCELORT	brocatel
ABCELOST	obstacle
ABCELOTU	bluecoat
ABCELRSW	bescrawl
ABCELRTT	bractlet
ABCELTTU	table-cut
ABCEMNRU	cream bun
ABCEMORS	cramboes
ABCENNOS	Besançon
ABCENOUY	buoyance
ABCENTUX	excubant
ABCEORRY	boy racer
ABCEOSUX	saucebox
ABCERRTU	carburet
ABCERSTU	sabre-cut
ABCERTUU	cubature
ABCESSTU	subcaste
ABCESTUU	subacute
ABCFFOTU	buff-coat
ABCFHOTW	fob-watch
ABCFIKLL	backfill
ABCFIKLP	backflip
ABCFIKLT	backlift liftback
ABCFILOS	bifocals
ABCFKLLU	full back
ABCFKLLY	black fly
ABCFKLOX	black-fox
ABCFKOST	softback
ABCFLLLU	bull-calf
ABCFLMOX	flax-comb
ABCGGIMO	gambogic
ABCGHINT	batching
ABCGHKOS	hog's-back
ABCGHNPU	punch-bag
ABCGIKLN	blacking
ABCGIKNR	king crab ring back
ABCGIKNW	wing back
ABCGILNO	log cabin
ABCGILRU	Bulgaric
ABCGKLPU	gulp back
ABCGKLUY	lucky bag
ABCGLNOX	clangbox
ABCGSUZZ	scuzzbag
ABCHHIIS	hibachis
ABCHIIPS	biphasic
ABCHIKLS	blackish
ABCHIKRS	brackish
ABCHILMO	choliamb
ABCHILOO	coolibah
ABCHIMOR	choriamb
ABCHIMRU	brachium
ABCHIMTU	a bit much
ABCHINOR	bronchia
ABCHIOOR	borachio
ABCHIRRT	tribrach

ABCHKLOT	hackbolt
ABCHKMPU	humpback
	hump-back
ABCHKOOP	chapbook
ABCHKOOS	cash-book
ABCHKSUW	buck-wash
ABCHLLUU	club-haul
ABCHLNRU	bar lunch
ABCHMOTX	matchbox
ABCHOPTX	patch box
ABCHOTWX	watchbox
ABCHRRSU	crush bar
ABCIIKRR	air-brick
ABCIINNO	in bianco
ABCIINOT	cibation
ABCIINSS	abscisin
ABCIINTU	bucatini
ABCIIORS	isobaric
ABCIIRST	tribasic
ABCIIRTU	Curitiba
ABCIISTY	basicity
ABCIITUX	bauxitic
ABCIKKLL	kickball
ABCIKLLL	back-lill
ABCIKLLT	back-lilt
ABCIKLST	backlist
ABCIKMRS	Bismarck
ABCIKNPS	backspin
ABCILLNY	billy-can
ABCILLRU	lubrical
ABCILLSU	bacillus✧
ABCILLSY	syllabic
ABCILMMO	cimbalom
ABCILMOO	Colombia
ABCILMOU	Columbia
ABCILMSU	subclaim
ABCILNNV	vin blanc
ABCILNPU	publican
ABCILOOR	coolibar
ABCILOSY	sociably
ABCILRRU	rubrical
ABCIMMSU	cambiums
ABCIMORR	microbar
ABCIMRTU	umbratic
ABCINORU	conurbia
ABCINPUY	panic-buy
ABCINRSU	Brancusi
ABCINRVY	vibrancy
ABCIORRS	barricos
ABCIORSU	caribous
ABCIOSSU	scabious
ABCIRSTT	abstrict
ABCJKOOT	boot-jack
	jackboot
ABCKKLOO	look back
ABCKKORW	backwork
	work back
ABCKLLOR	rollback
ABCKLLOS	ballocks
ABCKLLPU	pull back
	pullback
ABCKLOPT	blacktop
ABCKLORT	black rot
ABCKLOSW	slowback
ABCKLOTU	black out
	blackout
ABCKMOOR	back room
	backroom
ABCKMORR	brockram
ABCKMOSS	mossback
ABCKMOST	backmost
ABCKNOOT	back onto
ABCKNRTU	turn back
	turnback
	turn-back
ABCKOORU	buckaroo
ABCKOPST	backstop
ABCKORSS	rock bass
ABCKORUY	buckayro
ABCKRSTU	Starbuck
ABCLLNOR	cornball
ABCLLPUY	culpably
ABCLMNOU	Columban
ABCLMOOO	coloboma
ABCLMOSY	cymbalos
ABCLMSUY	scybalum
ABCLNORY	carbonyl
ABCLORXY	carboxyl
ABCLOSUV	subvocal
ABCLPRUW	pub-crawl
ABCLRSTU	Arts Club
ABCLSSSU	subclass
ABCLSUUU	subucula
ABCMOOPT	boot camp
ABCMOORT	mobocrat
ABCNNORU	conurban
ABCNORTY	corybant
ABCNOUYY	buoyancy
ABCNRSTU	crab-nuts
ABCORRSS	crossbar
ABCORRTU	turbo car
	turbocar
ABCORSSU	scabrous
ABCOSSTU	subcosta
ABCOSTTU	cottabus
ABCRSTTU	subtract
ABDDDEET	addebted
ABDDDGIY	big Daddy
ABDDEEHT	deathbed
ABDDEEKN	naked bed
ABDDEENR	reed-band
ABDDEERR	debarred
	Redbeard
ABDDEEST	bedstead
	bestadde
ABDDEHMO	hebdomad
ABDDEHOY	hobdayed
ABDDEILS	disabled
ABDDEILU	buddleia
ABDDEINR	brandied
ABDDEINS	sideband
ABDDEINV	divan-bed
ABDDEINW	wideband
ABDDELOT	dead-bolt
ABDDELRY	bladdery
ABDDENNU	unbanded
ABDDENOR	dead-born
ABDDERSW	bedwards
ABDDFORR	Bradford
ABDDHIOR	rhabdoid
ABDDILMO	lambdoid
ABDDILRY	ladybird
ABDDIMNO	bondmaid
ABDDINNW	wind band
ABDDIRRY	yardbird
ABDDLOUZ	Zola Budd
ABDEEEFL	feedable
ABDEEEFN	bedeafen
ABDEEEKR	Baedeker
ABDEEENR	Aberdeen
ABDEEERV	beavered
	bereaved
ABDEEEYY	beady eye
ABDEEFLM	flambéed
ABDEEFNR	reef band
ABDEEGGL	bedaggle
ABDEEGHR	herbaged
ABDEEGLN	gable end
ABDEEGLR	Belgrade
ABDEEGRU	bedeguar
ABDEEHNO	bonehead
ABDEEHRT	breathed
ABDEEHST	bethesda✧
ABDEEHTT	behatted
ABDEEILN	deniable
ABDEEILR	bride-ale
	rideable
ABDEEILT	delibate
	editable
ABDEEILW	bewailed
ABDEEIRT	Abderite
	ebriated
ABDEEIST	diabetes
ABDEEKLL	Lake Bled
ABDEEKMR	bedmaker
	embarked
ABDEEKNR	bedarken
ABDEEKNS	seed bank
ABDEELLL	labelled
ABDEELLN	lendable
ABDEELLW	weldable
ABDEELMN	mendable
ABDEELNO	Denebola
ABDEELNS	sendable
ABDEELNT	bandelet
ABDEELOR	lee-board
ABDEELPT	bedplate
ABDEELRZ	blazered
ABDEELZZ	bedazzle
ABDEEMNS	beam-ends
	bedesman
ABDEEMRR	embarred
ABDEENNR	bannered

ABDEEPRS bespread
ABDEEPRX pax-brede
ABDEERRY ryebread
ABDEERST breasted
ABDEERTT battered
drabette
ABDEERTW water bed
ABDEFFST bed-staff
ABDEFHLR half-bred
ABDEFHOO boofhead
ABDEFILN findable
ABDEFILR leafbird
ABDEFINO bona fide
ABDEFLLO foldable
ABDEFLNU fundable
unfabled
ABDEFLOR fordable
ABDEFNRU faburden
ABDEFOWY Bay of Dew
ABDEGGIL diggable
ABDEGGOR Eggboard
ABDEGIIO Gobiidae
ABDEGILN blindage
ABDEGILU guidable
ABDEGIMR Ambridge
game bird
ABDEGIMX mixed bag
ABDEGINO gabioned
ABDEGINS debasing
ABDEGIRR abridger
ABDEGLOT globated
ABDEGLRY badgerly
ABDEGLSU slug-a-bed
ABDEGNOR bondager
ABDEGNOS dog'sbane
ABDEGNOW wagon bed
ABDEGOOT a good bet
ABDEGOPR pegboard
ABDEGRSU subgrade
ABDEHILL billhead
ABDEHILS dishable
ABDEHITU habitude
ABDEHKLU bulkhead
ABDEHLLN handbell
ABDEHLLU bullhead
ABDEHLOT bolthead
ABDEHMOO head-boom
ABDEHNSU Dushanbe
ABDEHNTU unbathed
ABDEHORR abhorred
ABDEHOSW beshadow
ABDEHOTT to the bad
ABDEHOTY Body Heat
ABDEHTTU butthead
head-butt
ABDEIIRT diatribe
ABDEIKMN Medibank
ABDEIKNU baudekin
ABDEIKQU quad bike
ABDEILLS slidable
ABDEILMN mandible
ABDEILNP pedal bin
ABDEILNR bilander
ABDEILNT bidental
ABDEILNY deniably
ABDEILOV voidable
ABDEILRS bar slide
ABDEILRV drivable
ABDEILRY diablery
ABDEILTU dutiable
ABDEIMNR brideman
ABDEIMOO amoeboid
ABDEIMOR amberoid
ABDEIMRU Drambuie®
ABDEIMST best maid
ABDEINOR debonair
ABDEINPP pipe band
ABDEINRR Birendra
ABDEINRS air-bends
brandise
ABDEINSU unbiased
ABDEINTU unbaited
ABDEIRRR rare bird
ABDEIRRW war bride
ABDEIRTY Darbyite
ABDEISSU disabuse
ABDEITTU dubitate
ABDEKLMO make bold
ABDEKLNP plank bed
ABDEKLSW skewbald
ABDEKNNU unbanked
ABDEKNRU unbarked
ABDEKNSU sunbaked
ABDEKORY keyboard
ABDELLOR bead-roll
ABDELLOT balloted
ABDELLPU balled-up
ABDELLUY Du Bellay
ABDELMNO lemon dab
ABDELMNU unblamed
ABDELNOR banderol
ABDELNRY bylander
ABDELNSS baldness
ABDELORU laboured
ABDELOSW Bode's law
ABDELOTT do battle
ABDELPTY play-debt
ABDEMNOR Doberman
ABDEMNRU Bermudan
ABDEMOOR rood beam
ABDEMRSU Bermudas
ABDEMRTU drumbeat
umbrated
ABDEMRUV ad verbum
ABDENNOS noseband
ABDENNRW brand-new
ABDENORR Dearborn
ABDENORW bear down
rawboned
ABDENORY boneyard
ABDENOTW beat down
downbeat
ABDENRRU unbarred
ABDENRSS drabness
ABDENRST bandster
ABDENRTU breadnut
turbaned
ABDENTTU debutant
débutant
ABDEORRU arboured
ABDEORRW wardrobe
ABDEORSW sowbread
ABDEORTU obdurate
ABDEORUX Bordeaux
ABDEPSTU Budapest
ABDEPSTW debt swap
ABDERSSU surbased
ABDERSTU surbated
ABDERSTW bedstraw
ABDERTUW draw-tube
ABDESTTU taste bud
ABDFFLOY badly off
ABDFFOOR off-board
ABDFHINS bandfish
ABDFLOOT foldboat
ABDFNORU funboard
ABDFNUYY Fundy Bay
ABDGGGOY doggy-bag
ABDGHINR hangbird
ABDGIINR braiding
ABDGILLY dilly bag
ABDGILNR bardling
ABDGILOR gaolbird
ABDGIMRU guimbard
ABDGINNY bandying
ABDGINOR boarding
ABDGINST dingbats
ABDGITTY ditty bag
ABDGJOOO a good job
ABDGLOOR logboard
ABDGOOUY a good buy
ABDHHSSU shadbush
ABDHIIST dishabit
ABDHILLN handbill
ABDHILNS blandish
ABDHINRS brandish
ABDHIORS broadish
ABDHIPRS bardship
ABDHIRSU Hudibras
ABDHIRTY birthday
ABDHKNOO book-hand
handbook
ABDHLNOS ash-blond
ABDHLOPR Bardolph
ABDHLORW blowhard
ABDHLOSW shadblow
ABDHMOTU badmouth
ABDHSTTU dust-bath
ABDIIJLR jailbird
ABDIILLR billiard
ABDIIMNR midbrain
ABDIIMRS Braidism
ABDIIMSU basidium

ABDIINOS	obsidian
ABDIINRR	rainbird
ABDIINTT	banditti
ABDIIRTY	rabidity
ABDIKLNR	blinkard
ABDILOOS	diabolos
ABDILORW	wild boar
ABDILOST	blastoid
ABDILOTY	tabloidy
ABDILRRY	ribaldry
ABDILRZZ	blizzard
ABDILSTU	subtidal
ABDIMNRY	myna bird
ABDINOPR	pair-bond
	pinboard
ABDINORY	Robin Day
ABDINOTY	antibody
ABDINOUU	Baudouin
ABDINRTY	banditry
ABDIORRU	Borduria
ABDIOSUU	subaudio
ABDIPRTT	Brad Pitt
ABDIRRUY	ribaudry
ABDISTUU	Daibutsu
ABDKLNOO	bookland
ABDKNNOW	bank down
ABDKOOOR	road book
ABDLLNOS	slobland
ABDLLSTU	dust-ball
ABDLMNOW	lamb down
ABDLNOOS	ob and sol
ABDLNOSW	sand blow
ABDLOOTX	blood-tax
ABDLRSUU	subdural
ABDLRSUY	absurdly
ABDLSTUU	subadult
ABDMNNOS	bondsman
ABDMNOOR	moor-band
ABDMNOUW	mawbound
ABDMOOPR	mopboard
ABDMRSSU	bass drum
ABDNNORW	own-brand
ABDNOORR	barn door
ABDNORSU	baudrons✧
ABDNORUY	boundary
ABDOORTU	board out
	outboard
ABDOOSSW	basswood
ABDOPRWY	body wrap
ABEEEERT	bee-eater
ABEEEFLT	leaf beet
ABEEEFRS	freebase
ABEEEGLT	bel étage
ABEEEGRS	bargeese
ABEEEGRV	beverage
ABEEEHTT	hebetate
ABEEEKLP	keepable
ABEEELNS	Lebanese
ABEEELPS	bel paese
ABEEELRR	real beer
ABEEEMRT	beam tree
ABEEENRR	near beer
ABEEENRT	bean tree
	tenebrae✧
ABEEENRV	bereaven
ABEEENST	absentee
ABEEEPRU	beau-pere
ABEEERRT	terebrae
ABEEFFTU	beauffet
ABEEFILN	fineable
ABEEFILR	afebrile
	bale-fire
ABEEFILS	feasible
ABEEFILT	flea-bite
ABEEFIRS	sea brief
ABEEFLLL	fellable
ABEEFLLN	befallen
ABEEFLOS	beefalos
ABEEFORR	forebear
ABEEGGNR	green-bag
ABEEGHRT	berthage
ABEEGINR	baregine
	bergenia
ABEEGIRV	verbiage
ABEEGKLR	leg break
ABEEGKNN	gene bank
ABEEGLLR	gabeller
ABEEGLTT	gettable
ABEEGMRY	emery bag
ABEEGMTY	megabyte
ABEEGNNR	green ban
ABEEGNOS	Gabonese
ABEEGOSZ	gazeboes
ABEEGRST	absterge
ABEEGTTU	baguette
ABEEHILR	hireable
ABEEHINT	thebaine
ABEEHIRS	Hebraise
ABEEHIRZ	Hebraize
ABEEHLLL	heelball
ABEEHLLP	helpable
ABEEHLLR	beerhall
	harebell
ABEEHLMO	La Bohème
ABEEHLRU	blue hare
ABEEHMOS	home base
ABEEHNOP	Phoebean
ABEEHNOT	The Beano
ABEEHNPP	behappen
ABEEHNSS	has-beens
ABEEHNTT	hebetant
ABEEHOTV	have to be
	the above
ABEEHQTU	bequeath
ABEEHRRT	breather
ABEEHRST	hartbees
ABEEHSTT	the Beast
ABEEIIMN	bien-aimé
ABEEIKLL	likeable
ABEEIKLT	Bakelite®
ABEEIKRT	tie-break
ABEEILLR	reliable
ABEEILLV	leviable
	liveable
ABEEILMN	mineable
ABEEILNN	Biennale
ABEEILNP	plebeian
ABEEILNS	Balinese
	baseline
ABEEILNU	banlieue
ABEEILNV	enviable
ABEEILNZ	Belizean
ABEEILPW	wipeable
ABEEILPX	expiable
ABEEILRT	liberate
ABEEILST	seablite
ABEEILSV	evasible
ABEEILSZ	seizable
	sizeable
ABEEILTV	evitable
ABEEILVW	viewable
ABEEIMRT	amberite
ABEEINSU	Eusebian
ABEEINTY	ayenbite
ABEEIPRS	bepraise
ABEEIRTT	batterie
ABEEIRTV	breviate
ABEEISSV	abessive
ABEEISTU	beauties
ABEEITUX	beauxite
ABEEJKLO	Joe Blake
ABEEJMNT	Betjeman
ABEEJMOR	jamboree
ABEEJNPU	Punjabee
ABEEKLOT	keelboat
ABEEKMNR	embanker
ABEEKMRR	re-embark
ABEEKOOP	peekaboo
ABEEKPST	keep tabs
ABEEKRST	bestreak
ABEELLLR	labeller
ABEELLLS	sellable
ABEELLLT	tellable
ABEELLMT	meltable
ABEELLOT	ballotee
ABEELLOV	loveable
ABEELLTT	lettable
ABEELMMR	embalmer
	emmarble
ABEELMNO	bone meal
ABEELMOV	moveable
ABEELMPR	preamble
ABEELMRT	atremble
ABEELMSS	assemble
	assemblé
	beamless
ABEELMTT	embattle
ABEELNOP	beanpole
	openable
ABEELNRT	rentable
ABEELNTU	tuneable
ABEELOPR	operable
	ropeable

ABEELOPS poseable
ABEELORX exorable
ABEELRRY ale-berry
ABEELRSU reusable
ABEELRSV beslaver
ABEELRTT batteler
ABEELRTU bateleur
bleuâtre
ABEELSSS baseless
ABEELSST bateless
ABEELSSU sublease
ABEELSTT seat belt
testable
ABEELSUX saxe blue
ABEELTTW wettable
ABEEMMNR membrane
ABEEMMRU bummaree
ABEEMNOR bemoaner
ABEEMNOS mason bee
ABEEMNQU Queen Mab
ABEEMNST basement
ABEEMNTT abetment
batement
ABEEMPTU beat-'em-up
ABEENNOT nota bene
ABEENNRT banneret
ABEENNRU eburnean
ABEENNTU unbeaten
ABEENORS seaborne
ABEENOTZ benzoate
ABEENRRT banterer
ABEENRSS bareness
ABEENSSS baseness
ABEEORRV overbear
ABEEORST rebatoes
ABEEORTV overbeat
ABEEOSTU see about
ABEEPRRY peaberry
ABEERRRT barterer
ABEERRST terebras
ABEERRSY sea-berry
ABEERRTT barrette
batterer
ABEERRTV vertebra
ABEERRTY betrayer
teaberry
ABEERSTU suberate
ABEERTTY terabyte
ABEESTTT beta test
beta-test
ABEESTWY sweet bay
ABEFFKOR break off
breakoff
off break
ABEFFLLO off-label
ABEFGLLR bergfall
ABEFGLLU blue flag
ABEFHILS fishable
ABEFHLLU half-blue
ABEFHOOT hoofbeat
ABEFILLL fallible
ABEFILLM filmable
ABEFILLR fireball
ABEFILLT liftable
ABEFILOT lifeboat
ABEFILRS false rib
ABEFILSU fabulise
ABEFILSY feasibly
ABEFILUZ fabulize
ABEFIRRT firebrat
ABEFITUY beautify
ABEFKLNT Left Bank
left-bank
ABEFLLMU blameful
full beam
ABEFLLTU tableful
ABEFLMOR formable
ABEFLNRU funebral
ABEFLRTU Flaubert
ABEFMORX box-frame
ABEFMRSU subframe
ABEFOORT barefoot
ABEFRRUY February
ABEGGHLU huggable
ABEGGILN beagling
ABEGGITY gigabyte
ABEGGLLU luggable
ABEGGLOS gas-globe
ABEGGLRY beggarly
ABEGGNOS bang goes
ABEGHILP philabeg
ABEGHILR alberghi
ABEGHINT in the bag
ABEGHINZ Benghazi
ABEGHNNO Ben Hogan
ABEGHNOY honey-bag
ABEGHORR begorrah
ABEGHRRY hagberry
ABEGHRST barghest
ABEGIILV give bail
ABEGIINO ibogaine
ABEGIKNN bean-king
ABEGIKNR breaking
ABEGILNN enabling
ABEGILNS singable
ABEGILNT bleating
tangible
ABEGILOT obligate
ABEGIMUX giambeux
ABEGINOR aborigen
ABEGINRS base ring
bearings
ABEGINTT abetting
ABEGINTW wingbeat
ABEGIPPR bagpiper
ABEGIPPS bagpipes
ABEGIRTU auger-bit
ABEGJLLY jelly bag
ABEGKMPR Bergkamp
ABEGKMRY gybe mark
ABEGKORS grosbeak
ABEGLLLU glueball
gullable
ABEGLLOR bargello
ABEGLLRU Llaregub
ABEGLLRY Llaregyb
ABEGLMUY mealy bug
ABEGLNOS noble gas
ABEGLORW growable
ABEGLPRU Paul Berg
ABEGLRUU blagueur
ABEGLSTU gustable
ABEGMNNU mung bean
ABEGMNOS gambeson
ABEGMNOY bogeyman
money bag
ABEGMORT bergamot
ABEGNOOR Gaborone
ABEGNRST bangster
ABEGNRTU burganet
ABEGNSTU subagent
ABEGOORS bargoose
ABEGORRW row barge
ABEGOTTU get about
ABEGPTTY Petty Bag
ABEGRRUV burgrave
ABEGRTUW water bug
ABEGSSTU substage
ABEHIJST the basij✧
ABEHILLR hairbell
ABEHILNR hibernal
ABEHILTT tithable
ABEHIMMS memsahib
ABEHIMNO bohemian✧
ABEHIMOS obeahism
ABEHIMRS Hebraism
ABEHINST absinthe
ABEHIOPU euphobia
ABEHIORS raise hob
ABEHIORV behavior
ABEHIRST Hebraist
ABEHJORS job share
jobshare
job-share
ABEHKLLW hawkbell
ABEHKLST the balks
ABEHKNOR hornbeak
ABEHKNST thanks be
ABEHKSTU Kate Bush
ABEHLLRT bethrall
ABEHLMMU hummable
ABEHLMSS shambles
ABEHLNOT benthoal
ABEHLOTY hylobate
ABEHLSSS bashless
ABEHLSVY by halves
ABEHMNOR hornbeam
ABEHMOOR rehoboam
ABEHMOPT Baphomet
ABEHMSTU bushmeat
ABEHNSTU sunbathe
ABEHOOST boat shoe
ABEHORRR abhorrer✧

	harborer
ABEHORST	bathorse
ABEHOSTU	house bat
ABEHRSST	the brass
ABEHRSSU	sea shrub
ABEHRTUY	Bayreuth
ABEHTWYY	by the way
ABEIILMT	imitable
ABEIILNN	biennial
ABEIILNR	bilinear
	Liberian
ABEIILNV	inviable
ABEIILPT	pitiable
ABEIILRR	libraire
ABEIILRS	biserial
ABEIILRT	Blairite
ABEIILST	albitise
	sibilate
ABEIILTV	live bait
	vitiable
ABEIILTZ	albitize
ABEIINNS	Ibsenian
ABEIIRST	Tiberias
ABEIJLNO	joinable
ABEIJLTU	jubilate✧
ABEIJMNN	benjamin✧
ABEIJMRR	J M Barrie
ABEIKLLM	lamb-like
ABEIKLLN	balkline
	linkable
ABEIKLLY	likeably
ABEIKLNS	sinkable
ABEIKLRU	buik-lear
ABEIKLSS	kissable
ABEIKMRR	rim brake
ABEIKNOR	beak-iron
ABEIKNRS	bearskin
ABEIKNTT	Kabinett
ABEIKRST	breaskit
ABEILLLM	millable
ABEILLLT	tillable
ABEILLLW	willable
ABEILLMM	limbmeal
ABEILLMT	time ball
ABEILLOS	isolable
ABEILLOV	violable
ABEILLQU	liquable
ABEILLRR	brailler
ABEILLRY	Bareilly
	beryllia
	blearily
	reliably
ABEILLST	bastille✧
	listable
ABEILLTT	tiltable
ABEILMNT	bailment
ABEILMOR	bromelia
ABEILMSS	missable
ABEILMST	timbales
ABEILNNW	winnable
ABEILNOP	opinable
ABEILNPT	pintable
ABEILNRS	rinsable
ABEILNRU	ruinable
ABEILNSS	albiness
	bassline
ABEILNST	instable
ABEILNSU	sabuline
ABEILNTV	bivalent
ABEILNUV	unviable
ABEILNVY	enviably
ABEILOTV	bloviate
ABEILPPT	tippable
ABEILPRT	partible
ABEILPRZ	prizable
ABEILPSS	passible
ABEILPST	epiblast
ABEILRRU	reburial
ABEILRTT	title bar
ABEILRTW	writable
ABEILRYY	bi-yearly
ABEILSSU	issuable
	suasible
ABEILSTU	suitable
ABEILSTY	beastily
ABEILSUX	bisexual
ABEILSYZ	sizeably
ABEIMRRU	Brumaire
ABEIMRTV	ambivert
	verbatim
ABEIMSSU	iambuses
ABEINNOR	Brian Eno
ABEINNOS	besonian
ABEINNOZ	bezonian
ABEINNPR	brine-pan
ABEINNRR	inner bar
ABEINNRU	Bruneian
	inurbane
ABEINOOT	Boeotian
ABEINORR	airborne
ABEINORS	sea robin
ABEINORT	baritone
	obtainer
ABEINOST	botanise
	obeisant
ABEINOTT	à bientôt
ABEINOTZ	botanize
ABEINQSU	basquine
ABEINRST	banister
ABEINRSU	urbanise
ABEINRTU	braunite
	urbanite
ABEINRUZ	urbanize
ABEINSST	bassinet
ABEINSTU	base unit
ABEINSTW	waste bin
ABEINTTU	intubate
ABEIORST	sabotier
ABEIORTT	Taborite
ABEIORTV	abortive
ABEIPQSU	squab pie
ABEIPRRS	spare rib
ABEIRRRS	barriers
ABEIRRVY	breviary
ABEIRSTY	bestiary
	sybarite✧
ABEIRTTY	ytterbia
ABEITTTU	titubate
ABEJKLOU	kabeljou
ABEJLMPU	jumpable
ABEJMOOR	jeroboam✧
ABEJMPSU	base jump
ABEJNORS	Sobranje
ABEJORUU	beau jour
ABEKLMOS	smokable
ABEKLNOW	knowable
ABEKLNRY	bankerly
ABEKLNRZ	Karl Benz
ABEKLOOR	book-lear
ABEKLORW	workable
ABEKLRSS	barkless
ABEKMOOT	book-mate
ABEKNNOT	banknote
ABEKNSSY	sneaksby
ABEKNSTW	West Bank
ABEKOORY	yearbook
ABEKORTU	break out
	breakout
	outbreak
ABEKORVW	break-vow
ABEKRSTY	basketry
ABELLLMU	labellum
ABELLLOR	rollable
ABELLLOT	tollable
ABELLLSY	syllable
ABELLMOR	ombrella
ABELLMRU	umbellar
	umbrella
ABELLMSS	mass-bell
ABELLNOS	bonsella
ABELLNOT	ballonet
ABELLNOW	own-label
ABELLNRU	Brunella
	rubellan
ABELLOOT	loo-table
ABELLOSV	solvable
ABELLOTU	lobulate
ABELLOTW	well boat
ABELLRVY	verbally
ABELLSUW	blue laws
ABELMNNO	nobleman
ABELMNOP	Belmopan
ABELMNOZ	emblazon
ABELMNST	semblant
ABELMNTU	Nembutal®
ABELMOOT	mootable
ABELMOVY	moveably
ABELMPTU	plumbate
ABELMRTY	Bartlemy
ABELMSSY	assembly✧
ABELNNOR	bannerol
ABELNNRU	lean-burn
	runnable

ABELNORT	noble art
ABELNORW	brown ale
ABELNORZ	blazoner
ABELNOST	neoblast
	notables
ABELNQTU	blanquet
ABELNRSY	Barnsley
ABELNRTY	Blantyre
ABELNRUY	urbanely
ABELNRYZ	brazenly
ABELNSTU	unstable
ABELNSTY	absently
ABELNSUU	unusable
ABELNUVY	navy blue
ABELOOST	boot sale
ABELOPRT	portable
ABELOPRU	pourable
ABELOPRV	provable
ABELOPRW	below par
ABELOPTT	table top
	top table
ABELOPTX	box-pleat
ABELOQTU	quotable
ABELORRU,	labourer
ABELORST	sortable
	storable
ABELORSV	absolver
ABELORTX	alert box
ABELORWX	ox-warble
ABELOSSU	sabulose
ABELOSTU	absolute✧
ABELOSTW	bestowal
ABELOSTZ	to blazes
ABELPRTU	pubertal
ABELQSUU	subequal
ABELRRTU	barrulet
ABELRSTU	baluster
ABELRTTU	burletta
	rebuttal
ABELSTUU	subulate
ABELTTUU	tubulate
ABEMMNOO	moonbeam
ABEMNNOR	mean-born
ABEMNOTU	umbonate
ABEMNPRU	penumbra
ABEMNSUY	sunbeamy
ABEMNTTU	abutment
ABEMORRS	embrasor
ABEMORSU	amberous
ABEMORTZ	barometz
ABEMRRUW	raw umber
ABENNOTU	nanotube
ABENNRUV	Van Buren
ABENOPRU	bear upon
ABENOPSU	subpoena
ABENOPTU	beat up on
ABENORSS	baroness
ABENORSY	Sobranye
ABENORTT	betatron
ABENORTV	bevatron
ABENORTW	banewort
ABENORTY	barytone
ABENOSSW	sawbones
ABENOSTY	bayonets
ABENRRTU	burnt-ear
ABENRRYZ	brazenry
ABENRSTU	unbraste
ABEOOSST	sea boots
ABEOPPRY	paperboy
ABEORRSS	braseros
ABEORRSU	à rebours
ABEORRTU	outer bar
ABEORSTU	saboteur
ABEORTTU	obturate
	tabouret
ABEORTUV	outbrave
ABEORTWX	water box
ABEOSSST	asbestos
ABEOSTTU	set about
ABEOSTUV	subovate
ABEPRSSY	passer-by
ABEPRSTT	best part
ABEQRSUU	arquebus
ABERRTYY	tayberry
ABERRWXY	waxberry
ABERSSTU	abstruse
ABERSTUW	water bus
ABERTTUY	butyrate
ABERTUXY	X-ray tube
ABESSTTU	substate
ABFFGIJY	Jiffy bag®
ABFFGILN	baffling
ABFFKLNO	blank off
ABFFLLPU	puffball
ABFFLOST	blast off
	blast-off
ABFFNOTU	bouffant
ABFFORSS	brass off
ABFGLLLO	golf ball
ABFGLLOO	goofball
ABFGNOTU	fungo bat
ABFGORUU	faubourg
ABFHIIST	baitfish
ABFHILLS	fishball
ABFHINNO	infobahn
ABFHIORS	boarfish
ABFHLOOT	half-boot
ABFHLSUX	flax-bush
ABFHLTTU	half-butt
ABFHOOTT	footbath
ABFIILLR	fibrilla
ABFIILMR	fimbrial
ABFILLLY	fallibly
ABFILNSU	basinful
ABFILRTT	T-bar lift
ABFILSTU	fabulist
ABFIMORS	fibromas
ABFIRTTU	fruit bat
ABFJORSU	frabjous
ABFKLLOR	korfball
ABFLLOOT	football
ABFLLORU	four-ball
ABFLLOST	softball
ABFLLSSU	fuss-ball
ABFLLUZZ	fuzz-ball
ABFLMRSY	lamb's fry
ABFLOSTU	boastful
ABFLOSUU	fabulous
ABFMOORT	from A to B
ABFNORTU	turbofan
ABFNORTW	brown fat
ABFORSTU	surf boat
ABGGGINR	bragging
ABGGIJNN	jingbang
ABGGILMN	gambling
ABGGILNR	garbling
ABGGNOOT	toboggan
ABGGRSUU	Augsburg
ABGHHIKN	bank-high
ABGHHILL	highball
ABGHHMRU	Hamburgh
ABGHILRT	Albright
ABGHINWZ	whizbang
ABGHIOPR	biograph
ABGHMORU	brougham
ABGHNRUV	Vanbrugh
ABGIILNS	saibling
ABGIILOT	obligati
ABGIIMST	bigamist
ABGIINNO	bignonia
ABGIINOR	aborigin
ABGIINSS	biassing
ABGIKLNN	blanking
ABGIKNOR	bank giro
ABGIKNRR	ring-bark
ABGILLLR	ball-girl
ABGILLMN	lambling
ABGILMNR	marbling
	rambling
ABGILMNW	wambling
ABGILNNT	bantling
ABGILNOT	bloating
	bog-Latin
	obligant
ABGILNRT	bratling
ABGILNRW	brawling
	warbling
ABGILNST	blasting
	stabling
ABGILNTT	blatting
ABGILNTY	tangibly
ABGILOOT	obligato
ABGILORW	brigalow
ABGIMORU	Maori bug
ABGIMOSU	bigamous
	subimago
ABGINNOR	aborning
ABGINNPU	nip a bung
ABGINNRX	banxring
ABGINOOT	tabooing
ABGINOST	boasting
	bostangi
ABGINSTW	batswing

ABGINTTU abutting
ABGIRRSS rib-grass
ABGLLLOY globally
ABGLLNOW ball-gown
ABGLLORU globular
ABGLLRUY bullyrag
ABGLMOPU plumbago✧
ABGLMOSU lumbagos
ABGLNOOT longboat
ABGLNORU rub along
ABGLNOUW bungalow
ABGLOOOO boogaloo
ABGLOOTY batology
ABGLORSU glabrous
ABGLRRUY burglary
ABGLRSUZ Salzburg
ABGMNOOR gambroon
ABGNNOTU baton gun
ABGNOOST boat-song
ABGNOOWX box-wagon
wagon box
ABGNORSU osnaburg
ABGNOSWY bowyangs
ABGOORST botargos
ABGORSSX grass box
ABGSTTUU bust a gut
ABHHOSTU hush-boat
Shabuoth
ABHHRSTU hatbrush
ABHIINRS brainish
ABHIIORZ rhizobia
ABHIKLOR kohlrabi
ABHILLPT pithball
ABHILNOT biathlon
ABHILOPS basophil
ABHILOTT hit a blot
ABHILRTW whirlbat
ABHILSST stablish
ABHIMMST bathmism
ABHINORT hot-brain
ABHIOSTU hautbois
ABHIOSTV Tisha Bov
ABHIRRSU airbrush
ABHIRSTT brattish
ABHISTTZ sitz-bath
ABHKLMOR Karl Böhm
ABHKLSUW bushwalk
ABHKNOST bank shot
ABHKOOOT boathook
book-oath
ABHKORSU kourbash
ABHLLMOT mothball
ABHLLNTU hunt ball
ABHLLOOY ballyhoo
ABHLLPSU push-ball
ABHLORTW whorlbat
ABHLOSST sash bolt
ABHLOSTT hot blast
ABHLOSWW washbowl
ABHLSSTU saltbush
ABHMNOTY bothyman
ABHMNSUU subhuman
ABHMOORT bathroom
ABHNORSS bass horn
ABHNORSY A S Hornby
ABHNORTX Bronx hat
ABHOORST tarboosh
ABHOOSST Basothos
ABHOOSTW Show Boat
showboat
ABHOPSTT stop bath
ABHORSTU tarboush
ABHRRSTU tar brush
ABHRSTTU Bathurst
ABIIIKRT Kiribati
ABIIILNT Libitina
ABIIINOT ab initio
ABIIINRY biriyani
ABIIKLSS basilisk
ABIILLMR millibar
ABIILLTY lability
ABIILMNO binomial
ABIILMNS albinism
ABIILMRS Blairism
ABIILNNP blini pan
ABIILNOT libation
ABIILNOV Bolivian
ABIILNRZ brazilin
ABIILNST sibilant
ABIILPTY pitiably
ABIILRTU air-built
ABIIMNOT ambition
ABIIRRTZ Biarritz
ABIIRSSV vibrissa
ABIJLMPU jump bail
ABIJLNTU jubilant
ABIJNOOT jobation
ABIJNOPT paint job
ABIJNOST banjoist
ABIKLMNS lambskin
ABIKLNRY byrlakin
ABIKMNNR brinkman
ABIKNORR ironbark
ABIKRSTZ britzska
ABILLLLM ball mill
ABILLLPY playbill
ABILLOTT toll bait
ABILLOVY violably
ABILLRTY tribally
ABILMNOU olibanum
ABILMOOT tail boom
ABILMOPS bioplasm
ABILMOTU bumaloti
ABILNOOT lobation
oblation
ABILNORU unilobar
ABILNOTU ablution
abutilon
ABILNRTU tribunal
turbinal
ABILNSTU Istanbul
stub-nail
ABILOPST bioplast
ABILORST strobila
ABILORTY libatory
ABILOSSV bass viol
ABILOTTT tilt-boat
ABILPSSY passibly
ABILRSSY brassily
ABILRSUV subviral
ABILRTUY ruby-tail
ABILSSUY issuably
ABILSTUY suitably
ABIMMNOO mainboom
ABIMNOOW obi-woman
ABIMNOSU bimanous
ABIMNPRS snap-brim
ABIMNRSU urbanism
ABIMNRTU tamburin
ABIMORSU biramous
ABIMRSST strabism
ABINNORW Brownian
ABINNRSU Burnsian
ABINOOQU a quoi bon?
ABINOORT abortion
ABINOPTU Pinatubo
ABINOPTX paintbox
ABINORTU tabourin
ABINORWY rainbowy
ABINOSTT botanist
ABINOTTX Tobin tax
ABINRSTU urbanist
ABINRTUY urbanity
ABINTTTU titubant
ABIOPRSU biparous
ABIOPSTU subtopia
ABIORRST arborist
rib-roast
ABIORRTV vibrator
ABIORSTV vibratos
ABIORTUY obituary
ABIPRSUU ubi supra
ABIPSSTT Baptists
ABIRRSTU airburst
ABIRSSUZ subsizar
ABJLLMPU jump ball
ABKKMOOR bookmark
ABKLLMSU musk-ball
ABKLLNOR bankroll
ABKLNOTU blank out
ABKLOOPY playbook
ABKLORWY workably
ABKMOOSS mass-book
ABKNOPST stopbank
ABKNPRTU bankrupt
ABKOOPSS passbook
ABKOORTW workboat
ABKOOSTT kottabos
ABLLLOOW wool ball
ABLLMNOO moon-ball
ABLLMOOR ballroom
ABLLMOPW blowlamp
ABLLNOSW snowball✧

ABLLOORT root ball
ABLLORST borstall
ABLLRTUY brutally
ABLLSSUY syllabus
ABLMMOOY may bloom
ABLMNRUU alburnum
laburnum
ABLMOSTY myoblast
ABLNORYZ blazonry
ABLNOSUZ subzonal
ABLNRSUU sublunar
ABLNSUUY unusably
ABLOORST bar stool
ABLOORTY oblatory
ABLOOSTT bootlast
ABLOOSTZ zooblast
ABLOPRSU subpolar
ABLOPRVY provably
ABLOPSUU pabulous
ABLOPSYY boy's play
ABLOQTUY quotably
ABLORSSU subsolar
ABLOSSUU sabulous
ABLOSTTU subtotal
ABLOSTTY stay bolt
ABLPRTUY abruptly
ABMMORTY tommy bar
ABMNTTUY buttyman
ABMOORTW warm boot
warm-boot
ABMOOTTT at bottom
ABNOORRT roborant
ABNORRTW brown rat
ABNORTUU runabout
ABNORXYY Baryonyx
ABNOSSSU bonassus
ABOORRSU arborous
ABOPRSST top brass
ABOPTTUU put about
ABRRSTUY star ruby
ACCCDEIO Coccidae
ACCCDIIO coccidia✧
ACCCENPY peccancy
ACCCFIIL calcific
ACCCHILO colchica
ACCCIILT calcitic
ACCCIIPR capricci
ACCCILLY cyclical
ACCCIOPU capuccio
ACCDDEEN cadenced
ACCDDEKO cockaded
ACCDDIIT didactic
ACCDEEEU deuce-ace
ACCDEEIN ice dance
ACCDEEPT accepted
ACCDEERU cardecue
ACCDEHIL chaliced
ACCDEILO dice-coal
ACCDEILU caudicle
ACCDEILY delicacy
ACCDEINT accident
ACCDEIRT accredit
ACCDEISU caudices
ACCDELLY calycled
ACCDELSU cul-de-sac
ACCDELSY Cyclades
ACCDEORR accorder
ACCDERSU accursed
ACCDESUU caduceus
ACCDGHOO coachdog
ACCDHIIR diarchic
ACCDHIIS Chasidic
ACCDHIMO dochmiac
ACCDHIOT cathodic
ACCDHLOR clochard
ACCDHPTU Dutch cap
ACCDIIRU uric acid
ACCDIIST dicastic
ACCDIITY dicacity
ACCDIKOR acid rock
ACCDILOY calycoid
ACCDILTY dactylic
ACCDINOR cancroid
draconic✧
ACCDIOOR coracoid
ACCDIORS sarcodic
ACCDIOST sticcado
ACCDITUY caducity
ACCDKLOP cold pack
ACCDLLOY clay-cold
ACCDOOST stoccado
ACCDOOXY cacodoxy
ACCDOSUU caducous
ACCEEHIT hiccatee
ACCEEHLO cochleae
ACCEEHRT ceterach
ACCEEHST seecatch
ACCEEIKR rice cake
ACCEEILR celeriac
ACCEEILS ecclesia
ACCEEIMR ice cream
ACCEEKLN necklace
ACCEELNR clarence✧
ACCEELOS coalesce
ACCEELRT calcrete
ACCEENNS nascence
ACCEENPR crepance
ACCEENST acescent
ACCEEORT croceate
ACCEEPRT accepter
ACCEFFIY efficacy
ACCEFILS fascicle
ACCEFIRT ice craft
ACCEFKSU suck face
ACCEGINO Cocaigne
ACCEGKMO gamecock
ACCEGKOS sage cock
ACCEGNOY co-agency
ACCEGPRU grace cup
ACCEHHIW Chichewa
ACCEHHKO chechako
ACCEHIJT hic jacet
ACCEHIKP chickpea
pea-chick
ACCEHILM alchemic
chemical
ACCEHILP cephalic
ACCEHILT hectical
ACCEHIMN mechanic
ACCEHIMS sachemic
ACCEHINO anechoic
ACCEHINR chicaner
ACCEHINT catechin
chance it
ACCEHITY ice yacht
ACCEHKRT the crack
ACCEHLOR cochlear
ACCEHLOT catechol
ACCEHMNO Comanche
ACCEHNNO chaconne
chance on
no chance
ACCEHNNY cynanche
ACCEHNOR charneco
encroach
ACCEHNOT conchate
ACCEHNRY chancery✧
ACCEHOPT cachepot
ACCEHRST cratches
ACCEIIST caecitis
ACCEIKRT ice track
ACCEILLN cancelli
ACCEILLR clerical
ACCEILLU caulicle
ACCEILLV clavicle
ACCEILNS scenical
ACCEILNT canticle✧
ACCEILNV clavecin
ACCEILNY calycine
ACCEILOS calicoes
ACCEILRV cervical
ACCEIMRS ceramics
ACCEINNR cancrine
ACCEINOT Coctaine
ACCEINRT Nearctic
ACCEINRY Cyrenaic
ACCEINTU cuneatic
ACCEIOPR cecropia
ACCEIOTV coactive
ACCEIPRS Caprices
ACCEIPRT practice
ACCEIPSV peccavis
ACCEIRRR ricercar
ACCEIRTU cruciate
ACCEISTT ecstatic
ACCEITTV civet cat
ACCEKKOR rock cake
ACCEKLNR cracknel
ACCEKNOR corn-cake
ACCEKNOY Cockayne
ACCEKOPY peacocky
ACCEKRRS crackers
ACCELLOR Roccella

ACCELLUY	calycule
ACCELMNY	cyclamen
ACCELNOV	conclave
ACCELNRU	caruncle
ACCELNTU	clean-cut
ACCELRSY	scarcely
ACCELRTU	clear-cut
ACCELSSU	saccules
ACCELWYY	cycleway
ACCENNSY	nascency
ACCENORR	cornacre
ACCENORT	accentor
ACCENOST	cosecant
ACCENOSU	concause
ACCEOPRT	acceptor
ACCEOPTU	occupate
ACCEORST	ectosarc
ACCEORTU	accouter
	accoutre
ACCEPRSW	cap screw
	screw cap
ACCESSTU	cactuses
ACCFFLTU	calc-tuff
ACCFFNPR	CFP franc
ACCFHKLO	half-cock
ACCFHLTY	catchfly
ACCFIILT	lactific
ACCFIKLL	calflick
ACCFLNOO	confocal
ACCFOORT	cofactor
ACCGHINO	coaching
ACCGHINT	catching
ACCGHIOR	choragic
ACCGIKMR	gimcrack
ACCGIKNR	cracking
ACCGINSU	accusing
ACCGLOOY	cacology
ACCHHIMT	catch him
ACCHHITT	chitchat
ACCHHMOS	camshoch
ACCHHMOU	muchacho
ACCHIIRT	rachitic
ACCHIIST	chiastic
ACCHILNO	chalonic
ACCHILNY	chancily
ACCHILOR	orichalc
ACCHILOT	catholic✧
ACCHINNO	cinchona
ACCHINOS	chicanos✧
ACCHINPU	capuchin✧
ACCHIORT	thoracic
	trochaic
ACCHIPTT	catch-pit
ACCHIRRT	carritch
ACCHKLOR	charlock
ACCHKMOR	arch-mock
ACCHKORT	hock-cart
ACCHLOOT	cacholot
ACCHLOPT	cloth cap
	cloth-cap
ACCHMORS	caschrom
ACCHMRTY	McCarthy
ACCHNNOT	Connacht
ACCHNNUY	unchancy
ACCHNOOR	coronach
ACCHNOTU	couchant
ACCHOPRS	cash crop
ACCHORTU	cartouch
ACCHOTTU	catch out
ACCHRSTY	scratchy
ACCIIIOT	oiticica
ACCIILLN	clinical
ACCIILMT	climatic
ACCIILRT	critical
ACCIIMNN	cinnamic
ACCIINNO	aniconic
ACCIINOT	aconitic
ACCIINPU	Puccinia
ACCIIPST	pasticci
ACCIIRTX	cicatrix
ACCIJKMR	jimcrack
ACCIKKNN	nick-nack
ACCIKKRR	rick-rack
ACCIKKTT	tick-tack
ACCIKLOT	cocktail
ACCIKNST	canstick
ACCIKOPR	apricock
ACCIKPRT	practick
ACCIKSTT	cat-stick
ACCILMOS	cosmical
ACCILMOX	cacomixl
ACCILNOT	ciclaton
ACCILNOV	volcanic
ACCILNUV	vulcanic✧
ACCILORR	Carl Cori
ACCILORT	cortical
ACCILPRY	caprylic
ACCILRRU	circular
ACCILSSS	classics
ACCIMMOS	Occamism
ACCIMNOS	moccasin
ACCIMNTU	canticum
ACCIMORR	microcar
ACCIMORU	coumaric
ACCIMOST	Occamist
ACCIMPSU	capsicum
ACCIMSTY	cymatics
ACCINOOS	occasion
ACCINOOT	coaction
ACCINORT	cratonic
	narcotic
ACCINORV	cavicorn
ACCINOST	canticos
	Scotican
ACCINOTY	canticoy
	cyanotic
ACCIOPST	spiccato
ACCIORST	acrostic
	Socratic
ACCIORSY	isocracy
ACCIOSTT	sticcato
ACCIOSTU	acoustic
ACCIOTTT	tic-tac-to
ACCIPRST	practics
ACCIRRTT	tric-trac
ACCIRSTY	scarcity
ACCKKRSU	rucksack
ACCKMMRU	crummack
ACCKNRSU	sun crack
ACCKOOOT	cockatoo
ACCKOPRT	crackpot
ACCKORST	stock car
ACCLLOOR	coll'arco
ACCLLOSU	occlusal
ACCLLSUU	calculus
ACCLMOOP	coco-palm
ACCLMOSU	Moluccas
ACCLNOOT	col canto
ACCLOPRU	cup coral
ACCLSSUU	sacculus
ACCMNOOR	Moroccan
ACCMOSTU	accustom
ACCNOOTU	cocoanut
ACCNOPRU	acorn-cup
ACCNOPRW	crown cap
ACCNOPTU	occupant
ACCNORTT	contract
ACCNOSTU	accounts
ACCOQSSU	squaccos
ACCORRTY	carrycot
ACCORSTU	scout car
ACDDDEIT	addicted
ACDDDEKU	dead duck
ACDDEEES	deceased
ACDDEEFR	red-faced
ACDDEEHT	detached
ACDDEEIT	dedicate
ACDDEEIU	deciduae
ACDDEELR	declared
ACDDEENR	credenda
ACDDEENT	decadent
ACDDEERR	red cedar
ACDDEERT	dead cert
ACDDEESU	Sadducee
ACDDEETU	educated
ACDDEFGO	dog-faced
ACDDEHKN	deck hand
ACDDEHLO	head cold
ACDDEIIL	deicidal
ACDDEIIM	medicaid✧
ACDDEILU	decidual
ACDDEINR	cider-and
	riddance
ACDDEINT	dedicant
ACDDEISU	deciduas
ACDDEKLO	deadlock
	dead-lock
	deck-load
ACDDEKOR	raddocke
ACDDENTU	adducent
ACDDFOOR	food-card
ACDDGILN	cladding
ACDDGLOR	gold card

ACDDHIIO	diadochi
ACDDHIMR	didrachm
ACDDHKOS	shaddock
ACDDIIOR	cardioid
ACDDILNY	candidly
ACDDILRW	wild card
ACDDILTY	didactyl
ACDDINNU	uncandid
ACDDINSY	discandy
ACDDIOOW	wood acid
ACDDIOPR	acid drop
ACDDKLNO	dockland
ACDDKORY	dockyard
ACDDORTU	adductor
ACDDOTTY	toddy cat
ACDEEEFT	defecate
ACDEEEKS	seedcake
ACDEEEMR	reed-mace
ACDEEENT	antecede
ACDEEERS	decrease
ACDEEESS	seedcase
ACDEEFFT	affected
ACDEEFIN	defiance
ACDEEFRS	frescade
ACDEEFRY	federacy
ACDEEGGN	egg dance
ACDEEGKM	deck game
ACDEEGLO	edge coal
ACDEEGLY	delegacy
ACDEEHKO	cokehead
ACDEEHMR	démarche
ACDEEHNR	enarched
ACDEEHNS	enchased
ACDEEIIP	epicedia
ACDEEILR	I declare!
ACDEEILT	delicate
ACDEEIMN	Medicean
ACDEEIMR	ceramide
	medicare✧
ACDEEIMT	decimate
	medicate
ACDEEINN	enneadic
ACDEEINR	déraciné
ACDEEINU	audience
ACDEEINV	deviance
	vice-dean
ACDEEIPR	Percidae
ACDEEIPS	dispeace
ACDEEIRT	tide race
ACDEEJKT	jacketed
ACDEEKNR	cankered
ACDEEKPT	tape deck
ACDEELNR	calender
	encradle
ACDEELNT	lanceted
ACDEELRR	declarer
ACDEELRT	decretal
ACDEELRV	calvered
ACDEELSS	déclassé
ACDEEMNO	codename
ACDEENNT	tendance
ACDEENNY	cayenned
ACDEENOT	anecdote
	toe dance
	toe-dance
ACDEENRS	ascender
	reascend
ACDEENRT	crenated
	decanter
	nectared
ACDEENRV	caverned
ACDEENRZ	credenza
ACDEENTT	dancette
	dancetté
ACDEENYY	eye candy
ACDEEOPS	peasecod
ACDEEORT	decorate
ACDEEOST	seed coat
ACDEEPRT	carpeted
ACDEERRT	terraced
ACDEESUX	caudexes
ACDEESUY	causeyed
ACDEFGIP	pig-faced
ACDEFGPU	pug-faced
ACDEFHLN	flanched
ACDEFIIL	deifical
ACDEFILL	ill-faced
ACDEFILN	canfield
ACDEFILR	card file
	fricadel
ACDEFNOW	face down
ACDEFOTW	two-faced
ACDEFRSU	surfaced
ACDEFRTU	furcated
ACDEGGRS	scragged
ACDEGHIL	Gadhelic
ACDEGHOP	dog-cheap
ACDEGIIL	algicide
ACDEGIKM	magicked
ACDEGIMR	decigram
ACDEGINU	guidance
ACDEGIRS	disgrace
ACDEGLLO	gold lace
ACDEGLOU	cloudage
ACDEGNRS	scrag-end
ACDEGNRU	ungraced
ACDEGORS	God's acre
ACDEGORY	Gray code
ACDEGOTT	cottaged
ACDEHHTT	thatched
ACDEHIIP	aphicide
ACDEHILL	Helladic
ACDEHILR	Heraclid
	heraldic
ACDEHILT	dithecal
ACDEHIMS	schiedam
ACDEHIOP	Phocidae
ACDEHIRS	rachides
ACDEHIRT	thridace
	tracheid
ACDEHKLO	headlock
ACDEHKNU	unhacked
ACDEHKOV	havocked
ACDEHKRU	archduke
ACDEHKSS	cash desk
ACDEHLNP	planched
ACDEHLNR	chandler✧
ACDEHLOR	hole card
	Rochdale
ACDEHNOR	rondache
ACDEHNSU	uncashed
ACDEHORR	hard core
	hard-core
ACDEHORT	chordate
ACDEHORW	cowheard
ACDEHORY	ad hocery
ACDEHOTT	cot death
ACDEHPRU	upcheard
ACDEHPST	despatch
ACDEHPTU	death cup
ACDEHPUW	chawed up
ACDEHRST	starched
ACDEIIMU	aecidium
ACDEIINR	acridine
ACDEIINS	sciaenid
ACDEIINT	actinide
	ctenidia
	diactine
	indicate
ACDEIINU	induciae
ACDEIITV	cavitied
	vaticide
ACDEIJNU	jaundice
ACDEIKMN	main-deck
ACDEIKNP	panicked
ACDEIKNT	anticked
ACDEILLM	medallic
ACDEILLN	declinal
ACDEILLR	caller ID
ACDEILLV	cavilled
ACDEILMN	medcinal
ACDEILMO	cameloid
	melodica
ACDEILMT	maledict
ACDEILNP	panicled
ACDEILNU	Claudine
	Dulcinea
ACDEILNV	vine-clad
ACDEILNY	lycaenid
ACDEILOR	Cordelia
ACDEILPS	displace
ACDEILPT	plicated
ACDEILPY	dice-play
ACDEILRT	articled
ACDEILRU	auricled
	radicule
ACDEIMNO	comedian
	daemonic
	demoniac
	mid-ocean
ACDEIMNP	pandemic
ACDEIMOR	Mordecai
ACDEIMRT	dermatic

	timecard
ACDEIMSU	Muscidae
ACDEINNR	crannied
ACDEINOP	canopied
ACDEINOS	diocesan
	oceanids✧
ACDEINOT	catenoid
	DA-Notice
ACDEINOV	voidance
ACDEINPT	pedantic
	pentadic
ACDEINRT	crinated
	dicentra
ACDEINSS	acidness
ACDEINST	distance
ACDEINTV	ci-devant
	Vedantic
ACDEINVY	deviancy
ACDEIOPS	diascope
	Psocidae
ACDEIORS	idocrase
ACDEIORT	ceratoid
ACDEIORV	Corvidae
ACDEIOSU	edacious
ACDEIOTT	Cottidae
ACDEIPSS	spadices
ACDEIPST	spicated
ACDEIQRU	acquired
ACDEIRSS	Cressida
ACDEIRTT	tetracid
	tetradic
ACDEISTT	acid test
ACDEKLMU	lame duck
ACDEKLTW	tack-weld
ACDEKNOT	tacked-on
ACDEKNPU	unpacked
ACDEKNRU	unracked
ACDEKOST	stockade
ACDEKPRS	spar deck
ACDELLNU	uncalled
ACDELLOR	carolled
	collared
ACDELLOS	so-called
ACDELMRU	ad clerum
ACDELMSU	muscadel
ACDELMUU	cum laude
ACDELNOO	canoodle
ACDELNOP	Copeland
ACDELNOR	colander
ACDELNPU	unplaced
ACDELNRY	calendry
	dry-clean
ACDELNSU	unscaled
ACDELOPT	clodpate
ACDELOPU	cupolaed
ACDELORR	red coral
ACDELORV	overclad
ACDELOTU	oculated
ACDELOUZ	Lucozade®
ACDELOVW	cold wave
ACDELRSY	sacredly
ACDELSTU	sulcated
ACDEMMRS	scrammed
ACDEMOPR	compadre
ACDEMORT	democrat✧
ACDEMSTU	Muscadet
ACDENNOR	ordnance
ACDENNOT	cantoned
ACDENNST	scandent
ACDENNSU	sun dance
ACDENOPR	endocarp
ACDENORS	endosarc
ACDENORY	deaconry
ACDENOSU	au second
ACDENOSY	cyanosed
ACDENOTU	outdance
	uncoated
ACDENPPU	uncapped
ACDENPST	Pandects
ACDENRTU	cedar-nut
	underact
	untraced
ACDENRVY	verdancy
ACDENSUU	uncaused
ACDENTTY	dancetty
ACDEOOPP	Copepoda
ACDEOORS	doorcase
ACDEOPRU	croupade
ACDEOPRY	copyread
ACDEOPTT	capotted
ACDEORRT	redactor
ACDEORSS	Sarcodes
ACDEORTU	educator
ACDEORTV	card-vote
ACDEOSTT	costated
ACDEPPRS	scrapped
ACDEPTTU	duct tape
ACDEQTUU	aqueduct
ACDERRSU	crusader
	sure card
ACDERRTU	traducer
ACDERSSU	Crusades
ACDERSTT	test card
ACDERTTU	tear duct
ACDERTUV	curvated
ACDFFHNU	handcuff
ACDFFIRT	diffract
ACDFFLOS	scaffold
ACDFGOOT	act of God
ACDFIILU	fiducial
ACDFILOU	fucoidal
ACDFLRTU	turf-clad
ACDFNORR	Cranford
ACDGHOTW	dogwatch
	watchdog
ACDGIILO	dialogic
ACDGILNR	cradling
ACDGILNS	scalding
ACDGIMOT	dogmatic
ACDGIOPR	podagric
ACDGKLOO	good-lack
ACDGLLTU	gall duct
ACDGLNOO	Golconda
ACDGNRRU	grand cru
ACDGNRTU	dung-cart
ACDHHNTU	unhatch'd
ACDHIINT	tachinid
ACDHIIOT	thio-acid
ACDHIISS	Hassidic
ACDHIKNP	hand-pick
ACDHIKOR	chokidar
ACDHILMN	man-child
ACDHILPR	pilchard
ACDHILPS	clapdish
ACDHINOR	hadronic
	rhodanic
ACDHINRY	dinarchy
ACDHINSW	sandwich✧
ACDHIOPS	scaphoid
ACDHIORY	hyracoid
ACDHIPST	dispatch
ACDHIRRS	Richards
ACDHKKUW	duck-hawk
ACDHKLRU	hard luck
ACDHKORR	hard rock
ACDHKOSY	Hock-days
ACDHLLOP	clap hold
ACDHLNOR	chaldron
	chlordan
	chondral
ACDHLOPT	pad-cloth
ACDHMNTU	Dutchman
ACDHMORU	mouchard
ACDHNORW	chawdron
ACDHNOSW	cash down
ACDHOOQU	quoad hoc
ACDHOOTW	woodchat
ACDHOPRY	hard copy
	hard-copy
ACDHOPTU	touch pad
ACDHORSS	sash cord
ACDHORSW	show card
ACDHORSY	dyschroa
ACDHRTUW	Dutch War
ACDIIILN	indicial
ACDIIIPR	diapiric
ACDIIJLU	judicial
ACDIILMS	disclaim
ACDIILNO	conidial
ACDIILNS	scaldini
ACDIILSU	suicidal
ACDIILTY	calidity
	dialytic
ACDIILVY	civil day
ACDIIMNO	daimonic
	Dominica
ACDIIMOR	dioramic
ACDIIMOT	diatomic
	midi-coat
ACDIIMSU	ascidium
ACDIINNT	indicant
ACDIINOP	pinacoid
ACDIINOT	actinoid

	diatonic
ACDIINPR	Pindaric
ACDIIOPR	DiCaprio
ACDIIOSS	acidosis
ACDIIRST	carditis
ACDIIRTY	acridity
ACDIISST	sadistic
ACDIKKPS	disk pack
ACDIKLTU	duck-tail
ACDIKMOO	cookmaid
ACDIKRRY	rickyard
ACDILLOU	caudillo
	lodicula
ACDILLPY	placidly
ACDILMOR	dromical
ACDILMTU	Talmudic
ACDILNOO	conoidal
ACDILNOR	iron-clad
ACDILNOS	scaldino
ACDILNSY	syndical
ACDILNUU	nudicaul
ACDILOPY	polyacid
ACDILOUV	oviducal
ACDILPSU	cuspidal
ACDILSTY	Dactylis
ACDILSUU	Claudius
ACDIMNOO	codomain
	monoacid
ACDIMNSU	muscadin
	scandium
ACDIMNSY	dynamics
ACDIMOSY	docimasy
ACDINOPS	spondaic
ACDINORS	sardonic
ACDINORT	tornadic
ACDINORW	cordwain
ACDINSTY	dynastic
ACDINTUY	aduncity
ACDIOPRS	sporadic
ACDIORTT	dictator
ACDIOSTX	doxastic
ACDIOSTY	dystocia
ACDIPRST	adscript
ACDIPSSU	Dipsacus
ACDIRSTT	distract
ACDKLMUY	Lady Muck
ACDKMMOR	drammock
ACDKORRT	track rod
ACDKSSSU	duck's ass
ACDLLNOW	call down
ACDLLOSW	cold slaw
ACDLMNOW	calm down
ACDLNNOR	cornland
ACDLNOPR	cropland
ACDLNOPS	cold snap
ACDLNORU	cauldron
ACDLNORY	condylar
ACDLNOST	Scotland
ACDLOOOR	Colorado
ACDLOOOW	wood coal
ACDLOORT	doctoral
ACDLOORW	wool card
ACDLORUW	war cloud
ACDLORWY	cowardly
ACDLOSTU	coal dust
ACDMMNOO	commando
ACDMNORY	dormancy
	mordancy
ACDMOOPR	macropod
ACDNOORR	roncador
ACDNOORV	cordovan
ACDNOOTU	ducatoon
ACDNORRW	wardcorn
ACDNOSTW	cast down
	downcast
ACDNOSUU	aduncous
ACDOOOPT	Octopoda
ACDOOPPR	podocarp
ACDOOPSU	docusoap
ACDOOPTY	octapody
ACDOORST	ostracod
	scordato
ACDOPRST	postcard
ACDORRWY	cowardry
ACDORSSU	crusados
ACDORSUZ	cruzados
ACDORTUY	court-day
ACDOSTTU	dustcoat
ACDRSTTU	dustcart
ACDRSTUW	draw cuts
ACEEEFRR	carefree
ACEEEGLN	elegance
ACEEEGRS	cargeese
ACEEEIPR	earpiece
ACEEEIPS	sea piece
ACEEEKNT	neckatee
ACEEEKPP	keep pace
ACEEEKPV	keep cave
ACEEELMR	cameleer
ACEEENRS	encrease
ACEEENSV	evanesce
ACEEERRT	recreate
ACEEERTT	et cetera
	etcetera
ACEEERTX	execrate
ACEEFFIN	caffeine
ACEEFFLT	left face!
ACEEFFRT	affecter
ACEEFHWY	whey-face
ACEEFILM	malefice
ACEEFIMT	face time
ACEEFIOP	of a piece
ACEEFKOR	ecofreak
ACEEFLOS	lose face
ACEEFLPU	peaceful
ACEEFLRT	tree calf
ACEEFLSS	faceless
ACEEFPRT	perfecta
	praefect
ACEEFPTY	typeface
ACEEFRSU	farceuse
ACEEGHNR	encharge
	Grenache
ACEEGHNX	exchange
ACEEGHRR	recharge
ACEEGILS	elegiacs
ACEEGIMY	magic eye
ACEEGINS	Genesiac
ACEEGIRS	Graecise
ACEEGIRZ	Graecize
ACEEGKNR	neckgear
ACEEGKRW	wreckage
ACEEGLNY	elegancy
ACEEGLPU	pucelage
ACEEGNOZ	cozenage
ACEEGNRY	reagency
ACEEGNSV	scavenge
ACEEGORR	racegoer
ACEEGORV	coverage
ACEEHHRU	heuchera
ACEEHHST	the chase
ACEEHIMN	Manichee
ACEEHINT	echinate
ACEEHIPT	petechia
ACEEHIRV	achiever
	chivaree
ACEEHITV	atchieve
ACEEHKLO	cake hole
ACEEHKNS	skeechan
ACEEHKTT	hackette
ACEEHLLL	HeLa cell
ACEEHLLN	Chellean
ACEEHLMP	empleach
ACEEHLMW	cam-wheel
ACEEHLNR	Charlene
ACEEHLOS	shoelace
ACEEHLRS	Heracles
ACEEHLSW	eschewal
ACEEHLTV	chevalet
ACEEHMNP	camphene
ACEEHMNR	menarche
ACEEHMRS	cashmere
	marchese
	search me
ACEEHNNR	enhancer
ACEEHNRV	revanche
ACEEHOOT	oothecae
ACEEHOPT	tape echo
ACEEHORT	ochreate
ACEEHPRR	preacher✧
ACEEHPRS	sea perch
ACEEHPRT	ethercap
ACEEHRRR	rere-arch
ACEEHRRS	research
	re-search
	searcher
ACEEHRRT	treacher
ACEEHRST	cheaters
ACEEHRTT	catheter
ACEEHRTY	cheatery
ACEEHSST	sea chest
ACEEHSTT	tea chest
ACEEHSTU	the sauce

ACEEHSTX cathexes
ACEEIKNP peacenik
ACEEIKRR creakier
ACEEIKST ice skate
ice-skate
ACEEILMN cameline
ACEEILMT emetical
ACEEILNP capeline
ACEEILNR cinereal
reliance
ACEEILNS salience
ACEEILPS especial
ACEEILRS escalier
ACEEILRV receival
ACEEIMOT acoemeti
ACEEIMRR creamier
rearmice
ACEEIMRS casimere
racemise
ACEEIMRT cemitare
ACEEIMRZ racemize
ACEEINNR narceine
ACEEINPS sapience
ACEEINPT patience
ACEEINRS increase
resiance
ACEEINRT centiare
creatine
increate
iterance
ACEEINSS Essencia
ACEEINST cineaste
cinéaste
ACEEINTV enactive
ACEEINTX exitance
ACEEIPPS pipe-case
ACEEIPST speciate
ACEEIPSY say-piece
ACEEIRSU causerie
ACEEIRSW wiseacre
ACEEIRTV creative
reactive
ACEEIRTW ice water
water ice
ACEEISTV vesicate
ACEEJKRT jack-tree
ACEEKLMP keep calm
ACEEKLMR mackerel
ACEEKLRW eelwrack
ACEEKMPT empacket
ACEEKNRW neckwear
ACEEKRRT racketer
ACEEKRST sack tree
ACEELLNT lancelet
ACEELLOS Elo scale
ACEELLOT ocellate
ACEELLOV Lovelace
ACEELLPT capellet
ACEELLRR cellarer
ACEELLRT cellaret
ACEELMNO cameleon
ACEELMNP placemen
ACEELMRS sclerema
ACEELNPT pentacle
ACEELNRR larcener
ACEELNRS cleanser
ACEELNRU cerulean
Laurence
ACEELNRW Lawrence
ACEELNSU nuclease
ACEELNTT tentacle
ACEELNTU nucleate
ACEELOPS escalope
ACEELORS escarole
ACEELORT relocate
ACEELOSV vocalese
ACEELPRR replacer
ACEELPRV Perceval
ACEELPSY clap eyes
cypselae
ACEELPTU peculate
ACEELPTY clypeate
ACEELRSS careless
ACEELRST scelerat
ACEELRSV cleavers
ACEELRTT raclette
ACEELRTU ulcerate
ACEELRTV cervelat
ACEELRTX excretal
ACEELSTT telecast
ACEEMNNS sceneman
ACEEMNOT meconate
ACEEMNST casement
ACEEMOPR camporee
ACEEMOPT copemate
ACEEMORS racemose
ACEEMRRS screamer
ACEEMRRY creamery
ACEENNPZ Penzance
ACEENNRT entrance
ACEENORT carotene
one-acter
ACEENOST notecase
ACEENPPR crêpe pan
ACEENPRR parcener
ACEENPRT perceant
ACEENPST Netscape®
ACEENRRS Sancerre
ACEENRRT recanter
recreant
Terrance
ACEENRST reascent
sarcenet
ACEENRTT entr'acte
ACEENRTU enacture
uncreate
ACEEORST creasote
ACEEOSTT ecostate
ACEEPRSU crease up
ACEEPRTT ettercap
ACEEPRTU peracute
ACEEPRTX excerpta
ACEEPSTT spectate
ACEEPSTY type case
ACEERRST terraces
ACEERRSU écraseur
ACEERRTU creature
ACEERRUV verrucae
ACEERSST cateress
cerastes
ACEERSSU surcease
ACEERSSV crevasse
ACEERTTU eructate
ACEESSTT cassette
test case
ACEFFHRU chauffer
ACEFFHRY chaffery
ACEFFILS sea cliff
ACEFFILT facelift
ACEFFIMS caffeism
ACEFFLLU full-face
ACEFFLOR clear off
ACEFFMOR cream off
ACEFGLNO long face
ACEFGLRU graceful
ACEFHIKS fish cake
ACEFHIRT car-thief
ACEFHISV cavefish
ACEFHNTY the fancy
ACEFHORU farouche
ACEFIIPR pacifier
ACEFIIRT artifice
ACEFILLY facilely
ACEFILMT calf-time
ACEFILOP epifocal
ACEFILOS fasciole
focalise
ACEFILOZ focalize
ACEFILRY fire clay
ACEFIMPR campfire
ACEFINNR Francine
ACEFINNS finances
ACEFINOR café noir
ACEFINRX carnifex
ACEFIORR air force✧
air-force
ACEFIOSS fiascoes
ACEFIRRT craftier
ACEFIRTT trifecta
ACEFIRTY feracity
ACEFKLRY cly-faker
ACEFLLOT alto clef
ACEFLLOV calf-love
ACEFLLRU leaf curl
ACEFLLSS calfless
ACEFLMNO flamenco
ACEFLNOR falconer
ACEFLNOT conflate
falconet
ACEFLNRY cranefly
ACEFLORS alfresco
ACEFLRTU crateful
fulcrate

ACEFMNOO moonface
ACEFMNOR Francome
ACEFNORV conferva
ACEFNPRT pencraft
ACEFOOPT footpace
ACEFOORT acre-foot
foot-race
ACEFOPST postface
ACEFORST forecast
ACEFRRRY car ferry
ACEFRRSU surfacer
ACEFRRTU fracture
ACEGGHPS pasch-egg
ACEGGILN cageling
glacéing
ACEGGIOP epagogic
ACEGGIRR craggier
ACEGHILN leaching
ACEGHILT lichgate
ACEGHINR in charge
reaching
ACEGHINT cheating
teaching
ACEGHJNO John Cage
ACEGHLRS schläger
ACEGHLRU rugelach
ACEGHLTY lychgate
ACEGHLUY Caughley
ACEGHMMU chummage
ACEGHMNO manchego
ACEGHMOR echogram
gramoche
ACEGHNPU change up
change-up
ACEGHNRU uncharge
ACEGHOPT chota peg
ACEGHRSU Gaucher's
ACEGIIMP epigamic
ACEGIINV vicinage
ACEGIIRS Gaiseric
ACEGILLO collegia
ACEGILLR allergic
ACEGILMU mucilage
ACEGILNN cleaning
ACEGILNR clearing
ACEGILNV cleaving
ACEGILNW lacewing
ACEGILPS Pelasgic
ACEGILRV claviger
ACEGILRY glyceria
ACEGILSS glacises
ACEGILST gelastic
ACEGIMMP gimme cap
ACEGIMMT tagmemic
ACEGIMNN menacing
ACEGIMNR Germanic
ACEGIMNT magnetic
ACEGIMOX exogamic
ACEGIMRR grimacer
ACEGIMRS Graecism
ACEGIMTY megacity
ACEGINNO canoeing
ACEGINNT enacting
ACEGINRT catering
citrange
ACEGINRU Guernica
ACEGINSS caginess
ACEGINSW wing case
ACEGINTX exacting
ACEGIOTT cogitate
ACEGIPRS spageric
ACEGIPRT price tag
ACEGIRST agrestic
ACEGIRTT tiger cat
ACEGJMRU cream jug
ACEGKLOT lock gate
ACEGKLOV gavelock
ACEGKORW cagework
ACEGKRTU truckage
ACEGLLNO collagen
ACEGLLSY scaly-leg
ACEGLNOO log-canoe
ACEGLOPS go places
ACEGMMPU gemma-cup
ACEGMNOY geomancy
ACEGMOPS compages
ACEGMORS scarmoge
ACEGMRRY gramercy
ACEGNNOR en garçon
ACEGNNOY cyanogen
ACEGNNTY tangency
ACEGNSSY cagyness
ACEGOOPS goose-cap
ACEGOORS cargoose
ACEGOPRY geocarpy
ACEGORST escargot
ACEGORTT cottager
ACEGORTY category
grey-coat
ACEGOTTY cottagey
ACEHHIPS cheapish
ACEHHIRR hierarch
ACEHHIRT the chair
ACEHHIST shechita
ACEHHKLT the Chalk
ACEHHLST The Clash
ACEHHLSU shauchle
ACEHHMNN henchman
ACEHHNRT ethnarch
ACEHHNSV Cheshvan
ACEHHPRT heptarch
ACEHHRTT thatcher✧
ACEHHRTY hatchery
thearchy
ACEHHTTY hatchety
ACEHIIMS ischemia
ACEHIINR Reichian
ACEHIIRT hieratic
ACEHIJKR hijacker
ACEHIJNT Jacinthe
ACEHIJPT Japhetic
ACEHIKLP kephalic
ACEHIKLW lichwake
ACEHIKRT thick ear
ACEHILLS Achilles
ACEHILLT hellicat
ACEHILMN inchmeal
ACEHILMO cholemia
ACEHILMP impleach
ACEHILMS camelish
ACEHILNP cephalin
ACEHILNT chainlet
chatline
chat-line
ethnical
ACEHILOR halicore
heroical
ACEHILPR parhelic
ACEHILSS Lachesis
ACEHILTT athletic
thetical
ACEHIMNN Eichmann
ACEHIMNP camphine
ACEHIMNT anthemic
ACEHIMNU achenium
ACEHIMPR camphire
ACEHIMPT empathic
emphatic
ACEHIMRS marchesi
ACEHIMRT rhematic
ACEHIMSS chamises
ACEHIMST misteach
tachisme
ACEHIMTT thematic
ACEHINNT in the can
ACEHINOT inchoate
ACEHINPT inch-tape
ACEHINRU echiuran
ACEHINRV vacherin
ACEHINSS Anchises
ACEHINST asthenic
ACEHINSY synechia
ACEHIOPS po'chaise
ACEHIOST toiseach
ACEHIPPW Chippewa
ACEHIPRS aspheric
parchesi
seraphic
ACEHIPRT chapiter
phreatic
pie chart
ACEHIPRW pew-chair
ACEHIPST pastiche
ACEHIPTT pathetic
ACEHIPTW whitecap
ACEHIRRS Chris Rea
ACEHIRSS rachises
ACEHIRST Charites
ACEHIRSU eucharis
ACEHIRSV archives
ACEHIRSW archwise
ACEHIRTT theatric
ACEHISST chastise

ACEHISTT tachiste
ACEHISTX cathexis
ACEHKLOV havelock
ACEHKLPR kreplach
ACEHKLSS shackles
ACEHKLTY latchkey
ACEHKMPU muckheap
ACEHKMRT techMARK®
ACEHKOTU tuckahoe
ACEHKRSW skew arch
ACEHKRTW thwacker
what reck?
ACEHKTWY watch key
ACEHLLLS shell-lac
ACEHLLMO mallecho
ACEHLLOO coal hole
ACEHLLOR orchella
ACEHLLPP Chappell
ACEHLLSU halluces
ACEHLMOT chamelot
ACEHLMPR carl-hemp
ACEHLNNS channels
ACEHLNOR Loch Earn
ACEHLNOU eulachon
ACEHLNOY Halcyone
ACEHLNPT planchet
ACEHLNRU launcher
relaunch
ACEHLNST stanchel
ACEHLORT chelator
chlorate
trochlea
ACEHLORU leachour
ACEHLOST eschalot
ACEHLOTT tea cloth
ACEHLOWW cow whale
ACEHLPRT chaptrel
ACEHLPRY chapelry
ACEHLPSS chapless
ACEHLRTU archlute
trauchle
ACEHLSSS cashless
ACEHLSTY chastely
ACEHMNRT merchant
ACEHMNSS chessman
ACEHMORT chromate
ACEHMPRS champers
ACEHMSTU mustache
ACEHNNOP pancheon
ACEHNNOT nanotech
ACEHNNPT penchant
ACEHNOPR canephor
Cape Horn
car phone
chaperon
ACEHNOPT cenotaph✧
ACEHNORR ranchero
ACEHNORT anchoret
ACEHNOSY honey-sac
ACEHNPRT pentarch
ACEHNPRU unpreach
ACEHNQUU Quechuan
ACEHNRSS archness
ACEHNRST snatcher
stancher
ACEHNRTT tranchet
ACEHNRTU chaunter
ACEHNSTU unchaste
ACEHNSTZ schantze
ACEHOPRR reproach
ACEHOPRT arch-poet
ACEHORRS horsecar
ACEHORRV overarch
ACEHORST charoset
thoraces
ACEHORTT theocrat
ACEHORTU outreach
ACEHOSST case-shot
ACEHOSSW showcase
ACEHOSTU cathouse
soutache
ACEHOTWW cow-wheat
ACEHPPRU preach up
ACEHPPSS chappess
ACEHPRRT Petrarch
ACEHPRSU purchase
ACEHPRTY patchery
petchary
ACEHRRST Chartres
starcher
ACEHRRTT tetrarch
ACEHRSSU chasseur
ACEHRSTW war chest
ACEHRSTY Strachey
ACEHRTTY chattery
trachyte
ACEHSSSU chausses
ACEHSTTU cathetus
ACEHTTUZ zuchetta
ACEIIKNT akinetic
ACEIILMN limacine
ACEIILNR irenical
ACEIILNS salicine
Sicelian
ACEIILNT Catiline
ACEIILST silicate
ACEIIMRV viraemic
ACEIIMSS aseismic
ACEIIMTU maieutic
ACEIINPS piscinae
ACEIINPT in capite
ACEIINRT anti-icer
ACEIINST canities
ACEIINTV inactive
ACEIINTZ anticize
ACEIIRRT criteria
ACEIISTT Atticise
ACEIITTZ Atticize
ACEIJKNP jack pine
ACEIJMST majestic
ACEIJNRR jerrican
ACEIKKLS sacklike
ACEIKLMR Milk Race
ACEIKLPS Special K
ACEIKLRY creakily
ACEIKMNN nickname
ACEIKMRV maverick✧
ACEIKNPS capeskin
ACEIKNRR crankier
ACEIKNRS skincare
ACEIKNRW wine rack
ACEIKNSW wine cask
ACEIKORR croakier
ACEIKOTW Katowice
ACEIKPPR pipe rack
ACEIKRRV vraicker
ACEIKSST sea stick
ACEIKSTT tackiest
ACEILLLT clitella
ACEILLMN cane-mill
ACEILLMR micellar
millrace
ACEILLMT calltime
metallic
ACEILLMY mycelial
ACEILLNT cliental
ACEILLOP calliope✧
ACEILLOR rocaille
ACEILLOS localise
ACEILLOT teocalli
ACEILLOZ localize
ACEILLPR calliper
ACEILLPS allspice
ACEILLPY epically
ACEILLRS Carlisle
ACEILLRV caviller
ACEILMMO camomile
ACEILMNN clinamen
ACEILMNO coalmine
ACEILMNP manciple
ACEILMNS mescalin
ACEILMOS camisole
ACEILMPS misplace
ACEILMPT pelmatic
ACEILMRS miracles
ACEILMRT metrical
ACEILMRY creamily
ACEILMST clematis
ACEILMSU musicale
ACEILMTU amuletic
ACEILNNP pannicle
pinnacle
ACEILNNR encrinal
ACEILNOR acrolein
Caroline
Cornelia
creolian
lonicera
ACEILNOT lace into
ACEILNPT ice plant
ice-plant
pectinal
planetic

ACEILNRT	clarinet
ACEILNSS	laciness
ACEILNSU	aesculin
ACEILNSY	saliency
ACEILOPP	Coppélia
ACEILOPR	capriole
ACEILOPT	poetical
ACEILORR	carriole
ACEILORT	erotical
	loricate
ACEILORV	arvicole
ACEILOST	societal
ACEILOSU	eusocial
ACEILOSV	vocalise
ACEILOTV	locative
ACEILOVZ	vocalize
ACEILPPY	clay pipe
	pipeclay
ACEILPRS	calipers
	spiracle
ACEILPRT	particle
	prelatic
ACEILPRU	peculiar✧
ACEILPRV	Percival
ACEILPSS	slipcase
ACEILPST	tie clasp
ACEILPTY	etypical
ACEILPXY	epicalyx
ACEILRRW	crawlier
ACEILRST	altrices
	articles
	selictar
ACEILRSV	visceral
ACEILRTT	tractile
ACEILRTU	Lucretia
	reticula
ACEILRTV	vertical
ACEILRTY	literacy
ACEILSST	Alcestis
ACEILSUV	vesicula
ACEILTVY	actively
ACEIMMNP	pemmican
ACEIMMOS	semicoma
ACEIMMRS	racemism
ACEIMNOO	Monoecia
ACEIMNOR	coramine
ACEIMNRU	manicure
ACEIMNST	semantic
ACEIMNSU	semuncia
ACEIMNSY	sycamine
ACEIMOPT	poematic
ACEIMOTX	toxaemic
ACEIMOTZ	metazoic
ACEIMPRR	mericarp
ACEIMPSS	escapism
ACEIMPST	campsite
ACEIMPTU	pumicate
ACEIMRRW	war crime
ACEIMRST	ceramist
	matrices
ACEIMRTT	trematic
ACEIMRTU	muricate
ACEIMSST	ascetism
	casteism
ACEINNOS	canonise
ACEINNOT	enaction
ACEINNOZ	canonize
ACEINNST	ancients
	insectan
	instance
ACEINNSU	nuisance
ACEINNTU	uncinate
ACEINOPR	apocrine
	caponier
	ice apron
	procaine
ACEINOPS	caponise
ACEINOPZ	caponize
ACEINORS	scenario
ACEINORT	actioner
	anoretic
	creation✧
	reaction
ACEINORV	Corvinae
	veronica✧
ACEINORX	anorexic
ACEINOST	canoeist
ACEINOTT	taconite
ACEINOTV	conative
ACEINOTX	exaction
ACEINPTT	pittance
ACEINPUY	picayune
ACEINRRU	curarine
ACEINRRY	cinerary
ACEINRSS	raciness
ACEINRST	canister
	cisterna
ACEINRTT	interact
ACEINRTU	Teucrian
ACEINRTV	navicert
ACEINRTX	xerantic
ACEINRVY	vicenary
ACEINSST	scanties
ACEINSSU	issuance
ACEINSTU	Anicetus
ACEINSTV	cistvaen
	vesicant
ACEINTTU	tunicate
ACEINTTX	excitant
ACEINTTY	tenacity
ACEINTUV	unactive
ACEIOPRT	operatic
ACEIORRT	race riot
ACEIORRV	air-cover
ACEIORSV	varicose
ACEIOSSU	caesious
ACEIOSTT	oscitate
ACEIOTTX	ex tacito
ACEIOTVV	vocative
ACEIOVVV	viva voce
ACEIPPRR	pericarp
ACEIPRRS	perisarc
ACEIPRRW	price war
ACEIPRST	crispate
	practise
ACEIPRTV	practive
ACEIPRTY	apyretic
ACEIPSST	escapist
ACEIPSSU	auspices
ACEIRRSU	curarise
ACEIRRSW	airscrew
ACEIRRTT	retraict
ACEIRRTX	creatrix
ACEIRRTY	retiracy
ACEIRRUZ	curarize
ACEIRSST	Castries
ACEIRSSV	vicaress
ACEIRSTT	cristate
ACEIRSTU	actus rei
	suricate
ACEIRSTZ	craziest
ACEIRTTU	urticate
ACEIRTTV	tractive
ACEIRTUV	curative
ACEIRTVY	veracity
ACEISSST	ecstasis
ACEISSSU	saucisse
ACEISSTU	sauciest
	suitcase
ACEISTTU	eustatic
ACEISTTW	scawtite
ACEJKOOR	jackeroo
ACEJLORY	cajolery
ACEJMRST	scramjet
ACEJNNOO	joncanoe
ACEJNRRY	jerrycan
ACEKKMRU	muck-rake
ACEKKNRS	knackers
ACEKKNRY	knackery
ACEKLLOV	lack-love
ACEKLLOY	Yale lock
ACEKLLRY	lay clerk
ACEKLMOO	Lake Como
ACEKLMPU	packmule
	plum-cake
ACEKLNTU	untackle
ACEKLORV	laverock
ACEKLPRS	sprackle
ACEKLSSS	sackless
ACEKNNOW	acknowne
ACEKNNSW	swan neck
ACEKNORT	one-track
ACEKNPRU	unpacker
ACEKNPSU	sneak-cup
ACEKNRRT	rack-rent
ACEKOORW	cookware
ACEKOPRW	capework
ACEKOPRY	Cape York
ACEKORRV	overrack
ACEKORSW	casework
ACEKORTU	rout-cake
ACEKPSSY	skyscape
ACEKQRUY	quackery

ACEKRRTY	racketry
ACEKRSTU	ruckseat
ACEKSSUW	waesucks
ACELLLLW	cell wall
ACELLLRU	cellular
ACELLMST	mast cell
ACELLMSU	sacellum
ACELLNOT	call-note
	Lancelot
ACELLNRU	nucellar
ACELLOPS	collapse
	escallop
ACELLORR	caroller
ACELLORV	call over
	coverall
	overcall
ACELLOSW	coleslaw
ACELLOTU	loculate
ACELLOVY	coevally
ACELLPRU	Lupercal
ACELLRTY	rectally
ACELLSSW	clawless
ACELLSTU	scutella
ACELLTWY	cetywall
ACELMMOU	mameluco
ACELMNOR	amelcorn
	Calormen
	cornmeal
ACELMNRU	crumenal
ACELMNSS	calmness
ACELMNSU	Uncle Sam
ACELMOPT	compleat
ACELMORS	scleroma
ACELMORY	claymore
ACELMOST	molecast
ACELMOSU	maculose
ACELMPSY	eclampsy
ACELMSTU	muscatel
ACELMSUU	saeculum
ACELMTUU	cumulate
ACELNNRS	scrannel
ACELNORV	novercal
ACELNOSU	lacunose
ACELNOSZ	calzones
ACELNOTT	Toltecan
ACELNOTU	clean out
	clean-out
ACELNOTV	covalent
ACELNOVY	conveyal
ACELNRVY	cravenly
ACELNSSU	scalenus
ACELNSTY	secantly
ACELOPPU	populace
ACELOPRS	parclose
ACELOPRT	pectoral
ACELOPRU	opercula
ACELOPTU	copulate
	outplace
ACELOPTY	calotype
ACELORRT	rectoral
ACELORSS	lacrosse
ACELORST	sectoral
ACELORSU	carousel✧
ACELORSY	coarsely
ACELORTU	clear out
	clear-out
ACELOSST	coatless
ACELOSTT	salt-cote
ACELOSTU	lacteous
	locustae
	osculate
ACELPPRS	clappers
	scrapple
ACELPPRU	parcel up
ACELPRSS	claspers
ACELPRST	sceptral
	spectral
ACELPRSU	specular
	sur place
ACELPTUU	cupulate
ACELPTUY	eucalypt
ACELQRUU	claqueur
ACELQSUY	lacqueys
ACELRRSW	scrawler
ACELRSSS	scarless
ACELRSTT	clatters
	Scarlett
	scrattle
ACELRTTU	cultrate
ACELRTTY	clattery
ACELSSTT	tactless
ACELSSUU	Aesculus
ACEMMOTY	mycetoma
ACEMNOOR	Cameroon
	con amore
ACEMNOPV	camp oven
ACEMNORR	romancer
ACEMNOST	camstone
ACEMNPSS	campness
ACEMNRSU	sun cream
ACEMNRTU	cream-nut
ACEMNRUY	numeracy
ACEMNSSU	mancuses
ACEMOORS	acrosome
ACEMOOST	comatose
	moot case
ACEMOPRS	mesocarp
ACEMORRT	cremator
	Mercator
ACEMORSW	case-worm
ACEMORSY	sycamore
ACEMORTY	cometary
ACEMORUX	morceaux
ACEMPSSU	campuses
ACENNNOU	announce
ACENNOSS	canoness
ACENNOTT	cotenant
ACENNOTV	covenant
ACENNOTZ	canzonet
ACENNPRY	pernancy
ACENNPTU	pecan nut
ACENNSUY	seacunny
ACENOOPX	Copaxone®
ACENOORT	coronate
ACENOOTZ	ectozoan
ACENOPRT	portance
ACENOPST	capstone
	open-cast
ACENOPTW	Cape Town
ACENOPUX	ponceaux
ACENOQTU	cotquean
ACENORRT	Torrance
ACENORRW	careworn
ACENORSS	narcoses
ACENORST	ancestor
	sarconet
	sortance
ACENORSU	carneous
	nacreous
ACENORTT	contrate
ACENORTU	courante
	outrance
ACENORUY	eucaryon
ACENOSST	contessa
ACENOSSV	cavesson
ACENOSTT	constate
ACENOSTV	centavos
ACENOTTT	tent coat
ACENOTTU	toucanet
ACENPRSU	encarpus
ACENPTTU	punctate
ACENRSTT	transect
ACENRSTU	Centaurs
	Etruscan
	recusant
ACENRSTY	ancestry
ACENRTTU	truncate
ACENRTUY	centaury
	cyanuret
ACENSSTW	newscast
ACEOOPSU	poaceous
ACEOORTV	evocator
	overcoat
ACEOPPRS	copperas
ACEOPRRT	recaptor
ACEOPRTT	attercop
ACEOPSTU	space out
ACEORRSU	carouser
ACEORRTT	retroact
ACEORRTU	Eurocrat
ACEORRVW	overcraw
ACEORSSS	cross sea
ACEORSST	Socrates
ACEORSTT	sectator
ACEORSTV	overcast
ACEORTTV	overt act
ACEORTUV	à couvert
	carve out
ACEORTUY	eucaryot
ACEORTWW	water cow
ACEOSSTU	Sea Scout
ACEOSSUY	soy sauce
ACEOSTTU	outcaste

Words marked ✧ can also be spelled with one or more capital letters

ACEPPRRS scrapper
ACEPPRSU scrape up
ACEPPRTU per caput
ACEPRRTU capturer
ACEPRSTW screw tap
ACEPSTTY typecast
ACERRSUV verrucas
ACERRUVZ Veracruz
ACERSSTY actressy
ACERSSUY Syracuse
ACERSTTU crustate
ACERSTTY scattery
ACERTTUW cutwater
ACESSTTT Test Acts
ACFFGHIN chaffing
ACFFHNOR chaffron
ACFFIILO official
ACFFILNU fanciful
ACFFKLOS slack off
ACFFLORR Carl Orff
ACFFLOSW scofflaw
ACFFORRY carry off
ACFGHINS Fasching
ACFGHITT cat-fight
ACFGIIMN magnific
ACFGIIPR caprifig
ACFGIKLS sick flag
ACFGIKNR fracking
ACFGINNY fancying
ACFGINRS scarfing
ACFGITUY fugacity
ACFGKNOP packfong
ACFGLNOR cornflag
ACFGLORT golf cart
ACFHHILN half-inch
ACFHHINW hawfinch
ACFHIJKS jackfish
ACFHILNO falchion
ACFHILNU faulchin
ACFHILOS coalfish
ACFHILTW with calf
ACFHINOU fauchion
ACFHIRSS scarfish
ACFHIRSW crawfish
ACFHIRSY crayfish
ACFHLMRU charmful
ACFHLNPU flanch up
ACFHLOSW cash flow
ACFHLTUW watchful
ACFHMNOR chamfron
ACFHORRT Rh-factor
ACFIILST fistical
ACFIILSV salvific
ACFIILTY facility
ACFIIMPS pacifism
ACFIIPST pacifist
ACFIISST Fascisti
ACFIKLNS calfskin
ACFILLSY fiscally
ACFILNOR fornical
ACFILNOT Califont®

ACFILNPU cup final
ACFILORT trifocal
ACFILRTY craftily
ACFILSSY classify
ACFIMNRU francium
ACFIMOSS Fascismo
ACFIMRTY city farm
ACFINORT factor in
fraction
ACFINPRS scarf-pin
ACFINSTY sanctify
ACFIOPRY fair copy
ACFIOSTU factious
ACFIRTUY furacity
ACFISSST fascists✧
ACFJKLOO Jack-fool
ACFKLLOR rockfall
ACFKLOPW wolf pack
ACFKLORS forslack
ACFKLOST lockfast
ACFKLRUW wrackful
ACFKLSSU sackfuls
ACFKOORR Afro-rock
roof rack
ACFKOPRU four-pack
ACFKOSTT fat stock
fatstock
ACFLLMRU cramfull
ACFLMNOO mooncalf
ACFLNORY falconry
ACFLOOPS foolscap
fool's cap
ACFLOOTW claw-foot
ACFLORSU scrofula
ACFLOTUU Foucault
ACFLRRUU furcular
ACFLRSTU cartfuls
ACFMOTTU factotum
ACFNRSTU fructans
ACFOOSTT cat's-foot
ACFORSTU scarf out
ACGGGILN clagging
ACGGIINT gigantic
ACGGIIOS isagogic
ACGGILNN clanging
glancing
ACGGIOOR coraggio
ACGGLNOU glucagon
ACGGLRSY scraggly
ACGHHIJK highjack
jack-high
ACGHHIMP high camp
ACGHHINT hatching
ACGHIIMN Michigan
ACGHIKNW whacking
ACGHILLR gill arch
ACGHILNS clashing
ACGHILNY achingly
ACGHILOR oligarch
ACGHILRT arc-light
ACGHILRU lug-chair

ACGHIMNR charming
ACGHIMNT matching
ACGHINNR ranching
ACGHINNU unaching
ACGHINOP poaching
ACGHINPT nightcap
patching
ACGHINRR charring
ACGHINRS crashing
ACGHINRU churinga
nuraghic
ACGHINST scathing
ACGHINTT chatting
ACGHINTU Taichung
ACGHINTW watching
ACGHINTY yachting
ACGHIPRS graphics
ACGHIQTU acquight
ACGHLLOR gralloch
ACGHLOOY chaology
ACGHNTUU uncaught
ACGHORSU choragus
ACGHPTUU upcaught
ACGIILNO logician
ACGIIMOS isogamic
ACGIIMST sigmatic
ACGIINRT granitic
ACGIIPRS spagiric
ACGIJJKO jickajog
ACGIKKLO goal kick
ACGIKLNN clanking
ACGIKLNT tackling
talcking
ACGIKLNU caulking
ACGIKLRY garlicky
ACGIKMNS smacking
ACGIKNOR croaking
ACGIKNRT tracking
ACGIKNST stacking
ACGIKPRS gripsack
ACGILLLR call-girl
ACGILLNS call sign
ACGILMMN clamming
ACGILNOZ Ozacling®
ACGILNPP clapping
ACGILNPS clasping
scalping
ACGILNRW crawling
ACGILNRY caringly
ACGILRSU surgical
ACGIMMNR cramming
ACGIMNOS coamings
ACGIMNPR cramping
ACGIMNPS scamping
ACGIMNSY gymnasic
syngamic
ACGIMORS orgasmic
ACGIMRTU Targumic
ACGINNNS scanning
ACGINNPR prancing
ACGINNRU uncaring

ACGINNUV	vauncing
ACGINORY	congiary
ACGINOST	agnostic
	coasting
ACGINPPR	crapping
ACGINPRS	scarping
	scraping
ACGINRRS	scarring
ACGINRRY	carrying
ACGINSTT	scatting
ACGIOORS	gracioso
ACGIORST	orgastic
ACGIORSU	gracious
ACGIORUW	Guicowar
ACGIPRSY	spagyric
ACGJKLPU	jack plug
ACGJLNOU	conjugal
ACGJLNRU	Carl Jung
ACGKLMOR	glam rock
	glam-rock
ACGLMOUU	coagulum
ACGLNORU	clangour
ACGLNOTU	cut along
ACGLOORY	arcology
ACGLOSUU	glaucous
ACGLSSTU	cut glass
	cutglass
ACGNNOOT	contango
ACGNORST	congrats
ACGORSSW	cowgrass
ACGPPSUU	scuppaug
ACHHHOTT	hot hatch
	hot-hatch
ACHHILPT	phthalic
ACHHINTW	whinchat
ACHHINTY	hyacinth
ACHHIOWW	aich whow
ACHHIPPR	hipparch
ACHHLLOT	challoth
ACHHLMOS	mashloch
ACHHLNOR	rhonchal
ACHHLPRY	phylarch
ACHHLSUY	shauchly
ACHHNTTU	nuthatch
	unthatch
ACHHOSTW	chat show
ACHHPTUZ	chutzpah
ACHHRSTU	crush hat
ACHHSTTU	such that
ACHIIKNN	china ink✧
ACHIILMS	chiliasm
ACHIILST	chiliast
ACHIIMNS	Mishnaic
ACHIIMRT	Mithraic
ACHIINPS	Hispanic
ACHIINPT	anti-chip
ACHIINRT	trichina
ACHIINSU	Chisinau
ACHIIRRS	Irish car
ACHIIRST	rachitis
ACHIIRSU	ischuria
ACHIJKPW	whipjack
ACHIKKNS	knackish
ACHIKKSW	kickshaw
ACHIKLLW	hickwall
ACHIKLPT	chalkpit
ACHIKNOP	pachinko
ACHIKNOT	hack into
ACHIKQSU	quackish
ACHIKRSW	rickshaw
ACHIKRTT	hat trick
ACHILLOR	orchilla
ACHILLRT	clithral
ACHILLTY	city hall
ACHILMOP	omphalic
ACHILMRS	chrismal
ACHILMTY	mythical
ACHILNNS	clannish
ACHILNOO	hoolican
ACHILNOS	lichanos
	Nicholas
ACHILNPS	clanship
ACHILOPR	rhopalic
ACHILORT	acrolith
ACHILPSY	physical
ACHILPTY	patchily
ACHILRUY	chyluria
ACHILRVY	chivalry
ACHILTTY	chattily
ACHIMMOS	machismo
ACHIMMST	mismatch
ACHIMNNW	winchman
ACHIMNOP	champion
ACHIMNOR	choirman
	harmonic
ACHIMNPT	pitchman
ACHIMNSU	inasmuch
ACHIMOPR	amphoric
ACHIMOSS	chamisos
	isochasm
ACHIMPSS	scampish
ACHIMRST	chartism✧
ACHIMSSU	chiasmus
ACHIMTUY	cyathium
ACHINNOP	panchion
ACHINOPR	parochin
ACHINORT	anorthic
ACHINOST	chitosan
ACHINOTZ	hoactzin
ACHINQUU	Quichuan
ACHINSTY	Scythian
ACHIOPRT	atrophic
ACHIORSS	coarsish
ACHIORST	actorish
ACHIORTV	tovarich
ACHIPPSS	sapphics✧
ACHIPRRT	parritch
ACHIPTTU	chupatti
ACHIRRSY	Syriarch
ACHIRRTY	triarchy
ACHIRSTT	chartist✧
	straicht
ACHISTTY	chastity
ACHJNORY	John Cary
ACHKKORW	hackwork
ACHKLOTU	chalk out
ACHKLSTU	stulchak
ACHKMORS	shamrock
ACHKNNUU	nunchaku
ACHKNOOT	canthook
ACHKOPTW	top whack
ACHKORSW	cow shark
ACHKOSSY	hassocky
ACHLLNWY	lynch-law
ACHLLORY	chorally
ACHLMSTZ	schmaltz
ACHLNOOU	oulachon
ACHLNSTY	stanchly
ACHLOOTY	holy coat
ACHLOPRT	calthrop
ACHLOPRY	polyarch
ACHLOPTT	potlatch
ACHLOTWX	waxcloth
ACHLPRTU	Plutarch
ACHMNNSU	Schumann
ACHMNOOR	Monarcho
ACHMNORS	Romansch
ACHMNORY	monarchy
	nomarchy
ACHMNOSU	Monachus
ACHMNRSU	Rumansch
ACHMNRTU	truchman
ACHMOORT	chat room
ACHMOPST	camp-shot
ACHMORTU	outmarch
ACHMOSTY	stomachy
ACHMOTTU	outmatch
ACHMPRTU	thrum cap
ACHNNORU	unanchor
ACHNOOOT	Ochotona
ACHNOPRU	up-anchor
ACHNPPSS	schnapps
ACHNRRTU	run chart
ACHNRSTU	unstarch
ACHNRSYY	synarchy
ACHNRTUY	chauntry
ACHOORTU	co-author
ACHOORTY	chayroot
ACHOPRTY	toparchy
ACHOPSST	spot cash
ACHORSTU	crash out
ACHOTTUW	outwatch
	watch out
	watch-out
ACHPRSTU	push-cart
	sharp-cut
ACHRSTTU	straucht
ACIIILMN	inimical
ACIIILNS	Sicilian
ACIIILNV	civilian
ACIIINST	Sinaitic
ACIIKLNO	kaolinic
ACIIKNNN	cannikin

ACIIKNPT	pack it in
ACIIKNTY	kyanitic
ACIIKPRT	paitrick
ACIILLOV	villiaco
ACIILLSU	silicula
ACIILLTV	villatic
ACIILLVW	civil law
ACIILMNR	criminal
ACIILNOR	ironical
ACIILNOT	talionic
ACIILNPT	platinic
ACIILNSU	Siculian
ACIILNTX	Calixtin
ACIILOSV	viliacos
ACIILRTT	tritical
ACIILRTU	uralitic
ACIILRVW	civil war
ACIILSST	Silastic®
	silastic
ACIIMNOR	morainic
ACIIMNOS	simoniac
ACIIMNOT	amniotic
ACIIMNST	actinism
ACIIMNSU	musician
ACIIMNTU	actinium
ACIIMNTY	imitancy
	intimacy
	minacity
ACIIMOST	iotacism
ACIIMOTT	amitotic
ACIIMPRT	primatic
ACIIMPRV	vampiric
ACIIMRST	scimitar
ACIIMRTU	muriatic
ACIIMSTT	Atticism
ACIIMSTV	activism
ACIIMTUV	viaticum
ACIINNOP	Panionic
ACIINNOS	Socinian
ACIINNOT	inaction
	nicotian
ACIINNQU	cinquain
ACIINNTT	incitant
ACIINNTY	caninity
ACIINOPT	optician
ACIINORZ	zirconia
ACIINOSS	Ossianic
ACIINOSV	avionics
ACIINOTT	citation
ACIINPRS	Crispian
ACIINPSS	piscinas
ACIINRSS	narcissi
ACIINRTU	uranitic
ACIIOPST	apositic
ACIIORST	aoristic
ACIIORTV	victoria✧
ACIIOSTT	Taoistic
ACIIOTWY	Iowa City
ACIIPPST	papistic
ACIIRSST	Triassic
ACIIRSTT	artistic

ACIISTTU	autistic
ACIISTTV	activist
ACIITTVY	activity
ACIITVVY	vivacity
ACIJKKPS	skipjack
ACIJKLMR	Jim Clark
ACIJKNOT	jack into
ACIJKSTW	stickjaw
ACIJNNOR	A J Cronin
ACIJRSSU	Jurassic
ACIKLLST	salt lick
ACIKLMST	malstick
ACIKLNOT	anti-lock
ACIKLNRY	crankily
ACIKLNSU	Nicklaus
ACIKLORY	croakily
ACIKMNTY	nicky-tam
ACIKMPST	mapstick
ACIKNNPR	crank pin
ACIKNPST	panstick
ACIKPPTU	pack it up
ACILLLMY	clay-mill
ACILLLOP	pollical
ACILLLPS	clap-sill
ACILLMMY	clammily
ACILLMOS	localism
ACILLNOO	colonial
ACILLNOR	carillon
ACILLNOS	scallion
ACILLOOZ	colzaoil
ACILLOQU	coquilla
ACILLORT	clitoral
ACILLORY	collyria
ACILLOST	localist
ACILLOSY	socially
ACILLOTY	locality
ACILLOUV	colluvia
ACILLSSY	classily
ACILMNNO	non-claim
ACILMNOP	complain
ACILMNOS	laconism
ACILMOOS	scolioma
ACILMOPR	proclaim
ACILMOPT	compital
ACILMOSV	vocalism
ACILMPTU	placitum
ACILMSSS	classism
ACILMSTY	mystical
ACILMTUY	ultimacy
ACILNOOT	location
ACILNOOV	vocalion
ACILNOPS	salpicon
ACILNOPT	platonic✧
ACILNORS	clarinos
ACILNORT	cilantro
	contrail
ACILNORY	iron-clay
ACILNOSU	unsocial
ACILNOSV	Slavonic
	Volscian
ACILNOUV	univocal

ACILNPSS	scalpins
ACILNRSU	cislunar
ACILNRUY	culinary
	uranylic
ACILNSTU	sultanic
ACILNSTY	scantily
ACILOPRT	tropical
ACILORRV	corrival
ACILORST	calorist
ACILORTV	vortical
ACILORYZ	zircaloy
ACILOSTV	vocalist
ACILOTVY	vocality
ACILPPST	split cap
ACILPRSU	spicular
ACILPRTU	pictural
ACILPSST	plastics
	slip-cast
ACILRSTU	rustical
ACILRTUV	cultivar
	curvital
ACILSSST	classist
ACILSTTY	scattily
ACILSTUV	victuals
ACILSTUX	Calixtus
ACILSTVY	sylvatic
ACIMMOSS	acosmism
ACIMMTUY	cymatium
ACIMNNNO	cinnamon
ACIMNOOR	acromion
	Comorian
ACIMNORT	romantic
ACIMNORU	conarium
	coumarin
ACIMNORY	acrimony
ACIMNOSS	mocassin
ACIMNOST	monastic
ACIMNOSU	un-Mosaic
ACIMNOTU	aconitum
ACIMNPTY	tympanic
ACIMNRSU	craniums
ACIMNSTU	Antmusic
ACIMOOST	scotomia
ACIMORST	acrotism
ACIMORSY	cramoisy
ACIMOSST	acosmist
	massicot
ACIMOSTT	masticot
	stomatic
ACIMPPTU	camp it up
ACIMPRSU	rap music
ACIMRRSY	miscarry
ACINNOOT	conation
	intonaco
ACINNORR	naricorn
ACINNOSS	scansion
ACINNOST	canonist
	sanction
ACINNOSU	Asunción
ACINNOTU	continua
ACINNRTY	tyrannic

ACINNSTY	instancy
ACINOOPR	picaroon
ACINOOTV	vocation
ACINOPPT	panoptic
ACINOPRS	parsonic
	Scorpian
ACINOQUV	coq au vin
ACINORRT	contrair
ACINORSS	narcosis
ACINORST	cantoris
	cast iron
	cast-iron
ACINORTT	traction
ACINOSSS	cassinos
ACINOSSY	cyanosis
ACINOSTT	oscitant
ACINOSTU	anticous
ACINOSTW	wainscot
ACINOSWX	coxswain
ACINOTTX	toxicant
ACINPQUY	piquancy
ACINPSTY	synaptic
ACINRSST	Sanscrit
ACINRSTU	saturnic
ACINRTTU	taciturn
	urticant
ACINSTTY	sanctity
	scantity
ACINSTYY	syncytia
ACIOOPST	scotopia
ACIOOPTX	Cotopaxi
ACIOOTYZ	zoocytia
ACIOPRST	piscator✧
ACIOPRTT	protatic
ACIOPRTY	poticary
ACIOPSST	potassic
ACIOPSSU	spacious
ACIOPSTU	captious
ACIOPTTU	autoptic
ACIORSSU	scarious
ACIORSTU	Air Scout
	Suctoria
ACIORTTY	atrocity
	citatory
ACIORTVY	voracity
ACIOSTUU	cautious
ACIPRRUU	pirarucu
ACIRRTTX	tractrix
ACIRRTUX	curatrix
ACIRSSTY	sacristy
ACISTTUY	astucity
ACJKORZZ	jazz-rock
ACKKLORR	rock lark
ACKKMOPR	pockmark
ACKKORRW	rackwork
ACKLLPSU	skullcap
ACKLMNOS	locksman
ACKLMORU	rock-alum
ACKLOOPW	woolpack
ACKLOOSW	woolsack✧
ACKLORST	rock salt
ACKMNOST	stockman
ACKMNRTU	truckman
ACKMOORT	tack room
ACKMOPRW	work camp
ACKMSUVY	musk-cavy
ACKNOPSW	snowpack
ACKOPRRT	traprock
ACKOPSTT	tap stock
ACKORSTW	catworks
ACKPRSTU	Turk's cap
ACLLLLOR	roll-call
ACLLLLOT	toll call
ACLLLNOY	clonally
ACLLLNUU	Lucullan
ACLLMNOU	columnal
ACLLMORU	corallum
ACLLMOSU	Mollusca
ACLLNOPU	call upon
ACLLNORW	Cornwall
ACLLOORT	collator
ACLLOOSS	colossal
ACLLOPTY	tall copy
ACLLORUY	ocularly
ACLLPPSU	pull caps
ACLLRTUU	cultural
ACLMMNOU	communal
ACLMNOOO	coolamon
ACLMNORU	columnar
ACLMNORY	normalcy
ACLMORTU	crotalum
ACLMPRSU	scalprum
ACLMRSUU	muscular
ACLMSUUV	vasculum
ACLNOORT	colorant
ACLNOOSY	Colonsay
ACLNOPSY	syncopal
ACLNOPTW	cow-plant
ACLNORSU	consular
ACLNORSW	Corn Laws
ACLNORTU	calutron
ACLNOSTU	consulta
	osculant
ACLNPTUU	punctual
ACLNSSUY	unclassy
ACLOOOTV	ovo-lacto
ACLOOPRR	corporal
ACLOOPRT	Coalport
ACLOPPRY	Polycarp
ACLOPRRW	prowl car
ACLOPRST	caltrops
ACLOPRXY	xylocarp
ACLOPSSY	calypsos
ACLOPSUU	opuscula
ACLORRTU	torcular
ACLORSTU	Crotalus
ACLORTUW	lawcourt
ACLOSSTT	cast lots
ACLOSSTU	outclass
	soul-scat
ACLOSTUW	scout law
ACMMNOSY	scammony
ACMMNOYY	myomancy
ACMNNOOW	con woman
ACMNOOPR	monocarp
ACMNOORR	cromorna
ACMNOORT	monocrat
ACMNOOYZ	zoomancy
ACMNOPUY	Apocynum
ACMNORTU	Turcoman
ACMNOSST	Scotsman
ACMOOPRS	coprosma
ACMOORRT	motor car
ACMOOSST	scotomas
ACMORRTY	Cromarty
ACMORSTW	wormcast
ACMORSTY	costmary
ACMSUVVY	cum-savvy
ACNNNORY	cannonry
ACNNOSST	Constans
ACNNOSTT	constant
ACNOOORT	octaroon
ACNOORRY	coronary
ACNOORST	corantos
	ostracon
ACNOORSU	canorous
ACNOORTY	octonary
ACNOPSTW	snow-capt
ACNORRTY	contrary
ACNORSTT	contrast
ACNORSWW	crown saw
ACNORTTU	turncoat
ACNORTUY	noctuary
ACNPRSUY	sprauncy
ACNPRSYY	syncarpy
ACNRRTUY	curranty
ACOOPRRS	corporas
ACOORSTU	touracos
ACOPRRTT	protract
ACOPRSUU	à coup sûr
ACOPRTUY	pay court
ACORRSTT	tractors
ACORRSUW	currasow
ACORRTUY	carry out
	carry-out
	curatory
ACORRTUZ	razor cut
	razor-cut
ACORSSTU	tau cross
ACORSSUW	curassow
ACORSSWY	crossway
ACORSTTY	cryostat
ACPSSTUY	pussy-cat
ACRRSTUU	Arcturus
ADDDEEGR	degraded
ADDDEEIM	diademed
ADDDEELR	laddered
ADDDEENR	reddenda
ADDDEINW	dead-wind
ADDDEMNU	addendum
ADDDENRU	deuddarn
ADDDEOOW	dead wood
	dead-wood

ADDDEOPR	drop dead
	drop-dead
ADDDEORS	addorsed
ADDEEEFH	feed-head
ADDEEENR	deadener
	endeared
ADDEEEPR	deep-read
ADDEEFIL	defilade
ADDEEFIR	dead-fire
ADDEEFRY	defrayed
ADDEEFTT	defatted
ADDEEGHR	hard edge
ADDEEGLN	danegeld
ADDEEGMU	gude-dame
ADDEEGNR	deranged
ADDEEGOR	dog-eared
ADDEEGSW	saw-edged
ADDEEHLY	aldehyde
ADDEEHNR	hardened
ADDEEILN	deadline
ADDEEILP	deep-laid
ADDEEILT	detailed
ADDEEINO	one-idea'd
ADDEEISS	diseased
ADDEEIST	steadied
ADDEELLM	medalled
ADDEELLP	pedalled
ADDEELMS	alms-deed
ADDEELNU	unleaded
ADDEEMNN	demanned
ADDEEMNR	demander
ADDEEMNU	ad eundem
ADDEENPX	expanded
ADDEENRR	reed-rand
ADDEENRW	wandered
ADDEENSS	deadness
ADDEENTT	dentated
ADDEENTU	denudate
ADDEENWX	waxed end
ADDEEOPR	dead-rope
ADDEEPRV	depraved
ADDEERRT	retarded
ADDEFIIL	ladified
ADDEFILT	dead-lift
ADDEFILY	field day
	ladyfied
ADDEFLRU	dreadful
ADDEFNOW	fade down
	fade-down
ADDEFORW	word-deaf
ADDEFRRW	red dwarf
ADDEGHOR	Drogheda
ADDEGIRS	disgrade
ADDEGMOO	good-dame
ADDEGNRU	ungraded
ADDEGRRU	Red Guard
ADDEHHIN	hindhead
ADDEHHLN	handheld
	hand-held
ADDEHHNS	shedhand
ADDEHHSY	Eddy Shah
ADDEHILR	dihedral
ADDEHIMS	made dish
ADDEHINW	headwind
ADDEHLNR	land-herd
ADDEHLOS	shedload
ADDEHMRU	drumhead
ADDEHNNY	dandy-hen
ADDEHNSU	undashed
	unshaded
ADDEHNTY	The Dandy
ADDEHORW	headword
ADDEHOST	dead shot
ADDEHPRU	purdahed
ADDEHSTU	Thaddeus
ADDEIITV	additive
ADDEIKRV	A V Kidder
ADDEILNS	landside
ADDEILNT	tideland
ADDEIMNN	in demand
ADDEIMOS	sodamide
ADDEIMRS	misdread
ADDEIMTT	admitted
ADDEINOS	adenoids
ADDEIOPR	parodied
ADDEIORS	roadside
	sideroad
ADDEIPPR	didapper
ADDEIPRS	dispread
ADDEIPSS	dipsades
ADDEIPST	dead spit
ADDEIQSU	squaddie
ADDEIRSW	sideward
ADDEIRVZ	vizarded
ADDEISSU	dissuade
ADDEKNVY	vandyked
ADDEKORW	dead-work
ADDEKOST	take odds
ADDELLOR	dollared
ADDELLPU	dead-pull
ADDELMOS	dolmades
ADDELNOU	duodenal
	unloaded
ADDELNPU	pudendal
ADDELNSU	unsaddle
ADDELOOR	El Dorado
	Eldorado
ADDELOSS	dead loss
ADDELPRS	paddlers
ADDELPSU	saddle up
ADDELRST	straddle
ADDELRSW	swaddler
ADDELRSY	saddlery
ADDELRTW	twaddler
ADDEMMNU	undammed
ADDEMNNO	on demand
ADDEMNNU	undamned
ADDEMNPU	undamped
ADDEMRYY	Mary Eddy
ADDENNSU	sand-dune
ADDENORU	unadored
ADDENPRU	undraped
ADDENRST	darndest
	stranded
ADDENRTU	untraded
ADDENRUW	unwarded
ADDENRYY	yarn-dyed
ADDEOTTU	outdated
ADDEPRSU	superadd
ADDFFILO	daffodil
ADDFFINR	dandriff
ADDFFNRU	dandruff
ADDFORRT	Dartford
ADDGGILN	gladding
ADDGGORU	guard dog
ADDGIILN	daidling
ADDGILNP	paddling
ADDGILNW	waddling
ADDGINOR	daring-do
ADDGIOSY	dog-daisy
ADDGLORU	old guard
ADDGMRUU	mudguard
ADDGOQSU	God squad
ADDGORSW	godwards
ADDHHLNO	handhold
ADDHHLOR	hold hard
	hold hard!
ADDHIKRS	hard disk
ADDHIMOO	maidhood
ADDHINRW	hindward
ADDHINSY	dandyish
ADDHIOTY	hydatoid
ADDHLOOY	ladyhood
ADDHNNOW	hand down
ADDHOORW	hardwood
ADDIIKMZ	zaddikim
ADDIILUV	dividual
ADDIINOT	addition
ADDIINRT	Trinidad
ADDIINTV	dividant
ADDIJMNY	jim-dandy
ADDIKORS	skid road
ADDILLNW	wildland
ADDILMNS	midlands✧
ADDILNNW	landwind
ADDIMNSY	dandyism
ADDIMPSY	Paddyism
ADDINNOO	Dodonian
ADDINNOR	ordinand
ADDINORS	disadorn
ADDINOSS	Addison's
ADDINQUY	quiddany
ADDINRWW	windward
ADDIORRT	dirt road
ADDIORSY	Doris Day
ADDIPTUY	duty-paid
ADDISSTV	St David's
ADDKMORT	Mark Todd
ADDKNRRU	drunkard
ADDLLNOR	landlord
ADDLNNOW	downland
ADDLNOOW	download
	woodland

ADDLNORS landdros
ADDLOOSS soldados
ADDLORSY Lord's Day
ADDMMOOY moody-mad
ADDMNOPW damp down
ADDMOOSY doomsday
ADDNOPUY pound day
ADDNOPWY pandowdy
ADDNORWW downward
drawdown
ADDOORRY door-yard
ADDOORWW woodward
ADDOORWY woodyard
ADEEEFFR affeered
ADEEEFLR lead-free
ADEEEFLS seed leaf
ADEEEFNY fedayeen
ADEEEFRT federate
ADEEEGLR red eagle
ADEEEGLT delegate
ADEEEGNR renegade
ADEEEGNT teenaged
ADEEEGPS gapeseed
ADEEEGRS degrease
ADEEEHKT take heed
ADEEEHRX exhedrae
ADEEEHSY eyeshade
ADEEEIMR dearie me
ADEEEINT detainee
ADEEEIUV eau de vie
ADEEEKNY naked eye
ADEEEKWY weak-eyed
ADEEELPY pale-eyed
ADEEELRT lead tree
ADEEELST teaseled
ADEEELTV elevated
ADEEEMNT emendate
ADEEEMRU emeraude
ADEEEMRY armed eye
ADEEENRS serenade
ADEEENTT attendee
edentate
ADEEENTV even date
ADEEEPRS rapeseed
ADEEEPRT repeated
ADEEERTT date tree
ADEEFFIR effraide
ADEEFHNR free hand
freehand
ADEEFHOR forehead
ADEEFHRT earth-fed
ADEEFILN enfilade
ADEEFINR fredaine
ADEEFIOR foedarie
ADEEFIRR rarefied
ADEEFIRY reaedify
ADEEFLMS self-made
ADEEFLOR freeload
ADEEFLRR deferral
ADEEFLRT deflater
ADEEFLRW weel-far'd
ADEEFLSS fadeless
ADEEFLSX flaxseed
ADEEFMNR freedman
ADEEFMTU deaf-mute
ADEEFNOT tone-deaf
ADEEFNRU unfeared
ADEEFNSS deafness
ADEEFORR foreread
ADEEFORT foredate
ADEEFOYY eye of day
ADEEFRRT raftered
ADEEFRRY defrayer
federary
ADEEGILO ego ideal
ADEEGILR edge rail
ADEEGIRS disagree
ADEEGIRT gaitered
ADEEGIST get ideas
ADEEGITT tide gate
ADEEGLLT galleted
ADEEGLLU De Gaulle
ADEEGLNR enlarged
ADEEGLNT danegelt
ADEEGLSV selvaged
ADEEGMNR gendarme
ADEEGMNY Ganymede
megadyne
ADEEGMOP megapode
ADEEGMOS megadose
ADEEGNNR endanger
ADEEGNNV vendange
ADEEGNOR renegado
ADEEGNRR gardener
ADEEGNRU dungaree
under age
under-age
ungeared
ADEEGNRV engraved
ADEEGNSS agedness
ADEEGORT derogate
ADEEGOTW goatweed
ADEEGPRT pargeted
ADEEGRRR regarder
ADEEGRRT garreted
ADEEGRRU redargue
ADEEGRRV Redgrave
ADEEGRSS dressage
ADEEGRTT targeted
ADEEGRTY get ready
ADEEGSWY edgeways
ADEEGTTZ gazetted
ADEEHHST sheathed
ADEEHIKP pike-head
ADEEHIKZ Zedekiah
ADEEHILN headline
ADEEHILS deisheal
ADEEHIPR pierhead
ADEEHIRR deer-hair
ADEEHIRT head-tire
ADEEHISV adhesive
ADEEHKWW hawkweed
ADEEHKWY hawk-eyed
ADEEHLLW wellhead
ADEEHLNO dane-hole
ADEEHLNP hen-padle
ADEEHLNR rehandle
ADEEHLNU unhealed
ADEEHLSS headless
ADEEHLTW the Weald
ADEEHMMO home-made
ADEEHMNN menhaden
ADEEHMRT The Dream
ADEEHNOT headnote
ADEEHNOV have done
ADEEHNRR hardener
ADEEHNRT adherent
head rent
neat-herd
threaden
ADEEHNTU unheated
ADEEHOPR headrope
ADEEHORS sorehead
ADEEHORV overhead
ADEEHRRS redshare
ADEEHRRT threader
ADEEHRST headrest
ADEEHRTW red wheat
wreathed
ADEEHRTY the ready
ADEEIILS idealise
ADEEIILZ idealize
ADEEIINT Tineidae
ADEEIIPR Pieridae
ADEEIIRS dies irae
ADEEIITV ideative
ADEEIJMR jeremiad
ADEEIKLS lakeside
ADEEIKSW weak side
ADEEILLN Danielle
lead-line
ADEEILLO oeillade
ADEEILMN endemial
Madeline
ADEEILMR remedial
ADEEILMT lead time
meal-tide
ADEEILMV medieval
ADEEILNT date line
dateline
lineated
ADEEILNU eau de Nil
ADEEILPR pedalier
ADEEILPS Pleiades
ADEEILPT depilate
pileated
ADEEILRR derailer
ADEEILRS sidereal
ADEEILSS idealess
ADEEILSV disleave
sea devil
ADEEIMNT dementia
ADEEIMNW made wine

Words marked ✧ can also be spelled with one or more capital letters

ADEEIMRS	maderise
ADEEIMRT	diameter
	remediat
ADEEIMRZ	maderize
ADEEIMST	side meat
ADEEIMTT	meditate
ADEEINNR	Adrienne
ADEEINNS	andesine
ADEEINOP	Oedipean
ADEEINPR	pindaree
ADEEINPT	diapente
ADEEINRS	arsenide
	draisene
	nearside
ADEEINRT	detainer
ADEEINSS	à dessein
ADEEINST	andesite
ADEEIPRS	airspeed
ADEEIPSS	speisade
ADEEIPSV	Vespidae
ADEEIPTT	tape-tied
ADEEIQUV	quae vide
ADEEIRST	readiest
	siderate
	steadier
ADEEIRSV	readvise
ADEEIRTV	derivate
ADEEISST	East Side
	set aside
	set-aside
ADEEISSV	adessive
ADEEISTV	sedative
ADEEITVW	tidewave
ADEEJLUV	juve lead
ADEEJNOT	Joe Dante
ADEEKKPR	keep dark
ADEEKLNS	sand leek
ADEEKMRR	remarked
ADEEKNPW	knapweed
ADEEKPRR	deer-park
ADEEKRST	streaked
ADEELLLP	lapelled
ADEELLMT	metalled
ADEELLMU	medullae
ADEELLMW	well-made
ADEELLNP	panelled
ADEELLNY	leadenly
ADEELLPR	pedaller
	predella
ADEELLPT	palleted
	petalled
ADEELLQU	equalled
ADEELLRS	sardelle
ADEELLRV	ravelled
ADEELLRW	well-read
ADEELLSS	leadless
ADEELLTY	elatedly
ADEELLVY	day-level
ADEELLWY	walleyed
ADEELMMR	mal de mer
ADEELMNO	lemonade
ADEELMNR	aldermen
ADEELMNS	emendals
ADEELMNT	lamented
ADEELMOS	somedeal
ADEELMRS	demersal
ADEELNNU	unaneled
ADEELNOR	De Lorean®
	oleander
ADEELNRS	Landseer
ADEELNRT	antlered
ADEELNRV	lavender
ADEELNRY	Alderney
ADEELNSU	unleased
	unsealed
ADEELNSV	enslaved
ADEELNTT	talented
ADEELNTU	unelated
ADEELOPR	lop-eared
ADEELOPS	pedaloes
ADEELORS	lease-rod
ADEELORU	aureoled
ADEELORV	overlade
ADEELOST	desolate
ADEELPPT	lappeted
ADEELPRS	relapsed
ADEELPST	pedestal
ADEELPTY	pedately
ADEELRRR	larderer
ADEELRRT	red alert
	treadler
ADEELRST	Lestrade
ADEELRTV	traveled
ADEELSST	dateless
	tasseled
ADEELSTY	sedately
ADEEMMSS	mesdames✧
ADEEMMXY	myxedema
ADEEMNNR	mannered
	Menander
ADEEMNOR	demeanor
ADEEMNOT	nematode
ADEEMNPY	ependyma
ADEEMNRS	meanders
ADEEMNSS	seedsman
ADEEMNST	stamened
ADEEMNSU	unseamed
ADEEMNTW	metewand
ADEEMNYY	many-eyed
ADEEMORS	seadrome
ADEEMORT	moderate
ADEEMPST	stampede
	stepdame
ADEEMRRY	dreamery
ADEEMRSU	measured
ADEEMRTY	meteyard
ADEENNRS	Andersen
ADEENNRU	unearned
ADEENNUW	unweaned
ADEENNUY	unyeaned
ADEENOPW	weaponed
ADEENORS	reasoned
ADEENORV	endeavor
ADEENORY	aerodyne
ADEENOSS	seasoned
ADEENOTT	denotate
	detonate
ADEENPPR	endpaper
ADEENPPS	sand-peep
ADEENPRU	unreaped
ADEENPRX	expander
	re-expand
ADEENPTT	pattened
ADEENRRW	wanderer✧
ADEENRSS	dearness
ADEENRSU	undersea
ADEENRSW	Rwandese
ADEENRTT	attender
	nattered
ADEENRTU	denature
ADEENSSU	danseuse
	Sudanese
ADEENSTU	unseated
ADEENSVY	seven-day
ADEENTTV	vendetta
ADEEOPRR	paderero
ADEEORRV	overread
ADEEORTT	tree toad
ADEEPPRR	prepared
ADEEPRRS	spreader
ADEEPRRT	departer
ADEEPRRU	upreared
ADEEPRST	pederast
ADEEPRSU	persuade
ADEEPRSW	perswade
ADEEPRTU	depurate
ADEEPSST	stapedes
ADEEPSWY	speedway
ADEEQRTU	détraqué
ADEERRRT	retarder
ADEERRRW	rereward
	rewarder
ADEERRST	serrated
ADEERRTW	redwater
ADEERTTT	tattered
ADEERTWW	wartweed
ADEERVYY	everyday
ADEESTTT	attested
ADEFFORT	trade off
	trade-off
ADEFFOSW	sawed-off
ADEFGILO	foliaged
ADEFGILR	Garfield
ADEFGILS	gasfield
ADEFGIMN	defaming
ADEFGIRS	gas-fired
ADEFGIRT	driftage
ADEFGITU	fatigued
ADEFGLLO	gold leaf
	gold-leaf
ADEFGLLU	full-aged
ADEFGLOT	gatefold
ADEFGLRU	feldgrau

ADEFGNOR	frondage
ADEFGNUW	wage fund
ADEFGOOW	a good few
ADEFHILS	dealfish
ADEFHILT	half-tide
ADEFHILY	hayfield
ADEFHIMS	famished
ADEFHKOR	forkhead
ADEFHLNO	half-done
ADEFHLNT	left-hand
ADEFHLRT	hard left
ADEFHLTU	deathful
ADEFHNOR	forehand
ADEFHNRR	hard-fern
ADEFHOST	softhead
ADEFIILR	airfield
ADEFIILS	salified
ADEFIIMR	ramified
ADEFIIRT	ratified
ADEFIIRX	fixed air
ADEFIKLY	fail-dyke
ADEFILLR	all-fired
ADEFILLT	ill-fated
ADEFILMN	inflamed
ADEFILNR	filander
ADEFILNT	inflated
ADEFILNY	fine lady
ADEFILOT	foliated
ADEFIMPR	fire damp
	firedamp
ADEFINRR	infrared
ADEFINRU	Freudian
ADEFINRW	fine-draw
ADEFINYZ	denazify
ADEFIORS	foresaid
ADEFKMOU	fumed oak
ADEFLLLU	ladleful
ADEFLLOR	fal de rol
ADEFLLRY	alder-fly
ADEFLLST	stall-fed
ADEFLLUY	feudally
ADEFLMRU	dreamful
ADEFLNNR	fern land
ADEFLNOR	foreland
ADEFLNRU	dearnful
ADEFLNRY	lady fern
ADEFLNUU	unfeudal
ADEFLNUW	unflawed
ADEFLOOR	real food
ADEFLOPR	drop-leaf
ADEFLORT	deflator
ADEFLPRS	feldspar
ADEFLPSU	spadeful
ADEFLRTU	tradeful
ADEFLRTW	leftward
ADEFMNRU	unframed
ADEFMOSU	fumadoes
ADEFNNNU	unfanned
ADEFNOOV	Vodafone®
ADEFNSST	daftness
ADEFORRR	forrader
ADEFORRW	foreward
ADEFORRY	foreyard
ADEFORUV	favoured
ADEFSSTT	stedfast
ADEGGJLY	jaggedly
ADEGGLRU	leg-guard
ADEGGLRY	raggedly
ADEGGMOY	demagogy
ADEGGNUU	ungauged
ADEGGOPY	pedagogy
ADEGGORT	Great Dog
ADEGGPRS	spragged
ADEGGRTY	gadgetry
ADEGHHOS	hogshead
ADEGHILR	head girl
ADEGHILT	alighted
	gilt-head
ADEGHINR	headring
ADEGHINS	sheading
ADEGHIRT	Third Age
ADEGHITY	eight-day
ADEGHLNO	headlong
	long-head
ADEGHMNO	hog-maned
ADEGHMOY	hey-go-mad
ADEGHNNU	unhanged
ADEGHNOY	hyena dog
ADEGHNPU	dungheap
ADEGHOOP	pagehood
ADEGHORT	goatherd
ADEGHOTW	dog-wheat
ADEGHRTU	daughter
ADEGHUYY	hay-de-guy
ADEGIILN	gliadine
ADEGIILP	diplegia
ADEGIINO	Ganoidei
ADEGIIRT	digerati
ADEGIITT	digitate
ADEGIJSW	jigsawed
ADEGIKOR	Oak Ridge
ADEGILLO	gladiole
ADEGILLR	grillade
ADEGILMN	medaling
ADEGILNO	galenoid
ADEGILNP	pedaling
	pleading
ADEGILNR	dearling
	dragline
	Reginald
ADEGILNS	dealings
	signaled
ADEGILNY	delaying
ADEGILOU	dialogue
ADEGILRS	Griselda
ADEGILRZ	Grizelda
ADEGILSS	glissade
ADEGILSV	disgavel
ADEGIMNR	dreaming
	margined
ADEGIMOR	ideogram
ADEGINNR	in danger
ADEGINOR	organdie
ADEGINOS	agonised
	diagnose
	San Diego
ADEGINOZ	agonized
ADEGINPU	anguiped
ADEGINRR	drearing
ADEGINRT	derating
	gradient
	red giant
	treading
ADEGINRY	readying
ADEGINST	d'Estaing
	steading
ADEGINSU	agnus dei✧
ADEGINYZ	zygaenid
ADEGIORT	ergatoid
ADEGIRWY	ridgeway
ADEGISSU	disusage
ADEGKLOY	dekalogy
ADEGKMOO	make good
ADEGLLNO	Legoland
ADEGLLNU	glandule
	ungalled
ADEGLMOS	gladsome
ADEGLMPU	plumaged
ADEGLMUY	amygdule
ADEGLNOS	dal segno
ADEGLNOY	gondelay
ADEGLNPS	spangled
ADEGLNRS	glanders
ADEGLNSS	gladness
ADEGLNUZ	unglazed
ADEGLRYY	Lady Grey
ADEGMNOY	endogamy
ADEGMNUU	ad unguem
ADEGMORW	wordgame
ADEGMOST	dog's-meat
ADEGNNOR	androgen
	dragonné
	end organ
ADEGNNPU	unpanged
ADEGNOPU	poundage
ADEGNORT	dragonet
ADEGNORW	gear down
ADEGNPUY	pyengadu
ADEGNRRU	grandeur
ADEGNRUU	unargued
ADEGNRUZ	gazunder
	ungrazed
ADEGOORY	goodyear
ADEGOOSW	wood sage
ADEGOPRR	prograde
ADEGORRT	garroted
ADEGORST	goadster
ADEGORTT	garotted
ADEGORTU	grade out
ADEGORTW	water dog
	water god
ADEGORWY	dog-weary
ADEGOSTY	go steady

Words marked ✧ can also be spelled with one or more capital letters

ADEGPRRU upgrader
ADEGRRST dragster
ADEGTTTU guttated
ADEHHIPR rhaphide
ADEHHIPS headship
ADEHHLOY Holyhead
ADEHHNTU headhunt
ADEHHOST headshot
ADEHIILT The Iliad
ADEHIIPS Pheidias
ADEHIITZ thiazide
ADEHIKLV khedival
ADEHIKNS skinhead
ADEHILLM Heimdall
mill-head
ADEHILLP phialled
pillhead
ADEHILNN hand line
ADEHILNP delphian✧
ADEHILNR hard line
hardline
ADEHILNU unhailed
ADEHILOX ox-halide
ADEHIMRS misheard
ADEHIMRT hard time
ADEHIMRY hydremia
ADEHINNR rein-hand
ADEHINOP diaphone
ADEHINOS adhesion
ADEHINPS deanship
ADEHINPU dauphine
ADEHINRS Sheridan
ADEHINRU unhaired
ADEHINST handiest
ADEHIOTT athetoid
ADEHIPRS raphides
Sephardi
ADEHIPST sidepath
ADEHIRVW hiveward
ADEHISSW Swadeshi
ADEHJLOT jolthead
ADEHKLNU lunkhead
ADEHKLOT take hold
ADEHKNRS red shank
redshank
ADEHKNSU skean-dhu
unshaked
ADEHKORW headwork
ADEHLLOW hallowed
ADEHLLPY lady-help
ADEHLLRS hard sell
ADEHLLRW hellward
ADEHLMNO homeland
ADEHLMOY holydame
ADEHLNNO lone hand
ADEHLNRW Landwehr
ADEHLNSS handless
ADEHLNST shetland✧
Stendhal
ADEHLNSU unhalsed
ADEHLOPS asphodel
pholades
ADEHLRRY heraldry
ADEHMMMO Mohammed
ADEHMNOS handsome
ADEHMNOT methadon
thanedom
ADEHMNRS herdsman✧
ADEHMNRU unharmed
ADEHMNSU unshamed
ADEHMOOR headroom
ADEHMORT mort-head
ADEHMORW homeward
ADEHMOST headmost
ADEHMOSU madhouse
ADEHMPPU pump-head
ADEHNNSW hand-sewn
ADEHNORV hand over
handover
overhand
ADEHNOSS sandshoe
ADEHNOSU seahound
ADEHNPSU unshaped
ADEHNPTU unpathed
ADEHNRSS hardness
ADEHNRSU unshared
ADEHNRSW swanherd
ADEHNRTU unthread
ADEHNSSU sunshade
unsashed
ADEHNSUV unshaved
ADEHNSUW unwashed
ADEHNTTU unhatted
ADEHNTTX text-hand
ADEHNTUW unthawed
ADEHOORT Dorothea
Theodora
ADEHOORW harewood
ADEHOPRS pad-horse
rhapsode
ADEHOPXY hexapody
ADEHORSW shadower
ADEHORTT throated
ADEHORTW death row
ADEHPRSU Phaedrus
ADEHPSUW washed-up
ADEHRTTW thwarted
ADEIILMN limnaeid
ADEIILMS idealism
ADEIILNN in denial
ADEIILNT in detail
ADEIILPR peridial
ADEIILRS Disraeli
ADEIILST idealist
ADEIILTV dilative
ADEIILTY ideality
ADEIIMNN indamine
Indiamen
ADEIIMNR meridian
ADEIIMPR impaired
ADEIIMRS semi-arid
ADEIIMVW a dim view
ADEIINNS sanidine
ADEIINOT ideation
taenioid
ADEIINRS draisine
ADEIINRU uredinia
ADEIINST adenitis
ADEIINUV induviae
ADEIIPRR perradii
prairied
ADEIIPRS presidia
ADEIIRST Aristide
ADEIITTV tidivate
ADEIITUV auditive
ADEIJMSS Sid James
ADEIJOSV Joe Davis
ADEIJRSU Judaiser
ADEIJRUZ Judaizer
ADEIKLLO keloidal
ADEIKLLY ladylike
ADEIKLNS sand-like
ADEIKLSW sidewalk
ADEIKMRT tidemark
ADEIKORT keratoid
ADEILLMY medially
ADEILLNN land-line
ADEILLNO load line
ADEILLNU unallied
ADEILLOR arillode
ADEILLOV live load
ADEILLPS spadille
ADEILLRT trialled
ADEILLRV rivalled
ADEILLSW sidewall
ADEILMNN landmine
ADEILMNO melanoid
ADEILMNU unmailed
ADEILMNY maidenly
medianly
ADEILMOS damoisel
soda lime
ADEILMPP palmiped
ADEILMPS misplead
ADEILMRW wild mare
ADEILMRY dreamily
ADEILMSS maidless
ADEILMST medalist
misdealt
ADEILMSV Maldives
ADEILMSY dysmelia
ADEILNNR inlander
ADEILNOP palinode
ADEILNOS Leonidas
nodalise
ADEILNOT delation
dial tone
ADEILNOZ nodalize
ADEILNPT pantiled
ADEILNPU paludine
ADEILNRS islander
ADEILNST tail ends
ADEILNSU unsailed

ADEILNSW Denis Law
ADEILNTU untailed
ADEILNTV divalent
ADEILOPR Leopardi
ADEILOPS episodal
opalised
sepaloid
ADEILOPT petaloid
ADEILOPZ opalized
ADEILOQU odalique
ADEILORS solidare
soredial
ADEILORT idolater
tailored
ADEILORV overlaid
ADEILORX exordial
ADEILOST diastole
isolated
sodalite
solidate
ADEILOSV De Valois
ADEILOTT datolite
ADEILOTV dovetail
ADEILPPP pedipalp
ADEILPRT dipteral
tripedal
ADEILPRU epidural
laired up
ADEILPRV deprival
ADEILPSS despisal
ADEILPTU plaudite
ADEILQSV Q D Leavis
ADEILRRY drearily
ADEILRSU residual
ADEILRSY dialyser
ADEILRTT detrital
ADEILRTY dielytra✧
ADEILRUV Duvalier
ADEILRVY variedly
ADEILRYZ dialyzer
ADEILSSY dialyses
ADEILSTY diastyle
steadily
ADEILSUV disvalue
ADEILSXY dyslexia
ADEILTTU altitude
latitude
ADEIMMNU unmaimed
ADEIMMST mismated
ADEIMMSZ Mazdeism
ADEIMNNO demonian
mondaine
ADEIMNNT in tandem
ADEIMNOP dopamine
ADEIMNOR Armenoid
ADEIMNOS nomadise
ADEIMNOT dominate
nematoid
ADEIMNOZ nomadize
ADEIMNRR manrider
ADEIMNRZ zemindar
ADEIMNSS sidesman
ADEIMNST tidesman
ADEIMNSY dynamise
ADEIMNSZ man-sized
ADEIMNTY dynamite
ADEIMNYZ dynamize
ADEIMORR airdrome
ADEIMORT mediator
ADEIMOSS sesamoid
ADEIMPRR rampired
ADEIMPST impasted
ADEIMRRS disarmer
ADEIMRSS sidearms
ADEIMRTU muriated
ADEIMRXY ready-mix
ADEINNOT Anointed
antinode
ADEINNOV Devonian
ADEINNPT pinnated
ADEINNPU unpained
ADEINNRW new dinar
ADEINNRZ rendzina
ADEINNSU unsained
ADEINNSX disannex
ADEINNTU inundate
ADEINOPT antipode✧
ADEINORR ordainer
reordain
ADEINORT deration
ordinate
read into
Rodentia
ADEINORU douanier
ADEINORZ arid zone
ADEINOST astonied
sedation
ADEINOTT antidote
tetanoid
ADEINOTV donative
ADEINOTW wade into
ADEINPPS sand pipe
ADEINPPX appendix
ADEINPRT dipteran
ADEINPRU unpaired
unrepaid
ADEINPSS in spades
ADEINPSV spavined
ADEINRRS serranid
ADEINRRW draw rein
ADEINRSS aridness
sardines
ADEINRST randiest
strained
ADEINRSU denarius
Eridanus
unraised
ADEINRSV sandiver
ADEINRSY synedria
ADEINRTT Andretti
ADEINRTU daturine
indurate
ADEINRUV unvaried
ADEINRVY vineyard
ADEINSSV avidness
vanessid
ADEINSTU sinuated
ADEINSTY desyatin
ADEINSVW swan dive
ADEIOPRS diaspore
ADEIOPST dioptase
ADEIOPTV adoptive
ADEIORST asteroid
ADEIORTT teratoid
ADEIORTV deviator
ADEIPRST spirated
tarsiped
ADEIPRSU upraised
ADEIPRTU eupatrid
ADEIPSTU put aside
ADEIPTTU aptitude
ADEIQRRU quarried
ADEIQSUY quayside
ADEIRRTW tawdrier
ADEIRRWW wiredraw
ADEIRSST disaster
ADEIRSSU radiuses
ADEIRSTT striated
tardiest
ADEIRTUV durative
ADEIRVWY driveway
ADEISSST assisted
ADEISSTT distaste
ADEISSWY sideways
ADEISTTU situated
ADEITTTU attitude
ADEJKORS soda jerk
ADEJLMPU jump lead
ADEJNRUW under-jaw
ADEJOPRY jeopardy
ADEJRSTU adjuster
readjust
ADEKLMRY markedly
ADEKLNSU unslaked
ADEKMNOW make down
ADEKMNRU Nurek Dam
unmarked
ADEKMNSU unmasked
ADEKMORS darksome
ADEKNNSS dankness
ADEKNOTW take down
take-down
ADEKNPTU tanked up
ADEKNRSS darkness
ADEKNRSU Dean Rusk
ADELLMRU medullar
ADELLMSU medullas
ADELLNNU annulled
ADELLNPS spendall
ADELLNSS landless
ADELLNSW wallsend✧
ADELLNTT Lettland
ADELLNUW unwalled

 Words marked ✧ can also be spelled with one or more capital letters

ADELLOSV lad's love
ADELLOTT allotted
totalled
ADELLOTU ladle out
ADELLOVY lady-love
ADELLOWW wallowed
ADELLRWW draw-well
ADELMNOS lodesman
sand mole
ADELMOOW woodmeal
ADELMOPR Palme d'Or
ADELMOST salt dome
ADELMOTU modulate
ADELMPTU date plum
ADELMRRU demurral
ADELMSUY amusedly
ADELNNNU unnaneld
ADELNNOT lentando
ADELNOOR Leonardo
ADELNOPR Polander
ponderal
ADELNORS Roseland
solander
ADELNORU Euroland
unloader
urodelan
ADELNORV overland
rondavel
ADELNORY read-only
ADELNOSS sand sole
ADELNPRS spandrel
ADELNPRU pendular
underlap
uplander
ADELNPRY panderly
ADELNPSY dyspneal
ADELNPUY unplayed
ADELNRSY Lysander
ADELNRTY ardently
ADELNRUY Dunleary
lay under
underlay
ADELNSTU unsalted
ADELNSTW westland
wetlands
ADELNTUU undulate
ADELNUUV unvalued
ADELNUZZ undazzle
ADELOOPV levodopa
ADELOORV overload
ADELOOTW late wood
ADELOOWW woodwale
ADELOPSU paludose
ADELOPSY sepalody
ADELOPTY petalody
ADELORRV overlard
Rod Laver
ADELORSS roadless
ADELORST lodestar
ADELORTW leadwort
ADELOVWY avowedly

ADELPPRY dapperly
ADELPRTY dry-plate
ADELRRTU ultrared
ADELRSTT startled
ADELRTUY adultery
ADELSTTY statedly
ADEMNNNU unmanned
ADEMNNOR on remand
ADEMNNOU unmoaned
ADEMNNRU underman
ADEMNNSU Amundsen
ADEMNOPR name-drop
pardon me
pomander
ADEMNOST stone-mad
ADEMNOWY dey-woman
ADEMNPPU unmapped
ADEMNPSS dampness
ADEMNPUU unmade-up
ADEMNRRU underarm
unmarred
ADEMNRTU undreamt
ADEMNRUW unwarmed
ADEMNSUU unamused
ADEMOORT moderato
ADEMOPRY pyoderma
ADEMOPST stampedo
ADEMOPSU mousepad
ADEMORRU armoured
Dr Moreau
ADEMORRW Romeward
ADEMORTW wardmote
ADEMOSSU Asmodeus
ADEMPRUW warmed-up
ADEMRSTY dry steam
ADENNNTU untanned
ADENNORS Anderson
ADENNOTU unatoned
ADENNRUW unwarned
ADENNTUW unwanted
ADENOOPS epanodos
ADENOORW wanderoo
ADENOPRR pardoner
ADENOPRS San Pedro
Sarpedon
ADENOPRW pare down
ADENOPRX expandor
ADENOPSS spadones
ADENOPSU unsoaped
ADENOPSY dyspnoea
ADENOPTT not-pated
ADENORTW Danewort
tear down
ADENORUX rondeaux
ADENORWW wear down
ADENOSSY Odyssean
ADENOSTW down east
ADENOSTY steady on!
ADENOTUY autodyne
ADENOUVW unavowed
ADENOVWW wave down

ADENPPSU unsapped
ADENPPTU untapped
ADENPRRU under par
ADENPRSU unspared
ADENPRTU depurant
ADENPRTY pedantry
ADENPRUW unwarped
ADENPRUY underpay
ADENQRSU squander
ADENRRTU untarred
ADENRRWY wardenry
ADENRSTU transude
ADENRSUY undersay
ADENRUWY under way
underway
ADENSTTU unstated
untasted
ADENSTUW unwasted
ADENSTUY unstayed
unsteady
ADENSUWY unswayed
ADEOORRT toreador
ADEOOTTT tattooed
ADEOPPRR pear drop
ADEOPRRS eardrops
ADEOPRRT parroted
predator
tear drop
ADEOPRTT tetrapod
ADEOPRUV vapoured
ADEOPSTT despotat
postdate
ADEOPTTU up to date
up-to-date
ADEORRST roadster
ADEORRVW overdraw
ADEORSST assorted
ADEORSTT road test
road-test
ADEORSTX extrados
ADEORSUV savoured
ADEOSSTT assotted
ADEPPRST strapped
ADEPRRTU raptured
ADEPRTTU tarted-up
ADEQSTTU squatted
ADERRSSW wardress
ADERRSTT redstart
ADERSTTU statured
ADERSTWW westward
ADESSTUY Tuesdays
ADFFGIIR giraffid
ADFFGORU off guard
ADFFHIRS draffish
ADFFHNOS hands off
hands-off
ADFFLRUU fraudful
ADFFNNOO off and on
off-and-on
on and off
on-and-off

ADFFNOST stand off
standoff
stand-off
ADFFNSTU and stuff
ADFFOOST fast food
ADFFORST Stafford
ADFFORSW off-wards
ADFGIINR infra dig
ADFGILRT drag lift
ADFGINNU unfading
ADFGLNOW flag down
ADFGLOUW god-awful
ADFGMNOO man of God
ADFHILNS land-fish
ADFHIORV VHF radio
ADFHIOST toadfish
ADFHIRSW dwarfish
ADFHISTY day shift
ADFHLLNU full hand
ADFHLNSU handfuls
ADFHLOOR half-door
ADFHLOST holdfast
ADFHORRT Hartford
ADFIILPY lapidify
ADFIILRT Id al-Fitr
ADFIIORX radio fix
ADFIIRST first aid
ADFIIRSU Firdausi
ADFILLLN landfill
ADFILLMN filmland
ADFILLNW windfall
ADFILLRU ill-faurd
ADFILMNO manifold
ADFIMNRW wind farm
ADFIMORY fairydom
ADFIMRSW dwarfism
ADFIORSV disfavor
ADFIRSTY first-day
ADFIRTWY drift-way
ADFKLLNO folkland
ADFLLNOU all found
ADFLLNOW downfall
ADFLMNOR landform
ADFLMNOY manyfold
ADFLMOPR frampold
ADFLOOWY floodway
ADFMORST Stamford
ADFMRSTU studfarm
ADFNOORT to and fro
ADFNOORZ forzando
ADFNOSTU Dan Fouts
ADFORRSW forwards
frowards
ADGGGINR dragging
ADGGGINS daggings
ADGGIIMO DiMaggio
ADGGILNN dangling
ADGGINNU Gunga Din
ADGGLRSU sluggard
ADGGORSS dog-grass
ADGHHHIN high hand

ADGHHILN highland✧
ADGHHINN nigh-hand
ADGHHIOR highroad
ADGHILLS Dalglish
ADGHILNN handling
ADGHILOS hidalgos
ADGHILPY diaglyph
ADGHILTY daylight
ADGHIMNS Gandhism
ADGHINOR hoarding
ADGHINPR handgrip
ADGHINST Gandhist
ADGHISTY day-sight
ADGHITTW tightwad
ADGHKNOT thank God
ADGHKNOZ Dzongkha
ADGHLNNO longhand
ADGHNOTU do-naught
ADGHNRTU drag hunt
ADGHOOPR odograph
ADGHORST drag-shot
ADGHPSYY dysphagy
ADGHRSTU draughts
ADGHRTUY draughty
ADGIILLN dialling
ADGIILLO gladioli
ADGIILMR Grimaldi
ADGIILNO gonidial
ADGIILNP plaiding
ADGIILNR ring dial
ADGIILPY pygidial
ADGIILTY algidity
ADGIIMNR admiring
ADGIIMOR idiogram
ADGIIMST digamist
ADGIINNT gin and it
ADGIINNY digynian
ADGIINRY dairying
ADGIINSV advising
ADGIJNRU adjuring
ADGIKLNR darkling
ADGILLNO oil gland
ADGILLNR land girl
ADGILLNW windgall
ADGILLNY dallying
ADGILMNU Maudling
ADGILMOR marigold
ADGILNNS sandling
ADGILNNU unlading
ADGILNOT dog Latin
ADGILNRY daringly
ADGILNZZ dazzling
ADGILOOS solidago
ADGILOPR prodigal
ADGILORY goliardy
gyroidal
ADGILOTW wild goat
ADGILRSY Ygdrasil
ADGIMNNO Mandingo
ADGIMOSU digamous
ADGIMOTX Dogmatix

ADGINNST standing
ADGINNTU daunting
ADGINOOP poignado
ADGINOOR rigadoon
ADGINOOT goad into
ADGINORR ring road
ADGINORS road sign
ADGINOTY toadying
ADGINRSW drawings
ADGIORTT Titograd
ADGKOOSZ gadzooks
ADGLOOPR drop goal
ADGLOORY gardyloo
ADGLOPSW gold-wasp
ADGLOSTY salty dog
ADGMNORU gourmand
Rogun Dam
ADGNNOQU quandong
ADGNNORS grandson
ADGNNRYY gynandry
ADGNOOOP Podogona
ADGNOORU go-around
ADGOOPRS gospodar
ADGOPRST postgrad
ADGOPRSU podargus
ADGORTUU outguard
ADHHINPW whip hand
ADHHIPRS hardship
ADHHNNOR hand-horn
ADHHNORU hour hand
ADHHNRTY hydranth
ADHIIMMS Mahdiism
ADHIIMSS Hasidism
ADHIIMST Mahdiist
ADHIINOP ophidian
ADHIINRW whiniard
ADHIIRRU Ruaidhri
Ruairidh
ADHIISST Hasidist
ADHIISTW had-I-wist
ADHIJNNO join-hand
ADHIKKOO Hokkaido
ADHIKNNT handknit
hand-knit
ADHILLMN hand-mill
millhand
ADHILLMO hollidam
ADHILLNS sandhill
ADHILLOP phalloid
ADHILLOT thalloid
ADHILMOO homaloid
ADHILMSS alms-dish
ADHILNPS land-ship
ADHILNST handlist
ADHILOOW Hailwood
ADHILOPS shipload
ADHILOPY haploidy
ADHILOSY holidays
ADHILPSY ladyship
ADHIMNOS admonish
ADHIMNOU humanoid

ADHIMNRT third man
ADHIMOPP amphipod
ADHIMRTY myriadth
ADHINNOR iron hand
ADHINPRW wind harp
ADHINRWY whinyard
ADHINSST standish
ADHINSSY sandyish
ADHINSTU dianthus
ADHIOPSS soap dish
ADHIOSTY toadyish
ADHIPRSW wardship
ADHIPRSY shipyard
ADHIPSTY dispathy
ADHIQSTU hit squad
ADHIRSTW wash-dirt
ADHIRTWW withdraw
ADHIRTWY third way
ADHKNORW handwork
ADHLLNOS Hollands
ADHLLNOY Holy Land
ADHLLOOR hall-door
ADHLLOPY hold play
ADHLLOTY tally-ho'd
ADHLMNOO hand-loom
ADHLMORT thraldom
ADHLNOPR Randolph
ADHLNORW waldhorn
ADHLNOUW downhaul
ADHLORRY Old Harry
ADHLOSWY hold sway
ADHMOOPS shampoo'd
ADHMOPRS dram-shop
ADHMOPRU road hump
ADHMORTT dart-moth
ADHNNOOR honorand
ADHNNORU Honduran
ADHNOOPR poor hand
ADHNOPST hand-post
ADHNORSU Honduras
ADHNOSTU thousand
ADHNOSUW unshadow
ADHNOSWW downwash
wash down
ADHOOPRS hospodar
ADHOORSW roadshow
ADHOORYZ hydrozoa✧
ADHOPRST potshard
ADHOPRSY rhapsody
ADHORSTU toadrush
ADHORSWY showyard
ADHPSTYY dyspathy
ADHRSTUY Thursday
ADIIIKNN india ink✧
ADIIINRV viridian
ADIIIQRU daiquiri
ADIIISST it is said
ADIIKLMM milkmaid
ADIIKLST tailskid
ADIIKNOP pinakoid
ADIIKNST antiskid
ADIILLMR milliard
ADIILLNY idyllian
ADIILLOR arilloid
ADIILLUV diluvial
ADIILMRV Vladimir
ADIILNOT dilation
ADIILNSU indusial
ADIILNSW windsail
ADIILNTW tail wind
ADIILNTY daintily
Ladinity
ADIILNUV diluvian
induvial
ADIILOPP diplopia
ADIILRST distrail
ADIILSSY dialysis
ADIILTVY validity
ADIIMNOT Domitian
ADIIMPSU aspidium
ADIINNOT nidation
ADIINNOZ diazinon
ADIINOSY Dionysia
ADIINOTU audition
ADIINRST distrain
ADIIOPRS sporidia
ADIIOPRT tapiroid
ADIIORST tarsioid
ADIIPRTY rapidity
ADIIPSTY sapidity
ADIIPTVY vapidity
ADIIRSTT distrait
triadist
ADIKKLRY Kirkaldy
ADIKKRRW kirkward
ADIKKRRY kirkyard
ADIKLLOR road kill
ADIKLNPS landskip
ADIKLNPY Pink Lady
ADIKLORW laid work
ADIKNNNU dunnakin
ADIKNNST inkstand
ADIKNOPY pyinkado
ADIKNPRW wind park
ADIKNRST stinkard
ADILLLPY pallidly
ADILLMNR mandrill
ADILLMOU allodium
ADILLMOV villadom
ADILLMSY dismally
ADILLNPS landslip
ADILLOOP poloidal
ADILLOPS spadillo
ADILLOSW disallow
ADILLOSY disloyal
ADILLRWY willyard
ADILLSTY distally
ADILMMOS modalism
ADILMNNO mandolin
ADILMNOS salmonid
ADILMOOR modiolar
ADILMOOW lima-wood
ADILMOPR mail drop
ADILMOPT diplomat
ADILMOPY olympiad✧
ADILMORU ordalium
ADILMOST modalist
ADILMOTY modality
ADILMPSU paludism
ADILMRUW wild arum
ADILNNNU nundinal
ADILNNOW nail down
ADILNNSU disannul
ADILNOOR doornail
ADILNOOV vindaloo
ADILNOPY palinody
ADILNORS Rosalind
ADILNOST stand oil
ADILNOTY nodality
ADILNPRS spandril
ADILNPST displant
ADILNRWY inwardly
ADILNSSW windlass
ADILOOPR Polaroid®
ADILOOPZ diplozoa
ADILOORT idolator
toroidal
ADILOPRS slip road
ADILOPRT tripodal
ADILOPSS disposal
ADILOQSU squaloid
ADILORSY solidary
ADILORTY adroitly
dilatory
idolatry
ADILOSTW wild oats
ADILOSTY sodality
ADILPPSY disapply
ADILPSTU plaudits
ADILRTTY tilt yard
ADILRTWY tawdrily
ADILRWYZ wizardly
ADIMMNOO ammonoid
ADIMMNOS monadism
nomadism
ADIMMNSY dynamism
ADIMMOOR Maoridom
ADIMMOST amidmost
ADIMMOTU domatium
ADIMNNOR Mondrian
ADIMNNOT dominant
ADIMNOOR maindoor
ADIMNOST donatism
saintdom
ADIMNOWW widowman
ADIMNRSY misandry
ADIMNSTY dynamist
ADIMOPRY myriapod
ADIMOPST impasto'd
ADIMOPSY sympodia
ADIMOSTY toadyism
ADIMOTUX Taxodium
ADIMPRSY pyramids✧

ADIMRSUU sudarium
ADIMSSTU stadiums
ADINNNTU inundant
ADINNOOT donation
nodation
ADINNORS iron-sand
ADINNORT ordinant
ADINNORY non-dairy
ADINNOTU nudation
ADINOOPS isopodan
ADINOOPT adoption
ADINOORT tandoori
ADINOOTT dotation
ADINOPRR raindrop
ADINOPST pintados
ADINORRY ordinary
ADINORST intrados
ADINORSU dinosaur
ADINORSV virandos
ADINORTU duration
ADINORWZ Zionward
ADINOSTT Donatist
ADINOSTU sudation
ADINOSTY dystonia
ADINRSUV DNA virus
ADINRUVZ unvizard
ADIOOPSS apodosis
ADIOPPST post-paid
ADIOPRST parodist
Port Said
ADIOPRSV privados
ADIOPRTY podiatry
ADIOPSTT toad spit
ADIOPSTY dystopia
ADIOQSUV quo vadis?
ADIORRST stair rod
ADIORRTT traditor
ADIORSTT stradiot
ADIORSVY advisory
ADIORTUY auditory
ADIORWWW war widow
ADIPRRTU purtraid
ADIRRWYZ wizardry
ADJKNRUY junkyard
ADJORSTU adjustor
ADKLMNSU slam dunk
slam-dunk
ADKLNOTW talk down
ADKLOOPT polka dot
polka-dot
ADKLOORW woodlark
workload
ADKMNORW mark down
mark-down
ADKMOORR darkroom
ADKNOPRT drop tank
ADKNRSTU stunkard
ADKOORRW roadwork
ADKORWYY worky-day
ADKRSSWY skywards
ADLLLNOR land-roll
ADLLLOOY doolally
ADLLLORY Lollardy
ADLLNORU all-round
ADLLNOSW Lowlands
ADLLORSU US dollar
ADLLORSY dorsally
ADLMMOOP doom-palm
ADLMMOPU doum-palm
ADLMNOOR moorland
ADLMNOOV Moldovan
ADLMNOOW old woman
ADLMNORY randomly
ADLMNOSS mossland
ADLMOOOR Aldo Moro
ADLMOORU malodour
ADLMOPRW moldwarp
ADLMOPSY psalmody
ADLMSTTU malt-dust
ADLNNOTW townland
ADLNNTUU undulant
ADLNOOPR land-poor
ADLNOORW loan word
ADLNOPRT portland✧
ADLNOPRU pauldron
ADLNOPSW slap down
ADLNOPWY downplay
play down
ADLNORWY onwardly
ADLNOSTU outlands
ADLNOSTW salt down
stand low
ADLOOOPW wood opal
ADLOOPTY Tylopoda
ADLOORWW woolward
ADLOPRWY wordplay
ADLOPSUU paludous
ADLOQSUW old squaw
oldsquaw
ADLORRWW World War
ADLORSTW draw lots
last word
ADLORSWW sword-law
ADLORTWY towardly
ADLOSSTW St Oswald
ADLPRUWY upwardly
ADMMMSUU ad summum
ADMMNOOS doomsman
ADMMNORU Omdurman
ADMMNTUU mutandum
ADMMRSSU Drum Mass
ADMNNORY monandry
ADMNNOSU soundman
ADMNNOTU notandum
ADMNOOOT odontoma
ADMNOORS doorsman
doors-man
madroños
Rosamond
ADMNOOST mastodon
ADMNOOSW woodsman
ADMNOOSX Saxondom
ADMNOPTW tamp down
ADMNORRU round-arm
ADMNORSU Rosamund
ADMNORSW sandworm
swordman
ADMNORWW warm down
warm-down
ADMNPPSU sandpump
ADMOORRW wardroom
ADMOPPPU poppadum
ADMORRSW sword-arm
ADNNORTY dynatron
ADNNOTWW want down
ADNOOPRS spadroon
ADNOOPRV Andropov
ADNOOQRU quadroon
ADNOORST tornados
ADNOORTY donatory
ADNOOSVW advowson
ADNOPRUW draw upon
ADNOPRUY pay round
ADNOPSSW pass down
ADNOQRSU squadron
ADNORSTW Dr Watson
sandwort
ADNORSXY sardonyx
ADNORTTU Turandot
ADNORTUW untoward
ADNORWWY wanwordy
ADNOSTTU outstand
stand out
standout
ADNRSSUW sunwards
ADOOPPRU pauropod
ADOOPRRT trapdoor
ADOOPRST post road
ADOOPRSU sauropod
ADOOPSWW wood wasp
ADOPPPYY Poppy Day
ADOPPRST Stoppard
ADOPRRWW word wrap
ADOPRSSW password
ADOPSSSU soapsuds
ADORRSTU dartrous
ADORRSTY dry-roast
ADORSTUW outwards
ADORSTUY sudatory
ADORTUVY advoutry
ADPRRTUY purtrayd
ADRSSTTU stardust
ADSSTUWY sawdusty
AEEEEGLY eagle eye
AEEEELRS releasee
AEEEFGRT great fee
AEEEFMRS seamfree
AEEEFMRT meat-free
AEEEFRRW freeware
AEEEFRTY aftereye
AEEEGGLU lee gauge
AEEEGGNR re-engage
AEEEGHLT The Eagle

AEEEGLLS legalese
AEEEGLMR Meleager
AEEEGLNR generale
AEEEGLRT eglatere
regelate
relegate
AEEEGLRV leverage
AEEEGLSV selvagee
AEEEGLTV vegelate
AEEEGNPR pea-green
AEEEGNRS sea green
sea-green
AEEEGNRT generate
green tea
renegate
teenager
AEEEGNTW tweenage
AEEEGRST steerage
AEEEGRSW sewerage
AEEEGTTV vegetate
AEEEHLRT ethereal
AEEEHLTW wheat eel
AEEEHMPR ephemera
AEEEHMRS same here
AEEEHNRS enhearse
AEEEHRRS rehearse
AEEEHRRT reheater
AEEEHRST shea tree
AEEEHSTT aesthete
AEEEIKLR Lake Erie
AEEEIMNX examinee
AEEEJNRY Jane Eyre
AEEEJNTT jeanette✧
AEEEKKPS keepsake
AEEEKLNS snake eel
AEEEKLRY Lake Eyre
AEEEKMSY make eyes
AEEEKNRW weakener
AEEEKPRT peat-reek
AEEELLPP appellee
AEEELLST telesale
AEEELLSV sea level
AEEELMRT meal-tree
AEEELNOR Eleanore
AEEELNPS Nepalese
AEEELNRS ens reale
AEEELNRV venereal
AEEELNST selenate
AEEELPRR repealer✧
AEEELPRS eel-spear
AEEELPRY pearl-eye
AEEELPST paste-eel
AEEELQSU sequelae
AEEELRRS releaser
AEEELRRV revealer
AEEELRST teaseler
AEEELRSW weaseler
AEEELRTX axle-tree
AEEELSSS easeless
AEEELSTW sweet ale
wet lease
wet-lease
AEEELSVY eye-salve
AEEEMMRT metamere
AEEEMNRT Nemertea
AEEEMNST easement
AEEEMPRS permease
AEEEMPRT permeate
AEEENNRV venerean
AEEENPTT patentee
AEEENRST serenate
AEEENRTT enterate
AEEENRTV enervate
venerate
AEEEPPRS Praesepe
AEEEPRRT pear-tree
repartee
repeater
AEEEPSTW sweet pea
AEEERRST arrestee
AEEERSST esterase
tesserae
AEEERTWY eye-water
AEEFFKNR frank-fee
AEEFFLLR free fall
free-fall
AEEFFLOV leave off
AEEFFLRT tafferel
AEEFFNRT afferent
AEEFGILN Fine Gael
AEEFGILR filagree
AEEFGILT get a life
AEEFGINR Faringee
AEEFGINT gate-fine
AEEFGIRR ferriage
AEEFGLLS false leg
AEEFGLSU fuselage
AEEFGPRS Graf Spee
AEEFHLLS selfheal
AEEFHLMS false hem
AEEFHLNW fan wheel
AEEFHLST self-hate
AEEFHRTY feathery
AEEFHRVY hay fever
AEEFHSTT the Fates
AEEFIINR inferiae
AEEFIKLL leaflike
AEEFIKRT take fire
AEEFIKRW wakerife
AEEFIKTV take five
AEEFILLR real life
AEEFILMN filename
AEEFILMT metafile
AEEFILNR flânerie
AEEFILNV vine-leaf
AEEFILPR pea-rifle
AEEFILRS fire sale
serafile
AEEFILRT frailtee
AEEFIPSW spaewife
AEEFKMNT fakement
AEEFKOPR forepeak
AEEFLLMR femerall
AEEFLLMT flamelet
AEEFLLNV evenfall
AEEFLLRW farewell
AEEFLLSS leafless
AEEFLMNR male-fern
AEEFLMOS fleasome
AEEFLMSS fameless
selfsame
AEEFLNOS nose-leaf
AEEFLNRU funereal
AEEFLORS rose leaf
AEEFLORV overleaf
AEEFLOSW see a wolf
AEEFLOTV love-feat
AEEFLRRR referral
AEEFLRSS fearless✧
AEEFLRTW weel-far't
AEEFMNOR foremean
forename
AEEFMORS fearsome
AEEFMORT free atom
AEEFMRRT tree farm
AEEFMRTY femetary
AEEFNRST fastener
fenestra
AEEFNRTT fattener
AEEFNSSS safeness
AEEFOSTU feateous
AEEFRSTU features
AEEFTTUV fauvette
AEEGGHIW weighage
AEEGGINR agreeing
AEEGGIRV aggrieve
AEEGGKOR oak egger
AEEGGLOU aeglogue
AEEGGLPP egg-apple
AEEGGNNR gangrene
AEEGGNOS gasogene
AEEGGNOZ gazogene
AEEGGPRU puggaree
AEEGHHTU The Hague
AEEGHILN Hegelian
AEEGHIRT heritage
AEEGHLLT hell-gate
AEEGHLOT helotage
AEEGHLRS shearleg
AEEGHLRW ragwheel
AEEGHMOP home page
AEEGHMPR grapheme
AEEGHNRS shagreen
AEEGHPRT the grape
AEEGHRRT gatherer
regather
AEEGHRTT the great
AEEGIINR aegirine
AEEGIIRT aegirite
AEEGILLS legalise
AEEGILLZ legalize
AEEGILMN liegeman
AEEGILNR algerine✧

AEEGILNS ensilage
AEEGILNT galenite
gelatine
get a line
legatine
AEEGILNU in league
AEEGILNV inveagle
AEEGILPR perigeal
AEEGILRS gaselier
AEEGILRT litreage
AEEGILST elegiast
AEEGILSY lay siege
AEEGILTV levigate
AEEGIMNR germaine✧
AEEGIMNT geminate
AEEGIMRT emigrate
remigate
AEEGINPR perigean
AEEGINRR regainer
AEEGINRS gesneria
AEEGINRT enargite
gratinée
AEEGINSS assignee
AEEGINST sagenite
AEEGINSV envisage
AEEGINTV agentive
gate-vein
negative
AEEGINTX exigeant
AEEGIPQU equipage
AEEGIRSS greasies
AEEGIRTT aigrette
AEEGIRTV ergative
AEEGKRWY Greek way
AEEGKSTY key stage
AEEGLLNR allergen
AEEGLLOW eagle-owl
AEEGLMOV love game
AEEGLMRT telegram
AEEGLMRY meagrely
AEEGLNNO Angeleno
AEEGLNNR enlargen
AEEGLNNT entangle
AEEGLNOS gasolene
AEEGLNOT elongate
AEEGLNRR enlarger
AEEGLNST Gnetales
AEEGLNSY Anglesey
AEEGLNVY evangely
AEEGLORT alter ego
AEEGLOST segolate
AEEGLRRY Earl Grey
AEEGLRSS eelgrass
gearless
largesse
AEEGLRSY grey seal
AEEGLRTU regulate
AEEGLRUX exergual
AEEGLSST gateless
AEEGLSSW wageless
AEEGLSSY eyeglass
glass eye
AEEGLTTU tutelage
AEEGLTUV evulgate
AEEGMMOS gamesome
AEEGMNNR green man
AEEGMNOR argemone
AEEGMNRS agrémens
AEEGMNRT agrément
AEEGMNSS gameness
AEEGMNTT tegmenta
AEEGMNTZ gazement
AEEGMOST somegate
AEEGMRRS Grasmere
AEEGMRRY grey mare
AEEGMRSS mess gear
AEEGMRST gamester
gas meter
AEEGMSSS messages
AEEGMSSU messuage
AEEGNNNO enneagon
AEEGNNRT generant
AEEGNNRU enraunge
AEEGNNRV engraven
AEEGNNSS sans gêne
AEEGNOST Stone Age
stone-age✧
AEEGNPRS sap-green
AEEGNRRT étranger
AEEGNRRV engraver
AEEGNRRY green ray
AEEGNRST estrange
segreant
sergeant
sternage
AEEGNRSV nerve gas
AEEGNRTU gauntree
AEEGNRWY green way
AEEGNRYZ Zane Grey
AEEGNSSS sageness
AEEGNSUY Guyanese
AEEGNTTV vegetant
AEEGOPRV overpage
AEEGORSY easy-goer
AEEGORTT great toe
AEEGPRRS asperger
presager
AEEGPRRT pargeter
AEEGPRSS asperges
AEEGRRRT regrater
AEEGRSST Argestes
AEEGRSSW sewer gas
AEEGRSTT greatest
AEEGRSTW strewage
AEEGSSTW sweet gas
AEEHHHNT heath-hen
AEEHHHSS hasheesh
AEEHHIKZ Hezekiah
AEEHHIMN Nehemiah
AEEHHLNZ hazel hen
AEEHHNST ensheath
heathens
AEEHHOOP pahoehoe
AEEHHORT the Horae
AEEHHRTY heathery
AEEHHSST the Ashes
AEEHIJMR Jeremiah
AEEHIKRS shikaree
AEEHILNP elaphine
AEEHILRS shiralee
AEEHILRT etherial
AEEHILSW sei whale
AEEHILTW white ale
AEEHILVY lie heavy
AEEHIMPT epithema
AEEHIMPU Euphemia
AEEHIMTT hematite
AEEHINPS Ephesian
AEEHINRS an-heires
inhearse
AEEHINRT atherine
AEEHINTT Theatine
AEEHIPRS Pharisee
AEEHIPST aphetise
hepatise
AEEHIPTT hepatite
AEEHIPTZ aphetize
hepatize
AEEHIRST hearties
AEEHIRSV shivaree
AEEHIRTU Eutheria
AEEHISST esthesia
AEEHISTT athetise
hesitate
AEEHISTV heaviest
AEEHISTW White Sea
AEEHITTZ athetize
AEEHKLLR rakehell
AEEHKLLU keelhaul
AEEHKLNT Kathleen
AEEHLLRS ear-shell
AEEHLLRT all there
hall tree
AEEHLLSS seashell
AEEHLMNW wheelman
AEEHLMNY hymeneal
AEEHLMOS healsome
AEEHLMPT helpmate
AEEHLNPT elephant
AEEHLNRT leathern
AEEHLNSS haleness
AEEHLNST St Helena
AEEHLNTV halve-net
AEEHLNVY heavenly
AEEHLOPT peat-hole
AEEHLORV overhale
AEEHLORW Earl Howe
AEEHLOSU alehouse
AEEHLPPT the Apple
AEEHLPRT pleather
The Pearl
AEEHLPST pleaseth
AEEHLPTT telepath

AEEHLRST halteres
leathers
AEEHLRTT heartlet
AEEHLRTY leathery
AEEHLSST hateless
the seals
AEEHLSTW what else?
AEEHLTTY ethylate
AEEHMMRR hammerer
AEEHMNNY hymenean
AEEHMNRT three-man
AEEHMNTX exanthem
AEEHMPSS emphases
AEEHMRTY erythema
AEEHMTUX exhumate
AEEHNNSS sneeshan
AEEHNNTX xanthene
AEEHNNVW New Haven
Newhaven
AEEHNOPR earphone
AEEHNPST stephane
AEEHNRST hastener
AEEHNRSU unhearse
AEEHNRTT haterent
threaten
AEEHNRTU urethane
AEEHNRTW waterhen
wreathen
AEEHNRWY anywhere
AEEHNSSS Esha Ness
AEEHNSTU uneathes
AEEHNSTW enswathe
AEEHOPRT ephorate
AEEHORRV overhear
AEEHORSS seahorse
seashore
AEEHORTV overheat
AEEHOSTU tea house
AEEHPRRS rephrase
AEEHPRST rap sheet
spreathe
AEEHPSTY pay-sheet
AEEHRRTU urethrae
AEEHRRTW wreather
AEEHRTVW whatever
AEEHRTWY three-way
AEEHSTVW The Waves
AEEHTVWY heavy wet
AEEIILLV live a lie
AEEIIMRT métairie
AEEIKKLM make like
AEEIKKLW likewake
AEEIKLMU leukemia
AEEIKLNW wine lake
AEEIKLOS Leo Esaki
AEEIKLPT tapelike
AEEIKLVW wavelike
AEEIKMMR merimake
AEEIKMMT make time
AEEIKMNT ketamine
AEEIKNRT ankerite
kreatine
AEEIKPTT keep at it
AEEIKRST take rise
AEEILLNT tenaille
AEEILLVX live axle
AEEILMMN melamine
AEEILMMT mealtime
AEEILMNS Milanese
AEEILMNT melanite
AEEILMRS measlier
AEEILMRT eremital
materiel
matériel
realtime
AEEILMSV malvesie
AEEILMTZ metalize
AEEILNNS selenian
AEEILNPR perineal
AEEILNPS penalise
sepaline
AEEILNPT petaline
tapeline
AEEILNPZ penalize
AEEILNRT elaterin
entailer
treenail
AEEILNRV Verlaine
AEEILNSV Vaseline®
AEEILNTV elvanite
ventaile
AEEILORT aerolite
AEEILOTT etiolate
AEEILPPP apple-pie
AEEILPPS seal-pipe
AEEILPPT pie plate
AEEILPRS espalier
pearlies
AEEILPRT pearlite
AEEILPST please it
AEEILPSW palewise
AEEILQSU equalise
AEEILQUX exequial
AEEILQUZ equalize
AEEILRRS realiser
AEEILRRT retailer
AEEILRRZ realizer
AEEILRST earliest
AEEILRSV velarise
AEEILRTT laterite
literate
AEEILRTV levirate
relative
AEEILRVW liveware
reviewal
AEEILRVZ velarize
AEEILSVW alewives
AEEILTTV levitate
AEEILTXX tax exile
AEEIMMNT mean time
meantime
AEEIMNNV Menevian
AEEIMNRT antimere
AEEIMNRX examiner
AEEIMNST seminate
AEEIMNUV mauveine
AEEIMORV Aviemore
AEEIMOSS ameioses
AEEIMRST reamiest
AEEIMRTV viameter
AEEIMSTT estimate
étatisme
meatiest
AEEIMSTW teamwise
AEEINNRR inner ear
AEEINNRS anserine
AEEINNSS in a sense
AEEINNTV Aventine
Venetian
AEEINPRT aperient
AEEINPRV pea-viner
AEEINPSS sea snipe
AEEINPTT pianette
AEEINRRT Eritrean
rain tree
retainer
AEEINRST arsenite
resinate
sin-eater
stearine
Teresina
AEEINRSU Irenaeus
AEEINSSS easiness
AEEINSSV vainesse
AEEINSSW sea swine
AEEINSTT anisette
tetanise
AEEINSVW sine wave
AEEINTTZ tetanize
AEEIOOPP epopoeia
AEEIORST etaerios
Oresteia
AEEIPPST appetise
AEEIPPSU eupepsia
AEEIPPTT appetite
AEEIPPTZ appetize
AEEIPRRR rare-ripe
repairer
AEEIPRTV perviate
AEEIPSST epitases
AEEIQTUV equative
AEEIRRTT retraite
AEEIRSTT treatise
AEEIRSTW as it were
AEEIRSVV aversive
AEEISTTT étatiste
steatite
AEEISTTV estivate
AEEITTUX eutaxite
AEEITUVX exuviate
AEEJLLSY sea jelly
AEEJLNPT jet plane
jetplane

AEEJLOSU jealouse
AEEJLRVW jaw lever
AEEJNRST serjeant
AEEJOPRT pejorate
AEEJRTTW water-jet
AEEKKLWY lykewake
AEEKKPSY keepsaky
AEEKLLNY Allen key
Keneally
AEEKLLPU Paul Klee
AEEKLLST skeletal
AEEKLMMU Mameluke
AEEKLMOP meal-poke
AEEKLMRT telemark
AEEKLMSS makeless
AEEKLPTY key-plate
AEEKLSSW wakeless
AEEKLSTY eyestalk
AEEKMNSW man-weeks
AEEKMORV make over
makeover
AEEKMOTY yoke-mate
AEEKMPRW keep warm
AEEKMRRR remarker
AEEKMRRT marketer
AEEKMRSU make sure
AEEKNNNS nankeens
AEEKNOTT take note
AEEKNPST Netspeak
AEEKNPSU sneakeup
AEEKNPSW newspeak✧
AEEKNSSW weakness
AEEKNSTT stake net
AEEKORRV overrake
AEEKORST keratose
kreasote
AEEKORTV overtake
take over
takeover
AEEKQRSU squeaker
AEEKRRST streaker
AEEKRTWY water key
AEELLLTT telltale
AEELLMMS mamselle
AEELLMNW mean well
AEELLMRT Tremella
AEELLMYY all my eye
AEELLNOT let alone
let-alone
AEELLNOV novellae
AEELLOTT allottee
AEELLPTT platelet
AEELLPTY teleplay
AEELLRRT terrella
AEELLRTW wall tree
AEELLSST satelles
tessella
AEELLSSZ zealless
AEELLSTT stellate
AEELLSWY weaselly
AEELLTVV valvelet

AEELMMNT Emmental
AEELMMNU Emmanuel
AEELMMTU malemute
AEELMNOS sea lemon
AEELMNOT lemon tea
AEELMNPS ensample
AEELMNSS lameness
maleness
maneless
nameless
AEELMNST steelman
AEELMNSU Menelaus
AEELMNTT mantelet
AEELMNTV lavement
AEELMORY moray eel
AEELMOTT matelote
AEELMPRT palm tree
AEELMPRX exemplar
AEELMPRY empyreal
AEELMPTT palmette
template
AEELMSSS seamless
AEELMSST mateless
meatless
tameless
AEELNNRT lanneret
AEELNNSS leanness
AEELNOPR peroneal
AEELNOPT antelope
AEELNORU aleurone
AEELNPPR en rappel
AEELNPPS spalpeen
AEELNPQU Palenque
AEELNPRS laser pen
AEELNPSS paleness
AEELNPST steel pan
AEELNQSU squalene
AEELNRSS realness
AEELNRSV enslaver
AEELNRTV levanter✧
relevant
AEELNRTX external
AEELNSST lateness
AEELNSSV vaneless
AEELNSWY Wesleyan
AEELNTUV eventual
AEELNTVY ventayle
AEELOPQU à l'époque
AEELOPRV overleap
AEELORRS releasor
AEELORRT Al Oerter
AEELORST oleaster
AEELORTT tolerate
AEELORTV elevator
AEELORTW toleware
AEELOSTV love seat
AEELOTTT teetotal
AEELOTTW tea towel
AEELOTUV leave out
AEELPRRS relapser
AEELPRRT palterer

AEELPRSU pleasure
AEELPRSV vesperal
AEELPRTU tape-lure
AEELPRTY pterylae
AEELPSST spätlese✧
tapeless
AEELPSTV septleva
AEELPTTU Paulette
AEELPTTW wet plate
AEELQRSU squealer
AEELQSTU L'Estaque
AEELRRSV reversal
slaverer
AEELRRTU ureteral
AEELRRTV traveler
AEELRSST tearless
tesseral
AEELRSSW wareless
AEELRSTT Letraset®
AEELRSTU resalute
AEELRSTW slew rate
AEELRSTY easterly
AEELRSVY aversely
AEELRVWY Waverley
AEELSSST sateless
seatless
AEELSSVW waveless
AEEMMNRS meresman
AEEMMNRT meter man
AEEMMNTZ mazement
AEEMMSST messmate
AEEMNNOT mean-tone
AEEMNNRT remanent
AEEMNNSS meanness
AEEMNORV overname
AEEMNORZ armozeen
AEEMNPRT peterman
peter-man
AEEMNPRY empyrean
AEEMNPTV pavement
AEEMNQUY May queen
AEEMNRSU username
AEEMNRSV verse-man
AEEMNRSW Answer Me
menswear
AEEMNRTU numerate
AEEMNRTV averment
AEEMNRUV maneuver
AEEMNRVY everyman✧
AEEMNSSS sameness
AEEMNSST tameness
AEEMNSSX Essex Man
AEEMNSTU mansuete
AEEMORST Masorete
AEEMORSU mouse-ear
AEEMOSSU sea mouse
AEEMPPRR pamperer
AEEMPRRT tamperer
AEEMPRSU Serapeum
AEEMPRTT attemper
AEEMPSTW swap meet

Words marked ✧ can also be spelled with one or more capital letters

AEEMQRRU	remarque
AEEMQTTU	maquette
AEEMRRST	remaster
	streamer
AEEMRRSU	measurer
AEEMRSSS	Ramesses
AEEMRSST	masseter
	seamster
AEEMRSSU	measures
	reassume
AEEMRSTT	teamster
AEEMRSTW	stemware
AEEMRSVY	very same
AEEMSSSU	masseuse
AEEMSSTT	Ames test
AEEMSSTU	meatuses
AEEMSTTU	amusette
AEENNNPS	Sean Penn
AEENNORS	Roseanne
AEENNPRY	Pyrenean
AEENNRSS	nearness
AEENNRTU	enaunter
AEENNRTV	revenant
AEENNRUX	annexure
AEENNSSS	saneness
AEENNSST	neatness
AEENNSTT	se-tenant
AEENOORT	aerotone
AEENOPPT	not a peep
AEENOPRS	personae
AEENOPRU	European
AEENOPRV	Eva Perón
AEENOPST	pea-stone
AEENORRS	reasoner
AEENORSS	seasoner
AEENORST	resonate
AEENORTV	overneat
	renovate
AEENORVW	ovenware
AEENOSTX	axe-stone
	stone axe
AEENPPRT	Peter Pan
AEENPPTT	appetent
AEENPQTU	pétanque
AEENRRRW	warrener
AEENRRSS	rareness
AEENRRSW	answerer
	reanswer
AEENRRTT	natterer
AEENRRTV	taverner
AEENRSSS	searness
AEENRSST	assenter
	sarsenet
AEENRSTT	seat rent
AEENRSTU	Sauterne
AEENRSVW	never-was
AEENRTTV	antevert
AEENRTTX	externat
	extranet
AEENRTTY	entreaty
AEENRTUV	aventure
AEEOPRRT	paterero
	perorate
AEEOPRST	protease
	soap tree
AEEOPRSW	sea power
AEEOPRTT	operetta
AEEOPRTW	power tea
AEEORRST	ore-stare
AEEORRSU	rearouse
AEEORRSV	Averroës
	sea rover
AEEORRSW	sowarree
AEEORRTV	over rate
	overrate
AEEORRTZ	zero-rate
AEEORRVV	rave over
AEEORRVW	overwear
AEEORRVY	overyear
AEEORSSV	over seas
	overseas
AEEORSTT	sea otter
AEEORSTU	Euroseat
AEEORSVY	easy over
AEEORTTX	Taxotere®
AEEOSTTU	tease out
AEEPPRRR	preparer
AEEPPRSU	à peu près
AEEPRRRT	parterre
AEEPRRTT	patterer
AEEPRRTU	aperture
AEEPRSSS	Passeres
AEEPRSSU	sea purse
AEEPRSTU	superate
	upas-tree
AEEPSSWW	sweep-saw
AEEQRRUV	quaverer
AEERRRST	arrester
	rearrest
AEERRSST	asserter
	reassert
AEERRSSU	reassure
AEERRSTU	treasure
AEERRSTV	traverse
AEERRSTW	sewer rat
AEERSSSS	reassess
AEERSSST	see stars
AEERSTTT	attester
AEERTTTZ	terzetta
AEERVWYY	everyway
AEFFFLOR	flare off
AEFFGILR	fire-flag
AEFFGOST	off-stage
AEFFGRSU	suffrage
AEFFHIKY	kaffiyeh
AEFFHILL	half-life
AEFFHKOS	off-shake
	shake off
AEFFIILR	fife rail
AEFFILLT	flat file
AEFFILRT	life raft
AEFFILUV	effluvia
AEFFIMRR	affirmer
	reaffirm
AEFFKLRU	freakful
AEFFKOST	stake off
AEFFLNOW	waffle on
AEFFLNTU	affluent
AEFFLORU	four-leaf
AEFFLOSS	off-sales
AEFFLOVV	valve off
AEFFLSTU	feastful
	sufflate
AEFFMRSU	earmuffs
AEFFNNSS	naffness
AEFFNORT	affronté
AEFFOPRT	taper off
AEFFORST	afforest
AEFFORSW	swear off
AEFFOSTV	stave off
AEFFRTTU	tartuffe✧
AEFGHIMS	game fish
AEFGHINR	hang fire
	hangfire
AEFGHIST	sea-fight
AEFGHITT	tea fight
AEFGHMOR	hog-frame
AEFGHTTU	fughetta
AEFGIIRS	gasifier
AEFGILNR	finagler
AEFGIMTU	fumigate
AEFGINST	feasting
AEFGINTU	fantigue
AEFGIORS	foie gras
AEFGIRRU	argufier
AEFGIRTU	figurate
	fruitage
AEFGISTU	fatigues
AEFGJRRZ	J G Frazer
AEFGLLOP	flagpole
AEFGLLPU	full-page
AEFGLMNU	flame gun
	fugleman
AEFGLMOP	megaflop
AEFGLNOR	angle for
AEFGLNSS	fangless
AEFGLOPR	leapfrog
AEFGLORU	Laforgue
AEFGLORW	garefowl
AEFGLRTU	grateful
AEFGMNOR	forgeman
AEFGMNRT	fragment
AEFGNNOT	fontange
AEFGNORT	frontage
AEFGOOPT	footpage
AEFGOORT	footgear
AEFGOPRX	fox-grape
AEFGOSSU	fougasse
AEFHHLOS	half-hose
AEFHIIST	Shafiite
AEFHIKLP	half-pike
AEFHIKNY	hay knife
AEFHIKRS	freakish

AEFHIKSW weakfish
AEFHILLN fellahin
AEFHILLT tefillah
AEFHILMS fishmeal
AEFHILMT half-time
AEFHILNW fin whale
AEFHILOR forhaile
AEFHILOX hexafoil
AEFHILPP half-pipe
AEFHILSZ half-size
AEFHIRRT The Friar
AEFHLLOS half-sole
AEFHLMRT half-term
AEFHLMSU shameful
AEFHLNOT half-note
half-tone
AEFHLPST half step
AEFHLRTY fatherly
AEFHLTTX half-text
AEFHLTWY wheat fly
AEFHMMOR home farm
AEFHMNRS freshman
AEFHMORS for shame
AEFHNRSW fernshaw
AEFHOORT hare-foot
AEFHORST sea froth
AEFHORTX fox-earth
AEFHRSTT farthest
AEFIIKLW waiflike
AEFIILLN nail file
AEFIILNS finalise
AEFIILNZ finalize
AEFIILRR air rifle
AEFIILRS Fair Isle
Fair-Isle
AEFIIMNS infamise
AEFIIMNZ infamize
AEFIIMRR Frimaire
AEFIINRS Friesian
AEFIINST fainites
AEFIIPRT aperitif
apéritif
AEFIIRRT ratifier
AEFIIRST Rifaites
AEFIITVX fixative
AEFIJLRZ jalfrezi
AEFIKKLV Keflavik
AEFIKLPR Parklife
AEFIKLRW fire-walk
AEFIKLTY fly a kite
AEFIKMNN knife-man
AEFIKMRR firemark
AEFIKRUW waukrife
AEFILLLN fall line
AEFILLNT flatline
AEFILLOS leaf soil
AEFILLRW firewall
AEFILLST ill-faste
AEFILLSV all-fives
AEFILMNR inflamer
rifleman
AEFILMNS misfalne
AEFILMNT filament
AEFILMTY femality
AEFILNNR infernal
AEFILNOT olefiant
AEFILNPS lifespan
AEFILNPY play fine
AEFILNRT inflater
AEFILNRU fräulein✧
AEFILOOR aerofoil
AEFILOPR fire opal
AEFILORS foresail
AEFILPSW swap file
AEFILRSV F R Leavis
AEFILRTT filtrate
AEFILRTU filature
AEFILRUW weariful
AEFILSTU fistulae
AEFILSTV festival
AEFILSTW flatwise
AEFILTUU fauteuil
AEFIMMMR mammifer
AEFIMNST manifest
AEFIMORR aeriform
AEFIMORT for a time
formiate
AEFIMRRS firearms
AEFIMRRW firmware
AEFINNSS fainness
AEFINOPR pinafore
AEFINORS farinose
AEFINRSS fairness
sanserif
AEFINRST fine arts
AEFIOPRR Porifera
AEFIORRT Rotifera
AEFIORTV favorite
AEFIPRRT firetrap
AEFIRRRY farriery
AEFIRSTW wastrife
AEFIRTTU fruit tea
AEFIRTUX fixature
AEFJMOSX James Fox
AEFKLLOT folk tale
AEFKLMRY flymaker
AEFKLNRU Faulkner
AEFKLNSY snake fly
AEFKLOTU flake out
AEFKLRUW wreakful
AEFKLSTT talkfest
AEFKNORR fore-rank
AEFKNORS forsaken
AEFKOPRS forspeak
AEFKORRS forsaker
AEFKORRW workfare
AEFKORTU freak out
freak-out
AEFLLLOR leaf roll
AEFLLMMU flammule
AEFLLMNU full name
AEFLLNNS flannels
AEFLLNNU unfallen
AEFLLNRY fernally
AEFLLORV fall over
overfall
AEFLLPTU plateful
AEFLLRUX flexural
AEFLLSSW flawless
AEFLLSTY festally
AEFLMNOT matfelon
AEFLMORU formulae
fumarole
AEFLMOSS foamless
AEFLMOTU flame out
flameout
AEFLMPRR frampler
AEFLNNOT fontanel
AEFLNNTY fentanyl
AEFLNOPR foreplan
AEFLNOPT pantofle
AEFLNORS farnesol
AEFLNOSW snow flea
AEFLNRTU flaunter
AEFLNSST flatness
AEFLNSUY unsafely
AEFLOORS sea floor
AEFLOPPT petaflop
AEFLOPRT teraflop
AEFLOPST leaf spot
AEFLORRW elf-arrow
AEFLORST forestal
AEFLORSU fusarole
AEFLORTU flare-out
AEFLORTW fleawort
AEFLOSSU fossulae
AEFLOSTT falsetto
AEFLPPRY flypaper
AEFLPSUU pauseful
AEFLRSTT fattrels
AEFLRTTU aflutter
AEFLRTTY flattery
flat tyre
AEFLRTWY water fly
AEFLSSTU flatuses
AEFLSTTT flattest
AEFLSTTU tasteful
AEFLSTUW wasteful
AEFMNNOT font name
AEFMNORW men-of-war
AEFMNRRY ferryman
AEFMORRT reformat
AEFMORST foremast
mort-safe
AEFMORVW waveform
AEFMOSTT soft meat
AEFMOSTU fat mouse
AEFNNSTU unfasten
AEFNOPRR profaner
AEFNORRW forewarn
AEFNORRY yearn for
AEFNORST seafront
AEFNOSTW feast-won

AEFNPRST far-spent
AEFNRRST transfer
AEFNRRTU run after
AEFNRRUY funerary
AEFNRSTU aftersun
AEFNSSST fastness
AEFNSTUY unsafety
AEFOORTW footwear
AEFOPRRT forepart
raft-rope
AEFOPRST forepast
AEFOPTUU pot-au-feu
AEFORRSW forswear
AEFORRUV favourer
AEFORRWY forweary
AEFORSTW forwaste
software
AEFORSTY forestay
AEFOSSWY fosse way✧
AEFOSTUU featuous
AEFOSTUV voutsafe
AEFPRSST pressfat
AEGGGINN engaging
AEGGGLSS egg glass
AEGGHHIR high gear
high-gear
AEGGHMSU meshugga
AEGGHOPY geophagy
AEGGHORU roughage
AEGGILLR grillage
AEGGILMN gleaming
AEGGILNN gleaning
AEGGILOT Taleggio
AEGGILOU oil gauge
AEGGIMRT gregatim
AEGGINNV avenging
AEGGINOR Georgian
Georgina
AEGGINOS sea-going
AEGGINST Gigantes
AEGGIOPR arpeggio
geropiga
AEGGIRRU garrigue
AEGGIRWY earwiggy
AEGGLNOT get along
AEGGLNPT eggplant
AEGGLORY gargoyle
AEGGLPUW wage plug
AEGGLRST straggle
AEGGMORR ergogram
AEGGMORT mortgage
AEGGNORV overgang
AEGGNORW waggoner✧
AEGGNRST gangster
AEGGNRTU great gun
AEGGNSST ants'-eggs
AEGGOPRU age group
groupage
AEGGRSST staggers
AEGHHILS Ashleigh
AEGHHISS high seas
AEGHHORS shear-hog
AEGHHORT earth-hog
AEGHILLM megillah
AEGHILLS shigella
AEGHILMT megalith
AEGHILNR narghile
nargileh
AEGHILNS shealing
AEGHILNT atheling
AEGHILPS shagpile
AEGHILRT litharge
thirlage
AEGHIMMT gimme hat
AEGHIMPS mageship
AEGHINNT naething
AEGHINPT night-ape
AEGHINRS shearing
AEGHINRT ingather
AEGHINRV Havering
AEGHINRY Haringey
AEGHINTT gnathite
AEGHIORT eight-oar
AEGHIPPR epigraph
pie graph
AEGHIPRT graphite
AEGHLLOT all the go
AEGHLLSS gas shell
AEGHLMTU the mulga
AEGHLNTT at length
AEGHLOPY hypogeal
AEGHLOSV go halves
AEGHLOSW show a leg
AEGHLOUW Lough Awe
AEGHLRTU laughter
AEGHLRTY lethargy
AEGHMNOP phenogam
AEGHMOPT apothegm
AEGHMOSW game show
AEGHNNOR hanger-on
AEGHNNST hangnest
AEGHNNSY Shenyang
AEGHNOPT heptagon
pathogen
AEGHNOPY hypogean
AEGHNORT horn gate
on the rag
AEGHNORV hang over
hangover
overhang
AEGHNOTW the Wagon
AEGHNPSW spanghew
AEGHNRSS gnashers
AEGHOPPR prophage
AEGHOPPY apophyge
AEGHOPXY exophagy
AEGHORSS go shares
AEGHORST shortage
AEGHOSTT Tashtego
AEGHPRTU upgather
AEGHRSYY ashy-grey
AEGHRTTU urge that
AEGIILLU aiguille
AEGIILMN e-mailing
AEGIILMR remigial
AEGIILMT age limit
AEGIILNT e-tailing
AEGIILPS Spigelia
AEGIILRT Galtieri
AEGIILTT litigate
AEGIIMNN Geminian
AEGIIMNR imaginer
migraine
AEGIIMNS imagines
AEGIIMNT gain time
AEGIIMTT mitigate
AEGIINNN nennigai
AEGIINNR arginine
Nigerian
AEGIIRRT irrigate
AEGIISTV vestigia
AEGIJRTU Gujerati
AEGIKLNR King Lear
AEGIKLNW weakling
AEGIKMNS skin game
AEGIKMNW make wing
AEGIKMRW wig-maker
AEGIKNNS sneaking
AEGIKNNW wakening
AEGIKNPS speaking
AEGIKNRT retaking
AEGIKNTW take wing
tweaking
AEGILLMS legalism
AEGILLNO goal line
lie along
AEGILLNV vine-gall
AEGILLNY genially
AEGILLPR pillager
AEGILLPS spillage
AEGILLRU guerilla
AEGILLRV all-giver
villager
AEGILLST legalist
stillage
AEGILLSU ill-usage
AEGILLTU ligulate
AEGILLTY legality
AEGILMMR aglimmer
lammiger
AEGILMNR germinal✧
maligner
malinger
AEGILMNS Galenism
AEGILMNT ligament
metaling
AEGILMRS regalism
AEGILMRX lexigram
AEGILNNR learning
AEGILNNT gantline
AEGILNNU ungenial
AEGILNNW weanling
AEGILNNY yeanling

AEGILNOR	geraniol
	regional
AEGILNOS	gasoline
AEGILNOT	gelation
	legation
	Lion Gate
AEGILNPR	pearling
AEGILNPS	pleasing
AEGILNRR	gnarlier
AEGILNRS	salering
	Salinger
	sanglier
	seal ring
	signaler
AEGILNRT	integral
	triangle
AEGILNRX	relaxing
AEGILNRY	layering
	yearling
AEGILNSS	gainless
	glassine
AEGILNST	eastling
	Galenist
	genitals
	stealing
AEGILNSV	Gil Evans
	leavings
	Svengali
AEGILNSW	swealing
AEGILNTV	valeting
AEGILNUV	vaginule
AEGILOPS	spoilage
AEGILOPT	pilotage
AEGILORS	gasolier
	girasole
	seraglio
AEGILPPS	slippage
AEGILPPU	pupil age
	pupilage
AEGILPSU	Pelagius
AEGILPSW	wage slip
AEGILRST	regalist
AEGILRSU	Galerius
AEGILRSY	greasily
AEGILRTT	aglitter
AEGILRTU	Gaultier
	ligature
AEGILRTY	regality
AEGILRVW	lawgiver
AEGILSST	Glassite
AEGILSSU	Gelasius
AEGIMMRS	Grammies
AEGIMNRT	emigrant
AEGIMNRU	geranium
AEGIMNRY	Imre Nagy
AEGIMNSS	gaminess
AEGIMNST	steaming
AEGIMNSV	veganism
AEGIMOPT	magot-pie
AEGIMORR	armigero
AEGIMORW	wagmoire
AEGIMPRU	umpirage
AEGIMQRU	quagmire
AEGIMRRT	ragtimer
AEGIMRST	magister
	sterigma
AEGIMRSV	give arms
AEGIMRTT	Magritte
AEGIMSSU	misusage
AEGIMSTY	Gay Times
AEGINNOT	Antigone
	negation
AEGINNPS	sneaping
AEGINNRS	earnings
AEGINNRV	ravening
AEGINNRY	renaying
	yearning
AEGINNST	steaning
AEGINNSU	sanguine
AEGINOPT	pinotage
AEGINORR	Rogerian
AEGINORS	ignaroes
	organise
AEGINORZ	organize
AEGINOTV	go native
AEGINPPR	papering
AEGINPRT	tapering
AEGINPRY	repaying
AEGINPTY	Egyptian
AEGINRRV	averring
AEGINRSS	assigner
	reassign
AEGINRST	astringe
	ganister
	inert gas
	rangiest
AEGINRSW	swearing
AEGINRTT	treating
AEGINRTV	vintager
AEGINRTW	watering
AEGINRVW	wavering
AEGINRVY	vinegary
AEGINRWY	wearying
AEGINSST	giantess
AEGINSSY	essaying
AEGINSTT	tangiest
AEGINSTU	sautéing
AEGINSTW	sweating
AEGIOPRR	progeria
AEGIORRT	riot gear
AEGIORSV	viragoes
AEGIOSTU	agouties
AEGIOSTX	geotaxis
AEGIPPRT	griptape
AEGIPRTY	pterygia
AEGIPRVY	grape ivy
AEGIQRSU	squirage
AEGIRRTY	argyrite
AEGIRSTT	strigate
AEGIRTTT	great tit
AEGJLTUU	jugulate
AEGKKKNO	angekkok
AEGKLORY	Key Largo
AEGKMNRU	gunmaker
AEGKOPRS	gas poker
AEGKORWW	wage work
AEGLLLMU	glumella
AEGLLLOR	l'allegro
AEGLLLSS	gall-less
AEGLLNOV	longeval
AEGLLNPS	langspel
AEGLLNST	St Gallen
AEGLLOPR	galloper
AEGLLORS	allegros
AEGLLORV	overgall
AEGLLORY	allegory
AEGLLOSS	goalless
AEGLLOST	log-slate
AEGLLOTT	tollgate
AEGLLRVY	gravelly
AEGLLSSU	galluses
AEGLMNNO	mangonel
AEGLMNOT	go mental
AEGLMNOW	leg-woman
AEGLMNTU	gunmetal
AEGLMOTV	megavolt
AEGLMSSU	gaumless
AEGLNNOR	Algernon
AEGLNNPT	plangent
AEGLNNSY	lang syne
AEGLNNTU	untangle
AEGLNOPT	gantlope
AEGLNORV	Lavengro
AEGLNORY	yearlong
AEGLNOST	tangelos
AEGLNOSZ	Gonzales
AEGLNOVW	long-wave
AEGLNPRS	spangler
	sprangle
AEGLNPSS	pangless
AEGLNPST	spanglet
AEGLNRRW	wrangler
AEGLNRST	strangle
AEGLNRSY	larynges
AEGLNRUY	gunlayer
AEGLNTTU	gauntlet
AEGLNTUU	ungulate
AEGLOOOZ	zoogloea
AEGLOOPU	apologue
AEGLOORY	aerology
AEGLOPRW	grow pale
AEGLOPRY	glory-pea
	play-goer
AEGLORSU	glareous
AEGLORTU	outglare
AEGLORTV	travelog
AEGLORTW	waterlog
AEGLORTY	geolatry
AEGLOSSW	galowses
AEGLOSUY	gealousy
AEGLOTUV	tog value
AEGLPPRR	grappler
AEGLPRSU	Spergula

AEGLPSSU	plussage
AEGLRSTU	gestural
AEGLRTUY	argutely
AEGLSTUU	glutaeus
AEGMMNOR	gammoner
AEGMMPRU	Pergamum
AEGMMRRU	rummager
AEGMNNOT	magneton
AEGMNOOT	moon gate
AEGMNOPR	Pergamon
AEGMNORV	mangrove
	venogram
AEGMNORY	rag-money
AEGMNOST	magnetos
AEGMNOTU	Montague
AEGMNOXY	xenogamy
AEGMNRTU	argument
AEGMNSSY	gamyness
AEGMOPRW	gapeworm
AEGMORRW	worm gear
AEGMORSS	gossamer
AEGMPSTU	stumpage
AEGNNOPT	pentagon✧
AEGNNORT	negatron
AEGNNPRT	pregnant
AEGNNRTY	gannetry
AEGNOORS	oreganos
AEGNOPRR	parergon
AEGNORRY	orangery
AEGNORST	ragstone
	stonerag
AEGNORTT	on target
	tetragon
AEGNORTU	outrange
AEGNORTY	negatory
AEGNORUV	vargueño
AEGNOSSX	nox gases
AEGNOTUY	autogeny
AEGNPRSU	spear gun
AEGNPRYY	panegyry
AEGNRRST	stranger
AEGNRSTU	straunge
AEGNRSUZ	sungazer
AEGNRSYY	asynergy
AEGNRTUW	water gun
AEGNSSST	gastness
AEGNSTTZ	Stan Getz
AEGOORSV	voragoes
AEGOOSWY	waygoose
AEGOPPST	stoppage
AEGOPPSU	suppeago
AEGOPRTU	portague
AEGOPSST	gestapos
AEGOPSSU	spousage
AEGOPSTT	gatepost
AEGORRRT	regrator
AEGORRSY	Rose Gray
AEGORRTT	garotter
	garrotte
AEGORSTU	goat's-rue
AEGORTTU	tutorage
AEGORUVY	voyageur
AEGOSSTV	gas stove
AEGPRRSU	spur gear
AEGQRTUU	truquage
AEGRRSSY	rye grass
AEGRRSUV	verrugas
AEGRRTUW	water rug
AEGRSTTY	strategy
AEHHHIST	shehitah
AEHHIKNS	Shekinah
AEHHIMTW	hamewith
AEHHIPSW	peishwah
AEHHISVY	yeshivah
AEHHLLST	the halls
AEHHLNTU	unhealth
AEHHNOPT	Phaethon
AEHHNRSW	hernshaw
AEHHNTTW	what then?
AEHHOPTT	At the Hop
AEHHORST	haroseth
AEHHORTW	Heathrow
AEHHRRST	thrasher
AEHIIKLR	hairlike
AEHIIKRT	terakihi
AEHIIKST	shiitake
AEHIILMO	hemiolia
AEHIILNR	hairline
AEHIIMNT	thiamine
AEHIIMOP	hemiopia
AEHIINNT	ianthine
AEHIINRT	in the air
AEHIINTZ	thiazine
AEHIIOPT	Ethiopia
AEHIIPTX	pixie hat
AEHIIRRW	wire-hair
AEHIIRSS	Irish Sea
AEHIISTV	Shaivite
	Shivaite
AEHIKKLW	hawklike
AEHIKKNN	Häkkinen
AEHIKLLT	lathlike
AEHIKLNP	kephalin
AEHIKLTT	like that
AEHIKLTW	what-like
AEHIKNSS	sneakish
AEHIKNST	heat sink
AEHIKPRS	her paiks
AEHIKPST	take ship
AEHILLNO	nail-hole
AEHILLNT	thalline
AEHILLOS	oil shale
	shale oil
AEHILLOW	whale oil
AEHILMNY	hymenial
AEHILMOT	halimote
AEHILMSW	Lewisham
	limewash
AEHILNOP	aphelion
AEHILNOS	shoe nail
AEHILNOT	Iolanthe
AEHILNRU	inhauler
AEHILNTX	anthelix
AEHILNTZ	zenithal
AEHILOOZ	Heliozoa
AEHILORT	aerolith
AEHILOTZ	thiazole
AEHILOVY	heavy oil
AEHILRSS	hairless
AEHILRST	last heir
AEHILRSV	shrieval
AEHILRTT	The Trial
AEHILRTY	earthily
	heartily
AEHILTWW	Whitelaw
AEHIMMNN	Mannheim
AEHIMMNP	Memphian
AEHIMMNR	hammer in
AEHIMNNU	inhumane
AEHIMNOR	Maori hen
AEHIMNRS	shireman
AEHIMNRT	theramin
AEHIMNSS	shamisen
AEHIMNSU	humanise
AEHIMNTU	inhumate
AEHIMNTW	white man
AEHIMNUZ	humanize
AEHIMPPT	pita-hemp
AEHIMPRS	samphire
	seraphim
AEHIMPRT	teraphim
AEHIMPSS	emphasis
	misshape
AEHIMPST	mateship
	shipmate
AEHIMRRS	marshier
AEHIMRTW	white arm
AEHIMSST	mathesis
AEHIMTTW	what time
AEHINNTX	xanthein
	xanthine
AEHINOPT	The Piano
AEHINOPU	euphonia
AEHINORT	anti-hero
	on the air
AEHINPPY	epiphany✧
AEHINPRS	parishen
	seraphin
	shear pin
AEHINPRT	perianth
AEHINPRX	xeraphin
AEHINPST	thespian✧
AEHINRSV	enravish
	vanisher
AEHINRSW	sherwani
AEHINRTU	haurient
AEHINRTW	in the raw
	tarwhine
	wear thin
AEHINRTZ	Hertzian
AEHINSST	anthesis
AEHINSSV	Shiv Sena
AEHINSSZ	haziness

Words marked ✧ can also be spelled with one or more capital letters

AEHINSTT hesitant
AEHINSTW inswathe
AEHINTTT antithet
AEHINTTW white ant
AEHINTWY in the way
AEHIOPRS aphorise
AEHIOPRU euphoria
AEHIOPRZ aphorize
AEHIORRV overhair
AEHIORSU air-house
AEHIORTU thiourea
AEHIPPRS papisher
sapphire
AEHIPPST peatship
AEHIPRRT rathripe
AEHIPRTT threapit
AEHIPSTT Peshitta
AEHIPSWW washwipe
AEHIPTVY Have Pity!
AEHIRRST trashier
AEHIRRSV ravisher
AEHIRRSY Ayrshire
AEHIRRVV River Váh
AEHIRSTU thesauri
AEHIRSTW waterish
AEHIRSTY hysteria✧
AEHIRTTW white rat
AEHIRTYZ yahrzeit✧
AEHISSSY essayish
AEHISSTU hiatuses
AEHISSVY yeshivas
AEHITWWX white wax
AEHJNNOS johannes
AEHJNORT on the jar
AEHJNRSY Jean Rhys
AEHJPRSW jews'-harp✧
jew's harp
jew's-harp✧
AEHKLLRS ark-shell
AEHKMOPW mopehawk
AEHKNNSU unshaken
AEHKNRST the narks
the ranks
AEHKNSTT Tashkent
AEHKNSWW newshawk
AEHKOSTU shake out
shake-out
AEHLLLTY lethally
AEHLLMOP lamphole
AEHLLNRT enthrall
Hartnell
AEHLLOSY sea holly
AEHLLSWW wash well
AEHLMMNS helmsman
AEHLMMOT meal moth
AEHLMMPP hemp-palm
AEHLMNOO home loan
AEHLMNOT methanol
on the lam
AEHLMNSW Welshman
AEHLMNUY humanely
AEHLMOTT hot metal
hot-metal
AEHLMPPT pamphlet
AEHLMRSS harmless
AEHLMRST thermals
AEHLNPRS shrapnel
AEHLNPTY enthalpy
AEHLNRTU Lutheran
AEHLNSST less than
nathless
AEHLNSTY naythles
AEHLNTUZ hazelnut
AEHLOPRT plethora
AEHLOPTT hotplate
AEHLORSY hoarsely
AEHLORTY the royal
AEHLORUV overhaul
AEHLORYY Holy Year
AEHLPPRT thrapple
AEHLPRSS splasher
AEHLPSST pathless
AEHLPSTU sulphate
AEHLRRTU urethral
AEHLSSTW thawless
AEHLSTTY stealthy
AEHLSTUU the usual
AEHMMRRU Muharrem
AEHMNNPY nymphean
AEHMNOPR morphean
AEHMNOPT on the map
AEHMNORS horseman
shoreman
AEHMNOSU houseman
AEHMNOTT on the mat
AEHMNOTW the woman
AEHMNPRU prehuman
AEHMNPSY sea nymph
AEHMNSTW new maths
AEHMOPRT metaphor
AEHMORST Masoreth
AEHMOSTW somewhat
AEHMPPTU heat pump
AEHMPRST hampster
AEHMPRTT The Tramp
AEHMRRTY rat-rhyme
AEHMRSSY Myra Hess
AEHMSSSU shamuses
AEHMSTTW Matthews
AEHMSTTY amethyst
AEHMSTUV must-have
AEHMSUZZ mezuzahs
AEHNNOPT pantheon✧
AEHNNORV Hannover
AEHNNOTY honey ant
AEHNNPRU nenuphar✧
AEHNNPSU unshapen
AEHNNSUV unshaven
AEHNNSUW unwashen
AEHNOOPT hanepoot
not a hope
AEHNOPPY payphone
AEHNOPRS Orpheans
AEHNOPRT hapteron
AEHNOPST stanhope
Stephano
AEHNOPTY Typhoean
AEHNOPXY xenophya
AEHNOQTU haqueton
AEHNORST North Sea
Sheraton
AEHNORTT Atherton
AEHNOSTV have-nots
AEHNOTWY on the way
AEHNPRTY hen party
AEHNRSSS rashness
AEHNRTTU earth-nut
AEHNSSTT thatness
AEHNSSTU shea nuts
AEHNSSTW whatness
AEHNSTUW unswathe
AEHNSTWW what's new?
AEHNTTWX what next?
AEHOPPRS prophase
AEHOPRST potshare
AEHOPSST pot ashes
pot-ashes
spathose
AEHOPSTT heatspot
AEHOPSTU phase out
taphouse
AEHOPSTW two-phase
AEHOPTVY top-heavy
AEHOQRUU huaquero
AEHORRRT or rather
AEHORRSS rose rash
AEHORRSV overrash
AEHORRSW warhorse
AEHORRTT heart-rot
AEHORSST short sea
AEHORSSW sawhorse
AEHORSTT rheostat
AEHORSTU arthouse
share-out
AEHORSTX thoraxes
AEHORSVW overwash
AEHORSWY horseway
AEHORTTW hot water
AEHOSSTU South Sea
AEHOSTUX house-tax
AEHPPRSU pear-push
AEHPRSST sharp-set
AEHPRSUX haruspex
AEHPRSUY euphrasy
AEHPSSTW The Wasps
AEHQRSSU squasher
AEHRRSTU urethras
AEHRRSTY trashery
AEHRRTTW thwarter
AEHRSTTY shattery
AEIIINTT initiate
AEIIIRRT retiarii
AEIIKLLT tail-like

Words marked ✧ can also be spelled with one or more capital letters

AEIIKLNS	Sikelian
AEIIKLNT	kalinite
AEIIKNRS	kaiserin
AEIIKNSS	akinesis
AEIIKRTY	teriyaki
AEIILLMR	milliare
	Ramillie
AEIILLRV	live-rail
AEIILLTV	illative
AEIILMNN	main line
	mainline
AEIILMNS	alienism
	Milesian
AEIILMPR	imperial
AEIILMRS	Ramilies
AEIILMSS	Islamise
AEIILMST	Islamite
AEIILMSZ	Islamize
AEIILMTT	militate
AEIILNPR	plein-air
AEIILNQU	aquiline
AEIILNRR	airliner
AEIILNRT	air inlet
	inertial
AEIILNRW	wire nail
AEIILNST	alienist
	Latinise
	Taliesin
AEIILNSW	Lewisian
AEIILNTZ	Latinize
AEIILOTT	Italiote
AEIILPPT	tailpipe
AEIILPRT	liparite
	Reptilia
AEIILRST	listeria
AEIILRSV	rivalise
AEIILRTT	literati
AEIILRVZ	rivalize
AEIILSTV	vitalise
AEIILTVZ	vitalize
AEIIMMRT	maritime
AEIIMMSX	maximise
AEIIMMXZ	maximize
AEIIMNSZ	simazine✧
AEIIMNTT	intimate
AEIIMNTU	minutiae
AEIIMNTV	vitamine
AEIIMOSS	ameiosis
AEIIMPRR	impairer
AEIIMRST	seriatim
AEIIMSSX	semi-axis
AEIINNRS	sirenian
AEIINNRT	Neritina
	triennia
AEIINNTV	innative
AEIINPRS	Piranesi
AEIINPST	pianiste
AEIINRRV	riverain
AEIINRSS	airiness
AEIINRST	rainiest
AEIINRSY	yersinia
AEIINRTZ	Nazirite
	triazine
AEIINSST	sanitise
AEIINSTZ	sanitize
AEIINSVV	invasive
AEIINTTT	titanite
AEIINTTU	uintaite
AEIIPRSW	pairwise
AEIIPRTZ	trapezii
AEIIPRZZ	pizzeria
AEIIPSST	epitasis
AEIIRRTT	irritate
AEIIRSST	satirise
	Tiresias
AEIIRSTW	wisteria
AEIIRSTZ	satirize
AEIIRTTT	tritiate
AEIIRTVZ	vizirate
AEIISTVZ	izvestia
AEIITTTV	titivate
AEIITTVV	vitative
AEIJKLMR	Jim Laker
AEIJKLTV	jive talk
AEIJLOSU	jalousie
AEIJLSTU	Julia set
AEIJMNRU	Jean Muir
AEIJMORR	Marjorie
AEIJMORT	Majorite
AEIJORST	jarosite
AEIKKLLW	likewalk
AEIKKLOO	kalookie
AEIKKLPR	parklike
AEIKKLST	take silk
AEIKKLUV	Lake Kivu
AEIKKMNO	kakiemon✧
AEIKKMRT	Kite mark
	Kitemark
	kite-mark
AEIKLMTT	talktime
AEIKLNNP	pannikel
AEIKLNOS	snake-oil
AEIKLNPS	skiplane
AEIKLNRS	near-silk
AEIKLNSS	sealskin
AEIKLNSW	swanlike
AEIKLNSY	sneakily
AEIKLPRT	traplike
AEIKLPSW	wasp-like
AEIKLRST	starlike
AEIKLRTW	wartlike
AEIKLRVY	Valkyrie
AEIKLRWY	Walkyrie
AEIKLSSS	saikless
AEIKMMRT	mark time
AEIKMNPR	pin-maker
AEIKMNST	mankiest
	mistaken
AEIKMPSS	misspeak
AEIKMSTW	mawkiest
AEIKNPST	snake-pit
AEIKNRTW	knitwear
AEIKNSTV	kistvaen
AEIKPRSS	apres-ski
	après-ski
AEIKPTTY	take pity
AEIKRSST	asterisk
AEIKRSTW	water-ski
AEILLLNY	lineally
AEILLLTW	wall tile
AEILLMNS	Sam Neill
AEILLMNY	menially
AEILLMSY	mesially
AEILLNNO	all in one
	all-in-one
	lanoline
AEILLNNS	nainsell
AEILLNNU	unlineal
AEILLNOP	Apolline
AEILLNOR	allerion
AEILLNPS	splenial
AEILLNQU	quinella
AEILLNRY	linearly
AEILLNSS	nailless
	sensilla
AEILLNSW	Wellsian
AEILLNVY	venially
AEILLOSS	loessial
AEILLOTV	volatile
AEILLOVZ	Vellozia
AEILLPPR	apperill
AEILLPRS	pis aller
AEILLPST	pastille
AEILLPSV	lipsalve
AEILLQTU	tequilla
AEILLRRY	raillery
AEILLRSS	railless
AEILLRSY	serially
AEILLRTT	ill-treat
AEILLRTU	tailleur
AEILLSSS	sailless
AEILLSST	tailless
AEILLSTT	sittella
AEILLSUU	Eulalius
AEILLSUV	allusive
AEILLSYZ	sleazily
AEILLTUZ	lazulite
AEILMMNS	melanism
AEILMMNT	immantle
AEILMMNU	Immanuel
AEILMMNY	immanely
AEILMMOR	memorial
AEILMMOT	immolate
AEILMMRT	trilemma
AEILMMSS	melismas
AEILMNNO	minneola
AEILMNNP	impannel
AEILMNNS	linesman
AEILMNOS	laminose
	semolina
AEILMNOT	time loan
AEILMNPR	Palmerin
AEILMNPW	palm wine

Words marked ✧ can also be spelled with one or more capital letters

	wine palm
AEILMNRT	terminal
	tramline
AEILMNRU	lemurian
	run a mile
AEILMNSS	islesman
AEILMNST	manliest
	salt-mine
AEILMOPR	proemial
AEILMOPS	semi-opal
AEILMORS	moralise
AEILMORZ	moralize
AEILMPRS	pile arms
AEILMPRV	primeval
AEILMPSS	pessimal
AEILMPST	petalism
	septimal
AEILMPTT	petit mal
AEILMPTY	playtime
AEILMRSY	smearily
AEILMRTT	remittal
AEILMRUV	velarium
AEILMSTT	metalist
	smaltite
AEILMSTU	simulate
AEILMSTY	steamily
AEILMTTU	mutilate
	ultimate
AEILNNOS	solanine
AEILNNOT	Neo-Latin
AEILNNPP	panel pin
AEILNNRT	internal
AEILNNSU	Linnaeus
AEILNNSY	insanely
AEILNNTW	New Latin
AEILNNTY	innately
AEILNOPR	lone pair
AEILNOPT	Antilope
	antipole
AEILNOPU	poulaine
AEILNORR	Lorraine
AEILNORS	Rosaline
AEILNORT	oriental✧
	relation
	taileron
	Tirolean
AEILNORV	overlain
AEILNOST	insolate
AEILNOSV	Slovenia
AEILNOSX	siloxane
AEILNOTT	tonalite
AEILNOTV	Olivetan
	Ovaltine®
AEILNPPT	pie-plant
AEILNPRS	pearlins
AEILNPRT	trapline
	triplane
AEILNPSS	painless
AEILNPSW	swap line
AEILNPTT	tinplate
AEILNRSS	rainless
AEILNRST	entrails
AEILNRSY	snailery
AEILNRTT	rattline
	trail-net
AEILNRTU	retinula
	tenurial
AEILNRTV	interval
AEILNRTY	interlay
AEILNSST	eastlins
AEILNSSZ	laziness
AEILNSTT	Intelsat
AEILNSTU	insulate
AEILNSUY	uneasily
AEILNTTU	Lutetian
AEILNTVY	natively
	venality
AEILNUVV	univalve
AEILOORV	ovariole
AEILOPPR	oil paper
AEILOPPT	oppilate
AEILOPRS	polarise
AEILOPRT	epilator
	petiolar
	tail rope
AEILOPRZ	polarize
AEILOPST	spoliate
AEILORSS	solarise
AEILORST	soterial
AEILORSV	oversail
	valorise
AEILORSY	royalise
AEILORSZ	solarize
AEILORTT	literato
AEILORTV	violater
	Voltaire
AEILORTZ	triazole
AEILORVZ	valorize
AEILORYZ	royalize
AEILOSTT	totalise
AEILOTTV	volitate
AEILOTTZ	totalize
AEILPPQU	appliqué
AEILPPST	split pea
AEILPRRS	reprisal
AEILPRST	pilaster
	plaister
AEILPRSW	slipware
AEILPRXY	pyrexial
AEILPSTY	ptyalise
AEILPSUV	plausive
AEILPTYZ	ptyalize
AEILQRSU	squailer
AEILQRTU	quartile
	requital
AEILQSUY	queasily
AEILQTUY	equality
AEILRRSU	ruralise
AEILRRTT	rattlier
AEILRRTY	literary
AEILRRUZ	ruralize
AEILRSST	slaister
AEILRSSV	rivaless
AEILRSUU	Aurelius
AEILRSWY	lyra-wise
AEILRTTY	alterity
AEILRTUZ	lazurite
AEILRTVV	trivalve
AEILRTVY	at livery
AEILRTXZ	zelatrix
AEIMMMRZ	mamzerim
AEIMMNNT	immanent
AEIMMNOT	ammonite
AEIMMPST	psammite
AEIMMRTU	immature
AEIMNNNR	inner man
AEIMNNOT	nominate
AEIMNNRS	reinsman
AEIMNNWZ	Weizmann
AEIMNOPP	Pompeian
AEIMNOPT	ptomaine
	Tom Paine
AEIMNORS	Romanise
AEIMNORT	Maronite
AEIMNORZ	armozine
	Romanize
AEIMNOST	Masonite®
	somniate
AEIMNOSW	womanise
AEIMNOTZ	monazite
AEIMNOWZ	womanize
AEIMNPRS	per minas
AEIMNPRT	tripe-man
AEIMNPRZ	prizeman
AEIMNQRU	ramequin
AEIMNRRV	riverman
AEIMNRSS	near miss
AEIMNRSU	aneurism
	Sumerian
	Suriname
AEIMNRSY	seminary
AEIMNRTT	martinet
AEIMNRTU	ruminate
AEIMNRTW	wariment
AEIMNRTY	tyramine
AEIMNSST	mantises
	matiness
AEIMNSSZ	maziness
AEIMNTTU	matutine
AEIMNTVZ	vizament
AEIMOPTT	optimate
AEIMORST	amortise
	atomiser
	Timor Sea
AEIMORTT	amoretti
AEIMORTZ	amortize
	atomizer
AEIMOSST	amitoses
AEIMOTTT	Ottamite
AEIMOTTV	motivate
AEIMPRRT	imparter
AEIMPRST	apterism
	Primates

AEIMPRTT part-time
AEIMPRTU apterium
AEIMPRTW time warp
AEIMPRTX mixer tap
AEIMQRSU marquise
AEIMQSUU Esquimau
AEIMRSST asterism
AEIMRSSY emissary
AEIMRSTT master it
mistreat
teratism
AEIMRSTU semitaur
AEIMRSTX matrixes
AEIMRSTY symitare
AEIMRSWW swimwear
AEIMSSTT misstate
AEIMSSTZ mestizas
AEIMTTUV mutative
AEINNNOR Neronian
AEINNNOS Senonian
AEINNNOX annexion
AEINNOOS sea onion
AEINNOPV pavonine
AEINNORS in reason
raisonné
AEINNORT anointer
inornate
AEINNOSS in season
AEINNOST Estonian
AEINNOTT intonate
AEINNOTV innovate
venation
AEINNRRT inerrant
AEINNRSU unarisen
AEINNRTT intranet
AEINNSSV vainness
AEINNSSZ zaniness
AEINNSTT stannite
AEINNSUV Venusian
AEINNTUV unnative
Venutian
AEINOPPR roanpipe
AEINOPPT antipope
AEINOPRT atropine
AEINOPST saponite
AEINOPTZ topazine
AEINOQTU equation
AEINORRT anterior
AEINORRW ironware
wear iron
AEINORSS sensoria
AEINORST arsonite
notarise
rosinate
señorita✧
AEINORSV aversion
AEINORTT tear into
tentoria
AEINORTV Orvietan
AEINORTZ notarize
AEINOSST assiento
AEINOSSX Saxonise
AEINOSTV stovaine
AEINOSTX saxonite
AEINOSXZ Saxonize
zone axis
AEINOTTZ Zantiote
AEINOTVX vexation
AEINPPPS Pan-pipes
AEINPPRT taper pin
AEINPPSY Pepysian
AEINPPTX Xantippe
AEINPPTZ Zantippe
AEINPRRT Terrapin®
terrapin
AEINPRRU unrepair
AEINPRST pinaster
pristane
AEINPRSU unpraise
AEINPRTT triptane
AEINPRTU painture
AEINPRTX expirant
AEINPRUV Peruvian
AEINPSST steapsin
AEINPSTU supinate
AEINPSTY epinasty
AEINPTTY antitype
AEINQSTU quantise
AEINQTTU equitant
AEINQTUZ quantize
AEINRRST restrain
strainer
trainers
transire
AEINRRTU Etrurian
AEINRRTV veratrin
AEINRRTW interwar
AEINRSST artiness
AEINRSSU anuresis
senarius
AEINRSSW wariness
AEINRSSX xeransis
AEINRSTT straiten
AEINRSUZ suzerain
AEINRTTU tainture
AEINSSST saintess
AEINSSTT Titaness
AEINSSVW waviness
AEINSSWX waxiness
AEINSTTV tastevin
AEINSTUV suivante
AEINSTWY Steinway
AEINSUVV vesuvian✧
AEINTTUU autunite
AEIOPPST apposite
AEIOPRRT Pretoria
priorate
AEIOPRRW air-power
AEIOPRST Isoptera
AEIOPRSV vaporise
AEIOPRTX expiator
AEIOPRVZ vaporize
AEIOPTTV optative
AEIORRRS arrieros
AEIORRUV au revoir
AEIORSTT toastier
AEIORSVY sea ivory
AEIORTTV rotative
AEIPPRRS appriser
AEIPPRRZ apprizer
AEIPQRTU pratique
AEIPRSST Tarsipes
AEIPRSTV privates
AEIPRSTY asperity
AEIPRSVY vespiary
AEIPSSTU tap issue
AEIPTTUV putative
AEIQRRRU quarrier
AEIQRRTU quartier
AEIRRRTV river-rat
AEIRRSSY siserary
AEIRRTTT retraitt
AEIRRTTY tertiary✧
AEIRRTVY River Tay
AEIRRVWY riverway
AEIRSSST assister
AEIRSSTW waitress
AEIRSTTT rattiest
tartiest
AEIRSTVY vestiary
AEIRSWWY waywiser
AEIRTTTW atwitter
AEISSSTY essayist
AEISSTTT tastiest
AEISTTTT tattiest
AEJKMORY major key
AEJKNOOR Jean Rook
AEJLLNPY jelly-pan
AEJLOSUY jealousy
AEJLOSUZ azulejos
AEJMPSTU jump seat
AEJMSSST St James's
AEJNNNOS Ann Jones
AEJNOOPP Pope Joan
AEJNORSZ zanjeros
AEKKLLWY lykewalk
AEKKMNOO kakemono
AEKLMNOS monk seal
AEKLMRUW lukewarm
AEKLMRUY yarmulke
AEKLNNSS lankness
AEKLNORW walker-on
AEKLNOSY ankylose
AEKLNOTW wale knot
AEKLNSST tankless
AEKLOPRW rope-walk
AEKLOPTY kalotype
AEKLORTV overtalk
talk over
AEKLORVW walk over
walkover
AEKLOSST stalkoes
AEKLPRRS sparkler

AEKLPRST	sparklet
AEKLQRUY	Quakerly
AEKMNRSU	unmasker
AEKMOPRT	topmaker
AEKMORTW	teamwork
	workmate
AEKMPRRV	verkramp
AEKMPRSU	musk pear
AEKMPRTU	upmarket
AEKNNRSS	rankness
AEKNORRV	overrank
AEKNORUY	eukaryon
AEKNOTTU	outtaken
AEKOORTT	take root
AEKOPSTU	outspeak
	speak out
	speakout
AEKOPSTW	weak spot
AEKORRWW	workwear
AEKORSTV	overtask
AEKORTUY	eukaryot
AEKOSTTU	stake out
	stake-out
AEKQRSUW	squawker
AEKRRSST	starkers
AELLLRTU	tellural
AELLLSSW	wall-less
AELLLSUV	vulsella
AELLMNOW	lemon law
AELLMNOZ	manzello
AELLMNTY	mentally
AELLMORR	moraller
AELLMORS	slalomer
AELLMORT	martello
AELLMOTY	tomalley
AELLMPUU	plumulae
AELLMRSY	mersalyl
AELLNOOT	all to one
AELLNOPV	volplane
AELLNORS	llaneros
AELLNOST	Stallone
AELLNOWW	enwallow
AELLNPRU	prunella✧
AELLNPSS	planless
AELLNPTT	plantlet
AELLNPTU	plantule
AELLNRUY	neurally
	unreally
AELLNRVY	vernally
AELLNSST	tallness
AELLNSWZ	Lenz's law
AELLNTTY	latently
AELLNTUU	lunulate
AELLNTWW	wall newt
AELLOOPY	alley-oop
AELLOPRS	Parolles
	reposall
AELLOPRW	walloper
AELLOPRY	role-play
AELLORSS	all roses
AELLORSV	overalls

AELLORSW	Rosewall
AELLORTY	alley-tor
AELLORWW	wallower
AELLOSUV	alveolus
AELLPPSU	sell a pup
AELLQRSU	squaller
AELLRRTY	retrally
AELLRTTY	latterly
AELLRTVY	trevally
AELLRWYY	lawyerly
AELLSSST	saltless
AELLSSTY	tasselly
AELLSUVV	valvules
AELLSUXY	sexually
AELMMORW	mealworm
AELMMOSY	myelomas
AELMMRST	strammel
	trammels
AELMMRSU	merum sal
AELMNNOP	neon lamp
AELMNNOT	non-metal
AELMNNOU	noumenal
AELMNNRY	mannerly
AELMNNTU	unmantle
AELMNOPS	neoplasm
	pleonasm
AELMNORT	Montreal
AELMNOST	salmonet
AELMNOSU	melanous
AELMNOYY	yeomanly
AELMNRSU	mensural
	numerals
AELMNSST	St Anselm
AELMNSUY	Süleyman
AELMOOPT	omoplate
AELMOORS	saleroom
AELMOPRR	premolar
AELMOPRT	prometal
	temporal
AELMOPSX	exoplasm
AELMOPSY	playsome
AELMOPTT	metaplot
	palmetto
	pot metal
AELMORSU	ramulose
AELMORTU	emulator
AELMOSSS	molasses
AELMOSTU	soul mate
AELMOSTY	atmolyse
AELMOTVZ	mazel tov
	mazeltov
AELMOTYZ	atmolyze
AELMPRRT	trampler
AELMPRSY	lampreys
	samplery
AELMPSUX	amplexus
AELMQSUU	squamule
AELMRSTT	maltster
AELMRSTY	masterly
AELMRTUY	maturely
AELMSSST	mastless

AELNNNPU	unpannel
AELNNOOP	napoleon✧
AELNNOOX	naloxone
AELNNOPP	open-plan
AELNNOPT	pentanol
AELNNORU	neuronal
AELNNOSU	annulose
AELNNRTU	unlearnt
AELNOOTV	à volonté
AELNOOTZ	entozoal
AELNOPPR	propenal
AELNOPRS	personal
	psoralen
AELNOPST	lapstone
	pleonast
AELNOPTW	towplane
AELNORTT	tetronal
	tolerant
AELNORTU	outlearn
AELNORTY	ornately
	Tyrolean
AELNOSSV	ovalness
AELNPPSY	spy plane
AELNPRSU	purslane
	supernal
AELNPRTY	plenarty
AELNPSSS	spanless
AELNPSSU	spansule
AELNPTTU	petulant
AELNPTTY	patently
AELNRRTY	errantly
AELNRRUV	nervular
AELNRSTT	slattern
AELNRSVY	sylvaner✧
AELNRSXY	larynxes
AELNRTTW	trawl-net
AELNRUWY	unwarely
AELNSSST	saltness
AELNSUUX	unsexual
AELNTTUX	exultant
AELOOPPT	tape loop
AELOOPRZ	zooperal
AELOORRS	roseolar
AELOORTW	Waterloo
AELOORTZ	zoolater
AELOPPRS	prolapse
	sapropel
AELOPPSU	papulose
AELOPPTU	populate
AELOPPXY	apoplexy
AELOPQUY	opaquely
AELOPRRV	reproval
AELOPRST	petrosal
	Pole Star
AELOPRSU	leaprous
AELOPRVY	overplay
AELOPSSS	soapless
AELOPSSU	espousal
	sepalous
AELOPSTU	petalous
AELORRSS	Rosslare

AELORSSU Larousse
AELORSTU rosulate
AELORSUU rouleaus
AELORTTV varletto
AELORTTW water lot
AELORTUV ravel out
AELORTWW low water
AELORTYZ zealotry
AELORUUX rouleaux
AELOSSTU assolute
AELOSSTY asystole
AELOSTTW wastelot
AELOSTUY autolyse
AELOTUUV outvalue
AELOTUYZ autolyze
AELPRRSW sprawler
AELPRRTT prattler
AELPRSSY sparsely
AELPRSTT splatter
sprattle
AELPRSTU aplustre
AELPRSTY plastery
psaltery✧
AELPSSSS passless
AELQRSUY squarely
AELQSTTU squattle
AELRRSTT startler
AELRRTVY varletry
AELRSSST starless
AELRSSTW wartless
AELRSSUU russulae
AELRSTTU lustrate
AELRSTTY slattery
AELRSTUV vestural
AELRSUVY surveyal
AELRTTTW twattler
AELRTTUX textural
AELRTTUY tutelary
AELRTTWY Wat Tyler
AELSSSTU saltuses
AELSSSTY stayless
AELSTTUY astutely
AEMMMOTU ommateum
AEMMMRTY mammetry
AEMMNNOY moneyman
AEMMNRRY merryman
AEMMNRTU ramentum
AEMMOORT roommate
AEMMORST marmoset
AEMMOSTU mousemat
AEMMRTUY maumetry
AEMMRTWY mawmetry
AEMNNOOW one-woman
AEMNNOPW penwoman
AEMNNORS Norseman
AEMNNORT ornament
AEMNNORW Morwenna
AEMNNOWW new woman✧
AEMNNPRU per annum
AEMNOORR marooner
AEMNOORT anteroom
AEMNOORY aeronomy
AEMNOOTZ metazoon
AEMNOPRS proseman
prose-man
AEMNOPRT empatron
AEMNOPRW manpower
AEMNORRS ransomer
AEMNORST monstera
on stream
on-stream
storeman
AEMNORSU neuromas
AEMNORSV oversman
AEMNORTT Martenot
no matter
AEMNORTU routeman
AEMNORTY monetary
AEMNORYY yeomanry
AEMNOSTU seamount
AEMNPRSS pressman
AEMNPRSU superman
AEMNPSST passment
AEMNPSTU spumante
AEMNRRUY numerary
AEMNRSSW warmness
AEMNRSTU menstrua
transume
AEMNRSTW transmew
trewsman
AEMNRSTX Max Ernst
AEMNRSUY aneurysm
AEMNSTUW mute swan
AEMOOPRT peat moor
AEMOOPST pomatoes
AEMOORTT amoretto
AEMOOSST maestoso
AEMOOSTT tomatoes
AEMOOSTU autosome
AEMOOTTY tomatoey
AEMOPPRS pamperos
AEMOPPRW power-amp
AEMOPRTW pomwater
tapeworm
AEMOPSST peat moss
AEMOQSSU squamose
AEMORRRU armourer
AEMORRST rearmost
AEMORRSY Mary Rose
rosemary
AEMORRTU Euromart
AEMORSST maestros
sea storm
AEMORSSY mayoress
AEMORSTV overmast
AEMORTTU tautomer
AEMOSSTT eastmost
AEMOSSWY someways
AEMOTTZZ mozzetta
AEMPRRSY spermary
AEMPRSTU upstream
AEMPRSUX supermax
AEMQRSSU marquess
AEMRRRTT R R Marett
AEMRRTUV veratrum
AEMRSSST rest mass
AEMRSSTT mattress
AEMRSSUU Sarum use
AEMRSTTU testamur
AEMRTUUX trumeaux
AEMSTTTU testatum
AENNNOTU Nuneaton
AENNNTTU untenant
AENNOPRT patronne
AENNOPST pentosan
AENNOPUW unweapon
AENNORST norteñas
resonant
AENNORSU unreason
AENNORVY novenary
AENNORWY Norweyan
AENNOSSU unseason
AENNOSTU tonneaus
AENNOSTW tenon saw
AENNOTUX tonneaux
AENNRSWY swannery
AENNRTTY tenantry
AENOOPST teaspoon
AENOORRT ratooner
AENOPPRW power nap
AENOPRRY rope yarn
AENOPRSS personas
Responsa
AENOPRTT patentor
AENOPRWY weaponry
AENOPSTT ante-post
AENORRST antrorse
AENORSST assentor
AENORSTW answer to
stoneraw
AENORSUV ravenous
AENORTTX tetraxon
AENORTTY attorney
AENOSSTW saw-tones
stone saw
AENOSSTZ stanzoes
AENOSSUU nauseous
AENPRRST partners
AENPRSTT transept
AENPRSTU persaunt
AENPRSTY Strepyan
AENPSSSY synapses
AENPSSTW waspnest
AENPSSTZ spetsnaz✧
AENPSTZZ spetznaz✧
AENQRRTU quartern
AENQSTTU questant
AENRRRTY errantry
AENRRSSU Serranus
AENRSSTT tartness
AENRSSTU anestrus
AENRSSTV servants
AENRSTWY sternway

AENRTUVY	vauntery
AENRTUWY	unwatery
AENSSSTV	vastness
AENSSSTW	wastness
AENSSTTU	tautness
AEOOPPPS	pappoose
AEOOPRRT	operator
	poor rate
AEOOPSTT	potatoes
AEOORRST	sororate
AEOORTTT	tattooer
AEOORTTV	rotovate
AEOPPRRV	approver
AEOPPSUY	pea-soupy
AEOPQRTU	paroquet
AEOPRRRT	parroter
AEOPRRST	Raptores
AEOPRRTV	overpart
AEOPRRUV	vapourer
AEOPRRVW	overwrap
	wrapover
AEOPRSST	espartos
	protases
AEOPRSSU	asperous
AEOPRSSV	overpass
	Passover
	pass over
AEOPRSTT	prostate
AEOPRSTU	apterous
AEOPRSTV	overpast
AEOPRTTW	water pot
AEOPRTWX	waterpox
AEOPSSTT	soap test
AEOPSTTU	put to sea
AEOPTTUY	autotype
AEOQRSTU	quaestor
AEOQRSUV	vaqueros
AEOQRTTU	torquate
AEOQRTUZ	quatorze◇
AEORRRST	arrestor
AEORRSST	assertor
	assorter
	oratress
AEORRSTT	rostrate
AEORRSTV	at rovers
AEORRTUV	avoutrer
AEORRTZZ	terrazzo
AEORSSSS	assessor
AEORSSTT	stratose
AEORSSTV	votaress
AEORSSUU	Rousseau
AEORSTTT	attestor
	testator
AEORSTTU	Eurostat
	outstare
	rout-seat
	sea trout
	stare out
AEORSTUW	outswear
AEORSTVY	overstay
	stay over
AEORSUVW	waverous
AEORSVWY	oversway
AEORTUWY	outweary
	weary out
AEORTVXY	vexatory
AEOSTTUY	tousy tea
AEPPRRST	strapper
AEPQRSUU	square up
AEPRSSST	trespass
AEPRSSTT	pattress
AEPRSTTU	stuprate
AEPRSTTY	tapestry
AEPRSTUX	supertax
AEPRTUVY	pyruvate
AEQRRSTU	quarters
AEQRSTTU	squatter
AEQRTTTU	quartett
AERRSSTT	starters
AERRSSTU	serratus
AERRSTUY	treasury◇
AERRSTWY	rye-straw
AERSSSTY	satyress
AERSSSUU	Saussure
AERSSTUU	Tauruses
AERSTTVY	travesty
AERTTUXY	textuary
AESSSTTU	statuses
AFFFFGGI	giff-gaff
AFFFFINN	niffnaff
AFFFFIRR	riff-raff
AFFGHIRT	affright
AFFGHLOU	laugh off
AFFGIIRT	graffiti
AFFGILMN	maffling
AFFGILNW	waffling
AFFGIMRS	misgraff
AFFGIORT	graffito
AFFGLNRU	far-flung
AFFHILLS	fallfish
AFFHILST	flatfish
AFFHILTU	faithful◇
AFFHIMRS	fish farm
AFFHKOST	off-shakt
AFFHORRT	far-forth
AFFIINTY	affinity
AFFILLMM	flimflam
AFFILLPP	flip-flap
AFFILNOW	Wolffian
AFFILORT	trail off
AFFILSUX	suffixal
AFFIMRST	stiff-arm
AFFINORR	forfairn
AFFINOSU	affusion
AFFIPSTT	tipstaff
AFFKOPRS	spark off
AFFLLLOU	foul fall
AFFLLOOT	footfall
AFFLLOST	stall off
AFFLLTUU	faultful
AFFLOOOT	foalfoot
AFFLOOTT	flat-foot
AFFLORTU	forfault
AFFLRRUU	furfural
AFFMORRY	marry off
AFFNORSY	saffrony
AFFNRRUU	furfuran
AFFRTTUU	Truffaut
AFGGGILN	flagging
AFGGGINR	fragging
AFGGILOP	gigaflop
AFGGINOT	fagoting
AFGGINRT	grafting
AFGHILLN	halfling
AFGHILNS	flashing
AFGHILNT	fanlight
AFGHILPS	flagship
AFGHINOT	of a night
AFGHINRT	farthing
AFGHINRW	wharfing
AFGHINST	shafting
AFGHIOST	goatfish
AFGHLLUU	laughful
AFGHLNSU	flashgun
AFGHLSTU	ghastful
AFGIILRS	flag iris
AFGIINNT	fainting
AFGIKORT	koftgari
AFGILLNT	flatling
AFGILMNO	flamingo
AFGILNOS	sol-faing
AFGILNOT	floating
AFGILNPP	flapping
AFGILNTT	flatting
AFGILORW	gairfowl
AFGILSSY	glassify
AFGIMNTU	fumigant
AFGIMORS	gasiform
AFGIMRST	misgraft
AFGINNNS	fannings
AFGINPPR	frapping
AFGINRTU	figurant
AFGINSUY	sanguify
AFGIPRTW	gift-wrap
AFGJNRUU	Jungfrau
AFGLLNOT	flatlong
AFGLLNPU	pang-full
AFGLLRUU	fulgural
AFGLLRUY	frugally
AFGLLSSU	glassful
AFGLLSTU	gastfull
AFGLMORW	flag-worm
AFGLNNOO	gonfalon
AFGLNORU	groanful
AFGLNOUW	wagonful
AFGNNNOO	gonfanon
AFGOOORT	go too far
AFGOORTZ	zoograft
AFGORTUW	tug-of-war
AFHHIKSW	fish-hawk
AFHHLORU	half-hour
AFHHLOST	hot flash
AFHIILRS	frailish

AFHIILSS sailfish
AFHIILST fishtail
AFHIIMST misfaith
AFHIINST faintish
AFHIKLPS hip flask
AFHIKNRS Frankish
AFHILLNS halflins
AFHILLSW wallfish
AFHILLSY flashily
AFHILNPT half-pint
AFHILNTT half-tint
AFHILOSY oafishly
AFHILOTW with foal
AFHILSST saltfish
AFHILSTT flattish
AFHIMNST manshift
AFHINOSS fashions
AFHINSTU tuna fish
AFHIOSSU fashious
AFHIOTTW what of it?
AFHIRSST starfish
AFHKLNTU thankful
AFHKMOOR hoof-mark
AFHKORSX foxshark
AFHLLOTU loathful
AFHLMNOO half-moon
AFHLMORS flash ROM
AFHLMOTU Falmouth
AFHLOSTU outflash
AFHLRTUW wrathful
AFHLRTUY hurt a fly
AFHNOOST fantoosh
AFHNORRT Far North
AFHOOPTT footpath
AFHORSTU Far South
AFHORTTU of a truth
AFIIILNP Filipina
AFIIKMRS fakirism
AFIILLLY filially
AFIILLNU unfilial
AFIILMMS familism✧
AFIILMNS finalism
AFIILMST Familist
AFIILNRU unifilar
AFIILNST finalist
AFIILNTY finality
AFIIMRSY fairyism
AFIINNOS sainfoin
sinfonia
AFIINOTX fixation
AFIINSTW Swiftian
AFIIORRT triforia
AFIJMNOR Janiform
AFIKLLMO milk loaf
AFIKLNNR franklin✧
AFIKLORT forktail
AFIKORST ask for it
AFIKRSTY karstify
AFILLLMX flax-mill
AFILLLOT flotilla
AFILLLSU full sail
AFILLLXY flax-lily
AFILLNPU plainful
AFILLOST sail loft
AFILLTUY faultily
AFILMNOR formalin
informal
AFILMOPR paliform
AFILMOSS sol-faism
AFILMRST film star
AFILNORT flatiron
inflator
AFILNPPT flippant
AFILNPST flat spin
AFILNRUY unfairly
AFILNSTU inflatus
AFILORTY filatory
AFILOSST sol-faist
AFILRSTU fistular
AFILSSTU fistulas
AFILSTTU flautist
AFIMMNOR maniform
AFIMMORR ramiform
AFIMNNOS man of sin
AFIMNOPR napiform
AFIMNORR raniform
AFIMNORT farm into
natiform
AFIMNOSU infamous
AFIMNTUU Funtumia
AFIMORRU auriform
AFIMORRV variform
AFIMORSV vasiform
AFINNOTU fountain
AFINNRTY infantry
AFINOPSY saponify
AFINORUV in favour
AFINQTUY quantify
AFINRSTX transfix
AFINRSUX Fraxinus
AFIORRST air frost
AFIORSTZ sforzati
AFIRSTTY stratify
AFJKNUZZ jazz-funk
AFJMNORU Januform
AFKLLMOS alms-folk
AFKLNOTU outflank
AFKLNPRU prankful
AFKLNSTU tankfuls
AFKMOORT footmark
AFKMORST soft mark
AFLLLORY florally
AFLLLPUY play full
AFLLLUWY lawfully
AFLLMNUY manfully
AFLLMORY formally
AFLLMRSY small fry
AFLLNOPU fall upon
AFLLNOSW snowfall
AFLLNUUW unlawful
AFLLOOTW footwall
AFLLOPUY foul play
AFLLORSU all-fours
AFLLRTUY artfully
AFLLSTUW wastfull
AFLMNORU unformal
AFLMOPRT platform
AFLMORRU formular
AFLMORSU formulas
AFLMORTU foulmart
AFLMORTW flatworm
AFLMOSUY famously
AFLNOOPR floor pan
AFLNOOST soft loan
AFLNOPRU apronful
AFLNRTUU unartful
AFLNTUUV vauntful
AFLNTUUY unfaulty
AFLOOSTT salt-foot
AFLOSTUU flatuous
AFLPRSYY flyspray
AFLRSTTU startful
AFLRSTUY trayfuls
AFMNNNUY funny man
AFMNNOOS son of man
AFMNNORT front man
frontman
AFMNOOSS Son of Sam
AFMNORTU farm-toun
AFMOOPRR pro forma
pro-forma
AFMOORTZ from A to Z
AFMOORUU amour fou
AFMORTUY fumatory
AFMOSSTU sfumatos
AFNNOPUW fawn upon
AFNOOPRS span roof
AFOOPRRT ratproof
AFOOPRRW war-proof
AFOOPSST soft soap
soft-soap
AFOORSTT root-fast
AFOORSTZ sforzato
AFOPRRTT raft-port
AFOPRRTU four-part
AFORSTTU tartufos
AFORSTTW forswatt
AFOSSTUU fastuous
AFPPPTUY puppy fat
AGGGGILN gaggling
AGGGHINS shagging
AGGGILNN gangling
AGGGILNS slagging
AGGGINNS snagging
AGGGINSW swagging
AGGGIYZZ zigzaggy
AGGGLNPU gang plug
AGGHHINT night-hag
AGGHILNT Lagthing
AGGHILNU laughing
AGGHILST gaslight
AGGHILSY shaggily
AGGHINNS gnashing

hangings
AGGHISTT gas-tight
AGGHJMNO mah-jongg
AGGHLOOT Golgotha
AGGHMOSS moss hagg
AGGHOOTT gag-tooth
AGGIILNS silaging
AGGIILNV gingival
AGGIINNR graining
AGGIINNS gainings
AGGIJLNN jangling
AGGILLMN gang mill
AGGILMNO gloaming
AGGILMPS gig-lamps
AGGILNNO ganglion
AGGILNNS slanging
AGGILNNT gnatling
tangling
AGGILNNW wangling
AGGILNOT goatling
AGGILNPY gapingly
AGGILNRY grayling
ragingly
AGGINNOR groaning
AGGINNOT tangoing
AGGINNTW twanging
AGGINOOR Gorgonia
AGGINOWY way-going
AGGINPRS grasping
AGGINRSS grassing
AGGINRSU sugaring
AGGIRTUZ ziggurat
AGGJLNOO jog along
AGGKLNNU angklung
AGGLLLOY lollygag
AGGLLOOY algology
AGGLLOSS log-glass
AGGLMOOR logogram
AGGLOORY agrology
AGGLRSTY straggly
AGGMRSUU sugar gum
AGGNUWZZ zugzwang
AGHHIILT hightail
AGHHIMSS High Mass
AGHHINOP Haiphong
AGHHLOTU although
AGHHNOUZ Hangzhou
AGHHORRT Hrothgar
AGHHOSTU as though
AGHIILOS Laoighis
AGHIILRT light air
AGHIINRT night air
AGHIIPRR hair grip
hairgrip
AGHIIRTT airtight
AGHIJNRT nightjar
AGHIJNUZ Zhu Jiang
AGHIKLRU Gurkhali
AGHIKNNT thanking
AGHIKNRS sharking
AGHILLNT allnight
all-thing
AGHILLRT all right
all-right
AGHILMTY almighty✧
AGHILNOO hooligan
AGHILNOR long-hair
AGHILNOS shoaling
AGHILNOT loathing
AGHILNPS plashing
AGHILNRS ringhals
AGHILNRY narghily
AGHILNSS lashings
slangish
slashing
AGHILNSU languish
AGHILNSW shawling
AGHILRSY garishly
AGHILRTY graithly
AGHILSUY aguishly
AGHILTWX wax light
AGHIMMNS shamming
AGHIMMNW whamming
AGHIMNNT night-man
AGHIMNPR pharming
AGHIMNRS Ram Singh
AGHIMNSS smashing
AGHIMNTY thingamy
AGHIMPRU graphium
AGHIMRRT right arm
AGHINNTU haunting
AGHINNTY anything
AGHINORS orangish
AGHINPPW whapping
AGHINPRS harpings
phrasing
sharping✧
AGHINPRY Phrygian
AGHINRRY harrying
AGHINSST hastings✧
AGHINSSW swashing
washings
AGHINUZZ huzzaing
AGHIPRRT trigraph
AGHIPSSW pig's-wash
AGHIRSTT straight
AGHIRUUW Wahiguru
AGHISSTT tight ass
AGHLLMPU gallumph
AGHLLNOU long haul
long-haul
AGHLMOOR hologram
AGHLNOSU shogunal
AGHLNSUY nylghaus
AGHMMOOY homogamy
AGHMNPSU sphagnum
AGHMOOPY omophagy
AGHMOORR Gomorrah
AGHMOOTT goat-moth
AGHMOPRY myograph
AGHNNOOT hang onto
AGHNNRUY an hungry
an-hungry
AGHNNSTU shantung
AGHNOORS shagroon
AGHNORST staghorn
AGHNPRSY syngraph
AGHNSTTU stag hunt
AGHNTTUU untaught
AGHOOPYZ zoophagy
AGHOPSSW swagshop
AGHRSTTU straught
AGIIINNS insignia
AGIIINRV Virginia
AGIIIRSY Sigiriya
AGIIKNPR king pair
AGIILLOV villagio
villiago
AGIILLTT gilt-tail
AGIILMNS misalign
AGIILNNP plaining
AGIILNNU inguinal
AGIILNNY inlaying
AGIILNOR original
AGIILNOT intaglio
ligation
taglioni
AGIILNOX gloxinia
AGIILNPT pig Latin
plaiting
AGIILNQU quailing
AGIILNRS railings
AGIILNRT ringtail
ring-tail
trailing
AGIILNRV virginal
AGIILNST tailings
AGIILNTT litigant
AGIILNTV vigilant
AGIILORU oliguria
AGIILTVY vagility
AGIIMNNR ring main
AGIIMNSS amissing
AGIIMNST giantism
AGIIMNTT mitigant
AGIINNNO Annigoni
AGIINNOV Giovanni
AGIINNPT painting
AGIINNRT training
AGIINNST staining
AGIINNSW swaining
AGIINORS signoria
AGIINORT rigatoni
AGIINPRS aspiring
praising
AGIINRTT attiring
AGIINRTY Tigrinya
Trigynia
AGIISSTV visagist
AGIJNNTT tjanting
AGIJNNTU jaunting
AGIJNRSU Juan Gris
AGIKKNNS skanking

AGIKLMOR	kilogram
AGIKLNNO	Algonkin
AGIKLNNP	planking
AGIKLNOP	polkaing
AGIKLNRW	ring walk
AGIKLNST	stalking
AGIKLNTY	takingly
AGIKLORY	kilogray
AGIKMNNS	king's-man
AGIKMNNU	unmaking
AGIKMNPU	upmaking
AGIKMNRR	ring mark
AGIKMNRS	markings
AGIKMRUU	kauri gum
AGIKNNPP	knapping
AGIKNNPR	pranking
AGIKNNPS	spanking
AGIKNNSW	swanking
AGIKNOST	goatskin
AGILLMNU	mulligan
AGILLMNY	malignly
AGILLMSU	Gaullism
AGILLNOT	long-tail
AGILLNPR	grill pan
AGILLNPS	spalling
AGILLNRU	alluring
	lingular
AGILLNRW	ring wall
AGILLNRY	nargilly
	rallying
AGILLNST	stalling
AGILLNSY	sallying
	signally
	slangily
AGILLNTY	tallying
AGILLOOR	gillaroo
AGILLOPT	gallipot
AGILLPRY	playgirl
AGILLPUY	plaguily
AGILLRUU	augur ill
AGILLSSY	glassily
AGILLSTU	Gaullist
AGILMMNS	slamming
AGILMNNT	mantling
AGILMNOO	Mongolia
AGILMNPS	sampling
AGILMNQU	qualming
AGILMOPR	lipogram
AGILMORS	algorism
AGILNNNP	planning
AGILNNOP	pangolin
AGILNNPT	planting
AGILNNRS	snarling
AGILNNST	slanting
AGILNNUY	ungainly
AGILNOOO	oogonial
AGILNOOS	isogonal
AGILNORT	trigonal
AGILNOSS	glossina
	lassoing
AGILNOTW	wagon-lit
AGILNOTY	antilogy
AGILNPPS	slapping
AGILNPPY	applying
AGILNPRS	sparling
	springal
AGILNPTT	platting
AGILNRST	slant rig
	starling
AGILNRSU	singular
AGILNRTT	rattling
AGILNRTW	trawling
AGILNRVY	ravingly
AGILNRWX	wraxling
AGILNSVY	savingly
AGILNSWY	swayling
AGILNTTT	tattling
AGILNTTW	wattling
AGILNTUV	vaulting
AGILNTWZ	waltzing
AGILOORS	gloriosa
AGILOOXY	axiology
AGILORSS	grass-oil
AGILOSTU	Ustilago
AGILQUUY	Guyaquil
AGILSYYZ	syzygial
AGIMMNPS	spamming
AGIMMNRT	tramming
AGIMMNUX	Maxim-gun
AGIMMOSY	misogamy
AGIMNNRU	manuring
AGIMNOPW	pig-woman
AGIMNORR	Morrigan
AGIMNORS	Orangism
	organism
AGIMNORU	origanum
AGIMNORY	agrimony
AGIMNPRT	tramping
AGIMNPST	stamping
AGIMNRRY	marrying
AGIMNRSW	swarming
AGIMNSSU	assuming
AGIMORRT	migrator
AGIMQRUY	quagmiry
AGINNNNY	nannying
AGINNNOY	annoying
AGINNNPS	spanning
AGINNNSW	swanning
AGINNOPT	poignant
AGINNOPU	gain upon
AGINNORT	ignorant
	Tir nan-Og
	Tir-na-nOg
AGINNPPS	snapping
AGINNPSW	spawning
	wingspan
AGINNRTU	naturing
AGINNSTU	unsating
AGINNTTU	taunting
AGINNTUV	vaunting
AGINNVVY	navvying
AGINOORT	rogation
AGINORRS	garrison
AGINORRY	iron-gray
AGINORSS	assignor
AGINORST	organist
	roasting
AGINORTV	graviton
AGINORTY	gyration
	organity
AGINOSTT	tangoist
	toasting
AGINPPRT	trapping
AGINPPRW	wrapping
AGINPPSW	swapping
AGINPPUY	appuying
AGINPRRS	sparring
AGINPRRY	parrying
AGINPRSS	raspings
AGINQRSU	squaring
AGINRRST	starring
AGINRRTY	tarrying
AGINRSST	nit-grass
	star sign
AGINRSTT	starting
AGINRSTV	starving
AGINRSTY	stingray
	straying
AGINSTTW	swatting
AGIOORSU	oragious
AGIOORSZ	grazioso
AGIOORTU	autogiro
AGIOPPRT	agitprop✧
	agit-prop✧
AGIORRTT	grattoir
AGIRSSTU	sastrugi
AGIRSTUZ	zastrugi
AGIRTTUY	gratuity
AGJLOSUV	Jugoslav
	Jugo-Slav
AGJNOPST	jog pants
	jogpants
AGKLMNOR	long mark
AGKMMORY	kymogram
AGKORSSW	gasworks
AGLLLNOW	longwall
AGLLMOPW	glowlamp
AGLLOOSW	slag wool
AGLLOOTU	go all out
AGLLOSSW	Owl-glass
AGLLPRSU	spur-gall
AGLLPRUW	Rawlplug®
AGLLPSTU	salt plug
AGLLRUVY	vulgarly
AGLMOOTY	atmology
AGLMOOYY	Mayology
AGLMOPYY	polygamy
AGLNNOPS	span-long
AGLNNORU	run along
AGLNOSST	glasnost
AGLNOSTY	long-stay
AGLNOSWY	longways
AGLNRUUV	unvulgar

AGLNRUVY ungravly
AGLNSSSU sunglass
AGLNSTUY yglaunst
AGLOOPST goalpost
AGLOOTUY autology
AGLOPRSS lopgrass
AGLOPRTU Portugal
AGLORSSY glossary
AGLOSUVY Yugoslav
Yugo-Slav
AGLPSSSY spyglass
AGLRTTUU guttural
AGLSTUUY augustly
AGMMNOOR monogram
nomogram
AGMMNOOY monogamy
AGMMOORT tomogram
AGMMOORU Mormugao
AGMNNOSW gownsman
AGMNNOUY young man
AGMNOORS sonogram
AGMNOORY agronomy
AGMNORST Ångström
angstrom
AGMNSSTY syntagms
AGMOOOSU oogamous
AGMOOPRY porogamy
AGMOORST gas-motor
AGMOOTVY vagotomy
AGNNOQTU quantong
AGNNOSSW swan song
swansong
AGNOPRST part-song
AGNORTUY nugatory
AGNOSSTW towns gas
AGNPPRSU upsprang
AGNPRSUY spray gun
AGNRSSTU nut-grass
AGOORRTY rogatory
AGOORTUY autogyro
AGOPPRRU rap group
AGORRSST grossart
rotgrass
AGORRTYY gyratory
AGORSTTY gyrostat
AGSSTUUU Augustus
AGSSTUUV Gustavus
AHHHOOOW whoa-ho-ho
AHHIKLSS shashlik
AHHILNPT phthalin
AHHILOST hailshot
AHHILPSW whiplash
AHHIMMSS mishmash
AHHIMMWW whim-wham
AHHIMSST smash hit
AHHIPRSS sharpish
AHHISSWW wish-wash
AHHITTTW with that
AHHJNNOS John Nash
AHHKMOTW hawk moth
AHHKRSTU kashruth✧

AHHLMRTY rhythmal
AHHLNOPT naphthol
AHHLOOPU hula hoop
AHHMNOTW than whom
AHHMPRRU harrumph
AHHNORTW hawthorn
AHHOOSST shatoosh
AHHOPSTU aphthous
AHHOSTTW how's that
AHHOSTUV Shavuoth
AHIIKMRS Kashmiri
AHIIKPSS his paiks
AHIILNPS plainish
AHIILOST haliotis✧
AHIILPPP Philippa
AHIILPRS Aprilish
AHIILPTW whiptail
AHIILRTY hilarity
AHIIMNOT himation
AHIIMNRS Irishman
AHIIMNST Ian Smith
isthmian
AHIIMNTV vitamin H
AHIIMSSV Shaivism
Shivaism
AHIINOPT photinia✧
AHIINPST antiship
AHIINSST saintish
AHIINSSW swainish
AHIIOPST hospitia
AHIJNNOW John Wain
AHIKLNNS Shanklin
AHIKLNRS rinkhals
AHIKLORS shark oil
AHIKLRSY rakishly
AHIKMSST Shaktism
AHIKNPRS prankish
AHIKORRW hair-work
AHIKOSST Skiathos
AHIKPRSS sparkish
AHIKRSSW Sikh Wars
AHILLMOU halloumi
AHILLMPS phallism
AHILLMSS smallish
AHILLMTU thallium
AHILLNRT in thrall
inthrall
AHILLNSW Swan Hill
AHILLNTW wanthill
AHILLPST tall ship
AHILLSTT talliths
AHILLSVY lavishly
AHILMNOT Hamilton
AHILMOPT philamot
AHILMOST mailshot
AHILMQSU qualmish
AHILMSST Stahlism
AHILNOPS siphonal
AHILNOPT oliphant
AHILNORT horntail
AHILOORT Lothario

AHILOPST hospital
AHILOSTT thio-salt
AHILOSTU halitous
AHILPSSY physalis
AHILRSTY trashily
AHILRTWY wrathily
AHIMMNSU humanism
AHIMMORZ mahzorim
AHIMMOSV moshavim
AHIMNORS Romanish
AHIMNOST hoistman
AHIMNOSW womanish
AHIMNOTW wham into
AHIMNRTU Mathurin
AHIMNSTU humanist
AHIMNTUX Xanthium
AHIMNTUY humanity
AHIMOPRS aphorism
AHIMOPST opsimath
AHIMORRW hairworm
AHIMPPSS sapphism✧
AHIMPRST trampish
AHIMRSST smartish
AHIMRSTT marsh tit
AHIMRSTY Rhytisma
AHIMSTVZ mitzvahs
AHINNNOR Rhiannon
AHINNNSY nannyish
AHINNOPT antiphon
AHINNORU Huronian
AHINOPRU ophiuran
AHINOPTY Hay Point
AHINORRS Harrison
AHINORST trahison
AHINOSST astonish
AHINPPSS snappish
AHINPRST tranship
AHINQSUV vanquish
AHINRRUY in a hurry
AHIOOPPT photopia
AHIOORRT root hair
AHIOPRST aphorist
AHIORSTV tovarish
AHIOSTWY hoistway
AHIPPSST sapphist
AHIPRSST starship
AHIQRSSU squarish
AHIRSSTT startish
AHJLNOPU John Paul
AHJMNOSS Mass-John
AHJNNOOT Jonathon
AHJOOTTW jaw-tooth
AHKLLOOY holly-oak
AHKLOPST shop talk
talk shop
AHKLOSTW talk show
talkshow
AHKMNOST Tom Hanks
AHKMORTU Khartoum
AHKNOOPT Pakhtoon
AHKNOOST Shotokan

AHKNOTUY	thank you
	thankyou
AHKNPSTU	Pakhtuns
AHLLMOOT	hall-moot
	moot hall
AHLLNOOS	shalloon
AHLLNOTW	town hall
AHLLNOUW	unhallow
AHLLOSSW	shallows
AHLLOSTU	thallous
AHLLOSTY	tally-hos
AHLLPRYY	phyllary
AHLMMOPY	lymphoma
AHLMNOOR	hormonal
AHLMNOTU	luna moth
AHLMOOPS	omphalos
AHLMOPRU	lamp-hour
AHLMOPTY	polymath
AHLMPSYY	Symphyla
AHLMSTYZ	shmaltzy
AHLNNORT	lanthorn
AHLOPRSU	Sholapur
AHLOPSST	slapshot
AHLOPSUZ	Zalophus
AHLORRTY	harlotry
AHLRSTUY	lathyrus
AHLRTTWY	thwartly
AHMNNNOU	non-human
AHMNNORT	Northman
AHMNNSTU	huntsman
AHMNOPTY	phantomy
AHMNORRS	ram's-horn
AHMNORSU	man-hours
AHMOOPPT	photomap
AHMOOPSS	shampoos
AHMOORSW	washroom
AHMOPTYY	myopathy
AHMORRST	shortarm
AHMORSST	R S Thomas
AHMORSSU	sour mash
AHMORSTY	harmosty
AHMORTTW	tamworth◇
AHMOSTTW	mostwhat
AHMPSTYY	sympathy
AHMQSSUU	musquash
AHNNSTYY	synanthy
AHNOOPSU	aphonous
AHNOOPTU	upon oath
AHNOORRY	honorary
AHNOPPSW	pawnshop
AHNOPPSY	pansophy
AHNOPSST	snapshot
AHNOPSTT	hot pants
AHNORSTV	Torshavn
	Tórshavn
AHNORTWW	wanworth
AHNOSSTW	swan-shot
AHNOSTUX	xanthous
AHNOSTUZ	Zoanthus
AHNPSSTU	Pashtuns
AHOOPRWW	war whoop
AHOOPTYZ	zoopathy
	Zoophyta
AHOOSSTY	soothsay
AHOOSTTW	sawtooth
AHOPPRRY	Porphyra
AHOPPSSW	swap-shop
AHOPSTUW	southpaw
AHORTTUW	watt-hour
AHOSSTUY	southsay
AIIILLVX	lixivial
AIIILRVZ	vizirial
AIIIRSSS	siriasis
AIIJKMOT	komitaji
AIIJNRTX	janitrix
AIIKKSUY	sukiyaki
AIIKLLST	silktail
AIIKLNRR	larrikin
AIIKMNNN	mannikin
AIIKNNNP	pannikin
AIIKNRST	Kristina
AIIKORTY	yakitori
AIIKTTZZ	tzatziki
AIILLLMT	milltail
AIILLLUV	illuvial
AIILLMRY	milliary
AIILLNNV	vanillin
AIILLNOP	pollinia
AIILLNOT	illation
AIILLNRY	Illyrian
AIILLNVY	villainy
AIILLPRS	sliprail
	spirilla
AIILLWWW	williwaw
AIILMMSS	Islamism
AIILMNOR	iron-mail
AIILMNOT	limation
	miltonia
AIILMNPS	alpinism
AIILMNPT	palmitin
AIILMNST	Latinism
AIILMNTT	militant◇
AIILMPUV	impluvia
AIILMRST	mistrial
	trialism
AIILMRTX	trail mix
AIILMRTY	limitary
	military
AIILMSST	Islamist
AIILMSTV	vitalism
AIILNOPS	Pasolini
AIILNOPT	oil paint
AIILNOPV	pavilion
AIILNORT	train-oil
AIILNOSV	visional
AIILNPST	alpinist
	tailspin
AIILNQRU	Quirinal
AIILNRSU	Silurian
AIILNSTT	Latinist
AIILNSTY	salinity
AIILNTTY	Latinity
AIILOPPS	papilios
AIILRSTT	trialist
AIILRTTY	triality
AIILRTVY	rivality
AIILSTTV	vitalist
AIILSTTW	wait list
	wait-list
AIILTTVY	vitality
AIIMMNNY	minyanim
AIIMMNRS	Marinism
AIIMMNRT	minimart
AIIMMNTY	immanity
AIIMMSTX	maximist
AIIMNNOS	insomnia◇
AIIMNPSS	sinapism
AIIMNPSX	panmixis
AIIMNRST	Marinist
AIIMNRSU	Arminius
AIIMNSST	saintism
	samnitis
AIIMNSTT	titanism◇
AIIMNSTV	nativism
AIIMNTTU	titanium
AIIMOPSX	apomixis
AIIMORTT	imitator
	timariot
AIIMOSST	amitosis
AIIMPPRS	priapism
AIIMPRSS	Parsiism
AIIMPRTY	imparity
AIIMRSTU	tiramisu
AIIMRUVV	vivarium
AIIMSSTT	mastitis
AIINNNOO	Anonioni
AIINNOPS	pianinos
AIINNORT	Tironian
AIINNOSV	invasion
AIINNQTU	quintain
AIINNSTU	Tunisian
AIINNSTY	insanity
AIINOOSV	avoision
AIINORTT	antiriot
	tritonia
AIINORTZ	Trizonia
AIINPRST	Pristina
AIINRRTT	irritant
AIINSSST	assist in
AIINSTTV	nativist
	visitant◇
AIINSTWX	twin axis
AIINTTVY	nativity◇
AIIORSTT	aortitis
AIIORSTV	ovaritis
AIIORTTV	vitiator
	Vittoria
AIIPRRST	airstrip
AIIPRVVY	vivipary
AIIRSSTT	satirist
AIISSSTY	syssitia
AIJKKNOU	kinkajou
AIJKLMNU	junk mail

AIJLLOOR	jillaroo
AIJLLOVY	jovially
AIJLNOPT	lap joint
AIJLNTUY	jauntily
AIJMMORS	Majorism
AIJMNOOR	Joan Miró
AIJMNOSS	Joan Sims
AIJMORSV	vis major
AIJMORTY	majority
AIJNNNOU	Junonian
AIJNOPPY	popinjay
AIJNOTTU	jato unit
AIKKLLMW	milk-walk
AIKKLLRW	Kirkwall
AIKKLOSY	silky oak
AIKKLTUW	Kwakiutl
AIKKNOTY	kantikoy
AIKKOPSY	kopiykas
AIKKRTUZ	zikkurat
AIKLLLMW	walkmill
	walk-mill
AIKLLMNT	malt-kiln
AIKLLMRR	rillmark
AIKLLMUW	waukmill
AIKLLRSS	all-risks
AIKLMMRW	milk-warm
AIKLMOSY	soya milk
AIKLMPTU	kalumpit
AIKLMWYY	Milky Way
AIKLNNPS	snap-link
AIKLNNPT	ink plant
AIKLNOPS	Polanski
AIKLNOTT	talk into
AIKLNOTW	walk into
AIKLNPST	lantskip
AIKLNRTU	kail-runt
AIKLOSUV	souvlaki
AIKLOTTW	kilowatt
AIKMMNOO	makimono
AIKMMNRT	mint mark
AIKMNOOY	yakimono
AIKMORSS	komissar
AIKNNOOS	nainsook
AIKNNSSW	swanskin
	swan-skin
AIKNORST	skiatron
AIKNORTY	karyotin
AIKNOSTT	stotinka
AIKNPSST	ski pants
AIKNRRSU	run a risk
AIKNRSST	Sanskrit
AIKNRSSU	Russniak
AIKRSSTY	satyrisk
AILLLMMT	malt-mill
AILLLNOO	linalool
AILLMMSY	smalmily
AILLMNOT	Montilla
AILLMNQU	quillman
AILLMOOV	Malvolio
AILLMOSS	Limassol
AILLMOST	misallot
AILLMOSY	loyalism
AILLMOTY	molality
AILLMPRY	primally
AILLMRUY	arum lily
AILLMUUV	alluvium
AILLNOPP	papillon
AILLNORT	anti-roll
AILLNOST	stallion
AILLNOSU	allusion
AILLNOTW	Low Latin
AILLNOUV	alluvion
AILLNPTY	pliantly
AILLNTUW	wall unit
AILLOPPS	slop pail
AILLOPUZ	pulza-oil
AILLOQTU	toquilla
AILLORSY	sailorly
AILLORTT	littoral
	tortilla
AILLORVY	lyra viol
	lyra-viol
AILLOSTY	loyalist✧
AILLPPRU	pupillar
AILLPPSU	supplial
AILLPPSY	playslip
AILLPRSY	spirally
AILLPRTY	paltrily
AILLPSTY	playlist
AILLPSWY	spillway
AILLRSTY	rallyist
AILLRTUY	ritually
AILLRTWY	willyart
AILLSUVY	visually
AILMMNOO	monomial
AILMMNUU	aluminum
AILMMOOR	mailroom
AILMMORS	moralism
AILMMORT	immortal
AILMMRSY	smarmily
AILMMSTU	summital
AILMNNOT	mannitol
AILMNNTU	luminant
AILMNOOP	palomino
AILMNOOR	monorail
AILMNOOS	moonsail
AILMNOOT	motional
AILMNOPR	prolamin
AILMNOPT	pilotman
AILMNOPY	Olympian
	palimony
	Polymnia
AILMNORT	torminal
AILMNORY	Mirna Loy
AILMNPTU	platinum
AILMNRUY	luminary
AILMNSTU	simulant
AILMOORS	sailroom
AILMOORT	motorail
	motorial
AILMOPRX	proximal
AILMORSS	solarism
AILMORST	moralist
AILMORSU	solarium
AILMORSY	royalism
AILMORTY	molarity
	morality
AILMOSTU	solatium
AILMOSTV	voltaism
AILMPPSY	misapply
AILMPSST	psalmist✧
AILMPSTY	ptyalism
AILMRRSU	ruralism
AILMRSSU	surmisal
AILMRSTU	altruism
	muralist
	ultraism
AILMRSTY	army list
AILNNOOP	Polonian
AILNNOOS	Solonian
AILNNOOT	notional
AILNNOSU	unisonal
AILNNOSW	son-in-law
AILNNOTU	lunation
	Ultonian
AILNNPTU	unpliant
AILNOOPT	optional
AILNOOST	solation
AILNOPRU	unipolar
AILNOPTY	ponytail
AILNORTW	owl-train
AILNORTZ	trizonal
AILNOSSS	sassolin
AILNOSUV	avulsion
AILNOSVY	synovial
AILNOTTV	volitant
AILNOTTY	tonality
AILNOTUX	luxation
AILNPPSY	snappily
AILNPRSU	purslain
AILNPRUV	pulvinar
AILNPSTU	nuptials
AILNPSUU	nauplius
AILNPTTU	tulipant
AILNQRTU	tranquil
AILNQTUY	quaintly
AILNRRTU	trial run
AILNRSTU	lunarist
AILNRTTU	rutilant
	turn tail
AILNRUWY	unwarily
AILNSSTU	stunsail
AILNSSUV	Silvanus
AILNSTTU	lutanist
AILNSTUU	nautilus
AILNSTVY	navy list
AILOOPRT	troopial
AILOOPST	sola topi
AILOOPZZ	Paolozzi
AILOORRS	sororial
AILOORST	isolator
AILOORTV	violator
AILOPRRV	proviral

Words marked ✧ can also be spelled with one or more capital letters

AILOPRST strap-oil
AILOPRSU pliosaur
AILOPRTU troupial
AILOPRTV Port-Vila
AILOPRTY polarity
AILOPRUY polyuria
AILORSST solarist
AILORSTT orlistat
AILORSTU sutorial
AILORSTY royalist✧
solitary
AILORTTU tutorial
AILORTUV outrival
AILOTTTY totality
AILPPRUY pupilary
AILPRRSU spur-rial
AILPRSTU stipular
AILPSTUY playsuit
AILRRSTU ruralist
AILRRSTY starrily
AILRRTUY rurality
AILRSTTU altruist
ultraist
AILRSTTY straitly
AILRSUVV survival
AILRTTUY titulary
AIMMMNOU ammonium
AIMMMSUX maximums
AIMMNORS Romanism
AIMMNORT mortmain
AIMMOSST somatism
AIMMOSSU miasmous
AIMMRRSY mismarry
AIMMRSUU masurium
AIMMXXYY mixy-maxy
AIMNNOOU uno animo
AIMNNOPT point man
AIMNNOSS mansions
AIMNNOTU mountain✧
AIMNNOTY antimony
antinomy
AIMNNRTU ruminant
AIMNOOOZ zoonomia
AIMNOORV Monrovia
AIMNOOTY myotonia
AIMNOPTV pivot-man
AIMNOQRU maroquin
AIMNORST Romanist
AIMNORTU Minotaur
AIMNORTY minatory
AIMNOSST stasimon
AIMNOSSX Saxonism
AIMNOTTU Mount Tai
mutation
AIMNPRSU up in arms
AIMNPRYY paynimry
AIMNPSTU sumpitan
AIMNRSTT Tantrism
transmit
AIMNRSTU naturism
AIMOPRSS prosaism
AIMOPRST atropism
AIMOPSST impastos
AIMOPSSY symposia
AIMORRST armorist
AIMORRSU rosarium
AIMORRUV variorum
AIMORSSU ossarium
AIMOSSTT somatist
AIMOSTTW Tom Waits
AIMPPRST strip map
AIMPPRUU puparium
AIMPRSTY partyism
AIMRRSTT Tristram
AIMRSTTU striatum
AIMRTTUY maturity
AINNNOST santonin
AINNOOTT notation
AINNOOTV novation
AINNOOTZ zonation
AINNORTU art union
AINNOTTU nutation
AINNPPSS snip-snap
AINNRSTU insurant
AINNRSTY tyrannis
AINNSSTT instants
AINNSTTY nystatin
AINOOPTT potation
AINOORTT rotation
AINOOSTT ostinato
AINOOTTV ottavino
AINOPPRT parpoint
AINOPPTU pupation
AINOPRTV proviant
AINOPSTT at points
postnati
AINOPSTW swaption
AINOPTTX tax point
AINOPTUW wait upon
AINOPTWY way point
AINOQRSU narquois
AINORRSW warrison
AINORRTU urinator
AINORSST arsonist
AINORSTT strontia
AINORSTU sutorian
AINORTVY Vanitory®
vanitory
AINOSSTX Saxonist
AINOSTTU titanous
AINPPRTT trippant
AINPRSST spraints
AINPRSSU Prussian
AINPRSTU Rasputin
AINPSSSY synapsis
AINPSSTU puissant
AINPSTTU pantsuit
AINQTTUY quantity
AINRSTTT Tantrist
AINRSTTU antirust
naturist
AINRSTTY tanistry
AINRTUXY X-ray unit
AIOOORRT oratorio
AIOORSUV ovarious
AIOPRRSS Pissarro
AIOPRRTT parrot it
portrait
AIOPRSST prosaist
protasis
AIOPRSTT Protista
AIOPSTTU utopiast
AIORRSTV varistor
AIORRTWY ryotwari
AIORSTTV votarist
AIORSTUV virtuosa
AIOSSSTY isostasy
AIPPRSTT Trappist
AIPPRSTY papistry
AIPPTTTY pitty-pat
AIPRRTTU Partitur
AIPRRTTY tray-trip
AIPRSSTU upstairs
AIPRSSTY sparsity
AIRRSTTY artistry
AJKLNSTU salt-junk
AJKNNOOU junkanoo
AJLLNOOS Al Jolson
AJLMPUWY lumpy jaw
AJMNSSTU Jan Smuts
AJMPRSTU star jump
AJMRSTUY jurymast
AJORRTUY juratory
AKKORSTW taskwork
AKLLMRUY mullarky
AKLLNOTW wall knot
AKLLNPRU pull rank
AKLMNOOW moonwalk
AKLNNOPT plankton
AKLNOTTW town talk
AKLOORWY look awry
AKLPRRSU larkspur
AKMMNOOR monomark
AKMMNRSU Murmansk
AKMNORTU Turkoman
AKMNRSTU Turkmans
AKMOPRST postmark
AKNNOSTZ Konstanz
AKNOORST ostrakon
AKNOOUYZ yokozuna
AKNOPSTW swankpot
AKOPQRTU top quark
AKOPRRTW partwork
AKOPRSTU spark out
AKORSWWX waxworks
ALLLOOPU Ullapool
ALLLOSSU All Souls
ALLLPRUY plurally
ALLMNORY normally
ALLMOPSX smallpox
ALLMORTY mortally
ALLMOSSW wall moss
ALLMOUWY mulloway

ALLMPRUU plumular
ALLMTUUY mutually
ALLNOOPY Apollyon
ALLNOPRS snap roll
ALLNORSS lasslorn
ALLOPSTY postally
ALLORSST allsorts
ALLORTWW wallwort
ALLRUUVY uvularly
ALMMMOOW Mo Mowlam
ALMMNRUU nummular
ALMMNSUU Musulman
ALMMOOPR lamp-room
ALMMORTW maltworm
ALMNNOOR non-moral
ALMNORTY matronly
ALMNORYY Myrna Loy
ALMOOPRY playroom
ALMOORTU alum-root
ALMOPPST lamppost
ALMORSUU ramulous
ALMOSTTU mulattos
sum total
ALMPSSTY symplast
ALMRTUUY tumulary
ALNNOOPR nonpolar
ALNNOTWY wantonly
ALNOOPPR propanol
ALNOOPRT portolan
pronotal
ALNOOPXY polyaxon
ALNOOPYZ polyzoan
ALNOPPTT plant pot
pot plant
ALNOPPUY play upon
ALNOPRST plastron
ALNOPRTU portulan
ALNOPTTU plant out
ALNORRWY narrowly
ALNORSVY sovranly
ALNOTWWY tawny owl
ALNPPSTU supplant
ALNRRTUU nurtural
ALOOOPRT Portaloo®
ALOOPPRS proposal
ALOOPRST postoral
ALOOPRSW poor laws
ALOOPRTU uprootal
ALOORSUV valorous
ALOORTYZ zoolatry
ALOPPRYY polypary
ALOPPSSU supposal
ALOPPSUU papulous
ALOPRRSU sporular
ALOPRSTT portlast
ALOPRSTU postural
pulsator
ALOPRSTY pastorly
ALOPSSSU spousals
ALOPSSTT last post
ALOPSTUU patulous
ALORRSUY surroyal
ALORSTTW saltwort
ALORSUVY savourly
ALORTUWY outlawry
ALPPSTUY platypus
ALPRRSUY spur-ryal
ALPRSTUU pustular
ALRSSSUU russulas
ALSSSSUW suss laws
AMMNOORT motorman
AMMNPTUY tympanum
AMMORRWY army worm
AMNNOOTT montanto
AMNNORSW mansworn
AMNNORSY mansonry
AMNNOSSU mass noun
AMNNOSTW townsman
AMNNOTTU mountant
AMNNOTYY antonymy
AMNNPSTU puntsman
AMNNSTTU stuntman
AMNOOPPS pompanos
AMNOOPTU Mount Apo
AMNOORTY many-root
AMNOOTUY autonomy
AMNOOTWY toywoman
AMNOOTXY taxonomy
AMNOPRYY paronymy
AMNOTTUU To Autumn
AMNOTTUY tautonym
AMOOORSS amorosos
AMOOPRSY Pyrosoma
AMOORRRT rotor arm
AMOORRTY moratory
AMOORSTZ smorzato
AMOORTWY motorway
AMOOSSTU astomous
AMOOTTUY autotomy
AMOPRRST marsport
AMOPRSTT tram-stop
AMOPRSXY paroxysm
AMOPSTTU stamp out
AMOQSSUU squamous
AMORRTUY mortuary
AMORSTTU outsmart
AMORTTUY mutatory
ANNOOQTU non-quota
ANNOORST sonorant
ANNOPRTY non-party
ANNOSSTU stannous
ANNPRSUY spunyarn
ANOOPPPS pap-spoon
ANOOPRRT pronator
ANOOPRSS sopranos
ANOOPRTT pro tanto
ANOORSUU anourous
ANOOSTTY not to say
ANOPPPRT proppant
ANOPPSSU pass upon
ANOPRSTU stroupan
ANOPRTTU trapunto
ANOPSTUY stay upon
ANOQRSSU squarson
ANORSTVY sovranty
ANPRSTUU pursuant
ANRRSTTU star turn
ANRRTTUY truantry
ANRSSTYY synastry
AOOOPRST soaproot
AOOOPRSZ Sporozoa
AOOOPRTZ protozoa✧
AOOPPRSY apospory
AOOPRSSU saporous
AOOPRSTT pot roast
pot-roast
AOOPRSTU atropous
AOOPRSTW soapwort
AOOPRSUV vaporous
AOOPRTTY potatory
AOORRTTY rotatory
AOORSSUV savorous
AOPPRSST passport
AOPPSTTU put a stop
AOPQRTTU quart-pot
AOPRRRTY parrotry
AOPRRTUY pourtray
AOPRSSTT starspot
AOPRSTTY pyrostat
AORRSSYY say sorry
AORRSTTW starwort
AORRTTWW wartwort
AORSSTTU stratous
AORSSTTY starosty
AORSTTTU start out

B

BBBCEOWY cobwebby
BBBEINOT bobbinet
BBBELRUY blubbery
BBBEOOTU boob tube
BBBGILNU blubbing
BBBHNOOY hobnobby
BBBHOOUU hubbuboo
BBBIITTY bit by bit
BBBINOPY bobby pin
BBBLMOPU plumb bob
BBBLOOXY box-lobby
BBBMOUZZ buzz bomb
BBCDEILR cribbled
BBCDERSU scrubbed
BBCDIMOY bombycid
BBCEILRS scribble
BBCEKLUU bluebuck
BBCELOPU cobble up
BBCELORS cobblers
BBCELORY cobblery
BBCEMNOU buncombe
BBCENSUU snub cube
BBCERRSU scrubber
BBCGIINR cribbing
BBCGIKSU big bucks
BBCGILNO cobbling

BBCGILNU	clubbing
BBCHILSU	clubbish
BBCHILUY	chubbily
BBCHKOOS	boschbok
BBCHKSUU	bushbuck
BBCILMSU	clubbism
BBCILRSY	scribbly
BBCILSTU	clubbist
BBCKLOOU	book club
BBDDEEIR	bride-bed
BBDDEEMO	demobbed
BBDDEEYY	beddy-bye
BBDDENUU	undubbed
BBDEEMNU	benumbed
BBDEENUW	unwebbed
BBDEERSU	subbreed
BBDEGIRU	Burbidge
BBDEHORT	throbbed
BBDEILLN	bellbind
BBDEILLR	bellbird
BBDEILMY	Dimbleby
BBDEILRR	dribbler
BBDEILRT	dribblet
BBDEILRU	bluebird
BBDEILRY	dry-bible
BBDEIMOV	dive-bomb
BBDEINOR	dobber-in
BBDEINRU	unribbed
BBDEKOOT	book-debt
BBDELLMU	dumb-bell
BBDELLOO	bobolled
BBDELSTU	stubbled
BBDENRUU	unrubbed
BBDGINRU	drubbing
BBDILORT	bird-bolt
BBDLOOWY	body blow
BBDOSUYY	busybody
BBEEEHRR	herb-beer
BBEEFLLU	bull-beef
BBEEGLOS	Goebbels
BBEEHINS	nebbishe
BBEEHLOW	bobwheel
BBEEHMOR	Beerbohm
BBEEHNOT	on the ebb
BBEEHTYY	by the bye
BBEEIIRR	beri-beri
BBEEIMTT	bimbette
BBEEIRRS	berberis
BBEEISTV	Tibb's Eve
BBEELLLU	bluebell
BBEEOPPR	bebopper
BBEFILRR	fribbler
BBEFIMOR	firebomb
BBEGIIST	gibbsite
BBEGILNP	pebbling
BBEGILRY	glibbery
BBEGLOPU	gobble up
BBEGRRUY	berry bug
BBEHIOTW	bobwhite
BBEILLNO	bonibell
BBEILNOW	wibble on
BBEILQRU	quibbler
BBEILRRY	bilberry
BBEILRST	stibbler
BBEIMMOT	time bomb
BBEIMOPP	pipe bomb
BBEIMOST	bombsite
BBEINOVY	Bevin boy
BBEIRSTU	subtribe
BBEISTTU	tubbiest
BBEKLOOU	blue book
BBEKNOOT	bontebok
BBELLORU	boerbull
BBELLOUY	bell buoy
BBELLRUY	lubberly
BBELNRUU	burn blue
BBELORSY	slobbery
BBENOORT	born to be
BBENOOTX	bento box
BBENORSY	snobbery
BBEORSUV	sub verbo
BBEOSTUU	Subbuteo®
BBERRRUY	Burberry®
BBFFLOUW	bluff bow
BBFGILNU	flubbing
BBGGINRU	grubbing
BBGHILNO	hobbling
BBGIIJNS	jibbings
BBGIILMN	blimbing
BBGIILNN	nibbling
BBGILMNU	bumbling
BBGILNOW	wobbling
BBGILNOY	lobbying
BBGILNRU	burbling
BBGILNSU	slubbing
BBGILRUY	grubbily
BBGINNSU	snubbing
BBGINSTU	stubbing
BBHILOSS	slobbish
BBHIMOSY	hobbyism
BBHINOOT	Hobbiton
BBHINOSS	snobbish
BBHINSSU	snubbish
BBHIOOSY	boobyish
BBHIORTY	hobbitry
BBHIOSTY	hobbyist
BBHIRSUY	rubbishy
BBHRSSUU	subshrub
BBIKLLOO	billbook
BBIKLNOO	bobolink
BBILLOYY	billyboy
BBILOSTY	lobbyist
BBILOSUU	bibulous
BBIMNOOR	bob minor
BBIMNOSS	snobbism
BBIMOOSY	boobyism
BBINORRY	ribbonry
BBLLNNUU	buln-buln
BBLLOUYY	bully boy
	bully-boy
BBNORSTU	stubborn
BCCCIILY	bicyclic
BCCDHIKO	dobchick
BCCEEIRR	cerebric
BCCEHIOY	by choice
BCCEHIRU	cherubic
BCCEHKOX	check box
BCCEIIIS	cicisbei
BCCEIILO	libeccio
BCCEIIOS	cicisbeo
BCCEIKLO	ice block
BCCEILRU	crucible✧
BCCEMRUU	cucumber
BCCIIMOR	microbic
BCCIISTU	cubistic
BCCILMOU	columbic
BCCILOOR	broccoli
BCCIMNUU	Buccinum
BCCINORR	corncrib
BCCIRTUU	cucurbit
BCCKLMOU	bum-clock
BCCOSTUU	Cub Scout
BCCSSUUU	succubus
BCDDEHIL	childbed
BCDEEEHR	breeched
BCDEEEMR	December
BCDEEHNR	bedrench
BCDEEHOU	débouché
BCDEEIKN	Benedick
BCDEEILR	credible
BCDEEILU	educible
BCDEEINT	benedict✧
BCDEEIRS	describe
BCDEEKRU	reedbuck
BCDEELOR	corbeled
BCDEEMRU	cumbered
BCDEEORV	bedcover
BCDEEOTT	obtected
BCDEFKLO	flock-bed
BCDEHINS	disbench
BCDEHLOT	blotched
BCDEIILR	bird-lice
BCDEIIPR	bid price
BCDEIIRR	ricebird
BCDEIKRR	brick-red
	red brick
	redbrick
BCDEILRY	credibly
BCDEIMNO	combined
BCDEIMOS	side comb
BCDEINOU	icebound
BCDEIRSU	curbside
BCDEKLUU	blue duck
BCDEKOOO	codebook
BCDEKOSS	bedsocks
BCDEMNOU	uncombed
BCDENRUU	uncurbed
BCDHIORR	birch rod
BCDHORSU	subchord
BCDIIKRT	tick bird
BCDIIMOR	bromidic
BCDIIPSU	bicuspid
BCDIKLLU	duckbill

BCDIKMOY Moby Dick
BCDIKORR rock-bird
BCDILMOY molybdic
BCDILORU colubrid
BCDIMORS scombrid
BCDINRUU rubicund
BCDLOOOT cold boot
cold-boot
BCEEEFIN benefice
BCEEEFKN neckbeef
BCEEEHRS breeches
BCEEEINR Berenice
BCEEEIRR rice beer
BCEEELRU Bruce Lee
BCEEENRS bescreen
BCEEEQRU Quebecer
BCEEERSU berceuse
BCEEFILN fencible
BCEEFNOR corn-beef
BCEEGLLU glee club
BCEEHILO beech-oil
BCEEHKSU buckshee
BCEEHNRU unbreech
BCEEHNTU beechnut
BCEEHPSY by-speech
BCEEIILM imbecile
BCEEINOT cenobite
BCEEIORR Corbiere
BCEEIRTT brettice
BCEEKNNO neck-bone
BCEELLOT bellcote
BCEELOOR borecole
BCEELRTU tubercle
BCEEMNOW Newcombe
BCEEMNRU encumber
BCEEMRRU cerebrum
cumberer
BCEEPRTY cyberpet
BCEERRSU Cerberus
BCEERSTU suberect
BCEERSXY cybersex
BCEFFIIR febrific
BCEFHISU subchief
BCEFILOR forcible
BCEFIMNO fine comb
BCEFLSUU Blefuscu
BCEGIINO biogenic
BCEGIMNO becoming
BCEGLNOO conglobe
BCEHILPU blue-chip
BCEHIMOT Chimbote
BCEHIMRS besmirch
BCEHIMRU cherubim
BCEHINRU cherubin
BCEHINSY by inches
BCEHIRST britches
BCEHIRTY bitchery
BCEHMSTU besmutch
BCEHNRSU Burschen
BCEHORRU brochure
BCEHORTY botchery
BCEHRSTU butcher's
Schubert
BCEHRTTU Cuthbert
BCEHRTUY butchery
BCEIIKLN iceblink
BCEIILMS miscible
BCEIILNV vincible
BCEIILST bit-slice
BCEIIMRS imbrices
BCEIINRS inscribe
BCEIKLOO booklice
BCEIKNOR beck-iron
BCEILLNU club-line
BCEILMRU Mulciber
BCEILNRU runcible
BCEILORW rice bowl
BCEILOTU tubicole
BCEILPRU republic
BCEIMNRU incumber
BCEIMOSW combwise
BCEIMRRU crumbier
BCEINOVX biconvex
BCEIOOPS bioscope
BCEIOOVX voice box
BCEIOPSX spice box
BCEIORRS cribrose
BCEIORST bisector
BCEJNOOT no object
BCEJOORT objector
BCEKLNOT bloncket
BCEKLNUU unbuckle
BCEKLSUY Buckley's
BCEKMSTU stembuck
BCEKOORU buckeroo
BCELLRUW well curb
BCELMOSS combless
BCELORTU clotebur
BCELORUV overclub
BCELRSSU curbless
BCEMNOOY cob money
BCEMOORS rose comb
BCEMOORV comb over
combover
BCENORRY by-corner
BCENOSTX scent box
BCEOORTU cube root
BCEORRSU obscurer
BCEORRWY cowberry
BCFGLLOU golf club
BCFHILRY birch fly
BCFIIMOR morbific
BCFIIORT fibrotic
BCFILORY forcibly
BCFIMORU cubiform
BCFLOOTU club foot
BCFLRTUU Turf Club
BCFOORRU curb-roof
BCGHIINT bitching
BCGHINNU bunching
BCGHINOT botching
BCGHINTU butching
BCGIIKNR bricking
BCGIIKST big stick
BCGIILMN climbing
BCGIINRS scribing
BCGIKKRU grub kick
BCGIKLNO blocking
BCGIKLNU buckling
BCGIKLOW wig block
BCGIKNOR brick-nog
BCGILOPU go public
BCGIMNOS combings
BCGINNOU bouncing
BCHIILTY bitchily
BCHIISSU hibiscus✧
BCHIKLOS blockish
BCHIOORY choirboy
BCHKNORU buckhorn
BCHKOSTU buckshot
BCHLMNOY lynch mob
BCHLNOUX lunch box
BCHLOOTX box-cloth
BCHLRSUU clubrush
BCHNOORS bronchos
BCHNORSU bronchus
BCHOOTUX touch-box
BCIIKNOR bick-iron
BCIILLSY sibyllic
BCIILNPU in public
BCIIMNOO bionomic
BCIIMORU ciborium
BCIIMRSS scribism
BCIINORV vibronic
BCIIORST sorbitic
BCIIOSTT biscotti
BCIISTUY biscuity
BCIKKNSU buckskin
BCIKLNOT block-tin
BCIKLOOT bootlick
BCIKORRW cribwork
BCILLORW crow-bill
BCILLPUY publicly
BCILMOSY symbolic
BCILNOUY bouncily
BCILOORU bicolour
BCIMORSU microbus
BCIMOSUX music box
BCINOSSU subsonic
BCINOSTU subtonic
BCINOSUU incubous
BCIOORST robotics
BCIOOSTT biscotto
BCIORRSS cross-rib
BCIORRSU cribrous
BCKKOOOO cookbook
BCKLLOUY bullocky
BCKLNOSU sunblock
BCKLOOTU block out
BCKOOOPY copybook
BCKOSTTU buttocks
BCLMOOOW wool comb
BCLMOORU clubroom

Words marked ✧ can also be spelled with one or more capital letters

BCLMOSSU club moss
BCLMOSUU Columbus
BCLOORTU clubroot
BCMORSUU cumbrous
BCNOORWW Brown Cow
BCNORSSU cross bun
BCOOORTW crow boot
BCOORSSW crossbow
BCOOSTUY Boy Scout
BCORSTTU obstruct
BCRSSTUU subcrust
BDDDEENU unbedded
BDDDEIRY red biddy
BDDDENUU unbudded
BDDEEELL debelled
BDDEEFIL field bed
BDDEEFLU befuddle
BDDEEGIR begirded
BDDEEGTU budgeted
BDDEEIMM bedimmed
BDDEEIMO embodied
BDDEEINT indebted
BDDEEINW bindweed
BDDEEIRR reed-bird
BDDEEIRS birdseed
BDDEEIRY bird-eyed
BDDEELMU bemuddle
BDDEENNU unbended
BDDEEORR bordered
BDDEESSU debussed
BDDEGINR Bridgend
BDDEGNOU Don Budge
BDDEGORY Derby dog
BDDEILNR brindled
BDDEILOO bloodied
BDDEIMUX mixed bud
BDDEINNU unbidden
BDDEINOU unbodied
BDDEINRU underbid
BDDEIORS disorbed
BDDEIOWY widebody
BDDELOOR blood-red
BDDEOTYY Teddy boy
BDDGINOR brodding
BDDGOOSY dogsbody
dog's-body
BDDGUUYY Buddy Guy
BDDHIIRY dihybrid
BDDHIMSU Buddhism
BDDHISTU Buddhist
BDDIMNOY mind-body
BDDINOOW woodbind
BDDINPUU pudibund
BDDMNOUW dumb down
BDEEEGNO edgebone
BDEEEGRU budgeree
BDEEEHST bed-sheet
BDEEEHTU hebetude
BDEEEINS beniseed
BDEEEIRV Bedivere
BDEEELLR rebelled
BDEEELLV bevelled
BDEEELOS seed-lobe
BDEEELPU Deep Blue
BDEEELUW blueweed
BDEEEMMR membered
BDEEENOS Bodensee
BDEEERTT bettered
BDEEERTV breveted
BDEEETTW bewetted
BDEEFFRU buffered
BDEEFILR belfried
BDEEFINN befinned
BDEEFINR befriend
BDEEFITT befitted
BDEEFOOR forebode
BDEEFOOW beefwood
BDEEGGIW bewigged
BDEEGGNU unbegged
BDEEGGRU begrudge
debugger
BDEEGILN bleeding
BDEEGINR breeding
BDEEHIRS Hebrides
BDEEHLLR hell-bred
BDEEHLNO beholden
BDEEHLOR beholder
BDEEHMOR home-bred
BDEEHNST the bends
BDEEHORV hover-bed
BDEEHRTY The Derby
BDEEIILN inedible
BDEEIINY bindi-eye
BDEEIKRS kerbside
BDEEILLL libelled
BDEEILLT billeted
BDEEILLU eludible
BDEEILMR mild beer
BDEEILNN bed linen
BDEEILNO bone-idle
BDEEILNV vendible
BDEEILOR erodible
BDEEILRW bewilder
BDEEIMRT timbered
BDEEINOT obedient
BDEEINSW bendwise
BDEEIORS osier-bed
BDEEIORU bouderie
BDEEIRRV river bed
BDEEIRST bestride
BDEEIRSY bird's-eye
BDEEISTU besuited
BDEEKNRU bunkered
debunker
BDEELLOW bowelled
BDEELLRW well-bred
BDEELLRY redbelly
BDEELMNO embolden
BDEELMOR rebeldom
BDEELMPU beplumed
BDEELNTU unbelted
BDEELORU redouble
BDEELORX box elder
BDEELOSU besouled
BDEEMNOT bodement
BDEEMORR emborder
BDEEMORY re-embody
BDEEMOSS embossed
BDEEMSSU embussed
BDEENNOT bonneted
BDEENOUY unobeyed
BDEEOPRW bepowder
BDEEORRR borderer
BDEEORST bestrode
BDEEORTU outbreed
BDEEOSSY boss-eyed
BDEEOSTT besotted
BDEEPRRU pure-bred
BDEEPRSS press bed
BDEERRTU true-bred
BDEERRWY dewberry
BDEERTTU rebutted
BDEFFTUU Dubuffet
BDEFIILR bird-life
BDEFIIRR fire-bird
BDEFIIRU rubified
BDEFILSU subfield
BDEFINRR fernbird
BDEFOORY fore-body
BDEGGNOU egg-bound
BDEGHHIR high-bred
BDEGHILT blighted
BDEGHIRT bedright
BDEGILNN blending
BDEGINRW berg wind
BDEGINSY by design
BDEGIORX Oxbridge
BDEGLLOY belly-god
BDEGLNOU bludgeon
BDEGLOOR Belgorod
BDEGNOOY go beyond
BDEGORRY dogberry✧
BDEGORSU budgeros
BDEGORUW budgerow
BDEHILNT the blind
BDEHIMOR home bird
BDEHIRST The Birds
BDEHJOOT do the job
BDEHKOOR herd-book
BDEHKOOY hooked by
BDEHLSUV bushveld
BDEHMOOY home body
BDEIIKLR birdlike
BDEIIKRT dirt bike
BDEIILMR bird-lime
BDEIILTY debility
BDEIIRRW wire bird
BDEIKNOR brodekin
BDEIKNSU buskined
BDEILLMU bdellium
BDEILLOW billowed
BDEILMOS semibold
BDEILMRT timbrel'd

BDEILMSU sublimed
BDEILNOU unilobed
BDEILNOY bodyline
BDEILNPW Blind Pew
BDEILNRS blinders
BDEILNRU unbridle
BDEILNVY vendibly
BDEILORT trilobed
BDEILORV lovebird
BDEILOSS bodiless
BDEILOSW disbowel
BDEILRRY lyrebird
BDEILRST bristled
BDEIMNOR Benidorm
BDEIMNSU nimbused
BDEIMNUU unimbued
BDEIMORR imborder
BDEIMORY embryoid
BDEINOOW woodbine✧
BDEINORV bind over
ovenbird
BDEINOSU bedouins✧
BDEINRSU burnside
BDEINRTU turbined
BDEINRUU unburied
BDEINTTU unbitted
BDEIORRY broidery
BDEIORTW word bite
BDEIOSUX suboxide
BDEIRSSU disburse
BDEKLMOO blokedom
BDEKNOOU unbooked
BDEKOOPU booked-up
BDELLOOR bordello
doorbell
BDELLOOT let blood
BDELLOUZ bulldoze
BDELMRUU delubrum
BDELNNUU unbundle
BDELNOOW new blood
BDELNOSS boldness
BDELNOTU unbolted
BDELNOUU undouble
BDELNOUW unblowed
BDELNPUU bundle up
BDELOORV overbold
BDELOPUU double up
BDELORTU troubled
BDELORUU doublure
BDELPSUU subduple
BDEMNOTU untombed
BDEMNSSU dumbness
BDEMOOSY somebody
BDEMOOTT bottomed
BDENNOTU Dubonnet
BDENNOUY ybounden
BDENNRUU unburden
unburned
BDENOORU Eurobond
BDENOOTW bentwood
BDENORUY under-boy
BDENOSTU bone-dust
BDENPRUU burned up
BDENRSUU unbrused
BDENRUUY underbuy
BDEOORRW borrowed
BDEOPTTU put to bed
BDEOPTYY type-body
BDEORRSU suborder
BDEORRTU obtruder
BDERSTUU subtrude
BDFFIPRU puffbird
BDFGNOOU fogbound
BDFILLLO billfold
BDFILNOO bloodfin
BDFINORU unforbid
BDFINRUU furibund
BDFIRRSU surfbird
BDFIRTUU fruit-bud
BDFLOTUU doubtful
BDFORSUY bodysurf
BDGGIINR bridging
BDGHOOUY doughboy
BDGIIKNR kingbird
BDGIILNN blinding
BDGIILNU building
BDGIINRW birdwing
BDGILNNU bundling
BDGILNOU doubling
BDGILNTU blind gut
BDGINNOU bounding
unboding
BDGINOOR brooding
BDGINOOY boodying
BDGINORS birdsong
songbird
BDGINOTU doubting
BDGIRSUU Duisburg
BDGNRUUY burgundy✧
BDHIIPRW whipbird
BDHIMOOR rhomboid
BDHIMORT birthdom
BDHIMSUU subhumid
BDHIORST birdshot
BDHKOORU Dukhobor
BDHLOOOT blood-hot
BDHMOSUW dumbshow
BDHNRSUU unshrubd
BDHOOPSY body shop
BDIIINRS brindisi✧
BDIIJOTU Djibouti
BDIILLRT drill bit
BDIILOQU obliquid
BDIIMRUU rubidium
BDIIOOSW wood ibis
BDIIOOTX idiot box
BDILLLOO ill blood
BDILLOOY bloodily
BDILMORY morbidly
BDILNNSU sunblind
sun-blind
BDILNOOW boil down
BDILNORW wild-born
BDILNOWW windblow
BDILNPRU purblind
BDILOORY broodily
BDILOOTW blood-wit
BDILORRT Lord Birt
BDILRTUY turbidly
BDIMNORU moribund
BDIMOOSS disbosom
BDIMOSTU misdoubt
BDINNRUW windburn
BDINORSW snowbird
BDINRTUU unturbid
BDIOORTY botryoid
BDIOSTUY bodysuit
BDIOTTXY ditty box
BDJKNNOU junk bond
BDKNOOOR doorknob
BDKOOORW wordbook
BDKOORWY bodywork
BDKOOSTU studbook
BDLLOTUY dolly tub
BDLLSTUU bulldust
BDLNOOOU doubloon
BDLNOOUY unbloody
BDLNOOWW blow down
blowdown
BDLOSTTU stud bolt
BDLOSTUW dust bowl✧
BDMOORRS smørbrød
BDNNOOTU bunodont
BDNNORUW burn down
BDNOOORW wood-born
BDNOOPTU pot-bound
BDNOOSUW sound bow
BDNOOSUX soundbox
BDNOOTUU outbound
BDORUWZZ buzz word
buzzword
BEEEEFLN enfeeble
BEEEENQU queen bee
BEEEENRT terebene
BEEEENRZ ebenezer
BEEEFLSS feblesse
BEEEGIRS besieger
BEEEGRTT begetter
BEEEHIST bheesite
bheestie
BEEEHLNO heel-bone
BEEEHLRT herbelet
BEEEHLWW webwheel
BEEEHNOY honey bee
BEEEHOSU bee-house
BEEEILLL libellee
BEEEILRV believer
BEEEINNS Beninese
BEEEINRT bien-être
BEEEINST ébéniste
BEEEKLRY Berkeley
BEEELLRR rebeller
BEEELLRT belleter

BEEELLRV beveller
BEEELLUV belle vue
BEEELMNS ensemble
BEEELMRS resemble
BEEELMSY beseemly
BEEELMZZ embezzle
BEEELRVY Beverley
BEEEMMRR remember
BEEEMNSU unbeseem
BEEEMRSS Bessemer
BEEENSST sebesten
BEEEPPPR bepepper
BEEEPRST bepester
BEEEPRUZ breeze up
BEEERSST bretesse
BEEERSTT besetter
BEEESSST tsessebe
BEEFFLMU bemuffle
BEEFGHNU hung-beef
BEEFGINR befringe
BEEFHILS feeblish
BEEFILLT lifebelt
BEEFILLX flexible
BEEFILNU unbelief
BEEFIORT fire-bote
BEEFIRTU fire-tube
BEEFLORW beflower
BEEFNORR Born Free
freeborn
BEEFNRRY fen-berry
BEEFNRTU unbereft
BEEGHILW big wheel
BEEGHLMR bergmehl
BEEGHLRU Breughel
BEEGIILL eligible
BEEGIILX exigible
BEEGILLR gerbille
gill beer
BEEGILNT beetling
BEEGILRU beguiler
BEEGINNR beginner
BEEGINSW beeswing
BEEGINUU Eugubine
BEEGKLUY keybugle
BEEGLNOR belonger
Grenoble
BEEGLRUY blue-grey
BEEGMRSU submerge
BEEGNOOW wobegone
BEEGNOTT begotten
BEEGNRSU subgenre
sungrebe
BEEGORTT go better
BEEHHMOT behemoth
BEEHIJST jib sheet
BEEHILMN Blenheim
BEEHLLNT hell-bent
BEEHLOOR borehole
BEEHLOVY behovely
BEEHLRSS herbless
BEEHLRST blethers
BEEHLSTU the blues✧
BEEHMORW home-brew
BEEHNOOP neophobe
BEEHNORS nose-herb
BEEHNOTY the Boyne
BEEHNRRT brethren
BEEHNRVZ Brezhnev
BEEHORTX The Boxer
BEEIILNZ zibeline
BEEIILST Tebilise®
BEEIILTZ Tebilize®
BEEIINOS ebionise
BEEIINOT Ebionite
BEEIINOZ ebionize
BEEIINRT bénitier
BEEIINST Ibsenite
BEEIISTZ bitesize
BEEIJSTU bejesuit
Jebusite
BEEIKLTU tubelike
BEEIKLWY bi-weekly
BEEILLLR libeller
BEEILLNO lobeline
BEEILLNU blue line
Blue Nile
Nile blue
BEEILLTT belittle
BEEILMOS embolise
BEEILMOZ embolize
BEEILMPR periblem
BEEILMPU umble-pie
BEEILNSS sensible
BEEILNST stilbene
tensible
BEEILNSU nebulise
BEEILNUZ nebulize
BEEILOTV lovebite
BEEILRRT terrible
BEEILRYZ breezily
BEEIMRRU umbriere
BEEIMRTT embitter
BEEINNSS beinness
BEEINNSV Ben Nevis
BEEINORT tenebrio✧
BEEIOQSU obsequie
BEEIORSS soberise
BEEIORSZ soberize
BEEIORTV overbite
BEEIRSSU suberise
BEEIRSUZ suberize
BEEIRTVY every bit
BEEISSUU Eusebius
BEEJLOWX jewel box
BEEKMOPR pembroke
BEEKNOPS bespoken
BEEKNORZ Brezonek
BEEKNOST steenbok
BEELLNTT bell tent
BEELLOPR bell-rope
BEELLORW bellower
rebellow
BEELLOSS lobeless
BEELLSUY Bullseye
bull's-eye
BEELLTUW tube well
BEELMMOP bepommel
BEELMNNO noblemen
BEELMRRT trembler
BEELMRRU lumberer
BEELMRST trembles
BEELMRTT Mt Elbert
BEELNNOT Ben Elton
BEELNOSS boneless
noblesse
BEELNOSU bluenose✧
BEELNOTU blue note
BEELNSSU blueness
BEELNTTU betel nut
BEELNTUY butylene
BEELOOST obsolete
BEELOPTU bleep out
BEELOQRU breloque
BEELOSTW steelbow
BEELPRUV buplever
BEELRSSV verbless
BEELRTUU true blue
true-blue
BEELSSTU tubeless
BEEMNORV november✧
BEEMNRRU numberer
renumber
BEEMOPRT obtemper
BEEMORSS embosser
BEEMPPRU beer pump
BEEMQSUU embusqué
BEEMRSSU submerse
BEEMRSTU bum steer
BEEMRTTU umbrette
BEEMRTUZ zerumbet
BEENNOOY one by one
BEENNOSW E W Benson
BEENORSS en brosse
BEENORTU bountree
BEENORTV verboten
BEENOSTU tubenose
BEENPRST besprent
BEENRSTW bestrewn
BEENRTTU brunette
BEENSSTU subtense
BEENSTTX next best
BEEOORRT boortree
root beer
BEEOORTT beetroot
boot-tree
BEEORRSV observer
BEEORRTU bourtree
BEEORSSU suberose
BEEORSTU to be sure
tuberose
BEEORSTW bestower
BEEPRSTY presbyte
BEERRSTW brewster

BEERRTTU rebutter
BEERSSUV subserve
subverse
BEERSTTY by-street
BEESTTTU test tube
BEFGIILL fillibeg
BEFGIINR briefing
BEFGILNU fungible
BEFHILSU bluefish
BEFHINOS bonefish
fish-bone
BEFHIRSU bushfire
BEFIKNOX knife-box
BEFIKNOY knife-boy
BEFILLMU blue film
BEFILLXY flexibly
BEFILMOR forelimb
BEFILNOO oil of ben
BEFILOUY lifebuoy
BEFILRST Filberts
BEFILSTY by itself
BEFINNOO bonne foi
BEFIORTT forebitt
BEFKLNUU blue funk
BEFLLLUY bellyful
BEFLLORU full-bore
BEFLNORS self-born
BEFLOOOT lobe-foot
BEFLORUW furbelow
BEFLSTUU tubefuls
BEFNOORR forborne
BEFOOTTU tube foot
BEFORRXY foxberry
BEGGINRS Ginsberg
BEGGOOOS goosegob
BEGHIILP philibeg
BEGHIIRT Ghiberti
BEGHILRT blighter
therblig
BEGHINOR neighbor
BEGHINRT brighten
BEGHIOSU big house
BEGHITWY by weight
BEGHLNOU bunghole
BEGHNOTU boughten
BEGHOSTU besought
BEGHOSUU bughouse
BEGIIISS sigisbei
BEGIILLN ill-being
libeling
BEGIILLY eligibly
BEGIINOS big noise
BEGIINRZ zingiber
BEGIIOSS sigisbeo
BEGIJORR jig borer
BEGILLLU bluegill
gullible
BEGILLNU bullgine
BEGILLNY bellying
BEGILNNU Nibelung
BEGILNNY benignly
BEGILNOS Gobelins
BEGILNOV beloving
BEGILNSS blessing
glibness
BEGILNTT bletting
BEGILNUW bluewing
BEGILRST best girl
BEGIMNOS besoming
BEGIMNOY big money
BEGIMOST misbegot
BEGIMOSY bogeyism
BEGINNNU unbenign
BEGINNOR ringbone
BEGINNOT not-being
BEGINNTU Tübingen
BEGINOOS besognio
BEGINORS Gisborne
sobering
BEGINRRY berrying
BEGLLORY gor-belly
BEGLLOTU globulet
BEGLMRRU grumbler
BEGLNOOR long robe
BEGLNOOU Boulogne
BEGLNOUW bluegown
BEGLOOVX glove box
BEGNNRRU Nürnberg
BEGNNTUV bung-vent
BEGNOORU bourgeon
BEGNORTU burgonet
BEGNSSUU subgenus
BEGPRSUU superbug
BEHHOTUW who but he
BEHIKLOS blokeish
BEHIKPSU pushbike
BEHILLMR herb mill
BEHILLOS shoebill
BEHILLTY blithely
BEHILMRW whimbrel
BEHILNPY biphenyl
BEHILORR horrible
BEHILPRU bhelpuri
BEHILRTU thurible
BEHIMNOO bonhomie
BEHINNOS shinbone
BEHINOSW wishbone
BEHINOTT on the bit
BEHINRTW new birth
BEHINRTY the briny
BEHIOOPR biophore
BEHIOTWY Whiteboy
white boy
BEHJLNOU blue john
BEHJNOOT on the job
on-the-job
BEHLLNOR hell-born
BEHLLOOT bolthole
BEHLLOOW blowhole
BEHLLOPS shop bell
BEHLLPSU bell push
BEHLOOPY hypobole
lyophobe
BEHLOOTT bottle-oh
BEHLOSSU sloebush
BEHMNOOR home-born
BEHMOOOX homeobox
BEHNNOUY honeybun
BEHNOOTT on the bot
BEHNORTX The Bronx
BEHOOOST boothose
BEHOORST horse bot
theorbos
BEHOORSX horse box
BEHOORSY horse-boy
BEHOOSUY houseboy
BEHOPRSU bush-rope
BEHORRST brothers
BEHORSSU rosebush
BEIIIKMN minibike
BEIIKRTZ kibitzer
BEIILLMT time bill
BEIILMMO immobile
BEIILMOS mobilise
BEIILMOZ mobilize
BEIILNNR bin-liner
BEIILNRS rinsible
BEIILOPR periboli
BEIILRST trilbies
BEIILRSU Liberius
BEIILRSX ex libris
ex-libris
BEIILRTT libretti
BEIILRUZ bruilzie
BEIILSSU Sibelius
BEIILSSV visibles
BEIILSTT stilbite
BEIIMNNR renminbi✧
BEIIMNOS ebionism
BEIIMNSS Ibsenism
BEIIMRTT imbitter
BEIINNOS Beninois
BEIINPRT brine-pit
BEIINSTT stibnite
BEIIRSTU Tiberius
BEIISSTU subitise
BEIISTUZ subitize
BEIJMOSU jumboise
BEIJMOUZ jumboize
BEIJNORW bijwoner
BEIKLMOW womblike
BEIKLMRY Kimberly
BEIKLNRS blinkers
BEIKLOTY kilobyte
BEIKNNOR broken-in
BEIKNOPY bony pike
BEIKNOST steinbok
BEIKNRRY inkberry
BEIKOORT brookite
BEILLMNO bone-mill
BEILLMSS limbless
BEILLMSU semibull
BEILLNTU bulletin

BEILLRTU true bill
BEILMMOS embolism
BEILMNOR bromelin
BEILMNOU nobelium
BEILMNRU in lumber
unlimber
BEILMNTU tumble in
BEILMNUU nebulium
BEILMPRU limber up
BEILMPTU plumbite
BEILMRSS brimless
BEILNNTU buntline
BEILNOOV Benvolio
BEILNOPS bonspiel
BEILNORV live-born
BEILNOST Nobelist
BEILNOVY bovinely
BEILNRUU blue ruin
BEILNSSY sensibly
BEILOORV boil over
boilover
overboil
BEILOPPW blowpipe
BEILOPSS possible
BEILORST strobile
BEILORTT libretto
BEILOTTT bottle it
BEILRRTY terribly
BEILRSTY blistery
BEILRTTY bitterly
BEILSTTU subtitle
BEIMNSSU nimbuses
BEIMOORS ribosome
BEIMORRV brim over
overbrim
BEIMORTX mitre box
BEIMORTY biometry
BEIMORYZ ribozyme
BEIMOTVY by-motive
BEIMRSTU resubmit
BEINNOSS boniness
BEINNRYZ zebrinny
BEINORST ribstone
BEINORTW brow-tine
BEINORTZ bronzite
BEINOSSX boxiness
BEINRRSY nisberry
BEINRSTU Burnsite
turbines
BEINSSSU business
BEIOORST robotise
BEIOORTZ robotize
BEIOQTUU boutique
BEIORRSU boursier
BEIORRTU roburite
BEIORSTU to-bruise
BEIORSTY sobriety
BEIOTTZZ bozzetti
BEIRRTTU tributer
BEJJMOTU jumbo jet
BEJKOOST jestbook
BEJNOORW Joe Brown
BEJNOSSW Job's news
BEJORTTU turbojet
BEKLLLPU bull kelp
BEKLNORY brokenly
BEKLOOOR booklore
BEKLOOOT look to be
BEKLOORT brooklet
BEKLOOSS bookless
BEKLORUV overbulk
BEKLSSUY Sky blues
BEKMOOPS spekboom
BEKMOOSX smokebox
BEKNNORU unbroken
BEKNOOOP open book
BEKNOOOT notebook
BEKNOORT to-broken
BEKOOORV overbook
BEKOORST bookrest
BEKOOTTX textbook
BELLLLPU bell pull
BELLMNOU Léon Blum
BELLMORT mortbell
BELLMORU umbrello
BELLMOSW swell-mob
BELLMRUY lumberly
BELLNORW well-born
BELLNOSU bullnose
BELLNTUY tunbelly
BELLOPTY pot-belly
BELLORTW bellwort
BELLOSTW two bells
BELLOSWX swell box
BELLOTUY belly out
BELMNOSU nelumbos
BELMOORS bloomers
BELMOORY bloomery
BELMORST temblors
BELMORSY sombrely
BELMORUW rumbelow
BELMOSST tombless
BELMPRUY plumbery
BELMPTUU tumble up
BELMRRUY mulberry
BELMRSSU slumbers
BELMRSTU Mt Elbrus
stumbler
BELMRSUY slumbery
BELNNOWW new-blown
BELNOORT noble rot
BELNOSUU nebulous
BELNSTUU unsubtle
BELOOOSX loose box
BELOOPRT bolt rope
BELOORSW rosebowl
BELOORVW blow over
bowl over
overblow
BELOOSST bootless
BELOOSVY boy's love
BELOOTUV obvolute
BELOPTTU bottle up
BELORRTU troubler
BELORSSW browless
BELOSSUY bless you!
BELOSTUY obtusely
BELPRSUY superbly
BELRSSSU Brussels
BELRSTTU rust belt✧
rust-belt
BELRSTUY blustery
BELSSTUY substyle
BELSTTUY subtlety
BEMNNSSU numbness
BEMNOORT trombone
BEMNOORW new broom
BEMNOOXY money box
BEMNOPRU rump bone
BEMNORSY embryons
BEMOORRS sombrero
BEMOOSTU besom out
BEMORTUW tube worm
worm tube
BEMRSSTU bumsters
BEMRTUZZ buzz term
BENNNOTU unbonnet
BENNNOTY Tony Benn
BENNNPUY penny-bun
BENNOOPU bone up on
BENNOORS Sorbonne
BENNOOTU boutonné
BENNOSSU snub nose
BENORRSU suborner
BENORRTU true-born
BENORRUV overburn
BENORSTU rubstone
BENORSTW bestrown
BENORSUU burnouse
BENORTTU rebutton
BENRRSUY sunberry
BENRRTUY by return
BENSSSUY busyness
BEOORRRW borrower
reborrow
BEOORRVW overbrow
BEOORSTY botryose
BEOOTTZZ bozzetto
BEOPRRSV Proverbs
BEOPRSSX press box
BEORSSSU sorbuses
BEORSSUU suberous
BEORSTUU tuberous
BEORSUVY overbusy
BEPRTTUU butter up
BERRSTUU surrebut
BERSSTTU buttress
BERSSTUV subverst
BFFFLMUU bumfluff
BFFGINOR bring off
BFFHORSU brush off
brush-off
BFFIISTT stiff bit

BFFLLOUY bully off
bully-off
BFFNOORU rub off on
BFFNOSUX snuffbox
BFFOSSTU sob stuff
BFGHINTU bun fight
BFGIKOOT gift-book
BFGIORRU Fribourg
BFGLLORU bullfrog
BFHIILLS billfish
BFHILOSW blowfish
BFHLLOOU bull-hoof
BFHLLSUU blushful
BFHLOSUX flush-box
BFHORSUX fox-brush
BFIIORSS fibrosis
BFILLMRU brim-full
BFILLSSU blissful
BFILOOST soft-boil
BFIMNORU nubiform
BFIMORTU tubiform
BFINORYZ bronzify
BFIORSTU four bits
BFLLNOWY flyblown
BFLLOSUW bowlfuls
BFLNOOOR born fool
fool-born
BFLOORSU subfloor
BGGGINOR brogging
BGGIILNO obliging
BGGIILNY gibingly
BGGIINNR bringing
BGGIINRU briguing
BGGILNNU bungling
BGGINOOT toboggin
BGGINRSU Ginsburg
BGHHINOR high-born
BGHHIORW highbrow
BGHHIOTY high toby
BGHHIRUY Highbury
BGHIINRT birthing
BGHILMNU humbling
BGHILNSU blushing
BGHILOTX light box
BGHILRTY brightly
BGHIMOTU bigmouth
BGHINORT Brighton
BGHINRSU brushing
BGHIORSU broguish
BGHIRSTY by rights
BGHJNNOY John Byng
BGHNNUUY bunny hug
bunny-hug
BGHNOTUU unbought
BGHOOPTU boughpot
BGHOPRSU grub shop
BGIIKLNN blinking
BGIILNRS brisling
BGIIMMNR brimming
BGIINNSW swingbin
BGIINRSU bruising
BGIIPRTU Tubigrip®
BGIKLNOT kingbolt
BGIKNSTU stink bug
BGILLNOU globulin
BGILLNRU bullring
BGILLNUY bullying
BGILMMNU mumbling
BGILMNOO blooming
BGILMNPU plumbing
BGILMNRU rumbling
BGILMNTU tumbling
BGILMORY gorblimy
BGILNNOS snobling
BGILNORT ringbolt
BGILNORY boringly
BGILNOTT blotting
BGILNOTU boulting
BGILNRRU blurring
BGILNRTU blurting
BGILNSTU bustling
BGINNORW browning✧
BGINNORZ bronzing
BGINORST strobing
BGINORSW browsing
BGINORTU bring out
BGKLNOOU book lung
lung-book
BGKNOOOS songbook
BGLOORXY glory box
BGLOORYY bryology
BGOPRSUU subgroup
BGRRUUWZ Würzburg
BHHOOTUU tohu bohu
BHIIKRSS briskish
BHIILMPS blimpish
BHIIMRST misbirth
BHIIOPRT prohibit
BHIJNORT John Birt
BHIKLLOO billhook
BHILLNOR hornbill
BHILLOSW show bill
BHILLPUW bullwhip
BHILNSTU bluntish
BHILORRY horribly
BHILOSYY boyishly
BHILPRSU lip brush
BHIMNORT thrombin
BHIMOOPR biomorph
BHINOPSU unbishop
BHINORSW brownish
BHIOPSSY ship's boy
BHIORRST short rib
BHJLLNOU John Bull
BHKMNOOY hymn-book
BHKNOOOR hornbook
BHKOOOOT boot-hook
BHKOOOPS bookshop
BHLLNORU bullhorn
BHLLOSTU bullshot
BHLMNOOR Bornholm
BHLOOOTT tolbooth
BHLRSUUY bulrushy
BHMMOTTU Tom Thumb
BHMNTTUU thumbnut
BHMOPTTU thumbpot
BHMORSTU thrombus
BHMPSTUU thumbs up
thumbs-up
BHMPTTUU tub-thump
BHMRRSUU rum shrub
BHNNOPUY bunny hop
BHNOORTX boxthorn
BHNOSSUW snow bush
snowbush
BHOOSSST boss shot
BIIKLLLL Kill Bill
BIIKMRSS Simbirsk
BIIKNOOT bootikin
BIILLMOR morbilli
BIILLNOS billions
BIILLNQU quill-nib
BIILMOTY mobility
BIILNOOV oblivion
BIILNOTY nobility
BIILNTUY nubility
BIILORST strobili
BIILORSU Orbilius
BIILOSSU sibilous
BIILOSSY biolysis
BIILSTTW witblits
BIIMMNSY nimbyism
BIIMMOSZ zombiism
BIINRSTU burinist
BIIORSTT botritis
BIIQTUUY ubiquity
BIIRSSTU bursitis
BIJMNORW Jim Brown
BIJMORST storm jib
BIKLNNSU sun-blink
BIKMTTUU Timbuktu
BIKOOUUZ bouzouki
BILLMSUY bullyism
BILLMWYY by my will
BILLNOOU bouillon
BILLNOTU bull into
BILLSTUU Tibullus
BILLSTUW swill-tub
BILMMPSU plumbism
BILMOSTU botulism
BILNOSUU nubilous
BILOORST sorbitol
BILOPSSY possibly
BILOPSUY Polybius
BILORSST bristols
BIMNOOOR boom-iron
BIMNOPTU bump into
BIMNORSW Brownism
BIMNORSY Byronism
BIMNOSTY symbiont
BIMNRRUU muirburn
BIMNRUUV viburnum
BIMOSSTY sybotism

BINNORTW twin-born
BINOORST isobront
BINORSTW Brownist
BIOOPSTT post-obit
BIOPRRSU subprior
BIOPRSTW bowsprit
BIORRSTU burritos
BIORSTTY Botrytis
BIORSTUY bistoury
BIOSTTUY obtusity
BIRSSTTU subtrist
BJOOPSST Job's post
BJOPPTUU put-up job
BKKOOORW bookwork
workbook
BKLNOORY Brooklyn
BKMOOORW bookworm
BKMOORUZ zomboruk
BKOOOPST book-post
BKORSUWY busywork
BLLLLOOY loblolly
BLLMOORW bollworm
BLLOOPSW slop bowl
BLMOOOST tombolos
BLMOOOTY lobotomy
BLMOOSSY blossomy
BLMOPSUU plumbous
BLNOOPUW blow upon
BLNOORWW brown owl✧
BLNORSUW slow burn
slow-burn
BLOOSSTY slyboots
BLORSTUY robustly
BLORTTUU blurt out
BLOSTUUU tubulous
BMNOOOOT moon boot
BMNOOOTW boom town
BMNOORRU moorburn
BMNOOSST bons mots
BMNORTUW mowburnt
BMOOPTTU bottom-up
BMOORSSU sombrous
BMOORSTU motor bus
BMOORTTY bottomry
BMORSSTU strombus
BNNORTUW nut-brown
BNNOTTUU unbutton
BNNRSTUU sunburnt
BNOOOSTW snowboot
BNOOOSUY sonobuoy
BNOORRTW brown rot
BNOORTUW brownout
BNOPTTUU button up
BNORRUUW unburrow
BNRSSTUU sunburst
BOOOPRSX poor's-box
BOOORRTW to borrow
BOORSSTY sob story
BOOTTWWY two by two
BOPRRTUY ruby port
BORSTTUU outburst

C

CCCDIILY dicyclic
CCCEEILT eclectic
CCCEGOSY coccyges
CCCEIIRT eccritic
CCCEILNY encyclic
CCCEILUY eucyclic
CCCHIORY chiccory
CCCIINSU succinic
CCCILNOY cyclonic
CCCILOPY cyclopic
CCCINSTU succinct
CCCIOORS scirocco
CCCKOORW cock-crow
CCCKOOWY cow cocky
CCCLOSUU Cocculus
CCDDKLOU cold duck
CCDEEENR credence
CCDEEHIL clichéed
CCDEEINS scienced
CCDEEIOP codpiece
CCDEEKOY cockeyed
CCDEENOR conceder
CCDEHIPU hiccuped
CCDEHLTU declutch
CCDEHORS scorched
CCDEHORT crotched
CCDEHRTU crutched
CCDEIILO cleidoic
CCDEIINO coincide
CCDEIIRT cricetid
CCDEILOS scolecid
CCDEINOR corniced
CCDEINOT occident✧
CCDEIOPR cercopid
CCDEIOPU occupied
CCDEIPRU cider-cup
CCDELNOU conclude
CCDELORU occluder
CCDELOTU occulted
CCDENOOR Concorde
CCDEORRU occurred
CCDEOSTU stuccoed
CCDHIIKP dipchick
CCDHIILO cichloid
CCDHIIOR dichroic
CCDHIIOT dichotic
CCDHINOO conchoid
CCDIINOO conoidic
CCDIINOS scincoid
CCDIINST discinct
CCDIIORT dicrotic
CCDINOTU conducti
CCDKOOOW woodcock
CCDLOSTU cold cuts
CCDOOOOW coco-wood
CCEEEEHH chee-chee
CCEEGINR recceing
CCEEHINZ zecchine
CCEEHKKY check-key
CCEEHKNS schnecke
CCEEHKRS checkers
CCEEHLOW cow-leech
CCEEHMOO ecce homo
CCEEHRSY screechy
CCEEILNR encircle
CCEEILNT elenctic
CCEEILPY epicycle
CCEEILRT electric
lectrice
CCEEIMNU ecumenic
CCEEINOR cicerone
CCEEINOV conceive
CCEEIORV coercive
CCEEIRSV cervices
crescive
CCEEITTU eutectic
CCEEKLOR cockerel
CCEEKNRW crew neck
CCEELMNY clemency
CCEELOSS scoleces
CCEEMMNO commence
CCEEMMOR commerce
CCEEMOPS compesce
CCEENNOS ensconce
CCEENORT concrete
CCEENRST crescent
CCEEOORT coco-tree
CCEFFHKO check off
check-off
CCEFIIPS specific
CCEFIRRU crucifer
CCEFLLOU floccule
CCEFLOOS floccose
CCEGHIOR choregic
CCEGIKLN clecking
CCEGILOO ecologic
CCEGILRY glyceric
CCEGINNO congenic
CCEGINRY reccying
CCEGNOOS cognosce
CCEHIIMR chimeric
CCEHIIMS ischemic
CCEHIINZ zecchini
CCEHIKSU chuckies
CCEHILNR clincher
CCEHILOR choleric
CCEHILOY choicely
CCEHINOR corniche
enchoric
CCEHINOZ zecchino
CCEHINST technics
CCEHIORT ricochet
CCEHKLRU chuckler
CCEHKMSU checksum
CCEHKOTU check out
checkout
check-out
CCEHLMOR cromlech
CCEHLNNU unclench
CCEHLRUY cleruchy

CCEHLSTU clutches
CCEHNRRU cruncher
CCEHORRS scorcher
CCEHORTT crotchet
CCEHRSTU scutcher
CCEHRTUY cutchery
CCEIIKLN nickelic
CCEIILNT enclitic
CCEIILNU culicine
CCEIILOR licorice
CCEIILPT ecliptic
CCEIILST scilicet
CCEIILTU leucitic
CCEIINNR encrinic
CCEIINOR ciceroni
CCEIIRRT circiter
CCEIIRSS eccrisis
CCEIIRTT rectitic
CCEIIRTU eucritic
CCEILMOO coelomic
CCEILMOP complice
CCEILNOR cornicle
CCEILNUY unicycle
CCEILOSS scolices
CCEILRRU curricle
CCEILRSY cresylic
CCEILRTY tricycle
CCEILRUU curlicue
CCEIMNOO economic
CCEIMOST cosmetic
CCEIMRRU mercuric
CCEINNOS insconce
CCEINNOV convince
CCEINOOR coercion
CCEINOOZ Cenozoic
CCEINOPR cecropin
CCEINOPT concepti
CCEINORT concerti
necrotic
CCEINOST C-section
CCEINOTT concetti
tectonic
CCEINOTU cut no ice
CCEINOTY conceity
CCEINPRT precinct
CCEINRTU cincture
CCEINSTY synectic
CCEINSZZ Szczecin
CCEIOORT crocoite
CCEIOOTX ecotoxic
CCEIOOTZ ectozoic
CCEIOPRT ectropic
CCEIOPRU occupier
CCEIORST cortices
CCEIOSTT Scottice
CCEIPRTU cut-price
CCEKORRY crockery
CCEKORSU cocksure
CCELMOPT complect
CCELOPSY cyclopes✧
CCELOSSY cycloses

CCENOORT concerto
CCENOOTT concetto
CCENORRU corn-cure
CCENORTY cornetcy
CCENRRUY currency
CCEOOORR corocore
CCEOORSU croceous
CCEOPRUY reoccupy
CCEORSSU crocuses
CCEORSTU stuccoer
CCFFHKOU chuck off
CCFFKLOO clock off
CCFIINOR cornific
CCFIIRUX crucifix
CCFIKNOY cocknify
CCFILLOU flocculi
CCFILNOT conflict
CCFKLLOU full-cock
CCFKLOOT cockloft
CCFLOOOO locofoco✧
CCFNOOOU con fuoco
CCGHHIOU hiccough
CCGHIINN cinching
CCGHINOU couching
CCGIIKLN clicking
CCGIILNR circling
CCGIKLNO clocking
cockling
CCGILLOY glycolic
CCGILNOY glyconic
CCGILOSU glucosic
CCGINOTW twoccing
CCHHIINN chin-chin
CCHHIITY ichthyic
CCHHINOT chthonic
CCHHLRUY churchly
CCHHNRUU unchurch
CCHHOOOO choo-choo
CCHHOOPP chop-chop
CCHHOOWW chow-chow
CCHIIKLT chick lit
CCHIINUZ zucchini
CCHIIORT orchitic
CCHIISTU Cushitic
CCHIKMPU chipmuck
CCHILMOW milch-cow
CCHINOSU scuchion
CCHINOTY Tychonic
CCHIPSSY psychics
CCHKLOSY schlocky
CCHKOOST cockshot
CCHKOPTU putchock
CCHKOSTU cockshut
CCHKOTUU chuck out
CCHLNTUU unclutch
CCHNRSUY scrunchy
CCIIKKTT tick-tick
CCIIKNPY picnicky
CCIILLRY Cyrillic
CCIILNOP clip coin
CCIIMNSY cynicism

CCIINNOP no picnic
CCIINNSU cicinnus
CCIINORZ zirconic
CCIINRSU Circinus
CCIIRTUY circuity
CCIKKLOP lockpick
picklock
CCIKKOTT tick-tock
CCIKLOSW cow's lick
CCIKNOPR princock
CCIKNORT con trick
CCIKOPRS cropsick
CCILLLUU Lucullic
CCILLOPP clip-clop
CCILNSUY succinyl
CCILOOPS piccolos
CCILORUU curculio
CCILOSSY cyclosis
CCIMNRUU curcumin
CCINOPRT procinct
CCINOPSY syncopic
CCINORSY cryonics
CCIOOPST scotopic
CCIOORSS siroccos
CCIOOTXY oxytocic
CCIRSSUY circussy
CCJNNOTU conjunct
CCKKLMUU muckluck
CCKKOOOR rock cook
CCKKOORR rock cork
CCKLOOTU clock out
CCKMMORU crummock
CCKMOOOR moorcock
CCKNORTU turncock
CCKOOPST stopcock
CCKOPRSU cockspur
CCLLOOPP clop-clop
CCLLOTUY occultly
CCLMOOPU cocoplum
CCLNOOOR concolor
CCLOOOSZ zoccolos
CCLOORSU occlusor
CCMOOORS moroccos
CCNOORSU concours
CCOOOORR corocoro
CCOOSSUU couscous
CCOOTTUU tucotuco
CCORSSTU crosscut
CCOTTUUU tucutuco
CCRSUUUU surucucu
CDDDIIOY diddicoy
CDDEEEFN defenced
CDDEEEJT dejected
CDDEEENT decedent
CDDEEHIT cheddite
CDDEEILP pedicled
CDDEEIRS descried
CDDEEKNU undecked
CDDEEKOT docketed
CDDEEKUW duckweed
CDDEELMO comeddle

CDDEELSU	secluded	CDEEGIIR	regicide	CDEEIRUY	Eurydice
CDDEELUX	excluded	CDEEGINO	genocide	CDEEKLLW	well deck
CDDEELUY	deucedly	CDEEGINR	receding	CDEEKLPS	speckled
CDDEERUV	decurved	CDEEGIOS	geodesic	CDEEKMSS	mess deck
CDDEFIIO	codified	CDEEGIOT	geodetic	CDEEKNRU	unrecked
CDDEHIRT	Redditch	CDEEHIKL	helideck	CDEEKOPT	pocketed
CDDEHISU	chuddies	CDEEHILN	lichened	CDEEKORV	deck over
CDDEIKOS	dockside	CDEEHILP	cheliped	CDEEKORW	rockweed
CDDEILNU	included	CDEEHIPR	decipher	CDEEKOST	socketed
CDDEKNOU	undocked	CDEEHITW	itchweed	CDEEKRSU	suckered
CDDEKOSU	dock-dues	CDEEHKOS	deck shoe	CDEELLPU	cupelled
CDDELLOW	cold-weld	CDEEHLMO	leechdom	CDEELNOV	Clevedon
CDDEMNOU	duncedom	CDEEHLSU	schedule	CDEELNPU	peduncle
CDDEOORW	codeword	CDEEHNNU	Duchenne	CDEELNTY	decently
CDDGHILO	godchild	CDEEHNRR	drencher	CDEELOOW	locoweed
CDDGHIOT	ditch-dog	CDEEHNUW	unchewed	CDEELOPU	decouple
CDDGILNO	clodding	CDEEHRTW	wretched	CDEELORV	clovered
CDDGILOS	gold disc	CDEEHSSU	duchesse	CDEELOST	closeted
CDDGINSU	scudding	CDEEIILR	Eric Idle	CDEELPRU	preclude
CDDHHISU	shidduch	CDEEIIMN	medicine	CDEELRUX	excluder
CDDHIIRY	dihydric	CDEEIIMP	epidemic	CDEEMORT	ectoderm
CDDHILOS	cloddish	CDEEIINT	indictee	CDEENNOS	condense
CDDIISTY	dytiscid	CDEEIISV	decisive	CDEENNOU	denounce
CDDIKLUW	wild duck	CDEEIITT	dietetic	CDEENNPY	pendency
	wild-duck	CDEEIJMU	me judice	CDEENNTU	undecent
CDDKNOPU	duck-pond	CDEEIKLN	nickeled	CDEENNTY	tendency
CDDKOOUW	wood duck	CDEEIKLR	deer lick	CDEENORR	cornered
CDDMMOUU	mocuddum	CDEEIKNV	invecked	CDEENORS	seconder
CDDOOORW	cordwood	CDEEIKPT	picketed		seed corn
CDEEEGIL	ice-ledge	CDEEIKRW	wickered	CDEENORT	centrode
CDEEEHRT	the Creed	CDEEILNP	pendicle	CDEENOSY	ecdysone
CDEEEINV	evidence	CDEEILNR	reclined	CDEENOTX	coextend
CDEEEIPS	epicedes	CDEEILNS	licensed	CDEENOVX	convexed
CDEEEIRV	deceiver		silenced	CDEENPRU	prudence
	received	CDEEILNT	denticle	CDEENRUV	verecund
CDEEEKNR	deer-neck	CDEEILNU	nucleide	CDEENSTY	encysted
CDEEEKNW	neckweed	CDEEILRS	sclereid	CDEEOOTV	dovecote
CDEEELLX	excelled	CDEEILRT	derelict	CDEEOPPS	speed-cop
CDEEELOS	coleseed	CDEEILSU	Seleucid	CDEEOPRS	proceeds
CDEEELST	deselect	CDEEIMNR	endermic	CDEEORRR	recorder✧
	selected	CDEEIMOR	mediocre		rerecord
CDEEELUX	excludee	CDEEIMOT	time code	CDEEORRT	tre corde
CDEEEMRS	Mercedes	CDEEIMPR	premedic	CDEEORTT	detector
CDEEENNT	tendence	CDEEIMRS	miscreed	CDEEPRST	sceptred
CDEEENOS	secondee	CDEEIMRV	decemvir	CDEERRRU	recurred
CDEEEPTX	expected	CDEEINNT	indecent	CDEERRUV	recurved
CDEEERRS	screeder	CDEEINPS	dispence	CDEERTUV	curveted
CDEEERSS	recessed	CDEEINPT	depeinct	CDEFHILL	elf-child
CDEEFFOR	coffered	CDEEINTU	inductee	CDEFHIMO	chiefdom
	force-fed	CDEEINTV	invected	CDEFIIIL	filicide
CDEEFIIL	field ice	CDEEIORV	divorcee	CDEFIIIT	citified
	icefield		divorcée	CDEFIIOR	codifier
CDEEFIIT	feticide	CDEEIPRS	précised	CDEFIIRT	drift ice
CDEEFIRR	Frederic	CDEEIPRT	decrepit	CDEFIITY	cityfied
CDEEFKLR	freckled		depicter	CDEFILSW	W C Fields
CDEEFKOR	foredeck	CDEEIPRU	pedicure	CDEFINNO	confined
CDEEFLOT	cold feet	CDEEIRRT	redirect	CDEFINNU	infecund
CDEEFNNU	unfenced	CDEEIRST	discreet	CDEFINOR	confider
CDEEFORS	frescoed		discrete	CDEFLORY	forcedly
CDEEFORT	defector	CDEEIRSV	descrive	CDEFNORU	unforced
CDEEGHLO	dog-leech	CDEEIRSY	Criseyde	CDEFNOSU	confused

CDEFOSSU focussed
CDEGIILO Goidelic
CDEGIINO Diogenic
CDEGILOO Coolidge
CDEGINRU reducing
CDEGINRY decrying
CDEGINSU seducing
CDEGINSY dysgenic
CDEGNOOR Congo red
CDEGORSW scrowdge
CDEHHNOO honchoed
CDEHHOTU Dutch hoe
CDEHIILO helicoid
CDEHIIMO homicide
CDEHIIMR chimerid
CDEHIINO echinoid
CDEHIIRT Dietrich
CDEHIKOT Hock-tide
CDEHIKRW herdwick
CDEHILMR merchild
CDEHILNR children
CDEHILOR chloride
CDEHILRT eldritch
CDEHIMOT methodic
CDEHINNR indrench
CDEHINOS hedonics
CDEHIOOR ochidore
CDEHIOTY theodicy
CDEHISTT stitched
CDEHKLSU shelduck
CDEHLOOS deschool
schooled
CDEHNOOP chenopod
CDEHOORR rheocord
CDEHORRS Schröder
CDEHORSU chorused
CDEHOSSU hocussed
CDEIIILS silicide
CDEIIIMT miticide
CDEIIIRV viricide
CDEIIITV viticide
CDEIIKKS sidekick
CDEIIKLS sicklied
CDEIIKMM mimicked
CDEIIKNR ciderkin
CDEIIKRS dricksie
CDEIILMO domicile
CDEIILNN inclined
CDEIILNO indocile
CDEIILOT idiolect
CDEIILPS disciple
CDEIILPU pediculi
pulicide
CDEIILRU ridicule
CDEIILRW wild rice
CDEIIMOS dioecism
CDEIIMRT dimetric
CDEIINNT incident
CDEIINOS decision
CDEIINRT indicter
indirect

CDEIINTY cytidine
CDEIIOPR periodic
CDEIIOPS episodic
CDEIIOPT epidotic
CDEIIPRR cirriped
CDEIIRTU diuretic
CDEIIRUV virucide
CDEIJPUU juiced up
CDEIKLNU unlicked
CDEIKLOS sidelock
CDEIKLOT tide lock
CDEIKLRU luderick
CDEIKLWY wickedly
CDEIKNPU unpicked
CDEIKNTU tunicked
CDEIKORR Roderick
CDEIKOST die-stock
CDEIKSTY city desk
CDEILLOR collider
CDEILLOU lodicule
CDEILLPU pellucid
CDEILMOP complied
CDEILMOS melodics
CDEILMRU dulcimer
CDEILMSY dysmelic
CDEILNOS closed-in
CDEILNRY cylinder
CDEILNSU unsliced
CDEILOOW woodlice
CDEILOPS scopelid
CDEILOPU clupeoid
CDEILORS scleroid
CDEILORU crude oil
CDEILORV coverlid
CDEILOSS disclose
CDEILPPR crippled
CDEILRTY directly
CDEILSXY dyslexic
CDEIMNRU mind-cure
CDEIMOST Docetism
domestic
CDEIMPRS scrimped
CDEINNOU uncoined
CDEINNOW wind cone
CDEINOOZ endozoic
CDEINORR cordiner
CDEINORS consider
CDEINORT centroid
doctrine
CDEINORU decurion
CDEINOST deontics
CDEINOTU eduction
CDEINOUV unvoiced
CDEINPRS prescind
CDEINPRU unpriced
CDEINPSY dyspneic
CDEINRRU incurred
CDEINRUV incurved
CDEINSTY syndetic
CDEIOPRT depictor
CDEIOPST despotic

CDEIOPTY copy-edit
CDEIORRT creditor
director
CDEIORRV co-driver
divorcer
CDEIORSU discoure
CDEIORSV discover
CDEIORSY decisory
CDEIOSTT Docetist
CDEIPRST scripted
CDEIPRSY cyprides
CDEIRSTU crudités
CDEKLMOR clerkdom
CDEKLMOU duckmole
CDEKLMRU mud-clerk
CDEKLNOU unlocked
CDEKLOPU uplocked
CDEKLORY yeldrock
CDEKNOOU uncooked
CDEKNSUU unsucked
CDEKNTUU untucked
CDEKOOPP poop deck
CDEKOORV rock dove
CDELLNOU Culloden
CDELLNUU unculled
CDELLOOP clodpole
CDELLORS scrolled
CDELLORU colluder
CDELLOTU cloudlet
CDELMNOO monocled
CDELMNOU columned
CDELMPRU crumpled
CDELNOSS coldness
CDELNOSU unclosed
CDELNOSY secondly
CDELNOUW uncowled
CDELNOWW clew down
CDELNRUU uncurled
CDELNSUY secundly
CDELOORS cold sore
CDELOORU coloured✧
decolour
CDELORSS cordless
CDELRSUY cursedly
CDELRTUU cultured
CDELSSTU ductless
CDELSSUY cussedly
CDEMMRSU scrummed
CDEMNOOW come down
comedown
down-come
CDEMNOTU document
CDEMNSUU secundum
CDEMOOPS composed
CDEMOPRU core dump
CDEMOSTU costumed
customed
CDENNOUY uncoyned
CDENOORR on record
CDENOORT creodont
CDENOOST secodont

CDENORTU	cornuted
CDENRSUU	sun-cured
CDENRTUU	undercut
CDENRUUV	uncurved
CDEOOPST	postcode
CDEOORSU	decorous
CDEOPRRU	producer
CDEORRSS	Red Cross
CDEORSST	doctress
CDEORSTU	seductor
CDEOSSTU	custodes
CDEPRUUV	upcurved
CDERSTTU	destruct
CDFFILOR	Clifford
CDFHILOS	cold fish
CDFIILSU	fluidics
CDFIKORS	disfrock
CDFKOORR	Rockford
CDFKRSUU	surf duck
CDFNNOOU	confound
CDGHIILN	childing
CDGHINOR	chording
CDGHKOOS	shock dog
CDGIINOS	discoing
CDGIKLNU	duckling
CDGIKLOR	gridlock
CDGIKORT	dog-trick
CDGILNOS	scolding
CDGILNOU	clouding
CDGILOOU	I could go
CDGINOUU	unco guid
CDHHIILS	childish
CDHIILTW	twichild
CDHIIOOR	chorioid
CDHIIORT	hidrotic
	trichoid
CDHIIOSZ	schizoid
CDHIISST	distichs
CDHILOOP	chilopod
CDHILOOS	dolichos✧
CDHIMNOR	Richmond
CDHIMOSU	dochmius
CDHINNOR	chondrin
CDHIOOPW	woodchip
CDHIOORT	trochoid
CDHIOPRW	whipcord
CDHIOPRY	hydropic
CDHIOPSY	psychoid
CDHIORRT	trichord
CDHIOSUV	disvouch
CDHKKOOU	duck hook
CDHKOSTU	duck-shot
CDHLOOPY	copyhold
CDHLOTUW	Low Dutch
CDHNORSU	chondrus✧
CDHOORRU	urochord
CDIIIMNS	MiniDisc®
CDIIIMNU	indicium
CDIIIORT	dioritic
CDIIKMNO	Dominick
CDIIKPST	dipstick

CDIILOTY	docility
CDIILTUY	lucidity
CDIIMNOU	conidium
	oncidium
CDIIMORS	Doricism
CDIINOOS	isodicon
	oniscoid
CDIINPRY	cyprinid
CDIINSTT	distinct
CDIIOORS	soricoid
CDIIOPRT	dioptric
CDIIORSU	Dioscuri
	sciuroid
CDIIPTUY	cupidity
	pudicity
CDIIRSTT	district
CDIJNSTU	disjunct
CDIKKNOW	kickdown
CDIKKOPR	drop kick
	drop-kick
CDIKLOPS	slip-dock
CDIKLPUY	lucky dip
CDIKNORW	wind rock
CDIKNOSW	windsock
CDIKNOTW	tick down
CDIKOOTW	wood tick
CDILLOTU	dulcitol
CDILLOUY	cloudily
CDILOOPS	podsolic
CDILOORS	discolor
CDILOORT	lordotic
CDILOOTY	cotyloid
CDILOPSW	cowslip'd
CDILOSST	disclost
CDILOSTY	scolytid
CDIMMOSU	modicums
CDIMOORT	microdot
CDIMTTUU	ut dictum
CDINNQUU	quidnunc
CDINOOOR	coronoid
CDINORSW	discrown
CDINORTU	inductor
CDINOSTU	discount
CDINOSTY	dystonic
CDIOOOPT	octopoid
CDIOOPRS	prosodic
CDIOORRR	corridor
CDIOPRSU	cuspidor
CDISSTUY	Dytiscus
CDJLNOUY	jocundly
CDKKMSUU	musk duck
CDKLMORU	Lord Muck
CDKLOOPR	drop lock
CDKLOORW	cold work
	cold-work
CDKMMORU	drummock
CDKOOORW	corkwood
	rock wood
CDKOPSUU	duck soup
CDLLLOOP	clodpoll
CDLNOOOW	cool down

CDLNOUUY	uncloudy
CDLOOOTW	coltwood
CDLOORSU	sour-cold
CDLOORTY	doctorly
CDLOOSTU	outscold
CDLOOSTW	Cotswold
CDLOPRUW	World Cup
CDMMOOSU	Commodus
CDMNOOPU	compound
CDMNOPSU	pond scum
CDMNORUU	corundum
CDNNOOOT	conodont
CDOORRUY	corduroy
CDOORTUW	crowd out
CDORSSUW	cussword
CDORSTUW	sword-cut
CEEEEIPY	eyepiece
CEEEELST	selectee
CEEEEPRS	preceese
CEEEFFIR	effierce
CEEEFFRT	effecter
CEEEFINR	enfierce
CEEEFNOR	conferee
CEEEGINX	exigence
CEEEGITX	exegetic
CEEEGMNR	mergence
CEEEGNRV	vergence
CEEEHIPT	the piece
CEEEHIST	cheese it
	ice sheet
CEEEHKOR	Cherokee
CEEEHLRV	cheverel
CEEEHLTT	the elect
CEEEHNNP	penneech
CEEEHNNY	Cheyenne
CEEEHRSS	secesher
CEEEHRSW	eschewer
CEEEHRVY	cheverye
CEEEIJTV	ejective
CEEEILNN	lenience
CEEEILNS	licensee
CEEEILNT	telecine
CEEEILRT	erectile
CEEEILTV	cleveite
	elective
CEEEIMNN	eminence
CEEEIMPR	empierce
CEEEIMRR	rere-mice
CEEEINNT	enceinte
CEEEINOP	one-piece
CEEEINPR	piecener
CEEEINRS	ceresine
CEEEIOPT	toe-piece
CEEEIPRR	creepier
	creperie
CEEEIPRV	perceive
CEEEIPST	set piece
	set-piece
CEEEIRRV	receiver
CEEEIRSX	exercise
CEEEIRTT	et ceteri

CEEEIRTV	erective
CEEEJRRT	rejecter
CEEEKNNP	penneeck
CEEELLNR	crenelle
CEEELOST	Eteocles
CEEELPRT	pre-elect
CEEELRST	reselect
CEEELRTT	electret
	tercelet
CEEEMNRT	cementer
	cerement
CEEEMRTY	cemetery
CEEEMSUX	excuse me
	excuse-me
CEEENNPT	tenpence
CEEENNST	sentence
CEEENNSV	Cévennes
CEEENPRS	presence
CEEENPRT	pretence
CEEENQSU	sequence
CEEENRRS	screener
CEEENRRT	recentre
CEEENRTW	New Crete
CEEENSST	centeses
CEEEPRTX	expecter
CEEERRSV	screever
CEEERRTX	excreter
CEEERSSS	recesses
CEEERSST	sesterce
CEEERSWY	screw eye
CEEERTTV	crevette
CEEERTUX	executer
CEEESSSX	excesses
CEEFFINT	in effect
CEEFFORT	effector
CEEFHIKR	kerchief
CEEFHILS	ice shelf
	shelf ice
CEEFHIRY	chiefery
CEEFHISS	chiefess
CEEFHIST	chiefest
CEEFHLRT	fletcher
CEEFHLRU	cheerful
CEEFIINT	inficete
CEEFIKKR	free kick
CEEFILRT	telferic
CEEFILRY	fiercely
CEEFINPP	fippence
CEEFINRT	frenetic
CEEFIPRT	perfecti
CEEFIRTY	free-city
CEEFKLSS	feckless
CEEFLLLU	fuel cell
CEEFLNOR	florence✧
CEEFLNTU	feculent
CEEFLRUU	flue-cure
CEEFNORR	confrère
	enforcer
	renforce
CEEFNRVY	fervency
CEEFOPRR	perforce
CEEFOPRT	perfecto
CEEFORRS	frescoer
CEEFORSS	frescoes
CEEFORST	cost-free
	free-cost
	of secret
	scot-free
CEEGGILS	egg slice
CEEGHINR	cheering
CEEGHLOW	cogwheel
CEEGILOT	eclogite
CEEGILRT	telergic
CEEGILRU	rice glue
CEEGIMNS	miscegen
CEEGINOR	erogenic
CEEGINPR	creeping
CEEGINRT	gentrice
CEEGINST	genetics
CEEGINSU	eugenics
CEEGINXY	exigency
CEEGIORX	exoergic
CEEGKNOR	Greenock
CEEGKNOS	Geckones
CEEGLLMR	germ cell
CEEGLLOR	colleger
CEEGMMOR	commerge
CEEGNNOO	oncogene
CEEGNNOR	congener
CEEGNNPU	pungence
CEEGNOOS	Congoese
CEEGNORT	congreet
	coregent
CEEGNORV	Congreve
	converge
CEEGNOTY	ectogeny
CEEGNRVY	vergency
CEEHHIRS	Cheshire
CEEHHLRS	Herschel
CEEHIIST	ethicise
CEEHIITZ	ethicize
CEEHIKLY	cheekily
CEEHIKNW	cheewink
CEEHILLM	Michelle
CEEHILLN	chenille
	Hellenic
CEEHILLS	shell-ice
CEEHILLV	cheville
CEEHILRT	telechir
CEEHILRV	cheveril
CEEHILRW	clerihew
CEEHILRY	cheerily
CEEHILSW	swelchie
CEEHILTV	Helvetic
CEEHIMRT	hermetic
CEEHINOR	coinhere
CEEHINPR	encipher
CEEHINPT	phenetic
CEEHINST	sithence
CEEHINTT	enthetic
CEEHIORS	cheerios
CEEHIOSU	ice house
CEEHIOSV	cohesive
CEEHIPRT	herpetic
CEEHIRSS	richesse
CEEHIRTT	tetchier
CEEHIRTU	heuretic
CEEHISTT	esthetic
	techiest
CEEHKLRT	The Clerk
CEEHKNOR	Honecker
CEEHKRSS	Cherkess
CEEHKRST	sketcher
CEEHKRTV	kvetcher
CEEHLLOR	Rochelle
CEEHLNOO	Holocene
CEEHLNOT	enclothe
CEEHLNPU	penuchle
CEEHLNSU	elenchus
CEEHLORT	reclothe
CEEHLOSS	echoless
CEEHLRSU	Hercules
CEEHLTUW	wheel-cut
CEEHMMOO	come home
CEEHMNOR	chromene
CEEHMORT	comether
CEEHNNOW	nowhence
CEEHNNRT	entrench
CEEHNORT	coherent
CEEHNORV	cheveron
CEEHNQRU	quencher
CEEHNRRT	retrench
	trencher
CEEHNRST	Trenches
CEEHOPRY	coryphee
	coryphée
CEEHOPTT	pochette
CEEHORRS	cosherer
CEEHORRT	hectorer
	torchère
CEEHORVW	chew over
CEEHPRRY	perchery
CEEHQRSU	chequers
CEEHRSTU	the curse
CEEHRTTU	teuchter
CEEHTTTU	cut teeth
CEEIIKLV	vicelike
CEEIIMNP	mince pie
CEEIIMPR	epimeric
CEEIIMRT	eremitic
CEEIINPS	in pieces
	in specie
CEEIINRT	icterine
CEEIINST	niceties
CEEIINVV	evincive
CEEIIPTU	cutie-pie
CEEIIRST	sericite
CEEIJLLO	Jellicoe
CEEIJLNO	Joceline
CEEIJNOT	ejection
CEEIJORR	rejoicer
CEEIJRUV	verjuice
CEEIKLNN	neckline

Words marked ✧ can also be spelled with one or more capital letters

CEEIKLPR pickerel
CEEIKNRS sickener
CEEIKPRT picketer
CEEILLLN cell line
CEEILLLP pellicle
CEEILLNT lenticel
lenticle
CEEILMOR comelier
CEEILMPS semplice
CEEILNNT centinel
CEEILNNY leniency
CEEILNOP Pliocene
CEEILNOT coteline
election
CEEILNOV violence
CEEILNPT Pentelic
CEEILNPX cineplex
CEEILNRR recliner
CEEILNRS licenser
silencer
CEEILNRU cerulein
CEEILNRV vernicle
CEEILORR recoiler
CEEILOSS solecise
CEEILOSZ solecize
CEEILPRS Pericles
CEEILPRY creepily
CEEILQSU liquesce
CEEILRST sclerite
CEEILRSU ciseleur
ciselure
CEEILRSV versicle
CEEILRTU reticule
CEEILRTY celerity
CEEILSSV viceless
CEEILSTT telestic
testicle
CEEIMMPY empyemic
CEEIMMRS mesmeric
CEEIMNNY eminency
CEEIMNPS specimen
CEEIMORT meteoric
CEEIMRTY my certie
CEEIMSTT smectite
CEEINNOP pine cone
CEEINNOT neotenic
CEEINNPR en prince
CEEINNPZ pince-nez
CEEINNRS incenser
CEEINNRT incentre
CEEINNSS niceness
CEEINNST nescient
CEEINORR encierro
CEEINORT erection
neoteric
CEEINORV overnice
CEEINORX exocrine
CEEINOSS senecios
CEEINOST icestone
seicento
CEEINOTV evection
CEEINPRT prentice
'prentice
CEEINPST pectines
CEEINPSX sixpence
CEEINRST in secret
scienter
secretin
CEEINRSU insecure
sinecure
CEEINRTT reticent
CEEINRTU ceinture
enuretic
CEEINSST centesis
CEEINSSX in excess
CEEINSTY cysteine
CEEIOPPR pericope
CEEIOPPS episcope
CEEIOPST to pieces
CEEIOPTU piece out
CEEIOPTW two-piece
CEEIORST esoteric
CEEIORSX exorcise
CEEIORTT erotetic
CEEIORTX exoteric
CEEIORXZ exorcize
CEEIOSTV covetise
CEEIPPRT precepit
CEEIPPTU eupeptic
CEEIRRTU ureteric
CEEIRSSV services
CEEIRSTU cerusite
CEEIRSTV vertices
CEEIRSVX cervixes
CEEISUVX excusive
CEEJKOTT jockette
CEEJORRT rejector
CEEKKNOS knee sock
CEEKKNPS kenspeck
CEEKLRSS clerkess
reckless
CEEKNORR reckoner
CEEKNRSU suckener
CEEKOPRX oxpecker
CEEKORRT corktree
rocketer
CEEKOSTT sockette
CEELLMOU molecule
CEELLMST stem cell
CEELLNOU nucleole
CEELLORT récollet
CEELLRRU crueller
CEELLRVY cleverly
CEELLSSU clueless
CEELMOPT complete
CEELMORW welcomer
CEELMOST telecoms
CEELMRTU electrum
CEELNNOP penoncel
CEELNNOT centonel
non-elect
CEELNOPU opulence
CEELNOPY lycopene
CEELNORS encloser
CEELNORT electron
CEELNORU encolure
CEELNOSS Les Noces
CEELNPTU centuple
CEELNRTU relucent
CEELNRTY recently
CEELNSTU esculent
CEELORSS coreless
sclerose
CEELORST corselet
electros
selector
CEELORTV coverlet
CEELOSST close-set
CEELOSSU coleuses
CEELRRTU lecturer
CEELRSST lectress
CEELRSSU cureless
CEELRSTY secretly
CEELRSUY securely
CEELSSUU Seleucus
CEEMMNTU cementum
CEEMNOOR once more
CEEMNORR cremorne
CEEMNORW newcomer
CEEMNORY ceremony
CEEMNOSW Newcomes
CEEMNOYZ coenzyme
CEEMOORV come over
overcome
CEEMOORW owrecome
CEEMORTU come true
CEENNOOS nose cone
CEENNORS on-screen
CEENNORT cretonne
CEENNORU renounce
CEENNORV convener
CEENNOST centones
CEENOORV once-over
CEENOPRU en croupe
en cuerpo
CEENOPTW two pence
twopence
CEENORST ten-score
CEENORSV conserve
converse
CEENORTT trecento
CEENORTU en croûte
CEENORVY conveyer
reconvey
CEENPPTU tuppence
CEENPRST percents
CEENPSSU suspence
CEENRSTU unsecret
CEENSSTU cuteness
CEEOORRW orecrowe
CEEOORST creosote
CEEOPRRT receptor
CEEOPRTX exceptor

CEEOPRTY	cerotype
CEEOQTTU	coquette
CEEORRRS	sorcerer
CEEORRST	secretor
CEEORRSU	recourse
	resource
CEEORRVY	recovery
CEEORSSS	Scorsese
CEEORSSY	cross-eye
CEEORSTX	cortexes
CEEORTTV	corvette
CEEORTUX	executor
CEEOSSTX	to excess
CEEPPSTY	type spec
CEEPRRSU	precurse
CEEPRSST	respects
CEERRSST	rectress
CEERRSTU	rest cure
CEERRTUZ	creutzer
CEERSSTW	setscrew
CEERSTTU	cruet set
CEERTUXY	executry
CEFFFHOT	fetch off
CEFFHKOO	choke off
CEFFIORU	coiffeur
	coiffure
CEFFIRSU	sufficer
CEFFLORU	forceful
CEFFLRSU	scuffler
CEFFMOOR	off-comer
CEFFOORS	score off
CEFGHINT	fetching
CEFGLNUY	fulgency
CEFHIIMS	mischief
CEFHILNR	flincher
CEFHILRT	flichter
	rich-left
CEFHINOT	infotech
CEFHINSU	fuchsine
CEFHISTU	fuchsite
CEFHKOOR	forehock
CEFHLSTU	chestful
CEFHOSSU	sous-chef
CEFHOTTU	fetch out
CEFIILMN	cine film
CEFIILNO	olefinic
CEFIILST	felsitic
CEFIILTY	felicity✧
CEFIIOPR	opificer
CEFIIPRT	petrific
CEFIIRRT	ferritic
	terrific
CEFIKLOR	firelock
CEFILLLO	follicle
CEFILMRU	crimeful
	merciful
CEFILNOT	flection
CEFILOPY	file copy
CEFILOUV	voiceful
CEFINNOR	confiner
CEFINNOS	confines
CEFINORS	forensic
	forinsec
CEFINORT	ice front
	infector
CEFINOTT	confetti
CEFIOORT	Corfiote
CEFIOPRS	forcipes
CEFIORTY	ferocity
CEFIRSTU	frutices
CEFIRTUV	fructive
CEFKLLOS	elflocks
CEFKLOOR	forelock
CEFKLPSY	fly-speck
CEFKLRUW	wreckful
CEFLLOSU	floscule
CEFLNRUU	furuncle
CEFLNSTU	scentful
CEFLNUWY	Cynewulf
CEFMORRY	for mercy
CEFOORRV	cover for
CEFOORST	soft-core
CEFOORSU	of course
CEFORSTU	fructose
CEGGILOO	geologic
CEGGILRS	scriggle
CEGGINOO	geogonic
CEGGIORS	Georgics
	scroggie
CEGGLNOY	glycogen
CEGHHHIT	high tech
	high-tech
CEGHHIMO	come high
CEGHHIPS	high spec
CEGHHOTU	the cough
CEGHIINY	hygienic
CEGHIKLN	heckling
CEGHILNT	letching
CEGHIMNS	scheming
CEGHINPR	perching
CEGHINVY	Givenchy
CEGHIRTU	theurgic
CEGHMRUY	chemurgy
CEGHNORS	groschen✧
CEGHOORS	hog-score
CEGHORSU	choregus
CEGIIKNV	vice-king
CEGIILNT	gentilic
CEGIILOP	epilogic
CEGIILOS	logicise
CEGIILOZ	logicize
CEGIINNT	enticing
CEGIINOS	isogenic
CEGIINPR	piercing
CEGIINRV	vice ring
CEGIINSS	gneissic
CEGIINTX	exciting
CEGIIOST	egoistic
CEGIJLOU	logjuice
CEGIKKLN	keckling
CEGIKLNR	reckling
CEGIKNRW	wrecking
CEGILNOO	neologic
CEGILNPU	cupeling
CEGILNRY	glycerin
CEGILNTU	cultigen
CEGIMNOS	genomics
CEGIMNOY	myogenic
CEGIMNUY	gynecium
CEGINNRT	centring
CEGINNST	scenting
CEGINNSY	ensigncy
CEGINOOP	geoponic
CEGINOOR	orogenic
CEGINOOZ	zoogenic
CEGINOPY	pyogenic
CEGINORT	gerontic
CEGINORV	covering
CEGINOTV	Viet Cong
	Vietcong
CEGINRST	cresting
CEGINRSU	rescuing
CEGINRSW	screwing
CEGINRSY	synergic
CEGIRSTU	scutiger
CEGLLNOO	col legno
CEGLLOOU	collogue
CEGLLORY	glycerol
CEGLLRYY	glyceryl
CEGLNOTY	cogently
CEGLOOOY	oecology
CEGLOOTY	cetology
CEGMNNOO	cognomen
CEGNNPUY	pungency
CEGNOOTY	gonocyte
CEGNORSS	congress✧
CEGNORSU	scrounge
CEGNORYY	cryogeny
CEGORRSU	scourger
	scrouger
CEHHHIOW	heich-how
CEHHHITW	the which
CEHHINPY	hyphenic
CEHHLOTT	the cloth
CEHHNORU	hurcheon
CEHHOPTY	hypothec
CEHIILLS	chillies
CEHIILMO	hemiolic
CEHIILNN	lichenin
CEHIILNT	lecithin
CEHIILOT	eolithic✧
CEHIILPS	Iphicles
CEHIIMOP	hemiopic
CEHIIMOS	isocheim
	isochime
CEHIIMPT	mephitic
CEHIIMST	ethicism
CEHIIMTT	itch-mite
CEHIINNN	nine-inch
CEHIIOPT	Ethiopic
CEHIIRSS	Chrissie
CEHIIRST	christie✧
CEHIIRTT	trichite

CEHIISTT ethicist
itchiest
theistic
CEHIITVY Vichyite
CEHIKLPT klephtic
CEHIKLRS clerkish
CEHIKLSU such like
suchlike
CEHIKMOS homesick
CEHIKOST thickoes
CEHIKSTT thickset
CEHIKTTY thickety
CEHILLRS schiller
CEHILMMS schimmel
CEHILMTW witch-elm
CEHILMTY methylic
CEHILNOP phenolic
pinochle
CEHILNOR chlorine
CEHILNPY phenylic
CEHILNSS chinless
CEHILOOS schoolie
CEHILOPT chipotle
CEHILORT chlorite
clothier
CEHILORY heroicly
CEHILPTY phyletic
CEHILSTW switchel
CEHILSTY chestily
Lecythis
CEHILTTY tetchily
CEHIMNOP phonemic
CEHIMNOR Nichrome®
CEHIMNOW chow mein
CEHIMNSU munchies
CEHIMNTZ Chemnitz
CEHIMOOT homeotic
CEHIMORT chromite
trichome
CEHINNRT intrench
CEHINOOS cohesion
CEHINOPS Echinops
CEHINOPT phonetic
Pinochet
CEHINOPU euphonic
CEHINORU unheroic
CEHINOSY hyoscine
CEHINOTY onychite
CEHINPRS pinchers
pinscher
CEHINPRU uncipher
CEHINRSS richness
CEHINRST christen
snitcher
CEHINRSW Schwerin
CEHINRTU ruthenic
CEHIOORS isochore
CEHIOPRS sopheric
CEHIOPRU euphoric
CEHIOPST postiche
CEHIOPTW Otchipwe

CEHIORRT rhetoric
torchier
CEHIORSS orchesis
CEHIORTT trochite
CEHIORTU touchier
CEHIPRSS spherics
CEHIPRST spitcher
CEHIRSTT stitcher
CEHIRSTW switcher
CEHIRSTY hysteric
CEHIRTTW twitcher
CEHIRTWY witchery
CEHISSTU cushiest
CEHISSUW suchwise
CEHKLLOS skelloch
CEHKLORS sherlock✧
CEHKLOSU suck-hole
CEHKNORW rock-hewn
CEHKNPUY key punch
keypunch
CEHKRSTU huckster
CEHLLMSU schellum
CEHLLOUY louchely
CEHLMNOU homuncle
CEHLMSSU much less
CEHLNNOU luncheon
CEHLNOSS Loch Ness
CEHLNOTU unclothe
CEHLORSU sloucher
CEHLORTY hectorly
CEHLOSTU selcouth
CEHLPPSY schleppy
CEHLQSUY squelchy
CEHLRRSY Chrysler®
CEHLSTUY lecythus
CEHMNRTU truchmen
CEHMNSSU muchness
CEHMOORS smoocher
CEHMOOSZ schmooze
CEHMORUV overmuch
CEHMRSTU chetrums
CEHNNNOU nuncheon
CEHNNOPU puncheon
CEHNNOSU nonesuch
unchosen
CEHNOORS schooner
CEHNOPTU putcheon
CEHNORTU chounter
hen-court
CEHNORVY chevrony
CEHNSSSU suchness
CEHNSTTU chestnut
CEHOOORZ zoochore
CEHOOPST post-echo
CEHOORSU ocherous
ochreous
CEHOORTU cute hoor
CEHOOSTU cot-house
CEHOOSUW cowhouse
CEHOPPRS choppers
CEHOPPRY prophecy

CEHOPSTW Chepstow
CEHOPSUY chop suey
CEHORSSZ scherzos
CEHORSTU scouther
CEHORSTW scowther
CEHOTTUZ zuchetto
CEHRSTTY stretchy
CEIIILMN Milicien
CEIIILSV civilise
CEIIILVZ civilize
CEIIIMNT ciminite
CEIIINOS Ionicise
CEIIINOZ Ionicize
CEIIINSS sinicise
CEIIINSV incisive
CEIIINSZ sinicize
CEIIJSTU Jesuitic
CEIIKLMR limerick
rice milk
CEIIKLNR licker-in
CEIIKMMR mimicker
CEIIKNSS kinesics
CEIIKNST kinetics
CEIIKRRT trickier
CEIIKSST ekistics
stickies
CEIILLMT mellitic
CEIILLOP pollicie
CEIILLPT elliptic
CEIILLSU silicule
CEIILMNT limnetic
CEIILMNY myelinic
CEIILMOT cimolite
CEIILNNP pencil in
CEIILNNR incliner
CEIILNOS isocline
silicone
CEIILNQU clinique
CEIILNSS enclisis
CEIILOPP epiploic
epipolic
CEIILOPS policies
CEIILORT elicitor
CEIILOST Siceliot
CEIILOTZ zeolitic
CEIILPRT perlitic
CEIILPRU pirlicue
CEIILPTX explicit
CEIILPTY pyelitic
CEIILRTV verticil
CEIILSSS scissile
CEIIMNOT emiction
CEIIMOPT epitomic
CEIIMORS isomeric
CEIIMOST semiotic
CEIIMPRR crimpier
CEIIMRRT trimeric
CEIIMRST meristic
trisemic
CEIIMSST Semitics
CEIINNOP nepionic

CEIINNOR irenicon
CEIINNOS oscinine
CEIINNOT cotinine
nicotine
CEIINNRT intrince
CEIINNST inscient
CEIINOPS epinosic
CEIINOPT epitonic
ice point
CEIINORS recision
soricine
CEIINOSX excision
CEIINOTV eviction
CEIINPPR Príncipe
CEIINPRT prince it
CEIINRSU incisure
sciurine
CEIINRTU neuritic
CEIINSTU cutinise
CEIINSTY cytisine
syenitic
CEIINTUZ cutinize
CEIIOPRS iriscope
CEIIOPRT periotic
CEIIOPTT picotite
CEIIOSTV sovietic
CEIIPRRS crispier
CEIIPRST priciest
CEIIQRTU critique
CEIIRSTT rectitis
CEIIRSTV veristic
CEIISTVV vivisect
CEIJLNOS Joscelin
CEIJMOOU moo-juice
CEIJNORT injector
CEIJNOUV cunjevoi
CEIJRSTU justicer
CEIKKLOR rocklike
CEIKKNRS knickers
CEIKKRRS skerrick
CEIKLMNY McKinley
CEIKLNPS spicknel
CEIKLOSV lovesick
CEIKLRST stickler
strickle
CEIKLRSY sickerly
CEIKLRTT tricklet
CEIKMNOR monicker
CEIKMOPT impocket
CEIKMORS ockerism✧
CEIKMPPU pick-me-up
CEIKMRSU musicker
CEIKMSTU muckiest
CEIKNNSU insucken
CEIKNOPT in pocket
CEIKNORT Cronkite
CEIKNOST sick note
CEIKNOTY cytokine
CEIKNRST stricken
CEIKNRSU unsicker
CEIKNSSS sickness

CEIKOPRV pick over
CEIKORTV tick over
tick-over
CEIKPPRU picker-up
CEIKQSTU quickset
CEIKRRTY trickery
CEIKRTTY ricketty
CEILLLOY ice lolly
CEILLNOU nucleoli
CEILLNTU unit cell
CEILLOPS pollices
CEILLOQU coquille
CEILLORS orsellic
CEILLORY colliery
CEILLOTU coutille
CEILLRTU telluric
CEILMMUY mycelium
CEILMNOP compline✧
CEILMNOT monticle
CEILMNSU muscle in
CEILMOPR compiler
complier
CEILMOPS polemics
CEILMOSS solecism
CEILMOSU coliseum✧
CEILMPUU peculium
CEILMTUU lutecium
CEILNNOT contline
non licet
CEILNNSY syncline
CEILNOOS colonise
eclosion
CEILNOOZ colonize
CEILNOPR percolin
replicon
CEILNOPT leptonic
CEILNORS incloser
licensor
CEILNOSU leucosin
CEILNPRY princely
CEILNRTU lincture
CEILNRUV culverin
CEILNSUU unsluice
CEILOPPS Popsicle®
CEILOPRT petrolic
CEILOPRV proclive
CEILOPST top-slice
CEILOPTU epulotic
poultice
CEILOPTY epicotyl
CEILORST cloister
coistrel
creolist
CEILORTY cryolite
CEILOSST solecist
solstice
CEILOSSU coulisse✧
CEILOTVY velocity
CEILPPRR crippler
CEILPPRS clippers
CEILPRSU surplice

CEILPRUU purlicue
CEILRRSU scurrile
CEILRSTU curliest
CEIMMNNO mnemonic
CEIMMNOU encomium
meconium
CEIMMORT recommit
CEIMMRRU crummier
CEIMMRSY merycism
CEIMNNOO encomion
CEIMNNOY neomycin
CEIMNOOT come into
emoticon
CEIMNOPT pentomic
CEIMNOPY eponymic
CEIMNORS cremosin
sermonic
CEIMNORT intercom
CEIMNOST centimos
CEIMNPSU music pen
CEIMNRST centrism
CEIMNSSU meniscus
CEIMOOSZ Mesozoic
CEIMOOUZ zooecium
CEIMOPRS comprise
CEIMORRT morticer
CEIMORST ice storm
CEIMORSX exorcism
CEIMORSY isocryme
CEIMORTU Mercutio
CEIMORTY emictory
CEIMOSSS cosmesis
CEIMRRSU scrimure
CEIMRRTU turmeric
CEIMSSTY systemic
CEINNNOT innocent✧
CEINNNOU inconnue
CEINNORS incensor
CEINNORU neuronic
CEINNORV conniver
CEINNOTU continue
CEINNOTW Newtonic
CEINOOPR pecorino
CEINOOTZ entozoic
enzootic
CEINOPPR cornpipe
CEINOPRS conspire
incorpse
CEINOPRT entropic
inceptor
CEINOPRU in cuerpo
CEINOPRV province
CEINOPTT entoptic
CEINOPTU put on ice
unpoetic
CEINORRS resorcin
CEINORRT tricorne
CEINORSS necrosis
CEINORSU in course
CEINORTT contrite
cornetti

Words marked ✧ can also be spelled with one or more capital letters

CEINORTU neurotic
CEINORTV contrive
CEINOSSS cosiness
CEINOSSX coxiness
CEINOSTT centoist
stenotic
CEINOSTY cytosine
CEINOTTU Teutonic
CEINPRSS princess
CEINRSTT centrist
CEINRSVV crivvens
CEINRTTU intercut
tincture
CEIOOPTV co-optive
CEIOOTUV outvoice
CEIOOTXX exotoxic
CEIOPPSY episcopy
CEIOPRRU croupier
CEIOPRST persicot
CEIOPRSU precious
rice soup
CEIOPRTU eutropic
outprice
CEIOPRTY Cypriote
CEIOPSSU specious
CEIORRTU courtier
CEIORRTW co-writer
CEIORRUZ cruzeiro
CEIORSST crosstie
CEIORSSX sixscore
CEIORSTU citreous
CEIORSTV vortices
CEIORSTX exorcist
CEIORTTU toreutic
CEIPRRST rescript
CEIPRSTU crepitus
pictures
piecrust
CEIPRSUU Epicurus
CEIRRRSU scurrier
CEIRRSTT restrict
CEIRRSTU crustier
CEIRSSSU scissure
CEIRSSTU rictuses
CEIRSSTV victress
CEIRSTUV curviest
CEIRSTUY security
CEISSSTU cistuses
CEJLMOUU Leucojum
CEJLOOSY jocosely
CEJNORRU conjurer
CEJNRTUU juncture
CEKKNORS knockers
CEKKNTUY Kentucky
CEKLLNOR roll-neck
CEKLLOOV lovelock
CEKLLOSS lockless
CEKLLSSU luckless
CEKLNOOP polo neck
CEKLNOST stenlock
CEKLOORS cork-sole
CEKLOORV overlock
CEKLOPST lockstep
CEKLRRTU truckler
CEKLRSSU sucklers
CEKNOPRU reckon up
CEKNOPST penstock
CEKNORTU cokernut
CEKNOSTU unsocket
CEKNRSTU strucken
CEKOOORV overcook
CEKOORRS rock rose
CEKOORRW co-worker
CEKOPRST sprocket
CEKORRTY rocketry
CEKPPRUU pucker up
CELLMORW Cromwell
CELLNSUU nucellus
CELLNTUU luculent
CELLOOQU colloque
CELLOSSY cloyless
CELLRSUY scullery
CELMNOTU Uncle Tom
CELMNOTY cloyment
CELMNOUY uncomely
CELMNTUU muculent
CELMOOOT locomote
CELMOOSY cloysome
CELMOPSU compulse
CELMOPSY symploce
CELMOSUU cumulose
CELMPRSU scrumple
CELMPRTU plectrum
CELMPSUU speculum
CELNNOTY nocently
CELNNOUV uncloven
CELNOORS consoler
CELNOORT contrôlé
CELNOORU encolour
CELNOOSS coolness
CELNOOVV convolve
CELNOPRT plectron
CELNOPUU uncouple
CELNORSU close-run
run close
CELNORTW crownlet
CELNORWY clownery
CELNOSUV convulse
CELNOSVY solvency
CELNOVXY convexly
CELNPTUU punctule
CELOOORV over-cool
CELOOPSS cesspool
CELOORRU colourer
CELOORTW colewort
CELOORVY overcloy
CELOOSTU cut loose
loose-cut
CELOPSSU Scopelus
CELOPSUU opuscule
CELOPTTU octuplet
CELORSST crosslet
CELORSSU sclerous
CELORSTY coystrel
CELORSUU Coelurus
ulcerous
urceolus
CELORSUY crousely
CELORTTU courtlet
CELORTVY covertly
CELOSTTU culottes
CELPRRSU scrupler
CELPRSSU scruples
CELPRSUY sprucely
CELRSTTU scuttler
CELRSTUY clustery
CEMMNOOR commoner
CEMMNOOS consommé
CEMMNOOY commoney
CEMMORTU commuter
CEMNOOPU come upon
CEMNOORR cromorne
CEMNOOTY monocyte
CEMNOPTT contempt
CEMNORSU consumer
mucrones
CEMNRSTU centrums
CEMOOPRS composer
CEMOORST Rome-scot
CEMOORSY sycomore
CEMOOSTY cytosome
CEMOPRSS compress
CEMOPRTU computer
CEMORRSU Mercosur
CEMORSTU costumer
customer
CEMPRSTU spectrum
CENNOOPR corn pone
corn-pone
CENNOORU couronne
CENNOORV convenor
CENNOOSW snow cone
CENNORRT corn rent
CENNORTU nocturne✧
CENNOSTT contents
CENOOOTZ ectozoon
CENOOPRT Eton crop
CENOOPST scoop net
CENOORRT tenor cor
CENOORSU corneous
CENOORTT cornetto
CENOORVY conveyor
CENOPRSY necropsy
CENOQSTU conquest✧
CENORRTU trouncer
CENORSTU construe
CENORSUU cernuous
coenurus
CENORSUY cynosure
CENORTUY Courtney
CENORTVY Coventry
CENOSSTU countess
CENPRTUU puncture

CENRSSTU curtness
CEOOOPST otoscope
CEOOPRRV overcrop
CEOORRVW crow over
overcrow
CEOORSTU outscore
score out
CEOORSTW two-score
CEOOSTUV covetous
CEOPPRST prospect✧
CEOPRRRU procurer
CEOPRSTT Prescott
CEOPRSTW screwtop
CEOPRSUU cupreous
CEOPRTUW power cut
CEOQRTUY coquetry
CEORRSSU cursores
CEORRSTY corsetry
CEORSSTU crustose
CEORSTUY courtesy
CEORSUWY screw you
CEPPRSSU scuppers
CEPPRSUU spruce up
CEPPRTUU uppercut
CEPRSTUU cutpurse
CERSSUUX excursus
CFFFHOOO choof off
CFFGIINO coiffing
CFFGIMNU McGuffin
CFFGINOS scoffing
CFFHINOS chiffons
CFFHKOSU shuck off
CFFHOOTU touch off
CFFIKLNU cuff link
CFFIRTUY fructify
CFFKKNOO knock off
CFFKLOPU pluck off
CFGHIILN filching
CFGIKNOR frocking
CFGINORT crofting
CFGINOSU focusing
CFHIINOO finochio
CFHIIORR horrific
CFHIKORS rockfish
CFHILPTY flypitch
CFHIMOSS scomfish
CFHIMSSU scumfish
CFHLOPUU pouchful
CFIIILSY silicify
CFIIKNYZ zinckify
CFIIKQUX quick-fix
CFIILOPR prolific
CFIILPSU pulsific
CFIIMNOS somnific
CFIIMORT mortific
CFIINOPT pontific
CFIINORT friction
CFIISSTU Sufistic
CFIKKORS for kicks
CFIKLSTU stickful
CFIKPSTU puckfist
CFILLMTU cult film
CFILMOOR coliform
CFIMNOOR coniform
CFIMNORU unciform
CFINNOTU function
CFIORSST Scots fir
CFIOSTTY Scottify
CFKKLOOR folk rock
CFKOORST soft rock
CFLLOPRU cropfull
CFLMRSUU fulcrums
CFLNOORT cornloft
CFLNORSU scornful
CFLOOPSU scoopful
CFLOPRSU cropfuls
CFNNOORT confront
CFOOORTW crowfoot
CFOOPSTY soft copy
CFOORTUY out of cry
CFRSTUUU usufruct
CGGGHINU chugging
CGGHINOU coughing
CGGIINNR cringing
CGGILRSY scriggly
CGGINORS scroggin
CGHHIIKK high kick
CGHHINSU Shu Ching
CGHIILLN chilling
CGHIINNP pinching
CGHIINPP chipping
CGHIINPR chirping
CGHIINPT pitching
CGHIINTW witching
CGHIKNNU chunking
CGHIKNOS shocking
CGHIKNSU shucking
CGHILNNY lynching
CGHILNOT clothing
CGHIMMNU chumming
CGHIMNPU chumping
CGHIMPSY sphygmic
CGHINNOT notching
CGHINNRU churning
CGHINOPP chopping
CGHINORT torching
CGHINOSU hocusing
CGHINOTU touching
CGHINPTU pinchgut
CGHINRSU crushing
CGHINSSU Cushing's
CGHIORRW grow rich
CGHLOOST shot-clog
CGHNOOSU souchong
CGHORTUU rough cut
CGIIILNT lignitic
CGIIKLNN clinking
CGIIKLNS slicking
CGIIKLNT tickling
CGIIKMMY gimmicky
CGIIKNNZ zincking
CGIIKNPR pricking
CGIIKNPS pickings
CGIIKNRT tricking
CGIIKNST sticking
CGIILMOS logicism
CGIILNPP clipping
CGIILORU oliguric
CGIILOST logicist
logistic
CGIILRTU liturgic
CGIIMNNO incoming
CGIINOOS isogonic
CGIINORT trigonic
CGIKKNNO knocking
CGIKLNOR rockling
CGIKLNSU suckling
CGIKMNOS smocking
CGIKNORW king-crow
CGIKNOST stocking
CGIKNRTU trucking
CGIKNSTU gunstick
CGILLNSU sculling
CGILLNUY cullying
CGILMNOO Mongolic
CGILMNPU clumping
CGILMNSU muscling
CGILMNUU cingulum
glucinum
CGILNNOW clowning
CGILNOOY cooingly
CGILNOPU coupling
CGILNOSW scowling
CGILNOTT clotting
CGILOORU urologic
CGILPSTY glyptics
CGIMMNSU scumming
CGIMNNOO gnomonic
oncoming
CGIMNOPU upcoming
CGIMNTUY gym tunic
CGIMRRUY micrurgy
CGINNOOR crooning
CGINNORS scorning
CGINNORW crowning
CGINOOPS scooping
CGINOOTV cognovit
CGINOPPR cropping
CGINORSS crossing
CGINORSU coursing
scouring
sourcing
CGINORTU courting
CGINOSTU scouting
CGINOUVY Young Vic
CGINRRUY currying
CGINSTUU Tungusic
CGKLOSTU gust-lock
CGKNOORS rock song
CGKNOSTU gunstock
CGKOOPRR prog rock
CGLLOSYY glycosyl
CGLMOOYY mycology

CGLNOOOY oncology
CGLOOOTY tocology
CGLOOTYY cytology
CGLRSUUY Lycurgus
CGMNNOOR mongcorn
CGMNNORU mungcorn
CHHIIKST thickish
CHHIILTY hitchily
CHHIINPT pinch-hit
CHHIIPST phthisic
CHHILRSU churlish
CHHIMRTY rhythmic
CHHIOPPS chip shop
CHHIOPST chip shot
CHHNORSU rhonchus
CHHOOPTT hotchpot
CHIIKLST ticklish
CHIIKRST trickish
CHIIKSTU Kushitic
CHIILLLY chillily
CHIILMSY hylicism
CHIILNNP linchpin
CHIILOST holistic
CHIILPRY chirpily
CHIILQSU cliquish
CHIILSTY hylicist
CHIIMPRU pichurim
CHIINOPS siphonic
CHIINORT ornithic
CHIIORSS chorisis
CHIIORST historic
orchitis
CHIIPPRU hippuric
CHIIRSTT tristich
CHIKLLOY hillocky
CHIKLNUY chunkily
CHIKLOOP clip-hook
CHIKLORS Horlicks®
CHIKMNNU munchkin
CHIKMNPU chipmunk
CHIKMNTU mutchkin
CHIKNNOP phinnock
CHIKOPST tick shop
CHIKOPTY kyphotic
CHIKORST trochisk
CHIKPSYY physicky
CHILLOOT oilcloth
CHILLOTU chill out
chill-out
CHILMMUY chummily
CHILMOPS complish
CHILMOSU scholium
CHILNNPY lynchpin
CHILNOOS scholion
CHILNOSW clownish
CHILNPSY lip-synch
CHILOOOZ holozoic
CHILOOPT holoptic
CHILOPPY choppily
CHILOSSU Huis Clos
CHILOSYY coyishly

CHILOTUY touchily
CHILOTYY holy city
CHILRSTY Christly
CHIMMORU chromium
CHIMNOOR hormonic
CHIMNORW inch-worm
CHIMNOSU insomuch
CHIMNOUY onychium
CHIMOORU mouchoir
CHIMORST christom
CHIMPSSY psychism
CHINOORT orthicon
CHINOORZ C-horizon
CHINOPTY hypnotic
pythonic
typhonic✧
CHINORSU in chorus
CHINORTU cothurni
CHINOSTW switch on
CHINOSTZ schizont
CHINOSUY cushiony
CHINSTTU unstitch
CHIOOPPT photopic
CHIOORSU ichorous
CHIOORSZ chorizos
CHIOORTT orthotic
CHIOPRST strophic
CHIOPSTY hypocist
CHIORSSS crossish
CHIOSSTT Scottish
CHIPRRUY chirrupy
CHIPRTTY triptych
CHIPSSTY psychist
CHIPSTTU stitch up
stitch-up
CHIRRSSU scirrhus
CHIRSSTU Christus
CHKMMOUY hummocky
CHKNORSU cornhusk
CHKOOOPS cook shop
CHKOOPPR pork-chop
CHKOPSTU tuck shop
CHKORRTU Thurrock
CHLNOOOP colophon
CHLNORUW churn-owl
CHLOORSU chlorous
CHLOPSTY splotchy
CHLORTUY choultry
CHMNOORT cornmoth
CHMNORRU crumhorn
CHMNORSU Rumonsch
CHMNPRUU rum punch
CHMOORSU chromous
CHMOOSSU so much so
CHMOOSYZ schmoozy
CHNOOPTT top-notch
CHNOPTUU punch out
CHNORSTU cothurns
CHNORTUU churn out
CHOOORTY choy-root
CHOOORYZ zoochory

CHOOPSTU octopush
CHOPSSTU cost push
CHOPSTUY psych out
CHORSTTU cut short
short cut
short-cut
CIIIKNTU cuitikin
CIIILMPT implicit
CIIILMSU silicium
CIIILNSU Licinius
CIIILPST spilitic
CIIILSTV civilist
CIIILTVY civility
CIIIMNSS Sinicism
CIIIMNSV incivism
CIIINNOS incision
CIIINTVY vicinity
CIIIRSSU Siricius
CIIJRSTU juristic
CIIKKSST ski stick
CIIKLLOS oil slick
CIIKLLSY sicklily
CIIKLOPT politick
CIIKLPST lipstick
CIIKLRTY trickily
CIIKLSST sick list
CIIKLSTY stickily
CIIKMNPX pick'n'mix
CIIKNOOT cootikin
CIIKNORS iron-sick
CIIKNPPR pinprick
CIIKNPST stick pin
CIILLNOP pollinic
CIILMNOT Miltonic
CIILMOPY impolicy
CIILMOSS sciolism
CIILMQSU cliquism
CIILMRSY lyricism
CIILNOOT noctilio
CIILNOPS psilocin
CIILOOPT politico
CIILOOTZ zoolitic
CIILOPPT poplitic
CIILOPST politics
psilotic
CIILORST clitoris
coistril
CIILOSST sciolist
CIILOSTY solicity
CIILOSVV slivovic
CIILRSTY lyricist
CIILRTUU utriculi
CIIMNOOS isonomic
CIIMNOST monistic
nomistic
CIIMORST trisomic
CIIMOSST misticos
stoicism
CIIMRSTY myristic
CIIMRTTU Triticum
CIINNNOO non-ionic

CIINNSTT instinct
CIINOOST isotonic
CIINOOTZ zoonitic
CIINOPSS psionics
CIINOPSU opinicus
CIINORST crostini
CIINORSY incisory
CIINOSSS scission
CIINOSTT stiction
CIINOSTV Visconti
CIINOTTY tonicity
CIINPSTU sinciput
CIIOOPST isotopic
CIIOPRST poristic
CIIOQTUX quixotic
CIIORRWW wirricow
CIIOTTXY toxicity
CIIPRRTU pruritic
CIIPRSTU puristic
CIIRSTTU truistic
CIISSTTY cystitis
CIJKLMUY Lucky Jim
CIJKOSTY joystick
CIJNNOOT conjoint
CIJNNOTU junction
CIJOOSTY jocosity
CIKKLOOS look sick
CIKKNRTU kick turn
CIKKOPST spot kick
CIKLLMTU tuck-mill
CIKLLOPR killcrop
CIKLLPUY pluckily
CIKLNORS corn silk
CIKLNOST linstock
CIKLNOTU luck into
CIKLOSSU soul-sick
CIKLOSTY stockily
CIKLRSSU kiss-curl
CIKMOORS sickroom
CIKMOPST mopstick
CIKNNOOS coonskin
CIKNNOST non-stick
CIKNORST corn-kist
CIKNOTTU tuck into
CIKOPRTU prick out
CIKOPSTT pot stick
CIKORTTU trick out
CIKOSSTT stockist
CIKOSTTU stick out
CIKPSSTU up sticks
CILLMNOR cornmill
CILLMSUY clumsily
cullyism
CILLNOOT cotillon
CILLNORS inscroll
CILLNOSU scullion
CILLOOOT ocotillo
CILLOOPW wool clip
CILLOORS criollos
CILMNOPU pulmonic
CILMNOUU inoculum
CILMNUUV vinculum
CILMOORS miscolor
CILMOPSY olympics✧
CILMPRSY scrimply
CILMPSUU spiculum
CILNOORU colour in
unicolor
CILNOOST colonist
CILNOOTU locution
CILNOPTU plutonic✧
CILNORTU Trinculo
CILNOSUY cousinly
CILNPSTU insculpt
CILOOPTW cow-pilot
CILOOPYZ polyzoic
CILOORRT tricolor
CILOORST cortisol
CILOORYZ Zircoloy®
CILOOSSU sciolous
CILOPPRY propylic
CILORSTY coystril
CILOSSTY systolic
CILOSSUU luscious
CILPRSTU spit curl
CILPSSTU sculpsit
CILRSTTY strictly
CILRSTUY crustily
CILRSUVY scurvily
CIMMNNOO in common
CIMMORSS Commissr
CIMNOOOZ zoonomic
CIMNOORU coronium
CIMNOOTY myotonic
CIMNOPRT comprint
CIMNORSY cronyism
CIMNOSTU miscount
CIMNOSUU mucinous
CIMNOSUY syconium
CIMOOOTZ zootomic
CIMOORSS moriscos✧
CIMOPPSU pop music
CIMOSTUU muticous
CIMOSTUY mucosity
CIMRRSUU Micrurus
CINNOOSS scoinson
CINNOOST scontion
CINNOOTU continuo
CINNOOTX non-toxic
CINNOSTY syntonic
CINNQUUX quincunx
CINOOOPT co-option
CINOOOTZ zoonotic
CINOOPRS scorpion✧
CINOOPRT protonic
CINOOSUV covinous
CINOOTXY oxytocin
oxytonic
CINOPSSY pycnosis
CINOPSTY synoptic
CINORSTT contrist
CINORSTU ructions
CINORSUY cousinry
CINOSTTU unit cost
CINOSTUV viscount✧
CINRSTTU instruct
CINRSTUY scrutiny
CIOOPRSS Scorpios
CIOOPRST porticos
CIOOPTYZ zootypic
CIOOQSTU coquitos
CIOORRWW worricow
CIOORSSU scorious
CIOOSSTU stocious
CIOPRSSU Scorpius
CIORRSTU cursitor
CIORSSSS scissors
CIOTTTUU cut it out
CIPPRRUU purpuric
CIQRSTUY cry quits
CIRSSTUY citrussy
CJNOORRU conjuror
CJRSUUUU sucurujú
CKKNOOTU knock out
knockout
CKKNOPRU punk rock
CKKOORRW rockwork
CKLMMOSU slummock
CKLNOOTY Tony Lock
CKLNOPUU luck upon
CKLOOORW rock wool
CKMMNOOO mock moon
CKMMORUW muck-worm
CKMNOOOR moonrock
CKMOOOOR cookroom
CKNOOSTT Stockton
CKNRSTUU unstruck
CKOOPSTT stockpot
CKORTTUW tow truck
CKOSSTUY tussocky
CLLLOOPT clotpoll
CLLOOQUY colloquy
CLMMNOOY commonly
CLMMOOOS Comsomol
CLMOOOTY colotomy
CLNOOOWY cony-wool
CLNOORTU controul
countrol
CLNOSTUY uncostly
CLOOOPRT protocol
CLOOPRUU colour up
CLOORTUY locutory
CLOOSSSU colossus
CLOOSSTU soul-scot
CLOPRSTU sculptor
CLOPSSTU cost plus
cost-plus
CLOSSTUY Scolytus
CLRSSUUU surculus
CMMNNOOU uncommon
CMMOOPST Postcomm
CMNOOOTY oncotomy
CMNOORRW cornworm

CMNOPSTU consumpt
CMOOPRSS moss-crop
CMOPRSUX scrumpox
CNNOOORT contorno
CNNOOOTT cotton on
CNNOORSW corn snow
CNOOOORT octoroon
CNOORRSW corn rows
CNOORRTW crown rot
CNOORRTY cryotron
CNOORSTU cornutos
outscorn
CNOOTTUU count out
count-out
CNOSTUUU unctuous
COOOPRRT root crop
COOOPSYZ zooscopy
COOPRSUU croupous
COOPRSUY uroscopy
COORRSSW cross-row
COORRWWY worrycow
COORSSTU outcross
COORTTYZ trot-cozy

D

DDDDEEOR doddered
DDDEEEES deseeded
DDDEEEFN defended
DDDEEENU undeeded
DDDEEEPY deep-dyed
DDDEEHRS shredded
DDDEENOR reddendo
DDDEENUW unwedded
DDDEEORR dodderer
DDDEIINV dividend
DDDEILNU unlidded
DDDEIMOS dismoded
DDDEINOR dendroid
DDDEINRU underdid
DDDENORW drownded
DDDIIOOR doridoid
DDEEEFLX deflexed
DDEEEFNR defender
DDEEEFRR deferred
DDEEEGNR degender
gendered
DDEEEHNU unheeded
DDEEEIMR remedied
DDEEEIWY wide-eyed
DDEEELSS deedless
DDEEEMNT demented
DDEEEMRS demersed
DDEEENNU unneeded
DDEEENRZ Enzedder
DDEEENSU unseeded
DDEEENTT denetted
DDEEENTX extended
DDEEENUW unweeded
DDEEEOVY dove-eyed
DDEEERRT deterred
DDEEERST deserted
DDEEERSV deserved
DDEEEWYY dewy-eyed
DDEEFFNO offended
DDEEFGIT fidgeted
DDEEFILW field-dew
DDEEFINR friended
DDEEFINU undefide
undefied
DDEEFIPR drip-feed
DDEEFMOR deformed
DDEEFNRU underfed
DDEEFORR fodderer
DDEEGHNU unhedged
DDEEGINR enridged
DDEEGOPS godspeed✧
DDEEGOTW two-edged
DDEEGPRU dredge up
DDEEHRRS shredder
DDEEIIJM Medjidie
DDEEIINT inedited
DDEEIIRV redivide
DDEEILLV devilled
DDEEILMN meddle in
DDEEILMW mildewed
DDEEILRW wildered
DDEEILWY wild-eyed
DDEEIMOS Diomedes
DDEEINNT indented
intended
DDEEINOS one-sided
DDEEINRT dendrite
DDEEINTU unedited
DDEEIPRV deprived
DDEELLMO modelled
DDEELLOP deed poll
DDEELLUY dull-eyed
DDEELOPX exploded
DDEEMNOR endoderm
DDEEMRRU demurred
DDEENNOR donnered
DDEENNOY endodyne
DDEENNTU untended
DDEENOPR perdendo
DDEENOPW deep down
pondweed
DDEENORR reed-rond
DDEENORS endorsed
DDEENORW wondered
DDEENRSU sundered
DDEEOPRW powdered
DDEERRUV verdured
DDEFFISU diffused
DDEFIILM midfield
DDEFIIMO modified
DDEFIIMW midwifed
DDEFLNOU unfolded
DDEFLRUU udderful
DDEFNNUU unfunded
DDEGGIOU guide dog
DDEGGLOY doggedly
DDEGGNOO doggoned
DDEGHINS shedding
DDEGILMN meddling
DDEGILNP peddling
DDEGILNS sledding
DDEGILNU ungilded
DDEGILOS dislodge
DDEGILRY gliddery
DDEGINOR der-doing
DDEGINRU ungirded
DDEGINUU unguided
DDEGIORT dog-tired
DDEGIOSV give odds
DDEGLNOS gold-ends
DDEGNORU grounded
underdog
DDEGOOOR do-gooder
DDEGOOWW Wedgwood®
DDEGRRUY drudgery
DDEHIISS side dish
DDEHILNY hiddenly
DDEHILOO idlehood
DDEHINNU unhidden
DDEHINOR dihedron
DDEHLPUU huddle up
DDEHNOOU unhooded
DDEHNPUU uphudden
DDEHNRSU hundreds
DDEHNTUY the nuddy
DDEHOOOO hoodooed
DDEHOOSW woodshed
DDEHOOWY how-d'ye-do
DDEHORSU shrouded
DDEHRSUY shuddery
DDEIIKNY dinky-die
DDEIILNR dieldrin
DDEIILRT tiddlier
DDEIIMVW midwived
DDEIINSW side wind
wind side
DDEIIOOX ox-iodide
DDEIIOPS diopside
DDEIIRSV dividers
DDEIIRUV reduviid
DDEIKMOT Mike Todd
DDEILMOV devildom
DDEILMSU mudslide
DDEILNPS splendid
DDEILNRU unriddle
DDEILOPS displode
lopsided
DDEILOSY dysodile
DDEILQRU quiddler
DDEILRST striddle
DDEILRSY sliddery
DDEILRTW twiddler
DDEIMMNU undimmed
DDEIMNNU unminded
DDEIMNUV videndum
DDEIMOQU idem quod
DDEIMOSU medusoid
DDEIMRSU side drum

DDEIMSTU	muddiest
DDEINNRU	unridden
DDEINNTU	undinted
DDEINORW	ride down
	wind-rode
DDEINOSW	disendow
	downside
DDEINOWW	windowed
DDEINPPU	undipped
DDEINRST	stridden
DDEINRSU	sun-dried
DDEINRUV	dun-diver
DDEIOORS	side door
DDEIOPRS	dropsied
DDEIOPRV	provided
DDEIOPSS	disposed
DDEIOQUV	quod vide
DDEIORRS	disorder
DDEIOSTW	two-sided
DDEIRSSU	druidess✧
DDEIRSTU	ruddiest
	sturdied
DDELLNUU	undulled
DDELMPUU	muddle up
DDELNORU	unlorded
DDELNSUY	suddenly
DDELOORW	dowel-rod
DDELOOWY	wool-dyed
DDELORST	stroddle
DDELOSYY	dysodyle
DDEMNOOU	undoomed
DDEMNOST	oddments
DDEMNOUU	duodenum
DDEMNPUU	pudendum
DDEMNSTU	St Edmund
DDEMOOTU	outmoded
DDENNOSU	unsodden
DDENNOSW	send down
DDENOOPR	Don Pedro
DDENOOUW	unwooded
DDENORSW	send word
DDENORUW	unworded
DDENSTUY	suddenty
DDEOORWW	rowdedow
DDFGIILN	fiddling
DDFGILNU	fuddling
DDFIIOSU	fiddious
DDFMNOUU	dumfound
DDGGINNO	ding-dong
DDGHIINW	whidding
DDGHINTU	thudding
DDGHLOOO	hold good
DDGIIINO	indigoid
DDGIIINV	dividing
DDGIIKNS	skidding
DDGIILMN	middling
DDGIILNP	piddling
DDGIILNR	riddling
DDGILNOP	plodding
DDGILNOT	toddling
DDGILNPU	puddling
DDGIMNUY	muddying
DDGIMRSU	drudgism
DDGINNOU	ding doun
DDGINOPR	prodding
DDGINPSU	puddings
	spudding
DDGINPUY	puddingy
DDGINRUY	ruddying
DDGINSTU	studding
DDGIORTY	dirty dog
DDGLNOOS	long odds
DDGLOSTU	gold dust
DDGOORSY	dry goods
DDHIJNOR	John Ridd
DDHILOSY	shoddily
DDHIOSWY	dowdyish
DDHLLOOO	dollhood
DDHLNOOW	hold down
DDHLORRU	Lord Hurd
DDIIIIVV	dividivi
DDIILOPY	diploidy
DDIIMMUY	didymium
DDIIMRSU	druidism✧
	siddurim
	siddur-im
DDIINOPU	dupondii
DDIIQTUY	quiddity
DDILOOPP	diplopod
DDILOOWW	wildwood
DDILORSY	sordidly
DDIMOSUY	didymous
DDIMOSWY	dowdyism
DDINNOWW	downwind
	wind down
	wind-down
DDINOOOT	odontoid
DDINOOWW	woodwind
DDLLOORW	Old World
	old-world✧
	world-old
DDLMORSU	doldrums
DDMNOOTY	Tom-noddy
DDMNORTU	Dortmund
DDNOOPRW	drop down
	drop-down
DDNOORTW	down-trod
DDNOOSSW	doss down
DDNOOUWY	Dunwoody
DDOORWWY	rowdydow
DEEEEFRR	free reed
	free-reed
DEEEEFRZ	defreeze
DEEEEGKR	kedgeree
DEEEEKNP	knee-deep
DEEEEMRR	redeemer✧
DEEEEMST	esteemed
DEEEFGIR	fire-edge
DEEEFGOR	fore-edge
DEEEFIIX	idée fixe
DEEEFILN	feed-line
	line feed
DEEEFINR	needfire
	redefine
DEEEFIPP	feed-pipe
DEEEFIRR	free ride
DEEEFIRW	fireweed
DEEEFIRY	fire-eyed
DEEEFITU	Fête-Dieu
DEEEFKST	keftedes
DEEEFLLR	refelled
DEEEFLOS	felo de se
DEEEFLPT	deepfelt
DEEEFLRX	reflexed
DEEEFMNR	freedmen
DEEEFNRS	fern-seed
	seed fern
DEEEFNRT	deferent
DEEEFNST	enfested
DEEEFORV	overfeed
DEEEFRRR	deferrer
	referred
DEEEFRRT	ferreted
DEEEGHTW	the wedge
DEEEGIPR	pedigree
DEEEGISW	edgewise
DEEEGLSS	edgeless
DEEEGLSV	selvedge
DEEEGMRR	demerger
DEEEGNNR	engender
DEEEGRYY	grey-eyed
DEEEHKPS	sheep ked
DEEEHLMT	helmeted
DEEEHLNO	dene-hole
DEEEHLRT	Ethelred
DEEEHLRW	wheedler
DEEEHLSS	heedless
DEEEHMPS	hempseed
DEEEHNTY	the needy
DEEEIKLS	seedlike
DEEEILNS	selenide
DEEEILRV	relieved
DEEEILTV	deletive
DEEEILVW	weeviled
DEEEILVY	evil-eyed
DEEEIMST	seed time
DEEEINRR	reindeer
DEEEINRS	nereides
DEEEINTV	eventide
DEEEIPPR	reed pipe
DEEEIPTX	expedite
DEEEIRRR	derrière
DEEEIRSS	diereses
DEEEIRST	reediest
DEEEIRTW	tweedier
DEEEISST	Teesside
DEEEJLLW	jewelled
DEEEJNRU	déjeuner
DEEEKOPW	pokeweed
DEEELLLV	levelled
DEEELLNT	dentelle
DEEELLNW	newelled
DEEELLPR	repelled

DEEELLPX expelled
DEEELLRV revelled
DEEELMOS somedele
DEEELMOY mole-eyed
DEEELMRU mule deer
DEEELNPU unpeeled
DEEELNSS needless
seldseen
DEEELNTU undelete
DEEELOPV develope
DEEELOSY sloe-eyed
DEEELPST steepled
DEEELRSS redeless
DEEELRTT lettered
DEEELRTU dule-tree
DEEELRTW tweedler
DEEELSSS seedless
DEEELSSW weedless
DEEELTVV velveted
DEEEMNNT needment
DEEEMPRT tempered
DEEEMRRU murderee
DEEEMRST deemster
DEEENNRT entender
DEEENNRV nerve end
DEEENNUW unweened
DEEENOPY open-eyed
DEEENORS endorsee
DEEENPRT repetend
DEEENPRU unpeered
DEEENPRX expender
DEEENPSS deepness
DEEENRRR renderer
DEEENRRT tenderer
DEEENRRV reverend✧
DEEENRRW reed-wren
DEEENRTX extender
DEEENRUV revenued
DEEENSSS seedness
DEEENSUV vendeuse
DEEEOPRR pederero
DEEEOPRT deportee
DEEEOSTY seedy-toe
DEEERRRV verderer
DEEERRST deserter
DEEERRSV deserver
reserved
reversed
DEEERRTV reverted
DEEERSTT streeted
DEEERSTX exserted
DEEERTTV revetted
DEEESTTU suedette
DEEFFGLU effulged
DEEFFINT infefted
DEEFFIRS seriffed
DEEFFMOR form feed
DEEFFNOR offender
reoffend
DEEFGINR fingered
DEEFGIUW gudewife
DEEFGLOO feelgood
feel-good
DEEFGLSY sedge fly
DEEFGLUW gulfweed
DEEFHILT The Field
DEEFHISS seed-fish
DEEFHLOR freehold
DEEFHLRS feldsher
DEEFHORR Hereford
DEEFIILN fedelini
DEEFIINT definite
DEEFIIPT tepified
DEEFIIRS fireside
DEEFIIRV verified
DEEFIKRR Frederik
DEEFILLT filleted
DEEFILNS Seinfeld
DEEFILNX inflexed
DEEFILWX flix-weed
DEEFIMTU tumefied
DEEFINRR inferred
DEEFINRZ frenzied
DEEFIORS foreside
DEEFLLNU unfelled
DEEFLLUY full-eyed
DEEFLNOR forelend
DEEFLNTU defluent
DEEFLORW deflower
flowered
DEEFLPSU speedful
DEEFMORR deformer
reformed✧
re-formed
DEEFMPPU feed-pump
DEEFMPRU perfumed
DEEFNRRU refunder
DEEFNSST deftness
DEEFOPRR free drop
DEEFORST deforest
forested
DEEFRTUY duty-free
DEEGGHHO hedgehog
DEEGGHIP hedgepig
DEEGGIJR jiggered
DEEGGKOR Greek god
DEEGGLOR doggerel
DEEGGNOR engorged
DEEGHHOP hedge-hop
DEEGHOPS sheepdog
DEEGHORW hedgerow
DEEGHUYY hey-de-guy
DEEGIINN indigene
DEEGIISS diegesis
DEEGILMO liegedom
DEEGILMP impledge
DEEGILNO legioned
DEEGILNR engirdle
reedling
DEEGILNS seedling
DEEGILRW weregild
DEEGILRY greedily
DEEGIMRU demiurge
DEEGINPS speeding
DEEGINRS designer
redesign
resigned
DEEGINSS edginess
DEEGINST signeted
DEEGIRST digester
Erdgeist
estridge
DEEGIRSU gudesire
DEEGJPRU prejudge
DEEGKMOR Greekdom
DEEGLNOU engouled
DEEGLNOZ lozenged
DEEGLNRU elder-gun
DEEGLNRY legendry
DEEGLOOT edge tool
DEEGLOPR pledgeor
DEEGLOPS dogsleep
DEEGLORV groveled
DEEGMNRU dungmere
DEEGNNOY endogeny
DEEGNNPU genned up
DEEGNOOV good-even
DEEGNPSU speed gun
DEEGOOST go to seed
DEEGORVY dove grey
DEEGOTUW goutweed
DEEGRRTU Gertrude
DEEHHNPY hyphened
DEEHHPRS shepherd✧
DEEHILNS enshield
DEEHILNW New Delhi
DEEHILOT The Oldie
DEEHILRS shielder
DEEHILST the slide
DEEHILSV dishevel
DEEHIMOP hemipode
DEEHIMRT Meredith
DEEHINNT in the end
DEEHINRR hinderer
DEEHINRS drisheen
DEEHINRT in the red
DEEHINST disthene
DEEHIPPS sheep-dip
DEEHIPRS hesperid
perished
shred-pie
DEEHIRRS redshire
DEEHIRRT ditherer
DEEHIRSV shrieved
DEEHIRSW shrewdie
DEEHIRTW withered
DEEHIRTY heredity
third eye
DEEHITTY the Deity
DEEHKLOP keep hold
DEEHKLPS helpdesk
DEEHKNOS keeshond
DEEHKNSU skene-dhu

DEEHLLOV hovelled
DEEHLMNU unhelmed
DEEHLMOT The Model
DEEHLMSW Weldmesh®
DEEHLNPU unhelped
DEEHLORS led horse
DEEHLORV verdelho
DEEHNORR deer horn
deer-horn
dehorner
DEEHNORT dethrone
threnode
DEEHNOSY hony-seed
DEEHNOWY honeydew
DEEHOORT Theodore
DEEHORRT dehorter
DEEHORSU house red
rose-hued
shore due
DEEHOSUY dye-house
DEEIILMT idle time
DEEIILNS sideline
DEEIILRV liveried
DEEIIMRS dimerise
DEEIIMRZ dimerize
DEEIINOS deionise
DEEIINOZ deionize
DEEIINSX endeixis
DEEIIPRS Pierides
DEEIIPRU prie-dieu
DEEIIRSS dieresis
DEEIIRST siderite
DEEIIRSV derisive
DEEIIRSW weirdies
DEEIISSS disseise
DEEIISSW sidewise
DEEIISSZ disseize
DEEIISVW side view
DEEIKLLR killdeer
DEEIKLMW milk-weed
DEEIKLNN enkindle
DEEIKLNR rekindle
DEEIKLOV dovelike
DEEIKLSW silkweed
DEEIKNPS skin-deep
DEEIKNPY pink-eyed
DEEIKNRS deerskin
DEEIKPSS deep kiss
DEEIKSTT diskette
DEEILLMN Medellín
DEEILLMP impelled
milleped
DEEILLNO nielloed
DEEILLOR orielled
DEEILLPR perilled
DEEILLRT tredille
DEEILLRV rivelled
DEEILLST let slide
DEEILMNU demilune
DEEILMOS melodise
DEEILMOZ melodize
DEEILNOT deletion
DEEILNRU lie under
underlie
DEEILNSS idleness
DEEILNST lintseed
tinseled
DEEILNUV unveiled
DEEILOPT lepidote
petioled
DEEILORT dolerite
DEEILORV evil-doer
DEEILOTT toileted
DEEILPRU lie perdu
DEEILPSY speedily
DEEILRSU leisured
DEEILRSV desilver
DEEILRTT littered
DEEILRTV let drive
DEEILRVY delivery
DEEILSST tideless
DEEILSSV deviless
DEEILSUV delusive
DEEILTUY yuletide✧
DEEILTWY tweedily
DEEIMMNS endemism
DEEIMMOS semi-dome
DEEIMMRS immersed
DEEIMNOO Idomeneo
DEEIMNOR domineer
DEEIMNOS demonise
DEEIMNOZ demonize
DEEIMNPT pediment
DEEIMNRR reminder
DEEIMNRV vermined
DEEIMNST sediment
DEEIMNSU semi-nude
DEEIMNSY mind's eye
DEEIMNTT mittened
DEEIMOST tedisome
DEEIMPRR periderm
DEEIMPRS premised
DEEIMRST demister
DEEIMRTT remitted
DEEINNRT indenter
intender
DEEINNRU unreined
DEEINNST desinent
DEEINNUV unenvied
DEEINOPS disponee
open side
DEEINOPW wide open
wide-open
DEEINORT oriented
DEEINORV Don Revie
DEEINOST sidenote
side tone
DEEINOSV nosedive
DEEINPSS dispense
piedness
DEEINPSU unespied
DEEINQSU sequined
DEEINRRT interred
trendier
DEEINRRW rewinder
DEEINRSS direness
DEEINRST inserted
resident
DEEINRSU uredines
DEEINRSV versed in
DEEINRTV inverted
DEEINRTW wintered
DEEINRTX dextrine
DEEINSSW dewiness
wideness
DEEINSUZ unseized
DEEINTUV duvetine
DEEINUVW unviewed
DEEIOPRT peridote
DEEIOPRX peroxide
DEEIORRV override
DEEIORSV over side
overside
DEEIORTU étourdie
DEEIORTV tide over
DEEIOTVX videotex
DEEIPPQU equipped
DEEIPPRZ zippered
DEEIPRSS despiser
disperse
DEEIPSST sidestep
DEEIPSTU deputise
DEEIPTUZ deputize
DEEIQRRU required
DEEIQRTU requited
DEEIQRUV quivered
DEEIQTUU quietude
DEEIRRRV Red River
DEEIRRST destrier
DEEIRRTV verditer
DEEIRSST dress tie
editress
DEEIRSSV disserve
dissever
DEEIRSVX sex drive
DEEIRTTV rivetted
DEEISSTW West Side
DEEJKNTU junketed
DEEJLNOY Joe Lyden
DEEJPRRU perjured
DEEKKOOY okey-doke
DEEKLLNY Ned Kelly
DEEKMRSU musk deer
DEEKNNNU unkenned
DEEKNOPW keep down
DEEKNOTW knotweed
DEEKNSSW news desk
DEEKOOTY yoke-toed
DEELLMOR modeller
DEELLNOR enrolled
DEELLNOW well done
well-done
DEELLORW rowelled

 Words marked ✧ can also be spelled with one or more capital letters

	well-doer
DEELLORY	yodeller
DEELLOTW	towelled
DEELLOTX	extolled
DEELLOVW	vowelled
DEELLOVY	volleyed
DEELLSSW	weldless
DEELLSUX	duxelles
DEELMNOO	melodeon
DEELMNOW	new-model
DEELMNTU	unmelted
DEELMNTW	weldment
DEELMOOS	dolesome
DEELMOOV	Love Me Do
DEELMOPR	empolder
DEELMOPY	employed
DEELMOSU	duelsome
DEELMRUY	demurely
DEELNNTU	tunneled
DEELNOOS	loose end
DEELNORT	redolent
DEELNORV	overlend
DEELNPRS	resplend
DEELNRTU	underlet
DEELNRTY	tenderly
DEELNSSW	lewdness
DEELNWWY	newly-wed
DEELNXYY	lynx-eyed
DEELOPRX	exploder
DEELOPRY	redeploy
DEELOPST	seed plot
DEELORRS	solderer
DEELORSV	resolved
DEELORTT	dotterel
DEELORTV	revolted
DEELORTY	deletory
DEELORUV	louvered
DEELPRTU	drupelet
DEELPRUX	duplexer
DEELPTTY	pettedly
DEELRSTU	ulstered
DEELRSTW	lewdster
DEEMMORS	mesoderm
DEEMMRRU	dummerer
DEEMNNTU	tenendum
DEEMNOOS	moonseed
DEEMNOOY	moon-eyed
DEEMNOQU	queendom
DEEMNORT	entoderm
DEEMNORY	no remedy
DEEMNOSS	demoness
	enmossed
DEEMNOTT	dome tent
DEEMNOTW	teem down
DEEMOORT	odometer
DEEMOPST	deepmost
DEEMORRW	dewormer
DEEMORSW	wormseed
DEEMORTU	udometer
DEEMPRST	dempster
DEEMRRRU	demurrer
	murderer
DEEMSSTY	systemed
DEENNNOP	pennoned
DEENNNPU	unpenned
DEENNOPT	deponent
DEENNOPU	unopened
DEENNORW	renowned
DEENNOSS	doneness
DEENNOSZ	endzones
DEENNOVW	even-down
DEENNRTU	untender
DEENNRUV	unnerved
DEENNSSU	nudeness
	unsensed
DEENNTTU	unnetted
	untented
DEENNTUV	unvented
DEENOORV	overdone
DEENOOST	Oostende
DEENOPRR	ponderer
DEENOPRS	rope's end
	rope's-end
DEENOPRW	pre-owned
DEENORRS	endorser
DEENORRW	New Order
	wonderer
DEENORSU	see round
DEENORTU	deuteron
DEENOSST	stenosed
DEENOSWY	eyes down
DEENRRSU	sunderer
DEENRSSU	rudeness
DEENRSTU	dentures
	sederunt
	underset
	undesert
DEENRSUU	underuse
DEENRSUV	unversed
DEENSTTU	untested
DEENTTUV	unvetted
DEENTTUW	unwetted
DEENTUVY	duvetyne
DEEOORRT	rood-tree
DEEOORRV	overdoer
	overrode
DEEOORSV	overdose
DEEOPPST	estopped
DEEOPRRR	preorder
DEEOPRST	reed stop
DEEOPRSY	eye-drops
DEEOPRUZ	douzeper
DEEOPSTU	outspeed
DEEORRRV	verderor
DEEORRTT	retorted
DEEORRTU	red route
DEEORRUV	devourer
DEEORSTT	rosetted
DEEORSTX	dextrose
DEEORSTY	storeyed
DEEORSUY	sour-eyed
DEEORTTT	tottered
DEEOSTUX	tuxedoes
DEEPRSTU	pertused
DEEPRSUY	pseudery
DEEPRUVV	revved-up
DEERRTTU	turreted
DEERRTUX	extruder
DEERSSST	de-stress
	stressed
DEERSSUV	suversed
DEERSTUV	vestured
DEERTTUX	textured
DEFFHILW	whiffled
DEFFILNU	Nuffield
DEFFILOV	fivefold
DEFFIORS	offsider
DEFFIORV	off drive
DEFFIRSU	diffuser
DEFFLRTU	truffled
DEFFORUV	duff over
DEFFPPUU	puffed up
DEFFSTUY	dyestuff
DEFGHILT	flighted
DEFGIILN	fielding
DEFGIINY	deifying
	edifying
DEFGIIST	digestif
DEFGILNU	field gun
DEFGILOS	dog's life
	God's life
DEFGILTY	giftedly
DEFGINOX	fog index
DEFGINTU	ungifted
DEFGIOOW	goodwife✧
DEFGJORU	forjudge
DEFGLOOY	old fogey
DEFGMOOY	fogeydom
DEFGNORU	unforged
DEFHIINS	fiendish
	finished
DEFHIISV	fish-dive
DEFHILLO	lifehold
DEFHILSS	disflesh
DEFHINSU	unfished
DEFHIOOW	wifehood
DEFHIRST	red shift
DEFHLOOS	selfhood
DEFHLOOT	the Flood
DEFHMOOU	fume hood
DEFHOORS	serfhood
DEFHORRT	Hertford
DEFHORTT	Thetford
DEFHORTW	the F-word
DEFIIILV	vilified
DEFIIKLS	disk file
DEFIILLO	oilfield
DEFIILLP	filliped
DEFIILLW	wildlife
DEFIILMS	misfield
DEFIILOR	oil-fired
DEFIILPS	flipside
DEFIILRW	wildfire

DEFIILSU fluidise
DEFIILTY fidelity
DEFIILUZ fluidize
DEFIIMOR modifier
DEFIINOT notified
DEFIINRW Winifred
DEFIINTU finitude
DEFIINTY identify
DEFIIOSS ossified
DEFIIOTV videofit
DEFIIPRU purified
DEFIIPSS fissiped
DEFIIPTY typified
DEFILLNU unfilled
DEFILMNU unfilmed
DEFILMOW demi-wolf
DEFILNNO ninefold
DEFILNOP pond-life
DEFILNRS flinders
DEFILNRU unrifled
urnfield
DEFILNRY friendly
DEFILORU fluoride
DEFILORW dire wolf
DEFILOTU outfield
DEFILPRU prideful
DEFILPTU uplifted
DEFILRRU flurried
DEFILRVY fervidly
fly-drive
DEFIMNOR informed
DEFIMORY remodify
DEFIMRRU drumfire
DEFIMRSU Dumfries
DEFINNOW fine down
DEFINNRU reinfund
unfriend
DEFINORW forewind
DEFINRTT drift net
DEFINSTU unsifted
DEFINSYY Disneyfy
DEFINTTU unfitted
DEFIOORR fire door
DEFIOORT to die for
DEFIOORW firewood
DEFIOOST side-foot
DEFIORRU froideur
DEFIORRV Fervidor
DEFIOTXY detoxify
DEFIRSSU fissured
DEFKLORY forkedly
DEFLLOOR folderol
DEFLNORU flounder
unfolder
DEFLNORY drone fly
DEFLNRUY fly-under
DEFLNSSU fundless
DEFLOORT foretold
DEFLOORV overfold
DEFLOOSS foodless
DEFMNORU unformed
DEFMOOOR foredoom
DEFNNORT frondent
front-end
DEFNNOSS fondness
DEFNNOUW new-found
DEFNOOPS spoonfed
spoon-fed
DEFNOORS frondose
DEFNOORU unroofed
DEFNOORV overfond
DEFNOOTU unfooted
DEFNOPRS forspend
DEFNORRU frondeur
DEFNORTU fortuned
DEFNORUV overfund
DEFNOSSW dowfness
DEFNRRUU underfur
unfurred
DEFOORRW foreword
DEFOPRST Stepford
DEGGHRSU shrugged
DEGGILNS sledging
DEGGINOV God-given
DEGGINRU unrigged
DEGGINUW unwigged
DEGGIORS disgorge
DEGGIPRS sprigged
DEGGLMSU smuggled
DEGGLRUY ruggedly
DEGGNORU ungorged
DEGHHIIT high tide
DEGHILNS shingled
DEGHILPT plighted
DEGHILRT red light
red-light
DEGHINNU unhinged
DEGHINRU hired gun
DEGHINTT tight end
DEGHIOPS dogeship
DEGHIPST despight
DEGHKLOW dog-whelk
DEGHLNOR horngeld
DEGHLORY hydrogel
DEGHLOSU sloughed
DEGHNORT thronged
DEGHNORY hydrogen
DEGHOOST the goods
DEGHOOSU doghouse
house-dog
DEGIIIRS rigidise
DEGIIIRZ rigidize
DEGIIIST digitise
DEGIIITZ digitize
DEGIILNR gridelin
DEGIILNS sideling
DEGIILNT diligent
DEGIILNV deviling
DEGIILNY yielding
DEGIILTY gelidity
DEGIIMNP impeding
DEGIIMSU misguide
DEGIINNR nidering
DEGIINNT indigent
DEGIINNX indexing
DEGIINOS indigoes
DEGIINOV videoing
DEGIINRS ringside
DEGIINRT dirigent
DEGIINST indigest
DEGIISSU disguise
DEGIJMSU misjudge
DEGIKLNU dukeling
DEGIKLOV kid glove
DEGIKNRY ring dyke
DEGILLNU duelling
DEGILLNW dwelling
DEGILMNO gold mine
modeling
DEGILNOP diplogen
DEGILNOS long side
sidelong
DEGILNPS spelding
DEGILNRU indulger
DEGILNRY yeldring
DEGILNWY wingedly
DEGILOOR goodlier
DEGILOOY ideology
DEGILORW gold wire
DEGILOST godliest
DEGILOSZ goldsize
DEGILPSU pulsidge
DEGILRZZ grizzled
DEGIMNOS smidgeon
DEGIMOOT goodtime
DEGIMOOY geomyoid
DEGINNNU unending
DEGINNPS spending
DEGINNRU enduring
unringed
DEGINNSU unsigned
DEGINNTU untinged
DEGINNUW unwinged
DEGINOPS disponge
DEGINORR ordering
DEGINORU guéridon
DEGINORV ringdove
DEGINPRS springed
DEGINPSU dispunge
DEGINRRU Gurinder
DEGINRRY grindery
DEGINRSS dressing
DEGINRST stringed
DEGINRSY synergid
DEGINTTU duetting
DEGIOORS goodsire
DEGIOPRR porridge
DEGIOPSS gossiped
DEGIORRV river god
DEGIORST grodiest
DEGJMNTU judgment
DEGLLNOY goldenly
DEGLLOPS Godspell

DEGLLOSS goldless
DEGLMNOT lodgment
DEGLMOOY demology
DEGLNOOT gold note
DEGLNOUV ungloved
DEGLNRTU gruntled
DEGLOOPY pedology
DEGLOOSU dog-louse
DEGLOOUU duologue
DEGLORUV love-drug
DEGMMNUU ungummed
DEGNNOPY penny-dog
DEGNNORU grounden
DEGNNOUW ungowned
DEGNOORS drongoes
DEGNOOSS dog's-nose
goodness
DEGNOOST stegodon
DEGNOPSU pug-nosed
DEGNORRU grounder
DEGNORTU get round
trudgeon
DEGNORUU unrouged
DEGNORYY gyrodyne
DEGNPRUU unpurged
DEGOOPPU gooped up
DEGOORTT grottoed
DEGOORVY very good
DEHHILOY hidy-hole
DEHHILTW withheld
DEHHMRTY rhythmed
DEHIILLS hillside
DEHIILSV devilish
DEHIIMRU mudirieh
DEHIIMST ditheism
DEHIINNW whinnied
DEHIINSU Hinduise
DEHIINUZ Hinduize
DEHIIOTT The Idiot
DEHIIRST disherit
DEHIISTT ditheist
DEHIJMNO demijohn
DEHIKMOS sheikdom
DEHIKNOW Windhoek
DEHIKNRT the drink
DEHIKPSU dukeship
DEHIKSST the skids
DEHILLOP phelloid
DEHILLRT thrilled
DEHILMOS demolish
DEHILMTY dimethyl
DEHILNOR inholder
DEHILNOW Whieldon
DEHILNPY diphenyl
DEHILOOR heliodor
DEHILOPS polished
DEHILPSU sulphide
DEHILPSY sylphide
DEHILRTW writhled
DEHILSTW whistled
DEHIMNOS hedonism
Sondheim
DEHIMPSY demyship
DEHINOPR nephroid
DEHINOPS sphenoid
DEHINOST hedonist
DEHINSUW unwished
DEHIOOVW wivehood
DEHIOPRS spheroid
DEHIOPRT trophied
DEHIORSS dishorse
DEHIORST Rhodites
DEHIORTY thyreoid
DEHIOSSU dishouse
DEHIOSSW sideshow
DEHIOTWW the Widow
DEHIPSSU pseudish
DEHIRRST Red Shirt
DEHIRTWW withdrew
DEHKLNOU elkhound
DEHLLOPY phyllode
DEHLMOOR Lord Home
DEHLMORY hydromel
DEHLNOOS lens hood
DEHLNOOW downhole
DEHLOOOW woodhole
DEHLOORV hold over
holdover
overhold
DEHLOORW Lord Howe
DEHLOOSS hoodless
DEHLOOST tool shed
DEHLOOSW woolshed
DEHLOPRU upholder
DEHLORSU shoulder
DEHLOSTU dust-hole
DEHLRSWY shrewdly
DEHMMRTU thrummed
DEHMNOOW down-home
DEHMNOOY homodyne
DEHMNRUY unrhymed
DEHMOORW whoredom
DEHMOPRY hypoderm
DEHMORUU humoured
DEHNNOOT on the nod
DEHNNTUU unhunted
DEHNOORU honoured
DEHNOOTT on the dot
DEHNORSU enshroud
DEHNORSY enhydros
DEHNORTW nowt-herd
DEHNORTY threnody
DEHNOSTU Southend
DEHNOSTW the Downs
DEHNOSUU unhoused
DEHNOTWY the downy
DEHNRTUY thundery
DEHOOOPP popehood
DEHOOPRT theropod✧
DEHOORST The Doors
DEHOORTU out-Herod
DEHOPPPU hopped-up
DEHOPRST potsherd
DEHOPTTU hotted-up
DEHORRST redshort
DEHRRSTU druthers
DEIIINSV divinise
DEIIINVZ divinize
DEIIIRTV viridite
DEIIISVV divisive
DEIIKLNN in kindle
DEIIKLNS disliken
DEIIKLNV devilkin
DEIILLMP milliped
DEIILLMT ill-timed
tidemill
DEIILMRU delirium
DEIILMSV devilism
DEIILNNU induline
DEIILNPV vilipend
DEIILNVY divinely
DEIILORS idoliser
DEIILORZ idolizer
DEIILPSS sideslip
DEIILRST redistil
DEIIMMRS dimerism
DEIIMMST mistimed
DEIIMMTT immitted
DEIIMNRT diriment
DEIIMNTU mutinied
DEIIMNUV venidium
DEIIMPRU peridium
DEIIMSVW midwives
DEIINNPP pinniped
DEIINNUV undivine
DEIINOPR pied noir
DEIINORS derision
Ironside
resinoid
DEIINORT retinoid
DEIINOST sedition
DEIINOSV visioned
DEIINOTV dive into
DEIINPPW windpipe
DEIINPRS inspired
DEIINPRT intrepid✧
DEIINPRY pyridine
DEIINPTU unpitied
DEIINQSU quinsied
DEIINRST disinter
DEIINRSU disinure
DEIINSST tidiness
DEIINSTU disunite
nudities
DEIINTTU intuited
DEIINTTY identity
DEIIOPRS presidio
DEIIOPZZ pezizoid
DEIIORRV voir dire
DEIIORSX oxidiser
DEIIORTX trioxide
DEIIORTY iodyrite
DEIIORXZ oxidizer

DEIIPRST spirited
DEIIPRSZ disprize
DEIIPRVZ Zip® drive
DEIIPTTY tepidity
DEIIQSTU disquiet
DEIIRRVV viverrid
DEIIRSSU diuresis
DEIJMORU demi-jour
DEIJNOPU joined-up
DEIJORRY joyrider
DEIKKLNO klondike✧
DEIKLLOR lordlike
DEIKLMNU unmilked
DEIKLNNU unlinked
DEIKLNOR Kol Nidre
DEIKLNRW wrinkled
DEIKLNSS kindless
DEIKLORS Roskilde
DEIKLSSS diskless
DEIKMNOO kimonoed
DEIKNNPU unpinked
DEIKNNSS kindness
DEIKNORU Iron Duke
DEIKNORV overkind
DEIKNSSU unkissed
DEIKPRSU prusiked
DEIKRSSU Rusedski
DEIKRSVY skydiver
DEILLMNU unmilled
DEILLNOR old-liner
DEILLNTU untilled
DEILLNUW unwilled
DEILLOOV livelood
DEILLOPW pillowed
DEILLOVW low-lived
DEILLOWW willowed
DEILLSTU duellist
DEILMNOO melodion
DEILMNSS mildness
mindless
DEILMNSU muslined
DEILMOOT dolomite
DEILMOOW lime-wood
DEILMOPR impolder
DEILMORT old-timer
DEILMORU lemuroid
mouldier
DEILMOST melodist
DEILMOSU emulsoid
DEILMOTV demi-volt
DEILMPPU plumiped
DEILMPSU displume
DEILMPTU multiped
DEILMSSY demissly
DEILNNOT indolent
DEILNNOW down-line
DEILNOOS solenoid
DEILNOPW dowel-pin
DEILNORS disenrol
DEILNOSU delusion
unsoiled
DEILNOVV involved
DEILNOVW live down
DEILNPRS speldrin
DEILNPRU underlip
DEILNPST split end
DEILNRSS rindless
DEILNRSW swindler
DEILNRTY trendily
DEILNSSV vildness
DEILNSSW wildness
windless
DEILNSTU unlisted
DEILNTTU untitled
DEILNTUY unitedly
DEILNUWY unwieldy
DEILOOPS poolside
DEILOOPW woodpile
DEILOOVW wood-evil
DEILOPPS dip-slope
DEILOPPY polypide
DEILOPRU preludio
DEILOQRU liquored
DEILORSU souldier
DEILORSY soldiery
DEILOSSV dissolve
DEILOSTU solitude
DEILPPST stippled
DEILPPSU supplied
DEILPPTU pulpited
DEILPRSU serpulid
DEILPSTT splitted
DEILPSTU stipuled
DEILPTTU uptilted
DEILPTWY wild type
DEILRSVY diversly
DEILRTVY deviltry
DEILSTUY sedulity
DEILSTWW Wild West
DEIMMNOS demonism
DEIMMNPU mine dump
DEIMMOST immodest
DEIMMPST misdempt
DEIMMRRU mire-drum
DEIMNNOP open mind
DEIMNNOS misdonne
DEIMNNOU unmonied
DEIMNNOY Endymion
DEIMNOOS dominoes
DEIMNOOT demotion
DEIMNOOX monoxide
DEIMNOPT piedmont
DEIMNOPU opium den
DEIMNORT dormient
DEIMNOST demonist
DEIMNOSW Wodenism
DEIMNOTW downtime
DEIMNPRU unprimed
DEIMNPSS misspend
DEIMNPTU impudent
DEIMNRTU rudiment
DEIMNSSU unmissed
DEIMOOSS sodomise
DEIMOOST moodiest
sodomite✧
DEIMOOSZ sodomize
DEIMOOTW wood mite
DEIMORRR mirrored
DEIMORRS misorder
DEIMORSS Messidor
DEIMORSU dimerous
soredium
DEIMORUX exordium
DEIMOSTT demotist
DEIMRSUU residuum
DEINNNOT Nintendo®
DEINNNOU innuendo
DEINNNPU unpinned
DEINNNTU untinned
DEINNOOR red onion
DEINNOOT noontide
DEINNORT indentor
DEINNORU unironed
DEINNOSW snowed in
DEINNOWW winnowed
DEINNPRU underpin
DEINNRSU in sunder
DEINNRTV TV dinner
DEINNRUU uninured
DEINNRUV undriven
DEINOOPS Poseidon
DEINOOPW pinewood
DEINOOTV devotion
DEINOPPW downpipe
pipe down
DEINOPRS disponer
DEINOPRU ride upon
DEINOPRY pyrenoid
DEINOPSS dopiness
DEINOPSU unpoised
DEINOPTW dewpoint
DEINORRV River Don
DEINORSU sourdine
DEINORSW disowner
wind rose
DEINORTT intorted
DEINORTU diner-out
DEINORTW tire down
DEINORVW overwind
DEINOSSV voidness
DEINOSSZ doziness
DEINOSWZ downsize
DEINOTTU duettino
DEINPPRU unripped
DEINPRRU Rupinder
DEINPRUZ unprized
DEINRRTU intruder
DEINRSSU sundries
DEINRSTT strident
DEINRSTU sit under
DEINRTUW underwit
DEINSSSY syndesis
DEINSTUU unsuited

DEIOORTV overdo it
DEIOPPRR drop-ripe
DEIOPRRV provider
DEIOPRSS disposer
DEIOPRST dipteros
DEIOPRSV disprove
DEIOPRSW dropwise
DEIOPSST side post
topsides
DEIOPTUW wiped out
DEIORRSY derisory
DEIORRTU outrider
DEIORSSU desirous
DEIORSTU outsider
DEIORTUV outdrive
DEIORTUW weird out
DEIOSSTU outsides
DEIOSTUZ outsized
DEIPPRST stripped
DEIPPTTU titupped
DEIPRSSU dispurse
DEIPRSTU disputer
DEIPSTUV stived-up
DEIPTTTU tittuped
DEIRRRSY dry riser
DEIRSSST distress
DEIRSSTU diestrus
DEIRSTTU detritus
DEISTTTU duettist
DEJKLLRY Dr Jekyll
DEJLOOOR jordeloo
DEJMPPUU jumped-up
DEJNOPRU June drop
DEJOOOTY Ode to Joy
DEKKLNOY klondyke✧
DEKKORSW desk-work
DEKLNOOU unlooked
DEKLOOPR Old Poker
DEKMNOSU unsmoked
DEKMORSY smoke-dry
DEKNORUW unworked
DEKNRSUY undersky
DEKNSSSU duskness
DEKORSWY dye-works
DELLLOOP lolloped
DELLMOOS modellos
DELLMOSW swelldom
DELLNOPU unpolled
DELLNORW rowndell
DELLNPUU unpulled
DELLNSSU dullness
DELLOOTW well-to-do
DELLOPTU polluted
DELLORRY drollery
DELLORSS lordless
DELLOSTY Old Style
DELLOTUW outdwell
DELMNOOV noveldom
DELMNORY modernly
DELMNOSU unseldom
DELMNOTW melt down
meltdown
DELMNPUU pendulum
DELMORSU smoulder
DELMOSTY modestly
DELNNOOR Londoner
DELNOORS Old Norse
DELNOORW Lord Owen
DELNOOSU nodulose
DELNOOWY woodenly
DELNOPPU unlopped
DELNOPRS splendor
DELNOPTW pelt down
DELNORSU unsolder
DELNORSY Reynolds
DELNORTU roundlet
DELNORWW New World
DELNORYY yonderly
DELNOSSU loudness
DELNOSUU undulose
unsouled
DELNOSUV unsolved
DELNRRTU trundler
DELOOOOT toodle-oo
DELOOPTU tooled up
DELOORRV overlord✧
DELOORRW wordlore
DELOORSV oversold
DELOORTY rootedly
DELOORUV overloud
DELOOSSW woodless
DELOPSTU postlude
DELOPSTW spot-weld
DELORSSW wordless
DELORSUY delusory
DELOSSUU sedulous
DELOTUVY devoutly
DELPRTUU pultrude
DELSSSTU dustless
DELSTUUV Deus vult
DEMMNOOO monomode
DEMMNSUU unsummed
DEMMRSTU strummed
DEMNNOOT Edmonton
DEMNOOOP monopode
DEMNORSY syndrome
DEMNORUW unwormed
DEMNOSTU mudstone
DEMNOSUU mouse-dun
DEMOOPRR prodrome
DEMOORST doomster
DEMOORSU dormouse
DEMOORTY odometry
DEMPRSTU dumpster
DENNNSUU unsunned
DENNOOOZ endozoon
DENNOORW no wonder
DENNOOTW tone down
DENNOPTU pound net
tend upon
ten-pound
DENNORST tendrons
DENNOTUW unwonted
DENNPRUU unpruned
DENNRRUU underrun
DENNRTUU unturned
DENOOOPR open door
open-door
DENOOOTW woodnote
DENOOOVW ovenwood
DENOOPRS prodnose
DENOOPRZ drop zone
DENOOPTU dote upon
DENOORRS endorsor
DENOORTU unrooted
DENOORTX next door
next-door
DENOORWW wood wren
DENOOSSW woodness
DENOOTVW vote down
DENOPPRU pop-under
DENOPRUV unproved
DENOPSTU outspend
unposted
DENOPSTW step down
step-down
stewpond
DENOPSUW snowed up
DENOQTUU unquoted
DENORRSU rounders
DENORRUU roundure
DENORSSU dourness
DENORSTU tonsured
unsorted
DENORSTY dry-stone
DENORSUU unroused
unsoured
DENORTTU unrotted
DENORTUW under tow
undertow
DENOSTUU unsued-to
DENOTUUV undevout
DENPRTUU upturned
DENRRSUY dry-nurse
sur-reyn'd
DENRSSSU sundress
DENSTTUY studenty
DEOOORSW rosewood
DEOOOSWW woodwose
DEOOPPRT pteropod
DEOOPRRS rose drop
DEOOPRRV provedor
DEOOPRST doorstep
torpedos
DEOORRSW sorrowed
DEOORRVW overword
DEOORRWW owreword
DEOOSTWW Westwood
DEOPPRST stropped
DEOPPRSU purposed
DEOPPSSU supposed
DEOPPSUU souped-up
DEOPRRTU protrude

Words marked ✧ can also be spelled with one or more capital letters

DEOPRSST top-dress
DEOPRSTT drop test
DEOPRSTU sprouted
DEORRSTU detrusor
DEORRTTU tortured
DEORSTUV overdust
DEORSTUX dextrous
DEORSTVY dry-stove
DEOSSSUY Odysseus
DEOSSTTU testudos
DEPPSSYY dyspepsy
DEQRSUUY surquedy
DERSTTTU strutted
DFFHIOOS food-fish
DFFIILUY fluidify
DFFIIRTY triffidy
DFFIKNOR drink off
DFFINOOZ Dino Zoff
DFFINPSU dip snuff
DFFLMPUU plum-duff
DFFLOORU fourfold
DFFLORTU to ruffl'd
DFFNOORU round off
DFFNOOSU sound off
DFFOORUW woodruff
DFGGHIOT dogfight
DFGGIOST God's gift
DFGHILOS goldfish
DFGIIIRY rigidify
DFGIILRY frigidly
DFGIINNS findings
DFGILLOO gold foil
DFGILMNU fling mud
DFGILNNO fondling
DFGILNOO flooding
DFGINNOU founding
DFGINOOR fordoing
DFGKLOOO good folk
DFGKNORU dung-fork
DFGLNOOR Longford
DFGMOOOR good form
DFGOOOST God's foot
DFHIIMUY humidify
DFHIMRSU drumfish
DFHINOOT hindfoot
DFHINOPS fish pond
DFHJNOOR John Ford
DFHLOOOT foothold
DFHNOOUX foxhound
DFIIINVY divinify
DFIILMTU multifid
DFIILOSY solidify
DFIILTUY fluidity
DFIINPRT driftpin
DFIKNOOS skinfood
DFILLOOT floodlit
DFILLORY floridly
DFILLOWW wildfowl
DFILNOTW lift down
DFILORTU old fruit
DFIMNORW firm down
DFIMOOOR iodoform
DFINRSUW windsurf
DFIOOPRS disproof
DFJKNOOU junk food
DFLNOOWW downflow
wolf down
DFLOOORT rood loft
DFLOOOSU soul food
DFLOPRUU proudful
DFNOOPRU profound
DFOOOORW woodroof
DFOOOSTW softwood
DGGGIINS diggings
DGGGINRU drugging
grudging
DGGHINOT night-dog
DGGIILNR ridgling
DGGIINNR grinding
DGGIINNW wingding
DGGILNOS lodgings
DGGINRTU trudging
DGGIRSTU druggist
DGHIILNS hidlings
DGHIIMNT midnight
DGHIIMST misdight
DGHIINNW hindwing
DGHIINPS sphingid
DGHIINRT thirding
DGHIISST dissight
DGHIKNOO kinghood
DGHIKNOS Hodgkin's
DGHILLNU dunghill
DGHILLOT Old Light
DGHILNOS holdings
DGHILNOT old thing
DGHILNRU hurdling
DGHILOOR girlhood
DGHILRTY dry light
DGHIMOST god-smith
DGHIOORS droogish
DGHLORSU gold rush
DGHNOOTU do-nought
DGHNOTUU doughnut
DGHOOOSW good show
DGHOOOTT dogtooth
DGHORRUY rough-dry
DGHORTUY droughty
DGIIIMRS dirigism
DGIIIRTY rigidity
DGIIKLNN kindling
DGIIKNNR drinking
DGIILLNR drilling
DGIILLOU liguloid
DGIILLRR drill rig
DGIILNOS disloign
DGIIMNOS misdoing
DGIIMNOU gonidium
DGIIMPUY pygidium
DGIINNOP poinding
DGIINNOR Girondin
non-rigid
DGIINNRW windring
DGIINNSS sindings
DGIINORR gridiron
DGIINOSV voidings
DGIINOTT dittoing
DGIINPPR dripping
DGIINRTY dirtying
DGIINVVY divvying
DGIINYZZ dizzying
DGIIOTTW two-digit
DGIKLOOY kidology
DGIKNOOR drooking
DGIKNOOW kingwood
DGIKNORU drouking
DGILLNOR drolling
lordling
DGILLOOW goodwill
DGILMNOU moulding
DGILMNPU dumpling
DGILMNSU sling mud
DGILMSUY smudgily
DGILNOOW woolding
DGILNOOY Indology
DGILNORS lordings
DGILNORY yoldring
DGILNOTY dotingly
DGILOOTW giltwood
DGILOPSU solpugid
DGILOSTY stodgily
DGILRTUY turgidly
DGIMMNRU drumming
DGINNOPU pounding
DGINNORU rounding
DGINNORW drowning
ring down
DGINNOSU sounding
DGINNOUW wounding
DGINNSSY syndings
DGINOOPS spongoid
DGINOPPR dropping
DGINOPRW prig down
DGINORTU grind out
DGINOSUY digynous
DGINSTUY studying
DGIOSUYZ dizygous
DGKLOORW goldwork
DGKNOOSW God knows
DGLLOORY Old Glory
DGLNOPUW gulp down
DGLOOOPY podology
DGLOOOSY dosology
DGLOOOXY doxology
DGMOPSYY gypsydom
DGNNORUU unground
DGNOOORV Novgorod
DGNOORTU good turn
DGNOOTYZ zygodont
DGOPPPUY puppy-dog
DHHILOTW withhold
DHIIIMNS diminish
minidish

DHIIIOST histioid
idiotish
DHIIKWZZ whizz kid
DHIILOSS solidish
DHIIMNOO hominoid
DHIIMNSU Hinduism
DHIIMPSS midships
DHIIMTUY humidity
DHIINPSW windship
DHIINSTW whinid'st
DHIINTWW withwind
DHIIOPRU ophiurid
DHIIORSS hidrosis
DHIKNOOW hoodwink
DHIKORSY hydroski
DHILLNOW downhill
DHILLOPY phylloid
DHILLORS drollish
DHILLOST tolldish
DHILMOPY lymphoid
DHILMOSY modishly
DHILNOPY lindy hop
DHILNTUW Wild Hunt
DHILOPRS lordship
DHILOPSS slipshod
DHILORRY horridly
DHIMNOST hindmost
DHIMNOSU unmodish
DHIMOOOY omohyoid
DHIMOOSS misshood
DHIMOPPY hippydom
DHINNOOR Rhinodon
DHINOORS dishonor
DHINORSU roundish
DHINOTUW whodunit
DHIOOPRZ rhizopod
DHIOPRSU proudish
DHIORSTY thyrsoid
DHIORSWY rowdyish
DHJNNOOP John Pond
DHJNOORY John Dory
DHJOPRSU jodhpurs
DHKMNOOO monkhood
DHLLNOUW hull-down
DHLLOPYY phyllody
DHLNOOWW howl down
DHLNORTU Lord Hunt
DHLNOSTU shouldn't
DHLOOORT roothold
DHLOOORY holy-rood
DHLORXYY hydroxyl
DHLOSSTU shouldst
DHMNOOOT homodont
DHMNOSTU Mt Hudson
DHMOOPPU pumphood
DHMORSYY Hydromys
DHMORTUW throw mud
DHMORTUY drymouth
DHNNOTUW hunt down
DHNOOPRU Proudhon
DHNOOSWW showdown
DHNORSUU unshroud
DHNORSUW downrush
DHNOSTUW shut down
shutdown
DHOOOPRT orthopod
DHOOORTX orthodox✧
DHOOPRST drop-shot
DHOORSUW woodrush
DHOPRSYY hydropsy
DHOSSTTU dust-shot
DIIIKMNS minidisk
DIIILLQU illiquid
DIIILRSW wild iris
DIIILTVY lividity
DIIIMOST idiotism
DIIIMTTY timidity
DIIINOSV division
DIIINTVY divinity
DIIIPRST dispirit
DIIIRTVY viridity
DIIITVVY vividity
DIIJNOST disjoint
DIIKLLNY kindlily
DIIKLLSW wild silk
DIILLMNR millrind
DIILLMNW windmill
DIILLMPY limpidly
DIILLQUY liquidly
DIILLSTY idyllist
DIILMOSS solidism
DIILMOTY mytiloid
DIILMUUV diluvium
DIILNOTU dilution
DIILNOUV diluvion
DIILNOXY xyloidin
DIILNTUY untidily
DIILOPRT triploid
DIILOPSY ypsiloid
DIILORSU siluroid
DIILOSST solidist
DIILOSTY solidity
DIILQSUU liquidus
DIIMMNOU dominium
DIIMNNOO dominion
in Domino
DIIMNNSU undinism
DIIMNOPT midpoint
mid-point
DIIMNSUU indusium
DIIMOPRS prismoid
DIIMPUXY pyxidium
DIIMRUUV duumviri
DIIMTTUY tumidity
DIINNORS Dinornis
DIINNOSU disunion
DIINOORT Triodion
DIINOSSU sinusoid
DIINSTUY disunity
DIIOPRTY pityroid
DIIOPRVZ Pozidriv®
DIKLMOOW milkwood
DIKLNNOW downlink
DIKLNNUY unkindly
DIKLNOOP kilopond
DIKLRUUU durukuli
DIKMOORW Mirkwood
DIKNOOSW woodskin
DIKNORTU outdrink
DIKOOSTU ditokous
DILLMNOP millpond
DILLNOPY pond lily
DILLOORS door-sill
DILLOSTY stolidly
DILMNOOS smilodon
DILMNORW lindworm
DILMNOSW slim down
DILMNUUX lux mundi
DILMOOSU modiolus✧
DILNOPSU lispound
DILNOUWY woundily
DILOOPPY polypoid
DILOOPRY droopily
DILOORSS lordosis
DILOORSU louis-d'or
DILOOSUY odiously
DILOOTUV volutoid
DILOPRTY torpidly
DILORRTY torridly
DILORSWY drowsily
DILPRTUY putridly
DILPSTUY stupidly
DILRSTUY sturdily
DIMMNORY myrmidon✧
DIMMNOTY to my mind
DIMMOOSU isodomum
DIMNOOOS isodomon
DIMNOOST monodist
DIMNORSV Mordvins
DIMNOSTU dismount
DIMNOSUW unwisdom
DIMNPPUW wind pump
DIMNSSTU Stundism
DIMOOPPU Pompidou
DIMOOPRR prodromi
DIMOOPRY myriopod
DIMOORTW modiwort
DIMOPRSU dum spiro
misproud
DIMORRTU Durmitor
DIMORSWY rowdyism
DIMOSTUY dumosity
DIMRSUUV duumvirs
DINNOORS rondinos
DINNOOST tondinos
DINNORUW win round
DINOOORW ironwood
DINOOPSU dipnoous
DINOORSU nidorous
DINOOSTT odontist
DINOOSTY nodosity
DINOPRTY dry-point
DINORSTU sturnoid

DINOSSUY Dionysus
DINPRTUY punditry
DINRSTUY industry
DINSSTTU Stundist
DIOOPRRT dirt-poor
proditor
DIOOPRRV providor
DIOORSTT ridottos
DIOSSTUU studious
DIRSSTTU distrust
DJRTUUYY jury duty
DKMNOOOR komondor✧
DKNNOOTW don't-know
DKNORSUW sow-drunk
DKOOORWW woodwork
DKORSTUW studwork
DLLMOOPY dolly-mop
DLLMORRU drum roll
DLLMORSU slumlord
DLLNOORY Lord Lyon
DLLNOPUW pull down
pull-down
DLLNORUY unlordly
DLMNOOTY mylodont
DLMORSUY smouldry
DLNOOPRU pouldron
DLNOOSUU nodulous
DLNOOSWW slow down
slowdown
DLNORTUY rotundly
DLNOSUUU undulous
DLOOOORS doloroso
DLOOOOWW wood wool
DLOOORSU dolorous
DLOOPPUW pulpwood
wood pulp
DLOOPPYY polypody
DLOORSTY old story
DMMNRUUY dummy run
DMNNOOOT monodont
DMNOORWY on my word
DMNOOSTW downmost
DMOOORWW woodworm
wormwood
DMOPPPUU puppodum
DMOPPPUY puppydom
DMPPPUUY mudpuppy
DNNOOPRU pundonor
DNNOOPUW down upon
DNNOORTW torn-down
DNNOOSSU od's nouns
DNNOOTWW down town
downtown✧
DNNORTUW downturn
turn down
turn-down
DNOOOOPW poon-wood
DNOOPPRU propound
DNOOPRSW snowdrop
DNOOPRTU round top
DNOOPRUW downpour
DNOOPSTW stop down
DNOOPSUW up so down
DNOOPTUW two pound
DNOORSUW wondrous
DNOORTUU round out
DNOOSTUU sound out
DNOOSTWW stowdown
DNOPRSSU sundrops
DNORRSUU surround
DNORSSUY undrossy
DOOOPRST doorpost
doorstop
DOOORSTU outdoors
DOOORSUW sourwood
DOOPPRTU top-proud
DOOPRRSY rosy drop
DOOPRRTW dropwort
DOOPSWWY powsowdy
DOORRSUU ordurous
DOORRTTU trout rod
DOORSSUU sudorous

E

EEEEFFLR feel free
EEEEFNRZ enfreeze
EEEEFRRZ refreeze
EEEEGGRR greegree
EEEEGMRR re-emerge
EEEEGNRY greeneye
EEEEGNSV Genevese
EEEEGQSU squeegee
EEEEHRSW see where
EEEEHRTV The Reeve
EEEELLPX expellee
EEEELLVY eye level
eye-level
EEEELMST let me see
teleseme
EEEELNRW ne'er-weel
EEEELNSV sleeveen
EEEEMNRT neem tree
EEEENNVV even-even
EEEENRRV veneerer
EEEEOTYY eye to eye
EEEEPPSW peesweep
EEEEPRRV repreeve
EEEEPTTW peetweet
EEEFFGIR fee-grief
EEEFFLOR forefeel
EEEFFLTY effetely
EEEFFNOR Freefone®
EEEFFNRT efferent
EEEFFORT forefeet
EEEFFRVW feverfew
EEEFHLTT the Fleet
EEEFIKLL feel like
EEEFILPR life peer
EEEFINRT Tenerife
EEEFIPRR repriefe
EEEFLMOS feme sole
EEEFLORV free love
EEEFLRSX reflexes
EEEFLSST feetless
EEEFNNPY penny fee
penny-fee
EEEFNORS foreseen
EEEFNRRT referent
rent-free
tree fern
EEEFNRSS freeness
EEEFNRTT enfetter
EEEFNRTY entry fee
EEEFNRUZ unfreeze
EEEFORRV overfree
EEEFORTV free vote
EEEFPRUZ freeze-up
EEEFRRRR referrer
EEEFRRRT ferreter
EEEGGILN negligee
negligée
EEEGGLPY Peggy Lee
EEEGHINT eighteen
EEEGHLRS sheerleg
EEEGHORS here goes!
EEEGHORV hog-reeve
EEEGHRTT get there
EEEGILNV enveigle
EEEGILPS espiègle
EEEGIMTV Vegemite®
EEEGINNR engineer
EEEGINRS energise
greenies
EEEGINRV engrieve
EEEGINRZ energize
EEEGIRTY tiger eye
EEEGISSX exegesis
EEEGISTV egestive
EEEGITVV vegetive
EEEGKKRY Greek key
EEEGLMOS gleesome
EEEGLNRT greenlet
EEEGMNRT emergent
EEEGMNRU merengue
EEEGMORT geometer
EEEGNNRS sengreen
EEEGNOSV Genovese
EEEGNRRU reneguer
EEEGNRRV revenger
EEEGNRRY greenery
EEEGNRSV revenges
EEEGOPRT protégée
EEEGQQUU Queequeg
EEEGRRST regreets
EEEHILRW erewhile
while-ere
wire-heel
EEEHIRST etherise
EEEHIRTZ etherize
EEEHITWY white-eye
EEEHKLNO kneehole
EEEHLMPT helpmeet
EEEHLNTV eleventh

EEEHLNTY ethylene
EEEHLNXY hexylene
EEEHLOPP peephole
EEEHLOPW weephole
EEEHLORS hose reel
lee shore
EEEHMNTV vehement
EEEHMNTY the enemy
EEEHMRYY eye-rhyme
EEEHNNPT nepenthe
EEEHNNQU henequen
EEEHNPPS sheep-pen
EEEHNPRS ensphere
EEEHNRSS hereness
EEEHNRTT Ethernet
EEEHNRVW whenever
EEEHORRS Hereroes
EEEHORST shoetree
EEEHPRST spreethe
EEEHRRVW wherever
EEEHRTVV The Verve
EEEIKLMS misleeke
EEEIKLPS Spike Lee
EEEIKLRT treelike
EEEIKMPT keep time
EEEIKNPS Pekinese
EEEILLRV reveille
EEEILMMN Emmeline
EEEILMRS seemlier
EEEILMRT lime-tree
EEEILNNO éolienne
EEEILNPR pelerine
EEEILNRS Ernie Els
EEEILNRT tree line
EEEILNRY eyeliner
EEEILNST selenite
EEEILORS Rosie Lee
EEEILRRV reliever
EEEILRTT teil tree
EEEILSSW elsewise
EEEILSTV televise
EEEILTVW teleview
EEEIMNRS Ménière's
EEEIMNRU meunière
EEEIMPRR premiere
première
EEEIMPRS emperise
EEEIMPRZ emperize
EEEIMRRS miserere✧
EEEIMRTT remittee
EEEINNNT nineteen
EEEINNRT internee
EEEINNSS Siennese
EEEINNST seine net
EEEINNSV Viennese
EEEINNSY nine-eyes
EEEINPRT perentie
pine tree
EEEINQTU queenite
EEEINRSS eeriness
EEEINRST eternise
EEEINRTT reinette
EEEINRTV en vérité
EEEINRTZ eternize
EEEINTUX euxenite
EEEIPPRT pipe-tree
EEEIPRRV reprieve
EEEIQSUX exequies
EEEIRRSV rerevise
EEEIRRTV retrieve
EEEIRRVW reviewer
EEEIRRVX River Exe
EEEIRTVX exertive
EEEJKKNR knee-jerk
EEEJLLRW jeweller
EEEKKNSY Ken Kesey
EEEKLLSS keelless
EEEKLNNR enkernel
EEEKLORV keel over
EEEKLPSW ekpweles
EEEKMNSS meekness
EEEKMRSS kermesse
EEEKNNSS keenness
EEEKNORS kerosene
EEEKNORV overkeen
overknee
EEEKNRTY enter key
EEEKNSWW Newsweek
EEEKOPRV overkeep
EEEKPPST keep step
EEELLLRV leveller✧
EEELLLSW sewellel
EEELLNOR enrollee
EEELLNQU quenelle
EEELLNSW well seen
well-seen
EEELLPRR repeller
EEELLPRX expeller
EEELLRRT reteller
EEELLRRV reveller
EEELLVWY wye-level
EEELMNST elements
steelmen
EEELMOPP empeople
EEELMOPY employee
EEELMORT telomere
EEELMOTT omelette
EEELMPRS REM sleep
EEELMRTU muleteer
EEELMSSS seemless
EEELMSST teemless
EEELNOPP Penelope
EEELNOPR open-reel
EEELNOPV envelope
EEELNOSV novelese
EEELNQTU queenlet
EEELNRSW newsreel
EEELNRSY serenely
EEELNRTV nervelet
EEELNRTY Terylene®
EEELOPPR repeople
EEELORST sloetree
EEELPRSS peerless
EEELPRSY sleepery
EEELPTTY Teletype®
EEELRRTT letterer
EEELRSST treeless
EEELRSTT resettle
EEELRSTV verselet
EEELRSVY severely
EEELRTVV velveret
EEELSSTW weetless
EEELSTVY steevely
EEELTTTX teletext
EEEMMRUZ mezereum
EEEMNNTT tenement
EEEMNORZ mezereon
EEEMNRST entremes
EEEMNSST meetness
EEEMORRV evermore
EEEMORST stereome
EEEMORTV overteem
EEEMPRRT temperer
EEEMPRSS empressé
EEEMRRTX extremer
EEEMRSST semester
EEEMRSTX extremes
EEEMRTTW wet meter
EEENNOPR neoprene
EEENNRST étrennes
EEENNRTV nerve net
EEENNSSV evenness
EEENOPRR reopener
EEENOPRV peen over
EEENORSV overseen
Veronese
EEENORVW overween
EEENORVY everyone
EEENPPRS prepense
EEENPRRT repenter
EEENPRSS ens per se
EEENPRST pre-teens
pretense
EEENPRSY Pyrenees
EEENPSSX expenses
EEENPSTW sweep-net
EEENRRST resenter
EEENRRSV renverse
EEENRRTU returnee
EEENRRTV reverent
EEENRSTV Serevent®
EEENRSTY yestreen
EEENSSTW tweeness
EEEOPPSY pope's eye
EEEOPRRV overpeer
EEEORRST rose tree
EEEORRSV overseer
EEEPPPRR pepperer
EEEPPSTU steepeup
EEEPRRST pesterer
EEEPRRSU reperuse
EEEPRRSV perverse
preserve

EEEPRRTW pewterer
EEEPSTTT septette
EEEQRRUV verquere
EEEQRSUZ squeezer
EEERRRSV reserver
reverser
EEERRSSV reserves
EEERRSTT resetter
EEERSTVX vertexes
EEERSTWZ tweezers
EEESSTTT sestette
EEESTTTX sextette
EEFFFGLU gefuffle
EEFFFIPR Pfeiffer
EEFFFKLU kefuffle
EEFFGIIS effigies
EEFFGIRR greffier
EEFFGIRT free gift
EEFFGORY Geoffrey
EEFFHIKY keffiyeh
EEFFHORS sheer off
EEFFILLS self-life
EEFFISUV effusive
EEFFKLOR folk-free
EEFFLLOV level off
EEFFLLST self-left
EEFFLNTU effluent
EEFFLOPS sleep off
EEFFLORT forefelt
EEFFMORR free-form
EEFFRRSU sufferer
EEFGIILR filigree
EEFGILNR fleering
EEFGILNS feelings
EEFGILNT fleeting
EEFGINRR refringe
EEFGINRZ freezing
EEFGIRRU refigure
EEFGLNOW gene flow
EEFGLNRY greenfly
EEFGLNUV vengeful
EEFGNOOR foregone
EEFGOORR foregoer
EEFGORRT tree frog
EEFHHLNS hen-flesh
EEFHILLR hellfire
hell-fire
EEFHILMO home-life
EEFHILST The Flies
EEFHIMOR home-fire
EEFHIORS fire hose
EEFHIRSV feverish
EEFHIRTY etherify
EEFHLLPS self-help
EEFHLLWY flywheel
EEFHLMOT homefelt
EEFHLMST themself
EEFHLNOS one flesh
EEFHLSTY flysheet
EEFHMORR herefrom
EEFHNORT forehent
EEFHNRSW fresh-new
EEFHORRT therefor
EEFHORRW wherefor
EEFHORST free-shot
shot-free
EEFHORSW foreshew
EEFIIKLL lifelike
EEFIIKLW wifelike
EEFIILLN lifeline
EEFIILMT lifetime
EEFIILSZ life-size
EEFIIMNN feminine
EEFIIMNS feminise
EEFIIMNZ feminize
EEFIIRRV verifier
EEFIJNNR Jennifer
EEFIKLLS self-like
EEFIKLRS serflike
EEFIKNNP penknife
EEFILLMR Mill Reef
EEFILLMT telefilm
EEFILLOV love life
EEFILLRW free will
free-will
EEFILLSS lifeless
EEFILMOS lifesome
EEFILMST fistmele
EEFILMTX Flextime®
EEFILNRT life-rent
EEFILNSS fineless
EEFILNUV nieveful
EEFILORS free-soil
EEFILPPU flue pipe
EEFILPRR pilferer
EEFILRSS fireless
EEFILRST free list
EEFILRSU fusileer
EEFILSSW wifeless
EEFIMORT foretime
EEFIMSTU time fuse
EEFINNSS fineness
EEFINNTU fine-tune
EEFINOPR open fire
EEFINORV overfine
EEFINRRY refinery
EEFINRSS finesser
rifeness
EEFINRSU reinfuse
EEFIPRST fire-step
EEFIRRSU sure-fire
EEFIRSTT frisette
EEFIRSTY esterify
EEFIRSUW fuse wire
EEFIRTTZ frizette
EEFISSSW fess-wise
EEFKNORT reef knot
EEFKOPRS for keeps
EEFLLLNU Fluellen
EEFLLNSS fellness
EEFLLORT foretell
toll-free
EEFLLOSV self-love
EEFLLRSU self-rule
EEFLLRXY reflexly
EEFLLSSS selfless
EEFLMMSY me myself
EEFLMNSU menseful
EEFLMORU fumerole
EEFLNORT forelent
EEFLNORW enflower
EEFLNOSS one's self
EEFLNOST felstone
EEFLNRTU refluent
EEFLNSSS selfness
EEFLNSSU senseful
EEFLNTUV eventful
EEFLORRW flowerer
reflower
EEFLORTV leftover
EEFLORTW floweret
EEFLORWW werewolf
EEFLOSUX flexuose
EEFLRSST fretless
EEFMNORT fomenter
EEFMORRR reformer✧
EEFMPRRU perfumer
EEFNNORS enfrosen
EEFNORST enforest
softener
EEFNORTU fourteen
EEFNORTW forewent
Freetown
EEFNQRTU frequent
EEFNRTTU unfetter
EEFOORRT rooftree
EEFOPRRT Freeport
free port
EEFOPRST Freepost®
post-free
EEFORRST forester✧
fosterer
reforest
EEFORRSU ferreous
EEFORRTY feretory
EEFORSUV feverous
EEFORSUY four-eyes
EEFOSSTT fossette
EEGGGOOS goose-egg
EEGGHITW egg white
EEGGHLLS eggshell
EEGGHLOR hoggerel
EEGGHMSU meshugge
EEGGIJRR rejigger
EEGGIKNR greeking✧
EEGGILNR legering
EEGGIMNR emerging
EEGGIMRT egg timer
EEGGINNR greening
EEGGINRS greesing
EEGGINRT greeting
EEGGINSU segueing
siege-gun

EEGGLOOR geologer
EEGGORTT go-getter
EEGGPRRS preggers
EEGGPRSU egg purse
EEGGPSUY Peggy Sue
EEGGQRSU squegger
EEGHHIKN knee-high
EEGHHINT heighten
EEGHIILS Sieg Heil
EEGHIIST eighties
EEGHIKRS Greekish
EEGHILNW wheeling
EEGHILRS sleigher
EEGHILTW white-leg
EEGHINPT phengite
EEGHINRS greenish
EEGHINST seething
sheeting
EEGHINTT teething
EEGHINWZ wheezing
EEGHIOTT goethite
EEGHISST sightsee
EEGHISTY eyesight
EEGHLNNT lengthen
EEGHMNOY hegemony
EEGHNNRU enhunger
EEGHNOOP geophone
EEGHNOPS phosgene
EEGHNOPY hypogene
EEGHNSSU hugeness
EEGHOPTY geophyte
EEGHORTT together
EEGHOSTT ghettoes
EEGHRSTY the Greys
EEGHRTTY The Tyger
EEGIIKTW Ewigkeit
EEGIILNR lingerie
EEGIILNV give line
inveigle
EEGIINNR Nigerien
EEGIINRT re-ignite
EEGIINRV give rein
EEGIINTV genitive
EEGIIRSV give rise
EEGIJOPR jerepigo
EEGIKLNS sleeking
EEGIKLOT eklogite
EEGILLTT Gillette
EEGILMNR germ line
EEGILNOR eloigner
EEGILNPS sleeping
EEGILNRR lingerer
EEGILNRU reguline
EEGILNST steeling
EEGILNSV sleeving
EEGILOPU epilogue
EEGILOSU eulogies
eulogise
EEGILOUZ eulogize
EEGILQSU squilgee
EEGILRSU regulise
EEGILRTV verligte
EEGILRTY legerity
EEGILRUZ regulize
EEGIMNNS meninges
EEGIMNRT regiment
EEGIMNRU meringue
EEGIMNSU eugenism
EEGINNQU queening
EEGINNRS sneering
EEGINNRT entering
EEGINNRW renewing
EEGINNRY enginery
EEGINNST steening
EEGINNSU unseeing
EEGINNSV evenings
EEGINNSZ sneezing
EEGINNTV eventing
EEGINOPR perigone
EEGINOPS epigones✧
EEGINORR erigeron
EEGINORV virogene
EEGINOST egestion
EEGINPSW sweeping
EEGINQUU queueing
EEGINRRS resigner
EEGINRST steering
streigne
EEGINRSU seigneur
EEGINRSW sewering
EEGINRTU geniture
EEGINRTX genetrix
EEGINRUZ Zigeuner
EEGINSSU geniuses
EEGINSTU eugenist
EEGINSTV steeving
EEGINSTW sweeting
EEGINSUU Eugenius
EEGINTTV vignette
EEGINTUX teguexin
EEGINTVV give vent
EEGIOPRS perogies
EEGIOPSU epigeous
EEGIORST ergotise
EEGIORTZ ergotize
EEGIORVV give over
overgive
EEGIPPSU Giuseppe
EEGIPRST prestige
EEGIRRST register
EEGIRSTT grisette
EEGJORSU goujeers
EEGKNSSS Skegness
EEGLMNOP emplonge
EEGLMNTU emulgent
EEGLMOSS glosseme
EEGLNNTU ungentle
EEGLNOOP gene pool
EEGLNOPY polygene
EEGLNOTY telegony
EEGLOOST Togolese
EEGLORRV groveler
EEGMMOSU gemmeous
EEGMNOST emongest
gemstone
EEGMNTTU tegument
EEGMORSU gruesome
EEGMORTY geometry
EEGMSTUW sweet gum
EEGNNORT roentgen✧
EEGNNOSS goneness
EEGNNOSV evensong
EEGNOORV engroove
EEGNOOST osteogen
EEGNOPTY genotype
EEGNORST estrogen
EEGNORSU generous
EEGNORSY eryngoes
EEGNOTYZ zygotene
EEGNPRTY Peer Gynt
EEGNPRUX expunger
EEGNRSSY greyness
EEGNRSUY guernsey✧
EEGNRTTU tung tree
EEGNRTUV Turgenev
EEGOPRSU superego
EEGOPRTU Portugee
EEGORRST ostreger
EEGORSTU urostege
EEHHILTW the while
EEHHIPSS sheepish
EEHHIRST The Shire
this here
EEHHIRTW herewith
EEHHLLLO hellhole
EEHHLMOP home help
EEHHLRST threshel
EEHHNOSU hen house
EEHHOORS horse hoe
EEHHORTT the other
EEHHOSTU the House
EEHHRRST thresher
EEHIIKLV hivelike
EEHIILTW white lie
EEHIINNR inhere in
EEHIITTW white tie
white-tie
EEHIKLLL like hell
EEHIKLLT hell-kite
EEHIKLMO homelike
EEHIKRRS shrieker
EEHIKTWW Whit week
EEHILLMS shlemiel
EEHILLNP helpline
EEHILMNU helenium
EEHILNNO nine-hole
EEHILNOP neophile
EEHILNPW pinwheel
EEHILOPS pile shoe
EEHILORT hotelier
hôtelier
EEHILRSS heirless
EEHILRST St Helier

EEHILSSV hiveless
EEHILWYZ wheezily
EEHIMMOT home time
EEHIMMPT Memphite
EEHIMNOR Hermione
EEHIMNRT theremin
EEHIMPRS emperish
EEHIMPST epithems
EEHIMQUV Vehmique
EEHIMRST erethism
etherism
The Miser
EEHIMRTT thermite
EEHIMSTT The Times
EEHIMTTW meet with
EEHINNQU henequin
EEHINNRS enshrine
EEHINNRT inherent
EEHINNSS sneeshin
EEHINORT etherion
hereinto
EEHINPRS insphere
EEHINPRT nephrite
prehnite
trephine
EEHINRTT thirteen
EEHINRTW whitener
EEHINSTT sheet tin
EEHINSTV hive-nest
EEHIOPPS hosepipe
EEHIORST isothere
theorise
EEHIORTZ theorize
EEHIPPST psephite
EEHIPPTY epiphyte
EEHIPRRS perisher
EEHIPRSS Hesperis
EEHIPRST treeship
EEHIPRTT perthite
pith-tree
tephrite
threepit
EEHIPSST steepish
EEHIPSUU euphuise
EEHIPUUZ euphuize
EEHIQRSU queerish
EEHIRRSV shiverer
EEHIRRSW wherries
EEHIRSTT etherist
tee shirt
EEHIRTVY thievery
EEHISSTW sweetish
EEHJLOWY joy-wheel
EEHKLOOR look here!
EEHKLOWY Holy Week
EEHKMOST the smoke✧
EEHLLLOW well hole
EEHLLMSS helmless
EEHLLNTW well then
EEHLLORV hoveller
EEHLLPSS helpless
EEHLLSTW the wells
EEHLMOOS holesome
EEHLMOPS so help me
EEHLMORU home rule✧
EEHLMOSS homeless
EEHLNOTT telethon
EEHLNOTV the novel
vent-hole
EEHLNSST St Helens
EEHLOPSS hopeless
EEHLORST hosteler
EEHLORSV shoveler
EEHLOSSS shoeless
EEHLOTUW wheel out
EEHLPPRS shlepper
EEHLPRSU spherule
EEHLPRTY three-ply
EEHLRSTY sheltery
EEHLSSTW thewless
EEHMMOPR morpheme
EEHMMORT ohmmeter
EEHMNOOS moonshee
EEHMNOOZ home zone
EEHMNOSW somewhen
EEHMOOPS some hope
EEHMOORT rheotome
EEHMORST rest home
EEHMORVW whomever
EEHMSSTU the Muses
EEHNNORT enthrone
EEHNNPPU unheppen
EEHNNSSS neshness
EEHNNSTU unnethes
EEHNOORS one-horse
EEHNOORU honouree
EEHNOPRU hereupon
EEHNOPST poshteen
EEHNOPSX phone sex
EEHNOPTY hypnotee
neophyte
EEHNORST the Norse
EEHNORSW heronsew
EEHNORTU hereunto
EEHNORTV overhent
EEHNPRSU sheep run
unsphere
EEHNPRYY Henry Pye
EEHNPSTU Pentheus
EEHNRRTY Tyrrhene
EEHNRTTU untether
EEHOOPRS oosphere
EEHOORSV overshoe
over-shoe
EEHOOTTY eye tooth
EEHOPPSW peepshow
EEHOPPSX sheep-pox
EEHOPRST sheep-rot
EEHOPRVY overhype
EEHORRTX exhorter
EEHORSVW whosever
EEHORTTU thereout
EEHORTUW whereout
EEHPRSST the press
EEHPRSSU Hesperus
EEHPRSTY physeter
EEHRSSSU usheress
EEHSSTTY Thyestes
EEIIKLPP pipelike
EEIIKLSW likewise
wise-like
EEIILLMM millième
EEIILLMT melilite
EEIILLOP eolipile
EEIILMNN nine-mile
EEIILMNT ilmenite
line item
melinite
timeline
EEIILMRT timelier
EEIILMSS emissile
EEIILNNO lie in one
EEIILNNT Leninite
EEIILNPP pipeline
EEIILNRW wire line
EEIILNTV lenitive
EEIILRVW live wire
EEIILSTW lewisite
EEIIMMTT mimetite
EEIIMNOT meionite
EEIIMNTW meet in wi'
EEIIMRST itemiser
EEIIMRTZ itemizer
EEIIMSST Semitise
EEIIMSSV emissive
EEIIMSTZ Semitize
EEIINNST Einstein
nineties
EEIINORT erionite
EEIINPPR piperine
EEIINPPW pipe-wine
EEIINPRV viperine
EEIINRRV riverine
EEIINRSS in series
resinise
sirenise
EEIINRSZ resinize
sirenize
EEIINRTT intertie
retinite
EEIINSSV inessive
EEIIOPTZ epizoite
EEIIPRTT epitrite
EEIIQSTU equities
EEIIQTUV quietive
EEIIRRTV tirrivee
EEIIRSTV verities
EEIJKRST jet-skier
EEIJLNNU julienne
EEIJLNRT jetliner
EEIJLNUV juvenile
EEIJNNOR enjoiner
EEIJUUVX vieux jeu

EEIKLLRY	kyrielle
EEIKLMRT	milk-tree
EEIKLNSS	likeness
EEIKLNST	nestlike
EEIKLORS	roselike
EEIKLORT	lorikeet
EEIKLPST	spikelet
EEIKLRST	triskele
EEIKMNOP	open-mike
EEIKNORS	kerosine
EEIKNPRT	Peterkin
EEIKNRRT	tinkerer
EEIKNRST	Kirsteen
EEIKOQUV	equivoke
EEIKPPRR	kipperer
EEIKRSTU	keiretsu
EEILLLVW	live well
	live-well
EEILLMPR	impeller
EEILLMRU	reillume
EEILLNST	stelline
EEILLNSY	ley lines
	senilely
EEILLNVV	venville
EEILLORS	orseille
EEILLPSS	ellipses
EEILLPSY	sleepily
EEILLRTY	tree lily
EEILLSSV	veilless
EEILLTTV	Villette
EEILLTVY	velleity
EEILLVWY	weevilly
EEILMNNO	limonene
EEILMNNU	enlumine
EEILMNOP	pemoline
EEILMNOS	Seminole
EEILMNRU	lemurine
	relumine
EEILMNSU	selenium
	semilune
EEILMOPS	polemise
EEILMOPZ	polemize
EEILMORT	motelier
EEILMOST	lose time
	mesolite
	misletoe
EEILMSST	timeless
EEILMSUV	emulsive
EEILMSVV	Mevlevis
EEILNNOR	one-liner
EEILNNST	sentinel
EEILNOPR	leporine
EEILNORS	Elsinore
EEILNOST	noselite
EEILNOSV	novelise
EEILNOVZ	novelize
EEILNPPZ	zeppelin✧
EEILNPRS	pilsener✧
EEILNPRU	perilune
EEILNPRV	replevin
EEILNRSS	reinless
EEILNRST	enlister
	Leinster
	listener
	re-enlist
EEILNRTW	welter in
EEILNRTY	entirely
	lientery
EEILNRUV	unveiler
EEILNSSV	evilness
	vileness
EEILNSTT	settle in
EEILORRT	loiterer
EEILORRV	overlier
EEILORST	literose
	Tirolese
EEILORSV	relievos
EEILORVV	overlive
	overveil
EEILOSTW	sweet-oil
EEILOSVW	vowelise
EEILOTTT	toilette
EEILOVWZ	vowelize
EEILPPSS	pipeless
EEILPPSY	epilepsy
EEILPRST	epistler
EEILPSSV	pelvises
EEILPSTY	epistyle
EEILRSST	riteless
	tireless
EEILRSSW	wireless
EEILSSTW	witeless
EEILSSVW	viewless
EEILSTVY	stievely
EEIMMORS	memorise
EEIMMORZ	memorize
EEIMMOST	sometime
EEIMMRST	meristem
	mimester
	mismetre
EEIMMRSU	eumerism
EEIMMRTT	term-time
EEIMMSTU	semi-mute
EEIMNNOO	eo nomine
EEIMNOPS	episemon
EEIMNORS	emersion
EEIMNORT	timoneer
EEIMNORV	vomerine
EEIMNOST	monetise
	semitone
EEIMNOTX	xenotime
EEIMNOTZ	monetize
	time zone
EEIMNPRU	perineum
EEIMNPST	sepiment
EEIMNQSU	mesquine
EEIMNRRT	terminer
EEIMNRTU	mutineer
EEIMNRTV	virement
EEIMNSSS	Essenism
EEIMOPRS	promisee
	reimpose
EEIMOPST	epsomite
EEIMORST	Timorese
	tiresome
EEIMORTV	overtime
EEIMORTX	oximeter
EEIMOSSW	somewise
EEIMPPRS	episperm
EEIMPPST	pipe-stem
EEIMPRRS	simperer
EEIMPRSS	impresse
	mesprise
	premises
EEIMPRSZ	mesprize
EEIMPSSY	empyesis
EEIMQSTU	mesquite
EEIMRRST	merriest
EEIMRRSV	River Ems
EEIMRRTT	remitter
	trimeter
EEIMRSTU	emeritus
EEIMRTTU	true time
EEIMRTTY	temerity
EEIMSSST	messiest
EEINNNPS	Pennines
EEINNOPT	en pointe
EEINNPTT	penitent
EEINNRSW	new-risen
EEINNRTT	internet✧
	renitent
	tin terne
EEINNRTV	in ventre
	reinvent
EEINNRUX	xenurine
EEINNSTT	sentient
EEINOPPR	peperino
	peperoni
	ronepipe
EEINOPRS	isoprene
EEINORRS	no sirree
EEINORRT	reorient
EEINORSS	essoiner
EEINORST	serotine
EEINORSV	eversion
EEINORTT	tenorite
EEINORTX	exertion
EEINOSST	essonite
EEINOSTT	noisette
	teosinte
EEINPPRW	pen-wiper
EEINPPTV	vent-pipe
EEINPPTZ	Zentippe
EEINPRSS	ripeness
EEINPRSU	resupine
EEINPRTX	expert in
	inexpert
EEINPSTT	spinette
EEINQRRU	enquirer
EEINQRSU	squireen
EEINRRST	inserter
	reinsert
EEINRRSU	reinsure

EEINRRTV inverter
EEINRRTW winterer
EEINRRTX interrex
EEINRSST interess
EEINRSSU enuresis
EEINRSTT insetter
interest
sternite
EEINRSTU esurient
EEINRSTV reinvest
servient
sirvente
EEINRSTX intersex
EEINRSTY serenity
EEINRSUV universe
EEINRSWW newswire
wire-sewn
EEINRTTY entirety
eternity
trey-tine
EEINSSSW wiseness
EEINSSSX sexiness
EEINSTTW tentwise
twenties
EEINSTTX existent
EEIOPPRR ropé-ripe
EEIOPPRS epispore
EEIOPRRT portière
EEIOPRRV overripe
EEIOPRRW wire rope
EEIOPRST poetries
EEIORRTV overtire
EEIORRTX exterior
EEIORRUV ouvrière
EEIORSST erotesis
EEIORSVW overwise
EEIORSVZ oversize
EEIORVVW overview
EEIORVWW wirewove
EEIPPQRU equipper
EEIPPRRS perspire
EEIPPRTY peripety
EEIPRRTT preterit
EEIPRSTT pretties
EEIPRSTX pre-exist
EEIPRSTY perseity
EEIPRTUV eruptive
EEIPSSTW stepwise
EEIPSTUY Puseyite
EEIQRRRU requirer
EEIQRRTU requiter
EEIQRRUV verquire
EEIQRTUY queerity
EEIQSSSU esquisse
EEIRRSST resister
EEIRRSSV reversis
EEIRRSTV reverist
EEIRRTTT titterer
EEIRRVWY River Wye
EEIRSSTV serve its
EEIRSTVY severity
EEIRTTTZ terzetti
EEISSTTT testiest
EEJJLNUY jejunely
EEJKMOOS jokesome
EEJKNRTU junketer
EEJLLORY jolleyer
EEJLPSTU pulsejet
EEJMORST St Jerome
EEJPRRRU perjurer
EEJPRSTU superjet
EEKKORWW workweek
EEKLLNRY kernelly
EEKLLPTW well-kept
EEKLNNNU unkennel
EEKLNOST skeleton
EEKLNOSV velskoen
EEKLORST Koestler
EEKLORTW telework
EEKMNOYY key money
EEKNOPST knee-stop
EEKNOSTY keystone
EEKNSSSW skewness
EEKOORST kreosote
EEKORSTV overkest
EEKRRTUZ kreutzer
EELLLLMP pell-mell
EELLLLWW well, well
EELLLNWY Llewelyn
EELLMPTU plumelet
EELLNOOS Ole Olsen
EELLNORR enroller
EELLNOUV nouvelle
EELLNPRU prunelle
EELLNSSW wellness
EELLNSTU entellus
EELLOOST let loose
EELLOPTV top-level
EELLORST solleret
EELLORSV oversell
EELLORTX extoller
EELLORVW well over
EELLORVY volleyer
EELLOSSV loveless
EELLOSUV levulose
EELLOSWY Wolseley
EELLOTUV level out
EELLRSSU ruleless
EELLRVWY very well
EELMMPUX exemplum
EELMNOOS lonesome
EELMNRTT Lent term
EELMNSUY unseemly
EELMNTTU temulent
EELMNTUY unmeetly
EELMOOSV lovesome
EELMOPRY employer
EELMOPSY polyseme
EELMORST molester
EELMORTY remotely
EELMOSSV moveless
EELMOTVW twelvemo
EELMPPRU empurple
EELMPRTU plum tree
EELMRRTU murrelet
EELMRSST termless
EELMRSTY smeltery
EELMRTUX luxmeter
EELMSSST stemless
EELNNOSS loneness
EELNNRTU tunneler
EELNNUVY unevenly
EELNOORS loosener
EELNOPPU unpeople
EELNOPRT petronel
EELNOPTT tent pole
EELNOPTY polytene
EELNOQTU eloquent
EELNORST entresol
EELNORTT teletron
EELNORTV overlent
EELNOSSS noseless
soleness
EELNOSST noteless
toneless
EELNOSSU selenous
EELNOSSZ zoneless
EELNOSTV love nest
EELNOTVV evolvent
on velvet
EELNSSSW newsless
EELNSSTT tentless
EELNSSTU tuneless
EELNSSTV ventless
EELNSTTU unsettle
EELNSTWY New Style
EELOOPRT Peterloo
EELOPPST estoppel
EELOPRRX explorer✧
EELOPRTT teleport
EELOPSTU outsleep
sleep out
sleepout
EELOQRUY requoyle
EELORRSV resolver
EELORRTV revolter
EELORRUV overrule
rule over
EELORRVV revolver
EELORSSS roseless
EELORSTU resolute
EELORSTY Tyrolese
EELORTTU roulette
EELORTUV revolute
truelove
EELOSSTU setulose
EELOSSTV voteless
EELOSTTX sextolet
EELPPSTU septuple
EELPRTXY expertly
EELPSSUX plexuses
EELPSTTU settle up
EELPSTUX sextuple

EELQSUUU Equuleus
EELRRSTW wrestler
EELRSSST restless
EELRSSTU streusel
EELRSSTY tyreless
EELRSTWY westerly
EELSSTTX textless
EEMMNOOP menopome
EEMMNOST mementos
EEMMNOTV movement
EEMMNRRY merry men✧
EEMMOORS merosome
EEMNNRSU Mensuren
EEMNOOPT tone poem
EEMNORRS sermoner
EEMNORST sermonet
EEMNORSU mounseer
EEMNPRTU erumpent
untemper
EEMNRSTU Muenster
EEMNSSTU muteness
tenesmus
EEMNSTTV vestment
EEMOOPRT proteome
EEMOORRV moreover
EEMOORTT roomette
EEMOORVV move over
EEMOOSSX exosmose
EEMOPRRS premorse
EEMOQRSU Moresque
EEMOQTTU moquette
EEMORRTU mouterer
outremer
EEMORSST somerset✧
tree moss
EEMORSTU temerous
EEMOTTTU teetotum
EEMPRRSU presumer
EEMPRSST sempster
EEMRRSTU musterer
EEMRRTTU mutterer
EEMRSSTT set terms
EENNNOOO one-on-one
EENNNOSS nonsense
EENNNOTV non-event
EENNNPTY tenpenny
EENNNPWY new penny
EENNOOOT one-to-one
EENNOOPT open note
EENNOORT rotenone
EENNOOTT ten to one
EENNOPSS openness
EENNOPTX exponent
EENNORRW renowner
EENNSSTX nextness
EENOORST oestrone
roestone
EENOORTV overtone
EENOORUZ Eurozone
EENOPPRS propense
EENOPRSS response
EENOPRST protense
EENOPRSU peroneus
EENOPRTT entrepot
entrepôt
tent rope
EENOPRXY pyroxene
EENOPSTU set one up
EENORSSS soreness
EENORSSU neuroses
EENORSTT onsetter
setter-on
EENORSTX extensor
EENORTVW overwent
EENOSSST stenoses
EENOSSWY snow-eyes
EENPPRTU upper ten
EENPRSST pertness
presents
EENPRSSU pureness
EENPRSTT strepent
EENPRSTU purse-net
EENPSSSU suspense
EENPSTTU petuntse
EENPTTUZ petuntze
EENRRRTU returner
EENRRSTV renverst
EENRRTUV venturer
EENRSSSU sureness
EENRSSTU trueness
EENRSTUW wet nurse
wet-nurse
EEOOOTTT toe to toe
toe-to-toe
EEOOPRRV pore over
EEOOPRST proteose
EEOOPRSX exospore
EEOOPRTZ zoetrope
EEOORRVV rove-over
EEOORRVW overwore
EEOORRZZ zero-zero
EEOPPRSS porpesse
EEOPRRRT reporter
EEOPRRRV reprover
EEOPRRSU reposure
EEOPRRTT potterer
EEOPRRTX exporter
re-export
EEOPRSSS espresso
EEOPRSST portesse
EEOPRSSU espouser
repoussé
EEOPRSSX expresso
EEOPRSTV overstep
EEOPRSTW power set
EEOPRSTY serotype
EEOPRSUX exposure
EEOPRTTU peter out
EEOPRTVY overtype
EEOPSSTW sweetsop
EEOPTTTW top tweet
EEOQRTTU roquette
EEORRRST resorter
restorer
retrorse
EEORRRTT retorter
EEORRSSV reversos
EEORRSTX extrorse
EEORRTTT totterer
EEORRTTU teru-tero
EEORRTTX extorter
EEORRTUV overture
trouvère
EEORSTUV serve out
EEORSTVX vortexes
EEORTTTZ terzetto
EEOSSTTT sestetto
EEPQRRUU perruque
EEPRRSSU pressure
EEPRSTTU setter-up
upsetter
EERRSSTU tressure
EERRSTUV vesturer
EERRSTVY revestry
EERRSUVY resurvey
EERSTTTU utterest
EFFGHIOW weigh off
EFFGHIRT the griff
EFFGILRU griefful
EFFGINOR offering
EFFGIOTT get it off
EFFHIILS filefish
EFFHIISW fishwife
EFFHIITT fiftieth
EFFHILRW whiffler
EFFHIOTW off-white
EFFHLLSU shelf-ful
EFFHLLSY flesh-fly
EFFHLRSU shuffler
EFFHOORS offshore
EFFHOOSV shove off
EFFIINSS iffiness
EFFIKOSV skive off
EFFILNRS sniffler
EFFILNSS sniffles
EFFILORT forelift
EFFILRSU siffleur
EFFIMOST smite off
EFFINOSU effusion
EFFIOPRS pifferos
EFFIOPST off-piste
EFFIORST forfeits
EFFIORTW write off
write-off
EFFIQRSU squiffer
EFFLMNUU unmuffle
EFFLNRSU snuffler
EFFLNRUU unruffle
EFFLNSSU snuffles
EFFLOOPS slope off
EFFNRSSU snuffers
EFFOOORT forefoot
EFFOORSW worse off

Words marked ✧ can also be spelled with one or more capital letters

EFFORRUV overruff
EFGGIINN feigning
EFGGILOS solfeggi
EFGGIORU go figure
EFGGIRTU eggfruit
EFGGORRY froggery
EFGHHIIL high life
EFGHHIIV high five
high-five
EFGHIILR Hilfiger
EFGHIINR Feringhi
EFGHILSU fish-glue
EFGHINOT night-foe
EFGHINRT frighten
EFGHINSU feng shui
EFGHIOSY fogeyish
EFGHIRSY grey-fish
EFGHNOTU foughten
EFGHORST The Frogs
EFGIILNU figuline
EFGIIMNS misfeign
EFGIINNR infringe
refining
EFGIINRS fire sign
EFGIINRU figurine
EFGIINRY reifying
EFGIITUV fugitive
EFGIKNOR foreking
EFGILLNO lifelong
long-life
EFGILLNU fuelling
EFGILLUU guileful
EFGILMOR filmgoer
EFGILNOR florigen
EFGILNTT fettling
EFGILNTW left wing
left-wing
EFGILPRU fireplug
EFGIMOSY fogeyism
EFGIMRUU refugium
EFGINNNP pfenning
EFGINOOR go on fire
EFGINORV forgiven
EFGINORW forewing
EFGINPUY pinguefy
EFGINRRY ferrying
EFGINRTT fretting
EFGINRTY gentrify
EFGIOPTT pettifog
EFGIORRV forgiver
EFGIORTT forget it
EFGKMOOS fog-smoke
EFGLOOVX foxglove
EFGLORWY grey wolf
EFGLRSUU surgeful
EFGLSSTU slugfest
EFGNOSST songfest
EFGNSSUU funguses
EFGORSTT frog test
EFHHILTT the filth
EFHHIRSS freshish
EFHIILMN Niflheim
EFHIILNS line-fish
EFHIILST tilefish
EFHIINRS finisher
EFHIIPPS pipefish
EFHIIPRS fireship
EFHIIRSS Friesish
EFHIIRSW fish-weir
EFHIKOOR fire-hook
EFHIKSTY shift key
EFHILTWY whitefly
EFHIOOOR forhooie
EFHIOPRS foreship
EFHIORSS rosefish
EFHIORSV overfish
EFHIORTT fortieth
EFHIPRSS serfship
EFHIRRTU thurifer
EFHIRTTZ the fritz
EFHISSTW fish-stew
EFHKLNOU funkhole
EFHKLOOR folk hero
EFHLLLSU shellful
EFHLLMOR from hell
EFHLNORS hornfels
EFHLNOTY on the fly
EFHLOOSS hoofless
EFHLOOST elf-shoot
EFHLOPST flesh pot
top-shelf
EFHLORSY horsefly
EFHLORVY hoverfly
EFHLOSTU flesh out
EFHLOSUU houseful
EFHLOSUY housefly
EFHNRRSU fresh-run
EFHOORSW foreshow
EFHOOSST soft-shoe
EFHORRTY frothery
EFHORSTT set forth
EFHORTTY the Forty
EFHRSTTU furthest
EFIIILRV vilifier
EFIIINNT infinite
EFIIIRVV vivifier
EFIIKRRS fire-risk
EFIILLNT tefillin
EFIILLRS frillies
EFIILNST in itself
EFIILNTY felinity
finitely
EFIILOQU filioque
EFIILPRT rifle pit
EFIILRSU fusilier
EFIILSTT fitliest
EFIILSTY feistily
EFIIMMNS feminism
EFIIMNOS fisnomie
EFIIMNST feminist
EFIIMNTY feminity
EFIIMRSS miss fire
EFIINNNS Sinn Fein
EFIINORR inferior
EFIINORT notifier
EFIINPSV fivepins
EFIINPSX spinifex
EFIINRRT ferritin
EFIINRSY resinify
EFIINSUV infusive
EFIIPRRU purifier
EFIIPRST spitfire✧
EFIIPRTY typifier
EFIIPRXX prix fixe
EFIIRTUV fruitive
EFIIRVVY revivify
EFIJLORS frijoles
EFIKLLOW wolflike
EFIKLOOR rooflike
EFIKLORW life-work
EFIKLRUY like fury
EFIKNNOS finnesko
EFIKNORS foreskin
EFIKNRSU refusnik
EFIKORRW firework
EFIKRTUY key-fruit
EFILLLNU fluellin
EFILLLSW self-will
Will Self
EFILLMSU smileful
EFILLMTU full time
full-time
EFILLOOR Fiorello!
EFILLORV overfill
EFILLORW low-lifer
EFILLORZ Florizel
EFILLOSU fusel-oil
EFILLRUY irefully
EFILLSTY stellify
EFILLTUY futilely
EFILMRSS firmless
EFILMSUY emulsify
EFILNNTU fluent in
influent
EFILNORU fluorine
EFILNOST soft line
EFILNOSU noiseful
EFILNPSY snipe fly
EFILNRTT flittern
EFILNUWY unwifely
EFILOORT roof tile
EFILOPRR profiler
pro-lifer
EFILOPRW fire-plow
EFILOPST sept-foil
EFILORTU fluorite
EFILPPSU pipefuls
EFILPRTU uplifter
EFILPSTU spiteful
EFILPSTY self-pity
EFILRSST riftless
EFILRSTT flitters
EFILRSTW fewtrils

EFILRTTU fruitlet
EFILSTTW swiftlet
EFIMNORR informer
reinform
reniform
EFIMNORS ensiform
EFIMNRSS firmness
EFIMORRT retiform
EFIMORRW fireworm
EFIMORST setiform
EFIMOSST semi-soft
EFIMOSTT ofttimes
EFIMRSTU fremitus
EFINNOOT nine-foot
EFINNORS infernos
EFINNPSU finespun
EFINOPTX pontifex
EFINORRT frontier
EFINORSU refusion
EFINOSSX foxiness
EFINOSSZ foziness
EFINRSST snifters
EFIOPRRT port-fire
profiter
EFIORRTT retrofit
EFIPPRRY frippery
EFIPRRUY repurify
EFIPRSTU superfit
EFIPRTTY prettify
EFIRRRUY furriery
EFIRRTUY fruitery
EFIRSTTU turfiest
EFKLLOOR folklore
EFKLMNOS menfolks
EFKLNOTU folk tune
EFKLORUW fluework
EFKNOORW foreknow
EFKOORRV fork over
EFKOOTUY out of key
EFKORRTW fretwork
EFLLLOOW woolfell
EFLLLOWY fellowly
EFLLLPSU spellful
EFLLLPTU full pelt
full-pelt
EFLLNOOW lone wolf
EFLLNSSU fullness
EFLLNTUY fluently
EFLLOORW follower
EFLLOOTW footwell
EFLLORUV overfull
EFLLOSST self-lost
soft sell
soft-sell
EFLLOUWY woefully
EFLLRUUY ruefully
EFLLSUUY usefully
EFLMMRUY flummery
EFLMNRUU frenulum
EFLMOOTW Tom Wolfe
EFLMORRY formerly
EFLMORSS formless
EFLNOOSU felonous
EFLNOOTW wolf note
EFLNORTT frontlet
EFLNOSST soft lens
EFLNOSSU foulness
EFLNOSSW self-sown
EFLNOSTY stonefly
EFLNSUUU unuseful
EFLOORSS roofless
EFLOORSW foreslow
EFLOORTU footrule
EFLOORVW overflow
EFLOOSST footless
EFLOPRUW powerful
EFLOPSTU flue stop
EFLOPSTW fowl-pest
EFLORRUY ryeflour
EFLORSUY yourself
EFLORTWY fly-tower
EFLOSUUX flexuous
EFLPRSSU pressful
EFLPRSUU purseful
EFLRSTUU frustule
EFLRSTUY flustery
EFLRTTUY fluttery
EFMMORST stem form
EFMNORTY fromenty
EFMNRTUY frumenty
furmenty
EFMOORST foremost
EFMOORSU foursome
EFNNOOOR forenoon
EFNNORST fornenst
EFNNORUZ unfrozen
EFNOOOTT footnote
EFNOOPRT pentroof
EFNOOSST eftsoons
EFNOPRST forspent
EFNOPSTU soften up
EFNORRST renforst
re'nforst
EFNOSSST softness
EFOOOPRT foot-rope
EFOOORST footsore
EFOOPRSY spoofery
EFOOPSTT footstep
EFOORRSW forswore
EFOORSST soft sore
EFOORSTT footrest
EFOOSTUU out of use
EFOPRRSU profuser
EFORRSST fortress
EFORRSTW frowster
EFORRSTY forestry
EFORSSST fostress
EGGGILNS leggings
EGGGNNOR ronggeng
EGGGOOOS goosegog
EGGGORRY groggery
EGGHIINW weighing
EGGHIKSW egg whisk
EGGHIRWY Whiggery
EGGHOOTT egg tooth
EGGHRTUY thuggery
EGGIINNS singeing
EGGIINNT tingeing
EGGIJPRU jigger up
EGGIKNOS gingkoes
ginkgoes
EGGILLNY gingelly
EGGILNNU lungeing
EGGILNRS sniggler
EGGILNRU grueling
EGGILNRY gingerly
EGGILQSU squiggle
EGGILRRW wriggler
EGGIMSTU muggiest
EGGINORR gorgerin
EGGINOST set going
EGGINOUV vogueing
EGGINPRU ginger up
EGGINRSS gressing
EGGINSSU guessing
EGGIPRRY priggery
EGGJLRUY jugglery
EGGLLNOS long-legs
EGGLMOOY gemology
EGGLMRSU smuggler
EGGLORUY gurgoyle
EGGLRSTU struggle
EGGMNTUY nutmeggy
EGGMSSTU smuggest
EGGNOOPS egg spoon
EGGNOOST geognost
EGGNOOSY geognosy
EGGNORST gongster
EGGNORTW get wrong
EGGNRSUY snuggery
EGGNSSTU snuggest
EGGOORSU gorgeous
EGHHHIOS high shoe
EGHHIIMT high time
EGHHIIRS high-rise
EGHHIIRW high wire
EGHHILNO high-lone
EGHHILTY eighthly
EGHHINNT hen night
EGHHINSS highness✧
EGHHINTT The Night
the thing✧
EGHHIPRU higher-up
EGHHIPTY type-high
EGHHISTT high-test
EGHHLOOW whole-hog
EGHHORUW rough-hew
EGHIILNR hireling
EGHIILNS sheiling
shieling
EGHIINTV thieving
EGHIINTW in weight
EGHIIPTT tithe-pig

EGHIIRST tigerish
EGHIKLTY key light
EGHILLNS shelling
EGHILLNW well-nigh
EGHILMOR homegirl
EGHILNOT hoteling
EGHILNPT light pen
penlight
EGHILNRS shingler
EGHILNSS shingles
EGHILNSV shelving
EGHILNSY Yenglish
EGHILNTU tile-hung
EGHILNTW New Light
EGHILNUW glühwein✧
EGHILORT regolith
EGHILPRT plighter
EGHILSTT set light
EGHIMPRU grumphie
EGHIMSTT mightest
EGHINNOY honeying
EGHINNSS nighness
EGHINNST sennight
se'nnight
EGHINOST histogen
EGHINOSU ginhouse
EGHINPSS sphinges
EGHINRSU ushering
EGHINRSW Gershwin
EGHINRTW New Right
EGHINSTT The Sting
EGHINTTW whetting
EGHIOPSU pishogue
EGHIORRV river-hog
EGHIOSTV eightvos
EGHIOTUW outweigh
weigh out
weigh-out
EGHIQRTU requight
EGHIRRUY hierurgy
EGHIRSTT streight
EGHJNNOW Gwen John
EGHLLNUW well-hung
EGHLLOPU plughole
EGHLMNOO long home
EGHLMNOP phlegmon
EGHLNRUY hungerly
EGHLOOOR horologe
EGHLOORY rheology
EGHLOOSU log-house
EGHLOOTY ethology
theology
EGHLOPRU plougher
EGHLORST short leg
EGHMNOOY homogeny
EGHMNORS gemshorn
EGHMOPUY hypogeum
EGHMOSUU mug-house
EGHNOOPR prong-hoe
EGHNOOPT photogen
EGHNOOST The Goons
EGHNOOTY theogony
EGHNORUV hung over
overhung
EGHNOSUU gunhouse
EGHNOTUU Huguenot
EGHNOTUY the young
EGHNRSTT strength
EGHOOOSW hoosegow
EGHORRTW regrowth
EGIIKKLN kinglike
EGIIKLLO killogie
EGIIKLNW winglike
EGIIKNSZ king-size
EGIILMMN immingle
EGIILMTW lime-twig
EGIILNNU linguine
EGIILNOR niger oil
religion
EGIILNRS Riesling
EGIILNRT girtline
tinglier
tireling
EGIILNRV reviling
EGIILNSW wiseling
EGIILRTZ glitzier
EGIIMNNU ingenium
EGIIMNOR in gremio
EGIIMNPR impinger
EGIIMNRS Isengrim
semi-ring
EGIIMNRT ring-time
EGIIMNST mingiest
EGIIMNSV misgiven
EGIIMNTT emitting
EGIIMOPT impetigo
EGIIMORR grimoire
EGIIMRST tigerism
EGIINNPR repining
EGIINNPW Winnipeg
EGIINNRT integrin
EGIINNST steining
EGIINOPR peignoir
EGIINORS seignior
EGIINOTV give into
EGIINPRX expiring
EGIINQTU quieting
EGIINRRT retiring
EGIINRST strigine
EGIINRSU signieur
EGIINRSW ringwise
EGIINRTU intrigue
EGIINRTV riveting
EGIINRTX genitrix
EGIINRVV reviving
EGIIOPRS pirogies
EGIIPTUV give it up
EGIIRTTU te igitur
EGIITUXY exiguity
EGIJMMNY jemmying
EGIJNQRU jerquing
EGIKKNRT trekking
EGIKLNOS songlike
EGIKLNPS skelping
EGIKLNSS kingless
EGIKLNSY Kingsley
EGIKNORV overking
EGIKNPPS skepping
EGILLMNS smelling
EGILLNNO long-line
EGILLNOR Negrillo
EGILLNOV livelong
EGILLNOW Lilongwe
EGILLNPS spelling
EGILLNSW swelling
EGILLNTU glutelin
EGILLOOR gloriole
EGILLOTT little go
EGILMMRY glimmery
EGILMNOT long-time
EGILMNPU implunge
EGILMNST smelting
EGILMOOR oligomer
EGILMOUU eulogium
EGILNNNO long-nine
EGILNNST nestling
EGILNOPP popeling
EGILNORW lowering
EGILNOSU ligneous
EGILNOSW longwise
EGILNOTW toweling
EGILNOVW long view
EGILNPRS sperling
springle
EGILNPRY replying
EGILNRRY erringly
EGILNRSS ringless
EGILNRST lingster
ringlets
sterling✧
EGILNRSW newsgirl
EGILNSSS signless
EGILNSSU ugliness
EGILNSSW wingless
EGILNSTT settling
EGILNSUW Lewis gun
EGILNVXY vexingly
EGILOOSU isologue
EGILOOTY etiology
EGILORTY gyrolite
EGILOSTU eulogist
EGILRRZZ grizzler
EGILRTTY glittery
EGIMMNST stemming
EGIMMRST grimmest
EGIMNNNO mignonne
EGIMNOOR Geronimo
EGIMNOSU geminous
EGIMNPRU impugner
EGIMNPTT tempting
EGIMNPTY emptying
EGIMNRSS grimness
EGIMNRSU gum resin

EGIMNRUY	eryngium
EGIMORST	ergotism
EGIMOSTW	twigsome
EGINNNUY	ennuying
EGINNORS	nose-ring
EGINNORT	nitrogen
	ringtone
EGINNORV	vigneron
EGINNPPY	penny-pig
EGINNRRU	unerring
EGINNRTV	ventring
EGINOORV	ingroove
EGINOOSS	gooiness
EGINOPRU	Perugino
EGINOPRY	pigeonry
EGINOPUV	give upon
EGINOPXY	epoxying
EGINORRY	iron-grey
EGINORSS	goriness
EGINORST	Negritos
EGINORSV	sign over
EGINORSY	seignory
EGINORTU	outreign
	routeing
EGINORTW	towering
EGINORUV	vin rouge
EGINORVW	overwing
	wingover
EGINOTTU	tongue it
EGINPPPR	prepping
EGINPPST	stepping
EGINPRRS	springer
EGINPRSS	pressing
EGINPRTU	reputing
EGINPRYY	perigyny
EGINQRUY	querying
EGINQSTU	questing
EGINRRST	restring
	ringster
	stringer
EGINRRTU	ring true
EGINRRTY	retrying
EGINRSST	trigness
EGINRSSY	syringes
EGINRSTW	strewing
EGINRSVW	swerving
EGINRTTU	tiger nut
	uttering
EGINSTTT	stetting
EGIOPRTU	portigue
EGIORSST	strigose
EGIORSSU	griseous
EGIORSTV	vertigos
EGIORSTY	oystrige
EGIORSUV	grievous
EGIOSUUX	exiguous
EGIRRSTY	registry
EGIRSTTT	grittest
EGISSYYZ	syzygies
EGISTTTU	guttiest
EGJLNORU	jongleur
EGJLNOTU	jelutong
EGJNORSS	Sjögren's
EGLLMORW	gromwell
EGLLNNWY	Nell Gwyn
EGLLNSSU	lungless
EGLLOOPY	pelology
EGLMMSTU	glummest
EGLMNOOS	longsome
EGLMNOOY	menology
EGLMNORT	long-term
EGLMNSSU	glumness
EGLMOPRU	promulge
EGLMORSS	gormless
EGLNNOOR	longeron
	no longer
EGLNNOSS	longness
EGLNNTUY	ungently
EGLNOOOY	oenology
EGLNOOPR	prolonge
EGLNOOPY	penology
EGLNOORV	overlong
EGLNOOSV	love-song
EGLNOPYY	polygeny
EGLNORUU	longueur
EGLNOSSS	songless
EGLNOSYY	lysogeny
EGLNPTUV	vent-plug
EGLNRSSU	rungless
EGLNRTUY	urgently
EGLOOORY	oreology
EGLOOPRU	prologue
EGLOOPTY	logotype
EGLOORSY	serology
EGLOOSXY	sexology
EGLOPRTU	grouplet
EGLORRWY	growlery
EGLORSUU	rugulose
EGLORSUY	rugosely
EGMMNOTT	Mt Egmont
EGMNNOOY	monogeny
	nomogeny
EGMNOOOS	mongoose
EGMNOORY	merogony
EGMNOOSU	mungoose
EGMNRSSU	grumness
EGMNSSSU	smugness
EGNNOOTY	ontogeny
EGNNOSTU	gunstone
EGNNOTTU	ungotten
EGNNOTUV	Vonnegut
EGNNRSUY	Grey nuns
EGNNSSSU	snugness
EGNNSTTU	tungsten
EGNOORRV	governor
EGNOOTUX	ox-tongue
EGNOPPRU	oppugner
EGNORRST	stronger
EGNORSST	songster
EGNORSTT	tongster
EGNORSTU	sturgeon
EGNORSTY	sentry-go
EGNOSTUY	youngest
EGNPRSUU	supergun
EGNSSTUU	Tunguses
EGOOPRRU	prorogue
EGOORRVW	overgrow
EGOORSTT	grottoes
EGOPRRSS	progress
EGOPRRSU	groupers
EGOPSSUY	gypseous
EGOSSTUU	outguess
EHHIIPRS	heirship
EHHIISTV	thievish
EHHILMNT	helminth
EHHINOPT	thiophen
EHHINSTY	the shiny
EHHIOPRS	heroship
EHHIORTT	hitherto
EHHIOTTW	white-hot
EHHIRSSW	shrewish
EHHJMNOU	John Hume
EHHKLSTU	the hulks
EHHLOOST	shothole
EHHLTUXY	T H Huxley
EHHMNOTT	The Month
EHHMOOSW	show home
EHHMPRUY	Humphrey
EHHNOOPT	on the hop
EHHNOORS	shoehorn
EHHNOOSS	Shoshone
EHHNORTT	the North
EHHNOTTT	to the nth
EHHNSSUY	hen-hussy
EHHOOPSS	shoe shop
EHHOOPST	theosoph
EHHOOSTU	hothouse
EHHORSTU	shouther
EHHOSTTU	the South
EHHOSTUV	Shevuoth
EHIIKLNS	Helsinki
EHIIKLPT	pithlike
EHIIKLPW	whiplike
EHIIKLRS	Irish elk
EHIIKMNO	Khomeini
EHIIKNSV	Kishinev
EHIILMST	Eli Smith
EHIILMTT	the limit
EHIILNOX	ex nihilo
EHIILNRS	linisher
EHIILOSS	heliosis
EHIILRSV	liverish
EHIIMNNT	Nethinim
EHIIMPST	mephitis
EHIINNOS	inhesion
EHIINNQU	heniquin
EHIINNRS	inshrine
EHIINRRT	hirrient
EHIINSVX	vixenish
EHIIPRST	ship-tire
EHIIPRSV	viperish
EHIIRRTX	heritrix
EHIIRSSU	huissier

EHIIRSTT thirties
EHIISTTX sixtieth
EHIJLSWY Jewishly
EHIJNOTT the joint
EHIJOSTV Jehovist
EHIKKNST The Kinks
EHIKLLNO kiln-hole
EHIKLNOS sink hole
sinkhole
EHIKLOSY yokelish
EHIKLRSU rushlike
EHIKMNST methinks
EHIKNRRS shrinker
EHIKNRSU shuriken
EHIKOPRS pokerish
EHIKRSSW whiskers
EHIKRSWY whiskery
EHILLLMO molehill
EHILLMOP Philomel
EHILLMOT mote-hill
EHILLMOY homelily
EHILLNSW Shinwell
EHILLOPY lyophile
EHILLPTY phyllite
EHILLRRT thriller✧
EHILLRTY litherly
EHILLSSW swellish
EHILLSWW well-wish
EHILMMST Mel Smith
EHILMOOR heirloom
EHILMOST helotism
EHILMPSY symphile
EHILMQUU umquhile
EHILNOOP oenophil
EHILNOPT thole pin
EHILNOSS holiness✧
EHILNOST Holstein
the Lions
EHILNOSV novelish
EHILNOTX xenolith
EHILNPSY sylphine
EHILNSWY newishly
EHILOOPZ zoophile
EHILOOST Holostei
EHILOPRS pilhorse
polisher
EHILOPRT heliport
EHILOPSS slip-shoe
EHILOPST helistop
isopleth
EHILORTY rhyolite
EHILPSSS shipless
EHILPSST pithless
EHILPSSW whipless
EHILPSTU sulphite
EHILRSST thrissel
EHILRSTT thristle
EHILRSTW whistler✧
EHILRSTY slithery
EHILRTTW whittler
EHILRTTY triethyl

EHIMMNUY hymenium
EHIMMRSY shimmery
EHIMNOPR morphine
EHIMNORT thermion
EHIMNOSU hemionus
EHIMNOTT monteith
EHIMNOTU home unit
EHIMNPRS phrenism
EHIMNPST shipment
EHIMNRRU murrhine
EHIMNRRY myrrhine
EHIMOOSS homeosis
EHIMOOST smoothie
EHIMOPRS sopherim
EHIMOPST Mephisto
EHIMORST isotherm
EHIMORTU mouthier
EHIMOSTT mothiest
EHIMPPSS psephism
EHIMPRRS shrimper
EHIMPRSU murphies
EHIMPSTU set him up
EHIMPSUU euphuism✧
EHIMPTTU umptieth
EHIMRSST smithers
EHIMRSTY smithery
EHIMSSTU mushiest
EHIMSSTY methysis
EHINNOPR phoner-in
EHINNOPU Huon pine
EHINNOTU the Union
EHINNOTW non-white
EHINNRST thinners
EHINNSST thinness
EHINNSSU sunshine
EHINNSTT thinnest
EHINOOPT in the poo
EHINOPPR hornpipe
EHINOPRT triphone
EHINOPRY Hyperion
EHINOPST siphonet
EHINORRT thornier
EHINORSS herisson
EHINORTT no-hitter
EHINOSTU outshine
EHINPRSU punisher
EHINPSSX sphinxes
EHINSSST thisness
EHINSTTW the Twins
EHIOOPSW whoopsie
EHIOORTT toothier
EHIOOSST stooshie
EHIOPPPS popeship
EHIOPPST poetship
EHIOPPSU eohippus
EHIOPSTT Peshitto
EHIOPTTW whitepot
EHIORSTT theorist
EHIORSTW worthies
EHIORTWZ howitzer
EHIOSSTU house-sit

EHIOSTVY yeshivot
EHIOTTUW white out
white-out
EHIPQSUY physique
EHIPRSST hipsters
thripses
EHIPRSTW whipster
EHIPRSWY whispery
EHIPSTUU euphuist
EHIRRSTT thirster
EHIRSTTW whitster
EHIRTTTW whittret
EHISSTUW thuswise
EHISTTTW the twist
EHJKMNOP John Kemp
EHJKNORR John Kerr
EHJLNOOW John Lowe
EHJMNOSS Mess-John
EHJNNNOV John Venn
EHKLNOOT knothole
EHKLOSTY lekythos
EHKMMNOR Mon-Khmer
EHKMOORW homework
EHKMOOSS smoke-hos
EHKMORSU humoresk
EHKMORSW mesh-work
EHKNNOTW the known
EHKNNRSU shrunken
EHKORSTW the works
EHLLLOWY Holywell
EHLLMOPY phyllome
EHLLNSTU nutshell
EHLLOOOP loophole
EHLLOPST top-shell
EHLLOSTU shell out
EHLMNOTU mole hunt
EHLMNOUY unhomely
EHLMOORW wormhole
EHLMORTY motherly
EHLMOSUU Mulhouse
EHLNNOPU unholpen
EHLNOOSW snow-hole
EHLNOPSU sulphone
EHLNORSS hornless
EHLNOSTY honestly
on the sly
EHLNSSSU lushness
shunless
EHLOOPRT porthole
potholer
EHLOOPST post hole
the pools
EHLOOPTY holotype
EHLOPPRT thropple
EHLOPRTY prothyle
EHLORSTT throstle
EHLORSTY hostelry
EHLORTTT throttle
EHLOSSTW thowless
EHLOSSTY thyloses
EHLRSSTU hurtless

	ruthless
EHMMOOPR	romp home
EHMMRRTU	thrummer
EHMNNPSU	sunn hemp
EHMNOOST	smoothen
EHMNOOTW	home town
EHMNOOTY	hot money
	theonomy
EHMNOPSU	homespun
EHMNPRYY	hypernym
EHMOOOTZ	zoothome
EHMOOPRT	home port
EHMOOPTY	homotype
EHMOORST	smoother
EHMOORSZ	shmoozer
EHMOPRST	the Proms
EHMOPRSU	Morpheus
EHMORRSU	Rushmore
EHMORSTY	smothery
EHMORTUV	vermouth
EHMOSTTU	Thutmose
EHMOTUWY	Weymouth
EHMOTUZZ	mezuzoth
EHMRTUYY	eurythmy✧
EHMSSTUY	thymuses
EHNNOOPX	Xenophon
EHNNOPRT	penn'orth
EHNNORRT	northern✧
EHNNORTU	on the run
	unthrone
EHNNOSTU	unhonest
EHNOOPPS	open shop
EHNOOPTY	honeypot
EHNOORRU	honourer
EHNOORST	hen roost
EHNOORSW	whoreson
EHNOORTW	honewort
EHNOORVZ	Voronezh
EHNOOSSW	snowshoe
EHNOPRST	Strephon
EHNOPSSS	poshness
EHNORSTT	thornset
EHNORSTU	southern✧
EHNOSTUU	nuthouse
EHNRSSTU	huntress
EHNSSSTU	thusness
EHOOPRTY	orthoepy
EHOOPSTU	housetop
	pothouse
EHOOPTYZ	zoophyte
EHOORRUZ	zero hour
EHOORSST	orthoses
EHOORSTV	overshot
EHOORSTW	two-horse
EHOORSUU	Our House
EHOORSUW	row house
EHOORSVW	show over
EHOORTWW	woe worth
EHOOSTUU	outhouse
EHOPPRSY	prophesy
EHOPRSST	hot press
	hot-press
EHOPRSTY	trophesy
EHOPRSUV	pushover
EHOPRTUY	eutrophy
EHOPSTUY	Typhoeus
EHORRSTY	herstory
EHORSTTT	the trots
EHORSTUY	try house
EHRRSTTU	thruster
EIIILMNN	in limine
EIIILMSS	similise
EIIILMSZ	similize
EIIILPPR	liripipe
EIIIMMNS	minimise
EIIIMMNZ	minimize
EIIIRRTV	tirrivie
EIIJKNRT	jirkinet
EIIKKLLM	milklike
EIIKKLLS	silk-like
EIIKKLNS	skin-like
EIIKKNOP	Kip Keino
EIIKLLLN	kill line
EIIKLLMN	limekiln
EIIKLLMT	kill time
	kill-time
EIIKLLNO	lionlike
EIIKLMRS	misliker
EIIKLNOR	ironlike
EIIKLOPS	spike oil
EIIKLOST	Sikeliot
EIIKNNSS	inkiness
EIIKNNSW	wineskin
EIIKNRST	strike in
EIIKRSST	riskiest
EIIKSSVV	skivvies
EIILLLVY	livelily
EIILLMMR	millirem
EIILLMNR	milliner
EIILLMNS	slimline
EIILLMNU	illumine
EIILLNOT	lino tile
EIILLNPR	lip liner
EIILLNST	niellist
EIILLNSU	suilline
EIILLNTT	in little
EIILLNTV	vitellin
EIILLOOV	olive oil
EIILLPSS	ellipsis
EIILLSUV	illusive
EIILMMOT	immotile
EIILMNNS	Leninism
EIILMNNT	liniment
EIILMNOT	limonite
EIILMNSS	liminess
EIILMNTT	melittin
EIILMOPT	impolite
EIILMPST	slime pit
EIILMSTT	mistitle
EIILMSTY	myelitis
EIILNNOT	lenition
EIILNNST	enlist in
	Leninist
	listen in
EIILNOPT	pile into
	pile it on
EIILNORS	lioniser
EIILNORV	Rivelino
EIILNORZ	lionizer
EIILNOSS	oiliness
EIILNOTT	toilinet
EIILNQTU	quintile
EIILNSSW	wiliness
EIILNSTW	wine list
EIILNSTY	senility
EIILNSVY	sylviine
EIILNTTU	intitule
EIILNTUV	vituline
EIILNTVY	Vinylite
EIILOPPS	soil pipe
EIILOPST	pisolite
EIILORTT	troilite
EIILOTVV	volitive
EIILPRSU	plurisie
EIILPRTT	let it rip
EIILPSST	pitiless
EIILPSTY	pyelitis
EIILPSUZ	spuilzie
EIILPTUV	live it up
EIILRSTU	utiliser
EIILRTUZ	utilizer
EIIMMNNO	Menomini
EIIMMNNT	imminent
	miniment
EIIMMNSU	immunise
EIIMMNTU	imminute
EIIMMNUZ	immunize
EIIMMPRU	imperium
EIIMMSSS	seismism
EIIMMSST	Semitism
EIIMNNOR	iron-mine
EIIMNOPT	pimiento
EIIMNORT	Minorite
EIIMNOSS	emission
EIIMNOST	Timonise
EIIMNOSV	visnomie
EIIMNOTV	monitive
EIIMNOTZ	Timonize
EIIMNRSS	miriness
EIIMNRST	minister
EIIMNRTT	intermit
EIIMNRTX	intermix
EIIMNSTT	mintiest
EIIMNTTU	time unit
EIIMOPRX	mirepoix
EIIMOPST	optimise
EIIMOPTZ	optimize
EIIMOSSV	omissive
EIIMOSUX	eximious
EIIMOTVV	vomitive
EIIMPRSS	misprise
EIIMPRSZ	misprize
EIIMQSTU	quietism

EIIMRSTT metritis
EIIMRSTW miswrite
EIIMRSTZ trim size
EIIMSSSV missives
EIIMSSTT mistiest
Semitist
EIINNNPS ninepins
EIINNOSU unionise
EIINNOSV envision
EIINNOSW in no wise
EIINNOUZ unionize
EIINNPSS spinnies
EIINNRRV River Inn
EIINNRST sinner it
EIINNRTV invertin
EIINNSST tininess
EIINNSTT tinniest
EIINNSTV invest in
EIINOPRS ripienos
EIINOPST sinopite
EIINOPTT petition
EIINORRT interior
EIINORSV revision
visioner
EIINORTW wire into
EIINPRRS inspirer
EIINPRST pristine
EIINPSTZ pint-size
EIINPTUV punitive
EIINQRRU inquirer
EIINQTUY equinity
inequity
EIINRSST sinister
EIINRSSW wiriness
EIINRSTT sitter-in
EIINRSTU neuritis
EIINSSSZ siziness
EIIOPRST Poitiers
EIIOPSTV positive
EIIORSTT rise to it
EIIOSSTT osteitis
EIIOTTTV totitive
EIIPPRRT trippier
EIIPPRTV pit viper
EIIPRRTW tripwire
EIIPRSTT rispetti
EIIPRSTY pyritise
EIIPRTYZ pyritize
EIIPSSTT stipites
tipsiest
EIIQRSTU Quirites
EIIQSTTU quietist
EIIRSTTU uteritis
EIIRSTTZ ritziest
EIJJNTUY jejunity
EIJKNOSS jokiness
EIJKORRS skijorer
EIJLNSTU St Julien
EIJLOOSU Joe Louis
EIJLOPTT pilot jet
EIJMNPSS jimpness
EIJNORTU jointure
EIJNOSTT jettison
EIJRSTUY Jesuitry
EIKKLLOO look like
EIKKLNNY Kilkenny
EIKLLMSS milkless
EIKLLNTW well-knit
EIKLLNUY unlikely
EIKLLOOW wool-like
EIKLLORV overkill
EIKLLSSS skilless
EIKLMNOS moleskin
EIKLMORW wormlike
EIKLMOSS mosslike
EIKLNOOR oerlikon✧
EIKLNOSU leukosin
EIKLNOSW snowlike
EIKLNPRS sprinkle
EIKLNRST linkster
strinkle
EIKLNRTW twinkler
EIKLNSSS skinless
EIKLNSTT knittles
EIKLOORT rootlike
EIKLOPRW pilework
EIKLOPSS ski slope
EIKLSSTT skittles
EIKMNOPT Potemkin
EIKMNORY minor key
EIKMNOST tokenism
EIKMNOSU mousekin
EIKMOPSS misspoke
EIKMORSV skim over
EIKMORTW time-work
EIKMSSTU muskiest
EIKNNOST inkstone
EIKNNPSS pinkness
EIKNOPRS rose-pink
EIKNOPSZ skip zone
EIKNORST on strike
strike-on
EIKNPRST Pinkster
EIKNPRTU turnpike
EIKNRRTU returnik
EIKNSSTT skin test
EIKOPPRW pipework
EIKOPRSV overskip
skip over
EIKORRWW wirework
EIKPRRSU spruiker
EIKPRSTU strike up
EIKPSTYY tipsy key
EILLLNTY lent lily
EILLLOVY lovelily
EILLLPUV pulville
EILLLSSW will-less
EILLMNOS Sémillon
EILLMNOU linoleum
EILLMOPS plimsole
EILLMORV mill over
EILLMOTT Little Mo
EILLMPSS misspell
psellism
EILLMPTU multiple
EILLMUVX vexillum
EILLNOOP loop-line
EILLNOPY epyllion
EILLNOST stellion
EILLNOTU luteolin
EILLNPQU quill-pen
EILLNPST ill-spent
EILLNPUU lupuline
EILLNPUW well up in
EILLNSTY silently
tinselly
EILLNSVY snivelly
EILLNUVY unlively
EILLOOSW woollies
EILLOPPR Pipe Roll
EILLOPRW lower lip
EILLOPTX exit poll
EILLOPTY politely
EILLORST trilloes
trollies
EILLORTT tortelli
EILLOSSS soilless
EILLOSST toilless
EILLOTUY I tell you
EILLRSTT testrill
EILLRSVY silverly
EILLSSST listless
EILLSTUV vitellus
EILMMNOU Moulmein
EILMMSST slimmest
EILMNOOR iron-mole
Leo Minor
EILMNOSU emulsion
EILMNOSV novelism
EILMNOTU moulinet
EILMNOTY mylonite
EILMNPSS limpness
EILMNPSU splenium
EILMNPTU tumpline
EILMNRST minstrel
EILMNSSS slimness
EILMNSTU muslinet
EILMNTUY minutely
untimely
EILMOOPS liposome
EILMOOST toilsome
EILMOPRR implorer
EILMOPRS pelorism
sperm oil
EILMOPRW pile-worm
EILMOPST milepost
polemist
EILMOSTT time slot
EILMOSUV volumise
EILMOUVZ volumize
EILMPPRU impurple
EILMPRUY impurely
EILMPSST misspelt

Words marked ✧ can also be spelled with one or more capital letters

EILMRSSY remissly
EILMRSUU Merulius
EILMTTUU lutetium
EILMTTUY multeity
EILMTUUZ zulu time
EILNNOST insolent
EILNNOSW snowline
EILNNOTV Ventolin®
vinolent
EILNNPTY in plenty
EILNNSTW twin-lens
EILNNTTY intently
EILNOOPP epiploon
EILNOOPS polonise
EILNOOPW pine-wool
EILNOOPZ polonize
EILNOOST oilstone
EILNOOTT Ottoline
EILNOPPS plenipos
EILNOPPY polypine
EILNOPRT Interpol
topliner
EILNOPRU neuropil
EILNOPTU unpolite
EILNOPTY Linotype®
EILNORRT ritornel
EILNORTT trotline
EILNOSSW lewisson
EILNOSTV novelist
EILNOSUV evulsion
EILNOSWW low wines
EILNOTUV involute
EILNOTXY Xylonite®
xylonite
EILNOTYZ zylonite
EILNPRST splinter
EILNPSSU splenius
EILNPSTU listen up
EILNPSTW split-new
EILNPSUY supinely
EILNQUUY uniquely
EILNRSTU insulter
lustrine
result in
EILNRSTY tinselry
EILNRSUU Ursuline
EILNRTUV virulent
EILNRTWY winterly
EILNSSTT tintless
EILNSSTW westlins
EILNSTTU lutenist
EILNSUWY unwisely
EILOOPTZ zopilote
EILOORST oestriol
EILOORTV overtoil
EILOORWW wire wool
EILOOSTY otiosely
EILOPPTY polypite
EILOPRSS oil press
EILOPRSU perilous
EILOPRSV overslip
slip-over
EILOPRTW pilewort
EILOPSTT pistolet
EILOPSUV Pluviôse
pluviose
EILORRTU ulterior
EILORRTV liver rot
EILORSTU Ortelius
EILORTTY toiletry
EILOSTTT stiletto
EILOSTUV love-suit
solutive
EILPPPRU upper lip
EILPPPRY preppily
EILPPRRT trippler
EILPPRST stippler
EILPPRSU periplus
supplier
EILPPRSY slippery
EILPPRTU pulpiter
EILPPSSU supplies
EILPRSTT splitter
EILPRSTY priestly
spritely
EILPRSUU purlieus
EILPRSUY pleurisy
EILPRTTY prettily
EILQRRSU squirrel
EILQRSUY squirely
EILQSTUU lustique
EILRRTWY writerly
EILRSSST stirless
EILRSSTY sisterly
EILRSTTU surtitle
EILRSTTW wristlet
EILRSTTZ strelitz
EIMMMNOT immoment
EIMMMORZ momzerim
EIMMNNOT moniment
EIMMNNTU muniment
EIMMNORS misnomer
EIMMOPRU emporium
EIMMOPST metopism
EIMMOSTT totemism
EIMMPRST primmest
EIMMPRSU premiums
EIMMPSSU pessimum
EIMMRRST Strimmer®
EIMMRSUY Erysimum
EIMMSSTU mumsiest
EIMNNOOT noontime
EIMNNOPT imponent
EIMNNOPY pin money
EIMNNOTT ointment
EIMNNOUY euonymin
EIMNOOPS empoison
EIMNOORS moonrise
EIMNOORT remotion
EIMNOORV omnivore
EIMNOPRS Peronism
EIMNOPRT orpiment
EIMNOPSS mopiness
EIMNOPST nepotism
pimentos
EIMNOPTT impotent
EIMNORSS Minoress
EIMNORSU inermous
monsieur✧
EIMNORTW time-worn
EIMNORTY enormity
EIMNPRSS primness
EIMNPSST misspent
EIMNRSST trimness
EIMNRSTU muster in
terminus✧
EIMNRSTY entryism
misentry
EIMOORST motorise
roomiest
EIMOORTZ motorize
EIMOOTTT Ottomite
EIMOPPRR improper
EIMOPRRS primrose
promiser
EIMOPRRT importer
reimport
EIMOPRRV improver
EIMOPRSS semi-pros
EIMOPRST imposter
EIMOPRUU europium
EIMOPSTT post time
EIMOPSTY peyotism
EIMOPTTU up to time
EIMOQSTU misquote
EIMORRST mortiser
EIMORRTT remittor
EIMORRWW wireworm
EIMORSTU misroute
moisture
EIMORSTV mist over
EIMORSTY isometry
EIMORSVW overswim
EIMORTTW two-timer
EIMOSSST mossiest
EIMOSSTU mousiest
EIMOSSTZ mestizos
EIMOSTTT totemist
EIMOSTTU titmouse
EIMPSSTY emptysis
EIMPSSUY Puseyism
EIMPSTTU tumpiest
EIMQSTUY mystique
EIMRRSSU surmiser
EIMRSSST mistress✧
EIMSSTTU mustiest
EIMSTUZZ muzziest
EINNOORZ zero in on
EINNOOTX neotoxin
EINNOPRS in person
EINNORST inter nos
EINNORSV environs
EINNORTT tontiner

EINNORTU neutrino
EINNORTV inventor
noverint
EINNORWW winnower
EINNOSSS nosiness
EINNOSSU non-issue
EINNOSTT tinstone
EINNPRSY spinnery
EINNPSSU puniness
EINNPSSY spinneys
EINNPSXY sixpenny
EINNRRTU in return
EINNRSTU runniest
sturnine
EINNRTTU nutrient
EINOOPRS poisoner
EINOOPSS opsonise
EINOOPSZ opsonize
EINOOPTT on tiptoe
EINOORSZ ozoniser
EINOORZZ ozonizer
EINOOSSZ ooziness
EINOOTXX exotoxin
EINOPPRV vine-prop
EINOPQRU in querpo
EINOPRRS prisoner
EINOPRSS poriness
pression
ropiness
EINOPRST Peronist
pointers
EINOPRSU pruinose
EINOPRSV overspin
EINOPRSY Epyornis
EINOPRTU eruption
EINOPRTW port wine
EINOPSTT nepotist
point set
set point
step into
step on it
stone pit
EINOPSWX swine-pox
EINOQSTU question
EINOQTTU quotient
EINORRST introrse
EINORRTV invertor
EINORSSS rosiness
EINORSSU neurosis
resinous
EINORSTT tenorist
EINORSTU rinse out
EINORSTV investor
EINORSTY tyrosine
EINORSUV souvenir
EINORTTU ritenuto
EINORTTW witter on
EINOSSSS sessions
EINOSSST stenosis
EINOSSSU Senoussi
EINOSTTU Eton suit

EINOSTUU tenuious
EINOSTVY venosity
EINPPRRT pre-print
EINPPSTY snippety
EINPRRST sprinter
EINPRRTU prurient
EINPRRTY printery
EINPRSST spinster
EINPRSTU unpriest
EINPRSTW wrest pin
EINPRTTU inputter
EINPSTTX spintext
spin-text
EINQRSTU squinter
EINQRTTU quit-rent
EINQTTTU quintett
EINRSSST instress
EINRSSXY syrinxes
EINRSTTY entryist
EINRTUUV unvirtue
EINSSSSU Senussis
EINSSTUX unsexist
EINSSTWY swine-sty
EINSSTXY syntexis
EIOOPPRS porpoise
EIOOPPST opposite
EIOOPRST portoise
EIOORRSS sororise
EIOORRSZ sororize
EIOORSTT rootiest
tortoise
EIOPPRTW pipewort
EIOPPTTY tippy-toe
EIOPRRSS prioress✧
EIOPRRSU superior
EIOPRRTV overtrip
EIOPRSTT rispetto
EIOPRSTV sportive
EIOPRSUV pervious
previous
viperous
EIOPRTTT triptote
EIOPRTTY petitory
EIOPRTUZ outprize
EIOPSTTY peyotist
EIORRRST errorist
EIORRRTU roturier
EIORRRTV Retrovir®
EIORRSST resistor
sorriest
EIORRSTV servitor
EIORRSVY revisory
EIORSSTT Rossetti
EIORSSTY serosity
EIORSTTU tutorise
EIORSTUV virtuose
vitreous
EIORTTUW write out
EIORTTUZ tutorize
EIPPRRST stripper
EIPPRRTY trippery

EIPQRSTU quipster
EIPRRRSU spurrier
EIPRRSSU surprise
EIPRRSTZ spritzer
EIPRSVVY spivvery
EIQRRSTU squirter
EIQRSSSU squiress
EIQRUYZZ quizzery
EIRRSTTU trustier
EIRSSSTU suitress
EIRSSTTU rustiest
EIRTTTUY tityre-tu
EIRTTTWY twittery
EIRTTUWZ wurtzite
EISSUUVV Vesuvius
EJLOOOSV Joe Slovo
EJLOPSTU pulsojet
EJMNOOST Tom Jones
EJMOORTT motor-jet
EJMOPPRU jump rope
EJMOPRUV overjump
EJNOOORT Joe Orton
EJNORSUY journeys
EJNSSSTU justness
EKKLRUUX Ku Kluxer
EKKMORSY kromesky
EKLMNOSS Smolensk
EKLNOOOR looker-on
onlooker
EKLNOOTV love-knot
EKLNOSST knotless
EKLOOORV look over
overlook
EKLOOPSW slowpoke
EKLORSST Klosters
EKLORSSW workless
EKLSSSTU tuskless
EKMMORSU murksome
EKMNRSTU Turkmens
EKMOOPRR morepork
EKMOORSW worksome
EKMOOSTU smoke out
EKMORSSU musk rose
EKMRSTUY musketry
EKNNOPSU unspoken
EKNOOPRW openwork
EKNOORST rose knot
strooken
EKNORTTW tent-work
EKOOPRRV provoker
EKOOPRRW ropework
EKOOPRSY spookery
EKOORRVW overwork
work over
work-over
EKOORTWW kowtower
EKOPPRST Prospekt
EKOPRSTU upstroke
EKORRUVY kurveyor
ELLLMOWY mellowly
ELLLNSUY sullenly

ELLLNWYY Llywelyn
ELLMNOSY solemnly
ELLMNOTY moltenly
ELLMNPUY lumpenly
ELLMOORS morellos
ELLMOORW well room
ELLMORUV mull over
ELLMOSTU smell out
ELLMPPUW pump-well
ELLNNSSU nullness
ELLNOORV lovelorn
ELLNOPRU prunello
ELLNORRT rent roll
ELLNORWW well-worn
ELLNOSVY slovenly
ELLNOUVY unlovely
ELLOOPRT Trollope
ELLOORRV roll over
roll-over
ELLOPRST pollster
ELLOPRTU polluter
ELLOPRUV pull over
pullover
ELLOPSST plotless
ELLOPSTU spell out
ELLORRST stroller
ELLORSTY trolleys
ELLOSSSU soulless
ELLOSTUW outswell
ELLPPSUY supplely
ELLSSSTU lustless
ELMMNOTU lomentum
ELMMNOTY momently
ELMMRSTU strummel
ELMMRSUY summerly
ELMNNOSU unsolemn
ELMNOOOP monopole
ELMNOOSS moonless
ELMNOOSZ zoom lens
ELMNOPSU pulmones
ELMNUUZZ unmuzzle
ELMOOORV loom over
ELMOOPPS pompelos
ELMOOPSY polysome
ELMOORST tremolos
ELMOORSY morosely
ELMOOSSY lysosome
ELMOPRTY metopryl
ELMOPRYY polymery
ELMOPSYY polysemy
ELMOSYYZ lysozyme
ELMPRSSU rumpless
ELMRRTUU multurer
ELNNOOSU unloosen
ELNNOPTU nonuplet
ELNOOPSU loosen up
ELNOOSST solonets
ELNOOSTZ solonetz
ELNOOSUV nuevo sol
ELNOPPTU punt-pole
ELNOPTTY potently
ELNORSTU turnsole
ELNORSVY slovenry
ELNORTTY rottenly
ELNOSSSW slowness
snowless
ELNOSSTW townless
wontless
ELNPPSUU unsupple
ELNPRTUU purulent
ELOOPRSU superloo
ELOOPRUW owerloup
ELOOPSSS sesspool
ELOORSST rootless
ELOORSTU torulose
ELOORSUV oversoul
ELOOSSST sootless
ELOOSTUU Toulouse
ELOPPRRY properly
ELOPRRTY porterly
ELOPRSTY prostyle
ELOPRSUV overplus
ELOPRSYY pyrolyse
ELOPRXYY pyroxyle
ELOPRYYZ pyrolyze
ELOPSSST spotless
stopless
ELORSTUY souterly
urostyle
ELORTTTU troutlet
ELOSSTUU setulous
ELPRSSSU spurless
ELPRSTTU splutter
ELPRSTUU rustle up
ELRSSSTU rustless
ELRSTTUY sluttery
ELSSSTUY styluses
EMMMNOTU momentum
EMMNNOTU monument
EMMNOOOS monosome
EMMNOOSY monosemy
EMMNORSU summoner
EMMNORYY meronymy
EMMNOTTU tomentum
EMMNOTYY metonymy
EMMOOORS roomsome
EMMOORRS Mrs Moore
EMMOORSS mess-room
EMMOPTTY pommetty
EMMPRSUU supremum
EMMRRRUU murmurer
remurmur
EMMRRSTU strummer
EMMRSTYY symmetry
EMNNNOOU noumenon
EMNNOOOT monotone
EMNOOPTY Monotype®
monotype
Moon type
EMNOORST mesotron
monteros
Montrose
EMNOORSU enormous
nemorous
EMNOORSW newsroom
EMNOORTY noometry
EMNOOSUV venomous
EMNOOTTY tenotomy
EMNOOTUV outvenom
EMNOPSYY spy-money
EMNORSTT sortment
EMNORSUU numerous
EMNORTUX Montreux
EMNOSUUY euonymus
EMNRSSTU sternums
EMNRSTTU stem turn
EMOOPRRT promoter
EMOOPRSY pyrosome
EMOOPRSZ zoosperm
EMOOPSSU espumoso
EMOORRST rest room
EMOORSSS moss rose
EMOORTYZ zoometry
EMOPPRRT prompter
EMOPRSSU spermous
supremos
EMORRRUU rumourer
EMORSSTU strumose
EMOSSTTW westmost
EMOSSTVZ zemstvos
EMPRRTUY trumpery
EMPRSTTU strumpet
EMPRSTUU muster up
ENNNORTY non-entry
ENNNOSTY Tennyson
ENNOOORT tenoroon
ENNOOOTZ entozoon
ENNOOPPT opponent
ENNOOPTW open town
ENNOORST norteños
ENNOORTV non-voter
ENNOOSTT nonettos
ENNOPRSU unperson
ENNOPRUV unproven
ENNOPTWY twopenny
ENNORSST sternson
ENNORSTU one's turn
ENNORTTU unrotten
ENNOSSTU sunstone
ENNPPTUY tuppenny
ENNPRRUU runner-up
ENOOORTW one or two
ENOOOSSZ zoonoses
ENOOPPRU pore upon
ENOOPPST postpone
ENOOPRSS poorness
ENOOPSTT potstone
top stone
ENOORRVW overworn
ENOORSTT rot-stone
ENOPPRRU unproper
ENOPPRUY prey upon
ENOPRTTU putter-on

ENOPRTUW uptowner
ENOPSSSY synopses
ENOPSTTU outspent
ENORRTUU tournure
ENORRTUV overturn
turn over
turnover
ENORSSSU sourness
ENORSTTU stentour
ENORSTTY snottery
ENORSTUV ventrous
vent'rous
ENOSSSUU sensuous
ENPRSSSY spryness
ENPRTTUY unpretty
ENRRRTUU nurturer
EOOOPRRT proto-ore
EOOOPRSS soporose
EOOOPRSZ zoospore
EOOOPRTZ zootrope
EOOORRST roseroot
EOOPPRRS proposer
Prospero
EOOPPSST postpose
EOOPPTTY topotype
EOOPRRTU Europort
outroper
uprooter
EOOPRSTU porteous
EOOPRSTV overpost
post over
stop over
stopover
EOOPRTUW outpower
EOORRRSW sorrower
EOORSSTU oestrous
EOORTTUV outvoter
EOOSTTTW set to two
EOPPRRTY property
EOPPRSSU purposes
supposer
EOPPSSSU supposes
EOPRRSST portress
EOPRRSTU posturer
EOPRRUVY purveyor
EOPRSSTT rest stop
EOPRSTTZ St-Tropez
EOPSTUUY set you up
EOQQTUUU tu quoque
EORRRTTU torturer
EORRSSST stressor
trossers
EORRSSTU trousers
EORRSSTW trowsers
EORRSTTT trotters
EORRSUVY surveyor
EORRTUUV trouveur
EORSSTTU tutoress
EORSSTWY Oswestry
EORSTTUW outwrest
EORSTUUV vertuous
EPPPRTUY puppetry
EPPRSSSU suppress
EPPRSSUY superspy
EPPRTTUY pretty up
EPRSTTUY sputtery
EQRRTUUU truqueur
ERRSTTTU strutter

F

FFFFPPUU puff-puff
FFFGHIOT fight off
FFFMOOTU footmuff
FFGGIILN gliffing
FFGHIINW whiffing
FFGHIORS frogfish
FFGHIORT right off
FFGHIRSU gruffish
FFGHORSU shrug off
FFGIILNP piffling
FFGIINNS sniffing
FFGIINPS spiffing
FFGILNOS sling off
FFGILNRU ruffling
FFGINNSU snuffing
FFGINORW wring off
FFGINSTU stuffing
FFHIIOTT hit it off
FFHIISST stiffish
FFHIISTY fiftyish
FFHILORW whirl off
FFHILOSU foul-fish
FFHILOSW wolffish
FFHILOSY offishly
FFHIOPSS spoffish
FFHIRSSU surffish
FFHLORTY froth-fly
FFHMOOTU mouth off
FFHOOOST offshoot
shoot off
FFHOORTW throw off
FFHOSTTU hot stuff
FFIILMOR filiform
FFIILNSY sniffily
FFIILNTY flintify
FFIINOOS soffioni
FFIIRSTX first fix
FFIKLORT fork-lift
FFIKLRSU friskful
FFILLOPP flip-flop
FFILLTUY fitfully
FFILOPST split-off
FFILRTUU fruitful
FFILRTUY fruit fly
FFILSTUY stuffily
FFIMORSU fusiform
FFINOPRT offprint
FFIOPRST strip off
FFIOSTTW twist-off
FFIOSTWX swift fox
FFKLORSU forkfuls
FFLMNOOU moufflon
FFLNORTY fly front
FFLNOTUU fountful
FFLORRUU furfurol
FFNOSTUU snuff out
FFNSTUUY unstuffy
FFOOORTU four-foot
FFOORRUU frou-frou
FFOORSST off-sorts
FFOSTUUY stuff you
FGGGILNO flogging
FGGGINOR frogging
FGGHIINT fighting
FGGHILOT fog light
FGGHINTU gunfight
FGGIILNN flinging
FGGILNOR frogling
FGGINOOR forgoing
FGHHISTY fight shy
FGHIIKNS kingfish
FGHIILNT in-flight
FGHIINST shifting
FGHILLTU lightful
FGHILMTU mightful
FGHILNSU flushing✧
lungfish
FGHILNTY night-fly
FGHILRTU rightful
FGHINOST of nights
FGHIOPST giftshop
FGHIOTTU outfight
FGHISSTU fish-guts
FGHLORUU furlough
FGHNOTUU unfought
FGIIKNRS frisking
FGIILLNR frilling
FGIILLNS fillings
FGIILLRT lift-girl
FGIILNOO folioing
FGIILNPP flipping
FGIILNRT flirting
trifling
FGIILNST stifling
FGIILNTT flitting
FGIILOSU Luis Figo
FGIINNUY unifying
FGIINRTT fritting
FGIINRTU fruiting
FGIINSST siftings
FGIINSTT fittings
FGIIRSTU figurist
FGILLNOW wolfling
FGILMNOR long-firm
FGILNNTU gunflint
FGILNOOR flooring
FGILNOOT footling
FGILNOOZ foozling
FGILNOSS flossing
FGILNOST softling
FGILNOTU fling out
outfling
FGILNPRU purfling

FGILNTYY fly-tying
FGINNORW frowning
FGINOOPR proofing
FGINORRT ring fort
FGINORST frosting
FGIOPRST frog-spit
FGJNNORY Fjorgynn
FGKLNOOS folk song
FGLLMOOU gloomful
FGLNORUW wrongful
FGLOOOST footslog
FGMNOORS song form
FGNOORTU unforgot
FHHIKOOS fish-hook
FHHLOSTU hot flush
FHHOORST shofroth
FHIIKLMS milkfish
FHIIKNSS fishskin
FHIILLTY filthily
FHIILMNT thin-film
FHIILRST flirtish
FHIILSTY shiftily
FHIINPSU finish up
FHIISSTY hissy fit
FHIKLLLO hillfolk
FHIKLSWY fly whisk
FHIKMNOS monkfish
FHIKNORT forthink
FHILLOOT foothill
FHILLORT hill-fort
FHILMPSU lumpfish
FHILMRTU mirthful
FHILOPST shoplift
FHILORSU flourish
FHILORTY frothily
FHIMNOOS moonfish
FHIMPRSU frumpish
FHINRTTU unthrift
FHIOOPTT Photofit®
photofit
FHIORSTY fortyish
FHLLLOTU lothfull
FHLLOSTU slothful
FHLMOTUU mouthful
FHLOOSTU soothful
FHLOOTTU toothful
FHLORTTU trothful
FHLORTUW worthful
FHLORTUY fourthly
FHLOSTUU flush out
outflush
FHLOTUUY youthful
FHLRTTUU truthful
FHOOORST forsooth
FHOORRST for short
FHOPRTTU put forth
FIIILNOP Filipino
FIIINNTY infinity
FIIJNORT joint-fir
FIIKLRSY friskily
FIILLMSY flimsily
FIILLMTU multifil
FIILLNTY flintily
FIILMNOR film noir
FIILMNRY infirmly
FIILMOPR piliform
FIILMPSY simplify
FIILTTUY futility
FIIMOPRS pisiform
FIIMOSTY moistify
FIINNOSU infusion
FIINORTU fruition
FIINTUXY unfixity
FIIQUYZZ quizzify
FIKKLNOS kinsfolk
FIKLLLSU skillful
FIKLLOSX flox silk
FIKLNOSW wolfskin
FIKNORSW forswink
FILLLTTU full tilt
full-tilt
FILLLUWY wilfully
FILLNORS no frills
no-frills
FILLNSUY sinfully
sulfinyl
FILLNUUW unwilful
FILLOPPY floppily
FILLOPSU spoilful
FILMNOPR porn film
FILMOPRS slipform
FILMORRY lyriform
FILMOSSU mofussil
FILMPPTU lift pump
FILNNOOY onion fly
FILNOSUX fluxions
FILORSTY frostily
FILRSTTU tristful
FILSTTUY stultify
FIMMNOOR omniform
FIMMORRU muriform
FIMOPRRY pyriform
FIMORTUY fumitory
FIMOSTUY fumosity
FIMRSTUU futurism✧
FINOORST soft iron
FINOPRTZ zip-front
FINORRTU run for it
FINORSUY infusory
FIOORSSU furiosos
FIORTTUY fortuity
FIPRSSUY Prussify
FIRSTTUU futurist
FIRTTUUY futurity
FJLLOUYY joyfully
FJLNOUUY unjoyful
FKKLOORW workfolk
FKKOORTW koftwork
FKLMOOOT folkmoot
FKLNOTUU flunk out
FKLNRTUU trunkful
FKLOORWW workflow
FKMOORRW formwork
FKNORSUW forswunk
FKOOORTW footwork
FLLMNOOU full moon
FLLNOOOW follow on
follow-on
FLLNOSUY sulfonyl
FLLOOPUW follow up
follow-up
upfollow
FLLOPSTU full stop
FLLOSSTU full toss
FLMNORUU mournful
FLMOOORW moorfowl
FLMOORSU roomfuls
FLMOOSSW moss-flow
FLMORSTU stormful
FLNOOPSU spoonful
FLNOOSTU snootful
FLOOOPTT poltfoot
FLOOPTTY toplofty
FLOORSUY soy flour
FLOOSSTW soft-slow
FLOPRSTU sportful
FLORTTUU troutful
FLRSTTUU trustful
FMNOOOOR moonroof
FMOOPPTU footpump
FMOORSSU Formosus
FMRSSTUU frustums
FNNOOORT frontoon
FNOOORTW footworn
FNOOPRSU sunproof
FNOORRSW forsworn
FNOORRTW front row
FNOORTUW outfrown
FNOSSTUY not fussy
FOOOPSTT footpost
FOOPSSTT soft spot

G

GGGGIILN giggling
GGGGILNO goggling
GGGGILNU glugging
GGGHIILN higgling
GGGHIINT thigging
GGGHIINW whigging
GGGHINOS shogging
GGGIILNN niggling
GGGIINPR prigging
GGGIINRT trigging
GGGIINSW swigging
GGGIINTW twigging
GGGIJLNO joggling
GGGIJLNU juggling
GGGILNOS slogging
GGGILNPU plugging
GGGILOOR go-go girl
GGGILORY groggily
GGGINNSU snugging
GGGINORT trogging

GGHHIINS	high sign
GGHHIISW	Whiggish
GGHHISTU	thuggish
GGHIILNT	lighting
GGHIIMSW	Whiggism
GGHIINRT	righting
GGHIINST	sighting
GGHIIPRS	priggish
GGHILSSU	sluggish
GGHIMSTU	thuggism
GGHINOST	ghosting
GGHINSTU	gunsight
GGHKNNOO	Hong Kong
GGHMOSTU	ghost gum
GGHNORUY	go hungry
GGHOOPRS	grog-shop
GGHOTUUY	tough guy
GGIIKLNN	kingling
GGIILLNR	grilling
GGIILMNN	mingling
GGIILMNY	ginglymi
GGIILNNP	pingling
GGIILNNS	gin sling
	singling
GGIILNNT	tingling
GGIIMPRS	priggism
GGIINNNR	grinning
GGIINNOR	groining
GGIINNOW	wongiing
GGIINNRW	wringing
GGIINNSS	sing-sing
GGIINNST	stinging
GGIINNSW	swinging
GGIINNUV	ungiving
GGIINPPR	gripping
GGIIRRSS	grisgris
	gris-gris
GGIKKNNO	King Kong
GGILLNUW	gull-wing
GGILMMNO	glomming
GGILMNOO	glooming
GGILNNOU	lounging
GGILNNPU	plunging
GGILNORW	growling
GGILNORY	glorying
GGILNTTU	glutting
GGILQSUY	squiggly
GGINNOOS	goings-on
	ongoings
GGINNOPP	Ping-Pong®
GGINNOSS	singsong
GGINNOTU	tonguing
GGINNRTU	grunting
GGINOOTU	outgoing
GGINOPRS	proggins
GGINOPRU	grouping
GGINORTU	grouting
GGLLOPUW	glow plug
GGLLPUUY	plug-ugly
GGLNOOST	long-togs
GGNNOUUY	young gun
GGOOOORR	groo-groo
GHHIIKRS	high-risk
GHHIILST	lightish
GHHIIPSW	Whigship
GHHIIRST	rightish
GHHIISTT	tightish
GHHIJMPU	high jump
GHHILOSU	ghoulish
GHHIMOST	highmost
GHHINNOO	high noon✧
GHHIOPST	high spot
GHHIORSU	roughish
GHHIOSTU	toughish
GHHOORTU	thorough✧
GHHOSTTU	thoughts
GHIIJNOS	jingoish
GHIIKNNT	thinking
GHIIKNPS	kingship
GHIIKNSW	whisking
GHIILLNS	shilling
GHIILMST	mislight
GHIILMTY	mightily
GHIILNOT	lithoing
GHIILNRW	whirling
GHIILNST	tinglish
GHIILNSY	Yinglish
GHIILNTW	whitling
GHIILTTW	twilight
GHIIMMNW	whimming
GHIIMRST	rightism
GHIINNNT	thinning
GHIINOST	hoisting
GHIINPPS	shipping
GHIINPPW	whipping
GHIINRRS	shirring
GHIINRRW	whirring
GHIINRST	shirting
GHIINRSV	shriving
GHIINRTV	thriving
GHIINRTW	writhing
GHIINSSW	swishing
GHIINTTW	twi-night
GHIINWZZ	whizzing
GHIIORSU	Ishiguro
GHIIORSV	vigorish
GHIIOSTV	Visigoth
GHIIRSTT	rightist
GHIISTTT	sit tight
GHIJKNNO	King John
GHIKLNTY	knightly
GHIKLSTY	skylight
GHIKMRUU	Gurmukhi
GHIKNNTU	unknight
GHILLOTW	lowlight
	owl-light
GHILLSTY	slightly
GHILMPSU	glumpish
GHILNOPS	longship
GHILNOPU	plough in
GHILNOPY	hopingly
GHILNOSS	sloshing
GHILNOSU	housling
GHILNOTW	night owl
GHILNRUY	hungrily
GHILNSTU	hustling
	sunlight
GHILOPRS	shop girl
GHILORSW	showgirl
GHILOSSU	sloughis
GHILOTTU	light out
GHILPRTY	triglyph
GHIMNOPR	morphing
GHIMNOPU	gumphion
GHIMNPTU	thumping
GHIMNSTU	gunsmith
GHINNNOT	non-thing
GHINNNSU	shunning
GHINNORT	northing
GHINNSTU	shunting
GHINOOPW	whooping
GHINOOST	shooting
	soothing
GHINOPPS	shopping
GHINOPPW	whopping
GHINOPSS	shop sign
GHINORTW	ingrowth
	throwing
	Worthing
GHINOSSU	housings
GHINOSTT	shotting
GHINOSTU	shouting
	southing
GHINOSTW	wing shot
	wing-shot
GHINOSUY	youngish
GHINOTTU	night out
	outnight
GHINPPUW	whupping
GHINRRSU	rush ring
GHINRRUY	hurrying
GHINSSTU	hustings
GHINSTTU	shutting
GHIORTTU	outright
	right out
GHIOSTTU	outsight
GHIPRSUU	guruship
GHJNRUUY	hung jury
GHLMOOOY	homology
GHLNNOOR	longhorn
GHLNOOPU	plough on
GHLNOORU	hourlong
GHLNOOST	long shot
GHLNORSU	slughorn
GHLNOTYY	yongthly
GHLOOORY	horology
GHLORTUU	turlough
GHMNNOTU	Thom Gunn
GHMPSSUY	sphygmus
GHNOPYYY	hypogyny
GHNOSTUU	unsought
GHOOOSTW	go to show
GHOORTUU	rough out

Words marked ✧ can also be spelled with one or more capital letters

rough-out
GHOORTUY yoghourt
GHOOTTUU tough out
GHOPRTUW upgrowth
GHORRTUW throw rug
GIIILMNT limiting
GIIILNNU linguini
GIIILOTV vitiligo
GIIILSUV Vigilius
GIIINNOT ignition
GIIINNTV inviting
GIIINRSS grissini
GIIINRTV virgin it
GIIINSTV visiting
GIIJMNOS jingoism
GIIJNNOT jointing
GIIJNNOW jowing-in
GIIJNOST jingoist
GIIKKLNP kingklip
GIIKKNNS skinking
GIIKLLNS skilling
GIIKLNNO on liking
GIIKLNNS sling ink
GIIKLNNT tinkling
GIIKLNRS skirling
GIIKMMNS skimming
GIIKMNPS skimping
GIIKMNRS smirking
GIIKNNNS skinning
GIIKNNST stinking
GIIKNNTT knitting
GIIKNPPS skipping
GIIKNRST skirting
striking
GIILLLMR mill girl
GIILLNPS spilling
GIILLNQU quilling
GIILLNRT trilling
GIILLNST stilling
GIILLNSW swilling
GIILLNTT littling
GIILLOPW polliwig
GIILLPSW pig swill
pigswill
GIILLTUY guiltily
GIILLTYZ glitzily
GIILMMNS slimming
GIILMNPS simpling
GIILMNPY implying
GIILMNZZ mizzling
GIILMPSU pugilism
GIILNNSY lyings-in
GIILNNTW twinling
GIILNNUV unliving
GIILNPPR rippling
GIILNPPS slipping
GIILNPRS slip ring
spirling
GIILNPRT tripling
GIILNQSU quisling
GIILNQTU quilting
GIILNRST Stirling
GIILNRVY virginly
GIILNSST listings
GIILNSTT slitting
stilting
GIILNSTU linguist
GIILNSTY stingily
GIILNSZZ sizzling
GIILORRT riot girl
GIILPSTU pugilist
GIILRTTY grittily
GIIMMNPR primming
GIIMMNRT trimming
GIIMMNSW swimming
GIIMNNOY ignominy
GIIMNOPS imposing
GIIMNOTT omitting
GIIMNOTV vomiting
GIIMNSSW swingism
GIIMORRS rigorism
GIINNNOT intoning
GIINNNPS spinning
GIINNNSW winnings
GIINNNTW twinning
GIINNOPT pointing
GIINNOQU quoining
GIINNORS nigrosin
GIINNORT ignitron
GIINNPPS snipping
GIINNPRT printing
GIINNRSS rinsings
GIINNRTU untiring
GIINNSTT stinting
GIINOPST positing
GIINOPTV pivoting
GIINORSS grissino
GIINORST roisting
GIINPPRT tripping
GIINPRSS rispings
GIINPRST striping
GIINPRSU uprising
GIINPRXY pixy-ring
GIINPSTT spitting
GIINPTTU tituping
GIINQTTU quitting
GIINQUZZ quizzing
GIINRRST stirring
GIINRSTV striving
GIINRSTW writings
GIINSSSW swissing
GIINSSTU suitings
GIINSTTW twisting
GIINTTTW twitting
GIIORRST rigorist
GIIPRSTZ spritzig
GIJKLNOY jokingly
GIJKNNRU junk-ring
GIJLLNOY jollying
GIJLNOST jostling
GIJLNSTU junglist
GIKKLNSU skulking
GIKLNNOP plonking
GIKLNNRU knurling
GIKLNNUY unkingly
GIKLNOPR porkling
GIKLORRW workgirl
GIKNNOPR pronking
GIKNNOST Kingston
stonking
GIKNNOTT knotting
GIKNNRTU trunking
GIKNOPST kingpost
GIKNORRW ringwork
GIKNORST stroking
GIKNORSW workings
GILLMOOY gloomily
GILLNOPS long slip
GILLNORT trolling
GILLNOST longlist
GILLNOSY losingly
GILLNOVY lovingly
GILLNPRU ring pull
GILLNPUY pulingly
GILLNSUY sullying
GILLOOPW polliwog
GILLOPSS lip gloss
GILLOPWY pollywig
GILLORVY gillyvor
GILLOSSY glossily
GILMMNSU slumming
GILMMTUY multigym
GILMNOPY mopingly
GILMNORT mortling
GILMNOSS moslings
GILMNOTT mottling
GILMNOTU moulting
GILMNOVY movingly
GILMNSUY musingly
GILMOOSY misology
GILMPRUY grumpily
GILNNOOR long iron
GILNNORU iron lung
GILNNOSU Longinus
GILNNOTW townling
GILNNOUV unloving
GILNNRSU nursling
GILNOOSY Sinology
GILNOOVY vinology
GILNOOWY wooingly
GILNOPPP plopping
GILNOPPS slopping
GILNOPRW prowling
GILNOPSY posingly
spongily
GILNOPTT plotting
GILNORVY rovingly
GILNOSTT slotting
GILNOSTU long suit
GILNOTUY outlying
GILNPRSU spurling
GILNPRYY pryingly
GILNPSSU plus sign

	plussing
GILNPUZZ	puzzling
GILNRRSU	slurring
GILNRSTU	lustring
	rustling
GILNRTTU	turtling
GILNRTYY	tryingly
GILNTUUY	unguilty
GILOOORS	rosoglio
GILOOOST	oologist
GILOORSU	glorious
GILOORVY	groovily
	virology
GILOOSSS	isogloss
GILOOSTY	sitology
GILORRRT	riot grrl
GILOSTUY	gulosity
GIMMMNUY	mummying
GIMMNRUY	gin rummy
GIMMNSTU	stumming
GIMMOSSU	gummosis
GIMNNORS	mornings
GIMNNORU	mourning
GIMNNOTU	mounting
GIMNNOUV	unmoving
GIMNOOOU	oogonium
GIMNOOPS	spooming
GIMNOORS	moorings
GIMNOPTU	gumption
GIMNORRW	ringworm
GIMNORST	storming
GIMNOSYY	misogyny
GIMNPRTU	trumping
GIMPSSYY	gypsyism
GINNNSTU	stunning
GINNOOSW	swooning
GINNOOTU	go in unto
GINNOPRS	spring on
GINNOPSS	sponsing
GINNOPSY	pyonings
GINNOPTU	gunpoint
GINNORST	snorting
GINNPRSU	spurning
GINNRSTU	turnings
	unstring
GINOOPPS	opposing
GINOOPST	stooping
GINOORTW	grow into
GINOPPPR	propping
GINOPPST	stopping
	toppings
GINOPPSW	swopping
GINOPRST	sporting
GINOPSST	signpost
GINOPSTT	spotting
GINOPSTU	spouting
GINORRWY	worrying
GINORSTT	Storting
GINORSTW	strowing
GINORSTY	roysting
	storying
GINORTTT	tottring
	trotting
GINORTTU	trouting
	tutoring
GINORTUW	wring out
GINOSTTW	swotting
GINOSTUW	outswing
GINPPRSU	upspring
GINPRRSU	spurring
GINPRSTU	string up
GINPRSUU	pursuing
	usurping
GINPTTUY	puttying
GINRSSTU	trussing
GINRSTTU	trusting
GIOOORSV	vigoroso
GIOOPRRS	porrigos
GIOORRSU	rigorous
GIOORSTU	goitrous
GIOORSUV	vigorous
GIOPRRSU	prurigos
GIOPRSST	Strigops
GIOPRSSY	gossipry
GIOPRSTU	groupist
GIORSTUY	rugosity
GJLMNOPU	long jump
GKLOOOTY	tokology
GLLNOSUW	low-slung
GLLOOPTY	polyglot✧
GLLOOPWY	pollywog
GLLOOXYY	xylology
GLMNOOOT	monoglot
GLMNOOOY	monology
	nomology
GLMNOOSS	long moss
GLMNORUW	lungworm
GLMNRTUU	ngultrum
GLMOOOPY	pomology
GLMOORWW	glow-worm
GLMOOYYZ	zymology
GLNNOPSU	long-spun
GLNOOOSY	nosology
GLNOOOTY	ontology
GLNOOPST	long stop
	long-stop
GLNOOPYY	polygony
GLNOPRSU	longspur
GLNOPYYY	polygyny
GLNORSTY	strongly
	strongyl
GLNORTUW	lungwort
GLNOSSUV	Volsungs
GLNOTTUY	gluttony
GLOOOPSY	posology
GLOOOPTY	optology
	topology
GLOOORUY	ourology
GLOOPSSY	gossypol
GLOOPTYY	typology
GLOORSUU	orgulous
GMMNOTUY	tommy gun
GMNNOOOY	monogony
GMNNOOYY	monogyny
GNNPRSUU	unsprung
GNNRSTUU	unstrung
GNOOOTTW	go to town
GNOORSUW	wrongous
GNPPRSUU	upsprung
GNPRSTUU	strung up
GOOPPPRU	pop group
GOORSSTU	gross out
	gross-out
	outgross
GOORTTUW	goutwort

H

HHHHSSUU	hush-hush
HHIIKKOO	Khoikhoi
HHIILOPT	thiophil
HHIINNST	thinnish
HHIIOORT	Hirohito
HHIIPSST	phthisis
HHIISTTW	with this
HHILPSSY	sylphish
HHIMNPSY	nymphish
HHIMPSSU	sumphish
HHINOOSS	Shoshoni
HHINOOSW	nohowish
HHIORSST	shortish
HHJNNOTU	John Hunt
HHJNORTU	John Hurt
HHJNOSSU	John Huss
HHKKSSUU	khuskhus
HHKOOOST	hook shot
HHMRSTUY	rhythmus
HHOOOOPP	pooh-pooh
HHOOPPRS	phosphor✧
HHOORSTT	hot-short
HHORRSUU	rush hour
	rush-hour
HIIILMNS	nihilism✧
HIIILNST	nihilist
HIIILNTY	nihility
HIIIMRSS	Irishism
HIIINRST	rhinitis
HIIJNOPT	hip joint
HIIKMNST	misthink
HIIKMRSS	skirmish
HIIKOPRS	piroshki
HIIKOPRZ	pirozhki
HIIKQRSU	quirkish
HIIKSSTT	skittish
HIILLNSW	Whin Sill
HIILMMSS	slimmish
HIILMOST	homilist
HIILMPSU	silphium✧
HIILMPSY	impishly
HIILMSWY	whimsily
HIILMTUY	humility
HIILNOPS	Sinophil
HIILPSST	thlipsis
HIILPSSY	syphilis

HIILRSTY shirtily
HIILSSTT stiltish
HIILSSTW wish list
HIIMNSTT tinsmith
HIIMOPSS phimosis
HIIMOPST Ophitism
HIIMORTU Hiri Motu
HIINORST histrion
HIINPRST shirt pin
HIINPSTW twinship
HIIORSST histrios
HIIPPQSU quippish
HIIPPRSU Hippuris
HIISSSSY sissyish
HIJMPPSU jump ship
HIKKNOST kink-host
HIKMNSUU minshuku
HIKNOOST in shtook
HIKNOTTU outthink
think out
HIKOOPRT trip-hook
HIKOOPSS spookish
HIKOORSU Kuroshio
HIKOPSSY kyphosis
HILLLOSU Solihull
HILLMOOT moot-hill
HILLMSUY mulishly
HILLNOUY unholily
HILLOOPT lopolith
HILLOOST lithosol
HILLOSWY owlishly
silly-how
HILMNOOT monolith
HILMOOPT philomot
HILMOPSY mopishly
HILMPPSU plumpish
HILMPRTU philtrum
HILMPSYY symphily
HILNOPSU unpolish
HILNOSTY tonishly
HILOOPYZ zoophily
HILOORST short-oil
HILOOTTY toothily
HILOPPSU polish up
HILOPPSY popishly
HILORSUU urushiol
HILORTUX Ulothrix
HILORTWY holy writ✧
worthily
HILOSSTY thylosis
HILOSTYY toyishly
HILPPRSU purplish
HILPPSUY uppishly
HILSSTTU sluttish
HIMMOPRU phormium✧
HIMNOPRX phorminx
HIMNOPSY phisnomy
HIMNORRS horn-rims
HIMOOPRS isomorph
HIMOOSTT smooth it
HIMOPRSW shipworm
HIMOPRWW whipworm
HIMORSTU humorist
HIMOTTVZ mitzvoth
HINNOSTW thin-sown
HINNPSTU thin-spun
HINNPSUY shinny up
HINNSSUY sunshiny
HINOORST hornitos
HINOORSU Honorius
HINOPSSY hypnosis
HINOPSTW township
HINORTXY thyroxin
HINOSTTU Tithonus
HIOOPRTT poortith
HIOORSST orthosis
HIOOSSTT shootist
HIOPPSST post ship
HIOPRSUZ rhizopus
HIOPSSTY phytosis
HIOQSUWZ quiz show
HIORRSSY sorryish
HIOSSTTU stoutish
HIPPPSUY puppyish
HIPSSSUY Sisyphus
HIPSUYZZ zizyphus
HJKNNOOX John Knox
HJKNOPSU junk shop
HJMOPSTU jump shot
HJMOPSUW showjump
HJNOOOPR poor-John
HJNOOOTT Otto John
HJNOORSS John Ross
HKKLOOYZ kolkhozy
HKKOOPYY hoky-poky
HKMNORRU krumhorn
HKMOOORW hookworm
HKNOORRW hornwork
HKOOPRSW workshop
HLLLOOWY hollowly
HLLMNOOU monohull
HLLNOOUU Honolulu
HLLOPPRY prophyll
HLLPPSUU push-pull
HLMOOSTY smoothly
HLMOPTUY Plymouth
HLNOOPPY polyphon
HLNOOPRY Rohypnol®
HLNOOSUW Hounslow
HLOOPPSS slop-shop
HLOOPRRY lorry-hop
HLOOSSTU soul-shot
HLPRSUUY sulphury
HMMNOOYY homonymy
HMMOORSU mushroom
HMMRSTUU humstrum
HMNOOOST moonshot
HMNOOOTY homotony
HMNOORRW hornworm
HMNOOSTU unsmooth
HMNOPSYY symphony
HMNOPYYY hyponymy
HMOOOPRZ zoomorph
HMOOORSW showroom
HMOOPTYY homotypy
HMOORSUU humorous
HMOPSSTU puss-moth
HMOPTTUU thump out
HNOOOOPR oophoron
HNOOPPRS porn shop
HNOOPRST post horn
HNOOPRSW shopworn
HNOOPRTU horn pout
horn-pout
HNOORRTW hornwort
HNOORSTT short ton
HNOORSTU southron✧
HNORRSTU run short
HNORTUWY unworthy
HNPSSTUU Pushtuns
HOOOOTTT hoot-toot
HOOOSTTU outshoot
shoot-out
HOOPPSTY photopsy
HOOPRRST porthors
HOORTTUW outworth
throw out
throw-out
HOOTTTUU hout-tout
HOPPRRYY porphyry✧
HOPRRSTU Portrush
HOPRRSUY pyrrhous
HPRSTTUU upthrust

I

IIIIPPRR piri-piri
IIIKLNPS spilikin
IIIKMNSS mini-skis
IIILLMNP minipill
IIILLMNU illinium
IIILLNOS Illinois
illision
IIILMRSV virilism
IIILMUVX lixivium
IIILNOPP Pilipino
IIILRTVY virility
IIIMMMNS minimism
IIIMMNST intimism
minimist
IIIMMPRS imprimis
IIIMNSTT intimist
IIIMNTTY intimity
IIIMOPRS Prosimii
IIINORRS irrision
IIINPRST inspirit
IIINQTUY iniquity✧
IIINSSTU sinuitis
IIIOSTTU ouistiti
IIJJSTUU jiu-jitsu
IIJKNNSY Nijinsky
IIJLNOOT joint-oil
IIJNNSTU ninjitsu
IIJRSSUU sui juris

IIKKLMMS	skim milk
IIKKLMNR	kirn-milk
IIKKORSS	Sikorski
IIKLLNOS	skillion
IIKLLNSY	slinkily
IIKLMPSY	skimpily
IIKLMRSY	smirkily
IIKLNPPS	pink slip
	pink-slip
IIKLQRUY	quirkily
IIKMNNOO	monokini
IIKNNSTU	sink unit
IIKNOPST	Tok Pisin
IIKNOSTT	stotinki
IILLLPTU	Lilliput
IILLLPUV	pulvilli
IILLMNOS	millions
IILLMRTU	trillium
IILLMUUV	illuvium
IILLNOOR	orillion
IILLNORT	trillion
IILLNOST	stillion
IILLNOSU	illusion
IILLOPQU	piquillo
IILLOPUV	pulvilio
IILMMNOS	Molinism
IILMMPSS	simplism
IILMMSUU	simulium
IILMNORT	mirliton
IILMNOST	Molinist
IILMNOSU	Limousin
IILMNSTU	luminist
IILMORST	troilism
IILMOTTY	motility
IILMPSST	simplist
IILMRSSY	missilry
IILNNOOT	nolition
IILNOORS	rosin oil
IILNOOST	inositol
IILNOOTV	volition
IILNOQRU	in liquor
IILNPPST	split pin
IILNRTWY	wintrily
IILOOPPR	liripoop
IILOPSSS	psilosis
IILOPSST	ptilosis
IILOPSTY	pilosity
IILORSTT	troilist
IILPRSSY	prissily
IILRSSTU	silurist✧
IILSTUUV	uvulitis
IILSTUVV	vulvitis
IIMMMNSU	minimums
IIMMNOST	Timonism
IIMMNTUY	immunity
IIMMOPST	optimism
IIMMOPSU	opiumism
IIMMSTTU	mittimus
IIMNNOOT	monition
IIMNNOSU	unionism✧
IIMNNOTU	munition
IIMNOOSS	omission
IIMNOPRS	imprison
IIMNOPST	mispoint
IIMNORTT	intromit
IIMNORTY	minority
IIMNOSST	simonist
IIMNOSTT	Timonist
IIMNPRST	misprint
IIMNPTUY	impunity
IIMNRSTY	ministry
IIMOPSTT	optimist
IIMORSSU	Missouri
IIMOSSTY	myositis
IIMOTTVY	motivity
IIMPRTUY	impurity
IIMRRTTU	Trimurti
IIMRRTUV	triumvir
IIMSSTUW	swimsuit
IINNOPPT	pinpoint
IINNOPTU	punition
IINNOSTU	inustion
	unionist✧
IINNPSST	tinsnips
IINNRTTU	turn it in
IINNSTTU	tinnitus
IINOOPST	position
IINOSTVY	vinosity
IINPRSTW	wrist pin
IINQRSUU	Quirinus
IINRTTUY	triunity
IIOOPPUU	piou-piou
IIOOPSTV	oviposit
IIOOQRSU	Iroquois
IIOOSTTY	otiosity
IIOPPSTV	pop-visit
IIOPRRTY	priority
IIORRRSY	irrisory
IIORRSSU	risorius
IIORSTUV	virtuosi
IIPRSSTU	spiritus
IJLLMNOR	Mjöllnir
IJLLORTU	Trujillo
IJMOPTTU	jump to it!
IJMPSTUU	jump suit
IJNNSTUU	ninjutsu
IKKLNORW	linkwork
IKKLNOSY	kolinsky
IKKNORTW	kirk town
IKKORSSY	sikorsky✧
IKLLMORW	millwork
IKLLOOTV	kilovolt
IKLLOSSY	kyllosis
IKLMORSW	silkworm
IKLMORTW	milkwort
IKLNOOOT	look into
IKLNOOPR	rink polo
IKLNOOSW	skin wool
IKLNOPST	slipknot
IKLNOTTY	knottily
IKLNPSSU	spun silk
IKLOOPSY	spookily
IKLOPSTY	sky pilot
IKNNOPSY	ponyskin
IKNNRSTU	turnskin
IKNOOPRT	pinkroot
IKNOORRW	ironwork
IKNOORTW	work into
IKNOPSTT	stink pot
	stinkpot
IKNOPSTW	townskip
IKNORSTW	tin works
IKNOSTTU	stink out
IKORSSTU	kurtosis
ILLLMOOW	wool mill
ILLLMOPS	plimsoll
ILLLMPPU	pulpmill
ILLLOOPP	lollipop
ILLMOPRW	pillworm
ILLMOPST	post mill
ILLMOSSY	lissomly
ILLMPSUY	psyllium
ILLMPTUY	multiply
	multi-ply
ILLOOPRT	Portillo
ILLOOPRW	poorwill
ILLOORSZ	zorillos
ILLOPPSS	slipslop
ILLOPPSY	sloppily
ILLOPRTW	pillwort
ILLOPRXY	prolixly
ILLOPSTT	pot still
	pot-still
ILLORSTU	trollius
ILLORSUY	illusory
ILLOSTUW	swill out
ILLOTTWY	wittolly
ILLRSTUY	sultrily
ILMNOOPS	polonism
ILMNOOPU	polonium
ILMNOSUU	luminous
ILMOPPSU	populism
ILMOPSTU	Psilotum
ILMORSTY	stormily
ILMOSTUV	volumist
ILMOSTUY	timously
ILMPPTUU	pulpitum
ILMPSTUY	stumpily
ILMSSTUU	stimulus
ILMSTTUY	smuttily
ILNNOTUW	until now
ILNOOPSU	Polonius
ILNOOPSV	volpinos
ILNOOPSY	spoonily
ILNOORTW	toilworn
ILNOOSTT	slot into
ILNOOSTU	solution
ILNOOSTY	snootily
ILNOOTTT	tint tool
ILNOOTUV	volution
ILNOPSSW	snowslip
ILNOPSTU	Plotinus
	unspoilt

ILNORSTY nitrosyl
ILNORTXY nitroxyl
ILNOSSTW stowlins
ILNOSTTY snottily
ILNPSUUV pulvinus
ILOOPPPY poppy-oil
ILOOPPRS propolis
ILOORSTU risoluto
ILOPPSTU populist
ILOPQRUU liquor up
ILOPRSTY sportily
ILOPSTTY spottily
ILOPSUUV pluvious
ILOQRTUU loquitur
ILPPRTUY pulpitry
ILRSTTUY trustily
ILRSTUUX luxurist
IMMOORTU motorium
IMMRSTUY summitry
IMMRTTUU rum-ti-tum
IMNNOOTT monotint
IMNNOSUU numinous
IMNOOPSU opsonium
IMNOORST trominos
IMNOORTY monitory
IMNOORVY omnivory
IMNOPPRU pump iron
IMNOSTUU mutinous
IMNRSTUU untruism
IMOOPRRS promisor
IMOOPRST impostor
IMOOPRTU muir-poot
IMOOPSSU più mosso
IMOOQSTU mosquito
IMOORSTT motorist
IMOORSTU sumotori
timorous
IMOORSTY morosity
IMOORTVY vomitory
IMOOSSTY myosotis
IMOPRRSY primrosy
IMOPRTUU muir-pout
IMORSTTU tutorism
IMORSTTZ St Moritz
IMPPPSUY puppyism
IMRSSTTU mistrust
IMRSSTTY mistryst
INNNNOOU non-union
INNNORTU trunnion
INNNOSTY syntonin
INNOOPSS sponsion
INNOOPSU unpoison
INNOORST notornis
INNOPRSU unprison
INNORTTU turn into
INNOTTWW twin town
INNPRRTU print run
INNPRSTU sun print
INOOOSSZ zoonosis
INOOOTXZ zootoxin
INOOPRST positron
sorption
INOOPSTT spittoon
INOOPTTU outpoint
point out
INOORSTY sonority
INOPRTTU print out
printout
INOPRTUY punitory
INOPRTWY port-winy
INOPSSSY synopsis
INORSSUV sun visor
INORTUVY ivory-nut
INPPRRUU purpurin
INPRSTTU turnspit
INPRTTUU turn it up
IOOPRRSV provisor
IOOPRSSV provisos
IOOPRSSY isospory
IOOPRSTY isotropy
porosity
IOORRSTY sorority
IOORRTTT trottoir
IOORSSTT risottos
IOORSSUV voussoir
IOORSTTU tortious
IOORSTUV virtuoso
IOORSUUX uxorious
IOOSSTTU stotious
IOOSTTUZ zoot suit
IOPRRSUV provirus
IOPRSSUU spurious
IOPRSTTU outstrip
strip out
IOPRSTUU poursuit
IOPRSTUY pyritous
IOPRSUVX poxvirus
IOQRTUXY quixotry
IORRSUVV survivor
IORSSUUU usurious
IORSTTUY touristy
yttrious
IORSTUUV virtuous
IPRRSTUU pruritus

J

JLNSTUUY unjustly
JLOOSUYY joyously
JMNPRTUU jump-turn
JMOORRUY jury room
JNNOORRU nonjuror✧
JNOOSUUY unjoyous

K

KKNOORTW knotwork
KKOOSSUU kouskous
KLLMNSUU numskull
KLMMOOOS Komsomol
KLMMPSUU musk-plum
KLNORSTY klystron
KLOOORWW woolwork
KLOOPRSW slopwork
KMOOORRW workroom
KNOOOOOR Oroonoko
KNOOORTT root-knot
KNOOPRUW work upon
KNOORTWY Yorktown
KNOPSTUU spunk out
KNRRTTUU turn Turk
KOORSTUW outworks

L

LLNOORST stroll on!
LLOOPRTY trollopy
LLOOPRYY roly-poly
LLOOSSTU lost soul
LLOSUUVV volvulus
LMMPSSUU slump sum
LMNOOOOP moon pool
LMNOOOPY Monopoly®
monopoly
LMNOOPYY polyonym
LMOOOORT toolroom
LMOOPRTU Pulmotor®
LMOOPSYY polysomy
LMOORSWW slowworm
LMOOSSSU molossus
LMOPPRTY promptly
LMRSSTUU lustrums
LNOOOPRT poltroon
LNOOOPYZ polyzoon
LNOOPPRY propylon
LNOOSWWY snowy owl
LOOOORSS olorosos
LOOOPSST solo stop
LOOOPSTT tool post
LOOPPSUU populous
LOOPPSUY polypous
LOOPSSST stop-loss
LOPSSTUW plus twos
LORSSTUU lustrous

M

MMNOOOSY monosomy
MMOOPPRU pump room
MMOORTTY tommyrot
MNNOOOTY monotony
MNNOSYYY synonymy
MNOOORST Nostromo
MNOOORTW moonwort
MNOOORXY oxymoron
MNOOPRTU pronotum
MNOOPTYY toponymy
MNOPRSTU no-trumps
MNORSTUU surmount
MNOSTUUU Mount Usu
MOOOOPRT moor-poot
MOOOPRRT promotor
MOOOPRTU moor-pout
MOOORRTW tomorrow
MOORRSUU rumorous
MOORSTUU tumorous
MOORSTUY urostomy

MOPPRSTU rump-post
MOPSTTUU stump out
MORSSTUU strumous
MSSTTUUU tsutsumu

N

NNOOOPST spontoon
NNOORTUU run out on
NNOPRTUU turn upon
NOOOPPRS prosopon
NOOORSSU sonorous
NOOPSTTW post town
NOPRSTUU Portunus
NRSTTUUY untrusty

O

OOOOPPWW Woop Woop
OOOPPRRT prop-root
OOOPRSSU soporous
OOOTTTUU out to out
OOPRSTTU outsport
OORRTUWY worry out
OORSTTUU tortuous
OORSTTYY Toy Story
OPRSSSUU sourpuss

R

RRSSSUUU susurrus

9 letters

A

AAAABCLLV balaclava✧
AAAABCLMN balmacaan
AAAABDDHM Ahmadabad
AAAABDHLL Allahabad
AAAABENNT Nabataean
AAAABIKLL balalaika
AAAABIRRT Barataria
AAAABJLMY jambalaya
AAAACCHMT tacamahac
AAAACCHRR arracacha
AAAACCLLR Caracalla
AAAACDDNY Canada Day
AAAACDIMM macadamia
AAAACDJNR jacaranda
AAAACDKLY alack-a-day
AAAACEHNP panachaea
AAAACGILT agalactia
AAAACIRRU araucaria✧
AAAACLNRT Alcantara®
AAAACLRRZ alcarraza
AAAACMNRT catamaran
AAAADILLM Dalai Lama
AAAAFHTUU Taufa'ahau
AAAAGHJMN Mahajanga
AAAAGLPRT alpargata
AAAAGNPRU Paranagua
AAAAHHJMR maharajah
AAAAHLPTU Atahualpa
AAAAHMNPT panama hat
AAAAHMNRT maranatha
AAAAILLPR paralalia
AAAAINSST Anastasia
AAAAJMRSY Arya Samaj
AAAAKKNRT Karnataka
AAAALLMMY Malayalam
AAAAMNPRY pranayama
AAAAMPRTT paramatta
AAAANRRTT tantarara
tarantara
AAAANRRTV Navaratra
AAAARRSSS sassarara
AAABBDEIS Adis Abeba
AAABBDINR Barbadian
AAABBINRR barbarian
AAABBLMOX Balaam-box
AAABCCEMN Maccabean
AAABCCHHR bacharach
AAABCCHLN bacchanal✧
AAABCCHNR charabanc
char-à-banc
AAABCDEIR Carabidae
AAABCDIIT adiabatic
AAABCDRRU barracuda
AAABCEIRS scarabaei
AAABCEKKM make a back
AAABCEKKT take aback
AAABCELTT cabaletta
AAABCELTU acetabula
AAABCEMRT carbamate
AAABCENRS sarbacane
AAABCHIRT batrachia✧
AAABCHNNR anabranch
AAABCHNRU carnahuba
AAABCIKTT katabatic
AAABCILNT abactinal
AAABCIMOR Maracaibo
AAABCINPR Pan-Arabic
AAABCIQTU aquabatic
AAABCISST catabasis
AAABCISTT ciabattas
AAABCKNNT cantabank
AAABCLMOR carambola
AAABCLMOZ Cambazola
AAABCLMRU ambulacra
AAABCLNOT canal-boat
AAABCNORR carbonara
AAABDDERW draw a bead
AAABDEEHH dahabeeah
AAABDEGRV bavardage
AAABDEHNR bear a hand
AAABDEINT Tabanidae
AAABDELNR Aldebaran
AAABDELPT adaptable
AAABDENNR naan bread
AAABDENRS sarabande
AAABDGIMR Digambara
AAABDHHIY dahabiyah
AAABDHHKS Ashkhabad
AAABDIKMR Kariba Dam
AAABDILLS sabadilla
AAABDILMS Islamabad
AAABDINWY in a bad way
AAABDLNNO à l'abandon
AAABDLORY lay aboard
AAABDOQRU aquaboard
AAABEEMNO amoebaean
AAABEGHLL gallabeah
AAABEGMSS ambassage
AAABEHHSV have a bash
AAABEHLLV have a ball
AAABEHSTV have a stab
AAABEILLV available
AAABEILMN alabamine
AAABEILMT Balaamite
AAABEKLOR koala bear
AAABEKPRR parabrake
AAABEKRWY break away
breakaway
AAABELLNN Annabella
AAABELLPT palatable
AAABELMOT Ametabola
AAABELMSS amassable
AAABELNST Alan Bates
AAABELRRT terra alba
AAABELRST alabaster
AAABELSSY assayable
AAABELWYZ blaze away
AAABGGOTU gaga about
AAABGHILL gallabiah
AAABGHILY galabiyah
AAABGILLY gallabiya
AAABGINRS barasinga
AAABGLORR algarroba
AAABGLWYY Galway Bay
AAABGNNOS go bananas
AAABHISTV Tisha Baav
AAABHLRST balthasar✧
AAABHLRTZ balthazar✧
AAABHNOST Naas Botha
AAABIKSST katabasis
AAABILLTV ablatival
AAABILLVY availably
AAABILMNS Balsamina
AAABILNNO banana oil
AAABILNRR Brian Lara
AAABILQRU Aqua Libra®
AAABINNSU banausian
AAABIPRSS parabasis
AAABJLMNO jambolana

AAABKLNRW Balkan War
AAABLLPTY palatably
AAABLOPRS parabolas
AAABMNRTU marabunta
AAABMNSTY Tasman Bay
AAABNNOPT top banana
AAACCCEET Cactaceae
AAACCHHH cha-cha-cha
AAACCCKNR crack a can
AAACCDELV cavalcade
AAACCDHMN camanachd
AAACCDILR cardiacal
AAACCDRSU cascadura
AAACCEEER Aceraceae
AAACCEEHR Characeae
AAACCEHIM cachaemia
AAACCELLN calcaneal
AAACCELNN calcanean
AAACCELNV calavance
AAACCELPR palace-car
AAACCELRT calcarate
AAACCENRV caravance
AAACCFLOT catafalco
AAACCGNOU Aconcagua
AAACCHKMT tacmahack
AAACCHNNR cranachan
AAACCHTWY catch away
AAACCILLU acalculia
AAACCINSU Caucasian
AAACCIRTT ataractic
AAACCLMNO calamanco
AAACCLMST cataclasm
AAACDDILN dandiacal
AAACDDNRY Canada Dry®
AAACDEGGP Cape dagga
AAACDEHLN Chaldaean
AAACDEINR acaridean
AAACDEIRS Ascaridae
AAACDEKMR make a card
AAACDENRV caravaned
AAACDENWY Dance Away
AAACDHIKT kadaitcha
AAACDHINR Arachnida
AAACDHNRS sandarach
AAACDIINR acaridian
AAACDILNR calandria
AAACDLMRU dulcamara
AAACDLRST cadastral
AAACDNRSS Cassandra
AAACEEFKM make a face
AAACEEHLP Acalephae
AAACEEHRV have a care
AAACEEIOZ Aizoaceae
AAACEELMV Malvaceae
AAACEELRU Lauraceae
AAACEENNO Anonaceae
AAACEENRS Caesarean
AAACEGLNT at a glance
AAACEGNRT Cartagena
AAACEGORT Arctogaea
AAACEHLNP acalephan
AAACEHLNV avalanche
AAACEHRTT Tracheata
AAACEILTV Via Lactea
AAACEIMNR Americana
AAACEIMNT catamenia
AAACEIMPR paramecia
AAACEIMTT atacamite
AAACEINOR oceanaria
AAACEINRS Caesarian
AAACELLPP a cappella
AAACELRWY clear away
AAACEMMNR cameraman
AAACENRRV caravaner
AAACENRSY sea canary
AAACFILNT fanatical
AAACGHLLN Callaghan
AAACGILNT agnatical
AAACGILRS sacralgia
AAACGILSU causalgia
AAACGINRU Nicaragua
AAACGLLSW scallawag
AAACGLNRS Carl Sagan
AAACGNORT Angora cat
AAACHHKKN Chaka Khan
AAACHILNR anarchial
AAACHILNW Walachian
AAACHIMNT matachina
AAACHIMNU naumachia
AAACHIMST chiasmata
AAACHINRS anacharis✧
AAACHIRSZ Zacharias
AAACHJLNP Jan Palach
AAACHKKMT Kamchatka
AAACHLLLT call a halt
AAACHLMNT nachtmaal
AAACHLNRT charlatan
AAACHLPRR chaparral
AAACHLRRT catarrhal
AAACHNPTY panchayat
AAACHNRSU Huascarán
AAACHOPRT cataphora
AAACHOSUY ayahuasco
AAACIIRSS acariasis
AAACILLMR camarilla
AAACILNOR Aaronical
AAACILNPT aplanatic
AAACILNRT lactarian
AAACILNRU lacunaria
AAACILNST Castalian
satanical
AAACILRTU actuarial
AAACINOPR paranoiac
AAACINOTT catatonia
AAACINRSU casuarina
AAACINSTT anastatic
AAACKLLNR Alan Clark
AAACKLSWY slack away
AAACLLLMR alarm call
call alarm
AAACLLPTU culpa lata
AAACLMMPW macaw-palm
AAACLMNPU campanula
AAACLMPST cataplasm
AAACLRSUV avascular
AAACMORST sarcomata
AAACMRSST camass-rat
AAACMRTUX taraxacum
AAACRRWYY carry away
AAADDEHIL Eid al-Adha
AAADDEILN daedalian✧
AAADDHMRY hamadryad
AAADDILNR Dalradian
AAADDINNR Dardanian
AAADDLSSY salad days
AAADEEINR Araneidae
AAADEFFNR fanfarade
AAADEFGMR megafarad
AAADEFIST asafetida
AAADEGKLR Lake Garda
AAADEGLMY amygdalae
AAADEGNPP appanaged
AAADEGNTV advantage
AAADEHRTV Theravada
AAADEINRV Varanidae
AAADELMMR marmalade
AAADELNRX Alexandra
AAADEMNOT adenomata
AAADEMNSU ad nauseam
AAADEOPTZ zapateado
AAADEPRST tapaderas
AAADFFLNU falun dafa✧
AAADFNRSY András Fay
AAADGLRVX gravadlax
AAADGMMNR grandmama
AAADGNNRT D'Artagnan
AAADGNPPR grandpapa
AAADHHPRZ haphazard
AAADHIMYY Ahmadiyya
AAADHIOPR adiaphora
AAADHLMRS dharmsala
AAADHMRSS madrassah
AAADHMRSY hamadryas
AAADHNNTY at any hand
AAADHPRYZ hazard pay
AAADILLNP Palladian
AAADILMNT Dalmatian
AAADILPRS paradisal
AAADINNOS Adansonia
AAADINRYY a rainy day
AAADIOPPR parapodia
AAADKMNRS Samarkand
AAADLLMNS Landsmaal
AAADLMMNN landamman
AAADLMNTY adamantly
AAADLMPRY lampadary
AAADLNNSY analysand
AAADLOPRX paradoxal
AAADLORTY Dolayatra
AAADMNRTY mandatary
AAADNRSSS Sassandra
AAADORSVY Sarvodaya
AAADPRRRT radar trap

AAAEEEGNS	Aegean Sea
AAAEEGRRR	arrearage
AAAEEGRTW	agateware
AAAEEHMNR	maharanee
AAAEEKKLT	take a leak
AAAEEKLMM	make a meal
AAAEEKNRS	area-sneak
AAAEEKSTT	take a seat
AAAEFGMNU	megafauna
AAAEGGLRV	galravage
AAAEGGRTV	aggravate
AAAEGILNS	analgesia
AAAEGIQRU	aqua regia
AAAEGLLLT	talegalla
AAAEGLLPR	paralegal
AAAEGLMNU	malagueña
AAAEGLMTU	Guatemala
AAAEGLNNS	salangane
AAAEGLSSV	vassalage
AAAEGMNNT	manganate
AAAEHHLMR	Halmahera
AAAEHIKKT	kahikatea
AAAEHLNNT	Nathanael
AAAEHLPVW	alpha wave
AAAEHMMOT	haematoma
AAAEHMNST	anathemas
AAAEHMNTT	Matthaean
AAAEHRTTW	aware that
AAAEIKLNZ	Elia Kazan
AAAEILMRS	lamaserai
AAAEILPRX	paralexia
AAAEILQRU	laquearia
AAAEIMNPS	spanaemia
AAAEIMNRS	Amerasian
AAAEIMPRS	sapraemia
AAAEINPRS	Asian pear
AAAEIQTUV	aqua vitae
AAAEKLMPY	make a play
AAAEKLNSY	Lake Nyasa
AAAEKMPSS	make a pass
AAAEKPRTT	take apart
AAAELLNPT	panatella
AAAELMMRT	alma mater
AAAELNNTT	antenatal
	Atlantean
	Tantalean
AAAELNPQU	aquaplane
AAAELNTTT	tantalate
AAAELPRST	palaestra
AAAEMNSST	Tasman Sea
AAAEMPRST	aspartame
AAAEMRRRT	terramara
AAAENRRTT	Tartarean
AAAENRTTY	at any rate
AAAEPRRTT	tear apart
AAAEPRSSS	apsarases
AAAESTWWY	waste away
AAAFFNNOR	fanfarona
AAAFGHNRW	Afghan War
AAAFGLRRT	Trafalgar
AAAFGMSTU	Famagusta
AAAFIKNRS	Afrikaans
AAAFILNUV	avifaunal
AAAFINORS	Afro-Asian
AAAFINRSS	in as far as
AAAFIRRST	rastafari✧
AAAFLLPRT	fall apart
AAAFLMRSY	Alf Ramsay
AAAFLORST	solfatara
AAAFRSSSS	sassafras
AAAGGLOPS	Galápagos
	galapagos
AAAGGMRSS	gama grass
AAAGGNRTU	Gargantua
AAAGHHOTY	hatha yoga
AAAGHJNNT	Jagannath
AAAGHLLNP	phalangal
AAAGHMPRS	Sarah Gamp
AAAGHPPRR	paragraph
AAAGILLMO	alalagmoi
AAAGILLRT	alligarta
AAAGILOPR	paralogia
AAAGILRST	astragali
	tarsalgia
AAAGIMNOT	angiomata
AAAGIMNRV	gravamina
AAAGIMRRT	margarita✧
AAAGINNRV	Varangian
AAAGINRRT	rangatira
AAAGJNNRU	Nagarjuna
AAAGLLMOS	alalagmos
AAAGLNPTY	Anaglypta®
AAAGLNRSU	Alan Sugar
AAAGLOSVV	vasovagal
AAAGLRSST	astragals
AAAGMMRSY	gamma rays
AAAGMNPTY	pantagamy
AAAGMTTUZ	Muz Tag Ata
AAAGNORRT	Tarragona
AAAGORSSS	Saragossa
AAAGPRRSS	pará grass
AAAGPRSSU	asparagus
AAAHHHJNS	Shah Jahan
AAAHHHPRT	Haphtarah
AAAHHIMNS	shamianah
AAAHHKMNS	khansamah
AAAHHLLMS	mashallah
AAAHHMSTY	hay asthma
AAAHIKKLT	kathakali✧
AAAHIKNRT	Katharina
AAAHILMNY	Himalayan
AAAHILMST	Tashi Lama
AAAHILMSY	Himalayas
AAAHIMNRS	Narasimha
AAAHIMNRU	marihuana
AAAHINSVV	Vaishnava
AAAHJNRST	Rajasthan
AAAHKLMNS	Lakshmana
AAAHKNNOR	Hank Aaron
AAAHKNRST	astrakhan
AAAHLLOTY	ayatollah✧
AAAHLLSTT	as all that
AAAHLOPSS	Lhasa Apso
AAAHLPRSY	alpha rays
AAAHMNNTT	Manhattan
AAAHMNPST	phantasma
AAAHMNRTT	harmattan
AAAHNOPTT	apathaton
AAAHSSTWY	stash away
AAAHTTUYY	Ayutthaya
AAAIIJNRY	Irian Jaya
AAAIILLLP	palilalia
AAAIILMNR	Laminaria
AAAIINQTU	Aquitania
AAAIINRST	sanitaria
AAAIJMNRU	marijuana
AAAIJPPRT	Prajapati
AAAIKKLMR	kalamkari
AAAILLMPR	alla prima
AAAILMMMN	mammalian
AAAILMNPR	palmarian
AAAILMNSY	Malaysian
AAAILMORT	amatorial
AAAILNNOT	Anatolian
AAAILNNPR	planarian
AAAILNNTT	Tantalian
AAAILNPPT	antipapal
AAAILNRST	artisanal
AAAILNRSU	Laurasian
AAAILNSST	assailant
AAAILPPRS	appraisal
AAAILRSTU	Australia
AAAILRTWY	trail away
AAAIMNNOZ	Amazonian
AAAIMNNRT	amarantin
AAAIMNNST	Tasmanian
AAAIMNNTZ	manzanita
AAAIMNORT	amatorian
	inamorata
AAAIMNOST	Toamasina
AAAIMNRST	Samaritan
	Sarmatian
AAAINNNTZ	Tanzanian
AAAINNSSS	Sassanian
AAAINOPRS	saponaria
AAAINORST	sanatoria
AAAINORTT	natatoria
AAAINPSSU	Pausanias
AAAINPSTV	vanaspati
AAAINQTTU	aquatinta
AAAINRRTT	Tartarian
AAAINRRTV	Navaratri
AAAINRSTT	astrantia
AAAINSSST	anastasis
AAAIPPRZZ	paparazzi
AAAIPRSTX	parataxis
AAAIPSTTZ	Zapatista
AAAIRSSTV	Sarasvati
AAAKMRSTU	Kama Sutra
	Kamasutra
AAAKMSTTU	Takamatsu
AAALLMPSS	Las Palmas
AAALMNRSY	salaryman

Words marked ✧ can also be spelled with one or more capital letters

AAALMORTX malaxator
AAALNNOPT Alan Paton
AAALNPSTY anaplasty
AAALNRSSV salvarsan
AAALNRTTU tarantula✧
AAALOOPPS Appaloosa
AAALPPRTY play a part
AAAMMNRST man-at-arms
AAAMNNOTZ amazon ant
AAAMNRSTU Amarantus
AAAMNSTVY a vast many
AAANNNPRU Annapurna
AAANPRTUV paravaunt
AAANRSSTT tarantass
AAANRTTTX Tartan tax
AAAOPPRZZ paparazzo
AAAPPRSTU apparatus
AAARRSSSU sussarara
AABBBEHTY Bath Abbey
AABBCCIRR bricabrac
bric-à-brac
AABBCCKRY crack baby
AABBCDEIL abdicable
AABBCDKLN blackband
AABBCDKOR backboard
AABBCEHLL beach-ball
AABBCEINR Caribbean
AABBCEKKR breakback
AABBCEKLN black bean
AABBCEKLR black bear
AABBCEOOT babacoote
AABBCILMS cabbalism
AABBCILST cabbalist
AABBCKLLL blackball
AABBCKLRT Black Bart
AABBCKLSS black bass
AABBCKMRR barmbrack
AABBCORSS barbascos
AABBDDNOR broadband
AABBDEELT debatable
AABBDEKNR bandbrake
AABBDEKOR bakeboard
AABBDENOR broad bean
AABBDEORS Barbadoes
baseboard
AABBDGNRY baby grand
AABBDLLNY bandy-ball
AABBDNOST bandobast
AABBDNRSS brass band
AABBEEKLR breakable
AABBEEKRT breakbeat
AABBEELLM blameable
AABBEELRT rebatable
AABBEFFGL bafflegab
AABBEGLNR Alban Berg
AABBEHHST Bathsheba
AABBEHILL habilable
AABBEHILT habitable
AABBEHIST Tisha be'Ab
AABBEIILT bilabiate
AABBEILLL ballabile

AABBEINOY Iona Abbey
AABBEINRT Barnabite
rabbinate
AABBEINST sabbatine
AABBEIRRS barbarise
AABBEIRRZ barbarize
AABBEISST sabbatise
AABBEISTZ sabbatize
AABBEKMMO make a bomb
AABBELLMY blameably
AABBELOTW at a low ebb
AABBELRST barbastel
AABBEORST absorbate
AABBFFINY Baffin Bay
AABBHHIST Tishah b'Ab
AABBHILTY habitably
AABBHIRRT bara brith
AABBHOSTT Shabbatot
AABBIILLL ballabili
AABBIMRRS barbarism
AABBIMSST sabbatism
AABBIRRTY barbarity
AABBIRSSU babirussa
AABBLRSUY balas ruby
AABBMOORT bamboo rat
AABBNOTYY Botany Bay
AABBNRTYY Bantry Bay
AABBORRSU barbarous
AABCCCCEI beccaccia
AABCCDEFR crab-faced
AABCCEEMS Maccabees
AABCCEFKL blackface
AABCCEHLT catchable
AABCCEHNT bacchante
AABCCEKLM camelback
AABCCEKPS backspace
AABCCEKRT trace back
AABCCELST cablecast
AABCCELSU accusable
AABCCHHKT hatchback
AABCCHIKN back-chain
AABCCHKKU huckaback
AABCCHLOR carbachol
AABCCHNOW chawbacon
AABCCHNST bacchants
AABCCIKKP pickaback
AABCCILOT catabolic
AABCCIORT acrobatic
AABCCJKKL blackjack
AABCCKKRT backtrack
AABCCKLLO coal-black
AABCCKLRW back-crawl
AABCCKRRY carry back
carry-back
AABCCNNOR crab canon
AABCCNORR carbon arc
AABCDDEFL bald-faced
AABCDDENN dance band
AABCDDORR cardboard
AABCDEEFR barefaced
AABCDEEHH beachhead

AABCDEELN danceable
AABCDEETY beta decay
AABCDEHKL blackhead
AABCDEILL cable-laid
cebadilla
AABCDEILN Alice band
AABCDEIMR carbamide
AABCDEIRR barricade
AABCDEKLL blacklead
AABCDEKLP back-pedal
AABCDEKLR lack-beard
AABCDELNR barnacled
AABCDELOY adobe clay
AABCDELPR clapbread
AABCDELRT card-table
AABCDEMRV vambraced
AABCDEMSU ambuscade
AABCDENNO abondance
AABCDENNR barn dance
AABCDENNU abundance
AABCDENOR carbonade
AABCDENPS space band
AABCDFRRT bard-craft
AABCDHILN baldachin
AABCDHILR Archibald
AABCDHKLN black hand✧
AABCDILMS labdacism
AABCDIMNO Cambodian
AABCDIORR barricado
AABCDIORS scaraboid
AABCDIORT abdicator
AABCDKLMP black damp
AABCDKRSW backwards
AABCDLNSS scablands
AABCDLOPR clapboard
AABCDLSUU subcaudal
AABCDMOSU ambuscado
AABCDNNUY abundancy
AABCDNOOR carbonado
AABCDNORT cant-board
AABCDORST broadcast
AABCEEEEN Ebenaceae
AABCEEELP peaceable
AABCEEHLR reachable
AABCEEHLT teachable
AABCEEHRS sea breach
AABCEEHRW beachwear
AABCEEIRU Rubiaceae
AABCEEKLS leaseback
AABCEEKNR canebrake
AABCEELLR care label
clearable
lacerable
AABCEELLV cleavable
AABCEELMS scale beam
AABCEELNT enactable
AABCEELPS escapable
AABCEELPY peaceably
AABCEELRS calabrese
AABCEELRT creatable
traceable

AABCEELTT cabalette
AABCEELTX exactable
AABCEENPR bean caper
AABCEENRR aberrance
AABCEERRT crab-eater
AABCEERTT bracteate
AABCEFILN fanciable
AABCEFIRT fabricate
AABCEFOSU fabaceous
AABCEFOTU about-face
AABCEGIKV give a back
AABCEGILR algebraic
AABCEGKLM blackgame
AABCEGKST backstage
AABCEGLMR cablegram
AABCEGPRT carpetbag
AABCEHILR Hebraical
AABCEHINR branchiae
AABCEHIRT brachiate
AABCEHITZ chabazite
AABCEHKLW whaleback
AABCEHLMP Palm Beach
AABCEHLMT matchable
AABCEHLNY chalybean
AABCEHLPT patchable
AABCEHLTW watchable
AABCEILLM claimable
AABCEILLN caballine
AABCEILMN imbalance
AABCEILMP impacable
AABCEILMR bicameral
AABCEILNP incapable
AABCEILNT cantabile
AABCEILRT bacterial
calibrate
AABCEILST Baltic Sea
AABCEIMNR mainbrace
AABCEIMTT metabatic
AABCEINOR anaerobic
AABCEINRR carabiner
AABCEINRS braincase
AABCEINRT bacterian
AABCEIORT aerobatic
AABCEISSS abscissae
AABCEJKMR amberjack
AABCEKKLS slack-bake
AABCEKLPT backplate
AABCEKLRT trackable
AABCEKLST stackable
AABCEKMPR break camp
AABCEKPPR paperback
AABCEKRRR barracker
AABCEKRTW back water
backwater
AABCELLLO allocable
AABCELLNO en caballo
AABCELLOR caballero
AABCELLOT locatable
AABCELLSS classable
AABCELMMR crammable
AABCELMNU ambulance
AABCELMOR carambole
AABCELNNO on balance
AABCELNNS scannable
AABCELNNU unbalance
AABCELNOR Barcelona
AABCELNPU uncapable
AABCELNRS barnacles
AABCELNTU unactable
AABCELOOS calaboose
AABCELORR barcarole
AABCELORZ carbazole
AABCELPPR crab-apple
AABCELRST Castlebar
AABCELRTT tractable
AABCELRTU trabecula
AABCELRTY traceably
AABCEMORX box camera
AABCEMOST emboscata
AABCENORT carbonate
AABCENRRY aberrancy
AABCENRTV vantbrace
AABCEORST ascorbate
AABCEORTU care about
AABCEORTZ Azobacter
AABCEOSTU sauce boat
AABCEOTUV a cut above
AABCEPRRT barret-cap
AABCERRTU carburate
AABCFGKLL black flag
black-flag
AABCFHKLS flashback
AABCFHLOT batch loaf
AABCFINRT fabricant
AABCFKSTU a fast buck
AABCFLLNY fancy ball
AABCGILLN caballing
AABCGILSS basic slag
AABCGIMRU gum arabic
AABCGKLMR black gram
AABCGKLNS back-slang
AABCGLRSS glass-crab
AABCGNORS gas-carbon
AABCGRRSS crab grass
AABCHHIRT bath chair✧
AABCHHOTT hatch boat
AABCHIKNR china bark
AABCHILNR branchial
AABCHIMNR Brahmanic
AABCHKLSS backslash
AABCHKLSW blackwash
AABCHMNOS hansom-cab
AABCHRRUY Brachyura
AABCIILLS basilical
AABCIILNS basilican
AABCIINOT anabiotic
AABCIKLLM blackmail
AABCIKLNR lack-brain
AABCILLRY bacillary
AABCILLSY basically
AABCILMNO cobalamin
AABCILNOT botanical
AABCILNPY incapably
AABCILOPR parabolic
AABCILOST bicoastal
AABCILPSU subapical
AABCILRUV vibracula
AABCILSST basic salt
AABCIMNOR macrobian
AABCIMORZ Mozarabic
AABCINNOR carbanion
AABCINORR Carbonari
AABCIOQRU aquarobic
AABCISSSS abscissas
AABCKKLMR black mark
AABCKLLLS All Blacks
AABCKLLMP lampblack
AABCKLLRT trackball
AABCKLLST backstall
AABCKLMSS black mass
AABCKLNSW black swan
AABCKLPSU back-spaul
AABCKLRSY scaly-bark
AABCKMPRR crampbark
AABCKORRZ razorback
AABCKORTT track-boat
AABCKRSTW swart-back
AABCKSSTY backstays
AABCLLMPR cramp ball
AABCLLNUV Naval Club
AABCLLOTU Cat Ballou
AABCLMNOR Marc Bolan
AABCLMOOZ Cambozola®
AABCLORSS coal-brass
AABCLORUV vocabular
AABCLRSSU subsacral
AABCLRTTU Clara Butt
AABCLRTTY tractably
AABCMNOTT combatant
AABCNOORR barracoon
AABCNORRS barrancos
AABCNORTX carbon tax
AABCOSTTU cast about
AABDDEEHR breadhead
AABDDEGLS saddlebag
AABDDEHOR headboard
AABDDEHRY Hyderabad
AABDDEIKR dika-bread
AABDDEINR brain-dead
AABDDELPT baldpated
AABDDELRS saddle bar
AABDDENNO abandoned
AABDDEORS soda bread
AABDDHORR hardboard
AABDDHORS dashboard
AABDDNNST bandstand
AABDDORRT dartboard
AABDEEFKR brake-fade
AABDEEGLL bald eagle
AABDEEILU beau ideal
AABDEEKLN Baekeland
kneadable
AABDEELLP pleadable

AABDEELLR balladeer
AABDEELMN amendable
AABDEELNS lease-band
AABDEELRT tradeable
AABDEEMNO endamoeba
AABDEEMSS embassade
AABDEENNO abandonee
AABDEERTT trabeated
AABDEFGLR fardel-bag
AABDEFHKL half-baked
AABDEFLNU unfadable
AABDEFLOR broad-leaf
loaf-bread
AABDEFLRT flatbread
AABDEGINO gabionade
AABDEGINR gabardine
AABDEGLRU guardable
AABDEGMOR board game
AABDEGMOS gambadoes
AABDEGNRR bargander
AABDEHHIY dahabiyeh
AABDEHJLL djellabah
AABDEHKNR handbrake
AABDEHKRU Ehud Barak
AABDEHLNR handlebar
AABDEHLRS salad herb
AABDEHLSY abashedly
AABDEHLTW bald wheat
AABDEHNSU unabashed
AABDEIILN inaidable
AABDEIINO Anobiidae
AABDEIKNU aduki bean
AABDEILLN balladine
AABDEILLT dilatable
AABDEILMR admirable
AABDEILMT table maid
AABDEILNR bird-alane
drainable
AABDEILNU unaidable
AABDEILOV avoidable
AABDEILRV adverbial
AABDEILSV advisable
AABDEINNR Nandi bear
AABDEINRS bandeiras
AABDEINST bastinade
AABDEIPRT pita bread
AABDEKNRS sand break
AABDEKOPR Broad Peak
AABDEKORW wakeboard
AABDEKPRS brake pads
AABDELLNT tableland
AABDELLST ballasted
stable lad
AABDELNOR bandalore
AABDELNRU burd-alane
AABDELNST sand table
AABDELPPY dapple-bay
AABDELRTW Bretwalda
draw-table
AABDELTWY twayblade
AABDEMNNR brand name
name brand
AABDEMORT dreamboat
AABDEMRTU adumbrate
AABDENSTW sweat band
AABDEORST adsorbate
AABDEORSV bravadoes
AABDEQRTU quadrate B
AABDERRSS debarrass
AABDFHLOR half board
AABDFKNRT bank draft
AABDGGNOR gangboard
AABDGIILR garibaldi✧
AABDGJLLR J G Ballard
AABDGLNOR Langobard
AABDGLOOR blood agar
AABDGNNOW bandwagon
AABDHIORZ biohazard
AABDHLRSU Hasdrubal
AABDHLSWY wash badly
AABDHORSW washboard
AABDHRSUY subahdary
AABDIJNOR jaborandi
AABDILLST balladist
AABDILMNO abdominal
AABDILMRY admirably
AABDILNQU baldaquin
AABDILNST stand bail
AABDILORS bad sailor
sailboard
AABDILORT broadtail
tailboard
AABDILOVY avoidably
AABDILSVY advisably
AABDINNRT trainband
AABDINOST bastinado
AABDINPRT in bad part
AABDINSTW waistband
AABDKLNRW draw blank
AABDKLORW boardwalk
AABDKMRST Bratsk Dam
AABDLLORW wallboard
AABDLLOSW salad bowl
AABDLNORX Arnold Bax
AABDLNSST sandblast
AABDLOOSW balsawood
AABDLORUY day-labour
Labour Day
AABDMNNOY man and boy
AABDNORTU bat around
AABDORRST starboard
AABDORSWY broadways
AABEEEGLR agreeable
AABEEENST sea-beaten
AABEEFLLT table leaf
AABEEFNST beanfeast
AABEEGGLU gaugeable
AABEEGILM imageable
AABEEGLLL glabellae
AABEEGLLT bagatelle
AABEEGLMT table game
AABEEGLRR barrelage
AABEEGLRY agreeably
AABEEGLSZ sleazebag
AABEEGLTT get-at-able
AABEEGMSS embassage
AABEEGRRT Great Bear
AABEEHKLS shakeable
AABEEHLLX exhalable
AABEEHLMS shameable
AABEEHLPS shapeable
AABEEHLRS shareable
AABEEHLRT herbal tea
AABEEHNSU hause-bane
AABEEHRRS earbasher
AABEEHRST sea-bather
tabasheer
AABEEHRTT heartbeat
AABEEILLN alienable
AABEEILRS raiseable
AABEEINRS béarnaise✧
AABEEKLPP bakeapple
AABEEKLPS speakable
AABEEKORR aerobrake
AABEEKPTY keep at bay
AABEELLLM malleable
AABEELLMT labelmate
AABEELLNN Annabelle
AABEELLNR learnable
AABEELLRT alterable
relatable
AABEELLRV alla breve
AABEELMMT emblemata
AABEELMPR praeamble
AABEELMST base metal
AABEELNTU uneatable
AABEELORT elaborate
AABEELPRR reparable
AABEELPRS separable
AABEELPRY repayable
AABEELPST baseplate
AABEELQTU equatable
AABEELRTT treatable
AABEELRTV avertable
AABEELRTW tableware
AABEELTTX battle axe
battle-axe
AABEEMNOT entamoeba
AABEEMNST abasement
AABEEMNTT abatement
AABEEMRTY yerba maté
AABEEQRSU arabesque
AABEERRTV beaver rat
AABEERRTW water bear
AABEFGILT fatigable
AABEFILRU Albufeira
AABEFKRST breakfast
AABEFLLMM flammable
AABEFLLMU album-leaf
AABEFLLOT floatable
AABEFLLPP flappable
AABEFLMSU flambeaus
AABEFLMUX flambeaux

AABEFLORV	favorable
AABEFLOST	sofa table
AABEGGINO	gabionage
AABEGGMNR	beggar-man
AABEGHILL	gallabieh
AABEGHIMT	The Gambia
AABEGHLLU	laughable
AABEGHORR	harborage
AABEGIILL	bailliage
AABEGILNV	navigable
AABEGINRR	bargainer
AABEGIRRT	arbitrage
AABEGKLOR	break gaol
	gaolbreak
AABEGKMRS	bergamask✧
AABEGKNNT	bank-agent
AABEGLLLR	glabellar
AABEGLMNP	Palembang
AABEGLNOR	Bangalore
AABEGLNRT	grantable
AABEGLPRS	graspable
AABEGLRTT	rattlebag
AABEGMNRT	bar magnet
AABEGNNOT	tonga-bean
AABEGNORT	abnegator
AABEGNRSU	sugar bean
AABEGNRUZ	Aurangzeb
AABEGORTW	wager boat
AABEGPSSY	by-passage
AABEHHNPR	Aphra Behn
AABEHHRTT	earth-bath
AABEHIITW	Wahabiite
AABEHINRR	herbarian
AABEHISTV	Tisha Be'Av
AABEHITTU	habituate
AABEHLOTW	whaleboat
AABEHLSSS	abashless
AABEHMNST	abashment
AABEHMSTT	steam bath
AABEHOPQU	aquaphobe
AABEHRTTW	water bath
AABEIILLS	labialise
AABEIILLZ	labialize
AABEIIMNR	bain-marie
AABEIIMNS	baisemain
AABEIIRTU	aubrietia
AABEIIRTV	bivariate
AABEIJKLR	break jail
	jailbreak
AABEIJMNS	semi-bajan
AABEIKLNS	balkanise✧
	lake-basin
AABEIKLNZ	balkanize✧
AABEIKNRR	karabiner
AABEILLLR	albarelli
AABEILLLT	talliable
AABEILLMN	laminable
AABEILLNR	ballerina
AABEILLNS	Sabellian
AABEILLPP	appliable
AABEILLRT	bilateral
	trailable
AABEILMNR	lamebrain
AABEILMNU	unamiable
AABEILNOT	anabolite
AABEILNPT	paintable
AABEILNRT	Albertina
	trainable
AABEILNRZ	balzarine
AABEILPST	basipetal
AABEILRSU	subaerial
AABEILSTT	stabilate
AABEILTTW	wait table
AABEIMNOT	abominate
AABEIMNRT	bairn-team
AABEIMSST	metabasis
AABEINORS	arabinose
AABEINRRV	verbarian
AABEINRST	abstainer
AABEINRVW	brainwave
AABEINSST	Sebastian
AABEIRRTT	arbitrate
AABEKKNRR	break rank
AABEKLLTT	table talk✧
AABEKLMNU	unmakable
AABEKLNST	beanstalk
AABEKLRTY	Art Blakey
AABEKMNRS	brakesman
AABEKNNOT	tonka-bean
AABEKNPPR	bank paper
	bank-paper
AABEKNSTT	state bank
AABEKOSTT	stake boat
AABEKPPRR	paperbark
AABEKPRRT	Pat Barker
AABELLLMR	alarm-bell
AABELLLMY	malleably
AABELLLOR	albarello
AABELLLOW	allowable
AABELLLVV	ball valve
AABELLMNY	Ballymena
AABELLNNR	bannerall
AABELLNPT	plantable
AABELLNSU	unsalable
AABELLPPR	palpebral
AABELLSTT	table salt
AABELLSTU	blastulae
AABELLSUV	valuables
AABELMNNU	unnamable
AABELMNST	stableman
AABELMNTU	untamable
AABELMQSU	bal masqué
AABELMRSS	lamb's ears
AABELMRTU	maturable
AABELMRTW	beam trawl
AABELMSSU	assumable
AABELNPUY	unpayable
AABELNRTY	bay-antler
AABELNSTU	unsatable
AABELNSUY	unsayable
AABELOPRR	polar bear
AABELOPRV	vaporable
AABELORRZ	razorable
AABELORST	astrolabe
AABELORTT	rotatable
AABELORTW	bloatware
AABELPRRY	reparably
AABELPRSY	separably
AABELPRYY	play by ear
AABELRRST	arblaster
AABELRSSU	assurable
AABELRSTU	saturable
AABELRTTU	tablature
AABELTTWX	wax tablet
AABEMNRTT	rabatment
AABEMOSTT	steamboat
AABEMRRSS	embarrass
AABENNSTV	Van Basten
AABENORSU	buona sera
AABEOPPRT	approbate
AABEOPRRS	boar-spear
AABEORTUV	rave about
AABEOSTTU	about east
	eastabout
AABERRSSW	brassware
AABERSTUX	beaux arts✧
AABFFFOTU	faff about
AABFGILSU	basifugal
AABFIIMNS	Fabianism
AABFIINST	Fabianist
AABFIKNRS	Fairbanks
AABFILMRS	balsam fir
AABFIMORT	fibromata
AABFLLOTU	fall about
AABFLORVY	favorably
AABFNORSZ	Franz Boas
AABGGIMNO	gambogian
AABGGRRYY	argy-bargy
AABGHIRST	barghaist
AABGHLLUY	laughably
AABGHNOTU	hang about
AABGHOPRR	barograph
AABGIINWY	in a big way
AABGILNRU	Bulgarian
AABGILNVY	navigably
AABGILRRT	Gibraltar
AABGIMOSU	ambagious
AABGINNOR	born-again
AABGINORU	baragouin
AABGINRTT	rabatting
AABGINTVY	vanity bag
AABGJSTYY	Jay Gatsby
AABGLOORR	algarrobo
AABGNORSZ	garbanzos
AABGNRRUW	burrawang
AABGOORRT	abrogator
AABGORTVY	gravy boat
AABHHIKSU	hibakusha
AABHHIMSW	Wahhabism
AABHHISTV	Tishah B'Av
AABHIILRZ	bilharzia✧
AABHIIMNP	amphibian
AABHIIMSW	Wahabiism

AABHIIOPP apiphobia
AABHIIRSW waribashi
AABHIMMRU Hammurabi
AABHIMNOT Ian Botham
AABHIMSSW bashawism
AABHINNOT Bathonian
AABHINOPP panphobia
AABHINRSW brainwash
AABHINSSW washbasin
AABHIPRRV vibraharp
AABHKKLNU Kubla Khan
AABHKLRRT Karl Barth
AABHLLOWX boxwallah
AABHLSSTT bath salts
AABHMRRTU barathrum
AABHOTTUW what about
AABHRSUWY brush away
AABIIILMR mirabilia
AABIIKNNS Iain Banks
AABIILLMS labialism
AABIILNOT notabilia
AABIILNRR librarian
AABIILNRZ Brazilian
AABIILNST balanitis
AABIIMNSS Sabianism
AABIINNRT Britannia
AABIINOSS anabiosis
AABIINRTT Brittania
AABIINRTV bivariant
AABIINRZZ Zanzibari
AABIJNOTW jawbation
AABILLLOW allow bail
AABILLNPT paintball✧
AABILLNST in ballast
AABILLORS isallobar
AABILMNOS anabolism
AABILMNRU manubrial
AABILMOPY amblyopia
AABILMORS ambrosial
AABILMPST baptismal
AABILNOTT battalion
AABILRRSU bursarial
AABILRTUU Tubularia
AABILSVWY Walvis Bay
AABIMNNOU buonamani
AABIMNORS ambrosian✧
AABIMORSU simarouba
AABINORTT boat train
AABINOSTW boatswain
AABIOSTTW waistboat
AABIOTTUW wait about
AABIRRRTY arbitrary
AABIRTTTU ribattuta
AABISTTTU Batistuta
AABJJLLNU Ljubljana
AABKLORTU lark about
AABKLOTTU talk about
AABKLOTUW walkabout
AABKMOORZ zamboorak
AABLLLOWY allowably
AABLLMOTZ matzo ball
AABLLMSYY abysmally
AABLLNTTY blatantly
AABLLORSY aryballos
AABLLOSTV Balto-slav
AABLLRSTU blastular
AABLLRSYY syllabary
AABLLRTUY tabularly
AABLLSSTU blastulas
AABLMNORY myrobalan
AABLMNRWY byrlaw-man
AABLMNTUY untamably
AABLMOOPS opobalsam
AABLMORTT altar-tomb
AABLMORTU ambulator
AABLMOSST blastomas
AABLMSSUY assumably
AABLNOORS saloon bar
AABLNORTU Ulan Bator
AABLOPTUY play about
AABLORSST albatross
AABLORTTU tabulator
AABLRSSTU subastral
AABLSSSUV subvassal
AABMMOSTY Ambystoma
AABMNNOOU buonamano
AABMNOSTW batswoman
AABMOPSTW swamp boat
AABNNOSTW Botswanan
AABNNSTTU Bantustan
AABNOOSSV bossa nova
AABNOSTTY stay-on tab
AABNOSTUW swan about
AABNRSSTV vantbrass
AABORRTUY abortuary
AABRSSTTU status bar
substrata
AACCCEHIM cachaemic
AACCCEIRS casarecci
AACCCHIOP capocchia
AACCCHIRS saccharic
AACCCIOPR carpaccio
AACCDDEIR caddie car
AACCDDINY candidacy
AACCDEELT calceated
AACCDEHKR crackhead
AACCDEIIR acaricide
AACCDEIMS academics
AACCDEIRV cadaveric
AACCDEJNY adjacency
AACCDELPR cradle cap
place card
AACCDERST sacred cat
AACCDHLOO coachload
AACCDHLRU archducal
AACCDHOOR coach road
AACCDIINR circadian
AACCDIIRU auric acid
AACCDIMNO mandiocca
AACCDIOSU Caucasoid
AACCDKNRS sand crack
AACCDNORT accordant
AACCDORSS as accords
AACCEEEIR Ericaceae
AACCEEFMR face cream
AACCEEHIN echinacea
AACCEEIRR cercariae
AACCEEIST Cistaceae
AACCEEJNU Juncaceae
AACCEEKMR cream cake
AACCEELNR clearance
AACCEEMNV cave canem
AACCEEMPP peace camp
AACCEENOR Cornaceae
AACCEENRT cancerate
reactance
AACCEEPRS space race
AACCEFGOU cacafuego
AACCEFHKL chalkface
AACCEFHNT fat chance
AACCEFIIP pacificae
AACCEFKNY fancy cake
AACCEGHPR charge-cap
AACCEGIRS cigar case
AACCEGORU accourage
AACCEHHQU chechaqua
AACCEHILL cailleach
AACCEHINR cane-chair
AACCEHJKP cheap Jack
cheap-jack✧
AACCEHMRU cauchemar
AACCEHRRT character
AACCEHRTY yacht race
AACCEHSTW watchcase
AACCEIILN caecilian
AACCEILMT acclimate
AACCEILNR calcarine
AACCEILNT analectic
AACCEILST ascetical
AACCEILTU aciculate
AACCEINNR Cancerian
AACCEINRR cercarian
AACCEINRS Saracenic
AACCEINTV vaccinate
AACCEIRRT ricercata
AACCEJKLN lancejack
AACCEJKRR carjacker
AACCEJKSU Jack-sauce
AACCEKNRS crankcase
AACCEKRRT racetrack
AACCELLLN canal-cell
AACCELLTU calculate
AACCELMNU calcaneum
AACCELMTY cyclamate
AACCELNSU calcaneus
AACCELNTU accentual
AACCELSTU sacculate
AACCEMRTY cyma recta
AACCENPTT acceptant
AACCEORTT coarctate
AACCEPRTU cut a caper
AACCERSSY accessary
AACCERSTU Crustacea

AACCFGOOS cacafogos
AACCFHIRT fair catch
AACCFIILP pacifical
AACCFMPRT campcraft
AACCGHHIN cha-chaing
AACCGINRR racing car
AACCHIILL cailliach
AACCHIKSW Chickasaw
AACCHILMO mail-coach
AACCHILNY china clay
AACCHIMPR camp-chair
AACCHIMSY sciamachy
AACCHINRS saccharin
AACCHINRT anthracic
AACCHIRTT cathartic
AACCHIRTU autarchic
AACCHKKSY Hacky Sack®
AACCHMRSU saccharum✧
AACCHNNWY wanchancy
AACCHORTU raccahout
AACCIILNT anaclitic
AACCIILNV vaccinial
AACCIILST ascitical
sciatical
AACCIINPS capsaicin
AACCIINTT tactician
AACCIKKPP pickapack
AACCILLNO cloacalin
cloacinal
laconical
AACCILLNY calycinal
AACCILLSS classical
AACCILLUV clavicula
AACCILMNU cacuminal
AACCILNNO canonical
AACCILNOR acronical
AACCILNRU canicular
AACCILOOS Colocasia
AACCILPRT practical
AACCILSTT stalactic
AACCILTTY catalytic
AACCIMNOR carcinoma
macaronic
AACCINORV Cracovian
AACCINOTT catatonic
toccatina
AACCINPRT pancratic
AACCINPTY captaincy
AACCINRTT Antarctic
AACCIOOPT cacotopia
AACCIOPRT capacitor
AACCIOPSU capacious
AACCIORST Costa Rica
AACCIRSST sarcastic
AACCKMNRS cracksman
AACCKRRTT cart-track
AACCLLLLO local call
AACCLLRUY calculary
AACCLMORY cyclorama
AACCLMSTY cataclysm
AACCLNORY acronycal
AACCLORRV carvacrol
AACCMNOPY accompany
AACCOPRRS sarcocarp
AACCORTUY autocracy
AACCOSSTT staccatos
stoccatas
AACDDEETU decaudate
AACDDEFHR hard-faced
AACDDEHLS scaldhead
AACDDEHMR dead march
AACDDEHRS shade card
AACDDEINR Decandria
AACDDEINT candidate
AACDDEIRT radicated
AACDDELNO do a candle
AACDDELOP decapodal
AACDDENNS sand dance
AACDDENOP decapodan
AACDDENSU Sadducean
AACDDENTU aduncated
AACDDEOPT coadapted
AACDDGNOT cat-and-dog
AACDDHIMR didrachma
AACDDHIMV David Mach
AACDDIIST Dadaistic
AACDDLMNO MacDonald
AACDDMORU docudrama
AACDDNRTY dandy-cart
AACDEEEFT defaecate
AACDEEEHP headpeace
AACDEEFLN lean-faced
AACDEEFLT defalcate
AACDEEHHR headreach
AACDEEHRS scare-head
AACDEEHTY decay heat
AACDEEIIR Iridaceae
AACDEEILM Camelidae
AACDEEIMT acetamide
emaciated
AACDEEIRT eradicate
AACDEEKPP peaked cap
AACDEELRT lacerated
AACDEELTU aculeated
AACDEEMNS damascene✧
AACDEEMRT camerated
demarcate
AACDEEMST casemated
AACDEENRV readvance
AACDEENTT decantate
AACDEEPRS sacred ape
AACDEETUX excaudate
AACDEFFHL half-faced
AACDEFFIN affianced
AACDEFFIR fair-faced
AACDEFGRU face-guard
AACDEFHRS headscarf
AACDEFIKR acid freak
AACDEFIST fasciated
AACDEFLRS false card
false-card
AACDEGILT glaciated
AACDEGINY Decagynia
AACDEGIOT dacoitage
AACDEGLNO decagonal
AACDEGNOS gasconade
AACDEGNST stag-dance
AACDEHHIR headchair
AACDEHHRS head-crash
AACDEHILN enchilada
AACDEHKMS smackhead
AACDEHKSW hacksawed
AACDEHLLN dance hall
AACDEHLRT cathedral
AACDEHMMT cat-hammed
AACDEHORT octahedra
AACDEHPST pas de chat
AACDEHRSU hard sauce
AACDEIINU audiencia
AACDEIIPR epicardia
AACDEIIRT Arctiidae
AACDEILLN dalliance
AACDEILLT dialectal
AACDEILLV cevadilla
AACDEILMR creamlaid
AACDEILNO Laodicean
AACDEILNT cadential
AACDEILPS asclepiad
AACDEILTU acidulate
AACDEIMMS academism
AACDEIMNO Macedonia
AACDEIMNR admirance
cardamine
AACDEIMNY cyanamide
AACDEIMPR epic drama
paramedic
pre-adamic
AACDEIMSS camisades
AACDEIMST academist
Steadicam®
AACDEINNR rain dance
AACDEINNV in advance
AACDEINOR androecia
AACDEINOT diaconate
AACDEINOV avoidance
AACDEINPS cispadane
AACDEINRT carinated
eradicant
AACDEIRSS ascarides
AACDEJKLL jackalled
AACDEJKMP jam-packed
AACDEKLRY lardy-cake
AACDEKMRT tarmacked
AACDELLNU calendula
AACDELMNO Damoclean
AACDELMNS Candlemas
slam-dance
AACDELNNS sand lance
AACDELNOT anecdotal
AACDELNPR lap dancer
AACDELNPS landscape
AACDELNRR Carl Andre
AACDELNRT declarant

AACDELPRU Paul Dacre
AACDELRRS laser card
AACDEMNTU manducate
AACDEMOPR campeador
AACDEMORS cream soda
AACDENNNO cannonade
AACDENNST adnascent
ascendant
AACDENORR carronade
AACDENOSS cassonade
AACDENOTU coadunate
AACDENPRT tap-dancer
AACDENSSV canvassed
AACDEOPRT drape coat
AACDERSTT castrated
AACDERSWY Sacred Way
AACDERTTV cravatted
AACDERTTX taxed cart
AACDFHLRS flash card
AACDFHNRT handcraft
AACDFHRST hard facts
AACDFIILT fatidical
AACDFIRRY Friday car
AACDFLNOO food canal
AACDFORRT roadcraft
AACDGHINR drag-chain
AACDGIILL diallagic
AACDGILRY cardialgy
AACDGINOR carangoid
AACDGLMOR cladogram
AACDHHNSS shadchans
AACDHIILR rachidial
AACDHIILS dichasial
AACDHIINR rachidian
AACDHIIRR Richardia
AACDHILMS Chaldaism
AACDHILMY chlamydia
AACDHILOP phacoidal
AACDHINNP cap in hand
AACDHINOR arachnoid
AACDHINOT acanthoid
AACDHINRT cantharid
AACDHIRSY chairdays
AACDHLLLO hold a call
AACDHLNPS clap hands
handclasp
AACDHLNPU launch pad
AACDHLNRS crash-land
AACDHLNTY land-yacht
AACDHNSTY sand yacht
sand-yacht
AACDHPRRS card-sharp
AACDIIIMR miracidia
AACDIILNT diactinal
AACDIIMNO amino acid
AACDIINNR cnidarian
AACDIINRR Ricardian
AACDIIPRS paradisic
AACDIISST diastasic
AACDIISTT diastatic
AACDILLRU cuadrilla
AACDILLRY radically
AACDILMNO monadical
AACDILMNY dynamical
AACDILMRU caldarium
AACDILMSU caladiums
AACDILNTY dilatancy
AACDILOPR parodical
AACDILOPX doli capax
AACDILPRU Paul Dirac
AACDILRRU radicular
AACDIMORY myocardia
AACDIMOSS camisados
AACDIMRST dramatics
AACDINNOR draconian✧
AACDINNOT contadina
AACDINORS Sarcodina
AACDINORT Octandria
AACDINRTU Traducian
AACDIOSUU audacious
AACDIPRTY cryptadia
AACDIQRTU quadratic
AACDIRSSY dyscrasia
AACDIRSTY caryatids
AACDJNTUY adjutancy
AACDJNUVY adjuvancy
AACDKMRRY Mark Darcy
AACDKNSST caskstand
AACDKORRT trackroad
AACDKRSTY stackyard
AACDLMORS rascaldom
AACDLNORS corn-salad
AACDLNOST coastland
AACDMMOST datacomms
AACDMRRST smart card
AACDNOSTT coatstand
AACDOOPRW carap-wood
AACDOORST Ostracoda
AACDOORTV advocator
AACDORSTW coastward
AACDPRRSY scrapyard
AACEEEGNR careenage
AACEEEGNT Gnetaceae
AACEEEILM Meliaceae
AACEEEKMP make peace
make-peace
AACEEELMN Lemnaceae
AACEEFFLS false face
AACEEFINN fainéance
AACEEFIRT cafeteria
AACEEFKMS make faces
AACEEFKRW wafer cake
AACEEFLLS scale leaf
AACEEFLMR lace-frame
AACEEFLPT faceplate
AACEEFLRT leaf trace
AACEEFLUV face value
AACEEFRRT aftercare
AACEEFRSV face-saver
AACEEGHNS sea change
AACEEGILL elegiacal
AACEEGKLN angel cake
AACEEGKNO Genoa cake
AACEEGKPR repackage
AACEEGLLR cellarage
AACEEGNRR carrageen
AACEEGPSS gas escape
AACEEHHRT heartache
AACEEHIPT Hepaticae
AACEEHLNR Heraclean
AACEEHLNU Acheulean
AACEEHLPT cephalate
AACEEHLPV have place
AACEEHPRT eparchate
AACEEHPTY Typhaceae
AACEEHRTT tracheate
AACEEHRTV cave-earth
AACEEHRTX exarchate
AACEEHSUV have cause
AACEEIILL Liliaceae
AACEEIILT Tiliaceae
AACEEILMU leucaemia
AACEEILOV Violaceae
AACEEJKPT pea jacket
AACEEJLTU ejaculate
AACEEKLPT take place
AACEEKLRY layer cake
AACEEKMPR pacemaker
AACEEKMRS casemaker
AACEEKNPT keep an act
AACEEKRRT caretaker
AACEELLMU melaleuca
AACEELMNP place name
AACEELNPS pleasance
AACEELNPT placentae
AACEELNRT nectareal
AACEELNRU caerulean
AACEELNST elastance
AACEELNTU anucleate
AACEELPPR lace-paper
AACEELPRT paraclete✧
AACEELRRY relay race
AACEELRTT altercate
AACEELRTY clay eater
AACEELSTW weasel cat
AACEEMNNU amenaunce
AACEEMNNY Mycenaean
AACEEMORW cameo ware
AACEEMRRW creamware
AACEEMRTW macaw-tree
AACEEMRTY Myrtaceae
AACEENNRT nectarean
AACEENRSV cesarevna
AACEENRTU centaurea
AACEENRTX excarnate
AACEENSTY cast an eye
AACEEOPRS aerospace
AACEEPPRS paper-case
AACEEPRSS cassareep
AACEEPRSV parasceve
AACEERSTT estate car
AACEERTTU reactuate
AACEFFIRT affricate

AACEFFMOR off camera
AACEFGLNR flagrance
AACEFGNRR fragrance
AACEFGOPR forage cap
AACEFGORT factorage
AACEFGOSU fagaceous
AACEFHLLW calf whale
whale calf
AACEFHLST half-caste
AACEFIKRY fairy cake
AACEFILPR prefacial
AACEFINNY faineancy
AACEFINPT face paint
AACEFINRR Africaner
AACEFINST fascinate
AACEFKMPR packframe
AACEFLLPU pull a face
AACEFLLTU falculate
AACEFLMPR farm-place
AACEFLPRT after-clap
AACEGHIMR archimage
AACEGHINR chain-gear
AACEGHLNR archangel
AACEGHLTT Gaeltacht
AACEGHMNP champagne
AACEGHMNR charge-man
AACEGHNOR anchorage✧
AACEGHRST gatecrash
AACEGILLN angelical
englacial
Galenical
AACEGILNP gin palace
AACEGILNS analgesic
AACEGILRS Algeciras
AACEGILRT cartilage
AACEGILST agelastic
AACEGIMNO come again?
egomaniac
AACEGINNO once again
AACEGISTT castigate
AACEGKRWY graywacke
AACEGLLSS lace glass
AACEGLMOU guacamole
AACEGLORT cataloger
AACEGLOST galactose
AACEGLOSU coagulase
AACEGLOTU catalogue
coagulate
AACEGLSSS case glass
glass case
AACEGNORR arrogance
AACEGNORT cartonage
Goa trance
AACEGNRSS cane grass
AACEGNRSU cane sugar
sugar cane
sugarcane
AACEGOPST scapegoat
AACEGORTT greatcoat
AACEHHINS shanachie
AACEHHIRZ Zechariah

AACEHHMRR March hare✧
AACEHIIMS ischaemia
AACEHIIRT hieratica
AACEHIKRT a thick ear
AACEHILLN Achillean
AACEHILLO echolalia
AACEHILMO cholaemia
AACEHILMR camel hair
AACEHILMT malachite
AACEHILNS selachian
AACEHILNT châtelain
AACEHILNU Acheulian
AACEHILPT caliphate
hepatical
AACEHILRT theriacal
AACEHIMNN Manichean
AACEHIMNR Charmaine
AACEHIMNT machinate
AACEHIMNU achaenium
AACEHIMTT athematic
AACEHINNT acanthine
AACEHINRR rancheria
AACEHINRS anarchise
AACEHINRT catarhine
Catharine
Catherina
AACEHINRW chinaware
AACEHINRZ anarchize
AACEHIOPT apothecia
AACEHIOST Taoiseach
AACEHIPRS hair space
praiseach
AACEHIPST chapaties
AACEHIPTT apathetic
AACEHIRRS archaiser
AACEHIRRZ archaizer
AACEHIRST catharise
AACEHIRSY easy chair
AACEHIRTZ catharize
AACEHIRZZ chiarezza
AACEHKLNO kalanchoe
AACEHKMOR hackamore
AACEHKMPU Kampuchea
AACEHKRSV haversack
AACEHKRTY Thackeray
AACEHKTTT the attack
AACEHLLLR Clare Hall
AACEHLMPP peach-palm
AACEHLMRS mareschal
AACEHLMUU chalumeau
AACEHLRTT clathrate
AACEHMNPR marchpane
AACEHMRSY camera-shy
AACEHNNPS snaphance
AACEHNNSY seannachy
AACEHNOPR canephora
AACEHNORS sea anchor
AACEHNOTV anchoveta
AACEHNPTY tachypnea
AACEHNRRT Hart Crane
AACEHNRST cane-trash

AACEHNSSS Sassenach
AACEHPPRS scrapheap
AACEHPRTU parachute
AACEHPRTW Cape Wrath
AACEHRRTY tracheary
AACEHRSST catharses
AACEIILNT laciniate
AACEIINRR cineraria
AACEIINRS raise Cain
AACEIIRTV vicariate
AACEIJKRT air-jacket
AACEIJLRS Aljeciras
AACEIKNPS sink-a-pace
AACEILLPT capitella
AACEILLRS rascaille
AACEILLRV varicella
AACEILLTV laticlave
vacillate
AACEILMMN immanacle
AACEILMNN Alemannic
AACEILMNP campanile
AACEILMPS eclampsia
AACEILMST mica-slate
AACEILMTV calmative
AACEILNNR carnelian
AACEILNNT cantilena
lancinate
AACEILNPP appliance
AACEILNPT analeptic
AACEILNRS arsenical
carnalise
AACEILNRT lacertian
nectarial
AACEILNRZ carnalize
AACEILNSU saliaunce
AACEILNTV venatical
AACEILORT aleatoric
AACEILPPT applicate
AACEILPSS asclepias
AACEILPTU apiculate
AACEILRRT erratical
AACEILRSS sacralise
AACEILRST sectarial
AACEILRSZ sacralize
AACEILRTY aliteracy
AACEILSSU casualise
AACEILSTU actualise
AACEILSTX catalexis
AACEILSUZ casualize
AACEILTTU actualité
AACEILTUZ actualize
AACEIMNNW Ian McEwan
AACEIMNOR Americano
AACEIMNPS spanaemic
AACEIMNPT mancipate
AACEIMNTU acuminate
AACEIMOPR paroemiac
AACEIMPRS sapraemic
AACEIMPRT metacarpi
AACEIMRSS Caesarism
AACEIMRST marcasite

AACEIMSTT masticate
AACEINNRT incarnate
AACEINNSY in any case
AACEINOPR paranoeic
AACEINOPT copataine
AACEINOST caseation
AACEINPRT Patna rice
AACEINRRT tarriance
AACEINRRV arrivance
AACEINRST ascertain
Cartesian
sectarian
AACEINTTV native cat
AACEIORRT acroteria
AACEIOSST associate
Scotia Sea
AACEIPPRT per capita
AACEIPRSS cassaripe
AACEIPSTU auspicate
AACEIPTTV captivate
AACEIRSST Caesarist
staircase
AACEISTUV causative
AACEJKKLN ankle-jack
AACEJKLNP jack plane
AACEJKLNT Jack-a-Lent
AACEJKLPP apple-jack
AACEJKLSV Jack-slave
AACEJKMOT Mao-jacket
AACEKLPRT plate rack
AACEKLPSW space walk
space-walk
AACEKMRST caste-mark
AACEKNPSW spawn cake
AACEKNRRS ransacker
AACEKPPTY pay packet
AACEKPSTT peat-stack
AACEKRSTW water cask
AACELLLRU acellular
AACELLLUV vallecula
AACELLMNR cellarman
AACELLMNS call names
AACELLNOR lanceolar
olecranal
AACELLNOT all at once
AACELLNOW allowance
AACELLNPT placental
AACELLNRY Carlylean
AACELLNST castellan
AACELLOPT coal-plate
AACELLPSW wall space
AACELLSTY clay-slate
AACELLSUU clausulae
AACELLTUV clavulate
AACELMNNU unmanacle
AACELMNOR roman à clé
AACELMNST calmstane
AACELMNTT cattleman
AACELMOOT Coelomata
AACELMOST steam coal
AACELMRST smart alec✧
smart-alec✧
AACELMSST classmate
AACELNNTU antelucan
cannulate
AACELNORT anorectal
AACELNOTT Canaletto
AACELNPST placentas
AACELNRST ancestral
Lancaster
AACELNSTU Anacletus
AACELNTTU tentacula
AACELOPPR paper-coal
AACELOPRT acropetal
cleopatra✧
AACELORST escalator
AACELOSTT cattaloes
AACELOTUV autoclave
vacuolate
AACELPPRT apple-cart
AACELPRTY calyptera
caprylate
AACELPSTU aspectual
capsulate
AACELPSTY catalepsy
AACELPTXY cataplexy
AACELRRTU creatural
AACELRRTY carrytale
AACELRSTY catalyser
AACELRTUW caterwaul
AACELRTUX curtalaxe
AACELRTYZ catalyzer
AACEMNNRU manurance
AACEMNOPR campanero
AACEMNORY aeromancy
AACEMNPRT mercaptan
AACEMNPRV camper van
AACEMNRST sacrament
AACEMNSTU caumstane
AACEMOPRT cameo-part
come apart
AACEMORRT macerator
AACEMRSTY camsteary
AACENNNOY annoyance
AACENNOSS assonance
AACENORST ostracean
AACENORTU à outrance
AACENPPRY apparency
AACENPRRY parcenary
AACENRSSU anacruses
assurance
AACENRSSV canvasser
AACENRTTU cauterant
AACENSSTT castanets
AACEOOPPT apocopate
AACEORTUV evacuator
AACEORTVX excavator
AACEORWWY cower away
AACEOSSUY soya sauce
AACEOSTTV cast a vote
AACEOSTUX taxaceous
AACERRTTW water cart
AACERSTTW cast water
AACFFFFRS scaff-raff
AACFFINRY fancy fair
AACFFJKST jack-staff
AACFFKPST packstaff
AACFGILRY fly agaric
AACFGLNRY flagrancy
AACFGNRRY fragrancy
AACFHIMNR chamfrain
AACFHJKST jack shaft
jackshaft
AACFHKLRT half-track
AACFHNTTY fancy that
AACFIILNN financial
AACFIILRT trifacial
AACFILNOT factional
falcation
AACFILORT factorial
AACFILORV varifocal
AACFINSTT fantastic
AACFIPRRS friar's cap
AACFJNOOR Joan of Arc
AACFKLPRT flaptrack
AACFKNNPY fanny pack
AACFKRSTT fast track
fast-track
AACFMNRRZ Franz Marc
AACFMNRST craftsman
AACGGHINN chain gang
AACGGHPSY shaggy cap
AACGGIKNP packaging
AACGGIOPR paragogic
AACGHHIRY hagiarchy
AACGHIIMN Chiang Mai
AACGHILPR graphical
AACGHIMNP champaign
AACGHIMOR Archimago
AACGHINRR Garrincha
AACGHMORT tachogram
AACGHMPRY cymagraph
AACGHNORS charangos
AACGHOPSZ gazpachos
AACGHORSU guacharos
AACGILLLY glacially
AACGILLMR calligram
AACGILLMY magically
AACGILLOS scagliola
AACGILLRT Largactil®
AACGILNNR ring-canal
AACGILNOR organical
AACGILOST costalgia
AACGIMMRT grammatic
AACGIMOTU autogamic
AACGIMPRT pragmatic
AACGINORV Craigavon
AACGIOSSU sagacious
AACGLLSSY lacy glass
AACGLLSWY scallywag
AACGLNOOT octagonal
AACGLNOTU coagulant
AACGLOORY acarology

AACGLSSUY Gay-Lussac
AACGMORRT cartogram
AACGNNSTY stagnancy
AACGNRRTY Cary Grant
AACGORSTU sugar-coat
AACGPRRSS grass carp
AACHHHIUU chihuahua
AACHHKKNU Chanukkah
AACHHLNOO hoolachan
AACHHNSSS Hans Sachs
AACHIILMN chain mail
AACHIILPT aliphatic
AACHIIMNT matachini
AACHIIMRS mariachis
AACHIINRT Carinthia
AACHIIPRS pharisaic
AACHIIRRV charivari
AACHIKMSY skiamachy
AACHILMRS marischal
AACHILNOZ chalazion
AACHILNPS ship canal
AACHILOPR parochial
AACHILOPT chipolata
AACHILORS Charolais
AACHILPST asphaltic
AACHILSST thalassic
AACHIMNOR harmonica
AACHIMNRR Charminar
AACHIMNRS anarchism
AACHIMRRT matriarch
AACHIMRST Catharism
AACHIMSTT asthmatic
AACHINOPR anaphoric
pharaonic
AACHINORT Tocharian
AACHINPRS parischan
AACHINRST anarchist
cantharis
AACHIOPPT apophatic
AACHIORST cash ratio
AACHIPRRT patriarch
AACHIPRSS chaprassi
AACHIPSTT chapattis
AACHIRRST Aristarch
AACHIRSST catharsis
AACHIRSTT Catharist
AACHKKLLT chalk talk
AACHKSSTY Haystacks
AACHLLMRY lachrymal
AACHLLPTY cataphyll
AACHLLRTW wallchart
AACHLMNOR monarchal
AACHLMOST stomachal
AACHLMPTY match play
matchplay
AACHLMRSY marshalcy
AACHLOPVY play havoc
AACHMMNSY Sammy Cahn
AACHMNNOR anchor man
anchor-man
AACHMNORW charwoman
AACHMNSTY yachtsman
AACHMPRST march past
AACHMRRTU MacArthur
AACHNNOTY anthocyan
AACHNOPRT anthocarp
AACHNOSTU acanthous
AACHNOTTY chatoyant
AACHNPRTY pyracanth
AACHNRSTU cantharus
AACHOPPRY apocrypha✧
AACHPRSSY chaprassy
AACHQSSTU sasquatch
AACIIILNS siciliana
AACIIINTV Vatican II
AACIILLRT altricial
AACIILMNP campanili
AACIILMRS racialism
AACIILMST ismatical
lamaistic
AACIILNPT ancipital
AACIILNPU Paulician
AACIILNST Castilian
AACIILNTV vaticinal
AACIILPRT piratical
AACIILRST racialist
satirical
AACIILSTV viaticals
AACIIMMST miasmatic
AACIIMOTX axiomatic
AACIINNOP poinciana
AACIINNOT nicotiana
AACIINNST antiscian
AACIINORT raciation
AACIINPRT patrician✧
AACIINRTZ Nazaritic
AACIIPRRY air-piracy
AACIIPRST parasitic
AACIIRRTU urticaria
AACIIRTVY air-cavity
AACIISTTV atavistic
AACIJNOTT jactation
AACIKLLNT lack-Latin
AACIKMNNY kanamycin
AACIKNPRT pack-train
AACIKRTTX taxi track
AACILLLLY calla lily
AACILLLQU quail-call
AACILLMMN Macmillan
AACILLMNY manically
AACILLMPS small pica
AACILLNOR Corallian
AACILLNOT allantoic
AACILLNRY ancillary
cranially
AACILLNTV vacillant
AACILLNTY actinally
AACILLOXY coaxially
AACILLPRY capillary
AACILLPTY capitally
AACILMNRS carnalism
AACILMOSW Mosaic Law
AACILMPST plasmatic
AACILMRRY lacrimary
AACILMRSS rascalism
AACILMRSU simulacra
AACILMRTU matricula
AACILMSSU casualism
AACILNNOR non-racial
AACILNNOV volcanian
AACILNNUV vulcanian✧
AACILNOPT pactional
placation
AACILNORT cantorial
AACILNOTT lactation
AACILNOTV clavation
AACILNOTY claytonia
AACILNPPT applicant
AACILNPSV Pan-Slavic
AACILNQTU quantical
AACILNRST carnalist
AACILNRTY carnality
AACILNRUV navicular
AACILNRUY caulinary
AACILNTTY latitancy
AACILOPRS prosaical
AACILORSW Social War
AACILORTU auctorial
caliatour
AACILOSSU salacious
AACILOSTT coat tails
AACILPRSU spiracula
AACILPRTU capitular
AACILPRTY paralytic
AACILQTTU acquittal
AACILRRTU articular
AACILRRUU auricular
AACILRSTT cart's-tail
Scarlatti
AACILRSTY rascality
sacrality
satyrical
AACILSSTY catalysis
AACILSTTT Attic salt
AACILSTTU actualist
AACILSTUY causality
AACILTTUY actuality
AACIMMOPS mosaic map
AACIMNNNU Mancunian
AACIMNNOY cynomania
AACIMNOPR panoramic
AACIMNORR Armorican
AACIMNORS macaronis
AACIMNORT manticora
AACIMNOST anosmatic
AACIMNOTT mactation
AACIMNPST campanist
AACIMORSX macro-axis
AACIMORTU amaurotic
AACIMOTTU automatic
AACIMPSST spasmatic
AACIMRRSU sacrarium
AACIMRSTY camstairy

AACIMRTTU	traumatic
AACINNOPT	pontianac
AACINNORT	carnation
AACINNOST	santonica
AACINNPRT	captain RN
AACINOOTV	avocation
AACINOOTZ	Actinozoa
AACINOPRS	caparison
AACINOPRT	paratonic
AACINOPRV	avoparcin
AACINOPST	capitanos
AACINORRV	Carnivora
AACINORTU	arcuation
AACINORTV	covariant
AACINOSST	cassation
AACINOSTU	causation
AACINOTTU	actuation
AACINOTUV	vacuation
AACINPRTY	captainry
AACINRRVY	arrivancy
AACINRSST	sacristan
AACINRSSU	anacrusis
AACIOPRSU	rapacious
AACIOPSTT	apostatic
AACIORTTV	activator
AACIOSTTW	waistcoat
AACIPRSSU	paracusis
AACIRSSUU	Carausius
AACJKPRST	Jack Sprat
AACJKRSTW	Jack Straw
	jack-straw
AACJKSSTY	jack-stays
AACJLORTU	jaculator
AACKLMNPX	Max Planck
AACKMRSST	stack arms
AACKORSTT	toast rack
AACLLLMOS	small-coal
AACLLMNOR	Mallorcan
AACLLMNTY	clamantly
AACLLMPSS	small caps
AACLLNOPT	coal plant
AACLLOPRS	collapsar
AACLLOPRY	allocarpy
AACLLPRTY	party-call
AACLLRSTU	claustral
AACLLRSUU	clausular
AACLLTTUY	tactually
AACLMORRZ	razorclam
AACLMRRYY	lacrymary
AACLNOORS	saloon car
AACLNOORT	root canal
AACLNOPTU	cantaloup
AACLNRUUV	avuncular
AACLOOPST	tapacolos
AACLOORTX	toxocaral
AACLOPRRR	parlor car
AACLOPRRT	patrol car
AACLOPRTU	portulaca
AACLOPRTY	placatory
	play-actor
AACLOPSTU	tapaculos
AACLORSTV	slavocrat
AACLPRSUY	capsulary
	scapulary
AACLRRTUY	cartulary
AACMMOORS	cosmorama
AACMNORST	stramaçon
AACMNOTTU	catamount
AACMOOSTT	scotomata
AACNNOSTT	Constanta
AACNOPRST	not a scrap
AACNORTUU	au courant
AACNOSTTY	at any cost
AACNPRSTU	carap-nuts
AACNRSTUY	sanctuary
AACNRSTUZ	Santa Cruz
AACOOPSTT	capotasto
AACORRSTU	Tuscarora
AACORRTTT	attractor
	tractator
AACORSSTT	castratos
AACORSSWY	cassowary
AACPRSSTU	Spartacus
AADDDELPS	pad-saddle
AADDDGNRY	grandaddy
AADDEEFHT	fat-headed
AADDEEHPS	sapheaded
AADDEEILV	dead-alive
AADDEEMRY	ready-made
AADDEENRU	Audenarde
AADDEERTW	dead-water
AADDEFHLR	half-adder
AADDEGMNU	undamaged
AADDEGRTU	graduated
AADDEHHIR	hardihead
AADDEHHMN	ham-handed
AADDEHIOR	Radiohead
AADDEHIRV	David Hare
AADDEHLNN	lend a hand
AADDEHMNR	hermandad
AADDEHMPT	death-damp
AADDEHRTW	dead thraw
	deathward
AADDEILNO	adenoidal
AADDEILNV	David Lean
AADDEINNV	Nanda Devi
AADDEINRT	andradite
AADDEINRW	Edwardian
AADDEIOPZ	Zapodidae
AADDEKLNY	naked lady
AADDELLNS	sandalled
AADDELLPS	saddle-lap
AADDELMNN	landdamne
AADDELMNR	dreamland
	raddleman
AADDELORU	read aloud
AADDELRST	astraddle
AADDEMNNT	demandant
AADDEMNOR	andromeda✧
AADDENNOO	Dodonaean
AADDENPTU	unadapted
AADDEORST	roadstead
AADDEOSTU	Adeodatus
AADDEPRST	dead's part
AADDERRTY	day trader
AADDGHOOS	had as good
AADDGMNNO	man-and-dog
AADDHLLOR	Roald Dahl
AADDHNNST	handstand
AADDHNRRW	hard-drawn
AADDIIMNY	Didynamia
AADDIIMRY	dairymaid
AADDIINRV	Dravidian
AADDILMSY	dismal day
	lady's-maid
AADDINORS	Diana Dors
AADDINPRT	dandiprat
AADDIORST	stadia rod
AADDLLRUW	auld-warld
AADDLNRSW	landwards
AADDLORSW	word salad
AADDLRSTY	dastardly
AADDNPRTY	dandyprat
AADDNRSST	standards
AADEEEHLS	headlease
AADEEELRT	tea-dealer
AADEEEMMN	âme damnée
AADEEFHMR	headframe
AADEEFLPR	flap-eared
AADEEGHMT	megadeath
AADEEGHNP	phagedena
AADEEGHRS	shag-eared
AADEEGHST	Gateshead
AADEEGLMN	magdalene✧
AADEEGNOR	orangeade
AADEEGNPP	appendage
AADEEGNRT	Great Dane
	tea garden
AADEEHHKS	headshake
AADEEHHLW	whale-head
AADEEHHRX	hexahedra
AADEEHHTT	heat death
AADEEHILN	line ahead
AADEEHINY	Hyaenidae
AADEEHISV	have ideas
AADEEHKNS	snakehead
AADEEHLSW	alewashed
AADEEHPRS	spearhead
AADEEHPST	heapstead
AADEEHRRT	heart-dear
AADEEHRTT	death rate
AADEEHRTW	headwater
	water head
AADEEIKWW	wide awake
	wideawake
AADEEILMV	mediaeval
AADEEILPV	Deepavali
AADEEIMNT	deaminate
AADEEIRRT	reradiate
AADEEISVW	wave aside
AADEEJMNS	James Dean
AADEEKMNS	damaskeen
AADEEKMRY	make ready

	make-ready
AADEELLMN	allemande
AADEELLNV	Dave Allen
AADEELLSW	sea-walled
	Swaledale
AADEELMRY	ready meal
AADEELNNR	lend an ear
AADEELNPS	esplanade
AADEELNRX	Alexander
AADEELORT	areolated
AADEELPRR	ale-draper
AADEELRRY	lay reader
AADEELRST	trade sale
AADEELTUV	devaluate
	value date
AADEELTVW	delta wave
AADEEMMRT	dream team
AADEEMNRT	tradename
AADEEMNST	Seated Man
AADEEMPRR	map-reader
AADEEMRSU	admeasure
AADEEMRTW	medaewart
AADEENSST	sense data
AADEEORTT	toad-eater
AADEEPPRT	parapeted
AADEEPPST	peat-spade
AADEEPRST	estrapade
	paederast
AADEERRTT	retardate
AADEERSTY	Easter Day
AADEESTTV	devastate
AADEFGLNN	fandangle
AADEFGRSU	safeguard
AADEFHILS	had as lief
AADEFHNOR	aforehand
AADEFHNPS	fan-shaped
AADEFILNT	fantailed
AADEFILTT	fat-tailed
AADEFINNR	farandine
AADEFINST	fantasied
AADEFIORS	aforesaid
AADEFIRRT	fair trade
	fair-trade
AADEFJNNO	Jane Fonda
AADEFLNOR	farandole
AADEFLNSW	false dawn
AADEFLORY	yard of ale
AADEFMPRT	after-damp
AADEFMRST	farmstead
AADEFNNRU	Anna Freud
AADEFOSTU	autos-da-fé
AADEFOSWY	Days of Awe
AADEFRRTW	afterward
AADEFSSTT	steadfast
AADEGGLNU	languaged
AADEGGRTU	true dagga
AADEGHNRU	harangued
AADEGHNRY	hydrangea
AADEGHNST	stage hand
AADEGIINU	Iguanidae
AADEGIIRT	dei gratia
AADEGILLR	gaillarde
AADEGILRT	taligrade
AADEGIMNT	diamagnet
AADEGINNR	Grenadian
AADEGINRR	darraigne
AADEGINRT	tragedian
AADEGINTV	vaginated
AADEGIPRS	disparage
AADEGIQRU	quadrigae
AADEGLLOP	gallopade
AADEGLLSS	lead glass
AADEGLNNR	engarland
	rangeland
AADEGLNNT	land agent
AADEGLNRT	tear gland
AADEGLNRV	landgrave
AADEGLNST	standgale
AADEGLNTU	angulated
AADEGLOTV	dataglove
AADEGLRSS	gala-dress
AADEGLRUX	axle-guard
AADEGLRVW	waldgrave
AADEGMNNR	danger man
AADEGMNNU	unmanaged
AADEGMOSV	savagedom
AADEGMSUU	gaudeamus
AADEGNORS	sea dragon
AADEGNORT	road agent
AADEGNRRT	regardant
AADEGORSS	dogaressa
AADEGRRRT	rag-trader
AADEGRRRU	rearguard
AADEGRRSS	as regards
AADEGRRVY	graveyard
AADEGRSTU	date-sugar
AADEHHITV	have had it
AADEHHKNS	handshake
AADEHHRRT	had rather
AADEHHRTW	hard wheat
AADEHILRR	diarrheal
AADEHIMOT	haematoid
AADEHIMPS	Phasmidae
AADEHIMRY	hydraemia
AADEHINNO	anhedonia
AADEHINRS	Adar Sheni
AADEHINRX	Hexandria
AADEHIORR	diarrhoea
AADEHIPRT	apartheid
	hit parade
AADEHIRST	stairhead
AADEHIRZZ	hazardize
AADEHKMST	death mask
AADEHLLLL	hallalled
AADEHLLPU	pull ahead
AADEHLLST	headstall
AADEHLMNN	manhandle
AADEHLMPS	lampshade
AADEHLMRT	hard-metal
AADEHLMSY	ashamedly
AADEHLNNP	panhandle
AADEHLNRT	heartland
AADEHLOPX	hexapodal
AADEHMNOW	head-woman
AADEHMNST	deathsman
AADEHMNSU	unashamed
AADEHMRTT	Mad Hatter
AADEHNNSW	as and when
AADEHNORT	rhodanate
AADEHNPPR	hand-paper
AADEHORRW	arrowhead
AADEHPRST	hard-paste
AADEHPRTT	deathtrap
AADEHRRTW	earthward
AADEHRSTT	death star
	head start
AADEHRSWY	ready-wash
AADEIILMM	Media Mail
AADEIILRS	radialise
AADEIILRZ	radialize
AADEIINRT	dietarian
AADEIIPRT	tepidaria
AADEIIPTU	Tupaiidae
AADEIIRRT	irradiate
AADEIIRTV	radiative
AADEIJNPS	jaspidean
AADEIKNRS	sneak-raid
AADEILLPT	dial-plate
AADEILLRT	arillated
	lardalite
AADEILMNN	almandine
AADEILMNR	Alderamin
AADEILMNS	ladies' man
AADEILMNT	laminated
AADEILMRT	diametral
AADEILNNN	annelidan
AADEILNNR	Adrenalin®
	adrenalin
AADEILNNS	Inland Sea
AADEILNPT	lead-paint
AADEILNSS	sea-island
AADEILNST	tanalised
AADEILNSV	vandalise
AADEILNTZ	tanalized
AADEILNVZ	vandalize
AADEILPPR	laid paper
AADEILPRR	perradial
AADEILPRU	praeludia
AADEILPRY	Pyralidae
AADEILPSS	palisades
AADEILPST	stapedial
AADEILRSY	daysailer
AADEILRTT	rat-tailed
AADEILRTV	travailed
AADEILRTY	radiately
AADEILTUV	laudative
AADEILTVW	tidal wave
AADEIMMNO	demomania
AADEIMMNR	Dramamine®
AADEIMMSS	mass media
AADEIMNNP	pandemian
AADEIMNNR	mandarine
	meandrian

AADEIMNSW	Adam's wine
AADEIMRRR	ram-raider
AADEIMRSS	Midas's ear
AADEIMRST	dramatise
AADEIMRTZ	dramatize
AADEINPTT	patinated
AADEINRST	steradian
AADEINRTT	antitrade
	attainder
AADEIOPTU	audiotape
AADEIORVW	radio wave
AADEIPPRS	disappear
AADEIPRST	disparate
AADEIPRTY	paediatry
AADEJRUVY	Yajurveda
AADEKKLRR	Karl Radek
AADEKMORR	road maker
AADEKMRRT	trade mark
	trademark
AADEKMRTY	market-day
AADEKNNSS	sand-snake
AADEKNNYY	Danny Kaye
AADELLMNR	mallander
AADELLMPY	medal play
	medalplay
AADELLMRY	alarmedly
AADELLNNO	one and all
AADELLNNP	land-plane
AADELLNPR	Laplander
AADELLNTU	landaulet
AADELLNUV	land-value
AADELLNUY	unallayed
AADELLQRU	quadrella
AADELMMOR	melodrama
AADELMNOR	ealdorman
AADELMNRS	malanders
AADELMORT	road metal
AADELMORV	ad valorem
AADELMPSU	Lampedusa
AADELNNTU	annulated
AADELNQUY	Dan Quayle
AADELNRRU	Laura Dern
	rural dean
AADELNRSU	Ausländer
AADELNSTW	wasteland
AADELPPRU	applauder
AADELPRST	lat spread
AADELPRTW	draw-plate
AADELRRSS	ressaldar
AADELRSTT	trade-last
AADELRSWY	seawardly
AADELRSYY	early days
AADELRTTY	latter-day
AADEMMNOR	memoranda
AADEMMNOW	made woman
AADEMMRST	Amsterdam
AADEMNOOR	enamorado
AADEMNOPT	tamponade
AADEMNPRS	ampersand
AADEMNPRZ	amperzand
AADEMNPSS	spadesman
AADEMNRST	tradesman
AADEMOQRU	aquadrome
AADEMORTT	Trematoda
AADEMOTTU	automated
AADEMPRSS	pas d'armes
AADEMPSTT	date-stamp
AADEMRRTU	dura mater
AADEMSTTU	State Duma
AADENNPPT	appendant
AADENNRST	Santander
AADENNTTT	attendant
AADENPPRS	sandpaper
AADENPRTU	pandurate
AADENRRTT	retardant
AADENRRTW	warranted
AADENRSST	sea strand
AADENRSTT	Ständerat
AADENRWWY	way warden
AADENSSTY	stand easy
AADENSSUY	unassayed
AADEOPRRS	paradores
AADEOPRRX	paradoxer
AADEOPRST	tapaderos
AADEOPSSS	passadoes
AADEORSTW	soda water
AADERRSVY	adversary✧
AADERSSTW	eastwards
AADERSTTU	saturated
AADERSTWW	war-wasted
AADFFHNST	handstaff
AADFFIITV	affidavit
AADFGNNOS	fandangos
AADFGNORR	Fragonard
AADFHHLRY	half-hardy
AADFHILNT	lift a hand
AADFIILNN	Finlandia
AADFILNRY	fairyland✧
AADFIMNRY	Man Friday
AADFIMRRY	dairy farm
AADFINNSS	ifs and ans
AADFKLLNS	Falklands
AADFLLUWY	lawful day
AADFMNRST	draftsman
AADFMNRSU	fraudsman
AADFNRRST	transfard
AADFNSSTT	stand fast
AADGGHIST	Haggadist
AADGGHLRY	haggardly
AADGGIINR	Diana Rigg
AADGGINNR	randan gig
AADGGLLRY	laggardly
AADGGLNOR	galdragon
AADGHHINS	shanghai'd
AADGHIJRR	jaghirdar
AADGHILNP	phalangid
AADGHILRS	harigalds
AADGHIMPR	diaphragm
AADGHINRT	Adi-Granth
AADGHIOPR	pariah dog
AADGHIPSY	dysphagia
AADGHIRRU	guard hair
AADGHLNSS	hand glass
AADGHNNOR	hand organ
AADGHRRSS	hardgrass
AADGILMNY	amygdalin
AADGILNOR	girandola
AADGILORT	gladiator✧
AADGILRRU	guardrail
AADGIMMMR	mridamgam
AADGIMMNO	gammadion
AADGIMMNR	mridangam
AADGIMNRU	marauding
AADGIMNRV	raving mad
AADGIMORR	radiogram
AADGIMORU	audiogram
AADGIMRRS	Mardi Gras
AADGINNRS	sand grain
AADGINORT	gradation
	indagator
AADGINRWY	grind away
AADGJPRUU	Durga-puja
AADGLLNRU	glandular
AADGLLNSY	Sandy Gall
AADGLLOPR	dollar gap
AADGLLRUY	gradually
AADGLLRWY	wallydrag
AADGLMNRS	grand slam
AADGLMSUY	Amygdalus
AADGLNNRT	land grant
AADGLNOOW	wagonload
AADGLNRRY	garlandry
AADGLNRSS	grassland
AADGLNSSS	sandglass
AADGMNORS	dragomans
AADGMNRSU	guardsman
AADGMRRTU	dramaturg
AADGNNRTU	grand-aunt
AADGNRSSS	sand grass
AADGNRSUV	guard's van
AADGORRTU	graduator
AADGORRTY	gradatory
AADGORSST	toadgrass
AADHHINRS	Nadir Shah
AADHHMNUW	hum and haw
AADHILLSS	allis shad
AADHILRST	tahsildar
AADHIMMST	Adam Smith
AADHIMOPP	Amphipoda
AADHINNNY	in any hand
AADHINNOT	danthonia
AADHINOTT	thanatoid
AADHINPSU	Upanishad
AADHIPSSY	dysphasia
AADHJMNOS	John Adams
AADHKLNRS	land-shark
AADHKMNTU	Kathmandu
AADHKNRTU	Hardaknut
AADHLLMNS	small-hand
AADHLLNST	hallstand
AADHLMNRS	marshland
AADHNSSTW	washstand
AADHORRSU	hadrosaur

AADHORSUZ hazardous
AADHPRRST hardparts
AADIIKLNU Niki Lauda
AADIIKLRY kailyaird
AADIILLMY Daily Mail
AADIILMNV Maldivian
AADIILRRT triradial
AADIILRTY radiality
AADIILSUV visual aid
AADIIMMOT ommatidia
AADIIMMST Adamitism
AADIIMNNO dinomania
AADIIMNRY dimyarian
AADIIMNRZ zamindari
AADIIMPTU Itaipu Dam
AADIINNNT Dinantian
AADIINNRS Sardinian
AADIINNRW Darwinian
Indian War
AADIINORT radiation
AADIINPRY pray in aid
AADIINRRT irradiant
Triandria
AADIIORTU auditoria
AADIISSST diastasis
AADIJNNOR Jordanian
AADIKLORT talk radio
AADILLMOR armadillo
AADILLMOY amyloidal
AADILLMPS Aldis lamp
AADILLMPU palladium✧
AADILLMRY amaryllid
AADILLMSW Will Adams
AADILLNNS land snail
AADILLNOT allantoid
AADILLNPU paludinal
AADILLOPS sapodilla
AADILLSSU Ladislaus
AADILMNNO adnominal
AADILMNOR Maoriland
AADILMNSU sudaminal
AADILMNSV vandalism
AADILMNTU Tamil Nadu
AADILMOPS plasmodia
AADILMORT maladroit
AADILMOST mastoidal
AADILMPRY pyramidal
AADILMPST lampadist
AADILNNOT antinodal
Daltonian
AADILNNPR plain-darn
AADILNOPT antipodal✧
AADILNOTT antidotal
AADILNOTU adulation
laudation
AADILNRTY radiantly
AADILNSWZ Swaziland
AADILORSY daysailor
AADILORTT dilatator
AADILOSVW disavowal
AADILPSSY dysplasia
AADILRSTY Daily Star
AADIMNNOR Dan Marino
Monandria
AADIMNNOT damnation
AADIMNOTV Vaiont Dam
AADIMNQSU damasquin
AADIMNRYZ zamindary
AADIMNSUV avisandum
AADIMNUVZ avizandum
AADIMOPRY Myriapoda
AADIMORSS madarosis
AADIMQRSU maquisard✧
AADIMRSTT dramatist
AADINNNOT andantino
AADINNOPT pandation
AADINNORS sardonian
AADINNORY Indo-Aryan
AADINOORT adoration
AADINORRT road train
AADINORSS Diana Ross
AADINPRRT drain-trap
AADINPSSS spadassin
AADINSSTY saint's day
AADINSTTX taxi stand
AADIORRST radio star
AADIORRTY radiatory
AADIPRSXY dyspraxia
AADIPSSUY ups-a-daisy
AADIRSWXY Six-Day War
AADISSTUY tayassuid
AADKLNPRS parklands
AADKLORSV volksraad✧
AADKLPSUU Paul Dukas
AADKLRWWY awkwardly
AADKPRRSW parkwards
AADLLLMSY small lady
AADLLNOOY lay on load
AADLLOPSU palladous
AADLLSWWY Wladyslaw
AADLMMPSU plumdamas
AADLMNPSW swampland
AADLMOORV Almodovar
AADLMPSUY mal du pays
AADLOORRY royal road
AADLORTUY adulatory
laudatory
AADLRWWYY waywardly
AADMMNOOR monodrama
AADMMNOTT Matt Damon
AADMNNOSS sand mason
AADMNORTY damnatory
mandatory
AADMNOSTY Tony Adams
AADMNQRUU quadruman
AADNNORSU anandrous
AADNOOPSW sapanwood
AADNOORRS Aaron's rod
AADNORTWY Tony Award
AADOOPPRU Pauropoda
AADOPPRST strappado
AADQRSTUU quadratus
AADRSSTUY Saturdays
AAEEEKLTV take leave
take-leave
AAEEELMPS pease-meal
AAEEELSTV tea leaves
AAEEEMRTT meat-eater
AAEEFFLLM flame-leaf
AAEEFGMRT aftergame
AAEEFGRST fare stage
AAEEFHNRT fan heater
AAEEFHNSV safe haven
AAEEFHRTT afterheat
AAEEFINNS feiseanna
AAEEFKMRT make after
AAEEFKRTT take after
AAEEFLLMP maple leaf✧
AAEEFLLMT leaf-metal
AAEEFLOTV faveolate
AAEEFLRSW self-aware
AAEEFLRTW water flea
water leaf
AAEEFMNRT name after
AAEEGGGRT aggregate
AAEEGGLLN galengale
AAEEGGMMS Sam Gamgee
AAEEGGRTW water gage
AAEEGHKLS shake a leg
AAEEGHKLW eagle-hawk
AAEEGHRST gas heater
AAEEGIJMR jigamaree
AAEEGILMR real image
AAEEGILNR generalia
AAEEGILTV laevigate
AAEEGIMNR Gramineae
AAEEGINRT Reaganite
AAEEGINTV evaginate
AAEEGIRTV variegate
AAEEGIRTW waiterage
AAEEGKLNO Lake Onega
AAEEGLLRY legal year
AAEEGLMNP panel game
AAEEGLMNT mental age
AAEEGLNST sea tangle
AAEEGLNSU Elaeagnus
AAEEGLPPS sage apple
AAEEGLPRV pea gravel
AAEEGLRST great seal✧
AAEEGLRSW real wages
AAEEGLRVV valve gear
AAEEGLRVY averagely
AAEEGLSVW wage slave
AAEEGLTVV gate valve
AAEEGMMNX Gammexane®
AAEEGMNNR enneagram
AAEEGMNNS manganese
AAEEGMNOP Agapemone
AAEEGMNST stage name
AAEEGMRRV Mr Average
AAEEGNORS sea orange
AAEEGNORV on average
AAEEGNPRT parentage

AAEEGNRRR rearrange
AAEEGNRRS sea ranger
AAEEGNRRT ergataner
AAEEGNRTT gnateater
AAEEGNRTU guarantee
AAEEGPRSS repassage
sea grapes
AAEEGPRSU gaspereau
AAEEGRRTY great year
AAEEGRTTW Watergate
water gate
AAEEGSTTW waste gate
AAEEHIKKT take a hike
AAEEHIMTT haematite
AAEEHIRTT eat the air
AAEEHISST aesthesia
AAEEHKLOT Lake Tahoe
AAEEHKMRS rakeshame
AAEEHKMST make haste
AAEEHKNNT Akhenaten
AAEEHKPST take shape
AAEEHKRTT take heart
AAEEHLMNY hymenaeal
AAEEHLMTW wheatmeal
AAEEHLRRS rehearsal
AAEEHMNNT enanthema
AAEEHMNNY hymenaean
AAEEHMNTT hetmanate
AAEEHMNTU Athenaeum
AAEEHMNTX exanthema
AAEEHMPST metaphase
AAEEHNRST hare-stane
AAEEHNSTU euthanase
AAEEHPPST shape tape
AAEEHPSVW waveshape
AAEEHRRRT rare earth
AAEEHRRSW shareware
AAEEHRSTT seat earth
AAEEHRSWY sheer away
AAEEHRTWY thereaway
AAEEHRWWY where away?
AAEEIJLNS Jean Alesi
AAEEIKLMU leukaemia
AAEEILLMN El Alamein
AAEEILLRV lavaliere
AAEEILLST ill at ease
AAEEILLTV alleviate
AAEEILMNS Melanesia
AAEEILMPP mealie pap
AAEEILNTV aventaile
AAEEILRTT aliterate
retaliate
AAEEIMNRT reanimate
AAEEIMNTV emanative
AAEEIMNTX examinate
exanimate
AAEEINRST arseniate
AAEEINSTW Taiwanese
AAEEIPPRS appraisee
AAEEIPTTX expatiate
AAEEIRRRV River Aare

AAEEISTTV aestivate
AAEEJLMSX Alex James
AAEEJNPSS Japaneses
AAEEKLNNP palankeen
AAEEKMMOV make a move
AAEEKMRTW make water
AAEEKMSVW make waves
AAEEKNPTW wapentake
AAEEKPRRT parrakeet
AAEEKPSSY speakeasy
AAEELLLMT lamellate
AAEELLLTT tell a tale
AAEELLMNS sallee-man
AAEELLNRW wellanear
AAEELLOTV alveolate
AAEELLPPT appellate
AAEELLPTT patellate
AAEELLQRU aquarelle
AAEELLRST all-seater
AAEELMNPS pleaseman
AAEELMNPT nameplate
AAEELMPTT meat plate
AAEELMRTW metalware
AAEELMSST matelasse
matelassé
AAEELMSTT stalemate
AAEELNOPR aeroplane
AAEELNRTT alternate
AAEELNRTV ervalenta
revalenta
AAEELOPPU à la poupée
AAEELPPRR reapparel
AAEELPPSX sex appeal
AAEELPRRV palaverer
AAEELPRST lapse rate
AAEELPSTV Laptev Sea
AAEELRSST sea slater
AAEELRSTW water seal
AAEELRSWY sea lawyer
AAEELRTTZ lazarette
AAEELRTUV revaluate
AAEELRTUY aureately
AAEEMMNNS name names
AAEEMMNTZ amazement
AAEEMMPTZ temazepam✧
AAEEMNNSS anamneses
AAEEMPRRT parameter
AAEEMPSTT meat paste
AAEEMRRRT terramare
AAEEMRSTT masterate
AAEEMRTTX taxameter
AAEENNPRY Pyrenaean
AAEENRRTW warrantee
AAEENRSSW awareness
AAEENTTTU attenuate
AAEEOPRTV evaporate
AAEEPPPRT paper tape
AAEEPPRRW paperware
AAEEPRRTY ratepayer
AAEEPRSST separates
AAEEPSSYY easy-peasy

AAEEPSTTU put at ease
AAEERRTTW water rate
AAEERSSTY sea satyre
AAEERSTTT tea taster
AAEERTVWW water wave
water-wave
AAEFFGLNO Fongafale
AAEFFHLMR half-frame
AAEFFIILT affiliate
AAEFFILRS Rafflesia
AAEFFINPR paraffine
AAEFFINRT raffinate
AAEFFLNUZ affluenza
AAEFGHLNT hang a left
AAEFGHMNR Fermanagh
AAEFGILTT flagitate
AAEFGINRS seafaring
AAEFGIRSX saxifrage
AAEFGLMOR megaflora
AAEFGLRTW water flag
AAEFGLRVW flag-waver
AAEFGMORU au fromage
AAEFGORRS farragoes
AAEFHIKLT khalifate
AAEFHKRRT hark after
AAEFHLLPT half-plate
AAEFHLLRT All-father
earthfall
AAEFHLPRT flare path
AAEFHLRST flatshare
AAEFHLRTX earthflax
AAEFHMRTT aftermath
hamfatter
AAEFHMSST shamefast
AAEFHRSTT earthfast
AAEFIINST Fantaisie
AAEFIKNNR Frankenia
AAEFIKNRR Afrikaner
AAEFIKPRS speak fair
AAEFILMRR fire alarm
AAEFILNNR Falernian
AAEFILNPU epifaunal
AAEFILNTX antefixal
AAEFILPTT palafitte
AAEFILRTY fairy tale
fairytale
AAEFIMMNR mainframe
AAEFIMNOU meiofauna
AAEFINNRS safranine
AAEFINSST fantasise
AAEFINSTZ fantasize
AAEFINTTU infatuate
AAEFJLLNW jaw-fallen
AAEFKLLST leaf-stalk
AAEFKMSSU make a fuss
AAEFKNNNR Anne Frank
AAEFLLLRY fallalery
AAEFLLPSY play false
AAEFLLRTW waterfall
AAEFLLSTU at full sea
AAEFLNRRT fraternal

AAEFLORTU autoflare
AAEFLORTZ Fortaleza
AAEFLRRST flare star
AAEFLSSTU sulfatase
AAEFMNSTY safetyman
AAEFMRRTX tax farmer
AAEFNQSTU fantasque
AAEFOOSVZ Sea of Azov
AAEFPRRTT Pat Rafter
AAEGGILLN galingale
AAEGGILNT gangliate
AAEGGILNW Galwegian
AAEGGILRV gilravage
AAEGGIMMY Maggie May
AAEGGINNT gigantean
AAEGGINOR Georgiana
AAEGGINRR gregarian
Gregarina
AAEGGINRU rain gauge
AAEGGIRRS gargarise
AAEGGIRRZ gargarize
AAEGGIRST garagiste
AAEGGLLNO gallonage
AAEGGLNSU slanguage
AAEGGMMSU a mug's game
AAEGGMSSU megagauss
AAEGGOPRU paragogue
AAEGHIILM hemialgia
AAEGHILNR angel hair
AAEGHILRT Thargelia
AAEGHIMSS mishegaas
AAEGHINXY Hexagynia
AAEGHLLPY hypallage
AAEGHLNOR hare along
AAEGHLNOX hexagonal
AAEGHLNPR phalanger
AAEGHLNPS phalanges
AAEGHLOPY hypogaeal
AAEGHLPRT tragelaph
AAEGHLRTW waghalter
AAEGHMNOP phaenogam
AAEGHMSSU meshugaas
AAEGHNOPR orphanage
AAEGHNOPY hypogaean
AAEGHNRRU haranguer
AAEGHOPRR aerograph
AAEGHOPRY aerophagy
AAEGHORRT Harrogate
AAEGHRTWY gather way
AAEGIILMO oligaemia
AAEGIILNT genitalia
AAEGIILQU aquilegia
AAEGIITTV agitative
AAEGIKNNW awakening
AAEGILLNT allegiant
AAEGILLNV villanage
AAEGILMRR armigeral
AAEGILNNN annealing
AAEGILNNT galantine
AAEGILNOS analogise
AAEGILNOZ analogize

AAEGILNPP appealing
lagniappe
AAEGILNPS Pelasgian
AAEGILNRU neuralgia
AAEGILNSV galvanise
AAEGILNUV vaginulae
AAEGILNVZ galvanize
AAEGILRST agrestial
AAEGILRSU Aula Regis
AAEGILRTT tailgater
AAEGIMMNS mismanage
AAEGIMNNS magnesian
AAEGIMNNT man-eating
manganite
AAEGIMNOR ergomania
AAEGIMNQZ Q Magazine
AAEGIMNRR margarine
AAEGIMNRS Reaganism
sea margin
AAEGIMNRT marginate
AAEGIMRRT margarite
AAEGIMRSY Magyarise
AAEGIMRYZ Magyarize
AAEGINNRT Argentina
tanagrine
AAEGINNRW Wagnerian
AAEGINORT aragonite
AAEGINORV over again
AAEGINOTV evagation
AAEGINPPS appeasing
AAEGINPTY Aegyptian
AAEGINPTZ Gaziantep
AAEGINRRR arraigner
AAEGINRRT gear train
AAEGINRSU guaranies
AAEGINRSY asynergia
gainsayer
AAEGINRTT gratinate
AAEGINRTU ruin agate
AAEGIORRT gear ratio
AAEGIPRST pargasite
AAEGIRTTV gravitate
AAEGISTTT sagittate
AAEGJLNSS Jena glass
AAEGKNOSS Agnes Oaks
AAEGKRRSS grass-rake
AAEGLLNOV longaeval
AAEGLLNRY laryngeal
AAEGLLRTW Great Wall
water gall
AAEGLLSTZ salt glaze
AAEGLMNSS Amen glass
AAEGLMNST gas mantle
AAEGLMORT gremolata
AAEGLMPSY play games
AAEGLMTTU glutamate
AAEGLNOPU a plague on
AAEGLNOSV saga novel
AAEGLNRTU granulate
AAEGLOPRS pearl-sago
AAEGLPRRY pearl-gray

AAEGLPRSV palsgrave
AAEGLPRVY pay gravel
AAEGLPSTY stage play
AAEGLRRUV Vulgar era
AAEGLRSSW glassware
AAEGLRSTY slate-gray
AAEGLRTTU gratulate
AAEGMMNNO Agamemnon
AAEGMMNOR anemogram
AAEGMNNOR Orangeman
AAEGMNNPR Pan-German
AAEGMNOPT tamponage
AAEGMNORT matronage
AAEGMNOTW meat wagon
AAEGMNPRT pentagram
AAEGMNPSU sagapenum
AAEGMNRTT target man
termagant
AAEGMOSST moss agate
AAEGMPRST strap-game
AAEGMRRTT tetragram✧
AAEGMRSTT stratagem
AAEGMRSTU gastraeum
AAEGNNOOT Notogaean
AAEGNOPRS parsonage
AAEGNOPRT patronage
AAEGNPRTY pageantry
AAEGNRSTV Stavanger
AAEGNRTTU great-aunt
AAEGOPPRT propagate
AAEGOPRSU Areopagus
AAEGPRSST tape grass
AAEGPRSTT Apgar test
AAEGPRSTU pasturage
AAEGRRSTZ stargazer
AAEHHIMNN Minnehaha
AAEHHIMTV have-at-him
AAEHHINPZ Zephaniah
AAEHHLNOT halothane
AAEHHLPTT phthalate
AAEHHOPTW what a hope
AAEHHOSTV have a shot
AAEHHRTTX hearth-tax
AAEHIKNRT Katharine
AAEHIKNSZ Ashkenazi
AAEHILLLU alleluiah
AAEHILLNN Annie Hall
AAEHILMMS hamamelis✧
AAEHILMNR harmaline
AAEHILNNT Nathaniel
AAEHILNTV leviathan✧
AAEHILORT hariolate
AAEHILRST hare's-tail
AAEHILRTW heir-at-law
AAEHILWWY while away
AAEHIMMNR Mariehamn
AAEHIMNOT theomania
AAEHIMNOV haoma vine
AAEHIMNPS Emin Pasha
AAEHIMRST ashramite
AAEHINPRT panta rhei

AAEHINPSY synapheia
AAEHIPRRS parrhesia
AAEHIPRSU euphrasia
AAEHIPSUU Euphausia
AAEHIRRVW hair-waver
AAEHIRSTW Artie Shaw
AAEHJNNNO Johannean
AAEHKLNRS ranshakle
AAEHKMRRS Marrakesh
AAEHKMRSY haymakers
AAEHKNOSW oakenshaw
AAEHKNSYZ Ashkenazy
AAEHLLMSU alum-shale
AAEHLLPUY Up-Helly-Aa
AAEHLLSTU haustella
AAEHLLTWY all the way
AAEHLMMNO namma hole
AAEHLMNOY hyalonema
AAEHLMSTU steam-haul
AAEHLNPPT pentalpha
AAEHLNPSX phalanxes
AAEHLNSTT Athelstan
AAEHLOPPR phalarope
AAEHLOTTT total heat
AAEHLPRST asphalter
AAEHLPSTT alpha test
alphatest
AAEHLTTWX wealth tax
AAEHMMMNR hammerman
AAEHMNOSU A E Housman
AAEHMNPRS phraseman
AAEHMNRSS sharesman
AAEHMNRSW washerman
AAEHMNTTU Nahum Tate
AAEHMOPST hepatomas
AAEHMORST atheromas
AAEHMOSTT haemostat
AAEHMPRRY pararhyme
AAEHMRSTU shamateur
AAEHNNTUY Netanyahu
AAEHNOOPT haanepoot
AAEHNPSST pheasants
AAEHNPSWW wapenshaw
AAEHNRRTX Xenarthra
AAEHNRSTT attrahens
AAEHNRTTT attrahent
AAEHNSSTY sea shanty
AAEHNSTUY euthanasy
AAEHPPRTY parhypate
AAEHPRSVY heavy spar
AAEHRRSTT earth-star
AAEIIKNRT air-intake
AAEIILMNS animalise
AAEIILMNZ animalize
AAEIILMRT marialite
AAEIILNRT inter alia
AAEIILNRZ alizarine
AAEIILNST Salientia
AAEIILPTX epitaxial
AAEIILRST aerialist
AAEIILRTY aeriality
AAEIIMNNT inanimate
AAEIIMNRS semi-Arian
AAEIIMRST artemisia✧
AAEIINNOS Ionian Sea
AAEIINNPR Napierian
AAEIINNRT Aretinian
AAEIINSST taeniasis
AAEIINSTT insatiate
AAEIIRTVV variative
AAEIJLNNP plain Jane
plain-Jane
AAEIJNNST satin jean
AAEIJRRSY Sir A J Ayer
AAEIKKRST take a risk
AAEIKKRTY Kartikeya
AAEIKLLRZ lazar-like
AAEIKLMRS sailmaker
AAEIKLMTU Mt Kilauea
AAEIKLTTV talkative
AAEIKMNRR rainmaker
AAEIKMNTX Max Aitken
AAEIKMSST take amiss
AAEIKNPRT partake in
AAEIKNPST take pains
AAEIKNRSU Euskarian
AAEIKPRRY perikarya
AAEIKRSTT karateist
AAEILLMMM mammillae
AAEILLMMT mamillate
AAEILLMNP mail-plane
AAEILLMNT alimental
AAEILLNPS sailplane
AAEILLNPT tailplane
AAEILLNTT Late Latin
AAEILLNTV élan vital
AAEILLPPT papillate
AAEILLPRR arpillera
AAEILLPRT plate rail
prelatial
AAEILLPSS paillasse
palliasse
AAEILLRTV relatival
AAEILMMNO melomania
AAEILMMST melismata
AAEILMNNP main plane
AAEILMNRU melanuria
AAEILMNSS Messalina
AAEILMNST stamineal
AAEILMNTU aluminate
AAEILMOPR paroemial
AAEILMPRV primaeval
verapamil
AAEILMPTT palmitate
AAEILMRST mare's-tail
materials
AAEILMRTU tularemia
AAEILNNSU annualise
AAEILNNUZ annualize
AAEILNOPS neoplasia
AAEILNORT alienator
rationale
AAEILNPRT perinatal
AAEILNSSS Salesians
AAEILNSTT tantalise
AAEILNTTT tantalite
AAEILNTTZ tantalize
AAEILORTV variolate
AAEILPPTT palpitate
AAEILPRST psalteria
AAEILPRTZ trapezial
AAEILRRTW trialware
water rail
AAEILRRVV Vaal River
AAEILRSSW wassailer
AAEILRSTU estuarial
AAEILRSTW altarwise
water sail
AAEIMMRRS marmarise
AAEIMMRRZ marmarize
AAEIMNNNR in a manner
AAEIMNNOO oenomania
AAEIMNNOT emanation
AAEIMNNOX xenomania
AAEIMNNSS anamnesis
AAEIMNNTX examinant
AAEIMNOST anatomise
AAEIMNOTZ amazonite
anatomize
AAEIMNPRR repairman
AAEIMNRTW water main
AAEIMNSTT emanatist
staminate
AAEIMORST aromatise
AAEIMORTZ aromatize
AAEIMPRRS spermaria
AAEIMPRRV primavera✧
AAEIMPRST spermatia
AAEIMRRST airstream
AAEIMRRTZ terza rima
AAEINNORT arenation
AAEINNRSW raw sienna
AAEINORRT aerotrain
AAEINORTX exaration
AAEINPPRT appertain
AAEINPRST septarian
AAEINPRTU input area
AAEINPSSV Vespasian
AAEINQTTU antiquate
AAEINRRRS in arrears
AAEINRRTV narrative
AAEINRRTW rainwater
AAEINRSST star anise
star-anise
AAEINRSTU estuarian
AAEINRSTZ St-Nazaire
AAEINRTVW wave train
AAEINSTTT satinetta
AAEINSTTU unsatiate
AAEIORSTX aerotaxis
AAEIPPRRS appraiser
AAEIPSSTV passivate
AAEIRRRSV River Saar

AAEIRRSTT tartarise
AAEIRRTTZ tartarize
AAEIRSSTV aviatress
AAEIRTWWY write away
AAEISSSUV assuasive
AAEISTTTW wait state
AAEJKLRWY jaywalker
AAEJMNOST jasmonate
AAEJMORTT état-major
AAEJMSTTW James Watt
AAEJNOPTU Jean Patou
AAEJPPRWW wapper-jaw
AAEJRTTTU jettatura
AAEKKPRST skatepark
AAEKKTYYY yakety-yak
AAEKLLOTV Lake Volta
AAEKLLSST sales talk
AAEKLMPRT platemark
AAEKLMPRY playmaker
AAEKLOPST Lake Patos
AAEKLOPTU Lake Taupo
AAEKLPRST lapstrake
lapstreak
AAEKMMNRT market-man
AAEKMMORR make or mar
AAEKMQRSU marsquake
AAEKMRRTW watermark
AAEKMRSTY staymaker
AAEKNNRTU nunataker
AAEKNORRW Korean War
AAEKNPRST Pasternak
AAEKNRTTU take a turn
AAEKORSTT at a stroke
AAELLLMOR malleolar
AAELLLNRY allenarly
AAELLLPTW wall plate
AAELLLRTY laterally
AAELLMNTT maltalent
AAELLMNTY allayment
AAELLMPTY palmately
AAELLMQSU squamella
AAELLMRST smell a rat
AAELLMSTU alum-slate
AAELLMSWY may as well
AAELLNPPT appellant
AAELLNPSW penal laws
AAELLNSTT neat-stall
AAELLOPRW wall a rope
AAELLPPRW wallpaper
AAELLPRTT tell apart
AAELLQRSU all square
AAELLSUXY asexually
AAELMMNOS melanomas
AAELMMORR marmoreal
AAELMMOTY myelomata
AAELMMOTZ matzo meal
AAELMMPST metaplasm
AAELMMRST Martlemas
AAELMNNRY nearly man
AAELMNNRZ ranzelman
AAELMNOSS sea salmon
AAELMNOSU mausolean
AAELMNRSY man-slayer
AAELMOPPR palampore
AAELMOPRT atemporal
AAELMOPRZ lorazepam
AAELNNOPT pantaleon
AAELNNPTU pennatula
AAELNNRTT alternant
AAELNOPRT rotaplane
AAELNORTZ Lanzarote
AAELNORZZ lazzarone
AAELNPPRU unapparel
AAELNPPSS sans-appel
AAELNPRTY planetary
AAELNPSTT pantalets
AAELNPSUX pansexual
AAELNRRUY lunar year
AAELNRSTT translate
AAELNRSTX transaxle
AAELNRTUU au naturel
AAELNSTTU sultanate
AAELNSTTX sextantal
AAELNUUVV Vanua Levu
AAELOOPRT tropaeola
AAELOPPRY propylaea
AAELOPRST pastorale
AAELOPSSU asepalous
AAELOPSTU apetalous
AAELORRSU rearousal
AAELORRSY solar year
AAELORTTZ lazaretto
AAELORTUV evaluator
AAELPPRRS pearl-spar
AAELPPRST star-apple
AAELPPRTT apple-tart
AAELPRRSY paralyser
AAELPRRYZ paralyzer
AAELPSTTU spatulate
AAELRRSTV traversal
AAELRSSTU assaulter
australes
saleratus
AAELRSTTW saltwater
AAELSSSSV vassaless
AAELSSTWY leastways
AAEMMNSST amassment
AAEMMORTT mattamore
AAEMNORST manor-seat
AAEMNORTU neuromata
AAEMNORTY emanatory
AAEMNORTZ Mozartean
AAEMNPRTT apartment
AAEMNPSST passament
AAEMNQRSU Marquesan
AAEMNRRTY arrayment
AAEMNRSST stearsman
AAEMNRSSW wasserman
AAEMNSSTT statesman
AAEMORSTT amarettos
teratomas
AAEMPRRTY prayer mat
AAEMPRSTT steam trap
AAEMPRSTU separatum
AAEMPRSTY paymaster
AAEMRSSTY say-master
AAENNNRST transenna
AAENNNRTY antennary
AAENNPSST en passant
AAENNTTTU attenuant
AAENOPRRT pro re nata
AAENORRTV Terranova
AAENPRSST apartness
AAENPRSTY peasantry
AAENPSSTY synaptase
AAENRRRST Stranraer
AAENRRRTW warranter
AAEOOPPRS soap opera
AAEOOPSTT sea potato
AAEOPRRST sea parrot
separator
AAEOPRRVW vaporware
AAEOPRSTT pastorate
AAEPPPRSW paper wasp
AAEPPRRST spare part
AAEPRSSTW pass water
AAFFFGLST flagstaff
AAFFGNRSU suffragan
AAFFIIRRS fair's fair
AAFFILNOT afflation
AAFFIMNRT affirmant
AAFFINPRY paraffiny
AAFGHLORT half groat
AAFGHLORU for a laugh
AAFGILMNS falangism✧
AAFGILNRS franglais✧
AAFGILNST falangist✧
AAFGINRRW warfaring
AAFGINRWY wayfaring
AAFGIORSS ossifraga
AAFGLLMNO fall among
AAFGLLORT allograft
AAFGLMOSS foam glass
AAFGLORSU loaf sugar
sugarloaf
AAFGORTTU autograft
AAFHHNNUY funny ha-ha
AAFHILNST anti-flash
AAFHLLORY half-royal
AAFHLMOTU Fomalhaut
AAFHLNRSS Frans Hals
AAFHLSTTT that's flat
AAFIIMNNO infomania
AAFIIRRYY airy-fairy
AAFILLNOP Fallopian
plain loaf
AAFILMMNY family man
AAFILMNOR foraminal
AAFILNOTX aflatoxin
AAFILORUW Rauwolfia
AAFIMORRW Mia Farrow
AAFIMORTU fumatoria
AAFINORSS in so far as

Words marked ✧ can also be spelled with one or more capital letters

AAFINRTTU	Tartufian
AAFINSSTT	fantasist
AAFIOTTTU	tout à fait
AAFKLNOTT	float tank
AAFKLNOUU	Nuku'alofa
AAFLLMORS	of all arms
AAFMORRTW	marrowfat
AAFNORRTW	of warrant
AAFNRSTTY	fantastry
AAFORRSTT	for a start
AAFRRTTYY	arty-farty
AAGGHHORS	Sarah Hogg
AAGGIMNOR	angiogram
AAGGIMNPR	rampaging
AAGGIMRRS	gargarism
AAGGINOST	go against
AAGGINSSU	assuaging
AAGGKLNNP	gangplank
AAGGLLLSS	glass-gall
AAGGLNOSY	synagogal
AAGGORSSS	sago grass
AAGHHILRT	high altar
AAGHIILMP	Malpighia
AAGHIJRTU	Gujarathi
AAGHIKMNY	haymaking
AAGHIKMOS	Kagoshima
AAGHIKPRS	skiagraph
AAGHILLLN	halalling
AAGHILNRS	ashlaring
	Shangri-la
AAGHILORS	Haloragis
AAGHIMOOP	omophagia
AAGHIMPRR	marigraph
AAGHINNNY	nannyghai
AAGHINNRU	Hungarian
AAGHINPRS	phansigar
AAGHINRSS	harassing
AAGHIORST	goat's-hair
AAGHIRRSS	hair-grass
AAGHIRTWY	right away
AAGHJNNTU	jugannath✧
AAGHKMRUW	Mark Waugh
AAGHLLOPR	allograph
AAGHLNPRY	pharyngal
AAGHLOPXY	Xylophaga
AAGHNOOPR	angophora
AAGHNOOPZ	zoophagan
AAGHNPRST	strap-hang
AAGHOPRTU	autograph
AAGHOPTUY	autophagy
AAGIIKNNS	Kisangani
AAGIIMMNS	magianism
AAGIIMNNT	animating
AAGIIMNRY	imaginary
AAGIIMRST	Stigmaria
AAGIINOTT	agitation
AAGIINPPR	Agrippina
AAGIINRTT	antitragi
AAGIIRRTU	air guitar
AAGIJLORY	Loya Jirga
AAGIJNNNP	japanning
AAGIKLNNO	Algonkian
AAGIKMRSS	kissagram
AAGIKNPRT	partaking
AAGILLNOZ	gallinazo
AAGILLNPP	appalling
AAGILLNTV	gallivant
AAGILLNVY	vaginally
AAGILLORT	alligator
AAGILLPSW	galliwasp
AAGILMMNU	magnalium
AAGILMNNO	agnominal
AAGILMNNS	signalman
AAGILMNNT	malignant✧
AAGILMNOO	logomania
AAGILMNSV	galvanism
AAGILMNSY	gymnasial
AAGILMNYZ	amazingly
AAGILMOPY	Polygamia
AAGILMORS	sialogram
AAGILMRST	magistral
AAGILNORU	urolagnia
AAGILNOST	analogist
	nostalgia
AAGILNRUU	inaugural
AAGILNRUV	vulgarian
AAGILNSTV	galvanist
AAGILNWYY	waylaying
AAGILQUUY	Guayaquil
AAGILSSTV	Vita glass®
AAGIMMMST	magmatism
AAGIMMNOT	gammation
AAGIMMRSY	Magyarism
AAGIMNOSY	anisogamy
AAGIMNPRS	Grampians
AAGIMNPRT	ptarmigan
AAGIMSSST	massagist
AAGINNRTU	turn again
	turnagain
AAGINNSYY	naysaying
AAGINOPRS	sporangia
AAGINORTV	navigator
AAGINPSTU	up against
AAGINPTXY	tax-paying
AAGINRSTT	giant star
AAGINSTTU	sitatunga
AAGIORSUV	vagarious
AAGIPSSTY	paysagist
AAGIRSTTY	sagittary
AAGKMORRY	karyogram
AAGKMORYY	karyogamy
AAGKNNOTW	tank wagon
AAGKNNRUU	Guru Nanak
AAGKNOORS	kangaroos✧
AAGLLLNTY	gallantly
AAGLLMPSS	lamp-glass
AAGLLNNTU	ungallant
AAGLLNOPY	play along
AAGLLNRSU	slangular
AAGLLNRTY	gallantry
AAGLLNRUY	angularly
AAGLLOPSS	opal glass
AAGLLRSUY	sugarally
AAGLMMMOY	mammalogy
AAGLMNORU	granuloma
AAGLMPRSU	palm sugar
	sugar palm
AAGLNNNOO	nonagonal
AAGLNOOSU	analogous
AAGLNOOUZ	guanazolo
AAGLNRRUY	granulary
AAGLNRTTU	gratulant
AAGLOPSSS	glass soap
AAGMMMMOR	mammogram
AAGMNNOST	mangostan
AAGMNNOSU	manganous
AAGMOOPSU	apogamous
AAGMRSSSU	sargassum
AAGNNNOTY	nanny goat
AAGNNORTU	orang-utan
AAGNNOTUY	agony aunt
AAGNORRTU	guarantor
AAGNORSTU	Angostura
	Argonauts
AAGNOTTUV	avant-goût
AAGNPRSSU	sugar snap
AAGNRUUUY	Uruguayan
AAGOOUWYY	away you go!
AAGOPRSSU	sugar soap
AAGORSSSS	sargassos
AAGPRSTTY	stag party
AAGRRSSST	star grass
AAGRRSSSU	rusa grass
AAHHHOPRT	Haphtorah
AAHHIIMRS	maharishi
AAHHIJPRS	rajahship
AAHHILLLS	shillalah
AAHHILLNS	inshallah
AAHHIMRTY	arhythmia
AAHHJNOOR	John O'Hara
AAHHKMRSW	marsh hawk
AAHHORSTT	Ashtaroth
AAHHSTTTT	that's that
AAHHSTTWW	what's what
AAHIILLNT	Anita Hill
AAHIILNTU	Lithuania
AAHIKMNNR	Imran Khan
AAHIKNORT	Tokharian
AAHIKOPRS	Rakaposhi
AAHIKRSST	katharsis
AAHIKRSTY	Kshatriya
AAHILMNOT	Malathion®
AAHILMTUZ	azimuthal
AAHILNORT	inhalator
AAHILNSTU	ailanthus
AAHILORST	sailor hat
AAHILORTU	authorial
AAHILPSXY	asphyxial
AAHILRWWY	whirl away
AAHIMMNSS	shamanism✧
AAHIMNOPY	hypomania
AAHIMNOST	Thomasina
AAHIMNPST	phantasim

AAHIMNSST shamanist
AAHIMNSTT thanatism
AAHIMNSTU amianthus
AAHIMNTTU thaumatin
AAHIMRRYY hairy Mary
AAHINOORR honoraria
AAHINOPRT parathion
Phanariot
AAHINORRV Harrovian
AAHINPSWW wapinshaw
AAHINPTTY antipathy
AAHINRRTU Arthurian
AAHINSTTT thanatist
AAHIOPPSS apophasis
AAHIORSTU haustoria
AAHIPRRSY hairspray
AAHKKMORS mako shark
AAHKLMORS shoal mark
AAHKLNORS loan shark
AAHKLNOTT talkathon
AAHKLNOTW walkathon
AAHKLRSTT talk trash
AAHKOPRST Kárpathos
AAHLLMOSW Hallowmas
AAHLLOPTY allopathy
AAHLLSTTT Hallstatt
AAHLMNNTU lanthanum
AAHLMPSTU asphaltum
AAHLMRSST salt marsh
AAHLOPRST alphasort
AAHLPPPSY slap-happy
AAHMNNSSU Haussmann
AAHMNNSTY shantyman
AAHMNOSTX xanthomas
AAHMNOUVX vox humana
AAHMNPPRY paranymph
AAHMOPPRR paramorph
AAHMOPRRX Harpo Marx
AAHNNOSTU ananthous
AAHNORTUX Xanthoura
AAHNOTTWY at a why-not
AAHNPPRSY nappy rash
AAHNRSTUY Thysanura
AAHORTWWY throw away
throwaway
AAIIILMNS Ismailian
AAIIILMRT militaria
AAIIILMSY Ismailiya
AAIIKNNNR Ian Rankin
AAIIKNNRU Ukrainian
AAIIKNPST Pakistani
AAIIKPRTT tripitaka✧
AAIILLMNS snail mail
AAIILMMNS animalism
AAIILMNRT mail-train
AAIILMNST animalist
AAIILMNTY animality
AAIILMPRT impartial
primatial
AAIILNNPU Paulinian
AAIILNOSU Louisiana

AAIILNPPZ Lippizana
AAIILNRTV antiviral
AAIILNSTU Lusitania
AAIILOPZZ pizzaiola
AAIILORTV viatorial
AAIILRRRS arris rail
AAIILRUXY auxiliary
AAIIMMNST animatism
AAIIMNNOT animation
AAIIMNRTU Mauritian
AAIIMNRVZ zanamivir
AAIIMORST Timisoara
AAIIMPPRR primipara
AAIINNRTU unitarian✧
AAIINNRTV invariant
AAIINOPRT topiarian
AAIINORTV variation
AAIINOSTT satiation
AAIINPRRU Ripuarian
AAIINPSTT antipasti
AAIINRRTU Ruritania
AAIIQRSTU aquariist
AAIIQRTZZ Tariq Aziz
AAIJMMNNT Jan Timman
AAIJMORSX major axis
AAIJMRSSW swarajism
AAIJNNOST Saint Joan
AAIJNRSSY janissary
AAIJRSSTW swarajist
AAIKKKORW krakowiak
AAIKKTYYY yakity-yak
AAIKLLMRY Rik Mayall
AAIKLLOSS alkalosis
AAIKLLPRV Villa Park
AAIKLMMNS slammakin
AAIKLMNPU nikau palm
AAIKLNNRS Sri Lankan
AAIKLNORW walk on air
AAIKLNOSV Slovakian
AAIKLOSUV souvlakia
AAIKMNRTW Mark Twain
AAIKNNOPT pontianak
AAIKNQRTU antiquark
AAIKRRRST ra-ra skirt
AAIKRSTTU autarkist
AAILLLMUX maxillula
AAILLLNOT lallation
AAILLMMRY mamillary
AAILLMMXY maximally
AAILLMOPP papilloma
AAILLMORT tamarillo
AAILLMRRY armillary
AAILLMRSY amaryllis
AAILLMRTY maritally
martially
AAILLMRXY maxillary
AAILLNOPT Altiplano
AAILLNOST allantois
AAILLNPRU nullipara
AAILLNSST All Saints
AAILLNTVY valiantly

AAILLOPTZ zapotilla
AAILLOPXY polyaxial
AAILLPPRY papillary
AAILLPRTY partially
AAILLPSTY spatially
AAILMMORS amoralism
AAILMNNPS plainsman
AAILMNOPT palmation
AAILMNORS sailor-man
AAILMNORT laminator
AAILMNORW railwoman
AAILMNOST atonalism
AAILMNPRU manipular
AAILMNSST talismans
AAILMNSTT tantalism
AAILMNTTU matutinal
AAILMORST amoralist
AAILMORSU malarious
AAILMORTY amorality
AAILMPRRS spiral arm
AAILMPRSU marsupial
AAILMPRTU multipara
AAILNNOPS Annapolis
AAILNNOPT planation
AAILNNOST santolina
AAILNNOSV Slavonian
AAILNNOTW Waltonian
AAILNNPQU palanquin
AAILNNPRU uniplanar
AAILNOOTV ovational
AAILNOPPT palpation
AAILNOPSS passional
sponsalia
AAILNOPUW paulownia
AAILNOPVV Pavlovian
AAILNORST rationals
AAILNORTT latration
AAILNORZZ lazzaroni
AAILNOSTT atonalist
saltation
stational
AAILNOSTV salvation
AAILNOSXZ zonal axis
AAILNOTTY atonality
AAILNOTUV valuation
AAILNPPST spinal tap
AAILNPPTT palpitant
AAILNPRTU tarpaulin
unpartial
AAILNPSUV V S Naipaul
AAILNPTTY antitypal
AAILNSSTW Stanislaw
AAILOORRT oratorial
AAILOORTZ zoolatria
AAILOPRRT raptorial
AAILOPRRY pair-royal
AAILOPRST pastorali
AAILOPRSX polar axis
AAILORRST sartorial
AAILPPRRU pluripara
AAILPRSSY paralysis

AAILPRTWY parity law
AAILRRRTY tirra-lyra
AAILRSSWY wassailry
AAIMMNNOO monomania
AAIMMNOSY Yanomamis
AAIMMNRST Martinmas
AAIMMORRT Mt Roraima
AAIMMORRY myriorama
AAIMMRSSU Marasmius
AAIMNNORS San Marino
AAIMNNORU Roumanian
AAIMNOOPS opsomania
AAIMNOORT inamorato
AAIMNOPRY pyromania
AAIMNOPTY typomania
AAIMNORTZ Mozartian
AAIMNOSTT anatomist
AAIMNRSTT tarantism
AAIMNRSTX marxisant
AAIMOORRT moratoria
AAIMORRSW Maori Wars
AAIMORSSU amaurosis
AAIMQRSUU aquariums
AAINNNSSY sannyasin
AAINNNTTU annuitant
AAINNORRT narration
AAINNORTT Tarantino
tarnation
AAINNPRSY spin a yarn
AAINNRSTU Saturnian
AAINOORRT oratorian✧
AAINOPSTT antipasto
AAINOPSTU sapi-outan
AAINORRST sartorian
AAINORSSY Yossarian
AAINPRSST satin spar
AAINPSSTT antispast
AAINPSTXY anaptyxis
AAINQRTUY antiquary
AAINSSSTT assistant
AAIOPPRRT apparitor
pro patria
AAIOPQRTU paraquito
AAIOPRRST aspirator
AAIOPRTTV Pavarotti
AAIOPSTTU autopista
AAIORRTTT trattoria
AAIPPRSSU pari passu
AAIPRRSTT rap artist
trap-stair
AAIPRRTTU partitura
AAIPSSTWW wasp waist
AAIPSTWYY pay its way
AAJLOPRTY A J P Taylor
AAJMORRSU Ursa Major
AAJNORRTW Trojan War
AAJOPRRTW parrot-jaw
AAKKMMOOS mako-makos
AAKLLLMST small talk
AAKLNNOTT Alan Knott
AAKNOOSST saskatoon✧
AALLLMMSS small slam
AALLLMOPS alloplasm
AALLMMRSS small arms
AALLMOPRY royal palm
AALLMRSYY Sally Army
AALLNNOPY pollyanna✧
AALLNRTUY naturally
AALLNSTUY Aunt Sally
AALLOPRTY allopatry
AALLORRUY aurorally
AALLORSST solar salt
AALLORSVY Yaroslavl
AALLPPRTU pull apart
AALLPRSTU palustral
plaustral
AALLPRTWY party wall
AALMMNOSW alms-woman
AALMNNPST plantsman
AALMNOOSU anomalous
AALMNOPRT patrolman
AALMNOPTU Pulmonata
AALMNOTTU Mount Taal
AALMNPRTY rampantly
AALMOOSTU autosomal
AALMOQSSU squamosal
AALMORSTY royal mast
AALMORTYY mayoralty
AALNNNORY Nolan Ryan
AALNNOOPT pantaloon✧
AALNNOTUV anovulant
AALNNRTUU lunarnaut
unnatural
AALNOOPZZ pozzolana
AALNOPRTT Port Natal
AALNOPSST postnasal
AALNOPSTT postnatal
AALNOPUZZ puzzolana
AALNOSTTU tantalous
AALNPRTWY lawn party
AALNSSTWY slantways
AALNSSUYZ lazy Susan
AALOPRRST polar star
AALOPRRTY portrayal
AALORSSVV valvassor
AALORSTTY saltatory
AALORSTVY salvatory
AALORTTUY autolatry
AALPRSTYY satyr play
AALRSSTTW last straw
AAMMNNOWX Manxwoman
AAMMNOOSY Yanomamos
AAMNNOTUY any amount
AAMNNOTWX montan wax
AAMNNPRTY pantryman
AAMNOORSW oarswoman
AAMNOOTTU automaton
AAMNOPRTU paramount
AAMNOPSSW mason wasp
AAMNORSTZ stramazon
AAMNQRRUY quarryman
AAMNQRTUY Mary Quant
AAMOPRTTU amputator
AANNOORTT annotator
AANNORSTT stannator
AANOOPVZZ pavonazzo
AANORRRTW warrantor
AANORRRTY narratory
AANORRTWY Norway rat
AANORSTTU astronaut
AANPRSSSU Parnassus
AAOORRTTV Rotavator®
rotavator
AAOPRRSTY raspatory
AAOPRSTWY sport away
AAORRSTTU saturator
AAPQRRSUY quarry-sap
AARRSSTTW swart star
ABBBCELLU clubbable
ABBBCELRU bubble car
ABBBCFLOY bobby calf
ABBBDOTTU Bud Abbott
ABBBEHLOT bobble hat
ABBBEILRU air-bubble
ABBBELSUY baby blues
ABBBEMNOO Bob Beamon
ABBBGGUYY Baby Buggy®
ABBBIRTTY Babbittry
ABBBNOSUY baby bonus
ABBCCEHKN back-bench
ABBCCKKLO back-block
ABBCCKKLU blackbuck
ABBCDEKNO backboned
ABBCDEKOW bow-backed
ABBCDELRY crabbedly
ABBCDIKLR blackbird
ABBCDKLOY black body
ABBCDKORU buckboard
ABBCDLOOY clabby-doo
ABBCEEKLR black beer
ABBCEELNU Benbecula
ABBCEIKLL black bile
ABBCEIKRT backbiter
ABBCEILLM climbable
ABBCEILRS scribable
ABBCEILRU Cuba libre
ABBCEIRST crabbiest
ABBCEKLLT black belt
ABBCEKLLU blue-black
ABBCEKLNO bone-black
ABBCEKLUY Lubeck Bay
ABBCELRRS scrabbler
ABBCEMORR car-bomber
ABBCGINRS scrabbing
ABBCHIKRR birchbark
ABBCHIKRT bath-brick
ABBCHJKOS Jack Hobbs
ABBCHNRSU subbranch
ABBCIIOSU bibacious
ABBCILPRU public bar
ABBCIMOST bombastic
ABBCKKLOO black book
ABBCKLLUY buckyball

ABBCKLNRU Blackburn
ABBCKLOOT bootblack
ABBCKLTTU black butt
ABBCMOOST cost a bomb
ABBDDOORY body board
ABBDEEERT breed-bate
ABBDEELNO blade-bone
ABBDEELRU bluebeard✧
ABBDEESTY bestead by
ABBDEGILR bridgable
ABBDEGINR Banbridge
ABBDEGLNU bugle-band
ABBDEIKLN bake blind
ABBDEILNO bon diable
ABBDEILOT bobtailed
ABBDEILRT bird table
ABBDEILTU dubitable
ABBDELLNY belly-band
ABBDELORU double bar
ABBDELOTU doubtable
ABBDELSUU subduable
ABBDENNTU but and ben
ABBDGIILN ad-libbing
ABBDGILNR drabbling
ABBDHLOOT bloodbath
ABBDHNNOO hob-and-nob
ABBDHOOTY tabbyhood
ABBDIINRR birdbrain
ABBDILLOR billboard
broadbill
ABBDILNUY Dublin Bay
ABBDILTUY dubitably
ABBDIMORR broad-brim
ABBDKLNOO blood bank
ABBDKNORU bark-bound
ABBDLLORU bull-board
ABBDMNOOR bombardon
ABBDMOQSU bomb squad
ABBDRRSUY Bradburys
Bradbury's
ABBEEEHRS Beersheba
ABBEEELRT table beer
ABBEEFIRT Beta fibre
ABBEEHLRT the rabble
ABBEEKLRU rebukable
ABBEELLMS semblable
ABBEELOPR probeable
ABBEELRRS slabberer
ABBEELRRY blaeberry
ABBEENORS bare bones
ABBEENRRY baneberry
ABBEENRST Ernst Abbe
ABBEEORRS sea robber
ABBEERRRY bearberry
ABBEGHIRT Big Bertha
ABBEGIJNR jabbering
ABBEGINRT rabbeting
ABBEHINOS Hobbesian
ABBEHLOTU tabbouleh
ABBEHOSUY baby house
ABBEIINRT rabbinite
ABBEIKNRU Burkinabé
ABBEILMOT bombilate
ABBEILMSU Abu Simbel
ABBEILMUY bum-baylie
ABBEILOST biostable
ABBEIMNOR Barenboim
ABBEIMNOS bombasine
ABBEIMNOT bombinate
ABBEIMNOZ bombazine
ABBEINORT barbitone
barbotine
ABBEIRRTX Rex rabbit
ABBEJLLYY jelly baby
ABBEKKLRU break bulk
ABBEKLOOT table book
ABBEKNORY Broken Bay
ABBEKOOSY absey book
ABBELLMSY semblably
ABBELMOOZ bamboozle
ABBELMORY Bob Marley
ABBELORSW browsable
ABBELOSTY stableboy
ABBELQRSU squabbler
ABBELSTTU battlebus
taste bulb
ABBEMORTU obumbrate
ABBENOORY baboonery
ABBENORRW brown bear
ABBENORST absorbent
ABBENORSU Enobarbus
ABBEORSWY Bob Sawyer
ABBERSUUU subbureau
ABBFHLLSU flashbulb
ABBGHMSUU ambush bug
ABBGIILOT obbligati
ABBGIINNO Gibbonian
ABBGILLNO billabong
ABBGILMNR brambling
ABBGILOOT obbligato
ABBGINORS absorbing
ABBGORTUU grub about
ABBHINOOS baboonish
ABBHIOPST abbotship
ABBHIQSSU squabbish
ABBHISTUY bathybius
ABBHMOPPY bomb-happy
ABBHOOTTY baby tooth
ABBIIMNRS rabbinism
ABBIINRST rabbinist
ABBILLORU bilobular
ABBIMMOXY Bombay mix
ABBIMNNOR Ribbon-man
ABBJMRUUU Bujumbura
ABBLLMOOR broomball
ABBLLOOTX ballot box
ABBLOOSTU slob about
ABBMMORST smart bomb
ABBMSTTUY Matt Busby
ABBOOORTW a bob or two
ABBOOPRTY booby trap
booby-trap
ABBOORRWY barrow boy
ABBOOSSTU boss about
ABBORSSTU Russ Abbot
ABCCCEFIO beccafico
ABCCCKKLO blackcock
ABCCDIIOR boric acid
ABCCDIRUY cubic yard
ABCCEEEHS escabeche
ABCCEEFRY cybercafé
ABCCEEHKL checkable
ABCCEEIKP backpiece
ABCCEENRU buccaneer
ABCCEGIMU magic cube
ABCCEHKKO choke back
ABCCEINOV biconcave
ABCCEINRU buccanier
ABCCEINRW cabin crew
ABCCELNOT cancelbot
ABCCELNRU carbuncle
ABCCEMNRU cumbrance
ABCCEMNTU accumbent
ABCCEOOST tobaccoes
ABCCFHIKS backfisch
ABCCFIINO Fibonacci
ABCCFIMOR bacciform
ABCCGHLTU clutch bag
ABCCHHKNU hunchback
ABCCHKLOT back-cloth
ABCCHKNOT notchback
ABCCHKOTU touchback
ABCCHLOOT coach bolt
ABCCHLORS Carl Bosch
ABCCHLTUY yacht club
ABCCHNOOR Conchobar
ABCCIIJNO Jacobinic
ABCCIIJOT Jacobitic
ABCCIILOU coulibiac
ABCCIKKLS slick back
ABCCIKLLO acock-bill
ABCCIKLRY brickclay
ABCCIKRST crab stick
crabstick
ABCCILLOU bucolical
ABCCILLUY cubically
ABCCILNOO obconical
ABCCILORU corbicula
ABCCILPTU public act
ABCCINOOS cocoa nibs
ABCCIRSTU subarctic
ABCCJKKLO jack-block
ABCCKKKNO knock back
knock-back
ABCCKKOOR crookback
ABCCKLLOO block-coal
ABCCKNOTU countback
ABCCKORSS back-cross
ABCCKORTU backcourt
ABCCLLSSU club class
ABCCMOORY mobocracy
ABCDDEEHU debauched
ABCDDEEIL decidable

ABCDDEFLO boldfaced
ABCDDEILU adducible
ABCDDEIRR cedar-bird
ABCDDEIRT debit card
ABCDDKORU duck-board
ABCDEEEHU debauchee
ABCDEEGRR berg-cedar
ABCDEEHMR chambered
ABCDEEHPT bepatched
ABCDEEHRU debaucher
ABCDEEIKR bridecake
ABCDEEILM medicable
ABCDEEILR calibered
ABCDEEIMR Barmecide
ABCDEEJKT bed-jacket
ABCDEEPRT carpet-bed
ABCDEESSS abscessed
ABCDEFIKL backfield
ABCDEFOOT boot-faced
ABCDEGIKR ridgeback
ABCDEGIMR Cambridge
ABCDEHIPS chip-based
ABCDEHIRT crib death
ABCDEHIRU Bruchidae
ABCDEHKLO blockhead
ABCDEIJLU judicable
ABCDEIKLS backslide
ABCDEIKRS disc brake
ABCDEIKRU baudricke
rudbeckia
ABCDEILNO balconied
ABCDEILRS crab-sidle
ABCDEILRV devil-crab
ABCDEIORT bacteroid
ABCDEIORZ bezoardic
ABCDEIRRV cab-driver
ABCDEKKNU buck naked
ABCDELLNO blond-lace
ABCDELLNU bull-dance
ABCDELLOT cold table
ABCDELMNO Candomble
Candomblé
ABCDELOSU cloud base
ABCDELOTU double act
ABCDENORR bread-corn
cornbread
ABCDENORS absconder
ABCDENOSU case-bound
subdeacon
ABCDEOORT obcordate
ABCDEOSST bad cess to
ABCDFLNOU calf-bound
ABCDGIPSU capsid bug
ABCDGKLLO black gold
ABCDHINRS disbranch
ABCDHIOPR chipboard
ABCDHIRSY Charybdis
ABCDHNRTU Dutch barn
ABCDIKRRY brickyard
ABCDILLNO blind coal
ABCDILMOR Lombardic
ABCDILOOT baldicoot
ABCDILOPR clipboard
ABCDILORU colubriad
ABCDILSUY subacidly
ABCDINOOT bandicoot
ABCDINOTU abduction
ABCDINTUY dubitancy
ABCDIOOSU bodacious
ABCDKLOOR roadblock
ABCDKLOOW blackwood✧
ABCDKLOPR black drop
ABCDKOORR corkboard
ABCDKOOSW backwoods
ABCDKORSW backsword
ABCDLNRSU scrubland
ABCDNOOXX Box and Cox
ABCDNORSS crossband
ABCEEELLR cerebella
ABCEEELLT electable
ABCEEELPR perceable
ABCEEELRT celebrate
erectable
ABCEEELRX execrable
ABCEEENRR cerberean
ABCEEERRR rerebrace
ABCEEERRT cerebrate
ABCEEFFGO coffee bag
ABCEEFFOR coffee bar
ABCEEFIRS briefcase
ABCEEFKLT Blackfeet
ABCEEFLTU flûte-à-bec
ABCEEFORR fore-brace
ABCEEGHRR herb-grace
ABCEEGKNR back green
greenback
ABCEEHIOT cohabitee
ABCEEHIRT Rechabite
ABCEEHKRT Chet Baker
ABCEEHLLY bellyache
ABCEEHLNU Cuban heel
ABCEEHLRS bleachers
ABCEEHLRY bleachery
ABCEEHMRR chamberer
March beer
ABCEEHMST beech mast
ABCEEHNST bench seat
ABCEEHPSS sheep scab
ABCEEHRST bretasche
ABCEEILLS sliceable
ABCEEILMR merciable
ABCEEILNV bivalence
ABCEEILRT recitable
ABCEEILSX excisable
ABCEEILTX excitable
ABCEEIMRV embracive
ABCEEINOS obeisance
ABCEEINRR carbineer
cerberian
ABCEEIRST bacterise
ABCEEIRTZ bacterize
ABCEEKKNR breakneck
ABCEEKPRS backspeer
ABCEEKPSW sweepback
ABCEELMNS semblance
ABCEELNRT celebrant
ABCEELNST albescent
ABCEELNUU nubeculae
ABCEELOPS placeboes
ABCEELORT bracteole
ABCEELORV coverable
revocable
ABCEELOSU leuco-base
ABCEELOTV covetable
ABCEELRSU rescuable
securable
ABCEELRSW screwable
ABCEELRXY execrably
ABCEELSUX excusable
ABCEEMMOR Morecambe
ABCEEMMRT Camembert
ABCEEMORR embraceor
ABCEEMORT embrocate
ABCEEMRRY embracery
ABCEENRTY cybernate
ABCEENSTT tabescent
ABCEEORST obsecrate
ABCEEOSSU sebaceous
ABCEEPRRU cupbearer
ABCEERSSY crab's-eyes
ABCEERSTT bescatter
ABCEFFHNO Offenbach
ABCEFFRTU buffet car
ABCEFHILT batch file
ABCEFHLSU flashcube
ABCEFILRU febricula
ABCEFINOR forecabin
ABCEFIRTU bifurcate
ABCEFOSTU obfuscate
ABCEFRTTU brute fact
ABCEGHILN bleaching
ABCEGHLNO Long Beach
ABCEGHORV Gorbachev
ABCEGILOR bricolage
ABCEGILOT cogitable
ABCEGIMNR cambering
embracing
ABCEGIMRT bregmatic
ABCEGKMSU megabucks
ABCEGKRTU tuckerbag
ABCEGLLLU bugle-call
ABCEGNOPU pounce bag
ABCEGNSUY subagency
ABCEGPRTU carpet bug
ABCEGRSUU sugar-cube
ABCEHILTY chalybite
ABCEHIMRS chime bars
ABCEHINNO bone china
ABCEHINOT aitchbone
ABCEHINRT Brechtian
ABCEHIOOP ecophobia
ABCEHIORT cohabiter
ABCEHKLLL hell-black

ABCEHKLLO	black hole✧
ABCEHKLLS	shellback
ABCEHKLOS	shockable
	shoeblack
ABCEHKMNR	benchmark
ABCEHKORS	horseback
ABCEHKRRY	hackberry
ABCEHKSTU	ash-bucket
ABCEHKTUW	buckwheat
ABCEHLMPU	beach plum
ABCEHLNRT	branchlet
ABCEHLOPW	peach-blow
ABCEHLOTU	touchable
ABCEHLRSU	crushable
ABCEHMNOR	bon marché
ABCEHMSSU	subschema
ABCEHNOOR	Orobanche
ABCEHNRRY	branchery
ABCEHOQRU	quebracho
ABCEHORRS	shore crab
ABCEHOSTU	touch base
ABCEHPRSU	caper-bush
ABCEHRSTU	Bucharest
ABCEIILNS	sibilance
ABCEIILRS	irascible
ABCEIIMRS	bias crime
ABCEIIMRT	imbricate
ABCEIINRR	carbinier
ABCEIJLNU	jubilance
ABCEIJNOT	abjection
ABCEIKLOV	olive-back
ABCEIKMQU	quickbeam
ABCEIKPRS	backspeir
ABCEIKRTW	write-back
ABCEIKSSU	back issue
ABCEILLOS	obeliscal
ABCEILLRR	cribellar
ABCEILLSS	classible
ABCEILMOT	metabolic
ABCEILMST	cembalist
ABCEILNNU	incunable
ABCEILNOT	balection
ABCEILNRU	incurable
ABCEILNVY	bivalency
ABCEILORT	cabriolet
ABCEILOTT	cobaltite
ABCEILRSX	Brix scale
ABCEILRTU	lubricate
ABCEILRUX	Excalibur
ABCEILSTU	Baculites
	bisulcate
ABCEILTXY	excitably
ABCEIMMUX	excambium
ABCEIMNOT	combinate
ABCEIMNOX	excambion
ABCEIMOTV	combative
ABCEIMRTU	bacterium
ABCEIMSTU	beat music
ABCEINORS	carbonise
	escribano
ABCEINORV	Avicebrón
ABCEINORZ	carbonize
ABCEINRTY	cabinetry
ABCEIORRS	barricoes
ABCEIRRSU	carburise
ABCEIRRTU	rubricate
ABCEIRRUZ	carburize
ABCEISSSS	abscisses
ABCEJNSTU	subjacent
ABCEJOSSU	jacobuses
ABCEKKORR	rock brake
ABCEKLLNR	bell crank
ABCEKLNSS	blackness
ABCEKLOPP	Black Pope
ABCEKLPRU	parbuckle
ABCEKNORR	cornbrake
ABCEKNRSS	brass neck
ABCEKOPRR	break crop
ABCEKORTU	outbacker
ABCEKPSTW	sweptback
ABCEKRTUW	waterbuck
ABCELLRSU	subcellar
ABCELLRSW	screwball
ABCELLRUV	curveball
ABCELLSTU	slate club
ABCELMNOY	belomancy
ABCELMOOR	rocambole
ABCELMOPT	comptable
ABCELMORU	calembour
ABCELMOSY	cymbaloes
ABCELMOTU	columbate
ABCELMPRU	clamber up
ABCELMRRS	scrambler
ABCELMRTU	tumble car
ABCELNOST	constable✧
ABCELNOTU	countable
ABCELNRUU	uncurable
ABCELORSU	crab-louse
ABCELORVY	revocably
ABCELOSTT	ectoblast
ABCELRSST	bractless
ABCELRSTU	scrutable
ABCELRTTY	battle-cry
ABCELRTUU	lucubrate
ABCELSSUU	subclause
ABCELSUXY	excusably
ABCEMNOPR	cramp-bone
ABCEMOOTU	come about
ABCEMORSS	crossbeam
ABCEMORSY	embryo-sac
ABCEMPRRU	bumper car
ABCEMRSUV	Verbascum
ABCENNRRU	cab-runner
ABCENORTY	baronetcy
ABCENORYZ	crazy bone
ABCENRRRY	cranberry
ABCENRTUU	Bucentaur
ABCENRTUY	cybernaut
ABCENSSTU	substance
ABCEOOPRS	baroscope
ABCEOPRRY	reprobacy
ABCEORSST	caber toss
ABCEORSTU	base-court
ABCEOSTUV	suboctave
ABCFFHNOR	branch off
ABCFFIRRU	fur fabric
ABCFGHIKT	fight back
	fightback
ABCFHIKLS	blackfish
ABCFHIKST	back-shift
ABCFHIKSY	fishyback
ABCFHRSTU	bushcraft
ABCFIMMOR	cambiform
ABCFKLOOT	Blackfoot
ABCGGIKPY	piggyback
ABCGHIKLT	back-light
ABCGHIKST	backsight
ABCGHINNR	branching
ABCGHLOOS	schoolbag
ABCGIINRT	racing bit
ABCGIKLNS	slingback
ABCGIKNOR	king cobra
ABCGIKNPU	backing-up
ABCGIKNSW	backswing
	swing-back
ABCGILMNS	scambling
ABCGIMNOT	combating
ABCGINNOS	sonic bang
ABCGKLLNU	black lung
ABCGKLORU	bulk cargo
ABCGKNOUW	buck-wagon
ABCHHIKSS	backshish
ABCHHKSUW	bushwhack
ABCHIIKTT	a bit thick
ABCHIILLN	chilblain
ABCHIIMNR	Brahminic
ABCHIINPS	cabin ship
ABCHIIOST	isobathic
ABCHIKRST	britschka
ABCHILLTW	watch bill
ABCHILMOS	shambolic
ABCHILNOR	bronchial
ABCHILNOT	chain bolt
ABCHILORR	charbroil
ABCHILTUV	Lubavitch
ABCHIOORS	borachios
ABCHJNOOT	John Cabot
ABCHKLLUW	bullwhack
ABCHKLORT	bark-cloth
ABCHKMOOT	matchbook
ABCHKMTTU	thumbtack
ABCHKNORT	thornback
ABCHKORTW	throw back
	throwback
ABCHLLNPU	punch-ball
ABCHLLOTT	latch bolt
ABCHLMORT	barm-cloth
ABCHNORRS	cornbrash
ABCHNORTU	branch out
ABCIIIKLW	bailiwick
ABCIIILPT	bicipital
ABCIIKLRS	Black Iris
ABCIIKNRS	brainsick

ABCIILLMU umbilical
ABCIILLST ballistic
ABCIILMOR microbial
ABCIILNOS basilicon
ABCIILNOT albinotic
ABCIILNSY sibilancy
ABCIILRSY irascibly
ABCIIMNOR microbian
ABCIINNRT Britannic
ABCIINRRU rubrician
ABCIINRTT Brittanic
ABCIINSSS abscissin
ABCIIOPRY biopiracy
ABCIIRSTY sybaritic✧
ABCIJLNUY jubilancy
ABCIKKOTU kick about
ABCIKLLRW brickwall
ABCIKLLST blacklist
ABCIKNORS rock-basin
ABCILLMRU lumbrical
ABCILLORU bilocular
ABCILLPUW public law
ABCILLSSY syllabics
ABCILMNOO Colombian
ABCILMNOU Columbian
ABCILMOPY amblyopic
ABCILMSTY cymbalist
ABCILMSUX subclimax
ABCILNNOU connubial
ABCILNOPT panic-bolt
ABCILNORU binocular
ABCILNRTU lubricant
ABCILNRUY incurably
ABCILOPSY polybasic
ABCILORRU courbaril
orbicular
ABCILORTU tubicolar
ABCILPRTU public art
ABCIMNOOS monobasic
ABCIMOSTU subatomic
ABCIMRSTY cambistry
ABCINNNOT cannon bit
ABCINORTU incubator
ABCINOSTU subaction
ABCINOSTY obstinacy
ABCINTTUY titubancy
ABCISTUVY subcavity
ABCKKLMNO black monk✧
ABCKKNOST bank-stock
ABCKLLLOP blackpoll
ABCKLLOOP Blackpool
ABCKLOOSS class-book
ABCKLOPST black spot
ABCKMOTUU muck about
ABCKNORRW crown-bark
ABCKNORSU Osnabrück
ABCKNORUY Ayckbourn
ABCKNRSTU burnt sack
ABCKOOPRS scrapbook
ABCKORSTY back story
ABCKORSUY buckayros
ABCKRSTUY rusty-back
ABCLLORRS scroll bar
ABCLLSUZZ scuzzball
ABCLMNNOT Mont Blanc
ABCLMNOUW clubwoman
ABCLMORSU Lambrusco
ABCLMORUY columbary
ABCLNOORW brown coal
ABCLNOWYY Colwyn Bay
ABCLOORRU colour bar
ABCLORSUU subocular
ABCLOSSTU subcostal
ABCLOSSUY scybalous
ABCMOSSUU submucosa
ABCMRRTUY crumb-tray
ABCNNOOXY box canyon
ABCNORSTU obscurant
subcantor
ABCNORSTY corybants
ABCRSSTTU substract
ABDDDEELR bladdered
ABDDDHLOU Old Buddha
ABDDDIPRY paddy-bird
ABDDEEEST besteaded
ABDDEEEYY beady-eyed
ABDDEEGHI bigheaded
ABDDEEGRR berg-adder
ABDDEEIRT diet-bread
ABDDEELLU deludable
ABDDEELMO beadledom
ABDDEELZZ bedazzled
ABDDEENRR brandered
ABDDEENRU unbearded
ABDDEENSU undebased
ABDDEEPRS bedspread
ABDDEERTY teddy bear
ABDDEGGOR badger-dog
ABDDEGLLO dodgeball
ABDDEHMNO mob-handed
ABDDEIILV dividable
ABDDEIIMR bridemaid
ABDDEILNT blind date
ABDDEILSS slab-sided
ABDDEINRR red riband
ABDDEINRU unbraided
ABDDEIORS broadside
sideboard
ABDDEIRRU ribaudred
ABDDELOPX paddle-box
ABDDELOSW saddlebow
ABDDEMRUU mud dauber
ABDDENNRU unbranded
ABDDFILOR forbiddal
ABDDGORUY bodyguard
ABDDHINTW bandwidth
ABDDILNNS sand-blind
ABDDILNOR blind road
ABDDJMNOO odd-jobman
ABDDNRSTU dust-brand
ABDEEEFLR deferable
ABDEEEGLL delegable
ABDEEELMN emendable
ABDEEELRY blear-eyed
ABDEEEMOU âme de boue
ABDEEERRT bread tree
ABDEEFHLR half-breed
ABDEEFILN definable
ABDEEFLTU debateful
ABDEEFORR freeboard
ABDEEFRST breastfed
ABDEEGGLR bedraggle
ABDEEGHIN beheading
ABDEEGINR gaberdine
ABDEEGLLN glebe land
ABDEEGMOR embargoed
ABDEEGNRR bergander
ABDEEGORR garderobe
ABDEEGRRY greybeard
ABDEEGRSY sage Derby
ABDEEHINR haberdine
Hebridean
ABDEEHLLT death-bell
ABDEEHLNW band-wheel
ABDEEHMOS besom-head
ABDEEHOSU bead-house
ABDEEHRRT earth-bred
ABDEEHRSW shewbread
ABDEEHRTT had better
ABDEEIILR diablerie
ABDEEILLR ébrillade
ABDEEILLW wieldable
ABDEEILLY yieldable
ABDEEILMS Ambleside
demisable
ABDEEILMT bedlamite
ABDEEILNO Belonidae
ABDEEILNR bandelier
breadline
ABDEEILNS disenable
ABDEEILRS desirable
ABDEEILRV derivable
driveable
ABDEEILST side table
ABDEEILSV devisable
ABDEEILTT tide table
ABDEEINST besainted
ABDEEINSW basen wide
Wiesbaden
ABDEEINTT bidentate
ABDEEINTU butadiene
ABDEEITTU beatitude
ABDEELLLY Leadbelly
ABDEELLPS speedball
ABDEELLRR barrelled
ABDEELLRV verballed
ABDEELLTY belatedly
ABDEELMTT embattled
ABDEELNOP pedal-bone
ABDEELNOR banderole
bandoleer
ABDEELNOT denotable
ABDEELNPR prebendal

ABDEELNPS spendable
ABDEELNRU endurable
ABDEELNST steel band
ABDEELOPS deposable
ABDEELOUX double-axe
ABDEELRSS beardless
ABDEELRSY Beardsley
ABDEEMNOT abodement
ABDEEMNOU beau monde
ABDEEMNRT debarment
ABDEEMNSU sunbeamed
ABDEEMPRT bad temper
ABDEEMRRW bed-warmer
ABDEEMRSY Ember-days
ABDEENOPS spade bone
ABDEENOTY bayoneted
ABDEENQTU banqueted
ABDEENRRT bartender
ABDEENRRU underbear
ABDEENRTU unrebated
ABDEENTTU debutante
débutante
ABDEEOPST speedboat
ABDEEORRU bordereau
ABDEERRST redbreast
ABDEESTUY use-by date
ABDEFFGLU duffel bag
ABDEFFLNU unbaffled
ABDEFGILM film badge
ABDEFIISX basifixed
ABDEFILNY definably
ABDEFINOS bona fides
ABDEFINRR firebrand
ABDEFLTUY by default
ABDEFOOPR bead-proof
ABDEFORRT fretboard
ABDEGGGIN debagging
ABDEGGHOR hog badger
ABDEGGLSU sluggabed
ABDEGGMOR beggardom
ABDEGGMRU Magdeburg
ABDEGIINN Big-endian
ABDEGIINU biguanide
ABDEGIIRR air-bridge
brigadier
ABDEGILNY Dingle Bay
ABDEGIMOY body image
ABDEGINRR debarring
ABDEGIORS raised bog
ABDEGLLMO gambolled
ABDEGLNOU go a bundle
ABDEGLNRU ungarbled
ABDEGNNOR dannebrog
ABDEGNOST Edgbaston
ABDEGNSTU Bundestag
ABDEGRSUU drug abuse
ABDEGRTUY budgetary
ABDEHHIRT heathbird
ABDEHIINR Hebridian
ABDEHILNO hobnailed
ABDEHIRTW wheat bird
ABDEHLLNS bandshell
ABDEHLNOS ash-blonde
ABDEHLOOT blood heat
ABDEHLORT holderbat
ABDEHLOTW deathblow
ABDEHLRSU subhedral
ABDEHNORT heart-bond
ABDEHNRRT brandreth
ABDEHOOST beasthood
ABDEHORSW showbread
ABDEHRRSY shadberry
ABDEHRRTY Bert Hardy
ABDEHRTYY by the yard
ABDEIIKLR like a bird
ABDEIILNU inaudible
ABDEIILOS diabolise
ABDEIILOZ diabolize
ABDEIILTV devil a bit
ABDEIINSW basin-wide
ABDEIJNNO Jean Bodin
ABDEIKLNR drinkable
ABDEIKMRS disembark
ABDEIKNRS snakebird
ABDEIKNRW break wind
break-wind
windbreak
ABDEIKRST Dekabrist
ABDEILLLO labelloid
ABDEILLOY Old Bailey
ABDEILLTU dilutable
ABDEILMMS bedlamism
ABDEILMOR bromeliad
ABDEILNNO bandoline
ABDEILNOR bandolier
bird-alone
ABDEILNRU unridable
ABDEILORV olive drab
olive-drab
ABDEILRRY early bird✧
ABDEILRSY desirably
ABDEILRVY derivably
ABDEILRWY bridleway
ABDEIMNRS bridesman
bride's-man
ABDEIMNRU Bermudian
ABDEIMPPT bit-mapped
ABDEINNPW pin and web
web and pin
ABDEINORW rainbowed
ABDEINOST bastioned
ABDEINRSS rabidness
ABDEINSSU unbiassed
ABDEINSSW bawdiness
ABDEIOORT boodie-rat
ABDEIORSW broadwise
ABDEIPRRU upbraider
ABDEIRRTW water bird
ABDEJMNOS James Bond
ABDEJORTT objet d'art
ABDEKLORW bladework
ABDEKLRSU Dark blues
ABDEKMRRU brake drum
drum brake
ABDEKNORW break down
breakdown
ABDEKNOSY naked boys
ABDEKOORT book trade
ABDEKORRW wordbreak
ABDEKORSY keyboards
ABDELLLSY syllabled
ABDELLMOU mouldable
ABDELLMRU umbrella'd
ABDELLOTU lobulated
ABDELLRSS ball-dress
ABDELMNOY baldmoney
ABDELMORV modal verb
ABDELMOTY molybdate
ABDELMRSU subdermal
ABDELMRTU drum table
ABDELNNOO bandoleon
ABDELNNSS blandness
ABDELNOOR bandolero
ABDELNOST endoblast
ABDELNOSV bond-slave
ABDELNOUW woundable
ABDELNRUY endurably
ABDELNSTU Dunstable
ABDELOOPS paso doble
ABDELORUV boulevard
ABDELTTUU tubulated
ABDEMNNOR Dobermann
ABDEMNRRT Rembrandt
ABDEMNSTY Stand by Me
ABDEMOORR breadroom
ABDENNNOO bandoneon
ABDENNOST band-stone
ABDENOORR road-borne
ABDENOPPR bond paper
ABDENOPSU subpoena'd
ABDENORRW Rob Andrew
Wonderbra®
ABDENORRY errand boy
ABDENORSS broadness
ABDENORST adsorbent
ABDENORSW sword-bean
ABDENOSTU eastbound
ABDENRRST St Bernard
ABDENRSTU Bundesrat
ABDENRSTY bystander
stander-by
ABDENRSUW subwarden
ABDEOORRT breadroot
ABDEOORRV overboard
ABDEOORWZ zebrawood
ABDEORRRW wardrober
ABDERRUYY rybaudrye
ABDFGLMOO Lamb of God
ABDFHILLN half-blind
ABDFHLLOO half-blood
ABDFHLNOU half-bound
ABDFIIRRR friarbird
ABDFLLNUY full and by

ABDFLLORU full board
ABDFOOORR roof board
ABDFOOORT board-foot
footboard
ABDFORRSU surfboard
ABDGHINSU sgian-dubh
ABDGHLLOU doughball
ABDGHORTU go hard but
ABDGIILNY abidingly
ABDGILNNR brandling
ABDGILNOU bungaloid
ABDGILOOX dialog box
ABDGILOOY diabology
ABDGINNOU abounding
ABDGINOOR Brigadoon
ABDGINORR organ-bird
ABDGINORS signboard
ABDGINOXY Boxing Day
ABDGINRRY brigandry
ABDGIRRSS grassbird
ABDGIRRSU sugar bird
ABDGKOORU guard-book
ABDGLNOOR Longobard
ABDHIINNR hindbrain
ABDHIMNRY mynah bird
ABDHIMORY hybridoma
ABDHIMRTY dithyramb
ABDHINRST shirtband
ABDHIOPRS shipboard
ABDHLNSUY husbandly
ABDHLOOOT blood oath
ABDHMOOST smooth dab
ABDHNOORU boar-hound
ABDHNOSUY Hudson Bay
ABDHNRSUY husbandry
ABDHOOPRS shopboard
ABDHOOSWX shadow box
shadow-box
ABDHPRSUU purdah bus
ABDIIILLN libidinal
ABDIILLRS billiards
ABDIILMOS diabolism
ABDIILMTU ad libitum
ABDIILNUY inaudibly
ABDIILOST diabolist
idioblast
ABDIIMPRY bipyramid
ABDIIMRST tribadism
ABDIINRST satin bird
ABDIKOOOU audio book
ABDILLMOR millboard
ABDILNOOR Bardolino
blood-rain
ABDILOPRS slip-board
ABDILOTUW wild about
ABDILRRRY Larry Bird
ABDILRSSU disbursal
ABDILRYZZ blizzardy
ABDIMNNOT badminton
ABDIMNOPU dumb piano
ABDIMNOTT Tom and Tib
ABDIMPQSU damp squib
ABDIMRSSU absurdism
ABDINNNOO bandonion
ABDINNOOS dona nobis
ABDINNORR brand-iron
ABDINNORU rain-bound
ABDINNRUU Burundian
ABDINOORT à bon droit
ABDINORRY by-ordinar
ABDINORWW window bar
ABDINOWWY bay window
ABDINRSTW wristband
ABDIRSSTU absurdist
ABDIRSTUY absurdity
ABDJMOPRU broad jump
ABDKLNOOR blank door
ABDKLNORW World Bank
ABDKNOOST bookstand
ABDLMOOOR broadloom
ABDLMOORW warmblood✧
ABDLOOPRY polar body
ABDLOPPRU pulpboard
ABDLORSSU subdorsal
ABDMMNOSU ombudsman✧
ABDMNNOOW bondwoman
ABDMNOOWY woman-body
ABDMNORTU Dumbarton
ABDMNORUU bum around
ABDMOOORR boardroom
ABDNNOSTY on stand-by
ABDNOORSW snow board
snowboard
ABEEEEFRT beefeater
ABEEEERSZ sea breeze✧
ABEEEFKRR break free
ABEEEFKST beefsteak
ABEEEFLOS beefaloes
ABEEEFLRR referable
ABEEEFLRZ freezable
ABEEEGGRT egg beater
ABEEEGLLR relegable
ABEEEGLNR generable
ABEEEGLNS Bengalese
ABEEEGLNV vengeable
ABEEEGLRR lager beer
ABEEEGLRU beleaguer
ABEEEGLRV bevel gear
ABEEEGLTV vegetable
ABEEEGNNR green bean
ABEEEGSTU beau geste✧
ABEEEHJST the baseej✧
ABEEEHLSW wheelbase
ABEEEHMRT embreathe
ABEEEHRVY heavy beer
ABEEEILLM belle amie
ABEEEKLST eel-basket
ABEEEKNRV break even
breakeven
break-even
ABEEEKNTY Yankee bet
ABEEEKPRR barkeeper
ABEEELLSV base-level
ABEEELMPR permeable
ABEEELMST steel beam
ABEEELMTY may beetle✧
ABEEELNRT enterable
ABEEELNRV venerable
ABEEELNRW renewable
ABEEELNSU unseeable
ABEEELRRV reverable
ABEEELRST steerable
ABEEELRSV severable
ABEEEMRST bee-master
ABEEENNTV an even bet
ABEEERRTT terebrate
ABEEERRTV verberate
vertebrae
ABEEERTUX exuberate
ABEEERWYZ breezeway
ABEEFFILN ineffable
ABEEFFLOR offerable
ABEEFGLOR forgeable
ABEEFIKRR firebreak
ABEEFILLT life table
ABEEFILNR inferable
ABEEFILRS bas-relief
ABEEFKLRU beakerful
ABEEFLORY lay before
ABEEFLRSU refusable
ABEEFLRTU refutable
ABEEFLSSU self-abuse
ABEEFORST roast beef
ABEEGGINU béguinage
ABEEGGLMR Lambegger
ABEEGHILW weighable
ABEEGHNOR habergeon
ABEEGILLR Gabrielle
ABEEGILLV levigable
ABEEGILNN bengaline
ABEEGILRT leger bait
ABEEGIMTU image tube
ABEEGINRS Bering Sea
ABEEGINRU aubergine
ABEEGKORR brokerage
ABEEGLLMO Malebolge
ABEEGLLRU regulable
ABEEGLMNR embrangle
ABEEGLNPR pregnable
ABEEGLNPS bespangle
ABEEGLNSU bel sangue
ABEEGLNVY vengeably
ABEEGLOPR bargepole
porbeagle
ABEEGLRTU butlerage
ABEEGLSSU guessable
ABEEGLTVY vegetably
ABEEGMNRW wambenger
ABEEGMORS embargoes
ABEEGNNRT rennet-bag
ABEEGNORS Boanerges
ABEEGNORZ Bronze Age
ABEEGNRSU subgenera

ABEEGOOPR	goober pea
ABEEGORUY	be your age!
ABEEGRSTU	beet sugar
	sugar beet
ABEEHHKSS	baksheesh
ABEEHHLLT	heath bell
ABEEHHNST	Hans Bethe
ABEEHHSTT	bath sheet
ABEEHILMT	Mehitabel
ABEEHILRT	heritable
ABEEHILST	Elisabeth
ABEEHILTT	biathlete
ABEEHILTZ	Elizabeth
ABEEHIMNR	Brahminee
ABEEHIMSV	misbehave
ABEEHIMTW	whitebeam
ABEEHINRT	hibernate
	inbreathe
ABEEHIRRS	Hebraiser
ABEEHIRRZ	Hebraizer
ABEEHIRTW	white bear
ABEEHKORS	brake shoe
ABEEHKOSU	bakehouse
ABEEHLLNS	shell bean
ABEEHLLUW	blue whale
ABEEHLMPS	blaspheme
ABEEHLNOW	whalebone
ABEEHLRRT	blatherer
ABEEHLTTT	The Tablet
ABEEHMNOT	on the beam
ABEEHNORS	horse bean
	share bone
ABEEHNORT	bone-earth
ABEEHNORY	honey bear
ABEEHNOTT	on the beat
ABEEHNSTU	Bhutanese
ABEEHOOPR	aerophobe
ABEEHORTU	hereabout
ABEEHPRTU	breathe up
ABEEHRVYY	Hervey Bay
ABEEIINRT	inebriate
ABEEIKLST	beastlike
ABEEIKMRT	breaktime
ABEEIKNST	snakebite
ABEEILLMR	mirabelle
ABEEILLNR	ballerine
ABEEILMNO	Meliboean
ABEEILMRS	miserable
ABEEILMST	estimable
ABEEILMTT	timetable
ABEEILNNT	intenable
ABEEILNPS	albespine
ABEEILNQU	inequable
ABEEILNRR	inerrable
ABEEILNRS	baseliner
	rinseable
ABEEILNTW	table wine
ABEEILPPT	appetible
ABEEILPRT	pier table
ABEEILPRX	expirable
ABEEILQTU	equitable
ABEEILRRW	rewirable
ABEEILRSV	revisable
	verbalise
ABEEILRTT	albertite
ABEEILRTV	avertible
	veritable
ABEEILRVV	revivable
ABEEILRVZ	verbalize
ABEEILSSW	Lewis base
ABEEILSTW	tablewise
ABEEIMNNO	bonne amie
ABEEIMNSS	beaminess
ABEEIMSTT	it beats me
ABEEINOST	seine boat
ABEEINRTV	binervate
ABEEINSST	asbestine
ABEEINSSZ	assez bien
ABEEIORSV	rise above
ABEEIPRST	rebaptise
ABEEIPRTZ	rebaptize
ABEEIRRSS	brasserie
	brassiere
	brassière
ABEEIRRST	biserrate
ABEEJKLOS	Joe Blakes
ABEEJLLNO	banjolele
ABEEJLLNU	banjulele
ABEEJLLNY	jelly bean
ABEEJLNOY	enjoyable
ABEEJNPUU	Punjaubee
ABEEKLMOS	smokeable
ABEEKLNSS	bleakness
ABEEKLORV	revokable
ABEEKLOSU	leuko-base
ABEEKLRSS	brakeless
ABEEKLSTW	skew-table
ABEEKMORR	robe maker
ABEEKNOST	bakestone
ABEEKNPSU	unbespeak
ABEEKOTUW	week about
ABEEKPRST	break step
ABEEKRRSU	Sue Barker
ABEELLLMS	smellable
ABEELLLMT	bell-metal
ABEELLLPS	spellable
ABEELLMRS	small beer
ABEELLMSS	blameless
ABEELLMTU	umbellate
ABEELLORT	tolerable
ABEELLOVV	evolvable
ABEELMMOR	memorable
ABEELMNRU	numerable
ABEELMORU	belamoure
ABEELMORV	removable
ABEELMOSV	moveables
ABEELMPRT	Temple Bar
ABEELMPRY	permeably
ABEELMPTT	temptable
ABEELMRSS	assembler
ABEELMRSU	resumable
ABEELMRTW	Bartlemew
ABEELNNTU	untenable
ABEELNPSU	spulebane
ABEELNPSY	albespyne
ABEELNQUU	unequable
ABEELNRTU	tenurable
ABEELNRTZ	bez-antler
ABEELNRVY	venerably
ABEELOPRV	proveable
ABEELOPSX	exposable
ABEELOSTT	seabottle
ABEELPRRV	preverbal
ABEELPRST	beplaster
ABEELPRSU	superable
ABEELPRTU	reputable
ABEELRRTV	vertebral
ABEELRSSZ	brazeless
ABEELRTTU	utterable
ABEELRTUW	blue water
ABEEMMNTY	embayment
ABEEMNTTT	battement
ABEEMORRT	barometer
ABEEMRRSU	embrasure
ABEEMRRUZ	embrazure
ABEEMRSTW	webmaster
ABEENNORV	raven-bone
ABEENNSTU	sunbeaten
ABEENORWY	bone-weary
ABEENQRTU	banqueter
ABEENQTTU	banquette
ABEENRRST	sternebra
ABEENRRSY	naseberry
ABEENRRTT	terebrant
ABEENRSST	steenbras
ABEENRTUX	exuberant
ABEEOPRRT	perborate
	reprobate
ABEEOPRSW	power base
ABEEOPRTT	peter-boat
ABEEOSTUU	beauteous
ABEEPRSTT	bespatter
ABEERRRTT	barretter
ABEEUUXXY	beaux yeux
ABEFFILNY	ineffably
ABEFFLOSU	buffaloes
ABEFGHILT	fightable
ABEFGILLN	befalling
ABEFGILNR	frangible
ABEFGILRU	figurable
ABEFHILST	shiftable
ABEFHIMRS	amber-fish
ABEFHLRTU	breathful
ABEFHLSTU	flash tube
ABEFIILLR	fibrillae
ABEFIILNU	unifiable
ABEFIILOT	bifoliate
ABEFIIMRT	fimbriate
ABEFILLRT	filtrable
ABEFILNRU	funebrial
ABEFILRST	fire-blast
ABEFILTUU	beautiful
ABEFINORR	forebrain

ABEFIRRTU bear fruit
ABEFKLORT flat broke
ABEFKLSTU basketful
ABEFKOORT footbrake
ABEFKRSTU busk after
ABEFLLLMU flabellum
ABEFLLLUY balefully
ABEFLLNUY banefully
ABEFLLRRU barrefull
barrelful
ABEFLLRWY warble fly
ABEFLLSTY stable fly
ABEFLNOSW wolfsbane
wolf's bane
ABEFLOSUW blow a fuse
ABEFLRTUY refutably
ABEFOORST bear's-foot
ABEFORRTY ferry-boat
ABEFRTTTU butterfat
ABEGGINSS bagginess
ABEGGNOPS spongebag
ABEGHHILT high table
ABEGHIKUW weigh-bauk
ABEGHILLP phillabeg
ABEGHILRT rightable
ABEGHILST sightable
ABEGHINRR harbinger
ABEGHINRT breathing
ABEGHMRRU hamburger
ABEGHRSSU sagebrush
ABEGIILLT litigable
ABEGIILMT mitigable
ABEGIILNS abseiling
ABEGIILNT ignitable
ABEGIILNW bewailing
ABEGIILRR irrigable
ABEGIINOR aborigine✧
baignoire
ABEGIINOS a big noise
ABEGIKMNR embarking
ABEGILLLN labelling
ABEGILLMN emballing
ABEGILLNR ring a bell
ABEGILLOS globalise
ABEGILLOZ globalize
ABEGILLST Bill Gates
ABEGILMMN embalming
ABEGILMNR imbrangle
ABEGILMNY beamingly
ABEGILMRT Tiger balm®
ABEGILNOR ignorable
ABEGILOTT toilet bag
ABEGILRSU Bulgarise
ABEGILRUZ Bulgarize
ABEGIMNNO bemoaning
ABEGIMNRR embarring
ABEGIMRRS ambergris
gris-amber
ABEGINNNT benignant
ABEGINNRT bantering
ABEGINNRU unbearing
ABEGINNTT battening
ABEGINORT barge into
ABEGINOST obsignate
ABEGINRSW sabrewing
ABEGINSST beastings
ABEGINSTW swingbeat
ABEGIORRY Yogi Berra
ABEGJLRRS Jarlsberg®
ABEGJORTU objurgate
ABEGJSTUU subjugate
ABEGKLLRU bulk large
ABEGKMNOY monkey bag
ABEGKMORS bergomask✧
ABEGKRSTU grubstake
ABEGLLLSS bell-glass
ABEGLLORS bargellos
ABEGLLOST log tables
ABEGLLSWY swag-belly
ABEGLMORU beglamour
ABEGLMUZZ muzzle-bag
ABEGLNORU lounge-bar
ABEGLNRRU gun barrel
ABEGLOPRU groupable
ABEGLOSTT bottle gas
gas-bottle
ABEGLRSSU bluegrass
ABEGMMMRU brummagem✧
ABEGMNNOO moong bean
ABEGMNOOR boomerang
ABEGMNOOW wagenboom
ABEGMNOSY moneybags
ABEGNOOVY bon voyage
ABEGNRRSU gas-burner
ABEGNRSST bent grass
ABEGOORST botargoes
ABEGORSTU subrogate
ABEGORTTU Goa butter
ABEHHLLOZ Hezbollah
ABEHHLOOP halophobe
ABEHHNOST on the bash
ABEHHOSTU bathhouse
bath-house
ABEHIINNR Hibernian
ABEHIINRT inhabiter
reinhabit
ABEHIITTW whitebait
ABEHIKLNT thinkable
ABEHIKNTT bethankit
ABEHILLLY Bill Haley
ABEHILLRS shillaber
ABEHILMOP amphibole
ABEHILMRS herbalism
ABEHILMSU Basil Hume
ABEHILOTT batholite
ABEHILPPS shippable
ABEHILRST herbalist
ABEHILRSY bearishly
ABEHILRTY breathily
heritably
ABEHILSST establish
ABEHILTTY bathylite
ABEHIMRRU herbarium
ABEHINOOP neophobia
ABEHINOST on the bias
ABEHINRTT tithe barn
ABEHIOPRU euphorbia
ABEHIORRV herbivora
ABEHIORUV behaviour
ABEHIPRRS herb Paris
ABEHIRRTT birth rate
ABEHISSTW whitebass
ABEHKLLRS shellbark
ABEHKLRSU blue shark
ABEHKNNOS shankbone
ABEHKNRSS Hans Krebs
ABEHLLLUW bull whale
ABEHLLNOT on the ball
ABEHLLOST blast-hole
ABEHLLSTU sublethal
ABEHLMNSU bushelman
ABEHLMORT alembroth
ABEHLMOTU mouthable
ABEHLMPSY blasphemy
ABEHLMSTU bush-metal
ABEHLNNSU shunnable
ABEHLNORW Brehon Law
ABEHLOOST shootable
ABEHLOOTT tholobate
ABEHLOPRY hyperbola
ABEHLORST sloth bear
ABEHLORTT betrothal
ABEHLORTW bowler hat
bowler-hat
ABEHLOSTY Hylobates
ABEHLOTTW bath-towel
ABEHMOORT Theobroma
ABEHNOOST bean shoot
ABEHNORRT abhorrent
earthborn
ABEHNORTT breton hat✧
ABEHNOSTT Bath stone
ABEHNOTTU thenabout
ABEHNRRTU heartburn
ABEHNRSSS brashness
ABEHNRSTU sunbather
ABEHOORST horse boat
shore boat
ABEHOOSTU boathouse
houseboat
ABEHORRRU harbourer
ABEHORTUW web author
ABEHQRSUU harquebus
ABEIIILRR librairie
ABEIIKLNR bairnlike
ABEIIKLRT trail bike
ABEIIKMNR minibreak
ABEIILLLR illiberal
ABEIILLMN Minié ball
ABEIILLMT limitable
ABEIILLRT biliteral
ABEIILMNR birlieman
ABEIILMSS amissible

ABEIILMTV lambitive
ABEIILNOS ionisable
ABEIILNOZ ionizable
ABEIILNRT nail-biter
ABEIILNRZ brazilein
ABEIILRRT irritable
ABEIILRTV vibratile
ABEIILSST stabilise
ABEIILSTV visitable
ABEIILSTZ stabilize
ABEIIMMNO meibomian
ABEIIMNRT bairn-time
ABEIINNPT bipinnate
ABEIINNRT inebriant
ABEIIPRTT bipartite
ABEIIRSSV vibrissae
ABEIIRTVV vibrative
ABEIJMRTX Jim Baxter
ABEIKLLNU unlikable
ABEIKLNSS balkiness
ABEIKMORR biomarker
ABEIKMSTY by mistake
ABEIKNNRT interbank
ABEIKNORT break into
ABEIKNORW wake-robin
ABEIKNRRV riverbank
ABEILLLMS slimeball
ABEILLLNT libellant
ABEILLLRY liberally
ABEILLNOT note a bill
tabellion
ABEILLNPU unpliable
ABEILLNUV unlivable
ABEILLPSU plausible
ABEILLRTX Bellatrix
ABEILLSSU subsellia
ABEILLSSY syllabise
ABEILLSYZ syllabize
ABEILMMOV immovable
ABEILMMSW swimmable
ABEILMMTU immutable
ABEILMNNO nominable
ABEILMNOR bromelain
ABEILMNSS balminess
ABEILMOPS imposable
ABEILMORT Baltimore
ABEILMPTU imputable
ABEILMRSV verbalism
ABEILMRSY miserably
ABEILMRTU umbratile
ABEILMSTU sublimate
ABEILMSTY estimably
ABEILNORR rail-borne
ABEILNOSS bonilasse
ABEILNPRT printable
ABEILNPSU subalpine
ABEILNRRY inerrably
ABEILNRSS brainless
ABEILNRSU insurable
sublinear
ABEILNRTU untirable
ABEILNSUV subniveal
ABEILNSUZ unsizable
ABEILOQSU obsequial
ABEILORRT liberator
ABEILORST strobilae
ABEILORTT trilobate
ABEILORTU Labourite
ABEILPPST blast-pipe
ABEILPRST periblast
ABEILPRTY bit player
ABEILQTUY equitably
ABEILRRYZ bizarrely
ABEILRSTU brutalise
ABEILRSTV verbalist
ABEILRTTY at liberty
ABEILRTUZ brutalize
ABEILRTVY verbality
veritably
ABEILRVVY revivably
ABEILSTTW twistable
waistbelt
ABEILSUVY abusively
ABEILTTTT tittlebat
ABEIMMNRT timberman
ABEIMNOST absit omen
ABEIMNRSS barminess
ABEIMNRST brainstem
tribesman
ABEIMNRSU submarine
ABEIMNRTU inumbrate
ABEIMNRUV brevi manu
ABEIMOTTU about time
time about
ABEIMPRST rebaptism
ABEIMSSST Miss Bates
ABEINNOPT pinto bean
ABEINNORR no-brainer
ABEINNORS Serbonian
ABEINNOST sanbenito
ABEINNRRV River Bann
ABEINNRST bannister✧
ABEINNSTT abstinent
ABEINNSUV subnivean
ABEINNTYZ Byzantine
ABEINOORT aerobiont
reboation
ABEINOPRT bioparent
ABEINORTT torbanite
ABEINOSTT obstinate
ABEINPRST breastpin
stepbairn
ABEINPTUZ unbaptize
ABEINRSST banisters
ABEINRTTU tribunate
turbinate
ABEIOPRTV probative
ABEIORRTV riverboat
ABEIPSSTT se-baptist
ABEIRRRST barrister
ABEIRRSST arbitress
ABEIRRTTW wart-biter
ABEIRTTTU attribute
ABEJKLOUW kabeljouw
ABEJLNOYY enjoyably
ABEJMORST job-master
ABEJORSST Job's tears
ABEKKMOOR bookmaker
ABEKKOOPR poke borak
ABEKLLMOS smoke ball
ABEKLLNSU bull snake
ABEKLLNTY belly tank
ABEKLLPRU pull baker
ABEKLNNSS blankness
ABEKLNOOT ankle-boot
ABEKLNOST Léon Bakst
ABEKLOOPT bookplate
ABEKLOOUV book value
ABEKLORST strokable
ABEKLORSU bark-louse
ABEKLORTW table-work
worktable
ABEKMNNOR broken man
ABEKMNPRS sperm bank
ABEKMOORT bootmaker
ABEKNNNPY penny-bank
ABEKNORSW snow brake
ABEKOOSTW waste book
ABELLLMRU larum-bell
ABELLLOWW blow a well
ABELLMMNO lemon balm
ABELLMNTY lambently
ABELLMORS small-bore
ABELLNOOP noble opal
ABELLNOSU unlosable
ABELLNOUV unlovable
ABELLORTY tolerably
ABELLORUY royal blue
ABELLOSWY Boyle's law
ABELLOVVW blow-valve
ABELLRSST Tsar's Bell
ABELLRTUW water bull
ABELMMNRU lumberman
ABELMMORY memorably
ABELMNORY embryonal
ABELMNOTU mountable
ABELMNOUV unmovable
ABELMNPRU penumbral
ABELMNRTT tremblant
ABELMNRUY numerably
ABELMNSTT blastment
ABELMNSTU submental
ABELMOORT motorable
ABELMORVY removably
ABELMOSST mesoblast
ABELMPSSU subsample
ABELNNORV non-verbal
ABELNNTUU untunable
ABELNOPTU unpotable
ABELNORUW New Labour
ABELNOSST slabstone
ABELNOSTT entoblast
ABELNOSUV snob value

ABELNOSUX Saxon blue
ABELNOSYZ lazybones
ABELNPTUY untypable
ABELNRSTU subaltern
ABELNRSUU subneural
ABELNRTTU turntable
ABELNSTUU sublunate
ABELOOPPS opposable
ABELOOTVY obovately
ABELOPPRS sorb-apple
ABELOPRST sportable
ABELOPRTU port a beul
ABELOPRTY pot barley
ABELOPRVY proveably
ABELOPTTY talbotype
ABELOSSST boastless
ABELOSTTY stylobate
ABELPRSUU pursuable
ABELPRSUY superably
ABELPRTUY reputably
ABELRSSUV subversal
ABELRSTTU trustable
ABELRSUYY Aylesbury
ABEMNNOSY by no means
ABEMNORSW Sam Browne
ABEMNORWY byrewoman
ABEMOOPRR broomrape
ABEMOOSTT sea bottom
ABEMOPRTY ambrotype
ABEMORRTU arboretum
ABEMORRTY barometry
ABEMOSSTU mess about
ABEMRSSTU truss beam
ABENNNNOY Anne Bonny
ABENNORTW war bonnet
ABENNSTTU subtenant
ABENOOSTT stoneboat
ABENOPRRS barperson
ABENORSTV observant✧
ABENOSSST stone bass
ABEOOPRTW powerboat
ABEOORRSU arboreous
ABEOPRRSY soapberry
ABEOQRSUU bourasque
ABEOSSSTU asbestous
ABEOSTTUW westabout
ABEOTUUYY you beauty
ABEPPRRSU bar supper
ABEPRRRSY raspberry
ABEPRRSTU superbrat
ABEPRSSSY passers-by
ABEPRTTTU butter pat
ABERSSTTU substrate
ABERTTTUW water butt
ABFGGHILT flight bag
ABFGIOPSY Bay of Pigs
ABFHLLSUY bashfully
ABFHLNRSU flash burn
ABFHLNSUU unbashful
ABFHLRSTU flat brush
ABFHSTTTU butt-shaft
ABFIILLRR fibrillar
ABFIIORSU bifarious
ABFILLSYY syllabify
ABFILMSUY subfamily
ABFILNSSU basinfuls
ABFLLLSTU full blast
full-blast
ABFLLOOPR ball-proof
ABFNOPPRZ Franz Bopp
ABGGIINPP bagpiping
ABGGIKNPY piggy bank
ABGGILNNR brangling
ABGGINNRS bangsring
ABGGINORT tarboggin
ABGGINRST string-bag
ABGGLOORY garbology
ABGGNTTUY butty-gang
ABGHIKNRT right-bank
ABGHILLLT light-ball
ABGHILLNO bingo hall
ABGHILMNS shambling
ABGHINORR abhorring
ABGHINWZZ whizz-bang
ABGHIOPRY biography
ABGHQSSUU squash bug
ABGHRSSUU sugar bush
ABGIILLNU bilingual
ABGIIMTUY ambiguity
ABGIJNNOW jawboning
ABGIKLLNY balkingly
ABGILLMOS globalism
ABGILLNOT balloting
ABGILLOST globalist
ABGILLOTY billy goat
ABGILNOSX signal box
ABGILNRTT brattling
ABGILOORT obligator
ABGILOOST obligatos
ABGIMOSSU subimagos
ABGIMOSUU ambiguous
ABGINOPSV bog spavin
ABGINOSTW swingboat
ABGLLNOOW bowl along
ABGLMNOOS boomslang
ABGLMOPSU plumbagos
ABGLOOTTY battology
ABGLORSUW sugar bowl
ABGLRSSUY ruby glass
ABGOPRSTU gastropub
ABHHHIKSS bakhshish
ABHHIIRUV bahuvrihi
ABHHILLOZ Hizbollah
ABHHILLUZ Hizbullah
ABHHILOTT batholith
ABHHILTTY bathylith
ABHHIPSSU subahship
ABHHIRRSU hairbrush
ABHIILLMS bismillah
ABHIINORT inhabitor
ABHIKLLSW hawksbill
ABHIKMRRT birthmark
ABHILMNTU thumbnail
ABHILMOPY amphiboly
ABHILNOOT halobiont
ABHILNRSU nailbrush
ABHILNRTY labyrinth
ABHILRTTY trilby hat
ABHILTTTY Blyth Tait
ABHIMPTUW with a bump
ABHINORRS rhino bars
ABHIOOOPZ zoophobia
ABHIOPSTU about-ship
ABHJNORRY Barry John
ABHKLLRSU bull shark
ABHKMMRTU thumb mark
ABHLLMSTU all thumbs
ABHLOPSTY hypoblast
ABHLOSSTT shot-blast
ABHMNOSUW bushwoman
ABHMNRTUY urban myth
ABHNORRUU unharbour
ABHOOPTUY autophoby
ABHOPRTYY Bryophyta
ABIIIKMRS Karisimbi
ABIIILLTY liability
ABIIILMRS mirabilis✧
ABIIILNTY inability
ABIIILTVY viability
ABIILLLRY Billy Liar
ABIILLNRT brilliant
ABIILLRST Braillist
ABIILMNNO binominal
ABIILMNOS albinoism
ABIILMRST tribalism
ABIILNOOT abolition
ABIILNOOV boliviano
ABIILNORT libration
ABIILNORY nobiliary
ABIILORST sibilator
ABIILORTT Trilobita
ABIILRRTY irritably
ABIILRSTT tribalist
ABIILSTTY stability
ABIILSTUY suability
usability
ABIIMOSTU ambitious
ABIIMRRTU arbitrium
ABIINNNUV Ivan Bunin
ABIINOOTV obviation
ABIINORTV vibration
ABIINSTVW bavin wits
ABIIORSTT barotitis
ABIJNRRRY brinjarry
ABIKLLNST stink ball
ABIKLNOPS spoil bank
ABIKMNRUU Burakumin
ABILLMOTU mill about
ABILLMSSY syllabism
ABILLNOPT ballpoint
ABILLNPUY unpliably
ABILLOPRX pillar box
ABILLORRZ razorbill

ABILLPSUY plausibly
ABILMMOTU bummaloti
ABILMMOVY immovably
ABILMMTUY immutably
ABILMNOUV ovalbumin
ABILMOORS ribosomal
ABILMORSU labourism
ABILMORXY xylorimba
ABILMPTUY imputably
ABILMRSTU brutalism
ABILNOPRS Planorbis
ABILNOPSS slop basin
ABILNORTY Tony Blair
ABILNOSTU ablutions
sublation
ABILNRTUZ Brazil nut
ABILNRTVY vibrantly
ABILOOPTT pilot-boat
ABILOORSU laborious
ABILORRTY libratory
ABILORSTU labourist
ABILRSSUY Salisbury
ABILRSTTU brutalist
ABILRSTUY salubrity
ABILRTTUY brutality
ABIMMNRUU manubrium
ABIMNORTU tambourin
ABIMNORTY abnormity
ABIMNQRTU Qutb Minar
ABIMNTUYZ Byzantium
ABIMORRTT Britomart
ABIMRSTUX submatrix
ABINNNORU Brunonian
ABINNOTVV bon vivant
ABINOOPRT probation
ABINOOPST spoonbait
ABINOPRTU abruption
ABINOPSTU subtopian
ABINOTVXY vanity box
ABINRRTTU turribant
ABIORRSUV arbovirus
ABIORRTVY vibratory
ABIORSTTU stirabout
ABIPRSTTY baptistry
ABIRRTTUY tributary
ABJLLOOTY jollyboat
ABJOSTTUU just about
ABKLLOOST bookstall
ABKLMOOPS psalm-book
ABKOQSUWX squawk box
ABLLLOOST stoolball
ABLLMOOSW lamb'swool
ABLLNORWW wall brown
ABLLOORTU roll-about
ABLLOPTUU pull about
ABLMNORSU subnormal
ABLMNOUVY unmovably
ABLNNTUUY untunably
ABLNORSUU alburnous
ABLNRSUUY sublunary
ABLOOPTYY play booty
ABLRSSTUY substylar
ABMNNOORW woman-born
ABMNOOOTU moon about
ABMNOORSU abnormous
ABMNORRST barnstorm
ABMNOSTUY Mounts Bay
ABMOOORTT motorboat
ABMPRSTTU bump-start
ABNOORSUY sonar buoy
ABNOPRRSW brown spar
ABNORTTUU about-turn
turn about
turnabout
ABNOSTTUU nuts about
ABOOPRRTY probatory
ABOOPRSTT bootstrap
ABOORRTTU obturator
ABORSSSTW straw boss
ABRRSSTTU starburst
ABRRSTTUW bratwurst
ACCCCEHIT cachectic
ACCCDEEEN accedence
ACCCDEEIN accidence
ACCCDHLOT catch cold
ACCCDIIMU mucic acid
ACCCDILOY cacodylic
ACCCDKLOR clock card
ACCCEEENS acescence
ACCCEELRY cycle race
ACCCEENSY acescency
ACCCEGLOY coccygeal
ACCCEHITT cathectic
ACCCEIIPV cevapcici
ACCCEIIRT cicatrice
ACCCEILLO calcicole
ACCCEIOPT copacetic
ACCCENOPU occupance
ACCCGINOY coccygian
ACCCHIKNP pack-cinch
ACCCHKMOT cockmatch
ACCCHKOOR cockroach
ACCCHNOTY cony-catch
ACCCHOPRT catch-crop
ACCCIILLY alicyclic
ACCCIILMT climactic
ACCCIIOPR capriccio
ACCCILMPY cyclic AMP
ACCCNOPUY occupancy
ACCDDEEEN decadence
ACCDDEENY decadency
ACCDDEHOR decachord
ACCDDEILS discalced
ACCDDIIST didactics
ACCDDIORS disaccord
ACCDDKNOY dandy-cock
ACCDEEEHN déchéance
ACCDEEHIK chickadee
ACCDEEHTW catchweed
ACCDEEINR ice dancer
ACCDEEIST desiccate
ACCDEELLN cancelled
ACCDEFILS fascicled
ACCDEFILY decalcify
ACCDEGKOR deck-cargo
ACCDEGLNO clogdance
ACCDEHIIL Cichlidae
ACCDEHIKR deckchair
ACCDEHILR child care
ACCDEHIST decastich
ACCDEHKOT cocked hat
ACCDEHPTU Cape Dutch
ACCDEIIIM Cimicidae
ACCDEIILN Icelandic
ACCDEIILO oleic acid
ACCDEIILT dialectic
ACCDEIILU Culicidae
ACCDEILLO lead colic
ACCDEILLP piccadell
ACCDEILNR calendric
ACCDEINST desiccant
ACCDEIORW cowardice
ACCDEKLOP cock-padle
ACCDEKOSS cassocked
ACCDELMOR cold cream
ACCDELNOY calcedony
ACCDELPUU caudle cup
ACCDEMNOO cacodemon
ACCDEMOOR macrocode
ACCDEMOPT compacted
ACCDEMORR camcorder
ACCDEMORY democracy✧
ACCDENORS arcsecond
ACCDENPSU dunce's cap
ACCDENSUU unaccused
ACCDEORRS scorecard
ACCDEORSW sacred cow
ACCDEORTU accoutred
ACCDFIILO folic acid
ACCDFILLY flaccidly
ACCDGINOR according
ACCDHHLOT catch hold
ACCDHHRUY archduchy
ACCDHIIIS ischiadic
ACCDHIIOR radicchio
ACCDHIISS Chassidic
ACCDHIKLS clackdish
ACCDHINOR chancroid
ACCDHIRTU cri du chat
ACCDHMORT match-cord
ACCDHNPRU cardpunch
punch-card
ACCDHOOOW coachwood
ACCDHOORT octachord
ACCDHORTW catchword
ACCDIIINT diactinic
ACCDIIIRT diacritic
ACCDIILLP piccadill
ACCDIILST cladistic
ACCDIIMOS osmic acid
ACCDIIOPT apodictic
ACCDIIOSU dicacious
ACCDIKLOR cocklaird

ACCDILLOY cycloidal
ACCDIMORR microcard
ACCDINOOR accordion
ACCDINORT dracontic✧
ACCDIOOPT octapodic
ACCDIOSST sticcados
ACCDKNORW crack down
crackdown
ACCDKNORY rock candy
ACCDKPSUU scaup duck
ACCDLOPTU cloud-capt
ACCDLORSW scald-crow
ACCDLORUY dulocracy
ACCDNOORT concordat
ACCDOOOOW cocoa-wood
ACCDOOSST stoccados
ACCDORRTU court card
ACCEEEHSX cache-sexe
ACCEEEINP cane piece
ACCEEELNR canceleer
ACCEEELRS recalesce
ACCEEENRR recreance
ACCEEESSY access eye
ACCEEGLMY megacycle
ACCEEHHKO cheechako
ACCEEHIKR chickaree
ACCEEHILR chelicera
ACCEEHIST catechise
ACCEEHITY haecceity
ACCEEHITZ catechize
ACCEEHKMN namecheck
ACCEEHKMT checkmate
ACCEEHLOR cochleare
ACCEEHLOT cochleate
ACCEEHNPR perchance
ACCEEHOST cacoethes
ACCEEHPST speech act
ACCEEIKPS spice cake
ACCEEILLS ecclesial
ACCEEILMU leucaemic
ACCEEILNR arc-en-ciel
cancelier
ACCEEILRT clericate
ACCEEILST Celtic Sea
ACCEEIPTV acceptive
ACCEEIQSU acquiesce
ACCEEIRRR ricercare
ACCEEIRTV accretive
ACCEEISTX exsiccate
ACCEEKLOR ear-cockle
ACCEEKLOT cockateel
ACCEELLNR canceller
ACCEELLNY cycle lane
ACCEELLOR clearcole
ACCEELMNO come clean
ACCEELNOR concealer
ACCEELNPR pre-cancel
ACCEELPST spectacle
ACCEELRTY recyclate
ACCEENNST canescent
ACCEENORT concreate
ACCEENRRY recreancy
ACCEENRSU recusance
securance
ACCEEOPRS praecoces
ACCEEOPSU cepaceous
ACCEEORSU ceraceous
ACCEEOSTU cetaceous
ACCEESSUU Ceausescu
ACCEFFFIL cliff-face
ACCEFFHNO off chance
off-chance
ACCEFGILU calcifuge
ACCEFHIRT catch fire
ACCEFHLNU chanceful
ACCEFHLOT facecloth
ACCEFIIRS sacrifice
ACCEFILSS fascicles
ACCEFILSU fascicule
ACCEGHLNO chalcogen
ACCEGHOSU gauchesco
ACCEGIKNO Cockaigne
ACCEGINOR acrogenic
ACCEGIOPR geocarpic
ACCEGIORT categoric
ACCEGIOTT geotactic
ACCEHHIOR coach-hire
ACCEHHIRT thearchic
ACCEHHIST schechita
ACCEHHKOT heathcock
ACCEHHLRU church-ale
ACCEHHNOW how chance?
ACCEHHOQU chechaquo
ACCEHIIMS ischaemic
ACCEHIIRV vice-chair
ACCEHIKLR checkrail
ACCEHIKNR raincheck
ACCEHILMO cholaemic
ACCEHILNO coachline
cochineal
ACCEHILNT technical
ACCEHILOR choleraic
oricalche
ACCEHILRU cleruchia
ACCEHIMNS mechanics
mischance
ACCEHIMST catechism
schematic
ACCEHINNO chaconine
ACCEHINOR anchor-ice
ice anchor
ACCEHINRY chicanery
ACCEHIRTT architect
the Arctic
ACCEHIRVZ czarevich
ACCEHISTT catechist
ACCEHJKKT Jack Ketch
ACCEHKLOT cockle hat
ACCEHKMPR crack-hemp
ACCEHKOPT patchocke
ACCEHKPSS pass-check
ACCEHLNOR chloracne
ACCEHLOOT chocolate
ACCEHLOPT catchpole
ACCEHLPTY cyclepath
ACCEHMMNU mumchance
ACCEHMNOS Comanches
ACCEHMNTT catchment
ACCEHNORS charnecos
ACCEHNRRU cranreuch
ACCEHORRT torch-race
ACCEHORTU cartouche
ACCEHORTV overcatch
ACCEHORTY theocracy
ACCEHRRST scratcher
ACCEHRSST scratches
ACCEIILMN calcimine
ACCEIILRT icterical
ACCEIIMNR cineramic
ACCEIIMNT cinematic
ACCEIINOS cocainise
ACCEIINOT ice-action
ACCEIINOZ cocainize
ACCEIINRT circinate
ACCEIIPRT accipiter
ACCEIIRST cicatrise
ACCEIIRTZ cicatrize
ACCEIISTV siccative
ACCEIKKLP place kick
ACCEIKLOT cockatiel
ACCEIKPRR rack price
ACCEIKPRS spice rack
ACCEIKRSW wisecrack
ACCEILLOT laccolite
ACCEILLRS clericals
ACCEILMPT eclamptic
ACCEILNRT centrical
ACCEILNST canticles✧
ACCEILNTU inculcate
ACCEILOPR precocial
ACCEILPST sceptical
ACCEILRTU circulate
ACCEIMNPT impeccant
ACCEIMOSU micaceous
ACCEIMSSU music case
ACCEINNOS accension
ACCEINOOZ Caenozoic
ACCEINORT accretion
anorectic
ACCEINOSS accession
ACCEINSTU encaustic
succinate
ACCEINSTX exsiccant
ACCEINTXY excitancy
ACCEIOPST copasetic
ACCEIORTT corticate
ACCEIPRVY pervicacy
ACCEIPSTY cityscape
ACCEJKOPY jockey cap
ACCEJKRSW jack screw
screw jack
ACCEJORYY Joyce Cary
ACCEKLMNO cockleman

ACCEKLNRS cracknels
ACCEKMORS smock-race
ACCEKNORR corncrake
ACCEKOPRR crack-rope
ACCEKORTW water cock
ACCELLLOS close call
ACCELLOOT collocate
ACCELLOSU calculose
ACCELLTUU cucullate
ACCELNOOR con calore
ACCELNOPY cyclopean
ACCELNOTU cancel out
ACCELNOVY concavely
covalency
ACCELNPTY peccantly
ACCELOTUY autocycle
ACCELPRTU claret cup
ACCEMNORY ceromancy
ACCEMNRTY McCartney
ACCEMOPRR cremocarp
ACCEMOPRT recompact
ACCEMORTY macrocyte
ACCENNOSS non-access
ACCENNOST Constance
ACCENNOTY cotenancy
ACCENNRST CT scanner
ACCENOORS coenosarc
ACCENOOTV convocate
ACCENORSU cancerous
ACCENRSUY recusancy
ACCEORRSW scarecrow
ACCEORRUY Eurocracy
ACCEORSSY accessory
ACCEORSTU coruscate
court case
ACCEPRSTU cut capers
ACCFFHHIN chaffinch
ACCFIILOR calorific
ACCFIILSS classific
ACCFIILSU fasciculi
ACCFIISST fascistic
ACCFIITTY facticity
ACCFIKNSY fancy-sick
ACCFIMORS sacciform
ACCFIMORT cactiform
ACCFINNOU Confucian
ACCFIORTX arctic fox
ACCFKOORT coat-frock
frock-coat
ACCFLLORU floccular
ACCGHHNNU Changchun
ACCGHIIKN chiacking
ACCGHIINN chicaning
ACCGHIIRR chiragric
ACCGHLNOO cacholong
ACCGIKLNR crackling
ACCGLORTU cargo cult
ACCGNORYY gynocracy
ACCHHIILR chiliarch
ACCHHIINP Pichincha
ACCHHIIOP chipochia
ACCHHIOPW coachwhip
ACCHHLORS scholarch
ACCHHMNRU churchman
ACCHHMOSU muchachos
ACCHHNOOR coach-horn
ACCHHORRS Rorschach
ACCHHRUWY churchway
ACCHIIIST ischiatic
ACCHIILRV chivalric
ACCHIINNP chincapin
ACCHIKLNO lock-chain
ACCHIKPST chapstick
ACCHILLOO alcoholic
ACCHILLOT laccolith
ACCHILNOR chronical
ACCHILNUU Cuchulain
ACCHILOPR roach clip
ACCHILOPS slip-coach
ACCHILORT Holarctic
ACCHILOTU acoluthic
ACCHILPSY psychical
ACCHIMNOR monarchic
ACCHIMNSY mischancy
ACCHIMOPR camphoric
ACCHIMORT chromatic
ACCHIMORX Chico Marx
ACCHIMOST stomachic
ACCHIMPPT pitch camp
ACCHINORT archontic
ACCHINPSU Capuchins
ACCHIOSTT octastich
ACCHIRTTY trachytic
ACCHJKLNY Jack Lynch
ACCHKLMOT matchlock
ACCHKLOPT packcloth
ACCHKLOST sackcloth
ACCHKLSTU saltchuck
ACCHKNPRU rack-punch
ACCHKOOOP cock-a-hoop
ACCHKOORW coachwork
ACCHLLOPT catchpoll
ACCHLOOPS school cap
ACCHLOORT colcothar
ochlocrat
ACCHLOOSW slowcoach
ACCHLOOTY chocolaty
ACCHMNOST Scotchman
ACCHNOOPY cacophony
ACCHNOPYY phycocyan
ACCHNORSU chancrous
ACCHOORTU coach tour
ACCHOSSTU succotash
ACCHPRSUU crush a cup
ACCIIILNN clinician
ACCIIINTV anticivic
ACCIILLPP Callippic
ACCIILLSY salicylic
ACCIILLVY civically
ACCIILNOR conciliar
ACCIILOPT occipital
ACCIILORV aciclovir
ACCIILTVY acclivity
ACCIIMNOS cocainism
ACCIIMNPT panmictic
ACCIIMNUV vaccinium
ACCIIMOPT apomictic
ACCIIMOSV vis comica
ACCIIMQSU caciquism
ACCIINOOZ Cainozoic
ACCIINOST cocainist
ACCIINRTY intricacy
ACCIIOPST pasticcio
ACCIIORST isocratic
ACCIIOSTT isotactic
ACCIIRSUV via crucis
ACCIISSTU casuistic
ACCIITTTY tacticity
ACCIJKKXY Jacky Ickx
ACCIKMRSU music rack
ACCIKNOSW cockswain
ACCILLMOY comically
ACCILLNOY conically
ACCILLNYY cynically
ACCILLRUY crucially
ACCILNOPY cyclopian
ACCILNORV clavicorn
ACCILNOTU ciclatoun
noctiluca
ACCILORTU coticular
ACCILORVY acyclovir
ACCILOSUV acclivous
ACCILPRTY cryptical
ACCILRRUU curricula
ACCILRTUU cuticular
ACCIMNOPS pancosmic
ACCIMNORY acronymic
ACCIMOORS crocosmia
ACCIMORTY timocracy
ACCIMPRTU practicum
ACCIMPSSU capsicums
ACCINNNOU uncanonic
ACCINOOSS occasions
ACCINOPRR Capricorn
ACCINOSTY canticoys
oscitancy
ACCINOSTZ scazontic
ACCINOTVY concavity
ACCINSTTY syntactic
ACCIOPRST sarcoptic
ACCIOPRTT catoptric
ACCIOPRTY procacity
ACCIOPSST spiccatos
ACCIOSSTT sticcatos
ACCIOSSTU acoustics
ACCJKORSS crossjack
ACCKKMMUU muck-a-muck
ACCKLLOPS scalp lock
ACCKLOORR coral-rock
ACCLLOSUU calculous
ACCLLSUUY calyculus
ACCLMNOTY Tom Clancy
ACCLMOPTY compactly

ACCLNNNOO colcannon
ACCLORTUY clay court
ACCLRSSUU succursal
ACCMMOORS macrocosm
ACCMNOORY monocracy
nomocracy
ACCMNOTUY contumacy
ACCMOOPRT compactor
ACCMOOPRY macrocopy
ACCMOORST cosmocrat
ACCNNOOTU no-account
on account
ACCNNOSTY constancy
ACCNOORTT contactor
ACCNOOTTU to account
ACCNORSTU coruscant
ACCNORTTU cunctator
ACCOOOOPP poco a poco
ACCOPRRUY procuracy
ACCOPRSTY cystocarp
ACCORSSTU cut across
ACDDDEEIT dedicated
ACDDEEEIT dedicatee
ACDDEEFNU undefaced
ACDDEEIMT medicated
ACDDEEITU deciduate
ACDDEELNN candle-end
ACDDEEMNO code-named
ACDDEENUY undecayed
ACDDEEORT decorated
ACDDEFGOO goodfaced
ACDDEFHIS dish-faced
ACDDEFIII acidified
ACDDEFLPU fuddle-cap
ACDDEFNTU ducted fan
ACDDEFORY forecaddy
ACDDEGIRU guide card
ACDDEGLLO gold-laced
ACDDEGNOO dodecagon
ACDDEGNRU dance drug
ACDDEHILY aldehydic
ACDDEHNRU dude ranch
ACDDEHRRU hard-cured
ACDDEIINS discandie
ACDDEIITV addictive
ACDDEIJNU jaundiced
ACDDEIKLU luckie-dad
ACDDEIMOP campodeid
ACDDEINRX card index
card-index
ACDDEIORT dedicator
ACDDEIORV video card
ACDDEITUV adductive
ACDDEKOST deadstock
ACDDELNRU underclad
ACDDELOPT clodpated
ACDDELRSU scuddaler
ACDDENRRU undercard
ACDDEOORW cedarwood
ACDDFILSY caddis fly
ACDDHHNSU dachshund
ACDDHIILM maid-child
ACDDHILSY caddishly
ACDDHIRRU arch-druid
ACDDIILOS discoidal
ACDDIILRU druidical
ACDDIIMOU diacodium
ACDDIINOO diacodion
ACDDIINOT addiction
ACDDIIORT idiot card
ACDDIIOSU audio disc
ACDDILNPU duplicand
ACDDIMSSU Sadducism
ACDDINOTU adduction
ACDDLLNOU cloudland
ACDDLNORW cold-drawn
ACDDMOORT mad-doctor
ACDDNOORR donor card
ACDDNOORT doctorand
ACDDNORSU soundcard
ACDDNRTUY cut and dry
ACDEEEHIP headpiece
ACDEEEHNR adherence
ACDEEELRY clear-eyed
ACDEEELSS déclassée
ACDEEEMRT decametre
ACDEEENTT dancettee
ACDEEEPPS deep space
ACDEEEPRT deprecate
ACDEEEPRV Cape Verde
ACDEEERST decastere
desecrate
ACDEEERTU re-educate
ACDEEFFLS self-faced
ACDEEFFNU uneffaced
ACDEEFGKU fudge cake
ACDEEFHMR chamfered
ACDEEFHWY whey-faced
ACDEEFIKR friedcake
ACDEEFIRR Frederica
ACDEEFKRT afterdeck
ACDEEFNTU fecundate
ACDEEFORT defecator
ACDEEFRRT redecraft
refracted
ACDEEGLOU decalogue✧
ACDEEGNNO endecagon
ACDEEGNRR green card
ACDEEGOPU decoupage
découpage
ACDEEGPRU peace drug
ACDEEHIIL Helicidae
ACDEEHINT echinated
ACDEEHIOR Orchideae
ACDEEHIOV head voice
ACDEEHIPP epedaphic
ACDEEHIRT tracheide
ACDEEHKNY hackneyed
ACDEEHLLN chandelle
ACDEEHLLT death cell
ACDEEHLOS closehead
ACDEEHLPT chapleted
ACDEEHLRT the cradle
ACDEEHNNT enchanted
ACDEEHNRU unreached
ACDEEHNRV chavender
ACDEEHNST chastened
ACDEEHPSY speech day
ACDEEHRRT chartered
three-card
ACDEEHRRY cherryade
ACDEEIILP epicedial
ACDEEIINP epicedian
ACDEEIIRT Icteridae
ACDEEIJTV adjective
ACDEEILMN demi-lance
endemical
ACDEEILMR declaimer
ACDEEILNN celandine
decennial
line dance
ACDEEILNR Icelander
ACDEEILNT declinate
ACDEEILNU Euclidean
ACDEEILPU Clupeidae
ACDEEILRS d'escalier
ACDEEILRT decalitre
ACDEEILTU elucidate
ACDEEIMNO macédoine
ACDEEIMNP impedance
ACDEEIMPR carpe diem
ACDEEINOS oceanides
ACDEEINRS Ecardines
ACDEEINSX index case
ACDEEIOPR adipocere
ACDEEIPRT predicate
ACDEEIPTU paedeutic
ACDEEIRRT traceried
ACDEEIRST c'est-à-dire
ACDEEIRTW iced water
ACDEEISST ecstasied
ACDEEITUV educative
ACDEEKKNR knackered
ACDEEKPPR prepacked
ACDEEKRTW water deck
ACDEELLMR marcelled
ACDEELLNV Cleveland
ACDEELLOT decollate
ocellated
ACDEELLPR parcelled
ACDEELLST steel-clad
ACDEELNNU uncleaned
ACDEELNNW new candle
ACDEELNOP penal code
ACDEELNRR calendrer
ACDEELNRS esclandre
ACDEELNRU uncleared
ACDEELNTT tentacled
ACDEELNTU nucleated
ACDEELORR Carol Reed
ACDEELORS seed coral
ACDEELORW coral weed
ACDEELRST decretals✧

ACDEELSTY	decastyle
ACDEELTTU	Claudette
ACDEELTUV	cut-leaved
ACDEEMMUV	vade-mecum
ACDEEMNOR	Decameron
ACDEEMNRU	unamerced
ACDEENNRU	endurance
ACDEENNRY	decennary
ACDEENNST	ascendent
ACDEENNTU	dance tune
ACDEENOPR	rope dance
ACDEENOSS	deaconess
ACDEENPST	step dance
ACDEENRTU	uncreated
ACDEENRTY	day centre
ACDEEOPRR	crop-eared
ACDEEORRR	care order
ACDEEORRW	cowardree
ACDEEPRRT	red carpet
	red-carpet
ACDEERRTT	retracted
ACDEERSST	Descartes
ACDEERSTT	scattered
ACDEERSTU	reductase
ACDEESSTU	decussate
ACDEFFILT	afflicted
ACDEFFIST	disaffect
ACDEFFLLU	full-faced
ACDEFFMOR	cofferdam
ACDEFGLNO	long-faced
ACDEFGMSU	smug-faced
ACDEFHINR	arch-fiend
ACDEFHINT	thin-faced
ACDEFHLTU	Dutch leaf
ACDEFIIIL	edificial
ACDEFIIIR	acidifier
ACDEFIILR	clarified
ACDEFIILT	feticidal
ACDEFIIRS	sacrifide
	scarified
ACDEFILLO	coalfield
ACDEFILOO	oil of cade
ACDEFILOR	coal-fired
ACDEFILRU	cauldrife
ACDEFILUV	adviceful
ACDEFINNU	unfancied
ACDEFINRT	infracted
ACDEFKLNO	folk dance
ACDEFLLOR	called-for
ACDEFLMOR	cold frame
ACDEFLNOR	force-land
	landforce
ACDEFLOOS	Sea of Cold
ACDEFLORZ	calfdozer
ACDEFMNOO	moon-faced
ACDEFORSS	cross-fade
ACDEGGIMO	demagogic
ACDEGGIOP	pedagogic
ACDEGGIRT	cat-rigged
ACDEGGOOR	good grace
ACDEGHINR	chagrined
ACDEGHIRS	discharge
ACDEGHNNU	unchanged
ACDEGHNRU	uncharged
ACDEGHOOP	good-cheap
ACDEGIILR	regicidal
ACDEGIIRT	citigrade
ACDEGILNO	genocidal
ACDEGILOO	logaoedic
ACDEGIMNO	endogamic
ACDEGINNR	ring dance
ACDEGINNS	ascending
ACDEGINOY	gynaecoid
ACDEGINST	singed cat
ACDEGIRRS	disgracer
ACDEGIRRT	cartridge
ACDEGLLRU	guard cell
ACDEGLNOU	Langue d'oc
ACDEGLOOS	gas-cooled
ACDEGMNOO	come and go
	come-and-go
ACDEGMORY	God-a-mercy
ACDEGNNOU	undecagon
ACDEHHIKT	thickhead
ACDEHHIRS	rhachides
ACDEHHKOS	shock-head
ACDEHHLOT	cloth head
	headcloth
ACDEHHNTU	unhatched
ACDEHHORX	hexachord
ACDEHIINS	side chain
ACDEHIIRR	diarrheic
ACDEHIITT	diathetic
ACDEHIKLN	kneidlach
ACDEHIKMR	march-dike
ACDEHIKST	headstick
ACDEHILLO	cheloidal
ACDEHILMN	name-child
ACDEHINNO	anhedonic
ACDEHINNR	hindrance
ACDEHINNU	unchained
ACDEHINRT	theandric
ACDEHINSV	cavendish
ACDEHIORT	Trochidae
ACDEHIOSU	acid house
	acid-house
ACDEHIPRS	Sephardic
ACDEHIPRT	dirt cheap
ACDEHIPST	cadetship
ACDEHIRSV	crash dive
	crash-dive
ACDEHKMOP	chokedamp
ACDEHKMRY	march-dyke
ACDEHKOST	headstock
ACDEHLLRT	dratchell
ACDEHLMSY	chlamydes
ACDEHLNOR	chlordane
ACDEHLNOT	decathlon
ACDEHLNRY	chandlery
ACDEHLPRY	parchedly
ACDEHLRSU	schedular
ACDEHLRWY	wych-alder
ACDEHMMOS	sachemdom
ACDEHMNRU	uncharmed
ACDEHMNTU	unmatched
ACDEHMOST	stomached
ACDEHMPRY	pachyderm
ACDEHNNRT	trenchand
ACDEHNOOT	chaetodon
ACDEHNOPR	cardphone
	phonecard
ACDEHNORW	crown-head
ACDEHNOTU	head count
ACDEHNRRT	trenchard
ACDEHNRSW	hand-screw
ACDEHNRTU	uncharted
ACDEHNRUY	hue and cry
ACDEHNSTU	unscathed
ACDEHNTUW	unwatched
ACDEHOOPT	chaetopod
ACDEHOOPW	peach-wood
ACDEHORRV	hardcover
ACDEHORSS	crosshead
ACDEIIINT	dietician
ACDEIILMN	adminicle
	medicinal
ACDEIILNO	lidocaine
ACDEIILNT	identical
ACDEIILNX	indexical
ACDEIILPU	Pulicidae
ACDEIILRV	larvicide
	veridical
ACDEIILST	deistical
ACDEIILSW	Lewis acid
ACDEIILTW	twice-laid
ACDEIIMMY	immediacy
ACDEIIMNR	Amerindic
ACDEIIMRT	diametric
	matricide
ACDEIINOR	Crinoidea
ACDEIINOS	sciaenoid
ACDEIINOT	dianoetic
ACDEIINPY	Cynipidae
ACDEIINRS	inside-car
ACDEIINST	andesitic
	Dianetics®
ACDEIINTV	vindicate
ACDEIIOPR	aperiodic
ACDEIIPRR	parricide
ACDEIIPRT	patricide
ACDEIIPTU	paideutic
ACDEIIPTY	diapyetic
ACDEIIRSU	Sciuridae
ACDEIKLLP	pickadell
ACDEIKMPR	rampicked
ACDEIKRST	sidetrack
ACDEIKTTY	ticket day
ACDEILLMY	decimally
	medically
ACDEILLOU	lodiculae
ACDEILLTY	edictally
ACDEILMNU	unclaimed
	undecimal

ACDEILNNP pinnacled
ACDEILNNT declinant
ACDEILNOU Deucalion
ACDEILNTU acidulent
ACDEILNVY divalency
ACDEILOOP alopecoid
ACDEILOOR air-cooled
ACDEILORX Delacroix
ACDEILOST dislocate
ACDEILOSY Lycosidae
ACDEILOTV dolce vita
ACDEILOTY Dicotylae
ACDEILPRU pedicular
ACDEILPTU duplicate
ACDEILRSS laser disc
ACDEIMNNO dominance
ACDEIMNNT mendicant
ACDEIMNOP companied
compendia
ACDEIMNSU muscadine
ACDEIMNTY mendacity
ACDEIMORT decimator
ACDEIMORU ami de cour
ACDEIMOSY Samoyedic
ACDEIMRTU muricated
ACDEINNOR ordinance
ACDEINNOT contadine
ACDEINNTU uncinated
ACDEINORR coriander
ACDEINORS Dinoceras
iron-cased
ACDEINORT redaction
ACDEINOTU education
Noctuidae
ACDEINOTV advection
ACDEINPRT predicant
tap cinder
ACDEINRTY Antrycide®
ACDEINSTY asyndetic
cystidean
syndicate
ACDEINTTU tunicated
ACDEIOORS Dioscorea
ACDEIORST Cordaites
ACDEIOSTY Cystoidea
ACDEIPRST practised
ACDEIPRSW card swipe
swipe card
ACDEIPRTY predacity
ACDEIPSTU cuspidate
ACDEIQSUV vice squad
ACDEIQTTU acquitted
ACDEIRSTY dicastery
ACDEIRTTU dictature
ACDEIRTTX direct tax
tax credit
ACDEIRUVY ayurvedic✧
ACDEISSTY ecdysiast
ACDEITTTW cat-witted
ACDEKMOOS mockadoes
ACDEKMSTU duck's-meat
ACDEKNOPU pound cake
ACDEKNRSW sneck draw
ACDEKNRTU untracked
ACDEKNRUV raven-duck
ACDEKRSSS sack dress
ACDELLOPS scalloped
ACDELLORR corralled
ACDELMOPR placoderm
ACDELMORY comradely
ACDELMTUU cumulated
ACDELNNOO colonnade
ACDELNNOR clarendon
ACDELNNTU candlenut
ACDELNOOT loden coat
ACDELNOOW lancewood
ACDELNORS Androcles
ACDELNOSU unsolaced
ACDELNOSW downscale
scale down
ACDELNOTU unlocated
ACDELNRSU sclaunder
ACDELNRTY trancedly
ACDELNRUY underclay
ACDELNSSU unclassed
ACDELOPSW slow-paced
ACDELOPTU cupolated
ACDELORTW cold water
ACDELPRSY clepsydra
ACDELRTTU cultrated
ACDEMMMNO commendam
ACDEMMNOR commander
ACDEMMOOR macrodome
ACDEMNNOS second man
ACDEMNOPR compander
ACDEMOORT motorcade
ACDEMORSU Scudamore
ACDEMORTY democraty
ACDENNNSU unscanned
ACDENNOSY nose candy
ACDENNRST transcend
ACDENOORT coronated
ACDENOOSS soda scone
ACDENOOTT cottonade
ACDENOPST spot dance
ACDENORST Doncaster
ACDENORSW sword-cane
ACDENORSY secondary✧
ACDENORTU undercoat
ACDENPTTU punctated
ACDENRRSU run scared
unscarred
ACDENRRTU undercart
ACDENRSSW sand-screw
ACDENRSTU undercast
ACDENRTTU reductant
truncated
ACDEOORRT decorator
ACDEOORTT doctorate
ACDEOPRRT carpet-rod
ACDEOPSTU spaced out
ACDEOPTTU coup d'état
ACDEORRST co-starred
store card
ACDEORRSW score draw
ACDEORRTT detractor
ACDEORSST coat-dress
dress coat
ACDEORSTU ceratodus
croustade
ACDEORSUU rudaceous
ACDEORSUZ cruzadoes
ACDEORTUY educatory
ACDERSTTU crustated
ACDESSTUY case-study
ACDFFHNSU handcuffs
ACDFHILSS scaldfish
ACDFHINOO food chain
ACDFIIILP lapidific
ACDFIIRUY fiduciary
ACDFIKLNO Nick Faldo
ACDFINNOT confidant
ACDFINTUY facundity
ACDFNORSW scarf down
ACDFNTTUY candytuft
ACDFOORTW woodcraft
ACDGGINOR dog racing
ACDGHIMOY dichogamy
ACDGHIPSY dysphagic
ACDGIILOR goliardic
ACDGIINNR dining-car
ACDGIINNY cyaniding
ACDGIIRST digastric
ACDGILNSS scaldings
ACDGIMORW magic word
ACDGIMOST dogmatics
ACDGINRTU traducing
ACDGLLOOR dog collar
ACDGLOOST Gold Coast
ACDGMNORU conga drum
ACDGNOPRU grand coup
ACDGORRSS cord grass
ACDHIIIRR Richard II
ACDHIIIST stichidia
ACDHIILMO homicidal
ACDHIILOP acidophil
ACDHIILST distichal
ACDHIIMOR chromidia
ACDHIIMSS Chasidism
ACDHIIMSU dichasium
ACDHIKLNO knaidloch
ACDHIKORW chowkidar
ACDHIKPRT pitch-dark
ACDHILLTU Auld Licht
ACDHILMUY diachylum
ACDHILNOY diachylon
ACDHILPSS scaldship
ACDHILRSY chrysalid
ACDHILRUY hydraulic
ACDHILSTT last-ditch
ACDHIMNOR man-orchid
ACDHIMORT chromatid
dichromat

ACDHINNOW chain down
ACDHINORS disanchor
ACDHINORY diachrony
ACDHINRTW wind chart
ACDHIOPRS rhapsodic
ACDHIORSY dyschroia
ACDHIOSUV disavouch
ACDHIRRSU churidars
ACDHLOOSY day school
schoolday
ACDHLORTU Coulthard
ACDHLORTY cloth-yard
ACDHMOOTW doomwatch
matchwood
ACDHNORRU roundarch
ACDHNORTU court hand
ACDHOOPPS scaphopod
ACDHOORRU Urochorda
ACDHORRTU hard court
Tudor arch
ACDHORTWW watchword
ACDIIILMT miticidal
ACDIIILOT idiotical
ACDIIILRV viricidal
ACDIIIMOT idiomatic
ACDIIJLRU juridical
ACDIIJMOT comitadji
ACDIIJRUY judiciary
ACDIIJSTU Judaistic
ACDIIKLLP pickadill
ACDIIKNOS Dicksonia
ACDIILLTY callidity
ACDIILMNO dominical
ACDIILNOR crinoidal
ACDIILOSS dissocial
ACDIILOST diastolic
ACDIILPTY placidity
ACDIILRUV virucidal
ACDIILSTU dualistic
ACDIIMNNO Dominican
ACDIIMPRY pyramidic
ACDIIMRTY mydriatic
ACDIINNOT contadini
ACDIINORS radionics
ACDIINORT indicator✧
ACDIINOSY Dionysiac
ACDIINOTT dictation
ACDIINRTY rancidity
ACDIIOPRT diatropic
ACDIIRTTX dictatrix
ACDIJORTU judicator
ACDIKKLRY Kirkcaldy
ACDIKKNST kickstand
ACDIKLLPR pack-drill
ACDIKLRTW wild track
ACDIKNQSU quicksand
ACDIKNRST rickstand
ACDIKRRTT dirt track
ACDIKRSTY yardstick
ACDILLLOO colloidal
ACDILLLUY ludically
ACDILLOOR coralloid
ACDILLORY cordially
ACDILLOSU caudillos
ACDILMNOO monodical
ACDILMOPS psalmodic
ACDILMOPY diplomacy
ACDILMOTU comatulid
ACDILNOOR coordinal
co-ordinal
ACDILNORT doctrinal
ACDILNORU rain-cloud
uncordial
ACDILNOSY synodical
ACDILNPRS land-scrip
ACDILOOPT octaploid
ACDILOORT doctorial
ACDILOPRS dropsical
ACDILORSW crowd sail
ACDILORSY corydalis
ACDILOSTU custodial
ACDILOSUU acidulous
ACDILOTUV oviductal
ACDILRTTY tridactyl
ACDILSTTY dactylist
ACDIMNNOY dominancy
ACDIMNORS Draconism
ACDIMOPSS spasmodic
ACDIMORTY mordacity
ACDINNOOT contadino
ACDINOSTU custodian
ACDIORTTY dictatory
ACDJLNTUY adjunctly
ACDJOORTU coadjutor
ACDKLLORR Lord Clark
ACDKLMOSY lady-smock
ACDKLORTU truckload
ACDKMNNOO monadnock
ACDKNORTW track down
ACDKORRSW sword-rack
ACDKORSTY stockyard
ACDLLNORU call round
Lord Lucan
ACDLMNOOY condyloma
ACDLMNOPW clamp down
clampdown
ACDLMNORU round clam
ACDLNNORW crown land
ACDLNNUUY undulancy
ACDLNSTYY syndactyl
ACDLOOPPY clappy-doo
ACDLORSSW word class
ACDLORSTT cold start
ACDMMNOOS commandos
ACDMMNORU communard✧
ACDMNOOPR compandor
ACDMOOPRR comprador
ACDMOOSUV muscovado
ACDMPRRTU trump card
ACDNNOOPR pro and con
ACDNNORUU uncandour
ACDNNRTUU cut and run
ACDOORRSS crossroad
ACDOORSTW saw doctor
ACDORRTUY courtyard
ACEEEFHLP feel cheap
ACEEEFIRS ceasefire
ACEEEFIRT cafetière
ACEEEFLNR freelance
ACEEEFPRS free space
free-space
ACEEEGHKU Aguecheek
ACEEEGHPR repechage
ACEEEGLNY eye-glance
ACEEEGNNV vengeance
ACEEEGRST secretage
ACEEEHHRW eachwhere
ACEEEHIPT petechiae
ACEEEHIRV echeveria
ACEEEHLRW wheel race
ACEEEHNPR cheapener
ACEEEHPRT peach-tree
ACEEEHSTV cheesevat
ACEEEILMP piecemeal
ACEEEIMPT peacetime
ACEEEINPT epaenetic
ACEEEIPPP peace pipe
ACEEEIPRT piece rate
ACEEEJLSW jewel case
ACEEEKNQU queen-cake
ACEEEKPSY escape key
ACEEEKRRT racketeer
ACEEELNRT crenelate
ACEEELNRV relevance
ACEEELNTU enucleate
ACEEELNTY acetylene
ACEEELPRT peat-creel
ACEEELPSS peaceless
ACEEELPSV cap sleeve
ACEEELRST scelerate
ACEEELSSS ceaseless
ACEEEMNNR remanence
ACEEEMNPR permeance
ACEEENPPT appetence
ACEEENPRS esperance
ACEEENPRT pecan tree
ACEEENRSV severance
ACEEENRTW new-create
ACEEERSTT etceteras
ACEEERSUY saucer eye
ACEEFFHRR chafferer
ACEEFFHRU réchauffé
ACEEFFITV affective
ACEEFFLMT maleffect
ACEEFFLNU affluence
ACEEFFLTU effectual
ACEEFFNRY fancy-free
ACEEFGMOO come of age
ACEEFHHKL half-cheek
ACEEFHITW whiteface
ACEEFHLNP halfpence
ACEEFHLPR parfleche
ACEEFHORR forereach

ACEEFHORT foreteach
ACEEFHSTT fact sheet
ACEEFIKNS case-knife
ACEEFILNR rail-fence
ACEEFILNV venefical
ACEEFILPR fireplace
ACEEFINRT interface
re infecta
ACEEFINRY in-yer-face
ACEEFIRSS fricassee
ACEEFKOPR poker face
ACEEFKORW weak force
ACEEFLLLS leaf cells
ACEEFLNRS scale fern
ACEEFLORR coral reef
ACEEFLOTV volte-face
ACEEFLRRX reflex arc
ACEEFMORT come after
forcemeat
ACEEFMPRV camp-fever
ACEEFNORV confervae
ACEEFRRST scart-free
ACEEFRRSU resurface
ACEEGHHNT the change
ACEEGHIOR heroic age
ACEEGHIRU gaucherie
ACEEGHISV give chase
ACEEGHLLN challenge
ACEEGHNRX exchanger
ACEEGHNSX sex change
sex-change
ACEEGHOPT go the pace
ACEEGHRST the Graces
ACEEGIILS gaelicise
ACEEGIILZ gaelicize
ACEEGILNR generical
ACEEGILNS Cingalese
ACEEGILNT clientage
genetical
ACEEGILNV evangelic
ACEEGILPV give place
ACEEGILRS sacrilege
ACEEGILRV vice-regal
ACEEGIMNR Germanice
ACEEGIMRU megacurie
ACEEGINOR recoinage
ACEEGINPS peace sign
ACEEGINRV grievance
ACEEGIRRT cigar tree
ACEEGIRRV caregiver
ACEEGIRTT cigarette
ACEEGKRWY greywacke
ACEEGLLOU colleague
ACEEGLNRT rectangle
ACEEGLRSS graceless
ACEEGLRSY greyscale
ACEEGMNOR geomancer
ACEEGMNUY gynaeceum
ACEEGMOPS megascope
ACEEGNNPR pregnance
ACEEGNORT grace note
ACEEGNORU encourage
ACEEGNRSV scavenger
ACEEGNRSY sergeancy
ACEEGNSSY cageyness
ACEEGOOPR cooperage
ACEEGOPPR Copper Age
ACEEGORST escortage
ACEEGPRSU grease cup
ACEEGRTTU curettage
ACEEHHLRW wheel arch
ACEEHHORT each other
ACEEHHRRT the Archer
ACEEHHRST the Arches
ACEEHHRTW what cheer?
ACEEHHTUX Hexateuch
ACEEHIIPR hairpiece
ACEEHILMS alchemise
ACEEHILMZ alchemize
ACEEHILPT petechial
ACEEHILRT cheralite
etherical
heretical
ACEEHILRV chevalier
ACEEHIMNS achimenes
mechanise
ACEEHIMNT the cinema
ACEEHIMNZ mechanize
ACEEHIMPR impeacher
ACEEHIMPS hemispace
ACEEHIMRT hate crime
ACEEHINNS sennachie
ACEEHINNV enhancive
ACEEHINPT phenacite
ACEEHINRR rancherie
ACEEHINRT Catherine
china tree
ACEEHINST hesitance
ACEEHIPRS Parcheesi®
ACEEHIRRS cashierer
ACEEHIRTW white race
ACEEHISTT aesthetic
ACEEHKOPR choke-pear
ACEEHKPST packsheet
ACEEHKPTW keep watch
ACEEHLMNO chameleon✧
ACEEHLMOO haemocoel
ACEEHLMPV champlevé
ACEEHLNNR channeler
ACEEHLNRU herculean✧
ACEEHLNSS seneschal
ACEEHLNTU Neuchâtel
ACEEHLORT trochleae
ACEEHLPSS chapeless
ACEEHLRSS reachless
ACEEHLRTW cartwheel
ACEEHLRTY teacherly
ACEEHLSST teachless
ACEEHMMRT machmeter
ACEEHMNRY arch-enemy
ACEEHMOTY haemocyte
ACEEHMRST The Scream
ACEEHMRSU charmeuse
ACEEHMTTU humectate
ACEEHNNOS encheason
ACEEHNNRT enchanter
ACEEHNOPR canephore
chaperone
ACEEHNOTW cone wheat
ACEEHNPSS cheapness
ACEEHNRST chastener
ACEEHNRTT entrechat
ACEEHNRTY Cytherean
ACEEHNSTU chanteuse
ACEEHOPRR orepearch
ACEEHORRS horse race
racehorse
ACEEHORRV overreach
ACEEHORST escheator
ACEEHOSTU theaceous
ACEEHPRTY archetype
ACEEHRRRT charterer
recharter
ACEEHRRSS archeress
ACEEHRRTT chatterer
ACEEHRRTY treachery
ACEEHRSUV ever such a
ACEEIILPT tailpiece
ACEEIINPT epainetic
ACEEIJQRU jacquerie✧
ACEEIKLLS scalelike
ACEEIKLMU leukaemic
ACEEIKLSV sick leave
ACEEIKMNZ Mackenzie
ACEEIKRST creakiest
ice-skater
ACEEILLNP capelline
ACEEILLPP peace pill
ACEEILLRT reticella
ACEEILLST celestial
ACEEILLTV vellicate
ACEEILMNS mescaline
ACEEILMOV come alive
ACEEILMRR reclaimer
ACEEILMRT carmelite✧
ACEEILMST timescale
ACEEILMTT telematic
ACEEILNOR Coleraine
ACEEILNOS Seneca oil
ACEEILNPR percaline
Periclean
ACEEILNPT pectineal
ACEEILNPW wipe-clean
ACEEILNRS scare-line
ACEEILNRT interlace
lacertine
reclinate
ACEEILNTY ceylanite
ACEEILOPV piacevole
ACEEILPRR real price
ACEEILPRS periclase
sale price
ACEEILPRT replicate

ACEEILPTX explicate
ACEEILRST cartelise
cerealist
ACEEILRTZ cartelize
zelatrice
ACEEILSTV c'est la vie
ACEEILSUV vesiculae
ACEEILSWX excise law
ACEEIMMNN immanence
ACEEIMMNT mincemeat
ACEEIMMRT metameric
ACEEIMNPR mepacrine
ACEEIMNRT incremate
ACEEIMNSX exciseman
ACEEIMPRT imprecate
ACEEIMPST empaestic
space-time
ACEEIMRRS careerism
ACEEIMRSS cassimere
ACEEIMRST creamiest
miscreate
stream-ice
ACEEIMRTT metricate
ACEEIMRVW crime wave
ACEEINNPS spinacene
ACEEINNRT nectarine
ACEEINNTU enunciate
ACEEINOPR caponiere
ACEEINPRU epicurean✧
ACEEINPTT pectinate
ACEEINRRS increaser
ACEEINRSS scenarise
ACEEINRST cisternae
ACEEINRSZ scenarize
ACEEINRTT Encratite
ACEEINSSV ascensive
ACEEIORST esoterica
ACEEIORTX excoriate
ACEEIOSSS écossaise
ACEEIOTVV evocative
ACEEIPPRR rice paper
ACEEIPRTT crepitate
ACEEIPRTV precative
ACEEIPSTX expiscate
ACEEIQRRU reacquire
ACEEIRRST careerist
ACEEIRRTW rice water
water rice
ACEEIRSSV caressive
ACEEIRSTU cauterise
ACEEIRSTV viscerate
ACEEIRSVV vice versa
ACEEIRTTX extricate
ACEEIRTUZ cauterize
ACEEISSST ecstasise
ACEEISSTZ ecstasize
ACEEISTXX excise tax
ACEEJNRSY serjeancy
ACEEKKPRT keep track
ACEEKLNNR enranckle
ACEEKMOPS Cape smoke
ACEEKORST sea rocket
ACEEKORTV take cover
ACEELLLOT locellate
ACEELLLSU cellulase
ACEELLNRU la lucerne
ACEELLORT electoral
ACEELLPSS placeless
ACEELLRSY Carlylese
ACEELLRTW water cell
ACEELLSSS scaleless
ACEELMNPT placement
ACEELMNRT recalment
ACEELMNST selectman
ACEELMNTU ante lucem
ACEELMOOR cameo-role
ACEELMOOT coelomate
ACEELMOPS someplace
ACEELMORT latecomer
ACEELMRSW male screw
ACEELNNOR ale-conner
ACEELNNRU cannelure
ACEELNNSS cleanness
ACEELNORT coeternal
tolerance
ACEELNOST Slate Cone
ACEELNPRT percental
ACEELNPTU petulance
ACEELNRSS clearness
ACEELNRTU calenture
crenulate
ACEELNRTW law centre
ACEELNRVY relevancy
ACEELNSSW Wenceslas
ACEELNSTT latescent
ACEELNSTW Newcastle
ACEELNTUX exultance
ACEELOOSU oleaceous
ACEELOPRT percolate
ACEELORRT coral tree
correlate
ACEELORSS casserole
ACEELORSW lower-case
ACEELORTT lectorate
ACEELORTU urceolate
ACEELOSST lose caste
ACEELPSSS scapeless
spaceless
ACEELPSTU speculate
ACEELPSTY type scale
ACEELPTUX exculpate
ACEELQRRU lacquerer
ACEELRRTT clatterer
ACEELRSST traceless
ACEELRTTU reluctate
ACEELRTUY electuary
ACEELSSST casteless
ACEELSSSU causeless
sauceless
ACEELSSTT cast-steel
ACEEMNNRY remanency
ACEEMNNTT enactment
ACEEMNPST scapement
ACEEMNRRY mercenary
ACEEMNTTX exactment
ACEEMOPRT Mecoptera
ACEEMOPST copes-mate
ACEEMORRS sarcomere
ACEEMORTT octameter
ACEEMORVW creamwove
ACEEMOVZZ mezza voce
ACEEMRRST cremaster
ACEEMRRTU mercurate
ACEEMRSTV Steve Cram
ACEEMRSTY mercy-seat
ACEENNNOR cannoneer
ACEENNNTT annectent
ACEENNOPR can-opener
ACEENNORS resonance
ACEENNOST caen-stone
Cantonese
ACEENNOSV sovenance
ACEENNOTT centonate
ACEENNRST renascent
ACEENNRTY centenary
ACEENORTZ Zenocrate
ACEENPPTY appetency
ACEENPRRT carpenter
ACEENPTTX exceptant
expectant
ACEENRRTU crenature
ACEENRSSY necessary
ACEENRSTV Cervantes
ACEENRTTU utterance
ACEENSSTU acuteness
ACEENSSTX exactness
ACEENTTUX executant
ACEEOOPRT cooperate
co-operate
ACEEOPRRT procreate
ACEEOPRSS spore case
ACEEOPRTV patercove
ACEEORRTT rectorate
ACEEORRTV overreact
ACEEORRTW water core
water-core
ACEEORTUY eucaryote
ACEEORTVX over-exact
ACEEOSSTU setaceous
ACEEPPRSU upper-case
ACEEPRRTU recapture
ACEEPRSSV cap verses
ACEERRSST creatress
ACEERRSTT scatterer
streetcar
ACEERRSTY secretary
ACEERRTUW water cure
ACEERSSTT tesseract
ACEERSSTU secateurs
ACEERSSTX exactress
ACEFFFLRU carfuffle
ACEFFGINT affecting
ACEFFHRUU chauffeur

Words marked ✧ can also be spelled with one or more capital letters

ACEFFIIOT officiate
ACEFFIKMR mafficker
ACEFFINOT affection
ACEFFIOPY pay-office
ACEFFIORT forficate
ACEFFIORW War Office
ACEFFMPRU cream puff
ACEFFOSTU suffocate
ACEFGHINT Night Café
ACEFGHIRT right face!
ACEFGHLNU changeful
ACEFGHLRU chargeful
ACEFGIRTU fruit cage
ACEFGLNOR gerfalcon
ACEFHIINT chieftain
ACEFHILPR half-price
ACEFHILSS scale fish
ACEFHINRS franchise
ACEFHIPRY preachify
ACEFHIRRU fraîcheur
ACEFHIRTU faith cure
ACEFHIRTW watch fire
ACEFHLLOS half-close
ACEFHLNOR arch-felon
ACEFHLNWX flax-wench
ACEFHLSTU scatheful
ACEFHMNNR Frenchman
ACEFHMORT homecraft
ACEFHOSUV vouchsafe
ACEFHRTTY fratchety
ACEFIILLS Filicales
ACEFIILMS facsimile
ACEFIILRR clarifier
ACEFIILRT laticifer
ACEFIINNR financier
ACEFIIRRS scarifier
ACEFIIRRT artificer✧
ACEFIIRTV fricative
ACEFIISST satisfice
ACEFIITTV factitive
ACEFIJKKN jackknife
ACEFIKRTU fruitcake
ACEFILLPR filler cap
ACEFILLSS life class
ACEFILNNO falconine
ACEFILNRZ frenzical
ACEFILNSS fanciless
ACEFILNTT fat client
ACEFILOPR caprifole
ACEFILORT fortalice
ACEFILOSU filaceous
ACEFILOTV olfactive
ACEFIMORT formicate
ACEFINORT fornicate
ACEFINRTU canefruit
ACEFINSTT fatiscent
ACEFINSTU infuscate
ACEFINTTV ventifact
ACEFIOPRT forcipate
ACEFIORST factorise
ACEFIORSU feracious
ACEFIORTZ factorize
ACEFIOSTU facetious
ACEFIRSSW scarfwise
ACEFIRSTT craftiest
ACEFJLNOR jerfalcon
ACEFKLNOR cornflake
ACEFKLORS foreslack
ACEFKORST task force
ACEFLLLSU full-scale
ACEFLLMRU full-cream
ACEFLLPSU pull faces
ACEFLLRUY carefully
ACEFLMNOS flamencos
ACEFLMOPY pomace-fly
ACEFLMOTU camouflet
ACEFLNORR conferral
coral fern
ACEFLNRUU uncareful
ACEFLPTUU teacupful
ACEFLRRUY curry-leaf
ACEFLRSST craftless
ACEFLRSTU cratefuls
ACEFLRSUU saucerful
ACEFLTTUU fluctuate
ACEFNORSU surf canoe
ACEFNORSV confervas
ACEFNRRTU runecraft
ACEFNRSTT transfect
ACEFOOPRS roofscape
ACEFOPRRT after-crop
ACEFORRRT refractor
ACEFOSTUU tufaceous
ACEFRTTUU fructuate
ACEGGHLRU ruggelach
ACEGGINOR racegoing
ACEGGINOS Gascoigne
ACEGGIRST craggiest
ACEGHHILP high-place
ACEGHHMSU camsheugh
ACEGHHOPR echograph
ACEGHHPTU Hugh Capet
ACEGHILRT lethargic
ACEGHILSU Ausgleich
ACEGHILTT tight-lace
ACEGHIMPR graphemic
ACEGHIMPS game chips
ACEGHIMRS mischarge
ACEGHINPR preaching
ACEGHINRS searching
ACEGHIRST Reichstag
ACEGHLNOR anchor leg
ACEGHLOOS school age
school-age
ACEGHLORT cole-garth
ACEGHMNOS cheongsam
ACEGHMORT hectogram
ACEGHMORY hercogamy
ACEGHNRRU grauncher
ACEGHOPRR cerograph
ACEGHOPTU Hugo Capet
ACEGHOPTY phagocyte
ACEGHRRSU surcharge
ACEGIILLS gallicise✧
silica gel
ACEGIILLZ gallicize✧
ACEGIILMO oligaemic
ACEGIILMS gaelicism
ACEGIILNS anglicise
ACEGIILNT genitalic
ACEGIILNV vigilance
ACEGIILNZ anglicize
ACEGIIMNT enigmatic
ACEGIINNT antigenic
ACEGIINRR rice grain
ACEGIINST sagenitic
ACEGIIRRT geriatric
ACEGIKPRR ragpicker
ACEGIKRST gear-stick
ACEGILLLO collegial
ACEGILLNO collegian
ACEGILLOR allegoric
ACEGILLOT colligate
ACEGILNNO congenial
ACEGILNNS cleansing
ACEGILNRU neuralgic
ACEGILNRW clearwing
ACEGILNSS cassingle
ACEGILNTU cingulate
ACEGILRTU curtilage
Géricault
graticule
ACEGIMMRS scrimmage
ACEGIMMST tagmemics
ACEGIMNOT geomantic
ACEGIMNRS screaming
ACEGIMNRT centigram
ACEGIMNST magnetics
ACEGIMNTU mutagenic
ACEGIMNUY gynaecium
ACEGIMTUZ zeugmatic
ACEGINNOR ignorance
ACEGINNOT négociant
ACEGINNSU unceasing
ACEGINOOT Notogaeic
ACEGINOSU cousinage
ACEGINOTU autogenic
ACEGINPRT carpeting
ACEGINPRY panegyric
ACEGINRRT terracing
ACEGINRSS caressing
ACEGIOPRR paregoric
ACEGIOSTT geostatic
ACEGIPPRS scrippage
ACEGIRRSS rice grass
ACEGIRSTT strategic
ACEGJLNTU jungle cat
ACEGJLRTU claret jug
ACEGJNOTU conjugate
ACEGKOORS gas cooker
ACEGLMNOO come along
ACEGLMNRY clergyman
ACEGLNNOU uncongeal

ACEGLNNPY plangency
ACEGLNOSU consulage
ACEGLNOTY cognately
ACEGLORST L'Escargot
ACEGMMNOO commonage
ACEGMMRSU scrummage
ACEGNNOTT cotangent
ACEGNNPRY pregnancy
ACEGORRTU corrugate
ACEGORSST get across
ACEGPRSTU scrapegut
ACEHHHINS Shechinah
ACEHHHIST shechitah
ACEHHILPS chelaship
ACEHHIRRY hierarchy
ACEHHIRSS rhachises
ACEHHIRST The Chairs
ACEHHISTX hexastich
ACEHHJNOP cheap John
ACEHHLSTT shtetlach
ACEHHLWYZ wych-hazel
ACEHHMNTT hatchment
ACEHHMOTY theomachy
ACEHHMRTW Wehrmacht
ACEHHMSSY Hesychasm
ACEHHNRTY ethnarchy
ACEHHOOTT toothache
ACEHHORST charoseth
ACEHHPRTY heptarchy
ACEHHSSTY Hesychast
ACEHIILTU halieutic
ACEHIIMRU hieracium
ACEHIINNP Phenician
ACEHIINPP epiphanic
ACEHIINPR chain pier
ACEHIINRT trichinae
ACEHIIPPT epitaphic
ACEHIIRST charities
ACEHIISTT atheistic
ACEHIJNTU China jute
ACEHIKKLL chalklike
ACEHIKNOV Chekovian
ACEHIKNPP Peckinpah
ACEHIKORT artichoke
ACEHIKRST heartsick
ACEHILLLY helically
ACEHILLRT cleithral
ACEHILLTY ethically
ACEHILMMO chamomile
ACEHILMRT thermical
ACEHILMST alchemist
ACEHILMTW witchmeal
ACEHILNNO chelonian
ACEHILNOR enchorial
ACEHILNOT chelation
ACEHILNPR Prince Hal
ACEHILNRU chain rule
ACEHILNSS chainless
ACEHILNTU unethical
ACEHILNTY thylacine
ACEHILOOT coolie hat
ACEHILOPT phacolite
ACEHILORR Charleroi
ACEHILORW archilowe
ACEHILOST the social
ACEHILOTW white coal
ACEHILPRS spherical
ACEHILPRY preachily
ACEHILRSU Heraclius
ACEHILRUV vehicular
ACEHILSTT athletics
ACEHILTTY tachylite
ACEHIMMNS mechanism
ACEHIMNRY machinery
ACEHIMNST mechanist
ACEHIMOPT omphacite
ACEHIMORY cherimoya
ACEHIMRTU rheumatic
ACEHINNOP open-chain
ACEHINNOT oenanthic
ACEHINNRY Hercynian
ACEHINNST encanthis
ACEHINOPR parochine
Phonic Ear®
ACEHINORS China rose
ACEHINORT anchorite
antechoir
ACEHINORX chronaxie
ACEHINOSV schiavone
ACEHINRRU hurricane✧
raunchier
ACEHINRSS chariness
ACEHINRSU sea urchin
ACEHINRTT in the cart
ACEHINSTY hesitancy
ACEHINTTU authentic
ACEHINTUY Eutychian
ACEHIOOTZ zoothecia
ACEHIOPRY coryphaei
ACEHIORRT hierocrat
ACEHIORST rhotacise
ACEHIORTZ rhotacize
ACEHIOSTT athetosic
ACEHIOTTT athetotic
ACEHIOTTW whitecoat
ACEHIPPSS spaceship
ACEHIPRSS ecphrasis
ACEHIPRTY architype
ACEHIPRUY eucryphia
ACEHIPSST pastiches
ACEHIPSTT pathetics
ACEHIRRRT trierarch
ACEHIRRST Reichsrat
ACEHIRSST chastiser
ACEHIRSTT theatrics
ACEHIRSTU Eucharist
ACEHIRSTV tsarevich
ACEHIRSTX exarchist
ACEHJLNOR John Clare
ACEHJNNOO John Canoe
ACEHKLNSU unshackle
ACEHKLOSU hause-lock
ACEHKMORY chromakey
ACEHKNORT on the rack
ACEHKOPRS packhorse
ACEHKORST shortcake
track shoe
ACEHKORVY heavy rock
ACEHKOSVW shock wave
ACEHLLLMS clamshell
ACEHLLLOR chlorella
ACEHLLNOP phone call
ACEHLLOOR Local Hero
ACEHLLOSU call house
house call
ACEHLMOPR polemarch
ACEHLMORU chermoula
ACEHLMORV love-charm
ACEHLMOSS Mohs scale
ACEHLMOST moschatel
ACEHLMOTV love match
ACEHLMRSS charmless
ACEHLMSST matchless
ACEHLMSSY chlamyses
ACEHLNNOY Lon Chaney
ACEHLNNPU up-Channel
ACEHLNNRU uncharnel
ACEHLNOSY anchylose
ACEHLNPSU spleuchan
ACEHLNPTY phlyctena
ACEHLOOSU coalhouse
ACEHLOPSU cephalous
ACEHLOPSW showplace
ACEHLORRT trochlear
ACEHLORST cloth-ears
ACEHLORSU house-carl
ACEHLORTT charlotte✧
ACEHLPRSU sprauchle
ACEHLPSSU sphacelus
ACEHLRSST chartless
ACEHLRSVY cry halves
ACEHLSSUY Aeschylus
ACEHLTTYY tachylyte
ACEHMMTUY tummy ache
ACEHMNOPY cymophane
ACEHMNORR cream horn
ACEHMNOTY theomancy
ACEHMNPRT parchment
ACEHMNRST Ernst Mach
ACEHMNSTY scytheman
ACEHMNTTU humectant
ACEHMORST stomacher
ACEHMORTV overmatch
ACEHMOSTT chemostat
ACEHMOSTU moustache
ACEHMPRTY champerty
ACEHMSSTU mustaches
ACEHMSTTT test match
ACEHNNRTT trenchant
ACEHNOQTU hacqueton
ACEHNORRS rancheros
ACEHNORSS anchoress
ACEHNORST archstone

ACEHNORTU near touch
ACEHNORTW wheat corn
ACEHNORTY honey-cart
ACEHNOSTT stonechat
The Cantos
ACEHNOSTU ceanothus
ACEHNPPRS schnapper
ACEHNPPTU tape punch
ACEHNPRTY pentarchy
ACEHNRSST chantress
ACEHNRSTU stauncher
ACEHNRSUZ schnauzer
ACEHNSTUW cashew nut
ACEHOOSTU housecoat
ACEHOPRRS sharecrop
ACEHOPRST chaseport
ACEHOPRSU proseucha
ACEHOPRTW wheat crop
ACEHOPRTY pothecary
ACEHOPSST chassepot
ACEHORRST cart-horse
orchestra
ACEHORRTU treachour
ACEHORSTU cart-house
search out
ACEHORSTY theocrasy
ACEHORSXY xerochasy
ACEHORTTY athrocyte
ACEHORTVW overwatch
watch over
ACEHOSSUW show cause
ACEHOSTUY easy touch
ACEHPRRSU purchaser
ACEHPRTTT Pratchett
ACEHPRTTU ratchet up
ACEHPSTTT patch test
ACEHPSTTY petty cash
ACEHRRTTU the cratur
ACEHRRTTY tetrarchy
ACEHRSSTT crash-test
ACEHRSTTT test chart
ACEHSTTUZ zuchettas
ACEIIILNS siciliane
ACEIIILST italicise
ACEIIILTZ italicize
ACEIIINNP epinician
ACEIIKLMS sicklemia
ACEIIKLNT kinetical
ACEIIKMNT kinematic
ACEIILLNN canellini
ACEIILLOT ciliolate
ACEIILLTV levitical
ACEIILMMT mimetical
ACEIILMOV voice mail
voicemail
voice-mail
ACEIILMPR empirical
ACEIILMPT implicate
ACEIILMSS seismical
ACEIILMST climatise
ACEIILMSV vicesimal

ACEIILMTZ climatize
ACEIILNNT anticline
ACEIILNNV vicennial
ACEIILNPS cisalpine
in special
ACEIILNST inelastic
sciential
ACEIILNTX Calixtine
ACEIILORT aerolitic
ACEIILOSS socialise
ACEIILOST socialite
ACEIILOSV viliacoes
ACEIILOSZ socialize
ACEIILPRT pearlitic
ACEIILRST eristical
realistic
ACEIILRTT lateritic
triticale
ACEIILRVY civil year
ACEIILSTV calvities
ACEIIMMNR Cimmerian
ACEIIMMRU americium
ACEIIMNOT emication
ACEIIMNRT antimeric
criminate
metrician
ACEIIMNSS messianic✧
ACEIIMPTT impactite
ACEIIMPTV impactive
ACEIIMRST armistice
ACEIIMSTU maieutics
ACEIINNOT aconitine
ACEIINNRT incertain
ACEIINOTV noviciate
ACEIINPRS periscian
precisian
ACEIINPRT pictarnie
ACEIINPST epinastic
ACEIINRTT intricate
triactine
ACEIINRTY itineracy
ACEIINTTT nictitate
ACEIIOSTV sociative
ACEIIPRST peirastic
ACEIIPSTT epistatic
ACEIIRSTT ceratitis
ACEIIRSTV variscite
ACEIISTTT steatitic
ACEIISTVV vae victis
ACEIITTUX eutaxitic
ACEIJKNPS jacksnipe
ACEIJKRRV river-jack
ACEIJLPTU juliet cap
ACEIJMRRY Jim Carrey
ACEIJNOSU jouisance
ACEIKKLPT kick pleat
ACEIKLLNN lack-linen
ACEIKLLTT all-ticket
ACEIKLMNS sickleman
ACEIKLNNS cleanskin
ACEIKLNPR Cal Ripken

ACEIKLNPT tan pickle
ACEIKLNRS clearskin
ACEIKLPRS spraickle
ACEIKLPST skeptical
ACEIKLRYZ like crazy
ACEIKNOQU a quick one
ACEIKNPTW pack-twine
ACEIKNRST crankiest
ACEIKNSST tackiness
ACEIKNSSW wackiness
ACEIKOPRT air-pocket
ACEIKOPST kopasetic
ACEIKORST croakiest
ACEIKPPRT pipe-track
ACEIKPRRT peritrack
ACEIKPSTY tipsy cake
ACEIKSSTT seat-stick
ACEILLLMS millscale
ACEILLLRT clitellar
ACEILLLXY lexically
ACEILLMOP polemical
ACEILLMOT collimate
local time
ACEILLNOR collinear
coralline
ACEILLNOT Collatine
ACEILLNPS spellican
ACEILLNPT plant lice
ACEILLORS localiser
ACEILLORT corallite
ACEILLORZ localizer
ACEILLOST oscillate
tesla coil
ACEILLOTV collative
ACEILLPRS callipers
ACEILLPSY specially
ACEILLPTY plicately
ACEILLRST cellarist
ACEILLRSW Carl Lewis
ACEILLSSU sulcalise
ACEILLSUZ sulcalize
ACEILMMNO Commelina
melomanic
ACEILMMOX meloxicam
ACEILMMSS mescalism
ACEILMNNU luminance
ACEILMNOP policeman
ACEILMNOR coalminer
ACEILMNOT melanotic
ACEILMNPS camel spin
ACEILMNRU melanuric
numerical
ACEILMNSU masculine
semuncial
ACEILMNTU culminate
ACEILMOPT Ptolemaic
ACEILMOSS coseismal
ACEILMOSU limaceous
ACEILMPST emplastic
ACEILMPTV palm civet
ACEILMRRU mercurial✧

ACEILMRST	cartelism
ACEILMRSU	simulacre
ACEILMRTU	climature
	tularemic
ACEILMSTU	salicetum
ACEILNNOR	cornelian
ACEILNNOT	octennial
ACEILNNTY	anciently
ACEILNOPR	porcelain
ACEILNOPT	point-lace
ACEILNOPZ	clozapine
ACEILNORS	censorial
ACEILNORT	clarionet
	crotaline
ACEILNOST	coastline
	sectional
ACEILNOSV	volcanise
ACEILNOTU	inoculate
ACEILNOVZ	volcanize
ACEILNPRT	replicant
ACEILNPST	split cane
ACEILNPTU	inculpate
ACEILNRST	larcenist
ACEILNRSW	screw nail
ACEILNRTU	centurial
ACEILNRTY	certainly
ACEILNSSS	scaliness
ACEILNSUV	vulcanise
ACEILNTUV	vulcanite
ACEILNTXY	inexactly
ACEILNUVZ	vulcanize
ACEILOPPS	episcopal
ACEILOPRT	precoital
ACEILOPSS	Asclepios
ACEILOPST	scapolite
ACEILOQUV	equivocal
ACEILORRT	rectorial
ACEILORST	sclerotia
	sectorial
ACEILORSV	vocaliser
ACEILORTT	tectorial
ACEILORTV	vectorial
ACEILORVZ	vocalizer
ACEILOTTU	autotelic
ACEILOTVY	coevality
ACEILOTWY	wyliecoat
ACEILPPPR	paper clip
ACEILPRTU	plicature
ACEILPRTW	W particle
ACEILPRTX	X-particle
ACEILPRTZ	Z particle
ACEILPSSU	Asclepius
	capsulise
ACEILPSTU	spiculate
ACEILPSTY	specialty
ACEILPSUZ	capsulize
ACEILPTUY	eucalypti
ACEILRRTU	curtailer
	recruital
	reticular
ACEILRSSZ	Carl Zeiss
ACEILRSTT	cartelist
ACEILRSTU	sterculia
ACEILRSTV	cat-silver
ACEILRSTW	crawliest
ACEILRSUV	vesicular
ACEILRTTT	cat litter
ACEILRTUV	lucrative
	revictual
ACEILSSTU	cause list
ACEILTTUV	cultivate
ACEIMMNNY	immanency
ACEIMMNOT	comminate
ACEIMMOSS	come amiss
ACEIMMOST	mesic atom
ACEIMNNOO	Neocomian
ACEIMNNOT	monactine
ACEIMNOPS	campesino
ACEIMNORT	cremation
	manticore
ACEIMNOST	encomiast
ACEIMNOTT	omittance
ACEIMNOTX	income tax
ACEIMNPTU	pneumatic
ACEIMNRST	Encratism
	miscreant
ACEIMNRSU	muscarine
ACEIMNSST	semantics
ACEIMNSTU	mint sauce
ACEIMNTYZ	enzymatic
ACEIMOPRS	premosaic
ACEIMORST	Masoretic
ACEIMORTU	autocrime
ACEIMORVW	microwave
ACEIMOSST	as it comes
ACEIMPRRU	per curiam
ACEIMPRST	spermatic
ACEIMRSTU	cauterism
	cerastium
ACEIMRTTU	micturate
ACEINNNOR	cannonier
ACEINNNSS	canniness
ACEINNOOV	Novocaine®
ACEINNORS	censorian
ACEINNORT	container
	crenation
	narcotine
ACEINNOSS	ascension✧
ACEINNOST	cantonise
ACEINNOTZ	cantonize
ACEINNRRY	inerrancy
ACEINNRSU	insurance
	nuisancer
ACEINNRTU	encurtain
	runcinate
	uncertain
ACEINNRTY	ancientry
ACEINNSST	cantiness
	incessant
ACEINOOST	iso-octane
ACEINOOTV	evocation
ACEINOPRT	recaption
ACEINOPST	stenopaic
ACEINOPTY	cytopenia
ACEINORRT	cinerator
ACEINORRV	carnivore
ACEINORSS	scenarios
ACEINORST	narcotise
ACEINORTT	carnotite
ACEINORTU	cautioner
	Cointreau®
ACEINORTZ	narcotize
ACEINOSST	cessation
ACEINOSTU	tenacious
ACEINOSUV	vinaceous
ACEINOTTY	to a nicety
ACEINPRRY	pericrany
ACEINPRSS	scarpines
ACEINPRTT	crepitant
ACEINPRUY	pecuniary
ACEINPSSU	puissance
ACEINQTTU	quittance
ACEINRSSS	scariness
ACEINRSST	scenarist
ACEINRSSZ	craziness
ACEINRSTU	securitan
ACEINRSTY	insectary
ACEINRTTY	certainty
ACEINRTUV	incurvate
ACEINSSSU	sauciness
ACEINSSTT	cattiness
	tacitness
ACEINSTTY	intestacy
ACEINSTWX	wax insect
ACEIOPRRS	acrospire
ACEIOPRST	patricoes
ACEIOPRSU	auriscope
	parecious
ACEIOPRTV	proactive
ACEIOPSTV	vitascope
ACEIOPTTT	petticoat
ACEIORSST	ostracise
	Socratise
ACEIORSTZ	ostracize
	Socratize
ACEIORSUV	veracious
ACEIOSSTW	coastwise
ACEIPQRTU	practique
ACEIPRRST	practiser
ACEIPRSTT	scarpetti
ACEIPSSTU	spacesuit
ACEIQSTUY	sequacity
ACEIRSTTU	rusticate
ACEIRSUWY	cruiseway
ACEIRTUVV	curvative
ACEISSTTU	suscitate
ACEISTTTY	city state
ACEJKKMOS	smoke-jack
ACEJKKRSY	skyjacker
ACEJKLOTW	jack towel
ACEJKMOOS	James Cook
ACEJKNOST	jackstone
ACEJLMSUU	majuscule

ACEKKLNOS	ankle sock
ACEKKMRRU	muck-raker
ACEKKNORS	rock snake
ACEKKOSTT	stocktake
	take stock
ACEKLLMMU	mallemuck
ACEKLLMSW	well smack
ACEKLLPSS	plackless
ACEKLNPSU	slacken up
ACEKLNSSS	slackness
ACEKLNSTU	snake cult
ACEKLOPRS	slack rope
ACEKLOPRW	workplace
ACEKLORST	lose track
ACEKLORSW	scalework
ACEKLORTW	towel-rack
ACEKLRSST	trackless
ACEKMORRR	rocker arm
ACEKMSTUW	mucksweat
ACEKNNORS	corn snake
ACEKNNRSS	crankness
ACEKNORSU	cankerous
ACEKOPPRW	power pack
ACEKOPTWX	wax pocket
ACEKORRTW	rockwater
ACEKPRSSU	sapsucker
ACEKRSTUW	awe-struck
ACELLLMOU	columella
ACELLLNUU	Lucullean
ACELLLORS	solar cell
ACELLMNOY	call-money
ACELLMORS	all comers
	allcomers
ACELLMORU	molecular
ACELLMRSU	Marcellus
ACELLMRSW	swarm-cell
ACELLMSTU	castellum
ACELLNNUY	uncleanly
ACELLNOPS	pollen sac
ACELLNORU	nucleolar
ACELLNOSS	localness
ACELLNOTU	Launcelot
ACELLNRTY	centrally
ACELLNRUY	unclearly
ACELLOOTV	local veto
ACELLOPRS	scalloper
ACELLOQUY	coequally
ACELLORSS	sclerosal
ACELLORST	sclerotal
ACELLORSU	cellarous
ACELLORSV	coveralls
ACELLPSSS	scalpless
ACELLPUUV	Vulpecula
ACELLRSSW	wall cress
ACELLRSTU	scutellar
ACELLRSUY	secularly
ACELLSSSS	classless
ACELMMNOS	commensal
ACELMMNSU	muscleman
ACELMMOSU	mamelucos
ACELMNOOR	clean room

ACELMNOST	calmstone
ACELMNTUU	tenaculum
ACELMOOSU	coal mouse
ACELMOPST	ectoplasm
ACELMORRU	clamourer
ACELMORSS	scleromas
ACELMORSU	Mucorales
ACELMOSSS	scale moss
ACELMOSUU	ulmaceous
ACELNNOOR	olecranon
ACELNNOPT	non placet
ACELNNOTU	Launceton
ACELNOORW	coal owner
ACELNOOST	consolate
	stone coal
ACELNOOSV	volcanoes
ACELNOPRV	Provençal
ACELNORSU	larcenous
ACELNORTU	nucleator
	recountal
ACELNORUV	rounceval
ACELNOSSV	vocalness
ACELNOSTU	consulate
ACELNOTUU	outlaunce
ACELNPRTU	crapulent
ACELNPTUY	petulancy
ACELNRSUU	unsecular
ACELNRTTU	reluctant
ACELNSTTU	castle nut
ACELNTUXY	exultancy
ACELOOOTT	toto caelo
ACELOOPRR	car-pooler
	corporeal
	Poor Clare
ACELOORTW	water-cool
ACELOOSST	cast loose
ACELOOSTT	coelostat
ACELOPRRU	opercular
	preocular
ACELOPRTU	outplacer
	parcel out
	peculator
ACELOPSTU	scopulate
ACELORRST	stercoral
ACELORRSU	carrousel
ACELORRTY	lay rector
ACELORSSU	caroluses
ACELORSSV	overclass
ACELOSSTU	cassoulet
	lost cause
ACELOSTTY	coat-style
	octastyle
ACELOSTUU	cautelous
ACELPPRRU	curlpaper
ACEMMMSUY	mummy-case
ACEMMNOOR	Common Era
ACEMMOTTU	commutate
ACEMNNOOY	oenomancy
ACEMNNORR	corner-man
ACEMNOOPS	moonscape
ACEMNOORU	coumarone

ACEMNOPSS	encompass
ACEMNORTU	mucronate
ACEMNOSTU	caumstone
ACEMOOPSS	somascope
ACEMOOPSU	pomaceous
ACEMOORSU	moraceous
ACEMOOSSW	Moscow Sea
ACEMOOTYZ	Mycetozoa
ACEMOPSSS	compasses✧
ACEMORRSU	sour cream
ACEMORRTY	crematory
ACEMORSTU	castoreum
ACEMOSSUU	musaceous
ACEMOSTVY	vasectomy
ACEMPRSUY	supremacy
ACENNNORU	announcer
ACENNOOPR	cornopean
ACENNOOTT	connotate
	Notonecta
ACENNORTU	connature
ACENNOSTZ	canzonets
ACENNPTUU	nuncupate
ACENNSSST	scantness
ACENNSSTU	uncessant
ACENOOPRT	co-operant
ACENOORST	corantoes
ACENOOTTY	tycoonate
ACENOPRRT	copartner
	per contra
	procreant
ACENOPRST	sportance
ACENOPSSW	snowscape
ACENOPSTW	townscape
ACENOPSTY	syncopate
ACENOPTYY	cyanotype
ACENOQRTU	croquante
ACENORRTU	raconteur
ACENORSTU	courtesan
	nectarous
ACENORSUV	cavernous
ACENORTUZ	courtezan
ACENORUVV	Vancouver
ACENOSSST	contessas
ACENOSSTT	stonecast
ACENOSSTZ	scazontes
ACENOSTTU	En-Tout-Cas®
	en tout cas
ACENOSTUU	cutaneous
ACENPRRTY	carpentry
ACENPRSUU	pursuance
ACENPTTUU	punctuate
ACENRRSTU	Cresta Run
ACENRRSUY	cursenary
ACENRSSSS	crassness
ACENRSTUU	Centaurus
ACEOOPRRT	corporate
ACEOOPRSS	ascospore
ACEOORSSU	rosaceous
ACEOORSTU	root cause
ACEOORTVY	evocatory
ACEOPPRST	spaceport

ACEOPPRSU après coup
ACEOPRRTY precatory
ACEOPRSST Sarcoptes
ACEOPRSSY caryopses
ACEOPRSTT scarpetto
spectator
ACEORRRTT retractor
ACEORRRVY carry over
carry-over
overcarry
ACEORRSTU craterous
ACEORRTTX extractor
ACEORSSTW worst case
worst-case
ACEORSSUU au secours
ACEORSTTY astrocyte
ACEORSTUU rutaceous
ACEORTVWY covert way
ACEQRSTUU square-cut
ACERRSSTW wart cress
ACERRTUUV curvature
ACERSSTUU actus reus
ACFFGHILN cliffhang
ACFFGIMNU MacGuffin
ACFFIILNO officinal
ACFFIINOT officiant
ACFFIINRT traffic in
ACFFILMOR falciform
ACFFILORU Forficula
ACFFIMNPU muffin-cap
ACFFLOSTW cowl-staff
ACFGHILNN flanching
ACFGHINRT fratching
ACFGHMORR frogmarch
ACFGIIMNO magnifico
ACFGIKLNY cly-faking
ACFGIKLST flagstick
ACFGIKNRT kingcraft
ACFGINORT factoring
ACFGINRRS scarf-ring
ACFGINRSU surfacing
ACFGIOSUU fugacious
ACFGLNORY gyrfalcon
ACFGLORYZ crazy golf
ACFGNORST songcraft
ACFHHHILT half hitch
ACFHHILPS flash chip
ACFHIILRT chairlift
ACFHILNOU faulchion
ACFHILORS coral-fish
ACFHILPRT flip chart
ACFHIMPRS cramp-fish
ACFHIPRSS fish-scrap
ACFHKLLUW full whack
ACFHKORST rockshaft
ACFHLLORT call forth
ACFHLMRSU scrum half
ACFHLNORW half-crown
ACFHLNOTU flanch out
ACFHLORTW flow chart
ACFHMORSU forasmuch
ACFHOOSTU out of cash
ACFHOPRST craft shop
ACFIIILMR mirifical
ACFIIILOR orificial
ACFIIISST fasciitis
ACFIILLNY finically
ACFIILNOT fictional
ACFIILOPR caprifoil
ACFIILRSU surficial
ACFIILTUV fluviatic
ACFIIMNOR aciniform
ACFIINSTU faunistic
ACFIIOPRS saporific
ACFIIOPRV vaporific
ACFIJKRTU jack-fruit
ACFIKNRSS scarfskin
ACFIKRRTU Friar Tuck
ACFILLOPT floptical
ACFILMNOR lanciform
ACFILMORU cauliform
formulaic
fumarolic
ACFILMORV claviform
ACFILNNOR francolin
ACFILNOOT olfaction
ACFILNPPY flippancy
ACFILNRTY franticly
ACFILNRUU funicular
ACFILORST trifocals
ACFILOSTU clafoutis
ACFIMNORT formicant
ACFIMOOST motoscafi
ACFIMOPRR capriform
ACFIMORRY formicary
ACFINORRT infractor
ACFINORTU furcation
ACFINRSST St Francis
ACFIOOPST ipso facto
ACFIORSTU fractious
ACFIORSUU furacious
ACFJKORST Jack Frost
ACFKMORST stock farm
ACFKMRRTU truck-farm
ACFKNORWY fancywork
ACFKORRTW craftwork
ACFLLORSS crossfall
ACFLLORSU floscular
ACFLLOSWW wolf's claw
ACFLLTTUY tactfully
ACFLMNOOR conformal
ACFLMORSS form class
ACFLNTTUU fluctuant
ACFLOORTY olfactory
ACFLORRTY carrot fly
ACFMOOOST motoscafo
ACFMORSUX Marcus Fox
ACFMOSTTU factotums
ACFOORRUY Fourcroya
ACFOORTTU factor out
ACFOOSTUU autofocus
ACFORTTUY outcrafty
ACFRRTUUY fructuary
ACGGGINRS scragging
ACGGHNNPU gang-punch
ACGGIIKMN magicking
ACGGIIOSS isagogics
ACGGILRSY scraggily
ACGGIMNOP go camping
ACGGNORTY Tony Cragg
ACGHHHIIR highchair
ACGHHILNT hatchling
ACGHHILSS high-class
ACGHHINTT thatching
ACGHIIJKN hijacking
ACGHIILNO chiliagon
ACGHIIMOY chiyogami
ACGHIINRW wing chair
ACGHIIPRT graphitic
ACGHIKNOV havocking
ACGHIKNTW thwacking
ACGHILLRR chargrill
ACGHILNNO long-chain
ACGHILNSS glass chin
ACGHILORY oligarchy
ACGHILPRY graphicly
ACGHILSTT cast light
ACGHIMMOO homogamic
ACGHIMOOP omophagic
ACGHIMOSW magic show
ACGHINNOT gnathonic
ACGHINNST stanching
ACGHINRTT night-cart
ACGHLMNOP Longchamp
ACGHLMOOY logomachy
ACGHLOORY archology
ACGHMOPRY cymograph
ACGHMOPYY mycophagy
ACGHMRSTU starch gum
ACGHNTUUZ Chuang-tzu
ACGHOOOST go cahoots
ACGHOPSSY psychogas
ACGHORSTU roughcast
ACGIIIMST imagistic
ACGIIKNNP panicking
ACGIIKNNT anticking
ACGIIKNRV vraicking
ACGIILLLO illogical
ACGIILLMS gallicism✧
ACGIILLNV cavilling
ACGIILLOR cigarillo
ACGIILMNS anglicism
ACGIILNST anglicist
ACGIILRTY gracility
ACGIIMSTT stigmatic
ACGIINNOR inorganic
ACGIINNRT nigricant
ACGIINOST agonistic
ACGIIORST orgiastic
ACGIJKPRU jack-up rig
ACGIKNNPU unpacking
ACGILLLOY logically
ACGILLNOR carolling

ACGILLNOU unlogical
ACGILLOOO oological
ACGILLOOY caliology
ACGILLOST collagist
ACGILMOPY polygamic
ACGILNNST scantling
ACGILNNTY cantingly
ACGILNOST gnostical
nostalgic
ACGILNOXY coaxingly
ACGILNPRY carpingly
ACGILNRSW scrawling
ACGILRRYZ Girl Crazy
ACGIMMNOO monogamic
ACGIMMNRS scramming
ACGIMMORR microgram
ACGIMNNOO cognomina
ACGIMNNOP companing
ACGIMNNOR romancing
ACGIMNOOR agronomic
ACGIMNORR cairngorm
ACGIMNOSS gasconism
ACGIMNOTU contagium
ACGIMNPRR cramp-ring
ACGIMNSTY gymnastic
nystagmic
ACGIMOOPR porogamic
ACGIMOORS sociogram
ACGIMOPRT pictogram
ACGIMOTYZ zygomatic
ACGINNNOT cantoning
ACGINNNOY canyoning
ACGINNOOT cognation
contagion
ACGINNOPY canopying
poignancy
ACGINNOST cognisant
ACGINNOTZ cognizant
ACGINOOTY Octogynia
ACGINOPSW coping-saw
ACGINOPTT capotting
ACGINORTU Agincourt
ACGINPPRS scrapping
ACGINPTUY pugnacity
ACGIOORSS graciosos
ACGIOORTT cogitator
ACGJNNOTU conjugant
ACGJNORRU currajong
ACGKLNOOW wagon lock
ACGKNOORU rock guano
ACGLLNORW crown gall
ACGLLORWY gally-crow
ACGLMNOOS Cosmo Lang
ACGLMOORU colour-mag
ACGLMOORY macrology
ACGLNOOST long-coats
ACGLNOOSY cosy along
ACGLOOPRY carpology
ACGLOORSY sarcology
ACGLOORTY cartology
ACGLOOSTY scatology
ACGMNNOOR Cro-Magnon
ACGMNORYY gyromancy
ACGMOPRTY cryptogam
ACGNNOOST contangos
ACGNORRUW currawong
ACGORRSUY surrogacy
ACHHIIRST rhachitis
ACHHIKLSS shashlick
ACHHILNOR rhonchial
ACHHILOPT phacolith
ACHHILORT haircloth
ACHHIMRTY arhythmic
ACHHINNOT chthonian
ACHHINOST chainshot
ACHHIORST Tocharish
ACHHIPRSU pushchair
ACHHISTTW witch's hat
ACHHLLLOT cloth-hall
ACHHLOSTU slouch hat
ACHHLOSTW washcloth
ACHHLPRYY phylarchy
ACHHNORTY Rhynchota
ACHHNRSTY chrysanth
ACHIIKNNP chinkapin
ACHIILMOS isochimal
ACHIILMST cash limit
ACHIILMSW whimsical
ACHIILOTT halitotic
ACHIILRTY chirality
ACHIIMNST machinist
ACHIIMORY chirimoya
ACHIINPSY physician
ACHIINRST Christian
Christina
trichinas
ACHIIOPST pistachio
ACHIIPRSV vicarship
ACHIIPRTU upaithric
ACHIIRRTT arthritic
ACHIIRSTT citharist
trachitis
ACHIIRSTV archivist
ACHIJKMST jacksmith
ACHIKKNPT pick-thank
ACHIKKSSW kickshaws
ACHIKLMST mahlstick
ACHIKMMOS Ockhamism
ACHIKMNOS Chomskian
ACHIKMOST Ockhamist
ACHIKMSWY whisky mac
ACHIKNORW chainwork
ACHIKPRUY Puck-hairy
ACHILLLOY allicholy
ACHILLMOY ohmically
ACHILLMSU music hall
music-hall
ACHILLNTY Chantilly
ACHILLOST sailcloth
ACHILMNPY nymphical
ACHILMPTY lymphatic
ACHILNNPU nail punch
ACHILNOPT haplontic
piña-cloth
ACHILNORT antichlor
ACHILNORV Lochinvar
ACHILNRUY raunchily
ACHILNSTU clianthus
ACHILNSTY snatchily
ACHILOPRT arctophil
ACHILOPTU patchouli
ACHILORST choralist
ACHILORTV archivolt
ACHILORUZ rhizocaul
ACHILOSST scholiast
ACHILOSSU à huis clos
ACHILPSSY physicals
ACHILPSTU sulphatic
ACHILRSSY chrysalis
ACHILRSTY starchily
ACHILSTTY cattishly
ACHIMMNOS monachism
ACHIMMORZ machzorim
ACHIMMOSS masochism
ACHIMNOPY hypomanic
ACHIMNORS harmonics
ACHIMNORT chromatin
ACHIMNOST macintosh
monachist
ACHIMNPPU chain pump
ACHIMNSTW switchman
ACHIMOOTX homotaxic
ACHIMORST rhotacism
ACHIMORYZ mycorhiza
ACHIMOSST masochist
ACHIMOSTU mustachio
ACHIMRSST Christmas
ACHIMRSSW scrimshaw
ACHINNOST stanchion
ACHINNOTW Chinatown
ACHINNSTY synanthic
ACHINOORT chinaroot
ACHINOOST in cahoots
ACHINOPPS pansophic
ACHINOPRT anthropic
rhapontic
ACHINOPST Cashpoint®
cashpoint
ACHINORRU hurricano
ACHINORST thrasonic
ACHINOSTU Antiochus
ACHINPRST chinstrap
ACHINRSTU trachinus
ACHINRSTY strychnia
ACHINRTUY uncharity
ACHIOOPST sociopath
ACHIOPPRS hippocras
ACHIOPRRZ rhizocarp
ACHIORSTV tovarisch
ACHIOSSTU astichous
ACHIPRSUY haruspicy
ACHIQRRSU squirarch
ACHISTUWZ Auschwitz

ACHKLMNOO kloochman
ACHKLNOOS solonchak
ACHKMNOSY Chomskyan
ACHKMORTU touch mark
ACHKNORRW hornwrack
ACHKOPRTW patchwork
ACHLLMOPS small chop
ACHLLOOPT photo call
ACHLLORSY scholarly
ACHLMNOOS schoolman
ACHLMOORR Loch Morar
ACHLMORSW slow march
slow-march
ACHLMOSTW slow match
ACHLMSTYZ schmaltzy
ACHLNOTUU launch out
outlaunch
ACHLNSSSU Anschluss
ACHLNSTUY staunchly
ACHLOOSTU holocaust✧
ACHLOPRYY polyarchy
ACHLOPTUY patchouly
ACHLORTTY tray cloth
ACHMMNOOY monomachy
ACHMMSSUY Symmachus
ACHMNORSU Roumansch
ACHMNRSTU truchmans
ACHMOOPRS promachos
ACHMOORRT chart-room
ACHNOOPRY acrophony
ACHNOPSTY sycophant
ACHNSTUYZ Zacynthus
ACHOOPRST crapshoot
ACHOORSTT short-coat
ACHOPRSTU stroupach
ACHOPSTTW stopwatch
ACHOPSTUY hypocaust
ACHORTTTU cut-throat
ACHPRSSUY chuprassy
ACIIILMST Islamitic
Italicism
ACIIILNOS siciliano
ACIIILNRT triclinia
ACIIILNTT latticini
ACIIIMNST animistic
ACIIINPPR principia
ACIIINPST pianistic
sincipita
ACIIISSTV Sivaistic
ACIIJRSTU justiciar
ACIIKMNRT Minitrack®
ACIIKNOOZ Kainozoic
ACIIKPRRT Prakritic
ACIILLNOS isoclinal
ACIILLNST scintilla
ACIILLOPT political
ACIILLPRS Priscilla
ACIILMNPU municipal
ACIILMNSU un-Islamic
ACIILMNSV Calvinism
ACIILMNTY militancy
ACIILMOSS socialism
ACIILMOSU malicious
ACIILMQTU quitclaim
ACIILMRSU curialism
ACIILNOOT coalition
ACIILNOPT plication
ACIILNOSX clinoaxis
ACIILNOTT latticino
tonalitic
ACIILNOVV convivial
ACIILNOVY inviolacy
ACIILNPPR principal
ACIILNPST cisplatin
ACIILNSTV Calvinist
ACIILOPRT pictorial
ACIILORST soritical
ACIILOSST socialist
ACIILOSTY sociality
ACIILOSVV slivovica
ACIILPRTY pyritical
ACIILQUZZ quizzical
ACIILRSTU curialist
rusticial
ACIILSTTT tactilist
ACIILTTTY tactility
ACIIMMOSS mosaicism
ACIIMMPST psammitic
ACIIMNNOS aniconism
insomniac
ACIIMNNOT antimonic
antinomic
ACIIMNOPT impaction
ACIIMNORT mortician
ACIIMNOSU minacious
ACIIMNOTT manicotti
ACIIMOPRS micropsia
ACIIMOPST simpatico
ACIIMORTT triatomic
ACIIMOSST mosaicist
ACIIMOSTT atomistic
ACIIMOTTY atomicity
ACIIMPRST prismatic
ACIIMPSSS sic passim
ACIIMRSSY Syriacism
ACIIMRSTY Myristica
ACIIMSTUV viaticums
ACIINNORU Uriconian
ACIINNOST aniconist
onanistic
Toscanini
ACIINNOTT nictation
ACIINNOTU incaution
ACIINOORT octonarii
ACIINOOST sociation
ACIINOPST panoistic
ACIINORTV Victorian
ACIINOSTT actionist
ACIINOTTX antitoxic
ACIINOTTY atonicity
ACIINPRTU Paricutin
Paricutín
puritanic
ACIINPTTY antitypic
ACIINRRTY irritancy
ACIIOPRST psoriatic
ACIIOPRTT patriotic
ACIIOPSTX optic axis
ACIIOPTZZ pizzicato
ACIIORSTZ zoiatrics
ACIIORSUV vicarious
ACIIOSSTT isostatic
ACIIOSUVV vivacious
ACIIPRSTT patristic
ACIIPRSTX piscatrix
ACIIPTTVY captivity
ACIISSTTT statistic
ACIJKLOPT pilot jack
ACIJKNNOU Union Jack
ACIKKMOPU pick oakum
ACIKKNNOT antiknock
ACIKKRSTT kick-start
ACIKLLSST Catskills
ACIKLMPTU multipack
ACIKLMSTU maulstick
ACIKLNOOP plain cook
plain-cook
ACIKLOPRS spark coil
ACIKLOSTT tailstock
ACIKLPSST slapstick
ACIKLPSTY plasticky
ACIKNORST Kit Carson
ACIKNRTTW twin-track
ACIKOPSSY skiascopy
ACIKPRSTT trap stick
ACIKRSTTU tracksuit
ACILLLNUU Lucullian
ACILLLOUV colluvial
ACILLLRYY lyrically
ACILLLTYY lytically
ACILLMORT millocrat
ACILLMRSY Carlylism
ACILLMSUY musically
ACILLNNSY synclinal
ACILLNOOT collation
ACILLNOTU clout-nail
ACILLOOQU colloquia
ACILLOPTY optically
topically
ACILLORST cloistral
ACILLORTV Victrolla®
ACILLOSTY callosity
stoically
ACILLOTXY toxically
ACILLPTYY typically
ACILLSSST class list
ACILLSSTU Callistus
ACILMMOTT committal
ACILMNNTU culminant
ACILMNOOS Salomonic
ACILMNOPT complaint
compliant
ACILMNOSV volcanism✧

ACILMNOUY	Alcyonium
ACILMNSUU	unmusical
ACILMNSUV	vulcanism✧
ACILMOORS	lacrimoso
ACILMOPRS	comprisal
ACILMORST	crotalism
ACILMORSY	isocrymal
ACILMPTUU	capitulum
ACILMSSTU	simulcast
ACILNNNUY	uncannily
ACILNNOTU	continual
ACILNNQTU	clinquant
ACILNNRUU	ranunculi
ACILNOORR	carron oil
ACILNOPRT	prolactin
ACILNOPST	Platonics
ACILNORTT	contralti
ACILNORTY	latrociny
ACILNOSTU	sulcation
ACILNOSTV	volcanist✧
ACILNOTTU	luctation
ACILNPTUY	untypical
ACILNRSTU	lincrusta
ACILNRSWY	scrawnily
ACILNSTUV	vulcanist✧
ACILNSTYY	syncytial
ACILOOPRS	acropolis✧
ACILOOPST	apostolic
ACILOORST	castor oil
ACILOOSSU	solacious
ACILOPPPU	Lucia Popp
ACILOPPST	cap pistol
ACILOPRTY	placitory
ACILOQTUY	loquacity
ACILORRSU	cursorial
ACILORRVY	corivalry
ACILORSSU	ossicular
ACILORSTU	ocularist
	suctorial
ACILOTTUY	autolytic
ACILPPRSY	scrappily
ACILPPSTU	supplicat
ACILPSTTY	styptical
ACILRRTUU	utricular
ACILSSTTY	systaltic
ACIMMNOOT	monatomic
ACIMMNOTY	myomantic
ACIMMORRS	Camorrism
ACIMMORSS	commissar
ACIMNNOOP	companion
ACIMNNOOX	monaxonic
ACIMNNOPY	in company
	in-company
ACIMNNOTY	antonymic
ACIMNOOST	onomastic
ACIMNOOTU	autonomic
ACIMNOOTX	taxonomic
ACIMNOOTZ	zoomantic
ACIMNOPRR	cramp-iron
ACIMNOPRY	parcimony
ACIMNORST	narcotism
ACIMNOSUU	acuminous
ACIMNOSUV	Muscovian
ACIMNOUVX	nux vomica
ACIMNTTUY	Mutiny Act
ACIMOPSSY	symposiac
ACIMORRST	Camorrist
ACIMORSST	ostracism
ACIMORSTT	stromatic
ACIMOSTTU	comitatus
ACIMPRSTY	sympatric
ACIMRSTTU	strumatic
ACINNNOOT	connation
ACINNORST	constrain
	transonic
ACINNQSUY	squinancy
ACINNRTUU	uncurtain
ACINOORRS	corrasion
ACINOORST	consortia
	Ostracion
ACINOOSST	iconostas
ACINOPRRS	scrap iron
ACINOPSTU	acupoints
ACINOPSUU	usucapion
ACINORSST	croissant
ACINORSTT	narcotist
	Nostratic
	stratonic
ACINORSTU	suctorian
ACINORSTY	carnosity
ACINORTTU	curtation
	ructation
ACINORTUV	curvation
ACINORTUY	cautionry
ACINOSSSU	sans souci
	saucisson
ACINPRSTY	St Cyprian
ACINPRSUW	Punic Wars
ACINPRTUU	curtain up
ACINRSSSU	narcissus
ACINRSSUU	uraniscus
ACIOOPPTT	apoptotic
ACIOOPRSU	paroicous
ACIOOPRSZ	saprozoic
ACIOOPRTT	copatriot
ACIOORSTU	atrocious
ACIOORSUV	voracious
ACIOOTTUX	autotoxic
ACIOPRSSY	caryopsis
ACIOPRSTT	prostatic
ACIOPRSTY	piscatory
ACIOSSTUU	astucious
ACIPSSTTU	Psittacus
ACIRRSTYZ	stir-crazy
ACIRSSTUY	casuistry
ACJKOPRST	jock strap
	jockstrap
ACJLLORUY	jocularly
ACJLOORTU	joculator
ACKKMNOPY	pockmanky
ACKLLNPSU	knapscull
ACKLLNRTU	trunk call
ACKLMOOOR	cloakroom
ACKLNOPRT	rock plant
ACKLNORST	cornstalk
ACKLORRWY	warlockry
ACKLORSST	cross-talk
ACKLORSSW	crosswalk
ACKLORSTW	slow track
ACKMOORST	stackroom
ACKMOPRRS	crop-marks
ACKMOPRSW	scamp-work
ACKRSTTUY	Cutty Sark
	cutty-sark
ACLLLOOOP	local loop
ACLLLOSUY	callously
ACLLMNOSU	molluscan
ACLLNOOPT	locoplant
ACLLOOPRT	practolol
ACLLOORRY	corollary
ACLLORSSW	scroll saw
ACLMMNOOW	common law
ACLMMOTUU	commutual
ACLMNOORU	colourman
	monocular
ACLMOOOPR	Marco Polo
ACLMOOPST	camp-stool
ACLMOORSS	classroom
ACLMOORSU	clamorous
ACLMOPRTU	palm court
	palm-court
ACLMOPSTY	cytoplasm
ACLMRSTUU	claustrum
ACLMSSUUV	vasculums
ACLNNORTU	nocturnal
ACLNOORTT	contralto
ACLNOORTU	colourant
ACLNOPSTY	nyctalops
ACLOOORRT	coralroot
ACLOOOSTV	ovo-lactos
ACLOOPRST	coral spot
ACLOORRTW	coralwort
ACLOORSUU	oraculous
ACLOORUWY	colourway
ACLOPRSTU	Patroclus
ACLOPRSTY	pyroclast
ACLOPRSUU	crapulous
ACLOPRTTU	plutocrat
ACLOPRTUY	culpatory
ACLOPSTTU	Paul Scott
ACLORSUUY	raucously
ACLOSTUUY	Autolycus
ACLOSUUVY	vacuously
ACMMNOORT	commorant
ACMNNOOST	oncostman
ACMNOORRT	cormorant
ACMNOORRW	acorn worm
ACMNOOSTU	cosmonaut
ACMNOPRYY	pyromancy
ACMNOPTTU	computant
ACMNORSTU	Turcomans
ACMOPRRSY	army corps
ACMORRSUU	macrurous

ACMORSTUY customary
ACMRSTUUY custumary
ACNNNOOST consonant
ACNOOPRRY procaryon
ACNOOPRST corposant
ACNOOPRTV provocant
ACNOORRSU rancorous
ACNOPRTTU punctator
ACNORRSSU run across
ACNORSTTY contrasty
ACOOPPRRS sporocarp
ACOOPSTUY autoscopy
ACOORSSTU autocross
ACOPRRRTY parrot-cry
ACOPRRSST sports car
ACOPRSSTU put across
ACORRRSUY cursorary
ACORRSSTT star-crost
ACORRSTTU scrutator
ACORSSSWY crossways
ACOSSTTTY statocyst
ADDDEEEHR red-headed
ADDDEEHNR redhanded
ADDDEEKLS skedaddle
ADDDEELMN demand-led
ADDDEENRU undreaded
ADDDEERSS addressed
ADDDEFIIN dandified
ADDDEGINO dead-doing
ADDDEGLOP dog-paddle
ADDDEGMNO goddamned
ADDDEIINS disdained
ADDDEIIOP Dipodidae
ADDDEIIOR Dorididae
ADDDEIMNO diamonded
ADDDEKNRU dead drunk
ADDDELNSU unsaddled
ADDDEMORR ramrodded
ADDDHMNOO hodmandod
ADDEEEGRY degree day
ADDEEEHRT hederated
ADDEEELLV dead-level
ADDEEEMNR meandered
ADDEEENRR end-reader
ADDEEEPRT depredate
ADDEEERRT retreaded
ADDEEERSS addressee
ADDEEFFNR affrended
ADDEEFIIX fixed idea
ADDEEFNNT defendant
ADDEEFNSS fadedness
ADDEEFRRU defrauder
ADDEEGHIP pigheaded
ADDEEGHRU rug-headed
ADDEEGILM middle-age
ADDEEGINN deadening
ADDEEGINR André Gide
ADDEEGJMU judge-made
ADDEEGLNR glandered
ADDEEGLNS sedgeland
ADDEEGNSW sand wedge

ADDEEHHOT hotheaded
ADDEEHILL ill-headed
ADDEEHIRR drerihead
red-haired
ADDEEHLNP hen-paddle
ADDEEHLNR elder hand
ADDEEHMNT the damned✧
ADDEEHMOP mop-headed
ADDEEHNNO one-handed
ADDEEHNOT not-headed
ADDEEHNTU the undead
ADDEEHOSU deadhouse
ADDEEHOTW tow-headed
two-headed
ADDEEHRSS headdress
ADDEEHRTY dehydrate
ADDEEIINX Dixie Dean
ADDEEILMR middle ear
ADDEEILRV dare-devil
ADDEEIMTT meditated
ADDEEINTY tie-and-dye
ADDEEIOTX deoxidate
ADDEEIPRR draperied
ADDEEJNSS jadedness
ADDEELMNR reddleman
ADDEELMNT addlement
ADDEELNUY undelayed
ADDEELOPR pre-loaded
ADDEELPPW dewlapped
ADDEELRSS dreadless
ADDEEMNNU unamended
ADDEEMNOS Desdemona
ADDEEMNRU undreamed
ADDEEMNST damnedest
ADDEEMORR dromedare
ADDEENNPT dependant
ADDEENORU Oudenarde
ADDEENOST stone-dead
ADDEENPRW deep-drawn
ADDEENSWY Wednesday
ADDEEOPRS desperado
ADDEEORTV overdated
ADDEEPRSS adpressed
ADDEEPRTY Pat Eddery
ADDEEPSUX pas de deux
ADDEERRSS addresser
readdress
ADDEERSSS addresses
ADDEFFHNO offhanded
ADDEFFLOS offsaddle
ADDEFFPRU puff adder
ADDEFHILN field hand
ADDEFIIPT pedatifid
ADDEFILRW fieldward
ADDEFINNR Ferdinand
ADDEFINSS faddiness
ADDEFIRSV Fred Davis
ADDEGGINR degrading
ADDEGGOOT dog eat dog
dog-eat-dog
ADDEGHILT deadlight

ADDEGHINR hag-ridden
ADDEGIITT digitated
ADDEGIMNN demanding
maddening
ADDEGIRRS disregard
ADDEGKNRU grand duke
ADDEGLLMO gold medal
ADDEGLNOT long-dated
ADDEGLRUY guardedly
ADDEGNOOR gadrooned
ADDEGNORR Red Dragon
ADDEGNORW downgrade
ADDEGNRRU undergrad
ADDEGNRUU unguarded
ADDEHHOTY hydathode
ADDEHIILP Didelphia
ADDEHIMUV David Hume
ADDEHINRY anhydride
ADDEHINSY hendiadys
ADDEHIOPV David Hope
ADDEHIRRV hard drive
ADDEHIRRW hard-wired
ADDEHIRTW deid-thraw
ADDEHLNNU unhandled
ADDEHLRRU hard-ruled
ADDEHNNRU underhand
ADDEHNORS hardnosed
ADDEHNORU Roundhead
ADDEHNOTW two-handed
ADDEHOOTT do to death
ADDEHTTUY death duty
ADDEIIIMT dimidiate
ADDEIILNX Dixieland
ADDEIIMNR air-minded
ADDEIINNR Indian red
ADDEIKNPP kidnapped✧
ADDEILLNS landslide
ADDEILMMN middleman
ADDEILMNO Domdaniel
ADDEILMNR midlander
ADDEILNNO dandelion
ADDEILNPS saddle pin
ADDEILNRU underlaid
ADDEILNSV sand-devil
ADDEILNSY deadly sin
ADDEILOSV David Sole
ADDEILPSY displayed
ADDEILSVY advisedly
ADDEIMMNN man-minded
ADDEIMNOT demantoid
ADDEIMNRU unadmired
ADDEIMNSY many-sided
ADDEIMORT dermatoid
ADDEINNRU undrained
ADDEINOPT dead point
ADDEINOUV unavoided
ADDEINOVW David Owen
ADDEINPRS sand pride
ADDEINPRU underpaid
ADDEINRTT dittander
ADDEINRTU indurated

ADDEINRTW trade wind
ADDEINSUV unadvised
ADDEIRSSU dissuader
ADDEIRSSW sidewards
ADDELMMOU mould-made
ADDELMNOO doom-laden
ADDELMNRU ruddleman
ADDELNOTU nodulated
ADDELNSUW unswaddle
ADDELNTUU undulated
ADDELNUZZ undazzled
ADDELOSSU Dead Souls
ADDEMORRY dromedary
ADDENNORU unadorned
ADDENNRTU redundant
ADDENNTUU undaunted
ADDENOORT deodorant
ADDENOPTU unadopted
ADDENORTW trade down
ADDENORUY duodenary
ADDENORVW dove-drawn
ADDENOSTU astounded
ADDENRRUW underdraw
ADDENRRUY Dundreary
ADDEOORRV drove road
ADDEOORST door-stead
ADDEORRSS addressor
ADDEORRTW adderwort
ADDEPQRUU quadruped
ADDFIIQRU quadrifid
ADDFILNRT drift-land
ADDFKNNUY dandyfunk
ADDFLLNOO land-flood
ADDFLNNOO land of Nod✧
ADDGGINRR Gradgrind
ADDGHNOOS good hands
ADDGHNORU draghound
ADDGILMNY maddingly
ADDGILNTW twaddling
ADDGNOOST stand good
ADDGQRSUU drug squad
ADDHHINRT third-hand
ADDHHIOOR hardihood
ADDHHLNOS hold hands
ADDHIKNSW wind-shak'd
ADDHLOOTU adulthood
ADDHNNORU roundhand
ADDHNNOSW hands down
ADDHNORSW sword-hand
ADDHORRSW hard words
ADDIIIOPS aspidioid
ADDIIKOSU audio disk
ADDILOOPP Diplopoda
ADDINNNOU Dundonian
ADDINORSU diandrous
ADDINRSWW windwards
ADDLLNORY dandy-roll
ADDLMOPTY toddy-palm
ADDLNOOSW woodlands
ADDLNORST landdrost
ADDMNOOTU odd man out
ADDNNOPUW up and down
up-and-down
ADDNNOSTW stand down
stand-down
ADDNORSWW downwards
ADDRSSTUY Dryasdust
ADEEEEGLY eagle-eyed
ADEEEELNR leaderene
ADEEEFHRT feathered
ADEEEFIRR federarie
ADEEEFIRY reaedifye
ADEEEFLLT leafleted
ADEEEFNRR referenda
ADEEEFRRT free trade
ADEEEFRTU defeature
ADEEEFRTW feed-water
ADEEEGGRT gadgeteer
ADEEEGJNR jade green
ADEEEGLPR pearl-edge
ADEEEGLRV everglade✧
leveraged
ADEEEGORT to a degree
ADEEEGPRS grapeseed
ADEEEGTTV vegetated
ADEEEHINT The Aeneid
ADEEEHLRT Aethelred
ADEEEHLST sheet lead
steelhead
ADEEEHPRT Peterhead
ADEEEHRST heartseed
shade tree
ADEEEHRTW weathered
ADEEEIIPR Epeiridae
ADEEEILMN madeleine
ADEEEILNT delineate
ADEEEIMRT remediate
ADEEEINRU Uredineae
ADEEEIRSS diaereses
ADEEEKKNW weak-kneed
ADEEEKNSW snakeweed
ADEEELLMN enamelled
ADEEELLNS lease-lend
lend-lease
ADEEELLST teaselled
ADEEELNRV land-reeve
ADEEELNTT dae-nettle
ADEEELPRS seed pearl
ADEEELPRY pearl-eyed
ADEEELRUV rue-leaved
ADEEEMNTT dementate
ADEEEMOST edematose
ADEEEMPRU âme perdue
ADEEEMRSV Mesa Verde
ADEEENRRS serenader
ADEEENRST East-ender
ADEEEPPRR paper-reed
ADEEEPRST desert pea
desperate
ADEEEQRTU détraquée
ADEEERRTW water deer
ADEEERTTU deuterate
ADEEERTWW waterweed
ADEEFFILR fieldfare
ADEEFGGLR reflagged
ADEEFGGRR defragger
ADEEFGINN deafening
ADEEFGLLR Lagerfeld
ADEEFHILR had liefer
ADEEFHIRT death-fire
ADEEFHNRS hands-free
ADEEFIISV five-a-side
ADEEFIKLW Wakefield
ADEEFIKRR firedrake
ADEEFILMS Masefield
ADEEFILOR Florideae
ADEEFILOT defoliate
ADEEFILRS feralised
ADEEFILRW weel-faird
ADEEFILRZ feralized
ADEEFILSU feudalise
ADEEFILUZ feudalize
ADEEFIMST defeatism
ADEEFINOR Freedonia
ADEEFIORT foederati
ADEEFIRTX fixed-rate
ADEEFISTT defeatist
ADEEFJNRT Fred T Jane
ADEEFLLMW well-famed
ADEEFLLST stall-feed
ADEEFLNNR Fernandel
ADEEFLNOS leaf-nosed
ADEEFLORT deflorate
floreated
ADEEFLOTW two-leafed
ADEEFLPRY palfreyed
ADEEFLRTU defaulter
ADEEFLRTW Delftware
ADEEFLRUW weel-faur'd
ADEEFMNOR forenamed
ADEEFMORR reformade
ADEEFNOST stone-deaf
ADEEFOPPY peep of day
ADEEGGINR gingerade
ADEEGGINS disengage
ADEEGGIRV aggrieved
ADEEGGITU tide gauge
ADEEGGJLT jet-lagged
ADEEGGLNO golden age
ADEEGGLOT lodge-gate
ADEEGGMOU demagogue
ADEEGGNNU unengaged
ADEEGGNRR Red Grange
ADEEGGOPU pedagogue
ADEEGGRST staggered
ADEEGHNNR greenhand
ADEEGHNOR negrohead
ADEEGHNRU ahungered
ADEEGHRST the grades
ADEEGILLR galleried
ADEEGILLT get laldie
ADEEGILNR Geraldine
ADEEGILNW wide-angle

ADEEGILOU idealogue
ADEEGILRS sea girdle
ADEEGIMOV video game
ADEEGIMOY Geomyidae
ADEEGINNR endearing
engrained
grenadine✧
ADEEGINPU anguipede
ADEEGINRR grenadier
ADEEGINRT denigrate
ADEEGINST designate
ADEEGIRSV graveside
ADEEGISTV stage-dive
ADEEGIUVW waveguide
ADEEGLLLY allegedly
ADEEGLLRV gravelled
ADEEGLNNR Englander
Greenland
ADEEGLNOR long-eared
ADEEGLNOT elongated
ADEEGLNRY legendary
ADEEGLOOW eaglewood
ADEEGLPRU red-plague
ADEEGLTTU tegulated
ADEEGMNRR germander
ADEEGMNRS gendarmes
ADEEGMNRT garmented
ADEEGMNTU augmented
ADEEGMRRU demurrage
ADEEGNNRS greensand✧
ADEEGNNUV unavenged
ADEEGNORR green road
reed organ
ADEEGNORS renegados
ADEEGNQRU drag-queen
ADEEGNRST estranged
ADEEGNRSU dungarees
ADEEGNRSV Gravesend
ADEEGORRZ razor edge
ADEEGPRTT pargetted
ADEEGRRSS deergrass
reed-grass
ADEEGRSUY Argus-eyed
ADEEGSTTU degustate
ADEEHHITW whitehead
ADEEHHLLT hell-hated
ADEEHHLRT The Herald
ADEEHHLSW dash-wheel
ADEEHHMRY head-rhyme
ADEEHHNOP headphone
ADEEHHNPY hedyphane
ADEEHHOPT The Phaedo
ADEEHHRSY A D Hershey
ADEEHIKLT deathlike
ADEEHIKTV khedivate
ADEEHILMO Ideal Home
ADEEHILNP hen-paidle
ADEEHILNR headliner
ADEEHILNS headlines
ADEEHILRV had liever
ADEEHILTW white lead
ADEEHIMNV mid-heaven
ADEEHIMOR Homeridae
ADEEHINOR rhoeadine
ADEEHINRT herniated
ADEEHINSS headiness
ADEEHIRRT threadier
ADEEHIRRV river head
ADEEHIRTV rivet head
ADEEHKLRS sheldrake
ADEEHLLNS hanselled
ADEEHLLOS leasehold
ADEEHLLST date-shell
ADEEHLMOR dreamhole
ADEEHLORW rowel-head
ADEEHLSSS shadeless
ADEEHLSST deathless
ADEEHMNOT methadone
ADEEHMNOY head money
ADEEHMOST homestead
ADEEHNOST headstone
ADEEHNPPR apprehend
ADEEHNPSW sweep hand
ADEEHNRSU unhearsed
ADEEHNRTU unearthed
ADEEHNRTW The Warden
ADEEHOPPS pope's head
ADEEHORSU eard-house
ADEEHORSV overheads
overshade
ADEEHOSWY eyeshadow
ADEEHPRSY sharp-eyed
ADEEHRRTY rehydrate
ADEEHRSTT shattered
ADEEHRSTW draw-sheet
watershed
ADEEHSTUX exhausted
ADEEIILRS idealiser
ADEEIILRZ idealizer
ADEEIIMMT immediate
ADEEIIMST mediatise
ADEEIIMTV mediative
ADEEIIMTZ mediatize
ADEEIINRT Neritidae
ADEEIIPRS raised pie
ADEEIIPRV Viperidae
ADEEIIRSS diaeresis
ADEEIKLPS spadelike
ADEEIKSST take sides
ADEEILLMW well-aimed
ADEEILLNT niellated
ADEEILLNY delay line
ADEEILLSS idealless
ADEEILMNN Mendelian
ADEEILMNR madrilène
ADEEILMNS Mélisande
ADEEILMPP palmipede
ADEEILMPR epidermal
impleader
ADEEILMRS misleader
misleared
ADEEILMTY mediately
ADEEILNOV devil a one
ADEEILNRT interdeal
tail-ender
ADEEILOTT etiolated
ADEEILPRR lip-reader
ADEEILPRS pearlised
ADEEILPRZ pearlized
ADEEILPSS displease
ADEEILPST side plate
ADEEILRRT irrelated
ADEEILRSV velarised
ADEEILRVZ velarized
ADEEILSVV side valve
ADEEILTUY eudialyte
ADEEILVVY ivy-leaved
ADEEIMMNR mermaiden
ADEEIMMNS misdemean
ADEEIMMRT dreamtime
meter maid
ADEEIMNNO menadione
ADEEIMNOS Maeonides
ADEEIMNRR remainder
ADEEIMNRT minareted
ADEEIMNST Mendaites
semantide
ADEEIMOPR Meropidae
ADEEIMPPR pipe dream
ADEEIMPRY Empire Day
ADEEIMSST demitasse
ADEEIMSSY seamy side
ADEEINNOS adenosine
ADEEINNPR panniered
ADEEINPRR Periander
ADEEINPRW warden pie
ADEEINPST di penates
pedantise
ADEEINPTZ pedantize
ADEEINRSS readiness
ADEEINRTT denitrate
ADEEINRUW unwearied
ADEEINSTT destinate
ADEEINTVV adventive
ADEEIOPRT periodate
ADEEIOPTV videotape
ADEEIORST sorediate
ADEEIPPSS passepied
ADEEIPPST peptidase
ADEEIPRRS draperies
ADEEIPRSS sea spider
spear side
ADEEIPRSV eavesdrip
ADEEIPRTU repudiate
ADEEIPRTV predative
tape drive
ADEEIPSTW waist-deep
ADEEIRRSY Easy Rider
ADEEIRSTV advertise
ADEEIRSTW waterside
ADEEIRTTT tetradite
ADEEIRTTW tidewater
ADEEIRTTX extradite

ADEEIRTVZ advertize
ADEEISSTT stateside✧
steadiest
ADEEISTTW statewide
ADEEITUVX exudative
ADEEJLNRY Leyden jar
ADEEJMRSU mudéjares✧
ADEEJOPRR jeoparder
ADEEJRSTU Judas tree
ADEEKLMRT market-led
ADEEKLSST seed-stalk
ADEEKLSTY stalk-eyed
ADEEKMNOY Yankeedom
ADEEKMRSS dressmake
ADEEKNNSS nakedness
ADEEKNNUW unwakened
ADEEKNRTU undertake
ADEEKNRUW unwreaked
ADEEKORRT take order
ADEEKRRST redstreak
ADEELLLRU laurelled
ADEELLMNR mallender
ADEELLMRT martelled
ADEELLMRV marvelled
ADEELLMTU medullate
ADEELLNNP pannelled
ADEELLNRY learnedly
ADEELLORV overalled
ADEELLPPR rappelled
ADEELLRTV travelled
ADEELLRVV varvelled
ADEELLRVW draw level
ADEELLRXY relaxedly
ADEELLSST tasselled
ADEELLSTT stellated
ADEELLTXY exaltedly
ADEELMMOP melampode
ADEELMMOR melodrame
ADEELMNOP pademelon
ADEELMNPY ependymal
ADEELMOPS mole spade
ADEELMORR male order
ADEELMORU remoulade
rémoulade
ADEELMORX exodermal
ADEELMRSS dreamless
ADEELNNRU unlearned
ADEELNNRV never land✧
ADEELNORV Eve Arnold
overladen
ADEELNOST endosteal
ADEELNPST seed-plant
ADEELNPSU unpleased
ADEELNPTU pendulate
unpleated
ADEELNRRS slanderer
ADEELNRRU launderer
ADEELNRSU under seal
underseal
ADEELNRTT latter end
ADEELNRTU unaltered
unrelated
ADEELNRUX unrelaxed
ADEELNSSV Valdenses
ADEELNSSW Waldenses
ADEELNSTY Steely Dan
ADEELNTTY day-nettle
ADEELNTUX unexalted
ADEELOPRV overpedal
paloverde
ADEELORST desolater
ADEELOTVW two-leaved
ADEELPRST plastered
ADEELPSSU pas de seul
ADEELRRSS redressal
ADEELRRTT red rattle
ADEELRRTU adulterer
ADEELRSST tradeless
ADEELRSTY steelyard
ADEELRSVY adversely
ADEELRTVY avertedly
ADEEMMNNT amendment
ADEEMMNQU quand même
ADEEMMORT dermatome
ADEEMMOXY myxoedema
ADEEMNOPR open-armed
promenade
ADEEMNORT emendator
Notre-Dame
ADEEMNORU demeanour
enamoured
ADEEMNOUY eudaemony
ADEEMNRRU maunderer
ADEEMNRUW E W Maunder
ADEEMOORR aerodrome
ADEEMOPRR madrepore
ADEEMORRX xeroderma
ADEEMORTT trematode
ADEEMORUW meadow-rue
ADEEMOSTU edematous
ADEEMPSTU despumate
steamed up
ADEEMQRRU remarqued
ADEEMRSTW smartweed
ADEENNORR non-reader
ADEENNPRT trepanned
ADEENNQRU quarenden
ADEENNRTU underta'en
undertane
ADEENNTTX extendant
ADEENOPRT ponderate
ADEENORSS road sense
ADEENORUV endeavour✧
ADEENORVY oven-ready
ADEENOSSU Soudanese
ADEENPPRU unpapered
ADEENPRSS panderess
ADEENPRTT patterned
ADEENPSST adeptness
ADEENQRRU quarender
ADEENQSTU Dantesque
ADEENRRTU underrate
ADEENRRUW underwear
ADEENRSTW newstrade
ADEENRSTY sedentary
ADEENRSUY undersaye
ADEENRTTU untreated
ADEENRTTV advertent
ADEENRTUV adventure
ADEENRTUW unwatered
ADEENSSST satedness
ADEENSSUY unessayed
ADEEOOPPR peraeopod
ADEEOPRSV eavesdrop
ADEEOPSTT despotate
ADEEORRRS rear-dorse
ADEEORRTV overtrade
ADEEORRTZ zero-rated
ADEEPPRSS appressed
ADEEPPRST speed trap
ADEEPQRTU parqueted
ADEEPRRSU persuader
ADEEPRRTU departure
ADEEPRSTU depasture
ADEEPRSTY pederasty
ADEEQRRTU quartered
ADEERRSTT desert rat
ADEERRSTV traversed
ADEERSTTW wadsetter
ADEERSTYY yesterday✧
ADEESSTUU assuetude
ADEFFHNOR harden off
ADEFFIILR fair field
ADEFFIILS falsified
ADEFFINOR rained off
ADEFFNORS saffroned
ADEFFNORT affronted
ADEFFOORR off-roader
ADEFGGOTU fagged out
ADEFGHORT godfather
ADEFGIIMN magnified
ADEFGIIRT gratified
ADEFGILLO field goal
ADEFGILLS gas-filled
ADEFGILRU lifeguard
ADEFGILRY field gray
ADEFGINRY defraying
ADEFGINTT defatting
ADEFGIRRU fireguard
ADEFGLLOO goodfella
ADEFGLOOT floodgate
ADEFGLRRU regardful
ADEFGNSUW wages fund
ADEFHIIPT Edith Piaf
ADEFHIMST ham-fisted
ADEFHINRT threadfin
ADEFHIPSS spadefish
ADEFHIRST head first
ADEFHLNOZ half-dozen
ADEFHLOOR floorhead
ADEFHLOOS falsehood
ADEFHLOOW whale food
ADEFHLPST feldspath

ADEFHNORU unheard-of
ADEFIILMP amplified
ADEFIILQU qualified
ADEFIILRT Eid al-Fitr
ADEFIINRV vide infra
ADEFIIPRR rapid fire
rapid-fire
ADEFIISST dies fasti
satisfied
ADEFIKKLR frikkadel
ADEFIKLLR field lark
ADEFIKLMR field mark
ADEFIKNRT after kind
ADEFILLSU fusillade
ADEFILMNS fieldsman
Mansfield
ADEFILMSU feudalism
ADEFILNNR Finlander
ADEFILNNZ zinfandel✧
ADEFILNOR floridean
ADEFILNOT deflation
defoliant
ADEFILNRS filanders
ADEFILNTU in default
ADEFILNTY defiantly
ADEFILORT floriated
ADEFILSTU feudalist
ADEFILTUY feudality
ADEFIMOTY time of day
ADEFINNRW fine-drawn
ADEFINOPR pinafored
ADEFINRST stand fire
ADEFITTTW fat-witted
ADEFKNNRU unfranked
ADEFLLLSU ladlefuls
ADEFLLMOU leaf mould
ADEFLLMSY damselfly
ADEFLLTUW waldflute
ADEFLMMOR malformed
ADEFLNOTU on default
ADEFLNOWY Fay Weldon
ADEFLOPST soft pedal
soft-pedal
ADEFLORWY dayflower
ADEFLOTTW twa-lofted
ADEFLPSSU spadefuls
ADEFLRRUW rewardful
ADEFLRSTW leftwards
ADEFMNNTU fundament
ADEFMOORR doorframe
reformado
ADEFMORTT formatted
ADEFNNOSU nefandous
ADEFNORRW forwander
ADEFOOORT oar-footed
ADEFOOPRR proofread
ADEFOOPST spade foot
ADEFOOTTU out of date
out-of-date
ADEFORRRW forwarder
ADEFORRTV overdraft
ADEFORRTW afterword
Waterford
ADEFORTUY feudatory
ADEFPRSTU turf spade
ADEFRRSTU fraudster
ADEGGGIZZ zigzagged
ADEGGHHIR high-grade
ADEGGHILN hang-glide
ADEGGIITZ dziggetai
ADEGGILLM gall midge
ADEGGILNR langridge
ADEGGINNR gardening
ADEGGINRR regarding
ADEGGINUW wind gauge
ADEGGMNOR doggerman
ADEGGNORU groundage
ADEGHHILT headlight
ADEGHIILV Diaghilev
ADEGHILPT glide path
ADEGHINNR hardening
ADEGHINRS degarnish
ADEGHINSU anguished
ADEGHIOPR eidograph
ideograph
ADEGHIRRT Third-Ager
third gear
ADEGHIRST sight-read
ADEGHLNOO angelhood
ADEGHLNTY day-length
ADEGHLORS gasholder
ADEGHMORU home guard✧
ADEGHNNOS Ogden Nash
ADEGHNNRU anhungred
ADEGHNOPR hop-garden
ADEGHNOPY endophagy
ADEGHNOST death-song
ADEGHNOUZ gaze-hound
ADEGHORST God's heart
ADEGHRRSS herd grass
ADEGHRRTU draughter
ADEGIILOS dialogise
ADEGIILOT dialogite
ADEGIILOZ dialogize
ADEGIILRU guide rail
ADEGIINNR ingrained
ADEGIINPR diapering
ADEGIINRS grain side
ADEGIIORS go airside
ADEGIKLNV gavelkind
ADEGILLMM gimmalled
ADEGILLMN medalling
ADEGILLNN all-ending
ADEGILLNO glenoidal
ADEGILLNP pedalling
ADEGILLNS signalled
ADEGILMOR Golda Meir
ADEGILNNU unaligned
ADEGILNOR girandole
negroidal
ADEGILNOS alongside
ADEGILNPS pleadings
ADEGILNRT treadling
triangled
ADEGILNRU gerundial
ADEGILNST desalting
ADEGILNTW delta wing
ADEGILORV Gore Vidal
ADEGILPRW wild grape
ADEGILRVW wildgrave
ADEGILTUV divulgate
ADEGIMNNN demanning
ADEGIMNRS ganderism
semi-grand
ADEGIMNTU magnitude
ADEGIMORV videogram
ADEGIMOST dogmatise
ADEGIMOTZ dogmatize
ADEGIMRRS misregard
ADEGINNRT integrand
ADEGINNRW wandering
ADEGINORR Rio Grande
ADEGINORS dragonise
grandiose
organised
ADEGINORZ dragonize
organized
ADEGINOSS diagnoses
ADEGINOYZ zygaenoid
ADEGINPRS spreading
ADEGINPRT departing
ADEGINRRS grandsire
ADEGINRRW rewarding
ADEGINRTU giant rude
ADEGINSSU gaudiness
ADEGINSTY steadying
ADEGIOPRS posigrade
ADEGIORRS rodgersia
ADEGIORUX aigre-doux
ADEGIOTUU autoguide
ADEGIPRRT partridge
ADEGIRRUW wire guard
ADEGIRTTU gratitude
ADEGLLNOO gallooned
ADEGLLOPT gold plate
gold-plate
ADEGLMNOO moon-glade
ADEGLNNSU Langesund
ADEGLNNTU untangled
ADEGLNOST Gladstone
ADEGLNPUU unplagued
ADEGLNRUX grand luxe
ADEGLNSTU angel dust
ADEGLOOPY paedology
ADEGLOOUV good value
ADEGLORST old stager
ADEGLRSSU guardless
ADEGMNOOZ Mao Zedong
ADEGMNORU round game
ADEGMNRTU Nemrut Dag
ADEGMOPRR deprogram
ADEGNNOPR pendragon
ADEGNNORY androgyne

ADEGNNRSS grandness
ADEGNOORS goosander
ADEGNOPRT godparent
ADEGNORSS dragoness
ADEGNORSU dangerous
ADEGNORTU get around
nature-god
ADEGNOSTW downstage
ADEGNRSSU ungrassed
ADEGOOPRW Goa powder
ADEGOORST stage door
ADEGOORSY goodyears
ADEGOOSTT good taste
ADEGORRTT garrotted
ADEHHIPRS rhaphides
ADEHHISTW death wish
ADEHHLLRS hardshell
ADEHHNOOT thanehood
ADEHHNORY hornyhead
ADEHHORST short-head
ADEHHOTUY youthhead
ADEHIIIPX Xiphiidae
ADEHIIIPZ Ziphiidae
ADEHIIKLV khedivial
ADEHIILLR ill-haired
ADEHIILNP delphinia
ADEHIILRS hair slide
ADEHIIMMS midmashie
ADEHIIMNO Hominidae
ADEHIIMNS maidenish
ADEHIINRU Hirudinea
ADEHIIPRT rhipidate
ADEHIIRRR hairdrier
ADEHIISST diathesis
ADEHIJMNU mujahedin
ADEHIKLOR Lake Ohrid
ADEHIKMOT The Mikado
ADEHIKNPS handspike
ADEHIKNRT in the dark
ADEHIKNSW windshake
ADEHILLOW lowlihead
ADEHILLST still-head
ADEHILLSW shield law
ADEHILMNS mishandle
ADEHILMOT ethmoidal
ADEHILMRS shield-arm
ADEHILMSY shield-may
ADEHILNOR hodiernal
ADEHILNPR philander✧
ADEHILNRR hardliner
ADEHILNRS hard lines
ADEHILNST Nithsdale
ADEHILOPX hexaploid
ADEHILRRT trihedral
ADEHILRST tehsildar
ADEHILSTU lustihead
ADEHILTWY white lady✧
ADEHIMMNO ad hominem
ADEHIMNOR rhodamine
ADEHIMNRS Sanhedrim
ADEHIMNRT hardiment
ADEHIMOPP hippodame
ADEHIMOSU housemaid
ADEHIMPRS Sephardim
ADEHIMPSS misshaped
ADEHIMPTW white damp
ADEHIMRST Hard Times
ADEHIMRTY diathermy
ADEHINNRS Sanhedrin
ADEHINNSS handiness
ADEHINNST set in hand
ADEHINOPU audiphone
ADEHINORS rhodanise
Rhodesian
ADEHINORT in the road
ADEHINORZ rhodanize
ADEHINOSS adhesions
ADEHINPRS inspheаr'd
ADEHINPRT printhead
ADEHINRSS hardiness
ADEHINRST interdash
tarnished
ADEHINRSW wind shear
ADEHINRTY anhydrite
ADEHINRYZ hydrazine
ADEHINSSS shadiness
ADEHINTWY win the day
ADEHIOPRS do a perish
ADEHIOPRT Aphrodite
atrophied
ADEHIPPRS sapphired
ADEHIPRST therapsid
ADEHIPRSY Syrphidae
ADEHIPSSY diaphyses
ADEHIPSUU euphausid
ADEHIRRRY hairdryer
ADEHIRRTT third-rate
ADEHIRSTW dishwater
ADEHIRSVW hivewards
ADEHIRSVY yravished
ADEHIRTVW third wave
ADEHISSST das heisst
ADEHISSTY dysthesia
ADEHJLLOY jollyhead
ADEHJLOSU judas hole✧
ADEHJNNOR John André
John Arden
ADEHKLORW Lord Hawke
ADEHKNNTU unthanked
ADEHKNOSW hawk-nosed
shake down
shakedown
ADEHKORRS dark horse
ADEHKORSU dark-house
ADEHKRSTU Turk's head
ADEHLLNOR Hollander
ADEHLLNSS shell-sand
ADEHLLORT death roll
ADEHLLOTY tally-hoed
ADEHLLRSW hellwards
ADEHLNOTW handtowel
ADEHLNSST Shetlands
ADEHLOPRY polyhedra
ADEHLORST Aldershot
ADEHLORSY hydrolase
ADEHLORTW hold water
ADEHMMOTU mouth-made
ADEHMNORY hard money
ADEHMNOTU haut monde
ADEHMNRUV Van der Hum
ADEHMNSTU them and us
ADEHMOOPS shampooed
ADEHMOORT Motorhead
ADEHMOORV Hoover Dam
ADEHMOPRY hypoderma
ADEHMORSW homewards
ADEHNNOST stonehand
ADEHNNTUU unhaunted
ADEHNOOPV Vodaphone
ADEHNOORT on the road✧
ADEHNORST stone-hard
ADEHNORTU under oath
ADEHNORTW two-hander
ADEHNORUV have round
ADEHNORVY hydrovane
ADEHNPPRU upper hand
ADEHNPRSS hand-press
ADEHNPRSU urn-shaped
ADEHOOPRT Theropoda
ADEHOORSU roadhouse
ADEHOORTW heartwood
ADEHOOSSW wood ashes
ADEHOOSTT statehood
ADEHOPPPY poppy-head
ADEHOPPTY heptapody
ADEHORRSW shoreward
ADEHORRSY dray-horse
ADEHORSUY dayr'house
ADEHORSVW have words
ADEHOSTUW washed-out
ADEHRSTUY Dusty Hare
ADEHTUVYY heavy-duty
ADEIIILNT initialed
ADEIIINNS Indianise
ADEIIINNZ Indianize
ADEIIINPR peridinia
ADEIIINTT dietitian
ADEIILLMS misallied
ADEIILLNY leylandii
ADEIILMNN Mindelian
ADEIILMNV vindemial
ADEIILMOZ imidazole
ADEIILMST Miltiades
ADEIILMTY Mytilidae
ADEIILNPT pintailed
ADEIILNRT deliriant
drain-tile
ADEIILNRU uredinial
ADEIILNST disentail
ADEIILOOR Oriolidae
ADEIILOPS apsidiole
episodial
ADEIILORT editorial

ADEIILPPP Pedipalpi
ADEIILPRS presidial
ADEIILPTU Tipulidae
ADEIILPTX pixilated
ADEIILQTU liquidate
qualitied
ADEIILRSU Siluridae
ADEIILSVY Sylviidae
ADEIIMNOT mediation
ADEIIMNRT ad interim
ADEIIMNRZ zemindari
ADEIIMOTT diatomite
ADEIIMRTX mediatrix
ADEIIMSSV admissive
misadvise
misavised
ADEIINNOS Indonesia
ADEIINNOU Unionidae
ADEIINORR ordinaire
ADEIINOTV deviation
ADEIINPPR drainpipe
ADEIINPRS Pindarise
ADEIINPRZ Pindarize
ADEIINRTT Titian red
ADEIINRVV vivandier
ADEIINSTU indusiate
ADEIINTUV induviate
ADEIIOPTT idiot tape
ADEIIOTVX oxidative
ADEIIPRRS disrepair
ADEIIPRSS dispraise
ADEIIPSST dissipate
ADEIIPSSY diapyesis
ADEIIRSST Aristides
ADEIIRSTT disattire
distraite
ADEIIRTTV traditive
ADEIISUXZ diazeuxis
ADEIJLMNS James Lind
ADEIJLOSU jalousied
ADEIKKSST kidstakes
ADEIKLNPU plaid-neuk
ADEIKLRSS laser disk
ADEIKMORS kaiserdom
ADEIKNNNP pen-and-ink
ADEIKNPPR kidnapper
ADEIKNPRS spikenard
ADEIKNPRT predikant
ADEIKNRRR rank-rider
ADEIKRSTW water-ski'd
ADEILLLMO lamelloid
ADEILLMNN ill-manned
ADEILLMNO médaillon
medallion
ADEILLMOT metalloid
ADEILLMRT treadmill
ADEILLMST medallist
ADEILLNNV Ivan Lendl
ADEILLNRW well drain
ADEILLNST installed
ADEILLORS dollarise
ADEILLORZ dollarize
ADEILLOVW video wall
ADEILLPRU preludial
ADEILLPSY Psyllidae
ADEILLQRU quadrille
ADEILLRSY Sally Ride
ADEILLRTW dill-water
ADEILMNNO denominal
mandoline
ADEILMNOR Madrileño
mole drain
ADEILMNOV movieland
ADEILMNRT tramlined
ADEILMNST dismantle
ADEILMNTU datum line
dentalium
ADEILMOPT diplomate
ADEILMOPY polyamide
ADEILMORR mail order
mail-order
ADEILMPTU amplitude
ADEILMSTU simulated
ADEILNNPU unplained
ADEILNNRU underlain
ADEILNOPP panoplied
ADEILNOPS delapsion
ADEILNOPT planetoid
ADEILNOPU aneuploid
ADEILNPPU unapplied
ADEILNPRU Paludrine®
ADEILNPSU unpalsied
ADEILNPTU unplaited
ADEILNRRT interlard
ADEILNRSU under sail
ADEILNRSY synedrial
ADEILNRTT tridental
ADEILNRTU uitlander
ADEILNRUY unreadily
ADEILNSSV validness
ADEILOPRS polarised
ADEILOPRT depilator
ADEILOPRZ polarized
ADEILOPSU lapideous
ADEILOQSU odalisque
ADEILORST steroidal
ADEILORVY olive-yard
ADEILPRSS dispersal
ADEILPRSY displayer
ADEILPSSS sapidless
ADEILPTTU platitude
ADEILRSXY Xyridales
ADEILRTTU rutilated
ADEILRTVV trivalved
ADEILRTWW wild water
ADEILSSTU lassitude
ADEILSTTU altitudes
ADEIMMRST midstream
ADEIMNNOR Normandie
ADEIMNNTU indumenta
ADEIMNOPR meropidan
ADEIMNOPT ademption
ADEIMNORS masonried
randomise
ADEIMNORZ randomize
ADEIMNOSS mid-season
ADEIMNOST Maidstone
staminode
ADEIMNPRR Parminder
reprimand
ADEIMNPRS panderism
Spider-Man
spiderman
ADEIMNPRU drepanium
ADEIMNPST pedantism
ADEIMNRRU murrained
unmarried
ADEIMNRSU nursemaid
ADEIMNRSY year's mind
ADEIMNRTY dynamiter
ADEIMNRYZ zemindary
ADEIMNSTV Adventism
Vedantism
ADEIMOORV road movie
ADEIMOPST impastoed
ADEIMORTT meditator
trematoid
ADEIMORTY mediatory
ADEIMPRST red-tapism
spermatid
ADEIMPRSY pyramides
ADEIMRRUU Du Maurier
ADEIMRTTU diatretum
ADEIMRTUX admixture
ADEIMRTXY taxidermy
ADEINNNPS inspanned
ADEINNNTT intendant
ADEINNOTT dentation
ADEINNPTU unpainted
ADEINNRRW inner ward
ADEINNRSS randiness
ADEINNRTU untrained
ADEINNSSS sandiness
ADEINNSTU unstained
ADEINNTTU untainted
ADEINOOPS poinadoes
ADEINOPPT appointed
ADEINOPRR preordain
ADEINOPRT predation
ADEINOPSS passioned
ADEINOPST antipodes✧
ADEINORRS serranoid
ADEINORST soda nitre
ADEINORSU deinosaur
ADEINORTT Andreotti
ADEINORTY arytenoid
ADEINORUZ Zonuridae
ADEINOTUX exudation
ADEINPPRS sandpiper
ADEINPPST standpipe
ADEINPRSS rapidness
ADEINPRSU unpraised
ADEINPRTT trepidant

Words marked ✧ can also be spelled with one or more capital letters

ADEINPSSS sapidness
ADEINPSSV vapidness
ADEINPSVY vin de pays
ADEINRRSV river sand
ADEINRRTV driver ant
ADEINRRTY Tyrian red
ADEINRRWW wiredrawn
ADEINRSST tardiness
ADEINRSTU Sturnidae
turn aside
ADEINRTTU unattired
ADEINSSST staidness
ADEINSSTU sustained
ADEINSTTU disattune
ADEINSTTV Adventist
ADEIOPRST parotides
ADEIOPRSU deiparous
ADEIOPRSV privadoes
ADEIOPRTT dioptrate
ADEIOPRTZ trapezoid
ADEIORSTT storiated
ADEIORTVY deviatory
ADEIOSSST toss aside
ADEIPPRSU dispauper
ADEIPPSSY dyspepsia
ADEIPRRSU perradius
ADEIPRRVW warp drive
ADEIPRSTT red-tapist
ADEIPRSTU drape suit
ADEIPRSUU Epidaurus
ADEIPRSUV vide supra
ADEIPRTVY depravity
ADEIPSSTU stapedius
ADEIPSSUX pseudaxis
ADEIRRSUY residuary
ADEIRSSTU auditress
ADEIRSTTW tawdriest
ADEIRSTVY adversity
ADEISTTUV vastitude
vedutista
ADEJLMPSU jump leads
ADEJMMOOR major mode
ADEJNOSVY Davy Jones
ADEKLNNPU unplanked
ADEKLNOSY ankylosed
ADEKLORUY royal duke
ADEKMNNOY donkey-man
ADEKMNOST don't ask me!
ADEKMOQRU Quakerdom
ADEKMRSWY dyke swarm
ADEKNNRRU dak runner
ADEKNOOSW snakewood
ADEKNOOTW tae kwon do
ADEKNORSW dear knows
ADEKNOTTX detox tank
ADEKNSTUU Eduskunta
ADEKOPRRW draw poker
ADEKOPRSW spadework
ADELLLOWY allowedly
ADELLMRUY medullary
ADELLNOOT Donatello
ADELLNOPR landloper
land-loper
ADELLNORW lowlander✧
new dollar
ADELLNOUY unalloyed
ADELLNPSU all ends up
ADELLNSTW stand well
ADELLNSYY Sandy Lyle
ADELLNTUU lunulated
ADELLOORW low-loader
ADELLOPRT patrolled
ADELLORRT tall order
ADELLRRWY dry-waller
ADELLRTXY dextrally
ADELMNNOS Mandelson
ADELMNNUY mundanely
ADELMNOPS endoplasm
ADELMNOPY padymelon
ADELMNORS red salmon
ADELMORST old master✧
ADELMORSU asmoulder
ADELMSSUY assumedly
ADELNNNPU unplanned
ADELNNNPY pennyland
ADELNNORW landowner
ADELNNPTU unplanted
ADELNOOST loadstone
ADELNOPSY dyspnoeal
ADELNORRV Land Rover®
ADELNORTU outlander
ADELNORUY roundelay
ADELNOSSW Les Dawson
ADELNPRUY underplay
ADELNRRUY Drury Lane
ADELNRSSU laundress
ADELNRTVY verdantly
ADELNSSTU dauntless
ADELNSTUU unsaluted
ADELOOOSW aloes-wood
ADELOOPRT door-plate
ADELOORRY early door
ADELOORST desolator
ADELOORWY early wood
ADELOPTUY played-out
ADELPQRUU quadruple
ADELPRSSY sparsedly
ADELRRSTY drysalter
ADELRSSUY assuredly
ADELSTTTW Weltstadt
ADEMMNOPP mappemond
ADEMMORST masterdom
ADEMNNORT adornment
ADEMNNOST most an end
ADEMNNRUU unmanured
ADEMNORST transomed
ADEMNORSU meandrous
ADEMNPSTU unstamped
ADEMNRRSU snare drum
under arms
ADEMNRTUU unmatured
ADEMNSSUU unassumed
ADEMOORRT moderator
ADEMOORST astrodome
moderatos
ADEMOORSY doomsayer
mooseyard
ADEMORRSW Romewards
ADEMORRTT Rotterdam
ADEMOSTTW two-masted
ADENNNSTU suntanned
ADENNOPSS senna pods
ADENNORRU do a runner
ADENNOSST sandstone
ADENNOSTY asyndeton
ADENNSSTW news-stand
ADENNTTWY and twenty
ADENOORST tornadoes
ADENOORTT detonator
ADENOORTW to a wonder
ADENOOSTT toadstone
ADENOOSVW wood avens
ADENOOTWZ zante-wood
ADENOOWWX woodwaxen
ADENOPPTY pentapody
ADENOPRSU panderous
ADENOPRTV davenport
ADENOPRUV up-and-over
ADENOPRUZ Ezra Pound
ADENOPSTW paste-down
ADENORRUY year-round
ADENORRUZ unrazored
ADENORSTV overstand
stand over
ADENORSTW stare down
ADENORTTU rotundate
ADENORTWW water down
ADENOSTTW downstate
ADENOSUVW sound wave
ADENOTTWY wyandotte✧
ADENPRRTU underpart
ADENPRSSU underpass
ADENQRSUU unsquared
ADENRRSTW sternward
ADENRRTUY day return
ADENRSSTW St Andrews
ADENRSSUU unassured
ADEOOPPRT Pteropoda
ADEOOPPRW wood paper
ADEOPPRTT tappet-rod
ADEOPRRTU depurator
ADEOPRRTW top drawer
top-drawer
water drop
ADEOPRRTY predatory
ADEOPRSTU outspread
ADEOPRTTW two-parted
ADEOPRTTY tetrapody
ADEOQRTTU torquated
ADEORRSTT rostrated
ADEORRSWW swear-word
ADEORRTUV advoutrer
ADEORRTUW outer ward

ADERRSTWY stewardry
ADERSSTWW westwards
ADFFFFRUU ruff-a-duff
ADFFGIIOR giraffoid
ADFFHRSTU hard stuff
ADFFIIMRS disaffirm
ADFFILNTU find fault
find-fault
ADFFOOSST fast foods
ADFFORRST Strafford
ADFFSTTUY staff duty
ADFGHIOOT good faith
good-faith
ADFGHIRSU Fishguard
ADFGIIINN Indian fig
ADFGILNOU fungoidal
ADFGILORY fairy gold
ADFGINORS sangfroid
ADFGINOWY Fay Godwin
ADFGLNORY dragonfly
ADFGOORRU roof guard
ADFGOORSW dogs of war
ADFHINRST first-hand
ADFHIOORY fairyhood
ADFHLNOPU half-pound
ADFHLNORU half-round
ADFHLOORY foolhardy
ADFHLORSW half-sword
ADFHNOOTU out of hand
ADFIILNOT latifondi
ADFIILOOP filopodia
ADFIILRST drift-sail
ADFILLMTU adult film
ADFILLOTW tidal flow
ADFILMNOS manifolds
ADFILMSUY dismayful
ADFILNOOV flavonoid
ADFILRSTY first lady✧
ADFIMNRST stand firm
ADFINOORX Oxfordian
ADFINORSZ sforzandi
ADFINRRTU turf drain
ADFIORRSW fair words
ADFIORSUV disfavour
ADFIRRSTT stardrift
ADFKLMOOR floodmark
ADFLLLOOW floodwall
ADFLLMOOP flood lamp
ADFLLOOOS Adolf Loos
ADFLLOOST faldstool
ADFLORRWY forwardly
frowardly
ADFLORUUY Raoul Dufy
ADFMOOPPR damp-proof
ADFNOORSZ sforzando
ADFNORRTW frontward
ADGGIILNN ding-a-ling
ADGGILNRY niggardly
ADGGILRSY Yggdrasil
ADGGINRRU guard ring
ADGGLOORV Volgograd
ADGGMNORU gum dragon
ADGHHILNS Highlands
ADGHHINRT right-hand
ADGHHIRRT hard right
ADGHHOOPR hodograph
ADGHIIMNS Gandhi-ism
ADGHIIOPR idiograph
ADGHIKOOW gawkihood
ADGHILLLU guildhall
ADGHILNRV grindhval
ADGHILNSY dashingly
ADGHIMNOR harmdoing
ADGHIMOSU Mogadishu
ADGHINNST and things
ADGHINOOT gianthood
ADGHINORS dragonish
ADGHINORT Arondight
ADGHINOSW shadowing
ADGHINPRS handgrips
ADGHINRSU shin guard
ADGHINRTU indraught
ADGHINRTW nightward
ADGHIPRSU guardship
guard-ship
ADGHIRRTW rightward
ADGHLOPUY playdough
ADGHNORSU ground-ash
ADGHNORTU on draught
ADGHNOSTU staghound
ADGHNSSUW swung dash
ADGHORRUW rough-draw
ADGHORTUX draught ox
ADGHPRTUU up-draught
ADGIIILNT digitalin
ADGIIILST digitalis
ADGIIJNNO adjoining
ADGIILMOS sigmoidal
ADGIILNSS glissandi
ADGIILOSS diglossia
ADGIILOST dialogist
ADGIIMNNR manriding
ADGIIMNRS disarming
ADGIIMNRU Inguri Dam
ADGIIMNSY dismaying
ADGIIMNTT admitting
ADGIINNNT indignant
ADGIINNRW in drawing
ADGIINORT granitoid
ADGIINOSS diagnosis
ADGIINRTY dignitary
ADGIINSSV dissaving
ADGIIRTVY gravidity
ADGIKLLMN milk-gland
ADGIKLLNS silk gland
ADGIKLNRS darklings
ADGILLNUY languidly
ADGILLOSU gladiolus
ADGILMNOW wild mango
ADGILMNRU grund mail
ADGILMNSU guildsman
ADGILNNOU unloading
ADGILNNST Landsting
ADGILNOPT gold paint
ADGILNORY adoringly
ADGILNOSS glissando
God's nails
ADGILNPRS springald
ADGILNRTY dartingly
ADGILOORY radiology
ADGILOOSS solidagos
ADGILOOUY audiology
ADGIMMOST dogmatism
ADGIMNNOS Mandingos
ADGIMNORS dragonism
ADGIMOSTT dogmatist
ADGINNNUW undawning
ADGINNOOU iguanodon
ADGINNOPR pardoning
ADGINNRST ringstand
ADGINOPRY parodying
ADGINPRRX grand prix✧
ADGINPRSY dayspring
ADGJNRRUY grand jury
ADGKLMNSU musk gland
ADGKNOORU ground oak
ADGKNRRTU Grand Turk
ADGLMNOOS dog-salmon
ADGLNOORY andrology
ADGLNOOTY odontalgy
ADGLNOUYY young lady
ADGMNNORU groundman
ADGMOOPRS spodogram
ADGMOORRU guardroom
ADGMOORTY dogmatory
ADGMRRSTU smart drug
ADGNNNNOU Dungannon
ADGNNNOOO go on and on
ADGNNORYY androgyny
ADGNOORTU a good turn
ADGNORRTU Grand Tour
ADGNORSUW snow guard
ADGOOORST a good sort
ADGOOPRST gastropod
ADGOOPRSU podagrous
ADGOORSUW wood sugar
ADHHIMOPR rhamphoid
ADHHIORRT Thora Hird
ADHHNOORU hoarhound
ADHHNOOTT hot-and-hot
ADHHNORST shorthand
ADHHOPRSS sharp-shod
ADHIIJMNU mujahidin
ADHIIKLNR drink-hail
ADHIILLOT lithoidal
ADHIILOPU audiophil
ADHIILOPX xiphoidal
ADHIILORZ rhizoidal
ADHIILPRS lairdship
ADHIILRRT third rail
ADHIIMMRS Midrashim
ADHIIMPSS amidships
ADHIIMSSS Hassidism

Words marked ✧ can also be spelled with one or more capital letters

ADHIIOPSU aphidious
ADHIIOPTY idiopathy
ADHIIPSSY diaphysis
ADHIKLPSS skaldship
ADHIKMNNU humankind
ADHIKNORW handiwork
ADHIKNSSS kiss hands
ADHILLMNO Damon Hill
ADHILLOSW dishallow
ADHILMNPY nymphalid
ADHILMOOP omphaloid
ADHILNNUY unhandily
ADHILNOOY on holiday
ADHILNOPY hypnoidal
ADHILNPSU uplandish
ADHILOPTY typhoidal
ADHIMNOSY Mondayish
ADHIMNRST thirdsman
ADHIMORSS Hormisdas
ADHIMSTYY dysthymia
ADHINNPRT handprint
ADHINNRTU hit-and-run
ADHINOORT radiothon
ADHINOOST sainthood
ADHINOPSY dysphonia
ADHINORTY hydration
ADHINRTWW withdrawn
ADHINSTTW withstand
ADHIOOPRZ Rhizopoda
ADHIOPRSY dysphoria
ADHISTWWY widthways
ADHJNOORW Jonah word
ADHKMOSTY Thomas Kyd
ADHKNORWY handywork
ADHLLMORT thralldom
ADHLLNOOY lay hold on
ADHLMNOUY lyam-hound
ADHLNNORT northland
ADHLNOOWY any old how
ADHLNORUU haul round
ADHLNOSTU southland
ADHLOTTUW would that
ADHMNOOOW womanhood
ADHMOORSY hydrosoma
ADHNNRSTU handsturn
hand's turn
ADHNOORYZ hydrozoan
ADHNORRTW northward
ADHNORSUY anhydrous
ADHNORTUY hydronaut
ADHNOSSTT stand shot
ADHNOSSTU thousands
ADHOOPRRT arthropod
ADHOOSTTW what's to do?
ADHORSTTY hydrostat
ADHORSTUW southward
ADHRSSTUY Thursdays
ADIIIKNNN indian ink✧
ADIIIMPRS diapirism
ADIIINNRV indinavir
ADIIINNST Indianist
ADIIINORS Isidorian
ADIIINOSZ isoniazid
ADIIIOSSX ixodiasis
ADIIJKSST disjaskit
ADIIKKRRY kirkyaird
ADIILLNTU lunitidal
ADIILLNVY invalidly
ADIILLOPR radio pill
ADIILLOPS spadillio
ADIILLPTY pallidity
ADIILMNNO mandilion✧
ADIILMOPS idioplasm
ADIILMPVY impavidly
ADIILMSSS dismissal
ADIILMSTY dismality
ADIILNOPT platinoid
ADIILNOPU nauplioid
ADIILNOQU quinoidal
ADIILNOTU nautiloid
ADIILOORV varioloid
ADIILOPRS sporidial
ADIILOWWW widow wail
ADIIMNOSS admission
ADIIMNOST staminoid
ADIIMNOTT admit into
ADIIMNPRS Pindarism
ADIIMNRSW Darwinism
ADIIMOSTT diatomist
ADIIMRSSY mydriasis
ADIINNOST disanoint
ADIINNOSY Dionysian
ADIINOOTX oxidation
ADIINOQTU quotidian
ADIINORTT tradition✧
ADIINORTV divinator
ADIINOSST soi-disant
stasidion
ADIINPRST Pindarist
ADIINRSTT distraint
ADIINRSTU saturniid
ADIINRSTW Darwinist
ADIIOPSTY adiposity
ADIIPRSTY disparity
ADIISSTUY assiduity
ADIISTTVY vastidity
ADIJKSSSU Judas kiss
ADIJMOPSU Poujadism
ADIJOPSTU Poujadist
ADIKKNNSY Kandinsky
ADIKLMNRS alms-drink
ADIKMNNOW womankind
ADILLLPSU spauld-ill
ADILLMNOO almond-oil
ADILLNOPT land-pilot
ADILLNOPU planuloid
ADILLNRUY diurnally
ADILLOPRS Paris doll
ADILLOPTW tallow dip
ADILLORRX rix-dollar
ADILLQSUY squalidly
ADILMMSTU Talmudism
ADILMNNOY mandylion✧
ADILMNOOS salmonoid
ADILMNOST daltonism✧
ADILMNRUU Duralumin®
duralumin
ADILMOPSY sympodial
ADILMRUUV duumviral
ADILMSTTU Talmudist
ADILNNNOO Londonian
ADILNNOPS pond snail
ADILNOOST isodontal
ADILNOPSY on display
ADILNORSW solar wind
ADILNPSWY wild pansy
ADILNRTUU diuturnal
ADILNSTTY distantly
ADILOOPRS prosodial
ADILOPRSV disproval
ADILOPRXY pyridoxal
ADILORRWW World War I
ADILORSTW swordtail
ADIMNNNOU anno mundi
ADIMNNTUY mundanity
ADIMNOOOP monopodia
ADIMNOORT admonitor
dominator
ADIMNOOSY moon daisy
ADIMNOPRY pyramidon
ADIMNOSTY staminody
ADIMNOSWW widow's man
ADIMOOORR radio room
ADIMOOQSU Quasimodo
ADIMORRTY Amy Dorrit
ADIMORTTX dot matrix
ADIMORTUW moudiwart
ADIMORTWW mowdiwart
ADINNNOUZ D'Annunzio
ADINNORTW down-train
train down
ADINNOSST dissonant
ADINNPRTU tip-and-run
ADINNPSTU stand up in
ADINOOPRS prosodian
ADINOOSTT odonatist
ADINOOSTW satinwood
ADINOPSTY dystopian
ADINORSTW downstair
ADINOTWWX window tax
ADINPSTTU disputant
ADINPSUVY vin du pays
ADIOOOPRT patio door
ADIOOPSTU adoptious
ADIORRSTT traditors
ADIOSSSUU assiduous
ADIPSSUYY upsy-daisy
ADJMMOOOR major-domo
ADJMMORRU drum-major
ADKLMORRS Lord Marks
ADKLNNOPW plank down
ADKLNORTU talk round
ADKNORRTU trunk road

ADKNORRWW drawn work
ADKOORRSW roadworks
ADLLLORRY Lollardry
ADLLNOSTU Lotus-land
ADLLNSSUV Sundsvall
ADLLOPRWY play-world
ADLMNORTY mordantly
Tom Landry
ADLMNRSTU Landsturm
ADLMOOPRR prodromal
ADLMOORRY Lord Mayor
ADLMOORTU modulator
ADLMOPRUW mouldwarp
ADLNOPRUY play round
ADLNOPRYY polyandry
ADLNOSUWY Low Sunday
ADLNRSSTU Stralsund
ADLOOOSTT toadstool
ADLOORRST Lord Astor
ADLOPRSWY swordplay
ADLORSUUY arduously
ADLORTUWY outwardly
ADLPPSUYY supply day
ADLPQRUUY quadruply
ADMMORRTY martyrdom
ADMNNORSU roundsman
ADMNNOSSY synodsman
ADMNOOOST odontomas
ADMNOORSZ smorzando
ADMNOORTY dynamotor
ADMNOOSUV novodamus
ADMNORSST sandstorm
ADMNORSSW swordsman
ADMOOPPRU pompadour
ADMOOPSTW wood stamp
ADMORRTUY Mary Tudor
ADMPSTTUY stamp duty
ADNNOOOTT Notodonta
ADNNOPSTU stand upon
ADNNORRUU runaround
ADNNOSSWW swansdown
swans-down
ADNNSSTTU St Dunstan
ADNOOSSST dos Santos
ADNOOTTUU out-and-out
ADNOPQRSU porn squad
ADNOPRRTY protandry
ADNOPRRUW wrap round
wrapround
ADNOPRSSU pass round
ADNOPRSTU Port Sudan
ADNOPSSTU sandspout
ADOOORRWW arrowwood
ADOPRRTUY pourtrayd
AEEEEHMPR ephemerae
AEEEEHRRW here we are
AEEEELMRS Release Me
AEEEELRRS rerelease
AEEEELRTV re-elevate
AEEEELSSV sea sleeve
AEEEEPPSW peaseweep

AEEEETTTT tête-à-tête
AEEEFFLRT feel after
AEEEFGLNR leaf-green
AEEEFGLRT telferage
AEEEFGNRR free-range
AEEEFGNRT free agent
AEEEFGRTV gate fever
AEEEFHLLN fellaheen
AEEEFHRRT heart-free
hereafter
AEEEFHRTV fever-heat
AEEEFINRR a free rein
AEEEFIRRT fire-eater
AEEEFKRST seek after
AEEEFLMRT flame-tree
AEEEFLMRZ ramfeezle
AEEEFLRUV value-free
AEEEFNNST Fasten-e'en
AEEEFSTTT estafette
AEEEGGGNR greengage
AEEEGGILR gier-eagle
AEEEGGNNR engrenage
AEEEGGNPR pre-engage
AEEEGGNRS sage green
sage-green
AEEEGGRST Easter egg
segregate
AEEEGHLRW gearwheel
AEEEGHPRT page three
page-three
AEEEGIKNV give a knee
AEEEGIMNR menagerie
AEEEGINTX exigeante
AEEEGJNNT Jean Genet
AEEEGKRTW Great Week
AEEEGLLNV vellenage
AEEEGLRRV gear-lever
AEEEGLRTT letter-gae
AEEEGLSTW sweet gale
sweet-gale
AEEEGMNNP empennage
AEEEGMNRT agreement
égarement
AEEEGNRRT étrangère
AEEEGNRSS eagerness
AEEEGNRTW tweenager
AEEEGNSTV Stevenage
AEEEGPRRT grapetree
AEEEGRRRT garreteer
AEEEGRRTT targeteer
AEEEGRSST res gestae
AEEEGRSTT streetage
AEEEGRTTZ gazetteer
AEEEGRTUZ gauze-tree
AEEEHHNST ensheathe
AEEEHHRTT tree heath
AEEEHKNRR hearkener
AEEEHLLMN mallee-hen
AEEEHLMPR ephemeral
AEEEHLMRS Haslemere
AEEEHLPRR Harper Lee

AEEEHMNST mane-sheet
AEEEHMPRS ephemeras
AEEEHMPST sheep meat
AEEEHMRTX hexameter
AEEEHNNRT enhearten
AEEEHNRTW enwreathe
AEEEHPRTT threepeat
AEEEHRRRS rehearser
AEEEHRSTT tearsheet
AEEEILLOT elaeolite
AEEEILLRU Laurie Lee
AEEEILNPY pineal eye
AEEEILRTT elaterite
AEEEIMNRX re-examine
AEEEIMRRT Téméraire
AEEEINRRR en arrière
AEEEIPPRT papeterie
AEEEIRRTT reiterate
AEEEJNNTT Jeannette
AEEEKLTTT tea kettle
AEEEKMNSS make sense
AEEEKMPRT keep a term
AEEEKMRRT marketeer✧
tee marker
AEEEKNRST tree snake
AEEEKNRTT entertake
AEEEKNSSY snake eyes
AEEEKRSWX weaker sex
AEEELLMNR enameller
AEEELLMNT elemental
AEEELLMNY my lee-lane
AEEELLNRS all serene
AEEELLRST teaseller
AEEELLRSW weaseller
AEEELLSST telesales
tessellae
AEEELMPTT metapelet
AEEELMSTW sweetmeal
AEEELNNPP peneplane
AEEELNPRT plane tree
AEEELNSTT sea nettle
AEEELNUVZ Venezuela
AEEELPPRT apple tree
AEEELPTTU epaulette
AEEELRSTT sea letter
AEEELRSTW steelware
AEEEMMNST semanteme
AEEEMNNRT nemertean
AEEEMNRST erasement
AEEEMNRTU enumerate
AEEEMORRT aerometer
areometer
AEEEMPRTT temperate
AEEEMRRSU remeasure
AEEEMRTVW wavemeter
AEEEMSTTW sweetmeat
AEEENNNQU Queen Anne
AEEENNPRT perennate
AEEENOPVW open-weave
AEEENORTX exonerate
AEEENPRTT penetrate

AEEENPRTU Euterpean
AEEENRRST easterner✧
AEEENRRTW treenware
AEEENRTTV eventrate
AEEENSSSV Seven Seas
AEEENTTUV eventuate
AEEENTTUX extenuate
AEEEOPPTU a peepe out
AEEEQRSTU tee-square
AEEERSTTW Teeswater
AEEESSTTY essayette
AEEFFFMUW fee-faw-fum
AEEFFILRT afterlife
AEEFFNORT affrontee
affrontée
AEEFFRSTT staff-tree
AEEFGGLUU fuel gauge
AEEFGHILS fish eagle
AEEFGILMS self-image
AEEFGILPR pilferage
AEEFGINRS far-seeing
AEEFGIRRT fire-grate
AEEFGLLOT flageolet
AEEFGLMOR foregleam
AEEFGLNNW newfangle
AEEFGLNUV avengeful
AEEFGLORV gaol-fever
AEEFGLORW flowerage
AEEFGLSTT stage left
AEEFGLSTW sweet flag
AEEFGORRT frog-eater
AEEFGORST forestage
fosterage
AEEFGRRSU sugar-free
AEEFHHRTT The Father
AEEFHIKPT keep faith
AEEFHIRSS sea-fisher
AEEFHLLNT the fallen
AEEFHLMST flesh-meat
AEEFHLRTT heartfelt
AEEFHORTT at the fore
AEEFHOSSU safe house
AEEFIJLRV jail-fever
AEEFILLMN en famille
AEEFILLTT title leaf
AEEFILMNR leaf miner
AEEFILMNT fine metal
AEEFILMPR relief map
AEEFILNRT interleaf
AEEFILNSS leafiness
AEEFILOTX exfoliate
AEEFILPPR paper-file
AEEFILPPW apple-wife
AEEFILRST reistafel
AEEFILRSV life-saver
AEEFILRTX tax relief
AEEFILRWY life-weary
AEEFIMMRT timeframe
AEEFIMORT aforetime
AEEFIMRTT aftertime
AEEFINRTU feature in
AEEFINSTT festinate
AEEFINSTX antefixes
AEEFIORRT free-to-air
AEEFIQTUW quite a few
AEEFIRRTW firewater
AEEFIRSTT feast-rite
AEEFIRSTW wasterife
AEEFKLOVW folk-weave
AEEFKOPRS forespeak
AEEFLLLMS feel small
AEEFLLMSS flameless
AEEFLLNNW new-fallen
AEEFLLOOS loose-leaf
AEEFLMNRT Fremantle
AEEFLMOSV false move
AEEFLNRST fenestral
AEEFLNSSS falseness
AEEFLORSS Flores Sea
AEEFLORST foresteal
AEEFLOSTV love feast
AEEFLPSST false step
AEEFLRRTT flatterer
AEEFLRTUW weel-faurt
AEEFLRTUY featurely
AEEFMNNRU unfreeman
AEEFMNORS freemason✧
AEEFMNORW freewoman
AEEFMPTTT tempt fate
AEEFMRRSS farmeress
AEEFNNORT foreanent
AEEFNRRTW water fern
AEEFNSTTY safety net
AEEFOPRRT perforate
AEEFORSTT foretaste
AEEFPRSSU supersafe
AEEFPRSTU perfusate
AEEGGILNO galiongee
AEEGGILNR ginger ale
AEEGGINNS gas engine
AEEGGINRR gregarine
AEEGGINRS sea ginger
AEEGGIRUW wire gauge
AEEGGLNOY genealogy
AEEGGMNRR green gram
AEEGGMORT mortgagee
AEEGGNPRY energy gap
AEEGGNRSU grease gun
AEEGGORRT toeragger
AEEGGRRST staggerer
AEEGGRRSW swaggerer
AEEGGRTUY tyre gauge
AEEGHHNOV hog heaven
AEEGHILST Eastleigh
AEEGHIMRT hermitage
AEEGHINNU guinea hen
AEEGHINRR rehearing
AEEGHINRS garnishee
AEEGHIRTW agree with
AEEGHLLMS shell game
AEEGHLMST gas helmet
AEEGHLORU auger-hole
AEEGHLOST segholate
AEEGHLPRT telegraph
AEEGHLRSS shearlegs
AEEGHLRWY grey whale
AEEGHLTTW get the law
AEEGHMNOP megaphone
AEEGHMNOR home range
AEEGHMNOT on the game
AEEGHMRRT Margrethe
AEEGHMRTW wheat germ
AEEGHMRTZ megahertz
AEEGHNRSW greenwash
AEEGHNRSY ashen-grey
AEEGHOSTU gatehouse
AEEGHSSTU the usages
AEEGIILNS genialise
AEEGIILNZ genialize
AEEGIIMNR gaminerie
imagineer
AEEGIINNR air-engine
AEEGILLMS misallege
AEEGILLNS all-seeing
AEEGILLNV villenage
AEEGILLRT treillage
AEEGILLRV villagree
AEEGILLST legislate
AEEGILMMR mailmerge
AEEGILMNN malengine
meningeal
AEEGILMNR greenmail
AEEGILMNS semiangle
AEEGILMSS imageless
AEEGILNNR e-learning
in general
AEEGILNNT eglantine
inelegant
AEEGILNNV leavening
AEEGILNRV revealing
AEEGILNST anglesite
teaseling
AEEGILNSW anglewise
AEEGILNTV elevating
AEEGILPTT title page
AEEGILRSV Silver Age
AEEGILRTU gauleiter
AEEGILUVY Ivy League
AEEGIMMTV gemmative
AEEGIMNNN engine-man
AEEGIMNNV given name
AEEGIMNRS Germanise
AEEGIMNRT germinate
AEEGIMNRZ Germanize
AEEGIMNSS gessamine
AEEGIMNST magnesite
magnetise
AEEGIMNSW new ageism✧
AEEGIMNTT magnetite
AEEGIMNTZ magnetize
AEEGIMOST isogamete
AEEGIMPTT pegmatite
AEEGIMRRT remigrate

AEEGIMRTT	tiger team
AEEGIMRTU	mugearite
AEEGINNRR	engrainer
AEEGINNRT	argentine✧
	tangerine✧
AEEGINNSU	Gneisenau
AEEGINNUW	New Guinea
AEEGINNYZ	zygaenine
AEEGINOPP	pigeon pea
AEEGINOPS	espionage
AEEGINOTT	negotiate
AEEGINPRT	interpage
	pignerate
	repeating
AEEGINPRV	grapevine
AEEGINRST	stingaree
AEEGINRTT	argentite
	integrate
AEEGINRTW	Wagnerite
AEEGINSTU	sautéeing
AEEGIOPSU	epigaeous
AEEGIPSUV	give pause
AEEGIQRSU	squireage
AEEGIRUWZ	wire gauze
AEEGISTTV	gestative
AEEGJLMOU	megajoule
AEEGJNORR	jargoneer
AEEGLLNOR	organelle
AEEGLLNRY	generally
AEEGLLNTY	elegantly
AEEGLMNNT	gentleman
AEEGLMNRY	germanely
AEEGLMNST	segmental
AEEGLMNTT	tegmental
AEEGLMOOS	mesogloea
AEEGLMORT	glomerate
AEEGLMORU	Rogue Male
AEEGLMRRY	germ layer
AEEGLNNOS	Angelenos
AEEGLNNPT	pentangle
AEEGLNNTT	tangle net
AEEGLNOPR	range pole
AEEGLNOPS	espagnole
AEEGLNORS	sloganeer
AEEGLNRRT	L'Étranger
AEEGLNRSS	angerless
	largeness
AEEGLNTTU	languette
AEEGLOPRT	petrolage
AEEGLORST	alter egos
AEEGLORVZ	glaze over
	overglaze
AEEGLPRRY	pearl-grey
AEEGLPRSS	grapeless
AEEGLQRSU	square leg
AEEGLRSSV	graveless
AEEGLRSTY	slate-grey
	steel-gray
AEEGLSSSY	glass eyes
AEEGMNNRU	ungermane
AEEGMNOSS	on-message
AEEGMNOTY	gate-money
AEEGMNRRS	merganser
AEEGMNRST	agréments
AEEGMNRTU	augmenter
AEEGMNSSY	gameyness
AEEGMOOTZ	zoogamete
AEEGMOPRS	megaspore
AEEGMORST	gasometer
	megastore
AEEGNNSTW	newsagent
AEEGNOPRS	personage
AEEGNOPST	open stage
AEEGNORRT	generator
AEEGNORTT	teratogen
AEEGNORTU	entourage
AEEGNOTTW	wagonette
AEEGNOTXY	oxygenate
AEEGNPRSS	passenger
AEEGNRRST	estranger
AEEGNRRVY	engravery
AEEGNRSST	greatness
AEEGNRSSV	graveness
AEEGNSSST	gastnesse
AEEGNSSUV	vagueness
AEEGOOPRV	go ape over
AEEGOOSSW	wasegoose
AEEGOPPST	estoppage
AEEGOPRRT	porterage
	reportage
AEEGORRTV	overgreat
AEEGORRVZ	overgraze
AEEGORTTW	gate-tower
AEEGPQRSU	square peg
AEEGPRRSS	Asperger's
AEEGPRRTT	pargetter
AEEGPRTUX	expurgate
AEEGRRSST	grass tree
AEEHHINST	insheathe
AEEHHIPRU	Uriah Heep
AEEHHITTW	white heat
AEEHHJLRR	lehrjahre✧
AEEHHKNRS	Shere Khan
AEEHHKSST	the shakes
AEEHHLLPS	shell heap
AEEHHLOSW	hawsehole
AEEHHNNPT	naphthene
AEEHHNPTY	hyphenate
AEEHHNRTY	heathenry
AEEHHNSTU	unsheathe
AEEHHOOVY	yo-heave-ho
AEEHHPSSW	sheep-wash
AEEHHRRTT	the rather
AEEHIILPT	epithelia
AEEHIKNPT	phenakite
AEEHIKNRT	Katherine
AEEHIKRSS	Erika Hess
AEEHIKTTW	white teak
AEEHILLNW	whale line
AEEHILLRS	raise hell
AEEHILLTW	tailwheel
AEEHILMNS	shale mine
AEEHILMNW	meanwhile
AEEHILNRS	Earl Hines
AEEHILNSS	Sinhalese
AEEHILNTV	Helvetian
AEEHILORV	overhaile
AEEHILPRS	Pele's hair
AEEHILPST	ephialtes
AEEHILRRS	shirralee
AEEHILRTT	theralite
AEEHILSTW	white sale
AEEHILTTV	let have it
AEEHIMNNT	in the mean
AEEHIMNST	mainsheet
AEEHIMPRR	epirrhema
AEEHIMPRT	Hemiptera
AEEHIMPRY	hyperemia
AEEHIMPSS	emphasise
AEEHIMPST	empathise
AEEHIMPSZ	emphasize
AEEHIMPTZ	empathize
AEEHIMRST	hetaerism
	timeshare
AEEHIMSTW	white seam
	white-seam
AEEHIMTTT	at the time
AEEHIMTTW	white meat
AEEHINPRS	Hesperian
	seraphine
AEEHINPST	Stephanie
AEEHINRSV	haversine
AEEHINRTT	Henrietta
AEEHINRTU	eutherian
AEEHINRTW	inwreathe
	near-white
AEEHINSSV	heaviness
AEEHINSTU	euthanise
AEEHINTUZ	euthanize
AEEHIPPRT	epitapher
AEEHIPPSW	hawsepipe
AEEHIPRRT	ratheripe
	three-pair
AEEHIPRSS	apheresis
AEEHIPRST	sphaerite
AEEHIRSTT	hetaerist
AEEHIRTWW	whiteware
AEEHIRTWY	either way
AEEHISSST	aesthesis
AEEHISSTT	athetesis
AEEHKLLRS	lark's-heel
AEEHKLLRY	rakehelly
AEEHKLPSW	sheepwalk
AEEHKMMOR	homemaker
AEEHKMNOT	on the make
AEEHKMORS	shoemaker
AEEHKMPRT	theme park
AEEHKNOTT	on the take
AEEHKORRS	horse rake
AEEHKORST	take horse
AEEHLLMOW	wholemeal
AEEHLLNOW	Hallowe'en
AEEHLLORS	aeroshell

AEEHLLOSW wholesale
AEEHLLPRT Peter Hall
AEEHLLRST tear shell
AEEHLMMNT Emmenthal
AEEHLMNOO Home Alone
AEEHLMNSW wheelsman
AEEHLMNSY hymeneals
AEEHLMOPT home plate
AEEHLMPRY melaphyre
AEEHLMRTY erythemal
AEEHLMSSS shameless
AEEHLMTTY methylate
AEEHLNOPS anopheles
AEEHLNOPT phenolate
AEEHLNRST hesternal
AEEHLNSST natheless
AEEHLOPST telophase
AEEHLORST lose heart
trehalose
AEEHLORTW water hole
AEEHLOTTU out at heel
AEEHLPSSS phaseless
shapeless
AEEHLPTTY telepathy
AEEHLRSST hartlesse
heartless
AEEHLRSTW star wheel
AEEHLRTTT The Tatler
AEEHLRTWY weatherly
AEEHLSTTT the latest
AEEHLSTTW whet-slate
AEEHLSTXY hexastyle
AEEHMMORT hammer-toe
AEEHMMPSY emphysema
AEEHMNNOP phenomena
AEEHMNOPT Amenhotep
AEEHMNORR menorrhea
AEEHMNORT nathemore
AEEHMNOTT moth-eaten
AEEHMNSTX exanthems
AEEHMOPRS semaphore
AEEHMORST heartsome
horsemeat
AEEHMORSU mouse hare
AEEHMOSTU house-mate
AEEHMPRST petersham
AEEHMRRTU Arthur Mee
AEEHMRTTT the matter
AEEHMSSST the masses
AEEHMSTTW Westmeath
AEEHNNRVY Henry Vane
AEEHNOOPR aerophone
AEEHNOORT Oenothera
AEEHNOPTX toxaphene
AEEHNORTT earth-tone
AEEHNOSTU neat-house
AEEHNPRRS sharpener
AEEHNPTTU up the ante
AEEHNRSWY anywheres
AEEHNRTTT tenth-rate
AEEHNRTTY Henry Tate
AEEHNRTUW unwreathe
AEEHNSTTY Thyestean
AEEHOPRTY aerophyte
AEEHOPSSY Soay sheep
AEEHORRRS rearhorse
AEEHORRST heart-sore
AEEHORRSW raree-show
AEEHORSTV overhaste
AEEHORSTW whatsoe'er
AEEHORSUW warehouse
AEEHPRRTT three-part
AEEHPRSTU superheat
AEEHRRSTT ratherest
shatterer
three-star
AEEHRRSTV harvester
AEEHRSTUX exhauster
AEEHSSTTT the States
AEEIIINRS niaiserie
AEEIIKRST Erik Satie
AEEIILLOP aeolipile
AEEIILMNT eliminate
AEEIILNRS linearise
AEEIILNRZ linearize
AEEIILQRU reliquiae
AEEIILRSS serialise
AEEIILRST Israelite
AEEIILRSZ serialize
AEEIILSTV Leavisite
AEEIIMNRR marinière
AEEIIMNST amenities
AEEIINNOT neoteinia
AEEIINNTV Vientiane
AEEIINRSY yersiniae
AEEIINRTT itinerate
AEEIIPPRT peripetia
AEEIIPRTV aperitive
AEEIIRSTV varieties
AEEIIRTTV iterative
AEEIIRTVZ vizierate
AEEIJLNQU Jaqueline
AEEIJLRSS jaileress
AEEIJMNSS jessamine
AEEIJPRSS jasperise
AEEIJPRSZ jasperize
AEEIKKLNS snakelike
AEEIKLLPT plate-like
AEEIKLMUW Milwaukee
AEEIKLNNP Lenin Peak
AEEIKLNPR Keplerian
AEEIKLNPS aspen-like
AEEIKLNSS leakiness
AEEIKLRTW like water
AEEIKLSTY yeastlike
AEEIKMNOT ketonemia
AEEIKMNSY Yankeeism
AEEIKNNSY Keynesian
AEEIKNPPS pipe snake
AEEIKNPPW wink-a-peep
AEEIKNRRS ink-eraser
AEEIKNSSW snakewise
AEEIKOPRS aerospike
AEEIKRRSS seraskier
AEEIKRSTW awe-strike
AEEIKSSTU take issue
AEEILLMNT metalline
AEEILLMOT emolliate
AEEILLMOZ Emile Zola
AEEILLMST metallise
AEEILLMTZ metallize
AEEILLNOT lineolate
linoleate
AEEILLNST sea lentil
AEEILLNTT littleane
AEEILLOPY aeolipyle
AEEILLPST palletise
AEEILLPTT paillette
AEEILLPTZ palletize
AEEILLSTT satellite
AEEILLTTV Little Eva
AEEILLTVW wavellite
AEEILMMRS marmelise
AEEILMMRZ marmelize
AEEILMMST lemmatise
semi-metal
AEEILMMTZ lemmatize
AEEILMNNT alinement
lineament
AEEILMNNU eumelanin
AEEILMNRY minelayer
AEEILMNSS mealiness
AEEILMORT meliorate
AEEILMOSS sesame oil
AEEILMPSS misplease
AEEILMPST time-lapse
AEEILMRST misrelate
salimeter
AEEILMRTT altimeter
AEEILMRTU elaterium
AEEILMRTW limewater
AEEILMSST measliest
AEEILMSTV live steam
AEEILMTUV emulative
AEEILNNPP peneplain
AEEILNNPR perennial
AEEILNNSX sexennial
AEEILNNTV levantine✧
valentine✧
AEEILNOPX pleonexia
AEEILNORR earlier on
AEEILNOTV elevation
AEEILNPPP pineapple
AEEILNPRU epineural
AEEILNPRX explainer
AEEILNPST Palestine
AEEILNPSX expansile
AEEILNRRV River Lena
AEEILNRSS earliness
AEEILNRST la trenise
AEEILNRSU unrealise
AEEILNRSV in several
vernalise

AEEILNRTU retinulae
AEEILNRTV eviternal
intervale
AEEILNRTW waterline
AEEILNRUZ unrealize
AEEILNRVZ vernalize
AEEILNSST essential
AEEILNSSV aliveness
AEEILNTTV ventilate
AEEILOPTT petiolate
AEEILORRT arteriole
AEEILPPRY pipe-layer
AEEILPRRV reprieval
AEEILPRST prelatise
AEEILPRTZ prelatize
AEEILQRSU equaliser
AEEILQRUZ equalizer
AEEILQUVV equivalve
AEEILRRTT air letter
AEEILRRTV retrieval
AEEILRSSW weariless
AEEILRSTU Aleurites
at leisure
AEEILRSTV versatile
AEEILRSTY seriately
AEEILRTTU elutriate
AEEILSSTW leastwise
AEEILSSUX sexualise
AEEILSUXZ sexualize
AEEILSVVY evasively
AEEILTUVX exit value
AEEIMNNOX xenomenia
AEEIMNNPP Menippean
AEEIMNNPT impennate
AEEIMNNRT nemertian
AEEIMNNRV venireman
AEEIMNNZZ mezzanine
AEEIMNOTT at one time
AEEIMNPRU perinaeum
AEEIMNRRU numeraire
numéraire
AEEIMNRTT terminate
AEEIMNRTV verminate
AEEIMNSSS seaminess
AEEIMNSST meatiness
AEEIMNSTT estaminet
AEEIMNSTV avisement
AEEIMNTVV vivamente
AEEIMOPPR peperomia
AEEIMORRS Marie Rose
Rosemarie
AEEIMORSS isomerase
AEEIMORST osmeteria
AEEIMORSW wearisome
AEEIMPRRT prime rate
AEEIMPRRU au premier
AEEIMPRSS Parseeism
AEEIMPRST spare time
spare-time
AEEIMPRTT impetrate
AEEIMRSTT tasimeter
AEEIMRTTX extra time
taximeter
AEEINNNPS Apennines
AEEINNNSS inaneness
AEEINNPST septennia
AEEINNRRW innerwear
Wernerian
AEEINNRST in earnest
AEEINNRTT entertain
Terentian
AEEINNRTV innervate
AEEINNSST antisense
insensate
AEEINNSSV naiveness
naïveness
AEEINNSTT intensate
AEEINOPPT appointee
AEEINOPSW weaponise
AEEINOPWZ weaponize
AEEINORTT orientate
AEEINPPST pepsinate
AEEINPRSS parenesis
passerine
AEEINPRST pistareen
sparteine
AEEINPRTU petaurine
AEEINPSVX expansive
AEEINRRTT reiterant
AEEINRRTV veratrine
AEEINRSST irateness
AEEINRSSW weariness
AEEINRSTT reinstate
AEEINRSTU estuarine
AEEINRSTV invertase
AEEINRSTY eyestrain
AEEINRSUV A Universe
AEEINRTVW water vine
AEEINSSTV assentive
AEEINSTTT enstatite
intestate
satinette
AEEINSTTU austenite
AEEINTTTV attentive
tentative
AEEIOPRTV evaporite
operative
AEEIPPRST appetiser
AEEIPPRSU pauperise
AEEIPPRTW water pipe
AEEIPPRTZ appetizer
AEEIPPRUZ pauperize
AEEIPPSTW waste pipe
AEEIPPTTU paupiette
AEEIPRRST sparterie
AEEIPRRTV privateer
AEEIPRSSV aspersive
AEEIPRSTW taperwise
AEEIPRSVV pervasive
AEEIPRTTX extirpate
AEEIPSSST epistases
AEEIRRSST rasterise
AEEIRRSTV arrestive
East River
AEEIRRSTZ rasterize
AEEIRSSTT sestertia
AEEIRSSTV assertive
AEEIRSTTT tiers état
AEEIRSUUX au sérieux
AEEJKRRTW jerkwater
AEEJLLMTY meat jelly
AEEJLMRSU Jerusalem
AEEJMORTT majorette
AEEJMRSTT jet stream
jetstream
AEEJNNORT Janet Reno
AEEJNRSST jesserant
AEEJNRSTY serjeanty
AEEKKMORS kermes oak
AEEKLLNSY Sean Kelly
AEEKLLPSW sleepwalk
AEEKLLSSS slakeless
AEEKLMNNN kennelman
AEEKLMORV lovemaker
AEEKLOPST Lake poets
AEEKLRSSW wreakless
AEEKLRTTW war kettle
AEEKLSTTW sweet talk
sweet-talk
AEEKMMNOY make money
AEEKMMRRY make merry
merry-make
AEEKMMRST make terms
AEEKMNPRR marker pen
AEEKMNRTT tentmaker
AEEKMNRTW newmarket✧
AEEKMOPRR rope-maker
AEEKMOPST peat-smoke
AEEKMORST tear smoke
AEEKMRSTY master-key
AEEKNORTV overtaken
AEEKOPRSU Eurospeak
AEEKORSST keratoses
AEEKORSTV skate over
AEEKORTUY eukaryote
AEEKPSSTT take steps
AEEKQRSSU Quakeress
AEEKQRSUY squeakery
AEELLLMOS lamellose
AEELLLSTT tell tales
AEELLLSUV vulsellae
AEELLMNTW well-meant
AEELLMRSS realmless
AEELLNPRT repellant
AEELLNPTX expellant
AEELLNRRT rentaller
AEELLNRST entralles
AEELLNRTY eternally
AEELLOPPV love apple
AEELLOPST Sellotape®
sellotape
soleplate
AEELLOSUV laevulose

AEELLOSWY Yellow Sea
AEELLRRTV traveller
AEELLRSST tessellar
AEELLRSVY severally
AEELLRTTU tellurate
AEELLSSUV valueless
AEELLSSVV valveless
AEELMMNRT entrammel
AEELMNOPR melon-pear
AEELMNOST molten sea
telamones
AEELMNPSS ampleness
AEELMNRTV ravelment
AEELMNSTT mental set
AEELMOPPR palempore
AEELMORST elastomer
AEELMORTW water mole
AEELMOSWY awesomely
AEELMPRST emplaster
AEELMPRXY exemplary
AEELMPSSY esemplasy
AEELMPTTY type metal
AEELMRRST real terms
AEELMRSST semestral
AEELMRSTT streamlet
AEELMRTTU tremulate
AEELMRTTW melt-water
AEELNNNPY Penny Lane
AEELNNNTU antennule
AEELNNOSS aloneness
AEELNNPRY arle-penny
AEELNNRTU neural net
AEELNNRTY Anne Tyler
AEELNOPST pleonaste
AEELNOSUV leavenous
AEELNOSYY lay eyes on
AEELNPRRV pre-vernal
AEELNPRTV prevalent
AEELNPRTY net-player
AEELNQSSU equalness
AEELNRSST alertness
AEELNRSTW water lens
AEELNRSTX externals
AEELNRSTY earnestly
AEELNRTTV tervalent
AEELNRTTY ternately
AEELNRTUV vulnerate
AEELNSSST staleness
AEELNSTVX sexvalent
AEELNSUVW news-value
AEELNTTVV velvet ant
AEELOOPST sola topee
AEELOPPRS rose apple
AEELOPRSU leaperous
AEELOPRTY epeolatry
AEELOPSTT salopette
AEELOPSUY please you
AEELORRTV revelator
AEELORSTU teleosaur
AEELORSTY areostyle
AEELORTVW water vole
AEELORTVY elevatory
AEELORUVV overvalue
AEELOSTUW weasel out
AEELPPRRU puerperal
AEELPPRSS paperless
AEELPPRTU perpetual
AEELPQTTU plaquette
AEELPRRST plasterer
AEELPRRSU pleasurer
reperusal
AEELPRRTU prelature
AEELPRSSS spareless
AEELPRSST prelatess
AEELPRSTT saltpeter
saltpetre
steel trap
AEELPRSTU pulse-rate
AEELPRTUY eutrapely
AEELPSSSU pauseless
AEELPSUVW pulse-wave
AEELQSTUZ quetzales
AEELQUVZZ Velázquez
AEELRRSTU serrulate
AEELRSSTV varletess
AEELRSSTW waterless
AEELRSTTU sea turtle
AEELRSTUY austerely
AEELRSTVY every last
severalty
AEELSSSTT stateless
tasteless
AEEMMNORT manometer
AEEMMNSTU amusement
AEEMMORTT atmometer
AEEMMPRUY empyreuma
AEEMMRRST stammerer
AEEMNNNTX annexment
AEEMNNOPR praenomen
AEEMNNORT nanometre
AEEMNNOTT atonement
AEEMNNPRT permanent
AEEMNOPRT treponema
AEEMNOPST steam open
AEEMNOPSU menopause
AEEMNOPYZ apoenzyme
AEEMNORTW worm-eaten
AEEMNORUV manoeuvre
AEEMNOSYY easy money
AEEMNPRTY pentamery
repayment
AEEMNPSST passement
AEEMNQRSU queen's-arm
AEEMNQRUY Queen Mary
AEEMNRSST mare's-nest
steersman
AEEMNRTTT treatment
AEEMNSSSY sameyness
AEEMNSSTT means test
means-test
AEEMNSSTY mateyness
AEEMNSTTT statement
testament✧
AEEMOPRTW pome-water
AEEMOPSSU mesopause
AEEMORRSU rearmouse
AEEMORRTT Rotameter®
AEEMORRTY aerometry
AEEMORSST Massorete
AEEMORTTU amourette
AEEMORTUX auxometer
AEEMPRRTU premature
AEEMPRSUU measure up
AEEMPRTTT attempter
reattempt
trampette
AEEMPRTTU permutate
AEEMPTTXX tax-exempt
AEEMRRSTT smatterer
AEEMRSSTT smear test
AEEMRSSTY easy terms
AEEMRTTTW wattmeter
AEENNNPTY penny ante
penny-ante
ten a penny
AEENNOPST pentosane
AEENNOPTT panettone
AEENNORTT neon tetra
AEENNPRRT trepanner
AEENNPRSY Pyreneans
AEENNPRTT penetrant
repentant
AEENNRRTT re-entrant
AEENOPPRT notepaper
AEENOPRST Esperanto
personate
AEENOPTTT potentate
AEENORRST nor'-easter
AEENORRTV venerator
AEENORRTW rowan tree
AEENORSTW stoneware
AEENPPRRT entrapper
AEENPPRRU unprepare
AEENPPRSW newspaper
AEENPRRTU enrapture
AEENPRSSS spareness
AEENPRSST apertness
taperness
AEENPRSTT at present
AEENPRSTY septenary
AEENPRTTY Pernettya
AEENRRSTU saunterer
AEENRRTUV Eva Turner
nervature
AEENRSSTU Sauternes
AEENRSTUV rune-stave
AEENSSSTT net assets
AEENSSSTW wasteness
AEEOOPRTZ azeotrope
AEEOORRTT root eater
AEEOPPRRV paper over
AEEOPPRSU pea-souper
AEEOPPRVW wove paper

AEEOPPSSU pease-soup
AEEOPRRST patereros
AEEOPRRTW water pore
AEEOPRSTT poetaster
AEEOPRSTX extrapose
AEEOPRTTW water poet
AEEOPRVWW wave power
AEEORRSTT erostrate
AEEORRSTV overstare
AEEORRSTW rosewater
AEEORRSVW overswear
AEEORRTUV avouterer
AEEORRTUW outerwear
AEEORRTVW overwater
AEEORRVWY overweary
AEEORSTTV overstate
AEEORSTTW twoseater
AEEORSUWY as you were
AEEPPRSSU pauperess
AEEPPRSTT test paper
AEEPRRSTU repasture
AEEPRRSTY spare tyre
AEEPRSTTU pertusate
AEEPRSTXY apteryxes
AEEQRSSTU sequestra
set square
AEEQRTTTU quartette
AEEQRTUUX exequatur
AEERRRSSU reassurer
AEERRRSTT restarter
AEERRRSTU serrature
treasurer
AEERRRSTV traverser
AEERRTTVX extravert
AEESTTTTU statuette
AEFFFLTUW Luftwaffe
AEFFGHORS shroffage
AEFFGIINR giraffine
AEFFGNNPY penny gaff
AEFFHILRS flash fire
AEFFHIORT off the air
AEFFHMOPT off the map
AEFFIILRS falsifier
AEFFIIPRR pifferari
AEFFIJMOR fife-major
AEFFIKPST pikestaff
AEFFILLUV effluvial
AEFFILORT firefloat
AEFFILOWY way of life
AEFFINORS raffinose
AEFFIOPRR pifferaro
AEFFIORRT forfaiter
AEFFIRSTW stiffware
AEFFKMNOU make fun of
AEFFLLRUY fearfully
AEFFLLTUY fatefully
AEFFLNOPT pantoffle
AEFFLNRUU unfearful
AEFFLORSW safflower
AEFFLORTT rattle off
AEFFMORST off-stream
AEFFNOOSS offseason
AEFFOQRSU square off
AEFFORSTV overstaff
AEFFPPSTU puff paste
AEFGHILNS angelfish
AEFGHILST safe light
AEFGHILTW white flag
AEFGHINST night safe
AEFGHIRST gearshift
AEFGHLOSU house flag
AEFGHLRTU flaughter
AEFGHORRT forgather
AEFGIILNR filigrane
AEFGIIMNR magnifier
AEFGIIRRT gratifier
AEFGILLNN Llangefni
AEFGILLRY fragilely
AEFGILNRT faltering
AEFGILORT fortilage
AEFGILOSU Solifugae
AEFGILRUY lay-figure
AEFGIMORT fogramite
AEFGINNRU unfearing
AEFGINNST fastening
AEFGINNTT fattening
AEFGINRRT raftering
AEFGINRRY rarefying
AEFGINRST afterings
AEFGINRTU figurante
AEFGIORSS foies gras
ossifrage
AEFGIRRRY grey friar✧
AEFGIRRST first gear
AEFGIRSTT gas-fitter
AEFGISTTU fustigate
AEFGKLNRU Garfunkel
AEFGKSUWY Guy Fawkes
AEFGLLLMU flagellum
AEFGLLMNU flugelman
AEFGLNOST flagstone
AEFGLORTW afterglow
AEFGLRTUU fulgurate
AEFGNOPRT front-page
AEFGNORRT frontager
AEFGNORTX xenograft
AEFGOOPPR page-proof
AEFGOOPRU ague-proof
AEFHHISST sheatfish
AEFHHLLLS half-shell
AEFHHLLTU healthful
AEFHHLMRY half-rhyme
AEFHHLOTW heath-fowl
AEFHIINRS sherifian
AEFHIKMST makeshift
AEFHILLMR half-miler
AEFHILLTT half-title
AEFHILMNU Human Life
AEFHILMRT half-timer
AEFHILORS loaferish
AEFHILPST fishplate
AEFHILSST faithless
AEFHIMNRS fisherman
AEFHINORS fashioner
refashion
AEFHINRTW wafer-thin
AEFHINTTT antitheft
AEFHIORRS horse fair
AEFHIPRSS fish-spear
spearfish
AEFHKLMRS shelf mark
AEFHLLTTU at the full
AEFHLLTUY hatefully
AEFHLNNPY halfpenny
AEFHLNOTU Fluothane®
AEFHLNSSW newsflash
AEFHLORSV flash-over
AEFHLORTW earthwolf
AEFHLOSTV love-shaft
AEFHLRTTU threatful
AEFHLSSST shaftless
AEFHMNRRS marsh fern
AEFHMORSU farmhouse
AEFHNRTTU hunt after
AEFHOOPRT heatproof
AEFHOORST hare's-foot
AEFHORSTU frat house
AEFHOSSST sheaf toss
AEFHOSTTW soft wheat
AEFIIKLRY fairylike
AEFIILMNS semifinal
AEFIILMPR amplifier
AEFIILNNT infantile
AEFIILNQU equifinal
AEFIILNTV inflative
AEFIILQRU qualifier
AEFIILRRT air filter
fire trail
trial-fire
AEFIIMNNS Fenianism
AEFIINNNT infantine
AEFIINNRT train fine
AEFIINRTU infuriate
AEFIIRSST satisfier
AEFIJLRST rijstafel
AEFIKLMMR film-maker
AEFIKLNSS flakiness
AEFILLMNS misfallen
AEFILLNRT flatliner
AEFILLNSS self-slain
AEFILLNTU faultline
AEFILLOOT foliolate
AEFILLUVZ avizefull
AEFILMMOR oriflamme
AEFILMNOS Isle of Man
AEFILMNTU fulminate
AEFILMORS formalise
AEFILMORZ formalize
AEFILMRSW welfarism
AEFILNNUZ influenza
AEFILNORT reflation
AEFILNOTX exfoliant
AEFILNRSS frailness

AEFILOPRR poriferal
AEFILORRT rotiferal
AEFILORTU foliature
AEFILPRST strip-leaf
AEFILPRSU praiseful
AEFILRRTV river flat
AEFILRSTW welfarist
AEFIMMNRT firmament
AEFIMNORW firewoman
AEFIMNOSS foaminess
AEFIMNOST manifesto
AEFIMNOTX tamoxifen
AEFIMNOTY fiat money
AEFIMNRST first name
AEFIMORSS misfeasor
AEFIMORTV formative
AEFINNSST faintness
AEFINOPRR poriferan
AEFINORSU nefarious
AEFINPSTY safety pin
AEFINRRTY fairy tern
AEFINRRWY fairy wren
AEFINRSSS sans serif
AEFINRTZZ frizzante
AEFINSSTT fattiness
AEFIORRRW fire-arrow
AEFIORRST forestair
AEFIORTUV favourite
AEFIORTVY of a verity
AEFIPRSUW superwaif
AEFIRRSTT first-rate
AEFKKRRTW Kraftwerk
AEFKLLUWY wakefully
AEFKLNOSW snowflake
AEFKLOORT look after
AEFKLOOST sootflake
AEFKLORSV slave-fork
AEFKLORSW falsework
AEFKMNNOT Man of Kent
AEFKMORRW framework
AEFKNNRSS frankness
AEFKOORST forest-oak
AEFLLLNNY flannelly
AEFLLLOOS loose fall
AEFLLMNOW fellow man
AEFLLNTTU flatulent
AEFLLORST astrofell
forestall
AEFLLRTUY tearfully
AEFLLSSTU faultless
AEFLMOOST fool's mate
AEFLMORTU formulate
AEFLMORWY mayflower✧
AEFLMRSTU masterful
AEFLMRTTU matterful
AEFLNOOSS aloofness
AEFLNOOTW now of late
AEFLNOPRY profanely
AEFLNOPTU pantoufle
AEFLNORRY royal fern
AEFLNOSTU sulfonate
AEFLNOTVW flat-woven
AEFLNSSUW awfulness
AEFLOOPRT roof plate
AEFLOOPTT footplate
AEFLORRTY ray floret
AEFLORRWY ray flower
AEFLORSSV favorless
AEFLORSTW forest law
AEFLORTWW water flow
waterfowl
AEFLORWWX wax flower
AEFLOSSTT falsettos
AEFLOSSTU fossulate
AEFLPRRUY prayerful
AEFLPSTTU step fault
AEFLRSTTU flustrate
lust after
AEFLRSTUW wasterful
AEFMNOORW forewoman
AEFMORRRT terraform
AEFMORRST store farm
AEFMORRTT formatter
term of art
AEFMORSTT aftermost
AEFNNOORT afternoon
AEFNOPRRS perforans
AEFNOPRRT perforant
AEFNORRSW answer for
AEFNORSTU Nosferatu
AEFNORTTU fortunate
AEFNORTVW wavefront
AEFNRSSTT sternfast
AEFNRSSTU transfuse
AEFOPRRTY prefatory
AEFOPSSTT soft-paste
AEFPRSSTU superfast
AEFRRSTTU frustrate
AEGGGINRU ring gauge
AEGGGLPUU plug gauge
AEGGHIKNT knightage
AEGGHINRT gathering
nightgear
AEGGHIRTZ gigahertz
AEGGHJMOS James Hogg
AEGGHOPRR ergograph
AEGGHOPRY geography
AEGGIILNS silageing
AEGGIINPU guinea pig
AEGGIIOTV give it a go
AEGGILLNT galleting
AEGGILNNS gleanings
AEGGILNOO geologian
AEGGILPSU slip gauge
AEGGIMNSS messaging
AEGGIMOPT maggot-pie
AEGGINNRV engraving
AEGGINOOR gorgoneia
AEGGINORR Gregorian
AEGGINORT going rate
AEGGINOSY easy-going
AEGGINPRT pargeting
AEGGINRRT regrating
AEGGINTTZ gazetting
AEGGIOPRS arpeggios
AEGGLNNOR long-range
AEGGLNRRY glengarry
AEGGLRRST straggler
AEGGMORRT mortgager
AEGGNORTW water gong
AEGGNOSUY synagogue
AEGGNPRSS press gang
press-gang
AEGGORRSS aggressor
AEGGORUVY gyrovague
AEGHHINST sheathing
AEGHHIPRT high-taper
AEGHHIRTV have right
AEGHHIRTW high water
AEGHHNNOY Honeyghan
AEGHHOPTY theophagy
AEGHHRRTU hearth rug
AEGHIILNS Ghislaine
AEGHIJNNZ Zhenjiang
AEGHIJRTU Gujerathi
AEGHIKLMT make light
AEGHIKNNR hankering
AEGHIKNPR phreaking
AEGHIKNRS ring-shake
shrinkage
AEGHILLMS megillahs
AEGHILLNY healingly
AEGHILNOX holing-axe
AEGHILNRS ashlering
shearling
AEGHILNRT earthling
heartling
AEGHILNSV shaveling
AEGHILRRT rear light
AEGHILRSS Alger Hiss
AEGHILRTY light-year
AEGHILSTT set alight
AEGHIMMNR hammering
AEGHIMNRS Germanish
AEGHIMNRT nightmare
AEGHIMNST eightsman
AEGHIMNWY Hemingway
AEGHIMORR hierogram
AEGHIMOTT Gothamite
AEGHIMPPR epiphragm
AEGHIMPRT tephigram
AEGHINNPP happening
AEGHINOPS siphonage
AEGHINORT a right one
AEGHINPPU upheaping
AEGHINRRS garnisher
AEGHINRST earth sign
AEGHINRSV haverings
AEGHINRTW nightwear
AEGHINSTT tea things
AEGHIOOPS oesophagi
AEGHIOPST hospitage
AEGHIORWY go haywire

AEGHIPPRY epigraphy
AEGHIPRRS serigraph
AEGHIPSTT spaghetti
AEGHISSTU Aegisthus
AEGHISTVW what gives?
AEGHKMORY herkogamy
AEGHLMNNT lengthman
AEGHLMOSU laughsome
AEGHLMOSY Moygashel®
AEGHLMPRU galumpher
AEGHLNOOS hang loose
AEGHLNORU hour-angle
AEGHLNOST angel shot
angle shot
AEGHLNPRY nephralgy
AEGHLOOPR oleograph
AEGHLOORR logorrhea
AEGHLOOTY atheology
AEGHLOPXY xylophage
AEGHLORTT larghetto
AEGHLRSTU slaughter
AEGHMNOPR nephogram
AEGHMOPUY hypogaeum
AEGHMORST short game
AEGHMPRYY hypergamy
AEGHNNPRU pergunnah
AEGHNOORR gonorrhea
AEGHNOPRT pot-hanger
AEGHNOPTY pathogeny
AEGHNORVW have wrong
AEGHNOSTU shogunate
AEGHNPRSY pharynges
AEGHNSSST ghastness
AEGHOORTT go to earth
AEGHOPRST grapeshot
AEGHOPRXY xerophagy
AEGHOPSSU esophagus
AEGHORRTU ore-raught
AEGHRSUVY Shug Avery
AEGHRTTUX extraught
AEGIILLNN lilangeni
AEGIILLRS grisaille
AEGIILLRT argillite
AEGIILLSS gallisise
AEGIILLST sigillate
AEGIILLSZ gallisize
AEGIILMNR regiminal
AEGIILMSV vigesimal
AEGIILNPS Spigelian
AEGIILNRS realising
AEGIILNRV Vergilian
AEGIILNRZ realizing
AEGIILNSS signalise
AEGIILNSZ signalize
AEGIILNTV genitival
vigilante
AEGIILNTY geniality
AEGIILRTT tiger tail
AEGIILSTV vestigial
AEGIIMMRT immigrate
AEGIIMMTT migmatite
AEGIIMNNX examining
AEGIIMNRS migraines
AEGIIMSSV give a miss
AEGIINNRR ingrainer
AEGIINNST sin-eating
AEGIINORT originate
AEGIINOSV voisinage
AEGIINOTT goniatite
AEGIINRRU Guarnieri
AEGIINRST granitise
AEGIINRTT granitite
AEGIINRTW waitering
AEGIINRTZ granitize
AEGIINSTT instigate
AEGIINTTU tinguaite
AEGIIRSTT Stagirite
AEGIISSTV visagiste
AEGIJNNTU juneating
AEGIJNORS jargonise
AEGIJNORZ jargonize
AEGIKKMNR kingmaker
AEGIKKNNS king snake
AEGIKLLSS glasslike
AEGIKLLST Gaitskell
AEGIKLNPP king-apple
AEGIKLOSW go walkies
AEGIKLRSS grass-like
AEGIKMMRS skrimmage
AEGIKMNNP Peking man
AEGIKMNRT marketing
AEGIKNNRS ring snake
AEGIKNQSU squeaking
AEGIKNRST streaking
AEGIKNSSW gawkiness
AEGILLLLY illegally
AEGILLLNU gallinule
AEGILLLRY regal lily
AEGILLMNT metalling
AEGILLMRU malgré lui
AEGILLNNP panelling
AEGILLNOS lignaloes
lign-aloes
AEGILLNPR pellagrin
AEGILLNPS langspiel
slip angle
AEGILLNQU equalling
AEGILLNRS signaller
AEGILLNRV ravelling
AEGILLNSU Gallienus
AEGILLNTU lingulate
AEGILLPPU pupillage
AEGILLPRS aspergill
AEGILLPSX Plexiglas®
AEGILLRRU guerrilla
AEGILLRST allergist
AEGILLRVY villagery
AEGILMMOR malgré moi
AEGILMNNT alignment
lamenting
AEGILMNNY meaningly
AEGILMNOS mal soigné
AEGILMNPT pigmental
AEGILMNRY malingery
Mayerling
AEGILMNSU San Miguel
AEGILMNTU glutamine
AEGILMORR rigmarole
AEGILMORS glamorise
AEGILMORZ glamorize
AEGILMRUW mulga wire
AEGILNNOO neologian
AEGILNNOR angle iron
AEGILNNRV navel ring
AEGILNOOT go it alone
AEGILNORS seignoral
AEGILNORT Elo rating
AEGILNORU neuroglia
AEGILNORY legionary
AEGILNOSS sloganise
AEGILNOSZ sloganize
AEGILNPRS pearlings
relapsing
AEGILNQSU equal sign
squealing
AEGILNRSS grass line
AEGILNRST gnarliest
triangles
AEGILNRSV slavering
AEGILNRSY syringeal
AEGILNRTU granulite
traguline
AEGILNRTV traveling
AEGILNRTY ingrately
AEGILNRWY wearingly
AEGILNSST eastlings
tasseling
AEGILNSSW wineglass
AEGILNSTX single tax
AEGILNSTY teasingly
AEGILNSUV vaginules
AEGILOOPS apologise
AEGILOOPZ apologize
AEGILOOTY aetiology
AEGILORSS seraglios
AEGILORST goslarite
AEGILORSU glaireous
AEGILORTU trialogue
AEGILPPRR papergirl
AEGILPPTU plague-pit
AEGILPRSS pier glass
AEGILPRTV gravel-pit
AEGILPRTY pterygial
AEGILPSSW wages slip
AEGILRRRU irregular
AEGILRRTW writ large
AEGILRSSW wire glass
AEGILRSUV vulgarise
AEGILRTUV virgulate
AEGILRUVZ vulgarize
AEGIMMNOT gemmation
AEGIMMNRS Germanism
AEGIMMNRU germanium

AEGIMMNRY yammering
AEGIMMNST magnetism
AEGIMMNSU magnesium
AEGIMNNNO no-meaning
AEGIMNNNS Minnesang
AEGIMNNNU unmeaning
AEGIMNNOR omnirange
AEGIMNNOT Montaigne
AEGIMNNRT germinant
AEGIMNNSS manginess
AEGIMNNSY gymnasien
AEGIMNNTU Augmentin®
AEGIMNOPS panegoism
AEGIMNOPT game point
AEGIMNORS Orangeism
AEGIMNORT morganite
AEGIMNPRT tampering
AEGIMNRST Germanist
mastering
streaming
AEGIMNRSU measuring
AEGIMNRSW Wagnerism
AEGIMNSTT agistment
magnetist
AEGIMPRST mag-stripe
AEGIMRSTU sugar mite
AEGIMRSTY magistery
AEGINNNOR anno regni
AEGINNOPS sapogenin
AEGINNORS reasoning
AEGINNORT Argentino
AEGINNORW Norwegian
AEGINNORZ organzine
AEGINNOSS seasoning
AEGINNOTT negotiant
AEGINNPPR Perpignan
AEGINNPRT parenting
AEGINNRSS angriness
ranginess
AEGINNRST gannister
AEGINNRTT integrant
rattening
AEGINOPPR organ-pipe
pipe organ
AEGINOPPT Giant Pope
AEGINOPRS Singapore
AEGINOPRT operating
orange-tip
pignorate
AEGINORRS organiser
AEGINORRV granivore
overgrain
AEGINORRY regionary
AEGINORRZ organizer
AEGINORSV sea-roving
AEGINORTT riot agent
AEGINORTU outraigne
AEGINORTY iatrogeny
AEGINOSST agonistes
AEGINOSTT gestation
AEGINPRST string pea
trapesing
AEGINPRSU sugar pine
AEGINPSSS gaspiness
AEGINQRUV quavering
AEGINRRST arresting
astringer
AEGINRRTU garniture
AEGINRSTU signature
AEGINRSTW Wagnerist
water sign
AEGINRTTY yattering
AEGINRWZZ zwanziger
AEGINSSSS gassiness
AEGINSSST staginess
AEGINSSUZ gauziness
AEGINSTUU Augustine
AEGIORSTV vis a tergo
AEGIORTVY ivory gate
AEGIPRTUV purgative
AEGIRRRST registrar
AEGIRRSSW wire grass
AEGIRSTTY Stagyrite
AEGISTTUV gustative
AEGJNOTYY get any joy
AEGKLPRSU sugar kelp
AEGKNQRUU Quaker gun
AEGKOPRRW parge-work
AEGLLMOOR loom large
AEGLLNOPW alpenglow
AEGLLNORV governall
AEGLLNOST gallstone
AEGLLOPRS gallopers
AEGLLORTU lager lout
AEGLLOSSW gallowses
Owle-glass
AEGLLRRUY regularly
AEGLLRTUY tegularly
AEGLLRUUW augur well
AEGLMMPRS germ plasm
AEGLMNOOY anemology
AEGLMNORW angleworm
lawmonger
Low German
AEGLMOPRY pyelogram
AEGLMRSSY lyme-grass
AEGLMRTUU Metal Guru
AEGLNOPRY gyroplane
AEGLNOPTT patent log
AEGLNOPTY pentalogy
AEGLNORSU granulose
AEGLNOSTU langouste
AEGLNOSTV Galveston
AEGLNPSTU staple gun
AEGLNRRST strangler
AEGLNRSST strangles
AEGLNRSTY strangely
AEGLOORTV gloat over
AEGLOOSUV volageous
AEGLOPPRU propagule
AEGLOPRSS glass-rope
AEGLORRTU regulator
AEGLORTTY tetralogy
AEGLPRSSS graspless
AEGLRSSSS grassless
AEGLRSSSU sugarless
AEGMMOPRR programme
AEGMNNORT magnetron
AEGMNOORW woomerang
AEGMNORRU neurogram
AEGMNORRW warmonger
AEGMNORTU augmentor
AEGMNOSTU mangouste
AEGMNOTTU mangetout
AEGMNRTTU gutter-man
AEGMOOSUX exogamous
AEGMOPRRR reprogram
AEGMOPRRT petrogram
AEGMORRUW auger-worm
AEGMORSSY gossamery
AEGMORSTY gasometry
AEGNNNOTU agent noun
AEGNNORSU non-usager
AEGNNPRTU repugnant
AEGNNSSTU gauntness
AEGNOOSSW swan-goose
AEGNOOSWY go one's way
AEGNOPRTU grate upon
AEGNORRWY garryowen
AEGNORSUV vargueños
AEGNRSSTU assurgent
AEGNSTTTU tungstate
AEGOOPRRT prorogate
AEGOOSTTW go to waste
AEGOOSWYZ wayzgoose
AEGOPRRSS grass rope
AEGOPRRTY partygoer
AEGOPRRUW groupware
AEGOPRSTU après-goût
AEGOPRTTY a pretty go
AEGORRRTT garrotter
AEGORRSSV overgrass
AEGORRSTT gas-retort
AEGORRSTU surrogate
AEGORSSTU stegosaur
AEGORSTTY gestatory
AEGPRRRUY prayer rug
AEHHHITTY hit the hay
AEHHILLLT ill health
AEHHILLOP halophile
AEHHILLPT tephillah
AEHHILLTW Whitehall
AEHHILLTY healthily
AEHHILNPT phthalein
AEHHILSST the Salish
AEHHIMPRS Hampshire
AEHHINPST thaneship
AEHHIORRS horsehair
AEHHIPPSS shipshape
AEHHIRRST ratherish
AEHHISSTW white hass
AEHHISSVY yeshivahs
AEHHISTWW whitewash

AEHHKLRSU	shear-hulk
AEHHLLMST	Stahlhelm
AEHHLLPRS	harp-shell
AEHHLNTUY	unhealthy
AEHHLOPTY	halophyte
AEHHLOSTV	shovel hat
AEHHLPRSW	Welsh harp
AEHHMOOPT	homeopath
AEHHMORRT	Rotherham
AEHHMOTTW	wheat moth
AEHHNOOPT	Theophano
AEHHNOPTY	theophany
AEHHNORSW	heronshaw
AEHHNORTW	Hawthorne
AEHHNRSSS	harshness
AEHHOPPST	phosphate
AEHHOPRSS	share shop
AEHHOPTTY	theopathy
AEHHORSTT	Ashtoreth
AEHHOSSUW	washhouse
AEHIIKNRT	heartikin
AEHIILMTU	humiliate
AEHIILNOP	neophilia
AEHIILNSY	hyalinise
AEHIILNTX	antihelix
AEHIILNYZ	hyalinize
AEHIIMNNT	in the main
AEHIIMNST	histamine
AEHIIMNTT	a thin time
AEHIIMOPS	hemiopsia
AEHIIMRST	hetairism
AEHIIMRTY	Himyarite
AEHIINOPT	Ethiopian
AEHIINRSS	hairiness
AEHIINTTU	uintahite
AEHIIPSTT	hepatitis
AEHIIRSTT	hetairist
AEHIJLOSU	jailhouse
AEHIJNNNO	Johannine
AEHIKKLMS	milk shake
AEHIKLMNU	humanlike
AEHIKLNOR	Heraklion
AEHIKLOST	like a shot
AEHIKMNPS	phenakism
AEHIKMRSS	Shakerism
AEHIKMRTW	mark-white
AEHIKNPSV	knaveship
AEHIKNPSW	whip snake
AEHIKNRST	heartsink
AEHIKNSSS	shakiness
AEHIKPRSS	ekphrasis
AEHIKQRSU	Quakerish
AEHILLMOP	Philomela
AEHILLMOV	villa home
AEHILLMSZ	shlimazel
AEHILLNSV	Nashville
AEHILLPRY	Phillyrea
AEHILLPTY	philately
AEHILLTTY	lethality
AEHILLTWW	whitewall
AEHILLTWY	wealthily
AEHILMNOP	nemophila
AEHILMNOS	Holmesian
AEHILMNPS	nephalism
AEHILMPSS	sisal hemp
AEHILMRTY	tail rhyme
AEHILNNOT	anthelion
	on the nail
AEHILNOOZ	heliozoan
AEHILNOPP	philopena
AEHILNOPR	parhelion
AEHILNOPS	phaseolin
AEHILNORS	horse nail
AEHILNORT	lion-heart
AEHILNOST	hailstone
AEHILNPRS	planisher
	Spinhaler®
AEHILNPST	nephalist
AEHILNQRU	harlequin✧
AEHILNSVY	Lev Yashin
AEHILOPPS	spoil heap
AEHILOPST	hospitale
AEHILORST	horsetail
	isotheral
AEHILORTT	The Tailor
AEHILOSSW	shoalwise
AEHILOSTT	heliostat
	lie at host
AEHILOSTY	isohyetal
AEHILPPST	plate-ship
AEHILPPTY	epiphytal
AEHILPRRV	River Alph
AEHILPRST	prelatish
AEHILPSSV	slave ship
AEHILRSTV	The Rivals
AEHILRSTY	hairstyle
AEHILSTTW	white salt
AEHIMMNNT	Tim Henman
AEHIMMRTU	Mithraeum
AEHIMNNOT	anthemion
AEHIMNORS	harmonise
AEHIMNORT	Harmonite
AEHIMNORZ	harmonize
AEHIMNOST	shame into
AEHIMNPPS	mishappen
AEHIMNPSS	misshapen
AEHIMNPST	pantheism
AEHIMNRST	mishanter
AEHIMNRTU	Mathurine
AEHIMNSST	in the mass
AEHIMOPXY	hypoxemia
AEHIMORST	Aerosmith
AEHIMPRSS	seraphims
AEHIMPSST	steamship
AEHIMQSSU	squeamish
AEHIMRSST	marshiest
AEHIMRTUZ	rheumatiz
AEHINNORS	senhorina
AEHINNOST	Esthonian
AEHINNRSS	in harness
AEHINNRTU	Hunterian
	Ruthenian
AEHINOPST	pantihose
	siphonate
AEHINORSS	hoariness
AEHINORST	Senhorita
AEHINORTT	anorthite
AEHINOTVW	have in tow
AEHINPPRT	paper-thin
AEHINPPSS	happiness
AEHINPPTT	tappit hen
AEHINPPTX	Xanthippe
AEHINPRSS	seraphins
AEHINPSSS	apishness
AEHINPSSY	Sisyphean
AEHINPSTT	pantheist
AEHINRRST	tarnisher
AEHINRRSV	varnisher
AEHINRRTY	erythrina
AEHINRSST	starshine
AEHINRSSW	sherwanis
AEHINSSST	hastiness
AEHINSSSW	washiness
AEHINSTTY	Thyestian
AEHIOPPRY	hyperopia
AEHIOPRRS	aphoriser
	pair-horse
AEHIOPRRZ	aphorizer
AEHIORRTT	throatier
AEHIORSTT	hesitator
AEHIORSTU	authorise
AEHIORSTX	rheotaxis
AEHIORTTV	hortative
AEHIORTUZ	authorize
AEHIOSSTT	athetosis
AEHIOTTUV	have it out
AEHIPRSTT	therapist
AEHIPRSTW	ship water
AEHIRRSTT	trashtrie
AEHIRSSTT	trashiest
AEHIRTTWW	whittawer
AEHJKMOOS	James Hook
AEHJKNOST	John Keats
AEHJLNOPP	apple-John
	John-apple
AEHJLNOWY	John Elway
AEHJMNSTU	James Hunt
AEHJNNOOS	John Soane
AEHJNNOWY	John Wayne
AEHKLNORU	Lake Huron
AEHKLNSST	thankless
AEHKLOOSW	Hooke's law
AEHKLRRSU	Karlsruhe
AEHKMMOPR	hammerkop
AEHKMNORR	horn-maker
AEHKMORST	shotmaker
AEHKNOOPS	hoop-snake
AEHKNOSTW	stone hawk
AEHKORRTW	earthwork
AEHKORSTT	take short
AEHKOSSTW	two shakes
AEHLLLMPS	lamp-shell
AEHLLLMRS	shell-marl

Words marked ✧ can also be spelled with one or more capital letters

AEHLLMOST	homestall
AEHLLMRTY	thermally
AEHLLNNOT	non-lethal
AEHLLNOOP	allophone
AEHLLNOVY	Lon Halévy
AEHLLOORW	holloware
AEHLLOPTY	hell to pay
AEHLLPRTY	L P Hartley
AEHLLPRUX	prehallux
AEHLLPSSU	phalluses
AEHLLPSSY	haplessly
AEHLLPTUW	up the wall
AEHLLRSST	shell star
	star shell
AEHLLSSSW	shawlless
AEHLLSSTU	thalluses
AEHLMNOPY	palm-honey
AEHLMOOST	loathsome
AEHLMOPSU	palmhouse
AEHLMOPTY	ampholyte
AEHLMORST	malt-horse
AEHLMOSSU	almshouse
AEHLMOSTU	malt-house
AEHLMRSTU	salt rheum
AEHLNNOPR	alpenhorn
AEHLNNOPT	panthenol
AEHLNOPTT	Pentothal®
AEHLNOSSS	shoalness
AEHLNPSUY	unshapely
AEHLNRTUY	unearthly
AEHLNSTUV	slave-hunt
AEHLNSTUW	Welsh aunt
AEHLOPPSY	polyphase
AEHLOPRST	astrophel
AEHLOPRSY	horseplay
AEHLOPRTU	hourplate
AEHLOPRTY	ephoralty
AEHLOPSUY	playhouse
AEHLORSST	salt horse
	short sale
AEHLORSTY	the royals✧
AEHLORTUU	outhauler
AEHLORTWY	holy water
AEHLOSTTT	to the last
AEHLPRRSU	spherular
AEHLRSSTU	Althusser
AEHLRSSTW	wrathless
AEHLRSTUW	The Walrus
AEHMMNOTY	mythomane
AEHMMNPUY	nymphaeum
AEHMMOORT	harmotome
AEHMMORTU	hammer out
AEHMNNSSU	humanness
AEHMNOOPS	monophase
	moonphase
AEHMNOOTT	not at home
AEHMNOPST	phantosme
AEHMNORSS	shoresman
AEHMNRRWY	wherryman
AEHMNRSTU	transhume
AEHMOOPRS	shampooer
AEHMOOPRT	Homoptera
AEHMOORSS	smasheroo
AEHMOPPRT	top hamper
AEHMOPRST	Tom Sharpe
AEHMORRTW	earthworm
AEHMORSTW	what's more
AEHMORTWW	wheatworm
AEHMOSSTU	masthouse
AEHMOSTTT	at the most
AEHMOSTTW	Thomas Tew
AEHMPRRTY	hypermart
AEHMPRTUU	Mt Ruapehu
AEHMSSSTY	Smyth's Sea
AEHNNOPRT	Parthenon
AEHNNRSSU	unharness
AEHNNSTUW	whunstane
AEHNOOPRR	harpooner
AEHNOOPSX	saxophone
AEHNOORST	hoar-stone
AEHNOPRTU	neuropath
AEHNOPRTY	honey-trap
AEHNOPSSU	saphenous
AEHNOPSTY	pantyhose
AEHNORSTT	north-east
AEHNPRSSS	sharpness
AEHNPRSXY	pharynxes
AEHOOORRT	otorrhoea
AEHOOPRRY	pyorrhoea
AEHOOPSTT	osteopath
AEHOOPTTT	the potato
AEHOORSTX	orthoaxes
AEHOORUWY	how are you?
AEHOOSSTU	oast house
AEHOPPRVY	overhappy
AEHOPPSSY	apophyses
AEHOPRSSU	rasp-house
AEHOPRSTU	put ashore
AEHOPSSTT	posthaste
AEHOPSSTW	sweat shop
AEHORSSTU	authoress
AEHORSTTW	water-shot
AEHORSTVW	short wave
	short-wave
AEHORSTVY	overhasty
AEHORSTWY	seaworthy
AEHOSSSTU	South Seas
AEHOSSTTU	south-east
AEHRSSTUU	thesaurus
AEIIIKNNP	epinikian
AEIIILMNP	epilimnia
AEIIILNTW	lie in wait
AEIIILRVZ	vizierial
AEIIILTVX	lixiviate
AEIIIMPRT	primitiae
AEIIIMTTV	imitative
AEIIINTVV	vivianite
AEIIJLNUV	juvenilia
AEIIKKTTW	kittiwake
AEIIKLLNS	snail-like
AEIIKLLTT	take it ill
AEIIKLNOS	kaolinise
AEIIKLNOT	kaolinite
AEIIKLNOZ	kaolinize
AEIIKLNPS	spike-nail
AEIIKLNST	saintlike
AEIIKLRST	triskelia
AEIIKLRTV	larvikite
AEIIKMRSS	kaiserism
AEIIKNPRU	kauri-pine
AEIIKRRST	air-strike
AEIIKRSTT	keratitis
AEIILLMNN	millennia
AEIILLMNR	Millerian
AEIILLMRS	Ramillies
AEIILLMRT	mitraille
AEIILLNTY	lineality
AEIILLTTT	titillate
AEIILMMOZ	milo maize
AEIILMNNR	mainliner
AEIILMNNT	eliminant
AEIILMNPS	maniplies
AEIILMNRT	train mile
AEIILMNRU	luminaire
AEIILMNSU	aluminise
AEIILMNUZ	aluminize
AEIILMOSV	malvoisie
AEIILMRSS	serialism
AEIILMRTT	literatim
	time trial
AEIILNNOP	neopilina
AEIILNNOT	lineation
AEIILNNRT	triennial
AEIILNNSV	venial sin
AEIILNNSY	asininely
AEIILNOPT	epilation
	polianite
AEIILNORV	live on air
	Oliverian
AEIILNOTV	inviolate
AEIILNPRT	reptilian
AEIILNPST	platinise
	spaniel it
AEIILNPTV	plaintive
AEIILNPTZ	platinize
AEIILNRRT	interrail
	trilinear
AEIILNRST	Latiniser
	Listerian
AEIILNRSU	uniserial
AEIILNRTY	in reality
	linearity
AEIILNRTZ	Latinizer
AEIILNSTW	waistline
AEIILNSVY	Sylviinae
AEIILNTVY	veniality
AEIILORST	solitaire
AEIILORSV	Lavoisier
AEIILORTV	variolite
AEIILOSSZ	assoilzie
AEIILOSTV	isolative
AEIILOTVV	violative
AEIILPPQU	quail-pipe

AEIILQSTU qualities
AEIILRRST arris tile
AEIILRRTY irreality
AEIILRSST serialist
AEIILRSTU ritualise
uralitise
AEIILRSTV vitaliser
AEIILRSTY seriality
AEIILRTUZ ritualize
uralitize
AEIILRTVZ vitalizer
AEIILSSUV visualise
AEIILSUVZ visualize
AEIIMMRSS Semiramis
AEIIMMRSX maximiser
AEIIMMRXZ maximizer
AEIIMNPRS mainprise
AEIIMNPST impatiens
AEIIMNPTT impatient
AEIIMNRRT Mt Rainier
AEIIMNRTU miniature
AEIIMOPRS Prosimiae
AEIIMPRRS impresari
AEIIMPRSS mispraise
AEIIMPRSV vampirise
AEIIMPRVZ vampirize
AEIIMPSSV impassive
AEIIMQTTU quia timet
AEIIMRRSV arrivisme
AEIIMRSTV vi et armis
AEIINNNTV antivenin
AEIINNOPT inopinate
AEIINNOST antinoise
AEIINNOTV evanition
AEIINNPTT in-patient
AEIINNQTU inquinate
AEIINNRSS raininess
AEIINNRTT itinerant
nitratine
AEIINNRTU uraninite
AEIINNSTU insinuate
AEIINNSWY in any wise
AEIINNSZZ Aziz Nesin
AEIINOPRW piano wire
AEIINOPTX expiation
AEIINORST seriation
AEIINORTT iteration
AEIINOTTV evitation
novitiate
AEIINPPTT petit pain
AEIINPRTV in private
AEIINRRTY itinerary
AEIINRSST sanitiser
AEIINRSSY yersinias
AEIINRSTZ sanitizer
AEIINRTUV urinative
AEIINSTTU inusitate
AEIINSTTY insatiety
AEIIPRSTV privatise
AEIIPRTTV partitive
AEIIPRTVV privative
AEIIPRTVZ privatize
AEIIPSSST epistasis
AEIIPSSTX epistaxis
AEIIPSTTT stipitate
AEIIRRRVV River Ravi
AEIIRRSTT arteritis
AEIIRRSTU retiarius
AEIIRRSTV arriviste
AEIIRSSTW stairwise
AEIIRTTVW writative
AEIISTVYZ izvestiya
AEIITTTTV tittivate
AEIITTTUV attuitive
AEIJKKRVY Reykjavík
AEIJKLNRR Kilner jar®
AEIJKLNSU Seljukian
AEIJMNNSS Jansenism
AEIJMOPPR pipe major
AEIJNNNRZ Zrenjanin
AEIJNNSST Jansenist
AEIJNRSST janitress
AEIJNSSZZ jazziness
AEIKKLLOO lookalike
AEIKKLMNS milk snake
AEIKKNNSS snakeskin
AEIKLLNNP pannikell
AEIKLLNPT plant-like
AEIKLLNRY Killarney
AEIKLLOOV look alive
AEIKLLPTY kallitype
AEIKLLTTU little auk
AEIKLMNNU unmanlike
AEIKLMNOS Kalsomine®
AEIKLMNOW womanlike
AEIKLMNWY milken-way
AEIKLMOSS smoke-sail
AEIKLNNSS lankiness
AEIKLNORT oil tanker
AEIKLNRSS larkiness
AEIKLNRUW unwarlike
AEIKLPRSS sparklies
AEIKLQSUY squeakily
AEIKLRSTW strawlike
AEIKLRSTY streakily
AEIKLRSVY Valkyries
AEIKMQRSU Quakerism
AEIKNNPRS spinnaker
AEIKNNSSS snakiness
AEIKNOOST Isokontae
AEIKNOPTW weak point
AEIKNORSU urokinase
AEIKNORTU ketonuria
AEIKNOTTW take in tow
AEIKNPSSW pawkiness
AEIKNQSSU quakiness
AEIKNRSSS sarkiness
AEIKOPRST periaktos
AEIKOPRSV perovskia
AEIKORSST keratosis
AEIKPPQSU pipsqueak
AEIKPRSTY strike pay
AEILLLPPU papillule
AEILLLRTY literally
AEILLLTVY live tally
AEILLMMST small-time
AEILLMNRY millenary
AEILLMNSY seminally
AEILLMNTT little man
AEILLMPPR paper mill
AEILLMRTW water mill
AEILLMSSY aimlessly
AEILLMSTT metallist
AEILLNNOT tenaillon
AEILLNNRW inner wall
AEILLNOPS Pisanello
AEILLNOPT pollinate
AEILLNORW Orwellian
AEILLNPRY plenarily
AEILLNPST panellist
AEILLNPTT pétillant
AEILLNRST installer
reinstall
AEILLNRTU ill nature
tellurian
AEILLNRTW trawl-line
AEILLNSTY saliently
AEILLOPPS papillose
AEILLOPPT papillote
popliteal
AEILLOPST apostille
AEILLORTW towel-rail
AEILLOSTY loyalties
AEILLPPTU pupillate
AEILLPRSU pluralise
AEILLPRUZ pluralize
AEILLPSTU pulsatile
AEILLQSSU sea squill
AEILLRRTY artillery
AEILLRRVW river wall
AEILLRSST trailless
AEILLRSSV rivalless
AEILLRSTW stairwell
AEILLRTVY vitellary
AEILLRTWY water lily
AEILLRVXY vexillary
AEILLSTTY statelily
AEILMMNPS pelmanism✧
AEILMMNST mentalism
Simmental
AEILMMORS memorials
AEILMNNOT melatonin
AEILMNNPS pennalism
plainsmen
AEILMNNPY penny mail
AEILMNNSS manliness
AEILMNOOT emotional
AEILMNOPR prolamine
AEILMNOPT emptional
AEILMNORS normalise
Orleanism
AEILMNORT lion-tamer
mentorial

AEILMNORZ normalize
AEILMNOSS loaminess
melanosis
AEILMNOTU emulation
AEILMNPRT reimplant
AEILMNPSU asplenium
AEILMNPSY manyplies
AEILMNPTU penultima
AEILMNRST tramlines
AEILMNRSU semilunar
unrealism
AEILMNRVY liveryman
AEILMNSTT mentalist
AEILMNTTY mentality
AEILMORRS moraliser
AEILMORRZ moralizer
AEILMORST mortalise
solar time
AEILMORTZ mortalize
AEILMOSTU mousetail
AEILMOSTZ zealotism
AEILMPRST prelatism
AEILMRTTY altimetry
AEILMSSUX sexualism
AEILMSSVY massively
AEILMSTTU stimulate
AEILMSTUU mutualise
AEILMTUUZ mutualize
AEILNNNOR non-linear
AEILNNNOV novennial
AEILNNOPR nonpareil
AEILNNOST tensional
AEILNNOSV Slovenian
AEILNNOSY lyonnaise✧
AEILNNOTV anti-novel
Valentino
AEILNNPSS plainness
AEILNNPSU peninsula✧
AEILNNPTU pinnulate
AEILNNPTW twin plane
AEILNNPTY panty line
pinnately
AEILNNRST internals
AEILNNTUV univalent
AEILNOOPS polonaise
AEILNOORS erosional
AEILNOPPR piperonal
AEILNOPRT prelation
rantipole
AEILNOPRV prevail on
AEILNOPST Platonise
sealpoint
AEILNOPTT potential
AEILNOPTU epulation
peanut oil
AEILNOPTZ Platonize
AEILNORSS sensorial
AEILNORST Orleanist
relations
serotinal
tensorial
AEILNORSV versional
AEILNORTT natrolite
tentorial
AEILNORTU outlinear
AEILNORTV ravel into
AEILNOSSS sessional
AEILNOSSV Slavonise
AEILNOSVZ Slavonize
AEILNPRST strapline
AEILNPRTY interplay
painterly
party line
AEILNPSTU spinulate
AEILNPSTY sapiently
AEILNPTTX plain text
AEILNPTTY patiently
AEILNPTUV pulvinate
AEILNQTUY antiquely
AEILNRRTU retinular
AEILNRSST trainless
AEILNRSTT sterilant
AEILNRSUV universal
AEILNRTTV trivalent
AEILNRTUV avirulent
AEILNRTUY unreality
AEILNRTVY vernality
AEILNSSST saltiness
slatiness
stainless
AEILNSSTT taintless
AEILNSSTW slantwise
AEILNSTUY sinuately
AEILNSTVY sylvanite
AEILNSUUX unisexual
AEILNTUVW wine vault
AEILOOSTT ostiolate
AEILOPRRS polariser
AEILOPRRZ polarizer
AEILOPRST saprolite
AEILOPRTT portatile
AEILOPRTV prolative
AEILOPTYZ zelotypia
AEILOQRUU Euraquilo
AEILORRTT literator
AEILORSST tailoress
AEILORSTT Aristotle
totaliser
AEILORTTV levitator
AEILORTTX textorial
AEILORTTZ totalizer
AEILOSSST sassolite
AEILPPRST periplast
AEILPPRTU preputial
AEILPPSST split peas
AEILPQRSU pasquiler
AEILPQSTU plastique
AEILPRSTT prelatist
AEILPRSVY privy seal✧
AEILPRTVY privately
AEILPSSVY passively
AEILPSTTU stipulate
AEILPSTUV pulsative
AEILQRRUY reliquary
AEILRRTWW law-writer
AEILRRUVY River Yalu
AEILRSSTT last rites
AEILRSSTV Silvestra
AEILRSSTY lay sister
slaistery
AEILRSTTT rattliest
AEILRSTTU literatus
AEILRTTTW latter-wit
AEILRTTVY reality TV
AEILRTUUX luxuriate
AEILSSSTV vistaless
AEILSSSTW waistless
AEILSSTUX sexualist
AEILSSUVY suasively
AEILSTUXY sexuality
AEIMMMNOT mammonite
AEIMMNNNO Memnonian
AEIMMNNOO monoamine
AEIMMNNRS mannerism✧
AEIMMNNTU minuteman✧
AEIMMNOPT pantomime
AEIMMRSSU summarise
AEIMMRSUZ summarize
AEIMMSTUV summative
AEIMNNNOO neonomian
AEIMNNNQU mannequin
AEIMNNOPU pneumonia
AEIMNNORS Normanise
AEIMNNORZ Normanize
AEIMNNOST Minnesota
AEIMNNOSY anonymise
AEIMNNOSZ neo-Nazism
AEIMNNOTT mentation
AEIMNNOYZ anonymize
AEIMNNPTY inpayment
AEIMNNRST mannerist✧
AEIMNOORV Maori oven
AEIMNOPRT protamine
AEIMNOPTU upon a time
AEIMNORRS Romaniser
rosmarine
AEIMNORRZ Romanizer
AEIMNORST main store
matronise
steam iron
AEIMNORSW womaniser
AEIMNORTV normative
AEIMNORTW tire-woman
AEIMNORTZ matronize
AEIMNORWZ womanizer
AEIMNOSST Samsonite®
AEIMNOSSX Semi-Saxon
AEIMNOSWW wise woman
AEIMNOTUY you name it
AEIMNPRRY a merry pin
AEIMNPRST spearmint
AEIMNRRST ranterism
AEIMNRRSU Surinamer

AEIMNRSTT stream-tin
AEIMNRSTU antiserum
misaunter
AEIMNRSTX Axminster
AEIMNRTTY maternity
AEIMNSSSS massiness
AEIMNSTTT mint state
AEIMNSTUX Maxentius
AEIMNTTUX tant mieux
AEIMOPRRT imperator
AEIMOPRTX proximate
AEIMOPSTT optimates
AEIMORRSV Averroism
AEIMORSTT East Timor
estimator
AEIMORSTV movie star
AEIMORTTU autotimer
AEIMPPRSU pauperism
AEIMPRRTT part-timer
AEIMPRSSY pyramises
AEIMPRSTU septarium
AEIMPRTTY Party Time
AEIMPRTUZ trapezium
AEIMQRSSU marquises
AEIMQSTUU quaesitum
AEIMQSUUX Esquimaux
AEIMRRRTU terrarium
AEIMRRRUV River Amur
AEIMRRSTY martyrise
AEIMRRTTY termitary
AEIMRRTYZ martyrize
AEIMRSTUU auteurism
AEIMSSTTU mussitate
AEINNNOOT one-nation
AEINNNOTW Newtonian
AEINNNPTU Neptunian
AEINNOPRT near point
AEINNOPSX expansion
AEINNOPTT panettoni
AEINNORST Nestorian
rain-stone
Rosinante
AEINNORTU neuration
AEINNORTV nervation
vernation
AEINNORTZ Rozinante
AEINNOSST sensation
AEINNOSTW wantonise
AEINNOSWY in one's way
AEINNOTTT attention
tentation
AEINNOTWZ wantonize
AEINNPPSS nappiness
AEINNPRRT inner part
AEINNPSST inaptness
AEINNRRTU Turnerian
AEINNRSTT instanter
transient
AEINNRSTU saturnine
AEINNRSTY tyrannise
AEINNRTYZ tyrannize
AEINNSSST nastiness
AEINNSSTT nattiness
AEINNSSTW tawniness
AEINOOPRT operation
AEINOOPST a top noise
AEINOOPSU ionopause
AEINOORTX exoration
AEINOPPPR Popperian
AEINOPPRT appointer
reappoint
AEINOPRSS aspersion
AEINOPRST isopteran
patronise
Peronista
AEINOPRSV pervasion
AEINOPRSY Aepyornis
AEINOPRTT reptation
tritanope
AEINOPRTU epuration
épuration
AEINOPRTV overpaint
AEINOPRTZ patronize
AEINOPSSS soapiness
AEINOPSTT septation
AEINOQRTU inquorate
ortanique
AEINOQTTU totaquine
AEINORRST serration
AEINORRTV overtrain
AEINORRVV River Avon
AEINORSST assertion
AEINORSSU arsenious
AEINORSTT stationer
AEINORSTV overstain
AEINOSSST assientos
AEINOSTTT testation
AEINPPPSS Pan's pipes
AEINPPSSS sappiness
AEINPRRST transpire
AEINPRSST paintress
AEINPRTTY paternity
AEINPRTWY wine party
AEINPSSST pastiness
AEINRRSST tarriness
AEINRRSTT restraint
AEINRRSVW Swan River
AEINRRTTV travertin
AEINRRTWW Winter War
AEINRSSTT rattiness
resistant
tartiness
AEINRSSTU sustainer
AEINRSTTT in tatters
AEINRSTWW straw wine
AEINSSSSS sassiness
AEINSSSTT tastiness
AEINSSTTT tattiness
AEIOPRRSS aspersoir
AEIOPRRSV vaporiser
AEIOPRRVZ vaporizer
AEIOPRSUY Praise You
AEIOPRTTV portative
vaporetti
AEIOPRTXY expiatory
AEIOQTTUV quotative
AEIORRRWZ razor wire
AEIORRSTV Averroist
AEIORRTTT trattorie
AEIORTUVV uvarovite
AEIOSSSTT steatosis
AEIOSSTTT toastiest
AEIOSTUVX vexatious
AEIPPRRTY Tipperary
AEIPPRSTU peripatus✧
AEIPRRSST spiraster
AEIPRRSTT tear strip
AEIPRRSTU rapturise
AEIPRRTUZ rapturize
AEIPRRTVY Varityper®
AEIPRSSTU prussiate
AEIPRSTTU petaurist
AEIPRSTUZ trapezius
AEIPRSTWY pit-sawyer
AEIPRSTYZ party-size
AEIPSSTTV tipstaves
AEIQRRTTU triquetra
AEIQRRTUU quaeritur
AEIQRSSTU sea squirt
AEIQRTTTU quartetti
AEIQRTTUZ quartzite
AEIRRSSSY sisserary
AEIRRSSTT traitress
AEIRRSTTU striature
AEIRRTTTU triturate
AEIRSSTTU tessitura
AEIRSSTUV Evaristus
AEIRSTTTX testatrix
AEIRSTTUU auteurist
AEIRSTTUY austerity
AEISSTTUW sweat suit
sweatsuit

AEJKMNORY monkey jar
AEJKSSUYZ Aujeszky's
AEJLLOSUY jealously
AEJLNOPSU Paul Jones
AEJLNOSUU unjealous
AEJLORSUV salvo jure
AEJMMORRT major term
AEJMNOORT major tone
AEJMNOSTW Jamestown
AEJMPRTUW water jump
AEJNNOPRU Juan Perón
AEJOPRSSU jasperous
AEJOPSTUX juxtapose
AEKKLRRSY skylarker
AEKKMNOOS kakemonos
AEKKORTUY turkey oak✧
AEKLLSSST stalkless
AEKLMOORT toolmaker
AEKLMORSS lossmaker
AEKLMORTW metalwork
AEKLOOOPP Lake Poopó

AEKLOSSTW	Stokes' law
AEKLPRSSS	sparkless
AEKMMNOSS	monk's seam
AEKMNOOQU	moonquake
AEKMNOORR	moonraker✧
AEKMNOPRS	pranksome
AEKMNOPSS	spokesman
AEKMNOPTW	kept woman
AEKMNORSY	sokemanry
AEKMOORSY	karyosome
AEKMPRRSS	pressmark
AEKMPRSTU	rump steak
AEKNOORST	snakeroot
AEKNPRRST	prankster
AEKNRSSST	starkness
AEKNRSTTU	take turns
AEKOOPSST	soopstake
	so to speak
AEKOORRST	stroke oar
AEKOPPRRW	paperwork
AEKOPRTYY	karyotype
AEKORRTWW	waterwork
AEKORRWWX	waxworker
AELLLMOSU	malleolus
AELLLMOWY	Amy Lowell
AELLLNSSW	Snell's law
AELLLOPRR	lap-roller
AELLLPPSY	play-spell
AELLLPTUU	pullulate
AELLLRSTU	stellular
AELLLSSWY	lawlessly
AELLMMOPY	polylemma
AELLMNOSZ	manzellos
AELLMNOTT	allotment
AELLMNOWW	well woman
AELLMNRUY	numerally
AELLMNSSS	smallness
AELLMOPRY	permalloy
AELLMORST	martellos
AELLMORTU	Tullamore
AELLMORTY	allometry
AELLMPRST	smell-trap
AELLMPTUU	plumulate
AELLMQSSU	qualmless
AELLNNOOR	all-or-none
AELLNOORT	lanterloo
AELLNOPRT	plant-lore
AELLNOSTT	attollens
AELLNOSTW	stonewall
AELLNOTTT	attollent
AELLNPSST	plantless
AELLNQUUY	unequally
AELLNRTUY	neutrally
AELLNRTVY	ventrally
AELLNSSUY	sensually
AELLOOPRT	allotrope
AELLOPRRT	patroller
AELLOPRTW	pot-waller
AELLOPRTY	prolately
AELLOPTUV	pole vault
	pole-vault
AELLORRST	rostellar
AELLORSTY	allostery
AELLORSWW	swallower
AELLORTTY	allottery
AELLOSUYZ	zealously
AELLRSSTY	artlessly
AELLRSTUW	Ullswater
AELLTTUXY	textually
AELMMNOST	malmstone
AELMMOOPS	amplosome
AELMMORST	maelstrom✧
AELMMOSUU	mausoleum
AELMMRSTY	symmetral
AELMNNNTU	annulment
AELMNNOOP	monoplane
AELMNNOPX	xenon lamp
AELMNOOPR	lampooner
AELMNOORT	monolater
AELMNOORY	monolayer
AELMNOPPY	empanoply
AELMNOPTU	pulmonate
AELMNORST	marlstone
AELMNORTT	lemon tart
	tremolant
AELMNORWW	lawnmower
AELMNOSSW	womanless
AELMNOSTU	alum-stone
AELMNOSTY	salt-money
AELMNOTTU	outmantle
AELMNPSTU	psalm-tune
AELMNRSTU	menstrual
	Ulsterman
AELMNRTTU	tremulant
AELMNSTTY	Mt Stanley
AELMOOPRT	plate-room
AELMOORSS	salesroom
AELMOORSW	Moore's law
AELMOPRSS	slope arms
AELMOPSTT	palmettos
AELMOSTTU	mulattoes
AELMPRSTU	per saltum
AELMRTWXY	myrtle-wax
	wax myrtle
AELNNPTWY	twalpenny
AELNOPRSS	personals
AELNOPRSY	layperson
AELNOPTTU	tau lepton
AELNORSTU	Solutrean
AELNORTVW	navelwort
AELNOSUUZ	unzealous
AELNOTUVV	vol-au-vent
AELNPRSUU	Paul Nurse
AELNRRSSU	ruralness
AELNRRUVY	vulnerary
AELNRSTTU	resultant
AELNSSSTU	sultaness
AELNSSSUU	usualness
AELOOPRSU	leaporous
AELOOPRSX	exosporal
AELOOPRTW	water polo
AELOOPRVY	parleyvoo
AELOORRTT	tolerator
AELOORRVW	love-arrow
AELOOSSTY	stay loose
AELOPPRWY	powerplay
AELOPPSTU	soup plate
AELOPRRTW	pearlwort
AELOPRRTY	proletary
	pyrolater
AELOPRSTU	sporulate
AELOPRSTV	overplast
AELOPRTUY	autoreply
AELOPRTWY	polywater
AELOPSSSU	espousals
AELOPSTTU	postulate
AELORRSTW	laserwort
AELORRSTX	extrorsal
AELORSTTY	lay to rest
AELORTTUV	outtravel
AELPPPPRU	paper-pulp
AELPPRRUU	purpureal
AELPPRTUW	Wuppertal
AELPRSSST	psaltress
	strapless
AELPRSSTU	pertussal
	supersalt
AELPSTTUU	pustulate
AELQRRTUY	quarterly
AELRSSSTW	strawless
AELRSSTVY	Sylvestra
AEMMNNOTY	momentany
AEMMNORRW	marrow-men
AEMMNORTY	manometry
	momentary
AEMMNOTUZ	Montezuma
AEMMNRSTU	sarmentum
AEMMOORST	steam room
AEMMORSSY	massymore
AEMMRSTYY	asymmetry
AEMNNORST	ornaments
	semantron
AEMNNORTT	remontant
AEMNNOSWW	newswoman
AEMNNOTTU	Mount Etna
AEMNOOPRT	protonema
AEMNOORTT	Nototrema
AEMNOORTX	taxonomer
AEMNOPSTT	stamp note
AEMNORRTU	numerator
AEMNORRYY	Romany rye
AEMNORSTU	anoestrum
AEMNORSTV	transmove
AEMNORSTY	monastery
AEMNPPRSY	panspermy
AEMNPRSTU	smarten up
AEMNPRTUY	prytaneum
AEMNRSSST	smartness
AEMNRSTTU	transmute
AEMNRSTVY	vestryman
AEMOOORRT	aeromotor
AEMOOPRRS	spare room
AEMOOPRTT	proto team✧

AEMOORRSS	morass ore
AEMOORSTT	stateroom
AEMOORSTX	xerostoma
AEMOOSSST	maestosos
AEMOPPRXZ	Zeppo Marx
AEMOPRRTY	temporary
AEMOPRSTT	steam port
AEMOPRSTU	mousetrap
AEMOPSTTY	asymptote
AEMORSTTW	two-master
AEMORSTWY	Tom Sawyer
AEMPPRTUW	pump-water
	water pump
AEMPRRSTU	supermart
	supertram
AEMPRSSTY	spymaster
AEMPRTUXZ	Max Perutz
AEMQRRTUY	marquetry
AEMRRSSTU	surmaster
AEMRSSTTW	straw-stem
AENNOOPPR	propanone
AENNOOSWY	on one's way
AENNOPTWY	two a penny
AENNORRST	resnatron
AENNORSTY	sonnetary
AENNPSSTU	unaptness
AENNRSSTY	tyranness
AENNRSTTU	transeunt
AENNSSTUY	Sun Yat-Sen
AENOOPPRT	protanope
AENOOPSST	soapstone
AENOORRST	resonator
AENOORRTV	renovator
AENOORSTV	oven-roast
AENOPPRRT	en rapport
AENOPRRTW	part-owner
AENOPRSST	patroness
	transpose
AENOPRSUV	supernova
AENOPSSTU	sponte sua
AENORRTWW	water-worn
AENORSSTT	starstone
AENORSSTU	anoestrus
AENORSTTY	attorneys
AENORSTWW	snow-water
AENOSSTWX	West Saxon
AENPSSSTW	wasps' nest
	wasp's nest
AENQSSSTU	squatness
AENRRSTVY	servantry
AENRRTTUX	tax return
AENRSSSTW	swartness
AENRSSTTV	transvest
AEOOPPRRT	porporate
AEOOPRSTZ	rose topaz
AEOOPRTTV	vaporetto
AEOORRSTV	overroast
AEOORRSTZ	Zoroaster
AEOORTTUU	autoroute
AEOPQRRTU	parroquet
AEOPRRRTY	portrayer
AEOPRRSSY	aspersory
AEOPRRSTT	prostrate
AEOPRRSTU	prosateur
	pterosaur
AEOPRRSTW	spearwort
AEOPRSTTY	poetastry
AEOPRSTWY	top-sawyer
AEOQRRSSU	squarrose
AEOQRSTUZ	quartzose
AEOQRTTTU	quartetto
AEORRSSTY	assertory
AEORRSTTV	start over
AEORRSTZZ	terrazzos
AEORSSTUU	trousseau
AEORSTTVW	straw vote
AEPPRSTUU	suppurate
AEPQRRTUY	parquetry
AEPRRSSTU	superstar
AEPRSTTUX	Apex Trust
AEQRRSTUY	try square
AERRSSTUU	susurrate
AERRSSVYY	arsy-versy
AERRSTTWY	stewartry
AFFFFINNY	niff-naffy
AFFGIIRST	sgraffiti
AFFGIKNOT	taking-off
AFFGIORST	sgraffito
AFFHHILST	half-shift
AFFHILRSY	raffishly
AFFHIPSTW	whipstaff
AFFIILNPT	plaintiff
AFFILLNTY	flay-flint
AFFILNOUX	affluxion
AFFILNRUY	ruffianly
AFFIMMNNU	muffin man
AFFIMNNPU	muffin pan
AFFIMORRT	far from it
AFFIPSSTT	tipstaffs
AFFKNORRT	Frankfort
AFFKNRRTU	Frankfurt
AFFLLORUV	flavorful
AFFLOOTTU	foot fault
	footfault
AFFMNNRUY	funny farm
AFFMOORST	staffroom
AFGGGINOT	faggoting
AFGGIINTU	fatiguing
AFGGILNOS	fog signal
AFGGLNNOU	falun gong✧
AFGHHILLT	half-light
AFGHHIRST	fish-garth
AFGHIIMNS	famishing
AFGHILLNS	halflings
AFGHILLNT	nightfall
AFGHILNRS	ring flash
AFGHILSTT	light-fast
AFGHINOSU	fish-guano
AFGHIPRTW	whip graft
	whip-graft
AFGHLLSTU	ghastfull
AFGHMOORT	homograft
AFGHNRTUU	unfraught
AFGHORSTU	far-sought
AFGIIILNR	filigrain
AFGIILNNU	unfailing
AFGIILNSY	salifying
AFGIILRTY	fragility
AFGIIMNRS	misfaring
AFGIIMNRY	ramifying
AFGIIMSTU	fastigium
AFGIINRRY	fairy ring
AFGIINRTY	ratifying
AFGIKNORS	forsaking
AFGIKNRST	skin graft
AFGILLMNY	flamingly
AFGILLNRY	flaringly
AFGILLNST	flatlings
AFGILLNUY	gainfully
AFGILLOPT	pilot flag
AFGILMNOS	flamingos
AFGILMNOY	foamingly
AFGILNNOU	union flag
AFGILNNTU	flaunting
AFGILNNUU	ungainful
AFGILNNWY	fawningly
AFGILNORV	flavoring
AFGILNRTZ	Fritz Lang
AFGILRSTU	frugalist
AFGILRTUY	frugality
AFGIMNORU	anguiform
AFGIMORTU	fumigator
AFGIMORTY	fogramity
AFGINNPRY	frying-pan
AFGINOORT	frigatoon
AFGIOSTTT	fagottist
AFGLLNORU	full organ
AFGLLSSSU	glassfuls
AFGLNRTUU	fulgurant
AFGNNOOSU	son of a gun
AFGNOOORW	wagon roof
AFGNOPRSW	frogspawn
AFGNRSUUY	ray fungus
AFGOORSTU	sugar foot
AFGORSSST	soft-grass
AFHHLRTTU	half-truth
AFHIIKNOP	kniphofia
AFHIILNSS	snailfish
AFHIILPRS	April-fish
AFHIINNOS	in fashion
AFHIKLOTT	of that ilk
AFHILORSY	royal fish
AFHILRSTW	trawl-fish
AFHIMNOSW	fish-woman
AFHIORRSZ	razorfish
AFHIORSTY	forsythia
AFHIORTTW	throw a fit
AFHIRSTTU	Tartufish
AFHLLMRUY	harmfully
AFHLLORST	fall short
	shortfall
AFHLMNRUU	unharmful
AFHLOOPPY	fool-happy

AFHOORRST hoarfrost
AFHOOSSTT soothfast
AFHOPPRST prop shaft
AFIIILNOT filiation
AFIIILNPS Filipinas
AFIILNNOT inflation
AFIILNOOT foliation
AFIILRSTT stairlift
AFIIMNRRY infirmary
AFIINNOST saintfoin
AFIINORSU infusoria✧
AFIIOORRT a fortiori
AFIIORRTU fioritura
AFIIORTTW wait for it!
AFIJKORST forjaskit
AFIKLLMOT milk float
AFIKLORTY forky-tail
AFILLLOPY Polyfilla®
AFILLNOUX fluxional
AFILLNPTU plaintful
AFILLNPUY painfully
AFILLOOPR April fool
AFILLRTUW wall fruit
AFILMMORS formalism
AFILMNNTU fulminant
AFILMNOOW Naomi Wolf
AFILMOPRS salpiform
AFILMORRV larviform
AFILMORST formalist
AFILMORTY formality
AFILNNPUU unpainful
AFILNOOTT flotation
AFILNORST frost-nail
AFILNOSTU sulfation
AFILNQUUY unqualify
AFILOORSS fossorial
AFILOSTTY fatty oils
AFIMMMMOR mammiform
AFIMNNORT informant
AFIMNOORT formation
AFIMORRTU tauriform
AFIMORSSY fairy moss
AFIMRSTTU Tartufism
AFINOOPRR rainproof
AFINOPRTY profanity
AFIOORSTT stairfoot
AFIORTTTT tit for tat
tit-for-tat
AFIOSTTUU fatuitous
AFIRRSTTU star fruit
AFIRRTTTU fruit tart
AFKLLMRSU full marks
AFKLMNOOS moon flask
AFKLOOSTT footstalk
AFKMOOPRR proof-mark
AFKNNORRT front-rank
AFKOORRTW work of art
AFLLLPUYY playfully
AFLLMNOSY salmon fly
AFLLMNOUY moanfully
AFLLMOOPR floor lamp
AFLLMOORT malt-floor
AFLLNOOPR floor plan
AFLLOOSTT foot-stall
AFLMNORSY salmon fry
AFLMORRUY formulary
AFLNOOPTU puftaloon
AFLOOPSTY splay foot
splay-foot
AFLOOPTUY out of play
AFLOORSUV flavorous
AFLOORSUY soya flour
AFLOPRRSU fluorspar
AFMNORRST transform
AFMNORRTW warm front
AFMOORSTY Styrofoam®
styrofoam
AFMOPRRTY for my part
AFMORRTTU trout farm
AFNORSTWY frontways
AFOOPRRST star-proof
AFOORSSTZ sforzatos
AFORRSTTU AstroTurf®
AGGGILLNY laggingly
AGGGINPRS spragging
AGGGINRSY Ryan Giggs
AGGHHILSY haggishly
AGGHHNOTU hang tough
AGGHHNRTU Hugh Grant
AGGHILOOY hagiology
AGGHILSWY waggishly
AGGHINSTT stag night
AGGHIRSTY gay rights
AGGHLOOPR logograph
AGGIIIMNN imagining
AGGIILNNS signaling
AGGIILNNT ting-a-ling
AGGIILNVW lawgiving
AGGIIMNST gigantism
AGGIIMNTY gigmanity
AGGIINNOS agonising
AGGIINNOZ agonizing
AGGIINNTV vintaging
AGGIKNORT go-karting
AGGILLLNY gallingly
AGGILLNOP galloping
AGGILLNRY glaringly
AGGILNNOS ganglions
sing along
singalong
AGGILNNPS spangling
AGGILNNRW wrangling
AGGILNNTW twangling
AGGILNOPY play-going
AGGILNPSY gaspingly
AGGILNRTY gratingly
AGGILOORY agriology
AGGIMMNNO gammoning
AGGINNOOR gorgonian
AGGINORRS grosgrain
AGGINORRT garroting
AGGINORTT garotting
tog rating
AGGMOORRT mortgagor
AGGMOSTYY mystagogy
AGGNNOPYY Pyongyang
AGGNORRWY grow angry
AGGOORSST go to grass
AGHHIISTW waist-high
AGHHIKNTW nighthawk
AGHHILRTU ultra-high
AGHHILTUY haughtily
AGHHINRST thrashing
AGHHLOOPR holograph
AGHHMOOPR homograph
AGHIILLNP phialling
AGHIILLTT tail light
AGHIILNRT night-rail
AGHIIMMMN Immingham
AGHIINNNT tanghinin
AGHIINNSV vanishing
AGHIINPST giantship
AGHIINRSV ravishing
AGHIINRTT raintight
AGHIINRTW Ian Wright
AGHIIORSV viragoish
AGHIIRRST hairst-rig
AGHIKLNTW night-walk
AGHIKMNOW Wokingham
AGHIKNNST thankings
AGHIKNOSU Kaohsiung
AGHIKRRTW Arkwright
AGHILLLOP Gallophil
AGHILLMPT lamplight
AGHILLNOP anglophil✧
AGHILLNRY narghilly
AGHILLNTY haltingly
AGHILLORY holy grail✧
AGHILMORT algorithm
logarithm
AGHILNPSS Spanglish
splashing
AGHILNPTY plaything
AGHILNSTT last thing
AGHILNTUY naughtily
AGHILOOPT Lotophagi
AGHILOSTY goatishly
AGHILPRTT light trap
AGHILRSTT starlight
AGHIMNNRU unharming
AGHIMNRST hamstring
AGHIMNRTY nightmary
AGHIMNSST sightsman
AGHIMOPRY amphigory
AGHIMORST histogram
AGHIMOSTT Gothamist
AGHIMSTTU mistaught
AGHINNOTT not a thing
AGHINNSTU unhasting
AGHINNTTU unhatting
AGHINOQSU qinghaosu
AGHINORRW harrowing
AGHINORTU authoring

AGHINPSUW washing-up
AGHINRRSY garnishry
AGHINRTTW thwarting
AGHIPRSUU augurship
AGHJNOORS rogan josh
AGHKKOSYZ kok-saghyz
AGHKMOPRY kymograph
AGHKOORSS grasshook
AGHLLOOPY haplology
AGHLMNOPU ploughman
AGHLMOOPR lagomorph
AGHLMOOTU goalmouth
AGHLNOOTY anthology
AGHLNOPSU push along
AGHLNOSTU onslaught
AGHLOOPTY pathology
AGHLOPPRY polygraph
AGHLOPPYY polyphagy
AGHLOPRXY xylograph
AGHLORSSU hourglass
AGHLORSSY holy grass
AGHMNOOPR monograph
nomograph
phonogram
AGHMNOOPY monophagy
AGHMNRSTU hamstrung
AGHMOOPRT photogram
tomograph
AGHMOPRYY myography
AGHMORSST grass moth
AGHNOOPRS sonograph
AGHNOOTTW wang tooth
AGHNOPSSU sphagnous
AGHNOPTUU Putonghua
AGHNORSST stag's horn
AGHNPRSUW spur-whang
AGHOOPRRT rotograph
AGHOOPRRY orography
AGHOOPRYZ zoography
AGHOOSSTU Oshogatsu
AGHOPRRUY urography
AGHORSTTY hygrostat
AGIIILNRV Virgilian
AGIIIMNPR impairing
AGIIIMNST imaginist
AGIIINNNS sinningia
AGIIINNRT Nigritian
AGIIINNRV Virginian
AGIIINSTV vaginitis
AGIIKLMNR grimalkin
AGIIKMNNP pin-making
AGIIKMNPR King Priam
AGIIKMNST mistaking
AGIILLMMR milligram
AGIILLNOR gorillian
AGIILLNRT trialling
AGIILLNRV rivalling
AGIILLNRY railingly
AGIILLNUV ingluvial
AGIILLNWY wailingly
AGIILLRSY sigillary
AGIILMNTY malignity
AGIILNNPT pantiling
AGIILNNST saintling
AGIILNNSW wing snail
AGIILNNWZ Zwinglian
AGIILNORS originals
sailoring
signorial
AGIILNORT largition
tailoring
AGIILNORU Liguorian
AGIILNOST intaglios
AGIILNQSU squailing
AGIILNRSV virginals
AGIILNSSS isinglass
AGIILNTWY waitingly
AGIILORTT litigator
AGIIMMNRT immigrant
AGIIMMSST sigmatism
AGIIMNORT migration
AGIIMNOST sigmation
AGIIMNRST maistring
AGIIMNSSS misassign
AGIIMNSSY missaying
AGIIMORTT mitigator
AGIIMRSTT trigamist
AGIINNNTW wanting in
AGIINNORS signorina✧
AGIINNPSS in passing
AGIINNRST straining
AGIINNRTT intrigant
AGIINNRTY trigynian
AGIINORST trisagion
AGIINPPRS apprising
AGIINPPRZ apprizing
AGIINPRST traipsing
AGIIORRRT irrigator
AGIIRSSTT gastritis
AGIIRSTTU guitarist
AGIJLNRRY jarringly
AGIJNORST jargonist
AGIKLLMSS milk glass
AGIKLLPSS skills gap
AGIKLMRSU milk sugar
AGIKLMRVY milk gravy
AGIKLNOSY soakingly
AGIKLNOTT talking-to
AGIKLNPRS sparkling
AGIKLNPTU uptalking
AGIKLNQUY quakingly
AGIKLRSSS silk-grass
AGIKMNNSU unmasking
AGIKMNOPT topmaking
AGIKMORSS kissogram
AGIKNNPRW king prawn
AGIKNQSUW squawking
AGILLLNRU all-ruling
AGILLLNUY lingually
AGILLLOPY palillogy
AGILLMNRS ring-small
AGILLMNSS sing small
AGILLMRSU sugar mill
AGILLNNNU annulling
AGILLNNPT plantling
AGILLNOPW walloping
AGILLNOTT allotting
totalling
AGILLNOWW wallowing
AGILLNQSU squalling
AGILLNSTY lastingly
AGILMMRSW Grimm's law
AGILMNNOO Mongolian
AGILMNNOT lamington
AGILMNOPS panlogism
AGILMNOPY Pygmalion
AGILMNPRT trampling
AGILMNSUY amusingly
AGILMOORS lagrimoso
AGILMOORY Mariology
AGILMRSUV vulgarism
AGILNNOPS plainsong
AGILNNOQU Algonquin
AGILNNOTY atoningly
AGILNNPTY pantingly
AGILNNRTY rantingly
AGILNNRWY warningly
AGILNNWYY yawningly
AGILNOOTT agnolotti
AGILNOPYY Polygynia
AGILNORRY roaringly
AGILNORSY soaringly
AGILNORVY vainglory
AGILNOSTW wagon-lits
wagons-lit
AGILNPRSW sprawling
AGILNPRSY raspingly
sparingly
AGILNPRTY pratingly
AGILNPRYY prayingly
AGILNPSTT splatting
AGILNPSUY pausingly
AGILNRSTT startling
AGILNRSTY staringly
strayling
AGILNTTTW twattling
AGILOOPST apologist
AGILOPRUY uropygial
AGILOQRSU gas-liquor
AGILRRTUY garrulity
AGILRTUVY vulgarity
AGIMMNOPV moving map
AGIMMNSUY gymnasium
AGIMNNOOR marooning
AGIMNNOOY Monogynia
AGIMNNORS amornings
AGIMNNSUU unamusing
AGIMNNSUY synangium
AGIMNORST sigmatron
AGIMNORSU ignoramus
AGIMOOSSU isogamous
AGIMOPRRS spirogram
AGIMORRTY migratory

AGIMORSTU	trigamous
AGIMRSTTU	Targumist
AGINNNOPY	non-paying
AGINNORRW	narrowing
AGINNORST	on a string
AGINNOSTU	Antigonus
AGINNOSUV	Sauvignon
AGINNPRSU	unsparing
AGINNRUVY	unvarying
AGINNSTUU	Tungusian
AGINNSTUW	unwasting
AGINNSTUY	unstaying
AGINOOPSS	poison gas
AGINOORRT	Tongariro
AGINOPPRV	approving
AGINOPRRT	parroting
AGINOPRTT	pottingar
AGINOPRTU	purgation
AGINOPRUV	vapouring
AGINORRTV	gravitron
AGINORSTY	signatory
AGINOSTTU	gustation
AGINOTTTU	guttation
AGINPPRST	strapping
	trappings
AGINPPRSW	wrappings
AGINPRSTU	upstaring
AGINQRRUY	quarrying
AGINQSTTU	squatting
AGINSTTUU	situtunga
AGIOORSTU	autogiros
AGIOPRRSY	spirogyra
AGIPRSSTY	spagyrist
AGIQRSSTU	grassquit
AGJKNORRU	kurrajong
AGKLMNOOY	golomynka
AGKLOORYY	karyology
AGKLORSSW	glasswork
AGKLPPRSU	spark plug
AGKMNOPRU	Mungo Park
AGKNORSST	knotgrass
AGKOPRSTU	task group
AGLLLNOOR	roll along
AGLLNOOPY	polygonal
AGLLOOSSW	glass wool
AGLMOORSU	glamorous
AGLMOORYY	Maryology
AGLMOPRUU	glamour up
AGLMPRSUU	lump sugar
	sugar-lump
	sugarplum
AGLNOORUY	uranology
AGLNORSUU	granulous
AGLNOSTYZ	lazy tongs
	lazy-tongs
AGLOOPRTY	patrology
AGLOORSST	glossator
AGLOORSTY	astrology
AGLOOTTUY	tautology
AGLOPPRUY	playgroup
AGLOPRSST	grass-plot
AGLORRSSU	grossular
AGLORRSUU	garrulous
AGLORSSTW	glasswort
AGLOSUYYZ	azygously
AGMMNOORS	groomsman
AGMMOSTUU	gummatous
AGMNNORST	strongman
AGMNORRST	strongarm
AGMNOSSUY	syngamous
AGMNRTUYZ	zygantrum
AGMNSSTUY	nystagmus
AGMOOOSUZ	zoogamous
AGMOORRSS	moor grass
AGMORRSSW	worm grass
AGNNOPPTU	oppugnant
AGNOQUUVX	vu quang ox
AGNPRSSUU	spun sugar
AGNPSSTUW	wasp-stung
AGNRRSTUY	strangury
AGOORSTUY	autogyros
AGOPRRTUY	purgatory✧
AGOPRSUVY	gravy-soup
AGORSTTUY	gustatory
AGRSTTTTU	Stuttgart
AHHHOOSST	shahtoosh
AHHIIMORS	Hiroshima
AHHIIRRST	hair shirt
AHHIKLSWY	hawkishly
AHHIKORST	Tokharish
AHHILLOPY	halophily
AHHILLRRY	Harry Hill
AHHILLWWY	whillywha
AHHILMOPT	philomath
AHHILTTUW	withhault
AHHIMSSST	Smash Hits
AHHIORSTU	authorish
AHHLORSTU	short-haul
AHHMOPRTU	mouth harp
AHHMOSTUW	mouthwash
AHHNORRST	hartshorn
AHHNRSTTU	ant thrush
AHHOOPRSS	Oh So Sharp
AHHOOSTTW	toothwash
AHHOPPRUY	happy hour
AHHORSTTU	thrash out
AHIIIKLSW	Kiswahili
AHIIILSST	lithiasis
AHIILLMTT	tallithim
AHIILLOST	sialolith
AHIILLTWW	with a will
AHIILMNTU	humiliant
AHIILNOPS	Ian Hislop
AHIILOOPZ	zoophilia
AHIILORSU	hilarious
AHIILOSST	halitosis
AHIILPRSV	rivalship
AHIILRSTT	shirt tail
AHIIMMRST	Mithraism
AHIIMMSUZ	Mizushima
AHIIMRSTT	Mithraist
AHIINOPPR	Hipparion
AHIINORST	historian
AHIINPSST	Hispanist
	saintship
AHIIPPRTY	hippiatry
AHIIPRSSZ	sizarship
AHIIRRSTT	arthritis
AHIJMNNNO	John Inman
AHIJMOPRS	majorship
AHIJNNOST	Ian St John
AHIKKNNTT	think tank
AHIKKNRSS	sharkskin
AHIKLMSWY	mawkishly
AHIKLNSVY	knavishly
AHIKLRSTU	hula skirt
AHIKNOTWW	I know what
AHILLNRTT	thrillant
AHILLOORS	hors la loi
AHILLOPRT	prothalli
AHILLOPSV	Slavophil
AHILLOSSW	sallowish
AHILLOSTW	tallowish
AHILLPSSY	splashily
AHILLPSTW	whipstall
AHILLSSTY	saltishly
AHILLSSVY	slavishly
AHILMNNSY	mannishly
AHILMNNUY	inhumanly
AHILMOPRS	rhopalism
AHILMOPSY	syphiloma
AHILMORST	hailstorm
AHILMPRTU	triumphal
AHILMRSTY	lathyrism
AHILNOPTY	notaphily
AHILNORTT	triathlon
AHILNPPUY	unhappily
AHILOORST	Lotharios
AHILOPPTY	Hippolyta
AHILORSTW	show trial
AHILORTTY	throatily
AHILOSTTT	statolith
AHILPSSWY	waspishly
AHILQSSUY	squashily
AHILRSSTT	startlish
AHILRSTWY	swarthily
AHIMMMNOS	mammonish
AHIMMMOSS	shammosim
AHIMMNORU	harmonium
AHIMMOPRS	amorphism
AHIMNNORY	inharmony
AHIMNOOSU	homousian
AHIMNOPRS	orphanism
AHIMNORST	harmonist✧
AHIMNPPSU	upmanship
AHIMNPSTY	sympathin
AHIMNRSTU	Mathurins
AHIMNRTUU	anthurium
AHIMOOSTX	homotaxis
AHIMOPRSY	mayorship
AHIMOPSTY	opsimathy
AHIMOPSUX	amphioxus
AHIMORRSW	marrowish

AHIMORSTU	authorism
AHINNOOPT	phonation
AHINNOPTY	antiphony
	typhonian✧
AHINNOTTU	Huttonian
AHINOOPRR	orpharion
AHINOOPTY	hypotonia
AHINOORTT	hortation
AHINOPRSS	parsonish
AHINPRSST	transship
	trans-ship
AHIOOPPST	photopsia
AHIOORSTX	orthoaxis
AHIOPPRRY	porphyria
AHIOPPRST	parish top
AHIOPPSSY	apophysis
AHIOPRSTU	out-parish
AHIOPRSUV	vapourish
AHIOPRSUX	Xiphosura
AHIOPSTXY	hypotaxis
AHIORRSST	arthrosis
AHIORRTWY	airworthy
AHIORTTUY	authority
AHJJMNOOR	John Major
AHJKNNOOO	John Kanoo
AHJLMNOOU	Jonah Lomu
AHJMNOOWY	John Mayow
AHJNNOOSS	Johansson
AHJNNORWY	Johnny-raw
AHJOPSSWY	phossy jaw
AHKLOOPRS	look sharp
AHKLOOSTU	akoluthos
AHKMOORSW	Hawksmoor
AHKNOOPST	Pakhtoons
AHKNPRSTU	Pankhurst
AHKORSSWW	swashwork
AHKORSTUW	Southwark
AHLLLOSWY	shallowly
AHLLMOOPR	allomorph
AHLLMORUY	humorally
AHLLOPSTY	tallyshop
AHLLOPSUY	aphyllous
AHLMNOSWY	showmanly
AHLMOOOPR	homopolar
AHLMOOPSY	homoplasy
AHLMOOPTY	homotypal
AHLMOPSUX	Max Ophuls
AHLMOPTYY	polymathy
AHLMORSTY	solar myth
AHLNOTXXY	xanthoxyl
AHLNOTXYZ	zanthoxyl
AHLOPSSTU	splash out
AHLORSTTW	stalworth
AHLORSTUW	twalhours
AHMMNOTTU	mutton ham
AHMNOOPTY	taphonomy
AHMOOPRSU	amorphous
AHMOPRTTU	mouthpart
AHMORRSTW	marshwort
AHNNNOOTY	hootnanny
AHNOOPRTY	phonatory
AHNOOPTUY	autophony
AHNOPSTYY	hyponasty
AHNORRSTT	North Star
AHNORRTTY	thyratron
AHOOOPTTT	hot potato
AHOOPRRTX	prothorax
AHOOPRTTU	autotroph
AHOOPRTUX	auxotroph
AHOOPSTTT	Photostat®
AHOORRSTW	arrow-shot
AHOORRTTY	hortatory
AHOORTWWX	thorow-wax
AHOPQSSTU	squat shop
AHPRSSTTU	push-start
AIIILLNTY	initially
AIIILMMSS	Ismailism
AIIILMNST	laminitis
AIIILMPRT	primitial
AIIIMNNOT	miniation
AIIIMNOTT	imitation
AIIIMPRST	primitias
AIIINNNOT	inanition
AIIINNSTY	asininity
AIIINORST	irisation
AIIINORTT	initiator
AIIINOTTV	vitiation
AIIJKKKNU	Kinkakuji
AIIJLOTVY	joviality
AIIJMRSTU	jus mariti
AIIJNNSTU	Justinian
AIIKLMNRT	milk train
AIILLMMNY	minimally
AIILLMRSY	similarly
AIILLNTUV	villa unit
AIILLPRRS	spirillar
AIILLPRST	pillarist
AIILLPSTU	it is all up
AIILLRSTT	triallist
AIILLRTVY	trivially
AIILMMNUU	aluminium
AIILMNNOT	Miltonian
AIILMNORT	trinomial
AIILMNPSU	Paulinism
AIILMNRTY	matriliny
AIILMNSST	Stalinism
AIILMOSST	altissimo
AIILMPRRY	primarily
AIILMPRSS	spiralism
AIILMPRTY	primality
AIILMRSTU	ritualism
AIILNOOST	isolation
AIILNOOTV	violation
AIILNOPST	pianolist
AIILNOQTU	liquation
AIILNORSV	livraison
AIILNOSTT	siltation
AIILNOTTU	tuitional
AIILNPRST	air-splint
AIILNPRTY	patriliny
AIILNPSTU	Paulinist
AIILNRSST	sinistral
AIILNSSTT	Stalinist
AIILOPRST	air pistol
AIILPRRTT	trial trip
AIILPRSST	spiralist
	spritsail
AIILPRSTU	spiritual
AIILPRSTY	spirality
AIILRSTTU	ritualist
AIILSSTUV	visualist
AIILSTUVY	visuality
AIIMMPRSV	vampirism
AIIMNNORS	Rosminian
AIIMNNTUY	unanimity
AIIMNOPRS	prosimian
AIIMNOPSS	impassion
AIIMNORSX	minor axis
AIIMNOSTY	animosity
AIIMNPSTT	timpanist
AIIMNRSSY	Syrianism
AIIMOPRRS	apriorism
AIIMPSSSV	passivism
AIIMRSTUU	Mauritius
AIIMRSUVV	vivariums
AIINNNOOT	Antonioni
AIINNOPRS	sopranini
AIINNORST	Santorini
AIINNORTT	nitration
AIINNORTU	ruination
	urination
AIINNOSTU	sinuation
AIINNOTTX	antitoxin
AIINNPRRT	rain-print
AIINNQQUU	quinquina
AIINNRSTT	in transit
	St Trinian
AIINOOQRU	Iroquoian
AIINOPRST	spiration
AIINOPRTT	partition
AIINOPRTV	privation
AIINORRTV	ritonavir
AIINORSTT	striation
AIINORSVY	visionary
AIINORTTT	attrition
	titration
AIINOSTTU	situation
AIINOSTXX	saxitoxin
AIINOTTTU	attuition
AIINQTTUY	antiquity
AIINRSTUV	antivirus
AIINRTUVV	Vitruvian
AIIOPRRST	apriorist
AIIOPRRTY	apriority
AIIOPRSSS	psoriasis
AIIOPRSTT	parotitis
	topiarist
AIIOPRTVY	oviparity
AIIORRRTT	irritator
AIIORSTTV	visitator
AIIPPRRST	parti pris
AIIPRTTUY	pituitary
AIIPSSSTV	passivist

 Words marked ✧ can also be spelled with one or more capital letters

AIIPSSTVY passivity
AIJMORSTU major suit
AIJNNNOOS Jonsonian
AIKKLNORS Raskolnik
AIKKNOSTY kantikoys
AIKLLLMUW waulkmill
AIKLLMMOR milk-molar
AIKLMNNNS Klinsmann
AIKLMNRTU trunk-mail
AIKLMSTTU multitask
AIKLNOPRW plainwork
AIKLNOSSY ankylosis
AIKLNOSTT klinostat
AIKLRRUVY Valkyriur
AIKMMNOOS makimonos
AIKMMRRST trim marks
AIKMNNOSW kinswoman
AIKMORSSV visor-mask
AIKMPRSTZ Mark Spitz
AIKNNOOST isokontan
AIKNOOOPS poison oak
AIKNOPRTW paintwork
AIKNPSSTU Skupstina
AIKORRSTW stairwork
AIKPRSTTU put at risk
AILLLMTUW multi-wall
AILLLPRUV pulvillar
AILLMMORY immorally
AILLMMPST stamp mill
AILLMNNOY nominally
AILLMNOUV voluminal
AILLMOOPS liposomal
AILLMOOTT tomatillo
AILLMOPPT pilot lamp
AILLMOPTY optimally
AILLMPRST strip mall
AILLMPRSU pluralism
AILLNNSTU uninstall
AILLNOOPR piano roll
AILLNORST tonsillar
AILLNORSU lunisolar
AILLNOSSW snail-slow
AILLNOSUV villanous
AILLNOTUU ululation
AILLNRSUY insularly
AILLOPPSU papillous
AILLOPRST Tirol Alps
AILLOPSST plastisol
AILLOPTVY pivotally
AILLORUXY uxorially
AILLPPRUY pupillary
AILLPRRWY Will Parry
AILLPRSTU pluralist
AILLPRTUY plurality
AILLRTTUY titularly
AILLRTUVY virtually
AILMMOORT immolator
AILMMORST immortals✧
AILMMRSUY summarily
AILMMSTUU mutualism
AILMMTTUU ultimatum
AILMNOOPS palominos
AILMNOOSS Molossian
AILMNOPRT trampolin
AILMNOPSS spoilsman
AILMNOPST Platonism
AILMNOPSU Paul Simon
AILMNOPSY amylopsin
AILMNORTY normality
trionymal
AILMNORUV mournival
AILMNOSUU aluminous
AILMNSTTU stimulant
AILMOORRT rail-motor
AILMOPRVY ivory-palm
AILMOPSSY symposial
AILMORSST storm sail
AILMORSTU simulator
AILMORTTU mutilator
AILMORTTY mortality
AILMOSSTY atmolysis
AILMPRSTY palmistry
AILMSTTUU mutualist
AILMTTUUY mutuality
AILNNOPTU Plutonian
AILNNOSSW sons-in-law
AILNNSTTU insultant
AILNNSTTY instantly
AILNNSTUY unsaintly
AILNOOPRT portolani
prolation
AILNOORST tonsorial
torsional
AILNOOSTV solvation
AILNOOTUV ovulation
AILNOPSTT Platonist
AILNOPSTU platinous
pulsation
put on sail
AILNOQRTU tan liquor
AILNORSTU insulator
Solutrian
AILNOSUXY anxiously
AILNOTTWZ waltz into
AILNPPSTU suppliant
AILNPQTUY piquantly
AILNRSTUY rusty nail
AILNRTUUX luxuriant
AILOOPRST spoliator
AILOOPTTU autopilot
AILOORRTT tail rotor
AILOORSSS rosa-solis
AILOORSUV variolous
AILOOTTUV voilà tout
AILOPRSTV postviral
AILORRSTW arrow-slit
AILORRSUV rivalrous
AILORRTTY traitorly
AILORSUVY savourily
variously
AILOSSTUY autolysis
AILPRRSSU surprisal
AILPRSTUY stipulary
AILQRSTUY squiralty
AIMMMMNOS mammonism
AIMMMNOST mammonist
AIMMNNOOT motion-man
AIMMNNORS Normanism
AIMMNNOST Montanism
AIMMNOOTY amniotomy
AIMMNORTY matrimony
AIMMNOSTU summation
AIMMPRSUU marsupium
AIMMRRTUY martyrium
AIMMRSSTU summarist
AIMNNOORT nominator
AIMNNOPST pointsman
AIMNNOSTT Montanist
AIMNNOSUU unanimous
AIMNNOTYY anonymity
AIMNOPRSY parsimony
AIMNOPRTT important
AIMNOPRTY patrimony
AIMNORRST rainstorm
AIMNORRSU Ursa Minor
AIMNORRTU ruminator
AIMNORRTY marry into
AIMNORSUU uniramous
AIMNORTTW taint-worm
AIMNOSSSY Simon says
AIMNPSTTY tympanist
AIMNRSSTU saturnism
AIMOOPRUZ Mario Puzo
AIMOORSTY amorosity
AIMOORTTV motivator
AIMOPRSUW Opium Wars
AIMOPSSTU potassium
AIMORRSSU rosariums
AIMORSTUV vis mortua
AIMPSSSTU assumpsit
AIMQRSTUU Utraquism
AIMSSSSTY miss stays
AINNNNOTU nunnation
AINNNOSTU Antoninus
unisonant
AINNOOOTZ ozonation
AINNOOPRS sopranino
AINNOOPRT pronation
AINNOORTT intonator
AINNOORTV innovator
AINNOPRSV prison van
AINNORSTT start in on
strontian
AINNOSUUX unanxious
AINNOTTWW witwanton
AINOOPPRT appointor
apportion
AINOOPRRT proration
troparion
AINOOPRST rat-poison
AINOOPTTU autopoint
AINOOQTTU quotation
AINOORSTT sortation

AINOOSSTT	ostinatos
AINOOSTTV	ottavinos
AINOOTTUX	autotoxin
AINOPRSST	sopranist
AINOPRSTU	Proustian
	put on airs
	supinator
AINOPRSUU	uniparous
AINORSTTU	outstrain
AINORSTUU	souari-nut
AINPSSTTU	pants suit
AINPSSTUU	puissaunt
AINRSSTTU	saturnist
AINRSTTTU	antitrust
AIOOORRST	oratorios
AIOOPPSST	apoptosis
AIOOPPTTT	potato pit
AIOOPRRTV	oviraptor
AIOOPRSTV	protoavis
AIOOPRSUV	apivorous
	oviparous
AIOOSTTTT	tattooist
AIOPPRSTT	pop artist
AIOPRSSTT	spit-roast
AIOPRTTUX	à tout prix
AIORRSSTU	sartorius
AIORRSTUV	rotavirus
AIPPRSSTT	Trappists
AIPRRSTTU	rapturist
AIQRSTTUU	Utraquist
AJMNORUWY	jurywoman
AJMPRSTTU	jump-start
AJPRRTUYY	party-jury
AKKLLNPSU	knapskull
AKKLLOSTY	yolk stalk
AKLLLMOOS	look small
AKLLMMOWY	mollymawk
AKLLMNOSU	molluskan
AKLMNORWY	workmanly
AKLMNPSTU	musk-plant
AKLMOORST	look smart
AKLORSSTW	saltworks
AKMNOORWW	workwoman
AKMNORSTU	Turkomans
AKMORRSWY	marrowsky
AKNNORSYY	synkaryon
AKNOOPRRY	prokaryon
AKOOPRRTY	prokaryot
AKOOPRSSW	soap-works
AKOPRRSTW	strap work
AKOPRRTWY	work party
AKORRSTWW	straw-work
ALLLNNSUY	Sally Lunn
ALLMNOSSY	All My Sons
ALLMNOSTW	small-town
ALLMOOSSY	lysosomal
ALLNOOPTY	polytonal
ALLNOOPYZ	polyzonal
ALLNOPTTU	pollutant
ALLNORUYY	unroyally
ALLNSUUUY	unusually
ALLOOPRTY	allotropy
ALLOPPRUY	popularly
ALLOPRSTW	straw poll
ALLOPRSTY	sallyport
ALLOPSUWW	swallow up
ALLRSTUUY	suturally
ALMMNRUUY	nummulary
ALMMNSSUU	Mussulman
ALMNNOOOS	monsoonal
ALMNNOUWY	unwomanly
ALMNOOPTY	toponymal
ALMNOORTY	monolatry
ALMNOPRUY	pulmonary
ALMNOPSST	mossplant
ALMOOPRYY	polyamory
ALMOORSUY	amorously
ALMOPSTYY	polymasty
ALNNOOPST	loon-pants
ALNNOPSTW	snow plant
ALNOOOPRT	portolano
ALNOOPPTU	top-up loan
ALNOOPSST	salt spoon
ALNOOPSTT	tonoplast
ALNOPPRUU	unpopular
ALNOPRRSU	sun parlor
ALNOPSTTU	postulant
ALNORTUVY	voluntary
ALNPSTTUU	pustulant
ALOOOPRTZ	protozoal
ALOOPRRTW	owl-parrot
ALOOPRSTV	Stavropol
ALOOPRTUV	pot valour
ALOOPRYYZ	polyzoary
ALOOPSTYZ	zooplasty
ALOOPTTTU	total up to
ALOORTUVY	ovulatory
ALOPPRSSU	prolapsus
ALOPRRSUY	spur-royal
ALOPRRTYY	pyrolatry
ALOPRSTTU	Port Salut
ALOPRSTUY	pulsatory
AMMNPSTUY	tympanums
AMNNOOSUY	anonymous
AMNNOOSWW	Woman's Own
AMNOOOPRT	Monotropa
AMNOOPSTW	postwoman
	woman post
AMNOORSTY	astronomy
AMNOOSSTU	Mount Ossa
AMNOPRSST	sportsman
AMNOTTUYY	tautonymy
AMNPRSTTU	transumpt
AMOOORSTV	vasomotor
AMOORRRWW	arrowworm
AMORRSTWW	strawworm
AMORSSTTY	storm-stay
AMPRSTUUY	sumptuary
ANNOOPRSU	nonparous
ANNORSTUY	tyrannous
ANNRRTTUU	nurturant
ANOOOPRSZ	sporozoan
ANOOOPRTZ	protozoan
ANOOPSSWY	spoonways
ANOORSTWY	Stornoway
ANOPRRSTT	transport
ANORSUUVY	unsavoury
ANRRSSTUU	susurrant
AOOOPRTTT	potato rot
AOOORRRTW	arrowroot
AOOORRTTV	Rotovator®
	rotovator
AOOPRRSTT	protostar
AOOSTTUUV	tout à vous
AOPRRSTTW	strapwort
AOPRRSTUU	rapturous
AOQSSTTUU	status quo✧
AORRRTWWY	worrywart
AORSTTTUY	statutory

B

BBBCKOOSY	bobbysock
BBBDEELRU	blubbered
BBBEEELMU	bumblebee
BBBEEELUZ	Beelzebub
BBBEEILLT	Bible belt
BBBEEJLTU	bubble-jet
BBBEELORS	beslobber
BBBEELRSU	beslubber
BBBEGLMUU	bubble gum
BBBEHJOOR	hobjobber
BBBEIKORS	skibobber
BBBEINNOT	bobbin net
BBBGINOOS	Bob Gibson
BBCCHKLOU	chubb-lock
BBCCKLSUU	Buck's Club
BBCDIRRSU	scrub bird
BBCEHKMOT	bomb-ketch
BBCEHLOTY	Toby Belch
BBCEHLOUY	cubby-hole
BBCEHORRY	bob-cherry
	cherry-bob
BBCEILRRS	scribbler
BBCEIRSSU	subscribe
BBCEKTUUY	buckytube
BBCGILMOO	logic bomb
BBCGINRSU	scrubbing
BBCIIILMS	biblicism
BBCIIILST	biblicist
BBCILLOSY	Bill Cosby
BBCKKLOOO	block-book
	book block
BBDDEELOU	double bed
BBDDEESYY	beddy-byes
BBDDEJOOR	odd-jobber
BBDDILLUY	Billy Budd
BBDDILOOR	blood-bird
BBDEEHMTU	bethumbed
BBDEELMTU	betumbled
BBDEELOTT	bed-bottle
BBDEGIMNO	demobbing
BBDEHMOPT	depth bomb
BBDEIMRRU	umber-bird

Words marked ✧ can also be spelled with one or more capital letters

BBDEINORR red ribbon
BBDEIORRW bowerbird
BBDELLOOU blue blood
BBDELMMOU Bumbledom
BBDIMORTY dirty bomb
BBDNOORUW brow-bound
BBDNOSTUU bundobust
BBDOORRUU Borobudur
BBEEEEINR bebeerine
BBEEEGGLR beglerbeg
BBEEEHLMU humble-bee
BBEEEHTYY bye the bye
BBEEEINRR berberine
BBEEELLRY beer belly
BBEEELRTU Blue Beret
BBEEFHORT beef broth
BBEEFINTY benefit by
BBEEFIORT to be brief
BBEEFLLUY bully-beef
BBEEGILNO gobbeline
BBEEHINRS nebbisher
BBEEILLNO bellibone
BBEEINOSV bene vobis
BBEEINRTZ rebbetzin
BBEEIRRSU rubberise
BBEEIRRUZ rubberize
BBEELRRUY blueberry
BBEELTTUY Betty Blue
BBEFLORRY robber fly
BBEGGLOWY wobbly egg
BBEGGNOOW wobbegong
BBEGHIIRS gibberish
BBEGHILOS bobsleigh
BBEGINSSU gubbinses
BBEGLMTUU tumblebug
BBEGNRRUU burger bun
BBEGORTTU bog-butter
BBEHHIOTT The Hobbit
BBEHKOOTY by the book
BBEHLLMOS bombshell
BBEHLNOOY honey-blob
BBEHLOSSY hobbyless
BBEHRRSUY shrubbery
BBEILLNNO bonnibell
BBEINNOSS nobbiness
BBEINSSTU tubbiness
BBEJNORTU nutjobber
BBEKMMOOS smoke bomb
BBELORSUW rub elbows
BBEMNORUX box number
BBEMNRSUY by numbers
BBENORSSW brown Bess
BBEOORVVY bovver boy
BBEORTTUX butter-box
BBERRTTUU butterbur
BBFGIILNR fribbling
BBFHIILRS fribblish
BBFJKOOOO Book of Job
BBFMOOOPR bombproof
BBGGIJMOU jiggumbob
BBGHILLTU light bulb
BBGHILNOO hobgoblin
BBGHIMOST bombsight
BBGHINORT throbbing
BBGIIILMN bilimbing
BBGIILNQU quibbling
BBGIINQSU squibbing
BBGIIOSTY gibbosity
BBGILLNOO bobolling
BBGILNOSY sobbingly
BBGILOSUY gibbously
BBGJNOORR Björn Borg
BBGOORTUY rugby boot
BBHILLNOO Hobbinoll
BBHILOSYY yobbishly
BBHILRSUY rubbishly
BBHIOOPSY boy bishop
BBIIILNRU bilirubin
BBIIKMTUZ kibbutzim
BBIIMNORS Ribbonism
BBIKMNOST stink bomb
BBILLMMOS Mills bomb
BBILLNORW brown bill
BBILOSTUY bulbosity
BBLLOSUUY bulbously
BCCCHIINU cubic inch
BCCCIMOOX coxcombic
BCCCKMOOS cockscomb
cock's-comb
BCCDEHKOY body-check
BCCDKLMUU dumb-cluck
BCCDKLOOY body clock
BCCDKOOUU cuckoo-bud
BCCEEIKTU ice bucket
BCCEEILOR coercible
BCCEEKOOU cuckoo bee
BCCEFIOOR coco fibre
BCCEHIILO libecchio
BCCEHIKNP pinchbeck
BCCEHKKOO checkbook
BCCEIIILM imbecilic
BCCEIILOS libeccios
BCCEILORY coercibly
BCCEINNOU concubine
BCCEINORS conscribe
BCCEINSUU succubine
BCCEKLORU cocklebur
BCCEKOSTU stock cube
BCCFIOOTU cubic foot
BCCGHHINU chinch bug
BCCHKOORT cock-broth
BCCIILSTY bicyclist
BCCIKLLOY billycock
BCCIKMOOO comic book
BCCIORSTU scorbutic
BCCKOOSSY boss cocky
BCCKORSSU crossbuck
BCCMOORXY coxcombry
BCCMORRUY currycomb
BCCOOOSSU osso bucco
BCCOSSUUU succubous
BCDDEEILU deducible
BCDDIIKRY Dicky Bird
dicky-bird
BCDDLLOOO coldblood
BCDEEEEHS beseeched
BCDEEEFIN beneficed
BCDEEEINO obedience
BCDEEHIIR herbicide
BCDEEHOOW beechwood
BCDEEIIRV verbicide
BCDEEIKRU Die Brücke
BCDEEILRU reducible
BCDEEILSU seducible
BCDEEINOT Cobdenite
BCDEEIRRS describer
BCDEEIRSU rescue bid
BCDEEJSTU subjected
BCDEELLOR corbelled
BCDEELOST bed-closet
BCDEELRTU tubercled
BCDEEMNTU decumbent
BCDEFILLU field club
BCDEHINPT pitch bend
BCDEHLOSV boschveld
BCDEIILNO indocible
BCDEIILNU inducible
BCDEIJSUU sub judice
BCDEIKOWY dickey bow
BCDEILMNU unclimbed
BCDEILOOR bicolored
BCDEILSTU bile ducts
BCDEIMNOS Cobdenism
BCDEIMRSU discumber
BCDEISTUU decubitus
BCDELLLOO blood cell
BCDELNRUU underclub
BCDEORRSS crossbred
BCDEORRUY body-curer
BCDGIKLOR gold brick
gold-brick
BCDHHIIOT dhobi itch
BCDHKNOUU buckhound
BCDIIMMUY cymbidium
BCDIINNOO ionic bond
BCDIKRSTU brick-dust
BCDILLORY colly bird
BCDILMNOW climb down
climb-down
BCDIMOORS scombroid
BCDIOPSUW Cupid's bow
BCDKLOOOW woodblock
BCDKNOOOS boondocks
BCDKNOORU rock-bound
BCDNOOPRU cropbound
BCDNOOTTU cotton bud
BCDNOOTUY body count
BCDOOOOSY Scooby Doo
BCDOPRTUY by-product
BCEEEEHRS beseecher
BCEEEEHRT beech tree
BCEEEEHTT tête-bêche
BCEEEFHNR beech fern

	free-bench
BCEEEFHNS	bench fees
BCEEEGHIS	big cheese
BCEEEHKNO	cheekbone
BCEEEKLPS	bespeckle
BCEEEKQRU	Quebecker
BCEEELQRU	becquerel
BCEEFFGOU	coffee bug
BCEEFILRU	febricule
BCEEFKRUV	buck fever
BCEEGHINR	breeching
BCEEGIINR	bigeneric
BCEEGINRS	big screen
	big-screen
BCEEHHLNO	bench-hole
BCEEHILOS	cohesible
BCEEHIORS	bee-orchis
BCEEHIRRS	Schreiber
BCEEHIRRT	birch tree
BCEEHKOOR	chokebore
BCEEHNSTT	bench test
	bench-test
BCEEHORTT	brochette
BCEEHPRUY	hypercube
BCEEHRTTU	trebuchet
BCEEIIJTV	bijective
BCEEIIKNN	Nickie-ben
BCEEIILNV	evincible
BCEEIILRT	Celtiberi
BCEEIJOTV	objective
BCEEIKNST	Steinbeck
BCEEILLLV	Clive Bell
BCEEILLMO	ill become
BCEEILLOR	corbeille
BCEEILLOS	bellicose
BCEEILLRU	rubicelle
BCEEILMNY	Cymbeline
BCEEILRTY	celebrity
BCEEIMMOS	misbecome
BCEEIMNOR	recombine
BCEEINOOT	coenobite
BCEEINRTT	centre bit
BCEEINRWY	Eric Newby
BCEEIOQSU	Québecois
BCEEIORSX	boxercise
BCEEIPRRS	prescribe
BCEEIPSSU	sub specie
BCEEISSUV	subsecive
BCEEJNORT	job centre
	jobcentre✧
BCEEJOSTX	sex object
BCEEKNORZ	Zernebock
BCEEKPRTU	Peter Buck
BCEELMRRY	Brylcreem®
BCEELNOSY	obscenely
BCEELOOSS	obsolesce
BCEELORVX	box clever
BCEELRTUU	tubercule
BCEEMNRTU	recumbent
BCEEMRRSU	cerebrums
BCEENPSTU	pubescent
BCEENRSTU	rubescent
BCEEORTTU	courbette
BCEFFIOOX	box office
	box-office
BCEFFIOOY	office boy
BCEFFIOSU	suboffice
BCEFFLOOR	corbel off
BCEFIIKRR	firebrick
BCEFIIRTY	febricity
BCEFIJOTY	objectify
BCEFIORTY	fibrocyte
BCEFKLTUU	bucketful
BCEGHORRU	Cherbourg
BCEGIIKTT	big-ticket
BCEGIKNTU	bucketing
BCEGILNOR	corbeling
BCEGKTTUU	gutbucket
BCEGLOOSU	goose-club
BCEGRRSUW	grub screw
BCEHIIOST	bioethics
BCEHIKRST	sick berth
BCEHILNTU	in the club
BCEHIMRSU	cherubims
BCEHINNOT	benthonic
BCEHINOOP	neophobic
BCEHIOQUU	chibouque
BCEHIPSSU	spicebush
BCEHKLLOO	blockhole
BCEHKMRUU	humbucker
BCEHKNORW	workbench
BCEHLLNPU	bell-punch
BCEHLNOOR	reblochon
BCEHLNORY	Chernobyl
BCEHLNOTU	on the club
BCEHLOSUU	clubhouse
BCEHLRTUY	butcherly
BCEHMNOOY	honeycomb
BCEHMSTUY	set much by
BCEHRSSTU	the Scrubs
BCEIIINOT	ebionitic
BCEIIIRST	Briticise
BCEIIIRTZ	Briticize
BCEIIJNOT	bijection
BCEIIJSTU	Jebusitic
BCEIILNVY	evincibly
BCEIILPSU	publicise
BCEIILPUZ	publicize
BCEIIMORT	biometric
BCEIINOST	bisection
BCEIINRRS	inscriber
BCEIINSSU	subincise
BCEIIOPRT	prebiotic
BCEIISSTU	Ctesibius
BCEIJLOPU	Joe Public
BCEIJNOOT	objection
BCEIKKORX	kick boxer
BCEIKLLNO	line block
BCEIKLPUY	public-key
BCEIKNOST	steinbock
BCEIKNSTU	steinbuck
BCEIKOOPR	book price
BCEILLMRU	cribellum
BCEILMNOU	columbine✧
BCEILMOPT	comptible
BCEILMORY	cor blimey
BCEILMOTU	columbite
BCEILMRSU	crumblies
BCEILNOOT	bolection
BCEILNORU	colubrine
BCEILOOPT	optic lobe
BCEILPSTU	spec-built
BCEIMNNOU	uncombine
BCEIMNNTU	incumbent
BCEIMNOOU	coenobium
BCEIMNORY	embryonic
BCEIMORRW	microbrew
BCEIMORTY	embryotic
BCEIMRSTU	crumbiest
BCEINORRW	brown rice
BCEINORTW	twice-born
BCEINOSTY	obscenity
BCEINSSUU	incubuses
BCEIOPRRS	proscribe
BCEIOPTTU	optic tube
BCEIORSST	crossbite
BCEIORSTT	obstetric
BCEIPRSTY	presbytic
BCEJLLMOY	comb jelly
BCEJNSTUU	unsubject
BCEKLOOTV	block vote
BCEKLOPTY	block type
BCEKNPRUY	cyberpunk
BCEKOORRR	corkborer
	rock borer
BCEKORTUX	tuckerbox
BCEKORUWY	wreck buoy
BCELMOOTY	lobectomy
BCELNOSSU	Luc Besson
BCELOORTU	corbel out
BCELOOSSU	colobuses
	lobscouse
BCELORSTW	screw bolt
BCELORSUY	obscurely
BCEMMORTU	combretum
BCEMOORSY	corymbose
BCEMOTTUY	tubectomy
BCEMRTYYY	by my certy
BCENOOPUX	pounce box
BCENOORRR	cornborer
BCENOORRY	corner-boy
BCENORSTU	curbstone
BCEOOPRRY	cryoprobe
BCEOORTTY	boycotter
BCEORRRWY	crowberry
BCEORSTUX	subcortex
BCEPRTTUU	buttercup
BCFFIKSTU	buff-stick
BCFHILLNU	bullfinch
BCFIKSUZZ	buck's fizz✧
BCFIMMORY	cymbiform
BCFIMOORR	cobriform
BCFLORSUW	scrub fowl

BCGHILNOT blotching
BCGHILNTU nightclub
BCGHORSSU scrog-bush
BCGIIMNNO combining
BCGIKRSUV Vicksburg
BCGILMNSU scumbling
BCGKNOPRU prongbuck
BCGNOOOTT bog cotton
BCGNOORTU Croton bug
BCGORSSSU scrog-buss
BCHHIIISU shibuichi
BCHHIKSSU buckshish
BCHIILLNY chilly bin
BCHIIOPRS bishopric
BCHIIRSTU hubristic
BCHIKLOPS blockship
BCHIKLSUY buckishly
BCHILOOPY lyophobic
BCHINORTY Brythonic
BCHKNORSU buck's-horn
BCHKNORTU buckthorn
BCHKOOTTU bucktooth
BCHLNOOPU bolo punch
BCHLNOPUW punchbowl
BCHLOOOSY schoolboy
BCHLOORTW blowtorch
BCHLOTUUY youth club
BCHMOOOTT toothcomb
BCIIIMRST Briticism
BCIIKKLNR brick-kiln
BCIILMSUU umbilicus
BCIILPSTU publicist
BCIILPTUY publicity
BCIILRTUY lubricity
BCIIMMNOR born mimic
BCIIMNOOS bionomics
BCIIMOSTY symbiotic
BCIINORTT Brittonic
BCIIOOOTZ zoobiotic
BCIIOOPRT probiotic
BCIKKNOST knobstick
BCIKKNSSU buckskins
BCIKKORRW brickwork
BCIKLNOTT tint block
BCIKNNRSU Innsbruck
BCIKNOOOR Robin Cook
BCIKNOQRU quick-born
BCIKNRSUW Brunswick
BCILLORSS cross bill
crossbill
BCILLORSW crow's-bill
BCILMMOUU columbium
BCILMNOOZ zinc-bloom
BCILMOSSY symbolics
BCILMRSUU lumbricus
BCILORSUU lubricous
BCILPRSTU strip club
BCIMNOOOS sonic boom
BCIMNORSU submicron
BCIMOOTTU Timbuctoo
BCIOOPRSS proboscis
BCIOORSTT Octobrist
BCIOPRSTU subtropic
BCIORSTUY obscurity
BCIPRSSTU subscript
BCJKLOOSS joss-block
BCKKLOORW blockwork
BCKNORRTU burnt cork
burnt-cork
BCMNOOORR broom-corn
BCMOORSTU combustor
BCMOSSUUU submucous
BCOOSSTUY Boy Scouts
BCRSSTTUU substruct
BDDDEEINR bedridden
BDDDEIIOS disbodied
BDDDEILOY Bo Diddley
BDDEEEINZ bedizened
BDDEEGIMN embedding
BDDEEGIRR Redbridge
BDDEEGIRS sedge bird
BDDEEGORX dredge-box
BDDEEIRSU debruised
BDDEELNNU unblended
BDDEELRRU de-blurred
BDDEENORT betrodden
BDDEENRRU underbred
BDDEEOPPR bedropped
BDDEEORTU redoubted
BDDEFILOW fiddle-bow
BDDEFINOR forbidden
BDDEFIORR forbidder
BDDEFLOOU blood-feud
BDDEFNOOW bed of down
BDDEGINRU unbridged
BDDEGLOOU doodlebug
BDDEHINOU hidebound
BDDEHLOOS bloodshed
BDDEIILLO Bill Oddie
BDDEIILNS blind side
blind-side
BDDEIISUV subdivide
BDDEILNNU unblinded
BDDEILNRU unbridled
BDDEILOPU double dip
double-dip
BDDEIMOSY disembody
BDDEINRSU disburden
BDDEIRSTU disturbed
BDDEKNOSU deskbound
desk-bound
BDDELNOOU unblooded
BDDELSUUY subduedly
BDDEMNORU odd number
BDDENNOUU unbounded
BDDENORUY underbody
BDDENOTUU undoubted
BDDENSUUU unsubdued
BDDFGIOOR God forbid
BDDFILLNO blindfold
BDDFMNOUU dumbfound
BDDHISSTU Buddhists
BDDIILRSW wild birds
BDDIIORWW widow bird
BDDILLORY dolly bird
BDDILNORW word-blind
BDDIMNORU mound-bird
BDDINNOUW windbound
BDDLOOOOW bloodwood
BDDLOOSTU blood-dust
BDDNOORUW wordbound
BDDNOOSUY sound body
BDDNOTUUY duty-bound
BDEEEELRV belvedere
BDEEEENNS benne-seed
BDEEEESTT bed-settee
BDEEEFINT benefited
BDEEEGHOT hedge-bote
BDEEEGLUW bugle-weed
BDEEEGRSY by degrees
BDEEEHNST sheet bend
BDEEEHTTW wet the bed
BDEEEINNS benni-seed
BDEEEIOTW woe betide
BDEEELNOS nosebleed
BDEEELORT dor-beetle
BDEEELSTT settle-bed
BDEEEMMNT embedment
BDEEENRTU debenture
BDEEERRRY deerberry
BDEEERSTW bestrewed
BDEEERTTV brevetted
BDEEFIILS disbelief
BDEEFILRT filter bed
BDEEFIORR fire-robed
BDEEFLLOW bedfellow
BDEEFLORW flower-bed
BDEEFOORR foreboder
BDEEFOOTW webfooted
BDEEGGLOW bow-legged
BDEEGHILL hedgebill
BDEEGHINT benedight
benighted
BDEEGHNOR hedge-born
BDEEGILLN debelling
BDEEGINOR ridge bone
BDEEGMRSU submerged
BDEEGOORU bodeguero
BDEEHILPS bedelship
BDEEHIORT bodhi tree
BDEEHNOTY the beyond✧
BDEEHORTT betrothed
BDEEIILLN indelible
BDEEIILOS biodiesel
BDEEIILRS derisible
BDEEIINNZ benzidine
BDEEIKLNR blinkered
BDEEILLRW bridewell
BDEEILLUV blue devil
BDEEILMSS dissemble
BDEEILRTV belt drive
drive belt
BDEEIMMRS dismember

BDEEIMORR embroider
BDEEINORT bonetired
BDEEINOSS sidebones
BDEEINOTT debit note
BDEEINRRT interbred
BDEEINRTU underbite
BDEEINTUY Debye unit
BDEEIORRR broiderer
BDEEIOTUV video tube
BDEEIPRSW spider web
BDEEIRSTT bedsitter
BDEEKNRUU unrebuked
BDEEKOORW brookweed
BDEELLSSY blessedly
BDEELNOUV unbeloved
BDEELNRRU blunderer
BDEELNSSU unblessed
BDEELOORT blootered
BDEELORST bolstered
BDEEMPPSU speed bump
BDEEMRSSU submersed
BDEEMSTTU besmutted
BDEENNOOY beyond one
BDEEOPSTT bespotted
BDEEORSTY oyster-bed
BDEEORVYY everybody
BDEEPRRTU perturbed
BDEFFLNOU bundle off
BDEFGILRY flybridge
BDEFIILRR rifle bird
BDEFIIRTU brutified
BDEFIKLOO field book
BDEFILLOO lifeblood
BDEFILLSU self-build
BDEFILNOO blood-fine
BDEFILRTU flute-bird
BDEFINORY boyfriend
BDEFIOORW wood fibre
BDEFIRTTU drift tube
BDEFLLORU full-orbed
BDEFLORUW flower-bud
BDEFLOSTU self-doubt
BDEGGGINU debugging
BDEGGHMUU humbugged
BDEGGINTU budgeting
BDEGGNUUY dune-buggy
BDEGHILNO beholding
BDEGHILNR Lindbergh
BDEGHILSU shield bug
BDEGHINRU Edinburgh
BDEGIIILR dirigible
BDEGIILOS disoblige
BDEGIIMMN bedimming
BDEGIIPPR big dipper✧
BDEGIKOOU guidebook
BDEGILNNY bendingly
BDEGIMNOY embodying
BDEGINNNU unbending
BDEGINOSS debossing
BDEGINSSU debussing
BDEGIORRX box girder
BDEGLLOOU double-log
BDEGLNOOY golden boy
BDEGLOOOR gore-blood
BDEGMMTUU mum-budget
BDEGMOSUX smudge box
BDEGORSUW budgerows
BDEHIIINT inhibited
BDEHIIRSY hybridise
BDEHIIRYZ hybridize
BDEHILNRU Brunhilde
BDEHINORY honey-bird
BDEHINRRY hindberry
BDEHIORRS shorebird
BDEHIORSU bird-house
BDEHLLOSY bodyshell
BDEHLMNUU unhumbled
BDEHMNOOU homebound
BDEHNOSTU South Bend
BDEHNOTUY bountyhed
BDEHNRSUU unbrushed
underbush
BDEHORTWY bed-worthy
BDEIIILSV divisible
BDEIIILTY edibility
BDEIILLNY indelibly
BDEIILSTV devil's-bit
BDEIINOSU sine dubio
BDEIIRTTU turbidite
BDEIISSSU subsidise
BDEIISSUZ subsidize
BDEIKLLRR kerb drill
BDEILLNOO bloodline
BDEILLNPS spellbind
BDEILLNSS blindless
BDEILMNOW Wimbledon
BDEILMOOR Dormobile®
BDEILMPRU plume-bird
BDEILMSSY dissembly
BDEILNNSS blindness
BDEILNRSU Dubliners
BDEILOOTW blood-wite
BDEILOQTU quodlibet
BDEILORRV bird-lover
BDEILORSU bird-louse
BDEILORUV overbuild
BDEIMNOST disentomb
BDEIMORSU mousebird
BDEIMSTTU submitted
BDEINNORW windborne
BDEINOOST do one's bit
BDEINORTX tinderbox
BDEINORTZ Trebizond
BDEINOSST dib-stones
BDEINOSTU sound bite
soundbite
BDEINRSST bird's-nest
BDEINRSSU sideburns
BDEINRSUU unbruised
BDEINRTUW winter bud
BDEINRUZZ unbrizzed
BDEIOORRW brier-wood
BDEIORSTU subeditor
BDEIPRSTU buprestid
BDEIRRSSU disburser
BDEIRRSTU disturber
BDEIRRSUV bus-driver
BDEIRSTTY bide tryst
BDEKOOORR order book
BDEKOOOTU booked-out
BDELLMOSY symbolled
BDELLMOUU blue mould
BDELLMRUY drum-belly
BDELLNOSU bull-nosed
BDELLOORS bordellos
BDELLOOSS bloodless
BDELLOPUW Bud Powell
BDELLORUZ bulldozer
BDELMNPUU unplumbed
BDELMNTUU untumbled
BDELMRTUY tumble-dry
BDELNNRUU unbundler
BDELNNTUU unblunted
BDELNOOTU doubleton
BDELNOSSU boundless
BDELNOTTU unblotted
BDELNOTUU bundle out
BDELOOPRU pure-blood
BDELOOPTU double top
BDELOOPTY blood type
BDELOOSTT blood test
BDELOOTUV obvoluted
BDELOOUUY double-you
BDELOPRSU superbold
BDELORRWY blow-dryer
BDELORSTW sword-belt
BDELOSSTU doubtless
BDEMMNOSU ombudsmen✧
BDEMNOOTT bottom end
BDENNOOST bondstone
BDENNOPUU upbounden
BDENNOSSU snub-nosed
BDENNOTTU obtundent
BDENNRSUU sunburned
BDENOORUV overbound
BDENORSUU burdenous
BDENORTUU burned out
BDENOSTUW westbound
BDEOOOPTT top-booted
BDEOOORRV brood over
BDEOOORRW wood-borer
BDEOOPRWX powder box
BDEOPRTUY dub poetry
BDEORSSTU sodbuster
BDFHIILNS blindfish
BDFHNOOOU hoof-bound
BDFHOORTY body forth
BDFIIINOR fibrinoid
BDFILORTT drift-bolt
BDFIOORST birdsfoot
BDFIORTUY fruit body
BDFLLLOOU full-blood
BDFLLNOUU full-bound

BDFLOOORU foul-brood
BDFOOOTUY out-of-body
BDGGILOOY Golgi body
BDGHIINRT nightbird
BDGIILLNO ill-boding
BDGIINNNU unbinding
BDGILNOOY bloodying
BDGINNORW bring down
BDGINORTU obtruding
BDGMNOORU bongo drum
BDHIIMRSY hybridism
BDHIIRRTY trihybrid
BDHIIRTYY hybridity
BDHIMOOPS bishopdom
BDHINOOOR Robin Hood
BDHINORRT thornbird
BDHIORSUY hybridous
BDHKOOORU Doukhobor
BDHKOORSU Dukhobors
BDHLOOOST bloodshot
BDHOORSUW brushwood
BDHRSSTUU dust-brush
BDIIILSVY divisibly
BDIIINNRU indirubin
BDIIKNOSS 'sbodikins
BDIIKNOST sit bodkin
BDIIKNRST stinkbird
BDIILRSTT stiltbird
BDIIMORTY morbidity
BDIINOSUU indubious
BDIIOSTUY dubiosity
BDIIRTTUY turbidity
BDIKKNRSU skunkbird
BDIKNORUV Dubrovnik
BDILLORSW swordbill
BDILMNNOO moonblind
BDILMNORW blindworm
BDILNNOSW snow-blind
BDILNNOWW windblown
BDILNOOSU soil-bound
BDILNOPST blind spot
BDILOOPST spit blood
BDILOSUUY dubiously
BDIMORRST stormbird
BDINNOORU iron-bound
BDINNOPUU bound up in
BDINNRTUW windburnt
BDINOOWWW bow window
BDINOOWWX window box
BDIORRSTU subtorrid
BDLLOOOWY Bollywood
BDLLOOSTU bloodlust
BDLMOOORW bloodworm
BDLMOOSUY molybdous
BDLNOOPSU Lob's pound
BDLNOORRY Lord Byron
BDLOOOORT bloodroot
BDLOOSSUU subdolous
BDMNOOOOR doornboom
BDMNORTUU B rotundum
BDNNOORRY brondyron
BDNNOOSUW snowbound
BDNNSTUUY dust bunny
BDNOOORTU rootbound
BDNOOSTUU outbounds
BDNORSTUW downburst
BEEEEEKPR beekeeper
BEEEEHNRS shebeener
BEEEEILNV bien élevé
BEEEEKMRW Ember-week
BEEEELLMR belle-mère
BEEEFFLOT beetle off
BEEEFGLOR leg before
BEEEFHILT the belief
BEEEFILOV beef olive
BEEEFLNOS be oneself
BEEEFLORW bee-flower
BEEEGGRUZ Zeebrugge
BEEEGIKLL bilge keel
BEEEGIMNS beseeming
BEEEGLNRT green belt
BEEEGLNRU blue-green
BEEEGLTUX Betelgeux
BEEEGNNOR green-bone
BEEEGNOOW woebegone
BEEEGNOTW go between
go-between
BEEEGRSTU guest beer
BEEEHHLMT Bethlehem
BEEEHLLOR hellebore
BEEEHLPSU blue sheep
BEEEHLRRT bletherer
BEEEHLRTT Ethelbert
BEEEHNOTV Beethoven
BEEEHORSU beer house
BEEEHPRRT herb Peter
BEEEHRSSW Hebrewess
BEEEIILNV believe in
BEEEIKLLR rebel-like
BEEEILLOT oil beetle
BEEEILMMS emblemise
BEEEILMMZ emblemize
BEEEILMNT belemnite
BEEEILNUV unbelieve
BEEEILRRV River Elbe
BEEEILRSV eversible
BEEEIMMSS misbeseem
BEEEIMRSV semibreve
BEEEINNTW in-between
BEEEINORT bête noire
BEEEINRSS beeriness
BEEEISTUV sieve tube
BEEEJKORS jobseeker✧
BEEEKOPRX boxkeeper
BEEEKORRT Robert Kee
BEEEKRRRS berserker
BEEELLMRU blue merle
BEEELLSTU steel-blue
BEEELMNTV bevelment
BEEELMRRS resembler
BEEELMRZZ embezzler
BEEELPRTU Blue Peter
BEEELSSSU sublessee
BEEEMNORY beer money
BEEEMNSTT besetment
BEEEMPRST September
BEEENORST tenebrose
BEEENOSSS obeseness
BEEENOSXZ sneeze box
BEEENRRSY neesberry
BEEFFGIRU febrifuge
BEEFFHLUW buff-wheel
BEEFFORTT better off
BEEFFOSTW web offset
BEEFGIILR Félibrige
BEEFGLOST self-begot
BEEFHLOUV behoveful
BEEFHLRTY The Belfry
BEEFHOTTT theft-bote
BEEFIILMS misbelief
BEEFILRSS briefless
fiberless
fibreless
BEEFINRSS briefness
BEEFIRRTU fruit beer
BEEFKLRUU rebukeful
BEEFLNNUW funnel-web
BEEFLNOSY by oneself
BEEFLORTW left bower
BEEFNNRUU unberufen
BEEFNORTU befortune
BEEFOORTY freebooty
BEEGGIINS besieging
BEEGGINTT begetting
BEEGGNRTU Gutenberg
BEEGHIILN Ghibeline
BEEGHINNT benighten
BEEGHINRT benighter
BEEGHIRTY eyebright
BEEGIILLL illegible
BEEGIILNV believing
BEEGIIMNN mining bee
BEEGIINOT Gibeonite
BEEGILLNR rebelling
BEEGILLNV bevelling
BEEGILLNW wellbeing
BEEGILNNN Nigel Benn
BEEGILNRS inselberg
BEEGILNSS beingless
BEEGILNUU unbeguile
BEEGILPRS Spielberg
BEEGINNSS beingness
BEEGINRTT bettering
BEEGINRTV breveting
BEEGINSST beestings
BEEGINSTT besetting
BEEGKLNTU kent-bugle
BEEGKORRS go berserk
BEEGLNOOS bolognese✧
BEEGMNRRU Nuremberg
BEEGMSTUY be my guest
BEEGNRSUV Venusberg
BEEHIINRS hibernise

BEEHIINRZ hibernize
BEEHIIRTX exhibiter
BEEHIKRRS Berkshire
BEEHILLMS embellish
BEEHILMPU humble pie
humble-pie
BEEHILNOR heliborne
BEEHILTUZ Buthelezi
BEEHIMRSW Hebrewism
BEEHINRTT terebinth
BEEHIOPRS biosphere
BEEHIORRS herborise
BEEHIORRV herbivore
BEEHIORRZ herborize
BEEHIRRRT rebirther
BEEHJKLNO John Keble
BEEHLLRSU busheller
BEEHLLTTU the bullet
BEEHLMSSU humblesse
BEEHLOPRY hyperbole
BEEHLOTTT the bottle
BEEHMORUY homebuyer
BEEHNNOOT on the bone
BEEHNOOPX xenophobe
BEEHNOOTT to the bone
BEEHOOPRU Europhobe
BEEHOOSTU house-bote
BEEHORSUW brew-house
BEEHORTWY the Bowery
BEEIILLNZ zibelline
BEEIILNNT intenible
BEEIILNRT libertine
BEEIILRST liberties
BEEIINRTY inebriety
BEEIKLMRU berkelium
BEEIKLMRY Kimberley
BEEIKLRTU brutelike
BEEIKLSSU blue-skies
BEEIKOSTV Steve Biko
BEEIKPRSU superbike
BEEILLNOR rebellion
BEEILLNTU ebullient
BEEILLORT bolletrie
BEEILLRTU bulletrie
rubellite
BEEILMNPU numble-pie
BEEILMNSS nimblesse
BEEILMOUV blue movie
BEEILMPRU lumber-pie
BEEILMRRT tremblier
BEEILMRTT embrittle
BEEILNNOZ benzoline
BEEILNOPX exponible
BEEILNOSS nobilesse
BEEILNPRU prenubile
BEEILNRSU blue rinse
blue-rinse
nebuliser
BEEILNRUZ nebulizer
BEEILORSV brisé volé
BEEILOTTU oubliette
BEEILPRST bel esprit
BEEILRRSV vers libre
BEEILRSST tribeless
BEEILSTUV vestibule
BEEIMNNNO bonne mine
BEEIMNRST tenebrism
BEEIMRRSU reimburse
BEEINNOTT bentonite
BEEINNRST Bernstein
BEEINNRTU inner tube
BEEINORST tenebrios
BEEINRRWY wineberry
BEEINRSTT tenebrist
BEEINRSTU subentire
Trubenise
BEEINRTTU butterine
BEEINRTTY tenebrity
BEEINRTUZ Trubenize®
BEEIOQSSU obsequies
BEEIORRRV River Ebro
BEEIOSSSV obsessive
BEEIQRTTU briquette
BEEIRRTTU retribute
BEEIRSSSU subseries
BEEISSTTV St Tib's Eve
BEEJNRRUY Juneberry
BEEJOOSST Jesse Boot
BEEJOSSTV Steve Jobs
BEEKLRRSY berserkly
BEEKLRRUY Kerry blue
BEEKNOPSU unbespoke
BEEKNORST kerbstone
BEEKOPRRY pokeberry
BEELLLMUU umbellule
BEELLORRW well-borer
BEELLORSU resoluble
re-soluble
BEELLORTW bell tower
BEELLRTUY bully-tree
BEELMNORU Melbourne
BEELMNOTY money belt
BEELMOORT bolometer
BEELMORST temblores
BEELMRRSU slumberer
BEELNNOSS nobleness
BEELNOORS rose noble
BEELNOPSU spulebone
BEELNOSTU bluestone
BEELORSVY obversely
verbosely
BEELORTTX letterbox
BEELOSSTU boletuses
BEELQRSUU burlesque
BEELRRSTU blusterer
BEELRSTTU subletter
BEEMMNNOR non-member
BEEMNNORU number one
BEEMNNRTU Number Ten
BEEMNORST bemonster
Mrs Beeton
BEEMNRTTU rebutment
BEEMOPRRY pre-embryo
BEENNOOTU boutonnée
BEENNOTUV ben venuto
BEENOQSTU obsequent
BEENORRST resorbent
BEENORSSS soberness
BEENORSTU tenebrous
BEENORSUU eburneous
BEENRSSTU bruteness
BEENRSTUU subtenure
BEEOORRSW boerewors
BEEOPPPRX pepper box
BEEOPPRSY presbyope
BEEORSSUU subereous
BEEORSTTU soubrette
BEEORSTTY streetboy
BEEPRRRTU perturber
BEEPRRSTY presbyter
BEERRSTUV subverter
BEFFGINTU buffeting
BEFFHINTU in the buff
BEFFHIOTT off the bit
BEFFIILLR fibrefill
BEFFINOTT bitten off
BEFFLNSSU bluffness
BEFFLOOTT bottle off
BEFFMNORU number off
BEFGHILOS globe fish
BEFGIINTT befitting
BEFGILNSU fungibles
BEFGLNRSU Flensburg
BEFHIRRSU brush fire
furbisher
refurbish
BEFHKLOOS bookshelf
BEFHOOTTT theftboot
BEFIILNOR fibroline
BEFIILNSU infusible
BEFIILORT fibrolite
BEFIILRTY febrility
BEFILLSTU self-built
BEFILNOOR foilborne
BEFILNTTY fly-bitten
BEFILRWYY fly-by-wire
BEFINOPRU ibuprofen
BEFIORSTT frostbite
BEFLLLOPY belly flop
belly-flop
BEFLLLSUU full blues
BEFLLOTTU bottleful
BEFLORRWY wolfberry
BEFLRTTUY butterfly
BEFNNNOUY funny bone
BEFOORSUW subwoofer
BEGGGGINO go begging
BEGGGILNY beggingly
BEGGGLOOX goggle-box
BEGGHMRUU humbugger
BEGGIINNN beginning
BEGGIINOO boogieing
BEGGINOSS bogginess

BEGGIOORV go over big
BEGGJLOOS Joe Bloggs
BEGHHILST high-blest
BEGHHINOT thigh bone
BEGHHOTTU bethought
BEGHIILLP phillibeg
BEGHIIRRT bier right
BEGHIIRTT big hitter
BEGHIIRTV give birth
BEGHILLNT night-bell
BEGHIMNOR bring home
BEGHINORT night-robe
BEGHINORU neighbour
BEGHINTTU butt hinge
BEGHIORSU brogueish
BEGHLNORU bugle-horn
BEGHNRTUU bug-hunter
BEGHOORTT borghetto
BEGHORRUX Roxburghe
BEGIIILNT ignitible
BEGIILLLN libelling
BEGIILLLY illegibly
BEGIILLNT billeting
BEGIIMNRT timbering
BEGIINNTY benignity
BEGIINSST biestings
BEGIINSTT besitting
BEGIJRTTU jitterbug
BEGILLNOW bowelling
BEGILLOTU globulite
BEGILMNOS Mel Gibson
BEGILMNRT trembling
BEGILMNRU lumbering
BEGILMOOR embroglio
BEGILMORY gorblimey
BEGILMPPU bilge-pump
BEGILMRRU Limburger
BEGILNNNO ennobling
BEGILNSSU bulginess
BEGILRSTW W S Gilbert
BEGILRTTU litterbug
BEGIMNOSS embossing
BEGIMNSSU embussing
BEGINOOSS besognios
BEGINOOSU biogenous
BEGINORRV bring over
BEGINORSU subregion
BEGINORSV observing
BEGINOSTT besotting
BEGINRTTU rebutting
BEGIOORSU bourgeois
BEGLLOPUY go belly up
BEGLMORTY bog myrtle
BEGLOORTT globe-trot
BEGNOOORX orgone box
BEGPRRSSU Pressburg
BEHHLLORT hell-broth
BEHHLMOTU thumb hole
BEHHMOOOP homophobe
BEHHORSSU shoe brush
BEHHOSSUU bush-house
BEHHOSTUW who but she
BEHIIINRT inhibiter
BEHIILPST phlebitis
BEHIILRTV live birth
BEHIIMNOY yohimbine
BEHIIORTX exhibitor
BEHIIRRST Britisher
BEHIIRSTT bitterish
BEHIKLMTU thumblike
BEHIKLOSV bolshevik✧
BEHIKLRSU shrublike
BEHIKOOTW white book
BEHILLNNY Benny Hill
BEHILLNTY thin-belly
BEHILMNRU rhumb line
BEHILNOOT on the boil
BEHILNOPS bisphenol
BEHILNORS Niels Bohr
BEHILNORW whirl bone
BEHILNSUW blush wine
BEHILPRSU publisher
republish
BEHIMMNOO bonhommie
BEHIMRRWY whimberry
BEHINRRSU burnisher
BEHINRRWY whinberry
BEHINSSSU bushiness
BEHIOPSSS bishopess
BEHIORRST herborist
BEHIORRVY herbivory
BEHIORSTT theorbist
BEHIRRSTT Herb Ritts
BEHIRRSUW wire brush
BEHJNNORY Johnny Reb
BEHJNORSU John Rebus
BEHKMOSSU smoke bush
BEHKNOSUU bunkhouse
BEHKSUVYY Kuybyshev
BEHLLSSSU blushless
BEHLMSSTU thumbless
BEHLOOTTU Bluetooth®
BEHLORRTY brotherly
BEHLORSST throbless
BEHLORSSU blush-rose
BEHLRSSSU shrubless
BEHMOOOOX homoeobox
BEHMOORST thrombose
BEHMORSSU rhombuses
BEHNNORTU Bunthorne
BEHNNRTUU unburthen
BEHNOOORT on the broo
BEHNOOPXY xenophoby
BEHNORSTU buhrstone
BEHOOPTTU phototube
BEHOPRTYY bryophyte
BEIIILNSV invisible
BEIIKLLSS Bill Sikes
BEIILLNSY sibylline
BEIILMOPU epilobium
BEIILMORS mobiliser
BEIILMORZ mobilizer
BEIILMOSS omissible
BEIILMRSX ex-librism
BEIILMSSU sublimise
BEIILMSUZ sublimize
BEIILNRTT litter bin
BEIILOOPR periboloi
BEIILORTT trilobite
BEIILOTVZ Leibovitz
BEIILRSTX ex-librist
BEIILSSTU subtilise
BEIILSTUZ subtilize
BEIINNRSS brininess
BEIINOOVV ovibovine
BEIINORSU inebrious
BEIINRTTU Tribunite
BEIIORSST sorbitise
BEIIORSTY ebriosity
BEIIORSTZ sorbitize
BEIIPRTTT bitter-pit
BEIJLLLOY Billy Joel
BEIKLMOOR brooklime
BEIKLNOTT ink-bottle
BEIKLNSSU bulkiness
BEIKLOORT robot-like
BEIKMOORT motorbike
BEIKNORRU Ernö Rubik
BEIKNOSSS boskiness
BEIKNRSSS briskness
BEIKRSTTU tube skirt
BEILLLOSU libellous
BEILLLTUW well-built
BEILLMNOY money bill
BEILLMNPU plumb line
BEILLMRUY beryllium
BEILLMSUY sublimely
BEILLNOSU insoluble
BEILLOQUY obliquely
BEILLRTTY brittlely
BEILLSSSS blissless
BEILMMNUU nelumbium
BEILMNOSW women's lib
BEILMOPTT bottle-imp
BEILMOSSY symbolise
BEILMOSYZ symbolize
BEILNOPSS sponsible
BEILNORRU oil-burner
BEILNORTU in trouble
BEILNORTY On Liberty
BEILNPRTU blueprint
BEILNRSSU burliness
BEILOOPRS peribolos
BEILOOPRT potboiler
BEILOPRSU peribolus
BEILOPSSS possibles
BEILORSSU subsoiler
BEILORSTT librettos
BEILORTTU butter oil
BEILSSTTU subtitles
BEIMMNORR merbromin
BEIMNNRSU in numbers
BEIMNORST brimstone

BEIMNOSSU	omnibuses
BEIMNPSSU	bumpiness
BEIMOSSTW	misbestow
BEIMRSTTU	submitter
BEIMRTTUY	ytterbium
BEINNNOSS	bonniness
BEINNOOTT	obtention
BEINNOOTV	obvention
BEINNRSUW	Swinburne
BEINOOPRT	obreption
BEINOORSS	biosensor
BEINOORSV	obversion
BEINOOSSS	obsession
BEINOOSSZ	booziness
BEINORSST	Britoness
BEINORSUU	rubineous
BEINORUVV	bon viveur
BEINOSSSS	bossiness
BEINOTTWY	bytownite
BEINRRSUU	rus in urbe
BEINRSSUU	subursine
BEIOOPRRU	pourboire
BEIOORRRT	brier-root
BEIOPRSTU	bite or sup
BEIOPTTTU	Pitot tube
BEIOQRSTU	sobriquet
BEIORSSST	sob sister
BEIORSTUV	obtrusive
BEIORSTVY	verbosity
BEIPRSSTU	Buprestis
BEIPRSTUY	superbity
BEIRRSTUW	bierwurst
BEJLNOORW	jobernowl
BEJNNNOOS	Ben Jonson
BEKKNOOOT	book token
BEKLMOORS	Mel Brooks
BEKLOOOSU	booklouse
BEKLOOSTY	stylebook
BEKNNNOUW	unbeknown
BEKOOORST	bookstore
BEKOOPRSS	press book
BELLMOOSS	bloomless
BELLMPRUU	plumb rule
BELLMPSSU	plumbless
BELLOOTWY	welly-boot
BELLOOWYY	yellow-boy
BELMMOOSS	emblossom
BELMNOOPR	no problem
BELMNOOST	most noble
BELMOOORW	elbow-room
BELMOORSS	reblossom
BELMOORTY	bolometry
BELMOOTTY	Bottomley
BELMOPSUU	plumbeous
BELMORSTT	storm belt
BELMOSSXY	sex symbol
BELNNSSTU	bluntness
BELNOORVW	overblown
BELNOOTVV	obvolvent
BELNRTTUU	turbulent
BELOOTTTU	bottle out
BELOOTTTW	two-bottle
BELOPPPUY	blue poppy
BELOPRSTU	bolster up
BELOPRSUW	Super Bowl®
BELORSSSU	sublessor
BELQRSUUY	brusquely
BEMMNSTUU	submentum
BEMNOORSU	unbosomer
BEMNOOSTT	tombstone
BEMNORTUU	outnumber
BEMNORTUW	number two
BEMNOSSUX	buxomness
BEMOOPRRY	proembryo
BEMOORRSS	sombreros
BEMRRTTUU	rum butter
BEMSSSTUY	subsystem
BENNNOSTU	sun bonnet
BENNORSSW	brownness
BENOOSTUU	bounteous
BENOPSTTU	subpotent
BENORRSTU	burrstone
BENORRSWY	snowberry
BENORSTTU	obstruent
BENORSTXY	sentry box
BENRRRTUY	Turnberry
BENRTTTUU	butternut
	nutbutter
BEOOPRSTY	poster boy
BEOOPSTTX	set-top box
BEOPPRSYY	presbyopy
BFFIIMORR	fibriform
BFGHILLTU	bullfight
BFGIIJLNY	flying jib
BFGIINRUY	rubifying
BFGLORSUW	Wolfsburg
BFGNOORSU	Bofors gun
BFHHIORRT	frithborh
BFHIRSTUU	bush-fruit
BFIIILLNR	fibrillin
BFIILMORY	myofibril
BFIINORSU	fibrinous
BFILNOTUU	bountiful
BFIMORRSU	bursiform
BFINORRST	first-born
BFJKOOORW	job of work
BFLLLNOUW	full-blown
BFLLOORTU	flour bolt
BFMMOOORR	bromoform
BFOORTUWY	four-by-two
	two-by-four
BGGHIILNT	blighting
BGGILLNUY	bulgingly
BGGILMNRU	grumbling
BGGINOSUY	Guy Gibson
BGHHILNOW	high-blown
BGHHIOOTT	thigh boot
BGHIINRST	birth sign
BGHILMNTU	thumbling
BGHILOPRU	rib-plough
BGHIMNRTU	thumb ring
BGHINORTU	inbrought
BGHINRSTU	sunbright
BGHLOOPUY	ploughboy
BGHOPRTUU	upbrought
BGHORRSUU	Burroughs
BGIIIKPRR	Kirbigrip®
	kirbigrip
BGIIIMNNO	biomining
BGIIKPRRY	kirby grip
BGIILLNOW	billowing
BGIILMNSU	subliming
BGIILMOOR	imbroglio
BGIILNRST	bristling
BGIILOOST	biologist
BGIIMNRUY	minirugby
BGIINNNRU	inburning
BGIKNOPRS	springbok✧
BGILLNSTU	stingbull
BGILMNNUY	numbingly
BGILMNOOY	myoglobin
BGILNNRUY	bunny girl✧
	burningly
BGILNORTU	troubling
BGILNORTW	wring bolt
BGILNUYZZ	buzzingly
BGILOORTY	tribology
BGILOOSTY	globosity
BGINNORTU	binturong
BGINNPRUU	upburning
BGINOORRW	borrowing
BGINOPRSX	box spring
	spring box
BGINORSTW	bowstring
BGLLOOSUU	globulous
BGLMOOPUY	bumpology
BGLMOOSYY	symbology
BGLNNORUW	brown lung
BGNOORSTX	strongbox
BGNOOTUYY	Toby Young
BGNORSTUW	bowstrung
BHHIMORTY	biorhythm
BHHIRSSTU	bush shirt
BHHNORSTU	thornbush
BHIIINORT	inhibitor
BHIIKLMPY	Kim Philby
BHIILLLLY	hillbilly
BHIILLNOT	billionth
BHIILLPRT	birth pill
BHIIMORUZ	rhizobium
BHIINRSTU	un-British
BHIINRTTW	twin birth
BHIKMNSTU	thumbkins
BHIKNNSUU	shubunkin
BHIKNOOSU	unbookish
BHILLLSUY	bullishly
BHILLNORT	thornbill
BHILMNOTY	bimonthly
BHILMOOPR	ombrophil
BHILOORSY	boorishly
BHILOPSTU	bush pilot
BHILRSTUY	brutishly
BHIMOOSTY	tomboyish

BHIMOOTTT hit bottom
BHIORRTTW birthwort
BHIOSWYZZ showbizzy
BHJOORSTW jobsworth
BHKMNOTTU thumb knot
BHKORRSUW brushwork
BHLLLOORS loll-shrob
BHLLOOOTT tollbooth
BHLMPSUUY subphylum
BHMNOOOSU bonhomous
BHNOORSTW snow-broth
BHNOOTTTU hot button
BIIILNSVY invisibly
BIIINQTUU ubiquitin
BIIIORSSV vibriosis
BIIKNNRSY skinny-rib
BIILLOSUY biliously
BIILLSSTY Sibyllist
BIILMSTUY sublimity
BIILOOSUV oblivious
BIILOQTUY obliquity
BIIMMNORS brominism
BIIMNOORR Borromini
BIIMNRSTU Tribunism
BIIMOPRTY improbity
BIIMOSSSY symbiosis
BIINSSSTU subsist in
BIISSTTYY itsy-bitsy
BIITTTTYY itty-bitty
BIKLNNOSW snowblink
BILLNOOPS spoonbill
BILLNOPTU bull point
BILLNORST stillborn
BILLNOSUY insolubly
BILLOPSTU slop-built
BILMMOSSY symbolism✧
BILMOORST Stromboli
BILMOQSTV Blomqvist
BILMOSSTY symbolist
BILMSSSUY submissly
BILNNOTUU unbuilt-on
BILOOPRTU Politburo
BILOOSUVY obviously
BILORSSTU strobilus
BIMNOPSSU mons pubis
BIMNORSTY brimstony
BIMNORTTU Tim Burton
BIMOPSTUU bumptious
BINOOOSUX obnoxious
BINOORSST Sorbonist
BINOORSTU obtrusion
BINOOSTVY Boston ivy
BINOOSUUV unobvious
BIOOPRRTW borrow pit
BIOORSTUV boot virus
BKLLMNSUU numbskull
BKLLOORUY bully-rook
BKMOORUUZ zumbooruk
BKOOORSTY storybook
BLLLOOSUW bull's wool
BLLORTTUU bull trout
BLMORSSUU slumbrous
BLOORSTUU troublous
BLORSSTUU blustrous
BLRSTTUUW blutwurst
BLSSSTUUU subsultus
BMOOOTTTU bottom out
BMOOPPRTX prompt box
BMOOPSTTU bottoms up
BOOOORRSU ouroboros
BOOPPRRTU turboprop

C

CCCCILNOY concyclic
CCCDIIMOU coccidium
CCCEEILST eclectics
CCCEEINRT eccentric
CCCEELLLY cell cycle
CCCEIILPY epicyclic
CCCEIINOR Ciceronic
CCCEILOOT coccolite
CCCENOORT concocter
CCCGINOOO gonococci
CCCHHIKOT Hitchcock
CCCHIINNO cinchonic
CCCHIKNOP pinchcock
CCCHILMOU colchicum
CCCHILOOT coccolith
CCCIILMSY cyclicism
CCCIILNOZ zinc colic
CCCIILOSY isocyclic
CCCIILRTY tricyclic
CCCIILTYY cyclicity
CCCIOORSS siroccos
CCCNOOORT concoctor
CCDDEKOUY decoy-duck
CCDDELNOU concluded
CCDEEEHKR checkered
CCDEEEINS decencies
CCDEEERSU succeeder
CCDEEHIKM chemicked
CCDEEHIKW chickweed
CCDEEHKNU unchecked
CCDEEHORT crocheted
CCDEEIINN incidence
CCDEEIINT endeictic
CCDEEINNY indecency
CCDEEINOT conceited
CCDEEINSU succeed in
CCDEEIOPR Price Code
CCDEEIOTV decoctive
CCDEEKNOS scene dock
CCDEELLOT collected
CCDEEMOOR coco-de-mer
CCDEENNOR concerned
CCDEENNOT connected
CCDEENORS crescendo
CCDEENORT concerted
CCDEEORTU decocture
CCDEFIIRU crucified
CCDEHIIOR De Chirico
CCDEIIKNP picnicked
CCDEIILPR dip-circle
CCDEIKLNU uncle Dick✧
CCDEILOOR crocodile
CCDEILOOS scolecoid
CCDEILSTY dyslectic
CCDEIMOOR microcode
CCDEINOOT decoction
CCDEINOUV conducive
CCDEINRTU cinctured
CCDEISTTY dystectic
CCDEKORSS dock-cress
CCDELNOTU occludent
CCDENORRU concurred
CCDHHIRSU dischurch
CCDHIIMOR dichromic
CCDHIKLLO child lock
CCDHKOOUW woodchuck
CCDIILNRY cylindric
CCDIIOORT corticoid
CCDIIOPST optic disc
CCDKKLNOO knock cold
CCDKLLOUY cuckoldly
CCDKLMOOU cuckoldom
CCDKLORUY cuckoldry
CCDNOORTU conductor
CCDNOSTUU conductus
CCDOOOSUW cocuswood
CCEEEFLNU feculence
CCEEEHHRR recherché
CCEEEHNOR coherence
CCEEEHRRS screecher
CCEEEIKNP neckpiece
CCEEEINNS nescience
CCEEEINRT reticence
CCEEELLOR clerecole
CCEEELORT rectocele
CCEEEMMOR e-commerce
CCEEFFOPU coffee cup
CCEEFHHRT cherchef't
CCEEFHKOR forecheck
CCEEFILLY life cycle
CCEEFLNUY feculency
CCEEGINOR concierge
CCEEGINOT ectogenic
CCEEGINTY cynegetic
CCEEHIKNR checkrein
CCEEHIKOY ice hockey
CCEEHILMY hemicycle
CCEEHKNNS schnecken
CCEEHKORV overcheck
CCEEHLORT cerecloth
CCEEHNORY coherency
CCEEHORRT crocheter
CCEEHOTTU couchette
CCEEIINNS inscience
CCEEIIPPR precipice
CCEEIKRRT cricketer
CCEEILNNO on-licence
CCEEILNOR reconcile
CCEEILOST scolecite
CCEEILPRY pericycle

CCEEILRST electrics
CCEEIMNOU oecumenic
CCEEIMNSU ecumenics
CCEEINNNO innocence
CCEEINORS cicerones
CCEEINORT ectocrine
CCEEINRTX excentric
CCEEINRTY reticency
CCEEIRRST rectrices
CCEEIRSTT tectrices
CCEEJKOOR Joe Cocker
CCEELLORT recollect
re-collect
CCEELOSTY cystocele
CCEELOTUY leucocyte
CCEELPRSU crepuscle
CCEEMMORT T-commerce
CCEENNORT concenter
concentre
connecter
reconnect
CCEENOOTY coenocyte
CCEFFIIIL felicific
CCEFHILOU choiceful
CCEFHIOOR for choice
CCEFIIRRU crucifier
CCEFIKLLT left-click
CCEFKNOYY cockneyfy
CCEFOSSUU succès fou
CCEGGHOST Scotch egg
CCEGHIMRU chemurgic
CCEGIIKLN Cecil King
CCEGILOOO oecologic
CCEGINNOO oncogenic
CCEGINOPS pigsconce
CCEGINORY cryogenic
CCEGLNOSY song cycle
CCEHHILNO El Chichon
CCEHHKLOU chuckhole
CCEHHKRUY church key
CCEHHNRTU the crunch
CCEHHNRUW New Church
CCEHIKLLT check-till
CCEHIKLOO chokecoil
CCEHIKLST checklist
CCEHIKNNO no chicken
CCEHILNOR chronicle
CCEHILNPU cup lichen
CCEHILORU euchloric
CCEHILRTU hut-circle
CCEHINOSZ zecchinos
CCEHINRRU crunchier
CCEHINRSU scrunchie
CCEHIOOPR pro-choice
CCEHIORST orchestic
CCEHKLNOT neckcloth
CCEHKLORS schlocker
CCEHKMOOR checkroom
CCEHKOORS cockhorse
CCEHKOPRR rock perch
CCEHKOPST spot check
spot-check
CCEHLMOST Scotch elm
CCEHLOSTY cholecyst
CCEHLOTTU the occult
CCEHLPSUY push-cycle
CCEHNNOOS sconcheon
CCEHNNOSU scuncheon
CCEHNOSTU scutcheon
CCEHORTTY crotchety
CCEHOTTUZ zucchetto
CCEHRRTUY cutcherry
CCEIIIPRT epicritic
CCEIIIRST criticise
sericitic
CCEIIIRTZ criticize
CCEIIKNPR picnicker
CCEIILMST Celticism
CCEIILNOT niccolite
CCEIILNYZ cyclizine
CCEIILRTY clericity
CCEIILSTT Celticist
CCEIIMOPR epicormic
CCEIIMOSS coseismic
CCEIINORS crescioni
CCEIINRTW new critic
CCEIINSTU succinite
CCEIKLLOY kilocycle
CCEIKLMOT time clock
CCEIKLOSW clockwise
CCEIKNOSS cockiness
CCEILNOSY concisely
CCEILNOTY cyclonite
CCEILOOST sociolect
CCEILORST sclerotic
CCEILOSUV occlusive
CCEILRRTY tricycler
CCEILRSTY recyclist
CCEILSSUU Leuciscus
CCEIMNOOS economics
CCEIMNRUU curcumine
CCEIMORTY microcyte
CCEIMOSST cosmetics
CCEINNNOY innocency
CCEINNORT in concert
CCEINNORV convincer
CCEINNOST conscient
CCEINNOTT conticent
CCEINOOSS consocies
CCEINORRT incorrect
CCEINOSTT tectonics
CCEINPRST precincts
CCEINRSTY syncretic
CCEINSSTY synectics
CCEINSTTY syntectic
CCEIOPPRS porcpisce
CCEIOPRST cost price
CCEIOPRTY precocity
CCEKLOOUZ ouzel-cock
CCEKNOOPS scoop neck
CCEKORRSS rock cress
CCEKORRSW corkscrew
CCELLNOOY colonelcy
CCELLOORT collector
CCELMNOOY monocycle
CCELMOOTY colectomy
CCELNSTUU succulent
CCELOPRSU corpuscle
CCELOPSSY Cyclopses
CCELORRTY correctly
CCELORTUU coculture
CCENNNORU unconcern
CCENNOORT connector
CCENNOPTU connect up
CCENNOSTU concentus
CCENOOORY cocoonery
CCENOORST concertos
CCENOORSU concourse
CCENOORTV convector
CCENOPSTU conceptus
CCENORRTU occurrent
CCENORSTU succentor
CCENSSSUU unsuccess
CCEOOORSS Socceroos
CCEOOPRRV cover crop
CCEOOPRSY cryoscope
CCEOORRRT corrector
CCEOPPRUY preoccupy
CCEORRSUU succourer
CCEORSSSU successor
CCEOSSUUX exsuccous
CCFGHIKOT cockfight
CCFGKLLOO clock-golf
CCFHIINOO finocchio
CCFHIORST Scotch fir
CCFHKKORU fork-chuck
CCFHKLLOU chock-full
CCFHKLLUU chuck-full
CCFIILOOR colorific
CCFIMORRU cruciform
CCFINOSUU Confucius
CCFKLOOUY cuckoo fly
CCFKOOOST cocksfoot
CCFLLOSUU flocculus
CCFLOOOOS locofocos✧
CCGHHINOU chincough
CCGHHINRU churching
CCGHIIKLN chickling
CCGHIINPU hiccuping
CCGHIKLNU chuckling
CCGHILOOP chop logic
choplogic
CCGHINORS scorching
CCGHINSTU scutching
CCGIINOPP coppicing
CCGILLLOY glycollic
CCGILMOOY mycologic
CCGILNOTU occulting
CCGINNOOO cocooning
CCGINOPUY occupying
CCGINORRU occurring
CCGLLLOOY glycocoll
CCHHIIKKT hitch kick

Words marked ✧ can also be spelled with one or more capital letters

CCHHILLRU Churchill
CCHHIMRSU churchism
CCHHINUUU Chu'un Ch'iu
CCHHLORUW Low Church
CCHHOOPST hopscotch
CCHIIIRTT trichitic
CCHIILORT chloritic
trochilic
CCHIIMOPR microchip
CCHIINOOP Pinocchio
CCHIINOOR chorionic
CCHIINOST conchitis
CCHIINSUZ zucchinis
CCHIIOORS isochoric
CCHIIORRT cirrhotic
trichroic
CCHIKLLOO cook-chill
CCHIKOPST chopstick
CCHILLOTY cyclolith
CCHILNRUY crunchily
CCHILOORT chlorotic
CCHINNOOR cornichon
CCHINRSTY strychnic
CCHIOPSTY psychotic
CCHJKKOOS shock jock
CCHKNORSU corn shuck
CCHKOOOST cock-shoot
CCHKOOPSY chopsocky
CCHLNOOTY colocynth
CCHOORRSU Corchorus
CCIIILNOS isoclinic
CCIIILNRT triclinic
CCIIILOST silicotic
CCIIILOSU cilicious
CCIIIMRST criticism
CCIIINNOT nicotinic
CCIIKKNST nickstick
CCIIKKRST rickstick
CCIIKLLOP pillicock
CCIILLLOU colliculi
CCIILNNOU in council
CCIILNOTY clonicity
CCIILOOST scoliotic
CCIILOPRT proclitic
CCIIMOSST Scoticism
CCIINNNSU cincinnus
CCIINNOOS concision
CCIINOPSY isopycnic
CCIIORRTT tricrotic
CCIIOSSTT Scotistic
CCIIRRTUY circuitry
CCIKKORSS cross-kick
CCIKMORSU rock music
CCILMOSTU occultism
CCILNOOPY polyconic
CCILNOORU councilor
CCILNOOSU occlusion
CCILNOOTY oncolytic
CCILOOORT colicroot
CCILOORST colostric
CCILORSUU curculios
CCILOSTTU occultist
CCILOTTYY cytolytic
CCIMMOORS microcosm
CCIMOOPRY microcopy
CCINOOSSU conscious
CCINOPRST conscript
CCINOPSTY syncoptic
CCINORSTT constrict
CCIOOOPRZ coprozoic
CCIOOOPST otoscopic
CCIOOOPSZ zooscopic
CCIOOPRSU uroscopic
CCIOOTTXY cytotoxic
CCJKOOSTT Jock Scott
CCJKOOSYY cocky's joy
CCKKLOORW clockwork
CCKKLOOST stocklock
CCKKNOOPY knock copy
CCKKOORSS rock socks
CCKMOORST stormcock
CCKNOORRW crown cork
CCKOOPPPY poppycock
CCLNOORTY cyclotron
CCNORSTTU construct
CCOOOORRS corocoros
CCOOPRSYY cryoscopy
CCOOSTTUU tucotucos
CCOSTTUUU tucutucos
CDDDEEENS descended
CDDDEEILY decidedly
CDDDEEINU undecided
CDDDEILNO condiddle
CDDDELORS scroddled
CDDDENRUU uncrudded
CDDDKRUUY ruddy duck
CDDEEEFLT deflected
CDDEEEIIW weedicide
CDDEEENRS descender
redescend
CDDEEGLLU cudgelled
CDDEEHHIU cuddeehih
CDDEEHLSU scheduled
CDDEEIKRU eider duck
CDDEEILSY Clydeside
CDDEEISST dissected
CDDEEITUV deductive
CDDEEKNRU underdeck
CDDEELNOS closed-end
CDDEEMNNO condemned
CDDEEMNRU credendum
CDDEENNOS condensed
CDDEENRUU unreduced
CDDEENSUU unseduced
CDDEHIILP didelphic
CDDEHIJNU Judi Dench
CDDEHKLSU sheldduck
CDDEHORRT Dordrecht
CDDEIILMO domiciled
CDDEIINRT dendritic
CDDEIIOSV videodisc
CDDEIIRST discredit
CDDEILTUU dulcitude
CDDEIMOOU duodecimo
CDDEINOTU deduction
CDDEIOSUU deciduous
CDDELNOUU unclouded
CDDELNRUU uncurdled
CDDELOOOP opodeldoc
CDDENORUW uncrowded
CDDGHLOTU Dutch gold
CDDHHILOO childhood
CDDHIILLW wild child
CDDHIIORY hydriodic
CDDHIIQTU quidditch
CDDHINOOR chondroid
CDDHLLOTU Dutch doll
CDDILNOOY condyloid
CDDILORSW Discworld
CDEEEEFNR deer fence
deference
CDEEEEIRU idée reçue
CDEEEEKNW ewe-necked
CDEEEEPRR creepered
CDEEEFFOR force-feed
CDEEEFITV defective
CDEEEFLRT reflected
CDEEEFORW cowfeeder
CDEEEGINR decreeing
CDEEEGINX exceeding
CDEEEHKNP henpecked
CDEEEHKRT three-deck
CDEEEHNRU uncheered
CDEEEHORR decoherer
CDEEEHPRU upcheered
CDEEEHQRU chequered
CDEEEILRS sclereide
CDEEEIMRR remercied
CDEEEIMRT decimeter
decimetre
CDEEEINNS desinence
CDEEEINPT centipede
CDEEEINRS residence
CDEEEINRT intercede
CDEEEINUV undeceive
CDEEEIPTV deceptive
CDEEEIRST decistere
CDEEEIRTV decretive
CDEEEITTV detective
CDEEEKNTW 'tween-deck
CDEEELLNR crenelled
CDEEELLOT décolleté
CDEEELNOR redolence
CDEEELNTU unelected
CDEEELORT electrode
CDEEEMNRT decrement
CDEEEMNTU educement
CDEEENPRT precedent
CDEEEOPRR proceeder
CDEEEOPRU doucepere
CDEEEORRT retrocede
CDEEEPRST sceptered
CDEEFIILR rice field

CDEEFIIMR	mercifide
CDEEFIINT	deficient
CDEEFIIOT	foeticide
CDEEFIIPS	specified
CDEEFIIRT	certified
	rectified
CDEEFIKRR	Frederick
CDEEFILTU	deceitful
CDEEFILUV	deviceful
CDEEFINOT	defection
CDEEFIORT	fore-cited
CDEEFKLOT	fetlocked
CDEEFKNSU	fen-sucked
CDEEFKOST	feedstock
CDEEFLORT	deflector
CDEEFLRUU	flue-cured
CDEEFNORR	conferred
CDEEFNOSS	confessed
CDEEGHOOR	good cheer
CDEEGIILN	ceilinged
	diligence
CDEEGIIMR	germicide
CDEEGIINN	indigence
CDEEGILOR	Coleridge
CDEEGILRY	glyceride
CDEEGINNO	endogenic
CDEEGINOP	pedogenic
CDEEGINPR	preceding
CDEEGINRS	screeding
CDEEGIOST	geodetics
CDEEGLLRU	cudgeller
CDEEGNOST	congested
	decongest
CDEEHHIRS	cherished
CDEEHIINN	echidnine
CDEEHIKRS	shickered
CDEEHIKTT	thicketed
CDEEHIKTW	the wicked
CDEEHIKTY	thick-eyed
CDEEHILLS	chiselled
CDEEHILSW	disc wheel
CDEEHINOT	ethnocide
CDEEHINST	dehiscent
CDEEHIORT	ditrochee
CDEEHKOOR	door-cheek
CDEEHKOSU	deckhouse
CDEEHLORY	hydrocele
CDEEHLPPS	schlepped
CDEEHLRSU	scheduler
CDEEHNORV	chevroned
CDEEHOPRS	cosphered
CDEEHPPRU	up-perched
CDEEHRRRY	cherry red
CDEEHRSTT	stretched
CDEEIILRT	deciliter
	decilitre
CDEEIILTV	videlicet
CDEEIIMNR	mediciner
CDEEIIMNT	menticide
CDEEIIMPR	epidermic
CDEEIIMPU	epicedium
CDEEIIMRT	cetrimide
CDEEIIMRV	decemviri
	vermicide
CDEEIIPRR	cirripede
CDEEIIPST	pesticide
CDEEIIPTV	depictive
CDEEIIRTV	directive
CDEEIISTT	dietetics
CDEEIJNOT	dejection
CDEEIJPRU	prejudice
CDEEIJRUV	verjuiced
CDEEIKKNR	knickered
CDEEIKLLN	nickelled
CDEEIKLRS	slickered
CDEEIKMRY	Dick Emery
CDEEIKQUY	quick-eyed
CDEEIKSST	stickseed
CDEEIKSTW	stickweed
CDEEILLNP	pencilled
CDEEILNNO	indolence
CDEEILNPR	pendicler
CDEEILNST	stenciled
CDEEILORR	Cordelier
CDEEILOTX	ex delicto
CDEEILPRT	predilect
CDEEILSTU	celsitude
CDEEILTXY	excitedly
CDEEIMMXY	myxedemic
CDEEIMNNU	decennium
CDEEIMNPU	impudence
CDEEIMRSV	decemvirs
CDEEINNOR	endocrine
CDEEINNSU	secundine
CDEEINOPT	deception
CDEEINORT	recondite
CDEEINOSS	decession
CDEEINOTT	detection
CDEEINPRU	unpierced
CDEEINQUY	De Quincey
CDEEINRRS	discerner
CDEEINRST	stridence
CDEEINRSY	residency
CDEEINTTX	extincted
CDEEINTUX	unexcited
CDEEIORRS	crosiered
CDEEIOTTU	eutectoid
CDEEIPRRT	predicter
CDEEIPRTU	depicture
CDEEIRSTT	decretist
CDEEIRSUV	decursive
CDEEIRTTU	certitude
	rectitude
CDEEIRTUV	reductive
CDEEISTUV	seductive
CDEEJORTY	dejectory
CDEEKLNOW	low-necked
CDEEKLORW	lower deck
	lower-deck
CDEEKLPRS	spreckled
CDEEKMNRU	muckender
CDEEKNORS	knee-cords
CDEEKNRWY	wry-necked
CDEEKOPRR	peck order
CDEEKORTW	two-decker
CDEELLMOP	compelled
CDEELLNRU	cullender
CDEELLOST	cold steel
CDEELMNTU	demulcent
CDEELMOPT	completed
CDEELMOPX	decomplex
CDEELNORY	redolency
CDEELOPPY	pelecypod
CDEELORSS	sclerosed
CDEELORST	corsleted
CDEELOSST	closed set
CDEELRSTU	clustered
CDEEMMNOR	recommend
CDEEMNOOS	comedones
CDEEMNORU	come under
CDEEMOOPS	decompose
CDEEMOORS	Morse code
CDEENNORS	condenser
CDEENNORT	contender
CDEENNORU	denouncer
CDEENNOTT	contented
CDEENNSTU	unscented
CDEENOOPS	endoscope
CDEENOORT	coroneted
CDEENOPRS	drop-scene
CDEENORRV	nerve cord
CDEENORUV	uncovered
CDEENOSSU	douceness
CDEENOSTT	contested
CDEENPRTY	encrypted
CDEENRRTU	decurrent
CDEENRSSU	crudeness
CDEENRSUU	unsecured
CDEEOPRRR	prerecord
CDEEOPRRU	procedure
	reproduce
CDEEOPRSS	processed
CDEEOPRTT	protected
CDEEOPRTY	deceptory
CDEEOQTTU	coquetted
CDEEORRTY	decretory
CDEEORSSY	cross-eyed
CDEEPRSSU	percussed
CDEEPSSTU	suspected
CDEEPSTUY	speedy cut
CDEERTTUV	curvetted
CDEFFIIIL	difficile
CDEFFIKOT	ticked off
CDEFGIINU	fungicide
CDEFGLOOR	cold forge
CDEFHIILL	Lichfield
CDEFHIILW	child-wife
CDEFHIORS	cod-fisher
CDEFHITUW	Dutch wife
CDEFHLNOR	Old French
CDEFIIIST	fideistic
CDEFIINNO	confide in
CDEFIINST	disinfect

CDEFIIOST Scotified
CDEFIKLOR frolicked
CDEFILNOR cornfield
CDEFIMNOR confirmed
CDEFINNOT confident
CDEFINOSX second fix
CDEFINTUY fecundity
CDEFKNORU unfrocked
CDEFLORUU cul-de-four
CDEFNOORW downforce
CDEFNOSUU unfocused
CDEGGLNOU unclogged
CDEGHHIIV high-viced
CDEGIIINV ice diving
CDEGIILOO ideologic
CDEGIIMRU demiurgic
CDEGIINNY indigency
CDEGIKNOT docketing
CDEGILNUX excluding
CDEGILOOP logopedic
police dog
CDEGILOSU glucoside
CDEGILOSY glycoside
CDEGIMOUW cowdie-gum
CDEGINNOS consigned
CDEGINORR recording
CDEGINORU ground ice
CDEGINOTY dictyogen
CDEGINRSY descrying
CDEGINSSY dysgenics
CDEGLORST goldcrest
CDEHHOORR rheochord
CDEHIIKLL childlike
CDEHIILNO lichenoid
CDEHIIOPT pithecoid
CDEHIIORT dichroite
CDEHIIORU echiuroid
CDEHIKLSU shielduck
CDEHIKNOT in the dock
CDEHIKOOY doohickey
CDEHIKPSY physicked
CDEHILLOV love child
CDEHILLSS childless
CDEHILNSS childness
CDEHILPST stepchild
CDEHINORT chondrite
threnodic
CDEHINOSU cushioned
CDEHINOUU eunuchoid
CDEHINSTU in the scud
CDEHINSTW wind chest
CDEHIOORT Theodoric
CDEHIORSV dish-cover
CDEHIORTW dowitcher
CDEHIOSTU dithecous
CDEHISTTY dysthetic
CDEHKLLSU shellduck
CDEHKMMOU hummocked
CDEHKNOOW choke down
CDEHKNOSU unshocked
CDEHKOSUV duckshove
CDEHLNORU chondrule
CDEHLNOTU unclothed
CDEHLOOSU coldhouse
CDEHLOSTU The Clouds
CDEHNNORU chunder on
CDEHNOOTT thecodont
CDEHNOTUU untouched
CDEHNOTUV Dutch oven
CDEHNSTUY unscythed
CDEHOOOPS hodoscope
CDEIIILSV civilised
CDEIIILVZ civilized
CDEIIIRST sideritic
CDEIIKMTW mid-wicket
CDEIIKRST sick-tired
CDEIILLNO decillion
CDEIILNNU include in
CDEIILNTU inductile
CDEIILOPR prolicide
CDEIILORT doleritic
CDEIILOSU delicious
CDEIILPUV vulpicide
CDEIILRRU ridiculer
CDEIILTVY declivity
CDEIIMNOS meniscoid
CDEIIMNTU ctenidium
CDEIIMNTY mendicity
CDEIIMRST miscredit
misdirect
CDEIINNOT incondite
nicotined
CDEIINNTU unincited
CDEIINOPT depiction
CDEIINORT cretinoid
direction
CDEIINOXZ zinc oxide
CDEIINRTT interdict
CDEIINTUV inductive
CDEIIOOSU dioecious
CDEIIOPRT peridotic
CDEIIORUX uxoricide
CDEIIORVV divorcive
CDEIIRRTX directrix
CDEIJNNOO conjoined
CDEIKKNPU Pekin duck
CDEIKLNSU klendusic
unsickled
CDEIKNSTY sticky end
CDEIKPPRU up-pricked
CDEILLLOU Celluloid®
celluloid
CDEILLORV Lord Clive
CDEILNNOY indolency
CDEILNOPU unpoliced
CDEILNORY cordyline
CDEILNOTU Dulcitone®
CDEILNPPU unclipped
CDEILNSSU lucidness
CDEILOOPS scopeloid
CDEILOOPU coup d'oeil
CDEILOSUU I could use
CDEILOSUV declivous
CDEILOTTW twice-told
CDEILPRSU surpliced
CDEILPSUU pediculus✧
CDEILRTUY credulity
CDEIMMNOO incommode
CDEIMMORY myrmecoid
CDEIMMOTT committed
CDEIMMSUY music-demy
CDEIMNNOT condiment
CDEIMNOPR princedom
CDEIMNORU indecorum
CDEIMNOSU Nicodemus
CDEIMNRRU mind-curer
CDEIMORTU udometric
CDEIMOSST domestics
CDEINNOTU continued
unnoticed
CDEINOPRT procident
CDEINOPSY dyspnoeic
CDEINORSU decursion
CDEINORTU introduce
reduction
CDEINORTV contrived
CDEINOSTU seduction
CDEINPPRR Dr Crippen
CDEINPRTU unpredict
CDEINRSSU curdiness
CDEINRSTY stridency
CDEINTTUV ventiduct
CDEIOOPRT porticoed
CDEIOORST scorodite
CDEIOPRRT predictor
CDEIOPRST dip-sector
CDEIOPRSU cuspidore
CDEIORRST recordist
CDEIORRTY directory✧
CDEIORSST dissector
CDEIORSSU discourse
CDEIORSTU custodier
CDEIORSTV discovert
CDEIORSVY discovery✧
CDEIOSSTT Docetists
CDEIPPSTY dyspeptic
CDEIRSSSU discusser
CDEKLNPUU unplucked
CDEKLOOPR orlop deck
CDEKLOORY crookedly
CDEKNOORU undercook
CDEKNOSTU unstocked
CDEKOOSTV stock dove
CDELLOSSU cloudless
CDELMNORU lemon curd
CDELMOOPU coupledom
CDELMOOWY low comedy
CDELNNOOT condolent
CDELNOOOR con dolore
CDELNOORT decontrol
CDELNOORU undercool
CDELNOOST stone-cold
CDELNOOSW close down

closedown
CDELNOOTY cotyledon
CDELNOPUU uncoupled
CDELNORSU scoundrel
CDELOORSU coloureds
CDELOORUV cloud over
overcloud
CDELOPRSU supercold
CDELORSUU credulous
CDEMMOOOR commodore
CDEMNOORU come round
CDENNORUW uncrowned
CDENNOTUU uncounted
CDENOOPRS drop scone
CDENOOPSY endoscopy
CDENOORRS scorrendo
CDENOORRT corrodent
CDENOORST consorted
CDENOORSW second row
second-row
CDENOORTT contorted
CDENOORTU contoured
CDENOPPRU uncropped
CDENORSSU uncrossed
CDENORSUU unscoured
unsourced
CDENORSWW screw-down
CDENPRTUU punctured
CDEOOOPST octopodes
CDEOOOPSW copsewood
CDEOOPPRR pop record
CDEOORRVW overcrowd
CDEOORSST doctoress
CDEOORSWW woodscrew
CDEORSTUV dust cover
CDFFIILTU difficult
CDFFNOOOR cordon off
CDFGHILNO goldfinch
CDFGIINNO confiding
CDFGIINOY codifying
CDFGIOOTY city of God
CDFHINORY chondrify
CDFIILOOR dolorific
CDFIIMOST discomfit
CDFIIORSU sudorific
CDFILOSTU old fustic
CDFIMMOOY commodify
CDFIMOORR cordiform
CDFIORRTU Fructidor
CDFKOOSTU duck's-foot
CDFLNOORT cold front
CDFOOORTU food court
CDGHHHITU High Dutch
CDGHIILLO chilli dog
CDGHIILNS chidlings
CDGHIILNY chidingly
CDGHILLOT cold light
CDGHLLOOT gold-cloth
CDGHNOOUW cough down
CDGHOOPRU cough drop
CDGIILNNU including
CDGIIOTYZ dizygotic
CDGIKLOST goldstick
CDGILNNOY condignly
CDGLNOORW gold crown
CDGOOSTTU Doug Scott
CDHHIILTW with child
CDHHIIOTY ichthyoid
CDHHILOST dishcloth
CDHHRSTUU Dutch rush
CDHIIINOT chitinoid
CDHIILLNW wind chill
CDHIIMOPR dimorphic
CDHIIMORS dichroism
CDHIIORRS scirrhoid
CDHIIORST orchidist
CDHIIPSTW DIP switch
dipswitch
CDHIIRRTY trihydric
CDHIKNPTU Dutch pink
CDHILOSTU dish-clout
CDHIMNOOR monorchid
CDHIMOOTY dichotomy
CDHIMSTYY dysthymic
CDHINOPSY dysphonic
CDHIOOPRR cirrhopod
CDHIOOPRY chiropody
CDHIOOPSZ schizopod
CDHIOPRSY dysphoric
CDHIOPRTY hydroptic
CDHIOPRWY whipcordy
CDHKOOOSW woodshock
CDHLLOOOS old school
old-school
CDHLOORST cold-short
CDHLOORTU hold court
CDHMNOOOR monochord
CDHMNOOST D C Thomson
CDHNNOOOU coonhound
CDHNOOORT notochord
CDHNOOTUW touch down
touchdown
CDHOOORTW torchwood
CDHOOOTUW touch wood
touchwood
CDHOORRST short-cord
CDIIILMNS diclinism
CDIIINNOT indiction
CDIIINOOT idioticon
CDIIIORST dioristic
CDIIISTVY viscidity
CDIIJOSUU judicious
CDIILMOOT dolomitic
CDIILNOPT diplontic
CDIILNOSU diclinous
CDIILPTUY duplicity
CDIILTTUY ductility
CDIIMMORU cormidium
CDIIMNPUY pycnidium
CDIIMOOST sodomitic
CDIIMORST dicrotism
CDIINNOOT condition
CDIINNOTU induction
CDIINOPRY cyprinoid
CDIINTWYY Windy City
CDIIOOPRS scorpioid
CDIIOPRST dioptrics
CDIIORRTT tortricid
CDIIPRSTU tricuspid
CDIJNOTUY jocundity
CDIKLLORR rock drill
CDIKLNOSW slick down
CDIKLOORS rock-solid
CDIKMRSTU drumstick
CDIKOOPRW prickwood
CDILLNOOO collodion
CDILOOOPT octoploid
CDILOORSU discolour
CDILOOSTY scolytoid
CDILORSUU ludicrous
CDIMMNOOS discommon
CDIMMOOTY commodity
CDIMNOORU doronicum
CDIMNORSY syndromic
CDIMOOPRR prodromic
CDINNOOPU pound coin
CDINOOPRY procyonid
CDINORSSW crosswind
CDIOORRRS corridors
CDIOORSSU Dioscorus
CDIOORSTU dicrotous
CDIRRSTUU duricrust
CDIRSSSUU discursus
CDKKNNOOW knock down
knock-down
CDKKNOOOR doorknock
CDKKNOOOW knock wood
CDKLNOPUW pluck down
CDKMPRTUU dump truck
CDLNOOTUW cloudtown
CDLOOORTU Oort cloud
CDMNNORUU conundrum
CDMNOOPQU compound Q
CDMNORSUW scrumdown
CDMOOORTY cordotomy
CDNNOOTUW count down
countdown
CDNOOOPST stop codon
CDOORRSSW crossword
CDOORRSUY corduroys
CEEEEEHSW ewe-cheese
CEEEEFFNR efference
CEEEEFNRR reference
CEEEEGMNR emergence
CEEEEHILP heel-piece
CEEEEHMNV vehemence
CEEEENRRV reverence
CEEEEORRV recoveree
CEEEFFITV effective
CEEEFFLNU effluence
CEEEFFORY rye coffee
CEEEFFOST coffee set
CEEEFHLTT flechette

flèchette
CEEEFILNN line-fence
CEEEFINNR inference
CEEEFINPV fivepence
CEEEFLNRU refluence
CEEEFLNSS fenceless
CEEEFLRRT reflecter
CEEEFNORR ferrocene
re-enforce
CEEEFNQRU frequence
CEEEFPRRT perfecter
CEEEGILNT telegenic
CEEEGIMNS miscegene
CEEEGINRT energetic
CEEEGISTX exegetics
CEEEGLMNU emulgence
CEEEGLNOR conger-eel
CEEEGLNRT neglecter
CEEEGMNRY emergency
CEEEHILPS sheep-lice
CEEEHILST scheelite
CEEEHINNR inherence
CEEEHINPS nipcheese
CEEEHIPST tip-cheese
CEEEHLNTY entelechy
CEEEHLOPR creep-hole
CEEEHLRSS cheerless
rechlesse
CEEEHLRUV chevelure
CEEEHMNVY vehemency
CEEEHNRST the screen
CEEEHNRVW whencever
CEEEHOPRS ecosphere
pre-echoes
CEEEHOPST sheepcote
CEEEHPRST the creeps
CEEEHPSST set speech
CEEEHQRUX exchequer✧
CEEEHRTTV chevrette
CEEEIIMPT timepiece
CEEEIINRV vicereine
CEEEIJRTV rejective
CEEEIKPRR pickeerer
CEEEILLNT clientele
clientèle
CEEEILNOP Pleiocene
CEEEILNST celestine✧
CEEEILOPP pole piece
CEEEILPSS epicleses
pieceless
CEEEILPSY eye splice
CEEEILRST electrise
Leicester
CEEEILRTT tiercelet
CEEEILRTZ electrize
CEEEILSTT celestite
CEEEILSTV selective
CEEEIMNTT cementite
CEEEIMRRS mercerise
CEEEIMRRZ mercerize
CEEEINNNP ninepence
CEEEINNPT penitence
CEEEINNRT centenier
CEEEINNSS in essence
CEEEINNST sentience
CEEEINOPS nosepiece
CEEEINPRT epicenter
epicentre
CEEEINQUV vice-queen
CEEEINRSU esurience
CEEEINSTX existence
CEEEIPRRV perceiver
CEEEIPRST creepiest
CEEEIPRSU précieuse
CEEEIPRTV receptive
CEEEIPTVX exceptive
CEEEIRRSX exerciser
CEEEIRSSV recessive
CEEEIRSSX exercises
CEEEIRSTV secretive
CEEEIRSVV Vic Reeves
CEEEIRSVX ex-service
CEEEIRTVX excretive
CEEEISSVX excessive
CEEEITUVX executive
CEEEJMNTT ejectment
CEEEJMORR Joe Mercer
CEEEJMOTZ J M Coetzee
CEEEKNRSV neckverse
CEEEKORRT rocketeer
CEEEKOSTY eye socket
CEEELLNRV nerve cell
CEEELLNTX excellent
CEEELMNTU temulence
CEEELMSUY eye muscle
CEEELNOQU eloquence
CEEELNOSY Ceylonese
CEEELOPRS crêpe sole
CEEELOPST telescope
CEEELORTV clove-tree
CEEELOTTT côtelette
CEEELPRST preselect
CEEELRSST electress
CEEEMNRRT recrement
CEEEMNRTX excrement
CEEEMSTUY Eumycetes
CEEENNORV reconvene
CEEENNRST secernent
sentencer
CEEENNSST senescent
CEEENNSSU unessence
CEEENORTT entrecôte
CEEENOSTY synoecete
CEEENQRSU sequencer
CEEENRSST erectness
CEEEOPSTT escopette
CEEEORRRV recoverer
CEEEPRRST respecter
CEEEPRSTU persecute
CEEFFFORT for effect
CEEFFIINT efficient
CEEFFILOR life-force
CEEFFIMOT Met Office
CEEFFIOOR o're-office
CEEFFIORS Escoffier
CEEFFIOSU coiffeuse
CEEFFNORS screen off
CEEFFNORT off-centre
CEEFFOOPT coffee pot
CEEFGHILN fleeching
CEEFGIKPR fig-pecker
CEEFGINNR ring-fence
CEEFGLNTU genuflect
CEEFHIIST fetichise
CEEFHIITZ fetichize
CEEFHILRS fish-creel
CEEFHILSS chiefless
CEEFHIPSY speechify
CEEFHLNRU free lunch
CEEFHLPSU speechful
CEEFIILRT feliciter
CEEFIINTV infective
CEEFIIRRT certifier
rectifier
CEEFIKRTV tick fever
CEEFILNNU influence
CEEFILNRT ferntícle
CEEFILRTY electrify
CEEFIMNOR confirmee
CEEFIMORT focimeter
CEEFIMPRT imperfect
CEEFINORR confrérie
reinforce
CEEFINORT refection
CEEFINTTU fettucine
CEEFIRRST firecrest
CEEFKLLSS fleckless
CEEFKNNSU sunk fence
CEEFKORRV Rock fever
CEEFLNORT tenor clef
CEEFLNRSU screenful
CEEFLOORS foreclose
CEEFLORRT reflector
CEEFLORSS forceless
CEEFLORSU fluoresce
CEEFLPRTY perfectly
CEEFMNORW worm fence
CEEFNNOSW snow fence
CEEFNOPRU fourpence
CEEFNORRR conferrer
CEEFNPRTU unperfect
CEEFNQRUY frequency
CEEFNRSTT TFT screen
CEEFNRSTU rufescent
CEEFOPRRT perfector
CEEFOPRSS forcepses
CEEFOPRST perfectos
CEEFORRTY refectory
CEEFORSTW crow's-feet
CEEGGILRS egg slicer
CEEGHIMNO hegemonic
CEEGHINNO hecogenin
CEEGHINRW Greenwich

CEEGHORRT The Grocer
CEEGIILPS spicilege
CEEGIIMNS miscegine
CEEGIINRS isenergic
CEEGIINRV receiving
CEEGIINST Genesitic
CEEGIIOVV give voice
CEEGILLNX excelling
CEEGILNOO Oligocene
CEEGILNOT telegonic
CEEGILNRY glycerine
CEEGIMORT geometric
CEEGINNOS consignee
CEEGINNRS screening
CEEGINNRT centering
centreing
CEEGINNST ignescent
CEEGINNSY syngeneic
CEEGINOOT oogenetic
CEEGINORS congeries
recognise
CEEGINORX exergonic
CEEGINORZ recognize
CEEGINPRS cee-spring
CEEGINPTX excepting
expecting
CEEGINRSV screeving
CEEGIORRS groceries
CEEGJKLOT jockteleg
CEEGKNOOS goose-neck
CEEGLNOOS Congolese
CEEGLNOSU gene locus
CEEGLRTTU leg-cutter
CEEGMNNTU cement gun
CEEGNNORR green corn
CEEGNOPRR green crop
CEEGNOPSY engyscope
CEEGORTTU courgette
CEEHHIRVW whichever
CEEHHOPST hope chest
CEEHIILNP Chile pine
cinephile
CEEHIILRU Richelieu
CEEHIILTT helictite
CEEHIIMRR rime riche
CEEHIIPTT epithetic
CEEHIIRTT erethitic
CEEHIKKNT thick knee
CEEHIKLNO choke line
CEEHIKNRT kitchener
thickener
CEEHIKPPR pike-perch
CEEHIKPRY cipher key
CEEHIKPST sheep tick
CEEHILLMS schlemiel
CEEHILLRS chiseller
CEEHILLTW white cell
CEEHILMNY Michel Ney
CEEHILNOS lichenose
CEEHILNRS schlieren
CEEHILPRT telpheric
CEEHILRSV cleverish
CEEHILSTT telestich
CEEHIMPRY hyperemic
CEEHIMPTY chemitype
CEEHIMRST hermetics
CEEHIMRSW shrewmice
CEEHIMTUV humective
CEEHINNRY inherency
CEEHINPRT phrenetic
CEEHINPST phenetics
CEEHINPSU euphenics
CEEHINQTU technique
CEEHINRTT threnetic
CEEHINRTY hercynite
CEEHINRVY every inch
CEEHINSST techiness
CEEHINSSW chewiness
CEEHINSTU euthenics
CEEHINSTZ Nietzsche
Zechstein
CEEHINSUU eunuchise
CEEHINUUZ eunuchize
CEEHIOPSW showpiece
CEEHIORRT torchière
CEEHIORSS coheiress
CEEHIORTT heterotic
theoretic
CEEHIPRRY cherry-pie
CEEHIPRTT pitch-tree
CEEHISTTT tetchiest
CEEHJLNOO Joel Cohen
CEEHKLLOW wheel lock
CEEHKLMNN H L Mencken
CEEHKNNOR Chernenko
CEEHLLNOP cellphone
CEEHLLNOS cone shell
CEEHLLNOV Loch Leven
CEEHLMTUY the Lyceum
CEEHLORSU lecherous
CEEHLORTV Chevrolet®
CEEHLPPRS schlepper
CEEHLPRSU sepulcher
sepulchre
CEEHLQRSU squelcher
CEEHLRSST retchless
CEEHMMOOR home-comer
CEEHMNORZ chernozem
CEEHMOORZ zoechrome
CEEHMORTT ectotherm
CEEHMORTY ecothermy
CEEHMRSTW screw them
CEEHNOPRR percheron
CEEHNOPRY coryphene
CEEHNOSTT chest-note
chest tone
CEEHOPRRV overperch
CEEHOPRSU proseuche
CEEHOPTTY ectophyte
CEEHORRST Rochester
CEEHORRTU retoucher
CEEHPRRSY sprechery
CEEHRRSTT stretcher
CEEIIJLMU lime juice
CEEIIJNOR rejoice in
CEEIIJNTV injective
CEEIIKLNN nickeline
CEEIIKLNS nickelise
CEEIIKLNZ nickelize
CEEIILMST time slice
CEEIILNPR pericline
CEEIILNRT lienteric
CEEIILNST insectile
selenitic
CEEIILPPT epileptic
CEEIILPRX pre-exilic
CEEIILPSS epiclesis
CEEIIMMNN imminence
CEEIIMNRS reminisce
CEEIIMNST centesimi
CEEIIMOST semeiotic
CEEIIMPRS imprecise
CEEIIMPST epistemic
CEEIIMRST metricise
CEEIIMRTZ metricize
CEEIINNOR eirenicon
CEEIINNRS insincere
CEEIINNRT encrinite
CEEIINNTV incentive
CEEIINPRT recipient
CEEIINPTV inceptive
CEEIINPTX excipient
CEEIINRST cretinise
CEEIINRSV in service
in-service
CEEIINRTZ cretinize
CEEIINSST scientise
CEEIINSTZ scientize
CEEIINTVV invective
CEEIIOPST poeticise
CEEIIOPTZ poeticize
CEEIIORRT écritoire
CEEIIORST eroticise
CEEIIORTZ eroticize
CEEIIPRSS Persicise
CEEIIPRSU epicurise
CEEIIPRSV precisive
CEEIIPRSZ Persicize
CEEIIPRUZ epicurize
CEEIIQSTU equisetic
CEEIIRRTT trieteric
CEEIJLOUV love-juice
CEEIJLSSU juiceless
CEEIJNORT rejection
CEEIJNRTT interject
CEEIJRRRY Jerry Rice
CEEIKKLLR clerklike
CEEIKKSSS skeesicks
CEEIKMSTT metestick
CEEIKNOPS kinescope
CEEIKNQRU quickener
requicken
CEEIKOPRW piecework

	workpiece
CEEILLLNO	lioncelle
CEEILLLOV	level-coil
CEEILLLTU	cellulite
CEEILLNNT	centinell
CEEILLNOR	Corneille
CEEILLNPR	penciller
CEEILLNSW	clew-lines
CEEILLNTT	intellect
CEEILLOTV	covellite
CEEILMNNT	inclement
CEEILMNPR	Crimplene®
CEEILMNSU	luminesce
CEEILMORS	misoclere
CEEILMOST	comeliest
CEEILMRSS	crimeless
	merciless
CEEILMRUV	vermicule
CEEILNNOS	insolence
CEEILNOPR	crepoline
	pencil-ore
CEEILNORS	scoreline
CEEILNORT	centriole
CEEILNOST	selection
CEEILNOTT	Nicolette
CEEILNOTY	ceylonite
CEEILNPRT	princelet
CEEILNPST	splenetic
CEEILNRSU	licensure
CEEILNRSY	sincerely
CEEILNRTV	ventricle
CEEILNRUV	virulence
CEEILOPRS	soil creep
CEEILOPTT	pectolite
CEEILOPTU	poeticule
CEEILORRT	terricole
CEEILORSX	excelsior✧
CEEILOSSS	isosceles
CEEILOSSV	voiceless
CEEILPRSS	priceless
CEEILPRST	Triple sec
CEEILPRSW	screw-pile
CEEILPRSY	precisely
CEEILRSTW	crewelist
CEEILRSUV	reclusive
CEEILSSUV	seclusive
CEEILSUVX	exclusive
CEEIMMNSU	ecumenism
CEEIMMOTT	committee
CEEIMNNRT	increment
CEEIMNOOS	economies
	economise
CEEIMNOOZ	economize
CEEIMNOPT	impotence
CEEIMNOST	centesimo
CEEIMNOWX	New Mexico
CEEIMNSTU	intumesce
CEEIMORST	core times
CEEIMRRSU	mercurise
CEEIMRRUZ	mercurize
CEEINNORS	ninescore
	recension
CEEINNOVX	connexive
CEEINNPTY	penitency
CEEINNRTY	renitency
CEEINNSTT	insect net
CEEINNSTY	sentiency
CEEINOPRS	pericones
	preconise
CEEINOPRT	in pectore
	reception
CEEINOPRZ	preconize
CEEINOPTX	exception
CEEINORRS	encierros
CEEINORRT	tierceron
CEEINORSS	recession
CEEINORST	necrotise
	resection
	secretion
CEEINORSU	cinereous
CEEINORTV	covin-tree
CEEINORTW	write-once
CEEINORTX	excretion
CEEINORTZ	necrotize
CEEINOSSS	secession
CEEINOSSY	synoecise
CEEINOSTX	exsection
CEEINOSYZ	synoecize
CEEINOTUX	execution
CEEINPRRU	prurience
CEEINPRSS	crepiness
	princesse
CEEINPRST	prescient
	reinspect
CEEINPRSU	unprecise
CEEINPRSW	screw pine
CEEINPRTT	intercept
CEEINQRTU	quercetin
CEEINQSTU	quiescent
CEEINRRSV	scrivener
CEEINRSTT	intersect
CEEINRSTV	virescent
CEEINRSUV	sine curve
CEEINRSUY	esuriency
CEEINSSTY	necessity
CEEIOORTZ	ozocerite
CEEIOORVV	voice-over
CEEIOOTVV	voice vote
CEEIOPPRS	periscope
CEEIOPRRV	overprice
CEEIOPSST	cespitose
CEEIORRST	corsetier
CEEIORRSX	exorciser
CEEIORRXZ	exorcizer
CEEIORSST	sectorise
CEEIORSSU	sericeous
CEEIORSTV	vectorise
CEEIORSTZ	sectorize
CEEIORTVW	twice over
CEEIORTVZ	vectorize
CEEIPRRWZ	prize crew
CEEIPRSST	tricepses
CEEIRRRTU	recruiter
CEEIRRSUV	recursive
CEEIRSSTU	cerussite
CEEIRSUVX	excursive
CEEIRTUXX	executrix
CEEJORRTT	retroject
CEEKKKNNO	knock-knee
CEEKLOTUY	leukocyte
CEEKLPSSS	speckless
CEEKLRUVY	culver-key
CEEKNOPTU	keep count
CEEKNPRTU	nutpecker
CEEKOOPRT	Peter Cook
CEEKOSSTT	socket set
CEELLLOSU	cellulose
CEELLMNTY	clemently
CEELLMOPR	compeller
CEELLMOWY	welcomely
CEELLMPRS	sperm cell
CEELLNNOT	centonell
CEELLNORS	ensorcell
CEELLNOST	stone cell
CEELLOPTU	locuplete
CEELLORTU	Courtelle®
CEELLRSTU	cruellest
CEELLRSUY	reclusely
CEELMMPTU	emplectum
CEELMNOPT	emplecton
CEELMNOUW	unwelcome
CEELMNTUY	temulency
CEELMOOTU	leucotome
CEELMOPRT	completer
CEELNNNOP	pennoncel
CEELNORSU	enclosure
CEELNOSSS	closeness
CEELNOSTU	consultee
CEELNPRUU	purulence
CEELNRSSU	cruelness
CEELNSSST	scentless
CEELNSTTU	lutescent
CEELOPRRT	prelector
CEELOPSTY	telescopy
CEELORSSS	scleroses
	scoreless
CEELORSUU	ceruleous
CEELORSUX	exclosure
CEELORTTU	court-leet
CEELOSTTU	select out
CEELOSTTZ	cloze test
CEELRSSST	crestless
CEELRSSTU	truceless
CEEMMNORT	commenter
CEEMNNORT	contemner
CEEMNOORT	oncometer
CEEMNOPRT	contemper
CEEMNOPTT	competent
CEEMNOQYZ	coenzyme Q
CEEMNORSU	cornemuse
CEEMNSTTU	tumescent
CEEMOOPRS	recompose
CEEMOORSS	Morescoes

CEEMORRTY	cryometer
CEEMORSUV	curvesome
CEEMORTTY	cytometer
CEEMOSSTY	ecosystem
CEEMPRTUX	excerptum
CEEMQRTUU	quercetum
CEENNORRT	rencontre
CEENNORRU	renouncer
CEENNORTU	encounter
CEENNRSSU	sunscreen
CEENOOPRS	open score
CEENOOPST	copestone
CEENOORSV	e converso
CEENOORTV	cover note
CEENOORTX	neocortex
CEENOPRRT	precentor
CEENOPRST	copresent
CEENOPSTT	Pentecost
CEENOQRRU	reconquer
CEENORRSV	conserver
	converser
CEENORRTV	converter
	reconvert
CEENORSTT	contester
CEENORSTW	sweetcorn
CEENRRRTU	recurrent
CEENRRTUX	excurrent
CEEOORRRV	recoveror
CEEOORRST	core store
CEEOORRSV	overscore
CEEOORRVV	overcover
CEEOPPRRT	preceptor
CEEOPRRSS	reprocess
CEEOPRRTX	excerptor
CEEOPRSTT	top secret
CEEOPRSTU	prosecute
CEEOQRTTU	croquette
CEEORRSSS	sorceress
CEEORRSST	crosstree
	rectoress
CEEORRSSU	resources
CEEORRSTW	worcester✧
CEEORRSTY	secretory
CEEORRSUV	verrucose
CEEORRSVW	screw over
CEEORRTUV	coverture
CEEORRTXY	excretory
CEEORSSTT	crossette
CEEORTUXY	executory
CEEPRRRRU	precurrer
CEEPRRSSU	repercuss
CEERRRSTU	resurrect
CEFFFFLUU	cuffuffle
CEFFFLRUU	curfuffle
CEFFHINRY	Frenchify
CEFFHNOTU	on the cuff
CEFFHNRRY	French fry
CEFFIILLO	ill office
CEFFIINOT	coffinite
CEFFIIOOX	ex officio
CEFFIKNST	stiff neck
CEFFIMOOT	come off it!
CEFFLPSUU	scuffle up
CEFFORTTU	off-cutter
CEFGHIILN	chiefling
CEFGHILNT	fletching
CEFGIKLNR	freckling
CEFGINORS	frescoing
CEFGINORU	configure
CEFHHIIPS	chiefship
CEFHIILSS	fish slice
CEFHIIMST	fetichism
CEFHIINNP	pine-finch
CEFHIIOTT	fiochetti
CEFHIISTT	fetichist
CEFHIITWW	witch-wife
CEFHIKRSW	wreck fish
	wreckfish
CEFHILMOR	cheliform
CEFHINORS	rosefinch
CEFHKLLOU	choke-full
CEFHKOORS	foreshock
CEFHLOORT	forecloth
CEFHMOORT	forthcome
	home-croft
CEFHNOPRX	French pox
CEFHOORSU	corfhouse
CEFHPRRSU	surfperch
CEFIIKNTY	finickety
CEFIIKQRU	quick fire
	quick-fire
CEFIIKRST	fire-stick
CEFIILNPV	pelvic fin
CEFIILNRT	inflicter
CEFIILNRU	luciferin
CEFIILTWY	Wyclifite
CEFIINNOT	infection
CEFIINOPT	pontifice
CEFIINTTU	cut it fine
	fettucini
CEFIIORRS	scorifier
CEFIKORSS	fossicker
CEFIKRRTU	fire truck
CEFILORRU	rice flour
CEFIMNORR	confirmer
	reconfirm
CEFIMNORT	cteniform
CEFIMNORU	cuneiform
CEFIMOPRR	perciform
CEFIMORRU	eruciform
CEFIMORTT	tectiform
CEFIMORTU	comfiture
CEFINNNOU	unconfine
CEFINOORT	confiteor✧
CEFINORSS	forensics
CEFINORSU	confiseur
CEFINORTU	confiture
CEFIOORSU	ferocious
CEFIORRSS	crossfire
CEFIORSST	frescoist
CEFIORSTU	fruticose
CEFIPRRSU	spruce fir
CEFKLNOSW	snowfleck
CEFKLOPTU	pocketful
CEFKLORSS	frockless
CEFKOORRW	workforce
CEFLLORSU	full score
CEFLNNOTU	confluent
CEFLNOSTY	confestly
CEFLOORSU	soul-force
CEFMNOORR	conformer
CEFMOORRT	comforter✧
	recomfort
CEFNNOORT	confronté
CEFNOORSS	confessor
CEFOOPSTY	fetoscopy
CEFOORRSU	fourscore
CEFOORRTU	forecourt
CEFOORSTV	softcover
CEGGIOORR	Correggio
CEGHIILOP	geophilic
CEGHIINPR	ciphering
CEGHIINSY	hygienics
CEGHIIOST	gothicise
CEGHIIOTZ	gothicize
CEGHIKNST	sketching
CEGHILLOU	guilloche
CEGHILMTU	gemütlich
CEGHILNTV	vetchling
CEGHILOOR	rheologic
CEGHILOOT	ethologic
	theologic
CEGHINNQU	quenching
CEGHINNRW	wrenching
CEGHINOOT	Neo-Gothic
	theogonic
CEGHINORS	coshering
CEGHINORT	hectoring
CEGHIOPTY	geophytic
CEGHKNORU	roughneck
CEGHLOOUY	euchology
CEGHMNOOR	chromogen
CEGIIJNOR	rejoicing
CEGIIKLNN	nickeling
CEGIIKNNS	sickening
CEGIIKNPT	picketing
CEGIILNNR	reclining
CEGIILNSY	lysigenic
CEGIIMNOT	mitogenic
CEGIINOTV	cognitive
CEGIINPRR	price ring
CEGIINPRS	précising
CEGIIOSTT	egotistic
CEGIKLLNR	clerkling
CEGIKNNOR	reckoning
CEGIKNOPT	pocketing
CEGIKNOST	socketing
CEGILLMOU	collegium
CEGILLNPU	cupelling
CEGILLORV	gill cover
CEGILMMNO	commingle
CEGILMNOW	welcoming
CEGILNNOS	long since

Words marked ✧ can also be spelled with one or more capital letters

CEGILNOPY polygenic
CEGILNOST closeting
CEGILNRSU surcingle
CEGILNSTU single-cut
CEGILOOOZ zoogloeic
CEGILOORS serologic
CEGILOOST ecologist
CEGILORRV cover girl
CEGIMNNOO monogenic
CEGIMNOOR ergonomic
CEGIMNOUY gynoecium
CEGIMNOYZ zymogenic
CEGINNOOT ontogenic
CEGINNORS consigner
CEGINOOPR coopering
CEGINOOPS geoponics
CEGINOPPR coppering
CEGINOPRY pyrogenic
CEGINOPTY genotypic
CEGINORRT corrigent
CEGINORTV vectoring
CEGINOSTT stegnotic
CEGINRRRU recurring
CEGINRTUV curveting
CEGIOOPRT geotropic
CEGLNOORY necrology
CEGMNNOOS cognomens
CEGMNOOSY cosmogeny
CEGNNOORR negro-corn
CEGNNORTU congruent
CEGNOORSU Coregonus
CEGNORRSU scrounger
CEGNORSUY surgeoncy
CEGOOPRSY gyroscope
CEHHHIIKT hitch-hike
CEHHIIMST hemistich
CEHHILLMS schlemihl
CEHHILLOT cholelith
CEHHIMOST shochetim
CEHHIMRRY rich rhyme
CEHHIMSTT hemstitch
CEHHLOOTU touch hole
CEHHOOPSU chophouse
chop-house
CEHIIILPT epilithic
CEHIIILST cheilitis
CEHIIKLRS lickerish
CEHIIKLTW witchlike
CEHIIKTTW hit wicket
CEHIILMNS lichenism
CEHIILMOT homiletic
CEHIILNOT ichnolite
Neolithic
CEHIILNST lichenist
CEHIILOOZ heliozoic
CEHIILOST Elohistic
CEHIIMMPT Memphitic
CEHIIMMRS chimerism
CEHIIMNST ethnicism
CEHIIMSTY mythicise
CEHIIMTYZ mythicize
CEHIINNOT on thin ice
CEHIINPPT pitchpine
CEHIINPRT nephritic
phrenitic
CEHIINRST Christine
CEHIINSST itchiness
CEHIINTTY ethnicity
CEHIINTWZ zinc white
CEHIIPPPT pitchpipe
CEHIIPPST psephitic
CEHIIPPTY epiphytic
CEHIIPRRT peritrich
CEHIIPRTT perthitic
tephritic
CEHIIRSTT thersitic✧
CEHIIRSTU heuristic
CEHIIRTTW twitchier
CEHIJPSTW Jew's-pitch
CEHIKLMTV milk vetch
CEHIKLPRS clerkship
CEHIKLSTY sketchily
CEHIKNPRT phrentick
CEHIKNSST thickness
CEHIKOPPR hop-picker
CEHIKOPPT hip pocket
CEHIKORTW work ethic
CEHIKOTTT hot ticket
CEHIKPRSW shipwreck
CEHIKSSTT the sticks
CEHILLNSS chillness
CEHILMNTU lunchtime
CEHILMOOS molochise
CEHILMOOZ molochize
CEHILNNPU punchline
CEHILNOOR holocrine
CEHILNOOU cohune oil
CEHILNOPR necrophil
CEHILNOSU lichenous
CEHILNOTU touchline
CEHILNPSU siphuncle
uncleship
CEHILNSTZ schnitzel
CEHILOOPS heliscoop
CEHILOPPT pitch-pole
CEHILOPRT plethoric
CEHILORTW wire cloth
CEHIMMOPR morphemic
CEHIMMORS micromesh
CEHIMNNOU ichneumon
CEHIMNOPS phonemics
CEHIMNOSS mochiness
CEHIMNSUU eunuchism
CEHIMOOOT homoeotic
CEHIMOPRT morphetic
CEHIMOPXY hypoxemic
CEHIMORRT trichrome
CEHIMORST hectorism
CEHIMORTT thermotic
CEHIMPRUY hypericum✧
CEHIMPTYY chemitypy
CEHIMRSTY chemistry
CEHIMSTTY methystic
CEHINOORS isochrone
CEHINOPRT nephrotic
CEHINOPRU neurochip
CEHINOPST phonetics
CEHINOPTY neophytic
CEHINORST sticheron
CEHINOSTU cushionet
CEHINPRST sphincter
CEHINRSST snitchers
CEHINSSSU cushiness
CEHINSTTY synthetic
CEHIOOPRT orthoepic
CEHIOORRT coheritor
CEHIOPPRS copperish
CEHIOPPRT prophetic
CEHIOPRTT prothetic
CEHIOPRTU eutrophic
Petruchio
CEHIOPRTV overpitch
CEHIOPRTY hypocrite
CEHIORRST chorister
CEHIORSUV ECHO virus
echovirus
CEHIOSSST schistose
CEHIOSTTU touchiest
CEHIPRRSU superrich
CEHIPRRTY cherry-pit
CEHIRSSTY hysterics
CEHIRSTTY stitchery
CEHITTTWY witchetty
CEHJKLNOO John Locke
CEHJLNOOT John Colet
CEHKLNORS schnorkel
CEHKLOOOV clove-hook
CEHKLOOSU lockhouse
CEHKLORSU suck-holer
CEHKOOOSU cookhouse
CEHKOOPPT hop-pocket
CEHKOORSU rock house
CEHKRSTUY huckstery
CEHLLOOPT photocell
CEHLLORUY holy-cruel
CEHLMNOSU homuncles
CEHLMNOUU homuncule
CEHLNOSZZ schnozzle
CEHLNOTTT tent cloth
CEHLOOOSU coolhouse
CEHLOOPRS preschool
CEHLOOPSS Sophocles
CEHLOORSY schoolery
CEHLOOSTU clout-shoe
CEHLOPSST slop-chest
CEHLOSSTU touchless
CEHMMNOOT the common
CEHMOOPRT ectomorph
CEHMOORRU urochrome
CEHMOORST come short
CEHMOORSZ schmoozer
CEHMOTTYY thymocyte
CEHMRSTTU schmutter

CEHNNNORU	chunner on
CEHNNORTU	chunter on
	truncheon
CEHNNRTUW	nut-wrench
CEHNOOPPT	technopop
CEHNOOPPY	phenocopy
CEHNOORTY	Tony Roche
CEHNOOTTU	Touchtone®
	touchtone
CEHNOOTYZ	zootechny
CEHNORRRS	schnorrer
CEHOOOPRS	horoscope
CEHOORSTU	court shoe
CEHOPSSSY	psychoses
CEHOPTTUY	touch-type
CEHORSTUY	scouthery
CEHOSTTUZ	zuchettos
CEIIILMNS	Miliciens
CEIIILMTV	civil time
CEIIILNRU	Ricinulei
CEIIILRSV	civiliser
CEIIILRVZ	civilizer
CEIIIMNRS	irenicism
CEIIIMSTV	victimise
CEIIIMTVZ	victimize
CEIIINNOP	epinicion
CEIIINNPT	incipient
CEIIINRSU	cuisinier
CEIIIPSTT	pietistic
CEIIJLSUV	jus civile
CEIIJNNOT	injection
CEIIJNSSU	juiciness
CEIIJNSTU	injustice
CEIIKLMPS	mispickel
CEIIKLMQU	quicklime
CEIIKLNNP	ink pencil
CEIIKLNRR	crinklier
CEIIKLRTY	ricketily
CEIIKMQTU	quick time
CEIIKNNPR	princekin
CEIIKNPRT	nit-picker
CEIIKNRST	Rick Stein
CEIIKRRST	tricksier
CEIIKRSTT	trickiest
CEIIKRSTU	Turkicise
CEIIKRTUZ	Turkicize
CEIILLMNT	Millicent
CEIILMNSU	miniscule
CEIILMORT	microlite
CEIILMOSV	Milosevic
CEIILMPSS	simplices
CEIILNNOR	crinoline
CEIILNPPR	principle
CEIILNSUV	inclusive
CEIILOPST	epistolic
CEIILOQRU	liquorice
CEIILOSSU	siliceous
CEIILPRST	list price
	price list
CEIILPRTU	pleuritic
CEIILRSST	scleritis
CEIILSTTY	sectility
CEIILSTUV	Leviticus
CEIIMMNNY	imminency
CEIIMNNOS	sonic mine
CEIIMNOST	semitonic
CEIIMNOVY	in my voice
CEIIMNRST	cretinism
CEIIMNSST	scientism
CEIIMOPST	impeticos
	poeticism
CEIIMORRW	microwire
CEIIMORST	eroticism
	isometric
	meroistic
CEIIMOSST	semiotics
CEIIMOSTX	exoticism
CEIIMPRST	crimpiest
CEIIMPRSU	epicurism
CEIIMRRTT	trimetric
CEIIMRSTT	metricist
CEIIMTTUV	viticetum
CEIINNOPT	inception
CEIINNORT	incretion
CEIINNOST	insection
CEIINNRTY	inner city
	inner-city
CEIINOPPW	wincopipe
CEIINOPRS	precision
CEIINOPRT	proteinic
CEIINORRT	criterion
	tricerion
CEIINORTV	victorine
CEIINPRSS	priciness
CEIINPRTU	unit price
CEIINPSSS	spiciness
CEIINRSTT	sternitic
CEIINRSTX	extrinsic
CEIINRSTY	sincerity
CEIINRSUV	incursive
CEIINRTTY	Intercity®
	intercity
CEIINRTYZ	citizenry
CEIINSSTT	scientist
CEIIOOPTZ	epizootic
CEIIORSST	isosteric
CEIIORSTT	eroticist
CEIIORSTU	triecious
CEIIPPTTY	pepticity
CEIIPRSST	crispiest
CEIIPSTTY	septicity
CEIIRSSTU	rusticise
CEIIRSTUZ	rusticize
CEIIRTTVY	verticity
CEIJKMOSY	jockeyism
CEIJKNOST	Jock Stein
CEIJNORTT	introject
CEIKLNNPY	lickpenny
CEIKLNOPV	clove pink
CEIKLNORT	interlock
CEIKLNOST	close-knit
CEIKLNOSU	nickelous
CEIKLNSSS	slickness
CEIKLNSSU	luckiness
CEIKLOPST	stockpile
CEIKLORTU	courtlike
CEIKLOSTV	livestock
CEIKLRSST	trickless
CEIKMNORS	misreckon
CEIKMNSSU	muckiness
CEIKMORST	tricksome
CEIKMPSTU	stick 'em up!
CEIKMRSTU	semi-truck
CEIKNOOPS	koniscope
CEIKNORSS	corkiness
	rockiness
CEIKNOSTT	stockinet
CEIKNOSTV	vine-stock
CEIKNQSSU	quickness
CEIKNRSSU	sicknurse
CEIKOPRRT	rock tripe
	rope trick
CEIKOPTTU	picket out
CEIKORRTV	overtrick
CEIKPPRSU	pick-purse
CEIKPQSTU	quickstep
CEIKPRSTW	Prestwick
CEIKRRSTT	trickster
CEILLLMTU	clitellum
CEILLMOOW	come-o'-will
CEILLNOOR	corolline
CEILLNOUV	involucel
CEILLOPPT	pole-clipt
CEILLOQSU	coquilles
CEILLOSUV	collusive
	colluvies
CEILLPRST	strip cell
CEILLPSTY	sylleptic
CEILMNNOO	monocline
CEILMNOOS	semicolon
CEILMNOPU	encolpium
CEILMNOPY	money clip
CEILMNOTU	monticule
CEILMNSUU	minuscule
CEILMOPRY	micropyle
	polymeric
CEILMOPTY	lipectomy
CEILMOSST	Scots mile
CEILMRTUU	reticulum✧
CEILNNOOP	encolpion
CEILNNOOS	cloisonné
CEILNNOTU	countline
CEILNOORS	coloniser
CEILNOORZ	colonizer
CEILNOOTU	elocution
CEILNOPSY	Polynices
CEILNORST	sclerotin
CEILNORSU	Cornelius
	inclosure
	reclusion
CEILNORUV	involucre
	volucrine
CEILNOSSU	seclusion

CEILNOSUX exclusion
CEILNPRSY lip-syncer
CEILNRSSU curliness
CEILNRUVY virulency
CEILNSSTU linctuses
CEILOOPRT coprolite
CEILOORSU colourise
CEILOORUZ colourize
CEILOPPRT proleptic
CEILOPRSU supercoil
CEILOPRSV coverslip
slip cover
CEILORRTU courtlier
CEILORSSS sclerosis
CEILOSSSU coulisses
CEILOSTVY costively
CEILRSTUU Lucretius
CEILRSUVY cursively
CEIMMNNOS mnemonics
CEIMMNOOR monomeric
CEIMMNOOS economism
monoecism
CEIMMNOSU communise
encomiums
CEIMMNOTU comminute
CEIMMNOTY metonymic
CEIMMNOUZ communize
CEIMMOORS microsome
CEIMMOORT microtome
CEIMMORTT committer
CEIMMRSTU crummiest
CEIMMRSTY symmetric
CEIMNNOOY coin money
CEIMNNOPU pneumonic
CEIMNNORS encrimson
CEIMNNORT Comintern
CEIMNNOTU emunction
CEIMNOOPT coemption
CEIMNOORT microtone
CEIMNOOST economist
CEIMNOOSU monecious
CEIMNOPTY impotency
CEIMNORTT metric ton
CEIMNOSSY synoecism
CEIMNRTUV centumvir
CEIMOOPRR micropore
poromeric
CEIMOOPRT compotier
CEIMOOPST composite✧
CEIMOORSS moriscoes✧
CEIMOORTZ zoometric
CEIMOOSTX exosmotic
CEIMOPRST prime cost
CEIMOPRSX proxemics
CEIMOPRTU ectropium
CEIMOPSUU pumiceous
CEIMORSTU costumier
Tom Cruise
CEIMOSSTU customise
CEIMOSTUV muscovite✧
CEIMOSTUZ customize

CEINNNOOX connexion
CEINNNOTT continent✧
CEINNNOTV connivent
CEINNOOTV connotive
CEINNOPRT Princeton
CEINNORSS corniness
CEINNORSY incensory
CEINNORTU centurion
continuer
CEINNOSTT centonist
CEINNOTTX in context
CEINNRRTU incurrent
CEINNSTTV St Vincent
CEINNTTUX unextinct
CEINOOPRT ectropion
CEINOORST cortisone
CEINOORTU co-routine
CEINOORTV cover into
CEINOPPRU porcupine
CEINOPRRS conspirer
CEINOPRRT intercrop
CEINOPRST inspector
CEINOPRSV provinces
CEINOPRTT cotter-pin
CEINOPRXY pyroxenic
CEINOPSST Scots pine
CEINOPSTT entoptics
CEINOPSUU pecunious
CEINORRRS serricorn
CEINORRSU recursion
CEINORRTV contriver
CEINORRTW town crier
CEINORSTT cornetist
CEINORSTU cretinous
CEINORSUX excursion
CEINOSTUV contusive
CEINOTVXY convexity
CEINPRRUY pruriency
CEINPRSSS crispness
CEINRSSUV curviness
CEINRSTWW twin-screw
CEIOOPRSS coreopsis
CEIOOPRST porticoes
CEIOOPRTZ zoetropic
CEIOORRSV corrosive
CEIOORSTV vorticose
CEIOPPRRT periproct
CEIOPRRTY procerity
CEIOPRSSU prescious
CEIOPRSTY serotypic
CEIOPRTUY eurytopic
CEIORRSSS scissorer
CEIORRSTT tortrices
trisector
CEIORRSTU scrutoire
CEIORRSUZ cruzeiros
CEIORRTUU couturier
CEIORSSSW crosswise
CEIORSSTV victoress
CEIORSTTU toreutics
CEIPPRRST prescript

CEIPRRSTU scripture✧
CEIRRSTTU stricture
CEIRSSTTU crustiest
CEJKOOTUY outjockey
CEJNOPRUU conjure up
CEJOOPRRT projector
CEKKNOPRU knocker-up
CEKKORSTY skyrocket
CEKLMNOOR rock melon
CEKLNNPUY luck-penny
CEKLNORTW town clerk
CEKLORSUW worse luck
CEKLOSSST stockless
CEKMNORTU mockernut
CEKNORSTU orestunck
CEKOORSTV overstock
CEKORTTUU tucker out
CELLMOORY Collymore
CELLMOPXY complexly
CELLMSTUU scutellum
CELLNOSUU nucleolus
CELLOOPTY collotype
CELLORTUY clouterly
CELMNOOOT melocoton
CELMNOSUU lucumones
CELMNOTUY contumely
CELMNPRUU uncrumple
CELMOOPRY copolymer
co-polymer
CELMOOSSU colosseum
CELMOOTUY leucotomy
CELMOPRUU operculum
CELMOPSUX complexus
CELMOSTUU muscle out
CELMOTTYY tylectomy
CELMPRSTU plectrums
CELNOORSU counselor
CELNOOSTU consolute
lose count
CELNOOTUV convolute
CELNOPRST plectrons
CELNOPRTU corpulent
CELNORSSW crownless
CELNORSTU consulter
CELNOSSTU countless
CELNPRUUY purulency
CELNRRTUY currently
CELNRTTUU truculent
CELNTTTUU nut cutlet
CELOOPRSU supercool
CELOOPRTU turcopole
CELOORTUY elocutory
CELOOSTTY octostyle
CELORRSUU soul-curer
CELORRSUY reclusory
CELORSSUU surculose
CELORSTUV cover-slut
CELORSUXY exclusory
CELPRSTUU sculpture
CELPRTTUU clutter up
CELRSSSTU crustless

CEMMNNOOT no comment
CEMMNOORT commentor
CEMNNOOPT component
CEMNNOORT contemnor
CEMNOOOQU monocoque
CEMNOOORS monoceros
CEMNOOOSU OncoMouse®
CEMNOORST storm cone
CEMNOORTY necrotomy
CEMNORSUY mercy on us
CEMNORTUY emunctory
CEMOOPRST composter
CEMOOPRSU composure
CEMOOPSTU mutoscope
CEMOOPSYZ zymoscope
CEMOOPTTY topectomy
CEMORRSUU mercurous
CEMORRSWW screw-worm
CEMORTTYY cytometry
CEMPRSTUU prescutum
CENNNORSU Cernunnos
CENNOOPPY opponency
CENNOOPRU pronounce
CENNOORST cornstone
CENNORSTU Nocturnes
CENNOSSSU consensus
CENNRRTUU uncurrent
CENOOPPTU pounce pot
CENOOPRST stonecrop
CENOOPRTT entoproct
CENOOPRTU open court
CENOOQRRU conqueror✧
CENOORRST consorter
CENOORRTV convertor
CENOORTUV overcount
CENOORTYY tycoonery
CENORRSTU construer
CENORSSSS crossness
CENORSSTW crow's-nest
CENORSTXY xenocryst
CENPRRTUU puncturer
up-current
CENPSSTUU unsuspect
CENRRSTUW turn-screw
CENRSSSTU curstness
CEOOOPPRS poroscope
CEOOOSTTV sotto voce
CEOOPPRSY pyroscope
CEOOPRRRT prorector
CEOOPRRSS processor
CEOOPRRST prosector
CEOOPRRSU Eurocorps
CEOOPRRTT protector✧
CEOOPSSTU octopuses
CEOORRSSS rose cross
CEOORRSSU sorcerous
CEOORRSSV crossover
CEOORSTTY trot-cosey
CEOORSTUU courteous
outsource
CEOPPSSTU posset cup
CEOPRRRSU precursor
CEOPRRRTU corrupter
CEOPRRRUU procureur
CEOPRRSSU percussor
procuress
CEOPRSSTU susceptor
CEOPRSSTW crow-steps
CEORRSUUV verrucous
CEPRSSSUU Cupressus
CERRSTTUU structure
CFFFIISTU fisticuff
CFFGIINSU sufficing
CFFHIOSTW switch off
CFFIIOOSU officious
CFFILRSUY scruffily
CFFLOOORU off colour
off-colour
CFFMORSTU storm cuff
CFFOOSSTU soft focus
soft-focus
CFFORRSSU cross-ruff
CFGHIILNN flinching
CFGHIILNS clingfish
CFGIIIKNN finicking
CFGIIINSS significs
CFGIILLMN clingfilm
CFGIINNNO confining
CFGILNNOU flouncing
CFGINNOSU confusing
CFGINOSSU focussing
CFGNPSUUU cup fungus
CFHIIKLMT thick film
CFHIIKSST fish stick
CFHIINNOO finnochio
CFHIINOOR honorific
CFHIINPST pinchfist
CFHIKOPRT pitchfork
CFHIKOSST stockfish
CFHILLPTU full pitch
CFHILOORT choir loft
CFHILORSY fly orchis
CFHINNOSW snow finch
CFHINORSY rosy finch
CFHIOPRST first chop
CFHIORSSS crossfish
CFHKLNORU fork lunch
CFHLOOOTT footcloth
CFHLOPSUU pouchfuls
CFHOOSTTU soft touch
CFIIKKLNS skinflick
CFIILMMOR microfilm
CFIILNORT inflictor
CFIILORST floristic
CFIIMOPRS pisciform
CFIIMORRR cirriform
CFIIOOPRS soporific
CFIKLLNOT flintlock
CFIKLLOOR folkloric
CFIKLMOSU folk music
CFIKLNOSW snowflick
CFILLNRUY in full cry
CFILNNORT flint corn
CFILNSUUU funiculus
CFIMMNOOR Cominform
CFIMMOORR microform
CFIMNOORR confirmor
corniform
CFIMORRUV curviform
CFIMORSTU scutiform
CFIMORSTY cystiform
CFINNOOSU confusion
CFINOOOPR proof coin
CFIOOPRRY corporify
CFKLOORRU rock flour
CFKNOORSW forswonck
CFLLOORUU colourful
CFLNOORRU cornflour
CFLOOORTU court fool
CFLOOOSTT coltsfoot
CFLOOPSSU scoopfuls
CFLOORTUU out of curl
CFMNNOORU unconform
CFNOOSTUY out of sync
CFOOORSTW crowfoots
crow's-foot
CFORSTUUU fructuous
CGGHIKNNU Chungking
CGGHINNOQ Chongqing
CGGIKNOST gong-stick
CGHHHIINS Shih Ching
CGHHINNOO honchoing
CGHHIORSS high cross
CGHHIORTU high court
CGHIILLNS schilling
CGHIILNST chitlings
CGHIILORR choirgirl
CGHIIMOST Gothicism
CGHIINSTT stitching
CGHIINSTW switching
CGHIINTTW twitching
CGHIIOSTT Gothicist
CGHIKKNOU kink-cough
CGHILLOPU gill pouch
CGHILNOOS schooling
CGHILNOOY ichnology
CGHILNOSU slouching
CGHILOOOR horologic
CGHILOORY chirology
CGHILORUY grouchily
CGHINNOPU pounching
CGHINORSU chorusing
CGHINORTW night-crow
CGHINOSSU hocussing
CGHIOPRTY copyright
CGHKLOTUU tough luck
CGHLLNOOT longcloth
CGHLOOORY chorology
CGHLOOPYY phycology
CGHNOORST torch song
CGIIIKMMN mimicking
CGIIILNNN inclining
CGIIKLNPR prickling

 Words marked ✧ can also be spelled with one or more capital letters

CGIIKLNRT	trickling
CGIIKMMRY	gimmickry
CGIIKMNSU	musicking
CGIILMNNY	mincingly
CGIILMNUU	glucinium
CGIILNNWY	wincingly
CGIILNPPR	crippling
CGIILNPSW	clip wings
CGIILOSST	logistics
CGIILRSTU	liturgics
CGIIMNNOS	comings-in
CGIINNOOT	cognition
	incognito
CGIINNOUV	unvoicing
CGIINNRRU	incurring
CGIJNNORU	conjuring
CGIKLMNOY	mockingly
CGIKLNRTU	truckling
CGIKNOPRS	prick-song
CGIKNOSST	stockings
CGIKOOPST	pogo stick
CGILLNORS	scrolling
CGILLNOYY	cloyingly
CGILMNOOO	monologic
CGILMNOOY	cynomolgi
CGILMNOPY	complying
CGILMNPRU	crumpling
CGILMOORY	micrology
CGILMOOYZ	zymologic
CGILNNNUY	cunningly
CGILNNOOR	longicorn
CGILNNRUU	uncurling
CGILNOOOT	ontologic
CGILNOOOY	iconology
CGILNOORU	colouring
CGILNOPUV	loving cup
CGILNORTU	courtling
CGILNTTUY	cuttingly
CGILOOOPT	topologic
CGILOOOSY	sociology
CGILORSTU	Girl Scout
CGIMMNNOO	commoning
CGIMMNNOU	communing
CGIMMNRSU	scrumming
CGIMMNSSU	scummings
CGIMNNOOS	gnomonics
CGIMNNOSU	consuming
CGIMNOPTU	computing
CGINNOORS	consignor
CGINNOOTT	cotton gin
CGINNORTU	trouncing
CGINOPRRU	procuring
CGINORRSS	ring-cross
CGINORSSU	scourings
CGINORTUY	congruity
CGLMOOOSY	cosmology
CGLMOOSUY	muscology
CGLOOOPRY	coprology
CGMNOOOSY	cosmogony
CGNNOOTTU	guncotton
CGNOORSUU	congruous

CGOOORTTU	go to court
CHHHIIMNO	Ho Chi Minh
CHHILOOST	soothlich
CHHIMRSTY	rhythmics
CHHINTTUW	witch hunt
CHHIOPSUU	Ophiuchus
CHHKLLOOY	hollyhock
CHHLNORUU	lunch hour
CHIIILPPP	philippic✧
CHIIILRTT	trilithic
CHIIKKNST	thickskin
CHIIKLPST	thick-lips
CHIIKLSSY	sickishly
CHIIKLSTY	kitschily
CHIIKNNOV	chinovnik
CHIILLOPY	lyophilic
CHIILMORT	microlith
CHIILOOTT	otolithic
CHIILOOTZ	zoolithic
CHIILORTU	urolithic
CHIILORTY	rhyolitic
CHIILOSTW	wholistic
CHIILPTTY	typhlitic
CHIILTTWY	twitchily
CHIIMMNSU	Munichism
CHIIMMSTY	mythicism
CHIIMOSTT	Thomistic
CHIIMPSSY	physicism
CHIIMSTTY	mythicist
CHIINOPTT	pitch into
CHIINOSTU	chitinous
CHIINOSTY	onychitis
CHIIOPSST	sophistic
CHIIORRSS	cirrhosis
CHIIORSST	Irish Scot
	trichosis
CHIIORSTY	hircosity
CHIIORTTY	rhoticity
CHIIPSSTY	physicist
CHIIRSSTT	strictish
	tristichs
CHIKLMNPU	milk punch
CHIKLMNRU	churnmilk
CHIKLMOST	locksmith
CHIKLOOSS	ski school
CHIKNOSTW	thick-sown
CHIKNOTTW	witchknot
CHIKOOPTT	pick-tooth
	toothpick
CHIKOPSTW	stock whip
	whipstock
CHILLNOOT	loincloth
CHILLOPPT	pitch-poll
CHILLORTY	torch-lily
CHILLOSTY	coltishly
CHILMNOUU	homunculi
CHILOOPRT	coprolith
CHILOOPTY	holotypic
CHILOORSS	chlorosis
CHILOPRTU	Turcophil
CHILORSTU	trochilus

CHILORTUY	ulotrichy
CHILOSTTY	cystolith
	lithocyst
CHILPRSUU	sulphuric
CHILRRSUY	currishly
CHIMMNOOY	homonymic
CHIMNOOOT	homotonic
CHIMNOOPT	monopitch
CHIMNOORY	chironomy
CHIMNOOST	monostich
CHIMNOPSY	symphonic
CHIMNORSU	unchrisom
CHIMOOPRT	morphotic
CHIMOOPTY	homotypic
CHIMPSTYY	symphytic
CHIMRSTYY	chymistry
CHINOOPST	photonics
CHINOOPTY	hypotonic
CHINOORTZ	chorizont
CHINOPPTU	pitch upon
CHINOPRRY	Pyrrhonic
CHINOPSTU	countship
CHINPSTUY	physic nut
CHINSSSYY	synchysis
CHIOOOPRZ	zoophoric
CHIOOPRTT	orthoptic
CHIOOPSSY	sciosophy
CHIOOPTYZ	zoophytic
CHIOORSTT	orthotics
CHIOPRSTU	courtship
CHIOPRSYY	hypocrisy
CHIOPSSSY	psychosis
CHIORRSSU	scirrhous
CHIOSSSTU	schistous
CHIPSSTTU	putschist
CHJNORRUY	John Curry
CHKLMOOST	Stockholm
CHKLNOORS	lock horns
CHKMOPSUU	musk-pouch
CHKNOORST	stockhorn
CHKOPRSTU	truck shop
CHLMOORTT	mortcloth
CHLNOOOPY	colophony
CHLNOORSU	school run
CHLNOTUUY	uncouthly
CHLOOPPSU	slop-pouch
CHLOOPTYY	hypocotyl
CHLOPPTYY	polyptych
CHMNOOORT	monotroch
CHMNOOPYY	cohyponym
CHMOORRSU	crush room
CHMORRRUW	churr-worm
CHNNORSYY	synchrony
CHNOOPTUU	touch upon
CHNOPPPRU	punch-prop
CHNOPSSTY	post-synch
CHNORSTUU	cothurnus
CHOOOPPTY	photocopy
CHOOOPRSY	horoscopy
CIIILLLTY	illicitly
CIIILLSTV	civil list

CIIILMNOT limonitic
CIIILMOPT impolitic
CIIILOPST pisolitic
CIIILORTV vitriolic
CIIILOSSS silicosis
CIIILOSSU silicious
CIIIMMNOR micro-mini
CIIIMRSTT triticism
CIIIMSTTW witticism
CIIINNRST intrinsic
CIIIOSTVY viciosity
CIIJLNOPT clip joint
CIIKLRSTY tricksily
CIIKNNOPT nickpoint
CIIKNNOTY cytokinin
CIIKOPPRT rock pipit
CIILLNOOP cipollino
CIILLNOOS collision
CIILLNOOT cotillion
octillion
CIILLNPUU lupulinic
CIILLNUVY uncivilly
CIILLOPTY politicly
CIILMNOTY mylonitic
CIILMPRSY scrimpily
CIILNNOSU inclusion
CIILNOOST colonitis
noctilios
CIILNOPTU punctilio
unpolitic
CIILOOPST politicos
CIILOORST solicitor
CIILOOSSS scoliosis
CIILOPRSS proclisis
CIILOSUVY viciously
CIILSSTTY stylistic
CIIMMSSTY mysticism
CIIMNORSU criminous
CIIMNORUZ zirconium
CIIMOOSST isosmotic
CIIMORSTV vorticism✧
CIIMRSSTU rusticism
CIINNNOTU inunction
CIINNORSU incursion
CIINNOSST consist in
CIINNOSSW Wisconsin
CIINNOTUY innocuity
CIINOOPRT inotropic
CIINOPSSU suspicion
CIINORSUU incurious
CIINORTTU Tuticorin
CIINOSTVY synovitic
CIINPSSTU sinciputs
CIINRTUVY incurvity
CIIOOPRST isotropic
CIIOPRSTT proctitis
protistic
tropistic
CIIORSTTU touristic
CIIORSTTV vorticist
CIIORSTUV virtuosic
CIIORSTUY curiosity
CIIORTTVY vorticity
CIIOSSTVY viscosity
CIIOSTUXY Sioux City
CIIRSTTUY rusticity
CIJKOSSST joss stick
CIJNNOTTU T-junction
CIKKOOSSU Kosciusko
CIKKORSTW stickwork
CIKLLMMOS smock mill
CIKLLNUUY unluckily
CIKLNORSS cross-link
CIKLNOSTT lintstock
CIKLOSSTT stocklist
CIKOPSSST poss-stick
CIKPPRRSU prick spur
CILLLNOUY cullionly
CILLMORSU music roll
CILLMORUY collyrium
CILLMOUUV colluvium
CILLNOOSU collusion
CILLOOORU oil colour
CILLOOOST ocotillos
CILLOOOTY coyotillo
CILLOPPUW pillow-cup
CILLOQRUW crow-quill
CILLORSSS cross-sill
CILMNOOOS Solomonic
CILMNOSTU columnist
CILMOORSU miscolour
CILMOSSUU soul music
CILMOTYYZ zymolytic
CILNOOORT croton oil
CILNOORUU unicolour
CILNOOSSY oncolysis
CILOOPSUY copiously
CILOORRTU tricolour✧
CILOORSTU colourist
CILOPPTYY polytypic
CILOPRTYY pyrolytic
CILOPRXYY pyroxylic
CILORRSUY cursorily
CILORSUUY curiously
CILOSSTYY cytolysis
CILRSTTUU culturist
CILRSTUUU utriculus
CIMMMNOSU communism✧
CIMMNNOOU communion
CIMMNOOOS monosomic
CIMMNOOOT commotion
CIMMNOSTU communist✧
CIMMNOTUY community
CIMMOORSU music room
CIMMOORTY microtomy
CIMMOPPRU micropump
CIMNNOOOT monotonic
CIMNNOSYY synonymic
CIMNNOTUU continuum
CIMNOOOPP nicompoop
CIMNOOPTY monotypic
toponymic
CIMNOOTXY mycotoxin
CIMNSTUYY syncytium
CIMOOTUYZ zoocytium
CIMOPRSSU promuscis
CIMOPSTTU computist
CIMOPSTTY symptotic
CIMORSUXY Roxy Music
CINNOOPRU pronuncio
CINNOORRW Iron Crown
CINNOORST in consort
CINNOOSTU continuos
contusion
CINNOOSUU innocuous
CINOOOPRT co-portion
CINOOORRS corrosion
CINOOPRST optronics
CINOORRSS Iron Cross
CINOOSSUY synoicous
CINOOTTXY cytotoxin
CINOPRRTU incorrupt
CINOPSSTT Scots pint
CINORSUUU uncurious
CINOSTUVY viscounty
CIOOOPRSZ zoosporic
CIOOOPRTZ protozoic
CIOOPPRSU Procopius
CIOOPSSTU posticous
CIOPPRRST proscript
CIOPRRSTY scriptory
CIORRRSUU scurriour
CIORRSTUY cursitory
CKKOORSTW stockwork
CKLLNOORR rock'n'roll
CKMMTTUUY tummy tuck
CKMNOOOTU Mount Cook
CKMOOORST stockroom
CKNOOOSTW Cookstown
CKNOORRWW crownwork
CKNRSSTUU sunstruck
CKOOORSTT rootstock
CKOOORSTU Cook's tour
CKOOPRSTT Stockport
CKOPRSTTU truck stop
CLLMOOPRT comptroll
CLLOORRTU court-roll
CLMOOOORT locomotor
CLMOOOSTY colostomy
CLMOORSTU colostrum
CLMOPSUUU opusculum
CLMOSSUUU musculous
CLNOOPRSU proconsul
CLNOORSTU consultor
CLNOORTUY Lyon Court
CLNOOSUUY nocuously
CLNORTUUY uncourtly
CLOOPRSUU colour-sup
CLOPRRTUY corruptly
CMMNOOORS Roscommon
CMNOOORST cosmotron
CMNOPRTYY cryptonym
CMOOORRTU courtroom

Words marked ✧ can also be spelled with one or more capital letters

CMOOORSST motocross
CMOOORTTU moot court
CMOOSTTYY cystotomy
CNNNOOTUU count noun
CNNOOORST contornos
CNNOOOSSU consonous
CNOOOPRSS cosponsor
CNOOORTUZ corozo nut
CNOOPPPRY corn poppy
CNOOPRSTW crown-post
CNOORSSTW crosstown
CNOPRRTUU uncorrupt
CNOPRTUUY up-country
COOOOPPPS poop scoop
COOOPPRSY poroscopy
COOOPRSUY ouroscopy
COOPRRRTU corruptor
COOPRSSTY sporocyst
COOPSSTUY Octopussy
COORRSSSY rosy cross
COORRSSTW crosswort
COORRSTUU sour-crout
COORTTTUU tout court

D

DDDDEGIOS disgodded
DDDEEHILL ill-hedded
DDDEEISTU Deusdedit
DDDEELNUU undeluded
DDDEEMNRU reddendum
DDDEENORS reddendos
DDDEFIOSX fixed odds
DDDEGINOR doddering
DDDEHIILP didelphid
DDDEIILVY dividedly
DDDEIINUV undivided
DDDILLOOP doddipoll
DDDLLOOPY doddypoll
DDEEEEHLR red-heeled
DDEEEEHLY heddle-eye
DDEEEFILP deep field
DDEEEFILS seed-field
DDEEEFNRS defenders✧
DDEEEFNRU underfeed
DDEEEGGLR red-legged
DDEEEGIPR pedigreed
DDEEEHNPR deprehend
DDEEEILRS red diesel
DDEEEILTT title deed
DDEEEIMMS misdeemed
DDEEEINRX Dexedrine®
DDEEEIRTU deuteride
DDEEELOPV developed
DDEEENNOP open-ended
DDEEENNPT dependent
DDEEENOPT deep-toned
DDEEENPRT pretended
DDEEEPRSS depressed
DDEEERSWY dyer's-weed
DDEEERTTX Ted Dexter
DDEEESTUU desuetude
DDEEFGHNU hedge fund
DDEEFGLNU unfledged
DDEEFGNOR Fredegond
DDEEFIIMY demi-deify
DDEEFILNU undefiled
DDEEFINNU undefined
DDEEFINOP dope-fiend
DDEEFIRTW drift-weed
DDEEFNNOR end for end
DDEEGGGLO doglegged
DDEEGGILT gilt-edged
DDEEGGLOS dog sledge
DDEEGHILT delighted
DDEEGINNP depending
DDEEGLNPU unpledged
DDEEGLOOT edged tool
DDEEGOOPS good-speed
DDEEHIINT hiddenite
DDEEHINNR hinder-end
DDEEHNOOY needy-hood
DDEEHNORU deerhound
DDEEHNRRU hundreder
DDEEIILMV demi-devil
DDEEIILNS sidelined
DDEEIINRV I never did!
DDEEIIOSX deoxidise
DDEEIIOXZ deoxidize
DDEEIIPPT dipeptide
DDEEIKLNN enkindled
DDEEILLLY ill-deedly
DDEEILLPS dispelled
DDEEILLRS seed drill
DDEEILLRV drivelled
DDEEILRSV Red Devils
DDEEIMMNO demi-monde
DDEEIMNPU unimpeded
DDEEIMNRR dendrimer
DDEEIMRST dermestid
DDEEINNUX unindexed
DDEEINOPS dispondee
DDEEINORW eiderdown
DDEEINPSS dispensed
DDEEINRSU underside
undesired
DDEEINRTT tridented
DDEEIOORS deodorise
DDEEIOORZ deodorize
DDEEIPRRS red spider
DDEEIRSSS side-dress
DDEEKLOOR red-looked
DDEELLOPR red-polled
DDEELOTVY devotedly
DDEELRSSU udderless
DDEELRSWY dyer's-weld
DDEENNORU underdone
DDEENNOUW unendowed
DDEENORRT retrodden
DDEENORRU underdoer
unordered
DDEENORTU outredden
DDEENORUY round-eyed
DDEENPSSU suspended
DDEENRSSU undressed
DDEEORSTY destroyed
DDEERRSTU Red Duster
DDEERSTTU trust deed
DDEFFIINT diffident
DDEFFLOOT toddle off
DDEFFMORU dufferdom
DDEFGGIOT God-gifted
DDEFGIIIN dignified
DDEFGILLO goldfield
DDEFGINOR foddering
DDEFGINRU drug fiend
DDEFIIMNU mundified
DDEFILOOT floodtide
DDEFINNUX index fund
DDEFIRSTY dry-fisted
DDEFLLOOW Oddfellow
DDEFNNOUU unfounded
DDEFNNRUU underfund
DDEGGNRUU ungrudged
DDEGHHIIR high-dried
DDEGHINRS shredding
DDEGIIIRW rigwiddie
DDEGIIMSU misguided
DDEGIINNR niddering
DDEGIINOR indigo red
DDEGIINSS giddiness
DDEGIISSU disguised
DDEGIJLLU ill-judged
DDEGIKMNO kingdomed
DDEGILRTY Teddy girl
DDEGINNPU puddening
DDEGINORR derring do
derring-do
DDEGINPRU redding-up
DDEGINRRU undergird
DDEGIOOSZ good-sized
DDEGIORRU Ruddigore
DDEGISSTU disgusted
DDEGLNNUU delundung
DDEGLNOOR goldenrod
DDEGLOOOP poodle-dog
DDEGNOOOR godrooned
DDEGNOVWY down-gyved
DDEGOOORY do-goodery
DDEHHNRTU hundredth
DDEHIILPS Didelphis
DDEHIIRSY Yiddisher
DDEHILPSY Didelphys
DDEHIORSW drowsihed
DDEHIORXY hydroxide
DDEHLOOST the old sod
DDEHNORRU hundredor
DDEHOORRT hot-rodder
DDEIIKLNR kiln-dried
DDEIIKNRT diet-drink
DDEIIKRSV disk drive
DDEIILLST distilled
DDEIILLSU disillude
DDEIILRST estrildid

DDEIILSTT tiddliest
DDEIIMTTW dim-witted
DDEIINORS iron-sided
DDEIINPRS spin-dried
DDEIINSST dissident
DDEIKLNNU unkindled
DDEILLNRU undrilled
DDEILMNOT Middleton
DDEILMNOW low-minded
DDEILNRRU unriddler
DDEILNTUU undiluted
DDEILORWW worldwide
DDEILSTUV dust devil
DDEILSTUY studiedly
DDEIMMOSU desmodium
DDEIMNSSU muddiness
DDEINOSSW dowdiness
DDEINRSSU dissunder
ruddiness
DDEINSTUU unstudied
DDEIOPPRU proud-pied
DDEIOPRRU Dr Proudie
DDEIOPRSV disproved
DDEIORSSW sword side
DDEIORSTT distorted
DDELMNOOO noodledom
DDELMNOUU unmoulded
DDELOORTT odd-lotter
DDENNORSU send round
DDENNORTU untrodden
DDENNORTW downtrend
DDENNORUU unrounded
DDENNORUW down under
undrowned
DDENNOSUU unsounded
DDENNOUUW unwounded
DDENOOOTU odd one out
DDENOORSW do wonders
DDENOORUW underwood✧
DDENOPSUU pudendous
DDENORSSW dress down
DDEOOPPSU pseudopod
DDEOORRRW word order
DDFGILORU Guildford
DDFIOORTW driftwood
DDGGINOOO do-gooding
DDGIIKLNY kiddingly
DDGIILMNS middlings
DDGIILNRS riddlings
DDGIILNTW twiddling
DDGIINORR riding rod
DDGILNNOY noddingly
DDGIMOOOS do-goodism
DDGINNORW grind down
DDHIOOOWW widowhood
DDHLMOOOU hood-mould
DDHOORSST short odds
DDIIKKNWY kiddywink
DDIILMSTU Ludditism
DDIIOSUUV dividuous
DDILLOPRR drop-drill
DDIMNOOUY do you mind?
DDIMPTUYY iddy-umpty
DDINNORUW wind round
DDINOPSUU dupondius
DDINOSTUY noddy suit
DDIORRTWY dirty word
DDNNOORUW round down
round-down
DDNOOORUW roundwood
DDOOORWWW row-dow-dow
DEEEEFHST sheet-feed
DEEEEFNRV enfevered
DEEEEGHLW wedge heel
DEEEEGNRW greenweed
DEEEEGNRY green-eyed
DEEEEHPRT three deep
DEEEEJLWW jewel-weed
DEEEEKLTY delete key
DEEEEKNRW weekender
DEEEFGIKN knife-edge
DEEEFIIRR re-edifier
DEEEFIJOU feu de joie
DEEEFIKNR reed-knife
DEEEFINPR predefine
DEEEFINSV defensive
DEEEFIRRR free-rider
DEEEFIRRV free-diver
DEEEFLLNU needleful
DEEEFLRUX deflexure
DEEEFMNOR enfreedom
DEEEFMNRT deferment
fermented
DEEEFPRRR preferred
DEEEFRRYZ freeze-dry
DEEEGGHIR Heidegger
DEEEGGLNO one-legged
DEEEGHNOT on the edge
DEEEGIKLW wedge-like
DEEEGILSW Wild Geese
DEEEGIMNR redeeming
DEEEGISWW wedgewise
DEEEGKLNT kentledge
DEEEGLNNU needle-gun
DEEEGLNOY GoldenEye
golden-eye
DEEEGLOSV sleeve dog
DEEEGMNST segmented
DEEEGNNRU engendure
DEEEGNOST set on edge
DEEEGNPSU gens de peu
DEEEGNRSW sedge wren
DEEEGNRTT detergent
DEEEGRRTT regretted
DEEEHILLW idle wheel
DEEEHILMS seemlihed
DEEEHILPS ephelides
DEEEHILSW side-wheel
DEEEHILTT dithelete✧
DEEEHIMPR ephemerid
DEEEHINPR ephedrine
DEEEHINSS heediness
DEEEHISTT diet sheet
DEEEHLMSY seemlyhed
DEEEHLRST sheltered
DEEEHMNRU enrheumed
DEEEHMRSS medresseh
DEEEHNOSY honey-seed
DEEEHNPRR reprehend
DEEEHNRRU hereunder
DEEEHORSW shoreweed
DEEEIILSS dieselise
DEEEIILSZ dieselize
DEEEILLMP millepede
DEEEILLVW weevilled
DEEEILNNT needle-tin
DEEEILNRT tree-lined
DEEEILPRU lie perdue
DEEEILPRV replevied
DEEEILPTV depletive
DEEEILRRV deliverer
redeliver
DEEEILSSW edelweiss
DEEEIMNRT determine
DEEEIMNSU Eumenides
DEEEIMSST disesteem
DEEEINNNZ endenizen
DEEEINNSS neediness
DEEEINNTV net-veined
DEEEINPST steeped in
DEEEINPTX expedient
DEEEINQSU queenside
DEEEINRRS reindeers
DEEEINRRV River Eden
DEEEINRSS reediness
DEEEINRST tenderise
teredines
DEEEINRTZ tenderize
DEEEINSSS seediness
DEEEINSSW weediness
DEEEIPRTX expediter
DEEEIRRVW riverweed
DEEEIRSTV detersive
DEEEISTTW tweediest
DEEEKLLNN kennelled
DEEEKNPRU keep under
underkeep
DEEELLPSW speedwell
DEEELLRVV vervelled
DEEELMNOW lemon-weed
DEEELMOPS sleep mode
DEEELNOPV enveloped
DEEELOPPV développé
DEEELOPRV developer
redevelop
DEEELORRS rose elder
DEEELPSSS speedless
DEEELRRTT red-letter
DEEELRSTW sweltered
DEEEMNNOV envenomed
DEEEMNOSY seed money
DEEEMNRTT determent
DEEEMOPRT pedometer

DEEEMORST dose-meter
DEEEMORSU deer mouse
mouse-deer
DEEEMPRST destemper
DEEENNQUU unqueened
DEEENNRTU unentered
DEEENNRUW unrenewed
DEEENNSSS denseness
DEEENORRS re-endorse
DEEENPPRU underpeep
DEEENPRRT pretender
DEEENRRSV renversed
DEEENRRTT deterrent
DEEENRSUV undeserve
unsevered
DEEENSSVX vexedness
DEEEOORVW woodreeve
DEEEOPRRS pedereros
DEEEOPRTV predevote
DEEEORRRS reredorse
DEEEORRSS reredosse
DEEEORRST ore-rested
DEEEORSTV stevedore
DEEEORSUV désoeuvré
DEEEORSVX oversexed
DEEEPPPRR red pepper
DEEEPRRSS derepress
repressed
DEEEPRRTV perverted
DEEEPRSST speedster
DEEEPRSSU supersede
DEEERRRSS redresser
DEEERRSTT red setter
DEEFFFSTU feedstuff
DEEFFHILS Sheffield
DEEFFILLT left-field
DEEFFINRT different
DEEFFNORU unoffered
DEEFFOPRR proffered
DEEFGIILN Englified
DEEFGIILR filigreed
DEEFGIIRS Siegfried
DEEFGILNY feignedly
DEEFGILRY field grey
DEEFGINNR finger-end
DEEFGINNU unfeigned
DEEFGINRR deferring
DEEFGIRRU red-figure
DEEFGJORU forejudge
DEEFGLNNO dog fennel
DEEFGLORV gold-fever
DEEFGNNRU green fund
DEEFHINRT The Friend
DEEFHLLUY heedfully
DEEFHLNSU unfleshed
DEEFHLNUU unheedful
DEEFHLOPS sheepfold
DEEFHLORT threefold
DEEFHLORY Fred Hoyle
DEEFIIKLN fiendlike
DEEFIILMN minefield
DEEFIILNR infielder
DEEFIILQU liquefied
DEEFIILSZ life-sized
DEEFIINNS definiens
DEEFIINRS densifier
DEEFIIPRT petrified
DEEFIIPSS fissipede
DEEFIIRRT terrified
DEEFIIRSV versified
DEEFIISST dies festi
DEEFIISTT testified
DEEFILLOV fieldvole
DEEFILNOP open-field
DEEFILNOX deflexion
DEEFILNRY refinedly
DEEFILORT trefoiled
DEEFILPRS self-pride
DEEFILRSV self-drive
DEEFILSTT field test
field-test
DEEFIMPST septemfid
DEEFIMRSU frusemide
DEEFINNPR pen friend
DEEFINNRU unrefined
DEEFINRRU under fire
underfire
DEEFINRUV under-five
DEEFINSST fetidness
DEEFINSSX fixedness
DEEFIOPRT torpefied
DEEFIORRT torrefied
DEEFIPRRV perfervid
DEEFIPRTU putrefied
DEEFIPSTU stupefied
DEEFIRSTU surfeited
DEEFKKLRW F W de Klerk
DEEFLLNNU funnelled
DEEFLLNUU unfuelled
DEEFLLNUY needfully
DEEFLLPSU full-speed
DEEFLNNUU unneedful
DEEFLNOSV sevenfold
DEEFLNRSU underself
DEEFLNRTU underfelt
DEEFLOOTW Fleetwood
DEEFLORRW Free World
DEEFNOOPS spoon-feed
DEEFNOPRS forespend
DEEFNORRU refounder
DEEFNOSTU fondue set
DEEFNRTTU unfretted
DEEFNRTUU unrefuted
DEEFOPRSS professed
DEEFORRST defroster
DEEFPRRRY Fred Perry
DEEGGIMOR demi-gorge
DEEGGIRSU ruggedise
DEEGGIRUZ ruggedize
DEEGGLOTW two-legged
DEEGGMNTU nutmegged
DEEGGOPRW egg powder
DEEGHHIPS high-speed
DEEGHHSTU Ted Hughes
DEEGHILNW wheedling
DEEGHINNU unheeding
DEEGHINUW unweighed
DEEGHOORS gooseherd
DEEGIILNS ingle-side
DEEGIILNU guideline
DEEGIILRT ridge tile
DEEGIINTY tie-dyeing
DEEGIISTV digestive
DEEGIJLNU line judge
DEEGIKLNT kintledge
DEEGILLOR liege-lord
DEEGILMNW winged elm
DEEGILNNS single-end
DEEGILNOS gens de loi
DEEGILNOU euglenoid
DEEGILNRT ringleted
DEEGILNSS gelidness
DEEGILNST legendist
DEEGILOOU ideologue
DEEGILOPR ridgepole
DEEGILPRS spider leg
DEEGILRSY lysergide
DEEGILSSU guideless
DEEGIMNPT depigment
pigmented
DEEGIMNRY remedying
DEEGIMORT geometrid
DEEGINNRR rendering
DEEGINNRS Red Ensign
DEEGINNRT tendering
DEEGINNTT denetting
DEEGINNTW net-winged
DEEGINORT de integro
redingote
DEEGINPRS predesign
DEEGINRRR derringer
DEEGINRRT deterring
DEEGINRSV deserving
DEEGINRTU negritude
DEEGINRTV divergent
DEEGINRUV gerundive
DEEGIOPRR ridge rope
DEEGIOPRU guide rope
DEEGIOSST geodesist
DEEGIPRST predigest
DEEGIRRUU de rigueur
DEEGJMNTU judgement
DEEGKLNNO dog-kennel
DEEGKLNOW knowledge
DEEGKOPRW powder keg
DEEGLLOOP lodgepole
DEEGLLORV grovelled
DEEGLMNOT lodgement
DEEGLNNOW Gwendolen
DEEGLNOOW wooden leg
DEEGLNTTU englutted
DEEGLORTT dog letter
DEEGNNNOU endungeon

DEEGNNORU dungeoner
gone under
undergone
DEEGNOORW greenwood
DEEGNOOSS good sense
DEEGNORRU reguerdon
DEEGNORSS engrossed
DEEGNORWW weed-grown
DEEGNOUYY young-eyed
DEEGNSSUU unguessed
DEEGORRSU red grouse
DEEHHILNW hind-wheel
DEEHHILOY hidey-hole
DEEHHIMRY hemihedry
DEEHHIORS horsehide
DEEHHMOTT the method
DEEHHPSTT the depths
DEEHIINPT pethidine
DEEHIKRSW whiskered
DEEHILNUY unheedily
DEEHILORU hierodule
DEEHILOTU hôtel-Dieu
DEEHILPRS eldership
DEEHILRSV shriveled
DEEHILSTV The Devils
DEEHIMOOV home video
DEEHIMORV drive home
DEEHIMOST methodise
DEEHIMOTZ methodize
DEEHINNOV Eindhoven
DEEHINOOP ideophone
DEEHINORT dinothere
DEEHINOST on the side
DEEHINRRV hen-driver
DEEHINRSW swineherd
DEEHINRTY enhydrite
DEEHINTTW hen-witted
DEEHIOPRT herpetoid
the period
DEEHIORSS shoreside
DEEHIOTTW to the wide
DEEHJNOWY John Dewey
DEEHLLOSU houselled
DEEHLLOSV shovelled
DEEHLNOOT on the dole
DEEHLNOPR penholder
phenol red
DEEHLOPRW pew-holder
DEEHLORST holstered
DEEHLPSST depthless
DEEHLRSSS shredless
DEEHMNNOT on the mend
DEEHMNORT den mother
endotherm
DEEHMOORT hodometer
DEEHMORST smothered
DEEHMRTUY thrum-eyed
DEEHNNOPS sphendone
DEEHNOOQU queenhood
DEEHNOPTY endophyte
DEEHNORRT dethroner
DEEHNORTY the yonder
DEEHNRRTU thunderer
DEEHNRSUU unushered
DEEHOOPRT heteropod
DEEHOORTX heterodox
DEEHOOSUV dove-house
DEEHOPSTU Deep South
DEEHRSTTU shuttered
DEEHSSTTU dustsheet
DEEIIINPR pieridine
DEEIIKNRS die-sinker
DEEIILLMP millipede
DEEIILLOS diesel oil
DEEIILMRT delimiter
DEEIILNSS sidelines
DEEIIMNTT midinette
DEEIIMPQU demipique
DEEIIMPRS epidermis
DEEIIMRTV drive time
DEEIIMSSV demissive
DEEIINNPP pinnipede
DEEIINNRT interdine
DEEIINPST desipient
DEEIINRTU inerudite
DEEIIOPRS periodise
DEEIIOPRZ periodize
DEEIIOPST epidosite
DEEIIPPPR pied piper
DEEIIPRSU Euripides
DEEIIPSSW sideswipe
DEEIIRRSV riverside✧
DEEIIRRTV river-tide
DEEIIRTVV divertive
DEEIISSSU side issue
DEEIJNORR rejoinder
DEEIJNRTV jet-driven
DEEIJPRUZ prejudize
DEEIKLLNR knee-drill
DEEIKLLRS killdeers
DEEIKLNSW slinkweed
DEEIKLNSX sex-linked
DEEIKLOVY yoke-devil
DEEIKNORV overinked
DEEIKNORY kidney ore
DEEIKNSTW stinkweed
DEEILLLNT lintelled
DEEILLLNW well-lined
DEEILLLOW well-oiled
DEEILLMNO ill-omened
DEEILLMST mild steel
DEEILLMTW well-timed
DEEILLNRT red lentil
DEEILLNRV Rivendell
DEEILLNRW indweller
DEEILLNST tinselled
DEEILLNSV snivelled
DEEILLNTT little end
DEEILLNTV divellent
DEEILLRRT tredrille
DEEILLRRV driveller
DEEILLRST stellerid
trellised
DEEILLRSU slide rule
DEEILLRSV ill-versed
DEEILLRTU telluride
DEEILLRTW well-tried
DEEILLRVY deliverly
DEEILLSSW wieldless
DEEILLSVW swivelled
DEEILMMNS Mendelism
DEEILMNOV dime novel
DEEILMNOY idle money
DEEILMNTV devilment
DEEILMOTV demi-volte
DEEILMPTU multipede
DEEILNNPU penduline
DEEILNNRU underline
DEEILNOPT depletion
diplotene
DEEILNOTV delve into
DEEILNPTU plenitude
DEEILNRTU interlude
DEEILNRUV live under
DEEILNSSX indexless
DEEILNTVY evidently
DEEILOPPS dispeople
DEEILOPRS despoiler
pelorised
DEEILOPRZ pelorized
DEEILPPRS slippered
DEEILPRSS prideless
DEEILRRSS riderless
DEEILRRTY retiredly
DEEILRSST slide rest
DEEILRSVY diversely
DEEILRTUY eruditely
DEEIMMOOR Demi Moore
DEEIMNNPT impendent
DEEIMNNRU undermine
DEEIMNNRV never mind
DEEIMNORS demersion
modernise
DEEIMNORZ modernize
DEEIMNOSS Des Moines
DEEIMNOSU Idomeneus
DEEIMNPTU unemptied
DEEIMNRTT detriment
DEEIMNRTU undertime
unmerited
DEEIMNSSX mixedness
DEEIMOORT meteoroid
DEEIMOPRR peridrome
DEEIMORST dime store
dosimeter
DEEIMORSX exodermis
DEEIMPRST distemper
DEEIMPRTT permitted
DEEIMRSST misdesert
DEEIMRSTU Demetrius
DEEIMRTUU deuterium
DEEINNNPU unpennied
DEEINNOOY onion-eyed

 Words marked ✧ can also be spelled with one or more capital letters

DEEINNORT internode
DEEINNOTT detention
DEEINNPRU unripened
DEEINNQSU sequinned
DEEINNRST dinner set
DEEINNRTU indenture
DEEINNSSS snideness
DEEINNSUW unsinewed
DEEINOPPR drone-pipe
DEEINOPRT terpenoid
DEEINOPTX pentoxide
DEEINORST desertion
deterision
DEEINORSW rosinweed
DEEINPRRU under-ripe
DEEINPRRV pen-driver
DEEINPRSS dispenser
DEEINPRST president
DEEINPRUX unexpired
DEEINPSST tepidness
DEEINRRSU surreined
DEEINRSST dissenter✧
tiredness
DEEINRSSW weirdness
DEEINRSTT trendiest
DEEINRSUV unrevised
DEEIOOPPR pereiopod
DEEIOOPTX exopodite
DEEIOPPRW piepowder
DEEIOPRTX expeditor
DEEIOPRVW power dive
power-dive
DEEIORRRV overrider
River Oder
DEEIORRVV overdrive
DEEIORSVZ oversized
DEEIORTTX tetroxide
DEEIOTTVX videotext
DEEIPRRSS disperser
DEEIPRSTU disrepute
DEEIQRTTU requitted
DEEIRSTTV test drive
test-drive
DEEIRSTUV divesture
servitude
DEEIRTTXY dexterity
DEEISTTTU destitute
DEEJMOSTU jeu de mots
DEEJNORUY journeyed
DEEJOORVY overjoyed
DEEKKOOYY okey-dokey
DEEKLLNNU unknelled
DEEKLNOSV veldskoen
DEEKNORST stonkered
DEEKNORUV unrevoked
DEEKRRTUY Turkey red
DEELLMMOP pommelled
DEELLMMPU pummelled
DEELLMOOR role model
DEELLMRTU red mullet
DEELLMSSU musselled
DEELLNNTU tunnelled
DEELLNOVW level down
DEELLNQUU unquelled
DEELLNRSU undersell
DEELLNRSY slenderly
DEELLNSSY endlessly
DEELLOPPR propelled
DEELLOPRT petrolled
DEELLORST Lord Steel
DEELLORTW trowelled
DEELMNORS mesne lord
DEELMOORV velodrome
DEELMOPRU loup de mer
DEELMRSTU steel drum
DEELNNOOS Londonese
DEELNNPST splendent
DEELNNPTY pendently
DEELNOOST lodestone
DEELNOPPU unpeopled
DEELNPRRU plunderer
DEELNRSTU end result
DEELNSTTU unsettled
DEELOOPRS rope-soled
DEELOORSV Dover sole
DEELOPRSY reposedly
DEELOPRTY depletory
DEELORRSS orderless
DEELORSSW dowerless
DEELPRTUY reputedly
DEEMMOOSS desmosome
DEEMNNOTW endowment
DEEMNNOUY unmoneyed
DEEMNOOSS endosmose
DEEMNOPRS endosperm
DEEMNOPSU spodumene
DEEMNORTT tormented
DEEMNORUV unremoved
DEEMNOSTU endosteum
DEEMNPTTU untempted
DEEMNSSTU must needs
needs must
DEEMOORST osteoderm
DEEMPRTTU trumpeted
DEEMRRSSU murderess
DEENNORTU undernote
undertone
DEENNOSST notedness
DEENNRSTU nurse-tend
DEENNRTUW underwent
DEENOOPRR open order
DEENOOPRS endospore
DEENOPRRS responder
DEENOPRRV provender
DEENOPRSV overspend
DEENOPRUX expounder
DEENOPSUX unexposed
DEENORSTU run to seed
DEENPRSSU suspender
unpressed
DEENRRRSU surrender
DEENRRSTU unredrest
DEENRRTTU Ted Turner
DEENRSSTT tent dress
DEENRSSTU untressed
DEENRSTTU Ernst Udet
DEENRSTUV undervest
DEENRSTYY dysentery
DEENRTTUU unuttered
DEEOOPRRT torpedoer
DEEOOPRRV provedore
DEEOOPRST torpedoes
DEEOOSTWW sweetwood
DEEOPPPSY poppy seed
DEEOPPSTU up to speed
DEEOPRRSS depressor
DEEOPRSSW prowessed
DEEOPRSUZ douzepers
DEEOPSSSS possessed
DEEORRSSV overdress
DEEORRSTU trousered
DEEORRSTX dextrorse
DEEORRSTY destroyer
DEEORSTUX dexterous
DEERRSSTU tressured
DEFFGINNO offending
DEFFIIORT fortified
DEFFIISUV diffusive
DEFFILLLU fulfilled
DEFFILNTU diffluent
DEFFILSUY diffusely
DEFFIMRSU dufferism
DEFFINOOT fin-footed
DEFFLNRUU unruffled
DEFFLORTU toruffled
DEFFNNSUU unsnuffed
DEFFNSTUU unstuffed
DEFFOPTUU puffed out
DEFFPSTUU stuffed up
DEFGGIINT fidgeting
DEFGGILLN fledgling
DEFGGIOOR good grief
good grief!
DEFGGLRUU grudgeful
DEFGHILOT eightfold
DEFGIIILN lignified
DEFGIIINS signified
DEFGIILOR glorified
DEFGIINNR friending
DEFGIIRSU disfigure
DEFGILLNO long field
DEFGILNSU designful
DEFGINOTW get wind of
DEFGINRRY finger-dry
DEFGINRUU unfigured
DEFGNNORU underfong
DEFGOOPRR drop-forge
DEFHHLOOS fleshhood
DEFHIIILT lithified
DEFHIILSV devilfish
DEFHIIORR horrified
DEFHILLOY Holyfield
DEFHINRSU furnished

underfish
DEFHIORRS rodfisher
DEFHLOOOW wholefood
DEFHNORRY Henry Ford
DEFIIINRT nitrified
DEFIIIPST tipsified
DEFIIIRTV vitrified
DEFIIISSS sissified
DEFIIJSTU justified
DEFIILLMO mollified
DEFIILLNU nullified
DEFIILLRR fire drill
DEFIILMRU Muirfield
DEFIILMSU semifluid
DEFIILOSX fixed oils
DEFIILPRT field trip
DEFIIMMMU mummified
DEFIIMNNY indemnify
DEFIIMORT mortified
DEFIIMRWY midwifery
DEFIIMSTY mystified
DEFIINRTY denitrify
DEFIINSST disinfest
DEFIIRSSU Russified
DEFIIRSVY diversify
DEFIIRTVY devitrify
fervidity
DEFIKLORW fieldwork
DEFIKORTW twiforked
DEFILLNNO linen-fold
DEFILLORR filler rod
DEFILLRUY direfully
DEFILMNRU remindful
DEFILMORT mitre fold
DEFILMSUY demulsify
DEFILNORT interfold
DEFILNOSW snowfield
DEFILNOUX defluxion
DEFILNSSU fluidness
DEFILNSTU disfluent
unstifled
DEFILORSX dorsiflex
DEFILRSST driftless
DEFIMNNOO of one mind
DEFIMNORT dentiform
DEFIMNORU uniformed
DEFIMORRT triformed
DEFIMORTW twiformed
DEFIMORTY deformity
DEFIMSTYY demystify
DEFIOOPSS dispose of
DEFIORSST disforest
DEFIORTTU fortitude
DEFIOSTTW two-fisted
DEFKOORTW two-forked
DEFKORTWY twyforked
DEFLLLOOW old fellow
DEFLLLOUY dolefully
DEFLLNOUW well-found
DEFLLORSW self-rowld
DEFLLRSSU full dress
full-dress
DEFLNOORU unfloored
DEFLNOORW new for old
DEFLNORUW underflow
wonderful
DEFLOORRT Lord Forte
DEFLOPRWY fly powder
DEFLSSTUY self-study
DEFMOORRR order form
DEFMORRSS dress form
DEFMORTWY twyformed
DEFNOORRU under-roof
DEFNOORTU underfoot
DEFNOOSST soft-nosed
DEFNORRSW sword fern
DEFNORSSU foundress
DEFNORSUU unsued-for
DEFNOSSTU not fussed
DEFOOOSTV dove's-foot
DEFOOOTTW two-footed
DEGGGIMRU gum-digger
DEGGHILOS dog sleigh
DEGGHLORU Lough Derg
DEGGHOORT hot-dogger
DEGGIILRU Girl Guide
DEGGIINNS designing
DEGGIINRV diverging
DEGGINOSS dogginess
DEGGLMORU mudlogger
DEGGLNPUU unplugged
DEGHHINOT high-toned
DEGHHOTTU thoughted
DEGHIILNS shielding
DEGHIILNT delight in
DEGHIILPR hip-girdle
DEGHIILST sidelight
DEGHIINST nightside
DEGHIINTT night-tide
DEGHIIPSU guideship
DEGHIIRST right side
DEGHIISTT tight side
DEGHIJPSU judgeship
DEGHIKORY hygrodeik
DEGHILMSU gumshield
DEGHILNTU undelight
unlighted
DEGHILOTW white gold
DEGHILPTU uplighted
DEGHILSTU light-dues
DEGHIMNRU humdinger
DEGHINOWW weigh down
DEGHINRTU ungirthed
DEGHINSTU unsighted
DEGHIORTV overdight
DEGHKOORU hooked rug
DEGHMOORR herd-groom
DEGHMOORT godmother
DEGHNNRUU underhung
DEGHNORUW grewhound
DEGHNORUY greyhound
DEGHOOOTT to the good
DEGHOORSS dogshores
DEGIIIMRS dirigisme
semi-rigid
DEGIIIRST digitiser
dirigiste
DEGIIIRTZ digitizer
DEGIIKNSZ king-sized
DEGIILLNV devilling
DEGIILNNR niderling
red-lining
DEGIILNNU indulge in
DEGIILNOV evil-doing
DEGIILNRW wildering
DEGIIMNNP impending
DEGIIMRSU misguider
DEGIINNOS diosgenin
DEGIINNSS dinginess
DEGIINOSS gneissoid
DEGIINOST digestion
DEGIINRRS ringsider
DEGIINRSS rigidness
DEGIINRTU nigritude
DEGIINRTV diverting
DEGIINSTU distingué
DEGIIOORW rigwoodie
DEGIIRRSV verdigris
DEGIIRSSU disguiser
DEGIKLNOU ungodlike
DEGIKMOOS Eskimo dog
DEGIKNNRU underking
DEGILLMNO modelling
DEGILLNOV long-lived
DEGILLNOW dowelling
well-doing
DEGILLOTT Little Dog
DEGILMNNU unmingled
DEGILMNOR goldminer
DEGILNNRU underling
DEGILNNTU indulgent
DEGILNNYY denyingly
DEGILNOOR gondolier
DEGILNORS soldering
DEGILNOSS godliness
DEGILNOST Odelsting
DEGILNOTU longitude
DEGILNPRS speldring
DEGILOOST goodliest
DEGILOOSW wild goose
DEGILOOTV dog violet
DEGILOSTT glottides
DEGIMNRRU demurring
DEGIMOORT good-timer
DEGIMRSUU demiurgus
DEGINNORW wondering
DEGINNRRU under-ring
DEGINNRSU sundering
undersign
DEGINNRUW underwing
DEGINNSSY dyingness
DEGINOOSS goodiness
DEGINOPSS podginess

DEGINORRW reworded
DEGINORSW wrong side
DEGINORUV devouring
DEGINPSSU pudginess
DEGIOORRR giro order
DEGIOORTW tigerwood
DEGIOPRTY pterygoid
DEGIOPSTU guidepost
DEGIORRTW grow tired
DEGKLORTU Kurt Gödel
DEGLLOOWY yellow dog
DEGLLOSSY godlessly
DEGLMORUY grey mould
DEGLNNOOZ long dozen
DEGLNNOPY gold penny
DEGLNOOST goldstone
DEGLNOOUZ Zeuglodon
DEGLNORSU groundsel
DEGLNOSSU unglossed
DEGMNOORU ungroomed
DEGMOPSTU smudge pot
DEGNNORSU undersong
DEGNNORUW undergown
DEGNOORRW wrongdoer
DEGNOOSTT stegodont
DEGNOPRUW gunpowder
DEGOORUVW vogue word
DEGORRSTU drugstore
DEHHIKMOS sheikhdom
DEHHINOSY hoydenish
DEHHIOPPS phosphide
DEHHLLNOU hellhound
DEHHLOOSU household✧
DEHHLORST threshold
DEHHNOORU horehound
DEHHORSTU the Shroud
DEHIIINST histidine
DEHIILMST dithelism✧
DEHIILOOP iodophile
DEHIILPSV devilship
DEHIILRSS disrelish
DEHIILSVY shield ivy
DEHIIMNSU disinhume
DEHIIMNTY thymidine
DEHIIMOPP hippiedom
DEHIINNRU hirundine
DEHIINNTW in the wind
DEHIINOOP idiophone
DEHIIOOPX pixie hood
DEHIIOPST it is hoped
DEHIIOSTY hideosity
DEHIIPRST petri dish✧
DEHIIPSTY diphysite✧
DEHIIRSSV disshiver
DEHIISTWW widthwise
DEHIKKOOZ Kozhikode
DEHIKLNOR inkholder
DEHILLLOR drillhole
DEHILMNOU lime-hound
DEHILMTWY wild thyme
DEHILNOPT dolphinet
DEHILNOWY wild honey
DEHILNPSU Delphinus
DEHILOORT rhodolite
DEHILORRT Lord Reith
DEHILOSTW dishtowel
DEHILOSUY hideously
DEHILRRUY hurriedly
DEHIMMOST Methodism
DEHIMNORT Trondheim
DEHIMNOSY hoydenism
DEHIMNSSU humidness
DEHIMORRT thermidor✧
DEHIMOSTT methodist✧
DEHIMOSTU Methodius
DEHINNOOR Rhineodon
DEHINNOPR endorphin
DEHINOORT rhodonite
DEHINOOSW swinehood
DEHINORRT trihedron
DEHINORST disthrone
DEHINORVW windhover
DEHINOSST dishonest
DEHINPPUW unwhipped
DEHINRRUU unhurried
DEHINRSUV unshrived
DEHINRTTU thunder it
DEHIOORSW Isherwood
DEHIOOSST sideshoot
DEHIOOTWW howtowdie
whitewood
DEHIORSTY hysteroid
DEHIORSUY yird-house
DEHJNNNOO John Donne
DEHKLOOST stokehold
DEHKMOOOS smokehood
DEHKNOOOS hook-nosed
DEHLLOOSU dollhouse
DEHLMNOPY endolymph
lymph node
DEHLMNOUY lyme-hound
DEHLMOORU hordeolum
DEHLMOORW wormholed
DEHLNOORW horned owl
DEHLNOOSU sound hole
DEHLNOSSW seldshown
DEHLOOPRT pot holder
DEHLORSYY hydrolyse
DEHLORTYY hydrolyte
DEHLORYYZ hydrolyze
DEHLOSSTU shouldest
DEHLPRSUU desulphur
DEHMMOPRU Prudhomme
prud'homme
DEHMNOOPR endomorph
DEHMOORSY hydrosome
DEHMOORTY hodometry
DEHMOPPRU mudhopper
DEHMORRWY rhyme word
DEHNNNSUU unshunned
DEHNNOOPS sphenodon✧
DEHNNOSUW newshound
DEHNOOOWY wood honey
DEHNOOPRS horsepond
DEHNOORWY Henry Wood
DEHNORSTU undershot
DEHNORSUY enhydrous
DEHNPRTUU upthunder
DEHOOOPPT hooped-pot
DEHOOORSW woodhorse
DEHOOOSUW woodhouse
DEHOOPRTY orthopedy
DEHOORSTU Herodotus
DEHOOSSSU dosshouse
DEHORSSTU stud horse
DEHOSTUUY house-duty
DEHRRRSYY dry sherry
DEIIIKNTT Identi-Kit
identikit
DEIIILLMT illimited
DEIIILMSS dissimile
DEIIILQSU liquidise
DEIIILQUZ liquidize
DEIIILRSV virilised
DEIIILRVZ virilized
DEIIINNQU quinidine
DEIIINSSS disseisin
DEIIINSSZ disseizin
DEIIINSTV disinvite
DEIIIPSTX ipse dixit
DEIIKKLNR kilderkin
DEIIKLNNX index-link
DEIIKNRSV skin-diver
DEIILLMPY impliedly
DEIILLMTY limitedly
DEIILLNOT tellinoid
DEIILLNST instilled
DEIILLOPR pilloried
DEIILLOPS ellipsoid
DEIILLOVW wild olive
DEIILLRST distiller
DEIILMNTU unlimited
DEIILMOPY polyimide
DEIILMOSS semisolid
DEIILMQUU deliquium
DEIILMRSU deliriums
DEIILNNUV unlived-in
DEIILNOPR iprindole
DEIILNOTU toluidine
DEIILNOXY xyloidine
DEIILNSSV lividness
DEIILOPRT reptiloid
DEIILORSU delirious
DEIILPPTU lippitude
DEIILPTTT tip-tilted
DEIILSUVV divulsive
DEIIMMRSU disimmure
DEIIMNNOS dimension
DEIIMNNST misintend
DEIIMNNTY indemnity
DEIIMNOSS demission
DEIIMNOSX endomixis
DEIIMNPUX mixed up in

DEIIMNRSS minidress
DEIIMNRTW mid-winter
DEIIMNRUU uredinium
DEIIMNRUW Edwin Muir
DEIIMNSST timidness
DEIIMORTV dormitive
DEIIMPRSS misprised
DEIIMPRSU presidium
DEIIMPRTU Pteridium
DEIIMRTTY tridymite
DEIINNNOT indention
DEIINNOOP opinioned
DEIINNORS Deinornis
DEIINNORT rendition
DEIINNOSU unionised
DEIINNOTT dentition
DEIINNOTV vendition
DEIINNOUZ unionized
DEIINNRTW interwind
DEIINNSSW windiness
DEIINNSTV disinvent
DEIINNTUV uninvited
DEIINOORX iron oxide
DEIINOPRT perdition
DEIINOPSS indispose
DEIINORSS Ironsides
DEIINORST disorient
DEIINORSV diversion
DEIINORTT detrition
DEIINORTU erudition
DEIINOSTU inside out
outside in
DEIINOTTZ Donizetti
DEIINPRRS spin drier
DEIINPSTU in dispute
DEIINPSTZ pint-sized
DEIINRSST dirtiness
DEIINSSTV disinvest
DEIINSSVV vividness
DEIINSSZZ dizziness
DEIINSTUV unvisited
DEIINTTTW nitwitted
DEIIOPRSS presidios
DEIIORSSS disseisor
siderosis
DEIIORSSZ disseizor
DEIIOSSTU seditious
DEIIOSTTY tediosity
DEIIPRRST priest-rid
DEIIPRSTT dipterist
DEIIRSTVY diversity
DEIIRSUVV redivivus
DEIISTTUV vedutisti
DEIJLNNNY Jenny Lind
DEIJNNOTU unjointed
DEIJNNRUU uninjured
DEIKKLNOR klondiker
DEIKKNOOP pondokkie
DEIKLLNSU unskilled
DEIKLLOSV Volkslied
DEIKLNSTU Kunstlied
DEIKLORSW swordlike
DEIKMMNSU unskimmed
DEIKMNNOW womenkind
DEIKNNNSU unskinned
DEIKNSSSU duskiness
sun-kissed
DEIKORSST disk store
DEILLLPUV pull devil
pulvilled
DEILLMNOU mullioned
DEILLMNUU unillumed
DEILLNORW world line
DEILLNOSS dolliness
DEILLNPSU unspilled
DEILLNSTU unstilled
DEILLNSUU unsullied
DEILLOPST pistolled
DEILLORSY soldierly
DEILLPRTU uptrilled
DEILLSTTY stiltedly
DEILMMOTU multimode
DEILMNOPT implodent
DEILMNUXY unmixedly
DEILMOOST Dolomites
DEILMOOSU melodious
DEILMOPSY disemploy
DEILMORSW idle worms
DEILMOSTU mouldiest
DEILMOUVV luvviedom
DEILMPRSY Simply Red
DEILMTTUU multitude
DEILNNOOS Londonise
DEILNNOOZ Londonize
DEILNOORS soldier on
DEILNOPSU unspoiled
DEILNOPTU unpiloted
DEILNOPTY pointedly
DEILNORSU undersoil
DEILNOSSS solidness
DEILNOSVW devil's own
DEILNOTUV involuted
DEILNRSSU luridness
DEILNSTTY stintedly
DEILOOPPT toodle-pip
DEILOORTW Lowrie-tod
Tod-lowrie
DEILOPPTW two-lipped
DEILORRWY worriedly
DEILORVWW world-view
DEILOSSTU dissolute
DEILOSTUY tediously
DEILOSUVY deviously
DEILRSSTU dislustre
DEIMMMRSU midsummer
DEIMMNOOR minor mode
DEIMMNORS modernism✧
DEIMMNOUY neodymium
DEIMMNRTU untrimmed
DEIMMNSSU dumminess
DEIMMOSTY immodesty
DEIMNNOOO onion dome
DEIMNOOSS moodiness
DEIMNOPRU impounder
DEIMNOPSU unimposed
DEIMNORST modernist✧
DEIMNORTY modernity
DEIMNOTUV unmotived
DEIMNPRTU imprudent
DEIMNPSSU dumpiness
DEIMNRSTU rudiments
DEIMNRSTY trendyism
DEIMNRSUY synedrium
DEIMNSSTU tumidness
DEIMOOORT ideomotor
DEIMOORTY iodometry
DEIMOPPUY yuppiedom
DEIMOPRRS primrosed
DEIMOPRSS sporidesm
DEIMOPSST despotism
DEIMOQRSU squiredom
DEIMORSTY dosimetry
DEIMORSUX exordiums
DEINNNOSU innuendos
DEINNOORW in one word
DEINNOOTU dine out on
DEINNOPTU unpointed
DEINNORRV non-driver
DEINNORSU unrosined
DEINNORSY synedrion
DEINNOSSW downiness
DEINNOSTU tendinous
DEINNPRTU unprinted
DEINNRSUU uninsured
DEINNRTTU undertint
DEINNSSUY sunny side
DEINNSTTU unstinted
DEINOOPRT portioned
DEINOORST detorsion
DEINOORTT detortion
DEINOOSSW woodiness
DEINOOSTV devotions
DEINOPPRR properdin
DEINOPRST dripstone
DEINOPRSV disproven
DEINOPRTV provident
DEINOPRUV unprovide
DEINOPRWW wind power
DEINOPSTU put on side
DEINORRUW unworried
DEINORRVW downriver
DEINORSSW rowdiness
wordiness
DEINORSTU detrusion
DEINORSUU uredinous
DEINORSWZ downsizer
DEINORTWW write down
write-down
DEINOSSTT dottiness
DEINOSTTU duettinos
DEINOTUWX exit wound
DEINPRRSY spin dryer
DEINPRSTU unstriped

DEINPSTWW windswept
DEINRRSTU unstirred
DEINRSTTY dentistry
DEINSSSSU dissensus
DEINSSSTU dustiness
DEINSTTUW untwisted
DEIOOPRST depositor
DEIOOPRSV disproove
DEIOOPRTX protoxide
DEIOOPSTW woodspite
DEIOOPSUW pousowdie
DEIOPRRST postrider
DEIOPRSSU disposure
DEIOPRSTU dipterous
DEIOPRTTU torpitude
DEIORSSTU dioestrus
outsiders
DEIORSSUU residuous
DEIOTTTUW outwitted
DEIPPTTTU tittupped
DEIPRRSSU surprised
DEIPRRSTU disrupter
DEIPRSUVY dispurvey
DEIPRTTUU turpitude
DEIRSSSTU dress suit
DEJKMNORU Junkerdom
DEKKLNORY klondyker
DEKLNNRUY drunkenly
DEKMNOOPY monkey pod
DEKNOORTU undertook
DEKNOOTUZ zonked out
DEKNORRUW underwork
DEKOPRSTU stud poker
DELLMOSWY Lymeswold®
DELLNOPSW spelldown
DELLNORSS drollness
DELMNOOOV moon-loved
DELMNOOOW lemonwood
DELMNOOPR lemon drop
DELMNOUVY unmovedly
DELMNPRUU unrumpled
DELMNPSUU pendulums
DELMNUUZZ unmuzzled
DELMOOORX loxodrome
DELMOPUZZ puzzledom
DELMRTTUU mud turtle
DELNNOOOS solenodon
DELNNOPSU nonplused
DELNOORWW low-downer
DELNOPRSU splendour
DELNOPRTU underplot
DELNOPSUU pendulous
DELNORRUY unorderly
DELNORTWX next world
DELNOSSSU soundless
DELNOSSUW woundless
DELNPRTUY prudently
DELOOORRV drool over
DELOOOSUW woodlouse
DELOOPRRS Lord Soper
DELOORSSU odourless
DELOORSUU urodelous
DELORSSSW swordless
DELORSTUY desultory
DELORSTWW Westworld
DELOSTUUY duteously
DELPRSUUY usurpedly
DEMMMOOTT tom-tommed
DEMMOOSTU stomodeum
DEMNNOOWY money down
DEMNNORUU unmourned
DEMNNOTUU unmounted
DEMNOOPSU sound poem
DEMNOPSUY pseudonym
DEMNORRTU tenor drum
DEMNORSTU undermost
DEMOOORTW two-roomed
DEMOOOSUW woodmouse
DEMOOPPRU propodeum
DEMORRSUU murderous
DEMPPRTUU trumped-up
DENNOOSST snot-nosed
DENNOOSTU do one's nut
DENNOOTTU tend out on
DENNORSSU roundness
DENNORSUW snow under
sundowner
DENNOSSSU soundness
DENOOOPPR propodeon
DENOOOPRS droop nose
DENOOOPTW woodentop
DENOOORST doorstone
DENOOOSTW woodstone
DENOOPPSU unopposed
DENOOPRSS sponsored
DENOOPRST dropstone
DENOOPRSU ponderous
DENOOPRTV devonport
DENOOPSTU sound poet
DENOORSTU tournedos
DENOORSUW wonderous
DENOORUVW overwound
DENOPPPRU unpropped
DENOPPRRU underprop
DENOPPSTU unstopped
DENOPRSSU proudness
DENOPSTTU unspotted
DENORTTUU untutored
DENOSTUUU unduteous
DENPRSUUU unpursued
DENRRRSUY surrendry
DENRSSTUU untrussed
DENRSTTUY studentry
DEOOORRTW rood-tower
DEOOPRRUV overproud
DEOORRSTU Tudor rose
DEOPPPRTU rod puppet
DEOPPRRSS drop-press
DEORRSUUV verdurous
DEORSTUVY overstudy
DEPPTTTUU put-putted
DEPRSSSTU press stud
DEQRRSUUY surquedry
DFFFOOSTU foodstuff
DFFGINPUU duffing-up
DFFGOOSTU good stuff
DFFHINSSU snuff-dish
DFFIINOSU diffusion
DFFIKSSTU kids' stuff
DFGHIILRT frithgild
DFGIIIMNW midwifing
DFGIIINNY indignify
DFGIIIRTY frigidity
DFGIILNNO infolding
DFGIIMNOY modifying
DFGIINNUY undignify
DFGILNNOU foundling
unfolding
DFGILNNOY goldfinny
DFGLLOOOS fool's gold
DFGLOOOPT pot of gold
DFGOOOSST soft goods
DFHHINOSU houndfish
DFHHLOORT hold forth
DFHILOORY hydrofoil
DFHINORSU round fish
DFHINOSTW downshift
shift down
DFHIORSSW swordfish
DFHLNOOUW wolfhound
DFHLNSSUU slush fund
DFIILORTY floridity
DFIINPRST spindrift
DFIINSTWW wind-swift
DFIIOPRST disprofit
DFIKLNOPY Pink Floyd
DFIKNORST soft drink
DFIKOOPRS skidproof
DFILLMNUY mindfully
DFILLTUUY dutifully
DFILMNNUU unmindful
DFILMNOSU sound film
DFILNTUUU undutiful
DFIMNOOTU out of mind
DFINOOPRW windproof
DFINORSTW snowdrift
DFIOORTUW fruitwood
DFLLMOOTU mould-loft
DFLOOORUW wood flour
DFNOOOPTU foot-pound
DFNOOORRT front door
DFNRSTTUU trust fund
DFOOOORTU out-of-door
DFOOPRSTU dustproof
DFOOSTTUY dusty-foot
DGGHILOST God's light
DGGHILOSY doggishly
DGGHINOOT goodnight
DGGHNOORU groundhog
DGGIILLNY glidingly
DGGIILNOW go wilding
DGGILNORS gold rings
DGGINNOOW down-going

DGGINNORU grounding
DGHHIINST hindsight
DGHHINOOT thinghood
DGHHINOPT diphthong
DGHHIORSW high words
DGHHKOOOU dough hook
DGHHOORSU roughshod
DGHIINTTW windtight
DGHIKNOOS king's-hood
DGHIKNOOT think good
DGHILMOST goldsmith
DGHILNOPU upholding
DGHILOTUY doughtily
DGHIMOPSY sphygmoid
DGHINNOOT do-nothing
DGHINOOOO hoodooing
DGHINORSU shrouding
DGHINORTW downright
right down
right-down
DGHINTTUY night duty
DGHIOOSTW wish to God
DGHJNNOOO John Ogdon
DGHLOOOTT gold tooth
DGHLOORYY hydrology
DGHOOOSTT dog's-tooth
DGHOORSTW ghost word
DGHOORSUU sourdough
DGHORSTTU God's truth
DGHRRTTUU truth drug
DGIIIMNVW midwiving
DGIIINNOT indigotin
DGIIINNRT nitriding
DGIIINNTY indignity
DGIIJNORY joyriding
DGIIKNRSY dry skiing
DGIIKNSVY skydiving
DGIILLNSY slidingly
DGIILLOOR gorilloid
DGIILNNPS spindling
DGIILNNRY dry lining
DGIILNNSW swindling
DGIILNNWY windingly
DGIILNRST stridling
DGIILOORY iridology
DGIIMNORS Girondism
DGIIMNSSU Sigismund
DGIINNNUW unwinding
DGIINNOWW windowing
DGIINOPRV providing
DGIINOPSS disposing
DGIINORST Girondist
DGIINSSTU in disgust
DGIIRTTUY turgidity
DGIJMNOOR Jo Grimond
DGIKLNNOR long drink
DGIKLNOPS goldspink
DGIKNOPSW gowdspink
DGILLLORY dolly girl
DGILLNORW worldling
DGILLNOUY ungodlily
DGILLOOWY good-willy
DGILLOPSY splodgily
DGILMNOOO mongoloid✧
DGILNNORY droningly
DGILNNOSY goldsinny
DGILNNOWY down-lying
DGILNNUYY undyingly
DGILNOOPT gold point
DGILNORRW Ringworld
DGILOOOSY dosiology
DGILOOTTY dittology
DGIMNRSUY Grundyism
DGINNOPSU pound sign
DGINNOSSU soundings
DGINNOSWW downswing
DGINOORSW swing door
DGINOPPRS droppings
DGINORSTU strouding
DGINORUVY ground ivy
ground-ivy
DGKLOOOOS good looks
DGKOOORSW good works
DGLNOOPTY Glyptodon
DGMNNSUUU mundungus
DGMOORRUW gourd-worm
DGMOORSTU stud groom
DGNNORRUU ground run
DGNNORTUU groundnut
DGNOOOOUY good on you
DGOORRSUU sour-gourd
DHHIKNSUU Hindu Kush
DHHLOORST shorthold
DHHOOOTUY youthhood
DHIIILSTT lithistid
DHIIIMPRU rhipidium
DHIIINOPR rhipidion
DHIIIPSTY hispidity
DHIIJNNOS Jin Shin Do®
DHIILLPRS drillship
DHIILNRWW whirlwind
DHIILOPSY syphiloid
DHIINOORT ornithoid
DHIINTWWY withywind
DHIIOOPRU ophiuroid
DHIIOSTTU dish it out
DHIKLSSUY duskishly
DHILLOSTY doltishly
DHILMOOYY mylohyoid
DHILMPSUY dumpishly
DHILNNOOS Londonish
DHILNORSY dronishly
DHILOOSTU lustihood
DHILPRSUY prudishly
DHIMNOSTY hymnodist
DHIMORSTW wordsmith
DHIMORSUU dishumour
DHINNOTUW whodunnit
DHINOOPRS rhodopsin
DHINOOPTY hypnotoid
DHINOORSU dishonour
DHINOPPSU shippound
DHINOPRUW whip-round
DHINORTWW windthrow
DHIOOSTTW withstood
DHIOOTTUW do without
DHIORRTTW throw dirt
DHIRSSTTU shirt stud
DHJNNOORS Dr Johnson
DHKMNOOOS monkshood
DHKNORUYY hunky-dory
DHLLOOOWY Hollywood
DHLLOOPPY phyllopod
DHLLOOPSY dolly-shop
DHLLOOSTY dolly shot
DHLMOOTUU loudmouth
DHLNOOOPT lophodont
DHLNOORRT Lord North
DHLNOOSUW slow-hound
DHLOPRTUY hydropult
DHMNOOPWY wood nymph
DHMOOPTUY Humpty Doo
DHNNOORTW North Down
DHNOOORYZ hydrozoon
DHNOOOSTW shoot down
DHNOORSUW show round
DHNOORTWW downthrow
throw down
throw-down
DHNOOSTUW down south
shout down
Southdown
DHNORSTUU thundrous
DHOOORTXY orthodoxy
DHOOPPPUY puppyhood
DHOPRSTYY dystrophy
DIIIKMRST midi-skirt
DIIILMNOX minoxidil
DIIILMPTY limpidity
DIIILNPSY insipidly
DIIILQTUY liquidity
DIIINOSSU insidious
DIIINOSUV invidious
DIIKKNNRY rinky-dink
DIIKNNPSY skinny-dip
DIILLMNOO modillion
DIILMNPST split mind
DIILNOSUV divulsion
DIILOPRTY triploidy
DIILOSTTY stolidity
DIIMNNOOS dominions
DIIMNNPTU put in mind
DIIMNOORT dormition
DIIMOORTY iridotomy
DIIMOPRSU sporidium
DIIMORSSY dimissory
DIIMPRTUU tripudium
DIINNOOQU quinonoid
DIINOPRSS disprison
DIINOPRXY pyridoxin
DIINOPTTW tip it down
DIINOSSUY Dionysius
DIIOPRTTY torpidity

DIIORRTTY	torridity
DIIPRTTUY	putridity
DIIPSTTUY	stupidity
DIJNOTUWW	jut-window
DIKLMNORU	milk round
DIKLOORTY	dirty look
DIKNNOOTW	I don't know
DIKNNOPPU	pink pound
DIKNOOSTW	stinkwood
DIKORRTWY	dirty work
DILLNOSUY	unsolidly
DILLOOPPY	polyploid
DILLOOPTT	dottipoll
DILLORSWY	sword lily
DILMNNOOS	Londonism
DILMNOOOP	monoploid
DILMNOORU	iron mould
DILMNPUUU	impundulu
DILMOOPPY	polypidom
DILNNOOVY	London ivy
DILNOOOPZ	diplozoon
DILNOPSUX	spondulix
DILNOQTUW	down-quilt
DILOOOPYZ	polyzooid
DILOOPTUW	tulipwood
DIMMNNOUW	mud minnow
DIMMNORSY	Myrmidons
DIMMOPSUY	sympodium
DIMNOPRUU	purdonium
DIMNORSTW	windstorm
DIMOOOOSV	voodooism
DIMOOOSSU	isodomous
DIMOORRTY	dormitory
DIMOORTUW	moudiwort
DIMOORTWW	mowdiwort
DINOOORST	toison d'or
DINOOORSU	inodorous
DINOOPRST	piston rod
DINOPRRTU	round trip
	round-trip
DINOPRSTW	strip down
DINOPTTUY	point duty
DINORTTUY	rotundity
DINOSTTWW	twist down
DIOOOOSTV	voodooist
DIOOOPSSU	isopodous
DIOOPRRTY	proditory
DIOOPRSST	prosodist
DIOPRRSTU	disruptor
DIOPRRSTW	wrist drop
DKLNOOORU	look-round
DKNOORSTW	sword knot
DKORSTUWY	work study
DLLNOPRUU	pull round
DLLNORUWY	unworldly
DLMOOORXY	loxodromy
DLNNOSUUY	unsoundly
DLNOOOSTW	down tools
DLOOORSUY	odorously
DMNNOOSTW	Mt Snowdon
DMNOORRUW	roundworm
DMOOORRST	storm door
DMOOPRRSU	prodromus
DMORSSTTU	dust storm
DNNORRTUU	turn round
	turnround
DNOOORRTU	ororotund
DNOOPRSUW	upon words
DNOOPSSTU	sound post
DNOOPSTUW	downspout
DNOORRWWY	worry down
DNOORTUWW	woundwort
DOOORSTUY	outdoorsy
DOOSTTTUU	out to stud

E

EEEEELRTY	eyeleteer
EEEEFHLRW	freewheel
EEEEFHRST	freesheet
EEEEFRRSV	free verse
EEEEFRRTV	fever tree
EEEEGGRRS	greegrees
EEEEGHINT	tee-heeing
EEEEGINVV	Genevieve
EEEEGJNOR	Joe Greene
EEEEGKLNR	green leek
EEEEGNRRV	evergreen
EEEEHLMPT	telepheme
EEEEHLRSW	elsewhere
EEEEIJLNN	Jennie Lee
EEEELLRSZ	Zeller See
EEEELMPTY	Eye Temple
EEEELMRTT	telemeter
EEEELNSSV	elevenses
EEEELNTVV	velveteen
EEEEMNNTV	événement
EEEENNSST	Tennessee
EEEENNSTV	seventeen
EEEENOPRY	eye-opener
EEEENPRST	presentee
EEEENRSTW	sweetener
EEEEPRRSV	persevere
EEEERSTVY	yestereve
EEEFFINRT	fifteener
EEEFFMNOT	Toffeemen
EEEFFMTTU	muffettee
EEEFGHINR	Feringhee
EEEFGIKRR	Greek fire
EEEFGKNRU	fenugreek
EEEFHIRTT	tithe-free
EEEFHLLTW	left wheel
EEEFHLORW	fore-wheel
EEEFHNOPR	freephone
EEEFHNRRS	freshener
	refreshen
EEEFHORRT	therefore
EEEFHORRW	wherefore
EEEFHORST	foresheet
EEEFHORSU	free house
EEEFHORTT	foreteeth
EEEFHRRRS	refresher
EEEFILLOV	I Feel Love
EEEFILLTU	feuilleté
EEEFILMPS	fee simple
EEEFILRRS	serrefile
EEEFILRRV	free-liver
EEEFILRVX	reflexive
EEEFINRRT	interfere
EEEFISSSW	fesse-wise
EEEFLLNRU	fullerene
EEEFLLOTT	tête folle
EEEFLNSST	fleetness
EEEFLORRV	free-lover✧
EEEFLRSTY	freestyle
EEEFLRTTU	fleurette
EEEFMNORW	freewomen
EEEFMNRRT	fermenter
EEEFNORST	freestone
EEEFORTUZ	freeze out
	freeze-out
EEEFPRRRR	preferrer
EEEGGORTT	georgette
EEEGHLRSS	sheerlegs
EEEGHOPRS	geosphere
EEEGIJNNT	jet engine
EEEGIKLSY	klieg eyes
EEEGIKNPS	Pekingese
EEEGILLNR	leger line
EEEGILLSS	liegeless
EEEGILMNR	lime green
	lime-green
EEEGILMNS	gelsemine
EEEGILNNR	Nile green
EEEGILNRS	Green Isle
EEEGINNOT	eigentone
EEEGINNRV	veneering
EEEGINPRR	peregrine
EEEGINRRZ	energizer
EEEGINRST	Serengeti
EEEGINRUV	Guinevere
EEEGINRVV	revengive
EEEGIRSSV	egressive
EEEGIRSTY	geyserite
	tiger's eye
EEEGISTTX	exegetist
EEEGKLLNY	Gene Kelly
EEEGKLRSS	Greekless
EEEGKNORS	Greek nose
EEEGKNRSS	Greekness
EEEGLLNTY	genteelly
EEEGLMNNT	gentlemen
EEEGLNNTU	ungenteel
EEEGLRSTY	steel-grey
EEEGMNNRU	energumen
EEEGMNNTV	vengement
EEEGMNRSS	messenger
EEEGMORRT	ergometer
EEEGNNRSS	greenness
EEEGNORRV	overgreen
EEEGNPRSU	supergene
EEEHHIRST	Shere Hite
EEEHIKLPS	sheeplike
	spike heel

EEEHILLNS hellenise✧
EEEHILLNZ hellenize✧
EEEHILMTT Thelemite
EEEHILNNP nepheline
EEEHILNPT nephelite
EEEHILNST Heseltine
EEEHILPRT three-pile
EEEHILRTU eleutheri
EEEHILRWW wire wheel
EEEHIMPRS ephemeris
EEEHIMPSU euphemise
EEEHIMPUZ euphemize
EEEHIMSTT time sheet
EEEHJSTTT the jet set
EEEHKLOSU house leek
EEEHKOPSU keep house
EEEHLLSSW wheel-less
EEEHLMNTT thelement
EEEHLMNTY methylene
EEEHLMSST themeless
EEEHLNOPT telephone
EEEHLNOSW nose wheel
EEEHLNRST enshelter
EEEHLNSST netheless
EEEHLOPPT The People
EEEHLOPSU peel-house✧
pele-house✧
EEEHLRRST shelterer
EEEHLTTVW the Twelve
EEEHMMNTY enthymeme
EEEHMNOPR ephemeron
EEEHMNTTU theme tune
EEEHMORRT rheometer
EEEHMORST threesome
EEEHMORSW somewhere
EEEHNNPST Nepenthes
EEEHNORSW whensoe'er
EEEHNRSSS sheerness✧
EEEHNRSST thereness
threeness
EEEHNRSSW whereness
EEEHNRVWY everywhen
EEEHNSSTW news-sheet
EEEHOPRSX exosphere
EEEHORSTU ethereous
tree house
EEEHPRSST Herpestes
EEEHRRSTW tree shrew
EEEHRSTTU usherette
EEEIIKLNV keelivine
EEEIIKLSV sieve-like
EEEIIKRST kieserite
EEEIIMPRS epimerise
EEEIIMPRZ epimerize
EEEIINRSW Ernie Wise
EEEIKLNQU queen-like
EEEIKLNVY keelyvine
EEEIKMRST kermesite
EEEIKNNPR innkeeper
EEEIKPQTU keep quiet
EEEILLLMR Lee Miller
EEEILLMRV vermeille
EEEILLPST pelletise
EEEILLPTZ pelletize
EEEILLSUV veilleuse
EEEILMNRV envermeil
EEEILMNTX exilement
EEEILMSST seemliest
EEEILNNRV enlivener
EEEILNPRS perseline
pre-senile
EEEILNSTX extensile
EEEILORTV olive tree
EEEILOSTT Teleostei
EEEILPTVX expletive
EEEILRSTV televiser
EEEILRSTX exsertile
EEEILRSVY silvereye
EEEILSVWY swivel-eye
EEEIMMNNO menominee✧
EEEIMMRSS mesmerise
EEEIMMRSZ mesmerize
EEEIMMSST misesteem
EEEIMNNRT nemertine
nine-metre
EEEIMNRSW mere swine
EEEIMNRTX extermine
EEEIMORRT eriometer
EEEIMORTT meteorite
EEEIMPRRT perimeter
EEEIMRRTZ terze rime
EEEIMRSTV serve time
EEEINNPRS persienne
EEEINNRTV intervene
EEEINNSTT St-étienne
EEEINORRT orienteer
EEEINORST neoterise
EEEINORTZ neoterize
EEEINPRRS reserpine
EEEINPRTY pyreneite
EEEINPSSW weepiness
EEEINPSVX expensive
EEEINQSUZ queen-size
EEEINRRTW wernerite
EEEINRSST interesse
EEEINRSTT serinette
EEEINRSTV resentive
EEEINRSTX sixteener
EEEINRTTV retentive
EEEINSSTV seventies
EEEINSTVX extensive
EEEIPRRTT pierrette
preterite
EEEIPRSTX expertise
EEEIPRTXZ expertize
EEEIQTTTU etiquette
EEEIRRRTV retriever
EEEIRRSSY yes sirree
EEEIRRSTV River Tees
EEEIRRTVV revertive
EEEIRSTTV serviette
EEEJKNRTU junketeer
EEEJLLRWY jewellery
EEEJLNOSY jeely nose
EEEJNRSWY New Jersey
EEEJRSTTT jet-setter
EEEKLLNSW knee-swell
EEEKLNSSS sleekness
EEEKMMORT mekometer
EEEKMORST smoke tree
EEEKMRSTU musketeer
EEEKNOPST open-steek
EEEKNOSTY synoekete
EEEKOOPRZ zookeeper
EEELLMNOP lemon peel
EEELLNPRT repellent
EEELLNPTX expellent
EEELLNSSV levelness
EEELLPSSS sleepless
EEELMMNOP Melpomene
EEELMNOPT elopement
EEELMNORT lemon tree
EEELMNSSS menseless
EEELMOPPR merpeople
EEELMRTTY telemetry
EEELMRTXY extremely
EEELNNPTY pentylene
EEELNOPTT leptotene
EEELNORVW wolverene
EEELNOSTT solenette
EEELNOTTV novelette
EEELNQSSU queenless
EEELNRRTY terrenely
EEELNRSSV nerveless
EEELNSSSS senseless
EEELNSSST tenseless
EEELNSSTV eventless
EEELNSTUV sleeve nut
EEELOPRSV oversleep
sleep over
sleepover
EEELOPRTW peel-tower✧
pele-tower✧
EEELRRSVY reversely
EEELRSTTT letterset
EEEMMNOST mementoes
EEEMMNPRS per mensem
EEEMMOPRT emmetrope
EEEMNNOVY even money
EEEMNNRTU enurement
EEEMNOORT oenometer
EEEMNOPRT treponeme
EEEMNORRS sermoneer
EEEMNORRV nevermore
EEEMNORST merestone
EEEMNOXYZ exoenzyme
EEEMNRSTT entremets
EEEMNRSTY mesentery
EEEMNRTTV revetment
EEEMNRTUX unextreme
EEEMOPRTX extempore
EEEMORRSU reremouse
EEEMRSTTV Mt Everest

EEEMRSTTX extremest
EEENNORST sonneteer
EEENNSSST tenseness
EEENOPPRW pew-opener
EEENOPRTY tree peony
EEENORSUV venereous
EEENOSSTY set eyes on
EEENPRRST presenter
represent
re-present
EEENPRRTV preventer
EEENPRSUV supervene
EEENPSSST steepness
EEENPSTUW sweeten up
EEENQRSSU queerness
EEENRRSTW westerner✧
EEENRRSUV unreserve
EEENRSSST terseness
EEENSSSTW sweetness
EEEOPRRTV portreeve
EEEOPRSST poetresse
EEEORRSTV oversteer
EEEORRTVX overexert
EEEPPPRTU puppeteer
EEEPRRRSS represser
EEEPRRRSV preserver
EEEPRRRTV perverter
EEEPRRSSV preserves
EEEPRRSSX expresser
EEEPRSTTU superette
EEEQRRSTU requester
EEEQRSSTU sequester
EEERRTTUX retexture
EEFFFKLRU kerfuffle
EEFFFMNOT feoffment
EEFFFOORT for toffee
EEFFGHIRT free fight
EEFFGHOPT off the peg
off-the-peg
EEFFGINOT teeing-off
EEFFGLNTU effulgent
EEFFHILLS shelf life
EEFFHINTT fifteenth
EEFFHLRSU reshuffle
EEFFILSSU siffleuse
EEFFIMNRU muffineer
EEFFINOST Fifteen O's
EEFFINOSV offensive
EEFFINRST stiffener
EEFFIORRT forfeiter
EEFFJNORS Jefferson
EEFFLOOTT fleet-foot
EEFFOPRRR profferer
EEFFORSTT off-street
setter-off
EEFGGIKRT Greek gift
EEFGGOORX George Fox
EEFGHIORW foreweigh
EEFGHIRRT freighter
EEFGILLNR refelling
EEFGILLNY feelingly
EEFGILNNU unfeeling
EEFGILRSS griefless
EEFGIMRUV vermifuge
EEFGINORR foreigner
EEFGINRRR referring
EEFGINRRT ferreting
EEFGIORTV forgetive
EEFGIPRRU prefigure
EEFGLLLUY gleefully
EEFGLNRTU refulgent
EEFGLRRTU regretful
EEFGORRTT forgetter
EEFHHISST the Fishes
EEFHIIKLT thieflike
EEFHIISST fetishise
EEFHIISTZ fetishize
EEFHIJLSW jewelfish
EEFHIKLLS shelflike
EEFHIKSTV the five Ks
EEFHILLRS shellfire
EEFHILMST sheet film
EEFHILOTT to the life
EEFHIMORS home fries
EEFHINPRY hyperfine
EEFHINQSU queenfish
EEFHINSST heftiness
EEFHIORSU firehouse
EEFHIOSUW housewife
EEFHIPRSV ship fever
EEFHIQRSU queer fish
EEFHIRSTU the Furies
EEFHISSTW sweetfish
EEFHLLSSS fleshless
EEFHLLTUW Ethelwulf
EEFHLMNST fleshment
EEFHLMOTU mouthfeel
EEFHLORUW four-wheel
EEFHLOSTW flow sheet
EEFHMORRT therefrom
EEFHMORRW from where
wherefrom
EEFHNORSW foreshewn
EEFHNPRSU freshen up
EEFHNRSSS freshness
EEFHOORRS fore-horse
foreshore
EEFHOORTT three-foot
to the fore
EEFHORRTU three-four
EEFHORRTW free throw
EEFHRRRTU furtherer
EEFIIKKLN knifelike
EEFIIKLLS like flies
EEFIILLNP fillipeen
EEFIILMTX flexitime
EEFIILNRT infertile
interfile
EEFIILQRU liquefier
EEFIILRST fertilise
EEFIILRTZ fertilize
EEFIIMNRY fiery mine
EEFIIMNTY femineity
EEFIIMRRT metrifier
EEFIINRSS fieriness
EEFIINRTT Nefertiti
EEFIIPRTW tripe-wife
EEFIIRRRT terrifier
EEFIIRRSV versifier
EEFIIRSTT testifier
EEFIKLMRV milk fever
EEFIKLNSS knifeless
EEFIKLRTY kite-flyer
EEFIKNRST knife-rest
EEFIKNRSU refusenik
EEFILLLOS filoselle
EEFILLORW low relief
EEFILLPTY pelletify
EEFILLRTY fertilely
EEFILLSTY lifestyle
EEFILMPXY exemplify
EEFILNNPU pie funnel
EEFILNORX reflexion
EEFILNRUX inflexure
EEFILNTUW wulfenite
EEFILORTU outrelief
EEFILSTVY festively
EEFIMNRTT refitment
EEFINNPVY fivepenny
EEFINOPRT reef point
EEFINORST firestone
forestine
set on fire
EEFINORTU refine out
EEFINPRSU superfine
EEFINRRST renfierst
EEFINRSTU interfuse
EEFIOPRRT profiteer
EEFIOPRRW firepower
EEFIOSTTV set to five
EEFIPPRRR fripperer
EEFIPRSTU stupefier
EEFIPRSUV perfusive
EEFIRRRTT fritterer
EEFIRRRTU fruiterer
EEFIRRSTU surfeiter
EEFIRRTTU fruit tree
EEFKLLTTU kettleful
EEFKNOORT foretoken
EEFLLNPSU spleenful
EEFLLOPWW pew-fellow
EEFLMORTW flowmeter
EEFLNNNTU funnel-net
EEFLNOPSU up oneself
EEFLNOSTU nose-flute
EEFLNRSTU resentful
EEFLNRTVY fervently
EEFLOPRSU reposeful
EEFLORRTX retroflex
EEFLORSTV leftovers
EEFLRSTTU streetful
EEFLSSTTY tsetse fly
EEFLSTTYZ tzetse fly

EEFLTTYZZ tzetze fly
EEFMNOORW forewomen
EEFMNORRT fermentor
EEFMOPRRR performer
EEFMORRST E M Forster
EEFMORRVW worm fever
EEFMPRRUY perfumery
EEFNNOSST oftenness
EEFNOPRST forespent
EEFOPRRRV perfervor
EEFOPRRTY ferrotype
EEFPRSSUU superfuse
EEGGGIPRS gripe's egg
EEGGHORSW whore's egg
EEGGIILNT gelignite
EEGGIKLNR Greekling
EEGGILMNR gemel-ring
EEGGILNNR greenling
EEGGILNNT negligent
EEGGILNSS legginess
EEGGILOOS geologise
EEGGILOOZ geologize
EEGGINNPU pug-engine
EEGGINNRV revenging
EEGGINRRS sniggerer
EEGGINRST gee-string
EEGGINRTT gettering
EEGGIORSU egregious
EEGGNNORW green gown
EEGGNOOOS gone goose
EEGGOORRV overgorge
EEGGOORSY grey goose
EEGGORSST St George's
EEGGRSSTU suggester
EEGHHIITT eightieth
EEGHHILLV high-level
EEGHHIRTT thegither
EEGHIIKLM Mike Leigh
EEGHIKNTW weeknight
EEGHIKPST keep sight
EEGHILMNT metheglin
EEGHILNNT enlighten
EEGHILNRS Englisher
EEGHIMMST the gimmes
EEGHIMOST egotheism
eightsome
EEGHINNSS sneeshing
EEGHINPST phengites
EEGHINRRR herringer
EEGHINRTT tightener
EEGHINSST see things
EEGHIORVW overweigh
EEGHIOSTT ghettoise
The Egoist
EEGHIOTTZ ghettoize
EEGHIPPST peep sight
EEGHIRSST sightseer
EEGHLLNOP phellogen
EEGHLNOPS long sheep
EEGHLOORT theologer
EEGHLOOTT logothete
EEGHLOOTU theologue
EEGHLOOTV go the vole
EEGHLORTY leg theory
EEGHMNOST theme song
EEGHNNORR greenhorn
EEGHNOOPS geophones
EEGHNOOPT photogene
EEGHNORTU toughener
EEGHOPSTU The Pogues
EEGHRTTTU the gutter
EEGIIKNNP in keeping
EEGIILMNT gmelinite
EEGIILNNO oil engine
EEGIILNRV inveigler
relieving
EEGIILNST gentilise
EEGIILNTZ gentilize
EEGIILOPS epilogise
EEGIILOPZ epilogize
EEGIILORS religiose
EEGIILPRV privilege
EEGIILRUX religieux
EEGIINNNO ion engine
EEGIINNST Genistein®
EEGIINRSU signeurie
EEGIINSTV ingestive
EEGIIOPRS pierogies
EEGIISTTZ zeitgeist✧
EEGIJLLNW jewelling
EEGIJLNRY jeeringly
EEGIJNNNT jenneting
EEGIJOPRS jerepigos
EEGIKLNNU ingleneuk
EEGIKNNRT Kentigern
EEGILLLNV levelling
EEGILLNPR repelling
EEGILLNPX expelling
EEGILLNRV Grenville
revelling
EEGILLNRY leeringly
reelingly
EEGILLNVW well-given
EEGILLSSU guileless
EEGILMMSU gelsemium
EEGILMNSY seemingly
EEGILNNRT relenting
EEGILNNST single ten
EEGILNNUY genuinely
EEGILNOOS neologise
EEGILNOOZ neologize
EEGILNORV line-grove
EEGILNPWY weepingly
EEGILNRST steerling
EEGILNRTT lettering
EEGILNRTW weltering
EEGILNRVY veeringly
EEGILNSSX single-sex
EEGILNTVV velveting
EEGILNTWY weetingly
EEGILNTXY exigently
EEGILOPSS gospelise
EEGILOPSZ gospelize
EEGILORST sortilege
EEGILRSSX Essex Girl
EEGILRTVY Trygve Lie
EEGILSTTW Weltgeist
EEGIMNNSU unseeming
EEGIMNPRR Preminger
EEGIMNPRT tempering
EEGIMOORV moviegoer
EEGINNNUU ungenuine
EEGINNSSV givenness
EEGINNTUW unweeting
EEGINOOSS oogenesis
EEGINORSS egression
EEGINORSV sovereign
EEGINOSSS gneissose
Sosigenes
EEGINOSXY oxygenise
EEGINOTTU tongue-tie
EEGINOXYZ oxygenize
EEGINPPPR peppering
EEGINPRSS speerings
EEGINPSSW sweepings
EEGINQSUZ squeezing
EEGINRRST restringe
tree rings
EEGINRRSV reversing
EEGINRSSY synergise
EEGINRSTW swingtree
westering
EEGINRSTY eye-string
EEGINRSUY seigneury
EEGINRSYZ synergize
EEGINRTTV revetting
vignetter
EEGIOPRSS serpigoes
EEGIORSTV vertigoes
EEGIRRSSU régisseur
EEGISSTUW guestwise
EEGKNNORZ Egon Krenz
EEGLLLPRU leg-puller
EEGLLMORU glomerule
EEGLLOOTY teleology
EEGLLOPRS gospeller
EEGLLORRV groveller
EEGLMNNOO Ogen melon
EEGLMNORT long metre
EEGLMOORY mereology
EEGLNOOVV oven glove
EEGLNORTT lorgnette
EEGLNOSSX sex on legs
EEGLNOTTU tonguelet
EEGLNSSUY glueyness
EEGLOOPST go to sleep
EEGLOORVZ gloze over
EEGLPPUZZ puzzle-peg
EEGLPRSUU superglue
EEGLRSSSU surgeless
EEGLRSSUU reguluses
EEGMMNTTU tegmentum
EEGMNNOTU engoûment

EEGMNOORR greenroom
EEGMNORSS moss green
EEGMORSTZ Esztergom
EEGNOORST oestrogen
EEGNOORSU erogenous
EEGNOOSTY osteogeny
EEGNOOSUX exogenous
EEGNOPRRR porrenger
EEGNORRSS engrosser
EEGNORSSV governess
EEGNORSTY greystone
EEGNPSTUY type genus
EEGNRRSTU resurgent
EEGOOPSST goose step
goose-step
EEGOPPRRU peer group
EEGOPRSTU guest rope
EEGOPRTUU Portuguee
EEGOQRSTU grotesque
EEGORRTTU tregetour
EEHHILOTW white hole
EEHHINOPT thiophene
EEHHINOSS shoeshine
EEHHINOVY hive-honey
EEHHINPSY hyphenise
EEHHINPYZ hyphenize
EEHHIOPTW white hope
EEHHIORTT thio-ether
EEHHIOSTW white-shoe
EEHHIRSST the Shires
EEHHIRTTW therewith
EEHHIRTWW wherewith
EEHHKLRSU sheer-hulk
EEHHKOOPS sheep-hook
EEHHLLLOS shell-hole
EEHHMNORT mother hen
EEHHNOPPS phosphene
EEHHOORSS horseshoe
EEHIIKLRS heli-skier
EEHIILMTW white lime
EEHIILNTW white line
White Nile
EEHIILRTT Hitlerite
EEHIINNRW Rhine wine
EEHIINNTT ninetieth
EEHIINPTW white pine
EEHIINTWW white wine
EEHIIPSST epithesis
EEHIIRSTT there it is
EEHIIRSTW where it is
EEHIIRTTW witherite
EEHIJNOPS Josephine
Joséphine
EEHIKLLLS shell-like
EEHIKMNSV Menshevik
EEHIKNPSS sheepskin
EEHILLLMS shell lime
EEHILLLMW millwheel
EEHILLLSV live shell
EEHILLMNS Hellenism
EEHILLMRT The Miller
EEHILLNST Hellenist
EEHILMNOP Philomene
EEHILMOST lithesome
EEHILMOSW somewhile
EEHILMTUV helvetium
EEHILNNOO hole in one
EEHILNNOS nineholes
EEHILNNOT on the line
EEHILNOOP oenophile
EEHILNOPX xenophile
EEHILNORS shoreline
EEHILNOSU house-line
EEHILNPRS replenish
EEHILNPSS spleenish
EEHILNPSW wheel spin
EEHILNRST inshelter
EEHILNSSS shineless
EEHILNSST litheness
EEHILOPRU Europhile
EEHILOPRX xerophile
EEHILOPTY heliotype
EEHILORTV rivet hole
EEHILPRTU Prue Leith
EEHILPSST slip sheet
EEHILPSVY peevishly
EEHILRSTW erstwhile
EEHIMMOOV home movie
EEHIMMPSU euphemism
EEHIMNRRT herriment
EEHIMOPRT hemitrope
EEHIMOSTV the movies
EEHIMPRRW whimperer
EEHIMRSST hermitess
EEHINNORT threonine
EEHINNOTZ in the zone
EEHINOPST phonetise
EEHINOPSU euphonise
pine-house
EEHINOPTT epitheton
EEHINOPTZ phonetize
EEHINOPUZ euphonize
EEHINOPVW viewphone
EEHINORST on the rise
sheet iron
EEHINORSV overshine
EEHINORTT thereinto
EEHINORTW whereinto
EEHINOSST hessonite
EEHINOSUW house wine
EEHINPQSU queenship
EEHINPRRT trephiner
EEHINPRSS phrenesis
EEHINRTTW white rent
EEHINSSTW whiteness
EEHINSTTU euthenist
EEHINSTTX sixteenth
EEHINTTTW twentieth
EEHIOPRTT tephroite
EEHIOQRTU theorique
EEHIORRSS hors série
EEHIORRST rhetorise
theoriser
EEHIORRTZ rhetorize
theorizer
EEHIORSST heterosis
EEHIORSTW otherwise
white rose
EEHIPPRRT The Ripper
EEHIPPRRY periphery
EEHIPPSSY epiphyses
EEHIPRRSW whisperer
EEHIPRSUV superhive
EEHIQRSTU The Squire
EEHIRRSST heritress
EEHIRRTTY erythrite
EEHIRTVWY every whit
EEHJKNOPS John Speke
EEHKLLNOY knee-holly
EEHKLMOOS smoke hole
EEHKLOORW look where
EEHKLOOST stokehole
EEHKLORWW wheelwork
EEHKMPSSU musk-sheep
EEHKNRTUY turkey hen
EEHKORSTW worksheet
EEHLLLNVY Helvellyn
EEHLLLSSS shell-less
EEHLLMMRU hummeller
EEHLLORST hosteller
EEHLLORSV shoveller
EEHLLORTY holly tree
EEHLLOSUW wellhouse
EEHLMOOSU mouse hole
EEHLMOOSW wholesome
EEHLMORRU home-ruler
EEHLMORSW shrew mole
EEHLMORTY mother lye
EEHLMORVW overwhelm
EEHLMORWW worm wheel
EEHLMOSZZ shemozzle
EEHLMPSSY emphlyses
EEHLMRSSY rhymeless
EEHLNOOOZ ozone hole
EEHLNOOTW whole note
whole tone
EEHLNOPTY polythene
telephony
EEHLNOSSW wholeness
EEHLNOSSY honeyless
EEHLNSSSW Welshness
EEHLNSTVY seventhly
EEHLOOPTT telephoto
EEHLOPPTU up the pole
EEHLOPSTW whole step
EEHLORSSS horseless
shoreless
EEHLORSTT short leet
EEHLOSSST hostlesse
EEHLOSSSU houseless
EEHLPPRTU the purple
EEHLPRSUW spur wheel
EEHMMOORY homeomery

EEHMNOOPR pheromone
EEHMNOORW homeowner
EEHMNOOTT nomothete
EEHMNOOTV on the move
EEHMNOPRT phonmeter
EEHMNORRY Henry More
EEHMNORSU home nurse
EEHMNORTY heteronym
EEHMNPTTU umpteenth
EEHMNPTTY nymphette
EEHMNRRTY herryment
EEHMOOSUV move house
EEHMOPSTY mesophyte
EEHMORRST smotherer
EEHMRRRTU murtherer
EEHMRRSTY rhymester
EEHMRRTUY eurytherm
EEHMSSTTY the system✧
EEHNNOORT none other
EEHNNOOST hone-stone
on the nose
EEHNOOPRS noosphere
EEHNOOPSU open house
EEHNOPPTY phenotype
EEHNOPRRS prehensor
EEHNOPRTU thereupon
EEHNOPRUW whereupon
EEHNOPSTU penthouse
EEHNOPTTX textphone
EEHNOPTTY entophyte
EEHNORRST shortener
EEHNORRTT thorntree
EEHNORSST otherness
EEHNORTTU thereunto
EEHNORTUW whereunto
EEHNOSTTW whetstone
EEHNPPRSU pen-pusher
EEHNSSSTY syntheses
EEHOOPRRT rheotrope
EEHOOPRSU rope house
EEHOORSSV over-shoes
EEHOORSVW howsoever
whosoever
EEHOPRRSU superhero
EEHOPRSTY hey presto
EEHOPRTXY xerophyte
EEHOPSSTU pesthouse
EEHORRRTT the Terror
EEHORSSTT sort these
these sort
EEHORSSTU rest house
EEHORSTTX hors texte
EEHORSTTY set theory
EEHORTTVX The Vortex
EEHPRTTXY hypertext
EEIIKLLMN Nellie Kim
EEIIKLRRV riverlike
EEIIKMRRV River Kemi
EEIIKNNTZ zinkenite
EEIIKPPRT kipper tie
EEIILLMRT millerite
EEIILLMTW willemite
EEIILLNTV vitelline
EEIILMSTT timeliest
EEIILNNRT interline
EEIILNOTV olivenite
EEIILNQSU Esquiline
EEIILNRRV River Nile
EEIILNRST resilient
EEIILNSTU luteinise
EEIILNTUZ luteinize
EEIILOPST sepiolite
EEIILRSST Listerise
sterilise
EEIILRSSV silverise
EEIILRSTZ Listerize
sterilize
EEIILRSVZ silverize
EEIIMMPRS epimerism
EEIIMMPRT prime time
prime-time
EEIIMMRST eremitism
EEIIMNOPT in epitome
EEIIMNOST Simeonite
EEIIMNPRS mire-snipe
EEIIMNRSU menuisier
EEIIMOPST epitomise
EEIIMOPTZ epitomize
EEIIMORSS isomerise
EEIIMORSZ isomerize
EEIIMRSSV remissive
EEIINNNPT penninite
EEIINNRTV intervein
EEIINNSTT intestine
EEIINNSTV intensive
EEIINNTTV intentive
EEIINNTVV inventive
EEIINPRRS reinspire
EEIINRRVV viverrine
EEIINRSTT enteritis
EEIINRSTW winterise
EEIINRSVV inversive
EEIINRTVW interview
EEIINRTWZ winterize
EEIINSSST sensitise
EEIINSSTV sensitive
EEIINSSTZ sensitize
EEIINSSVW viewiness
EEIIOPQSU equipoise
EEIIOSSTV sovietise
EEIIOSTVZ sovietize
EEIIPRSSW spirewise
EEIIPSUXZ epizeuxis
EEIIQRSTU requisite
EEIIQSTUX exquisite
EEIIRSSTV resistive
EEIJKKNRR ink-jerker
EEIJKNNOT knee joint
EEIJKNRSS jerkiness
EEIJLLMOR Joe Miller
EEIJMMNSS jemminess
EEIJNSSTT jettiness
EEIKKLMOS like smoke
EEIKKNRST steenkirk
EEIKLLMPW Will Kempe
EEIKLMORT kilometre
EEIKLNRSU nurselike
EEIKLRSST triskeles
EEIKLRTWY tri-weekly
EEIKMNORT konimeter
EEIKNOPSS open skies
EEIKNPRSS perkiness
EEIKNRRTT trinketer
EEIKNSTTX sex kitten
EEIKOORTZ ozokerite
EEIKOPSSW spokewise
EEILLMNOT emollient
EEILLMNPT impellent
EEILLMOPR millepore
EEILLMPRT ill temper
EEILLMSSS smileless
EEILLNNPU plenilune
EEILLNNTY leniently
EEILLNRSV sniveller
EEILLOPSW powellise
EEILLOPTU petiolule
EEILLOPTW powellite✧
EEILLOPWZ powellize
EEILLORTT title role
EEILLOTTT little toe
EEILLRSTT rillettes
EEILLRSTU tellurise
EEILLRSUV surveille
EEILLRSUY leisurely
EEILLRSVY servilely
EEILLRTTU tellurite
EEILLRTUZ tellurize
EEILLSSTT titleless
EEILLSUVY elusively
EEILLTTTU tuillette
EEILMMNPT implement
EEILMMNSY immensely
EEILMMORS sommelier
EEILMMORT milometer
EEILMMPSU semiplume
EEILMNNOT eloinment
EEILMNNTY eminently
EEILMNORT Nilometer
EEILMNOSS solemnise
EEILMNOST limestone
milestone
EEILMNOSZ solemnize
EEILMNPPR pimpernel
EEILMNSTU musteline
EEILMOPRY pleiomery
EEILMOPST septimole
EEILMOPTT title poem
EEILMORTT tremolite
EEILMORUX Émile Roux
EEILMOSTT mistletoe
EEILMOSVW semivowel
EEILMOTVY emotively
EEILMPSSS simplesse

EEILMRSTY lysimeter
EEILNNPSS penniless
EEILNNSTY intensely
EEILNOORS oleoresin
EEILNOOTY eye lotion
EEILNOPPS plenipoes
EEILNOPRS sine prole
EEILNOPRT interlope
repletion
terpineol
EEILNOPRV polverine
EEILNOPRW power line
EEILNOPST sleep on it
EEILNOPSX Polixenes
EEILNOPTT telepoint
EEILNORSV noveliser
EEILNORVV reinvolve
EEILNORVW wolverine
EEILNORVZ novelizer
EEILNOSSS noiseless
EEILNOSSU selenious
EEILNOSTT tile stone
EEILNOSTV novelties
EEILNOTUV veloutine
EEILNPRUV pulverine
EEILNPSSS spineless
EEILNPSTT pestilent
EEILNPSVY pensively
EEILNRSTU unsterile
EEILNRSVY inversely
EEILNSSSW sinewless
EEILNTUVW nut-weevil
EEILOPRST epistoler
pistoleer
EEILOPRTX exploiter
EEILOPSST politesse
EEILOPSSW slopewise
EEILOPSTT epistolet
EEILOPSVX explosive
EEILORRTT Tortelier
EEILORSTV televisor
EEILORTTT ottrelite
EEILOSTTT toilet set
EEILOTUVV evolutive
EEILPPRTU pulpiteer
EEILPRSSS spireless
EEILPRSTU serpulite
EEILPRSTY peristyle
Priestley
EEILPRSUV prelusive
pulverise
repulsive
EEILPRTTU tulip tree
EEILPRUVZ pulverize
EEILPSSTU sleepsuit
EEILPSUVX expulsive
EEILRRSSV riverless
EEILRSTUX extrusile
EEILRSTVY restively
EEILRSUVV revulsive
EEILSSSSU issueless
EEILSTTTU suttletie
EEIMMMRSS mesmerism
EEIMMNNOS menomines
EEIMMNRRT merriment
EEIMMNRTT remitment
EEIMMORRS memoriser
EEIMMORRT memoriter
EEIMMORRZ memorizer
EEIMMORST meteorism
EEIMMOSST sometimes
EEIMMPRST mistemper
EEIMMRSST mesmerist
EEIMMRSTU summiteer
EEIMMRSTW swimmeret
EEIMMRSTX extremism
EEIMNNNOT Mennonite
EEIMNNORW mine owner
EEIMNNOST minestone
EEIMNNRTT interment
EEIMNNRTU inurement
EEIMNNSTT sentiment
EEIMNOPTX exemption
EEIMNORSS sermonise
EEIMNORST neoterism
EEIMNORSZ sermonize
EEIMNOSTX sixteenmo
EEIMNOSYZ isoenzyme
EEIMNPQTU equipment
EEIMNPRRU en primeur
EEIMNPRSS primeness
EEIMNPSST emptiness
EEIMNRRSS merriness
EEIMNRRTU intermure
EEIMNRTTT remittent
EEIMNSSSS messiness
EEIMNSTTV vestiment
EEIMOORTZ merozoite
EEIMOPRST peristome
temporise
EEIMOPRTZ temporize
EEIMOQSTU quietsome
EEIMORRTV overtimer
EEIMORSST esoterism
EEIMORSTT meteorist
EEIMPPRRS perisperm
EEIMPRRTT permitter
pretermit
trip meter
EEIMPRRTY perimetry
EEIMPRSTV septemvir
EEIMPSSTU impetuses
EEIMQSTUU equisetum
EEIMRRSTT trimester
EEIMRSSSU messieurs✧
EEIMRSSTY mysteries
EEIMRSTTX extremist
EEIMRTTXY extremity
EEIMSSSTY systemise
EEIMSSTTU sutteeism
EEIMSSTYZ systemize
EEINNNNPY ninepenny
EEINNNOPS en pension
EEINNNRSS innerness
EEINNNRSU nunneries
EEINNOORT tree onion
EEINNOPPS Nipponese
EEINNOPRS pensioner
EEINNOPRT interpone
tin-opener
EEINNOPST penistone
stone pine
EEINNORTT enter into
retention
EEINNORTZ interzone
EEINNOSST sonnetise
EEINNOSTV veinstone
EEINNOSTW wine-stone
EEINNOSTX extension
in extenso
EEINNOSTZ sonnetize
EEINNPRST spinneret
EEINNPRTT pertinent
EEINNPRTY perennity
EEINNPSST ineptness
EEINNPSVY penis envy
EEINNPSWY penny wise
EEINNRSST inertness
EEINNRSSV Inverness
nerviness
EEINNSSSW newsiness
EEINOPPPR pepperoni
EEINOPPST peptonise
pipestone
EEINOPPTZ peptonize
EEINOPRRV overripen
EEINOPRSS personise
EEINOPRST interpose
EEINOPRSZ personize
EEINOPSTT potentise
EEINOPSUZ seize upon
EEINOPTTZ potentize
EEINOQRUV véronique✧
EEINORRSV reversion
versioner
EEINORRTU routineer
EEINORSTT neoterist
EEINORSTX exsertion
EEINOSSTV ostensive
EEINOSTTU Teutonise
EEINOTTUZ Teutonize
EEINPRRRT reprinter
EEINPRRTT interpret
EEINPRSSW winepress
EEINPRTTY Intertype®
EEINPSSSW spewiness
EEINPSSTT pettiness
EEINQSSTU quietness
EEINQSTUY squint-eye
EEINQTTTU quintette
EEINRRRSU reinsurer
EEINRRSTT intersert
EEINRRTTW rewritten

EEINRRTVY River Tyne
EEINRSSSW sweirness
EEINRSSSY syneresis
EEINRSSTT resistent
triteness
EEINRSSTW witnesser
EEINRSSUV Severinus
EEINRTTTX intertext
EEINSSSTT testiness
EEINSTTXY extensity
EEIOOPRSV overpoise
EEIOPPSTV stovepipe
EEIOPRRVZ overprize
EEIOPRTTU pirouette
EEIOPSTTT pettitoes
EEIOQQUUV equivoque
EEIORRRST roisterer
terrorise
EEIORRRSV reservoir
EEIORRRTZ terrorize
EEIORRSTX exteriors
EEIORRSUV River Ouse
EEIORRTTV retortive
EEIORRTVW overwrite
EEIORRTVY ivory-tree
EEIORSSUV overissue
EEIORSTTT storiette
EEIORSTVX extorsive
EEIORTTVX extortive
EEIPPRRTY periptery
EEIPRRSTT preterist
EEIPRRSVY River Spey
EEIPRSSST priestess
EEIPRSSUV supervise
EEIPRSTTT pet-sitter
EEIPRTTWY typewrite
EEIQRSSSU esquiress
EEIRRSSTV reservist
EEIRRSSTW writeress
EEIRRTTTW twitterer
EEIRSSSTT tristesse
EEIRSTTTU restitute
EEIRSTTUV vestiture
EEIRSTTUX texturise
EEIRSTUVX extrusive
EEIRTTUXZ texturize
EEJLNOPRU pleno jure
EEJMMNOPY jemmy open
EEJMNNOTY enjoyment
EEJMPQUUU queue-jump
EEJNNNRWY jenny-wren
EEJNOQSUU Junoesque
EEJNORRUY journeyer
EEJNOSSTW Jew's-stone
EEJPSSTUW Jesus wept
EEKKORRWY keyworker
EEKKORSTY keystroke
EEKLLMOSS sell smoke
EEKLMOOTU leukotome
EEKLMOSSS smokeless
EEKLNOOTV love-token
EEKLNPRSU spelunker
EEKLORSTW steelwork
EEKMNOPSS spokesmen
EEKMORRTY kryometer
EEKMOSSTT smoke test
EEKNOOTTV token vote
EEKNORRTW networker
EEKNRRTTU tree trunk
EEKNRRTUY return key
EEKORRSWX sex worker
EEKPPPUYY keepy-uppy
EELLLMSSS smell-less
EELLLNOSU Olenellus
EELLMNOOS lemon sole
EELLMPSSU plumeless
EELLNNRTU tunneller
EELLNORRS norseller
EELLNPSTW well-spent
EELLOOPRT trollopee
EELLOOSTT tool steel
EELLOOSTW steel wool
EELLOPPRR propeller
EELLOPPRX prepollex
EELLORRTW troweller
EELLORSSV loverless
EELLORSVW overswell
EELLOSSVW vowelless
EELLPRSSU supersell
EELLPSSSU pulseless
EELLPSSSY syllepses
EELLPSTUW well-set-up
EELLSSSTY styleless
EELLSSSUY uselessly
EELLSSSXY sexlessly
EELMMNOTU emolument
EELMMRSUW Welsummer
EELMNNORT enrolment
EELMNOOTY teleonomy
EELMNOSSS solemness
EELMNOSSY moneyless
EELMNOTTX extolment
EELMNPSTU Sun Temple
EELMOOPST leptosome
EELMOOPTT totem pole
EELMOOSTY toylesome
EELMOPPRY pre-employ
EELMOPRTU petroleum
EELMOPRTX metroplex
EELMORTTV voltmeter
EELMORTUV volumeter
EELMORTXY xylometer
EELMOSTVW twelvemos
EELMPRSUY supremely
EELNNNTTU tunnel net
EELNNOPRS personnel
EELNNQUUY unqueenly
EELNOOSSS looseness
EELNOPPRY propylene
EELNOPSTU plenteous
EELNOPSTW newel post
EELNORSSW ownerless
EELNORSTV resolvent
EELNORTUV volunteer
EELNOSSST stoneless
EELNPPRUX unperplex
EELNPRSTY presently
EELNQSTUY sequently
EELOOPRSY operosely
EELOORSTV Roosevelt
EELOPPRSS prolepses
EELOPRRSY leprosery
EELOPRRTU pétroleur
poulterer
EELOPRSSW powerless
EELOPRSTY polyester
proselyte
EELOPRTXY expletory
EELORRRSS errorless
EELORRRUV overruler
EELORRTUV revel-rout
EELORSSST ostleress
EELORSSTW towerless
EELORSSUV ourselves
EELPPSTTU septuplet
EELPRSSXY expressly
EELPRSTUU sepulture
EELPSTTUX sextuplet
EELRSSTTU utterless
EELRSSTVY Sylvester
EEMMMRSTU Mummerset
EEMMNNOSY Mnemosyne
EEMMNOORT metronome
monometer
monotreme
EEMMOORST osmometer
EEMMORTYZ zymometer
EEMMRSSTU summerset
EEMNNOPRY Rome-penny
EEMNNOPST penstemon
EEMNOORTT tonometer
EEMNOOSTT tomentose
EEMNOPQRU prom queen
EEMNOPRYZ proenzyme
EEMNORRTT tormenter
EEMNORRTY Monterrey
EEMNORSTU rousement
EEMNRSTTW strewment
EEMOOOSTT osteotome
EEMOOPPRS prose poem
EEMOOPRTT optometer
potometer
EEMOORSTU meteorous
EEMOPPRRT pre-emptor
EEMOPRRTY pyrometer
EEMORRRVY overmerry
EEMOSTTTU teetotums
EEMPRRTTU trumpeter
EEMPRSSTT temptress
EEMPRSTTU tree stump
EENNNPRTY penny-rent
EENNOOPRS one-person
EENNOOPRT pontoneer

EENNOOSTU neotenous
EENNOPRSS proneness
EENNOPRTU enter upon
EENNORSTU entre nous
EENNOSSTV Stevenson
EENNOTTWY twenty-one
EENNPRTUY truepenny
EENNRSSST sternness
EENOOPPSS pope's nose
EENOORRSU erroneous
EENOORSTV overtones
EENOPPRTT prepotent
EENOPQSTU queen post
EENOPRRSS responser
EENOPRSTV overspent
EENOPRSTW Peter Snow
EENOPSSTT step stone
EENOPSTTY Stenotype®
EENOPSTUW sweet upon
EENOQRSTU on request
EENORRSTW nor'wester
nor'-wester
EENORRTUY tourneyer
EENORSSSW worseness
EENORSSUY Norueyses
EENORSTUU souteneur
EENORTTTU neutretto
EENOSSSTX sextoness
EENPRRSTY serpentry
EENPRRTUV unpervert
EENPRSSSU suspenser
EENRSSTTU utterness
EEOOPRRVW overpower
EEOORRTVW overtower
tower over
EEOOSSSTX exostoses
EEOOSSTTV ovotestes
EEOPPPPRT pepper pot
EEOPPRSSU superpose
EEOPRRRSS repressor
EEOPRRRTY repertory
EEOPRRSST porteress
EEOPRRSSV overpress
EEOPRRSTT protester✧
EEOPRRSUW power user
EEOPRSSSS espressos
repossess
EEOPRSSTU pesterous
proteuses
EEOPRSTTU route-step
EEOPRSTUX exposture
EEOPSSTTU poussette
EEOPSSTTW sweet spot
EEORRRSTY roysterer
EEORRRTTV retrovert
EEORRSSTU retroussé
EEORRSTTU teruteros
EEORRSTUV overtures
EEORRSTVW overstrew
overwrest
EEORRTTVX extrovert
EEORSSTTU roussette
EEORSSTUW sou'wester
EEORSTTTU setter-out
tetterous
Tourette's
EEORSTTTY storyette
EEORSTTTZ terzettos
EEORSTTWW sweetwort
sweet-wort
EEOSSSTTT sestettos
EEPRRSSSU pressures
EEPRRSTTU sputterer
EERRSTTTU stutterer
EFFFLORTU effortful
EFFGGILNU effulging
EFFGGINOR goffering
EFFGGLOOT toggle off
EFFGHIIRT firefight
EFFGINORS offerings
EFFGINRSU suffering
EFFGLOOSV gloves-off
EFFGLORTU forgetful
EFFGNOOPS sponge off
EFFGNRSSU gruffness
EFFHIIKNS fish knife
EFFHIKSWW skew-whiff
EFFHILRSY fly-fisher
EFFHILRWY whifflery
EFFHINSSU huffiness
EFFHLLSSU shelf-fuls
EFFHMSTTU stuff them
EFFIIMNSS miffiness
EFFIIORRT fortifier
EFFIKLORT off kilter
EFFIKORST strike off
EFFILLLRU fulfiller
EFFILMUUV effluvium
EFFILNOUX effluxion
EFFILRSTU strifeful
EFFINOOSS noises off
EFFINPSSU puffiness
EFFINSSST stiffness
EFFINSTUV veinstuff
EFFIOOPRR fireproof
EFFIORRTY refortify
EFFIORTVY forty-five✧
EFFISSUUV suffusive
EFFLLRTUY fretfully
EFFLORRUU furfurole
EFFLORSTY forest-fly
EFFNOORRT forefront
EFFOORRTY offertory
EFFOPRTTU off-putter
EFFORSTUV overstuff
EFGGIINNR fingering
EFGGILOOS solfeggio
EFGGINOOR foregoing
EFGGINOSS fogginess
EFGGINSSU fugginess
EFGHHIILR high-flier✧
EFGHHILRY high-flyer✧
EFGHIILNT nightlife
EFGHIILOT eightfoil
EFGHIILRT firelight
EFGHIINRT nightfire
EFGHIIRST tiger fish
EFGHILLNS fleshling
EFGHILNSS fleshings
EFGHILPRT preflight
EFGHILTWY flyweight
EFGHINORT forenight
EFGHIOOSS goose-fish
EFGHIOOTT eight-foot
EFGHIORST foresight
gift horse
grief-shot
EFGHIORTV give forth
EFGHLLNTU lengthful
EFGHLNRUU hungerful
EFGIIINRS signifier
EFGIILLNT filleting
EFGIILNPR pilfering
EFGIINNRR inferring
infringer
EFGIINNSS finessing
EFGIINPRT fingertip
EFGIINPTY tepifying
EFGIINRTT refitting
EFGIINRVY verifying
EFGIKLNOT Folketing
EFGIKNOTT gift token
EFGILNORW flowering
reflowing
EFGILORTW tiger wolf
EFGILOSTY festilogy
EFGILRTUU fulgurite
EFGIMNTUY tumefying
EFGINNOST softening
EFGINOOSS goofiness
EFGINORST fostering
EFGIORRUV frugivore
EFGIORTUU figure out
EFGLLNORU gronefull
EFGLLNTUY fulgently
EFGLNOPUW gowpenful
EFGLNORSW self-wrong
EFGLOOSTY festology
EFGLOOTUV tug-of-love
EFGMNORSU form genus
EFGNOORTT forgotten
EFGOOOOST goosefoot
EFHHIISTW white fish
whitefish
EFHHILLSS shellfish
EFHHKLOOS flesh-hook
EFHHNOOOT on the hoof
EFHIIKPSS spikefish
EFHIIMSST fetishism
EFHIINPSS snipefish
EFHIINSSS fishiness
EFHIINSSW swine-fish
EFHIIRRTT thriftier

EFHIISSTT fetishist
EFHIJLLSY jellyfish
EFHIKNORT forethink
EFHILLORS fill-horse
EFHILLSSY selfishly
EFHILMNOS lemonfish
EFHILNSSU unselfish
EFHILNSTT flesh-tint
EFHILOOSS loose fish
EFHILORST rifle shot
short-life
EFHILOSSU fish louse
EFHILSSST shiftless
EFHINORRT firethorn
EFHINOSST stonefish
EFHINRRSU furnisher
refurnish
EFHIOPSTT stop thief!
EFHIORRST shotfirer
EFHLLLOTU lothefull
EFHLLNORY holly-fern
EFHLLNPUU unhelpful
EFHLLNSUY unfleshly
EFHLLOPUY hopefully
EFHLLORTW well forth
EFHLLOSST soft-shell
EFHLLOSUU full house
EFHLLOSUV shovelful
EFHLLOTTU to the full
EFHLLTTWY twelfthly
EFHLMOORS shelfroom
EFHLMORSW fleshworm
EFHLNNSSU nun's-flesh
EFHLNOPUU unhopeful
EFHLNSSSU flushness
EFHLOOPSU flophouse
EFHLOOSTU Lofthouse
EFHLOPSST flesh pots
EFHLORSST frothless
EFHLORSTW self-worth
EFHLORSUV overflush
EFHLORSUW showerful
EFHLOSSUU housefuls
EFHMOORRS form horse
EFHNOORSW foreshown
EFHNORTUX foxhunter
EFHOOORST horse-foot
EFHOOORTT foretooth
EFHOORRSU four-horse
EFHORSSTU short fuse
EFHOSTTUU theftuous
EFIIJRSTU justifier
EFIIKLOUY if you like
EFIIKNNOT knife into
EFIILLLST still life
still-life
EFIILLMOR mollifier
EFIILLNRU nullifier
EFIILLORT oil filter
EFIILLRST fillister
EFIILMNSS filminess
EFIILMOTT leitmotif
EFIILNNOX inflexion
EFIILOPSV spoilfive
EFIILOSSS fossilise
EFIILOSSZ fossilize
EFIILPRTT filter tip
EFIILRRSV silver fir
EFIILRTTY fertility
EFIIMORRT mortifier
EFIIMRSTT first-time
EFIIMRSTY mystifier
EFIINNPRT fine print
EFIINNRTU run it fine
EFIINNSST niftiness
EFIINNSTY intensify
EFIINOPRX prefixion
EFIINORRS fire irons
EFIINRTUV vine fruit
EFIINSSZZ fizziness
EFIIORRTU fioriture
EFIISTTVY festivity
EFIJKORST forjeskit
EFIJLLMOR jelliform
EFIKLNSSU flukiness
EFIKLORST frostlike
EFIKMNNOO moon knife
EFIKNNOTX next of kin
EFIKNNSSU funkiness
EFIKNORSS forkiness
EFIKOOPRV Prokofiev
EFIKORRST foreskirt
EFIKORRSW fireworks
EFILLMOPU filoplume
EFILLMRTU full-timer
EFILLNOWY yellowfin
EFILLNPTU plentiful
EFILLOOOS foliolose
EFILLOORT floor tile
EFILMNORT lentiform
EFILMNOSY solemnify
EFILMOPRV pelviform
EFILMOPRX plexiform
EFILMORSU formulise
Isle of Rum
EFILMORUZ formulize
EFILNNOOS no flies on
EFILNNORT front line
front-line
EFILNOORS solferino
EFILNOOSU felonious
EFILNOOTU out of line
EFILNORST frost line
EFILNORTW interflow
EFILNOSST loftiness
EFILNRSTU run itself
EFILOPSST soft spile
EFILOPSSU self-pious
EFILORSTY life story
EFILORSVX silver fox
EFILORTTU filter out
EFILOSSTU fistulose
EFILOTUZZ fizzle out
EFILPPUUY yuppie flu
EFILPRSTU spriteful
EFILQRUUV quiverful
EFILRSSTU fruitless
EFILRTUVY furtively
EFIMMORRS reformism
EFIMMORRV vermiform
EFIMNNOPR penniform
EFIMNNOTY Tom Finney
EFIMNNRTU furniment
EFIMOOTTU out of time
EFIMOPRST septiform
EFIMORRST fire-storm
reformist
restiform
EFIMORRSV versiform
EFINNNSSU funniness
EFINNORTU infortune
EFINNSSTU unfitness
EFINOOPRT forepoint
EFINOOSTT set foot in
EFINOPRSU perfusion
EFINOPRSY personify
EFINOPRTY prenotify
EFINORRST frontiers
EFINORSTW frontwise
EFINORTUZ fortunize
EFINRRSSU furriness
EFINRRTUU furniture
EFINRSSTU turfiness
EFINSSSSU fussiness
EFINSSSTU fustiness
EFINSSSTW swiftness
EFINSSUZZ fuzziness
EFIOORSTX six-footer
EFIOORSUV oviferous
EFIOPRTTU petit four
EFIORTTTU outfitter
EFIOSSTUV festivous
EFJNOOORT not for Joe
EFKLMNOOW womenfolk
EFKLMORUW fluke-worm
EFKNNOORW foreknown
EFKNOOPRS spoken for
EFLLMOSTU molestful
EFLLMOSUY fulsomely
EFLLMSUUY musefully
EFLLNOOTY loony left
EFLLNTUUY tunefully
EFLLOOVWW vow-fellow
EFLLORRUY Roy Fuller
EFLLRSTUU resultful
EFLLRSTUY restfully
EFLLSTUYZ zestfully
EFLNNOOYZ no-fly zone
EFLNNTUUU untuneful
EFLNOORVW overflown
EFLNOOSTW flowstone
EFLNOPRTU profluent
EFLNORSST frontless

EFLNORSUW sunflower
EFLNOSSUW wofulness
EFLNRSTUU unrestful
EFLOOOOST footloose
EFLOOPRSS proofless
EFLOOPRTW flowerpot
EFLOOSTTW Lowestoft
EFLOPRSTY flyposter
EFLOPRSUY profusely
EFLORRRTU terrorful
EFLORSSST frostless
EFLPRSUUX superflux
EFLRSSSTU stressful
EFLRSSTTU self-trust
EFMNORRTY entry form
EFNNNRRUU fun runner
EFNNOOOSW of one's own
EFNNOOSTT font-stone
EFNNOPRUY fourpenny
EFNNORTUU unfortune
EFNOOOSTT set on foot
EFNOORSST foster-son
EFNOOTTUU out of tune
EFOOOPRRV over proof
overproof
EFOOPPRSU of purpose
EFOOPRRSS professor
EFOOPRSTW soft power
EFOOPRTTX proof text
EFOOPSSTT footsteps
EFOOPSTTU out of step
EFOOQRRTU Roquefort
EFOORRSUV fervorous
EFOORTTUU out of true
EFOPRSSTU supersoft
EGGGILMSU misguggle
EGGGINOTT go-getting
EGGGINQSU squegging
EGGHHIILN in high leg
EGGHIILNS sleighing
EGGHIINNW whingeing
EGGHIINTW weighting
EGGHIJNOR John Greig
EGGHILORU Lou Gehrig
EGGHINORR hog-ringer
EGGIILNNR lingering
EGGIINNSW swingeing
EGGIINOOR Giorgione
EGGILLNOS single-log
EGGILLNRU gruelling
EGGILNORV groveling
EGGILOORS goose-girl
EGGILOOST geologist
EGGILOPRW porwiggle
EGGIMNNOR mongering
EGGIMNSSU mugginess
EGGINNNOR Groningen
EGGINNNPU genning up
EGGINNORV governing
EGGINNPTU tuning peg
EGGINNRTU ginger nut
EGGINOORS gorgonise
EGGINOORV going-over
overgoing
EGGINOORZ gorgonize
EGGINOOSS geognosis
EGGINOOSW goose-wing
EGGINOPPR ginger pop
EGGINORSU gingerous
EGGINORTY Tony Greig
EGGINOSSS sogginess
EGGINRTTU guttering
EGGINSSTU gusseting
EGGIORRTU outrigger
EGGJLMNUY jungle gym
EGGLMMOOY gemmology
EGGLRRSTU struggler
EGHHHIORS high horse
EGHHIKNTT The Knight
EGHHILNTU Leigh Hunt
EGHHILOST sight-hole
EGHHINRST threshing
EGHHIORTU eight-hour
EGHHMOTTU methought
EGHHNORUW rough-hewn
EGHHNOTTU thoughten
EGHHNOUZZ Zhengzhou
EGHIIKNRS shrieking
EGHIILLMT limelight
EGHIILMTT light time
EGHIILNNT night-line
EGHIILNRT girthline
EGHIILNST gentilish
sightline
EGHIILNTV the living
EGHIILPPT pipe-light
EGHIILTWY weightily
EGHIIMNTT night-time
EGHIINNTW whitening
EGHIINOTW weigh into
EGHIINPRS perishing
EGHIINRSV shivering
EGHIINRTV the Virgin
EGHIINRTW withering
EGHIINSTY hygienist
EGHIINTWW whitewing
EGHIIRSTZ rightsize
EGHIKLOST ghostlike
EGHILLMOT megilloth
EGHILLNOT hotelling
oil length
EGHILLNSW wing shell
EGHILLNTY lengthily
EGHILLOOP logophile
EGHILLOOY heliology
EGHILLOSU gill-house
EGHILLOTV lovelight
EGHILLSST lightless
EGHILMOST lightsome
EGHILNNOR Lohengrin
EGHILNNOT neon light
EGHILNNSU un-English
EGHILNOPR negrophil
EGHILNOPW longe whip
EGHILNPTU lighten up
EGHILNPUW lunge whip
EGHILNRSY Englishry
EGHILNRTU night-rule
EGHILNSST lightness
nightless
EGHILNSTU hung tiles
EGHILOORY hierology
EGHILOSST lose sight
EGHILOSTW go whistle
EGHILPRTU uplighter
EGHILRSST rightless
EGHILRTVY Very light
EGHILSSST sightless
EGHIMNORT mothering
EGHIMNOST something✧
EGHIMORTT tiger moth
EGHIMPPSU pemphigus
EGHINNOTW on the wing
EGHINNSST thingness
EGHINORSU rehousing
EGHINORSW showering
EGHINORTV overnight
EGHINOSTY histogeny
EGHINPTTU tighten up
EGHINRSST rightness
EGHINRSTT night-rest
EGHINRSTU sure thing
EGHINRTUW wuthering
EGHINSSTT tightness
EGHIOPRSU rogueship
EGHIOPRTT tightrope
EGHIORSTU righteous
EGHIORSTV oversight
EGHIRSTTU theurgist
EGHJLNNNO John Glenn
EGHLLLOUY gully-hole
EGHLLOORY glory hole
EGHLMNOPU ploughmen
EGHLMOOOU homologue
EGHLNNRTU run length
EGHLNOOPY nephology
phenology
EGHLNOORS longshore
EGHLNOOSU longhouse
EGHLNOOTY ethnology
EGHLNOPYY phylogeny
EGHLNORSU slughorne
EGHLOOORR horologer
EGHLOOOSS goloshoes
EGHLOORTY therology
EGHLOOTUV tough love
EGHLOOTYY hyetology
EGHLOSUUY hugeously
EGHMNOORW home-grown
EGHMNRTUU mug-hunter
EGHMOOPSS gomphoses
EGHNNOPYY hypnogeny
EGHNOOOPR gonophore

EGHNOOPRY gynophore
EGHNOOPTY photogeny
EGHNOPTYY phytogeny
EGHNORSSU roughness
EGHNOSSTU oughtness
toughness
EGHOOPSUY hypogeous
EGHOPTYYZ zygophyte
EGIIINRTV Irvingite
EGIIKLNSV king's evil
EGIIKNNRT tinkering
EGIIKNRSS Kissinger
EGIIKRSTZ sitzkrieg
EGIILLMNP impelling
EGIILLNNO nielloing
EGIILLNOR gorilline
EGIILLNPR perilling
EGIILLRTY tiger lily✧
EGIILMNST gentilism
EGIILMORS mirligoes
EGIILMPRR pilgrimer
EGIILNNPP lippening
EGIILNNST tinseling
EGIILNNUV unveiling
EGIILNORT loitering
EGIILNOST gilsonite
EGIILNOSU uliginose
EGIILNPSS singspiel
EGIILNRSV silvering
EGIILNRVW liverwing
EGIILNSTT tingliest
EGIILNSUV ingluvies
EGIILNTTY gentility
EGIILOORS religioso
EGIILOPST epilogist
EGIILORSU religious
EGIILSTTZ glitziest
EGIIMNNPT impingent
EGIIMNNSS minginess
EGIIMNORS Origenism
EGIIMNPRS simpering
EGIIMNRSS griminess
EGIIMNRTT remitting
EGIIMOPST impetigos
EGIIMSTUV vestigium
EGIINNORS nigrosine
signorine
EGIINNOST ingestion
EGIINNOSU ingenious
EGIINNRRT interring
EGIINNRSW inswinger
EGIINNSTT insetting
EGIINNTUY ingenuity
EGIINOPTT tiptoeing
EGIINORST Origenist
EGIINORSY seigniory
EGIINPPQU equipping
EGIINPRRZ prize ring
EGIINPRSS speirings
EGIINQRRU requiring
EGIINQRUV quivering
EGIINRRTU intriguer
EGIINRSST sistering
EGIINRSTT string tie
EGIINRTTT tittering
EGIINRTTV rivetting
EGIINRTTY integrity
EGIJKNNTU junketing
EGIJLLNOY jolleying
EGIJLNSTY jestingly
EGIKLNNOO inglenook
EGIKNNORT token ring
EGIKNNTUY tuning key
EGIKNOOSS goose-skin
EGIKNORRW reworking
EGILLLNTY tellingly
EGILLMNTY meltingly
EGILLMORU glomeruli
EGILLMOTU guillemot
EGILLNNOR enrolling
long-liner
EGILLNORS Negrillos
EGILLNORW rowelling
EGILLNOTT ill-gotten
EGILLNOTW towelling
EGILLNOTX extolling
EGILLNPTY peltingly
EGILLNPUW upwelling
EGILLOSSY syllogise
EGILLOSYZ syllogize
EGILLSSTU guiltless
EGILMNOOS Mongolise
neologism
EGILMNOOZ Mongolize
EGILMOOSY semiology
EGILMOSUU eulogiums
EGILNNNTU tunneling
EGILNNOSS lessoning
EGILNNOST singleton
EGILNNOTX Lexington
EGILNNOUY Neil Young
EGILNNRSU nurseling
EGILNOORY irenology
EGILNOOST neologist
EGILNOOSU Sinologue
EGILNOPRX exploring
EGILNORSU ring ousel
EGILNORTV revolting
EGILNORUZ ring ouzel
EGILNORVV revolving
EGILNORVY overlying
EGILNOSSX long sixes
long-sixes
EGILNOTVY longevity
EGILNPRST springlet
EGILNRSTU resulting
EGILNRSTW wrestling
EGILNSSST stingless
EGILNSUVW swivel-gun
EGILOOPRS prologise
EGILOOPRZ prologize
EGILOORTT Rigoletto
EGILOPRRW girl power
EGILORSTY sortilegy
EGILORTUV voltigeur
EGILOSSTT glottises
EGIMMNNOU immunogen
EGIMMNORS monergism
EGIMMNRSU summering
EGIMMNSSU gumminess
EGIMNNORS sermoning
EGIMNNORT mentoring
EGIMNNORY ring money
EGIMNNOSS no messing
EGIMNNTUU minute gun
EGIMNORSV misgovern
EGIMNORTW wit-monger
EGIMNOSTT misgotten
EGIMNOTUY timenoguy
EGIMNPRSU presuming
EGIMNRSSY synergism
EGIMNRTTU muttering
EGIMORRTW tiger worm
EGIMPRTUY pterygium
EGINNNRUV unnerving
EGINNNUVY unenvying
EGINNOSTT onsetting
EGINNOSUU ingenuous
EGINNOTTW towing net
EGINNPRUY penguinry
EGINNRSTT stringent
EGINNRSTU insurgent
unresting
EGINNRTUV venturing
EGINNTTUV vingt-et-un
EGINOOPRT protogine
EGINOOPSS goopiness
spongiose
EGINOOSSU isogenous
EGINOPPPR poppering
EGINOPPRS pop singer
EGINOPPST estopping
EGINOPRRR porringer
EGINOPRRT reporting
EGINOPRRV reproving
EGINOPRST progestin
EGINOPRTT pottering
pottinger
repotting
EGINOPSSY gossypine
EGINOPSUY epigynous
EGINORRST rostering
EGINORRTV Vortigern
EGINORRTW intergrow
EGINORSTT gritstone
rosetting
EGINORSUY Sigourney
EGINORTTT tottering
EGINOSSST stegnosis
EGINOSSTU goutiness
EGINPSTTU upsetting
EGINPSTWW sweptwing
EGINPSTXY sex typing

EGINRSSTU	russeting
EGINRSSTY	synergist
EGINRSUVY	surveying
EGINSSSTU	gustiness
	gutsiness
EGINSTTTU	tungstite
EGIOORSUV	ovigerous
EGIPPRTTU	gruppetti
EGIPSTUZZ	Zugspitze
EGKORSSUW	guesswork
EGLLLOORR	logroller
EGLLMNORY	mongrelly
EGLLSSTUY	gutlessly
EGLMNOOOU	monologue
EGLMOOORV	overgloom
EGLMOORTY	metrology
EGLMOOSUY	museology
EGLMOOTYY	etymology
EGLNNOSUU	sun lounge
EGLNNOTUY	Tony Leung
EGLNNPTUY	pungently
EGLNOOOPY	poenology
EGLNOOPRR	prolonger
EGLNOORUY	neurology
EGLNOOSUV	longevous
EGLNORSTY	strongyle
EGLNORSUU	longueurs
EGLNOSTUU	glutenous
EGLNRTTUY	turgently
EGLOOORTY	erotology
EGLOOOSTY	osteology
EGLOOPRTY	petrology
EGLOOPSTY	pestology
EGLOORSSV	gloss over
EGLOPSTYY	pygostyle
EGMNOOOSS	mongooses
EGMNOORRS	Gros Morne
EGMOORSTU	guest-room
EGMOPRSYZ	zygosperm
EGNNNRRUU	gunrunner
EGNNORSSW	wrongness
EGNNOSSUY	youngness
EGNOOOSSW	snow goose
EGNOOOSUZ	zoogenous
EGNOOPRSS	prognoses
EGNOOPRSY	sporogeny
EGNOOPSSU	spongeous
EGNOORRVW	overgrown
EGNOORSUU	urogenous
EGNOOSUXY	oxygenous
EGNOOTTUU	outtongue
EGNOPRSUW	newsgroup
EGNORSSSS	grossness
EGNORSSTT	strongest
EGNORSTUY	youngster
EGNPRSSUU	sun spurge
EGNRRTTUU	turret gun
EGOOOPRTV	go to prove
EGOOPRSST	go to press
EGOOPRSYZ	zygospore
EGOPPRTTU	gruppetto
EHHIIRTTT	thirtieth
EHHIJNORT	John Reith
EHHILLLSY	hellishly
EHHILMOOP	homophile
EHHILOPRS	philhorse
EHHILOTTT	to the hilt
EHHILSTTW	the whilst
EHHIMNPSY	hyphenism
EHHIMRSTY	rhythmise
EHHIMRTYZ	rhythmize
EHHINOPPS	phosphine
EHHINORTW	no whither
	nowhither
EHHIOPPST	phosphite
EHHIOPRSW	horsewhip
EHHIOSTVY	yeshivoth
EHHIPRSSU	ushership
EHHJNNORY	John Henry
EHHKLOOSW	Welsh hook
EHHLOOOPT	holophote
EHHLOOPTY	holophyte
EHHLOPTYY	hylophyte
EHHLOSSUU	lush-house
EHHMNNOPP	Phnom Penh
EHHMNOOOP	homophone
EHHMNOSUY	hush money
EHHMOOOST	shoot home
EHHMORTTU	home truth
EHHMRTUYY	eurhythmy✧
EHHNOORTU	on the hour
EHHNOSTUU	house-hunt
EHHOOPSTY	theosophy
EHHOOSSUW	show house
EHHORSTTU	thrust hoe
EHIIILMRS	Irish mile
EHIIINRVY	Henry VIII
EHIIJNORT	joint heir
EHIIKLMTW	milk-white
EHIIKNNPT	in the pink
EHIIKNSTT	kittenish
EHIILLNPT	tephillin
EHIILLNSS	hilliness
EHIILLRSW	ill-wisher
EHIILLTWY	lily-white
EHIILMRST	Hitlerism
EHIILNOPS	Sinophile
EHIILNTTW	lintwhite
EHIILOOPT	ophiolite
EHIILPRST	Philister
EHIILPSSY	syphilise
EHIILPSYZ	syphilize
EHIILRSTT	Hitlerist
EHIILRSTW	Wiltshire
EHIILSTTW	whitelist
EHIIMMPST	mephitism
EHIIMNSTW	in the swim
EHIIMRSTT	tritheism
EHIINNSSS	shininess
EHIINNSSW	whininess
EHIINOPST	Tisiphone
EHIINORRT	inheritor
EHIINORTW	white iron
EHIINPPRW	whipper-in
EHIINPRST	nephritis
	phrenitis
EHIINPSST	pithiness
EHIINRSSS	Irishness
EHIINSTUV	Vishnuite
EHIIOORRV	Ohio River
EHIIPPRTU	hippurite
EHIIPPSSY	epiphysis
EHIIPRSTT	the Spirit
EHIIQRSUV	quiverish
EHIIRRSTT	thirstier
EHIIRSSTW	Irish stew
EHIIRSTTT	tritheist
EHIIRSTTZ	zitherist
EHIJKMOST	jokesmith
EHIJMNOTU	Jotunheim
EHIJNOPPR	John Piper
EHIKLLMOW	whole milk
EHIKLLNPS	shell pink
	shell-pink
EHIKLLPSY	sylphlike
EHIKLMNPY	nymphlike
EHIKLMOSU	milk-house
EHIKLMPST	klephtism
EHIKLNPRY	hyperlink
EHIKLOOTT	toothlike
EHIKLORSW	shriek-owl
EHIKLORTZ	kilohertz
EHIKLRTTU	truthlike
EHIKMNOSY	monkeyish
EHIKNNOTW	in the know
EHIKNOOPR	pinhooker
EHIKNORTV	think over
EHIKNPRRS	pre-shrink
EHIKNSSSU	huskiness
EHIKORRSY	Yorkshire
EHIKPRSSU	spike-rush
EHIKRSWYY	rye whisky
EHILLMORS	horse mill
	mill-horse
EHILLNOPT	on the pill
EHILLOPSU	Lusophile
EHILLOSTY	hostilely
EHILLOSWY	yellowish
EHILLPSSU	slush pile
EHILLRSTU	Ruth Ellis
EHILLSSTU	shell suit
EHILMNPTU	in the lump
EHILMOOTT	lithotome
EHILMOSZZ	shimozzle
EHILMPPRY	perilymph
EHILMPSSY	emphlysis
EHILMRSST	mirthless
EHILMRSTU	Lutherism
EHILMRTTY	trimethyl
EHILNNOOP	phelonion
EHILNOOPT	in the loop
	lithopone
	phonolite

EHILNOOPY oenophily
EHILNOSTU shoutline
EHILNOSUY heinously
EHILNRTWY Henry Wilt
EHILOPRXY xerophily
EHILOPSSU Sophus Lie
EHILOPTYY heliotypy
EHILPRRSU rulership
EHILPSTTY pettishly
EHILPSTUW whistle up
EHILRSSST shirtless
EHILRSTTU Lutherist
EHIMNNOOR monorhine
EHIMNNOOS moonshine
EHIMNOPRS premonish
EHIMNOPST phonetism
EHIMNOPSU euphonism
EHIMNOPSY ship money
EHIMNOPUU euphonium
EHIMNORST horsemint
EHIMNPRST shrimp net
EHIMNRTUU ruthenium
EHIMNSSSU mushiness
EHIMNSTTU tunesmith
EHIMOOOSS homoeosis
EHIMOORST shire-moot
EHIMOOSTZ zootheism
EHIMOPPRR perimorph
EHIMORRRT The Mirror
EHIMORSTT short time
short-time
EHIMORTTW mother wit
EHIMORTWW white worm
EHIMOSTTU mouthiest
EHIMPRRTU triumpher
EHIMRRSTY erythrism
EHINNOPSS phoniness
EHINNORSS horniness
EHINNOSTW whinstone
EHINNRSUV unshriven
EHINNSSTU Nissen hut
EHINOOOPR ionophore
EHINOOPST point shoe
EHINOORRS iron horse
EHINOORST Hortensio
EHINOOSST shot noise
EHINOPRSS nephrosis
EHINOPRSW ownership
shipowner
EHINOPSTT phonetist
EHINOPSTU in the soup
EHINOPSTY hypnotise
EHINOPSVY envoyship
EHINOPTYZ hypnotize
EHINORRSU nourisher
EHINORSSS horsiness
EHINORSTT thorniest
EHINORTXY thyroxine
EHINOSSSW showiness
EHINOSTWW snow-white
EHINOTTUW withouten
EHINPRRTY pyrethrin
EHINPRSTU superthin
EHINPSSSU pushiness
EHINPTTWY petty whin
EHINQRSTU Rehnquist
EHINRSSSU rushiness
EHINSSSTY synthesis
EHINSTTWY twentyish
EHIOOPRST Pooterish
EHIOOPRTW poor white
wirephoto
EHIOOSTTT toothiest
EHIOPPRST tripe-shop
EHIOPRSST prothesis
sophister
store ship
EHIOPRTTW white port
EHIORRSTV overshirt
EHIORSTTU stouthrie
EHIPRSTTY prettyish
EHIQSSTTU the squits
EHIRRRRUV River Ruhr
EHJLNNOOT Elton John
EHJLNORTY John Tyler
EHJNNOOST Johnstone
EHJNORSTW Jews' thorn
EHJOOSSSU joss house
EHJOPRRSY jerry-shop
EHKKLOOSZ kolkhozes
EHKLLORSW shellwork
EHKLLSSTU tusk shell
EHKLOOOST tokoloshe
EHKLOTTYY thelytoky
EHKMRSSUW musk shrew
EHKNORSTU trunk hose
EHKOOOSTT theotokos
EHKOORRSW workhorse
EHKOORSUW housework
workhouse
EHLLMOPSY mesophyll
EHLLNOPTU on the pull
EHLLOOSTU tollhouse
EHLLORSST sell short
EHLLORTWW well worth
EHLMMOPTU plume-moth
EHLMORSSU humorless
EHLMOSSTU mouthless
EHLNNOTTU Len Hutton
EHLNOOPPY polyphone
EHLNOOPRT north pole
EHLNOOPXY xylophone
EHLNOORST sloethorn
EHLNOOSTY holystone
EHLNORRTY northerly
EHLNORSST thornless
EHLOOOSTU toolhouse
EHLOOPSTU south pole
spout-hole
EHLOOPSTV hovel-post
EHLOOPSTY photolyse
EHLOOSSTT toothless
EHLOPRSTU upholster
EHLOPSTYY hypostyle
EHLORRTTT throttler
EHLORSSTT trothless
EHLORSSTW worthless
EHLORSTUY southerly
EHLPRSTUU sulphuret
EHLRSSTTU truthless
EHMMNOORY monorhyme
EHMMOOORT motor home
EHMMOOPRS mesomorph
EHMNNOOOY honeymoon
EHMNORRST Ernst Röhm
EHMNOSTUU mouse-hunt
EHMNPRYYY hypernymy
EHMOOOPRS sophomore
EHMOOORSU houseroom
EHMOOOSTT toothsome
EHMOOOSTU moot house
EHMOOPRRX xeromorph
EHMOOPSTU shoot-'em-up
EHMOOPTTY mythopoet
EHMOORRTY horometry
EHMOOSTUY youthsome
EHMORRSTT short-term
EHMPRRTUY pyrethrum✧
EHNNOORST hornstone
EHNNOOTTW on the town✧
EHNNORTTU on the turn
EHNOOOPPR phonopore
EHNOOOPPT optophone
EHNOOORTT orthotone
EHNOOPPRY pyrophone
EHNOOPPTY phonotype
EHNOOPRTW throw open
EHNOOPSTT on the spot
on-the-spot
EHNOOPSTY honeypots
EHNOORTTT on the trot
EHNOOSSTT stoneshot
EHNOOSTUW town house
townhouse
EHNOOTTTT hottentot✧
EHNOPRTTU pot-hunter
EHNOPSSTY pythoness✧
EHNORRTTU true north
EHNORSSST shortness
EHNORSTTW north-west
EHNRSTTUU unshutter
EHOOOPRSU poorhouse
EHOOORSTU root house
EHOOORSTV overshoot
EHOOPPTTY phototype
EHOOPRRTV hoverport
EHOOPRSST posthorse
EHOOPRSTU porthouse
EHOOPSSTU posthouse
EHOORRTVW overthrow
throw over
EHOORSSTT sort those
those sort

EHOORSTTW shot tower
EHOPPSSTU set up shop
EHOPRSSTT step short
EHORRSTTW throwster
EHOSSTTUW south-west
EIIIKNNOP epinikion
EIIILLLOP illipe oil
EIIILMMTT time limit
EIIILNNQU inquiline
EIIILNNSV live in sin
EIIILNTZZ tin lizzie
EIIILSTTU utilities
EIIIMMNRS minimiser
EIIIMMNRZ minimizer
EIIIMNSTT intimiste
EIIIMPRTV primitive✧
EIIINNPST insipient
EIIINPRST ripienist
EIIINRSTT retinitis
EIIINTTUV intuitive
EIIJLMSSU Miss Julie
EIIJMSSTU Jesuitism
EIIJNNORT interjoin
EIIJNOSSU join issue
EIIJQRTUY jequirity
EIIKKLNST like stink
EIIKKNNSS kinkiness
EIIKKNRST steinkirk
EIIKLLORT kilolitre
EIIKLMNSS milkiness
EIIKLNNRT interlink
EIIKLNRSW wrinklies
EIIKLNSSS silkiness
EIIKLORST strike oil
EIIKNNOPS pink noise
EIIKNNPPR nipperkin
EIIKNNPSS pinkiness
EIIKNNRTT interknit
EIIKNPSSS spikiness
EIIKNRSSS riskiness
EIILLLMMO millimole
EIILLMNRU illuminer
EIILLMNRY millinery
EIILLMOST mollities
EIILLMSST limitless
EIILLNNOP penillion
EIILLNOOR neroli oil
EIILLNOPT pointillé
EIILLNSSS silliness
EIILLOPRS pillorise
EIILLOPRZ pillorize
EIILLSTUV Vitellius
EIILMMORS meliorism
EIILMNOPS moniplies
EIILMNOPT impletion
EIILMNOPX implexion
EIILMNORV vermilion
EIILMNOSU limousine
EIILMNPPS mislippen
EIILMNPRU primuline
EIILMNSSS sliminess
EIILMOPPS epipolism
EIILMOPRV Primo Levi
EIILMOPSV implosive
EIILMORST meliorist
EIILMORTY meliority
EIILMOTTV leitmotiv
EIILMPRSU puerilism
EIILMPSST simpliste
EIILMPSTT split time
EIILMPSUV impulsive
EIILMRSST Listerism
EIILMRSSV servilism
EIILMRSSY missilery
EIILNNOQU quinoline
EIILNOSSS soiliness
EIILNOTTV volitient
EIILNPSST splenitis
EIILNPSTY pensility
EIILNPTUV vulpinite
EIILNQTUY inquietly
EIILNRTUY neurility
EIILNSTTY tensility
EIILNSTVY sylvinite
EIILNTUVY unitively
EIILOPQTU politique
EIILOPSST spilosite
EIILOQSSU siliquose
EIILORSTV Vitreosil®
EIILORTTV Vitrolite®
EIILPRSTU pleuritis
spirituel
EIILPRSTZ prize list
EIILPRTUY puerility
EIILRSSUV Silverius
EIILRSTTY sterility
EIILRSTTZ strelitzi
EIILRSTVY servility
EIIMMMORS memoirism
EIIMMNORS immersion
EIIMMNOSS misoneism
EIIMMNRST minim rest
terminism
EIIMMNRSU immuniser
EIIMMNRUZ immunizer
EIIMMNSTY immensity
EIIMMORSS isomerism
EIIMMORST memoirist
EIIMMOSTV emotivism
EIIMMPSSS pessimism
EIIMMPSUY epimysium
EIIMMRTUX immixture
EIIMNNORR iron-miner
EIIMNNRTU triennium
EIIMNOPST impsonite
pimientos
EIIMNORSS missioner
remission
EIIMNORST Minorites
EIIMNORSV Minervois
EIIMNOSST misoneist
EIIMNOSTU minutiose
EIIMNOSUV vimineous
EIIMNOTZZ mizzonite
EIIMNPRST Petrinism
strip mine
EIIMNPRSU supermini
EIIMNRSTT terminist
EIIMNSSST mistiness
EIIMOPRST optimiser
EIIMOPRSU imperious
EIIMOPRSV improvise
EIIMOPRTZ optimizer
EIIMOPSTT epitomist
EIIMOSSTV sovietism
EIIMOSTTV emotivist
EIIMOTTVY emotivity
EIIMPSSST pessimist
EIINNNOST intension
EIINNNOTT intention
EIINNNOTV invention
EIINNNSST tinniness
EIINNORST insertion
EIINNORSV inversion
EIINNOSSS in session
noisiness
EIINNPPSS nippiness
EIINNPSSS spininess
EIINNRSTT internist
EIINNSSTT insistent
tintiness
EIINNSTTY intensity
EIINNSTXY sixty-nine
EIINOPRSV prevision
EIINOPTVW viewpoint
EIINORSSS resinosis
EIINORSTU routinise
EIINORSTY seniority
EIINORTUZ routinize
EIINPPRST pinstripe
EIINPRSST persist in
EIINPSSST tipsiness
EIINPSSSW wispiness
EIINQTTTU quintetti
EIINRSSTU siren suit
EIINRSSTZ ritziness
EIINRSTUV intrusive
EIINRTTUV nutritive
vetturini
EIINSSSSS sissiness
EIINSSSYZ synizesis
EIINSSTTW wittiness
EIINSTTTU institute
EIIOPPSTT petit pois
EIIORRTUV voiturier
EIIORSSTT sottisier
EIIPPRSTT trippiest
EIIPRRTUV irruptive
EIIQRRSTU quirister
EIIRSSSTV visitress
EIJJKNOTU juke-joint
EIJKLLOOU kilojoule
EIJKMNRSU Junkerism

EIJKMPRSU ski jumper
EIJKNNSSU junkiness
EIJLLLMOV Jim Lovell
EIJLLMNOT jolliment
EIJLLNOSS jolliness
EIJLMNPTU mint julep
EIJLNOSST jointless
EIJMNPSSU jumpiness
EIJNNOSST jointness
EIJNORRSU surrejoin
EIJNORSST jointress
EIJPRTTUY petit jury
EIKKNOOSS kookiness
EIKLLLSSS skill-less
EIKLLNOTY not likely
EIKLLRTUW Kurt Weill
EIKLMMORZ klezmorim
EIKLMNOSS moleskins
EIKLMNOSW Monk Lewis
EIKLMORSY irksomely
EIKLNNOOT kilotonne
EIKLNNRTU trunk line
EIKLNNRUW unwrinkle
EIKLNOTUW winkle out
EIKLNPRRS sprinkler
EIKLNSSSU sulkiness
EIKLRSSST skirtless
EIKMMNOSY monkeyism
EIKMNNORT Komintern
EIKMNNOST Minkstone
EIKMNOORS monoskier
EIKMNOPSS misspoken
EIKMNORSY risk money
EIKMNOSSS smokiness
EIKMNOSTY Mike Týson
EIKMNOTTT Tom Kitten
EIKMNRSSU murkiness
EIKMNSSSU muskiness
EIKNNOPRT pinkerton✧
EIKNNOSSW wonkiness
EIKNNPSSU punkiness
EIKNOORST sooterkin
EIKNORRTW interwork
EIKNORSTV overstink
EIKNRRTTY trinketry
EIKOPQRUW piqué work
EIKORRSTV overskirt
EIKORRSTW workerist
EIKORSTTU outstrike
strike out
strikeout
EILLLOTTW little owl
EILLMNORW mill owner
EILLMNOST millstone
EILLMNSSU sensillum
EILLMOPSW Powellism
EILLMORTU multirole
EILLMORTW tower mill
EILLMOSSY lissomely
EILLMPTTU multiplet
EILLMPTUX multiplex
EILLMRTUU tellurium
EILLNOPRU nullipore
EILLNORRT ritornell
EILLNORST stornelli
EILLNORTU tellurion
EILLNOSSW lowliness
EILLNOSTY stone-lily
EILLNOTVY violently
EILLNPTUY puy lentil
EILLNPUUV pulvinule
EILLNSSST stillness
EILLNSSSY sinlessly
EILLOOPRV Liverpool
EILLOPRST postiller
EILLOPRSV overspill
spill over
spillover
EILLOPRTY pellitory
EILLOPRWW willpower
EILLOPSST pilotless
EILLOPTUV pollutive
EILLOSTTY stylolite
EILLPSSSY syllepsis
EILLSSTWY witlessly
EILMMMOSS Moslemism
EILMMNNUU nummuline
EILMMNTUU nummulite
EILMMOPSY misemploy
EILMNOOSY noisomely
EILMNOPST simpleton
EILMNOPSU on impulse
EILMNOPSY monyplies
EILMNORST line-storm
EILMNORTT tormentil
EILMNOSTY solemnity
EILMNOSWY winsomely
EILMNPSSU lumpiness
EILMOOSTY ileostomy
EILMOPSVW simple vow
EILMORSUV volumiser
EILMORUVZ volumizer
EILMOSTUY timeously
EILMRSTUU multiuser
EILNNOOQU quinolone
EILNNOOSS looniness
EILNNOPTT nilpotent
EILNNOQTU non liquet
EILNNOSTV insolvent
EILNNPSTU unslept-in
EILNOOPSS loopiness
EILNOOPSX explosion
EILNOOTUV evolution
EILNOPRRU purloiner
EILNOPRSU repulsion
EILNOPSST pointless
EILNOPSSU spinulose
EILNOPSTT Intelpost
EILNOPSTV pontlevis
EILNOPSUX expulsion
EILNORSSY sensorily
EILNORSTY storyline
EILNORSUV revulsion
EILNORTUY routinely
EILNOSSSU lousiness
EILNOSSTT siltstone
EILNOSUVY enviously
EILNPPSSU pulpiness
EILNPQTUU quintuple
EILNPRSST printless
EILNPRSTY splintery
EILNQTUUY unquietly
EILNRSSSU surliness
EILNRSSUU Ursulines
EILNRSTTU turnstile
EILNRTUUV vulturine
EILNSSSTT stintless
EILNSSSTU lustiness
EILOPPRSS prolepsis
EILOPPRTY propylite
EILOPRSTV liver spot
EILOPRSTY leprosity
EILOPRTVY livery pot
EILOPSTTT test pilot
EILOPSTUY piteously
EILORRTVW liverwort
EILORSSUY seriously
EILOSSTTT stilettos
EILQRRSUY squirrely
EILRRTUWZ Wurlitzer®
EIMMNNOST mnemonist
EIMMNNSTU muniments
EIMMNOORS Monroeism
EIMMNOORT Mormonite
EIMMNOPRS persimmon
EIMMNORRT minor term
EIMMNRSSU rumminess
EIMMOOPRU pomoerium
prooemium
EIMMOORST timorsome
EIMMOPRSU emporiums
EIMMOPSTU impostume
EIMNNOORT minor tone
EIMNNOOTZ monzonite
EIMNNOPRT prominent
EIMNNORST innermost
EIMNNPTUU neptunium
EIMNNRTTU nutriment
EIMNNSTTU unsmitten
EIMNOOOPR prooemion
EIMNOOPRS Peronismo
EIMNOOPRT minor poet
premotion
EIMNOORSS roominess
EIMNOORST Monroeist
trominoes
EIMNOPRSU Simon Pure
simon-pure
EIMNOPRTU entropium
importune
EIMNOQRUY querimony
EIMNORRTW worriment
EIMNORSST monitress

Words marked ✧ can also be spelled with one or more capital letters

EIMNORSSU sensorium
EIMNORSSW worminess
EIMNORSUV verminous
EIMNORTTU tentorium
EIMNOSSSS mossiness
EIMNOSSST moistness
EIMNOSSSU mousiness
EIMNOSTTU Teutonism
EIMNOSTTY testimony
EIMNOSTUU untimeous
EIMNOTTZZ mezzotint
EIMNSSSSU mussiness
EIMNSSSTU mustiness
EIMNSSUZZ muzziness
EIMOOPRST Pooterism
EIMOOPRTV promotive
EIMOORRSW worrisome
EIMOORSSU isomerous
EIMOOSSSX exosmosis
EIMOPRRST misreport
EIMOPRSTU imposture
EIMOPRTYZ prozymite
EIMOPSTUU impetuous
EIMORRRST terrorism
EIMORRSSY remissory
EIMORRSTU trimerous
EIMORRTTW mitre-wort
EIMORSUVY voyeurism
EIMOSTTTT motettist
EIMPRSTTY prettyism
EIMPRSTUY supremity
EINNNOTTY nonentity
EINNNSSSU sunniness
EINNOOPPS poison pen
EINNOOPRT entropion
pontonier
prenotion
EINNOORST ironstone
serotonin
EINNOPTTU unipotent
EINNORSTU neutrinos
EINNORTVY inventory
EINNOSSST stoniness
EINNOSSSW snowiness
EINNOSSTX non-sexist
EINNOSSTY syntonise
EINNOSTYZ syntonize
EINNOSUUV unenvious
EINNPRSTW newsprint
EINNPSTTU Neptunist
EINNQSTTU St-Quentin
EINNRTTUW unwritten
EINNSSTTU nuttiness
sustinent
EINOOPPRT preoption
EINOOPRRS prerosion
EINOOPRRT portioner
EINOOPRST sore point
EINOOPSSW spoonwise
EINOORRST retorsion
EINOORRSW no worries
EINOORRTT retortion
EINOORTTX extortion
EINOORTTY notoriety
EINOOSSST sootiness
EINOOSSWZ wooziness
EINOPPQUU pique upon
EINOPPSSS soppiness
EINOPRRTV overprint
EINOPRSSS prosiness
EINOPRSTU pertusion
EINOPRSUU penurious
EINOPRTUW power unit
EINOPSSSS possess in
EINOPSSSY synopsise
EINOPSSTT pottiness
EINOPSSYZ synopsize
EINOQTTTU quintetto
EINORRSSS sorriness
EINORRTTV introvert
EINORRTUU nouriture
EINORSSUU unserious
EINORSTTU ritenutos
EINORSTUX extrusion
EINORTTUV vetturino
EINOSSTUU Suetonius
EINOSTTTU Teutonist
EINOSTTVY ventosity
EINPRRTTU interrupt
EINPRSSSU pursiness
EINRRSSTU run-resist
EINRSSSTU rustiness
EINRSTTUY strenuity
EIOOPRRST posterior
repositor
EIOOPRSSV provisoes
EIOOPRSTX expositor
EIOOPRSTY operosity
EIOOPRSTZ zooperist
EIOOSSSTX exostosis
EIOOSSTTV ovotestis
EIOPPRRTY propriety
EIOPPRSUV purposive
EIOPPTTUX Tipp-Ex out
EIOPRRTTV vertiport
EIOPRSTTU proustite
EIOPRSTTY posterity
EIOQRSTUU turquoise
EIORRRSTT terrorist
EIORRRTTY territory✧
EIORRSUVX River Oxus
EIORRTVWY River Towy
EIPQRTTUY triptyque
EIPRRRSSU surpriser
EIPRSSSTU pertussis
EIQRSSTTU questrist
squitters
EIRRSTVXY River Styx
EIRSSTTTU trustiest
EJLLOSSYY joylessly
EJLOOPPSY sloppy joe
EJMNORUWY jurywomen
EJMNRRTUW J M W Turner
EJMPRSTUW jews'-trump✧
jew's-trump✧
EJNOORRSU sojourner
EJOPRRSUU perjurous
EJPRTTUYY petty jury
EKKOOPRRW poker work
EKLLNNOWW well-known
EKLMMNOSU musk melon
EKLMOOTUY leukotomy
EKLNOOORS lookers-on
EKLNRSSTU trunkless
EKMMOOORS smoke room
EKMNNOORS non-smoker
EKMNNORUY monkey run
EKMNNOTUY monkey nut
EKMNNOTYY teknonymy
EKMNOOPSY pyknosome
EKMNOOPTY monkey pot
EKMNOOSTU musketoon
EKNOOPRUV unprovoke
EKNOOPSTU outspoken
EKNOORSTW stonework
EKNORSSTU sunstroke
EKNORSTUV overstunk
EKOOPRRSW ropeworks
EKOORRTUW outworker
EKOORSTTU stroke out
EKOORSTTW set to work
twostroke
EKOPRRSSW presswork
EKORRTTUW tutworker
ELLLMSUUV vulsellum
ELLMNOOPY poll-money
ELLMNOORT Mellotron®
ELLMOOTUW mellow out
ELLMOPSUU plumulose
ELLMORSTU rostellum
ELLMOSUUY emulously
ELLMRSTUU surmullet
ELLNOORST stornello
ELLNOPPUV pulp novel
ELLNOPRSU prunellos
ELLNOPTUW well put on
ELLNOPTUY opulently
ELLNOTTTY Lyttelton
ELLOOSTUU luteolous
ELLOPSTYY polystyle
ELLORSTUU tellurous
ELMMNSSUU Mussulmen
ELMNNOOST somnolent
ELMNOOPSU monopulse
ELMNOOSTY monostyle
ELMNOOSVW solemn vow
ELMNOPPUU plume upon
ELMNOPSTU plum-stone
ELMNPPSSU plumpness
ELMOOOPRW power loom
ELMOORSTW lowermost
ELMOORSUY lyomerous
ELMORSSST stormless

ELMORSTUU	tremulous
ELMPSSTTU	slump test
ELNOOOPRV	provolone
ELNOORSTU	turn loose
ELNOORSUY	onerously
ELNOPPSTU	pulpstone
ELNORSUVY	nervously
ELNOSTUUY	tenuously
ELOOPPTTT	pottle-pot
ELOORSTUW	lousewort
ELOORSTVY	love-story
ELOPPPUVY	puppy love
ELOPPRSUY	purposely
ELOPRRSUW	rowel-spur
	spur rowel
ELOPRRSUY	prelusory
ELOPRSSST	sportless
ELOPRSUUV	pulverous
ELOPSSSTU	spoutless
ELOPTUUZZ	puzzle out
ELOQRSUUU	querulous
ELORSSTTU	troutless
ELORSTTUU	outlustre
ELORSTUVY	overlusty
ELPPRSSUU	superplus
ELPRSTTUY	spluttery
ELRSSSTTU	trustless
EMMNOOOSS	meno mosso
EMMNOOSTU	momentous
EMMNORTTU	tormentum
EMMNOSSSU	summonses
EMMNRSTUU	menstruum
EMMOORSTY	osmometry
EMNNOOOST	moonstone
EMNNOORUU	numero uno
EMNNRRRUU	rum runner
EMNOOOPST	mote spoon
EMNOOOPTT	monoptote
EMNOOPSUY	eponymous
EMNOORRTT	tormentor
EMNOORSTT	mort-stone
EMNOORTTY	tonometry
EMNOORTUV	overmount
EMNOORTUY	neurotomy
EMNOORTWY	moneywort
EMNOOSTTU	tomentous
EMNOPRRTU	no-trumper
EMNOPRSSU	responsum
EMNOPSTUY	pumy stone
EMNORSSTT	sternmost
EMNRSTUUV	Vertumnus
EMOOORRST	storeroom
EMOOOSTTY	osteotomy
EMOOPRRSS	pressroom
EMOOPRTTY	optometry
EMOOPSSSU	espumosos
EMOORSTTU	outermost
EMOORTTUY	uterotomy
EMOPPRRTU	prompture
EMOPPRSTU	uppermost
EMOPRRTUV	overtrump
EMOPRRTYY	pyrometry
EMORSTTTU	uttermost
EMORSTTUU	muster out
ENNNOOOSW	on one's own
ENNNOOPRS	non-person
ENNNORRTU	non-return
ENNNPRTUY	turn-penny
ENNOOOPRT	pontooner
ENNOOPPRT	proponent
ENNOOPRTV	not proven
ENNOPPSTY	penny-post
ENNOPRTWY	pennywort
ENNORRTUU	outrunner
ENNORSTTU	turnstone
ENNPRRSUU	runners-up
ENOOPPRST	postponer
ENOOPPRSU	on purpose
ENOOPPRTU	opportune
ENOOPRRSS	responsor
ENOOPRRTU	root-prune
ENOORSSTY	ostensory
ENOORSTTT	Otto Stern
ENOORSTTW	stonewort
ENOOSSTTU	sostenuto
ENOPPRSSU	press upon
ENOPPRSTU	unstopper
ENOPRRSTT	sternport
ENOPRSSSU	suspensor
ENOPRSSTT	sternpost
ENOPRSTTY	post-entry
ENOPSTTYY	stenotypy
ENORSSTUU	strenuous
ENORSTTUY	out-sentry
ENORSTUUV	venturous
ENOSSSTTU	stoutness
ENOTTTWWY	twenty-two
ENRRSSTUU	untrusser
EOOOPRRTU	Europoort
	outrooper
EOOORTUVY	over to you!
EOOPPRRSS	oppressor
EOOPPRRST	prepostor
EOOPPRTTY	prototype
EOOPRRSTT	protestor✧
EOOPRRTTU	out-porter
EOOPRRTUU	outpourer
EOOPRSSSS	possessor
EOOPRSTUU	eutropous
EOORSTTWY	two-storey
EOPPRRSTU	supporter
EOPPRSSST	stop press
	stop-press
EOPRTTTUU	putter-out
EORRSSSST	strossers
EORRSTTUV	overtrust
EORRSTUXY	extrusory
EORSSSTTU	stress out

F

FFFHIINOS	finish off
FFFILMNSU	snuff film
FFGHIILNW	whiffling
FFGHIISTT	fistfight
FFGHILNSU	shuffling
FFGHILOST	slight off
FFGHILRTU	frightful
FFGHLOOSU	slough off
FFGIILLNU	in full fig
FFGILLLNU	full fling
FFGILNNSU	snuffling
FFGILNOXY	flying fox
FFGILNPUY	puffingly
FFGILNRTU	truffling
FFGIMNORU	fungiform
FFGINOPRS	offspring
FFGNOSTUW	stuff gown
FFHHILSUY	huffishly
FFHILOOPS	polish off
FFHINOOPS	siphon off
FFHLORSUU	four-flush
FFHMOORTY	froth-fomy
FFIILMOST	off limits
	off-limits
FFIIMNNTU	muffin tin
FFIINOSUX	suffixion
FFIIOPRST	spirit off
FFILLMNSU	snuff mill
FFILMOORR	floriform
FFINOSSUU	suffusion
FFIOORSTT	first-foot
FFIOOSTTW	swift-foot
FFIORSTTU	soft fruit
FFLLMNSUU	snuff-mull
FFLLNORTU	full-front
FFLMNOOSU	moufflons
FFLOOOOPR	foolproof
FFLOOOSTW	wolf's foot
FFNOPSTUU	up to snuff
FFNRRSTUU	surf'n'turf
FFORRSUUU	furfurous
FGGHIIRTW	fright wig
FGGIINORV	forgiving
FGGNOOUYY	young fogy
FGHHILNOW	high-flown
FGHHIOOPR	high-proof
FGHHIOSTW	show fight
FGHIIINNS	finishing
FGHIILLLT	fill light
FGHIILLTY	flightily
FGHIINSST	stingfish
FGHIKLORT	folk-right
FGHILLPTU	plightful
FGHILNOTW	night-fowl
FGHILOOTT	footlight
	light-foot
FGHILOPTT	top-flight
FGHINORTT	fortnight
FGHINOSTT	soft thing
FGHLNORTU	throngful
FGHMOORTU	frogmouth
FGIIILLNN	infilling
FGIIILLNP	filliping

FGIIILNVY vilifying
FGIIINNPR firing pin
FGIIINVVY vivifying
FGIIKLNSY ski-flying
FGIILLLRT flirt-gill
gillflirt
FGIILLNPU upfilling
FGIILLNRU in full rig
FGIILMNOR ligniform
FGIILNNOW inflowing
FGIILNNOY foiningly
FGIILNOPR profiling
FGIILNPTU uplifting
FGIILNRST firstling
FGIILNSTY siftingly
FGIILNTTY fittingly
FGIILRTUU ugli® fruit
FGIINNOPT fining-pot
FGIINNOTY notifying
FGIINNTTU unfitting
FGIINOPRT profiting
FGIINOSSY ossifying
FGIINPRUY purifying
FGIINPTYY typifying
FGIKLLNOS golf links
FGILLNOOW following
FGILLNOWY flowingly
FGILNNRUY Funny Girl
FGILNRRUY flurrying
FGILOOSTU ufologist
FGILSSTUU fustilugs
FGIMNORUU unguiform
FGINOSTUY fungosity
FGLLNORUW full-grown
FGLLNOSUY songfully
FGLOORSUU fulgorous
FGLORSUUU fulgurous
FGNOOORTW wrong-foot
FHHIOOSTT toothfish
FHHIORTTW forthwith
FHHOORSTW show forth
FHIIIKLLS killifish
FHIIJNOST fish-joint
FHIILOPST pilot fish
FHIILRTTY thriftily
FHIIORSTX hit for six
FHIIORSTY historify
FHIKNRSTU trunkfish
FHIKORSTW shift work
FHILLOOST foothills
FHILLOOSY foolishly
FHILLOSWY wolfishly
FHILLSUWY wishfully
FHILMORST short film
FHILNSUUW unwishful
FHILOPPSY foppishly
FHILORSUY flourishy
FHILRSTTU thirstful
FHIMORSTX sixth form
FHINNRSUU unfurnish
FHINNSTUY tunny fish
FHINOOPRT hoofprint
FHINRTTUY unthrifty
FHIOOOTTT hotfoot it
FHIORRSTT stir forth
FHLLPSUUY pushfully
FHLLRTUUY hurtfully
ruthfully
FHLMOORTU flour moth
FHLMOSTUU mouthfuls
FHLNRTUUU unhurtful
FHLOOOPRS shop floor
shop-floor
FHLOOORSW floor show
FHLOOOTTW wolf tooth
FHMOOOPRT mothproof
FHNOOPRST shopfront
FHNORRTTU turn forth
FHOOOPRST shotproof
FHOOPRRTU pour forth
FHOORRSUU four-hours
FHOORRTTW Fort Worth
FIIIKRTUW kiwi fruit
FIIILNOPS Filipinos
FIIILSSTY fissility
FIIIMNRTY infirmity
FIIJLLLRT jillflirt
FIIKLNNST skinflint
FIILLMORV villiform
FIILLMOTU multifoil
FIILLPTUY pitifully
FIILMORTU trifolium
FIILMPRST filmstrip
FIILNNOUX influxion
FIILNPTUU unpitiful
FIILOPRST profilist
FIILORSUV filovirus
FIILORTVY frivolity
FIILPRSTU spiritful
FIIMMNORS misinform
FIIMMORRT mitriform
FIIMNOPRS spiniform
FIIMNOSSU fusionism
FIIMORRTU triforium
FIIMORRTV vitriform
FIINOSSTU fusionist
FIIORSTUY furiosity
FIJMNOTUU Mount Fuji
FIKKLNOSS kinsfolks
FIKLLLSUY skilfully
FIKLLNSUU unskilful
FIKLLOSSS floss silk
FIKMMNOOR Kominform
FILLLMORU flour mill
FILLLPSTU full split
full-split
FILLNOPTU full point
FILLSTUWY wistfully
FILMMORSU formulism
FILMMORTU multiform
FILMNORUY uniformly
FILMNOSUU fulminous
sulfonium
FILMORSTU formulist
FILMORSTY styliform
FILMORUVV vulviform
FILNPRTUY turnip fly
FILOOOPRT portfolio
FILOORSSU fluorosis
FILOORSUV frivolous
FILORRSTY floristry
FILORSUUY furiously
FILOSSTUU fistulous
FIMMMMORU mummiform
FINNOOPRT non-profit
FINOOPRSU profusion
FINOOPRTT footprint
FIOPRSSTT first post
FKKLOORSW workfolks
FKLNOOSTW townsfolk
FKLNRSTUU trunkfuls
FKLOORSTY folk story
FKMNOOSTY moskonfyt
FKOOORTUW out of work
out-of-work
FKOORRSTW frostwork
FLLLOSUUY soulfully
FLLLSTUUY lustfully
FLLNOORRY forlornly
FLLOOOTUW follow out
FLMNOOOOS of Solomon
FLNOOPSSU spoonfuls
FLOOOOSTT footstool
FLOOOPPRT plot-proof
FLOOOPTTU poultfoot
FLOORRSUW sorrowful
FLOPRSSUU plus fours
FMMOOSTTY soft tommy
FMOORRTTU form tutor
FNNOOPRUW frown upon
FNOOOTTUW out-of-town
FOOPRRSTU rustproof
FOOPSSTUY pussyfoot

G

GGGHINRSU shrugging
GGGIILNNS sniggling
GGGIILNRW wriggling
GGGIINPRS sprigging
GGGIINRST strigging
GGGILMNSU smuggling
GGGILNTUY tuggingly
GGHHHIILT highlight
GGHHILOSY hoggishly
GGHHINORW high-grown
GGHHOORTU go through
GGHIIILRW whirligig
GGHIILNNS shingling
GGHIILNNT lightning
GGHIILNST slighting
GGHIILNSY sighingly
GGHIILPSY piggishly
GGHIINNSU unsighing

GGHIINRTW	right wing right-wing
GGHIINSST	sight-sing
GGHILNNOT	nightlong
GGHILNOPU	ploughing
GGHILNSUY	gushingly
GGHILOOPR	logogriph
GGHINNORT	thronging
GGHINNOTW	nightgown
GGHINPSUU	upgushing
GGHLOORYY	hygrology
GGIIIMNNP	impinging
GGIIIMNSV	misgiving
GGIIJNNOR	jingo-ring
GGIILNNRY	ringingly
GGIILNNSW	swingling
GGIILNNSY	singingly
GGIILNPRY	gripingly
GGIIMNOSS	go missing
GGIINNORW	ingrowing
GGIINNPRS	springing
GGIINNRST	stringing
GGIINNSWW	swing-wing
GGIINOPSS	gossiping
GGIINOTUV	outgiving
GGILLNNOY	longingly
GGILLNOWY	glowingly
GGILMNSUY	ginglymus
GGILMOOSY	gismology
GGILMOOYZ	gizmology
GGILNNOUY	youngling
GGILNOPRY	gropingly
GGIMNOORS	Gongorism
GGINOORST	Gongorist
GGINOOSTU	goings-out outgoings
GGINOPRUW	upgrowing
GGLNNORUW	lung-grown
GHHIIMST	Highsmith
GHHIIJKNS	high jinks
GHHIILPST	lightship
GHHIILSST	slightish
GHHIINOPT	high point
GHHILOPRY	hygrophil
GHHILOSTW	light show
GHHILRSTU	rushlight
GHHINOTTU	in thought
GHHLOOSTY	Holy Ghost
GHHLORTUY	throughly
GHHMNORUU	Hugh Munro
GHHMOOSTT	ghost moth
GHIIILNNS	linishing
GHIIKNNRS	shrinking
GHIIKNSTT	skintight
GHIIKNTTT	tight-knit
GHIILLLMT	light-mill
GHIILLNRS	shrilling
GHIILLNRT	thrilling
GHIILLRSY	girlishly
GHIILNNSY	shiningly
GHIILNNTY	hintingly
GHIILNNWY	whiningly
GHIILNOST	night-soil
GHIILNOTT	light into
GHIILNSSY	hissingly
GHIILNSTW	whistling
GHIILNTTW	whittling
GHIILRSTY	tigrishly
GHIIMNPRS	shrimping
GHIINNNST	thinnings
GHIINNNWY	whinnying
GHIINNPSU	punishing
GHIINNRSU	inrushing
GHIINNSUW	unwishing
GHIINOPPT	piping hot
GHIKLNNOT	think long
GHIKNORTW	night-work
GHILLOOPT	loop-light
GHILLOOPY	philology
GHILLOOTY	lithology
GHILLOSTW	lowlights
GHILMNNOT	monthling
GHILMNOOT	moonlight
GHILNOOPT	potholing
GHILNOORY	rhinology
GHILNOPTU	light upon
GHILNOPYY	philogyny
GHILNOSST	slingshot
GHILNOSTW	long whist
GHILNPSUY	pushingly
GHILNSTUY	unsightly
GHILOOOPY	ophiology
GHILOOPPY	hippology
GHILOOSTY	histology
GHILOPSTT	spotlight stoplight
GHILORSUY	roguishly
GHILOSTTU	lights out
GHILPRSTY	sprightly
GHILPRTUY	uprightly
GHIMMNRTU	thrumming
GHIMMNTUY	thingummy
GHIMNOOST	smoothing
GHIMNOSST	songsmith
GHIMOOPSS	gomphosis
GHIMORSTW	misgrowth
GHINOPRST	hot spring
GHINOPRTY	trophying
GHINOPSTT	nightspot
GHINORRTT	troth ring
GHINORSST	strongish
GHINORSTT	Storthing
GHINORTUW	inwrought
GHINOTUWY	with young
GHINRSTTU	thrusting
GHIOOTTUW	go without
GHIOPSTTT	tight spot
GHIORRSTY	hygristor
GHIORSTTW	growthist
GHJLNNOOS	long johns
GHLLOOOPY	hoplology
GHLMNOOYY	hymnology
GHLMOOTYY	mythology
GHLNOOOPY	phonology
GHLNOOPYY	hypnology
GHLNOSSTU	slung shot
GHLNOSTUY	unghostly
GHLNOTUYY	youngthly
GHLOOPTYY	phytology
GHMNOOPSY	gymnosoph
GHMNOOSUU	humongous
GHMNOSUUU	humungous
GHMOPSTYY	gypsy moth
GHNNOOPRR	pronghorn
GHNOORSTW	shortgown
GHNOOSTTW	ghost town
GHNORRSUW	rush-grown
GHNORTUUW	unwrought
GHOOORSTT	Ostrogoth
GHOORTTUW	outgrowth
GHOPRTUUW	upwrought wrought-up
GIIIKKNST	ski-kiting
GIIIKLMNS	misliking
GIIIKMNSV	vikingism
GIIILOSTU	litigious
GIIIMMNTT	immitting
GIIIMNRSV	Irvingism
GIIIMNRUV	virginium
GIIIMRSST	mistigris
GIIINNORS	signorini
GIIINNOSV	visioning
GIIINNPRS	inspiring
GIIINNQRU	inquiring
GIIINOSSS	Issigonis
GIIINPRST	spiriting
GIIINRTVY	virginity
GIIJKLMNO	Kim Jong Il
GIIJKNORS	skijoring
GIIKLLLNY	killingly
GIIKLMNSU	Kim Il-sung
GIIKLNNPU	uplinking
GIIKLNNTW	twinkling
GIIKLNNWY	winkingly
GIIKNNNUW	unwinking
GIIKNNORW	inworking
GIIKNPRSU	prusiking
GIIKNRSST	skirtings
GIILLLNWY	willingly
GIILLLSST	gill slits
GIILLMNPY	limpingly
GIILLMNSY	smilingly
GIILLMRST	grist-mill
GIILLNNUW	unwilling
GIILLNPSY	lispingly
GIILMNNSU	unsmiling
GIILMNOPR	imploring
GIILMNSSY	missingly
GIILNNNWY	winningly
GIILNNOST	Islington
GIILNNOTU	untoiling
GIILNNPPY	nippingly
GIILNNSTU	insulting

GIILNNTWY	twiningly
GIILNORST	oil string
GIILNOSUU	uliginous
GIILNPPRY	rippingly
GIILNPPST	stippling
GIILNPRST	split ring
	stripling
GIILNPRSY	springily
GIILNPSTT	splitting
GIILNPTYY	pityingly
GIILNRSTY	stringily
GIILNTTWY	wittingly
GIILOOSTY	sitiology
GIILOSSST	glossitis
GIILPRTTU	guilt trip
GIILRSTTU	liturgist
GIIMMNRST	trimmings
GIIMNNOOR	rooming-in
GIIMNNSSU	minus sign
GIIMNNTUY	mutinying
GIIMNOPRS	promising
GIIMNOPRV	improving
GIIMNORRR	mirroring
GIIMNOTTW	two-timing
GIIMNRSSU	surmising
GIIMPRSTU	spirit gum
GIINNNOWW	winnowing
GIINNNPTU	tuning pin
GIINNOORS	signorino✧
GIINNOPRU	inpouring
GIINNOSTT	sting into
GIINNPPRU	unripping
GIINNPRST	sprinting
GIINNPTTU	inputting
GIINNPTUY	unpitying
GIINNQSTU	squinting
GIINNRSSU	Rising Sun
	sunrising
GIINNRTUW	unwriting
GIINNSSTU	unsisting
GIINNSTUU	unsuiting
GIINNTTUW	unwitting
GIINOPRTT	trig point
GIINPPRST	stripping
GIINPPTTU	titupping
GIINPSTTU	upsitting
GIINPTTTU	tittuping
GIINQRSTU	squirting
GIINRSUVV	surviving
GIIORRSUU	irriguous
GIIPRSTTW	twist grip
GIJKLNORW	J K Rowling
GIJLLNOTY	joltingly
GIJLNTTUY	juttingly
GIJNNNORU	nonjuring
GIKKNORST	King Stork
GIKLLORRW	grillwork
GIKLNNNSY	King's Lynn
GIKLNNOOO	onlooking
GIKLNNOWY	knowingly
GIKLNOOOY	koniology
GIKNNNOUW	unknowing
GIKNNORUW	unworking
GIKNNOSTW	Kingstown
GIKNOOPRV	provoking
GILLLLNOY	lollingly
GILLLNOOP	lolloping
GILLMNOOY	limnology
GILLMOORR	grill room
GILLMOSSY	syllogism
GILLNOPSY	slopingly
GILLNORST	strolling
GILLNORUY	louringly
GILLOOOPY	oligopoly
GILLOORSU	orgillous
GILMMNOOS	mongolism✧
GILMNNOTY	Lymington
GILMNOPRY	rompingly
GILMOOSTY	myologist
GILNNNPUY	punningly
GILNNNRUY	runningly
GILNOORUY	urinology
GILNOPPTY	toppingly
GILNOPTUY	poutingly
GILNORSUY	rousingly
GILNORTTU	troutling
GILNOSTUU	glutinous
GILNPPSUY	supplying
GILNPRRUY	purringly
GILNSSTUU	singultus
GILOOORST	orologist
GILOOOSSU	isologous
GILOOOSTT	otologist
GILOOOSTZ	zoologist
GILOORSTU	urologist
GILORRRRT	riot grrrl
GILPRSSTU	gilt spurs
GIMMNPSUU	summing-up
GIMMNRRUU	murmuring
GIMMNRSTU	strumming
GIMMOSTUY	gummosity
GIMNNOORS	Monsignor
GIMNNORSU	mournings
GIMNOORSU	ginormous
GIMNOPPRT	prompting
GIMOPRUUY	uropygium
GIMOPSSUY	Gossypium
GIMOPSTUU	gumptious
GINNNOOTV	non-voting
GINNNRTUU	unturning
GINNOOPRT	Orpington
GINNORSST	no strings
	no-strings
GINNPRTUU	upturning
GINOOPRSS	prognosis
GINOOPRST	gros point
GINOOPRTU	uprooting
GINOOPSSU	spongious
GINOORRSW	sorrowing
GINOORSTU	trigonous
GINOPPPTU	topping-up
GINOPPRST	stropping
GINOPPSSU	supposing
GINOPRSST	Stringops
GINOPRSTU	outspring
	sprouting
GINOPTTTU	totting-up
GINOPTTUW	tuptowing
GINORRTTU	torturing
GINORSTTU	string out
GINORSTUY	trigynous
GINPPTTUU	up-putting
GINQRSTUU	squirt gun
GINRSTTTU	strutting
GIOSTTTUU	guts it out
GKNORRTUW	grunt work
GKNORTUUY	young turk✧
GKOOPRRUW	group work
	groupwork
	workgroup
GLLOOPTTY	polyglott
GLLOOPTUY	plutology
GLMNOOPUY	polygonum
GLNOOOSTY	nostology
GLOOOPRTY	tropology
GLOORSSSS	gross loss
GMNOORSSW	moss-grown
GNOOOOSUZ	zoogonous
GNOOOPRSY	sporogony
GNOOPRTYY	protogyny
GNOORRSTY	Roy Strong
GNORSTTUU	strung out
GOORSSTUU	goustrous
GOPRSTWYY	gypsywort
GORRSTUWY	worryguts

H

HHHMNNOUY	Houyhnhnm
HHIILNORT	rhinolith
HHIIOOSTY	Yoshihito
HHIIRSTTY	thirtyish
HHIJMNOST	John Smith
HHILOOPPT	photophil
HHILORSWY	whorishly
HHIMOOSST	smoothish
HHIMRSTTY	rhythmist
HHIORTTWW	Whitworth
HHLMOOPYY	homophyly
HHMMOOOPR	homomorph
HHMMOSTUU	mushmouth
HHMNOOOPY	homophony
HHMNOORTT	thorn moth
HHNOORRST	shorthorn
HHPPPSUUY	hush puppy
HIIIPRSVZ	vizirship
HIIKMSTWY	tim-whisky
HIILLMNOT	millionth
HIILLMSTW	Will Smith
HIILLNOTZ	zillionth
HIILLOOOP	hoi polloi
HIILLOSWW	willowish
HIILMPSSU	silphiums
HIILMPSWY	wimpishly

HIILNOPSY	Sinophily
HIILNORTT	trilithon
HIILNSSWY	swinishly
HIILNTYZZ	Thin Lizzy
HIILOPSST	pisoliths
HIILOQRSU	liquorish
HIILOSTTY	hostility
HIILPPPSU	pupilship
HIILPSTTY	typhlitis
HIILRSTTY	thirstily
HIIMNOPRS	minorship
HIIMNORST	ironsmith
HIIMNOSST	Shintoism
HIIMNSSUV	Vishnuism
HIIMOPSTU	hospitium
HIIMORSSS	Irish moss
HIIMORSST	historism
	hit-or-miss
HIIMRSSTU	hirsutism
HIIMSSSTU	Hussitism
HIINOPSSY	hypinosis
HIINORSST	histrions
HIINOSSTT	Shintoist
HIIOPPRRS	priorship
HIIOTTTUW	out with it!
HIJLLMNOS	John Mills
HIKLMNOSY	monkishly
HIKLMOOTT	milk tooth
HIKNNOPTU	think upon
HIKNNORST	stinkhorn
HIKNNOSSY	hyson-skin
HILLLMTUU	multihull
HILLLOOST	tol-lolish
HILLMOOTT	mill-tooth
HILLMORUU	ill-humour
HILLMPSUY	lumpishly
HILLNPSUY	sulphinyl
HILLNSTTU	still hunt
	still-hunt
HILLOOPPW	hop pillow
HILLOOPRW	whirlpool
HILLOSTUY	loutishly
HILLOSVWY	wolvishly
HILLSSTYY	stylishly
HILMMPSUY	mumpishly
HILMOOSYZ	hylozoism
HILMOOTTY	lithotomy
HILMOPRSY	rompishly
HILNNOSTY	tonnishly
HILOOPRST	polo shirt
HILOOPTXY	toxophily
HILOOSSTW	solo whist
HILOOSTYZ	hylozoist
HILOPRSST	short slip
HILOPRSSU	Russophil
HILORSSTT	short list
	short-list
HILORSSUY	sourishly
HILOSSTTY	sottishly
HILRSTUUV	vulturish
HIMNNOOSY	moonshiny
HIMNOPSTY	hypnotism
HIMOOPRSS	morphosis
HIMOOPRST	motor-ship
HIMOSSTTU	Tuthmosis
HIMOSTTUU	Mutsuhito
HIMPSSSYY	symphysis
HINNOOPSU	union shop
HINNOOPTT	thin on top
HINOORRST	short iron
HINOPPRRY	porphyrin
HINOPPRST	print shop
HINOPSTTY	hypnotist
HINORSTTU	North Uist
HIOOPPRRY	porphyrio
HIOOPPRST	troopship
HIOOPPTUW	whoop it up
HIOOPRRST	rotor ship
HIOORSTTT	orthotist
HIOPRSSTY	sophistry
HIOPRSTTU	tutorship
HIORRSTTY	thyristor
HIORSSTTW	wrist shot
HIOSSTTUU	South Uist
HJJMNOOST	J J Thomson
HJJNNOORU	John Junor
HJNOOPSWY	John Powys
HKKNNOOTY	honky-tonk
HKLMMORUZ	krummholz
HKMMNORRU	krummhorn
HKNOOOOPS	spoonhook
HLLNOPSUY	sulphonyl
HLLOOOTUW	hollow out
HLLPRSUUY	sulphuryl
HLMOOPPRY	polymorph
HLMOOPPXY	pompholyx
HLNOOPPYY	polyphony
HLOOOSSTU	sloosh out
HLOOPPRSY	sporophyl
HMMOOPSTY	tommy shop
HMMPSTUYY	Symphytum
HMNNOOOPY	monophony
HMNOOOSUV	novus homo
HMNOORSTT	northmost
HMOOOPRTU	poor-mouth
HMOOOPRYZ	zoomorphy
HMOOPTTYY	phytotomy
HMOOSSTTU	southmost
HNNOOOPRS	horn spoon
HNOOORTTW	throw onto
HNOOPPTYY	phonotypy
HNOOPRTTY	phytotron
HNOORSTUU	Southroun
HOOOPRSUZ	zoophorus
HOOOPRTYZ	zootrophy
HOOORTTTT	hot to trot
HOOORTTTW	toothwort
HOOPPTTYY	phototypy
HOOPRSSTT	shortstop
	stop short
HOOPRSTTU	Southport

I

IIIKLLNPS	spillikin
IIIKMNRST	miniskirt
IIILNOSTV	violinist
IIILNTTUY	inutility
IIILOSUVX	lixivious
IIIMMNOSS	immission
IIIMNOSVX	vision mix
IIIMPRSST	spiritism
IIIMRRTUV	triumviri
IIINNNRTT	Rin Tin Tin
IIINNOTTU	intuition
IIINNRRTT	trinitrin
IIINNSSSU	Sisinnius
IIINOSSTV	visionist
IIINPRSST	in spirits
IIINPRSSU	nisi prius
IIINPRTTU	pituitrin
IIINSSSTU	sinusitis
IIIOSTTVY	vitiosity
IIIPRSSTT	spiritist
IIJLLNOTW	joint will
IIJLMOOTU	joliotium
IIJNORSUU	injurious
IIJNORTUY	juniority
IIKKLNNSS	slinkskin
IIKLNORST	nitro-silk
IIKNNNOOS	onion-skin
IIKNTTTUU	Inuktitut
IILLLOPUV	pulvillio
IILLMNOPU	pollinium
IILLMPRST	strip mill
IILLMPRSU	spirillum
IILLNNNOO	nonillion
IILLNOQSU	squillion
IILLNORST	trillions
IILLOPQSU	piquillos
IILLOPSSY	lipolysis
IILLOSTVY	villosity
IILLOTTWW	willow tit
IILMMMSSU	Muslimism
IILMMNOST	Miltonism
IILMMPUUV	impluvium
IILMNOOPS	implosion
IILMNOPSU	impulsion
IILMNOSSU	Mussolini
IILMNOSTV	voltinism
IILMNPSUV	vulpinism
IILMOPSSS	solipsism
IILMOPSUY	impiously
IILMPSSTT	splittism
IILNNOSTU	union list
IILNOOPST	postilion
IILNSSTUY	insulsity
IILNTTUWY	unwittily
IILOOPSTY	isopolity
IILOPRTXY	prolixity
IILOPSSST	solipsist
IILORTTTY	tortility
IILOSTVVZ	slivovitz

IILOSTVWZ slivowitz
IILPSSTTT splittist
IIMNNOSTU munitions
IIMNOOSSU simonious
IIMNOOSTT motionist
IIMNOPSSZ Spinozism
IIMNORSTU minor suit
routinism
IIMOPRTXY proximity
IIMOQSTUX quixotism
IIMORSTTU tutiorism
IIMRRSTUV triumvirs
IIMRRTUVY triumviry
IIMRSSTTU strumitis
IINNOOPRT Pinot Noir
IINNOOPTT pin it onto
IINNOORST intorsion
IINNOORTT intortion
IINNOOSTT notionist
IINNOOSUX innoxious
IINNORSTU intrusion
IINNORTTU nutrition
IINNOSTUU union suit
IINOOPRSV provision
IINOOPSVY poison ivy
IINOOQTTU quotition
IINOORSTT sortition
IINOPRRTU irruption
IINOPSSTY spinosity
IINOPSSTZ Spinozist
IINORSTTU introitus
routinist
IINOSSTUY sinuosity
IINOSSTVY synovitis
IIOOPRSST spiritoso
IIOPRSSTU spiritous
IIOPSTTTU spit it out
IIORSTTTU tutiorist
IIRSTUUVV Vitruvius
IJMNOOPSS O J Simpson
IJMNOORTW jointworm
joint-worm
IKKNOOPRT Kropotkin
IKLMOSTTU milk stout
IKMOPPRUY Yom Kippur
IKNOORRSW ironworks
IKORSSTTU outskirts
ILLLOOPPS lollipops
ILLLPSUUV pulvillus
ILLMOORST stillroom
ILLNOOPSU pollusion
ILLNOOPTU pollution
ILLNOORTT tortillon
ILLNOPVYY polyvinyl
ILLOOQSUY soliloquy
ILLOQRTUW quillwort
ILLORSSSW Swiss roll
ILMNOOOPY polyomino
ILMNOOPRT Port Limon
ILMNOOSUY ominously
ILMNOPSTU Plutonism
ILMNOPTUU plutonium
ILMNOPXYY polymyxin
ILMOSSYYZ zymolysis
ILMRSTUUV vulturism
ILNNOSSTW stownlins
ILNOOPRST Prontosil®
ILNOOPRSU prolusion
ILNOOSUXY noxiously
ILNOPRXYY pyroxylin
ILNOPSSUU spinulous
ILNOPSTTU Plutonist
ILNORSUUY ruinously
ILNOSSUUY sinuously
ILNPQTUUY quintuply
ILOOPPRSY isopropyl
ILOOPPSSY polyposis
ILOOPPUVX vox populi
ILOOPQRTU pot liquor
ILOOPRSTU Port Louis
ILOOPRTTU tulip root
ILOOPSTXY pixy-stool
ILOORRTTT tilt-rotor
ILOORSSTU torulosis
ILOORSTUY riotously
ILOPRSSYY pyrolysis
ILORSSUVW slow virus
ILORSUUUX luxurious
IMMMNOORS Mormonism
IMMMPSSUU mumpsimus
IMMOPPRTU impromptu
IMMOPSSUY symposium
IMMPSSSUU sumpsimus
IMNNOOPTW topminnow
IMNNOOSTU Mount Sion
IMNNOOTUZ Mount Zion
IMNOOOPRT promotion
IMNOOOPTT moot point
IMNOOOSSU isonomous
IMNOOOSTZ zoonomist
IMNOORSTU torminous
IMNORRRSS Mrs Norris
IMNORSTTU strontium
IMOOOSTTZ zootomist
IMOOPPSTY pomposity
IMOOPRRSS promissor
IMOOQSSTU mosquitos
IMOORSSTU sumotoris
IMOPSSSTY symptosis
IMORSUVXY myxovirus
INNOOPSTU poison-nut
INNOOQRTU quintroon
INNOOSSUU unisonous
INOOOPSSU poisonous
INOOORSTU notorious
INOOPPRTU pourpoint
INOOPPTTU put option
INOOPRSSU prisonous
INOOSTTWW in two twos
INOPPRTTU turnip top
INOPPSTTU pint-stoup
INOPSSTTY synoptist
INRSTTTUU unit trust
IOOORRRST orris-root
IOOPPRRTU potpourri
IOOPPRSST proptosis
IOOPRRSVY provisory
IOORSSTUV virtuosos
IOPRSSTTU posturist
IOPRSTTUU poursuitt

J

JKOORSSTU Kurt Jooss

K

KKNORRTUW trunkwork
KMOPRSTUW stump work
KOOPRSSTY sky troops

L

LLOOOPRRS poor's-roll
LMMOPSTUY Mt Olympus
LMNNOOOXY monoxylon
LMNOOPTUY plutonomy
LMNOOPYYY polyonymy
LMOOPPSUY pompously
LOOPPRRSU propulsor
LOOPPRSUY Polyporus
LOOPRRSUY prolusory
LOORSTUUY routously
LOPSSTUUU pustulous
LORSTUUUV vulturous

M

MMORRSUUU murmurous
MNNOOOPSY monopsony
MNOOOPRSW spoonworm
MNOORSSTU monstrous
MNOORSSTW snowstorm
MOPSSTUUU sumptuous

N

NNOOOPPRT non troppo
NNOOSSTUY syntonous
NOOOOPRTV Porto Novo
NOOOOPRTZ protozoon
NOOOPPSSU soupspoon
NOPPRSUUU usurp upon

O

OOPRRSTVY provostry
OOPRSSTUU stuporous
OORRSTTUU torturous

10 letters

A

AAAAABCCRS asarabacca
AAAAALLMMY Malayaalam
AAAABBDDIS Addis Ababa
AAAABCCEMN Maccabaean
AAAABCCLNS Casablanca
AAAABCEKNN banana cake
AAAABCENRS scarabaean
AAAABCHNST Athabascan
AAAABDFILS Faisalabad
AAAABDFRTW Bafta Award
AAAABDLNNN Bananaland
AAAABEHNNT Nabathaean
AAAABEINRS Arabian Sea
AAAABEMPRT parabemata
AAAABHJRSY Rajya Sabha
AAAABHKNST Athabaskan
AAAABHMMNR Abraham-man
AAAABILMRV Ambarvalia
AAAABLMRRT Malabar-rat
AAAABLRSTU tabula rasa
AAAACCILPR carapacial
AAAACDEEIN Naiadaceae
AAAACDGMNS Madagascan
AAAACDGMRS Madagascar
AAAACDMMRT tarmacadam
AAAACEEILR Araliaceae
AAAACFLLNR alla Franca
AAAACGMNRT Magna Carta
AAAACHNPST Athapascan
AAAACILLMR alla marcia
AAAACLMNRT almacantar
AAAADELLLN Allan-a-Dale
AAAADEMNNS Andaman Sea
AAAADEMNNT adamantean
AAAADFNRWY far and away
AAAADGLNNR Angaraland
AAAADHMRUZ Ahura Mazda
AAAAEEGLOP palaeogaea
AAAAEFRRSU Arafura Sea
AAAAEGLMMT amalgamate
AAAAEHMNNV Ahvenanmaa
AAAAEIKLMS Lake Saimaa
AAAAELMNQU aquamanale
AAAAFNOQTU aqua Tofana
AAAAGGGGWW Wagga Wagga
AAAAGGLLNN alang-alang
AAAAGHJNNT Jagannatha
AAAAGHRSTY satyagraha
AAAAGNORSX Anaxagoras
AAAAGNPRUY Paraguayan
AAAAHHLLLL a hall, a hall
AAAAHIMMRS Amarasimha
AAAAHIMNRS masa harina
AAAAHINNST Athanasian
AAAAHIPPRS paraphasia
AAAAHKNPST Athapaskan
AAAAHRRTTY Rathayatra
AAAAILNRTT tartanalia
AAAAILRTTV La Traviata
AAAAIMMNRV Ramanavami
AAAAIMNNNP Panamanian
AAAAIMNRST Santa Maria
AAAALLORTV Alvar Aalto
AAAALMNRSZ salmanazar✧
AAAALPRSTT parastatal
AAAAMNRSTT Santa Marta
AAAAMPRRTT parramatta
AAABBCEEGS sea cabbage
AAABBCILST sabbatical
AAABBDHSTY Sabbath-day
AAABBDNRYY Barnaby Day
AAABBDRRST bastard-bar
AAABBEPRRY Barbary ape
AAABBGJNOU baba ganouj
AAABBHMRUU baba au rhum
AAABBMPRRY Barbara Pym
AAABBORRSS Barbarossa
AAABCCCHRT catch a crab
AAABCCEHLN Bacchanale
AAABCCENOS cacao beans
AAABCCHLNS bacchanals
AAABCCKNSV canvasback
AAABCCLMTU catacumbal
AAABCDEENR dance a bear
AAABCDEIRS scarabaeid
AAABCDELNR candelabra
AAABCEGGGR baggage-car
AAABCEGGNR garbage can
AAABCEGILN Balenciaga
AAABCEGMRS bergamasca
AAABCEHLMR beach-la-mar
AAABCEHLTT attachable
AAABCEKKNT taken aback
AAABCEKLTT attackable
AAABCELLLR clarabella
AAABCELRTU acetabular
AAABCELSTT cabalettas
AAABCEORRS Broca's area
AAABCERSSU scarabaeus
AAABCHILNR abranchial
AAABCHINRT batrachian
AAABCIKKNN banana kick
AAABCIKLMR black Maria
AAABCIKRSS cassia-bark
AAABCIQSTU aquabatics
AAABCJMMNO Jacob Amman
AAABCLLMRU ambulacral
AAABCORRTU barracouta
AAABDDEINT aid and abet
AAABDDHIRY bad hair day
AAABDEEGLM damageable
AAABDEGGNR garage band
AAABDEHLRZ hazardable
AAABDEILNN alabandine
AAABDEILNT alabandite
AAABDKLNRW draw a blank
AAABDLMSSU Abdus Salam
AAABDLRRUY à la Dubarry
AAABDMNRSY Bryan Adams
AAABDMORSS ambassador
AAABDNNSYY banyan days
AAABDNSTTY stand at bay
AAABDORRST astarboard
AAABEEGLMN manageable
AAABEEKKMR make a break
AAABEELLPP appealable
AAABEELMNS able seaman
AAABEELPPS appeasable
AAABEERVWY beaver away
AAABEGGGWY way baggage
AAABEGGMNR garbageman
AAABEGIMNR mangabeira
AAABEGLLSU Elagabalus
AAABEGLMNY manageably
AAABEHHMST The Bahamas
AAABEHLNPT analphabet
AAABEIJNRZ Azerbaijan
AAABEIKKLL Lake Baikal
AAABEILLSS assailable
AAABEILNTT attainable
AAABEINPST anabaptise
AAABEINPTZ anabaptize
AAABEKKORR karaoke bar
AAABELLNPS basal plane
AAABELLNSY analysable
AAABELLNYZ analyzable
AAABELLRST alablaster
AAABELMNST Abel Tasman
AAABELNRRT narratable
AAABEMRSTV Svetambara
AAABERRTWY barter away
AAABFHILXY Halifax Bay
AAABGHILLY gallabiyah
AAABGHINRS barasingha
AAABGLNNPU banana plug
AAABHIOPQU aquaphobia
AAABHNRSSU sub-Saharan
AAABIKNNNS banana skin
AAABILRSTV Bratislava
AAABIMNPRS Pan-Arabism
AAABIMNPST anabaptism
AAABIMOPRR Paramaribo
AAABINPSTT anabaptist✧
AAABKNOSTT tanka boats
AAABLMOSTT blastomata
AAABMORRTU barotrauma
AAACCCEEIR Caricaceae
AAACCCIORT cacciatora
AAACCCJKKR crackajack

Words marked ✧ can also be spelled with one or more capital letters

AAACCDEHIR Characidae
AAACCDEILM academical
AAACCDEINR Canada rice
AAACCEEILS Salicaceae
AAACCEFHNT a fat chance
AAACCEHNNT catananche
AAACCEHRSS saccharase
AAACCEHRST saccharate
AAACCEIILR alcaicería
AAACCEIPTT capacitate
AAACCENOSU acanaceous
AAACCHILNR anarchical
AAACCHKKMT hackmatack
AAACCHPRTT cataphract
AAACCILLPR Callicarpa
AAACCILLRS cascarilla
AAACCILNST anaclastic
AAACCILRSV calcar avis
AAACCILSST cataclasis
AAACCIMORT acroamatic
AAACCINRTT Antarctica
AAACCIPRTT paratactic
AAACCIRRTU caricatura
AAACCLMNOS calamancos
AAACCMOPRR macrocarpa
AAACDDENSU Sadducaean
AAACDDJKNY Jack-a-dandy
AAACDEGINR Carangidae
AAACDEHLPY alpha decay
AAACDEIMMS macadamise
AAACDEIMMZ macadamize
AAACDEKNPY Pancake Day
AAACDELMNR calamander
AAACDELMRS salad cream
AAACDEMNNV advance man
AAACDENNRV caravanned
AAACDGIILR cardialgia
AAACDHINNR arachnidan
AAACDIILMT Adamitical
AAACDIIPRS paradisaic
paradisiac
AAACDIKLSY lackadaisy
AAACDILLNY Canada lily
AAACDILLTY call it a day
AAACDILMRT dramatical
AAACDILNOP pina colada
piña colada
AAACDILRTY caryatidal
AAACDIMNRU anacardium
AAACDLRSUW casual ward
AAACDOQRSU quoad sacra
AAACEEENVV venae cavae
AAACEEGNOR Onagraceae
AAACEEHMNR Rhamnaceae
AAACEEILMS Alismaceae
AAACEENPPR appearance
AAACEENRRV caravaneer
AAACEEOPST Sapotaceae
AAACEFILTU café au lait
AAACEFKNTY take a fancy
AAACEFLQTU catafalque
AAACEGHLPR cephalagra
AAACEGNORT Arctogaean
AAACEHIMNN Manichaean
AAACEHIMNU naumachiae
AAACEHIRRT Trachearia
AAACEILMNT catamenial
AAACEINNRT catenarian
AAACEINPRS parascenia
AAACEINPSS Caspian Sea
AAACEINPST anapaestic
sea captain
AAACEINRRS sarracenia
AAACEINRTV at variance
AAACEJKNPS jackanapes
AAACEKLSST take a class
AAACELLNPT aplacental
AAACELMPRT metacarpal
AAACELPSTY acatalepsy
AAACENNRRV caravanner
AAACESSTUY satay sauce
AAACFGHNOT Afghan coat
AAACFINNPR Pan-African
AAACFKNPRR Frank Capra
AAACFMNORU macrofauna
AAACGGILNO anagogical
AAACGGILOP apagogical
AAACGGIORV Caravaggio
AAACGHNRTT tragacanth
AAACGHOPRS Sarcophaga
AAACGILLNO analogical
AAACGILMRT ragmatical
AAACGIMRRV Marcgravia
AAACGINNRU Nicaraguan
AAACGINNRV caravaning
AAACHIINPT Cap Haitian
AAACHILLNW Wallachian
AAACHIMNRT marchantia
AAACHIMNSU naumachias
AAACHINORT Tocharian A
AAACHIPPRS paraphasic
AAACHJOPRS chaparajos
AAACHLMNNR manna-larch
AAACHLNOTU anacolutha
Talcahuano
AAACHLRSSU Sarah Lucas
AAACHNPRTY pyracantha
AAACHOSSUY ayahuascos
AAACHQTUUU chautauqua✧
AAACIILRUV Avicularia
AAACIINNPR Incaparina
AAACIIRSSS ascariasis
AAACIJMMRU Jamaica rum
AAACIKLMNP pack animal
AAACIKLMNR Lamarckian
AAACIKLRTU autarkical
AAACILLMNU animalcula
AAACILLMNY maniacally
AAACILLNTY analytical
AAACILLNUV Vulcanalia
AAACILLRTU Ural-Altaic
AAACILMMNO ammoniacal
AAACILMNOT anatomical
AAACILNORY Alcyonaria
AAACILNPST anaplastic
AAACILNRSS carnassial
AAACILNRST scarlatina
AAACILORRT crotalaria
AAACILRTTU Articulata
AAACIMMORZ macrozamia✧
AAACIMNNOR narcomania
AAACIMNPTY Panama City
AAACINNPRT pancratian
AAACINRRTT tractarian✧
AAACISSSTT catastasis
AAACJKNPUY Puncak Jaya
AAACLLPSST Pallas's cat
AAACLMNPRU campanular
AAACLMNPSU campanulas
AAACLMNRTU almucantar
AAACLMNRVY cavalryman
AAACLNSSTU Santa Claus
AAACLPRRSW wrap-rascal
AAACMNNRTT marcantant
AAACMRRTWY tramway car
AAACMRSSTY Mary Cassat
AAACNNOPTT panna cotta
AAACNRSTUX crux ansata
AAACNRTTTT attractant
AAACPRSTWW Warsaw Pact
AAADDEEMNV Adam and Eve
AAADDEGNTV advantaged
AAADDEIMNN anandamide
AAADDEINRW Edwardiana
AAADDELMPT maladapted
AAADDELNOT adelantado
AAADDGIRRT Tardigrada
AAADDHMRSY hamadryads✧
AAADEEGHNP phagedaena
AAADEEKRST take as read
AAADEFIOST asafoetida
AAADEFISST assafetida
AAADEFNNRR far and near
AAADEGGLNR garlandage
AAADEGGRTV aggravated
AAADEGINRV devanagari✧
AAADEGKLLO Lake Ladoga
AAADEGLMTY amygdalate
AAADEGNRRV Ava Gardner
AAADEGNRTV avant-garde
AAADEHINRS raise a hand
AAADEHINTW what an idea!
AAADEHLPRT hard palate
AAADEHLSTY alas the day
AAADEIINST Anita Desai
AAADEILNRX Alexandria
AAADEIMNNT adamantine
amantadine
AAADEIMNRZ mazarinade
AAADEIMSTT diastemata
AAADEINPRS paradisean
AAADEINSSS Sassanidae
AAADEIPTTV adaptative

AAADEIRRSV	adversaria
AAADEKMNST	make a stand
AAADELLORR	dollar area
AAADELLPST	salad plate
AAADELMNRS	salamander
AAADELMNSS	Ansel Adams
AAADELMPPS	Adam's apple
AAADELMPRY	A Dream Play
AAADELRSTY	lead astray
AAADENNWWX	wax and wane
AAADEOPSTZ	zapateados
AAADFMNNSY	Fanny Adams
AAADGHIRSW	sharawadgi
AAADGIILLR	gaillardia
AAADGILLNR	granadilla
AAADGINNPT	giant panda
AAADGLLNOR	allargando
AAADGMMMNR	grandmamma
AAADGMNORR	mandragora
AAADGNOPPR	propaganda✧
AAADHHLMRS	dharmshala
AAADHLLNTT	and all that
AAADHLLNTW	and what all
AAADIILNPR	lapidarian
AAADIILORR	Radiolaria
AAADIILPRS	paradisial
AAADIIMMNR	Maid Marian
AAADIINNST	Saint Aidan
AAADIINPRS	paradisian
AAADIIOSTU	Said Aouita
AAADIKLPST	Das Kapital
AAADILMORR	alarm radio
	alarm-radio
	radio alarm
AAADILNNSU	Andalusian
AAADILNOPR	paranoidal
AAADILOPPR	parapodial
AAADIMNOTT	datamation
AAADINOPTT	adaptation
AAADIORSSY	radio assay
AAADKNNNOR	Donna Karan
AAADLLNPST	salad plant
AAADLMMNNN	landammann
AAADLNORSV	Salvadoran
AAADLNQRTU	quadrantal
AAADMNQRUU	Quadrumana
AAADNNNORX	anax andron
AAADNOTUWY	out and away
AAADNPRRTT	art and part
AAADORSTTU	autostrada
AAADQRRTUU	quadratura
AAAEEGGLRS	garage sale
AAAEEGNRST	arena stage
AAAEEGPSSS	sea passage
AAAEEGRRTT	target area
AAAEEHHRTV	have a heart
AAAEEHIRRS	raise a hare
AAAEEILMMN	melanaemia
AAAEEIMMNR	à main armée
AAAEFGLLLT	Flagellata
AAAEFJLLPS	false jalap
AAAEFJNOPS	Sea of Japan
AAAEFLLMRS	false alarm
AAAEFLMNST	malfeasant
AAAEGGIMNT	gametangia
AAAEGHLLNP	phalangeal
AAAEGHTTWW	wag-at-the-wa'
AAAEGILMNR	managerial
AAAEGILPPR	paraplegia
AAAEGINPRS	asparagine
AAAEGIPRSS	air-passage
AAAEGLMNTU	Guatemalan
AAAEGLMTTU	malaguetta
AAAEGLMTXY	metagalaxy
AAAEGMRRTV	margravate
AAAEGNNTTT	at a tangent
AAAEGPSSWY	passageway
AAAEHHLNNT	Nathan Hale
AAAEHIMRTU	haematuria
AAAEHINSTU	euthanasia
AAAEHIRSTW	washateria
AAAEHJNPRT	japan-earth
AAAEHKNOTT	take an oath
AAAEHLMRSS	Marshalsea
AAAEHMMRWY	hammer away
AAAEHMOPTT	hepatomata
AAAEHMORTT	atheromata
AAAEHNOPPR	epanaphora
AAAEHPPRRS	paraphrase
AAAEHRRSTT	start a hare
AAAEIILNTT	Italianate
AAAEIKLLMW	Lake Malawi
AAAEIKLMST	Alaska Time
AAAEILLPST	palatalise
AAAEILLPTZ	palatalize
AAAEILMNQU	aquamanile
AAAEILMPST	metaplasia
AAAEILMRTU	tularaemia
AAAEILNPPR	parapineal
AAAEILNPRT	planetaria
AAAEILNPTT	palatinate
AAAEIMNNRT	amarantine
AAAEIMNPRS	paramnesia
AAAEIMNQRU	aquamarine
AAAEIMNRSW	Samian ware
AAAEIMNRTU	Mauretania
AAAEINNPPR	Paraná pine
AAAEINNRTV	Tananarive
AAAEINRRTU	a natura rei
AAAEKLNPRR	Alan Parker
AAAEKLPRRW	parawalker
AAAEKMPRST	pasta maker
AAAELLNRRZ	Ranzellaar
AAAELLNRTT	tarantella
AAAELLPRST	palaestral
AAAELMMNOT	melanomata
AAAELMNRSS	salmanaser✧
AAAELMNRTT	atramental
AAAELMPRRT	parametral
AAAELMRSTT	metatarsal
AAAELNPQRU	aquaplaner
AAAELPRSTY	pray a tales
AAAELSSTWY	leastaways
AAAEMORTTT	teratomata
AAAENNORSS	Nasoraeans
AAAENRSTUW	at unawares
AAAEQRSUWY	square away
AAAFFIILNN	Fianna Fáil
AAAFFKKNRZ	Franz Kafka
AAAFGINNUU	anguifauna
AAAFHKNORR	Frank O'Hara
AAAFIJNNRS	Rafsanjani
AAAFIKPRRS	safari park
AAAFILMMNR	Animal Farm
AAAFKNPPRZ	Frank Zappa
AAAFLORSST	solfataras
AAAGGHIRSW	sharawaggi
AAAGGILLNO	algolagnia
AAAGGILRST	gastralgia
AAAGGMRRSS	grama grass
AAAGGNNRTU	gargantuan✧
AAAGGNPRST	gangsta rap
AAAGHILRRT	arthralgia
AAAGHIMRRT	margharita
AAAGHIOPTU	autophagia
AAAGHIRSTY	satyagrahi
AAAGHLLMOP	Mallophaga
AAAGHNPPRT	pantagraph
AAAGHNPSTU	agapanthus
AAAGIILMNR	marginalia
AAAGIILMST	galimatias
AAAGIIRSTT	Sagittaria
AAAGIKKKOS	Soka Gakkai
AAAGILLMNO	Gallomania
AAAGILMNNO	anglomania✧
AAAGIMMNRR	grammarian
AAAGIMNORT	Maoritanga
AAAGIMNSTT	anastigmat
AAAGINNOPT	Patagonian
AAAGKORTYY	Yogyakarta
AAAGLNRSTU	natural gas
AAAGLOPRSS	paraglossa
AAAGLRSSTU	astragalus✧
AAAGMNNRSS	manna-grass
AAAGMNSTTY	syntagmata
AAAGPRRSSS	sparagrass
AAAHHIMNSY	shamiyanah
AAAHHNOPRT	Pharaoh ant
AAAHIIJMRY	jamahiriya
AAAHIILPPR	paraphilia
AAAHIKMNRT	Karmathian
AAAHILMRRS	air-marshal
AAAHILNSST	thalassian
AAAHIMNNOT	anthomania
AAAHIMNSTY	Mahayanist
AAAHINOPPR	paraphonia
AAAHINORTZ	Zoantharia
AAAHINRRTU	Arthuriana
AAAHINSSTU	Athanasius
AAAHIPRRRT	pararthria
AAAHKKNSTZ	Kazakhstan
AAAHLMNPST	phantasmal
AAAHLNPXYY	anaphylaxy

Words marked ✧ can also be spelled with one or more capital letters

AAAHLOPSSS Lhasa Apsos
AAAHMNOTTX xanthomata
AAAHMNRSTU Amaranthus
AAAHPPRRST paraphrast
AAAIIJNNRZ janizarian
AAAIILLMRR armillaria
AAAIILLNTT natalitial
AAAIILMNNR laminarian
AAAIILNRTW Italian War
AAAIIMNPRS Arimaspian
AAAIIMNRTU Mauritania
AAAIINNRST sanitarian
AAAIIRRTWY raiyatwari
AAAIKLNOOV valonia oak
AAAIKMMRSW Wasim Akram
AAAILLMNNZ manzanilla
AAAILLMNPR rampallian
AAAILLMRTW martial law
AAAILLORTV lavatorial
AAAILLRRST altar-rails
AAAILMNORZ Mario Lanza
AAAILMNOTX malaxation
AAAILMNPST aplanatism
AAAILMNRWY railwayman
AAAILMRRTT martial art
AAAILNORTT natatorial
AAAILNRSTU Australian
saturnalia✧
AAAILOPRSV Valparaiso
Valparaíso
AAAIMNORST inamoratas
AAAIMORTTV ottava rima
AAAIMRTTTV amritattva
AAAINNOTTT Anatotitan
AAAINNPRSS Parnassian
AAAINSSSTU Anastasius
AAAJKNNORV von Karajan
AAAKKMORTT Mt Krakatoa
AAALLLLLPY all-play-all
AAALLNRTUW natural law
AAALMNOPRR paranormal
AAALNNOSST assonantal
AAALNOORSV Savonarola
AAALNPRSSY nasal spray
AAAMNNORTT tramontana
AAAMNPSSTU Maupassant
AAAMNRRTTY Tartan army
AAAMRTZZZZ razzmatazz
AAANNOTWWY wanton away
AABBBBHHUU hubba hubba
AABBBEILTV babblative
AABBBELORS absorbable
AABBCCKKOT back-to-back
AABBCDEEGR red cabbage
AABBCDEEKR barebacked
AABBCDEKLR Blackbeard
black bread
AABBCDKLOR blackboard
AABBCDNRSU unscabbard
AABBCEFGLY cabbage-fly
AABBCEILRS ascribable
AABBCELMOT combatable
AABBCELNRU Crab Nebula
AABBCIILNR rabbinical
AABBCIJKRT jack rabbit
AABBDDEORR breadboard
AABBDDEORS broad-based
AABBDDNNYY bandy-bandy
AABBDEEELT debateable
AABBDEEKNS baked beans
AABBDEEKRR break bread
AABBDEGILR abridgable
AABBDEGORR bargeboard
AABBDEILRY abbey-laird
AABBDELORS adsorbable
AABBDENNTU a but and ben
AABBDEOORV above board
above-board
AABBDLLNRY brandy-ball
AABBDNOTUY bandy about
AABBDRSTUY Bustard Bay
AABBEEELRT rebateable
AABBEEFLST beast fable
AABBEEGILT aglet babie
AABBEEGLRU Aberglaube
AABBEEHLRT breathable
AABBEEIRTV abbreviate
AABBEEKLRS breakables
AABBEELLRS baseballer
AABBEELLRT barbellate
AABBEELMRV beaver lamb
AABBEELNRU unbearable
AABBEELNTU unbeatable
AABBEEMUXY Meaux Abbey
AABBEGIRST sage rabbit
AABBEGLLUZ Bella Abzug
AABBEHRTTY The Tar Baby
AABBEIISSS babesiasis
AABBEILLLS ballabiles
AABBEILLNU unbailable
AABBEILMNO abominable
AABBEILNOT obtainable
AABBEILRRT arbitrable
AABBEIMNWZ Zimbabwean
AABBEINNRV Brian Bevan
AABBEINRST Barnabites
AABBEKLLST basketball
AABBEKLORT Béla Bartók
AABBEKLRWY baby-walker
AABBELLMNU unblamable
AABBELNRUY unbearably
AABBELORYY Royal Abbey
AABBEPRRRU pará rubber
AABBERSSTY baby's-tears
AABBGGILNR Balbriggan
AABBHIRRSU burra sahib
AABBHORRRU harbour-bar
AABBIKORUY Aboukir Bay
AABBILLNTU balibuntal
AABBILLOOT Italo Balbo
AABBILMNOY abominably
AABBILNNOY Babylonian
AABBIORSSU babiroussa
AABBLLMNUY unblamably
AABBLLORRW ball-barrow
AABBLMMNOP napalm bomb
AABBMMNPYY namby-pamby
AABBNNUUYY bunya-bunya
AABCCCIKRR crack a crib
AABCCCKWYY wacky baccy
AABCCDEFKL blackfaced
AABCCDELOR accordable
AABCCEEHHT The Bacchae
AABCCEELPT acceptable
AABCCEHILN chain cable
AABCCEHKNY hackney cab
AABCCEHNST bacchantes
AABCCEILLN calcinable
AABCCEILPT accept bail
AABCCEIMRT cambric tea
AABCCEKKPR backpacker
AABCCEKPRS backspacer
AABCCELLLU calculable
AABCCELOST accostable
AABCCELPTY acceptably
AABCCENOOS cocoa beans
AABCCGIKLM black magic
AABCCHINST catch-basin
AABCCHKKLL black chalk
AABCCHKLTW Black Watch
AABCCIILST cabalistic
AABCCIINNR cinnabaric
AABCCIINRT bacitracin
AABCCIJLOR Carl Jacobi
AABCCIKLLL Cilla Black
AABCCIKNRR crackbrain
AABCCILNSS cabin class
AABCCIMORT imbroccata
AABCCINOTU accubation
AABCCIORST acrobatics
AABCCLLLUY calculably
AABCDDEHKN backhanded
AABCDDEHKR hardbacked
AABCDDEKLR ladder-back
AABCDDEKLS saddleback
AABCDDORRY cardboardy
AABCDEEHLT detachable
AABCDEEHRT cheat bread
AABCDEEILR eradicable
AABCDEEKNR breakdance
AABCDEELLR declarable
AABCDEELNS ascendable
AABCDEELTU educatable
AABCDEERSU bread sauce
AABCDEFNRY fancy bread
AABCDEFRSS brass-faced
AABCDEGKNR back garden
AABCDEHKLT black death✧
AABCDEHKNR back-hander
AABCDEIILS Alcibiades
AABCDEIILT diabetical
AABCDEILMR Barmecidal
AABCDEILMT decimal tab

AABCDEIOTV advice-boat
AABCDEKSWY swaybacked
AABCDELMNU manducable
AABCDELNNU unbalanced
AABCDELNSU subdecanal
AABCDELORS scale board
AABCDELPRW parcel-bawd
AABCDENNOR carbonnade
AABCDERSTT abstracted
AABCDGKLRU blackguard
AABCDHIINR Dibranchia
AABCDHINRY Charybdian
AABCDHKLOR chalkboard
AABCDHMORT matchboard
AABCDHOPRT patchboard
AABCDIILLO diabolical
AABCDIINOT abdication
AABCDILMMS lambdacism
AABCDINRRY canary-bird
AABCDIORRS barricados
AABCDKLPSU back-spauld
AABCDKLRWY backwardly
AABCDLLNPU cup-and-ball
AABCDMNOPY bad company
AABCDMNRRY marc brandy
AABCDMOSSU ambuscados
AABCDNNORT contraband
AABCDNOORS carbonados
AABCEEEFFL effaceable
AABCEEELMR amerceable
AABCEEELTU Betulaceae
AABCEEEMRR mace-bearer
AABCEEERTT ebracteate
AABCEEERTU Tuberaceae
AABCEEERTX exacerbate
AABCEEFNRZ brazen-face
AABCEEGHLN changeable
AABCEEGHLR chargeable
AABCEEGKLL black eagle
AABCEEGKRT age-bracket
AABCEEHILV achievable
AABCEEHLMP peach Melba
AABCEEHLNS encashable
AABCEEHLNT the Balance
AABCEEHLRS searchable
AABCEEHLTY chalybeate
AABCEEHRST sabretache
AABCEEILMR amerciable
AABCEEIMRT bacteremia
AABCEEINRR carabineer
AABCEEIRTU eubacteria
AABCEEIRTV abreactive
AABCEEKLMR marble cake
AABCEEKSST basket case
AABCEELLLR recallable
AABCEELLNS cleansable
AABCEELLOT locateable
AABCEELMOT come-at-able
AABCEELMSU melba sauce
AABCEELNRT tabernacle
AABCEELPST aspectable
AABCEELRTU trabeculae
AABCEEMRTU camera tube
AABCEESTTU subacetate
AABCEFFLNO off balance
AABCEFIILP pacifiable
AABCEFIILT beatifical
AABCEFLORT factorable
AABCEGHKNR bank charge
AABCEGHLNY changeably
AABCEGHLRY chargeably
AABCEGHMRS gas chamber
AABCEGIRRR carrier bag
AABCEGKLLR Clark Gable
AABCEGKRST gas-bracket
AABCEGLLOU coagulable
AABCEGLMNN blancmange
AABCEGLSUV Savage Club
AABCEGNORU beau garçon
AABCEHHMST hatch beams
AABCEHIIMM Miami Beach
AABCEHIKNR chainbrake
AABCEHILMN machinable
AABCEHILNN Balanchine
AABCEHILPT alphabetic
AABCEHILRT charitable
AABCEHINRT branchiate
AABCEHINTU habitaunce
AABCEHJNOT Jacobethan
AABCEHKLRT black earth
blackheart
AABCEHKMNR harman-beck
AABCEHKORS ahorseback
AABCEHLMNR chambranle
AABCEHLMRR Marble Arch
AABCEHLNST stanchable
AABCEHLOUV avouchable
AABCEHLRUY Chaleur Bay
AABCEHMNOR à bon marché
AABCEHPSTY bathyscape
AABCEHQRSU shabracque
AABCEIILLM bacillemia
AABCEIINRR carabinier
AABCEIINTU beautician
AABCEILLMP implacable
AABCEILLPP applicable
AABCEILLPS slip a cable
AABCEILMOT ametabolic
AABCEILMST masticable
AABCEILNOT actionable
AABCEILOSS associable
AABCEILOTT catabolite
AABCEILPSZ capsizable
AABCEILQRU acquirable
AABCEINNOS ocean basin
AABCEINORR carabinero
AABCEINORT abreaction
AABCEINSTT state cabin
AABCEIORST aerobatics
AABCEIRRRT Barrier Act
AABCEIRSTT tetrabasic
AABCEKKLNS black snake
AABCEKKMRR backmarker
AABCEKLPPR black paper
AABCEKLRTW blackwater
AABCEKNORS rackabones
AABCEKNRSW answer back
AABCEKOPTT packet-boat
AABCEKPRRT brat packer
AABCELLLOT collatable
AABCELLMOR collar beam
AABCELLNSU unscalable
AABCELLORR barcarolle
AABCELLORS caballeros
AABCELMOPR comparable
AABCELMTUU acetabulum
AABCELNOTU outbalance
AABCELNRTY Central Bay
AABCELRRTU trabecular
AABCENORST castor bean
AABCEOPRRT Robert Capa
AABCERRSTT abstracter
AABCERRTUU bureaucrat
AABCERSTUU subarcuate
AABCFIKLRR black friar✧
AABCFIORRT fabricator
AABCFLNORU confabular
AABCFNORRU carbofuran
AABCGHINPT bathing cap
AABCGIILLM galliambic
AABCGIKMNR back margin
AABCGIKNRR barracking
AABCGILLSU subglacial
AABCGILPST plastic bag
AABCGINORT boat racing
AABCGKMMNO backgammon
AABCGLRRTU cat-burglar
AABCHHIMPR amphibrach
AABCHILRTY charitably
AABCHINOOP canophobia
AABCHINORT Tocharian B
AABCHINOTT cohabitant
AABCHIOOPR acrophobia
AABCHIOPQU aquaphobic
AABCHIRSXY brachyaxis
AABCHKLMOR Bramah-lock
AABCHKLPSS splashback
AABCHLMNPR palm branch
AABCHLNOOR halocarbon
AABCHLRRUY brachyural
AABCHMNORW Brahman cow
AABCHMORUY moucharaby
AABCHORTTU ratch about
AABCIIKLOU koulibiaca
AABCIILLMY iambically
AABCIILNOT anabolitic
AABCIILPTY capability
AABCIILTTY actability
AABCIIOPRT parabiotic
AABCIKRSST backstairs
AABCILLLSY syllabical
AABCILLMPY implacably
AABCILLNNY cannibally

AABCILLPPY	applicably
AABCILMORU	columbaria
AABCILMOST	catabolism
AABCILMRTU	umbratical
AABCILNNNO	cannabinol
AABCILNNUU	incunabula
AABCILNORR	brain coral
AABCILNOTY	actionably
AABCILNRSU	subcranial
AABCILNSUV	subclavian
AABCILORRT	calibrator
AABCILOTUV	cavil about
AABCILRSTU	arcubalist
	ultrabasic
AABCIMMNOZ	Mozambican
AABCIMOORT	macrobiota
AABCIMORST	acrobatism
AABCINRSST	cat's-brains
AABCIOQRSU	aquarobics
AABCIQSTUU	subaquatic
AABCKLMOOR	blackamoor
AABCKRSSST	brass tacks
AABCLLNNNO	cannonball
AABCLMMRUU	ambulacrum
AABCLMOPRU	labour camp
AABCLMOPRY	comparably
AABCLNOOVY	Volcano Bay
AABCLORUVY	vocabulary
AABCLRSTTY	abstractly
AABCNORSST	contrabass
AABCORRSTT	abstractor
AABDDDEEHL	bald-headed
AABDDEEEHR	bareheaded
AABDDEEGLR	degradable
AABDDEEHNR	barehanded
AABDDEELMN	demandable
AABDDEELNR	bandleader
AABDDEGGNS	sandbagged
AABDDEHLMO	hebdomadal
AABDDEHLRS	balderdash
AABDDEHMOR	hebdomadar
AABDDEILRR	air-bladder
AABDDEILRY	daily bread
AABDDEIMNR	madbrained
AABDDEINST	bastinaded
AABDDELOPR	pedal-board
AABDDELOPT	paddle boat
AABDDEORRT	trade board
AABDDEORRY	day-boarder
AABDDILLMO	lambdoidal
AABDDINORR	drainboard
AABDDKLNUY	Dundalk Bay
AABDDMRSUU	ad absurdum
AABDEEELMS	sealed-beam
AABDEEELOR	à la dérobée
AABDEEFLRY	defrayable
AABDEEGHNR	headbanger
AABDEEGLRR	regardable
AABDEEGNRR	bear garden
AABDEEGNRS	greaseband
AABDEEHKKW	hawk-beaked
AABDEEHRRT	threadbare
AABDEEILNT	detainable
AABDEEILRU	Baudelaire
AABDEEINPR	pea-brained
AABDEEKPRR	parbreaked
AABDEELNOR	ordeal bean
AABDEELNPX	expandable
AABDEELNRU	unreadable
AABDEELPRS	spreadable
AABDEELRRV	laver bread
	laverbread
	ravel bread
AABDEELRRW	rewardable
AABDEEMNOV	above-named
AABDEEMRRS	embarras de
AABDEEPRRY	prayer bead
AABDEEQRSU	arabesqued
AABDEFFLOR	affordable
AABDEFINRT	fatbrained
AABDEFIRSY	fairy-beads
AABDEFKORY	break of day
AABDEGGINR	brigandage
AABDEGGNRS	sandbagger
AABDEGGORU	broad-gauge
AABDEGHLNR	grab handle
AABDEGHLNS	Bangladesh
AABDEGHNSU	husbandage
AABDEGIMNR	brand-image
AABDEGIMRR	Bridgerama
AABDEGIMRS	bragadisme
AABDEGLNOY	Donegal Bay
AABDEGLNRY	by and large
AABDEGLPRU	upgradable
AABDEGMNNR	German band
AABDEGORST	goat's-beard
AABDEGORSW	board-wages
AABDEGRRSS	beard-grass
AABDEHINNR	bear in hand
AABDEHINRT	brain death
AABDEHINWY	win by a head
AABDEHJLNS	J B S Haldane
AABDEHKNST	hand-basket
AABDEHKRSW	hawksbeard
AABDEHNSTW	sweath-band
AABDEHORRT	earth-board
AABDEHRRTW	draw breath
AABDEIJMRS	James Braid
AABDEIKKOR	Kodiak bear
AABDEIKNSU	adsuki bean
AABDEIKNUZ	adzuki bean
AABDEILLLU	illaudable
AABDEILLNR	banderilla
AABDEILLSY	dialysable
AABDEILLYZ	dialyzable
AABDEILMTT	admittable
AABDEILNOR	ordainable
AABDEILNOT	dealbation
AABDEILOST	Blastoidea
AABDEINNNT	en badinant
AABDEINNOR	Aberdonian
AABDEINRSU	Diane Arbus
AABDEINRTZ	bartizaned
AABDEINSST	bastinades
AABDEIPRTT	pitta bread
AABDEIRSST	bastardise
AABDEIRSTZ	bastardize
AABDEJLSTU	adjustable
AABDEKLLMS	masked ball
AABDEKLLNR	randle-balk
AABDEKMNOW	Meadowbank
AABDEKORST	skateboard
AABDELLNNO	belladonna
AABDELNOPR	pardonable
AABDELNUWY	bundle away
AABDELORRZ	razor blade
AABDELRSTU	balustrade
AABDEMNNNO	one-man band
AABDEMNNRS	bad manners
AABDEMNOSW	beadswoman
AABDEMNRST	bandmaster
AABDEMORRT	Robert Adam
AABDEMORSS	embassador
AABDEOPPRR	paperboard
AABDEOPRST	pasteboard
AABDFHLNOT	not half bad
AABDFHLORS	flashboard
AABDFLOORT	float-board
AABDGHRRTU	draught-bar
AABDGIILNW	law-abiding
AABDGIKMNR	barking mad
AABDGIKNOS	baking soda
AABDGILNOY	loading bay
AABDGNOORT	dragon boat
AABDHLORRU	hard labour
AABDHMNNSU	husbandman
AABDHNORRW	hand-barrow
AABDHNORTT	throatband
AABDIILNST	tidal basin
AABDIINNRR	brain drain
AABDILLLUY	illaudably
AABDILLORY	aryballoid
AABDILMNRU	mandibular
AABDILNRRY	DNA library
AABDILOOPR	paraboloid
AABDIMNRRU	barramundi
AABDIMRSST	bastardism
AABDIORRST	stir abroad
AABDJLSTUY	adjustably
AABDLNNTUY	abundantly
AABDLNOPRY	pardonably
AABDLOORRW	barrowload
AABDLORRTY	bardolatry
AABDLORSTY	astral body
AABDMQRTUU	B quadratum
AABDNNORRW	narrowband
AABDNNPRSY	brandy snap
AABDOORRRW	broad arrow
AABDORRSTW	strawboard
AABEEEKRRX	axe-breaker
AABEEELLPR	repealable
AABEEELLRS	releasable
	resealable

AABEEELLRV revealable
AABEEELPRT repeatable
AABEEELPST pâte sablée
AABEEELRRT talebearer
AABEEFIKRT take a brief
AABEEFILRR rarefiable
AABEEFLLLT flabellate
AABEEGILNR regainable
AABEEGKRST break gates
AABEEGLLRS greaseball
AABEEGLLST Bagatelles
AABEEGLMSS assemblage
AABEEGLOVY voyageable
AABEEGLRTT targetable
AABEEGNNRU near-begaun
AABEEGNORT baronetage
AABEEGRSUV subaverage
AABEEHIRTT beat the air
AABEEHKRRT heartbreak
AABEEHKRTT take breath
AABEEHLLNU unhealable
AABEEHLQTU bequeathal
AABEEHLRTT earth-table
AABEEHMMMR hammer beam
AABEEHMRTW amber wheat
AABEEHNRTY Theban year
AABEEHPRTT beat the rap
AABEEHRRTV Braveheart
AABEEHRTTW beware that
AABEEILLRS realisable
AABEEILLRZ realizable
AABEEILMNX examinable
AABEEILNRS inerasable
AABEEILNRT retainable
AABEEILPRR repairable
AABEEINRRR arrière-ban
AABEEINRTV native bear
AABEEJKMRS James Baker
AABEEJKNRT Janet Baker
AABEEJKRRW jaw-breaker
AABEEJKRST break a jest
AABEEKLLRT Lake Albert
AABEEKLMRR remarkable
AABEEKLMRT marketable
AABEEKLRRW lawbreaker
AABEEKMRRT bear market
AABEEKPRRS Breakspear
AABEEKRRTW breakwater
water break
AABEELLLSZ sleazeball
AABEELLMNT lamentable
AABEELLNPT plane table
AABEELLNSU unsaleable
AABEELLPRR pall-bearer
AABEELMNNU unamenable
unnameable
AABEELMNTU untameable
AABEELMRRU rumble area
AABEELMRSU measurable
AABEELMSTT metastable
stablemate
AABEELNNTT tenantable
AABEELNORS reasonable
AABEELNOSS seasonable
AABEELNPTT patentable
AABEELNRSU unerasable
AABEELNRSW answerable
AABEELNRTU untearable
AABEELNRUW unwearable
AABEELNTTT tablanette
AABEELOPRV evaporable
AABEELPPRY prepayable
AABEELRRST arbalester
arrestable
AABEELRSST assertable
AABEELRTTW table water
water table
AABEELRTTY Earl Beatty
AABEELSSSS assessable
AABEELSTTT attestable
AABEEMNOPW beam weapon
AABEENRSST Barents Sea
AABEEORTVW above water
AABEEQRSSU Arabesques
AABEERRTTV Vertebrata
AABEFFIILL affiliable
AABEFFILLR fair befall
AABEFFILMR affirmable
AABEFFLLLW baffle wall
AABEFFOPRU opera buffa
AABEFGILTU fatiguable
AABEFGKLNR klangfarbe
AABEFGKLST flag-basket
AABEFHLMOT fathomable
AABEFHOSTY Bay of Heats
AABEFIILLS salifiable
AABEFIILRT ratifiable
AABEFILLMN inflamable
AABEFILLNT inflatable
AABEFILPPR papal brief
AABEFIMORS framboesia
AABEFINRRT Barnet Fair
AABEFLORUV favourable
AABEFNORRT forbearant
AABEGGORRT Greta Garbo
AABEGHILLY gallabiyeh
AABEGHINRS earbashing
AABEGHINST sea-bathing
AABEGHNORT Orange Bath
AABEGHOOPR agoraphobe
AABEGHORRU harbourage
AABEGIILMN imaginable
AABEGILNOZ zabaglione
AABEGILNRT able rating
AABEGILNRV Belgravian
AABEGILNSS assignable
AABEGILRST algebraist
AABEGINNOT abnegation
AABEGINRRU rue-bargain
AABEGIORTV abrogative
AABEGIRRRT arbitrager
AABEGKRRSU sugar-baker
AABEGLNORW brown algae
AABEGLNRUU unarguable
AABEGLOPPR propagable
AABEGMNRSU submanager
AABEGPSSUY Pegasus Bay
AABEHIILTT habilitate
AABEHIKMRT habit-maker
AABEHILORV behavioral
AABEHINRRT Herbartian
AABEHIOOPR aerophobia
AABEHKLNSU unshakable
AABEHKRRSZ zebra shark
AABEHLQSSU squashable
AABEHLRSZZ belshazzar✧
AABEHQRSSU squabasher
AABEHRRSTW water brash
AABEIILNRV invariable
AABEIILNST insatiable
AABEIILNTU unilabiate
AABEIILRSV braaivleis
AABEIILSST assibilate
AABEIIMNSS baisemains
AABEIIMOSS amoebiasis
AABEIINNST in absentia
AABEIJLOSU Beaujolais
AABEIKLMST mistakable
AABEIKLNRT retail bank
AABEIKNNRV knave-bairn
AABEILLLST La Bastille
AABEILLMNU unmailable
AABEILLMPP impalpable
AABEILLNRS ballerinas
AABEILLNUV invaluable
AABEILLORV labiovelar
AABEILLRSY realisably
AABEILLRYZ realizably
AABEILMMRU barium meal
AABEILMNTU albuminate
AABEILMNTV ambivalent
AABEILMPRT impartable
AABEILMPSS impassable
AABEILMSUX ambisexual
AABEILNNOT balneation
AABEILNRSU Belarusian
AABEILNRSY inerasably
AABEILNRUV unvariable
AABEILNSTU unsatiable
AABEILNTTT batteilant
AABEILOPRS parabolise
AABEILOPRZ parabolize
AABEILQRRU quarriable
AABEILRRST arbalister
breastrail
AABEILRSTU tabularise
AABEILRSVY abrasively
AABEILRTTT titratable
AABEILRTUZ tabularize
AABEIMNORU Maria Bueno
AABEIMPRTV vampire bat
AABEINORRT aberration
AABEINORTT trabeation

AABEINRRTW	water-brain
AABEINSSTT	bastnäsite
AABEIORRTV	arbor vitae
AABEKKMNRR	banker-mark
AABEKKNRRS	break ranks
AABEKLLNNR	rannel-balk
	rannle-balk
AABEKLLNRT	rantle-balk
AABEKLLNSU	unslakable
AABEKLMRRY	remarkably
AABEKLRTTW	wattlebark
AABEKNNRRU	run a banker
AABEKOPRRT	parrot-beak
AABELLLORS	albarellos
AABELLLPRY	ball-player
AABELLMNSY	by all means
AABELLMNTY	lamentably
AABELLNPUY	unplayable
AABELLNUUV	unvaluable
AABELLRRSY	salal berry
AABELLRSTW	breast wall
AABELLSSST	stable lass
AABELMNNOT	Monte Albán
AABELMNORS	ransomable
AABELMNOTU	ablutomane
AABELMNSUU	unamusable
AABELMNTUY	untameably
AABELMOSTT	melba toast
AABELMPRSU	Peru balsam
AABELMRSUY	measurably
AABELNNOTU	unatonable
AABELNORSY	reasonably
AABELNOSSY	seasonably
AABELNPRST	Barnstaple
AABELNPRTZ	zebra plant
AABELNPSSU	unpassable
AABELNRRTY	aberrantly
AABELNRSWY	answerably
AABELNSUWY	unswayable
AABELOORRT	elaborator
AABELOPPRV	approvable
AABELOPRRT	proratable
AABELPPRSY	parablepsy
AABELPRSST	brass plate
AABELPRSTU	pasturable
AABELPSSSY	les Pays Bas
AABELSTTTU	statutable
AABEMMORVY	Emma Bovary
AABEMNNSYY	by any means
AABEMRSTTU	masturbate
AABEORTTUW	water about
AABFFIILTY	affability
AABFHLOSTU	flash about
AABFILLOTU	flail about
AABFLMNOTY	flamboyant
AABFLORUVY	favourably
AABFNNOTUY	fanny about
AABGGHINSY	gay-bashing
AABGGLRRTY	braggartly
AABGHILOOP	algophobia
AABGHMMSUY	Sammy Baugh
AABGIILMNY	imaginably
AABGIILNOR	aboriginal✧
AABGIKLLMT	Kimball tag
AABGIMNPTW	gambit-pawn
AABGIMORTY	ambagitory
AABGINNOOT	Tobagonian
AABGINNOTW	angwantibo
AABGINOORT	abrogation
AABGINORTU	outbargain
AABGINRSSU	sugar basin
AABGIOSSSS	bagassosis
AABGIRSSTU	bass guitar
AABGLNRSUU	subangular
AABGLNRUUY	unarguably
AABGLOORRS	algarrobos
AABGNRTTTY	Grant Batty
AABHHIPSSW	bashawship
AABHIIKLMS	Lakshmi Bai
AABHIINNTT	inhabitant
AABHIINOTT	habitation
AABHIKKLNU	Kublai Khan
AABHIKKPSU	pukka sahib
AABHILLTUY	habitually
AABHILORTY	habilatory
AABHIMMNRS	Brahmanism
AABHIMRSTV	Bar Mitsvah
	Barmitsvah
	Bar-Mitsvah
AABHIMRTVZ	Bar Mitzvah
	Barmitzvah
	Bar-Mitzvah
AABHIMSSTV	Bas Mitsvah
	Basmitsvah
	Bas-Mitsvah
AABHIMSTTV	Bat Mitsvah
	Batmitsvah
	Bat-Mitsvah
AABHIMSTVZ	Bas Mitzvah
	Basmitzvah
	Bas-Mitzvah
AABHIMTTVZ	Bat Mitzvah
	Batmitzvah
	Bat-Mitzvah
AABHINOOPP	panophobia
AABHIOOPTU	autophobia
AABHKLNSUY	unshakably
AABHLLLOOU	hullabaloo
AABHLPSSYY	hypabyssal
AABHNOTTUU	haunt about
AABHOPRTUV	vapour-bath
AABHOSTTUW	whatabouts
AABIIILMTY	amiability
AABIIINNPR	bipinnaria
AABIIKMNNS	Iain M Banks
AABIILLSTY	salability
AABIILMTTY	tamability
AABIILNRVY	invariably
AABIILNSTY	insatiably
AABIILRTTY	ratability
AABIILTTXY	taxability
AABIIMNOSS	bonamiasis
AABIINNSSU	Sabinianus
AABIINNSSY	Abyssinian
AABIINPRST	bipartisan
AABIINQRUU	ubiquarian
AABIIOPRSS	parabiosis
AABIJNORTU	abjuration
AABIKLMNTU	Mt Kinabalu
AABIKLMOST	katabolism
AABIKLMSTY	mistakably
AABIKMNRTU	Kutab Minar
AABIKNOPRT	Portakabin®
AABILLMNUY	bimanually
AABILLMPPY	impalpably
AABILLMSST	lamb's-tails
AABILLNNUY	biannually
AABILLNOOT	oblational
AABILLNRUY	binaurally
AABILLNUVY	invaluably
AABILLRUVV	bivalvular
AABILMNOTU	ambulation
AABILMPSSY	impassably
AABILMPSTY	lay baptism
AABILMRSST	strabismal
AABILNOORT	abortional
AABILNOTTU	tabulation
AABILNRTUU	tubularian
AABILOPRST	parabolist
AABILOSTTU	battailous
AABILPRTUY	patibulary
AABIMNOOQS	Mina Qaboos
AABIMNOORT	abominator
AABINPRRST	bairn's-part
AABINRRSTY	binary star
AABIORRRTT	arbitrator
AABIRSSSTT	Bass Strait
AABKKOORRU	kookaburra
AABLLMNORY	abnormally
AABLLMOSTU	salbutamol
AABLLNOPST	planoblast
AABLLPPYYY	play-by-play
AABLMMOSTY	Amblystoma
AABLMMPSTU	stamp album
AABLMORTUY	ambulatory
AABLNRSTUU	subnatural
AABLOORRTY	laboratory
AABLOPRRRU	bar-parlour
AABLOPRRTY	Labor Party
AABLORTTUY	tabulatory
AABLOSSTTT	statoblast
AABLRSSTTU	substratal
AABLSTTTUY	statutably
AABMORRRTW	barrow-tram
AABNOORRTW	narrowboat
AABNORRSSW	Barons' Wars
AABORRRSTU	barratrous
AABORRSSUU	Barosaurus
AACCCDEIIT	acetic acid
AACCCDENOR	accordance
AACCCDIILT	lactic acid
AACCCDIINY	cyanic acid
AACCCDNORY	accordancy

AACCCEEILO Lee Iacocca
AACCCEENPT acceptance
AACCCEILTT catalectic
AACCCEIORT cacciatore
AACCCEKRRT cat-cracker
AACCCENPTY acceptancy
AACCCEOSTU cactaceous
AACCCHIRRT arctic char
AACCCIJKLO Calico Jack
AACCCILRSS classic car
AACCCINRUY inaccuracy
AACCDDEHKN cack-handed
AACCDDEIRT caddie cart
AACCDDEISS caddis-case
AACCDDIIIP adipic acid
AACCDDIILS didascalic
AACCDDIILT didactical
AACCDEENNS ascendance
AACCDEENSU succedanea
AACCDEEPST space cadet
AACCDEERRZ care-crazed
AACCDEGHRR charge card
AACCDEHIRS saccharide
AACCDEHNOR archdeacon
AACCDEIILM maleic acid
AACCDEILNT accidental
AACCDEILTU aciculated
AACCDEIMNU unacademic
AACCDEIMRS disc camera
AACCDEIORT coradicate
co-radicate
AACCDEJNOT coadjacent
AACCDELLNO candle-coal
AACCDELLTU calculated
AACCDELRST card-castle
cat's-cradle
AACCDELSTU sacculated
AACCDEMNOO cacodaemon
AACCDENNSY ascendancy
AACCDENRRW Cancer Ward
AACCDEORSS access road
AACCDERSTY scaredy-cat
AACCDGIILL gallic acid
AACCDHIILN Chalcidian
AACCDHILMO dochmiacal
AACCDHINRT catch-drain
AACCDHIORS saccharoid
AACCDHNOST coach-stand
AACCDHPRST scratch pad
AACCDIIILS sialic acid
AACCDIILLY acidically
AACCDIILOX oxalic acid
AACCDIILRU lauric acid
AACCDIINNT tannic acid
AACCDIIRTY caryatidic
AACCDIISTU diacaustic
AACCDIMORY myocardiac
AACCDNOTUY account day
AACCEEELRT accelerate
AACCEEEPRY Cyperaceae
AACCEEFFOT face to face
face-to-face
AACCEEFGHN change face
AACCEEFHSS chasse-café
AACCEEGPRS scapegrace
AACCEEIKNP pancake ice
AACCEEIMNR cine camera
ciné camera
AACCEEIMRY Myricaceae
AACCEEINPU Punicaceae
AACCEEIRTU Urticaceae
AACCEEKLTT cattle cake
AACCEELLNT cancellate
AACCEELLOT calceolate
AACCEELNRT accelerant
AACCEENTTU accentuate
AACCEEORSU aceraceous
AACCEEORTV coacervate
AACCEEPRSU caper-sauce
AACCEFGORT act of grace
AACCEFGOSU cacafuegos
AACCEFHHLN half-chance
AACCEFIIPT pacificate
AACCEFLORT calefactor
AACCEFPRST spacecraft
AACCEGHKNT change tack
AACCEGHOST stagecoach
AACCEGIORT Arctogaeic
AACCEGLLNO glance-coal
AACCEHIJKN Jackie Chan
AACCEHILLM alchemical
AACCEHILMN mechanical
AACCEHILOR Cochlearia
AACCEHIMNN main chance
AACCEHINNT cachinnate
AACCEHINNW wanchancie
AACCEHINRS saccharine
AACCEHINRU Chaucerian
AACCEHIRRT arctic hare
AACCEHIRSS saccharise
AACCEHIRST chaise-cart
AACCEHIRSV viscachera
AACCEHIRSZ saccharize
AACCEHLNOT coelacanth
AACCEHLNRT lancet arch
AACCEHLPRT chapel cart
AACCEHNNOT not a chance
AACCEHNOTY chatoyance
AACCEHORSS saccharose
AACCEHRRTT rat-catcher
AACCEHRRTY charactery
AACCEIKMMO cockamamie
AACCEILLNO cloacaline
AACCEILOPR praecocial
AACCEILPTT cataleptic
AACCEINNOT canonicate
AACCEINORV covariance
AACCEINOSU acinaceous
AACCEINPRT pancreatic
AACCEINPTV captivance
AACCEINRTT cantatrice
AACCEINRTU inaccurate
AACCEIORTT aerotactic
AACCEIRRTU caricature
AACCEIRRUV River Cauca
AACCEISTUV accusative
AACCEJKKOR crack a joke
AACCEKLLVV clack valve
AACCEKORRT carrot cake
AACCELLLOR coal cellar
AACCELLNNO cannel-coal
AACCELLOTT toccatella
AACCELLTUY calyculate
AACCELMTUU accumulate
AACCELORSU calcareous
AACCELPRSW crawlspace
AACCELRTUY accurately
AACCENNRST CAT scanner
AACCENRSTU crustacean
AACCFHIRSY saccharify
AACCFHKLOT at half-cock
AACCFIIPRW Pacific War
AACCFILLRY farcically
AACCFILRSU fascicular
AACCFINNRS Franciscan
AACCGHHLNS Nachschlag
AACCGHIORY hagiocracy
AACCGHIPRY graphicacy
AACCGHLOSS glass-coach
AACCGHOPRY cacography
AACCGIIILP I Pagliacci
AACCGIJKNR carjacking
AACCGIKLNO caking coal
AACCHHIINN chinachina
AACCHHINTW watch chain
AACCHIIMRS archaicism
AACCHIIRST archaistic
AACCHILNPY chaplaincy
AACCHIMORT achromatic
AACCHINNOR anachronic
AACCHINOPT cataphonic
AACCHIOPRT cataphoric
AACCHKLLUW chuckwalla
AACCHKNPPU pack a punch
AACCHKOSST Cossack hat
AACCHLNORY acronychal
AACCHLOPTY Phytolacca
AACCHMORSU scaramouch✧
AACCHNORST cast anchor
AACCHNOTYY chatoyancy
AACCHOPRTY coach party
AACCIILLMT climatical
AACCIILLNU canaliculi
AACCIILORS sacroiliac
AACCIINORV Cavicornia
AACCIINPRT practician
AACCIINPTY incapacity
AACCIINRSS circassian✧
AACCIIOSTT stiacciato
AACCIJNOPR Canopic jar
AACCILLMOT malo-lactic
AACCILLRUV clavicular
AACCILLTTY tactically

AACCILMMUY immaculacy
AACCILMNOR romancical
AACCILNNOS canonicals
AACCILNNOT Clactonian
AACCILNOOS occasional
AACCILOSTU acoustical
AACCILPRST practicals
AACCILPTTU catapultic
AACCILRTUY articulacy
AACCIMNORS carcinomas
macaronics
AACCINNRSZ cancrizans
AACCINOOPT cacotopian
AACCINORST Costa Rican
AACCINORTV vaccinator
AACCINOSTU accusation
AACCINPTTY anaptyctic
AACCINRSTU anacrustic
AACCINRTTU act curtain
AACCINSTTY asyntactic
AACCIOPTTY to capacity
AACCIORTTU autocratic
AACCKLLMOR alarm clock
AACCLLOORS sarcocolla
AACCLLORTU calculator
AACCLLRTUU accultural
AACCLNOTTU contactual
AACCLNRRUU caruncular
AACCLORSVY slavocracy
AACCMNNOPY capnomancy
AACCMNNOTT contact man
AACCMNOPTT accomptant
AACCMNORTY cartomancy
AACCNNOTTU accountant
AACCNORSST sacrosanct
AACCORSTUY accusatory
AACDDEEHLR decahedral
AACDDEEIMP aide-de-camp
AACDDEEIRT eradicated
AACDDEERRR card reader
AACDDEGINR cardiganed
AACDDEHKKN kack-handed
AACDDEIJTU adjudicate
AACDDEINNR decandrian
AACDDEINSV disadvance
AACDDEKLPS packsaddle
AACDDELLNS scandalled
AACDDELOTW clawed toad
AACDDGLNRU grand-ducal
AACDDHKPWY paddy-whack
AACDDIOTTU autodidact
AACDEEEERS Resedaceae
AACDEEEFNS defeasance
AACDEEELST de-escalate
AACDEEEMNS damasceene
AACDEEFFLS false-faced
AACDEEFHMS shamefaced
AACDEEFHNR face-harden
AACDEEFPPR paper-faced
AACDEEGIRU grâce à Dieu
AACDEEGLLN lead glance
lead-glance
AACDEEGMMR decagramme
AACDEEGNOT anecdotage
AACDEEHLRT thread-lace
AACDEEHNRS case-harden
AACDEEHRRT race hatred
AACDEEHRTT tracheated
AACDEEHRTX ex cathedra
ex-cathedra
AACDEEIINS Sciaenidae
AACDEEIINT taeniacide
AACDEEIKTV take advice
AACDEEILNY Lycaenidae
AACDEEILRT dilacerate
AACDEEIMNR maiden race
AACDEEINRT deracinate
ecardinate
AACDEEIPTT decapitate
AACDEEIRXY Xyridaceae
AACDEEITTV deactivate
AACDEEKNNS snake dance
AACDEELNRR calendarer
AACDEELNTU anucleated
AACDEELOSS escaladoes
AACDEELRRW declare war
AACDEEMPRS dreamscape
AACDEENNRR ance-errand
AACDEENNTT attendance
AACDEENRSY canary-seed
AACDEEOPRS escape road
AACDEEOPSS escapadoes
AACDEESUWY causewayed
AACDEFFIRT affricated
AACDEFGLSS glass-faced
AACDEFINRR Africander
AACDEFINRU fricandeau
AACDEFJNSU Janus-faced
AACDEFLNNO flanconade
AACDEFLORT defalcator
AACDEFPSTY pasty-faced
AACDEFRRTT tradecraft
AACDEGGIOP paedagogic
AACDEGHHNR charge-hand
AACDEGHINS casinghead
AACDEGINNY decagynian
AACDEGLNNY land agency
AACDEGLSSS cased glass
AACDEGNORS gasconader
AACDEHHMTT deathmatch
AACDEHHTTW deathwatch
AACDEHIINT Tachinidae
AACDEHILMY chlamydiae
AACDEHILNR Heraclidan
AACDEHINRS sedan chair
AACDEHIORS icosahedra
AACDEHIORY Hyracoidea
AACDEHJKLT Jack the lad
AACDEHKPRT packthread
AACDEHLLPY lady chapel
AACDEHLMTY chlamydate
AACDEHLNNR Archenland
AACDEHLNNS clean hands
AACDEHLORT octahedral
AACDEHMNOR Andromache
AACDEHNTTU unattached
AACDEHOOPT Chaetopoda
AACDEIILNT laciniated
AACDEIILPR epicardial
AACDEIILRS radicalise
AACDEIILRZ radicalize
AACDEIILUV Aviculidae
AACDEIIMNR marine acid
AACDEIINRR irradiance
AACDEIIPRT paediatric
AACDEIIRRT irradicate
AACDEIIRTV divaricate
AACDEIJLTV adjectival
AACDEIKLLP Lake Placid
AACDEILLLN candelilla
AACDEILMNO demoniacal
AACDEILMNR aldermanic
AACDEILMNT declaimant
AACDEILMRY acrylamide
AACDEILNNO Caledonian
AACDEILNOR androecial
AACDEILNPS snail-paced
AACDEILNPT led captain
pedantical
AACDEILNSS scandalise
AACDEILNSZ scandalize
AACDEILORT Crotalidae
AACDEIMNNO Macedonian
AACDEIMNRU admiraunce
AACDEIMNTT admittance
AACDEIMNTU acuminated
AACDEIMOPR paramedico
AACDEIMPRS paramedics
AACDEIMRRY dairy cream
AACDEINORU Ecuadorian
AACDEINQTU acquainted
AACDEINQUY inadequacy
AACDEINRRW warrandice
AACDEINRST discarnate
AACDEINRTX taxi dancer
AACDEINSUV disavaunce
AACDEIORRT Cortaderia
eradicator
AACDEIOSST associated✧
AACDEIRSTY caryatides
AACDEJLNTY adjacently
AACDEKLLRW cradlewalk
AACDELLSTY Lady Castle
AACDELMNNU unmanacled
AACDELMNPY maple candy
AACDELMNRS slam dancer
AACDELMOPR camelopard
AACDELMRSU clear as mud
AACDELNPPY candy apple
AACDELNSST sandcastle
AACDELOPRT leopard cat
AACDELORRT declarator
AACDELORST sacerdotal

AACDELORSU lardaceous
AACDELOTUV vacuolated
AACDELPSTU scapulated
AACDELRTWY tawdry lace
AACDEMMNRU ad crumenam
AACDEMOOPR Adam Cooper
AACDEMRRST MasterCard®
master-card
AACDENNTTY attendancy
AACDENRSSU sand saucer
AACDENTTUU unactuated
AACDEOPRRS radarscope
AACDEORRVW draw a cover
AACDEORSUV cadaverous
AACDFGILRS fiscal drag
AACDFHINRT handicraft
AACDFIILLS falsidical
AACDFIINOO aficionado
AACDFIINOR Africanoid
AACDFIMNRT frantic-mad
AACDFIMORR microfarad
AACDFISTTY fatty acids
AACDFLOORT load factor
AACDGGINRR drag-racing
AACDGHHINR Chandigarh
AACDGHIIPR diagraphic
AACDGHMNRR grand march
AACDGHRTUW watchguard
AACDGIKOSS sick as a dog
AACDGILMOT dogmatical
AACDGILNNP lap dancing
AACDGILOPR podagrical
AACDGIMORR cardiogram
AACDGINNPT tap-dancing
AACDGNRSUY sugar candy
sugar-candy
AACDGORSTU coastguard
AACDHHIMNS shadchanim
AACDHHINNS cash in hand
cash-in-hand
AACDHIIKNR Dinah Craik
AACDHIINSY daisy chain
daisy-chain
AACDHIIRRS I A Richards
AACDHIKRTU kurdaitcha
AACDHILLMY chlamydial
AACDHILMSY chlamydias
AACDHINORT anthracoid
AACDHIRRSU Charadrius
AACDHJMMNO John McAdam
AACDHLMNRS marchlands
AACDHLORSY day-scholar
AACDHMNORR orchardman
AACDHNNORY chardonnay
AACDHOSSTW shadowcast
AACDIILLRV larvicidal
AACDIILMRS Radicalism
AACDIILMRT matricidal
AACDIILNOP pinacoidal
AACDIILPRR parricidal
AACDIILPRT patricidal
AACDIILRTY radicality
AACDIILSTT diastaltic
AACDIIMNRY Adriamycin®
AACDIINORS Icosandria
AACDIINORT radication
AACDIINRRY irradiancy
AACDIJLLUY Judaically
AACDILLMTU Talmudical
AACDILLNRY cardinally
AACDILLOOR local radio
AACDILMNNO calamondin
AACDILMORY myocardial
AACDILNOPS spondaical
AACDILNORS sardonical
AACDILNSTY dynastical
AACDILOPRS sporadical
AACDIMMRSU music drama
AACDIMNRTU undramatic
AACDINNORT octandrian
AACDINNOST contadinas
AACDINOOTV advocation
AACDINORRT ration card
AACDINORST Sadi Carnot
AACDINRRSW Drawcansir
AACDIQRSTU quadratics
AACDJKNORU jack around
AACDJNOTTU coadjutant
AACDKLMORY Lord Mackay
AACDLMORRU armour-clad
AACDLNOSSU scandalous
AACDLOPRST postal card
AACDLOSTUY adactylous
AACDMMNNOT commandant
AACDNOORST ostracodan
AACDNOORWY canary-wood
AACDNORRSS crossandra
AACDNORRTU cart around
AACDNORSTU cast around
AACDOOPRRT paradoctor
AACDOOPRST capodastro
AACDOORTVY advocatory
AACDORRSTU scordatura
AACDORSSTW coastwards
AACEEEGHST escheatage
AACEEEGLLN allegeance
AACEEEIOST Isoetaceae
AACEEEIPPR Piperaceae
AACEEEKMPR peacemaker
AACEEEKNSY eye askance
AACEEELMNP elecampane
AACEEELMRT telecamera
AACEEELNOP Palaeocene
AACEEEOPRT Proteaceae
AACEEFFLTT caffè latte
AACEEFGSTY safety cage
AACEEFHRRT reach after
AACEEFQRSU square-face
AACEEFRRTV crave after
AACEEGGHNR change gear
gearchange
gear-change
AACEEGHKRT take charge
AACEEGHNRR carragheen
AACEEGHRUV Che Guevara
AACEEGILLN allegiance
AACEEGILNS Genesiacal
AACEEGKPPR prepackage
AACEEGKPTW wage packet
AACEEGLLNR Angel Clare
AACEEGLLRS large-scale
AACEEGLNTU acute angle
AACEEGLNUY launcegaye
AACEEGMOST escamotage
AACEEGMPRS megaparsec
AACEEHHLRT healthcare
AACEEHILMU leuchaemia
AACEEHILNR Heracleian
AACEEHILNT châtelaine
AACEEHINNS seannachie
AACEEHINRY Rhyniaceae
AACEEHKPST cheapskate
AACEEHLLSW Lech Walesa
AACEEHLMNO chamaeleon✧
AACEEHLMNR menarcheal
AACEEHLNPT antechapel
AACEEHLORV coal heaver
AACEEHLPST sphacelate
AACEEHLRTT trachelate
AACEEHLRTY Lythraceae
AACEEHMNRY aerenchyma
AACEEHMPPR paper-mâché
AACEEHMRVY heavy cream
AACEEHNNRT anthracene
AACEEHOPRS sea poacher
AACEEHPPRS paper chase
AACEEHPRTW peach-water
AACEEHRTTT tear the cat
AACEEIJNNR Jean Racine
AACEEIKNPS sinke-a-pace
AACEEILMRS caramelise
AACEEILMRZ caramelize
AACEEILNPR Alpine race
AACEEILNRR air cleaner
AACEEILNRV en cavalier
AACEEILPRT altarpiece
AACEEILRTV lacerative
AACEEILSTT elasticate
AACEEIMMOS Mimosaceae
AACEEIMNPT emancipate
AACEEIMNTX Mexican tea
AACEEIMSST Siamese cat
AACEEINPRT Capernaite
paraenetic
AACEEIPPRT appreciate
AACEEIPSSY assay-piece
AACEEIRTTV reactivate
AACEEITUVV evacuative
AACEEKLRRT crater lake✧
AACEEKLRRW race-walker
AACEEKMPRT meat packer
AACEELLLUV valleculae
AACEELLNOT lanceolate

AACEELLORT reallocate
AACEELLPRT carpellate
AACEELLPUV place value
AACEELMRVW Marcel wave
AACEELMSTU emasculate
AACEELNNRT alternance
AACEELNOSU sauce-alone
AACEELNPPS spaceplane
AACEELNTTT neat-cattle
AACEELOPRT capreolate
AACEELOPRY Pyrolaceae
AACEELOPSU paleaceous
AACEELPPSU apple sauce
AACEELRTVY acervately
AACEEMRRST master race
AACEENNRSS arcaneness
AACEENORSU arenaceous
AACEENOSSY Sean O'Casey
AACEENOSUV avenaceous
AACEENRRTV veteran car
AACEENRRTW water crane
AACEEOPPRS space opera
AACEEPPRTY peace-party
AACEEPRSTT peat-caster
AACEERSSTV stavesacre
AACEFFGINY faying-face
AACEFFGLOS scaffolage
AACEFFIMNR affirmance
AACEFGINSV face-saving
AACEFGLMOU camouflage
AACEFGNRSU gas-furnace
AACEFGRSTT stagecraft
AACEFHIMNX fax machine
AACEFHLLNP chapfallen
AACEFHLLNR fallen arch
AACEFHLMNR arch-flamen
AACEFHRSTY safety arch
AACEFHRTTW watch after
AACEFIILLM maleficial
AACEFIILTT facilitate
AACEFIIMPR prima facie
AACEFIINRS Africanise
AACEFIINRZ Africanize
AACEFIINST fanaticise
AACEFIINTZ fanaticize
AACEFILMOS leaf mosaic
AACEFILNSU final cause
AACEFILRSY fiscal year
AACEFINORT arefaction
AACEFINRRU Eurafrican
AACEFJKKLT flak jacket
AACEFJKRRT jack-rafter
AACEFKLRST flare stack
AACEFLLLOR flea collar
AACEFLLLPR cellar-flap
AACEFLLOTW tallow face
AACEFLMNOR roman à clef
AACEFLMORT malefactor
AACEFLRRTU Fratercula
AACEFLRSTU sucralfate
AACEFMNRSU surfaceman
AACEFNRRTY fan tracery
AACEFRRRTY refractary
AACEFRRTTW watercraft
AACEFRSTTT statecraft
AACEGHILNR alcheringa
AACEGHILNW ca'ing whale
AACEGHINOR archegonia
AACEGHINRT chain grate
AACEGHLNRY Clayhanger
AACEGHLRSW scrag-whale
AACEGHMOPR macrophage
AACEGHNORT coathanger
AACEGHOTTT act the goat
AACEGIINRR Craig Raine
AACEGILLPR pre-glacial
AACEGILMNN malignance
AACEGILMNT magnetical
AACEGILORT categorial
AACEGILOTZ catalogize
AACEGILPPR paraplegic
AACEGIMNOR ergomaniac
AACEGIMNPR campaigner
AACEGINRTV vintage car
AACEGIPPRR paper-cigar
AACEGIRRRS carrier gas
AACEGJNOTU Conjugatae
AACEGLMNOR carmagnole
AACEGLMORY acromegaly
AACEGLORTU cataloguer
AACEGMNNNO cannon-game
AACEGMNRTY termagancy
AACEGNNORT cartonnage
AACEGOPRRS Apgar score
AACEGORTUY act your age!
AACEHHHNUV have a hunch
AACEHHILRR hierarchal
AACEHHKLMS hamshackle
AACEHHLMPT health camp
AACEHHMNTT hatchet man
AACEHIIMNR hemicrania
AACEHIIMNT haematinic
AACEHIIPRR hiera-picra
AACEHIKLMR like a charm
AACEHIKLNN ankle-chain
AACEHILLLY heliacally
AACEHILMMS Michaelmas
AACEHILMPR alphameric
AACEHILMPT alphametic
emphatical
AACEHILMRS camel's hair
AACEHILNOP Cephalonia
AACEHILNRS Lancashire
AACEHILNTX hexactinal
AACEHILOPT apothecial
AACEHILPRS aspherical
seraphical
AACEHILPRX hexaplaric
AACEHILPST chaptalise
AACEHILPTT pathetical
AACEHILPTZ chaptalize
AACEHILRTT theatrical
AACEHIMMNN machineman
AACEHIMMPR amphimacer
AACEHIMMTT mathematic
AACEHIMNOO haemoconia
AACEHIMNOT theomaniac
AACEHIMNRT carthamine
Rachmanite
AACEHIMNRW war machine
AACEHIMNSU Manichaeus
naumachies
AACEHINNOU ouananiche
AACEHINPRS parischane
AACEHINPTY pay the cain
AACEHINRRT catarrhine
AACEHINRST Charentais
China aster
AACEHINRTT anthracite
AACEHINSTT in that case
AACEHINSTU Eustachian
AACEHIOPRX echopraxia
AACEHIORST Oireachtas
AACEHIPRRT arch-pirate
AACEHIPRSS Caesarship
AACEHIPSTT chapatties
AACEHIRRTV architrave
AACEHJKMMR jackhammer
AACEHJOPRS chaparejos
AACEHKLMRS ramshackle
AACEHKLNRS ranshackle
AACEHKMMRT matchmaker
match-maker
tack hammer
AACEHKMNNY hackneyman
AACEHKMRTW watchmaker
AACEHKOPRT karate chop
karate-chop
AACEHKORVW wreak havoc
AACEHLLPSU Alcelaphus
AACEHLMMRW claw hammer
AACEHLMUUX chalumeaux
AACEHLNPRT plane chart
AACEHLNPTY phlyctaena
AACEHLNRRU neural arch
AACEHLOPSU acephalous
AACEHLOPTY Polychaeta
AACEHLPRRT Petrarchal
AACEHLPRTY archetypal
AACEHLRRSY Ray Charles
AACEHLRSTT scarlet hat
AACEHMNPRY parenchyma
AACEHMNRRT Carmarthen
AACEHMNRTY athermancy
AACEHMNTTT attachment
AACEHMOPRT camphorate
AACEHNNPSU snaphaunce
AACEHNOPTY tachypnoea
AACEHNORTT archontate
AACEHNPRRT Petrarchan
AACEHNPSWW wapenschaw
AACEHNSSTU acanthuses
AACEHOPPRS approaches

AACEHOPRTY apothecary
AACEHPPRTW watch paper
AACEHRSTTT at a stretch
AACEIILLPR capillaire
AACEIILLRT Lacertilia
AACEIILPST capitalise
AACEIILPTZ capitalize
AACEIIMNOT emaciation
AACEIIMPRT parmacitie
AACEIINNRV invariance
AACEIINORT acieration
AACEIINPTT anticipate
AACEIINTTV inactivate
vaticinate
AACEIIOPSS Cassiopeia
AACEIIPRRS persicaria
AACEIIPRTT patriciate
AACEIJLMST majestical
AACEIKLLRS rascal-like
AACEIKLRTT racket-tail
AACEILLMNU animalcule
AACEILLNOS escallonia
AACEILLNPT planetical
AACEILLNRT carnallite
AACEILLNTT cantillate
AACEILLOSU alliaceous
AACEILLPRT prelatical
AACEILLPRU Lupercalia
AACEILLRRV varicellar
AACEILLRTU calliature
AACEILLRVY cavalierly
AACEILLSTY salicylate
AACEILMMNO melomaniac
AACEILMMTU immaculate
AACEILMNOR camino real
AACEILMNOT Celtomania
noematical
AACEILMNPR imparlance
AACEILMNPS campaniles
AACEILMNRT reclaimant
AACEILMNRU unicameral
AACEILMNSU main clause
AACEILMNTU calumniate
AACEILMRRT tricameral
AACEILMRTU tularaemic
AACEILNORT creational
laceration
reactional
AACEILNOST escalation
AACEILNPSS snail's pace
AACEILNPSU Esculapian
AACEILNPTU paniculate
AACEILNRRT intercalar
AACEILNRTU retinacula
AACEILOOPZ Palaeozoic
AACEILORRT acroterial
AACEILPRST palaestric
AACEILPTTU capitulate
AACEILRSST scale stair
AACEILRTTU articulate
AACEILRTUU auriculate
AACEILSTTT stalactite
AACEILSTTU actualités
AACEILTTTW tattie-claw
AACEIMMPRU paramecium✧
AACEIMNNOR Cameronian
necromania
AACEIMNNRU un-American
AACEIMNNST anamnestic
AACEIMNORS Americanos
macaronies
AACEIMNORT cameration
maceration
racemation
AACEIMNORU oceanarium
AACEIMNRRW Crimean War
AACEIMNRSS Saracenism
AACEIMNRWX Mexican War
AACEIMOPST aposematic
AACEIMORRT crematoria
AACEIMPRRT parametric
AACEIMRSTU metri causa
AACEIMSTTT metastatic
AACEINNNTU annunciate
AACEINNOTT catenation
AACEINNOWY once in a way
AACEINNPRT pancreatin
AACEINNRTU centaurian
AACEINORTU aeronautic
AACEINORTV acervation
vacationer
AACEINOTUV evacuation
AACEINOTVX excavation
AACEINPRST Persian cat
AACEINPRTY at any price
AACEINQRTU reacquaint
AACEINRSST incrassate
Isaac Stern
AACEINSSST assistance
AACEINSTVY vanity case
AACEIORSTT aerostatic
AACEIOSTVV vasoactive
AACEIPRTTV private act
AACEIRTTTV attractive
AACEJKNNVY Jan van Eyck
AACEJKNRRW Jack Warner
AACEJKNRTT natterjack
AACEJLMORS major scale
AACEJLORTU ejaculator
AACEKKMRST make tracks
AACEKLLPUW wake-up call
AACEKLMRST smart Aleck
smart-Aleck
AACEKLNORS coral snake
AACEKLOOPR opera cloak
AACEKLRRTY tracklayer
AACEKLRSTW slack water
slack-water
AACEKLSTTY stay-tackle
AACEKMORRW camerawork
AACELLLMPS plasma cell
AACELLLMSS small-scale
AACELLLORT collateral
AACELLLRST saltcellar
AACELLLRUV vallecular
AACELLPRRY carpellary
AACELLPSST cast a spell
AACELMMORS sarcolemma
AACELMNOPT complanate
AACELMNOPZ clonazepam
AACELMNORS roman à clés
AACELMOPSU palmaceous
AACELMORST coalmaster
scleromata
AACELMOSUV malvaceous
AACELMOSUY amylaceous
AACELMPRST campestral
scrap metal
AACELMRRSU secular arm
AACELMRTUU maculature
AACELNNORU neurocanal
AACELNNOST stone canal
AACELNNOTV covenantal
AACELNNUVY Uncle Vanya
AACELNOPTU cantaloupe
AACELNORTU à l'outrance
AACELNOTTV octavalent
AACELNPSTU pulsatance
AACELNRRUV vernacular
AACELNRTTU tentacular
AACELNSSSU casualness
AACELOPPSY apocalypse✧
AACELOPRSU acarpelous
AACELORSTY escalatory
AACELORSUU lauraceous
AACELORSUY lay a course
AACELPRSSU Paracelsus
AACELPRTTY calyptrate
AACELSTTUU auscultate
AACEMNOPRS campaneros
mascarpone
AACEMNOPRT compearant
AACEMNOPSW spacewoman
AACEMNORST Sacramento
AACEMPRSTU metacarpus
AACENNOOSU anonaceous
AACENNORRV Caernarvon
AACENNOTTZ canzonetta
AACENNSSTV vacantness
AACENOPPRV approvance
AACENOTTUZ Uto-Aztecan
AACENRRSSU sarus crane
AACENRSTTY Stan Tracey
AACENRTTTX extractant
AACEOOPRTT potato race
AACEORRTTT terracotta
AACEPSTTTU statute cap
AACFFIINPR paraffinic
AACFFIJMRT traffic jam
AACFFIRTWY way traffic
AACFGIILMN magnifical
AACFGIIMNT Magnificat
AACFGILLNW wall-facing

AACFGILNRT flat racing
AACFGILRTW tragic flaw
AACFGLRSTU Carl Gustaf
AACFHKNRST crankshaft
AACFHLLOTW fallow-chat
AACFHLNORW half-a-crown
AACFIIILRT artificial
AACFIILLMN flaminical
AACFIILLSV salvifical
AACFIILNOR California
AACFIILNRV acriflavin
AACFIILSTT fatalistic
AACFIIMNRS Africanism
AACFIIMNST fanaticism
AACFIIMORR formicaria
AACFIINOST fasciation
AACFIINPSU piscifauna
AACFIINRST Africanist
AACFILLMOU claim a foul
AACFILLOSU fallacious
AACFILMOOT coat of mail
AACFILMORT matrifocal
AACFILMPRU falciparum
AACFILNORT fractional
AACFILOPRT patrifocal
AACFILORST solfataric
AACFILORSV varifocals
AACFILRTTY fractality
AACFILTTUY factuality
AACFIMNORU microfauna
AACFINORST fascinator
AACFINORTY factionary
AACFINOSTT fantastico
AACFJLMMRY clamjamfry
AACFLLMRST small craft
AACFLLORSS fall across
AACFLMOORR macroflora
AACFLNNOTU non-factual
AACFMNNOWY fancy woman
AACFMOORST coat of arms
AACFNRSTTU surfactant
AACFOPSSUY cup of assay
AACFRRTTYY arty-crafty
AACGGIILOS sialagogic
AACGGLLMNO McGonagall
AACGHHINPR Chinagraph®
AACGHHOPRT tachograph
AACGHHPRTY tachygraph
AACGHILLOR oligarchal
AACGHILNPY anaglyphic
AACGHILRRT arthralgic
AACGHILRTV galravitch
AACGHINORR chair-organ
AACGHINRSS China grass
AACGHIOPRS sarcophagi
AACGHLMRUU chaulmugra
AACGHLSSTW watchglass
AACGHMMOSY chasmogamy
AACGHNNSUU Anschauung
AACGHNRTTT Gantt chart
AACGHOPSTY scatophagy
AACGIILLST glacialist
AACGIILNOT glaciation
AACGIIMRRT margaritic
AACGIIMSTT astigmatic
AACGIINNOS San Ignacio
AACGIKMNRT tarmacking
AACGILLLNS call signal
AACGILLMNR margin call
AACGILLRSW Gallic Wars
AACGILLRTY tragically
AACGILMNNY malignancy
AACGILMRTU Targumical
AACGILNORS cor anglais
AACGILNPTY anaglyptic
play-acting
AACGILOPRT proctalgia
AACGILORWY cog railway
AACGILPRSY spagyrical
AACGIMNORT morganatic
AACGIMPRST pragmatics
AACGIMRSTY magistracy
AACGINNSSV canvassing
AACGINORTU argonautic
AACGINOUUV Nova Iguacu
AACGINPRSS panic-grass
AACGINRTTT attracting
AACGINRTTV cravatting
AACGIORSTT castigator
AACGKQRSSU quack grass
AACGKRRSSW grasswrack
AACGLLMOOY malacology
AACGLNORTU octangular
AACGLOORTU coagulator
AACGLOOSTY astacology
AACGNOPRST cargo pants
AACHHHIKSU shakuhachi
AACHHILNPT naphthalic
AACHHIMNNU human chain
AACHHIORTZ chota hazri
AACHHNNPSU snaphaunch
AACHHOPRTY Charophyta
AACHIIINPR caipirinha
AACHIILLOR allochiria
AACHIILNOP canophilia
AACHIILORS arachis oil
AACHIIMNPS amphiscian
AACHIINNOT Antiochian
AACHIINPTT antipathic
AACHIKMORT Marita Koch
AACHILLOPT allopathic
AACHILLORS Charollais
AACHILMNOR harmonical
monarchial
AACHILNNPT plainchant
AACHILNPRY chaplainry
AACHILNPSY Lychnapsia
AACHILOPRY acarophily
AACHILPRSU haruspical
AACHIMMNOO monomachia
AACHIMMNRS Rachmanism
AACHIMNNOR anharmonic
Monarchian
AACHIMNNRU Manchurian
AACHIMNOOS monochasia
AACHIMNOPR anamorphic
AACHIMNORS maraschino
AACHIMNORT achromatin
machinator
AACHIMNORW chairwoman
AACHIMNPST phantasmic
AACHIMNSSU in as much as
inasmuch as
AACHIMPRST pharmacist
AACHIMRRTY matriarchy
AACHIMRSTT Maastricht
AACHINOPPR paraphonic
AACHINOPRY paronychia✧
AACHINPSTT phantastic
AACHINPSWW wapinschaw
AACHINRSTU Carthusian
AACHIPRRTY patriarchy
AACHIPRSTY parastichy
AACHIRSTTU autarchist
AACHLLMRSY lachrymals
AACHLLOPRT phallocrat
AACHLLORTT altar-cloth
AACHLMMOOS schoolma'am
AACHLMRRYY lachrymary
AACHLNNNOT nonchalant
AACHLOPPRY apocryphal
AACHLRRTUY chartulary
AACHMNNORR Norman arch
AACHMOOPRT apochromat
AACHMORTUY tauromachy
AACHNOOPST Pocahontas
AACHORRSTU catarrhous
AACHPRSTTW watchstrap
AACIIIMSST Asiaticism
AACIILLNNT anticlinal
AACIILLNOS salicional
AACIILLOPT apolitical
AACIILMNOS simoniacal
AACIILMNPS panislamic
AACIILMNST talismanic
AACIILMNTX anticlimax
AACIILMPRT primatical
AACIILMPST capitalism
AACIILNNOR Carolinian
AACIILNNST annalistic
AACIILNOPT capitolian
AACIILNORS salicornia
AACIILNOST antisocial
AACIILNPST capital sin
AACIILNRTT triactinal
AACIILPPST papistical
AACIILPSTT capitalist
AACIILRRTU urticarial
AACIILRSTT artistical
AACIIMNRST anti-racism
AACIIMNSTT Instamatic®
AACIIMNSTV Vaticanism
AACIIMOSTX axiomatics

AACIINNPTT anticipant
AACIINNRRT trinacrian✧
AACIINOPRT aprication
AACIINOPTT capitation
AACIINORTV victoriana✧
AACIINOTTV activation
cavitation
AACIINRRTU air curtain
AACIINRSTT anti-racist
AACIINSTTT antistatic
AACIINSTTV Vaticanist
AACIIORSUV avaricious
AACIJLMMPU jump a claim
AACIJLNOTU jaculation
AACIJMNORS Canis Major
AACIJPRSTV JavaScript®
AACIKLLMRY karmically
AACIKLMMRS Lamarckism
AACIKLMRST smart Alick
smart-Alick
AACIKNSSTY Kansas City
AACILLMORT matrilocal
AACILLMOSY mosaically
AACILLMOTY atomically
AACILLNOOT allocation
locational
AACILLNOPT Platonical
AACILLNORS rascallion
AACILLNTUY nautically
AACILLOOPR coprolalia
AACILLOPRT allopatric
patrilocal
AACILLOPTT to cap it all
AACILLPTYY atypically
AACILLRWXY wax lyrical
AACILLSTTY statically
AACILLTVWY cavity wall
AACILMNNOT monactinal
AACILMNORT romantical
AACILMNOST monastical
AACILMNOTU maculation
AACILMNOTY claymation
AACILMOPSX axoplasmic
AACILMOSTU calamitous
AACILMPPRY paralympic
AACILMPSTU capital sum
AACILMRRTU matricular
AACILMSTTU sal Atticum
AACILNNOPT action plan
AACILNNOSV Sclavonian
AACILNNRTY tyrannical
AACILNNTUY unanalytic
AACILNOOTV vocational
AACILNOPPT panoptical
AACILNOPRS parsonical
AACILNOPTY nyctalopia
play action
AACILNORSS scansorial
AACILNORTT tractional
AACILNPTTU capitulant
AACILNRSUZ Salina Cruz
AACILOORRT oratorical
AACILOPPRT applicator
AACILOPRTT optical art
AACILOPSTU apolaustic
AACILOPTTU autoptical
AACILORRTU curatorial
AACILORSTU lactosuria
AACILPRRSU spiracular
AACILPRRTU particular
AACILPRSTT plastic art
AACILPRTUY capitulary
AACILPSSUW wassail cup
AACILTTTUY tactuality
AACIMMMNOU ammoniacum
AACIMMNNOO monomaniac
AACIMNNOXY axinomancy
AACIMNOOPS opsomaniac
AACIMNOPRY pyromaniac
AACIMNPRTU pancratium
AACIMOPRSU rampacious
AACIMORRST Camorrista
AACIMORSTT masticator
AACIMRRTUU atracurium
AACINNOORT octonarian
AACINNORRT contrarian
AACINNORTT incantator
AACINNOSTT Constantia
AACINNQTUU unacquaint
AACINOOPTT coaptation
AACINOOSTV Nova Scotia
AACINORSTT castration
AACINORTTT attraction
AACINORTUY auctionary
cautionary
AACINPPRST Capri pants
AACINPRSTT pancratist
practisant
AACIOOPPRT apotropaic
AACIOOPTVZ Octavio Paz
AACIOORSST associator
AACIORRSTT aristocrat
AACIOSSUVX saxicavous
AACIPPRSST Paris Pacts
AACIPRSSTT Spartacist
AACJKRSSTW Jack Straws
AACJLMMPRU jumar clamp
AACJLMRSUU majuscular
AACJLNORSU Juan Carlos
AACJLORTUY jaculatory
AACKLLNPSW Planck's law
AACKLNOTUY you can talk
AACKNORSVW canvas-work
AACLLMNPRU Pullman car
AACLLMORST call to arms
AACLLORRUY oracularly
AACLLOSSTT at all costs
AACLLRSUVY vascularly
AACLMMOPSY mycoplasma
AACLMNNOSW clanswoman
AACLMOPRSS sarcoplasm
AACLMPSTUY Paul McStay
AACLNNORTU connatural
AACLNNORVW naval crown
AACLOOPRRT parrot-coal
AACLOORRTU coloratura
AACLOPPRSS papal cross
AACLOPRRRU parlour car
AACMMNNOPY company man
AACMNNOPRU manna-croup
AACMNOOPST campo santo
AACMNOPRUY paramouncy
AACMNRSSUU cassumunar
AACMOOPRRT comparator
AACMOORRTU coat-armour
AACMOPSSSW compass saw
AACNNNOSTT constantan
AACNNOPTTU put on an act
AACNNORSTY Nancy Astor
AACNOORSST Cosa Nostra
AACNORRSTT transactor
AACNORRSTW narrowcast
AACOOPPRSU apocarpous
AACOOPSSTT capotastos
AACOPRRSTU artocarpus
AACORRSTTT stratocrat
AADDDDGNRY granddaddy
AADDDEEHHR hard-headed
AADDDEEHRT death adder
AADDDEELLR all-dreaded
AADDDEELPT addle-pated
AADDDEELUV value added
AADDDEHHNR hard-handed
AADDDEILPR paradiddle
AADDDEILRT taradiddle
AADDDGRSUY sugar daddy
AADDDHNNYY handy-dandy
AADDDILUVV David Duval
AADDEEEHKW weak-headed
AADDEEFHIR fair-headed
AADDEEGGRS Edgar Degas
AADDEEGHST stag-headed
AADDEEGMNR grande dame
AADDEEHHOR hoar-headed
AADDEEHHOT head to head
head-to-head
AADDEEHHST death's-head
AADDEEHILN nail-headed
AADDEEHIMN maidenhead✧
AADDEEHIRR drearihead
AADDEEHKNW weak-handed
AADDEEHMNY many-headed
AADDEEHNNT neat-handed
AADDEEHNRR hard-earned
AADDEEHNRV verandahed
AADDEEHORR roadheader
AADDEEILST St Adelaide
AADDEEIRST desiderata
AADDEEIRWY day-wearied
AADDEEISTT state-aided
AADDEEKLMR madder-lake
AADDEELRRW Edward Lear
AADDEEMRRY daydreamer

AADDEENORU	Oudenaarde
AADDEEPPRT	preadapted
AADDEFHNST	fast-handed
AADDEFINRW	far and wide
AADDEFLSST	saddle-fast
AADDEGGLRY	ragged-lady
AADDEGGNRT	egg-and-dart
AADDEGHLNR	glad-hander
AADDEGHNOR	dragonhead
AADDEGIILT	digladiate
AADDEGIMMR	diagrammed
AADDEGIMNV	Magen David
AADDEGINRT	grant-aided
AADDEGIRRT	tardigrade
AADDEGMNOR	Armageddon
AADDEGNNOR	dragonnade
AADDEHIILP	Diadelphia
AADDEHIMNN	handmaiden
AADDEHNORS	Esarhaddon
AADDEHNRUZ	unhazarded
AADDEHQSTU	death squad
AADDEHRSTW	deathwards
AADDEIILPT	dilapidate
AADDEIIMNP	indapamide
AADDEILMMY	midday meal
AADDEILMRR	red admiral
AADDEIMMTV	David Mamet
AADDEIMNTT	additament
AADDELLNOR	Elland Road
AADDELMRSS	maladdress
AADDELMUWY	muddle away
AADDELOPSS	saddle soap
AADDELPRRT	trap-ladder
AADDENPRTU	pandurated
AADDFLNORY	yard of land
AADDGHIOSY	siddha yoga
AADDGIILLO	diallagoid
AADDGILMOY	amygdaloid
AADDGINRTY	day trading
AADDGNNRST	grandstand
AADDGNOPWY	paddy wagon
AADDGNRSTU	stand guard
AADDHHINNN	hand in hand
	hand-in-hand
AADDHHNNOT	hand to hand
	hand-to-hand
AADDHIKSSY	say Kaddish
AADDHNNRSY	shandrydan
AADDIILNOT	additional
AADDIIMNNY	didynamian
AADDIJNOSV	David Jason
AADDILLLOV	Valladolid
AADDILNORR	Lord Adrian
AADDILNOSS	Sado Island
AADDILNRSZ	sand lizard
AADDIMNRTY	dynamitard
AADDINORRT	ritardando
AADDINPRTY	paddy train
AADDKNORYY	Dan Aykroyd
AADDLLNORS	sand dollar
AADDLNOOSW	sandalwood
AADDMOORSY	Roodmas Day
AADDNNRRUU	Duran Duran
AADDNPRSUW	and upwards
AADEEEGLMR	game-dealer
AADEEEJLUV	eau de Javel
AADEEELNPT	peel-and-eat
AADEEELRSY	day release
	day-release
AADEEEPRRT	tape reader
AADEEFGHOR	forge ahead
AADEEFGLRT	deflagrate
AADEEFGRRU	Edgar Faure
AADEEFILRR	fair-leader
AADEEFLNRT	trade-falne
AADEEGGINR	reading age
AADEEGGOPU	paedagogue
AADEEGHLNT	death angel
	get a handle
AADEEGINSV	Geena Davis
AADEEGINYZ	Zygaenidae
AADEEGIRTV	variegated
AADEEGKLRS	Greek salad
AADEEGLLNU	Land League
AADEEGLNRS	green salad
AADEEGLRVW	Waldegrave
AADEEGMNRW	game warden
AADEEGNRRU	daguerrean
AADEEGNRST	degreasant
	garden seat
AADEEGNRTU	guaranteed
AADEEGNSYY	gey and easy
AADEEGOPRT	pagoda-tree
AADEEHHLRX	hexahedral
AADEEHHMMR	hammerhead
AADEEHIMTV	have it made
AADEEHINOV	have no idea
AADEEHIRTW	head waiter
AADEEHKKOV	have a dekko
AADEEHKNRT	header tank
AADEEHKNSS	snake's-head
AADEEHLMTT	death metal
AADEEHLNVY	heavy-laden
AADEEHLORS	Rhoeadales
AADEEHLPPT	lappet-head
AADEEHLRTT	rattlehead
AADEEHLTWY	lead the way
AADEEHMNTY	name the day
AADEEHMRST	headmaster
	head-stream
AADEEHMRVY	heavy-armed
AADEEHNPRT	pentahedra
AADEEHNRVW	heavenward
AADEEHPPRS	pear-shaped
AADEEHPRSS	press ahead
AADEEHQRSU	headsquare
AADEEHRRTT	tetrahedra
AADEEHRSTT	strae death
AADEEHRTTY	at the ready
AADEEIILMN	Limnaeidae
AADEEIINNV	Idaean vine
AADEEIKLNS	Neil Sedaka
AADEEIKNST	steak diane
AADEEILMNN	Madelenian
AADEEILMNT	delaminate
AADEEILNNR	adrenaline
AADEEILNST	desalinate
AADEEILRSW	ladieswear
AADEEILRTV	revalidate
AADEEIMMNN	maiden name
AADEEIMNOT	Nematoidea
AADEEIMNOU	eudaemonia
AADEEIMNRU	Muraenidae
AADEEIMPRS	emparadise
AADEEIMPRT	pre-Adamite
AADEEINNNR	Enneandria
AADEEINQTU	inadequate
AADEEINRRS	Serranidae
AADEEINRST	Diana's tree
AADEEIORST	Asteroidea
AADEEIPRST	deaspirate
AADEEIQTUV	adequative
AADEEIRRWW	war-wearied
AADEEIRSTT	asteriated
AADEEJMRSW	James Dewar
AADEEKKKOT	take a dekko
AADEEKMMNS	make amends
AADEEKNNUW	unawakened
AADEEKOTWY	a week today
AADEELLLMT	lamellated
AADEELLLPR	paralleled
AADEELLOTW	a lead towel
AADEELLPPR	apparelled
AADEELLPRY	playleader
AADEELLRRS	serradella
AADEELNNNU	unannealed
AADEELNNRT	neandertal✧
AADEELNNWZ	New Zealand
AADEELNRSX	alexanders
AADEELOPRS	sea leopard
AADEELPRTT	trade plate
AADEELQRSU	square deal
AADEELQTUY	adequately
AADEELRSSV	salsa verde
AADEELRSSW	easselward
AADEELRSTV	slave trade
AADEELRTTU	adulterate
AADEEMNNOY	anadyomene
AADEEMNSSZ	amazedness
AADEEMPRRT	Dermaptera
AADEEMQRSU	masquerade
AADEEMQSTU	desquamate
AADEENPPSU	suppedanea
	unappeased
AADEENRRWY	wander year
AADEENSTVZ	Zend-Avesta
AADEENTTTU	attenuated
AADEEPPRRT	trade paper
AADEERRTTW	tread water
AADEFFNORT	fore-and-aft
AADEFGLNRT	garden flat
AADEFGNNOS	fandangoes
AADEFGRRTU	after-guard

AADEFHIIRR	fair-haired
AADEFHLNOZ	half-a-dozen
AADEFHLNRT	fatherland
AADEFHRSTY	Father's Day
AADEFIKNRR	Afrikander
AADEFILLRT	falderal it
AADEFIMNOT	defamation
AADEFINNRR	farrandine
AADEFINTTU	infatuated
AADEFKLNOR	do a flanker
AADEFKLRSW	dewar flask✧
AADEFMORTY	defamatory
AADEFNRRSW	Dawn Fraser
AADEFRRSTW	afterwards
AADEGGILLT	daggle-tail
AADEGGILNT	gangliated
AADEGGINRS	aggrandise
AADEGGINRZ	aggrandize
AADEGGLORT	data logger
AADEGGMOTT	tagged atom
AADEGGOSSU	sausage dog
AADEGHHINS	shanghaied
AADEGHHIRS	shag-haired
AADEGHIINR	hearing aid
AADEGHNNRT	Ndrangheta
	'Ndrangheta
AADEGHNOTY	death-agony
AADEGHNPRT	garden path
AADEGIIMPR	pie diagram
AADEGIINTV	indagative
AADEGILLNR	grenadilla
AADEGILMNN	leading man
AADEGILMNR	lead-arming
AADEGILPRR	paraglider
AADEGILRST	saltigrade
AADEGILTTY	agitatedly
AADEGIMNPR	map-reading
AADEGIMNRS	smaragdine
AADEGIMNRT	marginated
AADEGIMRST	smaragdite
AADEGINOTT	toad-eating
AADEGINRRS	disarrange
AADEGIOPRR	radiopager
AADEGIORST	Deo gratias
AADEGIPRRS	disparager
AADEGKNPRT	peg-tankard
AADEGLLNRU	eglandular
AADEGLLSTZ	salt-glazed
AADEGLNNRS	rangelands
AADEGLNOPR	pedal-organ
AADEGLNQRU	quadrangle
AADEGLNSTW	sweat gland
AADEGMRRSY	Gerry Adams
AADEGMRRTU	dramaturge
AADEGNNRRU	unarranged
AADEGNOPRR	grand opera
AADEGNORSS	Sangradoes
AADEGNSSUU	unassuaged
AADEGOORVV	avvogadore
AADEGRRTUW	water guard
AADEHHRTWY	the hard way
AADEHIILOT	Haliotidae
AADEHIILRS	dish aerial
AADEHIIMNR	maidenhair
AADEHIINRT	antheridia
AADEHIIPRS	sphaeridia
AADEHIKNNT	take in hand
AADEHILMNS	Mahe Island
AADEHILMRT	diathermal
AADEHILNNT	lanthanide
AADEHILNRT	Thailander
AADEHILORR	diarrhoeal
AADEHILRSW	hawser-laid
AADEHIMRSY	Hardy Amies
AADEHINNRX	hexandrian
AADEHINOTZ	Zoanthidae
AADEHINPRT	Heptandria
AADEHINRSS	hansardise
AADEHINRSZ	hansardize
AADEHINRTV	Theravadin
AADEHINSSW	Sandie Shaw
AADEHIOPST	Hitopadesa
AADEHIPRST	Therapsida
AADEHIPRSU	saphir d'eau
AADEHISTTW	twaite shad
AADEHJNRRW	Wanderjahr
AADEHKMRRT	thread mark
AADEHLLMRS	marshalled
AADEHLNNPR	panhandler
AADEHLNPRR	Ralph Nader
AADEHLNPST	shade plant
AADEHLRSSY	harassedly
AADEHLSTTY	the Last Day
AADEHMNNST	the sandman
AADEHMNOSY	Moshe Dayan
AADEHMNRST	master-hand
AADEHMPRSS	Sam Shepard
AADEHNNSTT	thé dansant
AADEHNSSTV	handstaves
AADEHPRSST	star-shaped
AADEHRRSTW	earthwards
AADEIILMNN	Indian meal
AADEIILNOT	ideational
AADEIILNTV	invalidate
AADEIIMNNR	Amerindian
AADEIIMNNT	diamantine
	maintained
AADEIIMNST	disanimate
	mediastina
AADEIIMPRS	imparadise
AADEIIMRTV	admirative
AADEIINNST	East Indian
AADEIINNTV	vanadinite
AADEIINORT	eradiation
AADEIINPPR	India paper
AADEIINPTV	inadaptive
AADEIINRST	asteridian
AADEIINTTV	adventitia
AADEIIRRTT	triradiate
AADEIKLNSW	Wake Island
AADEIKSSTU	diaskeuast
AADEILLMMT	mamillated
AADEILLMTU	Adullamite
AADEILLPPT	papillated
AADEILLQSU	quesadilla
AADEILLRRS	serradilla
AADEILLRTU	laurdalite
AADEILMMST	Lammas-tide
AADEILMNNR	mainlander
AADEILMNNT	nidamental
AADEILMNOR	Adrian Mole
AADEILMNOS	Salmonidae
AADEILMNPT	Dame Pliant
AADEILMNTY	animatedly
AADEILMORT	tailor-made
AADEILMRTX	taxidermal
AADEILNNSW	Waldensian
AADEILNNTV	native land
AADEILNPRS	palisander
AADEILNPRT	land-pirate
AADEILNRSU	unsalaried
AADEILNRTW	land-waiter
AADEILNSSU	unassailed
AADEILNSTU	andalusite
AADEILOPSS	palisadoes
AADEILOQSU	Squaloidea
AADEILORRR	railroader
AADEILORST	asteroidal
AADEILPPRS	disapparel
AADEILPTVY	adaptively
AADEILRRTY	radial tyre
AADEIMMNNO	domain name
AADEIMMNOT	ammoniated
AADEIMNNSW	swan-maiden
AADEIMNNTU	maiden aunt
	unanimated
AADEIMNRTV	animadvert
AADEIMNSUX	à deux mains
AADEIMORST	steam radio
AADEINNOPT	antipodean✧
AADEINNPRT	Pentandria
AADEINNQRU	quadrennia
AADEINNRTY	Tyrannidae
AADEINNRWW	win and wear
AADEINORRT	tread on air
AADEINORTY	arytaenoid
AADEINPQSU	pasquinade
AADEINPRSU	unparadise
AADEINPTTY	day-patient
AADEINQTTU	antiquated
AADEINRRTT	Tetrandria
AADEINRSTT	antitrades
AADEINSTTU	unsatiated
AADEIOPQRU	radiopaque
AADEIORSTV	advisorate
AADEIPPTTT	pit-a-patted
AADEIPRRTU	pietra dura
AADEIPRSST	disparates
AADEIRSSTU	raise a dust
AADEISTTVV	devastavit
AADEJNORST	Oranjestad
AADEJPRRSU	Raj Persaud
AADEKKNRST	stark-naked

Words marked ✧ can also be spelled with one or more capital letters

AADEKLLMNS Dan Maskell
AADEKLMORW meadow lark
AADEKMORSS damask rose
AADEKMRRTT dark matter
AADEKNPTTU put-and-take
AADEKNRSTT start-naked
AADELLLMTY Tam Dalyell
AADELLMNOS all and some
AADELLMNRS mallanders
AADELLMNRY aldermanly
AADELLMORT mortadella
AADELLNPPU unappalled
AADELLNPTT platteland
AADELLNRTY Talleyrand
AADELLNSUV land-values
AADELLORSV El Salvador
AADELLPRUU Paul Eluard
AADELLRTTY tally trade
AADELMMNOY Meal Monday
AADELMNPTU datum plane
paludament
AADELMNRRY aldermanry
AADELMORST loadmaster
AADELNNOST stand-alone
AADELNNPSV Vanden Plas®
AADELNNSUY unanalysed
AADELNNUYZ unanalyzed
AADELNOPRS personal ad
AADELNRTTU adulterant
AADELORSVW aardwolves
AADELORTTX extradotal
AADELRRTUX extradural
AADELRSTWY eastwardly
AADEMMNSSU mandamuses
AADEMMORTU trou-madame
AADEMNOORS enamorados
AADEMNOQRU Andromaque
AADEMNORTY amendatory
AADEMNQRUU quadrumane
AADEMNRRRW Andrew Marr
AADEMOQRTU Torquemada
AADEMRRSTY yard-master
AADENNRTTU denaturant
AADENOPRSU andropause
AADENORRRY Ray Reardon
AADENPPRSY sandpapery
AADENPPSSW passed pawn
AADENQRSTU quadrantes
AADENRSTTT stand treat
AADENRSTTU transudate
AADEOPRRUX paradoxure
AADEORSTTV devastator
AADEQRRSUY square yard
AADEQRRTUU quadrature
AADEQRRTUY quarter day
AADFFFNORU faff around
AADFFGHNSY shandygaff
AADFFHNSST handstaffs
AADFGLNOPR flap-dragon
AADFHIKLOR Frida Kahlo
AADFHLLLOR half-dollar
AADFIILMPT palmatifid
AADFIILNTU latifundia
AADFILMRYY My Fair Lady
AADFILRSTU fruit salad
AADFIMNRSY Man Fridays
AADFLNRSTT strandflat
AADGGILMNY damagingly
AADGHHLNSU Lughnasadh
AADGHIILRU Dhaulagiri
AADGHIMNNT hand mating
AADGHINSWY washing-day
AADGHIOPRR radiograph
AADGHIOPRU audiograph
AADGHIPRSY dysgraphia
AADGHLLNOP hand gallop
AADGHMNRTU draughtman
AADGHNNORU hang around
AADGIIIRSS giardiasis
AADGIIMNNT data mining
AADGIIMNRR ram-raiding
AADGIINNOT indagation
AADGIINNRT grant-in-aid
AADGIINNSU ungainsaid
AADGIINOTV divagation
AADGIJNORU jaguarondi
AADGIJNRUU jaguarundi
AADGIKMNOR road-making
AADGILLNOY diagonally
AADGILMNSU salmagundi
AADGILMRSU gradualism
AADGILNOOT odontalgia
AADGILNOSY disanalogy
AADGILNPPU applauding
AADGILORTY gladiatory
AADGILRSTU gradualist
AADGILRTUY graduality
AADGIMNRST magistrand
AADGINNOPR grand piano
AADGINOPST spatangoid
AADGINORRY Dorian Gray
AADGINORTU graduation
AADGINORTY indagatory
AADGLLNORR Lord Raglan
AADGLMNORY Gary Oldman
AADGLMNSUY salmagundy
AADGLNORTT grand total
AADGMNNORT Montagnard
AADGMNORRU dragon arum
AADGMRRTUY dramaturgy
AADGMRSSTU mustard gas
AADGNNOPRS snapdragon
AADGNRSSSU Sudan grass
AADGOOPRST Gastropoda
AADHIILNSW India shawl
AADHIIMNRR Harimandir
AADHIIOPRS aphrodisia
AADHIKRSWW awkwardish
AADHILLMOO homaloidal
AADHILLNPS Laplandish
AADHILOTXY tax holiday
AADHILRTWW withdrawal
AADHIMNNOS madonnaish
AADHIMNORY hydromania
AADHINOOPR adiaphoron
AADHINOPSU diaphanous
AADHINORRS hard as iron
AADHINORSW rain shadow
AADHINPSSU Upanishads
AADHIOTWWY do away with
AADHIRRSTY dysarthria
AADHKMORSW shadow mark
AADHKMOSSW shadow mask
AADHLLLLNO allhallond
AADHLLNNOS on all hands
AADHLNNOSY lay hands on
lay on hands
AADHLNORWY Andy Warhol
AADHLOPSWY shadow play
AADHOOPRRT Arthropoda
AADIIINSTT antiaditis
AADIIKLNOP pinakoidal
AADIILLNST tillandsia
AADIILNNSS Nias Island
AADIILNOPT lapidation
AADIILNOTT dilatation
AADIILNOTV validation
AADIILNPRW Rawalpindi
AADIILORTU auditorial
AADIILPRST lapidarist
triapsidal
AADIILQRUV quadrivial
AADIILRTTU audit trail
AADIIMMNNU anima mundi
AADIIMNOPS dipsomania
AADIIMNORT admiration
AADIINNRRT triandrian
AADIINNSST Sandinista
AADIINORSU Dinosauria
AADIIOPRST parasitoid
AADIIPRSST aspidistra
AADIIRRSTV Stradivari
AADIJNORTU adjuration
AADIKMNOSS Damaskinos
AADIKMRSVZ vizard-mask
AADILLLRWZ wall lizard
AADILLMOPS plasmodial
AADILLMORS armadillos
AADILLOPSU palladious
AADILLORWY Roy Laidlaw
AADILNNNOS On an Island
AADILNOPRY Polyandria
AADILNOPTT top and tail
AADILNORST Rota Island
AADILNORTU durational
AADILNRSTT stand trial
AADILNSSUW duniwassal
AADILORSTU Australoid
AADILPRRTU ultra-rapid
AADIMMSSVY Sammy Davis
AADIMNNOOX Monaxonida
AADIMNNOPR prima donna
AADIMNNRST sand martin

AADIMNOOQU	quoad omnia
AADIMNORWY	dairywoman
AADIMNOSTY	mastodynia
AADIMNOSYZ	Ozymandias
AADIMNPRTY	pantrymaid
AADIMOPPRU	parapodium
AADINNNOST	andantinos
AADINORRUV	ouvirandra
AADINORTUW	wait around
AADIOOPSSY	oops-a-daisy
AADIOPRSTX	paradoxist
AADIOQRSUY	Quai d'Orsay
AADIORSTVY	advisatory
AADIQRRTUX	quadratrix
AADJMNNPRU	panjandrum
AADJMNOOSY	Joy Adamson
AADJORRTUY	adjuratory
AADKLMMPSU	damask plum
AADKLMNORW	random walk
AADKLNOOSY	look and say
	look-and-say
AADKLNORUW	walk-around
AADKMORSTU	durmast oak
AADLLNNOPT	Dalton plan
AADLLNOSTW	Dalton's law
AADLMNNNOS	No Man's Land
	no-man's-land
AADLMNNRUY	laundryman
AADLMNORTU	Laundromat®
AADLMNPSUY	Palm Sunday
AADLNOPRUY	play around
AADLNOQRSU	squadronal
AADLNSUYYZ	Lazy Sunday
AADMNOOOTT	odontomata
AADMNOORSU	anadromous
AADMNPSSUY	ampussy-and
AADNNORSUW	swan around
AADNOOPPSW	sappanwood
AADNOPRRUW	wraparound
AADOPPRSST	strappados
AAEEEFHRST	sea feather
AAEEEGGLLL	legal eagle
AAEEEGGLNR	green algae
AAEEEGGMMT	megagamete
AAEEEGGRTX	exaggerate
AAEEEGINRT	teeing area
AAEEEGKLNV	Lake Geneva
AAEEEGLLMT	mallee gate
AAEEEGLNOP	Palaeogene
AAEEEGLNRT	generalate
AAEEEGLSST	easselgate
AAEEEGMNRU	Eugene Aram
AAEEEGNRRW	wage-earner
AAEEEHHLRT	heather ale
AAEEEHKKMT	ka me, ka thee
AAEEEHRSST	heartsease
	heart's-ease
AAEEEILLMM	mealie meal
AAEEELLNOV	leave alone
AAEEELNPRS	paraselene
AAEEELRSTT	real estate
	real-estate
AAEEEMNNOS	sea anemone
AAEEEMORRT	araeometer
AAEEENRSST	Eastern Sea
AAEEENRSTU	ease nature
AAEEEPRSTX	exasperate
AAEEERSSTV	asseverate
AAEEFFGPRT	gaffer tape
AAEEFGIMRT	after-image
AAEEFGINTU	taeniafuge
AAEEFGLLLT	flagellate
AAEEFGMRSW	sewage farm
AAEEFGNNTT	enfant gâté
AAEEFHHLST	leaf-sheath
AAEEFHHSTW	wheat sheaf
AAEEFHLMSS	false shame
AAEEFHRSTV	aftershave
AAEEFKKQSU	Kafkaesque
AAEEFKLMRT	flea market
AAEEFKMMRR	frame-maker
AAEEFLLPRS	false pearl
AAEEFLMRTV	Malta fever
AAEEFLRSST	aftersales
AAEEFLRSSV	Lassa fever
AAEEFMRRTW	water frame
AAEEFOSSVW	Sea of Waves
AAEEFRSTTT	aftertaste
AAEEGGIPRT	arpeggiate
AAEEGGKORR	Karageorge
AAEEGGMSTU	steam gauge
AAEEGGPPRU	paper-gauge
AAEEGGRTUW	water gauge
AAEEGHLLRT	all the rage
AAEEGHLNOT	halogenate
AAEEGHLPRY	harpy eagle
AAEEGHRTWW	weather gaw
AAEEGIJNPT	Jean Piaget
AAEEGIKMMR	image-maker
AAEEGILMNN	emalangeni
AAEEGILNRV	evangeliar
AAEEGILNTT	gelatinate
AAEEGIMNRT	emarginate
AAEEGIMRRR	remarriage
AAEEGIMSSX	Sexagesima
AAEEGINPRT	repaginate
AAEEGINRTV	vegetarian
AAEEGIOPRT	Areopagite
AAEEGJMPST	James Paget
AAEEGKLRST	Great Lakes
AAEEGKMRRV	grave-maker
AAEEGLMNOP	epagomenal
AAEEGLMNPS	panel games
AAEEGLMPRS	palm-grease
AAEEGLNNNO	enneagonal
AAEEGLNRTW	angel-water
AAEEGLNTWY	tawny eagle
AAEEGMMNNT	management
AAEEGMMORR	aerogramme
	aérogramme
AAEEGMNNTT	game tenant
AAEEGMNRSS	manageress
AAEEGMPRST	master page
AAEEGNPRRR	prearrange
AAEEGNRSXY	sexagenary
AAEEGNSSSV	savageness
AAEEGQRRTU	quarterage
AAEEHHILRT	hartie-hale
AAEEHIKNST	take a shine
AAEEHIKRTT	take the air
AAEEHILLNN	Nehallenia
AAEEHILRTX	exhilarate
AAEEHIMPRY	hyperaemia
AAEEHIMPTT	epithemata
AAEEHIMRTT	Metatheria
AAEEHINSST	anesthesia
AAEEHIPRSS	aphaeresis
AAEEHIRSTW	washeteria
AAEEHKLORT	oak leather
AAEEHKPRTT	take the rap
AAEEHKQRTU	earthquake
	heart-quake
AAEEHLLMST	all the same
AAEEHLLNNT	Ethan Allen
AAEEHLLRTW	all-weather
AAEEHLMTVY	heavy metal
AAEEHLNNST	The Annales
AAEEHLNSTT	Aethelstan
AAEEHLNTTT	latent heat
AAEEHLNTVX	hexavalent
AAEEHLPRTT	earth-plate
AAEEHLSTTT	at the least
AAEEHMNORR	amenorrhea
AAEEHMNRTW	weatherman
AAEEHMPRST	metaphrase
AAEEHMPRTW	weather map
AAEEHNNRSW	Shane Warne
AAEEHNOSTT	eat one's hat
AAEEHNPRSV	Enver Pasha
AAEEHPTVWY	pave the way
AAEEHRRSTW	shearwater
AAEEHRRTTW	heartwater
AAEEHRTVWY	heavy water
AAEEIILNRS	Eilean Siar
AAEEIKLMNS	seamanlike
AAEEIKMNOS	make a noise
AAEEIKMNOT	ketonaemia
AAEEIKSTTY	take it easy
AAEEILLLRV	lavallière
AAEEILLMNN	nail enamel
AAEEILLQTU	illaqueate
AAEEILLRTT	alliterate
AAEEILMNNS	Melanesian
AAEEILMNSU	aes alienum
AAEEILMORT	ameliorate
AAEEILNPRT	penetralia
AAEEILNPVW	plain weave
AAEEILPRTU	eutrapelia
AAEEILRTTV	alterative
AAEEILRTVX	relaxative
AAEEILTUVV	evaluative
AAEEIMNNSX	Anaximenes
AAEEIMNRRW	Weimaraner

AAEEIMNRSU in a measure
AAEEIMPRSV sea vampire
AAEEIMRTWZ water maize
AAEEINPPRV papaverine
AAEEINPRRT pea-trainer
AAEEINPRSS paraenesis
AAEEINPRST inseparate
AAEEINSTUV nauseative
AAEEIOPRRS opera seria
AAEEIPPRRS reappraise
AAEEIPQRTU equiparate
AAEEIPRRTT repatriate
AAEEIPRRTV reparative
AAEEIPRSTV separative
AAEEIPRTTX expatriate
AAEEJJMNSS James Jeans
AAEEJLMNPR Jane Marple
AAEEJLRTVW Javel water
AAEEJNNSTU Jane Austen
AAEEJNPQSU Japanesque
AAEEJNPRSY Japanesery
AAEEJNQTTU Jaquenetta
AAEEJPRRSW jasperware
AAEEKLLRWY lake-lawyer
AAEEKLMPRT platemaker
AAEEKLMRYY Mary Leakey
AAEEKLNNRV Lake Vänern
AAEEKLNRSS Lake Nasser
AAEEKLPRSV parkleaves
AAEEKMMORR Mark O'Meera
AAEEKMMRTT meat market
AAEEKMPPRR paper-maker
AAEEKNRSTW water snake✧
AAEEKPRTTU take-up rate
AAEEKQRTUW waterquake
AAEELLLRVW Earl Wavell
AAEELLMSST matellasse
AAEELLNNSW Anna Sewell
AAEELLPRTY platelayer
AAEELLTTTT tattletale
AAEELMNOPT Ptolemaean
AAEELMNRST man-stealer
AAEELMPRRT marprelate
AAEELMPRTY team player
AAEELMPSTY Sympetalae
AAEELMQRSU square meal
AAEELMRRTT maltreater
tetrameral
AAEELNNPTU pennatulae
AAEELNPRRT parenteral
AAEELNPRTT tea planter
AAEELNPRTW water plane
AAEELNRRRW Earl Warren
AAEELOPPTY palaeotype
AAEELORSTY araeostyle
AAEELPRSTU at pleasure
AAEELPRSTY separately
AAEELPRTTT rattlepate
AAEELPRTTW water plate
AAEELRSTTZ lazarettes
AAEEMMNRRT rearmament
AAEEMNNSSU amanuenses
AAEEMNSSTT estatesman
man's estate
AAEEMORRTY araeometry
AAEEMRSSTT stearsmate
AAEEMSSSTT metastases
AAEENNPRSY Pyrenaeans
AAEENORRYY year-on-year
AAEENQRTTU quaternate
AAEENRRTTT retreatant
AAEENRSSTV tsesarevna
AAEENRSTTY asynartete
AAEENRSTVW water avens
AAEENRTTUV at a venture
AAEEPPRSTT state paper
AAEEPPRSTW waste paper
AAEEPRSSTW pease-straw
AAEERRSTXX Artaxerxes
AAEFFFTTTU tuftaffeta
AAEFFGILNY yaffingale
AAEFFHLLMO hall of fame
AAEFFHRSTT aftershaft
AAEFFILLNR farfalline
AAEFFILORV love affair
AAEFGGHRTU fraughtage
AAEFGHILNU half guinea
AAEFGIISTT fastigiate
AAEFGIMNOS Foaming Sea
AAEFGINNPR frangipane
AAEFGLLLNS Angel Falls
AAEFGLLLNT flagellant
AAEFGLMNRT fragmental
AAEFGLORWW wager of law
AAEFGLPRRY prayer flag
AAEFGPRRST grasp after
AAEFGRRSST aftergrass
AAEFHHLMRT health farm
AAEFHINRTT faint-heart
AAEFHKOORT heart of oak
AAEFHLLRYY half-yearly
AAEFHLNRRZ Franz Lehár
AAEFHPRSST spear-shaft
AAEFHRTTTY fatty heart
AAEFIKRRTT traik after
AAEFILLMTV vital flame
AAEFILLNRX fraxinella
AAEFILMMNY family name
AAEFILMNOU meiofaunal
AAEFILNNOT La Fontaine
AAEFILNNOV vienna loaf✧
AAEFIMRRRT terra firma
AAEFINPRST afterpains
AAEFKLOPSS soap flakes
AAEFKMNRRT tank-farmer
AAEFKPPRRT kraft paper
AAEFLLNOPT float plane
AAEFLLNPTU fault plane
AAEFLLNRST fallen star
AAEFLLNSTU fustanella
AAEFLLORRS solar flare
AAEFLLRSTW Fats Waller
AAEFLMPSTY safety lamp
AAEFLOPSTT soft palate
AAEFLOPSTZ false topaz
AAEFLRSSTT false start
AAEFMRRSTW afterswarm
AAEFMRSSTT fast stream
AAEFORRSTT after a sort
AAEGGGLNUV luggage-van
AAEGGGLSSU gauge glass
AAEGGHMNSY shaggy mane
AAEGGILLRV gillravage
AAEGGILNSW Glaswegian
AAEGGILOSU sialagogue
AAEGGILRRV gilravager
AAEGGIMNSV saving game
AAEGGINORT agrégation
AAEGGNOSTT gens togata
AAEGGPRRSU grape sugar
AAEGHHINRS shanghaier
AAEGHHIRTV have a right
AAEGHIKNTW wake a night
AAEGHILLSS Galashiels
AAEGHILMPS phlegmasia
AAEGHILNPR nephralgia
AAEGHILNRS angel's hair
AAEGHILORT hagiolater
AAEGHILPSY hypalgesia
AAEGHILRTU gaultheria
AAEGHIMMNO hemangioma
AAEGHINNNS shenanigan
AAEGHINNRT a near thing
AAEGHINNXY hexagynian
AAEGHINPTY Heptagynia
AAEGHIRSTT Ishtar Gate
AAEGHKLNRS angelshark
AAEGHKNOOR kohanga reo
AAEGHLMMNO gnamma hole
AAEGHLNNRS Langerhans
AAEGHLNOPT heptagonal
AAEGHLNPRY pharyngeal
AAEGHLOSTU hasta luego
AAEGHLPPSS splash page
AAEGHLPTWY play the wag
AAEGHMNOPR anemograph
phanerogam
AAEGHNPPRT pentagraph
AAEGHOPRRY aerography
areography
AAEGHORRTW growth area
AAEGHPPPRR graph paper
AAEGHRSSSV shave-grass
AAEGHRSUVY heavy sugar
AAEGHSSTUX exhaust gas
AAEGIILLNT genitalial
AAEGIILLNV villainage
AAEGIILPRS plagiarise
AAEGIILPRZ plagiarize
AAEGIIMNRR inmarriage
AAEGIINNTV invaginate
AAEGIINRTT ingratiate
AAEGIKLMPR magpie lark

AAEGIKMMRR magi-marker
AAEGILLMNO Galia melon
AAEGILLMNT ligamental
AAEGILLMQU maquillage
AAEGILLNOT allegation
AAEGILLPRS aspergilla
AAEGILLRSU sugarallie
AAEGILMNRT martingale
AAEGILMRRV River Glåma
AAEGILMSTT stalagmite
AAEGILNNTT tangential
AAEGILNOPT palagonite
AAEGILNRST sternalgia
AAEGILNRSV galvaniser
AAEGILNRVZ galvanizer
AAEGILNSWX sealing wax
AAEGILOPRS paralogise
AAEGILOPRZ paralogize
AAEGILPRTY apterygial
AAEGILRSSY Gail Sayers
AAEGIMNRRS misarrange
AAEGIMNRRV margravine
AAEGIMNRUV Ivan Mauger
AAEGIMNRVY Marvin Gaye
AAEGIMPRST pragmatise
Sparagmite
AAEGIMPRTZ pragmatize
AAEGIMRSTT magistrate
sterigmata
AAEGINNOST antagonise
AAEGINNOTZ antagonize
AAEGINNPTY Pentagynia
AAEGINNSTU nauseating
AAEGINOPRT paragonite
AAEGINORRT arragonite
AAEGINPRST paste-grain
AAEGINRTTV Gravettian
AAEGINRTTY Tetragynia
AAEGINRTUU inaugurate
AAEGINSSTT set against
AAEGINSTTT tea-tasting
AAEGIORRTV variegator
AAEGIRRSTV stravaiger
AAEGIRSTTV give a start
AAEGJORRST storage jar
AAEGKLLRVW gravel-walk
AAEGKLMNOS maskalonge
AAEGKLNSSS glass snake
AAEGKMNNOS maskanonge
AAEGKNRSSS grass snake
AAEGLLPSST plate glass
plate-glass
AAEGLLRRTY art gallery
AAEGLMNORT moral agent
AAEGLMORSU megalosaur
AAEGLMPRSU maple sugar
sugar maple
AAEGLNNOPT pentagonal
AAEGLNORRS argon laser
AAEGLNORTT tetragonal
AAEGLNRRTU granulater
AAEGLOPRSS opera glass
AAEGLPPRSS glasspaper
AAEGLPPRSU sugar apple
AAEGLPRRYY Gary Player
AAEGLRSSTW water glass
waterglass
AAEGMMNOST Mostaganem
AAEGMMPPUW wampumpeag
AAEGMNORST steam organ
AAEGMOPRSU rampageous
AAEGMRRSTT St Margaret
AAEGNNNORY nonagenary
AAEGNOPRST apron-stage
AAEGNORTWW water wagon
AAEGOPPRRT rapportage
AAEGOPRTTY Apterygota
AAEGPPRRSU sugar paper
AAEGPRRSSS spear grass
AAEHHILLLU halleluiah
AAEHHINTWY The Hay Wain
AAEHHJLLLU hallelujah
AAEHHKLRSW whale shark
AAEHHLLRTY Hal Hartley
AAEHHLNOPY hyalophane
AAEHHLPRTY hypaethral
AAEHHMNSTU Haemanthus
AAEHHRRSTU Arthur Ashe
AAEHIILMNS leishmania
AAEHIILNNT annihilate
AAEHIILRSV Rhea Silvia
AAEHIILTWW wait-a-while
AAEHIIMNOP hemianopia
AAEHIINOPT Aethiopian
AAEHIINPPT epitaphian
AAEHIIPSTT hepatitis A
AAEHIIRRRS hair-raiser
AAEHIKMNSZ Ashkenazim
AAEHIKPPSS speak a ship
AAEHIKRRST hairstreak
AAEHILLOPT palaeolith
AAEHILMMNP Manila hemp
AAEHILMNST The Animals
AAEHILNNOT anhelation
AAEHILNOPR eolian harp
AAEHILNOTX exhalation
AAEHILNRTX exhilarant
AAEHILRSVY Rhea Sylvia
AAEHIMMNOT methomania
AAEHIMNPRU Amphineura
AAEHIMNPRY hypermania
AAEHIMNPSS seamanship
AAEHIMNPST phantasime
AAEHIMNSTY myasthenia
AAEHIMOPXY hypoxaemia
AAEHIMOSST haematosis
AAEHIMRSTU amateurish
AAEHIMSTTU thaumasite
AAEHINNORV Hanoverian
AAEHIOTUVX à haute voix
AAEHIPPRTY apitherapy
AAEHIPRSST parathesis
AAEHIPSTXY asphyxiate
AAEHISTTTW tattie-shaw
AAEHISTTUW Watteauish
AAEHJLNORW Jean Harlow
AAEHJNOVYY have any joy
AAEHKLLMRT market-hall
AAEHKLNRRR Karl Rahner
AAEHLLMNOY hyalomelan
AAEHLLMRRS marshaller
AAEHLLRSWW wallwasher
AAEHLMOOPR Alpha Romeo®
AAEHLMRTTT lattermath
AAEHLNNOSS Hans Sloane
AAEHLNOPSY synaloepha
AAEHLNRRTX xenarthral
AAEHLOPPSY apophyseal
AAEHLORSTW shoal water
AAEHLORSUZ lazar house
AAEHLORTTY lay to heart
AAEHLPSSTU sulphatase
AAEHLPSSTW swash plate
AAEHLPSTTU spathulate
AAEHLSTTTX stealth tax
AAEHMNORRT marathoner
AAEHMNORST Thomas Arne
AAEHMNORTW earthwoman
woman-hater
AAEHMNRSST harassment
AAEHMNRSTV harvestman
AAEHMORTTX metathorax
AAEHMOSTTY stay-at-home
AAEHMPRSTT metaphrast
AAEHNNRSTU Tannhäuser
AAEHNOPRST anastrophe
AAEHNOPSWW weapon-shaw
AAEHNPPSWW wappenshaw
AAEHNPRSSS sans phrase
AAEHNPRSST trans-shape
AAEHNPRSTY pheasantry
sharny peat
AAEHPPRSSY paraphyses
AAEHPRRTTY art therapy
AAEIIILNST Italianise
AAEIIILNTZ Italianize
AAEIIKLLNS alkalinise
AAEIIKLLNZ alkalinize
AAEIIKLPRT trail a pike
AAEIIKNNTV take in vain
AAEIILLPTV palliative
AAEIILMMRT immaterial
AAEIILMNRS laminarise
seminarial
AAEIILMNRT Terminalia
AAEIILMNRZ laminarize
AAEIILMPTV ampliative
AAEIILMSST assimilate
AAEIILNNOT alienation
alineation
AAEIILNNST salientian
AAEIILNPST sapiential
AAEIILNPSY Ian Paisley

Words marked ✧ can also be spelled with one or more capital letters

AAEIILNSTV	insalivate
AAEIILPRST	partialise patrialise
AAEIILPRTZ	partialize patrialize
AAEIIMNNNR	Riemannian
AAEIIMNNRS	seminarian
AAEIIMNNRT	maintainer
AAEIIMNSST	Asian Times
AAEIIMOSTX	axiomatise
AAEIIMOTXZ	axiomatize
AAEIIMPPRR	primiparae
AAEIINRTUV	univariate
AAEIIPPRSV	appraisive
AAEIIPRSST	parasitise
AAEIIPRSTZ	parasitize
AAEIJLMNNV	javelin-man
AAEIJLNNUV	Juvenalian
AAEIJLNPPU	Alain Juppé
AAEIJLNRUY	Julian year
AAEIKLMNOZ	Amazon-like
AAEIKLMORT	tailormake
AAEIKLMRTY	Lake Taimyr
AAEIKLNSTY	like a tansy
AAEIKMNOPT	make a point
AAEIKMNPRR	Mark Napier
AAEIKMRSST	samarskite
AAEIKNNNOT	Neo-Kantian
AAEIKNPRST	painstaker
AAEIKNPRTT	take part in
AAEILLLMUX	maxillulae
AAEILLLNPR	in parallel
AAEILLLRST	saltarelli
AAEILLMNOP	animal pole
AAEILLMNOT	malleation
AAEILLMNPT	palliament
AAEILLMPRX	premaxilla
AAEILLMRTY	materially
AAEILLNORT	relational
AAEILLNRRT	all-terrain
AAEILLNRTU	unilateral
AAEILLNSTW	Eatanswill
AAEILLORTV	alleviator
AAEILLPRSU	au pis aller
AAEILLRRTT	trilateral
AAEILLRTTY	laterality
AAEILLRTVY	varietally
AAEILMMNNT	immanental
AAEILMNNSS	Las Meninas
AAEILMNNSU	semi-annual
AAEILMNPRT	parliament
AAEILMNPTU	manipulate
AAEILMNRRT	interramal mineral tar
AAEILMNRSU	aneurismal
AAEILMNRTT	alternatim
AAEILMNRTU	unmaterial
AAEILMNRTY	alimentary
AAEILMNRUV	Verulamian
AAEILMNRWX	mineral wax
AAEILMNSST	assailment
AAEILMORRT	Mariolater
AAEILMPRRT	premarital
AAEILMPRTU	multiparae
AAEILMPSST	metaplasis
AAEILMRSST	mare's-tails
AAEILMSTWW	Mawlawites
AAEILNNOPT	neapolitan✧
AAEILNNOTV	venational
AAEILNNRTU	Laurentian
AAEILNNRTW	Lawrentian
AAEILNOORT	areolation
AAEILNOPRS	personalia
AAEILNOPST	spaniolate
AAEILNOQTU	equational
AAEILNORST	senatorial
AAEILNORTT	alteration
AAEILNORTU	laureation
AAEILNORTV	venatorial Voltairean
AAEILNORTX	relaxation
AAEILNOTTX	exaltation
AAEILNOTUV	evaluation
AAEILNPRST	psalterian
AAEILNPSTT	plastinate
AAEILNRSTT	tantaliser
AAEILNRSTU	naturalise
AAEILNRSTW	water snail
AAEILNRTTZ	tantalizer
AAEILNRTUZ	naturalize
AAEILOPRRT	praetorial
AAEILOQRTU	equatorial
AAEILORRTT	retaliator
AAEILPPRRT	paper trail
AAEILPPRSS	paralipses
AAEILPPRST	epiplastra
AAEILPPRYZ	play a prize
AAEILPPSUV	applausive
AAEILPRRTV	River Plata
AAEILPRTVW	private law
AAEILQRSSU	square-sail
AAEILRSTTT	state trial
AAEILRSTTU	australite
AAEILSSTUV	assaultive
AAEILSTUXY	asexuality
AAEIMMNORT	metromania
AAEIMMNRST	main stream mainstream
AAEIMMNTTY	Tammanyite
AAEIMMPRTU	at a premium
AAEIMMRSTU	amateurism
AAEIMNNOPR	Pomeranian praenomina
AAEIMNNOSY	mayonnaise
AAEIMNNOTT	antimonate
AAEIMNNSSU	amanuensis
AAEIMNNTTT	attainment
AAEIMNOOQU	aequo animo
AAEIMNOORT	erotomania
AAEIMNOPPT	Papiamento
AAEIMNOPRS	marine soap
AAEIMNORTX	examinator
AAEIMNPPRS	panspermia
AAEIMNPRTZ	nitrazepam
AAEIMNQSTU	antimasque
AAEIMNRTTT	antimatter
AAEIMNRTVW	Vietnam War
AAEIMOSTTU	automatise
AAEIMOTTUZ	automatize
AAEIMPRSST	separatism
AAEIMQRSTU	marquisate
AAEIMQRSUU	seaquarium
AAEIMRRSST	Ramsar site
AAEIMRSTTU	traumatise
AAEIMRTTUV	maturative
AAEIMRTTUZ	traumatize
AAEIMSSSTT	metastasis
AAEINNNOTX	annexation
AAEINNNTTU	annuntiate
AAEINNORRT	enarration
AAEINNOTTV	annotative
AAEINNQRTU	quarantine
AAEINNRSST	Stannaries
AAEINNRTUV	avanturine
AAEINNSSST	Saint-Saëns
AAEINOPRRT	praetorian reparation
AAEINOPRST	separation
AAEINOPSST	passionate
AAEINOSTVX	tax evasion
AAEINPPRST	satin paper
AAEINPRRSW	Persian War
AAEINPRSTU	Pasteurian
AAEINQTTTU	quantitate
AAEINRRSTW	warrantise
AAEINRRTTZ	tartrazine
AAEINRSSTU	Russian tea
AAEINRTTTT	tarte tatin
AAEINRTTTU	attainture
AAEIOPRTTX	expatiator
AAEIOPSSTT	apostatise
AAEIOPSTTZ	apostatize
AAEIPRRSTX	separatrix
AAEIPRRTVW	private war
AAEIPRSSTT	separatist
AAEIPRSSTX	Paris, Texas
AAEIQRSSUU	Aquariuses
AAEJMMNOSS	James Mason
AAEJMNNOOT	Joe Montana
AAEJRSTTYY	Jay's Treaty
AAEKKMMRRS	maker's mark
AAEKKOSTTT	take to task
AAEKLLMNOR	Karl Malone
AAEKLMMORS	smoke alarm
AAEKLMRTYY	Lake Taymyr
AAEKLNPRST	ankle strap
AAEKMMRSST	mass market mass-market
AAEKMPRSTU	take up arms
AAEKMRSSTT	taskmaster
AAEKRRSTUU	sauerkraut
AAELLLLPRY	parallelly
AAELLLMNOS	salmonella

Words marked ✧ can also be spelled with one or more capital letters

AAELLLNPRU	unparallel
AAELLLORST	saltarello
AAELLLPSTT	stall plate
AAELLMNOPS	salmon leap
AAELLMNRTY	maternally
AAELLMORTT	martellato
AAELLMORZZ	mozzarella
AAELLMPPSU	slap-up meal
AAELLMPRTY	malapertly
AAELLMRSSW	small wares
AAELLNOPRS	solar panel
AAELLNOPRT	alloparent
AAELLNOSSY	seasonally
AAELLNPPRW	parpen-wall
AAELLNPRTY	parentally paternally
AAELLNPSTY	pleasantly
AAELLNRSTU	Stan Laurel
AAELLOSSWW	sea swallow
AAELLPRUVY	Paul Valéry
AAELLRSTTT	Tattersall
AAELMMPRTT	tramp metal
AAELMNNORT	ornamental
AAELMNNPUW	Paul Newman
AAELMNNRTU	unmaternal
AAELMNOPPW	apple-woman
AAELMNOPSU	menopausal
AAELMNORVV	removal van
AAELMNOSSW	saleswoman
AAELMNRRTW	trawlerman
AAELMNRSUY	aneurysmal
AAELMOOPTZ	Pelmatozoa
AAELMORRSS	serrasalmo
AAELMRRTUX	extramural
AAELNNNPRU	penannular
AAELNNOSSU	unseasonal
AAELNNPRTU	unparental
AAELNNPSTU	pennatulas unpleasant
AAELNNRRTU	Lana Turner
AAELNOPRUV	no par value
AAELNORRTT	alternator
AAELNORSTT	altar-stone
AAELNPPRTY	apparently
AAELNPPTTY	tap penalty
AAELNPRRSU	suprarenal
AAELNPRSTT	transeptal
AAELNPRSTY	pleasantry
AAELNPRTTW	water plant
AAELNPSTTY	yeast plant
AAELNRSTUV	transvalue
AAELNRSTUX	transexual
AAELOOPSTT	apostolate
AAELOPPRST	poles apart
AAELOPRSST	pastorales
AAELOPTTUU	plateau out
AAELORRSTX	extra-solar
AAELORRTTV	travelator
AAELORSTTZ	lazarettos
AAELPRRSTU	superaltar
AAELPRRTTT	rattletrap
AAELPRSSTY	party sales
AAELPRSSUU	as per usual
AAELSTTTUW	statute law
AAEMNNORTT	tramontane
AAEMNNRSTV	man-servant servant-man
AAEMNOOSST	anastomose
AAEMNPRSTT	apartments
AAEMNSTVVY	steam navvy
AAEMOORRST	motor areas
AAEMOPSSZZ	passamezzo
AAEMPPPRST	stamp paper
AAEMPRSSTT	past master
AAEMRSSTTU	metatarsus
AAENNNSTTY	nanny state
AAENNPPRTU	unapparent
AAENOPSWYY	pay one's way
AAENORRSSW	narrow seas
AAENORSSTT	assentator
AAENORTTTU	attenuator
AAENORTUUV	Art Nouveau
AAENPSSTTW	sweatpants
AAENQRRTUY	quaternary✧
AAENRRSTTU	restaurant
AAEOOPRRTV	evaporator
AAEOPPRRRT	preparator
AAEOPPRSUV	papaverous
AAEOPRRRTY	reparatory
AAEOPRRSTY	separatory
AAEOPRRUVW	vapourware
AAEOQRRTTU	a quarter to
AAEORRRSST	terra rossa
AAEORRSTTU	tartareous
AAEQRRSTUW	quarter-saw
AAEQRSTUUY	quaestuary
AAFFGIMNRU	ragamuffin✧
AAFFILLRTW	tariff wall
AAFFINRTTU	Tartuffian
AAFGGILNVW	flag-waving
AAFGIINNPR	frangipani
AAFGIJNNOU	Juan Fangio
AAFGILMNNT	Flamingant
AAFGINNRRT	infragrant
AAFGKLNRUU	Aufklärung
AAFGLLNRTY	flagrantly
AAFGLLOSST	float glass
AAFGLNNRTY	granny flat
AAFGLNRRTY	fragrantly
AAFGLORSST	float grass
AAFHHLRRSY	flash Harry
AAFHIINNOS	in a fashion
AAFHIMNNRU	infrahuman
AAFHIMORRS	Omar Sharif
AAFHLLORTT	for all that
AAFIIILRSS	filariasis
AAFIILLMRY	familiarly
AAFIILMNRU	unfamiliar
AAFIINRRTU	fruitarian
AAFIINRTVY	Vanity Fair
AAFIIRSSTU	safari suit
AAFILLLOPS	Pilao Falls
AAFILNOOTT	floatation
AAFILOPRSS	passiflora
AAFIMMORRS	samariform
AAFIMOORRS	afrormosia
AAFIOQRSTU	aqua fortis aquafortis
AAFMNOORST	sonata form
AAFMNORSTW	man of straw
AAFNRSTTTY	trans-fatty
AAGGHHINRT	hang a right
AAGGHINNRU	haranguing
AAGGHLNNSW	slang-whang
AAGGIILLNN	ilang-ilang
AAGGIINNRR	arraigning
AAGGIINNSY	gainsaying
AAGGIINRRT	air-grating
AAGGINRSTZ	stargazing
AAGGLLLOSS	galloglass
AAGGLLNNYY	ylang-ylang
AAGGMNOORR	organogram
AAGGNNOOWW	wonga-wonga
AAGGRRSSSU	sugar grass
AAGHHILLMR	Graham Hill
AAGHHIMNWY	highwayman
AAGHHJMNOR	John Graham
AAGHIIKNNT	think again
AAGHIILMNP	Malpighian
AAGHIINRVW	hair-waving
AAGHIKNQSU	quaking ash
AAGHILLLLN	hallalling
AAGHILMNPU	gnaphalium
AAGHILMNSW	Walsingham
AAGHILNPPR	planigraph
AAGHILNPST	phalangist
AAGHILOPPY	polyphagia
AAGHILORTY	hagiolatry
AAGHIMNORS	Ngaio Marsh
AAGHINNOST	Gosainthan
AAGHINPRSS	springhaas
AAGHIPPRSY	pasigraphy
AAGHLMOOPR	Lagomorpha
AAGHLNOPXY	xylophagan
AAGHMMMOPR	mammograph
AAGHMMNTUX	xantham gum
AAGHMNNTUX	xanthan gum
AAGHMOORTT	Otto Graham
AAGHMORSTY	Thomas Gray
AAGHNOPPRT	pantograph
AAGHNOPPTY	pantophagy
AAGHNRTUUU	Tungurahua
AAGHOPRSTY	Pythagoras
AAGHOPRTUY	autography
AAGIIILNRT	tagliarini
AAGIIINNRV	viraginian
AAGIIKLMNS	sailmaking
AAGIIKMNNR	rainmaking
AAGIIKNPRT	parakiting
AAGIILLNOT	alligation
AAGIILLNVY	availingly
AAGIILMPRS	plagiarism
AAGIILNNPS	salpingian

AAGIILNNUV unavailing
AAGIILNSSW wassailing
AAGIILPRST plagiarist
AAGIIMNOPR Parmigiano
AAGIIMNRST stigmarian
AAGIINNOPT pagination
AAGIINNOST sagination
AAGIINNOTV navigation
AAGIINPSTT pit against
AAGIJKLNWY jaywalking
AAGIKMNRST king-at-arms
AAGILLLNUU Anguillula
AAGILLMNRY alarmingly
marginally
AAGILLNOSZ gallinazos
AAGILLORSS glossarial
AAGILLSTTY sagittally
AAGILMNNSU sign-manual
AAGILMNOOR agronomial
AAGILMNORS organismal
AAGILMOPRS paralogism
AAGILNNOQU Algonquian
AAGILNNOTU angulation
AAGILNNRTU Alan Turing
AAGILNOPRS sporangial
AAGILNORTY gyrational
AAGILNOSTV solivagant
AAGILNPRTU tarpauling
AAGILNRRTU triangular
AAGILNRTUY angularity
AAGILOSUVY Yugoslavia
AAGILRSSSS sisal grass
AAGIMMNRWY Mary Wigman
AAGIMMPRST pragmatism
AAGIMMRSTT grammatist
AAGIMNNNRY Mary Anning
AAGIMNNOST antagonism
AAGIMNNPRW warming pan
AAGIMNPRSU sparganium
AAGIMNSSTY gymnasiast
AAGIMPRSTT pragmatist
AAGINNOOPR piano organ
AAGINNORTW wagon train
AAGINNOSTT antagonist
stagnation
AAGINNRRTW warranting
AAGINNRSUY sanguinary
AAGINOOPRZ Zaporogian
AAGINOORRT arrogation
AAGINOPRSS paragnosis
AAGINRRTVY gravy train
AAGINRSTTU antitragus
AAGLLMOOSU allogamous
AAGLLNOPTT topgallant
AAGLLNOSTT at long last
AAGLLNRRUY granularly
AAGLLOOSTW goat-sallow
AAGLMMOPSY plasmogamy
AAGLMNORSU granulomas
AAGLMOPSTY plastogamy
AAGLNNOOSX Anglo-Saxon
AAGLNNSTTY stagnantly
AAGLNOOSTY satanology
AAGLNORRTU granulator
AAGLNORRTY arrogantly
AAGLNOSTTY at long stay
AAGLNOTUVW wagon vault
AAGMMMNOWY mammy-wagon
AAGMOOSTUU autogamous
AAGOOPPRRT propagator
AAGOOPRRST Protagoras
AAGOOPSUYY pay-as-you-go
AAGORRRSSW arrow-grass
AAGRRRSSST starr grass
AAHHILMOPT ophthalmia
AAHHILORST aloha shirt
AAHHIMMMSS shammashim
AAHHIMRRTY arrhythmia
AAHHLORSTT throatlash
AAHHLOSSTT hash totals
AAHHLRRSTU last hurrah
AAHIIKLLMT Mikhail Tal
AAHIILLNOR rhinolalia
AAHIILNNOT inhalation
AAHIILNNTU Lithuanian
AAHIILNOPS Hispaniola
AAHIIMNOPP hippomania
AAHIIMNPRS airmanship
AAHIIMPRSS pharisaism
AAHIKNOOST Takashi Ono
AAHILLOPRT prothallia
AAHILLOPTW topi-wallah
AAHILMNSTU Malthusian
AAHILMOOTX homotaxial
AAHILMTTUZ altazimuth
AAHILNNOPT antiphonal
AAHILOPPSY apophysial
hypoplasia
AAHIMMNOTY mythomania
AAHIMOOPPR apomorphia
AAHINOPSTX xanthopsia
AAHINOSSTT thanatosis
AAHINPSTXY asphyxiant
AAHINRSTUV hantavirus
AAHIPPRSSY paraphysis
AAHISSTTTY it says that
AAHJKMPRRU rajpramukh
AAHKKNNPYY hanky-panky
AAHKLLLOOR Lalla Rookh
AAHKLMRSSY sky marshal
AAHKLORRSW ashlar-work
AAHKMORSTY matryoshka
AAHKOPTUUW pohutukawa
AAHLLLLNOW allhallown
AAHLLMOPSY hyaloplasm
AAHLLORSTU at all hours
AAHLMOPSTU potash alum
AAHLMOPSTY staphyloma
AAHLOPRSTY hyoplastra
AAHLPRTTWY Twyla Tharp
AAHMMNNOST Thomas Mann
AAHMNNORSW Norman Shaw
AAHMOOSTWY smooth away
AAHMOPRSST Ramphastos
AAHNNNOOTY hootananny
AAHNNRSTUY thysanuran
AAHNOPRTTU naturopath
AAHNORRSTU anarthrous
AAHNPRSTTY phantastry
AAHOPRRTTU Utahraptor
AAHPRSTTUU tatpurusha
AAHRSTTWWY thwartways
AAIIILMMNT militiaman
AAIIILMMNX Maximilian
AAIIILMNRT limitarian
AAIIILMNST Italianism
AAIIILNQRU Quirinalia
AAIIILNSTT Italianist
AAIIJJPPPP jippi-jappa
AAIIJKNSTT Tajikistan
AAIIJLNORT janitorial
AAIIJMOQRU Jamiroquai
AAIIKLLNTY alkalinity
AAIIKMNNST Kantianism
AAIILLNOPT palliation
AAIILLNPST plastilina
AAIILLNUXY uniaxially
AAIILMMNRT minimal art✧
AAIILMMRST martialism
AAIILMMSTX maximalist
AAIILMNNOT antimonial
lamination
AAIILMNOPT ampliation
AAIILMPRST partialism
patrialism
AAIILMRSTT martialist
AAIILNNSTT instantial
AAIILNNSTU Lusitanian
AAIILNORRT irrational
AAIILNORST solitarian
AAIILNORTV Voltairian
AAIILNOSTV salivation
AAIILNOTTT latitation
AAIILNPPZZ Lippizzana
AAIILNPSTU Paulianist
AAIILNRSTY sanitarily
AAIILNSTTV vital stain
AAIILPPRSS paralipsis
AAIILPRSTT partialist
AAIILPRTTY partiality
patriality
AAIILPSTTY spatiality
AAIILRRRRT tirra-lirra
AAIIMMNNOT immanation
AAIIMMNRST Martin Amis
AAIIMMNRSX Marxianism
AAIIMNNNOT antinomian
AAIIMNNOPT impanation
AAIIMNNRTU Ruminantia
AAIIMNPRTU panaritium
AAIIMNRSST Marianists
AAIIMNRSTU sanitarium
AAIIMNRSTZ Nazaritism

AAIIMNRTTV intra vitam
AAIIMPPRRS primiparas
AAIIMPRSST parasitism
AAIINNNOST nanisation
AAIINNNOTZ nanization
AAIINNOPTT patination
AAIINNOSTT sanitation
AAIINNQQUU quinaquina
AAIINNRRTU Ruritanian
AAIINNRSTY insanitary
AAIINNRTUV univariant
AAIINOPPRT apparition
AAIINOPRST aspiration
AAIINOPRTT patriation
tritanopia
AAIINORSTT air station
AAIINPTTVY Patavinity
AAIINQRSUV saquinavir
AAIINRSSTT sanitarist
AAIIPRSTTV vita patris
AAIIPRSTWY spirit away
AAIIRSSSTY satyriasis
AAIKKMORSV maskirovka
AAIKLPRSTV vital spark
AAIKORRSTW tarsia-work
AAILLLOPVW pillow lava
AAILLLPSTU Pulsatilla
AAILLMNNOZ Manzanillo
AAILLMORST tamarillos
AAILLMPRUU Plumularia
AAILLNNOOP Apollonian
AAILLNNOTY nationally
AAILLNNOVV Villanovan
AAILLNNSTT installant
AAILLNOPST spallation
AAILLNORTY notarially
rationally
AAILLOPRTY palliatory
AAILLRSTUY salutarily
AAILMMNNSU Mina Sulman
AAILMNNOPR nominal par
AAILMNNORS Roman snail
AAILMNOPRU Pulmonaria
AAILMNOTTU mutational
AAILMNPSSV Pan-Slavism
AAILMNRRTU intramural
AAILMNRSTU naturalism✧
AAILMNSSTU Stan Musial
AAILMOPPRX approximal
AAILMOPSTY polymastia
AAILMORRTY Mariolatry
AAILMPRSTU multiparas
AAILNNNOTU annulation
AAILNNOOTT notational
AAILNNOPTT plantation
AAILNNORRV non-arrival
AAILNNORTZ intrazonal
AAILNNOSTT altisonant
AAILNNOTTT altitonant
AAILNNOTTU nutational
AAILNNRTUY annularity
AAILNOORTT rotational
AAILNOPPTU papulation
AAILNOPRST Alain Prost
AAILNOPTTV pot-valiant
AAILNOPTUV vapulation
AAILNOPVVV Ivan Pavlov
AAILNOSTTU salutation
AAILNPQSTU pasquilant
AAILNPRSTU palustrian
AAILNPSSTV Pan-Slavist
AAILNRSSUY uranalysis
AAILNRSTTU naturalist
AAILNRSTUY insalutary
AAILNSSSTU Stanislaus
AAILOORRTV variolator
AAILOPRTTU partial out
AAILORSTTT altostrati
AAILPRSTTW straw-plait
AAILRSSTTY Lysistrata
AAILRSSTUV visual arts
AAIMMMNSTY Tammanyism
AAIMMORRSS marmarosis
AAIMMOSSTU miasmatous
AAIMMOSTTU automatism
AAIMMRSTTU traumatism
AAIMNNOOST nostomania
AAIMNNOOSW Ian Woosnam
AAIMNNORSY mansionary
AAIMNOORST inamoratos
AAIMNOOTTU automation
AAIMNOPRUV Paavo Nurmi
AAIMNOPTTU amputation
AAIMNOQSTU squamation
AAIMNORSTU sanatorium
AAIMNORTTU maturation
natatorium
AAIMNOSTUV mauvais ton
AAIMOORSTU amatorious
AAIMOSTTTU automatist
AAINNNOOST San Antonio
AAINNNOOTT annotation
AAINNORSXY synaxarion
AAINNRSTUY unsanitary
AAINOOPPRT protanopia
AAINOORSTT trio sonata
AAINOPRSSY passionary
AAINOPRSTW waist apron
AAINOPSTTY pay station
AAINOQRTTU quartation
AAINOQRTUZ quatorzain
AAINORSTTU saturation
AAINORSTTV starvation
AAINORSTTY stationary
AAINORSTUU saouari-nut
AAINOSTTWY way station
AAINPPRSTY spray paint
spray-paint
AAINPSTTWY panty-waist
AAIOPQRSTU paraquitos
AAIOPRRSTY aspiratory
AAIORRSTTT trattorias
AAJKKLNRSY Karl Jansky
AAKKLLTTYY talky-talky
AAKKLLTWYY walky-talky
AAKLMOPRSY karyoplasm
AAKLNORSUY ankylosaur
AAKMMNORSS mason's mark
AAKMMNORSW markswoman
AAKMNNORTY Mark Antony
AAKORRTTTU Turko-Tatar
AALLLLNNUU nulla-nulla
AALLLLOTWW wall-to-wall
AALLLMTUUW mutual wall
AALLMNORUY monaurally
AALLMNOTWY tallywoman
AALLMNTUUY autumnally
AALLOOSTTY loyal toast
AALLOPRSTY pastorally
AALLORSSUU Allosaurus
AALLPSSWYY palsy-walsy
AALLRSTTWY stalwartly
AALMMOOPSS plasmosoma
AALMNORSTY Lyon-at-arms
AALMOOPPRS malapropos
AALMOOPRTY laparotomy
AALMOPRSXY paroxysmal
AALMORRTYY Maryolatry
AALMPQRTUZ quartz lamp
AALNNNORTU non-natural
AALNNOOPST pantaloons
AALNNPRSTT transplant
AALNNRRSTU translunar
AALNOOPPRV on approval
AALNOOPUZZ pozzuolana
AALNOPRSST transposal
AALNOPRSTU unpastoral
AALNORRSTT translator
AALNPRRSUU supralunar
AALNPRTTUY play truant
AALOORRTTV travolator
AALOPRRSTU Australorp
AALOPSTTUY autoplasty
AALORRSTTY astrolatry
AALORSTTUY salutatory
AAMNNOTTTU tantamount
AAMNOOPRSY paronomasy
AAMNOOSTTU automatons
AAMNOPRTTU portmantua
AAMOOSSTTU astomatous
AAMORSSSUU Mosasaurus
AANOOPRSTU anatropous
AAOOPPRRST paratroops
AAOOPPRTTT potato trap
ABBBBEEYYY Bye Bye Baby
ABBBBEHLTU bubble bath
ABBBBINORY baby-ribbon
ABBBCEILNO bobbin lace
ABBBCEKLPU bubble pack
ABBBCEORRR robber crab
ABBBCIKRTU buck-rabbit
ABBBCLMOOT cobalt bomb
ABBBDDRUUU rub-a-dub-dub

ABBBDENRRU rubber band
ABBBDNOSSY Bobby Sands
ABBBDOORVY Bobby Davro
ABBBEELMNT babblement
ABBBEELORU Eurobabble
ABBBEELRSU sea blubber
ABBBEILNRU unbribable
ABBBEIRRRT Brer Rabbit
ABBBELOPSU soap bubble
ABBBELPRUW bubble wrap
ABBBEMOORY baby boomer
ABBBIIMSTT Babbittism
ABBCCDEKMO backcombed
ABBCCEKNOU bounce back
ABBCCKKLOS back-blocks
ABBCDEEHMR bedchamber
ABBCDEEILR edible crab
ABBCDEIMOY Bombycidae
ABBCDEKLOU double back
ABBCDELMNO candle bomb
ABBCDEMRRU breadcrumb
ABBCDKLOOR blockboard
ABBCDKMOUY Bombay duck
ABBCEEEIPY abbey-piece
ABBCEGGHUY beach buggy
ABBCEHLORS Bob Charles
ABBCEIKLOR back boiler
ABBCEILMNO combinable
ABBCEILRSU subcaliber
subcalibre
ABBCEINRSS crabbiness
ABBCEINSSS scabbiness
ABBCEINSTU subcabinet
ABBCEJKORW jabberwock✧
ABBCEJLLOT object ball
ABBCEKKLOR brake block
ABBCEKKSTU buck-basket
ABBCEKLRRY blackberry
ABBCEKMNRU back number
ABBCEKNRRU back burner
back-burner
ABBCELLNUU unclubable
ABBCELLOTU cobalt-blue
ABBCELMOPR parcel bomb
ABBCELNRUU uncurbable
ABBCELNUYY Cluny Abbey
ABBCEMOPRT carpet-bomb
ABBCENORSY absorbency
ABBCGIIKNT backbiting
ABBCGIIORT gabbroitic
ABBCHHOOTY booby hatch
ABBCIILLLY biblically
ABBCIILLNU unbiblical
ABBCIIRRTU barbituric
ABBCIKLNOR black robin
ABBCIKORRT rock rabbit
ABBCIMMOOT atomic bomb
ABBCKLLLUY black-bully
ABBCKNOTTU button-back
ABBCMOOOTT combat boot
ABBCNOORST Boston crab
ABBDDEEILO able-bodied
ABBDEEELNR Ben Bradlee
ABBDEEGILR bridgeable
ABBDEEHLPS pebbledash
ABBDEEIRRW barbed wire
ABBDEEKNOR doner kebab
ABBDEELNNU unbendable
ABBDEENORR bearer bond
ABBDEENRRU unbarbered
ABBDEERRRY breadberry
ABBDEFIORR fiberboard
fibreboard
ABBDEHINRS behind bars
ABBDEHIORY ride a hobby
ABBDEHRRRU hard rubber
ABBDEILLOR Barbie doll®
ABBDEILNRU blue riband
blue-riband
ABBDEILOUY Douay Bible
ABBDEILSUU subaudible
ABBDEIMNRY baby-minder
ABBDEIMORR bombardier
ABBDEINRSS drabbiness
ABBDEJLNOR land-jobber
ABBDEKLNOU double-bank
ABBDEKNNSU Bundesbank
ABBDELLNRU land-lubber
ABBDELNOST blond beast✧
ABBDELORSY absorbedly
ABBDELOSSU double bass
ABBDENORRW brown bread
ABBDGILLNY dabblingly
ABBDHORRSU broadbrush
ABBDILLNRT Bill Brandt
ABBDIMMORU radium bomb
ABBEEEILLV believable
ABBEEEJMSW James E Webb
ABBEEEKLLR bell beaker
ABBEEEKLRT bark-beetle
ABBEEELPRW pebble-ware
ABBEEELQSU babelesque
ABBEEELRRR beer-barrel
ABBEEELRRY barley-bree
ABBEEERTTT a better bet
ABBEEGILLR Gibberella
ABBEEGLMNT gabblement
ABBEEGNRTT Battenberg
ABBEEIKRRW Karrie Webb
ABBEEILLRR bearer bill
ABBEEILPPR Bible paper
ABBEEKRTTU butter-bake
ABBEELLRTT better-ball
ABBEELMNRT rabblement
ABBEELORSV observable
ABBEELRSTU bluebreast
ABBEELRTTU rebuttable
ABBEENORST breastbone
ABBEENORTW browbeaten
ABBEENRRSU base-burner
ABBEENRTTU butter bean
ABBEEORRTW browbeater
ABBEERRRUW rubberwear
ABBEFGNOOS bag of bones
ABBEFILNSS flabbiness
ABBEFMORRU foam rubber
ABBEGGLLRU bull-beggar
ABBEGKLNOT blanket bog
ABBEGNORTT Battonberg
ABBEGNRTTU Battenburg
ABBEHHIKSS shish kebab
ABBEHIKMOT Thabo Mbeki
ABBEHILORT rabbit hole
ABBEHINSSS shabbiness
ABBEHLLSUW Hubble's law
ABBEHLRSSU sable brush
ABBEHNORTW Bob Newhart
ABBEHOPRRS barbershop
barber-shop
ABBEHRSSUY Rhesus baby
ABBEIILMNO bibliomane
ABBEIIOSSS babesiosis
ABBEILLMSU sublimable
ABBEILMOPR improbable
ABBEILNORS ribbon-seal
ABBEILNOTU obnubilate
ABBEILNSSS slabbiness
ABBEILNTTU balbutient
ABBEILOPSY Bob Paisley
ABBEIRSTTY baby-sitter
ABBEJMPRUY baby-jumper
ABBEKLLRRU barrel-bulk
ABBEKLNOTT bottle bank
ABBEKLNOTX blanket box
ABBELLRSTU ball-buster
ABBELLRTTU butterball
ABBELMOORZ bamboozler
ABBELMSSUU subsumable
ABBELOORRY barley-broo
ABBELOPRTW pot-wabbler
ABBELORRTU rabble rout
ABBELORSVY observably
ABBEORTTTU butter-boat
ABBERRTTUY buttery-bar
ABBFFIILMU bumbailiff
ABBFHIIRST rabbitfish
ABBFILORST fibroblast
ABBGHINOTX bathing box
ABBGHINRRU rhubarbing
ABBGILNSTY stabbingly
ABBGILOOST obbligatos
ABBGINORTU bring about
ABBGINORTY bring to bay
ABBHIIMNOS Hobbianism
ABBHILMSUU Lubumbashi
ABBHILNOSY Babylonish
ABBHJNORTY John Bratby
ABBIILLORR Barbirolli
ABBILMOPRY improbably
ABBILORSTU suborbital
ABBIMMOSUX bob maximus
ABBINOPRTU rabbit upon
ABBLLNOTTU buttonball

ABCCCEFIOS beccaficos
ABCCCEMNUY accumbency
ABCCDEEIRT brecciated
ABCCDELNRU carbuncled
ABCCDHLNTU band-clutch
ABCCDIIINO niobic acid
ABCCDIIMOR bromic acid
ABCCDIIORS sorbic acid
ABCCDKNOOY cock-a-bondy
ABCCEEEIRT Rebeccaite
ABCCEEELNS albescence
ABCCEEENST tabescence
ABCCEEILMP impeccable
ABCCEEILSS accessible
ABCCEEIMRS Rebeccaism
ABCCEEIMRT bacteremic
ABCCEEKNRT centre-back
ABCCEELLOY bel-accoyle
ABCCEELLRY recyclable
ABCCEEPRSY cyberspace
ABCCEFFIKO back-office
ABCCEGOOTT cob cottage
ABCCEHILRU cherubical
ABCCEHIMOR ceramic hob
cibachrome
ABCCEHNNOO en cabochon
ABCCEIKKLN nickelback
ABCCEILLRU circulable
ABCCEILMPY impeccably
ABCCEILNOU bon accueil
ABCCEILORU corbiculae
ABCCEILSSY accessibly
ABCCEINOSU suboceanic
ABCCEIRSTU Beta Crucis
ABCCEKLOOT cockle boat
ABCCEKNORR cornerback
ABCCHIILMO choliambic
ABCCHIIMOR choriambic
ABCCHIIRRT tribrachic
ABCCHIKLNO block-chain
ABCCHIKLPT pitch-black
ABCCHIKSTT backstitch
ABCCHIKSTW switchback
ABCCHILOSU calico-bush
ABCCHILOTU coachbuilt
ABCCIKLTTU Kitcat Club
ABCCILLOSU social club
ABCCILNORU Bar Council
ABCCILORXY carboxylic
ABCCILRTUU cucurbital
ABCCIMOORT mobocratic
ABCCINORTU buccinator
ABCCINORTY corybantic
ABCCKLLOUY cockabully
ABCCMOPSTU subcompact
ABCCNOOPRY carbon copy
carbon-copy
ABCCNOORSY snobocracy
ABCDDEEHLU club-headed
ABCDDEEORR barred code
ABCDDEFIKL fiddleback
fiddle-back
ABCDDEIRUV David Bruce
ABCDDEKLOR badderlock
ABCDEEEELR decreeable
ABCDEEEILV deceivable
ABCDEEELLT delectable
ABCDEEELPR deprecable
ABCDEEELRT celebrated
ABCDEEELTT detectable
ABCDEEHLNU unbleached
ABCDEEHNRU unbreached
ABCDEEHRUY debauchery
ABCDEEIKRS bride's-cake
ABCDEEILLN declinable
ABCDEEILNS ascendible
ABCDEEILNU ineducable
ABCDEEILPR predicable
ABCDEEILPS despicable
ABCDEEILRT creditable
ABCDEEILVY deceivably
ABCDEEIOPR broadpiece
ABCDEEKLRV backvelder
ABCDEEKNOT boat-necked
ABCDEELLNO blonde-lace
ABCDEELLNY belly dance
ABCDEELLTY delectably
ABCDEELLUX excludable
ABCDEELMRS descramble
ABCDEELNUU uneducable
ABCDEELORR recordable
ABCDEENRTY cybernated
ABCDEFIKNR back-friend
ABCDEFIRTU bifurcated
ABCDEFOSTU obfuscated
ABCDEGKMOS gobsmacked
ABCDEGKORR rock-badger
ABCDEHIILR herbicidal
ABCDEHILSU child abuse
ABCDEHKMPU hump-backed
ABCDEHMORY brachydome
ABCDEHNNRU unbranched
ABCDEHOOPX pochade box
ABCDEHORSS chessboard
ABCDEHORSY body search
ABCDEIILMO biomedical
ABCDEIILNT indictable
ABCDEIILNV vindicable
ABCDEIIORT aborticide
bacterioid
ABCDEIKLRS backslider
ABCDEIKOUV bivouacked
ABCDEIKRST breadstick
ABCDEILLNU includable
ABCDEILORU Colubridae
ABCDEILPSY despicably
ABCDEILRTU traducible
ABCDEILRTY creditably
ABCDEILSTU subdialect
ABCDEIMORS Scombridae
ABCDEINORY binary code
ABCDEIPRRS crispbread
spider crab
ABCDEIRRRS bird-scarer
ABCDEIRSUV scuba diver
ABCDEJKOOT jackbooted
ABCDEKLOTU bucketload
ABCDEKMOSS mossbacked
ABCDEKOPRY body packer
ABCDEKORSU sea burdock
ABCDELMNRU Cumberland
ABCDELNNOO condonable
ABCDELRRSY scaldberry
ABCDEOORRS scoreboard
ABCDEOPRTY body carpet
ABCDEORSTU subcordate
ABCDGKNORU background
ABCDHIILNR brainchild
ABCDHINNRU nudibranch
ABCDHINORU chairbound
ABCDHIOOPR brachiopod
ABCDHLOORT broadcloth
ABCDHNOORT notch-board
ABCDHNOPRU punchboard
ABCDIILLSY disyllabic
ABCDIILNNU Indian club
ABCDIIMNOY biodynamic
ABCDIIMPRT bird impact
ABCDIIRSTY scabridity
ABCDIISTUY subacidity
ABCDIKLOWW black widow
ABCDIKOPRR drop a brick
ABCDILNOST cnidoblast
ABCDIOTVYY body-cavity
ABCDLMNOUY Monday Club
ABCDNNORRY cornbrandy
ABCDOORSST Broad Scots
ABCEEEELSS Celebes Sea
ABCEEEFFNO coffee bean
ABCEEEFLTT beef cattle
ABCEEEHLRW wheel brace
ABCEEEIKRR icebreaker
ABCEEEILNT enticeable
ABCEEEILPR pierceable
ABCEEEILRV receivable
ABCEEEINNS bienséance
ABCEEEJLRT rejectable
ABCEEELLRR cerebellar
ABCEEELLST selectable
ABCEEELNRS screenable
ABCEEELPTX expectable
ABCEEELTUX executable
ABCEEENRUX exuberance
ABCEEFHNNR French bean
ABCEEFIILN beneficial
ABCEEFINRV cabin fever
ABCEEFNORT benefactor
ABCEEGILLR clergiable
ABCEEGLLRY clergyable
ABCEEGNNOR bonne grâce
ABCEEHHKSS backsheesh
ABCEEHILNR hibernacle
ABCEEHJOPS Jacob sheep

ABCEEHKLPS	black sheep
ABCEEHKLST	sketchable
ABCEEHKNQU	bank cheque
ABCEEHKRTU	hackbuteer
ABCEEHLLRY	bellyacher
ABCEEHLLTT	bell the cat
ABCEEHLMRY	chamber-lye
ABCEEHLNQU	quenchable
ABCEEHLNSU	Chelsea bun
ABCEEHLSTU	subchelate
ABCEEHNORR	abhorrence
ABCEEHNRRY	cherry bean
ABCEEHORSU	herbaceous
ABCEEHRRST	Barchester
ABCEEIJLNT	injectable
ABCEEIKLNR	linebacker
ABCEEILLNR	reclinable
ABCEEILLNS	licensable
ABCEEILLPX	explicable
ABCEEILMMT	emblematic
ABCEEILMRR	Eric Ambler
ABCEEILNNU	enunciable
ABCEEILNOT	noticeable
ABCEEILNTU	binucleate
ABCEEILRTX	extricable
ABCEEIMNPR	cembra pine
ABCEEINNOZ	benzocaine
ABCEEINNST	abstinence
ABCEEIOPRV	above price
ABCEEJKLTU	bluejacket
ABCEEJMRSU	James Bruce
ABCEEJNSST	abjectness
ABCEEKLRTT	backletter
ABCEEKORRV	break cover
ABCEEKRRRY	crakeberry
ABCEEKRSTT	backstreet
ABCEEKSTTU	bucket seat
ABCEELLORT	brocatelle
ABCEELLPUX	exculpable
ABCEELLRRY	cerebrally
ABCEELNNOV	convenable
ABCEELNOTT	balconette
ABCEELNOVY	conveyable
ABCEELNRRU	uncerebral
ABCEELNRSU	censurable
ABCEELOPRU	recoupable
ABCEELOPRW	pace-bowler
ABCEELORRT	celebrator
ABCEELORTV	table cover
ABCEELOSTT	case-bottle
ABCEELPTXY	expectably
ABCEELRTVV	velvet-crab
ABCEEMRSTU	Burmese cat
ABCEENOPRR	reprobance
ABCEENOPRS	spaceborne
ABCEENOPRT	Cape Breton
ABCEENORSV	observance
ABCEENRUXY	exuberancy
ABCEEOPPRS	space probe
ABCEEPRSTT	spectre bat
ABCEERRRTU	carbureter
ABCEFFHISS	Schiff base
ABCEFHINOR	chief-baron
ABCEFHINRZ	zebra finch
ABCEFHNORT	beachfront
ABCEFIKLPU	backup file
ABCEFILLOT	olfactible
ABCEFILNNO	confinable
ABCEFILORT	clofibrate
ABCEFLNOSU	confusable
ABCEFLNOTU	confutable
ABCEFRSSUU	subsurface
ABCEGGKLOU	block gauge
ABCEGHIMNR	chambering
ABCEGHISTT	the big cats
ABCEGILNOS	cognisable
ABCEGILNOZ	cognizable
ABCEGINNNY	benignancy
ABCEGKLOSW	swage block
ABCEGLNOOT	conglobate
ABCEGNOORR	Roger Bacon
ABCEHHJOTT	hatchet job
ABCEHHLLTU	health club
ABCEHHNNOU	haunch bone
ABCEHHORTY	Tycho Brahe
ABCEHIIMRS	Hebraicism
ABCEHIIRST	Hebraistic
ABCEHIKLNT	in the black
ABCEHIKNRS	Reichsbank
ABCEHIKPST	chip basket
ABCEHIKRRT	brick-earth
ABCEHILNNR	branch line
ABCEHILORW	elbow-chair
ABCEHILPRT	birthplace
ABCEHILRST	Christabel
ABCEHIMNOR	Mainbocher
ABCEHIMNRT	Chambertin
ABCEHIMNTU	Buchmanite
ABCEHIMOPT	baphometic
ABCEHIMORT	bichromate
ABCEHIMRRT	hermit crab
ABCEHINNRV	vine-branch
ABCEHINORR	chairborne
ABCEHINRRY	chinaberry
ABCEHIOOPR	aerophobic
ABCEHIPPRR	paper-birch
ABCEHIPRRY	hyperbaric
ABCEHIPRTY	hyperbatic
ABCEHJKSTU	bush jacket
ABCEHKLORT	heart block
ABCEHKLOSU	black house
ABCEHKPRSY	Becky Sharp
ABCEHLLNTU	lunch-table
ABCEHLLOTT	tablecloth
ABCEHLMOOP	peach-bloom
ABCEHLNRSS	branchless
ABCEHLPSUU	Bucephalus
ABCEHMMNRU	Mach number
ABCEHMOPRT	chamberpot
ABCEHMORST	storm beach
ABCEHNORRY	abhorrency
ABCEHNRSTU	subchanter
ABCEHOQRSU	quebrachos
ABCEHORTTX	chatterbox
ABCEHPRSTU	subchapter
ABCEHRRSTU	subcharter
ABCEHRSTTU	bruschetta
ABCEIIJNOS	Jacobinise
ABCEIIJNOZ	Jacobinize
ABCEIILLMT	bimetallic
ABCEIILLNN	inclinable
ABCEIILLNR	brilliance
ABCEIILMTU	umbilicate
ABCEIILNOS	insociable
ABCEIILPST	epiblastic
ABCEIINTUV	incubative
ABCEIIOORT	aerobiotic
ABCEIISSTU	sea biscuit
ABCEIISTTU	tea biscuit
ABCEIJLOTV	objectival
ABCEIKKMRR	brickmaker
ABCEIKKRST	strike back
ABCEIKKSTY	stickybeak
ABCEIKLNPU	unpickable
ABCEIKLRRY	bricklayer
ABCEIKLRSV	silverback
ABCEIKNNOV	Kevin Bacon
ABCEIKNPRU	Purbeckian
ABCEILLMOP	compliable
ABCEILLNOU	inoculable
ABCEILLNPU	Alpine Club inculpable
ABCEILLNRS	cranesbill crane's bill crane's-bill
ABCEILLSSU	casus belli
ABCEILLSUV	Savile Club
ABCEILLTUV	cultivable
ABCEILMOPT	compatible
ABCEILMRUY	embryulcia
ABCEILMSTU	table music
ABCEILNNSU	incunables
ABCEILNOSU	unsociable
ABCEILNOTY	noticeably
ABCEILNPRU	republican✧
ABCEILNRRU	incurrable
ABCEILPRTY	liberty cap
ABCEILRSTU	subarticle
ABCEIMNRTT	mitten-crab
ABCEIMOORT	macrobiote
ABCEIMORRT	barometric
ABCEINNSTY	abstinency
ABCEINORSS	escribanos
ABCEINOSTU	Count Basie
ABCEINRRST	transcribe
ABCEIOORRT	bioreactor
ABCEIORSUU	rubiaceous
ABCEIRRRSU	subcarrier
ABCEJKLMRU	lumberjack
ABCEJKLOTT	bottle jack
ABCEKKLMOS	smoke-black
ABCEKKORRW	backworker
ABCEKKORST	backstroke

Words marked ✧ can also be spelled with one or more capital letters

ABCEKLLNOP	block plane
ABCEKLLNOU	unlockable
ABCEKLLOOR	cellar-book
ABCEKLLOWY	yellowback
ABCEKLMNOY	black money
ABCEKLNNPY	penny black
ABCEKLNORU	coal bunker
ABCEKLNOST	Black Stone
ABCEKLOPRW	black power✧
ABCEKLPRSU	Pearl S Buck
ABCEKLRTTU	turtleback
ABCELLLORS	scrollable
ABCELLLORU	blue-collar
ABCELLNOOR	collarbone
ABCELLNOOS	consolable
ABCELLOORS	Carlos Belo
ABCELLOORU	colourable
ABCELLOOST	blastocoel
ABCELLOSTU	leucoblast
ABCELLRTUU	culturable
ABCELMMNOO	commonable
ABCELMMOTU	commutable
ABCELMMPRU	lumber-camp
ABCELMNOSU	consumable
ABCELMNRSU	unscramble
ABCELMOPTU	computable
ABCELMOSTU	customable
ABCELMRSTU	clubmaster
ABCELMRTTU	tumble cart
ABCELNORRY	barleycorn
ABCELNOSTU	locust bean
ABCELNRSTU	subcentral
ABCELNRSUU	subnuclear
ABCELNRSUY	censurably
ABCELOOPRV	provocable
ABCELOPPRY	clapperboy
ABCELOPRRU	procurable
ABCELORRRY	coral berry
ABCELRRTUU	tubercular
ABCELSTUUY	subacutely
ABCEMNRRTU	burnt cream
ABCEMOOPRT	amboceptor
ABCEMOSSUU	submucosae
ABCEMTUUUV	vacuum tube
ABCENNNNOO	cannon bone
ABCENNSSTU	subnascent
ABCENNSTUY	subtenancy
ABCENOOPTU	ponce about
ABCENOPUUY	upbuoyance
ABCENORSST	crab-stones
ABCENORSTY	corybantes
ABCENORSUW	brown sauce
ABCENORSVY	observancy
ABCENORTTU	obtruncate
ABCENPSSTU	substance P
ABCENRRTUY	canterbury✧
ABCEOORRST	Serbo-Croat
ABCEORRRTU	carburetor
ABCEORRRTY	Robert Cray
ABCEOSSSUY	byssaceous
ABCERRSTTU	subtracter
ABCFGHIIIO	Fabio Chigi
ABCFILMORU	baculiform
ABCFKLORST	black frost
ABCGHIIOPR	biographic
ABCGHIKLLT	black light
ABCGHKLOPU	plough back
ABCGHLORYY	brachylogy
ABCGHNORYZ	zygobranch
ABCGHNRSSU	bunch grass
ABCGIILLOO	biological
ABCGIINRTT	bratticing
ABCGIKNOPX	packing box
ABCGILMNRS	scrambling
ABCGILNOSY	cognisably
ABCGILNOYZ	cognizably
ABCGKLNORT	block grant
ABCHHILOTT	habit-cloth
ABCHHIOPRS	archbishop
ABCHHJNNOU	John Buchan
ABCHHLMTTU	thumb latch
ABCHIILMOP	amphibolic
ABCHIILOOT	halobiotic
ABCHIILOPS	basophilic
ABCHIILOTT	batholitic
ABCHIILTTY	bathylitic
ABCHIINOTU	tibouchina
ABCHIKLMST	blacksmith
ABCHIKLRST	Black Shirt
	Blackshirt
ABCHILTTUY	yacht-built
ABCHIMMNSU	Buchmanism
ABCHIMNORW	brahmin cow
ABCHIMOORZ	Chimborazo
ABCHIMORSU	choriambus
ABCHINOOPY	cynophobia
ABCHIOPPSS	bishop's cap
ABCHIORTYY	charity-boy
ABCHJKNOSU	John Backus
ABCHKKOOTU	chukka boot
ABCHKLLOTU	tchoukball
ABCHKLNORT	blackthorn
ABCHKNORRW	branch-work
ABCHKOOSTW	swatchbook
ABCHNOORSY	Anchor Boys
ABCHNOORUY	anchor buoy
ABCHNORRTU	turnbroach
ABCIIILNST	albinistic
ABCIIINOTT	antibiotic
ABCIIJMNOS	Jacobinism
ABCIIJMOST	Jacobitism
ABCIILLNRY	brilliancy
ABCIILLOTY	biotically
ABCIILLSST	ballistics
ABCIILMOPS	bioplasmic
ABCIILNOOT	bilocation
ABCIILRTUY	curability
ABCIIMNOSS	Ambisonics®
ABCIIMOORT	microbiota
ABCIIMRSST	strabismic
ABCIINNOTU	incubation
ABCIINORRT	cribration
ABCIINOSSS	abscission
ABCIINRSTU	urbanistic
ABCIJKKLSY	Jack S Kilby
ABCIJKOOTT	jackboot it
ABCIJNNOTU	abjunction
ABCIKLLORY	rockabilly
ABCIKLMOTV	black vomit
ABCIKLORVY	ivory-black
ABCIKNNORS	carbon sink
ABCIKNORRT	rick-barton
ABCIKNPRSW	spawn brick
ABCILLMOSY	symbolical
ABCILLNPUY	inculpably
ABCILLRRUY	rubrically
ABCILLRTUU	bicultural
ABCILMOPTY	compatibly
ABCILMOSTY	myoblastic
ABCILMOSUX	musical box
ABCILMRUUV	vibraculum
ABCILNNOPT	Pinot Blanc
ABCILNOORS	Sorbonical
ABCILNOOTT	bolt-action
ABCILNORSU	binoculars
ABCILNOSUY	unsociably
ABCILORRTU	lubricator
ABCILORTUY	royal cubit
ABCILOSTUV	vocabulist
ABCIMNOORS	coram nobis
ABCIMOSSTU	subatomics
ABCINORTUY	incubatory
ABCIORRRTU	rubricator
ABCIPPRSUU	suprapubic
ABCKKNOOTU	knock about
	knockabout
ABCKLLOOWY	woollyback
ABCKLMPSTU	black stump
ABCKNPRTUY	bankruptcy
ABCKOOSSUY	ya-boo sucks
ABCKPRSTUY	bucks party
	bucks' party
	buck's party
ABCLLOORUY	colourably
ABCLMMRUUU	umbraculum
ABCLMOSSUU	submucosal
ABCLNOOTUW	clown about
ABCLORRTUU	lucubrator
ABCLORRTUY	Rotary Club
ABCLORSSUY	scabrously
ABCLOSSTTY	blastocyst
ABCLPRSTTU	Pratt's Club
ABCLRSSTUU	subcrustal
ABCNNOOPTU	punto banco
ABCNNRRTUU	currant bun
ABCNOORRTU	court-baron
ABCOOSTTUU	scout about
ABCORRSTTU	subtractor
ABDDDENORW	Edward Bond
ABDDEEEFLN	defendable
ABDDEEEHNO	bone-headed
ABDDEEELNP	dependable
ABDDEEGGLR	bedraggled

ABDDEEGHIR bridgehead
ABDDEEGIOR biodegrade
ABDDEEGIRR Red Brigade
ABDDEEHLLU bull-headed
ABDDEEHLOO beadlehood
ABDDEEHMOR hebdomader
ABDDEEIMNS base-minded
ABDDEEINTT bidentated
ABDDEEIRTT bearded tit
ABDDEELNPY dependably
ABDDEELRST bestraddle
ABDDEENRRU undebarred
ABDDEFILSS bass fiddle
ABDDEGHKOU dough-baked
ABDDEGILNR land bridge
ABDDEGINRU unabridged
ABDDEGIORR road bridge
ABDDEGIRRW drawbridge
ABDDEHHINN behindhand
ABDDEHILLR hard-billed
ABDDEHILNR bridle-hand
ABDDEHILOR hard-boiled
ABDDEHNORY hard done by
ABDDEIIMRS bridesmaid
bride's-maid
ABDDEIIOVW David Bowie
ABDDEILLLS saddlebill
ABDDEILORR bridle-road
ABDDEINNRS sand-binder
ABDDEINRVY David Byrne
ABDDEIORSS sideboards
ABDDELMORU Boulder Dam
ABDDELNOOS Dane's blood
ABDDELNORR borderland
ABDDELNRTU bladder nut
ABDDELORSW sword-blade
ABDDENORRU under-board
ABDDERSSSU address bus
ABDDERSTUY bread study
ABDDFGLNOO Band of Gold
ABDDGGINPU pudding bag
ABDDHHIIRW whidah bird
ABDDHHIRWY whydah bird
ABDDHLNOOY bloody hand
ABDDHNRSUY dandy-brush
ABDDIIOORT idiot board
ABDDILLORR dollarbird
ABDDINOORU in bad odour
ABDDLMOORU mouldboard
ABDDNOORSU soundboard
ABDDOORRSW broadsword
ABDEEEEHLT beetlehead
ABDEEEELMR redeemable
ABDEEEFHRT feather bed
featherbed
ABDEEEFILS defeasible
ABDEEEFLRR deferrable
ABDEEEFRST breastfeed
ABDEEEGGLR barelegged
ABDEEEGLLP pledgeable
ABDEEEGNRR beer garden
ABDEEEHLNT needle-bath
ABDEEEHNRV heaven-bred
ABDEEEILLL belle laide
belle-laide
ABDEEEILLN delineable
ABDEEEILMR remediable
ABDEEEILRT deliberate
ABDEEEINRV aberdevine
ABDEEEKLNN needle bank
ABDEEELLPT depletable
ABDEEELLVV bleed valve
ABDEEELMRY redeemably
ABDEEELNPX expendable
ABDEEELNRR renderable
ABDEEELNRZ land breeze
ABDEEELNTX extendable
ABDEEELRYY bleary-eyed
ABDEEELSTT detestable
ABDEEEMNST debasement
ABDEEEMNTT debatement
ABDEEENRTT Bernadette
ABDEEENRUV unbeavered
ABDEEEPRST breast-deep
ABDEEERSTW sweetbread
ABDEEFFHLU bufflehead
ABDEEFGILN bad feeling
ABDEEFGILR leaf-bridge
ABDEEFHNOR beforehand
ABDEEFIKNR bread knife
ABDEEFLMOR deformable
ABDEEFLNRU refundable
ABDEEFOORT barefooted
ABDEEFRSST Fred Basset
ABDEEGGIRT tiger badge
ABDEEGHIRT big-hearted
ABDEEGHNRR herb garden
ABDEEGHRRR herb Gerard
ABDEEGILNS designable
ABDEEGILRT ledger bait
ABDEEGINNW winged bean
ABDEEGLNOR Golden Bear
ABDEEGLNUW unwedgable
ABDEEGLORT gold-beater
ABDEEGORRV verge-board
ABDEEHIKNR Birkenhead
ABDEEHILLS déshabillé
ABDEEHILLT billet-head
ABDEEHILLV ill-behaved
ABDEEHILPS beadleship
ABDEEHILRR halberdier
ABDEEHIMRT timberhead
ABDEEHIMSV misbehaved
ABDEEHIRTW whitebeard
white bread
ABDEEHJRST J H Breasted
ABDEEHLLPS bell-shaped
ABDEEHLLTU bullet-head
ABDEEHLOTT bottle-head
table d'hôte
ABDEEHLTTY hye-battel'd
ABDEEHMMRU head-bummer
ABDEEHNNOT bonnethead
ABDEEHNRTU unbreathed
ABDEEHORRS horse-bread
ABDEEHORST broadsheet
ABDEEIILTT debilitate
ABDEEIKNNY kidney bean
ABDEEILLMR mallee-bird
ABDEEILLST ill bestead
ABDEEILMRY remediably
ABDEEILNNU undeniable
ABDEEILNRU unrideable
ABDEEILNUW unbewailed
ABDEEILORR rear-boiled
ABDEEILPRU repudiable
ABDEEILPRV deprivable
ABDEEILPSS despisable
ABDEEIMNTY amenity bed
ABDEEIMRRT time-barred
ABDEEIMRTX ambidexter
ABDEEINNOR debonnaire
Edna O'Brien
ABDEEINNRR Bernardine
ABDEEIOPRT paedotribe
ABDEEIORUV de Beauvoir
ABDEEIRRVW weaver bird
ABDEEISTTU beatitudes
ABDEEISTTV Bette Davis
ABDEEKLOOS sealed book
ABDEEKLOTU double take
ABDEEKOPPY Pobedy Peak
ABDEEKORRY keyboarder
ABDEEKRRRT kerb-trader
ABDEELLLNU unlabelled
ABDEELLMRU umbrellaed
ABDEELLMTU umbellated
ABDEELLOPR deplorable
ABDEELLOUX double axel
ABDEELLPSU spuleblade
ABDEELLSTY sell-by date
ABDEELMRRU demurrable
ABDEELNOPR ponderable
ABDEELNORS endorsable
ABDEELNPXY expendably
ABDEELOPTX box-pleated
ABDEELORTT battledore
ABDEELPRRU perdurable
ABDEELRSTU balustered
ABDEELRTUX extrudable
ABDEELSTTY detestably
ABDEEMOOOR oboe d'amore
ABDEEMORRY emery board
ABDEENOPSU subpoenaed
ABDEENOSSY beyond seas
ABDEENPRRY prebendary
ABDEENRSUY subdeanery
ABDEENRTTU unbattered
ABDEENRTUY unbetrayed
ABDEEOORVW beaver-wood
ABDEFFRSTU breadstuff
ABDEFGIRRT raft-bridge
ABDEFHILLN fall behind

ABDEFHILOR hold a brief
ABDEFHNOOP Band of Hope
ABDEFIILMO modifiable
ABDEFIIMRT fimbriated
ABDEFIKLRU brake fluid
ABDEFIKNOR knife-board
ABDEFILMOR formidable
ABDEFILMRU amber fluid
ABDEFILNOS bed of nails
ABDEFINRSS Fassbinder
ABDEFIRRRT rafter-bird
ABDEFIRRTU breadfruit
ABDEFLLOTU double flat
ABDEFLNORU unfordable
ABDEFLOORT after blood
ABDEFLORST Stableford
ABDEGGIRRU budgerigar
ABDEGGNOOT tobogganed
ABDEGHINSU subheading
ABDEGHIORW weighboard
ABDEGHOOTT go to the bad
ABDEGHORTU dearbought
ABDEGIILOR Logie Baird
ABDEGIINNR brigandine
ABDEGILNSY debasingly
ABDEGILNTY debatingly
ABDEGIMNRT abridgment
ABDEGIMRRU Bermuda rig
ABDEGINORY reading-boy
ABDEGIRRTW Bridgwater
ABDEGLMMRU lambeg drum✧
ABDEGLOSTT bottled gas
ABDEHIILLS dishabille
ABDEHIKLLW hawk-billed
ABDEHILNSU Danish blue
ABDEHILPRT bridlepath
ABDEHIMRTU thumb a ride
ABDEHINORT hot-brained
ABDEHINRRS brandisher
ABDEHINRTT hard-bitten
ABDEHIORTW whiteboard
ABDEHIRRSU airbrushed
ABDEHIRSSU brush aside
ABDEHLLOOY ballyhooed
ABDEHLOORT heart-blood
ABDEHNORRS shard-borne
ABDEHNORTU earthbound
ABDEHNRSTU Bundesrath
subtrahend
ABDEHNRTUY Thunder Bay
ABDEHOPRUY Prudhoe Bay
ABDEHORRST shortbread
ABDEHORTTU outbreath'd
ABDEHOSUWY bawdy-house
ABDEIIKLLS dislikable
ABDEIILMPS bipedalism
ABDEIILMSS admissible
ABDEIILNOT delibation
ABDEIILOST tabloidise
ABDEIILOSX oxidisable
ABDEIILOTZ tabloidize
ABDEIILOXZ oxidizable
ABDEIILPSS dissipable
ABDEIIMNNR bear in mind
ABDEIITTUV dubitative
ABDEIKLNNS blind snake
ABDEIKNNRR André Brink
ABDEIKQRRU Quaker-bird
ABDEIKRTTU dika-butter
ABDEILLLNY blind alley
blind-alley
ABDEILLLSY disyllable
ABDEILMNRT timberland
ABDEILMSTU sublimated
ABDEILNNUY undeniably
ABDEILNOPY pineal body
ABDEILNORY debonairly
ABDEILNRSW swear blind
ABDEILNSUY unbiasedly
ABDEILOPRV providable
ABDEILOPSS disposable
ABDEILORTT trilobated
ABDEILPSTU disputable
ABDEILRTTW wattlebird
ABDEIMNRST disbarment
ABDEIMNSTU submediant
ABDEIMORZZ morbidezza
ABDEIMRRTY timberyard
ABDEIMRSSY bradyseism
ABDEIMRTUW dumb waiter
ABDEINNOTU unobtained
ABDEINOSSU buenos dias
ABDEINPSTU bite and sup
unbaptised
ABDEINPTUZ unbaptized
ABDEINRTTU turbinated
ABDEJORSTT objets d'art
ABDEKLLOTU Double Talk
double-talk
ABDEKLOPRU double-park
ABDEKMOORS smokeboard
ABDEKNNRSU sand bunker
ABDELLNSUY buy and sell
ABDELLOOPT blood-plate
ABDELLOPRY deplorably
ABDELLOPUY double play
ABDELLORST Lord's table
ABDELLOSTU double salt
ABDELMMOOT Tom o' Bedlam
ABDELMNOUY Blue Monday
ABDELMOPUY Paul Dombey
ABDELMORST blastoderm
ABDELMRRUY lumber-yard
ABDELNOORS bandoleros
ABDELNOPSU spauld-bone
ABDELNORTU round table✧
round-table
ABDELNORUU unlaboured
ABDELNOSUV unabsolved
ABDELOORST stable door
ABDELOORTT battledoor
ABDELOOSTW sweat blood
ABDELORSTU double star
ABDELORTUY obdurately
ABDELPRRUY perdurably
ABDEMNORRS roberdsman
ABDEMORRWY body-warmer
ABDENOORUV overabound
ABDENOPPRU paperbound
ABDENORRST sternboard
ABDENORTUW bound water
water-bound
ABDENRSSSU absurdness
ABDENRSSTY standers-by
ABDENSSTUY Sunday best
ABDEOORRTT otter-board
ABDEOORRTU order about
ABDEOPRRST port de bras
spot-barred
ABDEORRSWY worry beads
ABDERRTTYY dry battery
ABDFGIINOR fair-boding
ABDFGOORSX Oxford bags
ABDFILMORY formidably
ABDFILNORU floribunda
ABDFINSSTU ifs and buts
ABDFLOOORR floorboard
ABDFNORRWW brown dwarf
ABDGGINORR bordraging
ABDGHOORTY Dorothy bag
ABDGIINPRU upbraiding
ABDGINNRST band-string
string band
ABDGINORTU groundbait
ABDGLLNOTU bulldog ant
ABDGLNOOOW blood-wagon
ABDGLOORSU blood sugar
ABDGNORRUU grub around
ABDGNORSSU ground-bass
ABDHHILORT rhabdolith
ABDHIIINOT adhibition
ABDHIKLNRS blind shark
ABDHILMOOR rhomboidal
ABDHINOOUU Nouadhibou
ABDHINRTUY unbirthday
ABDIIILRTY ridability
ABDIIILSTY disability
ABDIIILTUY audibility
ABDIIIRSTT diatribist
ABDIIJNOTU Djiboutian
ABDIIKNNRY bradykinin
ABDIILLLNN inland bill
ABDIILMNOU albuminoid
ABDIILMOTY bimodality
ABDIILNOOS obsidional
ABDIILORRT tailorbird
ABDIILPTUY dupability
ABDIILRTUY durability
ABDIINOTTU dubitation
ABDIIRSSUY subsidiary
ABDIKLLNOU load in bulk
ABDILLNOST Bollandist
ABDILLRYZZ blizzardly

ABDILNOOST	bloodstain
ABDILNORSU	subordinal
ABDILNRUZZ	Buzz Aldrin
ABDILOORTY	botryoidal
ABDILOORWZ	brazil-wood
ABDILPSTUY	disputably
ABDIMNOOSU	abdominous
ABDIMNRRUU	burramundi
ABDINOORTU	obduration
ABDINOPRRS	parson-bird
ABDINRRTTY	tyrant bird
ABDINRSTTU	disturbant
ABDKLNOORS	Brooklands
ABDLLOOORY	blood-royal
ABDLMNOOTT	bottom-land
ABDLMOORYY	bloody Mary
ABDLNOORSU	slob around
ABDMNNOOSW	bondswoman
ABDMNNPRUU	bump and run
ABDMOORRUY	body armour
ABDNOORSSU	boss around
ABDNOORTUU	round about
	roundabout
ABDOORRSTY	storyboard
ABDOORRTUU	troubadour
ABDOOTTTUY	dotty about
ABEEEEFLLT	flea-beetle
	leaf beetle
ABEEEERRTV	beaver-tree
ABEEEFIKLM	make-belief
ABEEEFILLY	F Lee Bailey
ABEEEFLLRU	refuelable
ABEEEFLPRR	preferable
ABEEEFLRRR	referrable
ABEEEFMRST	beefmaster
ABEEEFNRTW	far between
ABEEEGGLRS	segregable
ABEEEGIMNN	beam-engine
ABEEEGLLNR	green label
ABEEEGLSTT	stag beetle
ABEEEHKLRW	brake-wheel
ABEEEHKRRS	break sheer
ABEEEHLRTT	Aethelbert
ABEEEHLSTT	The Beatles
ABEEEHRRRT	rebreather
ABEEEHRRWY	Hebrew year
ABEEEHRSTT	hartebeest
ABEEEIKLNR	Berkeleian
ABEEEIKRRT	tiebreaker
ABEEEILLRV	relievable
ABEEEILMRR	irremeable
ABEEEILRRV	livebearer
ABEEEILRRW	rewireable
ABEEEILRVW	reviewable
ABEEEIPRST	pâte brisée
ABEEEKLPRT	Peter Blake
ABEEELLLPX	expellable
ABEEELLSTT	settleable
ABEEELMNNT	enablement
ABEEELMNRU	enumerable
ABEEELMPRT	temperable
ABEEELMRSS	reassemble
ABEEELNPRT	penetrable
ABEEELNPRU	unpeerable
ABEEELNRSW	renewables
ABEEELQSUZ	squeezable
ABEEELRRSV	reservable
ABEEELRSTW	beware lest
ABEEEMMNST	embasement
ABEEEMNRTT	rebatement
ABEEEMRSTT	beetmaster
ABEEEMRSTY	Mersey beat
ABEEENNOZZ	azobenzene
ABEEENORST	absente reo
ABEEENQRTU	banqueteer
ABEEEOPRSS	pease-brose
ABEEEORSTT	stereobate
ABEEERRSST	Basseterre
	Basse-Terre
ABEEERRTTV	vertebrate
ABEEFFHMOT	off the beam
ABEEFFLMNT	bafflement
ABEEFFLOST	offsetable
ABEEFFLRSU	sufferable
ABEEFGILNR	Bengal fire
ABEEFHLMTY	fly the beam
ABEEFHLRST	self-breath
ABEEFHLRTT	better half
ABEEFHORTT	before that
ABEEFIILNS	infeasible
ABEEFIILRV	verifiable
ABEEFIIRTU	beautifier
ABEEFIKLNT	table knife
ABEEFIKRST	fire-basket
ABEEFILLLR	refillable
ABEEFILLRT	filterable
ABEEFILNOR	Froebelian
ABEEFILNRR	inferrable
ABEEFILNSU	unfeasible
ABEEFILNTT	flea-bitten
ABEEFINRRV	brain fever
ABEEFJNORS	Josef Beran
ABEEFKKLOR	Beaker Folk
ABEEFKLRSU	beakerfuls
ABEEFLLNSU	self-unable
ABEEFLMORR	reformable
ABEEFLOPRR	perforable
ABEEFLORRU	free labour
ABEEFLORSW	safe-blower
ABEEFLORTU	Earl of Bute
ABEEFLPRRY	preferably
ABEEFLRSSU	self-abuser
ABEEFLSTTY	safety belt
ABEEFMOOTT	beef tomato
ABEEGHIOPR	biographee
ABEEGHLLNR	bellhanger
ABEEGHNRRS	Hans Berger
ABEEGHNTTU	beat the gun
ABEEGIINRS	raising-bee
ABEEGIKNNN	bank engine
ABEEGILLMP	bell magpie
ABEEGILMNR	germinable
ABEEGILNOT	negotiable
ABEEGILNRT	integrable
ABEEGILNSS	Albigenses
ABEEGILRTU	glauberite
ABEEGILRTW	bilge-water
ABEEGIRSTU	aubergiste
ABEEGLNOPS	spongeable
ABEEGLNORV	governable
ABEEGLNPUX	expugnable
ABEEGLNRRY	angleberry
ABEEGLNSTW	West Bengal
ABEEGLORRT	Albert Gore
ABEEGMMNNO	gombeen-man
ABEEGMOSSX	message box
ABEEGMOSSY	message-boy
ABEEGNRSTT	abstergent
ABEEHILLRS	relishable
ABEEHILORT	heriotable
ABEEHILPRS	perishable
ABEEHIMNTT	Benthamite
ABEEHINOTT	hebetation
ABEEHKLOSU	Bleak House
ABEEHKNORS	boneshaker
ABEEHLLNPU	unhelpable
ABEEHLLOST	ballet shoe
ABEEHLLRRY	Halle Berry
ABEEHLLRST	three balls
ABEEHLLSTT	all the best
ABEEHLMPRS	blasphemer
ABEEHLNOSW	whale's bone
ABEEHLRSST	breathless
ABEEHMORTT	bathometer
ABEEHMRTTY	bathymeter
ABEEHNNORV	heaven-born
ABEEHOORRS	seborrhoea
ABEEHORSTU	hereabouts
ABEEHORTTU	outbreathe
	thereabout
ABEEHORTUW	whereabout
ABEEHORTWW	weather bow
ABEEHORTWX	weather box
ABEEHPRRSV	verb phrase
ABEEHPRRSY	barysphere
ABEEHQRSUU	harquebuse
ABEEHRRTTT	Brett Harte
ABEEHRRTWY	wheat berry
ABEEHRSTTT	breath test
ABEEHRSTTU	shea butter
ABEEIIJLLN	Billie Jean
ABEEIILLMN	eliminable
ABEEIILLNS	isabelline
ABEEIILLRS	liberalise
ABEEIILLRZ	liberalize
ABEEIILNPX	inexpiable
ABEEIILNRS	inerasible
ABEEIILNTV	inevitable
ABEEIILSST	bestialise
ABEEIILSTZ	bestialize
ABEEIIRRRZ	bizarrerie
ABEEIJMOSW	James Bowie
ABEEIKLLLS	Klebsiella

ABEEIKLLNU unlikeable
ABEEIKLLSZ like blazes
ABEEIKLNRT ankle-biter
ABEEIKNNRT barkentine
ABEEILLMNR bellarmine
ABEEILLNNT table linen
ABEEILLNOR neoliberal
ABEEILLNRU unreliable
ABEEILLNST listenable
ABEEILLNTV ventilable
ABEEILLNUV unliveable
ABEEILLRSU leisurable
ABEEILLRTT Little Bear
ABEEILLSTU beatus ille
ABEEILMMOV immoveable
ABEEILMNRT terminable
ABEEILMNSU albumenise
ABEEILMNUZ albumenize
ABEEILMOST metabolise
ABEEILMOTT metabolite
ABEEILMOTZ metabolize
ABEEILMRRY irremeably
ABEEILMRTT remittable
ABEEILMSTV semblative
ABEEILNNTV inventable
ABEEILNNUV unenviable
ABEEILNOPR inoperable
ABEEILNORV verbena-oil
ABEEILNORX inexorable
ABEEILNPSX expansible
ABEEILNRSS bleariness
ABEEILNRST insertable
ABEEILNRWY barley wine
ABEEILNSTV investable
ABEEILNSUZ unseizable
unsizeable
ABEEILORTT obliterate
ABEEILPRRS respirable
ABEEILPRRT Liber Pater
ABEEILPRTX extirpable
ABEEILQRRU requirable
ABEEILQRTU requitable
ABEEILRRTU tree burial
ABEEILRRTW rewritable
ABEEILRSSU reissuable
ABEEILSSTW sweet basil
ABEEIMMRRT timber-mare
ABEEINNPRR pine-barren
ABEEINPTUY pine beauty
ABEEINRTUX exurbanite
ABEEIORTTX exorbitate
ABEEIRRSTW sweetbriar
ABEEIRSSTV abstersive
ABEEJLLMSU jumble sale
ABEEJMMNNT enjambment
ABEEJMPRSU base jumper
ABEEKKMRRT kerb-market
ABEEKLLMRT market-bell
ABEEKLLPRS spell baker
ABEEKLNRSV blank verse
ABEEKLNTTW wet blanket
ABEEKLOORS break loose
ABEEKLORST strokeable
ABEEKLRSTU blue streak
ABEEKMMNNT embankment
ABEEKMMNRT embarkment
ABEEKNORST stonebreak
ABEEKNRSTW West-Banker
ABEEKOPRRW power brake
ABEELLLNSU unsellable
ABEELLLNTU untellable
ABEELLMNOT noble metal
ABEELLMNTU antebellum
Blue Mantle
ABEELLMOPY employable
ABEELLMORU bellamoure
ABEELLNOUV unloveable
ABEELLNRUV vulnerable
ABEELLNTTU unlettable
ABEELLNTTY Betty Allen
ABEELLORSV resolvable
ABEELLORVV revolvable
ABEELLPRUV pulverable
ABEELMMMNT embalmment
ABEELMNORZ emblazoner
ABEELMNOTY table money
ABEELMNOUV unmoveable
ABEELMNPRU rumple-bane
ABEELMNRRU real number
ABEELMNRST resemblant
ABEELMNRSU Lebensraum
mensurable
ABEELMNTTT battlement
ABEELMORST astrobleme
blastomere
ABEELMORSW seam bowler
ABEELMPRSU presumable
ABEELMPRTU permutable
ABEELMRSSY reassembly
ABEELMRSTU rumble seat
ABEELNNNOY Anne Boleyn
ABEELNNTUU untuneable
ABEELNOPRS personable
ABEELNORTV verbal note
ABEELNOSST oblateness
ABEELNPRTY penetrably
ABEELNQTTU blanquette
ABEELNRRTU returnable
ABEELNRTUU neural tube
ABEELNRTUY untyreable
ABEELNSSST stableness
ABEELNSSSU usableness
ABEELOOPPT boat people
ABEELOPRRR beer parlor
ABEELOPRRT reportable
ABEELOPRRV reprovable
ABEELOPRTX exportable
ABEELORRST restorable
ABEELORTTT tear bottle
ABEELORTUY leery about
ABEEMMSSTY beam system
ABEEMNNNOT abonnement
ABEEMNORTY embryonate
ABEEMNRUVW wave number
ABEEMRRSTW brewmaster
ABEENNNORT Anne Brontë
ABEENNNRRU runner bean
ABEENNORSV raven's-bone
ABEENNRRSS barrenness
ABEENNRRSU baserunner
ABEENNRSSU urbaneness
ABEENNRSSZ brazenness
ABEENNRSUV uneven bars
ABEENORRTW waterborne
water-borne
ABEENORSST baronetess
ABEENORSTU Eastbourne
ABEENRRSTU subterrane
ABEEOPRRRT reprobater
ABEEOPRRTX exprobrate
ABEEORRSTW water brose
ABEEPRRTTU perturbate
ABEFFGILRU febrifugal
ABEFFHIOTW Wife of Bath
ABEFFILLOR ball of fire
bill of fare
ABEFFILNST snaffle-bit
ABEFFLLLOU foul befall
ABEFFLNRUU unruffable
ABEFFLRSUY sufferably
ABEFGILORV forgivable
ABEFGILRSS fiberglass
fibreglass
glass fibre
ABEFGINORR forbearing
ABEFHIRRTT afterbirth
ABEFHIRRTZ Fritz Haber
ABEFHKORRT break forth
ABEFHRRSTU surf-bather
ABEFIILLLN infallible
ABEFIILLRT fibrillate
ABEFIILNOT notifiable
ABEFIILNTU infibulate
ABEFIKLNRS fire blanks
ABEFILLLNU unfallible
unfillable
ABEFILLLOS bill of sale
ABEFILMORR moral fibre
ABEFILOPRT profitable
ABEFIMMOOR amoebiform
ABEFKLSSTU basketfuls
ABEFKNORRT break-front
ABEFKOOORZ Book of Ezra
ABEFLLLMUY blamefully
ABEFLLLORW ball-flower
ABEFLLMORU formulable
ABEFLLOORT footballer
ABEFLLRRSU barrelfuls
ABEFLORSTW fast bowler
ABEFLOSTTY safety bolt
ABEFNORSTY Fray Bentos
ABEFNORTUY Fortune Bay
ABEFNRRRYY Bryan Ferry

ABEGGGGINO go a-begging
ABEGGIMNOR embargoing
ABEGGNOORT tobogganer
ABEGGNOOSU gauge boson
ABEGGNOPSS spongebags
ABEGGNRSTU gangbuster
ABEGHHIRST breast-high
ABEGHIKLRT brake light
ABEGHIKSUW weigh-bauks
ABEGHILLTT late blight
light table
ABEGHILNTT night table
ABEGHIMNNU human being
ABEGHINOOP genophobia
ABEGHINRTU thunbergia
ABEGHIOOPR ergophobia
ABEGHIOPRR biographer
ABEGHLLLUY belly laugh
ABEGHLLOOP Gallophobe
ABEGHLLOPU ploughable
ABEGHLNOOP anglophobe✧
ABEGHLNPTU plunge bath
ABEGHMRRSU Gasherbrum
ABEGHNOPST sponge bath
ABEGHNRRSU bushranger
ABEGHQSUUU usquebaugh
ABEGHRSTTU bestraught
ABEGHRSTUV harvest bug
ABEGIIJNTW Jew-baiting
ABEGIILNNT intangible
ABEGIILNRT Gilbertian
ABEGIIMNRT reaming-bit
ABEGIINNRT brigantine
ABEGIINOST abiogenist
ABEGIKLNNT blanketing
ABEGILLLRT ballet-girl
ABEGILLNOY all-obeying
ABEGILLNRV verballing
ABEGILLOSU Bela Lugosi
ABEGILMNPU impugnable
ABEGILNNTU untangible
ABEGILNRSS singles bar
ABEGILNRSW swingle-bar
ABEGILRRSU burglarise
ABEGILRRUZ burglarize
ABEGIMORSU seaborgium
ABEGINNNOR non-bearing
ABEGINNORS Bergsonian
ABEGINNQTU banqueting
ABEGINNRST string bean
ABEGINOPRV Gabon viper
ABEGINRSSU ear-bussing
ABEGINRSTU gas turbine
ABEGLLNOOY balneology
ABEGLNORRY loganberry
ABEGMNOOTY Montego Bay
ABEGMORRSS brome-grass
ABEGMORSUU umbrageous
ABEGNNSTTU subtangent
ABEGNOORST brant goose
ABEGNOORTU Baton Rouge
ABEGNORRTU gubernator
ABEHHILLST sheathbill
ABEHHIOOPT theophobia
ABEHHMRTTY beta rhythm
ABEHHORRTT heart-throb
ABEHHORSTW shower bath
ABEHIIILPS bailieship
ABEHIILMNT habiliment
ABEHIIPSTT hepatitis B
ABEHIJNNOR John Braine
ABEHIKLNRS shrinkable
ABEHIKLSTT basket-hilt
ABEHIKNOOP kenophobia
ABEHIKNRRS shin-barker
ABEHILLOPS polishable
ABEHILMPRS blepharism
ABEHILMSTY basil thyme
ABEHILNPSU punishable
ABEHILOOPZ zelophobia
ABEHILOPST hospitable
ABEHILORTV Bath Oliver
ABEHILPRSY perishably
ABEHILPSTT battleship
ABEHILPSTU bisulphate
ABEHILRSTV silver-bath
ABEHIMMNST Benthamism
ABEHIMNNST banishment
ABEHIMRRSU herbariums
ABEHINNORT on the brain
ABEHINOOPX xenophobia
ABEHINOPRV vibraphone
ABEHINORTW The Rainbow
ABEHIOOPRU Europhobia
ABEHIRRTTW water birth
ABEHIRRTWY Barry White
ABEHIRSSTW white brass
ABEHJNNORS John Barnes
ABEHKLRSUW bushwalker
ABEHKOOPRS phrase book
ABEHLMOOST smoothable
ABEHLMORTW Bartholmew
ABEHLMOTTU ethambutol
ABEHLNOORS El Brooshna
ABEHLNOORU honourable✧
ABEHLNORSW Brehon Laws
ABEHLOOPSV Slavophobe
ABEHLOPRSY hyperbolas
ABEHLORRTY lay brother
ABEHLORTTU bluethroat
ABEHLOSTTW wash-bottle
ABEHLRSUWY bush-lawyer
ABEHLRTTTU truth table
ABEHMMNSTU ambushment
ABEHMNOOTY bay the moon
ABEHMORSTU a sore thumb
ABEHMRSSTU bushmaster
ABEHMRTTYY bathymetry
ABEHNOPRTY hyperbaton
ABEHNORRTW brown earth
ABEHNORSST basset horn
stonebrash
ABEHNOSTTU thenabouts
ABEHOOPTUY up the booay
ABEHOORSTT sabretooth
ABEHOORSTW showboater
ABEHORRSSS horse brass
ABEHPRSUZZ buzz phrase
ABEHQRSSUU harquebuss
ABEIIILMNT inimitable
ABEIIILMRT mirabilite
ABEIIILNNZ Leibnizian
ABEIIILNSS sensibilia
ABEIILLMRS liberalism
ABEIILLNNY biennially
ABEIILLNOV inviolable
ABEIILLRST liberalist
ABEIILLRTY liberality
ABEIILLSTT ballistite
ABEIILLSTU utilisable
ABEIILLTUZ utilizable
ABEIILMNSS lesbianism
ABEIILMNSU albuminise
ABEIILMNUZ albuminize
ABEIILMPRT impartible
ABEIILMPSS impassible
ABEIILMRST bimestrial
ABEIILMSST bestialism
ABEIILNORT liberation
ABEIILNOTT nobilitate
ABEIILNPRS inspirable
ABEIILNPXY inexpiably
ABEIILNRSY inerasibly
ABEIILNTTU intuitable
ABEIILNTTY tenability
ABEIILNTVY inevitably
ABEIILQTUY equability
ABEIILRSST stabiliser
ABEIILRSSU Belisarius
ABEIILRSTZ stabilizer
ABEIILSTTY bestiality
ABEIILSTUY sueability
ABEIIMNTTU bituminate
ABEIINNRRT interbrain
ABEIINNRSS braininess
ABEIINNRTW New Britain
ABEIINRRSV river basin
ABEIINRSTU urbanities
ABEIINRTTU abiturient
ABEIIOORSS aerobiosis
ABEIJLNOTT join battle
ABEIJMNOST James Tobin
ABEIKLNNSU unsinkable
ABEIKLNRTW water blink
ABEIKNOPRT break point
breakpoint
ABEIKNORTU break out in
ABEIKNSTUZ Uzbekistan
ABEILLLNRW Berlin Wall
ABEILLLNTU untillable
ABEILLMMOS embolismal
ABEILLMNRT Martin Bell
ABEILLMSTU stimulable

ABEILLNORT Lionel Bart
ABEILLNOSV insolvable
ABEILLNOSW Boswellian
ABEILLNSSS ballsiness
ABEILLNSTU insultable
ABEILLRSUY leisurably
ABEILLSUXY bisexually
ABEILMMOST metabolism
ABEILMMOSV immovables
ABEILMNQRU lambrequin
ABEILMNRRU ruin marble
ABEILMNRTY liberty-man
terminably
ABEILMNSSU unmissable
ABEILMNSSW wambliness
ABEILMOOTU automobile
ABEILMOPRT importable
ABEILMOPRV improvable
ABEILMORTY traymobile
ABEILMRSSU surmisable
ABEILNNORS Selbornian
ABEILNNOSS bonnilasse
ABEILNNRUY inurbanely
ABEILNNUVY unenviably
ABEILNOOPS poisonable
ABEILNOPRY inoperably
ABEILNORXY inexorably
ABEILNPRUZ unprizable
ABEILNPSXY expansibly
ABEILNSTUU unsuitable
ABEILOOPRS soap boiler
ABEILOPRRV proverbial
ABEILOPSTU bipetalous
ABEILORRTY liberatory
ABEILORSTT strobilate
ABEILORSUV Ebola virus
ABEILORTVY abortively
ABEILRSTUV vestibular
ABEILRSUVV survivable
ABEIMMNRUU Mare Nubium
ABEIMMOQUZ Mozambique
ABEIMNNOTT obtainment
ABEIMNOORR Brian Moore
ABEIMNORTT montbretia
ABEIMNORTU tambourine
ABEIMNRRSU submariner
ABEIMOSSTU abstemious
ABEINNOPRU bear in upon
ABEINNOPSV bone spavin
ABEINNORTU eburnation
ABEINNORTV native-born
ABEINNOSST sanbenitos
ABEINNOSTT abstention
ABEINNRRTU interurban
ABEINNRSSW brawniness
ABEINOOSTU noise about
ABEINOPPTT bon appetit
ABEINOPRRW brainpower
ABEINORSST abstersion
ABEINORTTX exorbitant
ABEINPRRSU superbrain
ABEINRRSTU subterrain
ABEINRSSSS brassiness
ABEIOOORST rooibos tea
ABEIOPPRSY presbyopia
ABEIOPRSTV absorptive
ABEIORRRST rib-roaster
ABEIORRSTT birostrate
ABEIOSSSST asbestosis
ABEIPRRSTT bitter-spar
ABEIPRSTTY baptistery
ABEIRSTUVY subvariety
ABEJMNORSW James Brown
ABEKKMOORR bookmarker
ABEKKORSTW basketwork
workbasket
ABEKLLMRTU bull market
ABEKLLOSTU leukoblast
ABEKLNNOUW unknowable
ABEKLNOPTT knap-bottle
ABEKLNORUW unworkable
ABEKLOOPRV provokable
ABEKLOPRRR pork barrel
ABEKMMNORY memory bank
ABEKMNNOTU mountebank
ABEKMNOOTY monkey boat
ABEKMORRST Bram Stoker
ABEKMORRUY marker buoy
ABEKNNORSW brown snake
ABEKNOPRRW pawnbroker
ABEKNORSTT breast-knot
ABEKNORSTY oyster-bank
ABEKNRSTTU tankbuster
ABEKOOPRRY prayer book
ABEKORRSTW breastwork
ABELLLLORR rollerball
ABELLLLOVY volleyball
ABELLLORRR barrel roll
ABELLLOSUW Saul Bellow
ABELLLPSSY Bell's palsy
ABELLMNOYY Ballymoney
ABELLMOSTY myeloblast
ABELLNOSUV unsolvable
ABELLOORWY woolly bear
ABELLORRRU bull-roarer
ABELLOSTUY absolutely
ABELLRSSTU substellar
ABELLSSSUY syllabuses
ABELMMNOSU somnambule
summonable
ABELMMPTUW wampum belt
ABELMNNOOW noblewoman
ABELMNOOST monostable
ABELMNORXY onyx marble
ABELMNORYZ emblazonry
ABELMNOUVY unmoveably
ABELMNPRRU lamp-burner
ABELMOOPRT promotable
ABELMOORSU laboursome
ABELMOORTW water bloom
ABELMPRSUY presumably
ABELMPRTTU palm-butter
ABELNNORUV verbal noun
ABELNNRTUU unturnable
ABELNOOPST tablespoon
ABELNOPRUV unprovable
ABELNOPTXY penalty box
ABELNOQTUU unquotable
ABELNORRTT latter-born
ABELNORRTW brow-antler
ABELNORSTU neuroblast
ABELNOSUXY Saxony blue
ABELNPRTUY trypan blue
ABELNRRTUU nurturable
ABELNRSSTU substernal
ABELOOPPRS proposable
ABELOOPRST blastopore
ABELOOPSST Sebastopol
ABELOORRUV overlabour
ABELOOSSTT osteoblast
ABELOOTTUW out at elbow
ABELOPPSSU supposable
ABELOPRSTT table-sport
ABELOPRTTX prattlebox
ABELOPSTTU postal tube
ABELORRTUX Albert Roux
ABELORSTYY lay store by
ABELRSSTUY abstrusely
ABELRSTTTU salt-butter
ABELRTTUUU tubulature
ABEMMNNRSU numbers man
ABEMMNORSU membranous
ABEMMNRSSU mass number
ABEMNNORSS sans nombre
ABEMNNOSTU submontane
ABEMNOOPRT proton beam
ABEMNOORRW marrow-bone
ABEMNOORTY Moreton Bay
ABEMNOORWW bowerwoman
ABEMNORRST robertsman
ABEMPPRSTU breast pump
ABENNOPRSX box-spanner
ABENOORTTV ben trovato
ABENOPPRRW brown paper
ABENOPRSTU bean sprout
ABENORRRTW barrenwort
ABENORRRWY rowan-berry
ABENORRSTZ Bronze Star
ABENPRRTTU perturbant
ABENPRSSTU abruptness
ABEOOPRRRT reprobator
ABEOORRSTV observator
ABEOORSTUU rouseabout
ABEOPSTTUY beauty spot
ABEOQRRTUY quarter-boy
ABEOQSSUUU subaqueous
ABERRRSTWY strawberry
ABFFGILLNY bafflingly
ABFFLNOTUU buffalo-nut
ABFFMOORST broomstaff
ABFGHOORRU farborough
ABFGILNOTW batfowling
ABFGILNOTY flying-boat

ABFGOPRRSU up for grabs
ABFHILMTTU thumb a lift
ABFHIOSTTU shift about
ABFIIILRTY friability
ABFIILLLNY infallibly
ABFIILLRRY fibrillary
ABFIILNORV riboflavin
ABFILOPRTY profitably
ABFILOSTUY fabulosity
ABFIMNORRY binary form
ABFINORRST Fortinbras
ABFJLORSUY frabjously
ABFKMOOOOS Book of Amos
ABFKNNORRU Frank Bruno
ABFLLOSTUY boastfully
ABFLLOSUUY fabulously
ABFLNOSTUU unboastful
ABGGGILNRY braggingly
ABGGGINORW growing-bag
ABGGILLMNO gambolling
ABGGILLNRU Raging Bull
ABGHHINTTU bathing hut
ABGHIIMMNR Birmingham
ABGHIINOTX Thai boxing
ABGHIJNORS job sharing
ABGHIMNSTU mashing-tub
ABGHINNSTU sunbathing
ABGHINOOPY gynophobia
ABGHIOPRRV vibrograph
ABGHIORTTU right about
ABGHIRRRSU Harrisburg
ABGHIRRSTT star-bright
ABGHLORRUY royal burgh
ABGHOORRUY Yarborough
ABGIIILNNT nail-biting
ABGIILNNTY intangibly
ABGIILNOOT obligation
ABGIIMNNOO Mabinogion
ABGIIMNNST bantingism
ABGIIMNORS Grobianism
ABGIIMNPPT bit-mapping
ABGIINNORU Bourignian
ABGIKKMNOO bookmaking
ABGIKMNOOT bootmaking
ABGILLLNOW lowballing
ABGILLMNOU lumbang-oil
ABGILLMNRY ramblingly
ABGILLMNWY wamblingly
ABGILLNNOO ballooning
ABGILLNRWY warblingly
ABGILLNSUU sublingual
ABGILMOSUY bigamously
ABGILNSSUY busy signal
ABGILOORTY obligatory
ABGILOOSTT batologist
ABGIMOOTTW witgatboom
ABGINNORRT Barrington
ABGINNRRSU nursing-bra
ABGINOORRT roborating
ABGINOORRY roaring boy
ABGINOORTW rowing boat
ABGINORRTU barring-out
ABGINRSSST string bass
ABGJORSTUU subjugator
ABGKLOORTU Olga Korbut
ABGKNOPRTU go bankrupt
ABGLLLORUY globularly
ABGLMOORUY glamour boy
ABGLNOORUY urbanology
ABGMOPRRSU subprogram
ABGNORRSUW brown sugar
ABGORRSSTU Strasbourg
ABHHIMOOOP homophobia
ABHHNORSSW hash browns
ABHHORRSUW bush-harrow
ABHIIMMNRS Brahminism
ABHIIMNSST absinthism
ABHIIMOPSU amphibious
ABHIIOOPST sitophobia
ABHIIOOPTX toxiphobia
ABHIIRSSTY sybaritish✧
ABHIKNOTTU think about
ABHILLRSTW whirlblast
ABHILLTTUY I'll buy that
ABHILNRSTY Labyrinths
ABHILOOSTU Louis Botha
ABHILOPSTY hospitably
ABHILORTUW whirl-about
ABHILOSSTT histoblast
ABHIMNOOOP monophobia
ABHIMNOPTU thumb piano
ABHIMNORRS marsh-robin
ABHIMOOPSY mysophobia
ABHINOOOPS nosophobia
ABHINPRSTU paintbrush
ABHIOOPPRY pyrophobia
ABHIPRRSSU bursarship
ABHJNNNOUY John Bunyan
ABHLLLORSU loll-shraub
ABHLLMSTTU thumbstall
ABHLMOOSTY homoblasty
ABHLNOORUY honourably
ABHLORRRUW hurlbarrow
ABHNOORTTU northabout
ABHNOTTTUW not but what
ABHOORTTUW throw about
ABHOOSTTUU southabout
ABHORRTTUY rubythroat
ABIIIKLLTY likability
ABIIILLPTY pliability
ABIIILLTVY livability
ABIIILMNTY inimitably
ABIIILMSST stibialism
ABIIILNOST sibilation
ABIIINOSST antibiosis
ABIIIORSTT tibiotarsi
ABIIJLNOTU jubilation
ABIILLLMNT Bill Tilman
ABIILLMNSU subliminal
ABIILLNOVY inviolably
ABIILLNSTY sibilantly
ABIILLOTVY lovability
ABIILMOTVY movability
ABIILMPRTY impartibly
ABIILMPSSY impassibly
ABIILMTTUY mutability
ABIILNNOTY non-ability
ABIILNOOSV bolivianos
ABIILNOTTY bitonality
notability
ABIILNPRST split-brain
ABIILOPRTY bipolarity
ABIILORSTY sibilatory
ABIIMRSSTY sybaritism✧
ABIINNOTTU intubation
ABIINNRTUY inurbanity
ABIINORSTV vibrations
ABIINOTTTU titubation
ABIINRTTYY Trinity Bay
ABIIORSTTU obituarist
ABIIQRTUUY ubiquitary
ABIJLLNTUY jubilantly
ABIJNOORTU objuration
ABIKLNNOPT point-blank
ABIKNOOORT ration book
ABIKNOPRTU prink about
ABILLLOOSV Villa-Lobos
ABILLMORRR mirror ball
ABILLMRRUY Bill Murray
ABILLNOOST balloonist
ABILLNOOTU lobulation
ABILLNORUU unilobular
ABILLNOSVY insolvably
ABILLOORSZ Laszlo Biro
ABILLOPRRT parrot-bill
ABILMNOOTU out on a limb
ABILMNOSUU albuminous
ABILMNOTUW woman-built
ABILMOPRVY improvably
ABILMOPSSY Amblyopsis
ABILMOSSTU absolutism
ABILNNOORU labor union
ABILNOOSTU absolution
ABILNOTTUU tubulation
ABILNSTUUY unsuitably
ABILOORSTV absolvitor
ABILORSSUU salubrious
ABILOSSTTU absolutist
ABILRTTUUY tubularity
ABIMMNRSUU manubriums
ABIMNNOOTU umbonation
ABIMNOPTTU Mt Pinatubo
ABIMNORRST brainstorm
ABIMRSSSTU strabismus
ABINNOPSVY bony spavin
ABINNORSTW town's-bairn
ABINNRSTTU subintrant
ABINOOPRST absorption
ABINOORRST torsion bar
ABINOORTTU obturation
ABINOOSSST bassoonist
ABINOPRRSS prison bars
ABINORSTTY bryostatin

ABINOSSTTU	substation
ABJLNOORUX	journal-box
ABLMMOOSSY	may blossom
ABLOOPRTTT	Port Talbot
ABLOORSTUY	absolutory
ABLOPPSSUY	supposably
ABLOPSTTUY	tuboplasty
ABLORRSUWW	law-burrows
ABLORRTTUU	turbulator
ABMOORSTTY	strabotomy
ABMRSSTTUU	substratum
ABNOORRSTU	brontosaur
ABOOPTTTUY	potty about
ABOORSTTUU	roustabout
ACCCCIKKLL	click-clack
ACCCDEIIPT	pectic acid
ACCCDEIIRU	erucic acid
ACCCDHIILO	cholic acid
ACCCDIIIPR	picric acid
ACCCDIIIRT	citric acid
ACCCEEEKLS	Eccles cake
ACCCEEELNS	calescence
ACCCEEENNS	canescence
ACCCEEHITT	catechetic
ACCCEENRST	accrescent
ACCCEFHKOR	cockchafer
ACCCEGINOS	cacogenics
ACCCEHIKOR	Chick Corea
ACCCEHILOT	chalcocite
ACCCEHIPRT	ecphractic
ACCCEHKOPT	patchcocke
ACCCEHLNOO	Coco Chanel
ACCCEHORSW	coach screw
ACCCEHORTW	cowcatcher
ACCCEHORUU	accoucheur
ACCCEIILRT	cicatricle
ACCCEIIRST	cicatrices
ACCCEIKORT	cockatrice
ACCCEILLNY	encyclical
ACCCEILMOP	accomplice
ACCCEIMNPY	impeccancy
ACCCELMORY	macrocycle
ACCCENOPRT	concept car
ACCCGLNOOO	gonococcal
ACCCHHIIMR	arch-chimic
ACCCHHILOO	chocaholic
ACCCHINOOP	cacophonic
ACCCHKLOTW	watch clock
ACCCHKOPST	spatchcock
ACCCHLOORY	ochlocracy
ACCCHOOTUU	caoutchouc
ACCCHORSTT	Scotch cart
ACCCIILLOT	laccolitic
ACCCIIOPRS	capriccios
ACCCIKKLRT	click-track
ACCCIKMORR	microcrack
ACCCILLLYY	cyclically
ACCCILMOOX	coxcomical
ACCCILMOPY	complicacy
ACCCILMORY	cycloramic
ACCCINOPPU	cappuccino
ACCDDEEINT	accidented
ACCDDEEIRT	accredited
ACCDDEEIST	desiccated
ACCDDEEKNT	canted deck
ACCDDEIILL	cicadellid
ACCDDEINOS	disco dance
ACCDDEIRRT	credit card
ACCDDEKLOP	cock-paddle
ACCDDIIMOO	domoic acid
ACCDEEENNS	ascendence
ACCDEEHLOT	cochleated
ACCDEEHQRU	cheque card
ACCDEEIIRT	Cricetidae
ACCDEEINNS	incandesce
ACCDEEINRS	dancercise
ACCDEELLPY	pedal cycle
ACCDEELPST	spectacled
ACCDEELPTY	acceptedly
ACCDEELRTY	trade cycle
ACCDEENNST	candescent
ACCDEENNSY	ascendency
ACCDEENNTU	unaccented
ACCDEEORTU	accoutered
ACCDEFHKLO	half-cocked
ACCDEFIIRR	ferric acid
ACCDEFILNO	diclofenac
ACCDEFKMOS	smock-faced
ACCDEGHNOS	dog's chance
ACCDEGIINN	ice dancing
ACCDEGLNOR	clog dancer
ACCDEHISST	decastichs
ACCDEHLNOY	chalcedony
ACCDEHNORT	torch-dance
ACCDEIILNY	indelicacy
ACCDEIILST	dialectics
ACCDEIIMOY	Cecidomyia
ACCDEIIOPT	apodeictic
ACCDEIITUZ	diazeuctic
ACCDEIKLNW	candlewick
ACCDEIKLOP	cock-paidle
ACCDEIKLOT	cocktailed
ACCDEIKNOP	cock and pie
ACCDEILLOP	peccadillo
ACCDEILNOO	calcedonio
ACCDEILNOT	occidental✧
ACCDEILOPY	cyclopedia
ACCDEIMNNY	mendicancy
ACCDEIMNSU	dance music
ACCDEIMORT	democratic
ACCDEIMORY	mediocracy
ACCDEINNTU	inductance
ACCDEINOPR	endocarpic
ACCDEIORST	desiccator
ACCDEIORTT	corticated
ACCDEIOSST	sticcadoes
ACCDELLTUU	cucullated
ACCDELOPSU	cloudscape
ACCDELOPTU	coup d'éclat
ACCDELRSUY	accursedly
ACCDEMOSTU	accustomed
ACCDENORTT	contracted
ACCDEOOPRT	Cape doctor
ACCDEOPRST	cadet corps
ACCDFIILTY	flaccidity
ACCDFIIMOR	formic acid
ACCDGNOOOR	raccoon-dog
ACCDHHNOST	Scotch hand
ACCDHHRRUW	churchward
ACCDHHRRUY	churchyard
ACCDHIINOR	diachronic
ACCDHILNOO	conchoidal
ACCDHILORR	clarichord
ACCDHILORV	clavichord
ACCDHLORST	Old Scratch
ACCDIIINQU	quinic acid
ACCDIIINRT	nitric acid
ACCDIILLOP	piccadillo
ACCDIILLPY	piccadilly
ACCDIILNOO	conoidical
ACCDIILNOY	cycloidian
ACCDIILOTU	toluic acid
ACCDIILSST	cladistics
ACCDIIMOST	docimastic
ACCDIINNOO	diaconicon
ACCDIIOSTU	diacoustic
ACCDIKLOOR	clock radio
ACCDILNOOR	concordial
ACCDILOOOW	calico-wood
ACCDILORSU	sdrucciola
ACCDINORTT	contradict
ACCDLMNORU	card column
ACCDLOORSV	vocal cords
ACCDLOORUY	doulocracy
ACCDNNOORT	concordant
ACCEEEEHKS	cheesecake
ACCEEEHILR	chelicerae
ACCEEEHIST	seecatchie
ACCEEEHNNV	even chance
ACCEEEHRTY	eye-catcher
ACCEEELMNU	Clemenceau
ACCEEELNST	latescence
ACCEEELPRT	receptacle
ACCEEENNRS	renascence✧
ACCEEENPTX	expectance
ACCEEFHLRT	leechcraft
ACCEEFINST	fatiscence
ACCEEFIRRU	Cruciferae
ACCEEGINSY	gay science
ACCEEGLLOP	college cap
ACCEEHHKLO	cheechalko
ACCEEHHKOS	cheechakos
ACCEEHHLOW	coach-wheel
ACCEEHIIMN	ice machine
ACCEEHILLR	cheliceral
ACCEEHILNP	encephalic
ACCEEHINSV	chevisance
ACCEEHIRST	catechiser
ACCEEHIRSV	cesarevich
ACCEEHIRSW	cesarewich
ACCEEHIRTZ	catechizer
ACCEEHISST	catechesis
ACCEEHKKRT	check-taker

Words marked ✧ can also be spelled with one or more capital letters

ACCEEHLNSS	chanceless
ACCEEHMNTU	catechumen
ACCEEHNOPR	ocean perch
ACCEEHNORR	encroacher
ACCEEILLRT	electrical
ACCEEILMNU	ecumenical
ACCEEILMOT	ecoclimate
ACCEEILMRS	cream-slice
ACCEEILNPS	pencil-case
ACCEEILNTV	Venice talc
ACCEEILNTY	acetylenic
ACCEEILORT	calico-tree
ACCEEILORV	varicocele
ACCEEILSST	ecclesiast
ACCEEIMNRS	miscreance
ACCEEIMOPR	comice pear
ACCEEIMSST	access time
ACCEEINPQU	cinque-pace
ACCEEIORST	Eric Coates
ACCEEIORSU	ericaceous
ACCEEIRRSV	service car
ACCEEIRTUX	excruciate
ACCEEKOOPR	peacock ore
ACCEEKOPRY	peacockery
ACCEELLNRT	call centre
ACCEELNOST	coalescent
ACCEELNOSV	convalesce
ACCEELNPRU	crapulence
ACCEELNRTU	reluctance
ACCEELNRUX	Clarenceux
ACCEELNSST	accentless
	scent scale
ACCEELNSTT	lactescent
ACCEELNSTU	caulescent
ACCEELPSST	spectacles
ACCEELRTWY	water cycle
ACCEEMNRST	marcescent
	scarcement
ACCEEMNSTU	accusement
ACCEEMOSTY	ascomycete
ACCEENNNOV	convenance
ACCEENNOVY	conveyance
ACCEENOPRR	coparcener
ACCEENOPSS	open access
ACCEENORST	consecrate
ACCEENOTTY	eye contact
ACCEENPTXY	expectancy
ACCEENRSSS	scarceness
ACCEENTUXY	executancy
ACCEEOPPRS	Peace Corps
ACCEEORRSU	racecourse
	Sacre Coeur
ACCEEORSTU	cretaceous✧
ACCEFFIINY	inefficacy
ACCEFFIITY	efficacity
ACCEFHLRTY	flycatcher
ACCEFIILPS	specifical
ACCEFIIRRS	sacrificer
ACCEFIKNRT	fan-cricket
ACCEFILLOR	calciferol
ACCEFILMOR	calceiform
ACCEFILRSU	flea circus
ACCEFILRYY	fairy-cycle
ACCEFILSSU	fascicules
ACCEFINOST	confiscate
ACCEFLLOTU	flocculate
ACCEGHLNOO	cool change
ACCEGIINOR	cariogenic
ACCEGIKLNN	necklacing
ACCEGILLNN	cancelling
ACCEGILLNO	collagenic
ACCEGILLOO	ecological
ACCEGILNOT	lactogenic
ACCEGIMOPS	megascopic
ACCEGINNOR	carcinogen
ACCEGINNOS	cognisance
ACCEGINNOY	cyanogenic
ACCEGINNOZ	cognizance
ACCEHHHIST	schechitah
ACCEHHIIRR	hierarchic
ACCEHHIKNO	choke chain
ACCEHHIMRS	Carchemish
ACCEHHIPRT	heptarchic
ACCEHHMRSU	Schumacher
ACCEHHOORS	coach-horse
ACCEHHOOSU	coach house
ACCEHHRRTU	church-rate
ACCEHIILMR	chimerical
ACCEHIIMRT	chemiatric
ACCEHIINNT	technician
ACCEHIINPT	epicanthic
ACCEHIKLNU	Auchinleck
ACCEHIKOPS	peacockish
ACCEHILLMY	chemically
ACCEHILLOY	echoically
ACCEHILLTY	hectically
ACCEHILNST	technicals
ACCEHILPRS	Cecil Sharp
ACCEHILPRV	pelvic arch
ACCEHIMNNU	unmechanic
ACCEHIMNNY	chimney can
ACCEHIMNOO	maconochie
ACCEHIMPRT	emphractic
ACCEHIMRSU	Chaucerism
ACCEHINNRY	in chancery
ACCEHINNSS	chanciness
ACCEHINORT	Acherontic
	anchoretic
ACCEHINSST	catchiness
ACCEHIOPRV	pro hac vice
ACCEHIORRY	hierocracy
ACCEHIORST	escharotic
ACCEHIORTT	theocratic
ACCEHIRRTT	tetrarchic
ACCEHIRTVZ	czarevitch
ACCEHKLNOT	checklaton
ACCEHKLOST	Scotch kale
ACCEHKOORS	a-cockhorse
ACCEHKORSU	crack house
ACCEHLLNOR	chancellor
ACCEHLMOOR	homocercal
ACCEHLOOTY	chocolatey
ACCEHLORRY	cherry-coal
ACCEHLOSUY	chylaceous
ACCEHMNOOR	comanchero
ACCEHNNOPU	chance upon
ACCEHNNPTY	catchpenny
ACCEHNNRTY	trenchancy
ACCEHNOOTY	choanocyte
ACCEHNORTT	technocrat
	trench coat
ACCEHNORVX	convex arch
ACCEHOORSU	ochraceous
ACCEHOPSTT	Scotch tape®
ACCEHORRUW	crouch-ware
ACCEIILNOT	conciliate
ACCEIILNRS	circensial
ACCEIILRRT	rectricial
ACCEIILRTT	tectricial
ACCEIILSSS	classicise
ACCEIILSSZ	classicize
ACCEIIMRST	ceramicist
ACCEIIMSST	asceticism
ACCEIINNNT	cincinnate
ACCEIINNOR	Ciceronian
ACCEIINNRS	circensian
ACCEIINRST	Cistercian
ACCEIIRSTX	cicatrixes
ACCEIKLPRT	Celtic Park
ACCEIKMNNO	Connie Mack
ACCEIKRRTW	wit-cracker
ACCEILLLOR	claircolle
ACCEILLNRU	unclerical
ACCEILLNSY	scenically
ACCEILMMOR	commercial
ACCEILMNOO	economical
ACCEILMNOP	compliance
ACCEILMNOR	Colin McRae
ACCEILMOOT	coelomatic
ACCEILMOPT	complicate
ACCEILMORS	microscale
ACCEILMOST	cacomistle
	cosmetical
ACCEILNOSS	neoclassic
ACCEILNOTU	noctilucae
ACCEILNRST	calc-sinter
ACCEILNSST	lac insects
ACCEILOPPT	apoplectic
ACCEILOPRR	reciprocal
ACCEILOPRV	prevocalic
ACCEIMNORS	conacreism
ACCEIMNRSY	miscreancy
ACCEIMOOPR	comic opera
ACCEINNNOV	connivance
ACCEINNOOR	cancionero
ACCEINNOPR	Copernican
ACCEINNORT	concertina
ACCEINNSSY	incessancy
ACCEINOORS	occasioner
ACCEINOOST	consociate
ACCEINORST	Cestracion
ACCEINRRTT	arctic tern
ACCEINTTUV	cunctative

ACCEIOORSU	coriaceous
ACCEIOPPSY	episcopacy
ACCEIOPTUV	occupative
ACCEIORRTU	Eurocratic
ACCEIORSTX	exsiccator
ACCEIORTUY	eucaryotic
ACCEIOSSTT	sticcatoes
ACCEIOSSTU	cistaceous
ACCEIRRSTT	tractrices
ACCEJNOSUU	juncaceous
ACCEKKLMOR	clockmaker
ACCEKLORTW	water clock
ACCEKNOOTT	cotton cake
ACCEKNRRTU	nutcracker
ACCELLLLOR	collar cell
ACCELLNOSU	cancellous
ACCELLNRUY	lunar cycle
ACCELLOORT	colorectal
ACCELLSSUU	calculuses
ACCELMNOPT	complacent
ACCELMNORY	cleromancy
ACCELMOPRS	camel-corps
ACCELNOPTU	conceptual
ACCELNOTXY	nectocalyx
ACCELNRTUY	reluctancy
ACCELOOPST	lactoscope
ACCELOORSV	vocal score
ACCELORTTU	coal-cutter
ACCELRSSUU	succursale
ACCEMNNORY	necromancy
ACCEMOORSS	come across
ACCEMOPRTU	compacture
ACCEMORSTU	reaccustom
ACCENNNOOS	consonance
ACCENNNOST	connascent
ACCENNORSS	as concerns
ACCENOORRT	cancer root
ACCENOORSU	cornaceous
ACCENORSST	sector scan
ACCENORSTY	consectary
ACCENORTTU	counteract
ACCENRSUVY	Cyrus Vance
ACCEOOPRTT	Ectoprocta
ACCEOORTTV	covert coat
ACCEOPSSTU	scout's pace
ACCEORSUUV	curvaceous
ACCFFFFHHI	chiffchaff
ACCFFIOPRT	traffic cop
ACCFHIRTTW	witchcraft
ACCFIIIMPR	Pacific Rim
ACCFIIIMPS	pacificism
ACCFIIIPST	pacificist
ACCFIINNOT	fantoccini
ACCFILMORY	calyciform
ACCFILSSUU	fasciculus
ACCFIMNORR	cancriform
ACCFIMOPTY	compactify
ACCFNOORRT	corn-factor
ACCFNOORTU	account for
ACCFORRTTU	courtcraft
ACCFORSTTU	scoutcraft
ACCGGHILOO	cholagogic
ACCGHHILTT	catch light
ACCGHHIORT	Gothic arch
ACCGHHISTT	catch sight
ACCGHIILOR	oligarchic
ACCGHINRST	scratching
ACCGHIOPTY	phagocytic
ACCGHIRSTW	scratch-wig
ACCGHKNOUW	chuck wagon
ACCGHLOPRY	cyclograph
ACCGHORSSU	couch grass
ACCGIIMORT	tragicomic
ACCGIKLNOO	coking coal
ACCGIKLNRS	cracklings
ACCGILNSUY	accusingly
ACCGINNOTU	accounting
ACCGINORTU	accoutring
ACCGINORTY	gynocratic
ACCGOSTUYZ	zygocactus
ACCHHIILLN	chinchilla✧
ACCHHIILRY	chiliarchy
ACCHHILLSS	clish-clash
ACCHHMRRUY	Church Army
ACCHHORSST	cross-hatch
ACCHIIILST	chiliastic
ACCHIILOOT	Catholicoi
ACCHIILORT	acrolithic
ACCHIILTTY	tachylitic
ACCHIIMOSS	isochasmic
ACCHIIMSST	mica-schist
	schismatic
ACCHIINORT	anchoritic
ACCHIINRST	stracchini
ACCHIKMQRU	quick march
ACCHIKMQTU	quick-match
ACCHIKMSTT	matchstick
ACCHILLOTY	catholicly
ACCHILMOPS	accomplish
ACCHILNNPS	splanchnic
ACCHILNNUU	CúChulainn
ACCHILNOOT	catholicon✧
ACCHILOOST	Catholicos
ACCHILOOTU	acolouthic
ACCHILOSST	scholastic
ACCHILRSTY	scratchily
ACCHILSSTT	talc schist
ACCHILTTYY	tachylytic
ACCHIMNOOY	iconomachy
ACCHIMNORY	chiromancy
ACCHIMORST	chromatics
ACCHINOOPR	acrophonic
ACCHINORST	stracchino
ACCHIOPRSZ	schizocarp
ACCHIOPTTY	hypotactic
ACCHIOSSTT	stochastic
ACCHJKLNOO	John Alcock
ACCHKLMRUY	lucky charm
ACCHMOOORT	motorcoach
ACCHMORSST	cross-match
ACCHNOPSST	Scotch snap
ACCHNOPSYY	sycophancy
ACCHNORRST	cornstarch
ACCHOOPRTY	cacotrophy
ACCHOPRSST	crosspatch
ACCHORSTTU	scratch out
ACCIIILLLP	piccalilli
ACCIIINNNT	Cincinnati
ACCIILLLNY	clinically
ACCIILLNOY	iconically
ACCIILLRTY	critically
ACCIILMNOS	laconicism
ACCIILMORU	coumarilic
ACCIILMOTY	comicality
ACCIILMSSS	classicism
ACCIILNNOT	calcitonin
ACCIILNORY	conciliary
ACCIILNRTU	uncritical
ACCIILOPRT	pictorical
ACCIILORTY	caloricity
ACCIILSSST	classicist
ACCIIMNNNO	cinnamonic
ACCIIMNOOT	iconomatic
ACCIIMNOPS	misocapnic
ACCIIMNRSU	muscarinic
ACCIIMORTT	timocratic
ACCIINNOST	canonistic
ACCIINNOTY	canonicity
ACCIINNSST	scintiscan
ACCIINORSS	carcinosis
ACCIIOPRSU	capricious
ACCIIOTTVY	coactivity
ACCIISTTUY	causticity
ACCIJKNOSU	Cousin Jack
ACCIJMORRW	Jim Crow car
ACCIKKKKNN	knick-knack
ACCIKKRRTT	trick-track
ACCILLMORY	millocracy
ACCILLMOSY	cosmically
ACCILLRRUY	circularly
ACCILLSUUU	cauliculus
ACCILMNNOU	councilman
ACCILMNOOS	iconoclasm
ACCILMNOPT	complicant
ACCILMNOPY	compliancy
ACCILMORSS	crossclaim
	cross-claim
ACCILMOSUV	vocal music
ACCILMOUXY	oxy-calcium
ACCILNOOST	iconoclast
ACCILNOPTY	nyctalopic
ACCILNORTU	inculcator
ACCILNOSTV	conclavist
ACCILNOTUX	council tax
ACCILNSSTY	synclastic
ACCILOOOTT	loco citato
ACCILOPPRY	polycarpic
ACCILORRTU	circulator
ACCILRRRUU	curricular
ACCIMMOORS	cosmoramic
ACCIMNNOVY	vancomycin
ACCIMNOOPR	monocarpic
ACCIMNOOPT	compaction

ACCIMNOORT monocratic
ACCIMNOSUU cacuminous
ACCIMORSSY cosmic rays
ACCINNNOVY connivancy
ACCINNOOOS on occasion
ACCINNOPRU Canopic urn
ACCINNORTT contract in
ACCINNOTTU cunctation
ACCINOOPRU cornucopia
ACCINOOPTU occupation
ACCINOPRSY conspiracy
ACCINORSTY Carson City
ACCIOOPRSU procacious
ACCIOOPSTU autoscopic
ACCIOPRSTT catoptrics
ACCIORSUUV curvacious
ACCKKNOOOS cock a snook
ACCKLMOORU cockalorum
ACCKORSTTU track-scout
ACCKRRSTTY crack-tryst
ACCLOPRTUY plutocracy
ACCNNNOOSY consonancy
ACCNOOPRRY pornocracy
ACCNOORRTT contractor
ACCNORTTUY cunctatory
ACDDDEELLP padded cell
ACDDDEGIPY giddy-paced
ACDDDGIRTU drug addict
ACDDEEEIRT rededicate
ACDDEEEKNU Dundee cake
ACDDEEENNP dependance
ACDDEEENRT dead centre
ACDDEEGKLN angled deck
ACDDEEHLOO coolheaded
ACDDEEHLTY detachedly
ACDDEEHNOR decahedron
ACDDEEIIPT diapedetic
ACDDEEIITV dedicative
ACDDEEKORW Edward Coke
ACDDEELLOT decollated
ACDDEELLRY declaredly
ACDDEELLSY Clydesdale
ACDDEELNRU undeclared
ACDDEELNTY decadently
ACDDEENNRU redundance
ACDDEENNST descendant
ACDDEENNSU unascended
ACDDEENTUU uneducated
ACDDEESSTU decussated
ACDDEFGHOU doughfaced
ACDDEFNORU round-faced
ACDDEGHNNY cynghanedd
ACDDEGILNO Iceland-dog
ACDDEGILRR griddle car
ACDDEGINOT date coding
ACDDEHIIIP aphidicide
ACDDEHINTU The Dunciad
ACDDEHKLRU herald-duck
ACDDEHLORR card-holder
ACDDEHNNOS second hand
second-hand
ACDDEHNOOO deaconhood
ACDDEIIJTU dijudicate
ACDDEIILTU dilucidate
ACDDEIINOT dedication
ACDDEIIRRS Cader Idris
ACDDEIKLOR Carole Kidd
ACDDEIKNRS crank-sided
ACDDEILMOU duodecimal
ACDDEILPRU dual-priced
ACDDEINNSS candidness
ACDDEIOPSU pseudoacid
ACDDEIORTY dedicatory
ACDDEIPSTU cuspidated
ACDDEIRSTT distracted
ACDDEKLLNO landlocked
ACDDEKLORS dread locks
dreadlocks
ACDDELNNOO colonnaded
ACDDELNOOW candlewood
ACDDELNOPU candle-doup
ACDDENNORU round dance
ACDDENNRUY redundancy
ACDDENORSU decandrous
ACDDENORSW sword dance
ACDDEOOPSU decapodous
ACDDFHIORU chaudfroid
ACDDGHILNR grandchild
ACDDGHNRUY grand duchy
ACDDHILNVY David Lynch
ACDDIINOPS dispondaic
ACDDILNNUY uncandidly
ACDDIMNOTU diamond-cut
ACDDIMORSW caddis-worm
ACDDINORST discordant
ACDDIOSTTV David Scott
ACDDIPRSTU cupid's dart
ACDEEEEHHS cheese-head
headcheese
ACDEEEELNS needle-case
ACDEEEELRT decelerate
ACDEEEEPRS predecease
ACDEEEFHPS sheep-faced
ACDEEEFLNR fer-de-lance
ACDEEEFMNN defenceman
ACDEEEFMNT defacement
ACDEEEGNRY degeneracy
ACDEEEHHRS hard cheese
ACDEEEHLTT decathlete
ACDEEEHNRT head-centre
ACDEEEILSU Seleucidae
ACDEEEINRT Tenrecidae
ACDEEEIPRT depreciate
ACDEEELNRT candle-tree
ACDEEELSTT telecasted
ACDEEEMNST casemented
ACDEEENNTT antecedent
ACDEEENRTV advertence
ACDEEEORRT redecorate
ACDEEERRST desecrater
ACDEEERSUY saucer-eyed
ACDEEFFHRT far-fetched
ACDEEFFLOR declare off
ACDEEFFLTY affectedly
ACDEEFFNTU unaffected
ACDEEFGOOP peace of God
ACDEEFHITW white-faced
ACDEEFHORS horse-faced
ACDEEFIIRR Fredericia
ACDEEFIKLP packed file
ACDEEFINOT defecation
ACDEEFINWZ wizen-faced
ACDEEFIRSS fricasseed
ACDEEFKOPR poker-faced
ACDEEFLNOR confederal
ACDEEFLNOY falcon-eyed
ACDEEFLORS forced sale
ACDEEFMSST mass defect
ACDEEFOPRW face powder
ACDEEFORST forecasted
ACDEEGHINP phagedenic
ACDEEGHLLN challenged
ACDEEGHNNO hendecagon
ACDEEGHNOT on the cadge
ACDEEGIIMN mediagenic
ACDEEGIINT diagenetic
ACDEEGIKLR girdle cake
ACDEEGILMO geomedical
ACDEEGILNS side glance
ACDEEGILOS geodesical
ACDEEGILOT geodetical
ACDEEGIMMR decigramme
ACDEEGINNR grand-niece
ACDEEGINRR adrenergic
ACDEEGINRT centigrade
ACDEEGIORU aigre-douce
ACDEEGLLOU colleagued
ACDEEGLLRW well-graced
ACDEEGLNRT rectangled
ACDEEGORTY grey-coated
ACDEEHIINO Echinoidea
ACDEEHILNR chandelier
ACDEEHIMRS Archimedes
ACDEEHINNR hinderance
ACDEEHINOT theodicean
ACDEEHIORT cote-hardie
ACDEEHIRTW white cedar
ACDEEHKLLS shellacked
ACDEEHLLLY Hadley cell
ACDEEHLLMU chaud-mellé
ACDEEHLLNN channelled
ACDEEHLLRT thread-cell
ACDEEHLLST satchelled
ACDEEHLNRW D H Lawrence
ACDEEHLORT cloth-eared
ACDEEHLRRU hurdle-race
ACDEEHMNTT detachment
ACDEEHNNRS hand-screen
ACDEEHNRSU unsearched
ACDEEHNRTT tented arch
ACDEEHOPPR copperhead
ACDEEIILMP epidemical
ACDEEIILMS decimalise

medicalise
ACDEEIILMZ decimalize
medicalize
ACDEEIILNT indelicate
ACDEEIILTT dietetical
ACDEEIIMRT acidimeter
ACDEEIIMTV medicative
ACDEEIIRRV a rivederci
ACDEEIKLNR Eric Kandel
ACDEEIKPRR prick-eared
ACDEEILLNP lead pencil
pencil-lead
ACDEEILLNR Cinderella
ACDEEILLRS escadrille
ACDEEILLTY delicately
ACDEEILMNR endermical
ACDEEILMNT maledicent
ACDEEILMPR premedical
ACDEEILMRV decemviral
ACDEEILNRT credential
ACDEEILNSU Seleucidan
ACDEEILOSV devocalise
ACDEEILOVZ devocalize
ACDEEILPRY dice-player
icy-pearled
ACDEEILPTU pediculate
ACDEEILRTT red lattice
red-lattice
ACDEEIMMNT medicament
ACDEEIMNNO encomienda
ACDEEIMNOT nematocide
ACDEEIMNOU eudaemonic
ACDEEIMNRT endermatic
ACDEEIMOTT comedietta
ACDEEIMPRT mercaptide
ACDEEIMRST medicaster
miscreated
ACDEEIMSTU miseducate
ACDEEINNNT intendance
ACDEEINNTU denunciate
ACDEEINORS Deinoceras
ACDEEINOST cestoidean
ACDEEINOTV advice note
ACDEEINPPS appendices
ACDEEINPTT pectinated
ACDEEINRRW wire-dancer
ACDEEINSST desistance
ACDEEIORTV decorative
ACDEEIOTTX detoxicate
ACDEEIPRRT trade price
ACDEEIPRST pederastic
ACDEEIPSTU paedeutics
ACDEEIRTTV detractive
ACDEEITTUX exactitude
ACDEEKLNRY cankeredly
ACDEELLLPW well-placed
ACDEELLLTU cellulated
ACDEELLMOS scale model
ACDEELLMPU cul-de-lampe
ACDEELLNPS spancelled
ACDEELLNRU unrecalled
ACDEELLOPS escalloped
ACDEELLOTT dolcelatte
ACDEELMORT ectodermal
ACDEELMORU leucoderma
ACDEELMRTU emerald-cut
ACDEELNNOV decennoval
ACDEELNNSU uncleansed
ACDEELNOPR pole dancer
ACDEELNOPS leap second
ACDEELNORR corn-dealer
ACDEELNOST adolescent
coated lens
ACDEELNRRY dry-cleaner
ACDEELNRTU crenulated
ACDEELOORT decolorate
ACDEELOPPY Pelecypoda
ACDEELOPRV overplaced
ACDEELORTU edulcorate
ACDEELPRSY clepsydrae
ACDEELPRTU curled-pate
ACDEELRRTT letter-card
ACDEEMMNOR commandeer
ACDEEMMNPT decampment
ACDEEMNNOS second name
ACDEEMNOST second mate
ACDEEMNOTY adenectomy
ACDEEMORSU decamerous
ACDEENNOPR ponderance
ACDEENNORR once-errand
ACDEENNOST condensate
ACDEENNOTV covenanted
ACDEENNRSU sunderance
ACDEENNRTY dry canteen
ACDEENOPRR rope dancer
ACDEENOPRT Pete Conrad
ACDEENORST second-rate
ACDEENPRRU perdurance
ACDEENPRST stepdancer
ACDEENPRTU uncarpeted
ACDEENRRSZ Zener cards
ACDEENRSSS sacredness
ACDEENRTTU detruncate
ACDEENRTVY advertency
ACDEEOPRRT deprecator
tape-record
ACDEEOPRRY copyreader
ACDEEOPRSU predaceous
ACDEEORRST desecrator
stereocard
ACDEEORVWY covered way
ACDEFFIKRT trafficked
ACDEFFILNO land office
ACDEFFILRT fieldcraft
ACDEFFINRT fact-finder
ACDEFFLORS scaffolder
ACDEFFLOTU duffel coat
ACDEFGHILT light-faced
ACDEFGILNY defacingly
ACDEFGINOR dog-fancier
ACDEFGLLNO golden calf
ACDEFGLORW clawed frog
ACDEFHILNS candlefish
ACDEFHIRSS sacred fish
ACDEFHNNRW Dawn French
ACDEFHOSUV vouchsafed
ACDEFIIINT nidificate
ACDEFIILMS facsimiled
ACDEFIILOT foeticidal
ACDEFIILSS classified
ACDEFIINPU unpacified
ACDEFIINST sanctified
ACDEFIIRRT fratricide
ACDEFILMTU multifaced
ACDEFILSSY declassify
ACDEFINNOT confidante
ACDEFINORT deforciant
ACDEFIOPRT forcipated
ACDEFIRSSY decrassify
ACDEFLNOOR dance floor
ACDEFLNOOT foot-candle
ACDEFNORRU uncared-for
ACDEFNRRTU under-craft
ACDEFNRRUY furry dance
ACDEFNRSSY fancy dress
ACDEFNRSUU unsurfaced
ACDEFPTTUY putty-faced
ACDEGGIOPS pedagogics
ACDEGGNOOR go-go dancer
ACDEGGRSTU egg custard
ACDEGHHILP high-placed
ACDEGHILTT tight-laced
ACDEGHIRRS discharger
ACDEGHNNOW change down
ACDEGHNORW charge down
ACDEGHRRSU surcharged
ACDEGIILMN declaiming
ACDEGIILMR germicidal
ACDEGIINNN indignance
ACDEGIINOR radiogenic
ACDEGIINOT Cotingidae
ACDEGIINRS in disgrace
ACDEGIINST die-casting
ACDEGIIRRR cirrigrade
ACDEGILNRW arc welding
ACDEGILNTU cingulated
ACDEGILOOP logopaedic
ACDEGILOST decalogist
ACDEGILRTT cattle grid
ACDEGIMNOY geodynamic
ACDEGIMNRR grand merci
ACDEGINNOR androgenic
ACDEGINNST set dancing
ACDEGINORR corrigenda
ACDEGINRTT detracting
ACDEGINRTY garden city
ACDEGIORSU discourage
ACDEGJNOTU conjugated
ACDEGKNORR rock garden
ACDEGKORRT tracker dog
ACDEGLLOPR placer-gold
ACDEGLLPUY cudgel-play
ACDEGLNNRU grand-uncle

ACDEGLNNST scent gland
ACDEGLNORS cradle-song
ACDEGLOORS socdolager
ACDEGLTUYY legacy duty
ACDEGNOSUY decagynous
ACDEGOOPRS scrapegood
ACDEHHIMOR Hemichorda
ACDEHHNTTU unthatched
ACDEHHOPRT heptachord
ACDEHHORTY hydrotheca
ACDEHIILLO helicoidal
ACDEHIILTV civil death
ACDEHIIMRT diathermic
ACDEHIINNS disenchain
ACDEHIINRS Irish dance
ACDEHIINRV chain drive
ACDEHIIORR diarrhoeic
ACDEHIKPPU pick-up head
ACDEHILLMT ill-matched
ACDEHILMOT methodical
ACDEHILMRS Childermas
ACDEHILNRS Reichsland
ACDEHILNST Shetlandic
ACDEHILORT chloridate
ACDEHILRTW witch-alder
ACDEHIMORT dichromate
ACDEHINNST disenchant
ACDEHINOPS deaconship
ACDEHINOPT Dictaphone®
ACDEHINORT ditrochean
ACDEHINPRT cinder path
ACDEHINRSZ scherzandi
ACDEHIOPPT heptapodic
ACDEHIORRR hod carrier
Richard Roe
ACDEHIPRST dispatcher
ACDEHIPSST dispatches
ACDEHIRTTW ditchwater
ACDEHKLNSU unshackled
ACDEHKNNOS danke schön
ACDEHLLNPU punch-ladle
ACDEHLLNRY chandlerly
ACDEHLMOOS dame-school
school dame
ACDEHLMTTU Dutch metal
ACDEHLNOSY anchylosed
ACDEHLNRSU rush candle
ACDEHLOOPP cephalopod
ACDEHLRSTY starchedly
ACDEHMNOOT come to hand
ACDEHMOSTU moustached
ACDEHNNOOT cante hondo
ACDEHNNORU unanchored
ACDEHNNSTU unstanched
ACDEHNOORT octahedron
ACDEHNOPRT pentachord
ACDEHNOPRW preach down
ACDEHNORST on the cards
ACDEHNORSZ scherzando
ACDEHNRSTU unstarched
ACDEHOPRSY hydrospace
ACDEHOPRTU pouched rat
ACDEHORRSW wordsearch
ACDEHORRTT tetrachord
ACDEHRTTTU Dutch treat
ACDEIIILST idealistic
ACDEIIINNR Indian rice
ACDEIIINTV indicative
ACDEIIIPRR Cirripedia
ACDEIIJTUV judicative
ACDEIIKNNS Dickensian
ACDEIILLOT idiolectal
ACDEIILMMS decimalism
ACDEIILMMT dilemmatic
ACDEIILMRS disclaimer
ACDEIILMRT direct mail
ACDEIILMRV vermicidal
ACDEIILMST decimalist
ACDEIILNNT incidental
ACDEIILNOT Diocletian
ACDEIILOPR periodical
ACDEIILOPS episodical
ACDEIILORS cordialise
ACDEIILORZ cordialize
ACDEIILPST pesticidal
septicidal
ACDEIILPTU Pediculati
ACDEIIMNOT decimation
medication
ACDEIIMOST lastic mode
ACDEIIMPRU epicardium
ACDEIIMRTX taxidermic
ACDEIIMRTY acidimetry
ACDEIINNOR crinoidean
ACDEIINNRY incendiary
ACDEIINOSY isocyanide
ACDEIINPRY Cyprinidae
ACDEIIORSU iridaceous
ACDEIIOSST dissociate
ACDEIIPPRY cypripedia
ACDEIIPRST pediatrics
ACDEIIPSTU paideutics
ACDEIJNTUV adjunctive
ACDEIJRTUU judicature
ACDEILLORR cordillera
ACDEILLTUV victualled
ACDEILMNOR decinormal
ACDEILMNOS Colin Meads
ACDEILMOST domestical
ACDEILNNOR endocrinal
ACDEILNORT centroidal
declinator
ACDEILNORY corydaline
ACDEILNOSV volcanised
ACDEILNOVZ volcanized
ACDEILNPSS placidness
ACDEILNRTW winter-clad
ACDEILNSTY syndetical
ACDEILOPRR precordial
ACDEILOPST despotical
ACDEILORSU radiculose
ACDEILORSW Oscar Wilde
ACDEILORTU elucidator
ACDEILOSTU Locustidae
ACDEILOSTY Scolytidae
ACDEILOSUY edaciously
ACDEILOTTU colatitude
ACDEILPRSY disc player
ACDEILPSTU disculpate
ACDEILRTTW wildcatter
ACDEIMMORY immoderacy
ACDEIMNNNO demi-cannon
ACDEIMNNOP pandemonic✧
ACDEIMNNOR corn-maiden
ACDEIMNNST mendicants
ACDEIMNOPR incompared
ACDEIMNOPU coup de main
ACDEIMNORU androecium
ACDEIMNOSU mendacious
ACDEIMNRSU muscardine
ACDEIMOPRR madreporic
ACDEINNNTY intendancy
ACDEINNOSS dissonance
ACDEINNRSS rancidness
ACDEINOORT carotenoid
co-ordinate
decoration
ACDEINOPPT pentapodic
ACDEINOPRS scorpaenid
ACDEINOQRU quadricone
ACDEINORRW cordwainer
ACDEINORST draconites
ACDEINORTT detraction
ACDEINOSTT anecdotist
ACDEINOSTW wainscoted
ACDEINOTTX detoxicant
ACDEINPPTU painted cup
ACDEINPRST discrepant
ACDEINPSTT pandectist
ACDEINRTUV incurvated
ACDEINSTTU sanctitude
ACDEIOOPRS radioscope
ACDEIOPRST ceratopsid
ACDEIOPRSU predacious
ACDEIOPRTT tetrapodic
ACDEIOPSSU coup d'essai
spadiceous
ACDEIORRTT Attic order
ACDEIORSTU outside-car
ACDEIOSSTT tossicated
ACDEIOSTTT tosticated
ACDEIPQRSU quadriceps
ACDEIPRSTU custard pie
ACDEIQRSTU quadrisect
ACDEIRSSTT dictatress
ACDEIRSSTU crassitude
ACDEIRSSTY dyscrasite
ACDEIRSTTU rusticated
ACDEIRTTUV traductive
ACDEJKKNOY jack donkey
ACDEJKSTTU dust jacket
ACDEJNNOOT cante jondo
ACDEKKMOPR pockmarked

ACDEKLNOOS saloon deck
ACDEKMNORS second mark
ACDEKMORST dock-master
ACDEKMPRSU muckspread
ACDEKNRSSU sandsucker
ACDEKNRSUV raven's-duck
ACDEKORSTY rocksteady
rock-steady
ACDELLOORT decollator
ACDELLORSW worldscale
ACDELLORWY yellow card
ACDELMNOOR coromandel✧
ACDELMNOTU columnated
documental
ACDELMOPRR palmcorder
ACDELNNOOY Conan Doyle
ACDELNOORT decolorant
ACDELNOORW Noël Coward
ACDELNOOTY acotyledon
ACDELNORTU edulcorant
ACDELNPRUU peduncular
ACDELNRSSU underclass
ACDELOOPST postal code
ACDELOORRW wool-carder
ACDELOPPTU clapped-out
ACDELOPRRU procedural
ACDELOPRTT cattle prod
ACDELOSSTU outclassed
ACDELPRSSY clepsydras
ACDEMMNORY commandery
ACDEMMORRY memory card
ACDEMMOSTU custom-made
ACDEMNORST Doc Martens®
ACDEMNORTU mucronated
ACDEMOOPRR compradore
ACDEMOPRSU damp-course
ACDEMORRSS cross-armed
ACDEMPRSTU spermaduct
ACDENNNOOR ordonnance
ACDENNOPRY ponderancy
ACDENOPPSW snow-capped
ACDENOPSSU soundscape
ACDENOPSTY syncopated
ACDENORRTU underactor
ACDENORSTY candy store
ACDENORTTU tranced-out
ACDENRRRTU redcurrant
ACDENRRSTU transducer
ACDENRSTTU cruet-stand
ACDEOORRVW woodcarver
ACDEOPPRSU pseudocarp
ACDEOPRRTT protracted
ACDEOPRSUU drupaceous
ACDEORRTTY detractory
ACDFFHINSU handicuffs
ACDFGIIINY acidifying
ACDFGIILNU fungicidal
ACDFGILRTU craft guild
ACDFGLNORU calf-ground
ACDFGNOOSY fancy goods
ACDFIILLUY fiducially
ACDFIIMORR radiciform
ACDFILNOSU social fund
ACDFIMNNOR confirmand
ACDFLNOSSY candyfloss
ACDFLOORXY Oxford clay
ACDFORRSTW swordcraft
ACDGHIINNS Ding an sich
ACDGHINORR orcharding
ACDGHIOPRT Dictograph®
ACDGHIPRSY dysgraphic
ACDGHNOOTU touch and go
ACDGIIIMNR gramicidin
ACDGIILLRW wild garlic
ACDGIILOOR radiologic
ACDGIINORS disorganic
ACDGIINORT riding coat
ACDGIINOST diagnostic
ACDGIKNNNU King Duncan
ACDGILMOOS mosaic gold
ACDGILNOOT odontalgic
ACDGILOORY cardiology
ACDGIMMNNO commanding
ACDGINNPRU cup-and-ring
ACDGLNORUY clay-ground
ACDGLOTYYZ zygodactyl
ACDGMNOPRU campground
ACDGORRSSU cross guard
ACDHHLNOOR anchor-hold
ACDHIIIIRR Richard III
ACDHIIILRT crithidial
ACDHIIIOPT idiopathic
ACDHIILOSZ schizoidal
ACDHIIMSSS Chassidism
ACDHIINOTU Houdini act
ACDHILLPSY child's play
ACDHILLRYY hydrically
ACDHILMNOW woman-child
ACDHILMOOS schoolmaid
ACDHILNOOP chilopodan
ACDHILOORT trochoidal
ACDHILRSST third class
third-class
ACDHILRSSY chrysalids
ACDHILRSUY hydraulics
ACDHIMOSTU Midas touch
ACDHIMSTYY dysthymiac
ACDHINOOOP Ophiacodon
ACDHINOOOX chionodoxa
ACDHIOOPRR Cirrhopoda
ACDHIOOPRS Discophora
ACDHIOOPSZ Schizopoda
ACDHIOPRSW cowardship
ACDHIORRST orchardist
ACDHIORRSW disc harrow
ACDHIORTTY trachytoid
ACDHIRSSSW Swiss chard
ACDHKMNOOY Hock Monday
ACDHKORSST hard stocks
ACDHLLOOSU dual school
ACDHLOORRU urochordal
ACDHLOORSW schoolward
ACDHLOOSSY schooldays
ACDHMNOORS chondromas
ACDHMNORYY hydromancy
ACDHMNOTUW Dutchwoman
ACDHNORSUW dawn chorus
ACDIIIJLNU injudicial
ACDIIIMMRU miracidium
ACDIIINNOT indication
ACDIIJLLUY judicially
ACDIIJNOTU judication
ACDIIKLLOP pickadillo
ACDIIKLLPY pickadilly
ACDIIKMNPX pick-and-mix
ACDIILLOPR prolicidal
ACDIILLSUY suicidally
ACDIILMOPT diplomatic
ACDIILMOST modalistic
ACDIILNOSV Colin Davis
ACDIILOPRT dioptrical
ACDIILORST clostridia
ACDIILORTY cordiality
radiolytic
ACDIILORUX uxoricidal
ACDIIMNNOS Dominicans
ACDIIMNOOT coati-mondi
ACDIIMNORT antidromic
ACDIIMNOSY isodynamic
ACDIIMNOTU coati-mundi
ACDIIMNSTY dynamicist
dynamistic
ACDIINNNOR Indian corn
ACDIINNORY inordinacy
ACDIINOORT carotinoid
ACDIINOORV Ordovician
ACDIINOOST scotodinia
ACDIINORSU dinosauric
ACDIINORTV vindicator
ACDIINORTY dictionary
indicatory
ACDIINOSTT donatistic
ACDIINRTUY iracundity
ACDIIOORTX radiotoxic
ACDIIOPRST parodistic
ACDIIOSSSU Dio Cassius
ACDIJNNOTU adjunction
ACDIJORTUX coadjutrix
ACDIJORTUY judicatory
ACDIKKNORU kick around
ACDIKLORRZ rock lizard
ACDIKNNPTU nip and tuck
ACDIKNOTTY tick and toy
ACDIKNQSUY quick-sandy
ACDILLMNOT call to mind
ACDILLMNOU calmodulin
ACDILLOOST idoloclast
ACDILLOSTT St Clotilda
ACDILMPRUY Plaid Cymru
ACDILNOPRS spinal cord
ACDILNRSTU translucid
ACDILOOPRS prosodical
ACDILOOPTY octaploidy

Words marked ✧ can also be spelled with one or more capital letters

ACDILOPRTU	duplicator
ACDILORSSU	discoursal
ACDILPSSTY	dysplastic
ACDIMMORUY	myocardium
ACDIMNNOOT	codominant
ACDIMNORTU	Dracontium
ACDIMNSSTU	music stand
ACDIMOORSU	mordacious
ACDINNORSU	Andronicus
ACDINNOSSY	dissonancy
ACDINOORRT	rain-doctor
ACDINORSTY	syndicator
ACDINORTTU	traduction
ACDINSSSTU	discussant
ACDIOOPRSY	radioscopy
ACDIOOSTUU	outdacious
ACDIORRSTT	distractor
ACDJKLNNOO	Jack London
ACDKLMOSSY	lady's-smock
ACDKLORSTU	truckloads
ACDKMNORUU	muck around
ACDKNORSTU	soundtrack
ACDLLNNOOY	London Clay
ACDLLOOPSW	codswallop
	cod's-wallop
ACDLLOPTYY	polydactyl
ACDLLORSSW	world-class
ACDLLORSTU	collar stud
ACDLMNOOSY	condylomas
ACDLMNOOUV	mud volcano
ACDLNOOSTT	scot and lot
ACDLNSTYYY	syndactyly
ACDMMNNOOO	on commando
ACDMMNOOOT	common toad
ACDMNOOPSY	spodomancy
ACDMOOSSUV	muscovados
ACDNOORSTU	octandrous
ACDOORRSSS	crossroads
ACEEEEGHSS	sage cheese
ACEEEEGNPR	Greenpeace
ACEEEFFKTT	take effect
ACEEEFFMNT	effacement
ACEEEFFTTU	effectuate
ACEEEFGNRY	free agency
ACEEEFIPRS	fire escape
ACEEEFIPRT	afterpiece
ACEEEFKNNS	snake fence
ACEEEFLNRR	freelancer
ACEEEFMNNT	enfacement
ACEEEFORST	Sea of Crete
ACEEEFRSSX	excess fare
ACEEEGILNN	inelegance
ACEEEGILTX	exegetical
ACEEEGINRT	great-niece
ACEEEGNPRT	percentage
ACEEEGNRRY	regeneracy
ACEEEHILSV	chevesaile
ACEEEHIRTT	hereticate
ACEEEHKPRS	cash-keeper
ACEEEHLNST	clean sheet
ACEEEHLOTU	haute école
ACEEEHLPSW	scape-wheel
ACEEEHNNRV	en revanche
ACEEEHORRT	Heterocera
ACEEEHPSTT	set the pace
ACEEEHRRRS	researcher
ACEEEHRRRT	treacherer
ACEEEHRSTT	chaste tree
ACEEEIMRST	camsteerie
ACEEEINNNT	ante-Nicene
ACEEEINRRS	reincrease
ACEEEINRRT	reiterance
ACEEEINRSS	nécessaire
ACEEEIPPRV	apperceive
ACEEEIPRRV	Peace River
ACEEEIRRST	secretaire
ACEEEIRRTV	recreative
ACEEEIRSTV	eviscerate
	tea service
ACEEEIRTVX	execrative
ACEEEKPPPR	pepper-cake
ACEEELLNPR	repellance
ACEEELLNRT	crenellate
ACEEELMNNT	enlacement
ACEEELNPRV	prevalence
ACEEELNRTW	T E Lawrence
ACEEELORTT	electorate
ACEEELOSTT	steatocele
ACEEELPRVY	everyplace
ACEEELPSSS	escapeless
ACEEELRRST	steer clear
ACEEELRRTW	welter race
ACEEELRSTT	telecaster
ACEEELRTUX	exulcerate
ACEEELSTTU	sea lettuce
ACEEEMMNRT	amercement
ACEEEMNNPR	permanence
ACEEEMNNST	encasement
ACEEEMNPRT	temperance
ACEEEMNPST	escapement
ACEEEMNRST	meatscreen
ACEEEMNRTT	metacentre
ACEEEMNRTX	excrementa
ACEEENNOTV	covenantee
ACEEENNPRT	penetrance
	repentance
ACEEENNRRT	re-entrance
ACEEENNSTV	evanescent
ACEEENNTTW	wet canteen
ACEEEPPPRR	crêpe paper
ACEEEPRRTU	recuperate
ACEEEPRSTT	pace-setter
ACEEEPRSTU	pâte sucrée
ACEEERRTTT	terracette
ACEEFFFHOT	off the face
ACEEFFHLOT	halo effect
ACEEFFHLRS	schefflera
ACEEFFHSUU	chauffeuse
ACEEFFILRT	café filtre
ACEEFFIMNY	effeminacy
ACEEFFLOTY	feet of clay
ACEEFFLSST	affectless
ACEEFFNRSU	sufferance
ACEEFGIRST	siegecraft
ACEEFGPRST	perfect gas
ACEEFHHTTW	chew the fat
ACEEFHINPR	pine-chafer
ACEEFHINRS	franchisee
ACEEFHISSV	cavefishes
ACEEFHLNRT	centre-half
ACEEFHMNRS	French seam
ACEEFHNORT	technofear
ACEEFHORRS	rose chafer
	shear force
ACEEFHRTTU	feather cut
ACEEFIIILN	Filicineae
ACEEFIILTT	felicitate
ACEEFIILTV	active life
ACEEFIJKLT	life jacket
ACEEFIKLRT	filter cake
ACEEFILMNT	maleficent
ACEEFILNRT	frenetical
ACEEFILNSS	facileness
ACEEFILNST	leaf insect
ACEEFILRSU	luciferase
ACEEFIORTV	vociferate
ACEEFIRRTV	refractive
ACEEFKORRW	faceworker
ACEEFLLNTU	flatulence
ACEEFLLORV	cloverleaf
ACEEFLLPUY	peacefully
ACEEFLLSTY	safety cell
ACEEFLNPUU	unpeaceful
ACEEFLNRST	flat-screen
ACEEFLNSTV	flavescent
ACEEFLORST	forecastle
ACEEFLRTTU	leaf-cutter
ACEEFNOOST	to one's face
ACEEFNQRTU	queencraft
ACEEFOPSSU	pousse-café
ACEEFORRST	forecaster
ACEEFPRSTU	superfecta
ACEEFRRRTU	refracture
ACEEGGGINP	pace-egging
ACEEGGHOPR	egg poacher
ACEEGGILNO	genealogic
ACEEGGLPSU	egg capsule
ACEEGGNORT	congregate
ACEEGGRSTU	curate's egg
ACEEGHHRTW	chew the rag
ACEEGHIKMR	Graeme Hick
ACEEGHILNT	genethliac
ACEEGHINNX	in exchange
ACEEGHIRTX	exit charge
ACEEGHLLNR	challenger
ACEEGHLNRT	acre-length
ACEEGHLNSS	changeless
ACEEGHLRSS	chargeless
ACEEGHNNOP	Copenhagen
ACEEGHNORV	change over
	changeover
ACEEGHNRRT	rent-charge
ACEEGHORRV	overcharge

ACEEGIKNPS king's peace
ACEEGIKTTW get a wicket
wicket gate
ACEEGILLNR allergenic
ACEEGILLOT collegiate
ACEEGILLPR peelgarlic
ACEEGILNNY inelegancy
ACEEGILNTU geniculate
ACEEGILRRR career girl
ACEEGILSTU sluicegate
ACEEGIMNOR cinema-goer
ACEEGINNPT pangenetic
ACEEGINOPP Cape pigeon
ACEEGIOPTT cottage pie
ACEEGIORRT groceteria
ACEEGIORST categories
categorise
ACEEGIORTZ categorize
ACEEGIOTTX excogitate
ACEEGJNORS Grace Jones
ACEEGKLLRY Grace Kelly
ACEEGKNOPS sponge cake
ACEEGLLRTT target cell
ACEEGLMNOR camerlengo
ACEEGLNORS close-range
ACEEGLNORV glance over
overglance
ACEEGLNRTU great-uncle
ACEEGLNRTW clew-garnet
ACEEGLRTUV culvertage
ACEEGMMOSU gemmaceous
ACEEGMOTTY gametocyte
ACEEGNNORV governance
ACEEGNNPRU repugnance
ACEEGNNSWY news agency
ACEEGNORRU encourager
ACEEGNRSVY scavengery
ACEEGOPRST corpse-gate
ACEEHHILNW chainwheel
ACEEHHILRW wheelchair
ACEEHHIPRT chip heater
ACEEHHIRRS heresiarch
ACEEHHLMNT Cheltenham
ACEEHHLNNT the Channel
ACEEHHNNOT Ethan Cohen
ACEEHHNOPT on the cheap
ACEEHHPTTU Heptateuch
ACEEHIIPRT perithecia
ACEEHIKNTT kitchen tea
ACEEHILMNN manchineel
ACEEHILMRT hermetical
ACEEHILNNP encephalin
ACEEHILNNS channelise
ACEEHILNNZ channelize
ACEEHILNRT in the clear
ACEEHILNST anthelices
ACEEHILPTT telepathic
ACEEHILSSS chaiseless
ACEEHIMMNO home cinema
ACEEHIMNPZ chimpanzee
ACEEHIMNRZ mechanizer
ACEEHIMPRY hyperaemic
ACEEHIMPTT empathetic
ACEEHIMRTX hexametric
ACEEHIMSST schematise
ACEEHIMSTZ schematize
ACEEHIMTTT metathetic
ACEEHINNOT Antiochene
ACEEHINNPT phenacetin
ACEEHINOPR peacherino
ACEEHINPRS phrenesiac
ACEEHIORRT charioteer✧
ACEEHISSTT aesthetics
ACEEHISTUW white sauce
ACEEHKLNRT halter neck
ACEEHKMNSU hamesucken
ACEEHKMTTU make the cut
ACEEHKPRST sheeptrack
ACEEHLLMOS cameo-shell
ACEEHLLMPW wheel clamp
wheel-clamp
ACEEHLLNNR channeller
ACEEHLLNOP Cellophane®
ACEEHLLRTV latch lever
ACEEHLMSTU Telemachus
ACEEHLNNOP encephalon
ACEEHLNPRU leprechaun
ACEEHLNPRW leprechawn
ACEEHLNPTT planchette
ACEEHLNPTY phlyctenae
ACEEHLOPTY polychaete
ACEEHLOSSV close shave
ACEEHLRSSS searchless
ACEEHLRSST thale cress
ACEEHLRTVW lever-watch
ACEEHLSSST scatheless
ACEEHMMRSU meerschaum
ACEEHMNNST encashment
ACEEHMNPRT preachment
ACEEHMNRST Manchester
ACEEHMOPRS scrape home
ACEEHMOPRT chrome tape
ACEEHMOPSS mesoscaphe
ACEEHMORTT tachometer
ACEEHMPRTY pachymeter
ACEEHMRTTY tachymeter
ACEEHMSSTT steam chest
ACEEHNOPST peach-stone
ACEEHNPTTU Pentateuch
ACEEHNRSST stern-chase
ACEEHNSSST chasteness
ACEEHOPRRR reproacher
ACEEHOPRSU proseuchae
ACEEHOPTTY hepatocyte
ACEEHORRST trace-horse
ACEEHORRTT the Creator
ACEEHPPRSY hyperspace
ACEEHPRRSU repurchase
ACEEHPRTUY hyperacute
ACEEHPSTTU put the case
ACEEHRRSTU chartreuse✧
ACEEHRTTUW water chute
ACEEIILMRT eremitical
ACEEIILNPS in especial
ACEEIILNTT licentiate
ACEEIILPSS specialise
ACEEIILPSZ specialize
ACEEIILSST elasticise
ACEEIILSTZ elasticize
ACEEIIMNPT impatience
ACEEIIMNTT antiemetic
ACEEIIMPST episematic
ACEEIIMRRU Marie Curie
ACEEIINNRT creatinine
incinerate
ACEEIIPSST asepticise
ACEEIIPSTZ asepticize
ACEEIIRRST sericteria
ACEEIIRTTV recitative
ACEEIITTVX excitative
ACEEIJLMSV Clive James
ACEEIJLNQU Jacqueline
ACEEIJMOPR major piece
ACEEIKLMNS simnel cake
ACEEIKLMTT meal ticket
ACEEIKLNRT trancelike
ACEEIKLRRT craterlike
ACEEIKNNSS snick-a-snee
ACEEIKNOTT take notice
ACEEIKNRSS creakiness
ACEEIKPRTT ticker tape
ACEEILLMST mile-castle
ACEEILLMTY emetically
ACEEILLNRW wine cellar
ACEEILLORS El Escorial
ACEEILLORT electorial
ACEEILLPSY especially
ACEEILLPTT capelletti
ACEEILMMRS mesmerical
ACEEILMNNT Clementina
ACEEILMNOR ceremonial
real income
ACEEILMNOT colemanite
melaconite
ACEEILMNRT mercantile
ACEEILMNST centesimal
lemniscate
ACEEILMOSU meliaceous
ACEEILMPTT metaleptic
ACEEILMRST Carmelites
ACEEILMSTT telematics
telesmatic
ACEEILNNNT centennial
ACEEILNNPT Pentelican
ACEEILNNUV univalence
ACEEILNOPU leucopenia
ACEEILNORT neoterical
ACEEILNPRT epicentral
ACEEILNRRT centre-rail
ACEEILNRST centralise
ACEEILNRSU nuclearise
ACEEILNRTV cantilever
trivalence

ACEEILNRTZ centralize
ACEEILNRUZ nuclearize
ACEEILORTV corelative
ACEEILORTX exoterical
ACEEILPPRT preceptial
tea clipper
ACEEILPRSW parcelwise
ACEEILPRTT carpet tile
ACEEILRRSU curselarie
ACEEILRRTT retractile
ACEEILRSSU secularise
ACEEILRSUZ secularize
ACEEILRTTU reticulate
ACEEILRTUV ulcerative
ACEEILRTVY creatively
reactively
ACEEILSTUV vesiculate
ACEEIMNNRS Emi-Scanner®
ACEEIMNNST incasement
ACEEIMNORU Mucorineae
ACEEIMNRSS creaminess
ACEEIMNRSV serviceman
ACEEIMNRTT remittance
ACEEIMORRT aerometric
ACEEIMPRST spermaceti
ACEEIMRSTT tetrasemic
ACEEINNPRS inner space
Spencerian
ACEEINNRST transience
ACEEINOPST stenopaeic
ACEEINORRT recreation
ACEEINORST estanciero
ACEEINORTU auctioneer
ACEEINORTX execration
ACEEINPPRT apprentice
pine carpet
ACEEINPRST interspace
ACEEINRSST resistance✧
ACEEINRTTT tetractine
ACEEINRTUV unreactive
ACEEINRTVY inveteracy
ACEEINSSTV activeness
ACEEIOOPRS aeciospore
ACEEIOPPST episcopate
ACEEIOPSST caespitose
ACEEIOQTUV equivocate
ACEEIORTVV overactive
ACEEIPPRTY party piece
ACEEIPQRSU picaresque
ACEEIPRRSV riverscape
ACEEIQRSTU requiescat
ACEEIRRSUW cruisewear
ACEEIRRTTV retractive
ACEEIRSTTU Securitate
ACEEIRTTVX extractive
ACEEJJMOSY James Joyce
ACEEJKMSST mess jacket
ACEEJKNOTT Eton jacket
ACEEJLMNOT cajolement
ACEEKLLNNO kennel-coal
ACEEKLLOWY yellowcake
ACEEKLLRSS sales clerk
salesclerk
ACEEKLNOST nose tackle
ACEEKLOPPR pack or peel
ACEEKLRRTW water clerk
ACEEKNOPTT packet-note
ACEEKNRRRT rack-renter
ACEEKNRTTV track event
ACEEKORRRW careworker
ACEEKORRSW caseworker
ACEELLLMOU columellae
ACEELLMNRT recallment
ACEELLNOTU nucleolate
ACEELLNPRY repellancy
ACEELLNPST pallescent
ACEELLNRSW Allen screw
screen wall
ACEELLORTT collarette
ACEELLRSSY carelessly
ACEELLRSTY celery salt
ACEELLSTTU scutellate
ACEELMNOST solacement
ACEELMNOTY melanocyte
ACEELMOPRT clapometer
ACEELMORTT lactometer
ACEELNOPRV Provençale
ACEELNOPST opalescent
ACEELNORRT necrolater
ACEELNPRSU superclean
ACEELNPRSY screenplay
ACEELNPRVY prevalency
ACEELNRRTY recreantly
ACEELNSSUW Wenceslaus
ACEELOOPRT Coleoptera
ACEELOORSU oleraceous
ACEELOOSTW weasel coot
ACEELOPPRT Plecoptera
ACEELOPRTU operculate
ACEELOSSTT cassolette
ACEELPPRTU perceptual
ACEELPRSTW screw plate
ACEELQRRUU craquelure
ACEELRRTUY creaturely
ACEELRSSSU saucerless
ACEEMMNNPT encampment
ACEEMMNOTT commentate
ACEEMMORRY race memory
ACEEMMORSU commeasure
ACEEMNNPRY permanency
ACEEMNOPST compensate
ACEEMNORTY cyanometer
ACEEMNPRST escarpment
ACEEMOSTUZ eczematous
ACEENNOOSS on one's case
ACEENNOPRV provenance
ACEENNOPSU pennaceous
ACEENNORTV contravene
covenanter
ACEENNOTTZ canzonette
ACEENNPRST PET scanner
ACEENNPRTU purtenance
ACEENNPRTY penetrancy
ACEENNPRVY prevenancy
ACEENNRRTY re-entrancy
ACEENNRSSV cravenness
ACEENNSSTU sustenance
ACEENOOSTU coetaneous
ACEENOPRTT pernoctate
ACEENOPSST set one's cap
ACEENORSSS coarseness
ACEENORSST antecessor
ACEENORSTU nectareous
raconteuse
ACEENORSTX Xenocrates
ACEENPRRST Carpenters
ACEENPRSTT respectant
ACEENPRUVY purveyance
ACEENRRSTT arts centre
ACEENRRTUU nature cure
ACEENRSSST ancestress
ACEENRSSTW newscaster
ACEENRSUVY surveyance
ACEENSSTTV Cat Stevens
ACEEOPRSTU outer space
ACEEORRSTT stercorate
ACEEORRTVX extra cover
ACEEORRTXY execratory
ACEEOSSTTU testaceous
ACEEPRRRTU recapturer
ACEEPRSTUU superacute
ACEERRSSTW watercress
ACEFFGINSU suffigance
ACEFFGNSUU face-fungus
ACEFFHHILT Heathcliff
ACEFFHLNOR French loaf
ACEFFHLPSU shuffle-cap
ACEFFIILTV afflictive
ACEFFIIMNS caffeinism
ACEFFIIORR air-officer
ACEFFIKRRT trafficker
ACEFFILNOO loan-office
ACEFFILORW law-officer
ACEFFINSSU suffisance
ACEFFKLNOS slacken off
ACEFFLOOSS loss of face
ACEFFOSTUU tuffaceous
ACEFGHIRRT freight-car
ACEFGIKLRU craigfluke
ACEFGILNST self-acting
ACEFGINRRT refracting
ACEFGIRTUU cut a figure
ACEFGLLRUY gracefully
ACEFGLNRUU ungraceful
ACEFGLORUU courageful
ACEFHHIRRS archerfish
ACEFHHNRSS French sash
ACEFHIIMOR Maori chief
ACEFHIINTT fianchetti
ACEFHILNST lancet fish
ACEFHILPST felspathic
ACEFHILRTU ultrafiche
ACEFHINOTT fianchetto

ACEFHINRRS	franchiser
ACEFHIORSS	coarse fish
ACEFHIPSTT	the cap fits
ACEFHIRRSV	fish-carver
ACEFHKORST	aftershock
ACEFHLLNOP	chopfallen
ACEFHLOOTT	act the fool
ACEFHLOPSW	wolf's peach
ACEFHMPPTU	fetch a pump
ACEFHOORTU	out of reach
ACEFHORRTV	hovercraft
ACEFHORSTU	housecraft
ACEFIIILNN	filicinean
ACEFIIILST	facilities
ACEFIILMSS	facsimiles
ACEFIILNRU	Luciferian
ACEFIILORR	calorifier
ACEFIILPST	spiflicate
ACEFIILRSS	classifier
ACEFIINRST	sanctifier✧
ACEFIKLLNS	sick-fallen
ACEFIKLNPS	clasp knife
ACEFILMOTU	atomic fuel
ACEFILNORS	forinsecal
ACEFILNOST	self-action
ACEFILNTUU	funiculate
ACEFILOOSU	foliaceous
ACEFILORTV	vital force
ACEFILRSSY	reclassify
ACEFIMNOSS	Neofascism
ACEFINNPRY	Fanny Price
ACEFINORRT	for certain
	refraction
ACEFINORTV	vociferant
ACEFINORUY	in-your-face
ACEFINOSST	Neofascist
ACEFINRSST	craftiness
ACEFIRRRTV	rivercraft
ACEFIRRTTU	trifurcate
ACEFIRSSTU	first cause
ACEFJKLNOT	Jack of Lent
ACEFKLNORS	cornflakes
ACEFKLOPPR	flock-paper
ACEFKLOSTY	safety lock
ACEFKMORTY	Mary of Teck
ACEFLLNOOR	once for all
	once-for-all
ACEFLLNTUY	flatulency
ACEFLMORUU	camoufleur
ACEFLOOPTU	out of place
ACEFLPSTUU	teacupfuls
ACEFLRSSUU	saucerfuls
ACEFMNOORT	canto fermo
ACEFNNOSST	confessant
ACEFNOPRTT	Pontefract
ACEFNOPRTU	pot furnace
ACEFORRRTY	refractory
ACEFRRSSTU	surfcaster
ACEGGHILNN	changeling
ACEGGHIOPR	geographic
ACEGGHLOOU	cholagogue
ACEGGILLOO	geological
ACEGGINNOO	ocean-going
ACEGGINNSV	scavenging
ACEGGINRSS	cragginess
ACEGGIORRR	Roger Craig
ACEGGNNORT	congregant
ACEGHHIJKR	highjacker
ACEGHHILPS	high places
ACEGHHINOT	high-octane
ACEGHHLOOR	hog-cholera
ACEGHHOPRR	choregraph
ACEGHHOPRT	hectograph
ACEGHIILMT	megalithic
ACEGHIIMTW	white magic
ACEGHIINRS	cashiering
ACEGHIIPPR	epigraphic
ACEGHILMPT	phlegmatic
ACEGHILPSY	hypalgesic
ACEGHILRTT	tight-lacer
ACEGHILRTU	theurgical
ACEGHIMNNU	machinegun
ACEGHIMNOP	megaphonic
ACEGHIMNOX	Mexican hog
ACEGHIMPRS	graphemics
ACEGHINNNT	enchanting
ACEGHINOOS	China goose
ACEGHINOPT	pathogenic
ACEGHINOTT	Tao-te-ching
ACEGHINRTT	chattering
ACEGHIOOPS	hagioscope
ACEGHIORRT	tragic hero
ACEGHIRSTW	switchgear
ACEGHLOORY	archeology
ACEGHLORUY	Guy Laroche
ACEGHNOPSY	agency shop
ACEGHOPRRY	cerography
ACEGHOPRTV	vectograph
ACEGHORTUV	overcaught
ACEGHRRRSU	surcharger
ACEGIIKNST	ice-skating
ACEGIILLST	legalistic
ACEGIILMTY	legitimacy
ACEGIILNNO	agonic line
	lignocaine
ACEGIILOST	egoistical
ACEGIIMOST	isogametic
ACEGIIMOTT	Giacometti
ACEGIIMPTT	pegmatitic
ACEGIINNRS	increasing
ACEGIINORT	iatrogenic
ACEGIIOTTV	cogitative
ACEGIIPRST	epigastric
ACEGIIRRST	geriatrics
ACEGIIRRSU	Curia Regis
ACEGIKKLOR	goalkicker
ACEGIKLNNS	slackening
ACEGIKLNOR	Carole King
ACEGIKLNRY	creakingly
ACEGIKMRTY	kerygmatic
ACEGILLNOO	neological
ACEGILLNPR	parcelling
ACEGILLOOS	oligoclase
ACEGILLPRT	parcel-gilt
ACEGILMNNY	menacingly
ACEGILMNOR	camerlingo
ACEGILMRSS	melic-grass
ACEGILMSTU	gum elastic
ACEGILNNOR	iron-glance
ACEGILNNOT	congenital
ACEGILNOOP	geoponical
ACEGILNOPY	clay pigeon
ACEGILNOTU	glauconite
ACEGILNPPR	clappering
ACEGILNQRU	lacquering
ACEGILNRST	sternalgic
ACEGILNTXY	exactingly
ACEGILOOPT	apologetic
ACEGIMMMNO	mammogenic
ACEGIMMRRS	scrimmager
ACEGIMNRSU	Germanicus
	Marc Séguin
ACEGIMORST	gasometric
ACEGIMORSU	gracious me
ACEGINNNRT	entrancing
ACEGINNORU	guinea corn✧
ACEGINNOST	costeaning
ACEGINNRST	transgenic
ACEGINNRTU	uncreating
ACEGINNSTT	casting-net
ACEGINNTUX	unexacting
ACEGINOPRS	saprogenic
ACEGINOSTU	autogenics
ACEGINRSTT	scattering
ACEGIORSTT	categorist
ACEGIOSSTT	geostatics
ACEGIRSSTT	strategics
ACEGKLORRR	Roger Clark
ACEGKMNOOR	mock orange
ACEGKNORRT	garnet-rock
ACEGKNOSTT	stock agent
ACEGKORSTU	goatsucker
ACEGLLRTUU	culture lag
ACEGLMOSUU	glumaceous
ACEGLNNOUY	agony uncle
ACEGLNOOOY	oceanology
ACEGLOOPRT	colportage
ACEGLOOPSY	escapology
ACEGLOOTUY	autecology
ACEGLOPPRS	scrog-apple
ACEGLORSSV	cover glass
ACEGMMRRSU	scrummager
ACEGMNOORR	Greco-Roman
ACEGNNORST	scent organ
ACEGNNORTW	crown agent✧
ACEGNNPRUY	repugnancy
ACEGNOORSU	acrogenous
ACEGNOORTY	octogenary
ACEGNRSSUY	assurgency
ACEGNRSTTU	scatter-gun
ACEGOOPRRT	proctorage
ACEGOOPRRY	Gary Cooper
ACEGOORSUU	courageous

ACEGOPRRSU supercargo
ACEGORSTTT Great Scott!
ACEGPRRSTU gut-scraper
ACEHHIINRT in the chair
ACEHHIINTW China white
ACEHHIKNOV Chekhovian
ACEHHIKSTT hit the sack
ACEHHILOPT Achitophel
ACEHHILTWZ witch-hazel
ACEHHIMPSS sachemship
ACEHHINNPT naphthenic
ACEHHINOPT theophanic
ACEHHINORT rhinotheca
ACEHHIPTTW whip the cat
ACEHHIRRST Reichsrath
ACEHHKLLNS chank-shell
ACEHHLNNOP channel-hop
ACEHHLNOTT on the latch
ACEHHLOPRT heptachlor
ACEHHLSSTT thatchless
ACEHHMNNOW henchwoman
ACEHHMNORT on the march
ACEHHNORSU ranch house
ACEHHNOTTW on the watch
ACEHHORSTU charthouse
ACEHHOSTUW watch house
ACEHIILLPT philatelic
ACEHIILMOS isocheimal
ACEHIILMPT mephitical
ACEHIILMRT hermitical
ACEHIILNNO Heliconian
ACEHIILNOP neophiliac
ACEHIILNPR hair-pencil
ACEHIILNST Cisleithan
ACEHIILPST cephalitis
ACEHIILSTT theistical
ACEHIILSTU halieutics
ACEHIILTTY ethicality
ACEHIIMMNS Manicheism
ACEHIIMRTT arithmetic
ACEHIINNOP Phoenician
ACEHIINNRT Cerinthian
interchain
ACEHIINORT anti-heroic
ACEHIINOTV inchoative
ACEHIINTTT antithetic
ACEHIIOPST teichopsia
ACEHIIPRRT peritricha
ACEHIIRRRV River Chari
ACEHIIRSTT tracheitis
ACEHIKLNSS chalkiness
ACEHIKMNOS chain-smoke
ACEHIKMNTW Twickenham
ACEHIKMRRS reichsmark
ACEHIKNOPT Kate Chopin
ACEHIKPPST packet-ship
ACEHILLMSZ schlimazel
ACEHILLNTY ethnically
ACEHILLOOS alcoholise
ACEHILLOOZ alcoholize
ACEHILLORY heroically
ACEHILLOSU hellacious
ACEHILLPRY Caerphilly
ACEHILLTTY thetically
ACEHILMMST mischmetal
ACEHILMNOR chloramine
ACEHILMOOP phocomelia
ACEHILMORS male orchis
ACEHILMOTY haemolytic
ACEHILNNOT non-ethical
ACEHILNOPT phonetical
ACEHILNOPU euphonical
ACEHILNORT chlorinate
ACEHILNORU unheroical
ACEHILNOTY inchoately
ACEHILNPRS phrensical
ACEHILNSST schalstein
ACEHILOORZ coleorhiza
ACEHILOOTZ zoothecial
ACEHILOPRT arctophile
cartophile
ACEHILOPST telophasic
ACEHILORRT rhetorical
ACEHILPSST sales pitch
ACEHILRSTU Heraclitus
ACEHILRSTY hysterical
ACEHILSSST scaithless
ACEHIMMSST schematism
ACEHIMNNOR enharmonic
ACEHIMNOPT phonematic
ACEHIMNORS monarchise
ACEHIMNORU euharmonic
ACEHIMNORY hieromancy
ACEHIMNORZ monarchize
ACEHIMNOTT theomantic
ACEHIMNPRY hypermanic
ACEHIMNPTU unemphatic
ACEHIMNRST mischanter
ACEHIMNRSV revanchism
ACEHIMNSTY myasthenic
ACEHIMOPRS semaphoric
ACEHIMOPRT amphoteric
metaphoric
ACEHIMOPTU apothecium
ACEHIMOPXY hypoxaemic
ACEHIMORYZ mycorhizae
ACEHIMOSTX chemotaxis
ACEHIMPSTY metaphysic
ACEHIMRSTT chrematist
ACEHIMRSTU rheumatics
ACEHIMSSTT schematist
ACEHINNOST china stone
ACEHINNRST Ernst Chain
ACEHINOORT orthocaine
ACEHINOPSS poachiness
ACEHINOPTT heptatonic
ACEHINORRT chitarrone
ACEHINORST chain store
ACEHINORTV chevrotain
ACEHINPSTT pentastich
ACEHINPSTU epicanthus
ACEHINPTTU unpathetic
ACEHINQRSU square inch
ACEHINRSTU raunchiest
ACEHINRSTV revanchist
ACEHINRSTY tyre chains
ACEHINSSTT chattiness
ACEHIOPRRT Chiroptera
ACEHIOPRSX echopraxis
ACEHIOPSST post chaise
post-chaise
ACEHIOPSTY isopachyte
ACEHIORSTT rheostatic
ACEHIORSTY Sothic year
ACEHIPPSTT pettichaps
ACEHIPRRST arch-priest
ACEHIPRSSU haruspices
ACEHIPRSTU curateship
pasticheur
ACEHIPRSTW pear-switch
ACEHIPRSTY psychiater
ACEHIPRTTU picture hat
ACEHIQRRSU squirearch
ACEHIRRRTY trierarchy
ACEHIRSTTT tetrastich
ACEHIRSTTV tsarevitch
ACEHIRTTWW water witch
ACEHIRTVWY vichy water✧
ACEHJKNNOY johnny-cake✧
ACEHJRRSUW jaw-crusher
ACEHKLMMOR hammerlock
ACEHKLMOTY lackey moth
ACEHKLNNTZ lanzknecht
ACEHKLNOST chalkstone
Shackleton
shecklaton
ACEHLLMNOY melancholy
ACEHLLNORS acorn-shell
ACEHLLNSSY Nelly Sachs
ACEHLLOORS chloralose
real school
ACEHLLOSTY shellycoat
ACEHLLPRSU sepulchral
ACEHLMMORU chrome alum
ACEHLMNOOT monothecal
ACEHLMOOST schoolmate
ACEHLMORSY lachrymose
ACEHLNNOPT cannot help
ACEHLNOOPS Sophoclean
ACEHLNOOST stone loach
ACEHLNORSS anchorless
ACEHLNORST charleston✧
ACEHLNORUV overlaunch
ACEHLNSSST stanchless
ACEHLNSTUY unchastely
ACEHLOORST orthoclase
ACEHLOORSY school year
ACEHLOPPRT paper-cloth
ACEHLOPTTU touch-plate
ACEHLORRST Clare Short
orchestral
ACEHLOSTTW cattle show
ACEHLPRTYY phylactery

ACEHMMNOTU mean much to
ACEHMNNSUU Munchausen
ACEHMNOOST Mocha stone
ACEHMNORST march-stone
ACEHMNOSTY chemonasty
ACEHMNOTUV avouchment
ACEHMNPRTY parchmenty
ACEHMNRRTY merchantry
ACEHMOOTTT come to that
ACEHMOPRTT carpet-moth
ACEHMOPRTY chromatype
ACEHMORRTU route march
ACEHMORTTY tachometry
ACEHMOSSTU moustaches
ACEHMRTTYY tachymetry
ACEHNNORTT contrahent
ACEHNNSSST stanchness
ACEHNOOPRT Ctenophora
ACEHNOPRSU canephorus
ACEHNOPTYY cyanophyte
ACEHNORRTT trochanter
ACEHNORTTT Chatterton
ACEHNPRSTT stench trap
ACEHNRSSTU chauntress
ACEHNSSTUW cashew nuts
ACEHOOPPRR carpophore
ACEHOOPSTU tophaceous
ACEHOORRST Orthoceras
ACEHOPPRTU touchpaper
ACEHOPRSUY coryphaeus
ACEHOPSTUY typhaceous
ACEHORTTWW watchtower
ACEHPPSTTY petty-chaps
ACEHRSSSUU chaussures
ACEIIIKNST ekistician
ACEIIILMSS Islamicise
ACEIIILMSZ Islamicize
ACEIIILRST Israelitic
ACEIIINTTV incitative
ACEIIIRTTV recitativi
ACEIIISTTV activities
ACEIIJLSTU Jesuitical
ACEIIKMNST kinematics
ACEIIKNRTT kinetic art
ACEIIKRSTT rickettsia
ACEIILLLPT elliptical
ACEIILLNNN cannellini
ACEIILLNPR periclinal
ACEIILLNRY irenically
ACEIILLOSU liliaceous
ACEIILLOSV social evil
ACEIILLRTY illiteracy
ACEIILLSTT satellitic
ACEIILMMST melismatic
ACEIILMNST melanistic
ACEIILMNSU semi-uncial
ACEIILMOPT atomic pile
epitomical
ACEIILMPSS specialism
ACEIILNNRT encrinital
ACEIILNOPT capitoline✧

ACEIILNORV arvicoline
ACEIILNOSX saxicoline
ACEIILNOTT actinolite
ACEIILNPST Plasticine®
ACEIILNSTT static line
ACEIILNTVY inactively
ACEIILOSTU tiliaceous
ACEIILPPRT participle
ACEIILPRTT triplicate
ACEIILPSST plasticise
specialist
ACEIILPSTY speciality
ACEIILPSTZ plasticize
ACEIILRSSS scleriasis
ACEIILRSTT recitalist
ACEIILSTTV active list
ACEIILSTTY elasticity
ACEIIMMOTT atomic time
ACEIIMNORS Micronesia
ACEIIMNORT Marcionite
ACEIIMNPST emancipist
ACEIIMNRRU cinerarium
ACEIIMNRSU musicianer
ACEIIMOTTV comitative
ACEIIMPSST asepticism
ACEIIMRRST erraticism
ACEIIMRSTT tasimetric
ACEIINNNTV Vincentian
ACEIINNORT cineration
ACEIINNQRU quinacrine
ACEIINNRTY itinerancy
ACEIINOPST speciation
ACEIINORTT recitation
ACEIINOSTV vesication
ACEIINOTTX excitation
intoxicate
ACEIINPPRT principate
ACEIINPSTT antiseptic
psittacine
ACEIINRTVY inveracity
ACEIINSSTT sanctities
ACEIINSTTU austenitic
ACEIIORRRT certiorari
ACEIIORTTV recitativo
ACEIIPPSST epispastic
ACEIIRRSSU cuirassier
ACEIIRSTTV astrictive
ACEIIRTTVY creativity
reactivity
ACEIISSSTY essayistic
ACEIJKMNTU minute-jack
ACEIJKOPSX Joe Sixpack
ACEIJKPRST Jack-priest
ACEIJNORTT trajection
ACEIKKNNSS knackiness
ACEIKLRSTV travel-sick
ACEIKLRTTT title track
ACEIKMNOPT pockmantie
ACEIKMRRST arsmetrick
ACEIKNNRSS crankiness
ACEIKNORTV native rock

ACEIKNPSTT septic tank
ACEIKNPTTW pawnticket
ACEIKORTUY eukaryotic
ACEIKQRTUW quick-water
ACEILLLNPU Pulcinella
ACEILLLOPW lace-pillow
pillow lace
ACEILLLPRU pellicular
ACEILLMNSY miscellany
ACEILLMORT allometric
ACEILLMPTU capitellum
ACEILLMRTY metrically
ACEILLNNNO cannelloni
ACEILLNOOT ocellation
ACEILLNORT citronella
ACEILLNRTU lenticular
ACEILLOPSW pillowcase
ACEILLOPTY poetically
ACEILLOQTU colliquate
ACEILLORST allosteric
sclerotial
ACEILLORTV vorticella
ACEILLORTY erotically
ACEILLOSTY societally
ACEILLOTXY exotically
ACEILLPRUY peculiarly
ACEILLPSTY septically
ACEILLPSUV culpa levis
ACEILLRTUV victualler
ACEILLRTVY vertically
ACEILMMNNO mnemonical
ACEILMMNSS clamminess
ACEILMNOPR complainer
ACEILMNORS minor scale
sermonical
ACEILMNORT coterminal
ACEILMNRST centralism
ACEILMNRTU unmetrical
ACEILMNRUW lawrencium
ACEILMOORT recoil atom
ACEILMOPRR proclaimer
ACEILMOPRT pleromatic
ACEILMOPRY promycelia
ACEILMRRUV vermicular
ACEILMRSSU secularism
ACEILMRSUY early music
ACEILMSSTU salicetums
ACEILMTUUV cumulative
ACEILNNOOP Napoleonic
ACEILNNOTU nucleation
ACEILNNRTU unicentral
ACEILNNRUU uninuclear
ACEILNNUVY univalency
ACEILNOORT corelation
iconolater
relocation
ACEILNOORU Eriocaulon
ACEILNOPPS scaloppine
ACEILNOPRT pratincole
ACEILNOPST neoplastic
pleonastic

ACEILNOPTU peculation
unpoetical
ACEILNOPTY polyactine
ACEILNORTU ulceration
ACEILNORTY lectionary
ACEILNOSSS socialness
ACEILNOSTU inosculate
ACEILNOTUV novaculite
ACEILNPPPU Punic apple
ACEILNPPSU suppliance
ACEILNRSTT centralist
ACEILNRSTU lacustrine
ACEILNRTTY centrality
ACEILNRTVY trivalency
ACEILNRUUX luxuriance
ACEILNSSSS classiness
ACEILOOPRT laeotropic
ACEILOOSUV olivaceous
violaceous
ACEILOPPRS sapropelic
ACEILOPPRT police trap
ACEILOPRRT replicator
ACEILOPRTX explicator
ACEILOPTUV copulative
ACEILOQTUY coequality
ACEILORSSS cross aisle
ACEILORTTV tail covert
ACEILOSTWY Law Society
ACEILPPSTU supplicate
ACEILPRSTX lex scripta
ACEILPRTUU apiculture
ACEILRRSUV versicular
ACEILRRTUY reticulary
ACEILRSSTU secularist
ACEILRSTTU testicular
trisulcate
ACEILRSTUY secularity
ACEILRTUUV aviculture
ACEILRTUVY curatively
ACEIMMNORT manometric
ACEIMMPRTY campimetry
ACEIMMRSTY asymmetric
ACEIMNNOST cismontane
ACEIMNNRRS MRI scanner
ACEIMNNRUY innumeracy
ACEIMNOPRT importance
ACEIMNOPSS campesinos
ACEIMNOPTT Camptonite
pentatomic
ACEIMNORSU main course
ACEIMNORUY Aureomycin®
ACEIMNPPRS panspermic
ACEIMNPSTU pneumatics
ACEIMNQTTU acquitment
ACEIMNRRTY Terramycin®
ACEIMOOPST Compositae
ACEIMOPPPT apopemptic
ACEIMORRST miscreator
ACEIMORRTT meritocrat
ACEIMORRTU acroterium
ACEIMORSST Massoretic
ACEIMORSVW microwaves
ACEIMORTTT tetratomic
ACEIMORTTU tautomeric
ACEIMPPRSU music paper
ACEIMRSSTU cerastiums
ACEIMRSTUW water music✧
ACEIMSSTTY systematic
ACEINNNOSU uncanonise
unisonance
ACEINNNOUZ uncanonize
ACEINNOORT incoronate
nero-antico
ACEINNOPTT pentatonic
ACEINNORSU sea unicorn
ACEINNORTU enunciator
ACEINNOTTU continuate
ACEINNRRSU insurancer
ACEINNRSTY transiency
ACEINNRTUU nunciature
ACEINNSSST scantiness
ACEINNSSTT intactness
ACEINOORRT acroterion
e contrario
ACEINOORTV revocation
ACEINOPPST episcopant
ACEINOPRTU precaution
ACEINOPRTY capernoity
ACEINOPSSU spinaceous
ACEINOPSTT constipate
costean-pit
ACEINORRTT retraction
triaconter
ACEINORSSY cessionary
ACEINORSTU Carnoustie
recusation
ACEINORTTU eructation
ACEINORTTW tonic water
ACEINORTTX extraction
ACEINOSTTU unicostate
ACEINOSTTV constative
ACEINPSSUU puissaunce
ACEINPSTUU usucapient
ACEINRSTTU scaturient
ACEINRSUVV survivance
ACEINRTUVY unveracity
ACEINSSSTT scattiness
ACEIOOPRRT aerotropic
ACEIOOPRSU paroecious
ACEIOOPRTZ azeotropic
ACEIOOPTTV co-optative
ACEIOORRRW ecowarrior
ACEIOORTTU autoerotic
ACEIOPRRSU precarious
ACEIOQSSUU sequacious
ACEIORSTTT tricostate
ACEIORSTVY vesicatory
ACEIORTTXY excitatory
ACEIPPRSTT tapescript
ACEIPRRSTU crispature
ACEIPRSTTX spectatrix
ACEIRRSTUW rusticware
ACEJKLLOWY yellow Jack✧
ACEJKLMMNO Jack Lemmon
ACEJKLPPSU supplejack
ACEJKNOSST jackstones
ACEJNOSUUY jouysaunce
ACEJNOSUVY jovysaunce
ACEJORRTTY trajectory
ACEKKMOSST smokestack
ACEKLLLRTY tally clerk
ACEKLLORTW wall rocket
ACEKLLRSTU lackluster
lacklustre
ACEKLMNORT mantle rock
ACEKLNOPST alpenstock
ACEKLNORSS close ranks
ACEKLNPRTU panel truck
ACEKLOOPRW wool-packer
ACEKLORSTY York Castle
ACEKMNORRW cankerworm
ACEKOPSSST sack-posset
ACEKOSTTTY stotty cake
ACEKPRRSSY skyscraper
ACELLLMORU columellar
ACELLLORSS collarless
ACELLMNOTU loculament
ACELLMOSTU Samuel Colt
ACELLNOORT Eton collar
ACELLNOTVY covalently
ACELLOOOST osteocolla
ACELLOPRTY pectorally
ACELLOPSTU leucoplast
ACELLOPSTY closet play
ACELLOPTUY eucalyptol
ACELLORRTY trolley car
ACELLORSSW lower-class
ACELLORSUX sexlocular
ACELLPRSTY spectrally
ACELLSSTTY tactlessly
ACELMMNOOS common seal
ACELMMNOOW commonweal
ACELMNNOTT malcontent
ACELMNOORT Monte Carlo
ACELMNTTUU tentaculum
ACELNNNORU non-nuclear
ACELNNOOTT notonectal
ACELNNOSSU consensual
ACELNNOSTU Launceston
ACELNNOSUU noun clause
ACELNNOTUV conventual✧
ACELNOPRRU pronuclear
ACELNOPRSY narcolepsy
ACELNOPRTX contraplex
ACELNOPSTY nyctalopes
ACELNORRTY necrolatry
ACELNOTTUX contextual
ACELNOTTXY not exactly
ACELNPTTUU punctulate
ACELNRTTUY truncately
ACELOOPRRS Poor Clares
ACELOOPRRT coal-porter
percolator

ACELOORRTW watercolor
ACELOOSSTT osteoclast
ACELOPPRST parcel post
ACELOPPRTT carpet plot
ACELOPRSSU processual
ACELOPRSTU speculator
ACELOPRSUY pelycosaur
ACELOPRSWY cow-parsley
ACELOPSTTT cattle stop
ACELOPSTUU pultaceous
ACELORRSTY clearstory
ACELPPRSSU upper class
upper-class
ACELPRSSSU superclass
ACELPSTUUY eucalyptus
ACELRSSTTY crystal set
ACEMMMMOTY mammectomy
ACEMMNOORT Mt Cameroon
ACEMMNORTY commentary
ACEMMNOSTU consummate
ACEMMOSTTY mastectomy
ACEMNNNOTT cantonment
ACEMNNORST monstrance
ACEMNNORTU counterman
ACEMNOOPRT montero-cap
ACEMNOOTYZ mycetozoan
ACEMNOSTTY nematocyst
ACEMOOPRRS macrospore
ACEMOOPSST come to pass
ACEMOORSTU octamerous
ACEMOOSTTY come to stay
ACEMORSTUY myrtaceous
ACENNOORTU onocentaur
ACENNOORTV covenantor
ACENNORRWY Cannery Row
ACENNORSTV conservant
conversant
ACENNOSTTT contestant
ACENOOPPST pantoscope
ACENOOPRTT Entoprocta
ACENOOPRVY overcanopy
ACENOORRSZ scorzonera
ACENOPPRRY pyrenocarp
ACENOPRRTY copartnery
ACENOPRSTT par contest
ACENOPRTTT protectant
ACENORRSWY cornerways
ACENORSTYZ stone-crazy
ACENOSSSTT stone's-cast
ACENOSTTUY county seat
ACENPRSSTU percussant
ACENRSSTTU tersanctus
ACEOOOPRRT co-operator
ACEOOPPRST Psocoptera
ACEOOPRRRT procreator
ACEOOPRRSU porraceous
ACEOOPSSTT statoscope
ACEOORRTVY revocatory
ACEOORSSTU ostraceous
ACEOPRSTTY copy taster
ACEORRRSTY stercorary
ACEORSTUXY excusatory
ACFFGHILNY chaffingly
ACFFGIIKMN mafficking
ACFFGIILNT afflicting
ACFFHNRSTU churn-staff
ACFFHORSTT torch-staff
ACFFIILLOY officially
ACFFIILNNO coffin nail
ACFFIILNOT affliction
ACFFIILNOU unofficial
ACFFIILOTY officialty
ACFFIIOORT officiator
ACFFILLNUY fancifully
ACFFINOOTU auction off
ACFFINORTU curtain off
ACFFOPRSST staff corps
ACFFORSSST cross-staff
ACFGHILNNU flaunching
ACFGHMORRS frog's-march
ACFGIILNRY clarifying
ACFGIINRSY scarifying
ACFGILMNPY flying camp
ACFGILNNOO cooling fan
ACFGILOPRY profligacy
ACFGILRSTU gastric flu
ACFGINOORT foot-racing
ACFGNORRTW crown graft
ACFHIINPTU Punic faith
ACFHILNOPR francophil✧
ACFHIMORTY cyathiform
ACFHIMRSTT smithcraft
ACFHIOPRST factorship
ACFHKLSSUU Klaus Fuchs
ACFHKOOTUW out of whack
ACFHLLTUWY watchfully
ACFHLMOOST smooth calf
ACFHLMOSTU stomachful
ACFHLNTUUW unwatchful
ACFHMNOOTU not much of a
ACFHNOTUWY Yun-Fat Chow
ACFHOOPRRS crash-proof
ACFHOOSTTU a soft touch
ACFIIILMST familistic
ACFIIILNTY finicality
ACFIIIMNPR rifampicin
ACFIIIORTV factor VIII
ACFIILLOPR prolifical
ACFIILMMOR limaciform
ACFIILMNOT action film
ACFIILNOPT pontifical
ACFIILNORT frictional
ACFIINNORS infrasonic
ACFIINNORT infarction
infraction
ACFIINOSTT factionist
ACFIIOSTTU factitious
ACFIJNORST scarf-joint
ACFIKORRST risk factor
ACFILLLORU follicular
ACFILLORUY cauliflory
ACFILMOORR microflora
ACFILNNOOT conflation
ACFILNNOTU functional
ACFILNOOPT focal point
ACFILNOOST tonic sol-fa
ACFILORRSW friar's cowl
ACFILOSTUY factiously
ACFILRSSST first-class
ACFINNORTU craft union
ACFINNSTUY unsanctify
ACFINOORRT fornicator
ACFINOORSU facinorous
ACFINRSSSW Swiss franc
ACFLLOOPRT port of call
ACFLLOORSS collar of SS
ACFLNOORTW contraflow
ACFLNORRTW front crawl
ACFLNRRUUU furuncular
ACFLOORSTU colourfast
ACFMNOORSW can of worms
ACFOORRRTT rotorcraft
ACGGGILNRS scraggling
ACGGHHIRWY Whiggarchy
ACGGHIILOO hagiologic
ACGGHINNNU unchanging
ACGGHINOPY hypnagogic
ACGGHINOTT chittagong✧
ACGGIILLOT Glagolitic
ACGGIILNNO ganglionic
ACGGIILOOS sialogogic
ACGGIINRSU icing sugar
ACGGILLNNY glancingly
ACGGILLOOY glaciology
ACGGIMOSTY mystagogic
ACGHHIINRT night-chair
ACGHHILNTT night latch
ACGHHILTTW watch light
ACGHHIMUUV high-vacuum
ACGHHINRSU Hugh Cairns
ACGHHINTTW night-watch
watch night
ACGHHIOPRR chirograph
ACGHHNOSSU Hugh Casson
ACGHHORSYY hygrochasy
ACGHIIKNRS king's-chair
ACGHIILRTV gilravitch
ACGHIINPSW wishing-cap
ACGHIIOPPX xiphopagic
ACGHIKMNOR Rockingham
ACGHIKNNOR king-archon
ACGHIKNOPS hop-sacking
ACGHILMNRY charmingly
ACGHILNSST nightclass
ACGHILNSTY scathingly
ACGHILOOPT pathologic
ACGHILOOST chaologist
ACGHIMNNOP champignon
ACGHIMNNRU uncharming
ACGHIMOPRR micrograph
ACGHIMOPRY myographic
ACGHINNORR anchor-ring
ACGHINNPTU hunting-cap

ACGHINNSTU staunching
ACGHINNTTU hunting-cat
ACGHINOORR choir organ
ACGHINOPRT prognathic
ACGHINOPRZ zincograph
ACGHINPTUU caught up in
ACGHIOOPRR orographic
ACGHIOOPRZ zoographic
ACGHIOPPRT pictograph
ACGHIOPRRU urographic
ACGHIRRTTW cartwright
ACGHLLOOPR collograph
ACGHLLOSST glass-cloth
ACGHLOOPRY carphology
ACGHLORSST grass cloth
ACGHMMOORR chromogram
ACGHMNOORR chronogram
ACGHMOPRSY psychogram
ACGHOOPPRY coprophagy
ACGIIKKMNS sick-making
ACGIIKLLPR pilgarlick
ACGIILLMSU Caligulism
ACGIILLORS cigarillos
ACGIILLOST logistical
ACGIILLOTY logicality
ACGIILLRTU liturgical
ACGIILNOOR air-cooling
ACGIILNORY royal icing
ACGIILNOSU caliginous
ACGIILNPUU Pinguicula
ACGIILNRTU granulitic
ACGIILNRTY laryngitic
ACGIILNSST anglistics
ACGIIMMRRT trigrammic
ACGIIMMRSU sugar mimic
ACGIIMNORS organicism
organismic
ACGIIMNRST scintigram
ACGIINNOTT incogitant
ACGIINOOTT cogitation
ACGIINORST organicist
ACGIINOSST agonistics
ACGIINPRST practising
ACGIINQTTU acquitting
ACGIIORSTY graciosity
ACGIJKKNSY skyjacking
ACGIKKMNRU muck-raking
ACGIKLLNNY clankingly
ACGIKMNOPS smoking cap
ACGIKQRSSU quick grass
ACGILLMNOY gnomically
ACGILLMOOY limacology
myological
ACGILLNORR corralling
ACGILLNORW wing collar
ACGILLNRWY crawlingly
ACGILLOOOR orological
ACGILLOOOT otological
ACGILLOOOZ zoological
ACGILLOORU urological
ACGILLRSUY surgically
ACGILMNNOO cognominal
gnomonical
ACGILMOSTY clistogamy
ACGILNNPRY prancingly
ACGILNOORY craniology
ACGILNOPSS Panglossic
ACGILNOSST glasnostic
ACGILOORST astrologic
ACGILOOTTU tautologic
ACGILORSUU glucosuria
ACGILORSUY glycosuria
graciously
ACGILOSUVY Yugoslavic
ACGIMNNOPY companying
ACGIMNNORY nigromancy
ACGIMNOORS agronomics
ACGIMNOPSS compassing
ACGIMNORRS Cairngorms
ACGIMNSSTY gymnastics
ACGIMOOPRT gamotropic
ACGINNORRY carrying-on
ACGINNOSTW nowcasting
ACGINOOSTU contagious
ACGINOPRST Racing Post
ACGINOPSUU pugnacious
ACGINORRST co-starring
ACGINORRTU touring car
ACGINORSUU ungracious
ACGINPPRTU parting-cup
ACGINPRRST spring-cart
ACGIORSTTY gyrostatic
ACGJLLNOUY conjugally
ACGJLNNOUU unconjugal
ACGLLOOPRU Local Group
ACGLNOORSU clangorous
ACGLNORSSW crown glass
ACGMOPRRTY cryptogram
ACGMOPRTYY cryptogamy
ACGNNOPPUY oppugnancy
ACGOORRRTU corrugator
ACGORRSSTU grass court
ACHHIILPST phthisical
ACHHIIPRTU hupaithric
ACHHILMOPT ophthalmic
ACHHILMRTY rhythmical
ACHHILOOPS shopaholic
ACHHILOPTY halophytic
ACHHIMRRTY arrhythmic
ACHHINNOTT Antichthon
ACHHINOPRS archonship
ACHHIOPPRS Hipparchos
ACHHIOPPST phosphatic
ACHHJNNOSY Johnny Cash
ACHHNOOTTU autochthon
ACHHNOPRSY chrysophan
ACHHOPPSTY psychopath
ACHIIIMNST histaminic
ACHIIIMRTY Himyaritic
ACHIIIPPRT hippiatric
ACHIIIRSST trichiasis
ACHIIISSTV Shivaistic
ACHIIJKNRS jinricksha
ACHIIKLNNY kinchin-lay
ACHIIKMSTV hacktivism
ACHIIKNPSU puschkinia
ACHIIKSTTV hacktivist
ACHIILLMPS phallicism
ACHIILLNTW within call
ACHIILNOPT notaphilic
ACHIILNOPY cynophilia
ACHIILOOPR Ciliophora
ACHIILORST historical
ACHIILORTU thiouracil
ACHIIMNNOR inharmonic
ACHIIMNRSS sinarchism✧
ACHIIMNSTU humanistic
ACHIIMNSUV chauvinism
ACHIIMOPPP hippocampi
ACHIINNOOT inchoation
ACHIINNOPT antiphonic
ACHIINNORT Corinthian
ACHIINNPQU chinquapin
ACHIINORRT chitarroni
ACHIINORST sticharion
ACHIINORSU air-cushion
ACHIINPSUY picayunish
ACHIINRSST sinarchist
ACHIINRSTT Antichrist
ACHIINSTUV chauvinist
ACHIIOPRST aphoristic
ACHIIOPSST pistachios
ACHIISSSTU such as it is
ACHIJKKSWY whisky jack
ACHIJLNNOV John Calvin
ACHIJMNOTT match-joint
ACHIKKNPRS shrinkpack
ACHIKLOORW workaholic
ACHIKLPRSY prickly ash
ACHIKMNOST mackintosh
ACHIKMNOUU makunouchi
ACHIKMNRSS scrimshank
ACHILLMOOS alcoholism
ACHILLMORS chloralism
ACHILLMTYY mythically
ACHILLNNSY clannishly
ACHILLNOOP allophonic
ACHILLNOPY phonically
ACHILLOOYZ hylozoical
ACHILLOPRT prothallic
ACHILLOSTT lithoclast
ACHILLPSYY physically
ACHILMNOTY lithomancy
ACHILMOPTY polymathic
ACHILMORYZ mycorhizal
ACHILMPSSY scampishly
ACHILMRTTU thalictrum
ACHILNNOTU launch into
ACHILNOORS isochronal
ACHILNOSSY anchylosis
ACHILOPPSY polyphasic
ACHILOPRTY arctophily
cartophily

ACHILORSUV	chivalrous
ACHILOSTTW	waistcloth
ACHIMMNORS	monarchism
ACHIMMOOPR	Commiphora
ACHIMNNOOR	harmonicon
ACHIMNOOPS	monophasic
ACHIMNOOPT	taphonomic
ACHIMNOPTT	match point
ACHIMNOPTW	pitchwoman
ACHIMNOPTY	amphictyon
ACHIMNORST	monarchist
ACHIMNSSTU	miscanthus
ACHIMORRTT	trichromat
ACHIMORRYZ	mycorrhiza
ACHIMOSSTU	mustachios
ACHIMRSSTY	Christmasy
ACHINNOSSW	snow chains
ACHINOOPSX	saxophonic
ACHINOORST	cartoonish
ACHINORSTU	Sun Chariot
ACHINSTTUY	unchastity
ACHIOOPSTY	sociopathy
ACHIOPRSTY	physiocrat
ACHIOPRTTY	potty-chair
ACHIOPSTTY	hypostatic
ACHIORRSSS	cross hairs
ACHIPRSTYY	psychiatry
ACHIQRRSUY	squirarchy
ACHIRSTTWW	wristwatch
ACHJKNNOOR	John Cranko
ACHKLLOSST	shockstall
ACHKLMNOOT	klootchman
ACHKLMORSS	marshlocks
ACHKMOOOST	Thomas Cook
ACHKNOOTTU	Nouakchott
ACHLLLLOYY	allycholly
ACHLLLOOOW	low-alcohol
ACHLLNOTUY	county hall
ACHLLOOPSY	playschool
ACHLMMOORS	schoolmarm
ACHLMNORUU	homuncular
ACHLNNORSY	synchronal
ACHLOOOSTU	acolouthos
ACHLOORSUW	colourwash
ACHLORSTWZ	schwarzlot
ACHMOOSSTU	stomachous
ACHMOSSUYY	Hyoscyamus
ACHNNNOOST	cannon-shot
ACHNNORSYY	asynchrony
ACHNOOPPRY	apocryphon
ACHNOOPSYZ	scyphozoan
ACHOOPRSST	shoot craps
ACHOORSSTT	short coats
ACIIIILMST	Ismailitic
ACIIIKLNOT	kaolinitic
ACIIILLMNP	ampicillin
ACIIILLMNY	inimically
ACIIILMORT	miarolitic
ACIIILMSST	Islamicist
ACIIILNOPT	politician
ACIIILNORS	incisorial
ACIIILNOSS	sicilianos
ACIIILNOTT	latticinio
ACIIILNPPR	principial
ACIIILNPST	sincipital
ACIIILORTV	variolitic
ACIIILSTTV	vitalistic
ACIIIMNSTV	anticivism
ACIIINNOTT	incitation
ACIIINRSTT	inartistic
ACIIINSTTV	nativistic
ACIIINTTVY	inactivity
ACIIJLRSTU	juristical
ACIIJRSTUY	justiciary
ACIIKNRSST	Sanskritic
ACIIKTTUWY	Kuwait City
ACIILLMNRY	criminally
ACIILLMSSY	salicylism
ACIILLNNOS	Scillonian
ACIILLNORS	nicrosilal
ACIILLNORY	ironically
ACIILLNRUY	culinarily
ACIILLRTTY	tritically
ACIILMNORS	consimilar
ACIILMNOST	monistical
ACIILMNRTY	matricliny
ACIILMNSUY	musicianly
ACIILMORST	moralistic
ACIILMSTUY	musicality
ACIILNOORT	lorication
ACIILNOPPR	pilocarpin
ACIILNOPRV	provincial
ACIILNORTT	tinctorial
ACIILNOSTT	solicitant
ACIILNOTXY	anxiolytic
ACIILNPRTY	patricliny
ACIILOPRST	poristical
ACIILOPTTY	topicality
ACIILOSSUV	lascivious
ACIILPRSTU	puristical
ACIILPSTTY	plasticity
ACIILPTTYY	typicality
ACIILRSTTU	altruistic
ACIILRTTTY	tractility
ACIILSSTUV	vasculitis
ACIIMMNOPT	pantomimic
ACIIMMNSTU	numismatic
ACIIMNNORS	Canis Minor
ACIIMNORST	Marcionist
	Romanistic
ACIIMNPTTY	tympanitic
ACIIMNRSSS	narcissism
ACIIMNRSTU	manicurist
ACIIMOPRSS	prosaicism
ACIIMOPRST	porismatic
ACIINNOOTV	invocation
ACIINNOSTU	insouciant
ACIINNOTTX	intoxicant
ACIINOOSTT	oscitation
ACIINOOTTX	toxication
ACIINOPRST	ascription
	crispation
ACIINOPRTT	tritanopic
ACIINOPSTU	ancipitous
ACIINOPTTU	cuit à point
ACIINORSTT	astriction
ACIINORTTU	urtication
ACIINOSTUU	incautious
ACIINRSSST	narcissist
ACIINRSTTU	naturistic
	unartistic
ACIINRSTUY	cystinuria
ACIIOPRRST	scriptoria
ACIIOPSSUU	auspicious
ACIIOPSTZZ	pizzicatos
ACIIORSTVY	varicosity
ACIIPRSSTT	patristics
ACIIPSSTTY	spasticity
ACIIQRTTUZ	quartzitic
ACIISSSTTT	statistics
ACIJLORTUY	jocularity
ACIKKLMNOR	Kilmarnock
ACIKKOPRUW	kick up a row
ACIKLLNOPR	pink-collar
ACIKLMRTTU	multi-track
ACIKLNNOPT	planktonic
ACIKLOORSW	social work
ACIKLPRSTY	play tricks
ACIKOPRTYY	karyotypic
ACILLLNOOY	colonially
ACILLLOOQU	colloquial
ACILLMNNOO	monoclinal
ACILLMOORT	collimator
	mortal coil
ACILLMOPYY	myopically
ACILLMOTUU	altocumuli
ACILLMOTUV	multivocal
ACILLMSTYY	mystically
ACILLNOOPT	call option
ACILLNOOTU	allocution
ACILLNOPST	splint coal
ACILLNOQTU	colliquant
ACILLNORUU	unilocular
ACILLNORUV	involucral
ACILLNOSTU	Collatinus
ACILLNOSUY	unsocially
ACILLNOUVY	univocally
ACILLOOPRT	allotropic
ACILLOOPTY	play it cool
ACILLOORST	oscillator
ACILLOORUX	uxorilocal
ACILLOPRTY	tropically
ACILLORRTU	trilocular
ACILLORTVY	vortically
ACILLRSTUY	rustically
ACILMMNOOR	common rail
ACILMMOORS	microsomal
ACILMMRSUU	simulacrum
ACILMNOOOS	nosocomial
ACILMNOORT	microtonal
ACILMNORSY	Carly Simon
ACILMNORTY	matrocliny
ACILMNOSUU	calumnious

ACILMNOTUU cumulation
ACILMNRSUU minuscular
ACILMNSTUY stimulancy
ACILMOOOTZ zootomical
ACILMOOPRT compilator
ACILMOOPTY polyatomic
ACILMOPRRY micropylar
ACILMOPSTY polymastic
ACILMORSTU tacrolimus
ACILMORSUU miraculous
ACILMPRSUU spiraculum
ACILNNOOOT on location
ACILNNPSUU panniculus
ACILNOOORT coloration
ACILNOOPRR incorporal
ACILNOOPTU copulation
ACILNOOPXY polyaxonic
ACILNOOPZZ pozzolanic
ACILNOORSU Coriolanus
ACILNOORTU inoculator
ACILNOORTY iconolatry
ACILNOOSTU osculation
ACILNOOTTT cottontail
ACILNOPRTY patrocliny
ACILNOPSTY synoptical
ACILNORRTY contrarily
ACILNORSST Latin cross
ACILNORSTU ultrasonic
ACILNOSTTY oscitantly
ACILNPPSTU supplicant
ACILNRTTUY taciturnly
ACILNRUUXY luxuriancy
ACILOOPRRT proctorial
ACILOOPSTT postcoital
ACILOOPSTZ zooplastic
ACILOOQSUU loquacious
ACILOOSSUX saxicolous
ACILOPPRSU Pilocarpus
ACILOPSSUY spaciously
ACILOPSTTY calotypist
ACILOPSTUY captiously
ACILORRRVY corrivalry
ACILORRTTU trial court
ACILORRTUV vorticular
ACILORTTUV cultivator
ACILOSTUUY cautiously
ACILPPTUVY pulp cavity
ACILPRRSTU scriptural
ACILQRTUYZ crazy quilt
ACIMMNOOTU muonic atom
ACIMMNOPSS pancosmism
ACIMMNORTY matronymic
ACIMMOPRRS macroprism
ACIMMORSSY commissary
ACIMNNNOOR minor canon
ACIMNNORTU unromantic
ACIMNNOSTY sanctimony
ACIMNOOPRS comparison
ACIMNOOPSS compassion
ACIMNOORST astronomic
ACIMNOORTY craniotomy
ACIMNOOSST onomastics
ACIMNOOSTU autonomics
ACIMNOPPRS prison camp
ACIMNOPPTU pump-action
ACIMNOPRTY importancy
patronymic
pyromantic
ACIMNOPSST tonic spasm
ACIMNPRSTU manuscript
ACIMOOPRTT compatriot
ACIMOOPTTX Mt Cotopaxi
ACIMOORTVY varicotomy
ACIMOPRRRR mirror carp
ACIMOPSTTY asymptotic
ACINNNNOOT cannon into
ACINNNOSTT inconstant
ACINNNOTTU continuant
ACINNOOORT coronation
ACINNOOPPT panopticon
ACINNOPRST conspirant
ACINNOPTTU punctation
ACINNORSST transonics
trans-sonic
ACINNORSTT constraint
ACINNORTTU truncation
ACINNOTUWY you can't win
ACINNSTTYY nyctinasty
ACINOOOPTT co-optation
ACINOOPPRT protanopic
ACINOORSTT cartoonist
ACINOORSTU octonarius
ACINOORTVY invocatory
ACINOPPRSW cow parsnip
ACINOPRSTU Count Paris
ACINOPSTUU usucaption
ACINORSSTU Sanctorius
ACINORSTTU crustation
ACINPRRSTT transcript
ACIOORRSST cross-ratio
ACIOORSTVY Ivory Coast
ACIOPRRTTU pourtraict
ACIOPRSTTY pyrostatic
ACIORRSTTU rusticator
ACJKMMNOOR Jack Mormon
ACJNOORRTU conjurator
ACKKNRSTUW knackwurst
ACKLLOORRW collar-work
ACKLMNOORS rock salmon
ACKLOOPRUV vapour lock
ACKOOPRSTY pastrycook
ACKOQRRTUZ quartz-rock
ACKRRSSTTU star-struck
ACLLLLOORR rollcollar
ACLLLNOOPY polyclonal
ACLLLOOSSY colossally
ACLLLRTUUY culturally
ACLLMMNOUY communally
ACLLMNNOOO monoclonal
ACLLMORTUU multocular
ACLLMRSUUY muscularly
ACLLNPTUUY punctually
ACLLOOPRRY corporally
ACLLORRSSY rallycross
ACLLPRSTUU sculptural
ACLMMNOOTY commonalty
ACLMNORRUW mural crown
ACLMOORSTY cosmolatry
ACLNNOSTTU consultant
ACLNNOSTTY constantly
ACLNNOSTUV convulsant
ACLNNPTUUU unpunctual
ACLNNRSUUU ranunculus
ACLNOORSTT contraltos
ACLNOORSTY stony coral
ACLNOORSUY canorously
ACLNOOTTUV Count Volta
ACLNOPSTUY postulancy
ACLOOPRSTU postocular
ACLOOPRTUY copulatory
ACLOORSSST across lots
ACLOORSTUY osculatory
ACLRRSTTUU structural
ACMMOORTTU commutator
ACMMPPUUUV vacuum pump
ACMNNORTUY countryman
ACMNOOPRTU contour map
ACMNOORSUY acronymous
ACMNOOSSTW Scotswoman
ACMOOOPRTT compotator
ACMOOPRTTU computator
ACNNNNOOSW snow cannon
ACNNNOSTTU unconstant
ACNOOPPRRT contraprop
ACNOOPRRTY port-crayon
ACNOOPRSTY syncopator
ACNOORRSTW crown roast
ACNOPRSSUY syncarpous
ACNOPRTTUU punctuator
ACOOOPRRRT corporator
ACOOOPRRTV provocator
ACOOPRRRTT protractor
ACOOPRRRTU procurator
ACOOPRSSTT sports coat
ACOPRRSSTY cross-party
ACOPRSSSTT sportscast
ADDDEEEHIL idle-headed
ADDDEEEHNW hand-weeded
ADDDEEEHRT the dreaded
ADDDEEFHIL fiddlehead
ADDDEEGILM middle-aged
ADDDEEHLMU muddle-head
ADDDEEHNRU dunderhead
ADDDEEILSS sidesaddle
ADDDEEKLRS skedaddler
ADDDEELLPW well-padded
ADDDEERSSY dressed day
ADDDEFILPY paddy field
ADDDEGILOV David Lodge
ADDDEGINWY wedding day
ADDDEGNORU dead-ground
ADDDEILNOR dendroidal
ADDDELLOTY toddy-ladle

ADDDELOOPW paddle-wood
ADDEEEEPST deep-seated
ADDEEEERSW red seaweed
ADDEEEFHNR free-handed
ADDEEEFLRS saddle reef
ADDEEEFNTU undefeated
ADDEEEGHRY grey-headed
ADDEEEHNNV even-handed
ADDEEEHORS soreheaded
ADDEEEIMNW maidenweed
ADDEEEIRST desiderate
ADDEEELLSW Weddell Sea
ADDEEELNTT dead-nettle
ADDEEELRST saddletree
ADDEEELRTT dead-letter
ADDEEENNRU unendeared
ADDEEENRTV denervated
ADDEEFHLNT left-handed
ADDEEFHNOR forehanded
ADDEEFHOST soft-headed
ADDEEFIINN definienda
ADDEEFILOT defoliated
ADDEEFLPPR Def Leppard
ADDEEFMNOR foredamned
ADDEEFNRVY dandy-fever
ADDEEGGHLU head-lugged
ADDEEGGINS disengaged
ADDEEGHHOT the Godhead
ADDEEGHITW dead-weight
ADDEEGHLNO long-headed
ADDEEGHPRS sharp-edged
ADDEEGILMM middle game
ADDEEGILMS Middle Ages
ADDEEGINRR dead ringer
ADDEEGLRRU drug dealer
ADDEEGNRRU unregarded
ADDEEGOSSS sea goddess
ADDEEHLLNS handselled
ADDEEHLNRU unheralded
ADDEEHLNST eldest hand
ADDEEHLOOS hooded seal
ADDEEHNNOP open-handed
ADDEEHNNRU unhardened
ADDEEHNNSS handedness
ADDEEHNOOW woodenhead
ADDEEHNORV overhanded
ADDEEHNRTU unthreaded
ADDEEHRRTY dehydrater
ADDEEIIMMX mixed-media
ADDEEIINNR dinanderie✧
ADDEEIINRT ride and tie
ride-and-tie
ADDEEIIPSS diapedesis
ADDEEIIRUV Reduviidae
ADDEEIKMNW weak-minded
ADDEEILMMN middle name
ADDEEILMST Middle East
ADDEEILNSS deadliness
ADDEEILPSS displeased
ADDEEILSTV David Steel
ADDEEIMNRR mind-reader
ADDEEIMRXY ready-mixed
ADDEEINNRU unindeared
ADDEEIPPRV dive-dapper
ADDEEIPRSW widespread
ADDEEJNRUW underjawed
ADDEEKMNNU Edmund Kean
ADDEEKORST deadstroke
ADDEELLMTU medullated
ADDEELLSSS saddleless
ADDEELMNOR endodermal
ADDEELMNOY almond-eyed
ADDEELMOTU demodulate
ADDEELNOSS saddle-nose
ADDEELOPRR rope ladder
ADDEELORSS saddle sore
saddle-sore
ADDEELPRST stepladder
ADDEELPRVY depravedly
ADDEEMNNRU undernamed
ADDEEMNORR road mender
ADDEEMORRS rose madder
ADDEENNPUX unexpanded
ADDEENNTTU unattended
ADDEENORRU round-eared
ADDEENORST adderstone
ADDEENPRTU dunderpate
ADDEENPRUV undepraved
ADDEENQRSU squandered
ADDEENRRSS red sanders
ADDEENRRTU unretarded
ADDEENRRUW unrewarded
ADDEENSSWY Wednesdays
ADDEEOPRRT depredator
ADDEEOPRSS desperados
ADDEEPRSSY pressed day
ADDEFGLLNO oldfangled
ADDEFGLORR Gerald Ford
ADDEFHIINS dead-finish
ADDEFHILPS paddlefish
ADDEFHILRS fish-ladder
ADDEFHIRST hard-fisted
ADDEFHLLNU full-handed
ADDEFHNORU four-handed
ADDEFIIILP lapidified
ADDEFIIMNR fair-minded
ADDEFILRSW fieldwards
ADDEFJLLOR Alfred Jodl
ADDEFLLOOP flapdoodle
ADDEFLLRUY dreadfully
ADDEFLMNOY many-folded
ADDEFLOORS saddle roof
ADDEGGILNO leading dog
ADDEGHHHIN high-handed
ADDEGHILOO goodlihead
ADDEGHILST deadlights
ADDEGHLNOR dog handler
ADDEGHLOOY goodlyhead
ADDEGHLORT gold thread
ADDEGIKNNP padding-ken
ADDEGIKNRW King Edward
ADDEGIMNOV Mogen David
ADDEGINNRU undreading
ADDEGIORRS dorsigrade
ADDEGIORVW David Gower
ADDEGJMNTU adjudgment
ADDEGLLOPT gold-plated
ADDEGLMNNO gold-end-man
ADDEGMNNOR grand monde
ADDEGMNORR dendrogram
ADDEGMNORU made ground
ADDEGOPRST graded post
ADDEGORSSW war goddess
ADDEGPTUWY Deputy Dawg
ADDEGRRSSU dressguard
ADDEHHILNS shield-hand
ADDEHHPRSU hard-pushed
ADDEHIILMS shield-maid
ADDEHIILNP didelphian
ADDEHIJMNU mujaheddin
ADDEHILNNR hinderland
ADDEHIMNOO maidenhood
ADDEHINNOR iron-handed
ADDEHIOORR drearihood
ADDEHIORSW drowsihead
ADDEHIRSYZ hydrazides
ADDEHJMNNO John Madden
ADDEHKNORW handworked
ADDEHLLNOR landholder
ADDEHLORST stadholder
ADDEHMNNOW hand-me-down
ADDEHMNORY home and dry
ADDEHNOORT horned toad
ADDEHNORSW Howards End
ADDEHNORSY dandy-horse
ADDEHNOSUW unshadowed
ADDEHNOTUW death-wound
ADDEHORRTY dehydrator
ADDEHORSTT short-dated
ADDEHRSUWW Huw Edwards
ADDEIILLSV ill-advised
ADDEIILMPY epididymal
ADDEIIMSSV misadvised
ADDEIINNVV David Niven
ADDEIIORVY video diary
ADDEIIPSST dissipated
ADDEILMNOY Lydian mode
ADDEILMTTY admittedly
ADDEILNNRY dinner lady
ADDEILNOYZ daily dozen
ADDEIMNOOR Dorian mode
ADDEIMNRSW miswandred
ADDEIMNSUY undismayed
ADDEIMNTTU unadmitted
ADDEINNORU unordained
ADDEINNOTU denudation
ADDEINNRRU underdrain
ADDEINOORS radiosonde
ADDEINRSTU disnatured
ADDEIPRRSY spray-dried
ADDEJNSTUU unadjusted
ADDEKMNOOS make no odds
ADDELLMNPU demand pull

ADDELMNOPY paddymelon
ADDELMOORS saddleroom
ADDELMORRW dream-world
ADDELNNORW wonderland✧
ADDELNNRSU Sunderland
ADDELNOORW woodlander
ADDELNORRW Lord Warden
ADDENNOPRU unpardoned
ADDENNPRUU up-and-under
ADDENNRSTU understand
ADDENOQRSU squadroned
ADDEORRSTW adder's-wort
ADDEORRSTY dry-roasted
ADDFFILLOY daffodilly
ADDFGIOORY Good Friday
ADDFIILNSU disdainful
ADDFILMORY myriadfold
ADDFIORSTV David Frost
ADDFLLORWY Lydford law
ADDGGLOOOS good as gold
ADDGHHINRY high and dry
ADDGHIINRR hard-riding
ADDGHINNOT Haddington
ADDGILLNWY dawdlingly
ADDGILLOSS dildo-glass
ADDGIMNORR ramrodding
ADDGINNOPU up and doing
ADDGNOPRTU Pont du Gard
ADDGORRSUW sword-guard
ADDHHILNNO hold in hand
ADDHIILMOS old-maidish
ADDHILORSU shroud-laid
ADDIIILNUV individual
ADDIIINNOT in addition
ADDIILLNST distilland
ADDIILMMOS old-maidism
ADDIILMRTW draw it mild
ADDILLLLYY dilly-dally
ADDIMNOSUY didynamous
ADDINOORSU sound radio
ADDLNORWWY downwardly
ADDNNOOTUW down-and-out
ADDNOORSSU doss around
ADEEEEFHRT feed-heater
ADEEEEGNRT degenerate
ADEEEEHRTX exheredate
ADEEEELNRT enterdeale
ADEEEELRTT leaderette
ADEEEEMSSS sesame seed
ADEEEFIIRS dies feriae
ADEEEFIKNY Yankeefied
ADEEEFILLR file-leader
ADEEEFILMR readme file
ADEEEFILRS federalise
ADEEEFILRZ federalize
ADEEEFIRTV federative
ADEEEFKPRS speedfreak
ADEEEFLLTT leafletted
ADEEEFLORR freeloader
ADEEEFLORT tree of lead
ADEEEFMNNS defenseman
ADEEEFNOST East of Eden
ADEEEFNOTV Deo favente
ADEEEFRRRT free-trader
ADEEEGGGLT gate-legged
ADEEEGGLNR near-legged
ADEEEGHNRS shagreened
ADEEEGILMN gleemaiden
ADEEEGKNRR green-drake
ADEEEGLLNR generalled
ADEEEGLNTW tangleweed
ADEEEGLOPV Lope de Vega
ADEEEGLRSV everglades✧
ADEEEGLRTU deregulate
ADEEEGNNRR endangerer
ADEEEGPRSS pass degree
ADEEEGSTWX Texas wedge
ADEEEHHNRT hen-hearted
ADEEEHHPSS sheep's-head
ADEEEHHSST headsheets
ADEEEHILMS seemlihead
ADEEEHKLLR lark-heeled
ADEEEHLNOT heel and toe
ADEEEHLNSV sleevehand
ADEEEHLPSY sleepyhead
ADEEEHLRTT letterhead
ADEEEHLRTW treadwheel
ADEEEHNRTT threatened
ADEEEIKLRU Auld Reekie
ADEEEIKMMN maiden-meek
ADEEEINNTV Venetianed
ADEEEINSSV seven-a-side
ADEEEIOPSU peau de soie
ADEEEIORWW woe-wearied
ADEEEIPRRT pied-à-terre
ADEEEIPTTX expeditate
ADEEEIRRTT reiterated
ADEEEIRSTT Eastertide
ADEEEJKMRT jerked-meat
ADEEEJMPUU jeu de paume
ADEEEKNNUW unweakened
ADEEELLMNP empanelled
ADEEELLNRW well-earned
ADEEELLRSS leaderless
ADEEELNNSS leadenness
ADEEELNNUV unleavened
ADEEELNPRU unrepealed
ADEEELNRRT randle-tree
ADEEELNRSU underlease
unreleased
ADEEELNRSW newsdealer
ADEEELNRUV unrevealed
ADEEELNRUW Leeuwarden
ADEEELNSST elatedness
ADEEELPRTY repeatedly
ADEEELRRTW Walter Reed
water elder
ADEEEMNNRT endearment
man-entered
ADEEEMNRSU demeasnure
ADEEEMOOST oedematose
ADEEEMPRTT attempered
ADEEEMRRST streamered
ADEEENPRTT predentate
ADEEENPRTU unrepeated
ADEEENRRSW newsreader
ADEEENRSSS searedness
ADEEENSSST sedateness
ADEEEPPRWY wapper-eyed
ADEEEQRSUY square-eyed
ADEEERSSTU Easter dues
ADEEFFILOR foliar feed
ADEEFFLORU four-leafed
ADEEFGGLRT ragged left
ADEEFGHIRU figurehead
ADEEFGHRTU gude-father
ADEEFGLLSZ self-glazed
ADEEFGLNNW newfangled
ADEEFGLNRS self-danger
ADEEFGLRRS self-regard
ADEEFGMNRT defragment
fragmented
ADEEFHILNR hand relief
ADEEFHILTW wheatfield
ADEEFHLNRT left-hander
ADEEFHLORW flower-head
ADEEFHLRST self-hatred
ADEEFHNRTU unfathered
ADEEFILLNS self-denial
ADEEFILMRS federalism
ADEEFILOUX folie à deux
ADEEFILRSS self-raised
ADEEFILRST federalist
ADEEFILSSU diseaseful
ADEEFINNRR ferrandine
ADEEFINORT federation
ADEEFINORZ fazendeiro
ADEEFINRRW fire-warden
ADEEFIOPRS safe period
ADEEFIORSV fore-advise
ADEEFIPRTV five-parted
ADEEFIRSTU disfeature
ADEEFLLLNN flannelled
ADEEFLLORS self-loader
ADEEFLLORW fallow deer
ADEEFLLSSY fadelessly
ADEEFLMORY Adolf Meyer
ADEEFLORUV four-leaved
ADEEFMNORW freedwoman
ADEEFMNRRU underframe
ADEEFMNRTY defrayment
ADEEFMORRS reformades
ADEEFNNSTU unfastened
ADEEFNOPRR free pardon
ADEEFNRTUU unfeatured
ADEEFOPRRT perforated
ADEEFORSTU foederatus
ADEEGGHHRU head-hugger
ADEEGGHJRU jugged hare
ADEEGGHLOR loggerhead
ADEEGGHPTU depth gauge
ADEEGGJNSS jaggedness
ADEEGGLNNR green gland

ADEEGGNORS George Sand
ADEEGGNRSS raggedness
ADEEGGNRUY gaudy-green
ADEEGHHIRR high-reared
ADEEGHIKNW weak-hinged
ADEEGHILNY Headingley
ADEEGHILRT lethargied
ADEEGHIMTW wheat midge
ADEEGHIRRY grey-haired
ADEEGHISUY hay-de-guise
ADEEGHNNRU anhungered
ADEEGHNRRU eard-hunger
ADEEGHNRTU ungathered
ADEEGHNTUW the unwaged
ADEEGHSUYY hay-de-guyes
ADEEGIINSS diagenesis
ADEEGIIRRV River Adige
ADEEGIJLNR Darjeeling
ADEEGILLRT treillaged
ADEEGILNNR danger line
ADEEGILNOT delegation
ADEEGILNRR ringleader
ADEEGILNRY delayering
ADEEGILRSV Gail Devers
ADEEGIMNNR meandering
ADEEGIMORT diagometer
ADEEGINNOT denegation
ADEEGINNRS Grenadines
ADEEGINRRT gradienter
intergrade
ADEEGINRTU green audit
ADEEGINRTW dewatering
ADEEGIORTV derogative
ADEEGIRSTV stage-diver
ADEEGLLNOS golden seal
ADEEGLLNRY enlargedly
ADEEGLMNNO golden mean
ADEEGLMOST Maltese dog
ADEEGLNNPR preen gland
ADEEGLNORT goal-tender
ADEEGLNORZ angledozer
ADEEGLNPRU plunderage
ADEEGLNRUZ underglaze
ADEEGLNTTU gauntleted
ADEEGLORRR large order
ADEEGLORRW lower grade✧
ADEEGLORTY derogately
ADEEGLPPRY dapple-grey
ADEEGLRRSS regardless
ADEEGMNORT dermatogen
ADEEGMNRSS gensdarmes
ADEEGNNRRU ungarnered
ADEEGNNRTU underagent
ADEEGNORRS rose garden
ADEEGNORRT dragon-tree
ADEEGNRRSW greensward
ADEEGNRRTU ungartered
ADEEGOORSV overdosage
ADEEGOORSW greasewood
ADEEGORRRT retrograde
ADEEGORSTU uredo-stage
ADEEHHILMR hemihedral
ADEEHHILST heat shield
ADEEHHINST in the shade
ADEEHHISST dissheathe
ADEEHHLOSV shovelhead
ADEEHHMNOT heathendom
ADEEHHNOPS headphones
ADEEHHNORX hexahedron
ADEEHHNPTY hyphenated
ADEEHHNRTU headhunter
ADEEHHNSTU unsheathed
ADEEHHORTT death throe
ADEEHHOSTU death house
ADEEHHOTTT to the death
ADEEHHRRTW hetherward
ADEEHIIKRR Keir Hardie
ADEEHIIKTV khediviate
ADEEHIILLV livelihead
ADEEHIILPS aedileship
ADEEHIIRRW wire-haired
ADEEHIJKNR jerkinhead
ADEEHIKLRS shieldrake
ADEEHIKLRT threadlike
ADEEHILLOV lovelihead
ADEEHILMNR mind-healer
ADEEHILMRW dreamwhile
ADEEHILNOT endothelia
ethanediol
ADEEHILNTU heulandite
ADEEHILOPP paedophile
ADEEHILPPR hare-lipped
ADEEHILPRS dealership
leadership
ADEEHILSVY adhesively
ADEEHILSWY daisy-wheel
ADEEHIMNSU dehumanise
ADEEHIMNUZ dehumanize
ADEEHIMOTT dimethoate
ADEEHIMPRY hypermedia
ADEEHINRST dishearten
ADEEHINRSX share index
ADEEHINRTT thenardite
ADEEHINRTV thread vein
ADEEHINSTV Edith Evans
ADEEHIPRRS readership
ADEEHIRRSS sherardise
ADEEHIRRSZ sherardize
ADEEHIRRTY hereditary
ADEEHIRSTT threadiest
ADEEHJLORT jolterhead
ADEEHKLLNT death knell
ADEEHKLLRS shelldrake
ADEEHKNOOY hook and eye
ADEEHKNOTT death-token
ADEEHKORRW headworker
ADEEHLLNRT enthralled
ADEEHLLORY Lord Healey
ADEEHLLOWY yellowhead
ADEEHLNOTW down at heel
down-at-heel
ADEEHLNRST Shetlander
ADEEHLOOSX aldohexose
ADEEHLOPRT petrolhead
The Leopard
ADEEHLPUZZ puzzle-head
ADEEHLRRTU hurdle rate
ADEEHMMNOR remand home
ADEEHMMOTT homme d'état
ADEEHMNPRU unhampered
ADEEHMRTWY what remedy?
ADEEHNNRTU underneath
ADEEHNRRTU underearth
ADEEHNRRTW netherward
ADEEHNSTVY seventh day
seventh-day
ADEEHOOPRT Heteropoda
ADEEHOPPPT poppet-head
ADEEHOPRTT deep throat
ADEEHORTTY the year dot
ADEEHRRSTT Thar Desert
ADEEIIJLLO jolie laide
ADEEIIJNRR jardinière
ADEEIIKLMN maidenlike
ADEEIILMTT delimitate
ADEEIILNSS desalinise
ADEEIILNSZ desalinize
ADEEIILNTV delineavit
evidential
ADEEIILSTV devitalise
ADEEIILTVZ devitalize
ADEEIIMNRT intermedia
ADEEIIMNRU minauderie
ADEEIIMNTV vindemiate
ADEEIIMTTV meditative
ADEEIINORV Vireonidae
ADEEIINPST tinea pedis
ADEEIINRST distrainee
ADEEIINRVV vivandière
ADEEIINSST dessiatine
East Indies
ADEEIIRRVV Viverridae
ADEEIIRTTW tidewaiter
ADEEIIRTVV derivative
ADEEIJMNRS red jasmine
ADEEIJOPRS jeopardise
ADEEIJOPRZ jeopardize
ADEEIKKMRT kite-marked
ADEEIKKPRT keep it dark
ADEEIKLLWW weak-willed
ADEEIKLMNN kennelmaid
ADEEIKLRUW Die Walküre
ADEEIKNRRT dreikanter
tea drinker
ADEEIKRSST asterisked
ADEEIKRSTW water-skied
ADEEILLMRY remedially
ADEEILLMVY medievally
ADEEILLPRS espadrille
ADEEILLPTX pixellated
ADEEILLRRU dérailleur
ADEEILLSVV slide valve
ADEEILLUVV vaudeville

ADEEILMNPT pedimental
ADEEILMNRT derailment
ADEEILMNTY myelinated
ADEEILMORS demoralise
ADEEILMORU Lemuroidea
ADEEILMORZ demoralize
ADEEILMPRR peridermal
ADEEILMSTU Mustelidae
ADEEILNNRW Andrew Neil
New Ireland
ADEEILNNTT tendential
ADEEILNNTU unentailed
ADEEILNORT delineator
ADEEILNORU Le Douanier
ADEEILNPRT interplead
ADEEILNRSU unrealised
Uredinales
ADEEILNRTU adulterine
ADEEILNRUZ unrealized
ADEEILNSSV disenslave
ADEEILNTTT dilettante
ADEEILNTTW lean-witted
ADEEILOPPT deoppilate
ADEEILOPRS depolarise
ADEEILOPRZ depolarize
ADEEILOPTT petiolated
ADEEILORSV devalorise
ADEEILORVZ devalorize
ADEEILPRRV pearl diver
ADEEILPRST pilastered
ADEEILPRSU Serpulidae
ADEEILPRTU tulip-eared
ADEEILRSSU Aussiedler
ADEEILRSSV sales drive
ADEEILRSTU adulterise
ADEEILRTUZ adulterize
ADEEIMMNSS maimedness
ADEEIMMORT immoderate
ADEEIMMRSU immeasured
ADEEIMMUVW medium-wave
ADEEIMNNOT denominate
emendation
ADEEIMNNTT detainment
ADEEIMNNUX unexamined
ADEEIMNORV maiden over
ADEEIMNPRS Parmenides
ADEEIMNPRT pandermite
ADEEIMNRRT dreariment
ADEEIMNRRW new-married
ADEEIMNRSS dreaminess
ADEEIMNSTV advisement
ADEEIMNSTW tandemwise
ADEEIMORRS drearisome
ADEEIMORRT radiometer
ADEEIMORRX xerodermia
ADEEIMORTU audiometer
ADEEIMOTTV demotivate
ADEEIMQRRU quadrireme
ADEEIMRSST mediatress
sidestream
ADEEINOPRT Pontederia
ADEEINORTT orientated
ADEEINOTTV denotative
ADEEINPPSX appendixes
ADEEINPRRU unrepaired
ADEEINPRST pedestrian
ADEEINPTUX unexpiated
ADEEINRRSS dreariness
ADEEINRRST restrained
ADEEINRSTT straitened
ADEEINRSTU denaturise
ADEEINRTTT tridentate
ADEEINRTUZ denaturize
ADEEINSSST steadiness
ADEEINSSTY dessyatine
ADEEIOPRSX peroxidase
ADEEIOSSTY easy does it
ADEEIOSXYY ox-eye daisy
ADEEIPRRTY retired pay
ADEEIPRSTT tapestried
ADEEIPRTUV depurative
ADEEIRRRWW wiredrawer
ADEEIRRSTV advertiser
ADEEIRRTVW waterdrive
ADEEIRSSTT dissertate
ADEEIRSTTV travestied
ADEEISSTVV Steve Davis
ADEEJKLNRU junk-dealer
ADEEJKORRS soda jerker
ADEEJNOORR rejoneador
ADEEKLLMRW well-marked
ADEEKLMORU leukoderma
ADEEKMNRRU unremarked
ADEEKMNRSS markedness
ADEEKMRRSS dressmaker
ADEEKNNRTU undertaken
ADEEKNORST drakestone
ADEEKNRRTU undertaker
ADEEKORRST take orders
ADEELLMMRT trammelled
ADEELLMNRS mallenders
ADEELLMNTU unmetalled
ADEELLMORT mortadelle
ADEELLMTUV datum level
ADEELLNNPU unpanelled
ADEELLNQUU unequalled
ADEELLNRSS sallenders
ADEELLNRUV unravelled
ADEELLORSS loss-leader
ADEELLOSTY desolately
ADEELLQRRU quarrelled
ADEELMMORS mesodermal
ADEELMNNTU malentendu
unlamented
ADEELMNORT almond-tree
ADEELMNPUX unexampled
ADEELMNTZZ dazzlement
ADEELMORTY moderately
ADEELMRSUY measuredly
ADEELNNQSU Queensland
ADEELNNSUV unenslaved
ADEELNNTTU untalented
ADEELNOPRU endopleura
ADEELNORRV overlander
ADEELNRRUY underlayer
ADEELNRSTW westlander
ADEELNRTTU laundrette
ADEELNRUUV undervalue
ADEELOPPTU depopulate
ADEELOPRSS leopardess
ADEELOPRST spot dealer
ADEELPPRRY preparedly
ADEELRRSSW rewardless
ADEELRRSTU serrulated
ADEELRSSTU adulteress
ADEEMNNNRU unmannered
ADEEMNNTTT attendment
ADEEMNOPRR promenader
ADEEMNORST damson tree
sordamente
ADEEMNORTT Tate Modern
ADEEMNORTY emendatory
ADEEMNORYY ready money
ready-money
ADEEMNPPRU unpampered
ADEEMNPRTT department
ADEEMNRRTT retardment
ADEEMNRSTU unmastered
unstreamed
ADEEMNRSUU unmeasured
ADEEMNSSTU sense datum
ADEEMNSTUU mansuetude
ADEEMOOSTU oedematous
ADEEMOPRRT Dermoptera
ADEEMORRVW warmed-over
ADEEMORSST dermatoses
ADEEMRRSUY dry measure
ADEENNNTTU untenanted
ADEENNOPUW unweaponed
ADEENNORSU unreasoned
ADEENNOSSU unseasoned
ADEENNPRTT pretendant
ADEENNPRTU unparented
ADEENNPTTU unpatented
ADEENNRSUW unanswered
ADEENOOPRW wooden pear
ADEENOPRST personated
ADEENORSTW down-easter
ADEENPPRRS red snapper
ADEENPPRRU unprepared
ADEENPPRSS dapperness
ADEENPRRTU enraptured
ADEENPRSST depressant
ADEENPRSTY present-day
ADEENQRRRU quarrender
ADEENQRRSU squanderer
ADEENRRTUV adventurer
ADEENRRTUW under water
underwater
ADEENRSTTU understate
ADEENSTTTU unattested
ADEEOOPSTT seed potato
ADEEOPPRRR order paper

ADEEOPRRSV	overspread
	spread-over
ADEEOQRSTU	square-toed
ADEEORRRRT	rear-dorter
ADEEORRTTU	trade route
ADEEPQRTTU	parquetted
ADEEPRRSTU	departures
ADEERRSTTW	streetward
ADEERRSTYY	starry-eyed
ADEERSSSTW	stewardess
ADEERSSTVX	sex-starved
ADEERSSTYY	yesterdays
ADEESTTTUY	estate duty
ADEFFGGGIR	gaff-rigged
ADEFFGHIRT	affrighted
ADEFFGIIRT	graffitied
ADEFFIKLNR	Frank Field
ADEFFLOOTT	flat-footed
ADEFGGGINR	defragging
ADEFGGINOR	God-fearing
ADEFGHILPT	dip the flag
ADEFGHIRST	far-sighted
ADEFGHOORT	good-father
ADEFGIINOR	foreign aid
ADEFGILLSS	field glass
ADEFGILRSU	Life Guards
ADEFGIRTVY	gravity-fed
ADEFGLLOOS	GoodFellas
ADEFGNOORR	roof garden
ADEFHHLOOT	health food
ADEFHHOOPT	pad the hoof
ADEFHHOORT	fatherhood
ADEFHILMSS	damselfish
ADEFHILTTW	halfwitted
ADEFHINPRT	pathfinder
ADEFHIRSTV	drive shaft
ADEFHIRTWW	white dwarf✧
ADEFHLLPUX	half-duplex
ADEFHLOOSW	whale's food
ADEFHLTTWY	Twelfth Day
ADEFHMNOTU	unfathomed
ADEFHNNOOT	note of hand
ADEFHNNORY	Henry Fonda
ADEFHOORSW	foreshadow
ADEFHORRST	draft horse
ADEFIIILNN	Indian file
ADEFIIINNR	Indian fire
ADEFIILLNS	sildenafil
ADEFIILLRT	field trial
ADEFIILMST	mailed fist
ADEFIILNRS	flindersia
ADEFIILNRT	field train
ADEFIINOPS	saponified
ADEFIINRTU	unratified
ADEFIINRTW	draw it fine
ADEFIIRRST	first-aider
ADEFIIRSTT	stratified
ADEFIKLORT	fork-tailed
ADEFILLLRY	all-firedly
ADEFILLLSU	full-sailed
ADEFILLNNW	windfallen
ADEFILLNTY	inflatedly
ADEFILMNNU	uninflamed
ADEFILMNOR	manifolder
ADEFILMORS	Fidel Ramos
ADEFILNNTU	uninflated
ADEFILOORT	defoliator
ADEFILORTU	fluoridate
ADEFILPRSU	despairful
ADEFILRSTY	stray field
ADEFIMMSTU	deaf-mutism
ADEFIMRRRT	dirt farmer
ADEFINOORR	foreordain
ADEFINOPRS	infraposed
ADEFINORSZ	Sanforized®
ADEFINRRSU	fund-raiser
ADEFINRSST	draftiness
ADEFIRSSTX	fixed stars
ADEFKLNOTU	untalked-of
ADEFKLORST	tradesfolk
ADEFLLMNNU	full-manned
ADEFLLNNOW	downfallen
ADEFLLOSUU	useful load
ADEFLLRTWY	leftwardly
ADEFLMNORR	land reform
ADEFLNRTUU	fraudulent
ADEFLOORST	lord of seat
ADEFLOORTW	floodwater
	water flood
	waterflood
ADEFLOOSUV	food values
ADEFLOPRSY	self-parody
ADEFLORRTW	afterworld
ADEFMNORTU	undreamt-of
ADEFMOORRS	reformados
ADEFNNOPRU	unprofaned
ADEFNOORRW	for a wonder
ADEFNOOSTV	O's of Advent
ADEFOOPRWX	wax-proofed
ADEFOORSYY	days of yore
ADEFOPRRTU	four-parted
ADEFORSSTW	soft sawder
ADEFRRSTTU	frustrated
ADEGGGILNR	laggen-gird
ADEGGGINNR	darning egg
ADEGGHILNR	hang-glider
ADEGGHINOR	hearing dog
ADEGGHOOTT	gag-toothed
ADEGGHORUY	hydragogue
ADEGGHOSTU	shagged out
ADEGGIINRS	niggardise
ADEGGIINRZ	niggardize
ADEGGIMMOS	demagogism
ADEGGIMOPS	pedagogism
ADEGGIPRSW	digger-wasp
ADEGGLLNOO	golden goal
ADEGGLMNOR	golden gram
ADEGGLOORS	sogdolager
ADEGGMNORU	ground game
ADEGGNOPTU	get-up-and-go
ADEGGOORSV	grave goods
ADEGHHIIRS	high-raised
ADEGHHILNR	highlander✧
ADEGHHINST	nightshade
ADEGHHISTT	high-tasted
ADEGHILLNO	Heligoland
ADEGHILMRT	light-armed
ADEGHILNNR	rehandling
ADEGHILNOR	long-haired
ADEGHILNOW	Goldie Hawn
ADEGHILNSU	languished
ADEGHINNSW	hand-sewing
ADEGHINOSU	enough said
ADEGHINPRS	springhead
ADEGHIOPRY	ideography
ADEGHLNNRU	land-hunger
ADEGHLNORT	Grand Hotel
ADEGHLOOPY	edaphology
ADEGHLORSW	gold-washer
ADEGHLRTUY	daughterly
ADEGHMOPRY	demography
ADEGHNOPTU	upon the gad
ADEGHNORST	headstrong
	strong head
ADEGHNORTT	hard-gotten
ADEGHNRRUY	eard-hungry
ADEGHNRTTU	draught-net
ADEGHOOPTT	gap-toothed
ADEGHORRSY	Gary Rhodes
ADEGHORSUU	guardhouse
ADEGHRRSSS	herd's grass
ADEGIIILST	digitalise
ADEGIIILTZ	digitalize
ADEGIIIMNS	disimagine
ADEGIILLSU	seguidilla
ADEGIILMNS	misleading
ADEGIILNOT	deligation
	gadolinite
	gelatinoid
ADEGIILNPR	lip-reading
ADEGIILNRT	ring-tailed
ADEGIILTTY	digitately
ADEGIIMNNU	unimagined
ADEGIIMNRS	misreading
ADEGIINNRY	dye in grain
ADEGIINPRS	despairing
	spinigrade
ADEGIINRTT	dirt-eating
ADEGIIOPRR	prairie dog
ADEGIJKMNU	Kim Dae-jung
ADEGIJLNRS	J D Salinger
ADEGIKLNOR	dragonlike
ADEGILLNNY	Glyn Daniel
ADEGILLNOS	solid angle
ADEGILLNOU	Langue d'oïl
ADEGILLNPY	pleadingly
ADEGILLNYY	delayingly
ADEGILMNRY	dreamingly
ADEGILMRTU	multigrade
ADEGILNNNO	non-aligned
ADEGILNNNT	landing net
ADEGILNNOR	golden rain
ADEGILNNRS	sanderling

ADEGILNNUY undelaying
ADEGILNOSY agonisedly
ADEGILNOTT glottidean
ADEGILNOUU Langue d'oui
ADEGILNOYZ agonizedly
ADEGILNPPR dapperling
ADEGILNRRR errand girl
ADEGILNRTT glitterand
ADEGILNRUV gerundival
ADEGILORRY goliardery
ADEGILOSTW slow-gaited
ADEGILRSSW wired glass
ADEGIMNNOS Mandingoes
ADEGIMNNRU maundering
undreaming
ADEGIMNOPU impoundage
ADEGIMNORS gormandise
ADEGIMNORZ gormandize
ADEGIMOPSU pseudimago
ADEGIMORRV Roger Vadim
ADEGIMORST dogmatiser
ADEGIMORTZ dogmatizer
ADEGINNPRW drawing-pen
ADEGINNSSU unassigned
ADEGINOOPS poignadoes
ADEGINOORT derogation
Trogonidae
ADEGINORRT denigrator
ADEGINORRV overdaring
ADEGINORST designator
ADEGINORTX axe to grind
ADEGINPRSW wingspread
ADEGIORRTY argyrodite
ADEGIPRRST partridges
ADEGJLMNTU judgmental
ADEGJNRSSU grand jésus
ADEGKNNORT knot garden
ADEGKNRRRU Kruger Rand
krugerrand✧
ADEGLLMNOP Golden Palm
ADEGLLMOSY gladsomely
ADEGLMORST stream-gold
ADEGLNNORU round angle
ADEGLNORSU glanderous
ADEGLNPRUW wander plug
ADEGLNRSTY grand style
ADEGLOPRSY dog-parsley
ADEGMMOPRR programmed
ADEGMNNOOR gander-moon
ADEGMNNOYY dynamogeny
ADEGMNOOSU endogamous
ADEGMNORSS Dream Songs
ADEGNNORRU groan under
ADEGNOOORW orange-wood
ADEGNOOPST steganopod
ADEGNOORTU good nature
ADEGNOPRRS sandgroper
ADEGNORSSU sand grouse
ADEGNORUVW ground wave
ADEGNOSSTU sound stage
ADEGOOPRST gasteropod
ADEGOORRTY derogatory
ADEHHHNPRY hard hyphen
ADEHHIIORR hide or hair
ADEHHIIPRT diphtheria
ADEHHILNPW whip handle
ADEHHILPRS heraldship
ADEHHIORTT hit the road
ADEHHIRRTW hitherward
ADEHHIRSSW dishwasher
ADEHHLLOOR holohedral
ADEHHNOOPR rhodophane
ADEHHNOPRY hydrophane
ADEHHOSSTW The Shadows
ADEHIILMNR nihil ad rem
ADEHIILMST Delia Smith
ADEHIILOPU audiophile
ADEHIILPTW whiptailed
ADEHIIMNNP Indian hemp
ADEHIIMNOO Hominoidea
ADEHIIMRTT mithridate
ADEHIINNRU hirudinean
ADEHIINOTT dithionate
ADEHIIOPRU Ophiuridae
ADEHIIPSUU euphausiid
ADEHIKNNSW wind-shaken
ADEHILLLSW shieldwall
ADEHILLNTW thin-walled
ADEHILLORU loudhailer
ADEHILNNRS hinderlans
ADEHILNNRT hinterland
ADEHILNOPS sphenoidal
ADEHILNORT threnodial
ADEHILNORZ endorhizal
ADEHILNRST disenthral
ADEHILOPRS spheroidal
ADEHILPRUY hyperdulia
ADEHILPSTU disulphate
ADEHIMNNTU minute hand
ADEHIMNORY Rhodymenia
ADEHIMORTU rheumatoid
ADEHIMSSSW Swadeshism
ADEHINOOPR radiophone
ADEHINOSST astonished
ADEHINPRSW wardenship
ADEHINPSSU dauphiness
ADEHINRSST Sanhedrist
ADEHINRSUV unravished
ADEHIOOPRT orthopedia
ADEHIOORTW waiterhood
ADEHIOPRRW hair-powder
ADEHIOPRSS rhapsodise
ADEHIOPRST Portishead
ADEHIOPRSZ rhapsodize
ADEHIRRTWW withdrawer
ADEHKNORRW work-harden
ADEHLLMOPR lampholder
ADEHLLNOOR loan-holder
ADEHLLNORU hell around
ADEHLLNOUW unhallowed
ADEHLLOPRY polyhedral
ADEHLMNORT enthraldom
motherland
ADEHLMNOSY handsomely
ADEHLMNPPU pump-handle
ADEHLMOOSU Samuel Hood
ADEHLMOPRY hypodermal
ADEHLMOPTY methyldopa
ADEHLNOPRY hydroplane
ADEHLNRSTU Sutherland
ADEHLOSSSW shadowless
ADEHLRTTWY thwartedly
ADEHMMNOPR hammer-pond
ADEHMMOPRR drop-hammer
ADEHMNNOSU unhandsome
ADEHMNOTTU muttonhead
ADEHMOORST masterhood
ADEHMORRTW threadworm
ADEHMORSTU Thomas Edur
ADEHMORSTY Mother's Day
ADEHMRTUUW durum wheat
ADEHNNNOTW now and then
ADEHNNOOST to one's hand
ADEHNOOPRR androphore
ADEHNOOPRT parenthood
ADEHNOPPRS sandhopper
ADEHNOPRSS sharp-nosed
ADEHNORSUX hexandrous
ADEHNPPPTU hand puppet
ADEHNRRTTU Arthur Dent
ADEHOOPRTY orthopaedy
ADEHOORSVW overshadow
ADEHOORUWY how dare you!
ADEHOOSTTW saw-toothed
ADEHOPRRTU pourtrahed
ADEHOPTTTU put to death
ADEHORRSSW shorewards
ADEHORSTWW westward ho!✧
ADEIIIKNSS diakinesis
ADEIIILLNT initialled
ADEIIILMST Militiades
ADEIIILMSU Simuliidae
ADEIIIMNTT intimidate
ADEIIINNPP Indian pipe
Pinnipedia
ADEIIINNPR peridinian
ADEIIINOSZ isoniazide
ADEIIKMNNP maiden pink
ADEIIKNNOP Indian poke
ADEIIKNNST ink-stained
ADEIIKNSSY dyskinesia
ADEIILLMPX maxilliped
ADEIILLPTX pixillated
ADEIILLRTV vitrailled
ADEIILLSTT distillate
ADEIILMMTU multimedia
ADEIILMNOR meridional
ADEIILMNSU unidealism
ADEIILMRTW limited war
ADEIILMSSV Miles Davis
ADEIILNNPR dinner-pail
ADEIILNNSU Niue Island
ADEIILNOPT depilation

ideal point
ADEIILNORT deliration
ADEIILNOTV inviolated
ADEIILNRST disentrail
ADEIILNRTT intertidal
ADEIILNTTT dilettanti
ADEIILORST idolatrise
ADEIILORTZ idolatrize
ADEIIMNNOR iron maiden✧
ADEIIMNNOT antimonide
ADEIIMNOTT meditation
ADEIIMNOTV admonitive
dominative
ADEIIMNPRU unimpaired
ADEIIMNRST administer
ADEIIMNRTX mixed train
ADEIIMNSTY disamenity
ADEIIMORST Radio Times
ADEIIMPRSU praesidium
ADEIIMPRTU tepidarium
ADEIIMRSTT dermatitis
ADEIINNNOS Indonesian
ADEIINNORT inordinate
ADEIINNOTW nationwide
ADEIINNOTX indexation
ADEIINNOTZ denization
ADEIINNPPT pinnatiped
ADEIINNRST disentrain
ADEIINNRVY Andy Irvine
ADEIINNSST daintiness
ADEIINNSTW West Indian
ADEIINORST sideration
ADEIINORTV derivation
ADEIINPPRS drainpipes
ADEIINPTTU inaptitude
ADEIINRRST distrainer
ADEIINRTUV indurative
ADEIINTTUV unvitiated
ADEIIPRRSS dispraiser
ADEIIPRRSY presidiary
ADEIIPRTTU tripudiate
ADEIIPRTTW pittie-ward
ADEIIRRTVX Taxi Driver
taxi-driver
ADEIISSSUV dissuasive
ADEIJLNOPT lap-jointed
ADEIJMMNRW windjammer
ADEIJOPSSU jaspideous
ADEIKKLNTY take kindly
ADEIKLLLRY lady-killer
ADEIKLLMMT malted milk
ADEIKLLNUY unladylike
ADEIKLNOSU sound-alike
ADEIKLNRSY alkyd resin
ADEIKLNSTY litany-desk
ADEIKOPSWW widow's peak
ADEILLMORY Marie Lloyd
ADEILLMSTW Willemstad
ADEILLNOOS solenoidal
ADEILLNOPR Pirandello
ADEILLNOSS on all sides
ADEILLNOSU delusional
ADEILLNPRU unpillared
ADEILLNPSS pallidness
ADEILLNRRT tendrillar
ADEILLNRTU ill-natured
ADEILLNRUV unrivalled
ADEILLORSZ Leo Szilard
ADEILLPSTU plastidule
ADEILLQRRU quadriller
ADEILLRRST ill-starred
ADEILLRSUY residually
ADEILMNNOR molendinar
ADEILMNNUY unmaidenly
ADEILMNOPR palindrome
ADEILMNORS Madrileños
ADEILMNORT intermodal
tremolandi
ADEILMNRST dismantler
ADEILMNRTU rudimental
ADEILMNSSS dismalness
ADEILMNSTU dentaliums
ADEILMNTVY ivy-mantled
ADEILMOPSS psalmodise
ADEILMOPSZ psalmodize
ADEILMORSU modularise
ADEILMORUZ modularize
ADEILMPRUU praeludium
ADEILNNORT internodal
ADEILNNOXZ zonal index
ADEILNNPTU pinnulated
ADEILNOOST desolation
ADEILNOOTV devotional
ADEILNOPPT pedal point
pentaploid
ADEILNOPRR Lord Napier
ADEILNORTY ordinately
ADEILNOTUV unviolated
ADEILNPRTU prudential
ADEILNPTUV pulvinated
ADEILNQTUU unqualited
ADEILNRSTY strainedly
ADEILNSTTU testudinal
ADEILNSTUY unsteadily
ADEILNSTWY Walt Disney
ADEILOORST oestradiol
ADEILOPQRU quadripole
ADEILOPRTT tetraploid
ADEILOPRTW tidal power
ADEILOPRTY depilatory
ADEILOPSSU disepalous
ADEILOPSTU dipetalous
ADEILORSST idolatress
ADEILOSSTT solid-state
ADEILPPPSU pedipalpus
ADEILRRRSU Rural Rides
ADEILRSTTU stridulate
ADEILRTTXY dextrality
ADEIMMMSSU mass medium
ADEIMMNNTU nidamentum
ADEIMMNRST mastermind
ADEIMMNTTU manumitted
ADEIMMORST moderatism
ADEIMNNORT ordainment
ADEIMNNOSS idem sonans
ADEIMNNOTU mountained
ADEIMNNRSU unseminar'd
ADEIMNOORS moon-raised
ADEIMNOORT moderation
ADEIMNORRS randomiser
ADEIMNORRZ randomizer
ADEIMNORSW randomwise
ADEIMNORTW woman-tired
ADEIMNPRTU unimparted
ADEIMNRRRU red-murrain
ADEIMNRRTT Mitterrand
ADEIMNRSTY mistrayned
ADEIMOOOTZ diatom ooze
ADEIMORRTX moderatrix
ADEIMORRTY radiometry
ADEIMORSST dermatosis
ADEIMORSTT Mister Toad
ADEIMORTUW moudiewart
ADEIMORTUY audiometry
ADEIMORTWW mowdiewart
ADEIMRTUUV duumvirate
ADEINNOORS in one's road
ADEINNOOTT denotation
detonation
ADEINNOPWW windowpane
ADEINNORTU trade union
ADEINNOSTT Endostatin®
ADEINNRSSW inwardness
ADEINNRSTU unstrained
ADEINNTUUY annuity due
ADEINOOPRT readoption
ADEINOPRTU depuration
ADEINOPTTU deputation
ADEINORRUV River Donau
ADEINORRWW Rear Window
ADEINORSST adroitness
intradoses
ADEINORSUV adenovirus
ADEINORTUW autowinder
ADEINOSTVY video nasty
ADEINOSTWW window seat
ADEINPPRSU unapprised
ADEINPRSST dispersant
ADEINPRSSY dispensary
ADEINPRUUV unpurvaide
ADEINQRRUU unquarried
ADEINRSSTW tawdriness
ADEINRSTTU unstriated
ADEINRTTUW twi-natured
ADEINSSSTU unassisted
ADEINSSTTV Adventists
ADEIOPPRSV disapprove
ADEIOPRRTU repudiator
ADEIOPRSST pas de trois
ADEIOPRSTV adsorptive
ADEIOPRSTY depositary
ADEIORRSTT traditores
ADEIORSSTT siderostat

Words marked ✧ can also be spelled with one or more capital letters

ADEIPPRRTY day-tripper
ADEIRRSSTW ward sister
ADEIRSSTWY strideways
ADEJKNORRU jerk around
ADEJLNOPVY J P Donleavy
ADEJMNORZZ modern jazz
ADEJMNOSSY James Dyson
ADEJMNSTTU adjustment
ADEJOOPRSU jeopardous
ADEKMNORTW downmarket
ADEKNOPRST pond skater
ADEKNORSTU skate round
ADEKNORSUZ Konrad Zuse
ADEKOPRSTU sparked out
ADELLLORSS dollarless
ADELLMMSUY sell a dummy
ADELLNOOWY Woody Allen
ADELLNOPRU land-louper
ADELLNORRU all-rounder
ADELLNORWW Wonderwall
ADELLNOTTU unallotted
ADELLNTUUY undulately
ADELLOORRR road roller
ADELLOORST rolled oats
ADELMMNTUU nummulated
ADELMMOOSS desmosomal
ADELMMOPSS plasmodesm
ADELMNOORT tremolando
ADELMNORVY Very Old Man
ADELMNPRTU untrampled
ADELMOPSTU deutoplasm
ADELMORSST old masters
ADELNNNOOR nandrolone
ADELNNOOOR Lorna Doone
ADELNNOOST East London
ADELNNPRTU underplant
ADELNOPRSS pardonless
ADELNORSSU slanderous
ADELNOUVWY unavowedly
ADELNRSTTU delustrant
ADELNRSTUW wanderlust
ADELOORRSY early doors
ADELOORSTY desolatory
ADELOORTWY two-year-old
ADELOPQRUU quadrupole
ADELORRWWY world-weary
ADELORSTUU adulterous
ADELPQRTUU quadruplet
ADELPQRUUX quadruplex
ADELRRSTYY drysaltery
ADELRSTWWY westwardly
ADEMMMNORU memorandum
ADEMMOOSTU stomodaeum
ADEMMORTUX extra modum
ADEMNNORSS randomness
ADEMNNORSU unransomed
ADEMNOPRST pond-master
ADEMNORRUU unarmoured
ADEMNORSSU mess around
ADEMNORSTW downstream
ADEMNRRSSV Mrs Danvers
ADEMOQRTUY demy quarto
ADENNOOPRT pteranodon
ADENNOPTTU attend upon
ADENNORRRU roadrunner
ADENNOSTUW use and wont
ADENNPRSTU underpants
ADENNRRRSU run errands
ADENOORTUV over and out
ADENOPPRRU paper round
ADENOPPRUV unapproved
ADENOPRRST drop astern
ADENOPRSTV Van der Post
ADENORRSWY Roy Andrews
ADENORSSTW towardness
ADENPPRSTU unstrapped
ADENPRRSUW under wraps
ADENPRSSUW upwardness
ADENPRSTUU unpastured
ADENRRSSTW sternwards
ADENRRSUYY day nursery
ADENRTTUWY twy-natured
ADEOOPPRSW soap powder
ADEOPRRTUY depuratory
ADEOQRRSUW word square
ADEORRSTTW Rod Stewart
ADFFGIMNOP damping-off
ADFFGINOOR off-roading
ADFFHLLOOS flash flood
ADFFIIINRT triffidian
ADFFLLRUUY fraudfully
ADFGGINNPU gap funding
ADFGHHORTU hard-fought
ADFGHINORS dragon-fish
ADFGHORRTU rough-draft
ADFGIIINNT Indian gift
ADFGIILRRY Girl Friday
ADFGILMNOR glandiform
ADFGILNNUY unfadingly
ADFGILORSU Douglas fir
ADFGIMNRRY dry farming
ADFGIMNRTU Grand Mufti
ADFGINORRU fairground
ADFGINORRW forwarding
ADFGOORSTU footguards
ADFHIILRSZ lizardfish
ADFHILORYY Holy Friday
ADFHILRSWY dwarfishly
ADFHINNOOT infanthood
ADFHINNORU four-in-hand
ADFHNOORST and so forth
ADFIIILNOS solifidian
ADFIIILPTT Fittipaldi
ADFIIINNPT pinnatifid
ADFIIKMNRU fair dinkum
ADFIILMRSU disulfiram
ADFIILQSUY disqualify
ADFIIOSSTU fastidious
ADFIISSSTY dissatisfy
ADFILLMNOY manifoldly
ADFILLNOOP flood plain
ADFILMORRU raduliform
ADFILORSTY faldistory
ADFILOSTTU studio flat
ADFIMMNOOR monadiform
ADFIMNOOST Fats Domino
ADFIMOQRRU quadriform
ADFINNOOTU foundation
ADFINNORSU infrasound
ADFINRRTTU turn adrift
ADFINRSSTT stand first
ADFIOPRSUU pious fraud
ADFIPRRSTY spray drift
ADFKNNORSY Frank Dyson
ADFLNOOORU fool around
ADFLNORSTW strandwolf
ADFNOORSSZ sforzandos
ADFNOORTUY foudroyant
ADFNORRSTW frontwards
ADFOPRRTUW put forward
ADGGGINORU gauging-rod
ADGGHINOOT a good thing
ADGGHINTUY gaudy-night
ADGGHIRRTU right guard
ADGGILLRSY Yggdrasill
ADGGINNOOR gadrooning
ADGGINNORR ranging rod
ADGGINNORU gain ground
ADGGLLRSUY sluggardly
ADGGNOORRY Gordon Gray
ADGGNOORSY Gay Gordons
ADGHHIILOS hidalgoish
ADGHHILNOW high and low
ADGHHOPRRY hydrograph
ADGHIILLNN dining-hall
ADGHIILMOS hidalgoism
ADGHIINRSS disgarnish
ADGHIIOPRT graphitoid
ADGHIKMRTU khidmutgar
ADGHILNNST Landsthing
ADGHIMNOPP hopping mad
ADGHINNPRS handspring
ADGHINNSTT nightstand
ADGHINRRTW right-drawn
ADGHIRRSTW rightwards
ADGHIRSTTU distraught
ADGHLLMNPY lymph gland
ADGHLLNOPU ploughland
ADGHLMOOST Thomas Gold
ADGHLNOPSU sand plough
ADGHLOPRUY dray-plough
ADGHNOORRU honor-guard
ADGHOOPRXY doxography
ADGIIILLRS sigillarid
ADGIIILMNO Modigliani
ADGIIILNNV invaliding
ADGIIINNNS Indian sign
ADGIIINOTT digitation
ADGIIKNNPP kidnapping
ADGIIKNNRR rank-riding
ADGIILMNNN landmining
ADGIILMNOU gadolinium
ADGIILMNRY admiringly

ADGIIMNNRU unadmiring
ADGIIMNPRS rising damp
ADGIIMNRSW misdrawing
ADGIINNPRW drawing pin
ADGIINOOOZ zoogonidia
ADGIINPRTW writing pad
ADGIINQSTU giant squid
ADGIINRSST distringas
ADGIKLLRUW Karl Ludwig
ADGIKNORWY working day
working-day
ADGILLNNOS Long Island
ADGILLNRWY drawlingly
ADGILLNYZZ dazzlingly
ADGILLOPRY prodigally
ADGILMNORU ground mail
ADGILNNNOW land-owning
ADGILNNORT Darlington
ADGILNNPRS land-spring
ADGILNNTUU undulating
ADGILNOSSS glissandos
ADGILOOORS good sailor
ADGIMMNORS gormandism
ADGIMMNPUY mumping-day
ADGIMNNRSY gynandrism
ADGIMNOOSY doomsaying
ADGIMNOSTY nystagmoid
ADGINNOOTU go in and out
ADGINNOSTU astounding
ADGINNPSTU upstanding
ADGINOOPRT in good part
ADGINOORST goods train
ADGINOPRRR grand prior
ADGINOPRTU point guard
ADGINPRRSX grands prix✧
ADGINRRSTW drawstring
draw-string
ADGIORSSWW grass widow
ADGJNORRRU grand juror
ADGLLMOOSS small goods
ADGLLNOSUU glandulous
ADGLMNOOOY monadology
ADGLNNOPRU ground plan
ADGLNOPRUY playground
ADGLNOTUUY young adult
ADGMNNORSU groundsman
ADGMNORSSU groundmass
ADGMNORTUU mount guard
ADGNNORSUY gynandrous
ADGNOOORRT dragonroot
ADGNOPSTUW wasp-tongu'd
ADGORRSSSW sword grass
ADHHILLNOS Hollandish
ADHHJNOORW John Howard
ADHHMOOOST Thomas Hood
ADHHNOOOPR orphanhood
ADHHNOSTTU thousandth
ADHHOPRTYY hydropathy
ADHIIILSTT Lithistida
ADHIIKKNNT kith and kin
ADHIILLNOP phalloidin
ADHIILMNOT Midlothian
ADHIILNNTW within land
ADHIILNRST disinthral
ADHIIMMNPS midshipman
ADHIIMNSST hit-and-miss
ADHIIMSTTU humidistat
ADHIINNOST Indian shot
ADHIINNSTU Hindustani
ADHIJMORRT major third
ADHIKLNOTU think aloud
ADHILLNOPY hold in play
ADHILLNOSY Holy Island
ADHILLOPRS dollarship
ADHILLPRUW uphillward
ADHILNNOOT hand lotion
ADHILNOPYY hypolydian
ADHILNOSTU outlandish
ADHILOOPRS drosophila
ADHILORSTY thyrsoidal
ADHIMNORSY disharmony
ADHIMNOTWY Whit Monday
ADHIMOPRSY dysmorphia
ADHINNOOOT nationhood
ADHINOOPRT anthropoid
ADHINOOPRY hypodorian
radiophony
ADHINOOPSS soda-siphon
ADHINOPSTU Diophantus
ADHINOSSWW sash window
window sash
ADHINSTUWY Whit Sunday
Whitsunday
ADHIOPRSST rhapsodist
ADHIOPRSTY dystrophia
ADHIORSTXY hydrotaxis
ADHIPRRTTY third party
third-party
ADHIRRRTYY Dirty Harry
ADHJLNNOOT John Dalton
ADHJNOSSTY St John's Day
ADHLLOOPPY Phyllopoda
ADHLMOORST Thomas Lord
ADHLMOORSY hydrosomal
ADHLNOPSSW splash down
splashdown
ADHMNOOORT matronhood
ADHNOOPRSU shop around
ADHNOPRSUU push around
ADHNORRSTW northwards
ADHNORSTWW Wandsworth
ADHOORRTWY roadworthy
ADHORSSTUW southwards
ADIIIKNNNP Indian pink
ADIIILMNSV invalidism
ADIIILMRSS dissimilar
ADIIILNOSV divisional
ADIIILNTVY invalidity
ADIIINNOTV divination
ADIIINOTTV tidivation
ADIILLORTY dilatorily
ADIILMMNSU maudlinism
ADIILMMPSU impaludism
ADIILMNOXY mixolydian✧
ADIILMOPRR primordial
ADIILMOPRS prismoidal
ADIILMORSS solidarism
ADIILNNOTU nidulation
ADIILNORRY ordinarily
ADIILNOSSU sinusoidal
ADIILNRSTU diurnalist
industrial
ADIILOPPSY polydipsia
ADIILOQRTU liquidator
ADIILORRWW World War II
ADIILORSST solidarist
ADIILORSSY radiolysis
ADIILORSTY solidarity
ADIILQSTUY squalidity
ADIIMMMOTU ommatidium
ADIIMNNNOO anno Domini
ADIIMNNOOT admonition
domination
ADIIMNNOSS Sandinismo
ADIIMNOPRY pyramidion
ADIIMNORTX dominatrix
ADIIMNRSST misandrist
ADIIMOPRST diatropism
ADIIMORTUU auditorium
ADIIMPRSTY pyramidist
ADIIMQRUUV quadrivium
ADIINNNOTU inundation
ADIINNOORT ordination
ADIINNORRY in ordinary
ADIINNORTU induration
ADIINOPPST disappoint
ADIINOPSSS dispassion
ADIINORRST distrainor
ADIINORTVY divinatory
ADIINOSSSU dissuasion
ADIIOPRSTT podiatrist
ADIIPRRTUY tripudiary
ADIKLNORTZ Karl Dönitz
ADIKMORSTT ditto marks
ADILLLMORS Lollardism
ADILLLOSYY disloyally
ADILLMNORU mill around
ADILLMNOTT Matt Dillon
ADILLNNOST still and on
ADILLNSSTT stand still
standstill
still-stand
ADILLOSTYY disloyalty
ADILMMNNOO Moominland
ADILMMOPSU plasmodium
sodium lamp
ADILMNNOTY dominantly
ADILMNOOOP monopodial
ADILMNOOTU modulation
ADILMOPSST psalmodist
ADILMORRWZ worm lizard
ADILMORSTU mustard oil
ADILMORTUY modularity

ADILNNNOOT Anton Dolin
ADILNNOOTU nodulation
ADILNNOTUU undulation
ADILNOOVWW oval window
ADILNOPSUU paludinous
ADILNRSTTU stridulant
ADILOORSTU idolatrous
ADILOPRSTY Daily Sport
ADILOPRTUY plauditory
ADIMNNOOTW Tin Woodman
ADIMNNRSUY synandrium
ADIMNOORTY admonitory
ADIMNOPTTU datum point
ADIMNORRST storm drain
ADIMNORSSU misandrous
ADIMNRRTUV Trivandrum
ADIMOPSSST spasmodist
ADIMORSTUU sudatorium
ADIMQRRUUV quadrumvir
ADINNOPSTT standpoint
ADINNORRUY unordinary
ADINNOSSTU ins and outs
outs and ins
ADINNOSTTW stand to win
ADINOOPRST adsorption
ADINOPRRSY prison yard
ADINORRSTU triandrous
ADINORSSTW downstairs
ADIORSSSTU disastrous
ADIORSSSUY dissuasory
ADJLOPRTUU plat du jour
ADJMMOOORS major-domos
ADLLLNNOOW London Wall
ADLLMORSSW small sword
ADLLNOORSW Lord Lawson
ADLLNORRUY rally round
ADLLOOOTWW tallow wood
ADLLOORRTY lordolatry
ADLMOOORSU malodorous
ADLNOORRSS Ronald Ross
ADLNOOTUWW walnutwood
ADLNORSTUU ultrasound
ADLNORTUUY undulatory
ADLNORTUWY untowardly
ADMNNOOORU moon around
ADMNNOORSU monandrous
ADMOOOPSTT stomatopod
ADMPRSSTUW draw stumps
ADNNORRTUU turn around
turnaround
ADNNORSSUY synandrous
ADNOOSTUYY you don't say!
ADNOPSSTUY Sunday Post
AEEEEFGRWZ wage freeze
AEEEEFLLRT leafleteer
AEEEEGKMPR gamekeeper
AEEEEGKPRT gate-keeper
AEEEEGLNSS Senegalese
AEEEEGNRRT regenerate
AEEEEGRTTV revegetate
AEEEEHKLTT eat the leek
AEEEEHLLNR her lee-lane
AEEEEHMRTT meet the ear
AEEEEHRTWY weather eye
AEEEEKPRRT peat-reeker
AEEEELPRRS prerelease
AEEEENRTTX exenterate
AEEEESTTTT tête-à-têtes
AEEEFFGLRU effleurage
AEEEFFIMNT effeminate
AEEEFFKNOR offer a knee
AEEEFFMNRT affeerment
AEEEFGILNR Generalife
AEEEFGLNRU enfleurage
AEEEFGRSTV stage fever
AEEEFHINRS shereefian
AEEEFHLRST flesh-eater
AEEEFHLSTT false teeth
AEEEFHNPRT pen-feather
AEEEFHRRTT thereafter
AEEEFHRRTW whereafter
AEEEFILSTT life-estate
AEEEFINRTZ antifreeze
AEEEFJLNNR Jean Fernel
AEEEFKMRRT free market
free-market
AEEEFLLNST fenestella✧
AEEEFLLPTT plate-fleet
AEEEFLLTVV velvet-leaf
AEEEFLMNSS femaleness
AEEEFLNOOZ Zeno of Elea
AEEEFNRRST transferee
AEEEFNRSTT fenestrate
AEEEFNSSTV Fastens-eve
AEEEFRSSTT Free States
AEEEFRSTVX Texas fever
AEEEFRTTTU featurette
AEEEGGHLOR George Hale
AEEEGGMMRR mega-merger
AEEEGGMNNT engagement
AEEEGHILTW white eagle
AEEEGHINNT heat engine
AEEEGHLPRT telpherage
AEEEGHMNST Gethsemane
AEEEGHNRRT green earth
greenheart
AEEEGIKNPS seakeeping
AEEEGILNRS generalise
AEEEGILNRV vinegar-eel
AEEEGILNRZ generalize
AEEEGILNSV evangelise
AEEEGILNUV eigenvalue
AEEEGILNVZ evangelize
AEEEGIMNTT tea meeting
AEEEGINNOR aero-engine
AEEEGINNRT ingenerate
AEEEGINRTV generative
AEEEGITTVV vegetative
AEEEGKLOPR goalkeeper
AEEEGKNNRS green snake
AEEEGKNPRS greenspeak
AEEEGLMNRT regalement
AEEEGLNOPR orange peel
AEEEGLNOST eagle-stone
AEEEGLRRTU reregulate
AEEEGLRSSS greaseless
AEEEGLSSSY eyeglasses
AEEEGMNNRT enragement
AEEEGMNNTV avengement
AEEEGMNRSS meagreness
AEEEGMNSTT segmentate
AEEEGNNRTV nerve agent
AEEEGNORRT orange tree
AEEEGNPPRR green paper✧
AEEEGNRSSV avengeress
AEEEGNRVWY wave energy
AEEEGNSSSV Seven Sages
AEEEGPRSSX expressage
AEEEGQSTUU squeteague
AEEEHHINST heathenise
AEEEHHINTZ heathenize
AEEEHHISTV the heavies
AEEEHHLTTW at the wheel
AEEEHHPRST three-phase
AEEEHHRTTT the theatre
AEEEHIKLRS hearse-like
AEEEHILLNS his lee-lane
AEEEHIRSTW weatherise
AEEEHIRTWZ weatherize
AEEEHKRTTU take the rue
AEEEHLLRTY ethereally
AEEEHLMSTT sheet metal
AEEEHLNRTT The Eternal
AEEEHLNSST nathelesse
AEEEHLORSV shore leave
AEEEHLPSTT steeple hat
AEEEHLRSST shear-steel
AEEEHLRTWW water wheel
AEEEHMNORX hexaëmeron
AEEEHMPRTT heptameter
AEEEHMSSTT metatheses
AEEEHNNNPT nepenthean
AEEEHNNRTT thereanent
AEEEHNNSTV heaven-sent
AEEEHNORTY honeyeater
AEEEHNRRTT threatener
AEEEHORRUY here you are
AEEEHRSTTW sweetheart
AEEEIILRRS earlierise
AEEEIILRRZ earlierize
AEEEIIPPRT peripeteia
AEEEIKLPRT keep it real
AEEEIKNPRS speakerine
AEEEILLMRV à merveille
AEEEILLMSS Leslie Ames
AEEEILLSTT little-ease
AEEEILNRST eternalise
AEEEILNRTV interleave
AEEEILNRTZ eternalize
AEEEILPSTV sieve plate
AEEEILRTVV revelative
AEEEIMNNRT Nemertinea
AEEEIMNRTT intemerate

AEEEIMNSTV Vietnamese
AEEEIMPRTV permeative
AEEEIMRSTT Eastertime
AEEEINNNTV antivenene
AEEEINNRTT intenerate
AEEEINRRTT en retraite
AEEEINRSST easternise
AEEEINRSTZ easternize
AEEEINRTTV entreative
inveterate
AEEEINRTVV enervative
AEEEINRTVW interweave
AEEEIPRTVY private eye✧
AEEEJJMSSS Jesse James
AEEEJKRRRT tear-jerker
AEEEJMNRRV Jan Vermeer
AEEEJNRTUV rejuvenate
AEEEKKPPRR park-keeper
AEEEKLNUWY Lee Kuan Yew
AEEEKMRRSV verse-maker
AEEEKPSSTW sweepstake
AEEELLLRSV laser level
AEEELLLRTT tale-teller
AEEELLPSTT steel plate
AEEELLRTVW water level
AEEELLSSTT tessellate
AEEELMMNPT empalement
AEEELMMNRT Emmentaler
AEEELMNNTT lentamente
tenemental
AEEELMNPTU epaulement
AEEELMNRTT manteltree
terne metal
AEEELMNRTV revealment
AEEELMNRTY elementary
AEEELMORST telomerase
AEEELMPPRX par exemple
AEEELNNOSY anyone else
AEEELNNSTY enneastyle
AEEELNNUVZ Venezuelan
AEEELNORVV overleaven
AEEELNOSTT teleostean
AEEELNPRRV René Préval
AEEELNPRTT terne plate
AEEELPRRUV Paul Revere
AEEEMMNORT anemometer
AEEEMNNOTV envenomate
AEEEMNOPSS open sesame
AEEEMNPRTT pentameter
AEEEMNRRTU remunerate
AEEEMNRRUV maneuverer
AEEEMNRSTT street name
AEEEMORSTT taseometer
AEEEMPPRRY emery paper
AEEEMRRSTT Easter term
AEEEMRRTTT tetrameter
AEEEMRRTTW water meter
AEEEMRSSTT steersmate
AEEEMRSTTW watersmeet
AEEENNPSTT septennate
AEEENORSTT stone-eater
AEEENPRSST sea serpent
AEEENQRSUW Queen's ware
AEEENRRSTU entreasure
AEEENRSSSV averseness
AEEENRSTVY eye-servant
AEEEOPRRST patereroes
AEEEPPRRST Peter Pears
AEEEPPRRTT perpetrate
AEEEPPRTTU perpetuate
AEEEQRSSUY square eyes
AEEERRSTYY yesteryear
AEEERSSTTY easy street
AEEERSTTWW sweetwater
sweet-water
AEEFFGIRTU effigurate
AEEFFGMOSS off-message
AEEFFHORRT forefather
AEEFFLLORR free-for-all
AEEFFLSTUX exsufflate
AEEFFMORSU measure off
AEEFFMORTT team effort
AEEFFORRST reafforest
AEEFFSSTUY safety fuse
AEEFGGHIRT freightage
AEEFGHINRT feathering
AEEFGHIRRT heart-grief
AEEFGHLNRS green flash
AEEFGHORRT foregather
AEEFGILLNT leafleting
AEEFGILNRR rifle range
AEEFGILPRS persiflage
AEEFGILRRS Serge Lifar
AEEFGINORW orange-wife
AEEFGINRVW finger wave
AEEFGIRTTU Guttiferae
AEEFGLPRSU presageful
AEEFHHINRT Fahrenheit
AEEFHIKLRT fatherlike
AEEFHIKLTW flake-white
AEEFHIKNST sneak thief
AEEFHIKRTT thief-taker
AEEFHILRSS seal-fisher
AEEFHILRTU haut relief
AEEFHINPRT pin feather
AEEFHIRSST fish eaters
AEEFHIRSTX the fair sex
AEEFHIRTTW water thief
AEEFHLLTUW Aethelwulf
AEEFHLOPPR leaf-hopper
AEEFHLRSST fatherless
AEEFHMMORR fore-hammer
AEEFHMORSU frame-house
AEEFHMORTT fathometer
AEEFHMRRSV marsh-fever
AEEFHORRST Sefer Torah
AEEFHORRTW whore after
AEEFHPRSTT stepfather
AEEFHRRSTW freshwater
AEEFIIRRRS fire-raiser
AEEFIJORRZ Joe Frazier
AEEFIKKNST steak knife
AEEFIKLNPT knife pleat
AEEFIKLRRW fire-walker
AEEFIKNPPR paperknife
AEEFIKNRSS freakiness
AEEFIKOTTW take to wife
AEEFILLRSV silver leaf
AEEFILMRTY family tree
AEEFILNNTT life-tenant
AEEFILNORR free on rail
AEEFILNORX raloxifene
AEEFILNPRR palfrenier
AEEFILOPRT perfoliate
AEEFILPRSS self-praise
AEEFIMNRRT freemartin
AEEFIMRRST fire-master
AEEFIMRSTU misfeature
AEEFINRRST fraternise
AEEFINRRTZ fraternize
AEEFINRSTU tea infuser
AEEFINRSTY safety rein
AEEFIQRSUV five-square
AEEFKLLLRW fell-walker
AEEFKLMNOY leaf monkey
AEEFKLNORT Earl of Kent
AEEFLLLMOW mallee-fowl
AEEFLLMSST smell-feast
AEEFLLNNOT fontanelle
AEEFLLNRUY funereally
AEEFLLOPRT pâte frolle
AEEFLLRSSY fearlessly
self-slayer
AEEFLMOPRX for example
AEEFLMORSY fearsomely
AEEFLOSTUY feateously
AEEFMNORRT Formentera
AEEFMNRRST stern frame
AEEFMPRSVW swamp fever
AEEFNNSSSU unsafeness
AEEFNRRRST retransfer
AEEFORRSTU four-seater
AEEGGHILRT lighterage
AEEGGHOPRR geographer
AEEGGHORSW George Shaw
AEEGGIINSV ease-giving
AEEGGINOPR arpeggione
AEEGGINORS seignorage
AEEGGINRRS grangerise
AEEGGINRRZ grangerize
AEEGGINTTV vegetating
AEEGGINTVW get weaving
AEEGGIORRY George Airy
AEEGGIRSSV aggressive
AEEGGIRTTU egurgitate
AEEGGJORRY Joe Gargery
AEEGGMORRT remortgage
AEEGGNNOVW Geneva gown
AEEGGNORTV voetganger
AEEGGNORTY ergatogyne
AEEGGNRRSS grass-green
AEEGGORSSU sage grouse
AEEGHIIINP Iphigeneia

AEEGHIILMP	hemiplegia
AEEGHIILRT	aerie light
AEEGHIIRTV	give the air
AEEGHIJLNT	Janet Leigh
AEEGHIKMTW	make-weight
AEEGHIKNRS	sea gherkin
AEEGHILLTV	the Village✧
AEEGHILMNO	hegemonial
AEEGHILNPS	pea shingle
AEEGHILNRT	leathering
AEEGHILNSS	Singhalese
AEEGHILPST	legateship
AEEGHILRST	lethargise
AEEGHILRTZ	lethargize
AEEGHINNRT	heartening
AEEGHINPSW	weeping ash
AEEGHINRRS	rehearsing
AEEGHINRRV	Rhinegrave
AEEGHINRTV	Rh-negative
AEEGHINRTW	weathering
AEEGHINSTT	seeing that
AEEGHIPPRR	epigrapher
AEEGHKNNRS	greenshank
AEEGHLLLNS	hell's angel✧
AEEGHLLRSU	auger-shell
AEEGHLLSTU	The Seagull
AEEGHLMORT	geothermal
AEEGHLNOPR	lagerphone
AEEGHLNSTU	The Angelus
AEEGHLNTVW	wavelength
AEEGHLOOTT	theologate
AEEGHLORTT	altogether
AEEGHLPRTY	telegraphy
AEEGHLSSST	sheet-glass
AEEGHMNOOT	homogenate
AEEGHMNORT	hate-monger
	thereamong
AEEGHMORTY	game theory
	heterogamy
AEEGHNORTW	the Wagoner
AEEGHNOSTU	house agent
AEEGHORSST	stage horse
AEEGHORSTT	other gates
	othergates
AEEGHPRRSY	spreaghery
AEEGHSTUVW	Steve Waugh
AEEGIILLLS	illegalise
AEEGIILLLZ	illegalize
AEEGIILLNV	villeinage
AEEGIILMTT	legitimate
AEEGIILNST	gelatinise
AEEGIILNTZ	gelatinize
AEEGIIMNNT	ingeminate
AEEGIIMNST	enigmatise
AEEGIIMNTZ	enigmatize
AEEGIINRRT	garnierite
AEEGIINRST	siege train
AEEGIJLMNN	Jan Leeming
AEEGIJNNRS	Jean Ingres
AEEGIKLNSX	sex linkage
AEEGIKNNNT	tank engine
AEEGIKNRST	tiger snake
AEEGIKORTV	give or take
AEEGILLMNN	enamelling
AEEGILLNST	teaselling
AEEGILLORS	allegorise
AEEGILLORZ	allegorize
AEEGILLRTY	galleryite
AEEGILMNRR	malingerer
AEEGILMNRT	regimental
AEEGILMNRU	marine glue
AEEGILMNSV	evangelism
AEEGILNNSS	genialness
AEEGILNOPS	Anglepoise®
AEEGILNORT	regelation
	relegation
AEEGILNRRT	interregal
AEEGILNRST	easterling
	generalist
AEEGILNRTY	generality
AEEGILNSTV	evangelist✧
AEEGILNTVY	negatively
AEEGILOPTX	exploitage
AEEGILRRSU	regularise
AEEGILRRUZ	regularize
AEEGILRSTV	silver gate
AEEGILRTUV	regulative
AEEGIMNNRT	regainment
AEEGIMNNSV	Genevanism
AEEGIMNORT	ergotamine
AEEGIMNPRT	impregnate
AEEGIMNQSU	gaminesque
AEEGIMNRST	magnetiser
AEEGIMNRTZ	magnetizer
AEEGIMNSTU	mutagenise
AEEGIMNTUZ	mutagenize
AEEGIMORRT	morigerate
AEEGIMRRTU	marguerite
AEEGIMRRTV	gravimeter
AEEGIMSTTU	guestimate
AEEGINNNSU	ensanguine
AEEGINNORT	generation
	renegation
AEEGINNPSS	pangenesis
AEEGINNRRT	interregna
AEEGINNRST	Tangerines
AEEGINNRTT	entreating
AEEGINNRTV	enervating
AEEGINNSSY	Syngenesia
AEEGINNSUX	exsanguine
AEEGINORRS	reorganise
AEEGINORRZ	reorganize
AEEGINOSSV	Sangiovese
AEEGINOTTV	vegetation
AEEGINPRRS	Paris green
AEEGINPRSY	panegyrise
AEEGINPRYZ	panegyrize
AEEGINRRSY	ear syringe
AEEGINRRTX	generatrix
AEEGINRSSS	greasiness
AEEGINRSSV	vernissage
AEEGIPPRRT	paper tiger
AEEGIPRRTW	Gripe Water®
	gripe water
AEEGIPRSST	petrissage
AEEGJLLNOR	jargonelle
AEEGJLNORR	Joel Garner
AEEGKMRRTY	grey market
AEEGLLLOSW	gallows-lee
AEEGLLNOSS	Los Angeles
AEEGLLNRST	stallenger
AEEGLLORTT	allegretto
AEEGLLSTWY	galley-west
AEEGLMMNOR	meal-monger
AEEGLMNNTT	tanglement
AEEGLMNOST	tanglesome
AEEGLMNPRT	graplement
AEEGLMNTTU	tegumental
AEEGLMOPSU	plaguesome
AEEGLMRRSW	leg warmers
AEEGLNORST	estrangelo
AEEGLNORTU	outgeneral
AEEGLNORTV	graveolent
	lovat-green
AEEGLOPRSU	grapelouse
	plague-sore
AEEGLORTUV	travelogue
AEEGLORUUV	rogue value
AEEGLRRTUW	water gruel
AEEGMNNOOS	on one's game
AEEGMNNOST	mangosteen
AEEGMNNOTW	meganewton
AEEGMNOOTV	get a move on
AEEGMNOPRR	pearmonger
AEEGMNOQSU	Monegasque
AEEGMNOSWY	money wages
AEEGMNRRTU	garmenture
AEEGMNRSTY	segmentary
AEEGMOPRSU	soup meagre
AEEGMORRST	stereogram
AEEGMPRTUU	up a gum tree
AEEGMPSTTU	get up steam
AEEGMRRTTY	grey matter
AEEGNNORSS	sense organ
AEEGNNORTV	governante
AEEGNOPRST	grapestone
AEEGNOPRSW	spongeware
AEEGNOPSST	set a sponge
AEEGNORSSU	sea surgeon
AEEGNORSTV	gravestone
AEEGNORTTY	teratogeny
AEEGNOSTWY	get one's way
AEEGNPRRTU	page-turner
AEEGNPRRTY	Green Party
AEEGNPRSST	press agent
AEEGNRSSTU	arguteness
AEEGOORRRV	rare groove
AEEGOPRSSU	repoussage
AEEHHHINST	heathenish
AEEHHILTWW	white whale
AEEHHIMNST	heathenism
AEEHHINRRR	hen harrier
AEEHHINRST	earth-shine

AEEHHIRTTW white-heart
AEEHHISTUW white hause
AEEHHISTWW white hawse
AEEHHITTWW white wheat
AEEHHKNPSS sheepshank
AEEHHLLRST heart shell
AEEHHLLSST healthless
AEEHHLMOST healthsome
AEEHHLMSTU methuselah✧
AEEHHLORTW heart-whole
AEEHHLOTWW wholewheat
AEEHHLSSST sheathless
AEEHHMMMOR hammer home
AEEHHNOPRT open-hearth
AEEHHNORVX Enver Hoxha
AEEHHORSTU earth-house
AEEHHORSVY heavy horse
AEEHHPSSTU Hephaestus
AEEHIILLPT epithelial
AEEHIILMST Ishmaelite
AEEHIINPRR prairie hen
AEEHIISTTV hesitative
AEEHIJLPSW Jewish Pale
AEEHIKLMNW minke whale
AEEHIKLNNP enkephalin
AEEHILLMTT all the time
AEEHILLNSW snail wheel
AEEHILLORT heliolater
AEEHILLRRS hellraiser
AEEHILMNRS shale-miner
AEEHILMNTY ethylamine
AEEHILMOST mesothelia
AEEHILMPRT epithermal
hemipteral
AEEHILMRST thermalise
AEEHILMRSZ Alzheimer's
AEEHILMRTT Thermalite®
AEEHILMRTZ thermalize
AEEHILMTTW white metal
AEEHILNNOP anopheline
AEEHILNRUY euryhaline
AEEHILOPSU heliopause
AEEHILPPRR peripheral
AEEHILPPSY epiphyseal
AEEHILPRST sphalerite
AEEHILPRTW pearl-white
AEEHILRTTT triathlete
AEEHILSSTW sea whistle
AEEHILSTVW white slave
AEEHIMNOPP epiphonema
AEEHIMNPRT hemipteran
AEEHIMNSTW anthemwise
AEEHIMRRST time-sharer
AEEHIMRSTU rheumatise
AEEHIMRTUZ rheumatize
AEEHIMSSTT metathesis
AEEHIMSTTU The Timaeus
AEEHINNORW Erewhonian
AEEHINNPRT pantherine
AEEHINORTT aroint thee
AEEHINPRST interphase
AEEHINPSTT stephanite
AEEHINQTTU the antique
AEEHINRRTW Wertherian
AEEHINRSST earthiness
heartiness
AEEHINRTTU uintathere
AEEHINSSTT antitheses
AEEHIOPRST rosehip tea
AEEHIPPRRS periphrase
AEEHIPPRTW white paper✧
AEEHIRSTTW where it's at
AEEHIRTTWW white water
white-water
AEEHISTUVX exhaustive
AEEHJMNRSY Henry James
AEEHJORSTU Joshua tree
AEEHKKNRUZ Hakenkreuz
AEEHKLLOTW walk to heel
AEEHKLOSWY keyhole saw
AEEHKMMORT home market
AEEHKMORST earth-smoke
AEEHKNOSSU snake-house
AEEHKNSTTU take the sun
AEEHKOPSSV spokeshave
AEEHKORSTT heatstroke
AEEHKOSSTU steakhouse
AEEHLLLPRS pearl-shell
AEEHLLLSWY Wesley Hall
AEEHLLMOST sola helmet
AEEHLLOPTW whole-plate
AEEHLLORSW wholesaler
AEEHLLOSUW whale louse
AEEHLLSVWY heavy swell
AEEHLMMNOT mental home
AEEHLMMRSS hammerless
AEEHLMMRSY male rhymes
AEEHLMNNOP phenomenal
AEEHLMNPRT telpherman
AEEHLMORTX exothermal
AEEHLMPRSW sperm whale
AEEHLNORTT on the alert
AEEHLNOSTT on the slate
AEEHLNPPST sheep-plant
AEEHLNPSTT The Planets
AEEHLNRSTT nettle rash
AEEHLOPRTW power lathe
AEEHLOPSTT at the slope
AEEHLORSVW shovelware
AEEHLOSTWY lose the way
AEEHLPPSSS she's apples
AEEHLPRSSS phraseless
AEEHLPRTWY telpherway
AEEHLRSSTW Walter Hess
wreathless
AEEHLRSTTX tax shelter
AEEHLRSTTY Hattersley
AEEHLRTTTY tetraethyl
AEEHLSSSTT Lesh states
AEEHMNNSSU humaneness
AEEHMNOORR menorrhoea
AEEHMNOPRT Heptameron
Promethean
AEEHMNPTTY Pat Metheny
AEEHMOOSTT Etheostoma
AEEHMOPRRU ampere hour
AEEHMOPRST atmosphere
AEEHMORRRT arthromere
AEEHMORRST horse-tamer
AEEHMORRTV earthmover
AEEHMORSUX hexamerous
AEEHMORTTY metatheory
AEEHMRTTWY water thyme
AEEHNNOORT one another
AEEHNNOPSX Xenophanes
AEEHNNPRSY penny share
AEEHNOOPRR harpooneer
AEEHNOPPTY phaenotype
AEEHNORSSS hoarseness
AEEHNORSSZ shear zones
AEEHNORSTV note-shaver
AEEHNOSSST The Seasons
AEEHNPPTVY happy event
AEEHNPRSST pantheress
AEEHNRTUUY Euthyneura
AEEHOOPRRS horse opera
AEEHOOPRST peashooter
AEEHOOPRSU opera house
AEEHOOPSST apotheoses
AEEHORRSTW water horse
AEEHORRTVW or whatever
AEEHORSTTY here to stay
AEEHORSTVW whatsoever
AEEHORTTUW weather out
AEEHORTTXY heterotaxy
AEEHORTVWY over the way
wave theory
AEEHOSSTTU state house✧
AEEHPRRSTT three-parts
AEEHPRSTXY sex therapy
AEEHPRSUVY superheavy
AEEIIKNRST keratinise
AEEIIKNRTZ keratinize
AEEIILLRST literalise
AEEIILLRTT illiterate
AEEIILLRTZ literalize
AEEIILMNNT eminential
AEEIILMNRS mineralise
AEEIILMNRZ mineralize
AEEIILMRST serial time
AEEIILNNPR en plein air
AEEIILNNSU Eleusinian
AEEIILNPRX pre-exilian
AEEIILNRTT retinalite
trilineate
AEEIILNSTT lie in state
AEEIILOSST ateleiosis
AEEIILQRRU reliquaire
AEEIILRRTV irrelative
AEEIILRSTV relativise
revitalise
AEEIILRTVZ relativize
revitalize

AEEIIMNNST inseminate
AEEIIMNSTT anti-Semite
AEEIIMPRTV imperative
AEEIIMSTTV estimative
AEEIINNPRS Parisienne
AEEIINPPRT peripetian
AEEIINPPRZ piperazine
AEEIINPRSS Persianise
AEEIINPRSZ Persianize
AEEIINRRVV Viverrinae
AEEIINRSTU uniseriate
AEEIINRTWW wine waiter
AEEIINRTWX water nixie
AEEIINTTTV entitative
AEEIIPPTTV appetitive
AEEIIPRSST asperities
patisserie
pâtisserie
AEEIIRRRVZ River Zaire
AEEIJLLMNT Jean Millet
AEEIJMNOST Jamesonite
AEEIJNNORR Jean Renoir
AEEIJOPRTV pejorative
AEEIKKMSST Kiss Me Kate
AEEIKKRSTT take strike
AEEIKLLMTT make little
AEEIKLNOPU leukopenia
AEEIKLNSSW weakliness
AEEIKLOSSS sessile oak
AEEIKLRRWW wire-walker
AEEIKMMORV movie-maker
AEEIKMNNRR reim-kennar
AEEIKMNORS noisemaker
AEEIKNNSSS sneakiness
AEEIKNRRSV Snake River
AEEIKNRSTT kersantite
AEEIKRRSTW water-skier
AEEIKRSSTW weak sister
AEEILLLLNV villanelle
AEEILLMNST enamellist
AEEILLMRSS Marseilles
AEEILLNPRT Parnellite
AEEILLNTVV inlet valve
AEEILLPRST palletiser
AEEILLPRTZ palletizer
AEEILLPSTT stipellate
AEEILLRSSV Versailles
AEEILLRSTY Easter lily
AEEILLRTTY literately
AEEILLRTVY relatively
AEEILLSSTT satellites
AEEILLSTUV televisual
AEEILMMNPT impalement
AEEILMMNRU neurilemma
AEEILMNNOS Liam Neeson
AEEILMNNTT entailment
AEEILMNORS neorealism
AEEILMNPRT planimeter
AEEILMNRST streamline
AEEILMNRSW New Realism
AEEILMNRTT retailment
AEEILMNSSS measliness
AEEILMNSTU Mustelinae
semilunate
AEEILMORRS remoralise
AEEILMORRZ remoralize
AEEILMORTT meteorital
AEEILMPRRT perimetral
AEEILMPSST metalepsis
AEEILMQRSU square mile✧
AEEILMRSST semestrial
AEEILMRTTT littermate
AEEILNNNPY penny-a-line
AEEILNNPPR linen paper
AEEILNNPST septennial
AEEILNNRST real tennis
AEEILNNSTT sentential
AEEILNNTTU lieutenant
AEEILNOPRT peritoneal
AEEILNORST neorealist
AEEILNORTV revelation✧
AEEILNPRRU perineural
AEEILNPRSS pearliness
AEEILNPRST episternal
presential
AEEILNPRSU pleasure in
AEEILNPSTV splenative
AEEILNQSTU sequential
AEEILNQTUV equivalent
AEEILNRRTV irrelevant
AEEILNRSTT eternalist
AEEILNRSTU neutralise
AEEILNRTTY eternality
AEEILNRTUV unrelative
AEEILNRTUZ neutralize
AEEILNRVWY lawyer vine
AEEILNSSSU sensualise
AEEILNSSSZ sleaziness
AEEILNSSUZ sensualize
AEEILNSTVX sexivalent
AEEILOPRST periosteal
AEEILORRSV revalorise
AEEILORRVZ revalorize
AEEILOTTUV leave it out!
AEEILPPRRT peripteral
AEEILPPRTT Petri plate
AEEILPRRRV Pearl River
AEEILPRRSV reap-silver
AEEILPRRTV River Plate
AEEILPRSSS praiseless
AEEILPRSSY erysipelas
AEEILPRSTX aes triplex
Praxiteles
AEEILPSTTU estipulate
AEEILRRSVW silverware
AEEILRRTTU literature
AEEIMMMRST metamerism
AEEIMMOPRT emmetropia
AEEIMMORTV memorative
AEEIMMRSSU mismeasure
AEEIMNNORT enantiomer
AEEIMNNPRT pine marten
AEEIMNNRRV River Neman
AEEIMNNRTT retainment
AEEIMNNRTU innumerate
AEEIMNOPRT permeation
AEEIMNORTT marionette
AEEIMNOSTT maisonette
AEEIMNPRRU praemunire
AEEIMNRRRV River Marne
AEEIMNRRST Martin Rees
AEEIMNRSSS smeariness
AEEIMNRSST easternism
AEEIMNRSSU Surinamese
AEEIMNRSTT main street✧
martensite
misentreat
AEEIMNRTTT attirement
AEEIMNRTTV avertiment
AEEIMNSSST steaminess
AEEIMOPQSU semi-opaque
AEEIMOPRTU opium-eater
AEEIMORRTV variometer
AEEIMPRRSS spermaries
AEEIMPRSST passimeter
AEEIMQRSUV semiquaver
AEEINNNSSS insaneness
AEEINNNSST innateness
AEEINNNTTT tennantite
AEEINNNTVY in any event
AEEINNORTV enervation
veneration
AEEINNOTTT Antoinette
AEEINNPPTT inappetent
AEEINNPRSS Spenserian
AEEINNRTUV aventurine
AEEINNSSSU uneasiness
AEEINNSSTT assentient
AEEINNSSTV nativeness
AEEINOPRTX paroxetine
AEEINOPTTT potentiate
AEEINORRSV River Saône
AEEINPRSTU resupinate
AEEINQRSTU equestrian
AEEINQSSSU queasiness
AEEINQSTTU Titanesque
AEEINRRRST restrainer
AEEINRRSSU urea resins
AEEINRRTTT triternate
AEEINRRTTV travertine
AEEINRRTVY veterinary
AEEINRSSST reastiness
AEEINRSSSY synaeresis
AEEINRSSTU St Irenaeus
AEEINRSSTW ear-witness
wateriness
AEEINRSTTT interstate
AEEINRSTTV en travesti
AEEINRSTTW wine taster
AEEINRTTXY extraneity
AEEINSSSTW sweatiness
AEEINSSSTY yeastiness
AEEIOPRRSV overpraise

AEEIPPRRST perspirate
AEEIPPRRTW wiretapper
AEEIPPRVWY pay-per-view
AEEIPRSSTT striptease
AEEIPRSSTU pasteurise
AEEIPRSSUV persuasive
AEEIPRSTTX sexpartite
AEEIPRSTUZ pasteurize
AEEIPRTTUV reputative
vituperate
AEEIQRRTTU triquetrae
AEEIQRSSUW squarewise
AEEIRRRTVW river water
AEEIRRSTVW serve a writ
AEEIRRSTVY revestiary
AEEIRRTTWY Terry Waite
AEEJLNNYZZ Jan Zelezny
AEEJLNORSU journalese
AEEJMNORUU jeune amour
AEEJMORRST teres major
AEEJNRRSTY serjeantry
AEEKLLLSTY skeletally
AEEKLLMNOY Molly Keane
AEEKLLMNPR palm-kernel
AEEKLMMORY memory leak
AEEKLNNRRR Karl Renner
AEEKLOPRRW rope-walker
AEEKMMNORY moneymaker
AEEKMMNOTW weak moment
AEEKMMNPRY kempery-man
AEEKMMRRRY merrymaker
AEEKMNOPRT open market
AEEKMNORTY money-taker
AEEKMORRTU Euromarket
AEEKMORSTW water smoke
AEEKMPRRTV verkrampte
AEEKMRSTTT test-market
AEEKMSSTUY eyas-musket
AEEKNNOSST snakestone
AEELLLSTTU stellulate
AEELLLSTTY stellately
AEELLMMNOT Monel metal®
AEELLMMRRT trammeller
AEELLMNOTV malevolent
AEELLMNQRU man-queller
AEELLMNRTU allurement
AEELLMNSSY namelessly
AEELLMORTW tree mallow
AEELLMSSSY seamlessly
AEELLNOPRT petronella
AEELLNORSV lovers' lane
AEELLNOTTY Lotte Lenya
AEELLNRRUV unraveller
AEELLNRTVY relevantly
AEELLNRTXY externally
AEELLNSSTT talentless
AEELLNTUVY eventually
AEELLORRSU rose laurel
rose-laurel
AEELLORSTT rostellate
AEELLORTTU autoteller
AEELLORTTW tallow tree
AEELLORTTY tea trolley
AEELLOTTTY teetotally
AEELLPPPRW wall pepper
AEELLQRRRU quarreller
AEELLRSTTW Wall Street
AEELMMNORU neurolemma
AEELMMNORY memory lane
AEELMMNRTT trammel net
AEELMNNRSS mannerless
AEELMNOPRT planometer
AEELMNORSS moral sense
AEELMNORTV overmantel
AEELMNORTW water lemon
watermelon
AEELMNSTTV vestmental
AEELMOPPSS ampelopses
AEELMOPRSY polymerase
AEELMOPRTX extemporal
AEELMOPSTT palmettoes
AEELMORTTV voltameter
AEELMPRSTT streetlamp
AEELMRSSST masterless
streamless
AEELMRSSTT matterless
AEELMRSSTU emulatress
AEELMRSWYY Mary Wesley
AEELNNORSW New Orleans
AEELNNPRSY arles-penny
AEELNNPTTU antepenult
AEELNNQSTU lansquenet
AEELNNSSTT tenantless
AEELNOOPTX ox-antelope
AEELNOORYZ ozone layer
AEELNOPRST pearl-stone
AEELNOPSSW weaponless
AEELNORSSS reasonless
AEELNORSWY Ron Weasley
AEELNORTVZ zero-valent
AEELNOSSSS seasonless
AEELNOSTUV suaveolent
AEELNPRSST parentless
AEELNPRTTW wentletrap
AEELNPSTTY pentastyle
AEELNRRSVW Verner's law
AEELNRRTTY trey-antler
AEELNRSSSW answerless
AEELNRTUVY entry value
AEELOPPRRT poplar tree
AEELOPPRTU repopulate
AEELOPSSTT salopettes
AEELOQRRUU roquelaure
AEELORRTVY revelatory
AEELORSTTU lotus-eater
AEELORTUWZ water ouzel
AEELPPRRRU paper-ruler
AEELPRRSSY prayerless
AEELPRSSTY spray steel
AEELPRSTUX superexalt
AEELQRSSTU sequestral
AEELRRSTUW lustreware
AEELRSTTTY tetrastyle
AEEMMNORTT ante mortem
AEEMMNORTY anemometry
AEEMNNOOST to one's name
AEEMNNOPRS praenomens
AEEMNNOPRT Pentameron
AEEMNNORRT ornamenter
AEEMNNORUV mavourneen
AEEMNNPRTT entrapment
AEEMNNPRTW enwrapment
AEEMNNTTTU attunement
AEEMNOPPRR proper name
AEEMNOPPRY paper money
AEEMNOPRST treponemas
AEEMNOPTTT tapotement
AEEMNOQRSU Romanesque
AEEMNORRTU enumerator
AEEMNORRUV manoeuvrer
AEEMNORSST sarmentose
sea monster
AEEMNORSUV manoeuvres
AEEMNORSWW womenswear
AEEMNPPRST sapperment
AEEMNPPRTY prepayment
AEEMNPRSSX expressman
AEEMNRRSTT arrestment
AEEMNRSSTU matureness
AEEMNRSTTU menstruate
AEEMNSSSST assessment
AEEMOORTTT tree tomato
AEEMOPRSTW steam power
AEEMORRSTV overmaster
AEEMORRTTV overmatter
AEEMORSSTT eastermost
AEEMORSTUU measure out
outmeasure
AEEMORSTUW water mouse
AEEMPRRSTY Mary Peters
AEEMPRRTTU ear-trumpet
AEEMRSSSST seamstress
AEEMRSSWWY Wemyss ware
AEENNNPSTY penny-stane
AEENNOOPSS open season
AEENNORSST ornateness
AEENNRSSUW unwareness
AEENOORRTX exonerator
AEENOPQSSU opaqueness
AEENOPRRSU pure reason
AEENOPRRTT penetrator
AEENOPRRTU neuroptera✧
AEENOPRSUV supernovae
AEENORSTUX extraneous
AEENORTTUX extenuator
AEENPPRSTT step-parent
AEENPRSSSS sparseness
AEENQRSSSU squareness
AEENRRSSTV transverse
AEENRRSTUU untreasure
AEENRSSSTV Seven Stars
AEENSSSTTU astuteness
AEENSSTTTU sustentate

AEEOPPRRTU paper route
AEEOPRRSTT tetraspore
AEEOPRRTWW water power
AEEOPRSTTY poetastery
AEEOPRTTTT tetraptote
AEEOQRSSTU square-toes
AEEORRSSTW Sears Tower
AEEORRSTVY overstayer
AEEORRTTWW water tower
AEEORSTTWX Texas tower
AEEPPRRTUW Tupperware®
AEEPRRSSST trespasser
AEEPRRSSUV supersaver
AEEPRSSTTU superstate
AEEPRSSWXY expressway
AEEQRSSTUY satyresque
AEEQSSTTUU statuesque
AEESSSSTUX East Sussex
AEFFFGIRST Steffi Graf
AEFFFTTTUY tuftaffety
AEFFGGINRU gauffering
AEFFGHINRT affrighten
AEFFGHLLTY fly the flag
AEFFGKMNOY monkey-gaff
AEFFHIMRRS fish farmer
AEFFHKMORT off the mark
AEFFHLLOTW off the wall
AEFFIIINTV affinitive
AEFFIJLOSW Jaws of Life®
AEFFILMSTY safety film
AEFFILNORW waffle iron
AEFFILNSTU insufflate
AEFFILRSST tariffless
AEFFILRSTU false fruit
AEFFINORTV affrontive
AEFFKNRSTU snuff-taker
AEFFLLNTUY affluently
AEFFLLPPRY fly-flapper
AEFFLMOOPR flameproof
AEFFNPPRSU snuff-paper
AEFFNRSSTU staff nurse
AEFFOOSTTU affettuoso
AEFFRRTTUY Tartuffery
AEFGGGILNR reflagging
AEFGGILNSS flagginess
AEFGHHLLNT half-length
AEFGHIINSS sea-fishing
AEFGHIIRRT air freight
air-freight
AEFGHIKLTT take flight
AEFGHIKRTT take fright
AEFGHILLPT fill the gap
AEFGHILNRS angler fish
AEFGHILRTT after-light
AEFGHINORU fair enough
AEFGHINRRW wharfinger
AEFGHIRTWY way freight
AEFGHLSTTU self-taught
AEFGHNOORT gate of horn
AEFGHNORTU fearnought
AEFGHORTTU foretaught
AEFGIILLOR florilegia
AEFGIILMNN Ian Fleming
AEFGIILMST smifligate
AEFGIILNNR fingernail
AEFGIILNSV life-saving
AEFGIINRTX rate fixing
AEFGIINSTU ignes fatui
AEFGIIOPVW View of a Pig
AEFGIIRTUV figurative
AEFGIKMNRR fingermark
AEFGILLLMR flame-grill
AEFGILLNPY flying leap
AEFGILMNNU meaningful
AEFGILMNOR lageniform
AEFGILMNOS flamingoes
AEFGILMNRY ley-farming
AEFGILMRUV vermifugal
AEFGILNOUW guinea fowl
AEFGILNPRS leaf spring
AEFGILNRTT flattering
AEFGILNRTU ingrateful
AEFGILNRVY vinegar-fly
AEFGILOPRT profligate
AEFGIPRRTU grapefruit
AEFGIRRRSY Grey Friars
AEFGLLLOWY yellow flag
AEFGLLOPUW fowl-plague
AEFGLLRTUY gratefully
AEFGLMRSTU Gulf Stream
AEFGLNOOTT tanglefoot
AEFGLNRTUU ungrateful
AEFGLPSTUY safety plug
AEFGLSSTTU Gulf States
AEFGMORRRS ferrograms
AEFGNORSTW wafer tongs
AEFHHHISST sheathfish
AEFHHIMMRS hammer-fish
AEFHHIPRST fathership
AEFHHLNRTU half-hunter
AEFHHLORSY halfe-horsy
AEFHHLORTY Holy Father
AEFHHLOSSU flash-house
AEFHHORSST shaft-horse
AEFHIINRTT interfaith
AEFHIIRRTW white friar✧
AEFHIKLLRT half-kirtle
AEFHIKLRSY freakishly
AEFHILLLOW hail-fellow
AEFHILMNOT fathom line
AEFHILNRTT flint-heart
AEFHILNSSS flashiness
AEFHILNSSY Hessian fly
AEFHILPPRS flapperish
AEFHILRSST half-sister
AEFHIMMNST famishment
AEFHIMNRSU fish-manure
AEFHINOPTY in the pay of
AEFHINOSSS oafishness
AEFHIORSUY Fairyhouse
AEFHLLLOVY half volley
AEFHLLMSUY shamefully
AEFHLLNNOS half nelson
AEFHLMNTTW twelfth man
AEFHLMOSST fathomless
AEFHLNRTUY unfatherly
AEFHLOOSTT false tooth
AEFHLRSTVY harvest-fly
AEFHMOOPRS shame-proof
AEFHOOPSTU out of phase
out of shape
AEFHORRSTU after hours
AEFHORRTTU fourth-rate
AEFHORSSTU a short fuse
AEFHOSSTTY safety shot
AEFIIINNTT infinitate
AEFIILLTUV fluviatile
AEFIILMNTY feminality
AEFIILNOOS Isle of Iona
AEFIILNOTU unifoliate
AEFIILNRTT infiltrate
AEFIILORTT trifoliate
AEFIIMNNOS infamonise
AEFIIMNNOZ infamonize
AEFIIMNRRR infirmarer
AEFIINQRTU quantifier
AEFIINSTUZ fustianize
AEFIJLRSTT rijsttafel
AEFIKLNNRZ Franz Kline
AEFIKMOSUY if you ask me
AEFIKNOPRS fair-spoken
AEFILLLNOV fall in love
AEFILLMMOR malleiform
AEFILLNNRY infernally
AEFILLNNUZ influenzal
AEFILLRTVY rift valley
AEFILLRUWY wearifully
AEFILMNSTY manifestly
AEFILMORRT formaliter
life-mortar
AEFILMORTW wolframite
AEFILMRTTU left atrium
AEFILNNRTV ventral fin
AEFILNOOSV isoflavone
AEFILNORSU laniferous
AEFILNORTU fluorinate
AEFILNPRTU turnip flea
AEFILNSSTU faultiness
AEFILOORTX exfoliator
AEFILOPPUX faex populi
AEFILOQRTU quatrefoil
AEFILORSSU saliferous
AEFILPQRUY pre-qualify
AEFIMNORYY fairy-money
AEFIMNOSST manifestos
AEFIMORSTU fumatories
AEFIMRSSTU mutessarif
AEFINNRSSU unfairness
AEFINOOPRT fortepiano
pianoforte
AEFINOPRTT point after
AEFINORRST rainforest
AEFINORRSW wafer irons

AEFINORSTY fairy-stone
AEFINORTTU refutation
AEFINORTUV unfavorite
AEFINRRRTY train ferry
AEFINRRTTY fraternity
AEFIORRSUU auriferous
AEFIRRSTTW first water
AEFKLNORSY forsakenly
AEFKLOORSW sale of work
AEFKNNORSU unforsaken
AEFKORRSTW fast worker
AEFLLLOORV All for Love
AEFLLLOOSV of all loves
AEFLLLOPWY playfellow
AEFLLLORWW wallflower
AEFLLLPTTU at full pelt
AEFLLNNRTY lantern fly
AEFLLNOORT root-fallen
AEFLLNOSSW fallowness
AEFLLNSSUW lawfulness
AEFLLOORRY ferro-alloy
AEFLLORSSV flavorless
AEFLLPSUUY pausefully
AEFLLSSSTY Tysse Falls
AEFLLSTTUY tastefully
AEFLLSTUWY wastefully
AEFLMNNSSU manfulness
AEFLMOORSV flavorsome
AEFLMORRSV salverform
AEFLNOOSTT float-stone
AEFLNOPRRT prefrontal
AEFLNOTTTU flatten out
AEFLNRSSTU artfulness
AEFLNRSTUW wanrestful
AEFLNSTTUU untasteful
AEFLOOPPRT plate-proof
AEFLOORUVV love-favour
AEFLORRSTW starflower
AEFLORSSUV favourless
AEFLORSTTU flatterous
AEFLRSSTUU useful arts
AEFLRSTTWY fly swatter
AEFMNORRTU from nature
AEFMNOSSSU famousness
AEFMOORRTW foot-warmer
AEFMOPRRST permafrost
AEFMORRSTY oyster-farm
AEFMPRTUXZ Max F Perutz
AEFNNPPRUY funny paper
AEFNORRRST transferor
AEFNORRTTW waterfront
AEFNRRSSTU transfuser
AEFOOPRRRT perforator
AEFOOPRRTW waterproof
AEFOOQRSTU square foot
AEFOORRSTT tortfeasor
AEFOPRRSTU perforatus
AEFOQRRSUU four-square
AEGGGIINRW earwigging
AEGGGILNNY engagingly
AEGGGINRST staggering
AEGGGINRSW swaggering
AEGGGIRYZZ zigzaggery
AEGGHHIMNR High German
AEGGHHLNOU Lough Neagh
AEGGHIILRS geisha girl
AEGGHIINTW gain weight
AEGGHILNRT right angle
AEGGHIMOPS geophagism
AEGGHIMORW whiggamore
AEGGHINOVY heavy going
AEGGHINSSS shagginess
AEGGHIOPST geophagist
AEGGHIORST The Gorgias
AEGGHIRSTT stage right
AEGGHLOPTU ploughgate
AEGGHOOPSU geophagous
AEGGIILMPR pilgrimage
AEGGIILMTU limit gauge
AEGGIILNVW living wage
AEGGIJMRST jigger-mast
AEGGIKLNOS Ginkgoales
AEGGIKNNSS knagginess
AEGGILLNRV gravelling
AEGGILMNOS losing game
AEGGILOOSU sialogogue
AEGGIMNRRS Grangerism
AEGGIMNRRT triggerman
AEGGINNPRS gingersnap
AEGGINORSS aggression
AEGGINPRTT pargetting
AEGGINQSSU quagginess
AEGGIORRSU gregarious
AEGGJNRTUU juggernaut✧
AEGGKLNOSW walk on eggs
AEGGLLNOOY angelology
AEGGLMORTU Great Mogul
AEGGLNORST strong gale
AEGGLOORTY geratology
AEGGLRSUZZ gas-guzzler
AEGGMNNORR Greg Norman
AEGGMOSTUY mystagogue
AEGGNNOORY organogeny
AEGGNNORSU gangrenous
AEGGOORSSS goose-grass
AEGGORRSST great gross
AEGHHHLLSU Hughes Hall
AEGHHIIRRS High Sierra
AEGHHIKNRR high-ranker
AEGHHILLLS shillelagh
AEGHHILOPR heliograph
AEGHHILRTT earth-light
AEGHHILRTW right whale
AEGHHILRUU Hugh Laurie
AEGHHINOSS high season
AEGHHINRST hear things
AEGHHINSTW wing sheath
AEGHHIOPRR hierograph
AEGHHISSTW sash weight
AEGHHLORSU horselaugh
AEGHHMOPPT apophthegm
AEGHHNOPPR nephograph
AEGHHOPRTY hyetograph
AEGHHORTTU eat through
AEGHIILOST goliathise
AEGHIILOTZ goliathize
AEGHIINPPR piping hare
AEGHIINRSV vinegarish
AEGHIIPRST graphitise
AEGHIIPRTZ graphitize
AEGHIKMMNO homemaking
AEGHIKMNOS shoemaking
AEGHIKNRST Kentish rag
AEGHIKRRST tiger shark
AEGHILLLOP Gallophile
AEGHILLNNS hanselling
AEGHILLNOP anglophile✧
AEGHILLNRT allnighter
AEGHILMMNU humming ale
AEGHILMNNS Englishman
AEGHILMNOS home-signal
AEGHILMNRT lighterman
AEGHILMORT lithomarge
AEGHILNOOT theologian
AEGHILNORW wholegrain
AEGHILNRSU languisher
AEGHILNSSS gashliness
AEGHILNSTT stealthing
AEGHILOPRT light opera
AEGHILPRXY lexigraphy
AEGHILRTTW light water
AEGHIMMOPR mimeograph
AEGHIMMOPT magpie moth
AEGHIMNPST stamp hinge
AEGHIMSTTT steamtight
AEGHINNRTV night-raven
AEGHINPRRS rangership
spring hare
AEGHINPRSS springhase
AEGHINPRST strap hinge
AEGHINPRTT night-taper
AEGHINRSSS garishness
AEGHINRSTT shattering
straighten
AEGHINSTUX exhausting
AEGHIPRRSY serigraphy
AEGHIRSTUW white sugar
AEGHIRTTTW watertight
AEGHJLLPRY jellygraph
AEGHLLOSSW Howleglass
AEGHLMNNST lengthsman
AEGHLMNRST arms-length
AEGHLMOOOT homologate
AEGHLMOPTU plough-team
AEGHLMORTU largemouth
AEGHLNNOOP anglophone✧
AEGHLNOOPY phaenology
AEGHLNOORR gonorrheal
AEGHLNOORS alongshore
AEGHLNOOSU halogenous
AEGHLNSTWY lengthways
AEGHLOOORR logorrhoea
AEGHLOOPRY oleography

Words marked ✧ can also be spelled with one or more capital letters

AEGHLOOPTY hepatology
AEGHLOPSTY glyphosate
AEGHLORSTT larghettos
AEGHLORSUV overslaugh
AEGHLOSSSU glasshouse
AEGHLRSTUY slaughtery
AEGHMMORRT thermogram
AEGHMNOOPR Gramophone®
gramophone
AEGHMNOPRS sphenogram
AEGHNNOOTW on the wagon
AEGHNNOOWY honey-wagon
AEGHNOOORR gonorrhoea
AEGHNOORSW horse-gowan
AEGHNOPRRY granophyre
AEGHNOPRST Stenograph®
stenograph
AEGHNOPRVY venography
AEGHNORRST short-range
AEGHNOSUXY hexagynous
AEGHOOPRRY oreography
AEGHOOPRRZ zoographer
AEGHOOPSSU oesophagus
AEGHOOPSUX exophagous
AEGHOOPSUY hypogaeous
AEGHOORSTV shove-groat
AEGHOPPSTT stop the gap
AEGHOPRRXY xerography
AEGHORRTUV overraught
AEGHORSSUU sugarhouse
AEGIIILNRT taglierini
AEGIIILNTV invigilate
AEGIIIMTTV mitigative
AEGIIIRRTV irrigative
AEGIIJMNNZ Jiang Zemin
AEGIIKNRSS ear-kissing
AEGIILLLTY illegality
AEGIILLPTV pit village
AEGIILMNRT trigeminal
AEGIILMNST time signal
AEGIILMNSX maxi-single
AEGIILMPST split image
AEGIILMRTT Tamil tiger
AEGIILNOPR perigonial
AEGIILNOTV levigation
AEGIILNPPY pipe-laying
AEGIILNPRV prevailing
AEGIILRTTT glitterati
AEGIIMMNNO meningioma
AEGIIMNNOT gemination
AEGIIMNORT emigration
remigation
AEGIIMNRRU migraineur
AEGIIMNSTT enigmatist✧
AEGIIMNSTV negativism
time-saving
AEGIIMSSTT stigmatise
AEGIIMSTTZ stigmatize
AEGIINNOST isoantigen
AEGIINNPRT repainting
AEGIINNRTT intrigante
AEGIINOPPR pigeon pair
AEGIINORTV invigorate
AEGIINPPST appetising
AEGIINPPTZ appetizing
AEGIINPRTT petit grain
AEGIINRSTV gainstrive
AEGIINSTTV negativist
AEGIINTTVY agentivity
negativity
AEGIIRRSTT geriatrist
AEGIIRTTVY ergativity
AEGIKLLRST grillsteak
AEGIKLMMOR kilogramme
AEGIKLMNOV lovemaking
AEGIKLNNSY sneakingly
AEGIKLNPRY pearly king
AEGIKLNPSY speakingly
AEGIKLNRWW wing-walker
AEGIKMNNOS maskinonge
AEGIKMNOPR rope-making
AEGIKMNOTT Tom Keating
AEGIKNNPSU unspeaking
AEGIKNNSST takingness
AEGIKNPRSS king's-spear
AEGIKPRSSS spike grass
AEGILLLLNT all-telling
AEGILLLLNU Lingulella
AEGILLLNRU laurelling
AEGILLMNRV marvelling
AEGILLMNST single malt
AEGILLNORY orange-lily
regionally
AEGILLNOXY glyoxaline
AEGILLNPPR rappelling
AEGILLNPRU prelingual
AEGILLNPSY pleasingly
AEGILLNRST stallinger
AEGILLNRTV travelling
AEGILLNRTY integrally
AEGILLNSST tasselling
AEGILLNSTY stealingly
AEGILLOPTT epiglottal
AEGILLORST allegorist
legislator
AEGILLPSSX Plexiglass®
plexiglass
AEGILMMNNT malignment
AEGILMNNOR non-gremial
AEGILMNOOP monoplegia
AEGILMNORS rosemaling
AEGILMNORY mineralogy
AEGILMNRST streamling
AEGILMSSTT gestaltism
AEGILMSTTU multi-stage
AEGILNNOOT elongation
AEGILNNOSU lanuginose
AEGILNNPSS glans penis
AEGILNNPSU unpleasing
AEGILNNRTU unaltering
AEGILNNRYY yearningly
AEGILNNSSS slanginess
AEGILNNSUY sanguinely
AEGILNOOSU oleaginous
AEGILNORST Interlagos
AEGILNORSU lanigerous
AEGILNORTU regulation
urogenital
AEGILNORVY overlaying
AEGILNOSTU gelatinous
AEGILNPRRT large print
AEGILNPRST plastering
AEGILNPRTU tape luring
AEGILNPRTY taperingly
AEGILNQSSU equals sign
AEGILNRSTV starveling✧
AEGILNRVWY waveringly
AEGILNRWYY wearyingly
AEGILNSSSS glassiness
AEGILOORST aerologist
AEGILOPRTT graptolite
AEGILORRSS gressorial
AEGILORRVV River Volga
AEGILRRTUY lyre guitar
regularity
AEGILRSWWY lawyer's wig
AEGILSSTTT Gestaltist
AEGIMMNRST stammering
AEGIMMORSS seismogram
AEGIMNNORU enamouring
AEGIMNNPRT impregnant
AEGIMNNRSV serving-man
AEGIMNNSST assignment
AEGIMNOPRS angiosperm
AEGIMNORSU gramineous
AEGIMNORTW worm-eating
AEGIMNORUW guinea worm✧
AEGIMNPRTY pigmentary
AEGIMNPTTY mating type
AEGIMNRRST ringmaster
AEGIMNRSTT smattering
AEGIMOPRSU soup maigre
AEGIMORRSU armigerous
AEGIMORRTY emigratory
AEGIMOSSTT stigmatose
AEGIMRRTVY gravimetry
AEGINNNOSS Annie's Song
AEGINNNOTV non-vintage
AEGINNNPRT trepanning
AEGINNORRS engarrison
AEGINNPPRW enwrapping
AEGINNRSTT astringent
AEGINNRSTU sauntering
AEGINNRSUW unswearing
AEGINNRUVW unwavering
AEGINNRUWY unwearying
AEGINNSSSV savingness
AEGINOORTT negotiator
AEGINOPRSW Spiro Agnew
AEGINORRTT integrator
AEGINORRTZ zero-rating
AEGINORSUU aeruginous
AEGINPPRTT tappet-ring

AEGINPRRTW	tiger prawn
AEGINPRSTU	supergiant
AEGINPRSTY	panegyrist
AEGINPSTTU	Septuagint
AEGINQRRTU	quartering
AEGINRRRUV	Argun River
AEGINRRSSU	reassuring
AEGINRRSTT	registrant
AEGINRRSTU	austringer
AEGINRRSTV	traversing
AEGINRSSSS	grassiness
AEGINRSSSU	sugariness
AEGINRSTWW	water wings
AEGIOPRSTU	Portugaise
AEGIPRRTTU	gutter pair
AEGIRRRSTY	registrary
AEGIRRSTUV	River Tagus
AEGIRSSTTT	strategist
AEGJLOSUUY	Jealous Guy
AEGKLLMRSS	Mrs Gaskell
AEGKLLRRUY	gully-raker
AEGKLNOSVW	Volkswagen®
AEGKLPRRUU	Paul Kruger
AEGKMNOSXY	oxygen mask
AEGKMOORTT	go to market
AEGLLLLNNO	Llangollen
AEGLLMORRU	glomerular
AEGLLMORWY	galley-worm
AEGLLMRTUY	metallurgy
AEGLLNNPTY	plangently
AEGLLNOPST	long-staple
AEGLLNORSW	swell organ
AEGLLOPRSU	pellagrous
AEGLMNOOOV	avgolemono
AEGLMNOOSY	mosey along
AEGLMNOOTY	nematology
AEGLMNORSS	lemon grass
AEGLMOPRTU	promulgate
AEGLMORTTU	malgré tout
AEGLMPRSSU	plume-grass
AEGLNNOOST	logan-stone
AEGLNNPRTY	pregnantly
AEGLNOOOSS	solan goose
AEGLNOOPRT	prolongate
AEGLNOOSUV	longaevous
AEGLNOPRSU	a long purse
AEGLNSSSSU	sunglasses
AEGLOOOPTW	a peg too low
AEGLOORRST	astrologer
AEGLOORTTY	teratology
AEGLOPPSTU	plague-spot
AEGLORRTUY	regulatory
AEGLPRSSUU	surplusage
AEGLRSSSTY	grass style
AEGMMNRTUU	argumentum
AEGMMOPRRR	programmer
AEGMNOORST	gastronome
AEGMNORRST	starmonger
AEGMNORSTT	strong meat
AEGMNORTTU	Tantum ergo
AEGNNNPRTU	unpregnant
AEGNNRTUUY	unguentary
AEGNOOORRT	orange-root
AEGNOORRSU	sour orange
AEGNOORTXY	oxygenator
AEGNOORVWY	Now, Voyager
AEGNOOSTUU	autogenous
AEGNOPRSTT	patter-song
AEGNOPSTUW	wasp-tongue
AEGNRRSSST	transgress
AEGNSSSTUU	augustness
AEGNSTUVYY	Yves Tanguy
AEGOORSTUU	outrageous
AEGOPRRRTY	grey parrot
AEGOPRRSSU	sour grapes
AEGOPRRTUX	expurgator
AEGPRRSSSU	supergrass
AEHHHILOPT	Ahithophel
AEHHIKMNST	think shame
AEHHIKOOOS	Ooka Shohei
AEHHILNOPT	lithophane
AEHHILNSTU	Helianthus
AEHHIMNPST	hetmanship
AEHHINOPRT	hierophant
AEHHINPRST	pantherish
AEHHINRTWY	anywhither
AEHHIRSTTW	white trash
AEHHJNNOSY	John Haynes
AEHHLMMOPY	haemolymph
AEHHLNOPTT	heptathlon
AEHHLOOPRS	holophrase
AEHHLOPTTU	heath-poult
AEHHMOOOPT	homoeopath
AEHHMOOPTY	homeopathy
AEHHNNOOSS	Shoshonean
AEHHNOOPRT	anthophore
AEHHNOPRTY	hypaethron
AEHHOORSTT	root sheath
AEHHORTTWY	hateworthy
AEHHPSSTTU	Hatshepsut
AEHIIKLRTW	wraithlike
AEHIIKNPST	kinesipath
AEHIIKPRSS	kaisership
AEHIILLMNW	Wilhelmina
AEHIILNOPX	philoxenia
AEHIILNPST	Philistean
AEHIILOPRS	Hierapolis
AEHIILOPRZ	pileorhiza
AEHIILOSTX	heliotaxis
AEHIIMNORS	mashie iron
AEHIIMNSTT	antitheism
AEHIIMNSTU	humanities
AEHIINOSTT	hesitation
AEHIINPPRS	sapphirine
AEHIINPRTU	up in the air✧
AEHIINSSTT	antithesis
AEHIINSTTT	antitheist
AEHIIPPRRT	Rhipiptera
AEHIIPPSTT	epitaphist
AEHIIPRSTW	Paris white
AEHIJNNOPR	John Napier
AEHIKKNOPT	pinakothek
AEHIKLLLRW	hillwalker
AEHIKLNSSY	sneakishly
AEHIKLPPTY	play the kip
AEHIKLSSST	skaithless
AEHIKMNNST	Kentish-man
AEHIKMRRST	harem skirt
AEHIKMRSTV	Vikram Seth
AEHIKMSTWY	Wykehamist
AEHIKNRSSS	rakishness
AEHIKOPPRT	pork-pie hat
AEHIKORRST	hair stroke
AEHILLLNSS	snail-shell
AEHILLMOST	allotheism
AEHILLOOVW	view-halloo
AEHILLOPSV	Slavophile
AEHILLOPTW	pilot whale
AEHILLOPTY	polyhalite
AEHILLORSV	all-overish
AEHILLORTY	heliolatry
AEHILLOSTY	halloysite
AEHILLSTTY	stealthily
AEHILMMNST	Simmenthal
AEHILMMRTT	tilt hammer
AEHILMNNUY	inhumanely
AEHILMNOPY	anemophily
AEHILMNSTV	lavishment
AEHILMOPRT	hemitropal
AEHILMORST	isothermal
	thimerosal
AEHILMOSSY	haemolysis
AEHILMPSTU	multiphase
AEHILMRRTY	Hilary term
AEHILNNOOP	phaelonion
AEHILNNOPS	Alphonsine
AEHILNNOTV	on the anvil
AEHILNOOPP	philopoena
AEHILNOOST	shoot a line
AEHILNOPRZ	rhizoplane
AEHILNOPST	Polianthes
AEHILNOPTT	thiopental
AEHILNORSS	lion's share
AEHILNPSTY	staphyline
AEHILNSSSV	lavishness
AEHILNSTTY	hesitantly
AEHILNSTUW	Whitsun ale
AEHILOOPRT	ophiolater
AEHILOPRST	hospitaler
	trophesial
AEHILOPTVY	top-heavily
AEHILORRTY	hierolatry
AEHILPPRRT	triple harp
AEHILRSTVW	silver thaw
AEHILRSTVY	shrievalty
AEHIMMNORT	hammer into
AEHIMMPRRT	trip hammer
AEHIMMRSTU	rheumatism
AEHIMNNPPS	penmanship
AEHIMNNSTV	vanishment
AEHIMNNSUU	unhumanise
AEHIMNNUUZ	unhumanize
AEHIMNOPPS	hippomanes

AEHIMNORRS harmoniser
AEHIMNORRZ harmonizer
AEHIMNORUU iure humano
AEHIMNOTUX exhumation
AEHIMNRSSS marshiness
AEHIMNRSTV ravishment
AEHIMNSSTU enthusiasm
AEHIMOOPTY mythopoeia
AEHIMORRSV Averrhoism
AEHIMOSTTU autotheism
AEHIMPRSST mastership
shipmaster
AEHIMPSSTY sympathies
sympathise
AEHIMPSTYZ sympathize
AEHINNNOOT hootnannie
AEHINNOPPT happen into
AEHINNOPRT antiphoner
AEHINNPSTT tenantship
AEHINNRRTY Tyrrhenian
AEHINNRTVW wanthriven
AEHINOPRTU euphoriant
AEHINOPRTY hypertonia
AEHINOPSTT on the tapis
tip one's hat
AEHINORRTV hovertrain
AEHINORSTU house-train
AEHINOSTUX exhaustion
AEHINQRSUV vanquisher
AEHINRSSST trashiness
AEHINRSSTW wrathiness
AEHINSSTTU enthusiast
AEHIOOPSST apotheosis
AEHIOPPRRS repair-shop
AEHIORRSTU authoriser
AEHIORRSTV Averrhoist
AEHIORRTUZ authorizer
AEHIORSSST air hostess
AEHIORSTTT throatiest
AEHIORSTTY hesitatory
AEHIOSTTTU autotheist
AEHIRSSTTW sweatshirt
sweat-shirt
AEHIRSTTWW thwartwise
AEHJKNNOOS John a-Nokes
AEHJLNORTW John Walter
AEHKLMNORS lemon shark
AEHKLMNOTU Mount Hekla
AEHKLMRTUW lukewarmth
AEHKLNNSUY unshakenly
AEHKLNOSTY honey-stalk
AEHKLOPRSW shop walker
AEHKNOORRT North Korea
AEHKNORRST other ranks
AEHKNORSTT taken short
AEHKNRRSSU nurse shark
AEHKOORSTU South Korea
AEHKOPRSTU Petroushka
AEHLLMRSSY harmlessly
AEHLLMSTUU haustellum
AEHLLOOPRT Hartlepool
AEHLLOORWW hollow-ware
AEHLLOPRXY phylloxera
AEHLLORRSZ razor shell
AEHLLOSWWY yellow wash
AEHLMNOOPR pheromonal
AEHLMNORTT antler-moth
AEHLMNOSWW Welshwoman
AEHLMNPTTU pentathlum
AEHLMOOPRS Homorelaps
AEHLMOOSUX homosexual
AEHLMOPPTT lappet moth
AEHLMORRYY rhyme royal
AEHLMPSSYY symphyseal
AEHLNNOPTT pentathlon
AEHLNOPPRT thorn apple
AEHLNOPSTU house plant
plant-house
sulphonate
AEHLNOPTTY entophytal
AEHLNORTTT tetrathlon
AEHLOOPRRY pyorrhoeal
AEHLOORSSW wool shears
AEHLORRSVY overrashly
AEHLORSSTU authorless
AEHLORSTUV horse vault
AEHLPRSTUU sulphurate
AEHLRTTUUV truth value
AEHMMMTUWY mummy-wheat
AEHMMOORST More Thomas
Thomas More
AEHMNNOOSW one-man show
AEHMNOORSU manor-house
AEHMNOORSW horse-woman
AEHMNOOSUY shame on you
AEHMNOPRST smart phone
smartphone
AEHMNORRTT Matterhorn
AEHMNORTTU Mount Thera
AEHMNORTWY nameworthy
AEHMNPRSUU superhuman
AEHMNPRTWY water nymph
AEHMNRSTTU anthersmut
AEHMNRTTUY nature-myth
AEHMNSSTTY assythment
AEHMOOPSTT smoothpate
AEHMOORSTX mesothorax
AEHMOPRRTT Tetramorph
AEHMOPSTTU put to shame
AEHMORSTTT thermostat
AEHNNNOOTY hootenanny
AEHNNOOPST panton-shoe
AEHNNOPPPU happen upon
AEHNNOPRSU noun phrase
AEHNNORSTY Antony Sher
AEHNOOOPRT orthopnoea
AEHNOOPRST heart-spoon
AEHNOOPSSU sousaphone
AEHNOORSSX Saxon Shore
AEHNOPPRST Shepparton
AEHNOPRTUY neuropathy
AEHNORRTTU run to earth
AEHNORRTTW north water
AEHNORSTWW snow-wreath
AEHOOPPRST apostrophe
AEHOOPPRTY opotherapy
AEHOOPRRTT orthoptera✧
AEHOOPRTYZ zootherapy
AEHOOPRYZZ Zaporozhye
AEHOOPSSTY photo-essay
AEHOOPSSTZ zoothapses
AEHOOPSTTT toothpaste
AEHOOPSTTY osteopathy
AEHOORRSTT sore throat
AEHOORSSTY soothsayer
AEHOORSTTW water shoot
AEHOPPRSTY saprophyte
AEHOPRSTUV the vapours
AEHOPRSTUY house party
AEHOPSSSTY hypostases
AEHORRRSTW restharrow
AEHORRSTWY shower tray
AEHORRTTVW overthwart
AEHORSTTTW at the worst
AEHPPRRSSU supersharp
AEHPRSSTTY strathspey
AEIIIILNST initialise
AEIIIILNTZ initialize
AEIIIINTTV initiative
AEIIILLMTW Williamite
AEIIILMNOS isoaminile
AEIIILMRST militarise
AEIIILMRTZ militarize
AEIIILMSTV similative
AEIIILMTTV limitative
AEIIILRSTV trivialise
AEIIILRTVZ trivialize
AEIIILSTTV vitalities
AEIIIMMNPR imipramine
AEIIIMNRST ministeria
AEIIIMNSTV vitaminise
AEIIIMNTVZ vitaminize
AEIIIMRRTU iure mariti
AEIIIRRTTV irritative
AEIIISTTVV visitative
AEIIJMNRSW James Irwin
AEIIKLLNPR painkiller
AEIIKLLORS sailorlike
AEIIKLRSST strike sail
AEIIKLRTUV laurvikite
AEIIKMNTTY amenity kit
AEIILLLMMS millesimal
AEIILLLMNN millennial
AEIILLLTVY illatively
AEIILLMNOR mineral oil
AEIILLMNPP Pimpinella
AEIILLMNSS sinsemilla
AEIILLMNTU illuminate
AEIILLMPRY imperially
AEIILLMRST literalism
AEIILLMSWY Willie Mays
AEIILLNRTU uniliteral
AEIILLNSSV villainess

AEIILLOSTV	alveolitis
	volatilise
AEIILLOTVZ	volatilize
AEIILLPSTT	pistillate
AEIILLRRTT	triliteral
AEIILLRRTU	tirailleur
AEIILLRRTY	literarily
AEIILLRSTT	literalist
AEIILLRSTV	silvertail
AEIILLRTTY	literality
AEIILMMMOR	immemorial
AEIILMNNOS	nominalise
AEIILMNNOZ	nominalize
AEIILMNORT	eliminator
AEIILMNRST	mineralist
AEIILMNSTY	seminality
AEIILMNSZZ	mizzensail
AEIILMNTTY	intimately
AEIILMOPST	optimalise
AEIILMOPTZ	optimalize
AEIILMOSSS	isoseismal
AEIILMRSTV	relativism
AEIILMRSVV	revivalism
AEIILMSTUV	simulative
AEIILNNOPT	antilopine
AEIILNNORS	rosaniline
AEIILNNSSU	insulinase
AEIILNNSTT	intestinal
AEIILNOOTT	etiolation
AEIILNOPRT	oil painter
AEIILNOPSS	spaniolise
AEIILNOPSZ	spaniolize
AEIILNORRT	irrelation
AEIILNORST	inter alios
	Toni Sailer
AEIILNORSV	revisional
AEIILNORTT	literation
AEIILNORTV	leviration
AEIILNOSST	leontiasis
AEIILNOTTV	levitation
	tonalitive
	velitation
AEIILNPPRT	plain tripe
AEIILNPPRZ	Lippizaner
AEIILNPRZZ	Lipizzaner
AEIILNQTUY	inequality
AEIILNRSTY	silentiary
AEIILNRTTV	intervital
AEIILOPPTV	oppilative
AEIILOPSTV	spoliative
AEIILORTTV	vitriolate
AEIILRSSUV	visualiser
AEIILRSTTV	relativist
AEIILRSTTZ	strelitzia
AEIILRSTVV	revivalist
AEIILRSUVZ	visualizer
AEIILRTTVY	relativity
AEIIMMMNOR	in memoriam
AEIIMMNPRT	impairment
AEIIMMNRST	antimerism
AEIIMMNSSS	Messianism
AEIIMMRSTT	mime artist
AEIIMNNNOS	Nina Simone
AEIIMNNNOT	innominate
AEIIMNNOST	Noetianism
	semination
AEIIMNNOTT	antimonite
AEIIMNNOTV	nominative
AEIIMNOSTT	estimation
AEIIMNOSTV	somniative
AEIIMNPPRT	Martin Pipe
AEIIMNPQRU	primaquine
AEIIMNQRTU	Martinique
AEIIMNQTUY	equanimity
AEIIMNRSST	seminarist
AEIIMNRTUV	ruminative
AEIIMNSSST	Messianist
AEIIMNSSTX	antisexism
AEIIMOPRRS	impresario
AEIIMPRSTT	team spirit
AEIIMPTTUV	imputative
AEIINNOQTU	inequation
AEIINNOSST	enantiosis
AEIINNOTVV	innovative
AEIINNPRTT	tripinnate
AEIINNPSST	paintiness
AEIINNSTTX	inexistant
AEIINOPPST	inapposite
AEIINOPPTT	appetition
AEIINOPPTV	appointive
AEIINOPRTX	expiration
AEIINOPSTT	poinsettia
AEIINOPSTU	utopianise
AEIINOPTUZ	utopianize
AEIINOQTTU	equitation
AEIINOSTTV	estivation
AEIINOTUVX	exuviation
AEIINPRSTU	puritanise
AEIINPRTTU	unipartite
AEIINPRTUZ	puritanize
AEIINPSSST	antisepsis
	inspissate
AEIINQTTUV	quantitive
AEIINRRSTT	tristearin
AEIINRRSTV	intra vires
AEIINRRTTT	trinitrate
AEIINRSSSU	Russianise
AEIINRSSUZ	Russianize
AEIINRSTTV	revisitant
	transitive
AEIINSSTTX	antisexist
AEIIOPPRTT	propitiate
AEIIOPPSTV	appositive
AEIIOPRRSS	proairesis
AEIIPPSSSW	pipsissewa
AEIIPRRSTV	privatiser
AEIIPRRTTT	tripartite
AEIIPRRTVZ	privatizer
AEIIRRSTVZ	River Tisza
AEIJKLRSUZ	Jaruzelski
AEIJLNORSU	journalise
AEIJLNORUZ	journalize
AEIJLNOSSV	jovialness
AEIJMNOSSS	jam session
AEIJMNRRUV	River Jumna
AEIJMORSVY	James Ivory
AEIJNNSSTU	jauntiness
AEIJNOOPRT	pejoration
AEIJNORTTW	water joint
AEIJRSTTWW	jaw-twister
AEIKLLMNSU	muslin-kale
AEIKLLMPPR	lapper-milk
AEIKLMMNRS	slammerkin
AEIKLMNORT	matron-like
AEIKLMNORY	monkey rail
AEIKLMNOTY	monkey tail
AEIKLMNSTY	mistakenly
AEIKLMPPRR	ripple mark
AEIKLNPPRT	ripple tank
AEIKMNNRTU	Turkmenian
AEIKMNPRRT	printmaker
AEIKNNORRY	Ronnie Kray
AEIKNOPRRY	perikaryon
AEIKNORSTU	keratinous
AEILLLMOSU	Louis Malle
AEILLLMOTW	all-time low
AEILLLMSTT	little slam
AEILLLNQSU	line squall
	squall line
AEILLLOTWY	yellowtail
AEILLLSUVY	allusively
AEILLMMRST	millstream
	small-timer
AEILLMNPRS	Parnellism
AEILLMNPTU	multiplane
AEILLMNRTY	terminally
AEILLMPPSS	small-pipes
AEILLMPRVY	primevally
AEILLMRTTY	little Mary
AEILLMTTUY	ultimately
AEILLNNPRU	plenilunar
AEILLNNRTY	internally
AEILLNOPTT	potentilla
AEILLNORTY	orientally
AEILLNOTTT	not a little
AEILLNPSST	plaintless
AEILLNPSSY	painlessly
AEILLNRTTU	Tertullian
AEILLNRTUY	tenurially
AEILLOPSTT	postillate
AEILLORSSS	sailorless
AEILLORTUV	trouvaille
AEILLPPRTY	triple play
AEILLPSSTT	pastellist
AEILLQRRTU	quarter-ill
AEILLRRTTU	Turritella
AEILLRSSTV	liver salts
AEILLRSTTU	illustrate
AEILLRSTTW	still water
AEILMMNORT	montelimar
AEILMMNPRS	miner's lamp
AEILMMNSSS	smalminess
AEILMMPRSS	Miss Marple

AEILMMRTUY immaturely
AEILMNNOTY nominately
AEILMNNSTT instalment
AEILMNOPRS impersonal
AEILMNOPRT trampoline
AEILMNORTU tourmaline
AEILMNORTY monetarily
AEILMNOSST assoilment
AEILMNPRTY planimetry
AEILMNRRTY Martin Ryle
AEILMNRSTU neutralism
AEILMNRTTT latter-mint
AEILMNSSSU sensualism
AEILMNSSVY levy in mass
AEILMNSTTU last-minute
AEILMOORRT meliorator
AEILMOPPSS ampelopsis
AEILMOPRST peristomal
AEILMOPSST semipostal
AEILMOPSTT Ptolemaist
AEILMORSTV removalist
AEILMPPSST palimpsest
AEILMPRSST slipstream
AEILMPRSSU plumassier
AEILMPRSTU psalterium
AEILMPRTUU pari-mutuel
AEILMRRSSU surrealism✧
AEILMSTTUX textualism
AEILNNNPPY penny-plain
AEILNNNSTW lawn tennis
AEILNNOOPR pearl onion
AEILNNOPSY Polynesian
AEILNNORTT intolerant
AEILNNORTU neutralino
AEILNNORTZ interzonal
Lorentzian
AEILNNOSST nationless
AEILNNPRSU peninsular
AEILNNPRTT interplant
AEILNNPSST pliantness
AEILNNRRTU interlunar
AEILNNRSTT lanternist
AEILNOOPRT tropaeolin
AEILNOORSS solar noise
AEILNOORTT toleration
AEILNOOSTT nose to tail
AEILNOPPST pentapolis
AEILNOPRRT interpolar
AEILNOPRRV rain-plover
AEILNOPRST interposal
AEILNOPRTU eruptional
AEILNOPRTV portal vein
AEILNOPSTY toy spaniel
AEILNORRTT torrential
AEILNORRTY anteriorly
AEILNORTTV ventilator
AEILNORTWW in low water
AEILNOSTTU Titus Alone
AEILNOTTUX exultation
AEILNPPRTU prenuptial
AEILNPRSST paltriness
AEILNPRSTU palustrine
AEILNPSUUV unplausive
AEILNRRTUY unliterary
AEILNRSSVW swirl vanes
AEILNRSTTU neutralist
AEILNRSTUU Laurentius
laurustine
AEILNRTTUY neutrality
AEILNRTTWW written law
AEILNSSSTU sensualist
AEILNSSTUU nautiluses
AEILNSSTUY sensuality
AEILNSTUVW wine vaults
AEILOOPSST apostolise
AEILOOPSTT toilet soap
AEILOOPSTZ apostolize
AEILOOPTTZ topazolite
AEILOPPRST Leptospira
AEILOPPRSU popularise
AEILOPPRUZ popularize
AEILOPPSTY appositely
AEILOPRRST serial port
AEILOPRSSU plesiosaur
AEILOPRSTT tetrapolis
AEILOPRSTY epistolary
AEILOPTTVY optatively
AEILORRRTV retroviral
AEILORRTTU elutriator
AEILORRTVV River Volta
AEILORSTTU staurolite
AEILPRRSTY peristylar
AEILPRRTWY play-writer
AEILPRSSTU sur le tapis
AEILPRSSUV supervisal
AEILPRTTUV virtual pet
AEILPTTUVY putatively
AEILQRRTTU triquetral
AEILQRRTUY quarry tile
AEILRRSSTU surrealist
AEILRRSSTV Silver Star
AEILRRSTUV ultra vires
AEILSTTTUX textualist
AEIMMMNORY main memory
AEIMMNNRSS mismanners
AEIMMNORST monetarism
AEIMMNOTUU auto-immune
AEIMMNPRTT impartment
AEIMMNRSSS smarminess
AEIMMNRSTT mint master
AEIMMNRSTY symmetrian
AEIMMNRTTU manumitter
AEIMMNSTZZ mizzenmast
AEIMMOOPRR pro memoria
AEIMMPRRSU spermarium
AEIMMPRSTU spermatium
AEIMNNNORW inner woman
AEIMNNNOTT anointment
AEIMNNOPRR mainpernor
AEIMNNOPRS in personam
AEIMNNORTU numeration
AEIMNOOPZZ mezzo-piano
AEIMNOORST aeronomist
AEIMNOOTVW wave motion
AEIMNOPRTT armipotent
portamenti
AEIMNOPRTW tripe-woman
AEIMNOPRWZ prizewoman
AEIMNOPTTT temptation
AEIMNOQSUU equanimous
AEIMNORRST ironmaster
AEIMNORRTT terminator
AEIMNORSTT monetarist
AEIMNORSTU Mousterian
AEIMNOSSTU stamineous
AEIMNPPRST pentaprism
AEIMNPSSSW swampiness
AEIMNPSTTY tympanites
AEIMNRRRTY intermarry
AEIMNRRSTT retransmit
AEIMNRSSTU antiserums
AEIMOORSTX xerostomia
AEIMOOTTUV automotive
AEIMOPRRTU praetorium
AEIMPRSSST masspriest
AEIMPRSSTT spermatist
AEIMPRSSTU pasteurism
AEIMPRSTUZ trapeziums
AEIMPSSTUV assumptive
AEIMQRSTUZ quizmaster
AEIMRRRSTU terrariums
AEIMRRSTTT ritt-master
AEINNNOPST pensionnat
AEINNNOQSU sine qua non
AEINNOOPRZ Renzo Piano
AEINNOORST insane root
AEINNOORTV renovation
AEINNOPRSY pensionary
AEINNOPRWY Norway pine
AEINNOQRTU quaternion
AEINNORRSU raisonneur
AEINNORSTT stentorian
AEINNOSSTT satin stone
AEINNOSTTT attentions
AEINNQSSTU quaintness
AEINNRRTTU Tina Turner
AEINNRSSUW unwariness
AEINOOPPRT apoprotein
propionate
AEINOOPRRT peroration
AEINOORRTT orientator
AEINOPPPRR poprin pear
AEINOPPPRT preappoint
AEINOPPRRS Proserpina
AEINOPPRST spear-point
AEINOPRRST patroniser
periastron
AEINOPRRTW powertrain
AEINOPRRTZ patronizer
AEINOPRSSS rap session
AEINOPRSSU persuasion✧
AEINOPRSTT prestation
AEINOPRSTU superation

AEINOPRSTW	waitperson
AEINOPRTTU	reputation
AEINOPRTTY	potentiary
AEINOPTTTU	out-patient
AEINOQSTTU	at question
AEINORRSST	serrations
AEINORRSTU	souterrain
AEINORRSTV	overstrain
AEINORSSTY	tyrosinase
AEINORSTTY	stationery
AEINPPRSST	trappiness
AEINPPRSTW	wit-snapper
AEINPRRSTU	rupestrian
AEINPRRTTU	parturient
AEINPRSTTT	strepitant
AEINQRTTUY	quaternity
AEINRRSSST	starriness
AEINRSSSTT	straitness
AEINRSTUYZ	suzerainty
AEIOPRRRST	respirator
AEIOPRRTTX	extirpator
AEIOPRRTXY	expiratory
AEIORRRSSW	warrioress
AEIORSSTTT	Stratiotes
AEIOSTTTUW	sweat it out
AEIPRSTUUV	usurpative
AEIRSSSTUU	saussurite
AEIRSTTTWW	water twist
AEJLLLORYY	royal jelly
AEJLLMOSWW	Jews' mallow
	Jew's mallow
AEJLLSSTUW	just as well
AEJMNNORUY	journeyman
AEKKLRTTUY	talk turkey
AEKKMNRRTU	trunk maker
AEKLLMRUWY	lukewarmly
AEKLLOPSTU	leukoplast
AEKLMNOORW	moonwalker
AEKLMNOSTY	money talks
AEKLNOPRTT	petrol tank
AEKLNPRSTW	wrest plank
AEKLOPPPRR	Karl Popper
AEKLOPRSTY	stroke play
	strokeplay
AEKLORTTWW	wattlework
AEKMMSSSTY	MKSA system
AEKMNNOTUY	Mount Kenya
AEKMNOPRRU	remark upon
AEKMNORTTW	market-town
AEKMOORTTY	keratotomy
AEKMOPRSTT	spot market
AEKMORRSTW	masterwork
	workmaster
AEKMRRSSST	stress mark
AEKNNNOSTT	Stan Kenton
AEKNOOTTTW	take to town
AEKNOQRSTU	square knot
AEKOOPRRTY	prokaryote
AEKOPRRSTY	oyster-park
AEKORRSTWW	waterworks
AELLLMOTTU	outlet mall
AELLMNNOUY	noumenally
AELLMNORTY	trolley man
AELLMOORSW	rose mallow
AELLMOPRTY	temporally
AELLMOPSSY	plasmolyse
AELLMOPSYZ	plasmolyze
AELLMORSUV	marvellous
AELLNOOPRT	Trollopean
AELLNOPPRT	propellant
AELLNOPRSY	personally
AELLNOPSTU	plant louse
AELLNOPTVY	polyvalent
AELLNORTTY	tolerantly
AELLNOSSSW	sallowness
AELLNPRSUY	supernally
AELLNPTTUY	petulantly
AELLNRSTTY	slatternly
AELLNTTUXY	exultantly
AELLOOPSTW	wool staple
AELLOOPSWY	yellow soap
AELLOPPRSU	all-purpose
AELLOPRSUY	superalloy
AELLOPRTUV	plural vote
AELLPRSTUU	sepultural
AELLRTTUXY	texturally
AELMMNNOTU	monumental
AELMMNOSSS	solemn mass
AELMMNTTUZ	Muntz metal
AELMMOOPSS	plasmosome
AELMMOORRT	tremolo arm
AELMMOPRRW	palmer-worm
AELMMOSSUU	mausoleums
AELMMPRSTU	emplastrum
AELMNNNRUY	unmannerly
AELMNNOOTV	monovalent
AELMNNOSSS	Nelson Mass
AELMNOOOSS	Solomon Sea
AELMNOOPRT	monopteral
	protonemal
AELMNOOPRY	lampoonery
AELMNOPRST	emplastron
	Palmerston
AELMNOPRSU	neuroplasm
AELMNOPRTT	portmantle
AELMNOPRTU	Paul Merton
AELMNOPSTY	polysemant
AELMNORSSS	ransomless
AELMNPRSUU	Paul M Nurse
AELMNSSSUW	swan-mussel
AELMOOPPTT	tappet-loom
AELMOOPRTU	tropaeolum
AELMOPPRUY	propylaeum
AELMOPRTTU	petrolatum
AELMOPRTTY	temporalty
AELMOPSSST	Epsom salts
AELMOQSSUU	squamulose
AELMORRSSU	armourless
AELMORRSSW	marrowless
AELMORSSTU	somersault
AELMORSTTT	lattermost
AELMPPRSUY	maple syrup
AELMRSSTTU	mulattress
AELMTTTUUU	tumultuate
AELNNOORSZ	San Lorenzo
AELNNOPRYY	pennyroyal
AELNNORSTY	resonantly
AELNOOPRRT	rotor plane
AELNOOPRST	solo parent
AELNOOPSTT	postal note
AELNOPPRTW	power plant
AELNOPRSST	patronless
AELNOPRSTY	personalty
AELNOPSTTT	talent-spot
AELNOPSTTV	stove plant
AELNOPSTTW	staple town
AELNORSUVY	ravenously
AELNOSSUUY	nauseously
AELNPPRSTU	supplanter
AELNPRRSUU	superlunar
AELNPRTTYY	penalty try
AELOOOPRTY	aeolotropy
AELOOPRRSW	solar power
AELOOPSSTV	Sevastopol
AELOOPSTTV	postal vote
AELOPPRRRU	pourparler
AELOPRRSTW	law reports
AELOPRRSUY	super-royal
AELORRTTTW	otter-trawl
AELORSSSUV	savourless
AELPPPPTUY	puppet play
AELPPSSTUY	platypuses
AEMMNOPRSY	memory span
AEMMNOPRTU	map-mounter
AEMMNORRTT	Montmartre
AEMMNORSTY	Asymmetron
	smart money
AEMMNRSTYY	mystery-man
AEMMOSSTTU	stemmatous
AEMNNNOOSW	one's own man
AEMNNNOPTY	non-payment
AEMNNOOSST	stonemason
AEMNNORTTT	attornment
AEMNNORTTU	tournament
AEMNNRRSUY	nurseryman
AEMNOOPRTT	portamento
AEMNOORRST	astronomer
AEMNOPRRSY	Perry Mason
AEMNOPRSSW	presswoman
AEMNOPRSUW	superwoman
AEMNORRSTT	Montserrat
AEMNORRTUY	uranometry
AEMNORSSTT	assortment
AEMNORSSTU	sarmentous
AEMNRRSTTU	transmuter
AEMOOPSTTY	somatotype
AEMOORRTTW	water motor
AEMOPRRSSW	swarm-spore
AEMOPRSSTT	postmaster✧
AEMORRSTTW	masterwort
AEMORRSTTY	astrometry
AEMORRSTUX	extra muros

AEMPRSSSTU	pass muster
AENNNOSSTW	wantonness
AENNOPSTTY	stannotype
AENNORRSSW	narrowness
AENNORRSTT	non-starter
AENOOPRRST	personator
AENOOPRTXY	paroxytone
AENOOQRRTU	quarteroon
AENOORSSTU	anoestrous
	treasonous
AENOPRRSST	transposer
AENOPRSSUV	supernovas
AENOPRSTTT	protestant✧
AENORSTTUW	run to waste
AENPRRSTTU	transputer
AEOOPPRRRT	propraetor
AEOOPPRRST	praepostor
AEOOPPRSTU	tropopause
AEOOPRSTTV	vaporettos
AEOOQRRSTU	square root
AEOPPPRTWY	poppy water
AEOPPRRRTU	rapporteur
AEOPPRSTTW	potter wasp
AEOPRRSSTW	sportswear
AEOPRRSSUY	persuasory
AEOPRRTTTY	art pottery
	treaty port
AEOPRSTTUW	waterspout
AEOQRRSTUZ	rose quartz
AEORSSSTUU	trousseaus
AEORSSTUUX	trousseaux
AEPRRSTUUU	usurpature
AFFFFINNYY	niffy-naffy
AFFFGILLNO	falling-off
AFFGGNOORU	gang of four✧
AFFGIILNSY	falsifying
AFFGIINORT	forfaiting
AFFGIIRSTT	graffitist
AFFGIMRSSU	suffragism
AFFGINNORT	affronting
AFFGINRSTW	wring staff
AFFGIRSSTU	suffragist
AFFGNOORST	stroganoff
AFFHIINRSU	ruffianish
AFFHILLNOR	half florin
AFFHILLTUY	faithfully
AFFHILNTUU	unfaithful
AFFHIRSTTU	Tartuffish
AFFIIMNRSU	ruffianism
AFFILNOSTU	sufflation
AFFIMRSTTU	Tartuffism
AFFLLORUUV	flavourful
AFFPPRSTUY	puff pastry
AFGGGILNNU	unflagging
AFGGIIMNNY	magnifying
AFGGIINRTY	gratifying
AFGGILMNOR	gangliform
AFGGLLNSUU	fungus-gall
AFGHHILLST	flashlight
AFGHHILPTT	flight path
AFGHIIINRR	hiring fair
AFGHIILRTY	fairy light
AFGHIINNTY	if anything
AFGHIIRSTU	guitarfish
AFGHILLNPT	flight plan
AFGHILNPSU	upflashing
AFGHIORTWY	right of way
	right-of-way
AFGHLLSTUY	ghastfully
AFGHNOOSTU	Nothofagus
AFGIIKLMMN	film-making
AFGIILLNSY	sail-flying
AFGIILMNPY	amplifying
AFGIILNQUY	qualifying
AFGIILOSTU	flagitious
AFGIIMNOTU	fumigation
AFGIINORTU	figuration
AFGIINOTTU	fugitation
AFGIINSSTY	satisfying
AFGIKKNORU	King Farouk
AFGIKMNORS	king-of-arms
AFGILLNOTU	falling-out
AFGILLNOTY	floatingly
AFGILLNSST	flint glass
AFGILNORUV	flavouring
AFGIMNORTT	formatting
AFGIMORTUY	fumigatory
AFGINNOOPS	poison-fang
AFGIRRSTUU	fruit sugar
AFHHLLORUY	half-hourly
AFHIILMOPR	phialiform
AFHIILMTTU	multi-faith
AFHIINOSST	fashionist
AFHILLMORT	thalliform
AFHILLMOYY	Holy Family
AFHILNOPST	flashpoint
AFHILNPSSY	Spanish fly
AFHIOORTTY	tooth fairy
AFHIOPRRST	parrot-fish
AFHKLLNTUY	thankfully
AFHKLNNTUU	unthankful
AFHLLORSTY	sally forth
AFHLLORSUY	royal flush
AFHLLORTTU	throat-full
AFHLLORTUW	fourth wall
AFHLLRTUWY	wrathfully
AFIIINNNTT	infinitant
AFIIINNRTY	infinitary
AFIIKLORTT	forkit-tail
AFIILLLNUY	unfilially
AFIILLRRTY	fritillary
AFIILLSTUV	fluvialist
AFIILMNOSW	Wolfianism
AFIILNNOST	fontinalis
AFIILNORSU	infusorial
AFIILNORTT	filtration
	flirtation
AFIILRSUVV	flavivirus
AFIIMORSTV	favoritism
AFIINNORSU	infusorian
AFIINSSTTU	fustianist
AFIIORRSTU	trifarious
AFIJKOPRRT	JFK Airport
AFIKLLMNOS	man of skill
AFILLLLTYY	tilly-fally
AFILLMNORY	informally
AFILLMORTU	multiflora
AFILLMRSTU	small fruit
AFILLNOPRU	plain flour
AFILLNPPTY	flippantly
AFILLOSSUX	Sioux Falls
AFILMNOSUY	infamously
AFILMSSUUY	Yusuf Islam
AFILNORUXY	fluxionary
AFILNRSTZZ	Franz Liszt
AFILOPRSTY	filo pastry
AFIMMOQRSU	squamiform
AFIMMORTUU	fumatorium
AFIMNOORSU	foraminous
AFIMNRSTUU	rumfustian
AFIMOOPRRV	vaporiform
AFIMORRSTT	stratiform
AFIORRSTYY	fairy story
AFLLLNUUWY	unlawfully
AFLLMNNUUY	unmanfully
AFLLMNOUWY	womanfully
AFLLNOORSU	on all fours
AFLLNRTUUY	unartfully
AFLMOORRTU	formulator
AFLOOOPRSW	sloop-of-war
AFLOOOPRTT	foot-patrol
AGGGGIINZZ	zigzagging
AGGGIIINNV	gaingiving
AGGGILNNTU	gatling gun
AGGGILNRST	straggling
AGGGINNNRU	running gag
AGGHHOPRRY	hygrograph
AGGHIILLMN	Gillingham
AGGHIINNRS	garnishing
AGGHILLNUY	laughingly
AGGHILNNSY	gnashingly
AGGHILNNUW	whaling-gun
AGGHILNORT	light-organ
AGGHILNSST	night-glass
AGGHIORSTT	go straight
AGGHLOOPRY	graphology
	logography
AGGIIIMNNS	imaginings
AGGIIIMNTT	mitigating
AGGIILLNNS	signalling
AGGIILMMNR	gimmal ring
AGGIILMNSV	almsgiving
AGGIILNNTU	agglutinin
AGGIIMNNNS	singing-man
AGGIJLLMNU	malling jug
AGGILLNNSY	slangingly
AGGILLNNTY	tanglingly
AGGILLNORR	rag-rolling
AGGILLNOTY	gloatingly
AGGILLOOST	algologist
AGGILMORSY	gargoylism
AGGILNNORY	groaningly
AGGILNNTWY	twangingly

Words marked ✧ can also be spelled with one or more capital letters

AGGILNPRSY graspingly
AGGILOORST agrologist
AGGINNSSWW swing-swang
AGGINORRTT garrotting
AGGINOSSTU outgassing
AGGLNOOORZ Gorgonzola
AGGLOORSTY gastrology
AGGMOSSTUY mystagogus
AGGNORRSSW grass-grown
AGGNORSSTU sugar tongs
AGHHHOTTUW what though
AGHHIIILTT hightail it
AGHHIKNRST night shark
AGHHILOPRT lithograph
AGHHIOPPPY hippophagy
AGHHKORSST ghost shark
AGHHLOOPRY holography
AGHHNOOPPR phonograph
AGHHOOPPRT photograph
AGHHOOPRRT orthograph
AGHHOOPRRY horography
AGHHORTUWY throughway
AGHIILNORS Anglo-Irish
AGHIIMNNTT tithingman
AGHIINNRSV varnishing
AGHIINPRRS hairspring
AGHIINRTWW wainwright
AGHIKMNOST shotmaking
AGHIKMRTTU khitmutgar
AGHIKNRRTU King Arthur
AGHILLNOSW shallowing
AGHILLNOTY loathingly
tally-hoing
AGHILLOPTU plough-tail
AGHILMNSSY smashingly
AGHILNNTUY hauntingly
AGHILNPRST springhalt
AGHILNPSTY night-palsy
AGHILNRSTT stringhalt
AGHILOPPRY lipography
AGHILOPPSY gypsophila
AGHILPRTWY playwright
AGHILRSTTY straightly
AGHIMMOPRY mimography
AGHIMNNOTT Nottingham
AGHIMNOOPS siphonogam
AGHIMNPRTU upright-man
AGHINNOSTW Washington
AGHINNRTTU rat-hunting
AGHINOPTTW towing path
AGHINORSTT ghost train
AGHIOPPRRS spirograph
AGHIOPPSUX xiphopagus
AGHIOPSTTT a tight spot
AGHIPRSTTU straight up
AGHKMOPRYY kymography
AGHLMMOPRY lymphogram
AGHLMNOOYY Moholy-Nagy
AGHLMNOPTU thump along
AGHLNOOORT orthogonal
AGHLOPPRYY polygraphy
AGHLOPRSTY stylograph
AGHLOPRXYY xylography
AGHLORSTWY Galsworthy
AGHMMOOOSU homogamous
AGHMNOOPRY gramophony
monography
nomography
AGHMNOOPTY pathognomy
AGHMNOORTU mouth organ
AGHMOOOPSU omophagous
AGHMOOPRTY tomography
AGHNNOOPRU harpoon-gun
AGHNOOPRSY nosography
sonography
AGHNOORSTT goat's-thorn
AGHOOOPSUZ zoophagous
AGHOOPPRTY topography
AGHOOPRSST gastrosoph
AGHOPPRRYY pyrography
AGHOPPRTYY typography
AGIIIILNNT initialing
AGIIILMNNN mainlining
AGIIILNOTT litigation
AGIIILNSTV vitalising
AGIIILNTVZ vitalizing
AGIIIMNOTT mitigation
AGIIINNNRT in training
AGIIINORRT irrigation
AGIIINRRTT irritating
AGIIKKMNNR marking-ink
AGIIKNNNPR napkin ring
AGIILLMNSY misallying
AGIILLNNST installing
AGIILLNNUU unilingual
AGIILLNORY originally
AGIILLNRTU trilingual
AGIILLNRTY trailingly
AGIILLNRVY virginally
AGIILLNTVY vigilantly
AGIILLRTTY gratillity
AGIILNNORU unoriginal
AGIILNPRST springtail
AGIILNPRSY aspiringly
praisingly
AGIILNRSTY laryngitis
AGIILNSSTV vital signs
AGIILOOSTX axiologist
AGIIMMOSST misogamist
AGIIMMSSTT stigmatism
AGIIMNNPRS mainspring
AGIIMNORSU migrainous
AGIIMNOSSS Miss Saigon
AGIIMNSSUV vaginismus
AGIIMORTTY mitigatory
AGIIMSSTTT stigmatist
AGIINNNNPS inspanning
AGIINNNTTU untainting
AGIINNOORT ignoration
AGIINNORTV invigorant
AGIINNPRSU unaspiring
AGIINNRTTU intriguant
AGIINNSSTU sustaining
AGIINNSTUY sanguinity
AGIINOORRT originator
AGIINOPRRR rip-roaring
AGIINORSTT instigator
AGIINORSUV viraginous
AGIINPPRSW ripping-saw
AGIKKLNRSY skylarking
AGIKLMNNOS king salmon
AGIKLMNOOT toolmaking
AGIKLNNPRY prankingly
AGIKLNNPSY spankingly
AGIKLNOPRT parking lot
AGIKLNORST skirt along
AGIKMMORXY Maxim Gorky
AGIKMNNOOR moonraking
AGIKMNNORW working man
AGIKMNNOTU Kuomintang
AGIKMNNRTU marking-nut
AGILLLNRUY alluringly
AGILLLNRYY rallyingly
AGILLNNRSY snarlingly
AGILLNNSTY slantingly
AGILLNOPRT patrolling
AGILLNORTY trigonally
AGILLNRSUY singularly
AGILLNTTTY tattlingly
AGILLOOSSS isoglossal
AGILLOOSTT isoglottal
AGILLOOTWW goat-willow
AGILMNOPTU go platinum
AGILMNRSTY smartingly
AGILMNRTUU Triangulum
AGILMNSSUY assumingly
AGILMOOSTT atmologist
AGILMOOSTU gliomatous
AGILMOOSTY Mayologist
AGILMOPSTY polygamist
AGILNNNOPY non-playing
AGILNNNOYY annoyingly
AGILNNOPTY poignantly
AGILNNOPYY polygynian
AGILNNORTY ignorantly
AGILNNOSUU lanuginous
AGILNNPPSY snappingly
AGILNNTTUY tauntingly
AGILNNTUVY vauntingly
AGILNOOSTU antilogous
AGILNOPSST gloss paint
AGILNORTYY gyniolatry
AGILNOTUYY Young Italy
AGILNPRSST salt spring
AGILNRSTTY startingly
AGILOORSTY aristology
AGILORSSST glossarist
AGIMMNNORY May-morning
AGIMMNOOST monogamist
AGIMMNOSSU Simon Magus
AGIMMNSSUY gymnasiums
AGIMNNNNRU Running Man
AGIMNNNOOY monogynian

AGIMNNSSUU	unassuming
AGIMNOOPRU	amino group
AGIMNOORST	agronomist
AGIMNOOSST	not go amiss
AGIMNOPRSU	sporangium
AGIMOPRRST	stripogram
AGINNOOPRT	organ-point
AGINNOPTTU	at gunpoint
AGINNOPTTY	tantony pig
AGINNORRTW	Warrington
AGINNPPSUW	swan-upping
AGINNPRSUW	pruning saw
AGINNRSTUW	turning-saw
AGINOOOPRS	sporogonia
AGINOOPRTT	potato ring
AGINOORSUV	voraginous
AGINORRRST	Ringo Starr
AGINORSTTU	Titus Groan
AGINORSTZZ	strangozzi
AGINPRSSSU	surpassing
AGINSTYYYZ	antisyzygy
AGIORSTTUU	gratuitous
AGJLLLNOOY	jolly along
AGKLORSSSW	glassworks
AGKNNNORTY	granny knot
AGKNRSTYYZ	Kyrgyzstan
AGLLLLOPPU	Gallup poll
AGLLLOOPRY	pyrogallol
AGLLNOOPYY	palynology
AGLLRTTUUY	gutturally
AGLMNNOOTU	Mount Logan
AGLMOOOPTY	potamology
AGLMOOOSTY	somatology
AGLMOOOSUY	oogamously
AGLMOOPSUY	polygamous
AGLMOPPRUU	propagulum
AGLMORSSST	storm glass
AGLNOORSUU	languorous
AGLOOOSTUU	autologous
AGLOOPPRYY	papyrology
AGLORTTUUZ	Turgut Ozal
AGLSSTUUUU	Augustulus
AGMMNOOOSU	monogamous
AGMMNOPSUU	magnum opus
AGMNNOORWW	woman-grown
AGMNOORSTY	gastronomy
AGMOORSTTY	gastrotomy
AGMORRSTUU	surrogatum
AGNOPRUWWY	wrong way up
AGOORRSSST	grass-roots
AHHILLWWWY	whillywhaw
AHHILMOPTY	philomathy
AHHILOORTU	Holothuria
AHHILOPSTY	lithophysa
AHHIMNOPRY	rhinophyma
AHHIMNOPST	phantomish
AHHIMNOSTY	Mishnayoth
AHHIMNPTUY	hypanthium
AHHIOOPRRZ	Rhizophora
AHHIOPRSTU	authorship
AHHIPRSTTW	thwartship
AHHISSWWYY	wishy-washy
AHHLLMOOTY	homothally
AHHLLOOOPT	holophotal
AHHLMNNOTU	Holman Hunt
AHHMORRSTW	Harmsworth
AHIIIJKNRS	jinrikisha
AHIIILNPPP	Philippian
	philippina
AHIIILNPST	Philistian
AHIIIMMPSX	amphimixis
AHIIJKMNSW	Jim Hawkins
AHIIKMNRSS	Krishnaism
AHIILLNOPS	nail polish
AHIILMNORS	Sir Ian Holm
AHIILMORTU	humiliator
AHIILOOPPT	topophilia
AHIILPRSST	split hairs
AHIIMNNOTU	inhumation
AHIIMNNTUY	inhumanity
AHIIMNORSW	Irishwoman
AHIIMPSTTT	Patti Smith
AHIIRSSTTW	shirtwaist
AHIJKNNORW	John Kirwan
AHIJLLNOSW	John Wallis
AHIJMNNORT	John Martin
AHIJMORUUY	jumhouriya
AHIJNNNOOS	Johnsonian
AHIKKMNRSS	skrimshank
AHIKKSTUUY	Kitakyushu
AHIKLMSTWY	malt whisky
AHIKLPRSSY	sparkishly
AHIKMORSTY	matryoshki
AHIKNPRRSW	shrink-wrap
AHIKNPSSTU	Skupshtina
AHILLMQSUY	qualmishly
AHILLOPRTY	Phyllotria
AHILLORTTY	litholatry
AHILMMOPPS	psammophil
AHILMMORSU	humoralism
AHILMNNOOR	monorhinal
AHILMNOPYY	Polyhymnia
AHILMNOSWY	womanishly
AHILMORSTU	humoralist
AHILMPSSYY	symphysial
AHILNOORTZ	horizontal
AHILNOPSTU	sulphation
AHILNPPSSY	snappishly
AHILNPSSTU	sultanship
AHILOOPRTY	ophiolatry
AHIMNOOOSU	homoousian
AHIMNOORRU	honorarium
AHIMNOORSU	harmonious
AHIMNOPPSS	pansophism
AHIMNOPRST	matronship
AHIMNOPRTY	Amphitryon
AHIMNORTTU	Mount Thira
AHIMNPRTTU	triumphant
AHIMNPSTYY	in sympathy
AHIMORSTUU	haustorium
AHIMPPPRSU	parish pump
	parish-pump
AHINNNOOSU	Union Shona
AHINNOOPRT	Trophonian
AHINNOPRRY	Pyrrhonian
AHINOPPSST	pansophist
AHINOPRSTY	notaryship
AHINOPRSUX	xiphosuran
AHINPRSTTU	truantship
AHIOOPSSTZ	zoothapsis
AHIOOPSTTX	phototaxis
AHIOPPRSST	pastorship
AHIOPSSSTY	hypostasis
AHJKMNSSUY	J K Huysmans
AHJLNOORTY	John Taylor
AHJMNNOOSY	Amy Johnson
AHJMNNORTY	John Martyn
AHKKMOORRT	Mark Rothko
AHKLLOOPSU	All Shook Up
AHKLMOOSTT	smooth-talk
AHKLMOPRYY	karyolymph
AHKLOOOSTU	akolouthos
AHKMNNSTUU	Knut Hamsun
AHKMOOSTTU	husk-tomato
AHLLLLNOOW	allhollown
AHLLMMOSTU	smallmouth
AHLLMORSSU	small hours
AHLLOPRSST	sports hall
AHLLOPRSTU	prothallus
AHLLOPTXYY	phyllotaxy
AHLMMOOPSY	homoplasmy
AHLMNNORTU	lunar month
AHLMNOORST	solar month
AHLMOPPRUY	Paul Morphy
AHLMOPSSTY	Stymphalos
AHLMPRSUWY	Murphy's law
AHLNOOPRRT	north polar
AHLNOPSTUY	polyanthus
AHLOOPRSTU	south polar
AHLORRSTTU	ultrashort
AHMNNOORSU	honours-man
AHMNNOOSTU	Anthonomus
AHMNOOPRTU	protohuman
AHMNPSTUYY	unsympathy
AHMOOPRTYY	amyotrophy
AHMOOSSTTY	stay shtoom
AHMOPRSTTU	mouthparts
AHNNOSSTUY	synanthous
AHNNOSTTWY	shantytown
AHNOOPRRXY	oropharynx
AHNOOPRTYZ	zoanthropy
AHNOOPSTTY	nostopathy
	photonasty
AHNOOPTTUY	tautophony
AHNOPPRTTY	tryptophan
AHOOPPRRST	saprotroph
AHOOPPRTTY	protopathy
	Protophyta
AHOOPRRTXY	orthopraxy
AHOOPRTTUY	autotrophy
AHOORRTTTW	throatwort
AHPRSSTTTU	thrust past
AIIIILMNST	initialism

AIIIINNOTT	initiation
AIIILLMNTU	illuminati✧
AIIILLMNTY	liminality
AIIILLMRTY	militarily
AIIILLPPST	papillitis
AIIILMMMNS	minimalism
AIIILMMNST	minimalist
AIIILMMRST	militarism
AIIILMNOSS	moniliasis
AIIILMNOTT	limitation
AIIILMRSTT	militarist
AIIILMRSTV	trivialism
AIIILMRSTY	similarity
AIIILNOPTX	pixilation
AIIILORSTV	visitorial
AIIILRTTVY	triviality
AIIIMNNOTT	intimation
AIIIMNOPSS	pianissimo
AIIIMPRSVV	viviparism
AIIINNOOST	ionisation
AIIINNOOTZ	ionization
AIIINNOTTV	invitation
AIIINORRTT	irritation
AIIINORTTT	tritiation
AIIINORTTY	initiatory
AIIINOSTTV	visitation✧
AIIINOTTTV	titivation
AIIIPRSSTY	pityriasis
AIIIPRTVVY	viviparity
AIIJJLLMSW	J J Williams
AIIKLNOOSS	kaolinosis
AIILLLNOSU	illusional
AIILLMNNTU	illuminant
AIILLMNORY	millionary
AIILLMNTTY	militantly
AIILLNOOTV	volitional
AIILLNOSUV	villainous
AIILLNOSVY	visionally
AIILLNOTUV	outvillain
AIILLOORTV	volitorial
AIILLORSTY	solitarily
AIILLORTTT	titillator
AIILLOSSTT	solstitial
AIILLOTTVY	volatility
AIILLPRSTY	pistillary
AIILLSTUVV	valvulitis
AIILMMMORS	immoralism
AIILMMNNOS	nominalism
AIILMMNOOT	immolation
AIILMMNRSU	luminarism
AIILMMORST	immoralist
AIILMMORTY	immorality
AIILMNNOST	nominalist
AIILMNNOTU	lumination
AIILMNOORT	monitorial
AIILMNOSTU	simulation
AIILMNOTTU	mutilation
AIILMNRSSU	insularism
AIILMNRSTU	luminarist
AIILMNRTUY	unmilitary
AIILMNTTUY	utility man
AIILMOPTTY	optimality
AIILMORSTV	Voltairism
AIILMPPRST	spirit lamp
AIILMRRTUV	triumviral
AIILMRSTUV	virtualism
AIILNNNOTU	Latin Union
AIILNNOOST	insolation
AIILNNOSTU	insulation
AIILNOOPPT	oppilation
AIILNOOPST	positional
	spoliation
AIILNOOTTV	volitation
AIILNPTTUY	nuptiality
AIILNRSSUY	urinalysis
AIILNRSTUY	insularity
AIILORSSTU	sailor suit
AIILQRSTUY	squirality
AIILRSTTUV	virtualist
AIILRTTTUY	titularity
AIILRTTUVY	virtuality
AIIMMNNOTU	ammunition
AIIMMPRRTU	imprimatur
AIIMMRTTUY	immaturity
AIIMNNNOOT	nomination
AIIMNNOORS	Morisonian
AIIMNNORTU	rumination
AIIMNNOSTU	Mount Sinai
AIIMNNRSTT	ministrant
AIIMNOOTTV	motivation
AIIMNOPRTV	provitamin
AIIMNOPRTY	omniparity
AIIMNOPSTU	utopianism
AIIMNOPTTU	imputation
AIIMNORSSY	missionary
AIIMNPRSTU	puritanism✧
AIIMNPSSTU	impuissant
AIIMNPSTTY	tympanitis
AIIMNQRSSU	sinarquism✧
AIIMNRSSSU	Russianism
AIIMOPRSTT	patriotism
AIIMORRSTT	traitorism
AIIMOSSTTT	stomatitis
AIIMPRRSTT	tripartism
AIINNNOOTT	intonation
AIINNNOOTV	innovation
AIINNOORRT	iron ration
AIINNOPSTT	snap into it
AIINNOPSTU	supination
AIINNORSTT	transition
AIINNORSTU	insinuator
AIINNOSSTX	Six Nations
AIINNRSSTT	St Trinian's
AIINNRSTTU	in transitu
AIINNTTUVY	vanity unit
AIINOOPPST	apposition
AIINOPRRST	inspirator
AIINOPSSST	Passionist
AIINORTTUY	tuitionary
AIINORTTVY	invitatory
AIINQRSSTU	sinarquist
AIINQRSTUU	Tarquinius
AIINRSSSTU	Russianist
AIIOPRSUVV	viviparous
AIIPPRSSTU	Aristippus
AIIPRSTTVY	varitypist
AIJLMNORSU	journalism
AIJLNORSTU	journalist
AIJMNOQRTU	quint major
AIKKRRSTWY	Kirsty Wark
AIKLLLOPTW	pillow talk
AIKLLNOWWY	Willy Wonka
AIKLMNNOPS	pink salmon
	salmon pink
	salmon-pink
AIKLNORVVY	Ivan Krylov
AIKLOPSTUV	Volapükist
AIKLORSSYY	karyolysis
AIKMMNORSS	Simon Marks
AIKMMORRRS	Mark Morris
AIKNNOPRSS	Parkinson's
AIKNOPRSTW	paintworks
AIKNRSSTVY	Stravinsky
AILLLLTVYY	tilly-vally
AILLLMNOWY	Willy Loman
AILLMMORTY	immortally
AILLMNOOPY	polynomial
AILLMNPRST	small print
AILLMOOSTT	tomatillos
AILLMOPRTU	multipolar
AILLMOPRXY	proximally
AILLMOQRTU	malt liquor
AILLMQRTUZ	quartz-mill
AILLNNOOTY	notionally
AILLNNOSUY	unisonally
AILLNOOPRT	pollinator
	Trollopian
AILLNOOPTY	optionally
AILLNOOSTU	solutional
AILLNOPPTT	pilot-plant
AILLNORSTY	tonsillary
AILLNQRTUY	tranquilly
AILLOOPRRT	pillar-root
AILLOORRSY	sororially
AILLOQRSUW	liquor laws
AILLORSTTY	stillatory
AILLORTTUY	tutorially
AILMMNORTU	unimmortal
AILMNNOOOS	Solomonian
AILMNNOOPR	pronominal
AILMNNORSU	surnominal
AILMNNRTUY	ruminantly
AILMNOOPST	lampoonist
AILMNORTUY	unmorality
AILMOOPRRT	implorator
AILMOOPRST	prostomial
AILMOOPSTU	lipomatous
AILMOOSSUZ	Luis Somoza
AILMORSTTU	stimulator
AILMORSTUY	simulatory
AILMOSSSTY	asystolism
AILMPRTTUY	multiparty
AILNNOOPSS	sponsional

Words marked ✧ can also be spelled with one or more capital letters

AILNNQRTUU untranquil
AILNOOOPST piano stool
AILNOOPPTU population
AILNOOPRSS sponsorial
AILNOOTTUV volutation
AILNORSTTU lustration
AILNOSTTUU ustulation
AILNPRSSTU plus strain
AILNPSSTUY puissantly
AILOOPRSSU Paulo Rossi
AILOOPRSTY spoliatory
AILOPPRTUY popularity
AILOPRSTTU stipulator
AIMMNORSTU stramonium
AIMMOORRTU moratorium
AIMMTTXXYY mixty-maxty
AIMNOOPRSU omniparous
AIMNOORSTY somniatory
AIMNOOSTTU autonomist
AIMNOOSTTX taxonomist
AIMNOPSSTU assumption✧
AIMNORRSTU intra muros
AIMNRSTTUU nasturtium✧
AIMOOORTVY ovariotomy
AIMOPRSSTT prostatism
AIMOPSSSTY symposiast
AIMOQSSTUY squamosity
AINNOOPRSS sopraninos
AINNOOPRTT antiproton
AINNOORTVY innovatory
AINNOPRSTT strapontin
AINOOOPPRT pornotopia
AINOOPPSTW swap option
AINOOPPTTU up to a point
AINOOPRSTY anisotropy
AINOOPSSTU outpassion
AINOORRSUV ranivorous
AINOOSTTTU outstation
AINOPRSTTU stupration
AINOPRSTUU usurpation
AINOPRTTTY potty-train
AINOQSTTUU in statu quo
AINORRSSTT transistor
AINORRSTTY transitory
AINORSTTUU suturation
AINPRSTUUV pursuivant
AIOOPRRSUU uproarious
AIOOPRSTVY vaporosity
AIOOQSTTUU quotatious
AIOORRSTTU traitorous
AIOPPPRSUU pupiparous
AIOPPRRSTU air support
AIOPRRSUVV Parvo virus
parvovirus
AIORRRTTTU triturator
AKKKLLNUUX Ku Klux Klan
AKLLMMOSUW musk-mallow
AKLNOOPPSY look snappy
AKLOPRRSUY sky parlour
AKMNOORRUY on your mark
AKMNORTTUW tutworkman

ALLLLMNORU Ramón Llull
ALLMMORRSU Summar Roll
ALLMNOOSUY allonymous
ALLMOOOPRW palolo worm
ALLNOOOSTZ stanozolol
ALLOOPPRRT poll-parrot
ALLOORSUVY valorously
ALLOPRSTYY polystylar
ALLOPRTTUY plutolatry
ALMMNSSSUU Mussulmans
ALMMOOPTTU plum tomato
ALMNOORSTY monostylar
ALMOOPPRST protoplasm
ALMOPPSSUY play possum
ALMOPSTTUU postulatum
ALMRTTUUUY tumultuary
ALNOOOPRST portolanos
ALNPRSTUUY pursuantly
ALOOORSTUZ zoolatrous
ALOOPPRSTT protoplast
ALOOPPRTTY prototypal
ALOOPRSTTU postulator
ALOOPRSUVY vaporously
ALOPRTUUVY voluptuary
ALORSSTTUU Lotus Sutra
AMMNNOOTUY Mount Mayon
AMMOOSTUXY myxomatous
AMNNOOSTUY antonymous
AMNNOOSTWW townswoman
AMNNOSTTUW stuntwoman
AMNOOOSTUU autonomous
AMNOOPRSUY paronymous
AMOORSSTTU stromatous
AMOPPRRTUY promptuary
AMOPPRSTTU postpartum
post-partum
ANNOOPRSST transposon
ANOOOPRSTZ protozoans
AOOOPPRSSU aposporous
AOOOPPRSTU apotropous
AOOPRRRSTZ razor-strop
AOORRSSTUU Torosaurus
AOPRRSTUUY usurpatory

B

BBBCEEILRS bescribble
BBBCEEORWY cobwebbery
BBBCJKLOUY bubbly-jock
BBBDEEINOR beribboned
BBBEEIINRW winebibber
BBBEELORUV bubble over
BBBEHHLOSU hobble-bush
BBBEILNORU blue ribbon
blue-ribbon
BBBEJNOOSY Bobby Jones
BBBELORSTU bubble sort
BBBEMOOORY Bobby Moore
BBBENORSUY Bobby Unser
BBBEOORSXY bobbysoxer
BBBGHIJNOO hobjobbing
BBBGHINNOO hobnobbing

BBBGIIKNOS skibobbing
BBBHRSSUUY subshrubby
BBBLLOOWWY blow-by-blow
BBCCEEKOOY cockeye bob
BBCDEGILRU bridge club
BBCDEIKORR rock-ribbed
BBCDEINOOU cuboid bone
BBCDEIRSSU subscribed
BBCDELORRU cold rubber
BBCEEHOPRY cyberphobe
BBCEEKNRRU rubberneck
BBCEELNOOU bubonocele
BBCEHINSSU chubbiness
BBCEIKRSUU Rubik's Cube®
BBCEIRRSSU subscriber
BBCGIIINRT crib-biting
BBCGIILNRS scribbling
BBCGINORSY Bing Crosby
BBCHMRRSUU crumb-brush
BBCIILLLPU public bill
BBDDDDUUYY buddy-buddy
BBDDDEENOT bonded debt
BBDDEILNOU double bind
BBDDELMNOU dumb blonde
BBDDELNOOU double bond
BBDDELOOUY body double
BBDDGIJNOO odd-jobbing
BBDEEFLSTU stubble-fed
BBDEEGIILL big-bellied
BBDEEHIINS Bishen Bedi
BBDEEIMORV dive-bomber
BBDEEINORW ribbon-weed
BBDEEINSWY Sidney Webb
BBDEELNOTU bent double
BBDEGLNOOW gobble down
BBDEGMOORU drogue bomb
BBDEHNRSUU unshrubbed
BBDEIKNOOR bookbinder
BBDEILLLOU double bill
BBDEILLNOU I'll be bound
BBDEILORTT Lord Tebbit
BBDEIMNORT bond-timber
BBDEIRRTTU butter-bird
BBDEKLOOOU double-book
BBDELOPSUU pseudobulb
BBDHIILLRY hybrid bill
BBDHIIOPRS bishop-bird
BBEEEFGRRU beefburger
BBEEEFIRSW beef-brewis
BBEEEHNNRT herb bennet
BBEEEIRRTT bitter beer
BBEEELLSUV bull-beeves
BBEEELORTT beer bottle
BBEEERRRTU rubber tree
BBEEHLLORU lubber hole
BBEEHORRRT herb Robert
BBEEHORRST The Robbers
BBEEIKLLRU lubberlike
BBEEILLNRU Berlin blue
lubber line
BBEEISSTTV St Tibb's Eve

BBEELLOTTU bluebottle
BBEELMORTT letter bomb
BBEELMOSSV bomb-vessel
BBEELNNOTU blue-bonnet
BBEEMMNNTU benumbment
BBEFLMOOTU bumble-foot
BBEGHIORRT Big Brother
BBEGIILOPY bibliopegy
BBEGILNRSU slubbering
BBEGINRSSU grubbiness
BBEGLOOSSU subglobose
BBEHHILOST shibboleth
BBEHHOORSY hobby-horse
BBEHJNNOOW John Benbow
BBEHMOOOPR ombrophobe
BBEIILLOOP bibliopole
BBEIIORRTU urbi et orbi
BBEIKLLORR bill-broker
BBEIKLMOOO bookmobile
BBEIKNNOSS knobbiness
BBEILLNOSY Billy Bones
BBEILNOSSW wobbliness
BBEILNOSUY boys in blue
BBEINOORWX box Brownie®
BBEINSSSTU stubbiness
BBEIOOPRYZ booby prize
BBEKLORRUW rubblework
BBEKNORSTU bonkbuster
BBELMMSTUU stumblebum
BBELMOOPRT petrol bomb
BBELOOPRTW pot-wobbler
BBELOORRTT Robert Bolt
BBEMNRRTUU burnt umber
BBEMOORRRU rubber room
rubber-room
BBEMPRTTUU butter-bump
BBENORTTWY Brown Betty
BBEOORRRTU root rubber
BBFGILMNOY flying bomb
BBFHIINORS ribbonfish
BBFIMNOOSU fusion bomb
BBGGIILLNN bling bling
BBGHIINRSU rubbishing
BBGHILLNOY hobblingly
BBGHIMNOTU thingumbob
BBGIILLNNY nibblingly
BBGIILLOOY bibliology
BBGIKLNUUY bulk buying
BBGILNNSUY snubbingly
BBHIIILLOP bibliophil
BBHILNOSSY snobbishly
BBHJLNOOWY John Bowlby
BBHNOSTTUU buttonbush
BBIIIIMNOT imbibition
BBIIKKNTUZ kibbutznik
BBIILLOOPY bibliopoly
BBIIMNORST Tim Robbins
BBILLNORSY Bill Bryson
BBILLOSUUY bibulously
BBILMOOOTT bombolotti
BBIMNOORRW ribbon worm
BBIMNOORSU Bourbonism
BBIMNOOSUX omnibus box
BBINOORSTU Bourbonist
BBJMMMOOUU mumbo-
jumbo✧
BBLNORSTUY stubbornly
BBOOOSSSTY bossyboots
BCCDEEEMNU decumbence
BCCDEEILOT decoctible
BCCDEEJOOT object code
BCCDEEMNUY decumbency
BCCDEILNOU conducible
BCCDHIIPSY psychic bid
BCCEEEILLR cerebellic
BCCEEEMNRU recumbence
BCCEEENPSU pubescence
BCCEEGIINS big science
BCCEEIINOS bioscience
BCCEEIMRRY cybercrime
BCCEEIMRTU cubic metre
BCCEEINRTY cybernetic
BCCEEKLRSY Krebs cycle
BCCEEMNRUY recumbency
BCCEHIILOS libecchios
BCCEHIIMRU cherubimic
BCCEHKRRUY Chuck Berry
BCCEHNORSS crossbench
BCCEIIIMSS cicisbeism
BCCEIINOOT coenobitic
BCCEIINRTU cubic nitre
BCCEILORSU scrobicule
BCCEILORTU Bertolucci
BCCEIMNNUY incumbency
BCCEJKLOUY Jockey Club
BCCEKMOOPT pocket-comb
BCCESSSUUU succubuses
BCCHHIINNY inch by inch
BCCHIINORT bronchitic
BCCHLMORTU crumbcloth
BCCIIRSTUU subcircuit
BCCLNOOTTU Cotton Club
BCDDEEGIKR deck-bridge
BCDDEEILTU deductible
BCDDEIKLLU duck-billed
BCDDHIISTU Buddhistic
BCDEEEEHMR bêche-de-mer
BCDEEEFILT defectible
BCDEEEFIMN minced beef
BCDEEEFNOR corned beef
BCDEEEHNRU unbreeched
BCDEEEIINT benedicite✧
BCDEEEILPT deceptible
BCDEEEILTT detectible
BCDEEEIRRS redescribe
BCDEEEKLPS bespeckled
BCDEEELMRY Decemberly
BCDEEHLNNU unblenched
BCDEEHLOST bedclothes
BCDEEHOPRS beech-drops
BCDEEHORUU debouchure
BCDEEIILNR incredible
BCDEEIIPRR bride price
BCDEEILLUX excludible
BCDEEILNNZ zinc blende
BCDEEILNRU uncredible
BCDEEIMRST Decembrist
BCDEEINOPR probenecid
BCDEEINSSU subsidence
BCDEEINSTU Benedictus
BCDEEKLLNU bull-necked
BCDEEKLRTU truckle bed
BCDEEMNORU code-number
BCDEEMNRUU uncumbered
BCDEEMOORS rose-combed
BCDEENOSST second best
second-best
BCDEEORRSS crossbreed
BCDEFIIKLR brickfield
BCDEFLOOTU club-footed
BCDEHIILLR Bill Edrich
BCDEHILNOU double chin
BCDEHIRRRY bird-cherry
BCDEHLOORS school-bred
BCDEIILLNU includible
BCDEIILNRY incredibly
BCDEIILOOS obeliscoid
BCDEILOORR corrodible
BCDEILOORU bicoloured
BCDEILOPRU producible
BCDEIMNNOO income bond
BCDEINORTU counterbid
BCDEINSSUY subsidency
BCDEIRRRSU scrub rider
BCDEKLNOUW buckle down
BCDEKLOOOS closed book
BCDEKNOTUW bucket down
BCDEKORTTU butterdock
BCDELNOORU cordon bleu
BCDELNORSU Drones Club
BCDELORRUY cloudberry
BCDEMMNRUU cummerbund
BCDENORRWY Crown Derby
BCDENORSUU unobscured
BCDENRRSUU underscrub
BCDGIIOSTU dog biscuit
BCDHHIILRT childbirth
BCDHOOOPRU brood-pouch
BCDIIILOTY docibility
BCDIILMORU lumbricoid
BCDIIMMSUY cymbidiums
BCDIIOPRRT tropicbird
BCDIKKSTUU Dick Butkus
BCDILLOTUU cloud-built
BCDILOOSSU discobolus
BCDILORSTU locust bird
BCDINOSTUU subduction
BCDKLOOOST bloodstock
BCDKMRSTUU dumbstruck
BCDKORRUUW burrow-duck
BCDLNOOOTU blood count
BCDLOOORUY body colour
BCDLORSTUU cloudburst

BCDNORRSUU	scrub round
BCEEEEHLSU	blue cheese
BCEEEFFILT	effectible
BCEEEFINNT	beneficent
BCEEEFLLRT	treble clef
BCEEEFMOOR	come before
BCEEEGHINS	beseeching
BCEEEHLRSS	breechless
BCEEEIIKRT	riebeckite
BCEEEIJLRT	rejectible
BCEEEILLNU	ebullience
BCEEEILPRT	receptible
BCEEEIRSTU	erubescite
BCEEELLMRU	cerebellum
BCEEELLNRS	bell screen
BCEEELNRSU	blue screen
	blue-screen
BCEEENORRS	resorbence
BCEEENRSTU	erubescent
BCEEEPRRSU	spruce beer
BCEEFIINRT	tenebrific
BCEEFIKRTU	fire bucket
BCEEFIOPRS	fiberscope
	fibrescope
BCEEFORRTU	brute force
BCEEFPRSTU	subprefect
BCEEGHMOOU	gobemouche
BCEEGHNORS	Schoenberg
BCEEGIINOT	biogenetic
BCEEGINRSU	subgeneric
BCEEGLLLOT	goblet cell
BCEEGNNORR	Cronenberg
BCEEHHNNOT	on the bench
BCEEHIINPT	epibenthic
BCEEHIMPTU	thumbpiece
BCEEHIRTWY	bewitchery
BCEEHKLNOU	huckle-bone
BCEEHKLOSU	shoe buckle
BCEEHKOOQU	chequebook
BCEEHKORRY	chokeberry
BCEEHMNRSU	Übermensch
BCEEHMORUU	embouchure
BCEEHNOOPR	necrophobe
BCEEHNORRX	Bronx cheer
BCEEHNPRSS	bench press
BCEEHORRST	Borchester
BCEEHRSTTU	bruschette
BCEEIILPST	plebiscite
BCEEIILTYZ	Belize City
BCEEIIRRST	cerebritis
BCEEIJSTUV	subjective
BCEEIKLMNR	limberneck
BCEEILLMRU	Illecebrum
BCEEILLNPU	blue pencil
	blue-pencil
BCEEILLNUY	ebulliency
BCEEILLOOS	cellobiose
BCEEILMOST	comestible
BCEEILNORT	Colbertine
BCEEILNOTY	by-election
BCEEIMRTYY	by my certie

BCEEIPRRRS	prescriber
BCEEIPRRSY	spiceberry
BCEEIPSSSU	subspecies
BCEEJLOSST	objectless
BCEEKLLNNU	Kennel Club
BCEEKLNORV	nerve block
BCEEKLNOTT	bottleneck
BCEEKLORSW	skew-corbel
BCEEKLORTU	blue rocket
BCEELMRSSU	cumberless
BCEELNNRUY	Lenny Bruce
BCEELNOTTU	cuttle-bone
BCEELNQSUU	Queen's Club
BCEELNRTUU	turbulence
BCEELOPRST	corbel step
BCEEMMNRTU	cumberment
BCEEMMORSU	cumbersome
BCEEMOORTU	Umberto Eco
BCEEOOORRR	corroboree
BCEFFIKOOO	office-book
BCEFFINNOO	coffin bone
BCEFFIORSU	subofficer
BCEFHILLOX	Felix Bloch
BCEFHNNORT	front bench
	front-bench
BCEFIIMORR	microfibre
BCEFIIOPRT	fibre-optic
BCEFIJSTUY	subjectify
BCEFIKKLNO	knife block
BCEFILNORU	unforcible
BCEFILNOSU	confusible
BCEFKLSTUU	bucketfuls
BCEFLMORRU	Reform Club
BCEGHIINTW	bewitching
BCEGHIKNNS	King's Bench
BCEGHINRTU	butchering
BCEGIILNSU	subceiling
BCEGIILORR	corrigible
BCEGILLNOR	corbelling
BCEGILMNOY	becomingly
BCEGILOOOY	bioecology
BCEGIMNNOU	unbecoming
BCEGMORSSU	comburgess
BCEHHIIRTW	white birch
BCEHHNNOUY	honeybunch
BCEHIIIOTV	cohibitive
BCEHIIMOST	biochemist
BCEHIINSST	bitchiness
BCEHIIOPRS	biospheric
BCEHILNOOR	bronchiole
BCEHILOOPZ	zelophobic
BCEHILOPRY	hyperbolic
BCEHILOTTT	Tibet cloth
BCEHILSTUW	White's Club
BCEHINNSSU	bunchiness
BCEHINOOPX	xenophobic
BCEHINPRSU	subphrenic
BCEHKKOOST	sketch book
	sketchbook
BCEHKLNOOT	on the block
BCEHKLOORS	horse block

BCEHKLOOSU	blockhouse
BCEHKOORRT	Robert Koch
BCEHKOPSTU	bucket shop
BCEHLLLOOS	school bell
BCEHMRSTUW	thumbscrew
BCEHNORRTU	burnt ochre
BCEHOOOPST	Scotophobe
BCEHOOPRTU	Turcophobe
BCEIIILMMS	immiscible
BCEIIILMTY	imbecility
BCEIIILNNV	invincible✧
BCEIIKLLLS	sicklebill
BCEIIKLRRT	rib-tickler
BCEIILLOTT	Botticelli
BCEIILMMOS	embolismic
BCEIIMOQTU	coquimbite
BCEIIMORST	biometrics
BCEIINOOTX	xenobiotic
BCEIJNOSTU	subjection
BCEIKLOORT	bootlicker
BCEIKNRRRU	rick-burner
BCEIKOOTTY	tickety-boo
BCEILLMOOO	locomobile
BCEILMOORT	bolometric
BCEILMSSUU	blues music
BCEILNNSTU	tennis club
BCEILNORSU	Berlusconi
BCEILNPSSU	publicness
BCEILNRTUU	tuberculin
BCEILOORRS	corrosible
BCEIMOOPRR	microprobe
BCEIMOSTUV	combustive
BCEINNOSSU	bounciness
BCEINOPSTU	subception
BCEINORTTU	contribute
BCEINOSSTU	subsection
BCEIOPPRSY	presbyopic
BCEIOPRRRS	proscriber
BCEIORSSTT	obstetrics
BCEJKMPRUU	buck-jumper
BCEJLOOSTU	object-soul
BCEKKLNOUW	knuckle-bow
BCEKKOOOPT	pocketbook
BCEKLNRTUU	turnbuckle
BCEKLOOPRW	power block
BCEKLOORTW	tower block
BCEKLOPSTU	slop bucket
BCEKLORSTW	wrest block
BCEKOOORSU	coursebook
	sourcebook
BCEKORRTTU	rock butter
BCEKRSTTUU	rust bucket
BCELLNOTTU	button cell
BCELMOOORW	wool-comber
BCELMRTUUU	tuberculum
BCELNOOTTT	cotton belt✧
BCELNRTUUY	turbulency
BCELOORSSU	lob's course
BCELOPSTUU	suboctuple
BCELORSTTU	clotbuster
BCELRSTUUU	subculture

BCEMNOPRTU	procumbent
BCEMNOSSUV	Venus's comb
BCEMOORSSX	Scombresox
BCEMOOSSTT	Coombs test
BCENOOPTUX	pouncet-box
BCENOORSSS	crossbones
BCEOORRSSW	crossbower
BCEORRSTTU	obstructer
BCFIIMORRR	cribriform
BCFOSSSUUU	subfuscous
BCGHINNTUU	cub-hunting
BCGHINOOPY	gynophobic
BCGHORRTUU	burgh court
BCGHORTUUY	touch rugby
BCGIIKKNOX	kick boxing
BCGIKNPRSU	springbuck
BCHHIMOOOP	homophobic
BCHIIINOOT	cohibition
BCHIIMOOPR	biomorphic
BCHIINORST	bronchitis
BCHIIOPSSY	biophysics
BCHIKNNORY	Nick Hornby
BCHIMNOOOP	monophobic
BCHIMOORTT	thrombotic
BCHIOOPPRY	pyrophobic
BCHIORRSST	crossbirth
BCHKLOOOOS	school book
BCHNOOSTTU	cotton bush
BCIIILMMSY	immiscibly
BCIIILNNVY	invincibly
BCIIILORTT	trilobitic
BCIILNOPSY	psilocybin
BCIILORSUU	lubricious
BCIIOOPRST	probiotics
BCIKKORRSW	brickworks
BCIKLNOPTU	input block
BCIKMNOOTT	Nick Bottom
BCIKMOORST	broomstick
BCIKNOPTTU	pin-buttock
BCILNOOORT	biocontrol
BCILOOSTUU	tubicolous
BCIMNOOSTU	combustion
BCIMORRSTU	microburst
BCINOSSSTU	consubsist
BCIOPRSSTU	subtropics
BCKMOOORTT	rock bottom
	rock-bottom
BCKMOORUUZ	zumbooruck
BCKOORRTTU	rock turbot
BCLLNOOOTT	cotton boll
BCLMORSUUY	cumbrously
BCNOORRUWY	cony-burrow
BCNOORTUXY	country-box
BCOORRSTTU	obstructor
BDDDEEFNTU	funded debt
BDDDEEGINW	wedding bed
BDDDEEIIOW	wide-bodied
BDDDEEINTW	twin-bedded
BDDDEELOOR	red-blooded
BDDDEELOUY	double-dyed
BDDEEEILLS	Bill Deedes
BDDEEEILLV	bedevilled
BDDEEEILRW	bewildered
BDDEEELORU	double reed
BDDEEELOUY	double-eyed
BDDEEENRTU	debentured
BDDEEEOPRW	deep-browed
BDDEEGNTUU	unbudgeted
BDDEEIISSY	side by side
BDDEEIMMNU	unbedimmed
BDDEEIMNNR	mind-bender
BDDEEIMNOU	unembodied
BDDEEINNNU	unbedinned
BDDEEINRST	bestridden
BDDEEIORRV	overbidder
BDDEELMORU	dumbledore✧
BDDEELNRTU	trundle bed
BDDEELOOYY	bloody-eyed
BDDEENNRUU	unburdened
BDDEFILLLU	bull fiddle
BDDEFILLOU	full-bodied
BDDEFIOOST	soft-bodied
BDDEGILLOU	double-gild
BDDEHIIPPR	bird-hipped
BDDEHINOOR	behind-door
BDDEHLNOOR	bondholder
BDDEHLOOOT	hot-blooded
BDDEIIKNOR	ride bodkin
BDDEIIPRRS	bird-spider
BDDEIIRSUV	subdivider
BDDEIIRTTW	bird-witted
BDDEILMORW	middlebrow
BDDEILNOOU	unbloodied
BDDEILNRUU	underbuild
BDDEILOOSZ	blood-sized
BDDEIMNORU	dendrobium
BDDEIMOUVY	buddy movie
BDDEINNRUW	windburned
BDDELLORUW	dull-browed
BDDELMORRU	drumbledor
BDDELOOORU	double door
BDDFGIINOR	forbidding
BDDGIIINOR	indigo bird
BDDHLLOUYY	Buddy Holly
BDDHLNOOOU	bloodhound
BDDIIKNSSU	'sbuddikins
BDDIKLNNRU	blind-drunk
BDDLNOOOOR	blood donor
BDEEEEELTY	beetle-eyed
BDEEEEJLLW	bejewelled
BDEEEELRTW	beweltered
BDEEEEPRTY	Peter Debye
BDEEEFILNS	defensible
BDEEEFINRR	befriender
BDEEEFINTT	benefitted
BDEEEFITTW	beef-witted
BDEEEFLOTT	bottle-feed
BDEEEGHILR	Heidelberg
BDEEEGILRT	telebridge
BDEEEGINNS	gens de bien
BDEEEGINSW	beeswinged
BDEEEGLLOT	gold beetle
BDEEEGLNTU	dung-beetle
BDEEEGNNRU	Edenburgen
BDEEEHILTW	bleed white
BDEEEHLLNR	hellbender
BDEEEHMORW	home-brewed
BDEEEIILSV	disbelieve
BDEEEILLOS	Léo Delibes
BDEEEILNSS	edibleness
BDEEEILNTX	extendible
BDEEEILNUV	unbelieved
BDEEEILSTW	wildebeest
BDEEEIMRTT	embittered
BDEEEINNRZ	Benzedrine®
BDEEEINRRT	interbreed
BDEEEKLNOO	needle-book
BDEEEKNORR	broken reed
BDEEELLMOW	embowelled
BDEEELMNOR	emboldener
BDEEELMTUW	tumbleweed
BDEEELORTU	doubletree
BDEEELRRRY	elderberry
BDEEENRTTU	unbettered
BDEEEPRRSS	bedpresser
BDEEERRSVW	bed-swerver
BDEEFGGLOO	foolbegged
BDEEFGIINR	debriefing
BDEEFGNORU	ground beef
BDEEFIINST	disbenefit
BDEEFILNRS	self-binder
BDEEFILNSY	defensibly
BDEEFLOOOT	lobe-footed
BDEEFOORSS	bed of roses
BDEEFORRST	forest-bred
BDEEGHIRTT	get the bird
BDEEGIILST	digestible
BDEEGIINNR	inbreeding
BDEEGIIRRW	wire bridge
BDEEGIKRSW	skew bridge
BDEEGILLOR	gor-bellied
BDEEGILNUU	unbeguiled
BDEEGILRSS	bridgeless
BDEEGIMOSU	disembogue
BDEEGINRRT	regent-bird
BDEEGINTTW	bed-wetting
BDEEGIOPRR	rope bridge
BDEEGIORRV	overbridge
BDEEGIORST	Gobi Desert
BDEEGNNORY	bond energy
BDEEGNORSW	Swedenborg
BDEEGNOTXY	oxygen debt
BDEEGOORSU	bodegueros
BDEEHIIMNT	behind time
BDEEHILLLY	Delhi belly
BDEEHILLPS	bedellship
BDEEHIOPSW	bishopweed
BDEEHIRRSY	Derbyshire
BDEEHLNNOR	hornblende
BDEEHLNNOU	unbeholden
BDEEHNRSUW	Bundeswehr
BDEEHORRST	the Borders
BDEEIILLNU	ineludible

BDEEIILMOS	demobilise
BDEEIILMOZ	demobilize
BDEEIILNNR	inbred line
BDEEIILNNV	invendible
BDEEIILNRR	bridle-rein
BDEEIILRSW	bridle-wise
BDEEIILRTV	divertible
BDEEIILSTV	divestible
BDEEIINNOT	inobedient
BDEEILLNTU	tunbellied
BDEEILLOPT	pot-bellied
BDEEILLSUV	blue devils
BDEEILMOSU	semi-double
BDEEILMOSW	disembowel
BDEEILMOTU	double time
BDEEILMRSS	dissembler
BDEEILNNOS	disennoble
BDEEILNNUV	unvendible
BDEEILNORR	borderline
BDEEILNOTY	obediently
BDEEILNRSU	blue-rinsed
BDEEILORSW	bowdlerise
BDEEILORWZ	bowdlerize
BDEEIMMNOT	embodiment
BDEEIMNRTU	untimbered
BDEEIMOOSS	somebodies
BDEEIMORRS	besom-rider
BDEEIMORRY	embroidery
BDEEINNOTU	unobedient
BDEEIORRRT	Robert Reid
BDEEIORSSS	sobersides
BDEEIORVWY	review body
BDEEIPPPRR	bird-pepper
BDEEIRRSSU	redisburse
BDEEKNOOTY	ketone body
BDEEKNORRV	kerb-vendor
BDEELLNRUY	underbelly
BDEELMRRUU	blue murder
BDEELNNOPU	open bundle
BDEELNOSSU	doubleness
BDEELOORRT	Robert Dole
BDEELOPRUW	powder blue
BDEELORRSS	borderless
BDEELOSTTY	besottedly
BDEEMNNRUU	unnumbered
BDEEMNORSU	burdensome
BDEEMNSTUU	subduement
BDEENNNOTU	unbonneted
BDEENNORRU	underborne
BDEENOORTV	Denver boot
BDEENORRUV	overburden
BDEENORSUV	unobserved
BDEENOSTUW	unbestowed
BDEENRTTUU	unbuttered
BDEEOPRRSS	Beres drops
BDEEORSVWY	body swerve
	body-swerve
BDEFFIILSU	diffusible
BDEFFNOORW	browned off
BDEFGINOOR	foreboding
BDEFGIOORT	footbridge
BDEFGSSTUU	fussbudget
BDEFHLOORS	fresh blood
BDEFILLOST	soft-billed
BDEFILNORW	brownfield
BDEFILOOST	fieldboots
	soft-boiled
BDEFIOPRRY	bird of prey
BDEFKLLOOU	blood fluke
BDEFLOORUX	Oxford blue
BDEFNOORTW	bow-fronted
BDEGGGIINN	egg-binding
BDEGGLNOOO	boondoggle
BDEGHHIINR	highbinder
BDEGHIMOTU	bigmouthed
BDEGHINNOU	hinge-bound
BDEGHINNRU	Hindenburg
BDEGHINOPP	bed-hopping
BDEGHLNOUU	double-hung
BDEGHNORUU	underbough
BDEGIILLMR	limb-girdle
BDEGIILLNV	diving bell
BDEGIILNOU	indigo blue
BDEGIIMNTU	minibudget
	mini-budget
BDEGIINNRR	ring binder
BDEGIINORR	broidering
	Ironbridge
	riding robe
BDEGIKORRW	bridgework
BDEGILLNUW	winged bull
BDEGILLORR	bridge roll
BDEGILLORT	tollbridge
BDEGILNNOS	single bond
BDEGILNNOT	Bedlington
BDEGILNNRU	blundering
BDEGILNORU	bouldering
BDEGILNRRU	de-blurring
BDEGIMOORR	bridegroom
BDEGINNRRU	bring under
BDEGINOORY	gooneybird
BDEGINORTW	Bridgetown
BDEGINRRST	Strindberg
BDEGIOPRRT	Bridgeport
BDEGIORRTW	Trowbridge
BDEGLLLNOU	golden bull
BDEGLLNOOR	Gordon Bell
BDEGLMNTUU	tumbledung
BDEGLNORUU	blue ground
BDEGLOOPRU	blood purge
BDEHIILOST	hostile bid
BDEHIILPSU	bisulphide
BDEHIIMOOR	rhomboidei
BDEHIIRRSY	hybridiser
BDEHIIRRYZ	hybridizer
BDEHILLLOT	the Old Bill
BDEHIMNTUX	thumb index
	thumb-index
BDEHIMOORS	rhomboides
BDEHINNRUY	Hindenbury
BDEHINOPST	behind post
BDEHINRSTU	disburthen
BDEHIORRSW	whore's bird
BDEHIRSTTU	butter dish
BDEHKLOOOR	book-holder
BDEHLLNOSU	shellbound
BDEHLLOOOW	whole blood
BDEHLNOOUW	whole bound
BDEHLOOORS	blood horse
BDEHNOOSUU	housebound
BDEHNORTUX	thunderbox
BDEHNRRSUU	underbrush
	undershrub
BDEIIILNRV	biliverdin
BDEIIKRRST	bird strike
BDEIILLLNT	Bill Tilden
BDEIILLNOV	bidonville
BDEIILLNUY	ineludibly
BDEIILMORS	disembroil
BDEIILMRSS	missel-bird
BDEIIRSTTU	distribute
BDEIJNORSU	subjoinder
BDEIKLNOTU	double knit
	double-knit
BDEIKMRSTU	strike dumb
BDEIKNNORW	wind-broken
BDEILLMOTU	multilobed
BDEILLORWY	yellowbird
BDEILLOSSU	dissoluble
BDEILLOTUX	billet-doux
BDEILMNSUU	unsublimed
BDEILMOOSS	disselboom
BDEILMORSW	bowdlerism
BDEILNNOST	stone-blind
BDEILNNOTY	Enid Blyton
BDEILNOOSS	bloodiness
BDEILNOOWW	window-bole
BDEILNOPRT	triple bond
BDEILNORRY	orderly bin
BDEILORSTU	distrouble
BDEILOSSTU	blissed-out
BDEIMMNOUY	immune body
BDEIMMOOSS	disembosom
BDEIMNORSS	morbidness
BDEIMOORXY	oxy-bromide
BDEINOORSS	broodiness
BDEINRSSTU	turbidness
BDEIOORTTW	bitterwood
BDEKNNOORW	broken-down
BDEKOORRWY	bodyworker
BDELLNOPSU	spellbound
BDELLOORVY	overboldly
BDELLORRTU	Lord Butler
BDELLORTUY	troubledly
BDELMMNOUY	molybdenum
BDELMNOOOY	blood money
BDELMNOTUW	tumbledown
BDELNOOOST	bloodstone
BDELNORRTY	Robert Lynd
BDELNORTUU	untroubled
BDEMNNOOUY	money-bound
BDEMNOOTTU	unbottomed
BDEMOORRRS	smørrebrød

BDEMOORRSY dyer's-broom
BDENNOTTUU unbuttoned
BDENNRRTUU underburnt
BDENOOPRRU border upon
BDENOORRUW unborrowed
BDENOPRRUW powder burn
BDENOPTTUU buttoned up
buttoned-up
BDEOOPPPRY body-popper
BDFILOORST first blood
BDFLLOOUXY bloody flux
BDFLLOTUUY doubtfully
BDFLNOTUUU undoubtful
BDFNOORSTU frostbound
BDGHIILNNT night-blind
BDGHIILNST blindsight
BDGIIIKNRS bird-skiing
BDGIIKNNRY by-drinking
BDGIILLNNY blindingly
BDGIILNPUU upbuilding
BDGIINOORT riding boot
BDGIINORVX driving-box
BDGIINRSTU disturbing
BDGIKMNOSU subkingdom
BDGILLOOTU blood-guilt
BDGILNNNUU unbundling
BDGILNOORY broodingly
BDGILNORWY dry blowing
BDGILNOTUY doubtingly
BDGINNORRU bring round
BDGINNOTUU undoubting
BDGINOOORW wood-boring
BDGLNOOOUY young blood
BDGLOOOPRU blood group
BDGLRRSTUU Struldbrug
BDGMNOORSU bongo drums
BDGNOOORSW brown goods
BDHIIIINST disinhibit
BDHIILRRWY whirlybird
BDHILNOOOT in hot blood
BDHILOPRYY polyhybrid
BDHIMNOORY monohybrid
BDHINNOOPS in-bond shop
BDHIOSTTUU shut-out bid
BDHKOOORSU Doukhobors
BDHLNOOTTU buttonhold
BDHMNOSTUW thumbs down
thumbs-down
BDHNNOORTU northbound
BDHNOOSTUU southbound
BDHNORRSUU round brush
BDIIIILNST libidinist
BDIIILNOSU libidinous
BDIILOORST strobiloid
BDILLNPRUY purblindly
BDILMOOSSY molybdosis
BDILNOOOTW boil down to
BDILNRSTTU blind trust
BDIMNORTTU mutton bird
BDINNOORRU round robin✧
BDINNOOSTU Dobson unit
BDKNNOOORY donnybrook✧
BDMNOORSTU stormbound
BDNNOOTTUW button-down
BDNOOOTTUW buttonwood
BDNORSTUWY brown study
BEEEEEGHST The Bee Gees
BEEEEFLNSS feebleness
BEEEEGIKNP beekeeping
BEEEEGILLY eye-legible
BEEEEGINNR beer engine
BEEEEGLSTU Betelgeuse
BEEEEGNRRT Green Beret
BEEEEHLLRU blue heeler
BEEEEILNPT pine-beetle
BEEEELLNSW well-beseen
BEEEELORRT Robert E Lee
BEEEELORST rose beetle
BEEEELORTV rove beetle
BEEEELRSSZ breezeless
BEEEEMMRRR rememberer
BEEEERRSTT Beer Street
BEEEFILLRX reflexible
BEEEFILLSS beliefless
BEEEFILRRR referrible
BEEEFIMORT beforetime
BEEEFINRRV nerve fibre
BEEEFMMNNO bonne femme
BEEEFMRRUZ bumfreezer
BEEEFOORRT freebooter
BEEEGGINRR ginger beer
BEEEGGORST George Best
BEEEGGRRUV vegeburger
BEEEGHINNS shebeening
BEEEGHLOSU glebe-house
BEEEGIILLR re-eligible
BEEEGILNRS inselberge
BEEEGINRRW Weinberger
BEEEGMOORS ember-goose
BEEEGNOSTW go-betweens
BEEEGORRRT Grote Reber
BEEEHIILNW wheelie bin
BEEEHIPRST sheep-biter
BEEEHKNOTW bow the knee
BEEEHLLRST three bells
BEEEHLLRTW bellwether
BEEEIILMSV misbelieve
BEEEIILOSV I believe so
BEEEIKLLRR bierkeller
BEEEIKMNRT knee-timber
BEEEILNRUV unbeliever
BEEEILNSTX extensible
BEEEILRRSV reversible
BEEEILRRTV revertible
BEEEIMRRTT embitterer
timber tree
BEEEIMRSTT beetmister
BEEEINRRUV River Benue
BEEEINRSSZ breeziness
BEEEINTTWY betweenity
BEEEIRRSTW sweetbrier
BEEEKKOOPR bookkeeper
BEEEKLMSTU musk beetle
BEEELLPRSV vesper-bell
BEEELLRSST bestseller
BEEELLRTTU bullet-tree
BEEELLTUVV Blue Velvet
BEEELMMNST emblements
BEEELMMRSS memberless
BEEELMNOTU éboulement
BEEELNNOTV benevolent
BEEELNRSST trebleness
BEEELOPRRT Robert Peel
BEEELORTTT bottle tree
BEEEMMNRTU embruement
BEEEMNNRUV even number
BEEEMNRTTT betterment
BEEENNPRYZ benzpyrene
BEEENORSTT bonesetter
BEEENRRSTU subterrene
BEEENRSSTT betterness
BEEEOQSUXZ squeeze-box
BEEERRTTTU butter-tree
BEEFFHNOOT off the bone
BEEFFNORUZ buffer zone
BEEFGIINNT benefiting
BEEFGLNOOR before long
BEEFGRSTUU subterfuge
BEEFHORSTT for the best
BEEFIIKNOW bowie knife
BEEFIILLNX inflexible
BEEFIILNRR inferrible
BEEFIINRTV finite verb
BEEFILLMRU umbellifer
BEEFILMORS Froebelism
BEEFILNOST stifle bone
BEEFILRSTU subfertile
BEEFINNOTU bufotenine
BEEFIORRTT forebitter
BEEFIORSSU sebiferous
BEEFIRTTUW butter-wife
BEEFLLLORW bellflower
flower-bell
BEEGGGNORY George Byng
BEEGGHORSU George Bush
BEEGGIILLN negligible
BEEGGLOORT bootlegger
BEEGGNRRSU Regensburg
BEEGHIILLN Ghibelline
BEEGHIKNSU husking-bee
BEEGHIKRTW kerb weight
BEEGHILLLS sleigh bell
BEEGHILLST eight bells
BEEGHILNRT blethering
BEEGHMNRTU green thumb
BEEGHNOOPR negrophobe
BEEGHOOTTT get the boot
BEEGIIILLN ineligible
BEEGIILNRT Gilbertine
BEEGIILNST ingestible
BEEGIINOSS biogenesis
BEEGILLNRR bellringer
BEEGILMNOT obligement

BEEGILMNRS resembling
BEEGILNNNU Nibelungen
BEEGILNNSU Blue Ensign
BEEGINRTTV brevetting
BEEGINRTTW Wittenberg
BEEGIOORSU bourgeoise
BEEGLNOTUU blue tongue
blue-tongue
BEEGMNORYY embryogeny
BEEGNNOTTU unbegotten
BEEGNOORST brent goose
BEEGNSSSUU subgenuses
BEEGOORRSY gooseberry
BEEGPRRSTU Petersburg
BEEGRRSTTU Grub Street
Grubstreet
BEEHHLRSUW brushwheel
BEEHIIITVX exhibitive
BEEHILLOPT phlebolite
BEEHILMMOO mobile home
BEEHILMOST blithesome
BEEHILNSST blitheness
BEEHILOSSV Bolshevise
BEEHILOSVZ Bolshevize
BEEHIMMPRS membership
BEEHINOOST the boonies
BEEHINOPST epibenthos
BEEHINRRRY Rheinberry
Rhineberry
BEEHJLOSST the jobless
BEEHKMNOOR broken home
BEEHLLLLSS hell's bells
BEEHLMMOTU tumble home
tumblehome
BEEHLMNSSU humbleness
BEEHLMORRT Herbert Lom
BEEHLORSSU Blue Horses
BEEHLRSSTU bus shelter
BEEHMOORST bothersome
BEEHMOORTT mother-to-be
BEEHNOPRRS sphere-born
BEEIIJORTU bijouterie
BEEIIKLMRT kimberlite
BEEIILLLRV Libreville
BEEIILMMRS immersible
BEEIILMNRT timber line
BEEIILMRSS remissible
BEEIILNNSS insensible
BEEIILNNTV inventible
BEEIILNRTV invertible
BEEIILNSTV investible
BEEIILRSST resistible
BEEIILSSTX bissextile
BEEIIRRRTV River Tiber
BEEIKKNORR knobkerrie
BEEIKLLNRT Tinkerbell
BEEIKLNPRS besprinkle
BEEIKLPRTU Kuiper Belt
BEEILLLLRS bell-siller
BEEILLLNTU Lutine bell
BEEILLLOVW boll weevil
BEEILLLOWY yellow bile
BEEILLLRSV silver bell
BEEILLMNTU minute-bell
BEEILLOOTW wellie-boot
BEEILLOPRW pillow-beer
pillow-bere
BEEILLOPSX explosible
BEEILLORSU rebellious
BEEILLOSSW Boswellise
BEEILLOSWZ Boswellize
BEEILLRSTT belletrist
BEEILMNNRU number line
BEEILMNNSS nimbleness
BEEILMNRRU lime-burner
BEEILMNRSS limberness
BEEILMRSTT trembliest
BEEILNNSSU unsensible
BEEILNOPRZ Nobel prize✧
BEEILNOSST ostensible
BEEILNOTTW wine bottle
BEEILOOPST stobie pole
BEEILRRSVY reversibly
BEEILRSTUX extrusible
BEEILSSSSU subsessile
BEEIMMNRTU imbruement
BEEIMNNNRU number nine
BEEIMORRST sombrerite
BEEIMORRTT tribometer
BEEIMORRTV vibrometer
BEEIMORSSV misobserve
BEEIMORSTT timber-toes
BEEIMRRRSU reimburser
BEEINNORRT Norbertine
BEEINNPRSW web spinner
BEEINORRRU beurre noir
BEEINORRTT torbernite
BEEINORRVY River Boyne
BEEINORSTU tenebrious
BEEINRRTUV reverb unit
BEEINRSSTT bitterness
BEEINRSTTU burnettise
BEEINRTTUZ burnettize
BEEIPRSTUV subreptive
BEEIQRRSUU brusquerie
BEEIRSSUVV subversive
BEEJNNORSU Burne-Jones
BEEJNOSSTV Steven Jobs
BEEKLLOORS bookseller
BEEKLOORRV love-broker
BEEKNNOOPT poke bonnet
BEEKNNOPSU unbespoken
BEEKNNORSS brokenness
BEEKNOORST stone-broke
BEEKNORTTW know better
BEEKOOPRRT Peter Brook
BEEKORRTTT Robert Kett
BEELLNOPTU pollen tube
BEELLOOSTY obsoletely
BEELLOPRTU petrol blue
BEELLRRTTU bell-turret
BEELMMMNTU mumblement
BEELMMNSUW mumble-news
BEELMMORSU lumbersome
BEELMNNOOW noblewomen
BEELMNRSSU numberless
BEELMOQSUU Blue Mosque
BEELMORTUV tumble over
BEELNNOPST splent bone
BEELNOOSTT bottle-nose
BEELNPRTUU puberulent
BEELNSSSTU subtleness
BEELOQSTTU blottesque
BEELORSTUV oversubtle
BEEMMNNOTT entombment
BEEMMNOSST embossment
BEEMMOORRT ombrometer
BEEMMRRSSU bressummer
BEEMNORSSS sombreness
BEEMNOSTTW bestowment
BEEMOPRRSY pre-embryos
BEEMORSTTT bettermost
BEENOORRST stoneborer
BEENORRSTU burnet rose
BEENOSSSTU obtuseness
BEENPRSSSU superbness
BEENQSSTUU subsequent
BEENRRTTUY Tyburn-tree
BEEORSSTTY set store by
BEEPPRRTUY prepuberty
BEEPPSSTTY step by step
BEEPRRSTYY presbytery
BEFFIIMNTU mini-buffet
BEFFIJKNRU buff-jerkin
BEFFIKLOOO Book of Life
BEFFILLMNU muffin-bell
BEFFNOORUY buffoonery
BEFGHIILRT fire-blight
BEFGHIRRSU fishburger
BEFGIIKNRS king's brief
BEFGIINNOR fibrinogen
BEFGILNORW fingerbowl
BEFGINNOOR fibronogen
BEFGIRSUVY Rugby fives
BEFGKOOORR go for broke
BEFHHLORST flesh-broth
BEFHHLRSSU flesh-brush
BEFHIILLTT fit the bill
BEFHILLMTU thimbleful
BEFHILOSTT bottle-fish
BEFHINOSSY bony fishes
BEFHIRSTTU butterfish
BEFHLNORSW fresh-blown
BEFIILLNXY inflexibly
BEFIILLORS fibrillose
BEFIILRSTU filibuster
BEFILLRSTY blister fly
BEFILMORTW timber wolf
BEFIMORRTU tuberiform
BEFINORSUU nubiferous
BEFJKLOOOO Book of Joel
BEFLLMRSUU slumberful
BEFLLMRTUU tumblerful

BEFLLOSTTU bottlefuls
BEFLNOSTUY self-bounty
BEFNOORRST forest-born
BEGGHIINNT benighting
BEGGHMRUUY humbuggery
BEGGHNORTU Gothenburg
BEGGIILLNY negligibly
BEGGILNNOS belongings
BEGHHOOPRY hygrophobe
BEGHIILMRT thimblerig
BEGHIILNRT blithering
BEGHIINRRT rebirthing
BEGHILLNSU bushelling
BEGHILLSTU Light blues
BEGHILNORY neighborly
BEGHIMORST brightsome
BEGHINRSST brightness
BEGHIORRTW right bower
BEGHJMORTZ J B M Hertzog
BEGHNOSTUU unbesought
BEGHNRRTUU grubhunter
BEGHOORSTT borghettos
BEGHOORTUV overbought
BEGHRSTTUU shutterbug
BEGIIILLNY ineligibly
BEGIIILLTY legibility
BEGIIIMNRT ignimbrite
BEGIIKLRTZ blitzkrieg
BEGIIKMNOS Mike Gibson
BEGIIKNRTT bitter-king
BEGIILLNTT belittling
BEGIILMNTT timing belt
BEGIILMRTU limburgite
BEGIILNRST blistering
BEGIILNRTT bitterling
BEGIINORSU rubiginose
BEGIKLNRUY rebukingly
BEGIKNNOSU bousingken
BEGILLNORW well-boring
BEGILMNRSU slumbering
BEGILMOORS embroglios
BEGILNNNUY unbenignly
BEGILNORST bolstering
BEGILNORSY soberingly
BEGILNRSTU blustering
BEGILNSTTU subletting
BEGILOOOXY exobiology
BEGILPSTTU spittlebug
BEGIMNNORW embrowning
BEGIMNORSS Bergsonism
BEGINNORSS boringness
BEGINNORWZ bronze-wing
BEGINNOSTX nesting box
BEGINNOSUU nubigenous
BEGINOOOTT gnotobiote
BEGLMOORYY embryology
BEGLMORUUX Luxembourg
BEGMOOPSSU goose bumps
BEGNORRUYY youngberry
BEGOOPPRST gobstopper
BEHHIKRSSU bush-shrike
BEHHIOOPPP hippophobe
BEHHOOOPPT photophobe
BEHHOOPPSY hypsophobe
BEHIIIINTV inhibitive
BEHIIINOTX exhibition
BEHIIOPRRT prohibiter
BEHIIORTXY exhibitory
BEHIJLNOWY John Wilbye
BEHIKLLNOR Broken Hill
BEHIKLNNOT on the blink
BEHIKOPRRS shipbroker
BEHILLOPTT top the bill
BEHILLORWW willowherb
BEHILMOOPR ombrophile
BEHILMOOPS mobile shop
BEHILMOSSV Bolshevism
BEHILOSSTV Bolshevist
BEHILPRSTU butlership
BEHILRSTTU bur-thistle
BEHIMOPRUU euphorbium
BEHIMSSSTU miss the bus
BEHINORSTT birthstone
BEHINOSSSY boyishness
BEHIOPRSTT hop-bitters
BEHJJOSTTU just the job
BEHJNNNOOS Ben Johnson
BEHLMOOPTY phlebotomy
BEHLNOOTTU buttonhole
BEHLOOORRW borrow hole
BEHLOOPSTT bottle shop
BEHMNORTTU burnet moth
BEHMOOORST smooth-bore
BEHMOORSST thromboses
BEHMPRTTUU tub-thumper
BEHNOOORTU on the buroo
BEHOOPRSSU Russophobe
BEHRRSSUWY Shrewsbury
BEIIIIKLNN bikini line
BEIIILMMOS immobilise
BEIIILMMOZ immobilize
BEIIILNQTU biquintile
BEIIILNSSV invisibles
BEIIIMNOST ebionitism
BEIIIMNSTU bituminise
BEIIIMNTUZ bituminize
BEIIIOOPSS biopoiesis
BEIIKLLLOY like billy-o
BEIILLLPRT triple bill
BEIILLLRSV silverbill
BEIILLMOPR milliprobe
BEIILLNOTU ebullition
BEIILLOSSU solubilise
BEIILLOSUZ solubilize
BEIILMOPSS impossible
BEIILMRTUY muliebrity
BEIILNNSSY insensibly
BEIILNORST strobiline
BEIILORSTU boiler suit
BEIILPRSTU spirit-blue
BEIILRSSTY resistibly
BEIILRSTTT librettist
BEIILSUYZZ busy Lizzie
BEIIMSSSUV submissive
BEIINNOQUU ubiquinone
BEIINNSSSU in business
BEIINORSTY insobriety
BEIJLRRTUY jerry-built
BEIKLLLNSU sell in bulk
BEIKLLMOTT milk bottle
BEIKLMRTTU buttermilk
BEIKMNOOTU minute book
BEIKNNOOOS in one's book
BEIKNOORUY on your bike
BEILLLMMRU lumber-mill
BEILLMOSSW Boswellism
BEILLMSSUU subsellium
BEILLNOORW Berlin wool
BEILLNSUUU Luis Buñuel
BEILLOOTTU bouillotte
BEILLOPRST billposter
BEILMMNSUU nelumbiums
BEILMNOOSW snowmobile
BEILMNOOTT bottom line
BEILMOOORR boiler room
BEILMOOOST lobotomise
BEILMOOOTZ lobotomize
BEILMOOPRY biopolymer
BEILMOOSST obsoletism
BEILMOPRST problemist
BEILMORSSY symboliser
BEILMORSYZ symbolizer
BEILMPSUUY impulse buy
BEILMSTUUV vestibulum
BEILNNOPST splint bone
BEILNNSSUY unsensibly
BEILNOOOST obsoletion
BEILNOORST Orion's belt
BEILNOPRSW spin bowler
BEILNOPSSU unpossible
BEILNOSSTY ostensibly
BEILNOSTUY nebulosity
BEILNPRSUY ruby spinel
spinel ruby
spinel-ruby
BEILORSSTT lost tribes
BEILRRSUVY ruby silver
BEILSSTUUV subsultive
BEIMNNOOPT embonpoint
BEIMNORSSU submersion
BEIMOORSST boosterism
BEIMORRSTU Morris-tube
BEIMORSSTU bouts rimés
BEIMPRSSTY presbytism
BEINNOSTUV subvention
BEINNRSTTU sun bittern
BEINOPRSTU subreption
BEINORSSUV subversion
BEINORSTUU subroutine
BEINOSSSUU bonus issue
BEINOSSTWX witness box
BEINSSSTTU subsistent
BEIOOQSSUU obsequious

BEIOORRTTT bitter-root
BEIOORSSTU boisterous
BEIOQRSTUU soubriquet
BEIORRRTTU retributor
BEIORSTTUY tuberosity
BEISSTTTUU substitute
BEJKLNOTTU junk-bottle
BEJLLMRSYY Mrs Jellyby
BEKLNNORUY unbrokenly
BEKMNORSSU mossbunker
BEKMOORSTU muster book
BEKNOORSTY stony-broke
BELLMOPSTU post-bellum
BELLNNOOSU non-soluble
BELLNOSUUY nebulously
BELLOOSSTY bootlessly
BELLORSTUY trolleybus
BELMMOORRU lumber room
BELMOOSSTT bottomless
BELMORSSUU slumberous
BELNNRRUYY Yul Brynner
BELNOORSWW snowblower
BELNOPPRRU purple-born
BELOOPRSTT lobster pot
BELOORSTTU bolster out
BELOPRSUUU puberulous
BELORSSTUU blusterous
BELORSTTUU outbluster
BEMMOORTYY embryotomy
BEMNOOSSTT bottomness
BEMNOPRSUU penumbrous
BEMNOTTTUU mute button
BEMOOPRRSY proembryos
BENNOORSTW brownstone
BENOORRTTW torrent-bow
BENORSSSTU robustness
BEORRTTTUW butterwort
BFFFIOSTTU bit of stuff
BFFILOTTUU bluff it out
BFFNNORSUW snuff-brown
BFFOORRUUY four-by-four
BFGHILNTYY fly-by-night
BFGHINORRT bring forth
BFGIINRTUY brutifying
BFGILLMNUY fumblingly
BFHIMOOSTT bottom fish
BFHIRSSTUU bush fruits
BFHKOOORTU Book of Ruth
BFIIILSTUY fusibility
BFIIIORSST fibrositis
BFIIKORSTT bit of skirt
BFIILLORSU fibrillous
BFILLLSSUY blissfully
BFILLNSSUU unblissful
BFIOOPRSTX box profits
BFLLMOOTTU full-bottom
BGGGHIMNUU humbugging
BGGHINOOSS Higgs boson
BGGIIINNNR inbringing
BGGIIKNSSU kissing bug
BGGIILLNOY obligingly
BGGIINNPRU bringing up
upbringing
BGGILLNNUY bunglingly
BGHHIINRTT birthnight
BGHHIIRRTT birthright
BGHHIJNORT John Bright
BGHHORRTUU rub through
BGHIIKNOOT hiking boot
BGHIILNPSU publishing
BGHIIMRSTU British gum
BGHIINNRSU burnishing
BGHIJNOOPP job-hopping
BGHIJNOOSS Josh Gibson
BGHIKORRTW brightwork
BGHILLMNUY humblingly
BGHILLNSUY blushingly
BGHILNNSUU unblushing
BGHINNOTTU nothing but
BGHINNOTUX hunting-box
BGHINNRSTU Burns Night
BGHIPRSTTU Pittsburgh
BGHIRRSTUY rugby shirt
BGIIILNOTY ignobility
BGIIILNSTU bilinguist
BGIIKLNNNU unblinking
BGIILMNOWX mixing bowl
BGIILMOORS imbroglios
BGIILNNORU oil-burning
BGIILNOOPT potboiling
BGIILNOSSU subsoiling
BGIIMNSTTU submitting
BGIINNORRV virgin-born
BGIINORSUU rubiginous
BGIJLLMNUY jumblingly
BGILLMMNUY mumblingly
BGILLMNRUY rumblingly
BGILLMRSUU mulligrubs
BGILMNOOSS blossoming
BGILMOORTY timbrology
BGILOORSTY bryologist
BGILORSUUU lugubrious
BGIMNOOORR robing room
BGINNOOORU buon giorno
BGINNORUUY rugby union✧
BGINPRSTUU upbursting
BHHOORSTTU toothbrush
BHIIIINNOT inhibition
BHIIIMRSST Britishism
BHIIIMSSTU Mitsubishi®
BHIIINORTY inhibitory
BHIIKMNPSU bumpkinish
BHIIKMNSTU thumbikins
BHIILLRSTT stillbirth
BHIIOOPRRT prohibitor
BHIMNORSTY Robyn Smith
BHIMNPRTTU thumbprint
BHIMOORSST thrombosis
BHINORRSTW Brown Shirt
Brownshirt
BHINORTWWY whity-brown
BHJNNOORTU John Bruton
BHKNOOOTTU buttonhook
BHLLOOSSUU holus-bolus
BHLLRRUUYY hurly-burly
BHNOPSTTUU push-button
BHOOOOPSUZ zoophobous
BIIIILRSTY risibility
BIIIILSTVY visibility
BIIILMMMOS immobilism
BIIILMMOTY immobility
BIILLLLSYY silly-billy
BIILLNOSTU bullionist
BIILLOSTUY solubility
BIILLOTUVY volubility
BIILMOPSSY impossibly
BIIMNOSSSU submission
BIIMNOSTUU bituminous
BIINOSSSSY byssinosis
BIIOQSTUUU ubiquitous
BIKLLORSST storksbill
stork's bill
BIKLMNOOSU book-muslin
BIKLMNORTU Tom Kilburn
BILLMNORUU rumbullion
BILLMOORSU morbillous
BILLNOORTU tourbillon
BILMMNOOTU immunoblot
BILMMOOOSV Oblomovism
BIMNOORSTT trombonist
BIMOOPPRRU opprobrium
BINNOORSST Sorbonnist
BINOOORRSY Roy Orbison
BINOORRSSU Bruno Rossi
BINOPSSSUU subspinous
BIOORSSTUU robustious
BJLLNOORWY brown jolly
BKMOOOPPRT prompt book
BKOOORRTTU brook trout
BLLLMMOOOY Molly Bloom
BLLOOTTUWY woollybutt
BLMMOORSSU rum blossom
BLMOOOSSTU blossom out
BLORSSTUUY subsultory
BMMOOOSTTT bottommost
BMNOOOPTTU bottom upon
BNOORRTTUW brown trout
BNOORSTTUW brown stout

C

CCCCGINOOO gonococcic
CCCCIIMOOR micrococci
CCCDEILOPY cyclopedic
CCCDEIMRUU circumduce
CCCDHKLOTU Dutch clock
CCCDIMRTUU circumduct
CCCEEHKKLR checkclerk
CCCEEINNOS conscience
CCCEEINRST crescentic
CCCEEINTUY cecutiency
CCCEELNSUU succulence
CCCEENORRU occurrence
CCCEHIILMY hemicyclic

CCCEHIILNO colchicine
CCCEHIMOTY ecchymotic
CCCEHKORSS crosscheck
CCCEIILPRY pericyclic
CCCEIIMRSU circumcise
CCCEIIRSTY cysticerci
CCCEILLTYY lytic cycle
CCCEILNORR corn circle
CCCEILOPRR crop circle
CCCEILOTUY leucocytic
CCCEINNOOP Concepción
CCCEINNORT concentric
CCCEINOOSU coccineous
CCCEINOOTU coconut ice
CCCEINOOTV concoctive
CCCEINOOTY coenocytic
CCCEIOOPRT eccoprotic
CCCEKLNOOR corncockle
CCCELNSUUY succulency
CCCFHIIKKL chick flick
CCCGNOOOSU gonococcus
CCCHHILOOO chocoholic
CCCHIKOPST spitchcock
CCCHILMOOY homocyclic
CCCHILMOSU colchicums
CCCIIMORTY microcytic
CCCIINORVW civic crown
CCCILLOPYY polycyclic
CCCILMNOOY monocyclic
CCCILNSTUY succinctly
CCCINNOOOT concoction
CCCIOOPRSY cryoscopic
CCCLOORSSY cyclo-cross
CCDDEENNOS condescend
CCDDEIKMNO midden-cock
CCDDEKLORU curled dock
CCDEEEENPR precedence
CCDEEEFIIN deficience
CCDEEEHINS dehiscence
CCDEEEHRSU curd cheese
CCDEEEKNRW crew-necked
CCDEEENPRY precedency
CCDEEENRST crescented
decrescent
CCDEEERRSU recrudesce
CCDEEFIINY deficiency
CCDEEFINNO confidence
CCDEEGINSU succeeding
CCDEEHHTUW chew the cud
CCDEEHIORT ricocheted
CCDEEHMOSY ecchymosed
CCDEEHNOSY synecdoche
CCDEEHORTT crotcheted
CCDEEIIIPT epideictic
CCDEEIILRT dielectric
CCDEEIIOPS speciocide
CCDEEIIPPR precipiced
CCDEEIKLRV clever dick✧
CCDEEILMOO coomceiled
CCDEEIMORT ectodermic
CCDEEINNOR cinder cone
CCDEEINOPR procidence
CCDEEIORRU cri de coeur
CCDEEKLNOW cowl-necked
CCDEEKLOPS clock speed
CCDEELMOPT complected
CCDEELNNOO condolence
CCDEENNORT concentred
CCDEENORSS crescendos
CCDEENRRUY decurrency
CCDEEOORSU source code
CCDEEORTUU deuce court
CCDEFINNOY confidency
CCDEFKLLOU full-cocked
CCDEGHHIOU hiccoughed
CCDEGHIIKT check digit
CCDEHILLOS cold chisel
CCDEHKNOSU soundcheck
CCDEHLNTUU Dutch uncle
CCDEHNORSU unscorched
CCDEIIILOT idiolectic
CCDEIIKLSS dickcissel
CCDEIILOPY epicycloid
CCDEIINNOR endocrinic
CCDEIINNOT coincident
CCDEIINORT endocritic
CCDEIIOSTT Docetistic
CCDEIJKOSY disc jockey
CCDEIKLOSU cuckoldise
CCDEIKLOUZ cuckoldize
CCDEIMOOOT octodecimo
CCDEINNOST disconnect
CCDEINOOPS endoscopic
CCDEINOPUU unoccupied
CCDEINORST disconcert
CCDEINOTUV conductive
CCDEIORSTT direct cost
CCDEKMNOOY cockneydom
CCDEKORSTU scoter duck
CCDELOOORU colour code
colour-code
CCDEMOORTY cordectomy
CCDGIILOSU glucosidic
CCDGIILOSY glycosidic
CCDGILNNOU concluding
CCDGILOOOY codicology
CCDHHLNTUU Dutch lunch
CCDHIIIORT dichroitic
CCDHIIMOOT dichotomic
CCDHIINORT chondritic
CCDHNRRSUY scrunch-dry
CCDHORTUUY duchy court
CCDIMNOSTU misconduct
CCDIMOSSTU cosmic dust
CCDINNOOTU conduction
CCDLMMNOOO common cold
CCEEEEHIKP cheekpiece
CCEEEELLNX excellence
CCEEEENNSS senescence
CCEEEFFIIN efficience
CCEEEFNNOR conference✧
conférence
CCEEEGINOS geoscience
CCEEEHIKPS pick-cheese
CCEEEHINST the science
CCEEEIINPR recipience
CCEEEINPRS prescience
CCEEEINQSU quiescence
CCEEEINRSV virescence
CCEEEIOPSS ecospecies
CCEEEKLNOS skene-occle
CCEEELLNXY excellency✧
CCEEEMMNOR recommence
CCEEEMNOPR recompence
CCEEEMNOPT competence
CCEEEMNSTU tumescence
CCEEENOPRS copresence
co-presence
CCEEENRRRU recurrence
CCEEENRSTX excrescent
CCEEEORRUV crève-coeur
CCEEFFIINY efficiency
CCEEFFILNO off-licence
CCEEFHHRRU Free Church
CCEEFIKNRT fen-cricket
CCEEFINTTU fettuccine
CCEEFKLORS self-cocker
CCEEFLNNOU confluence
CCEEGHINOT geotechnic
CCEEGHLNSY sheng cycle
CCEEGIMNSU ecce signum
CCEEGINNOR congeneric
CCEEGINNOT congenetic
CCEEGINORT egocentric
geocentric
CCEEGLLOOW cow college
CCEEGNNORU congruence
CCEEHHIRST Chichester
CCEEHHKOPU cheekpouch
CCEEHIILRT telechiric
CCEEHIINST technicise
CCEEHIINTZ technicize
CCEEHILNRY Henry Cecil
CCEEHINOSS choiceness
CCEEHIOPTU touch-piece
CCEEHIOSTV chest voice
CCEEHKLLPS spellcheck
spell-check
CCEEHLORST Colchester
CCEEHLORSW screech owl
CCEEHNOSTU escutcheon
CCEEIIINNP incipience
CCEEIILMRS semicircle
CCEEIILPTU epicuticle
CCEEIINPRY recipiency
CCEEIIPRTT peritectic
CCEEIIRRTU circuiteer
CCEEIKLPUY lucky-piece
CCEEIKOORR rice cooker
CCEEILLOTV collective
CCEEILMNNY inclemency
CCEEILNOPT pleonectic
CCEEILNOPU leucopenic

CCEEILNORR reconciler
CCEEILNORT electronic
CCEEILOPST telescopic
CCEEILORVY coercively
CCEEINNNOT continence
CCEEINNNOV connivence
CCEEINNOTV connective
CCEEINNRRU incurrence
CCEEINNRST increscent
CCEEINNRTU encincture
CCEEINOPRT preconceit
CCEEINOPRW crown piece
CCEEINOPTV conceptive
CCEEINORST concertise
concretise
CCEEINORTV concretive
CCEEINORTZ concertize
concretize
CCEEINOSSV concessive
CCEEINOTVV convective
CCEEINQSUY quiescency
CCEEIOPRRV cover price
CCEEIOPRSS crosspiece
CCEEIORRTV corrective
CCEEISSSUV successive
CCEEJNORTU conjecture
CCEEKKLOYY cockyleeky
CCEELMORTY cyclometer
CCEELNOPRU corpulence
CCEELNORTY concretely
CCEELNRTUU truculence
CCEELOSTTU cos lettuce
CCEELPRSUU crepuscule
CCEEMNOPTY competency
CCEENOOSSX ex concesso
CCEENOPRRT preconcert
CCEENORSTT cost centre
CCEENRRRUY recurrency
CCEEOOPRST rectoscope
CCEFFFHNRU French cuff
CCEFHIIMOR microfiche
CCEFHIMOOR from choice
CCEFHKLOOT of the clock
CCEFIIINST scientific
CCEFIINPSU unspecific
CCEFIKORST stick force
CCEFILLLRU full-circle
CCEFILMRUX circumflex
CCEFILNOTU conceitful
CCEFIMRSUU circumfuse
CCEFINNOOT confection
CCEFLLNOTU flocculent
CCEFLSSSUU successful
CCEGGILNOY glycogenic
CCEGHHORRU churchgoer
CCEGHIIIOP pichiciego
CCEGHIIKMN chemicking
CCEGHIILNO conchiglie
CCEGHINORT crocheting
CCEGIIKNRT cricketing
CCEGIILNNR encircling
CCEGILLNOT collecting
CCEGILNOOR necrologic
CCEGIMNOOS cosmogenic
CCEGINNNOR concerning
CCEGINORSY cryogenics
CCEGNNORUY congruency
CCEHHIINOR heroin chic
CCEHHILOTV clove hitch
CCEHHIPSTU the hiccups
CCEHHLRSSU churchless
CCEHHRTTUX church text
CCEHIIIMOS isocheimic
CCEHIIMNST technicism
CCEHIIMOOR heroi-comic
CCEHIINNNO cinchonine
CCEHIINNOS cinchonise
CCEHIINNOZ cinchonize
CCEHIINSTT technicist
CCEHIIRSTU ischuretic
CCEHIKMOOR mock-heroic
CCEHIKNNRU chicken run
CCEHIKNOPT checkpoint
CCEHIKNOPX chickenpox
CCEHIKNOSY cockneyish
CCEHIKNOTU chicken out
CCEHIKPRRY cherry-pick
CCEHIKSSTT Schick test
CCEHILNORR chronicler
CCEHILNORS chronicles✧
CCEHILOOPR pleochroic
CCEHILOPRR perchloric
CCEHILORRU hour-circle
CCEHILORVW cow-chervil
CCEHIMOSSY ecchymosis
CCEHINOPST Scotch pine
CCEHINRSTU crunchiest
CCEHIOOPRR pro-choicer
CCEHIOPTTY ectophytic
CCEHIORRST orchestric
CCEHIORSST orchestics
CCEHKLOOST hot-cockles
CCEHKNOORY honey-crock
CCEHKNOOST chockstone
CCEHKORTUU chucker-out
CCEHLMOTYY cyclothyme
CCEHMOORTY cytochrome
CCEHNOPRUW cowpuncher
CCEHNORTVW crown vetch
CCEHNOSSST Scotchness
CCEHOORSST Scotch rose
CCEHOORTUU choucroute
CCEHOSTTUZ zucchettos
CCEIIILNOR ricinoleic
CCEIIINNPY incipiency
CCEIIINNRT encrinitic
CCEIIIRRST criticiser
CCEIIIRRTZ criticizer
CCEIIIRSTV cervicitis
CCEIILMNOR microcline
CCEIILMORT cliometric
CCEIILOSST solecistic
CCEIIMNOST misconceit
CCEIIMOORS seriocomic
CCEIIMOTXY Mexico City
CCEIIMPSST scepticism
CCEIINNOPT concipient
CCEIINOTVV convictive
CCEIINRTTY centricity
CCEIIOORST crocoisite
CCEIIOPPRS periscopic
CCEIIORTVY coercivity
CCEIIOSSTT Scotticise
CCEIIOSTTZ Scotticize
CCEIKKOPPT pickpocket
CCEIKLOTUY leukocytic
CCEIKMNOSY cockneyism
CCEIKNORTT not cricket
CCEIKNOSSS cocksiness
CCEILLLOSU cellulosic
CCEILLMTUY multicycle
CCEILLNOOT collection
CCEILLSSSU ill success
CCEILNNOSU nucleonics
CCEILNOSUV conclusive
vice-consul
CCEILOOQTU coquelicot
CCEILOORSU ice colours
CCEIMMRRUU circummure
CCEIMNNOOU uneconomic
CCEIMNORST concretism
CCEIMNOSTT concettism
CCEIMNRTUV circumvent
CCEIMOOPRS microscope
CCEIMOPRSU circumpose
CCEIMORRST miscorrect
CCEIMORRTY cryometric
CCEIMORTTY cytometric
CCEINNNOOT connection
CCEINNNOTY continency
CCEINNNOVY connivency
CCEINNOOPT conception
CCEINNOORT concertino✧
concretion
CCEINNOOSS concession
CCEINNOOTV convection
CCEINOOOPS iconoscope
CCEINOORRT correction
CCEINOORTY cryoconite
CCEINOPRSU Copernicus
CCEINORSTT concretist
CCEINOSSSU succession
CCEINOSSUV concussive
CCEINOSTTT concettist
CCEINOTUVY vice-county
CCEIOOPRSU precocious
CCEIOOTTXY exocytotic
CCEISSSUUV succussive
CCEKKORTUY turkey cock
CCEKLOORTW clock tower
CCEKLORSUY cocksurely
CCEKMOORST comstocker
CCEKNNOORY cockernony

CCEKORRTTU cork-cutter
CCELLOSTYY cyclostyle
CCELMOORTY motorcycle
CCELMOOSTY cyclostome
CCELNOPRUY corpulency
CCELNOSSTU occultness
CCELNRTUUY truculency
CCELOOOPPS colposcope
CCELOPRSUU corpuscule
CCELPRSTUU cluster-cup
CCEMNNOOPY componency
CCEMOSTTYY cystectomy
CCENNORRTU concurrent
CCENOOPPRT pop concert
CCENOOPRSY necroscopy
CCENOOPRTU contrecoup
CCENOPSSTU conspectus
CCENORRSTU cut corners
CCENORRTTU corn-cutter
CCEOOPSSTY cystoscope
CCEOORRRTY correctory
CCFFFFHHUU chuff-chuff
CCFGIINRUY crucifying
CCFHIMNOOR conchiform
CCFIILMORU culiciform
CCFIILNNOT in conflict
CCFIIMORRT form critic
CCFIMMORUU cucumiform
CCFKKMOORS smock-frock
CCFKLOOORU four-o'clock
CCGHHHHIRU High Church
CCGHHIKOTT chock-tight
CCGHIIKLRT right-click
CCGHLNOOOY conchology
CCGIIIKNNP picnicking
CCGIILMOOR micrologic
CCGIILNRTY tricycling
CCGIILOOOS sociologic
CCGIINNNOV convincing
CCGILLOTYY glycolytic
CCGILORSUU glucosuric
CCGILORSUY glycosuric
CCGIMNOOOS cosmogonic
CCGINNORRU concurring
CCGIOOPRSY gyroscopic
CCHHHOOPTT hotchpotch
CCHHIIOTTY ichthyotic
CCHHLOORUW wool church
CCHIIIRSTT tristichic
CCHIILNNOO conchiolin
CCHIILOPRY cryophilic
CCHIIMNNOS cinchonism
CCHIIMNOOR chironomic
CCHIIMORRT trichromic
CCHIIMPSSY psychicism
CCHIINORTY chronicity
CCHIIOPRTY hypocritic
CCHIIPSSTY psychicist
CCHIKLNQUU quick-lunch
CCHIKLOSTT lockstitch
CCHIKOPSST chopsticks
CCHILMNNOU column inch
CCHILOOPRY polychroic
CCHILORSTW scritch-owl
CCHIMNOOOR monochroic
CCHIMORTYY cymotrichy
CCHIMOSSTT Scotch mist
CCHINNORSY synchronic
CCHIOOOPRS horoscopic
CCHIORSSTU trochiscus
CCHIORSTTY trichocyst
CCHKLNOSUU no such luck
CCHKLOORRS schorl-rock
CCHKLOTUUY touch lucky
CCHMNOOPTU not much cop
CCHNOOSTUY coconut shy
CCHOOPSSUU hocus-pocus
CCIIILMORT microlitic
CCIIILOSST sciolistic
CCIIKKQRTU quick trick
CCIIKKQSTU quick-stick
CCIILLNOPY polyclinic
CCIILMNNOO monoclinic
CCIILMNNOY lincomycin
CCIILMOPTY complicity
CCIILOOPRT coprolitic
CCIILORTUV civil court
CCIILRSTTY tricyclist
CCIIMMOORT microtomic
CCIIMNOSTV convictism
CCIIMOPRST comic strip
CCIIMOSSTT Scotticism
CCIIMOSTUV Muscovitic
CCIINNNOTY concinnity
CCIINNOOTV conviction
CCIINOOPRS scorpionic✧
CCIIORSTUU circuitous
CCIKNOOPTU cuckoo pint
CCIKOOPSTU cuckoo-spit
CCILLLOSUU colliculus
CCILLNOORU councillor
CCILLOOPTY collotypic
CCILMNORUU corniculum
CCILMRRUUU curriculum
CCILNNOOSU conclusion
CCILNOOOTU coconut oil
CCILOOOPRT protocolic
CCILOOPRTY polycrotic
CCILOPSTYY polycystic
CCIMOOPRSY microscopy
CCINNNOOSU concinnous
CCINNOOSSU concussion
CCINOSSSUU succussion
CCINOSTUVY viscountcy
CCIOOOPPRS poroscopic
CCIOOPRTYZ cryptozoic✧
CCIOPPRRTY procryptic
CCIORRSSSS criss-cross
CCIORSSSTU scissor cut
CCJLNNOTUY conjunctly
CCLLOOORTU collocutor
CCLNOORSUY conclusory
CCLOOOPPSY colposcopy
CCNOORRTUW crown court
CCOOOSSUUU couscousou
CCOOPSSTYY cystoscopy
CCOORRSSTU cross-court
CDDDLRSUUY sculduddry
CDDEEEEGKL deckle-edge
CDDEEEELRR del credere
CDDEEEENNP dependence
CDDEEEINUV undeceived
CDDEEEJLTY dejectedly
CDDEEELNOR needlecord
CDDEEEMNTU deducement
CDDEEENNPY dependency
CDDEEENNST descendent
CDDEEENRSU descendeur
CDDEEENTTU undetected
CDDEEFFIIN diffidence
CDDEEGGKLU duck-legged
CDDEEGINNS descending
CDDEEIINSS dissidence
CDDEEIJPRU prejudiced
CDDEEILRSY Clydesider
CDDEEIMNOR endodermic
CDDEEINORS considered
CDDEEINRSU undescried
CDDEEINRTU uncredited
undirected
CDDEEINTUY Dundee City
CDDEEKMRXY Eddy Merckx
CDDEELLSUY secludedly
CDDEELMOSU cuddlesome
CDDEELNUUX unexcluded
CDDEENNOSU unseconded
CDDEENORRU unrecorded
CDDEEOOPSU pseudocode
CDDEFFHISU dischuffed
CDDEFKOOTU duck-footed
CDDEFKTTUU tufted duck
CDDEFNNOOU confounded
CDDEGIKLOR gridlocked
CDDEGKLNOU golden duck
CDDEGLOORR gold record
CDDEGNOORR corn dodger
CDDEHISTUY Thucydides
CDDEIINPRS disprinced
CDDEIKMMNU muck-midden
CDDEILOOUV loud-voiced
CDDEIMMNOS discommend
CDDEIMMOOS discommode
CDDEIMOOSU duodecimos
CDDEINNOSW second wind
CDDEINORUV undivorced
CDDELLLOOR cold-rolled
CDDELLSUUY Duc de Sully
CDDELOOORS closed-door
CDDEMNOOPU decompound
CDDENOORTU undoctored
CDDENOPRTU end-product
CDDENOPRUU unproduced
CDDFILORSU discordful

Words marked ✧ can also be spelled with one or more capital letters

CDDHHIIMSU shidduchim
CDDHIILORW wild orchid
CDDHILLOSY cloddishly
CDDHILSTUY child-study
CDDHOPRSTU Dutch drops
CDDIILNORY cylindroid
CDDIKOSTTY toddy-stick
CDDILNSUUU Didunculus
CDDILOOPSU diplodocus✧
CDDINNOOTY dicynodont
CDEEEEFFGT edge effect
CDEEEEGILP Ledge Piece
CDEEEEGNRT detergence
CDEEEEINPX expedience
CDEEEENRRT deterrence
CDEEEFFHOS cheesed off
CDEEEFFINR difference
CDEEEFFIST side effect
CDEEEFFNTU uneffected
CDEEEFHIKR kerchiefed
CDEEEFIILP fieldpiece
CDEEEFILST self-deceit
CDEEEFILTV deflective
CDEEEGIIPR ridgepiece
CDEEEGINRV divergence
CDEEEGNRTY detergency
CDEEEHINRS Chinese red
CDEEEHIPRR decipherer
CDEEEHKLOR cork-heeled
CDEEEHLNSU enschedule
CDEEEHLRSU reschedule
CDEEEHOOSW cheesewood
CDEEEIINNV in evidence
CDEEEIINPS desipience
CDEEEIINRS decree nisi
CDEEEILOPV velocipede
CDEEEILQSU deliquesce
CDEEEIMNNO comedienne
comédienne
CDEEEIMNNP impendence
CDEEEINNPZ pince-nezed
CDEEEINPXY expediency
CDEEEINRRT interceder
CDEEEINRSW widescreen
CDEEEINRUV unreceived
CDEEEINSST desistence
CDEEEIPRRU cire perdue
CDEEEKNSTW 'tweendecks
CDEEELLNUX unexcelled
CDEEELMNOT dolcemente
CDEEELMOPS Empedocles
CDEEELOPRS crêpe-soled
CDEEELORRT telerecord
CDEEELPTXY expectedly
CDEEEMNSTU seducement
CDEEENNORS recondense
CDEEENNRSU unscreened
CDEEENPTUX unexpected
CDEEENTUUX unexecuted
CDEEERRSTT street cred
street-cred

CDEEFFILOR force field
CDEEFFINRY differency
CDEEFIINRT dentifrice
CDEEFIIORS crise de foi
CDEEFIIPRX fixed-price
CDEEFILNOT deflection
CDEEFILNRT fernticled
CDEEFINNTU uninfected
CDEEFINTUV defunctive
CDEEFLNORY enforcedly
CDEEFLNOSS second self
CDEEFMORRY Cry Freedom
CDEEFNNORU unenforced
CDEEFNORSS forcedness
CDEEGHHIKN high-necked
CDEEGHHITT get hitched
CDEEGHIKQU quick-hedge
CDEEGIINOR Ceredigion
CDEEGIKNNR ring-necked
CDEEGILNNU indulgence
CDEEGILNOV Venice gold
CDEEGILNUV divulgence
CDEEGILPST get spliced
CDEEGINNOR endergonic
CDEEGINOPR proceeding
CDEEGINRRS screen grid
CDEEGINRVY divergency
CDEEGIOOPS piece goods
CDEEHHIKTT hit the deck
CDEEHIILOP ophicleide
CDEEHIILTT ditheletic✧
CDEEHIIPRR cirrhipede
CDEEHIMNOR echinoderm
CDEEHINNRU unenriched
CDEEHLNOSU on schedule
CDEEHLNOSV veldschoen
CDEEHLOORS deschooler
CDEEHLRTWY wretchedly
CDEEHMNOOS second home
CDEEHMNOPR comprehend
CDEEHNNQUU unquenched
CDEEHNNRTU untrenched
CDEEHNORTU untochered
CDEEHORRST Dorchester
CDEEHORTUU euchred out
CDEEIIILSV decivilise
CDEEIIILVZ decivilize
CDEEIIIMNT cimetidine
CDEEIIINSV indecisive
CDEEIILNNO Céline Dion
CDEEIILNRT credit line
CDEEIILSVY decisively
CDEEIIMNTY endemicity
CDEEIIMPRS spermicide
CDEEIINOPW cowdie-pine
CDEEIINPRX price index
CDEEIINRRR dernier cri
CDEEIINRST indiscreet
indiscrete
iridescent
CDEEIINSUV undecisive

CDEEIIORRT cordierite
Directoire
CDEEIIPRTV predictive
CDEEIIRSSV disservice
CDEEIIRSTV discretive
CDEEIISSTV dissective
CDEEIJNORU unrejoiced
CDEEIJNOST dejections
CDEEIKNNST deck tennis
CDEEIKNPSS pickedness
CDEEIKNSSW wickedness
CDEEILLNST stencilled
CDEEILMNOU undecimole
CDEEILNNOS declension
CDEEILNNSU unlicensed
CDEEILNNTY indecently
CDEEILNOOS decolonise
CDEEILNOOZ decolonize
CDEEILNOPY epicondyle
CDEEILNOSS disenclose
CDEEILNOSU nucleoside
CDEEILNOTU nucleotide
CDEEILNPSU uneclipsed
CDEEILNRTU interclude
CDEEILNRVY Inverclyde
CDEEILOORS decolorise
CDEEILOORZ decolorize
CDEEILORRS Cordeliers
CDEEILORST cloistered
CDEEILRRVY River Clyde
CDEEILRSTY discreetly
discretely
CDEEIMMOXY myxoedemic
CDEEIMNNPY impendency
CDEEIMNNTU inducement
CDEEIMNPRU imprudence
CDEEIMORRX xerodermic
CDEEINNOSS descension
CDEEINNRSW windscreen
CDEEINNSSU secundines
CDEEINOPRV providence✧
CDEEINORRS reconsider
CDEEINORTT credit note
CDEEINORUV undervoice
CDEEINPRSY presidency✧
CDEEINRSST directness
CDEEINRSTY dysenteric
CDEEIOPRRV overpriced
CDEEIOPSTU deceptious
CDEEIORRSV discoverer
rediscover
CDEEIORRVV cover drive
CDEEIORSTU courtesied
CDEEIPRRSS cider press
CDEEIPRSST disrespect
CDEEIRRSST directress
CDEEIRRSTT derestrict
restricted
CDEEIRRSVY dry service
CDEEIRSTTT crested tit
CDEEISTUXY excise duty

CDEEKKKNNO	knock-kneed
CDEEKLNRRU	under-clerk
CDEEKLTUVV	velvet-duck
CDEEKNNORU	unreckoned
CDEEKNPRUU	unpuckered
CDEEKNRTUU	untuckered
CDEEKOOORV	overcooked
CDEEKOOPRW	peckerwood
	woodpecker
CDEELLNOSU	counselled
CDEELMNOUW	unwelcomed
CDEELMORRS	scleroderm
CDEELNNOSU	unenclosed
CDEELNOVXY	convexedly
CDEEMMNOOR	common reed
CDEEMNNOOU	come undone
CDEEMNNOPR	precondemn
CDEEMNNOST	secondment
CDEEMNPRSU	screen dump
CDEEMOOPRS	decomposer
CDEEMOPRSS	compressed
	decompress
CDEENNNOTT	contendent
CDEENNORSU	uncensored
CDEENNORSY	condensery
CDEENNORTV	convertend
CDEENNRSUU	uncensured
CDEENOOOTT	odontocete
CDEENOORRS	rood screen
	screen door
CDEENOOSTT	cottonseed
CDEENOOTTW	cottonweed
CDEENORRSU	underscore
CDEENORRUV	under cover
	undercover
CDEENORSTU	uncorseted
	unescorted
CDEENOSTUU	consuetude
CDEENPRSTU	unsceptred
CDEENRRSTU	undercrest
CDEENRSSSU	cursedness
CDEENSSSSU	cussedness
CDEEOPRRRU	reproducer
CDEEOPRSSU	due process
CDEERSSSTU	seductress
CDEFFILNRU	undercliff
CDEFFINNOU	uncoffined
CDEFGHIKLT	flight deck
CDEFGOORTU	Truce of God
CDEFHINORU	four-inched
CDEFHIORRT	third force
CDEFHIORSY	cod-fishery
CDEFHLMORS	Chelmsford
CDEFHNOORR	French door
CDEFIIIILS	silicified
CDEFIIINPR	principled
CDEFIIOSTT	Scottified
CDEFILLOUV	full-voiced
CDEFILNOUU	fluid ounce
CDEFILNSUY	disfluency
CDEFILORSS	crossfield
CDEFILORST	disc floret
CDEFILORSW	disc flower
CDEFINNNOU	unconfined
CDEFINNORU	uninforced
CDEFINNOTU	defunction
CDEFINOORV	confervoid
CDEFIOSSTX	fixed costs
CDEFLNORUY	unforcedly
CDEFLNOSUY	confusedly
CDEFNNOSUU	unconfused
CDEFNOOPRU	pound force
CDEFNORRTU	undercroft
CDEFNOSSUU	unfocussed
CDEGGILLNU	cudgelling
CDEGHHIIPR	high-priced
CDEGHHIMOY	high comedy
CDEGHINOTT	dot-etching
CDEGHJOTUU	touch judge
CDEGHOOORT	tocher-good
CDEGIIILNNY	incedingly
CDEGIINNRS	discerning
CDEGIINOTU	digoneutic
CDEGIINSST	dissecting
CDEGIIORTY	ergodicity
CDEGIKKNPU	Peking duck
CDEGIKNOST	stockinged
CDEGILMMNO	commingled
CDEGILNNUY	indulgency
CDEGILNOPU	decoupling
CDEGILNSUY	seducingly
CDEGILOOPS	logopedics
CDEGILOORS	socdoliger
CDEGINNNOT	contending
CDEGINORSW	scowdering
CDEGIOORRR	corregidor
CDEGIORTUU	court guide
CDEGLOOORS	socdologer
CDEGMNORUU	curmudgeon
CDEGNNSTUU	St Cunegund
CDEGNOOORR	go on record
CDEGNORRUW	ground crew
CDEHHIILNS	Shieldinch
CDEHHIIPRT	diphtheric
CDEHHIIQSU	quiche dish
CDEHHIIRRT	Third Reich
CDEHHIJNOR	John Edrich
CDEHHOORRY	hydrochore
CDEHIIISTT	ditheistic
CDEHIILNNR	inner child
CDEHIILOPS	discophile
CDEHIILORS	chloridise
CDEHIILORZ	chloridize
CDEHIILPTY	diphyletic
CDEHIIMNSW	wind chimes
CDEHIINOST	hedonistic
CDEHIINRTY	enhydritic
CDEHIKMNOT	kitchendom
CDEHIKORTT	do the trick
CDEHILNRSU	nurse-child
CDEHILOOST	schooltide
CDEHILOPRY	polyhedric
CDEHILOPTW	low-pitched
CDEHILRRWY	wild cherry
CDEHILSTTU	Dutch tiles
CDEHIMNRSU	unsmirched
CDEHIMOPRY	hypodermic
CDEHINOOOV	novicehood
CDEHINOOPR	princehood
CDEHINOPTY	endophytic
CDEHINOSTW	switched on
CDEHIOOORW	hoodie crow
CDEHIOOPRT	orthopedic
CDEHIOORSU	orchideous
CDEHISSTTT	set-stitch'd
CDEHKOOOOR	cooker hood
CDEHKORSUV	duckshover
CDEHLNOORY	chlorodyne
CDEHLNOOSU	unschooled
CDEHLOOPPR	clodhopper
CDEHLOOPRY	copyholder
CDEHLOOPSS	closed shop
CDEHNOOORT	octohedron
CDEHNORSUU	chunderous
CDEHOOPRSY	hydroscope
CDEHPSTUUY	upsey Dutch
CDEIIIILNS	in deliciis
CDEIIILLST	stillicide
CDEIIILNNS	disincline
CDEIIILNOT	indicolite
CDEIIILNPS	discipline
CDEIIIMNSU	indie music
CDEIIIMRSV	recidivism
CDEIIINNOS	indecision
CDEIIINTVV	vindictive
CDEIIIRSTV	recidivist
CDEIIJNOST	disjection
CDEIIKLLLP	dill pickle
CDEIIKLSST	sick-listed
CDEIILNNOR	crinolined
CDEIILNOPU	unpolicied
CDEIILNOSS	disinclose
CDEIILNPPR	principled
CDEIILNRTY	cylindrite
	indirectly
CDEIILOSTU	solicitude
CDEIIMNNTT	indictment
CDEIIMNOST	midsection
CDEIIMOORT	iodometric
CDEIIMORRS	misericord
CDEIIMORRV	micro drive
CDEIIMORTY	iridectomy
	mediocrity
CDEIIMOSTT	demoticist
CDEIIMPPSU	piped music
CDEIIMPRTU	impictured
CDEIINOPRT	prediction
CDEIINORST	directions
	discretion
	soricident
CDEIINOSST	dissection
CDEIINSTTU	discutient
CDEIIOOPTX	exopoditic

CDEIIOORRS sororicide
CDEIIORSUV veridicous
CDEIIORTTY city editor
CDEIIPRSTU pedicurist
CDEIIRSSUV discursive
CDEIISSSUV discussive
CDEIKNRRTU undertrick
CDEIKNRSUW wind-sucker
CDEIKNSSTY sticky ends
CDEIKOORTW wicket door
CDEIKOPPRT cork-tipped
CDEIKOPPTT pockpitted
CDEIKOQSTU deck quoits
CDEIKORRST stock rider
CDEIKPTTUY picket-duty
CDEILLLOVY Clive Lloyd
CDEILLLPUY pellucidly
CDEILLNOOR corn-dollie
CDEILMOPPR crippledom
CDEILNNOSU uninclosed
CDEILNOSSU cloudiness
discounsel
CDEILNOTUU include out
CDEILOPRTU productile
CDEILOPSUU pediculous
CDEILORRUV Lord Cuvier
CDEILORSSS cross-slide
CDEILORSSU disclosure
CDEIMMNOPU compendium
CDEIMMNOTU comminuted
CDEIMNOOPS incomposed
CDEIMNOOST endosmotic
CDEIMNOOSY diseconomy
CDEIMNORSW mince words
CDEIMNOSTU undomestic
CDEIMNOSUU mucedinous
CDEIMOOPSS discompose
CDEIMORSTU Democritus
CDEIMOSSTU customised
CDEIMOSTUZ customized
CDEIMPRSTU spermiduct
CDEINNOSST disconsent
CDEINNOSTT discontent
CDEINNRTUU under-tunic
CDEINOORSU indecorous
CDEINOPRTY decryption
CDEINORRTU introducer
CDEINORSSX cross-index
CDEINORSTU discounter
rediscount
CDEINPRSTU unscripted
CDEIOOPRTY copy-editor
CDEIOPRRST descriptor
CDEIOPRRTU picture rod
CDEIOPRTUV productive
CDEIORRSSU discourser
CDEIRRSTTU strictured
CDEJNNOSSU jocundness
CDEKKNNORU knock under
CDEKLORTUY cold turkey
CDEKMMOOST mock-modest
CDEKNNRRUU runner duck
CDEKNORSTU understock
CDELLNOORT controlled
CDELLNOORU lend colour
CDELLOOOPS closed-loop
CDELMNOOOY old economy
old-economy
CDELMNOSUY consumedly
CDELMOOPSY composedly
CDELMOOPTT complotted
CDELNNOOSU unconsoled
CDELNOORUU uncoloured
CDELNOORUY Euroclydon
CDELNOOTUV convoluted
CDELNPRSUU unscrupled
CDELNRTUUU uncultured
CDELOOORUV dove-colour
CDELOORSUY decorously
CDELORRSSU russel-cord
CDELPRSTUU sculptured
CDEMMNOTUU uncommuted
CDEMMOOORS cosmodrome
CDEMNNOSUU unconsumed
CDEMNOOPRU compounder
CDEMNOSTUU uncustomed
CDENNOOPRU pronounced
CDENOOPRRS correspond
CDEOOOPSTU scooped-out
CDEOORRRTU court order
CDEOORTTUW woodcutter
CDEOPRRSTU cropduster
CDEORRSSSS cross-dress
CDEORRSSTU court dress
CDEORRSTTU destructor
CDERRSTTUU structured
CDFFIILTUY difficulty
CDFGHIINOS cod-fishing
CDFHILOOPR childproof
CDFHIOORST doctor-fish
CDFIIMNORS disconfirm
CDFILNOOSU cold fusion
CDFILOPPSY floppy disc
CDFIMOORST discomfort
CDFINNOOTU confound it
CDGHILNOTU night-cloud
CDGHILOORY hydrologic
CDGHILOPSU disc plough
CDGIIKNNOO in good nick
CDGIINOPRR riding crop
CDGIKLLOOS goldilocks
CDGILLNOSY scoldingly
CDGILMOOOY docimology
CDGINNOOPY pycnogonid
CDGINPPRUY dry-cupping
CDHHIILLSY childishly
CDHHIOORST Christhood
CDHIIIMSTU stichidium
CDHIILOOST Dolichotis
CDHIIMMORS dichromism
CDHIIMMORU chromidium
CDHIIMNOOR chironomid
CDHIIMOOTV victimhood
CDHIINORST chondritis
CDHIIOORTT diorthotic
CDHIIOSSTU distichous
CDHIKMORSU musk orchid
CDHILLNRRU churn-drill
CDHILLORSY Chris Lloyd
CDHILMNOOT codlin moth
CDHILOORSV dichlorvos
CDHILOOSSU holodiscus
CDHILOPRYY polyhydric
CDHILORSUU dolichurus
CDHILORTYY hydrolytic
CDHIMNOORY monohydric
CDHIMOPRSY dysmorphic
CDHINOOOSU cousinhood
CDHINOOPRY hydroponic
CDHIOOPRST doctorship
CDHIOPRSTY dystrophic
CDHKNNPRUU punch-drunk
CDHKNOORSU Rock Hudson
CDHLLMNOOO Loch Lomond
CDHLMMNOOO commonhold
CDHMOOORTY chordotomy
CDIIILNOTY indocility
CDIIIMPTUY impudicity
CDIIINNSTT indistinct
CDIIINOSSS discission
CDIIKNPRTU Dick Turpin
CDIIKPRSTU spirit duck
CDIIKRRTTY dirty trick
CDIILNOOSU nidicolous
CDIILNPSUU sipunculid
CDIILNSTTY distinctly
CDIILORSUU ridiculous
CDIINNOOST conditions
CDIINOPSUU cupidinous
CDIINORSSU discursion
CDIINOSSSU discussion
CDIIRSSSTU discursist
CDIJNORSTU disjunctor
CDIKORSSTW sword-stick
CDILLMOOSU molluscoid
CDILLOQUUY dulciloquy
CDILMOOORX loxodromic
CDILMOOPUY lycopodium✧
CDILMORSUW world music
CDILOOOPTY octoploidy
CDIMMOOOSU commodious
CDINNOOORS con sordino
CDINOOORTW citron wood
CDINOOPRST spin doctor
spin-doctor
CDINOOPRTU production
CDIOORSTUW citrus wood
CDIORRSSUY discursory
CDLMOORSTU storm cloud
CDLNOOORRT control rod
CDLNOORTUY old country
CDLOOOPRST Doctor Slop
CDLOORRTUW World Court

CDNOOOOTTW	cottonwood
CDNOOPSSTU	pound scots
CDOOOOPSTU	octopodous
CDOORRSTUW	court sword
CEEEEFFORT	coffee tree
CEEEEFFRSV	effervesce
CEEEEFHPRS	free speech
CEEEEFLLSS	fleeceless
CEEEEFLRST	free-select
CEEEEFNPRR	preference
CEEEEGIIPS	siege piece
CEEEEGIPTX	epexegetic
CEEEEHIMST	cheesemite
CEEEEHIPRT	three-piece
CEEEEHIRSW	cheesewire
CEEEEHNPRT	threepence
CEEEEIJLPY	jeely piece
CEEEEINPRX	experience
CEEEEIRSVY	eye-service
CEEEEKPRST	keep secret
CEEEELLNPR	repellence
CEEEELNORT	enterocele
CEEEELNRST	telescreen
CEEEELNRTT	telecentre
CEEEENNPSV	sevenpence
CEEEENNRST	resentence
CEEEENRRRV	reverencer
CEEEFFGLNU	effulgence
CEEEFFHNRR	Free French
CEEEFFKRRT	Kerr effect
CEEEFFLORS	effloresce
CEEEFFLSST	effectless
CEEEFGLNRU	refulgence
CEEEFHHLNR	French heel
CEEEFHIKNT	kitchen-fee
CEEEFHLMNT	fleechment
CEEEFHLRTT	three-cleft
CEEEFHNRTT	trench feet
CEEEFHOSST	soft cheese
CEEEFILRTV	reflective
CEEEFINNNS	Fescennine
CEEEFINORU	nourice-fee
CEEEFINRRS	firescreen
CEEEFINRRT	centre-fire
CEEEFINRSS	fierceness
CEEEFIPRTV	perfective
CEEEFLLOOW	fleece-wool
CEEEFMNRST	fremescent
CEEEFMORTV	feme covert
CEEEFNRSTV	fervescent
CEEEFPRRTU	prefecture
CEEEGGILNN	negligence
CEEEGHIKLN	ingle-cheek
CEEEGHINPT	eightpence
CEEEGHJOSU	chose jugée
CEEEGIINPT	epigenetic
CEEEGIINRS	genericise
CEEEGIINRZ	genericize
CEEEGILNTV	neglective
CEEEGINNOT	neogenetic
CEEEGINNOX	xenogeneic
CEEEGINOTX	exogenetic
CEEEGINRST	energetics
CEEEGINRTV	vicegerent
	viceregent
CEEEGINSTU	eugenecist
CEEEGKQRUY	grecque key
CEEEGLLNOW	New College
CEEEGLNORT	electrogen
CEEEGNORSS	Seger cones
CEEEGNRRSU	resurgence
CEEEHHLORS	horseleech
CEEEHHMRTU	Erechtheum
CEEEHHRSTU	Erechtheus
CEEEHIKNSS	cheekiness
CEEEHIMRST	crime sheet
CEEEHIMSTT	chemisette
CEEEHINPTT	epenthetic
CEEEHINRSS	cheeriness
CEEEHINSSS	cheesiness
CEEEHINSTT	teschenite
CEEEHJLNOS	John Cleese
CEEEHKNPRY	henpeckery
CEEEHKPRTU	up the creek
CEEEHKRSSS	Cherkesses
CEEEHLLSSY	Seychelles
CEEEHLMOOT	come to heel
CEEEHLPSSS	speechless
CEEEHMMNSY	mesenchyme
CEEEHMNOSW	somewhence
CEEEHMORTT	hectometre
CEEEHNOPQU	open cheque
CEEEHNOPSS	ecphoneses
CEEEHNORSS	chersonese
CEEEHOQRUU	Eurocheque
CEEEHORRST	threescore
CEEEHORSST	scoresheet
CEEEHORSTT	hectostere
CEEEHRRRTY	cherry tree
CEEEIILMPT	epimeletic
CEEEIILNRS	resilience
CEEEIINRTV	ciné vérité
CEEEIJLTVY	ejectively
CEEEIKKPTW	keep wicket
CEEEILLPRV	price level
CEEEILLTVY	electively
CEEEILMNNT	clementine✧
CEEEILMORT	ceilometer
CEEEILMRTT	telemetric
CEEEILNNRT	centreline
CEEEILNORT	re-election
CEEEILNPRT	percentile
CEEEILNPRY	celery pine
CEEEILNPST	pestilence
CEEEILNRTV	live centre
CEEEIMNNTT	enticement
CEEEIMNNTV	evincement
CEEEIMNRST	mesenteric
CEEEIMNRTT	centimeter
	centimetre
CEEEIMNTTX	excitement
CEEEIMOPSU	mousepiece
CEEEIMRRRS	merceriser
CEEEIMRRRZ	mercerizer
CEEEINNPPY	penny-piece
CEEEINNPRT	pertinence
CEEEINORRT	re-erection
CEEEINPRSS	creepiness
CEEEINPRTT	penteteric
CEEEINTTWY	winceyette
CEEEIORRST	corsetière
CEEEIORTVX	overexcite
CEEEIPPRTV	perceptive
	preceptive
CEEEIPRSTV	respective
CEEEKKLNPS	kenspeckle
CEEEKKLOPR	lock-keeper
CEEEKOPRRW	crow-keeper
CEEEKRRSSU	seersucker
CEEELLLNTT	nettle-cell
CEEELLNNOP	penoncelle
CEEELLNPRY	repellency
CEEELLRRWY	crewellery
CEEELMORRT	electromer
CEEELNRSSV	cleverness
CEEELNSSST	selectness
CEEELORSST	electoress
CEEELORSTT	corselette
CEEELPSSTX	exceptless
CEEELRRSSU	recureless
CEEEMNNRST	secernment
CEEEMNOPRS	recompense
CEEEMNORRT	centromere
CEEEMNOTYZ	ectoenzyme
CEEEMNRSTU	securement
CEEEMOPRSU	creepmouse
CEEENNRSST	recentness
CEEENOPPRT	prepotence
CEEENOPRST	open secret
CEEENORSSV	seven-score
CEEENORTTY	enterocyte
CEEENRRSTT	rest centre
CEEENRSSST	secretness
CEEENRSSSU	secureness
CEEENRSSTT	screen test
	screen-test
CEEERSSTUX	executress
CEEFFFIIOR	fire-office
CEEFFFLNOU	offenceful
CEEFFGOOPT	pogo effect
CEEFFHILNS	Schlieffen
CEEFFHIMOO	Home Office
CEEFFHNORU	forfeuchen
CEEFFHOOPS	coffee shop
CEEFFIIOPP	Pipe Office
CEEFFIKNST	skin effect
CEEFFILLMO	coffee mill
CEEFFINPTY	fifty pence
CEEFFIOORV	overoffice
CEEFFIOPRR	offer price
CEEFFMOOOR	coffee room
CEEFGHINNR	greenfinch
CEEFGILNRT	reflecting

CEEFGINOSU Cienfuegos
CEEFGINPRT perfecting
CEEFGINRTU centrifuge
CEEFGLLNTU neglectful
CEEFGLNRUY refulgency
CEEFHHNNRS French hens
CEEFHHNORT henceforth
CEEFHIPRTV fever pitch
CEEFHKLOPS folk-speech
CEEFHLLRUY cheerfully
CEEFHLNRUU uncheerful
CEEFHLOORS free school
CEEFHMNNOT fence month
CEEFHMNORW from whence
CEEFHNNRSS Frenchness
CEEFHNOORS forechosen
CEEFHORTTU fourchette
CEEFIILNRT ferniticle
CEEFIILNTV inflective
CEEFIIMNNU munifience
CEEFIINORS confiserie
CEEFIINPRT perficient
CEEFIJLNST self-inject
CEEFIJLORU rejoiceful
CEEFIKLNRT ferntickle
CEEFIKLNSS fickleness
CEEFIKLORT life-rocket
CEEFILMOOT come to life
CEEFILNNRU influencer
CEEFILNORT reflection
CEEFILNRTY fernyticle
CEEFILORVX flexi-cover
CEEFILRTTU file-cutter
CEEFINOORT fore-notice
CEEFINOPRT perfection
CEEFINOSUV veneficous
CEEFIORRSU ceriferous
CEEFKLLSSY fecklessly
CEEFKLORTT fetterlock
CEEFLNOORW coneflower
CEEFLNOPRU profluence
CEEFLNORST florescent
CEEFLPPRTU pluperfect
CEEFLPRSTU respectful
CEEFMNNORT conferment
CEEFNOPRST spent force
CEEFOORRSU forecourse
CEEFORRRSS cross-refer
CEEFORRSST C S Forester
CEEGHHOPTT get the chop
CEEGHIILMP hemiplegic
CEEGHIINPT nightpiece
CEEGHIMORT geothermic
CEEGHIMOST geochemist
CEEGHIOQRU giro cheque
CEEGHIORST eightscore
CEEGHLNORT greencloth
CEEGHLOPST clothes-peg
CEEGHNOPSS speech-song
CEEGIILNTV Gil Vicente
CEEGIINOST isogenetic
CEEGIINOTV give notice
CEEGIINPRV perceiving
CEEGIINSTT geneticist
CEEGIINSTU eugenicist
CEEGIKLNOR King Creole
CEEGILLOOT teleologic
CEEGILNNOT neglection
CEEGILNPRY creepingly
CEEGIMMNSU e e cummings
CEEGINNOOR coregonine
CEEGINNORU encoignure
neurogenic
CEEGINNQSU sequencing
CEEGINNRSS screenings
CEEGINNRST nigrescent
CEEGINNRSU insurgence
CEEGINNSTY syngenetic
CEEGINOORT erotogenic
orogenetic
CEEGINOOST osteogenic
CEEGINOPRS precognise
CEEGINOPRZ precognize
CEEGINORRS recogniser
CEEGINORRZ recognizer
CEEGINOSTV congestive
CEEGINPRST respecting
CEEGINPRTX excerpting
CEEGINRSTY synergetic
CEEGIOOPST go to pieces
CEEGKORRSS Greek cross
CEEGLLNNOS Glenn Close
CEEGLORSTU Gloucester
CEEGMOTYYZ zygomycete
CEEGNNORRW crown green
CEEGNNORTV convergent
CEEGNOOSTU ectogenous
CEEGNPRSUU upsurgence
CEEGNRSTTU turgescent
CEEHHIKMNO Hockenheim
CEEHHILNOY honey-chile
CEEHHILPTW pitch-wheel
CEEHHIMORT come-hither
CEEHHKOOTT cheektooth
CEEHHNOTTY theotechny
CEEHIIKNNS chinese ink✧
CEEHIILNOT Eneolithic
CEEHIIMRST erethismic
CEEHIIORSZ heroic size
CEEHIIOTVW white voice
CEEHIIPPRR peripheric
CEEHIIRRST heritrices
CEEHIIRSTT erethistic
CEEHIKLNOY hockey line
CEEHIKORST the Rockies
CEEHIKPPRS schipperke
CEEHILMNOP clomiphene
CEEHILNOPR necrophile
CEEHILNOPT telephonic
CEEHILNORU euchlorine
CEEHILOOPS helioscope
CEEHILOPRT helicopter
CEEHILORTT hectolitre
CEEHILOSVY cohesively
CEEHILPSST ecthlipses
CEEHILSSTY chessylite
CEEHIMMOOR homeomeric
CEEHIMMPSY emphysemic
CEEHIMNNRT enrichment
CEEHIMNRTT Metternich
CEEHIMNTTU technetium
CEEHIMOOPR heroic poem
CEEHIMOPTU mouthpiece
CEEHIMORRY cherimoyer
CEEHIMORTX exothermic
CEEHIMSSTU sheet music
CEEHINNORT incoherent
CEEHINOPPR Hippocrene
CEEHINOPSS ecphonesis
CEEHINORSS heroicness
CEEHINPPRW pipe-wrench
CEEHINRRST christener
rechristen
CEEHINRSTW Winchester®
winchester✧
CEEHINSSST chestiness
CEEHINSSTT tetchiness
CEEHIOPRSX exospheric
CEEHIOPSTT The Poetics
CEEHIORSTT theoretics
CEEHIPRRRY Cherry Ripe
CEEHIRRSTV Chris Evert
CEEHIRSTTY hysteretic
CEEHIRSTWZ Schweitzer
CEEHKKOOYY hokey cokey
CEEHKLNOTT kente cloth
CEEHKLOOPT pocket-hole
CEEHKNORSS horse's neck
CEEHLLMORT mother cell
CEEHLLNOSW well-chosen
CEEHLLNSUW Welsh uncle
CEEHLMORTY emery cloth
CEEHLMOSZZ schemozzle
CEEHLNOOPT technopole
CEEHLNORTY coherently
CEEHLNORWW crown-wheel
CEEHLNOTUW count wheel
CEEHLNQSSU quenchless
CEEHLORSST tocherless
CEEHMMOORR chromomere
CEEHMOOPRT hoc tempore
CEEHNOOPPS nephoscope
CEEHNOOPRT ctenophore
CEEHNOORTT heterocont
CEEHNOPRTY hypocentre
CEEHNORRYY Henry Royce
CEEHNORSTV chervonets
CEEHNPPRTU thruppence
CEEHOOPRRS horse-coper
CEEHOOPSST post-echoes
CEEHOPRSTY spherocyte
CEEIIILNNS sicilienne
CEEIIINNPS insipience

CEEIIINSTZ citizenise
CEEIIINTZZ citizenize
CEEIIJORST jeistiecor
CEEIIKLNPR princelike
CEEIIKLNPT picket line
CEEIILLLTV vitellicle
CEEIILLMRV vermicelli
CEEIILNOSU isoleucine
CEEIILNRSY resiliency
CEEIILNRTT centiliter
centilitre
CEEIILNSSX in excelsis
CEEIILPRSV lip service
CEEIILRTTY erectility
CEEIILTTVY electivity
CEEIIMMPRT metempiric
CEEIIMNNTT incitement
CEEIIMNOPR minor piece
CEEIIMNRTV ivermectin
CEEIIMORTT meteoritic
CEEIIMOSST semeiotics
CEEIIMPRRT perimetric
CEEIIMPSSS speciesism
CEEIIMPSST epistemics
CEEIIMQRSU semicirque
CEEIINNORV inner voice
CEEIINNPPR en principe
CEEIINNSST insistence
CEEIINOPRW cowrie-pine
CEEIINOSST sectionise
CEEIINOSTZ sectionize
CEEIINPPRT percipient
CEEIINPSTV inspective
CEEIINRSTT interstice
CEEIINSSTT seicentist
CEEIINSSTZ citizeness
CEEIINTTVX extinctive
CEEIIOPPSS episcopise
CEEIIOPPSZ episcopize
CEEIIORRST escritoire
CEEIIPSSST speciesist
CEEIIRSSTU securities
securitise
CEEIIRSTUZ securitize
CEEIJLOPRT projectile
CEEIJOPRTV projective
CEEIKLLLLR killer cell
CEEIKLNOPU leukopenic
CEEIKLNRSS silkscreen
CEEIKLSSTT ticketless
CEEIKNOTTZ zone-ticket
CEEIKNPRTY pernickety
CEEIKNRSSS sickerness
CEEILLNRST stenciller
CEEILLOOPT coleoptile
CEEILLORSS recoilless
CEEILLPRTT letter-clip
CEEILMNOOT teleonomic
CEEILMNOPT incomplete
CEEILMNORT clinometer
CEEILMNOSS comeliness
CEEILMNSTU semilucent
CEEILMOPRS microsleep
CEEILMOPTV completive
CEEILNNSTU inesculent
CEEILNOORS recolonise
CEEILNOORW wine cooler
CEEILNOORZ recolonize
CEEILNOPRT prelection
CEEILNOPSY Polyneices
CEEILNORST encloister
CEEILNORTT crinolette
CEEILNORVW corn weevil
CEEILNORVY overnicely
CEEILNQSTU liquescent
CEEILNRSUY insecurely
CEEILNRTTY reticently
CEEILNRTUV ventricule
CEEILORRST cloisterer
CEEILORSST sclerotise
CEEILORSTZ sclerotize
CEEILOSSUV vesiculose
CEEILPRSUV preclusive
CEEIMMOPRT emmetropic
CEEIMMORRT micrometer
micrometre
CEEIMNNOPR prominence
CEEIMNOORS economiser
CEEIMNOORT iconometer
CEEIMNOORZ economizer
CEEIMNOSST centesimos
CEEIMNSSSU meniscuses
CEEIMORSTV viscometer
CEEIMOSSTV vicomtesse
CEEIMPRRRU premier cru
CEEINNNOTV convenient
CEEINNOPST post-Nicene
CEEINNORTU recontinue
CEEINNOSTT cosentient
CEEINNPRTY pertinency
CEEINNPSST spinescent
CEEINOOPST teinoscope
CEEINOPPRT perception
CEEINOPRSS encopresis
precession
CEEINOPRTU pie-counter
CEEINOPRTV optic nerve
CEEINOPRTX excerption
CEEINORRSW cornerwise
CEEINORRTT citron tree
CEEINORSTV ventricose
CEEINORTTV convertite
CEEINORTTY coeternity
CEEINOSSTX exoticness
CEEINOSTTX coexistent
CEEINPPRSU spruce pine
CEEINPRRTX precentrix
CEEINPRSTU putrescine
CEEINPRTTU percutient
CEEINRRSTU scrutineer
CEEINRSSSW screwiness
CEEINRSSTY syncretise
CEEINRSTTT trecentist
CEEINRSTTV vitrescent
CEEINRSTUU secure unit
CEEINRSTYZ syncretize
CEEINRTTUX extincture
CEEIOPRRSV Pecos River
CEEIOPRTTV protective
CEEIOPRVWY review copy
CEEIOPSTTW cop it sweet
CEEIOPSTUX exceptious
CEEIORRTUU couturière
CEEIORSTTU tricoteuse
CEEIPRRSUV precursive
CEEIPRSSUV percussive
CEEIPSSTUV susceptive
CEEJNOOSSS jocoseness
CEEJOPRRTU projecture
CEEKLLMOST Tom Selleck
CEEKLLRSSY recklessly
CEEKLMOPRT rock temple
CEEKLNRTTU turtleneck✧
CEEKLOORRV overlocker
CEEKLOPSST pocketless
CEEKLOPSTU outspeckle
CEEKLORRWW crewelwork
CEEKLRSUVY culver-keys
CEEKNOORRV overreckon
CEEKOOPTTV pocket veto
CEEKOPRSTT step rocket
CEEKOPSTTV vest pocket
vest-pocket
CEELLMOPTY completely
CEELMMNOPT complement
CEELMNNOOS somnolence
CEELMNOOSU nucleosome
CEELMNOPTU couplement
CEELMNRSUU Uncle Remus
CEELMOORTU coulometer
CEELNORSVY conversely
CEELNORVVY revolvency
CEELOOORSV loose cover
CEELOOPRRT Cole Porter
CEELORRSTY clerestory
CEELORSTTU locust tree
CEEMMOORRY core memory
CEEMMOTXYY myxomycete
CEEMNNOOWY new economy
new-economy
CEEMNNSTTY encystment
CEEMNOOPSS meconopses
CEEMNOORST centrosome
CEEMNOORUV unovercome
CEEMNOOSTU coenosteum
CEEMNOPRSU preconsume
CEEMNOPRTU recoupment
CEEMNOPRTY pycnometer
CEEMNORTUY neurectomy
CEEMNPSSTU spumescent
CEEMOOPPRS precompose
CEEMOOPTTU outcompete
CEEMOORSTT come to rest

scotometer
CEEMOPRRSS recompress
CEEMORTTUY uterectomy
CEENNOPRTU centre upon
CEENNOQSTU consequent
CEENNORRTU rencounter
CEENNOSSVX convexness
CEENNPRSSY pennycress
CEENOOPPRS copper nose
CEENOORSVX ex converso
CEENOORTTT cotton tree
CEENOPPPRR peppercorn
CEENOPPRTY prepotency
CEENOPRSTT torpescent
CEENOQRSSU conqueress
CEENOQRSTU reconquest
CEENORRTUV rev counter
CEENORSTUU countersue
CEENORTTUX contexture
CEENPRRRTU percurrent
CEENPRSSSU spruceness
CEENPRSTTU putrescent
CEEOOPRSTV Vertoscope®
CEEOPPRRTY preceptory
CEEOPRRSTT retrospect
CEEOPRRSTU persecutor
CEEOPRSTTT Peter Scott
CEEPRRSSSW screw press
CEEPRTTTUY type cutter
CEERSSSUUX excursuses
CEFFFFHOTU off the cuff
CEFFFHIORS coffer-fish
CEFFGIILOR office girl
CEFFHIINOR chiffonier
CEFFHILOOY Holy Office
CEFFHINSSU chuffiness
CEFFHNOORR French roof
CEFFIIKKLN flick-knife
CEFFIILTWY Wycliffite
CEFFIINSTU sufficient
CEFFIOOPST post office✧
CEFFLLORUY forcefully
CEFGHILRTW flight crew
CEFGIIKNPR fingerpick
CEFGIINPSY specifying
CEFGIINRTY certifying
rectifying
CEFGINNORR conferring
CEFGLOORSU golf course
CEFHHINORT Richthofen
CEFHHNNORR French horn
CEFHHOOPRT for the chop
CEFHIIRRST First Reich
CEFHIKNRSS French kiss
CEFHIKRSSU suckerfish
CEFHILLOOS life school
CEFHILPRTU pitcherful
CEFHILPRTY flypitcher
CEFHILSTTU cuttlefish
CEFHLLNORR French roll
CEFHLMNPRU French plum
CEFHNOORTT trench foot
CEFIIILNTV inflictive
CEFIIILNTY infelicity
CEFIIIMNST feministic
CEFIIJRTUU fruit juice
CEFIIKLRRT rick-lifter
CEFIIKMNNY Mickey Finn
CEFIIKQRRU quick-firer
CEFIILNNOT inflection
CEFIILNOQU cinquefoil
CEFIILOPRY fire-policy
CEFIILOSTU felicitous
CEFIIMNNOT omnificent
CEFIIMNNTU munificent
CEFIINOPRT proficient
CEFIINOPST pontifices
CEFIINOSTU infectious
CEFIKLMOSU Isle of Muck
CEFIKLOORT foot-licker
CEFILLLOOS Isle of Coll
CEFILLMRUY mercifully
CEFILMNRUU unmerciful
CEFILMOORS frolicsome
CEFILMOPRY clypeiform
CEFILMOPXY complexify
CEFILOOPRR floor price
CEFILOPRRS rifle corps
CEFILORSUU luciferous
CEFIMORRSU securiform
CEFIMORSUU muciferous
CEFINNOOSS confession
CEFINOORSU coniferous
CEFINORSUU nuciferous
CEFINRSSSU scurfiness
CEFIOORSUV vociferous
CEFIORRSSY fiery cross
CEFKKORSTU sucket fork
CEFKLOPSTU pocket-fuls
CEFLLOORSU self-colour
CEFLLRSTUY cluster fly
CEFLLSTTUU scuttleful
CEFLNOORRW cornflower
CEFLNOORVW flown cover
CEFLOORRWW crow-flower
CEFLORSTUW cut flowers
CEFLPSSTUU suspectful
CEFOOOPSTY foetoscopy
CEGGHIMNUW chewing gum
CEGGHIORST ostrich-egg
CEGGIILNNR cringeling
CEGGILNOSS clogginess
CEGGIMNTTU gem-cutting
CEGGINNORV converging
CEGGINOOST geognostic
CEGHIIILLN ice hilling
CEGHIIKNNT thickening
CEGHIILLNS chiselling
CEGHIILOOR hierologic
CEGHIINNUY unhygienic
CEGHIINORZ rhizogenic
CEGHIINOST histogenic
CEGHIINPPR rechipping
CEGHIINRTT chittering
CEGHILMNOP phlegmonic
CEGHILNOOP nephologic
CEGHILNOOT ethnologic
CEGHILNOST close thing
CEGHILNPPS schlepping
CEGHILNQSU squelching
CEGHILOORR logorrheic
CEGHILOPRY hypergolic
CEGHIMMNOO homecoming
CEGHINNOPY hypnogenic
CEGHINOOPT photogenic
CEGHINOORR gonorrheic
CEGHINOORT orthogenic
CEGHINOPTY phytogenic
pythogenic
CEGHINORRU chirurgeon
CEGHINORTY trichogyne
CEGHIOPSSY geophysics
CEGHIRRRUY chirurgery
CEGHLNOOTY technology
CEGHLOOORY choreology
CEGHOOPRSY hygroscope
CEGIIIMNNT meningitic
CEGIIINOSV visiogenic
CEGIIINSST gneissitic
CEGIIJNORS rejoicings
CEGIIKLLNN nickelling
CEGIIKMNRS smickering
CEGIIKNNQU quickening
CEGIIKPRST pig-sticker
CEGIILLNNP pencilling
CEGIILNNPR princeling
CEGIILNNSS clinginess
CEGIILNNST stenciling
CEGIILNNTY enticingly
CEGIILNOSU genius loci
CEGIILNPRY piercingly
CEGIILNTXY excitingly
CEGIILOPTT epiglottic
CEGIILOSTU eulogistic
CEGIINNRSV scrivening
CEGIINNTUX unexciting
CEGIINOPRR Prince Igor
CEGIINOSST Gnosticise
CEGIINOSTZ Gnosticize
CEGIINRRTU recruiting
CEGIJNOPRT projecting
CEGIKNOOPR rock pigeon
CEGIKNORST stockinger
CEGIKNSTTU get stuck in
CEGILLMNOP compelling
CEGILLMOSU collegiums
CEGILLOOXY lexicology
CEGILMNOOP monoplegic
CEGILMOORT metrologic
CEGILNNOST clingstone
CEGILNORTU toe-curling
CEGILNORWY coweringly
CEGILNOTVY covetingly

CEGILNRSTU clustering
CEGILOORUV give colour
CEGILORSSS scissor-leg
CEGIMNNSSU McGuinness
CEGIMNOORS ergonomics
CEGIMNORTU tumorgenic
CEGINNNOTT contingent
CEGINNOOST congestion
CEGINNOQRU conquering
CEGINNORST constringe
CEGINNOSTT contesting
CEGINNRRUU unrecuring
CEGINNRSTY stringency
CEGINNRSUY insurgency
CEGINOORRV River Congo
CEGINOPRTT protecting
CEGINOQTTU coquetting
CEGINRTTUV curvetting
CEGIOORRUX Rouge Croix
CEGLMOOOTY cometology
CEGLMOOTYY mycetology
CEGLNNOORR long corner
CEGLNOOSYY synecology
CEGOOPRRTY gyrocopter
CEGORSSSTY Scots Greys
CEHHHIIKRT hitch-hiker
CEHHHKRSUV Khrushchev
CEHHIILMNT helminthic
CEHHILORSW shriche-owl
shriech-owl
CEHHIMRTUY eurhythmic
CEHHIOOPRT theophoric
CEHHIOOPST theosophic
CEHHIOPRST hectorship
CEHHIOPTTY hypothetic
CEHHKLLOSS shellshock
CEHHLLOOTW whole cloth
CEHHLOORST horse-cloth
CEHHLORTTW Letchworth
CEHIIINRST trichinise
CEHIIINRTZ trichinize
CEHIIJOSTV Jehovistic
CEHIIKLRST Christlike
CEHIIKNTTW think twice
CEHIIKRTTV Trevithick
CEHIIKRTTW whitterick
CEHIIKSTTW white stick
CEHIILLNSS chilliness
CEHIILLOOP oleophilic
CEHIILMORT Roche limit
CEHIILMOST homiletics
Mesolithic
CEHIILNNTT thin client
CEHIILNOOP oenophilic
CEHIILNORS chlorinise
CEHIILNORZ chlorinize
CEHIILNPST clientship
CEHIILOPTY heliotypic
CEHIILORTY leiotrichy
CEHIILPSST ecthlipsis
CEHIIMNNRS miner's inch
CEHIIMNORT thermionic
CEHIIMNORY Hieronymic
CEHIIMOPRT hemitropic
CEHIIMRSTY mythiciser
CEHIIMRTYZ mythicizer
CEHIIMSTTW time switch
CEHIINOPPR periphonic
CEHIINOPSV noviceship
CEHIINORST trichinose
CEHIINPRSS chirpiness
CEHIINPSST pitchiness
CEHIINSSTT in stitches
CEHIIOSTTY histiocyte
CEHIIPRSTY sphericity
CEHIIPSTUU euphuistic
CEHIIRRTTU urethritic
CEHIIRRTTY erythritic
CEHIIRSSTU heuristics
CEHIISTTTW twitchiest
CEHIJKOPSY jockeyship
CEHIJNNOPR Prince John
CEHIKNNSSU chunkiness
CEHIKOPSTW whip socket
CEHIKORRSW crow-shrike
CEHIKPSTTU up the stick
CEHIKRSTTU trekschuit
CEHIKRSTYY hystericky
CEHILLMSSU music-shell
CEHILMOOPR lipochrome
CEHILMOOST schooltime
CEHILMOPPY Polyphemic
CEHILMORUX Michel Roux
CEHILNOPRY necrophily
CEHILNOPST clothes-pin
CEHILNPRSY lip-syncher
CEHILNRSTT slit trench
CEHILOOPST Scotophile
CEHILOORST holosteric
CEHILOPRST lectorship
CEHILOPRTU Turcophile
CEHILORSTY chrysolite
chrysotile
CEHILRSSST Christless
CEHIMMNSSU chumminess
CEHIMMOPRS morphemics
CEHIMNOOPR microphone
CEHIMNOORR chironomer
CEHIMNOOTT nomothetic
CEHIMNOPTY chimney pot
chimney top
CEHIMNOPUY eponychium
CEHIMOOORT homoerotic
CEHIMOOPTY mythopoeic
CEHIMOOTUZ zoothecium
CEHIMOPRTY microphyte
CEHIMOPSTY mesophytic
CEHIMORSSU semichorus
CEHIMORSTT thermotics
CEHIMORTTY mother city
CEHIMOSSUU house music✧
music house
CEHIMRSTUY Eurythmics
CEHIMSSTTT stem stitch
CEHIMSSTTU miss the cut
CEHINNNPPY penny-pinch
pinchpenny
CEHINNOPTU unphonetic
CEHINNRSTU unchristen
CEHINNRSTY strychnine
CEHINOOPRS rhinoscope
CEHINOORRS rhinoceros
CEHINOORRT rhinocerot
CEHINOPPRR pronephric
CEHINOPPSS choppiness
CEHINOPPTY phenotypic
CEHINOPRSS censorship
CEHINOPRSY hypersonic
CEHINOPRTY hypertonic
CEHINOPSTT open-stitch
pitchstone
CEHINOPTTY entophytic
CEHINORSTU urosthenic
CEHINOSSSY coyishness
CEHINOSSTU touchiness
CEHINPSSSU Spheniscus
CEHINSTTTT tent stitch
CEHIOOPRRT rheotropic
CEHIOOPRRY pyorrhoeic
CEHIOOPRSY hieroscopy
CEHIOORRRT retrochoir
CEHIOPRRST rectorship
CEHIOPRSTT prosthetic
rope stitch
CEHIOPRSTW white crops
CEHIOPRTXY xerophytic
CEHIOPSSTU Picts' house
CEHIOQSTTU coquettish
CEHIORSTTU Theocritus
CEHIORSTVW switch-over
CEHKLMNOOT klootchmen
CEHKLNOSUY hony-suckle
CEHKNOORST on the rocks
CEHKNORRSU cornhusker
CEHKOOPPRR rockhopper
CEHKOORSST stockhorse
CEHKRSSSTU huckstress
CEHLMNOSUU homuncules
CEHLMOOPRY polychrome
CEHLMOORST school term
CEHLMOORXY xylochrome
CEHLMOPTYY lymphocyte
CEHLMPRRUY cherry plum
CEHLNOORTU coolhunter
CEHLNOPRUW power lunch
CEHLOOOPRT tocopherol
CEHLOOPPRS prep school
CEHLOPRSTY polychrest
CEHMMNOOOR monochrome
CEHMMOOORS chromosome
CEHMMOTTYY thymectomy
CEHMNOOTTU touch-me-not
CEHMOOPRTY chromotype

	cormophyte
	ectomorphy
CEHMPRTTUY	pretty much
CEHNNOSTUU	cohune nuts
CEHNOOPRTT	top-notcher
CEHNOORSST	on the cross
CEHNOOSTTU	touchstone✧
CEHNOPRSTU	Scunthorpe
CEHNOPRSTY	phenocryst
CEHNOPRTYY	pyrotechny
CEHOOPPRST	hot coppers
CEHOOPRSTU	octopusher
CEHOORRSST	short score
CEHOORSTUU	courthouse
CEHORSTTTU	outstretch
CEIIIILSTV	civilities
CEIIIKNOST	isokinetic
CEIIILLNNP	penicillin
CEIIILNOSU	Ion Iliescu
CEIIILNPTX	inexplicit
CEIIILNSVY	incisively
CEIIILOPST	politicise
CEIIILOPTZ	politicize
CEIIIMMPRS	empiricism
CEIIIMOSSS	isoseismic
CEIIIMPRST	empiricist
CEIIIMRRST	Sir Tim Rice
CEIIIMRSTV	victimiser
CEIIIMRTVZ	victimizer
CEIIIMSSTY	seismicity
CEIIINPPRT	precipitin
CEIIIQSTTU	quietistic
CEIIJNNTUV	injunctive
CEIIKKLNPT	tickle pink
CEIIKLMORT	kilometric
CEIIKLNRST	crinkliest
CEIIKLNSSS	sickliness
CEIIKLOPRT	politicker
CEIIKMPSST	skepticism
CEIIKNOSTT	kenoticist
	tokenistic
CEIIKNRSST	trickiness
CEIIKNSSST	stickiness
CEIIKRSSTT	tricksiest
CEIILLLSTU	cellulitis
CEIILLNNOT	centillion
CEIILLNRTU	citrulline
CEIILLORRT	Torricelli
CEIILLOSSU	siliculose
CEIILLPTXY	explicitly
CEIILMNNOU	lenocinium
CEIILMOPST	polemicist
CEIILMORTT	tremolitic
CEIILMSSTV	victimless
CEIILNNOST	consilient
CEIILNOPRU	rupicoline
CEIILNOSTU	licentious
CEIILNOSTV	novelistic
CEIILNQSSU	cliquiness
CEIILNRTUV	ventriculi
CEIILOOPRT	riot police
CEIILOOPST	politicoes
CEIILOPSTX	post-exilic
CEIIMMORSS	microseism
CEIIMNNOST	omniscient
CEIIMNNOTU	income unit
CEIIMNRSSU	sinecurism
CEIIMNRTUV	centumviri
CEIIMORSST	isometrics
CEIIMORSTT	cottierism
CEIIMOSTTT	totemistic
CEIINNOPST	cispontine
	inspection
CEIINNORSV	environics
CEIINNOTTX	extinction
CEIINNSSTY	insistency
CEIINOPRST	isentropic
	triniscope
CEIINOPRSU	pernicious
CEIINOPRTV	voiceprint
CEIINOPSTT	nepotistic
CEIINORSSS	rescission
CEIINORSTT	trisection
CEIINPRSSS	crispiness
CEIINPSSTU	suscipient
CEIINRSSTU	scrutinise
	sinecurist
CEIINRSTUY	insecurity
CEIINRSTUZ	scrutinize
CEIIOOPSTZ	epizootics
CEIIOORSTU	trioecious
CEIIOPRSTY	preciosity
CEIIOPSSTY	speciosity
CEIIORSTTU	triticeous
CEIIORSTVV	vivisector
CEIIPRSSSU	scrip issue
CEIIPSSTUY	Puseyistic
CEIIRRSTTX	trisectrix
CEIIRSSSUZ	Suez Crisis
CEIJNOOPRT	projection
CEIJNORSTU	surjection
CEIKKORRST	kicksorter
CEIKKORRWW	wickerwork
CEIKLLORTT	Little Rock
CEIKLMMNTY	Mt McKinley
CEIKLNNOST	clinkstone
CEIKLNOSST	slickstone
CEIKLNPSSU	pluckiness
CEIKLOOPRW	wool-picker
CEIKLOORTV	rock violet
CEIKLOPRSU	prick-louse
CEIKLOPSTT	slit pocket
CEIKMOPRTV	mock privet
CEIKNOPPRS	copperskin
CEIKNORRST	corn-kister
CEIKNORRWZ	zinc-worker
CEIKNOSSST	stockiness
CEIKOPSTTU	soup-ticket
CEIKOTTTTU	ticket tout
CEILLMNOOT	Monticello
CEILLMNORR	corn-miller
CEILLNOOPT	ponticello
CEILLNOORU	colour line
CEILLOOQSU	colloquise
CEILLOOQUZ	colloquize
CEILLORSSW	scrollwise
CEILMMNOPT	compliment
CEILMNOOPT	completion
CEILMNOOPX	complexion
CEILMNOOTT	melicotton
CEILMNORTY	clinometry
CEILMNOSSU	miscounsel
CEILMNPSSU	clumpiness
CEILMNSSSU	clumsiness
CEILMOOOTV	locomotive
CEILMOOPST	leptosomic
CEILMOOPTU	Police Motu
CEILMOPSTT	completist
CEILMOPSUV	compulsive
CEILMOPTXY	complexity
CEILMORSTU	sclerotium
CEILMORTUV	volumetric
CEILMOSTUU	meticulous
CEILNNNOTY	innocently
CEILNNOPTY	nilpotency
CEILNNOSVY	insolvency
CEILNNPRUY	unprincely
CEILNOOPRS	necropolis
CEILNOORRS	resorcinol
CEILNOOSTZ	solonetzic
CEILNOPRSU	preclusion
CEILNORSTU	uncloister
CEILNORTTY	contritely
CEILNOSSST	costliness
CEILNOSSTT	clottiness
CEILNOSTUV	consultive
CEILNOSUVV	convulsive
CEILNPRSSY	princessly
CEILOORTTT	troctolite
CEILOPRSUU	periculous
CEILOPRSUV	corpus vile
CEILOPRSUY	preciously
CEILOPSSUY	speciously
CEILORRTUY	courtierly
CEILORSSST	cloistress
CEILORSTTU	courtliest
CEIMMMNOOT	common time
CEIMMMNOTT	commitment
CEIMMNOORT	metronomic
	monometric
CEIMMNOQUU	communique
	communiqué
CEIMMNORTY	metronymic
CEIMMNRSSU	crumminess
CEIMMOOPRS	compromise
CEIMMOORST	osmometric
CEIMMOORTV	overcommit
CEIMMOPSTU	miscompute
CEIMMORRTY	micrometry
CEIMMORSSU	commissure
CEIMMORTUX	commixture
CEIMNNOPRY	prominency
CEIMNNOSTT	miscontent

CEIMNOOOSU monoecious
CEIMNOOPRT pome-citron
CEIMNOOPSS meconopsis
CEIMNOORTY iconometry
CEIMNOPRSU proscenium
CEIMNORSST misconster
CEIMNORSUU ceruminous
CEIMNPRSSS scrimpness
CEIMNRSSTY syncretism
CEIMOOPRRS microspore
CEIMOOPRST proteomics
CEIMOOPRSY myrioscope
CEIMOOPRTT competitor
optometric
CEIMOORSTU eco-tourism
CEIMOORSTY sociometry
CEIMOPRRTY pyrometric
CEIMORSTVY viscometry
CEIMORTTVY vitrectomy
CEIMQSUUUU cuique suum
suum cuique
CEINNNOOSS consension
CEINNNOOSX connexions
CEINNNOOTT contention
CEINNNOOTV convention✧
CEINNOORSV conversion
CEINNOORTT cornettino
CEINNOOSTY non-society
CEINNOPRTY encryption
CEINNOPSSU in one's cups
CEINNOPTUX expunction
CEINNOSSTT consistent
CEINOOPRRT correption
porrection
CEINOOPRSS procession
CEINOOPRTT protection
CEINOOPRTV cover point
provection
CEINOOPSTT stenotopic
CEINOORSSU censorious
CEINOORTTV contortive
CEINOORTUX neurotoxic
CEINOOSSUY synoecious
CEINOPRSSU croupiness
percussion
supersonic
CEINOPRSTT introspect
CEINOPRSTU supertonic
CEINOQRRTU quercitron
CEINOQTUYZ Quezon City
CEINORRSST intercross
CEINORSTTT cornettist
CEINORSTUV ventricous
CEINOSSTUU incestuous
CEINOSTTTU constitute
CEINPRRRTU rip current
CEINPRSTUU sun picture
CEINRSSSTT strictness
CEINRSSSTU crustiness
CEINRSSSUV scurviness
CEINRSSTTY syncretist

CEIOOPRRST proctorise
CEIOOPRRTU Puerto Rico
CEIOOPRRTY corporeity
CEIOOPRRTZ proctorize
CEIOORSSTT scooterist
CEIOORSTTU eco-tourist
CEIOOSSTXY exocytosis
CEIOPPRRTT protreptic
CEIOPRRTTX protectrix
CEIOPRRTUV corruptive
CEIOPRRTUZ prize court
CEIOPRRTWY copywriter
CEIOQRSSTU quit scores
CEIORRSSSY rescissory
CEIPPRSTTY typescript
CEIPRRSSTU scriptures✧
CEJJKMOPUY jump-jockey
CEJNOORRTU contre-jour
CEJNOORTUU conjure out
CEJOOORRSZ José Orozco
CEKLLLSSUY lucklessly
CEKLMOOORR locker room
CEKLMORTTU mock turtle✧
CEKLMPRSUU lumpsucker
CEKLNOORTY control key
CEKLNOSTUY lucky stone
CEKLOOORSW slow cooker
CEKLORSTUV lovestruck
CEKNNOPSTY penny stock
CEKOOPPRRW copperwork
CEKOORRSUW coursework
CEKOORSTTU stock route
CEKORRSTUV overstruck
CELLLNTUUY luculently
CELLNOORRT controller
CELLNOORSU counsellor
CELLOOORSU lose colour
CELLOOOSST close-stool
CELLOORRSY Rolls-Royce®
CELLOORSSU colourless
CELLORSUUY ulcerously
CELMMOOSUW Moscow Mule
CELMMOPTUY lumpectomy
CELMNNOOSY somnolency
CELMNOOOOT melocotoon
CELMNOOSSY Ceylon moss
CELMOOPRTY completory
CELMOORSTY sclerotomy
CELMOORTUY coulometry
CELNOOORTU tone colour
CELNOPRSUU pronucleus
CELNOPSTYY pycnostyle
CELNORSTUY Lucy Stoner
CELOOOPRSU procoelous
CELOOORRSU rose colour
CELOOORRUV overcolour
CELOOPRRTU colporteur
CELOORTUUZ zooculture
CELOOSSSSU colossuses
CELOOSTUVY covetously
CELOPPRTUU pop culture

CELPRSSSTU sculptress
CEMMNNOOSS commonness
CEMNOOORSU monocerous
CEMNOPRSTU sperm count
CEMOOPPRRW copperworm
CEMOOPRRSS compressor
CEMOOPRSTU composture
CENNNNOOTT non-content
CENNNORRTU non-current
CENNOOPPUU pounce upon
CENNOOPRRU pronouncer
CENOOOSSTT to one's cost
CENOOPPPRR corn popper
CENOOPPRSY pycnospore
CENOORRSSU Rouen cross
CENOORRTTV controvert
CENOORSSST cross-stone
CENOORSTTY Notoryctes
CENOPRSTUY counterspy
CEOOPPRRST prospector
CEOOPRRSTU prosecutor
CEOOPRRTTY protectory
CEOORRSTUV rover scout
CEOPPRSSTU prospectus
CEOPRRRSUY percursory
precursory
CEOPRRSSTU Procrustes
CEPPRRSTUU upper crust
upper-crust
CFFFIISSTU fisticuffs
CFFGIIIORR frigorific
CFFGIIKNOT ticking-off
CFFGILNOOO cooling-off
CFFGILNOSY scoffingly
CFFHIINOPS coffin ship
CFGHIILLNY filchingly
CFGIIKLNOR frolicking
CFGIIKNOSS fossicking
CFGIIMNNOR confirming
CFGIINNORU Finno-Ugric
Ugro-Finnic
CFGIINNOSY consignify
CFGIINOPRT forcing-pit
CFGIINOSTY Scotifying
CFGILOSUUU lucifugous
CFGILOUYZZ fuzzy logic
CFGIMNOORT comforting
CFGMMNOOOR common frog
CFGOOPRSUU focus group
CFHHIILRTY filthy rich
CFHIIKSSTT stick shift
CFHIMOPRSY scyphiform
CFHIOORSTT Otto Frisch
CFHKOOOPRS shockproof
CFHLLOOORT floorcloth
CFHLMOOORR chloroform
CFHNOOSTUY out of synch
CFHOOTTUUU out of touch
CFHOORRSTU fourscorth
CFIIILNNOT infliction
CFIIIMNORS incisiform

CFIIINOSTT fictionist
CFIIIOSTTU fictitious
CFIILMOOSU fimicolous
music folio
CFIILNOPRU unprolific
CFIILORSST floristics
CFIIMORRST cristiform
CFIINNNOOT non-fiction
CFIIOOPRRT torporific
CFIIOORRST Cristofori
CFIIRSTTUU futuristic
CFILLMOORU colour film
film colour
CFILLNOSUU full cousin
CFILMMORUU cumuliform
CFILMOOPRU poculiform
CFILMOORTY cotyliform
CFILMORRTU cultriform
CFILNOSTUU fonticulus
CFIMNOORST conformist
CFIMNOORTY conformity
CFKOOOSTTU out of stock
CFLLNORSUY scornfully
CFLLOOSSUU flosculous
CFLOOORRUU four-colour
CFLOOOSSTT coltsfoots
CFLOORSSUU scrofulous
CFOOORTTUU out of court
CGGHINNOTU hunting-cog
CGGIIKNPSU sucking-pig
CGGIILNNRY cringingly
CGGINNORSU scrounging
CGHHHILOOS high school
CGHHILLNTU light lunch
CGHHILOORU high colour
CGHHILORTT torchlight
CGHHINRRTU night-churr
CGHIIIOSTV Visigothic
CGHIIKLNOP holing-pick
CGHIIKNPSY physicking
CGHIIKNSTT nightstick
CGHIILLLNY chillingly
CGHIILLOOP philologic
CGHIILLOOT lithologic
CGHIILMORT microlight
CGHIILMSTU light music
CGHIILNNPY pinchingly
CGHIILNTWY witchingly
CGHIILOOOP ophiologic
CGHIILOOST histologic
CGHIILOPST phlogistic
CGHIILPRTY triglyphic
CGHIKLNOSY shockingly
CGHIKNORTW thick-grown
CGHILLOORS schoolgirl
CGHILMOOTY mythologic
CGHILNOSTT long stitch
CGHILNOTUY touchingly
CGHILNRSUY crushingly
CGHILOORTY trichology
CGHILOOSTY stichology
CGHILORRSU chorus girl
CGHILORSST crosslight
CGHIMNOORY chirognomy
CGHIMORSUU rough music
CGHINOOSYZ schizogony
CGHIOORTUV Victor Hugo
CGHLNOOORY chronology
CGHLNOOOSS song school
CGHLOOPSYY psychology
CGHNOOPSYY psychogony
CGHOPRTUUU cut up rough
CGIIIJNOST jingoistic
CGIIIKNNPT nit-picking
CGIIILLPUU Luigi Pulci
CGIIILNNTY incitingly
CGIIILNOST soliciting
CGIIILNSTU linguistic
CGIIILPSTU pugilistic
CGIIKLLNOR rollicking
CGIIKLNORV living rock
CGIIKNNOPR corking-pin
CGIIKNNOPY copying ink
CGIILMNOOV moving-coil
CGIILNPPRS spring clip
CGIILOOSTT isoglottic
CGIIMMNOTT committing
CGIIMNOSST Gnosticism
CGIIMNSSUW swing-music
CGIINNNOTU unnoticing
CGIINNOOST incognitos
CGIINOPPRW piping crow
CGIINOTTUY contiguity
CGIKLLNOOR rollocking
CGIKLNNOTU locking-nut
CGIKLNOPRS spring lock
CGIKNOSSTU King's Scout
CGIKNOSSTW swing-stock
CGILLNOSWY scowlingly
CGILLOSSYY glycolysis
CGILMOOSTY mycologist
CGILMOOSUY musicology
CGILNNOSTU consulting
CGILNOOOST nostologic
oncologist
CGILOOOPRT tropologic
CGILOOOTXY toxicology
CGILOOSTTY cytologist
CGIMNRRRUU curmurring
CGINOOPRST prognostic
CGINOOSTUU contiguous
CGINOPPTYY copy-typing
CGLMNOOSUY cynomolgus
CGLOOOPRTY proctology
CGLOOORTYY oryctology
CGLOOPRTYY cryptology
CGNOOOSTUY octogynous
CHHIIKPSTY phthisicky
CHHIIMRSST Chris Smith
CHHIIOSSTY ichthyosis
CHHIIPSTTW whipstitch
CHHILLRSUY churlishly
CHHILMOOPR chromophil
CHHILOOPSS school ship
CHHILOOPTY holophytic
CHHILORSTW shritch-owl
CHHIMNOOOP homophonic
CHHIMOPSSS schism shop
CHHIOOPPRS phosphoric
CHHLLOOPRY chlorophyl
CHHMMOOORY homochromy
CHIIIILNST nihilistic
CHIIILLOPP lipophilic
CHIIILOOPT ophiolitic
CHIIILPSTY syphilitic
CHIIINORST histrionic
CHIIINORTT trithionic
CHIIIPPRTU hippuritic
CHIIKLLSTY ticklishly
CHIIKLRSTY trickishly
CHIILMNOOT monolithic
CHIILMOOTT lithotomic
CHIILNOOPT phonolitic
CHIILNORTY chlorinity
CHIILOSTTY histolytic
CHIILPSSTT slip stitch
slip-stitch
CHIIMOOPRS isomorphic
CHIIMOPRRT trimorphic
CHIIMORRST trichroism
CHIIMORSST ostrichism
CHIIMORSTU humoristic
CHIINNOPPT pinchpoint
CHIINNOPSU pincushion
CHIINOPRSX crio-sphinx
CHIINOPSSU cousinship
CHIINORSTU trichinous
unhistoric
CHIIORSSSU rhoicissus
CHIIOSSSVY vichyssois
CHIIPRRSTY pyrrhicist
CHIIPRSTTW trip switch
CHIIRRSTUU Trichiurus
CHIKKLLSTU thick-skull
CHIKNOQRTU quickthorn
CHIKNORSWY corn whisky
CHIKOOPSST Pooh sticks
Poohsticks
CHIKORSSTW how's tricks?
CHIKORSTTW stitchwork
throw stick
CHILLMOPRY microphyll
CHILLNOSWY clownishly
CHILLOOPTT pilot cloth
CHILLOPSTY splotchily
CHILNOOPPY polyphonic
CHILNOOPXY xylophonic
CHILNOOQRU chloroquin
CHILNOPSSU consulship
CHILOOPPSY policy-shop
CHILOOPTTY photolytic
CHIMMNOORS monorchism
CHIMMOSTUU mouth music

CHIMNNOOOP	monophonic
CHIMNRSSTY	strychnism
CHIMOOOPRS	sophomoric
CHIMOOOPRZ	zoomorphic
CHIMOOPRSY	hypocorism
CHIMOORTTY	trichotomy
CHIMOSSSTT	moss stitch
CHINOOORTT	orthotonic
CHINOOPPTY	phonotypic
CHINOOPRSY	rhinoscopy
CHINOPRRST	corn thrips
CHINRSSSYY	synchrysis
CHIOOOPRTT	orthotopic
CHIOOOPRTZ	zootrophic
CHIOOPPRRY	pyrophoric
CHIOOPPTTY	phototypic
CHIOOPRSTT	orthoptics
CHIOOPTTXY	phytotoxic
CHIORSTTTW	stitchwort
CHKLMNOOST	monk's cloth
CHKLOOORSW	schoolwork
CHLMMMOTUY	mummy-cloth
CHLMNOSUUU	homunculus
CHLMOOOORS	schoolroom
CHLMOOPRYY	polychromy
CHLNOOTTUU	out to lunch
CHLOOOSTTT	colt's tooth
CHMMNOOORY	monochromy
CHMNOOPTTU	mutton chop
CHMOOPPPSY	psychopomp
CHNNOOORRT	chronotron
CHNOOORRTT	trochotron
CHOOOORSUZ	zoochorous
CHOOPRRSUY	cryophorus
CHOORTTUUY	youth court
CHORRSSTTU	shortcrust
CIIIIKLOPT	poikilitic
CIIIILMNPT	implicit in
CIIIILNNQU	inquilinic
CIIIILNTVY	incivility
CIIILLMPTY	implicitly
CIIILMNRTU	triclinium
CIIILMPSST	simplistic
CIIILMPSSU	Simplicius
CIIILMPSTY	simplicity
CIIILPRTTY	triplicity
CIIIMNNOST	nicotinism
CIIIMNORTU	tirocinium
CIIIMNPPRU	principium
CIIIMOPSTT	optimistic
CIIINNNOTT	intinction
CIIJMMORSW	Jim Crowism
CIIJNNNOTU	injunction
CIIKKNNOPT	knickpoint
CIIKMORRST	microskirt
CIIKNOSTTW	in two ticks
CIILLMOOSU	limicolous
CIILLNOOPS	cipollinos
CIILLNOOTU	illocution
CIILLOSTTY	stylolitic
CIILMMNTUU	nummulitic
CIILMNOPRS	Nicol prism
CIILMOOPRS	micropolis
CIILNOPSTU	punctilios
CIILNOSSYZ	zincolysis
CIILOOSSTU	solicitous
CIILOOSTUV	viticolous
CIILOPRTVY	proclivity
CIILRRSTUY	scurrility
CIILSSSTTY	stylistics
CIIMMNOOSS	commission
CIIMMNOOTX	commixtion
CIIMMOPRRS	microprism
CIIMNNOOTZ	monzonitic
CIIMNOPRRT	microprint
CIIMORRSTT	tricrotism
CIINNNOOPT	conniption
CIINNOORTT	contrition
CIINNOPRST	spintronic
CIINNOTTUY	continuity
CIINOOPRST	con spirito
CIINOOPRTX	picrotoxin
CIINOPRRST	corn spirit
CIINOSSSTY	cystinosis
CIIOORSTUV	victorious
CIIOPRSTTU	prosciutti
CIIOPSSSUU	suspicious
CIIPSTTTYY	stypticity
CIJKNOOSTT	joint-stock
CIJLNNOOTY	conjointly
CIKLLOSSTT	stock-still
CIKLNOOSTT	silk cotton
CIKLOOPSST	polo sticks
CIKMNOOPPU	nickumpoop
CIKNOPSTTU	put stock in
CIKOPRSTTU	up to tricks
CIKORRSTUW	rusticwork
CILLMNOOST	Tom Collins
CILLMNOOTT	cotton mill
CILLMOOQUU	colloquium
CILLMORSUY	collyriums
CILLMOSUUV	colluviums
CILLOOQSTU	colloquist
CILLOPRSTU	portcullis
CILLOPSTUY	Polyclitus
CILLOSSUUY	lusciously
CILMMOPUUV	compluvium
CILMNOOOOT	locomotion
CILMNOOPSU	compulsion
CILMNOOPYY	polyonymic
CILMNORUUV	involucrum
CILMNOSTUU	monticulus
CILMOOOPSS	cosmopolis
CILMOOSSTU	music stool
CILNNOOSUV	convulsion
CILOOPRSSY	corylopsis
CILOOPRSUU	rupicolous
CILORRSSUU	scurrilous
CIMNNOOOPP	nincompoop
CIMNNOSTUU	continuums
CIMNOOORXY	oxymoronic
CIMNOOPRSU	compursion
CIMNOOPSTY	toponymics
CIMNOORSST	consortism
CIMNOORSTU	consortium
CIMOOOPRST	compositor
CIMOORSSTU	roots music
CINNOOORTT	contortion
CINNOOPRSU	pronuncios
CINNOOSTUU	continuous
CINOOPPRRS	prison crop
CINOOPRRTU	corruption
CINOOPRSUY	urinoscopy
CINOORSSTY	consistory
CINOORSUUV	nucivorous
CINORRSTTU	instructor
CINORSSTUU	scrutinous
CINORSTTUY	Tony Curtis
CINOSTTUUY	unctuosity
CIOOPRSSTU	uroscopist
CIOOPRSTTU	prosciutto
CIOORRSTTU	tricrotous
CIOPPRRSSY	procrypsis
CIOPPRSSTT	PostScript®
	postscript
CIOPPSTTYY	copy typist
CIPPRRSTUU	stirrup cup
CKKNORSTUW	knockwurst
CKLLOORRSW	scrollwork
CKMNOORSTU	moonstruck
CKOOSSTUUY	sucks to you!
CKORSSTTTU	trust stock
CLLMOOPRUU	plum-colour
CLLMOOSSUU	molluscous
CLMMNNOOUY	uncommonly
CLMNOOOSUU	monoculous
CLMOOOORTU	oculomotor
CLMOOOORTY	locomotory
CLMOOPRSUY	compulsory
CLNOOOOTTW	cotton wool
CLNOOOPTTY	polycotton
CLNOORRTUU	turn colour
CLNOORSTUY	consultory
CLNOORTUWY	low-country
CLNOSTUUUY	unctuously
CLOOOPPSTY	coppy-stool
CLOOOPRRTU	prolocutor
CLOOOPSTUY	polytocous
CLOOORSSTU	colostrous
CLOOPPRSUU	colour-supp
CLOOSTTTUY	cutty-stool
CLOPRSSUUU	scrupulous
CMMMNOOOOR	common room
CMMNNNOOOU	common noun
CMNOOOOSTU	monotocous
CMNOOORTTW	cotton-worm
CMOOPPPRTY	prompt copy
CMOOSSTTYY	cystostomy
CNNOOTTUWY	county town
COOOPPRRRT	proproctor
COOORSSTTU	costus-root

D

DDDDDFUUYY fuddy-duddy
DDDDDHOOYY hoddy-doddy
DDDEEEFNNU undefended
DDDEEELORS Lord Deedes
DDDEEFIOST eisteddfod✧
DDDEEIINVX ex dividend
DDDEEINOSW disendowed
DDDEEINPRS dispredden
DDDEEIORRS disordered
DDDEFILOOW fiddlewood
DDDEGIIOOR didgeridoo
DDDEHLNORU Old Hundred
DDDEINOORW Edwin Drood
DDDELOORYY Roddy Doyle
DDDOORWWYY rowdy-dowdy
DDEEEEELTW tweedledee✧
DDEEEEMNRU unredeemed
DDEEEFGLNW new-fledged
DDEEEFIMNR free-minded
DDEEEGIINS inside edge
DDEEEGRSST get dressed
DDEEEHIRST three-sided
DDEEEHLNUY unheededly
DDEEEIMNNV even-minded
DDEEEIMNPT pedimented
DDEEEIMNRT determined
DDEEEIMNRU unremedied
DDEEEINNTX inextended
DDEEEINORZ Zener diode
DDEEEINRVY in very deed
DDEEEIRSSV dissevered
DDEEELMMOS meddlesome
DDEEELMNTY dementedly
DDEEELMTUW Tweedledum
DDEEELNTXY extendedly
DDEEELRSVY deservedly
DDEEENNRRU unrendered
DDEEENNRTU untendered
DDEEENNTUX unextended
DDEEENRRTU undeterred
DDEEENRSUV undeserved
DDEEENRSUX undersexed
DDEEEOOPRT deep-rooted
DDEEFFLNOY offendedly
DDEEFFNNOU unoffended
DDEEFGIILU field guide
DDEEFGIRRU red-figured
DDEEFHIRST red-shifted
DDEEFIIINT identified
DDEEFIILLN ill-defined
DDEEFIILMR midfielder
DDEEFIINSY Disneyfied
DDEEFIINTU definitude
DDEEFINNRU unfriended
DDEEFLMORY deformedly
DDEEGGHOOP hodgepodge
DDEEGGNNUU nudge, nudge
DDEEGGNOSS doggedness
DDEEGHNORY hodden-grey
DDEEGIINST indigested
DDEEGIIRUW wire-guided
DDEEGILNSY designedly
DDEEGILOSY god's eyelid
DDEEGILSTY digestedly
DDEEGINNSU undesigned
DDEEGINORR derring doe
DDEEGINSTU undigested
DDEEGJLLUW well-judged
DDEEHIILNP didelphine
DDEEHILNSU unshielded
DDEEHINNRU unhindered
DDEEHINNSS hiddenness
DDEEHINORR ride herd on
DDEEHLORSU shouldered
DDEEHNRTUY ythundered
DDEEIIKLLR riddle-like
DDEEIIKLMN like-minded
DDEEIILMNV evil-minded
DDEEIILNVW wild endive
DDEEIIMNOT demi-ditone
DDEEIIMOPR epidermoid
DDEEIIMRSU desiderium
DDEEIINRSW sidewinder
DDEEIIOPST epidotised
DDEEIIOPTZ epidotized
DDEEIIORSX deoxidiser
DDEEIIORXZ deoxidizer
DDEEIKMORS smoke-dried
DDEEIKORST desk editor
DDEEILLMNW well-minded
DDEEILLNRT tendrilled
DDEEILMMRT middle term
DDEEILMSTW Middle West
DDEEILNNTY intendedly
DDEEILNOSY one-sidedly
DDEEILNOTT dotted line
DDEEILSTTU lust-dieted
DDEEIMMOPR demirepdom
DDEEIMNNOP open-minded
DDEEIMNNRU underminde
DDEEIMNORS endodermis
DDEEIMNPRU epidendrum
DDEEIMNRTU undertimed
DDEEINNNTU unintended
DDEEINOOPT endopodite
DDEEINOPRS perdendosi
DDEEINORRV overridden
DDEEINPRUV undeprived
DDEEINRRUV underdrive
DDEEINRRUW underwired
DDEEINRSUZ undersized
DDEEINRTUV undiverted
DDEEINSTUV undivested
DDEEIOORRS deodoriser
DDEEIOORRZ deodorizer
DDEEIRSSST distressed
DDEELLOORW olde-worlde
DDEELNOPRU undeplored
DDEELNOPUX unexploded
DDEELRRSSU rudderless
DDEENNOPST despondent
DDEENNORTU undernoted
undertoned
DDEENNOSSS soddenness
DDEENNPRSU underspend
DDEENNSSSU suddenness
DDEENOOTTT dotted note
DDEENOPPST end-stopped
DDEENOPRUW unpowdered
DDEENRRSSU underdress
DDEEOORRSW o'er-drowsed
DDEEOORTTV dotted over
DDEEORSTTT dotted rest
DDEEORTVXY eddy vortex
DDEFFILSUY diffusedly
DDEFGIIIIR rigidified
DDEFHIIMUY dehumidify
DDEFHIRRSU rudderfish
DDEFHLNORU fundholder
DDEFIIILOS solidified
DDEFIILRUV fluid drive
DDEFIIMNOU unmodified
DDEFIIORSX dorsifixed
DDEFILLNOU ill-founded
DDEFILNNSU nun's-fiddle
DDEFIMNORR dendriform
DDEFINORRW word-finder
DDEFKNNRUU dunderfunk
DDEFLOOOTU flooded out
DDEFLORSSU Düsseldorf
DDEFMNORUU dumfounder
DDEGGGILOR gold-digger
DDEGHHIIMN high-minded
DDEGHILNNO Golden Hind
DDEGHINRSU shuddering
DDEGHMNOUU humdudgeon
DDEGHNORTU thunder god
DDEGIILNNR nidderling
DDEGIILNRY deridingly
DDEGIINPPU pudding-pie
DDEGILNNOW long-winded
DDEGILNORW welding rod
DDEGILNSUV devil's dung
DDEGILNUUV undivulged
DDEGILOORS dog-soldier
DDEGINNOPS desponding
DDEGINNORS dog's dinner
DDEGINNORU redounding
DDEGIOOPRR do porridge
DDEGLLLOOR rolled gold
DDEGLLNOUU loud-lunged
DDEGLNOORY dendrology
DDEGLNORUY groundedly
DDEGNNORUU ungrounded
DDEGNOORUV ground-dove
DDEGOOPSTT spotted dog
DDEGOORSSS dress-goods
DDEHHNOOOY hoydenhood
DDEHIIIMNS diminished
DDEHIIKNSY kidney dish
DDEHIILNOP delphinoid
DDEHIILNSW windshield
DDEHIILPSU disulphide

DDEHIIMOST Dodie Smith
DDEHILNOPS shield pond
DDEHILOPSU didelphous
DDEHIMNOST hiddenmost
DDEHINOPRS dendrophis
DDEHINOSSS shoddiness
DDEHIOOOPT photodiode
DDEHIORRRT third order
DDEHIORTTY do the dirty
DDEHJNNORY John Dryden
DDEHLOOSTU the ould sod
DDEIIIKKNW kiddiewink
DDEIIIMPSY epididymis
DDEIIINOTV divide into
DDEIIIPRST dispirited
DDEIIJNOST disjointed
DDEIIKNRRV drink-drive
DDEIIMNNOU diminuendo
DDEIINOPSS indisposed
DDEIINOSTU duodenitis
DDEIINOSUX unoxidised
DDEIINOUVZ zidovudine
DDEIINOUXZ unoxidized
DDEIIOPRSS dispersoid
DDEIIOPRSV disprovide
DDEIKNNOOS do one's kind
DDEIKNNRUW wunderkind
DDEILLNORV Lord Devlin
DDEILLNPSY splendidly
DDEILLOORS old soldier
DDEILLOPSY lopsidedly
DDEILLTTUW dull-witted
DDEILMMOST middlemost
DDEILOPSSY disposedly
DDEILORRSY disorderly
DDEILSSTUV devil's dust
DDEIMMOSSU desmodiums
DDEIMNOORR room-ridden
DDEINOORRW iron-worded
DDEINOPRUV unprovided
DDEINOPSSU undisposed
DDEINOPSUW upside down
upside-down
DDEINORSSS sordidness
DDEINPSTUU undisputed
DDEJRRRUUY jury-rudder
DDEKLNOOOW downlooked
DDELNORRUW underworld
DDENNOORSU round-nosed
DDENNOORUZ round dozen
DDENNORTUW downturned
DDENOOPRWW powder down
DDENOORSTU understood
DDENRSTUUY understudy
DDGGILNRUY drudgingly
DDGGOOOOYY goody-goody
DDGHIINOOR riding hood
DDGHIIRRYY hirdy-girdy
DDGHILNTUY thuddingly
DDGHLNOORU ground-hold
DDGHRRUUYY hurdy-gurdy
DDGIIILNOW wild indigo
DDGIILLMNY middlingly
DDGIILLNRY riddlingly
DDGIINNPSU spudding-in
DDGIKLMNOO Old Kingdom
DDGIKLNOOO odd-looking
DDGILLMNUY muddlingly
DDGILLNOPY ploddingly
DDGILMNOUW Ludwig Mond
DDGINOORSW dowsing rod
DDHIIIMSSY Yiddishism
DDHIIINORU hirudinoid
DDHILORRTW Third World
DDHINOOPTY diphyodont
DDHOOOOUWY how do you do?
how-do-you-do
DDIIIMNUUV individuum
DDIIKLNTWY tiddlywink
DDINNOOOTT notodontid
DDINOOOPRT diprotodon
DDINOPRSWY wind dropsy
DDOOOOORRT door-to-door
DEEEEEFPRZ deep-freeze
DEEEEENSWZ sneezeweed
DEEEEFFLRS self-feeder
DEEEEFILLN Lee Enfield
DEEEEFLRSS self-seeder
DEEEEFNRST enfestered
DEEEEFNRTT tenderfeet
DEEEEGINRS de-energise
DEEEEGINRZ de-energize
DEEEEGNNRR engenderer
DEEEEHLLLW well-heeled
DEEEEHMMOP homme d'épée
DEEEEIJLLL jellied eel
DEEEEILMNT needle time
DEEEEILNNP pine needle
DEEEEJOPWY joe-pye weed
DEEEELLSSW weeldlesse
DEEEELMNVY Mendeleyev
DEEEELMRSS redeemless
DEEEELSSSV seed vessel
DEEEEOPRRS pedereroes
DEEEFFOORR free-fooder
DEEEFFOORT free-footed
DEEEFGILNR greenfield
DEEEFHILNS needlefish
DEEEFHLNTU the needful
DEEEFHLORR freeholder
DEEEFHORSW foreshewed
DEEEFIJOUX feux de joie
DEEEFILLSX self-exiled
DEEEFILMNT defilement
DEEEFILNTV field event
DEEEFIMNNT definement
DEEEFJORTU jour de fête
DEEEFLORRW deflowerer
DEEEFMNORW freedwomen
DEEEFMNRRU referendum
DEEEFNORWZ freeze down
DEEEFNRTTU unfettered
DEEEFORRST deer forest
DEEEGGGLOY goggle-eyed
DEEEGHHHIL high-heeled
DEEEGHISUY hey-de-guise
DEEEGHSUYY hey-de-guyes
DEEEGIKNNW weekending
DEEEGILLNR ledger line
DEEEGILMTY gimlet-eyed
DEEEGILNRW Gene Wilder
DEEEGILNSY single-eyed
DEEEGIMORT Geodimeter®
DEEEGINRSS greediness
niger seeds
DEEEGINRSU under siege
DEEEGIPPPR pepperidge
DEEEGIRRST deregister
registered
DEEEGIRSSV degressive
DEEEGKMORS Greek modes
DEEEGLLOPR poll-degree
DEEEGLNORR gender role
DEEEGLNORV glendoveer
DEEEGLNRSS genderless
DEEEGLORRS gelder rose
DEEEGMNNOR mondegreen
DEEEGNNRRU engendrure
DEEEGNNRUV unrevenged
DEEEGNOPSU pseudogene
DEEEGNORSU degenerous
DEEEGORRVY overgreedy
DEEEHIKRRT Erik the Red
DEEEHILOTT diothelete✧
DEEEHILPRT three-piled
DEEEHIMNRT Methedrine®
DEEEHINORT deinothere
DEEEHINRST entrée dish
DEEEHIPRSS Hesperides
DEEEHJNTUZ Judenhetze
DEEEHLLRTY the elderly
DEEEHLLSSY heedlessly
DEEEHLLTWW well-thewed
DEEEHLMNTU unhelmeted
DEEEHLNORS lederhosen
DEEEHLOTTY dyothelete✧
DEEEHLOTUW wheedle out
DEEEHLOTWW two-wheeled
DEEEHLPRSU spur-heeled
DEEEHLPRTU The Prelude
DEEEHNORTY heterodyne
DEEEHNRRTU thereunder
DEEEHNRRUW whereunder
DEEEHNRTTU untethered
DEEEHOSSTW sow the seed
DEEEIIMNPR meperidine
DEEEIIPTVX expeditive
DEEEIKLLRW weedkiller
DEEEIKNPRS deep-sinker
DEEEILLMOS demoiselle
DEEEILLMST millet-seed
DEEEILMRSS remediless

DEEEILNRSS slenderise
DEEEILNRSZ slenderize
DEEEILNRUV unrelieved
DEEEILNSVW wind sleeve
DEEEILORRV Oliver Reed
DEEEILPRTT deep litter
DEEEILPTXY expeditely
DEEEILRRVY redelivery
DEEEILRSSS desireless
DEEEILRSVW silverweed
DEEEIMMPRS semper idem
DEEEIMNOST demonetise
DEEEIMNOTZ demonetize
DEEEIMNRRT determiner
DEEEIMNRRW Windermere
DEEEIMNRST densimeter
DEEEIMORTU eudiometer
DEEEIMPRTV redemptive
DEEEIMRSSY Merseyside
DEEEIMRSTV time-served
DEEEINNPTV pendentive
DEEEINORST désorienté
DEEEINPRST predestine
DEEEINPSSS speediness
DEEEINQSUZ queen-sized
DEEEINRRST residenter
tenderiser
DEEEINRRTZ tenderizer
DEEEINRSSV versed sine
DEEEINRSTT interested
DEEEINSSTW tweediness
DEEEIORRTU étourderie
DEEEIPRRTU pietre dure
DEEEIPRSSV depressive
DEEEIRRSSV redressive
DEEEIRRTVW River Tweed
DEEEIRSSTT side street
DEEEIRSTWX dexterwise
DEEEJKNNOY Joe Kennedy
DEEEKLLSYY skelly-eyed
DEEEKLNORW needlework
DEEEKOOPRR doorkeeper
DEEEKOPPST keep posted
DEEELLNORW ne'er-do-well
DEEELLNPRU unrepelled
DEEELLNSSY needlessly
DEEELLOWWY yellow-weed
DEEELNOOTV Deo volente
volente Deo
DEEELNRTTU unlettered
DEEELOPPRV predevelop
DEEELOPPTT pottle-deep
DEEELPPPRU Deep Purple
DEEELRRSVY reservedly
reversedly
DEEELRSSST desertless
DEEEMMOTTU tout de même
DEEEMNNOTT denotement
DEEEMNNOTU denouement
dénouement
DEEEMNOTTV devotement
DEEEMNPRTU untempered
DEEEMNRSSU demureness
DEEEMNSTTV vestmented
DEEENNPRTT pretendent
DEEENNPRTU unrepented
DEEENNRRUV unreverend
DEEENNRSST tenderness
DEEENNRSSU enuredness
undersense
DEEENNRSTU unresented
DEEENOOSWZ sneezewood
DEEENOPRRS drop serene
DEEENOPSTW steepdowne
DEEENOPTTT tête-de-pont
DEEENORTVX overextend
DEEENPPPRU unpeppered
DEEENPRSSU superdense
DEEENPSSTT pettedness
DEEENRRSTU understeer
DEEENRRSUV undeserver
unreserved
unreversed
DEEENRRTUV unreverted
DEEENRSSSS dress sense
DEEEOPSTTY eye-spotted
DEEEORRRRT reredorter
DEEEORSSTY seed oyster
DEEEPPRSSU superspeed
DEEEPRRSSU superseder
DEEFFLOOTT left-footed
DEEFFNORSS offendress
DEEFGGILLN fledgeling
DEEFGGLORU four-legged
DEEFGHINRT frightened
DEEFGIINRV free-diving
DEEFGILRSS Selfridges
DEEFGINNRS finger's-end
DEEFGINSST giftedness
DEEFGLNNOS dog's-fennel
DEEFGLNOOR golden orfe
DEEFHILNRS shield fern
DEEFHMORRS fresherdom
DEEFHOORSW foreshowed
DEEFIIINNP nifedipine
DEEFIIINNT indefinite
DEEFIIINRS resinified
DEEFIIINRT identifier
DEEFIIINTV definitive
DEEFIIIRVV revivified
DEEFIILLST stellified
DEEFIILNRS friendlies
DEEFIILNST inside left
DEEFIILNTY definitely
DEEFIINRUV unverified
DEEFIINRVW viewfinder
DEEFIKLLLS self-killed
DEEFILLLSW self-willed
DEEFILLLTW fillet weld
DEEFILLNTU unfilleted
DEEFILLRSU fleur-de-lis
DEEFILMMSU misdeemful
DEEFILMOSU fieldmouse
DEEFILNOST field notes
fieldstone
DEEFILNRSS friendless
DEEFILNRSV self-driven
DEEFILNRTU unfiltered
DEEFILOPSS self-poised
DEEFILORTU outfielder
DEEFILPSTU despiteful
DEEFINNRTX next friend
DEEFINOSST foetidness
DEEFINRSSV fervidness
DEEFKNORSS forkedness
DEEFLLLORS self-rolled
DEEFLLMORW well-formed
DEEFLLNOUW unfellowed
DEEFLLOTVW twelvefold
DEEFLLPSUY speedfully
DEEFLLRSUY fleur-de-lys
DEEFLLSSTY self-styled
DEEFLMNNOT enfoldment
DEEFLMRRSU self-murder
DEEFLOORVW overflowed
DEEFMNNRTU refundment
DEEFMNORRU unreformed
DEEFMNPRUU unperfumed
DEEFNNOSTU unsoftened
DEEFNOORTT tenderfoot
DEEFNORSTU unforested
unfostered
DEEFOOQRTU fore-quoted
DEEFOORSTU surefooted
DEEFORRUWW furrow-weed
DEEGGGIMRU Muggeridge
DEEGGGLLNO long-legged
DEEGGHNRTU thunderegg
DEEGGIIPRW periwigged
DEEGGINRSS dregginess
DEEGGLMNOR Greg LeMond
DEEGGNRSSU ruggedness
DEEGGRSTUY greedy guts
DEEGHHNORT thornhedge
DEEGHIKNRT The Red King
DEEGHINOTV give the nod
DEEGHINOUY honey guide
DEEGHINRRR red herring
DEEGHINSTT night-steed
DEEGHINSTU Gesundheit
DEEGHLNOOT gentlehood
DEEGHMORTU gude-mother
DEEGHNRRUY yerd-hunger
DEEGIIINNS indigenise
DEEGIIINNZ indigenize
DEEGIILPRV privileged
DEEGIIMMNS misdeeming
DEEGIINNRT ingredient
DEEGIINSTU distinguée
DEEGIIRSSV digressive
DEEGILLOPS glide slope
DEEGILNNRT tenderling
DEEGILNOPV developing

DEEGILNRSY resignedly
DEEGILNSSS designless
DEEGILOPSS gospel side
DEEGILRSST stridelegs
DEEGIMNNST designment
DEEGINNRWY wind energy
DEEGINOOPT pigeon-toed
DEEGINORSS degression
DEEGINOTTU tongue-tied
DEEGINPPSU speeding up
DEEGINPRSS depressing
DEEGINRTTW dew-retting
DEEGIORRST Rod Steiger
DEEGIOSTTU get outside
DEEGIRSSTU gude-sister
DEEGJJMORU Medjugorje
DEEGKNOTTT get knotted!
DEEGLLMNOO golden mole
DEEGLLMRRU Gerd Muller
DEEGLLNORU golden rule
DEEGLMSSSU smudgeless
DEEGLNOORS golden rose
DEEGLOOOPP good people
DEEGNNOOSU endogenous
DEEGNNOPRU green pound
DEEGNNORUV ungoverned
DEEGNOPRST serpent god
DEEGNORRUV undergrove
DEEGORRTXY dextrogyre
DEEHHIILMS Hildesheim
DEEHHIIRST hitherside
DEEHHIMNOR hemihedron
DEEHHRRSTU reed-thrush
DEEHIIKLLS shieldlike
DEEHIILOTT diothelite✧
DEEHIIRSTT hereditist
DEEHILLRSV shrivelled
DEEHILLSSS shieldless
DEEHILLSWW well-wished
DEEHILMORS demolisher
DEEHILNOTW The Wild One
DEEHILNRSU unrelished
DEEHILOOTT theodolite
DEEHILOPRS spider hole
DEEHILORTV hot-livered
DEEHILOTTY dyothelite✧
DEEHIMOOST the moodies
DEEHIMORST methodiser
DEEHIMORTZ methodizer
DEEHIMPRSS seed shrimp
DEEHIMRSTY Mister Hyde
DEEHINOOPV videophone
DEEHINORSV Devonshire
DEEHINORVV vinho verde
DEEHINPRSU unperished
DEEHINRSTU the insured
DEEHINRTUW unwithered
DEEHIOPPRS prophesied
DEEHIORRRS horse-rider
DEEHIORSTV Shrovetide
DEEHIRRTTU redruthite

DEEHJNNORS John Enders
DEEHJNNORV John Denver
DEEHKNOOSS hookedness
DEEHLLMOPR phelloderm
DEEHLLOOWY hollow-eyed
DEEHLMNOSW seldom when
DEEHLMNRUW underwhelm
DEEHLMOORT mother lode
DEEHLNOSUU unhouseled
DEEHLOOOPP peoplehood
DEEHLOPRTY type holder
DEEHLORSTW world sheet
DEEHLPPRUU purple-hued
DEEHMNORTU unmothered
DEEHMNORTY endothermy
DEEHMORRTY hydrometer
DEEHNOORTT heterodont
DEEHNOPRTU three-pound
DEEHNORSUW unshowered
DEEHNOSUWY Wendy House®
DEEHNRSSSW shrewdness
DEEHOORSUW dower house
DEEHOORTXY heterodoxy
DEEHOPPRSU dope pusher
DEEHOSSTYY The Odyssey
DEEIIIMNSV semi-divine
DEEIIIMPTV impeditive
DEEIIINPPR piperidine
DEEIIIOPRT epidiorite
DEEIIKLNRT tinder-like
DEEIIKLPRS spiderlike
DEEIILLMPR imperilled
DEEIILLNOS linseed oil
DEEIILLOPT lepidolite
DEEIILMNVW vine-mildew
DEEIILMPST speed limit
DEEIILMSTX sex-limited
DEEIILNNVY vinylidene
DEEIILNPRS spider line
DEEIILNSST distensile
DEEIILNSSW wieldiness
DEEIILNSTT disentitle
DEEIILORST siderolite
DEEIILPRRV pile-driver
DEEIILRSSV silverside
DEEIILRSVY derisively
DEEIIMMNPT impediment
DEEIIMNNRT dinner-time
DEEIIMNNTT inditement
DEEIIMNOST semi-ditone
DEEIIMPRST spider mite
DEEIINNRTT Tridentine
DEEIINNSSV divineness
DEEIINNSTW disentwine
DEEIINOPTX expedition
DEEIINPTTU ineptitude
DEEIINQSTU disquieten
DEEIINQTUU inquietude
DEEIINRSSV divineress
DEEIINRTTW wintertide
DEEIINSSST sensitised

DEEIINSSSY syneidesis
DEEIINSSTV distensive
DEEIINSSTW West Indies
DEEIINSSTZ sensitized
DEEIIOPRSX peroxidise
DEEIIOPRTT peridotite
DEEIIOPRXZ peroxidize
DEEIIOPSTV depositive
DEEIIPRSSV dispersive
DEEIIPRSSW sideswiper
DEEIJMNOSW jimson weed
DEEIJNORRU rejoindure
DEEIJPRSTU jeu d'esprit
DEEIKKNPRU dukkeripen
DEEIKLLOPW kewpie doll
DEEIKLNORT rodent-like
DEEIKMNNOS end in smoke
DEEIKNNRSU Iskenderun
DEEIKORSST sidestroke
DEEILLLPUY idle pulley
DEEILLMPSS misspelled
DEEILLNOOR Ile d'Oléron
DEEILLOWWW willow weed
DEEILLSUVY delusively
DEEILMMNPT dimplement
DEEILMNRTW wilderment
DEEILMOPRY polymeride
DEEILNNNRU underlinen
DEEILNNORT tenderloin
DEEILNNQTU delinquent
DEEILNNRSS dinnerless
DEEILNNSTU unlistened
DEEILNNTTU unentitled
DEEILNOPSV disenvelop
DEEILNORSU sourdeline
DEEILNPTTU plentitude
DEEILNRSSW wilderness
DEEILNRSUU unleisured
DEEILNRTVY invertedly
DEEILNSSTU diluteness
DEEILOPPRS rose-lipped
DEEILOPPRT dopplerite
DEEILORSSV redissolve
DEEILOSTTT stilettoed
DEEILRRSSV driverless
DEEIMMMRTU medium-term
DEEIMMMSUU dime museum
DEEIMMNOSU eudemonism
DEEIMMRSTU summertide
DEEIMNNNTT intendment
DEEIMNNOPR prime donne
DEEIMNNRRU underminer
DEEIMNNRTU underntime
DEEIMNNRUV menu-driven
DEEIMNOOPS empoisoned
DEEIMNOOTV Montevideo
DEEIMNOPRT redemption
DEEIMNOPTT idempotent
DEEIMNORRS moderniser
DEEIMNORRZ modernizer
DEEIMNORST insert mode

Words marked ✧ can also be spelled with one or more capital letters

DEEIMNORTV Monteverdi
DEEIMNRRUX index rerum
DEEIMNRSTW Midwestern
stemwinder
DEEIMNRSTY densimetry
DEEIMNRSWW Wim Wenders
DEEIMNRTTU unremitted
DEEIMNSTTV divestment
DEEIMOOSTU tediousome
DEEIMOPRRY pyromeride
DEEIMOPRSW disempower
DEEIMORTUY eudiometry
DEEINNNOSU innuendoes
DEEINNOPRS prednisone
DEEINNORRW irrenowned
DEEINNRSST trendiness
DEEINNRSSU inuredness
DEEINNRSTU indentures
DEEINNSSTU unitedness
DEEINNSTUV uninvested
DEEINOPRSS depression✧
DEEINOPSUW upsideowne
DEEINORRUY reioyndure
DEEINORSTT rose-tinted
DEEINPRRST rinderpest
DEEINPRRSU underprise
DEEINPRRUZ underprize
DEEINPRSTU unrespited
DEEINPRSTY predestiny
DEEINQRRUU unrequired
DEEINQRTUU unrequited
DEEINQSTUY squint-eyed
DEEINRRTUW underwrite
DEEINRSSSY synderesis
DEEINRSSTU unresisted
unsistered
DEEINSSTTU testudines
DEEIOPPRRT propertied
DEEIOPPRSS predispose
DEEIOPRSUX Oedipus Rex
superoxide
DEEIOPSSSU disespouse
DEEIOPSSTU despiteous
DEEIORRSTV overstride
DEEIORTTTX text editor
DEEIPPRRSU purse-pride
DEEIPRRTUY eurypterid
DEEIRRSSST distresser
DEEJMOSTUX jeux de mots
DEEJNPRRUU unperjured
DEEKLMRTTU kettledrum
DEEKLOPRUY dyke-louper
DEEKNOOTVY donkey vote
DEEKOORRVW overworked
DEELLMNOUW unmellowed
DEELLMOOSY dolesomely
DEELLMPUVY dumpy-level
DEELLNORTY redolently
DEELLNRTUW well-turned
DEELLORSVY resolvedly
DEELLORTUW out-dweller
DEELMMNOPU nom de plume
DEELMNOPTY deployment
DEELMNOPUY unemployed
DEELMNOSSS seldomness
DEELMNOSTU unmolested
DEELMOPRSU supermodel
DEELNNOOST selenodont
DEELNNOSSU unlessoned
DEELNNRTUY untenderly
DEELNOORRW one-worlder
DEELNOPRUX unexplored
DEELNORSUV unresolved
DEELNOSTTW settle down
DEELNOSTUU edentulous
DEELOORTTW letter-wood
DEELOOVVYY lovey-dovey
DEELOPRRTT drop-letter
DEELOPRRTY reportedly
DEELOPRSTW spot-welder
DEELORRRTU Lord Reuter
DEELORTTUV turtledove
DEEMMNRSUU unsummered
DEEMNNOPRT ponderment
DEEMNNORSS modernness
DEEMNNORTW wonderment
DEEMNNRSTU sunderment
DEEMNOORRY money order
DEEMNOPRTT deportment
DEEMNORSTU tremendous
DEEMNORTUV devourment
DEEMOOPRRT petrodrome
DEEMOORRST drosometer
DEEMOPRRTY redemptory
DEENNNORUW unrenowned
DEENNOOSSW woodenness
DEENNOPPRT propendent
DEENNOPRST respondent
DEENNOPRTU ten-pounder
DEENNORSVW newsvendor
DEENNOSSTW wontedness
DEENNRRTUU unreturned
DEENOOPPPT open-topped
DEENOOPRRV ponder over
DEENOOPRTT torpedo net
DEENOOPTWY wooden type
DEENOORSST rootedness
DEENOORSTU endorse out
DEENOPRRTU unreported
DEENOPRRUV unreproved
DEENOPRRUW under-power
DEENOQRTUU underquote
DEENORRSTU unrestored
DEENORSUVZ rendezvous
DEENOSSTUV devoutness
DEENPRSSSU suspenders
DEENPRUUVY unpurveyed
DEENRSSSTU unstressed
DEENRSUUVY unsurveyed
DEEOOPRRSU uredospore
DEEOORRSTT street door
DEEOPPRSSU superposed
DEEOPRRRSU superorder
DEEOQRSTUU Tudoresque
DEEPPRRSUU super-duper
DEEPPRSSSU suppressed
DEFFGGINOO Giffen good
DEFFGLORTU truffle dog
DEFFHIMORS sheriffdom
DEFFINNOST soft-finned
DEFFINOSUV snuff video
DEFFLNORTY fly-fronted
DEFFOOORTU four-footed
DEFFOOOSTT soft-footed
DEFFOORSWW of few words
DEFFOPPRUW powder puff
DEFGGILLRU full-rigged
DEFGGILNOR Goldfinger
DEFGHIILNT field night
DEFGHIILRT right-field
DEFGHIILTX fixed light
DEFGHILLTU delightful
DEFGHILNOR fingerhold
DEFGHINRTU unfrighted
DEFGHOOOSU house of God
DEFGIILNRR girlfriend
DEFGIILNYY edifyingly
DEFGIINNUY unedifying
DEFGIINRSS frigidness
DEFGILLNSU sdeignfull
DEFGILLNUW full-winged
DEFGIMNNPU Empfindung
DEFGINOOTW wing-footed
DEFGLLOOOW goodfellow
DEFGNOORRU foreground
DEFHIIIKSW whiskified
DEFHIIIMRU humidifier
DEFHIILNSY fiendishly
DEFHIINNSU unfinished
DEFHIINPRS friendship
DEFHIKLOTY Keith Floyd
DEFHILORRS Lord Fisher
DEFHILORSU flourished
DEFHLNOSUW flesh wound
DEFHLOPRSU proud flesh
proud-flesh
DEFHLORSSU Rudolf Hess
DEFHNOOORT horn-footed
DEFHNOOPRU unhoped-for
DEFHOOORSX Oxford shoe
DEFHOOPRRT for the drop
DEFHORRRTU rutherford✧
DEFIIILMPS simplified
DEFIIILNTY infidelity
DEFIIINNOT definition
DEFIIINNTU infinitude
DEFIIKLLSU dislikeful
DEFIILLNRY friendlily
DEFIILMNSY Disney film
DEFIILORSU fluoridise
DEFIILORUZ fluoridize
DEFIILSTTU stultified
DEFIINORST iron-fisted

DEFIINOSSU	unossified
DEFIINPRUU	unpurified
DEFIIOPRSU	perfidious
DEFIIRRRTV	river drift
DEFIKLORSW	fieldworks
DEFILLORWW	wild flower
	wildfowler
DEFILLPRUY	pridefully
DEFILNNRUY	unfriendly
DEFILNORSS	floridness
DEFILNORWW	windflower
DEFILNPTUU	unuplifted
DEFILOORSU	florideous
DEFILOORUX	ox-fluoride
DEFILOPRSW	wolf spider
DEFILPRSUU	superfluid
DEFIMMORSU	medusiform
DEFIMNNORU	uninformed
DEFIMRSTTU	Fred Titmus
DEFINOPRTU	unprofited
DEFINRRSUW	windsurfer
DEFIOPRSSS	disprofess
DEFKLMNOUY	flunkeydom
DEFLLMMSUU	full-summed
DEFLLOORRY	Lord Florey
DEFLLORRSU	full orders
DEFLNOORRU	underfloor
DEFLNOORTU	unforetold
DEFLNOORVY	overfondly
DEFLNOTTWY	twentyfold
DEFLOOOPTT	polt-footed
DEFLOOOSTW	slow-footed
DEFMNNOOUY	found money
DEFMNOORTT	De Montfort
DEFNNORTUU	unfortuned
DEFNOOORSW	of one's word
DEFNOOPRRU	under proof
	underproof
DEFNOORSTY	end of story
DEFNOORSUU	founderous
DEFNORRUUW	unfurrowed
DEFOOORRTU	out of order
DEFOOORSTY	rosy-footed
DEFOORSSTW	soft sowder
DEFOORTTTX	foxtrotted
DEGGHIILLR	hill-digger
DEGGHIIPRS	ship-rigged
DEGGIIKNSU	King's Guide
DEGGIILNRW	wild ginger
DEGGIJRRUY	jury-rigged
DEGGILLNOR	golden girl
DEGGILOORS	sogdoliger
DEGGINNOPU	gudgeon pin
DEGGINNORU	undergoing
DEGGINORUV	give ground
DEGGLOOORS	sogdologer
DEGGMNOOOR	Demogorgon
DEGGNOOSTU	dog's-tongue
DEGHHIIKLT	high-kilted
DEGHHILOSU	high-souled
DEGHIILLNS	shieldling
DEGHIILNRT	right-lined
DEGHIILTTW	twilighted
DEGHIIMOPP	pemphigoid
DEGHIINRRT	nightrider
DEGHIKNNTU	unknighted
DEGHIKNOST	hot desking
	hot-desking
DEGHILLNOS	Old English
DEGHILNNSU	unshingled
DEGHILNOOS	singlehood
DEGHILNOST	Odelsthing
DEGHINNORT	dethroning
DEGHINNRTU	thundering
DEGHINOSSU	doughiness
DEGHINRRUY	yird-hunger
DEGHINRSST	nightdress
DEGHIOOSTW	white goods
DEGHIORRRU	roughrider
DEGHLNOORU	golden hour
DEGHLNOPUU	unploughed
DEGHMNOORU	home ground
DEGHMOOORT	good-mother
DEGHNNRTUU	dung-hunter
DEGHNOPRTU	thronged up
DEGHPRRSUU	drug pusher
DEGIIIKNNS	die-sinking
DEGIIILNOT	indigolite
DEGIIINRST	rising tide
DEGIIKLLNS	deskilling
DEGIILLMRX	mixed grill
DEGIILLNNW	indwelling
DEGIILLNPS	dispelling
DEGIILLNRV	drivelling
DEGIILLNTY	diligently
DEGIILLNYY	yieldingly
DEGIILMNPY	impedingly
DEGIILNNTY	indigently
DEGIILNNUY	unyielding
DEGIILNORS	soldiering
DEGIILOOST	ideologist
DEGIIMNOOT	in good time
DEGIIMNRSY	semi-drying
DEGIINNORT	dinitrogen
DEGIINNOSU	indigenous
DEGIINNRSU	undesiring
DEGIINNSST	dissenting
DEGIINORRV	overriding
DEGIINORSS	digression
DEGIINOSST	disgestion
DEGIINPRST	spring tide
	springtide
DEGIINPTUU	pinguitude
DEGIJLNSTU	Jugendstil
DEGIKLMOOR	grimlooked
DEGIKLORST	strike gold
DEGIKMNNOW	New Kingdom
DEGILLMORS	miller's dog
DEGILLOOTY	deltiology
DEGILMNRSU	mudslinger
DEGILNNNUY	unendingly
DEGILNNORU	loundering
DEGILNNRUY	enduringly
	underlying
DEGILNOOSS	goodliness
DEGILNRSTU	disgruntle
DEGILOOOOZ	zoogloeoid
DEGILOOPST	pedologist
DEGIMNORTW	wrong-timed
DEGIMNSSSU	smudginess
DEGINNNORW	dinner-gown
DEGINNOPRU	ground pine
DEGINNORST	grindstone
	stringendo
DEGINNORSU	resounding
DEGINNRSSU	undressing
DEGINNRSTU	unstringed
DEGINOOOPW	wood pigeon
DEGINORSSU	gourdiness
DEGINORSTY	destroying
DEGINOSSST	stodginess
DEGINPRSUW	spur-winged
DEGINRSSTU	turgidness
DEGIOORSST	good-sister
DEGIOORSTW	Tiger Woods
DEGKLOOOOR	good-looker
DEGLLNORSU	groundsell
DEGLMNOOOY	demonology
DEGLMOOORT	motor lodge
DEGLNNRSUU	underslung
DEGLNOOOTY	deontology
DEGLNOORSU	lose ground
DEGLNOOTUZ	zeuglodont
DEGLNORRUU	ground rule
DEGLNORSSU	groundless
DEGLOOPSUY	pseudology
DEGLOORTTY	troglodyte
DEGLOORTUW	towel-gourd
DEGNNOOOTY	odontogeny
DEGNNOOPSW	sponge down
	sponge-down
DEGNNORRTU	ground rent
DEGNNORRUW	undergrown
DEGNNRRRUU	drug-runner
DEGNOOOPSW	spongewood
DEGNOORRUV	overground
DEGNOORRUZ	ground zero
DEGNOORTTU	get round to
DEGOOORSUW	woodgrouse
DEHHILNOTW	withholden
DEHHILNTUW	unwithheld
DEHHILOPRS	ship-holder
DEHHILORTW	withholder
DEHHLNOOOR	holohedron
DEHHLORRSU	rush holder
DEHHMOOORT	motherhood
DEHHMOOTTU	hot-mouthed
DEHHNOOPRY	hydrophone
DEHHOPRTYY	hydrophyte
DEHIIINRST	disinherit
DEHIIJKOOT	Hideki Tojo
DEHIIKLLOO	likelihood
DEHIILLOOV	livelihood

DEHIILLSVY devilishly
DEHIILMNPU delphinium
DEHIILMOST diothelism✧
DEHIILNNRS hinderlins
DEHIILNPSS displenish
DEHIILNPSY sylphidine
DEHIIMNOPR dimorphine
DEHIIMNPRU nephridium
DEHIINOPSY hypnoidise
DEHIINOPYZ hypnoidize
DEHIINORSS disherison
DEHIINRSSW widershins
DEHIIOPRST editorship
DEHIIOPSTY diophysite✧
DEHIIORRST disheritor
DEHIIRSTVW whist drive
DEHIJKNOPU John Updike
DEHIKOORSW woodshrike
DEHIKORSST kiss the rod
DEHILMOSTY dyothelism✧
DEHILNOPSU unpolished
DEHILNORSU shroud line
DEHILNORTU unitholder
DEHILNORTW in the world
DEHILOOPSS shopsoiled
DEHILORSTV short-lived
DEHIMMNORR horn-rimmed
DEHIMMPSSY dysphemism
DEHIMNORST hindermost
DEHIMNOSSS modishness
DEHIMNRTTU The Tin Drum
DEHIMOOPPR hippodrome
DEHIMOPRSY hypodermis
DEHINNORRU dinner hour
DEHINNORTU in the round
DEHINNPSUU unpunished
DEHINOORRS dishonorer
her indoors
DEHINOPRTU tripehound
DEHINORRSS horridness
DEHINORSTT threnodist
DEHINOSSTY dishonesty
DEHINRRSTU undershirt
DEHIOOPRST priesthood
DEHIOOQRSU squirehood
DEHIOORSST sisterhood
DEHIOOSSTU Theodosius
DEHIOPPRSW worshipped
DEHIOPRRTY pyrethroid
DEHIOPSTYY dyophysite✧
DEHIRRSSST dress shirt
shirt dress
DEHJLOOPRS Lord Joseph
DEHJNNOPPY Johnny Depp
DEHKNNORUW hunker down
DEHLLLLOOY Hello Dolly!
DEHLLMNOSU shell mound
DEHLLOOSSU doll's house
DEHLNOOPRY polyhedron
DEHLNOUUZZ unhouzzled
DEHLOOPRST postholder
DEHLOORRSY holy orders
DEHLOORRTW otherworld
DEHLORSSSU shroudless
DEHMMNOORY monorhymed
DEHMNOOPRY endomorphy
DEHMNOOSST The Osmonds
DEHMNOOSTU unsmoothed
DEHMOORSSY hydrosomes
DEHMORRTYY hydrometry
DEHMORTUWY wry-mouthed
DEHNNOORUU unhonoured
DEHNNORSUU nursehound
DEHNOOOPRS personhood
DEHNOOPRRW powder horn
DEHNOOPRTU horned pout
horned-pout
DEHNOORRSU horrendous
DEHNOORSTU undershoot
DEHNOORSUU roundhouse
DEHNOORTTU otter hound
DEHNORSTUU thunderous
DEHOOPPRTW hopped-wort
DEHOOPRRWY hydropower
DEHOOPRSUU house-proud
DEHOORRRST short order
short-order
DEIIILMQSU semi-liquid
DEIIILMSTU similitude
DEIIILNSST dissilient
DEIIILOPRT ripidolite
DEIIILQRSU liquidiser
DEIIILQRUZ liquidizer
DEIIILSVVY divisively
DEIIIMNORS iridosmine
DEIIIMNPRU peridinium✧
DEIIIMNPRY pyrimidine
DEIIIMNSSU Sinus Medii
DEIIIMNTUV diminutive
DEIIIMSSSV dismissive
DEIIINNSTT tendinitis
DEIIINORSV redivision
DEIIINORUV iure divino
DEIIJMNORS misjoinder
DEIIKLLNOR kirn-dollie
DEIIKLLNST linked list
DEIIKLNNSS kindliness
DEIIKLNNTU unit-linked
DEIILLMPTU multiplied
DEIILLNOPS spindle oil
DEIILLNORW iron-willed
DEIILLNUWY unwieldily
DEIILLOPST pistillode
DEIILLOSTV still video
DEIILLPSUV pulvilised
DEIILLPUVZ pulvilized
DEIILLQRUV quill drive
DEIILLRSTY distillery
DEIILMNOOT demolition
DEIILMNPSS limpidness
DEIILMNSTT distilment
DEIILMOOST dolomitise
DEIILMOOTZ dolomitize
DEIILNNRTY dirty linen
DEIILNOPTY yield point
DEIILNORRV Lord Irvine
DEIILNORST tin soldier
DEIILNOSVV disinvolve
DEIILNPRTY intrepidly
DEIILNQSSU liquidness
DEIILNSTUU unutilised
DEIILNTUUZ unutilized
DEIILPRSTY spiritedly
DEIILQSTUY disquietly
DEIIMMSSTY midi-system
DEIIMNOPRT diremption
DEIIMOPRSV disimprove
DEIIMORRRS side mirror
DEIIMOSTWW widow's mite
DEIIMPRSSU presidiums
DEIINNOQRU inquirendo
DEIINNORSV disenviron
DEIINNOSSS dissension
DEIINNOSST distension
DEIINNOSTT Dennis Tito
distention
tendonitis
DEIINNPRSU uninspired
DEIINNSSTU untidiness
DEIINOOPST deposition
in deposito
positioned
DEIINOPRSS dispersion
pieds noirs
DEIINOPRXY pyridoxine
DEIINORTTW iron-witted
DEIINPPRST pinstriped
DEIINPRSTU unspirited
DEIINRRSUV River Indus
DEIINRSSST in distress
DEIIOPSSTU dispiteous
DEIIORSTTV distortive
DEIIPRSTUV disruptive
DEIIPSSSTU spissitude
DEIJLNOOTW dowel-joint
DEIJNNNOOR non-joinder
DEIKKNNOPS kind-spoken
DEIKLLNORV Lord Kelvin
DEIKLMNOPS mild-spoken
DEIKLNNRUW unwrinkled
DEIKLNSTUY klendusity
DEIKLRTUWY wild turkey
DEIKMNNORY drink-money
DEIKMPPRSU mudskipper
DEIKNNNORR non-drinker
DEIKNNNSSU unkindness
DEIKNNRSUW swine-drunk
DEIKNORSTW strike down
DEIKNRRSTU underskirt
DEIKOPRRSW spiderwork
DEILLLNOOR Lord O'Neill
DEILLMMOSU slime mould
DEILLMNSSY mindlessly

DEILLMOPRW powder mill
DEILLNNOTY indolently
DEILLNOPUW unpillowed
DEILLNORSS lordliness
DEILLOPRRW power drill
DEILLORRST Lord Lister
DEILLPRRSS drill-press
DEILMMOSTY immodestly
DEILMNNOSU unsmiled-on
DEILMNOPRU unimplored
DEILMNOSSU mouldiness
DEILMNPTUY impudently
DEILNNNTUW wind tunnel
DEILNNOUVV uninvolved
DEILNOOOTT odontolite
DEILNOORWW wool-winder
DEILNOOTUV devolution
DEILNOQRUU unliquored
DEILNOSSST stolidness
DEILNOSSTV dissolvent
DEILNOSSWW windowless
DEILNPPSUU unsupplied
DEILNRSTTY stridently
DEILOOOTVW violet-wood
DEILOOPSSU solipedous
DEILOORRVW wool-driver
DEILOORSTY toy soldier
DEILOPRSUU preludious
DEILOPSSTY stylopised
DEILOPSTYZ stylopized
DEILORSSUY desirously
DEILORSUUY Louis Durey
DEIMMNNTUU indumentum
DEIMMNORSW simmer down
DEIMMOPSTU impostumed
DEIMNNNOOS on one's mind
DEIMNNOSTW disownment
DEIMNOOSSS endosmosis
DEIMNOPRSU unpromised
DEIMNOPRTU minute-drop
DEIMNOPRUV unimproved
DEIMNORSTU unmortised
DEIMNORSUX sound mixer
DEIMNORTYY dirty money
DEIMNRSSUU unsurmised
DEIMOORRTV motor drive
DEIMOORRTY odorimetry
DEIMOORTUW moudiewort
DEIMOORTWW mowdiewort
DEIMOPPRST prompt side
DEIMOPRSSU dispermous
DEIMRSSTTY mistrysted
DEINNNORTU trunnioned
DEINNNOSUW unsinnowed
DEINNNOUWW unwinnowed
DEINNOOPSU unpoisoned
DEINNOORST tension rod
DEINNOPRSU unprisoned
DEINNORTUW interwound
DEINOOPRSS droopiness
DEINOOPRST desorption
DEINOOQTUX Don Quixote
DEINOORRTZ torrid zone
DEINOORSWW rose window
DEINOOSSSU odiousness
DEINOPRSST torpidness
DEINOPSSSU suspensoid
DEINORRSST torridness
DEINORRTTT dirt-rotten
DEINORSSSS drossiness
DEINORSSSW drowsiness
DEINORSSUU undesirous
DEINPPRSTU unstripped
DEINPRSSTU putridness
DEINPSSSTU stupidness
DEINRSSSTU sturdiness
DEIOOPRRTV proveditor
DEIOOPRSTT torpedoist
DEIOOPRSTY depository
DEIOORRRUV River Douro
DEIOPRRSTW spiderwort
DEIOPSSSSS dispossess
DEIRRSSTTU distruster
DEJLLLMOUY jelly mould
DEJLNOOPUY Joey Dunlop
DEJNOORSSU de nos jours
DEKKNOORWY donkey-work
DEKLLMNSUU numskulled
DEKLORSSVV Sverdlovsk
DEKMNOPPUY donkey-pump
DEKNOOPRUV unprovoked
DEKNOOPTTT topknotted
DEKNOORRWW wonderwork
DEKNOORSTW downstroke
DEKOOORRWW woodworker
DEKOOSSTVY Dostoevsky
DELLLOPTUY pollutedly
DELLNOPTUU unpolluted
DELLOOOWWY yellow-wood
DELLORSSWY wordlessly
DELLOSSUUY sedulously
DELMOORRSS Lord Somers
DELNNOPSSU nonplussed
DELNNOTUWY unwontedly
DELNOOORTT rondoletto
DELNOOORTU root nodule
DELNOOPRTU pleurodont
DELNOPRSSU splendrous
DELNOPRSUU plunderous
DELOOORRSW wood sorrel
DELOOORRUV louver-door
louvre-door
DELOOPPRUW purple wood
DELOOPRRRT Lord Porter
DELOOPRRWW world power
DELOOPRTUU trou-de-loup
DELOPPSSUY supposedly
DELORRTTUY torturedly
DELORSTTUY Tudor-style
DELORSTUXY dextrously
DEMMNNNOUU nomen nudum
DEMMNNOSUU unsummoned
DEMMOORRWY word memory
DEMMOORSUW summerwood
DEMNOOOPST Podostemon
DEMNOOPRST post-modern
DEMNOPPRTU unprompted
DEMNORSTUU surmounted
DEMOOOPRRW powder room
DEMOOPRRWW worm powder
DENNOOPRSU pundonores
DENNORTUWY entry wound
DENNRRTUUU unnurtured
DENOOPPRRU propounder
DENOOPPRSU unproposed
DENOOPRSWW powder snow
DENOORRTUW round tower
DENOPPRSUU unpurposed
DENOPRRTTU protrudent
DENOPRSSUU supersound
DENOPSSTUU stupendous
DENORRSTUY understory
DENORRTTUU untortured
DEOORRSSUU uredosorus
DEOPPRRSUU purse-proud
DFFIIMORTY difformity
DFFIMNSTUU stud muffin
DFGGIIINNY dignifying
DFGHIINORS fishing-rod
rodfishing
DFGHIINSTY dying shift
DFGHILLOOT floodlight
DFGHILOOSY old-fogyish
DFGIIILLNR fringillid
DFGIIIMORT digitiform
DFGIILORSY disglorify
DFGIIMNNUY mundifying
DFGIINOSUU nidifugous
DFGIINRRSU surf-riding
DFGILMNPUY fly-dumping
DFGILSSTUU disgustful
DFGOOOORUY good for you
DFHIINRSSU disfurnish
DFHILLNOPY dolphin-fly
DFHILORTTY thirtyfold
DFHINOSSTU sound shift
DFHLLRSUYY sulfhydryl
DFHLOOOOPT photoflood
DFHNOOOSTU hounds-foot
DFIIKNRYZZ fizzy drink
DFIILMOOPU filopodium
DFIIOOOPRT idiot-proof
DFIKLOPPSY floppy disk
DFILORRSTW First World
DFIMNOOSTW of two minds
DFINOOPRST spoondrift
DFINOPRTUY profundity
DFLLNOPRUU roll-up fund
DFLNOOPRUY profoundly
DFLOOORTTU Rudolf Otto
DFNOOOPRSU soundproof
DFOOOORSTU out of doors
out-of-doors

DFOOOPRRSW swordproof
DFOORTTUUY tour of duty
DGGGHINOOT hot-dogging
DGGGILMNOU mudlogging
DGGGILNRUY grudgingly
DGGGINNRUU ungrudging
DGGHHIIINR riding high
DGGHINORRU rough-grind
DGGIIILMNO ginglimoid
DGGIIINSSU disguising
DGGIIKLNOO good-liking
DGGIILLNOW God willing
DGGIILNNRY grindingly
DGGIILNORV virgin gold
DGGIINSSTU disgusting
DGGILNNORU groundling
DGGILNOOTU outlodging
DGGINNNORU running dog
DGGINNOOOR godrooning
DGGINNOORW wrongdoing
DGGNOOORTU go to ground
DGHHIKNOOT knighthood
DGHHNOORTU nod through
DGHHNOORUU rough hound
DGHIIILOTT idiot light
DGHIIINPRW riding whip
DGHIIKLNOO kinglihood
DGHIILLNNO Hillingdon
DGHIILMNTY midnightly
DGHIILPRTY ditriglyph
DGHIINOORV virginhood
DGHILLNOOW go downhill
DGHINNNOTU Huntingdon
DGHINRRUYY yird-hungry
DGHJNNOOOR John Gordon
DGHLNOORST stronghold
DGHMOOORUU good humour
DGHNOORSUW showground
DGIIIJNNOS disjoining
DGIIIKNNSV skin diving
DGIIILLNST distilling
DGIIIMORTU digitorium
DGIIINPTUY pinguidity
DGIIINRSTU riding suit
DGIIINSTUV diving suit
DGIIKLOOST kidologist
DGIILLLNOV Living Doll
DGIILNOOST Indologist
DGIILNORSY drying oils
DGIILNOSSV dissolving
DGIILNYYZZ dizzyingly
DGIIMMNNOR mid-morning
DGIIMNNOOR dining room
DGIIMNORSW miswording
DGIINNOPRU pundigrion
DGIINNOSWZ downsizing
DGIIOOPRSU prodigious
DGILLNORSU groundsill
DGILLRTUUU Ruud Gullit
DGILNNOSUY soundingly
DGILNNOUWY woundingly
DGILNOOPRY droopingly
DGILOOOPST podologist
DGILOOPRTT proglottid
DGINNNOORW ring down on
DGINNOOPRU undrooping
DGINNOOPRW roping-down
DGINOOPRSW springwood
DGKNOORRUW groundwork
DGLNOOOOTY odontology
DGLNOOOPRU ground loop
DGLNOOPRTU groundplot
DGLNOOPTTY glyptodont
DGMOOOORRW good-morrow
DGNOOOOPTU up to no good
DGNOOPRRUX groundprox
DGOPRSTUUY study group
DHHILOPRYY hydrophily
DHHMOOOSST smooth-shod
DHHOORSTUW woodthrush
DHIIKNNOTT I don't think
DHIILOOPSS pholidosis
DHIIMMOPRS dimorphism
DHIIMNORRT minor third
DHIINOPRSU Irish pound
DHIINORSUU hirudinous
DHIIOORSST diorthosis
DHIIOPRSSW disworship
DHIIORSTTU struthioid
DHILMOOSTU Lithodomus
DHILORSSYY hydrolysis
DHIMMNNOST month's mind
DHIMMSTUWY dummy whist
DHIMOOPRSU dimorphous
DHINNNOSWY shinny down
DHINOOOPRT ornithopod
DHINOOPSWW shop window
window-shop
DHINOOSTWW shot window
DHINOPRSTY dystrophin
DHINORTUWY whodunitry
DHIOOOPTYZ zoophytoid
DHLOOORTXY orthodoxly
DHLOOPPRYY hydropolyp
DHMNOORTUU round mouth
DHMOOORRTY orthodromy
DHNNOSTUUW shunt-wound
DHNOOORTUX unorthodox
DHOORRSSTW shortsword
DHOORRSTWW Wordsworth
DIIIINPSTY insipidity
DIIILNOSTY insolidity
DIIILSTTUY disutility
DIIIMMORSU iridosmium
osmiridium
DIIIMNNOTU diminution
DIIIMNOSSS dismission
DIIIORRSUV iridovirus
DIIJMNSUUV jus divinum
DIILLMNOSY silly mid-on
DIILLNOSWW windowsill
DIILLRSTTW twist drill
DIILNOOPSS displosion
DIILNOSTUY unsolidity
DIIMMOPRRU primordium
DIIMMSUUVV dum vivimus
DIIMNNOSTW in two minds
DIIMOORSSS osmidrosis
DIIMORSSSY dismissory
DIINOOPSSU Posidonius
DIINOORSTT distortion
DIINOPRSTU disruption✧
DIINRTTUUY diuturnity
DIIOOPRSST dispositor
DIIOOPRSTW wood spirit
DILLMNOXYY nix my dolly
DILLNOORSW Lord Wilson
DILLOOPPYY polyploidy
DILMOOPPUY Polypodium
DILNOOPSTW splintwood
DILORSSTUU stridulous
DILOSSTUUY studiously
DIMMNOOOPU monopodium
DIMMOPPSUU sodium pump
DIMOPRSSUY dysprosium
DIMOPRTTUY import duty
DINOOOPRRS prison door
DINOORTTUY orotundity
DIOOPQQRUU quid pro quo
DKLNNOOOOW look down on
DLLOOORSUY dolorously
DLMOOOSTUY sooty mould
DLNOOPSSUY spondylous
DLNOORSUWY wondrously
DMNNOOORSY dry monsoon
DMNOOPRUWY upon my word
DNOOOOPRST droop snoot

E

EEEEEGPRST Pete Seeger
EEEEEGPSSX epexegeses
EEEEEHMTTY meet the eye
EEEEELMSSS seemelesse
EEEEEMPRST Peter-see-me
EEEEFFNSST effeteness
EEEEFGNRRY free energy
EEEEFKLRSS self-seeker
EEEEFLMSST self-esteem
EEEEFLRSSV self-severe
EEEEFPRSSX express fee
EEEEFRRRSV free-verser
EEEEGILNST genteelise
EEEEGILNTZ genteelize
EEEEGINNRR re-engineer
EEEEGIPSSX epexegesis
EEEEGNRTTV genevrette
EEEEHIMRSU euhemerise
EEEEHIMRUZ euhemerize
EEEEHIRRSV shire-reeve
EEEEHLLOTY eyelet-hole
EEEEHLMRWY emery wheel
EEEEHNPSST epentheses
EEEEHORRSW wheresoe'er

EEEEHPSSSY	sheep's eyes
EEEEHRRVWY	everywhere
EEEEIILLSW	Elie Wiesel
EEEEIIPSTW	sweetie-pie
EEEEIKKPPR	pike-keeper
EEEEIKMPRT	timekeeper
EEEEILLLOR	Lorelei Lee
EEEEILRTTV	televérité
EEEEILRTVW	televiewer
EEEEIMRSTT	semiterete
EEEEINPSSW	sweep-seine
EEEEIPRRVW	peer review
EEEEIPRTTT	Reet Petite
EEEEKLPRSS	keeperless
EEEEKMRRSY	kerseymere
EEEELLORRT	reel-to-reel
EEEELLSSSV	sleeveless
EEEELMNNTV	enlevement
	enlèvement
EEEELNRTTT	nettle-tree
EEEELORSVV	oversleeve
EEEEMNRSST	entremesse
EEEENNRRVV	never-never✧
EEEENNRSSS	sereneness
EEEENNSTVV	even-steven
EEEENNTWYY	teeny-weeny
EEEENRSSSV	severeness
EEEENRSTVY	yestereven
EEEEOPPRRT	peer-to-peer
EEEEPPPRRT	pepper tree
EEEERRRTTV	terre verte
EEEETTTTWW	tweet-tweet
EEEFFHINTT	the Fifteen
EEEFFHIRRS	free-fisher
EEEFFHLORT	off the reel
EEEFFIIMNS	effeminise
EEEFFIIMNZ	effeminize
EEEFFILORT	tree of life
EEEFFNOOST	toffee-nose
EEEFFOQSUZ	squeeze off
EEEFGIINNR	fire engine
EEEFGILNRR	rifle green
EEEFGINORS	foreseeing
EEEFGINRRT	fringe tree
EEEFGLNRUV	revengeful
EEEFHHRSTT	the three F's
EEEFHILSSV	sleeve fish
EEEFHOORRT	heretofore
EEEFHORSST	foresheets
EEEFIJLLNU	jeune fille
EEEFILLRSS	reliefless
EEEFILNRRT	life-renter
EEEFILORRS	free-soiler
EEEFILRRSV	file server
EEEFILRRTV	River Fleet
EEEFIMNNRT	refinement
EEEFIMNRTV	fermentive
EEEFINORRR	ferronière
EEEFINORRV	over-refine
EEEFINRRRT	interferer
EEEFINRSVW	swine fever
EEEFINSSSV	five senses
EEEFIORTVW	free-to-view
EEEFKNOPRS	free-spoken
EEEFLLMSTT	self-mettle
EEEFLLORRT	foreteller
EEEFLNOSST	set oneself
EEEFLOPRSS	self-repose
EEEFLORRVY	overfreely
EEEFLRRSTY	freestyler
EEEFLRSSTT	fetterless
EEEFMMORTT	femtometre
EEEFMNPRRT	preferment
EEEFNNORSU	unforeseen
EEEFNORRTU	fourteener
EEEFNQRRTU	frequenter
EEEFORRSTT	forest-tree
EEEGGHHNRU	Hugh Greene
EEEGGHRRTU	tree-hugger
EEEGGNOORS	Goose Green
	green goose
EEEGHHINTT	eighteenth
EEEGHIILTV	give the lie
EEEGHILNST	genteelish
EEEGHIMNOT	eighteenmo
EEEGHKLNNT	knee-length
EEEGHNNOST	Stonehenge
EEEGHNORSU	greenhouse
EEEGHNORTV	on the verge
EEEGHNORTW	get nowhere
EEEGHNORTY	heterogeny
EEEGHRRTWY	grey-wether
EEEGIILLNS	selegiline
EEEGIILRSU	religieuse
EEEGIINPSS	epigenesis
EEEGIINRSS	greisenise
EEEGIINRSU	seigneurie
EEEGIINRSZ	greisenize
EEEGIIPRSS	periegesis
EEEGILMNPW	weeping elm
EEEGILMNST	genteelism
EEEGILNNSS	engineless
EEEGILNORV	olive green
	olive-green
EEEGILNRST	singletree
EEEGILNSST	gentilesse
EEEGIMNNRT	enregiment
EEEGIMORST	geometrise
EEEGIMORTZ	geometrize
EEEGINNOPY	eye-opening
EEEGINNORS	rose engine
EEEGINNOSS	neogenesis
EEEGINNPTY	Gene Pitney
EEEGINNRRT	re-entering
EEEGINNSTW	sweetening
EEEGINOPRY	epeirogeny
EEEGINRRST	enregister
	interreges
EEEGIRRRST	reregister
EEEGIRRSSV	regressive
EEEGKLRSTY	Greek style
EEEGLLNRWY	green welly✧
EEEGLMNRTY	emergently
EEEGLNNSST	gentleness
EEEGLNOSTZ	seltzogene
EEEGLOPSTT	get to sleep
EEEGMNNOTU	engouement
EEEGNNORST	greenstone
EEEHHIMPRS	hemisphere
EEEHHISTTW	white sheet
EEEHHITTTW	White Teeth
EEEHHLLSTT	hell's teeth
EEEHHLORSW	wheelhorse
EEEHHLOSUW	wheelhouse
EEEHHLRTTY	ethyl ether
EEEHHORRTW	otherwhere
EEEHHRRSTT	the three R's
EEEHIKLNTT	kitten heel
EEEHIKLPRS	spherelike
EEEHIKPPRS	keepership
EEEHILLTWW	whewellite
EEEHILMORT	heliometer
EEEHILMRTW	mitre wheel
EEEHILNOTT	toe the line
EEEHILNOTV	the evil one
EEEHILNPRS	prehensile
EEEHILPSSS	lesseeship
EEEHILRRTV	River Lethe
EEEHILSTTT	title sheet
EEEHIMMRSU	Euhemerism
EEEHIMNRST	smithereen
EEEHIMNSTW	the Wise Men
EEEHIMPRST	ephemerist
EEEHIMRSTU	euhemerist
EEEHIMRTTW	white meter
EEEHINNNTT	nineteenth
EEEHINNTTV	in the event
EEEHINORSW	Eisenhower
EEEHINPRSV	prehensive
EEEHINPSST	epenthesis
EEEHINSSWZ	wheeziness
EEEHINSTTV	seventieth
EEEHJLOSUW	jewel-house
EEEHKLLOTT	kettle hole
EEEHKMNOST	The Monkees
EEEHKOPPRS	shopkeeper
EEEHLLMRUV	Leverhulme
EEEHLLNOTV	on the level
EEEHLLNTVY	eleventhly
EEEHLMNPTT	hemp-nettle
EEEHLMNTVY	vehemently
EEEHLMOPST	speleothem
EEEHLMSSTV	themselves
EEEHLNOPRT	telephoner
EEEHLOPSSU	sheep-louse
EEEHLORTWW	two-wheeler
EEEHLPRSSS	sphereless
EEEHLSSTTY	stylesheet
EEEHMMNNST	enmeshment
EEEHMNORRT	nethermore
EEEHMNORTV	veneer-moth
EEEHMOPRSS	mesosphere
EEEHMOPRSU	ephemerous

Words marked ✧ can also be spelled with one or more capital letters

EEEHMORRRT	Rothermere
EEEHMORTTY	hyetometer
EEEHMPRTTT	the Tempter
EEEHMPSTTT	The Tempest
EEEHNNPRTY	threepenny
EEEHNOPPRS	Persephone
EEEHNORRVW	or whenever
EEEHNORSSS	horse sense
EEEHNORSVW	whensoever
EEEHNOSTUY	See You Then
EEEHNOSTWY	honey-sweet
EEEHNPRSTT	the serpent
EEEHNRRVYY	Henry Every
EEEHNRSSTT	sternsheet
EEEHNSTTVY	the Seventy
EEEHOPPRRT	tree hopper
EEEHORRRVW	or wherever
EEEHORRTVY	every other
EEEHORSTTT	set to three
	store teeth
EEEIIMRSST	time series
EEEIINNSST	Eisenstein
EEEIINRRSV	River Seine
EEEIIPRTTV	repetitive
EEEIJNRSUV	rejuvenise
EEEIJNRUVZ	rejuvenize
EEEIKLLNTT	nettlelike
EEEIKLMSWY	semi-weekly
EEEIKLNNPR	pine kernel
EEEILLNRVW	well I never!
EEEILLNUVV	Villeneuve
EEEILLPTVV	velvet-pile
EEEILMMORT	mileometer
EEEILMNRTV	revilement
EEEILMNSSS	seemliness
EEEILMNSTY	mesitylene
EEEILMPRTV	pelvimeter
EEEILMPRTX	pleximeter
EEEILMRSST	missel-tree
EEEILNOPPS	penelopise
EEEILNOPPZ	penelopize
EEEILNPRRT	terreplein
EEEILNPSSS	sleepiness
EEEILNRRST	re-enlister
EEEILNSSST	sleetiness
	steeliness
EEEILOPRRS	leproserie
EEEILRRSTV	silver tree
EEEILRRTTW	telewriter
EEEIMMNNOS	Menominees
EEEIMMRRSS	mesmeriser
EEEIMMRRSZ	mesmerizer
EEEIMNNPRT	pre-eminent
	repinement
EEEIMNOPST	Piemontese
EEEIMNORST	remonetise
EEEIMNORTZ	remonetize
EEEIMNPRTX	experiment
EEEIMNRRTT	retirement
EEEIMNRSTT	tensimeter
EEEIMNRTVV	revivement
EEEIMOPRTZ	piezometer
EEEIMPPRTV	pre-emptive
EEEIMPSTTV	tempestive
EEEIMRRSTV	timeserver
EEEIMRRSUV	River Meuse
EEEINNPRSS	persiennes
EEEINNPRST	serpentine
EEEINNPRTV	prevenient
EEEINNRRTV	intervener
EEEINNRSST	entireness
EEEINOPPPR	pipe-opener
EEEINOQSTU	questionee
EEEINPPRSV	prepensive
EEEINPRRST	enterprise
EEEINPRSST	serpentise
EEEINPRSSU	purse-seine
EEEINPRSTT	Peter Stein
EEEINPRSTV	presentive
	vespertine
EEEINPRSTZ	serpentize
EEEINPRTVV	preventive
EEEINPSSST	steepiness
EEEINQTTTU	netiquette
EEEINRRRTV	irreverent
EEEINRSSTW	westernise
EEEINRSTWZ	westernize
EEEINSSTWY	eyewitness
EEEIOPRRRT	repertoire
EEEIPRRSSV	repressive
EEEIPRRSVV	perversive
EEEIPRRTTU	répétiteur
EEEIPRSSUV	supervisee
EEEIPRSSVX	expressive
EEEIRRRSVW	River Weser
EEEIRSSTTW	streetwise
EEEJJNNSSU	jejuneness
EEEJKMNORR	Jerome Kern
EEEJLNRSUV	Jules Verne
EEEJNOSSSW	Jesse Owens
EEEJNOSSTV	Steve Jones
EEEKLNOSST	sleekstone
EEEKLORRTW	teleworker
EEEKMNORTV	revokement
EEELLNPSSS	spleenless
EEELLNPSUV	eleven-plus
EEELLNRRTY	Ellen Terry
EEELLNRSST	relentless
EEELLNRTVY	entry-level
EEELLORTTV	love letter
EEELLPRSSY	peerlessly
EEELLRSSTT	letterless
EEELMMOSTT	mettlesome
EEELMNNRTT	relentment
EEELMNOPTU	Mount Pelée
EEELMNOSTT	nettlesome
EEELMNOTVV	evolvement
EEELMNSTTT	settlement
EEELMOOSTT	teleostome
EEELNNORST	lenten rose
EEELNOPRTT	open letter
EEELNOTTVW	twelve-note
	twelve-tone
EEELNPPRSY	prepensely
EEELNRRTVY	reverently
EEELNRSTTW	newsletter
EEELOOPPRV	overpeople
EEELOPRRRT	Peter Lorre
EEELOPRSTU	pétroleuse
EEELORRRST	sorrel tree
EEELORSVWW	werewolves
EEELPRRSVY	perversely
EEELPRSSTU	reputeless
EEELRSSSVW	swerveless
EEELRSTTTU	ulsterette
EEEMMNOTUV	mouvementé
EEEMMRRSTU	summer-tree
EEEMNNORST	mesenteron
EEEMNNRSTT	resentment
EEEMNNSSTU	unmeetness
EEEMNOPRST	treponemes
EEEMNORSST	remoteness
EEEMNORSTT	sermonette
EEEMNPRSTT	pesterment
EEENNNPSVY	sevenpenny
EEENNNSSUV	unevenness
EEENNRRTUV	unreverent
EEENORSSST	restenoses
EEENORSTWZ	sneezewort
EEENOSTTUW	outsweeten
EEENPRSSTX	expertness
EEEOOPRSVX	overexpose
EEEOPRRRTX	re-exporter
EEEOPRSTTY	stereotype
EEEOPRTTUV	éprouvette
EEEOSTTTVV	Steve Ovett
EEEPPRRRSU	rere-supper
EEEPRRSSUX	expressure
EEEPRSSTUW	supersweet
EEEPRSTTTY	typesetter
EEFFFFIMOU	fee-fi-fo-fum
EEFFGHILRT	free flight
EEFFGIINRV	fivefinger
	five-finger
EEFFGINORR	forefinger
EEFFGNRSTU	greenstuff
EEFFHHILTW	fifth wheel
EEFFHILNST	the sniffle
EEFFHLRRSU	refreshful
EEFFIILLNO	line of life
EEFFIILLRZ	Zeffirelli
EEFFIILNOR	line of fire
EEFFILLLRS	self-filler
EEFFILLSUU	useful life
EEFFILSUVY	effusively
EEFFIMNNTT	infeftment
EEFFIORRTU	forfeiture
EEFFLOORTT	left-footer
EEFFLORSST	effortless
EEFFNORRTY	effrontery
EEFFSSTTUW	sweet-stuff
EEFGGIILOS	Isle of Eigg
EEFGHHIILR	high relief

EEFGHHIITV five-eighth
EEFGHIKNST knight's fee
EEFGHILNOR fingerhole
EEFGHINRRS refreshing
EEFGHINRTV Night Fever
EEFGHLNOSU hug oneself
EEFGHLOOSS gooseflesh
EEFGIILLLN ill feeling
EEFGIILLNS single file
EEFGIILNRV free-living
EEFGIINRRT gentrifier
EEFGILLNRY fleeringly
EEFGILLNTY fleetingly
EEFGILNRSS fingerless
fringeless
EEFGILNRTW left-winger
EEFGINNRRT refringent
EEFGINPRRR preferring
EEFGJLMOPZ Jozef Glemp
EEFGKLLNOT gentlefolk
EEFGLLMNOR fellmonger
EEFGLLNUVY vengefully
EEFGLMNNTU engulfment
EEFGLNPRTU prefulgent
EEFGORRTTY forgettery
EEFHHILNST in the flesh
EEFHHIORST horse-thief
EEFHHIOTTV The Hot Five
EEFHHLNOST on the shelf
EEFHHLORSS horseflesh
EEFHIILNRS line-fisher
EEFHIKLSTT fish kettle
EEFHILLORW fellow heir
EEFHILNSSS fleshiness
EEFHILNSTT nettle-fish
EEFHILORSV fire-shovel
EEFHILRSVY feverishly
EEFHINOPRS infosphere
EEFHINRSTY net-fishery
EEFHIORSTT the Forties
EEFHLNOORS Holofernes
EEFHLPRSSS press flesh
EEFHMOORRT foremother
EEFHMOORST foster-home
EEFHNORTTU fourteenth
EEFHNPRSTY Stephen Fry
EEFHOOPRST proof sheet
EEFHOOPSST sheep's-foot
EEFHORRSTT for the rest
EEFHORRSUY ferry-house
EEFIIILMNR Minié rifle
EEFIIIRRTV River Teifi
EEFIIKLLNU unlifelike
EEFIIKLLNX Felix Klein
EEFIIKLNUW unwifelike
EEFIILMNNY femininely
EEFIILMRSU emulsifier
EEFIILNSSW wifeliness
EEFIILRRST fertiliser
EEFIILRRTZ fertilizer
EEFIIMNNNU unfeminine
EEFIINNNRS Sinn Feiner
EEFIINNOTV nine-to-five
EEFIINNSST finiteness
EEFIINSSST feistiness
EEFIIPRRST free spirit
EEFIKLLLRS self-killer
EEFIKLLRUV liver fluke
EEFIKLOSSY Isle of Skye
EEFIKMNNOY knife-money
EEFIKNNOPS fine-spoken
EEFILLLSSY lifelessly
EEFILLNOTU feuilleton
EEFILMNOQU mefloquine
EEFILMRSTU muster-file
EEFILNNNUW wine funnel
EEFILNNORT florentine✧
EEFILNOTUX fluoxetine
EEFILNPPTT felt-tip pen
EEFILNRRSV silver fern
EEFILNRSSU irefulness
EEFILNRTUV interfluve
EEFILNSSZZ fizzenless
EEFILOOPRR poor relief
EEFILOORSU oleiferous
EEFILOSTWX Felixstowe
EEFILPRRSU persifleur
EEFILQRTUU requiteful
EEFILRSSST strifeless
EEFIMNOSTT oftentimes
EEFINNOPRU refine upon
EEFINNORRT interferon
EEFINNQRTU infrequent
EEFINOPSST fesse-point
EEFINOSSTV five-stones
EEFINTTVWY twenty-five
EEFIORRRTX fox terrier
EEFIORRSTT forsterite
EEFIORSSTU setiferous
EEFIORSTWY oyster-wife
EEFIPRRTUX prefixture
EEFIRRSSTU fruiteress
EEFKLLOOWY yoke-fellow
EEFKLNOOST Folkestone
EEFLLLSSSY selflessly
EEFLLNNRRU fell-runner
EEFLLNTUVY eventfully
EEFLLORSSW flowerless
EEFLMORRSU remorseful
EEFLMORRTT form letter
EEFLNNSSTU fluentness
EEFLNNTUUV uneventful
EEFLNOSSUW woefulness
EEFLNQRTUY frequently
EEFLNRSSUU ruefulness
EEFLNSSSUU usefulness
EEFLRSSTTU streetfuls
EEFLRSSTUU futureless
EEFMOORTZZ mezzo-forte
EEFNNORRRU forerunner
EEFNNQRTUU unfrequent
EEFNOOPRRS foreperson
EEFNOORSTY festoonery
EEFOOPRSSX ex professo
EEFOPRRRUV perfervour
EEGGGHIMNU Guggenheim
EEGGGILMOS gigglesome
EEGGHILNRT green light
EEGGHINTUV give the gun
EEGGHMNNOO hogen-mogen
EEGGIINNRW ginger wine
EEGGIMNRST stem ginger
EEGGINOTUV give tongue
EEGGINRRTT regretting
EEGGISSTUV suggestive
EEGGLOPRSV plover's egg
EEGGNOORTW George Town
Georgetown
EEGHHILRTW right wheel
EEGHHINOTT eighth note
EEGHHIOSUW weigh-house
EEGHHIRSTT high street✧
high-street
EEGHHORRUW rough-hewer
EEGHHORSTU see through
see-through
EEGHHPSTTU get the push
EEGHIILTVW live weight
EEGHIKLRSU kieselguhr
EEGHILMRTT light meter
EEGHILNOOP pigeonhole
EEGHILNOPR negrophile
EEGHILNRST sheltering
EEGHILNSTW lengthwise
EEGHILNSTY seethingly
EEGHILNSWW swing-wheel
EEGHILNWYZ wheezingly
EEGHILOOST theologise
EEGHILOOTZ theologize
EEGHILOSTW lose weight
EEGHILRTVY Verey light
EEGHILSSTW weightless
EEGHIMMNOS hegemonism
EEGHIMNOOS homogenise
EEGHIMNOOZ homogenize
EEGHIMNOST hegemonist
EEGHINNORT one-nighter
EEGHINNPTY eightpenny
EEGHINPRST regentship
EEGHINRTVY everything
EEGHIORTVW overweight
EEGHIPRRSV vergership
EEGHKMORRU Khmer Rouge
EEGHLLNOUW well enough
EEGHLNOOSW go on wheels
EEGHLNORST Glenrothes
EEGHLOORTY heterology
EEGHLOPRSU sleep rough
EEGHLOPRTU plough-tree
EEGHMORRTY germ theory
hygrometer
EEGHNNRSTT strengthen
EEGHNOORTY heterogony

EEGHNOPSYZ zygosphene
EEGHNORSUU sure enough
sure-enough
EEGHNORTTU untogether
EEGHOORTUY there you go
EEGHORSSTU other guess
otherguess
EEGHOSSTUU guest-house
house guest
EEGIIILMST legitimise
EEGIIILMTZ legitimize
EEGIIKLPRS kriegspiel
EEGIILNNST lentigines
EEGIILNORR religioner
EEGIILNRVV ever-living
EEGIILNTVY genitively
EEGIILOPSU epiloguise
EEGIILOPUZ epiloguize
EEGIIMMNSS misseeming
EEGIINNOPR pioneering
EEGIINNQTU quietening
EEGIINPRSS serpigines
EEGIINRRRV River Niger
EEGIINRRTV retrieving
EEGIINRSSU sui generis
EEGIINRSSV ingressive
EEGIINRSTV vertigines
EEGIISTTYZ zeitgeisty
EEGIJNSTTT jet-setting
EEGIKLLNNN kennelling
EEGIKLNOTU tonguelike
EEGIKORSSW siegeworks
EEGILLOPSS gospellise
EEGILLOPSW Owlspiegle
EEGILLOPSZ gospellize
EEGILMMNNT minglement
EEGILMNNOT eloignment
EEGILMNORS mongrelise
EEGILMNORZ mongrelize
EEGILNNPPU pulp-engine
EEGILNNPRS leg spinner
EEGILNNPSU unsleeping
EEGILNNRSY sneeringly
EEGILNNSSS singleness
EEGILNOSST telegnosis
EEGILNPPRX perplexing
EEGILNPRVY replevying
EEGILNPSST single-step
EEGILNPSWY sweepingly
EEGILNRSTW sweltering
EEGILORRST sortileger
EEGIMNNOOR engine-room
EEGIMNNOTT mignonette
EEGIMNNRST resignment
EEGIMNNTTU integument
EEGIMNOORT goniometer
EEGIMNOPPT peeping Tom
EEGIMNOPRW Empire gown
EEGIMORSTT geometrist
EEGINNNOPY pony engine
EEGINNOOSS noogenesis
EEGINNOPPS pepsinogen
EEGINNORST röntgenise
EEGINNORTZ röntgenize
EEGINNPRUY penguinery
EEGINNPRUZ Prinz Eugen
EEGINNRRSU rune-singer
EEGINNSSSY syngenesis
EEGINNSSVX vexingness
EEGINOORSS orogenesis
EEGINOPSSY pyogenesis
EEGINORRRV River Negro
EEGINORRSS regression
EEGINORRWW wine-grower
EEGINORSTY generosity
EEGINPRRST perstringe
EEGINPRSTT presetting
EEGIOPPRRT ego-tripper
EEGIORSSTU setigerous
EEGIORSTTU urostegite
EEGJLORRUU El Guerrouj
EEGLLLOSWY yellowlegs
EEGLLMRTUY grey mullet
EEGLLNOOSY selenology
EEGLLNOTTW well-gotten
EEGLLOOPSY speleology
EEGLMMNOOY emmenology
EEGLMNOORV love-monger
EEGLMNOOVY glove-money
EEGLMNOPRT peltmonger
EEGLMNORRT long-termer
EEGLMORSUY gruesomely
EEGLNNOOSS on one's legs
EEGLNOOSTU telegonous
EEGLNOPPPR long pepper
EEGLNORSUY generously
EEGLNOSSTU tongueless
EEGLOORRST ergosterol
EEGMNNOORT Montenegro
EEGMNNORSW newsmonger
EEGMNNORTV government✧
EEGMNOOPRS spermogone
EEGMNOORUY rogue money
EEGMNOSSSU ugsomeness
EEGMOOORRR Roger Moore
EEGNNOOSUX xenogenous
EEGNNORSUU ungenerous
EEGNNOTTXY oxygen tent
EEGNORSSVY governessy
EEGNORSTTU tonguester
EEGNORSTWY snowy egret
EEGOPPRRRU Upper Roger
EEGOPRSTUU Portuguese
EEGORRRSST retrogress
EEHHIKMNTT methinketh
EEHHIKNRTT The Thinker
EEHHILLOST The Hollies
EEHHILMPTT pith helmet
EEHHILOPTY heliophyte
EEHHILORTW otherwhile
EEHHILPSSY sheepishly
EEHHIMNOST henotheism
EEHHINORSS shoeshiner
EEHHINOSTT henotheist
EEHHINRTTT thirteenth
EEHHIORRSS shire horse
EEHHIORSTW Whitehorse
white horse
EEHHIOSTUW house white
White House
EEHHIRSSTV the shivers
EEHHLNOOTW on the whole
EEHHLRSTTU The Hustler
EEHHMOOOSS Moshoeshoe
EEHHNOOSTU on the house
EEHHNRRRTU Herrnhuter
EEHHNRSTUY heresy-hunt
EEHHOOPRST theosopher
EEHHOORRSS horseshoer
EEHHOORSUW whorehouse
EEHHOPPRTT the Prophet
EEHHOPRSST short sheep
EEHHOPSSTY hypotheses
EEHIIKLNRS shrinelike
EEHIILLMNW Wilhelmine
EEHIILMPTU epithelium
EEHIILNOPR perihelion
EEHIILNTWY Eli Whitney
EEHIIMNNOT methionine
EEHIINNPPR epinephrin
EEHIINOSTW white noise
EEHIINRRRV River Rhine
EEHIINSTTU the unities
EEHIIPRSVW viewership
EEHIIRRSTX heritrixes
EEHIJNNNOR John Rennie
EEHIJNSSSW Jewishness
EEHIJRSTTT the jitters
EEHIKLMNOU unhomelike
EEHIKMORST strike home
EEHIKNOTTT tie the knot
EEHIKOSSTT to the skies
EEHILLLNSW Helen Wills
EEHILLLOSV olive-shell
EEHILLMRST mitre shell
EEHILLNSSS shelliness
EEHILLORTZ lherzolite
EEHILLPRST tellership
EEHILLRSWW well-wisher
EEHILMNOSS homeliness
EEHILMOPRT thermopile
EEHILMOSSW somewhiles
EEHILNNRTY inherently
EEHILNORTT enterolith
EEHILNOSTT on the tiles
EEHILNRTUW whereuntil
EEHILNSTUV Nevil Shute
EEHILOOPRT heliotrope
EEHILOPRST priest hole
EEHILOSTTU silhouette
EEHILPRSTT ship letter
EEHILPRSTU spherulite
EEHILPRSUX superhelix

EEHILRSSTV thriveless
EEHIMMNNST inmeshment
EEHIMMNORT ermine moth
EEHIMNNOTY in the money
EEHIMNNRTU minehunter
EEHIMNPRRT permethrin
EEHIMNPRST reshipment
EEHIMOOSUV movie house
EEHIMOPRST the Promise
EEHIMOPRSV empoverish
EEHIMRRSTW Wertherism
EEHIMRSSTV verse-smith
EEHINNOPRS prehension
EEHINNOPRT interphone
EEHINNORST enthronise
rhinestone✧
EEHINNORSU Inner House
EEHINNORTZ enthronize
EEHINNOSST tennis shoe
EEHINNOSTT to the nines
EEHINNSSSW newishness
EEHINOOPRS ionosphere
EEHINOQTTU on the quiet
EEHINORRRV River Rhône
EEHINORSTW no the wiser
EEHINPRSST in the press
EEHINSSSTX sixth sense
EEHINSSSTY synthesise
EEHINSSTTY synthetise
EEHINSSTYZ synthesize
EEHINSTTYZ synthetize
EEHIOPPRRS prophesier
EEHIOPPRST epistrophe
EEHIORRRSV river horse
EEHIORSTTU stoutherie
EEHIRSSSTY hysteresis
EEHJLNNOVY John Evelyn
EEHJLNOSWY John Wesley
EEHJNNOOSS Johnsonese
EEHJOSSSUW Jews' houses
EEHKKOOPYY hokey-pokey
EEHKLLORRW Heller work
EEHKLNORRV Herrenvolk
EEHKMOOPST keep shtoom
EEHKMOORRW homeworker
EEHKMOOSSU smokehouse
EEHKNOORTT heterokont
tenterhook
EEHKNORTUY Turkey hone
EEHLLLPSSY helplessly
EEHLLMNOOP mellophone
EEHLLMNOSY shell money
EEHLLMORTW Motherwell
EEHLLMOSZZ shlemozzle
EEHLLNSSUV Venus-shell
EEHLLOPSSY hopelessly
EEHLLORSTT otter shell
EEHLLORSTW tower-shell
EEHLMMNOTY lemon thyme
EEHLMNOOYZ holoenzyme
EEHLMNORTU mole hunter
EEHLMNSSTT Mt St Helens
EEHLMORSST motherless
EEHLMORVWY vowel-rhyme
EEHLNNNRYY Lenny Henry
EEHLNOOOST on the loose
EEHLNOOSSV shovelnose
EEHLNORSST throneless
EEHLOOPSTT telephotos
EEHLOORSTW towel-horse
EEHLOORSUW lower house
EEHLORSSSW showerless
EEHLOSSTUY house style
EEHMMOOORY homoeomery
EEHMMOPRTU prometheum
EEHMNNNOOP phenomenon
EEHMNNOOTY on the money
EEHMNOOPRT phonometer
EEHMNOORRY Henry Moore
EEHMNOORTY heteronomy
EEHMNOOSTT nomothetes
EEHMNOOSUY honey-mouse
EEHMNORSTT nethermost
EEHMOOPRTT photometer
EEHMOORSVW whomsoever
EEHMOOSSUU house mouse
EEHMOPRSTT stepmother
EEHMOPRSTU Prometheus
EEHMOPRSTY hypsometer
EEHMOQRSUU humoresque
EEHMORRSTT short metre
EEHMORSSUW shrewmouse
EEHMOSSTTT the mostest
EEHNNOOSTY honey-stone
EEHNNOPRTY Entryphone®
EEHNNOPSST Stephenson
EEHNNOPSSY phoneyness
EEHNNORRRT northerner✧
EEHNOOOPRR orpheoreon
EEHNOOPRST on the ropes
EEHNOORSST stonehorse
EEHNOORTTU on the outer
EEHNOPPRXY nephropexy
EEHNOPRRSY prehensory
EEHNOPRSUY Euphrosyne
EEHNOPSSTU penthouses
EEHNOPSTTU theopneust
EEHNOPSTUY hypotenuse
EEHNORRSTU southerner✧
EEHNPSSSTT St Stephen's
EEHOOPRRSW horsepower
EEHOOPRSUW powerhouse
EEHOOPRTTV over the top
over-the-top
EEHOOPSTTY osteophyte
EEHOORRSVW overshower
EEHOORRTTW two or three
EEHOORSSTU storehouse
EEHOORSTUU Outer House
EEHOOSTTTW sweet tooth
EEHOPPRSST prophetess
EEHOPPRSUU upper house
EEHOPRRSTV Shreveport
EEHOPRSSST prostheses
EEHOPSSTUU set up house
EEHORRSTTW otter shrew
EEIIIMMRSS immiserise
EEIIIMMRSZ immiserize
EEIIIMNRSS miniseries
EEIIJLNSUV juvenilise
EEIIJLNUVZ juvenilize
EEIIJMNNOT Meiji Tenno
EEIIKLLMRT time-killer
EEIIKLLNSS likeliness
EEIIKLNPRW periwinkle
EEIIKLPRST priest-like
EEIIKLQRSU squirelike
EEIIKLRSST sisterlike
EEIILLMMRT millimetre
EEIILLMNRU reillumine
EEIILLNSSV liveliness
EEIILMMNPT limpet mine
EEIILMMPST simple time
EEIILMNOSW Simone Weil
EEIILMNSST timeliness
EEIILMPRTT triple time
EEIILNNORT Tirolienne
EEIILNNRST listener-in
EEIILNOSTV television
EEIILNOSTX ex silentio
EEIILNOTTT toilinette
EEIILOPSST epistolise
EEIILOPSTZ epistolize
EEIILOPTVX exploitive
EEIILORRRV River Loire
EEIILORSTT toiletries
EEIILOSSUZ Louis-Seize
EEIILRRSST steriliser
EEIILRRSTZ sterilizer
EEIIMMNRTU meitnerium
EEIIMNNOST in one's time
EEIIMNNPTT impenitent
pentimenti
EEIIMNNTTV invitement
EEIIMNRSTX in extremis
EEIIMNRTTW wintertime
EEIIMNRTZZ intermezzi
EEIIMOPRST epitomiser
EEIIMOPRTZ epitomizer
EEIIMPRSSV impressive
permissive
EEIIMPRSTV septemviri
EEIINNNSTT insentient
EEIINNRTTW intertwine
EEIINNSSTT intestines
EEIINNSTTX inexistent
EEIINOPRTT petitioner✧
repetition
EEIINRSSST sensitiser
EEIINRSSTZ sensitizer
EEIINRTTVY eviternity
EEIIOPSTVX expositive
EEIIORRSST rotisserie

Words marked ✧ can also be spelled with one or more capital letters

rôtisserie
EEIIPQRSTU perquisite
EEIIPRSSTV persistive
EEIIRRSTTU ureteritis
EEIJKLNORU Julie Krone
EEIJKNPRTY perjinkety
EEIJLLNUVY juvenilely
EEIJLRRSWY Jerry Lewis
EEIJMNNNOT enjoinment
EEIKKLNNPS skip-kennel
EEIKLLNOSV slovenlike
EEIKLLNRSW well-sinker
EEIKLMMRSU summerlike
EEIKLNNSSU unlikeness
EEIKLNPSTT kettle-pins
EEIKLORRVW evil-worker
EEIKMNORRW mine worker
EEIKMORRTW time-worker
EEIKNORSTZ strike zone
EEIKOPRSTV perovskite
EEIKORRRWW wireworker
EEIKORRSTV overstrike
EEILLLLNTT Little Nell
EEILLLLRWW well-willer
EEILLLNOWY yellow line
EEILLLOTVW well-to-live
EEILLLPSTV split-level
EEILLLRSST tillerless
EEILLMMORT immortelle
EEILLMNSSS smelliness
EEILLMPPPR peppermill
EEILLMPRTW pewter-mill
EEILLMSSTY timelessly
EEILLNNOSS loneliness
EEILLNORRT ritornelle
EEILLNORVZ Zollverein
EEILLNOSSV loveliness
EEILLNSSTT littleness
EEILLOPRRT tiller-rope
EEILLORTWW willow tree
EEILLOTWYY yellow-yite
EEILLPRRUW wirepuller
EEILLRSSTU Russellite
EEILLRSSTY tirelessly
EEILLSSVWY viewlessly
EEILMMRTTU multimeter
EEILMNNOTT entoilment
EEILMNNSTT enlistment
EEILMNOPRT Montpelier
EEILMNORSS solemniser
EEILMNORSZ solemnizer
EEILMNOSSU mousseline
EEILMNOTTU Moulinette®
EEILMNPSSS simpleness
EEILMOOSTT Teleostomi
EEILMOPRSY polymerise
EEILMOPRYZ polymerize
EEILMORRSV River Mosel
EEILMORSTY tiresomely
EEILMORTVY overtimely
EEILMOSSTV motiveless
EEILMPRSTU pulsimeter
EEILMPRTVY pelvimetry
EEILMPRTXY pleximetry
EEILNNOQTU ineloquent
EEILNNORST liner notes
EEILNNORTY Tyrolienne
EEILNNPRSU spinnerule
EEILNNPTTY penitently
EEILNNSSST silentness
EEILNNSTTY sentiently
EEILNOOTVV evolve into
EEILNOPPTT poplinette
EEILNOPRRT interloper
EEILNOPSST politeness
EEILNORRVV river novel
EEILNORTVV intervolve
EEILNOSSTW stolenwise
EEILNPRSST tripleness
EEILNPRTXY inexpertly
EEILNRSSTW winterless
EEILNRSTUY esuriently
EEILOOPRST teliospore
EEILOOPSST Osteolepis
EEILOPPRSS Persepolis
EEILORRSTU irresolute
EEILORRTTW rottweiler✧
EEILORRTXY exteriorly
EEILORSTUV resolutive
EEILORSVWY overwisely
EEILPPRTXY perplexity
EEILPPSTUV suppletive
EEILPRRSTY sperrylite
EEILPRRSUV pulveriser
EEILPRRUVZ pulverizer
EEILPRSSST stripeless
EEILPRSTTU supertitle
EEILRSSSST resistless
sisterless
EEILRSSTTZ strelitzes
EEILRSSTUV virtueless
EEIMMMNRTU immurement
EEIMMMORSS mesomerism
EEIMMMRSTU summer time
summertime
EEIMMOPRRV prime mover
EEIMMORRSV River Somme
EEIMMORSTU osmeterium
EEIMMPRSTT stimpmeter
EEIMMRSSTY symmetrise
EEIMMRSTYZ symmetrize
EEIMNNNRTT internment
EEIMNNOPTT pentimento
EEIMNNORST minestrone
EEIMNNPSTU Pennisetum
septennium
EEIMNNSSTU minuteness
EEIMNNSTTV investment
EEIMNOPPRT pre-emption
EEIMNOPRTU peritoneum
EEIMNOPRYZ prize money
EEIMNOPSTU pumie stone
EEIMNORRRT in terrorem
EEIMNORRSS sermoniser
EEIMNORRST teres minor
EEIMNORRSZ sermonizer
EEIMNORRTT nitrometer
EEIMNORRTU urinometer
EEIMNORTTT Tintometer®
EEIMNORTZZ intermezzo
EEIMNOSSTX sixteenmos
EEIMNPPPRT peppermint
EEIMNPRSSU impureness
EEIMNPRSTU episternum
EEIMNRSSSS remissness
EEIMNRSSTU terminuses
EEIMNRSSTW westernism
EEIMNRSTUV misventure
EEIMOOPRST opisometer
opsiometer
EEIMOOPRSX peroxisome
EEIMOPRRRT reimporter
EEIMOPRRST spirometer
temporiser
EEIMOPRRTZ temporizer
EEIMOPRSTU periosteum
EEIMPPRRUU puerperium
EEIMPPRSTU suppertime
EEIMPRRSSU impressure
presurmise
EEIMPRSSTV septemvirs
EEIMPRSTUV resumptive
EEIMRSSTTU sestertium
EEINNNSSTT intentness
EEINNOPPRT porpentine
EEINNOPRSS presension
EEINNOPRST pretension
pre-tension
EEINNOPRTT ten-pointer
EEINNOPRTV prevention
EEINNOPSST stone snipe
EEINNORRSS orneriness
EEINNORRTV intervenor
EEINNOSSTT set in stone
EEINNOSSTW swinestone
EEINNOSSTX extensions
EEINNPRSSU unripeness
EEINNPRTTU turpentine
EEINNPSSSU supineness
EEINNQSSUU uniqueness
EEINNRSSTV inventress
EEINNSSSUW unwiseness
EEINOOPRSS pensieroso
EEINOOSSST otioseness
EEINOPPRSV propensive
EEINOPQTTU equipotent
EEINOPRRSS repression
EEINOPRRST interposer
EEINOPRRSV perversion
EEINOPRSSV responsive
EEINOPRSSX expression
EEINOPRSTV protensive
EEINOPRSXY epoxy resin

EEINOPRTXY	pyroxenite	EELLNOSSTY	tonelessly	EEMPRSSSST	sempstress
EEINOQRSTU	questioner	EELLNOSSWY	yellowness	EEMQRSSTUU	sequestrum
EEINORRSUV	overinsure	EELLNSSTUY	tunelessly	EENNNNOOSS	no-nonsense
EEINORRTVW	overwinter	EELLORSTUY	resolutely	EENNNOPSTY	penny-stone
EEINORSSST	restenosis	EELLPRTTWY	pretty well	EENNOOOSST	on one's toes
EEINPPPRSS	preppiness	EELLRSSSTU	lustreless	EENNOQRSTU	quernstone
EEINPRSSTT	persistent		resultless	EENNORRRUV	overrunner
	prettiness	EELLRSSSTY	restlessly	EENNORSSTT	rottenness
EEINPSSSUV	suspensive	EELMMNOPTY	employment	EENNOSSSTY	syntenoses
EEINQSSTUY	squint-eyes	EELMMNOSTU	emoluments	EENNRSSTUU	untrueness
EEINRRRTTV	River Trent	EELMNNOSSS	solemnness	EENOOPPRSU	repose upon
EEINRRSTWW	news-writer	EELMNNOSTU	ensoulment	EENOPPRRSS	properness
EEINRSSSTY	synteresis	EELMNOPPRT	propelment	EENOPRSTTY	stenotyper
EEINSSTTUV	sustentive	EELMNOPPSU	pumple-nose	EENOPRSTUU	soup tureen
EEIOPPRRST	Piesporter	EELMNPPSTU	supplement	EENORRRTUV	overturner
EEIOPPRSSV	oppressive	EELMNPTUZZ	puzzlement	EENORSTTTU	neutrettos
EEIOPRRSTV	resorptive	EELMOORRSS	more or less	EENPRRSSUU	supernurse
EEIOPRRTTU	pirouetter	EELMOPRSTU	pulsometer	EEOPPPRRTW	pepperwort
EEIOPRSSST	stereopsis	EELMORRSST	tremorless	EEOPPPRSSU	presuppose
EEIOPRSSSV	espressivo	EELMORSTTY	metrostyle	EEOPPRRSSW	power press
EEIOPRSTTT	operettist	EELMORSTUY	temerously	EEOPPRRSUW	superpower
EEIOPSSSSV	possessive	EELMORTVVW	velvet worm	EEOPPRSSSS	prepossess
EEIORRRRST	terroriser	EELMSSSSTY	systemless	EEOPRRSSTU	streperous
EEIORRRRTZ	terrorizer	EELNNORRTU	unrelentor		superstore
EEIPPRRSST	per stirpes	EELNNORTUU	Eurotunnel	EEOPRSTTYY	stereotypy
EEIPPRTTUY	perpetuity	EELNOPPRSY	propensely	EEORRSSSTV	overstress
EEIPQRRRUU	perruquier	EELNOPRSTW	spleenwort	EEORRSTTTW	setterwort
EEIPRRSSSU	pressurise	EELNPPSSSU	suppleness	EEPRRSTUUY	Eurypterus
EEIPRRSSUZ	pressurize	EELNRRSSTU	returnless	EESSSSTUWX	West Sussex
EEIPRRSTVY	perversity	EELOOPPSSS	opposeless	EFFFFHLOSU	shuffle off
EEIPRRTTWY	typewriter	EELOOPRSTT	protostele	EFFFHIPRSU	puffer fish
EEIPRSSSTT	stepsister	EELOOPRSTU	petroleous	EFFFILLLOU	full of life
EEIRRSSSTV	servitress	EELOOPRSTY	proteolyse	EFFFILNSSU	fluffiness
EEIRSSSTTU	sestertius	EELOPPSTTU	put to sleep	EFFFINOOOT	foot of fine
EEJLMNOSTT	jostlement	EELOPRSTTT	post letter	EFFGGIORRT	trigger off
EEJLMOSTTU	le mot juste	EELOPRUVZZ	puzzle over	EFFGHIINRS	fish finger
EEJLMRSTWY	Jew's-myrtle	EELOPSSSSU	spouseless	EFFGHNOORU	forfoughen
EEJNORRSTY	Terry Jones	EELORRRSST	terrorless	EFFGHORSTU	Geoff Hurst
EEKLLNOPSW	well-spoken	EELORRRSTY	retrorsely	EFFGIINNST	stiffening
EEKLLNORRS	snorkeller	EELORSSUVY	yourselves	EFFGILLNOT	telling-off
EEKLLNRSSU	Ken Russell	EELORSTTUW	wrestle out	EFFGILPRTU	truffle pig
EEKLOOORRV	overlooker	EELPPRSSSU	supperless	EFFGINOPRR	proffering
EEKLOOPPRW	workpeople	EELPRRSTTU	splutterer	EFFGIORRUU	four-figure
EEKLORSSTW	steelworks	EELRSSSSST	stressless	EFFHHKOOOT	off the hook
EEKMNNOOTY	token money	EEMMMTTUUU	meum et tuum	EFFHILOSTW	whistle off
EEKMNOOPRY	monkey rope	EEMMOORRTT	tromometer	EFFHINOSSS	offishness
EEKMNOPRTY	pyknometer	EEMMOORTUX	ex mero motu	EFFHISTTUW	white stuff
EEKMRSSTTU	musket-rest	EEMNNOPSTT	pentstemon	EFFHNOOSUU	House of Fun
EELLLOPRSS	slop-seller	EEMNNORRRU	Rome-runner	EFFIIKLOSS	kiss of life
EELLLOSSVY	lovelessly	EEMNOOPRTY	petromoney	EFFIIKNRTU	fruit-knife
EELLMMORSS	mess or mell	EEMNOORSSS	moroseness	EFFIINNSSS	sniffiness
EELLMNNORT	enrollment	EEMNOORTTY	enterotomy	EFFILLMNTU	fulfilment
EELLMNOOSY	lonesomely	EEMNOPRSSY	press money	EFFILLOSSU	fossil fuel
EELLMNOSSW	mellowness	EEMNOPSSTY	open system	EFFILMNRSY	filmy ferns
EELLMNTTUY	temulently	EEMNORRSTY	yestermorn	EFFILNSSTU	fitfulness
EELLMOSSVY	movelessly	EEMNPRRSTU	presternum	EFFILOPRST	self-profit
EELLNNSSSU	sullenness	EEMOOPPRRT	pro tempore	EFFIMNOSUV	snuff movie
EELLNNSSUW	unwellness	EEMOORRSTT	streetroom	EFFINNOOPS	pension off
EELLNOPPRT	prepollent	EEMOORSTTY	stereotomy	EFFINNOPRS	off spinner
	propellent	EEMOPPRRTY	peremptory	EFFINNSSSU	snuffiness
EELLNOQTUY	eloquently	EEMORSSTTW	westermost	EFFINORTTW	written off

EFFINSSSTU stuffiness
EFFLMOOTTY My Left Foot
EFFNNOOSTU off one's nut
EFGGHILOTV glove-fight
EFGGHINRTU gunfighter
EFGGIIILNV life-giving
EFGGIILNNR fingerling
EFGGIILNSV self-giving
EFGGIINNNU unfeigning
EFGGIINNRR ring finger
EFGGILOOSS solfeggios
EFGGINORSU ego-surfing
EFGGINORTT forgetting
EFGGNOOUYY young fogey
EFGHIIKNRS kingfisher
EFGHIILLNT flight line
EFGHIINNST net-fishing
EFGHIIPRTZ prizefight
EFGHILLSST flightless
EFGHILNSSW swing-shelf
EFGHILOPRU fire-plough
EFGHILORTV overflight
EFGHILSTTT flight test
flight-test
test flight
EFGHIMNORS fishmonger
EFGHIMORST frightsome
EFGHINORTT freight ton
EFGHIRSTTU fish-gutter
EFGHLLLNTU full-length
EFGHLLNORU flugelhorn
flügelhorn
EFGHLLOOUY Lough Foyle
EFGHNNOTUU unfoughten
EFGHOOPPRR frog-hopper
EFGIIILNNR firing line
EFGIIKLNTY kite-flying
EFGIILNQUY liquefying
EFGIILNRSS self-rising
EFGIILTUVY fugitively
EFGIIMNORS foreignism
EFGIINNNTU fine-tuning
EFGIINNOST in one's gift
EFGIINPRST firing-step
EFGIINPRSY presignify
EFGIINPRTY petrifying
EFGIINRRTY terrifying
EFGIINRSTU surfeiting
EFGIINRSVY versifying
EFGIINSTTY testifying
EFGIKLNORS folk-singer
EFGIKORRUW figurework
EFGILLLUUY guilefully
EFGILLNORR finger roll
EFGILLNOSV self-loving
EFGILLNRSU self-ruling
EFGILLORRW flower girl
EFGILMNORS Single Form
EFGILMNOSV self-moving
EFGILNNOTW fowling-net
EFGILNOOST single-foot
EFGILNORST fosterling
EFGIMNOPRR performing
EFGINNORUV unforgiven✧
EFGINOPRSS professing
EFGINOPRST fingerpost
EFGINOPRTY torpefying
EFGINORRTY torrefying
EFGINPRTUY putrefying
EFGINPSTUY stupefying
EFGJLLNOUW junglefowl
EFGLLLNOOW Longfellow
EFGLNOPRTU profulgent
EFGNOOPRTU Group of Ten
EFGNOPRSUU pore fungus
EFGOOOOSST goosefoots
EFHHIJNORS John Fisher
EFHHIOORTT hit the roof
EFHHNOPSTY soft hyphen
EFHIILNRST Flintshire
EFHIILNSST filthiness
EFHIILRSSV silverfish
EFHIINRSTT in the first
EFHIINSSST shiftiness
EFHIIRSTTT thriftiest
EFHIKLNSUY flunkeyish
EFHIKNORST frithsoken
EFHILLOPSW fellowship
EFHILMOOTY oil of thyme
EFHILOOPRT hop-trefoil
EFHILOOPSY shoofly pie
EFHILOPRST shoplifter
EFHILORRSU flourisher
EFHILORSTW fish-trowel
EFHILORSUX flexihours
EFHILORSWW werwolfish
EFHILPPRSU purple fish
EFHILRSSTT thriftless
EFHINORSST frothiness
EFHINORTTZ on the fritz
EFHIOPRTWY trophy wife
EFHIORRRTV River Forth
EFHIORSTTU stouthrief
EFHIORSTTW white frost
EFHJLNOOSW John Fowles
EFHLLMOOOW follow home
EFHLLOOPRS shellproof
EFHLLOSSUV shovelfuls
EFHLMOORTW moth-flower
EFHLMORSTY smother-fly
EFHLMOTTUU flutemouth
EFHLOORSWW flower show
EFHMMOORRT thermoform
EFHNRTTTUU tuft-hunter
EFHOOOPRSU proof-house
EFIIIINNTV infinitive
EFIIILLMOR millefiori
EFIIILMNTY feminility
EFIIILMPRS simplifier
EFIIILNNTY infinitely
EFIIIMMNNS femininism
EFIIIMNNTY femininity
EFIIKLLMMO milk of lime
EFIIKNNOPT knife-point
EFIIKNRSSS friskiness
EFIILLLSST still lifes
EFIILLLTTT tilt fillet
EFIILLMNST silent film
EFIILLORSV silver foil
EFIILMNSSS flimsiness
EFIILNNSST flintiness
EFIILNORRY inferiorly
EFIILOPRSU piliferous
EFIILRSTTU stultifier
EFIIMNNRSS infirmness
EFIIMOPRRV viperiform
EFIIMORRSU Fourierism
EFIINOPSTV Five Points
EFIINRSSTU fruitiness
EFIIORRSTU Fourierist
EFIIORSTUV vitiferous
EFIIPRRSTZ first prize
EFIKLMNSUY flunkeyism
EFIKLNOSSS folksiness
EFIKNPTTUY putty-knife
EFILLLMOSU Isle of Mull
EFILLMORST stelliform
EFILLNORTU ill fortune
EFILLNSSUW wilfulness
EFILLOOPRW low profile
low-profile
EFILLPSTUY spitefully
EFILLRSSTU full sister
EFILMNOOST self-motion
EFILMNOSUU fulmineous
EFILMOPRSU promiseful
EFILMORRTY elytriform
EFILMORSTW mist-flower
EFILNNSSSU sinfulness
EFILNOORSS solferinos
EFILNOOSSS foisonless
EFILNOPPSS floppiness
EFILNORTWW twinflower
EFILNOSSSU fusionless
EFILOPRSST profitless
EFIMNOORRV overinform
EFIMNOORSU omniferous
EFIMNORSTU misfortune
EFIMOOPRRT proteiform
EFIMOOPRSU pomiferous
EFINNORRTY forty-niner
EFINOOPRSS profession
EFINOPRRRT ferro-print
EFINORRRTV riverfront
EFINORRSTT strife-torn
EFINORRTUU fourniture
EFINORSSST frostiness
EFINORSSSW frowsiness
EFINORSSWZ frowziness
EFINORSTTU stone fruit
EFIOOPRRSU poriferous
EFIOORRSTU rotiferous
EFIOORSSSU ossiferous

EFIOPRRSTT	esprit fort
EFJLLORUWY	July-flower
EFJLNOSSUY	joyfulness
EFKLLOORWW	workfellow
EFKLMMOORY	folk-memory
EFKLMNOOSW	womenfolks
EFKLNOOPSU	foul-spoken
EFKMOOOPRS	smokeproof
EFKMOORSST	frost-smoke
EFKNOOPSST	soft-spoken
EFKOPPRRSU	fork supper
EFLLLNNOSU	full nelson
EFLLLOPSUY	spoylefull
EFLLMOOORW	room-fellow
EFLLMORSSY	formlessly
EFLLNNORRY	Errol Flynn
EFLLNSUUUY	unusefully
EFLLOPRUWY	powerfully
EFLMNOOORW	moonflower
EFLMOOORTY	tomfoolery
EFLNORSSUW	Sunflowers
EFLOOPRTUY	fluorotype
EFLOPPRSUU	purposeful
EFMMNOORYY	for my money
EFMNNNOUYY	funny money
EFMOOPRRTU	outperform
EFNNOORRSU	non-ferrous
EFNOORRSTT	storefront
EFNORRSTTU	soft return
EFNORTTUWY	twenty-four
EFOOOPPRRR	repro proof
EFOOPPRRSS	press proof
EFOOPRRSTU	four-poster
EGGGHILMSU	mishguggle
EGGGIINNRS	sniggering
EGGGIJJOTY	jiggety-jog
EGGGIMNNTU	nutmegging
EGGGINORSS	grogginess
EGGHHIMTTU	hug-me-tight
EGGHHIPRSU	hip-huggers
EGGHHORTTU	get through
EGGHIIKLLT	Kleig light
	Klieg light
EGGHIILNNT	lightening
EGGHIINNUW	unweighing
EGGHIKNRTY	grey knight
EGGHINNOTU	toughening
EGGHINOORS	shore-going
EGGHINSTTU	guest-night
EGGIILMMNR	glimmering
EGGIILNNST	glistening
EGGIILNRST	glistering
EGGIILNRTT	glittering
EGGIILNRVY	grievingly
EGGIINNOPW	pigeon-wing
EGGIINNRST	signet ring
EGGILLLNPU	leg-pulling
EGGILLNORV	grovelling
EGGILMOOST	gemologist
EGGILNNRSU	gunslinger
EGGILNNTTU	englutting
EGGILNOORT	toggle iron
EGGILNSSUY	guessingly
EGGILOORST	Georg Solti
EGGILORTUW	wriggle out
EGGINNOOOR	gorgoneion
EGGINNORSS	engrossing
EGGINOORSV	goings-over
EGGINOSSTU	suggestion
EGGIOPRSTT	get to grips
EGGLLOOOPX	googolplex
EGGLNOOOSY	gnoseology
EGGLOOPTYY	Egyptology
EGGLOORSUY	gorgeously
EGHHIILNTT	in the light
EGHHIILTTW	white light
EGHHIINNST	The Shining
EGHHIINRTT	in the right
EGHHIINTTW	white night
EGHHIIPRST	high priest
EGHHIITTWW	with weight
EGHHILLORR	high-roller
EGHHILOPRY	hieroglyph
EGHHILORST	light horse
EGHHILOSTU	lighthouse
EGHHIMORST	highermost
EGHHINNORT	night heron
EGHHINOSTU	night-house
EGHHIOPSTT	spot height
EGHHIOPTTW	hop the twig
EGHHOORSUU	rough house
	rough-house
EGHHOPRTYY	hygrophyte
EGHHORTTUW	wet through
EGHIIIKLNS	heli-skiing
EGHIIJNNOT	hinge joint
EGHIIJPSTU	the jig is up
EGHIILMNSS	Englishism
EGHIILNNPS	plenishing
EGHIILNNRT	inner light✧
EGHIILNRSV	shriveling
EGHIILNSST	sightlines
EGHIILRSTY	tigerishly
EGHIIMMNRS	shimmering
EGHIIMNPRW	whimpering
EGHIIMNSST	mightiness
EGHIINNPRT	trephining
EGHIINNPSS	ensignship
EGHIINNSST	thinginess
EGHIINNSTW	in the wings
EGHIINPPTW	whippeting
EGHIINPRSW	whispering
EGHIINRTTW	twi-nighter
EGHIINSTUX	extinguish
EGHIJLNOPR	John Pilger
EGHIKLNRTU	Luther King
EGHIKLNSST	knightless
EGHIKMOSTT	smoketight
EGHIKNNRVY	King Henry V
EGHIKNOTUW	huntiegowk
EGHILLNOST	hostelling
EGHILLNOSU	houselling
EGHILLNOSV	shovelling
EGHILLNPST	night-spell
EGHILLOOPR	philologer
EGHILLOOPU	philologue
EGHILLOOTV	light-o'-love
EGHILMOOOS	homologise
EGHILMOOOZ	homologize
EGHILNORST	Nigel Short
EGHILNORVY	hoveringly
EGHILNSSST	slightness
EGHILOOPPT	phlogopite
EGHILOOPSU	geophilous
EGHILOORST	rheologist
EGHILOOSTT	ethologist
	theologist
EGHILOPSUW	ploughwise
EGHILORSTV	slight over
EGHILORTTW	light-tower
EGHIMNOPRS	phorminges
EGHIMNORST	smothering
EGHIMNRRTY	merry-night
EGHIMOPPSU	pemphigous
EGHIMOSSTU	mouse-sight
EGHIMOSUYZ	hemizygous
EGHINNORST	shortening
EGHINNORTW	in the wrong
EGHINNRSTT	in strength
EGHINNRSTU	night nurse✧
EGHINOOSTT	theogonist
EGHINOPSST	open sights
EGHINORSST	shoestring
EGHINORSTU	southering
EGHINRSTTU	shuttering
EGHIORSTTW	ghost-write
EGHJMMNORU	John Gummer
EGHJMNPTUU	jump the gun
EGHJNOORRS	John Rogers
EGHLLMOOPU	mole plough
EGHLMOORTY	mythologer
	thermology
EGHLNOOPRY	nephrology
	phrenology
EGHLOOORTY	heortology
EGHLOOPPSY	psephology
EGHLOPPRTY	petroglyph
EGHMNOOOSU	homogenous
EGHMNOOPRY	morphogeny
EGHMOOOTYZ	homozygote
EGHMORRTYY	hygrometry
EGHMPRSWYY	pygmy shrew
EGHOOPRSUU	house group
EGHOORRTUW	ore-wrought
EGHOORRTVW	overgrowth
EGHOPRSTUU	supertough
EGHORRRSTU	Ruth Rogers
EGIIILMMST	legitimism
EGIIILMPRS	pilgrimise
EGIIILMPRZ	pilgrimize
EGIIILMSTT	legitimist
EGIIILNNPP	pipelining
EGIIILNORR	irreligion

EGIIIMNNST	meningitis
EGIIJNNOOS	Inigo Jones
EGIIKKLNNU	unkinglike
EGIIKLLLNW	well-liking
EGIIKLLTUY	guilty-like
EGIIKLNNRS	ink-slinger
EGIIKLNNSS	kingliness
EGIIKLNORV	King Oliver
EGIIKLNPRS	springlike
EGIIKNNRTT	trinketing
EGIIKNPPRS	skippering
EGIIKNPRST	priest-king
EGIILLMNSS	mis-selling
EGIILLNNST	tinselling
EGIILLNNSV	snivelling
EGIILLNOTU	guillotine
EGIILLNRSV	silverling
EGIILLNRVY	revilingly
EGIILLNSVW	swivelling
EGIILLRSTV	silver-gilt
EGIILNNPRS	spring line
EGIILNNPRY	repiningly
EGIILNPRST	priestling
EGIILNQRSU	squireling
EGIILNRRTY	retiringly
EGIILNRSSS	grisliness
EGIILNRSTU	linguister
EGIILNRTVY	rivetingly
EGIILNRVVY	revivingly
EGIILNSSTU	guiltiness
EGIILNSSTZ	glitziness
EGIILOPSTT	epiglottis
EGIIMNNRTU	unmeriting
EGIIMNOPRT	primogenit
EGIIMNOPRU	perigonium
EGIIMNPRST	springtime
EGIIMNPRTT	permitting
EGIIMNRSTU	trigeminus
EGIINNNPRU	unrepining
EGIINNOPTT	ignipotent
EGIINNORSS	ingression
EGIINNSSST	stinginess
EGIINNSTUU	Unigenitus
EGIINORRST	roistering
EGIINORRTT	intertrigo
EGIINRRSTW	sign-writer
EGIINRSSTT	grittiness
EGIINRTTTW	twittering
EGIINSTTTV	vignettist
EGIJKNNSTU	junketings
EGIJMNPRUU	gum juniper
EGIJMNSTUU	jus gentium
EGIJNNORUY	journeying
EGIJNOTTTU	outjetting
EGIKLLORRW	grille-work
EGIKLNNPSU	spelunking
EGIKLORRSW	silkgrower
EGIKNNNOST	Kensington
EGIKNNORTW	networking
EGIKNOOQSU	quink-goose
EGIKNOORST	go on strike
EGILLLNPSY	spellingly
EGILLLNSWY	swellingly
EGILLLORWY	yellow-girl
EGILLMMNPU	pummelling
EGILLNNNTU	tunnelling
EGILLNNOTW	wellington✧
EGILLNOPPR	propelling
EGILLNOPRT	petrolling
EGILLNORRR	ring roller
EGILLNORTW	trowelling
EGILLNORWY	loweringly
EGILLNPRSW	wellspring
EGILLNTUXY	exultingly
EGILLOOQSU	goose-quill
EGILLORSSY	syllogiser
EGILLORSYZ	syllogizer
EGILMMNORS	mongrelism
EGILMNOOOS	monologise
EGILMNOOOZ	monologize
EGILMNOOSS	gloominess
EGILMNOPRR	long primer
	longprimer
EGILMNOPSY	polygenism
EGILMNOPTT	melting-pot
EGILMNOSUU	leguminous
EGILMNPTTY	temptingly
EGILMOOSSY	seismology
EGILNNOSST	slingstone
EGILNNOSSV	lovingness
EGILNNRRUY	unerringly
EGILNNSTTU	unsettling
EGILNOOORY	oneirology
EGILNOOOST	oenologist
EGILNOOPST	penologist
EGILNOPRTT	Port Gentil
EGILNOPSTY	polygenist
EGILNORRUV	overruling
EGILNORRVW	liver-grown
EGILNORTWY	toweringly
EGILNOSSSS	glossiness
EGILNOSSUY	lysigenous
EGILNOSTTU	gluttonise
EGILNOSTUU	lounge suit
EGILNOTTUZ	gluttonize
EGILNPRSSS	springless
EGILNPRSSY	pressingly
EGILNQRUYY	queryingly
EGILNQSTUY	questingly
EGILNRSSST	stringless
EGILNRSTTU	lutestring
EGILOOORST	oreologist
EGILOOPRSU	prologuise
EGILOOPRUZ	prologuize
EGILOORSST	serologist
EGILOOSSTX	sexologist
EGILOPRRST	poster girl
EGILORSUVY	grievously
EGILOSUUXY	exiguously
EGIMMNNOOS	monogenism
EGIMMNNPTU	impugnment
EGIMNNOORR	ironmonger
EGIMNNOORS	Monsignore
EGIMNNOOST	monogenist
EGIMNNOOSU	omnigenous
EGIMNNORTT	tormenting
EGIMNOORST	ergonomist
EGIMNOORTY	goniometry
EGIMNPRSSU	grumpiness
EGIMNPRTTU	trumpeting
EGIMOOPRST	geotropism
EGIMOORRSU	morigerous
EGIMRSSTUY	Misery Guts
EGINNOPRSU	unreposing
EGINNOPSSS	sponginess
EGINNORRTW	intergrown
EGINNRSUVW	unswerving
EGINNSSTTU	sunsetting
EGINOOPPST	pigeon-post
EGINOOPRRT	progenitor
EGINOOPRTW	towing rope
EGINOORSSV	grooviness
EGINOPRRSS	in progress
EGINOPRSTY	serotyping
EGINOPRSUY	perigynous
EGINOPRTUW	pouring wet
EGINORRSTU	trousering
EGINORRSTW	songwriter
EGINORRUVY	Ivor Gurney
EGINORSSTT	grottiness
EGINORSTUW	outswinger
EGINOSTTTU	outsetting
EGINPRSTTU	sputtering
EGINRSSTTV	string vest
EGINRSTTTU	stuttering
	Turing test
EGIOPPRSUU	pupigerous
EGJLLOORRY	Jolly Roger
EGJLMNOPRU	long jumper
EGKNOORTUW	tongue-work
EGLLMORSUU	glomerulus
EGLLNOOPPU	plunge pool
EGLMNOOOTY	entomology
EGLMNOORUY	numerology
EGLMNOOYYZ	enzymology
EGLNNORSUU	sunlounger
EGLNOOOPRY	ponerology
EGLNOOPSUY	polygenous
EGLNOOSUXY	xylogenous
EGLOOORRWW	wool-grower
EGLOOPRTYY	pyretology
EGMMNOORTY	Montgomery
EGMMNOPRSY	gymnosperm
EGMMPRUUWY	mugwumpery
EGMNNOOOSU	monogenous
EGMOOORRSU	grouse moor
EGMORRSSTU	storm surge
EGNNORSSSU	Guns 'n' Roses
EGNOOPRSUY	pyrogenous
EGNOORRSTV	overstrong
EGNORRSTUV	overstrung
EGNORSSSST	songstress
EGNPQRRSUU	quersprung

EGOPPRRSUU supergroup
EGOPRSTTUY Pterygotus
EHHIILLMSW Wilhelm His
EHHIILOPPP hippophile
EHHIILSTVY thievishly
EHHIIMSTTW whitesmith
EHHILLORST thill-horse
EHHILMOPRT thermophil
EHHILMOSTY hylotheism
EHHILNOPTW help on with
EHHILOOPPS philosophe
EHHILOPRSU Herophilus
EHHILOPSTY lithophyse
EHHILOPTTY lithophyte
EHHILORTWW worth while
worthwhile
EHHILOSTTY hylotheist
EHHILRSSWY shrewishly
EHHIMOPRST mother ship
EHHIMORSTT hithermost
EHHINORTTW whitethorn
EHHIOOPRRZ rhizophore
EHHIOPPPTY hippety-hop
EHHIOPRRSS Shropshire
EHHIOPSSTY hypothesis
EHHJNNORTU John Hunter
EHHKLLMOTU Helmut Kohl
EHHLLOOSTT toothshell
EHHLMRSSTY rhythmless
EHHLOOOPPR lophophore
EHHMMOOOPR homeomorph
EHHMNNOOTY honeymonth
EHHMNORTTU moth-hunter
EHHMORSTTU home-thrust
EHHNOOOPPR phonophore
EHHNOOOPPT photophone
EHHNORSTUW run the show
EHHOOOPPRT photophore
EHHOOPPRST phosphoret
EHHOOPRRTY orthophyre
EHHOORRRST the horrors
EHHOPPRSTU phosphuret
EHHOPPSSYY hypophyses
EHIIILNPPP philippine✧
EHIIILNPST philistine✧
EHIIILPPPS Philippise
EHIIILPPPZ Philippize
EHIIIMRSST Irish Times
EHIIINRRTX inheritrix
EHIIIPRSVZ viziership
EHIIJMMTWY Jimmy White
EHIIKLNPSX sphinxlike
EHIIKMRRSS skirmisher
EHIIKMSTWY tim-whiskey
EHIILLLOWY Holy Willie
EHIILLMNOT the million
EHIILLNQTU in the quill
EHIILLOOPS Heliopolis
EHIILLOPSY lyophilise
EHIILLOPYZ lyophilize
EHIILLRSVY liverishly
EHIILMOPRT limitrophe
EHIILNOOPS eosinophil
EHIILNQRSU relinquish
EHIILNSTTW tin whistle
EHIILORTTT lithotrite
EHIIMNOPSX phoenixism
EHIIMNPSSS impishness
EHIIMNSSSW whimsiness
EHIIMOPRSV impoverish
EHIIMPPRSU umpireship
EHIIMPPSTY epiphytism
EHIINNPRST internship
EHIINNTTTW with intent
EHIINOOPSV visiophone
EHIINORSSS Oirishness
EHIINOSSTW on this wise
EHIINPPSSW whippiness
EHIINRSSST shirtiness
EHIIOPRSTV Rh-positive
EHIIOSSTTV stishovite
EHIIPPRRST tripperish
EHIIPPRSST priestship
EHIIPPRSTU Hippurites
EHIIPQRSSU squireship
EHIIPRRSTW writership
EHIIPRSTTY Triphysite
EHIIRRSTTU urethritis
EHIIRSSTTT thirstiest
EHIIRSSTTY hysteritis
EHIJKLNOSW John Wilkes
EHIJLLNOTT Little John
EHIKLMNOPY lymphokine
EHIKLNORTW Kenilworth
EHIKLOOSVW swivel-hook
EHIKLOPRSY pokerishly
EHIKMNOTTT kitten moth
EHIKOORSST sister hook
EHILLMNPUY phillumeny
EHILLNRSSS shrillness
EHILLNSTUV Huntsville
EHILLOSSTU stillhouse
EHILLPRYYZ zephyr lily
EHILMNOPST polishment
EHILMNSSSU mulishness
EHILMOPSTY polytheism
EHILNNOOSW Welsh onion
EHILNNORTU lion-hunter
EHILNNOSSU unholiness
EHILNOPRTU neutrophil
EHILNORRSV horn silver
EHILNOSSSW owlishness
EHILNSSSSU slushiness
EHILOOPRST strophiole
EHILOOPRTY heliotropy
EHILOOPSTU pilot house
EHILOPRSSU Russophile
EHILOPSTTY polytheist
EHILORRTTY erythritol
EHILOSSTTW sow thistle
EHILPRSSUU sulphurise
EHILPRSUUZ sulphurize
EHILRSSSTT thirstless
EHIMMNOOST monotheism
EHIMMOPRTU promethium
EHIMMOPSTU imposthume
EHIMNNOORS moonshiner
EHIMNNPSTU punishment
EHIMNOORTY herniotomy
EHIMNOOSTT monotheist
EHIMNOPRST mentorship
EHIMNOPSSS mopishness
EHIMNORTTW winter moth
EHIMOOPRRU eriophorum
EHIMOOTTYY Timothy Yeo
EHIMOPPRST prophetism
EHIMOPPSSU mesohippus
EHIMORRSTT thermistor
EHIMORRTUV river mouth
EHIMPRRTUY triumphery
EHIMRSTTTU time-thrust
EHINNORSST thorniness
EHINNOSSST tonishness
EHINOOPSUU euphonious
EHINOOPTTT to the point
EHINOOSSTT toothiness
EHINOPPRTY periphyton
EHINOPRRTY pyrrhotine
EHINOPRSTY hypnotiser
EHINOPRTYZ hypnotizer
EHINOPSSTX sextonship
EHINORSSTW worthiness
EHINORSTUU ruthenious
EHINOSSSTY toyishness
EHINPPSSSU uppishness
EHINPRSSST Ship's Stern
EHINPRSUYZ Zephyrinus
EHINRRTTUW Winterthur
EHINSSSTTY synthesist
EHINSSTTTY synthetist
EHIOOPPRRS spirophore
EHIOOPRSSU puir's-hoose
EHIOOPRSTT orthoepist
EHIOOPRTTX thixotrope
EHIOORSSTX six-shooter
EHIOPPRRSW worshipper
EHIOPPRRTY porphyrite
EHIOPRRSTY prehistory
EHIOPRRTTY pyrrhotite
EHIOPRSSST prosthesis
EHIOPRSSUU puir's-house
EHIORSSSTX short sixes
EHIPPRRSSU pursership
EHIPRRSTTU turret ship
EHIPRSSTUY suretyship
EHJLLORTTU Jethro Tull
EHJLNNNNOO John Lennon
EHJMNOORSS John Somers
EHJMOPRSUW showjumper
EHJNOOPRTT John Potter
EHJNOORRTY John Torrey
EHKMOOPRSU skeuomorph
EHKMOSSTTU musket-shot

Words marked ✧ can also be spelled with one or more capital letters

EHKNNNOTUW the unknown
EHKOPRSSTU push-stroke
EHLLLOORRY Holy Roller
EHLLNOOPPY polyphenol
EHLLNOOSSW hollowness
EHLLRSSTUY hurtlessly
ruthlessly
EHLMNOPPTY nympholept
EHLMNORTUY unmotherly
EHLMNOSSUY slush money
EHLMOOPPRY pleomorphy
EHLMOPPSUY Polyphemus
EHLMORSSUU humourless
EHLNOOOPTV photonovel
EHLNOOPRTW on the prowl
EHLNOORSSU honourless
EHLNORSTUY southernly
EHLOOPPRRY plerophory
EHLOOPRSTU toolpusher
EHLOORRRTY holy terror
EHLOORTVWY loveworthy
EHLOPPPSWY Welsh poppy
EHLOPRSTUY upholstery
EHMMOOPRSY mesomorphy
EHMMOORRSU mushroomer
EHMMOORSUU humoursome
EHMMORRSTU Mt Rushmore
EHMNOOORRT throne room
EHMNOOOSTU theonomous
EHMNOOPRTU mother upon
EHMNOOPRTY nephrotomy
EHMNOOSSST smoothness
EHMNOOSTTW smooth newt
EHMNOPSTTU on the stump
EHMOOORSTV smooth over
EHMOOPRSTT mother spot
EHMOOPRTTY photometry
EHMOORRTTW motherwort
EHMOPRSTYY hypsometry
EHMRRSTTUU truth serum
EHNNOPRTWY pennyworth
EHNNPPRTUY thruppenny
EHNOOPPRRS pronephros
EHNOORTTWY noteworthy
EHNOQSTTUU Quonset hut®
EHNORSTWWY newsworthy
EHOOOPPRRS sporophore
EHOOOPPRTT phototrope
EHOOOPRRST troop horse
EHOOOPRSSU poor's-house
EHOOPPRSTY sporophyte
EHOOPPRTTY protophyte
tropophyte
EHOPPPSTUW puppet show
EHOPRSSSTY hypostress
EHOPRSTTTU shot-putter
EHORRSTTUV overthrust
EHORSSTTUU trust house
EIIILLLMRT millilitre
EIIILMNNOP epilimnion
EIIILORSTV vitriolise
EIIILORTVZ vitriolize
EIIIMNNRST in terminis
EIIIMNOSSS missionise
EIIIMNOSSZ missionize
EIIIMPRSTT time spirit
EIIIMSSTVY emissivity
EIIINPRRST reinspirit
EIIIOPRRST prioritise
EIIIOPRRTZ prioritize
EIIJKNPRTY perjinkity
EIIJLNTUVY juvenility
EIIJMNORTT mitre-joint
EIIJMNRTUY injury time
EIIJMNSTTU just-in-time
EIIKKLOSSW Kieslowski
EIIKLLNRTW winterkill
EIIKLNNSSS slinkiness
EIIKLNORST triskelion
EIIKLNPSTT kittle-pins
EIIKLNRSSV silverskin
EIIKMNPSSS skimpiness
EIIKMOPRRS morris-pike
EIIKNNNSSS skinniness
EIIKNORSTT strike into
EIIKNQRSSU quirkiness
EIILLLNOTT Little Lion
EIILLLOSUV Louisville
EIILLLSUVY illusively
EIILLMMNNU millennium
EIILLMNOOT emollition
EIILLMNORV vermillion
EIILLMNOVY minivolley
EIILLMOPTY impolitely
EIILLMPRTU multiplier
EIILLNOPST septillion
EIILLNORRT ritornelli
EIILLNORSS Rossellini
EIILLNORTT tortellini
EIILLNOSTX sextillion
EIILLNPSTU illipe nuts
EIILLPPRSY slipperily
EIILLPSSTY pitilessly
EIILMMNNTY imminently
EIILMNNNUU unnilenium
EIILMNNSTT instilment
EIILMNOSST lentissimo
EIILMNOSTY mylonitise
EIILMNOTYZ mylonitize
EIILMORTTU outer limit
EIILMOSUXY eximiously
EIILNNOTUV univoltine
EIILNOPRST prosilient
EIILNORRTY interiorly
EIILNOSSSV visionless
EIILNPPSSS slippiness
EIILNRSSTY sinisterly
EIILNRSTUV lentivirus
EIILNSSSTT stiltiness
EIILOPRSTU reptilious
EIILOPSSTT epistolist
EIILOPSTVY positively
EIILORSTTY literosity
EIILPRSSST spiritless
EIIMMOPRSV misimprove
EIIMMORSTU immeritous
EIIMMPRSUY perimysium
EIIMNNORSU reunionism
EIIMNNORTU munitioner
EIIMNNOSTU Ismet Inönü
EIIMNNRSTU trienniums
EIIMNOPRSS impression
permission
EIIMNRSSST ministress
EIIMOOPSTY episiotomy
EIIMOPRRSV improviser
EIIMOPRSSV promissive
EIIMOPRSUV impervious
EIIMORRRST mirror site
EIIMORRRSW mirrorwise
EIIMORSSTU moisturise
EIIMORSTUZ moisturize
EIIMRSSSTT mistress it
EIINNNORTU interunion
EIINNNOSTT intentions
EIINNNRTTU innutrient
EIINNOPPSU union pipes
EIINNOQSTU in question
EIINNORSTU reunionist
EIINNRSSTW wintriness
EIINOOPRST positioner
reposition
re-position
EIINOOPSTX exposition
EIINOORSUV Eurovision
EIINOPPTTT petit point
EIINORSSTV versionist
EIINORSTVV inter vivos
EIINORTTWZ zwitterion
EIINPRSSSS prissiness
EIINPRSSST stripiness
EIINQSSUZZ quizziness
EIINRSSTTW twin sister
EIINRSTTTU instituter
EIINRSTTTW intertwist
EIINRSTUVY university
EIINRTTTWY nitwittery
EIINSSTTTU institutes
EIIOOPPSTV oppositive
EIIOOPRSSU uropoiesis
EIIOPPRRSX ex propriis
EIIOPPSSTT petits pois
EIIOQRRSTU requisitor
EIIORSTTVY vitreosity
EIIPRTTUVY eruptivity
EIJKLNORRT J R R Tolkien
EIJKNNORSY Roy Jenkins
EIJLMPPRTU triple jump
triple-jump
EIJNORSSTU jointuress
EIJOPRRSUU perjurious
EIKLLLOOVY look lively!
EIKLLMOORS Eskimo roll

EIKLLMORRW millworker
EIKLMNOSSY Lysenkoism
EIKLNNOPSS Leon Spinks
EIKLNSSTUZ klutziness
EIKLOSTTTU skittle out
EIKLRSSSTU tusser silk
EIKMNOORST moonstrike
EIKMNOSTUY monkey suit
EIKNNOSSTT knottiness
stinkstone
EIKNNPSSSU spunkiness
EIKNOOPSSS spookiness
EIKNOPPPRS skin-popper
EIKNOPRTTY kryptonite
EIKNORRUVY Yukon River
EIKOORRSTT strike root
EIKOPPRRST strip-poker
EIKORSTTTY Trotskyite
EILLLLSSWY will-lessly
EILLLOORTT toilet roll
EILLLSSSTY listlessly
EILLMNOSYY silly money
EILLMOOSTY toilsomely
EILLMPSSSU psellismus
EILLNNOSTY insolently
EILLNOOPSS pollenosis
EILLNOORRT ritornello
EILLNOOSSW woolliness
EILLNOPTUY unpolitely
EILLNORWWW willow wren
EILLNOSSTT stone-still
EILLNOSTVW Townsville
EILLNRTUVY virulently
EILLOOPPPS Lippes loop
EILLOORRTT rototiller
EILLOPPPPR pill-popper
EILLOPRSUY perilously
EILLOPSTTU spell it out
EILLORRTUY ulteriorly
EILLORTTTU litter lout
EILLQRRSUY squirrelly
EILMMNOOPU polemonium
EILMMNSSSU slumminess
EILMMOPRSY polymerism
EILMMSSSTU summitless
EILMNNOSTU insoulment
EILMNNRTUU unruliment
EILMNNSTTU insultment
EILMNOOOPS monopolise
EILMNOOOPZ monopolize
EILMNOOSST motionless
EILMNOPTTY impotently
EILMNOSSSS lissomness
EILMNRSSTY minstrelsy
EILMOOPRST metropolis✧
EILMOPPRRY improperly
EILMOPSUUX implexuous
EILMORSSTT moss-litter
EILMRSSSTY mistressly
EILMSSTTTU litmus test
EILNNNOOTV non-violent
EILNNOOSTW low-tension
EILNNOSTTW Tinseltown
EILNNRSSUU unruliness
EILNOOOPTV love potion
EILNOOPTVW vowel point
EILNOORSTU resolution
EILNOORTUV revolution
EILNOOSTUV evolutions
EILNOPPRTW nipplewort
EILNOPPSSS sloppiness
EILNOPPSTU suppletion
EILNOPRSST portliness
EILNOPRSSX prolixness
EILNOPRSUU unperilous
EILNOPRXYY pyroxyline
EILNORRSTY introrsely
EILNORSSUY neurolysis
resinously
EILNOSTUUV velutinous
EILNPQTTUU quintuplet
EILNPRRTUY pruriently
EILNPRSSTY spinsterly
EILNPRSTUY unpriestly
EILNRSSSTU sultriness
EILNRSSTUY unsisterly
EILOOPPRTY pleiotropy
EILOOPPSTY oppositely
EILOPPRSUV propulsive
EILOPRRSTU protrusile
EILOPRRSUY superiorly
EILOPRSSTY pterylosis
EILOPRSTUY pyrolusite
EILOPRSTVY sportively
Very pistol
EILOPRSUVY perviously
previously
viperously
EILORSSSTU soul sister
EILRRSTUVW liverwurst
EIMMNNORSW non-swimmer
EIMMNORRSW miner's worm
EIMMOPSSTY symptomise
EIMMOPSTYZ symptomize
EIMNNOOPTT omnipotent
EIMNNOPRST prisonment
EIMNNORSUU innumerous
EIMNNOSSYY synonymise
EIMNNOSYYZ synonymize
EIMNNRSTTU instrument
EIMNOOPPSU impose upon
EIMNOOPRRT premonitor
EIMNOOPRSS spoonerism
EIMNOORSST in some sort
EIMNOOSTTT tenotomist
EIMNOOTTZZ mezzotinto
EIMNOPRRTU importuner
EIMNOPRSTU resumption
EIMNORSSST storminess
EIMNORSSSU sensoriums
EIMNORSTUY numerosity
EIMNPSSSTU stumpiness
EIMNSSSTTU smuttiness
EIMOOQSSTU mosquitoes
EIMOOTTTWW two-two time
EIMOPRRSTU romper suit
EIMOPRRSTY spirometry
EIMORSSTUX sex tourism
EIMORSSTUY mysterious
EIMQRRTTUU triquetrum
EIMSSTUUVV Mt Vesuvius
EINNNOOPRT pontonnier
EINNNOPTTU intent upon
EINNNORSTU in one's turn
EINNOOPPRS open prison
propension
EINNOOPRST protension
EINNOOPSTU out-pension
EINNOOQSTU no question
EINNOORTUX neurotoxin
EINNOOSSST snootiness
EINNOPRSUU superunion
EINNOPSSSU suspension
EINNOSSSTT snottiness
EINNOSSSTY syntenosis
EINNOSSSUU insensuous
EINNOSSTTU sustention
EINNPRTTUY turpentiny
EINOOOPRTZ zero option
EINOOPPRSS oppression
EINOOPPRTW power point
EINOOPRRST resorption
EINOOPRSTU proteinous
EINOOPSSSS possession
EINOOPSTTT Post-it note®
EINOOPTTTT totipotent
EINOORSSST rootsiness
EINOORSSTU serotinous
EINOORTTTT Tintoretto
EINOORTTTX tetrotoxin
EINOPPRSTY propensity
EINOPRRRST ripsnorter
EINOPRSSST sportiness
EINOPRSTTY protensity
EINOPSSSTT spottiness
EINOQRTTUU tourniquet
EINORRRTUU nourriture
EINORSTTWW Twin Towers
EINPRSSSST spinstress
EINRSSSTTU trustiness
EIOOOPRSTZ sporozoite
EIOOPPRRRT proprietor
EIOOPPRRST prepositor
EIOOPRRSST posteriors
EIOOPRRSSU repoussoir
EIOOPRRSTY repository
EIOOPRSSTT strepitoso
EIOOPRSSTU isopterous
EIOOPRSTXY expository
EIOORRSSTU roisterous
EIOORRTVWY ivory tower
EIOORSTTUZ zootsuiter
EIOPPRRSTY prosperity

EIOPPRSTUV supportive
EIOPRRSSUV supervisor
EIOPRRSTTU tripterous
EIOPRRSTUV protrusive
EIOPRRTTVY protervity
EIOPRSSTTU strepitous
EIOPRSTTTU prostitute
EIORRRSTUV retrovirus
EIORRSTTTU restitutor
EIPPRRSUVY privy purse✧
EIPRSSTTUW supertwist
EJNNSSSTUU unjustness
EJNOOSSSUY joyousness
EKLMRSTTUU musk turtle
EKLNOOORWY looyenwork
EKLNOORSTV lover's knot
EKLOORRTUW work to rule
work-to-rule
EKMMNOPPUY monkey pump
EKNORRSSTW sternworks
EKOOPRSSTT spot stroke
EKOPPRRSUW upperworks
EKORRTTTUY turkey trot
ELLLOSSSUY soullessly
ELLMMPSSUU mussel-plum
ELLMORRSTU muster roll
ELLNNOPTUY polytunnel
ELLNOOSWWY yellow snow
ELLNPRTUUY purulently
ELLOOORTWY yellow-root
ELLOOOSTTY Leo Tolstoy
ELLOOPSTWY yellow spot
ELLOORTWWY yellow-wort
ELLOPPSSTT spellstopt
ELLOPSSSTY spotlessly
ELLORSTUWY yellow rust
ELMMOOPPSU pompelmous
ELMNOORSUY enormously
ELMNOOSUVY venomously
ELMNORSUUY numerously
ELMNPPSTUY supplyment
ELMOOPRSUY polymerous
ELMOOPRTUY pleurotomy
ELMOOPRTXY protoxylem
ELMOOPSSUY polysemous
ELMOPPPPUY plume poppy
ELMOPPPRTU petrol pump
ELMORSTTYY stylometry
ELNOOOPRTU poultroone
ELNOORSTUU ultroneous
ELNOPPRRUY unproperly
ELNOSSSUUY sensuously
ELNRRTTTUU turn turtle
ELOOORRSTW woolsorter
ELOORRSSSW sorrowless
ELOPPRSTUY Polypterus
suppletory
ELOPPRSUVY oversupply
ELOPRSTTUU turtle soup
EMMNOOOSSU monosemous
EMMNRSSTUU menstruums
EMMNRSTUYY unsymmetry
EMMOOPRSTT post mortem
post-mortem
EMNNOOOPRT monopteron
EMNNOOORTU motoneuron
EMNNOOOSTW wet monsoon
EMNNOOPTUY put money on
EMNOOOPRST monopteros
EMNOOPPRTT prompt-note
EMNOOQSTUU musquetoon
EMNOPPRSST promptness
EMNORRSTUU surmounter
EMNORSSTUU menstruous
EMNOSTTTUU mutton suet
EMOOOPRSTT protostome
EMOOORRSTV servomotor
EMOORRSTVY vestry-room
EMOORSSTTY root system
ENNNORRTUV Trevor Nunn
ENNOOPPRRU proper noun
ENOOPPRSST postperson
ENOOPRRSSY responsory
ENOOPRSSSU porousness
ENOOPRSTTU portentous
ENOORSTTTU troutstone
ENOOSSSSTY synostoses
ENOOSSSTTU sostenutos
ENOPRSSSUY suspensory
ENOPRSTTUU put to nurse
EOOOPRSSUX exosporous
EOOOSSTTTV voetstoots
EOOPPRRSSU prosperous
EOOPRRSSTU pro-oestrus
EOOPRSSSSY possessory
EOORRSSTTU stertorous
EOORRSSTUY roysterous
EOPPRRSSSU suppressor
EOPPRRSSTU supporters
EOPPRRSTUU supporture
EOPPRRSTUY upper story

F

FFFFIITTYY fifty-fifty
FFFNNSTUUY funny stuff
FFGGILNORY flying frog
FFGHIIINRS griffinish
FFGHIILNSY fly-fishing
flying fish
FFGHIIOPPR hippogriff
FFGHIMNRUU humgruffin
FFGHORSTUU rough stuff
FFGIIIMNRS griffinism
FFGIILLLNU fulfilling
FFGIILNNSY sniffingly
FFGIINORTY fortifying
FFGINOPTTU off-putting
FFIIRRSTTU first-fruit
FFILLRTUUY fruitfully
FFILNRTUUU unfruitful
FFILOORRST first floor
first-floor
FFIOOPRRST first proof
FFIORSSTTU soft fruits
FFNNOOPSSU snuff spoon
FGGHHIILNY high-flying
FGGHIIINNT infighting
in-fighting
FGGHINOORT forthgoing
going forth
FGGIIILNNY lignifying
FGGIIINNSY signifying
FGGIILNNWY flying wing
FGGIILNORY glorifying
FGHHIINSTT night shift
FGHHIMNOOR from on high
FGHHIORRTT forthright
FGHHLOTTUU thoughtful
FGHIIILNTY lithifying
FGHIILNSTU insightful
FGHIILRSTT first light
FGHIINNSTU unshifting
FGHIINORRY horrifying
FGHIINRSTT first night
first thing
FGHIINSSTW swing shift
FGHIIOTTTU fight it out
FGHILLRTUY rightfully
FGHILNOSTY flying shot
FGHILNRTUU unrightful
FGHILOOPRT light-proof
FGHILOOSTT footlights
FGHILPRSTU sprightful
FGHINNOORT for nothing
FGHINNOTUX foxhunting
FGHIOOSTTU out of sight
FGHMOORSTU frog's-mouth
FGIIINNRTY nitrifying
FGIIINPSTY tipsifying
FGIIJNSTUY justifying
FGIIKLNRSY friskingly
FGIILLMNOY mollifying
FGIILLNNUY nullifying
FGIILLNRTY flirtingly
triflingly
FGIILLNSTY stiflingly
FGIILMNORU linguiform
FGIILNOSUU fuliginous
FGIILNPPTY fly-tipping
FGIILNRSTU sling fruit
FGIILNSTUY flying suit
FGIIMMMNUY mummifying
FGIIMNORTY mortifying
FGIIMNSTYY mystifying
FGIIMORRST strigiform
FGIINOTTTU fitting-out
outfitting
FGIINRSSUY Russifying
FGIKLNOOOR looking-for
FGIKNNORTU tuning fork
FGIKNRSSUY sky surfing
FGILLNOTUY floutingly
FGILNNORWY frowningly

FGILNOOTUW	outflowing
FGILNOPSTY	flyposting
FGIMNOOPRS	spongiform
FGLLNORUWY	wrongfully
FGLOORTUUY	futurology
FGMNSSTUUU	smut fungus
FGNRSSTUUU	rust fungus
FHHIIINSTW	finish with
FHHIOPRSTT	thrift shop
FHIILLRRST	shirt frill
FHIILPSSTT	split shift
FHILLMRTUY	mirthfully
FHILMOORRR	horror film
FHILOORSTT	frithstool
FHILOPRSUW	worshipful
FHINORRSTT	shirt front
FHLLLOSTUY	slothfully
FHLLOTUUYY	youthfully
FHLLRTTUUY	truthfully
FHLNRTTUUU	untruthful
FHNOOOPRRT	thornproof
FHOOOPPSTU	hoppus foot
FIIJNORSTT	first joint
FIILLMOORT	floor limit
FIILMMNOOR	moniliform
FIILMMORTY	mytiliform
FIILMNOPPY	minifloppy
FIILMOPRSY	ypsiliform
FIILNOSTUX	fluxionist
FIIMNORTUY	uniformity
FIIMOORSST	fortissimo
FIIMORSTTU	fortuitism
FIINORTTUU	futurition
FIIORSTTTU	fortuitist
FIJNOOOTTU	out of joint
FIKLLLLSUY	skillfully
FIKLLOORST	folklorist
FIKNORSTWY	forty winks
FILLOOPTTY	toploftily
FILLOOSTUW	follow suit
FILNOORSUU	uniflorous
FILOOOPRST	portfolios
FIMNOSTTTU	mutton-fist
FINOOOPSTT	soft option
FINOOPRSTT	footprints
FINOOPRTTU	out of print
FIOORSTTUU	fortuitous
FJJMOOPRUY	jump for joy
FLLMNORUUY	mournfully
FLLMORSTUY	stormfully
FLLOPRSTUY	sportfully
FLLRSTTUUY	trustfully
FLNRSTTUUU	untrustful
FMOOOPRRST	stormproof
FNNOORSTTU	not for nuts
FOOORSSTTU	out of sorts

G

GGGHINOOTU	tough going
GGGIILLNNY	nigglingly
GGGIJLLNUY	jugglingly
GGGILNRSTU	struggling
GGHHHIILST	highlights
GGHHIIILNV	high living
GGHHIILNTT	night-light
GGHHIILSWY	Whiggishly
GGHHIILTTT	light-tight
GGHHIINNTT	night-night
GGHHIINSTT	night-sight
GGHHINRSTU	high-strung
GGHIILNPTU	lighting-up
GGHIILPRSY	priggishly
GGHIIPRRYY	higry-pigry
GGHILLSSUY	sluggishly
GGHILNOSTU	oughtlings
GGHINOOPPS	go shopping
GGHINORRTW	growth ring
GGIIIILLNO	gingili oil
GGIIIINSTV	gingivitis
GGIIINNRTU	intriguing
GGIILLMNNY	minglingly
GGIILLNNNO	long-lining
GGIILNNNRY	grinningly
GGIILNNSTY	stingingly
GGIILNNSWY	swingingly
GGIILNPPRY	grippingly
GGIKMNNOSU	smoking gun
GGILLLNOOR	logrolling
GGILLNNOUY	loungingly
GGILLNORWY	growlingly
GGILNNRTUY	gruntingly
GGILNOOOSY	gnosiology
GGIMORSSSU	Gus Grissom
GGINNNNRUU	gunrunning
GGLLNNOOOW	Wollongong
GGLLOOOSSY	glossology
GGLLOOOTTY	glottology
GGLNOOOPSY	spongology
GGMORRRUUW	gru-gru worm
GHHIIJNORU	junior high
GHHIILSTTY	tightishly
GHHIINRSTT	nightshirt
GHHIIPRSTW	shipwright
GHHILLOPTY	lithoglyph
GHHILLOSUY	ghoulishly
GHHIMOSTTU	misthought
GHHINOOSTU	hothousing
GHHINOPRTT	triphthong
GHHINORTUW	win through
GHHIOPPPRY	hippogryph
GHHLOOPPTY	photoglyph
GHHLOORTUY	thoroughly
GHHNOORTUU	unthorough
GHHNORRTUU	run through
	run-through
GHHNORSSTU	song thrush
GHHOORTTUU	throughout
GHHOPRTTUU	put through
	put-through
	throughput
GHIIKLNNTY	thinkingly
GHIIKNNNTU	unthinking
GHIIKNSSTT	skintights
GHIILLMRTW	millwright
GHIILLNOTW	Linlithgow
GHIILLNRWY	whirlingly
GHIILLOPTT	pilot light
GHIILNOPSS	polishings
GHIILNRTVY	thrivingly
GHIILNRTWY	writhingly
GHIILNWYZZ	whizzingly
GHIILOOSTY	histiology
GHIILPRSTT	strip light
GHIIMNNOST	nothingism
GHIIMNPRTU	triumphing
GHIINNNTTU	huntingtin
GHIINNORSU	nourishing
GHIKLNNTUY	unknightly
GHIKNOORTW	hot-working
GHIKNOPRTU	groupthink
GHILMNPTUY	thumpingly
GHILMOOORU	horologium✧
GHILNOOPRU	plough-iron
GHILNOOPST	phlogiston
GHILNOOPTU	plough into
GHILNOOSTT	night-stool
GHILNOOSTY	soothingly
GHILNORTTT	throttling
GHILNOSTTU	gluttonish
GHILNOSTUY	shoutingly
GHILNRRUYY	hurryingly
GHILOOORST	horologist
GHILOOPSYY	physiology
GHILOORSTT	grith-stool
GHIMMNOPTU	humming-top
GHINNOPTTU	pot-hunting
GHINNRRUUY	unhurrying
GHIOOTTTUU	tough it out
GHLLOOPTYY	typhlology
GHLMOOOOSU	homologous
GHLMOOOPRY	morphology
GHLNOOPSUW	snowplough
GHLOOOPRTY	trophology
GHMNOOPSYY	gymnosophy
GHMOOOSUYZ	homozygous
GHMOOPRYYZ	zygomorphy
GHNOOPSUYY	hypogynous
GHOORSSTTY	ghost story
GHOORTTUUW	outwrought
GIIIILNRSV	virilising
GIIIILNRVZ	virilizing
GIIIKNNRTW	writing-ink
GIIILLLNVW	living will
GIIILLNNST	instilling
GIIILNNPRT	tirling-pin
GIIILNNTVY	invitingly
GIIILNORSV	virgin soil
GIIIMNNNOR	iron-mining
GIIIMNNPRT	imprinting
GIIIMNRSTY	myringitis
GIIINNNTUV	uninviting
GIIINRSSTY	syringitis
GIIJKKNORS	skikjöring

Words marked ✧ can also be spelled with one or more capital letters

GIIJKMNPSU ski jumping
GIIKLLLNOO ill-looking
GIIKLLNNTY tinklingly
GIIKLLNRST kill string
GIIKLMMNSY skimmingly
GIIKLMNPSY skimpingly
GIIKLMNRSY smirkingly
GIIKLNNPRS sprinkling
GIIKLNNRST strinkling
GIIKLNNSTY stinkingly
GIIKLNPPSY skippingly
GIIKLNRSTY strikingly
GIIKMNNOOS monoskiing
GIIKNNORTV virgin knot
GIIKNORSTU ski touring
GIIKNRSTWY skywriting
GIILLLNOPU louping-ill
GIILLLNPUV pulvilling
GIILLNNOPR rolling pin
GIILLNOPRY pillorying
GIILLNOPST pistolling
GIILLNPPRY ripplingly
GIILLNSYZZ sizzlingly
GIILMMNRTY trimmingly
GIILMMNSWY swimmingly
GIILMNNOTW Wilmington
GIILMNOORV living room
GIILMNOPSY imposingly
GIILMOOSST misologist
GIILMOOSSY missiology
GIILNNNOTY intoningly
GIILNNOSTV Livingston
GIILNNPPSU unslipping
GIILNNRTUY untiringly
GIILNNSTTY stintingly
GIILNOOPST topsoiling
GIILNOORSU inglorious
GIILNOOSST Sinologist
GIILNOOSTV vinologist
GIILNPPRTY trippingly
GIILNPRSST slip-string
GIILNRRSTY stirringly
GIILNRSTUY linguistry
GIILNRSTVY strivingly
GIILNTTTWY twittingly
GIILOORSTV virologist
GIILOPPRST pistol grip
GIIMNNNORU in mourning
GIIMNNOORS Monsignori
GIIMNNOPSU unimposing
GIIMNOORRT tiring-room
GIIMNORRRW wing mirror
GIIMNOSSTY misogynist
GIINNNSTTU unstinting
GIINNOPRST piston ring
GIINNSTTUW untwisting
GIINOTTTUW outwitting
GIINPPRSST strippings
GIINPPTTTU tittupping
GIINPRRSSU surprising
GIJKMNPSUY skyjumping
GIJNNOORSU sojourning
GIJNOTTTUU outjutting
GIKKLLNSUY skulkingly
GIKMNNNOOS non-smoking
GIKNNOORTW Workington
GIKNNORSTT strong-knit
GILLNNOUVY unlovingly
GILLNOOPRT trolloping
GILLNOPRRS spring roll
GILLNOPRWY prowlingly
GILLNOPTTY plottingly
GILLNPUYZZ puzzlingly
GILLNRSTUY rustlingly
GILLOORSUY gloriously
GILMMNOOUY immunology
GILMNNORUY mourningly
GILMNNUUZZ unmuzzling
GILMNOOOST monologist
nomologist
GILMNOOSVW slow-moving
GILMOOOPST pomologist
GILMOOSTYZ zymologist
GILNNNOPSU nonplusing
GILNNNSTUY stunningly
GILNNOOSWY swooningly
GILNNORSTY snortingly
GILNOOOPSY oligopsony
GILNOOOSST nosologist
GILNOOOSTT ontologist
GILNOOPSTY stoopingly
GILNOPRSTY sportingly
GILNORRWYY worryingly
GILNPRSUUY pursuingly
usurpingly
GILNRSTTUY trustingly
GILOOOPSTT optologist
topologist
GILOOOPSTU goloptious
GILOOORSTY storiology
GILOOPRSTT proglottis
GILOOPSTTY typologist
GILOOPSTUU goluptious
GILOORRSUY rigorously
GILOORSUVY vigorously
GIMMMNOOTT tom-tomming
GIMMPPTUYY gippy tummy
GIMNNNRRUU rum-running
GIMNNOORSS Monsignors
GIMNOOQRTU Mount Qogir
GIMNOOSSUY misogynous
GINNOOPSTU unstooping
GINNOPPRSU spring upon
GINNOPRSTU unsporting
GINNRSSTUU untrussing
GINOOPPTTU topping-out
GINOOPRRSU ring-porous
GINOOPRRTU nitro-group
GINOOPRTUU outpouring
GINOPPRSTU supporting
GINOPRRSTW springwort
GINORSSTTU strong suit
GINPPTTTUU put-putting
GINTTTTTUU tut-tutting
GKMMNOOOPS Kompong Som
GKMORSSSUY Mussorgsky
GKOOORRTTW grotto-work
GLNOOPSUYY polygynous
GLNOORSUWY wrongously
GLNOOSTTUU gluttonous
GMMPPTUYYY gyppy tummy
GMNNOOOSUY monogynous
GMNOOOOPTY pogonotomy
GMNOOORRST strongroom

H

HHHMNNOSUY Houyhnhnms
HHIILOPPRT Philip Roth
HHIJKNOSWY whisky john
HHIKNNOOOS Nohon Shoki
HHILOOPPSY philosophy
HHILOOPPTY photophily
HHIMNOPSTX sphinx moth
HHIMOOOPPR ophiomorph
HHIMOOPRRZ rhizomorph
HHINOOPPSS shop-in-shop
HHIOPPSSYY hypophysis
HHIORSSTTW short whist
HHJNNOOSTU John Huston
HHLLOPPSYY hypsophyll
HHLMOPRTYY polyrhythm
HHNOOOPPTY photophony
HHOOOOPSTT photo shoot
HHOOPPRSSU phosphorus✧
HHOPPSSTUU shut up shop
HIIKLSSTTY skittishly
HIILLNORTT trillionth
HIILMMPSSY symphilism
HIILMOOPSZ zoophilism
HIILNOPRTT lithoprint
HIILOOPSTZ zoophilist
HIILOPPPSU Pliohippus
HIILOPPSTW pistol-whip
HIILOPRSTY Holy Spirit
HIILORTTTY lithotrity
HIILOSSSTY histolysis
HIIMMNOPRS morphinism
HIIMOPRSSW misworship
HIIMSSTTYY hitty-missy
HIINOORSST ornithosis
HIINOPPRSS prison ship
HIINORRSUV rhinovirus
HIIOOOPRST oophoritis
HIIOOTTTYY hoity-toity
HIJKNNORSU John Ruskin
HIJLMNNOOT John Milton
HIJMNNOOSS Johnsonism
HIJNOOPRSU junior soph
HIKLNORSTW thrown silk
HIKORSSUWY whisky sour
HILLNOTTUW Will Hutton
HILLOOPRST trollopish
HILLSSTTUY sluttishly

HILMNOOSTU lion's mouth
HILMNOPSUU sulphonium
HILMNORTTY trimonthly
HILMOPSSUY symphilous
HILNORTUWY unworthily
HILOOOPSUZ zoophilous
HILOOPRRTY lorry-hop it
HILOOPRSTY polyhistor
HILOOPSSTY photolysis
HILOPPSTUY Hippolytus
HIMMMOSTTY Tommy Smith
HIMMNOOTYY homonymity
HIMNNOOPSY symphonion
HIMNOOOOPR omophorion
HIMNOPRRSY Pyrrhonism
HIMNOPRTTU turnip moth
HIMNOPSSTY symphonist
HIMOOPRRST orthoprism
HINOOPTTXY phytotoxin
HINOPRRSTY Pyrrhonist
HINOPRSSUW sun worship
HINORSTTTU thrust into
HIOOOSTTTU shoot it out
HIOOPPRRSY porphyrios
HIOOPRSTTT orthoptist
HIOOPRTTXY thixotropy
HIORSSTTUU struthious
HJMNNOOORT John Morton
HKNOOOUWWY you-know-who
HLLOOPPRSY sporophyll
HLMOOOSTUY hylotomous
HLMOORSUUY humorously
HLMOPSSUYY symphylous
HLOPRSSUUU sulphurous
HMMNOOOSUY homonymous
HMMOOORTTU motormouth
HMNOOOOSTU homotonous
HMNOOORSTY Roy Thomson
HMOOPRSTTU Portsmouth
HMOOPSSTUU posthumous
HNNORSSTUY synthronus
HOOOOSSTTT hoots-toots
HOOOPPRRTT prototroph
HOOOPPRTTY phototropy
HOOOPRRTTY orthotropy
HOOOPRSTTY photo story
HOOPPRRSUY porphyrous
pyrophorus✧
HOORRSSTTY short story
HOOSSTTTUU houts-touts

I

IIIKLLNPSS spillikins
IIIKLLNPSW pilliwinks
IIILLMMMSU simillimum
IIILLMMNSU illuminism
IIILLMNSTU illuminist
IIILLNOPST pillionist
IIILMMOTTY immotility
IIILMNOPTT limit point
IIILNOSSTT tonsilitis
IIIMMNNOTU imminution
IIIMNOOPST imposition
IIIMNOPRSS misprision
IIIMOPSSTV positivism
IIINNOOPST opinionist
IIINOQRSTU inquisitor
IIINOQSTUU iniquitous
IIIOPSSTTV positivist
IIIOPSTTVY positivity
IIJMNORSSU junior miss
IIJNOPRSTT strip joint
IIKLLLMSTU multiskill
IIKLMNNOOT link-motion
IIKLOOPSTT Ostpolitik
IILLLLLPYY lilly-pilly
IILLLLNWYY willy-nilly
IILLLLWWYY willy-willy
IILLLOPPSW pillowslip
IILLLORSUY illusorily
IILLMOOSTU mollitious
IILLNOOPPS poison pill
IILLNOOPST postillion
IILMMNOOSU moliminous
IILMNOORSU Orimulsion®
IILMNOPSTY postliminy
IILMNOSTUY luminosity
IILMOSTUUV multivious
IILNNOOTUV involution
IILNNOPRSU proinsulin
IILNNOTTUY non-utility
IILNOOQRRU iron-liquor
IILOOPRSUV poliovirus
IILOOPRSUX prolixious
IILOPRSSTW low spirits
IIMMOORTUV vomitorium
IIMNNOOSSU insomnious
IIMNNOQRTU quint minor
IIMOOPRSST isotropism
IINOOOPPST opposition✧
IINOOPRSSV provisions
IINOOPRSTT portionist
IINORRSSSU Sinus Roris
IINORSSSTU sinistrous
IINORSTTTU institutor
IINORSTTUU nutritious
IIOOOPRSTV ovipositor
IIOOPPRSTU propitious
IIOPRSSSUU suspirious
IIOPRSSTUU spirituous
IIOPRSSTUY spuriosity
IIORSTTUVY virtuosity
IIOSSSTTTU tsotsi suit
IJLNOOOSTT joint-stool
IKKNOPRSTU prusik knot✧
IKLLOOPPSY look slippy
IKMORSSTTY Trotskyism
IKNOPRRSTW printworks
IKORSSTTTY Trotskyist
ILLMMORRUU rumour mill
ILLMNOSUUY luminously
ILLMOQTUUY multiloquy
ILLOPPPSSY slipsloppy
ILMMNOOOPS monopolism
ILMNOOOPST monopolist
ILMNOOOPSY polyominos
ILMNOOOSTW slow motion
slow-motion
ILMNOOQSUY somniloquy
ILMNOOSUUV voluminous
ILMNOSTUUY mutinously
ILMOORSTUY timorously
ILMORSTTUY multistory
ILNOOPPRSU propulsion
ILNOPRSTUU pultrusion
ILOOPPRSST spoilsport
ILOORSTTUY tortiously
ILOORSUUXY uxoriously
ILOPRSSUUY spuriously
ILORSSUUUY usuriously
ILORSTUUVY virtuously
ILPRSSTTTU split trust
IMMOOPRSTU prostomium
IMNNOSSTYY synonymist
IMNNOSTYYY synonymity
IMNOOOPSTT stop-motion
IMNOOORSUV omnivorous
IMOOORSTUV visuomotor
IMOOPRRSSY promissory
IMTUUYZZZZ tuzzi-muzzy
INOOOPPRRT proportion
INOOPRRSTU protrusion
INOOSSSSTY synostosis
INOPPPRRSU Rippon spur
INOQRSTUWY quinsy-wort
INORSTUUUV unvirtuous
IOOOPRSSSU isosporous
IOOOPRSSTU isotropous
IOOORSSSUV ossivorous
IOORSTTTUY tortuosity

L

LLLOOOORSS lollo rosso
LLOOPPSUUY populously
LLORSSTUUY lustrously
LMNOOOSUXY monoxylous
LMNOOPSUUY upon my soul!
LMOOORRRTY motor lorry
LMOOOSTUXY xylotomous
LMOSTTUUUU tumultuous
LNOOORSSUY sonorously
LNOOPPSUUU unpopulous
LOOPPRRSUY propulsory
LOOPSTUUUV voluptuous
LOORSTTUUY tortuously
LORRSTUUYY yours truly

M

MMOOPRRSUU rumpus room
MMPPPRUUYY rumpy-pumpy
MNNOOOOSTU monotonous
MNNOOSSUYY synonymous
MNOOOPRRTY promontory

Words marked ✧ can also be spelled with one or more capital letters

MNOORSSTUU monstruous
MTUUYYZZZZ tuzzy-muzzy

N

NOOOPRSTTU trout spoon
NOOORRTTWY not to worry

O

OOOOPRSSUZ zoosporous
OOPPPSSWYY popsy-wopsy
OPRSTTUVYY topsy-turvy

11 letters

A

AAAAABBCDRR abracadabra
AAAAABHHMRT Mahabharata
AAAAACLMNNP Panama Canal
AAAAADGJLRU Guadalajara
AAAAAGLMMRS garam masala
AAAAAHMNNST hasta mañana
AAAAANRRTTT taratantara
AAAABBBDNRS Bandar Abbas
AAAABBCELNR Calabar-bean
AAAABBCHILN Bahia Blanca
AAAABBDRRRW Barbara Ward
AAAABBINRST sabbatarian✧
AAAABCCHILN bacchanalia
AAAABCHINNS Sanni Abacha
AAAABCHINPT Captain Ahab
AAAABCIJKMR Jamaica bark
AAAABCNRUWX carnauba wax
AAAABDEKKLS baked Alaska
AAAABDGHMNR Grand Bahama
AAAABDIIRSU Saudi Arabia
AAAABGINRWY bargain away
AAAABGNNPRT Nanga Parbat
AAAABHHMMRS sham Abraham
AAAABHJMMRS Brahma Samaj
AAAABHKLLRU Allahu akbar
AAAABHLRSTT Shatt al-Arab
AAAABIJLMOR labia majora
AAAACCCELMN Malacca-cane
AAAACCEEHNT Acanthaceae
AAAACCEFILS false acacia
AAAACDEENNP Pandanaceae
AAAACDELRSS Caesar salad
AAAACDGLLNU Guadalcanal
AAAACDGMOSV Vasco da Gama
AAAACEELNPT Platanaceae
AAAACEEMNRT Marantaceae
AAAACEGLMNP à la campagne
AAAACEGMMMR gamma camera
AAAACEHKLLP Lake Chapala
AAAACEJNSTV Ajanta caves
AAAACFLMMOS fama clamosa
AAAACGHMNRT Magna Charta
AAAACGILPSS passacaglia
AAAACGINNRR Gran Canaria
AAAACILLMRS Maria Callas
AAAACKNPRRV caravan park
AAAACNRRSVY caravansary
AAAADEHRTVV Atharvaveda
AAAADELMRSS Dar es Salaam
AAAAEEHNNPT Panathenaea
AAAAEGPRTUY Paraguay tea
AAAAELMNNUZ Manuel Azaña
AAAAFGMNORT fata Morgana
AAAAFGNOSTT Antofagasta
AAAAFINRRST Ras Tafarian
rastafarian✧
AAAAFNNOQTU aqua fontana
AAAAGHIPPRR paragraphia
AAAAGJNNNRY Narayanganj
AAAAHHMRRST Maharashtra
AAAAHIPPRRX paraphraxia
AAAAILRSSTU Australasia
AAAAIMORRST Ars Amatoria
AAAALLLOOPZ lalapalooza
AAAALLMNRSY Allan Ramsay
AAAALNNOPVV Anna Pavlova
AAAAMRTZZZZ razzamatazz
AAABBCCEEMO Bombacaceae
AAABBCEELMN balance beam
AAABBCEGLMP cabbage palm
palm-cabbage
AAABBCEKLNN bank balance
AAABBCELLPS baseball cap
AAABBCHJKMR Jack Brabham
AAABBDELORZ blaze abroad
AAABBDILNST blind as a bat
AAABBDLMRST bastard balm
AAABBEEHRSZ Zaheer Abbas
AAABBEINRSS Bessarabian
AAABBGHNOSU baba ganoush
AAABBILMORT amobarbital
AAABBLNOPSY San Pablo Bay
AAABCCDLRRY Barclaycard
AAABCCEEILL Bacillaceae
AAABCCFIKLR Black Africa
AAABCCLLOWY Cab Calloway
AAABCDDIRRY bradycardia
AAABCDEEINR abecedarian
AAABCDEIORS scarabaeoid
AAABCDELNRS candelabras
AAABCDEMNOR bon camarade
AAABCDEMNRU maceranduba
AAABCDENORR radar beacon
AAABCDFIORS fascia-board
AAABCDGINRY Cardigan Bay
AAABCDKLNNT Black and Tan
black-and-tan
AAABCDLLLNW ball-and-claw
claw-and-ball
AAABCDLOOST bald as a coot
AAABCDNORSV canvas board
AAABCEEIMRT bacteraemia

AAABCEGILLR algebraical
AAABCEGKPSS back passage
AAABCEHINRT abranchiate
AAABCEHPRSU chapeau-bras
AAABCEIILLM bacillaemia
AAABCEIMPRT parabematic
AAABCEIRSST scarabaeist
AAABCEKLLNR canella bark
AAABCELLLOT allocatable
AAABCELRTTT attractable
AAABCHILMNR Brahmanical
AAABCHLLMPS paschal lamb
AAABCILLNTY abactinally
AAABCILLOPR parabolical
AAABCILNOTT ablactation
AAABCLLOPSS Pablo Casals
AAABCRRSTTT abstract art
AAABDEELRTW Walter Baade
AAABDEELRWY Delaware Bay
AAABDEGGLNU bad language
AAABDEGGNOV vagabondage
AAABDEGHMRR graham bread
AAABDEGIMNR brain damage
AAABDEILNPT inadaptable
AAABDEKRSTT bastard teak
AAABDELLOPR ballad opera
AAABDELNPTU unadaptable
AAABDELNRSS Abd al-Nasser
AAABDELORRS Labrador Sea
AAABDELORRT Labrador tea
AAABDENORRS Aaron's beard
AAABDEQRRTU a bad quarter
AAABDGNNOOU Oda Nobunaga
AAABEEGLLSV salvageable
AAABEEGLNRR arrangeable
AAABEEHLNPT analphabete
AAABEFLOTTU A Tale of a Tub
AAABEGILNPR plea bargain
plea-bargain
AAABEGKMNNR bank manager
AAABEGNOPRZ garbanzo pea
AAABEGOPSST passage-boat
AAABEHIMNPS amphisbaena✧
AAABEIIJNRZ Azerbaijani
AAABEIILNRS Rabelaisian
AAABEIILPTT battalia pie
AAABEILLMRT ambilateral
AAABEILLNUV unavailable
AAABEILLRTZ blaze a trail
AAABEILNRST alabastrine
AAABEILPPRS appraisable
AAABEKLLNOT Lake Balaton
AAABELLNPTU unpalatable
AAABELNNOTT annotatable
AAABELNRRTW warrantable
AAABELOORRT ora et labora
AAABEMRSTTT Stabat Mater
AAABENNOPRT Bonapartean
AAABEPPRRTY baryta paper
AAABFINNORT Fontarabian
AAABGHIOOPR agoraphobia
AAABGORSSZZ Zsa Zsa Gabor
AAABHIKRSTV svarabhakti
AAABHIOPRST astraphobia
AAABIILMNOR labia minora
AAABIINORST arabisation
AAABIINORTZ arabization
AAABILLNUVY unavailably
AAABILMNOTU ablutomania
AAABILNNPST banana split
AAABIMPPRST parabaptism
AAABINPSSTT Anabaptists
AAABLLLORTY ballat royal
AAABLLNPTUY unpalatably
AAABLNOPRSU parabolanus
AAABLNRRTWY warrantably
AAABLOSSTTU assault boat
AAABLPRRSTU tabular spar
AAACCCDEHHH cha-cha-chaed
AAACCCEILTT acatalectic
AAACCCEINPT capacitance
AAACCCILLTT catallactic
AAACCCILMST cataclasmic
AAACCCILSTT cataclastic
AAACCCISTTU catacaustic
AAACCDEEIPS Dipsacaceae
AAACCDEHRST saccharated
AAACCDEIIMN academician
AAACCDEILMS academicals
AAACCDHIRTY tachycardia
AAACCEEEHTY Cyatheaceae
AAACCEEELLN Canellaceae
AAACCEEHSTT attaché-case
AAACCEEKNPR pancake race
AAACCEEMRST carcase meat
AAACCEENOPY Apocynaceae
AAACCEENORS acne rosacea
AAACCEFLOST catafalcoes
AAACCEGLNST cast a glance
AAACCEHINPU ipecacuanha
AAACCEHNOPR achaenocarp
AAACCEILLOR calceolaria
AAACCEILNRS Saracenical
AAACCEILPRT Palaearctic
AAACCEILPTT acataleptic
AAACCELMNOS calamancoes
AAACCEMRSST carcass meat
AAACCEORTTV caveat actor
AAACCGHLLMR Marc Chagall
AAACCGILNPT pan-galactic
AAACCGLLMNO clog-almanac
AAACCGMNOTU Mt Aconcagua
AAACCHILLRY archaically
AAACCHILNRT charlatanic
AAACCHILRTT cathartical
AAACCHILRTU autarchical
AAACCIIKLSS Alick Isaacs
AAACCIKNPTT panic attack
AAACCILLNRU canalicular
AAACCILLPRT parallactic
AAACCILLSTT stalactical
AAACCILLTTY catalytical

AAACCILMNOT	acclamation
AAACCILRRTU	caricatural
AAACCILSTUV	accusatival
AAACCIMNORT	carcinomata
AAACCLMOPRT	caprolactam
AAACCLMORTY	acclamatory
AAACDDMNPTU	ad captandum
AAACDDNRSTT	CAT standard
AAACDEEEILP	Pedaliaceae
AAACDEEELTT	lead acetate
AAACDEEGKLP	package deal
AAACDEEIKMR	Madeira cake
AAACDEEILOX	Oxalidaceae
AAACDEEIMRR	camaraderie
AAACDEEKLNS	cakes and ale
AAACDEELLOV	Ada Lovelace
AAACDEELLST	alla Tedesca
AAACDEENPRW	War and Peace
AAACDEGLPRU	palace guard
AAACDEGNOOS	Canada goose
AAACDEHINRT	acidanthera
AAACDEHNRTU	Hardacanute
AAACDEIIRST	Adriatic Sea
AAACDEILMPR	paramedical
	pre-adamical
AAACDEILNRT	cardinalate
AAACDEINRTY	caryatidean
AAACDEINSTT	at a distance
AAACDEOOPRV	avocado pear
AAACDEPRTTU	data capture
AAACDGILNRT	crag-and-tail
AAACDGINSTT	datacasting
AAACDGMNNRY	Grand Cayman
AAACDHILNOR	arachnoidal
AAACDHILNRT	cantharidal
AAACDHNPRSY	pachysandra
AAACDIILRSX	radical axis
AAACDIIMNRS	Arcadianism
AAACDILMPRU	Paul A M Dirac
AAACDILOPRX	paradoxical
AAACDILORRR	railroad car
AAACDILQRTU	quadratical
AAACDNRRRTW	warrant card
AAACEEEGINR	Geraniaceae
AAACEEFIMRU	Fumariaceae
AAACEEFLMNS	malfeasance
AAACEEGILNO	Loganiaceae
AAACEEGNNRR	carrageenan
AAACEEILNOV	Valoniaceae
AAACEEILPRS	special area
AAACEELLNST	a clean slate
AAACEENRTTV	caravanette
AAACEFGILLN	facial angle
AAACEFIKNRT	African teak
AAACEFLRTTU	artefactual
AAACEGHILLP	cephalalgia
AAACEGHILNW	caa'ing whale
AAACEGILMNO	egomaniacal
AAACEGIRRWY	carriageway
AAACEGLLLRT	call-at-large
AAACEHILLPR	parheliacal
AAACEHILPTT	apathetical
AAACEHIMRRY	Mariah Carey
AAACEHINNPT	Panathenaic
AAACEHINRRT	trachearian
AAACEHKRTTT	heart attack
AAACEHLLVVV	Vaclav Havel
AAACEHLMNNP	Panchen Lama
AAACEIKLMST	stake a claim
AAACEILLMNR	all-American
AAACEILLMNY	anaemically
AAACEILLNPT	Placentalia
AAACEILMMNT	analemmatic
AAACEILNPRS	Paracelsian
AAACEILNPSU	Aesculapian
AAACEILORSU	araliaceous
AAACEIMNNPR	Pan-American
AAACEINORSZ	azione sacra
AAACEINPRRT	carpentaria
AAACEINRSTV	caravan site
AAACEIPPRRT	paraparetic
AAACEJKLMNR	Jean Lamarck
AAACELLMTUU	macula lutea
AAACELMNPTU	campanulate
AAACELMNRST	sacramental
AAACELMOPRT	paracetamol
AAACEMNNNNO	Anna Comnena
AAACERRSTTU	tartar sauce
AAACFGILNPT	flag-captain
AAACFIIORST	Afro-Asiatic
AAACFILLNTY	fanatically
AAACFILNSTT	fantastical
AAACFIMNNOR	francomania✧
AAACFIMNRRT	aircraftman
AAACFJLMNRY	clanjamfray
AAACGGILOPR	paragogical
AAACGHIPPRR	paragraphic
AAACGHLMOYZ	chalazogamy
AAACGHLOPRS	sarcophagal
AAACGHNOOTT	Chattanooga
AAACGIINNRU	Aurignacian
AAACGILLNTY	agnatically
AAACGILMMRT	grammatical
AAACGILMNNO	anglomaniac✧
AAACGILMPRT	pragmatical
AAACGILNNNP	Pan-Anglican
AAACGIMPRST	sparagmatic
AAACGINNNRV	caravanning
AAACGNRRSSY	canary-grass
AAACHHIPSTY	tachyphasia
AAACHIILPPR	paraphiliac
AAACHIILPRS	pharisaical
AAACHIKPPRT	apparatchik
AAACHILMRRT	matriarchal
AAACHILMSTT	asthmatical
AAACHILNOPR	anaphorical
AAACHILNOTU	anacoluthia
AAACHILPRRT	patriarchal
AAACHILRSWY	cash-railway
AAACHIMNNOT	anthomaniac
AAACHKMMNPR	Mark Chapman
AAACHLNRRTY	charlatanry

AAACHNQTUUU	Chautauquan
AAACIILMOTX	axiomatical
AAACIILNOTT	Taliacotian
AAACIILPRST	parasitical
AAACIIMNPST	Isaac Pitman
AAACIIMOSSV	Isaac Asimov
AAACIJLMMPU	Jamaica plum
AAACIKLMNNR	Alan Rickman
AAACIKLRRWY	rack railway
AAACILLMNRU	animalcular
AAACILLMPST	plasmatical
AAACILLNNPS	spinal canal
AAACILLNORV	Convallaria
AAACILLNOTT	lactational
AAACILLNSTY	satanically
AAACILLRTUY	actuarially
AAACILLSTTT	stalactital
AAACILMMNOS	sal ammoniac
AAACILMORSS	macassar oil
AAACILMOTTU	automatical
AAACILMPSST	spasmatical
AAACILNNORY	alcyonarian
AAACILNNRST	Lancastrian
AAACILNOSTU	causational
AAACILOPSTT	apostatical
AAACIMNNORY	acronymania
AAACINPRSTT	pancratiast
AAACINPSTUU	sapucaia-nut
AAACINQSTUU	aquanautics
AAACIRRTWYY	carry it away
AAADDDDEOOS	dead as a dodo
AAADDDEKPRT	dark-adapted
AAADDEGINST	dead against
AAADDEHLMOP	Adolphe Adam
AAADDEHMRSY	hamadryades
AAADDEHORTW	draw to a head
AAADDEIMNSV	David Seaman
AAADDEIMRRR	Madara Rider
AAADDEINORR	Andrea Doria
AAADDELNOST	adelantados
AAADDFHNRST	hard and fast
	hard-and-fast
AAADDHILNNS	Handa Island
AAADDIMNUVZ	ad avizandum
AAADDLLLNNO	Allan Donald
AAADEEFHHVW	have had a few
AAADEEGKNRT	take a gander
AAADEENRRTW	tear and wear
	wear and tear
AAADEENSSTT	stand at ease
AAADEFFNNOR	fanfaronade
AAADEFIOSST	assafoetida
AAADEFOPSST	deaf as a post
AAADEGHHMNS	Meghnad Saha
AAADEGILMNN	Magdalenian
AAADEGIMRUV	marivaudage
AAADEGINRSS	André Agassi
AAADEGLNRTV	landgravate
AAADEGMNORR	road manager
AAADEGNOTTV	to advantage
AAADEHHHTTV	have had that
AAADEHHMSTT	ashamed that
AAADEHIMPST	Phasmatidae
AAADEHINRTT	radiant heat
AAADEHINSTT	that's an idea
AAADEHLNOOV	have a load on
AAADEHLNPRS	Alan Shepard
AAADEHMNOWY	home-and-away
AAADEHMNRRW	hardwareman
AAADEHMOPST	Phasmatodea
AAADEHNRSWW	wash-and-wear
AAADEIINPRT	radiata pine
AAADEIKNNVV	Vivekananda
AAADEILLMNN	Daniel Malan
AAADEILMPTV	maladaptive
AAADEILMRRR	rear admiral
AAADEILNNRX	Alexandrian
AAADEILPRSS	Sal Paradise
AAADEILRRSV	adversarial
AAADEILRSUV	Laura Davies
AAADEIMNNNS	Sandemanian
AAADEIMNNRT	mandarinate
AAADEIMNNRX	Anaximander
AAADEISSTUY	Tayassuidae
AAADEKKNOTZ	Takada Kenzo
AAADEKLOPPY	Oak-apple Day
AAADELLMPRT	Mar del Plata
AAADENNNRST	transandean
AAADENNPRST	transpadane
AAADFFHHLLN	half-and-half
AAADFLNRRTU	auld-farrant
AAADGGINORT	aggradation
AAADGHHITWY	data highway
AAADGHILMPR	diaphragmal
AAADGIILMNR	madrigalian
AAADGIINTWY	Waitangi Day
AAADGILNORT	gradational
AAADGILORXY	radio galaxy
AAADGINNNOW	now and again
AAADGMMRRWY	Grammy Award
AAADHHLPRYZ	haphazardly
AAADHIIRSST	stadia hairs
AAADHILMMMU	Muhammad Ali
AAADHILNRSS	hard as nails
AAADHIMMMUZ	Muhammad Zia
AAADHISSSTY	Shasta daisy
AAADHLNNRUY	hardy annual
AAADHORSTTU	à tout hasard
AAADIILLNNS	Lanai Island
AAADIILNORR	radiolarian
AAADIILNORT	radiational
AAADIKLLMTW	walk Matilda
AAADILMOQRU	maquiladora
AAADILNORSV	Salvadorian
AAADIMOPRST	paramastoid
AAADJMNNPRU	panjandarum
AAADLLNRSTW	warts and all
AAADLNORSSV	San Salvador
AAADLOOPSTT	potato salad
AAAEEELNPRS	paraselenae
AAAEEGGMNST	stage-manage
AAAEEGHMNOP	Phaenogamae

AAAEEGINPRS paragenesia
AAAEEGMSSTU sausage meat
AAAEEGRTTVX extravagate
AAAEEHHRTTV have at heart
AAAEEHINSST anaesthesia
AAAEEHLLSST Tallahassee
AAAEEHLNRRS Alan Shearer
AAAEEHLQRTU aqualeather
AAAEEHMNTTX exanthemata
AAAEEISSTTU aetatis suae
AAAEELLNNRT à la lanterne
AAAEELNPRTY penalty area
AAAEERSTTVX extravasate
AAAEFFGJNOR Jaffa orange
AAAEFFIJNRX Jane Fairfax
AAAEFNRSSWY farawayness
AAAEGGINRST staging area
AAAEGHILNRT Argathelian
AAAEGHIMMNO haemangioma
AAAEGHIMSST Thai massage
AAAEGHKPSSW passage hawk
AAAEGHLPTUW what a plague
AAAEGHPPRRR paragrapher
AAAEGIILNRT egalitarian
AAAEGIKNSTT take against
AAAEGILMMNO megalomania
AAAEGILMNNT galantamine
AAAEGILMNRS Marginal Sea
AAAEGILNRWY in a large way
AAAEGIMRRTV margraviate
AAAEGINRRRV Angara River
AAAEGIPRRTT tirage à part
AAAEGJLMSWY James Galway
AAAEGLMNOUY Maya Angelou
AAAEGLOPRSS paraglossae
AAAEGMRSSSU massasauger
AAAEGNOSSTU not a sausage
AAAEGNRTTVX extravagant
AAAEGORSSSS Sargasso Sea
AAAEHHLNNPT naphthalane
AAAEHIILMPT epithalamia
AAAEHILMSST thalassemia
AAAEHILNOPR aeolian harp✧
AAAEHILNPRT paranthelia
AAAEHILNPRX hexaplarian
AAAEHIMNNRT amaranthine
AAAEHIMNRST Samian earth
AAAEHINPPRR paraphrenia
AAAEHINPPRT Aphaniptera
AAAEHLLMRRS Earl Marshal
AAAEHLLRSUY Laura Ashley
AAAEHLMNRSS Las Hermanas
AAAEHMNNOPP panomphaean
AAAEHPPRRRS paraphraser
AAAEILMNNOT emanational
AAAEILMNOPT petalomania
AAAEILMRRTW raw material
AAAEILNPWXY explain away
AAAEILPPRRS reappraisal
AAAEIMNNRTU Mauretanian
AAAEIMOPRRT amor patriae
AAAEINPRRRV River Paraná
AAAEINPRRTT partenariat
AAAEINSSSST assassinate
AAAEIPPRRSS paraparesis
AAAEJLLNPRU Japan laurel
AAAEKKLNRTU Lake Turkana
AAAEKLMNOOT malakatoone
AAAEKMMNRTU mantua-maker
AAAEKRRSTTT tartar steak
AAAELLMMMPS plasmalemma
AAAELLNNTTY antenatally
AAAELMMRSUZ Emma Lazarus
AAAELMNPRTT apartmental
AAAELNRRSTW warrant sale
AAAELNRRTUY natural year
AAAELPPSSTT Papal States
AAAEMRSSSTY assay-master
AAAEMRSSTUW Satsuma ware
AAAENNPRSTU Punta Arenas
AAAENPRSSTW Peasants' War
AAAEPPRSSTU apparatuses
AAAFFFILNST Falstaffian
AAAFFINPRWX paraffin wax
AAAFGHINNST Afghanistan
AAAFHINRSWZ Nawaz Sharif
AAAFILLMRTY family altar
AAAGGGINRTV aggravating
AAAGGHHIOPR Hagiographa
AAAGGINORTV aggravation
AAAGHHIIOPS Hagia Sophia
AAAGHIMNOPR graphomania
AAAGIILNPRS parasailing
AAAGIILNRST rail against
AAAGIIMNRRS agrarianism
AAAGIINNRSU sanguinaria
AAAGIINRSTT Sagittarian
AAAGILNNPQU aquaplaning
AAAGILNPRTV travail pang
AAAGILNPSSY gap analysis
AAAGIMMMRST agrammatism
AAAGIMNRRUY Nyamuragira
AAAGKNOOPRW kangaroo paw
AAAGKNOORRT kangaroo rat
rat-kangaroo
AAAGLLOPRSS paraglossal
AAAGLLORSSV Vargas Llosa
AAAGLMNORTU granulomata
AAAGLMNRSTU mangalsutra
AAAGMMRRRSS marram grass
AAAGMNNORST manna-groats
AAAGMPPRSSS pampas grass
AAAHHHNORSS Rosh Hashana
AAAHHNOPRST Pharaoh's ant
AAAHIILNNTT antithalian
AAAHIKKNSTZ Kazakhstani
AAAHIKMNRRS Ramakrishna
AAAHIKNRRSV Ravi Shankar
AAAHILMOPRT prothalamia
AAAHILNPSXY anaphylaxis
AAAHIMNNORT Marathonian
AAAHIMNRRUZ Ziaur Rahman

AAAHINNORTZ	zoantharian
AAAHINPSSTT	phantasiast
AAAHIPPRRSX	paraphraxis
AAAHKMMORYY	Omar Khayyám
AAAHLLMMNTY	Tammany Hall
AAAHNNOPSTY	satanophany
AAAIILLMMMR	mammillaria
AAAIILMNORU	ailuromania
AAAIILMPRSU	Marsupialia
AAAIILMRSST	Alastair Sim
AAAIILNNORT	national air
AAAIILNORTV	variational
AAAIILNPRTV	travail pain
AAAIILNPSTU	saintpaulia
AAAIIMNNRTU	Mauritanian
AAAIIMPRSTV	a prima vista
AAAIINNQRTU	antiquarian
AAAIINQRRRW	Iran-Iraq War
AAAIJRSTTYY	Satyajit Ray
AAAIKKNSTZZ	Kazantzakis
AAAIKNOPPST	spanakopita
AAAILLMNSWY	in a small way
AAAILLMORTY	amatorially
AAAILLNOTUV	valuational
AAAILLORSTT	saltatorial
AAAILMMORTU	Maria Mutola
AAAILMNPRTY	party animal
AAAILMRRSTT	martial arts
AAAILNNORTT	Nationalrat
AAAILNNRSTU	saturnalian
AAAILNORTVV	Navratilova
AAAILNPPRTY	play a part in
AAAILOPRRTT	raptatorial
AAAIMNNOOST	antonomasia
AAAIMNOOPRS	paronomasia
AAAJLLNOPTW	Japan tallow
AAAJMPPRTYY	pyjama party
AAAJNNNOOTV	Jana Novotna
AAAJOPRRSVW	Java sparrow
AAALLMMNOWX	Max Mallowan
AAAMNNNPRTU	Mt Annapurna
AAAMNORRTTU	Mount Ararat
AAAOPRSSTUU	Apatosaurus
AABBBCDEINR	bib and brace
AABBBCEKRST	backstabber
AABBBEHRSTY	baby's breath
AABBCCIILST	cabbalistic
AABBCCKLNOR	black carbon
	carbon black
AABBCDEEIRT	bacteria bed
AABBCDEINRT	brace-and-bit
AABBCEEEGRT	cabbage tree
AABBCEEELMR	embraceable
AABBCEEGORS	cabbage rose
AABBCEEKKRR	backbreaker
AABBCEGHMOT	cabbage-moth
AABBCEGMORW	cabbage-worm
AABBCEGNOTW	cabbagetown
AABBCEINORT	bicarbonate
AABBCEKLTUY	Black Beauty
AABBCEKNRUY	Banbury cake

AABBCFIOSYY	Bay of Biscay
AABBCKLLNOO	balloon-back
AABBCOORRTU	Barbour® coat
AABBDDDENOR	bed and board
AABBDEEGILR	abridgeable
AABBDEEHNTT	beat the band
AABBDEEKRST	breadbasket
AABBDEEORRV	Beaverboard®
	beaverboard
AABBDEFFLOR	baffle-board
AABBDEGLNRR	land-grabber
AABBDEGLORS	Barbados leg
AABBDEILLOR	Della-Robbia
AABBDEILSSY	Baily's beads
AABBDEINOTT	Diane Abbott
AABBDHLLOTY	bothy ballad
AABBDILMORU	Malibu board
AABBDLORSSS	bold as brass
AABBDRRRUYY	Ray Bradbury
AABBEEHHMXY	Hexham Abbey
AABBEEIRRTV	rebarbative
AABBEEKLLRR	ball-breaker
AABBEEKLNRU	unbreakable
AABBEEKLRRY	barley-brake
	barley-break
AABBEELLMNU	unblameable
AABBEELLRST	barbastelle
AABBEEQRRSU	barbaresque
AABBEFGLNOY	Bay of Bengal
AABBEFGLRST	flabbergast
AABBEGIINRT	bear-baiting
AABBEGILLNR	ball-bearing
AABBEHIILNT	inhabitable
AABBEHILLOS	abolishable
AABBEHILMNO	abhominable
AABBEHILNTU	unhabitable
AABBEHKLNTT	blanket bath
AABBEHLSSST	Sabbathless
AABBEHRRRSS	barber's rash
AABBEIILNOR	baron bailie
AABBEILRSST	Alberti bass
AABBEIMNRSS	Babes in Arms
AABBEIORRTV	abbreviator
AABBEIRRTTU	barbiturate
AABBELLMNUY	unblameably
AABBELORRSU	subarboreal
AABBFGIMNRY	baby-farming
AABBGLNNORY	Long Barnaby
AABBHHIOOPT	bathophobia
AABBHIKOSUZ	Bashi-Bazouk
AABBHLLMNRU	Brahman bull
AABBIIILMNO	bibliomania
AABBIIKLNTY	bankability
AABBIILMNOO	bona mobilia
AABBINNORRR	Brian Barron
AABBKLOORRW	barbola work
AABBLORRSUY	barbarously
AABCCCDEIIS	sebacic acid
AABCCCDIIOR	boracic acid
AABCCCHKRST	backscratch
	scratchback

AABCCDEEKLM camel-backed
AABCCDEHNRT cadet branch
AABCCDEKLOT black-coated
AABCCDHILNO baldacchino
AABCCDKLNOR Conrad Black
AABCCEEHMPY Campeche Bay
AABCCEEIMRT bacteraemic
AABCCEELLNO concealable
AABCCEHKLNN back channel
AABCCEILLRY acerbically
AABCCEILPRT practicable
AABCCEKLLTT black cattle
AABCCEKRSTT backscatter
AABCCELMNOU Molucca bean
AABCCELMOPT accomptable
AABCCELNOTT contactable
AABCCELNOTU accountable
AABCCELNSUU unaccusable
AABCCEORTTU cacao butter
AABCCERRUUY bureaucracy
AABCCGIKKNP backpacking
AABCCGILLNR calling-crab
AABCCHNORUY Baron Cauchy
AABCCIIJLNO Jacobinical
AABCCIIJLOT Jacobitical
AABCCIKLORT cocktail bar
AABCCILMOST saltimbocca
AABCCILPRTY practicably
AABCCKLLMSU Almack's Club
AABCCKNNOTU bank account
AABCCLNOTUY accountably
AABCCLNRRUU carbuncular
AABCCLNSUUY unaccusably
AABCDDEEHKL blackheaded
AABCDDEILRS discardable
AABCDDEORST broadcasted
AABCDDIKMNO diamondback
AABCDEEELLR leader-cable
AABCDEEFLRY barefacedly
AABCDEEFNRZ brazen-faced
AABCDEEHIRS raised beach
AABCDEEHRRT acre-breadth
AABCDEEILMT alembicated
AABCDEEKNRR breakdancer
AABCDEELNRT tabernacled
table-dancer
AABCDEENORT decarbonate
AABCDEEORRT beat a record
AABCDEFIIIL acidifiable
AABCDEFNOSU bauson-faced
AABCDEHIMMR chambermaid
AABCDEHLMTY Lady Macbeth
AABCDEHLOPR bachelor pad
AABCDEHNPRY peach brandy
AABCDEIKLSV black-a-vised
AABCDEILNRY clay-brained
AABCDEILNST elastic band
AABCDEINOOR radio beacon
AABCDEINORT debarcation
AABCDEINRRU unbarricade
AABCDEIORRS barricadoes
AABCDEKNRRS banker's card
AABCDELLNPS cap and bells
AABCDELMNRU candelabrum
AABCDEMOSSU ambuscadoes
AABCDENOORS carbonadoes
AABCDEORRST broadcaster
rebroadcast
AABCDFIKLLN back and fill
AABCDFIKLRY black Friday✧
AABCDGGIOOR braggadocio✧
AABCDGHKRTU back-draught
AABCDGIKLNO back-loading
AABCDHHNRST Brands Hatch
AABCDHHORTT thatch-board
AABCDHIOOPR Brachiopoda
AABCDHIRRSY Richards Bay
AABCDHMNORY rhabdomancy
AABCDIINNNO cannabinoid
AABCDIIQRTU biquadratic
AABCDILNOSU subdiaconal
AABCDILNRSU subcardinal
AABCDINOORR radiocarbon
AABCDINOUYY buoyancy aid
AABCDKLMNOY black Monday
AABCEEEENRV Verbenaceae
AABCEEEGINO Begoniaceae
AABCEEEHLST escheatable
AABCEEEIIRS Ribesiaceae
AABCEEEILLO Lobeliaceae
AABCEEEKLPY black-eye pea
AABCEEEKRRR career break
AABCEEELLPR replaceable
AABCEEELNPU unpeaceable
AABCEEELRRT retraceable
AABCEEERRSU Burseraceae
AABCEEFLRRT refractable
AABCEEFNORR forbearance
AABCEEGLLNO congealable
AABCEEHILMN machineable
AABCEEHILMP impeachable
AABCEEHKLRT leatherback
AABCEEHLNRU unreachable
AABCEEHLNTU unteachable
AABCEEHLORX Lochaber axe
AABCEEHMMRR hammer-brace
AABCEEHMNRT antechamber
AABCEEHMRST beach-master
AABCEEHORTT the Boat Race
AABCEEIINRR carabiniere
AABCEEILLMR reclaimable
AABCEEILMNV ambivalence
AABCEEILNPS inescapable
AABCEEILNQU equibalance
AABCEEILNRS increasable
AABCEEILPPR appreciable
AABCEEILRTU eubacterial
AABCEEKLLNP pancake bell
AABCEELMNSS assemblance
AABCEELNORV overbalance
AABCEELNPSS capableness
AABCEELNPSU unescapable

AABCEELNRST	scarlet bean
AABCEELNRTU	untraceable
AABCEELORTT	bracteolate
AABCEELRRTT	retractable
AABCEELRSTT	scatterable
AABCEELRTTU	trabeculate
AABCEELRTTX	extractable
AABCEFFLOPU	Cape buffalo
AABCEFIIRTV	fabricative
AABCEFILNOT	labefaction
AABCEFINOTT	tabefaction
AABCEFLMNOY	flamboyance
AABCEFLNOTU	confabulate
AABCEGHNORT	baton charge
	baton-charge
AABCEGILNNT	enabling act
AABCEGMNNSU	Angus McBean
AABCEHHPSTY	bathyscaphe
AABCEHIIMRT	Marie Bichat
AABCEHIINNT	inhabitance
AABCEHIKRST	basket chair
AABCEHILLRY	Hebraically
AABCEHILMNR	chamberlain✧
AABCEHILNRU	hibernacula
AABCEHILSST	chastisable
AABCEHIMNRR	rain-chamber
AABCEHINORT	haricot bean
AABCEHKORTT	back to earth
AABCEHLLMRS	Charles Lamb
AABCEHLMNTU	unmatchable
AABCEHLNNOR	horn balance
AABCEHLNSTU	staunchable
AABCEHLNTUW	unwatchable
AABCEHLOPRU	cheap labour
AABCEHLPRSU	purchasable
AABCEHMNRRT	merchant bar
AABCEHMRRST	star chamber✧
AABCEHNRRTW	branch water
AABCEIIINRR	carabinieri
AABCEIILNNS	cannibalise
AABCEIILNNZ	cannibalize
AABCEIIMRST	basmati rice
AABCEIINNNR	cinnabarine
AABCEIKLLMR	blackmailer
AABCEIKMRSS	Bismarck Sea
AABCEILLLOS	localisable
AABCEILLLOZ	localizable
AABCEILLMRY	reclaimably
AABCEILLNSU	suballiance
AABCEILLORY	aerobically
AABCEILLPRU	burial-place
AABCEILLRTU	articulable
AABCEILLSTY	syllabicate
AABCEILMNOP	companiable
AABCEILMNVY	ambivalency
AABCEILNNOT	containable
AABCEILNORT	baronetical
AABCEILNPSY	inescapably
AABCEILNRTT	intractable
AABCEILPPRT	parableptic
AABCEILPPRY	appreciably
AABCEIMNORT	embarcation
AABCEIMNPRR	Precambrian
AABCEINORRS	carabineros
AABCEINORTT	carbonatite
AABCEIRSTTV	abstractive
AABCEJLMORY	Jacob Marley
AABCEKKLMRT	black market
AABCEKLLRRT	trackerball
AABCEKLNNRT	central bank
AABCEKLNRRU	cab-rank rule
AABCEKMRUUV	vacuum brake
AABCEKORTTU	racket about
AABCEKQRRTU	quarterback
AABCELLLOPS	collapsable
AABCELLOORT	collaborate
AABCELLQRTU	racquetball
AABCELMNOTU	uncomatable
AABCELMOPSS	compassable
AABCELMRSTU	Albert Camus
AABCELMRTUU	umbraculate
AABCELNORTY	carbonylate
AABCELNRTTU	untractable
AABCELOORST	car boot sale
AABCEMMOPSS	beam compass
AABCENOPPRR	carbon paper
AABCENOPRST	absorptance
AABCENRRSSU	bancassurer
AABCEOORRSU	arboraceous
AABCEOORTTZ	Azotobacter
AABCFFJOSST	Jacob's staff
AABCFIINORT	fabrication
AABCFIKLRRS	Black Friars
AABCFIORRVY	Vicar of Bray
AABCFLMNOYY	flamboyancy
AABCGGGIKNN	back-ganging
AABCGHHNOWY	Hang-Chow Bay
AABCGHIOOPR	agoraphobic
AABCGHKLOQU	black quahog
AABCGIILLMS	galliambics
AABCGILLNRR	call-barring
AABCGILLOOT	batological
AABCHHIOOPT	tachophobia
AABCHIILMNR	Brahminical
AABCHIINNTY	inhabitancy
AABCHIINORT	brachiation
AABCHILLRTY	charity ball
AABCHJLNORY	John Barclay
AABCHNOPPRW	Cappah-brown
AABCIIILMTY	amicability
AABCIIJNNOT	antijacobin✧
	anti-Jacobin✧
AABCIILLPTY	placability
AABCIILLSTY	scalability
AABCIILMNNS	cannibalism
AABCIILNORT	calibration
AABCIILRSTY	sybaritical✧
AABCIIMNNOS	Baconianism
AABCILLMNTU	lactalbumin
AABCILLNOTY	botanically
AABCILLORSS	Carlo Blasis
AABCILLOSTV	Balto-slavic

Words marked ✧ can also be spelled with one or more capital letters

AABCILLRUWY	Railway Club
AABCILMNOST	saltimbanco
AABCILNNRUU	incunabular
AABCILNRTTY	intractably
AABCILOSTTY	biocatalyst
AABCIMNORRS	Carbonarism
AABCINNOORT	carbonation
AABCINORRTU	carburation
AABCINORSTT	abstraction
	in abstracto
AABCKLLLNOU	Alan Bullock
AABCKLLNTUW	black walnut
AABCKLLORWY	rock wallaby
AABCKMNORWY	Mackay Brown
AABCKMNSSTU	subtacksman
AABCKMOORRR	barrack-room
AABCLLLRSTY	crystal ball
AABCLPRSSUU	subcapsular
	subscapular
AABCMNNOOTY	botanomancy
AABCNOORSST	contrabasso
AABDDDELOPR	paddle-board
AABDDEEELRW	Edward Albee
AABDDEEGHLR	Hedda Gabler
AABDDEEHRST	hard bestead
AABDDEELNRR	brand leader
	dealer brand
AABDDEELORR	leaderboard
AABDDEELORV	broad-leaved
AABDDEELRSS	addressable
AABDDEEMNNR	bad-mannered
AABDDEGGORR	daggerboard
AABDDEGLLLR	gall bladder
AABDDEHHNRT	handbreadth
AABDDEHMORY	hebdomadary
AABDDEIILVY	David Bailey
AABDDEIINNR	Indian bread
AABDDEINOST	bastinadoed
AABDDEINOTV	David Beaton
AABDDELNNOY	abandonedly
AABDDERRRUW	Edward Burra
AABDDGLOORR	Labrador dog
AABDDGNORST	bog standard
AABDDHHIMOR	Bodhidharma
AABDDHLNNSU	husbandland
AABDDINRTVY	David Bryant
AABDDMNRSSU	drum and bass
AABDDNRSSTU	substandard
AABDEEEHKLW	beaked whale
AABDEEEHKRW	Rebekah Wade
AABDEEEKLRR	dealbreaker
AABDEEEMRTY	yerba de maté
AABDEEFGLLR	deflagrable
AABDEEGIMRR	marriage-bed
AABDEEGLPRU	upgradeable
AABDEEGNNSV	Geneva bands
AABDEEGPSSS	passage beds
AABDEEHHRRS	haberdasher
AABDEEHINRR	hare-brained
AABDEEHLSTY	beastly-head
AABDEEHNSTU	de haut en bas
AABDEEILLNS	aniseed ball
AABDEEILMNR	lamebrained
AABDEEINNRT	bandeirante
AABDEELLMRT	ballad metre
AABDEELMNNU	unamendable
AABDEELNRSS	Abdel Nasser
AABDEELPRSU	persuadable
AABDEELRSTW	wastel bread
AABDEEMRRSS	embarrassed
AABDEEPQSSU	pas de basque
AABDEEQRSUU	arquebusade
AABDEFIIMRR	aramid fibre
AABDEFILRST	bastard file
AABDEGGHINN	headbanging
AABDEGHMOUZ	Gezhouba Dam
AABDEGILMNN	landing-beam
AABDEGILNOR	load-bearing
AABDEGILNOS	diagnosable
AABDEGINOSV	vagabondise
AABDEGINOVZ	vagabondize
AABDEGMORTY	Tremadog Bay
AABDEGNORTU	unabrogated
AABDEHHIRRT	hairbreadth
AABDEHIINRR	hair-brained
AABDEHRSTWY	breadthways
AABDEIILNSV	inadvisable
AABDEIILRTY	readability
AABDEIJNNRU	Jean Buridan
AABDEIKNORT	debarkation
AABDEILLNOT	labiodental
AABDEILLRVY	adverbially
AABDEILLSTY	Bastille Day
AABDEILMNPS	Pemba Island
AABDEILMNTU	mandibulate
AABDEILNNRU	undrainable
AABDEILNOUV	unavoidable
AABDEILNSUV	unadvisable
AABDEILORRS	sailboarder
AABDEILORRT	labradorite
AABDEIMRTUV	adumbrative
AABDEINOORS	noise abroad
AABDEINOSST	bastinadoes
AABDEKNOORT	take on board
AABDEKNRRTZ	Bernard Katz
AABDELLNNRY	blarney-land
AABDELLNORR	Allan Border
AABDELLNSTU	unballasted
AABDELNNTUU	undauntable
AABDELNOPRU	Pablo Neruda
AABDELNRSST	sandblaster
AABDELNRSTU	salad burnet
AABDELORRUY	day-labourer
AABDEMNNNOT	abandonment
AABDFFOORWY	off-Broadway
AABDFGILLNN	falling band
	falling-band
AABDFIIINPS	spina bifida
AABDFILNORS	Island of Rab
AABDGGGHINN	handbagging
AABDGHIILNT	in a bad light
AABDGHINOSV	vagabondish

AABDGIILRTY gradability
AABDGIINNST bastinading
AABDGIINRSW bias-drawing
AABDGIMNOSV vagabondism
AABDGINRSTW bastard wing
AABDGKLNOUW dak bungalow
AABDGLNRSSY brandy glass
AABDHHOOPRR Rhabdophora
AABDHIILNTU habitudinal
AABDHIKLNOY bank holiday
AABDHINNOPS abandon ship
AABDHIOSTTV Bodhisattva
AABDHLOPRSS splashboard
AABDHMMOORY rhabdomyoma
AABDIILLTUY laudability
AABDIILMNTY damnability
AABDIILMOTT admit to bail
AABDIILMQRU Liquidambar
AABDIILNRSS Brian Aldiss
AABDIIMRRTU ad arbitrium
AABDILLMNOY abdominally
AABDILLRUXY axillary bud
AABDILNORTU Adrian Boult
AABDILNOUVY unavoidably
AABDILNSUVY unadvisably
AABDILOORRS boardsailor
AABDILOORRT orbital road
AABDIMNOOOW Amboina-wood
AABDIMNORTU adumbration
AABDIMPSSUY bumpsadaisy
AABDINRSSSU Buridan's ass
AABDIORRSST Broadstairs
AABDKMMOOOS Akosombo Dam
AABDLLMOOPS blood plasma
AABDLLNOOST boots and all
AABDLNOPRTY Portland Bay
AABDMNNOOPR moor-band pan
AABDMNOOOWY Amboyna-wood
AABDMOORRRT mortarboard
AABDNOOPRSX Pandora's box
AABDNOORRWW bow and arrow
AABDNOOTTUU out and about
AABDNRRRSTU surtarbrand
AABDOPRRSTY pastry board
AABEEEEGRRV eager beaver
AABEEEEKLST seakale beet
AABEEEFKRRS safe-breaker
AABEEEGLLTU league table
AABEEEGLNRU unagreeable
AABEEEHLRTW weatherable
AABEEEHMRTW weather beam
AABEEEKSTVW basketweave
AABEEELNPRT panel beater
AABEEELNRTT entreatable
AABEEENRRSW Benares ware
AABEEERRRTW Water Bearer
AABEEFFLLPT baffle-plate
AABEEFGIRRR barrage-fire
AABEEFORSTU Beaufort Sea
AABEEGGIIRR argie-bargie
AABEEGGLLRR argle-bargle
AABEEGHILNR Belgian hare
AABEEGILNRT talebearing
AABEEGINNRT annabergite
AABEEGKMRTU take umbrage
AABEEGLMNTU augmentable
AABEEGLNOSV noble savage
AABEEGLNTTU ungetatable
unget-at-able
AABEEGLOSTU absolute age
AABEEGMNOTU beaumontage
AABEEGMRRST bargemaster
AABEEHILNTZ Elizabethan
AABEEHILPST alphabetise
AABEEHILPTZ alphabetize
AABEEHIRRRT heat barrier
AABEEHKLNSU unshakeable
AABEEHLLTTY lay the table
AABEEHLRSTY breathalyse
AABEEHLRTYZ breathalyze
AABEEHSTTTY the Bay State
AABEEIILLNN inalienable
AABEEIILRTW water bailie
AABEEIKPRRR pereira bark
AABEEILLLQU illaqueable
AABEEILLNNU unalienable
AABEEILLNPX explainable
AABEEILLNRT inalterable
AABEEILMNSS amiableness
AABEEILNNRR inenarrable
AABEEILNORT inelaborate
AABEEILNPRS inseparable
AABEEILNRST line abreast
AABEEILNRUW unweariable
AABEEILORTV elaborative
AABEEILPRRR irreparable
AABEEINNNST Annie Besant
AABEEINRRRT train-bearer
AABEEINRRST brainteaser
AABEEINSSTT bastnaesite
AABEEKKMORR make or break
make-or-break
AABEEKKMRST basket-maker
AABEEKLLNSU unslakeable
AABEEKLNPSU unspeakable
AABEEKLPSTT plate-basket
AABEEKSSTTW waste basket
AABEELLLMNU unmalleable
AABEELLMNOT balletomane
AABEELLNPTT battleplane
AABEELLNRTU unalterable
AABEELLNSSS salableness
AABEELLNSSV Vanessa Bell
AABEELLORTY elaborately
AABEELLOTUV All About Eve
AABEELLPRRY pearl barley
AABEELLPRSU pleasurable
AABEELMNSST tamableness
AABEELMPPRR marble-paper
AABEELMPRTU perambulate
preambulate
AABEELMPTTT attemptable

AABEELMRRTW beam trawler
AABEELNORST treasonable
AABEELNORTU unelaborate
AABEELNPRSU unseparable
AABEELNRTTU entablature
untreatable
AABEELNRTUV unavertable
AABEELNSSSV savableness
AABEELPPRRW bale wrapper
AABEELPRSTT breastplate
AABEELRRRTW water barrel
AABEELRRSTT sabre-rattle
AABEELRRSTV traversable
AABEELRRTTU terebratula
AABEELRRTWY barley water
AABEELSSUUX sexual abuse
AABEEMMOPRT meprobamate
AABEEMNRTTT rabattement
AABEENNOTTY not bat an eye
AABEENRRSTU sauerbraten
AABEFFIILLS falsifiable
AABEFGIILMN magnifiable
AABEFGILLRU bella figura
AABEFHILNOS fashionable
AABEFHILPST half-baptise
AABEFHILPTZ half-baptize
AABEFIILLQU qualifiable
AABEFIILSST satisfiable
AABEFIKLMRY family baker
AABEFILLMMN inflammable
AABEFILMNOT lifeboatman
AABEFILORRS Isle of Barra
AABEFLLNPPU unflappable
AABEFLMNOTY flamboyante
AABEFLMNTUU funambulate
AABEFLNOPSY Bay of Naples
AABEGGGILLR galli-bagger
galli-beggar
AABEGGGLLRY gally-bagger
gally-beggar
AABEGGILMNT gaming-table
AABEGGINORY Georgian Bay
AABEGGINSST staging base
AABEGGLNSUU sublanguage
AABEGIILNNS Albigensian
AABEGIILNNV innavigable
AABEGIIMNRT time bargain
AABEGIIMRRV River Gambia
AABEGIINPRS base pairing
AABEGIJKNRW jaw-breaking
AABEGIKLMNW walking-beam
AABEGIKLNRW lawbreaking
AABEGIKNORR aerobraking
AABEGILNNUV unnavigable
AABEGILNORS organisable
AABEGILNORZ organizable
AABEGIRRRTU arbitrageur
AABEGJSSTUU assubjugate
AABEGKLOSTW blow a gasket
AABEGLLMOST megaloblast
AABEGLLRSTU Glauber salt
AABEGLMRTTU Galam butter
AABEGLNOPTU Paul Boateng
AABEGLNORRR barrel organ
AABEGLNPRSU ungraspable
AABEGLRRSUY barley sugar
barley-sugar
AABEHHIOPPT taphephobia
AABEHILNRST tarnishable
AABEHILORUV behavioural
AABEHIMNOOP anemophobia
AABEHIRRSVW Wabash River
AABEHKLLMTW Lambeth Walk
AABEHKLNSUY unshakeably
AABEHKLRRST Halbstarker
AABEHLOPRRR Pearl Harbor
AABEHLORRSU harbour seal
AABEHLPRRSV phrasal verb
AABEHMPRRSS Bramah-press
AABEHMRTTUU mahua butter
AABEIILLMSS assimilable
AABEIILLNNY inalienably
AABEIILLSTY saleability
AABEIILMMOR memorabilia✧
AABEIILMNPS animal bipes
AABEIILMNTY amenability
AABEIILMORT biomaterial
AABEIILMTTY tameability
AABEIILNRRT libertarian
AABEIILRTTY rateability
AABEIILRTWY wearability
AABEIIMNNOP Amboina pine
AABEIINPRRR pain barrier
AABEIINRTTT Tate Britain
AABEIJLMNRU Julian Bream
AABEIKLNNPT table napkin
AABEIKMNORT embarkation
AABEIKNPRTV private bank
AABEILLLRTY bilaterally
AABEILLMNPU manipulable
AABEILLMRRU air-umbrella
AABEILLNNUY unalienably
AABEILLNRTY inalterably
AABEILLRRST liberal arts
AABEILLRRTU Turbellaria
AABEILLRRTZ trailblazer
AABEILLRSUY subaerially
AABEILLRVZZ Brazzaville
AABEILMMOST ametabolism
AABEILMNPRS Persian lamb
AABEILMNRRU unmarriable
AABEILNNPTU unpaintable
AABEILNNSTU unstainable
AABEILNOORT elaboration
AABEILNORTT anteorbital
AABEILNPRSY inseparably
AABEILNRRTT rattlebrain
AABEILNRSSU Belarussian
AABEILNRSTT transitable
AABEILNRUWY unweariably
AABEILNSSTU sustainable
AABEILNTTVY vanity table

AABEILOPRSV vaporisable
AABEILOPRVZ vaporizable
AABEILPPRSS parablepsis
AABEILPRRRY irreparably
AABEILPRTYY play it by ear
AABEILRSTUU ritual abuse
AABEIMNRRTT arbitrament
AABEINNOORT anaerobiont
AABEINNORSV non-abrasive
AABEINNPRTT Brian Patten
AABEINOSSTT base station
AABEIOPPRTV approbative
AABEIOPRSST taboparesis
AABEJNOORRT Jean Borotra
AABEKLLLNNR rannell-balk
AABEKLNPSUY unspeakably
AABEKNORSTV karbovanets
AABEKOPTTUU take up about
AABELLLNOUW unallowable
AABELLLPRSU subparallel
AABELLLRRSY sallal berry
AABELLMNRTU umbrella-ant
AABELLNRTUY unalterably
AABELLOPPRT ballot paper
AABELLORSUV slave labour
AABELLORTTY battle royal
AABELLPRSUY pleasurably
AABELLRRTUV barrel vault
AABELMMNSSY assemblyman
AABELMNOSTT nematoblast
AABELMNSSTY Laban system
AABELMOOSTU ametabolous
AABELMPRRUY preambulary
AABELNOOTUY lay about one
AABELNORSTY treasonably
AABELNOSTUY beauty salon
AABELOORRTY elaboratory
AABELPRSSSU surpassable
AABFFGLNOTU buffalo gnat
AABFHILNOSY fashionably
AABFIKNORSU Burkina Faso
AABFILLMMNY inflammably
AABFLLLSTTU at full blast
AABFLLNPPUY unflappably
AABFLLOORTW Football War
AABFLMOPRTY bay platform
AABFLNOSTUU fantabulous
AABGGHINOTW go with a bang
AABGGIMRRST braggartism
AABGHHINRST Granth Sahib
AABGHHIOOPP phagophobia
AABGHIILNTY hangability
AABGHIJKLRT J K Galbraith
AABGHILLMRY Billy Graham
AABGHILLOOP Gallophobia
AABGHILNOOP anglophobia✧
AABGIILMNSU subimaginal
AABGIILNNVY innavigably
AABGIILNOST sailing boat
AABGIKLNSSW walking bass
AABGIKNNSSV savings bank
AABGILMNRSU submarginal
AABGILNRSTZ blazing star
AABGILRSUVV survival bag
AABGINNOSTW angwantibos
AABGINORSSU Sanguisorba
AABGINSSSSU assassin bug
AABGINSTTTU butt against
AABGLNSTUUU Subungulata
AABHHIMSTTV Bath Mitsvah
Bathmitsvah
Bath-Mitsvah
AABHHIMTTVZ Bath Mitzvah
Bathmitzvah
Bath-Mitzvah
AABHHIOOPPT pathophobia
taphophobia
AABHIILORTT habilitator
AABHIILSTWY washability
AABHIINOTTU habituation
AABHILLNRTY labyrinthal
AABHILOOPST Alpha Boötis
AABHIMNPSST batsmanship
AABHINOOPPT pantophobia
AABHJMMOORS Brahmo Somaj
AABHJMNORRT John Bartram
AABHKNOORTT katabothron
AABHMOOSSTU Matsuo Basho
AABHNOOPRTU harp on about
AABIIILRTVY variability
AABIIILSTTY satiability
AABIIKLLTTY talkability
AABIILLLMMW William Lamb
AABIILLNOOT abolitional
AABIILLNORT librational
AABIILLPPTY palpability
AABIILLSTVY salvability
AABIILMNRUU albuminuria
AABIILMOOTU automobilia
AABIILNORTV vibrational
AABIILORSTU atrabilious
AABIILOSTTU ablatitious
AABIILRRRTY arbitrarily
AABIIMMNORT timbromania
AABIIMNNOOT abomination
AABIINORRTT arbitration
AABIIRRRTTX arbitratrix
AABILLMNNRU Alan Milburn
AABILLMORSY ambrosially
AABILLMORTY balmorality✧
AABILLMPSTY baptismally
AABILLMRSUY syllabarium
AABILLNORRT anti-roll bar
AABILLOSSWW wassail bowl
AABILLRSUXY subaxillary
AABILMMNORS abnormalism
AABILMNORTY abnormality
AABILNOOPRT probational
AABILNORSTT trailbaston
AABILNORTUY ablutionary
AABILNSSTTU substantial
AABILOSSTUW wassail bout

AABIMMNOQUZ Mozambiquan
AABIMNOPRST Bonapartism
AABINNOPSTU subpanation
AABINOOPPRT approbation
AABINOPRSTT Bonapartist
AABINORRSTU saburration
subarration
AABLLNORSWW barn swallow
AABLMMNORSU somnambular
AABLNNORRTU natural-born
AABLOPRRTUY Labour Party
AABMORRSTTU masturbator
AABOOPPRRTY approbatory
AACCCCEHILT cachectical
AACCCDEJNOY coadjacency
AACCCDEOSUY cycadaceous
AACCCDHIILR radical chic
AACCCDHRRST scratchcard
AACCCDIILRY acrylic acid
AACCCEENTTU acute accent
AACCCEILPTT cataplectic
AACCCEINORT Arctic Ocean
AACCCEJKKRR crackerjack
AACCCGHIOPR cacographic
AACCCGIKNRT cat-cracking
AACCCGIORST cacogastric
AACCCHHILRS clairschach
AACCCHNOSTU cash account
AACCCHORSTT scratch coat
AACCCIIILRT cicatricial
AACCCIILLMT climactical
AACCCIILRTU cicatricula
AACCCILMSTY cataclysmic
AACCCINPRRU Crucian carp
AACCCNNOTUY accountancy
AACCDDEINOR endocardiac
AACCDEEHIOR Orchidaceae
AACCDEEILST discalceate
AACCDEELLNT cancellated
AACCDEELNOR accelerando
AACCDEHIRTT cathedratic
AACCDEIILLT dialectical
AACCDEIILPS Asclepiadic
AACCDEIILRV valeric acid
AACCDEIIMMS academicism
AACCDEIIPRR pericardiac
AACCDEIIRST stearic acid
AACCDEILLNR calendrical
AACCDEILNOT anecdotical
AACCDEILNST accidentals
AACCDEILOPY cyclopaedia
AACCDEIMNNO non-academic
AACCDEKORRS soda cracker
AACCDEMMOOT accommodate
AACCDENNORT contradance
AACCDENRTUV cut and carve
AACCDFIIMRU fumaric acid
AACCDGIIILN alginic acid
AACCDGILLNR calling card
AACCDGIORYZ zygocardiac
AACCDHIINOR characinoid
AACCDHIINRT cantharidic
AACCDHIINTX xanthic acid
AACCDHILNOR chancroidal
AACCDHILPSW chalcid wasp
AACCDHLOORT octachordal
AACCDHLPTYY pachydactyl
AACCDIIILRT diacritical
AACCDIIINTT titanic acid
AACCDIILMNO malonic acid
AACCDIILOPT apodictical
AACCDIINNST stannic acid
AACCDIOSSTU caustic soda
AACCDLMORTY macrodactyl
AACCDLNORTY accordantly
AACCDMOPRSS compass card
AACCEEFILNT calefacient
AACCEEFILTV calefactive
AACCEEFKRRS safe-cracker
AACCEEGHPRS space charge
AACCEEGNRTV grave accent
AACCEEHHPST escape hatch
AACCEEILRSV Alcaic verse
AACCEEILTTT atelectatic
AACCEEINPRS parascience
AACCEEINRRT incarcerate
AACCEEINRTV revaccinate
AACCEEJNOTU Jean Cocteau
AACCEEKLRRW crackleware
AACCEELLNOT collectanea
AACCEELLRTU recalculate
AACCEELMNRR Marcel Carné
AACCEELNSTU acaulescent
AACCEELORRT accelerator
AACCEELPRTU receptacula
AACCEEMNOPR compearance
AACCEENNOTT concatenate
AACCEFHSTTY safety catch
AACCEFIIRSS scire facias
AACCEFILNOT calefaction
AACCEFILSTU fasciculate
AACCEFINRTU café curtain
AACCEFKNRRS César Franck
AACCEFLORTY calefactory
AACCEGHILLP cephalalgic
AACCEGHILNR archangelic
AACCEGHNRTT gnatcatcher
AACCEGHOPRR cacographer
AACCEGIKNPS packing case
AACCEGILMOR acromegalic
AACCEGILNOS Nicolas Cage
AACCEGILORT categorical
AACCEGILOTT geotactical
AACCEGIMPRT magic carpet
AACCEGNORST scant-o'-grace
AACCEGORRTY ergatocracy
AACCEHHILNR Charlie Chan
AACCEHHIMNS cash machine
AACCEHHMOST stomachache
AACCEHHPRST catchphrase
AACCEHIIMNN mechanician
AACCEHIIMNR air-mechanic

AACCEHILMNS	mechanicals
AACCEHILMOT	machicolate
AACCEHILMRT	mail-catcher
AACCEHILMST	catechismal
	schematical
AACCEHINOPT	pinacotheca
AACCEHINRRT	in character
AACCEHIRSST	catachresis
	chaise-carts
AACCEHKLRRT	crack-halter
AACCEHLLORS	local search
AACCEHLNNNO	nonchalance
AACCEHMORSU	scaramouche✧
AACCEHNRRTY	carry the can
AACCEHNRTTW	want-catcher
AACCEHOPRSU	couch a spear
AACCEHORSTU	chartaceous
AACCEIILMST	acclimatise
AACCEIILMTZ	acclimatize
AACCEIINPRT	Capernaitic
AACCEIKLNSV	Salk vaccine
AACCEILLNST	Callanetics
AACCEILLSTY	ascetically
AACCEILLTUU	cauliculate
AACCEILLTUV	calculative
AACCEILMPRT	malpractice
AACCEILNORS	anisocercal
AACCEILORSS	accessorial
AACCEILOSSU	salicaceous
AACCEIMNOPR	accompanier
AACCEIMPRSU	America's Cup
AACCEINNORT	Anacreontic
	canceration
	Eric Cantona
AACCEINOPSV	Canopic vase
AACCEINOPTT	acceptation
AACCEINPTUV	captivaunce
AACCEINQTTU	acquittance
AACCEJKKORU	Jack Kerouac
AACCEKKTYYY	yackety-yack
AACCEKLLNOY	cycloalkane
AACCEKMNOTT	make contact
AACCEKNRRTU	currant cake
AACCELLMNOW	Ewan MacColl
AACCELLNTUY	accentually
AACCELLPPRW	clapperclaw
AACCELMNUUV	vacuum-clean
AACCELNORTU	real account
AACCELNRTUU	caruncleulate
AACCELPRSTU	spectacular
AACCELRTTUU	acculturate
AACCEMNOPRT	contra pacem
AACCEMNORRT	cartomancer
AACCENNORSS	Carcassonne
AACCENOPRRY	coparcenary
AACCENORSUY	sauce-crayon
AACCFHILMOY	family coach
AACCFIIILNR	carnificial
AACCFIIILRS	sacrificial
AACCFIILLPY	pacifically
AACCFIILRTY	farcicality
AACCFIIMNOR	acinaciform
AACCFIIOPRT	pacificator
AACCFILMORR	calcariform
AACCFINNRSS	Franciscans
AACCFORSTTY	Factory Acts
AACCGHIILRR	chiragrical
AACCGHIKNOT	hacking coat
AACCGHIMMOS	chasmogamic
AACCGHIMNNR	arm-chancing
AACCGHINRTT	rat-catching
AACCGILLNTU	calculating
AACCHHIINTU	t'ai chi ch'uan
AACCHIIMRST	charismatic
AACCHIINRST	anarchistic
AACCHIINRTT	anthracitic
AACCHILLOTY	chaotically
AACCHILLPTY	hypallactic
AACCHILMNOR	monarchical
AACCHILMOST	stomachical
AACCHILNOSV	volcanic ash
AACCHILNOTU	anacoluthic
AACCHILORRV	vicar-choral
AACCHILPRSU	Alpha Crucis
AACCHINOPST	cataphonics
AACCHIPPRSY	parapsychic
AACCHLLOTTW	tallow catch
AACCHLNSTUY	calycanthus
AACCHORRRTY	carry a torch
AACCIIILRST	racialistic
AACCIILLNTY	actinically
AACCIILLSTY	sciatically
AACCIILMNOT	acclimation
AACCIILMOPT	apomictical
AACCIILMPRT	impractical
AACCIILNNOT	calcination
AACCIILNORV	Clavicornia
AACCIILNSTT	Cisatlantic
AACCIILSSTU	casuistical
AACCIILSTTT	stalactitic
AACCIINNOTV	vaccination
AACCIINOPSU	incapacious
AACCIINOSTU	acoustician
AACCIINRSTY	actinic rays
AACCIINTTVY	Vatican City
AACCILLLNOR	clarion call
AACCILLLNOY	laconically
AACCILLLSSY	classically
AACCILLNNOY	canonically
AACCILLNOOT	local action
AACCILLNOTU	calculation
AACCILLNRTU	curtain call
AACCILLNSSU	unclassical
AACCILLNSUU	canaliculus
AACCILLOOPR	coprolaliac
AACCILLPRTY	practically
AACCILLPSTY	plastic clay
AACCILLSTUY	caustically
AACCILNNNOU	uncanonical
AACCILNOSST	class action
AACCILNOSTU	sacculation
AACCILNPRTU	unpractical

AACCILNSTTY syntactical
AACCILOPPTY apocalyptic
AACCILOPSUY capaciously
AACCILRRSUW circular saw
AACCILSSSUY Cassius Clay
AACCIMNOPST accompanist
AACCINOORTT coarctation
AACCINORTVY vaccinatory
AACCIOPRRST paracrostic
AACCIORRSTY aristocracy
AACCLMORTUU accumulator
AACCLNOOPRT Locarno Pact
AACCLNOPRTY plantocracy
AACCLNORTTU contractual
AACCLOORSST sacrocostal
AACCMOORRSZ Occam's razor
AACCMORSTUY accustomary
AACCORRSTTY stratocracy
AACDDDEINOR Dodecandria
AACDDEEEFNS defeasanced
AACDDEEEHLR clear-headed
AACDDEEHNRT dendrachate
AACDDEEHRTW Edward Teach
AACDDEEIMOP Campodeidae
AACDDEEIMPS aides-de-camp
AACDDEEIORR Eddie Arcaro
AACDDEFHNRT handcrafted
AACDDEGILNR leading card
AACDDEGINOY Dodecagynia
AACDDEGNNRY gandy dancer
AACDDEHINPP handicapped
AACDDEHKLNS slack-handed
AACDDEILNOR endocardial
AACDDEINRTU candidature
AACDDEINTUU nudicaudate
AACDDIIINSS candidiasis
AACDDIJORTU adjudicator
AACDDIKNORS Adirondacks
AACDDNORRTY dot and carry
AACDEEEFLSW weasel-faced
AACDEEEHHRT head teacher
AACDEEELNPS lance pesade
AACDEEEMPRS speed camera
AACDEEENSTV sede vacante
AACDEEEORRS Droseraceae
AACDEEEPPRT peace-parted
AACDEEFFINT caffeinated
AACDEEFILRR free radical
AACDEEGGLNW waggle dance
AACDEEGHINP phagedaenic
AACDEEGHNRR Grande Arche
AACDEEGILNS leading case
AACDEEGKPPR prepackaged
AACDEEGKPSS deck-passage
AACDEEHHIMN machine head
AACDEEHIIMR Chimaeridae
AACDEEHILMX hexadecimal
AACDEEHILNR Heracleidan
AACDEEHIMMN machine-made
AACDEEHIMNR Archimedean
AACDEEHLPST sphacelated
AACDEEHMOOT come to a head
AACDEEHNNOS Dean Acheson
AACDEEHRRST Sacred Heart
AACDEEHRSSV headscarves
AACDEEIILRS deracialise
AACDEEIILRZ deracialize
AACDEEIIRTV eradicative
AACDEEILNRS calendarise
AACDEEILNRZ calendarize
AACDEEILPST seed capital
AACDEEILRSS desacralise
AACDEEILRSZ desacralize
AACDEEILRTV declarative
AACDEEILSTT elasticated
AACDEEIMORV video camera
AACDEEINNNT dance in a net
AACDEEINPST encapsidate
AACDEEJKPRT drape jacket
AACDEEKLNPP pack and peel
AACDEELLMOS Camaldolese
AACDEELLNOT lanceolated
AACDEELLRSS class-leader
AACDEELLSTT castellated
AACDEELMOPR cameleopard
AACDEELPSTU decapsulate
AACDEEMNNTV advancement
AACDEEMNOSU Osmundaceae
AACDEENNOTV advance note
AACDEENNPRY penny arcade
AACDEENOPRR opera-dancer
AACDEENQRSU square dance
square-dance
AACDEENSSSV sedes vacans
AACDEENTUVX unexcavated
AACDEFFGLOS scaffoldage
AACDEFGORSY days of grace
AACDEFILNOT defalcation
AACDEFIMNOT madefaction
AACDEFINRUX fricandeaux
AACDEFLLNOR floral dance
AACDEFLLOTW tallow-faced
AACDEFORSTW face towards
AACDEGGILMO demagogical
AACDEGGILOP pedagogical
AACDEGGIORR carriage dog
AACDEGHHNNS change hands
AACDEGHIINT teaching aid
AACDEGHIPRS cigar-shaped
AACDEGHNPRT garden patch
AACDEGIIMNT diamagnetic
AACDEGIMNNS damascening
AACDEGLNRSU Angus Calder
AACDEGLRSTU castle-guard
AACDEGLRTTU cattle guard
AACDEGORSTU sugar-coated
AACDEHHNRRT charter-hand
AACDEHIIMRT adiathermic
AACDEHIINRT Trachinidae
AACDEHILORS icosahedral
AACDEHILRRX Richard Axel
AACDEHIMPRY pachydermia

AACDEHIMRTY diathermacy
AACDEHINOTT anticathode
AACDEHINPPR handicapper
AACDEHINRST cantharides
AACDEHINRTU Hardicanute
AACDEHIPPRT crappit-head
AACDEHIRRTV architraved
AACDEHJLMOT Maja Clothed
AACDEHKLNNR crankhandle
AACDEHLMPRY pachydermal
AACDEHLNOST close at hand
AACDEHLNRWX wax-chandler
AACDEHLOOPP Cephalopoda
AACDEHMNOTY one-day match
AACDEHMORSU Machaerodus
AACDEHMRRTT tetradrachm
AACDEHORSTY cathode rays
AACDEHPRRRS card-sharper
AACDEHRRTYY carry the day
AACDEIILMNO Iain MacLeod
AACDEIILMRT diametrical
AACDEIILMRV vice-admiral
AACDEIILPRR pericardial
AACDEIIMPRT pre-adamitic
AACDEIIMSTT diastematic
AACDEIINNNO Indian Ocean
AACDEIINNNR incarnadine
AACDEIINNRT incardinate
AACDEIINORT eradication
AACDEIINPRR pericardian
AACDEIIORTV radioactive
AACDEIIPRST paediatrics
AACDEIIPRSU parasuicide
AACDEIJRSTU res judicata
AACDEILLLTY dialectally
AACDEILLMOT Camaldolite
AACDEILLOTV La Dolce Vita
AACDEILMNOT declamation
AACDEILNOPT pedal-action
AACDEILNORT declaration
redactional
AACDEILNOTU educational
AACDEILNPRS Iceland spar
AACDEILNPTU paniculated
AACDEILNRRU ruridecanal
AACDEILNRSS radicalness
scandaliser
AACDEILNRST calendarist
AACDEILNRSZ scandalizer
AACDEILOPRR praecordial
AACDEILORRT redactorial
AACDEILPSSY display case
AACDEILRSTT strait-laced
AACDEILRTTU articulated
AACDEILRTTY dairy cattle
AACDEILRTUU auriculated
AACDEILSTTT stalactited
AACDEIMNNOP pandemoniac✧
AACDEIMNORT demarcation
AACDEIMNORY aerodynamic
AACDEIMNORZ Cameron Diaz
AACDEIMOPRS paramedicos
AACDEINNORT carnationed
AACDEINNOTT decantation
AACDEINOPRS caparisoned
AACDEINORST stenocardia
AACDEINOTUV coadunative
AACDEINRSST incrassated
AACDEIOPRTT parti-coated
AACDELLLMOY Ally Macleod
AACDELLMORY dolly camera
AACDELLNOTY anecdotally
AACDELMNNOR Roman candle
AACDELMORST closet drama
AACDELMORTY declamatory
AACDELNPTTY pentadactyl
AACDELOOPRT proctodaeal
AACDELORRTY declaratory
AACDELRTTTY tetradactyl
AACDEMNOSTU cat-and-mouse
AACDEMNPRTY payment card
AACDENNRSUV under canvas
AACDENOPRTT pedantocrat
AACDENPSTTU cut and paste
AACDEOPRRRS road scraper
AACDEOPRTTY party-coated
AACDEORRTVW draw a covert
AACDEPRSTUY carte du pays
AACDFFIINOO afficionado
AACDFIILLTY fatidically
AACDFIILRRT fratricidal
AACDFIINOOS aficionados
AACDFINNRYY Nancy Friday
AACDFINOOTY day of action
AACDGGHIIST Haggadistic
AACDGGHIKNU Dick Gaughan
AACDGHIOPRR cardiograph
AACDGHOPRSU cardophagus
AACDGIILNRS radical sign
AACDGILMNNS slam dancing
AACDGILNPRY playing-card
AACDGIMRRTU dramaturgic
AACDGINNSST sand-casting
AACDGLMORTY dactylogram
AACDGNNOOTY contango-day
AACDHIIMRTT mithradatic✧
AACDHIIOPRS aphrodisiac
AACDHIJMNSW jam sandwich
AACDHIKLLNO kachina doll
AACDHILMOPY holiday camp
AACDHILOPRS rhapsodical
AACDHIMMNTU I'm a Dutchman
AACDHIMNNSW sandwich man
AACDHIMORSU Machairodus
AACDHINPPTY pitch and pay
AACDHLNOSYY halcyon days
AACDHMOPRSY psychodrama
AACDHNQSSTU snatch squad
AACDHOORRTU Urochordata
AACDIIILMOT idiomatical
AACDIILMNRU adminicular
AACDIILMNTT mid-Atlantic

Words marked ✧ can also be spelled with one or more capital letters

AACDIILMPRY pyramidical
AACDIILNOPX doli incapax
AACDIILNSTV vandalistic
AACDIILORTT dictatorial
AACDIIMMRST dramaticism
AACDIIMNOPS dipsomaniac
AACDIINNORS icosandrian
AACDIIORTVY Victoria Day
AACDIJKKNSW Jack Dawkins
AACDIJNNORT cardan joint
AACDIKNNRRU rack and ruin
AACDILLLOOR coralloidal
AACDILLMNOY nomadically
AACDILLMNYY dynamically
AACDILLMOPS psalmodical
AACDILLNORS coral island
AACDILLRSTY drastically
AACDILMNSSU musical sand
AACDILMOPSS spasmodical
AACDILMPRSU Admiral's Cup
AACDILNPSST landscapist
AACDILORTTY artiodactyl
AACDILOSUUY audaciously
AACDIMMMRUX maximum card
AACDIMMOOTY mycodomatia
AACDIMNNOOR monocardian
AACDIMNNOTU manducation
AACDIMNORST nostradamic
AACDINNOOTU coadunation
AACDINNPPSS spic and span
AACDINOSTTU at a discount
AACDJKLNOSY Lady Jackson
AACDKLNOORT cool-tankard
AACDKNORRTW dock-warrant
AACDLLORTYY loyalty card
AACDLMNOOTY condylomata
AACDLMNORRS Lord Scarman
AACDMMNNOOP common panda
AACDMNORTUY manducatory
AACDMOORSTU catadromous
AACDOOPRSST capodastros
AACDRRSTTTU custard tart
AACEEEFINRS scène à faire
AACEEEGGLNU aleggeaunce
AACEEEHKKTT take the cake
AACEEEHKMPT make the pace
AACEEEHLMOT haematocele
AACEEEHLRSW Chelsea ware
AACEEEHMRTT tame cheater
AACEEEHPRST space heater
AACEEEIRRSV service area
AACEEEJMNTT ejectamenta
AACEEELNPSW a clean sweep
AACEEELPSVV escape valve
AACEEFFLLNN face flannel
AACEEFFMNRT Raman effect
AACEEFGORRY year of grace
AACEEFILLTT lattice-leaf
AACEEFILMTT acetate film
AACEEFIMNSS misfeasance
AACEEFIRRTV rarefactive
AACEEFKLMSU acesulfame K
AACEEFLLPTT cleft palate
AACEEFNNNOS non-feasance
AACEEFNORRT confarreate
AACEEFNORST Sea of Nectar
AACEEGGNRSW swagger cane
AACEEGHIMRS search image
AACEEGHLMNR Charlemagne
AACEEGHLMTU league match
AACEEGHLRST Castlereagh
AACEEGHNOPR chaperonage
AACEEGHNPRR crapehanger
AACEEGHRRST gatecrasher
AACEEGIKMNP peacemaking
AACEEGILLLY elegiacally
AACEEGILLNR Gracie Allen
AACEEGILLNV evangelical
AACEEGILMNS seaming lace
AACEEGIMNOR Moringaceae
AACEEGINNRR carrageenin
AACEEGINPRT paragenetic
AACEEGJMNSY James Cagney
AACEEGKORTT Cottage Rake
AACEEGKORTU take courage
AACEEGLLNOS collagenase
AACEEGMMORT macrogamete
AACEEGMNNOR German Ocean
AACEEGORTTV great octave
AACEEHHLTUX hexateuchal
AACEEHHMPTY chamaephyte
AACEEHILMNR Amelanchier
AACEEHILNRT Heraclitean
AACEEHILRRT clear the air
AACEEHILSTT aesthetical
AACEEHIMNPT tape machine
AACEEHIMPPR papier-mâché
AACEEHINSTT anaesthetic
AACEEHKLLSW Haeckel's law
AACEEHLLNRT chantarelle
AACEEHLMNNS channel seam
AACEEHLNNPY anencephaly
AACEEHLNNSV clean-shaven
AACEEHLNPTY phlyctaenae
AACEEHLNSTT The Analects
AACEEHLORTT leather-coat
AACEEHLPRRT arch-prelate
AACEEHLRTWY clear the way
AACEEHMNPPT appeachment
AACEEHMPRST spermatheca
AACEEHNRRSS harness race
AACEEHPSTTY stay the pace
AACEEHRRTTT tetrarchate
AACEEIILMRR Marie Claire
AACEEIIMNPR American Pie
AACEEIIMNRS Americanise
AACEEIIMNRZ Americanize
AACEEIIMNST Scitamineae
AACEEIIMPST septicaemia
AACEEIJLTUV ejaculative
AACEEIJMNPS Cape jasmine
AACEEIKKTTW take a wicket

AACEEIKLLRW Alice Walker
AACEEIKMNRT make certain
AACEEIKNSVW view askance
AACEEIKPTTV take captive
AACEEILLMNS mésalliance
miscellanea
AACEEILMMOT camomile tea
AACEEILMPRU Primulaceae
AACEEILMTVX exclamative
AACEEILNNRS encarnalise
AACEEILNNRZ encarnalize
AACEEILNRTT intercalate
AACEEILOPST Psilotaceae
AACEEILORST aeroelastic
AACEEILRRST secretarial
AACEEILRTTV altercative
AACEEILSSTT atelectasis
AACEEIMMNRT amerciament
AACEEIMMORS Mesoamerica
AACEEIMNNNT maintenance
AACEEIMNOTT matinée coat
AACEEIMNVWX Mexican wave
AACEEIMORRT araeometric
AACEEIMRSSU eremacausis
AACEEINNNRT centenarian
AACEEINNRRT reincarnate
AACEEINNRSS necessarian
renaissance✧
AACEEINRSTT tea canister
AACEEIPRRTV prevaricate
AACEEIRRRVW carrier wave
AACEEIRRSST tracasserie
AACEEIRRSTT secretariat
AACEEJJNQSU Jean Jacques
AACEEJKLNOS Leos Janácek
AACEEJKMSTT steam jacket
AACEEJKRTTW water jacket
AACEEKLLNST alkalescent
AACEEKLMPRT marketplace
AACEEKMPSTT steam packet
AACEEKNPRST carpet snake
AACEELLLTUV valleculate
AACEELLNRRW crawler lane
AACEELLORSV Ellora caves
AACEELMMRST steamer clam
AACEELMNPRU emparlaunce
AACEELMORST coarse metal
AACEELMORSY Mary Seacole
AACEELMPPSS sample space
AACEELNNPUZ Paul Cézanne
AACEELNOPSY play one's ace
AACEELNPSTU encapsulate
AACEELNSSTT sclate-stane
AACEELNTTTU tentaculate
AACEELPPRST spacer plate
AACEELPRSTV space travel
AACEELQRRUW lacquerware
AACEELRRTTT treacle tart
AACEELRSTTW Alec Stewart
AACEEMNORRW career woman
AACEEMNORST ocean-stream
AACEEMNOSTU amentaceous
AACEEMRRSVY cyma reversa
AACEENPRRTT pattern race
AACEENRRSSU reassurance
AACEENRRTUV averruncate
AACEFFHINRS affranchise
AACEFFIIIRS fieri facias
AACEFFIIRTV affricative
AACEFFILNOT affectional
AACEFFINOTT affectation
AACEFFIOSSY Assay Office
AACEFFKNORS saffron cake
AACEFGGHINR chafing-gear
AACEFGHINOR change of air
AACEFGHINRR far-reaching
AACEFGILNOR Fra Angelico
AACEFGINPRS spacefaring
AACEFGLNORT conflagrate
AACEFGLOOTT cottage loaf
AACEFHISSTW wash its face
AACEFHMSTTY safety match
AACEFIILLNS fiançailles
AACEFIILNRT interfacial
AACEFIILNRV acriflavine
AACEFILLLMY malefically
AACEFILLORR for all I care
AACEFILMNOT malefaction
AACEFILMRSU surface mail
AACEFILTTUV facultative
AACEFINORRT rarefaction
AACEFINORRV vicar-forane
AACEFINORSU farinaceous
AACEFINORTT fractionate
AACEFKNNRTU tank furnace
AACEFKRRSTT fast-tracker
AACEFLLORTY Carley float
AACEFLMNORS roman à clefs
AACEFLMORSU formal cause
AACEFLMORTY malefactory
AACEFLNSSTU factualness
AACEFMNRTUU manufacture
AACEFNPRRTT parentcraft
AACEFORRSTT fast reactor
AACEGGILPTU Tegucigalpa
AACEGGINRRU gun carriage
AACEGGINRSV saving grace
AACEGGMUUUV vacuum gauge
AACEGGORSTW swagger coat
AACEGHHNOTT chaetognath
AACEGHILLRT lethargical
AACEGHILNOR archegonial
AACEGHILOOT Oligochaeta
AACEGHILOPR archipelago✧
AACEGHILORT The Agricola
AACEGHIMNOP phaenogamic
AACEGHIOPRR areographic
AACEGHLLMNS small change
AACEGHLLSSV cheval-glass
AACEGHLOORY archaeology
AACEGHNORTU autochanger
AACEGHPRTTU gutta-percha

AACEGIILLPR	periglacial
AACEGIILMNT	enigmatical
AACEGIILNSV	vice anglais
AACEGIIMNNT	magnetician
AACEGIIMRRS	miscarriage
AACEGIIOPRT	Areopagitic
AACEGIKLNNW	walking-cane
AACEGIKLNRW	race-walking
	walking race
AACEGIKLNSW	walking case
AACEGIKMMRR	Magic Marker®
	magic marker
AACEGIKMNPT	meat packing
AACEGILLLNY	angelically
	englacially
AACEGILLLOR	allegorical
AACEGILLMMR	calligramme
AACEGILLMNN	name-calling
AACEGILLNPY	callipygean
AACEGILLOOR	aerological
AACEGILLOPS	plagioclase
AACEGILLRTV	village cart
AACEGILLTUV	victuallage
AACEGILNOVX	vox angelica
AACEGILNPRY	panegyrical
AACEGILOSTU	cataloguise
AACEGILOTUV	coagulative
AACEGILOTUZ	cataloguize
AACEGILRSTT	strategical
AACEGIMMNOR	micromanage
AACEGIMMNRT	engrammatic
AACEGIMNNOR	cinema-organ
AACEGIMNNPR	permanganic
AACEGIMNOPT	compaginate
AACEGIMNORS	Reaganomics
AACEGIMNRTY	city manager
AACEGIMQRSU	magic square
AACEGINNRTW	watering can
AACEGINPPRT	rate-capping
AACEGINPRTW	watering-cap
AACEGINPSTT	peat-casting
AACEGIRTTTU	acte gratuit
AACEGKOPRTU	package tour
AACEGLNOPRS	scrape along
AACEGLNRRTU	rectangular
AACEGMNOORR	Graeco-Roman
AACEGMNOSTY	gynaecomast
AACEGNNRRTY	gantry crane
AACEGNOORSU	onagraceous
AACEGRRSSTU	caster sugar
AACEHHILSTX	hexastichal
AACEHHINTTT	Cat in the Hat
AACEHIILLMV	Machiavelli
AACEHIILLOR	allocheiria
AACEHIILMPT	epithalamic
AACEHIILRSV	cavalierish
AACEHIILSTT	atheistical
AACEHIIMMNS	Manichaeism
AACEHILLMNO	melancholia
AACEHILLNPP	Ian Chappell
AACEHILLNTU	hallucinate
AACEHILLOSW	social whale
AACEHILLPTY	aphetically
AACEHILLRTW	Willa Cather
AACEHILMMNS	Mischa Elman
AACEHILMNNN	manna-lichen
AACEHILMRSV	vice-marshal
AACEHILMRTU	rheumatical
AACEHILMSST	thalassemic
AACEHILNPST	chainplates
AACEHILNRTT	intrathecal
AACEHILNTTU	authentical
AACEHILPPSS	Cephalaspis
AACEHILRRRT	trierarchal
AACEHILRSTT	theatricals
AACEHIMMSTT	mathematics
AACEHIMNNNO	nanomachine
AACEHIMNNOT	technomania
AACEHIMNNOY	haemocyanin
AACEHIMNRRS	in arm's reach
AACEHIMORST	achromatise
AACEHIMORTT	haematocrit
AACEHIMORTZ	achromatize
AACEHIMOSTT	haemostatic
AACEHINOPRS	coin a phrase
AACEHINOTTU	Teotihuacán
AACEHINOTTY	thiocyanate
AACEHINPPRR	paranephric
AACEHINPRRT	Petrarchian
AACEHIPRSTU	haruspicate
AACEHKMRRRT	Charter Mark
AACEHKNRSSS	harness-cask
AACEHKPRRST	carpet shark
AACEHLLOPRY	chapel royal
AACEHLLRSSW	Charles's law
AACEHLMNRTW	law-merchant
AACEHLMNSTU	steam launch
AACEHLMORSY	Charles Mayo
AACEHLNOPRT	anchor plate
AACEHLOOPRR	Rhopalocera
AACEHLOPTUY	autocephaly
AACEHLSSTTT	the last cast
AACEHMMNNRT	merchantman
AACEHMMOTWY	come what may
AACEHMNNRST	transmanche
AACEHMNORSU	rhamnaceous
AACEHMNPSTY	cash payment
AACEHNNORST	anthracnose
AACEHNOPRVY	anchovy-pear
AACEHNOPSWW	weapon-schaw
AACEHNOSTUY	an easy touch
AACEHNPPSWW	wappenschaw
AACEHOPRSTT	catastrophe
AACEHOPSSTU	spathaceous
AACEHPPRRST	starch paper
AACEHPRRSTY	search party
AACEHPRSTUX	purchase tax
AACEIIKLMNT	kinematical
AACEIILLMNS	misalliance
AACEIILLNRT	lacertilian
AACEIILLNRV	incarvillea
AACEIILLRTV	leviratical

AACEIILMRRR mail-carrier
AACEIILMRSV cavalierism
AACEIILNPRR pericranial
AACEIILNRRT interracial
AACEIILPPRR pericarpial
AACEIILPPTT Pitti Palace
AACEIILPPTV applicative
AACEIILPRSV avec plaisir
AACEIIMMNRS Americanism
AACEIIMNNPT mine-captain
AACEIIMNRST Americanist
AACEIIMNRTV carminative
AACEIIMQSTU semi-aquatic
AACEIINORTT ratiocinate
AACEIIOSSTV associative
AACEIIPPRTT participate
AACEIJLNOTU ejaculation
AACEIJQSTTU Jacques Tati
AACEIKLLOPU leucoplakia
AACEIKLRSTU Lake Scutari
AACEILLLSTY elastically
AACEILLMNOR mineral coal
AACEILLMNPT implacental
AACEILLMNRY clay mineral
AACEILLMNSU animalcules
AACEILLMPRY miracle play
AACEILLMPUX amplexicaul
AACEILLNPRU Lupercalian
AACEILLNTTY tetanically
AACEILLNTVY venatically
AACEILLOPRR Procellaria
AACEILLPRRT Caterpillar®
caterpillar
AACEILLPTVY capital levy
AACEILLRRTY erratically
AACEILLRSST rascalliest
AACEILMNOPT cleptomania
AACEILMNOPY alycompaine
AACEILMNORT reclamation
AACEILMNOTX exclamation
AACEILMNPTU pneumatical
AACEILMORRT crematorial
AACEILMOSSU alismaceous
AACEILMPRST spermatical
AACEILMPSTT metaplastic
palmatisect
AACEILMRTTU matriculate
AACEILNNOSS ascensional
AACEILNNPTT pentactinal
AACEILNNRTU antinuclear
AACEILNOPRT anaplerotic
AACEILNORST ancestorial
AACEILNORTT altercation
AACEILNPSTU incapsulate
AACEILNRRTU retinacular
AACEILNRRTY intercalary
AACEILNRTTT tetractinal
AACEILOPPTY palaeotypic
AACEILOPSST Castile soap
AACEILORTVV aortic valve
AACEILPRSTU spiraculate
AACEILPRTTU catapultier
particulate
tau particle
AACEILPSSUU Aesculapius
AACEILRSSUV vascularise
AACEILRSUVZ vascularize
AACEILSTUVY causatively
AACEIMMOSTT metasomatic
AACEIMNNOOR Cameroonian
AACEIMNNOTT contaminate
AACEIMNOORT erotomaniac
AACEIMNOPRT emancipator
AACEIMNORSU oceanariums
AACEIMNPRST campestrian
AACEIMNPRSU parascenium
AACEIMOPRTV comparative
AACEIMPRRRY primary care
AACEINNORTT recantation
AACEINNORTX excarnation
AACEINNOSTW Isaac Newton
AACEINNRSTU unsectarian
AACEINNRTTT interactant
AACEINOPRST ceratopsian
AACEINORRTU au contraire
AACEINORRTY reactionary
AACEINORSTU aeronautics
AACEINPQRTU preacquaint
AACEINRSSTU sanctuarise
AACEINRSTTY asynartetic
AACEINRSTUZ sanctuarize
AACEIOPPRRT appreciator
AACEIOPRSTT aspect ratio
AACEIORSSTT aerostatics
AACEIORSTTW coast-waiter
AACEIPRRSTT stair carpet
AACEJKQRRTU quarter-jack
AACEJLORTUY ejaculatory
AACEJNORUWY conjure away
AACEKKLNOOS look askance
AACEKKLRRTW track-walker
AACEKLMRSTY smart-alecky
AACEKLQRSUV quacksalver
AACELLLNOOV Leoncavallo
AACELLLORTT total recall
AACELLMMORS sarcolemmal
AACELLMNRSU Marcus Allen
AACELLMOSTV small octave
AACELLNRSTY ancestrally
AACELLOPRSU acarpellous
AACELLOPRTY acropetally
AACELMMRSUU mare clausum
AACELMNNNOT cannon-metal
AACELMORRSU scale armour
AACELMORSTU emasculator
AACELMORTXY exclamatory
AACELMRSSST master-class
AACELMRTTTX malt-extract
AACELNNORWY canon lawyer
AACELNNRSTT transcalent
AACELNOOSSU solanaceous
AACELNORSTT translocate

AACELOOPPRS laparoscope
AACELOPPRTU appeal court
AACELPRRSSU superscalar
AACELPRSSTT plaster cast
AACELPRSSTY play-actress
AACELQRTUUU aquaculture
AACELRSTUUV vasculature
AACEMNORRST Sam Torrance
AACEMNORSUY mornay sauce
AACEMOOSTTU tomato sauce
AACENNNORTW water cannon
AACENOOPSSU saponaceous
AACENORRTVY contrayerva
AACENORSSST ansate cross
AACEOOPSSTU sapotaceous
AACEOPPRRSW Cape sparrow
AACEOPPRSUY papyraceous
AACFFIINORT affrication
AACFFIOORTU Out of Africa
AACFFIORRTT trafficator
AACFFMORRTY factory farm
AACFGIINNST fascinating
AACFGILLSUU Iguaçu Falls
AACFGLNNORT conflagrant
AACFGLORRTY Carl Fogarty
AACFHIORSTU South Africa
AACFHORRTTU authorcraft
AACFHPSSTTU upcast-shaft
AACFIILLNNY financially
AACFIILNNOR Californian
AACFIILORTT facilitator
AACFIINNOST fascination
AACFIKRSTTT first-attack
AACFILLNOTV lactoflavin
AACFILLNRTY frantically
AACFILMORRS scalariform
AACFILNORST infracostal
AACFILRRRTU curtal friar
AACFIMMNOPR campaniform
AACFINORRTY fractionary
AACFKLMSUUV vacuum flask
AACFLNORRTU currant loaf
AACFMNORSTW craftswoman
AACFMNORTUY manufactory
AACFNORSTUU anfractuous
AACFOORRRTY carry too far
AACGGHHMOOR Graham Gooch
AACGGILLLOO algological
AACGGILLNPP call gapping
AACGGILLOOR agrological
AACGGILNOSY synagogical
AACGGILOPTY ptyalagogic
AACGHHILNOT Chilognatha
AACGHHPRTYY tachygraphy
AACGHIIPPRS pasigraphic
AACGHIKMMNT matchmaking
AACGHIKMNTW watchmaking
AACGHILLPRY calligraphy
graphically
AACGHILNNOT gnathonical
AACGHIMNNTW man-watching
AACGHIMNRSY gymnasiarch
AACGHINPPRY Phrygian cap
AACGHINRRST starch-grain
AACGHIOPRTU autographic
AACGHIPRRST graphic arts
AACGHKNPTUY naughty pack
AACGHLMOORU chaulmoogra
AACGHLNOORY arachnology
AACGHNOOPPR coprophagan
AACGHNOOPRR coronagraph
AACGHOPRRTY cartography
AACGHOPRSSU sarcophagus
AACGIILLMNS Gallicanism
AACGIILLNTV vacillating
AACGIILLNTW call waiting
AACGIILLOOX axiological
AACGIILMNNS Anglicanism
AACGIILMSTT stalagmitic
stigmatical
AACGIILNNNT lancinating
AACGIILNNOR Carolingian
AACGIILNOST agonistical
AACGIIMRSTT magistratic
AACGIINOSTT castigation
AACGIINPTTV captivating
AACGIINRSST staircasing
AACGIJNNRTU jaunting car
AACGIKLNRTY tracklaying
AACGILLNORY organically
AACGILLOPST post-glacial
AACGILMNOOR agronomical
AACGILMNSTY gymnastical
AACGILNOOTU coagulation
AACGILNORSS cors anglais
AACGILOORST acarologist
AACGILOSSUY sagaciously
AACGIMMMNOU gum ammoniac
AACGIMMNORR marconigram
AACGIMMNRTU ungrammatic
AACGIMNNRST canting arms
AACGIMNSTTY syntagmatic
AACGIMOPRTY Cryptogamia
AACGINNOTTV noctivagant
AACGINORSST nasogastric
AACGINPRVYZ crazy paving
AACGIORSTTY castigatory
AACGKMMOSST gamma stocks
AACGLLLRTUU cultural lag
AACGLLNOOTY octagonally
AACGLMNOOPY campanology
AACGLOORTUY coagulatory
AACGMNORSTY gastromancy
AACGNSSSTUU agnus castus
AACGORRSSTU castor sugar
AACGRSSSSTU tussac grass
AACHHIIMPPT amphipathic
AACHHINORRW chain harrow
AACHHJKMNOR John Rackham
AACHHLORTTT throatlatch
AACHIIINRST christiania✧
AACHIILLNRV arch-villain

AACHIILOPRT	arctophilia
AACHIILORST	ahistorical
AACHIILPPST	capital ship
AACHIIMNNOT	machination
AACHIIMNOPR	prochain ami
AACHIIMNSST	shamanistic
AACHIINPPST	captainship
AACHIINRSSU	saurischian
AACHIKLRTWY	charity walk
AACHIKMNORV	Markov chain
AACHIKNOOPT	Captain Hook
AACHIKORSTU	auto ricksha
AACHILLMNOP	Campion Hall
AACHILLMOPY	malacophily
AACHILLNOPV	Pancho Villa
AACHILLOPRY	parochially
AACHILMNOOS	monochasial
AACHILMOPPP	hippocampal
AACHILMOSTU	moustachial
AACHILNOPPS	pansophical
AACHILNOPRT	anthropical
AACHILNOPRY	paronychial
AACHILNORST	thrasonical
AACHILQRRSU	squirarchal
AACHIMMNOSS	Simon Schama
AACHIMMNOTY	mythomaniac
AACHIMMORST	achromatism
AACHIMNNORS	anachronism
AACHIMNNORV	Rachmaninov
AACHIMNOPRY	prochain amy
AACHIMNOPTT	phantomatic
AACHIMNORRU	chain armour
AACHIMNORSS	maraschinos
AACHIMNOTTY	Titanomachy
AACHIMOPPRR	paramorphic
AACHINNNOTY	anthocyanin
AACHINORSST	anthracosis
AACHINORSTW	waist anchor
AACHINRSSTU	Carthusians
AACHIORRRTT	arch-traitor
AACHIPPSSTY	pataphysics
	'pataphysics
AACHIPRSTTU	parachutist
AACHLLLMOOY	amyl alcohol
AACHLLLORSW	shawl collar
AACHLLOOSTU	holocaustal
AACHLMNOOPS	paschal moon
AACHLMORRTY	lachrymator
AACHLNNOOTU	anacoluthon
AACHLNOPSTU	Polacanthus
AACHLPPPPYY	happy-clappy
AACHMMRRSUU	harum-scarum
AACHMNNOORW	anchor-woman
AACHMNOSTWY	yachtswoman
AACHMOORSTU	achromatous
AACHMOSTTWY	cost what may
AACHNNOOPTT	not a patch on
AACHNNOORSU	anachronous
AACHNNOORTY	Anthony Caro
AACHORRSTTY	Thyrostraca
AACHQRTTUWZ	quartz watch

AACIIILNNOT	laciniation
AACIIILNOST	laicisation
AACIIILNOTZ	laicization
AACIIILNPST	initial caps
AACIIILPPRT	participial
AACIIJNOTTT	jactitation
AACIIKLNOPS	Nikola Pasic
AACIIKLPRST	risk capital
AACIILLMNRW	criminal law
AACIILLMRTU	multiracial
AACIILLNOOT	coalitional
AACIILLNOTV	cavillation
	vacillation
AACIILLNTTY	titanically✧
AACIILLPRTY	capillarity
	piratically
AACIILLRSTY	satirically
AACIILMNNOT	antinomical
AACIILMNOST	anomalistic
AACIILMNRRW	war criminal
AACIILMNSTT	Atlanticism
AACIILMPRST	prismatical
AACIILNNNOT	lancination
AACIILNOPPT	application
AACIILNPRTU	puritanical
AACIILNPRTY	patricianly
AACIILNPTTY	antitypical
AACIILNRSTU	unsatirical
AACIILNSTTT	Atlanticist
AACIILNTTYY	analyticity
AACIILOPRST	piscatorial
AACIILPRSTT	patristical
AACIILPRTUY	piacularity
AACIILRRTUU	utricularia
AACIILSSTTT	statistical
AACIIMNNOPT	mancipation
AACIIMNNORT	animatronic
AACIIMNNOTU	acumination
AACIIMNOOTX	toxicomania
AACIIMNOSTT	mastication
AACIIMORTTY	aromaticity
AACIINNNORT	incarnation✧
AACIINNNOTT	incantation
AACIINOOSST	association
AACIINOPRTT	anticipator
AACIINOPTTV	captivation
AACIINORTTV	vaticinator
AACIINOSTTV	vacationist
AACIINPPRTT	participant
AACIINPSSTT	antispastic
AACIIRSTTTY	triatic stay
AACIKLORSTT	tailor's tack
AACILLLMMSS	small claims
AACILLLOPST	alloplastic
AACILLMOSTY	somatically
AACILLNOPRS	rapscallion
AACILLNOPTY	polyactinal
AACILLNRTUW	curtain wall
AACILLOOPST	apostolical
AACILLOPRSY	prosaically
AACILLORTVY	vacillatory

AACILLOSSUY	salaciously
AACILLPRTUU	apicultural
AACILLPRTUY	capitularly
AACILLPSSTY	spastically
AACILLRRUUY	auricularly
AACILMNNOPT	complainant
AACILMNOOTU	autonomical
AACILMNOOTX	taxonomical
AACILMNOPRT	proclaimant
AACILMNOPST	complaisant
AACILMNORTU	calumniator
AACILMPPRSY	paralympics
AACILNNNOTU	cannulation
AACILNNOPSV	Pan-Slavonic
AACILNNOPSY	calypsonian
AACILNOORRT	al contrario
AACILNOOTUV	vacuolation
AACILNOPRTY	coplanarity
AACILNORTVY	clairvoyant
AACILOPPRTY	applicatory
AACILOPRSUY	rapaciously
AACILOPRTTU	capitulator
AACILOPSTTU	autoplastic
AACILORRTTU	articulator
AACILORRTUY	oracularity
AACILPPRSTW	plastic wrap
AACILRSTUVY	vascularity
AACIMNNNOTT	contaminant
AACIMNNOTTU	mountain cat
AACIMNOOSTT	anastomotic
AACIMNOPRTY	mancipatory
AACIMNPRSTT	transit camp
AACIMOPRSTT	comparatist
AACIMORSTTY	masticatory
AACINNNORTU	annunciator
AACINNORSTT	transaction
AACINNORTTY	incantatory
AACINNRRSTU	transuranic
AACINOOOPPT	apocopation
AACINOPPSTT	post captain
AACINOPRSTT	pantisocrat
AACINOPRSTU	carnaptious
AACINORSTTU	astronautic
AACINRSTTUY	Tracy Austin
AACKLNOTTUY	you can't talk
AACLMMOPSSY	mycoplasmas
AACLNNNOOST	consonantal
AACLNPSTTUU	Tantalus-cup
AACLOOORTVY	royal octavo
AACLOOPPRSY	laparoscopy
AACLOPRSSTU	supracostal
AACLORSTTUU	auscultator
AACMNOPPRTY	part company
AACMNOPRTUY	paramountcy
AACMOORSSTU	sarcomatous
AACMOORSTTY	astrocytoma
AACNOOPRRTT	Pantocrator
AADDDDEEEHL	addle-headed
AADDDEEHHRY	hydra-headed
AADDDEIILPT	dilapidated
AADDDEILRRT	tarradiddle
AADDDEIOPSY	Dasypodidae
AADDDELNORW	Donald Dewar
AADDDGNOPRR	drag and drop
	drag-and-drop
AADDDISSTVY	St David's Day
AADDEEEHHVY	heavy-headed
AADDEEELLRV	alder-leaved
AADDEEELMNS	Adam's needle
AADDEEFLLRR	Alfred Adler
AADDEEGHLNR	large-handed
AADDEEGHNNR	hand grenade
AADDEEGLRRW	Edward Elgar
AADDEEHHNVY	heavy-handed
AADDEEHHRRT	hard-hearted
AADDEEHHRTW	Edward Heath
AADDEEHKMRT	death-marked
AADDEEHLPRY	paraldehyde
AADDEEHORRW	arrow-headed
AADDEEIKLNS	naked ladies
AADDEEILRSY	sidereal day
AADDEEIMNOZ	a dime a dozen
AADDEEIMRST	dedramatise
AADDEEIMRTZ	dedramatize
AADDEEKMRRT	trademarked
AADDEEMMQUZ	queez-maddam
AADDEENRRTW	Dawn Treader
AADDEENRSSW	Sean Edwards
AADDEEPRRSS	dress parade
AADDEFFLPST	paddle-staff
AADDEFGMNNU	managed fund
AADDEFHLPST	paddle-shaft
AADDEFILMNN	final demand
AADDEGHINRR	hard-grained
AADDEGHIRSV	hard-visaged
AADDEGHNORS	dragon's-head
AADDEGHNRTU	dreadnaught
AADDEGILLNY	leading lady
AADDEGINORT	degradation
	gradationed
AADDEGIRTTY	tardy-gaited
AADDEGLLOOY	logodaedaly
AADDEGNNORS	dragonnades
AADDEHILLLN	hill and dale
AADDEHILLNV	de Havilland
AADDEHINNPT	hand-painted
AADDEHMOOST	ashamed to do
AADDEIILPPP	Pedipalpida
AADDEIKNPRR	park-and-ride
AADDEILNOPR	planar diode
AADDEILNPTY	painted lady
AADDEIMOPRR	period drama
AADDEINRSST	standardise
AADDEINRSTZ	standardize
AADDEIOPRSX	Paradoxides
AADDEIPRRSW	Edward Sapir
AADDEIQRSUY	Yardie squad
AADDEJLMSTU	maladjusted
AADDELLNNSU	unsandalled
AADDELNRSTW	land-steward
AADDELPQRUU	quadrupedal
AADDENRSSST	dastardness

AADDFHNNOOT hand and foot
AADDFILMOUV David Malouf
AADDFIORSTV Star of David
AADDGGHILNN glad-handing
AADDGHILNNR hard landing
AADDGHINRRY daring-hardy
AADDGIILNOV David Ginola
AADDGIILORT digladiator
AADDGJLNRUY Judy Garland
AADDGLMNNOR grand old man
AADDIIINNRT Trinidadian
AADDIILLLRR radial drill
AADDIILOPRT dilapidator
AADDILLNNOS Öland Island
AADDILLOOPR olla-podrida
AADDILMNRUY laundry-maid
AADDIMNOWWW Widow Wadman
AADDINORRST ritardandos
AADDINOTUYY day in, day out
AADDMNORRTY Raymond Dart
AADDNNNORST non-standard
AADEEEFHHRT feather-head
AADEEEFHLLN halfendeale
AADEEEFNRSY free and easy
free-and-easy
AADEEEGGHRS shagge-eared
AADEEEGGRTX exaggerated
AADEEEGLNRV garden leave
AADEEEGLPRS spread eagle
spread-eagle
AADEEEGMNRR Grande Armée
AADEEEHHLRT leather-head
AADEEEHKRTW weak-hearted
AADEEEHLNNR enneahedral
AADEEEHLPRT pale-hearted
AADEEEHMMNS Naseem Hamed
AADEEELNRSV sea lavender
AADEEEMNPRR André Ampère
AADEEEPPRTU depauperate
AADEEFGLLLT flagellated
AADEEFHHLRT half-hearted
AADEEFHIMOT ahead of time
AADEEFHKLOT Lake of Death
AADEEFHOSTT head of state
AADEEFILNRT anti-federal
AADEEFINNTT anti-feedant
AADEEFIRRST Fred Astaire
AADEEFLLNRT trade-fallen
AADEEFLMORT moral defeat
AADEEGHNNOT on the agenda
AADEEGHRTTU The Graduate
AADEEGIKKRR Kierkegaard
AADEEGIKNTV give and take
AADEEGILPSV pale-visaged
AADEEGILRRT laterigrade
AADEEGIMRRT tree diagram
AADEEGINPSU spade guinea
AADEEGINRTU aguardiente
AADEEGLLRUY leaguer-lady
AADEEHHPRST heart-shaped
AADEEHIINRT Atherinidae
AADEEHIMPSS spade mashie
AADEEHJNRRW Wanderjahre
AADEEHKMRRT threadmaker
AADEEHKORTT take the road
AADEEHKQRTU earthquaked
AADEEHLNNRT neanderthal✧
AADEEHLNPPT pad-elephant
AADEEHLNPRT pentahedral
AADEEHLRRTT tetrahedral
AADEEHLRTTT death rattle
AADEEHMNSSS ashamedness
AADEEHMRRTW warm-hearted
AADEEHNRSVW heavenwards
AADEEHPPRRT thread-paper
AADEEIILNNR Dáil Eireann
AADEEIKMNNR make a dinner
AADEEIKNNOT Diane Keaton
AADEEILLMVY mediaevally
AADEEILLNPR plain dealer
AADEEILMNOO Aeolian mode
AADEEILNNRX alexandrine✧
AADEEILNRRV red valerian
AADEEILNRTX alexandrite
AADEEILNSUV leave unsaid
AADEEINNNNR enneandrian
AADEEINPPSW weasand-pipe
AADEEINRSTT tear-stained
AADEEIPPRTV preadaptive
AADEEIRRTTV retardative
AADEEIRSTVV adversative
AADEEISTTVV devastative
AADEEJKMNRR Derek Jarman
AADEEJNOORR rejoneadora
AADEEJPPRWW wapper-jawed
AADEEKLMSST damask-steel
AADEEKMNRUY make unready
AADEELLNTTU landaulette
AADEELLPPPR pappardelle
AADEELMNRSU land-measure
AADEELNNORT alendronate
AADEELNOOST at a loose end
AADEELNPRSS lesser panda
AADEELNPTTT pantaletted
AADEELPRTTT rattle-pated
AADEELRRSTV slave-trader
AADEEMMNSSU assumed name
AADEEMNNNTU antemundane
AADEEMNNSSU Amundsen Sea
AADEEMORTWW water meadow
AADEEMQRRSU masquerader
AADEENNNORV ever and anon
AADEENNNTTT en attendant
AADEENNRTWY Tyne and Wear
AADEENPRSTU unseparated
AADEENRSTVY Veterans Day
AADEENRSWYY New Year's Day
AADEEORRRST rear-roasted
AADEEPQRSTU pas de quatre
AADEERSTTUV Deus avertat
AADEESSTTTY steady state
AADEFFGGRST ragged staff

AADEFGHNRRT grandfather
AADEFGIILNR fair-dealing
AADEFGIISTT fastigiated
AADEFGILNRR Garand rifle
AADEFGLORRT deflagrator
AADEFGLORSU sugar of lead
AADEFGMNNSU fun and games
AADEFHJOSTW jaws of death
AADEFHLLOTW wall of death
AADEFHLRSTV half-starved
AADEFIKLNNR rank and file
AADEFIMNORT foraminated
AADEFLLMMTU flammulated
AADEFLMNNTU fundamental
AADEFLSSTTY steadfastly
AADEFNRRSTY transfer day
AADEFNSSTTU unsteadfast
AADEGGHNRSS haggardness
AADEGGIINRR Gregarinida
AADEGGILLRT draggle-tail
AADEGGILNNR landing gear
AADEGGIORRY Yegor Gaidar
AADEGGLNRSS garden-glass
laggardness
AADEGGMRSST mad staggers
AADEGHIKLNT talking head
AADEGHINRRW hard-wearing
AADEGHINRTU The Guardian
AADEGHINSTY an eight days
AADEGHNRTTT granted that
AADEGIILLRS galliardise
AADEGIILNTT intagliated
AADEGIILPTW pied wagtail
AADEGIINNNT Indian agent
AADEGILLNNP pineal gland
AADEGILMNPR reading-lamp
AADEGILNNRV landgravine
AADEGILNPRT plantigrade
AADEGILNRVW waldgravine
AADEGIMNNRV Venn diagram
AADEGINNTUV unnavigated
AADEGINSTTV devastating
AADEGKLRSSS dark glasses
AADEGLLLORV Glad All Over
AADEGLLNRSS garlandless
AADEGLMMMNO Emma Goldman
AADEGLNRSSU gradualness
AADEGMNRRST Grand Master
grandmaster
AADEGMORSSW meadow-grass
AADEGNNOPRU unparagoned
AADEGNNPRRT grandparent
AADEGNPRRTY garden party
AADEGOOPRST Gasteropoda
AADEGOPPRTT targa-topped
AADEHIILNRT antheridial
AADEHIILOPP paedophilia
AADEHIINNRR Adrian Henri
AADEHIINPTY diaphaneity
AADEHILMMMO Mohammed Ali
AADEHILMNOP Monadelphia
AADEHILMNPY Nymphalidae
AADEHILRTTW Wild at Heart
AADEHIMNNOO hedonomania
AADEHINOPPY hypnopaedia
AADEHINOSTT head-station
AADEHIPSTXY asphyxiated
AADEHJMNORS John-a-dreams
AADEHKMNPPR Hampden Park
AADEHLMNRRS marshlander
AADEHLMNSUY unashamedly
AADEHLNORSV Harold Evans
AADEHLRRRUY Harry Lauder
AADEHLRSTVY harvest lady
AADEHNORSST hard as stone
AADEHNPTUWY unpathwayed
AADEHPPRSST strap-shaped
AADEHPRSSTT spatterdash
AADEIIIRRTV irradiative
AADEIILMNST mediastinal
AADEIILMORT mediatorial
AADEIILNOTU Nautiloidea
AADEIILNRRT interradial
AADEIILNSST stadia lines
AADEIIMNNOT deamination
AADEIINORRT reradiation
AADEIIPRSSS pass airside
AADEIIPRSTT paediatrist
AADEIKLNRSZ snake lizard
AADEIKMNNOY Diana monkey
AADEIKMNORT demarkation
AADEILLLMOT metalloidal
AADEILLMRTY diametrally
AADEILLNNPS land-spaniel
AADEILLNNRT rallentandi
AADEILLNOPT planetoidal
AADEILMMORY Memorial Day
AADEILMNRRT intradermal
AADEILMNRTY aldermanity
AADEILMOORV viola d'amore
AADEILNNQRU quadrennial
AADEILNOOTW Natalie Wood
AADEILNORST desalinator
AADEILNOTUV devaluation
AADEILNPPRR preprandial
AADEILNPPST planta pedis
AADEILNPSST displeasant
AADEILNRRST snail darter
AADEILNSSUW duniewassal
AADEILOPRTZ trapezoidal
AADEILORRSV River Salado
AADEILORRTV advertorial
AADEILOSTVW dovetail saw
AADEILPPRST applied arts
AADEILPRSTY disparately
AADEIMMNNOO demonomania
AADEIMMNRST disarmament
AADEIMNNNOP pandemonian✧
AADEIMNNOSW madonnawise
AADEIMNRSTV maidservant
servant-maid
AADEIMRSTTU traumatised

AADEIMRTTUZ	traumatized
AADEINNNPRT	pentandrian
AADEINNNRST	transandine
AADEINNRRTT	tetrandrian
AADEINNTTTU	unattainted
AADEINOPRTV	depravation
AADEINORRTT	retardation
AADEINORSST	diatessaron
AADEINORSTT	raison d'état
AADEINOSTTV	devastation
AADEINPQRSU	pasquinader
AADEINPRSTU	unaspirated
AADEINPRSUY	dyspareunia
AADEINRTTUV	durante vita
AADEIPSSTWW	wasp-waisted
AADEKLNNRRT	dark lantern
AADEKLNSUWY	D Wayne Lukas
AADEKNORSTU	skate around
AADEKNRSSWW	awkwardness
AADELLMNOSX	Alex Salmond
AADELLMNSTY	lady's-mantle
AADELLNNORT	rallentando
AADELLPUUVX	Paul Delvaux
AADELMMOPSS	plasmodesma
AADELMNOOSY	loadsamoney
AADELMNOPST	almond paste
AADELMNRRST	transdermal
AADELNNOOPT	pantalooned
AADELNOPQSU	Don Pasquale
AADELNPRSTU	pasture-land
AADELORRTTU	adulterator
AADELORSVWY	Oswald Avery
AADEMMNRRUU	Mare Undarum
AADEMNNNRWY	Randy Newman
AADEMNOOSTU	adenomatous
AADEMNORSTW	tradeswoman
AADEMOORRSU	Dromaeosaur
AADENNNOTTU	unannotated
AADENNRRTUW	unwarranted
AADENPRSTTT	standpatter
AADENRRSTTU	understrata
AADENRSSWWY	waywardness
AADENRSTTUU	unsaturated
AADEOQRRRTU	quarter-road
AADEORRRTTY	retardatory
AADFFIINOPR	paraffinoid
AADFFILORRX	Lord Fairfax
AADFFORRSTW	fast forward
	fast-forward
AADFGHHNNOU	Afghan hound
AADFGHILLNN	half-landing
AADFGHIMORR	rhagadiform
AADFGHINNST	handfasting
AADFGILLNNP	landing flap
AADFGILMORW	flow diagram
AADFHHILLOY	half-holiday
AADFHINRSTT	at first hand
AADFHKORRRW	hark forward
AADFHLNORSU	flash around
AADFILLNTWX	windfall tax
AADFILNSSUU	Susan Faludi
AADFIOORWWY	fairway wood
AADFKNOSUXY	Sandy Koufax
AADFLLLOOSY	All Fools' Day
AADFMNOORRS	mansard-roof
AADFNNNORUY	fanny around
AADFOPRRSSW	forward pass
AADGGGGMNOO	Gog and Magog
AADGGHILOSU	Douglas Haig
AADGGIILNPR	paragliding
AADGGIIMMNR	diagramming
AADGGIINOPR	radiopaging
AADGGIINPRS	disparaging
AADGGINPRSU	Pasir Gudang
AADGGKNOOOR	kangaroo dog
AADGGOOOUUU	Ouagadougou
AADGHHIILMR	high admiral
AADGHHIKNNS	handshaking
AADGHHILMNN	Highlandman
AADGHHOPRSW	shadowgraph
AADGHIIJNRV	Rajiv Gandhi
AADGHILNOST	hold against
AADGHINNOQU	Qinhuangdao
AADGHINOSSW	washing-soda
AADGHINRSWW	wash drawing
AADGHIOPRRY	radiography
AADGHLRRRYY	hydrargyral
AADGHMNOPRY	dynamograph
AADGHMNRSTU	draughtsman
AADGIIILORT	Giro d'Italia
AADGIIIMNTW	waiting-maid
AADGIIKLNNR	Kaliningrad
AADGIILLNOV	Gallovidian
AADGIILMRST	madrigalist
AADGIILNNNO	Anglo-Indian
AADGIILNRRU	Laura Riding
AADGIKLLNWY	walking lady
AADGIKLNOTW	walking toad
AADGILLNNST	all standing
AADGILNNOPS	span loading
AADGILNNOST	Gladstonian
AADGIMNRSUV	vanguardism
AADGINNOSTT	stand to gain
AADGINOPRTU	upgradation
AADGLLLNRUY	glandularly
AADGLLNPPUY	plug-and-play
AADHHINSTTT	this and that
AADHHKORSWW	Howard Hawks
AADHHMORSTY	Thomas Hardy
AADHHNOOPTW	wood naphtha
AADHIILMPRS	admiralship
AADHIILNOPR	dolphinaria
AADHIIMOPRS	adiaphorism
AADHIINOPRS	Aphrodisian
AADHIIOPRST	adiaphorist
AADHILNORSW	Rhodian laws
AADHILOPSTY	day hospital
AADHINNOSTT	station hand
AADHIOOPRSU	adiaphorous
AADHIOPPRTY	paratyphoid
AADHIOPPSSY	hypospadias
AADHIOPRRTY	parathyroid

AADHJMMNNOO	Joan Hammond
AADHKNOORTT	North Dakota
AADHKOOSTTU	South Dakota
AADHLMNOSTY	Dylan Thomas
AADHLNNOOSS	sandal shoon
AADHLOOPRRT	arthropodal
AADHLORSUYZ	hazardously
AADHMMNNOUY	human dynamo
AADHMOORSTY	hydrosomata
AADHNOPQRUY	quadraphony
AADHNORRRVY	Harry Vardon
AADHNORSUUZ	unhazardous
AADIIINNNOR	Indo-Iranian
AADIIINORRT	irradiation
AADIIJNOSTU	Judaisation
AADIIJNOTUZ	Judaization
AADIILLLMUW	William Laud
AADIILLMNSW	wild animals
AADIILLNTTU	altitudinal
	latitudinal
AADIILNOOTX	oxidational
AADIILNOPSS	anadiplosis
AADIILNORTT	traditional
AADIILNTTTU	attitudinal
AADIILOSUUV	audiovisual
AADIIMNOPST	adoptianism✧
AADIINNORSU	dinosaurian
AADIINNOTTX	antioxidant
AADIINOPSTT	adoptianist
AADIINOSTTV	idiot savant
AADILLLLNST	still and all
AADILLMNNOY	Madonna-lily
AADILLMNOOT	amontillado
AADILLMORTY	maladroitly
AADILLMPRYY	pyramidally
AADILMNORTY	mandatorily
AADILMOPRRT	port admiral
AADILMOPRRU	parlour-maid
AADILNNOPRT	Portlandian
AADILOOORSV	via dolorosa
AADILOORSTV	vasodilator
AADILOPPRSV	disapproval
AADIMNNOPRS	prima donnas
AADIMNNSSYY	syndyasmian
AADIMNORSTU	Surinam toad
AADINNSSTUY	Sunday saint
AADINOPPRST	post and pair
AADINOPRSSU	sauropsidan
AADINOPRTWX	twin paradox
AADINORRRYY	ordinary ray
AADIRRSSTUU	Straduarius
AADKMOORSTU	katadromous
AADKNNOPRSW	Sandown Park
AADLLLOSSUY	All Souls' Day
AADLLMORSWY	Mrs Dalloway
AADLLMRSTUW	wall mustard
AADLMOOPRWY	palmyra wood
AADLOPRRSTW	worlds apart
AADMNORSSTU	Nostradamus
AAEEEFFLMMT	femme fatale
AAEEEFGLNTT	fête galante
AAEEEFGNNTT	enfant gâtée
AAEEEFHPRTT	feather-pate
AAEEEGGHRTW	weather gage
AAEEEGHNSTV	Heaven's Gate
AAEEEGIIRSS	raise a siege
AAEEEGIPQTU	tea equipage
AAEEEGNNRSZ	Gene Sarazen
AAEEEGNSTTT	estate agent
AAEEEGRSSTU	sausage tree
AAEEEGRSTWY	steerage way
AAEEEHKPRSS	Shakespeare
AAEEEHLNPST	sea elephant
AAEEEHNNRTZ	the Nazarene
AAEEEHNRRTW	earthenware
AAEEEHNRTVW	weather vane
AAEEEHPRTTU	Therapeutae
AAEEEHRRTTW	water-heater
AAEEEIJMNNR	Marie-Jeanne
AAEEEILLSXY	Alexei Sayle
AAEEELMMMPP	mammee apple
AAEEELMNPPR	paper-enamel
AAEEELNOPPS	sleep apnoea
AAEEELNPPSS	epanalepses
AAEEEMNPPST	appeasement
AAEEEMPRSTU	tape measure
AAEEENRSSTU	aureateness
AAEEFFGILLO	foliage leaf
AAEEFGHLMRT	Magherafelt
AAEEFGIKMRU	make a figure
AAEEFGLLLNN	fallen angel
AAEEFGMRRRW	germ warfare
AAEEFHHILRT	faith healer
AAEEFHHLLRT	half-leather
AAEEFHILRRT	fair leather
AAEEFHILRTT	tail feather
AAEEFHIRRTW	fair-weather
AAEEFHKNRRT	hanker after
AAEEFHLMPRT	feather palm
AAEEFHLMRSU	half measure
AAEEFHLMTWY	meet halfway
AAEEFHLRRTT	flat-earther
AAEEFHMRRRS	sharefarmer
AAEEFHRRSTT	feather star
AAEEFIINNST	fainéantise
AAEEFIJLNTT	Jean Lafitte
AAEEFILMRRT	Fleet Air Arm
AAEEFIPRRST	aspire after
AAEEFKMRRTT	aftermarket
AAEEFLORSVY	vale of years
AAEEFLSTVVY	safety valve
AAEEFNRRSST	transferase
AAEEFPPRSTY	safety paper
AAEEGGGIRTV	aggregative
AAEEGGGLRTY	aggregately
AAEEGGGNNRS	gas gangrene
AAEEGGGNORT	on aggregate
AAEEGGHLORS	George Halas
AAEEGGIMNRV	graven image
AAEEGGINNRW	wage-earning
AAEEGGLMORT	agglomerate
AAEEGGMNNOT	megatonnage

AAEEGGNNORT	Agent Orange
AAEEGGNOORS	Osage orange
AAEEGGORRTX	exaggerator
AAEEGHHMORR	haemorrhage
AAEEGHILRTV	have it large
AAEEGHIMNRT	The Germania
AAEEGHINRST	heart-easing
AAEEGHKRSST	great shakes
AAEEGHLLRTW	weather gall
AAEEGHLMNUU	Human League
AAEEGHLMPTY	play the game
AAEEGHLNRSS	angels' share
AAEEGHLNRTW	Walter Hagen
AAEEGHLOOPS	oesophageal
AAEEGHNPPRR	paperhanger
AAEEGHNRRTT	greater than
AAEEGHRRTTX	tax gatherer
AAEEGIKLNTV	leave-taking
AAEEGIKNNRW	reawakening
AAEEGIKRRRV	Kagera River
AAEEGILLLNS	selaginella
AAEEGILLLTT	tagliatelle
AAEEGILLNNT	gentianella
AAEEGILMMNY	Amin Gemayel
AAEEGILMNNR	line manager
AAEEGILMNTT	latent image
AAEEGILMSSX	sexagesimal
AAEEGILNPPT	eating apple
AAEEGILNRVY	evangeliary
AAEEGILPRTT	tetraplegia
AAEEGINNOPS	neopaganise
AAEEGINNOPZ	neopaganize
AAEEGINPPTY	Egyptian pea
AAEEGINPRSS	paragenesis
AAEEGINPRST	grease paint
AAEEGINRRTW	graniteware
AAEEGINRTVY	vintage year
AAEEGKNRRST	garter-snake
AAEEGLLLSVY	galley slave
AAEEGLLRSSU	leaguer-lass
AAEEGLLRTTY	Tate Gallery
AAEEGLMMRSU	rummage sale
AAEEGLMNOPT	planogamete
AAEEGLNNORV	navel orange
AAEEGLNNPTT	Plantagenet
AAEEGLNRTTV	travel agent
AAEEGLNSSTV	vantageless
AAEEGLPRSTY	pearly gates
	stage-player
AAEEGLRSVWY	wage slavery
AAEEGMNNRRT	arrangement
AAEEGMNOPRT	pomegranate
AAEEGMNSSTU	assuagement
AAEEGMRSSSS	sesame grass
AAEEGNNPTTT	patent agent
AAEEGNNSUVZ	Suzanne Vega
AAEEGNPPRRT	garnet-paper
AAEEGNRSTTU	gutta serena
AAEEHHLNNPT	naphthalene
AAEEHHLRSTW	wash leather
AAEEHIILMNS	leishmaniae
AAEEHIKLMNO	make a hole in
AAEEHILLMNW	wheel animal
AAEEHILMOPR	hemeralopia
AAEEHILNNST	Saint Helena
AAEEHIMMNPT	amphetamine
AAEEHIMMSTT	mathematise
AAEEHIMMTTZ	mathematize
AAEEHIMNORT	etheromania
AAEEHIMNRTT	metatherian
AAEEHINPSST	panesthesia
AAEEHINRSTT	Anthesteria
AAEEHINSSST	anaesthesis
AAEEHIPRSST	paresthesia
AAEEHKMOPTY	take-home pay
AAEEHKMPRRS	phrasemaker
AAEEHKMRRST	market share
AAEEHKMRSTV	save the mark
AAEEHKORTTT	take to heart
AAEEHLLMNOY	hyalomelane
AAEEHLLMRSS	Marshallese
AAEEHLLSTTU	haustellate
AAEEHLMNRSS	Shalmaneser
AAEEHLSTTTT	at the latest
AAEEHMMMRST	steam hammer
AAEEHMMRRTW	water hammer
AAEEHMNOORR	amenorrhoea
AAEEHMNORST	roman à thèse
AAEEHNOSVWY	have one's way
AAEEHNPSSTT	The Peasants
AAEEHORRSTT	steatorrhea
AAEEHPRSTTT	shatter-pate
AAEEIILLTVV	alleviative
AAEEIILMRST	materialise
AAEEIILMRTZ	materialize
AAEEIILNSST	Ilie Nastase
AAEEIILRRST	arterialise
AAEEIILRRTZ	arterialize
AAEEIILRTTV	retaliative
AAEEIINRSSV	sansevieria
AAEEIIPTTVX	expatiative
AAEEIKKLRST	like a streak
AAEEIKLLMRT	alkalimeter
AAEEIKMNSST	skaines mate
AAEEIKNNSTV	vienna steak
AAEEILLLNRT	lateral line
AAEEILLLPRS	parallelise
AAEEILLLPRZ	parallelize
AAEEILLMPRX	premaxillae
AAEEILLNOTV	elevational
AAEEILLPPTV	appellative
AAEEILLPRRV	Pierre Laval
AAEEILLPRST	ipselateral
AAEEILLQRTU	equilateral
AAEEILMMPST	semipalmate
AAEEILNNPRT	penetralian
AAEEILNOPRT	peritonaeal
AAEEILNPPSS	epanalepsis
AAEEILNPRTX	Praxitelean
AAEEILNPTVX	explanative
AAEEILNRTTV	alternative
AAEEILPPRSS	paraleipses

AAEEILPSTTT latiseptate
AAEEIMNSSTV amativeness
AAEEIMOQSTU metasequoia
AAEEIMRTTVY variety meat
AAEEIMSSSTT metastasise
AAEEIMSSTTZ metastasize
AAEEINRRSTT tea-strainer
AAEEINRRTUX ex natura rei
AAEEIOPRTVV evaporative
AAEEIORSTTX stereotaxia
AAEEIPPRRRS reappraiser
AAEEIPPRRTV preparative
AAEEISTTTTV attestative
AAEEJKLMMNS James Kelman
AAEEKKMMRRT market maker
AAEEKLMRTUV market-value
AAEEKLNRSTT rattlesnake
AAEEKMNOSWY make one's way
AAEEKNOSTWY take one's way
AAEELLLMNOS salmonellae
AAEELLNPRTU neural plate
AAEELLNRTTY alternately
AAEELLNSTTV at all events
AAEELLOOSST a slate loose
AAEELLPRSTU pasteurella✧
AAEELLRRTUW laurel-water
AAEELMNPPRT apparelment
AAEELMNSTTT testamental
AAEELMPRRTW plate-warmer
AAEELNNPTTV pentavalent
AAEELNOPSVW weapon salve
AAEELNPQRRU quarrel-pane
AAEELNPRSSU sea purslane
AAEELNPRTTY penalty rate
AAEELNPSTTT pantalettes
AAEELNRRSTT retranslate
AAEELNRTTTV tetravalent
AAEELOPRTTX extrapolate
AAEELQRRSTU quarter-seal
AAEELRRSTTU serratulate
AAEELSSSTTV slave states
AAEEMMNNNTT Emma Tennant
AAEEMMPRRSU map-measurer
AAEEMMPRTUY empyreumata
AAEEMNOPRTT treponemata
AAEEMNORSTZ estramazone
AAEEMNORTUX auxanometer
AAEEMNPPRTT appartement
AAEEMNRSTTT testamentar
AAEEMORRSSY sea rosemary
AAEEMPPRSST Pete Sampras
AAEEMQRSSTU marquessate
AAEENNOPPRU pan-European
AAEENNRSSUW unawareness
AAEENORSTTV à votre santé
AAEENPRRTTT tetrapteran
AAEENPRSTTT transeptate
AAEENRRSTWY Ten Years' War
AAEEOPRRSTX exasperator
AAEEPPRSTTU pâte-sur-pâte
AAEFFFFTTTU tufftaffeta
AAEFFFILRSS self-affairs
AAEFFIIMRTV affirmative
AAEFGHILNRT farthingale
AAEFGIKLLNW walking leaf
AAEFGIKMOOT make a go of it
AAEFGILLNRT tear-falling
AAEFGILNNRT in flagrante
AAEFGILNOST olefiant gas
AAEFGILPRST septifragal
AAEFGLLLOPS false gallop
AAEFGLLLORT flagellator
AAEFGLLLSTU Tugela Falls
AAEFGLMNORY Morgan le Fay
AAEFGLNNNPT pennant flag
AAEFGLSSSTY safety glass
AAEFGMNRRTY fragmentary
AAEFHILLLNT hälleflinta
AAEFHILMRRS fire-marshal
AAEFHILNRTW father-in-law
AAEFHLMNOTW The Man of Law
AAEFHLMOPRT heart of palm
AAEFHLNOPST half past one
AAEFHLPRSTT patter flash
AAEFIIILMRS familiarise
AAEFIIILMRZ familiarize
AAEFIINNORT roi fainéant
AAEFIIORRSV savoir-faire
AAEFILMMNRT firmamental
AAEFILMNRTY filamentary
AAEFILNORRS Isle of Arran
AAEFILOPRRT prefatorial
AAEFIRRTTWY fritter away
AAEFLLMNNOW fallen woman
AAEFLLNRRTY fraternally
AAEFLLORRTX extrafloral
AAEFLNORTUW law of nature
AAEFLNRRRST transferral
AAEFLOPSTTY state of play
AAEFMMNORST foremastman
AAEFNNRRRST transfer RNA
AAEFORRSTYZ safety razor
AAEGGGINORT aggregation
AAEGGILLNOR lingoa geral
AAEGGILLNOW Gallowegian
AAEGGILNNVZ navel-gazing
AAEGGILNTTU agglutinate
AAEGGIMMNTU gametangium
AAEGGIMNNUZ magazine-gun
AAEGGINRSSU guinea grass✧
AAEGGINRSTU strain gauge
AAEGGLMMORU grammalogue
AAEGGLNPRTT garget plant
AAEGGLOPTUY ptyalagogue
AAEGGMMNRST gammerstang
AAEGGMNORST steganogram
AAEGGNORRSS orange-grass
AAEGGNORRUW narrow gauge
narrow-gauge
AAEGHHIIKST high as a kite
AAEGHHIPPRY hyperphagia
AAEGHIMNORR menorrhagia

AAEGHIMNPRS	managership
AAEGHINNNSS	shenanigans
AAEGHINOORT	Ornithogaea
AAEGHINPRRV	River Pahang
AAEGHKNOORS	kohanga reos
AAEGHLLNOXY	hexagonally
AAEGHLLOTWY	go all the way
AAEGHLMOOTY	haematology
AAEGHLMRSSW	Gresham's law
AAEGHLNNOPY	angelophany
AAEGHLOPTTY	play the goat
AAEGHLPSSTT	the last gasp
AAEGHMNOPRY	anemography
AAEGHMOPRRS	phraseogram
AAEGHMRTTUU	thaumaturge
AAEGHNOPRTY	Pythagorean
AAEGHNORSST	North Sea gas
AAEGHNPRRST	strap-hanger
AAEGHNSTTTU	set at naught
AAEGIIIMNTV	imaginative
AAEGIIKNOPP	a pig in a poke
AAEGIILMNPS	Pelagianism
AAEGIILMNRS	marginalise
AAEGIILMNRZ	marginalize
AAEGIILMRST	magisterial
AAEGIILNRRY	air layering
AAEGIILNRSU	Ligurian Sea
AAEGIIMMNRT	immarginate
AAEGIIMMNTV	megavitamin
AAEGIIMMRRS	mismarriage
AAEGIIMNSTT	against time
AAEGIIMRRTT	metri gratia
AAEGIINNNRT	Argentinian
AAEGIINNOTV	evagination
AAEGIINORTV	variegation
AAEGIIRTTVV	gravitative
AAEGIKLNPRS	spring a leak
AAEGIKLNPTU	Paul Keating
AAEGIKMNPPR	paper-making
AAEGIKMNPST	masking tape
AAEGIKNNNUW	unawakening
AAEGILLLNPR	paralleling
AAEGILLNPPR	apparelling
AAEGILLNPPY	appealingly
AAEGILMMNOS	Maglemosian
AAEGILMNNOS	nonagesimal
AAEGILMNPST	Leptis Magna
AAEGILMNRTV	malt vinegar
AAEGILMNRTY	ligamentary
AAEGILMNSTU	glutaminase
AAEGILMORSU	megalosauri
AAEGILNNPPU	unappealing
AAEGILNNRTT	alternating
AAEGILNOPRS	saprolegnia
AAEGILNOSTT	gestational
AAEGILNPPSY	appeasingly
AAEGILNPRSV	palsgravine
AAEGILNQRUU	equiangular
AAEGILNRTTU	triangulate
AAEGILNRTUV	granulative
AAEGILORSTT	gestatorial
AAEGILPRRSU	Spergularia
AAEGIMNNOPS	neopaganism
AAEGIMNNRRT	arraignment
AAEGIMNNTTU	antimutagen
AAEGIMORRTU	outmarriage
AAEGIMORSST	mesogastria
AAEGIMPRRST	pragmatiser
AAEGIMPRRTZ	pragmatizer
AAEGINNNPTY	pentagynian
AAEGINNOPRS	Singaporean
AAEGINNORSS	anagnorises
AAEGINNPPRT	parapenting
AAEGINNRTTY	tetragynian
AAEGINOPRST	aspergation
AAEGINORRTT	terra ignota
AAEGINOSTTV	vote against
AAEGINPRRTT	in great part
AAEGIOPPRTV	propagative
AAEGIOPSTTY	steatopygia
AAEGJNORSST	Jan Gossaert
AAEGKLLMNOS	maskallonge
AAEGKOPRSSW	passagework
AAEGLLNNSST	gallantness
AAEGLLNNTTY	tangentally
AAEGLLNOPTY	penalty goal
AAEGLLNORTY	angelolatry
AAEGLLORRST	Grallatores
AAEGLLORSSU	sausage roll
AAEGLLOSTTU	as all get-out
AAEGLMNRTTY	termagantly
AAEGLMOPRRU	parlour game
AAEGLMORSSU	megalosaurs
AAEGLNNPRTU	pentangular
AAEGLNOSSWY	one-way glass
AAEGLNRRSSV	vernal grass
AAEGLNRSTTU	strangulate
AAEGLORSSTT	tessaraglot
AAEGMMOPRSY	agamospermy
AAEGNNORTWY	orange-tawny
AAEGNOQRSSU	squarsonage
AAEGORRTUUV	autogravure
AAEGRRSTTUY	treasury tag
AAEHHIILMOP	haemophilia
AAEHHIKNRRS	Hare Krishna
AAEHHILNPST	naphthalise
AAEHHILNPTZ	naphthalize
AAEHHLLSSTT	health salts
AAEHHLMPSTT	health stamp
AAEHHLMRSTT	thrash metal
AAEHHMNOSST	Thomas Nashe
AAEHHOPPSST	phosphatase
AAEHHOTUVWY	what have you
AAEHIILLMRW	William Hare
AAEHIILMNSS	leishmanias
AAEHIIMNOPS	hemianopsia
AAEHIIMNSST	histaminase
AAEHIJLNNOU	Jean Anouilh
AAEHIJLNOPP	Japanophile
AAEHIKLNRRS	Lanarkshire
AAEHILLMMNP	Manilla hemp
AAEHILLPRRT	earth-pillar

AAEHILMNSTT	The Talisman
AAEHILNNNWZ	Hanni Wanzel
AAEHILNOOPY	hypoaeolian
AAEHILNOSTT	East Lothian
AAEHILNPSTW	Westphalian
AAEHILNSSTU	ailanthuses
AAEHILOORRS	sialorrhoea
AAEHILORRTX	exhilarator
AAEHILPPRSY	hyperplasia
AAEHILSTWWY	whistle away
AAEHILTTWWY	whittle away
AAEHIMOSSST	haemostasis
AAEHIMPRSST	metaphrasis
AAEHIMPRSTU	amateurship
AAEHINNNOOT	hootanannie
AAEHJNNORSU	Johannes Rau
AAEHKMPRSST	pass the mark
AAEHLLLLNOW	allhallowen
AAEHLLLOPTY	allelopathy
AAEHLLNPRRU	Ralph Lauren
AAEHLNPRSTY	phalanstery
AAEHLPPRTYY	play therapy
AAEHLPRRSWY	prayer shawl
AAEHLPRSSTW	water splash
AAEHMMORSST	atom-smasher
AAEHMNNRTUU	human nature
AAEHMNORSTT	Tam O'Shanter
AAEHMNORSTU	athermanous
AAEHMNORSWW	washerwoman
AAEHMOPRTTU	thaumatrope
AAEHNNPRRSW	Warren Spahn
AAEHNOPPRRS	paranephros
AAEHNRRRRWY	Harry Warren
AAEHNRRSTUV	Arthur Evans
AAEHOPRSTTW	potash water
AAEHPRRTXYY	X-ray therapy
AAEIIILRSUX	auxiliaries
AAEIIJMORRT	majoritaire
AAEIIKNRSST	raise a stink
AAEIILLMNNR	millenarian
AAEIILLMNRT	matrilineal
AAEIILLNNOT	allineation
AAEIILLNOPR	Apollinaire
AAEIILLNOTV	alleviation
AAEIILLNPRT	patrilineal
AAEIILLNRSV	Vallisneria
AAEIILLPRST	ipsilateral
AAEIILLPTXY	epitaxially
AAEIILMMRST	materialism
AAEIILMNNRS	marine snail
AAEIILMNNTY	inanimately
AAEIILMNRRT	air terminal
	matrilinear
AAEIILMPRTV	imperatival
AAEIILMRSTT	materialist
AAEIILMRTTY	materiality
AAEIILNNNTV	Valentinian
AAEIILNNOST	nationalise
AAEIILNNOTZ	nationalize
AAEIILNNPST	Palestinian
AAEIILNORST	rationalise
	realisation
AAEIILNORTT	retaliation
AAEIILNORTZ	rationalize
	realization
AAEIILNPRRT	patrilinear
AAEIILNRTTV	tire-valiant
AAEIILNSTTY	insatiately
AAEIILPPRSS	paraleipsis
AAEIILQTTUV	qualitative
AAEIIMNNORT	reanimation
AAEIIMNNOTT	antimoniate
AAEIIMNNOTX	examination
	exanimation
AAEIIMNRSST	Erastianism
AAEIINNPPRT	paripinnate
AAEIINNSTTT	instantiate
AAEIINOPTTX	expatiation
AAEIINOSTTV	aestivation
AAEIINPSSTT	sat sapienti
AAEIKKLLOPU	leukoplakia
AAEIKKLMNOU	kamelaukion
AAEIKLLMRTY	alkalimetry
AAEIKLLNOST	Nikola Tesla
AAEIKLLTTVY	talkatively
AAEIKLMNOPT	kleptomania
AAEIKLNOORT	Lake Ontario
AAEIKLPRRRT	trailer park
AAEILLLMPRS	parallelism
AAEILLLOSTV	sal volatile
AAEILLLPPTU	papillulate
AAEILLLPRST	parallelist
AAEILLMNORZ	Lorin Maazel
AAEILLMNOTT	no time at all
AAEILLMPRVY	primaevally
AAEILLMRTVV	mitral valve
AAEILLNNPTY	Tin Pan Alley
AAEILLNOPPT	appellation
AAEILLORTTU	ratatouille
AAEILLORTVY	alleviatory
AAEILLPPRST	epiplastral
AAEILLQRSTU	aquarellist
AAEILLRSUVZ	Luis Alvarez
AAEILMMNRST	maternalism
AAEILMMORRW	war memorial
AAEILMNNOTT	lamentation
AAEILMNNRSU	semi-annular
AAEILMNORST	monasterial
AAEILMNPRST	paternalism
AAEILMNPRTU	planetarium
AAEILMNRRSS	Silas Marner
AAEILMNRRTU	ultramarine
AAEILMNRSST	martialness
AAEILMNRTTY	amyl nitrate
AAEILMOORRT	ameliorator
AAEILMOPRTV	Parma violet
AAEILMOPTTT	totipalmate
AAEILNNOPSX	expansional
AAEILNNOPTX	explanation
AAEILNNORTT	alternation
AAEILNNOSST	sensational
AAEILNNOTTT	attentional

AAEILNNPRST	transalpine
AAEILNNPSST	plainstanes
AAEILNNPTTU	antenuptial
AAEILNOOPRT	operational
AAEILNOPPRY	piano-player
	player piano
AAEILNOPRRT	proletarian
AAEILNOPRSS	anaplerosis
AAEILNORTUV	revaluation
AAEILNOSSTY	seasonality
AAEILNPRTYZ	lazy painter
AAEILNPTTVY	vanity plate
AAEILNQRSTU	Latin Square
AAEILNRRSTT	intertarsal
AAEILNRRSTU	sertularian
AAEILNRRTTU	nature trail
AAEILNRRTVY	narratively
AAEILNRSTTV	at intervals
	translative
AAEILNRSTUX	intrasexual
	neutral axis
AAEILOPPRRS	paper-sailor
AAEILOPRRTT	proletariat
AAEILOQRSTU	quaestorial
AAEILORRTTY	retaliatory
AAEILORSSSS	assessorial
AAEILQRRRTU	quarter-rail
AAEILRRTVVV	River Vltava
AAEIMMNORUU	Naomi Uemura
AAEIMMOPSST	aposematism
AAEIMNNOSST	Samian stone
AAEIMNNOTTU	mountain tea
AAEIMNNRRST	transmarine
AAEIMNNSTTT	attainments
AAEIMNNTTTT	attaintment
AAEIMNORRVZ	River Amazon
AAEIMNRRUVY	River Yamuna
AAEIMOOPRSZ	azoospermia
AAEIMOPPRTX	approximate
AAEINNOPRSZ	Arno Penzias
AAEINNOPRTT	trepanation
AAEINNOSSTT	assentation
AAEINNOSTTT	nation state
AAEINNOTTTU	attenuation
AAEINNRRSVY	anniversary
AAEINOOPRTV	evaporation
AAEINOORSTT	aerostation
AAEINOPPRRT	preparation
AAEINOPRRST	reparations
AAEINORRSTT	arrestation
AAEINOSTTTT	attestation
AAEINPRRSSW	Persian Wars
AAEIOPPPRRT	appropriate
AAEIOPPRRSS	appressoria
AAEIOPRRRTT	repatriator
AAEIOPRRSTU	Pterosauria
AAEIOPRTTXY	expatiatory
AAEIORRTTVW	Ottawa River
AAEIORSSTTV	assortative
AAEJKLPRRSS	Karl Jaspers
AAEJLMNOPRT	major planet
AAEJLMORSTY	James Taylor
AAEJLNNRSTW	lantern jaws
AAEJLNRSTUU	jus naturale
AAEJMNOSSTW	James Watson
AAEJMRSSTTU	James Stuart
AAEKLLLORVW	walk all over
AAEKLNNRTTV	ventral tank
AAEKMMNORTW	market-woman
AAEKMNNOSTY	Satan monkey
AAELLLMNOSS	salmonellas
AAELLLNPRSU	sal prunella
AAELLLORSST	saltarellos
AAELLMMMORY	marmem alloy
AAELLMMORRY	marmoreally
AAELLMNOSTU	natale solum
AAELLMRSSTT	stallmaster
AAELLOPSSTT	Elastoplast®
AAELLORRSTT	stellarator
AAELLRSSTTT	Tattersalls
	Tattersall's
AAELMMNORSW	Woman's Realm
AAELMNOORSV	vomeronasal
AAELMNOPRSS	salmon spear
AAELMNOPRWY	Norway maple
AAELMNPQTUU	quantum leap
AAELMNRRTUY	Mary Renault
AAELMNSSTTY	statesmanly
AAELMOPQSTU	quota sample
AAELMOPRRTU	armour-plate
	plate armour
AAELMOPSTTW	saw palmetto
AAELMORRSSS	serrasalmos
AAELNNRSSTU	naturalness
AAELNOOPPRS	aplanospore
AAELNOPRTXY	explanatory
AAELNORSSTY	royal assent
AAELNRRSSTV	transversal
AAELNRRSTUV	transvaluer
AAELNRSSSTV	servant-lass
AAELNRSSTUX	transsexual
	trans-sexual
AAELOOPPPTT	potato apple
AAEMMNOORTT	Monotremata
AAEMMNORSST	master mason
AAEMMNPRSSU	Mare Spumans
AAEMMOPRRUV	Mare Vaporum
AAEMNNOOSTZ	amazon-stone
AAEMNNORTUV	verumontana
AAEMNOOPRTT	protonemata
AAEMNOOSSST	anastomoses
AAEMNOPRSTU	persona muta
AAEMNOPRTTU	portmanteau
AAEMNORSTTU	atramentous
AAEMNOSSTTW	stateswoman
AAEMNPPRTTY	part-payment
AAEMOOPRSTZ	spermatozoa
AAEMORSSTTT	toastmaster
AAENNNORSTY	Ayrton Senna
AAENNPPRTTU	appurtenant
AAENNPRRSTT	transparent
AAENNPRSTTU	supernatant

AAENQRRSTUW	quarter-sawn
AAEOOPPRRRT	paratrooper
AAEOPPRRRTY	preparatory
AAEOPPRRSTU	support area
AAEOPPRSSST	sea passport
AAEOPRRTUVW	water vapour
AAEOPRSSTTU	stratopause
AAEOPRSSTTW	potass water
AAEPQRRSTTU	quarter past
AAEQRRRTUWY	quarry-water
AAFFGGIMNRU	raggamuffin
AAFFGHHIINS	haaf-fishing
AAFFGILOPST	gaff-topsail
AAFFHIJNORX	John Fairfax
AAFFIIILNOT	affiliation
AAFFIILNOPR	paraffin oil
AAFFIIMNORT	affirmation
AAFFILMNPTY	Tiffany lamp
AAFFIMORRTY	affirmatory
AAFFNNNORTZ	Frantz Fanon
AAFGGGGILNW	flag-wagging
AAFGHIMRSTW	Graham Swift
AAFGHLMORRU	graham flour
AAFGIILNOTT	flagitation
AAFGIKLNSTT	fast-talking
AAFGIKMNNRT	tank-farming
AAFGILLMRUY	gallimaufry
AAFGILLNRST	falling star
AAFGILNNTUV	fan vaulting
AAFGILNOSTT	stagflation
AAFGINORRSU	farraginous
AAFGMNORRST	grant of arms
AAFHIINOSST	fashionista
AAFHILLLLSY	fallalishly
AAFHLMNORTY	not harm a fly
AAFHLOPSTTW	half past two
AAFIIIILLRRT	fritillaria
AAFIIILMRTY	familiarity
AAFIIIMNNRR	infirmarian
AAFIILLMTTW	William Taft
AAFIILNRSTU	fustilarian
AAFIINNOTTU	infatuation
AAFILLMNORW	laminar flow
AAFILMNOORT	formational
AAFIMNNNRTY	infantryman
AAFINNNOOTU	Aonian fount
AAFINNOOPRT	profanation
AAFIOPRSSTY	pair of stays
AAFIOQRSTTU	aquafortist
AAFKLPRSTYY	flaky pastry
AAFLNNOORST	nasofrontal
AAFNOOPRRTY	profanatory
AAFRRSSTTYY	artsy-fartsy
AAGGGHILNSU	laughing gas
AAGGGILNSSZ	glass-gazing
AAGGHHIINNS	shanghaiing
AAGGHHIOPRY	hagiography
AAGGHIINNRS	gain-sharing
AAGGHINOPRY	angiography
AAGGIINRRUY	Yuri Gagarin
AAGGILLNSTZ	salt glazing
AAGGILNNTTU	agglutinant
AAGGILNPUUU	Paul Gauguin
AAGGIMNRSTU	Gargantuism
AAGGINRSTTU	Gargantuist
AAGGLLLOSSW	gallowglass
AAGGNNOORTU	orang-outang
AAGHHLOPPRY	haplography
AAGHHOPPRTY	pathography
AAGHIIINRRS	hair-raising
AAGHIILLNOP	anglophilia✧
AAGHIILNRTV	rival-hating
AAGHIINRRST	right as rain
AAGHIKLNRTU	Laura Knight
AAGHIKMORST	Kashmir goat
AAGHILLMNPY	lymphangial
AAGHILLMNRS	marshalling
AAGHILNRSSY	harassingly
AAGHILOPRSY	sialography
AAGHILPPRSY	psaligraphy
AAGHIMNRSTT	straight man
AAGHIMRRSTT	straight-arm
AAGHINOPSSV	shaving-soap
AAGHINOSTTY	Stygian oath
AAGHIOPPRTY	typographia
AAGHIRSTTWY	straightway
AAGHKNOOOPR	kangaroo-hop
AAGHLNOOTTY	thanatology
AAGHLNOSTWY	galanty show
AAGHMMMOPRY	mammography
AAGHMMNOORR	harmonogram
AAGHMRTTUUY	thaumaturgy
AAGHNOPPRTY	pantography
AAGHNOPRRUY	uranography
AAGHOOPSTUU	autophagous
AAGIIILLNRS	sigillarian
AAGIIILMNRY	imaginarily
AAGIIIMNNOT	imagination
AAGIIJMMNNT	antijamming
AAGIIKNNPST	painstaking
AAGIILLLNWW	Wailing Wall
AAGIILMMNRS	marginalism
AAGIILMNNTY	animatingly
AAGIILMNORT	migrational
AAGIILMNRST	marginalist
AAGIILMNRTY	marginality
AAGIILNNSTT	tantalising
AAGIILNNTTZ	tantalizing
AAGIILOPRRT	gloria Patri
AAGIIMMNNTY	magnanimity
AAGIIMMSSTT	astigmatism
AAGIIMNNORT	margination
AAGIIMRSSUU	Gaius Marius
AAGIINNORSS	anagnorisis
AAGIINNOSST	assignation
AAGIINNOSTT	angiostatin
AAGIINNPTWX	wax painting
AAGIINNSTTU	unsatiating
AAGIINNSTUU	Augustinian
AAGIINORTTV	gravitation
AAGIINPPTTT	pit-a-patting
AAGIINPSTTU	up against it

AAGIIRSSTTU	Sagittarius
AAGIJKNOPRT	joking apart
AAGIKLNPRTW	walking part
AAGIKNORSTW	work against
AAGILLLNPPY	appallingly
AAGILLLOOSS	glossolalia
AAGILLMNNTY	malignantly
AAGILLMNOST	giant slalom
AAGILLMOORY	malariology
AAGILLNRTUV	Vulgar Latin
AAGILMMMOST	mammalogist
AAGILMNNOOR	Anglo-Romani
AAGILNNNRSU	annual rings
AAGILNNOPSS	Panglossian
AAGILNNORTU	granulation
AAGILNNOSST	glasnostian
AAGILNOOPRS	sporangiola
AAGILNOORSU	Louis Aragon
AAGILNOPSTY	angioplasty
AAGILNORSSU	agranulosis
AAGILNORSTV	vital organs
AAGILNORTTU	gratulation
AAGILNOSUVY	Yugoslavian
AAGILNRRTUY	granularity
AAGILOPRRTU	purgatorial
AAGIMMNNOSU	magnanimous
AAGIMOSTUUV	mauvais goût
AAGINNOPRST	roasting pan
AAGINNRSTTU	turn against
AAGINOOPPRT	propagation
AAGINOPRRTU	purgatorian
AAGINORRTUU	inaugurator
AAGLLLNNTUY	ungallantly
AAGLLMNORRS	Ragman Rolls
AAGLLMNRTUU	multangular
AAGLLNOOSUY	analogously
AAGLMNNNOOR	Anglo-Norman
AAGLMOOPSUY	apogamously
AAGLNOOPRTW	patrol-wagon
AAGLOOPRTXY	protogalaxy
AAGLORRTTUY	gratulatory
AAGLQRSSTUZ	quartz glass
AAGMNNOSTUY	Mount Sangay
AAGNNOSSSTU	Susan Sontag
AAGOPRSTTUU	Port Augusta
AAHHHLMPRTY	alpha rhythm
AAHHILMPRSS	marshalship
AAHHLLOPTTY	Thallophyta
AAHHMNOPRRY	Harry Hopman
AAHHMOPRSST	Rhamphastos
AAHHOPRRTTY	arthropathy
AAHIIKLMRWZ	al-Khwarizmi
AAHIILMMPXY	maximaphily
AAHIILMNNOT	Hamiltonian
AAHIILMNSST	Stahlianism
AAHIILNNORT	annihilator
AAHIILNNRSV	nail varnish
AAHIILNOORT	hariolation
AAHIILPRSWY	ship railway
AAHIIMNNPSS	Spanish Main
AAHIIMORSST	a hit or a miss
AAHIINNOTWW	with a wanion
AAHIINPRSST	antiphrasis
AAHIINPSTTT	antipathist
AAHIJKLMPSU	Lakshmi-puja
AAHIJNNNOOS	Johnsoniana
AAHIKKLNOSV	kalashnikov✧
AAHIKLNPSSW	Spanish walk
	Spanish-walk
	walk Spanish
AAHIKNOOPRS	Anish Kapoor
AAHILLLOPRT	prothallial
AAHILLMNOPY	phyllomania
AAHILLOPSTT	allopathist
AAHILLOPTXY	litholapaxy
AAHILLPSTVY	Sylvia Plath
AAHILMNTTWW	Walt Whitman
AAHILPPSSST	pissasphalt
AAHIMMNNOPY	nymphomania
AAHIMNNOPPT	phantom pain
AAHIMNNOSTU	mountain ash
AAHIMNOPRSS	oarsmanship
AAHIMRSSTTU	Mathias Rust
AAHINNOPRTY	antiphonary
AAHINOPPSSS	Spanish soap
AAHINOPSSTT	thanatopsis
AAHIOPRSTXY	asphyxiator
AAHIOSSTTTY	that is to say
AAHIOTUWWYY	away with you
AAHKLOPRRST	shark patrol
AAHKMNNTTUU	Tut'ankhamun
AAHKNOORTTV	katavothron
AAHKOPRRSWW	sparrowhawk
AAHLLMMORSW	marshmallow
	marsh-mallow
AAHLLMORTYY	Royal Lytham
AAHLLOPRSTY	hyoplastral
AAHMMNOORRY	Ram Mohan Roy
AAHMMNORSSY	Harmony Mass
AAHMMOORRTY	hoary marmot
AAHMNNRSTTU	transhumant
AAHMNOOPRSU	anamorphous
AAHMOOSTTWY	Thomas Otway
AAHMOSTTTWY	Thomas Wyatt
AAHNNOPRSXY	nasopharynx
AAHNOOPSTUU	autophanous
AAHNOPRTTUY	naturopathy
AAHOPRRSTTT	throatstrap
AAHORSSTTTY	at short stay
AAIIILNNORT	Italian iron
AAIIILNRTTU	utilitarian
AAIIIMMNNRS	Arminianism
AAIIIMNNNOT	inanimation
AAIIIMNNTTV	antivitamin
AAIIINNRRTT	Trinitarian
AAIIJKLMNOR	Kilimanjaro
AAIIKMNOPRT	imparkation
AAIILLLNPSU	sinupallial
AAIILLLPSUZ	lapis lazuli
AAIILLMMNOT	mamillation
AAIILLMPRTY	impartially
AAIILLNOPRS	Apollinaris

AAIILLNPRST pillar-saint
AAIILMMNORT matrimonial
AAIILMMNPSS panislamism
AAIILMNNOST nationalism
AAIILMNNOTV nominatival
AAIILMNOPRT patrimonial
AAIILMNOPST maintopsail
AAIILMNOPTU tulipomania
AAIILMNORST rationalism
AAIILMNPSST panislamist
AAIILMOOPPS spolia opima
AAIILMORSST assimilator
AAIILMORTTU ultima ratio
AAIILNNOSTT nationalist
AAIILNNOTTY nationality
AAIILNNPSTU Saint-Paulin
AAIILNOORTV variolation
AAIILNOPPTT palpitation
AAIILNORSTT rationalist
AAIILNORTTT attritional
AAIILNORTTY rationality
AAIILNOSTTU situational
AAIILNOTTTU attuitional
AAIIMMNORSV Moravianism
AAIIMNNORST Mastroianni
AAIIMNNOSTV Novatianism
AAIIMNOOSTT atomisation
AAIIMNOOTTZ atomization
AAIIMNOPRTT impartation
AAIIMNOPSTT impastation
AAIIMNORRST Rotarianism
AAIIMNPRTVY parvanimity
AAIIMNRSSTU sanitariums
AAIINNOQTTU antiquation
AAIINNOSTTV Novatianist
AAIINOPRSST aspirations
AAIINRSSTTV transit visa
AAIIOPRSSST parasitosis
AAIJMNNOTTW want jam on it
AAILLLOSTWW swallowtail
AAILLMNPRUU plumularian
AAILLNOPSTT at all points
AAILLNRUUVV univalvular
AAILLOOPRYZ polyzoarial
AAILLORRSTT latirostral
AAILLORRSTY sartorially
AAILLRRTUVV trivalvular
AAILMMNOSTU summational
AAILMMOPPRS malapropism
AAILMNOPRTU manipulator
AAILMNPSSTU nuptial Mass
AAILMNRSTTT transmittal
AAILMOPRSST pastoralism
AAILNNORSTT translation
AAILNNOSSTU anno salutis
AAILNOPPSSY passion play
AAILNOPSTTY PlayStation®
AAILNOPTUUV upvaluation
AAILNPPRSTY plain pastry
AAILOORSTTT totalisator
AAILOORTTTZ totalizator
AAILOPRRSUV larviparous
AAILOPRRTUV vapour trail
AAILOPRSSTT pastoralist
AAIMMNNOORY monomyarian
AAIMMNOPSTT maintopmast
AAIMMNOSSUY immunoassay
AAIMNNORSTT Aston Martin®
AAIMNOOOSTT somatotonia
AAIMNOOPSST pass a motion
AAIMNOOSSST anastomosis
AAIMNORSSTU sanatoriums
AAIMNORSTTU natatoriums
AAIMOOPPRST apotropaism
AAIMORRSTTU Moira Stuart
AAINNNOPRST non-partisan
AAINNOPRSTT patron saint
AAINOOPRSTT asportation
AAINOORRSTZ Zoroastrian
AAINORRSTTU instaurator
AAIOPPRSUVV papovavirus
AAKKNORRSSY Krasnoyarsk
AAKLLMPRUUU Kuala Lumpur
AAKLNNOOSSW also known as
AALLMNOOSUY anomalously
AALLMOQRSTU small quarto
AALLNNRTUUY unnaturally
AALMMMOPSTY mammoplasty
AALMMOOPSST somatoplasm
AALMMOPPRRS Mrs Malaprop
AALMNNOPSTW plantswoman
AALMNOOPRTW patrolwoman
AALMNOOPRTY protanomaly
AALMNOPRTUY paramountly
AALMNPRSTUY palmyra nuts
AALNNNORSTU non-naturals
AALNNRRSTUY translunary
AALNOORTUVY anovulatory
AALNOPRRSTT transportal
AALNOPRSTUY uranoplasty
AALNORRSTTY translatory
AALOOQRRTUY royal quarto
AALORSSTTTU altostratus
AAMNPRSSTTY smartypants
AAMOOPRRTUU out-paramour
AANNORRSTUY tyrannosaur
AANOOPPRSTV avant-propos
AANOOQRRTUW quo warranto
ABBBBEELRUY abbey-lubber
ABBBCELLNUU unclubbable
ABBBCENORUY baby-bouncer
ABBBDELOORW wobble board
ABBBDINOSST bits and bobs
ABBBEEHILRS Bible-basher
ABBBEELMNRT brabblement
ABBBEHITWYY Whitby Abbey
ABBBEHLMRSU bramble-bush
ABBBELNOOTY Bolton Abbey
ABBBENORUWY Woburn Abbey
ABBBERRRSSU brass rubber
ABBBINNRTUY bunny rabbit
ABBCCDEHKNU bunch-backed

ABBCCEEHKNR backbencher
ABBCCEEHKNS back benches
ABBCCEEHMOR beachcomber
ABBCCEEINOR bone-breccia
ABBCCEKKLOR back-blocker
ABBCCHIORTT Bob Cratchit
ABBCCNOORSY snobbocracy
ABBCDEEFIKO biofeedback
ABBCDEEILRS describable
ABBCDEEKRUV Dave Brubeck
ABBCDEENRSS crabbedness
ABBCDEENSSS scabbedness
ABBCDEIKLRR blackbirder
ABBCDEKLORW black-browed
ABBCDEMRRSU breadcrumbs
ABBCDGIKLNO black-boding
ABBCEEEHRRS bear's-breech
ABBCEEEKLLT black beetle
ABBCEEEKNRU Beckenbauer
ABBCEEGILOR corbie gable
ABBCEEKLORT beta-blocker
ABBCEELLORT corbel table
ABBCEHIIKLN kibble-chain
ABBCEHIILOT bibliotheca
ABBCEHILLMR bill-chamber
ABBCEHIOPRY cyberphobia
ABBCEHIRRRS Chris Barber
ABBCEHIRRST barber's itch
ABBCEIILNRS inscribable
ABBCEILLMNU unclimbable
ABBCEJKORWY jabberwocky✧
ABBCGIIIMNN minicabbing
ABBCHHIRTTU rabbit hutch
ABBCHIMNOOP Bob Champion
ABBCHINPRTU rabbit punch
ABBCIILLTUY clubability
ABBCIILMNOY bibliomancy
ABBCILMOPST plastic bomb
ABBCKLMOOTT black bottom
ABBCKLNORYY black bryony
ABBCKNNNORU Bannockburn
ABBCLLMOOOT cobalt bloom
ABBDDEEGNOT debt bondage
ABBDDEGIORR bridgeboard
ABBDDEIINRR birdbrained
ABBDDOOORWW Bob Woodward
ABBDEEEFINR beef-brained
ABBDEEILRST bestridable
ABBDEELORTU redoubtable
ABBDEEMORRR armed robber
ABBDEGILNOT bold-beating
ABBDEGIOOOR boogie board
ABBDEGIORSY Boys' Brigade
ABBDEGNNRRU Brandenburg
ABBDEHLLORU Deborah Bull
ABBDEIILNTU indubitable
ABBDEIINRRU India rubber
india-rubber
ABBDEILORTU boat-builder
ABBDEINRTTU tribute band
ABBDELNOTUU undoubtable
ABBDELNSUUU unsubduable
ABBDELORTUY redoubtably
ABBDEMMNORT bombardment
ABBDFFILORU buffalo-bird
ABBDGGINNOR Brobdingnag
ABBDGIIINNS bias binding
ABBDGIJLNNO land-jobbing
ABBDGMNOOOW go down a bomb
ABBDHLNORRU L Ron Hubbard
ABBDIILNTUY indubitably
ABBDMNOOSTU boom and bust
ABBEEEGILNV Geneva Bible
ABBEEEHLLRT bear the bell
ABBEEEHRRUV hevea rubber
ABBEEEILNRT beetlebrain
ABBEEFFNOOR baron of beef
ABBEEFIRRTV rabbit fever
ABBEEGILLNU Belgian Blue
ABBEEGINRTW tear webbing
ABBEEGKRSUY Sergey Bubka
ABBEEGLRTTY Betty Grable
ABBEEHJKMOO Jakob Boehme
ABBEEHMMORX Max Beerbohm
ABBEEKLLNTU Blue Blanket
ABBEEKLORRT Robert Blake
ABBEEKLRSTU stubble rake
ABBEELMSSSU subassemble
ABBEELOPRRS barber's pole
ABBEELORRSU rabble-rouse
ABBEELPRRTU perturbable
ABBEEMNSSTU subbasement
ABBEFFLOORU buffalo robe
ABBEFIILLMY family Bible
ABBEFNORRSY Bryan Forbes
ABBEGGHLMUU humbuggable
ABBEGIJLNRY jabberingly
ABBEGIKLMOO go like a bomb
ABBEGINORRT bring to bear
ABBEGINORTW browbeating
ABBEGIOOTUY I Got You Babe
ABBEGLORRSU Lagos rubber
ABBEGMMNOOT megaton bomb
ABBEHHIPRSU rubbish heap
ABBEHIIRTTW White Rabbit
ABBEHILLPSU publishable
ABBEHILRSTW Welsh rabbit
ABBEHIORRTY bribery-oath
ABBEHLORRTY barley-broth
ABBEHNOORTT Berthon-boat
ABBEIILLMOS mobilisable
ABBEIILLMOZ mobilizable
ABBEIILLORT bibliolater
ABBEIJNORTT rabbet-joint
ABBEIKLOORS Basil Brooke
ABBEILORTTY liberty-boat
ABBEIMNRRTU Martin Buber
ABBEINOQRUY Quiberon Bay
ABBEINRSSUU suburbanise
ABBEINRSTUU suburbanite
ABBEINRSUUZ suburbanize
ABBELLMRSUU subumbrella

ABBELMSSSUY subassembly
ABBELNPRRTU rubber plant
ABBELORRRTU retrobulbar
ABBELOSTTUU bustle about
ABBEMPRRSTU rubber stamp
rubber-stamp
ABBEOOSSSTU obsess about
ABBFILLNORS Ribbon Falls
ABBGGIRRRSY Barry Briggs
ABBGHIMNOTU thingumabob
ABBGHIMNOTY thingamybob
ABBGIILLNTU bull-baiting
ABBGIINSTTY baby-sitting
ABBGILLNSTU ball-busting
ABBGILNORSY absorbingly
ABBGINORRSS ribbon-grass
ABBGLLORSUU subglobular
ABBHILLMNRU brahmin bull
ABBHJNOORRU John Barbour
ABBIILLORTY bibliolatry
ABBIILMNOOT bombilation
ABBIILMOPRS probabilism
ABBIILOPRST probabilist
ABBIILOPRTY probability
ABBIIMNNOOT bombination
ABBIMNOORTU obumbration
ABBIMNRSSUU suburbanism
ABBINNOORRS Brian Robson
ABBINRSTUUY suburbanity
ABBLLLLOOYY loblolly bay
ABCCCCILORY carbocyclic
ABCCCELNORY carbon cycle
ABCCCHIJKOS Jacob Schick
ABCCCHKKLOO chock-a-block
ABCCCILMOOX coxcombical
ABCCCNOORTU coconut crab
ABCCDDHIIKY chick-a-biddy
ABCCDEEIIRT bactericide
ABCCDEENNOS abscondence
ABCCDEFHIKN finch-backed
ABCCDEHHKNU hunchbacked
ABCCDEHIRRT bird-catcher
ABCCDEIIILL bacillicide
ABCCDEIINOZ benzoic acid
ABCCDEIIRSU suberic acid
ABCCDEIKNRR carrick bend
ABCCDEKKOOR crookbacked
ABCCDEKLMOY black comedy
ABCCDHHORRU broad church✧
broad-church
ABCCDHOORST Broad Scotch
ABCCDIILMPU plumbic acid
ABCCDIIRTUY butyric acid
ABCCDKLLNOU cock-and-bull
ABCCDOPRRUY cry cupboard
ABCCEEERSTW Rebecca West
ABCCEEFFKLO black coffee
ABCCEEHHMOR echo chamber
ABCCEEHKLNU uncheckable
ABCCEEHNNNO bonne chance
ABCCEEILMRS marcescible
ABCCEEILNOO eccaleobion
ABCCEEILNOT Cecil Beaton
ABCCEEILNOV conceivable
ABCCEEKLOPU peacock-blue
ABCCEELLLOT collectable
ABCCEELNNOT connectable
ABCCEELORRT correctable
ABCCEEMNNRU encumbrance
ABCCEEMRSUU sea cucumber
ABCCEEPRRST spectre crab
ABCCEFILNOS confiscable
ABCCEFIORSU bacciferous
ABCCEGINNOU concubinage
ABCCEGKLLRY black clergy
ABCCEHIILMO biochemical
ABCCEHIKMRS sick chamber
ABCCEHILNNN Chenin Blanc
ABCCEHILSTT cable-stitch
ABCCEHINRTT tectibranch
ABCCEHKRSTT back stretch
ABCCEHLRSTU scratch blue
ABCCEHOORTT boot-catcher
ABCCEIILLNO conciliable
ABCCEIILPTY peccability
ABCCEIKKLPR prickleback
ABCCEIKKLST stickleback
ABCCEIKLMRT balm-cricket
ABCCEIKLNPR Black Prince
ABCCEILNOVY conceivably
ABCCEILNSSU cubicalness
ABCCEILORTU corbiculate
ABCCEILOSTT ectoblastic
ABCCEILRRUV cruciverbal
ABCCEINORRT centrobaric
ABCCEINRRTY barycentric
ABCCEIOOPPT tobacco pipe
ABCCELORSUU succourable
ABCCEOORTTU cocoa butter
ABCCGIKLRRU Garrick Club
ABCCGILNNNU Canning Club
ABCCHKLNOST snatch block
ABCCIIKRRTT carrick bitt
ABCCIILLNSU subclinical
ABCCIILRSTU subcritical
ABCCIIMOORT macrobiotic
ABCCIIORSSU scribacious
ABCCIKLMNOR cramboclink
ABCCIKMMORU cork cambium
ABCCIKORTTY Toby Crackit
ABCCILLLOUY bucolically
ABCCILNOOUY conical buoy
ABCCILORRSU scrobicular
ABCCILORSTU subcortical
ABCCINNORUY concubinary
ABCCINNOTTU concubitant
ABCCINOOSTT tobacconist
ABCCINORTUY buccinatory
ABCCIOORSUV baccivorous
ABCCKNOOOTU account book
book-account
ABCCKNORTUY back-country

ABCCLLNORTU Carlton Club
ABCCNNOOPTU puncto banco
ABCCNORSTTU subcontract
ABCDDEEELNS descendable
ABCDDEEFLOU double-faced
ABCDDEEHLUY debauchedly
ABCDDEEHNUU undebauched
ABCDDEEILNU undecidable
ABCDDEELNOS close-banded
ABCDDEFILRR fiddler crab
ABCDDEFINOR forbiddance
ABCDDEFLOOY bloody-faced
ABCDDEILNOO Blood and Ice
ABCDDEKNORU round-backed
ABCDDENORSS crossbanded
ABCDEEEERRT decerebrate
ABCDEEEHORS cheeseboard
ABCDEEEKORR code-breaker
ABCDEEFHILL bleach-field
ABCDEEFHNRR French bread
ABCDEEGINNR Grecian bend
ABCDEEHMNTU debauchment
ABCDEEIILMM immedicable
ABCDEEIILMN medicinable
ABCDEEIJKOR Derek Jacobi
ABCDEEILLMN clean-limbed
ABCDEEILMOW bid a welcome
ABCDEEILNRS rescindable
ABCDEEILORV divorceable
ABCDEEILPRT predictable
ABCDEEINORS decarbonise
ABCDEEINORZ decarbonize
ABCDEEIRRSU decarburise
ABCDEEIRRUZ decarburize
ABCDEELLNOW clean bowled
ABCDEELLNRU Leander Club
ABCDEELLNRY belly dancer
ABCDEELMMNO commendable
ABCDEELMNNO condemnable
ABCDEELMORU double cream
ABCDEELNNOS condensable
ABCDEELNRRY candleberry
ABCDEELOPSU double-space
ABCDEELORRS close-barred
ABCDEENORRT centreboard
ABCDEERRTTU carburetted
ABCDEFIINRR bird-fancier
ABCDEGHIINR chain bridge
ABCDEGHKLOT the black dog
ABCDEGILOOW W A B Coolidge
ABCDEHIILLN chilblained
ABCDEHIKPRS brick-shaped
ABCDEHILORR charbroiled
ABCDEHILSTW switchblade
ABCDEHIRRTW birdwatcher
ABCDEHLLOOR old bachelor
ABCDEHLMOOR bachelordom
ABCDEIILLRU billiard cue
ABCDEIILMRU Lumbricidae
ABCDEIILOSS dissociable
ABCDEIILTUY educability
ABCDEIINSTU subindicate
ABCDEIIORTT obiter dicta
ABCDEIIPSTU bicuspidate
ABCDEILOORT carbide tool
ABCDEILORRS soldier crab
ABCDEILPRTY predictably
ABCDEILRRST blister card
ABCDEILSSSU discussable
ABCDEINOORT noticeboard
ABCDEINRSTU disturbance
ABCDEINSSSU subacidness
ABCDEIOOPRS Proboscidea
ABCDEIORRSV scriveboard
ABCDEIPPRTY bradypeptic
ABCDEKLLORS balderlocks
ABCDEKLMRUX Max Delbrück
ABCDEKLOPRW black powder
ABCDELLORUY boulder clay
ABCDELMMNOY commendably
ABCDELMNRUU Cumbernauld
ABCDELNNORU banner cloud
ABCDELORRWY Clyde Barrow
ABCDENNORSY body scanner
ABCDENORSUY subdeaconry
ABCDEORRRSS crossbarred
ABCDFGKOOOR Back for Good
ABCDFIMOSSY body fascism
ABCDFIOSSTY body fascist
ABCDGHINOOV Bogdanovich
ABCDGIIILMN aid climbing
ABCDGIIKLNS backsliding
ABCDGIINSUV scuba diving
ABCDGIKNNOW backing-down
ABCDHIIMRTY dithyrambic
ABCDHIIRSTU Hudibrastic
ABCDHINOOPR branchiopod
ABCDHIOPSTX dispatch box✧
ABCDHIORSTW switchboard
ABCDHJNORUY John Cadbury
ABCDHLOOORS board-school
school board
ABCDHLOORRU cold harbour
ABCDHNOORRY hydrocarbon
ABCDIIILOST idioblastic
ABCDIILORYY ciliary body
ABCDIILOSSY dissociably
ABCDIIMNOSY biodynamics
ABCDILLNPSU public lands
ABCDINORSUY subordinacy
ABCDLMOSUUY Columbus Day
ABCDMNORRUU Carborundum®
ABCEEEFFKOR coffee break
ABCEEEFFLOT coffee table
ABCEEEFIINT beneficiate
ABCEEEFLNOR enforceable
ABCEEEFLOPR place before
ABCEEEGLLNT neglectable
ABCEEEHIKRT break the ice
ABCEEEHMNRT beech marten
ABCEEEILMPR imperceable
ABCEEEILNRX inexecrable

ABCEEEILPRV perceivable
ABCEEEILPTT battle-piece
ABCEEEILRSV receivables
serviceable
ABCEEEILRSX exercisable
ABCEEEINNSS bienséances
ABCEEELLNTU unelectable
ABCEEELMNRS resemblance
ABCEEELORRV recoverable
ABCEEELPRRU recuperable
ABCEEELPRST respectable
ABCEEEMMNRR remembrance✧
ABCEEEMMNRT embracement
ABCEEFGHORR herb-of-grace
ABCEEFHIKRR chief barker
ABCEEFHMMRU fume chamber
ABCEEFIILPS specifiable
ABCEEFIILRT certifiable
rectifiable
ABCEEFIINRY beneficiary
ABCEEFILLMR leaf-climber
ABCEEFINNOT benefaction
ABCEEFINRTU rubefacient
ABCEEFKORTY take by force
ABCEEFLNORR conferrable
ABCEEFNORTY benefactory
ABCEEGGILRS beggar's lice
ABCEEGHLLNT cable-length
ABCEEGIIKNR icebreaking
ABCEEGIIMPT gambit-piece
ABCEEGIINOT abiogenetic
ABCEEGIJMRR Jim Bergerac
ABCEEGILLOR cabriole leg
ABCEEGLNORS Serge Blanco
ABCEEHIILRR Cherie Blair
ABCEEHIKKMT kick the beam
ABCEEHIKLPU pickelhaube
ABCEEHILMST thimble case
ABCEEHIMNVY Maeve Binchy
ABCEEHINNRS Sennacherib
ABCEEHINPST spinach beet
ABCEEHINRRV River Chenab
ABCEEHINSSU bien chaussé
ABCEEHKLNOS shackle-bone
ABCEEHKLNQU blank cheque
ABCEEHLLLRS Charles Bell
ABCEEHLLORT cholera belt
ABCEEHLOOST Chelsea boot
ABCEEHMNRRW bench-warmer
ABCEEHMOSUU amuse-bouche
ABCEEHMRTTU butcher meat
ABCEEHNNRSW Ben Crenshaw
ABCEEHORRRT torchbearer
ABCEEIILNRT Celtiberian
ABCEEIILNTX inexcitable
ABCEEIJKKRT biker jacket
ABCEEIJOTTV objectivate
ABCEEILLMPT Campbellite
ABCEEILLNTU ineluctable
ABCEEILMRRS cerebralism
ABCEEILNOPT beneplacito
ABCEEILNORT celebration
ABCEEILNPSS Basil Spence
ABCEEILNSUX inexcusable
ABCEEILNTUX unexcitable
ABCEEILOOTT bootlace tie
ABCEEILOQSU oblique case
ABCEEILORRV irrevocable
ABCEEILPRVY perceivably
ABCEEILRRST cerebralist
ABCEEILRRSU irrecusable
ABCEEILRRTT retractible
ABCEEILRRTU recruitable
ABCEEILRSVY serviceably
ABCEEILRTTX extractible
ABCEEILSSST ecblastesis
ABCEEIMRTUU eubacterium
ABCEEINNOST incense-boat
ABCEEINNRTY bicentenary
ABCEEINORRT cerebration
ABCEEINORTX exorbitance
ABCEEIORSTT stereobatic
ABCEEIPRRTT carpet biter
ABCEEKKLNRU bareknuckle
ABCEEKKORRR rock breaker
ABCEEKLLRTT black letter
ABCEEKLLTVV black velvet
ABCEEKLPPPR black pepper
ABCEEKLRRRW kerb-crawler
ABCEELLLMOP compellable
ABCEELLMOPT completable
ABCEELLMRSU mallee scrub
ABCEELLOOST blastocoele
ABCEELLRRSW screwballer
ABCEELMNOPS compensable
ABCEELMORRV clamber over
ABCEELNOQRU conquerable
ABCEELNORST carbon steel
Eastern bloc
ABCEELNORSV conservable
conversable
ABCEELNOSTT contestable
ABCEELNOUVV valve bounce
ABCEELNRSSU curableness
ABCEELNRSTU cluster-bean
ABCEELOPRRR procerebral
ABCEELORRTY celebratory
ABCEELPRSTY respectably
ABCEELPSSTU suspectable
ABCEELRTTUU tuberculate
ABCEEMRRTTU butter cream
ABCEENNORTU bean counter
ABCEENORRST arborescent
ABCEENORSTU counterbase
ABCEENPRRTU perturbance
ABCEEORRRSS crossbearer
ABCEEORSTUU tuberaceous
ABCEEORSTUV Beaver Scout
ABCEERRRTTU carburetter
ABCEFFHISSS Schiff's base
ABCEFGIKLRU black-figure
ABCEFHIKLRS black-fisher

ABCEFHNOOPR francophobe✧
ABCEFIILLNT inflictable
ABCEFIILRTY certifiably
ABCEFIKORTZ Rifat Ozbeck
ABCEFILMNOR confirmable
ABCEFINORTU rubefaction
ABCEFKLLLOW black-fellow
ABCEFLMNOOR conformable
ABCEFLMOORT comfortable
ABCEFLMRRSU Farmers Club
ABCEFLOORRU labour force
ABCEGGIKRST beggar ticks
ABCEGHORRTU turbocharge
ABCEGIILMPU public image
ABCEGIILNOT incogitable
ABCEGILLMTU magic bullet
ABCEGILLNRS sacring bell
ABCEGILMNRY embracingly
ABCEGILNNOS consignable
ABCEGILNOPW pace-bowling
ABCEGILNOST blastogenic
ABCEGIMMNRU magic number
ABCEGIMNPRU bumping race
ABCEGJLOSST object-glass
ABCEGKLORSU black grouse
ABCEGLLORSU bogus caller
ABCEGORSTUY subcategory
ABCEHHIOOPT theophobiac
ABCEHHKRSUW bushwhacker
ABCEHHNNRSU Hans Buchner
ABCEHIIMRST Rechabitism
ABCEHIIMRSW Micawberish
ABCEHIIRTTV active birth
ABCEHIKNRSU Chris Eubank
ABCEHILMORS bachelorism
ABCEHILNORV olive branch
ABCEHILOPSU bicephalous
ABCEHILRTUV Lubavitcher
ABCEHIMORRT thermobaric
ABCEHIMRTTY bathymetric
ABCEHINNRST Ernst B Chain
ABCEHINOOPR necrophobia
ABCEHINPSTY spy in the cab
ABCEHIOPRRS broach-spire
ABCEHIORSSU Susie Orbach
ABCEHKLLOST shackle-bolt
ABCEHKLNOSU unshockable
ABCEHKOORTT rock the boat
ABCEHKPSSTU pass the buck
ABCEHLNNORU luncheon-bar
ABCEHLNOTUU untouchable
ABCEHLNRSUU uncrushable
ABCEHLORTTT bottle-chart
ABCEHMPRTTU Bach trumpet
ABCEHNOORRT Robert Cohan
ABCEHNOORRW bower-anchor
ABCEHRRSTTU chart-buster
ABCEHRSSTTU bruschettas
ABCEIIILLSV civilisable
ABCEIIILLVZ civilizable
ABCEIIILNSV basilic vein
ABCEIIIOSTV bisociative
ABCEIIJLSTU justiciable
ABCEIIKLNRT tickle-brain
ABCEIILMNRU Mulciberian
ABCEIILMRTY imbricately
ABCEIILNOSV cablevision
ABCEIILRTUV lubricative
ABCEIIMMRSW Micawberism
ABCEIIMNOTV combinative
ABCEIIORSST bacteriosis
ABCEIKLPRST blister pack
ABCEIKLRRRU bulk carrier
ABCEIKMMRSW backswimmer
ABCEIKNOOPT a bone to pick
ABCEIKNORTW cabinetwork
ABCEIKNSSWW Bewick's swan
ABCEILLLLLU Lucille Ball
ABCEILLLMRW wallclimber
ABCEILLLOPS collapsible
ABCEILLLOQU colliquable
ABCEILLMOOR Claire Bloom
ABCEILLMORU bimolecular
ABCEILLNTUY ineluctably
ABCEILLRTUV carvel-built
ABCEILMMOTT committable
ABCEILMOPRS comprisable
ABCEILMOPRT problematic
ABCEILMORST meroblastic
ABCEILMOSST mesoblastic
ABCEILNNOTU continuable
ABCEILNORTV contrivable
ABCEILNRSTU inscrutable
ABCEILNSUXY inexcusably
ABCEILOPTTV captive bolt
ABCEILORRSU orbiculares
ABCEILORRVY irrevocably
ABCEILORSTT obstetrical
ABCEILOSSUV subvocalise
ABCEILOSUVZ subvocalize
ABCEILPSTUU usucaptible
ABCEILRRSUY irrecusably
ABCEILRSTUU bursiculate
ABCEILRSTUV subvertical
ABCEILRTUVY Variety Club
ABCEIMNNORT recombinant
ABCEIMNOORT embrocation
ABCEINNORTY cybernation
ABCEINNSSTU in substance
ABCEINOORST obsecration
ABCEINOOSTT incest taboo
ABCEINORRTU carburetion
ABCEINORTXY exorbitancy
ABCEINRRRST transcriber
ABCEIOOPRRT bicorporate
ABCEIORSTUU cruise about
ABCEIRSTTUV subtractive
ABCEJMNORSU James Coburn
ABCEKKLLLNU knuckleball
ABCEKKLMORS black smoker
ABCEKLLMNOT mental block
ABCEKMORRRT RBMK reactor

ABCELLLMNOO collembolan
ABCELLLRSUU subcellular
ABCELLMNOOS salmon coble
ABCELLMOPRY Roy Campbell
ABCELLNSSTU sanctus bell
ABCELMORTUU tuberculoma
ABCELNNORTU contubernal
ABCELNNOTUU uncountable
ABCELNORSSU uncrossable
ABCELNORSTU construable
ABCELNORSVY conversably
ABCELORSSUU scaberulous
ABCENRRSTUY canterburys
ABCEOOORRRT corroborate
ABCEORRRTTU carburettor
ABCEORSTUUY butyraceous
ABCFGIIKLLN backfilling
ABCFGIIKNTT backfitting
ABCFGIKORST bag of tricks
ABCFHIKMOOO Book of Micah
ABCFHINOOST son of a bitch
ABCFIILLMOR bacilliform
ABCFIINORTU bifurcation
ABCFINOOSTU obfuscation
ABCFKNOORTT back to front
ABCFLMNOORY conformably
ABCFLMOORTY comfortably
ABCFOORSTUY obfuscatory
ABCGGHINNPU punching-bag
ABCGHIKKLNT black knight
ABCGHIKLPTU backup light
ABCGHIKNSUW buck-washing
ABCGHILNOOP anglophobic✧
ABCGHILNORU Brian Clough
ABCGHOORRSU Scarborough
ABCGIIKKMNR brickmaking
ABCGIIKLNRY bricklaying
ABCGIIKNOUV bivouacking
ABCGIILLOST go ballistic
ABCGIINNPUY panic-buying
ABCGIKNNNRU running back
ABCGIKNPSSU buck passing
buck-passing
ABCGILLMNSY scamblingly
ABCGILLOORY bryological
ABCHHIILOTT batholithic
ABCHHIILTTY bathylithic
ABCHHILOOOP ochlophobia
ABCHHLNOOPR lophobranch
ABCHIILNOOT halobiontic
ABCHIILNRTY labyrinthic
ABCHIILOPSY biophysical
ABCHIIOOPTX toxiphobiac
ABCHILLOOST holoblastic
ABCHILMNPSU clubmanship
ABCHILMOOST homoblastic
ABCHILNOORR bronchiolar
ABCHILNOPRT branch-pilot
ABCHILOPSTY hypoblastic
ABCHIMNORSU subharmonic
ABCHIMOTTUU much about it
ABCHIMPRRSY brachyprism
ABCHINOOPTY nyctophobia
ABCHINORRSY chrysarobin
ABCHIOOOPPS scopophobia
ABCHIOOOPST Scotophobia
ABCHIOOPRTU Turcophobia
ABCHKOOSSUY yah-boo sucks
ABCHLMNOPRU pulmobranch
ABCHLORSTUU Authors' Club
ABCHORRSUUY brachyurous
ABCHOSTTUWY cut both ways
ABCIIILNRTU tribunicial
ABCIIILOSTY sociability
ABCIIILRSTT tribalistic
ABCIIIMNORT imbrication
ABCIIINNRTU tribunician
ABCIIINOOST bisociation
ABCIIKLNRSY brainsickly
ABCIIKLNSUW Kiwanis Club
ABCIILLMRSU lumbricalis
ABCIILLPTUY culpability
ABCIILLRSTY trisyllabic
ABCIILLSTYY syllabicity
ABCIILNOPTU publication
ABCIILNORTU lubrication
ABCIILOOPRV Pico Bolívar
ABCIILORRSU orbicularis
ABCIIMNNOOT combination
ABCIINORRTU rubrication
ABCIINORSTT abstriction
ABCIIOOPRST saprobiotic
ABCIKLLMMSU Black Muslim
ABCIKLMOTTU buttock-mail
ABCILLNNOUY connubially
ABCILLNORUY binocularly
ABCILLNORYY Byronically
ABCILLORRUY orbicularly
ABCILMMNOSU somnambulic
ABCILMMORUU columbarium
ABCILMNNUUU incunabulum
ABCILMNOPUW public woman
ABCILMRSTUU rumbustical
ABCILNNOORS Sorbonnical
ABCILNORTUU lucubration
ABCILNRSTUY inscrutably
ABCILOPRSTU subtropical
ABCILORSUUV baculovirus
ABCIMNOORTY combinatory
ABCIMNORSTY corybantism
ABCIMOPSUVX pax vobiscum
ABCINNOORTU conurbation
ABCINNOPTTU panic button
ABCINOORSTU obscuration
ABCINORSTTU subtraction
ABCLLRSTUUU subcultural
ABCMNOORSSW crossbowman
ABCNOOORRRT corroborant
ABCNORRSTUY subcontrary
ABCORRSSTTU substractor
ABDDDEEEFLS false-bedded
ABDDDEGINNW wedding band

ABDDDEIMNOR broadminded
ABDDDIIMNOR diamond bird
ABDDEEEGLMR marble-edged
ABDDEEEILTY baddeleyite
ABDDEEELNOR bandoleered
ABDDEEELRTT treble-dated
ABDDEEEMPRT bad-tempered
ABDDEEENSSS debasedness
ABDDEEFLNRR bladder fern
ABDDEEGGLNY bandy-legged
ABDDEEHILLS shad-bellied
ABDDEEHLOSU double-shade
ABDDEEIIMNR bridemaiden
ABDDEEILNOR bandoliered
ABDDEEPRRRY drap-de-Berry
ABDDEFHLLOO half-blooded
ABDDEFILOTU fiddle about
ABDDEFLNORU fardel-bound
ABDDEGIKORR Dirk Bogarde
ABDDEGINNST standing bed
ABDDEHLLNOO lo and behold
ABDDEHNNSUU unhusbanded
ABDDEIIILNV individable
ABDDEIILNUV undividable
ABDDEILLNRU dull-brained
ABDDEILLOUY daily double
ABDDEILMRSW swim bladder
ABDDEILOPTU piddle about
ABDDEIMNNST disbandment
ABDDEINOWWY bay-windowed
ABDDEKOORSS address book
ABDDELMOORW warm-blooded
ABDDELMORRW bladderworm
ABDDELORRTW bladderwort
ABDDGIINNRV driving-band
ABDDGIINORV diving board
ABDDGINOORR dragoon-bird
ABDDHLOOORT Bardo Thodol
ABDDLNOOSUY body and soul
ABDEEEGLLOU double eagle
ABDEEEGLNUW unwedgeable
ABDEEEHILNV leave behind
ABDEEEHILRT hereditable
ABDEEEHIMRT ride the beam
ABDEEEHLLVW well-behaved
ABDEEEHLRST shard beetle
ABDEEEILLRV deliverable
ABDEEEILPPP apple-pie bed
ABDEEEIMNTW between-maid
ABDEEEKLNTW blanketweed
ABDEEELLOPV developable
ABDEEELMNRU denumerable
ABDEEELNSST belatedness
ABDEEELORSV sleeve board
ABDEEELRRRW reed warbler
ABDEEELRRSS redressable
ABDEEENRRRU underbearer
ABDEEEORRTT teeter-board
ABDEEEOTTTV vedette-boat
ABDEEEPRSTT bespattered
ABDEEERRTTV vertebrated
ABDEEFGIIRR fire brigade
ABDEEFGNOSU sang-de-boeuf
ABDEEFIILNN indefinable
ABDEEFIINRT defibrinate
ABDEEFILLTT battlefield
ABDEEFILNNU undefinable
ABDEEFILNRT Alfred Binet
ABDEEFLLNOR Alfred Nobel
ABDEEFLORRY Earl of Derby
ABDEEFNOORR free on board
ABDEEGGINRR gingerbread✧
ABDEEGHHOTY go by the head
ABDEEGHNORY honey badger
ABDEEGIKNRR barking deer
ABDEEGILLSW swag-bellied
ABDEEGIMNRT abridgement
ABDEEGINPRS bespreading
ABDEEGIRSSS asses' bridge
ABDEEGLNNRU urban legend
ABDEEGLNOTU double agent
ABDEEGLOSTU about-sledge
ABDEEHILRTW bridewealth
ABDEEHILSST established
ABDEEHIRSTW breadthwise
ABDEEHLOSTT tables d'hôte
ABDEEHLOTTU at the double
ABDEEHMRTTU beat the drum
ABDEEHNRRTU underbreath
ABDEEIIJMRS James Bridie
ABDEEIIKLLS dislikeable
ABDEEIILNOT obediential
ABDEEIILRST detribalise
ABDEEIILRTZ detribalize
ABDEEIILSST destabilise
ABDEEIILSTZ destabilize
ABDEEIKNRRW Windbreaker®
ABDEEILMNNO denominable
ABDEEILMNRS simnel bread
ABDEEILMNST disablement
ABDEEILMSSS disassemble
ABDEEILNNOO Daniel Boone
ABDEEILNNRT dinner table
ABDEEILNPSS dispensable
ABDEEILNRSU undesirable
ABDEEILNRTU unliberated
ABDEEILNRUV undriveable
ABDEEILNSSU audibleness
ABDEEILORRT deliberator
ABDEEILORTT obliterated
ABDEEIMNRST Namib Desert
ABDEEINNRRS Bernardines
ABDEEINNRRW breadwinner
ABDEEINRRUV River Danube
ABDEEIPRRSZ zebra spider
ABDEEIPRSTU Buprestidae
ABDEEIRTTTU deattribute
ABDEEISTTVY Betty Davies
ABDEEKLNOOR book-learned
ABDEEKLOPSU doublespeak
ABDEEKMNORY monkey bread
ABDEEKNORRT Derek Barton

Words marked ✧ can also be spelled with one or more capital letters

ABDEEKNORSZ	baker's dozen
ABDEELLLORR	Rollerblade®
	rollerblade
ABDEELLNOPW	Baden-Powell
ABDEELMNORZ	bronze medal
ABDEELMNOTU	demountable
ABDEELMNRUY	denumerably
ABDEELNNRRU	Blade Runner
ABDEELNNRUU	unendurable
ABDEELNOSST	bloatedness
ABDEELNRSSU	durableness
ABDEELNRSTW	waldsterben✧
ABDEELOPPTT	table-topped
ABDEELOPRSU	double spare
	pas redoublé
ABDEELORRTT	letter-board
ABDEELORRTW	world-beater
ABDEELORSTY	destroyable
ABDEELRSSTT	battledress
ABDEEMNORTY	embryonated
ABDEEMRSSUY	Burmese Days
ABDEENNORRT	André Breton
ABDEENORSTX	sandbox tree
ABDEEORRRSW	sword-bearer
ABDEEQRRRTU	quarter-bred
ABDEFFLORRU	luffer-board
ABDEFGIIRRT	frigate bird
ABDEFGINORR	fingerboard
ABDEFGIRSSU	figured bass
ABDEFHOORTT	footbreadth
ABDEFIILLRT	fibrillated
ABDEFIILNNY	indefinably
ABDEFILNOTY	field botany
ABDEFILNRRS	Flinders bar
ABDEFLLOTUU	double fault
	double-fault
ABDEGGILNOR	Goldbergian
ABDEGGILNOT	gold-beating
ABDEGGINORR	ragged Robin
ABDEGGINRWY	windbaggery
ABDEGHHILTT	high-battled
ABDEGHHOORU	headborough
ABDEGHINSTT	the dingbats
ABDEGHLOOPS	bog asphodel
ABDEGHLORSU	shoulder bag
ABDEGHMNRTU	bang the drum
ABDEGIILNNT	dining table
ABDEGIILSSU	disguisable
ABDEGIINPRT	paint-bridge
ABDEGIKNOOR	reading-book
ABDEGILLNRV	gravel-blind
ABDEGILNOWW	gable window
ABDEGILOOUX	dialogue box
ABDEGINNORS	Dennis Gabor
ABDEGINNPSW	spawning-bed
ABDEGKNORRU	break ground
ABDEGLMOOTT	bottom-glade
ABDEGLNOOOR	blood orange
ABDEGNOORUV	above-ground
ABDEGOOORRV	go overboard
ABDEGORRTTU	gutter board
ABDEHHMOORR	rhombohedra
ABDEHIINNTU	uninhabited
ABDEHIKLNSU	husbandlike
ABDEHILNOSU	unabolished
ABDEHKMMRTU	thumb-marked
ABDEHLLMOOR	hall-bedroom
ABDEHLLNRTU	Thunderball
ABDEHLNSSSU	husbandless
ABDEHLOORST	heart's-blood
ABDEHLOORSV	shovelboard
ABDEHLOPRSU	double-sharp
ABDEHMOORRT	motherboard
ABDEHNORRUU	unharboured
ABDEHNORTTU	Tudorbethan
ABDEHNOSSTU	basset hound
	basset-hound
ABDEHORRSUU	harbour dues
ABDEIIILNTY	deniability
ABDEIILLLST	distillable
ABDEIILLTWY	weldability
ABDEIILMNOT	indomitable
ABDEIILMQRU	amber liquid
ABDEIILRSTU	bridal suite
ABDEIIMNOST	demi-bastion
ABDEIINNRRY	Indian berry
ABDEIINRTTU	inturbidate
ABDEIKLNNRU	undrinkable
ABDEIKNORTW	break it down
ABDEIKORSTY	keyboardist
ABDEILLLSSY	dissyllable
ABDEILLOSSV	dissolvable
ABDEILMNOPU	impoundable
ABDEILMOTTU	tolbutamide
ABDEILMSSSY	disassembly
ABDEILNNORT	bonnet laird
ABDEILNPSSY	dispensably
ABDEILNRSUY	undesirably
ABDEILNSSUY	unbiassedly
ABDEILOPRSS	bolas spider
ABDEILOPRSV	disprovable
ABDEIMNOOST	mastoid bone
ABDEINNORWW	window-barne
ABDEINORSTU	subordinate
ABDEIPRSSST	striped bass
ABDEKMNOORY	monkey board
ABDEKMNOOTU	make no doubt
ABDELLLNSUY	unsyllabled
ABDELLMNRSU	slumberland
ABDELLNOORS	ob-and-soller
ABDELMOORST	bloodstream
ABDELNNOSUU	unsoundable
ABDELNNOUUW	unwoundable
ABDELNNRUUY	unendurably
ABDELNORRTY	Bernard Lyot
ABDELOORRUV	louver-board
	louvre-board
ABDELOORRWW	wood warbler
ABDELOOSTWY	bloody-sweat
ABDELOPRRTU	protrudable
ABDEMMOORRY	memory board
ABDEMNOORWW	meadow-brown

ABDENNORSTV bondservant
ABDENOORRSW snowboarder
ABDENOORTUW wonder about
ABDENOPRSUU superabound
ABDENORSTVY body servant
ABDEOOOPRTT torpedo boat
ABDEOPRRSST ports de bras
ABDEOPRTTUY probate duty
ABDFGHIILNN half-binding
ABDFGHIRRTY graft hybrid
ABDFIILLSYY disyllabify
ABDFIILNNUU infundibula
ABDFILMOORR dolabriform
ABDFKNNOORS Frank Dobson
ABDFLLOOORW follow-board
ABDFNOORUUX fauxbourdon
ABDGGHIKNOO badging-hook
ABDGGILNORS Ronald Biggs
ABDGHHJNOOO John Habgood
ABDGHIIINRT riding habit
ABDGHILNSTY sandy blight
ABDGHINNOSW bond-washing
ABDGHINPSSU spud-bashing
ABDGIIINRTY binary digit
ABDGIILLLNU all-building
ABDGIINNOPR pair-bonding
ABDGILLOOOY diabolology
ABDGILLORSW gallows-bird
ABDGILMORRU bur-marigold
ABDGILNNOSW snowblading
ABDGILNOPTT blotting-pad
ABDGINOPRRS springboard
ABDGINORRST stringboard
ABDGKNNOORS Gordon Banks
ABDGMOORRSS smörgåsbord
ABDGNNNORSY granny bonds
ABDHHIOOPRY hydrophobia
ABDHIMNNOPS bondmanship
ABDHIMOOOPR dromophobia
ABDHINOOPRS on shipboard
ABDHLMOOOST Thomas Blood
ABDIIILLLNY libidinally
ABDIIILRTVY drivability
ABDIIINNNOS Indian bison
ABDIIKLNOOS Bioko Island
ABDIILLMRWY William Byrd
ABDIILLMSSY disyllabism
ABDIILMNOTY indomitably
ABDIILNOTUZ Butazolidin®
ABDIINOORSY obsidionary
ABDIINOOSTY isoantibody
ABDIINORRSY Sir Robin Day
ABDIINOSTUU subaudition
ABDIKLNNOWW blank window
ABDILLNRTWY Willy Brandt
ABDILLORRRW drill-barrow
ABDILMNORUU burial mound
ABDILNNPRUW Dublin prawn
ABDILNOOPSV blood-spavin
ABDILNOPRSU spiral bound
ABDIMNNOSTU subdominant
ABDIMNOORTT motor-bandit
ABDINORRSUY subordinary
ABDLMOORRSU dorsolumbar
ABDLNOOOSTT odontoblast
ABDMOORRUZZ moorbuzzard
ABDNNOORSTU baton rounds
ABDNRRRSTUU surturbrand
ABEEEEFLORS foreseeable
ABEEEEGLNRR regenerable
ABEEEEIKLMV make believe
make-believe
ABEEEELRTTW water beetle
ABEEEEMNRTV bereavement
ABEEEERRRTV reverberate
ABEEEFFINOP banoffee pie
ABEEEFHIRRT breathe fire
ABEEEFIRRRR barrier reef
ABEEEFLLLRU refuellable
ABEEEFLMNRT fermentable
ABEEEFLPRRR preferrable
ABEEEGGILLN negligeable
ABEEEGGKLOR George Blake
ABEEEGIKSST siege basket
ABEEEGIRRTV verbigerate
ABEEEGLORSW elbow-grease
ABEEEGLRRTT regrettable
ABEEEHHINPR hebephrenia
ABEEEHHLLRT bell-heather
heather bell
ABEEEHINRRT Bertie Ahern
ABEEEHLRSTW breast wheel
ABEEEHMNRRV Bremerhaven
ABEEEHNNORT near the bone
ABEEEHNRRSY Barry Sheene
ABEEEHORRTV over-breathe
ABEEEIILNPS plebeianise
ABEEEIILNPZ plebeianize
ABEEEILLLMN Nellie Melba
ABEEEILLPRV repleviable
ABEEEILMMPR impermeable
ABEEEILMMST emblematise
ABEEEILMMTZ emblematize
ABEEEILNRSV inseverable
ABEEEILPRRY Pierre Bayle
ABEEEILRRTU Blaue Reiter
ABEEEILRRTV retrievable
ABEEEIMNRRU beurre manié
ABEEEIMNSST absenteeism
ABEEEINSTUV Sainte-Beuve
ABEEEJMMNNT enjambement
ABEEEKNRRSV reserve bank
ABEEEKRRSTT Baker Street
ABEEELLMNYY by my lee-lane
ABEEELMNNTT entablement
ABEEELMNRRU remunerable
ABEEELNNRUV unvenerable
ABEEELNNSST tenableness
ABEEELNPRST presentable
ABEEELNPRTV preventable
ABEEELNQSSU equableness
ABEEELPPRRT perpetrable

ABEEELPPRTU perpetuable
ABEEELPRRST Albert Speer
ABEEELPRRSV preservable
ABEEELPSTUY beauty sleep
ABEEEMOPRTT obtemperate
ABEEENQTUUY beauty queen
ABEEENRRRRW Werner Arber
ABEEENRRRTV reverberant
ABEEEPRRRSU purse-bearer
ABEEFFHLRTU buff-leather
ABEEFFILORT forfeitable
ABEEFFOOPRU opera bouffe
opéra bouffe
ABEEFFRSTTU buffer state
ABEEFGILNRR refrangible
ABEEFGLORTT forgettable
ABEEFGNORSV bag of nerves
ABEEFIILLQU liquefiable
ABEEFIKLNRT fire blanket
ABEEFILNRSS friableness
ABEEFILPRTU putrefiable
ABEEFILRRTU irrefutable
ABEEFKLMNNY Fanny Kemble
ABEEFLLNOOT footballene
ABEEFLLNSSU balefulness
ABEEFLMOPRR performable
ABEEFLNNSSU banefulness
ABEEFLORSUW sea furbelow
ABEEFNRRRTU afterburner
ABEEFOPRSTY beast of prey
ABEEGGIILLV give leg bail
ABEEGGILNPS sleeping bag
ABEEGGLRUUY rugby league✧
ABEEGHIKNST baking sheet
ABEEGHILPPT the Big Apple
ABEEGIIJNTW wag-'n-bietjie
ABEEGIILNRT libertinage
ABEEGIILNRV live-bearing
ABEEGIILRRS bersaglieri
ABEEGIINNRR bearing rein
ABEEGIINOSS abiogenesis
ABEEGIKLNNT telebanking
ABEEGILMNPR impregnable
ABEEGILMORT great mobile
ABEEGILNRUZ gaberlunzie
ABEEGILOTTT tattiebogle
tattie-bogle
ABEEGILRRST registrable
ABEEGINORRV overbearing
ABEEGLMOPPR problem page
ABEEGLNOSTU obtuse angle
ABEEGLRRTTY regrettably
ABEEGMMNRSU numbers game
ABEEGNORSST barge-stones
ABEEGORTTUW water bouget
ABEEHHPRSTY bathysphere
ABEEHIILNRT inheritable
ABEEHIKPRRS ship-breaker
ABEEHILLSTW whistleable
ABEEHILPRSS perishables
ABEEHILRSST establisher
re-establish
ABEEHILSTUX exhaustible
ABEEHIMOOPT emetophobia
ABEEHINPRSS spine-basher
ABEEHINRSSS bearishness
ABEEHINRSST breathiness
ABEEHIRRSST Barsetshire
ABEEHIRRTTT bitter-earth
ABEEHKNORRT heartbroken
ABEEHKOPRRS shopbreaker
ABEEHLLNOPT open the ball
ABEEHLNORTT the noble art
ABEEHLOORST Athole brose
ABEEHLORRSU barrelhouse
ABEEHLORRWW wheelbarrow
ABEEHLORSUY Aubrey holes
ABEEHLOSSTU bastel-house
bastle-house
ABEEHLOSTTU the absolute✧
ABEEHNOPRRY hyperborean
ABEEHNORSTW Noah Webster
ABEEHNORTTT on the batter
ABEEHORRSTT rother-beast
ABEEHORSTTU thereabouts
ABEEHORSTUW whereabouts
ABEEIILMNPS plebeianism
ABEEIILMNST inestimable
ABEEIILMPRV imperviable
ABEEIILNQTU inequitable
ABEEIILQRTU equilibrate
ABEEIKLLNSS likableness
ABEEIKLLRSV Baskerville
ABEEIKLMNRT blanket mire
ABEEIKLMORR boilermaker
ABEEIKLNNRX Karen Blixen
ABEEILLMOPT tempolabile
ABEEILLNORT intolerable
ABEEILLNPSS pliableness
ABEEILLNRSS liberalness
ABEEILLNRSU Lesbian rule
ABEEILLOPRT boilerplate
ABEEILLOPTX exploitable
ABEEILLOTTT toilet table
ABEEILLRSST Leisler's bat
ABEEILMMORS memorisable
ABEEILMMORZ memorizable
ABEEILMMOSV immoveables
ABEEILMMPRY impermeably
ABEEILMMRRU mare liberum
ABEEILMMSTT emblematist
ABEEILMNNOT mentionable
ABEEILMNNRU innumerable
ABEEILMNOOT emotionable
ABEEILMNRTU unmeritable
ABEEILMORRV irremovable
ABEEILMORST steam boiler
ABEEILNNOPS pensionable
ABEEILNNSTT table tennis
ABEEILNPRSU insuperable
ABEEILNQTUU unequitable
ABEEILNRTTU inutterable

	nattier blue
ABEEILNRTUV	unavertible
ABEEILNSSST	beastliness
ABEEILORSTT	bitter aloes
ABEEILORTUY	outer bailey
ABEEILPPRRS	perspirable
ABEEILPPRTT	bitter-apple
ABEEILPRSSU	persuasible
ABEEILPRTUV	vituperable
ABEEILRRTVY	retrievably
ABEEIMNNOTU	aminobutene
ABEEIMNRRTT	arbitrement
ABEEINNNPST	bien pensant
ABEEINNQRTU	barquentine
ABEEINORRTT	terebration
ABEEINORRTV	verberation
ABEEINORSSU	Buenos Aires
ABEEINORSTT	serotine bat
ABEEINRRSSZ	bizarreness
ABEEINRSSTW	bear witness
ABEEINSSSUV	abusiveness
ABEEIOPRRTV	reprobative
ABEEIORSTVV	observative
ABEEIQRRSUU	arquebusier
ABEEIRRTTTU	reattribute
ABEEJLNNOUY	unenjoyable
ABEEKLNORTV	overblanket
ABEEKLNORTW	T-Bone Walker
ABEEKLORTTU	take trouble
ABEEKMNOOSW	make one's bow
ABEEKMNORST	broken meats
ABEEKMORRRT	Robert Remak
ABEEKMOSSST	Moses basket
ABEEKNOOPTU	keep on about
ABEEKNOORUZ	Kenzaburo Oë
ABEEKRRRSTY	tarry breeks
ABEELLLMNOR	melon baller
ABEELLLMSSY	blamelessly
ABEELLLMTUY	umbellately
ABEELLNOSSV	lovableness
ABEELLORSST	Ballesteros
ABEELLRRTVY	vertebrally
ABEELMMNORU	unmemorable
ABEELMNORUV	unremovable
ABEELMNOSSV	movableness
ABEELMNPRTU	number plate
ABEELMNRRSU	real numbers
ABEELMNSSTU	mutableness
ABEELMNSTTT	battlements
ABEELNNOSST	notableness
ABEELNNSSTU	tunableness
ABEELNOOSTW	at one's elbow
ABEELNPRSTY	presentably
ABEELNRTTUU	unutterable
ABEELNRTUXY	exuberantly
ABEELOPRRRU	beer parlour
ABEELOPSSSS	possessable
ABEELORRRST	Earl Roberts
ABEELORTTTW	water bottle
ABEELOSTUUY	beauteously
ABEELPPRRTU	prepubertal
ABEELPPRTTU	apple butter
ABEELPRRSTY	presbyteral
ABEELPRTTTU	butter plate
ABEELQQRUUU	Albuquerque
ABEEMMNORSU	membraneous
ABEEMNORSTT	storm-beaten
ABEEMNRSSTU	surbasement
ABEEMORRSTT	strabometer
ABEENNORTUV	Bonaventure
ABEEOORSSTT	booster seat
ABEEOPRRTTU	protuberate
ABEEPPRRTTU	butter-paper
ABEFFGHLOTW	blow the gaff
ABEFFGLOOOR	beg for a fool
ABEFFIILORT	forfeit bail
	fortifiable
ABEFFLLNOSU	full of beans
ABEFFLNSTUU	subaffluent
ABEFGHRRRSU	Fraserburgh
ABEFGIIILNS	signifiable
ABEFGIILNNR	infrangible
ABEFGIINRST	giant fibres
ABEFGILNOSW	safe-blowing
ABEFGILNSST	self-basting
ABEFGLMOORR	gambrel roof
ABEFHHLORRT	half-brother
ABEFHKOOOOS	Book of Hosea
ABEFHLNSSSU	bashfulness
ABEFHNORRTW	Father Brown
ABEFHOORTTU	out of breath
ABEFHRSSTUY	Shaftesbury
ABEFIIILRTV	vitrifiable
ABEFIIILSTY	feasibility
ABEFIIJLSTU	justifiable
ABEFIILLOOT	bifoliolate
ABEFIILNORV	riboflavine
ABEFIILNOSS	fissionable
ABEFIKNOSSU	bank of issue
ABEFILLMRRU	umbrella fir
ABEFILLNOOR	fire-balloon
ABEFILLNRTU	unfiltrable
ABEFILLTUUY	beautifully
ABEFILNNNOR	Flann O'Brien
ABEFILNTUUU	unbeautiful
ABEFILRRTUY	irrefutably
ABEFIMORSST	asbestiform
ABEFIRRTTUY	fairy-butter
ABEFLLNOORT	frontal lobe
ABEFLMOORTT	foot-lambert
ABEFLMOOSTT	false bottom
ABEFLNNRSSU	branfulness
ABEFLNOPTYY	Bay of Plenty
ABEFLOOOTTU	footle about
ABEFNNNRUYY	Fanny Burney
ABEGGHILLNT	Bengal light
ABEGGHIMNRT	German Bight
ABEGGIILNOR	globigerina
ABEGGIKNRRS	Karen Briggs
ABEGGLMNRVY	Melvyn Bragg
ABEGGMNORRU	Munro-bagger
ABEGHIKMNNO	home banking

ABEGHILLPPT apple-blight
ABEGHILLRTY early blight
ABEGHILMNOO haemoglobin
ABEGHILNSTT sling the bat
ABEGHILNSUW washing-blue
ABEGHINNRTU unbreathing
ABEGHINOOPR negrophobia
ABEGHINRRSU rush bearing
ABEGHINRRTU Antiburgher
ABEGHLRTUUW bulgur wheat
ABEGHORSSTU burgess oath
ABEGIIILMMT immitigable
ABEGIIKLNNR brake lining
ABEGIIKLNNT inking-table
ABEGIIKMNRS Kim Basinger
ABEGIILMNTU unmitigable
ABEGIILNNPY belaying pin
ABEGIIMNSSU subimagines
ABEGIINRRUV River Ubangi
ABEGIIRRSTU subirrigate
ABEGIJMMNNU gum benjamin
ABEGIJMNNPU jumping bean
ABEGIJMNPSU base jumping
ABEGIJORTUV objurgative
ABEGIKMNORW working-beam
ABEGIKNOSST Basingstoke
ABEGILLLNOW will be along
ABEGILLNPSS passing bell
ABEGILLNSSU Sabine's gull
ABEGILMNOSW seam bowling
womb-leasing
ABEGILMNPRY impregnably
ABEGILNNNTY benignantly
ABEGILNNOTT toning table
ABEGILNNRTY banteringly
ABEGILNOORW wool-bearing
ABEGILNORSU subregional
ABEGILNOSUU albugineous
ABEGILOOORY aerobiology
ABEGILRRYZZ grizzly bear
ABEGINNNNTU unbenignant
ABEGINNORTU gubernation
ABEGINOOPRV gaboon viper
ABEGLLNOOPR prolongable
ABEGLLORSSW glass-blower
ABEGLLOSSTT bottle glass
ABEGLMNOSTU lamb's tongue
ABEGLNSTUUU subungulate
ABEGLOOOPTT potato bogle
ABEGMORRSTU burgomaster
ABEHHHRRSTU hearth-brush
ABEHHIIOOPR hierophobia
ABEHHILNNOS Hans Holbein
ABEHHJNORSY John Ashbery
ABEHIIILLPS baillieship
ABEHIILMNST habiliments
ABEHIILMOPT amphibolite
ABEHIILPRST blepharitis
ABEHIIMMNOS bohemianism✧
ABEHIIMORSV behaviorism
ABEHIINNORT hibernation
ABEHIINRSST inhabitress
ABEHIIORSTV behaviorist
ABEHIKLNNTU unthinkable
ABEHILLLRTY liberty hall✧
ABEHILMNOST abolishment
ABEHILNORSU nourishable
ABEHILOOPRU ailurophobe
ABEHILOPRSW worshipable
ABEHILPPRST slipper bath
ABEHILPSSTT battleships
ABEHIMOSSTT miss the boat
ABEHINOORTT botheration
ABEHINOOSST Hessian boot
ABEHINPRRTT birth parent
ABEHIOOOPRT erotophobia
ABEHJKNOPSS Joseph Banks
ABEHJLMNORT John Lambert
ABEHLLOORST Atholl brose
ABEHLMNOSUW bushelwoman
ABEHLMOORTW Bartholomew
ABEHLMOPSSU blasphemous
ABEHLMORTWY blameworthy
ABEHLNNNSUU unshunnable
ABEHLNORRTY abhorrently
ABEHLORRSSU harbourless
ABEHMOOTTVY bottom-heavy
ABEHMOTUWYY Weymouth Bay
ABEHNNOOTTY ethnobotany
ABEHNORSSSU bonus shares
ABEHNORSTTY east-by-north
north-by-east
ABEHOOORRTT orthoborate
ABEHOSSTTUY east-by-south
south-by-east
ABEHPRRRTUY Hubert Parry
ABEHRSTTWYY Aberystwyth
ABEIIIKLLTY likeability
ABEIIILLLMT illimitable
ABEIIILLMNN bimillennia
ABEIIILLNOR billionaire
ABEIIILLQRU equilibrial
ABEIIILLRTY reliability
ABEIIILLTVY liveability
ABEIIILMTTU Mutabilitie
ABEIIILNNTZ Leibnitzian
ABEIIINNORT inebriation
ABEIIJMRRRS Sir J M Barrie
ABEIILLLLRY illiberally
ABEIILLLMNU illuminable
ABEIILLMMST bimetallism
ABEIILLMNRY bimillenary
ABEIILLMPSU implausible
ABEIILLMSTT bimetallist
ABEIILLOTVY loveability
ABEIILLPRTV private bill
ABEIILLRSTT bristletail
ABEIILMNNNO innominable
ABEIILMNSTY inestimably
ABEIILMOTVY moveability
ABEIILMRSST miserablist
ABEIILNNOOP piano nobile

ABEIILNNSTV vinblastine
ABEIILNOPRT prelibation
ABEIILNQTUY inequitably
ABEIILNRRTT intertribal
ABEIILNRTTY rentability
ABEIILNSTUV unvisitable
ABEIILOPPRT propitiable
ABEIILOPRTY operability
ABEIILORTXY exorability
ABEIILRSSST stabilisers
ABEIILRSSTZ stabilizers
ABEIILRSTVY versability
ABEIILSTTTY testability
ABEIILSTUXY bisexuality
ABEIIMMMRRU Mare Imbrium
ABEIIMNORSV ambiversion
ABEIINNOSTT Sino-Tibetan
ABEIINRRSST bar-sinister
ABEIIRTTTUV attributive
ABEIJKRSSTU Jesuits' bark
ABEIKLLLSTT skittle-ball
ABEIKLLMRRS Barker's mill
ABEIKLLNOOT kite-balloon
ABEIKLNRSTW water blinks
ABEIKNNRRSU brankursine
ABEIKNRRSTW winter's bark
ABEILLLRSTY trisyllable
ABEILLMORTU Rambouillet
ABEILLMOTTU multilobate
ABEILLNNOOV balloon-vine
ABEILLNORTY intolerably
ABEILLNPSUU unplausible
ABEILLNRSSY brainlessly
ABEILLNRTTU bullet train
ABEILMNNRUY innumerably
ABEILMNRSTU subterminal
ABEILMOORTV Oliver Tambo
ABEILMORRVY irremovably
ABEILMORSUY Louis B Mayer
ABEILMOSSTW misbestowal
ABEILMRSTUU semi-tubular
ABEILNNORTT Leon Brittan
ABEILNNOSSU non-issuable
ABEILNNPRTU unprintable
ABEILNNRSUU uninsurable
ABEILNNSTTY abstinently
ABEILNOOSSS obsessional
ABEILNORSSU Belorussian
ABEILNOSTTY obstinately
ABEILNPRRST splinter bar
ABEILNPRSUY insuperably
ABEILOORRTT obliterator
ABEILOPRTUU Politbureau
ABEILORSSTW below stairs
belowstairs
ABEILQRSTUU square-built
ABEILRRSTTT brittlestar
ABEIMNNSSSU businessman
ABEIMNORRRY marionberry
ABEIMNORSTW tribeswoman
ABEIMNRTTTY Betty Martin
ABEINNNOQTU tonquin-bean
ABEINNNRSTU burnt sienna
ABEINNORSTV inobservant
ABEINOOPRRT probationer
reprobation
ABEINOORSTV observation
ABEINOOSTTT obtestation
ABEINOSSTTU abstentious
ABEINOSSTUU subitaneous
ABEINSSTTUV substantive
ABEIORRRSVZ Brazos River
ABEIRSSTTUV substrative
ABEJMORRTTU turbo-ram-jet
ABEKLLSSUWY blue-sky laws
ABEKLMNOPRT Belmont Park
ABEKMNOOTUY monkey about
ABEKMNORSSY brass monkey
ABEKMORSTTY take by storm
ABEKOOSTTTU statute book
ABEKORSTTTU trout basket
ABELLMOPPRY problem play
ABELLNNOTTY tantony bell
ABELLNOORTY balloon tyre
ABELMNOOPRT not a problem
ABELMNORRSY salmonberry
ABELMOOPSSS Peasblossom
ABELNOOPRST open borstal
ABELNOOPRSU Paul Robeson
ABELNOPPSTU unstoppable
ABELNOPRTTU pearl button
ABELNORRTUW Bruno Walter
ABELNORSTVY observantly
ABELNRTTUUY unutterably
ABELOPPRSTU supportable
ABELOPRTTTY bottle party
ABELRRSTTUU surrebuttal
ABEMNNOTTTU Mountbatten
ABEMNOORRSW marrow-bones
ABEMNORRRST barnstormer
ABEMNORTTUW butter-woman
ABEMNOSSSTU bums on seats
ABENNNOOSTT non obstante
ABENNOORSTU no reason but
ABENNORSTUV unobservant
ABENNOSSTUY buoyantness
ABENOPRRTTU protuberant
ABENOPSTTUU pause button
ABEOOPRRRTY reprobatory
ABEOORRSTVY observatory
ABEOPRRRTTU perturbator
ABEOPRSSTTX pattress box
ABERRSSTUUY subtreasury
ABFFFFILOTU a bit of fluff
ABFFFHILOSU buffalo fish
ABFFGHHIIIL high bailiff
ABFFILLMSTU bull-mastiff
ABFGHINRSTU surf-bathing
ABFGHIOORTU a bit of rough
ABFGHNOORRU Farnborough
ABFGIILNNRY infrangibly
ABFGIILNORT floating rib

ABFGILLNOOT footballing
ABFGILNOSTW fast bowling
ABFHJKNOOOO Book of Jonah
ABFHKMNOOOU Book of Nahum
ABFIIILLLMS fallibilism
ABFIIILLLST fallibilist
ABFIIILLLTY fallibility
ABFIIIMNORT fimbriation
ABFIIJLSTUY justifiably
ABFIILORSUY bifariously
ABFIINOOTTT not a bit of it
ABFILLLNSTU in full blast
ABFILLOOSTT footballist
ABFILMNSTUU funambulist
ABFLNOOORRS Flora Robson
ABGGGHIKNOO bagging-hook
ABGGGINNOOT tobogganing
ABGGGINNSTU gangbusting
ABGGHINNRTU burning ghat
ABGGHINOPPS shopping bag
ABGGILOOORY agrobiology
ABGGILOORST garbologist
ABGGINOOSTT tobogganist
ABGHHLLORTU through ball
ABGHHOORRTU tharborough
ABGHIILMNOR Lamborghini®
ABGHIINRSTT brattishing
ABGHIINSTTU bathing suit
ABGHIKLLNOO booking hall
ABGHIKLNORS goblin shark
ABGHIKLNSUW bushwalking
ABGHIKPRRST bright spark
ABGHILLNOOY ballyhooing
ABGHILMOOPY amphibology
ABGHILNOOPT haptoglobin
ABGHINNTTUY anything but
ABGHNOOPRSY snobography
ABGHNOPTUUU hung up about
ABGIIILMMTY immitigably
ABGIIILNTTY tangibility
ABGIIKNNORR barking iron
ABGIILLLNUY bilingually
ABGIILLNRST star billing
ABGIILMNTUY unmitigably
ABGIILNOOPS soap boiling
ABGIILNRTUV rib-vaulting
ABGIIMMNRTT trimming tab
ABGIINNOOST obsignation
ABGIINNPRTT bat printing
ABGIINORRST rib-roasting
ABGIIOOORRT Arrigo Boito
ABGIJNOORTU objurgation
ABGIJNOSTUU subjugation
ABGIKKLNOOT talking book
ABGIKLNOOTW walking boot
ABGIKNNOPRW pawnbroking
ABGIKNNSTTU tankbusting
ABGIKNRRSTY stringy-bark
ABGILLORTUY globularity
ABGILMMNOUU gum olibanum
ABGILMNOOST gonimoblast
ABGILMNOSUU lumbaginous
ABGILMOSUUY ambiguously
ABGILNNORUU unlabouring
ABGILORRSUU burglarious
ABGIMNOSUUU unambiguous
ABGINOORSTU subrogation
ABGINOORSTY obsignatory
ABGINOPRSST bring to pass
ABGJOORRTUY objurgatory
ABGLLOOPRYY pyroballogy
ABGLNORSTUY Glastonbury
ABGMMMNNOUU magnum bonum
ABGMOORSSTT bottom-grass
ABGOORRTTUW Otto Warburg
ABHHIILMOOS Homo habilis
ABHHIIOOOPP ophiophobia
ABHHIIOOPPP hippophobia
ABHHIKRSTTU Turkish bath
ABHHIMNPSSU bushmanship
ABHHINOOOPP phonophobia
ABHHIOOOPPT photophobia
ABHHIOOPPSY hypsophobia
ABHIIIOOPST sitiophobia
ABHIILNOSTT nihil obstat
ABHIIMRRSTW British warm
ABHIIORTUWY hairy woubit
ABHIKLLLNSY Bill Shankly
ABHIKNORSVY Baryshnikov
ABHILLMNOST in mothballs
ABHILMMNOPT phantom limb
ABHILMOOPSU amphibolous
ABHILRRSSTU Arthur Bliss
ABHIOOPRSSU Russophobia
ABHIOPRSSSW Bishops' Wars
ABHIORRSTUU airbrush out
ABHJMNNOOOR John Boorman
ABHLLMOPSTY lymphoblast
ABHLOOPRSTT trophoblast
ABHMNOORSTW Thomas Brown
ABHMORRSTTU Arthur's Tomb
ABHPRRSSTUY pastry brush
ABIIIILMTTY imitability
ABIIIILNTVY inviability
ABIIIKLLNOT Bikini Atoll
ABIIIKMMRST Mt Karisimbi
ABIIILLLMTY illimitably
ABIIILLOSTY isolability
ABIIILNNTWY winnability
ABIIILNOSTU antibilious
ABIIILNRTTU tribunitial
ABIIILNSTTY instability
ABIIILPRTTY partibility
ABIIILPSSTY passibility
ABIIILRTTVY vibratility
ABIIILSTTUY suitability
ABIIINNRTTU tribunitian
ABIIINOPRTT bipartition
ABIIKLORTWY workability
ABIILLLNRTY brilliantly
ABIILLMPSUY implausibly
ABIILLOSTVY solvability

ABIILMNOSTU sublimation
ABIILMOSTUY ambitiously
ABIILNOOQTU obliquation
ABIILNORTTU tribulation
ABIILNRSTUY insalubrity
ABIILOPRTTY portability
ABIILOQTTUY quotability
ABIILRRTTUY tributarily
ABIIMNNOORT bromination
ABIIMNNSTYZ Byzantinism
ABIIMNOOPRT improbation
ABIIMNORSTT nimbostrati
ABIIMNOSTUU unambitious
ABIINNORTTU turbination
ABIINNSTTYZ Byzantinist
ABIINOOPSTT obstipation
ABIINOORSTT abortionist
ABIINORTTTU attribution
ABIIORSSTTU tibiotarsus
ABIJLRRTUYY Trial by Jury
ABIJNOOORTT job rotation
ABILLNPSUUY unplausibly
ABILLOORSUY laboriously
ABILLOPRRSW sparrow-bill
ABILLORSTTU sublittoral
ABILMOORTUU taurobolium
ABILMORSTUU umbratilous
ABILNOORSUU unlaborious
ABILNOQTTUU button quail
ABILNOSTUUX subluxation
ABILNRSTTTU turntablist
ABILOOPRSTT post-orbital
ABINNOORSTU subornation
ABINOOOPRRS ora pro nobis
ABINRRSSTTU brains trust
ABJOQSTUUUU jusqu'au bout
ABLNOPPSTUY unstoppably
ABLOPPRSTUY supportably
ABMNOPPTTUY Natty Bumppo
ABMNORTTUXY braxy mutton
ABMOORSSTTY smarty-boots
ACCCCEEENRS accrescence
ACCCCHHOSTT Scotch catch
ACCCCILMOOR micrococcal
ACCCCILMORY macrocyclic
ACCCDEEENNS candescence
ACCCDEHILNO chalcedonic
ACCCDEIILNU nucleic acid
ACCCDEIIORT cerotic acid
ACCCDEIKRRT crack credit
ACCCDEILOPY cyclopaedic
ACCCDENNOOR concordance
ACCCDENNOTU conductance
ACCCDHIILOR chloric acid
ACCCDHIIMOR chromic acid
ACCCDIIIILS silicic acid
ACCCDIMOPST compact disc
ACCCEEELNOS coalescence
ACCCEEELNST lactescence
ACCCEEEMNRS marcescence
ACCCEEFNORT café-concert
ACCCEEHILRS ecclesiarch
ACCCEEHISTT catechetics
ACCCEEHMNOR chance-comer
ACCCEEHOSUU accoucheuse
ACCCEEILNRT eccentrical
ACCCEEILRRT electric arc
ACCCEELMNOP complacence
ACCCEELNOPT conceptacle
ACCCEENNNOS connascence
ACCCEFFHIOO coach-office
ACCCEGIILMR magic circle
ACCCEGILNRY cycle racing
ACCCEHIISTT catechistic
ACCCEHIKNOT check action
ACCCEHIMOTT chemotactic
ACCCEHLLOST Castell Coch
ACCCEHNORTY cony-catcher
technocracy
ACCCEIILMRT climacteric
ACCCEIINPRS picnic races
ACCCEIKNRST cancer stick
ACCCEILNPTY pentacyclic
ACCCEILORTU leucocratic
ACCCEILRTTY tetracyclic
ACCCEINNOTT tonic accent
ACCCEINORRT acrocentric
ACCCEKLLORT cartel clock
ACCCEKNORRR corn-cracker
ACCCELLLLOT call collect
ACCCELMNOPY complacency
ACCCELNORTY Carnot cycle
ACCCENNNORY concernancy
ACCCENNNOSY connascency
ACCCHHIINNO Cochin-China
ACCCHHIMPUU Machu Picchu
ACCCHIILLOT laccolithic
ACCCHILOORT ochlocratic
ACCCHOOPRTY ptochocracy
ACCCHORRSYY chrysocracy
ACCCIILLTYY cyclicality
ACCCIIOOPRS capriccioso
ACCCIKLMOOT atomic clock
ACCCILLOOSU calcicolous
ACCCIMMOORS macrocosmic
ACCCIMOOPRS macroscopic
ACCCIMOORST cosmocratic
ACCCINOPPSU cappuccinos
ACCCLOOOPRT protococcal
ACCCNOOSTTU cost-account
ACCDDEHLOOT cold cathode
ACCDDEHNPRU punched card
ACCDDEINORS discordance
ACCDDFIIISU fusidic acid
ACCDDIIIMST didacticism
ACCDDINORSY discordancy
ACCDEEEENNT antecedence
ACCDEEEFNRT face-centred
ACCDEEEKNNR crane-necked
ACCDEEELNOS adolescence
ACCDEEENRST crescentade
ACCDEEFHHKL half-checked

ACCDEEFHLNT fetch-candle
ACCDEEFNORY confederacy✧
ACCDEEFOPPR copper-faced
ACCDEEGIINU eugenic acid
ACCDEEGOPRU coup de grâce
ACCDEEHHKLU chuckle-head
ACCDEEHIMNO machine code
ACCDEEHINRS hard science
ACCDEEHIORS archdiocese
ACCDEEIILNS selenic acid
ACCDEEIILPT epic dialect
ACCDEEIINTX ex accidenti
ACCDEEIIRSU race suicide
ACCDEEIISTV desiccative
ACCDEEILNPR pencil-cedar
ACCDEEIMNOR decameronic
ACCDEEINOSS deaccession
ACCDEEINPRS discrepance
ACCDEEIORTT decorticate
ACCDEEKKNNN neck and neck
ACCDEELNNOU unconcealed
ACCDEEMNSUU succedaneum
ACCDEENNORT contredance
ACCDEEPPRSW screw-capped
ACCDEFHITTY chitty-faced
ACCDEFHMORR forced march
ACCDEFILNSS flaccidness
ACCDEFKLORU Fleur Adcock
ACCDEFNOSTU safe-conduct
ACCDEHHRSSU archduchess
ACCDEHILNOS closed-chain
ACCDEHILPRY diphycercal
ACCDEHIMPRY pachydermic
ACCDEHINORW choice-drawn
ACCDEHIRSSY Cyd Charisse
ACCDEHKLNPU packed lunch
ACCDEHLMORW clam-chowder
ACCDEHLNOXY chalcedonyx
ACCDEHNRSTU unscratched
ACCDEHPRTTU Dutch carpet
ACCDEIILLTY deictically
ACCDEIINOST desiccation
ACCDEIIOPRT pteroic acid
ACCDEIIPSTU suicide pact
ACCDEIKLNST candlestick
ACCDEIKNRRT cinder track
ACCDEILLMMU cadmium cell
ACCDEILLOPS peccadillos
ACCDEILMOPT complicated
ACCDEIMRSSU sacred music
ACCDEINNOOR co-ordinance
ACCDEINOOST consociated
ACCDEINOOTU coeducation
ACCDEINPRSY discrepancy
ACCDEIPRRTU picture card
ACCDEKNNOPR neck and crop
ACCDEKORRRT track record
ACCDELMOPTY compactedly
ACCDELNOSSS second class
second-class
ACCDEMNOORY demonocracy
ACCDEMNOPTU uncompacted
ACCDENORTUV cut and cover
ACCDFIIINOP Indo-Pacific
ACCDFIIKNRS Dick Francis
ACCDFKMOOOR crack of doom
ACCDGGILNNO clog dancing
ACCDGILNOOR cooling card
ACCDGILNORY accordingly
ACCDGINOORT according to
ACCDGINORRS scoring card
ACCDHHLRTUU Durchlaucht
ACCDHHNSSUU such-and-such
ACCDHHRRSUW churchwards
ACCDHIIILOP acidophilic
ACCDHIIMORT dichromatic
ACCDHILLOOT Old Catholic
ACCDHINORYY hydrocyanic
ACCDHIORTTY hydrotactic
ACCDIIINNOS scincoidian
ACCDIIKKNPP pick-and-pick
ACCDIILLLOU loculicidal
ACCDIILLNRY cylindrical
ACCDIILLORY codicillary
ACCDIILMNNY clindamycin
ACCDIILNOOR crocodilian
ACCDIIOOPRS radioscopic
ACCDIIOSSTU diacoustics
ACCDIIPRSSU prussic acid
ACCDIIPRUVY pyruvic acid
ACCDIKMOPST compact disk
ACCDILMNOUV volcanic mud
ACCDIMOSSTU disaccustom
ACCDLNRSUUU dracunculus✧
ACCDNNOOTTY cotton candy
ACCEEEEHMRS cream cheese
ACCEEEENNSV evanescence
ACCEEEFIKOP piece of cake
ACCEEEFILMN maleficence
ACCEEEFLNRT reflectance
ACCEEEGILMN game licence
ACCEEEHHKOS cheechakoes
ACCEEEHILRT chelicerate
ACCEEEHLLOP cephalocele
ACCEEEIKKLO cockaleekie
cock-a-leekie
ACCEEELLNPS pallescence
ACCEEELNOPS opalescence
ACCEEELNPST en spectacle
ACCEEELNRST recalescent
ACCEEFHPRST speechcraft
ACCEEFIIPST specificate
ACCEEFIIRTT certificate
ACCEEFIKRRR firecracker
ACCEEFINORV vociferance
ACCEEFIOSTY café society
ACCEEFLORST Corfe Castle
ACCEEFNRRST screencraft
ACCEEGHIKMN game-chicken
ACCEEGHILMO geochemical
ACCEEGHINTY eye-catching
ACCEEGHKRUY Chuck Yeager

ACCEEGHORRV cover charge
ACCEEGIINRS agriscience
ACCEEGILRRT great circle
ACCEEGLNSTU glaucescent
ACCEEHHIIRS Escherichia
ACCEEHHIRRT arch-heretic
ACCEEHHIRST Cheshire Cat
ACCEEHHKRSW screech-hawk
ACCEEHHNTTT catch-the-ten
ACCEEHILLMN Mechlin lace
ACCEEHILLPS Chelsea clip
ACCEEHILMNO chameleonic
ACCEEHILNRT chanticleer
ACCEEHILRST telearchics
ACCEEHIPRRT Pherecratic
ACCEEHIRRTU charcuterie
ACCEEHIRSTV cesarevitch
ACCEEHIRSTW cesarewitch
ACCEEHKLNNT lance-knecht
ACCEEHKLORT heart cockle
ACCEEHKORTW weathercock
ACCEEHLLNRY chancellery
ACCEEHLMORT molecatcher
ACCEEHLNOXY cyclohexane
ACCEEHMMORY cache memory
ACCEEHMNNOY coenenchyma
ACCEEHMNRSY sarcenchyme
ACCEEHMORSU escarmouche
ACCEEHNPRRT trencher cap
ACCEEIILMRR miracle rice
ACCEEIILNRT electrician
ACCEEIIMPST septicaemic
ACCEEIINQSU acquiesce in
ACCEEIISTVX exsiccative
ACCEEIKKLOP peacock-like
ACCEEIKKLPR place-kicker
ACCEEIKNPRS science park
ACCEEIKRRSW wisecracker
ACCEEILLLRT all-electric
ACCEEILLRST electricals
ACCEEILMNOU oecumenical
ACCEEILNNST incalescent
ACCEEILNORT electronica
ACCEEILNRUX Clarencieux
ACCEEILNSST scale insect
ACCEEILOOPR Alice Cooper
ACCEEILRRTU recirculate
ACCEEILRRTY electric ray
ACCEEIMNOPS CinemaScope®
ACCEEIMNRSU miscreaunce
ACCEEIMNRTT metacentric
ACCEEINNORV cracovienne
ACCEEINPRTT net practice
ACCEEINQSTU acquiescent
ACCEEIOPRRT reciprocate
ACCEEIORSSS accessorise
ACCEEIORSSZ accessorize
ACCEEIORTTX excorticate
ACCEELLOPRT leptocercal
ACCEELMNNOT concealment
ACCEEMNNORR necromancer
ACCEEMNOPPU comeuppance
ACCEEMOSSTY Ascomycetes
ACCEENNNOSV convenances
ACCEENNNOTU countenance
ACCEENNOPRT Canton crepe
ACCEENNORSV conservance
conversance
ACCEENNORTT concentrate
concertante
ACCEENNORVY conveyancer
ACCEENOPRRY coparcenery
ACCEENOPRTU counterpace
ACCEENORRRT catercorner
ACCEENORRTT concrete art
ACCEENPSSTU susceptance
ACCEEOPPRTU preoccupate
ACCEEOPRSUY cyperaceous
ACCEFFHNNRR French franc
ACCEFFHRTTU chaff-cutter
ACCEFFIIOSU efficacious
ACCEFFINORT traffic cone
ACCEFHHKLNR French chalk
ACCEFHIINTY chieftaincy
ACCEFHIKOPS peacock-fish
ACCEFHNORST soft chancre
ACCEFIIIMPT Pacific Time
ACCEFILORSU calciferous
ACCEFINORRT Afrocentric
Afro-centric
ACCEGGIKNRT get cracking
ACCEGHHITTW catchweight
ACCEGHHMNPU chump change
ACCEGHIINST catechising
ACCEGHIINTZ catechizing
ACCEGHIKNQU quick-change
ACCEGHILMRU chemurgical
ACCEGHINNPT catching pen
ACCEGHIOPRR cerographic
ACCEGHLLRTU gull-catcher
ACCEGHOPRRS crescograph
ACCEGIKMRRY gimcrackery
ACCEGILLOPY cycloplegia
ACCEGILOOTU autecologic
ACCEGILORSU calcigerous
ACCEGINORTU accoutering
ACCEGKLNOPS spang-cockle
ACCEHHIKKNW chicken hawk
ACCEHHISSTY Hesychastic
ACCEHHLOOST teach school
ACCEHHNSTTU catch the sun
ACCEHHRSTUV stave-church
ACCEHIILLRT Callitriche
ACCEHIILNST calisthenic
ACCEHIILOPT ophicalcite
ACCEHIILOST catholicise✧
ACCEHIILOTZ catholicize✧
ACCEHIIMNST mechanistic
ACCEHIIORRT hierocratic
ACCEHIIRSTU Eucharistic
ACCEHIKLNOR chain locker
ACCEHIKPRTY parity check

ACCEHILLMNO	melancholic
ACCEHILLNTY	technically
ACCEHILMOOZ	zoochemical
ACCEHILMOPR	microcephal
ACCEHILNNTU	untechnical
ACCEHILNOOT	Neo-Catholic
ACCEHILOOPZ	zoocephalic
ACCEHILOORT	chocolatier
ACCEHILOPPR	procephalic
ACCEHILPRTY	phylacteric
ACCEHILRRUU	curule chair
ACCEHILSSST	the Classics
ACCEHIMNNOR	chrominance
ACCEHIMNORT	mechatronic
ACCEHIMORTT	tachometric
ACCEHIMORTU	euchromatic
ACCEHIMPSTY	metapsychic
ACCEHIMRTTY	McCarthyite
	tachymetric
ACCEHKLNOST	schecklaton
ACCEHKOPPTT	patch pocket
ACCEHKOPTTW	watch pocket
ACCEHLLMNOY	collenchyma
ACCEHLLNNSW	Schwann cell
ACCEHLLNORT	concert hall
ACCEHLLNORY	chancellory
ACCEHLNOORT	torchon lace
ACCEHLRSSST	scratchless
ACCEHMNOORS	comancheros
ACCEHNOPRTU	coup the cran
ACCEHORRSSU	crash course
ACCEHRSSTTT	scratch test
ACCEIIILLNN	aclinic line
ACCEIIILMST	metasilicic
ACCEIIINPRT	accipitrine
ACCEIILLMRS	clericalism
ACCEIILLNPR	preclinical
ACCEIILLRST	clericalist
ACCEIILMSTU	caustic lime
ACCEIILNORR	cornice-rail
ACCEIILNSTV	clavecinist
ACCEIILNTUV	inculcative
ACCEIILPRRT	precritical
ACCEIILRRSU	circularise
ACCEIILRRUZ	circularize
ACCEIILRTTY	city article
ACCEIILRTUV	circulative
ACCEIIMNOST	cosmetician
	encomiastic
ACCEIIMORTT	Matteo Ricci
ACCEIINNOSU	insouciance
ACCEIINOSTX	exsiccation
ACCEIINRSST	Cistercians
ACCEIIPRTVY	pervicacity
ACCEIIPTTVY	acceptivity
ACCEIIRRSTT	criticaster
ACCEIKKOTTT	tick-tack-toe
ACCEIKLMRST	clickstream
ACCEIKLORTU	leukocratic
ACCEIKNRSSS	car-sickness
ACCEILLLMRS	small circle
ACCEILLLOTV	voltaic cell
ACCEILLMOST	somatic cell
ACCEILLMRRU	mural circle
ACCEILLNRTY	centrically
ACCEILLOPRR	polar circle
ACCEILLPSTY	sceptically
ACCEILMNOSS	comicalness
ACCEILMOPST	ectoplasmic
ACCEILMSSTU	multi-access
ACCEILNNOTY	anticyclone
ACCEILNNSSY	cynicalness
ACCEILNOORT	neocortical
ACCEILNOPRT	Eric Clapton
	narcoleptic
ACCEILNORTT	contractile
ACCEILNORTU	corniculate
ACCEILNSTTY	syntectical
ACCEILOPRST	ceroplastic
ACCEILOPSTT	ectoplastic
ACCEILOPTTU	octuplicate
ACCEILORSSY	accessorily
ACCEILORSTT	caloric test
ACCEIMMNOTU	communicate
ACCEIMNNORT	necromantic
ACCEIMNORTY	craniectomy
ACCEIMNOSTY	Actinomyces
ACCEIMNRSTU	trance music
ACCEIMORRTY	meritocracy
ACCEINNNOTU	continuance
ACCEINNOORS	cancioneros
ACCEINNORSU	coinsurance
ACCEINNORTV	contrivance
ACCEINOPRRT	reciprocant
ACCEINOPSUU	punicaceous
ACCEINORSTU	cater-cousin
ACCEINORTTV	contractive
ACCEINSSSTU	causticness
ACCEIOORSSU	scoriaceous
ACCEIORSSSS	scissor case
ACCEIORSTUU	urticaceous
ACCEJLNORTU	conjectural
ACCEKLLMNOT	mantel clock
ACCEKLMORST	master-clock
ACCEKLOPRTY	kleptocracy
ACCEKLSSTTU	scuttle cask
ACCEKNRRSTU	nutcrackers
ACCEKORRTTU	racket-court
ACCELLORSUY	sclerocauly
ACCELLOSTTU	coal scuttle
ACCELMMNOOP	commonplace
ACCELNNOSTT	contact lens
ACCELNOOORT	concolorate
ACCELPRRSUU	crepuscular
ACCEMNOOPRT	comportance
ACCEMNOPSST	compactness
ACCENNORSVY	conservancy
	conversancy
ACCENOOPRTU	pococurante
ACCENOORRST	consecrator
ACCENOPPRTU	preoccupant
ACCENOPRRTT	precontract

ACCENORRTTU contracture
ACCENORRTTY catty-corner
ACCENORSTTU counter-cast
ACCENPRTUUU acupuncture
ACCENRRSUVY Cyrus R Vance
ACCEORSSTUU crustaceous
ACCFGILOSUU calcifugous
ACCFHILLORT chill factor
ACCFHINSTTY fancy stitch
ACCFHIRSTTT stitchcraft
ACCFHLOORST schoolcraft
ACCFIILOPRY prolificacy
ACCFIIMOORR coraciiform
ACCFILMNNOO Finn mac Cool
ACCFILMORSU sacculiform
ACCFINOORST confiscator
ACCFINOPPRU Frappuccino®
ACCFLNORTUY calf-country
ACCGHIILRRU chirurgical
ACCGHIINNNO coaching inn
ACCGHIINPRV chip carving
ACCGHIIOOPS hagioscopic
ACCGHIOOPPR coprophagic
ACCGHRSSSTU scutch grass
ACCGIILNORV ganciclovir
ACCGIILNOTU glauconitic
ACCGIILNRTU circulating
ACCGIINNNOT canting-coin
ACCGIINNOTY incogitancy
ACCGIKNOPST stocking cap
ACCGILLMOOY mycological
ACCGILLNOOO oncological
ACCGILLOOTY cytological
ACCGILNOORY carcinology
ACCGIMOPRTY cryptogamic
ACCGINORSTU coruscating
ACCHHIIMNPT Mt Pichincha
ACCHHIINSTT chainstitch
ACCHHILNRTU Latin Church
ACCHHJKNNOO John Hancock
ACCHHLMOORS charm school
ACCHHLNNOOR Loch Rannoch
ACCHHMNORUW churchwoman
ACCHIIIMMPT amphimictic
ACCHIIIRSTT citharistic
ACCHIILMOST catholicism✧
ACCHIILOPRT cartophilic
ACCHIILOSST scholiastic
ACCHIILOTTY catholicity
ACCHIIMNORT chiromantic
ACCHIIMOSST masochistic
ACCHIINPSYY physiciancy
ACCHIIOOPST sociopathic
ACCHIIOPPRT Hippocratic
ACCHIIOPRRZ rhizocarpic
ACCHIIPRSTY psychiatric
ACCHILLNORY chronically
ACCHILLPSYY psychically
ACCHILMOTYY cyclothymia
ACCHILNNOOT non-Catholic
ACCHILNORSY Cornish clay
ACCHILOOSTU holocaustic
ACCHIMMRSTY McCarthyism
ACCHIMNORTY crithomancy
ACCHINNOPYY phycocyanin
ACCHINOOSTT octastichon
ACCHINOPSTT catch points
ACCHINOPSTY sycophantic
ACCHIOOPRRT prothoracic
ACCHIOOPTTT phototactic
ACCHIOORRSU chiaroscuro
ACCHIOPRSYY physiocracy
ACCHKNNOOTY Tony Hancock
ACCHKNOORST anchor-stock
ACCHKORRSTW scratch-work
ACCHLLOORSY chrysocolla
ACCHLNOSTWY Cathy's Clown
ACCHMNNOOYY onychomancy
ACCHMNOOSTW Scotchwoman
ACCHNOOOPSU cacophonous
ACCHOOOPTTU couch potato
ACCHOPRSTTU up to scratch
ACCIIIKKNPW Pickwickian
ACCIIILMNRT matriclinic
ACCIIILNPRT patriclinic
ACCIIILNSTV Calvinistic
ACCIIILOSST socialistic
ACCIIILRSTU curialistic
ACCIIILRSUV calicivirus
ACCIIILRTTY criticality
ACCIILLLNOX cloxacillin
ACCIILLNNNO non-clinical
ACCIILLOPTY occipitally
ACCIILMNORT matroclinic
ACCIILNNOTU inculcation
ACCIILNNQUU quincuncial
ACCIILNOORT conciliator
ACCIILNOPRT patroclinic
ACCIILNORTU circulation
ACCIILNOTVY volcanicity
ACCIILNTUVY vulcanicity
ACCIILOSTUV acclivitous
ACCIILRRTUY circularity
ACCIINNSTTY nyctinastic
ACCIINOORTT cortication
ACCIINORRSU Rosicrucian
ACCIJNNOTUV conjunctiva
ACCIKKKKNNY knick-knacky
ACCIKKOOTTT tick-tack-too
ACCIKLLORWW crack willow
ACCIKNPRSTU panic-struck
ACCILLMOSTY Ally McCoist
ACCILLNOOOT collocation
ACCILLNOSSU call cousins
ACCILLOOSUU caulicolous
ACCILLPRTYY cryptically
ACCILMNRRUU circumlunar
ACCILMOPRRU circumpolar
ACCILMOPSTY cytoplasmic
ACCILMORRSU circumsolar
ACCILMORSTU claims court
ACCILNOORSU corona lucis

ACCILNOOTTU occultation
ACCILNORTUY inculcatory
ACCILOOPSTV post-vocalic
ACCILOPRSTY pyroclastic
ACCILOPRTTU plutocratic
ACCILORRTUY circulatory
ACCIMMNNOTU communicant
ACCIMNNOOTT concomitant
ACCIMNOPTYY City Company
ACCIMNOTTUY contumacity
ACCINNNOSTY inconstancy
ACCINNOOOTV convocation
ACCINNOOPRU cornucopian
ACCINNOORTT contraction
ACCINOOPPST pantoscopic
ACCINOOPRSY cranioscopy
ACCINOORRRW carrion crow
ACCINOORSST cross action
ACCINOORSTU coruscation
ACCINOPRRSU Capricornus
ACCINOSTTUU cunctatious
ACCIORSSSTY sarcocystis
ACCKLLNOOTY Tony Allcock
ACCKLOQRTUZ quartz clock
ACCKLORRSTY rock crystal
ACCKOOPRRSW cock-sparrow
ACCKOOPSSST Cossack post
ACCLLLOOORU local colour
ACCLMNOOPTU coconut palm
ACCLNNOSTUY consultancy
ACCLNOOORTU octonocular
ACCLNORSUUU carunculous
ACCLOPRRSUU corpuscular
ACCNNNOOOTU on no account
ACCNOOORTVW crown octavo
ACCNOORTTTU contract out
ACCORSSSTUW crosscut saw
ACDDDEEKLOR dreadlocked
ACDDDEIKNUV duck and dive
ACDDDEINRTU cut and dried
ACDDDIKMNOU diamond duck
ACDDEEEEHST the deceased
ACDDEEEEPRS predeceased
ACDDEEFFIST disaffected
ACDDEEGIKLR griddle-cake
ACDDEEGIKNW wedding cake
ACDDEEHHIKT thickheaded
ACDDEEHHKOS shock-headed
ACDDEEHILOT load the dice
ACDDEEHIPPW widechapped
ACDDEEHLNOS close-handed
ACDDEEHLORT cold-hearted
ACDDEEHLOST dead-clothes
ACDDEEHLRUY curly-headed
ACDDEEHNORW crowned head
ACDDEEIINTU indeciduate
ACDDEEILPTU pediculated
ACDDEEIMRRV David Mercer
ACDDEEIMSSU Sadduceeism
ACDDEEINNNR dinner-dance
ACDDEELOSTY dodecastyle
ACDDEEMNNOR modern dance
ACDDEEMNRUV demand curve
ACDDEENNOPT co-dependant
ACDDEENORTU undecorated
ACDDEHIKNPR Cheddar pink
ACDDEHILMMR Middlemarch
ACDDEHILMTW middle watch
ACDDEHINSSS caddishness
ACDDEHKMORU archdukedom
ACDDEHLLOST saddlecloth
ACDDEHMNRUV Edvard Munch
ACDDEHNNOSS seconds hand
ACDDEHNOOPY dodecaphony
ACDDEHNORRU roundarched
ACDDEHOPPRR dropped arch
ACDDEIIKLMN Dickin medal
ACDDEIILNRT dendritical
ACDDEIJNNUU unjaundiced
ACDDEILLMSS middle class
middle-class
ACDDEILMOSU duodecimals
ACDDEILORRY Daily Record
ACDDEIMNORU endocardium
ACDDEIMNRST discardment
ACDDEINOOPT paedodontic
ACDDEIOPSTY Space Oddity
ACDDEKLOSST stock saddle
ACDDELLMNOU mould-candle
ACDDELNORSU Duc d'Orléans
ACDDELNORUU under a cloud
ACDDGIIIMNR gramicidin D
ACDDGIINNSY discandying
ACDDGIJKNPU Jack-pudding
ACDDGKLNOOP long paddock
ACDDHINOORS doch-an-doris
ACDDIIMORSU diascordium
ACDDILOSTUY didactylous
ACDEEEEHLRR cheerleader
ACDEEEFLNRT needlecraft
ACDEEEFLRST self-created
ACDEEEFNORT confederate✧
ACDEEEGIRVY gay deceiver
ACDEEEGLLOT décolletage
ACDEEEGLNOR grande école
ACDEEEHILPT Delta Cephei
ACDEEEHORRV overreached
ACDEEEIKLNS linseed-cake
ACDEEEILLPT pedicellate
ACDEEEILNRV deliverance✧
ACDEEEIMPRT premedicate
ACDEEEIMRTV decemvirate
ACDEEEINPRU preaudience
ACDEEEINRTV revendicate
ACDEEEIPRTT decrepitate
ACDEEEIPRTV deprecative
ACDEEEKNNPY Cape Kennedy
ACDEEELLNRT crenellated
ACDEEELLRVW cave-dweller
ACDEEELLSST Leeds Castle
ACDEEELORRT decelerator
ACDEEENNSTT antecedents

ACDEEERRSTT trade secret
ACDEEFFILLT ill-affected
ACDEEFFINOT affectioned
ACDEEFGINRU figure-dance
ACDEEFHLSTT flat-chested
ACDEEFILNRZ fence-lizard
ACDEEFLMOTT mottle-faced
ACDEEFLNRUU fraudulence
ACDEEFMORRS armed forces
ACDEEFNRRTU unrefracted
ACDEEFORRTT tractor feed
ACDEEGGNORT congregated
ACDEEGGNRSS craggedness
ACDEEGHHPRT depth charge
ACDEEGHILRS sledge-chair
ACDEEGHIRRR Richard Gere
ACDEEGHNRRU undercharge
ACDEEGILLMO medico-legal
ACDEEGILNNR calendering
ACDEEGILNTU geniculated
ACDEEGINPRT deprecating
ACDEEGINRTU nectar-guide
ACDEEGKLNOW acknowledge
ACDEEHHKNRR handkercher
ACDEEHIIMNT Medicine Hat
ACDEEHIITTV ethic dative
ACDEEHILLLM chilled meal
ACDEEHILLTV Edith Cavell
ACDEEHILNOP encephaloid
ACDEEHILNPP Chippendale
ACDEEHILPSY psychedelia
ACDEEHIMNOR Echinoderma
ACDEEHIMNPU unimpeached
ACDEEHIMNRS merchandise
ACDEEHIMNRZ merchandize
ACDEEHINRTW windcheater
ACDEEHIORTT octahedrite
ACDEEHKKLNU knuckle-head
ACDEEHKNNUY unhackneyed
ACDEEHLLOPR placeholder
ACDEEHLLOSU close-hauled
ACDEEHLNNTY enchantedly
ACDEEHLNPRR randle-perch
ACDEEHLRRRU hurdle-racer
ACDEEHMNORW reach-me-down
ACDEEHMNOSW Chad Newsome
ACDEEHNNNTU unenchanted
ACDEEHNNSTU unchastened
ACDEEHNPPTU punched tape
ACDEEHNPRSS parchedness
ACDEEHNRRTU unchartered
ACDEEHRRSTW screw thread
ACDEEIILLTV divellicate
ACDEEIILLTY eidetically
ACDEEIILMPR Émile Picard
ACDEEIILMTV maledictive
ACDEEIILPSS specialised
ACDEEIILPSZ specialized
ACDEEIILTUV elucidative
ACDEEIIMMNN medicine man
ACDEEIIMRST mediatrices
ACDEEIINPST pedanticise
ACDEEIINPTZ pedanticize
ACDEEIINRTV revindicate
ACDEEIIOPPS epidiascope
ACDEEIIPRTV predicative
ACDEEIIRRRV arrivederci
ACDEEIJLTVY adjectively
ACDEEIJPRTU prejudicate
ACDEEIKLRST stickleader
ACDEEIKMRTT dream ticket
ACDEEILLLLN Daniell cell
ACDEEILLMNY endemically
ACDEEILLMSU mal du siècle
ACDEEILLNRU clair de lune
ACDEEILLORS radicellose
ACDEEILMNRU unreclaimed
ACDEEILMORU leucodermia
ACDEEILMRTY Emerald City
ACDEEILNNST clandestine
ACDEEILNOTT delectation
ACDEEILNPST lapidescent
ACDEEILNRST credentials
ACDEEILNRTU declinature
ACDEEILNTTU denticulate
ACDEEILOOSS loco disease
ACDEEILPRTU reduplicate
ACDEEILRTTU reticulated
ACDEEILSTUV vesiculated
ACDEEIMNOSU eudaemonics
ACDEEIMNPRT predicament
ACDEEIMNRTY determinacy
ACDEEIMORRR microreader
ACDEEIMORST democratise
ACDEEIMORTZ democratize
ACDEEIMOSTT domesticate
ACDEEINNRRY yince-errand
ACDEEINNRST disentrance
ACDEEINOPRT capernoited
deprecation
ACDEEINORST considerate
desecration
ACDEEINORTU decurionate
re-education
ACDEEINORTV verde-antico
ACDEEIOPRRT depreciator
ACDEEIOPTTT petticoated
ACDEEIORRSV service road
ACDEEIORRTT directorate✧
ACDEEIPPRRT paper-credit
ACDEEJMNRTU muntjac deer
ACDEEKLLSTW well-stacked
ACDEEKMRSTU steamer duck
ACDEEKNRRSW sneck drawer
ACDEEKQRRTU quarterdeck
ACDEELLMORU leucodermal
ACDEELLNOTU nucleolated
ACDEELMMNOT telecommand
ACDEELMNOTU Claude Monet
ACDEELMNPRS sperm candle
ACDEELMORRS scleroderma
ACDEELMPRRU Marcel Dupré

ACDEELNOPRW	candle-power
ACDEELNOSTU	Doune Castle
ACDEELNPTUU	pedunculate
ACDEELOORTW	water-cooled
ACDEELOPRTU	operculated
ACDEELORSSV	cross-leaved
ACDEELRSTTY	scatteredly
ACDEELSSTUY	decussately
ACDEEMNRTTU	traducement
ACDEENORRST	second-rater
ACDEENORRTV	A/D converter
ACDEEOPRRTY	deprecatory
ACDEERRSSTT	detractress
ACDEFFHLOST	the scaffold
ACDEFFIIRTV	diffractive
ACDEFGHLLRU	full-charged
ACDEFGILRSU	disgraceful
ACDEFHILPST	feldspathic
ACDEFHMOOST	smooth-faced
ACDEFIIINNT	infanticide
ACDEFIIINOT	deification
	edification
ACDEFIILSTU	feudalistic
ACDEFIINPSU	fides Punica
ACDEFIIORTY	edificatory
ACDEFILNRUU	Lucian Freud
ACDEFILORST	Fidel Castro
ACDEFINNOTU	fecundation
ACDEFINNRUW	wind furnace
ACDEFINRSUW	surface wind
ACDEFIRRTTU	trifurcated
ACDEFLLMOTT	mottled calf
ACDEFLLNORU	full-acorned
	uncalled-for
ACDEFLMMNOS	self-command
ACDEFLNRUUY	fraudulency
ACDEFLOOSSU	Sea of Clouds
ACDEFMOORRW	come forward
ACDEGGHMRTU	grudge match
ACDEGGIIINT	giganticide
ACDEGGILMRS	clam-diggers
ACDEGHHIOWY	Highway Code
ACDEGHIILNP	hiding-place
ACDEGHIIOPR	ideographic
ACDEGHILLNT	candlelight
ACDEGHILLRR	chargrilled
ACDEGHILNNO	golden chain
ACDEGHILNNR	chandlering
ACDEGHILORR	cigar-holder
ACDEGHILORS	shared logic
ACDEGHIMOPR	demographic
ACDEGHINORS	code-sharing
ACDEGHLOORS	grade school
ACDEGHOORTU	rough-coated
ACDEGIIIMNR	graminicide
ACDEGIILLOO	ideological
ACDEGIILMRU	demiurgical
ACDEGIILNNN	line dancing
ACDEGIILSST	Distalgesic®
ACDEGIIMNPT	magnetic dip
ACDEGIIMNSU	misguidance
ACDEGIINNRW	wire-dancing
ACDEGIKLNTW	tack-welding
ACDEGIKNNPS	send packing
ACDEGIKPRTU	picket-guard
ACDEGILLOOP	pedological
ACDEGILNNRY	dry-cleaning
ACDEGILNOST	closing date
ACDEGILOOPS	logopaedics
ACDEGIMNOSY	geodynamics
ACDEGIMORTY	tragicomedy
ACDEGINNPST	stepdancing
ACDEGINOPRY	copyreading
ACDEGKLOORS	sockdolager
ACDEGLOORST	cold storage
ACDEGOORSTT	scattergood
ACDEGOPRRSU	producer gas
ACDEHHINRSS	Hans Driesch
ACDEHHLLORR	Lord Harlech
ACDEHIIIPRR	Cirrhipedia
ACDEHIIKMNT	kitchen-maid
ACDEHIILOPP	paedophilic
ACDEHIILORT	Trochilidae
ACDEHIIMNNW	wind machine
ACDEHIINNRV	chain-driven
ACDEHIIOPRT	diaphoretic
ACDEHIIPPRT	crappit-heid
ACDEHIKLNST	stickhandle
ACDEHIKOSTT	sick to death
ACDEHILLLPY	delphically
ACDEHILMPTY	itchy-palmed
ACDEHILOPSU	dicephalous
ACDEHILOPSY	psychodelia
ACDEHILRSSY	chrysalides
ACDEHILRSTT	stilted arch
ACDEHIMMNRU	drum machine
ACDEHIMOPRS	comradeship
ACDEHIMOSTU	mustachioed
ACDEHINNNTU	uninchanted
ACDEHINNORR	horned cairn
ACDEHINNOST	stanchioned
ACDEHINOORS	icosahedron
ACDEHINOPRT	pointed arch
ACDEHINSSTU	unchastised
ACDEHINSTUZ	unchastized
ACDEHIOOPRT	orthopaedic
ACDEHIOPRSW	shadow price
ACDEHIPSTTY	dyspathetic
ACDEHJLLNNO	John Cleland
ACDEHKLNNST	landsknecht
ACDEHKMRSTU	Deutschmark
ACDEHKOSTUY	Hock Tuesday
ACDEHLLLOPY	phylloclade
ACDEHLMORRR	Lord marcher
ACDEHLMOSUY	chlamydeous
ACDEHLNOOST	close to hand
ACDEHLNPRTU	thunderclap
ACDEHLOORST	trade school
ACDEHLORRUY	Harold C Urey
ACDEHLPRTYY	hyperdactyl
ACDEHMNNOOR	enchondroma
ACDEHMOOPST	smooth-paced

ACDEHMOORTW	doomwatcher
ACDEHNNSTUU	unstaunched
ACDEHNOOPRS	sancho-pedro
ACDEHNOORST	octahedrons
ACDEHNORSSZ	scherzandos
ACDEHNORTTW	ratchet down
ACDEHNPRSUU	unpurchased
ACDEHOORRTU	urochordate
ACDEHORRTWW	draw the crow
ACDEIIILMOT	domiciliate
ACDEIIINTVV	vindicative
ACDEIIJLPRU	prejudicial
	pre-judicial
ACDEIIKNRST	inside track
ACDEIILLMNY	medicinally
ACDEIILLNTY	identically
ACDEIILLORV	varicelloid
ACDEIILLRVY	veridically
ACDEIILLSTY	deistically
ACDEIILMNOT	malediction
ACDEIILMPRS	spermicidal
ACDEIILNNOS	Nico Ladenis
ACDEIILNNOT	declination
ACDEIILNORT	directional
ACDEIILNOTU	elucidation
ACDEIILNOTV	valediction
ACDEIILNPTU	in duplicate
	induplicate
ACDEIILOPRW	periodic law
ACDEIILORRT	directorial
ACDEIILPRSU	Pedicularis
ACDEIILPTUV	duplicative
ACDEIILRTUV	diverticula
ACDEIIMMNOS	demoniacism
ACDEIIMNPST	pedanticism
ACDEIIMORRT	radiometric
ACDEIIMORTU	audiometric
ACDEIIMPRRU	pericardium
ACDEIINNRSS	Indian cress
ACDEIINNRTY	tyrannicide
ACDEIINOPRT	predication
ACDEIINORRT	doctrinaire
ACDEIINPRSS	Princess Ida
ACDEIINRTTX	indirect tax
ACDEIIORRTT	Tortricidae
ACDEIIRSTTV	distractive
ACDEIJNPRTU	prejudicant
ACDEILLLMOY	melodically
ACDEILLNOOT	decollation
ACDEILLORRV	corrivalled
ACDEILMMNNO	command line
ACDEILMNOOR	Locrian mode
ACDEILMNOPS	endoplasmic
ACDEILMNOSS	Iceland moss
ACDEILMNOSU	Claude Simon
ACDEILMNOTU	columniated
ACDEILMOPRR	dimercaprol
ACDEILMORTY	maledictory
ACDEILNNOSY	Coney Island
ACDEILNOOPY	Lycopodinae
ACDEILNOOST	consolidate
ACDEILNOOSW	wood sanicle
ACDEILNOPRY	epicondylar
ACDEILNOPST	endoplastic
ACDEILNORSS	cordialness
ACDEILNORSY	secondarily
ACDEILNORTU	radiolucent
ACDEILNORTY	declinatory
ACDEILNOSTT	Scotlandite
ACDEILNOSUV	unvocalised
ACDEILNOTTU	tentaculoid
ACDEILNOUVZ	unvocalized
ACDEILNPRUY	Cyndi Lauper
ACDEILNRTUU	uncurtailed
ACDEILORTUY	elucidatory
ACDEILORTVY	valedictory
ACDEILPPSTY	dyspeptical
ACDEILPRTUU	duplicature
ACDEIMMMNNO	in commendam
ACDEIMNNOOP	companioned
ACDEIMNNOPU	uncompanied
ACDEIMNORRS	morris dance
ACDEIMORSTT	democratist
ACDEINNNOSU	uncanonised
ACDEINNNOUZ	uncanonized
ACDEINNOORT	incoronated
ACDEINNORST	constrained
ACDEINNORTU	denunciator
	underaction
ACDEINNRTUU	uncurtained
ACDEINOOPRS	scorpaenoid
ACDEINOOPRY	Procyonidae
ACDEINOORRT	Corrodentia
	recordation
ACDEINOORST	co-ordinates
	decorations
ACDEINOPRTY	trypanocide
ACDEINOPSTT	constipated
ACDEINORRWY	cordwainery
ACDEINORTUV	decurvation
ACDEINOSSTU	decussation
ACDEINOSTTU	outdistance
ACDEINOSTTW	wainscotted
ACDEINPRSTU	unpractised
ACDEINPRSTY	candy stripe
ACDEIOPPRRT	dipterocarp
ACDEIOPRRTY	predicatory
ACDEIOPRSSY	caryopsides
ACDEIOPRSTT	disceptator
ACDEIOPRTTY	Dictyoptera
ACDEIORSUXY	xyridaceous
ACDEIPRSSTU	custard pies
ACDEIRSTTUY	daisy-cutter
ACDEJORRTUU	carte du jour
ACDEJORSSTU	coadjutress
ACDEKLNNOST	Ken Scotland
ACDEKNRRRTU	dark current
ACDEKOPRSTT	spatterdock
ACDELLOORRT	call to order
ACDELLOPTTY	leptodactyl
ACDELMNOTTU	laced mutton
ACDELNOOPRS	scolopendra

ACDELNOOPRT panel doctor
ACDELNOORTU tan-coloured
ACDELNPTTUU punctulated
ACDELOORRTU edulcorator
ACDELOPRTTY pterodactyl
ACDEMMMNNOT commandment
ACDEMMNOORT commendator
ACDEMNNORTU countermand
ACDEMNORTUY documentary
ACDEMOOPRTU proctodaeum
ACDEMOORRST ostracoderm
ACDEMOPRSSU mass-produce
ACDENNNNOUU unannounced
ACDENNOOPRU ponce around
ACDENOORRSW no-score draw
ACDENORRTUW counterdraw
ACDENPRSSWY dawn cypress
ACDEOORRTTW water doctor
ACDEOPPRRSU à corps perdu
ACDEORRSSST star-crossed
ACDFFGIINNT fact-finding
ACDFFGILNOS scaffolding
ACDFFIILMOO officialdom
ACDFFIINORT diffraction
ACDFGHHIINS chafing-dish
ACDFGILMNOU mould-facing
ACDFHILPSTU dispatchful
ACDFHINORRT drift-anchor
ACDFKLOORRW lock forward
ACDFOORRTUW ward of court
ACDGGIILNNR dancing-girl
ACDGGIKNORV graving dock
ACDGGINOORR Gordon Craig
ACDGHHIMMNO high command
ACDGHIIINNR dining chair
ACDGHIIIOPR idiographic
ACDGHILNORR Richard Long
ACDGHIMOOSU dichogamous
ACDGHIOPRSY discography
ACDGIIILOST dialogistic
ACDGIIKLNOR riding cloak
ACDGIIKNPRS disc parking
ACDGIILLNOO loading coil
ACDGIILNPRU dual pricing
ACDGIILNPTU duplicating
ACDGIINOPRR road pricing
ACDGIINOSST diagnostics
ACDGIINRSTT distracting
ACDGIIORSSU disgracious
ACDGIKNNORW knowing card
ACDGILLOOOX doxological
ACDGILNOORW carding wool
wool-carding
ACDGILNRTUY traducingly
ACDGIMNNOPU up and coming
up-and-coming
ACDGINNOOPY Pycnogonida
ACDGINOORVW woodcarving
ACDGINORSST cross-dating
ACDGIOPRRTU agriproduct
ACDGLLOOTYY dactylology
ACDGLOORRUU colour guard
ACDGORSSSTU Scots Guards
ACDHHIILOTY ichthyoidal
ACDHHIKNRRU Richard Kuhn
ACDHHIOPRRS harpsichord
ACDHHIOPRTY hydropathic
ACDHHIORRSY Hydrocharis
ACDHIIIMRTT mithridatic✧
ACDHIILOOPR chiropodial
ACDHIILOPSU acidophilus
ACDHIIMNORS diachronism
disharmonic
ACDHIINNSTW sandwich tin
ACDHIINOOPR radiophonic
ACDHIIOPRST diastrophic
ACDHILNOPRS spinal chord
ACDHILOOPSZ schizopodal
ACDHIMNOORT trichomonad
ACDHIMNORSY dysharmonic
ACDHIMNORTY hydromantic
ACDHIMNRSSY scrimshandy
ACDHINNORYY cyanohydrin
ACDHINNPRTU pitch and run
ACDHINOOPRS discophoran
ACDHINOORSU diachronous
ACDHIOPRSTT drop a stitch
ACDHIORSTTY hydrostatic
ACDHLLOOOOW wood alcohol
ACDHLNNSUUY Sunday lunch
ACDHLNOOORT notochordal
ACDHLOORSSW schoolwards
ACDHNNPSUUY Sunday punch
ACDHNOPRSUY Hydnocarpus
ACDIIIJLRUY judiciarily
ACDIIILLNPS disciplinal
ACDIIILLOTY idiotically
ACDIIILMORY domiciliary
ACDIIILORST dioristical
ACDIIIMNOST diatonicism
ACDIIIMNOTU unidiomatic
ACDIIINNOTV vindication
ACDIIJLLRUY juridically
ACDIIKLOPST optical disk
ACDIIKNOOST dockisation
ACDIIKNOOTZ dockization
ACDIILLLLYY idyllically
ACDIILLORST clostridial
ACDIILMNOPR palindromic
ACDIILMNSSY syndicalism
ACDIILMOOST sodomitical
ACDIILMOPST diplomatics
ACDIILMSTTU Talmudistic
ACDIILNNOOT conditional
ACDIILNNOTU inductional
ACDIILNOOST dislocation
ACDIILNOPTU duplication
ACDIILNSSTY syndicalist
ACDIIMNORSS sardonicism
ACDIIMORSTY myocarditis
ACDIINNOSTY syndication
ACDIINOPRST adscription

ACDIINORSTT distraction
ACDIINORSTU nitrous acid
ACDIINORTVY vindicatory
ACDIIOORRRR air-corridor
ACDIIOORSSS sarcoidosis
ACDIKKPSTUU kick up a dust
ACDIKLNOOSS Cook Islands
ACDIKMORSTU stadium rock
ACDIKNOPRTW Downpatrick
ACDIKNORSTU stick around
ACDILLNORTY doctrinally
ACDILLNOSYY synodically
ACDILLORSTY crystalloid
ACDILNNORSS Corn Islands
ACDILNOSSTU locus standi
ACDILNOSUUU nudicaulous
ACDILOOPSTW plastic wood
ACDIMNOOPST spodomantic
ACDIMNOOSTT mastodontic
ACDIMNORSUY urodynamics
ACDIMOOORRT cardiomotor
ACDINNNOOOT condonation
ACDINOOORRT co-ordinator
ACDINOORSSU icosandrous
ACDINOPRRTU drop-curtain
ACDIRSTUVYY drusy cavity
ACDKKNNOORU knock around
ACDKLLNOORR rock and roll
ACDLLNOORTU dual control
dual-control
ACDLLOPTYYY polydactyly
ACDLMNOOTYY monodactyly
ACDLNNOORUW clown around
ACDLNOOORTY condolatory
ACDMMNOOPST command post
ACDMMNPTUUU pactum nudum
ACDMNOOOPUZ azo-compound
ACDNNOOPRSS pros and cons
ACDNOORSTUU scout around
ACDNORRSTTU transductor
ACDOOORSSTU ostracodous
ACDOPRRSTUY drop a curtsy
ACEEEEEKPPR peacekeeper
ACEEEEFLLNV Lee Van Cleef
ACEEEEFNNRT entrance fee
ACEEEEHKMSS make cheeses
ACEEEEHLPSW escape wheel
ACEEEEHPRRS cheeseparer
ACEEEEKPRST keep a secret
ACEEEELNNNR René Laënnec
ACEEEENPQSU queen's peace
ACEEEERSTWZ tweezer case
ACEEEFFFRTT after-effect
ACEEEFFGRTU Auger effect
ACEEEFFGSTT stage effect
ACEEEFFKMOR coffee-maker
ACEEEFFKNOT take offence
ACEEEFGMPRT perfect game
ACEEEFHLNRV French leave
ACEEEFIOPPP pipe of peace
ACEEEFLNOPS pace oneself
ACEEEFPRRTY perfect year
ACEEEGGORRY George Carey
ACEEEGHHRST chargesheet
ACEEEGHLLNR rechallenge
ACEEEGHNPRR crepehanger
ACEEEGILNRT energetical
ACEEEGIMNNR generic name
ACEEEGIMNRT race meeting
ACEEEGIMNST miscegenate
ACEEEGIMNTT metagenetic
ACEEEGLMNOU leucaemogen
ACEEEGLOTTT telecottage
ACEEEGMNOPR peace-monger
ACEEEGNORRU re-encourage
ACEEEGNRSTT centre stage
secret agent
ACEEEHHPRRT the Preacher
ACEEEHIIMPR epicheirema
ACEEEHILNNP encephaline
ACEEEHIMNTV achievement
ACEEEHINSST cenesthesia
ACEEEHIORVV overachieve
ACEEEHIPRTT epic theatre
ACEEEHKLNRT leatherneck
ACEEEHKMPRS speechmaker
ACEEEHLLNRT chanterelle
ACEEEHLMNOS chaenomeles
ACEEEHLNPST cheese plant
ACEEEHLNRTT centre lathe
ACEEEHLRSST teacherless
ACEEEHMNNNT enhancement
ACEEEHMNSTT escheatment
ACEEEHMORTT tacheometer
ACEEEHPRSTT teacher's pet
ACEEEHRRTTU the creature
ACEEEHRSSTW cheese straw
ACEEEILLMRR crémaillère
ACEEEILMNPS mise en place
ACEEEILMNPT mantelpiece
ACEEEILNPPR pipe-cleaner
ACEEEILNQUV equivalence
ACEEEILNRRV irrelevance
ACEEEIMPRST masterpiece
ACEEEINNPPT inappetence
ACEEEINRSSS necessaries
ACEEEINSSTT necessitate
ACEEEIPRRST respite care
ACEEEIPTTVX expectative
ACEEEJKLPST steeplejack
ACEEEJORSTT ejector seat
ACEEEKLLNRU Lake Lucerne
ACEEEKLORTW electroweak
ACEEEKPRSTV Everest pack
ACEEELLMNOV malevolence
ACEEELLPRRW wallcreeper
ACEEELLSSSY ceaselessly
ACEEELMMNPT emplacement
ACEEELMNPRT replacement
ACEEELMNRRT recremental
ACEEELMNRTX excremental
ACEEELNORST Rene Lacoste

ACEEELNOSUX exonuclease
ACEEELNPRST pearlescent
ACEEELQRRTU lacquer tree
ACEEEMNNRTT re-enactment
ACEEEMNORTY tea ceremony
ACEEEMNRTTW cement-water
water cement
ACEEENPPRTU perpetuance
ACEEENRRSSV screen saver
ACEEEOPRTTX expectorate
ACEEEPRSSTT streetscape
ACEEERRSTTY Carey Street
ACEEFFFNOOS off one's face
ACEEFFGHINN chaff-engine
ACEEFFHINOT in the face of
ACEEFFIILOS officialese
ACEEFFILNTU ineffectual
ACEEFFILTVY affectively
ACEEFFIOPPR paper-office
ACEEFFLLOST coffee stall
ACEEFFLLTUY effectually
ACEEFFLRRUV Laffer curve
ACEEFFMNORT afforcement
ACEEFFNOOSS off one's case
ACEEFHINNRS enfranchise
ACEEFHINRVW weaver finch
ACEEFHIRRTW fire-watcher
ACEEFHKLTTW Twelfth cake
ACEEFHLLOOR alcohol-free
ACEEFHLLPRS parcel shelf
ACEEFHLNPRT French pleat
ACEEFHLRRSU researchful
ACEEFHMORRT form teacher
ACEEFHNRRTU furtherance
ACEEFIISTTT testificate
ACEEFIKOPSS kiss of peace
ACEEFILLNVY venefically
ACEEFILLORT refocillate
ACEEFILNRRT central fire
ACEEFILNRSU increaseful
ACEEFILPRUU Cupuliferae
ACEEFILRSTV service flat
ACEEFIMNORS freemasonic
ACEEFIMNTTU tumefacient
ACEEFINOPTT tepefaction
ACEEFINORRT refectorian
ACEEFIORSSS Sea of Crises
ACEEFKMOPRT Pomfret cake
ACEEFLLNRST crestfallen
ACEEFLLNRUU nuclear fuel
ACEEFLNRSSU carefulness
ACEEFLOPRRT prefectoral
ACEEFLORRUV overcareful
ACEEFLORSUU ferulaceous
ACEEFLOTTUV octave-flute
ACEEFLPRRTU prefectural
ACEEFLRRSTY Carl Seyfert
ACEEFMNOPRR performance
ACEEFMNOPRY free company
ACEEFNNORSU run one's face
ACEEFOORTTU à toute force
ACEEFPPRSTT past perfect
ACEEGGIMMNO emmenagogic
ACEEGGIMNOT geomagnetic
ACEEGGIMRSU reggae music
ACEEGGLORSU George Lucas
ACEEGHHNOSU change-house
ACEEGHHORSU charge-house
ACEEGHHPRRY hypercharge
ACEEGHILLNR all-cheering
ACEEGHILMNO hegemonical
ACEEGHILOOT oligochaete
ACEEGHILPRT telegraphic
ACEEGHIMPRS magic sphere
ACEEGHINNOX ion-exchange
ACEEGHINNRT interchange
ACEEGHINORT atherogenic
ACEEGHKRSTU hucksterage
ACEEGHLNOOS loose change
ACEEGHLOPST close the gap
ACEEGHMMORT hectogramme
ACEEGHNRRSU chargenurse
ACEEGHPRRSU supercharge
ACEEGIILNNT geanticline
ACEEGIINPRR ear-piercing
ACEEGIKNNPP kneecapping
knee-capping
ACEEGIKNTTT ticket agent
ACEEGILLNOR collegianer
ACEEGILLNRS selling race
ACEEGILLNRY generically
ACEEGILLNTY genetically
ACEEGILLNUY eugenically
ACEEGILMMRT telegrammic
ACEEGILMNRS single cream
ACEEGILMOPS mesopelagic
ACEEGILMORT geometrical
ACEEGILNPRS sleeping car
ACEEGILNRRY gyre-carline
ACEEGILNSSV Venice glass
ACEEGILNSTT telecasting
ACEEGILOPSU specialogue
ACEEGILPRTT tetraplegic
ACEEGILSTTU gesticulate
ACEEGIMMNPT camp-meeting
ACEEGIMMNRT centigramme
ACEEGIMMORT microgamete
ACEEGIMNSUW New Age music
ACEEGINNORS Grecian nose
ACEEGINORST coasteering
ACEEGINORTT teratogenic
ACEEGIRRRTY cerargyrite
ACEEGIRSTTT strategetic
ACEEGKLNOOR cook-general
ACEEGKNORRT rocket range
ACEEGLLRSSY gracelessly
ACEEGLMNNOT congealment
ACEEGLMNOPR place-monger
ACEEGLMNORS camerlengos
ACEEGLNNSTU languescent
ACEEGMNORRS scaremonger
ACEEGMORSTU come a gutser

ACEEGNNORRS organ-screen
ACEEGNNOSST cognateness
ACEEGNNRSUY agency nurse
ACEEGNOORTT cottage orné
ACEEGNORSSV Geneva cross
ACEEGPPRRSU caper-spurge
ACEEGRRSSSU rescue-grass
ACEEHHIIRRS hierarchise
ACEEHHIIRRZ hierarchize
ACEEHHILPTW Whitechapel
ACEEHHIPRST teachership
ACEEHHIRTTT Thatcherite
ACEEHHITTTT hatchettite
ACEEHHLMRST crash-helmet
ACEEHHLORST hearse-cloth
ACEEHHLOSTT shoe latchet
ACEEHHMNRTT The Merchant
ACEEHHNORST sheet anchor
ACEEHHOPTTY hypothecate
ACEEHIILNNP Chilean pine
ACEEHIILNOT Aeneolithic
ACEEHIILNST antihelices
lecithinase
ACEEHIILPRT perithecial
ACEEHIILPTT epithetical
ACEEHIIMMNT time machine
ACEEHIIMRST hetaerismic
ACEEHIINNRT inheritance
ACEEHIIPPRT perihepatic
ACEEHIIRSTT theatricise
ACEEHIIRTTZ theatricize
ACEEHIKMNRT niche market
ACEEHIKNRTW kitchenware
ACEEHILLNNP panhellenic✧
ACEEHILLNSW Chinese wall
ACEEHILLOPR La Périchole
ACEEHILLRTY heretically
ACEEHILMNOW Michael Owen
ACEEHILMOPR hemeralopic
ACEEHILNPRT phrenetical
ACEEHILNRTT chain letter
threnetical
ACEEHILNSST ethicalness
ACEEHILOORZ coleorhizae
ACEEHILORTT theoretical
ACEEHILPSTT tip the scale
ACEEHILRSSV Charles Ives
ACEEHIMMNPT impeachment
ACEEHIMNNNT enchainment
ACEEHIMNNSU unmechanise
ACEEHIMNNUZ unmechanize
ACEEHIMNOPR rope machine
ACEEHIMNRST cashierment
ACEEHIMOORR Archie Moore
ACEEHIMORTT theorematic
ACEEHIMRRSW schwärmerei
ACEEHIMRRTT time charter
ACEEHIMRSTT catheterism
ACEEHIMRTTY erythematic
ACEEHIMSTTW witches' meat
ACEEHINNSTZ Nietzschean
ACEEHINORST heteroscian
ACEEHINORTT the Creation✧
Theocritean
ACEEHINOSTT action sheet
ACEEHINPRSS preachiness
ACEEHINPRTT parenthetic
ACEEHIOPRST spirochaete
ACEEHIPRRST Petrarchise
ACEEHIPRRTZ Petrarchize
ACEEHIPRTTU therapeutic
ACEEHIPRTVY hyperactive
ACEEHIRSSTV tsesarevich
ACEEHIRSSTW tsesarewich
ACEEHJKLLST shell jacket
ACEEHJLNORR John Le Carré
ACEEHKLLOPT placket-hole
ACEEHKLORRT rock leather
ACEEHKNOPST technospeak
ACEEHLLNTTU call the tune
ACEEHLLQRUW Raquel Welch
ACEEHLLRRST shell-crater
tracer shell
ACEEHLMMNSY mesenchymal
ACEEHLMNRUU Herculaneum
ACEEHLMOPSY mesocephaly
ACEEHLNOPSU encephalous
ACEEHLNPRTU place-hunter
ACEEHLOORRU leucorrhoea
ACEEHLOPRRT perchlorate
ACEEHLORSTT earth-closet
ACEEHMMNNRT merchantmen
ACEEHMNNNTT enchantment
ACEEHMNNRRT trencherman
ACEEHMNNSTT chastenment
ACEEHMOPTTY hepatectomy
ACEEHMOPXYY Myxophyceae
ACEEHMORRTY archeometry
ACEEHMORTTY tacheometry
ACEEHNNORRT archenteron
ACEEHNNOSTT chansonette
ACEEHNNRSST enchantress
ACEEHNOPRTT on the carpet
ACEEHNRRSST stern-chaser
ACEEHORRSTT orchestrate
Sacher torte
Sachertorte
ACEEHORRSTU treacherous
ACEEHORRTTU treachetour
ACEEIIKNNTZ Citizen Kane
ACEEIIKRSTT rickettsiae
ACEEIILLNPT penicillate
ACEEIILLNRT rectilineal
ACEEIILLPPT epileptical
ACEEIILMNRS criminalese
ACEEIILNNSU lean cuisine
ACEEIILNRRT rectilinear
ACEEIILPRSS specialiser
ACEEIILPRSU peculiarise
ACEEIILPRSZ specializer
ACEEIILPRTT periclitate
ACEEIILPRTV replicative

ACEEIILPRUZ peculiarize
ACEEIILPTVX explicative
ACEEIILRRST rectiserial
ACEEIIMNRRT recriminate
ACEEIIMPTTV captive time
ACEEIIMRSTV miscreative
ACEEIIMSSVW seismic wave
ACEEIINNTUV enunciative
ACEEIINOPRT capernoitie
ACEEIINRSST canisterise
insectaries
ACEEIINRSTZ canisterize
ACEEIINRTTV interactive
ACEEIIPPRTT peripatetic
precipitate
ACEEIIPRTTV crepitative
ACEEIIRSSTT cassiterite
ACEEIIRSTTV recitatives
ACEEIJNNRTT interjacent
ACEEIKLLMNN Ian McKellen
ACEEIKLMNSY McKinley Sea
ACEEIKMPRRT market-price
ACEEIKMRRSV service mark
ACEEIKNPSVY Kevin Spacey
ACEEIKNRSTW awe-stricken
ACEEIKNSSSS seasickness
ACEEILLLSTY celestially
ACEEILLNNRS Carl Nielsen
ACEEILLNNSS cleanliness
ACEEILLNPST slate pencil
splenetical
ACEEILLOPPR papier collé
ACEEILLOPST all to pieces
ACEEILLORST selectorial
ACEEILLORTV vorticellae
ACEEILLPPTT cappelletti
ACEEILLRTVY cleverality
ACEEILMNNRT incremental
ACEEILMNORT Trincomalee
ACEEILMNOSS Monica Seles
ACEEILMNRRY mercenarily
ACEEILMNRTT Central Time
ACEEILMORRT calorimeter
ACEEILMORST elastomeric
ACEEILMPSST esemplastic
ACEEILMPSTU time capsule
ACEEILMRTUV vermiculate
ACEEILNNORT intolerance
ACEEILNNOTU enucleation
ACEEILNNRST intercensal
ACEEILNNTUU uninucleate
ACEEILNNTUY lieutenancy
ACEEILNOPTX exceptional
ACEEILNORSS recessional
ACEEILNORST resectional
secretional
ACEEILNOSSS secessional
ACEEILNOSST coessential
ACEEILNPRRT pericentral
ACEEILNPRTT centripetal
ACEEILNPSSS specialness
ACEEILNPTTY pectinately
ACEEILNQUVY equivalency
ACEEILNRRVY irrelevancy
ACEEILNRSST treacliness
ACEEILNRSSY necessarily
ACEEILNSSST elasticness
ACEEILNSTTT client state
ACEEILNTTTU tentaculite
ACEEILOPSTT police state
ACEEILORRTV correlative
ACEEILORTUX executorial
ACEEILOTVVY evocatively
ACEEILPPRRW crippleware
ACEEILPRTTY rectipetaly
ACEEILPSTUV speculative
ACEEILSTTTU testiculate
ACEEIMMNORT anemometric
ACEEIMMNRRS mercenarism
ACEEIMMNRSU same numeric
ACEEIMMORST commiserate
ACEEIMNNOTT cementation
ACEEIMNORRT craniometer
ACEEIMNORTT actinometer
coterminate
ACEEIMNPRTT permittance
ACEEIMNQRTU acquirement
ACEEINNNSST ancientness
ACEEINNOPTZ pentazocine
ACEEINNORSS reascension
ACEEINNORST sanctioneer
ACEEINNPPTY inappetency
ACEEINNPTTX inexpectant
ACEEINNRRSU reinsurance
ACEEINNSSTX inexactness
ACEEINOORRU iure coronae
ACEEINOPTTX expectation
ACEEINORSST estancieros
ACEEINPRRST transpierce
ACEEINRRSTV transceiver
ACEEINRSTTX res extincta
ACEEIOOPRTT opere citato
ACEEIOOPRTV co-operative
ACEEIOPPRSU piperaceous
ACEEIOPRRTT apricot tree
ACEEIOPRRTV procreative
ACEEIORRSTV eviscerator
ACEEIORRTTV retroactive
ACEEIORSTTX stereotaxic
ACEEIPRRSTW space writer
ACEEIPRSTUV superactive
ACEEIRRSTUV River Escaut
ACEEIRSSTTU resuscitate
ACEEJMNNORS Carmen Jones
ACEEJNPRSTU superjacent
ACEEKKLMRSY mackerel sky
ACEEKKPRRRY Kerry Packer
ACEEKLMNRTT tracklement
ACEEKLNOPRR rocker panel
ACEEKLNOPRT rocket plane
ACEEKMNNSTT Mack Sennett
ACEEKMNOPPY keep company

ACEEKMRRSTW wreckmaster
ACEEKNRRTTU tenure track
ACEEKNRSTTV track events
ACEEKPRRSST racket-press
ACEELLLORST steel collar
ACEELLLORTY electorally
ACEELLMNRSS small screen
small-screen
ACEELLNNORS corneal lens
ACEELLNORTY coeternally
ACEELLNOSTT constellate
ACEELLOOPRT coleopteral
ACEELLOPTUY eucalyptole
ACEELLQRSUY Carlylesque
ACEELLRSSTY tracelessly
ACEELLSSSUY causelessly
ACEELMMNORS Carlos Menem
ACEELMNNOOV monovalence
ACEELMNOPTT contemplate
ACEELMPRRTY crape myrtle
ACEELNNNSSU uncleanness
ACEELNNRSSU unclearness
ACEELNOOPRT coleopteran
ACEELNOOSSS close season
ACEELNOPRTU counterplea
ACEELNOPSTT Pentecostal
ACEELNORSTU counterseal
ACEELNOSTWY wet one's clay
ACEELNPTTXY expectantly
ACEELOORRTW water cooler
ACEELOORSTW sea colewort
ACEELOPPPRT copperplate
ACEELOPPRTT Plectoptera
ACEELORSTTT store cattle
ACEELORSTTW water closet
ACEEMMMOORT commemorate
ACEEMMNNORT Roman cement
ACEEMMORRTY memory trace
ACEEMNNNOTU mountenance
ACEEMNNORTU connumerate
ACEEMNNRRUY unmercenary
ACEEMNORTTY cementatory
ACEEMOPRTTU computerate
ACEEMORSTTT stactometer
ACEENNNOPRU preannounce
ACEENNNORSY Sean Connery
ACEENNOPRTU counterpane
ACEENNORRTV contravener
ACEENNORSTT consternate
ACEENNPPRSY scrapepenny
ACEENNPRSST SPET scanner
ACEENNPTTUX unexpectant
ACEENNRSSUY unnecessary
ACEENOORSTT cotoneaster
ACEENOPRTTX expectorant
ACEEOOPRSTU proteaceous
ACEEOORSSTU ostreaceous
ACEEOPRRRTU recuperator
ACEEOPRSTUV superoctave
ACEEORRSTUW watercourse
ACEEORSSTUU ceteosaurus
ACEEPPRRTTU paper-cutter
ACEEPRRSSUU acupressure
ACEEPRSSSTT spectatress
ACEERRRTUUV recurvature
ACEFFFGILOR flag-officer
ACEFFFILOST facts of life
ACEFFFIMORS farm-offices
ACEFFGHILNR cliffhanger
ACEFFGILNTY affectingly
ACEFFGINNTU unaffecting
ACEFFGLORTU flag of truce
ACEFFHKORTT off the track
ACEFFIILPST spifflicate
ACEFFIITTVY affectivity
ACEFFIKOPRR park-officer
ACEFFILORTU forficulate
ACEFFILOSST last offices
ACEFFILRSST trafficless
ACEFFIMOPST stamp office
ACEFFIOSTUV suffocative
ACEFGGIMNOO coming-of-age
ACEFGHLLNOT focal length
ACEFGHLLNUY changefully
ACEFGHLNNOR Anglo-French
ACEFGHNNORT change front
ACEFGHOOPRR proof-charge
ACEFGIIINST significate
ACEFGIIMNNT magnificent
ACEFGIIMNOS magnificoes
ACEFGIINNNR refinancing
ACEFGIINNRT interfacing
ACEFGIKNORW working face
ACEFGILNRTU centrifugal
ACEFGILNTTU leaf-cutting
ACEFGINORTU configurate
ACEFGMNNORY fancy monger
ACEFGMNORSU Magnus force
ACEFHHINRSS Hans Fischer
ACEFHHINSTT snatch-thief
ACEFHIILNOR Nicole Farhi
ACEFHIILNPS pelican-fish
ACEFHIINRTY chieftainry
ACEFHIJLMOX Michael J Fox
ACEFHILMOOT Michael Foot
ACEFHILNOPR francophile✧
ACEFHILNOSU leaf-cushion
ACEFHILORRT trefoil arch
ACEFHILRSTY self-charity
ACEFHIRSTTY city fathers
ACEFHLLOOSU house of call
ACEFHLNNRSU channel-surf
ACEFHLNRTUY half-century
ACEFHLOPRRU reproachful
ACEFHMNNORW Frenchwoman
ACEFHMORRTT mothercraft
ACEFHNNOOPR francophone✧
ACEFHNORSTT French toast
ACEFHOORSTU house-factor
ACEFHOORSUU hour of cause
ACEFIIILNRT fairniticle
ACEFIIIMNRT rifacimenti

ACEFIIINORT reification
ACEFIIKLLRT flickertail
ACEFIILMNOR infomercial
ACEFIILMNRS crimen falsi
falsi crimen
ACEFIILNNOT final notice
ACEFIILNNSS finicalness
ACEFIILNRTV vertical fin
ACEFIILNRTY fairnyticle
ACEFIILPRSU superficial
ACEFIILRSTW welfaristic
ACEFIIMNORT rifacimento
ACEFIIMNOTT metafiction
ACEFIIMORRS formicaries
ACEFIINOPTT pontificate
ACEFIINORST fractionise
ACEFIINORSU facinerious
ACEFIINORTZ fractionize
ACEFIINRRTU curtain-fire
ACEFIIORRTY reificatory
ACEFIIPRRSS fiars prices
ACEFILLORUW cauliflower
ACEFILMMOTU comme il faut
ACEFILNORTT fractionlet
ACEFILORSST trace fossil
ACEFILORSTU lactiferous
ACEFILOSTUY facetiously
ACEFIMMNORT fair comment
ACEFIMNOTTU tumefaction
ACEFIMORRRT crateriform
ACEFINNORST for instance
ACEFINNOTTU functionate
ACEFINNRSST franticness
ACEFINOTTUV confutative
ACEFINPRSTY presanctify
ACEFINRRRTU franc-tireur
ACEFIOORRTV vociferator
ACEFIPRRSTT priestcraft
ACEFKLMORST flock-master
ACEFKMORRST stock-farmer
ACEFKMRRRTU truck-farmer
ACEFLLLOSSW class-fellow
ACEFLLMOORW cam follower
ACEFLLOORRW coral flower
ACEFLLRRUVY curry favell
ACEFLNNOOST stone falcon
ACEFLNSSTTU tactfulness
ACEFLOOPRRS polar forces
ACEFOOPRRTW power factor
ACEFOOPSTTX ex post facto
ACEGGHILLNN challenging
ACEGGHOPSUY psychagogue
ACEGGILLMOO gemological
ACEGGILLNOU colleaguing
ACEGGILNPRW crawling peg
ACEGGINNORU encouraging
ACEGGINRSSS scragginess
ACEGGKLORSU Georg Lukacs
Georg Lukács
ACEGGLNOOYY gynaecology
ACEGHHILOPR helicograph
ACEGHHILRST searchlight
ACEGHHIMORZ Chaim Herzog
ACEGHHINORW weigh anchor
ACEGHHLORTU leach-trough
ACEGHHMNRRU hunger march
ACEGHHNORST short-change
ACEGHHOOPRR choreograph
ACEGHHOPRRY choregraphy
ACEGHIILPRX lexigraphic
ACEGHIILRRU hierurgical
ACEGHIIPRRS serigraphic
ACEGHIKLLNS shellacking
ACEGHIKLNNT lance-knight
ACEGHIKMNOP epoch-making
ACEGHILLNNN channelling
ACEGHILLNRT night-cellar
ACEGHILLOOR rheological
ACEGHILLOOT ethological
theological
ACEGHILNOOT theogonical
ACEGHILNRSY searchingly
ACEGHILOOPR oleographic
ACEGHILOPSY geophysical
ACEGHILPSTY get physical
ACEGHIMMOOT homogametic
ACEGHIMNNRT merchanting
ACEGHIMNORU archegonium
ACEGHIMRSST great schism
ACEGHINNOPT change point
ACEGHINNPRU unpreaching
ACEGHINOPRV venographic
ACEGHINORRS horse-racing
ACEGHINORRV overarching
ACEGHINPRSS graphicness
ACEGHIOOPRR oreographic
ACEGHIOPRRX xerographic
ACEGHIRRTWY carry weight
ACEGHLOOSTY eschatology
ACEGHLOPTTY glyptotheca
ACEGHMOORSU hercogamous
ACEGHMORRSU rogues' march
rogue's march
ACEGHNOPRSY scenography
ACEGHOOPRSU creophagous
ACEGHOOPSTY phagocytose
ACEGHOPRRST port charges
ACEGIIKMNNT magnetic ink
ACEGIIKNPRS asking price
ACEGIILLNNV clean-living
ACEGIILLOTV colligative
ACEGIILOSTT egotistical
ACEGIILRSST sacrilegist
ACEGIIMNOST isomagnetic
ACEGIIMNRST Germanistic
ACEGIIMRRTV gravimetric
ACEGIINNORV organic vein
ACEGIINRRRR ring-carrier
ACEGIINRSTU cauterising
ACEGIINRSTW writing case
ACEGIINRTUZ cauterizing
ACEGIIPRRST perigastric

ACEGIJNOTUV conjugative
ACEGIKLNNOT Nat King Cole
ACEGIKMMRRW Mark McGwire
ACEGIKNORST orange stick
ACEGILLMRTU metallurgic
ACEGILLNNOR non-allergic
ACEGILLNNOY congenially
ACEGILLNNRU unrecalling
ACEGILLNOOO oenological
ACEGILLNOOP penological
ACEGILLNOSS logicalness
ACEGILLNTTU Luing cattle
ACEGILLOOOR oreological
ACEGILLOORS serological
ACEGILLOOSX sexological
ACEGILLRTVY gravity cell
ACEGILMNORS camerlingos
ACEGILMNRSY screamingly
ACEGILMOSTY cleistogamy
ACEGILNNNOU uncongenial
ACEGILNNOOS cloisonnage
ACEGILNNOOT congelation
ACEGILNNPRS spring-clean
ACEGILNNRTU clearing-nut
ACEGILNNSUY unceasingly
ACEGILNOORS Nicolas Roeg
ACEGILNORRS carol singer
ACEGILNORRT relict organ
ACEGILNOSUU cauligenous
ACEGILNPRSS spring scale
ACEGILNRSSY caressingly
ACEGILNRSTT scatterling
ACEGILNTUUU unguiculate
ACEGILOOPST apologetics
ACEGILOORTT teratologic
ACEGILORSUV clavigerous
ACEGILPRRSS garlic press
ACEGILRRTUU agriculture
ACEGIMNNOOT cognominate
ACEGIMNNOPR panic-monger
ACEGIMNNORT centi Morgan
ACEGIMNOOST somatogenic
ACEGIMNOOTZ zoomagnetic
ACEGIMORSST mesogastric
ACEGINNNOSU consanguine
ACEGINNOPRY panegyricon
ACEGINNORTY octingenary
ACEGINNRSST transgenics
ACEGINNRSTY astringency
ACEGINNSSTW newscasting
ACEGINOORTV overcoating
ACEGINORSTV overcasting
ACEGINOSTTV casting vote
ACEGINPRRRS scraper ring
ACEGINPSTTY typecasting
ACEGINRTTTU rate-cutting
ACEGIOORTTX excogitator
ACEGIOPRSSU scapigerous
ACEGIORSSTT get it across
ACEGKLNNOUW luckengowan
ACEGKLOPSST pocket-glass
ACEGKRSSTTU stage-struck
ACEGLLNOOSU collagenous
ACEGLLOSTYY glycosylate
ACEGLMNORWY clergywoman
ACEGLNOPRTY calyptrogen
ACEGLNORTUY granulocyte
ACEGLORRSSV clovergrass
ACEGLRSSTTU glass-cutter
ACEGMNNORSS Congressman
ACEGMNOORRR Roger Corman
ACEGMOPRRST spectrogram
ACEGMORSTTY gastrectomy
ACEGNOORRTT gerontocrat
ACEGNORRSST cross-garnet
ACEGOOPRSST gastroscope
ACEGRRSSTTU grass-cutter
scatter rugs
ACEHHIILMOP haemophilic
ACEHHIILMST hemistichal
ACEHHIIMRRS hierarchism
ACEHHIINNTY hyacinthine
ACEHHIINRTW within reach
ACEHHILLPRU Paul Ehrlich
ACEHHILNOTT chloanthite
ACEHHIMNOPS machine-shop
ACEHHIMOOPT homeopathic
ACEHHIMOSTT theomachist
ACEHHIMRSTT Thatcherism
ACEHHINOPPY phycophaein
ACEHHINOPTT Phaethontic
ACEHHINRRST Hans Richter
ACEHHINRRTU heart urchin
ACEHHIPRSTT heptarchist
ACEHHJLNORS John Charles
ACEHHKLRTUY hurly-hacket
ACEHHLMMORT hammercloth
ACEHHLNOORT anthochlore
ACEHHMNNSUU Munchhausen
ACEHHOORSTY chaos theory
ACEHHOPRTYY hypothecary
ACEHIIIMRST hetairismic
ACEHIIINPSS hispanicise✧
ACEHIIINPSZ hispanicize✧
ACEHIILLMOT homiletical
ACEHIILLNRT tiller-chain
trichinella
ACEHIILLOST isolecithal
ACEHIILMSTT athleticism
ACEHIILNOPR necrophilia
ACEHIILNPRT nephritical
ACEHIILOSTT chiastolite
ACEHIILPPTY epiphytical
ACEHIILRSTT thersitical✧
ACEHIILRSVW swivel-chair
ACEHIILSTWW welwitschia
ACEHIIMNOPR prochein ami
ACEHIIMNOPT hemianoptic
ACEHIIMRSTT theatricism
ACEHIIMSSST schismatise
ACEHIIMSSTZ schismatize
ACEHIINNOPT phonetician

ACEHIINNTTU inauthentic
ACEHIINORRT rhetorician
ACEHIINOSSU hoisin sauce
ACEHIINPRSS Spanish rice
ACEHIINPRSY physicianer
ACEHIINPSTT pantheistic
ACEHIKLLORS scholar-like
ACEHIKLLRWY illy whacker
ACEHIKLNORT Loch Katrine
ACEHIKLPRRS parish clerk
ACEHIKLPRTY prickly heat
ACEHIKMNORS chain-smoker
ACEHIKMNORW machine-work
ACEHIKMRTUY rheumaticky
ACEHIKRRSSS sherris-sack
ACEHIKRSSTW cat's-whisker
ACEHIKRSTTV harvest tick
ACEHILLMRTY thermically
ACEHILLOPRT plethorical
ACEHILLORTW white-collar
ACEHILLPRSY spherically
ACEHILMMNPY lamp chimney
ACEHILMNOOR melanochroi
ACEHILMNOOT machine tool
ACEHILMNOST slot machine
ACEHILMOPTU plaice-mouth
ACEHILMORTT thermotical
ACEHILMPSTW Limp Watches
ACEHILNORSU A Chorus Line
ACEHILNPRST sphincteral
ACEHILNSTTY synthetical
ACEHILOOPRT orthoepical
ACEHILOORRZ coleorrhiza
ACEHILOOTTU acolouthite
ACEHILOPPRT prophetical
ACEHILOPPRW coal-whipper
ACEHILOSSST cholestasis
ACEHILRRTUV River Clutha
ACEHILRSSSY chrysalises
ACEHIMMNSTU The Music Man
ACEHIMMOPRT metamorphic
ACEHIMNOPRY prochein amy
ACEHIMNOPSS championess
ACEHIMNORSS marchioness
ACEHIMNORTU euchromatin
ACEHIMNOSYY hyoscyamine
ACEHIMNOTTU humectation
ACEHIMNTTUW minute-watch
ACEHIMOOSTT homeostatic
ACEHIMOPRST atmospheric
ACEHIMORRST choirmaster
ACEHIMORRYZ mycorrhizae
ACEHIMORSST metachrosis
ACEHIMORTTX thermotaxic
ACEHIMPRRST Petrarchism
ACEHIMPSSTY metaphysics
ACEHIMPSTTY sympathetic
ACEHINNNORS chansonnier
ACEHINNNRTT intrenchant
ACEHINNOOTT canine tooth
ACEHINNOPTT pantothenic
ACEHINNRSSU raunchiness
ACEHINNSTTY synanthetic
ACEHINNTTUU unauthentic
ACEHINOOPRZ Phanerozoic
ACEHINOPRRS chairperson
ACEHINOPRRT chiropteran
ACEHINOPRTU neuropathic
ACEHINORRST orchestrina
ACEHINORRSU hurricanoes
ACEHINPSSTT pentastichs
ACEHINRSSST starchiness
ACEHINSSSTT cattishness
ACEHINSTUUY Eutychianus
ACEHIOOPSTT osteopathic
ACEHIOOPTTV photoactive
ACEHIOOPTTX hepatotoxic
ACEHIOORTTV cohortative
ACEHIOPPRST Hippocrates
ACEHIOPRRST creatorship
ACEHIOPRRTT Trichoptera
ACEHIORSSTY case history
ACEHIPRRSST strip search
strip-search
ACEHIPRRSTT Petrarchist
ACEHIPRSSUY hyperacusis
ACEHIQRRSUY squirearchy
ACEHJNNORYY Johnny Carey
ACEHKKLLMSU Muschelkalk
ACEHKKORTTY Korky the Cat
ACEHKKRRSSU sharksucker
ACEHKNORTUV have no truck
ACEHKNOSSTU Stockhausen
ACEHKOOPRSW Cooper's hawk
ACEHKORRTWW workwatcher
ACEHKRRSTTU heart-struck
ACEHLLMRSSY charmlessly
ACEHLLMSSTY matchlessly
ACEHLLOORRS horse-collar
ACEHLMNORST camel's thorn
ACEHLMNRSUY secular hymn
ACEHLMOOPTY cephalotomy
ACEHLMOSSST stomachless
ACEHLNNRTTY trenchantly
ACEHLNOPRTY lycanthrope
ACEHLNORSTW Charlestown
ACEHLNSSSTU staunchless
ACEHLOOPRSU colour phase
ACEHLOOSSTT state school
ACEHLOPSUXY sceuophylax
ACEHLORSTUY lythraceous
ACEHLPPPRTU purple patch
ACEHMNNSSUU Munchausen's
ACEHMNOPRSY prosenchyma
ACEHMNOPRTY tephromancy
ACEHMNRRTTU return match
ACEHMOOPPST compost heap
ACEHMOORTTY tracheotomy
ACEHMOPRSTU champertous
ACEHNNOOPRT ctenophoran
ACEHNNSSSTU staunchness
ACEHNOORSTT on that score

ACEHNOORTTU	tautochrone
ACEHNOPPRRT	proper chant
ACEHNPRSSTU	snatch-purse
ACEHOOPPSTY	hepatoscopy
ACEHOOPRRST	arthroscope
	crapshooter
	prothoraces
ACEHOPRRSSY	chrysoprase
ACEHOPRRTYY	cryotherapy
ACEHOPRSTUU	purchase out
ACEHORSSTTT	scattershot
ACEHORSSTTV	torch-staves
ACEHORSTUWY	water souchy
ACEIIIILNSV	civilianise
ACEIIIILNVZ	civilianize
ACEIIIKNRST	kinesiatric
ACEIIILLLNT	initial cell
ACEIIILMNRS	criminalise
ACEIIILMNRZ	criminalize
ACEIIILMPTV	implicative
ACEIIILNOTT	elicitation
ACEIIILPSTT	pietistical
ACEIIIMNNRT	incriminate
ACEIIIMNOST	semiotician
ACEIIIMNRTV	criminative
ACEIIIMNSTT	anti-Semitic
ACEIIINNNRZ	cinnarizine
ACEIIINNOSS	Socinianise
ACEIIINNOSZ	Socinianize
ACEIIIQSTUV	acquisitive
ACEIIKLLNNV	Calvin Klein
ACEIIKLLNTY	kinetically
ACEIIKLLOOR	kilocalorie
ACEIIKLRSTT	rickettsial
ACEIIKNOTTU	autokinetic
ACEIIKNRSSS	air-sickness
ACEIIKRSSTT	rickettsias
ACEIILLLTVY	levitically
ACEIILLMMTY	mimetically
ACEIILLMNNU	illuminance
ACEIILLMOTY	meiotically
ACEIILLMPRY	empirically
ACEIILLMSSY	seismically
ACEIILLNOTV	vellication
ACEIILLNRTV	intervallic
ACEIILLNRUV	curvilineal
ACEIILLNSTT	scintillate
ACEIILLOPST	epistolical
ACEIILLOPTV	voltaic pile
ACEIILLOSTV	oscillative
ACEIILLPRTU	pleuritical
ACEIILLRSTY	eristically
ACEIILMNNTU	culminate in
ACEIILMNPRT	planimetric
ACEIILMNSSU	masculinise
ACEIILMNSTT	mentalistic
ACEIILMNSUZ	masculinize
ACEIILMORST	isometrical
ACEIILMOTTU	itacolumite
ACEIILMPRSU	Laserpicium
ACEIILMPRTU	implicature
ACEIILMRRTT	trimetrical
ACEIILNNORT	reclination
ACEIILNOORT	coalitioner
ACEIILNOPPR	pilocarpine
ACEIILNOPRT	replication
ACEIILNOPTX	explication
ACEIILNOQTU	equinoctial
ACEIILNOSSV	Slavonicise
ACEIILNOSVZ	Slavonicize
ACEIILNOTUV	inoculative
ACEIILNPRUY	pecuniarily
ACEIILNRRUV	curvilinear
ACEIILNRSTT	clarinetist
ACEIILNRSTU	unrealistic
ACEIILNRSTX	extrinsical
ACEIILNRTTY	intricately
ACEIILOORVV	cavo-rilievo
ACEIILORRST	escritorial
ACEIILOSTUY	eusociality
ACEIILPPRST	psi particle
ACEIILPRRTU	picture rail
ACEIILPRSST	plasticiser
ACEIILPRSTT	peristaltic
ACEIILPRSTZ	plasticizer
ACEIILPRTUY	peculiarity
ACEIILRTTVY	verticality
ACEIIMMNOTV	comminative
ACEIIMMORSS	commissaire
ACEIIMMRRSU	Mare Crisium
ACEIIMNNORS	Micronesian
ACEIIMNNORT	incremation
ACEIIMNNRST	manneristic
ACEIIMNOPRT	imprecation
ACEIIMNORST	creationism✧
	miscreation
	reactionism
	romanticise
ACEIIMNORTT	interatomic
	metrication
ACEIIMNORTZ	romanticize
ACEIIMNPRRU	pericranium
	per incuriam
ACEIIMNPSSU	impuissance
ACEIIMNRSTT	martensitic
ACEIIMNRSTU	insectarium
ACEIIMNSSTT	semanticist
ACEIIMOPSSU	cassiopeium
ACEIINNNOST	incensation
ACEIINNNOTU	enunciation
ACEIINNOPST	case in point
ACEIINNOPTT	pectination
ACEIINNORRT	incinerator
ACEIINNORTT	interaction
ACEIINNPSTT	pinnatisect
ACEIINNRTTY	incertainty
ACEIINOORTX	excoriation
ACEIINOPRTT	crepitation
ACEIINOPSTT	pectisation
ACEIINOPSTX	expiscation
ACEIINOPTTZ	pectization
ACEIINORSTT	creationist

	reactionist
ACEIINORSTV	Insectivora
ACEIINORTTX	extrication
ACEIINPPRTT	precipitant
ACEIINPRTTY	antipyretic
	pertinacity
ACEIIOOPPST	aposiopetic
ACEIIORSTTV	recitativos
ACEIJKLOPTT	pilot jacket
ACEIJLMMPRU	claim-jumper
ACEIJLNTUUW	walnut juice
ACEIJMMRRTY	Jimmy Carter
ACEIJMNOQTU	Jacqueminot
ACEIKKLNPTY	penalty kick
ACEIKKNOSTT	take stock in
ACEIKLLPRTT	lick-platter
ACEIKLLPSTY	skeptically
ACEIKLORTTW	latticework
ACEIKLPPRRY	prickly pear
ACEIKMNORST	section mark
ACEIKMRSTTT	smart-ticket
ACEIKNOPSWY	pick one's way
ACEIKPRSSTU	Sitka spruce
ACEIKPSSSSY	Sissy Spacek
ACEIKQSSSTU	quick assets
ACEILLLMNOR	lamellicorn
ACEILLLMOPY	polemically
ACEILLLNORT	citronellal
ACEILLLNRUU	unicellular
ACEILLLPSTY	sylleptical
ACEILLLRSTW	Will Scarlet
ACEILLLRTUY	cellularity
ACEILLMMSTY	symmetallic
ACEILLMNNOT	non-metallic
ACEILLMNOOV	Monaco-Ville
ACEILLMNORW	Cromwellian
ACEILLMNOST	Callistemon
ACEILLMNRSU	Marcellinus
ACEILLMNRUY	numerically
ACEILLMNSUY	masculinely
ACEILLMOSUZ	Isla Cozumel
ACEILLMPRRY	primary cell
ACEILLMRRUY	mercurially
ACEILLNNOTY	octennially
ACEILLNOOPR	precolonial
ACEILLNOPTU	cupellation
ACEILLNORST	Sir Lancelot
ACEILLNOSTY	sectionally
ACEILLNOTTY	tonetically
ACEILLNRSTY	crystalline
ACEILLOPPRT	proleptical
ACEILLOPPSY	episcopally
ACEILLOQUVY	equivocally
ACEILLORSUV	varicellous
ACEILLORTVY	vectorially
ACEILLRRTUY	reticularly
ACEILLRSSTY	crystallise
ACEILLRSTTY	crystallite
ACEILLRSTYZ	crystallize
ACEILLRTUVY	lucratively
ACEILLSSTUV	victualless
ACEILMMNOSU	communalise
ACEILMMNOTY	metonymical
ACEILMMNOUZ	communalize
ACEILMMORRT	coal-trimmer
ACEILMMORTT	recommittal
ACEILMMRSTY	symmetrical
ACEILMNNORT	conterminal
ACEILMNNSUU	unmasculine
ACEILMNOOPS	scopolamine
ACEILMNOOPW	policewoman
ACEILMNOPTY	amylopectin
ACEILMNOTTU	monticulate
ACEILMNRTTU	curtailment
ACEILMNRTUU	retinaculum
ACEILMNSSSU	musicalness
ACEILMORRTY	calorimetry
ACEILMRRTUU	mariculture
ACEILNNNOOX	connexional
ACEILNNNOSS	nonsensical
ACEILNNNOTT	continental
ACEILNNOOPT	Neoplatonic
ACEILNNORTU	crenulation
ACEILNNRTUY	uncertainly
ACEILNNSSTY	incessantly
ACEILNOOPRR	incorporeal
ACEILNOOPRT	Neotropical
	percolation
ACEILNOORRT	correlation
ACEILNOORSU	arenicolous
ACEILNOORTU	unicolorate
ACEILNOOSTY	loan-society
ACEILNOPRRY	prince royal
ACEILNOPRTU	inter pocula
ACEILNOPSTU	speculation
ACEILNOPSTX	xenoplastic
ACEILNOPTUX	exculpation
ACEILNOQUUV	unequivocal
ACEILNORRTU	interocular
ACEILNORSTT	intercostal
ACEILNORTTU	reluctation
ACEILNORTUV	countervail
	involucrate
ACEILNOSSST	stoicalness
ACEILNOSTUY	tenaciously
ACEILNPSSTY	typicalness
ACEILNRRRTU	intercrural
ACEILNRRTUV	ventricular
ACEILOOOPRT	aeolotropic
ACEILOOPPRS	polariscope
ACEILOOPPRU	colour a pipe
ACEILOOSSST	osteoclasis
ACEILOPRRTT	protractile
ACEILOPRTXY	explicatory
ACEILORSUVY	veraciously
ACEILORTVYY	viceroyalty
ACEILPPRTUY	picture-play
ACEILPRSTTU	curtail-step
ACEILPRSTTY	spectrality
ACEILPRSTUX	speculatrix
ACEILPSSTTU	speculatist
ACEILQRTUUU	aquiculture

ACEILRRTTUU	turriculate
ACEIMMNOOST	mesonic atom
ACEIMMOOSSU	mimosaceous
ACEIMMORRTU	crematorium
ACEIMMOTTUV	commutative
ACEIMMPRSSU	supremacism
ACEIMMRSSTU	music master
ACEIMNNNOTT	containment
ACEIMNNOORY	oneiromancy
ACEIMNNORTT	coterminant
ACEIMNNORTW	New Romantic
ACEIMNOOPRS	rose campion
ACEIMNOORTX	axonometric
ACEIMNORRTU	mercuration
ACEIMNORRTW	Martin Crowe
ACEIMNORRTY	craniometry
ACEIMOOPRSZ	azoospermic
ACEIMOOPRTW	atomic power
ACEIMOORTVY	ovariectomy
ACEIMOPRRTY	cryptomeria
	imprecatory
ACEIMOPTTUV	computative
ACEIMORRSTT	astrometric
ACEIMORTTTU	tautometric
ACEIMPRSSTU	supremacist
ACEIMSSSTTY	systematics
ACEINNNNSSU	uncanniness
ACEINNNOSTT	Constantine
ACEINNOORTT	contorniate
ACEINNOOTTV	connotative
ACEINNORSTT	transection
ACEINNORTUY	enunciatory
ACEINNOSTTY	encystation
ACEINNPRSTU	Pentacrinus
ACEINNPTUUV	nuncupative
ACEINNRRTUW	currant-wine
ACEINNRSSSW	scrawniness
ACEINNRTTUY	uncertainty
ACEINOOOPRT	co-operation
ACEINOOPRRT	incorporate
	procreation
ACEINOOPRSS	sea scorpion
ACEINOOPRTU	aponeurotic
ACEINOORRTT	retroaction
ACEINOOSSST	iconostases
ACEINOPPRTY	cappernoity
ACEINOPRRTU	Puerto Rican
ACEINOPRSSS	prosaicness
ACEINOPRSTU	precautions
ACEINORRTTU	centuriator
ACEINORRTTY	contrariety
ACEINORSTTV	contrastive
ACEINORSUUV	unveracious
ACEINPPRSSS	scrappiness
ACEINPTTUUV	punctuative
ACEINRRTUUV	incurvature
ACEINRSSSSU	narcissuses
ACEINRSSTTU	resuscitant
ACEINRSSTTV	transvestic
ACEIOOPPRRS	Cooper pairs
ACEIOOPRRTV	corporative
ACEIOOPRTVV	provocative
ACEIOOQRTUV	equivocator
ACEIOPRRRTT	Port Cartier
ACEIOPRRSTT	tetrasporic
	triceratops
ACEIOPRRSTY	caryopteris
ACEIOPRRTTV	protractive
ACEIOPRSTUU	precautious
ACEIOPRSTXY	expiscatory
ACEIRSTTTUV	active trust
ACEJKLLRSSU	Jack Russell
ACEJKOPRSTY	jockey strap
ACEKKLOPTTU	take pot luck
ACEKKMORSTT	stock market
ACEKLLRSSTY	tracklessly
ACEKLPRRRTU	parrel truck
ACEKMNORRTU	countermark
ACEKMORRSST	market cross
ACEKMSSSTTY	stack system
ACEKNNNOPRT	pennant rock
ACEKOORTTTU	take to court
ACELLLMORUY	molecularly
ACELLMMNOSY	commensally
ACELLMNOPSU	nucleoplasm
ACELLMNORST	small cornet
ACELLMORRST	storm cellar
ACELLMPRTTU	trumpet call
ACELLMPSSSU	mussel-scalp
ACELLNORSUY	larcenously
ACELLNOSSSU	callousness
ACELLNRTTUY	reluctantly
ACELLOOPRRY	corporeally
ACELLSSSUUU	Aulus Celsus
ACELMNNOOPT	componental
ACELMNNOORT	nomenclator
ACELMNNOORU	mononuclear
ACELMNNOOVY	monovalency
ACELMNNOPTT	contemplant
ACELMNOOOTY	Monocotylae
ACELMOPSTUY	costume play
ACELMPSSSUU	mussel-scaup
ACELMRSTTUU	latus rectum
ACELMRSTUUU	musculature
ACELNNNOOOS	loose cannon
ACELNNOOPVX	plano-convex
ACELNNORRTW	crown antler
ACELNNOSTUV	Conventuals
ACELNNRSTTU	translucent
ACELNNRTTUU	unreluctant
ACELNOPRRST	corn plaster
ACELNORRWWY	crown lawyer
ACELNORSUUV	cavernulous
ACELNORSUVY	cavernously
ACELNOSSTTU	sansculotte
ACELNOSTTTU	talent scout
ACELNPPRTUU	prepunctual
ACELNPRTTTU	plantcutter
ACELOOPPRSS	pop-lacrosse
ACELOOPRRTT	protectoral
ACELOOPRRTY	corporately
ACELOORRSUU	coelurosaur

ACELOORRTUW watercolour
ACELOPPRSST parcels post
ACELOPRSTUY speculatory
ACELOPRTUXY exculpatory
ACELORSSTUY locust-years
ACELORSTTTW Walter Scott
ACEMMNOORTT commentator
ACEMMNOPRTT compartment
ACEMMOPRRUY marry come up
ACEMNOOPRST compensator
ACEMNOORRRW corn earworm
ACEMOOPRSSS compass rose
ACEMORRSUYY Seymour Cray
ACEMORSSTTU scoutmaster
ACENNOORRTT contra-tenor
ACENNOPRSTU span-counter
ACENNORRSTZ Rosencrantz
ACENNPRTTYY Nancy-pretty
ACENOOOPSTT potato scone
ACENOOPRRTY porte-crayon
ACENOORRSTV conservator
ACENOOSTTTW cotton waste
ACENOPPRSTU supportance
ACENOPRRSTU Procrustean
ACENOPRRSUU run up a score
ACENOPRRTTU counterpart
ACENOPRSTTU constuprate
ACENORSSSUU raucousness
ACENORSTTUY country seat
ACENOSSSUUV vacuousness
ACENPRRSSTU pass current
ACEOOPPRRSS carpospores
ACEOOPRRTUV provocateur
ACEOOPRSSTU stauroscope
ACEOPRRSSTT sportcaster
ACEORSSSSSY syssarcoses
ACERRSTTTUW straw-cutter
ACFFFIKKOOR for a kick-off
ACFFGIIKNRT trafficking
ACFFGINOSTU suffocating
ACFFHILLNOW fallow-finch
ACFFIIILMOS officialism
ACFFIIILOTY officiality
ACFFIIINOOT officiation
ACFFIILLNOY officinally
ACFFINOOSTU suffocation
ACFFKMNOORS mock saffron
ACFGHIIKNPS fish-packing
ACFGHINOSUV vouchsafing
ACFGIIINNST significant
ACFGIIINSST satisficing
ACFGIILNSSY classifying
ACFGIINNSTY sanctifying
ACFGIINSTTU fungistatic
ACFGILLMOPY Olympic Flag
ACFGILNTTUU fluctuating
ACFGINRSSTU surfcasting
ACFGLLOOOTY olfactology
ACFHIILNOOR honorifical
ACFHILSSSTU cutlass fish
ACFHIMORRST ostrich-farm
ACFHINNOTUX fucoxanthin
ACFHIOPRSTY factory ship
ACFHKOPRSWZ Schwarzkopf
ACFHLMOSSTU stomachfuls
ACFHOOPRSTY factory shop
ACFIIILLMRY mirifically
ACFIIILMSST facsimilist
ACFIIINNOTU unification
ACFIIINORTV vinificator
ACFIILMNORU californium
ACFIILMORST formalistic
ACFIILMSSSY misclassify
ACFIILNOPST pontificals
ACFIIMMORRU formicarium
ACFIIMNOORT formication
ACFIIMNORST informatics
ACFIIMNRSTU cantus firmi
ACFIINNOORT fornication
ACFIINOOPRT forcipation
ACFIIOPRRTU purificator
ACFIKKPSSUU kick up a fuss
ACFILLMOORR coralliform
ACFILLOOPTT toploftical
ACFILLOSTUU lactifluous
ACFILMNNOTU malfunction
ACFILMOORSS macrofossil
ACFILMOPRRS scalpriform
ACFILMORSUV vasculiform
ACFILMORTUY family court
ACFILNOTTUU fluctuation
ACFILORSTUY fractiously
ACFIMNOORRT confirmator
ACFINNOOTTU confutation
ACFINNORSTW Francistown
ACFINNORTUY functionary
ACFINOOOTTU out of action
ACFINORTTUU fructuation
ACFIOOTTTTU cut it too fat
ACFMNOOORRT conformator
ACFNNNOOOPR cannon-proof
ACFORRRUUVY curry favour
ACGGHHIIJKN highjacking
ACGGHIILNTT tight-lacing
ACGGHILOOPR graphologic
logographic
ACGGIIKKLNO goalkicking
ACGGIJNNOTU conjugating
ACGGIKNOSTZ gazing-stock
ACGGILOSTWY Glasgow City
ACGHHILOOPR holographic
ACGHHINOPRY ichnography
ACGHHIOPPTY phytophagic
ACGHHIOPRRY chirography
ACGHHMNORSU ramgunshoch
ACGHHNOOPRR chronograph
ACGHHNOOPYY onychophagy
ACGHHOOPRRY chorography
ACGHHOPPRSY psychograph
ACGHHORSTTU caught short
ACGHHOSTTTU thoughtcast
ACGHIILLNOP anglophilic✧

ACGHIILLRTV gillravitch
ACGHIILMORT algorithmic
logarithmic
ACGHIILNORT granolithic
ACGHIILRRTY charity-girl
ACGHIINPRTY pharyngitic
ACGHIIPRSST sphragistic
ACGHIKMOPRY kymographic
ACGHILLMOOO homological
ACGHILLOOOR horological
ACGHILMOOPR lagomorphic
ACGHILMOORT cologarithm
ACGHILMOOST logomachist
ACGHILNNOOP anglophonic✧
ACGHILNNSTY snatchingly
ACGHILNOOTU touch-in-goal
ACGHILNRSTT latchstring
ACGHILNRSTU nautch-girls
ACGHILOPPRY polygraphic
ACGHILOPRXY xylographic
ACGHIMNOOPR gramophonic
monographic
nomographic
ACGHIMOOPRT tomographic
ACGHIMOPRRY micrography
ACGHIMOPSTY mycophagist
phagocytism
ACGHIMORRST Christogram
ACGHINOOPRS nosographic
ACGHINOOPRY iconography
ACGHINOPRRY granophyric
ACGHINOPRYZ zincography
ACGHINORSTT short-acting
ACGHINPRSTW watchspring
ACGHIOOPPRT topographic
ACGHIOPPRTY pictography
typographic
ACGHIOPRSTY hypogastric
ACGHIQRSSTU quitch grass
ACGHIRSSTTW twitch grass
ACGHIRSTTTU straight-cut
ACGHLMMNOOU Chomolungma
ACGHMOOPRSY cosmography
ACGHMOORRUX Groucho Marx
ACGHNOOOPRR coronograph
ACGHOPPRRTY cryptograph
ACGIIILNOST logistician
ACGIIILNPST salpingitic
ACGIIJNORST jargonistic
ACGIIKLLPRY pilgarlicky
ACGIIKLMNPS lip-smacking
ACGIILLLLOY illogically
ACGIILLLNRW Will Carling
ACGIILLMNRZ crazing mill
ACGIILLMRST gastric mill
ACGIILLNOOS Sinological
ACGIILLNOOT colligation
ACGIILLNOST oscillating
ACGIILLNTUV victualling
ACGIILLOORV virological
ACGIILMNNOP complaining
ACGIILNNOOT cognitional
ACGIILOPRTT graptolitic
ACGIIMNOSST agnosticism
ACGIIMRSTTU Targumistic
ACGIINNNOST incognisant
ACGIINNNOTZ incognizant
ACGIINNOSTW wainscoting
ACGIINORRTY tragic irony
ACGIJJKMNPU jumping jack
ACGIJLNOTUY conjugality
ACGIJNNOOTU conjugation
ACGIJNNOPTU gap junction
ACGIKKNNORT knock-rating
ACGIKKNOSTT stocktaking
ACGILLLOOSS glossolalic
ACGILLMNOOO monological
nomological
ACGILLMOOOP pomological
ACGILLMOORS oscillogram
ACGILLMOOTY climatology
ACGILLMOOYZ zymological
ACGILLNOOOS nosological
ACGILLNOOOT ontological
ACGILLNOSTY gnostically
ACGILLNRRYY rallying-cry
ACGILLNRSWY scrawlingly
ACGILLOOOPS posological
ACGILLOOOPT topological
ACGILLOOPTY typological
ACGILLOPSUY callipygous
ACGILMOOOST somatologic
ACGILNNOORT gain control
ACGILNORSUY carousingly
ACGILOOPRST carpologist
ACGIMNNOORT morning coat
ACGIMNNOORY craniognomy
ACGIMNOOPRU carpogonium
ACGIMNOORRT motor racing
ACGIMNOORST gastronomic
ACGINNOPSTW townscaping
ACGINNORRSY carryings-on
ACGINOOPRTU action group
ACGINOORRST Corti's organ
ACGINOORRTU corrugation
ACGINOORSTY cosignatory
ACGINOOSTUV noctivagous
ACGIORSSTTY gyrostatics
ACGLLNOOOVY volcanology
ACGLLNOOUVY vulcanology
ACGLMNNOOUY agony column
ACGLNOOORRU colour organ
ACGMOOPRRTU compurgator
ACGMOOPRSSY gyrocompass
ACGNOORSSTT cotton grass
ACGRRSSSUVY scurvy grass
ACHHIILLPTY ithyphallic
ACHHIILMOPT philomathic
ACHHILLMOOT homothallic
ACHHILLOOOT thioalcohol
ACHHILOPRSS scholarship
ACHHINOORTX Xanthochroi

ACHHINSSTUZ schizanthus
ACHHIOPRSTY charity shop
ACHHIOPSTYZ Schizophyta
ACHHIORSTUY ichthyosaur
ACHHJKNOOST John Toshack
ACHHKLOORSS school shark
ACHHNOOOPRY Onychophora
ACHHNOOSTTU autochthons
ACHHNOOTTUY autochthony
ACHHNORRSST Scharnhorst
ACHHOPPSTYY psychopathy
ACHHORRSTWY crashworthy
ACHIIIMMRST Mithraicism
ACHIIIMNPSS hispanicism
ACHIIIPPRST hippiatrics
ACHIIJKNRSW jinrickshaw
ACHIILLLPTU Paul Tillich
ACHIILLMSWY whimsically
ACHIILMOSTT Thomistical
ACHIILMPSSY physicalism
ACHIILNOPST canophilist
ACHIILNRSTY Christianly
ACHIILOOPPR coprophilia
ACHIILOOPPS scopophilia
ACHIILOOPST Scotophilia
ACHIILOPRSV corivalship
ACHIILOPSST sophistical
ACHIILORRTU ritual choir
ACHIILPSSTY physicalist
ACHIILPSTYY physicality
ACHIIMNORST harmonistic
ACHIIMOPPRT amphiprotic
ACHIIMORRRS Morris chair
ACHIINNORST anno Christi
ACHIINNRSTU unchristian
ACHIINOORST chorisation
ACHIINOORTZ chorization
Zonotrichia
ACHIINOPRST spathic iron
ACHIINSSTTT satin stitch
ACHIIPRSSTY physiatrics
ACHIKKOSTVY Tchaikovsky
ACHILLMNOOP Champollion
ACHILLMOOPR allomorphic
ACHILLORSST choirstalls
ACHILMNOORT trichomonal
ACHILMOOPST homoplastic
ACHILMORRYZ mycorrhizal
ACHILNOOOPS piano-school
ACHILNOORRT chlorinator
ACHILNPPSUY supply chain
ACHILNPSTTW switch-plant
ACHILOOPTYZ zoophytical
ACHILOPPSTY hypoplastic
ACHILOSSTTW waistcloths
ACHIMMNOOSU monochasium
ACHIMNNNOOR non-harmonic
ACHIMNOORST Trichomonas
ACHIMNOPTYY amphictyony
ACHIMNPPSSY panpsychism
ACHIMOOOPST photomosaic
ACHIMOOPRSY hypocorisma
ACHIMOOPRTU automorphic
ACHIMOOPRTY amyotrophic
ACHIMOOSSST Schistosoma
ACHIMOPPPSU hippocampus
ACHIMOPRSSY symposiarch
ACHIMOPSSTY scyphistoma
ACHIMORRSTY chrismatory
ACHIMRSSSTY Christmassy
ACHINOOPRTZ zoanthropic
ACHINOOPSTT photonastic
ACHINOOPTTU tautophonic
ACHINORSSTU cushion star
ACHINPPSSTY panpsychist
ACHIOOPPRST apostrophic
ACHIOOPPRTT haptotropic
protopathic
ACHIOOPPSTT potato chips
ACHIOOPRTTU autotrophic
ACHIOORSTTT orthostatic
ACHIOPPRSTY saprophytic
ACHIOPRRSTU curatorship
ACHJMNNOOPY John Company
ACHKLMNOOST klootchmans
ACHKMMNOOSY Noam Chomsky
ACHKMNOOPRT Rockhampton
ACHLLNORSUY unscholarly
ACHLLOOPRST chloroplast
ACHLMMOOORS chromosomal
ACHLMNOORTU motor-launch
ACHLMOOPRST chromoplast
ACHLNOPRTYY lycanthropy
ACHLOOOSTTT a colt's tooth
ACHMMNOOORT monochromat
ACHMMOPPSTU stomach pump
ACHMNOOPSUY cymophanous
ACHMOOORTTY thoracotomy
ACHNNOSTTUY nyctanthous
ACHNOPRSTYY sycophantry
ACHOOPRRSTY arthroscopy
ACHOPRSTUXY choux pastry
ACIIIILMNTY inimicality
ACIIILLMOPT impolitical
ACIIILLMPTU capillitium
ACIIILLNORS nicrosilial
ACIIILLNOTV villication
ACIIILMNOPT implication
ACIIILMNRST criminalist
ACIIILMNRTY criminality
ACIIILMOPST apoliticism
ACIIILNNNOT inclination
ACIIILNNRST intrinsical
ACIIILNPSTU Paulinistic
ACIIILRSTTU ritualistic
ACIIIMNNORT crimination
ACIIIMNNOSS Socinianism
ACIIIMOSSVV vivacissimo
ACIIINNORTT titanic iron
ACIIINNOTTT nictitation
ACIIINOQSTU acquisition
ACIIINPRSST Priscianist

ACIIIOSSTTU ascititious
ACIILLLOPTY politically
ACIILLMNOOS colonialism
ACIILLMNOOT collimation
ACIILLMNOXY amoxycillin
ACIILLMNPUY municipally
ACIILLMOSUY maliciously
ACIILLMOTTY mitotically
ACIILLNNSTT scintillant
ACIILLNOOST colonialist
oscillation
ACIILLNOPTU unpolitical
ACIILLNORST carillonist
ACIILLNOVVY convivially
ACIILLNPPRY principally
ACIILLOPRTY pictorially
ACIILLPRSTU pluralistic
ACIILLQSTTU call it quits
ACIILLQUYZZ quizzically
ACIILMNNOPT incompliant
ACIILMNNOTU culmination
ACIILMNOOPT compilation
ACIILMNOPST Platonicism
ACIILMNORTU latrocinium
ACIILMNOSSU unsocialism
ACIILMNOSUU unmalicious
ACIILMNSSTU masculinist
ACIILMNSTUY masculinity
ACIILMOPRRY primary coil
ACIILMSTTUU mutualistic
ACIILNNOOTU inoculation
ACIILNNOPTU inculpation
ACIILNNORSY synclinoria
ACIILNNORTY inclinatory
ACIILNNSTTU instinctual
ACIILNOOOTT Otto Nicolai
ACIILNOSTUY unsociality
ACIILNOTTUV cultivation
ACIILOOPSST isapostolic
ACIILOPRRST scriptorial
ACIILORSSST scissortail
ACIILORSTTU staurolitic
ACIILORSUVY vicariously
ACIILOSUVVY vivaciously
ACIILPPSTUV supplicavit
ACIIMMMNOST mammonistic
ACIIMMNNOOT commination
ACIIMMNORST romanticism✧
ACIIMMNOSST monasticism
ACIIMMNSSTU numismatics
ACIIMMOOPRR comprimario
ACIIMNNOSTT Montanistic
ACIIMNOORSU acrimonious
ACIIMNORRTY criminatory
ACIIMNORSTT romanticist
ACIIMNPRTTU Mt Paricutin
ACIINNOOPTT action point
ACIINNORRTU iron curtain✧
ACIINNORTUV incurvation
ACIINOOPRST anisotropic
ACIINOOSSST iconostasis
ACIINOOSTTT tostication
ACIINOPRTTU unpatriotic
ACIINORSTTU rustication
ACIINOSSTTU suscitation
ACIINRTTTUY taciturnity
ACIIOPSSSTT psittacosis
ACIIORRRSTT cirro-strati
ACIIORRSTUU urticarious
ACIIRSSSTUU saussuritic
ACIJKLMNOST Milt Jackson
ACIJKLNNOTY Tony Jacklin
ACIJNNOORTU conjuration
ACIKOOPRRTY prokaryotic
ACILLMNOORY moronically
ACILLMNOPTY compliantly
ACILLMNSUUY unmusically
ACILLMOOSTY osmotically
ACILLMOPSTY plasmolytic
ACILLMOTYYZ zymotically
ACILLNNOOOP apollonicon
ACILLNNOTUY continually
ACILLNOOOPT local option
ACILLNOOPRR incorporall
ACILLOORSTY oscillatory
ACILMMMNOSU communalism
ACILMMNOOOT commotional
ACILMMNOOTY commonality
ACILMMNOSTU communalist
ACILMMORSSU commissural
ACILMMRSSUU simulacrums
ACILMNNOPTU uncompliant
ACILMNNOSYY synonymical
ACILMNOOPTY toponymical
ACILMNORTUY columnarity
ACILMNOSTUU musculation
ACILMOOPRTY compilatory
ACILMOOPSTX toxoplasmic
ACILMOPSSTY spasmolytic
ACILMORSSTU Lacus Mortis
ACILMORSTUY customarily
ACILMRSTUUY muscularity
ACILNNOOOST consolation
ACILNOOORTU colouration
ACILNOOPSTU unapostolic
ACILNOORRST conirostral
ACILNOORSTX consolatrix
ACILNOORTUY inoculatory
locutionary
ACILNOPRTUY inculpatory
ACILNORSSTU ultrasonics
ACILNPSTTUU punctualist
ACILNPTTUUY punctuality
ACILNRSTTWY twin crystal
ACILOOPRRTY corporality
ACILOORSTUY atrociously
ACILOORSUVY voraciously
ACILOPRSTUY crapulosity
ACILOSSTUUY astuciously
ACIMMNOORST common stair
ACIMMNOORTY comminatory
ACIMMNOOTTU commutation

ACIMMOPSTTY symptomatic
ACIMMORSTUU muscatorium
ACIMNNOOOST onomasticon
ACIMNNOOPRY Cypro-Minoan
ACIMNNOSTYY synonymatic
ACIMNOOOPRT compo ration
ACIMNOOOPTT compotation
ACIMNOOOSTT somatotonic
ACIMNOOPSSU poison sumac
ACIMNOOPTTU computation
ACIMNOPRTUY importunacy
ACIMOOPRRST corporatism
ACINNNNOOST inconsonant
ACINNNOOOTT connotation
ACINNNOPTUU nuncupation
ACINNOOPRTT contraption
ACINNOOPSTY syncopation
ACINNOORTTU continuator
ACINNOPTTUU punctuation
ACINNORSSST trans-sonics
ACINNOSSTTU Constantius
ACINOOOPRRT corporation
ACINOOOPRTV provocation
ACINOOPRRST conspirator
ACINOOPRRTT protraction
ACINOOPRRTU procuration
ACINOORRSTU contrarious
ACINOORRSUV carnivorous
ACINOPRSTUU curnaptious
ACIOOPRRSTT corporatist
ACIOPRSSTTU put it across
ACIORRSSTUU curious arts
ACIORSSSSSY syssarcosis
ACKLMNOORRT control mark
ACKOOPRRRSW rock sparrow
ACLLMNOORUY monocularly
ACLLMOORRST storm collar
ACLLMOORSUY clamorously
ACLLMOSTUUU altocumulus
ACLLNNORTUY nocturnally
ACLLOORSUUY oraculously
ACLLOPRSTYY polycrystal
ACLMNOORRST arms control
ACLMNOORSTY monocrystal
ACLMOOOPPRU coram populo
ACLNNNOOSTY consonantly
ACLNNOOPTTT cotton plant
ACLNOOORSTY consolatory
ACLNOOPRRSU proconsular
ACLNOORRSUY rancorously
ACLOOPPRSUY polycarpous
ACLOOPRRTUY colour party
ACLOOPRSUXY xylocarpous
ACLOORRSTUW straw-colour
ACMMNNOOPRW common prawn
ACMMNOORSTU consummator
ACMNNOORRSS Norman cross
ACMNOOOPRSU monocarpous
ACMOOOPRTTY compotatory
ACMOOOSSTTU scotomatous
ACNNOPRTUUY nuncupatory
ACNOOPRSSUU Uranoscopus
ACOOOPRRTVY provocatory
ACOOPRRRTUY procuratory
ADDDDEEGHIY giddy-headed
ADDDDEEHMUY muddy-headed
ADDDDENNOSS odds and ends
ADDDDNOOSSS odds and sods
ADDDEEFILMR field madder
ADDDEEHIILP Didelphidae
ADDDEEHNNRU underhanded
ADDDEEHNORU round-headed
ADDDEEHNSTU sudden death
ADDDEEIMMTU medium-dated
ADDDEEIMNST middenstead
ADDDEEINSUW duddie weans✧
ADDDEELNOSS saddle-nosed
ADDDEELOPRY delayed drop
ADDDEENRSSU unaddressed
ADDDEFGORRT draft-dodger
ADDDEGGINRY dandy-rigged
ADDDEGGLOPY doggy-paddle
ADDDEHNOORR rhododendra
ADDDEIMNOOV diamond dove
ADDDENOORWW dawn redwood
ADDDERSSTTU star-studded
ADDDHILMOOO old-maidhood
ADDDILQSTUY diddly-squat
ADDDIMNOSTU diamond-dust
ADDDNNOOSST do's and don'ts
ADDEEEEHKLS sleek-headed
ADDEEEEHLLV level-headed
ADDEEEEHLST steel-headed
ADDEEEFILLM E M Delafield
ADDEEEFILNO Daniel Defoe
ADDEEEFILSU defeudalise
ADDEEEFILUZ defeudalize
ADDEEEFPRRY deferred pay
ADDEEEFRRTW dwarfed tree
ADDEEEGGILN leading edge
ADDEEEGHPSW wedge-shaped
ADDEEEGILTW wedge-tailed
ADDEEEGLNTU undelegated
ADDEEEHHITT die the death
ADDEEEHHITW white-headed
ADDEEEHHNRT three-handed
ADDEEEHIKNS hide-and-seek
ADDEEEHILTV The Evil Dead
ADDEEEHLLPW paddle wheel
ADDEEEHLLSW swelled head
swell-headed
ADDEEEHLMTY metaldehyde
ADDEEEHMPTY empty-headed
ADDEEEHPRTT the departed
ADDEEEIMRST Dermestidae
ADDEEEIRTWW wide-watered
ADDEEELLLSW Weddell seal
ADDEEELLPST pedestalled
ADDEEENRRSW Dresden ware
ADDEEEOPRSS desperadoes
ADDEEFGHINN hand-feeding
ADDEEFGHIRT dead-freight

ADDEEFIIMNV five-and-dime
ADDEEFILLMS Fields Medal
ADDEEFMNORU undreamed-of
ADDEEFMNRTU defraudment
ADDEEFNORRW forwandered
ADDEEGGIRRV Edvard Grieg
ADDEEGHHILT light-headed
ADDEEGHILPY pigheadedly
ADDEEGHNORW wrong-headed
ADDEEGIISTT sedigitated
ADDEEGIKMNR redding-kame
ADDEEGIKNRS reading-desk
ADDEEGILMNR large-minded
ADDEEGILRST girdlestead
ADDEEGINORW edge in a word
ADDEEGINPRW deep drawing
deep-drawing
ADDEEGINRRW reed-drawing
ADDEEGIOSSS dog's disease
ADDEEGJMNTU adjudgement
ADDEEGNRSSU guardedness
ADDEEHHINTW white-handed
ADDEEHHNRTU thunderhead
ADDEEHIILNP Delphinidae
ADDEEHIKNRT kind-hearted
ADDEEHILMRT middle-earth✧
ADDEEHILNST in the saddle
ADDEEHIRTWW Edward White
ADDEEHISTTU death duties
ADDEEHLNORV overhandled
ADDEEHLORSS saddle horse
ADDEEHMNPTY empty-handed
ADDEEHNORTW downhearted
ADDEEHPPPUY puppy-headed
ADDEEHPRRSS hard pressed
hard-pressed
ADDEEIILRST Estrildidae
ADDEEIINNNW wine and dine
ADDEEILLSVW well-advised
ADDEEILNOSW Eddie Lawson
ADDEEILRRVY dare-devilry
ADDEEIMNORY ready-monied
ADDEEIMNTTU unmeditated
ADDEEIMRSTU desideratum
ADDEEINOPRT depredation
ADDEEINSSSV advisedness
ADDEEIRTTWY ready-witted
ADDEELLRSSY dreadlessly
ADDEELNORUV round-leaved
ADDEEMNNNRU undermanned
ADDEEMNPRRU underdamper
ADDEEMNRSTU undermasted
ADDEEMOORRT made to order
ADDEEMRSSTU Mustard-seed
ADDEENORTWW watered-down
ADDEENPRSUU unpersuaded
ADDEENRSTTU understated
ADDEEOPRRTY depredatory
ADDEFFHLNOY offhandedly
ADDEFFIISST distaff side
ADDEFGILNOU Dean of Guild
ADDEFGLORRR Gerald R Ford
ADDEFHILNTY find the lady
ADDEFHINSSS faddishness
ADDEFIIMOTW midwife toad
ADDEFLNOORT front-loaded
ADDEGGHORTU goddaughter
ADDEGGIIIRT digitigrade
ADDEGGILNRU drug dealing
ADDEGHHILNT light-handed
ADDEGHHINRT right-handed
ADDEGHILRST saddle-girth
ADDEGHNORTU dreadnought✧
ADDEGIIMNNR mind-reading
ADDEGILMNNY maddeningly
ADDEGIMNNNU undemanding
ADDEGIMNNOR road-mending
ADDEGINNOSU undiagnosed
ADDEGINNRST angst-ridden
ADDEGJMNTUY Judgment Day
ADDEGLLMNOU muddle along
ADDEGLLNOOW well and good
ADDEGLNRUUY unguardedly
ADDEGNOORTU good-natured
ADDEHHIOPRY Hydrophidae
ADDEHHLOORT hold the road
ADDEHHMORTU hardmouthed
ADDEHHNNORY horny-handed
ADDEHHNOOPR rhododaphne
ADDEHHNORST short-handed
ADDEHIILMOT thalidomide
ADDEHIKNNTT hand-knitted
ADDEHIKNRRR hard drinker
ADDEHILNNRS hinderlands
ADDEHILNORS Rhode Island
ADDEHILNSSS laddishness
ADDEHILOPSU diadelphous
ADDEHINORTY dehydration
hydrated ion
ADDEHLNOTWY two-handedly
ADDEHLOPRSU shoulder pad
ADDEHLORSTT stadtholder
ADDEHMNNOSW hand-me-downs
ADDEHMORSUY hydromedusa
ADDEHNOORTW down the road
ADDEHNRRTTU thunder-dart
ADDEHOPRSSW sword-shaped
ADDEIIIKLVW David Wilkie
ADDEIIINTUV individuate
ADDEIILLMNT Middle Latin
ADDEIILMNNO Neil Diamond
ADDEIIMMOSU sodium amide
ADDEIINOOTX deoxidation
ADDEIINORST disordinate
ADDEIJNOPRY pride and joy
ADDEIKMNRRR dram-drinker
ADDEILLMMNS small-minded
ADDEILLMORV David Mellor
ADDEILLNNST still and end
ADDEILMORSU modularised
ADDEILMORUZ modularized
ADDEILNSTUY dual-density

ADDEILNSUVY unadvisedly
ADDEIMNOORS rose diamond
ADDEINNOTVY Danny DeVito
ADDEIOOPPSU pseudopodia
ADDEIORSTVY David Storey
ADDEKLOOPTT polka-dotted
ADDELLNORVY Dolly Varden
ADDELMNOTUU unmodulated
ADDELMOORTU demodulator
ADDELNNRTUY redundantly
ADDELNNTUUY undauntedly
ADDELNOOPRS Donald Soper
ADDELNORRTY dendrolatry
ADDELOOOPRW leopard-wood
ADDELORRTWY Edward Tylor
ADDEMNOOORT rodomontade
ADDEMNOOPSU pseudomonad
ADDEMOSSTTY add-to system
ADDEMRSTUWY Muddy Waters
ADDENOORRRU order around
ADDENOORSSW sanderswood
ADDEOOPRRTY ready to drop
ADDEOOPSTTT toad-spotted
ADDFFLOORRT Old Trafford
ADDGGINOPSU sago pudding
ADDGHILLNNO landholding
ADDGHILNOOR roadholding
ADDGHLORSUU Douglas Hurd
ADDGHNORTUW down-draught
ADDGIMNNOPW damping-down
ADDGLNNOSUU Douglas Dunn
ADDHIILNOOV invalidhood
ADDHILNNOOS Hondo Island
ADDHJLNNOOW John Dowland
ADDHLLLOORY Harold Lloyd
ADDHLOOORYY Holy-rood Day
ADDHNOOSSUW sound shadow
ADDIIIIMNOT dimidiation
ADDIIIKLLMW William Kidd
ADDIIIORVZZ David Rizzio
ADDIIIOSTTU addititious
ADDIILNOSVW David Wilson
ADDIIMNNOOY Dominion Day
ADDIINORSTU suraddition
ADDIJNOSUWW judas window✧
ADDILLMNORS landlordism
ADDILLNNOUV null and void
ADDILMNORTY dirty old man
ADDILMRSTUW wild mustard
ADDLLOORRSW sword-dollar
ADDNNOPSSUW ups and downs
ADEEEEFGHRT feather-edge
ADEEEEFHLRT three-leafed
ADEEEEFHRRT free-hearted
ADEEEEFPPRR paper-feeder
ADEEEEGGRST desegregate
ADEEEEGINRR Reindeer Age
ADEEEEHIMPR Ephemeridae
ADEEEEHLRTV three-leaved
ADEEEELLNVV needle valve
ADEEEELNPPR needle paper
ADEEEEMMPRS semper eadem
ADEEEENNRTU nuée ardente
ADEEEFGNOSX fox and geese
ADEEEFHNRTU unfeathered
ADEEEFHNRTW weather-fend
ADEEEFIKVWY five-day week
ADEEEFILNRT deferential
ADEEEFIMORT fide et amore
ADEEEFINNRT terfenadine
ADEEEFINSTV defensative
ADEEEFNRRRY referendary
ADEEEFNRSSV vas deferens
ADEEEFNRSTT fenestrated
ADEEEGGHHOS sea hedgehog
ADEEEGGILNW eagle-winged
ADEEEGGLLNO golden eagle
ADEEEGGLMOR George Medal
ADEEEGGNNOT engaged tone
ADEEEGHLMPT dephlegmate
ADEEEGILMNR legerdemain
ADEEEGIMNRR gendarmerie
ADEEEGIMNST demagnetise
ADEEEGIMNTZ demagnetize
ADEEEGIMORT Geometridae
ADEEEGINNRT tragedienne
tragédienne
ADEEEGJMNNU Jean de Meung
ADEEEGKLNNR Kendal green
ADEEEGLLNRT legal tender
ADEEEGMNNRT derangement
ADEEEGMNRST désagrément
ADEEEGNNRTU grande tenue
ADEEEGNOTXY deoxygenate
ADEEEGNRRRT Grande-Terre
ADEEEHIIPRS Hesperiidae
ADEEEHILNSY Denis Healey
ADEEEHIMPSS de-emphasise
ADEEEHIMPSZ de-emphasize
ADEEEHIRSTW weather side
wise-hearted
ADEEEHIRTVY the very idea
ADEEEHLLORS leaseholder
ADEEEHLORRS horse-dealer
ADEEEHMORST homesteader
ADEEEHMRSTT three-masted
ADEEEHNNNOR enneahedron
ADEEEHNOPRT open-hearted
ADEEEHNRRSU unrehearsed
ADEEEHNRTUW unweathered
ADEEEHPPRTY deep therapy
ADEEEHPRRTT three-parted
ADEEEHPRSST spreadsheet
ADEEEHRRTTU true-hearted
ADEEEIILNTV delineative
ADEEEIIMMOR aide-mémoire
ADEEEIIMNRV Vendémiaire
ADEEEIINSSV vine-disease
ADEEEILLMNS linseed-meal
ADEEEILLMRS Emerald Isle
ADEEEILMNTY demyelinate
ADEEEILMSSY Lyme disease

ADEEEILNRRT interdealer
ADEEEILOPRS oilseed rape
rapeseed oil
ADEEEILSSUX desexualise
ADEEEILSUXZ desexualize
ADEEEIMNRTT determinate
ADEEEIMNSST mediateness
ADEEEIMPPRR pipe-dreamer
ADEEEIMPRTT premeditate
ADEEEINNRTV Venetian red
ADEEEINPRTW in deep water
ADEEEINRSVY never say die✧
ADEEEIORRTT deteriorate
ADEEEIPPRSU depauperise
ADEEEIPPRUZ depauperize
ADEEEIPRRST pieds-à-terre
ADEEEIRRSTV readvertise
ADEEEKKLNWY weak-kneedly
ADEEEKLLLRW lake-dweller
ADEEEKLRRST deerstalker
ADEEELLMRYY medley relay
ADEEELLNSWY Wensleydale
ADEEELLPSTT steel-plated
ADEEELLSSTT tessellated
ADEEELMNNOW needlewoman
ADEEELMNSST délassement
ADEEELMPRTY emerald type
ADEEELNNRSS learnedness
ADEEELNRSST relatedness
ADEEELNRTTU launderette
ADEEELNSSTX exaltedness
ADEEELORSTT sea dotterel
ADEEELPRSTY desperately
ADEEEMMNNRT reamendment
ADEEEMNNTTT attendement
ADEEEMNPRTT département
ADEEEMNPRTV depravement
ADEEEMNSTTT statemented
ADEEEMOSTWW meadowsweet
ADEEENOPRTU deuteranope
ADEEENRSSSV adverseness
ADEEENRSTTX next dearest
ADEEEPRSSSU supersedeas
ADEEFFHNOOS off one's head
ADEEFFIINRT differentia
ADEEFFILNRS false friend
ADEEFFLNNRW dwarf fennel
ADEEFGGLOPR leapfrogged
ADEEFGILNOR freeloading
ADEEFGINNRR rangefinder
ADEEFGINNRV never-fading
ADEEFGINORR forereading
ADEEFGIRTVY gravity-feed
ADEEFGKLNPR frank-pledge
ADEEFGMNOOW A Few Good Men
ADEEFHLLRTU full-hearted
ADEEFHORSTT soft-hearted
ADEEFIIINNT definientia
ADEEFIIMNOT animo et fide
ADEEFIINRST finasteride
ADEEFIINSST dies nefasti
ADEEFIKMNRS make friends
ADEEFILLNOX deflexional
ADEEFILNRST self-trained
ADEEFILNSUU unfeudalise
ADEEFILNUUZ unfeudalize
ADEEFILPRSS self-despair
ADEEFIMRSTU misfeatured
ADEEFINNRRT after-dinner
ADEEFINNSST defiantness
ADEEFINORSZ fazendeiros
ADEEFINRRTW water-finder
ADEEFIOPSST safe-deposit
ADEEFISSSTX fixed assets
ADEEFKLOOPR poodle-faker
ADEEFLLNPST self-planted
ADEEFLLOORR floor leader
ADEEFLLORSV severalfold
ADEEFLMSSSU self-assumed
ADEEFLOPPRR paper-folder
ADEEFLRRSSX flax-dresser
ADEEFLRSSSU self-assured
ADEEFMMNOOY made of money
ADEEFMNRRTU Fred Trueman
ADEEFMOORRS reformadoes
ADEEFNORSSV favoredness
ADEEFNRRRST transferred
ADEEFOOPRRR proofreader
ADEEFPRSTTU superfatted
ADEEGGGIRRV grave-digger
ADEEGGHHIRR Higher grade
ADEEGGHNSSS shaggedness
ADEEGGINRRU Ranger Guide
ADEEGGINUWZ gauze-winged
ADEEGGLORTW waterlogged
ADEEGGMNNOR garden gnome
ADEEGGMORUY demagoguery
ADEEGGNNORR green dragon
ADEEGGNORST tread on eggs
ADEEGGOPRUY pedagoguery
ADEEGHHHIRT high-hearted
ADEEGHIKLTT take delight
ADEEGHIKSTW weak-sighted
ADEEGHILSTY see daylight
ADEEGHINPRS grandeeship
ADEEGHINRST near-sighted
ADEEGHINSSV have designs
ADEEGHIRRST sight-reader
ADEEGHLNORS golden share
ADEEGHLRSTU slaughtered
ADEEGHMOPRR demographer
ADEEGHNNPRW grand-nephew
ADEEGHNOOSV good heavens
ADEEGHNOPRS hedge-parson
ADEEGHNORSU garden-house
ADEEGHNORSY hydrogenase
ADEEGHNORTY hydrogenate
ADEEGHNRRUY yeard-hunger
ADEEGIINNST indesignate
ADEEGIINSTV designative
ADEEGIIORRV Diego Rivera
ADEEGIIRSST great diesis

ADEEGIKNNRS	ringed snake
ADEEGILLNRY	legendarily
ADEEGILMNSW	seam welding
ADEEGILMORS	deglamorise
ADEEGILMORZ	deglamorize
ADEEGILNNOT	leading note
ADEEGILNNRY	endearingly
ADEEGILNNST	disentangle
ADEEGILNORS	Gorée Island
ADEEGILNTTU	deglutinate
ADEEGIMORRT	gradiometer
ADEEGINNNSU	ensanguined
ADEEGINNSUX	exsanguined
ADEEGJLMNTU	judgemental
ADEEGLLNOSU	eglandulose
ADEEGLNOSTT	Golden State
ADEEGLNOSTU	Tsung-Dao Lee
ADEEGLNRTUU	unregulated
ADEEGMMOPRR	deprogramme
ADEEGMNNORY	danger money
ADEEGMNNRTU	ungarmented
ADEEGMNNTUU	unaugmented
ADEEGMNRRRY	gerrymander
ADEEGMORTUY	deuterogamy
ADEEGNNRRST	transgender
ADEEGNNRSTU	stun grenade
ADEEGORSTUV	Gustave Doré
ADEEHHIIRTW	white-haired
ADEEHHIMRTY	hemihydrate
ADEEHHIMSST	missheathed
ADEEHHLORRS	shareholder
ADEEHHMMNOO	home-and-home
ADEEHHNOPRT	heptahedron
ADEEHHNORSX	hexahedrons
ADEEHHORTTY	the other day
ADEEHHPRSTU	The Phaedrus
ADEEHHRSSST	sheath dress
ADEEHIIKMNT	nikethamide
ADEEHIILTTW	white-tailed
ADEEHIIOPRS	isodiaphere
ADEEHIKNPPS	snake-hipped
ADEEHIKSTWY	this day week
ADEEHILLMOU	Émile Lahoud
ADEEHILLNOT	endothelial
ADEEHILMRTY	tailed rhyme
ADEEHILMTWW	wheat mildew
ADEEHILNOPT	elephantoid
ADEEHILNORT	lion-hearted
ADEEHILNPRR	philanderer
ADEEHILNRTW	draw the line
ADEEHILNSST	deathliness
ADEEHINNOTT	the Anointed
ADEEHINNRTW	near the wind
ADEEHINORRT	iron-hearted
ADEEHINRSST	threadiness
ADEEHINSTUX	inexhausted
ADEEHIORTTV	dehortative
ADEEHIRRRSS	hairdresser
ADEEHIRRRSW	washer-drier
ADEEHIRRSTW	Harris tweed
ADEEHIRSTTT	third estate
ADEEHKLORST	stakeholder
ADEEHKMNORT	mother-naked
ADEEHKORSTT	death-stroke
ADEEHKORTTW	take the word
ADEEHLLNOSV	love handles
ADEEHLLORSV	slaveholder
ADEEHLMMORT	emerald moth
ADEEHLMNOTT	mentholated
ADEEHLMOSTX	Texas hold 'em
ADEEHLNORTY	theory-laden
ADEEHLNOSST	loathedness
ADEEHLNPRTU	thunder peal
ADEEHLOORSZ	Dolores Haze
ADEEHLOORTW	leatherwood
ADEEHLORTUY	youth leader
ADEEHLSTUXY	exhaustedly
ADEEHMNNOST	and then some
ADEEHMNOPTU	pneumathode
ADEEHNNNOTY	Anthony Eden
ADEEHNNOPRT	pentahedron
ADEEHNNORVY	on every hand
ADEEHNNOSST	set one's hand
ADEEHNNPRSU	undershapen
	unsharpened
ADEEHNNRSSU	unharnessed
ADEEHNOOSWW	shawnee-wood
ADEEHNOOUVY	have you done?
ADEEHNOPRRT	The Pardoner
ADEEHNORRTT	tetrahedron
ADEEHNOSSTW	stonewashed
ADEEHNRRSTW	netherwards
ADEEHNRSTUV	unharvested
ADEEHNSTUUX	unexhausted
ADEEHRRRSWY	washer-dryer
ADEEIIKNPRT	take pride in
ADEEIILLMPX	maxillipede
ADEEIILLNRT	interallied
ADEEIILMMSV	medievalism
ADEEIILMMTY	immediately
ADEEIILMNOT	matinée idol
ADEEIILMNRT	intermedial
ADEEIILMSTV	medievalist
ADEEIILNNOT	delineation
ADEEIILNNST	desinential
ADEEIILNNSY	aniline dyes
ADEEIILNRST	residential
ADEEIILNSST	de-Stalinise
ADEEIILNSTZ	de-Stalinize
ADEEIIMMNPT	impedimenta
ADEEIIMNNPT	pentamidine
ADEEIIMNORT	remediation
ADEEIIMNRSS	in medias res
ADEEIIMNSST	disseminate
ADEEIIMRSTX	taxidermise
ADEEIIMRTXZ	taxidermize
ADEEIINOPRS	sideropenia
ADEEIINPSTT	stipendiate
ADEEIINRTVY	evidentiary
ADEEIIPRTUV	repudiative
ADEEIIPRTVV	deprivative
ADEEIKLLSSV	sleaved silk

ADEEIKLMORU leukodermia
ADEEIKNRRST dreikanters
ADEEIKRRSTV Kavir Desert
ADEEILLMNNR ill-mannered
ADEEILLMRSV silver medal
ADEEILLNRST stelleridan
ADEEILLNRTT trendle-tail
ADEEILMNNST enlisted man
ADEEILMNORR mole drainer
ADEEILMNORT endometrial
ADEEILMNRST streamlined
ADEEILMNRTT detrimental
ADEEILMNRVY delivery-man
ADEEILMOORT meteoroidal
ADEEILMOPST diplomatese
ADEEILMOSTV dame's-violet
ADEEILMPPUU ami du peuple
ADEEILMSTUU demutualise
ADEEILMTUUZ demutualize
ADEEILNNPRR linen-draper
ADEEILNNPRT dinner plate
ADEEILNNPTT pentlandite
ADEEILNNPUX unexplained
ADEEILNNRTT interdental
ADEEILNOTTV Tainted Love
ADEEILNPRSU under-espial
ADEEILNRSTW windlestrae
ADEEILNRSTY disentrayle
sedentarily
ADEEILNRUWY unweariedly
ADEEILNRVVY delivery-van
ADEEILOPPRT Lepidoptera
ADEEILPQSSU sesquipedal
ADEEILPRSSU displeasure
ADEEILRRSTV evil-starred
ADEEILRRSVV slave-driver
ADEEILRRTTU literatured
ADEEIMMNORS misdemeanor
ADEEIMMNOSU eudaemonism
ADEEIMMORST maisterdome
ADEEIMMSUVW medium waves
ADEEIMNNPTU antependium
ADEEIMNNRTT determinant
detrainment
ADEEIMNNTTU edutainment
ADEEIMNOPPR Pompeian red
ADEEIMNOPRT predominate
ADEEIMNOPSS empassioned
ADEEIMNOSTU eudaemonist
ADEEIMNRSTV steam-driven
ADEEIMNRSTY sedimentary
ADEEIMNRTWX Max de Winter
ADEEIMOPRRT madreporite
ADEEIMPRSSU mispersuade
ADEEIMRTTTY tetradymite
ADEEINNPRRV André Previn
ADEEINNRSSU unreadiness
ADEEINNRTTV inadvertent
ADEEINOPRST desperation
ADEEINOPTTT potentiated
ADEEINORRST raison d'être
ADEEINORTTU deuteration
ADEEINOSTTT detestation
ADEEINPPRRT Peter Pindar
ADEEINPRRSU underpraise
ADEEINQRTUV verd-antique
ADEEINRSTUV disaventure
ADEEIOPRSSU au désespoir
ADEEIPRRSTW water spider
ADEEIPRRTUY Eurypterida
ADEEJMNRRRY jerrymander
ADEEKLLMORU leukodermal
ADEEKLMMORY Melody Maker
ADEEKLOPRSU loudspeaker
ADEELLMRSSY dreamlessly
ADEELLNNRUY unlearnedly
ADEELLNRTUV untravelled
ADEELMNOORT demonolater
ADEELMOORST osteodermal
ADEELNNRSTU dental nurse
ADEELNOOPST aldopentose
ADEELNOOSST at loose ends
ADEELNOPRSU sleep around
ADEELNORSUW weasel round
ADEELNOSSST stoss and lee
ADEELNPRSTU unplastered
ADEELNRRUUV undervaluer
ADEELNRTTVY advertently
ADEELOPPRRW pearl-powder
ADEELOPPRTW plate-powder
ADEELOQSSTU soldatesque
ADEELORSSWW weasel words
ADEEMMNOORR more and more
ADEEMMNORTY dynamometer
ADEEMMOOSUW meadow mouse
ADEEMMORSTY maysterdome
ADEEMNNNSSU mundaneness
ADEEMNNOOOW wood anemone
ADEEMNNSSTU untamedness
ADEEMNOPPRR name-dropper
ADEEMNORSTT demonstrate
ADEEMNOSTVW woman-vested
ADEEMNPPSUU suppedaneum
ADEEMNPTTTU unattempted
ADEEMNRRRWY merry-andrew
ADEEMORSSUY Musée d'Orsay
ADEEMRRSTTU mustard tree
ADEENNNORSU enneandrous
ADEENNNPPSY spend a penny
ADEENNNRTTU undertenant
ADEENNOSWWY wend one's way
ADEENNPRTTU unpatterned
ADEENOORRVV over and over
ADEENOPSSUY pay one's dues
ADEENRRRSTU under arrest
ADEENRRSTUV untraversed
ADEENRRSUWY under-sawyer
ADEENRSSSSU assuredness
ADEENRSSTUV adventuress
ADEEOOPPRRV Depo-Provera®
ADEEOPRRRSW reed-sparrow
ADEEOPRSTWY yeast powder

ADEERRSSTTW streetwards
ADEFFGNRSTU garden stuff
ADEFFILNRTU fault-finder
ADEFFIORSST disafforest
ADEFFKNNOOR Frankenfood
ADEFFLLORTU altoruffled
ADEFGGINRRU fingerguard
ADEFGHLOOTT flog to death
ADEFGIINRTU ungratified
ADEFGILLNOS self-loading
ADEFGILMNNS self-damning
ADEFGILNOST folding seat
ADEFGILNRSY lady's finger
ADEFGITTUUY fatigue-duty
ADEFGKNOORS god-forsaken✧
ADEFGKOORSS for God's sake
ADEFGLLNSSU gladfulness
ADEFGLLRRUY regardfully
ADEFHIKOSST kiss of death
ADEFHILLORT Adolf Hitler
ADEFHILOORS foolhardise
ADEFHILOORZ foolhardize
ADEFHILOPST felspathoid
ADEFHILOSTU outside half
ADEFHINNOSU unfashioned
ADEFHIRUYZZ fuzzy-haired
ADEFHLMOPTU flap-mouthed
ADEFHLNOPRU half-pounder
ADEFHLOOPPR flapperhood
ADEFHORRTWW whet forward
ADEFIIILNOT defiliation
ADEFIILLQUY qualifiedly
ADEFIILLSUV visual field
ADEFIILNOOT defoliation
ADEFIILNQUU unqualified
ADEFIINNOTU infeudation
ADEFIINSSTU unsatisfied
ADEFILLORUV ill-favoured
ADEFILLRSTY lady-trifles
ADEFILMNOSU sulfonamide
ADEFILMNOSW fieldswoman
ADEFILMORSW words fail me
ADEFILMRRUY Murrayfield
ADEFILNOORT defloration
ADEFILNOSUX sulfadoxine
ADEFILSSTTU distasteful
ADEFIMNNORS Denis Forman
ADEFIMNOORT deformation
ADEFIMNORWW window frame
ADEFIORRSUV disfavourer
ADEFISSSTUU dies faustus
ADEFKLOPRSW powder flask
ADEFLLLOPRY Alfred Polly
ADEFLLNOSST dental floss
ADEFLNOORRS fool's errand
ADEFLNOORRT front-loader
ADEFLNORUUV unflavoured
ADEFLOOPSTY splay-footed
ADEFMNORRST transformed
ADEFMNORTTU unformatted
ADEFNOOPRSS ropes of sand
ADEFNORRSSW forwardness
frowardness
ADEFOORRRVW overforward
ADEGGGHIRRT ragged right
ADEGGHILNRT right-angled
ADEGGHIOPSU pedagoguish
ADEGGHLRSTU The Sluggard
ADEGGHNORRU Darren Gough
ADEGGIIJMOO Joe DiMaggio
ADEGGIINNRW wide-ranging
ADEGGIINRRV driving-gear
ADEGGILNNOT goal-tending
ADEGGILNOSV long-visaged
ADEGGILNRUU unguligrade
ADEGGILRRSU sugar glider
ADEGGILRSSU sluggardise
ADEGGILRSUZ sluggardize
ADEGGIMMOSU demagoguism
ADEGGIMOPSU pedagoguism
ADEGGINNRRU unregarding
ADEGGINOSTY steady-going
ADEGGKLOORS look daggers
ADEGGMNORST gangsterdom
ADEGGMNORTU unmortgaged
ADEGGNOORRU Rouge Dragon
ADEGGNORRYY Andy Gregory
ADEGHHILNNP helping hand
ADEGHHINNTU headhunting
ADEGHHINRRT right-hander
ADEGHHLNORU rough-handle
ADEGHHORTUW wade through
ADEGHIIKNNT The King and I
ADEGHIILMNN mind-healing
ADEGHIILNTV devil a thing
living death
ADEGHILLNNS handselling
ADEGHILNNOV hand in glove
ADEGHILNNSW swing-handle
swingle-hand
ADEGHIMNRST hamstringed
ADEGHINNNRU running head
ADEGHINNRSU ungarnished
ADEGHINOOPS in good shape
ADEGHINOORT in good heart
ADEGHJLNOTY John Lydgate
ADEGHLMOOST Thomas Lodge
ADEGHLMOOSU Douglas-Home
ADEGHMNNORT gander-month
ADEGHMNORRT grandmother
ADEGHMOPRRY dermography
ADEGHNOOPSU endophagous
ADEGHNOORWW Gwen Harwood
ADEGHNRRTUU run the guard
ADEGHOOPRRX doxographer
ADEGHOPPRSU pseudograph
ADEGHORRSSU horse guards✧
ADEGHORRTUV overdraught
ADEGHPRRTUY drug therapy
ADEGIIIKMNR Kimeridgian
ADEGIIINNRV Indian giver
ADEGIIJKNOS joking aside

ADEGIIKNNOS indigo snake
ADEGIILLMNT metalliding
ADEGIILMNPS mispleading
ADEGIILNNRW line drawing
ADEGIILNOSV video signal
ADEGIILNOTV dovetailing
ADEGIILNPSS displeasing
ADEGIILNSST sliding seat
ADEGIILOPRS prodigalise
ADEGIILOPRZ prodigalize
ADEGIILRSTU slide guitar
ADEGIIMNNRX margin index
ADEGIIMNORT demigration
ADEGIIMNOSS misdiagnose
ADEGIIMNPST die-stamping
ADEGIIMNRST mistreading
ADEGIIMNTTU unmitigated
ADEGIINNORS inorganised
ADEGIINNORT denigration
ADEGIINNORZ inorganized
ADEGIINNOST designation
ADEGIINNTUV undeviating
ADEGIINOPRR Perigordian
ADEGIINORSS disorganise
ADEGIINORSZ disorganize
ADEGIINRRVZ Grand Vizier
ADEGIINRRWW wiredrawing
ADEGIINRSTT giant stride
ADEGIINRSTV advertising
driving seat
ADEGIINRTTU ingratitude
ADEGIIPRSTV tripe-visag'd
ADEGIKMNRSS dressmaking
ADEGIKNNRTU undertaking
ADEGIKNRRST ring-straked
ADEGILLOSSU gladioluses
ADEGILLPTUY plead guilty
ADEGILMMNRY Me and My Girl
ADEGILNNRRR Ring Lardner
ADEGILNNRWY wanderingly
ADEGILNNSSU languidness
ADEGILNORSY grandiosely
ADEGILNOSTW long-waisted
ADEGILNPRSY spreadingly
ADEGILNPRTY panty girdle
ADEGILNPRVY depravingly
ADEGILNSTTY settling day
ADEGILOOPST paedologist
ADEGILOOPSU pseudologia
ADEGIMNOORR reading-room
ADEGIMNORRS gormandiser
ADEGIMNORRZ gormandizer
ADEGIMNORSU gourmandise
ADEGINNNORW dinner-wagon
ADEGINNNRUW unwandering
ADEGINNNTTU unattending
ADEGINNOPRT danger point
ADEGINNORSU unorganised
ADEGINNORUZ unorganized
ADEGINNQRSU squandering
ADEGINNRRUW unrewarding
ADEGINOORVW wood vinegar
ADEGINOPRTW giant powder
ADEGINORRRV river-dragon
ADEGINORRTV overtrading
ADEGINORSTY designatory
ADEGINOSTTU degustation
ADEGINPRSST tap-dressing
ADEGKLMNNOY monkey-gland
ADEGLLNORRW Lord Wrangel
ADEGLMOOPRT Good Templar
ADEGLMOORTY dermatology
ADEGLNNORVY Danny Glover
ADEGLNOPRTU ground plate
ADEGLNORSUY dangerously
ADEGMMMNOOR monogrammed
ADEGMNNOORS good manners
ADEGMNNOTUY many-tongued
ADEGNNOORSU androgenous
on one's guard
ADEGNNOPUUZ ungazed upon
ADEGNORRTUW ground water
ADEGNORSTTU ground state
ADEGNORSTUW waste ground
ADEGORSTTUY degustatory
ADEHHIINORR hide nor hair
ADEHHIIRSTW white radish
ADEHHILMNSU human shield
ADEHHILPRSY her ladyship
ADEHHIMNRTT The Third Man
ADEHHIMOORR haemorrhoid
ADEHHIOPPST phosphatide
ADEHHIORRSS horseradish
ADEHHIRRSTW hitherwards
ADEHHIRRTTW thitherward
ADEHHIRRTWW whitherward
ADEHHJNOPSY Joseph Haydn
ADEHHLMRTTY delta rhythm
ADEHHMMRTTU thrummed hat
ADEHIIMMPST midshipmate
ADEHIIMNOPR diamorphine
ADEHIIMNRST Damien Hirst
ADEHIIMNRTU antheridium
ADEHIIMPRSU sphaeridium
ADEHIIMRSTT Mithridates
ADEHIINNOPT Diophantine
ADEHIIOOPRU Ophiuroidea
ADEHIIOPRSS diaphoresis
ADEHIIOPSVV vaivodeship
ADEHIIORSTT historiated
ADEHIIPRSSV advisership
ADEHIKKLRTU the Auld Kirk
ADEHIKMRRTT Third market
ADEHIKNORSW whiskerando
ADEHIKNRSST strike hands
ADEHIKOORST Theodorakis
ADEHILLMMRR hammer drill
ADEHILLMOSW mishallowed
ADEHILLNRST disenthrall
ADEHILLOOPR haloperidol
ADEHILMNOOP Monodelphia
ADEHILMNRYY Myra Hindley

ADEHILNOPRU lie hard upon
ADEHILNPRYY hyperlydian
ADEHILORRVY Oliver Hardy
ADEHILORSTY hysteroidal
ADEHIMMPPUY happy medium
ADEHIMNOPRS hand-promise
preadmonish
ADEHIMNPSSS dampishness
ADEHIMOPRST Thomas Pride
ADEHIMORSTU diathermous
ADEHIMRRSTT third stream
third-stream
ADEHINNNSSU unhandiness
ADEHINNRSTU untarnished
ADEHINNRSUV unvarnished
ADEHINNRTTW handwritten
ADEHINOORTT dehortation
ADEHINOORTZ antherozoid
ADEHINOPRRY hyperdorian
ADEHINORRTT in order that
ADEHINORRTY rehydration
ADEHINOSSSW shadowiness
ADEHINOSTTT that's done it
ADEHINRSTTW withstander
ADEHIOPPSSY diapophyses
ADEHIOPRRTY pyritohedra
ADEHIORRSST arthrodesis
ADEHIPRSSTW stewardship
ADEHIPRSTTW sharp-witted
ADEHISTTTWY hasty-witted
ADEHJLNOOSW hold one's jaw
ADEHJLOOOSU jealoushood
ADEHJMNOOOR Mohenjo-daro
ADEHJMNOORS John o'dreams
ADEHKLOORTW The Woodlark
ADEHLLLMORS smallholder
ADEHLLLORST stallholder
ADEHLLLORTW all the world
ADEHLLNOSTW show-and-tell
ADEHLLOOSSU A Doll's House
ADEHLMOOPRT leopard moth
ADEHLNNORRT northlander
ADEHLNORSTU southlander
ADEHLORRSTV harvest lord
ADEHLORSTTW the last word
ADEHLORSTYY hydrolysate
ADEHLORTXYY hydroxylate
ADEHMNNORSS horn-madness
ADEHMNOORTY monohydrate
ADEHMNOORWY Woody Herman
ADEHMNORRSY Rodney Marsh
ADEHNNNOOSS on one's hands
ADEHNNOPSTU open-and-shut
ADEHNNORSTY try one's hand
ADEHNOORRSU horse around
ADEHNOORTTW down to earth
down-to-earth
ADEHNOPRSTU heptandrous
ADEHNORRSTW sand-thrower
ADEHOOPPRTY paedotrophy
ADEHOORRTTW tooth-drawer
ADEHOORRTTY dehortatory
ADEHOPRSSTW shop steward
ADEHORRUXYY hydroxyurea
ADEIIILMSST dissimilate
ADEIIIMMMST immediatism
ADEIIINNTTU uninitiated
ADEIIIOPSTV diapositive
ADEIIIPSSTV dissipative
ADEIIISSSTU assiduities
ADEIILLLNSS Ellis Island
ADEIILLLOPS ellipsoidal
ADEIILLMRSY Daisy Miller
ADEIILLMSTW Ted Williams
ADEIILLNNSS Line Islands
ADEIILLNPQU Daniel Quilp
ADEIILLNRSS Reil's island
ADEIILLNRTT trindle-tail
ADEIILLNRTU interludial
ADEIILLORTY editorially
ADEIILMNNOS dimensional
ADEIILMNRSU semi-diurnal
ADEIILMOPST diplomatise
ADEIILMOPTZ diplomatize
ADEIILMSSTU dissimulate
ADEIILNNORT internodial
ADEIILNNSSV invalidness
ADEIILNQTUU unqualitied
ADEIILRRTTY irritatedly
ADEIIMMNNOS demonianism
ADEIIMMNRST in midstream
ADEIIMMNSTU mediastinum
ADEIIMNNSSS Dennis Amiss
ADEIIMNOPSS impassioned
ADEIIMNORSS readmission
ADEIIMNPRST median strip
ADEIIMOPPTW meadow pipit
ADEIIMRSTTX taxidermist
ADEIINNNOTT indentation
ADEIINNOOPS Poseidonian
ADEIINNOOPT opinionated
ADEIINNOORY oneirodynia
ADEIINNORTT denitration
ADEIINNOSTT destination
ADEIINNOTTV venditation
ADEIINOOPRT periodontia
ADEIINOPRST stride piano
ADEIINOPRTT trepidation
ADEIINOPRTU repudiation
ADEIINOPRTV deprivation
ADEIINOPSST Passiontide
ADEIINORRTT traditioner
ADEIINORSTY seditionary
ADEIINORTTX extradition
ADEIINPRSTY stipendiary
ADEIINPSSST inspissated
ADEIINQSTTU equidistant
ADEIINRRSTU interradius
ADEIIOPRSTX ideopraxist
ADEIIPRSTTW twisted pair
ADEIIPSTTUV disputative
ADEIIRRSSTT Dire Straits

ADEIJNORRRV	River Jordan
ADEIJPRSSTU	Judas Priest
ADEIKLLNSST	kiss and tell✧
	kiss-and-tell
ADEIKNPPRSS	sand-skipper
ADEILLMNOPT	mal del pinto
ADEILLMRRST	drill-master
ADEILLNNRSU	disannuller
ADEILLNRSTW	stellar wind
ADEILLNRTTU	trundle-tail
ADEILLOPSSV	lap dissolve
ADEILLORSST	ill-assorted
ADEILLOSVWW	swallow-dive
ADEILLRSTTU	illustrated
ADEILLSSTUU	Iles du Salut
ADEILMNNORT	Modern Latin
ADEILMNNORW	annelid worm
ADEILMNNORY	molendinary
ADEILMNOPTU	deplumation
ADEILMNORSU	unmoralised
ADEILMNORUZ	unmoralized
ADEILMNTTUU	unmutilated
ADEILMORSTT	solid matter
ADEILNNNOSY	Sidney Nolan
ADEILNNOSTY	Lydian stone
ADEILNNSTUU	uninsulated
ADEILNNTTUY	untaintedly
ADEILNOOPRT	deploration
	periodontal
ADEILNOPPTY	pentaploidy
ADEILNOPRSU	unpolarised
ADEILNOPRUY	pleurodynia
ADEILNOPRUZ	unpolarized
ADEILNPPRST	spider plant
ADEILNPRSTU	prudentials
ADEILNQSSSU	squalidness
ADEILNRSTWW	windlestraw
ADEILNRSTWZ	Switzerland
ADEILNSSTUY	sustainedly
ADEILOPRRTY	predatorily
ADEILOPRTTY	tetraploidy
ADEILOPSTTT	toad spittle
ADEIMMNNOPU	pandemonium✧
ADEIMMNOOST	somatomedin
ADEIMMNSSTT	dismastment
ADEIMNNOORT	denominator
ADEIMNNOPRT	predominant
ADEIMNNORSU	unromanised
ADEIMNNORUZ	unromanized
ADEIMNNOTUW	mountain dew
ADEIMNNQRUU	quadrennium
ADEIMNOORST	moderations
ADEIMNOPSTU	despumation
ADEIMNORSTU	nematodirus
ADEIMNOTTUV	unmotivated
ADEIMNRRSUY	nurserymaid
ADEIMNRRTUY	rudimentary
ADEIMNRSTTT	transmitted
ADEIMNRSTUV	adventurism
ADEIMOPRTUY	apodyterium
ADEINNOOPRT	ponderation
ADEINNOPPTU	unappointed
ADEINNOPSSU	unpassioned
ADEINNOQRTU	quaternion'd
ADEINNORRWY	Winona Ryder
ADEINNORSTU	trades union
ADEINNPRRTY	dinner party
ADEINNQSTUU	unquantised
ADEINNQTUUZ	unquantized
ADEINNSSSTT	distantness
ADEINNSSSTU	unstaidness
ADEINNSSTUU	unsustained
ADEINOOPRTT	deportation
ADEINOPRRSS	Napier's rods
ADEINOPRRTU	perduration
ADEINOPRRTW	word-painter
ADEINOPRSST	dispensator
ADEINORRTXY	rotary index
ADEINPPPRUW	wrapped up in
ADEINPRSTUY	superdainty
ADEINQRRTUW	quarter-wind
ADEINRSTTUV	adventurist
ADEINRSTTUY	testudinary
ADEIOPRRTTY	trepidatory
ADEIORRSSTT	dissertator
ADEIPPSSTTU	past dispute
ADEJMNNORTU	adjournment
ADEJMNORRTY	Tom and Jerry
ADEJMOORRRS	major orders
ADELLMMORTY	troll-my-dame
ADELLMNORSW	small wonder
ADELLNOOSWW	wooden walls
ADELLNOSUWW	unswallowed
ADELLNSSTUY	dauntlessly
ADELLOORRSU	Euro-dollars
ADELMNOORST	tremolandos
ADELMNOORTY	demonolatry
ADELNOOPRSW	snow leopard
ADELNOPPTUU	unpopulated
ADELNORSWWY	Wayne's World
ADELOOPPRTU	depopulator
ADELOOPRRST	postal order
ADELOPPRSUU	dual-purpose
ADELOPRRRSY	Lord's Prayer
ADELOPRRSWY	swordplayer
ADEMMMNORSU	memorandums
ADEMMNNOOSS	moon-madness
ADEMMNNORSU	Donna Summer
ADEMMNNOSUU	ad unum omnes
ADEMMNNOUYY	maundy money
ADEMMNORTYY	dynamometry
ADEMMOPRSUU	Prado Museum
ADEMNNOPTWY	down payment
ADEMNNOSTTU	astoundment
ADEMNNOSTVY	Yves Montand
ADEMNOOPSSU	pseudomonas
ADEMNOORTTY	attorneydom
ADEMNOPRSTU	pound-master
ADEMORSSTTY	storm-stayed
ADENNNOORST	ondansetron
ADENNOPPSTT	pendant-post
ADENNOPRRST	transponder

Words marked ✧ can also be spelled with one or more capital letters

ADENNOPRSTU pentandrous
ADENOORTTUU out-and-outer
ADENOPPPRSY Podsnappery
ADENOPRRRTY proterandry
ADENOPRRSTT transported
ADENORRSTTU tetrandrous
ADENORSSSUU arduousness
ADENORSSTUW outwardness
ADENORSTUUV adventurous
ADENPRRSSUY sand spurrey
ADENPRSSSUU unsurpassed
ADENRSSTUWY dusty answer
ADENRSTTUUY nature study
ADEOOOPPSST as opposed to
ADEOOPRSTTU tetrapodous
ADFFGIINNRU Fair Funding
ADFFGNORSTU ground staff
ADFFHINOSST standoffish
ADFFLLLORTU all to ruffld
ADFFLNOOOOT offload onto
ADFGHHIOSTW shadow fight
ADFGHIINOOT in good faith
ADFGHLNOORY hand of glory
ADFGIIILNPY lapidifying
ADFGIIIMRRU frigidarium
ADFGIILLLNN landfilling
ADFGIINNRSU fund-raising
ADFGIINQRSU firing squad
ADFGILNNOST soft landing
ADFGILNQSUY flying squad
ADFGINORRWW wing forward
ADFGOOOORSS so far so good
ADFHHNOOSSW show of hands
ADFHHOORSTW shadow forth
ADFIIIKRSTT first aid kit
ADFIIILLNNU nullifidian
ADFIIIMNNTU ad infinitum
ADFIILMNTUU latifundium
ADFIINOOPRS India proofs
ADFILLMSUYY dismayfully
ADFIMNOPRRU panduriform
ADFINNOORRZ rinforzando
ADFINNOOSTU foundations
ADFKLOOORRW look forward
ADFLMNSTUUU mutual funds
ADFLMOORSUW world-famous
ADFMNOORSWY of many words
ADFOOPPRRRW prop forward
ADGGGHIILNN hang-gliding
ADGGHHIOORS road-hoggish
ADGGHIILNSW wash-gilding
ADGGHILMOTY God-almighty
ADGGIILNNOW wing loading
ADGGIINNNSS singing sand
ADGGIINNNWW wing-and-wing
ADGGIINRSTU guiding star
ADGGILLNOPT gold-plating
ADGGLMOOOTY dogmatology
ADGGLNORSSU ground glass
ADGHHIINRTT hard-hitting
ADGHHILNOPT diphthongal
ADGHHNORTUW handwrought
ADGHHOPRRYY hydrography
ADGHIILNNPS landing-ship
ADGHIINNRTW handwriting
ADGHIIRRSSU Irish Guards
ADGHIKNORRW hardworking
ADGHILLNNOS Hollands gin
ADGHILNNOTY any old thing
ADGHILRRTWY rightwardly
ADGHINNNNRU hand-running
running hand
ADGHINOOORU in a good hour
ADGHIOPRTTY dittography
ADGHMRRRUYY hydrargyrum
ADGHNOOOPRT odontograph
ADGHNOPRRSU sharp-ground
ADGIIILOOSS idioglossia
ADGIIINNNOT indignation
ADGIIINOOTT goniatitoid
ADGIIINSTVY visiting-day
ADGIILLMOSY sigmoidally
ADGIILNNNTY indignantly
ADGIILNNRWY lying-in ward
ADGIILNOTUV divulgation
ADGIILOORST radiologist
ADGIILOOSTU audiologist
ADGIILOPRTY prodigality
ADGIINNNOOV Don Giovanni
ADGIINNPPPR dripping-pan
ADGIINOPTUY audiotyping
ADGIINORRSS disgarrison
ADGIINORSTY grandiosity
ADGIJLOPRTU Judit Polgar
ADGIJNOPPRW jaw-dropping
ADGIKKLORSU Kirk Douglas
ADGIKNNOORT Gordian knot
ADGILMNNNOR morning-land
ADGILMNOSUW guildswoman
ADGILNNOOPS poison-gland
ADGILNOOPRS prodigal son
ADGILNOOSSY glossodynia
ADGILNOSSWW window glass
ADGIMMNORSU gourmandism
ADGIMNOORRW drawing room
ADGINNNOPRU unpardoning
ADGINNOSTTU outstanding
ADGINOORRTU ground-to-air
ADGINOPRRRY grand priory
ADGINOPRSTT trading post
ADGINPRRSYY spray drying
ADGINRSTTYY trysting-day
ADGIRSSSSUW Swiss Guards
ADGLNOOOOTY odonatology
ADGNNNOOTWW town and gown
ADGNNNOQTUU quandong-nut
ADGNNOORSUY androgynous
ADHHIMRSTYY dysrhythmia
ADHHJMNNOWY John Wyndham
ADHHMNOOTTU hand to mouth
hand-to-mouth
ADHHMPRUVYY Humphry Davy

ADHHOORRTXY hydrothorax
ADHIIIMOPRU ophidiarium
ADHIIMOPPST hippodamist
ADHIIOPPSSY diapophysis
ADHIIOPRSTU auditorship
ADHIIORRSST diarthrosis
ADHILLNNOSW Don Whillans
ADHILLOOPRT prothalloid
ADHILLORRRW drill-harrow
ADHILMNOOSW old-womanish
ADHILNNORST North Island
ADHILNOSSTU South Island
ADHIMMOOSVV moshav ovdim
ADHIMOOPPSU amphipodous
hippodamous
ADHINOOOPRT Ornithopoda
ADHINOOORTT orthodontia
ADHINOORRSY dishonorary
ADHINPPRSUW whip and spur
ADHIOOORRTT traitorhood
ADHIOPRTTTU hard put to it
ADHKLOOORRT Harold Kroto
ADHLNORRTWY northwardly
ADHLORSTUWY southwardly
ADHMNOPRTUU thump around
ADHNOOPQRUY quadrophony
ADHNOORRTUW throw around
ADIIIINORST iridisation
ADIIIINORTZ iridization
ADIIILLMSUV diluvialism
ADIIILLSTUV diluvialist
ADIIILNOOST idolisation
ADIIILNOOTZ idolization
ADIIILNOQTU liquidation
ADIIIMNORTT intimidator
ADIIIMOSSTT mastoiditis
ADIIINOOTXZ oxidization
ADIIINOPSST dissipation
ADIIINORSVY divisionary
ADIIIOPRSTT parotiditis
ADIIJLMMMSY dismal Jimmy
ADIILLMORTT midlittoral
ADIILLNOQRU quadrillion
ADIILMNNOST mandolinist
ADIILMOOSSY amyloidosis
ADIILMOPSTT diplomatist
ADIILNORTUY dilutionary
ADIILNRSSTU industrials
ADIIMMNNORY myrmidonian
ADIIMMNOSTU staminodium
ADIIMNNOOST dominations
ADIIMNOOPST adoptionism✧
ADIIMNOSTTU dismutation
ADIIMORSTUU auditoriums
ADIINNOORRT Torridonian
ADIINOOPSTT adoptionist
ADIINOPPPTU point d'appui
ADIINOPSTTU disputation
ADIIOOPRSUV avoirdupois
ADIIOPSTTUY audiotypist
ADIKLLLNSSU Skull Island
ADIKLOOSTVV Vladivostok
ADIKNOPRRSW Windsor Park
ADIKNORRSTU skirt around
ADILLMOPSYY sympodially
ADILLNORSSU Russian doll
ADILLNRSTUY laundry list
ADILMNNOPTW Piltdown man
ADILNNORTWY Tiny Rowland
ADILNNOSSTY dissonantly
ADILNOPRSSU Old Prussian
ADILNORSSTU Orust Island
ADILORRSTTU stridulator
ADILOSSSUUY assiduously
ADIMNOOOPRR Romano Prodi
ADIMPRRRSTU stirrup dram
ADINOOPRSSW Windsor soap
ADINOOPRTTW point toward
ADINRSTTTUY transit duty
ADKLNOOTUWY talk-you-down
ADLLOOOSWWW wood swallow
ADLNOOPRSUY polyandrous
ADLOOPRSTVY Lady Provost
ADLOPRRTUYY poultry yard
ADMNOOSVWXY Max von Sydow
ADMOOPPRSTT Tom Stoppard
ADNNORSSTTU toss and turn
ADNOOPRRSTU protandrous
ADNOORSUUYY you and yours
ADNOPRSSTUY Sunday Sport
ADNORRSTTUW turn towards
ADOOOPPRRSU prosauropod
ADOOOPRSSUU sauropodous
AEEEEFFMRRZ freeze-frame
AEEEEFGGLRU feeler gauge
AEEEEFGILPR life peerage
AEEEEFLNOSS ease oneself
AEEEEFNORYY eye for an eye
AEEEEGHHTTV get the heave
AEEEEGHLRSS grease-heels
AEEEEGKNRTV take revenge
AEEEEGLMSST Telemessage®
AEEEEGLNSUV seven-league
AEEEEGRRRSV reverse gear
AEEEEHHNSST heathenesse
AEEEEHILRST etherealise
AEEEEHILRTZ etherealize
AEEEEHLRTTT Leatherette®
AEEEEHMRSTU rheumateese
AEEEEHRRTTT The Retreate
AEEEEILMRST time-release
AEEEEJLMSST lese-majesté
AEEEEKNNOPY keep an eye on
AEEEEKNRSUV Keanu Reeves
AEEEELLMNOS leesome-lane
AEEEELMNRST releasement
AEEEELNPPQU queene-apple
AEEEELNRSUV lues venerea
AEEEEMMPRRT permeameter
AEEEENRSVWY New Year's Eve
AEEEEPRRSTV perseverate
AEEEESSTTTT têtes-à-têtes

AEEEFFHLRSZ flash-freeze
AEEEFFLOPPT toffee apple
AEEEFFNRRST transfer fee
AEEEFGIKNPS safekeeping
AEEEFGIRRRT refrigerate
AEEEFGLLNRX reflex angle
AEEEFHIKLRT featherlike
AEEEFHINRRT hereinafter
AEEEFHMPRRS sheep-farmer
AEEEFILNRRT referential
AEEEFILPRST steeple fair
AEEEFLLMPSX self-example
AEEEFLLNNTT flannelette
AEEEFLLRVVY valley fever
AEEEFLNOSWY feel one's way
AEEEFLORSSX Earl of Essex
AEEEFLRSSTU featureless
AEEEFNNRSST Fastern's-e'en
AEEEFPRSTTU superfetate
AEEEGGILNOS genealogise
AEEEGGILNOZ genealogize
AEEEGGIRSTV segregative
AEEEGGMMNOU emmenagogue
AEEEGHHLOTV heave the log
AEEEGHIKNST heat-seeking
AEEEGHLNRST The Gleaners
AEEEGHLPRRT telegrapher
AEEEGHNPRTW great-nephew
AEEEGHNPRTY gene therapy
AEEEGHORRTT theatre-goer
AEEEGHRSTTT the greatest
AEEEGIKKNNV Kevin Keegan
AEEEGILLNNR general line
AEEEGILMMRR lammergeier
AEEEGILMNNV evening meal
AEEEGILMNRR greenmailer
AEEEGILNRSV evangeliser
AEEEGILNRVZ evangelizer
AEEEGIMNNST steam engine
AEEEGIMNSST metagenesis
AEEEGINNRTW water engine
AEEEGINORTT renegotiate
AEEEGINPRRT peregrinate
AEEEGINRRTT reintegrate
AEEEGINRTTV vinegarette
AEEEGKLMNOU leukaemogen
AEEEGKNOOPR orange pekoe
AEEEGLLOPTV vegetal pole
AEEEGLMMRRY lammergeyer
AEEEGLMNNRT enlargement
Greenmantle
AEEEGLMSUUU amuse-gueule
AEEEGLNSSSS agelessness
AEEEGMNNRRU green manure
AEEEGMNNRSS germaneness
AEEEGMNPRST presagement
AEEEGMNQRSU Germanesque
AEEEGMSSTTX text message
AEEEGNORRRT regenerator
AEEEGNORSTW sweet orange
AEEEGNQRSUW Wagneresque
AEEEGNSSSTV St Agnes's Eve
AEEEHHLMMRV helve-hammer
AEEEHHLMRTW weather helm
AEEEHHLORST shoe leather
AEEEHHNNNPT phenanthene
AEEEHIKLNNP enkephaline
AEEEHIKLTTV take the veil
AEEEHILNNPT elephantine
AEEEHILNRTU eleutherian
AEEEHILPSTT telepathise
AEEEHILPTTZ telepathize
AEEEHILRTTY ethereality
AEEEHILSSTT telesthesia
AEEEHIMPRSS re-emphasise
AEEEHIMPRSZ re-emphasize
AEEEHIMRSTX hexametrise
AEEEHIMRTXZ hexametrize
AEEEHIMSSTT metathesise
AEEEHIMSTTZ metathesize
AEEEHIPRSST aspheterise
AEEEHIPRSTZ aspheterize
AEEEHIRSTWW weather-wise
AEEEHISSTTX The Exstasie
AEEEHKMOOPW make whoopee
AEEEHLLLRTW Lee Hartwell
AEEEHLLMPRY ephemerally
AEEEHLMMNRT Emmenthaler
AEEEHLMOPST spelaeothem
AEEEHLMPPRT pamphleteer
AEEEHLMRSTW master-wheel
AEEEHLNPTTT pentathlete
AEEEHLNTUVY lay the venue
AEEEHLORRTV overleather
AEEEHLPRRWY prayer wheel
AEEEHMPRSST sheep-master
AEEEHMRRSTT three-master
AEEEHNNORRW nowhere near
AEEEHNOPRTU The European
AEEEHNOSSTU senate-house
AEEEHNPRSST parentheses
AEEEHNRSTTW news-theatre
AEEEHOPQTUU haute époque
AEEEHOPRRTT Heteroptera
AEEEHORRTUY there you are
AEEEHORRTVW overweather
AEEEHORRUWY where you are
AEEEHPRRSTU superheater
AEEEHPRSSWW sweep-washer
AEEEHQRRSTU three-square
AEEEIINPPRT peripeteian
AEEEIINQSTU Equisetinae
AEEEIIRRTTV reiterative
AEEEILLLPWY peelie-wally
AEEEILMNRST mesenterial
AEEEILMNRTT melanterite
AEEEILMPRST time-pleaser ✧
AEEEILNORRS Sierra Leone
AEEEILNORTV re-elevation
AEEEILNRRTT interrelate
AEEEILNRRTV reverential
AEEEILNRSTV interleaves

AEEEILNRSTX externalise
AEEEILNRTXZ externalize
AEEEILNSTUV eventualise
AEEEILNTUVZ eventualize
AEEEILPRRTT preliterate
AEEEILQSSTU Equisetales
AEEEILRRSUW leisurewear
AEEEIMNPRTT impenetrate
intemperate
AEEEIMNRSSW Meissen ware
AEEEIMNRSTT Eastern Time
AEEEIMNRSUW wine measure
AEEEIMNRTTX exterminate
AEEEIMNRTUV enumerative
AEEEIMNRWZZ Ezer Weizman
AEEEIMPRTTV temperative
AEEEIMQRRTU marqueterie
AEEEINNRRTT entertainer
AEEEINOPRSU Europeanise
AEEEINOPRUZ Europeanize
AEEEINORRTT reorientate
AEEEINORTVX exonerative
AEEEINPRTTV penetrative
AEEEINSSSVV evasiveness
AEEEINTTUVX extenuative
AEEEJLMSSTY lese-majesty
AEEEJLMSTYZ leze-majesty
AEEEKLLOSTX exoskeletal
AEEEKLLPRSW sleepwalker
AEEEKMNPRVY Mervyn Peake
AEEEKMORRTT keratometer
AEEEKPSSSTW sweepstakes
AEEELLLMNTY elementally
AEEELLNSSVW lawn sleeves
AEEELLORRSV sallee-rover
AEEELLORSSW slow-release
AEEELLORTTT teetotaller
AEEELMMNNPT empanelment
AEEELMNNSTV enslavement
AEEELMNOPTT omelette pan
AEEELMNOSTV stove enamel
AEEELMPRTTY temperately
AEEELMRSSSU measureless
AEEELMSSSTV steam vessel
AEEELNNRSST eternalness
AEEELNOPPVY pay envelope
AEEELNOSSST set one's seal
AEEELNPQRUY pearly queen
AEEELNSSSSW awelessness
AEEELORSTUY see you later
AEEELPPRTVV velvet-paper
AEEELPQRSTU plateresque
AEEELPQSUYZ squeeze play
AEEELRRSSVX sex-reversal
AEEELRSTTUV street value
AEEEMMNPRTT temperament
AEEEMMNRSTU measurement
AEEEMNNNRST ensnarement
AEEEMNNRTTT entreatment
AEEEMNNRTTY tenementary
AEEEMNOSSSW awesomeness
AEEEMNRRTTT retreatment
AEEEMNRSSTT Mean Streets
AEEEMNRSTTT estreatment
restatement
AEEEMORRSUV overmeasure
AEEEMPRRTTU temperature
AEEEMQRRSTU square metre
AEEENNNRRST Ernest Renan
AEEENNRSSST earnestness
AEEENORRSTV overearnest
AEEENPRRSTV perseverant
AEEENRSSSTU austereness
AEEEOPPRRRV overprepare
AEEEORRSTUV auto-reverse
AEEEPPPRRTW water pepper
AEEEPRRSSSV reverse pass
AEEEQRSSTTU sequestrate
AEEFFGILLNR free-falling
AEEFFGMNOOS off one's game
AEEFFGRSTTU suffragette
AEEFFIKMOTT take time off
AEEFFILMRTU feature film
AEEFFILNNRS snaffle-rein
AEEFFILORTW water of life
AEEFFIRRTTU Tartufferie
AEEFFLMOSTT let off steam
AEEFFLNRSSU fearfulness
AEEFFLNSSTU fatefulness
AEEFGHHHIRT high feather
AEEFGHILLNS self-healing
AEEFGHILNRT half-integer
AEEFGHORRTT heterograft
AEEFGIIMNRS fair-seeming
AEEFGIKLNRS Finger Lakes
AEEFGIKNRST free skating
AEEFGILLNSS self-sealing
AEEFGILLNTT leafletting
AEEFGILMRRS Farmer Giles
AEEFGILNNNT giant fennel
AEEFGILNPRT fingerplate
AEEFGILNPRU plane figure
AEEFGILNRSS fragileness
AEEFGINRRRT refrigerant
AEEFGIPRRTU prefigurate
AEEFGLLNORW green fallow
AEEFGLLORSW gallows-free
AEEFGLMNRTU German flute
AEEFGLORSTW stage flower
AEEFGMNNRTT engraftment
AEEFGOOPRRS greaseproof
AEEFHHIKNST sheath knife
AEEFHHILMTT half the time
AEEFHHILRSW whale-fisher
AEEFHHORSTU house-father
AEEFHILNNPS halfpennies
AEEFHILNRST Riefenstahl
AEEFHILPRRS pearl-fisher
AEEFHIMNNOS anemone fish
AEEFHINRSTT the fine arts
AEEFHKLLRST shelftalker
AEEFHKLMRST flesh-market

AEEFHLLMNST	mantelshelf
AEEFHLMNORU	funeral home
AEEFHLNSSTU	hatefulness
AEEFHMORRRT	farthermore
AEEFHNNORTW	no fewer than
AEEFHORRSTU	frater-house
AEEFHORSSTU	the four seas
AEEFIILNNRT	inferential
AEEFIILOTVX	exfoliative
AEEFIILPRTV	private life
AEEFIKLLNWX	Felix Wankel
AEEFILLLMRT	filler metal
AEEFILLMORS	famille rose
AEEFILLNRST	self-reliant
AEEFILNSTTY	festinately
AEEFILOPRRT	proliferate
AEEFILOPSUY	if you please
AEEFILPPRRT	filter paper
AEEFIMMMRRZ	Zimmer® frame
AEEFIMNOSST	manifestoes
AEEFIMOPRRT	imperforate
AEEFIMORRTV	reformative
AEEFINORRRZ	Enzo Ferrari
AEEFINPRSTZ	zip fastener
AEEFINRRRST	fraterniser
AEEFINRRRTZ	fraternizer
AEEFIOPRRTV	perforative
AEEFIRRRRSV	Fraser River
AEEFIRRRSTT	Firestarter
AEEFKLNSSUW	wakefulness
AEEFKLORRWW	welfare work
AEEFLLORRST	forestaller
AEEFLLPRSUU	pleasureful
AEEFLMNORUV	roman fleuve
AEEFLMORRTU	reformulate
AEEFLMRSSTY	self-mastery
AEEFLNNOPRY	penny loafer
AEEFLNPRRSY	parsley fern
AEEFLNRSSTU	tearfulness
AEEFLOPPRRS	proper-false
AEEFLRRSSTT	self-starter
AEEFMMNRRSZ	Franz Mesmer
AEEFMNOPRTY	forepayment
AEEFMNORRSY	freemasonry✧
AEEFMORRRST	store farmer
AEEFMORRSTY	term of years
AEEFNNOPRSS	profaneness
AEEFNOPPRST	pop-fastener
AEEFNORRSVW	war of nerves
AEEFNRRRRST	transferrer
AEEFOPRRRTV	parrot fever
AEEFOQRRRTU	forequarter
AEEFPPRRSTU	aftersupper
AEEFPRSSTUY	supersafety
AEEFRSSSTUY	refuse stays
AEEGGGMOORW	George Gamow
AEEGGGNNRRZ	Grenzgänger
AEEGGHHMNSU	meshuggenah
AEEGGHNORTW	the Waggoner
AEEGGHORTUY	gauge theory
AEEGGIINORS	seigniorage
AEEGGIKORRS	Georg Kaiser
AEEGGILLNNR	generalling
AEEGGILMRSS	message-girl
AEEGGILNOST	genealogist
AEEGGIMNNPP	gene mapping
AEEGGIMNOSS	gamogenesis
AEEGGINORST	segregation
AEEGGINQSTU	gigantesque
AEEGGINRRSV	River Ganges
AEEGGIRRTTU	regurgitate
AEEGGORSTTY	geostrategy
AEEGHHINNRT	hang in there
AEEGHHITVWY	heavyweight
AEEGHHNRRTU	earth-hunger
AEEGHIILMNS	Hegelianism
AEEGHIKLLNU	keelhauling
AEEGHIKLNRR	lake herring
AEEGHILLMRT	hellgramite
AEEGHILLNPS	English Pale
AEEGHILMRWY	whigmaleery
AEEGHILNORY	oral hygiene
AEEGHILNPRS	generalship
AEEGHILNPSS	single-phase
AEEGHILRRTW	weathergirl
AEEGHIMMRTU	Megatherium
AEEGHIMPSTU	the game is up
AEEGHINNRTT	threatening
AEEGHINORTV	overheating
AEEGHINORVZ	Herzegovina
AEEGHINOSTU	eating-house
AEEGHINRSTW	weather sign
AEEGHIPPRTW	paperweight
AEEGHIPRRRS	serigrapher
AEEGHIQRSTU	eight-square
AEEGHLNNPTU	elephant gun
AEEGHLNOPRS	selenograph
AEEGHLNORST	estranghelo
AEEGHLNUVWY	Evelyn Waugh
AEEGHLORSUZ	hazel grouse
AEEGHLRRSTU	slaughterer
AEEGHMNNRSY	Syngman Rhee
AEEGHMOPTTY	gametophyte
AEEGHMORSTY	games theory
AEEGHNOOSTT	agonothetes
AEEGHNPRSTV	stevengraph
AEEGHNPRSTY	Stephen Gray
AEEGHOOPRST	ostreophage
AEEGHOPRRST	stereograph
AEEGIIIMNNR	Mare Ingenii
AEEGIIKLLLS	skilligalee
AEEGIILLSTV	legislative
AEEGIILLTTU	aiguillette
AEEGIILMNPT	leaping-time
AEEGIILNNOR	legionnaire
AEEGIILNORS	regionalise
AEEGIILNORZ	regionalize
AEEGIILNPPR	appleringie
AEEGIILNRST	gelatiniser
AEEGIILNRSU	seigneurial
AEEGIILNRTZ	gelatinizer
AEEGIIMNRTV	germinative

AEEGIINNRVW wine vinegar
AEEGIINPSTY Egyptianise
AEEGIINPTYZ Egyptianize
AEEGIINRTTV integrative
vinaigrette
AEEGIINSTTV investigate
AEEGIJKNRRT tear-jerking
AEEGIKLNRRY Gary Lineker
AEEGIKMNRSV verse-making
AEEGILLLNTT tale-telling
AEEGILLMNNP empanelling
AEEGILLMNNW well-meaning
AEEGILLNNTY inelegantly
AEEGILLNRVY revealingly
AEEGILLORRS allegoriser
AEEGILLORRZ allegorizer
AEEGILLRSTU legislature
AEEGILMNNRT engrailment
realignment
AEEGILMNNSS meaningless
AEEGILMNOSU Leguminosae
AEEGILMNRST regimentals
AEEGILNNNRW New Learning
AEEGILNNPRS Spenglerian
AEEGILNNPSY palingenesy
AEEGILNNRTT intertangle
AEEGILNNRUV unrevealing
AEEGILNRSTV everlasting✧
AEEGILRRSTW sweater-girl
AEEGIMMNSST mass meeting
AEEGIMMNSTY May-meetings
AEEGIMNOTTW witenagemot
AEEGIMNSSTU message unit
mutagenesis
AEEGIMPRRRT great primer
AEEGIMSSTTU guesstimate
AEEGINNNOTV non-negative
AEEGINNORST generations
nitrogenase
AEEGINNORTX Generation X
X-generation
AEEGINNPRTT penetrating
AEEGINNRSTV evening star
AEEGINNTTUX extenuating
AEEGINOPPRT oppignerate
AEEGINOPRRS opera singer
AEEGINOPRRZ Orange Prize
AEEGINORRRV Orange River
overgrainer
AEEGINORRTT interrogate
AEEGINOSSTU autogenesis
AEEGIOPRRTV prerogative
AEEGKORSSWW sewage works
AEEGLLMNNTY gentlemanly
AEEGLLMNOTY metallogeny
AEEGLLMNSTY segmentally
AEEGLLMORTU glomerulate
AEEGLLNSSTT tassell-gent
AEEGLLOOPSY spelaeology
AEEGLLOPSWY Yellow Pages®
AEEGLLORSTT allegrettos
AEEGLLORSTW gallows-tree
AEEGLMNNOTW gentlewoman
AEEGLMNOOPR prolegomena
AEEGLMNORSU long measure
AEEGLMNORSW wranglesome
AEEGLMNRSST garmentless
AEEGLNNOPRU enlarge upon
AEEGLNOORSS lose one's rag
AEEGLNOPRST general post
AEEGLNORRRR Errol Garner
AEEGLNORRSY solar energy
AEEGLOOPRRT Porto Alegre
AEEGMMOORRT meteorogram
AEEGMMOPRRR reprogramme
AEEGMNNOSST magnesstone
AEEGMNORRTV overgarment
AEEGMNORSTT state-monger
AEEGMNRTTUY tegumentary
AEEGMORRRTU guerre à mort
AEEGNNORTUV gouvernante
AEEGNNRSSST strangeness
AEEGNOORRTV governorate
AEEGNOOSSTT get one's oats
AEEGNOSSSSU gaseousness
AEEGOPRRSTT report stage
AEEGORRSSTU retroussage
AEEGPPPRRSS pepper grass
AEEHHHLLTTW what the hell
AEEHHHOSTTV have the hots
AEEHHILLLTW all the while
AEEHHILNSST healthiness
AEEHHILRTTW therewithal
whitleather
AEEHHILRTWW wherewithal
AEEHHIPRSTW weather ship
AEEHHIPSSTY hypesthesia
AEEHHIRRTTV rivet hearth
AEEHHIRSTTT shittah tree
AEEHHIRSTWW whitewasher
AEEHHLLMRST Stahlhelmer
AEEHHLMNPRY Henry Pelham
AEEHHMMNOST shame on them
AEEHHMNORTT the other man
AEEHHMNORTY hearth-money
AEEHHMORRTT earth mother
AEEHHMORSTV harvest home
AEEHHNNPRTY hearth-penny
AEEHHNORSTT hearthstone
AEEHHPRRSSU share-pusher
AEEHIIKNSST kinesthesia
AEEHIILMOPT epithelioma
AEEHIILNTWY lie in the way
AEEHIIMPRSS phariseeism
AEEHIINNORT anti-heroine
AEEHIINNOTV have it in one
AEEHIINPRST traineeship
AEEHIIPRSTT Petite Sirah
AEEHIKLLLRW killer whale
AEEHIKLMRRS sharemilker
AEEHIKMNRTT in the market
AEEHIKNSTTV have kittens

AEEHIKPPRSS speakership
AEEHIKRRSTT heart-strike
AEEHILLMOST mesothelial
AEEHILLMRUV humeral veil
AEEHILMMNTY methylamine
AEEHILNNOST stenohaline
AEEHILNPPRS planisphere
AEEHILNPSSS shapeliness
AEEHILNRSST earthliness
AEEHILNRSTU Lutheranise
AEEHILNRTUZ Lutheranize
AEEHILNSSTW wealthiness
AEEHILPPRST prelateship
AEEHILPSTTT telepathist
AEEHILRSSTY hysteresial
AEEHILRSTVW white slaver
AEEHIMMNRST Hammerstein
AEEHIMNNNRT in the manner
AEEHIMNNPST panentheism
AEEHIMNNRST Martin Sheen
AEEHIMNNSTV evanishment
AEEHIMNORRS horse marine
AEEHIMNPRSY hypermnesia
AEEHIMNSTTY amethystine
AEEHIMPPRSS pre-emphasis
AEEHIMPRSST aspheterism
AEEHIMRRSTV River Thames
AEEHIMRSTTT tetratheism
AEEHIMRSTTV harvest mite
AEEHIMRSTTX hexametrist
AEEHIMRTTTW white matter
AEEHINNPSTT panentheist
AEEHINORSTU heterousian✧
AEEHINPRSST parenthesis
AEEHINRRSTV varnish tree
AEEHINRRSVY River Seyhan
AEEHINRTTWW winter wheat
AEEHIOOPRTT heterotopia
AEEHIOOPSST apotheosise
AEEHIOOPSTZ apotheosize
AEEHIORSTTX heterotaxis
AEEHIORTTVX exhortative
AEEHIPPPRTY pay the piper
AEEHIPPRRSS periphrases
AEEHIPPSTUX exhaust pipe
AEEHJLLMOSW James Howell
AEEHJMRSSSU James Ussher
AEEHJMSSTTU just the same
AEEHJNNORTV John Tavener
AEEHKLOORRU leukorrhoea
AEEHKMMOSTT make the most
AEEHKMNORTT on the market
AEEHKMORSTU market-house
AEEHKMPRRTY hypermarket
AEEHKNNOSVW heaven knows
AEEHKOPRRTY keratophyre
AEEHLLMRSYY Mary Shelley
AEEHLLMSSSY shamelessly
AEEHLLNORTY lonely heart
lonely-heart
AEEHLLORRTW weather roll
AEEHLLORTWY yellow earth
AEEHLLPSSST sell the pass
AEEHLLPSSSY shapelessly
AEEHLLRSSTY heartlessly
AEEHLMNNRTT enthralment
AEEHLMNNRWY Hermann Weyl
AEEHLMNOOPR melanophore
AEEHLMOSSTV steam shovel
AEEHLMOSTTY stately home
AEEHLMRRTUY eurythermal
AEEHLNOPRST open slather
AEEHLNORTZZ on the razzle
AEEHLNPSSSS haplessness
AEEHLNSSSST hatlessness
AEEHLOOPRRT heteropolar
AEEHLOPPRTY pelotherapy
AEEHLPPRRTU purple heart✧
AEEHLPPRSTU persulphate
AEEHLPRRSTU spur leather
AEEHLRRTTTU turret lathe
AEEHLSSSTUX exhaustless
AEEHMMMORTT mammoth-tree
AEEHMMNORST stone hammer
AEEHMMNRTUX xeranthemum
AEEHMMORSTT smother mate
AEEHMMRSTUW summer wheat
AEEHMNNNOOP phaenomenon
AEEHMNOOPRT nematophore
AEEHMNOPRTY Hymenoptera
AEEHMNPRRTU preterhuman
AEEHMOPRSTU heptamerous
AEEHMORRRTT earth tremor
AEEHMORRSTT starter home
AEEHMORRSTW whoremaster
AEEHMORRTTW mother water
AEEHMORSSTU housemaster
AEEHMORSTTW weathermost
AEEHMORSTVW whatsomever
AEEHMPPRSTY spermaphyte
AEEHNNOPRSW answerphone
AEEHNOPRSTU houseparent
AEEHNOPRTTY enteropathy
AEEHNOPRTYZ zone therapy
AEEHNOQRSTU on the square
AEEHNORRSTT north-easter
AEEHNORRTWW weather-worn
AEEHNORSSTU Southern Sea
AEEHOOSTTTW a sweet tooth
AEEHOPRRSTY serotherapy
AEEHOQRTTUZ the Quatorze
AEEHORRSSTU house arrest
AEEHORSSTTU south-easter
AEEHPPPRRSU paper-pusher
AEEHRSSSTUU thesauruses
AEEIIILMNRT en militaire
AEEIIILMNTV eliminative
AEEIIILMPRS imperialise
AEEIIILMPRZ imperialize
AEEIIINNNST Einsteinian
AEEIIINRSTV vis inertiae
AEEIIJLMORV Jamie Oliver

AEEIIKLLNPS	spaniel-like
AEEIIKLNNST	in-line skate
AEEIIKMSSYY	Issey Miyake
AEEIILLMMPR	milliampere
AEEIILLRRST	literaliser
AEEIILLRRTZ	literalizer
AEEIILLRSTW	Water Lilies
AEEIILLRWWY	Weary Willie
AEEIILLSSTT	satellitise
AEEIILLSTTZ	satellitize
AEEIILMMORS	memorialise
AEEIILMMORZ	memorialize
AEEIILMNPRT	Latin Empire
AEEIILMNRRS	mineraliser
AEEIILMNRRZ	mineralizer
AEEIILMNRSW	Lewis Namier
AEEIILMORSU	Marie Louise
AEEIILMORTV	meliorative
AEEIILMRRST	semi-trailer
AEEIILNNPTT	penitential
AEEIILNNRRT	interlinear
AEEIILNNRST	internalise
AEEIILNNRTZ	internalize
AEEIILNNSST	inessential
AEEIILNORST	orientalise
AEEIILNORTZ	orientalize
AEEIILNRRRT	interrailer
AEEIILNSTTX	existential
AEEIILNTTTV	native title
AEEIILNTTVV	ventilative
AEEIILRSSTW	saltirewise
AEEIILRTTVY	iteratively
AEEIIMMNORT	Tammie Norie
AEEIIMMSSTT	misestimate
AEEIIMNNRTT	terminate in
AEEIIMNRTTV	terminative
AEEIIMPRTTT	petit maître
AEEIIMPRTTV	impetrative
AEEIINNSTTV	intensative
AEEIINNTTTV	inattentive
AEEIINOPRTV	inoperative
AEEIINORRTT	reiteration
AEEIINQSTTU	Titianesque
AEEIINSTUVV	vesuvianite
AEEIIOPRSST	sepiostaire
AEEIIPRRSTV	reprivatise
AEEIIPRRTVZ	reprivatize
AEEIIPRTTVX	extirpative
AEEIIPRTVVW	private view
AEEIKLLOSUY	Louis Leakey
AEEIKLMOPTZ	Emil Zatopek
AEEIKLNNPPR	ankle-nipper
AEEIKLNRSSW	warlikeness
AEEIKLNSTTW	Kate Winslet
AEEIKLPRSTT	strike plate
AEEIKMNNRTY	Yam Kinneret
AEEIKMNSTTU	minute steak
AEEIKMOTTTU	take time out
AEEIKNOPSSW	Passion week✧
AEEIKNQSSSU	squeakiness
AEEIKNRSSST	streakiness
AEEIKOPRRST	perestroika
AEEIKOPRSST	strike a pose
AEEILLLMNRW	mineral well
AEEILLLMPRT	pearl millet
AEEILLMMNPT	implemental
AEEILLMNOPS	psilomelane
AEEILLMPRXY	exemplarily
AEEILLNNPRY	perennially
AEEILLNNPTY	penalty line
AEEILLNNSXY	sexennially
AEEILLNOPPT	en papillote
AEEILLNOSTT	stellionate
AEEILLNRSST	literalness
AEEILLNRTVY	eviternally
AEEILLNSSTY	essentially
AEEILLPRSST	Peter Alliss
AEEILLPRSTV	silver plate
AEEILLRSSWY	wearilessly
AEEILLRSTVY	versatilely
AEEILLSTTVY	Vesta Tilley
AEEILMNNSTT	sentimental
AEEILMNORRS	renormalise
AEEILMNORRZ	renormalize
AEEILMNORST	salinometer
AEEILMNPRST	sempiternal
AEEILMNPRTV	prevailment
AEEILMNPTTU	penultimate
AEEILMNRSTX	externalism
AEEILMNSSSS	aimlessness
AEEILMNSSWY	Wesleyanism
AEEILMNSTTV	vestimental
AEEILMOPRRT	polarimeter
AEEILMORRST	solarimeter
AEEILMORSWY	wearisomely
AEEILMOSTTT	teetotalism
AEEILMPPRRS	perispermal
AEEILMPRSTY	semelparity
AEEILMPRTXY	exemplarity
AEEILMSTTTU	statute mile
AEEILNNNPRT	inner planet
AEEILNNNPRY	penny-a-liner
AEEILNNOOPT	napoleonite
AEEILNNOPTX	exponential
AEEILNNOSTX	extensional
AEEILNNPSTU	peninsulate
AEEILNNPSTW	twalpennies
AEEILNNRRTU	interneural
AEEILNNSSTU	unessential
AEEILNNSSTY	insensately
AEEILNOPRSS	personalise
AEEILNOPRSZ	personalize
AEEILNOPRTT	interpolate
AEEILNORRSV	reversional
AEEILNORSST	interosseal
AEEILNORSTV	Revelations
AEEILNPPRTW	winter apple
AEEILNPRSTT	interseptal
	septentrial
AEEILNPRSTV	vespertinal
AEEILNPSVXY	expansively
AEEILNRRSTT	intersertal

 Words marked ✧ can also be spelled with one or more capital letters

AEEILNRRSTU neutraliser
AEEILNRRTUZ neutralizer
AEEILNRSSSS airlessness
AEEILNRSTTX externalist
AEEILNRSTUX intersexual
AEEILNRTTXY externality
AEEILNSSSTT stateliness
AEEILNTTTVY attentively
tentatively
AEEILNTTUVY eventuality
AEEILOPPRST sapropelite
AEEILOPPRTT toilet paper
AEEILOPPSSU episepalous
AEEILOPPSTU epipetalous
AEEILOPRRVV prevail over
AEEILOPRTVX explorative
AEEILOPRTVY operatively
AEEILOPSTUY please it you
AEEILORSSTY areosystile
AEEILORSSXY Alexis Soyer
AEEILORTTTW toilet water
AEEILORTTVW water violet
AEEILPPPPST pipe-stapple
AEEILPPQRSU apple-squire
AEEILPPRRSV silver paper
AEEILPRSTUV superlative
AEEILPRSVVY pervasively
AEEILPSTTUX exstipulate
AEEILQRRTUV quarter-evil
AEEILQRSSTU sesquialter
AEEILRRRSTT terrestrial
AEEILRRSSVW Servile Wars
AEEILRRSTTW slate-writer
AEEILRRTTTU littérateur
AEEILRSSTVY assertively
AEEILRSTTUV resultative
AEEIMMNNPRT impermanent
AEEIMMNOPRR Roman Empire
AEEIMMNPRST pentamerism
AEEIMMQRSSU Requiem Mass
AEEIMMRRSTT tetramerism
AEEIMNNNOQU menaquinone
AEEIMNNNRTT entrainment
AEEIMNNOPRT prenominate
AEEIMNNORTU enumeration
mountaineer
AEEIMNNOSTT maisonnette
AEEIMNNPRTT intemperant
AEEIMNNSTTT instatement
AEEIMNOPRST impersonate
AEEIMNOPRSU Europeanism
AEEIMNOPRTU peritonaeum
AEEIMNORRST marine store
Rose Tremain
AEEIMNRRSTT tin-streamer
AEEIMNRSSST streaminess
AEEIMNRSTTV Steve Martin
AEEIMNRSTUV mensurative
AEEIMNSSSSV massiveness
AEEIMNSSSUV amusiveness
AEEIMOPRRST temporaries
AEEIMOPRRTV vaporimeter
AEEIMOPRSST Marie Stopes
AEEIMORRSTU temerarious
AEEIMQRSTTU marquisette
AEEIMSSSTTY systematise
AEEIMSSTTYZ systematize
AEEINNNOPRT perennation
AEEINNOORTX exoneration
AEEINNOPRSX re-expansion
AEEINNOPRTT penetration
AEEINNORSTV anteversion
AEEINNORSVV varsovienne
AEEINNORTTV eventration
AEEINNOTTUV eventuation
AEEINNOTTUX extenuation
AEEINNPPRTT appertinent
AEEINNQSSTU antiqueness
AEEINNTTTUV unattentive
AEEINOPRSTU Europeanist
AEEINOPRSTV personative
pet aversion
AEEINOPRTUV unoperative
AEEINOQSSSU Ossianesque
AEEINORRSST reassertion
AEEINORRSTV reservation
AEEINORTVXY over-anxiety
AEEINPRRSTT inter partes
AEEINPRSSST spessartine
AEEINPRSSTT Esperantist
AEEINPRSSTU septenarius
AEEINPRSSTV privateness
AEEINPSSSSV passiveness
AEEINRSSTUV unassertive
AEEINSSSSUV suasiveness
AEEIOOPPSSS aposiopeses
AEEIOPPRRTX expropriate
AEEIORRSTTV restorative
AEEIORSSTTX stereotaxis
AEEIPPRRSSU superpraise
AEEIPPRRTUW water purpie
AEEIPPRSSTU tissue paper
AEEIPRRSSTU pasteuriser
AEEIPRRSTTW water sprite
AEEIPRRSTUZ pasteurizer
AEEIPRSSSTT spessartite
AEEIPRSSTUZ trapeziuses
AEEJLLNRSSU Jane Russell
AEEJLLOSSTW Tessa Jowell
AEEJLNOSSSU jealousness
AEEJMMNOORS James Monroe
AEEJMNORSTY James Tyrone
AEEJMNORSUY Jane Seymour
AEEJNORRTUV rejuvenator
AEEKLLMOPSW mellowspeak
AEEKLLNORSW Ken Rosewall
AEEKLLORRST roller skate
roller-skate
AEEKLLPRSSW Kepler's laws
AEEKLMORRTW metalworker
AEEKLNORRST Lake Torrens
AEEKLOORRSY seal rookery

AEEKLORVXYY	Alexey Rykov
AEEKMMNORTY	money market
AEEKMMRSSTY	system-maker
AEEKMNORTWY	water monkey
AEEKMORRTTV	market overt
AEEKMORSTTT	staktometer
AEEKMPRRSTU	supermarket
AEEKNOPRRSY	nosey parker✧
AEEKNORSTVW	weaver's knot
AEEKNPRRSTU	supertanker
AEELLLLRVWY	all very well
AEELLLMOTWY	yellow metal
AEELLLMRSTT	small letter
AEELLLNPRSU	sal prunelle
AEELLLNPRTY	repellantly
AEELLLNSTTT	Tall Nettles
AEELLLORTWY	yellow alert
AEELLLRRSSU	Earl Russell
AEELLMMNOTU	emolumental
AEELLMMORWY	yellow-ammer
AEELLMNORTT	reallotment
AEELLMORRST	steam-roller
AEELLMPRSSU	pearl mussel
AEELLNORRTT	retrolental
AEELLNORSTW	stonewaller
AEELLNOSUVZ	allez-vous-en
AEELLNPRTVY	prevalently
AEELLNRSTWW	Western Wall
AEELLNSSSSW	lawlessness
AEELLOPRSTU	pastourelle
AEELLOPRTUV	pole-vaulter
AEELLPPRRUV	purple laver
AEELLPPRRUY	puerperally
AEELLPPRTUY	perpetually
AEELLPSSSUY	pauselessly
AEELLSSSTTY	tastelessly
AEELMMOOPPS	pampelmoose
AEELMMOPPSU	pampelmouse
AEELMMORSSU	Samuel Morse
AEELMNNORTT	Roman nettle
AEELMNNPRTY	permanently
AEELMNNRTUV	unravelment
AEELMNPRTTT	prattlement
AEELMNPSSTY	panel system
AEELMOORRSU	Olaus Roemer
AEELMOPRSSU	semelparous
AEELMOPRSTT	postal meter
AEELMOPRSTV	volt-amperes
AEELMOQRRSU	quarrelsome
AEELMPPSSUY	Samuel Pepys
AEELMPRRTUY	prematurely
AEELMPRSTTT	letter-stamp
AEELNNOOPST	on one's plate
AEELNNORTUZ	neutral zone
AEELNNPRTTY	repentantly
AEELNNRTTUW	water tunnel
AEELNNSSSSU	sensualness
AEELNOOSSWY	lose one's way
AEELNOPPRTT	rotten apple
AEELNOPRSSS	salesperson
AEELNOPRSST	prolateness
AEELNOPRTTU	outer planet
AEELNOSSSUZ	zealousness
AEELNPSSSSS	saplessness
AEELNRSSSST	artlessness
AEELNRSSSTV	servantless
AEELNSSTTUW	sweet sultan
AEELOOPSSUY	so please you
AEELOORSUVZ	over-zealous
AEELOPPPTVV	poppet-valve
AEELOPRRSTV	plaster over
AEELOPRRSTY	pearl oyster
AEELOPSTTUX	expostulate
AEELORRRSTV	resveratrol
AEELORRSTTT	telestrator
AEELORSSTTU	Lotus-eaters
AEELORSSTUU	Teleosaurus
AEELPPPTUVV	puppet-valve
AEELPPRRSTY	parsley pert
AEELPPRSSTU	russet apple
AEELPRRSSTU	raptureless
AEELPRRSTTU	perlustrate
AEELPRSSSTU	pastureless
AEEMMORRSTW	meteor swarm
AEEMNNOQRSU	Normanesque
AEEMNNORSTT	stone marten
AEEMNNRSSTV	men-servants
AEEMNOPRSTU	pentamerous
AEEMNOPRTVY	overpayment
AEEMNOQRTTU	Quantometer®
	quantometer
AEEMNORRRTU	remunerator
AEEMNORRSTT	remonstrate
AEEMNORSSTT	easternmost
AEEMNORTTYY	treaty money
AEEMNPRRSST	present arms
AEEMNRSSTTT	stentmaster
AEEMOPRRTXY	extemporary
AEEMORRSTTU	tetramerous
AEEMRRSSTTT	streetsmart
AEEMRSSSSTY	seamstressy
AEENNNPRTTU	unrepentant
AEENNOPPRST	parpen-stone
AEENNOPRRTU	neuropteran
AEENNORSSST	sarsen-stone
AEENOOPRSSU	aponeuroses
AEENOOSSTTT	to one's taste
AEENOPPRSUW	superweapon
AEENOPRRSTT	paternoster✧
AEENOPSTTVX	Steve Paxton
AEENOQRRTTU	quarter note
	quarter-tone
AEENORTTUXY	extenuatory
AEENPRRSSTT	serpent-star
AEENPRRSTUU	supernature
AEENPRSSTUW	pastures new
AEENPRSTTTT	test pattern
AEENQRSSTTU	sequestrant
AEENRRSSTTU	Saturn's tree
AEENRRTTUVY	at every turn
AEEOOPSTTTW	sweet potato
AEEOPPRRRTT	perpetrator

	prêt-à-porter
AEEOPPRRTTU	perpetuator
AEEOPRRRSTW	tree sparrow
AEEOQRRSTUU	terraqueous
AEEORRRSTVY	reservatory
AEEPRSSTTWY	sweet pastry
AEERSSTTTTU	trust estate
AEFFFFILOST	staff of life
AEFFFFTTTUY	tufftaffety
AEFFGHIINNT	infangthief
AEFFGHILRTU	fire-flaught
AEFFGHNOOTW	off the wagon
AEFFGIILNRT	lift a finger
AEFFGIMSTUU	suffumigate
AEFFHHILTTU	the faithful✧
AEFFHILORST	off the rails
AEFFHILORTU	rule of faith
AEFFHILRSTY	sheriffalty
AEFFHINRSSS	raffishness
AEFFHLNORSZ	flash-frozen
AEFFIIKLNRU	ruffianlike
AEFFIIMNORR	foraminifer
AEFFIORSTUU	fatuous fire
AEFFKLMORRS	Reform flask
AEFFKNRRRTU	frankfurter
AEFFLLNRUUY	unfearfully
AEFFLLORSUY	full of years
AEFFLOOSSTT	Feast of Lots
AEFFMSSSTTY	staff-system
AEFFNOOOSST	off one's oats
AEFGGHIIMNS	game fishing
AEFGGHILOPS	Phileas Fogg
AEFGGHIRSTT	stage fright
AEFGGIINOTV	not give a fig
AEFGGILNORU	a long figure
AEFGGILNRSS	fingerglass
AEFGGINRRSS	finger-grass
AEFGHHLORTU	leaf through
AEFGHHLOSTW	show the flag
AEFGHHORRTU	throughfare
AEFGHIILNSS	seal-fishing
AEFGHILLORT	fothergilla
AEFGHILMNRS	self-harming
AEFGHILSTTY	safety light
AEFGHLOPRXY	flexography
AEFGHOPRRRY	ferrography
AEFGHORRTTW	aftergrowth
AEFGHORRTUV	overfraught
AEFGHORSTTU	sought after
AEFGIIINRRS	fire-raising
AEFGIIKLNRW	fire-walking
AEFGIILNRSS	self-raising
AEFGIINNPRT	finger-paint
AEFGIJRRRSZ	Sir J G Frazer
AEFGIKLLLNW	fell-walking
AEFGIKLNNRW	walking fern
AEFGIKLNNSY	flying snake
AEFGILLMORU	Glumiflorae
AEFGILLNRST	fingerstall
AEFGILLNRTY	falteringly
AEFGILLOSTY	galley-foist
AEFGILNNOOR	gonfalonier
AEFGILNNRTU	unfaltering
AEFGILNNSSU	gainfulness
AEFGILNORSU	soul-fearing
AEFGILNOSTU	glufosinate
AEFGILNPPST	self-tapping
AEFGILNPRSU	Persian Gulf
AEFGINNNSSW	fawningness
AEFGINNORRW	forewarning
AEFGINORRSU	graniferous
AEFGINORSUU	guaniferous
AEFGINRRSTU	transfigure
AEFGIRRSSTU	sugar sifter
AEFGLLOOPRY	galley proof
AEFGLMNRRSU	farmer's lung
AEFHHIIRSTT	hatti-sherif
AEFHHLLLTUY	healthfully
AEFHHLLNTUU	unhealthful
AEFHIILMNPS	lifemanship
AEFHIINORTV	have it in for
AEFHIIRRSTW	White Friars
AEFHIKLNNRT	The Franklin
AEFHILLMRSS	slasher film
AEFHILLSSTY	faithlessly
AEFHILNNRST	lantern fish
AEFHIMNOPRS	HMS Pinafore
AEFHIMNORSW	fisherwoman
AEFHJNOPRSZ	Franz Joseph
AEFHKMNRSTY	Frank Smythe
AEFHKOORTTU	out of the Ark
AEFHLLOOPTY	play the fool
AEFHLMMORSY	flash memory
AEFHLMNRSSU	harmfulness
AEFHMORRSTT	farthermost
AEFHOOTTUWY	out of the way
	out-of-the-way
AEFIIKLNNRT	franklinite
AEFIILLNNOX	inflexional
AEFIILLNNTU	influential
AEFIILLNQUY	equifinally
AEFIILLOSSY	Isle of Islay
AEFIILNNORT	reinflation
AEFIILNNRTY	infernality
AEFIILNNTUY	life annuity
AEFIILNOOTX	exfoliation
AEFIILOPRRW	prairie fowl
	prairie wolf
AEFIIMNORTV	informative
AEFIINNOSTT	festination
	infestation
	sinfonietta
AEFIINNOSTV	Five Nations
AEFIINNRSTT	transfinite
AEFIINORSTT	fire station
AEFIKLRSTTU	strike fault
AEFIKMOORTW	a work of time
AEFIKOPRRTT	profit-taker
AEFILLLMMOR	lamelliform
AEFILLLMORS	Ormeli Falls
AEFILLMOPRT	patelliform
AEFILLNOORS	saloon rifle

AEFILLNORSW snail flower
AEFILLNRTTU intreatfull
AEFILLRRTTU ultrafilter
AEFILMNOSTU filamentous
AEFILMOPRTY play for time
AEFILMORRSU formularise
AEFILMORRUZ formularize
AEFILMPRSUY superfamily
AEFILNNPSSU painfulness
AEFILNOOPST point of sale
point-of-sale
AEFILNORSTW satin flower
AEFILNORSUY nefariously
AEFILOOPSTY play footsie
AEFILOPPSTV pop festival
AEFILOPRRTY prefatorily
AEFILOPRSSS press of sail
AEFILORSSTW fossil water
AEFILORSTTY foley artist
AEFIMMMORSU mammiferous
AEFIMNNNORT antenniform
AEFIMNNNRTY infantrymen
AEFIMNNOOTT fomentation
AEFIMNNORSU manniferous
AEFIMNOORRT reformation✧
re-formation
AEFIMOPRRTZ trapeziform
AEFINNNOPTU fountain pen
AEFINNRRRST transferrin
AEFINOOPRRT perforation
AEFINOOPRST pianofortes
AEFINOORSTT forestation
AEFINORSSWW sinews of war
AEFINORTUUV unfavourite
AEFINRSSTUV transfusive
AEFIOOPRSTW Tower of Pisa
AEFIOPPRSST pair of steps
AEFJMMNOORY money for jam
AEFKLLOORRW floorwalker
AEFKLLORSTW flower-stalk
AEFKNNORRRT front-ranker
AEFLLLNTTUY flatulently
AEFLLLOPRUW all-powerful
AEFLLLSSTUY faultlessly
AEFLLMRSTUY masterfully
AEFLLNPSSUY playfulness
AEFLLOOPRVY play for love
AEFLLORSSUV flavourless
AEFLLPRRUYY prayerfully
AEFLLRSTUWY wasterfully
AEFLMOORSUV flavoursome
AEFLNOOPSTU teaspoonful
AEFLNORTTUY fortunately
AEFLORRSTWW straw flower
strawflower
AEFMNORRRST transformer
AEFMNORRRTY ternary form
AEFMOOPPRRT tamper-proof
AEFMOOPRSTT foretopmast
AEFMOORRRTY reformatory
AEFNNORSTTU fast neutron
AEFNNORTTUU unfortunate
AEFNOOOSSTU out of season
AEFNOSSSTUU fatuousness
AEFORRRSSTT for starters
AEGGGNORSTU go great guns
AEGGHHIKNNS Genghis Khan
AEGGHHILOTV high-voltage
AEGGHIILNNT nightingale
AEGGHIILNSX Alex Higgins
AEGGHIIMMST Maggie Smith
AEGGHIINNRT ingathering✧
AEGGHIIRRRT hair trigger
hair-trigger
AEGGHIMNOSU gaming house
AEGGHINOOPT photo-ageing
AEGGHINSSSW waggishness
AEGGHIRSSTT stage rights
AEGGHKLNRSU Enghalskrug
AEGGHLOOPRR logographer
AEGGHMNORST Gormenghast
AEGGHMNORTU Grangemouth
AEGGHNNOOWY honey-waggon
AEGGIIKMNTT Mike Gatting
AEGGIIKNSST kissing gate
AEGGIILMPRR pilgrimager
AEGGIINRTTU ingurgitate
AEGGIJNNORS Jane Grigson
AEGGILMORTU Miguel Torga
AEGGILNNOPR ranging pole
AEGGILNNORW longwearing
AEGGILNNRSS glaringness
AEGGIMNOOTY geitonogamy
AEGGIMNORRW worm gearing
AEGGIMNRSST gangsterism
AEGGINNNRRU running gear
AEGGINORRVZ overgrazing
AEGGINORRZZ zero-grazing
AEGGINPRRSU spur gearing
AEGGINPSTUY paying guest
AEGGINRRTTU regurgitant
AEGGLNNOOST loggan-stone
AEGGLOORRST gastrologer
AEGGNRRSSTU Günter Grass
AEGHHIILLMT all-time high
AEGHHILMRTU Hugh Latimer
AEGHHILMTTY the Almighty
AEGHHILOPRY heliography
AEGHHINNOTV have nothing
AEGHHINORST high treason
AEGHHINORTV have no right
AEGHHINSSTU haughtiness
AEGHHIOPRRY hierography
AEGHHKOTTTU take thought
AEGHHLLOPUW Hugh Walpole
AEGHHLOPRSU ploughshare
AEGHHMOPRRT thermograph
AEGHHNOPRTY ethnography
AEGHHOOPRRR horographer
AEGHHOOPSTU theophagous
AEGHHOPRTYY hyetography
AEGHHORRTUW wear through

AEGHHOTTUVW thought wave
AEGHIIIJJNS Jiang Jieshi
AEGHIIKMNNT in the making
AEGHIILNNSW washing line
AEGHIIMNRST time-sharing
AEGHIINPSTT spaghettini
AEGHIINPTTY tithe-paying
AEGHIINRTTT night-attire
AEGHIINRTTW weight-train
AEGHIIPPRST epigraphist
AEGHIJMNPRU jumping hare
AEGHIJRSTTT straight-jet
AEGHIKLNRTW night-walker
AEGHIKNOOPR reaping-hook
AEGHIKNOPRT kinetograph
AEGHIKNRSTV thanksgiver
AEGHILLMPRT lamplighter
AEGHILLMSTW might as well
AEGHILLNNRT enthralling
AEGHILMNOPR Germanophil
AEGHILMOPSU meliphagous
AEGHILNOOST anthologise
AEGHILNOOTZ anthologize
AEGHILNOPSV leaving-shop
AEGHILNOTTU glutathione
AEGHILNSSST ghastliness
AEGHILPRSTY sight-player
AEGHIMMOPRR mimographer
AEGHIMNNRST garnishment
AEGHIMNORTV earthmoving
AEGHIMNRSTX German sixth
AEGHIMOPRSS seismograph
AEGHINNOSST night-season
AEGHINNRTTT tenant right
AEGHINNSSTU naughtiness
AEGHINNSTTU hunting-seat
AEGHINORSUW warehousing
AEGHINOSSST goatishness
AEGHINPRSTW spring wheat
AEGHINPRSTX Great Sphinx
AEGHINPRTTT patent right
AEGHINRRSTT heart-string
AEGHIRSTTWW strawweight
AEGHLLOOTTW go to the wall
AEGHLNOOORR gonorrhoeal
AEGHLNOOPTY pantheology
AEGHLOOPRSY phraseology
AEGHLOPPRYY pyelography
AEGHLOPRRXY xylographer
AEGHMMPRSUY Murphy's game
AEGHMNNORRY Henry Morgan
AEGHMNOOPRR monographer
nomographer
AEGHMNOOPTY entomophagy
AEGHMOOPRRT ergatomorph
AEGHMOPRSUY hypergamous
AEGHNOOPRRS nosographer
sonographer
AEGHNOOPSTU pathogenous
AEGHNOPRSTY stenography
AEGHNOPSTUY heptagynous
AEGHNORSTTU hart's tongue
AEGHNORSTTW strong wheat
AEGHNOSTTTU set at nought
AEGHOOPPRRT topographer
AEGHOOPRSTY osteography
ostreophagy
AEGHOORSTTW go to the wars
AEGHOPPRRRY reprography
AEGHOPPRRSS grasshopper
AEGHOPPRRTY petrography
typographer
AEGHRSSTTTU thrust stage
AEGIIIKLNRV Like a Virgin
AEGIIILLNTT gentilitial
AEGIIILMNPR primigenial
AEGIIILNNTT gentilitian
AEGIIILNORS seigniorial
AEGIIIMNPRT pairing-time
AEGIIINORTV originative
AEGIIINSTTV instigative
AEGIIKLLNRT giant-killer
AEGIIKLNSST glaikitness
AEGIIKNRSTW water-skiing
AEGIILLMMMR milligramme
AEGIILLNOST legislation
AEGIILLNTVY genitivally
AEGIILMNOPR primogenial
AEGIILMNORS regionalism
AEGIILMNTUV lignum vitae
AEGIILMNVVX mixing valve
AEGIILMOSST legatissimo
AEGIILNNRTU interlingua✧
AEGIILNORRY religionary
AEGIILNORST regionalist
AEGIILNRRSV silver-grain
AEGIILNRSSU singularise
AEGIILNRSUZ singularize
AEGIILNRTTY integrality
AEGIIMMMNUW minimum wage
AEGIIMMNNOS meningiomas
AEGIIMMORRR mirror image
AEGIIMMRSTU magisterium
AEGIIMNNNRU unremaining
AEGIIMNNORT germination
AEGIIMNNORV Merovingian
AEGIIMNNPRS spring a mine
AEGIIMNNRST instreaming
AEGIIMNOPRT impignorate
AEGIIMNORRT remigration
AEGIIMPRSTU epigastrium
AEGIINNNORT Ignorantine
AEGIINNNOST angiotensin
AEGIINNOOTT negotiation
AEGIINNORRS searing-iron
AEGIINNORST eating irons
resignation
AEGIINNORTT integration
AEGIINNORTU unoriginate
AEGIINNOSTT negationist
AEGIINNPRST sign-painter
AEGIINNRRST restraining

AEGIINNRTTU intriguante
AEGIINNSTTW wine tasting
AEGIINORTTX negotiatrix
AEGIINPPRTW wiretapping
AEGIINRRTVX extra virgin
extra-virgin
AEGIINRSSTW waitressing
AEGIJLMTTUU multijugate
AEGIJMNORTT majoretting
AEGIJNNNPST Pat Jennings
AEGIKLLNNST stalling-ken
AEGIKLMNOSS smoke signal
AEGIKLNOPRW rope-walking
AEGIKLNQSUY squeakingly
AEGIKMMNNOY moneymaking
AEGIKMMNRRY merrymaking
AEGIKNPRSTU purse-taking
AEGILLMMNRT trammelling
AEGILLMNNTY lamentingly
AEGILLMOOPS megalopolis
AEGILLMPRSU aspergillum✧
AEGILLMRSST millet-grass
AEGILLNNOPR pollen grain
AEGILLNNOSW Nigel Lawson
AEGILLNNRUV unravelling
AEGILLNOPRY role-playing
AEGILLNQRRU quarrelling
AEGILLNRSVY slaveringly
AEGILLOPRSW gallows-ripe
AEGILLOPSTV post village
AEGILLOSSTT toilet glass
AEGILLPRSSU Aspergillus
AEGILLRRRUY irregularly
AEGILMMNOTU gemmulation
AEGILMNNNUY unmeaningly
AEGILMNNOPS plasminogen
AEGILMNOORT glomeration
AEGILMNOPRU pelargonium
AEGILMNORST gila monster
AEGILMNOSTU ligamentous
AEGILMNRSTY streamingly
AEGILMNSSTU minute-glass
AEGILMOOPST plagiostome
AEGILMOOSSY semasiology
AEGILNNOSTU langoustine
AEGILNNPRTY trying plane
AEGILNNRSTV navel-string
AEGILNNSSST lastingness
AEGILNNSSTY assentingly
AEGILNOOPRS sporangiole
AEGILNOOSSX xenoglossia
AEGILNORSST Interglossa
AEGILNORSTU rogues' Latin
AEGILNOSTTU lotus-eating
AEGILNQRUVY quaveringly
AEGILNRRSTV servant-girl
AEGILNRRSTY arrestingly
AEGILNRSUUV unvulgarise
AEGILNRTTYY yatteringly
AEGILNRUUVZ unvulgarize
AEGILOOSTTU tautologise
AEGILOOTTUZ tautologize
AEGILPRTUVY purgatively
AEGILRSTTUU gutturalise
AEGILRTTUUZ gutturalize
AEGIMMMNORX maxim-monger
AEGIMMOPRSU gemmiparous
AEGIMNNNRTU running mate
AEGIMNOOPRS spermogonia
AEGIMNOPRRS Piers Morgan
AEGIMNORSSU ignoramuses
AEGINNNOPRS none-sparing
AEGINNNORSU unreasoning
AEGINNNPRRS ring spanner
AEGINNNPRTT pennant grit
AEGINNOOTXY oxygenation
AEGINNOPRST personating
AEGINNOPSST passing note
passing tone
AEGINNOPSTV paving-stone
AEGINNOPTUX expugnation
AEGINNORRTT interrogant
AEGINNOSSUU sanguineous
AEGINNPRSSS sparingness
AEGINOOPPRT oppignorate
AEGINOPRTTV vintage port
AEGINOPRTTW watering pot
AEGINOPRTUX expurgation
AEGINOPSTTV post-vintage
AEGINOQSTTU question tag
tag question
AEGINPRRSTW springwater
water spring
AEGINPRSSST trespassing
AEGINPRSTTY tapestrying
AEGINRRSTUV invert sugar
AEGINRSSTVW wring staves
AEGINRSTTVY travestying
AEGINSSTTUU St Augustine
AEGIPRRRTYY pyrargyrite
AEGIPRRSSSV viper's grass
AEGIRRRSTTU arris gutter
AEGKLORRSSW glassworker
AEGKMNORSSY monkey-grass
AEGLLNOOPTY planetology
AEGLLNOSSSW gallowsness
AEGLLOPRUYZ zygopleural
AEGLMNNOOTU Léon Gaumont
AEGLMNOORSW sea longworm
AEGLNNOOOTY neonatology
AEGLNNOTTUU notungulate
AEGLNNPRTUY repugnantly
AEGLNOOPRTT potter along
AEGMNOOOPTT potamogeton
AEGMNOORRST gastronomer
AEGNNNPRTUU unrepugnant
AEGNNOPSTUY pentagynous
AEGNNORRSTY röntgen rays
AEGNOOPRSSU saprogenous
AEGNOOPRSSY greasy spoon
AEGNOORSTTU tetragonous
AEGNORSTTUY tetragynous

AEGOORRRSST grass-rooter
AEGOORRRTUV rotogravure
AEGOORSTTWW grow to waste
AEGOPRRRUVY pyrogravure
AEGOPRRTUXY expurgatory
AEGORSSSTUU stegosaurus✧
AEHHHNOORRY Hoorah Henry
AEHHIILRTTT hit the trail
AEHHIIMPSSS Messiahship
AEHHIKMMSSY shimmy-shake
AEHHIKNSSSW hawkishness
AEHHILLNTUY unhealthily
AEHHILOPSTY lithophysae
AEHHIMMMRST Hammersmith
AEHHIMOPRTY hypothermia
AEHHIMRSTVY Harvey Smith
AEHHINNOPTY hyphenation
AEHHINOORRR rhinorrhoea
AEHHINOPRST on the parish
AEHHIOPPSST phosphatise
AEHHIOPPSTZ phosphatize
AEHHIOPRSST ship the oars
AEHHIORTTTW whitethroat
AEHHIOTUVWY have with you
AEHHLLOPTTY thallophyte
AEHHLLOSSTW the shallows
AEHHLMMOORT homothermal
AEHHLMOPRTY hypothermal
AEHHLOOPRTX axerophthol
AEHHLOPPSYY hypophyseal
AEHHMMORRTW hammer throw
AEHHMOOOPTY homoeopathy
AEHHMOOPRRT Theromorpha
AEHHMORSTWY shameworthy
AEHHNNOOPTY Anthony Hope
AEHHNOORRYY Hooray Henry
AEHHNOPPRTY nephropathy
AEHHNOPRRTY tenorrhaphy
AEHHNOPRTTY theanthropy
AEHHOOPPRST phosphorate
AEHHRRSTTUW water thrush
AEHIIILMTUV humiliative
AEHIIILRSST Israelitish
AEHIIKLLNTT in at the kill
AEHIIKMRSTT Mekhitarist
AEHIIKNPSTY kinesipathy
AEHIILLOPRU ailurophile
AEHIILLPSTT philatelist
AEHIILNPSTW White Plains
AEHIILOPRRT horripilate
retrophilia
AEHIILOPSST hospitalise
AEHIILOPSTZ hospitalize
AEHIILPRSTT peristalith
AEHIIMMRSTY Mare Smythii
AEHIIMNNORY Hieronymian
AEHIIMNRSTT martinetish
AEHIIMPPRST primateship
AEHIIMRSTUV Sivatherium
AEHIINOPRRS parishioner
AEHIINORTTT trithionate
AEHIIPPRRSS periphrasis
AEHIJLMNOST James Hilton
AEHIJLNOSST John a-Stiles
AEHIKLMRSUW lukewarmish
AEHIKMNNORT inkhorn-mate
AEHIKMNSSSW mawkishness
AEHIKMORSTY make history
AEHIKNNPPRT Pink Panther
AEHIKNNSSSS snakishness
AEHIKNNSSSV knavishness
AEHILLMTTUU ultima Thule
AEHILLNNSTU in a nutshell
AEHILLNOSST loathliness
AEHILLOPPTY apophyllite
AEHILLOPRST hospitaller
AEHILLPRSTU hill-pasture
AEHILLQSTUW white squall
AEHILMMOPPS psammophile
AEHILMNOPPY Polyphemian
AEHILMNORTW mother-in-law
AEHILMNOTTY methylation
AEHILMNPSSY misshapenly
AEHILMNRSTU Lutheranism
AEHILMQSSUY squeamishly
AEHILNOOPRS Sophia Loren
AEHILNOORST North Sea oil
AEHILNOPTXY phytoalexin
AEHILNORSST shorten sail
AEHILNOSTTW West Lothian
AEHILNPRRTY platyrrhine
AEHILNPRSST shinplaster
AEHILNSSSST saltishness
AEHILNSSSSV slavishness
AEHILOOPPRR plerophoria
AEHILOPPSST apostleship
AEHILOPRSTY physiolater
AEHILORRTTY theriolatry
AEHILORSTVY overhastily
AEHILORTTVY hortatively
AEHILPRSTWY whist-player
AEHILRSSTTT star thistle
AEHIMMNNNRY ninny-hammer
AEHIMNNNSSS mannishness
AEHIMNOOPPR apomorphine
AEHIMNOOPSS Homo sapiens
AEHIMNOPRST misanthrope
AEHIMNOPRSY hypersomnia
AEHIMNORSTU house martin
AEHIMOOSSST homeostasis
AEHIMOPRSTT metaphorist
AEHIMOPSSTY haemoptysis
AEHIMORSTTX thermotaxis
AEHIMPPRSTU hippeastrum
AEHIMPQSTUY sympathique
AEHIMPRSSTY sympathiser
AEHIMPRSTYZ sympathizer
AEHINNPPSSU unhappiness
AEHINNSSSTY synanthesis
AEHINOOPRST share option
AEHINOORSTT anorthosite
AEHINOORTTX exhortation

AEHINOPRSST senatorship
AEHINOPRSTT antistrophe
AEHINOPSSTT stephanotis
AEHINORRRSX Rex Harrison
AEHINORRSST enarthrosis
AEHINORSSTT throatiness
AEHINPPRRST partnership
transhipper
AEHINPRSSTV servantship
AEHINPSSSSW waspishness
AEHINQSSSSU squashiness
AEHINRSSSTW swarthiness
AEHIOOPRRTT Prototheria
AEHIOPPRRST praetorship
AEHIOPSSSTY hypostasise
AEHIOPSSTTY hypostatise
AEHIOPSSTYZ hypostasize
AEHIOPSTTYZ hypostatize
AEHIORSTVWY variety show
AEHIPPPRSSS ship's papers
AEHJJNOPRSS Jasper Johns
AEHJLNOSSTY John a-Styles
AEHJMNNNORS John Manners
AEHJMNNOOST John Smeaton
AEHJNOORRST Trojan horse
AEHKLLNSSTY thanklessly
AEHKLOOPRTT look the part
AEHKMMORRST mother's mark
AEHKMNOOSST smooth snake
AEHKMOPRTTU up to the mark
AEHKNOORRTY arrhenotoky
AEHKOORRSTT heart-strook
AEHKOPRSTTU take up short
AEHLLLMOOPR allelomorph
AEHLLLOOSWW swallow hole
AEHLLMOOSTY loathsomely
AEHLLMORRSY Larry Holmes
AEHLLNOSSSW shallowness
AEHLLOPRRST shell parrot
AEHLMNOQSSU lemon squash
AEHLMOPPRRY lamprophyre
AEHLNNOOPTT pantothenol
AEHLNOPSTTY penalty shot
AEHLNORRTUY lunar theory
AEHLNPRSTTU thrust plane
AEHLOPRSSTT short-staple
AEHLOPRTUUX Paul Theroux
AEHMMMORRUU Mare Humorum
AEHMMOOOPRT ommatophore
AEHMMOOORST Thomas Moore
AEHMMOPPSTY psammophyte
AEHMMRRRTUU heart murmur
AEHMNNOOPRY open harmony
AEHMNOORRSS harness-room
AEHMNOORSTV harvest moon
AEHMNOPPTTU put on the map
AEHMNOPRTTU put the arm on
AEHMNORSTTY thermonasty
AEHMOORRTTW to the marrow
AEHMORRSTTY Terry-Thomas
AEHNNOORSST Sharon Stone
AEHNNRRTUWY Arthur Wynne
AEHNOOPRRTT orthopteran
AEHNOOPRSST snapshooter
AEHNOOPRSTU Eoanthropus
AEHNOOPRSWW whooper swan
AEHNOORSSUY honours easy
AEHNOOTTUWY on the way out
AEHNOPPRSTT pattern-shop
AEHNOPPRTTY tryptophane
AEHNORSTUWY unseaworthy
AEHNPRRUXYY Eurypharynx
AEHOOPPQRTU quota-hopper
AEHOOPRRRST arthrospore
AEHOOPRRSTT trapshooter
AEHOOPRRSTX prothoraxes
AEHOORRTTXY exhortatory
AEHOPRRRTTY Harry Potter
AEHOPRRSTTT strep throat
AEHOQRRRTUU quarter hour
AEIIILLMNOR millionaire
AEIIILLMNST sillimanite
AEIIILLTTTV titillative
AEIIILMMPRS imperialism
AEIIILMNNOT elimination
AEIIILMNRST ministerial
AEIIILMPRST imperialist
AEIIILMPRTY imperiality
AEIIILMRRSV verisimilar
AEIIILMTTVY imitatively
AEIIILNNNRT nitraniline
AEIIILNPRST plein-airist
AEIIIMNNRST artemisinin
AEIIIMNNRTU in miniature
AEIIIMNORRT minoritaire
AEIIIMNOSTT itemisation
AEIIIMNOTTZ itemization
AEIIIMNRSTU miniaturise
AEIIIMNRTUZ miniaturize
AEIIINNORTT itineration
AEIIINNSTUV insinuative
AEIIINPRSTV inspirative
AEIIINQSTTU antiquities
AEIIKLLMNTW William Kent
AEIIKLLOPRT realpolitik
AEIIKLMNPRS marlinspike
AEIIKLNNRRT Link trainer
AEIIKLOSTUY As You Like It
AEIIKNOSSTU autokinesis
AEIIKNRRSTV River Kistna
AEIILLLLMTW William Tell
AEIILLLMNTU multilineal
AEIILLMMNNR man-milliner
AEIILLMMNRS millenarism
AEIILLMNNPW William Penn
AEIILLMNRTU multilinear
AEIILLMRRTU mitrailleur
AEIILLMRSTU multiserial
AEIILLMRSWX Rex Williams
AEIILLMSTTU satellitium
AEIILLNNRTY triennially
AEIILLNOPST pillion-seat

AEIILLNOSTX	lex talionis
AEIILLNOTVX	vexillation
AEIILLNOTVY	inviolately
AEIILLNPRTY	reptilianly
AEIILLNPTVY	plaintively
AEIILLNRSTV	Silver Latin
AEIILLNRSUY	uniserially
AEIILLNTUUX	luxulianite
AEIILLOORTV	alto-rilievo
AEIILLPRRSU	pluriserial
AEIILLRRSTT	artillerist
AEIILMMORST	immortalise
	memorialist
AEIILMMORTZ	immortalize
AEIILMNNOPS	Minneapolis
AEIILMNOORT	melioration
AEIILMNORST	misrelation
	Orientalism
	relationism
AEIILMNORTY	eliminatory
AEIILMNOSTT	testimonial
AEIILMNOSTV	love-in-a-mist
	neovitalism
AEIILMNPRRY	preliminary
AEIILMNPTTY	impatiently
AEIILMNRTTY	amyl nitrite
AEIILMOPRST	peristomial
AEIILMPRSTU	Laserpitium
AEIILMPSSVY	impassively
AEIILMQTTUY	quality time
AEIILMRRSTT	trimestrial
AEIILMRRSTY	literaryism
AEIILMSTTUV	stimulative
AEIILNNNOST	intensional
AEIILNNNOTT	intentional
AEIILNNORST	insertional
AEIILNNORTV	inventorial
AEIILNNOTTV	ventilation
AEIILNNPRST	interspinal
AEIILNNRSTT	transilient
AEIILNNRTTY	internality
	itinerantly
AEIILNNSSST	saintliness
AEIILNOOPSZ	apiezon oils
AEIILNOPRSV	previsional
AEIILNOPSTX	post-exilian
AEIILNORSSS	insessorial
AEIILNORSTT	Orientalist
	relationist
AEIILNORTTU	elutriation
AEIILNORTTY	orientality
AEIILNOSSUV	visual noise
AEIILNOSTTV	neovitalist
AEIILNPPRZZ	Lippizzaner
AEIILNPRSST	spinsterial
AEIILNQRTUZ	tranquilize
AEIILNRSSTV	silvestrian
	trivialness
AEIILNRSSTW	sister-in-law
AEIILORRRTT	territorial✧
AEIILORRSTV	servitorial
AEIILORSTTU	lateritious
AEIILPRSSST	peristalsis
AEIILPRTTVY	partitively
AEIILPRTVVY	privatively
AEIILRSTTVY	versatility
AEIILTTTUVY	attuitively
AEIIMMMNNST	immanentism
AEIIMMNNSSW	Weismannism
AEIIMMNNSTT	immanentist
AEIIMMNRSTT	martinetism
AEIIMMRRTTU	termitarium
AEIIMNNOPTT	omnipatient
AEIIMNNORST	inseminator
	nitrosamine
AEIIMNNORTT	termination
AEIIMNNORTV	vermination
AEIIMNOPRTT	impetration
AEIIMNPRRSS	primariness
AEIIMOPPRRT	impropriate
AEIIMOPRRSS	impresarios
AEIIMOPRSTV	improvisate
AEIIMRRTTUV	triumvirate
AEIINNNORST	Tironensian
AEIINNNORTV	innervation
AEIINNNOSVV	non-invasive
AEIINNNOTTT	inattention
AEIINNNQQUU	quinquennia
AEIINNOORTT	orientation
AEIINNOQRTU	enquiration
AEIINNORSST	ens rationis
AEIINNORSTT	reinstation
AEIINNPRSST	spinsterian
AEIINNRSSUV	Russian vine
AEIINOPPRTT	Point-a-Pitre
AEIINOPPSTT	peptisation
AEIINOPPTTZ	peptization
AEIINOPRRST	Airstrip One
	respiration
	retinispora
AEIINOPRRTT	partitioner
	repartition
AEIINOPRRTU	proteinuria
AEIINOPRSTU	utopianiser
AEIINOPRTTX	extirpation
AEIINOPRTTY	petitionary
AEIINOPRTUZ	utopianizer
AEIINORRSVY	revisionary
AEIINORRTTY	anteriority
AEIINPPRSTT	Trappistine
AEIINPRSSSU	Prussianise
AEIINPRSSUZ	Prussianize
AEIINPSTVXY	expansivity
AEIINSSTTUV	antitussive
AEIIOOPPSSS	aposiopesis
AEIIOOPRRST	a posteriori
AEIIOPRRTTY	iteroparity
AEIIORRSVVV	savoir-vivre
AEIIPRRSTTW	water spirit
AEIJJKNNPRU	Jan Purkinje
AEIJLNNPSSU	Juan-les-Pins
AEIJMNNNPTY	Jenny Pitman

AEIJMNNOORS Marion Jones
AEIJMNORSTT master-joint
AEIJMOSSSTT James Tissot
AEIJNNNOTTT joint tenant
AEIKKLMNORW workmanlike
AEIKLLRSTTW stilt-walker
AEIKLMORRVY River Kolyma
AEIKLMORSTW sea milkwort
sea-milkwort
AEIKLMPRRSU Muriel Spark
AEIKLNNOPPS plain-spoken
AEIKLNNSTTY skinny latte
AEIKLNOOSWY Wole Soyinka
AEIKLNOPSTT kinetoplast
AEIKMNNPRTU turnpike man
AEIKNOOTTTU take it out on
AEILLMNNSTT installment
AEILLMNOORW mineral wool
AEILLMNOOTY emotionally
AEILLMNOPRT Tempranillo
AEILLMNOTTW little woman
AEILLMNRTUV intervallum
AEILLMNTTUV multivalent
AEILLMOOSTT tomatilloes
AEILLMPRSST spill-stream
AEILLNNOOTV non-volatile
AEILLNNOPRT Anton Piller
AEILLNNOSTY tensionally
AEILLNOOTUV evolutional
AEILLNOPRRT paint roller
AEILLNOPTTY potentially
AEILLNORSSY sensorially
AEILLNOSSSY sessionally
silly season
AEILLNPSTTT patent still
AEILLNRSTUV surveillant
AEILLNRSUVY universally
AEILLNSSSTY stainlessly
AEILLNSSTTY taintlessly
AEILLNSUUXY unisexually
AEILLNTUUXY luxulyanite
AEILLORTTUV ultraviolet
AEILMMMSSTY symmetalism
AEILMMNORTY momentarily
AEILMMSTUYZ Mesut Yilmaz
AEILMNNNSSU unmanliness
AEILMNNOOPS Napoleonism
AEILMNNOOTU unemotional
AEILMNNOPRT minor planet
AEILMNNOSSW womanliness
AEILMNNRTTU nutrimental
AEILMNOORRT linear motor
AEILMNOOSTT molestation
AEILMNOOSTY Alison Moyet
AEILMNOPPRY propylamine
AEILMNOPRRT trampoliner
AEILMNOPRSS personalism
AEILMNORSTT Simon Rattle
AEILMNORTVY normatively
AEILMNOSSSU Susie Salmon
AEILMNPPRSU paper-muslin
AEILMNRSTWY Martyn Lewis
AEILMNTTUWZ Minute Waltz
AEILMOPRRSU leprosarium
AEILMOPRRTY polarimetry
temporarily
AEILMOPRTTY temporality
AEILMOPRTXY proximately
AEILMOQSTTU milquetoast✧
AEILMORRSVY Oliver's Army
AEILMPPRSTU litmus paper
AEILMRTTTWY Walter Mitty
AEILNNOPRSU unipersonal
AEILNNOPSST plainstones
AEILNNORSTY royal tennis
AEILNNORTUV vulneration
AEILNNRRTUY interlunary
AEILNNRSTTY transiently
AEILNNRSTUY saturninely
AEILNOOPRTX exploration
AEILNOPPRST epiplastron
AEILNOPPRUV prevail upon
AEILNOPPTTY platinotype✧
AEILNOPRRST tripersonal
AEILNOPRSST personalist
AEILNOPRSTY personality
AEILNOPRTUV pulveration
AEILNOPSSSS passionless
AEILNORRSTU serrulation
AEILNORTTVY ventilatory
AEILNOTTUVV voluntative
AEILNRSSTVY sylvestrian
AEILOOPRRRT reportorial
AEILOORRTTV Il Trovatore
AEILOPPPRST spoilt paper
AEILOPPRRSU populariser
AEILOPPRRUZ popularizer
AEILOPRSTTU tripetalous
AEILOPRSTTW water pistol
AEILOSTUVXY vexatiously
AEILRSSSTUV Lévi-Strauss
AEIMMNPPRSS panspermism
AEIMMNPRRTU trump marine
AEIMMNRSSSU summariness
AEIMMOPSTTU impostumate
AEIMMORSTTU tautomerism
AEIMMPRSSTU suprematism✧
AEIMMSSSTTY systematism
AEIMNNOORTY ration money
AEIMNNOPPTT appointment
AEIMNNORSTT ornamentist
AEIMNNORSTU mensuration
AEIMNNSSTTU sustainment
AEIMNOORSST astronomise
AEIMNOORSSU anisomerous
AEIMNOORSTZ astronomize
AEIMNOPPRRY open primary
AEIMNOPRTTU importunate
permutation
AEIMNORRTTY terminatory
AEIMNORSSTU stramineous
AEIMNORSTTY attorneyism

AEIMNORTTTU	mutteration
AEIMNOSSSTY	seismonasty
AEIMNPPRSST	panspermist
AEIMNRRSTTT	transmitter
AEIMOOPRRST	aerotropism
AEIMOORRTTY	arteriotomy
AEIMOORSTTU	autoerotism
AEIMOPRRSSU	aspersorium
AEIMOPRRSWY	primrose way
AEIMOPRRTTY	impetratory
AEIMOPSTTTU	temptatious
AEIMPRRTTUY	prematurity
AEIMPRSSTTU	suprematist✧
AEIMRRRRUVY	Murray River
AEIMSSSTTTY	systematist
AEINNNORSTY	Tyronensian
AEINNNORTTU	antineutron
AEINNOOPRST	personation
AEINNOOSTTT	ostentation
AEINNOPSTTY	spontaneity
AEINNOQRSTU	quaternions
AEINNORRTUV	nervuration
AEINNORSTUV	intravenous
AEINNORTTUU	tau neutrino
AEINNOSSSUX	anxiousness
AEINNRRSTTU	unrestraint
AEINNRSSSSU	Russianness
AEINOOPPRRT	reapportion
AEINOOPRRST	retinospora
AEINOOPRSSU	aponeurosis
AEINOOPRTTX	exportation
AEINOORRSTT	restoration✧
AEINOORSUVX	over-anxious
AEINOPPPQRU	appropinque
AEINOPPRSTT	poster paint
AEINOPRSSSV	vasopressin
AEINOPRSSTT	state prison
AEINOQRSTUY	questionary
AEINORRSSUW	war neurosis
AEINORSSSUV	savouriness
	variousness
AEINPRRSTTU	nature strip
AEINQSSSTTU	squattiness
AEIOOOPPPRS	prosopopeia
AEIOOPRRSTU	iteroparous
AEIOPPRRRTY	proprietary
AEIOPRRRSTY	respiratory
AEIOPRRRTTU	portraiture
AEIOPRRTTUV	vituperator
AEIOPRRTTXY	extirpatory
AEIPPRSTUUV	suppurative
AEJMMMOORRU	more majorum
AEJMNNOORTW	Trojan Women
AEKKLMMORSV	Volkskammer
AEKLLPRSSSY	sparklessly
AEKLMMORTWY	Tommy Walker
AEKLMOPRRSW	sampler-work
AEKLOPRRSTW	plasterwork
AEKLPPPRUWY	puppy-walker
AEKMNOOPSSW	spokeswoman
AEKOPRRSTTW	spatterwork
AELLMSSTTYY	tally system
AELLNNTTUUV	tunnel vault
AELLNOOPRTW	pot-walloner
AELLNOPRSTT	patent rolls
AELLNPRSTUU	ne plus ultra
AELLOOPPRTW	pot-walloper
AELLOOPRSTW	wool-stapler
AELLOPPRRUY	royal purple
AELLOPRSSUX	solar plexus
AELLOQRRSUU	quarrellous
AELMMOOPSSS	plasmosomes
AELMMRSSTUU	summersault
AELMNOORRRS	Roman sorrel
AELMNOPPRTU	trample upon
AELMNOPRRSU	supernormal
AELMNORSTUW	Ulsterwoman
AELMOOPRSTU	tropaeolums
AELMOPSSTUY	sympetalous
AELMORSSSTY	solar system
AELMPRSTYYY	mystery play
AELNNNOPRTW	town planner
AELNNSSSUUU	unusualness
AELNOPPSTTY	penalty spot
AELNOPRRTTY	entry portal
AELNOPRSTTY	oyster plant
AELNOPSSTTW	staple towns
AELNPRRSUUY	superlunary
AELOOPRRTXY	exploratory
AELOOPSSTTY	osteoplasty
AELOPPRRRSU	pourparlers
AELPPRSTUWY	water supply
AEMNNNOORST	Norman Stone
AEMNNORRSTT	remonstrant✧
AEMNOOPRSTY	trypanosome
AEMNOORSSSU	amorousness
AEMNOORSTWY	oyster-woman
AEMNOPPRRTY	property man
AEMNOPRTTWY	Pretty Woman
AEMNOSTTTUX	Mantoux test
AEMOOOPSTTU	mouse potato
AEMOOPPRRRU	amour-propre
AEMOQSSTTUY	quota system
AEMORRSTTTU	trout stream
AENNOOPRSSS	parson's nose
AENNOOPSSTU	spontaneous
AENNOPPRSST	Prestonpans
AENNORRSTTU	neutron star
AENOOPPRSTT	top one's part
AENOORSSTTW	at one's worst
AENOPRRRSTT	transporter
AENORRSTTTU	sternutator
AENORRTTUVX	turnover tax
AENORSSTTTU	sustentator
AENPPRSSSTU	suppressant
AEOOPPPRRTY	party-pooper
AEOOPRRSSSV	vasopressor
AEOPPPPRRTY	party popper
AEOPPRRTTVY	poverty trap
AEOPPRRTTXY	property tax
AEOPRRRSSTY	rotary press
AEOPRRSSTTW	water sports

AEOPRSTTTYY oyster-patty
AEOQRRSTTUU outquarters
AEPPPRRSTUY supper party
AFFFGHILRTU affrightful
AFFGGINORSU sugaring off
AFFGHIIMNRS fish farming
AFFGHIMNRUU humgruffian
AFFGHIORSTT straight off
AFFGHLLRTUU full-fraught
AFFGHLOPSTU plough-staff
AFFGIILMNRY affirmingly
AFFGIKNNSTU snuff-taking
AFFHIILLLNS fill-in flash
AFFHIKLOTWW walk off with
AFFIINOSTUX suffixation
AFFILLMMNNO non-flam film
AFFILNORSTU insufflator
AFFLLLNORTU full-frontal
AFFLMNOOPPU palm off upon
AFFOOORTUUV out of favour
AFFOOORTUWY four-foot way
AFGGHIINNRT nightfaring
AFGGHILOORT goliath frog
AFGGIILNTUY fatiguingly
AFGGIINSSTT gas-fittings
AFGGILNPRUX purging flax
AFGGINOORTZ zoografting
AFGHHHIINOS high fashion
AFGHHIILNTU highfalutin
AFGHHLLORTU fall through
AFGHIIKLNSW walking fish
AFGHIILRSTY fairy lights
AFGHILMOPRY filmography
AFGHIORSTWY right-of-ways
rights-of-way
AFGHJNNOOTU John of Gaunt
AFGHLORTTUU trough fault
AFGIIINNRTU infuriating
AFGIILLNNTY inflatingly
AFGIILLNNUY unfailingly
AFGIILMNNTU fulminating
AFGIILNNOTU antifouling
AFGIIMNORRT granitiform
AFGIIMORSTT sagittiform
AFGIINNNORU Finno-Ugrian
AFGIINNOPSY saponifying
AFGIINOSTTU fustigation
AFGIINPRRTY firing party
AFGIINRSTTY stratifying
AFGIINSSTUU ignis fatuus
AFGILLNNTUY flauntingly
AFGILMNOPRT platforming
AFGILMNORRU granuliform
AFGILNOORSW flooring saw
AFGILNORTUU fulguration
AFGILNPRTYY flying party
AFGILNRSTTY flying start
AFGINOOPPTT foot-tapping
AFGINRRSTTU frustrating
AFGLLOOOSTW gallows-foot
AFHHIORTTWY faithworthy
AFHIIINNSST satin finish
AFHIILOTTUW without fail
AFHIIMPRRSY fairy shrimp
AFHILNOPSSW Spanish fowl
AFHINORRSTU sharon fruit
AFHKORSSUUY Yousuf Karsh
AFHLLMNRUUY unharmfully
AFHLNOOOPRU lap of honour
AFHLOOPPRSS splashproof
AFHLOOSSTTY soothfastly
AFIIIILNNTV infinitival
AFIIILMNNST infantilism
AFIIILNNTTY infantility
AFIIILNRSTU fustilirian
AFIIIMPRSSS fissiparism
AFIIINNORTU infuriation
AFIIIPRSSTY fissiparity
AFIILLLMOPR lapilliform
AFIILLMMMOR mamilliform
AFIILLMOPPR papilliform
AFIILLMORTW Fort William
AFIILLNOSTU fusillation
AFIILMNNOTU fulmination
AFIILMNOPRU naupliiform
AFIILMNORTY informality
AFIILMOPRRS spiraliform
AFIILNORRTT infiltrator
AFIILORSTTU flirtatious
AFIIMNNOORT information
AFIIMNOORSU omnifarious
AFIIMNORRRS Friars Minor
AFIIMORSTUV favouritism
AFIINNORSTX transfixion
AFIIOPRSSSU fissiparous
AFILLMNOPRU planuliform
AFILLMOOPRT oil platform
AFILMMNOORS Milos Forman
AFILMNOORTU formulation
AFILMNORTUY fulminatory
AFILNNOOSTU sulfonation
AFILNORSTTU flustration
AFIMMNOPRTY tympaniform
AFIMMORSTUU fumatoriums
AFIMNOORRTY informatory
AFINNORSSTU transfusion
AFINOOPPRST Port of Spain
AFINOOPSTTU snap out of it
AFINORRSTTU frustration
AFKKLMPRTUU Kulturkampf
AFLLOPRUUXY lap of luxury
AFLMOPRRTUY poultry-farm
AGGGIIJNNOR jagging-iron
AGGGILNOOTY gigantology
AGGGILNSUZZ gas-guzzling
AGGHHIIKNNR high-ranking
AGGHHLOPPRY glyphograph
AGGHHNORTUU throughgaun
AGGHIIJMNTU thingumajig
AGGHIIJMNTY thingamyjig
AGGHIIKNNTW night-waking
AGGHIILNNSU languishing

AGGHIILOOST hagiologist
AGGHILNOOTW go along with
AGGHINORTWW wagonwright
AGGHKORSTUU August Krogh
AGGHLNOOPSY sphagnology
AGGHMMOPRSY sphygmogram
AGGIIKLNNWW wing-walking
AGGIIKLNTWW walking twig
AGGIILNNOSS sloganising
AGGIILNNOSY agonisingly
AGGIILNNOSZ sloganizing
AGGIILNNOYZ agonizingly
AGGIILNRSST tiring-glass
AGGIINNOPRT pig-ignorant
AGGIINNPRST part-singing
AGGIINORTTU gurgitation
AGGIKLNNOSW walking-song
AGGIKNNOSUW wauking-song
AGGILLMORRU glamour girl
AGGILLNNOPY long-playing
AGGILLNNTWY twanglingly
AGGILNNORST string along
AGGIMMNOPRR programming
AGGIMMOORTU maggotorium
AGGIMNORRSS gross margin
AGGINNRSTTU starting gun
AGGINOPSSTT staging post
AGGLLNOORYY laryngology
AGGLOOORSTY agrostology
AGHHIIMNRST nightmarish
AGHHIIRSSTT straightish
AGHHIJMNORS John Grisham
AGHHILOPRTY lithography
AGHHIMNRSTU human rights
AGHHKLORTTU talk through
AGHHKLORTUW walk-through
AGHHLOOPSUY hylophagous
AGHHLORTUWY laughworthy
AGHHMNOPRYY hymnography
AGHHMOPRTYY mythography
AGHHNOOPPRY phonography
AGHHOOPPRTY photography
AGHHOOPRRTY orthography
AGHHOORTUWX thoroughwax
AGHHOPPRSYY hypsography
AGHHOPPRTYY phytography
AGHHOPRSSTU pass through
through pass
AGHIIILLLNS Lillian Gish
AGHIIILMNTU humiliating
AGHIIILNPSS sailing ship
AGHIIKLLLNW hillwalking
AGHIILLNOOP philologian
AGHIILLPPSS Philip Glass
AGHIILMNOOS hooliganism
AGHIILMPRRS A Shrimp Girl
AGHIILNNSVY vanishingly
AGHIILNRSVY ravishingly
AGHIIMOSTTX thigmotaxis
AGHIIMRRTTU right atrium
AGHIINNOSST astonishing
AGHIINPRSTY pharyngitis
AGHIIPRSTTT straight tip
AGHIKLNOPST talking shop
AGHIKNORRSW work-sharing
AGHIKNORSUW waking hours
AGHILLNORTW All Right Now
AGHILLOPRST polar lights
AGHILMNNORY gymnorhinal
AGHILMNOOTY mythologian
AGHILMORRST moral rights
AGHILNOOSTT anthologist
AGHILNOPRTW whaling-port
AGHILNORRWY harrowingly
AGHILNRTTWY thwartingly
AGHILOOPSTT pathologist
AGHIMNNRSTY Granny Smith
AGHIMNNSSTU hunting-mass
AGHIMNOOPSY siphonogamy
AGHIMNOORRU hog in armour
AGHIMNOPRST prognathism
AGHIMOPRSTY myographist
Pythagorism
AGHINNOPPSW swan-hopping
AGHINOORSTW shooting war
AGHINOOSSTY soothsaying
AGHINOPRSTT parting shot
AGHINOPSSST passing shot
AGHINRRSTTY Starry Night
AGHIOOPPSUX xiphopagous
AGHIOOPRRST torsiograph
AGHIOOPRSTZ zoographist
AGHIOOPSTUX toxiphagous
AGHIOPPRRSY spirography
AGHIORSTTTU straight out
straight-out
AGHJMNNOOTU John Montagu
AGHLLOOPSSY hypoglossal
AGHLOOPPSUY polyphagous
AGHLOOPSUXY xylophagous
AGHLOPRSTYY stylography
AGHLOSSTTUV Gustav Holst
AGHMNOOOPSU monophagous
AGHMNOOSTUY Thomas Young
AGHNNOSSTUY syngnathous
AGHNOOPPRRY pornography
AGHNOOPRSTU prognathous
AGHNORRTUUY Arthur Young
AGHOOPRSSTY gastrosophy
AGHOORRSTTW groatsworth
AGIIIILLNNT initialling
AGIIIKLLNNP painkilling
AGIIILLMNST mailing list
AGIIILLNOST sigillation
AGIIILLNTTT titillating
AGIIILMNSTV vigilantism
AGIIILNNOPT oil painting
AGIIILNNORS original sin
AGIIILNORTV invigilator
AGIIILNORTY originality
AGIIILNPSST salpingitis
AGIIILNSTTW waiting list

AGIIILORSTV	toga virilis
AGIIIMMNORT	immigration
AGIIINNNSTU	insinuating
AGIIINNOORT	origination
AGIIINNOSTT	instigation
AGIIKKNNRST	skating rink
AGIIKNPRSSY	sky-aspiring
AGIILMNNOTY	longanimity
AGIILMNRSSU	singularism
AGIILMNSTTU	stimulating
AGIILMOOPST	Plagiostomi
AGIILMOORST	Mariologist
AGIILMOOSST	gliomatosis
AGIILNRSSTU	singularist
AGIILNRSTUY	singularity
AGIIMMNNTTU	manumitting
AGIIMNNOPTU	impugnation
AGIIMNNORTW	tiring-woman
AGIIMNOORTW	waiting room
AGIIMORRSTU	agritourism
AGIINNOOPRT	pignoration
AGIINNOPRST	patronising
AGIINNOPRTZ	patronizing
AGIINNSSSTU	unassisting
AGIINOORRTV	invigorator
AGIINORSTTT	tritagonist
AGIINPRRTTW	part-writing
AGIKKRSSUUY	kikuyu grass
AGIKLLNPRSY	sparklingly
AGIKLMSTTUV	Gustav Klimt
AGILLMNNOOU	monolingual
AGILLNOPSTU	post-lingual
AGILLNRSTTY	startlingly
AGILMMNPSUW	lignum-swamp
AGILMNNOOSU	longanimous
AGILMNNSUUY	unamusingly
AGILMNORSST	storm signal
AGILMNPPRSS	Palm Springs
AGILMNRSSUY	laryngismus
AGILMOOPRTY	primatology
AGILMOOSTTU	tautologism
AGILMORRRSS	mirror glass
AGILNNOSSUW	Angus Wilson
AGILNNPRSUY	unsparingly
AGILNOPPRVY	approvingly
AGILNOPRUVY	vapouringly
AGILNOSSSUU	salsuginous
AGILOORSSTT	astrologist
AGILOORSSYY	Assyriology
AGILOOSTTTU	tautologist
AGILPRTTUYY	guilty party
AGIMMNOORST	mooring mast
AGIMMOOPRST	gamotropism
AGIMNNNORRY	non-marrying
AGIMNNORRST	morning star✧
AGIMNOORRTT	Mt Tongariro
AGIMNORRSTU	gran turismo
	organistrum
AGINNOPPRUV	unapproving
AGINNOPRRST	apron-string
AGINNOPRSST	transposing
AGINNOQRRTU	quarrington
AGINOOOPRRT	prorogation
AGINOOPRSTT	protagonist
AGINOORRSTU	surrogation
AGINOORRSUV	granivorous
AGLLLNOOPYY	polygonally
AGLLLOOPTTY	polyglottal
AGLLMOORSUY	glamorously
AGLLOOPSTTT	glottal stop
AGLLORRSUUY	garrulously
AGLMNOOPTUY	polygonatum
AGLMNOORSUU	unglamorous
AGLMNOORTYY	laryngotomy
AGLMOOOSTTY	stomatology
AGLMOOPRRTU	promulgator
AGLMOORRTYY	martyrology
AGLMOPRSSUU	glamourpuss
AGLOOOSTTUU	tautologous
AGMOORSSTTY	gastrostomy
AGNOOPRRSSW	song sparrow
AHHIIIPRSST	phthiriasis
AHHIJKNNOSW	John Hawkins
AHHILLOOPSU	halophilous
AHHILLPSTUY	ithyphallus✧
AHHILMOPSTT	ophthalmist
AHHILMOPSTY	hylopathism
AHHILNOORTU	holothurian
AHHILOPPSYY	hypophysial
AHHILOPSTTY	hylopathist
AHHIMNNOOPR	harmoniphon
AHHIMNOPSSW	showmanship
AHHINORSTUZ	rhizanthous
AHHIPRSSTTW	thwartships
AHHJKNNOSWY	John Hawkyns
AHHKNORTTWY	thankworthy
AHHLLNOPTXY	xanthophyll
AHIIILMNOTU	humiliation
AHIIINNORTT	into thin air
AHIIIPPRSTT	hippiatrist
AHIIJNOPRST	janitorship
AHIIKLRRSTU	Turkish lira
AHIILLNOSTT	hill station
AHIILLNRTTY	Trinity Hall
AHIILLORSUY	hilariously
AHIILMNOPST	notaphilism
AHIILMORTUY	humiliatory
AHIILNOPRRT	horripilant
AHIILNOPSTT	notaphilist
AHIILOPSTTY	hospitality
AHIILPSSTTY	staphylitis
AHIILRSSTTY	hairstylist
AHIIMMNSSTU	shunamitism
AHIIMNNRRTU	antirrhinum
AHIIMNOOOSU	homoiousian
AHIIMOOPPPT	hippopotami
AHIIMRSSTUU	Mauritshuis
AHIINNSSTTT	this instant
AHIIOPRRSTT	traitorship
AHIKKOORRSW	kwashiorkor
AHIKLMOORSW	workaholism
AHIKMNOPRSW	workmanship

AHIKPPRRSTU Arthur Kipps
AHILLMOPRTU prothallium
AHILLNNOPSY pollyannish
AHILLOOPSWY woolly aphis
AHILLOPSTXY phyllotaxis
AHILMMOOPSU ammophilous
AHILMNPPRST shrimp plant
AHILMORTTUU multi-author
AHILNOPRSTY rhinoplasty
AHILOORRSTY oral history
AHILOORRTTY hortatorily
AHILOPPRSXY prophylaxis
AHILOPRSTYY history play
physiolatry
AHIMNOOPSTT taphonomist
AHIMNOORRSU honorariums
AHIMNOPRSTY misanthropy
AHIMNOPSSSS Spanish moss
AHIMOOOPSST opisthosoma
AHIMOORSTUZ rhizomatous
AHIMOPRSSTY stasimorphy
AHINNOORRST horrisonant
AHINNOPSSTW Spanish Town
AHINOOPPRST patroonship
AHINOOPSSTX saxophonist
AHINOORRSTU ornithosaur
AHINORSTTTT that's torn it!
AHIOOORRSST Horatio Ross
AHIOOPRRSTX orthopraxis
AHIOOPRSTTX trophotaxis
AHJKMNOOOSU Joshua Nkomo
AHJLLMNNOPU John Pullman
AHJMNNOORST John Marston
AHKKMNOOPRR Ankh-Morpork
AHKNOOTUWWY you-know-what
AHLLNOORSTW sallow-thorn
AHLMOOPPRST trophoplasm
AHLMOOPRSUY amorphously
AHLNOOPRSTY hyoplastron
AHLNOORSSTU last honours
AHLOPRRSTUU sulphurator
AHMNNOOPRTT Northampton
AHMNOOPSTTU Southampton
AHMOOPRRTTU parrot mouth
AHNORSSTUUY thysanurous
AHOOPPRSSTU apostrophus
AHOPRRSSTTY short pastry
AHQRSSTTTUU squat thrust
AIIIILNOTVX lixiviation
AIIIKLMNRRS larrikinism
AIIILLLNPTU lilliputian✧
AIIILLMPTTW William Pitt
AIIILLNOPTX pixillation
AIIILLNOQTU illiquation
AIIILLNOTTT titillation
AIIILLNOTUV illuviation
AIIILLRSTTV vitraillist
AIIILMNOSST in altissimo
AIIILNNOOST lionisation
AIIILNNOOTZ lionization
AIIILNNOTTU intuitional
AIIILNORSTT institorial
AIIILNOSTTU utilisation
AIIILNOTTUZ utilization
AIIIMNOPSSS pianissimos
AIIIMNRSTTU miniaturist
AIIIMPPRRTY primiparity
AIIIMPSSTVY impassivity
AIIINNNOQTU inquination
AIIINNNOSTU insinuation
AIIINNOPRST inspiration
AIIINNOQRTU inquiration
AIIINNOSTTU inusitation
unitisation
AIIINNOTTUZ unitization
AIIINOTTTTV tittivation
AIIJJLNNOPS Janis Joplin
AIIJLLMNSUV Jim Sullivan
AIIJLLMPRSW J P R Williams
AIIKNRSSSTT Sanskritist
AIILLMMNOTU multinomial
AIILLMNORTU illuminator
AIILLMPRSTU multispiral
AIILLNNOOPT pollination
AIILLNORSUY illusionary
AIILLNPRTUY nulliparity
AIILLNRSSTY sinistrally
AIILLPPRTUY pupillarity
AIILLPRRSTY spirit rally
AIILLPRSTUY spiritually
AIILMMORTTY immortality
AIILMNOOPRT imploration
AIILMNOOPST malposition
AIILMNOOSST solmisation
AIILMNOOSTZ solmization
AIILMNOPSSU Palus Somnii
AIILMNOSTTU stimulation
AIILMOOPSST lipomatosis
AIILMPRTTUY multiparity
AIILMRSSUVV survivalism
AIILNNOOSTT notionalist
AIILNNORTTU nutritional
AIILNOOPRSV provisional✧
AIILNOOPTTY optionality
AIILNOORTVY volitionary
AIILNOPRTUY unipolarity
AIILNOPSTTU stipulation
AIILNORTUUX luxuriation
AIILNOSSTTY stylisation
AIILNOSTTYZ stylization
AIILNPRSTUU unspiritual
AIILNQRTTUY tranquility
AIILPRSTTUY spiritualty
AIILRSSTUVV survivalist
AIIMMNNOSSU manumission
AIIMMNOPSTT pantomimist
AIIMMNSSTTU numismatist
AIIMNNOOSTU antimonious
AIIMNNRSSTU minus strain
AIIMNOOPRTT importation
AIIMNOOPRTX proximation
AIIMNOPRTTZ Martin Opitz

AIIMNOSSTTU mussitation
AIIMNOSTTTU mutationist
AIIMNPRSSSU Prussianism
AIIMOPPRRSU primiparous
AIIMOPPRRTU ipratropium
AIINNOOOPRT opinionator
AIINNOOOSTZ ozonisation
AIINNOOOTZZ ozonization
AIINNOORSTT nitrosation
AIINNORSTUY insinuatory
AIINNOTTTWW witwanton it
AIINOPRRSTY inspiratory
AIINOPRRSUU uriniparous
AIINOPRRTTU parturition
AIINOPRSSST inspissator
AIINOPRSSTU suspiration
AIINORRTTTU trituration
AIIOOPPRRTT propitiator
AIIOPRRSTTT portraitist
AIIOPRSSTTT prostatitis
AIIPPRRSTTY party spirit
AIKLMMSSTTU summit talks
AIKLNOPPRRU parlour pink
AIKMMNOSTTY Tommy Atkins
AIKNOORSTTW workstation
AILLLMNOOPP lollipop man
AILLLNOOPRU allopurinol
AILLLNOPTUU pullulation
AILLLNOSUVY villanously
AILLMOOPRST allotropism
AILLMOPSSSY plasmolysis
AILLMOPSTUY ampullosity
AILLNOORSTY torsionally
AILLNOOSTTY litany-stool
AILLNOPRSUU nulliparous
AILLNORTUVY voluntarily
AILLNPPSTUY suppliantly
AILLNRTUUXY luxuriantly
AILLOOPRSTT postillator
AILLOPPPRTU tulip poplar
AILLORRSTTU illustrator
AILMMNNOTUU nummulation
AILMMNOSTUU multanimous
AILMMOPSSTY polymastism
AILMNNOSTTU multisonant
AILMNNOSUUY unanimously
AILMNOOOPRT promotional
AILMNOORSTT monolatrist
AILMNOPRTTY importantly
AILMNORSTUV voluntarism
AILMOOPRRTY imploratory
AILMOOPRUYZ polyzoarium
AILMOPRSTUU multiparous
AILMORSTTUY stimulatory
AILNNOOPSTU postal union
AILNNORTUVY involuntary
AILNNRTUUUX unluxuriant
AILNOOPRSTU sporulation
AILNOOPSTTU postulation
AILNOPPSTTU post-nuptial
AILNOPSTTUU pustulation
AILNORSTTUV voluntarist
AILNORSUUVY unsavourily
AILNRSSTUUU laurustinus
AILOOPRSUVY oviparously
AILOPRSTTUY stipulatory
AILORSTTTUY statutorily
AIMMNORRTUU murmuration
AIMMOORRSTU moratoriums
AIMMOOSSTXY myxomatosis
AIMNNOOPTTU mountain-top
AIMNNOORRSV Van Morrison
AIMNNOOSTUU mountainous
AIMNNOPRTTU unimportant
AIMNOPPPRSY Mary Poppins
AIMOPPRRSTY post-primary
AINNOOOPPRT pornotopian
AINOOOPRRSW arrow-poison
AINOOPRRSTT prostration
AINOPPRSTUU suppuration
AINORRRTTTU turn traitor
AINORRSSTUU susurration
AJLLMOOPRYY jam roly-poly
AJMMNPQTUUU quantum jump
AJMMOOORRTW jam tomorrow
AKLNNOOOPTZ zooplankton
AKMNOORRSUY on your marks
AKMOQRSTUYZ smoky quartz
ALLNOOOPPRR propranolol✧
ALLNOPPRUUY unpopularly
ALLOOOPRSTU allotropous
ALLOORSTWWW swallow-wort
ALMMNOOTTWY Tommy Lawton
ALMMNOSSUUW Mussulwoman
ALMNNOOSUYY anonymously
ALMNOOORSTU monolatrous
ALMNOORSTTU salmon trout
ALMOOOPRSUY polyamorous
ALNNORSTUYY tyrannously
ALOOOPRSTUV pot-valorous
ALOOPRSTTUY postulatory
ALOPRRSTUUY rapturously
AMMNOOORRST Marston Moor
AMNNOOOPPRT ma non troppo
AMNOOPRSSTW sportswoman
AMNOOPRSTTU put to ransom
AMNOOPSSSST Samson's post
AMNOOSTTUUY tautonymous
AMOOPRRRTTY protomartyr
AMOOPRRSTTU stump orator
ANOOOPRRTTY protonotary
AOOOPPRSTTU à tout propos

B

BBBBDEEELRU beblubbered
BBBBNOOORSY Bobby Robson
BBBDEELNRUU bubble under
BBBEEHLLLSU bubble-shell
BBBEELMMORY lobby-member
BBBEGIIINNW winebibbing
BBBEINORRSU Robbie Burns
BBBELRRTUUY butyl rubber

Words marked ✧ can also be spelled with one or more capital letters

BBBEOORRRSU sorbo rubber
BBCCDEEKOOY cockeyed bob
BBCCEEHKLOR breechblock
BBCCEEHKRRU rubber check
BBCCEHIOPRY cyberphobic
BBCDEEORRRU rubber-cored
BBCDEGIKLNO bed-blocking
BBCDEHIIKRT thick-ribbed
BBCDEHIRRTU butcherbird
BBCDELLOOSU Boodle's Club
BBCDGIIMNNO comb binding
BBCEEEIKRRZ breeze brick
BBCEEEKLORZ breeze block
BBCEEEPRRRU crêpe rubber
BBCEEHHIRRT breech birth
BBCEEHNNOOU bonne bouche
BBCEEIKORRS Boris Becker
BBCEELNOOST cobblestone
BBCEEORRRTU Robert Bruce
BBCEGIIILOP bibliopegic
BBCEGINNOUV nubbing-cove
BBCEILMOSTU combustible
BBCEINRSSUU unsubscribe
BBCEJKOORST stockjobber
BBCEKLORSTU blockbuster
BBCELMORSTU cluster bomb
BBCGIILMNOY climbing boy
BBCGIINRSSU subscribing
BBCGIMOORRY borborygmic
BBCHJKLNOOU John Lubbock
BBCIIILLOOP bibliopolic
BBCKLOORSSU Brooks's Club
BBCOOOOSTWY cowboy boots
BBDDEEIKOOS bedside book
BBDDEELLOOU blue-blooded
BBDDEENOORR Broederbond
BBDDEILLNOU double-blind
BBDDEILORUY body-builder
BBDDENOOTUY beyond doubt
BBDEEELOSTV best-beloved
BBDEEELOUYY blue-eyed boy
BBDEEFILNRU lubber fiend
BBDEEGLOOUY double bogey
BBDEEHHLOOY hobbledehoy
BBDEEHILNUW Edwin Hubble
BBDEEHIRRSU shrubberied
BBDEELLORWY Lloyd Webber
BBDEFFLLOUU double bluff
BBDEGIIMNOV dive-bombing
BBDEGOORRSU rubber goods
BBDEIILRRST bristlebird
BBDEIKNOORY bookbindery
BBDELLNOOTT bottle-blond
BBDELNOOOSY bloody-bones
BBDELNRSSUU blunderbuss
BBDELRRSUUU Ruud Lubbers
BBDENOORRSY Robber Synod
BBDGHLOOOTU blood-bought
BBDGIIKNNOO bookbinding
BBDILNOORRS Lord Robbins
BBEEEHRRSTU sheet rubber
BBEEELNOPST pebble-stone
BBEEELORSTW beetle brows
BBEEGIILLNR gibberellin
BBEEGILMRSU submergible
BBEEHIIRTTT the biter bit
BBEEHLLORSU lubber's hole
BBEEIILRRRV River Ribble
BBEEILLMRTY belly-timber
BBEEILLNRSU lubber's line
BBEEILMRSSU submersible
BBEEILNSSSU subsensible
BBEEINNNOOR bonbonnière
BBEEINRRSSU rubberiness
BBEEKLNOOST skeleton bob
BBEELLLLNRU Bell Burnell
BBEELNORSTU rubble stone
BBEELOORRTY Robert Boyle
BBEENORRSYY boysenberry
BBEFGIIMNOR firebombing
BBEFILORSUU bulbiferous
BBEGGGILNOW begging bowl
BBEGHKOOOTY go by the book
BBEGIINSSSU big business
BBEGILMNOSX sembling box
BBEGINOSSSU gibbousness
BBEHIIILLOP bibliophile
BBEHIKLORST hobble skirt
BBEHINRSSSU shrubbiness
BBEHLORSTTU bottlebrush
BBEHMOORSTU bumbershoot
BBEIILMSSSU submissible
BBEILLNRTUY Billy Bunter
BBEILNNORUY bunny-boiler
BBEILNOPRTU burble point
BBEIMMOORRT Bob Mortimer
BBELLMOOSTT bell-bottoms
BBELLNOTTUY belly button
BBELMOSSTYY lobby system
BBELMPPPUUY bumble-puppy
BBELNOSSSUU bulbousness
BBEMNNOORTU neutron bomb
BBENOORRRTW Robert Brown
BBENORRRSTU Robert Burns
BBEOOORSTVV bovver boots
BBFIIMNOOSS fission bomb
BBFIKOOOOTT Book of Tobit
BBGHILNOORY hobgoblinry
BBGHILNORTY throbbingly
BBGHINNRSUU burning bush
BBGIILLNQUY quibblingly
BBGIKNOOORT bring to book
BBGILMNOTUX tumbling box
BBGINOPRSTU rubbing post
BBGMOORRSUY borborygmus
BBHIIILLOPY bibliophily
BBIILLLNTUY Billy Butlin
BBIKMNOOOSU omnibus book
BBILLNOOSTY Billy Boston
BBJMMMOOSUU mumbo-jumbos✧
BBLLLLOOOYY loblolly-boy
BCCCEHHHNRU church-bench

BCCCEIIKKLY	bicycle kick
BCCCEIILLPY	bicycle clip
BCCDEEHKLOU	double-check
BCCDEIKLLOU	double-click
BCCDEIKLNOR	cinder block
BCCDEILNOTU	conductible
BCCEEEEFINN	beneficence
BCCEEEENRSU	erubescence
BCCEEEHOPPR	copper-beech
BCCEEEIKLLT	click beetle
BCCEEEILRTY	tree bicycle
BCCEEENRSUY	erubescency
BCCEEHILRTU	The Crucible
BCCEEIILNOR	incoercible
BCCEEILLLOT	collectible
BCCEEILNNOT	connectible
BCCEEILNOSS	concessible
BCCEEILORRT	correctible
	Robert Cecil
BCCEEINRSTY	cybernetics
BCCEFFIKLOO	office block
BCCEFIIPSSU	subspecific
BCCEGILNOOS	cognoscible
BCCEHILLNTU	clench-built
BCCEHILPSUY	push-bicycle
BCCEHINOOPR	necrophobic
BCCEIIIRSTU	rice biscuit
BCCEIILNNOV	convincible
BCCEIINOOOT	biocoenotic
BCCEIINOORT	necrobiotic
BCCEIKLMORR	rock climber
BCCEIKLORSS	brissel-cock
BCCEILLOOPY	bicycle polo
BCCEILMPPUY	bicycle pump
BCCEIMNOOSU	subeconomic
BCCEINOOPPR	corncob pipe
BCCELLRTUUU	Culture Club
BCCFIIORSTY	fibrocystic
BCCGHLOORUU	Groucho Club
BCCHHILOOOP	ochlophobic
BCCHHOORSTT	Scotch broth
BCCHIOOOPST	Scotophobic
BCCLNORTUUY	country club
BCDDDEFOORR	Bedford cord
BCDDDELLOOO	cold-blooded
BCDDEEEILNS	descendible
BCDDEEIIRTT	direct debit
BCDDEEILOOS	close-bodied
BCDDEEINRSU	undescribed
BCDDEENORTY	body-centred
BCDDEFIKLLO	fiddle block
BCDDEGIMNOR	redding-comb
BCDDEHLOTUU	double Dutch
BCDDILLNOOO	in cold blood
BCDEEEEIRRS	decerebrise
BCDEEEEIRRZ	decerebrize
BCDEEEFINNU	unbeneficed
BCDEEEHIMRS	Decemberish
BCDEEEIINNO	inobedience
BCDEEEIINNT	Benedictine
BCDEEEIINTV	benedictive
BCDEEEIORRS	cerebroside
BCDEEEPRRSU	Breeder's Cup
BCDEEGGKLUU	duck-egg blue
BCDEEHILNPT	pitchblende
BCDEEHKLOOS	blocked shoe
BCDEEHMNOOY	honeycombed
BCDEEHMNOTU	debouchment
BCDEEIIILRT	liberticide
BCDEEIIIMNO	biomedicine
BCDEEIILNRS	discernible
BCDEEIILPRS	discerpible
BCDEEIILRRU	irreducible
BCDEEIILSST	dissectible
BCDEEIIMRSS	misdescribe
BCDEEIINNOT	benediction
BCDEEILNOSS	docibleness
BCDEEILNRUU	unreducible
BCDEEIMNRSU	disencumber
BCDEEIMRTUU	decumbiture
BCDEEINOPRY	beyond price
BCDEEINORSV	bond-service
BCDEEINORTY	benedictory
BCDEEIORTVY	brevity code
BCDEEJNSTUU	unsubjected
BCDEEKLNRUU	buckle under
BCDEELMNTUY	decumbently
BCDEFJNOOTU	found object
BCDEGHNRRSU	bergschrund
BCDEHILNNOR	hornblendic
BCDEHILORSU	subchloride
BCDEHINOSWW	widow's bench
BCDEHKOOTTU	bucktoothed
BCDEIIILRTY	credibility
BCDEIILNRSY	discernibly
BCDEIILOQTU	quodlibetic
BCDEIILRRUY	irreducibly
BCDEIILSSSU	discussible
BCDEIINNRSU	uninscribed
BCDEIKLOQUU	double-quick
BCDEINORRSS	incrossbred
BCDEIOOPRSS	proboscides
BCDEKLNOOOS	do one's block
BCDEKLOORSU	bloodsucker
BCDELMNOSUU	muscle-bound
BCDELOORSSU	double-cross
BCDENNOORTU	counterbond
BCDEOORRRSS	cross-border
BCDFIKORSUY	Dick Fosbury
BCDFILNPSUU	public funds
BCDGIIKMNOR	mockingbird
BCDGILLLOPU	bulldog clip
BCDHHIOOPRY	hydrophobic
BCDHIMOORRY	hydrobromic
BCDHLMOORSY	chord symbol
BCDIILMORTU	trombiculid
BCDIILOOPTY	body politic
BCDIINOORUX	doxorubicin
BCDIINRTUUY	rubicundity
BCDIIRSSTTU	subdistrict
BCDILLNOORU	colour-blind
BCDKLLLOORU	Lord Bullock

BCEEEEIJLTU Beetlejuice
BCEEEELMRRU crème brulée
crème brûlée
BCEEEELNNOV benevolence
BCEEEEMNOTW come between
BCEEEFFORRY coffee berry
BCEEEFILPRT perfectible
BCEEEGMNRSU submergence
BCEEEHHINPR hebephrenic
BCEEEHKLTUW bucket-wheel
BCEEEHNNQSU Queen's Bench
BCEEEHNORTT en brochette
BCEEEILPPRT perceptible
BCEEEILPRTX excerptible
BCEEEINNOPT bonnet-piece
BCEEEIRRUVZ Bézier curve
BCEEELLMRSU cerebellums
BCEEELLORSU cerebellous
BCEEENNOSSS obsceneness
BCEEENQSSUU subsequence
BCEEFFMOOST come off best
BCEEFHNRRRY French berry
BCEEFIIKNST sick benefit
BCEEFILORRW Wilberforce
BCEEFIMNORT Fibrocement®
BCEEFIMORRR cerebriform
BCEEFKLNRRU buckler fern
BCEEGHMOOSU gobe-mouches
BCEEGILNOST congestible
BCEEGIMNORY embryogenic
BCEEHHINPRS benchership
BCEEHHIOORT Cherie Booth
BCEEHHNOOPT technophobe
BCEEHIIINRS hibernicise✧
BCEEHIIINRZ hibernicize✧
BCEEHIIQTUU hic et ubique
BCEEHILPRTU The Republic
BCEEHIMNTTW bewitchment
BCEEHINNORT bon chrétien
BCEEHINNRSU Chinese burn
BCEEHIOORRS seborrhoeic
BCEEHIRSTWW witches' brew
BCEEHIRTTTV bitter vetch
BCEEHJKLOWY cheek by jowl
BCEEHKLRRUY huckleberry
BCEEHNOOPST benthoscope
BCEEIIJLLPU jubilee clip
BCEEIIJOSTV objectivise
BCEEIIJOTVZ objectivize
BCEEIILRSTV vitrescible
BCEEIINRRST interscribe
BCEEIJLOTVY objectively
BCEEIKOORSV service book
BCEEILLLOSY bellicosely
BCEEILMNNOT contemnible
BCEEILMNPUY public enemy✧
BCEEILMOSST comestibles
BCEEILNORST bristlecone
BCEEILNORTV convertible
BCEEILORRSU Le Corbusier
BCEEILORRTV Robert Clive
BCEEILPPRTY perceptibly
BCEEILPRSTU putrescible
BCEEILPSSTU susceptible
BCEEILRSTUU tuberculise
BCEEILRTUUZ tuberculize
BCEEINOOOSS biocoenoses
BCEEINSSSTU subsistence
BCEEIOPRSST corbie-steps
BCEEIPRRSSU superscribe
BCEEIPRTTUU picture tube
BCEEIRRSSTT bitter-cress
BCEEJLSSSTU subjectless
BCEEKKLNNOU knuckle-bone
BCEEKLLORTT block letter
BCEEKOORSTU Crookes tube
BCEELLMOSUU submolecule
BCEELLNORTU clenbuterol
BCEELMMOOTY embolectomy
BCEELMNRTUY recumbently
BCEELNOOSST obsolescent
BCEELNOSTTT scent bottle
BCEELORSTUU tuberculose
BCEELRRRUWY curlew-berry
BCEEMNORSTU obscurement
BCEEMNOSTTU obmutescent
BCEEMOPRRRU procerebrum
BCEENOORRTU counterbore
BCEENORSSSU obscureness
BCEFFKORSTU buffer stock
BCEFFNORTUU counterbuff
BCEFHIINORS bichon frise
BCEFIINNORT fibronectin
BCEFIIOPRST fibre optics
BCEGHHIMOWY High Wycombe
BCEGHILNNNU unblenching
BCEGHILOPRU police burgh
BCEGIILNOOY cinebiology
cinébiology
BCEGIIMMNOS misbecoming
BCEGIINRTTU butter icing
BCEGILLNSSU singles club
BCEGILMOORY embryologic
BCEHHIILOOP heliophobic
BCEHHIIMRTT timber hitch
BCEHHIIOOPR hierophobic
BCEHHIJNORR John Bircher
BCEHHILNOOT holobenthic
BCEHHJNNNOY Johnny Bench
BCEHIIIMNRS Hibernicism
BCEHIIKOOUZ Keizo Obuchi
BCEHIILRRSV silver birch
BCEHIINPRST bits per inch
BCEHIJLNOTU join the club
BCEHIJPSSTU subjectship
BCEHIKLMOOR hook-climber
BCEHILNORRU Ulrich Boner
BCEHILNOSST blotchiness
BCEHILOPSUU public house
BCEHIMNRSSU Burschenism
BCEHIMOORRS chrisom-robe
BCEHKLNOOTU luckenbooth

BCEHKMMORSU Kommersbuch
BCEHKOPRRTU pork-butcher
BCEHLMOPTYY B lymphocyte
BCEHLORRSYY chrysoberyl
BCEHLORTTTU butter cloth
BCEHMOORTTY thrombocyte
BCEHMORRSUU rhumb course
BCEIIIMMOST biomimetics
BCEIIINSTUW wine biscuit
BCEIIJMOSTV objectivism
BCEIIJOSTTV objectivist
BCEIIJOTTVY objectivity
BCEIIKLLRST billsticker
BCEIILLOSTY bellicosity
BCEIILLRSUW Bruce Willis
BCEIIMNOOST coenobitism
BCEIINOOOSS biocoenosis
BCEIINOORSS necrobiosis
BCEIIORRSTW Eric Bristow
BCEIJNSTUUV subjunctive
BCEIKLLMNOO nickel-bloom
BCEIKLLOSVW swivelblock
BCEIKMNORSU broken music
BCEIKOOPRTU picture book
BCEIKOOTTTY tickettyboo
BCEILLNOSUV convulsible
BCEILLORSSU brucellosis
BCEILMNNTUY incumbently
BCEILMNRSSU crumbliness
BCEILMOOPSS compossible
BCEILMOORRT root climber
BCEILMORTUU microtubule
BCEILNORTVY convertibly
BCEILOPRRTU corruptible
BCEILPPRSUU public purse
BCEILPSSTUY susceptibly
BCEIOOPRSSS proboscises
BCEIORSTTUV obstructive
BCEIPRSSSUY presbycusis
BCEKKLMNOOY monkey block
BCEKKOOOORY cookery-book
BCEKKOORRST stockbroker
BCEKLMOSSTY block-system
BCEKLOORRST rock lobster
BCEKRRSTUUY scrub turkey
BCELMOOOSTW come to blows
BCELNOORTUW counterblow
BCELORSTUUU tuberculous
BCELSTTTTUU scuttlebutt
BCEOOOPRSST stroboscope
BCEOORRSTTT Robert Scott
BCFIIILORTY forcibility
BCFILLOOSST bill of costs
BCFILMOORRU colubriform
BCGHILOORRU Lough Corrib
BCGHINOORSU Conisbrough
BCGHLOORSUY Rugby School
BCGIIIKLNRT rib-tickling
BCGIIKLNOOT bootlicking
BCGIILNNRTU cirl bunting
BCGIINOOOTT gnotobiotic
BCGIKLNOPPU upping-block
BCGILMNOOOW wool-combing
BCGILMNRSUU lignum-scrub
BCGILNOOPUX coupling-box
BCGILNOPRUW public wrong
BCGILOOORYY cryobiology
BCGINNNORTU corn bunting
BCGKLMOPSUY gypsum block
BCHHIOOOPPT photophobic
BCHIIIPSSTU ship biscuit
BCHIOOPRSSU Russophobic
BCHMOOOTTTU touch bottom
BCHNOORSSTU hot cross bun
BCHPRSSTUUY scrub typhus
BCIIIILMSTY miscibility
BCIIIILNTVY vincibility
BCIIILLORUU cuir-bouilli
BCIIINNOSSU subincision
BCIILLLNNOT Bill Clinton
BCIILLORSSS scissorbill
BCIILLORUUY cuir-bouilly
BCIILMMNOUU cumulonimbi
BCIILMOSSTY symbolistic
BCIINOORSTT obstriction
BCIIOORSTTU biscuit-root
BCIJNNOOTUX box junction
junction box
BCIJNNOSTUU subjunction
BCIKLLLOOPW pillow-block
BCIKLOPRSUW public works
BCILLORSUUY lubricously
BCILMOSTTUU custom-built
BCILOPRRTUY corruptibly
BCIMOOSSTUU combustious
BCINOOPRTTY cryptobiont
BCINOORRTTU contributor
BCINOORSTTU obstruction
BDDDEEEGLOU double-edged
BDDDEEEINRT interbedded
BDDDEEIIMOS disembodied
BDDDEEINRRU underbidder
BDDEEEIMMRS dismembered
BDDEEEIMNRT débridement
BDDEEELNORU double-ender
BDDEEFILLNS self-blinded
BDDEEFLSSUU self-subdued
BDDEEGIIRRV bridge-drive
BDDEEGINRRU underbridge
BDDEEGLLORU dole-bludger
BDDEEGNRTUU underbudget
BDDEEIINOST disobedient
BDDEEILLOSW disbowelled
BDDEEILLOUV double-lived
BDDEEILMNNO noble-minded
BDDEEILOOOS loose-bodied
BDDEEIMNORS sober-minded
BDDEEIMNRSU disemburden
BDDEEINOPPT peptide bond
BDDEEIOPRRT bordered pit
BDDEEKMNRUU Edmund Burke
BDDEEKNORYY donkey derby

BDDEELOOPRU pure-blooded
BDDEENNNOUY Bonny Dundee
BDDEENOORST bonded store
BDDEENSSSUU subduedness
BDDEFILNORY forbiddenly
BDDEFINNORU unforbidden
BDDEFLLLOOU full-blooded
BDDEFMNORUU dumbfounder
BDDEGGINORX dredging-box
BDDEGHHILOO highblooded
BDDEGIILOTU double-digit
BDDEGIIMNNN mind-bending
BDDEGIINORV overbidding
BDDEGINRUWY ruby wedding
BDDEGMOORRY Dogberrydom
BDDEHIMNSUZ Zen Buddhism
BDDEHINNOUU unhidebound
BDDEHINRRTU thunderbird
BDDEIINRSTU distribuend
BDDEILMOSUY middy blouse
BDDEINOOWWW bow-windowed
BDDEINRSTUU undisturbed
BDDELNNOUUY unboundedly
BDDELNOTUUY undoubtedly
BDDELOOORSU double doors
BDDFILLNNOU unblindfold
BDDGIINPSTU spudding bit
BDDGILNOOOP blood doping
BDDGILNOPUW pudding bowl
pudding-bowl
BDDGIMNNOUW dumbing-down
BDDIIKNOOSS od's bodikins
BDDIILNNOWW window blind
BDDIINPTUUY pudibundity
BDEEEEHIRST therebeside
BDEEEEHKNNT bend the knee
BDEEEEIIMRR Biedermeier
BDEEEEILRTV beetle drive
BDEEEEINRRS de Bernières
BDEEEEKNOPS keep one's bed
BDEEEFGINRW web-fingered
BDEEEFILOOU oeil-de-boeuf
BDEEEFILRRU reef-builder
BDEEEFINNTU unbenefited
BDEEEGINRSW web designer
BDEEEHIKRSW bewhiskered
BDEEEHILMTW thimbleweed
BDEEEHIMMNO homme de bien
BDEEEIILRSV disbeliever
BDEEEIIRRSV Sir Bedivere
BDEEEILLNPP bleed nipple
BDEEEILLNTU belle-de-nuit
BDEEEILLORV Old Believer
BDEEEILMNTV bedevilment
BDEEEILMPRT redemptible
BDEEEILMRTT Bette Midler
BDEEEILOSTW boiled sweet
BDEEEILPRSS depressible
BDEEEIMMRRS disremember
BDEEEIMNNTZ bedizenment
BDEEEIMORRR embroiderer
BDEEEINNNTU bien entendu
BDEEELLLOVW well-beloved
BDEEELNSSSS blessedness
BDEEELORTTX letterboxed
BDEEFFGIJRS Jeff Bridges
BDEEFHIILLS fish-bellied
BDEEFHIIRRT The Firebird
BDEEFIIINRS defibrinise
BDEEFIIINRZ defibrinize
BDEEFIIOTTT fit to be tied
BDEEFLLNORU bell-founder
BDEEGGHIIRW weighbridge
BDEEGGLLNOO Golden Globe
BDEEGHINNTU unbenighted
BDEEGHIORSU bridge-house
BDEEGHOORRT god-botherer
BDEEGHORRTU gude-brother
BDEEGIILLNR ill breeding
BDEEGIILLNV bedevilling
BDEEGIILNRW bewildering
BDEEGINNRTU reed bunting
BDEEGINORTU outbreeding
BDEEGINRRTT Trent Bridge
BDEEGLNORRY goldenberry
BDEEGMNRSUU unsubmerged
BDEEHHLLOTT hold the belt
BDEEHIILLTW white-billed
BDEEHILLOUX double helix
BDEEHILMNSU unblemished
BDEEHIMNOOT ethmoid bone
BDEEHIOPSSW bishop's weed
BDEEHISTTTU bite the dust
BDEEHLLMTUW well-thumbed
BDEEHNNRTUU unburthened
BDEEIILNNYZ benzylidine
BDEEIILNSST distensible
BDEEIIMRSTT disembitter
BDEEIINNRTW binder twine
BDEEIINOTTU boîte de nuit
BDEEIIRSTTU distributee
BDEEILLMOOS loose-limbed
BDEEILLNPRS spellbinder
BDEEILMNOTY molybdenite
BDEEILMRRTU tumble-drier
BDEEILNORST stereoblind
BDEEILNOSSV devil's bones
BDEEILORRSW bowdleriser
BDEEILORRWZ bowdlerizer
BDEEIMMNRUX mixed number
BDEEIMMORRV overbrimmed
BDEEIMNNRUX index number
BDEEINNRTTU underbitten
BDEEINNSSSU business end
BDEEIORSSTU sober-suited
BDEEJLORSTU Jules Bordet
BDEELLOORTT bloodletter
BDEELLOOSSV blood vessel
BDEELLORRRY roller derby
BDEELMRRTUY tumble-dryer
BDEELNOOSTT bottle-nosed
BDEELNORTUY double-entry

BDEELPRRTUY	perturbedly
BDEENNNORTU	under-bonnet
BDEENORSTTU	deobstruent
BDEENPRRTUU	unperturbed
BDEEOOPRTTU	torpedo tube
BDEEOORSSTT	desert boots
BDEFFLNNOUU	bundle of fun
BDEFHILMNOS	Flemish bond
BDEFHIORRST	for the birds
BDEFHLSSTUU	busted flush
BDEFHNOOORU	bed of honour
BDEFILORSTU	double first
BDEFLLNORTU	bull-fronted
BDEFLLNORUY	bell-foundry
BDEFLLOOORW	blood-flower
BDEFLNOOORZ	blood-frozen
BDEGGHIILLN	hedging-bill
BDEGGHLNOOU	golden bough
BDEGGIIIMNT	biting midge
BDEGGIINRSW	swing bridge
BDEGHIIIRRS	Irish bridge
BDEGHIIRSTW	bridge whist
BDEGHILNNOS	English bond
BDEGHKOOOOT	the Good Book
BDEGHOOORRT	good-brother
BDEGIIINNRW	wire binding
BDEGIILLNNS	single-blind
BDEGIILMNSS	dissembling
BDEGIINNRST	bird-nesting
BDEGIIOPRTV	pivot bridge
BDEGILNNNUY	unbendingly
BDEGILNTTUW	butt welding
BDEGIMORRSY	Dogberryism
BDEGINORSTW	bowstringed
BDEGIORRSTU	Stourbridge
BDEGLOORTTU	bottle-gourd
	gutterblood
BDEGLOOSSUY	God bless you!
BDEHHOOORRT	brotherhood
BDEHIIILNTY	inhibitedly
BDEHIIINNTU	uninhibited
BDEHIIKLLTY	Billy the Kid
BDEHIILORST	boiled shirt
BDEHIILPRSU	shipbuilder
BDEHIINNPTU	nip in the bud
BDEHIKLNOOY	blind hookey
BDEHIKLNOTU	doublethink
BDEHILNPSUU	unpublished
BDEHILOOPRY	hyperboloid
BDEHIMOORSU	rhomboideus
BDEHINNRSUU	unburnished
BDEHINNRTUW	burn-the-wind
BDEHLNORTTU	thunderbolt
BDEHMOOORST	smooth-bored
BDEHNORRSUY	hounds-berry
BDEIIIILNSV	indivisible
BDEIIIILNTY	inedibility
BDEIIILMSSS	dismissible
BDEIIILNTVY	vendibility
BDEIIISSUVV	subdivisive
BDEIILLLRWY	Billy Wilder
BDEIILMRSUU	subdelirium
BDEIINNRTUW	wind turbine
BDEIIRRSTTU	distributer
BDEIJNOTTTU	butted joint
BDEIKLOOSSV	devil's books
BDEIKNNORSZ	bronzed skin
BDEIKNORSTU	strikebound
BDEILLLNORR	rollerblind
BDEILLLORTU	double trill
BDEILLOSTUX	billets-doux
BDEILNNOOOS	in one's blood
BDEILNORSTY	blind-storey
BDEILNTTTUW	blunt-witted
BDEIMMNOPRU	Premium Bond
BDEIMNORSSY	bi syndromes
BDEINNORTTU	run into debt
BDEINORSTTU	Brotstudien
BDEINOSSSUU	dubiousness
BDEISSTTTUU	substituted
BDELLOSSTUY	doubtlessly
BDELNOOPRST	bloodsprent
BDELOOSTTUU	double-stout
BDEMOOOOPRT	torpedo boom
BDEMOOORSSY	rosy-bosomed
BDFGIIKNORS	king of birds
BDFIILLLNOO	billionfold
BDFILMOSTUU	misdoubtful
BDFKOOOORSW	book of words
BDFLNOOOOSY	nobody's fool
BDFLOOOORTU	out for blood
BDFNOOOSTUU	out of bounds
BDGGIIILNOS	disobliging
BDGGIIINNNR	ring binding
BDGGIIINNRS	singing-bird
BDGHIIMMNRU	Humming-Bird
	hummingbird
BDGIILMNNOW	mind-blowing
BDGIILNNORT	Bridlington
BDGIILNOTUU	outbuilding
BDGIIMMNNNU	mind-numbing
BDGILLOOTUY	blood-guilty
BDGILNOOPTY	blood typing
BDGINNOORRU	ground-robin
BDGINOOPPPY	body-popping
BDGNNOOORRW	Gordon Brown
BDGNORRSTUU	groundburst
BDHKOORSTUY	Dukhobortsy
BDHLMNOOTUV	von Humboldt
BDHNNOOORUU	honour-bound
BDIIIILNSVY	indivisibly
BDIIINOSSUV	subdivision
BDIILMMNSTU	blind summit
BDIIMNORTUY	moribundity
BDIIMOORRSS	bromidrosis
BDIIORRSTTU	distributor
BDINRSSTUUY	subindustry
BDLMNOOTTUU	button-mould
BDLOOOPRSST	blood sports
BEEEEFHRRSZ	fresh breeze
BEEEEGILRTT	tiger beetle
BEEEEGIMNST	besiegement

BEEEEHLLSVW	bevel wheels
BEEEEIMNTTW	betweentime
BEEEELPPPRT	betel pepper
BEEEENNSSTW	betweenness
BEEEFHINRSS	fines herbes
BEEEFLORRTU	troublefree
BEEEFOORRTY	freebootery
BEEEGGGLORS	beer goggles
BEEEGGIORST	Georgie Best
BEEEGGLOOOR	George Boole
BEEEGGOORRY	George Robey
BEEEGHILPST	The Big Sleep
BEEEGHILRTZ	light breeze
BEEEGHLOTTW	get the elbow
BEEEGIINNOR	bioengineer
BEEEGILLNPS	spelling bee
BEEEGILLNRT	belligerent
BEEEGILLNSS	legibleness
BEEEGILMNSY	beseemingly
BEEEGILMNTU	beguilement
BEEEGIMNNSU	unbeseeming
BEEEGIMPRSS	Bessemer pig
BEEEGINNNRZ	benzene ring
BEEEGINRRST	Steinberger
BEEEGLNORTT	bottle-green
	greenbottle
BEEEGNOORTT	go one better
BEEEHIKNTWY	in by the week
BEEEHILLMRS	embellisher
BEEEHILLNOR	helleborine
BEEEHILNPRS	prehensible
BEEEHLLRSTT	shelter belt
BEEEHLORTTT	three-bottle
BEEEHLPSSTU	steeplebush
BEEEHORRSTV	The Observer
BEEEIIJLMSU	semi-jubilee
BEEEIILMRSV	misbeliever
BEEEIKMORSU	boeremusiek
BEEEIKNRTTU	knee-tribute
BEEEILLRTYZ	leze-liberty
BEEEILMPPRT	pre-emptible
BEEEILNNORV	non-believer
BEEEILNPRTV	preventible
BEEEILPRRSS	repressible
BEEEILPRRTV	pervertible
BEEEILPRSSX	expressible
BEEEIMMMRRS	misremember
BEEEIMMNOTT	emboîtement
BEEEINNRSTV	Ernest Bevin
BEEEIOPRRRS	Robespierre
BEEEIOQRTUU	bouquetière
BEEEIRSTTTW	Bitter Sweet
	bittersweet
BEEELMMNOTW	embowelment
BEEELMMNRTT	tremblement
BEEELMNNNOT	ennoblement
BEEELNOSTTU	snout beetle
BEEELORSSWY	eyebrowless
BEEEMMNORTW	embowerment
BEEENOPPRTY	teeny-bopper
BEEENORSSSV	verboseness
BEEFFINNOOZ	Benioff zone
BEEFGIINNTT	benefitting
BEEFGINOORT	freebooting
BEEFGINRSUZ	subfreezing
BEEFGLLOORW	globeflower
BEEFHLLRRSU	fuller's-herb
BEEFIKNRTTU	butter knife
BEEFILNRRST	bristle-fern
BEEFILRSTTU	butterflies
BEEFKLLRUUY	rebukefully
BEEGGHORSUW	George W Bush
BEEGGIILNSY	besiegingly
BEEGGILSSTU	suggestible
BEEGGINSTTX	next biggest
BEEGGNOORRW	brown George
	George Brown
BEEGGNORRSU	George Burns
BEEGHIINPST	sheep-biting
BEEGHIISSTU	The Big Issue
BEEGHIKMOST	the big smoke✧
BEEGHILLLSS	sleigh bells
BEEGHILLNRT	ring the bell
BEEGHILNORT	bring to heel
BEEGHIMNNTT	benightment
BEEGHIMNRTU	number eight
BEEGHINNORR	herringbone
BEEGHLNOORT	the long robe
BEEGIILLNVY	believingly
BEEGIILNNUV	unbelieving
BEEGIILNQTU	quilting bee
BEEGIILNRST	Gilbertines
BEEGIIMNRTT	embittering
BEEGIIOORSU	bourgeoisie
BEEGIKKNOOP	bookkeeping
BEEGIKLNNSY	Ben Kingsley
BEEGILLMNOW	embowelling
BEEGILLNSST	bestselling
BEEGILLRRTY	Gilbert Ryle
BEEGILNNOSS	ignobleness
BEEGILNNPUU	blue penguin
BEEGILNSSSU	leg-business
BEEGIMNOSTT	misbegotten
BEEGINOPRRY	pigeon-berry
BEEGJRRSUYY	rugby jersey
BEEGNNOORTU	bonnet-rouge
BEEGNORRTUU	bourtree-gun
BEEGPRRRSSU	Pressburger
BEEHHISTTTW	with the best
BEEHIIKNNRS	Henrik Ibsen
BEEHIILNRRU	Henri Breuil
BEEHIIMSSST	Bessie Smith
BEEHIKLNRRT	Bert Hinkler
BEEHIKLORRT	brotherlike
BEEHIKORTUW	Bourke-White
BEEHILLSTTU	blue thistle
BEEHILMMNST	blemishment
BEEHILMNOOP	mobile phone
BEEHILNNPTT	Phil Bennett
BEEHILNOTTU	into the blue
BEEHILOPRSY	hyperbolise
BEEHILOPRYZ	hyperbolize

BEEHILOTTTW white bottle
BEEHILPRRSU republisher
BEEHIMNOORT theobromine
BEEHIMRRRUV River Humber
BEEHINNOTTW white bonnet
BEEHINSSSTU the business
BEEHIORRSST Borsetshire
BEEHIQRSTUY by the squire
BEEHJNORSTW John Webster
BEEHJOPSSUY Joseph Beuys
BEEHKMNORRY broken rhyme
BEEHKNOORSU house-broken
BEEHKOOORRT Robert Hooke
BEEHLLNOOPR Bellerophon
BEEHLMNORUW whole number
BEEHLOORSTW The Rose Bowl
BEEHLORSTTU the Troubles
BEEHLRRRTUY hurtleberry
BEEHLRRTTTU Rhett Butler
BEEHMNORTTT betrothment
BEEHMOORSTT mothers-to-be
BEEHNORRTUV overburthen
BEEHOPRRSTT stepbrother
BEEIIILPSTT epistilbite
BEEIILLORSS brise-soleil
BEEIILMPRSS impressible
permissible
BEEIILMPSUZ zum Beispiel
BEEIILNOPST bite one's lip
BEEIILNSSSV visibleness
BEEIIRRTTUV retributive
BEEIJLPRSTY J B Priestley
BEEIKLLNOTT Klein bottle
BEEIKOOPRRZ Booker Prize
BEEILLLNTUY ebulliently
BEEILLNRSTT Brinell test
BEEILLORRSU irresoluble
BEEILLRRRTU bull terrier
BEEILLRSTTT bellettrist
BEEILLSTTTY set little by
BEEILMMNORT embroilment
BEEILMNORTT bitter lemon
BEEILMNORTY Emily Brontë
BEEILMNSSSU sublimeness
BEEILNNOSTW tennis elbow
BEEILNOPRSS responsible
BEEILNOPRTU blue pointer
BEEILNOQSSU obliqueness
BEEILNOSTUY isobutylene
BEEILNPSSSU suspensible
BEEILNRRSSU blue rinsers
BEEILNRSSTT brittleness
BEEILORSSSV brisés volés
BEEILOSSSVY obsessively
BEEILPRRSSY repressibly
BEEIMMNPRRU prime number
BEEIMPRSSTT Septembrist
BEEINNOORTU boutonnière
BEEINNORRST Norbertines
BEEINORRSTT sternotribe
BEEINORSTTY tenebrosity
BEEINORTTTW twitter-bone
BEEINRRRTWY winterberry
BEEINRSSTTU butteriness
BEEINRSSTUV subservient
BEEINRTTUUV venturi tube✧
BEEJLNOSSSS joblessness
BEEJOORTTUV objet trouvé
BEEKMNOORRY money broker
BEEKMNOORTY more by token
BEEKOOPRRRW power broker
BEELLLLOWYY yellow-belly
BEELLMRSSSU slumberless
BEELLNOSSUV volubleness
BEELLPRTTUY belly putter
BEELMMORSSU slumbersome
BEELMNORTTU Mount Elbert
BEELMOORSTU troublesome
BEELOORSTTT bottle store
BEELPRSSTUU supersubtle
BEEMNORRRRY Rory Bremner
BEENNNOTTTY Tony Bennett
BEENOORRRST Robert Ensor
BEENQRSSSUU brusqueness
BEERRRSTTUU surrebutter
BEFGHILLRTU bullfighter
BEFGIILLNOR foreign bill
BEFGIILNORT bring to life
BEFGIILNTTY befittingly
BEFGIINNTTU unbefitting
BEFGILMRRUY mulberry fig
BEFHIILLLLT fill the bill
BEFHILLMSTU thimblefuls
BEFHILLOOTT foot the bill
BEFHILLOSSW bellows-fish
BEFHLLORRTU full brother
BEFHLMORTUU rule of thumb
rule-of-thumb
BEFHLOORRTW froth-blower
BEFIIILLTXY flexibility
BEFIILNORRU neurofibril
BEFILLOORST bill of store
BEFILMNRSSU brimfulness
BEFILMOORRT floor timber
BEFIMOORRSU morbiferous
BEFIMORRSUU umbriferous
BEFINORSTTT frostbitten
BEFKNOOORTU fortune book
BEFLLMRSTUU tumblerfuls
BEFLLOOPRTU bullet-proof
BEFOORRRSTT Robert Frost
BEGGGILNOOT bootlegging
BEGGHIINNOR neighboring
BEGGHILNORS Helsingborg
BEGGHINRRSY Henry Briggs
BEGGHNNRUUY bunny-hugger
BEGGIILLNNR bellringing
BEGGIILLNUY beguilingly
BEGGIINNNNU unbeginning
BEGGILNOOVX boxing glove
BEGGINOORRS Bognor Regis
BEGGOPRRSUU Bruges group

BEGHHIIRTTW birth weight
BEGHIILNTUW blue whiting
BEGHIINNOSW wishing-bone
BEGHILLNOSU bell-housing
BEGHILNOOSW bowling shoe
BEGHILNORUY neighbourly
BEGHINOPSTT betting shop
BEGHINRRSSU herring-buss
BEGHIPRRSTU superbright
BEGHORSSTTU ghostbuster
BEGIIIILLTY eligibility
BEGIILNOSTU biting louse
BEGIINRSTUV Vitus Bering
BEGIKLLNOOS bookselling
BEGILLMNRTY tremblingly
BEGILMNNRTU untrembling
BEGILNNORRY lingonberry
BEGILNORSVY observingly
BEGINNORSUV unobserving
BEGLNORRUWY Gurley Brown
BEGMNNORRUW wrong number
BEGMNOOORSU ombrogenous
BEHHIMORRTT birth mother
BEHHIOOPSTT theophobist
BEHHJNOOSTY John Sotheby
BEHIIIOPRTV prohibitive
BEHIIKLLLOY like billy-oh
BEHIILNOTTY the nobility
BEHIILPRSTY liberty ship
BEHIIMNPRRS brine shrimp
BEHIIMOSTWY whiteboyism✧
BEHIINPRSTU tribuneship
BEHIINRRTTY herb-trinity
BEHIINRSSST Britishness
BEHIKKOOSST kiss the book
BEHIKNOOSSS bookishness
BEHIKOOSTTX textbookish
BEHILLNSSSU bullishness
BEHILMNPSTU publishment
BEHILMOPRSY hyperbolism
BEHIMNNRSTU burnishment
BEHINOORSSS boorishness
BEHINORRTTW twin brother
BEHINORTWYY white bryony
BEHINRSSSTU brutishness
BEHIOORRSUV herbivorous
BEHJNNOOORS John Osborne
BEHKRRSTUUY brush turkey
BEHLLLSSSUY blushlessly
BEHLMOORSTT lobster moth
BEHLNOORTTU buttonholer
BEHLNORRTUY unbrotherly
BEHLOORRSTU soul brother
BEHMNOORTUU Bournemouth
BEHMOOOSTTU bottom house
BEHNNOOTTTU on the button
BEHNORSTTWY north-by-west
west-by-north
BEHOORRSSTX boxer shorts
BEHOSSTTUWY south-by-west
west-by-south
BEIIILMMORS immobiliser
BEIIILMMORZ immobilizer
BEIIILMNRST libertinism
BEIIILMQRUU equilibrium
BEIIILNSSTY sensibility
BEIIILNSTTY tensibility
BEIIILQRSTU equilibrist
BEIIILQRTUY equilibrity
BEIIILRRTTY terribility
BEIIILLORSSY berylliosis
BEIILLORSTV Orbitsville
BEIILLORTUV blue vitriol
BEIILMPRSSY permissibly
BEIILNOSSSU biliousness
BEIILNRSSST bristliness
BEIILRRSSTV verslibrist
BEIINNPSTXY sixpenny bit
BEIINORRTTU retribution
BEIINORSTUV inobtrusive
BEIKKLNPSUY sky-blue pink
BEIKLNNOOTW bowline knot
BEIKLNOSTTT ink-blot test
BEILLLLOSUY libellously
BEILLMPSTUU submultiple
BEILLNOPTTU bullet point
BEILLNORSVW Brownsville
BEILLNOSSSU bull session
BEILLORRSUY irresolubly
BEILLORSSTT stilbestrol
BEILMNOOOTT Milton Obote
BEILMNOOPSS monoblepsis
BEILMNOORTW winter-bloom
BEILMOORSTT mortise bolt
BEILMORRSTW bristle worm
BEILMORSSTU mossbluiter
BEILMPRRSTU rumble strip
BEILMSSTTUY system-built
BEILNOPRRTU pilot burner
BEILNOPRSSY responsibly
BEILOPRRSTU protrusible
BEILORSTUVY obtrusively
BEIMNOPSSTU montes pubis
BEIMNPPRTUU turbine pump
BEIMNSSSSSU submissness
BEIMOORRTTV river bottom
BEIMPSSTUUV subsumptive
BEINNOPTTWY twopenny bit
BEINOOSSSUV obviousness
BEINOPRRSTU stirrup bone
BEINORSTUUV unobtrusive
BEINPRRTTTU butter-print
BEINQRRSUYY quinsy-berry
BEINSSTTTUU substituent
BEIOPRRSSSU subprioress
BEIORRRTTUY retributory
BEIORSSTUUV subvitreous
BEKKMORTTUU kokum butter
BEKLMOPRRUW plumber-work
BEKNNNOSTUW unbeknownst
BEKNORRTUWY turkey brown
BELLMOSSSUY bless my soul!

BELLNRTTUUY turbulently
BELLORSSSTU Butler-Sloss
BELMNOOPRSU numbers pool
BELMNORSTUU Mount Elbrus
BELNNNOORSY Byron Nelson
BELNOOOPSTW blow one's top
BELNOORTTUW trouble-town
BELNOOSTUUY bounteously
BELOOPRSTTU trouble spot
BEMNNOORTUY money to burn
BEMOOPRRSTY Port Moresby
BENOPRSSTTU press button
press-button
BENPPRRSSUU Burns Supper
BERRSSTTTUU trustbuster
BFFGINOSTUX stuffing box
BFFHIMOPTTU buff-tip moth
BFFLOOPRSUY Fosbury flop
BFGHIILLOST bill of sight
BFGIIILNTUY fungibility
BFHILLORSTY Bill Forsyth
BFHKOOOORSU book of hours
BFILLNOTUUY bountifully
BFILOORSTUU tubiflorous
BFLLOORUUYY bully for you
BGGHIILLNTY blightingly
BGGILLMNRUY grumblingly
BGGINNOORUU bourguignon
BGGLMOOORSS grog-blossom
BGHHIIMORSW highbrowism
BGHHKOOORTU book through
BGHHLOORTTU through bolt
BGHIIINRRTV virgin birth✧
BGHIILLRTWY Billy Wright
BGHIINOPPWY whipping boy
BGHIKNOSTWY know by sight
BGHILOPRTTU bolt upright
BGHIMNPTTUU tub-thumping
BGHINOOOSTX shooting box
BGIIILLLTUY gullibility
BGIIKNOORTW writing-book
BGIILLNNPRU pruning bill
BGIILNNOPSW spin bowling
BGIILNNORRU burling-iron
BGIILOORSTT tribologist
BGIINOOOSST gnotobiosis
BGIINOSTTTW towing-bitts
BGIKNNOSTUY king's bounty
BGILLMNSTUY stumblingly
BGINNNOSTUW snow bunting
BGINOOOPPTT boot-topping
BGLLMOOOSYY symbolology
BGLMOOPRSUY symbol group
BHHMMOOPTUY hop-o'-my-thumb
BHIIIMOORTU Hirobumi Ito
BHIIINOOPRT prohibition✧
BHIIIOPRSTU triphibious
BHIILLLRSUY Silbury Hill
BHIILMOPRTY timbrophily
BHIILMRSTUW Wilbur Smith
BHIIOOPRRTY prohibitory
BHIJLLMNOSU John Bullism
BHIKNNOOSTW with knobs on
BHIKOOOTTUW without book
BHILMOOSTYY tomboyishly
BHIMNOOPRRT prothrombin
BHINORSTTTU shirt button
BIIILMOPSSS possibilism
BIIILOPSSST possibilist
BIIILOPSSTY possibility
BIIILORSTTY torsibility
BIIKLLMORST Bristol-milk
BIIKNOORSSV Novosibirsk
BIILLNOORTU tourbillion
BIILLOOSUVY obliviously
BIILMORRTUU lubritorium
BIILNRTTTUY tributyltin
BIILOOQSTUU obliquitous
BIIMNNOSTUU submunition
BIIMNOOSTUX moxibustion
BIIMOPRSSTU Möbius strip
BILMMOORSTT Mt Stromboli
BILMOPSTUUY bumptiously
BILNNOOORSU blouson noir
BILNOOOSUXY obnoxiously
BIMNNOORRSS Mrs Robinson
BIMNOPSSTUU subsumption
BIMORSSTUUU rumbustious
BINNOOOSUUX unobnoxious
BINOOPSSSTU Puss in Boots
BIOOOPPRRSU opprobrious
BLLMMOOPSSU plum-blossom
BLLMORSSUUY slumbrously
BLLOORSTUUY troublously
BLMNORSSUUU unslumbrous
BMMMMNOSUUU summum bonum
BMMNOTTTUUY tummy button
BNOORRSTUWW burrowstown

C

CCCCIMOORSU micrococcus
CCCCKKLOOOU cuckoo clock
CCCDDHOSTUY Scotch cuddy
CCCDEEIINNO coincidence
CCCDEHINOSY synecdochic
CCCDEIINNOY coincidency
CCCDENNOOTU unconcocted
CCCDGINOOOO gonococcoid
CCCDIIIOOSS coccidiosis
CCCDILOOPSU diplococcus
CCCEEEENRSX excrescence
CCCEEENRSXY excrescency
CCCEEFLLNOU flocculence
CCCEEIILMST eclecticism
CCCEEIINRTV civic centre
CCCEEINOORT enterococci
CCCEENNORRU concurrence
CCCEENNORST concrescent
CCCEFIINOPS conspecific
CCCEFILMRTU circumflect
CCCEHHIKLRS schrecklich
CCCEHIILPRT pitch circle

CCCEHILOSTY Sothic cycle
CCCEHKLLOTU collet chuck
CCCEIIMRRSU circumciser
CCCEIINNOPY concipiency
CCCEILORSST Celtic cross
CCCEIMPRSTU circumspect
CCCEINNOTTU Connecticut
CCCEINOOPRS necroscopic
CCCEIRSSTUY cysticercus
CCCENNORRUY concurrency
CCCGILOPRUY cyclic group
CCCHHORRTUU church court
CCCHIIINNNO cinchoninic
CCCHILMOTYY cyclothymic
CCCHKLLORSU scroll chuck
CCCIIMMOORS microcosmic
CCCIIMOOPRS microscopic
CCCINOOOSSU coconscious
CCCINORSTUY succinctory
CCCIOOPSSTY cystoscopic
CCCOOOPRSTU Protococcus
CCDDEEENORS decrescendo
CCDDEEENSUU unsucceeded
CCDDEKLNOUU uncuckolded
CCDEEEEINNR Nicene Creed
CCDEEEFHIKN chickenfeed
CCDEEEGINOT genetic code
CCDEEEHHSTU Dutch cheese
CCDEEEIINRS iridescence
CCDEEELLORT recollected
CCDEEENNORT concentered
CCDEEENRRST Red Crescent
CCDEEFFIKOR deck officer
CCDEEFINOOS food science
CCDEEGIMNOO comedogenic
CCDEEHILORS Cecil Rhodes
CCDEEHILPSY psychedelic
CCDEEHINORS Second Reich
CCDEEHIORTT ricochetted
CCDEEIIINST insecticide
CCDEEIILMRS semicircled
CCDEEIILRRR circle-rider
CCDEEIIRRST directrices
CCDEEILMORU leucodermic
CCDEEILNOTY conceitedly
CCDEEILRRSS dress circle
CCDEEIMOSTY discomycete
CCDEEINNOUV unconceived
CCDEEIOPPRU preoccupied
CCDEEIORRSU cris de coeur
CCDEELLLOTY collectedly
CCDEELLNOTU uncollected
CCDEELNNOOS condolences
CCDEELNNORY concernedly
CCDEELNNOTY connectedly
CCDEEMNNOTU conducement
CCDEENNNORU unconcerned
CCDEENNNOTU unconnected
CCDEENNORTU unconcerted
CCDEENORRTU uncorrected
CCDEFIMRSUU circumfused
CCDEHHIKLNO hold in check
CCDEHILOPSY psychodelic
CCDEHIOOPRS dichroscope
CCDEHLORTUV Dutch clover
CCDEIILNOPS condisciple
CCDEIILOORT crocidolite
CCDEIIMORRT microcredit
CCDEILNORRU circle round
CCDEILNOXYY doxycycline
CCDEIMNOORS microsecond
CCDEIMOOOST octodecimos
CCDEINNNOUV unconvinced
CCDEINNOTUV unconvicted
CCDEINOOTTY endocytotic
CCDEINORSTT constricted
CCDEIOPRRTU picture cord
CCDENOORTUY country code
CCDENORSSTU conductress
CCDENORSTTU deconstruct
CCDENORSUUU unsuccoured
CCDFGKLOOOR crock of gold
CCDFLMOOORT cold comfort
CCDGILNNOUY conducingly
CCDHHILLOOS schoolchild
CCDHHIOORRY hydrochoric
CCDHIILORWY wild chicory
CCDHILOOPYY hypocycloid
CCDHIOORTTW witch doctor
CCDHIOOSTUU studio couch
CCDHIOPRRTY cryptorchid
CCDHMMNOOOR common chord
CCDILLMNNOU Don McCullin
CCDKMOSUUVY muscovy duck
CCEEEEFMNRS fremescence
CCEEEEILLRT electric eel
CCEEEEILNST telescience
CCEEEEILRTY electric eye
CCEEEEINPRT centrepiece
CCEEEFHIKNR neckerchief
CCEEEFHIRTV hectic fever
CCEEEFIKNPT picket fence
CCEEEFLNORS florescence
CCEEEGINNRS nigrescence
CCEEEGINOTT ectogenetic
CCEEEGINRVY vicegerency
CCEEEGNNORV convergence
CCEEEGNRSTU turgescence
CCEEEHHLOST cheesecloth
CCEEEHIKKNP keep in check
CCEEEHINNOR coinherence
incoherence
CCEEEHIPRRS speech-crier
CCEEEHORRTT crotcheteer
CCEEEHORRTY heterocercy
CCEEEIINPPR percipience
CCEEEIKOPPT pocket-piece
CCEEEILNQSU liquescence
CCEEEILSTWY sweet cicely
CCEEEIMORRT coercimeter
CCEEEINNNOV convenience
CCEEEINNPSS spinescence

CCEEEINOPRV preconceive
CCEEEINOPSS cenospecies
CCEEEINOSTX coexistence
CCEEEINPRSU pure science
CCEEEINRRST Cirencester
CCEEEINRSTV vitrescence
CCEEEIRSTUX executrices
CCEEELORTTU electrocute
CCEEEMNPSSU spumescence
CCEEENNOQSU consequence
CCEEENOPRST torpescence
CCEEENPRSTU putrescence
CCEEFFHINPT pinch effect
CCEEFFIINOT coefficient
CCEEFFIINSU sufficience
CCEEFHNRRUV French curve
CCEEFIILMOR comic relief
CCEEFIIMNNO omnificence
CCEEFIIMNNU munificence
CCEEFIINOPR proficience
CCEEFILNOST self-conceit
CCEEFILOOPR police force
CCEEFINOSST soft science
CCEEFLNNORS self-concern
CCEEFLNOPST self-concept
CCEEFNORTTU counterfect
CCEEGHHKRRU Greek Church
CCEEGHINOST geotechnics
CCEEGINNNOT contingence
CCEEGINOOTT geotectonic
CCEEGINOTTY cytogenetic
CCEEGLLORSV clever clogs
CCEEGNNOOST cognoscente
CCEEGNNORVY convergency
CCEEGNOOPRS precognosce
CCEEGNOORRT concert-goer
CCEEGNRSTUY turgescency
CCEEHHINOTT theotechnic
CCEEHHKORRY chokecherry
CCEEHHLORSW schreech-owl
CCEEHIIKKNV chicken kiev
CCEEHIIKNRW chicken wire
CCEEHIKLNOR nickel-ochre
CCEEHILORST cholesteric
CCEEHIMORTT ectothermic
CCEEHINNORY incoherency
CCEEHINOPSY Chinese copy
CCEEHINORRS choirscreen
CCEEHINORTT theocentric
CCEEHKLLLOS cockleshell
CCEEHMOPTYY phycomycete
CCEEHNNPRTU centre punch
CCEEHNORSTU touch screen
touch-screen
CCEEHNRRSWW screw-wrench
CCEEIILNNOS consilience
CCEEIILNOSS soil science
CCEEIILORST isoelectric
CCEEIILRTTY electricity
CCEEIIMMNSU ecumenicism
CCEEIIMNNOS omniscience
CCEEIIMNOSV misconceive
CCEEIIMNRTT centimetric
CCEEIIMOSST cosmeticise
CCEEIIMOSTZ cosmeticize
CCEEIINOPTV nociceptive
CCEEIINPPRY percipiency
CCEEIINPRRT pericentric
CCEEIKLMORT mole cricket
CCEEILMORTY myoelectric
CCEEILNNORT non-electric
CCEEILNNOTV conventicle
CCEEILNOOPR cornice-pole
CCEEILNORST electronics
stone circle
CCEEILNORSY cycloserine
CCEEILNORTT telocentric
CCEEILNOSST conceitless
CCEEILNQSUY liquescency
CCEEILPPRRU upper circle
CCEEILPPRTU peptic ulcer
CCEEIMNOORT econometric
CCEEIMNRSTU music centre
CCEEINNNOVY conveniency
CCEEINNOQTU cinquecento
CCEEINNOSSS conciseness
CCEEINNOSST consistence
CCEEINOORTW once or twice
CCEEINORRTU Eurocentric
CCEEINOSSSX ex concessis
CCEEINOSTUV consecutive
CCEEIOPRSTU Eurosceptic
CCEEJNORRTU conjecturer
CCEEKOORRRV rocker cover
CCEELSSSSSU successless
CCEEMNNNORT concernment
CCEENOPSSTU conceptuses
CCEENORRSST correctness
CCEEOOPRSTV vectorscope
CCEEOORRRTV overcorrect
CCEFFIINSUY sufficiency
CCEFFINOORW Crown Office
CCEFGIKLNOS self-cocking
CCEFHHINPRT French pitch
CCEFHIIISTT fetichistic
CCEFHIIMORS microfiches
CCEFHIKNRST French stick
CCEFIIIPSTY specificity
CCEFIILNOTV conflictive
CCEFIINNOPS non-specific
CCEFIINOPRY proficiency
CCEFILMOORS scoleciform
CCEFINORSST cross-infect
CCEFIORRSUU cruciferous
CCEFKLLOORW flower-clock
CCEGHIIIOPS pichiciegos
CCEGHIILNOR cholinergic
CCEGHIINORT ricocheting
CCEGHIINOSZ schizogenic
CCEGHIKNRST check-string
CCEGHIMNOOR chromogenic
CCEGHINOPSY psychogenic

CCEGIINNORR cornice ring
CCEGIINOOTX toxicogenic
CCEGILNOORY eccrinology
CCEGILNOOSY synecologic
CCEGINNNORT concentring
CCEGINNNOTY contingency
CCEGINNOOST cognoscenti
CCEGINOPRTY cryptogenic
CCEHHHORSUU house church
CCEHHILNTTU in the clutch
CCEHHIMRSTU Church Times
CCEHHIOSSTT schottische
CCEHHKOOORT crochet hook
CCEHHLNOORY rhynchocoel
CCEHHMORSUU church mouse
CCEHHORRTUW church tower
CCEHIIKNNOV kinchin-cove
CCEHIILNOPR necrophilic
CCEHIILOOPS helioscopic
CCEHIIMORTU home circuit
CCEHIINPRST sphincteric
CCEHIIPRRTY hypercritic
CCEHIKKOSTY hockey stick
CCEHIKMOORS mock-heroics
CCEHIKNOOOR cornice-hook
CCEHIKNPTTU ticket punch
CCEHIKSSSTT Schick's test
CCEHILLNOOR clinochlore
CCEHILNOORT Technicolor®
CCEHILNOPTY polytechnic
CCEHIMNOORT homocentric
CCEHIMNOSTU technomusic
CCEHIMNOTYZ zymotechnic
CCEHIMOOPRT chemotropic
ectomorphic
CCEHIMOORTY orchiectomy
CCEHIMOOSTT cosmothetic
CCEHINNRSSU crunchiness
CCEHINOOSTZ zootechnics
CCEHINOPRTY pyrotechnic
CCEHIOOPRTT ectotrophic
CCEHIORRSUV hircocervus
CCEHKLOSTTU shuttlecock
CCEHKMOORTU Cockermouth
CCEHKNORRSU corn shucker
CCEHKNPRSUU sucker-punch
CCEHLNOOPSY lychnoscope
CCEHMOOOPRS chromoscope
CCEHNOOOPRS chronoscope
CCEIIILMOPU Emilio Pucci
CCEIIILRTUV live circuit
CCEIIIMPRTU empiricutic
CCEIIINSSTT scientistic
CCEIIJMNORT microinject
CCEIIKLRSTY city slicker
CCEIIKNSSTT stick insect
CCEIILMNORT clinometric
CCEIILMORST cliometrics
CCEIILOOPRT poliorcetic
CCEIIMMORRT micrometric
CCEIIMMOSST cosmeticism
CCEIIMOORST sociometric
CCEIIMORSTV viscometric
CCEIINNNOST inconscient
CCEIINOORST coercionist
CCEIINOPRTU open circuit
CCEIIOPRRTY reciprocity
CCEIJNNOTUV conjunctive
CCEIKLMOORT mortice lock
CCEIKLNOPRU cupronickel
CCEILLNOOST collections
CCEILMOORTU coulometric
CCEILMORUVV circumvolve
CCEILNNOTTU noctilucent
CCEILNOPRTY polycentric
CCEILNORRTU current coil
CCEILNORRTY incorrectly
CCEILOOPRTU police-court
CCEIMNNNOOO non-economic
CCEINNNOOST connections
CCEINNOORST concertinos
CCEINNOOSTU consecution
CCEINNOPRRW crown prince
CCEINNOSSTY consistency
CCEINOOPSTU conceptious
CCEJNNORTUU conjuncture
CCEKLORRTTU turret clock
CCEKMNOSTUU come unstuck
CCEKMOORSTY comstockery
CCELLNSTUUY succulently
CCELNOOOOPS colonoscope
CCELNOOPPRW copple-crown
CCELORSSSUU succourless
CCEMORRUYYY cry you mercy
CCENORRSTTU constructer
current-cost
reconstruct
CCEOOOPPRST proctoscope
CCEOOOPRRSS coprocessor
CCFGIILNNOT conflicting
CCFIIINORUX crucifixion✧
CCFIILNNOOT confliction
CCGGHHIINOU hiccoughing
CCGGHHINORU churchgoing
CCGHIIKLNOO choking coil
CCGHIIKMNOT thick-coming
CCGHILNOOOR chronologic
CCGHILNORSY scorchingly
CCGHILOOPSY psychologic
CCGHIOOPRSY hygroscopic
CCGIIINRRTU ring circuit
CCGIILOOOTX toxicologic
CCHHIIORSST Scotch-Irish
CCHHILOOORS choir school
CCHHMNOOPTU not much chop
CCHIIILMORT microlithic
CCHIIILNOPS silicon chip
CCHIIINORTT trichinotic
CCHIIIOSTTY histiocytic
CCHIILNOOOS Ionic school
CCHIILOOPPS scopophilic
CCHIILOOPST Scotophilic

CCHIIMNOOPR microphonic
CCHIIMOPRTY microphytic
CCHIIMORSTW microswitch
CCHIINOOPRS rhinoscopic
CCHILMNOORY chylomicron
CCHILMOOPRY polychromic
CCHIMMNOOOR monochromic
CCHIMNOOPSY psychonomic
CCHIMOOORRR horror comic
CCHIMOOPRTY cormophytic
mycotrophic
CCHIOOOPRST orthoscopic
CCHIOOPSTXY psychotoxic
CCHIOPRSSYY cryophysics
CCHIORRSSST Christ-cross
CCHIORSSSTT cross-stitch
CCIIINNOTVY convicinity
CCIIKKORSSS scissor kick
CCIIKKQSSTU quick-sticks
CCIILMORRUU cirro-cumuli
cumulocirri
CCIILOOPSSU piscicolous
CCIILOORSTU colouristic
CCIIMMNOORS in microcosm
CCIIMMNOSTU communistic
CCIINNOOSSU inconscious
CCIINOPRTTY nyctitropic
CCIINOPSTUY conspicuity
CCIJNNNOOTU conjunction
CCIKKPPRTUU pick-up truck
CCIKLMNOOTU coconut milk
CCIKMMOOSST comstockism
CCILMOORSUU colour music
CCILMRRSUUU curriculums
CCILNNOOTUW town council
CCILNOOSSUY consciously
CCILNOOSTUU noctilucous
CCILOOORSTU corticolous
CCIMNNOOPTU compunction
CCINNOOSSUU unconscious
CCINOOPSSUU conspicuous
CCINOORRSTT constrictor
CCINOORSSSU cross cousin
CCIOOPRSSTY sporocystic
CCKMMNOOOST common stock
CCKNOORRTUY country rock
country-rock
CCLLOOORTUY collocutory
CCLNNOOORWY crown colony
CCLNOOOOPSY colonoscopy
CCLNOOOORSU concolorous
CCLOOORRSSU cross colour
CCNOORRSTTU constructor
CCNOORRSTUW crown courts
CCNOORTTUUY county court
CCOOOPPRSTY proctoscopy
CDDDEEEEGKL deckle-edged
CDDDEEENNSU undescended
CDDDEEILNUY undecidedly
CDDDELLMOOU cold-moulded
CDDDELRSUUY sculduddery
CDDDGIKNNOU nodding duck
CDDEEEENPRT precedented
CDDEEEFFOPR pedder-coffe
CDDEEEILPRT predilected
CDDEEEINNUV unevidenced
CDDEEEIPRTU decrepitude
CDDEEENNOPS despondence
CDDEEENNOPT co-dependent
CDDEEEOPRRR prerecorded
CDDEEFILNSU self-induced
CDDEEHLNSUU unscheduled
CDDEEHNNRSU sundrenched
CDDEEILLLLR Eric Liddell
CDDEEIILMPR middle price
CDDEEIINORT rodenticide
CDDEEILTUVY deductively
CDDEEINNRSU undiscerned
unrescinded
CDDEEINPRRU underpriced
CDDEEMMNNOU uncommended
CDDEENNOPSY despondency
CDDEENORSSW crowdedness
CDDEENRRTUY eddy current
CDDEEOORRVW overcrowded
CDDEEOPPRTU topped crude
CDDEFIIKLST fiddlestick
CDDEFIIMOST discomfited
CDDEGIINPRU rice pudding
CDDEGILLNOW cold welding
CDDEHIILMNR childminder
CDDEHIINRTW witch-ridden
CDDEHIKLTUW The Wild Duck
CDDEIIILNNS disinclined
CDDEIILPPSS slipped disc
CDDEIINNOOT conditioned
decondition
CDDEIINOSUU indeciduous
CDDEIKOPSTT spotted dick
CDDEILNOOTY dicotyledon
CDDEILNOSSU undisclosed
CDDEILOORSU discoloured
CDDEIMMOORS desmodromic
CDDEINNOOST endodontics
CDDEINSSSUU undiscussed
CDDEIOPSTUU cut up didoes
CDDEKKNNOOW knocked-down
CDDELLLMOOY mollycoddle
CDDELNOORSW Second World
CDDELOOPPTU cloud-topped
CDDELOORRRW world record
CDDELOORRWY Lord Cowdrey
CDDGIKNNOPU ducking-pond
CDDGIKNOPPU pock-pudding
CDDHIILQTUU Dutch liquid
CDEEEEFFLNS self-defence
CDEEEEFHMNO home-defence
CDEEEEFLLST self-elected
CDEEEEFLNSS defenceless
CDEEEEFLORS close-reefed
CDEEEEGINRR regredience
CDEEEEHKORS rose-cheeked

CDEEEEHKRRT three-decker
CDEEEEINPRX experienced
CDEEEFHIMNR chemin de fer
CDEEEFHNRRT trencher-fed
CDEEEFHORUV chef d'oeuvre
CDEEEFIILNS fin de siècle
CDEEEFIILRT electrified
CDEEEFILSTX self-excited
CDEEEFILTVY defectively
CDEEEFIORRT fore-recited
CDEEEFKORST stock-feeder
CDEEEFLNRST self-centred
CDEEEFLNRTU unreflected
CDEEEFLORSV self-covered
CDEEEFMNORT deforcement
CDEEEFNPRTU unperfected
CDEEEGHRTTU hedgecutter
CDEEEGIIMNO geomedicine
CDEEEGILNOR congé d'élire
CDEEEGILNXY exceedingly
CDEEEGINORS derecognise
CDEEEGINORZ derecognize
CDEEEHKORSY rosy-cheeked
CDEEEHSSSTU duchesse set
CDEEEIINSST necessitied
CDEEEIIOPPR period piece
CDEEEIKLNST needlestick
CDEEEILLNTT intellected
CDEEEILMNOR microneedle
CDEEEILNOST deselection
CDEEEILNSTT delitescent
CDEEEILOPRV velocipeder
CDEEEILORTT lie detector
CDEEEILPTVY deceptively
CDEEEINNRTT intercedent
CDEEEINPRTU unreceipted
CDEEEINPRUV unperceived
CDEEEINRSUX unexercised
CDEEEINSSTX excitedness
CDEEEINSSTY needcessity
CDEEELLORVW well-covered
CDEEELNPRTY precedently
CDEEEMMNORR recommender
CDEEEMNNOOR encomendero
CDEEENNNSTU unsentenced
CDEEENNOPRS respondence
CDEEENORRTT retrocedent
CDEEENORRUV unrecovered
CDEEENPRSTU unrespected
CDEEEOOPRRW woodcreeper
CDEEEOPRRSS predecessor
CDEEFFIKNST stiff-necked
CDEEFFINORU unofficered
CDEEFFOPRRT Ford Prefect
CDEEFHIKLOY field hockey
CDEEFHOORUV forevouched
CDEEFIILNTY deficiently
CDEEFIIMNOX fixed income
CDEEFIINPSU unspecified
CDEEFIINRTU uncertified
unrectified
CDEEFIIORRX ferric oxide
CDEEFIKLNRT ferntickled
CDEEFILLTUY deceitfully
CDEEFILNNTU uninflected
CDEEFILNORT field cornet
CDEEFILNORU fleur de coin
CDEEFILNORY ecofriendly
CDEEFILOSST close-fisted
CDEEFIMNORT comet-finder
CDEEFINORRT Fredericton
CDEEFLNOSSY confessedly
CDEEFNNORST frondescent
CDEEFNNOSSU unconfessed
CDEEFNORSTT soft-centred
CDEEFOORRTU tour de force
CDEEFOPRRTW word-perfect
CDEEGGINTTU cutting edge
CDEEGGLORSS cross-legged
CDEEGHHLOOS hedge-school
CDEEGIINOPT doting-piece
CDEEGIINRSW screwing die
CDEEGIJLOPU police-judge
CDEEGINOPRS proceedings
CDEEGLMNOUU come unglued
CDEEGNOOSTT cotton sedge
CDEEGNOSSSU second-guess
CDEEHHNORRS horse-drench
CDEEHIILOTT diotheletic✧
CDEEHIINNOS Indo-Chinese
CDEEHIINNST indehiscent
CDEEHIKNNTU unthickened
CDEEHIKNTVY kidney vetch
CDEEHILMNNR men-children
CDEEHILOTTY dyotheletic✧
CDEEHIMNORT endothermic
CDEEHIMNOST Demosthenic
CDEEHIOOSSS choose sides
CDEEHIOPRTV overpitched
CDEEHIOQSTU discotheque
discothèque
CDEEHLNORTU underclothe
CDEEHNNORTU truncheoned
CDEEHNOORRT on the record
CDEEHNOORSU echo-sounder
CDEEHNORTUU unretouched
CDEEHORRSST the Red Cross
CDEEIIILNSS dissilience
CDEEIIIMPTY epidemicity
CDEEIIKLNSS slickenside
CDEEIILNORT dereliction
CDEEIILRSVW wild service
CDEEIIMNRST densimetric
CDEEIIMORRS misericorde
CDEEIIMORTU eudiometric
CDEEIIMOSST domesticise
CDEEIIMOSTZ domesticize
CDEEIINNOTT identic note
CDEEIINOPTV point-device
CDEEIINORRT redirection
CDEEIINPTUV input device
CDEEIINRSTV viridescent

CDEEIINRTTU incertitude
CDEEIIOORTV Côte d'Ivoire
CDEEIIPRSTV descriptive
discerptive
CDEEIISTTTV detectivist
CDEEIJKOOVY video jockey
CDEEIKLMORU leukodermic
CDEEIKLNNOO nickelodeon
CDEEIKNNQUU unquickened
CDEEIKOPSTZ pocket-sized
CDEEILLOPPS close-lipped
CDEEILNNQUY delinquency
CDEEILNOORT intercooled
CDEEILNORSS crossed line
CDEEILNORTY reconditely
CDEEILNSSTU ductileness
CDEEILOORSU decolourise
CDEEILOORUZ decolourize
CDEEILOPRST corps d'élite
CDEEILOPRSU supercoiled
CDEEILRSUVY decursively
CDEEILRTUVY reductively
CDEEILSTUVY seductively
CDEEIMNNORS encrimsoned
CDEEIMNNRST discernment
rescindment
CDEEIMNOPRS endospermic
CDEEIMNOPTY idempotency
CDEEIMNORTV divorcement
CDEEIMOOPST decomposite
CDEEIMOORST osteodermic
CDEEIMOOSTX sextodecimo
CDEEINNOSTU tendencious
CDEEINNPRST prescindent
CDEEINOORTT condottiere
CDEEINOPRTV open verdict
CDEEINORRTU reintroduce
CDEEINORSUU in due course
CDEEINPRSUU superinduce
CDEEIOOOPPS opeidoscope
CDEEIORRSVY rediscovery
CDEEIORRTXY ex-directory
CDEEIRRRSVW screwdriver
CDEEIRSTTUV destructive
CDEEJNOPRTU unprojected
CDEEKNNRSSU druckenness
CDEEKNOORSS crookedness
CDEEKORRSTY dyer's rocket
dyer's-rocket
CDEELLLOPUW well-coupled
CDEELLMNOPU uncompelled
CDEELMNNOOT condolement
CDEELMNOPTU uncompleted
CDEELNNOTTY contentedly
CDEELNORRTU rodent ulcer
CDEELNRRTUY decurrently
CDEELNRTTUU uncluttered
CDEELPSSTUY suspectedly
CDEEMNNNOTU uncontemned
CDEEMNOOPUY compound eye
CDEEMNOPRTU compte rendu
producement
CDEEMOORSTY Comedy Store
CDEENNOPRSY respondency
CDEENNOQRUU unconquered
CDEENNORRTU centre round
CDEENNORTUU unrecounted
CDEENNORTUV unconverted
CDEENNOSTTU uncontested
CDEENOPRSSU unprocessed
CDEENOPRTTU unprotected
CDEENORRTUV undercovert
CDEENPSSTUU unsuspected
CDEEOOPPSSU pseudoscope
CDEEOOPRRUV overproduce
CDEEOPPRSTW screw-topped
CDEFFGIOOOS good offices
CDEFFIORTUY duty officer
CDEFFLOOORU off-coloured
CDEFGLOOPRU cudgel-proof
CDEFHIINRTW witch-finder
CDEFHILLORW flower child
CDEFHILORST foster-child
CDEFHIOOPRT pitched roof
pitch-roofed
CDEFIINNTUY infecundity
CDEFIINORST disinfector
CDEFIINORTU countrified
CDEFILNNOTY confidently
CDEFIMNNORU unconfirmed
CDEFIMNNOTU ciment fondu✧
CDEFINNNOTU unconfident
CDEFINORTUY countryfied
CDEFLLNNOUU funnel cloud
CDEFLNOOORS second floor
second-floor
CDEFMNOORTU uncomforted
CDEGGLRSUUY sculduggery
CDEGHHHIIPT high-pitched
CDEGHILNOOS deschooling
CDEGHINORRS Schrödinger
CDEGHINOSST second sight
CDEGIILNNNU undeclining
CDEGIINNORS considering
CDEGIINOOOV in good voice
CDEGIINOPTY copy-editing
CDEGIINSTTU side cutting
CDEGIKLMNOO mode-locking
CDEGIKLOORS sockdoliger
CDEGIKMMNOO kingdom come
CDEGILMNOOO demonologic
CDEGIMNORRU corrigendum
CDEGINNNOSS condignness
CDEGINNOOOT odontogenic
CDEGINOOPPU coup de poing
CDEGKLOOORS sockdologer
CDEGMORRSUY dog's-mercury
CDEGNOORRUV ground cover
CDEHHIOORSU orchid-house
CDEHHNOOOPR chordophone
CDEHIIINNOR enchiridion
CDEHIIKLLNU unchildlike

CDEHIIKLPPT thick-lipped
CDEHIIKTTTW thick-witted
CDEHIILLNOT decillionth
CDEHIILOOTT theodolitic
CDEHIILOTTY dyothelitic✧
CDEHIIMOOST dichotomise
CDEHIIMOOTZ dichotomize
CDEHIIMOSTT Methodistic
CDEHIIOOPRT epitrochoid
CDEHIKLSTTU lick the dust
CDEHIKMNPRU Humperdinck
CDEHILMNOOP monodelphic
CDEHILMORSU music holder
CDEHILNOSTU in the clouds
CDEHILOOOOV Voodoo Chile
CDEHILOORXY oxy-chloride
CDEHILOPRST poster child
CDEHILPRTUU pulchritude
CDEHIMNOOPR endomorphic
CDEHIMNOOUX xenodochium
CDEHIMNORST Christendom
McIntosh red
CDEHIMORRTU thermoduric
CDEHIMORRTY hydrometric
CDEHINNOSUY Deinonychus
CDEHINOOPRT endotrophic
CDEHINOPRRY Pondicherry
CDEHIOOPRST orthopedics
CDEHIOPRRST short-priced
CDEHIORTTUY youth credit
CDEHKLOORST stockholder
CDEHLNOORSU under-school
CDEHLNOOSUY endochylous
CDEHOOORRST horse-doctor
CDEHPPRSTUU Dutch supper
CDEIIILMRTT credit limit
CDEIIILNPRS discipliner
CDEIIILNSUV uncivilised
CDEIIILNUVZ uncivilized
CDEIIILSTUV civil-suited
CDEIIIMMSTU mediumistic
CDEIIINNORT indirection
CDEIIINNTVY incendivity
CDEIIINORTX nitric oxide
CDEIIINSTTV distinctive
CDEIIIOPRTY periodicity
CDEIIIRTTVY directivity
CDEIIISSTUV vicissitude
CDEIIJNSTUV disjunctive
CDEIIKKLNPT tickled pink
CDEIIKQTTUW quick-witted
CDEIILLMNOS millisecond
CDEIILLOORV cod-liver oil
CDEIILLOSUY deliciously
CDEIILLPTUY pellucidity
CDEIILNOSTU unsolicited
CDEIILNRTUY incredulity
CDEIILNTUVY inductively
CDEIILOORST sclerotioid
CDEIILOPSSU pediculosis
CDEIILOSTUV declivitous
CDEIIMMOOST commodities
CDEIIMNORST modernistic
CDEIIMOSTTY domesticity
CDEIIMPPRUY cypripedium
CDEIINNOORT conditioner
recondition
CDEIINNORTU credit union
CDEIINNOSTU discontinue
CDEIINOORTT condottieri
CDEIINOPRST description
discerption
CDEIINORRTT interdictor
CDEIINORRTU irreduction
CDEIINRSTTU distincture
CDEIIOOPRTX dexiotropic
CDEIIORSSUV discoursive
CDEIJNNOOST second joint
CDEIJNRSTUU disjuncture
CDEIKLNORTW trickle-down
CDEILNNNOOU on cloud nine
CDEILNNOTUY continuedly
CDEILNOORUU unicoloured
CDEILNOORUX colour index
CDEILNOPSST split second
split-second
CDEILNORSUU incredulous
CDEILOORRTU tricoloured
CDEILORSTTY Ridley Scott
CDEIMMNOPSU compendiums
CDEIMMNOTTU uncommitted
CDEIMNOOPSU compendious
CDEIMNOOSTU Comte Dunois
CDEIMNOSSTY syndesmotic
CDEINNOPRST nondescript
CDEINNORTUV uncontrived
CDEINNRTTUU untinctured
CDEINOOPSST endoscopist
CDEINOOSSTY endocytosis
CDEINORSSSU unscissored
CDEINORSTTU destruction
CDEINORSTUY countryside
CDEINORTUWY countrywide
CDEIOPRRTUW word picture
CDEIORSSTUY discourtesy
CDEIORSSUWW widow's cruse
CDEKKLNNOUW knuckle down
CDEKKNOOORR doorknocker
CDEKLOORSUY sky-coloured
CDEKMMOOSTY mock-modesty
CDEKMPRRTUU dumper truck
CDELLLOSSUY cloudlessly
CDELLNORSUY scoundrelly
CDELLOOOPRT protocolled
CDELLOPRRUW crowd-puller
CDELLORSUUY credulously
CDELOOORTUW tow-coloured
CDELOORSSTU souter's clod
CDENNOORTTW content word
CDENOPRRTUU uncorrupted
CDEOPRRRUWY curry powder
CDFFIILLTUY difficultly

CDFGHIIINNO indigo finch
CDFGHLLOOOT cloth of gold
CDFGIILNNOY confidingly
CDFGIMNOOSY Song of my Cid
CDFHIMNNOOU confound him
CDFHLOOORTX Oxford cloth
CDFILLOSUUU dulcifluous
CDFINNOSTUY dysfunction
CDFNNOOOUUY confound you
CDGHHIINOPT diphthongic
CDGHILMNOOT codling moth
CDGHILNOOPP clodhopping
CDGHILOOORY orchidology
CDGIIKNNSUW wind-sucking
CDGIIKNSTTU sitting duck
CDGIILOOSUY suicidology
CDGIILOSSTY dyslogistic
CDGILNNOPRU curling pond
CDGILNOOOOT odontologic
CDGILOORTTY troglodytic
CDGINNOOOPY pycnogonoid
CDGINOOTTUW woodcutting
CDGINOPRSTU crop-dusting
CDGNOORSTUY God's country
CDHHIILOPRY hydrophilic
CDHHIIOPSTY ichthyopsid
CDHHIOPRTYY hydrophytic
CDHHNNOORTY rhynchodont
CDHIIIMOOPR idiomorphic
CDHIIIOORST choroiditis
CDHIILLNQUU liquid lunch
CDHIILPRSUU disulphuric
CDHIIMOOPPR hippodromic
CDHIIMOOSTT dichotomist
CDHIIMORRSU Iris Murdoch
CDHIIOOPRST chiropodist
CDHILLOSTWY dolly switch
CDHILOORSSS scissor hold
CDHILOOTTUW cold-without
CDHIMOOORRT orthodromic
CDHIMOOOSTU dichotomous
CDHINOOORTT orthodontic
CDHINOOPRSY hydroponics
CDHIOOPRRTY hydrotropic
CDHIORSSTUW discus throw
CDIIIJNOSUU injudicious
CDIIILNTTUY inductility
CDIIINNNOOT in condition
CDIIINNOSTT distinction
CDIIINTTUVY inductivity
CDIIJLOSUUY judiciously
CDIIJNNOSTU disjunction
CDIIKRRSTTY dirty tricks
CDIILMORSTU clostridium
CDIILMPSTUU multicuspid
CDIILNOPSTY spondylitic
CDIILNOPSUU sipunculoid
CDIILOPSTUU duplicitous
CDIIMMNNOOU condominium
CDIIMMNOOTY incommodity
CDIINNNOOOT on condition
CDIIOOOOSTV voodooistic
CDIKLNOPSSU spondulicks
CDILLOOORSU solid colour
CDILLORSUUY ludicrously
CDILMOOORSX loxodromics
CDILOOORUUU douroucouli
CDINNOOPRTY Cyprinodont
CDKKNNOOOOW knock on wood
CDMNOOOPUXY oxycompound
CDOORRSSSSW cross swords
CEEEEEGHNRS green cheese
CEEEEEGMNRR re-emergence
CEEEEEPRRRT tree creeper
CEEEEHHRRST three cheers
CEEEEHLMNOS lemon cheese
CEEEEHNRVWY everywhence
CEEEEHNSSTT set the scene
CEEEEHPRSSS cheesepress
CEEEEILNORT electioneer
CEEEEIMMNPT empiecement
CEEEEIMNNPR pre-eminence
CEEEEIMNNSS mise en scène
CEEEEINNPRV prevenience
CEEEEINPRRX experiencer
CEEEEINRRRV irreverence
CEEEEINRSTX re-existence
CEEEEIRRSTV service tree
CEEEEJNRSUV rejuvenesce
CEEEENNRRTV nerve centre
CEEEENPPRST Peter's pence
CEEEFFFLNOS self-offence
CEEEFFGINOV give offence
CEEEFFHIOTW white coffee
CEEEFFHOOSU coffee house
CEEEFFHORST shore effect
CEEEFFIINTV ineffective
CEEEFFILTVY effectively
CEEEFFIMORT moiré effect
CEEEFFLNOSS offenceless
CEEEFGLLNST self-neglect
CEEEFHIIPRS speechifier
CEEEFHNRRTV trench fever
CEEEFIILRRT electrifier
CEEEFIKQRUZ quick-freeze
CEEEFILRSSV self-service
CEEEFINNQRU infrequence
CEEEFINORRT refectioner
CEEEFKLLORR Rockefeller
CEEEFLMRTYY fly cemetery
CEEEFLPRSST self-respect
CEEEFLRRTUY cruelty-free
CEEEFMNNORT enforcement
CEEEFNPRSST perfectness
CEEEGGHINNS gegenschein
CEEEGGNORRR greengrocer
CEEEGHILNOS Egon Schiele
CEEEGHINRSW cheesewring
CEEEGHLOSTU The Eclogues
CEEEGIINOPR epeirogenic
CEEEGIINPST epigenetics
CEEEGIKNORT greenockite

CEEEGILMNNO	meningocele
CEEEGIMNORT	merogenetic
CEEEGINNNTV	Gene Vincent
CEEEGINNOSS	cenogenesis
CEEEGINNOTX	xenogenetic
CEEEGINORTV	eigenvector
CEEEGINOSST	ectogenesis
CEEEGLLNOOT	Eton College
CEEEHHINORT	Erechtheion
CEEEHHKLNOP	heckelphone
CEEEHHMMRSY	rhyme scheme
CEEEHHMOPRS	chemosphere
CEEEHHNRSTT	the trenches✧
CEEEHIKNTTT	kitchenette
CEEEHILORTT	heteroclite
CEEEHILRRSW	Lecher wires
CEEEHILSTTT	telesthetic
CEEEHIMNRTU	hermeneutic
CEEEHIMORST	heteroecism
CEEEHIMPRTY	hyperemetic
CEEEHINRSTT	in the secret
CEEEHINSSST	cenesthesis
CEEEHIORRSV	heroic verse
CEEEHIPRRSU	supercherie
CEEEHIQRSUW	chequerwise
CEEEHLLLPRT	helper T cell
CEEEHLLRSSY	cheerlessly
CEEEHLMORST	chrome steel
CEEEHLNPRSU	ensepulchre
CEEEHLOPRST	Cleethorpes
CEEEHLRTTUW	wheel-cutter
CEEEHMOPRSS	moss-cheeper
CEEEHNORRTT	corner teeth
CEEEHOPPRST	sheet copper
CEEEIIKLNTT	telekinetic
CEEEIILNRSV	service line
CEEEIIMNNPT	impenitence
CEEEIIMPRSV	misperceive
CEEEIIMRSTV	time-service
CEEEIINNNRT	internecine
CEEEIINNNST	insentience
CEEEIINNRTV	internecive
CEEEIINNSTX	inexistence
CEEEIIPPRSV	service pipe
CEEEIIPRRRU	Pierre Curie
CEEEIIPRRTV	irreceptive
CEEEIIRRSVW	service wire
	wire service
CEEEIJMNORT	rejoicement
CEEEIKLLNST	nickel steel
CEEEIKNNRSS	snickersnee
CEEEIKNQRTU	quicken-tree
CEEEILLORRT	electrolier
CEEEILLSTVY	selectively
CEEEILMORTV	velocimeter
CEEEILNNOQU	ineloquence
CEEEILNNOTV	non-elective
CEEEILNOPRT	pre-election
CEEEILNOPST	Pleistocene
CEEEILNORST	reselection
CEEEILNRRUV	culverineer
CEEEILNSTUV	unselective
CEEEILOSTVX	voix céleste
CEEEILPRTVY	receptively
CEEEILRSSSV	serviceless
CEEEILRSSVY	recessively
	sycee silver
CEEEILRSTVY	secretively
CEEEILSSVXY	excessively
CEEEILTUVXY	executively
CEEEIMMNRTX	cement mixer
CEEEIMMPSUU	museum piece
CEEEIMNNNST	incensement
CEEEINNOPRV	provenience
CEEEINNOSTV	venesection
CEEEINNRSSS	sincereness
CEEEINORTUX	executioner
CEEEINOSTVX	coextensive
CEEEINPRRSW	screen-wiper
CEEEINPRRTT	intercepter
CEEEINPRSSS	preciseness
CEEEINPRSST	persistence
CEEEINPRTUV	unreceptive
CEEEINRSTVV	revivescent
CEEEIOPRRSV	over-precise
CEEEIPPRSTV	perspective
CEEEIPPSSTY	type species
CEEEIPRSTUV	persecutive
CEEEIRRSSTT	street cries
CEEEIRSTUXX	executrixes
CEEEJNNSTUV	juvenescent
CEEEKLNOPSU	keep counsel
CEEEKMNORSS	smokescreen
CEEEKNPRSSY	cypress knee
CEEELLLNTXY	excellently
CEEELLNNNOP	pennoncelle
CEEELLNOPPR	prepollence
CEEELLORSTY	electrolyse
CEEELLORTTY	electrolyte
CEEELLORTYZ	electrolyze
CEEELMMOTTU	telecommute
CEEELMNOSSW	welcomeness
CEEELMNSSSU	muscle sense
CEEELMORRST	sclerometer
CEEELMPRRTY	crepe myrtle
CEEELNOQSTU	closet queen
CEEELNRSSSU	recluseness
CEEELOPRRST	preselector
CEEELOPRTTY	electrotype
CEEELORSTVW	twelve score
CEEELPRSSST	respectless
	scepterless
	sceptreless
CEEEMMNRTUX	excrementum
CEEEMNNNOTT	contenement
CEEEMNNOSTT	cement-stone
CEEEMNOPRRS	recompenser
CEEEMNORTTY	enterectomy
CEEEMNRTTTU	curettement
CEEEMOPRSTU	computerese
CEEENNNOQSU	non-sequence
CEEENNOPRTT	penteconter

CEEENNPTTWY	twenty pence
CEEENPRRSST	precentress
CEEENPRRSSU	superscreen
CEEEOOPRSST	stereoscope
CEEEPPRRSST	preceptress
CEEFFHIIORS	Irish coffee
CEEFFHINRRS	French fries
CEEFFIIINNT	inefficient
CEEFFIILNTY	efficiently
CEEFFIITTVY	effectivity
CEEFFILNOOR	line of force
CEEFFINQRUU	queer cuffin
CEEFFIOPRSS	press office
CEEFGHHIMRT	Fehmgericht
CEEFGIINSTU	insectifuge
CEEFGIMOORT	come to grief
CEEFGINNRRY	refringency
CEEFGINORRU	reconfigure
CEEFHHINRTW	French white✧
CEEFHHNORTT	thenceforth
CEEFHHNORTW	whenceforth
CEEFHIKNNRT	trench knife
CEEFHILORSU	cheliferous
CEEFHINNRSS	Frenchiness
CEEFHIPPRST	prefectship
CEEFHLOTUYY	touchy-feely
CEEFHMOORRR	ferro-chrome
CEEFHMOORRT	home-crofter
CEEFIIKLLRT	tickler file
CEEFIIKLNRT	fernitickle
CEEFIILNTVY	infectively
CEEFIIMNORR	Enrico Fermi
CEEFIINOSUV	veneficious
CEEFIIPRSSU	superficies
CEEFIKKLNOS	kick oneself
CEEFIKKNOPT	pocket knife
CEEFIKLNORR	ferro-nickel
CEEFIKLNRTY	fernytickle
CEEFIKOOPRW	piece of work
CEEFIKORRST	strike force
CEEFILLORSU	celliferous
CEEFILMPRTY	imperfectly
CEEFILNNOSS	confineless
CEEFILNORSU	fluorescein
CEEFIMNNNOT	confinement
CEEFINNQRUY	infrequency
CEEFINORTTU	counterfeit
CEEFINOSSTY	of necessity
CEEFINPRSTU	superinfect
CEEFKLMORSY	self-mockery
CEEFLLRSTUU	self-culture
CEEFLNNOSTT	self-content
CEEFLNORSTU	fluorescent
CEEFLNPRTUY	unperfectly
CEEFLOORRSU	foreclosure
CEEFLORRSUU	resourceful
CEEFMNNOTTU	confutement
CEEGGKMNOOR	George Monck
CEEGGKOPRRY	Gregory Peck
CEEGGOORRSS	George Cross
CEEGHHIMRTV	Vehmgericht
CEEGHIKNNRR	neck-herring
CEEGHIKNPSS	King's Speech
CEEGHILNRSS	Schlesinger
CEEGHIMNOOT	homogenetic
CEEGHIMNORT	thermogenic
CEEGHINOPST	pigeon chest
CEEGHINRSST	sight screen
CEEGIILNORS	ceiling rose
CEEGIILNSTY	lysigenetic
CEEGIIMNOTT	mitogenetic
CEEGIIMNSST	miscegenist
CEEGIINORTV	recognitive
CEEGIINPRST	string piece
CEEGIJJLNUU	jungle juice
CEEGIKNOPRW	weeping rock
CEEGILMNORR	relic-monger
CEEGILNNOSY	geosyncline
CEEGILNOPTY	polygenetic
CEEGILNOSTT	telegnostic
CEEGILNPTXY	expectingly
CEEGILOOOSS	sociologese
CEEGIMNNOOT	monogenetic
CEEGIMNORST	egocentrism
CEEGINNOOSS	oncogenesis
CEEGINNOOTT	ontogenetic
CEEGINOORST	oestrogenic
CEEGINOPRTY	pyrogenetic
CEEGINOSSTY	cytogenesis
CEEGIOPRRTU	picture-goer
CEEGKNORSST	green stocks
CEEGLLOORTY	electrology
CEEGLNNORTU	electron gun
CEEGLNRRSUY	curly-greens
CEEGMNOORYY	grey economy
CEEGMNORTTU	cement grout
CEEGMOSTYYZ	Zygomycetes
CEEGNNOORSU	congenerous
CEEHHIILPRS	helispheric
CEEHHIIMPRS	hemispheric
CEEHHILMOOR	heliochrome
CEEHHILNOPT	technophile
CEEHHIMNRST	cherishment
CEEHHIMNSTU	the munchies
CEEHHIORSVW	whichsoever
CEEHHIPSSTY	hypesthesic
CEEHHMORSTT	home stretch
CEEHHNNOPRS	henchperson
CEEHIIINORS	chinoiserie
CEEHIIKNOOS	cookie-shine
CEEHIIKNSTT	kinesthetic
CEEHIILLNST	Hellenistic
CEEHIILLRSS	schillerise
CEEHIILLRSZ	schillerize
CEEHIILMORT	heliometric
CEEHIIMNOPS	phonemicise
CEEHIIMNOPZ	phonemicize
CEEHIIMPRTU	perithecium
CEEHIIMPSTU	euphemistic
CEEHIIMPTTY	epithymetic
CEEHIIMRTTY	hermeticity
CEEHIINOOTW	within cooee

CEEHIINOPST phoneticise
CEEHIINOPTZ phoneticize
CEEHIINPPRR perinephric
CEEHIKNOORT kinetochore
CEEHIKNPSSS peckishness
CEEHIKNSSST sketchiness
CEEHIKORRTY hickory tree
CEEHIKORSST The Sick Rose
CEEHILLNOST clothesline
clothes-line
CEEHILMNORT thermocline
CEEHILMOPST pilot scheme
CEEHILMORRT chlorimeter
CEEHILNOOST the Colonies
CEEHILNORST cholesterin
CEEHILOPRST electorship
CEEHILOPSTT Philoctetes
CEEHILORTVW white clover
CEEHILPRSTU lectureship
CEEHIMMOOOR homoeomeric
CEEHIMOPRSS mesospheric
CEEHIMORRTX xerothermic
CEEHIMPTTUY emphyteutic
CEEHIMRRTUY eurythermic
CEEHINOORRT rhinocerote
CEEHINQSTTU queen-stitch
CEEHIOOPRTT heterotopic
CEEHIOPPRTW white copper
CEEHIOPRRST Terpsichore
CEEHIOPRTTY heterotypic
CEEHIORSTTX The Exorcist
CEEHJMNNOOR John McEnroe
CEEHKLNOSUY honeysuckle
honey-suckle
CEEHKNOOPPT pocketphone
CEEHKNORSTT netherstock
CEEHKNORSUY honey-sucker
CEEHKOQRRUW chequerwork
CEEHKRSSSTU hucksteress
CEEHLLNOOPW Enoch Powell
CEEHLLNOTTT nettle-cloth
CEEHLLOOPST clothes-pole
CEEHLLOORST cholesterol
CEEHLLOORUW colour wheel
CEEHLLORSUY lecherously
CEEHLMOOOST close to home
CEEHLMOORRT chlorometer
CEEHLMRSTWZ Weltschmerz
CEEHLNOOPRR chloroprene
CEEHLOOPRRS preschooler
CEEHLOORRTU three-colour
CEEHLRSSSTT stretchless
CEEHMNOORRT chronometer
CEEHMNOORST stenochrome
CEEHMNOPRTY nephrectomy
CEEHMNORSST tschernosem
CEEHMOOPRSS cosmosphere
CEEHMOOPRST thermoscope
CEEHMOORRTT trochometer
CEEHMOORSTU Homo erectus
CEEHMOPRSTY psychometer
CEEHMPPSSTU stump speech
CEEHNNORRTU truncheoner
CEEHNOOPRRY Henry Cooper
CEEHNOORRTT orthocentre
CEEHNOQSTTU the Conquest
CEEHNORRSTY cherry-stone
CEEHNORSTWY oyster-wench
CEEHNOSSTTY scythe-stone
CEEHOOPRRSU horse-couper
CEEHOOPSSTT stethoscope
CEEHOORRRST The Sorceror
CEEHORRSTTV overstretch
stretch over
CEEHORRTTYY erythrocyte
CEEIIINNSTV incentivise
CEEIIINNTVZ incentivize
CEEIIISTVVV vivisective
CEEIIKNRSST ricketiness
CEEIIKPRRST strike price
CEEIILMPRSY imprecisely
CEEIILMPRTX pleximetric
CEEIILMRTUV vermiculite
CEEIILNNRSY insincerely
CEEIILNRSTV virilescent
CEEIILSTTVY selectivity
CEEIIMMNOTT in committee
CEEIIMMPRST metempirics
CEEIIMNNPTY impenitency
CEEIIMNNRST reminiscent
CEEIIMOPTTV competitive
CEEIIMORSST esotericism
CEEIIMORSTT meteoritics
CEEIIMORSTX exotericism
CEEIIMPPRRS perispermic
CEEIIMRRSTU sericterium
CEEIINNNSTY insentiency
CEEIINNOSTV venisection
CEEIINNOTUX inexecution
CEEIINNPRST serpentinic
CEEIINORSTV insectivore
CEEIINPRSST resipiscent
CEEIINRSTVV reviviscent
CEEIIORSSTT esotericist
CEEIIPPTTUY eupepticity
CEEIIPRRTUW picture-wire
CEEIIPRTTVY receptivity
CEEIIRRSTTV restrictive
CEEIJNORRTT interjector
CEEIJRRSUVY jury service
CEEIKKLNRSS knickerless
CEEIKLLNRST skillcentre
CEEIKLMNORR microkernel
CEEIKLNORRT interlocker
CEEIKMMOSUY Mickey Mouse
CEEIKNNORSS snick or snee
CEEIKNOOPST kinetoscope
CEEIKNORSST stick or snee
CEEIKNOSTTT stockinette
CEEIKNRRSTU kernicterus
CEEIKORRTTV rover ticket
CEEILLMNNTY inclemently

CEEILLMRSSU music-seller
CEEILLMRSSY mercilessly
CEEILLPRSSY pricelessly
CEEILLSUVXY exclusively
CEEILMMNOPT compilement
CEEILMNNSTU luminescent
CEEILMNRSTU multiscreen
CEEILMOOPRU meo periculo
CEEILMOORRT colorimeter
CEEILMOPSTU Telescopium
CEEILMORTVY velocimetry
CEEILNNNOOT non-election
CEEILNNNOOV non-violence
CEEILNNOPST pencil-stone
CEEILNNOSST close tennis
CEEILNOOPRS necropoleis
CEEILNOORRT intercooler
CEEILNOPRTU neuroleptic
CEEILNORTTT electrotint
CEEILNPRSST split screen
split-screen
CEEILNPRSTU cluster pine
CEEILNPRSTY presciently
CEEILNQSTUY quiescently
CEEILNRSTUV ventricules
CEEILNSUUVX unexclusive
CEEILOOORST creosote oil
CEEILOORSTV locorestive
CEEILOORTTV toilet cover
CEEILOPSSTT telescopist
CEEILPPRSTY clyster-pipe
CEEILRRRUVW Curlew River
CEEILRRSTUU sericulture
CEEILRSUVXY excursively
CEEIMNNOOPT omnipotence
CEEIMNNOPTT incompetent
CEEIMNNORTU countermine
CEEIMNNSTTU intumescent
CEEIMNOORSU ceremonious
CEEIMNOPSTU pumice-stone
CEEIMNORTTU counter-time
CEEIMNRRTTU recruitment
CEEIMOOPSSS seismoscope
CEEIMOORRSV room service
service room
CEEIMOPRSSV compressive
CEEIMOPRSTU computerise
CEEIMOPRTUZ computerize
CEEINNNOSTT consentient
CEEINNOORRT reconnoiter
reconnoitre
CEEINNOOSTX coextension
CEEINOOPRST retinoscope
CEEINOORSST stereosonic
CEEINOPRRTT interceptor
CEEINOPRSTU persecution
CEEINOPRTTU tone picture
CEEINORRSST intercessor
CEEINORRSTU intercourse
CEEINORTUVW counter-view
CEEINOSSSTU necessitous
CEEINOSSSTV costiveness
CEEINPRSSTY persistency
CEEINPRSSVY cypress vine
CEEINRRSSTW winter cress
CEEINRSSSSW swine's cress
CEEIOPPRSTV prospective
CEEIOPRRTUV overpicture
CEEIOPRSSTT stereoptics
CEEIOPRSTTY stereotypic
CEEIORRTTTY yttrocerite
CEEIPQRSTUU picturesque
CEEIRSTTVVY civvy street
CEEJLNORSWW crown jewels
CEEJMNNORTU conjurement
CEEJMNOPRTT projectment
CEEKLRRSTVY vestry-clerk
CEEKMNOOPTY pocket money
CEEKMOOPSTU pocket mouse
CEEKOORRRTT retro-rocket
CEELLMNOUWY unwelcomely
CEELLNOORTT telecontrol
CEELLNOPPRY prepollency
CEELLRSSTUU cultureless
CEELMNNOOST consolement
CEELMNNOSTU locum tenens
CEELMNOPSSX complexness
CEELMNOPSTY splenectomy
CEELMNOPTTY competently
CEELMNSTTUY tumescently
CEELNNOSSTT contentless
CEELNOOOPRT coleopteron
CEELNOOPPST copple-stone
CEELNORSTTU tone cluster
CEELNORSTUW stone curlew
CEELNRRRTUY recurrently
CEELOPRTTYY electrotypy
CEELPRRTUUU pure culture
CEELPSSSSTU suspectless
CEEMMMNOORT common metre
CEEMMNNOOSS common sense
commonsense
CEEMMOOPRTT Comptometer®
CEEMMOORSTT come to terms
CEEMNNNOTTT contentment
CEEMNNOOOPY open economy
CEEMNNORTTU recountment
CEEMNNRSTTU encrustment
CEEMNOORTUV countermove
CEEMNOPRRTU procurement
CEEMNOPRSTT contretemps
CEEMNORRSTT storm centre
CEEMNORRTUU countermure
CEEMOPRRSSU compressure
CEENNOOPPST postponence
CEENNOORRST cornerstone
CEENNRRSSTU currentness
CEENOORRSTV controverse
seroconvert
CEENOORTTUV counter-vote
CEENOPPPRRY peppercorny
CEENOPQRSTU pre-conquest

CEENOQSSTUU	Queen's Scout
CEENORSTTTU	stonecutter
CEEOOPRSSTY	stereoscopy
CEEOPRRSSTT	protectress
CEEOPRRSTUY	persecutory
CEEORRRRSTU	resurrector
CEERRRSTTUU	restructure
CEFFFINOORT	front office
CEFFHIINNOR	chiffonnier
CEFFHIOORSU	office hours
CEFFHIRSSTT	festschrift
CEFFINRSSSU	scruffiness
CEFFIORRSUU	furciferous
CEFGGIINNNR	ring-fencing
CEFGHILMRTY	mercy flight
CEFGHIORTUV	gift voucher
CEFGIIINPRX	price-fixing
CEFGIKLLNOS	self-locking
CEFGILLNOSS	self-closing
CEFGIMOORSY	sycomore fig
CEFGNOORRST	strong force
CEFHIIISSTT	fetishistic
CEFHIIKNSTW	knife-switch
CEFHIILLMOS	Flemish coil
CEFHILLRTUY	filthy lucre
CEFHILNPPRU	purple finch
CEFHILORSUY	chyliferous
CEFHIMORSUY	chymiferous
CEFHKORSTUU	future shock
CEFHLLOORSU	flesh-colour
CEFIIKLORTT	tick trefoil
CEFIIMNORST	insectiform
CEFIINNOSTW	news fiction
CEFIINORSUZ	zinciferous
CEFIKNNOTUY	function key
CEFIKNOQRUZ	quick-frozen
CEFILLLOOSU	folliculose
CEFILLOOOSV	oil of cloves
CEFILMORSUU	culmiferous
CEFILNOORRT	fire control
CEFILNOORTU	counterfoil
CEFILNORTUY	Country Life
CEFILOORSUY	ferociously
CEFIMORRRUV	verruciform
CEFINNOOSSU	fusion cones
CEFINOORRSU	corniferous
CEFIOPRRSUU	cupriferous
CEFKOOOPTTU	out of pocket out-of-pocket
CEFLLNNOTUY	confluently
CEFLLNOORST	self-control
CEFLMOORSST	comfortless
CEFLOOOPRSU	fluoroscope
CEFMNOOORTZ	comfort zone
CEFNOORRTTU	counterfort
CEFNOPRRTUY	perfunctory
CEFOOORSTUU	out of course
CEGGHORRTUU	touch rugger
CEGHHIIOSTY	high society
CEGHHMOORTU	come through
CEGHIILNRST	Christingle
CEGHIILNRTT	chitterling
CEGHIINNRST	christening
CEGHIINNTTW	twin-etching
CEGHIKLNORS	Rock English
CEGHILLNOOY	lichenology
CEGHILLOORU	rough collie
CEGHILMOOOR	oligochrome
CEGHILMOOTT	come to light
CEGHILNOOOU	euchologion
CEGHILNOOPR	phrenologic
CEGHILNOOTV	Gothic novel
CEGHILOOORR	logorrhoeic
CEGHILORSTU	light source
CEGHIMNOOPR	morphogenic
CEGHIMOOOST	Moeso-gothic
CEGHIMORRTY	hygrometric
CEGHINOOORR	gonorrhoeic
CEGHINOORST	orthogenics
CEGHINORRST	torch singer
CEGHINORSSU	grouchiness
CEGHINORSTU	scouthering
CEGHINSUWZZ	zwischenzug
CEGHIOOPRST	geostrophic
CEGHLLNOOST	long-clothes
CEGHLNOOORR	chronologer
CEGHLNOOPST	sponge cloth
CEGIIILOPST	epilogistic
CEGIIINORST	Origenistic
CEGIIJLNORY	rejoicingly
CEGIIJNNORU	unrejoicing
CEGIIKLNNSY	sickeningly
CEGIIKLNSST	singlestick
CEGIILLNNST	stencilling
CEGIILMNOST	closing time
CEGIILMOOSS	seismologic
CEGIILNOOST	neologistic
CEGIILNOTVY	cognitively
CEGIILOOPST	geopolitics
CEGIIMMNNOU	immunogenic
CEGIIMNOORT	goniometric
CEGIIMNORTU	tumorigenic
CEGIINNOORT	recognition
CEGIINORRSU	crinigerous
CEGIINRSSTY	synergistic
CEGIJLMNSUU	jungle music
CEGIKKLNPSU	pig's knuckle
CEGIKLNOORV	overlocking
CEGILLLNNOO	colonelling
CEGILLMNOWY	welcómingly
CEGILLNNOSU	counselling
CEGILMNNOUW	unwelcoming
CEGILMNOSUU	lounge music
CEGILMOPSSU	gospel music
CEGILNOORST	necrologist
CEGILNOOSTY	insectology Scientology®
CEGILNORSSS	single-cross
CEGIMNNNOST	consignment
CEGIMNOOPRU	income group
CEGIMOOORRV	microgroove
CEGIMOOPRST	come to grips

CEGINNNNSSU cunningness
CEGINNNORTU incongruent
CEGINNOOPST coping-stone
CEGINNOPRTY corn in Egypt
CEGINNORSTU countersign
CEGINOORRSU cornigerous
CEGINOORRTY recognitory
CEGINOPPRST prospecting
CEGINORSTUY courtesying
CEGLMMOORYY myrmecology
CEGLMOOOSTY cosmetology
CEGLMOOSSTY glossectomy
CEGLNNORTUY congruently
CEGLNOOOSYY synoecology
CEGLNOORTUW counter-glow
CEGLOOPRSTY spectrology
CEGLOORSTUY Etruscology
CEGLOPRSUUU groupuscule
CEGNNOPPRSU scuppernong
CEGNOORRSUY cryosurgeon
CEGORRRSUYY cryosurgery
CEHHIILOTTY ichthyolite
CEHHIIMMOPR hemimorphic
CEHHIINORRT tichorrhine
CEHHIINPRTT pinch-hitter
CEHHILMOORY heliochromy
CEHHILMRSUY helichrysum✧
CEHHILOOSTT chisel tooth
CEHHILOSTTW wholestitch
CEHHILOTTYY the Holy City
CEHHIMMOORT homothermic
CEHHIMOOPRT theomorphic
CEHHIMOSSSU schism house
CEHHIMRSTUY eurhythmics
CEHHIOPRRST Christopher
CEHHIOPSTYZ schizophyte
CEHHIPRSTTY Pterichthys
CEHHLMOOSTT clothes moth
CEHHLOOOSSU school house
schoolhouse
CEHHMNORSSY synchromesh
CEHHMNORTTU trench mouth
CEHHMOOOPRR chromophore
CEHHMOOPRTY phytochrome
CEHHOOOPRRT trochophore
CEHIIILLMNT methicillin
CEHIIINPSTZ citizenship
CEHIIIORSST historicise
CEHIIIORSTZ historicize
CEHIIIRSTTT tritheistic
CEHIIJNNOTZ John Citizen
CEHIIJPSSTU justiceship
CEHIIKKNNST kitchen-sink
CEHIIKLLRSY lickerishly
CEHIIKLNOPS pick holes in
CEHIIKLORST ostrich-like
CEHIIKMNNUY chimney-nuik
CEHIIKNNTTU kitchen unit
CEHIIKNSSSS sickishness
CEHIIKNSSST kitschiness
CEHIILMNTTU multiethnic
CEHIILOOPRT heliotropic
CEHIILOPPRS scripophile
CEHIILPRSTU spherulitic
CEHIIMNOPST phonemicist
phoneticism
CEHIIMNOQTU monchiquite
CEHIIMNORST thermionics
CEHIIMOPPRR perimorphic
CEHIIMOSSUV mischievous
CEHIIMPRSST Mister Chips
CEHIINOOPRS ionospheric
CEHIINOORRT coinheritor
CEHIINOORSS isochronise
CEHIINOORSZ isochronize
CEHIINOPRST Eric Shipton
CEHIINOPRTY hyperinotic
CEHIINOPSTT phoneticist
CEHIINORSTU cushion-tire
CEHIIOOSTTZ zootheistic
CEHIIOPRRST prehistoric
CEHIIOPRSVY viceroyship
CEHIIOSSSVY vichyssoise
CEHIJRSSSTU Jesus Christ
CEHIKMNNOOY chimney-nook
CEHIKNOPSTU soup kitchen
CEHIKOOPRTT tooth-picker
CEHILLNNOPU Punchinello
CEHILLNOOPS colonelship
CEHILLOOTTT toilet cloth
CEHILLPRSSY Cypress Hill
CEHILMOOPPR pleomorphic
CEHILMOOPRS pleochroism
CEHILMOORST schorlomite
CEHILMORRTY chlorimetry
CEHILMORSTT stretch limo
CEHILMORTTY thermolytic
CEHILNOOPST technopolis
CEHILNOOQRU chloroquine
CEHILNOSSST coltishness
CEHILOOPSSY Coelophysis
CEHILOPRSUY perichylous
CEHILPSSTUU hic sepultus
CEHIMMOOPRS mesomorphic
CEHIMMOOSST cosmotheism
CEHIMNOOPRX xenomorphic
CEHIMNORRSS scrimshoner
CEHIMOOPRRX xeromorphic
CEHIMOOPRTT photometric
CEHIMOOPTTY mythopoetic
CEHIMOOSSST schistosome
CEHIMOOTTUW come out with
CEHIMOPPRST coppersmith
CEHIMOPRSTY hypsometric
CEHIMORSTTY stichometry
CEHINNORSSY synchronise
CEHINNORSYZ synchronize
CEHINOOPRRS coronership
CEHINOOPRST the Scorpion
CEHINOORRST orchestrion
CEHINOPPRST pitchperson
CEHINOPPRTU unprophetic

CEHINOPRSSY hypersonics
CEHINORSSSY synchoresis
CEHINORSTUY cushion-tyre
CEHINRRSSSU currishness
CEHIOOOPPRT photocopier
CEHIOOPSTTY osteophytic
CEHIOPRSSTT prosthetics
CEHKNOOSSTT on the stocks
CEHKNORRSTU return shock
CEHLLLOPRSY sclerophyll
CEHLMOORRTY chlorometry
CEHLMOPTTYY T-lymphocyte
CEHLNOORSSU school nurse
CEHLNOOSTUY honey locust
CEHLOOPPRST clothes-prop
CEHLOOPPRSU upper school
CEHLOOPRRUY hypercolour
CEHLOPPRSTU supper cloth
CEHLOPRSSUU sepulchrous
CEHMMNOOORS common-shore
CEHMMOOORSX X-chromosome
CEHMMOOORSY Y-chromosome
CEHMNOOOSTU monothecous
CEHMNOORRTY chronometry
CEHMNOORSTY stenochromy
CEHMNORRRUY horn mercury
CEHMOOSSTUU custom house
CEHMOPRSTYY psychometry
CEHNNOORTTY Henry Cotton
CEHNNORTTUU hunt counter
hunt-counter
CEHNNOSSTUU uncouthness
CEHNOORRRST short corner
CEHOOPSSTTY stethoscopy
CEHOORRSSTV cover shorts
CEIIILLMNPU Penicillium
CEIIILLNSST illicitness
CEIIILLPTTY ellipticity
CEIIILMORST melioristic
CEIIILMPRST simpliciter
CEIIILNNPPR in principle
CEIIILNNPTY incipiently
CEIIIMNOPRS imprecision
CEIIIMNOSST misoneistic
CEIIIMPSSST pessimistic
CEIIINNRSTV vincristine
CEIIINNRSTY insincerity
CEIIINNSTTV instinctive
CEIIINOPRTT peritonitic
CEIIINORSTU cineritious
CEIIINOSTVV vivisection
CEIIINPRSTV inscriptive
CEIIIOPRSTT periostitic
CEIIIORSTTU icteritious
CEIIJLOORTU Joliot-Curie
CEIIKKLNNNO Neil Kinnock
CEIIKKMQSSU kiss-me-quick
CEIIKLLPSTT lickspittle
CEIIKLNOORV olivine-rock
CEIIKLNPRSS prickliness
CEIIKLNPRST pencil skirt
CEIIKLOOPTY poikilocyte
CEIIKLQRSUV quicksilver
CEIIKLRSSTV silver-stick
CEIIKNOSSTY cytokinesis
CEIIKNRSSST tricksiness
CEIILLLSSSY Scilly Isles
CEIILLNSUVY inclusively
CEIILMSSUVX exclusivism
CEIILNNOPPR on principle
CEIILNOPRSY prosiliency
CEIILNRTUUV viniculture
CEIILOOPPRT pleiotropic
CEIILORSSTT sclerotitis
CEIILRTTUUV viticulture
CEIILSSTUVX exclusivist
CEIILSTUVXY exclusivity
CEIIMNOOPST incomposite
CEIIMNOOPTT competition
CEIIMNOPSUU impecunious
CEIIMNORRTT nitrometric
CEIIMNORSTU neuroticism
CEIIMNOSTTU Teutonicism
CEIIMNPRSSS scrimpiness
CEIIMOOPSTV compositive
CEIIMOPRRST spirometric
CEIIMOPRSST semi-tropics
CEIIMORRRTW microwriter
CEIIMORRSTU courtierism
CEIIMRRSTVY Mystic River
CEIINNNNOTT incontinent
CEIINNNORTU internuncio
CEIINOOSSSY synoeciosis
CEIINOPRSSS prescission
CEIINORRSTT restriction
CEIINOSSSUV viciousness
CEIINRRSSTU scrutiniser
CEIINRRSTUZ scrutinizer
CEIINRSTTUV instructive
CEIIOPPRSTU precipitous
CEIIORRRSTT terroristic
CEIIORSSSSW scissorwise
CEIIORSTUVY voyeuristic
CEIIPPRSTUY perspicuity
CEIJLLOOPRY Jilly Cooper
CEIJNNOQSUY Quincy Jones
CEIJOOORSSU jocoserious
CEIKKLRSTUY lucky strike
CEIKLMOORST mortise lock
CEIKLNNSSUU unluckiness
CEIKNNORSTU countersink
CEIKNORTWYY New York City
CEILLLNNORS linen-scroll
CEILLLNOOOV violoncello
CEILLLOSUVY collusively
CEILLNOOPST ponticellos
CEILLOORRUV liver-colour
CEILMMNOPST compliments
CEILMMOORSU Coulommiers
CEILMMOPRUY promycelium
CEILMOOOPST cosmopolite
CEILMOOPSTY compositely

CEILMOORRTY colorimetry
CEILMOPRTUU pomiculture
CEILMORSUUV vermiculous
CEILNNNOTTY continently
CEILNNOOPSU close in upon
CEILNNOORTU contour line
CEILNOOOTUV coevolution
CEILNOOPRTU perlocution
CEILNOPRRTW triple crown
CEILNORSSTU courtliness
CEILNPRSTUU insculpture
CEILNRSTUUV ventriculus
CEILOOOPRST protocolise
CEILOOOPRTZ protocolize
CEILOOPRRSS cross-or-pile
CEILOOPRRTU turcopolier
CEILOOPRTTY proteolytic
CEILOORRSTU terricolous
CEILOORRSVY corrosively
CEILORSSTVY victoryless
CEIMMNNOOUX excommunion
CEIMMNOOPRV common viper
CEIMMNORSSU consumerism
CEIMMOOPRRS compromiser
CEIMMOORRTT tromometric
CEIMNNOOPTY omnipotency
CEIMNOOPRSS compression
CEIMNOORSTU coterminous
CEIMNOPSSTU postscenium
CEIMNOPSTUV consumptive
CEIMNORSSTU consumerist
misconstrue
CEINNOORSSU connoisseur
CEINNOOSTTU contentious
CEINNORSTTU court tennis
CEINNOSTTTU constituent
CEINOOOPRSY oneiroscopy
CEINOOPPRST prospection
CEINOOPRRTU neurotropic
CEINOOPRSTT stenotropic
CEINOOPRSTU point source
prosecution
CEINOOPRSTY retinoscopy
CEINOOPSSSU copiousness
CEINOOPTTTY totipotency
CEINOPQRSTU Cinque Ports
CEINOPRSSSU supersonics
CEINORRSSSU cursoriness
CEINORSSSUU curiousness
CEINOSSSSUV viscousness
CEINOSSSTUV viscountess
CEIOOOPRRTZ Proterozoic
CEIOPPRSSUU perspicuous
CEIOPRRSTUX prosecutrix
CEIPPRRSSTU superscript
CEJOPRRSSUY jury-process
CEKKLLMOOPU poke mullock
CEKLLMPPTUU plume-pluckt
CEKLLNOORRR rock'n'roller
CEKLNORSTUY try one's luck
CEKMMORSSTU summer stock
CEKMOOORRTT rocket motor
CEKMRSSTTUY truck system
CEKNNORSTUU countersunk
CEKNOOPSSTU sucket spoon
CEKNOORRTUW counterwork
counter-work
CEKOOPPRRSW copperworks
CELLLOOOSTU Lou Costello
CELLMOOPRRT comptroller
CELLNNOOPTU pollen count
CELLNOORRTU counter-roll
CELLNOPRTUY corpulently
CELLNRTTUUY truculently
CELLOORTUVY courtly love
CELLOPRTUUY polyculture
CELMNNOORTT controlment
CELMNOORTUU monoculture
CELMOOORSUU mouse-colour
CELNNOOORTT tone control
CELNOOORSTU stone-colour
CELNOOPRTTU counter-plot
CELOOOPRRST coprosterol
CELOORSTUUY courteously
CELPPRSUUVY supply curve
CEMMNOOPRTT comportment
CEMMNOORRSU censor morum
CEMMOOOPRTY Tommy Cooper
CEMOOOPPSTY metoposcopy
CENNOOSSSUU nocuousness
CENNORRTTUU counter-turn
CENOOPRSSTT cotton press
CENOORRSTVY controversy
CENOORSTUUU uncourteous
CENOPRRRSUY corn spurrey
CENOPRRSSTU corruptness
CENORSTTUWY West Country
CEPRRSSTTUU superstruct
CFFGIIIOORR frigorifico
CFFGINOORSU offscouring
CFFHILMNOTU fifth column
CFFIIINOOSU inofficious
CFFIILOOSUY officiously
CFFIINOOSUU unofficious
CFFLNOORSUU snuff-colour
CFGGIILNOYY yogic flying
CFGHIIKNSSU sucking fish
CFGHIILLNNY flinchingly
CFGHIILNNNU unflinching
CFGHIMNOORT forthcoming
CFGHIMNORTU furthcoming
CFGIIIKNQRU quick-firing
CFGIIILMNOR microfiling
CFGIINOSTTY Scottifying
CFGIKMNOORR rock-forming
CFGILNNOSUY confusingly
CFGILNOPRSY Flying Corps
CFGIMNOPPRU forcing-pump
CFGINOSTUUY young fustic
CFHILOORSST first school
CFIIILOPRTY prolificity
CFIILMOORSS microfossil

CFIILNNOPTU inflict upon
CFIILNOPPTU pulp fiction
CFIIMNOSSUU fusion music
CFIINORSSTU first cousin
CFIKKNOORSX knock for six
CFILLLOOSUU folliculous
CFILLMOOORR corolliform
CFILMOOPPRY microfloppy
CFILNOOPRSY scorpion fly
CFILOOSSUVW viscous flow
CFINNOORSTU Inns of Court
CFINORSTUUU infructuous
CFKLNOORTUY country-folk
CFLLLOORUUY colourfully
CFLNORSUUUU furunculous
CFLOOOPRSUY fluoroscopy
CFMMMNOOORS common forms
CFNORSTUUUU unfructuous
CGGHILNOOOS schoolgoing
CGGIIIKNPST pig-sticking
CGGIINOORST Gongoristic
CGGILNOOOTT glottogonic
CGHHHIIIKNT hitch-hiking
CGHHIKOSTTU thought-sick
CGHHILNOOST night school
CGHHILOOTYY ichthyology
CGHHINNOSTU no such thing
CGHHIOPRTYY hygrophytic
CGHIIILRSTV civil rights✧
civil-rights
CGHIILOOPSY physiologic
CGHIILOORST chirologist
CGHIKNNORSU cornhusking
CGHILMOOOPR morphologic
CGHILOOORST chorologist
CGHILOOPSTY phycologist
CGHILOORSTY Christology
CGHIMNOORST shortcoming
CGHIMOOOTYZ homozygotic
CGHIMOOPRYZ zygomorphic
CGHINNOPRTU hunting-crop
CGHINOOPPSU posing pouch
CGHINOPTTUY touch-typing
CGHIOOORSTT Ostrogothic
CGHKOORSTTW growth stock
CGIIIKLNOPT politicking
CGIIILNSSTU linguistics
CGIIIMNOSTV cognitivism
CGIIINNPRTU unit-pricing
CGIIINOTTVY cognitivity
CGIIKKNOPST poking-stick
CGIIKLLMNTU tucking-mill
CGIIKLNOPST stockpiling
CGIIKNNRSSU sicknursing
CGIIKNOPSTT poting-stick
CGIILLOSSTY syllogistic
CGIILMMNOOU immunologic
CGIILMNOORY criminology
CGIILMOOOSS sociologism
CGIILMOORST micrologist
CGIILMOOTVY victimology
CGIILNNORVW crown living
CGIILNNOTTU linocutting
CGIILNOOOST iconologist
CGIILNSTTTU cutting list
CGIILOOOSST sociologist
CGIINNNNOUV unconniving
CGIINNORSST cross-tining
CGIINNORTUY incongruity
CGIINOPRTWY copywriting
CGIKLNOOORT rocking tool
CGIKNOPPSTU upping-stock
CGILLNNOORT controlling
CGILLNNOOSY consolingly
CGILLOOPTTY polyglottic
CGILMNNOPUY uncomplying
CGILMNNOSUY consumingly
CGILMNOOPTT complotting
CGILMOOOSST cosmologist
CGILNPRSTUU sculpturing
CGIMNOOOSST cosmogonist
CGIMNOOOTYZ monozygotic
CGIMNOORTTU cutting room
CGINNNOOPRU pronouncing
CGINNOORSUU incongruous
CGINOOPRSTY pyrognostic
CGINOORSSTU outcrossing
CGINOORSTUU outsourcing
CGLNOORSUUY congruously
CHHIILOOPPS philosophic
CHHIILOOPPT photophilic
CHHIILOPTTY lithophytic
CHHIIMORSTY isorhythmic
CHHIIMRTTYY rhythmicity
CHHIINORSTY ichthyornis
CHHILMOOPRY hylomorphic
CHHILMOORTY lithochromy
CHHILOPPSYY psychophily
CHHIMMOOOPR homomorphic
CHHINOOOPPT photophonic
CHHINORSSUW urchin-shows
CHHIOOPRRTY orthophyric
CHHIOORSTTY orthostichy
CHHKOOORRRS shock horror
shock-horror
CHHLLLOOPRY chlorophyll
CHHMOOOPRTY photochromy
CHHNORSUXYY oxyrhynchus
CHIIILORTTT lithotritic
CHIIIMMNRSU Michurinism
CHIIIMORSST historicism
CHIIINORSST histrionics
trichinosis
CHIIIORSSTT historicist
CHIIIORSTTY historicity
CHIIKMNNORT kinchin-mort
CHIIKNSSTTY shinty-stick
CHIILLLNOPS Phil Collins
CHIILLNOOTT octillionth
CHIILNOPSTY cynophilist
CHIILOOPRTT protolithic
CHIILOOSTYZ hylozoistic

CHIILOPPRSY scripophily
CHIIMNOORSS isochronism
CHIIMOOPRTX mixotrophic
CHIINOPSTTY hypnotistic
CHIIOOPRTTX thixotropic
CHIIOPPRRTY porphyritic
CHIIOPRSTVY victory ship
CHIIORSSTTU tristichous
CHIIOSSSTTY schistosity
CHIJLLNNOOS John Collins
CHIKNNOORST stock in horn
CHILMOOPPRY polymorphic
CHILMOOPRSY polychroism
CHILMOPRTUY Polytrichum
CHILMOPSTUY Polystichum
CHILNOOOPST school point
CHILOORSTUU ulotrichous
CHIMMNOOOPR monomorphic
CHIMNNOORTU unicorn-moth
CHIMNNORSSY synchronism
CHIMNOOPPPY hypnopompic
CHIMNOOPRRS prochronism
CHINOOORSSU isochronous
CHINOOORSTU ortho-cousin
CHINOORRSTU trichronous
CHIOOOPPRRS sporophoric
CHIOOOPPRTT phototropic
CHIOOOPRRTT orthotropic
CHIOOOPRSST horoscopist
CHIOOPPRRST proctorship
CHIOOPPRSTY sporophytic
CHIOOPPRTTY protophytic
tropophytic
CHIOPSTTTUY touch-typist
CHKMOOSSTTU tussock moth
CHKOOOPRSST shock troops
CHLMNOOTTTU mutton cloth
CHMNOOOTTTU cottonmouth
CHMNOOPTTUU not up to much
CHMOOOPRSTY psychomotor
CHNNOORRSTY synchrotron
CHNNOORSSUY synchronous
CHRRRRSUUYY hurry-scurry
CIIIIKKKLLN killikinick
CIIIIKKKNNN kinnikinick
CIIIILNOSTV violinistic
CIIIINNOPPR in principio
CIIIIPRSSTT spiritistic
CIIILLMOPTY impoliticly
CIIILLNOSTT tonsillitic
CIIILMNOSTY consimility
CIIILOPSSST solipsistic
CIIIMNORTTU micturition
CIIIMNOSSTY city mission
CIIINNOPRST inscription
CIIINOOSTTY isotonicity
CIIINOPSSTZ Spinozistic
CIIINORSTUY incuriosity
CIILLOORSTT torticollis
CIILMNNOTUU unniloctium
CIILMNOPRSS Nicol's prism
CIILNOOPSTU liposuction
CIILNOPSTUU punctilious
CIILNORSUUY incuriously
CIIMMNNOOTU comminution
CIIMMNOOTUX immunotoxic
CIIMMOORSTT microtomist
CIIMNOOOPST composition
CIIMNRSSTTU misinstruct
CIIMOPRRSTU scriptorium
CIIMOPRSTUY promiscuity
CIIMPRRSSTU scripturism
CIINNOOPSSU on suspicion
CIINNOPRSST spintronics
CIINNOPSSUU unsuspicion
CIINNORSTTU instruction
CIINOOPSSTY pinocytosis
CIINOPSSTTY synoptistic
CIIOOPRSSUV piscivorous
CIIOPRRSSUU corpus iuris
CIIPRRSSTTU scripturist
CIJKLNOOSWY Jocky Wilson
CIJLNOOPSTT Scott Joplin
CIKKMOOSSTU Mt Kosciusko
CIKNOOPRUWY pick-your-own
CILLMOOQSUU colloquiums
CILLMOORTUU multicolour
CILLOORRTVY victory roll
CILMNNOOOSU monoclinous
CILMNOOOSTU monticolous
CILMNOOSTUU monticulous
CILMOOPRSTU compulsitor
CILMOOPRSTY polycrotism
CILNNOOOTUV convolution
CILNNOORTTU control unit
CILNNOOSSUV convulsions
CILNNOOSUUY innocuously
CILNOOOPRTU colourpoint
prolocution
CILNOOORSUU unicolorous
CILNOPRRTUY incorruptly
CILOOOPRSTT protocolist
CILOOPRRTUX prolocutrix
CIMNNNOOSYY synonymicon
CIMNNOOPSTU consumption
CIMNOORSSTU consortiums
CIMNOPPSTUU suction pump
CIMOOOPRRSU microporous
CIMOOOPSSTU compositous
CIMOOPRSSUU promiscuous
CIMOPRSSTUU scrumptious
CINNOOORTTT nitrocotton
CINOOPSSTTU suction stop
CINOORSTTTU constitutor
CIOOPRSSTTU prosciuttos
CLLNOOSUUVV convolvulus
CLMNOOOORRT control room
CNNOORTTUWY country town

D

DDDDEEEEFIL fiddle-de-dee
DDDEEFIOSST eisteddfods

DDDEEGILORV devil-dodger
DDDEEGIMOSS demigoddess
DDDEEIILMSZ middle-sized
DDDEEIINNTV net dividend
DDDEEOPRWXY proxy-wedded
DDDEFHLNORU hundredfold
DDDEHLOOORT toddlerhood
DDDEIILNUVY undividedly
DDDEILLMORW middle-world
DDDEIMNOPRU proud-minded
DDDEKLRSUUY skulduddery
DDDENNOORTW downtrodden
DDEEEEILMRR riddle-me-ree
DDEEEFILLNW well-defined
DDEEEFIMNRS Defenderism
DDEEEFLNORU enfouldered
DDEEEFLOSTV self-devoted
DDEEEGHIRRT third degree
DDEEEGILNNS single-ended
DDEEEGIMNPT depigmented
DDEEEGINPRU unpedigreed
DDEEEGIOSTU outside edge
DDEEEGNOOWW wooden wedge
DDEEEHILLSV dishevelled
DDEEEHMOPTU deep-mouthed
DDEEEIIINRV Eddie Irvine
DDEEEIINPRS deserpidine
DDEEEILLRSW well-desired
DDEEEILLRVW well-derived
DDEEEILMNRT intermeddle
DDEEEILNRUV undelivered
DDEEEIMPRST distempered
DDEEEINNNPT independent✧
DDEEEINNOPR epidendrone
DDEEEINNPRT interdepend
DDEEEINORSV video sender
videosender
DDEEEKNNOUW Wounded Knee
DDEEELLNOWW well-endowed
DDEEELLORRW well-ordered
DDEEELLRSSW well-dressed
DDEEELNOPUV undeveloped
DDEEELNPRTY pretendedly
DDEEEMNORRT dendrometer
DDEEENOSSTV devotedness
DDEEENOSTWY sweeney todd✧
DDEEENPRSSU undepressed
DDEEENRRSSU unredressed
DDEEEORTTUV true-devoted
DDEEFFGLLLU full-fledged
DDEEFHILNOT on the fiddle
DDEEFIIIMNN indemnified
DDEEFIIIRSV diversified
DDEEFIIMNNU definiendum
DDEEFLLNOUW well-founded
DDEEFMMRUUV dumdum fever
DDEEGHIILMT middle eight
DDEEGHILLTY delightedly
DDEEGHILNTU undelighted
DDEEGHLLNNO Glenn Hoddle
DDEEGHLNOOR Golden Horde
DDEEGILLNOO golden oldie
DDEEGILNNPY dependingly
DDEEGILNOWW window ledge
DDEEGILORRY Roy Eldridge
DDEEGINNNPU undepending
DDEEGINNRSU undersigned
DDEEGINNRTY tender-dying
DDEEGINORRR derring-doer
DDEEGLNORRU ground elder
DDEEGMNNOSU gens du monde
DDEEGMNORRU Rumer Godden
DDEEGNNORUU unguerdoned
DDEEGNOPRSU groundspeed
DDEEHHIOSST do the dishes
DDEEHIILMNT in the middle
DDEEHIILRTY third eyelid
DDEEHILRSSS dress-shield
DDEEHIMPRUY Eddie Murphy
DDEEHINRSSS reddishness
DDEEHIORRST ride the rods
DDEEHMORSSU shuddersome
DDEEHOORSTV over the odds
DDEEIIKLNNX index-linked
DDEEIILNPSS spindle side
DDEEIIMNNOS dimensioned
DDEEIINRRST disinterred
DDEEIINRTUV derived unit
DDEEIIQSTUU disquietude
DDEEIKNNRSS kindredness
DDEEILMNNTW dwindlement
DDEEILMNPUY unimpededly
DDEEILMOPSY disemployed
DDEEILNNOTU tunnel diode
DDEEILNOPSU undespoiled
DDEEILNOSVZ devil's dozen
DDEEILPRSSY dispersedly
DDEEINNOORR Eriodendron
DDEEINNPSSU undispensed
DDEEINNRRUV under-driven
DDEEINRSSYY Sydneysider
DDEEINSSSTU studiedness
DDEEIOSSWWW widow's weeds
DDEELLNORTW well-trodden
DDEELLNORUW well-rounded
DDEELMOORUY Dudley Moore
DDEENNORSSU roundedness
DDEENNORSUW snowed under
DDEENNPSSUU unsuspended
DDEENOORSST send to dorse
DDEENORSTUY undestroyed
DDEENRRSSUU under duress
DDEEOOPPRST door-stepped
DDEEOORRSST Ordos Desert
DDEEOORRSVW over-drowsed
DDEFFIILNTY diffidently
DDEFGIIIINN indignified
DDEFGIIINNU undignified
DDEFHILNOOP phonofiddle
DDEFHILOOOS solid-hoofed
DDEFINOPRSU de profundis
DDEFLNNOUUY unfoundedly

DDEGGIINNRW wedding ring
DDEGHIILMNT light-minded
DDEGHIIMNRT right-minded
DDEGHILLSTU dull-sighted
DDEGHILNSTU Sudden Light
DDEGHILOTUY gilded youth
DDEGHIMNOTU tough-minded
DDEGHIOPSSS goddess-ship
DDEGHLNNORU long hundred
DDEGHLNOPRY dendroglyph
DDEGIILMSUY misguidedly
DDEGIILSSUY disguisedly
DDEGIIMNPTU pudding-time
DDEGIINORST Otis Redding
DDEGIINPPPU pudding-pipe
DDEGIINRSSV diving dress
DDEGIINSSUU undisguised
DDEGILMNOST dislodgment
DDEGILNNNOR Lord Denning
DDEGILNRSTU disgruntled
DDEGILPRSSU gilded spurs
DDEGILSSTUY disgustedly
DDEGIMNNORW wrong-minded
DDEGINNORUW round-winged
DDEGINOOOPT odontoid peg
DDEGINOOORR in good order
DDEGINORSWW winged words
DDEGINPSTUU suet pudding
DDEGMNOOOSS moon goddess
DDEGNNORRUU underground
DDEHHIIOPRT diphtheroid
DDEHHIIRSTT dish the dirt
DDEHIIKNPRS kindredship
DDEHIINRSSW widdershins
DDEHILNOTTY on the tiddly
DDEHILOOTWW The Wild Wood
DDEHINNOTWW down the wind
DDEHINORSSU disenshroud
DDEHINORSTW short-winded
DDEHIOOORWW widowerhood
DDEHJMNNOOR John Redmond
DDEHJNOOORW John Redwood
DDEHLLOORTW the Old World
DDEHLMOOTUU loudmouthed
DDEHNOORSTU do the rounds
DDEIIINORUX idoxuridine
DDEIIJLMMRY Jimmy Riddle
DDEIIKNRRRV drink-driver
DDEIILLNSTU undistilled
DDEIILLOPSS ill-disposed
DDEIILNOTTY old identity
DDEIIMNNOSU diminuendos
DDEIIMOORRV room-divider
DDEIKNRRRUV drunk-driver
DDEILMMNOSW slimmed-down
DDEILMNOWWY downy mildew
DDEILNNOOPR London pride✧
DDEILNOPSSU splendidous
DDEILNOSSUV undissolved
DDEIMNOORUZ zoodendrium
DDEINNOOPRV non-provided
DDEINORSTTU undistorted
DDELNNOORRY Londonderry
DDEMNOSTTUU Desmond Tutu
DDFGHILNNOU fundholding
DDFGILNOOOR folding door
DDFOOORRRWW word for word
DDGGGGIILNO gold-digging
DDGGHINOPSU hog's pudding
DDGIIINNNOV non-dividing
DDGIIINNORV divining rod
DDGIIKLMNPU milk pudding
DDGIILLMNRU drilling mud
DDGILMNOORR Lord Grimond
DDGILMNPPUU plum-pudding
DDGINNOORSU sounding rod
DDGINOOOORU in good odour
DDHIKOSTWYY whisky toddy
DDHIMOOORUW rhodium-wood
DDIIIMRTTUY rumti-iddity
DDIIKLNSTWY tiddlywinks
DDIILMNNOOO Old Dominion
DDINNOORUWW round window
DDINOOOPRTT diprotodont
DEEEEEFHRST sheet-feeder
DEEEEEHMRRT the Redeemer
DEEEEFGNRUV dengue fever
DEEEEFLNRUZ needle-furze
DEEEEFLORST Lee De Forest
DEEEEGGHLRT three-legged
DEEEEGGLLPV level-pegged
DEEEEGKLOPR lodge-keeper
DEEEEGKRTTX greeked text
DEEEEHILRSW side-wheeler
DEEEEHIMPRS ephemerides
DEEEEHLMOSW wheedlesome
DEEEEHLNRTU under the lee
DEEEEHNPRRR reprehender
DEEEEHNQRTU The Red Queen
DEEEEILRRRV redeliverer
DEEEEILSSSY sessile-eyed
DEEEEIMNRRT redetermine
DEEEEKNPRRU underkeeper
DEEEELLNRTW well-entered
DEEEELNRSUV undersleeve
DEEEEMOPRST speedometer
DEEEENNRSSW renewedness
DEEEENNSTUW unsweetened
DEEEENOPSTW steepedowne
DEEEENRRRSU surrenderee
DEEEEPRRSSU supersedere
DEEEEQRSSTU sequestered
DEEEFFFNOOS off one's feed
DEEEFFGILNS self-feeding
DEEEFFLOOTT fleetfooted
DEEEFFNOOST toffee-nosed
DEEEFFNORSX sex offender
DEEEFGINNSS feignedness
DEEEFGNORTU free-tongued
DEEEFHLNSSU heedfulness
DEEEFHLORUW four-wheeled
DEEEFHNRRSU unrefreshed

DEEEFIIJLLO fille de joie
DEEEFIILMPX exemplified
DEEEFILNSTV field events
self-evident
DEEEFILNSVY defensively
DEEEFINNRSS refinedness
DEEEFLLORRW elderflower
DEEEFLLOSVV self-evolved
DEEEFLMPSTT self-tempted
DEEEFLNNOSY deny oneself
DEEEFLNNSSU needfulness
DEEEFLOPRSW self-powered
DEEEFLORRTX retroflexed
DEEEFMNNRTU unfermented
DEEEFMNRRSU referendums
DEEEFMOORRV overfreedom
DEEEFNPRRRU unpreferred
DEEEGGILNSS gens d'église
DEEEGHHILLT light-heeled
DEEEGHIPRST hedge-priest
DEEEGHIRRTW hedge-writer
DEEEGIMNNRU mud engineer
DEEEGIMNRTV divergement
DEEEGINNNRV nerve ending
never-ending
DEEEGINOSXY deoxygenise
DEEEGINOXYZ deoxygenize
DEEEGINQSUU Queen's Guide
DEEEGKLNNOW long weekend
DEEEGLORRSU guelder rose
DEEEGLORRSV gold reserve
DEEEGMNNSTU unsegmented
DEEEGMNORRU nom de guerre
DEEEHHORSST The Red Shoes
DEEEHHPRSSS shepherdess
DEEEHIKRSTU the Dukeries
DEEEHILNPRS replenished
DEEEHILPRSW spider wheel
DEEEHILRSSY Iles d'Hyères
DEEEHIMRRSU Rudesheimer
Rüdesheimer
DEEEHIRSTTU three-suited
DEEEHKNOORT three-nooked
DEEEHLMNOTY the old enemy
DEEEHLNNORT Heldentenor
DEEEHLNRSTU unsheltered
DEEEHMNOSST Demosthenes
DEEEHMOPRTT hot-tempered
DEEEHNPRTXY hyperextend
DEEEHOSSSTW sow the seeds
DEEEIIJORVV joie de vivre
DEEEIILNSSW Denise Lewis
DEEEIILPSST epistle side
DEEEIILRSSV desilverise
DEEEIILRSVZ desilverize
DEEEIIMPRTX time-expired
DEEEIINNPTX inexpedient
DEEEIINSSST desensitise
DEEEIINSSTZ desensitize
DEEEIKLNRSV linked verse
DEEEILLMPRT ill-tempered
DEEEILLNNST sentinelled
DEEEILLNPPZ Led Zeppelin
DEEEILLNRSS elderliness
DEEEILLORWY lower eyelid
DEEEILMMNUV mendelevium
DEEEILNNOPT needlepoint
DEEEILNPRST spindle tree
DEEEILNPTXY expediently
DEEEILORSTU deleterious
DEEEILPPRUY upper eyelid
DEEEIMMPRST mistempered
DEEEIMNOPTT mont-de-piété
DEEEIMNPRTV deprivement
DEEEINPRRUV unreprieved
DEEEINPRTUX expenditure
DEEEINQSSUY Disneyesque
DEEEINRRSST retiredness
DEEEINRRSSV vine-dresser
DEEEINRRUVW underviewer
DEEEINRSSTW dessert wine
DEEEIOPRRSV preside over
DEEEIPPRSST sidestepper
DEEEKNOPPRU pound-keeper
DEEELLNRRSU underseller
DEEELLOPUUX poule de luxe
DEEELLPPRXY perplexedly
DEEELLRTTTU telluretted
DEEELMNNORY moneylender
DEEELMNOPTV development
DEEELMNOTVV devolvement
DEEELNNPRST resplendent
DEEELNNRSSS slenderness
DEEELNNSSSS endlessness
DEEELNPPRUX unperplexed
DEEELNRRTTU underletter
DEEELNSSSTT settledness
DEEELOOPRST rood-steeple
DEEELOOPRVV overdevelop
DEEELRRSSUV verdureless
DEEEMNNORST endorsement
DEEEMNNORTW re-endowment
DEEEMNORSSV removedness
DEEEMOPRRWY emery powder
DEEENNPRTUV unprevented
DEEENNRRSTU nurse-tender
DEEENOPRSSS reposedness
DEEENOPRSUX underexpose
DEEENOPSSSX exposedness
DEEENOPSTTU pedetentous
DEEENPRRTUV unperverted
DEEENPRSSUX unexpressed
DEEENRRRRSU surrenderer
DEEENRRSTTT trendsetter
DEEEOPRSTTY stereotyped
DEEEORRRTTV retroverted
DEEEORRTTVX extroverted
DEEEPRRSSST pre-stressed
DEEEPRRSSUU supersedure
DEEFFGILRSU self-figured
DEEFFIILOVW field of view
DEEFFIINNRT indifferent

DEEFFILNNOS find oneself
DEEFFILNRTY differently
DEEFFILOTVW View of Delft
DEEFFINORTU unforfeited
DEEFFINSSSU diffuseness
DEEFGGHHIIN high-feeding
DEEFGGILNOO good feeling
DEEFGHHIRST freight shed
DEEFGHHORTU feedthrough
DEEFGHILLST self-delight
DEEFGHIORST foresighted
DEEFGIINNRX index-finger
DEEFGIINSST fidgetiness
DEEFGIKNORW weeding-fork
DEEFGILNNSY self-denying
DEEFGILNNUY unfeignedly
DEEFGILNORS gird oneself
DEEFGIOORTT tiger-footed
DEEFHHLOOOW whole-hoofed
DEEFHIIKSWY whiskeyfied
DEEFHILPPRW Fred Whipple
DEEFHILTTTW Twelfthtide
DEEFHJNNORS John F Enders
DEEFHLLNUUY unheedfully
DEEFHLLOSST soft-shelled
DEEFHLOOOTW whole-footed
DEEFHLOOSTU lofted house
DEEFIIIMNNR indemnifier
DEEFIIINNST intensified
DEEFIILLMST self-limited
DEEFIILMRSU demulsifier
DEEFIILNQUU unliquefied
DEEFIILNSTV self-invited
DEEFIINOPRS personified
DEEFIINRRTU unterrified
DEEFIJOORST Jodie Foster
DEEFIKLORRW fieldworker
DEEFILLRSSU fleurs-de-lis
DEEFILMNNRU Dunfermline
DEEFILMOPSS self-imposed
DEEFILMSSSU self-misused
DEEFILNORWW Wilfred Owen
DEEFILNRSSU direfulness
DEEFILORSTY oyster-field
DEEFILOSTTU outside left
DEEFINNSSUX unfixedness
DEEFIORRTTT retrofitted
DEEFIPRRTUV putrid fever
DEEFKLMOPRU Rudolf Kempe
DEEFLLNNUUY unneedfully
DEEFLLNOSSU dolefulness
DEEFLLRSSUY fleurs-de-lys
DEEFLNOORST fender-stool
DEEFLNORRRW Lord Renfrew
DEEFLNRSTUU unflustered
DEEFLOPRSSY professedly
DEEFMNOPRRU unperformed
DEEFMORRRSS dress-reform
DEEFNOORSTT tenderfoots
DEEFNOPRSSU unprofessed
DEEFNOPRSTU turn of speed
DEEFNOPRTUY type founder
DEEFOORRTTW wood-fretter
DEEGGGHILLT light-legged
DEEGGGHLORU rough-legged
DEEGGHOOSTT get the goods
DEEGGIKNORW working edge
DEEGGILNORR dégringoler
DEEGGINNOOS goods engine
DEEGGINNOOV good-evening
DEEGGINOOSW goose-winged
DEEGGLLOORY Lloyd-George
DEEGGLNOOOS golden goose
DEEGHHILMTT high-mettled
DEEGHHINRST ring the shed
DEEGHHIOPRW high-powered
DEEGHHOPSSY hedge-hyssop
DEEGHIILLMT limelighted
DEEGHIINTWW white-winged
DEEGHIKNOOW weeding-hook
DEEGHILLNWY wheedlingly
DEEGHILLOSV glove-shield
DEEGHILLSST delightless
DEEGHILMOST delightsome
DEEGHILNNOT Len Deighton
DEEGHILNNSU un-Englished
DEEGHILNNTU unlightened
DEEGHILNNUY unheedingly
DEEGHINORSW Winged Horse
DEEGHINORSY hydrogenise
DEEGHINORYZ hydrogenize
DEEGHINRTUW underweight
DEEGHIORRRV red river hog
DEEGHLLLNOO golden hello
DEEGHLMOOPS so help me God
DEEGHLNRSST dress-length
DEEGHNORSTU groundsheet
DEEGHOOPSUW P G Wodehouse
DEEGIIINSTV indigestive
DEEGIIKLLNS sliding keel
DEEGIIKNPSS deep kissing
DEEGIILRRST lister ridge
DEEGIILSTVY digestively
DEEGIILTTUV deglutitive
DEEGIIMNNOR domineering
DEEGIINNNTW twin-engined
DEEGIIOPPRR Périgord pie
DEEGIJMNPRU jumping deer
DEEGILLNOSS single-soled
DEEGILLNPSS spindle-legs
DEEGILMNOOY endemiology
DEEGILMNTUV divulgement
DEEGILNORUV overindulge
DEEGILNRSVY deservingly
DEEGILNRTVY divergently
DEEGIMNNSST dessignment
DEEGIMNOPSY Gymnopédies
DEEGIMORSUU demiurgeous
DEEGINNOSTW get one's wind
DEEGINNRSUV undeserving
DEEGINNRTUU ungenitured
DEEGINORSTU dentigerous

DEEGINRSSST	de-stressing
DEEGJLRSSUU	Judges' Rules
DEEGJMNPRTU	prejudgment
DEEGLLMOORW	well-groomed
DEEGLNOSSSS	godlessness
DEEGLOOPSUU	pseudologue
DEEHHIIMMRS	hemihedrism
DEEHHILLNOT	hold the line
DEEHHLOORSU	householder
DEEHHNOORRS	horned horse
DEEHHOPRRSY	hydrosphere
DEEHIIKLNTW	like the wind
DEEHIILMSTT	ditheletism✧
DEEHIILNNRT	thin red line
DEEHIILOPRS	siderophile
DEEHIILSTTW	white-listed
DEEHIIMPRSU	hesperidium
DEEHIINNPSZ	denizenship
DEEHIIOPRSS	spheroidise
DEEHIIOPRSZ	spheroidize
DEEHIKLNRTU	thunderlike
DEEHILLNOPS	spindle hole
DEEHILLORTT	title-holder
DEEHILMNOTU	endothelium
DEEHILNNOTW	down the line
	down-the-line
DEEHILNOWWW	wheel window
DEEHIMNNOTW	Down the Mine
DEEHIMNOPWW	hempen widow
DEEHIMPRTUW	white-rumped
DEEHINNORST	disenthrone
DEEHINOPRRV	horned viper
DEEHINOPSTY	dehypnotise
DEEHINOPTYZ	dehypnotize
DEEHINOSSSU	hideousness
DEEHINOSSSV	doveishness
DEEHINRRSSU	hurriedness
DEEHIORSTTU	The Outsider
DEEHJKNNORW	John Kendrew
DEEHKLOPTUY	loup-the-dyke
DEEHKOOPRRT	red-hot poker
DEEHLLNRRTU	Ruth Rendell
DEEHLLOOSUW	whole-souled
DEEHLMNNOSS	Mendelssohn
DEEHLNORRTW	netherworld
DEEHLNORTWW	the New World
DEEHLNRSSTU	thunderless
DEEHLOPSUUX	duplex house
DEEHLORRSSU	elders' hours
DEEHLPRSTUU	sulphureted
DEEHMNOOPTU	open-mouthed
DEEHMOORRTY	hydrometeor
DEEHMOORSTU	The Dormouse
DEEHNNORSTU	underhonest
DEEHNNRSTUU	under the sun
DEEHNOOOPRT	open the door
DEEHNOOORSW	wooden horse
DEEHOORRSUV	hors d'oeuvre
DEEIIIKKNNX	Nikkei index
DEEIIIQSTUV	disquietive
DEEIIKLLMRV	milk-livered

DEEIIKLLMSS	semi-skilled
DEEIIKLLORS	soldierlike
DEEIIKLNPRS	kinderspiel
DEEIIKLNSSS	dislikeness
DEEIIKMMMSS	semi-skimmed
DEEIILLLRVY	lily-livered
DEEIILLNRSV	ill-versed in
DEEIILLPPQU	ill-equipped
DEEIILMNSST	limitedness
DEEIILMNSSU	disseminule
DEEIILMORTV	limited-over
DEEIILNOPRS	Lepidosiren
DEEIILOPRSY	erysipeloid
DEEIILRRSTT	retired list
DEEIILRSSSV	silversides
DEEIIMMNRST	determinism
DEEIIMMNRTU	intermedium
DEEIIMMPRSU	peridesmium
DEEIIMNNOPS	demi-pension
DEEIIMNOPTT	piedmontite
DEEIIMNPSST	dissepiment
DEEIIMNRRST	irredentism✧
DEEIIMNRSTT	determinist
DEEIIMNRSXY	misery index
DEEIIMNRTTT	intermitted
DEEIIMOPSTT	time deposit
DEEIIMORRST	deteriorism
DEEIINNNOTT	intentioned
DEEIINNSSTT	dissentient
DEEIINOPRRS	risperidone
DEEIINOPSTV	point-devise
DEEIINPRSTY	serendipity
DEEIINRRSTT	irredentist✧
DEEIINRSSTT	disinterest
DEEIINRTTXY	indexterity
DEEIIOPSTUX	expeditious
DEEIIOQSSUX	sesquioxide
DEEIIORRRTT	territoried
DEEIIORRTTV	detritivore
DEEIIORRTTY	deteriority
DEEIIRRRRVV	river-driver
DEEIIRSTTUV	divestiture
DEEIJLOOPRT	projet de loi
DEEIJMNOPSW	jimpson weed
DEEIJNOSSWW	Jesse window
DEEIJPRSTUX	jeux d'esprit
DEEIKLLORSV	Volkslieder
DEEIKLNORRS	Lord Erskine
DEEIKMNPPSU	pumpkinseed
DEEIKNNOSTY	kidney stone
DEEIKNORSTX	stroke index
DEEILLMPRRY	elderly prim
DEEILLNOPRU	perduellion
DEEILMMOSST	seldom-times
DEEILMNOPST	despoilment
DEEILMNRTUY	unmeritedly
DEEILMOSTUW	it would seem
DEEILNNORVY	non-delivery
DEEILNOPTUX	unexploited
DEEILNORRSS	orderliness
DEEILNSSSTT	stiltedness

DEEILOPPPTY	polypeptide
DEEILOPSSTU	Lepidosteus
DEEILORRSSW	World Series
DEEILQRRRSU	red squirrel
DEEIMMNORTU	endometrium
DEEIMNNNOTU	unmentioned
DEEIMNNOOTU	unemotioned
DEEIMNNOSST	set one's mind
DEEIMNNOSTU	unmoistened
DEEIMNOPRSY	money spider
DEEIMNORUYY	mind your eye
DEEIMNPRSSU	unimpressed
DEEINNNOPSU	unpensioned
DEEINNNORST	non-resident
DEEINNOPSST	pointedness
DEEINNOSTTU	tendentious
DEEINNPRSTU	superintend
DEEINNRRSUU	underinsure
DEEINNSSSTT	stintedness
DEEINNSSTUW	unwitnessed
DEEINOPRRVW	power-driven
DEEINORRRVW	owner-driver
DEEINORRTTV	introverted
DEEINORSSUW	series-wound
DEEINOSSSTU	tediousness
DEEINOSSSUV	deviousness
DEEINPPRTTU	reputed pint
DEEINPRRTTU	interrupted
DEEINRRRSTV	River Dnestr
DEEINRRRTUW	underwriter
DEEIOOPRRSU	urediospore
DEEIOOPRRTV	proveditore
DEEIOORSTUV	overtedious
DEEIOPRRTUY	eurypteroid
DEEIOPRSTUV	dispute over
DEEIOSTTTUU	tout de suite
DEEJKNNNOYY	jenny donkey
DEEKLNOORRU	underlooker
DEEKLRSSTTU	Studs Terkel
DEEKNNNRSSU	drunkenness
DEEKNORRRUW	underworker
DEELLLMRSUW	slum-dweller
DEELLNORTWW	town dweller
DEELLNSTTUY	unsettledly
DEELMNOOTTU	tout le monde
DEELMNORSSW	endless worm
DEELMNORTTY	tormentedly
DEELORSTTUV	turtle doves
DEELORSTUXY	dexterously
DEEMNNORTTU	untormented
DEEMNOORTUY	Deuteronomy
DEEMNORSSUY	Mersey sound
DEEMNOSSSSY	syndesmoses
DEENNSSSTTU	stuntedness
DEENOPRRRTU	under-report
DEENOPRSTTU	unprotested
DEENOPSSSSU	unpossessed
DEENOPSSSTT	spottedness
DEENORRRRSU	surrenderor
DEENORRRRTU	return order
DEENORRSTUY	understorey
DEENOSSSTUU	duteousness
DEEOOPPRRST	doorstepper
DEEOORSTTWY	two-storeyed
DEEORSSSTTU	stressed out
	stressed-out
DEERRSSTTTU	Sturt Desert
DEFFGHIORTU	right of feud
DEFFGINNNOU	unoffending
DEFFGINOORS	finger foods
DEFFGINORUV	duffing-over
DEFFHHIOORS	sheriffhood
DEFFHILOSSU	soufflé dish
DEFFIILORSS	fossil-fired
DEFFIILSUVY	diffusively
DEFFIINORSU	Rediffusion®
DEFFIINORTU	unfortified
DEFFILLLNUU	unfulfilled
DEFFILLNRUU	underfulfil
DEFFINPPRSU	snuff-dipper
DEFFIOOSTTW	swift-footed
DEFFKOORUWY	Woodruff key
DEFFNOOSSTU	do one's stuff
DEFGGGHIRTU	grudge fight
DEFGHIISTTT	tight-fisted
DEFGHILOOSY	old-fogeyish
DEFGHILOOTT	light-footed
DEFGHINORSU	unsighed-for
DEFGHIOORTT	right-footed
DEFGHMOOORT	Mother of God
DEFGHOOORTU	rough-footed
DEFGIIINNTY	identifying
DEFGIILNNSW	self-winding
DEFGIILNPRS	Springfield
DEFGIINNSYY	Disneyfying
DEFGIINORRR	firing order
DEFGIINORSZ	frigid zones
DEFGIINSTWW	swift-winged
DEFGILLNSUY	sdeignfully
DEFGILNRSSY	fly-dressing
DEFGINNORUV	overfunding
DEFHHLOORTT	hold the fort
DEFHILMNOSW	flemish down
DEFHIMNORTU	mouth-friend
DEFHINNRSUU	unfurnished
DEFHINORSTW	downshifter
DEFHINORSUW	unwished-for
DEFHINPRSTT	spendthrift
DEFHIOOPRST	fish-torpedo
DEFHIOORRSX	Oxfordshire
DEFHLLMOTUU	full-mouthed
DEFHLMOOTUU	foul-mouthed
DEFIIIMNSTY	misidentify
DEFIIINRTUV	unvitrified
DEFIIJNSTUU	unjustified
DEFIILLMNOR	ill-informed
DEFIILLNOPS	flip one's lid
DEFIILNOSSX	index fossil
DEFIILQSTUU	disquietful
DEFIIMNORTU	unmortified
DEFILMNNSSU	mindfulness
DEFILNSSTUU	dutifulness

DEFILNSTUXY flux density
DEFILOOORST foot soldier
DEFILOPPRVY floppy drive
DEFILOPRSST field sports
DEFILRSSSTU distressful
DEFIMNORSTU misfortuned
DEFINNNOPSU pension fund
DEFINNOORRU iron-founder
DEFINOSSSUW Swiss fondue
DEFIOOORRSU odoriferous
DEFIOORRSSU dorsiferous
DEFKLNOOORU unlooked-for
DEFLLNORUWY wonderfully
DEFLNOOSSTW twofoldness
DEFLNRTUUUV vulture fund
DEFLOOOOSTT footstooled
DEFLOORRTUW Tudor flower
DEFNOOPRRUU four-pounder
DEFNOPRTUYY type foundry
DEGGHHHIILT highlighted
DEGGHHHIIST high-sighted
DEGGHIILNTW light-winged
DEGGHIJLNOU John Gielgud
DEGGHILNOST long-sighted
DEGGHINOSSS doggishness
DEGGHOOOSTT go to the dogs
DEGGIIILNST single-digit
DEGGIILNNSY designingly
DEGGIILNORV riding glove
DEGGIILNRVY divergingly
DEGGIINNNSU undesigning
DEGGIJLLNUW well-judging
DEGGKLRSUUY skulduggery
DEGGLNNOOTU long-tongued
DEGHHHILRSU high hurdles
DEGHHIILMOT high old time
DEGHHIILRTY highly tried
DEGHHIINSTY high-density
DEGHHILNORT hold the ring
DEGHHILNOST shed light on
DEGHHLORSTU The Gold Rush
DEGHIIINRST inside right
DEGHIIINRTV divine right
DEGHIILLLPT gild the pill
DEGHIILLLTY gild the lily
DEGHIILNNRS hinderlings
DEGHIILNNRY hinderingly
DEGHIILPPTT tight-lipped
DEGHIIMNRRY riding-rhyme
DEGHIINNTTU hunting-tide
DEGHIINORRS horse-riding
riding horse
DEGHILMNOOP phlegmonoid
DEGHILNORSU shouldering
DEGHILNORTW downlighter
DEGHILOSSTW slow-sighted
DEGHINNOORY hydrogen ion
DEGHINNOOST do one's thing
DEGHINNOPRR herring pond
DEGHINNRSTU underthings
DEGHINOPSTT potting shed
DEGHINOPTUW pound weight
DEGHINORSTU ride shotgun
DEGHINOSSTU doughtiness
DEGHLMOOOTY methodology
DEGHNNOOPRR prong-horned
DEGHNNOORTU on the ground
DEGHNOOOSTT honest-to-God
DEGHNOOPTTU put on the dog
DEGHNOORSTU go the rounds
DEGHNOORSUY hydrogenous
DEGHNOORXYY oxy-hydrogen
DEGHNORRTUW undergrowth
DEGIIILNPRV pile-driving
DEGIIINNOST indigestion
DEGIIINQSTU disquieting
DEGIIKNRSTW writing desk
DEGIILLNPTW pit-dwelling
DEGIILLNRSU sliding-rule
DEGIILNOTTU deglutition
DEGIILNRTVY divertingly
DEGIIMNNNRU undermining
DEGIIMNNORT morningtide
DEGIINNRRUW underwiring
DEGIINNRTUV undiverting
DEGIINOPRVW power-diving
DEGIINPPRTW dripping wet
DEGIINRSSST distressing
DEGIINRSTTV driving test
DEGIJMMNSTU misjudgment
DEGIKLMNOSS kingdomless
DEGIKNNSTUU St Kunigunde
DEGILLNNTUY indulgently
DEGILLNOPRY deploringly
DEGILMNORSU smouldering
DEGILNNOPRY ponderingly
DEGILNNORWY wonderingly
DEGILNNOSSU ungodliness
DEGILNNOTTW letting down
DEGILNOPSSS splodginess
DEGILNORUVY devouringly
DEGILOOPRTY pteridology
DEGILORTTUY deglutitory
DEGIMMNORUU regium donum
DEGINNNSSUY undyingness
DEGINNOSTTW down-setting
DEGINOPRSST top dressing
DEGLLNORSUW groundswell
DEGLNOPRSUY golden syrup
DEGLOORSTTY Troglodytes
DEGNNOORSTU stoneground
DEGNOOOTUWY woody-tongue
DEHHIILMNOT helminthoid
DEHHILMOORS holohedrism
DEHHILOPRRS her lordship
DEHHLNOSTUU sleuth-hound
DEHHMMOSTUU mush-mouthed
DEHHNNORSUY Henry Hudson
DEHHOOOPPRT prophethood
DEHIIIJMNRX Jimi Hendrix
DEHIIILMSTT dithelitism✧
DEHIIKNNNST thin-skinned

DEHIILLMNPS	Mendip Hills
DEHIILMNPSU	delphiniums
DEHIILOPRSS	soldiership
DEHIILPRSTU	trisulphide
DEHIIMNORSW	in her wisdom
DEHIIMNORTU	dinotherium
DEHIINORSTZ	disthronize
DEHIINSTTUW	Whitsuntide
DEHIIOOPSVV	voivodeship
DEHIIOPRSTT	hot-spirited
DEHIKNSSSSU	duskishness
DEHILLMORUU	ill-humoured
DEHILLNOSSS	dollishness
DEHILNORTVY	thorny devil
DEHILNOSSST	doltishness
DEHILNOSSTY	dishonestly
DEHILNOSTTW	thistledown
DEHILNOTTWW	whittle down
DEHILNRRUUY	unhurriedly
DEHILPRSTUU	disulphuret
DEHIMMOPSTU	imposthumed
DEHIMNPSSSU	dumpishness
DEHIMNSSTYY	Sydney Smith
DEHINNORSSS	dronishness
DEHINNORSUU	unnourished
DEHINNRTTUW	turn the wind
DEHINOORRSU	dishonourer
DEHINOPRRST	third person
DEHINORRSUV	Hudson River
DEHINORSSSW	wordishness
DEHINORSSTU	drouthiness
DEHINPRSSSU	prudishness
DEHINPSSTTU	studentship
DEHINRRSTTU	underthirst
DEHIOOOPPRT	photoperiod
DEHIOOPRSTT	orthopedist
DEHLLNOOWWY	wholly-owned
DEHLNNOOOSW	hold one's own
DEHLNOOPRSY	polyhedrons
DEHMMORSTUW	mum's the word
DEHMOOPPRSU	pseudomorph
DEHNOOOOPRT	odontophore
DEHNOOPPPRY	horned poppy
DEHNORRSSTU	undershorts
DEHNRRSTTUU	underthrust
DEHOOOPRTTW	tooth powder
DEIIILLSSUV	disillusive
DEIIIMNPRSU	peridiniums
DEIIINNPSSS	insipidness
DEIIINNSSTV	disinvest in
DEIIINPRTTY	intrepidity
DEIIIOPSSTV	dispositive
DEIIKKLMMMS	skimmed milk
DEIILLMNNUU	unillumined
DEIILLMNTUY	unlimitedly
DEIILLOORRV	Lord Olivier
DEIILLORSUY	deliriously
DEIILLQRRUV	quill-driver
DEIILMMNPSS	Simple Minds
DEIILMPRSTW	limp-wristed
DEIILNOORWW	oriel-window
DEIILNOPRRY	pyrrolidine
DEIILNOSSTU	delusionist
DEIILOPRSTW	low-spirited
DEIILOSSTUV	dissolutive
DEIILOSSTUY	seditiously
DEIIMNOOSST	endomitosis
DEIIMNOOSTV	misdevotion
DEIIMNOPRTV	improvident
DEIIMNORTTT	intromitted
DEIIMQRTTUU	tertium quid
DEIINNOQRSU	inquirendos
DEIINOOSTTV	devotionist
DEIINOSSSTU	dissentious
DEIINOSTTTU	destitution
DEIIOQSSTUU	disquietous
DEIJKLNNORS	Lord Jenkins
DEIKLNNPRSU	unsprinkled
DEIKNRSTUYY	key industry
DEILLMOOSUY	melodiously
DEILLMRSTUY	dusty-miller
DEILLNORSSW	worldliness
DEILLNORSTU	tendrillous
DEILLNORSUY	unsoldierly
DEILLORSTUY	desultorily
DEILLORSWWY	worldly-wise
DEILLOSSTUY	dissolutely
DEILMNOORSW	one-worldism
DEILMNOOSUU	unmelodious
DEILMNPRTUY	imprudently
DEILNOPRTVY	providently
DEILNOPSTUY	pendulosity
DEILOOORSW	rosewood oil
DEILPPRSSUY	supply-sider
DEILPRRSSUY	surprisedly
DEIMMNNOPTU	impoundment
DEIMMNNSTUU	indumentums
DEIMMRSSTYY	dissymmetry
DEIMNNNOOVW	Devon minnow
DEIMNNOPSWY	penny-wisdom
DEIMNOOPRSU	imponderous
DEIMNOORRRS	minor orders
DEIMNOORRTV	motor-driven
DEIMNOPRSST	spinsterdom
DEIMNOPRSTT	disportment
DEIMNOSSSSY	syndesmosis
DEIMNPRRRTU	drum printer
DEIMOORRSUV	merdivorous
DEIMOPPRTTU	promptitude
DEINNOOPRTU	unportioned
DEINNOPRTUV	unprovident
DEINNPSSUUY	sunny side up
DEINOOPRSTU	torpedinous
DEINOOPRSTY	ponderosity
DEINOPSSTUU	stupendious
DEINOSSTUUW	wound tissue
DEINPRRSSUU	unsurprised
DEIOPPRRSTY	disproperty
DEKNOORRSWW	work wonders
DEKOORRSTWW	worsted-work
DELLLORRSSU	Lord Russell
DELLNOPSUUY	pendulously

DELLNOSSSUY soundlessly
DELMOOORRRY orderly room
DELMORRSUUY murderously
DELNOOORSTT rondolettos
DELNOOPRSSU splendorous
DELNOOPRSUY ponderously
DELNPPRSUUY undersupply
DELOOPRSTUU trous-de-loup
DELOPPRRSSU Lord's Supper
DELOPPRRTUY purportedly
DELOPRRUWZZ word-puzzler
DEMMOORSTYY Tommy Dorsey
DEMNORSXYYY XYY syndrome
DEMNOSSSTUY sound system
DEMOOPRRSTU Petrodromus
DEMOOPRTTUW trumpet wood
DEMOORSSSTT storm-tossed
DENNNOSSSUU unsoundness
DENNOOOOPSW wooden spoon
DENNOOSSTTY snotty-nosed
DENNORRSSUU Sensurround®
DENOOORSSSU odorousness
DENOOORSSTW do one's worst
DENOOORTTUU unrooted out
DENOOPPRRSW snow-dropper
DENOOPPRSTU petropounds
DENOPPRSTUU unsupported
DEOPPRRRSTU Rupert's drop
DEOPPRTTUWY putty-powder
DFFGHIJOORS Josh Gifford
DFFIIISTUVY diffusivity
DFFIILLMOSY silly mid-off
DFGGGHIINOT dogfighting
DFGGIIIINRY rigidifying
DFGGINOOPRR drop-forging
DFGHIIOPRRT right of drip
DFGIIILNOSY solidifying
DFGIIIMNNRT drift-mining
DFGIIKNNNSU sinking fund
DFGIILLNOWW wildfowling
DFGIILNQSUY flying squid
DFGIINNRSUW windsurfing
DFGLNOOORRU ground floor
DFGNOORRSTU ground frost
DFHHIILNOPS dolphinfish
DFHLOOORSST Lord of hosts
DFHLOORRTUW Fourth World
DFHMOOORTUW word-of-mouth
DFIILLLMNOO millionfold
DFIILMOSTUU multifidous
DFILLMNNUUY unmindfully
DFILLNTUUUY undutifully
DFILRSSTTUU distrustful
DFINNOORRUY iron-foundry
DGGHIIILNRT riding light
DGGHINNOOTU good hunting!
DGGHINNOSTU Hunting Dogs
DGGIIILLNRR drilling rig
DGGIIINNNRW ring-winding
DGGIILMNNSU mudslinging
DGGIKLNOOOO good-looking
DGGILNNORTU lodging turn
DGGIMNNOOOR good-morning
DGGINNNRRUU drug-running
DGHHHIOOPTU up to high doh
DGHHIINOSWW High Windows
DGHIIIIMNNS diminishing
DGHIIINSSTU distinguish
DGHIIMNNSTU midnight sun
DGHILLLOPRU drill-plough
DGHILLORTWY Lloyd Wright
DGHILMORSTY goldsmithry
DGHILOORSTY hydrologist
DGHILOPRTYY tyroglyphid
DGHLNOORSTU ground-sloth
DGIIIINPRST dispiriting
DGIIIKNRRST riding skirt
DGIIILOORST iridologist
DGIIINNORRV driving iron
DGIILLNRRST drill string
DGIILNNOPRU lip-rounding
DGIILNOPSSY disposingly
DGIIMNOOOUZ zoogonidium
DGIINNOSTTW down-sitting
DGIIOOPRSST good spirits
DGIKNNORRST strong drink
DGILNNOOOSY sindonology
DGILNOORSTY strongyloid
DGINNOOSTUU sounding out
DGINNORRSUU surrounding
DGLOORSUUXY luxury goods
DGNNOOORSTU Gordonstoun
DGNNOORRTUU run to ground
DHHIILOPRSS his lordship
DHHIOOPRTYY hypothyroid
DHHLLPRSUYY sulphhydryl
DHHMNOOOSTU smooth hound
DHHNOOOSTTU hound's-tooth
DHHNOOPRTYY hydrophyton
DHIIIMNOSSW in his wisdom
DHIIIMPSSTY Diphysitism
DHIIIORSTTY thyroiditis
DHIILMOOORS Moorish Idol
DHIIMOOSTTW shittim wood
DHILLNOOPPY podophyllin
DHILMOOOSTU lithodomous
DHIMOOOSTTW wisdom tooth
DHINNORTUWY whodunnitry
DHINOOSTTUW unwithstood
DHIOOORTTUW without-door
DHLLMOOPPUY Podophyllum
DHLMNOOORST Lord Thomson
DHLOOPRXYYY polyhydroxy
DHMNNOOSTUU Mount Hudson
DHNOOORTUXY unorthodoxy
DIIIILLQTUY illiquidity
DIIIIMNOSSV divisionism✧
DIIIINOSSTV divisionist
DIIIJNOOSVY Joy Division
DIIIKNOPSST od's pitikins
DIIILLNOSSU disillusion
DIIILNOSSUY insidiously

DIIILNOSUVY invidiously
DIIIMMNORTU tridominium
DIIIMNOPRSS disimprison
DIIIMNRSSUU Sinus Iridum
DIIINNOSSTU disunionist
DIIINNOSUUV uninvidious
DIIINOOPRSV pro indiviso
DIIINOOPSST disposition
DIILLMPTTUY put it mildly
DIILNOOSSTU dissolution
DIILNOPSSTY spondylitis
DIILOPRRSTW spirit world
DIINORSSTUU industrious
DIKNNOORSTW Windsor knot
DILMOOPSTUY stylopodium
DILNNOORSTW Lord Winston
DILNOOORSUY inodorously
DILNOOPSSSY spondylosis
DIMNOORSTWW storm window
DINOOPRTTTU punto dritto
DKLNNOOOOTW Don't Look Now
DLOOOPRRSTV Lord Provost
DNNOOOORSTV Rostov-on-Don

E

EEEEEEOSTYY see eye to eye
EEEEEGKNPRR green-keeper
EEEEENPRRST representee
EEEEFFLLNOS feel oneself
EEEEFHNRRRS refreshener
EEEEFIISTWW sweetie-wife
EEEEFILPRSS life peeress
EEEEFILQRTU téléférique
EEEEFLNNSTW sweet fennel
EEEEFLRSTTT Fleet Street
EEEEGGGNORR George Green
EEEEGIILPRS espièglerie
EEEEGILLNRW green-wellie
EEEEGLLNRVY energy level
EEEEGLNNSST genteelness
gentlenesse
EEEEGLNRSSV revengeless
EEEEGMNNRTV revengement
EEEEGNNQRTU queen-regent
EEEEGNPPPRR green pepper
EEEEHINNOTY one in the eye
EEEEHKLOPRT hotel-keeper
EEEEHKOPRSU housekeeper
EEEEHMOQSUZ squeeze home
EEEEHNNSTTV seventeenth
EEEEHORRSVW wheresoever
EEEEIINRTVW interviewee
EEEEIMNPRSW minesweeper
EEEEINOPPSY pipe one's eye
EEEEKOPRRST storekeeper
EEEELLNQRUY Ellery Queen
EEEELLRSTTV street-level
EEEELMNOOSS someone else
EEEELNOSSTV sleeve notes
EEEELNPRSST repleteness
EEEELRRSSSV reverseless
EEEELRRSTTT trestletree
EEEEMNPRSTT estrepement
EEEEMNRSSTX extremeness
EEEEMORRSTT stereometer
EEEENNSSTVV even-stevens
EEEENPPRRTU en pure perte
EEEENPRRRST representer
EEEEPPPRSTW sweet pepper
EEEEQRRSTTU Queer Street
EEEFFFMNNOT enfeoffment
EEEFFGILLNS self-feeling
EEEFFHILLOW wheel of life
EEEFFHILRTW whiffletree
EEEFFILLRST self-fertile
EEEFFILORTW Eiffel Tower
EEEFGIKLNSS self-seeking
EEEFGILLNSS feelingless
EEEFGJLNRUV jungle fever
EEEFGLLNSSU gleefulness
EEEFHIKNRRT freethinker
EEEFHILNSSY fisheye lens
EEEFHILRRSW Ferris wheel
EEEFHLLNOPS help oneself
EEEFHLMNNST enfleshment
EEEFHLORRTU rule of three
EEEFHLORRUW four-wheeler
EEEFHLORTTV over the left
EEEFHMNRRST refreshment
EEEFHOORRTT theretofore
EEEFIILMPRX exemplifier
EEEFIILORST Isle of Tiree
EEEFIILRRVX irreflexive
EEEFILLRSST self-sterile
EEEFILLRVXY reflexively
EEEFIMNNRRW Minenwerfer
EEEFINNORRR ferronnière
EEEFINPRRSU superrefine
EEEFINRRTTV vine-fretter
EEEFINSSSTV festiveness
EEEFIPRSSUY upsey Friese
EEEFLLNNRSS Fresnel lens
EEEFLLNOOSS lose oneself
EEEFLLORVWY yellow fever
EEEFLMPRSSU perfumeless
EEEFLORRWWY werewolfery
EEEFLPRSSSX self-express
EEEFMOORRRV for evermore
forevermore
EEEGGGOORRV George Grove
EEEGGHHMNSU meshuggeneh
EEEGGHIIRTW Reggie White
EEEGGHORTTT get together
get-together
EEEGGIINNNR engineering
EEEGGILLORS George Ellis
EEEGGILOORT George Eliot
EEEGGJLNNRU jungle-green
EEEGGMNNORT engorgement
EEEGHHILSTT see the light
EEEGHIIRTVW give the wire
EEEGHIKMNOP home-keeping

EEEGHIKNPRT keep the ring
EEEGHILNNRT enlightener
EEEGHIMNOST eighteenmos
EEEGHINOSST esthesiogen
EEEGHINTTVW get even with
EEEGIIKMNPT timekeeping
EEEGIILMNNS gelseminine
EEEGIILMORS Emilio Segrè
EEEGIILNTVW televiewing
EEEGIINPPRW weeping-ripe
EEEGIINPRSS perigenesis
EEEGIINPSST epigenesist
EEEGILLLNST teleselling
EEEGILLNNRT green lentil
EEEGILLNORU genouillère
EEEGILMNORS Simon Legree
EEEGILNNNRT green linnet
EEEGILNRSTW swingletree
EEEGIMNNSSS seemingness
EEEGIMNORSS merogenesis
EEEGIMNRSTU true-seeming
EEEGIMPRRST Peter Grimes
EEEGINNNSSU genuineness
EEEGINNORVW overweening
EEEGINNOSST seeing stone
EEEGINNOSSX xenogenesis
EEEGINNRRTW wintergreen
EEEGINPRRSV persevering
EEEGINRRSTT net register
EEEGIORRSST grossièreté
EEEGKMNNORY green monkey
EEEGLLNNTUY ungenteelly
EEEGLLNSSSS leglessness
EEEGLLOTVVV velvet glove
EEEGLMNNOTW gentlewomen
EEEGLNOORVY venereology
EEEGLNOPRRV green plover
EEEGLNRRTTU green turtle
EEEGMNNPTUX expungement
EEEGMNORRSV verse-monger
EEEGNOPPPRR Negro pepper
EEEGNORRSTU tree surgeon
EEEGRRRSTUY tree surgery
EEEHHILLLNP philhellene
EEEHHILOPRS heliosphere
EEEHHILPPTW Hepplewhite
EEEHHILRSTW elsewhither
EEEHHLLLMST helmet-shell
EEEHHLMOSST the homeless
EEEHHMOSTTT thesmothete
EEEHHNOSTTV The Hot Seven
EEEHHNPRSTY hypersthene
EEEHIILNNPT nephelinite
EEEHIINNPPR epinephrine
EEEHIKLNSTT kitten heels
EEEHILLMTTT tell the time
EEEHILLNPRT telpherline
EEEHILMNNRR Helen Mirren
EEEHILNPRRS replenisher
EEEHILPPRTW whippletree
EEEHILPRSSV sheep-silver
EEEHILRSSTV shirtsleeve
EEEHILRSTUU Eleutherius
EEEHIMMNPRT penthemimer
EEEHIMNNOPS phenomenise
EEEHIMNNOPZ phenomenize
EEEHIMNNPRT phentermine
EEEHIMNOPPR Oppenheimer
EEEHIMNOPRS merino sheep
EEEHIMNRSST smithereens
EEEHIMOOSTT so mote I thee
EEEHIMPRSSY hyperemesis
EEEHINPSSSV peevishness
EEEHINRSTUV The Universe
EEEHIPPPRTW white pepper
EEEHIRRRSTV Three Rivers
EEEHIRRSSST heritresses
EEEHKLMMOST smoke helmet
EEEHKLMNOWY monkey wheel
EEEHLLNOPTW Pelton wheel
EEEHLLRSSST shelterless
EEEHLMNOOTT monothelete✧
EEEHLMORTUV three-volume
EEEHLMRRTTY rhyme letter
EEEHLNNOSST none the less
nonetheless
EEEHLNRSTTT shelter tent
EEEHLORTTTT to the letter
EEEHMMORRTT thermometer
EEEHMNOQRTU queen mother
EEEHMOPRRST spherometer
EEEHNORSTTT on the street
EEEHNRSSSTT sternsheets
EEEHOORSSVW whosesoever
EEEHOPSTTUY up to the eyes
EEEHRRSSTWY sweet sherry
EEEIIKLNSST telekinesis
EEEIILLMPSS semi-ellipse
EEEIILMNRST Lise Meitner
EEEIIMNQRSU mesquinerie
EEEIINNPSVX inexpensive
EEEIINNRRST Niersteiner
EEEIINRRSTW Winterreise
EEEIINRRTTV irretentive
EEEIINRRTVW interviewer
EEEIIORRSTX exteriorise
EEEIIORRTXZ exteriorize
EEEIIPRRSTT peristerite
EEEIIPRRTTV preteritive
EEEIJNNOTUY Étienne Jouy
EEEIKLNNQUU unqueenlike
EEEIKLNOSST skeletonise
EEEIKLNOSTZ skeletonize
EEEIKLNPRST serpentlike
EEEIKMRRSTZ Imre Kertész
EEEIKRRRSTY Skye terrier
EEEILLLPRTY Peter Lilley
EEEILLMRUVX merveilleux
EEEILLRSSTV silver steel
EEEILMMNPRT implementer
EEEILMNNNTV enlivenment
EEEILMNNPRT Inner Temple

EEEILMNNTTT entitlement
EEEILMOORTT meteorolite
EEEILMPRSST plessimeter
EEEILNNOPSS in one's sleep
EEEILNNPSSS pensileness
EEEILNNQSSU queenliness
EEEILNPRRTT teleprinter
EEEILNPRTTV triple event
EEEILNPSVXY expensively
EEEILNRTTVY retentively
EEEILNSSSUV elusiveness
EEEILNSSTTT tensile test
EEEILNSSTVV velvetiness
EEEILNSTVXY extensively
EEEILQRSSTU requiteless
EEEIMMNNSSS immenseness
EEEIMMORSST seismometer
EEEIMNNNORT mentonnière
EEEIMNNNTTW entwinement
EEEIMNNRRTT reinterment
EEEIMNORSTT tensiometer
EEEIMNOSSTV emotiveness
EEEIMNQQRUU quinquereme
EEEIMNQRRTU requirement
EEEIMNQRTTU requitement
EEEIMOPRSTX extemporise
EEEIMOPRTXZ extemporize
EEEIMORRTTV terremotive
EEEIMRRRSVY River Mersey
EEEINNNSSST intenseness
EEEINNPRSTT presentient
spinnerette
EEEINNPRTUX unexperient
EEEINNPSSSV pensiveness
EEEINNPSUVX unexpensive
EEEINNRTTUV unretentive
EEEINORRRSV reversioner
EEEINPPPRSS pepperiness
EEEINPQRSTU Pinteresque
EEEINPRRRST enterpriser
EEEINPRRRTT interpreter
reinterpret
EEEINPRRSST intersperse
EEEINPRRSSU purse-seiner
EEEINPRSTTX pre-existent
EEEINRRRSVV River Severn
EEEINRSSSTV restiveness
EEEINRSTTWW winter-sweet
EEEIOPRRSSW power series
EEEKKLNOSTY skeleton key
EEEKLNOOSTX exoskeleton
EEEKLNRSTUV trunksleeve
EEEKLORRSTW steelworker
EEELLLNPRTY repellently
EEELLLPSSSY sleeplessly
EEELLNRSSVY nervelessly
EEELLNSSSSY senselessly
EEELLOOWXYY yellow ox-eye
EEELLOPRSSU soul-sleeper
EEELMNNOPTV envelopment
EEELMOOPPRV people mover
EEELMORRSSS remorseless
EEELMPRRSTY Meryl Streep
EEELMPSSTVY Empty Vessel
EEELNNOPSST spleenstone
EEELNNPTVWY twelve-penny
EEELNOPQTUV Pont-l'Évêque
EEELNSSSSSU uselessness
EEELNSSSSSX sexlessness
EEELOOOPRTT Peter O'Toole
EEELOOPPPRW people power
EEELORRSTVW overwrestle
EEELPRRSSTT letterpress
EEELRSSTTTY street style
EEELRSSTTUX textureless
EEEMMMRSTUU Terme Museum
EEEMMNOPRTV premovement
EEEMMNOPRTW empowerment
EEEMNNOSTUX exeunt omnes
EEEMNNPRSTT presentment
EEEMNORSTUV venturesome
EEEMNPRSSSU supremeness
EEEMNPRSTTY empty-nester
EEEMOQRRTTU torque meter
EEEMORRSTTY stereometry
EEEMPRRSSTX express term
EEEMPRRTTTU trumpet tree
EEENNPRSSST presentness
EEENOOPRSSS operoseness
EEENOPRRRST representor
EEENOQRSTTU request note
EEENPRSSSSX expressness
EEENQRRSTUU Turneresque
EEEOPPRRRTT Peter Porter
EEEOPPRRSTW pester power
EEEOPRRSTTY stereotyper
EEFFFHHLOST off the shelf
off-the-shelf
EEFFGHIILST gefilte fish
EEFFGHIIRRT firefighter
EEFFGIINRSV fivefingers
EEFFGILNRSU glue-sniffer
EEFFGLLNTUY effulgently
EEFFHILNSST the sniffles
EEFFHILNTTY fifteenthly
EEFFIILMOPR prime of life
EEFFIILRRVY River Liffey
EEFFIINNOSV inoffensive
EEFFILLPPTU fipple flute
EEFFILNOSVY offensively
EEFFINNOSUV unoffensive
EEFFIORRRSU ferriferous
EEFFLNRSSTU fretfulness
EEFFLOOPRRS self-reproof
EEFGGIOPRTT pettifogger
EEFGHHORTTU free-thought
EEFGHIILRRT firelighter
EEFGHIINRTW white finger
EEFGHIITTUV The Fugitive
EEFGHILLRTX reflex light
EEFGHINRRST frighteners
EEFGHIORRTV overfreight

EEFGHLMNORS fleshmonger
EEFGIILNOPR pigeon-flier
EEFGIINNRRT interfering
EEFGIKLNOTT Folketinget
EEFGILLLORW gelliflowre
EEFGILLNNUY unfeelingly
EEFGILLNRSY self-relying
EEFGILNNOPS self-opening
EEFGILNNOUX genuflexion
EEFGILNOPRY pigeon-flyer
EEFGILNORRW reflowering
EEFGILNRSSV self-serving
EEFGILORRTW tiger flower
EEFGIMMORSU gemmiferous
EEFGINNORSS foreignness
EEFGINORSSV forgiveness
EEFGINPRRSV spring fever
EEFGLLNRTUY refulgently
EEFGLLOORXY reflexology
EEFGLLRRTUY regretfully
EEFGLOOORSW goose-flower
EEFGMNOORTT forget-me-not
EEFHIIKNRST Kentish fire
EEFHIILNRSU Henri Fuseli
EEFHIIOSTTZ the size of it
EEFHIISTTVW the five wits
EEFHIKNORRT forethinker
EEFHILLNSSS fleshliness
EEFHILNSSSS selfishness
EEFHILOOPRT photo-relief
EEFHILORSTU lethiferous
EEFHILORSWW werewolfish
EEFHILOSUWY housewifely
EEFHIORSUWY housewifery
EEFHKLNNORR elkhorn fern
EEFHKOOSSUY House of Keys
EEFHLLNOOOP loop of Henle
EEFHLLNPSSU helpfulness
EEFHLNOPSSU hopefulness
EEFHMNOORRW from nowhere
EEFHMORRRTU furthermore
EEFHMORRSTU furthersome
EEFHNOORRST foreshorten
EEFHOORRSTW for the worse
EEFHORRSTTT setter-forth
EEFIIINNRST intensifier
EEFIIINNSTT infinite set
EEFIIISSTTV festivities
EEFIILNNNSS Niels Finsen
EEFIILNORRX irreflexion
EEFIILNRRTX life-rentrix
EEFIILRTVXY reflexivity
EEFIINNOPRR friponnerie
EEFIINOPRRS personifier
EEFIKLLNOWY Yellowknife
EEFIKNORSTY oyster-knife
EEFILLLMNTU mellifluent
EEFILLLMRSU mille fleurs
millefleurs
EEFILLMORSU melliferous
EEFILMNOSSS miss oneself
EEFILMORRTU fluorimeter
EEFILMORSST St Elmo's fire
EEFILMORSWW werewolfism
EEFILNNRTTU interfluent
EEFILNOPRST Fleet Prison
EEFILNORSSW floweriness
EEFILOOPRRT profiterole
EEFILOORSST loosestrife
EEFINRSSTUV furtiveness
EEFIOPRSSTU pestiferous
septiferous
EEFLLNORTTU fortune-tell
EEFLLNORUUV Ulf von Euler
EEFLLNRSTUY resentfully
EEFLLOPRSUY reposefully
EEFLMNORSTT self-torment
EEFLMNOSSSU fulsomeness
EEFLMNRSTTU flusterment
EEFLMOORRTU fluorometer
EEFLNNRSTUU unresentful
EEFLNNSSTUU tunefulness
EEFLNOPPSTW Steppenwolf
EEFLNOPRSUU unreposeful
EEFLNORSSTU fortuneless
EEFLNORSSUV overfulness
EEFLNPSSSUU suspenseful
EEFLNRSSSTU restfulness
EEFLNSSSTUZ zestfulness
EEFLOOPRRWW Flower Power
EEFLORRSTTU self-torture
EEFMOOPRTTU out of temper
EEFNOPRSSSU profuseness
EEFNORRSSTU foster-nurse
EEFOOPRRTUV vertue-proof
EEFOPRRRRSU fore-spurrer
EEGGGHINRTU tree-hugging
EEGGGIINRRT rigging-tree
EEGGGINNPTT tent-pegging
EEGGGNOORUY George Young
EEGGGOORRSZ George Grosz
EEGGHHLOORW whole-hogger
EEGGHIILNNT light engine
EEGGHIINSST sightseeing
EEGGHMNNOOS hogen-mogens
EEGGIJMNNPU jumping gene
EEGGILLNNTY negligently
EEGGILNNRVY revengingly
EEGGILORSUY egregiously
EEGGIMNOOTT go-to-meeting
EEGGNOOPRST progestogen
EEGHHIILNRT The Hireling
EEGHHILRTWW wheelwright
EEGHHIPPRST high-stepper
EEGHHIPSTUV give the push
EEGHHLLNOTW whole-length
EEGHHLLOPUW wheel plough
EEGHHOPPRTU peep-through
EEGHIIILNVV Vivien Leigh
EEGHIIKNPST keep in sight
EEGHIILPPRT pipe-lighter
EEGHIILPSTV give the slip

EEGHIINNSTW White Ensign
EEGHIINPRST ship it green
EEGHIINRSTW wishing tree
EEGHIINSSTW weightiness
EEGHIKNNPST Stephen King
EEGHIKNOPPS shopkeeping
EEGHILMMNOT gentilhomme
EEGHILNNRST netherlings
EEGHILNNSSS Englishness
EEGHILNNSST lengthiness
EEGHILNOOPR pigeonholer
EEGHILNOOPS pigeonholes
EEGHILNORSS English rose
EEGHILNOSSU single house
EEGHILNOSSY hylogenesis
EEGHILNRTTT night letter
EEGHILOORST theologiser
EEGHILOORSY heresiology
EEGHILOORTZ theologizer
EEGHILRSTTT streetlight
EEGHIMNNNTU unhingement
EEGHIMNOORS homogeniser
EEGHIMNOORZ homogenizer
EEGHIMNOOSS homogenesis
EEGHIMNOOTY homogeneity
EEGHIMOORST isogeotherm
EEGHINNPTWY pennyweight
EEGHINNSSTU sight unseen
EEGHINOOPSU pigeon-house
EEGHINOORTV in the groove
EEGHINORRTV overnighter
EEGHINRSTTY yesternight
EEGHLLMOTTU hot-melt glue
EEGHLMMORTU grummet-hole
EEGHLOOPRTY herpetology
EEGHMNOOOSU homogeneous
EEGHMNOORRW whoremonger
EEGHNORRTTU run together
EEGHNORSTYY hysterogeny
EEGHNOSSSUU hugeousness
EEGIIILNORS religionise
EEGIIILNORZ religionize
EEGIIIMNPST impetigines
EEGIIKLLLOS skilligolee
EEGIIKLPRSS kriegsspiel
EEGIILLNNTT intelligent
EEGIILLTVWY give it welly
EEGIILMNNRT intermingle
EEGIILNNOPT pilot engine
EEGIILNNOST lentiginose
EEGIILNOPSS lipogenesis
EEGIIMMNNPT impingement
EEGIIMMNRSS mesmerising
EEGIIMMNRSZ mesmerizing
EEGIIMNNNRS Minnesinger
EEGIIMNNOPT opening time
EEGIIMNNOST neostigmine
EEGIIMNRSTV time-serving
EEGIINNNRTV intervening
EEGIINNORST nitrogenise
EEGIINNORTZ nitrogenize
EEGIINNRSTT interesting
EEGIINNRTTW wire netting
EEGIINNRTUU unigeniture
EEGIINOPRTV progenitive
EEGIINPRRTY peregrinity
EEGIKKNORWW working week
EEGIKLNORTW teleworking
EEGIKMNOOPR keeping-room
EEGIKMNORRV Mekong River
EEGIKORRSVY Sergey Kirov
EEGILLLMNNR Glenn Miller
EEGILLLNPRY repellingly
EEGILLLSSUY guilelessly
EEGILLMOOST teleologism
EEGILLOOSTT teleologist
EEGILLORRRU guerrillero
EEGILMNNSST meltingness
EEGILMOOSTY etymologise
EEGILMOOTYZ etymologize
EEGILNNNRTU unrelenting
EEGILNNPRTY repentingly
EEGILNNRSTY resentingly
single-entry
EEGILNNTUWY unweetingly
EEGILNOPSSY polygenesis
EEGILNORSVY sovereignly
EEGILNPRSTY pesteringly
EEGILOPRSTT poltergeist
EEGIMMNOORT Montgomerie
EEGIMNNNORT Montenegrin
EEGIMNNOOSS monogenesis
EEGIMNNORSU Monseigneur
EEGIMNNOTTW town meeting
EEGIMNNPRTU untempering
EEGIMNNRRTU interregnum
EEGIMNORSTW swingometer
EEGIMNPRSST sempstering
EEGINNNPRTU unrepenting
EEGINNNRSTU unresenting
EEGINNOOSST ontogenesis
EEGINNPRSST Springsteen
EEGINNRRSTT restringent
EEGINOORRTU rouge-et-noir
EEGINOPRRTU progeniture
EEGINORRSTT register ton
EEGINORRSTU terrigenous
EEGINORSTVY sovereignty
EEGINPRSTTU guttersnipe
EEGINPSTTTY typesetting
EEGIOPRRSSV progressive✧
EEGKLLMNSUU muskellunge
EEGKORRSTUW guest worker
EEGLMOOORTY meteorology
EEGLNNNRRTU Glenn Turner
EEGLNOOSUXY exogenously
EEGLNORSTUY Lester Young
EEGLNSSSSTU gutlessness
EEGLOPPPTUV glove puppet
EEGLOQRSTUY grotesquely
EEGMNNORRST morgenstern
EEGMNNORSST engrossment

EEGMNOOPRSS spermogones
EEGNOOORSTU erotogenous
EEGNOOOSSTU osteogenous
EEGNOORRSTW grow on trees
EEGOQRRSTUY grotesquery
EEGPPRSTTUY petty spurge
EEGPRRSSTTU gutter press
EEHHIINNRSW Rhenish wine
EEHHIINRTTW therewithin
EEHHIJKOPST Keith Joseph
EEHHIKLOTTW the whole kit
EEHHILLNSSS hellishness
EEHHILLORTV over the hill
EEHHILMOPRT thermophile
EEHHILOPRST lithosphere
EEHHILORSTW otherwhiles
EEHHIMORSTW somewhither
EEHHINORSTT in the throes
EEHHINRTTUW white hunter
EEHHINSSSWY wheyishness
EEHHIOOPSST theosophise
EEHHIOOPSTZ theosophize
EEHHIOPRRSZ rhizosphere
EEHHIOPSSTY hypothesise
EEHHIOPSTTY hypothetise
EEHHIOPSTXY ex hypothesi
EEHHIOPSTYZ hypothesize
EEHHIOPTTYZ hypothetize
EEHHJNOPRSY Joseph Henry
EEHHLMOPRST mother's help
EEHHLMOPRTT port the helm
EEHHLORSUUY hurley-house
EEHHMOORSTU house-mother
EEHHMOPRTUV over the hump
EEHHNOORRTW whether or no
EEHHNOPSTUY hypothenuse
EEHHNORSTUU house-hunter
EEHHOOPPRST photosphere
EEHHOOPRRTT heterotroph
EEHHOPPRSTT the prophets
EEHIIIMPTTT it pitieth me
EEHIIJNOPST josephinite
EEHIIKNPSTY pie in the sky
EEHIIKNSSST kinesthesis
EEHIILLMNWW Wilhelm Wien
EEHIILMNTUW minute-while
EEHIILRSTVW silver white
silver-white
EEHIIMNORTY Hieronymite
EEHIIMPPRRS premiership
EEHIIMSSTTV Stevie Smith
EEHIINRRSST inheritress
EEHIIORSTTT historiette
EEHIIQRSTUW white squire
EEHIIRRSSTT Irish setter
EEHIJLMRRUV River Jhelum
EEHIJLNNNOT John Tenniel
EEHIKMNNOSY monkey shine
EEHIKNSTUWW Whitsun week
EEHILLMNRRY Henry Miller
EEHILLORSTT Little Horse
EEHILMMOSTU mesothelium
EEHILMNOOTT monothelite✧
EEHILMOPPRS spermophile
EEHILNOORST line-shooter
EEHILNOPPRS nephrolepis
EEHILNOPRRT leptorrhine
EEHILNOPSTT telephonist
EEHILNOSSTV thesis novel
EEHILNOSTTV novelettish
EEHILNSTTXY sixteenthly
EEHILOPRSST priest's hole
EEHILORRSTT horse-litter
EEHILSSTTUW shuttlewise
EEHIMMNNOPS phenomenism
EEHIMNNOPST phenomenist
EEHIMNOPRSS Shimon Peres
EEHIMNORRTW mine-thrower
EEHIMOPPRRS emperorship
EEHIMOPRSTU hemipterous
EEHIMPSSTUY emphyteusis
EEHINNOOPTT thiopentone
EEHINNORRST northernise
EEHINNORRTY Henry Ireton
EEHINNORRTZ northernize
EEHINNOSSSU heinousness
EEHINOPSTVY hypotensive
EEHINORRTTU rinthereout
EEHINORSSSW showeriness
EEHINORSSTU southernise
EEHINORSTUZ southernize
EEHINPSSSTT pettishness
EEHINRSSSTU hirsuteness
EEHINRSSSTY synthesiser
EEHINRSSTTY synthetiser
EEHINRSSTYZ synthesizer
EEHINRSTTYZ synthetizer
EEHIOORRSTW or otherwise
EEHIOPRRSST The Prioress
EEHIOPRRSTW tree worship
EEHIPRRSSUV herpes virus
EEHIPRSSTTU trusteeship
EEHJLOOPSSY Joseph Losey
EEHJNOPRRST Prester John
EEHJNORSSTU John Surtees
EEHKLLLMOSY Kelly Holmes
EEHKNOORSTT on the stroke
EEHKNOSTUVY Yevtushenko
EEHLLLMSSSU mussel-shell
EEHLLLRSTTU turtleshell
EEHLLMOOSWY wholesomely
EEHLLOOPSTT lose the plot
EEHLLORSSTY oyster-shell
EEHLLRRTTTU truth-teller
EEHLMMOOPRS pommel horse
EEHLMNOOSUW unwholesome
EEHLMNOTTVW twelvemonth
EEHLMORSSSU horse mussel
EEHLOOPRSVW power shovel
EEHLOPRRSTU reupholster
upholsterer
EEHLOPRSSTU Telesphorus

EEHLORSTTYY heterostyly
EEHLPRSSTUU supersleuth
EEHLRSSSTTU shutterless
EEHMMNORSTU The Summoner
EEHMMOOORSU homeomerous
EEHMMOOPRRT emperor moth
EEHMMORRTTY thermometry
EEHMMORSSUU summerhouse
EEHMNNOOORY honeymooner
EEHMNOOORTV over the moon
EEHMNOORSSX sex hormones
EEHMOPPRSTY spermophyte
EEHMORRRSTT short-termer
EEHNOOOPRSZ ozonosphere
EEHNOOPRSTY stereophony
EEHNOPQSTUY Pythonesque
EEHNOPSTTUY theopneusty
EEHNORRSTTW north-wester
EEHOOPPRRST troposphere
EEHOOPRRSTU porterhouse
porter-house
EEHOOPRRSTY heterospory
EEHOORRRTVW overthrower
EEHORSSTTUW south-wester
EEHPRRSSSTY hyperstress
EEIIIMNNSTU einsteinium
EEIIIMRRSSV irremissive
EEIIINNSSTV insensitive
EEIIINNSTTV intensitive
EEIIINSTTVV investitive
EEIIJKLNNNS Neil Jenkins
EEIIJLMSTUU juste milieu
EEIIJNRSSTT jitteriness
EEIIKLLNNNS Enniskillen
EEIIKLNNRTU interleukin
EEIILLNRSTY resiliently
EEIILLPPRST pipistrelle
EEIILLPRSTU spirituelle
EEIILLPRSTV spirit level
EEIILMMNPRT imperilment
EEIILMNOSSU emulsionise
EEIILMNOSUZ emulsionize
EEIILMNRSSS miserliness
EEIILMRSSVY remissively
EEIILNNPRRT line printer
EEIILNNRSST listeners-in
EEIILNNSTVY intensively
EEIILNNTVVY inventively
EEIILNRSSSV silveriness
EEIILNSSTVY sensitively
EEIILORSTUZ Louis-Treize
EEIILQRSTUY requisitely
EEIILQSTUXY exquisitely
EEIILRSSTUU leisure suit
EEIILRSSTVY resistively
EEIIMNNORTU munitioneer
EEIIMNNPRTT impertinent
EEIIMNOPRTV premonitive
EEIIMNORTTX Intoximeter®
intoximeter
EEIIMNPRRUU perineurium
EEIINNNORTV reinvention
EEIINNNOSTX inextension
EEIINNNTUVV uninventive
EEIINNOOPRT Pointe-Noire
EEIINNORRST reinsertion
EEIINNORRTT irretention
EEIINNPRRWZ prize-winner
EEIINNSSTUV unsensitive
EEIINOPRRTT preterition
EEIINPPRRST printer's pie
EEIINQRSTUU unrequisite
EEIINRSTTUV investiture
EEIINRTTTVY retentivity
EEIIOPPRRST proprieties
EEIIOPPRSTV prepositive
EEIIOPRSTTU repetitious
EEIIOPSSTVX sex-positive
EEIIORRTTXY exteriority
EEIIRSTTTUV restitutive
EEIJLNNOPRU en plein jour
EEIJLRRSTUV River Sutlej
EEIJMNORRSY Jeremy Irons
EEIKLLNORUV unloverlike
EEIKLNNNPWY pennywinkle
EEIKLNOSTTW twinkletoes
EEIKLOPPRSU purpose-like
EEIKMNORSSS irksomeness
EEILLMMSTUV summit-level
EEILLMNOPRT Montpellier
EEILLMNOTTW Little Women
EEILLMOOPRT trompe l'oeil
EEILLMPPRSY slippery elm
EEILLMPRTUX multiplexer
EEILLMRSSUW Weissmuller
EEILLNNOSWX Lennox Lewis
EEILLNOPQTU equipollent
EEILLNORRTU ritournelle
EEILLNOSSSY noiselessly
EEILLNPRRST print-seller
EEILLNPSSSY spinelessly
EEILLNPSTTY pestilently
EEILLNRSUUY unleisurely
EEILLOPSVXY explosively
EEILLORRVWY Yellow River
EEILLOSTWWW sweet willow
EEILLPRSUVY prelusively
repulsively
EEILMMNORRW Erwin Rommel
EEILMNNOOVW Women in Love
EEILMNNORTW winter melon
EEILMNNOTVV involvement
EEILMNOOSST emotionless
EEILMNOSSSS lissomeness
EEILMNRTTTY remittently
EEILMOOPRSU pleiomerous
EEILMOPRSSS promiseless
EEILMOPRTUV pluviometer
EEILMPRSSTY plessimetry
EEILMRRSSUV river mussel
EEILNNOPPTT plenipotent
EEILNNOPSSS pensionless

EEILNNOSSST	tensionless
EEILNNPRTTY	pertinently
EEILNNSSSSS	sinlessness
EEILNOOPRSS	il penseroso
EEILNOORSTV	Oliver Stone
EEILNOORTVV	overviolent
EEILNOPRTVY	poverty line
EEILNORRTTZ	Linzertorte
EEILNORSSSU	elusoriness
EEILNORSSTV	Silverstone
EEILNOSSTVY	ostensively
EEILNOSTTTV	novelettist
EEILNSSSSTW	witlessness
EEILOPPPPST	pipe-stopple
EEILOPRSSTY	proselytise
EEILOPRSTYZ	proselytize
EEILORSTVXY	extorsively
EEIMMMNOORT	memento mori
EEIMMMNPRSU	menispermum
EEIMMNOPRTV	improvement
EEIMMNPRSST	impressment
EEIMMNPRSTU	sempiternum
EEIMMORSSTY	seismometry
EEIMMORSTYZ	zymosimeter
EEIMMPRSUVV	sempervivum
EEIMNNNORTV	environment
EEIMNNOOSSS	noisomeness
EEIMNNOPRST	omnipresent
EEIMNNORSSV	mons veneris
EEIMNNOSSSW	winsomeness
EEIMNNRTTTU	unremittent
EEIMNNSSTTV	investments
EEIMNORSTTY	tensiometry
EEIMNORSTZZ	intermezzos
EEIMNORTTZZ	mezzotinter
EEIMNRSSTTW	Westminster
EEIMOOPRTVW	motive power
EEIMOPPRSSU	superimpose
EEIMPPRSTUV	presumptive
EEINNNORRTU	interneuron
EEINNNOSTTX	non-existent
EEINNOORTTX	enterotoxin
EEINNOPPRSS	nose-nippers
EEINNOPRSTT	septentrion
EEINNORRTTV	interventor
EEINNOSSSUV	enviousness
EEINNOSSTTU	sententious
EEINNQSSTUU	unquietness
EEINOORRTTX	extortioner
EEINOPRSSXY	epoxy resins
EEINOPRSTTU	pretentious
EEINOPSSSTU	piteousness
EEINORRSTUV	enterovirus
EEINORSSSSU	seriousness
EEINPRRRTTU	interrupter
EEINPRRRTUZ	Turner Prize
EEINPRTTTWY	typewritten
EEINRRSTUWW	wienerwurst
EEIOPRRRSTW	prose-writer
EEIOPRRSSSU	superioress
EEIOPRSSSTX	expositress
EEIPPRSSSUV	suppressive
EEJLNOSSSSY	joylessness
EEKKOORRRTV	voortrekker✧
EEKLLMOSSSY	smokelessly
EEKLMNNOSTU	smoke tunnel
EEKLORRSTTW	trestlework
EEKMNOOPRTV	provokement
EEKMNOOPSSW	spokeswomen
EEKNORSTTUY	Turkey stone
EEKOOORRSTV	overstrooke
EELLLMNOOWY	lemon-yellow
EELLLOORRTW	roller towel
EELLMPPRSTU	pullet-sperm
EELLNOORSSW	Orson Welles
EELLNOPSTUY	plenteously
EELLNORRSTW	western roll
EELLNPRTUUV	pulverulent
EELLOPRSSWY	powerlessly
	yellow press✧
EELLORRSTTY	storyteller
EELMMNOPTTU	Temple Mount
EELMMOOOPPS	pompelmoose
EELMMOOPPSU	pompelmouse
EELMMOORTUV	volumometer
EELMNOOPSTU	Neoptolemus
EELMNOSSSUU	emulousness
EELMOPRRSTT	storm petrel
EELNNORSSTV	R L Stevenson
EELNNSSSSSU	sunlessness
EELNOOPPSTW	townspeople
EELNOOPRSTV	stone plover
EELNOORRRTV	terror novel
EELNOORRSUY	erroneously
EELNOPRSTYY	polystyrene
EELNOPSSSST	toplessness
EELNORSTTTU	turtle-stone
EELOPPRSSSU	purposeless
EELOPRRSSUW	low-pressure
EELOPRSTUUV	supervolute
EEMMOORRSTT	meteor storm
EEMMORWZZZZ	Mezz Mezzrow
EEMNNRSTTTU	entrustment
EEMNOORSTTY	enterostomy
EEMNOPPRSUU	presume upon
EEMNOPRTTTU	trumpet tone
EEMNORSSTTW	westernmost
EEMOORRSTTU	torturesome
EEMOPSSTTTT	tempest-tost
EEMOPSSTTUU	tempestuous
EENNOORSSSU	onerousness
EENNOORSTTT	rottenstone
EENNOQRSUUY	Runyonesque
EENNORSSSUV	nervousness
EENNOSSSTUU	tenuousness
EENOOPPRRSW	personpower
EENOPPRSSXY	pony express
EEOOPRRSSSS	repossessor
EEOPPRRSTUY	upper storey
EEOPQRSSTTU	request stop
EEPPRRRSTUU	purpresture
EFFFGINORUU	figure of fun

EFFFLLORTUY effortfully
EFFGHHHIIRS high sheriff
EFFGHIINNOT in the offing
EFFGHNOORTU forfoughten
EFFGIINNORS sin-offering
EFFGIINORSY foresignify
EFFGIINRRST first finger
EFFGILNOORT roofing felt
EFFGIOOPRUV Group of Five
EFFGIORRSUU frugiferous
EFFGLLORTUY forgetfully
EFFHHIIPRSS sheriffship
EFFHHINSSSU huffishness
EFFHHKOOOST off the hooks
EFFHINOSSST toffishness
EFFHJMNOOST Jeff Thomson
EFFHLMOPRSU muffler shop
EFFHLORRSUU four-flusher
EFFILOORRSU floriferous
EFFIOORRSTT first-footer
EFFOOPRRTUU futureproof
EFGGHIINNRT frightening
EFGGHIIRRST triggerfish
EFGGLOOORST footslogger
EFGHHIILOPR high profile
high-profile
EFGHHIILTTW white flight
EFGHHOORTTU forethought
EFGHIIILNNS fishing-line
line-fishing
EFGHIILMRTY Light My Fire
EFGHIILNOST line of sight
EFGHIILNSST flightiness
EFGHIILORTT right-to-life
EFGHIILOSTW Isle of Wight
EFGHILNORSY flying shore
EFGHILNORTW night-flower
EFGHILNPSWY when pigs fly
EFGHINNOORT for one thing
EFGHINORSSU surgeonfish
EFGHLNRSTTU strengthful
EFGHNNOSUUY honey fungus
EFGIIILLNNR fringilline
EFGIIINNRSY resinifying
EFGIIINNRTW fine writing
EFGIIINPPTT pipe fitting
EFGIIINRRTW firewriting
EFGIIINRVVY revivifying
EFGIILLMORU florilegium
EFGIILLNPRY pilferingly
EFGIILLNSTY stellifying
EFGIILMNNOT filet mignon
EFGIILMNSTT filmsetting
EFGIILNPSTY self-pitying
EFGIINNNRRU running fire
EFGIINNPRRT fingerprint
EFGIINNSSTT fittingness
EFGIINOPRUW rouping-wife
EFGIKLLLNRU fell-lurking
EFGIKLNNOSW self-knowing
EFGIKNNOORW foreknowing
EFGILLLORWY gillyflower
EFGILLMNRUY flying lemur
EFGILLNNNRU fell-running
EFGILMNOORT montgolfier✧
EFGILMNSSUU slime fungus
EFGILMORSUU glumiferous
EFGILNNOSSW flowingness
EFGILNNPRSU self-pruning
EFGILNOORVW overflowing
EFGIMMORSUU gummiferous
EFGIMPSTTUU tempus fugit
EFGINNNOSTU unsoftening
EFGINOOORST fons et origo
EFGINORRSUU ferruginous
EFGIOPRSSUY gypsiferous
EFGIORSTTUU guttiferous
EFGLMNOOTTU leg-of-mutton
EFGLNNOSSSU songfulness
EFGMOPRRSTU Forrest Gump
EFGNNOORTTU unforgotten
EFHHIILSSTW whistle fish
EFHHOOPPRRT froth-hopper
EFHIILORSTY life history
EFHIINRSSTT thriftiness
EFHIIOPRRSW fire-worship
EFHIKORRSTW shift worker
EFHILLNSSUY unselfishly
EFHILLOSTWW wolf whistle
wolf-whistle
EFHILLSSSTY shiftlessly
EFHILNOOSSS foolishness
EFHILNOSSSU fushionless
EFHILNSSSUW wishfulness
EFHILOPRSSW self-worship
EFHIMNNRSTU furnishment
EFHIMORRSTX sixth-former
EFHIMPRSTTU trumpetfish
EFHINOPPSSS foppishness
EFHIORRSTTT thrift store
EFHIORRSTUU thuriferous
EFHLLNOPUUY unhopefully
EFHLNOOOPRR forlorn hope
EFHLNPSSSUU pushfulness
EFHLNRSSTUU hurtfulness
EFHLOSTTUUY theftuously
EFHMORRSTTU furthermost
EFHOOOPRRSW showerproof
EFIIILNRTTY infertility
EFIIIMNNNSS Sinn Feinism
EFIIINORRTY inferiority
EFIIJLNOSTT stifle-joint
EFIIKNORSUZ zinkiferous
EFIIKRRSSTT first strike
first-strike
EFIILMOORTZ zeolitiform
EFIILNNOOPS self-opinion
EFIILNPSSTU pitifulness
EFIIMMNORRS misinformer
EFIINNORSTU interfusion
EFIINOOPTVW point of view
EFIINOPRSSU spiniferous

EFIINORRSUU uriniferous
EFIINPRSSTU first supine
EFIKLLNSSSU skilfulness
EFIKLOORTTU out of kilter
EFILLLMOSUU mellifluous
EFILLLNPTUY plentifully
EFILLMNOTTV Nevill F Mott
EFILLNOOSUY feloniously
EFILLRSSTUY fruitlessly
EFILNORSTUU interfluous
EFILNSSSTUW wistfulness
EFILOOPRRSU proliferous
EFILOORSUUV ovuliferous
EFILORSSTUY styliferous
EFILPRSTUUY superfluity
EFIMNNORSSU uniformness
EFIMNOORSSU somniferous
EFIMOORRSTU mortiferous
EFINOOORSUZ ozoniferous
EFINOPRRSST first person
first-person
EFINOPRSSUU superfusion
EFINORSSSTW frowstiness
EFINORSSSUU furiousness
EFIOOPRRTUV virtue-proof
EFIORRSSTTY first storey
EFIORRSTTUY yttriferous
EFKMOOPRSTU musket-proof
EFKNNNOORUW unforeknown
EFLLNNTUUUY untunefully
EFLLNORSSTY frontlessly
EFLLNOSSSUU soulfulness
EFLLNSSSTUU lustfulness
EFLLOOPPRRU proof-puller
EFLLOORRTTU floor turtle
EFLNNOORRSS forlornness
EFLOPPRSSTU self-support
EFLOPRSSUUU superfluous
EFMMOOORTUY From Me to You
EFMNOOOPSTY pots of money
EFMNOOORRUY for our money
EFNNNORRRTU front-runner
EFNOOPRRTTY port of entry
EFOOPRSSTUY pussyfooter
EGGGIIINPRW periwigging
EGGGILNNOOS gone gosling
EGGGINOPRRU ginger group
EGGGLNOOSSW snow-goggles
EGGHHHIILRT highlighter
EGGHHIILTTW lightweight
EGGHHINORTU right enough
EGGHHINOSSS hoggishness
EGGHIILNNWY whingeingly
EGGHIINPSSS piggishness
EGGHIINRRTW right-winger
EGGHIINRSST sight-singer
EGGHILLNRRU herring gull
EGGHIORSSTW gross weight
EGGHLNOORSW hornswoggle
EGGHLNOOSTT go to lengths
EGGIIKLNTWY tiggywinkle
EGGIIKNNNPU king penguin
EGGIILLNNRY lingeringly
EGGIILNNSWY swingeingly
EGGIINNNORT ringing tone
EGGIINNORWW wine-growing
EGGIINNRTWW wringing wet
EGGIJLNOOTT toggle joint
EGGIKLMMORW glimmer-gowk
EGGILLLNRUY gruellingly
EGGILLNORWY gloweringly
EGGILMMOOST gemmologist
EGGLMMNOOOR gloom-monger
EGGLNOOORTY gerontology
EGHHHOORSTU hog-shouther
EGHHIIKNRST night-shriek
EGHHIIKNTTW white knight
EGHHIINNOST high-tension
EGHHILMOPRY high polymer
EGHHILNNORS English horn
EGHHILORTUV live through
EGHHILOSSTU house lights
EGHHIMNOSSU Simon Hughes
EGHHIMORRTT mother-right
EGHHINNRTTU night-hunter
EGHHIORTTWW throw weight
EGHHKNOTTUW hunt-the-gowk
EGHHLLORSTU sell through
sell-through
trough shell
EGHHLOSSTTU thoughtless
EGHIIIMNTTW whiting-time
EGHIIKLNNOT The Lion King
EGHIIKLNRSY shriekingly
EGHIIKNNRVY King Henry IV
King Henry VI
EGHIILLNRSV shrivelling
EGHIILLNSWW well-wishing
wishing well
EGHIILLOSSS shigellosis
EGHIILNNOST in one's light
EGHIILNNSST thingliness
EGHIILNPRSY perishingly
EGHIILNRSSS girlishness
EGHIILNRSVY shiveringly
EGHIILNRTWY witheringly
EGHIILNSSST sightliness
EGHIILOORST hierologist
EGHIIMNRRST miner's right
EGHIIMPRRST tiger shrimp
EGHIINNNSSS shiningness
EGHIINNOPSS sphingosine
EGHIINNORVY virgin honey
EGHIINNPRSU unperishing
EGHIINNRRVY Henry Irving
EGHIINNRTUW unwithering
EGHIINORSTU tiring-house
EGHIINRSSST tigrishness
EGHIINRSSTT night sister
EGHIINRSTTW the Writings
EGHIIPPRSSW pig's whisper
EGHIIRSSSTU rights issue

EGHIKMNOORW homeworking
EGHIKNORRTW night-worker
EGHILLMOSTY lightsomely
EGHILLSSSTY sightlessly
EGHILMNOORT moonlighter
EGHILMNOSTU unlightsome
EGHILMOOSTY Mythologies
mythologise
EGHILMOOTYZ mythologize
EGHILNOOPRT gerontophil
EGHILNOOPST nephologist
phenologist
EGHILNOOSTT ethnologist
EGHILNOOSTU lithogenous
EGHILNOSSST ghostliness
EGHILORSTUY righteously
EGHILPRSSST sprightless
EGHIMNNORSU nursing home
EGHINNNOSST nothingness
EGHINNOPTUW upon the wing
EGHINOORSUZ rhizogenous
EGHINOPPRSY prophesying
EGHINOPRRTT night-porter
EGHINOPRSSU springhouse
surgeonship
EGHINOPTTUW put on weight
EGHINORRRTT night terror
EGHINORRTTW intergrowth
EGHINORSSSU roguishness
EGHINORSTUU unrighteous
EGHINPRSSTU uprightness
EGHINRRTUWW wither-wrung
EGHIORRSTTW ghost-writer
EGHIORSSTTT set to rights
EGHKNOOPRSU rough-spoken
EGHLLNRTUUY gully-hunter
EGHLMNOOPSU phlegmonous
EGHLMOPRTUY methyl group
EGHLOPPRTYY petroglyphy
EGHNNOOPSUY hypnogenous
EGHOOPRRTUY group theory
EGHOORRTUVW overwrought
EGIIIKKLNNW like winking
EGIIIKLLMNT killing time
time-killing
EGIIIKLMMNT milking-time
EGIIIKNNOTY ignition key
EGIIILLMNPR imperilling
EGIIILMNORS religionism
EGIIILNNNRT interlining
EGIIILNNNST listening-in
EGIIILNORST religionist
EGIIILORRSU irreligious
EGIIILORSTY religiosity
EGIIIMNNRST ministering
EGIIIMNPRRW priming-wire
EGIIINNOPRT pre-ignition
EGIIINNOPTT petitioning
EGIIIRRRSTV River Tigris
EGIIKKLNRRS Kris Kringle
EGIIKLLNNSW well-sinking
EGIIKLMNOPS pigeon's milk
EGIIKLNOOSY kinesiology
EGIIKNORRWW wireworking
EGIILLMNPSS misspelling
EGIILLNNSSW willingness
EGIILLNORTY loiteringly
EGIILLNPRUW wirepulling
EGIILLNRSTW ill-wresting
EGIILLORSUY religiously
EGIILMNNSSS smilingness
EGIILMNPRSY simperingly
EGIILMOOSST semiologist
EGIILNNNSTU unlistening
EGIILNNNSUV nun's-veiling
EGIILNNOSTU lentiginous
EGIILNNOSTV Livingstone
EGIILNNOSUY ingeniously
EGIILNNTTUY ungentility
EGIILNORSUU unreligious
EGIILNOSTTT stilettoing
EGIILNQRUVY quiveringly
EGIILNRSSST gristliness
EGIILNRSSTY resistingly
EGIILNRTTTY titteringly
EGIIMNNNRTU running time
EGIIMNNOPPU impinge upon
EGIIMNNRTTU unremitting
EGIIMNOPRST temporising
EGIIMNOPRTZ temporizing
EGIIMNSTTTU Mistinguett
EGIINNNNSSW winningness
EGIINNNQRUU unenquiring
EGIINNOQSTU questioning
EGIINNOSTTU tentiginous
EGIINNPRSSS springiness
EGIINNPSTUU penguin suit
EGIINNRSSST stringiness
EGIINNRSSTU unresisting
EGIINOPRRTX progenitrix
EGIINOPRSSU serpiginous
spinigerous
EGIINORRSTT intertrigos
EGIINORSTUV vertiginous
EGIINPRTTWY typewriting
EGIIOPRSSTU prestigious
EGIKKNORSTY keystroking
EGIKLLLNOOW well-looking
EGIKLLNNORS snorkelling
EGIKLLNOSWY king's-yellow
EGIKLNRTUUV king-vulture
EGIKMNOOPSU go up in smoke
EGIKNNNORSU Gunn Erikson
EGIKNNNOSSW knowingness
EGIKNNORRTW ring network
EGIKNOORRVW working-over
EGILLLOOVXY vexillology
EGILLLSSTUY guiltlessly
EGILLNNORSW rolling news
EGILLNORTVY revoltingly
EGILMNOOOSU monologuise
EGILMNOOOUZ monologuize

EGILMNOORTY terminology
EGILMNPRSUY presumingly
EGILMNRTTUY mutteringly
EGILMOOORSU oligomerous
EGILMOORSTT metrologist
EGILMOOSSTU museologist
EGILMOOSTTY etymologist
EGILMOPRSUU plumigerous
EGILNNOSUUY ingenuously
EGILNNRSTTY stringently
EGILNNRSTUY unrestingly
EGILNNRTUVY venturingly
EGILNOOOPST stool pigeon
EGILNOORSTU neurologist
EGILNOPRRTY reportingly
EGILNOPRRVY reprovingly
EGILNOPRTTY potteringly
EGILNORTTTY totteringly
EGILNPRSTTU spluttering
EGILOOORSTY soteriology
EGILOOOSSTT osteologist
EGILOOPRSSY perissology
EGILOOPRSTT petrologist
EGILOOPSSTT pestologist
EGIMMNOSTUY gynostemium
EGIMNNOORRY ironmongery
EGIMNNPRSUU unpresuming
EGIMNOOORZZ Mezzogiorno
EGIMNOORRSV misgovernor
EGIMNOORRTT Trimetrogon
EGIMOPRRSSS progressism
EGINNNORRSU running sore
EGINNNORRUV overrunning
EGINNNRRTUU unreturning
EGINNNRTTUX running text
EGINNOORSTU nitrogenous
EGINNOPPSTU upping-stone
EGINNOPRRUV unreproving
EGINNOPRSTY trypsinogen
EGINOOPRRSS progression
EGINOPPRRST ring stopper
EGINORRSSTU trouserings
EGIOORRSSSU gressorious
EGIOPRRSSST progressist
EGLLNOPPRSU long-purples
EGMMMNSSUUU summum genus
EGMMNNOOTTU Mount Egmont
EGNNOOPRSUY young person
EGNOOOPRSSU sporogenous
EGNOOPRRTYY proterogyny
EGNOORSSTTY oyster-tongs
EGNOPRRSSTU superstrong
EHHIIMPSSTY physitheism
EHHIINRSSTW withershins
EHHIINSSSTW whitishness
EHHIJMOPSST Joseph Smith
EHHILMNOSTU helminthous
EHHILOOPPRS philosopher
EHHILOPTTTU up to the hilt
EHHIMOOPRRT theriomorph
EHHIMOOPSST theosophism
EHHIMRSTTUY eurhythmist
EHHINORSSSW whorishness
EHHIOOPPRSS phosphorise
EHHIOOPPRST phosphorite
EHHIOOPPRSZ phosphorize
EHHIOOPRRSW hero-worship
EHHIOOPSSTT theosophist
EHHIOPPPRST prophetship
EHHIOPSSSST hostess-ship
EHHIPPPSSUU Hush Puppies®
EHHLLNORTUY Holly Hunter
EHHLOOSTTUY youth hostel
EHHMMOOOOPR homoeomorph
EHHMMOOOPRY homeomorphy
EHHNNOPSTUU upon the shun
EHHNOOSSTTU shoot the sun
EHHOOPPRSTY hypostrophe
EHHOOPSSTTW stop the show
EHHOPPRRTYY hypertrophy
EHIIILLPPST phillipsite
EHIIILNPPPS Philippines
EHIIILOSSTT hostilities
EHIIIOPSTVV HIV positive
EHIIIPRSTTW white spirit
EHIIKLLMSTT milk thistle
EHIIKLNSTTY kittenishly
EHIIKLRSVWY whisky-liver
EHIIKNNPSSS pinkishness
EHIILMNNUUX unnilhexium
EHIILMRSSTV silversmith
EHIILNOOPRT heliotropin
EHIILNOOPST oenophilist
EHIILOOPTTX toxophilite
EHIIMNOSSTT smithsonite
EHIIMNPSSSW wimpishness
EHIIMNSSSSS missishness
EHIINNORSST in one's shirt
EHIINNSSSSW swinishness
EHIINOPRSSY hyperinosis
EHIINOPRTTY hyponitrite
EHIINPRSSST spinsterish
EHIINRSSSTT thirstiness
EHIIRRRSTVY River Irtysh
EHIJNNNOOSV John Nevison
EHIJNNNOSTU honest Injun
EHIKLMSSTTU musk thistle
EHIKLNSSSSU luskishness
EHIKLORRSTW silk-thrower
EHIKMNNOSSS monkishness
EHIKNNPSSSU punkishness
EHIKORSSUWY whiskey sour
EHILLMRSSTY mirthlessly
EHILLNRSTTU still-hunter
EHILLOPPSUY epiphyllous
EHILLORTTTW littleworth
EHILMMNOOST monothelism✧
EHILMMNOSTY semi-monthly
EHILMNOOPTY entomophily
EHILMNPSSSU lumpishness
EHILMOOSSTU Lossiemouth
EHILMOPTTUY Plymouthite

EHILMORSSTY thermolysis
EHILNOSSSTU loutishness
EHILNSSSSTY stylishness
EHILOOPRSST horse pistol
EHILOOPRSUX xerophilous
EHILOPRSSSW worshipless
EHILOPSSTTW whistle stop
whistle-stop
EHIMMNPSSSU mumpishness
EHIMMOOORST homoerotism
EHIMNNNOOOY honeymoon in
EHIMNNORRST northernism
EHIMNNORSTU nourishment
EHIMNOOPSTY monophysite✧
EHIMNOORTTU Nototherium
EHIMNOPRSSS rompishness
EHIMNORRSTU mothers' ruin
mother's ruin
EHIMNORRTUY erythronium
EHIMNORSSTU southernism
EHIMOOPRRST rheotropism
EHIMOOPRSTU hemitropous
EHIMOOPSTTY mythopoeist
EHIMOPRRTUV triumph over
EHIMPRSSTYY mystery ship
EHINNNNSSSU nunnishness
EHINNNOSSST tonnishness
EHINNOOPSTY hypotension
EHINNORSSTT short tennis
EHINOOPRRTT ornithopter
EHINOOPRSSU prison house
EHINORRSTTU North Utsire
EHINORSSTTU Struthiones
EHINOSSSSTT sottishness
EHIOOOPRRSU eriophorous
EHIOOOPRTTZ trophozoite
EHIOOPRSSTT photoresist
EHIOPRSSTTT prosthetist
EHIORRRTVWY riverworthy
EHIORSSTTUU South Utsire
EHJKLNNOOST John Skelton
EHJLLNORSSU John Russell
EHJLNOOPSSY Joseph Lyons
EHJNOORRSTV John Vorster
EHKLNOOPSSU lokshen soup
EHKLOOSTTUY thelytokous
EHKNNOOOSTT nook-shotten
EHKNOOPRSST short-spoken
EHKOORSTTUY turkey-shoot
EHLLNNNOOPY nonylphenol
EHLLOOOOPPT loop the loop
EHLLORSSTWY worthlessly
EHLMMOOOPRY homopolymer
EHLMNOORSTY monthly rose
EHLMNOPPSYY nympholepsy
EHLMNOPTUWY New Plymouth
EHLMOOOSTTY toothsomely
EHLMPPRSUUY superphylum
EHLNNOOSSTY Holy Sonnets
EHLNOOORRRV horror novel
EHLOOPRSTTY phytosterol
EHLOPRSSSTU upholstress
EHLOPRSSUUU sulphureous
EHMNNOORSTU hunter's moon
EHMNOOPSSUY honey possum
EHMNOORRSTT northermost
EHMNOORSTWY money's-worth
EHMOOOPRSTU homopterous
EHMOORSSTTU southermost
EHMOORSTTYY hysterotomy
EHNNOOPRTTW two-penn'orth
EHNOOOPRRTT orthopteron
EHNOOPRRTUY neurotrophy
EHNOOPSTTUY entophytous
EHNOORSSTTW stone's-throw
EHOOPPRRTTY hot property
EHOOPPRSSTU support hose
EHOOPPRSSTW show-stopper
EHOOQRTTUWY quoteworthy
EHOPRRSTUVY push-over try
EIIIINQSTUV inquisitive
EIIIKLNNPSW pilniewinks
EIIILMPRTVY primitively
EIIILNNPSTY insipiently
EIIILNTTUVY intuitively
EIIILORSSST listeriosis
EIIIMMNRSTU ministerium
EIIIMNORRSS irremission
EIIIMNORSSV revisionism
EIIIMNORSVX vision mixer
EIIINNOQRTU inquire into
EIIINOPRSTT peritonitis
EIIINOPSTTT petitionist
EIIINOQRSTU requisition
EIIINORRTTY interiority
EIIINORSSSY yersiniosis
EIIINORSSTV revisionist
EIIINRSSTTY sinisterity
EIIINSSTTVY sensitivity
EIIINSTTTUV institutive
EIIIOPRSSTT periostitis
EIIIRSSTTVY resistivity
EIIKKNORSSS kirk session
EIIKLLOPTTW Weltpolitik
EIIKLMRSTTU multistrike
EIIKLNNNPWY pinnywinkle
EIIKNNPRRST printer's ink
EIIKNOPRSSY pyrokinesis
EIILLLMSSTY limitlessly
EIILLMMNNSU millenniums
EIILLMPSUVY impulsively
EIILLOOQSSU soliloquise
EIILLOOQSUZ soliloquize
EIILLOPTTUY utility pole
EIILMNNOOTV I'm Not in Love
EIILMOPRSUY imperiously
EIILMORSTTU outer limits
EIILNNRSSVY vinyl resins
EIILNNSSTTY insistently
EIILNOOPPRT lipoprotein
EIILNOPPRTT triple point
EIILNOPRSTV silverpoint

EIILNOQSUUZ Louis-Quinze
EIILNRSTUVY intrusively
EIILNRTTUVY nutritively
EIILOPPRSTY propylitise
EIILOPPRTYZ propylitize
EIILORSTTVW Oliver Twist
EIILPRRTUVY irruptively
EIIMMNNNOST Mennonitism
EIIMNNOOPRT premonition
EIIMNNOOSTT set in motion
EIIMNNOPSTU pneumonitis
EIIMNOPSSST miss one's tip
EIIMNOPSSSU impiousness
EIIMNORRTTT intromitter
EIIMNRRTTTY Trinity term
EIIMOOPRSVX ex improviso
EIIMOORRSTU meritorious
EIIMOPPRRTY impropriety
EIIMOPRSSST prestissimo
EIIMOPSTTUY impetuosity
EIIMORRSSTU moisturiser
EIIMORRSTUZ moisturizer
EIINOOPPRST preposition
pre-position
EIINOORRRTV River Tornio
EIINOPRRSTY iron pyrites
EIINOPRSSUV supervision
EIINOPRSSUX isoxsuprine
EIINOQSSTTU questionist
EIINORRSSST sinistrorse
EIINORSTTTU restitution
EIIOPPRRRTX proprietrix
EIIOPPSSTUV suppositive
EIIOPQRRSTU perquisitor
EIIOPRRSSTX xerotripsis
EIIOPRRSTUY superiority
EIIOQRRSTUY requisitory
EIJJLLNNOOO Jonjo O'Neill
EIJKMMRSSUU Rijksmuseum
EIJLOOSTUUV Louis Jouvet
EIKKLRRSTUU Kulturkreis
EIKLLORRSTW trellis work
EIKMMOOPRSU opium-smoker
EIKMNORRSTY York Minster
EILLLLMNOOW woollen mill
EILLMOOPRST proso millet
EILLMOORSUV mellivorous
EILLMOPRTUX multiplexor
EILLNOOORVV Ivor Novello
EILLNOORRST ritornellos
EILLNOORTYY Tony O'Reilly
EILLNOPSSTY pointlessly
EILLOPRRSUY prelusorily
EILLOPRSTTV stilt-plover
EILLORRTTTY lily-trotter
EILMNNOPRTY prominently
EILMNOOOPRS monopoliser
EILMNOOOPRZ monopolizer
EILMNOPRTUY importunely
EILMNOPTTTU multipotent
EILMNOSTUUY untimeously
EILMOORRSWY worrisomely
EILMOOSSSTU tous-les-mois
EILMOPRSSTY proselytism
EILMOPSTUUY impetuously
EILMORSTTUY multistorey
EILNOOPRSST portionless
EILNOOSSTTU solution set
EILNOPRSUUY penuriously
EILNOQRTUVY ventriloquy
EILOOPRRSTY posteriorly
EILOOPRSSTY proteolysis
EILOPPRRSTW slipperwort
EIMMMNOOSTU immomentous
EIMMOOPRSUZ zoospermium
EIMNNOOSSSU ominousness
EIMNOOPPRUV improve upon
EIMNOOPRRTY premonitory
EIMNOOQSTTU mosquito net
EIMNOORSTTU neurotomist
EIMNOOSTTZZ mezzotintos
EIMNOPPRSTU presumption
EIMOOPRRSSX expromissor
EIMOOPRSTTT optometrist
EIMOORRSUVV vermivorous
EIMOPRSSTUV primus stove
EIMRRSSSSTU surmistress
EINNOOPPRTU inopportune
EINNOOPRSSS responsions
EINNOOPSSTT post-tension
EINNOOSSSUX noxiousness
EINNOQRSTUU non sequitur
EINNORSSSUU ruinousness
EINNOSSSSUU sinuousness
EINOOPRRSSV Provins rose
EINOORSSSTU riotousness
EINOPPRSSSU suppression
EINOPRRRTTU interruptor
EINOPSSTTTY stenotypist
EINORSSTTUY strenuosity
EIOPRRSSUVY supervisory
EIOQRRSTTUU triquetrous
EIORRSSTTUU trouser suit
EIORRSTTTUY restitutory
EJKNOORRUWY journey-work
EJMNNOORSTU sojournment
EKLLRRSSTUU Kurt Russell
EKLNOOPSTUY outspokenly
EKLNOORSTTY Leon Trotsky
EKMNNOOSTUY teknonymous
EKNNNNOSSUW unknownness
EKNOOPRRSTT porters' knot
ELLMNNOOSTY somnolently
ELLMORSTUUY tremulously
ELLNORTTUUW turn out well
ELLOPPRTTYY Pretty Polly
ELLOQRSUUUY querulously
ELMMNOOSTUY momentously
ELMMORRUUVW murmur vowel
ELMNNORSUYY Lynn Seymour
ELMNOPPSUYY money supply
ELMNORSTUUU untremulous

ELNNOORSTUW slow neutron
ELNOOOPRRTY poltroonery
ELNOOPPRTUY opportunely
ELNORSSTUUY strenuously
ELNORSTUUVY venturously
ELOPPRRSSTU purportless
ELOPPRSSSTU supportless
EMNOOPPSSSU pompousness
EMNOPPRSTTU supportment
EMOOOPRRSST mosstrooper
EMORRSTTUYY mystery tour
ENNOORSTTTU turn to stone
ENOORRSTTUU torrentuous
EOPPRRSSSTU supportress
EOPRRRTTUUW rupturewort

F

FFFGHIIMNTU muffin-fight
FFGGHIIINTT fighting fit
FFGGHIINORS fishing-frog
FFGHILLNSUY shufflingly
FFGHILLRTUY frightfully
FFIIRRSSTTU first-fruits
FFIMNORRUWY muffin-worry
FGGGIILNORT rigging loft
FGGHIILNNTY night-flying
FGGHIINNOTT nothing-gift
FGGHIINSTTU fish-gutting
FGGIIKKNNOS king of kings✧
FGGIIMNNORT morning gift
FGGIINNORUV unforgiving
FGGNNOOOSSS Song of Songs
FGHHIORSTTU sift through
FGHHNOOTTUU unthought-of
FGHIIINNNSU unfinishing
FGHIILLOPTW pillow-fight
FGHIILNOPST shoplifting
FGHIILNORSU flourishing
FGHIINNPSTU punt-fishing
FGHIINNRSSU furnishings
FGHIINOPSTT fitting-shop
FGHILLNOOWW Howling Wolf
FGHILNORTTY fortnightly
FGHILOPTTTU put to flight
FGHINNTTTUU tuft-hunting
FGIIILMNPSY simplifying
FGIIINNOPRT firing point
FGIILLLLMNU fulling-mill
FGIILLNNSUW in full swing
FGIILLNPTUY upliftingly
FGIILNNTTUY unfittingly
FGIILNOPPTT topping lift
FGIILNSTTUY stultifying
FGIIMNNNORU uninforming
FGIIMNOORTT fitting-room
FGIINNOPRTU unprofiting
FGIINNOPSTU fusing point
FGIINNORRTU turfing iron
FGIMNOOPRST post-forming
FGINNORSSUW snowsurfing
FGINOORTTTX foxtrotting
FGIOOPRRSST gross profit
FGIOORRSUUV frugivorous
FGLNOORRSTU strong flour
FHHIINOOPST photo finish
FHHIORRSSTT short shrift
FHIIKNOOTTT to think of it
FHIILNRTTUY unthriftily
FHIIOPRSTTW with profits
FHIKNOOPRRS shrink-proof
FHIMOORTTUW from without
FHJMNOOOPRU John Profumo
FHLLNRTUUUY unhurtfully
FHLPRSTTUUU sulphur tuft
FHMOOORTUUU out of humour
FHNOOOPRRST thornproofs
FIILLNOOSUX solifluxion
FIILLNPTUUY unpitifully
FIIMMNOORTY omniformity
FIIMOORSTTT fritto misto
FIIOOPPRRST proof spirit
FIIRTTTTTUU tutti-frutti
FIKLLLNSUUY unskilfully
FILLOORSUVY frivolously
FILMRSSTTUU mistrustful
FILNOORSSTY frontolysis
FKMNOOORRST Morton's fork
FLLOORRSUWY sorrowfully

G

GGGINNOORST going strong
GGHHHIORTUW highwrought
GGHHIILLNOR high-rolling
GGHHIINNNRU running high
GGHIILLNSTY slightingly
GGHIILNNPUW lunging whip
GGHILNOPSUW swing-plough
GGHINNNOSTU hunting-song
GGHINORRSTU rough string
GGHIOORSTUU Hugo Grotius
GGHLMOOPSYY sphygmology
GGIIINNRSTW sign-writing
GGIIKLNORRW working girl
GGIINNOSTUW outswinging
GGIINNPRSTU stringing up
GGIJLMNNOPU long jumping
GGILNNNNORU long-running
GGILNOOORWW wool-growing
GGIMNNNOORW morning gown
GGLMNNOOOOY gnomonology
GHHHOPRSTUU push through
GHHIIINSTTW within sight
GHHIIIPRSST high spirits
GHHIINNPTUW hunting-whip
GHHIKMORSTU skim through
GHHIKOPRSTU skip through
GHHILOPRTTT trothplight
GHHINNNORTU hunting-horn
GHHINOOPRTU thoroughpin
GHHIORSTTWY sightworthy
GHHKOORRTUW work through
GHHLLOPRTUU pull through

 Words marked ✧ can also be spelled with one or more capital letters

	pull-through
GHHLOOPPTYY	photoglyphy
GHHMNNOOOPT	monophthong
GHHMOOPRRTU	romp through
GHIIIKMNRSS	skirmishing
GHIIINNNOTT	nothing in it
GHIIINNOSTV	night vision
	vision thing
GHIIKLNNRSY	shrinkingly
GHIIKLNTTTY	tightly-knit
GHIIKNNNRSU	unshrinking
GHIILLLNRTY	thrillingly
GHIILLNNOTT	Notting Hill
GHIILLNSTWY	whistlingly
GHIILLOOPST	philologist
GHIILLOOSTT	lithologist
GHIILNNPSUY	punishingly
GHIILNOORST	rhinologist
GHIILNOPSTY	philogynist
GHIILOOOPST	ophiologist
GHIILOOPPST	hippologist
GHIILOOSSTT	histologist
GHIINNOOTTT	nothing to it
GHIINOPPPTW	whipping-top
GHIINOPPRSW	worshipping
GHIINOPTTUW	whiting pout
GHIJMNOPSUW	showjumping
GHIKNNNOOTW	know-nothing
GHIKNNOOPRU	pruning hook
GHILLOOOPST	hoplologist
GHILLOOPSYY	syphilology
GHILLOPSTTU	plough-stilt
GHILMMNRTUY	thrummingly
GHILMNOOSTY	hymnologist
GHILMOOSTTY	mythologist
GHILNOOOPST	phonologist
GHILNOOORTY	ornithology
GHILNOOPSUY	philogynous
GHILOOOPRTY	oligotrophy
GHILOOPSSUY	physiologus
GHILOOPSTTY	phytologist
GHIMNNOORRS	morsing-horn
GHIMNOOPSYY	physiognomy
GHIMOOOSSYZ	homozygosis
GHINNNOSTTU	Huntington's
GHINOORRTUW	wrought iron
	wrought-iron
GHIOPRSTTTU	put to rights
GHLLMOPUYYZ	Zygophyllum
GHMNNOOPSTU	Thompson gun
GIIIINNPRST	inspiriting
GIIIKLMNNSS	missing link
GIIIKNNNOPR	pinking iron
GIIIKNNNPRT	printing ink
GIIILLOSTUY	litigiously
GIIILNNPRSY	inspiringly
GIIILNNQRUY	inquiringly
GIIIMNNOOSU	ignominious
GIIIMNNOPRR	priming-iron
GIIINNNPRSU	uninspiring
GIIINNNQRUU	uninquiring
GIIKLLLNOSU	soul-killing
GIIKLNNNUWY	unwinkingly
GIIKLNPRSSU	prusik sling✧
GIIKMMNNOST	skimmington
GIIKNNOPPPS	skin-popping
GIILLLLMNOR	rolling mill
GIILLLNNUWY	unwillingly
GIILLMNNSUY	unsmilingly
GIILLMNOOST	limnologist
GIILLMNOPRY	imploringly
GIILLMNPTUY	multiplying
GIILLNNSTUY	insultingly
GIILLOOOPST	oligopolist
GIILMNOPRSY	promisingly
GIILMNOPRVY	improvingly
GIILNNOQTUY	longinquity
GIILNNPTUYY	unpityingly
GIILNNQSTUY	squintingly
GIILNNTTUWY	unwittingly
GIILNOORSUV	lignivorous
GIIMMNPPPRU	pump-priming
GIIMNNOPRSU	unpromising
GIIMNNOPRTU	importuning
GIIMNOORSTT	sitting room
GIIMOORRRST	rigor mortis
GIINNNOOPRS	spring onion
GIINNNOPPST	spinning top
GIINNNOPSTW	winning post
GIINNOPRRST	ripsnorting
GIINOOPRRSU	porriginous
GIINOORSTUV	vortiginous
GIINOPRRSUU	pruriginous
GIINRTTTTYY	nitty-gritty
GIJLMOSTUUU	multijugous
GIKLMORSTUW	silkworm-gut
GIKLNNNOUWY	unknowingly
GIKLNOOPRVY	provokingly
GIKMMNOOORS	smoking room
GIKNNNNORTU	running knot
GIKNNNOORUW	unknowing or
GIKNNOOPRUV	unprovoking
GILLLMNOSUU	slumgullion
GILLMNNOORR	morning roll
GILLNOSTUUY	glutinously
GILLNPRSSTU	pull strings
GILLOOPSTTU	plutologist
GILMMNRRUUY	murmuringly
GILMNOOOSTU	monologuist
GILNNNOPSSU	nonplussing
GILNORRTTUY	torturingly
GILNRSTTTUY	struttingly
GIMMNNOOORR	morning room
GIMMNNRRUUU	unmurmuring
GIMMNOORTYY	myringotomy
GIMMNOPRTUU	rumgumption
GIMNNORSTUU	surmounting
GIMNOOOPRSU	sporogonium
GIMNOORSTYY	syringotomy
GINNOOPRRTU	root-pruning
GINNOOPRSTT	strong point
	strongpoint

GINOOPPSTTU stopping-out
GNOOOPRSTUY protogynous
GOOPRSSTTUU gross output

H

HHIINOSSTWW wishtonwish
HHILMOOPSTY holophytism
HHIMNOOPPSU phosphonium
HHIMOOPPRSS phosphorism
HHKNOOOSWWW know who's who
HHMNOOOOPSU homophonous
HHMNOOORTUU mouth-honour
HHOOOPPRSSU phosphorous
HIIIKKLMNPS milk-kinship
HIIILMNOPSS Sinophilism
HIIIMNORSST histrionism
HIILLNNNOOT nonillionth
HIILLOPRSWW will-worship
HIILMNNOOPY hypolimnion
HIILMOOSTTT lithotomist
HIILNNPSSST shin splints
HIILOORRTTT lithotritor
HIILOPRSTTY lithotripsy
HIIMMOOPRSS isomorphism
HIIMMOPRRST trimorphism
HIIMNOOPRST monitorship
HIIOOPRSSTU Istiophorus
HIJMNNOOPSS John Simpson
HIJNOORRSSS Sir John Ross
HILLOOPSUXY xylophilous
HILLOPRSTUY triphyllous
HILMMOPSTUY Plymouthism
HILMOOOSTTU lithotomous
HILMOPSTTUY Plymouthist
HILNOOPPSTY polyphonist
Psilophyton
HILNOOPSTXY xylophonist
HILNOORSSTU honours list
HILOOPRSTYY polyhistory
HILOORTTWWW whitlow-wort
HIMMOOOPRSZ zoomorphism
HIMNOOPSSUY symphonious
HIMOOOPRSSU isomorphous
HIMOOPRRSTU trimorphous
HIMOOPSTTTY phytotomist
HIMOORTTTWY thirty-twomo
HINNOOOPRTU honour-point
HINOOORRSSU horrisonous
HINOOPPRSSS sponsorship
HINOOPPSTTY phonotypist
HINOOPRRTTY thyrotropin
HIOOPPRSSTV provostship
HIOOPPSSTYY hypotyposis
HIOPRRSSSTT sports shirt
HJNOORSSTTW St John's wort
HKRRRRSUUYY hurry-skurry
HLOOPRRSTUU sulphur-root
HLOPRRSTUUW sulphurwort
HMNNOOPTTYY Monty Python
HMOOOOPRSSU homosporous
HMOOOPPRRTY morphotropy
HOOOPPRRSUY pyrophorous
HOOOPPRRTTY prototrophy
HOOORRRRSTY horror story
HORRSTTTUWY trustworthy

I

IIIILMNNQSU inquilinism
IIIILNNQTUY inquilinity
IIIIMMPRSTV primitivism✧
IIIIMNSTTUV intuitivism
IIIIMPPSSSS Mississippi
IIIIMPRSTTV primitivist
IIIINNOQSTU inquisition✧
IIILLMNOPST pointillism✧
IIILLMNOSSU illusionism
IIILLNNOQTU quintillion
IIILLNOPSTT pointillist
IIILLNOSSTT tonsillitis
IIILLNOSSTU illusionist
IIILLOPRSSS spirillosis
IIILMNOSTUV multi-vision
IIILNNOQSUU inquilinous
IIINNNORTTU innutrition
IIINNOSTTTU institution
IIINOOOPSTV oviposition
IIINSSTTTTU institutist
IIJLNORSUUY injuriously
IILLNNOOOPP opinion poll
IILLOOQSSTU soliloquist
IILLORSSTUU illustrious✧
IILMOORTTUY utility room
IILNNOOSUXY innoxiously
IILNOOSSTTU solutionist
IILOOPRRSVY provisorily
IIMMNNOOTUX immunotoxin
IIMNOOPRSTU positronium
IIMNOPRTTUY importunity
IIMOOPRSSTT Soroptimist
IINNNNOOSTU non-unionist
IINNOOPRRTY non-priority
IINOOOPPRST proposition
IINOOPPSSTU supposition
IINOPPQRTUY propinquity
IINOPRRRSTU stirrup iron
ILLOPSSUWWY pussy willow
ILLORSUUUXY luxuriously
ILMMORSTUUW Wilms' tumour
ILMNOOOSTTY tonsilotomy
ILMNOOPSTTU plutonomist
ILMNOPRSSUU plus or minus
ILMOOOPRSST misoprostol
ILNNNOOSSTY Sonny Liston
ILNOOOPSSUY poisonously
ILNOOORSTUY notoriously
ILNORSUUUUX unluxurious
IMMOPSSUUUV opus musivum
IMNNOOOPSST monopsonist
IMNOOOPRSTY tropomyosin
IMNOOPPRSTU opportunism
IMNOORSSTTY monstrosity
IMOOOPPRRTU motu proprio

IMOOPPRSTTU pittosporum
IMOPSSTTUUY sumptuosity
IMPPPRRSTUU stirrup pump
INOOOPPRRST proportions
INOOPPRSTTU opportunist
INOOPPRTTUY opportunity
INOPPTTTUUU input/output
IOOPPRSSTUY suppository
IOOPRRSTTTU prostitutor

L

LMMORRSUUUY murmurously
LMNOOOPSUYY polyonymous
LMNOORSSTUY monstrously
LMOPSSTUUUY sumptuously

M

MOOOPRRSSTT storm troops

12 letters

A

AAAAAABCNNNN Canaan Banana
AAAAAADDDYYY yada yada yada
AAAAAALMRSTT taramasalata
AAAAABBNRRST Santa Barbara
AAAAABCDLMNS Canada balsam
AAAAACEEMNRT Amarantaceae
AAAAACINRRSV caravansarai
AAAAAEGNPSST apage Satanas
AAAABBDHMRRY Abraham Darby
AAAABBEKLMST Balaam-basket
AAAABBJMORRR Major Barbara
AAAABBLMMOSY Salaam Bombay!
AAAABCCELNRU baccalaurean
AAAABCCHILNN bacchanalian
AAAABCEHMNOT Acanthamoeba
AAAABCEILMNR Arabian camel
AAAABCIILLMT Balaamitical
AAAABCINNOTV bona vacantia
AAAABDEGNRRU guaraná bread
AAAABDEIKNNR Bandaranaike
AAAABDELNNNR Bananalander
AAAABDGGHITV Bhagavad Gita
AAAABDGILMOV viola da gamba
AAAABDIINRSU Saudi Arabian
AAAABDIKLQST Kitab al-Aqdas
AAAABDMNRSSU massaranduba
AAAABEELRSTU tabulae rasae
AAAABEIPRRRV pareira brava
AAAABGGILLNS basal ganglia
AAAABILNPRSV Bavarian Alps
AAAACCCCIRTU acciaccatura
AAAACCDEIJMR Jamaica cedar
AAAACCEEIMRT Tamaricaceae
AAAACCHINRTT anacathartic
AAAACCILMORT acroamatical
AAAACCILPRTT paratactical
AAAACCLLOSTT alla stoccata
AAAACCLMORST Malacostraca
AAAACCNSSSUU causa causans
AAAACDDEMRWY Academy Award
AAAACDIILPRS paradisaical
paradisiacal
AAAACDIIMORT acaridomatia
AAAACDIMMNTU macadamia nut
AAAACDIMOORT acarodomatia
AAAACEEEEGLN Elaeagnaceae
AAAACEEEPPRV Papaveraceae
AAAACEEIMRTT Marattiaceae
AAAACEILNPST anapaestical
AAAACEINRRSV caravanserai
AAAACELLLLPP alla cappella
AAAACGIMMNRT anagrammatic
AAAACHILNPPS Appalachians
AAAACHINRSST anacatharsis
AAAACHNNPRTT Panchatantra
AAAACILMNPRU Campanularia
AAAACIMNRSST antimacassar
AAAADEFHLSSZ Hafez al-Assad
AAAADEHMNOPR panorama head
AAAADEHMRSTT mad as a hatter
AAAADELNRSTW Anwar el-Sadat
AAAADEPQRRTU paraquadrate
AAAADILMNNRS salamandrian
AAAADILRSTUY Australia Day
AAAAEEHNNNPT Panathenaean
AAAAEFFHINRV have an affair
AAAAEFMMORRS Sea of Marmara
AAAAEFRRSSTY Yasser Arafat
AAAAEGGLNPRU paralanguage
AAAAEGILMMTV amalgamative
AAAAEGINPRSS asparaginase
AAAAEGNRTVXZ extravaganza
AAAAEGPPRSSU asparagus pea
AAAAEHILMSST thalassaemia
AAAAEIIMPRST parasitaemia
AAAAEIKNNNNR Anna Karenina
AAAAEIMMNRRT armamentaria
AAAAEINPRSTV pâte à savarin
AAAAFGILLNRS Niagara Falls
AAAAGHHMMRRT Martha Graham
AAAAGHHNRSUV Sarah Vaughan
AAAAGILMMNOT amalgamation
AAAAHILSSTTV hasta la vista
AAAAHIMNNOTT thanatomania
AAAAHIMNORRS Narasimha Rao
AAAAIILLMNRT antimalarial
AAAAILLPRRSS sarsaparilla
AAAAILNRSSTU Australasian
AAAAINNNNOVV Anna Ivanovna
AAAAINNNORTV Antananarivo

AAAALLLLOOPZ lallapalooza
AAABBBCHKLST Black Sabbath
AAABBBHHHLLL blah-blah-blah
AAABBCEEINRS Caribbean Sea
AAABBCEGHINR beanbag chair
AAABBCEGIRRY baby carriage
AAABBCORRSTY Barbary coast
AAABBDEENNNR banana-bender
AAABBEEFHMTT abaft the beam
AAABBEEIRTTX Beata Beatrix
AAABBEHLMTWY Waltham Abbey
AAABBEIILLOV bioavailable
AAABBELNSTTT Blatant Beast
AAABBGHHNOUZ baba ghanouzh
AAABBINRRSTU antibarbarus
AAABCCCDIIMR carbamic acid
AAABCCEHRRTT tab character
AAABCCEILLOX coaxial cable
AAABCCGILNNT balancing act
AAABCCIILLST cabalistical
AAABCDDILRVY David Barclay
AAABCDEELLNW weal-balanced
AAABCDEEMNRS danse macabre✧
AAABCDEILNPR balanced pair
AAABCDENNNOS second banana
AAABCDHHIPTT hit a bad patch
AAABCDHIINRT Dibranchiata
AAABCDHILLNN ball and chain
AAABCEEGILRR carriageable
AAABCEEGINOR Boraginaceae
AAABCEEHLRST calabash tree
AAABCEELLLRS clear as a bell
AAABCEERSSSU scarabaeuses
AAABCEGILMNR mariage blanc
AAABCEHILLPT alphabetical
AAABCEHILNPT analphabetic
AAABCEHIMRSU Beaumarchais
AAABCEHLOPPR approachable
AAABCEHPRSUX chapeaux-bras
AAABCEIILNRT celibatarian
AAABCEIILNSZ Isaac Albéniz
AAABCEIJMNOY Jamaica ebony
AAABCEILLNRT trial balance
AAABCEILLPSS Blaise Pascal
AAABCEILLRWY cable railway
AAABCEILMNRU air ambulance
AAABCEILNPTY Placentia Bay
AAABCEINSSTU satanic abuse
AAABCELLLNRU Lauren Bacall
AAABCELLQRUY Lyra Belacqua
AAABCELMMNNU ambulanceman
AAABCELMRTWY cable tramway
AAABCELNPSTT capstan table
AAABCELNRRTU tabernacular
AAABCGIINNRT Cantabrigian
AAABCGILLOTV Volga-Baltaic
AAABCHKKLRWW Black Hawk War
AAABCIILRRUV vibracularia
AAABCIINPSTT anabaptistic
AAABCIKPRRSU Cusparia bark
AAABCILNORUV vocabularian
AAABCLLORSUU casual labour
AAABCMNNORRS Baron Scarman
AAABDDEGIMNR brain-damaged
AAABDDELNTTW wattle and dab
AAABDDJNNORY Darby and Joan
AAABDEEFHLPT deaf alphabet
AAABDEEKKMNR make-and-break
AAABDEGILNRV Naval Brigade
AAABDEHLLNRY Albany herald
AAABDEILMNPR Brian De Palma
AAABDEILMRST dramatisable
AAABDEILMRTZ dramatizable
AAABDEINNTUX ex abundantia
AAABDELLLORY ballade royal
AAABDEMMORVY Madame Bovary
AAABDEMNRSSU masseranduba
AAABDEMRSSSS ambassadress
AAABDGHMNRSS smash-and-grab
AAABDIILNNQU banana liquid
AAABDIILPTTY adaptability
AAABDILLOOPR paraboloidal
AAABDILMRTYY Admiralty Bay
AAABDLLMNOOR abnormal load
AAABDNRRSSST Stars and Bars
AAABEEERRTTT beat a retreat
AAABEEGHINRT breathe again
AAABEEGIKNTT take a beating
AAABEEGILMRR marriageable
AAABEEGILRRV variable gear
AAABEEGLMNNU unmanageable
AAABEEHIMNPS amphisbaenae
AAABEEILNPPS inappeasable
AAABEELLNPPU unappealable
AAABEELLRTUV ratable value
AAABEELMNOSW able seawoman
AAABEELNPPSU unappeasable
AAABEFLMOTTZ Battle of Zama
AAABEGGGINRT baggage-train
AAABEGLMNNUY unmanageably
AAABEHHKKLLS Lake Balkhash
AAABEHIKPPPT Phi Beta Kappa
AAABEHIMNPSS amphisbaenas
AAABEHLMOSTT haematoblast
AAABEHMSSTTY that's as may be
AAABEIIJNRSZ Azerbaijanis
AAABEIILMNNT maintainable
AAABEILLMNOT balletomania
AAABEILLNSSU unassailable
AAABEILLRRUV Lualaba River
AAABEILMNPRR Parian marble
AAABEILNNTTU unattainable
AAABEILNORRT aberrational
AAABEILRRSTV variable star
AAABEINNSSST San Sebastian
AAABELLLPRRS parallel bars
AAABELLNNSUY unanalysable
AAABELLNNUYZ unanalyzable
AAABELLNRSSW ballanwrasse
AAABELLNRSTT translatable
AAABELLRSTTW water ballast
AAABELNOOPTY palaeobotany

AAABELQSTTUU	absquatulate
AAABEMNORTTW	water boatman
AAABFILMRRSS	friar's balsam
AAABGGLNNPRU	Luang Prabang
AAABGIILNRRT	Gibraltarian
AAABGLLMRRRU	burglar alarm
AAABHIILNOTT	habitational
AAABHIKLLMOR	Kimball O'Hara
AAABHINOOPST	satanophobia
AAABIIILLTVY	availability
AAABIILLPTTY	palatability
AAABIILNNOST	banalisation
AAABIILNNOTZ	banalization
AAABIILNRWXZ	Brazilian wax
AAABIKKLNOTU	Kota Kinabalu
AAABIKLNNNOT	national bank
AAABILLNQRRU	Barranquilla
AAABILNNOOTT	labanotation
AAABILNNTTUY	unattainably
AAABILNPRSSU	Assurbanipal
	sublapsarian✧
AAABIMMNORRT	tromba marina
AAABLLMOPPRS	balsam poplar
AAACCCDILLSY	saccadically
AAACCCEEIINV	Vacciniaceae
AAACCCGHHHIN	cha-cha-chaing
AAACCCHIPRTT	cataphractic
AAACCCILLSTT	catallactics
AAACCDDEIMNR	candid camera
AAACCDEEEIPR	Epacridaceae
AAACCDEEGNRS	Cascade Range
AAACCDEEIORT	Cordaitaceae
AAACCDEILLMY	academically
AAACCDEILMNO	decalcomania
AAACCDEILMRU	camera lucida
AAACCDGIIMNN	manganic acid
AAACCDGIIMRR	margaric acid
AAACCDHILORS	saccharoidal
AAACCDHILSTU	cactus dahlia
AAACCDHNRRSY	cash and carry
	cash-and-carry
AAACCDIILNTT	tantalic acid
AAACCDIINRRT	intracardiac
AAACCDIIPRST	aspartic acid
AAACCDIIRRTT	tartaric acid
AAACCEEEHISZ	Schizaeaceae
AAACCEELRSSU	Crassulaceae
AAACCEFHNNTT	café-chantant
AAACCEGILMTT	metagalactic
AAACCEHIPTTY	heat capacity
AAACCEHNOSTU	acanthaceous
AAACCEIIKLTT	Lake Titicaca
AAACCEIINPTT	incapacitate
AAACCEILLLNR	cancellarial
AAACCEILLNNR	cancellarian
AAACCEILLNTU	canaliculate
AAACCEINNQTU	acquaintance
AAACCFILNTTU	in actual fact
AAACCGHILLOT	galactic halo
AAACCGHILMOZ	chalazogamic
AAACCHILLNRY	anarchically
AAACCHILNPTY	anaphylactic
AAACCHILPSTY	cataphysical
AAACCIINNPTT	incapacitant
AAACCIINOPTT	capacitation
AAACCILORSTU	accusatorial
AAACDDEGNRUV	advance guard
AAACDDEHIIRR	Charadriidae
AAACDDEILNSV	Aladdin's cave
AAACDDHIMRRS	Richard Adams
AAACDDHNRTWW	watch and ward
AAACDEEGJLNU	Juglandaceae
AAACDEEHINVY	have a nice day
AAACDEEILNPS	Asclepiadean
AAACDEELNRRY	calendar year
AAACDEENNPST	Peasant Dance
AAACDEERSSWY	caraway seeds
AAACDEFILNOP	da capo al fine
AAACDEGIIPRR	carriage-paid
AAACDEGINNNO	once and again
AAACDEHMPRTY	Pachydermata
AAACDEILPSSU	Isla de Pascua
AAACDEINOTVX	tax avoidance
AAACDEINRSTT	tradescantia
AAACDELMORYY	Royal Academy
AAACDENNOPSU	pandanaceous
AAACDGHMNRSU	gum sandarach
AAACDGHNPRTU	Chandragupta
AAACDGIIMMRT	diagrammatic
AAACDGIIMPRT	paradigmatic
AAACDHIINNRT	cantharidian
AAACDHKKLLNT	chalk and talk
AAACDHOOPPRR	approach road
AAACDIINNNSV	Scandinavian
AAACDILLMRTY	dramatically
AAACDILORTTY	Artiodactyla
AAACDINOOPTT	coadaptation
AAACDLLMORUY	Lord Macaulay
AAACDLMMNOPY	lampadomancy
AAACDLNNOOPR	Aaron Copland
AAACDLNOORST	arco saltando
AAACDLRSTUWY	casualty ward
AAACEEEGINNT	Gentianaceae
AAACEEEHMNPY	Nymphaeaceae
AAACEEEILMRS	Marsileaceae
AAACEEENPPRR	reappearance
AAACEEFKMRWY	make a wry face
AAACEEGILMNO	Magnoliaceae
AAACEEGLLOPY	Polygalaceae
AAACEEGLNRRT	Angela Carter
AAACEEGNRTVX	extravagance
AAACEEHILNNP	anencephalia
AAACEEHINSST	East China Sea
AAACEEHIPSUU	Euphausiacea
AAACEEIILNSV	Salviniaceae
AAACEEILMNOR	American aloe
AAACEEILNPRT	paraenetical
AAACEEIMNRRT	retina camera
AAACEENORTTY	acetate rayon
AAACEENPRRTW	peace-warrant
AAACEERRSTTU	tartare sauce
AAACEFIJKRST	safari jacket

AAACEFILMRTT material fact
AAACEFIMNORR Afro-American
AAACEFINSTTT fantasticate
AAACEGGGLOTU galactagogue
AAACEGHKLMRR Grahame Clark
AAACEGIILMRR mail-carriage
AAACEGILMMNO megalomaniac
AAACEGIMNPRT paramagnetic
AAACEGNNOPRY paracyanogen
AAACEGNRTVXY extravagancy
AAACEHILLMPR alphamerical
AAACEHILMMTT mathematical
AAACEHILMSST thalassaemic
AAACEHILPRST share capital
AAACEHIMRRTT matriarchate
AAACEHIPRRTT patriarchate
AAACEHJMMMNS James Mancham
AAACEHKNSSTW Saskatchewan
AAACEHLLORRV alveolar arch
AAACEHLNPSTT capstan lathe
AAACEHNORSTU near as a touch
AAACEIILMNRT Latin America
AAACEIJLMORW majolicaware
AAACEILLNSTT Atlantic seal
AAACEILLPRST palaestrical
AAACEILMNNPR American plan
AAACEILMOOST osteomalacia
AAACEILMPRRT parametrical
AAACEILNNRST Lancasterian
AAACEILNORTU aeronautical
AAACEILOPPRT pearl-tapioca
AAACEILORSTT aerostatical
AAACEJJKMPTY pyjama jacket
AAACEJKLNNRT Jack-a-lantern
AAACEJLNPQRU Japan lacquer
AAACELLNOTWX tax allowance
AAACELLNRSTU natural scale
AAACELMORSUY Rose Macaulay
AAACELNOPSTU platanaceous
AAACELNOSSTU santalaceous
AAACELNPRSTT Lateran Pacts
AAACELOSTTUY autocatalyse
AAACELOTTUYZ autocatalyze
AAACEMNPRTTU catena patrum
AAACEMNRRSTY sacramentary
AAACFGILNNRU lingua franca
AAACFIINRRTT anti-aircraft
AAACFIMNRRST aircraftsman
AAACFLMNRTUU manufactural
AAACGGILLNOY anagogically
AAACGGILLOPY apagogically
AAACGIILLNNT anti-Gallican
AAACGIILNOTT Tagliacotian
AAACGIILNPST capital gains
AAACGIIMNSTT anastigmatic
AAACGIKNSSTT stack against
AAACGILLLNOY analogically
AAACGILLLNVY galvanically
AAACGILLMMMO mammalogical
AAACGILMNRTU natural magic
AAACGIMNOORS angiosarcoma
AAACHHIPRSTY tachyphrasia
AAACHIIKPPRT apparatchiki
AAACHIKPPRST apparatchiks
AAACHILMNPST phantasmical
AAACHILMNPTU human capital
AAACHILMNRST charlatanism
AAACHIMNORTU tauromachian
AAACHIMNSTTT antasthmatic
AAACHIPPRRST paraphrastic
AAACHLLPRTYY cataphyllary
AAACHMNNOPPR panpharmacon
AAACIIILNNRT Catilinarian
AAACIILLMNST talismanical
AAACIILNNOST canalisation
AAACIILNNOTZ canalization
AAACIILNNRRT intracranial
AAACIILOPRSX coaxial pairs
AAACILLLNNOT national call
AAACILLLNTYY analytically
AAACILLMNOTY anatomically
AAACILLMORTY aromatically
AAACILLMPSSU lapsus calami
AAACILLNNTUY unanalytical
AAACILMMNNOO monomaniacal
AAACILMNOPRY pyromaniacal
AAACILPPRTTY party-capital
AAACIMNNOTTU catamountain
AAACLLMNORSY nasolacrymal
AAACLMMOPSTY mycoplasmata
AAACMNOORRTV motor caravan
AAACNNNORTTT contranatant
AAADDDEEILNV dead-and-alive
AAADDDEIJMNV Javed Miandad
AAADDEEELPPS Dead Sea apple
AAADDEEGGLNU dead language
AAADDEELMMRS Esmeralda Dam
AAADDEGINSTV disadvantage
AAADDEGLLNNR adrenal gland
AAADDEGLLNSS leads and lags
AAADDEGLNOPT Ponta Delgada
AAADDEHHNNRT heart and hand
AAADDEJJNRWZ Andrzej Wajda
AAADDFHLLOOO all of a doodah
AAADDFLLORSW Waldorf salad
AAADDGILLMOY amygdaloidal
AAADDGLMOSSU Douglas Adams
AAADDGLNNNOW Gondwanaland
AAADDHLOPRSU Alpha Doradus
AAADDIINOPRX paradoxidian
AAADDILLMNPS Aladdin's lamp
AAADDILLORSV Salvador Dali
AAADDILMNORS salamandroid
AAADDKQRSUWW awkward squad
AAADDLMNPRST lamp-standard
standard lamp
AAADEEFGGLNU deaf language
AAADEEFNRRTU turn a deaf ear
AAADEEGMMRRT Margaret Mead
AAADEEHLRTUU à la hauteur de
AAADEEHMMNNS name and shame
AAADEEHRRSST Sahara Desert

AAADEEIILLNP India Pale Ale
AAADEEINRRSV Sierra Nevada
AAADEEIRRSST disaster area
AAADEEKMNNRR make an errand
AAADEELLNRTY early and late
AAADEELPPRST spread a plate
AAADEEMNNRSS André Masséna
AAADEFHILMNT time and a half
AAADEFIKMOTY make a day of it
AAADEFLLMNNS Adam's flannel
AAADEFNORRRR Andro Ferrara
AAADEFRSTTTU saturated fat
AAADEGIIMNNT time and again
AAADEGILNRTV landgraviate
AAADEGILPQRU quadraplegia
AAADEGIMQRSU Quadragesima
AAADEGLNNORR Ronald Reagan
AAADEGMNRRTU grand amateur
AAADEGNOSTUV advantageous
AAADEGNQRRUY quadragenary
AAADEHILNPRS nail-head-spar
AAADEHLNNOPT hand on a plate
AAADEHLNRTTU natural death
AAADEHMMMNRR Armand Hammer
AAADEHMPRRTY drama therapy
AAADEHNRRTTW death warrant
AAADEIILNNOP Palaeo-Indian
AAADEIILNPTT Adelina Patti
AAADEIIMNNST East-Indiaman
AAADEILMNNRS salamandrine
AAADEILNNPRT anteprandial
AAADEILORRRT arterial road
AAADEILRRRTY radial artery
AAADEIMMNRST near as dammit
AAADEIMNRRRV River Narmada
AAADEIMNRTTY Tetradynamia
AAADEIMORRTU radio amateur
AAADEINNOPRS Andrea Pisano
AAADEINOPRTT readaptation
AAADELMNRRUX André Malraux
AAADELMRSSTW Walter S Adams
AAADELNRSTUY Austen Layard
AAADEMNNSSWY ways and means
AAADEMNPSSTU De Maupassant
AAADFGINRRSS à grands frais
AAADFIINORST faradisation
AAADFIINORTZ faradization
AAADFINRSTWY waif and stray
AAADFKLLNRSW Falklands War
AAADGHHIMNSW Aswan High Dam
AAADGHIMNOOT agathodaimon
AAADGIILLORT gladiatorial
AAADGIILNORT gladiatorian
AAADGILLMNNR marginal land
AAADGILMNRRW marginal ward
AAADGIMNRSTV avant-gardism
AAADGINRSTTV avant-gardist
AAADGLMMMNRY mammary gland
AAADGLNQRRUU quadrangular
AAADGLOORSVW Avogadro's law
AAADGMPRSTUU Samudragupta
AAADHHMNRSTU Rhadamanthus
AAADHHMNRSTY Rhadamanthys
AAADHHNSTTTT and that's that
AAADHIILMNNP Milindapanha
AAADHIILNNNS Hainan Island
AAADHILLNRSW Hadrian's Wall
AAADIILLMNPS Palladianism
AAADIINNOPTT inadaptation
AAADILLMTTWZ waltz Matilda
AAADILLNPSSU Palau Islands
AAADILLNSSTY All Saints' Day
AAADILNRSSSU Russian salad
AAADINNORTTU Antoni Artaud
AAAEEEFNRRTU ferae naturae
AAAEEELQTUVV ave atque vale
AAAEEFILPRRS false pareira
AAAEEGGLMNTU metalanguage
AAAEEGGMNRST stage manager
AAAEEGGPRSSV passage grave
AAAEEGHMNOPR Phanerogamae
AAAEEGIKMPRS make a pig's ear
AAAEEGINNRSX sexagenarian
AAAEEGLMNOPT aplanogamete
AAAEEGMNNPRT permanganate
AAAEEHIMNSTT anathematise
AAAEEHIMNTTZ anathematize
AAAEEHIMRRST Maria Theresa
AAAEEHINPSST panaesthesia
AAAEEHIPRSST paraesthesia
AAAEEHLLNPST Pallas Athene
AAAEEILLNPRT earl palatine
AAAEEIPPRRTT pater patriae
AAAEEJLMRRSY James Earl Ray
AAAEEJNOPSST Japanese tosa
AAAEEKNRSTUW take unawares
AAAEEKRRSTTT steak tartare
AAAEELMMNSST meat-salesman
AAAEELMRRSTU Mare Australe
AAAEEMMMOPST mammee-sapota
AAAEFFIJLTVV Tel Aviv-Jaffa
AAAEFMOPRRTW marrowfat pea
AAAEGGPPRSTU egg apparatus
AAAEGHIMNOPR Phanerogamia
AAAEGHLLTTWW wag-at-the-wall
AAAEGHLOPPRY palaeography
AAAEGHNPPRRT pantagrapher
AAAEGILLMNRY managerially
AAAEGILLMOTT agalmatolite
AAAEGILLNORV all over again
AAAEGILMNPRS area sampling
AAAEGILMNRST marginal seat
AAAEGILRTTWW water wagtail
AAAEGINNNNOR nonagenarian
AAAEGJMOORSS José Saramago
AAAEGKLMMNOR make a long arm
AAAEGLOPRSST paraglossate
AAAEGNOPRRST persona grata
AAAEGNPPRSSU sugar snap pea
AAAEGNRSSSUU as sure as a gun
AAAEHHKLLNRS hallan-shaker
AAAEHIMNORTT theatromania

AAAEHINSSTTU euthanasiast
AAAEHKORSTUV katharevousa
AAAEHLNPRTTY natal therapy
AAAEHMNPPRTW Whatman paper®
AAAEHMOPRRTY aromatherapy
AAAEHNPRSTTY parasyntheta
AAAEIIKKNRTW Kiri Te Kanawa
AAAEIILNNRSS Alain Resnais
AAAEIILNQRTU equalitarian
AAAEIKLLLMST alkali metals
AAAEILLLNPRT antiparallel
AAAEILMNOPPR paralipomena
AAAEILMRRTTX extramarital
AAAEILNPPRRS prelapsarian
AAAEIMNNRRRW Marina Warner
AAAEIMNNRSST transaminase
AAAEIMNQRSTU à quatre mains
AAAEINRRSTWY sanitary ware
AAAELLLSSTVY Telly Savalas
AAAELMNOVYYZ Novaya Zemlya
AAAELPRSTTWY play at waster
AAAELQQRSUUV quaquaversal
AAAEMMRRSSTT master-at-arms
AAAENOPRSUYY pay-as-you-earn
AAAEPQRRSTTU a quarter past
AAAFGLNNOPRT platanna frog
AAAFHHLMNORT half-marathon
AAAFIILMNWYY in a family way
AAAFIKNNRRST Frank Sinatra
AAAFILLMRSTZ Mtarazi Falls
AAAFILMRRSSY Sir Alf Ramsay
AAAFILORSSSS sassafras oil
AAAFINNOPSTY Piano Fantasy
AAAFINRRSTTU trustafarian
AAAFLORRSTTT salt of tartar
AAAFMMNNORSW man-of-war's-man
AAAFNRSSSSTU sassafras nut
AAAGGIOPPRTU appoggiatura
AAAGGLNOSSUV Volsungasaga
AAAGHHIJKNNR Jahangir Khan
AAAGHIIMPRST amphigastria
AAAGHIMNPRST paragnathism
AAAGHIPPRRST paragraphist
AAAGHIRSTTWY straight away
straightaway
AAAGHNOPRSTU paragnathous
AAAGIILNNOTV navigational
AAAGILLLORRT grallatorial
AAAGILLPRSXY spiral galaxy
AAAGILMNRRSV larva migrans
AAAHHHHNORSS Rosh Hashanah
AAAHIILNNOTT antihalation
AAAHIIMMNORT arithmomania
AAAHIIMNNRTU humanitarian
AAAHIJNNPRSV Japan varnish
AAAHIKLTWWWY walk away with
AAAHINSSSTTU St Athanasius
AAAHKMMNOTUY thank-you-ma'am
AAAHLLMNPSTY phantasmally
AAAHLPPRRSYY happy as Larry
AAAIILLMMMRS mammillarias
AAAIILLNNOPR Apollinarian
AAAIILMPRRTY paramilitary
AAAIILNNNOTT anti-national
AAAIILNNOSST nasalisation
AAAIILNNOSTZ nasalization
AAAIILNOPPRT apparitional
AAAIILNOPRST aspirational
AAAIILNORTTT totalitarian
AAAIIMMNRSST Samaritanism
AAAIINPPRSST Patripassian
AAAIKLNNOPRT national park
AAAIKLNORSUY Ankylosauria
AAAILLNOSTTU salutational
AAAILMNORTTU maturational
AAAILNORSTTU salutatorian
AAAINNNRRSTU transuranian
AAAINORSSSST assassinator
AAALLLLOOOPZ lollapalooza
AAALLMMNPTTU tantalum lamp
AAALMMOOPSST plasmosomata
AAALNOPPSTZZ palazzo pants
AAALNORRRTWY royal warrant
AABBBCEEIKRR Caribbee bark
AABBBCGIKNST backstabbing
AABBBDEERTTY battered baby
AABBBEERRTTY baby-batterer
AABBCCEMOOSU bombacaceous
AABBCCIKOSST back to basics
AABBCCKKLLNO Black on Black
AABBCDEEEHRR bare-breached
AABBCDEKLLNU black-and-blue
AABBCDELRSSS scabbardless
AABBCDFHIRSS scabbard fish
AABBCEEEKLNY black-eye bean
AABBCEEGHITW cabbage-white
AABBCEEHINRT the Caribbean
AABBCEEHLNRU unbreachable
AABBCEEITUXY Citeaux Abbey
AABBCEEMMORY Morecambe Bay
AABBCEGIKKNR backbreaking
AABBCEGKKNSU skunk cabbage
AABBCEHNRSTY baby-snatcher
AABBCGIKLLLN blackballing
AABBCIIILMNO bibliomaniac
AABBCIILLNRY rabbinically
AABBCIIMORRX mixobarbaric
AABBCNOORSST contrabbasso
AABBDDEEHLVY badly-behaved
AABBDEEFLOTU feel bad about
AABBDEEHNNNR Brendan Behan
AABBDEELLRWY Redwall Abbey
AABBDEGNRRUY Barnaby Rudge
AABBDEHIORUV bad behaviour
AABBDEIMNRRY barmy-brained
AABBDGGILNNR land-grabbing
AABBDIILLLLR billiard ball
AABBDIILLRRS bar billiards
AABBDILMNOSU subabdominal
AABBEEEHLQTU bequeathable
AABBEEEHRTTY Abbey Theatre
AABBEEELNRSS bearableness

AABBEEGINORU Eugenio Barba
AABBEEGLMMRR amber gambler
AABBEEHKKNRT break the bank
AABBEEHLNRTU unbreathable
AABBEEHPRRSY Barbary sheep
AABBEEILPRRY repairable by
AABBEEIRRTUV abbreviature
AABBEEKLNNOR non-breakable
AABBEELLMNSS blamableness
AABBEGIKLLNR ball-breaking
AABBEGINRSTW rabbeting-saw
AABBEIILMNRZ Mazarin Bible
AABBEIINORTV abbreviation
AABBEILNNOTU unobtainable
AABBEILOSTUY A Suitable Boy
AABBEILRTTTU attributable
AABBEIMMNPSY namby-pambies
AABBEINRRRTW rabbit warren
AABBEIORRTVY abbreviatory
AABBELMOORTT Alberto Tomba
AABBFHOOORTY a broth of a boy
AABBHIIILTTY habitability
AABBIILNRRSU sublibrarian
AABBKKNOOPSS bank pass book
AABCCCDEIIOO oboe di caccia
AABCCCDIIISS abscisic acid
AABCCCDIILOR carbolic acid
AABCCCDIINOR carbonic acid
AABCCCDIIORS ascorbic acid
AABCCDEIILRT bactericidal
AABCCDEIKNRR crackbrained
AABCCDEILLSY decasyllabic
AABCCDELMMOO accommodable
AABCCDHLRTYY brachydactyl
AABCCDHORRST scratchboard
AABCCDIINOTU butanoic acid
AABCCEEEMORT Combretaceae
AABCCEEHHINU Chinua Achebe
AABCCEEHLNRT carte blanche
AABCCEEKKPSY backspace key
AABCCEEKLLRT black treacle
AABCCEELNPTU unacceptable
AABCCEELORST obstacle race
AABCCEENRRST breast cancer
AABCCEGLLNOT cobalt glance
AABCCEHHLPRY brachycephal
AABCCEHIINNT china cabinet
AABCCEHINOPR cancerphobia
AABCCEHOORTT tobacco-heart
AABCCEIINNSV Sabin vaccine
AABCCEILLLNU incalculable
AABCCEILLMOV clavicembalo
AABCCEILMNOR microbalance
AABCCEIMORTY mycobacteria
AABCCEIRRTUU bureaucratic
AABCCEJKMOTT combat jacket
AABCCEKLORTT crack a bottle
AABCCELNORTT contractable
AABCCENOORSU carbonaceous
AABCCFINNORS Francis Bacon
AABCCGIKKNRT backing track
backtracking
AABCCHHIIMPR amphibrachic
AABCCHHNORUY Boyana Church
AABCCHIINSTU antibacchius
AABCCIKLLOPT block capital
AABCCILLLNUY incalculably
AABCCILOOPRS carbolic soap
AABCCINRSTTU subantarctic
AABCCKLNRRTU blackcurrant
AABCCLNOOPTT tobacco plant
AABCDDDEEKLS saddlebacked
AABCDDEHIKMV David Beckham
AABCDDEJLORS Jacob's ladder
AABCDDEKLRRW bladderwrack
AABCDDEKLRST straddleback
AABCDDGINORR boarding card
AABCDDIILNRR cardinal-bird
AABCDDIKLMNO black diamond
AABCDEEEKLPY black-eyed pea
AABCDEEFLLNU balanced flue
AABCDEEHKLRT black-hearted
AABCDEEIILNR ineradicable
AABCDEEILLPS displaceable
AABCDEEKORRR break a record
AABCDEELLLNW well-balanced
AABCDEELLLSY decasyllable
AABCDEELLNRT ballet-dancer
AABCDEELLRTU Albert Claude
AABCDEELNNSU unascendable
AABCDEELRTTU trabeculated
AABCDEGGNNOS bacon-and-eggs
eggs-and-bacon
AABCDEGHIRTW with bad grace
AABCDEGIKLSV black-visaged
AABCDEGIKNNR breakdancing
AABCDEGILNNT table-dancing
AABCDEGINNRV Dancing Brave
AABCDEGLNSUV Vulcan's badge
AABCDEHIINRT dibranchiate
AABCDEHIKRTY birthday cake
AABCDEHMNORR rhabdomancer
AABCDEHNNRST bandersnatch
AABCDEHORRTY carbohydrate
AABCDEIILNRY ineradicably
AABCDEILORUV vocabularied
AABCDEINOSTU subdiaconate
AABCDEKNRSSW backwardness
AABCDELOPPRR clapperboard
AABCDELRSTTY abstractedly
AABCDENOPRSW bow and scrape
AABCDENRRRTU currant bread
AABCDEOPRRRS scraperboard
AABCDFHKNORT back and forth
AABCDGGIOORS braggadocios✧
AABCDGHIMNSU handbag music
AABCDGHINRTU Dutch bargain
AABCDGHKLRTU black draught
AABCDGIKLMOR block diagram
AABCDGINNORT carbon dating
AABCDGINORST broadcasting
AABCDGKLLRUY blackguardly

AABCDGLNRRSU Carl Sandburg
AABCDHINOOPR Branchiopoda
AABCDHINORSU subarachnoid
AABCDHIOPSTT dispatch-boat
AABCDIILLLOY diabolically
AABCDIMNORSY barodynamics
AABCDKLMRSTU black mustard
AABCDKMNOOSW backwoodsman
AABCDKMNORSW backswordman
AABCEEEEKPRR peace-breaker
AABCEEEELLRS cable release
AABCEEEFFILN ineffaceable
AABCEEEGHLNX exchangeable
AABCEEEGHLRR rechargeable
AABCEEEHLLNW balance wheel
AABCEEEHLNST balance sheet
AABCEEEHLRRS researchable
AABCEEEILMOR Bromeliaceae
AABCEEELORTT ebracteolate
AABCEEEMQRSU macaberesque
AABCEEENORTT betacarotene
AABCEEFFILNY ineffaceably
AABCEEFIPRRT prefabricate
AABCEEGGPRRT carpetbagger
AABCEEGHLNNU unchangeable
AABCEEGHLNXY exchangeably
AABCEEGIINNO Bignoniaceae
AABCEEGKLNRT angle bracket
AABCEEHIKNRR chain-breaker
AABCEEHILNNT in the balance
AABCEEHILNUV unachievable
AABCEEHILRRS Isabel Archer
AABCEEHLMNRT merchantable
AABCEEHLNRSU unsearchable
AABCEEHLOPRR reproachable
AABCEEIKMNRT cabinetmaker
AABCEEIKMNYZ Mackenzie Bay
AABCEEILLMMT emblematical
AABCEEILMNSS amicableness
AABCEEIMRRRR barrier cream
AABCEEINORTX exacerbation
AABCEEINOSST Sebastian Coe
AABCEEJNNORS Arne Jacobsen
AABCEEKLNPST space blanket
AABCEEKLSSTU basket clause
AABCEEKNNOPS pease-bannock
AABCEELLLMPR Earl Campbell
AABCEELLLNRU unrecallable
AABCEELLNOOT oblanceolate
AABCEELLNPSS placableness
AABCEELLNSSS scalableness
AABCEELLORRT correlatable
AABCEELMNOTU uncomeatable
AABCEELMNSSU assemblaunce
AABCEENNOSST as best one can
AABCEFGILNNR Belgian franc
AABCEFHIKLNW finback whale
AABCEFHLLORT bachelor flat
AABCEFHLMORT float chamber
AABCEFIILLSS classifiable
AABCEFIILLTY beatifically
AABCEFIILNST sanctifiable
AABCEFINORRS Franco Baresi
AABCEFKLORRT Roberta Flack
AABCEFLNRSTU blast furnace
AABCEFNNNORT Anne Bancroft
AABCEGGHINRR bring a charge
AABCEGHILMTW Abel Magwitch
AABCEGHILPTY bathypelagic
AABCEGHLLORS global search
AABCEGHLNNUY unchangeably
AABCEGHMNORR chamber organ
AABCEGIKLNNR clearing bank
AABCEGILLMNR all-embracing
AABCEGILLNOU incoagulable
AABCEGILLNTV galvanic belt
AABCEGILORRT carriage bolt
AABCEGLMMRUU album Graecum
AABCEGLNRRUU gubernacular
AABCEHHNOOPR arachnophobe
AABCEHIILNRT incharitable
AABCEHIILRST Hebraistical
AABCEHIILTTY teachability
AABCEHIIMNPS amphisbaenic
AABCEHILNRTU uncharitable
AABCEHIRRRRS crash barrier
AABCEHKLLOPR alpha-blocker
AABCEHKLNPRT Black Panther
AABCEHKMNNRT merchant bank
AABCEHKMPRRS spark chamber
AABCEHKNOPTT pat on the back
AABCEHLMNORS elasmobranch
AABCEHLNNSTU unstanchable
AABCEHLNRSUY unsearchably
AABCEHLRRRSY Charles Barry
AABCEHMNORRT Bonham Carter
Bonham-Carter
AABCEHNNRRTW bench-warrant
AABCEHOPRSSU habeas corpus
AABCEIIILPST capabilities
AABCEIILLNPP inapplicable
AABCEIILMMRS bicameralism
AABCEIILMNOT alembication
AABCEIILMRST bicameralist
AABCEIILPPRT participable
AABCEIILRTTY traceability
AABCEIINOORT anaerobiotic
AABCEIJLLNOY Jacobean lily
AABCEILLLLTY balletically
AABCEILLNPPU unapplicable
AABCEILLNSUV vulcanisable
AABCEILLNUVZ vulcanizable
AABCEILLTTUV cultivatable
AABCEILMNNOT contaminable
AABCEILMNOPR incomparable
AABCEILMORRT barometrical
AABCEILMORVW microwavable
AABCEILNNOST sanctionable
AABCEILNPSUZ uncapsizable
AABCEILNRSST bass clarinet
AABCEILRSSSY absciss layer
AABCEIMNNNOR cinnamon bear

AABCEINRRSTT scatterbrain
AABCEIORSTTT bacteriostat
AABCEKLQRRTU black-quarter
AABCEKNORTTU back to nature
back-to-nature
AABCELNNORTU Barcelona nut
AABCENORRSTY carry one's bat
AABCENRSSSTT abstractness
AABCFHINOOPR francophobia✧
AABCFHKMNNRU Frank Buchman
AABCFIILNRSY Francis Baily
AABCFIKLLSSY black salsify
AABCFILORSTU subfactorial
AABCFKLLNOPU fall back upon
AABCFLNOORTU confabulator
AABCGHHPRRYY brachygraphy
AABCGHIILOPR biographical
AABCGHIKRSTT back straight
AABCGHILNOOP anglophobiac✧
AABCGHKLLNOY by a long chalk
AABCGHNOPPRW Cappagh-brown
AABCGIKLNPPS back-slapping
AABCGIKNRSTT backstarting
AABCGILLLSUY subglacially
AABCGILLOOTT battological
AABCHHIIMOOP aichmophobia
AABCHIILTTWY watchability
AABCHIIMORTT microhabitat
AABCHIINOOTT cohabitation
AABCHILMNSTY Scythian lamb
AABCHILNRTUY uncharitably
AABCHIMNNORT cinnabar moth
AABCHLNRSTTU Stuart Blanch
AABCIIILNPTY incapability
AABCIIKLNPTT Paint It Black
AABCIILLNPPY inapplicably
AABCIILLPRSY parisyllabic
AABCIILMRSST strabismical
AABCIILRTTTY tractability
AABCIIMMNORT timbromaniac
AABCIKLNRSSU Black Russian
AABCIKMNOTTU back-mutation
AABCILLLLSYY syllabically
AABCILLNNOTU National Club
AABCILMNOPRY incomparably
AABCILMNOSST saltimbancos
AABCILOOPPSS Pablo Picasso
AABCILRRSUUU subauricular
AABCIMNOSSUZ scazon iambus
AABCIMOPRRSU coram paribus
AABCINORSTUU subarcuation
AABCLLOOORRT collaborator
AABCLNORSTUY constabulary
AABCMNNNOOTT non-combatant
AABCORRRTUYY carry your bat
AABDDDEEILNR addle-brained
AABDDDEEIMTY it may be added
AABDDDENRRST standardbred✧
AABDDEEEHRTW bearded wheat
AABDDEEEIKRR Baedeker raid
AABDDEEILLLN dead-ball line
AABDDEEKNRVY Vandyke beard
AABDDEELNNRS bladder senna
AABDDEFOORRT board of trade✧
AABDDEGLORSU Douglas Bader
AABDDEHHNRST hand's breadth
AABDDEHLLMOY hebdomadally
AABDDEHORRTW draw the board
AABDDEILLMVY David Bellamy
AABDDEILMNTU mandibulated
AABDDELLNOOW downloadable
AABDDELMNORS old man's beard
AABDDGHORRTU draughtboard
AABDDGINORRW drawing board
AABDDIJNRTTU adjutant bird
AABDDLMNOOTZ zalambdodont
AABDEEEGILRS disagreeable
AABDEEEKLLNO Leo Baekeland
AABDEEELNRSS readableness
AABDEEELPRRT Peter Abelard
AABDEEFLNOST leaf-nosed bat
AABDEEGILRSY disagreeably
AABDEEGINPTV paving debate
AABDEEGINRTU drainage-tube
AABDEEGMORSS message board
AABDEEHHRRSY haberdashery
AABDEEHLRTTW draw the table
AABDEEHORRTW weatherboard
AABDEEIILRSV adverbialise
AABDEEIILRVZ adverbialize
AABDEEILMNTT maiden battle
AABDEEILRTTX extraditable
AABDEEIRRRRT trade barrier
AABDEEJLMRSY James Bradley
AABDEEKLNRTU undertakable
AABDEEKORRST skateboarder
AABDEELLLMOT labelled atom
AABDEELLNSSU laudableness
AABDEELMNNSS damnableness
AABDEELNOPRS leopard's-bane
AABDEELNORSS adorableness
AABDEELNORTU unelaborated
AABDEEMNORTY Notre Dame Bay
AABDEEMORRSU board-measure
AABDEENNPRWY brandy-pawnee
AABDEENOORVV over and above
AABDEENRSSTU buenas tardes
AABDEFGILLMO balm of Gilead
AABDEFILLNOS Island of Elba
AABDEFKNRRST banker's draft
AABDEFLLNNOR flannelboard
AABDEGGLNOST Gladstone bag
AABDEGGLNOUY body language
AABDEGHINORT bring to a head
AABDEGIIMSTU disambiguate
AABDEGIJMORR brigade major
AABDEGIKNORW wakeboarding
AABDEGILNRTW drawing-table
AABDEGLLMNOR balladmonger
AABDEGLNNORY yard-long bean
AABDEGLOOSSU blood sausage
AABDEGMRRSSU Bermuda grass

AABDEHHIRRST hair's-breadth
AABDEHHORSTY by a short head
AABDEHIINSTT absinthiated
AABDEHILRRTW bridal wreath
AABDEHINTTUU unhabituated
AABDEHLNOSUW unshadowable
AABDEHRRSTTW straw-breadth
AABDEIILNRST distrainable
AABDEIJLMNSW James Baldwin
AABDEILLLOSW disallowable
AABDEILLNOSS ballon d'essai
AABDEILNNOTT national debt
AABDEILRSTTT bastard title
AABDEIMNNTUY unanimated by
AABDEIMNORRS dermabrasion
AABDEIMOPPST paedobaptism
AABDEIMRRSSS disembarrass
AABDEINOPPRT pipe and tabor
AABDEIOPPSTT paedobaptist
AABDELLNOSSU sound as a bell
AABDELMORTUY deambulatory
AABDELNNOPRU unpardonable
AABDELOPRRST plasterboard
AABDELOPRTTW draw-top table
AABDEMNORRRY Raymond Barre
AABDENNNOPRT broad pennant
AABDENNORTUV overabundant
AABDENRRRSSY Barry Sanders
AABDEPRSSTTY bastard types
AABDFFIILNNS Baffin Island
AABDFIMNORRW man-of-war bird
AABDGHINORSW washing-board
AABDGIILNORS boardsailing
sailboarding
AABDGIINNOST bastinadoing
AABDGILNNSST sandblasting
AABDGINOPRSS boarding pass
AABDHKNORRSU Honduras bark
AABDHLNNRSSU slash-and-burn
AABDHMMOORSY rhabdomyomas
AABDIIIINSTV absit invidia
AABDIIILLTTY dilatability
AABDIIILSTVY advisability
AABDIILMNRTY military band
AABDIILNSTUU Tubuai Island
AABDILNORRSX Sir Arnold Bax
AABDIMOOPSSY boomps-a-daisy
AABDINOOTTUY autoantibody
AABDLLNORTYY brand loyalty
AABDLMNNOORR Marlon Brando
AABDLNNOPRUY unpardonably
AABDLOORRSTU bardolatrous
AABEEEEIKLMN make a beeline
AABEEEFKMRRR frame-breaker
AABEEEGGLLTT gateleg table
AABEEEGHRRTT the Great Bear
AABEEEGIKMRR image breaker
AABEEEGLMPRS gas-permeable
AABEEEGLMRSS reassemblage
AABEEEGLTVWX vegetable wax
AABEEEHHLRTT heather-bleat
AABEEEHKRRRT heartbreaker
AABEEEHNOSVV heavens above
AABEEEILLPRR irrepealable
AABEEELLNPRU unrepealable
AABEEELLNRUV unrevealable
AABEEELLNSSS saleableness
AABEEELMNNSS amenableness
AABEEELMNRUV maneuverable
AABEEELMNRWY Wembley Arena
AABEEELMNSST tameableness
AABEEELNPRTU unrepeatable
AABEEELRRTTU terebratulae
AABEEEMORSUV above measure
AABEEFFLORST afforestable
AABEEFGIKNRS safe-breaking
AABEEFGILRRR irrefragable
AABEEFGILRRU Gabriel Fauré
AABEEFGLORSS A Glass of Beer
AABEEFHINRRT feather-brain
AABEEFILMNST manifestable
AABEEFJLNOTT Battle of Jena
AABEEFKRSSTT breakfast-set
AABEEFLLRSTY self-betrayal
AABEEFLMOSTV movable feast
AABEEFLNRRST transferable
AABEEGGGRSTU subaggregate
AABEEGGHOPRY Geographe Bay
AABEEGGLMORT mortgageable
AABEEGHHRRTT gather breath
AABEEGHIMRTY Hermitage Bay
AABEEGHNNORT groan beneath
AABEEGIILRTY agreeability
AABEEGILMNST magnetisable
AABEEGILMNTZ magnetizable
AABEEGILNNPT panel beating
AABEEGIMNORR marriage-bone
AABEEGIRRSTT Gastarbeiter
AABEEGLNNTUW Blaenau Gwent
AABEEGLNOUVY unvoyageable
AABEEGLRSTUW blue water gas
AABEEGMNOTUU beaumontague
AABEEHIILRTT rehabilitate
AABEEHILLSTW the Wallabies
AABEEHLMQRSU Alhambresque
AABEEHLNRRTY learn by heart
AABEEHLOSTTV above the salt
AABEEHLRRSTY breathalyser
AABEEHLRRTYZ breathalyzer
AABEEHNPSTTT beat the pants
AABEEIIKLRST Lake Tiberias
AABEEIILLRRS irrealisable
AABEEIILLRRZ irrealizable
AABEEIILPRRR irrepairable
AABEEIKKRRST break a strike
AABEEILLLNPP inappellable
AABEEILLNRSU unrealisable
AABEEILLNRUZ unrealizable
AABEEILLOPRT parietal lobe
AABEEILLPRRY irrepealably
AABEEILMMRSU immeasurable
AABEEILMNOTT antimetabole

AABEEILMRRSS Lesser Bairam
AABEEILNPRRU unrepairable
AABEEILNPRSS inseparables
AABEEILNRRST restrainable
AABEEILNRSSV variableness
AABEEILPTTTU Tibet Plateau
AABEEILRRRRY barrier layer
AABEEIMMRRRT Marie Rambert
AABEEINNNRUV Aneurin Bevan
AABEEINRRTTV Invertebrata
AABEEINRSSSV abrasiveness
AABEEKLLRTTW Bakewell tart
AABEEKLMNRRU unremarkable
AABEEKLMNRTU unmarketable
AABEELLMPPRY Bramley apple
AABEELLMRSTT ballet-master
AABEELLNPPSS palpableness
AABEELLNSSUV valuableness
AABEELMNNRST table manners
AABEELMNORUV manoeuvrable
AABEELMNRSUU unmeasurable
AABEELMPPRRR paper-marbler
AABEELNNNTTU untenantable
AABEELNNORSU unreasonable
AABEELNNOSSU unseasonable
AABEELNNRRUW urban renewal
AABEELNNRSUW unanswerable
AABEELNOSSVW avowableness
AABEELNPSSSS passableness
AABEELNRSTTU subalternate
AABEELOPRSTU pleasure boat
AABEELQRRSTU Albert Square
AABEELRRSTTU terebratulas
AABEELRSSUUX sexual abuser
AABEEMORRRRU armour-bearer
AABEENNRRSTU subterranean
AABEENNRTUUV Buenaventura
AABEENRRTTWY Warren Beatty
AABEERRTTTWY water battery
AABEFFIILRTW water bailiff
AABEFFLLORTU forfaultable
AABEFFLORTUW water buffalo
AABEFGILRRRY irrefragably
AABEFHLMNOTU unfathomable
AABEFIILNOPS saponifiable
AABEFIILNQTU quantifiable
AABEFILLLNOT flabellation
AABEFLLMMNNO non-flammable
AABEFLMOPRSU balsam of Peru
AABEFLMORRRU farm labourer
AABEFLNORUUV unfavourable
AABEFLNRSSTU transfusable
AABEGGILLNTU agglutinable
AABEGGINORRZ organizer-bag
AABEGHIINRRT air-breathing
AABEGHIKNORT oath-breaking
AABEGHIKNRTT breathtaking
AABEGHILLOSU Heliogabalus
AABEGHILNOST Althea Gibson
AABEGHIMNTTW bantamweight
AABEGHIMOPRR iambographer
AABEGHINNRSW weaning brash
AABEGHKMRSTU Hamburg steak
AABEGHLLTWWY wag-by-the-wall
AABEGHNORUUW Auberon Waugh
AABEGIILMNNU unimaginable
AABEGIILNNSS Albigensians
AABEGIINRRTT Great Britain
AABEGIINSSUU Guinea-Bissau
AABEGIJLNOTU Jubilate Agno
AABEGIKKMNST basket-making
AABEGILLOOPY palaebiology
AABEGILMNRTW beam trawling
AABEGILNNSSU unassignable
AABEGILNPPRT table-rapping
AABEGIMNRRSS embarrassing
AABEGIMNRRTT battering-ram
AABEGLLRSSTU Glauber's salt
AABEGLMMOPRR programmable
AABEGLMNORRU gobar numeral
AABEGLNOSTVY Galveston Bay
AABEHIIILNRS Isaiah Berlin
AABEHILLORVY behaviorally
AABEHILNQSUV vanquishable
AABEHILNSSTU habitualness
AABEHILOPSST base hospital
AABEHILORSTU authorisable
AABEHILORTUZ authorizable
AABEHIMMNOPR marimbaphone
AABEHINRRSTT shatter-brain
AABEHLLLMSSY assembly hall
AABEHLLMORST sal alembroth
AABEHLLNOTWY on the wallaby
AABEHLMRRRSW marsh warbler
AABEHLOPPSTU alphabet soup
AABEHLOPRRRU Pearl Harbour
AABEHMNOOTTY bay at the moon
AABEHNNRSUVV Vannevar Bush
AABEIIILLNTY alienability
AABEIIKLLLMW William Blake
AABEIILLLMTY malleability
AABEIILLMNSS Sabellianism
AABEIILLMRST bilateralism
AABEIILLNRTY learnability
AABEIILLORST isobilateral
AABEIILLRTTY alterability
AABEIILPRRTY reparability
AABEIILPRSTY separability
AABEIILRRRST barristerial
AABEIINOORSS anaerobiosis
AABEIINRRTTV Vera Brittain
AABEIJLNNRSU Julian Barnes
AABEIKLMNSTU unmistakable
AABEIKNPRRUV Peruvian bark
AABEILLMNNTU in all but name
AABEILLMNTVY ambivalently
AABEILLNRRTU turbellarian
AABEILLNRSSW Barnes Wallis
AABEILLPRRTY Liberal Party
AABEILMMRSUY immeasurably
AABEILNPRRST transpirable
AABEINNOPRWY binary weapon

AABEINOPRRTU bona peritura
AABEINSSTTTU substantiate
AABEJKLLMMTU Kemal Jumblat
AABEKLNPRSTY blanket spray
AABELLMNNRTY R M Ballantyne
AABELMMNOSTU somnambulate
AABELMNOOSSS beso las manos
AABELMNORRTT Robert Altman
AABELMNRSTTU transmutable
AABELMNRSUUY unmeasurably
AABELMOPRRTU perambulator
AABELMQRRSTU lamb's quarter
AABELNNORSUY unreasonably
AABELNNOSSUY unseasonably
AABELNNRSTTU subalternant
AABELNNRSUWY unanswerably
AABELNOPRSST transposable
AABELNSTTTUU unstatutable
AABELORRSTTY solar battery
AABEORRSSTUV à bras ouverts
AABFFGLORSSU buffalo-grass
AABFGGHIKOOO Book of Haggai
AABFHIIKOOOS Book of Isaiah
AABFHLMNOTUY unfathomably
AABFIILLMMTY flammability
AABFIILNORRT infraorbital
AABFLLMNOTYY flamboyantly
AABFLLMOOSTU balsam of Tolu
AABFLMNORTUU funambulator
AABFLNORUUVY unfavourably
AABGGIILLMRW William Bragg
AABGHHIOOPPR graphophobia
AABGHIINNRSW brainwashing
AABGHIKKNRSS basking shark
AABGHILLNOOP Bologna phial
AABGIIILNOUV bougainvilia
AABGIIILNTVY navigability
AABGIILLNOOT obligational
AABGIILLNORY aboriginally
AABGIILLNRTZ trailblazing
AABGIILMNNUY unimaginably
AABGILLMOOST glioblastoma
AABGILNORSUV labour-saving
AABGILNRSSTT star-blasting
AABHHIMOOPPS phasmophobia
AABHIIILNOTT habilitation
AABHIIILRSSZ bilharziasis
AABHIIINNOTT inhabitation
AABHIIKNRTYZ Yitzhak Rabin
AABHIILNNRTY labyrinthian
AABHIILOOPRU ailurophobia
AABHIKMNORSU Hosni Mubarak
AABHINORRSTU subarrhation
AABHINOSSTTU subhastation
AABIIILMNTUY unamiability
AABIIILNOSST assibilation
AABIIILNRTTY trainability
AABIIINQRTUU ubiquitarian
AABIIJMNOSSV Jonas Savimbi
AABIILLLOTWY allowability
AABIILLNSTUY unsalability
AABIILNNNTTU tintinnabula
AABIILNOORTY abolitionary
AABIILORSSTT stabilisator
AABIILORSTTZ stabilizator
AABIILRSTTUY saturability
AABIINNOORTT anti-abortion
AABIINNORSTU urbanisation
AABIINNORTUZ urbanization
AABIINOORRST arborisation
AABIINOORRTZ arborization
AABIKLMNSTUY unmistakably
AABILLLNOORT trial balloon
AABILLMRSUXY submaxillary
AABILLNOSTTU blastulation
AABILMNOORRS ribosomal RNA
AABILNPRRSUY binary pulsar
AABILNSSTTUV substantival
AABILOPRRSTU supraorbital
AABIMNORSTTU masturbation
AABINOOPRRTY probationary
AABLLLOOPSTT postal ballot
AABLLMMOSUXY xylobalsamum
AABLMMNNOSTU somnambulant
AABLMMNORSUY somnambulary
AABLMNRSTTUY transmutably
AABLNSTTTUUY unstatutably
AABLORRRSTUY barratrously
AABMNNOOTTUW man-about-town
AABMORRSTTUY masturbatory
AACCCDEEEMOR crème de cacao
AACCCDEHIMNR card mechanic
AACCCDIIIMNN cinnamic acid
AACCCDIIINOT itaconic acid
AACCCEEGHRSS access charge
AACCCEEHILMM Chemical Mace
AACCCEEHILTT catechetical
AACCCEEKMRRR cream cracker
AACCCEENNPTU unacceptance
AACCCEFIINOP Pacific Ocean
AACCCEGNORYY gynaecocracy
AACCCEHHKNOY hackney coach
AACCCEHILNOT coelacanthic
AACCCEHIRSTT catachrestic
AACCCEILRSSS classic races
AACCCEIRSSTT scare tactics
AACCCEKORRST stock car race
AACCCHILNOOP cacophonical
AACCCIOSSTTU catacoustics
AACCDDEHIIRS disaccharide
AACCDDEHKLNY cack-handedly
AACCDDHHNOOR doch-an-dorach
AACCDDIILLTY didactically
AACCDDIIOTTU autodidactic
AACCDDINORST disaccordant
AACCDEEFFNOT Coanda effect
AACCDEEFHHTT hatchet-faced
AACCDEEHHIKS sick headache
AACCDEEHKRTW cracked wheat
AACCDEEHLNRS Charles Dance
AACCDEEHMRRT dreamcatcher
AACCDEEIMORS ice-cream soda

AACCDEELLNTY cyclandelate
AACCDEFILSTU fasciculated
AACCDEFLOSVY self-advocacy
AACCDEGIMNRT magnetic card
AACCDEHHPRRU church-parade
AACCDEHIINOT ethanoic acid
AACCDEHILMOT machicolated
AACCDEHILTXY hexadactylic
AACCDEHINORS archdiocesan
AACCDEHIPSST dispatch case
AACCDEHNORRY archdeaconry
AACCDEIIILNT dialectician
AACCDEIILOPT apodeictical
AACCDEIKNOPT action-packed
AACCDEILLNTY accidentally
AACCDEILMORT democratical
AACCDEINNTUV unvaccinated
AACCDEIRTUUV curvicaudate
AACCDEKMPUUV vacuum-packed
AACCDELLNRSU Della-Cruscan
AACCDELLNTUU uncalculated
AACCDELORSTW Cawdor Castle
AACCDEMNORSS random access
AACCDENOPRTY pedantocracy
AACCDFKNNORY Fanny Cradock
AACCDGHIPRRS graphics card
AACCDGIILMTU glutamic acid
AACCDGINRRRY card-carrying
AACCDHIILNOR diachronical
AACCDIIILMPT palmitic acid
AACCDIIINOOP iopanoic acid
AACCDIIKPSTY disk capacity
AACCDIILNOTU claudication
AACCDIINNNOO nonanoic acid
AACCDIIOPRTT catadioptric
AACCDILLLTYY dactylically
AACCDILNNOSV volcanic sand
AACCDLLOORRY dollarocracy
AACCDLMORTYY macrodactyly
AACCDLNORTUU Count Dracula
AACCDMMOOORT accommodator
AACCEEEFIKOP a piece of cake
AACCEEEHIPRY Hypericaceae
AACCEEEILRTV accelerative
AACCEEEKLLNS alkalescence
AACCEEELMMRR crème caramel
AACCEEELPSSU escape clause
AACCEEGHIMNN Ian McGeechan
AACCEEHIILMN Michael Caine
AACCEEHILNNP anencephalic
AACCEEHIRRST characterise
AACCEEHIRRTZ characterize
AACCEEHMPPRR camp-preacher
AACCEEHNOPYY Cyanophyceae
AACCEEHRRSTT character set
AACCEEIILLPR capercaillie
AACCEEIILPRZ capercailzie
AACCEEILNORT acceleration
AACCEEILPSTT space lattice
AACCEEILRRTT recalcitrate
AACCEEKLLNSY alkalescency
AACCEELMMNTU calceamentum
AACCEELORRTY acceleratory
AACCEELPPSSU space capsule
AACCEELPRRTU receptacular
AACCEENRSSTU accurateness
AACCEERSSTTU Easter cactus
AACCEFFRRSTU surface-craft
AACCEFGIKNRS safe-cracking
AACCEFHLRRTU characterful
AACCEFILLORY Calyciflorae
AACCEGHIILMR agrichemical
AACCEGHIILPR archipelagic
AACCEGHILMOR agrochemical
AACCEGHLORRY charcoal grey
AACCEGIILMNR claiming race
AACCEGILLLNV galvanic cell
AACCEGILORSS social graces
AACCEHHIILRR hierarchical
AACCEHHILNTT chalcanthite
AACCEHHINPTY Cape hyacinth
AACCEHIIMNRV vice-chairman
AACCEHILLMNO melancholiac
AACCEHILLMNY mechanically
AACCEHILMNNU unmechanical
AACCEHILMOPY hypocalcemia
AACCEHILNORT anchoretical
AACCEHILORTT theocratical
AACCEHILPRTY archetypical
AACCEHILRRTT tetrarchical
AACCEHIMNNOT technomaniac
AACCEHIMORTT metathoracic
AACCEHIMPRTU pharmaceutic
AACCEHIMRRST characterism
AACCEHINORRT chain reactor
AACCEHLMNORT coal merchant
AACCEHLMNTYY calycanthemy
AACCEHLMOPRY macrocephaly
AACCEHLNORRS Rachel Carson
AACCEIILLNRT anticlerical
AACCEIILMRST acclimatiser
AACCEIILMRTZ acclimatizer
AACCEIIMRSUU amicus curiae
AACCEIKLOPST peacock's tail
AACCEIKNOOST take occasion
AACCEILLLMNR Carmen Callil
AACCEILLMSTU miscalculate
AACCEILLNNOT cancellation
AACCEILLNOSS neoclassical
AACCEILLOPPT apoplectical
AACCEILLOPSU capillaceous
AACCEILLPRSS preclassical
AACCEILLRSTU sella turcica
AACCEILLSTTY ecstatically
AACCEILMNOPS complaisance
AACCEILMOOST osteomalacic
AACCEILMTUUV accumulative
AACCEILNORVY clairvoyance
AACCEILNRRTT recalcitrant
AACCEILNRTUY inaccurately
AACCEILNTTUY accentuality
AACCEILSTUVY accusatively

AACCEIMRSSTT smear tactics
AACCEINNORST transoceanic
AACCEINNOTTU accentuation
AACCEINOORTV coacervation
AACCEINORRRT incarcerator
AACCEINORSTT caster action
AACCEIOPRTVY overcapacity
AACCEKNPRRRW prawn cracker
AACCELLOORSU corallaceous
AACCELLRRSTY crystal clear
AACCELNNOOPV plano-concave
AACCELNNORSU canon secular
AACCELNNRSTY transcalency
AACCENOOPSUY apocynaceous
AACCEORSSTUY styracaceous
AACCFIIINOPT pacification
AACCFIILMOPT fait accompli
AACCFIINPRST transpacific
AACCFIIOPRTY pacificatory
AACCFIIORRST scarificator
AACCFINNORSS San Francisco
AACCGHHIPRTY tachygraphic
AACCGHHLOPRY chalcography
AACCGHIILLOR oligarchical
AACCGHIILLPR calligraphic
AACCGHILOPTY phagocytical
AACCGHIOPRRT cartographic
AACCGIILMORT tragicomical
AACCGIILNSST actinic glass
AACCGILLOOPR carpological
AACCGILLOORT cartological
AACCGILLOOST scatological
AACCHHIILNOR Archilochian
AACCHIIINRTT antirachitic
AACCHIILMSST schismatical
AACCHIILNORT anchoritical
AACCHIILNOTT anticatholic
AACCHIILTTUX Ixtaccihuatl
AACCHIINNNOT cachinnation
AACCHIINRSTY saccharinity
AACCHILLLOTY catholically
AACCHILLOPRT phallocratic
AACCHILLOSST scholastical
AACCHIMNOPRT panchromatic
AACCHIMOOPRT apochromatic
AACCHINNORTY cachinnatory
AACCHIOPRSTT catastrophic
AACCHIOQRTTU a quattr'occhi
AACCHJKLNORT Jack Charlton
AACCHLLNORYY acronychally
AACCHLRSTTWY watch crystal
AACCHMMRRTYY Mary McCarthy
AACCHOPPRSUY pachycarpous
AACCIIILPSTT capitalistic
AACCIILLLMTY climatically
AACCIILLMSSS classicalism
AACCIILLSSST classicalist
AACCIILLSSTY classicality
AACCIILMORTT timocratical
AACCIILMPRST practicalism
AACCIILMRSST critical mass
AACCIILNRTUY inarticulacy
AACCIILNTTTY Atlantic City
AACCIILOPPRT paroccipital
AACCIILPRSTT practicalist
AACCIILPRTTY practicality
AACCIINNOPRR Capricornian
AACCIIORRSTT aristocratic
AACCIIRRSTTU caricaturist
AACCIJKKLNSU Jack Nicklaus
AACCIKKORSTY kakistocracy
AACCILLLNOVY volcanically
AACCILLNNOOP plano-conical
AACCILLNOOSY occasionally
AACCILLNORTY narcotically
AACCILLORSTY acrostically
Socratically
AACCILLOSTUY acoustically
AACCILMNNOOT conclamation
AACCILMNOTUU accumulation
AACCILMNPSUY scapulimancy
AACCILMOPRSS sarcoplasmic
AACCILNOOPTU occupational
AACCILNORVYY clairvoyancy
AACCILNRSTUU lunar caustic
AACCILOOPPRS laparoscopic
AACCILOPRSST capital cross
AACCIMNOPSTY accompanyist
AACCINOORSSY acrocyanosis
AACCINOORSTT castor action
AACCINOPRSTY pantisocracy
AACCIORRSTTT stratocratic
AACCLMNOPSUY scapulomancy
AACCLMOOSTTY Cyclostomata
AACCLNORRTTU contractural
AACCLORRSSVY Calvary cross
AACCOOOSSTTT coast-to-coast
AACCOQRSTTUY squattocracy
AACDDDEEHLOR dodecahedral
AACDDDEHIISV David Daiches
AACDDDHIKMUV David Duckham
AACDDDIIORRV David Ricardo
AACDDEEEHLTY acetaldehyde
AACDDEEFHNOT dance of death
AACDDEEHIMRR Richard Meade
AACDDEEHKLLS saddle hackle
AACDDEEIMPSV David Campese
AACDDEGILLOO logodaedalic
AACDDEGINNOY dodecagynian
AACDDEHNNOST at second hand
AACDDEIIJTUV adjudicative
AACDDEIILNOT dedicational
AACDDEIILORT dedicatorial
AACDDEIKLLRV David L Clarke
AACDDEILMNNR carnal-minded
AACDDEIMOOPR Macropodidae
AACDDEIORRTX dextrocardia
AACDDELOORTV Lord Advocate
AACDDGGHILNR Claddagh ring
AACDDGGLNNOO Donald Coggan
AACDDGIIKRRV David Garrick
AACDDIIJNOTU adjudication

AACDDIIKNORT Anita Roddick
AACDDIKMNNRU mandarin duck
AACDDLNORSTY Scotland Yard
AACDDNORSSTT standard cost
AACDEEEFFINT decaffeinate
AACDEEEHHRSZ Schéhérazade
AACDEEEHLRRS Charles Reade
AACDEEEHRRTT earth-created
AACDEEEIILMR Mircea Eliade
AACDEEELLPTV valet de place
AACDEEFFNORR force and fear
AACDEEFGLRRS Gerald Scarfe
AACDEEFHLMSY shamefacedly
AACDEEFHNORS Dean of Arches
AACDEEGHILMR Michael Grade
AACDEEGHINRS scare-heading
AACDEEGHLNNO hendecagonal
AACDEEGHLNTU langue de chat
AACDEEHIMSTT semi-attached
AACDEEHINSTZ zantedeschia✧
AACDEEHLLRTY Ely Cathedral
AACDEEHLNSST scandal sheet
AACDEEHNPSTT stand the pace
AACDEEIILLPR pedicellaria
AACDEEIILPST decapitalise
AACDEEIILPTZ decapitalize
AACDEEIKLRTT racket-tailed
AACDEEILLNNR calendar-line
AACDEEILLPRV pedal-clavier
AACDEEILMMNT medicamental
AACDEEILMNST maiden castle
AACDEEILMRVY devil-may-care
AACDEEILMSSU Luís de Camães
AACDEEILNOST de-escalation
AACDEEILNPRS lance prisade
AACDEEILNPSS displeasance
AACDEEILNRTT intercalated
AACDEEILRTTU dearticulate
AACDEEIMMSSU cuisse-madame
AACDEEIMNRTT readmittance
AACDEEJKLNNR clean and jerk
AACDEELNPTTY pentadactyle
AACDEELNRSTW candle-waster
AACDEFFILNNR Ann Radcliffe
AACDEFHISSTU fidus Achates
AACDEFHMORSY Marsh of Decay
AACDEFIILPTX fixed capital
AACDEFIKNRRS Francis Drake
AACDEFILLNRY Finlay Calder
AACDEFIMNRSU Francis Maude
AACDEGGHNNOR egg-and-anchor
AACDEGGINNTY dating agency
AACDEGILLNNP landing-place
AACDEGILLNNY cleaning lady
AACDEGILLOOP paedological
AACDEGILMNOY geodynamical
AACDEGILMORY cardiomegaly
AACDEGILNNOU Languedocian
AACDEGILNNPR candle-paring
AACDEGILNOTU longicaudate
AACDEGIMNNRY dynamic range
AACDEGINNPRS parascending
AACDEGLMNORT central dogma
AACDEGLNNRRY grand larceny
AACDEGLNOPRR drop a clanger
AACDEGLNOTUU uncatalogued
AACDEHHIMORT Hemichordata
AACDEHHLRTTY Lady Thatcher
AACDEHIILOPP paedophiliac
AACDEHIINNRT cantharidine
AACDEHILLLRY heraldically
AACDEHIMNRTY diathermancy
AACDEHINORRT ride at anchor
AACDEHJKPPRS Jack Sheppard
AACDEHLMOSUY achlamydeous
AACDEHLOPRRT procathedral
AACDEHLORRTT tetrachordal
AACDEHNOPPRU unapproached
AACDEHORRRTW Howard Carter
AACDEHPPRSST cash-strapped
AACDEIIIPRST parasiticide
AACDEIILLMSY salicylamide
AACDEIILMNOS Laodiceanism
AACDEIILMNTU adminiculate
AACDEIILNNRX cranial index
AACDEIILNORT dilaceration
AACDEIILNRTU clairaudient
AACDEIIMRSTY Armistice Day
AACDEIINNORT deracination
AACDEIINNOSS Isaac Dineson
AACDEIINOPTT decapitation
AACDEIINOTTV deactivation
AACDEIIOSSST disassociate
AACDEIJLLTVY adjectivally
AACDEIKMNNNR mandarin neck
AACDEIKNORRT dark reaction
AACDEILLMNOY demoniacally
AACDEILLMOST Camaldolites
AACDEILLNOSW disallowance
AACDEILLNPTY pedantically
AACDEILLPRRY dicarpellary
AACDEILLRSTY ideal crystal
AACDEILMMORT melodramatic
AACDEILNNOOT national code
AACDEILNOPRS lance prisado
AACDEILNOSTT anecdotalist
AACDEILNOSTW in a cold sweat
AACDEILNPPRU appendicular
AACDEIMNORSY aerodynamics
AACDEIMOOSTU diatomaceous
AACDEINNOSSY Ascension Day
Ascension-day
AACDEINNQTUU unacquainted
AACDEINOPSSU sapindaceous
AACDEINOSSTU unassociated
AACDEKKNRRSY knacker's yard
AACDELLLNOTW tallow candle
AACDELLORSTY sacerdotally
AACDELMNRSUU Samuel Cunard
AACDELNPTTYY pentadactyly
AACDELOORSTW draw to a close
AACDELPPRSTU custard apple

AACDELRTTTYY tetradactyly
AACDEMMNOPPR command paper
AACDEMMORSTU costume drama
AACDFFIINOOS afficionados
AACDFFIINRTY affinity card
AACDFGILNNRT landing craft
AACDFGIMNPRT camp-drafting
AACDFHIKNSTT thick and fast
AACDFIIILNNT infanticidal
AACDFJNOORRW Joan Crawford
AACDFLNOPRRU Rudolf Carnap
AACDFORRRRWY carry forward
carry-forward
AACDGGIILMOR logic diagram
AACDGHHOOPRT cathodograph
AACDGHIILTTW digital watch
AACDGHIIOPRR radiographic
AACDGHILNNPU launching-pad
AACDGHILNNRS crash-landing
AACDGHILNNTY land-yachting
AACDGHINNSTY sand-yachting
AACDGHIOPRRY cardiography
AACDGHORRRSS orchard-grass
AACDGIILLOOR radiological
AACDGIILLOOU audiological
AACDGIILRSTU gradualistic
AACDGIIMMPRY magic pyramid
AACDGILLMOTY dogmatically
AACDGILOOPST capital goods
AACDHIILNPRS cardinalship
AACDHIIMNOOR orchidomania
AACDHILMRRUY hydraulic ram
AACDHIMNOORT machairodont
AACDHIMRSSTY Christmas Day
AACDHINOPQRU quadraphonic
AACDHLLNOPSW slow handclap
AACDHLMNORUY dual monarchy
AACDIIINORTV divarication
AACDIILLMOPT diplomatical
AACDIILLNOTY diatonically
AACDIILLSSTY sadistically
AACDIILMNOST disclamation
AACDIILNNRTY tyrannicidal
AACDIILNOOOP Paolo Di Canio
AACDIILNOSTT donatistical
AACDIIMNRSTU Traducianism
AACDIINNORRT doctrinarian
AACDIINORSST dracontiasis
AACDIINORSTU action radius
AACDIINRSTTU Traducianist
AACDIKNNPPSS spick and span
AACDILLNORSY sardonically
AACDILLNSTYY dynastically
AACDILLOPRSY sporadically
AACDILNOORTT traction load
AACDILNOPRTY trypanocidal
AACDIMMNOORT monodramatic
AACDIMOOPRSS radio compass
AACDJLMOOQRU Jacquard loom
AACDKLNRRUYZ Darryl Zanuck
AACDLLNOSSUY scandalously
AACEEEEGINRS Gesneriaceae
AACEEEEHNNPT Nepenthaceae
AACEEEEIQSTU Equisetaceae
AACEEEFGIRRR carriage-free
AACEEEFHLOPS chapel of ease
AACEEEFLMRRX reflex camera
AACEEEFNOSSV save one's face
AACEEEGHNRTX exchange rate
AACEEEGILNRT angelica-tree
AACEEEGIRSTV ergative case
AACEEEGNSTTY estate agency
AACEEEHHOPPY Phaeophyceae
AACEEEHILNRT Heracleitean
AACEEEHKRRTT The Caretaker
AACEEEHLTTTY ethyl acetate
AACEEEHNPRRT Pherecratean
AACEEEILLOVZ Velloziaceae
AACEEEIPRRRT partie carrée
AACEEEIRRSSU air-sea rescue
AACEEEIRRSTT secretariate
AACEEEJMNRTT rejectamenta
AACEEELMMRSY Mary McAleese
AACEEELNORTT Coelenterata
AACEEEMORRST stereocamera
AACEEENPRSVY severance pay
AACEEFFHRTTT after the fact
AACEEFFINOTT affectionate
AACEEFGHKORT take charge of
AACEEFGIORRR forecarriage
AACEEFHILLMO Michael Foale
AACEEFHMNRTY Cathy Freeman
AACEEFHOSTVW have two faces
AACEEFIINRSV venire facias
AACEEFLPRSTU surface plate
AACEEFRRSTUW surface water
AACEEGGILLNO genealogical
AACEEGHILLNT genethliacal
AACEEGHILPST Satchel Paige
AACEEGHIMNTT team teaching
AACEEGHINNRR carragheenin
AACEEGHINORT archegoniate
AACEEGHINPST space-heating
AACEEGHNPRTX part-exchange
AACEEGHOPSTT The Scapegoat
AACEEGIILNRR carriage line
AACEEGIJLNSS Jessica Lange
AACEEGILLNRS clearing sale
AACEEGILNRRV vicar-general
AACEEGIMNPTT magnetic tape
AACEEGIMNRST East Germanic
AACEEGINNRTT cetane rating
AACEEGLLNNRT central angle
AACEEGLLPTTU cattle-plague
AACEEGLMORTT galactometer
AACEEGLMRSSU secular games
AACEEGLNOOPY Polygonaceae
AACEEGLNRTVY travel agency
AACEEHHHMRRT The March Hare
AACEEHHIKRTT take the chair
AACEEHHLLLRS Charles Hallé
AACEEHHLPTTU heptateuchal

AACEEHHRRTTW weather chart
AACEEHIILPRT perichaetial
AACEEHIINSTT aesthetician
AACEEHILLMNO melancholiae
AACEEHILMMOT chamomile tea
AACEEHILMRTX hexametrical
AACEEHILMTTT metathetical
AACEEHIMNORT etheromaniac
AACEEHIMNTTX exanthematic
AACEEHINSSTT anaesthetics
AACEEHINTTTU authenticate
AACEEHKMNRRS snake-charmer
AACEEHLLRSTT chattels-real
AACEEHLMPRST chapel master
spermathecal
AACEEHLNNNST channel stane
AACEEHLNNRTW water-channel
AACEEHLNOPRT another place
AACEEHLNOSST teach a lesson
AACEEHLNOTUV not have a clue
AACEEHLNPTTU pentateuchal
AACEEHLPPSSW cashew apples
AACEEHMNRTTT reattachment
AACEEHMORRTY archaeometry
AACEEHNNPPST happenstance
AACEEIILMSTT metasilicate
AACEEIILNSTT Elias Canetti
AACEEIILPRST recapitalise
AACEEIILPRTZ recapitalize
AACEEIINRSST sectarianise
AACEEIINRSTZ sectarianize
AACEEIIPPRTV appreciative
AACEEIJMRSSY Jeremy Isaacs
AACEEILLLNSW Wallace's line
AACEEILLLSWW Lewis Wallace
AACEEILLMPTT metaleptical
AACEEILLMSTT telesmatical
AACEEILLRRSX Alexis Carrel
AACEEILMPPRS pre-eclampsia
AACEEILMRRUV Maurice Ravel
AACEEILNNRRV cranial nerve
AACEEILNORRT recreational
AACEEILNRRRY Claire Rayner
AACEEILNTTVY vinyl acetate
AACEEILPRSTX extra-special
AACEEILPRTTU recapitulate
AACEEIMMNORS mesoamerican✧
AACEEIMNORRU Euro-American
AACEEIMNRRST Mare Nectaris
AACEEIMRRTTT tartar emetic
AACEEINPRSST paracentesis
AACEEIOPRSTT ectoparasite
AACEEIORSTTW waistcoateer
AACEEIPRRRRS spear carrier
AACEEIPRRSST separatrices
AACEEIRRRRTW Water Carrier
AACEEJKMNRVY every man Jack
AACEEJLLLMSV James Clavell
AACEEJLNOSSS San Jose scale
AACEEJMMNORS James Cameron
AACEEJORRRSS José Carreras
AACEEKLMRTTT cattle market
AACEEKLNQSUY squeaky clean
AACEEKNNRSTU take a scunner
AACEELLLNOTY lanceolately
AACEELMNPRSS plasma screen
AACEELMORSSU Coal Measures
AACEELNRRTUX extranuclear
AACEELNRSTUW nuclear waste
AACEEMNRRTTU trauma centre
AACEEMOPRTTV caveat emptor
AACEENNORTTW connate water
AACEENNPPRTU appurtenance
AACEENNPRRST transparence
AACEENNPRRTT carpenter-ant
AACEENOPRRSW narrow escape
AACEENPRRSSU preassurance
AACEEORRRTTW water reactor
AACEFFILNORV naval officer
AACEFFILRSTV slave traffic
AACEFFMORTTT matter-of-fact
AACEFFORSTTY safety factor
AACEFGHIMRRT graft chimera
AACEFGHLRRTY carry the flag
AACEFGIINNPT face painting
AACEFGLNORRT corneal graft
AACEFHILMNRY Michael Frayn
AACEFHINPSSU saucepan-fish
AACEFIIILTTV facilitative
AACEFIILNOST factionalise
AACEFIILNOTZ factionalize
AACEFILLMMSU musical flame
AACEFILNORRT refractional
AACEFINOSSTT fantasticoes
AACEFINOSSTU assuefaction
AACEFIORRSTU surface-to-air
AACEFLLNORTU call of nature
AACEFLLPRUWY pull a wry face
AACEFLNORRSU solar furnace
AACEFLOOSTVW law of octaves
AACEFMNRRTUU manufacturer
AACEFNORRTTX extractor fan
AACEGGHIINNR chain-gearing
AACEGGHILOPR geographical
AACEGGHINNPR crapehanging
AACEGGIIORRS Sergio Garcia
AACEGGINOPST scapegoating
AACEGHHIMORR haemorrhagic
AACEGHHPRRTY tachygrapher
AACEGHIIKLMN Lake Michigan
AACEGHIILPPR epigraphical
AACEGHILLMPT phlegmatical
AACEGHILLOOT atheological
AACEGHILLPRR calligrapher
AACEGHILOPRS archipelagos
AACEGHIMNOPR anemographic
phanerogamic
AACEGHIMOPTT apothegmatic
AACEGHJKNNNU Kanchenjunga
AACEGHMMOPRY Myrmecophaga
AACEGHMOPRRY ceramography
AACEGHNOOPRY oceanography

AACEGHNORSTT	Hattons Grace
AACEGHOPRRRT	cartographer
AACEGIIINRRT	geriatrician
AACEGIILLNNT	geanticlinal
AACEGIILLNRT	interglacial
AACEGIILLOOT	aetiological
AACEGIILMMRS	magic realism
AACEGIILMRST	magic realist
AACEGIILPRRS	slip-carriage
AACEGIIMMPRT	epigrammatic
AACEGIIMMRST	grammaticise
AACEGIIMMRTZ	grammaticize
AACEGIIMNNTT	anti-magnetic
AACEGIKLNPPR	parking place
AACEGIKNPPPR	packing-paper
AACEGILLMNRY	Germanically
AACEGILLMNTY	magnetically
AACEGILLMSST	Glamis Castle
AACEGILLNOSU	gallinaceous
AACEGILLNRTW	watering-call
AACEGILLOOPT	apologetical
AACEGILLORSU	argillaceous
AACEGILLORTY	categorially
AACEGILLPRSU	superglacial
AACEGILMNNRT	magic lantern
AACEGILMORST	gasometrical
AACEGILNOOST	A Song to Celia
AACEGILNRSST	tragicalness
AACEGILNRTUW	caterwauling
AACEGILNSSUV	saving clause
AACEGIMNORSU	graminaceous
AACEGIMNORUY	Young America
AACEGINNOORT	octogenarian
AACEGINNORTT	octane rating
AACEGINOOPTT	cottage piano
AACEGINOPRRY	pony carriage
AACEGINPPRRT	tracing paper
AACEGLLOPSSW	scapegallows
AACEGLMOORRU	moral courage
AACEGLNNORRU	canon regular
AACEGLNOOPSV	galvanoscope
AACEGLNORTTU	congratulate
AACEGLOPRSSV	salvage-corps
AACEGLRRSTYZ	crystal-gazer
AACEGMNOSTYY	gynaecomasty
AACEGMRRSUVY	Marcus Garvey
AACEHHHMOPRT	rhamphotheca
AACEHHIILMOP	haemophiliac
AACEHHILOPRZ	Rhizocephala
AACEHHKKLLTW	walk the chalk
AACEHIILLMNP	Michael Palin
AACEHIILLOPT	Palaeolithic
AACEHIILLPRS	Schiaparelli
AACEHIILMPRX	alexipharmic
AACEHIILMRTT	arithmetical
AACEHIILNTTT	antithetical
AACEHIILOPRS	parochialise
AACEHIILOPRZ	parochialize
AACEHIIMMNNS	Manicheanism
AACEHIINNRST	Anna Christie
AACEHIINPTTT	antipathetic
AACEHIINRRST	Christian era
AACEHIJLMMPR	clamjamphrie
AACEHIKMNPPS	Sam Peckinpah
AACEHIKMRSTT	strike a match
AACEHILLLNOY	Holy Alliance
AACEHILLLTTY	athletically
AACEHILLMPTY	empathically
	emphatically
AACEHILLMTTY	thematically
AACEHILLNRRV	Lachlan River
AACEHILLPRSY	seraphically
AACEHILLPTTY	pathetically
AACEHILLRTTY	theatrically
AACEHILMNNOR	enharmonical
AACEHILMNPRU	alphanumeric
AACEHILMOPRT	metaphorical
AACEHILMPSTY	metaphysical
AACEHILNOPST	sphacelation
AACEHILNRSSW	Charles's Wain
AACEHILQRRSU	squirearchal
AACEHILRSTTT	tetrastichal
AACEHIMMNNOR	harmonic mean
AACEHIMNORRT	North America
AACEHIMNORVW	harmonic wave
AACEHIMNPRTY	party machine
AACEHIMNRRRT	Archer Martin
AACEHIMORSTU	South America
AACEHIMPRSTT	metaphrastic
AACEHIMPRSTU	Ramapithecus
AACEHIOPRSST	cataphoresis
AACEHJKKNRSS	Jack Harkness
AACEHLLOOPRR	rhopaloceral
AACEHLLPRTYY	archetypally
AACEHLMORSST	scholar's mate
AACEHLRRTUYY	Arthur Cayley
AACEHMNNRSTU	transhumance
AACEHMNNRTVY	merchant navy
AACEHMNORRST	march-treason
	stream anchor
AACEHMOPRRSY	hypersarcoma
AACEHMORRRTY	charter mayor
AACEHNOPRRTY	narcotherapy
AACEHORSSTWY	across the way
AACEHPRRRTTY	charter party
	charterparty
AACEIIINPTTV	anticipative
AACEIIKLORTV	Lake Victoria
AACEIIKOPRTV	Victoria Peak
AACEIILLMMNT	Macmillanite
AACEIILLMNTU	nautical mile
AACEIILLMRTT	altimetrical
AACEIILLMRWY	William Carey
AACEIILMNTTT	Atlantic Time
AACEIILNOPPS	episcopalian
AACEIILNPRTT	antiparticle
AACEIILNRTTU	inarticulate
AACEIILRRUVY	River Ucayali
AACEIIMNNOPT	emancipation
AACEIIMNORST	racemisation
AACEIIMNORTZ	racemization
AACEIIMNRSST	Cartesianism

	sectarianism
AACEIIMRRSSY	seismic array
AACEIIMRTTVX	active matrix
AACEIINNNOTT	incatenation
AACEIINNNRTW	win in a canter
AACEIINNNTUV	annunciative
AACEIINOPPRT	appreciation
AACEIINORTTV	reactivation
AACEIINPRSTT	pancreatitis
AACEIINRSSTV	incrassative
AACEIJKRSTTT	straitjacket
AACEIJLLMSTY	majestically
AACEIJLRSSUU	Julius Caesar
AACEIKLLSTTY	Salt Lake City
AACEIKLMNOPT	kleptomaniac
AACEIKNOPRRT	Tarpeian Rock
AACEILLLLMTY	metallically
AACEILLLLOPV	Valpolicella
AACEILLLMORS	small calorie
AACEILLLPRTY	prelatically
AACEILLMMTUY	immaculately
AACEILLMNOTY	noematically
AACEILLMNSTY	semantically
AACEILLNNRSU	Carl Linnaeus
AACEILLNOORT	reallocation
AACEILLNOPRR	procellarian
AACEILLNOPST	pleonastical
AACEILLNOSTT	castellation
AACEILLNPRTU	unprelatical
AACEILLNPTUY	paniculately
AACEILLOPRTY	operatically
AACEILLRTTUY	articulately
AACEILLSTTUY	eustatically
AACEILMMNORT	manometrical
AACEILMMRSTY	asymmetrical
AACEILMNOSTU	emasculation
AACEILMOPRST	optical maser
AACEILMSSTTY	systematical
AACEILNNOPTT	placentation
AACEILNOORSY	Casino Royale
AACEILNOPRTU	precautional
AACEILNOPRTY	action replay
	Platonic year
AACEILNOSSTV	vacationless
AACEILNRTTUU	unarticulate
AACEILOPRRTY	tropical year
AACEILOPRSTT	spectatorial
AACEILOPRSUY	Pelycosauria
AACEILRSTTTU	straticulate
AACEILRTTTVY	attractively
AACEILSTTUUV	auscultative
AACEIMNNOOPT	companionate
AACEIMNOPRTY	emancipatory
AACEIMNPPRST	panspermatic
AACEINNNORST	non-sectarian
AACEINOPSSTT	space station
AACEINORRTTT	retractation
AACEINORRTUV	avant-courier
AACEINRTTTUV	unattractive
AACEIOPPRRTY	appreciatory
AACEIOPRRRTV	prevaricator
AACEJJKNNOST	Janet Jackson
AACEJKLNNORT	jack-o'-lantern✧
AACEJKOOPTTT	jacket potato
AACEJNNOPRRS	Jasper Conran
AACEJNNPRRTU	Japan Current
AACEKNNORSTU	cantankerous
AACELLLLORTY	collaterally
AACELLMNRTUY	Tracey Ullman
AACELLNNPRTU	carpal tunnel
AACELLNORWYY	canary yellow
AACELLNRRUVY	vernacularly
AACELLOOSSSU	salsolaceous
AACELLORRSST	cross-lateral
AACELMNNOSTU	Manon Lescaut
AACELMNOPPSS	compass plane
AACELMNORSTW	scarlet woman
AACELMORSTUY	emasculatory
AACELNNNORTW	Walter Cannon
AACELNORRSSU	oracularness
AACELNPRRSUU	supernacular
AACELOOPRRTU	corpora lutea
AACELOPPRSTU	appeals court
AACELPPPRRTY	claptrappery
AACEMMNRSSTU	crassamentum
AACEMNOORSTT	Entomostraca
AACEMNOPRTTU	Truman Capote
AACEMOOORSST	osteosarcoma
AACEMORRSTTY	cry roast-meat
AACENNPRRSTY	transparency
AACENNRRTTUZ	Zante currant
AACENORRRTUV	averruncator
AACEORRSSTUU	Ceratosaurus
AACFGHINRRRS	Ragnar Frisch
AACFGHOPRRTY	fractography
AACFGIIINOST	gasification
AACFGIILLMNY	magnifically
AACFHIMNPRST	craftmanship
AACFHINORSTU	South African
AACFIIIILNRT	inartificial
AACFIIILLRTY	artificially
AACFIIILMORR	microfilaria
AACFIIILNNST	financialist
AACFIIILNOPT	palification
AACFIIILNOST	salification
AACFIIILNOTT	facilitation
AACFIIILNRTU	unartificial
AACFIIILOSSS	fascioliasis
AACFIIIMNORT	ramification
AACFIIINNOPT	panification
AACFIIINNOTZ	Nazification
AACFIIINORTT	ratification
AACFIILLLSVY	salvifically
AACFIILMNOST	factionalism
AACFIILNNPTT	Captain Flint
AACFIILNOOST	focalisation
AACFIILNOOTZ	focalization
AACFIILNOSTT	factionalist
AACFIILOQRTU	qualificator
AACFIIMNSSTT	fantasticism
AACFIINNRSST	Saint Francis
AACFIINOSSTT	satisfaction

AACFILLLOSUY fallaciously
AACFILLNORTY fractionally
AACFILMOPSST foam plastics
AACFILMORSTT stalactiform
AACFINOORRTT fractionator
AACFIORSSTTY satisfactory
AACFLLMORTUY moral faculty
AACGGHHIIOPR hagiographic
AACGGHIILLOO hagiological
AACGGHIKNPSY shaggy ink-cap
AACGGHIMNOTY gigantomachy
AACGGIILLNTY gigantically
AACGGILMOSTY mystagogical
AACGHHOPRRTY chartography
AACGHILLNOOR grain alcohol
AACGHILLOOPT pathological
AACGHILMOPRY myographical
AACGHILNOPPR planographic
AACGHILOOPRR orographical
AACGHILOOPRZ zoographical
AACGHIMNOPRR marconigraph
AACGHIMNRSTT crash-matting
AACGHIMRTTUU thaumaturgic
AACGHINOPPRT pantographic
AACGHINOPRRU uranographic
AACGHLMOOPRY pharmacology
AACGHMMOORRT chromatogram
AACGHOOPPRSU carpophagous
AACGHOOPRSSU sarcophagous
AACGHOOPSSTU scatophagous
AACGIIKNNOTT action-taking
AACGIILNNORV Carlovingian
AACGIILNORTT coat-trailing
AACGIIMMMRST grammaticism
AACGIIMMRRTT trigrammatic
AACGIINNOSTT antagonistic
AACGIINORTTV virgo intacta
AACGIINOSTTW waistcoating
AACGIJKNORST roasting jack
AACGIKLMRSSU surgical mask
AACGIKLNQSUV quacksalving
AACGILLMOOST malacologist
AACGILLMORSY orgasmically
AACGILLOORST astrological
AACGILLOOTTU tautological
AACGILLORSTY orgastically
AACGILLRRTUU agricultural
AACGILMNORST marginal cost
AACGILNNOOTV long vacation
AACGILNRTTTY attractingly
AACGILOOSSTT astacologist
AACGIMMNOOUZ Giacomo Manzú
AACGIMMOPRRT programmatic
AACGIMNOPRTY cryptogamian
AACGINOOPRSU angiocarpous
AACGINOPPRTU group-captain
AACGLMOOSTUU glaucomatous
AACGLNNORTTU congratulant
AACHHIILNPPS chaplainship
AACHHIIMNPRS chairmanship
AACHHIJMNNNO John Chinaman
AACHHIKLNPSS Spanish chalk
AACHHILMOPTY hypothalamic
AACHHINOORTX xanthochroia
AACHHOOPPRST approach shot
AACHIILLNPSY Hispanically
AACHIILMNNOR inharmonical
AACHIILMOPRS parochialism
AACHIILMPRST palma Christi
AACHIILNNOPT antiphonical
AACHIILOORST aristolochia
AACHIILOPRTY parochiality
AACHIIMNNOST machinations
AACHIIMNOOPT potichomania
AACHIIMPRRST patriarchism
AACHIINOPRST Aristophanic
AACHIINPRSTT antiphrastic
AACHIINRRTTT antarthritic
AACHIJMMORTU Joachim Murat
AACHIKLLORST tailor's chalk
AACHIKLMOOTY Oklahoma City
AACHIKORSTUW auto rickshaw
autorickshaw
AACHILLMNORY harmonically
AACHILLRRSWY Wally Schirra
AACHILMMNOOT monothalamic
AACHILMNOOPT taphonomical
AACHILMNORTY lachrymation
AACHILOPRRSU scrophularia
AACHILOPSTTY hypostatical
AACHIMMNNOPY nymphomaniac
AACHIMNOPRRS parachronism
AACHIMOOPRST chromatopsia
AACHIMPPRSSY parapsychism
AACHINOORSSU honoris causa
AACHINOPRTTU naturopathic
AACHIRRSTTUZ Zarathustric
AACHKMOORRSZ Ockham's razor
AACHLLMNRRUY lachrymal urn
AACHLLNNNOTY nonchalantly
AACHLLOPPRYY apocryphally
AACHLMMNOOPY omphalomancy
AACHLMOPPRYY polypharmacy
AACHLMORRTYY lachrymatory
AACHMOORSTTU trachomatous
AACHNOOPRSTU anthocarpous
AACIIINNOPTT anticipation
AACIIINNOTTV inactivation
vaticination
AACIIINNRSSU uncinariasis
AACIIINSSTTT statistician
AACIIJMNORSS Canis Majoris
AACIIKLLLMRW William Clark
AACIIKLNNOPR Carolina pink
AACIILLLOPTY apolitically
AACIILLMMNSU animalculism
AACIILLMNOSY simoniacally
AACIILLMNSTU animalculist
AACIILLMOTTY amitotically
AACIILLNNOTT cantillation
AACIILLNOOST localisation
AACIILLNOOTV Italo Calvino

AACIILLNOOTZ	localization
AACIILLNOSTY	antisocially
AACIILLORSTY	aoristically
AACIILLPPSTY	papistically
AACIILLRSTTY	artistically
AACIILLSTTUY	autistically
AACIILMMNOPT	pantomimical
AACIILMMORSS	commissarial
AACIILMNNOTU	calumniation
AACIILMOPRST	porismatical
AACIILNNOOPS	Nicola Pisano
AACIILNOOSTV	vocalisation
AACIILNOOTVZ	vocalization
AACIILNOPTTU	capitulation
AACIILNORTTU	articulation
AACIILNPRRTU	in particular
AACIILNRSTTU	naturalistic
AACIILOOPRRV	corpora vilia
AACIILORSTTU	tralaticious
AACIILORSUVY	avariciously
AACIILPRRSUY	supraciliary
AACIILSTUUVY	visual acuity
AACIIMMORSST	commissariat
	marcatissimo
AACIIMNNORST	animatronics
AACIIMNOSSTU	causationism
AACIIMOTTTUY	automaticity
AACIINNNNOTU	annunciation✧
AACIINNNOOST	canonisation
AACIINNNOOTZ	canonization
AACIINNNQTUU	unacquaint in
AACIINNORSST	incrassation
AACIINOORRTT	ratiocinator
AACIINOOSSST	associations
AACIINOPRTTY	anticipatory
AACIINOSSTTU	causationist
AACIIOORSSTX	toxocariasis
AACIIOPPRRTT	participator
AACIJKKNPSTU	skipjack tuna
AACIJKPRRSSU	Jurassic Park
AACIKLNSSSTY	slack in stays
AACIKLOPRTYY	karyotypical
AACILLLNOPTY	call into play
	platonically
AACILLLRTVWY	cavalry twill
AACILLMNORTY	romantically
AACILLMNOSTY	monastically
AACILLMOSTUY	calamitously
AACILLNNRTYY	tyrannically
AACILLNOOTVY	vocationally
AACILLNORTTY	cantillatory
AACILLOORRTY	oratorically
AACILLOPTTUY	autoptically
AACILLPRRTUY	particularly
AACILMNNOOPT	complanation
AACILMNNORTU	unromantical
AACILMNOOPRT	proclamation
AACILMNOORST	astronomical
AACILMNORTUY	calumniatory
AACILMOPSTTY	asymptotical
AACILMORRTTU	court martial
	court-martial
	matriculator
AACILNORSTTU	claustration
AACILNOSTTUU	auscultation
AACILOPRTTUY	capitulatory
AACILORRTTUY	articulatory
AACIMMNOORTY	microanatomy
AACIMMOPSTTY	asymptomatic
AACIMNNOOPWY	companionway
AACIMNNOORTT	contaminator
AACIMNNOOTTU	cat o' mountain
	non-automatic
AACIMNOOPRST	paronomastic
AACIMOORSSST	sarcomatosis
AACINNNOSSTU	Austin canons
AACINNOOSTTT	constatation
AACINOORRTTT	tractoration
AACINORSSTTU	astronautics
AACINPPRRSSU	Prussian carp
AACIOPRRRTTY	pyrotartaric
AACLLNNORTUY	connaturally
AACLMNOPPSST	compass plant
AACLMOOPRRTY	proclamatory
AACLMORSTTUU	cumulostrata
AACLNNOPRTTU	contrapuntal
AACLNPRSTTYY	cryptanalyst
AACLORSTTUUY	auscultatory
AACLPRRSSTUU	supracrustal
AACMOOPRSSST	astrocompass
AACMOORSSTTY	astrocytomas
AACMOPRSSTUU	Camptosaurus
AADDDEEGHINN	hidden agenda
AADDDEEHLPSS	saddle-shaped
AADDDEIORSWY	Edward A Doisy
AADDDGLNORST	gold standard
AADDDHNOPSWY	Paddy Ashdown
AADDEEEEHRSV	A Severed Head
AADDEEEFLORV	leave for dead
AADDEEEGRRSV	Edgard Varèse
AADDEEEHHMMR	hammer-headed
AADDEEEHLLNW	wheel and deal
AADDEEEHLRTT	rattle-headed
AADDEEFGLRTU	Grateful Dead
AADDEEFHILNT	life-and-death
AADDEEFHRRTU	hard-featured
AADDEEFIRSTU	Dead Sea fruit
AADDEEGHILNT	death-dealing
AADDEEGHLSSY	glassyheaded
AADDEEGLLNRW	walled garden
AADDEEGMNRRW	Edward German
AADDEEHHNORV	hand over head
AADDEEHNSSWY	Ash Wednesday
AADDEEIIIPRS	pia desideria
AADDEEILNSST	land set-aside
AADDEEILOPRT	Port Adelaide
AADDEELLNRWY	Edward Alleyn
AADDEEMNORTU	Edouard Manet
AADDEFFIILST	fit as a fiddle
AADDEFFJRSTT	Jeddart staff
AADDEFHIINNN	finnan haddie
AADDEFHORRUV	hard-favoured

AADDEFILNOTV feal and divot
AADDEFINORTU defraudation
AADDEFISTUUX fidus et audax
AADDEFLLNOSU all of a sudden
AADDEFNNOSSU safe and sound
AADDEGGHIRRR Rider Haggard
AADDEGHLNNOV hand and glove
AADDEGLLOOSU logodaedalus
AADDEGNOPRRU parade ground
AADDEHHNNORV hand over hand
AADDEHMORSTW Edward Thomas
AADDEHNORRSZ Zandra Rhodes
AADDEHOORSTT at death's door
AADDEIILNRSV Sir David Lean
AADDEIIMNRSW Edwardianism
AADDEIINPRRV Pre-Dravidian
AADDEIKMNNOS diamond snake
AADDEIKMNNRT meat and drink
AADDEIKRSTVY David Starkey
AADDEILLLPRS saddle pillar
AADDEIMNRSTT standard time
AADDEINRRSST standardiser
AADDEINRRSTZ standardizer
AADDELLMNORS salmon ladder
AADDELMMOPRY lampadedromy
AADDEMNOSTTU dead as mutton
AADDENRSSTWY St Andrew's Day
AADDFMOORTYY from day to day
AADDGGLOOOSS as good as gold
AADDGHIIINNR Indira Gandhi
AADDGHINNRST hard-standing
AADDGIIILNOT digladiation
AADDGIIILORT digital radio
AADDGIINORST disgradation
AADDGILNOPRT parotid gland
AADDGILNORRZ dragon lizard
AADDGINNRSTW standard wing
AADDGINOOSTV A Song to David
AADDHINORSSS Sarah Siddons
AADDIIILNOPT dilapidation
AADDIILLNOTY additionally
AADDIILMNSWY Midway Island
AADDILNNSSSU Sunda Islands
AADDJLMNNOOR jordan almond✧
AADDKLNORRSU drunk as a lord
AADDLLNNRSUY all and sundry
AADDNNNNNOOO on and on and on
AADEEEEHHLTV heave the lead
AADEEEEJLLUV eau de Javelle
AADEEEFHLMRT female thread
AADEEEFHLRST false-hearted
AADEEEGGLOPR George Palade
AADEEEGGMNRR Graeme Garden
AADEEEGHKMRT make the grade
AADEEEGHLRRT large-hearted
AADEEEGHRRTT great-hearted
AADEEEGIPRSS seaside grape
AADEEEGIRRRR arrière-garde
AADEEEGLMORT moderate gale
AADEEEGLNNRS Greenland Sea
AADEEEGLNRSV lasagne verde
AADEEEGLOPSV pagoda sleeve
AADEEEGMMNNT endamagement
AADEEEHHRTVY heavy-hearted
AADEEEHIRSST heart disease
AADEEEHLLNWX wheel and axle
AADEEEHLRTWX waxed leather
AADEEEHNPRST reed-pheasant
AADEEEHRSSTT streets ahead
AADEEEILPRSS pearl disease
AADEEEILRRSY sidereal year
AADEEEKLMRRT market leader
AADEEELNNRRT neandertaler✧
AADEEELNNRWZ New Zealander
AADEEEMNPRTW deepwaterman
AADEEEMPRRTW Peter Medawar
AADEEENQSSTU adequateness
AADEEFFNORRT fore-and-after
AADEEFGHOSTT gates of death
AADEEFHINRTT faint-hearted
AADEEFIKORRT take for a ride
AADEEFILLMRT fleet admiral
AADEEFKLMORS Lake of Dreams
AADEEGGGIRST disaggregate
AADEEGGHINNR age hardening
AADEEGGLMORT agglomerated
AADEEGHHNNOS hang one's head
AADEEGHOPPRS go pear-shaped
AADEEGIILNNR radial engine
AADEEGIINNRT Argentinidae
AADEEGIKLMOR go like a dream
AADEEGIKNRRT take a grinder
AADEEGILNORT Daniel Ortega
AADEEGILNRRT grand atelier
AADEEGIMNOVY maiden voyage
AADEEGINRTUV unvariegated
AADEEGJLNRYY Lady Jane Grey
AADEEGKMNRRT market garden
market-garden
AADEEGKNOPTW take down a peg
AADEEGMNQRRU grande marque
AADEEHHINTTT in at the death
AADEEHHISTTT that's the idea
AADEEHHMRTTT The Mad Hatter
AADEEHIINRRT hereditarian
AADEEHIIPSUU Euphausiidae
AADEEHIIRSST radiesthesia
AADEEHILNNOS no sae Hieland
AADEEHILNPRT plain-hearted
AADEEHILNQRU harlequinade
AADEEHILNTTY late in the day
AADEEHIMMSTT mathematised
AADEEHIMMTTZ mathematized
AADEEHISSSTY dysaesthesia
AADEEHLLLNOT Land o' the Leal
AADEEHLNPTTY death penalty
AADEEHLNSTTW The Waste Land
AADEEHLPRSSV salver-shaped
AADEEHMMRSSY Dame Myra Hess
AADEEHMRRSSU hard measures
AADEEHOPRRTZ trapezohedra
AADEEHQRRSTU headquarters

AADEEHRRSTVY the Adversary
AADEEIIKMTVW take a dim view
AADEEIIKNPRT take a pride in
AADEEIILMMSV mediaevalism
AADEEIILMSTV mediaevalist
AADEEIIMNNRT antemeridian
AADEEIIMNSSZ maiden assize
AADEEIIMRRRV River Madeira
AADEEIIMTTUV taedium vitae
AADEEIKLLMNR aldermanlike
AADEEIKMNSST maiden stakes
AADEEILLLNVW alive and well
AADEEILLNNRV live and learn
AADEEILLNUVV vaudevillean
AADEEILMMPST semipalmated
AADEEILNNOWW in weal and woe
AADEEILNPRRY lead in prayer
AADEEILNQTUY inadequately
AADEEILNRSST Easter Island
AADEEILNRSTU denaturalise
AADEEILNRTUZ denaturalize
AADEEIMMNNRR remainder-man
AADEEIMMNNST misdemeanant
AADEEIMNRRTV animadverter
AADEEIMQSTUV desquamative
AADEEINNPPPS Pandean pipes
AADEEINOPRST endoparasite
AADEEINOPRTU deuteranopia
AADEEINPSSTV adaptiveness
AADEEJLNNRTW lantern-jawed
AADEELLLNPRU unparalleled
AADEELLNORRS Ronald Searle
AADEELLNPPRU unapparelled
AADEELLRZZZZ razzle-dazzle
AADEELMNPRTT departmental
AADEELNRTTUU unadulterate
AADEEMMNRSTW New Amsterdam
AADEEMNNRTUX extramundane
AADEEMNORSTY Easter Monday
AADEEMPRSSST passed master
AADEENRSSTUY Easter Sunday
AADEEQRRSTUW quarter-sawed
AADEFFIIILST disaffiliate
AADEFFIILNTU unaffiliated
AADEFFILLORR ride for a fall
AADEFGGHLORT dagger of lath
AADEFGILNORT deflagration
AADEFGIMNRRW drawing-frame
AADEFGIMNRST farm steading
AADEFGKMNNRS Frank Sedgman
AADEFHIIPRSS paradise fish
AADEFHILLMRS field marshal
AADEFHILLORT all of a dither
AADEFHINNOTU fountainhead
AADEFHLLNOTW law of the land
AADEFIILMMNT animated film
AADEFIILNSUZ sulfadiazine
AADEFIKMNORR Afrikanerdom
AADEFILMORTY defamatorily
AADEFILNORSS Faroe Islands
AADEFILNORTY deflationary
AADEFILNRRSS Fraser Island
AADEFILNRSTU Alfred Austin
AADEFILOSTTW Two Fat Ladies
AADEFLLMNOSW Owen Falls Dam
AADEFLMMNRTY Marty Feldman
AADEFLNOORRS a fool's errand
AADEFLNOOSST fast-and-loose
AADEGGGILNOU loading gauge
AADEGGILNNRR Darling Range
AADEGGILNNST landing stage
AADEGGILNTTU agglutinated
AADEGGLNNRST gangsterland
AADEGGMNOPRS Gaspard Monge
AADEGHIKLNST Talking Heads
AADEGHILLLOY legal holiday
AADEGHINNSTY Syngnathidae
AADEGHINRRSW hard swearing
AADEGHIOPPRR Herod Agrippa
AADEGHIOPRRR radiographer
AADEGHIPRSTU graduateship
AADEGHMNNNRU under-hangman
AADEGIIINRVW Virginia Wade
AADEGIILLNNP plain dealing
plain-dealing
AADEGIILPQRU quadriplegia
AADEGIIMMNST diamagnetism
AADEGIINPRST Giant Despair
AADEGIKLNRRY Reginald Kray
AADEGILLLRWY wallydraigle
AADEGILLNPRV all-pervading
AADEGILNSSST stained glass
AADEGIMNNOTV not give a damn
AADEGIMNNRRR Grand Marnier®
AADEGIMPRRTY Great Pyramid
AADEGINNSTVW standing wave
AADEGINOPPRS propagandise
AADEGINOPPRZ propagandize
AADEGINPPRRW drawing paper
AADEGINPRSST painted grass
AADEGLLNNSUY Auld Lang Syne
AADEGLNNOOST Golden Sonata
AADEGLNPRSST star-spangled
AADEGLNRSTTU strangulated
AADEGNNOSTUY Angus Deayton
AADEGNOORTTW go down a treat
AADEGOPRSTTU postgraduate
AADEGQRRRTUU quarter-guard
AADEHHIILLPP Philadelphia
AADEHIILMRTW white admiral
AADEHIIMNRSZ mazarine dish
AADEHIKLMORY holidaymaker
AADEHIKMRTTW marked with a T
AADEHILLOPPY Polyadelphia
AADEHILMNPRS aldermanship
AADEHILMRTTY the Admiralty
AADEHILNORRT enarthrodial
AADEHILORSST heads or tails
AADEHIMNNORS Rhodesian man
AADEHIMNOORZ mazarine hood
AADEHINOPPRS parasphenoid
AADEHINOPRST Herod Antipas

AADEHIOPRRTY radiotherapy
AADEHKLOPRRS leopard shark
AADEHKLRSTWW walk the wards
AADEHKMNORSU Ahmed Sukarno
AADEHLNORSTU heart and soul
AADEHMOOPSTT mashed potato
AADEHNNSSSTT thés dansants
AADEHNORSTUY thousand-year
AADEHPRRSTTU Uttar Pradesh
AADEIIILNOPP Papilionidae
AADEIIILNOST idealisation
AADEIIILNOTZ idealization
AADEIIJMORRS Morarji Desai
AADEIILLNNPR Pirandellian
AADEIILLNOTY ideationally
AADEIILLNTUV antediluvial
AADEIILLNUVV vaudevillian
AADEIILMNNNX Daniel Mannix
AADEIILMNNOT delamination
AADEIILMNRTY Lymantriidae
AADEIILMPRRY imperial yard
AADEIILNNOST desalination
AADEIILNNQRU quadriennial
AADEIILNNTUV antediluvian
AADEIILNORTV derivational
revalidation
AADEIILNRSTT interstadial
AADEIIMMMOUX axioma medium
AADEIIMNNNTU unmaintained
AADEIIMNOPRT pteridomania
AADEIIMNORST maderisation
AADEIIMNORTZ maderization
AADEIIMNRSTT administrate
AADEIINNNORW Neo-Darwinian
AADEIINNORST Tardenoisian
AADEIINOPRST deaspiration
AADEIIOTTUVX autoxidative
AADEIJMMNOSS James Madison
AADEIKLMNNRU Milan Kundera
AADEIKLMNRTW milk-and-water
AADEIKLNORSS Kosrae Island
AADEIKMNNOST and no mistake
AADEIKMNORRV Andrei Markov
AADEILLMOTTU ultimate load
AADEILLNPRSS Pearl Islands
AADEILMNNSTY Sidney Altman
AADEILNNNORR noradrenalin
AADEILNNPRSS salad spinner
AADEILNNSSTT Staten Island
AADEILNNSSUW dunniewassal
AADEILNORTTU adulteration
AADEILNQRTUV quadrivalent
AADEILNRTUVY valetudinary
AADEILOPRSST Paradise Lost
AADEILRSSTYY it's early days
AADEIMMNNOPU pandaemonium✧
AADEIMNNNRTU intramundane
AADEIMNNOPTW painted woman
AADEIMNOQSTU desquamation
AADEIMNORRTY Dean Moriarty
AADEIMORTTTV motivated art
AADEIMSSTTUX Texas Stadium
AADEINNOOPPS open diapason
AADEINOPRRTT anti-predator
AADEINOPRRUX paradoxurine
AADEINORSTTU desaturation
AADEINRRSTTT transit trade
AADEIPRRSSTY raised pastry
AADEJLNORRTU trade journal
AADELLMNOPRR Arnold Palmer
AADELLMRRUYY medullary ray
AADELLNNORST rallentandos
AADELLOORRST dorsolateral
AADELMMNOPRS random sample
AADELMMNPTUU paludamentum
AADELMNNRTUU ultramundane
AADELMOPRRTU armour-plated
AADELNNNPSTU sun-and-planet
AADELNNRSTTU untranslated
AADELNORRRTU natural order
AADEMMOOSTTU stomatodaeum
AADEMNNNRSTU transmundane
AADEMNNPRSUU supramundane
AADEMNOPPRTU put a damper on
AADEMOQRSTUY desquamatory
AADENRSTTUXY next Saturday
AADFFFHLNOST stand-off half
AADFFHLORRSW flash forward
flash-forward
AADFFKLNORRW flank forward
AADFGHILNNRT farthingland
AADFHILNOOSU Island of Oahu
AADFIILMNOSU Island of Maui
AADFILNNOOTU foundational
AADFILNRSSTT first and last
AADFINNOOSTU soda fountain
AADGGJNNNPUU Ujung Pandang
AADGHHILRSTZ hazard lights
AADGHHIMNNRT right-hand man
AADGHIIMMNNT might and main
AADGHIINPRSU guardianship
AADGHIKLLNNO Alan L Hodgkin
AADGHILLMPTY daylight lamp
AADGHILNORSZ losing hazard
AADGHILNORTT grind to a halt
AADGHINNORTY Tonya Harding
AADGHLNOOSTU Dougal Haston
AADGHMMNNOOR Hammond organ®
AADGIIIMPRRV primigravida
AADGIILMRTUV multigravida
AADGIILNNORT Darlingtonia
national grid
AADGIINNNORS Grandisonian
AADGIINNNPST sand painting
AADGIINNOOTU Antonio Gaudí
AADGILLNPPUY applaudingly
AADGILMPRSSY Glass Pyramid
AADGILNOOSSU disanalogous
AADGIMNOPPRS propagandism
AADGIMNPRSTT trading stamp
AADGIMRRSTTU dramaturgist
AADGINOOPRRT progradation

AADGINOORSTY Rogation Days
AADGINOPPRST propagandist
AADGLLNNOPTY long-day plant
AADGLMNNRRUY Gunnar Myrdal
AADGLNNNORUU ground annual
AADGLNOOPRST Portland sago
AADGLOOOPRXY paradoxology
AADGMNOORRSY Gordon Ramsay
AADHIIIIKNRS kaisar-i-Hindi
AADHIIILNNTW Withnail and I
AADHIILOPPSY diapophysial
AADHILMNOORY Roman holiday✧
AADHILNNOOTT tooth and nail
AADHILNOOPRT anthropoidal
AADHILNOPSUY diaphanously
AADHINORRTUY Arundhati Roy
AADHINPRSSTY Danish pastry
AADHLMORRSUV Harold Varmus
AADHLORSTUYY Holy Saturday
AADIIILNNNPS Plains Indian
AADIIILNNNST Tinian Island
AADIIILNNOPS Indianapolis
AADIIILNNOTV invalidation
AADIIILNORTV divinatorial
AADIIINNNORR Irina Rodnina
AADIIKNNRSST Kristiansand
AADIILLLLSWW Will Ladislaw
AADIILLLMSWY Lady Williams
AADIILLMNNOW Indian mallow
AADIILMNOQRU quadrinomial
AADIILNOOSTV vasodilation
AADIIMMNOSUV Mauvoisin Dam
AADIIMNNOOST nomadisation
AADIIMNNOOTZ nomadization
AADIIMNNRSTT administrant
AADIINOORSTT radio station
AADIINOOTTUX autoxidation
AADIINORRTTY traditionary
AADIIRRSSTUV Stradivarius
AADILLMNOOST amontillados
AADILLNNNOST still and anon
AADILMMOSTUY Sodium Amytal®
AADILMNNOSUY Mail on Sunday
AADILNOPPRST postprandial
AADILOORSTVY vasodilatory
AADIMNPSSTTT standpattism
AADINNORSTTU transudation
AADKLLNOOTYZ Zoltán Kodály
AADLMNNORUWY laundrywoman
AADMNOQRSUUU quadrumanous
AADNORRSTTUY transudatory
AAEEEEKKLLTT talkee-talkee
AAEEEEKNOSST take one's ease
AAEEEELLMNSV mean sea level
AAEEEFGILLOS Sea of Galilee
AAEEEFHLLNNV heaven-fallen
AAEEEFHMNPRT mean free path
AAEEEFLRSTTW welfare state
AAEEEFMMNSTV femme savante
AAEEEGGHMNRR Graham Greene
AAEEEGGHRTUW weather gauge
AAEEEGGILNSY geese a-laying
AAEEEGGIRTVX exaggerative
AAEEEGGLNNRT agent-general
AAEEEGHLMRTW weather gleam
AAEEEGNRRSTT Great Eastern
AAEEEGRRRRST arrester gear
AAEEEHHHRTTV have the heart
AAEEEHILSSTT telaesthesia
AAEEEHIMMSST haematemesis
AAEEEHINRSTT raise the ante
AAEEEHINSSTT anaesthetise
AAEEEHINSTTZ anaesthetize
AAEEEHKMRSST Seretse Khama
AAEEEHLLNPST elephant seal
AAEEEHLLPRTT plate-leather
AAEEEHLNPRST elephant's-ear
AAEEEHLNRSTT neat's leather
AAEEEHMNSSUY Seamus Heaney
AAEEEHNNOSST Sheena Easton
AAEEEHNORSTY easy on the ear
AAEEEHNPSSTY pheasant's-eye
AAEEEIKRRSST seraskierate
AAEEEILPRSTT tapsalteerie
AAEEEINNORRS Eero Saarinen
AAEEEIPRSTVX exasperative
AAEEEJLLRTVW Javelle water
AAEEEJMNNORU Jeanne Moreau
AAEEEKLMPUWY make up leeway
AAEEEKMMNNOS make one's name
AAEEEKMRSSTU take measures
AAEEEKNOSSTT take one's seat
AAEEEKPQRRTU keep a quarter
AAEEELLPRSTU pasteurellae✧
AAEEELOPRTTU poet laureate✧
AAEEEMPRRSTT tape streamer
AAEEEMPRSSSU passemeasure
AAEEEMRRSTUW water measure
AAEEENPRSSST separateness
AAEEFFFKSSTT Kaffe Fassett
AAEEFFGLNRST general staff
AAEEFFHLMNST fan the flames
AAEEFFHLNORT half after one
AAEEFFOSSSST Feast of Asses
AAEEFGHORRST hart of grease
AAEEFGHRRSST feather-grass
AAEEFGILMTTU metal fatigue
AAEEFHHLOTVW have the law of
AAEEFHHLRRST father-lasher
AAEEFHILMOTW whale of a time
AAEEFHILRRTU heart failure
AAEEFHLMRSSU half measures
AAEEFHLORSSV half-seas-over
AAEEFHLRTTUV have a flutter
AAEEFHNOPRTU herpetofauna
AAEEFHOSSSSU safe as houses
AAEEFHRSSTTV harvest-feast
AAEEFIILRRSS laisser-faire
AAEEFIILRSSZ laissez-faire
AAEEFIJLLMNU famille jaune
AAEEFILMPRSV false vampire
AAEEFLLPPSSU self-applause

AAEEFMNNRRTT tenant farmer
AAEEFNNOORTT afternoon tea
AAEEFNNPRSST snap-fastener
AAEEFQRRRTTU quarter after
AAEEGGGGLLRT raggle-taggle
AAEEGGGGPRRW wagger-pagger
AAEEGGGHMORR George Graham
AAEEGGIKLMOR Lake Maggiore
AAEEGGIMNOSS agamogenesis
AAEEGGIMNRTV gram-negative✧
AAEEGGINNRTU guaranteeing
AAEEGGINORTX exaggeration
AAEEGGLLNSSU languageless
AAEEGGLNNOTU tone language
AAEEGGMORRTT mortgage rate
AAEEGGOPRRST egg separator
AAEEGGORRTXY exaggeratory
AAEEGHHRRSST sage-thrasher
AAEEGHILMRTV give the alarm
AAEEGHILNNPT panel heating
AAEEGHILNPRT tragelaphine
AAEEGHILNRRT grain leather
AAEEGHILPRSY hyperalgesia
AAEEGHILRVWY Rayleigh wave
AAEEGHINRSTT thereagainst
AAEEGHINRSTW whereagainst
AAEEGHLMOPTY hepatomegaly
AAEEGHLNORTW weather along
AAEEGHLRSSTW weather glass
AAEEGHMNOPRT on the rampage
AAEEGHNORRST Sarah Egerton
AAEEGHNORRTT theatre organ
AAEEGIILMNPS Semi-Pelagian
AAEEGIILNNPS palingenesia
AAEEGIILNPRT patrilineage
AAEEGIILNSTU Ustilagineae
AAEEGIIMMNTZ Time Magazine
AAEEGIIMNNRY ayeremaining
AAEEGIKLLNTT take a telling
AAEEGIKLMNRS leasing-maker
AAEEGILMNNOT antilegomena✧
AAEEGILNNORT generational
AAEEGILNOPTV give on a plate
AAEEGILNOTTV vegetational
AAEEGILNRRST sterling area
AAEEGILRSSUV liver sausage
AAEEGIMNNSWZ news magazine
newsmagazine
AAEEGIMNOPRR open marriage
AAEEGIMNOPRS Angiospermae
AAEEGIMNORST ménage à trois
AAEEGIMNTTUV augmentative
AAEEGIMPSSTU Septuagesima
AAEEGIMRSSTW semiwater gas
AAEEGINNORSW Norwegian Sea
AAEEGINNRSTV Geraint Evans
AAEEGINNSTUX exsanguinate
AAEEGINPRSTX exasperating
AAEEGINRSSTV asseverating
AAEEGIPRSTYZ stargazey pie
AAEEGJLMNORR major-general
AAEEGKNOORRT tree kangaroo
AAEEGLLMNOTW Eton wall game
AAEEGLMNNORW New Mangalore
AAEEGLMNORTV galvanometer
AAEEGLMNPPST Pagan temples
AAEEGLMNRRTV Great Malvern
AAEEGLNNORRS Sloane Ranger
AAEEGLNNPRWY Penang-lawyer
AAEEGLNOOPTT goat-antelope
AAEEGLNORSSU Lorne sausage
AAEEGLOPRSSS opera glasses
AAEEGLRRRTUX extra-regular
AAEEGMNOPSSY passage-money
AAEEGMNOPTTU mangetout pea
AAEEGMRRRSTT garret-master
AAEEGNNNNRXY granny annexe
AAEEGNPRSSWY way passenger
AAEEGNPRSTUY septuagenary
AAEEGNRRSSTX Texas Rangers
AAEEHHILLSTW alas the while
AAEEHHIMPRTT amphitheatre
AAEEHHIPSSTY hypaesthesia
AAEEHHKNNSTV thank heavens
AAEEHHLMNNRS Helen Sharman
AAEEHHLNOTVW have the law on
AAEEHHMNRSTW what's-her-name
AAEEHHORRTTT heart-to-heart
AAEEHHOSSSST ashes to ashes
AAEEHIIKNSST kinaesthesia
AAEEHIILRTVX exhilarative
AAEEHIIMPRST hemiparasite
AAEEHIIPRRTW white pareira
AAEEHILMNNOP phaeomelanin
AAEEHILMNNRT Lemnian earth
AAEEHILOPRST heteroplasia
AAEEHILPRSTU laureateship
AAEEHIMMNNRR Hermann Maier
AAEEHIMNNPRS arsphenamine
AAEEHINNRSTU neurasthenia
AAEEHINORRST tear one's hair
AAEEHINORSST raise one's hat
AAEEHINPPRRT heir apparent
AAEEHINRSTTW weather stain
AAEEHINSSSTY synaesthesia
AAEEHINSSTTT anaesthetist
AAEEHIRRSSTY East Ayrshire
AAEEHKMNRRSS harness-maker
AAEEHKMORRTT katharometer
AAEEHLLNOPTW Lethal Weapon
AAEEHLMNOQTU methaqualone
AAEEHLMNPRRW Pelham Warner
AAEEHLNOPRST Earl Stanhope
AAEEHLOPPTXY heat-apoplexy
AAEEHLORRTTY Theatre Royal
AAEEHLORTTTT total theatre
AAEEHLSTUVVX exhaust valve
AAEEHMNORSUW warehouseman
AAEEHMNPRTTT The Apartment
AAEEHMOORSTT Heterosomata
AAEEHMSSTTUX exhaust steam
AAEEHOORRSTT steatorrhoea

AAEEHORSTTVY Savoy Theatre
AAEEHPRRSTTW sprat-weather
AAEEIIJNOPRS japonaiserie
AAEEIIKKLLTW walkie-talkie
AAEEIIKLRSTU Karelia Suite
AAEEIILLMRSS Marseillaise
AAEEIILLRTTV alliterative
AAEEIILMMNTU a mile a minute
AAEEIILMNTTV alimentative
AAEEIILMORTV ameliorative
AAEEIILPRRUV prairie value
AAEEIIMPRSST semiparasite
AAEEIINNRRTV veterinarian
AAEEILLLPRSW parallelwise
AAEEILLLRRSS laisser-aller
AAEEILLLRSSZ laissez-aller
AAEEILLMNPST planetesimal
AAEEILLNORTV revelational
AAEEILLNPRUV Paul Verlaine
AAEEILLPRSTT septilateral
AAEEILMNRRTW mineral water
AAEEILMNRSST materialness
AAEEILMNRSTT Samian letter
AAEEILMORRST alstroemeria
AAEEILNORRTT re-alteration
AAEEILNORSTT Aristotelean
AAEEILNORSTU teleosaurian
AAEEILNPRSST pleasantries
AAEEILNPRSTW water spaniel
AAEEILNSSTVX laxativeness
AAEEILOPRRTT proletariate
AAEEILQRSSTU sesquialtera
AAEEIMNNSTTV Venetian mast
AAEEIMNOPSST empassionate
AAEEIMNPPRST appraisement
AAEEIMNPPRTT apparent time
AAEEIMNPRSTV private means
AAEEIMNRSSUV Seven Samurai
AAEEINNNORTX reannexation
AAEEINOPRSTX exasperation
AAEEINOQTUVW wave equation
AAEEINORSSTV asseveration
AAEEINPPRRST paper-stainer
AAEEJKMMNRTZ katzenjammer
AAEEJMMNPRXY Jeremy Paxman
AAEEJMRSSTTW James Stewart
AAEEKKMMNORS make one's mark
AAEEKLLNOPST Lake Tonlé Sap
AAEEKLNNOOTW an oaken towel
AAEEKMNPRRTT pattern-maker
AAEEKMQRRSTU market square
AAEELLMMPRSU Samuel Palmer
AAEELLNNNTTU annual nettle
AAEELLNPRRTY parenterally
AAEELLPRSSTU pasteurellas✧
AAEELMMNRTTT maltreatment
AAEELMNPRSST malapertness
AAEELMNPRSTT saltpetreman
AAEELNNOPPRU European plan
AAEELNNPSSST pleasantness
AAEELORSSTYY araeosystyle
AAEELPQRRTTU quarter-plate
AAEEMMPRRSTT tramp steamer
AAEEMNNPPRSW newspaperman
AAEEMNNPRTWY permanent way
AAEEMNNSSTTW New Statesman
AAEEMNORSSTW Western Samoa
AAEEMNRSTTTY testamentary
AAEEMPRSSSUY passy-measure
AAEENNOSSSTU assentaneous
AAEENNPPRSST apparentness
AAEENNPRSTUU superannuate
AAEENPRRTWYY new year party
AAEENPRSTTWY Payne Stewart
AAEEOOPRSTTW ware potatoes
AAEEPRRSSTTT streets apart
AAEERRRSTTUU restaurateur
AAEFFFLNORSS false saffron
AAEFFGIMORRS fromage frais
AAEFFHLMNORS an arm of flesh
AAEFFHLORTTW half after two
AAEFFIIMNORR Foraminifera
AAEFFINPRSTT paraffin test
AAEFFQRRSTTU quarterstaff
AAEFGHHIILNT faith healing✧
AAEFGHILLNRT half-integral
AAEFGHIMNRRS sharefarming
AAEFGHLLNNPR flannelgraph
AAEFGIKLMNRW walking frame
AAEFGILLLNOT flagellation
AAEFGILLNOPT foliage plant
AAEFGILNNORY lay a finger on
AAEFGINNORTT engraftation
AAEFGINRRTUW fugie-warrant
AAEFGIPRTTUY fatigue-party
AAEFGKLNRRTU Art Garfunkel
AAEFGLLLORTY flagellatory
AAEFGLLMORSW gallows frame
AAEFGLMMOPRT platform game
AAEFGLMNOORR floor manager
AAEFGNNRRSST fragrantness
AAEFHHLOSUWY halfway house
AAEFHILLRSTT lateral shift
AAEFHILMNSSS fish-salesman
AAEFHILNOPST fashion plate
AAEFHILNRSTW fathers-in-law
AAEFHINPRSST fresh as paint
AAEFIILMORRV overfamiliar
AAEFIJNNNOOT Joan Fontaine
AAEFILLNSSSY self-analysis
AAEFILNORRTY reflationary
AAEFILNPRTVY trypaflavine
AAEFILNQRRTU quarter-final
AAEFIMRSSTTU mutessarifat
AAEFIPPRRSSU safari supper
AAEFKKLNORRW work a flanker
AAEFKLLLNPRU pull a flanker
AAEFKLMMNRRZ Franz Klammer
AAEFLLLNSSTY Stanley Falls
AAEFLLNOPSTU pull a fast one
AAEFLLOPPRSV self-approval
AAEFLMNOOPTT footplateman

AAEFLNOQRRTU quartern loaf
AAEFNNOOSSTT as often as not
AAEFOOPRSSUV Sea of Vapours
AAEGGGHILNRU laughing gear
AAEGGGIKMNRU marking gauge
AAEGGGILNNSU sign language
AAEGGHHIOPRR hagiographer
AAEGGHIRRSTT straight gear
AAEGGHLNNRSW slang-whanger
AAEGGHMNOPRT magnetograph
AAEGGHNOPRST steganograph
AAEGGHOPRSSU rough passage
AAEGGIIMNRRR marriage-ring
AAEGGIIMNRRS gregarianism
AAEGGIINOPRT arpeggiation
AAEGGIMRRRSY merry as a grig
AAEGGINRSTTT starting gate
AAEGGIOPPRTU appoggiature
AAEGGLLNORRY organ-gallery
AAEGHHIKNRST earthshaking
AAEGHHKMOSTU make as though
AAEGHHNNRUVY Henry Vaughan
AAEGHHOPPRRS phraseograph
AAEGHIILLMUW William Hague
AAEGHIILNRTX exhilarating
AAEGHIINORRT Te Rangi Hiroa
AAEGHIKNQRTU earthquaking
AAEGHILNORST solar heating
AAEGHIMMNPSS gamesmanship
AAEGHIMMORRT hierogrammat
AAEGHIMNPSTY Pythian games
AAEGHIMNRRTW heartwarming
AAEGHIMORRRT metrorrhagia
AAEGHINPPRSW paper-washing
AAEGHIOORSTT Horatio Gates
AAEGHKNOPRRU keraunograph
AAEGHLLNNOTT ten-gallon hat
AAEGHLMNRSTT at arm's length
AAEGHLMNRSTU manslaughter
slaughterman
AAEGHLMOPPRY ampelography
AAEGHLMRSTUV Gustav Mahler
AAEGHLOPRTTU Telautograph®
AAEGHMNOOPSU phaenogamous
AAEGHMNOSTTU metagnathous
AAEGHMNOTTUY thaumatogeny
AAEGHNNRRTTY Henry Grattan
AAEGHNOPPRRT pantographer
AAEGHNOPRRRU uranographer
AAEGHNOQRSSU orange squash
AAEGHNRRTUWY Hungary water
AAEGHOOPPRRV evaporograph
AAEGIIKKLLMN make a killing
AAEGIIKMNNSZ skin magazine
AAEGIILLMRRT Material Girl
AAEGIILLNNPS plane sailing
AAEGIILLNOST legalisation
AAEGIILLNOTZ legalization
AAEGIILMNORT emigrational
AAEGIILMRTUV virtual image
AAEGIILNNOTT gelatination
AAEGIIMMNNOT meningiomata
AAEGIIMMNRRS Mare Marginis
AAEGIIMNNORT emargination
AAEGIIMNNRSW Wagnerianism
AAEGIINNOPRT repagination
AAEGIINNPPRT appertaining
AAEGIJMOOPRS Jorge Sampaio
AAEGIKKMMNRT market-making
AAEGIKLNPRTV valet parking
AAEGIKNNOORV kangaroo vine
AAEGILLLQSSU Lalique glass
AAEGILLNNPUV Paul Langevin
AAEGILLNNTTY tangentially
AAEGILMNOPRS angiospermal
AAEGILMNPPUZ pulp magazine
AAEGILNNOPPR Angela Rippon
AAEGILNNPRTV vinegar-plant
AAEGILNNRRWY early-warning
AAEGILNNSTUY nauseatingly
AAEGILNPRTVY leaving party
AAEGILNPSTTU Septuagintal
AAEGIMMNNPRS Pan-Germanism
AAEGIMNNOTTU augmentation
AAEGIMNORRTY agrimonetary
AAEGIMNRRRTU ring-armature
AAEGIMNRRSTT transmigrate
AAEGIMNRSTTX taxing master
AAEGIMNSTTTY syntagmatite
AAEGIMRRSTTU magistrature
AAEGINNOPTTV vantage point
AAEGINOORRTT aerating root
AAEGINORSSTU stegosaurian
AAEGINPRRTTW water-parting
AAEGINPRSSST press against
AAEGINSSSTTW wasting asset
AAEGIRSTVVWY gravity waves
AAEGKLLMORSW gallows-maker
AAEGKNQRRSTU strange quark
AAEGLLNNOPTY pentagonally
AAEGLLNORTTY tetragonally
AAEGLLNPPPRT grapple-plant
AAEGLMNORTVY galvanometry
AAEGLMOOPSSU gamosepalous
AAEGLMOOPSTU gamopetalous
AAEGLMORSSUU megalosaurus
AAEGMOPPSSTT postage stamp
AAEGOPRRSSST esparto grass
AAEHHIIKLPTW whiptail hake
AAEHHIINRSTU hiatus hernia
AAEHHILMOPTX exophthalmia
AAEHHIMNSSTW what's-his-name
AAEHHIMRRRRS marsh-harrier
AAEHHINNOPST phonasthenia
AAEHHNOPRTTW on the warpath
AAEHIIILNNTV annihilative
AAEHIIKKKMNN Mika Häkkinen
AAEHIILMMPTU epithalamium
AAEHIILMNOPT epithalamion
AAEHIILNNRST Sir Nathaniel
AAEHIILNORTX exhilaration
AAEHIINOPRTZ azathioprine

AAEHIINOPSTT	hepatisation
AAEHIINOPTTZ	hepatization
AAEHIKNOSTTV	stakhanovite
AAEHILLMORSV	Villahermosa
AAEHILLNNNPY	phenylalanin
AAEHILLPSSWY	Paisley shawl
AAEHILMMRSTU	rheumatismal
AAEHILMNOTXY	haematoxylin
AAEHILMNPSSS	salesmanship
AAEHILMOSSTY	haematolysis
AAEHILMRSTUY	amateurishly
AAEHILNNOPRT	paranthelion
AAEHILNNRSTT	transleithan
AAEHILNOPPSS	Phalaenopsis
AAEHILORRTXY	exhilaratory
AAEHILRRRSTT	trailer trash
AAEHIMMRSSTU	shamateurism
AAEHIMNNORTU	mountain hare
AAEHIMNNSSSU	haussmannise
AAEHIMNNSSUZ	haussmannize
AAEHIMNORSTY	hysteromania
AAEHIMNPRSTW	watermanship
AAEHIMNSSTTW	what's-its-name
AAEHIMPPRRSY	primary phase
AAEHIMPRSTTW	Matthew Paris
AAEHINNOPTTY	enantiopathy
AAEHINNORTTW	Ian Trethowan
AAEHINNRSTUY	annuity share
AAEHINOPPRST	Siphonaptera
AAEHINOPRSST	Aristophanes
AAEHINOPSSTY	enhypostasia
AAEHIPPRRSST	star sapphire
AAEHJLLMOOST	hojatoleslam
AAEHJMMNSSTY	James Nasmyth
AAEHKKLLNPTW	walk the plank
AAEHKKMMNRUW	Kwame Nkrumah
AAEHLLMOPRSX	morphallaxes
AAEHLLMORSTW	Thomas Waller
AAEHLLNRSSTV	servants' hall
AAEHLMNNRSTU	Real Huntsman
AAEHLMNOOTXY	Haematoxylon
AAEHLMNOPTWY	play the woman
AAEHLNPRSTTW	shawl pattern
AAEHMMNOOPRT	Nematomorpha
AAEHMNOOPRRT	parathormone
AAEHMNOOPRSS	anamorphoses
AAEHMNOPSSYY	A Sea Symphony
AAEHMOOPRSTT	potato masher
AAEHMOORSTTU	atheromatous
AAEHMORSSTVY	Thomas Savery
AAEHNOPRRSTT	prostanthera
AAEHNOPRSTTY	Thysanoptera
AAEHOPPPRSSY	parapophyses
AAEIIILMSSTV	assimilative
AAEIIIMMNRSS	semi-Arianism
AAEIIJLLMMSW	William James
AAEIIKLLOTVW	A View to a Kill
AAEIIKMNRSTX	Sir Max Aitken
AAEIIKNRTTTW	Katerina Witt
AAEIIKORRTVW	River Waikato
AAEIILLLMPWY	William Paley
AAEIILLLNOST	Alan Sillitoe
AAEIILLMMRTY	immaterially
AAEIILLMNRTX	intermaxilla
AAEIILLMRTTX	extralimital
AAEIILLNOQTU	illaqueation
AAEIILLNORTT	alliteration
AAEIILLNPSTU	sinupalliate
AAEIILLNPSTY	sapientially
AAEIILMNNOTT	alimentation
AAEIILMNNRRT	interlaminar
AAEIILMNOORT	amelioration
AAEIILMNPTUV	manipulative
AAEIILMOPRRT	imperatorial
AAEIILMRTTUV	multivariate
AAEIILNNOPST	penalisation
AAEIILNNOPTZ	penalization
AAEIILNOPRST	epistolarian
AAEIILNOQSTU	equalisation
AAEIILNOQTUZ	equalization
AAEIILNORRST	rationaliser
AAEIILNORRTZ	rationalizer
AAEIILNORSTT	Aristotelian
	laterisation
AAEIILNORSTV	Itala version
	velarisation
AAEIILNORTTZ	laterization
AAEIILNORTVZ	velarization
AAEIILNPRSTT	interspatial
AAEIILPPRSVY	appraisively
AAEIIMNOPSST	impassionate
AAEIIMNOSSTV	avitaminoses
AAEIIMPPRSTU	Marius Petipa
AAEIIMRRRSTV	River Maritsa
AAEIINNOSTTT	tetanisation
AAEIINNOTTTZ	tetanization
AAEIINNRSSST	sanitariness
AAEIINOPQRTU	equiparation
AAEIINOPRRTT	repatriation
AAEIINOPRTTX	expatriation
AAEIINQTTTUV	quantitative
AAEIJLMNRSUZ	Jules Mazarin
AAEIJMSSTUUV	mauvais sujet
AAEIKLMMNNTU	Immanuel Kant
AAEIKLMNOTUU	Mount Kilauea
AAEIKMNPPSTY	make it snappy
AAEILLLMNOTW	an all-time low
AAEILLLMRTTU	multilateral
AAEILLLNORTY	relationally
AAEILLLNRTUY	unilaterally
AAEILLLRRTTY	trilaterally
AAEILLMNNOUV	nominal value
AAEILLMNNSUY	semi-annually
AAEILLMNRRTY	artilleryman
AAEILLMPRRXY	premaxillary
AAEILLNNNOTW	Antonine Wall
AAEILLNNTTTW	tenant at will
	tenant-at-will
AAEILLNORSTY	senatorially
AAEILLOQRTUY	equatorially
AAEILLPPSUVY	applausively
AAEILMMNNORR	Norman Mailer

AAEILMMNNOTU mountain meal
AAEILMMOPRTV primeval atom
AAEILMNNOSTT Lamentations
AAEILMNORRSY Royal Marines
AAEILMNORSTV malversation
AAEILMNPSSUX pansexualism
AAEILMNRSSTT mistranslate
AAEILMOPRTTY atemporality
AAEILMORSTTW Mariotte's law
AAEILNNNPSVY Pennsylvania
AAEILNNOPPTT pentapolitan
AAEILNNOPRTT replantation
AAEILNNOPTTX explantation
AAEILNNQTTUV quantivalent
AAEILNNRSTTU Saint Laurent
AAEILNNRSTUU unnaturalise
AAEILNNRTUUZ unnaturalize
AAEILNOPRTTT tetrapolitan
AAEILNOPSSTU antisepalous
AAEILNOPSSTY passionately
AAEILNOPSTTU antipetalous
AAEILNOPSTZZ Pestalozzian
AAEILNORSTTW law-stationer
AAEILNPPSUUV unapplausive
AAEILNPRRSUV spur valerian
AAEILNPRSSTT plaster saint
AAEILNPSSTUX pansexualist
AAEILNPSTUXY pansexuality
AAEILNQRRTTU Latin Quarter
AAEILNRSSSTU salutariness
AAEILORRSTTT latirostrate
AAEILPPRRUWY purple airway
AAEILQRRSUWY squirrel away
AAEIMMMOSSTT metasomatism
AAEIMNNORRRV River Marañón
AAEIMNNOTTUY ayuntamiento
AAEIMNOOOOPT onomatopoeia
AAEIMNORTTTU mutation rate
AAEIMQRRSTUX square matrix
AAEINNOPRSXY expansionary
AAEINNOPSSTU unpassionate
AAEINNOPTTTY pay attention
AAEINNORSSTU Austronesian
AAEINNPRRSTT trainer pants
AAEINOPRRSTU pterosaurian
AAEINOQRSTUY quaestionary
AAEINORRSTTU restauration
AAEINPPRRSTW water parsnip
AAEIOOPRRSTT root parasite
AAEIPPRRSTTV private parts
AAEIRRSSSTTU Erasistratus
AAEJKMNOOTTY Jomo Kenyatta
AAEJLLMNNOUY Joanna Lumley
AAEKLMNNORTU nomenklatura
AAEKLMORRTWW low watermark
low-water mark
AAEKLMRRRUWY Murray Walker
AAEKLNNOOPRT aeroplankton
AAEKLOPRSTTY keratoplasty
AAEKNOQRRSUW narrow squeak
AAEKNORRSTTT stratotanker
AAELLLNPRRTU parallel turn
AAELLLOPPRRT parallel port
AAELLMMNOSSU Seamus Mallon
AAELLMNNORTY ornamentally
AAELLMRRTUXY extramurally
AAELLNNPSTUY unpleasantly
AAELLNOPRSTT entoplastral
AAELLNRSSTUU ultrasensual
AAELMNNNORTU unornamental
AAELMNNORTTU ultramontane
AAELMNOOPRTT protonematal
AAELMOOPRSTZ spermatozoal
AAELNNOOPRTY pantaloonery
AAELNNOPRRTU annual report
AAELNNPRRSTT transplanter
AAELNNPRSTUY unpleasantry
AAELNOORRSUZ auroral zones
AAELNOPRTTWY Walter Payton
AAELNPRRSTUU supernatural
AAELNPRSSTUY sunray pleats
AAELNRSSSTTW stalwartness
AAELNRSSTUUU lusus naturae
AAELOOPRRTTX extrapolator
AAELOPRSSTUU Plateosaurus
AAEMMNOPRRTT Maarten Tromp
AAEMNNNORSTT transmontane
AAEMNNOORTUY neuroanatomy
AAEMNNOORUUV nouveau roman
AAEMNOOPRSTZ spermatozoan
AAEMNOPRSTTU portmanteaus
AAEMNOPRTTUX portmanteaux
AAEMNQSTTTUU quantum state
AAEMOORSTTTU teratomatous
AAEMOOSSTTTU steatomatous
AAEMQRRRSTUY quarrymaster
AAEOPPRSSTTU passe-partout
AAEOPRRRSSTW parrot-wrasse
AAEOPRRRTTTY pyrotartrate
AAFFFHJLNOST John Falstaff
AAFFGIKLNSTW walking-staff
AAFFGILLNNSY snaffling-lay
AAFFGILNSSTY Tiffany glass
AAFFLNOOPSTU pufftaloonas
AAFGHIMNRRST trash farming
AAFGHINNPRST span-farthing
AAFGIILMMNRR marginal firm
AAFGIKLMNNOR frankalmoign
AAFIIILNRTTU futilitarian
AAFIILLMNRUY unfamiliarly
AAFIILMMNNOT inflammation
AAFIILNNORTY inflationary
AAFIINRRSSTU Austin friars
AAFILLMMNOTU flammulation
AAFILMMNOORT malformation
AAFILMMNORTY inflammatory
AAFILMNNOTUX mountain flax
AAFILNNOOSTW law of nations
AAFILNNORTTU Fantin-Latour
AAFNOORRTTUW out of warrant
AAGGHNOOPRRY organography
AAGGIIILLNUV Luigi Galvani

AAGGIIINNRTT ingratiating
AAGGIIKLLNSS galligaskins
AAGGIKLLNRSS larking-glass
AAGGIKNQRSSU quaking-grass
AAGGLMMOORTY grammatology
AAGGNNOORTUU ourang-outang
AAGHHIINORRR rhinorrhagia
AAGHHMNOOPRR harmonograph
AAGHIILLRTWY light railway
AAGHIILMNRST animal rights
AAGHIINNNORT nothingarian
AAGHIINNOSTW washingtonia✧
AAGHIJLLNNOO John Galliano
AAGHIKLNNORS loan sharking
AAGHIKLNPSSY shaking palsy
AAGHIKLNRSTT trash talking
AAGHIKLRSTTT straight talk
AAGHILLNRTTU natural light
AAGHILMMNNOS Simon Langham
AAGHILMOORTY hamartiology
AAGHILPRSTTY straight play
AAGHIMNSSTTU assuming that
AAGHIMOOPRST Mastigophora
AAGHINOPPSTT pantophagist
AAGHINPRSSSS Spanish grass
AAGHIPRRSTTY stratigraphy
AAGHIRSSTTWY straightways
AAGHKNNNOSSS on Shanks's nag
AAGHLLMOOPSU mallophagous
AAGHLMOOTTUY thaumatology
AAGHLOOPPRRY polarography
AAGHMNRTTUUU Mt Tungurahua
AAGHMRSTTUUU thaumaturgus
AAGHNOOPPSTU pantophagous
AAGHOOPPRSSU saprophagous
AAGIIILLNNPS plain sailing
AAGIIILNORRT irrigational
AAGIIINNNOTV invagination
AAGIIINNORTT ingratiation
AAGIIKLNNORW walking on air
AAGIILLNNPTW wall painting
AAGIILMNNRTU marginal-unit
AAGIILNNRSUY sanguinarily
AAGIILNPPRSY appraisingly
AAGIILOSSSUZ Louis Agassiz
AAGIIMNNOTWW waiting-woman
AAGIIMNRSTTU traumatising
AAGIIMNRTTUZ traumatizing
AAGIINNOORST organisation
AAGIINNOORTZ organization
AAGIINNORTUU inauguration
AAGIINNSSTUU Augustinians
AAGIINORSSTV savings ratio
AAGIKLNRSTWW walking straw
AAGIKMMNORSS kissogram man
AAGIKMNNORSS a king's ransom
AAGIKNPPSSTW task swapping
AAGILLLORSSY glossarially
AAGILLMNORSY organismally
AAGILLMNTUWY mulligatawny
AAGILLNRRTUY triangularly
AAGILMNRSSUU uranium glass
AAGILNNORSTU granulations
AAGILNNSSTWY slantingways
AAGILNORSTTU gastrulation
AAGILOOPRSTY parasitology
AAGIMNNOOTTU mountain goat
AAGIMNNRRSTT transmigrant
AAGINNOOSTTW station wagon
AAGINNPRSTUU run up against
AAGINORRTUUY inauguratory
AAGLLNOOPSTT stoop-gallant
AAGLMNOPRSSY laryngospasm
AAGLMOORTTUY traumatology
AAGLOPRSSUZZ Zsuzsa Polgar
AAGMMNNOOOSY many moons ago
AAGOPRRRSSSW sparrow grass
sparrow-grass
AAHHIIMMSSSV Miss Havisham
AAHHIIMRRSTT hamarthritis
AAHHIINNRRSS Sirhan Sirhan
AAHHINNNOTTX anthoxanthin
AAHHINOPRSTT Parthian shot
AAHHIOPPRSTU phosphaturia
AAHHIORRTTWY Rita Hayworth
AAHHIRRRRSTU Arthur Harris
AAHHJLLMNORS John Marshall
AAHHLMOPSTUY hypothalamus
AAHIIILLOPRU ailurophilia
AAHIIILNNNOT annihilation
AAHIIILNSTTX Italian sixth
AAHIILMNORTU inhalatorium
AAHIIMNNOSTU humanisation
AAHIIMNNOTUZ humanization
AAHIIMNORSTU Ohinamatsuri
AAHIIMOPPRSS paraphimosis
AAHIINOPSTXY asphyxiation
AAHIINPPRSST partisanship
AAHIINPRRSTT panarthritis
AAHIJKMMMRSU Jammu-Kashmir
AAHIJLLMOOST hojatolislam
AAHIKMMNPRSS marksmanship
AAHIKMNNRSTU Turkish manna
AAHIKMNOSSTV stakhanovism
AAHILLMOPRSX morphallaxis
AAHILLNNOPSY pollyannaish
AAHILLNNOPTY antiphonally
AAHILLOPRSTX trophallaxis
AAHILMMOPRTU prothalamium
AAHILMNOOPRT prothalamion
AAHILNNNOTTU national hunt✧
AAHILOPPSSST hospital pass
AAHIMMOPPRRS paramorphism
AAHIMNOOPRSS anamorphosis
AAHINNORRTTU not turn a hair
AAHINOPPSSTZ Spanish topaz
AAHIOPPPRSSY parapophysis
AAHJLNOORTTV John Travolta
AAHKNNORSSUY Susannah York
AAHLMNOPRSUY orphan-asylum
AAHLNORRSTUY anarthrously
AAHLOPRRSTTY arthroplasty

AAHMNOORSTTW	Thomas Warton
AAHMNOOSTTUX	xanthomatous
AAHMNRRRSTUY	Harry S Truman
AAHMOQRRSSUW	marrow-squash
AAHNOPPRRSTU	paranthropus
AAIIILMNOSST	assimilation
	Islamisation
AAIIILMNOSTZ	Islamization
AAIIILMPRTTY	impartiality
AAIIILNNOSTT	Latinisation
AAIIILNNOSTV	insalivation
AAIIILNNOTTZ	Latinization
AAIIILNOSTTV	visitational
	vitalisation
AAIIILNOTTVZ	vitalization
AAIIILORSTTV	visitatorial
AAIIIMMNNORR	Marino Marini
AAIIIMMNOSTX	maximisation
AAIIIMMNOTXZ	maximization
AAIIIMNNRSTU	unitarianism✧
AAIIIMNOSSTV	avitaminosis
AAIIINNNOSTT	insanitation
AAIIINNOSSTT	sanitisation
AAIIINNOSTTZ	sanitization
AAIIINORSSTT	satirisation
AAIIINORSTTV	variationist
AAIIINORSTTZ	satirization
AAIIKLNRSSSY	risk analysis
AAIILLLMRWWY	William Lawry
AAIILLLNNPTY	plantain lily
AAIILLMOPRSY	mariposa lily
AAIILLMOSSTT	altaltissimo
AAIILLNNOSTT	installation
AAIILLNOOTTV	volitational
AAIILLNORRTY	irrationally
AAIILMNNOPTT	implantation
AAIILMNNOPTU	manipulation
AAIILMNOORST	moralisation
AAIILMNOORTZ	moralization
AAIILMNOOTTV	motivational
AAIILMNOSSTT	saltationism
AAIILMNOSSTV	Salvationism
AAIILMORSSTY	assimilatory
AAIILNNNOOTT	intonational
AAIILNNNOOTV	innovational
AAIILNNOPSTT	plastination
AAIILNNORSTT	transitional
AAIILNOOPPST	appositional
AAIILNOOPRST	polarisation
AAIILNOOPRTZ	polarization
AAIILNOORSST	solarisation
AAIILNOORSTV	valorisation
AAIILNOORSTZ	solarization
AAIILNOORTVZ	valorization
AAIILNOOSTTT	totalisation
AAIILNOOTTTZ	totalization
AAIILNORRSTU	ruralisation
AAIILNORRTUZ	ruralization
AAIILNOSSTTT	saltationist
AAIILNOSSTTV	Salvationist
AAIILNPTTVYY	nativity play
AAIILORSTTTU	tralatitious
AAIIMNNOORST	Romanisation
AAIIMNNOORTZ	Romanization
AAIIMNOORSTT	amortisation
AAIIMNOORTTZ	amortization
AAIINNNNOSTU	antoninianus
AAIINNOPRSTT	strain a point
AAIINNOQSTTU	quantisation
AAIINNOQTTUZ	quantization
AAIINNORSTTU	instauration
AAIINOOPRSTV	vaporisation
AAIINOOPRTVZ	vaporization
AAIJORRRSWZZ	Jazz Warriors
AAIKLNSSSTVY	Stanislavsky
AAILLMMNPPTU	platinum lamp
AAILLMNNOPSY	pollyannaism
AAILLMNOPRTT	all-important
AAILLMNOTTUY	mutationally
AAILLMNRRTUY	intramurally
AAILLMOPRTYY	morality play
AAILLNOOPTWW	wallop in a tow
AAILLOQTTTUY	total quality
AAILLORSTTUY	salutatorily
AAILMNOPRRSW	spinal marrow
AAILMNOPRTUY	manipulatory
AAILMOORRSTU	Mariolatrous
AAILOORSSTTU	saltatorious
AAIMMNOORRTU	Mount Roraima
AAIMNNOOPSTU	mountain soap
AAIMNNRRSTUU	transuranium
AAIMNOOSSTTT	somatostatin
AAINNORSTTUU	unsaturation
AAINORSSTTUU	Titanosaurus
AAIOOPPPRRRT	appropriator
AAKLNNNNOOPT	nanoplankton
AAKLNORSSUUY	Ankylosaurus
AALLMOOPPRST	protoplasmal
AALLNOORSWYY	Rosalyn Yalow
AALMMNNNOORT	Norman Lamont
AALMNOOPRSTY	trypanosomal
AALORSTTTUWY	statutory law
AAMMNNOOOTWW	woman to woman
ABBBBBBEEILL	bibble-babble
ABBBBEEGGILL	gibble-gabble
ABBBBEEILLRR	ribble-rabble
ABBBCEEHLNOT	technobabble
ABBBCEHLOPSY	psychobabble
ABBBCEILRSSU	subscribable
ABBBCEKLORRS	barber's block
ABBBCELNNORY	bonny-clabber
ABBBCIILLTUY	clubbability
ABBBDDEEEHLU	bubble-headed
ABBBDELORYZZ	bobby-dazzler
ABBBEELMRRRY	bramble-berry
ABBBEESTTTUY	test-tube baby
ABBBEGHIILNS	Bible-bashing
ABBBEHLMORTU	blabbermouth
ABBBGGIILNOS	Bilbo Baggins
ABBBGINRRSSU	brass rubbing
ABBBHIIILOOP	bibliophobia
ABBCCDIKLORW	cow blackbird

ABBCCEEHIIRR Berbice chair
ABBCCEGHIMNO beachcombing
ABBCCILMNOOV volcanic bomb
ABBCDEEHIMRR bride-chamber
ABBCDEEKKNOR broken-backed
ABBCDGIIKLNR blackbirding
ABBCEEEGGORR George Crabbe
ABBCEEEINRRU Eunice Barber
ABBCEEGGKLRU buckle-beggar
ABBCEEHHOSTY The Beach Boys
ABBCEEJKMORT bomber jacket
ABBCEEKLNOSS backboneless
ABBCEENORTUY abbey-counter
ABBCEFHILMNR bramble-finch
ABBCEFINORRS carbon fibres
ABBCEGHINNTU nubbing-cheat
ABBCEIKRRSTU rabbit-sucker
ABBCELOOORRR corroborable
ABBCFHKOOORU Book of Baruch
ABBCFIILORST fibroblastic
ABBCHIJKORSS Sir Jack Hobbs
ABBDDEEEILST bedside table
ABBDDEEKLNOU double-banked
ABBDDEEOORSS absorbed dose
ABBDDEGINORW Edward Gibbon
ABBDDEMNRRUU Edmund Rubbra
ABBDEEEGINRT bate-breeding
ABBDEEFLORSS self-absorbed
ABBDEEGIILRY Bailey bridge
ABBDEGHOORTY go by the board
ABBDEGNRRSUU garden suburb
ABBDEHIILRSY hybridisable
ABBDEHIILRYZ hybridizable
ABBDEILLMRRU umbrella bird
ABBDELLLNRUY land-lubberly
ABBDELNORTTY brandy-bottle
ABBDENORRSSU brass-bounder
ABBDENRRTTUY brandy butter
ABBDFFIILNOU bound-bailiff
ABBDHIKOORTY birthday-book
ABBDILMOOPSS bomb disposal
ABBDILOORRST Bristol board
ABBEEEELMMRR rememberable
ABBEEEFGGILR beggar belief
ABBEEEIILLMW William Beebe
ABBEEEILLNUV unbelievable
ABBEEELMMRRY rememberably
ABBEEELNRTTU unbetterable
ABBEEEMMNNOR membrane bone
ABBEEFLOORTW Tower of Babel
ABBEEFNRSSUY Furness Abbey
ABBEEGHILLNT bathing belle
ABBEEGMNORRR barber-monger
ABBEEGMORRTU Robert Mugabe
ABBEEHILNOOP belonephobia
ABBEEILLNUVY unbelievably
ABBEEILMRRSU reimbursable
ABBEEILNORSV inobservable
ABBEEILOPQRU equiprobable
ABBEEILRRTTU irrebuttable
ABBEEINNRTTY Tintern Abbey
ABBEELMNORST stone bramble
ABBEELNORSUV unobservable
ABBEELOPRSTV l'Abbé Prévost
ABBEELORRRSU rabble-rouser
ABBEELOSSSTU blue asbestos
ABBEELRRSTUV subvertebral
ABBEENNOTWWY Newtownabbey
ABBEFFLORRUY buffalo-berry
ABBEFFNNOSUX snuffbox bean
ABBEFHIIJSUU Jusuf Habibie
ABBEFHIORRSY Frobisher Bay
ABBEGHLNOORR Baron Holberg
ABBEGIILLLNN enabling bill
ABBEGIINNOTT babingtonite
ABBEHHMOOSST Thomas Hobbes
ABBEHIIMNOSS Hobbesianism
ABBEHIIRSTTW white rabbits
ABBEHIMNORUY Bohemian ruby
ABBEHIMORRRS Bomber Harris
ABBEILLMNOTU Bill Beaumont
ABBEILNOORTT borlotti bean
ABBEIMNNORTT Norman Tebbit
ABBEIMNNRRUY binary number
ABBELLLRSTUU tubular bells
ABBELLMRRSUU subumbrellar
ABBEMNNORRUY baryon number
ABBENNNOORST non-absorbent
ABBFIILLLPSU spill a bibful
ABBFLLOOOOTT football boot
ABBGHIILOPRY bibliography
ABBHINOOOPRT brontophobia
ABBHKMNORRSU monk's rhubarb
ABBHLOORTWWY throw a wobbly
ABBHMOOOOSST bamboo shoots
ABBIIIILMNOT imbibitional
ABBIILNNOOTU obnubilation
ABBIINOORTTU bioturbation
ABBIMRSSTTUY Sir Matt Busby
ABCCCEEHMNOY come-by-chance
ABCCCEHIILNY bicycle chain
ABCCCEKKLORT bracket clock
ABCCCHOOOPTU tobacco pouch
ABCCCINNOTUY concubitancy
ABCCDDIILMOY molybdic acid
ABCCDEEELPST bespectacled
ABCCDEEHILNN blanc-de-Chine
ABCCDEEHKKLU huckle-backed
ABCCDEEHKORR checkerboard
ABCCDEHILMNO chemical bond
ABCCDEHILORU coachbuilder
ABCCDEHLMORU cloud chamber
ABCCDEIKNOPY by cock and pie
ABCCDEILNOSU build a sconce
ABCCDEINOOSY occasioned by
ABCCDGHIINRT bird-catching
ABCCDHILNSUW club sandwich
ABCCDHILRSTU scratchbuild
ABCCDIIORRTU circuit board
ABCCDILNOORU council-board
ABCCDKLORUZZ buzzard-clock
ABCCEEEELRSU cause célèbre

ABCCEEEHLNRT treble chance
ABCCEEEILLNT table licence
ABCCEEEKPRRT bracket-creep
ABCCEEELNORT concelebrate
ABCCEEENORRS arborescence
ABCCEEGINNRU buccaneering
ABCCEEHINRSU buccaneerish
ABCCEEHKLOTT beat the clock
ABCCEEIILNSS inaccessible
ABCCEEIKKNRR Rickenbacker
ABCCEEIKLRTT cricket table
ABCCEEILLNOR reconcilable
ABCCEEIORRST Rebecca riots
ABCCEELMNRRU Bruce McLaren
ABCCEELNNORT concelebrant
ABCCEELORRSU clare-obscure
clear-obscure
ABCCEEMNNRRU encumbrancer
ABCCEENNOSTT contabescent
ABCCEENORRTU counterbrace
ABCCEHIILLNT chill cabinet
ABCCEHIIMNOS biomechanics
ABCCEHIKMRST chamber-stick
ABCCEHILLRUY cherubically
ABCCEHIMMRSU chamber music
ABCCEHINRTUW Bruce Chatwin
ABCCEHLNOOOS beacon school
ABCCEHLOOOTX chocolate-box
ABCCEHLORSTY Scotch barley
ABCCEIIILRST criticisable
ABCCEIIILRTZ criticizable
ABCCEIILNOOT coenobitical
ABCCEIILNSSY inaccessibly
ABCCEIINRRSU cabin cruiser
ABCCEIKLORRT erratic block
ABCCEILLNORY reconcilably
ABCCEILMMNOU communicable
ABCCEILNNOOS conscionable
ABCCEILNORTT contractible
ABCCEILORRSU clair-obscure
ABCCEILORSTU scrobiculate
ABCCEIOPRSSS basic process
ABCCEKLMNOOY black economy
ABCCELNOSTUY bouncy castle
ABCCENOORRRY raccoon-berry
ABCCGIKNORSS back-crossing
ABCCHHILOOOP ochlophobiac
ABCCHHIMOORT bathochromic
ABCCHHRRSSTU scratch brush
ABCCHILLMORU chlorambucil
ABCCHILRSTTU scratchbuilt
ABCCIILLSTUY cubistically
ABCCIILOPSTU suboccipital
ABCCIIMOORST macrobiotics
ABCCILLOOSTY octosyllabic
ABCCILMMNOUY communicably
ABCCILNNOOSY conscionably
ABCCKLNORTUY Black Country
ABCCKOOOSSST Cossack boots
ABCDDEHIILNR Hildebrandic
ABCDDGIKLNPU black pudding
ABCDEEEELRST sacred beetle
ABCDEEEHILPR decipherable
ABCDEEEHLORR breech-loader
ABCDEEEILNTT indetectable
ABCDEEEILNUV undeceivable
ABCDEEEINRTY Aberdeen City
ABCDEEELLNTU undelectable
ABCDEEELNRTU uncelebrated
ABCDEEELNTTU undetectable
ABCDEEGHLORU double-charge
ABCDEEGIKNOR code-breaking
ABCDEEHIINRU Richie Benaud
ABCDEEHIPPRR bread-chipper
ABCDEEHOQRRU chequerboard
red quebracho
ABCDEEIILLMN medicine ball
ABCDEEIILLNN indeclinable
ABCDEEILMNSS dissemblance
ABCDEEILMOST domesticable
ABCDEEILNNSU unascendible
ABCDEEILNORS considerable
ABCDEEILNRTU uncreditable
ABCDEEILORSV discoverable
ABCDEEIORRSV scrieveboard
ABCDEEKKLNRU bareknuckled
ABCDEEKKLORW break wedlock
ABCDEELLNORY beyond recall
ABCDEELMOOPS decomposable
ABCDEELRTTUU tuberculated
ABCDEEMNOOTT cane-bottomed
ABCDEFGIKLRU black-figured
ABCDEFKLRTTU flatbed truck
ABCDEFLOORRU forced labour
ABCDEFMOPRUU fume cupboard
ABCDEGHIILNR childbearing
child-bearing
ABCDEGHORRTU turbocharged
ABCDEGILNOTU double-acting
ABCDEHHLOOOR bachelorhood
ABCDEHIMNORY chimneyboard
ABCDEHINOOPS scaphoid bone
ABCDEHMOORST hors de combat
ABCDEHNOORRV chevron board
ABCDEHNORSTY body snatcher
ABCDEHNRRRYY cherry brandy
ABCDEIIILLRT liberticidal
ABCDEIILLNNY indeclinably
ABCDEIILRSTT distractible
ABCDEIINNSTZ Citizens' Band
ABCDEILLMNOT metallic bond
ABCDEILNORSY considerably
ABCDEILNOSTU discountable
ABCDEILORRTU direct labour
ABCDEILORSSS scissor blade
ABCDEILPSTUU subduplicate
ABCDEINOOPRS proboscidean
ABCDEINRSSSU business card
ABCDEIORSVYY Discovery Bay
ABCDEKLOORRU dock-labourer
ABCDELLNOOST second ballot
ABCDELMNOOPU compoundable

ABCDELNNOOTV covalent bond
ABCDELOOPRUV cupboard-love
ABCDENNOOTTU contend about
ABCDGHIINRTW birdwatching
ABCDGIILLNRS calling birds
ABCDGIKLNOOP blood packing
ABCDGIKNNOUW back-wounding
ABCDGINNORSS crossbanding
ABCDGINOORRS scoring board
ABCDHIIRSSTU Hudibrastics
ABCDHLNOORST chondroblast
ABCDIILLOPST diploblastic
ABCDIILMNOPU public domain
public-domain
ABCDIINOOPRS proboscidian
ABCDLLNOPRTU Portland Club
ABCDLNOOORRT control board
ABCEEEELPRTT carpet beetle
ABCEEEENPRRT carpenter-bee
ABCEEEFFIORR office-bearer
ABCEEEFNRSST benefactress
ABCEEEHHINPR hebephreniac
ABCEEEHPRRST breeches part
ABCEEEIILMPR impierceable
ABCEEEIKRRSV break service
ABCEEEILNTUX inexecutable
ABCEEEKLLORS block release
ABCEEEKLSTVY Steve Backley
ABCEEEKRRRTU truce-breaker
ABCEEELLMMNR cell membrane
ABCEEELMNORT electron beam
ABCEEELNNORU renounceable
ABCEEEMMNRRR remembrancer
ABCEEEMMNRRS remembrances
ABCEEEMNNRTU cetane number
ABCEEENORSUV verbenaceous
ABCEEFFIINRT febrifacient
ABCEEFIILLNY beneficially
ABCEEFIILNNU unbeneficial
ABCEEFILORRU air-force blue
ABCEEFINORST sorbefacient
ABCEEFLLOORS foreclosable
ABCEEGHLLNST cable's-length
ABCEEGHMRSTU guest-chamber
ABCEEGILLLNO eco-labelling
ABCEEGILNORS recognisable
ABCEEGILNORZ recognizable
ABCEEGLOPRSU barge-couples
ABCEEGNNORSS bonnes grâces
ABCEEHIKLMRU Michael Buerk
ABCEEHIKLNTT kitchen table
ABCEEHILLPST slip the cable
ABCEEHKMNRRT kerb-merchant
ABCEEHKMOSTT Becket Thomas
ABCEEHLMORRW lower chamber
ABCEEHLNNPTY penalty bench
ABCEEHLNNQUU unquenchable
ABCEEHMMNNRT embranchment
ABCEEHMORRSY Harry Secombe
ABCEEHMOSSUU amuse-bouches
ABCEEHMPPRRU upper chamber
ABCEEHMRSTTU butcher's meat
ABCEEHNNOSSU buenas noches
ABCEEHOPRRSS Haber process
ABCEEIILLNPX inexplicable
ABCEEIILLTTY electability
ABCEEIILNNNT bicentennial
ABCEEIILNRTX inextricable
ABCEEIINNNST inabstinence
ABCEEIJNOPST Jacob Epstein
ABCEEILLSSTU subcelestial
ABCEEILMMORS commiserable
ABCEEILMRRRY miracle berry
ABCEEILNNOTU unnoticeable
ABCEEILNNRST sentinel crab
ABCEEILNORSU ribonuclease
ABCEEILNOSSS sociableness
ABCEEILNPRRT Prince Albert
ABCEEILRSSTU resuscitable
ABCEEINNORSV inobservance
ABCEEINOORRT cerebrotonia
ABCEEINRRSTU canterburies
ABCEEIOPRSST step aerobics
ABCEEJKLMRTU lumberjacket
ABCEEJLMPRSU jumper cables
ABCEEKLNNORU unreckonable
ABCEEKLORRTW lower-bracket
ABCEEKPPRRTU upper-bracket
ABCEEKPRRSSU back pressure
ABCEELLLNOSU counsellable
ABCEELLMNOPT contemplable
ABCEELLMSTTU lamb's lettuce
ABCEELLNOOST console table
ABCEELLNPSSU culpableness
ABCEELLRRTTU tracer bullet
ABCEELLRSSSU Brussels lace
ABCEELMMMOOR commemorable
ABCEELMRRTTU marble-cutter
ABCEELOPRRSV procès-verbal
ABCEELOPRSTU prosecutable
ABCEEMNNORTU octane number
ABCEENNOORSX resonance-box
ABCEENNORSUV unobservance
ABCEENNORTUY Encounter Bay
ABCEENOPRRTU protuberance
ABCEEOOPRRRT baroreceptor
ABCEEORRSSUU burseraceous
ABCEFFINOORR baron-officer
ABCEFFKOOSST beat socks off
ABCEFHORRRTT craft brother
ABCEFIILOPRT optical fibre
ABCEFIIMOPRT Tampico fibre
ABCEFILNNNOU unconfinable
ABCEFILOPRTY cap of liberty
ABCEGGIKRSST beggar's ticks
ABCEGHIILNSS basic English✧
ABCEGHIKLLNS Black English
ABCEGHILLORR bachelor girl
ABCEGHILNORT bearing cloth
ABCEGHLNOOST hog-constable
ABCEGHORRRTU turbocharger
ABCEGIILNNOS incognisable

ABCEGIILNNOZ incognizable
ABCEGIIMNOST biomagnetics
ABCEGIINNORS in banco regis
ABCEGIJLMNOR crambo-jingle
ABCEGIKLNRRW kerb-crawling
ABCEGIKNORST backing store
ABCEGILMNOST single combat
ABCEGILNORSY recognisably
ABCEGILNORYZ recognizably
ABCEGILNPRUY burying place
ABCEGILOORTY bacteriology
ABCEGLLNOOTU conglobulate
ABCEGLMNRUUU gubernaculum
ABCEHHILLPTU public health
ABCEHHILOPRS bachelorship
ABCEHHINOOPT technophobia
ABCEHHRTTTUY buttery-hatch
ABCEHIILLNRY Hibernically
ABCEHIIMNPRU pichurim bean
ABCEHIJKNOTX jack-in-the-box✧
ABCEHIKNRSSS brackishness
ABCEHIKPPTTU pick up the tab
ABCEHIKSSTTT basket-stitch
ABCEHILLOPRY hyperbolical
ABCEHILMNRUU hibernaculum
ABCEHILSTTTY chastity belt
ABCEHIMPRRVY privy chamber
ABCEHINNOOTT ethnobotanic
ABCEHIRRRRSU crush barrier
ABCEHKLORTTT throttle back
ABCEHKLRSSUW swashbuckler
ABCEHKNORSTU sea buckthorn
ABCEHLLOOSTW blow the coals
ABCEHLMOOPSS peach blossom
ABCEHLNNQUUY unquenchably
ABCEIIILLRST liberalistic
ABCEIIILTTXY excitability
ABCEIIIMNORT biometrician
ABCEIIIMRSTU Marie biscuit
ABCEIILLMOWY William Boyce
ABCEIILLNPXY inexplicably
ABCEIILMNOPT incompatible
ABCEIILNOORU Luciano Berio
ABCEIILNRTUV vibratiuncle
ABCEIILNRTXY inextricably
ABCEIILOORST borosilicate
ABCEIILORSTT cristobalite
ABCEIILORTVY revocability
ABCEIILPRSTY plebiscitary
ABCEIINORRRS sonic barrier
ABCEIINORSTT obstetrician
ABCEIINORTTX Bettino Craxi
ABCEIIRSTTUW water biscuit
ABCEIKOSSTTT beat to sticks
ABCEILLNNOOS inconsolable
ABCEILLNORTU Oriental Club
ABCEILLNTUUV uncultivable
ABCEILMMNOTU incommutable
ABCEILMNNOSU inconsumable
ABCEILMNOPRU pre-Columbian
ABCEILMNOPTU incomputable
ABCEILMOPRST problematics
ABCEILNORTUU elucubration
ABCEILOOSSTT osteoblastic
ABCEILOPRRTT protractible
ABCEILOPSSST speiss cobalt
ABCEIMMNORTU atomic number
ABCEIPRSSSUY presbyacusis
ABCEKNNORSTU turn one's back
ABCELLLNOORT controllable
ABCELLLOOSTY octosyllable
ABCELMNOOPSU uncomposable
ABCELNNORTUY contubernyal
ABCELNOPRRUU unprocurable
ABCELNORSTTU counterblast
ABCELOPRRSUU subopercular
ABCEMNNORRRU Marcobrunner
ABCEMOOPSSSW bow-compasses
ABCENORSSSSU scabrousness
ABCENOSSTUUU subcutaneous
ABCEOOPRRTTU Probate Court
ABCFFHILOPSU buffalo chips
ABCFFKLLOOST block of flats
ABCFGHIIKLNS black-fishing
ABCFHIKOOORS Book of Sirach
ABCFLNOOORRU fluorocarbon
ABCGGHIIKLNT back-lighting
ABCGGIKNOPRU backing group
ABCGHHIKNSUW bushwhacking
ABCGHINRSTTU chart-busting
ABCGIIKLLNST blacklisting
ABCGIILLLMNW climbing wall
ABCGIILLLOOY biologically
ABCGILLMNRSY scramblingly
ABCGILNNOOOT conglobation
ABCGILOORSTU surgical boot
ABCGLMOOOSTY colostomy bag
ABCHHILOOOPS school phobia
ABCHIIKLOSTY shockability
ABCHIILLOSTU thiobacillus
ABCHIILOOPRU ailurophobic
ABCHIIOOOPTX toxicophobia
ABCHIMMOORTZ Mt Chimborazo
ABCHIMORSSTX Christmas box
ABCHIMOSTTTU Thomas Cubitt
ABCHIOOOPPST scoptophobia
ABCHLLLOOTUY butyl alcohol
ABCIIIILRSTY irascibility
ABCIIIKLSTTY stickability
ABCIIILMNOTU umbilication
ABCIIILNRTUY incurability
ABCIILLNRTTU brilliant-cut
ABCIILMNOPTY incompatibly
ABCIILNNOTUY connubiality
ABCIILNNSTUU incunabulist
ABCIILNOPPRY principal boy
ABCIILNPPRSU subprincipal
ABCIILORRTUY orbicularity
ABCIIMNNOOST combinations
ABCIINORSTUU turbinacious
ABCIJKMMRTUY Jimmy Tarbuck
ABCILLLMOSYY symbolically

ABCILLLOPSYY polysyllabic
ABCILLLRSTYY Billy Crystal
ABCILLMNOOSY monosyllabic
ABCILLNNOOSY inconsolably
ABCILMMNOSTU noctambulism
ABCILMMNOTUY incommutably
ABCILMNNOSUY inconsumably
ABCILMNOSTTU noctambulist
ABCILMORRTUU microtubular
ABCILNOPRTUY notary public
ABCILOOPRRTU public orator
ABCILOOPSSTU subapostolic
ABCIMNORSSTU obscurantism
ABCIMNORSTUU rambunctious
ABCINOPRRSTU burn to a crisp
ABCINORRTTUY contributary
ABCINORSSTTU obscurantist
substraction
ABCLLLNOORTY controllably
ABCOOOORRRRT corroborator
ABDDDEEEHLOU double-headed
ABDDDEEHLNOU double-handed
ABDDDEELRSSY badly-dressed
ABDDDEENOORW Edward De Bono
ABDDDEGINPRU bread pudding
ABDDDEGNOORS branded goods
ABDDEEEEEHLT beetleheaded
ABDDEEEGGGLR badger-legged
ABDDEEEGRRRU Gerard Debreu
ABDDEEEHIRTW white-bearded
ABDDEEEHLLTU bullet-headed
ABDDEEEHLNYZ benzaldehyde
ABDDEEEHLORU double-header
ABDDEEELLORU double-dealer
ABDDEEELNNPU undependable
ABDDEEFGILNS false bedding
ABDDEEFORRSW Edward Forbes
ABDDEEGGLORU double dagger
ABDDEEGLLOUZ double-glazed
ABDDEEILLNRU unriddleable
ABDDEEILRSWW Edward B Lewis
ABDDEEIMNNST absent-minded
ABDDEELMNNOU double-manned
ABDDEELOPRSU double spread
ABDDEGILNNPT bedding plant
ABDDEGILNPRS spring-bladed
ABDDEHIILRTV David Hilbert
ABDDEIILMRTV David Trimble
ABDDEILMNPST blind-stamped
ABDDEILNNSSY day-blindness
ABDDEILNOOST bloodstained
ABDDEKMOOOSY Domesday book
ABDDEMNNOOSY Dombey and Son
ABDDGIINNPSU pudding basin
pudding-basin
ABDDGIMNNPRU bump and grind
ABDDGINOORRU boudoir grand
ABDDGLNOOORS dragon's blood
ABDDHILMNNOO hoodman-blind
ABDDILNNOOOR blood and iron
ABDDKMOOOOSY Doomsday book
ABDDNOORTUUW Outward Bound®
outward-bound
ABDEEEEGGLOR George Beadle
ABDEEEEILMRR irredeemable
ABDEEEELLLSV base-levelled
ABDEEEELLRRT larder beetle
ABDEEEELMNRU unredeemable
ABDEEEFGNRST Stefan Edberg
ABDEEEFGRRRT ferret-badger
ABDEEEFIILNS indefeasible
ABDEEEFIRTTW battered wife
ABDEEEGHLRRW hedge warbler
ABDEEEGILLRT great-bellied
ABDEEEGLRRSW sedge warbler
ABDEEEHILRRS shield-bearer
ABDEEEHLLRTW well-breathed
ABDEEEIILMRR irremediable
ABDEEEIILRTV deliberative
ABDEEEILLRTY deliberately
ABDEEEILMNRT determinable
ABDEEEILMRRY irredeemably
ABDEEEILNRTU undeliberate
ABDEEEIMSTTW time-bewasted
ABDEEEKLORRR broker-dealer
ABDEEELMNTTT battlemented
ABDEEELMNTZZ bedazzlement
ABDEEENOOPTT open to debate
ABDEEEOPRRSU pas de bourrée
ABDEEFFJNTUU Jean Dubuffet
ABDEEFHILMRT half-timbered
ABDEEFHINORV heaven forbid
ABDEEFIIILNT identifiable
ABDEEFIILNSY indefeasibly
ABDEEFIIRRTY dietary fibre
ABDEEFILRTTY field battery
ABDEEFINRTTY Betty Friedan
ABDEEFINSTUU subinfeudate
ABDEEFLPRSST flat-bed press
ABDEEFNORTTU debt of nature
ABDEEGGHIPRT bridge the gap
ABDEEGHLNORT long-breathed
ABDEEGILLNPS speedballing
ABDEEGILMNRS disembrangle
ABDEEGIMNORT board meeting
ABDEEGINNRRU underbearing
ABDEEGINOPST speedboating
ABDEEGKLLNOW knowledgable
ABDEEGLNOSTU obtuse-angled
ABDEEHHOPRRS rhabdosphere
ABDEEHILLOTY the Old Bailey
ABDEEHILMRTW marbled-white
ABDEEHLRSTTU lust-breathed
ABDEEHNNORTU unbreathed-on
ABDEEHNORTUW weather-bound
ABDEEIIILTTV debilitative
ABDEEIIKLRST East Kilbride
ABDEEIILMRRY irremediably
ABDEEIILNORT deliberation
ABDEEIILRSST destabiliser
ABDEEIILRSTZ destabilizer
ABDEEIINORTY obedientiary

ABDEEIIPRSST	base-spirited
ABDEEILLMRTT	reimbattell'd
ABDEEILLNORR	banderillero
ABDEEILMNOPR	imponderable
ABDEEILMNRTY	determinably
ABDEEILMRSSS	disassembler
ABDEEILNNRRV	Bernard Levin
ABDEEILORRUV	boulevardier
ABDEEILPRSTU	disreputable
ABDEEIMNOOSS	sesamoid bone
ABDEEIMOPPRR	bromide paper
ABDEEINNORSS	debonairness
ABDEEINNRSTU	Nubian Desert
ABDEEINNSSSU	unbiasedness
ABDEEJNORTUY	journey-bated
ABDEEKLMNOOS	make old bones
ABDEEKLNNRTU	underblanket
ABDEEKNORRRS	banker's order
ABDEEKORRRSW	sword-breaker
ABDEELLLNOST	Lonsdale belt
ABDEELLLORRR	rollerblader
ABDEELLPRSTU	spurtle-blade
ABDEELMNORST	demonstrable
ABDEELMOPRRT	Peter Lombard
ABDEELNNORSU	danseur noble
ABDEENORSSTU	obdurateness
ABDEEOOPPSYY	Peep-o'-day Boys
ABDEEOORRSTT	bored to tears
ABDEFFGIILNR	diffrangible
ABDEFFHLORSU	shuffleboard
ABDEFGILNOTT	floating debt
ABDEFIIILLOS	solidifiable
ABDEFIIILNTY	definability
	identifiably
ABDEFIILMNOR	informidable
ABDEFIILMNOU	unmodifiable
ABDEFIILMNRR	rifleman bird
ABDEFIKLNOOO	Book of Daniel
ABDEFILMNORU	unformidable
ABDEFINOSTUU	subfeudation
ABDEFLLORRTY	flatbed lorry
ABDEFNORRSSU	brassfounder
ABDEFORSTUUY	subfeudatory
ABDEGGNOORUU	Bourdon gauge
ABDEGHINRSST	bathing dress
ABDEGHIRRSUU	Rubeus Hagrid
ABDEGIIILNTT	debilitating
ABDEGIIKNOPR	boarding-pike
ABDEGIINORUW	Rainbow Guide
ABDEGIKNOPRW	baking powder
ABDEGILLLNNY	belly landing
ABDEGILNORRU	organ-builder
ABDEGILNORTW	world-beating
ABDEGKLLNOWY	knowledgably
ABDEGLNNOQUU	blue quandong
ABDEGLNORTTU	battleground
ABDEGMNNNOOY	Benny Goodman
ABDEGNOPRSSY	Porgy and Bess
ABDEHHLMOORR	rhombohedral
ABDEHHNNOOTW	on the bow hand
ABDEHHNOSSUU	house-husband
ABDEHIIILMNS	diminishable
ABDEHIILNSUV	devil-in-a-bush
ABDEHIILSSST	disestablish
ABDEHILMNNST	blandishment
ABDEHILNOORS	dishonorable
ABDEHIMNNNOR	Hermann Bondi
ABDEHIMNRRST	Rembrandtish
ABDEHJNORSST	St John's bread✧
ABDEHLMMOUWY	double whammy
ABDEHLMOSSTU	Humboldt's Sea
ABDEHNNORSSU	rub one's hands
ABDEHNORUYZZ	honey buzzard
ABDEHORRTTUY	rubythroated
ABDEIIILMNSS	inadmissible
ABDEIIILMTXY	mixed-ability
ABDEIIILNOTT	debilitation
ABDEIIILRSTY	desirability
ABDEIIILRTVY	driveability
ABDEIILMNORT	Lamberto Dini
ABDEIILNPSTU	indisputable
ABDEIILORSTU	subeditorial
ABDEIILTTUVY	dubitatively
ABDEIIOOPRSS	basidiospore
ABDEIIRSTTUV	disturbative
ABDEILLOPRRX	pillar-box red
ABDEILMMNRTU	dumb terminal
ABDEILMNOPRY	imponderably
ABDEILMNSTUU	unsublimated
ABDEILPRSTUY	disreputably
ABDEIMMNRRST	Rembrandtism
ABDEIMORSTUX	ambidextrous
ABDEINORRRSU	sound barrier
ABDEINRTTTUU	unattributed
ABDEIOPSTTUU	dispute about
ABDEKNNORVWY	vandyke brown
ABDELMNORSTY	demonstrably
ABDELOOQRRTU	quarter-blood
ABDEMOORRTTW	bottom drawer
ABDENNOOPRUW	bear down upon
ABDENOORRRTU	Roberto Duran
ABDENOORSTWY	sword-bayonet
ABDENOPPRRTY	property band
ABDENOQRRTUU	quarter-bound
ABDENORRSTUY	Treasury bond
ABDFFILNOOWY	Wolffian body
ABDFGGINOORS	Frodo Baggins
ABDFGIILLLNO	bill of lading
ABDFGINORRRW	bring forward
ABDFGINORRSU	surfboarding
ABDFIILNNRUU	infundibular
ABDFIILNOOOV	bioflavonoid
ABDGGIILNNOR	bridging loan
ABDGHILNRTUY	burn daylight
ABDGHINOOSWX	shadow-boxing
ABDGIILLLOOR	Lollobrigida
ABDGIILOOORY	radiobiology
ABDGIINNNORR	branding-iron
ABDGIINNOORR	ironing-board
ABDGILNORRUU	burial ground
ABDGIMNNNORU	mourning band
ABDGINNNORRU	running board

ABDGINNOORSW snowboarding
ABDGINOQUUVV vu quang bovid
ABDHHINPSSSU ship's husband
ABDHIIMRSTTY dithyrambist
ABDHIIRSTTUY birthday suit
ABDHILNOORSY dishonorably
ABDHINOOOOPT odontophobia
ABDIIIILNTUY inaudibility
ABDIIILMNSSY inadmissibly
ABDIIILRSSUY subsidiarily
ABDIIIRSSTUY subsidiarity
ABDIILLMOTUY modulability
ABDIILNNNOSS Bonin Islands
ABDIILNPSTUY indisputably
ABDIIRRSTTUY distributary
ABDILLMNNOOS Mills-and-Boon
ABDINNOOPRSU onus probandi
ABDLMNNORSTU burnt almonds
ABDLNNOSSTTU nuts and bolts
ABDLNOORTUUY roundaboutly
ABDMNORRSTUW brown mustard
ABEEEEHLLNRY by her lee-lane
ABEEEELPRSUZ breeze up sale
ABEEEFHNOQSU Queen of Sheba
ABEEEFILLMRU Umbelliferae
ABEEEFILNSSS feasibleness
ABEEEFIRRTTV ratbite fever
ABEEEFLNOOSV above oneself
ABEEEGHLORTT Globe Theatre
ABEEEGILLOTV vegetable oil
ABEEEGILNORT renegotiable
ABEEEGILPRRT Peter Gabriel
ABEEEGILRSSS Gebrselassie
ABEEEGLRRSST Lee Strasberg
ABEEEGMOORRV beverage room
ABEEEHILLNSY by his lee-lane
ABEEEHILMPTU eat humble pie
ABEEEHILNOTV above the line
above-the-line
ABEEEHKKNNRT Kenneth Baker
ABEEEHKLRSTT bletherskate
ABEEEHKORRRS horse-breaker
ABEEEHKORRSU housebreaker
ABEEEHMNQTTU bequeathment
ABEEEHMORSTY Bayes' theorem
ABEEEHRSSTTY set by the ears
ABEEEIJMNNRT benjamin-tree
ABEEEIKLLNSS likeableness
ABEEEILLNRSS reliableness
ABEEEILLNRUV unrelievable
ABEEEILLPRSV replevisable
ABEEEILMNPRT impenetrable
ABEEEILMNRTX exterminable
ABEEEILMRRSS Balmer series
ABEEEILNNSSV enviableness
ABEEEILRRSTV silver-beater
ABEEEINNPRTV brevipennate
ABEEEINNRTTW winter-beaten
ABEEEINRRTTV invertebrate
ABEEEKNORRST stone-breaker
ABEEEKNRRSSV bank reserves
ABEEELLMRRTU umbrella tree
ABEEELLNOSSV loveableness
ABEEELLRSTTT trestle table
ABEEELLSTTVW Twelve Tables
ABEEELMMNTTT embattlement
ABEEELMNNORV lemon verbena
ABEEELMNOSSV moveableness
ABEEELNNNORW non-renewable
ABEEELNSSSSS baselessness
ABEEELQRSSTU sequestrable
ABEEEMMNQRTU embarquement
ABEEEMPRSTTU subtemperate
ABEEEOPRRSTT obstreperate
ABEEEORRRRTV reverberator
ABEEEPRRSTTY presbyterate
ABEEERRSSTWY brewer's yeast
ABEEFFILNRSU insufferable
ABEEFFLNRSUU unsufferable
ABEEFHILRTYZ Elizabeth Fry
ABEEFIILLMSU emulsifiable
ABEEFIILMNST manifestible
ABEEFIILNRUV unverifiable
ABEEFIILRRVY biliary fever
ABEEFILLMSTU fusible metal
ABEEFILLNOTT line of battle
ABEEFILLNRTU unfilterable
ABEEFILMOPRR imperforable
ABEEFILMORRR irreformable
ABEEFILNNRTY Albert Finney
ABEEFILNOTUY line of beauty
ABEEFKLNOORW foreknowable
ABEEFLLMNSSU blamefulness
ABEEFLLMSSSY self-assembly
ABEEFLLMSSUY fuel assembly
ABEEFLMNORRU unreformable
ABEEFLMORRST Forest Marble
ABEEFLRSTTUY sea butterfly
ABEEGGIILNOR globigerinae
ABEEGGILNRSS beggarliness
ABEEGGLNORST Glen T Seaborg
ABEEGHMNOOPR Germanophobe
ABEEGIILNSTV investigable
ABEEGIJNNNRT Jan Tinbergen
ABEEGIKNPSTU speaking tube
ABEEGILLMNRS Elgin marbles
ABEEGILLNORT bertillonage
ABEEGILNNPUX inexpugnable
ABEEGILNNSSS singableness
ABEEGILNNSST tangibleness
ABEEGILNORRT interrogable
ABEEGILNORRY Eleanor Rigby
ABEEGINOPRST pigeon breast
ABEEGINORRTT bitter orange
ABEEGLMRSSSU Burmese glass
ABEEGLNNORUV ungovernable
ABEEGLNNPUUX unexpugnable
ABEEGLRRRSTY Barry St Leger
ABEEGORRRSTV Robert Graves
ABEEHHIILOPP ephebophilia
ABEEHHOORSST horseshoe bat
ABEEHIILMPRS imperishable

ABEEHIKLRSTT blatherskite
ABEEHILLMORT thermolabile
ABEEHILLORTT Bertholletia
ABEEHILNORTT bletheration
ABEEHILNPRSU unperishable
ABEEHILPPRSU sapphire blue
ABEEHILPRSST pre-establish
ABEEHILRRSTW Welsh rarebit
ABEEHJJMNNOT John Betjeman
ABEEHJMRRSTU James Thurber
ABEEHKLMRSST bless the mark
ABEEHLLMRSTU The Umbrellas
ABEEHLLNSSTT St Benet's Hall
ABEEHLLOSTTW below the salt
ABEEHLLRSSTY breathlessly
ABEEHLMORSTT thermostable
ABEEHLNNOORR blennorrhoea
ABEEHLOPRSST blastosphere
ABEEHLORSTTW bottle-washer
ABEEHLORSTTY heteroblasty
ABEEHLRRTTUW Hubert Walter
ABEEHNNRRRUY Henry Raeburn
ABEEHNOPRRSY Hyperboreans
ABEEHNRRTTUW burn the water
ABEEIIILLLRS illiberalise
ABEEIIILLLRZ illiberalize
ABEEIIJLNSSU Jean Sibelius
ABEEIILLOSTT biosatellite
ABEEIILMNNRT interminable
ABEEIILMNORR marine boiler
ABEEIILMNSST imitableness
ABEEIILMNSSV visible means
ABEEIILMPRTY permeability
ABEEIILNNPSX inexpansible
ABEEIILNPRTX inextirpable
ABEEIILNPSST pitiableness
ABEEIILNRTWY renewability
ABEEIILORTTV obliterative
ABEEIILOSSUV Silva Eusebio
ABEEIILPRRRS irrespirable
ABEEIIMNNOST ambient noise
ABEEIIMRRVZZ River Zambezi
ABEEIJNORTUZ Benito Juárez
ABEEIKLRSTTT litter basket
ABEEIKMOPRRS break-promise
ABEEIKNNOPRR Bonnie Parker
ABEEIKNNORRR Ronnie Barker
ABEEIKNNRSTT bank interest
ABEEIKORRRST Robert Raikes
ABEEILLMNPRU umbrella pine
ABEEILLMNSSY assembly line
ABEEILLNNRUV invulnerable
ABEEILLNNSTU unlistenable
ABEEILLNOPRT interpolable
ABEEILLNOPSS belle passion
ABEEILLORRSV irresolvable
ABEEILLPRSUV pulverisable
ABEEILLPRUVZ pulverizable
ABEEILLRSTVY livery stable
ABEEILMMNRSU immensurable
ABEEILMMOORS aeroembolism
ABEEILMNPRTY impenetrably
ABEEILMNRRSU serial number
ABEEILMOPRST problematise
ABEEILMOPRTZ problematize
ABEEILMPRSTT beam splitter
ABEEILNOQSTU questionable
ABEEILNPSSSS passibleness
ABEEILNSSSTU suitableness
ABEEILOORSSV basso-relievo
ABEEILOPPRRX expropriable
ABEEILOPRRRV irreprovable
ABEEILORRTVY Trevor Bailey
ABEEILOTTTVV votive tablet
ABEEILPRRSTY presbyterial
ABEEILRRSTTW water blister
ABEEIMNNPRSU submarine pen
ABEEIMNNSSSU mean business
ABEEIMNOOSTT Moabite stone
ABEEIMNRSTTU steam turbine
ABEEINNNOTVV bonne vivante
ABEEINNOPRSS Napier's bones
ABEEINNORSTV Observantine
ABEEINORRTTV vertebration
ABEEINORSSTV abortiveness
ABEEINPRRRSY Persian berry
ABEEINPRRSTY presbyterian✧
ABEEINRRTTUW water turbine
ABEEIOPRRTVX exprobrative
ABEEIPRRTTUV perturbative
ABEEIPRSSTUX beaux esprits
ABEEJLLMOSSW James Boswell
ABEEKKLNNORS Blankers-Koen
ABEEKLLNOPST pollen basket
ABEEKLMORRTU troublemaker
ABEEKLNNOSSW knowableness
ABEEKLNORSSW workableness
ABEEKMRRSTUY buyers' market
buyer's market
ABEEKNORRRUV overrun brake
ABEEKNORSTTU Buster Keaton
ABEEKORRSSTT breaststroke
ABEELLLORTTY trolley table
ABEELLMNOPUY unemployable
ABEELLMOOPRT temporal lobe
ABEELLMRSTUU Samuel Butler
ABEELLNNRUUV unvulnerable
ABEELLNORSTW snowball tree
ABEELLNORSUV unresolvable
ABEELLNPRSUU unrepulsable
ABEELLORSTUW water-soluble
ABEELLORSTWW water bellows
ABEELMMNNOTZ emblazonment
ABEELMOOPSSS pease-blossom
ABEELMOPRRRT Robert Palmer
ABEELNNRRTUU unreturnable
ABEELNNSSSTU unstableness
ABEELNOPRRTU unreportable
ABEELNOPRRUV unreprovable
ABEELNOQSSTU quotableness
ABEELNOSSSTU absoluteness
ABEELNOSSTUV solvent abuse

ABEELNRSTTUU unutterables
ABEELOORSTUZ absolute zero
ABEELOPPRSSU superposable
ABEELORSTTTU trouble-state
ABEEMMRRSSTU breastsummer
ABEEMNQRRSUU square number
ABEENOPSSSTT past one's best
ABEENPRTTTUU peanut butter
ABEENRRSSTVY by transverse
ABEENRSSSSTU abstruseness
ABEERRRSSTUU subtreasurer
ABEFFIIILNTY ineffability
ABEFFILLLMOR flabelliform
ABEFFILNRSUY insufferably
ABEFFILOORST offers to bail
ABEFGIKNOSST king of beasts
ABEFGILNORRY forbearingly
ABEFGILNORUV unforgivable
ABEFGINNRRTU afterburning
ABEFHHILLLOT bill of health
ABEFHLLOOTTU Bat Out of Hell
ABEFIILMNOOR oil of mirbane
ABEFIIMNNORS Febronianism
ABEFILLORTUU Tubuliflorae
ABEFILMORRRY irreformably
ABEFILNOPRTU unprofitable
ABEFILNRSSTU transfusible
ABEFIMNOORRU neurofibroma
ABEFKNOORRST transfer book
ABEFLLOOORUV labour of love
ABEFLLOOOSTT Battle of Loos
ABEFLNOSSSTU boastfulness
ABEFLNOSSSUU fabulousness
ABEGGHILLLMN gambling hell
ABEGGHINORTV overnight bag
ABEGGHIOOPRY biogeography
ABEGGHNOORSS Baroness Hogg
ABEGGIILLNST billingsgate
ABEGHHINOOPP phengophobia
ABEGHHIOTTUV have bought it
ABEGHHKORRTU break through
breakthrough
ABEGHHLOPPRY phlebography
ABEGHHLRTUUW bulghur wheat
ABEGHIINNPSS spine-bashing
ABEGHIJNNORS Johannisberg
ABEGHIKNOPRS shopbreaking
ABEGHILNRRTW night-brawler
ABEGHINNRRTU heartburning
ABEGHINORTUW web authoring
ABEGHJNNORSU Johannesburg
ABEGHLOPRSTU breastplough
ABEGHNOOPRRS snobographer
ABEGHNOORTTU Attenborough
ABEGIILLNOUV Bougainville
ABEGIILNRTTW writing table
ABEGIINRSSSU agribusiness
ABEGIKLMNORT Goblin Market
ABEGIKLNNOOR book-learning
ABEGILLLNOWY bowling alley
ABEGILLMORSU semiglobular
ABEGILLNOOST balneologist
ABEGILMNNPUU unimpugnable
ABEGILNNNRUY running belay
ABEGILNNPUXY inexpugnably
ABEGILNNRTTU table-turning
ABEGILRRSSST bristle-grass
ABEGINNOSSTU seasoning-tub
ABEGINOQRTUU bouquet garni
ABEGINORSSSU agrobusiness
ABEGINPRSTUY spring beauty
ABEGLLLOSSSU soluble glass
ABEGLMORSUUY umbrageously
ABEGLNNOOOST Bologna stone
ABEGLNNORUVY ungovernably
ABEHIIILRTTY heritability
ABEHIIIMNNRS Hibernianism
ABEHIILMPRSY imperishably
ABEHIILNNRTY labyrinthine
ABEHIILNOPST inhospitable
ABEHIILPRSTT British plate
ABEHIIMORSUV behaviourism
misbehaviour
ABEHIIORSTUV behaviourist
ABEHIKLNNRSU unshrinkable
ABEHIKNRRSSS Sir Hans Krebs
ABEHILLNOPSU unpolishable
ABEHILNNPSUU unpunishable
ABEHILNOPSTU unhospitable
ABEHILNOPSTY hypnotisable
ABEHILNOPTYZ hypnotizable
ABEHILNORRTW brother-in-law
ABEHILOOOPRU ailourophobe
ABEHIMNOOOPT entomophobia
ABEHINNORSTU Born in the USA
ABEHJMNNORRY John Berryman
ABEHLMOPSSSY assembly shop
ABEHLORRSTTY erythroblast
ABEHMNOORSTW Thomas Browne
ABEHNORSTTUU hunt saboteur
ABEIIILLLRTY illiberality
ABEIIILLNNRT brilliantine
ABEIIILMRSUV mirabile visu
ABEIIILNRRTY inerrability
ABEIIILQTTUY equitability
ABEIIILRTVVY revivability
ABEIIJLNOTYY enjoyability
ABEIIKLLMRUW William Burke
ABEIIKMNNOTU mountain bike
ABEIIKNNPRRS Brian Perkins
ABEIILLLMPTU multipliable
ABEIILLORTTY tolerability
ABEIILMMORTY memorability
ABEIILMNNNOS innominables
ABEIILMNNRTY interminably
ABEIILMNOOST embolisation
ABEIILMNOOTZ embolization
ABEIILMNOPRS imprisonable
ABEIILMNOSST ambitionless
ABEIILMNRTUY numerability
ABEIILMORTVY removability
ABEIILMPTTTY temptability

ABEIILNNOSTU nebulisation
sublineation
ABEIILNNOTUZ nebulization
ABEIILNNTTUY untenability
ABEIILNOORTT obliteration
ABEIILNORRTT interorbital
ABEIILNORTTY Li-ion battery
ABEIILOORSSV basso-rilievo
ABEIILOQRRTU equilibrator
ABEIIMNNNRUY renminbi yuan
ABEIIMNRSTUU subminiature
ABEIINORSSTU suberisation
ABEIINORSTUZ suberization
ABEIJLMNOPSU jump one's bail
ABEIJLORRSTU Julia Roberts
ABEIJNNOOTTY bayonet joint
ABEIKMNNOTTU mountebank it
ABEIKNNOORZZ Zinzan Brooke
ABEIKNPRSSSU business park
ABEILLNNOPPT ballpoint pen
ABEILLNNRUVY invulnerably
ABEILLNOPPRT bipropellant
ABEILLNORRTU interlobular
ABEILLOPRRVY proverbially
ABEILLORRSVY irresolvably
ABEILLRRSTUY Treasury bill
ABEILMMNRSUU serum albumin
ABEILMNNOTUU Blue Mountain
mountain blue
ABEILMNOSUUX exalbuminous
ABEILMOSSTUY abstemiously
ABEILNNPSSSU business plan
ABEILNOQSTUY questionably
ABEILNORRTUY oriental ruby
ABEILNORSSUY Byelorussian
ABEILNORTTXY exorbitantly
ABEILNPRSSUU prussian blue✧
ABEILNRSTTUY subalternity
ABEILOPRRRVY irreprovably
ABEIMNRSSTYY binary system
ABEINOOPRRST reabsorption
ABEINOOPRRTX exprobration
ABEINOORRTTU tanto uberior
ABEINOPRRTTU perturbation
ABEKMNORSSSY brass monkeys
ABELLLLOPSYY polysyllable
ABELLLMNOOSY monosyllable
ABELLMMNOSSW swell-mobsman
ABELLMOOPPSS apple-blossom
ABELMMOORSSY assembly room
ABELMNORSTUU surmountable
ABELMPRRSTUY slumber party
ABELNOPPSSUU unsupposable
ABELOQRSSTTU squat lobster
ABEMOORSTTWY bottom-sawyer
ABEOOPRRRTXY exprobratory
ABEOPRRRTTUY perturbatory
ABFFGILNOSUW Buffalo wings
ABFFIKLOORRS Boris Karloff
ABFGHIIMNORT habit-forming
ABFGIIILNRTY frangibility
ABFGIIILRTUY figurability
ABFHILRSSTTU at first blush
ABFHJKOOOOSU Book of Joshua
ABFIIILLNORT fibrillation
ABFIIILLRTTY filtrability
ABFIIILNNOTU infibulation
ABFILLLORTUU tubulifloral
ABFILNOPRTUY unprofitably
ABFKLMOOOPSS Book of Psalms
ABGGGIMNNORU Munro-bagging
ABGGHIMNORUY Brigham Young
ABGGHINOORSU Gainsborough
ABGGHINORSTT bang to rights
ABGGIILNRSTT grit blasting
ABGGILLNOSSW glass-blowing
ABGGILNNRSSU burning-glass
ABGHHIKORTUW rough hawkbit
ABGHHILORRTU harbour-light
ABGHHINRSSUV shaving-brush
ABGHHJNNORUV John Vanbrugh
ABGHHOORSSTU thorough bass
ABGHIIILLLMW William Bligh
ABGHIILMNRSU rhumb-sailing
ABGHIIMMNSTW swimming-bath
ABGHILMNNOUW human bowling
ABGHILNOSSTT shot-blasting
ABGHILOOPTTT potato blight
ABGHILOORSTU Boutros-Ghali
ABGIIIILNTTY ignitability
ABGIIILLMNSU bilingualism
ABGIILLMRSUW Williamsburg
ABGIILLNORTT trolling-bait
ABGIILLOORTY obligatorily
ABGIINNORTUY Young Britain
ABGILMNOPSUU plumbaginous
ABGILNOORSTU urbanologist
ABGIMNNORRST barnstorming
ABGMMMNNOSUU magnum bonums
ABHIIILORSSZ bilharziosis
ABHIIKMNNPRS brinkmanship
ABHIILLMOOTW William Booth
ABHIILMOPSUY amphibiously
ABHIILNOPSTY inhospitably
ABHIIMNNORTT antithrombin
ABHIINOPRSTV vibraphonist
ABHIKLLNOOSW balloon whisk
ABHILNNPSUUY unpunishably
ABHIMNNORRTU Northumbrian
ABHIMNOOPRSS Spanish broom
ABHLNNNOTTUY Anthony Blunt
ABHLNNOOSUVW Hans von Bülow
ABIIIILMSSTY amissibility
ABIIIILRRTTY irritability
ABIIILLPPTUY pupilability
ABIIILLPSTUY plausibility
ABIIILMMOTVY immovability
ABIIILMMTTUY immutability
ABIIILMNOOST abolitionism
mobilisation
ABIIILMNOOTZ mobilization
ABIIILMPTTUY imputability

ABIIILNNOOTT nobilitation
ABIIILNOOSTT abolitionist
ABIIILNPRTTY printability
ABIIILNRSTUY insurability
ABIILLLMNSUY subliminally
ABIILLNOOPRT abortion pill
ABIILMMOOSTU automobilism
ABIILMNOORSV Simón Bolívar
ABIILMOOSTTU automobilist
ABIILNOORSTT strobilation
ABIILNORSSUU insalubrious
ABIILOOPPSTY opposability
ABIILOPRSTTY sportability
ABIIMNNORSTU omnibus train
ABIIMNORSTTU tambourinist
ABIIOPRSTTVY absorptivity
ABIKOPRSSSSY Boris Spassky
ABILLLMORTUU multilobular
ABILLLNOOOPT pilot balloon
ABILLORSSUUY salubriously
ABILMMMNOSSU somnambulism
ABILMMNOSSTU somnambulist
ABILMMPRSTUU Limbus patrum
ABILMNORSTUY subnormality
ABIMNNOORRSY Mary Robinson
ABIMNORSSTTU nimbostratus
ABINOORRTTUW rainbow trout
ABINOORSSSTU Russian boots
ABIOPRRSTTTU portrait-bust
ABKLLNOOSSTT lots to blanks
ABLLMOORSTYY symbololatry
ABLMOSSSTTUY status symbol
ABLOOOPRSSTU obstropalous
ABNOORRSSTUU brontosaurus✧
ACCCCDIIINSU succinic acid
ACCCCEIILRRT Arctic Circle
ACCCDEEEELNS decalescence
ACCCDEEENNOT once-accented
ACCCDEEIRSST direct access
ACCCDEIILRSY cresylic acid
ACCCDHIORTTU thoracic duct
ACCCDIIOOSTT coccidiostat
ACCCEEEELNRS recalescence
ACCCEEEGLNSU glaucescence
ACCCEEEILNNS incalescence
ACCCEEEINQSU acquiescence
ACCCEEELNORS calorescence
ACCCEEHKLTTU cut the cackle
ACCCEEHMNOTU accouchement
ACCCEEIILSST ecclesiastic
ACCCEEILLLTY eclectically
ACCCEELNOSTY nectocalyces
ACCCEEORSSSU access course
ACCCEGIINNOR carcinogenic
ACCCEHHILMOS chemical cosh
ACCCEHIILRTU cicatrichule
ACCCEHINORTT technocratic
ACCCEHINOSTU Echinocactus
ACCCEHIOORSU cichoraceous
ACCCEHKLORTW clock-watcher
ACCCEIJMNRTU circumjacent
ACCCEIKLMOSU caesium clock
ACCCEILNNORT central conic
concentrical
ACCCEIMNNOOT concomitance
ACCCEIMNRSTU circumstance
ACCCEINORSTU oceanic crust
ACCCEIRSTUUV caustic curve
ACCCENOPPRUY preoccupancy
ACCCFIIKNRRS Francis Crick
ACCCGHILOPRY cyclographic
ACCCGHINOSTU casting couch
ACCCHHIILLOT Chalcolithic
ACCCHIIOPRRT chiropractic
ACCCHIIOPRSZ schizocarpic
ACCCHIKOSSTT shock tactics
ACCCIILLNOUU Aulic Council
ACCCIILMNNOU councilmanic
ACCCIILNNOTY anticyclonic
ACCCIILNOOST iconoclastic
ACCCILLLNOYY cyclonically
ACCCIMNNOOSY coscinomancy
ACCCIMNNOOTY concomitancy
ACCCNOOORTTY cottonocracy
ACCDDDEHIIKL chick-a-diddle
ACCDDEEHINOR Eddie Cochran
ACCDDEEIIILN Cicindelidae
ACCDDEEINRTU unaccredited
ACCDDEHINOOP dodecaphonic
ACCDDEIIIOPR periodic acid
ACCDDEIINORT endocarditic
ACCDEEEELMNN Clemence Dane
ACCDEEEHLMNY chance-medley
ACCDEEEHLSSU duchesse lace
ACCDEEEHRRSS recessed arch
ACCDEEEILNPS lapidescence
ACCDEEEKSSTT cassette deck
ACCDEEELORSU cedrelaceous
ACCDEEENORST deconsecrate
ACCDEEFIIRTT certificated
ACCDEEFILLMS Macclesfield
ACCDEEGHILNO chalcogenide
ACCDEEGILNOT cladogenetic
ACCDEEHIILMX mixed chalice
ACCDEEHIILNP diencephalic
ACCDEEHLRSTY cradle-scythe
ACCDEEIIILPT epideictical
ACCDEEIIMORX ceramic oxide
ACCDEEIKNOPT patience-dock
ACCDEEILLOPS peccadilloes
ACCDEEILNOPY encyclopedia✧
ACCDEEINNNST incandescent
ACCDEEINNORS considerance
ACCDEEINNORT concertinaed
ACCDEEINORTX exotic dancer
ACCDEELMORTT clotted cream
ACCDEELMORTU clouted cream
ACCDEELNOPRS corpse candle
ACCDEELNPSTU unspectacled
ACCDEELOOPRU Cape Coloured
ACCDEENOSSUU succedaneous
ACCDEENRSSSU accursedness

ACCDEGHORTUU Dutch courage
ACCDEGIILRSY lysergic acid
ACCDEGIIMNST magnetic disc
ACCDEGNNORRT concert grand
ACCDEHHNRRUW churchwarden
ACCDEHIISTUW suicide watch
ACCDEHILMOOW chemical wood
ACCDEHILMOPS accomplished
ACCDEHIOORSU orchidaceous
ACCDEHLNNORR corn-chandler
ACCDEHNRRRUY hard currency
ACCDEHOPRRST Scotch draper
ACCDEIIILLNO linoleic acid
ACCDEIIILMST dialecticism
ACCDEIIILNOT Ionic dialect
ACCDEIIILNST insecticidal
ACCDEIIINORT retinoic acid
ACCDEIILLOPS piccadilloes
ACCDEIILLOPY epicycloidal
ACCDEIILLRTU telluric acid
ACCDEIILMOUX calcium oxide
ACCDEIILNNOT coincidental
ACCDEIILORST social credit✧
ACCDEIINORTT direct action
ACCDEILLNOTY occidentally
ACCDEILNOORU Cain-coloured
ACCDEILNOPSU nucleocapsid
ACCDEILNOPTU conduplicate
ACCDEILNORRU circle around
ACCDEILOOSUY calycoideous
ACCDEILRSSTU custard slice
ACCDEIMNOOST atomic second
ACCDEIMNORTU undemocratic
ACCDEINNORRT androcentric
ACCDEKKLMORU cuckold-maker
ACCDELNORTTY contractedly
ACCDEMNOSTUU unaccustomed
ACCDENNORTUY country dance
ACCDEOOPRSTY despotocracy
ACCDFFHIILRR Cliff Richard
ACCDFIIILMNU fulminic acid
ACCDFIIINOOT codification
ACCDFIILNOSU sulfonic acid
ACCDGIIKLLOT digital clock
ACCDGIINNNSS scanning-disc
ACCDGIINSTTU tungstic acid
ACCDGILOTYYZ zygodactylic
ACCDHHIIKKNT hitch and kick
ACCDHIIOOORT chorioid coat
ACCDHIKLNNWY Lynn Chadwick
ACCDHILLOOST Old Catholics
ACCDHILOOOSU I should cocoa
ACCDHILOORSU chlorous acid
ACCDHINOTTUU Dutch auction
ACCDHIORRSTT Richard Scott
ACCDIIIMRSTY myristic acid
ACCDIILOORSU radicicolous
ACCDIIMNNOOU incomunicado
ACCDIINOORST accordionist
ACCDILNOOSSS Cocos Islands
ACCDILNOSTUV volcanic dust
ACCDIMNOPSTU stand-up comic
ACCDINOORRTT contradictor
ACCDLNNOORTY concordantly
ACCDLOOPSTYY dactyloscopy
ACCEEEFFGILO Gaelic coffee
ACCEEEFFIOPR peace officer
ACCEEEFHIMRR crème fraîche
ACCEEEFHOPRT force the pace
ACCEEEGLLLOR Clare College
ACCEEEHILNPP epencephalic
ACCEEEHILPSV space vehicle
ACCEEEHILRRT electric hare
ACCEEEHINRST earth science
ACCEEEHLORRT heterocercal
ACCEEEILLRST electric seal
ACCEEEILSSST Ecclesiastes
ACCEEELNNORT lean concrete
ACCEEEMORSST remote access
ACCEEENNORVY reconveyance
ACCEEENORRST reconsecrate
ACCEEEOPPRSS peace process
ACCEEFGIIMNN magnificence
ACCEEFHHIRTT thief-catcher
ACCEEFHIIPST specific heat
ACCEEFHIMSTU face the music
ACCEEFIIMNPS specific name
ACCEEFIIPRRT fire practice
ACCEEFLNORRT central force
ACCEEGHILNOT geotechnical
ACCEEGHNNORX corn exchange
ACCEEGILNNOR congenerical
ACCEEGILNORT geocentrical
ACCEEGIMNORT magnetic core
ACCEEGINNORS recognisance
ACCEEGINNORZ recognizance
ACCEEGLNOPPR copper-glance
ACCEEGNORSTY escort agency
ACCEEHHILORT chalicothere
ACCEEHHIRSTV service hatch
ACCEEHHRRSTT charter-chest
ACCEEHIILNPT encephalitic
ACCEEHIKLRTY reality check
ACCEEHIKNSTU chuckie-stane
ACCEEHIKPSTT stick the pace
ACCEEHILMNRT thermic lance
ACCEEHILMOPS mesocephalic
ACCEEHILNRTU Chaunticleer
ACCEEHILRRST Richter scale
ACCEEHIMNRSW machine screw
ACCEEHIMORTT tacheometric
ACCEEHIMRSTU music teacher
ACCEEHIORSSS chassé-croisé
ACCEEHIORTTT heterotactic
ACCEEHIRRTTU architecture
ACCEEHLMNRSY sclerenchyma
ACCEEHLMORTY the real McCoy
ACCEEHMNNORT encroachment
ACCEEHORRSTW The Scarecrow
ACCEEIINNORT interoceanic
ACCEEIINNRSS circassienne
ACCEEIINPPRT precipitance

ACCEEIINRSTV sciatic nerve
ACCEEIJNNRTY interjacency
ACCEEIKLNRRW Carl Wernicke
ACCEEILLLRTY electrically
ACCEEILLMNUY ecumenically
ACCEEILLOPST telescopical
ACCEEILNPTTU centuplicate
ACCEEILNRTTY tetracycline
ACCEEINNPTXY inexpectancy
ACCEEINOPSTU pectinaceous
ACCEEINORSTV consecrative
ACCEEIORSTTT stereotactic
ACCEEKNOOPST peacock-stone
ACCEELLOORTT collectorate
ACCEELMPRTUU receptaculum
ACCEELNNOSTV convalescent
ACCEELNNRSTU translucence
ACCEELOPPSTU Cactus People
ACCEELPRRWYY creepy-crawly
ACCEEMNORTTU accouterment
accoutrement
ACCEEMNRSTTU accustrement
ACCEEMOOPPRR come a cropper
ACCEENNNORTU countenancer
ACCEENNORSTU unconsecrate
ACCEENOORRTU à contre coeur
ACCEENOPRRSU precancerous
ACCEENPRRSTY Spencer Tracy
ACCEFFHIORTW watch officer
ACCEFFIIJKNO jack-in-office✧
ACCEFGIIINNS significance
ACCEFHILMNSU mischanceful
ACCEFHILMRTU lucifer-match
ACCEFIIILNST scientifical
ACCEFIILLMRY family circle✧
ACCEFIILLPSY specifically
ACCEFIILLRRU circular file
ACCEFIILLRST self-critical
ACCEFILLOORW calico-flower
ACCEFILOPRST plastic force
ACCEFINRRTUY fiat currency
ACCEGGILNOOY gynaecologic
ACCEGHHIOPRT hectographic
ACCEGHILOOST eschatologic
ACCEGHINOPRS scenographic
ACCEGHLLOOOT chocolate log
ACCEGHLNOORU change colour
ACCEGIIJRSTU gastric juice
ACCEGIIKNRSW wisecracking
ACCEGIILMOST cleistogamic
ACCEGIINNNOS incognisance
ACCEGIINNNOZ incognizance
ACCEGIINRTUX excruciating
ACCEGIKLNRSU surgical neck
ACCEGILLLOOY ecologically
ACCEGILLNOOR necrological
ACCEGILNNNOU unconcealing
ACCEGILNNORT Anglocentric
ACCEGILNORSU lacing course
ACCEGILNOSUW wages council
ACCEGIMRRTUY circumgyrate
ACCEGINNNORS as concerning
ACCEGINNNOVY conveyancing
ACCEGNOORRTY gerontocracy
ACCEHHIIKNRT kitchen chair
ACCEHHIKPRTW crack the whip
ACCEHHILOSSZ eschscholzia
ACCEHHLOOOTT hot chocolate
ACCEHIILLMRY chimerically
ACCEHIILLNST callisthenic
ACCEHIILMOOR heroi-comical
ACCEHIILNOPR necrophiliac
ACCEHIILNORR rhinocerical
ACCEHIILNSST calisthenics
ACCEHIILNTTY technicality
ACCEHIIMRSTT chrematistic
ACCEHIIRRTTW carriwitchet
ACCEHIIRSTTT tetrastichic
ACCEHIKLMOOR mock-heroical
ACCEHIKMNSTY chimney stack
ACCEHILLLORY cholerically
ACCEHILMNOOR melanochroic
ACCEHILMOPRS accomplisher
ACCEHILMOPRY microcephaly
pyrochemical
ACCEHILNNNOT non-technical
ACCEHILNOOOT echo location
ACCEHILOORSU orichalceous
ACCEHILOOSST Catholicoses
ACCEHILOPRTY chalcopyrite
ACCEHIMNORST mechatronics
ACCEHIMOOPRT cecropia moth
ACCEHIMOORST mesothoracic
ACCEHIMORTTT thermotactic
ACCEHIMPSSTY metapsychics
ACCEHINNNOPT pantechnicon
ACCEHINOOPRT acrophonetic
ACCEHINORRTT trochanteric
ACCEHINRSSST scratchiness
ACCEHIOPSTVY psychoactive
ACCEHKLOOSVZ Czechoslovak
ACCEHLLLOOTY cetyl alcohol
ACCEHLNOPSUY Cynocephalus
ACCEHLOORSSU schorlaceous
ACCEHMNNORRT corn-merchant
ACCEHMNORRTU countercharm
countermarch
ACCEHMOPSTUU moustache cup
ACCEHMORSTTU scattermouch
ACCEHOOOPRST thoracoscope
ACCEHOOPRSTY tracheoscopy
ACCEIIILLLMW William Cecil
ACCEIIILNOTV conciliative
ACCEIIILPSST specialistic
ACCEIIIPSSSV vesica piscis
ACCEIIKKMNRS camiknickers
ACCEIILLLNTY enclitically
ACCEIILLOSST solecistical
ACCEIILMMORT microclimate
ACCEIILMNNOP incompliance
ACCEIILMOORS seriocomical
ACCEIILMOPTV complicative

ACCEIILMORRT	calorimetric
ACCEIILMRRSU	semicircular
ACCEIILNORTV	intervocalic
ACCEIILNRSST	criticalness
ACCEIILOPRRR	irreciprocal
ACCEIILOSSTV	viscoelastic
ACCEIILPRTUU	epicuticular
ACCEIILRSSTU	secularistic
ACCEIIMNOPRR	picrocarmine
ACCEIIMORRTT	meritocratic
ACCEIINORTUX	excruciation
ACCEIINPPRTY	precipitancy
ACCEIIOPRSUV	pervicacious
ACCEIIPPRSTY	perspicacity
ACCEIJNNOTUV	conjunctivae
ACCEIKKKKNNT	knick-knacket
ACCEIKKNNRSS	snicker-snack
ACCEIKLOPRTT	kleptocratic
ACCEILLMMORY	commercially
ACCEILLMNOOY	economically
ACCEILLMOORT	Camille Corot
ACCEILLMOSTY	cosmetically
ACCEILLNNORT	centroclinal
ACCEILLNOTTY	tectonically
ACCEILLNSTYY	synectically
ACCEILLOPRRY	reciprocally
ACCEILMMNORU	uncommercial
ACCEILMNNOOU	uneconomical
ACCEILMNORTU	counterclaim
ACCEILMOPRSU	microcapsule
ACCEILNNNOOT	connectional
ACCEILNNOOPT	conceptional
ACCEILNNOOTV	convectional
ACCEILNOORRT	correctional
ACCEILNORRTU	circular note
ACCEILNOSSSU	successional
ACCEILNOSSTU	acoustic lens
ACCEILOOSSTT	osteoclastic
ACCEILOPRSST	ceroplastics
ACCEIMNNOORT	concremation
ACCEIMNOSTTY	nematocystic
ACCEIMNRTTUU	circumnutate
ACCEINNNNOOS	inconsonance
ACCEINNOORST	consecration
ACCEINOOPRTU	reoccupation
ACCEINOORRSU	Enrico Caruso
ACCEINQRTTUY	cry quittance
ACCEIOOPRRRT	reciprocator
ACCEIORSTTUV	curvicostate
ACCEKNNORSTU	snack counter
ACCELLLOOOPU	Paolo Uccello
ACCELLMNOPTY	complacently
ACCELLMORSUU	ocular muscle
ACCELLNOPTUY	conceptually
ACCELLOOORSU	corollaceous
ACCELLOORTTX	tax collector
ACCELMNOOPSY	close company
ACCELMNOOSSY	economy-class
ACCELNNRSTUY	translucency
ACCELNOOPPRY	cyclopropane
ACCELNORTTWZ	concert waltz
ACCELNSSSTUY	successantly
ACCELOOOPSSU	scolopaceous
ACCEMOOSSTUY	ascomycetous
ACCENNOORRTT	concentrator
ACCENOOOPRRT	concorporate
ACCENOORRSTY	consecratory
ACCENOPRRSTU	counterscarp
ACCENOPRRTTY	concert party
ACCFGIIINNSY	significancy
ACCFHIINOPRT	North Pacific
ACCFHIIOPSTU	South Pacific
ACCFIIIINOTT	citification
ACCFIIINOTTY	cityfication
ACCFIIMNNOSU	Confucianism
ACCFIINNOOST	confiscation
ACCFIINNOSTU	Confucianist
ACCFILLNOOTU	flocculation
ACCFILNOORST	olfactronics
ACCFILNOORUW	council of war
ACCFINOORSTY	confiscatory
ACCGHHIINOPR	ichnographic
ACCGHHIIOPRR	chirographic
ACCGHHIOOPRR	chorographic
ACCGHHIORSTY	hygrochastic
ACCGHIIKLNOT	Catholic King
ACCGHIIKNORR	rocking chair
ACCGHIIMOPRR	micrographic
ACCGHIIMOTTT	thigmotactic
ACCGHIINOOPR	iconographic
ACCGHIINOPRZ	zincographic
ACCGHIIOPPRT	pictographic
ACCGHILLOOOR	chorological
ACCGHILLOOPY	phycological
ACCGHILNRSTY	scratchingly
ACCGHIMOOPRS	cosmographic
ACCGIIINORST	organicistic
ACCGIILLMOOR	micrological
ACCGIILLNOOO	iconological
ACCGIILLOOOS	sociological
ACCGIKLOPSST	glass cockpit
ACCGILLMOOOS	cosmological
ACCGILMNOOOS	cosmogonical
ACCGILNORTUY	granulocytic
ACCGILORSTTU	cargo cultist
ACCHHHIPRRSU	parish church
ACCHHIIIRSSS	rachischisis
ACCHHIILLNRU	Churchillian
ACCHHIINRTUY	churchianity
ACCHHILLOOTY	ichthyocolla
ACCHHINOORTX	xanthochroic
ACCHHIOPPSTY	psychopathic
ACCHHJMNORTY	John McCarthy
ACCHHLMNORUW	Low-Churchman
ACCHIIINSTUV	chauvinistic
ACCHIILOOPPS	scopophiliac
ACCHIILOPRTY	hypocritical
ACCHIIMMORST	chromaticism
ACCHIIMNOOST	iconomachist
ACCHIIMNOPTY	amphictyonic
ACCHIIMNORST	monarchistic
ACCHIIMOORST	isochromatic

ACCHIIMORRTT trichromatic
ACCHIIMORTTY chromaticity
ACCHIIOPRSTY physiocratic
ACCHILLNNOOO non-alcoholic
ACCHILLOPTTY phyllotactic
ACCHILNNORSY synchronical
ACCHILNOPRTY lycanthropic
ACCHILOOPRSS Los Caprichos
ACCHILOOPSSY psychosocial
ACCHILOPPRTY prophylactic
ACCHIMNOOPPT phonocamptic
ACCHINOOOPSU cacophonious
ACCHINOOPSTT phonotactics
ACCHIOOPRRRT chiropractor
ACCHIOOPRRST arthroscopic
ACCHIOOPRSTT octastrophic
ACCHIOOPRTTT trophotactic
ACCHIOORRSSU chiaroscuros
ACCHIOOSSTTU octastichous
ACCIIILMNPUV valium picnic
ACCIIILNNOOT conciliation
ACCIIINRSSST narcissistic
ACCIILLNRTUY uncritically
ACCIILLOPRTY pictorically
ACCIILMMOORT microtomical
ACCIILMNOOPT complication
ACCIILNOORTY conciliatory
ACCIILOPRSUY capriciously
ACCIIMOOPRTT compatriotic
ACCIINNOOOST consociation
ACCIINNOOPTU inoccupation
ACCIINOPRSST conspiracist
ACCIJKLNNOOS Colin Jackson
ACCIJLNNOTUV conjunctival
ACCIJMNNOSUU jus canonicum
ACCIJNNOOTTU joint account
ACCIJNNOSTUV conjunctivas
ACCIKLLNOUUY Lucky Luciano
ACCIKMMNNOOP common ink cap
ACCILLMNOOSU malocclusion
ACCILLNOOTTU colluctation
ACCILLORTUUV vocicultural
ACCILMOOPSST cosmoplastic
ACCILNOOPRSY cyclosporin A
ACCILNOPRSTY prostacyclin
ACCILNOSSTTU sansculottic
ACCILOPRSSTY pyroclastics
ACCIMMNOORTU communicator
ACCIMNOOSSTU cosmonautics
ACCIMNOOSTUU contumacious
ACCIMOOPRRTY McCoy Airport
ACCINNOPRTTT contact print
contact-print
ACCINOSSSTUU succussation
ACCIOOOPSTTU optoacoustic
ACCIOOPRSSTU stauroscopic
ACCKMMMNOOSU common as muck
ACCKMNOOPSTY stock company
ACCMNORSTUUU autumn crocus
ACCNOOPRSTTT contact sport
ACCNORSTTTUU trust account
ACDDDEEHNOOR dodecahedron
ACDDDEEINSST addictedness
ACDDDEFGINPU pudding-faced
ACDDDEGINOOR good riddance
ACDDDEGINRSW wedding cards
ACDDDENOORSU dodecandrous
ACDDEEEFLSTU self-educated
ACDDEEEHIMST semi-detached
ACDDEEEHNSST detachedness
ACDDEEELLTUW well-educated
ACDDEEEMNSSX excess demand
ACDDEEFIIRTT trade deficit
ACDDEEHILNRY cylinder head
ACDDEEHINNRS Dresden china
ACDDEEHINNST disenchanted
ACDDEEHLLNOR candle-holder
ACDDEEHORRST hard-sectored
ACDDEEIIMNST demi-distance
ACDDEEILNNOU duodecennial
ACDDEEILNTTU denticulated
ACDDEEIMOSSU Discomedusae
ACDDEEIMOSTT domesticated
ACDDEEIMPSST dissected map
ACDDEELLOORV collared dove
ACDDEELNPTUU pedunculated
ACDDEENNOSTV Second Advent
ACDDEFNNNOOR cannon fodder
ACDDEGHIMNPS camp-shedding
ACDDEGHIMNRW wedding march
ACDDEGHINRSU undischarged
ACDDEGHNRSSU grand duchess
ACDDEGIILLNO dialling code
ACDDEGIINNRS discandering
ACDDEGNOOSUY dodecagynous
ACDDEHIILMNO Donald Michie
ACDDEHIKLRUY hydraulicked
ACDDEHIKNOVY David Hockney
ACDDEHILSSTT saddle stitch
saddle-stitch
ACDDEHINORSU deuch-an-doris
ACDDEHINPSTU undispatched
ACDDEIIIPRSV disprivacied
ACDDEIIKNRST sick and tired
ACDDEIILNORT rodenticidal
ACDDEIILNORU radionuclide
ACDDEIILNPTU induplicated
ACDDEIINNOTV non-addictive
ACDDEIINORST endocarditis
ACDDEIINRTTY identity card
ACDDEILLOSTY dislocatedly
ACDDEILNOOST consolidated
ACDDEILRSTTY distractedly
ACDDEIMNOSSU discomedusan
ACDDEINNNSSU uncandidness
ACDDEINOOPST paedodontics
ACDDEINPRSTY candy-striped
ACDDEINRSTTU undistracted
ACDDEMOPRSSU mass-produced
ACDDENNNOOPR pro-and-conned
ACDDGIKLNOSU sack-doudling
ACDDHHIIMNOT diamond-hitch

ACDDHIILORRZ lizard orchid
ACDDHIIPRRTY Picardy third
ACDDHIMNORYY hydrodynamic
ACDDHJNNPUUY Punch and Judy
ACDDIIJNOTU dijudication
ACDDIIILNOTU dilucidation
ACDDILNORSTY discordantly
ACDDINNORSTU undiscordant
ACDDKLOOOPST paddock-stool
ACDDOOORRRUY corduroy road
ACDEEEEFFNOS feed one's face
ACDEEEEHKLPP apple-cheeked
ACDEEEFFFLST self-affected
ACDEEEFFLLTW well-affected
ACDEEEFFNSST affectedness
ACDEEEFLNNOZ zonal defence
ACDEEEFMOSUW meadow fescue
ACDEEEGINOPT paedogenetic
ACDEEEGINRTT cigarette end
ACDEEEGIRSVY gay deceivers
ACDEEEGKLLRT ledger tackle
ACDEEEGLNOOU eau de Cologne
ACDEEEGNNRRT garden centre
ACDEEEHIMNPS maiden speech
ACDEEEHINRUV underachieve
ACDEEEHKLNRT halter-necked
ACDEEEHLMNPU hempen caudle
ACDEEEHMNOSS damson cheese
ACDEEEIIPRTV depreciative
ACDEEEILLLRW well, I declare!
ACDEEEILNOPV velocipedean
ACDEEEILNORT deceleration
ACDEEEILNPRT precedential
ACDEEEILNPSS special needs
ACDEEEILNRST decentralise
ACDEEEILNRSU denuclearise
ACDEEEILNRTV cantilevered
ACDEEEILNRTZ decentralize
ACDEEEILNRUZ denuclearize
ACDEEEILNSST delicateness
delicatessen
ACDEEEINNRTV inadvertence
ACDEEEINRSSV disseverance
ACDEEEKNNRSS cankeredness
ACDEEELLNOOV leave one cold
ACDEEELNNOSU endonuclease
ACDEEELNNTTY antecedently
ACDEEEMNNOPS mend one's pace
ACDEEEMNNRRT remand centre
ACDEEENPRRST centre spread
ACDEEENRSTTU cetera desunt
ACDEEEOPRRRT tape recorder
ACDEEFFHOSTW shadow effect
ACDEEFFIIRTU feu d'artifice
ACDEEFFLNTUY unaffectedly
ACDEEFFNORRT Fort-de-France
ACDEEFGHIRSX fixed charges
ACDEEFGIILRS Gracie Fields
ACDEEFHHIKNR handkerchief
ACDEEFHILLRW child welfare
ACDEEFHNORRW henceforward
ACDEEFIILNSU unified scale
ACDEEFIINRRY ferricyanide
ACDEEFILLNOT deflectional
ACDEEFILMTTU multifaceted
ACDEEFILOPPR pride of place
ACDEEFIMMNNO Of Mice and Men
ACDEEFINORRY ferrocyanide
ACDEEFLMMNOO female condom
ACDEEFLMOOTW Fleetwood Mac
ACDEEFLORRTU federal court
ACDEEFNORRTU Tour de France
ACDEEFNRRSUU undersurface
ACDEEGGNRSSS scraggedness
ACDEEGHILRST clear-sighted
ACDEEGHLLNNU unchallenged
ACDEEGIINOPT doating-piece
ACDEEGIIRSTU Scutigeridae
ACDEEGILLOTY geodetically
ACDEEGILMNOY Ealing comedy
ACDEEGILNNRU Lucinda Green
ACDEEGILNORS close-grained
ACDEEGILNOSS cladogenesis
ACDEEGILNRSY decreasingly
ACDEEGILORVV gravel-voiced
ACDEEGINNNQU Dancing Queen
ACDEEGINPRRT cartridge pen
ACDEEGINRSSS dressing-case
ACDEEGKNOTTU tongue-tacked
ACDEEGMNOORR Grande Comore
ACDEEGNNORSS gas-condenser
ACDEEGNNORTV Covent Garden
ACDEEGNNOSTT decongestant
ACDEEGNOORVW covered wagon
ACDEEGNORSST get one's cards
ACDEEHHNRSTU under hatches
ACDEEHHOOPRY Rhodophyceae
ACDEEHIILLTT ditheletical✧
ACDEEHIINNRR Adrienne Rich
ACDEEHIINNRS Schneiderian
ACDEEHIIRSTT radiesthetic
ACDEEHIISSTT the die is cast
ACDEEHIKLPSS sickle-shaped
ACDEEHILLOOS de-alcoholise
ACDEEHILLOOZ de-alcoholize
ACDEEHILMNOR echinodermal
ACDEEHILNNOP diencephalon
ACDEEHILNNRT Netherlandic
ACDEEHILNNSS endless chain
ACDEEHIMNNSU unmechanised
ACDEEHIMNNUZ unmechanized
ACDEEHIMNRRS merchandiser
ACDEEHIMNRRZ merchandizer
ACDEEHINNRST disenchanter
ACDEEHINRRTV inverted arch
ACDEEHISSTTY dysaesthetic
ACDEEHKMRSTU Deutsche Mark
ACDEEHLLMSSU chauds-mellés
ACDEEHLNNOOR Leonard Cohen
ACDEEHLNOPRT elephant cord
ACDEEHLORTTY heterodactyl
ACDEEHMNORSW reach-me-downs

ACDEEHNNOPRU unchaperoned
ACDEEHNOPRRU unreproached
ACDEEHNRSSST starchedness
ACDEEIILLMPY epidemically
ACDEEIILLNTY indelicately
ACDEEIILLTTY dietetically
ACDEEIILNOPV velocipedian
ACDEEIIMNRTY intermediacy
ACDEEIINOPRT depreciation
ACDEEIINPRRR Pierre Cardin
ACDEEIINQSTU equidistance
ACDEEIINTTUX inexactitude
ACDEEIIOOPRS aecidiospore
ACDEEIJKNNRT dinner jacket
ACDEEIKLOOPS kaleidoscope
ACDEEIKNNNSS snick and snee
ACDEEILLNNOS declensional
ACDEEILLNRSY cylinder seal
ACDEEILLRTUV culvertailed
ACDEEILMNPST displacement
ACDEEILMORRS sclerodermia
ACDEEILMRTUV vermiculated
ACDEEILNNNOU non-Euclidean
ACDEEILNNOSS descensional
ACDEEILNOOPY Lycopodineae
ACDEEILNOSTT conseil d'état
ACDEEILNSSST distanceless
ACDEEILORRRS Sir Carol Reed
ACDEEILORTUV edulcorative
ACDEEILORTVY decoratively
ACDEEILRTTVY detractively
ACDEEILSTTTU testiculated
ACDEEIMNNOPR predominance
ACDEEIMOPRTU coup de maître
ACDEEIMORRTX xerodermatic
ACDEEINNOOTT Notonectidae
ACDEEINNOPRR preordinance
ACDEEINNORRT André Citroën
ACDEEINNRTVY inadvertency
ACDEEINOOPRT coin-operated
ACDEEINOOPRV overcanopied
ACDEEINOORRT redecoration
ACDEEINOPRTU deuteranopic
ACDEEINOSSSU edaciousness
ACDEEINOSUUV Dieu avec nous
ACDEEINRSSTV carte des vins
ACDEEIOPPRTU propaedeutic
ACDEEIOPRRTY depreciatory
ACDEEJKKNOTY donkey jacket
ACDEEKLLMMOR Derek Malcolm
ACDEEKLORTTW Derek Walcott
ACDEEKMPRRSU muckspreader
ACDEEKOPRRTY Peter Ackroyd
ACDEELMNNOTT malcontented
ACDEELNNNOTU non-nucleated
ACDEELNOOSSS closed season
ACDEELNOPRTU counter-paled
counterplead
ACDEELOPRRRY record player
ACDEELOPRRSW crowd-pleaser
ACDEELOPRTTY pterodactyle
ACDEEMNOPPTY appendectomy
ACDEEMNRRRSY merry dancers
ACDEEMOPSTTY stapedectomy
ACDEENNNOTUV uncovenanted
ACDEENNNRSTT transcendent
ACDEENNNRTUY undertenancy
ACDEENNOOPRV over-cannoped
ACDEENNORRTU centre around
ACDEENNORSTU second nature
ACDEENOORSTU Neoceratodus
ACDEEOORRSSU droseraceous
ACDEFFIINOST disaffection
ACDEFGHINNOW wind of change
ACDEFHHOORTT thatched roof
ACDEFHIINRSS disfranchise
ACDEFHINNRSU unfranchised
ACDEFHOORSSU house of cards
ACDEFIIIMOTV modificative
ACDEFIILMRTY family credit
ACDEFIILNNOT confidential
ACDEFIILNSSU unclassified
ACDEFIILNSTY sanctifiedly
ACDEFIINNSTT disinfectant
ACDEFIINNSTU unsanctified
ACDEFIINOORT deforciation
ACDEFILLLOTU folliculated
ACDEFILLOPSU Paul Scofield
ACDEFIMMOOPR campodeiform
ACDEFINORRSU François Rude
ACDEFIOPRRRW forward price
ACDEFLMNOOPU compound leaf
ACDEGGHLOORS ragged school
ACDEGHIILRSY Rayleigh disc
ACDEGHILNRRU hurdle-racing
ACDEGHIMNOTT method acting
ACDEGHIMOPRS demographics
ACDEGHINPRSY physic garden
ACDEGHIOPRRS discographer
ACDEGIIKMNST magnetic disk
ACDEGIILLNSS sliding scale
ACDEGIILPQRU quadriplegic
ACDEGIIMNNOR Indo-Germanic
ACDEGIINRRTT credit rating
ACDEGIIOOPRT diageotropic
ACDEGIKNNRSW sneck-drawing
ACDEGIKNRSSS dressing-sack
ACDEGILLOOTY dialectology
ACDEGILNNOST long-distance
ACDEGILNRTTY detractingly
ACDEGILNTUUU unguiculated
ACDEGIMMNRTU magnetic drum
ACDEGINORRSS cross-grained
ACDEGKLLOORS slockdolager
ACDEGKLNORTU ground tackle
ACDEGKNORRTU racket-ground
ACDEGNORRTUU counter-guard
ACDEHHHNOTTW down the hatch
ACDEHHIILNOR chiliahedron
ACDEHHILNPRS ship chandler
ACDEHHLORTTW draw the cloth
ACDEHHLOSTTU slouch-hatted

ACDEHHOOOPTT photocathode
ACDEHHOORRSU orchard-house
ACDEHIIILSTT ditheistical
ACDEHIIIRRTU Trichiuridae
ACDEHIILMMOT immethodical
ACDEHIIMNNOT indomethacin
ACDEHIIMNOOR Chironomidae
ACDEHIIMORST radiochemist
ACDEHIIPRTYY hyperacidity
ACDEHIKLMNOU Leonid Kuchma
ACDEHIKORRST strike a chord
ACDEHILLMOTY methodically
ACDEHILMNOTU unmethodical
ACDEHILNOPTT painted cloth
ACDEHILOOPRT orthopedical
ACDEHILORRRW Richard Lower
ACDEHILORSTY hydroelastic
ACDEHILRTTTY directly that
ACDEHIMNRRSS scrimshander
ACDEHIMOOPPR paedomorphic
ACDEHINNOPSW open sandwich
ACDEHINNRSTW sandwich tern
ACDEHINOORSS icosahedrons
ACDEHINOPTTU put the acid on
ACDEHINORRST Richard Stone
ACDEHIOOPRST orthopaedics
ACDEHJJNNORY John Jarndyce
ACDEHJNOOPRS Joseph Conrad
ACDEHKLLNOOU Cool Hand Luke
ACDEHLMOOSTU old moustache
ACDEHLPRTYYY hyperdactyly
ACDEHLPSTTTU Plattdeutsch
ACDEHMMNOORT doom-merchant
ACDEHMNNOORS enchondromas
ACDEHMOOOSTT smooth-coated
ACDEHMOPRSUY pachydermous
ACDEIIILNSTU unidealistic
ACDEIIILNTVY indicatively
ACDEIIILOSSS dissocialise
ACDEIIILOSSZ dissocialize
ACDEIIILRTVY veridicality
ACDEIIIMMORT radiomimetic
ACDEIIIMNNOT nicotinamide
ACDEIIIMNNRS incendiarism
ACDEIIIMNRST discriminate
ACDEIIIMORST isodiametric
ACDEIIINOPRT antiperiodic
ACDEIIINPPST appendicitis
ACDEIIINRSTT disintricate
ACDEIIINRTTU antidiuretic
ACDEIIIOPRTY aperiodicity
ACDEIIIOSSTV dissociative
ACDEIIIPRRST pericarditis
ACDEIIKLLOPS pickadilloes
ACDEIIKLMNNO Nicole Kidman
ACDEIIKLNOPR a rod in pickle
ACDEIIKLRSTT Lake District
ACDEIILLNNTY incidentally
ACDEIILLOPRY periodically
ACDEIILLOPSY episodically
ACDEIILMNOPT decimal point
ACDEIILNOPTU pediculation
ACDEIILNORST discretional
ACDEIILNOSSU unsocialised
ACDEIILNOSUZ unsocialized
ACDEIILNRSXY axis cylinder
ACDEIILRRTUV diverticular
ACDEIIMNOSTU miseducation
ACDEIIMOPRRT madreporitic
ACDEIINNNOTU denunciation
ACDEIINNOORT incoordinate
inco-ordinate
ACDEIINNOOTT conditionate
ACDEIINNOPRT pentacrinoid
ACDEIINNORTT indoctrinate
ACDEIINOORTV co-ordinative
ACDEIINOOTTX detoxication
ACDEIINOPSTT disceptation
ACDEIINORSTT at discretion
ACDEIINOSTTU educationist
ACDEIINRRSTU curtain-sider
ACDEIINRSSTV vindicatress
ACDEIIPRSTTU tricuspidate
ACDEIJLNTUVY adjunctively
ACDEIKNORSTT stock-in-trade
ACDEILLMOOSU Molluscoidea
ACDEILLMOSTY domestically
ACDEILLMRSUY scullery-maid
ACDEILLNSTYY syndetically
ACDEILLOOPSY Lycopodiales
ACDEILLOPSTU leucoplastid
ACDEILLOPSTY despotically
ACDEILMNOPRU unproclaimed
ACDEILMNOSUY mendaciously
ACDEILMOPSTU deutoplasmic
ACDEILMRSTXY mixed crystal
ACDEILNNOTWW lancet window
ACDEILNOOORT decoloration
ACDEILNOORTU edulcoration
ACDEILNOORTY co-ordinately
ACDEILNOOSST disconsolate
ACDEILNOPPPY Iceland poppy
ACDEILNOPRSS cross-and-pile
ACDEILNORSSW cowardliness
ACDEILNTTUUV uncultivated
ACDEILOORRUV varicoloured
ACDEILRRTTUU turriculated
ACDEIMMNNOOT commendation
ACDEIMMNORTY dynamometric
ACDEIMMOOORR air-commodore
ACDEIMNNNOOT condemnation
ACDEIMNNOPRY predominancy
ACDEIMNORRRS morris dancer
ACDEIMOORSTT domesticator
ACDEIMOPRSTU promuscidate
ACDEINNNOOST condensation
ACDEINNNOSTU unsanctioned
ACDEINNNOSTY Innocents' Day
ACDEINNORRTU counter-drain
ACDEINNORTTU detruncation
ACDEINNORTUY denunciatory
ACDEINOOPRRT incorporated

ACDEINOPRTTV privat-docent
ACDEINOPRTTY dictyopteran
ACDEINORRRSU sound-carrier
ACDEINORRTUV turacoverdin
ACDEINORSTTU decrustation
discount rate
ACDEIOOPRRST discorporate
ACDEIORRSTUV radius vector
ACDEIPRRTTVY party-verdict
ACDEJMNOOQSU Jacques Monod
ACDELLLOSTUW Ludlow Castle
ACDELMNOORUY many-coloured
ACDELMOPRTUW talcum powder
ACDELNOORTYY cotyledonary
ACDELNOPRRUU unprocedural
ACDELOPRRTTY protractedly
ACDEMMNOORTY commendatory
ACDEMNNOORTY condemnatory
ACDEMOOORRTU Doctor Moreau
ACDEMOPRRSSU mass producer
ACDENNORSTTU counter-stand
ACDENNORSTYY Sydney Carton
ACDENNPTTUUU unpunctuated
ACDENOSTTUUV cavendo tutus
ACDEOPRSTTUW waste product
ACDEORSTTTUU autodestruct
ACDFFILNOTUW Wolffian duct
ACDFGIKLNOOT floating dock
ACDFHHIINPSS fish and chips
ACDFIIIINNOT nidification
ACDFIIILNTVY divinity calf
ACDFIIIMNOOT modification
ACDFIMOORTY modificatory
ACDFIKMOPRRY Mary Pickford
ACDFILMOORTY family doctor
ACDFIMNNORTY Nancy Mitford
ACDGGHIINNNW wind-changing
ACDGGIINORSU discouraging
ACDGGIOOORSU good gracious
ACDGHHIOPRRY hydrographic
ACDGHILLOORY hydrological
ACDGHIMNOOTW doomwatching
ACDGHINNOSTW Washington DC
ACDGIIINRSTV visiting card
ACDGIIKLOSST digital socks
ACDGIIKNNRST skirt-dancing
ACDGIILOORST cardiologist
ACDGIIMRSTTU gratis dictum
ACDGILLOOTYY dactyliology
ACDGILMMNNOY commandingly
ACDGILMNOORR corn marigold
ACDGINNOPRST standing crop
ACDGINOOOPRT gonadotropic
ACDHHIIKNNTT thick-and-thin
ACDHHIILNTWY wild hyacinth
ACDHHIIOPSTY Ichthyopsida
ACDHHIIPSTTW with dispatch
ACDHHIMNOORR harmonichord
ACDHHINOOPRY hypochondria
ACDHHINOORTX xanthochroid
ACDHHINOOTWY wood hyacinth
ACDHIIMMORST dichromatism
ACDHIIMNOORT mitochondria
ACDHIINNORRX Richard Nixon
ACDHIINOOPRS radiophonics
ACDHIINORRSW Windsor chair
ACDHIIOPRSTT dictatorship
ACDHILNNOUWW launch window
ACDHILNOSSUY lady's-cushion
ACDHIMNOOPTY photodynamic
ACDHINNOORST chondrostian
ACDHINOOPQRU quadrophonic
ACDHINOPSSTT pitch-and-toss
ACDHINPPTTTU pitch and putt
ACDHIOPRRRRY Richard Pryor
ACDHIORSSTTY hydrostatics
ACDHKNNOORST stock and horn
ACDHLNOOSSUY Sunday school
ACDHNRSTTTUU cut and thrust
cut-and-thrust
ACDIIIJLLNUY injudicially
ACDIIILNNPST disciplinant
ACDIIILNPRSY disciplinary
ACDIIILOSSTY dissociality
ACDIIIMNNRST discriminant
ACDIIIMNORTV mid-Victorian
ACDIIINNOORT air-condition
ACDIIINOOSST dissociation
ACDIIIOSSTTU adscititious
ACDIILLMNPTU multiplicand
ACDIILLOOPSU lapidicolous
ACDIILMNOPTU undiplomatic
ACDIILMNPSTU platinum disc
ACDIILNOOQTU coloquintida
ACDIINNOOORT co-ordination
ACDIINORSSYY idiosyncrasy
ACDIIOOORTVW Victoria Wood
ACDIIOORRSUV radicivorous
ACDILLMOOORX loxodromical
ACDILLNOORWY Cowardly Lion
ACDILLOOPRSY prosodically
ACDILLOOPSUU paludicolous
ACDILMNSSTYY syndactylism
ACDILMOOPRSU cladosporium
ACDILMOORSUY mordaciously
ACDILNNOOSTU non-custodial
ACDILNOOORST consolidator
ACDILNOOPRTU productional
ACDILNORSUUU iracundulous
ACDILORSTTUY tridactylous
ACDIMMMOOTUY mycodomatium
ACDIMOORRRTY dormitory-car
ACDIMORRSSUU Sir Scudamour
ACDINNORSTTU transduction
ACDINOOQRSTU conquistador
ACDKLLNOOOPR droplock loan
ACDLLMNOOOPY Collop Monday
ACDLNNOOPTTU upland cotton
ACDLNOSSTUYY syndactylous
ACDLOOOPRSTT postdoctoral
ACDMMNNORTUU contra mundum
ACDNOOORSTTW Doctor Watson

ACEEEEEHKPPT keep the peace
ACEEEEFFMNTZ Zeeman effect
ACEEEEFJKRRT reefer jacket
ACEEEEGIKNPP peacekeeping
ACEEEEGILPTX epexegetical
ACEEEEHLPSST steeplechase
ACEEEEHRSSTT cheesetaster
ACEEEEILMRST Marie Celeste
ACEEEELMNRTT trace element
ACEEEELNORTT coelenterate
ACEEEELNPRRS real presence
ACEEEELNPRSS pearl-essence
ACEEEENPRRSV perseverance
ACEEEFFGHORR Roger Chaffee
ACEEEFILLNRS self-reliance
ACEEEFINNRTT Internet café
ACEEEFJMORRU force majeure
ACEEEFLNNOSV Anne of Cleves
ACEEEFLNPSSU peacefulness
ACEEEFLRRSTV scarlet fever
ACEEEFNNRRST transference
ACEEEGGHHLNT change the leg
ACEEEGGLORYY George Cayley
ACEEEGGORSTU secretagogue
ACEEEGHINNRS search engine
ACEEEGHINPRS cheeseparing
ACEEEGHNNRTU enterchaunge
ACEEEGIIMNNR ancien régime
ACEEEGIKNNRT ancient Greek
ACEEEGIKNRRT racketeering
ACEEEGILLTXY exegetically
ACEEEGIMNPPS specimen page
ACEEEGINNOSS caenogenesis
ACEEEGINRRST generatrices
ACEEEGLNSSTY Casey Stengel
ACEEEGNNRRUY unregeneracy
ACEEEHHILLLS Achilles' heel
ACEEEHHILNRS Charlie Sheen
ACEEEHHLNRTT health centre
ACEEEHHLRRTU eleutherarch
ACEEEHHLRTTW ratchet-wheel
ACEEEHHRRSST The Searchers
ACEEEHIISSTT aestheticise
ACEEEHIISTTZ aestheticize
ACEEEHIJNNRT Jean Chrétien
ACEEEHILSTTT telaesthetic
ACEEEHIMNQTU cinematheque
cinemathèque
ACEEEHINPPRS Chinese paper
ACEEEHIORRVV overachiever
ACEEEHIRRSTV heart-service
ACEEEHKLNRST Ernst Haeckel
ACEEEHLLOPST lose the place
ACEEEHLNNOPP epencephalon
ACEEEHMORRTT trocheameter
ACEEEHMORTTT cathetometer
ACEEEHNNPRST Stephen Crane
ACEEEHNOORRS one-horse race
ACEEEHNOORTT Heterocontae
ACEEEHNPRRTT The Carpenter
ACEEEHORRSTU terrace house
ACEEEHORRSUV have recourse
ACEEEHPRRSTU superteacher
ACEEEIIMNRTV cinéma vérité
ACEEEIJLLLOR Earl Jellicoe
ACEEEIJNOSTT ejection seat
ACEEEIKOPSTT take to pieces
ACEEEILLLNTT lenticellate
ACEEEILLNPST license plate
ACEEEILNNNSV Valenciennes
ACEEEILNNRTT canine letter
ACEEEILRTVXY execratively
ACEEEIMMNNPR impermanence
ACEEEIMNNPRS Prince Naseem
ACEEEIMNNPRT intemperance
ACEEEIMNNQSU main sequence
ACEEEIMNRSVX ex-serviceman
ACEEEINNPRST scene-painter
ACEEEINOPSSY say one's piece
ACEEEINRSSTV creativeness
reactiveness
ACEEEIOPRSTT tear to pieces
ACEEEIPPPRTV apperceptive
ACEEEIPRRTUV recuperative
ACEEEIRRRRTV river-terrace
ACEEEKNNNRTT Tennant Creek
ACEEEKNNOSSV save one's neck
ACEEELLOPRTT electroplate
ACEEELMOPRST spermatocele
ACEEELNNOVWY Evonne Cawley
ACEEELNNSTVY evanescently
ACEEELNOTXYY oxyacetylene
ACEEELNRSSSS carelessness
ACEEELORSSTT settle a score
ACEEELOSTUUV velouté sauce
ACEEEMNNNRTT entrancement
ACEEEMNPRSTT Terence Stamp
ACEEEMORRRTT meteor crater
ACEEEMORRSTY sycamore tree
ACEEEMRRSSTW screw steamer
ACEEENNNPRTU unrepentance
ACEEENNPSSST pass sentence
ACEEENNRRTTY tercentenary
ACEEENNRSTXY sexcentenary
ACEEENRRRSTU return crease
ACEEEPPPRRST pepper-caster
ACEEERRSSSTW watercresses
ACEEFFFGILNS self-effacing
ACEEFFFHIOTT fit of the face
ACEEFFGHILNO change of life
ACEEFFGLLOST staff college
ACEEFFGMNSTU Magnus effect
ACEEFFHOTTTT to that effect
ACEEFFIKLRTT raffle-ticket
ACEEFFILOPRS special offer
ACEEFFILSTUX exsufflicate
ACEEFFILTTUY effectuality
ACEEFFINOPTT Patent Office
ACEEFFINOTTU effectuation
ACEEFFLNNOSY fancy oneself
ACEEFFNNORSU on sufferance
ACEEFGHIMNST Gemeinschaft

ACEEFGHLLSST Gesellschaft
ACEEFGIINRSS fricasseeing
ACEEFGILLLNR clear felling
ACEEFGILLNNS self-cleaning
ACEEFGILNRST self-catering
ACEEFGIRRSTU figure-caster
ACEEFGIRRSTV gastric fever
ACEEFGLLNNOT falcon-gentle
ACEEFGLMORRT reflectogram
ACEEFGLNRSSU gracefulness
ACEEFGNNOOST age of consent
ACEEFHHIIRRS Archie Fisher
ACEEFHIINSST chieftainess
ACEEFHIKKMNT Mack the Knife
ACEEFHINNOSU finance house
ACEEFHIORSTU chaetiferous
ACEEFHLOPRRS self-reproach
ACEEFHLORRST Charles Forte
ACEEFHMNNRTT fent-merchant
ACEEFHNOOSSW show one's face
ACEEFHOPPRST part of speech
ACEEFIILNQTU liquefacient
ACEEFIILQTUV liquefactive
ACEEFIILRSTV Five Articles
ACEEFIIPRTTV petrifactive
ACEEFIKNNNRS frankincense
ACEEFILLNRTY frenetically
ACEEFILLRTTT cattle-lifter
ACEEFILMMOTU mute of malice
ACEEFILNNORT conferential
ACEEFILNORST self-creation
ACEEFILNPRST clip-fastener
ACEEFILOPRRT prefectorial
ACEEFILRRTVY refractively
ACEEFIMPRRTU picture frame
ACEEFINOPRTT perfectation
ACEEFINORSSU surface noise
ACEEFINPRTTU putrefacient
ACEEFINPSTTU stupefacient
ACEEFIPRTTUV putrefactive
ACEEFIPSTTUV stupefactive
ACEEFKMORRST market forces
ACEEFKNPRSSU Ferenc Puskas
ACEEFLLNPUUY unpeacefully
ACEEFLMOORTT olfactometer
ACEEFLOPPRST craftspeople
ACEEFMNORSST centre of mass
ACEEFNOOPSTU one's cup of tea
ACEEFNOPPRST copper-fasten
ACEEGGGHIMNU Maggie Cheung
ACEEGGHIINRV give in charge
ACEEGGHINNPR crepehanging
ACEEGGHLLPPR Greg Chappell
ACEEGGHNPRSS sprechgesang
ACEEGGINNRSV scavengering
ACEEGGIORRSU Georges Auric
ACEEGGIORSTT geostrategic
ACEEGGLMNOOR George Colman
ACEEGGMNORRW Ewan McGregor
ACEEGGMORRSU Sue MacGregor
ACEEGGNORTUU counter-gauge
ACEEGHIKMNPS speechmaking
ACEEGHIKNNRT kitchen-range
ACEEGHIKNPST packing-sheet
ACEEGHILLMNO Michelangelo
ACEEGHILLMNS mischallenge
ACEEGHILLOPR galilee porch
ACEEGHILNNOT genethliacon
ACEEGHILNNTW canting-wheel
ACEEGHILNOSU chaise-longue
ACEEGHILPRSY hyperalgesic
ACEEGHIMNPST camp-sheeting
ACEEGHINNRRT interchanger
ACEEGHINOPTT pathogenetic
ACEEGHIRRSST cash register
ACEEGHLLNSSY changelessly
ACEEGHLNRTUY legacy-hunter
ACEEGHLOPRRT electrograph
ACEEGHLORSTV grave-clothes
ACEEGHMNNORY moneychanger
ACEEGHNOPRRR necrographer
ACEEGHNOPSTX post exchange
ACEEGHPRRRSU supercharger
ACEEGHPRRSSS press charges
ACEEGIILMNSV evangelicism
ACEEGIILNSTV evangelistic
ACEEGIIMMNNT magnetic mine
ACEEGIIMNORT geometrician
ACEEGIINNOSS cainogenesis
ACEEGIINPRRT in great price
ACEEGIIOTTVX excogitative
ACEEGIKLNPRT tangle-picker
ACEEGIKMSSST message-stick
ACEEGIKNNRRV nerve-racking
ACEEGILLLOOT teleological
ACEEGILLLRTY telergically
ACEEGILLMNOT metallogenic
ACEEGILLMOOR mereological
ACEEGILLNRSV silver-glance
ACEEGILLNTUY geniculately
ACEEGILMNNST magnetic lens
ACEEGILNNPST nesting-place
ACEEGILNNSSU Alec Guinness
ACEEGILNNSSV evening class
ACEEGILNPRST resting place
ACEEGILNPSTT place setting
ACEEGILQRRSU squirrel cage
ACEEGIMNORST miscegenator
ACEEGIMNORTY atomic energy
ACEEGIMNRSTW West Germanic
ACEEGINNOSSY cyanogenesis
ACEEGINNRSTV ingravescent
ACEEGINNSSTX exactingness
ACEEGLLMMORU gram-molecule
ACEEGLMNOORT conglomerate
ACEEGLNOORTW Cologne water
ACEEGLNRSSTU Gunter's scale
ACEEGMMOPRTU computer game
ACEEGMNOPRRT carpetmonger
ACEEGMNPPSUV scavenge pump
ACEEGMOSTTUU Auguste Comte
ACEEGNNORTTU counter-agent

ACEEGNORRSSV governess car
ACEEGOPRRSSU supercargoes
ACEEHHILMSTT The Alchemist
ACEEHHIOPSTT Theopaschite
ACEEHHIOPTTT theopathetic
ACEEHHIPPRRS preachership
ACEEHHIPRRSU hire-purchase
ACEEHHIPSSTY hypaesthesic
ACEEHHIRSTVW weaver's hitch
ACEEHHLLORTT leathercloth
ACEEHHLMNRTY nychthemeral
ACEEHHLNORSU charnel house
ACEEHHLORRSY charley horse
ACEEHHLORTTW weathercloth
ACEEHHLOSTTU chattel house
ACEEHHMOPRTY chemotherapy
ACEEHHNOPRSU Schopenhauer
ACEEHHOPRSTU chapterhouse
ACEEHHOPRTTY tracheophyte
ACEEHHORRSTU Charterhouse
ACEEHHORSTTT cost the earth
ACEEHIIKNSTT kinaesthetic
ACEEHIILLNRT trichinellae
ACEEHIILMNOS isocheimenal
ACEEHIILNNOW once in a while
ACEEHIILNPST encephalitis
ACEEHIILPPRR peripherical
ACEEHIIMNNSS Meissen china
ACEEHIIMPRRT epirrhematic
ACEEHIIMPRTU perichaetium
ACEEHIIMSSTT aestheticism✧
ACEEHIINORTT theoretician
ACEEHIINRSTW white arsenic
ACEEHIINSTUU haute cuisine
ACEEHIISSTTT aestheticist
ACEEHIKKNNTV kitchen-knave
ACEEHIKLMNRT merchantlike
ACEEHIKMNOPR poker machine
ACEEHILLMORS Hemerocallis
ACEEHILLMRTY hermetically
ACEEHILLNSSW Chinese walls
ACEEHILLOPPT leptocephali
ACEEHILMNRRU machine-ruler
ACEEHILMORRT rheometrical
ACEEHILNORSS heroicalness
ACEEHILNPQSU Chaplinesque
ACEEHILNTVYY heavenly city
ACEEHILOORRZ coleorrhizae
ACEEHILOPRSX exospherical
ACEEHILPPRTU pupil teacher
ACEEHILPSSTT tip the scales
ACEEHILRRTTY Lyric Theatre
ACEEHIMNNRTW wine merchant
ACEEHIMNPRST parchmentise
ACEEHIMNPRTZ parchmentize
ACEEHIMNSSTT chastisement
ACEEHIMRSSTV Christmas eve
ACEEHIMRSTTU music theatre
ACEEHINNOSST inchoateness
ACEEHINNRSTU neurasthenic
ACEEHINORRRV River Acheron
ACEEHINORUUV nouveau riche
nouveau-riche
ACEEHINPRRTT interchapter
ACEEHINSSTTY synaesthetic
ACEEHIOOPRST aethrioscope
ACEEHIOPRRRV Pechora River
ACEEHIOPRTTU eutrophicate
ACEEHIPRRSTU creatureship
ACEEHIPRRTUY curietherapy
ACEEHIPRSTTU therapeutics
ACEEHIRSSTTV tsesarevitch
ACEEHIRSSTTW tsesarewitch
ACEEHKKLNNRT Kenneth Clark
ACEEHKKNORRS horse-knacker
ACEEHKLMORTW water hemlock
ACEEHLLLORST Rochelle-salt
ACEEHLLMOSTY Halley's Comet
ACEEHLLOORSV school-leaver
ACEEHLLOPSWY peach-yellows
ACEEHLLRRRUY cherry laurel
ACEEHLMNNOTU luncheon meat
ACEEHLMOPRTY cephalometry
ACEEHLNNNOST channel stone
ACEEHLNRSTTU turn the scale
ACEEHLOPRRSS reproachless
ACEEHLPSSTTU space shuttle
ACEEHMNNRSSU Scheuermann's
ACEEHNNORRST Hernán Cortés
ACEEHNNSSSTU unchasteness
ACEEHOORRSTW two-horse race
ACEEHOPPRRRS share cropper
sharecropper
ACEEHOPRSTTT The Spectator
ACEEHORTTUUU haute couture
ACEEIIILNPSS specialise in
ACEEIIILNPSZ specialize in
ACEEIIIMNOST semeiotician
ACEEIILLRTTV verticillate
ACEEIILMMPRT metempirical
ACEEIILMORTT meteoritical
ACEEIILMPRRT perimetrical
ACEEIILMRRSU mercurialise
ACEEIILMRRUZ mercurialize
ACEEIILMRSTY semiliteracy
ACEEIILNOPRS porcelainise
ACEEIILNOPRZ porcelainize
ACEEIILNORST neorealistic
ACEEIILNOSST sectionalise
ACEEIILNOSTZ sectionalize
ACEEIILPRSTZ particle size
ACEEIILPSSSU special issue
ACEEIIMMRSTT meristematic
ACEEIIMNNORT enantiomeric
ACEEIIMNORTT reaction time
ACEEIIMNPRSU Epicureanism
ACEEIINNORST containerise
ACEEIINNORTZ containerize
ACEEIINNRTUV renunciative
ACEEIINORSTV evisceration
ACEEIINORTTX exercitation
ACEEIINPPPRT appercipient

ACEEIINRRRRT cairn terrier
ACEEIINRRSST irresistance
ACEEIJMNSSST majesticness
ACEEIKLLTTTT kittle cattle
ACEEIKLMMNTY Mickey Mantle
ACEEIKNNOOTT take no notice
ACEEIKNOSSTT season ticket
ACEEIKNPRTTY necktie party
ACEEILLLNTTU intellectual
ACEEILLLORTY electorially
ACEEILLLPTTT Citlaltépetl
ACEEILLMMRSY mesmerically
ACEEILLMNORY ceremonially
ACEEILLMNSTY centesimally
ACEEILLMNTUV multivalence
ACEEILLMOPTV compellative
ACEEILLMORTY meteorically
ACEEILLNNORT crenellation
ACEEILLNOPRS porcellanise
ACEEILLNOPRT porcellanite
ACEEILLNOPRZ porcellanize
ACEEILLNORSS reliance loss
ACEEILLNORTY neoterically
ACEEILLNPSTT stencil plate
ACEEILLNRSUV surveillance
ACEEILLOPRSS solar eclipse
ACEEILLOPSTT total eclipse
ACEEILLORSTY esoterically
ACEEILLORTXY exoterically
ACEEILLPRSUV all-up service
ACEEILLRTTUY reticulately
ACEEILMMNORY claymore mine
ACEEILMMNPST misplacement
ACEEILMMRSTU cerium metals
ACEEILMNNOTV nomenclative
ACEEILMNOPRU police-manure
ACEEILMNOPTY pinealectomy
ACEEILMNPRST prince's metal
ACEEILNOPPRT perceptional
ACEEILNOPRRT electron pair
ACEEILNOPRSS precessional
ACEEILNOPRTU inoperculate
ACEEILNORTUX exulceration
ACEEILNRSSTV verticalness
ACEEILOOPRRS corporealise
ACEEILOOPRRZ corporealize
ACEEILOOPSST apostolic see
ACEEILOPPRRT preceptorial
ACEEILOSSTVX vox caelestis
ACEEILPPRSTV perspectival
ACEEILRRTTVY retractively
ACEEIMMMNOTT committeeman
ACEEIMMNNPRY impermanency
ACEEIMMNRSTT mince matters
ACEEIMMOOSST semicomatose
ACEEIMMPRTUY empyreumatic
ACEEIMNNOORR oneiromancer
ACEEIMNNORTT conterminate
ACEEIMNOPSTV compensative
ACEEIMNORSSX cross-examine
ACEEIMNORSVW servicewoman
ACEEIMNRTTUV centumvirate
ACEEIMOOPQRU opéra comique
ACEEIMOPPRRS Cape primrose
ACEEINNNPRSS Princess Anne
ACEEINNRRTTY tricentenary
ACEEINOORRTV overreaction
ACEEINOPPPRT apperception
ACEEINOPPRSU sea porcupine
ACEEINOPRRRT carton-pierre
ACEEINOPRRTU recuperation
ACEEINOPRSTT inspectorate
ACEEINOPSTTX expectations
ACEEINORRSSY recessionary
ACEEINORSTVV conservative✧
conversative
ACEEIORSTTUY stereoacuity
ACEEIRRSTTUY treasure-city
ACEEJJKNOSSS Jesse Jackson
ACEEJKKMNOTY monkey jacket
ACEEJKLLOTWY yellow jacket
ACEEJKMNORTY Monterey Jack
ACEEKKLNOPPR apple-knocker
ACEEKLLOSTTY cytoskeletal
ACEEKPRRTTUY Turkey carpet
ACEELLLMNSSU Munsell scale
ACEELLMMNOPT complemental
ACEELLMOPTTY patellectomy
ACEELLOOPRRT electropolar
ACEELMMNORTT Clément Marot
ACEELMMRSSUU Culm Measures
ACEELMNNORTU nomenclature
ACEELMNOOSTU lomentaceous
ACEELMNOPTTU outplacement
ACEELMNRSTTY Clytemnestra
ACEELMORSSST maltese cross✧
ACEELMPRRTUU permaculture
ACEELNOORRSS Eleanor Cross
ACEELNOPRRUW nuclear power
ACEELNOPSSTT Pentecostals
ACEELNPRTTYY petty larceny
ACEELNSSSSTT tactlessness
ACEELOOPPPTT Popocatepetl
ACEELOOPRSTY Astley Cooper
ACEELPPRSSSU upper classes
ACEELPPRSTTY spectral type
ACEELPSSTUUY eucalyptuses
ACEELRRTTUUW water culture
ACEEMMNOORST come on stream
ACEEMMNORSTU commensurate
ACEEMNNNNOTU announcement
ACEEMNNNOTUU mountenaunce
ACEEMNNORRST remonstrance
ACEEMNOOPRST compare notes
ACEEMNORRSST monstre sacré
ACEEMOPRSTTY spermatocyte
ACEENNOORTUV tonneau cover
ACEENOPRSTUU percutaneous
ACEEOOPRRTTT protectorate✧
ACEEOOPRRTTX expectorator
ACEEOPPPRRST pepper-castor
ACEEOPRRRTUY recuperatory

ACEEOPSTTTWZ Aztec two-step
ACEFFFFHIOST chief of staff✧
ACEFFFFIORST staff officer
ACEFFGILNNRU luffing crane
ACEFFGOOORST go off at score
ACEFFHILLLWY Wycliffe Hall
ACEFFIIILMOS semi-official
ACEFFIIKNNPS Pecksniffian
ACEFFIINRRTT intertraffic
ACEFFILNNSSU fancifulness
ACEFFORRSUUU furfuraceous
ACEFGHHLPRSU sprachgefühl
ACEFGHIINRTW fire-watching
ACEFGHILOPRX flexographic
ACEFGIIILMNS facsimileing
ACEFGIIKNNRV carving knife
ACEFGIILLNOT legal fiction
ACEFGILLNNOT falcon-gentil
ACEFGILMNTUX magnetic flux
ACEFGILNRSUY flying saucer
ACEFGILORSSU self-gracious
ACEFGLLNRUUY ungracefully
ACEFGLRRSTTU cluster graft
ACEFHHHIRSTY fish-hatchery
ACEFHHIMNSTY chimney shaft
ACEFHIIMNRTU fruit machine
ACEFHIMNOOPR machine proof
ACEFHJMNNOOR John Francome
ACEFHLNSSTUW watchfulness
ACEFHLOOSTTT cloth of state
ACEFHMNNNORR Norman French
ACEFHNORSTTU countershaft
ACEFHORRSSTU Rhesus factor
ACEFIIIKLNRT fairnitickle
ACEFIIILNOST fictionalise
ACEFIIILNOTT felicitation
ACEFIIILNOTZ fictionalize
ACEFIIINORTV verification
ACEFIIIPRTUV purificative
ACEFIIKLNRTY fairnytickle
ACEFIILLNNOT inflectional
ACEFIILLRRTY terrifically
ACEFIILMRRTU miracle fruit
ACEFIILNOOTT fail to notice
ACEFIILNOQTU liquefaction
ACEFIILORSTU laticiferous
ACEFIILORTUV curvifoliate
ACEFIILPRSSU superficials
ACEFIILSTTVY self-activity
ACEFIIMNNOST somnifacient
ACEFIIMNORTV confirmative
ACEFIINOORTV vociferation
ACEFIINOPRTT friction tape
petrifaction
ACEFIIORRSTV versificator
ACEFIIORRTVY verificatory
ACEFIIORSTTT testificator
ACEFIIOSSSTT fissicostate
ACEFIIRRTTUV vitrifacture
ACEFIIRRTTVY refractivity
ACEFILLMMOPY Olympic flame
ACEFILLNORSY forensically
ACEFILMNOPRT placentiform
ACEFILNNOOSS confessional
ACEFILNOOPST pelican's-foot
ACEFILNOPRST pectoral fins
ACEFILORRRTY refractorily
ACEFIMNORRST Afrocentrism
ACEFINNORSTT transfection
ACEFINNOTUVW wave function
ACEFINOORRTT torrefaction
ACEFINOPRTTU putrefaction
ACEFINOPSTTU stupefaction
ACEFINORRSST fornicatress
ACEFINOSSSTU factiousness
ACEFINOSTTTU Cosí Fan Tutte
così fan tutte
ACEFKLNOORRT control freak
ACEFKLOPTTTU futtock-plate
ACEFLLMOOPRW camp-follower
ACEFLLOORSSU false colours
ACEFLLOOSSTU out of all cess
ACEFLMOORTTY olfactometry
ACEFNOPRRSST craftsperson
ACEGGGHILMOP phlegmagogic
ACEGGHHHIINR high-reaching
ACEGGHINNNNY Chen Ning Yang
ACEGGHINRRTY gathering-cry
ACEGGHINSSTW gang switches
ACEGGIIKMNNR cringe-making
ACEGGIILLNSS glass ceiling
ACEGGIILNNST single-acting
ACEGGIKNNOOR cooking-range
ACEGGIKRSSTW swagger stick
ACEGGILLLOOY geologically
ACEGGILLMMOO gemmological
ACEGGILNOOST geognostical
ACEGGIMNORTY gyromagnetic
ACEGGINNOORT congregation
ACEGHHIILOPR heliographic
ACEGHHIIOPRR hierographic
ACEGHHINOPRT ethnographic
ACEGHHIOPRRR chirographer
ACEGHHIOPRTY hyetographic
ACEGHHNOPRTY technography
ACEGHHNORRST short-changer
ACEGHHOOPRRR chorographer
ACEGHHOOPRRY choreography
ACEGHIILLNYY hygienically
ACEGHIILLOOR hierological
ACEGHIILNPRS paring chisel
ACEGHIIMNOTV have it coming
ACEGHIIMOTTW atomic weight
ACEGHIKMNOPR epoch-marking
ACEGHIKNPRTT carpet-knight
ACEGHILLNNOU hallucinogen
ACEGHILLNOOP nephological
phenological
ACEGHILLNOOT ethnological
ACEGHILMOOOT Homage to Clio
ACEGHILMOPYY hypoglycemia
ACEGHILNNNTY enchantingly

ACEGHILNOPRV	graphic novel
ACEGHILNOPTT	Plectognathi
ACEGHILNRRTW	night crawler
ACEGHILOOPRS	phraseologic
ACEGHILOOPTY	hepaticology
ACEGHILOPRXY	lexicography
ACEGHILORSSU	surgical shoe
ACEGHIMOPRRR	micrographer
ACEGHINNRSTU	Gunter's chain
ACEGHINOOPRR	iconographer
ACEGHINOPRRZ	zincographer
ACEGHINOPRST	stenographic
ACEGHINORRTT	a tight corner
ACEGHIOPPRRR	reprographic
ACEGHIOPPRRT	petrographic
ACEGHIOPRRST	cerographist
ACEGHIORRSST	rags-to-riches
ACEGHIRRSTTT	garter-stitch
ACEGHLMNOOST	magnet school
ACEGHMNOOTTU	come to naught
ACEGHMOOPRRS	cosmographer
ACEGHMOOPRTY	cometography
ACEGHNOOPRSU	necrophagous
ACEGHOPPRRST	spectrograph
ACEGHOPPRTYY	ectypography
ACEGIIILLMTY	illegitimacy
ACEGIIILNNOV	vaginicoline
ACEGIIINOTTV	incogitative
ACEGIIINSTTV	negativistic
ACEGIIKKMNTY	mickey-taking
ACEGIILLLMOS	collegialism
ACEGIILLLOTY	collegiality
ACEGIILLMOOS	semiological
ACEGIILLOOPT	geopolitical
ACEGIILLOSTU	eulogistical
ACEGIILLOSTY	egoistically
ACEGIILNNNNS	line scanning
ACEGIILNNOST	single-action
ACEGIILNNOTU	geniculation
ACEGIILNNOTY	congeniality
ACEGIILNNRSY	increasingly
ACEGIILNPRSS	Alice Springs
ACEGIILORSSU	sacrilegious
ACEGIIMNOPTV	cognitive map
ACEGIIMNORRT	microgranite
ACEGIIMNORST	gastrocnemii
ACEGIIMNTTUY	mutagenicity
ACEGIINOOTTX	excogitation
ACEGIKLLNPRU	lurking-place
ACEGIKLLNSSS	gallsickness gall-sickness
ACEGIKLNOOPP	cooking apple
ACEGIKNNPRTY	necking party
ACEGIKNPPRSS	packing-press
ACEGILLLNOOY	neologically
ACEGILLMOORT	metrological
ACEGILLMOOSU	museological
ACEGILLMOOTY	etymological
ACEGILLNNOSY	geosynclinal
ACEGILLNNOTY	congenitally
ACEGILLNOORU	neurological
ACEGILLNORSY	early-closing
ACEGILLNORVW	wallcovering
ACEGILLNRTTY	clatteringly
ACEGILLOOOST	osteological
ACEGILLOOPRT	petrological
ACEGILLOOPST	pestological
ACEGILMMOPSY	Olympic games
ACEGILNNNRTY	entrancingly
ACEGILNNOTTU	conglutinate
ACEGILNOOOST	oceanologist
ACEGILNOOPRT	organoleptic
ACEGILNOOPTU	unapologetic
ACEGILNOORTW	water-cooling
ACEGILNOOSTW	sweat cooling
ACEGILNRSTTY	scatteringly
ACEGILOOPSST	escapologist
ACEGILORSTTU	gesticulator
ACEGIMNNORSU	cousin-german
ACEGIMNPRSUU	measuring cup
ACEGINNOPRST	precognisant
ACEGINNOPRTZ	precognizant
ACEGINNORRTU	raconteuring
ACEGINOPRRSU	superorganic
ACEGINORSSSU	graciousness
ACEGIOOOPPRT	apogeotropic
ACEGKLOORSSS	Crookes glass
ACEGLLNOOPTY	placentology
ACEGLMNORTYY	laryngectomy
ACEGLNOOPRSY	laryngoscope
ACEGLNOOPRTY	proteoglycan
ACEGLNOORSUY	acrogenously
ACEGLOORSUUY	courageously
ACEGOOPRSSTU	stegocarpous
ACEHHIIINRST	Chiantishire
ACEHHIILNOPT	technophilia
ACEHHIIMRSTT	Mechitharist
ACEHHIINOPRT	hierophantic
ACEHHILMOPTX	exophthalmic
ACEHHILMRTUY	eurhythmical
ACEHHILOOPST	theosophical
ACEHHILOPTTY	hypothetical
ACEHHIMNPRST	merchant ship
ACEHHIMOOOPT	homoeopathic
ACEHHINNOSTT	antichthones
ACEHHINOPRTT	theanthropic
ACEHHJLNNORY	John Charnley
ACEHHKLMORST	thermal shock
ACEHHKNNOOTV	Anton Chekhov
ACEHHKOPRSTY	shock therapy
ACEHHLLLOOTY	ethyl alcohol
ACEHHLLNNORY	Rhynchonella
ACEHHLLOSSTT	call the shots
ACEHHMORSTTY	chrestomathy
ACEHHNOOSTTU	autochthones
ACEHHOOPRTTY	hypothecator
ACEHHOPRTTUY	touch therapy
ACEHIIIKNPST	kinesipathic
ACEHIIINRSST	Christianise
ACEHIIINRSTZ	Christianize
ACEHIIINSTTT	antitheistic
ACEHIIJNPSSU	Spanish juice

ACEHIIKPRTTW Patrick White
ACEHIIKRRSWW Warwickshire
ACEHIILLNRST trichinellas
ACEHIILMNNTT anthelmintic
ACEHIILMNPRT mineral pitch
ACEHIILMOPSU pleiochasium
ACEHIILNOTUV cheluviation
ACEHIILNPPRS planispheric
ACEHIILNPRST sphincterial
ACEHIILOPRRT retrophiliac
ACEHIILPRSTY sphericality
ACEHIIMNNNRY Henry Mancini
ACEHIIMNOPTW white campion
ACEHIIMNORST monarchise it
ACEHIIMNORTZ monarchize it
ACEHIIMORSTT iatrochemist
ACEHIINNORST Neo-Christian
ACEHIINNPRRT chain printer
ACEHIINOPPPR hippocrepian
ACEHIINPRRST prechristian
pre-Christian
ACEHIINSSTTU enthusiastic
ACEHIINTTTUY authenticity
ACEHIIOPPRST Hippocratise
ACEHIIOPPRTZ Hippocratize
ACEHIIOPSSTT sophisticate
ACEHIIPPRRST periphrastic
ACEHIIPSSTUV Sivapithecus
ACEHIJLNNOOS Celia Johnson
ACEHIKLLLRRS Karl Schiller
ACEHIKLMNSTY chimney stalk
ACEHIKNPRRTY Patrick Henry
ACEHIKRRSSSW kirschwasser
ACEHILLMNNTU multichannel
ACEHILLMNOPY phonemically
ACEHILLNOPST plainclothes
ACEHILLNOPTY phonetically
ACEHILLNORUY unheroically
ACEHILLOPRUY euphorically
ACEHILLORRTY rhetorically
ACEHILLORSTU Ulotrichales
ACEHILLPRRSS schiller spar
ACEHILLRSTYY hysterically
ACEHILMNOOTT nomothetical
ACEHILMOORRT horometrical
ACEHILMOPSTW Sopwith Camel
ACEHILMORRRV cheval mirror
ACEHILNNNSSS clannishness
ACEHILNNORUW unicorn-whale
ACEHILNOORSW Nicholas Rowe
ACEHILNOPPTY phenotypical
ACEHILNPPRTT pitcher plant
ACEHILOOPSTT photoelastic
ACEHILOPRSTU tricephalous
ACEHILPPRSTY hyperplastic
ACEHIMMMNSTT mismatchment
ACEHIMMNNRSY Mercian Hymns
ACEHIMMNORST metachronism
ACEHIMNNORRT merchant iron
ACEHIMNPSSSS scampishness
ACEHIMOOOSTT homoeostatic
ACEHIMOORTTY atomic theory
ACEHIMOPRRTT tetramorphic
ACEHIMOPRSST atmospherics
ACEHIMOPSSTY scyphistomae
ACEHIMORSTTT thermostatic
ACEHIMPPRSTY spermaphytic
ACEHIMPRSTUY music therapy
ACEHIMRSSTTW master-switch
ACEHINOPPRTU hippocentaur
ACEHINOPRRTT trichopteran
ACEHINOPSSTY sycophantise
ACEHINOPSTTY enhypostatic
ACEHINOPSTYZ sycophantize
ACEHINORSSTT canister shot
ACEHINPRSSSS Spanish cress
ACEHIOPRRSTT orchestra pit
ACEHJLNNOORT John Coltrane
ACEHKMRRSSTT stretch marks
ACEHLLLLOPSS scallop shell
ACEHLLLMOSST small-clothes
ACEHLLLORRSS Charles Rolls
ACEHLLLPRSUY sepulchrally
ACEHLLMNOPSY shell company
ACEHLLMORSYY lachrymosely
ACEHLLORRSTY orchestrally
ACEHLMMNOOTW commonwealth
ACEHLMNOORSY close harmony
ACEHLMOORSST schoolmaster
ACEHLOPSSUXY psychosexual
ACEHMMNOOORT monochromate
ACEHMNOORTTT Cotton Mather
ACEHMNORRRTT trench mortar
ACEHMOORRTTY cherry tomato
ACEHMOORSTTY tracheostomy
ACEHMOORTTTY tetrachotomy
ACEHMOPRRTYY crymotherapy
ACEHMORRSSTU chorus master
ACEHNOOPPRRT torchon paper
ACEHNOPPRTTY carpet python
ACEHOORRRSTT orchestrator
ACEHOORSSTTY athrocytoses
ACEHPRRSTTUY trachypterus
ACEIIIKNRSST kinesiatrics
ACEIIILLMSTT elastic limit
ACEIIILLRSTT literalistic
ACEIIILMNNSS inimicalness
ACEIIILMNPSU municipalise
ACEIIILMNPUZ municipalize
ACEIIILMPRTY imperial city
ACEIIILNORTV Victoria Nile
ACEIIILNPRTT in triplicate
ACEIIILNSTTY inelasticity
ACEIIILRSTTV relativistic
ACEIIILRSTVV revivalistic
ACEIIIMNPRSS precisianism
ACEIIINNNORT incineration
ACEIIINNRSTT intrinsicate
ACEIIINPRSST precisianist
ACEIIJLLSTUY Jesuitically
ACEIIKOQQTUU quota quickie
ACEIILLLLPTY elliptically

ACEIILLLNSUV all-inclusive
ACEIILLMNSST miscellanist
ACEIILLMNTUU multicauline
ACEIILLMOSTY semiotically
ACEIILLMPTTU multiplicate
ACEIILLNORRT Torricellian
ACEIILLNORSW Willie Carson
ACEIILLNORTY collinearity
ACEIILLOQTUV colliquative
ACEIILMMNOPR clomipramine
ACEIILMMNRST mercantilism
ACEIILMMRRSU mercurialism
ACEIILMNORSS mini-lacrosse
ACEIILMNOSST sectionalism
ACEIILMNRSTT mercantilist
ACEIILMOPPSS episcopalism
ACEIILMOPRRT polarimetric
ACEIILMOPRST semi-tropical
ACEIILMRRSTU mercurialist
ACEIILMRRTUY mercuriality
ACEIILNNNRTU internuncial
ACEIILNNOPST inspectional
ACEIILNNRSTY transiliency
ACEIILNOORST creolisation
ACEIILNOORTZ creolization
ACEIILNOPRST inspectorial
ACEIILNORTTU reticulation
ACEIILNOSSTT sectionalist
ACEIILNOSTUV vesiculation
ACEIILNRSSSU arcus senilis
ACEIILNRSSTT triticalness
ACEIILNRSTTT clarinettist
ACEIILNRSTTU neutralistic
ACEIILNRSTVV civil servant
ACEIILNSSSTU sensualistic
ACEIILOPRSTT politicaster
ACEIILOQTUVY equivocality
ACEIILPRRSUY superciliary
ACEIILPSSTUY Puseyistical
ACEIILRRSSTU surrealistic
ACEIILRRTTTY retractility
ACEIIMMNNNOT antimnemonic
ACEIIMMNORTU communitaire
ACEIIMNORRRT recriminator
ACEIIMNORSTT cremationist
ACEIIMNOSSST seismonastic
ACEIIMNOSSTU scitamineous
ACEIIMNPTTUY pneumaticity
ACEIIMNRSSTU insectariums
ACEIIMOPRSTT peristomatic
ACEIINNNORTU renunciation
ACEIINNORTTU centuriation
ACEIINNOTTUV continuative
ACEIINOOQTUV equivocation
ACEIINOORSTV viscerotonia
ACEIINOPRRTT practitioner
ACEIINOPRSTU pertinacious
ACEIINORRSTW contrariwise
ACEIIOPPRRTT precipitator
ACEIIOPRRTTU picture ratio
ACEIIOQRTTUU autocritique
ACEIIORTTVVY overactivity
ACEIJKLLNOSV Jacksonville
ACEIJLNOOPRT projectional
ACEIJNNNOTTY joint tenancy
ACEIKKLNNSTY Kilkenny cats
ACEIKLNOOPRY plain cookery
ACEIKLOORRSW social worker
ACEIKLRRRTTU trailer truck
ACEIKMOOPRRT Patrick Moore
ACEIKNNORSST in one's tracks
ACEIKORRRTTT trick or treat
ACEILLLNRTUY lenticularly
ACEILLLORRSW Lewis Carroll
ACEILLMMNNOY mnemonically
ACEILLMMNOOT monometallic
ACEILLMMNOPT complimental
ACEILLMNOOPT compellation
ACEILLMNOOPX complexional
ACEILLMNORUU unimolecular
ACEILLMNRTTU multicentral
ACEILLMNRTUU multinuclear
ACEILLMNTUVY multivalency
ACEILLMORTUV volumetrical
ACEILLMORTUY molecularity
ACEILLMSTTUU multisulcate
ACEILLMTUUVY cumulatively
ACEILLNNORRU carillonneur
ACEILLNOPRTY entropically
ACEILLNOPTUY unpoetically
ACEILLNORTUY neurotically
ACEILLNOSTTU scutellation
ACEILLNOTTUY Teutonically
ACEILLOPTTYY type locality
ACEILLOPTUVY copulatively
ACEILLRRSTUU sericultural
ACEILMMMNOSS commensalism
ACEILMMNOORT monometrical
ACEILMMNOSTY commensality
ACEILMMOOTUV atomic volume
ACEILMNNOOPT componential
ACEILMNOOPTY come into play
ACEILMNOPSTY plastic money
ACEILMNSSSTY mysticalness
ACEILMOOPRRS corporealism
ACEILMOOPRTT optometrical
ACEILMOOPSTT leptosomatic
ACEILMOOSTTU coal titmouse
ACEILMOPRRTY pyrometrical
ACEILMOPRSUU primulaceous
ACEILMOPSTUV compulsative
ACEILMORTTTU Lucretia Mott
ACEILMOSTTTU multicostate
ACEILNNNOOTV conventional
ACEILNOOPRSS processional
ACEILNOOPRSU porcelainous
ACEILNOOPRTT lactoprotein
ACEILNOOPSTU option clause
ACEILNOORTUY elocutionary
ACEILNOPQTUU pauciloquent
ACEILNOPRRSU specular iron
ACEILNOPRSSU percussional

ACEILNOPRTTW Wilton carpet
ACEILNORSUXY exclusionary
ACEILNOSTTUV consultative
ACEILOOPRRST corporealist
prosectorial
ACEILOOPRRTT protectorial
ACEILOOPRRTV velociraptor
ACEILOOPRRTY corporeality
ACEILOOPSSTT osteoplastic
ACEILOPPRRTT protreptical
ACEILOPRRSUY precariously
ACEILOPSSTUU stipulaceous
ACEILOQSSUUY sequaciously
ACEILORRRSTT rectirostral
ACEILPPRSSTU superplastic
ACEILPRSSTTU special trust
ACEIMMNNOOTT commentation
ACEIMMNOSTUV consummative
ACEIMMOORRST commiserator
ACEIMMORRSTU crematoriums
ACEIMMORSTTY static memory
ACEIMNNNORTT conterminant
ACEIMNNOOPST companion set
compensation
ACEIMNNOOTUY caution money
ACEIMNNOPRTU unimportance
ACEIMNNOPRYZ pancreozymin
ACEIMNNOSTTT time constant
ACEIMNOOOOPT onomatopoeic
ACEIMNOOSSTT somatotensic
ACEIMNOPRSTY cryptomnesia
ACEIMNORRSST stercoranism
ACEIMNORSSTV conservatism✧
ACEIMNPSTTUU mispunctuate
ACEIMNSSTTUY unsystematic
ACEIMOOPRRTV Potomac River
ACEIMOOPRSTZ spermatozoic
zoospermatic
ACEIMOPRRSTU periostracum
ACEIMPRRRSTW writer's cramp
ACEINNNOOSTU Ion Antonescu
ACEINNNOOTTT contentation
ACEINNNORSTV inconversant
ACEINNOOPRTT pernoctation
ACEINNOORSTV conservation
conversation
ACEINNOOSTTT contestation
ACEINNORRSST contrariness
ACEINNORRTUY renunciatory
ACEINNORSTTU counterstain
encrustation
ACEINOOPPRSX praxinoscope
ACEINOORSSVY viscose rayon
ACEINOPPRRTU Port-au-Prince
ACEINOPPRSTU practise upon
ACEINOPSSSSU spaciousness
ACEINOPSSSTU captiousness
ACEINORRSSTT stercoranist
ACEINORRSTVX conservatrix
ACEINORRTTTU contriturate
ACEINORRTUUV vaunt-courier
ACEINOSSSTUU cautiousness
ACEIOOPRRRRT troop carrier
ACEIOOPRRRTT tricorporate
ACEIOOQRTUVY equivocatory
ACEIOORSTUUV overcautious
ACEIORRSSTTU resuscitator
ACEIORSSTUVW viscous water
ACEJKOPRSSTT sports jacket
ACEJLLNRRTUY currant-jelly
ACEKLNPRSTTU planet-struck
ACEKLOOQRRUU Quaker-colour
ACEKMMMNOORT common market✧
ACEKMMNORTUY mockumentary
ACEKMNORRTUY rockumentary
ACELLMNOOPRU cor pulmonale
ACELLMOPSUUU plumulaceous
ACELLNNOOPRT control panel
ACELLNNOSSUY consensually
ACELLNOOPRSU porcellanous
ACELLNORTTUY counter-tally
ACELLNOTTUXY contextually
ACELMMNOSTUY consummately
ACELMNOOPRTT contemplator
ACELMNPRSUUU supernaculum
ACELMOPRRSTU Marcel Proust
ACELNNPRTTUY century plant
ACELNNRSSUUU ranunculuses
ACELNOOPRSTU proconsulate
ACELNRRSSSUY nursery class
ACELOOOPSSTU octosepalous
ACELOOOPSTTU octopetalous
ACELOPRRSTTU court plaster
ACEMMMOOORRT commemorator
ACEMNOOPRRTY contemporary
ACEMNOOPRSTY compensatory
ACEMOOPRRSTU macropterous
ACEMPPRSSSWY cypress swamp
swamp cypress
ACEMPRRSTUXY X-ray spectrum
ACENNNORSTUV unconversant
ACENNOORSSSU canorousness
ACENNOORSTTU turn one's coat
ACENOOQRTTTU quattrocento
ACENOORRSTVY conservatory
ACENOPRRRTUY counter-parry
ACENOPRRSUWY Norway spruce
ACEOOPRRSTTT troposcatter
ACEOPRRSSSTT sportscaster
ACEPRRSTTTUY pastry cutter
ACFFGGHIILNN cliffhanging
ACFFHJNNORUY Johann Cruyff
ACFFIIILLOST official list
ACFFIILLNOUY unofficially
ACFFLOOORRTY factory floor
ACFGHOORRTTW growth factor
ACFGIIILNOTU uglification
ACFGIIINORST significator
ACFGIKMNRRTU truck-farming
ACFGILNPSTTU scalping-tuft
ACFGINOOORRT organ of Corti
ACFHHLNORSSY synchroflash

Words marked ✧ can also be spelled with one or more capital letters

ACFHIIIMNOTU humification
ACFHIILLORRY horrifically
ACFHIILNOSST slash fiction
ACFHILNNOOST infant school
ACFHLLNTUUWY unwatchfully
ACFIIIILNOTV vilification
ACFIIIIMNNOT minification
ACFIIIINNOTV vinification
ACFIIIINOTVV vivification
ACFIIILNOPST spiflication
ACFIIILNOTTY fictionality
ACFIIINNOOTT notification
ACFIIINNORTT antifriction
ACFIIINOOSST ossification
ACFIIINOPRTU purification
ACFIIINOPTTY typification
ACFIIINORTTV vitrifaction
ACFIIJORSTTU justificator
ACFIILLLOPRY prolifically
ACFIILLNOPTY pontifically
ACFIILNNNOOT non-fictional
ACFIILOSTTUY factitiously
ACFIIMNNOORT confirmation
ACFIIMNORRRT trinacriform
ACFIINORRTTU trifurcation
ACFIIOPRRTUY purificatory
ACFIKLLNOOTU out of all nick
ACFILLNNOTUY functionally
ACFILLOORRUU fluorouracil
ACFILMNOTUYY county family
ACFILORSTUUV virtual focus
ACFIMNNOOORT conformation
ACFIMNOORRTY confirmatory
ACFIMNRSSTUU cantus firmus
ACFIMORRSSUX Sir Marcus Fox
ACFKLNNOOOPR Norfolk capon
ACFMMNOOORTW comfort woman
ACFRRSTUUUUY usufructuary
ACGGHHIOPRRY hygrographic
ACGGHIISTTZZ zigzag stitch
ACGGHILNNNUY unchangingly
ACGGIILLLMOO Camillo Golgi
ACGGIILLOOST glaciologist
ACGGILLNOPRU group calling
ACGGILNPPSSU cupping-glass
ACGGILNSSTTU glass-cutting
ACGGINRSSTTU cutting grass
ACGHHHIOPTYY ichthyophagy
ACGHHHOPRTTU patch through
ACGHHIILOPRT lithographic
ACGHHINOOPPR phonographic
ACGHHINOORTT orthognathic
ACGHHIOOPPRT photographic
ACGHHIOOPRRT orthographic
ACGHHIOPPRTY phytographic
ACGHHLOOSTTU school-taught
ACGHHNOOPRRY chronography
ACGHHOPPRSYY psychography
ACGHHORRRTUY carry through
ACGHIIKNSSTV shaving-stick
ACGHIILLLOOP philological
ACGHIILLLOOT lithological
ACGHIILLNOOR rhinological
ACGHIILLOOOP ophiological
ACGHIILLOOST histological
ACGHIINNRRSU nursing chair
ACGHIINPRSTY scintigraphy
ACGHIIPRSSST sphragistics
ACGHIJMNNOOS Magic Johnson
ACGHIKNOOSTW what's cooking?
ACGHIKNORSTT tracking shot
ACGHILLMOOTY mythological
ACGHILLNOOOP phonological
ACGHILLOOPRS oscillograph
ACGHILLOOPTY phytological
ACGHILOPRSTY stylographic
ACGHIMNNORTW morning watch
ACGHIMOOPRSU microphagous
ACGHINNORRST anchor string
ACGHINOOPPRR pornographic
ACGHIOOPPRST coprophagist
ACGHIOOPSSTY phagocytosis
ACGHKLOPPUYY happy-go-lucky
ACGHLNOORSTU laugh to scorn
ACGHOOOPPRSU coprophagous
ACGHOPPRRTYY cryptography
ACGIIILLLOTY illogicality
ACGIIILLNSTU linguistical
ACGIIILLPSTU pugilistical
ACGIIILNOSTY caliginosity
ACGIIINNNRSS iris scanning
ACGIIINNOTTX intoxicating
ACGIIKKLNSTW walking stick
walking-stick
ACGIIKKNPRST kicking strap
ACGIIKLNNORU caulking-iron
ACGIIKNORSST stock-raising
ACGIILLLMNOO limnological
ACGIILLLOSTY logistically
ACGIILLLRTUY liturgically
ACGIILLMOOST limacologist
ACGIILLNORRV corrivalling
ACGIILMNOSUU mucilaginous
ACGIILMNSTTU multicasting
ACGIILNNNPTY city planning
ACGIILNOORST craniologist
ACGIILNOOSUV vaginicolous
ACGIILNPPSTU supplicating
ACGIILOOPPRT plagiotropic
ACGIIMNOORST gnomic aorist
ACGIIMORRTVY microgravity
ACGIINNNOOST consignation
ACGIINNNOOTT contignation
ACGIINNOOSTT contagionist
ACGIINNOSTTW wainscotting
ACGIKKMNOSST stocking mask
ACGIKLNORSSW working class
working-class
ACGILLLOOOYZ zoologically
ACGILLMNNOOY gnomonically
ACGILLNOOOST nostological
ACGILLNOOPST splat cooling

ACGILLOOOPRT tropological
ACGILNNNOTTU conglutinant
ACGILNOOSTUY contagiously
ACGILNOPSUUY pugnaciously
ACGILNORSUUY ungraciously
ACGILOPRSSTU postsurgical
ACGIMMOOPRRR microprogram
ACGIMNOOPRTU compurgation
ACGIMNOORSST gastronomics
ACGIMOPRSTTY cryptogamist
ACGINNOORSTY consignatory
ACGKORSSSSTU tussock grass
ACGLLNOORSUY clangorously
ACGLMOSSSUVY Muscovy glass
ACGLNOOPRSYY laryngoscopy
ACGMOOPRRTUY compurgatory
ACGMOOPRSTUY cryptogamous
ACHHHNOOPRRY Rhynchophora
ACHHHOOSSTTW chat-show host
ACHHIIINORST Ornithischia
ACHHIILMNOPR philharmonic
ACHHIIMNOPPS championship
ACHHIIMOSTTY stichomythia
ACHHIIMOSTYZ schizothymia
ACHHIKOOSSTV Shostakovich
ACHHILLMRTYY rhythmically
ACHHILLOPTTY thallophytic
ACHHILMNRTUY unrhythmical
ACHHILOOPRST holophrastic
ACHHILORTTYY ichthyolatry
ACHHIMNNOSTU Chimonanthus
ACHHIMNOSTTU insomuch that
ACHHINNOPTXY phycoxanthin
ACHHINOPRSTY christophany
ACHHINOPSSTY sycophantish
ACHHJLMNOUWY John W Mauchly
ACHHLOOORRSW Harrow School
ACHHNNOOOPRY onychophoran
ACHIIIINRSST trichiniasis
ACHIIILLOPRU ailurophilic
ACHIIILMSTWY whimsicality
ACHIIILNORST histrionical
ACHIIIMNPSSU musicianship
ACHIIIMNRSST Christianism
ACHIIINNNNOX Nixon in China
ACHIIINRSTTY Christianity
ACHIIKLMOPTT Machtpolitik
ACHIIKLNOTTY lay it on thick
ACHIILLLOSTY holistically
ACHIILLMOOTT lithotomical
ACHIILLNOSSU hallucinosis
ACHIILLORSTY historically
ACHIILNNOORT chlorination
ACHIILNOPRST rhinoplastic
ACHIILNORSTU unhistorical
ACHIILOOPPST scoptophilia
ACHIILOPRRSV corrivalship
ACHIILOPRSTT arctophilist
cartophilist
ACHIIMNOPRST misanthropic
ACHIIMOOPPPT hippopotamic
ACHIIMOPPRST Hippocratism
ACHIINNNORST non-Christian
ACHIINOPRSTT antistrophic
ACHIIPRSSTTY psychiatrist
ACHIKLLOOPST lock-hospital
ACHIKMORTUUV kurchatovium
ACHILLNOORSY isochronally
ACHILLNOPTYY hypnotically
ACHILLORSUVY chivalrously
ACHILMOOOPRS sophomorical
ACHILMOPPRRY lamprophyric
ACHILMORSTYY lachrymosity
ACHILNNOPSTU cushion-plant
ACHILNOOPPTY phonotypical
ACHILNORSUUV unchivalrous
ACHILOOOPTTV photovoltaic
ACHILOOPPRRS corporalship
ACHILORRSTTY Christolatry
ACHIMMOPPSTY psammophytic
ACHIMNNOORTY ornithomancy
ACHIMNNORSSY asynchronism
ACHIMNOOPRTY actinomorphy
ACHIMNOOPSSU poison sumach
ACHIMOPSSSTY scyphistomas
ACHINOOPTTUY autohypnotic
ACHINOOSTTTU Southcottian
ACHINOPRSSTY Cornish pasty
ACHIOOPPRRST saprotrophic
ACHIOOPRRSUZ rhizocarpous
ACHIOORSSTTY athrocytosis
ACHIOPRSSSTY astrophysics
ACHIQRSSTTUZ quartz-schist
ACHLLMNOOORS normal school
ACHLLOOPRSST chloroplasts
ACHMMNOOORSY monochromasy
ACHMOOORSTTY thoracostomy
ACHNNOORSSUY asynchronous
ACHOOPRRRTTU Port Harcourt
ACIIIILMRSTT militaristic
ACIIIILNOSTV civilisation
ACIIIILNOTVZ civilization
ACIIIILORSST sacroiliitis
ACIIIJLMSSTU justicialism✧
ACIIILLMPTTU multicipital
ACIIILMMNPSU municipalism
ACIIILMNNOST nominalistic
ACIIILMNOOST coalitionism
ACIIILMNPTUY municipality
ACIIILNOOSTT coalitionist
solicitation
ACIIILNOPRTT triplication
ACIIILNOSTVV convivialist
ACIIILNOTVVY conviviality
ACIIILNPPRTY principality✧
ACIIILQTUYZZ quizzicality
ACIIIMMNORST Marcionitism
ACIIIMNNORSS Canis Minoris
ACIIIMNORSTV Victorianism
ACIIIMPRSSTT patristicism
ACIIINNOOTTX intoxication
ACIIINNOSTTU cutinisation

Words marked ✧ can also be spelled with one or more capital letters

ACIIINNOTTUZ	cutinization
ACIIINOPSSUU	inauspicious
ACIIINPRRTTU	antipruritic
ACIIIPRSSSTY	scissiparity
ACIIJLLRSTUY	juristically
ACIIJLNORSTU	journalistic
ACIIKKKNPSTU	kick up a stink
ACIIKKPRSSTU	kick upstairs
ACIIKNOPSTTU	put a sock in it
ACIILLNOOQTU	colliquation
ACIILLNOPRVY	provincially
ACIILLNORSTT	scintillator
ACIILLNRTUUV	vinicultural
ACIILLOOPSTY	isotopically
ACIILLOQTUXY	quixotically
ACIILLOSSUVY	lasciviously
ACIILLPRSTUY	puristically
ACIILLRSSTTY	crystallitis
ACIILLRTTUUV	viticultural
ACIILMNNOOTU	columniation
ACIILMNORSTU	matriclinous
ACIILMOOPSST	apostolicism
ACIILMOPRTUV	victoria plum✧
ACIILNNOOOST	colonisation
ACIILNNOOOTZ	colonization
ACIILNNOOSTU	inosculation
ACIILNNOSTUY	insouciantly
ACIILNOORSST	consistorial
ACIILNOPPSTU	supplication
ACIILNOPRSTU	patriclinous
ACIILNORSSSS	nail scissors
ACIILNOSTUUY	incautiously
ACIILOOPSTTY	apostolicity
ACIILOPSSUUY	auspiciously
ACIILPRSTTUU	apiculturist
ACIIMMOOPRRS	comprimarios
ACIIMNOPRTTU	protactinium
ACIIMNOPSSSU	Passion-music
ACIINNNOOORT	incoronation
ACIINNNOOTTU	continuation
ACIINNOOPRST	conspiration
ACIINNOOPSTT	constipation
ACIINNOORSST	consistorian
ACIINNORSTTU	incrustation
ACIINOPRRSUV	picornavirus
ACIINOPSSUUU	unauspicious
ACIIOOPRRTTV	Port Victoria
ACIKLLPRSTUY	Turk's cap lily
ACIKLNOOPRST	split on a rock
ACIKMNNOORTU	mountain cork
ACILLLLOOQUY	colloquially
ACILLLMORTUU	multilocular
ACILLLOPRRUU	plurilocular
ACILLMNNOPSU	spinal column
ACILLMNOORTY	microtonally
ACILLMNOSUUY	calumniously
ACILLMOOOTYZ	zootomically
ACILLMORSUUY	miraculously
ACILLNNOOSUV	convulsional
ACILLNOORTTW	to crown it all
ACILLNOPSTYY	synoptically
ACILLOOPRRTY	proctorially
ACILLOOQSUUY	loquaciously
ACILLPRRSTUY	scripturally
ACILMMNNOOTT	non-committal
ACILMMNNOOUY	lay communion
ACILMNNSSTTU	CNS stimulant
ACILMNOOOPST	cosmopolitan✧
ACILMNOORSTU	matroclinous
ACILMNORSUUU	unmiraculous
ACILMOOPPRST	protoplasmic
ACILMOOPRRRT	Corporal Trim
ACILMOORRTVY	moral victory
ACILNNNOSTTY	inconstantly
ACILNNOOORTT	contortional
ACILNNOOSTTU	consultation
ACILNNOPTTUU	punctulation
ACILNOOPRSTU	patroclinous
ACILNPRRSTUU	unscriptural
ACILOOPPRSTT	protoplastic
ACILOOPPRTTY	prototypical
ACILOPPRSTUY	supplicatory
ACILORRRSTUV	curvirostral
ACILORSSSTTU	tourist class
ACIMMMNOPRUU	cuprammonium
ACIMMNNOOSTU	consummation
ACIMNNNOOPUY	company union
ACIMNNOOOPPT	pot companion
ACIMNOOPRSTY	trypanosomic
ACIMOOOPRSTT	somatotropic
ACINNNORSTTU	unconstraint
ACINNOORRSUV	oncornavirus
ACINNOPRTTUU	puncturation
ACINOOOPRRRT	incorporator
ACINOOOPRRTT	crop rotation
ACINOOPRRSTT	strip cartoon
ACINOPRSSTUU	transpicuous
ACIOOPPRSSTT	potato crisps
ACIORRRSSTTU	cirro-stratus
ACLLLMMOORWY	Malcolm Lowry
ACLLLPRSTUUY	sculpturally
ACLLMMMNOOOW	common mallow
ACLLMNOOORSU	salmon-colour
ACLLMNOORTUU	monocultural
ACLLNOOORTTT	control total
ACLLRRSTTUUY	structurally
ACLMOOPRSTUY	compulsatory
ACLNOORSTTUY	consultatory
ACMMNOORSTUY	consummatory
ACMMOPRTTUUU	caput mortuum
ACMNNNOOORWY	No Woman No Cry
ACMNNOORTUWY	countrywoman
ACMNOPRSTTUY	trust company
ACMOOORRRTTT	motor-tractor
ACNOOOPPRSTT	contrapposto
ACNOPRRTTUYY	country party
ADDDDEEEHLMU	muddle-headed
ADDDDEEEHNRU	dunderheaded
ADDDDEEFFILL	fiddle-faddle
ADDDEEEHNOOW	woodenheaded
ADDDEEFIOSTU	eisteddfodau
ADDDEEGHKNOU	dough-kneaded

ADDDEEHIILPY Didelphyidae
ADDDEEIIMPRS diadem spider
ADDDEEIMNNRV demand-driven
ADDDEELPRRSU rudder pedals
ADDDEEMNNOOS Ade Edmondson
ADDDEENNRSTU understanded
ADDDEFHIINNO findon haddie
ADDDEFIILMNO diamond-field
ADDDEFILNORU fiddle around
ADDDEGHILNOS load shedding
ADDDEILNNNOS Donald Sinden
ADDDENOORTTU dotted around
ADDDFGGINORT draft-dodging
ADDDIILLMNOR diamond-drill
ADDDINNORTWY down-and-dirty
ADDEEEEFLNRS self-endeared
ADDEEEEFNRRS ear defenders
ADDEEEFGNNOR Garden of Eden
ADDEEEFHILLT lead the field
ADDEEEFIIRTV additive-free
ADDEEEFIKLRR Freddie Laker
ADDEEEFILLNP fielded panel
ADDEEEFLLLRR Alfred Deller
ADDEEEFMNRRU ad referendum
ADDEEEGGHLOR loggerheaded
ADDEEEGINPRS speed reading
ADDEEEGLNNOU Angelo Dundee
ADDEEEGNNNRU unendangered
ADDEEEHHINOS hide one's head
ADDEEEHILPRT triple-headed
ADDEEEHINRST disheartened
ADDEEEHLNNVY even-handedly
ADDEEEHLPUZZ puzzle-headed
ADDEEEIIRSTV desiderative
ADDEEEIMPRTT premeditated
ADDEEEINSSSS diseasedness
ADDEEEJLLMSW James Weddell
ADDEEEJNNRRW Edward Jenner
ADDEEEKLNOOY Yankee-Doodle
ADDEEEKLPSST pedestal desk
ADDEEELLRRTW Edward Teller
ADDEEELNPTXY extended-play
ADDEEELORRSS sealed orders
ADDEEEMNORYY ready-moneyed
ADDEEENPPTXY expanded type
ADDEEENPRSSV depravedness
ADDEEEOPPRSV eavesdropped
ADDEEFFNRSTU understaffed
ADDEEFGILRRR larder fridge
ADDEEFGINOSY deed of saying
ADDEEFHLLNTY left-handedly
ADDEEFHLMORY formaldehyde
ADDEEFIKRRST Frederikstad
ADDEEFILLNRY friendly lead
ADDEEFILNORS self-ordained
ADDEEFIRRRST Freddie Starr
ADDEEFLNRSSU dreadfulness
ADDEEFNORSSW word deafness
ADDEEGGILLNN dingle-dangle
ADDEEGGILNOR dégringolade
ADDEEGHHLOUY oughly-headed
ADDEEGHILNNS single-handed
ADDEEGHKNRTU The Grand Duke
ADDEEGHMRSTU hedge-mustard
ADDEEGHNORTY hydrogenated
ADDEEGHNRRTU great hundred
ADDEEGIILNPT pleading diet
ADDEEGILNNPS landing-speed
ADDEEGINPPSU pease pudding
ADDEEGJMNTUY judgement-day
ADDEEGNORSTU adder's-tongue
ADDEEGOORWWW Wedgwood ware
ADDEEHHILPSS shield-shaped
ADDEEHHNNRTU the underhand
ADDEEHIILMNS shield-maiden
ADDEEHIILPRS shielded pair
ADDEEHILMNOW diamond-wheel
ADDEEHINNOOS do one's head in
ADDEEHINOPTY pointy-headed
ADDEEHLLMNOY Edmond Halley
ADDEEHLLNNSU unhandselled
ADDEEHLLOOWY woolly-headed
ADDEEHLNNOPY open-handedly
ADDEEHMNNORU dame d'honneur
ADDEEHMNOTTU muttonheaded
ADDEEHMORSUY Hydromedusae
ADDEEHOPRRTU proud-hearted
ADDEEIILNSVZ Denzil Davies
ADDEEIIMMNNO demi-mondaine
ADDEEIINOPRT Torpedinidae
ADDEEIINORST desideration
ADDEEIINORTT trade edition
ADDEEIKLMNWY weak-mindedly
ADDEEILLPSSY displeasedly
ADDEEILMNOOX lead monoxide
ADDEEILMSSTT Middle States
ADDEEILNRSST desert island
ADDEEILORRWW world-wearied
ADDEEIMNSSSY dismayedness
ADDEEINOPRST depredations
ADDEEINRSTUV disadventure
unadvertised
ADDEEKNRSTYY dry-stane dyke
ADDEELLMNRUW Edmund Waller
ADDEELNOSSTT staddle stone
ADDEELNRRUWY unrewardedly
ADDEENNORRUV over-and-under
under-and-over
ADDEENNORRVW Edward Vernon
ADDEENNRRSTU understander
ADDEENOSSTTU outdatedness
ADDEFGHHNOOT the hand of God
ADDEFGHORRYY Godfrey Hardy
ADDEFGIILLNN landing field
ADDEFGILNORY Golden Friday
ADDEFGILRRSU disregardful
ADDEFGLORRTU Artful Dodger
ADDEFHILNOOS Old Fashioned
old-fashioned
ADDEFHILOPST feldspathoid
ADDEFIIILQSU disqualified
ADDEFIIISSST dissatisfied

ADDEFINORRSW fire and sword
ADDEFLNNNOUW Newfoundland
ADDEFLNNOORT front-end load
ADDEGGINRRRY Gradgrindery
ADDEGHIINRRT third reading
ADDEGHILNORS Das Rheingold
ADDEGHILRRUW Ludwig Erhard
ADDEGIINORSS disorganised
ADDEGIINORSZ disorganized
ADDEGILNNOSU sounding lead
ADDEGILNOPRS spring-loaded
ADDEGILNORRR Lord Gardiner
ADDEGILNPPTU pudding-plate
ADDEGILNPRSS saddle spring
ADDEGINNRRUW underdrawing
ADDEGIOORUZZ Guido d'Arezzo
ADDEHHLORRSU hard shoulder
ADDEHHOSSTTW what's the odds?
ADDEHIILPPRZ lizard-hipped
ADDEHILNORRZ horned lizard
ADDEHIMNNOSU unadmonished
ADDEHINNORTW down the drain
ADDEHINPRRWY whip-and-derry
ADDEHIOPRTTV provided that
ADDEHLLMNSTU St Edmund Hall
ADDEHLNORTUW Edward Hulton
ADDEHMNOOORT rhodomontade
ADDEHMNORSUY hydromedusan
ADDEIIIQTTUV quidditative
ADDEIILLLSVY ill-advisedly
ADDEIILLNSSV Devil's Island
ADDEIILMOPRY dipyridamole
ADDEIILMSSVY misadvisedly
ADDEIILNQTUU unliquidated
ADDEIILPSSTY dissipatedly
ADDEIINOPPST disappointed
ADDEILMNNSTU undismantled
ADDEILMNOOTU demodulation
ADDEILMNOPRS promised land
ADDEILMNSSTW West Midlands
ADDEILNORSWW Edward Wilson
ADDEILOOPRSU au poids de l'or
ADDEIMMMRSUY Midsummer day
ADDEIMNNORRW narrow-minded
ADDEINNOOOTT Notodontidae
ADDEINOOPRTT traded option
ADDEINRRSUVY Sunday driver
ADDEMNOOORRT rodomontader
ADDEMNOOPRSU pseudorandom
ADDEMNOOPSSU pseudomonads
ADDENNOORTUW down-and-outer
ADDENNORSSWW downwardness
ADDFHIIMORTY hydatidiform
ADDFHLNOOSTU thousandfold
ADDFIILLNSUY disdainfully
ADDFILLNOOTW Donald Wolfit
ADDFLMNOORYY Raymond Floyd
ADDFLNNOOSTU lost-and-found
ADDGGHNOORUY Groundhog Day
ADDGHILNORTY thyroid gland
ADDGHIMNOORU rough diamond
ADDGHINPSTUY hasty pudding
ADDGIILNSSTU studdingsail
studding-sail
ADDGKMNOOOOR Komodo dragon
ADDGLLNOSSUY Guys and Dolls
ADDHIILLMOSY old-maidishly
ADDIIIINNOPR diprionidian
ADDIIILLNUVY individually
ADDIKLMNOOOS Komodo Island
ADDILLMOOSTY till doomsday
ADDILNOORRRY Lord Ordinary
ADDILNRRTUYY dirty laundry
ADEEEEFHNPRT pen-feathered
ADEEEEGINRTV degenerative
ADEEEEGLMNRR emerald green
ADEEEEGLNRRT gentle reader
ADEEEEGLNRTY degenerately
ADEEEEGNNRRT grande entrée
ADEEEEGRRRSV reserve grade
ADEEEEHHNRRT here and there
ADEEEEHKNOPS keep one's head
ADEEEEILMRST timed-release
ADEEEEKMMNST make ends meet
ADEEEEMNPRTW deepwatermen
ADEEEFFIINRT differentiae
ADEEEFFPRRTY deep-fat fryer
ADEEEFGHINTV heaven-gifted
ADEEEFGIKNNO on a knife-edge
ADEEEFGILNRR rifle grenade
ADEEEFGLNNRR Fernand Léger
ADEEEFGNORST drag one's feet
ADEEEFHIKLTT take the field
ADEEEFHILSSV self-adhesive
ADEEEFHINPRT pin-feathered
ADEEEFILLRST alder-liefest
ADEEEFIMTUUX faute de mieux
ADEEEFINPRRR referred pain
ADEEEFLPPRRS self-prepared
ADEEEFNNOSST tone-deafness
ADEEEFRSVWYY every few days
ADEEEGGHILST eagle-sighted
ADEEEGGINNRT degenerating
ADEEEGGNRSTU unsegregated
ADEEEGHIRRST head register
ADEEEGHLMMRS sledgehammer
ADEEEGHLPRSY hedge-parsley
ADEEEGILOPRS grapeseed-oil
ADEEEGIMNRST demagnetiser
disagreement
ADEEEGIMNRTZ demagnetizer
ADEEEGINNORT degeneration
ADEEEGINOPSS paedogenesis
ADEEEGINPRST predesignate
ADEEEGINRRTT redintegrate
ADEEEGLNNNRW New Englander
ADEEEGLNNRSS enlargedness
ADEEEGLNRSTW strangle-weed
ADEEEGMNNNRT endangerment
ADEEEGNOQRUW queen dowager
ADEEEGOPRSTW two-speed gear
ADEEEHHILRST heater-shield

ADEEEHHLORTW wholehearted
ADEEEHHNNRTT then and there
there and then
ADEEEHHRTTTW draw the teeth
ADEEEHIIMNPR ephemeridian
ADEEEHIMNRTT hereditament
ADEEEHINORTX exheredation
ADEEEHINSSSV adhesiveness
ADEEEHIRRTTT tetrahedrite
ADEEEHKNOOPS poke one's head
ADEEEHLNNRRT Netherlander
ADEEEHLNOOSS lose one's head
ADEEEHLNPRTT the Red Planet
ADEEEHLRSTTX tax-sheltered
ADEEEHNNRTTU unthreatened
ADEEEHNOORSV over one's head
ADEEEIILMNRS demineralise
ADEEEIILMNRZ demineralize
ADEEEIILMRST sidereal time
ADEEEIILNPTX expediential
ADEEEIILSSSW Weil's disease
ADEEEIIMMNRT ante meridiem
ADEEEIIMMRST semi-diameter
ADEEEIIMNRTT intermediate
ADEEEIIORRST aerosiderite
ADEEEIKLLPWY walleyed pike
ADEEEIKLRRTW Kielder Water
ADEEEILLMMOS mademoiselle✧
ADEEEILLMNOP lepidomelane
ADEEEILMNORT radioelement
ADEEEILNPRRT interpleader
ADEEEILNRRTT interrelated
ADEEEILRRRTW leader-writer
ADEEEILRRTTY reiteratedly
ADEEEIMMORTT Edmé Mariotte
ADEEEIMPRSTT distemperate
ADEEEIMRSSST mediatresses
ADEEEINPRSTT predestinate
ADEEEINPRSTW in deep waters
ADEEEJNOORRS rejoneadores
ADEEEKLLMRSS Skelmersdale
ADEEEKLLNOST endoskeletal
ADEEEKOSTTWY two-eyed steak
ADEEELLMNNRW well-mannered
ADEEELLMNOSV dolman sleeve
ADEEELNNQRSU Queenslander
ADEEELNOORSU Eleonora Duse
ADEEELNOSSST desolateness
ADEEELOPPRST tradespeople
ADEEEMNOOPST someone taped
ADEEEMNORSST moderateness
ADEEEMNPPRSS pamperedness
ADEEENNTTUUX unextenuated
ADEEENOPPRRT preponderate
ADEEENPPRRSS preparedness
ADEEENPRRTUV peradventure
ADEEENRRTTWW Derwent Water
ADEEENRSSVYY everydayness
ADEEEOPPRRRV overprepared
ADEEEOPPRRSV eavesdropper
ADEEEOPRRSUV overpersuade
ADEEFFGHINRT affrightened
ADEEFFHILORT thread of life
ADEEFFHIRSTT stiff-hearted
ADEEFFHOORST Feast of Herod
ADEEFFIILNRT differential
ADEEFFLLNOOR noodle farfel
ADEEFFLNRSVY sandfly fever
ADEEFGHHORTT The Godfather
ADEEFGHILNRS hard feelings
ADEEFGILLLMR flame-grilled
ADEEFGILLSSS field glasses
ADEEFGINNORT finger-and-toe
ADEEFGINNRST free-standing
ADEEFGIRSSTU fatigue-dress
ADEEFGLLNNWY newfangledly
ADEEFGLNORRW flower-garden
ADEEFGNORSVY Godfrey Evans
ADEEFHILLNOT lie of the land
ADEEFHILLPTY play the field
ADEEFHILNRRY Harry Enfield
ADEEFHILNRTT flint-hearted
ADEEFHILRSTV harvest-field
ADEEFHIMOTTY the time of day
ADEEFHINNOSW new-fashioned
ADEEFHLORRWW wheel forward
ADEEFHMOORST head foremost
ADEEFHRSTTUU death futures
ADEEFIILLNPS field-spaniel
ADEEFIKLNRSY Alfred Kinsey
ADEEFILLRSSY Alfred Sisley
ADEEFILMOSSV devil of a mess
ADEEFILNNOST self-anointed
ADEEFILNPTXY fixed-penalty
ADEEFILORUVV evil-favoured
ADEEFIMOPRRT imperforated
ADEEFINNRSTU Frauendienst
ADEEFINORSTV arfvedsonite
ADEEFKKMNORR Frank Kermode
ADEEFLLORUVW well-favoured
ADEEFLLPRSTU apfel strudel
ADEEFMORRSTT terms of trade
ADEEFNNORRUW unforewarned
ADEEFNOPRRTU unperforated
ADEEFNORSSUV favouredness
ADEEGGGNNOTU egg-and-tongue
ADEEGGHHILRY highly geared
ADEEGGHIRSTT straightedge
ADEEGGIILNRT trailing edge
ADEEGGILLLST all edges gilt
ADEEGGILNNRR angle grinder
ADEEGGIQRRSU square-rigged
ADEEGGLNOPPR doppelganger
doppelgänger
ADEEGGORSSTY St George's Day
ADEEGHHILRTT light-hearted
ADEEGHHINOSS high-seasoned
ADEEGHHINRSS shearing shed
ADEEGHHINSTW sheath-winged
ADEEGHIKLMOY like hey-go-mad
ADEEGHILNORS horse-dealing
ADEEGHILNSTW swing the lead

ADEEGHIMNOST homesteading
ADEEGHINNRRT heart-rending
ADEEGHLMOPRT dephlegmator
ADEEGHLNOSST The Golden Ass
ADEEGHLOORST leathergoods
ADEEGHNORSTT dragon's teeth
ADEEGHOPRRSW hedge sparrow
ADEEGHPRSTTU stepdaughter
ADEEGIIILLTV give it laldie
ADEEGIILLRSS Gilles de Rais
ADEEGIILNNRS leading reins
ADEEGIINRSST ringside seat
ADEEGIINRSTT disintegrate
ADEEGIIPPRTW periwig-pated
ADEEGIJNNRWW wandering Jew✧
ADEEGIKLLLNW lake dwelling
ADEEGIKLNRST deerstalking
ADEEGIKMMOOT make good time
ADEEGIKNNRRT kindergarten
ADEEGIKNPSST speed skating
ADEEGIKNRRST ring-streaked
ADEEGIKPRRRU Gerard Kuiper
ADEEGILLNOPR Reginald Pole
ADEEGILLORVY gaol delivery
ADEEGILNNRSU undersealing
ADEEGILNOORV lead-in groove
ADEEGILNORTU deregulation
ADEEGILORTVY derogatively
ADEEGIMNNNRU undermeaning
ADEEGINNRRTW winter garden
ADEEGINNRTTU unintegrated
ADEEGIOPRRTV prerogatived
ADEEGLLNOTTW golden wattle
ADEEGLLRRSSY regardlessly
ADEEGLMNNRRY merry England
ADEEGLMNOSSS gladsomeness
ADEEGLNNORSY General Synod
ADEEGLORRRTY retrogradely
ADEEGLPRSSSS pressed glass
ADEEGLRSTUVV velvet-guards
ADEEGMNNOORR gander-mooner
ADEEGMNNRRTU undergarment
ADEEGMNORRST Modern Greats
ADEEGNOORRVW wood engraver
ADEEGNPRTUUX unexpurgated
ADEEGORRTTXY dextrogyrate
ADEEHHHILLST The Hill-Shade
ADEEHHIKNRRS headshrinker
ADEEHHILLSTU hail the dules
ADEEHHILTTVW what the devil
ADEEHHLOOTTW toothed whale
ADEEHHMORTTY rhyme to death
ADEEHHNNNOOT on the one hand
ADEEHHNNPTUY unhyphenated
ADEEHHNOOSSW show one's head
ADEEHIILMNTY diethylamine
ADEEHIILRRTY hereditarily
ADEEHIINNRSS rise and shine
ADEEHIINRSTW raise the wind
ADEEHIKLNOOP kaleidophone
ADEEHILLPTVY play the devil
ADEEHILMNRRV Helmand River
ADEEHILMORTT maître d'hôtel
ADEEHILNPSTY synadelphite
ADEEHIMNPPRS misapprehend
ADEEHIMRSSST headmistress
ADEEHINNOOST Hindoostanee
ADEEHINORSTU house-trained
ADEEHIOSTTTU at the outside
ADEEHKKMORST Thomas Dekker
ADEEHLLNNRTU unenthralled
ADEEHLMMOTUY mealy-mouthed
ADEEHLMOOSTV smooth-leaved
ADEEHLPPRSSU pedal pushers
ADEEHLPRSTUU desulphurate
ADEEHMNNOSSS handsomeness
ADEEHMNORRSY dysmenorrhea
ADEEHMOPRTTY dermatophyte
ADEEHNNOPRST pentahedrons
ADEEHNNORSTU turn one's head under one's hat
ADEEHNOPSTTY spotted hyena
ADEEHNORRSTT tetrahedrons
ADEEHNORSTTY stony-hearted
ADEEHORRSSTT tear to shreds
ADEEHORSSTUW house-steward
ADEEHORSTTTU stout-hearted
ADEEIIILMRST demilitarise
ADEEIIILMRTZ demilitarize
ADEEIIILMTTV delimitative
ADEEIIILORST editorialise
ADEEIIILORTZ editorialize
ADEEIIJLLOSS jolies laides
ADEEIIJLLRVY jail delivery
ADEEIIJNOORR Rio de Janeiro
ADEEIIKPRSTW weak-spirited
ADEEIILLNNTT Little-endian
ADEEIILLNTVY evidentially
ADEEIILMMNPT impedimental
ADEEIILMNNRX index mineral
ADEEIILMNNSS maidenliness
ADEEIILMTTVY meditatively
ADEEIILNNRST internalised
ADEEIILNNRTZ internalized
ADEEIILNPRST presidential
ADEEIILOPPTV deoppilative
ADEEIILRTVVY derivatively
ADEEIIMNNOTV denominative
ADEEIIMNNRSU unseminaried
ADEEIIMNOPTT monte di pietà
ADEEIIMNPRST mean-spirited
ADEEIIMNRRTY intermediary
ADEEIIMPQRTU quare impedit
ADEEIINNPPST painted snipe
ADEEIINNPSTT patent inside
ADEEIINNRRVW Andrew Irvine
ADEEIINOPTTX expeditation
ADEEIINORSTT disorientate
ADEEIINPSSTV dispensative
ADEEIINRRSTT endarteritis
ADEEIINRRSTY residentiary
ADEEIINRRTVW water diviner

ADEEIIPPRSSU dispauperise
ADEEIIPPRSUZ dispauperize
ADEEIIRSSSUV virus disease
ADEEIIRSSTTV dissertative
ADEEIJLNRSUW Julie Andrews
ADEEIKKOSSSW Kwok's disease
ADEEIKLLMPPR lappered-milk
ADEEIKLLNSSY ladylikeness
ADEEIKLMPPRR ripple-marked
ADEEIKNRRRTW water-drinker
ADEEILLNNRST lantern slide
ADEEILLNOTTU andouillette
ADEEILLORSTV travel-soiled
ADEEILLOSTVW old wives' tale
ADEEILLPRSTV silver-plated
ADEEILMMORTY immoderately
ADEEILMNTTTU multidentate
ADEEILMPRTTY timely-parted
ADEEILNNTTUV unventilated
ADEEILNOPPRT lepidopteran
ADEEILNOPRTT latent period
ADEEILNOTTVY denotatively
ADEEILNRRSTY restrainedly
ADEEILORRSTW water soldier
ADEEILPRSSXY Daily Express
ADEEIMMNORSU misdemeanour
ADEEIMNNNRTU intermundane
ADEEIMNNRTTU unterminated
ADEEIMNOPTTU meditate upon
ADEEIMNRSTUV misadventure
ADEEINNOOPRU Indo-European
ADEEINNOPRST respondentia
ADEEINNRRSTU unrestrained
ADEEINNSSSTU unsteadiness
ADEEINORRSTV overstrained
ADEEINRRSSTY Syrian Desert
ADEEINSSSTTU situatedness
ADEEINSSTTTU United States
ADEEIOPSSSTT Pott's disease
ADEEIRRRSTTW water strider
ADEEJMNRSTTU readjustment
ADEEKLNORRSW Arnold Wesker
ADEEKNORSSYY donkey's years
ADEELLMMNRTU untrammelled
ADEELLMNORRT tandem roller
ADEELLMORUZZ muzzle-loader
ADEELLNNSSSS landlessness
ADEELLPPRSTU apple strudel
ADEELMMNORWY New Model Army
ADEELMNOSTTT Old Testament
ADEELMOPRSTU deuteroplasm
ADEELNOPRSSU poles asunder
ADEELNPPRRUY unpreparedly
ADEELOOPRRSW solar-powered
ADEELRSSSSTY lady's tresses
ADEEMMOSTUXY myxedematous
ADEEMNNNORTU unornamented
ADEEMNNOSSWY mend one's ways
ADEEMNNPRSUU supermundane
ADEEMNNPRTUY underpayment
ADEEMNOPPRSW newspaperdom
ADEENNOORRST androsterone
ADEENNOPPRRT preponderant
ADEENOORSSTW eat one's words
ADEENORSSSST assortedness
ADEENORSSTUW sweet-and-sour
ADEEPQRRTTUU reputed quart
ADEFFGHIINRR Henri Giffard
ADEFFGHILRTY affrightedly
ADEFFGINORRT foreign draft
ADEFFGNOORSU off one's guard
ADEFFHHRSTTU the hard stuff
ADEFFHNNOOSS off one's hands
ADEFFHORSSTT short-staffed
ADEFFIKKNNOR knife-and-fork
ADEFGGIINNNR rangefinding
ADEFGHHILNOT height of land
ADEFGHIKORSY skreigh of day
ADEFGHILNRTT right-and-left
ADEFGHILNSUW Ludwigshafen
ADEFGHIORSUW shadow figure
ADEFGHLNOSTY length of days
ADEFGIIILLNR Fringillidae
ADEFGIIKLLNW field walking
ADEFGIIKNNRW drawing-knife
ADEFGIILLNPY playing field
ADEFGIIMMNRX mixed farming
ADEFGIINRRST first reading
ADEFGILNNSST self-standing
ADEFGILNORSU glandiferous
ADEFGILNRSSY lady's fingers
ADEFGINNNSSU unfadingness
ADEFGINOOPRR proofreading
ADEFHHLNRSTU thunderflash
ADEFHILNNOST lift one's hand
ADEFHILNORRS Ronald Fisher
ADEFHIMNOORS fore-admonish
ADEFHINORSTV hand over fist
ADEFHINRSSSW dwarfishness
ADEFHLLORTTU full-throated
ADEFHLOORRWY Howard Florey
ADEFHOOORTTU out of the road
ADEFIIILNNOT definitional
ADEFIIILQRSU disqualifier
ADEFIIKLLPRW wildlife park
ADEFIIKNRSTT after its kind
ADEFIILLMNSU seminal fluid
ADEFIILMRSST disaster film
ADEFIILNOSTT deflationist
ADEFIILNPRSU Freudian slip
ADEFIIMNNORS fide non armis
ADEFIINNQTUU unquantified
ADEFIINRSTTU unstratified
ADEFILMNNOSS manifoldness
ADEFILMNORSU unformalised
ADEFILMNORUZ unformalized
ADEFILMNRTUU mutual friend
ADEFINNOORTU foundationer
refoundation
ADEFINOPRRSY Person Friday
ADEFLLLMNORS Moll Flanders
ADEFLLNRTUUY fraudulently

ADEFLMNORTUU unformulated
ADEFLMOOOPPS apple of Sodom
ADEFLNOOORTU footle around
ADEFLOOORRSW loose forward
ADEFOPRRRSSW press forward
ADEGGGGINORR gagging order
ADEGGHIILLNT leading light
ADEGGHIINRST sight-reading
ADEGGHILNRTU daughterling
ADEGGHINORRU rough-grained
ADEGGHNORRTU gather ground
ADEGGIILLMNR milling grade
ADEGGIILLNNP gliding plane
ADEGGIILNRTW water-gilding
ADEGGIINNRRV driving range
ADEGGIINORST disgregation
ADEGGINNORRR organ-grinder
ADEGGLNNNOUY Young England
ADEGHHHORSUW Howard Hughes
ADEGHHILNORS shareholding
ADEGHHIPRSST sharp-sighted
ADEGHHOPRRRY hydrographer
ADEGHHORRSTU draught horse
ADEGHHORSTUU draught-house
ADEGHIINNPRT printing-head
ADEGHIINRRSS hairdressing
ADEGHIINRRST in this regard
ADEGHILLNOSV slaveholding
ADEGHILNNPSU Penghu Island
ADEGHIMNOPRY Phrygian mode
ADEGHINORRST horse-trading
ADEGHINRSSTU draughtiness
ADEGHLLNORST stranglehold
ADEGHLNOSSTU thousand-legs
ADEGHMOPRSUW dowager's hump
ADEGHNOPRSTU sharp-tongued
ADEGHOPPRSUY pseudography
ADEGIIIKMMNR Kimmeridgian
ADEGIIILLOTV village idiot
ADEGIIILNRTT interdigital
ADEGIILLMNSY misleadingly
ADEGIILLNNOT dialling tone
tone dialling
ADEGIILLNNTU dentilingual
ADEGIILMNNRT mind-altering
ADEGIILMNORS demoralising
ADEGIILMNORZ demoralizing
ADEGIILNOOTT go into detail
ADEGIILNORSS digressional
ADEGIILNPRSY despairingly
ADEGIILNRRRV Darling River
ADEGIIMNRRST riding master
ADEGIINNORTU unoriginated
ADEGIINNPRSU undespairing
ADEGIINOORRT granodiorite
ADEGIINRSSTT giant's stride
ADEGIJKNNOST standing joke
ADEGILLNORUZ lounge lizard
ADEGILNNORUY Young Ireland
ADEGILNNRSSW drawlingness
ADEGILNOOTUZ Zeuglodontia
ADEGILNPRUVY pulvering day
ADEGILNRRSTY Land Registry
ADEGILOORRTY derogatorily
ADEGIMNNOPPR name-dropping
ADEGIMNORRSU measuring-rod
ADEGINOPRSTU outspreading
ADEGINORSTUU Auguste Rodin
ADEGIORRSSWW grass widower
ADEGJLLMNTUY judgmentally
ADEGLLMNNOOS golden salmon
ADEGMNOORSTW go downstream
ADEGNOOORSTU stooge around
ADEHHILLPPSU philadelphus✧
ADEHHIMOORRS haemorrhoids
ADEHHINNORTY hither and yon
ADEHHINORTTW Edith Wharton
ADEHHIRRSTTW thitherwards
ADEHHIRRSTWW whitherwards
ADEHHLMORRTY hydrothermal
ADEHHLORSTTX tax threshold
ADEHHNNOOSSW show one's hand
ADEHHOOPRSTT sharp-toothed
ADEHHOPRRTYY hydrotherapy
ADEHIIIMRSTT mithridatise
ADEHIIIMRTTZ mithridatize
ADEHIIKLMOOW Mike Hailwood
ADEHIILNSTTT dilettantish
ADEHIIMMNSSU his name is mud
ADEHIIMNORRT Thermidorian
ADEHIIMNORSS disharmonise
ADEHIIMNORSZ disharmonize
ADEHIIMOPRST mediatorship
ADEHIINOORTT Theriodontia
ADEHIIOPPRRT Rhipidoptera
ADEHIIORSSTU disauthorise
ADEHIIORSTUZ disauthorize
ADEHIJLOPSUU Philo Judaeus
ADEHIKLMNNOY milk and honey
ADEHIKLMRTUW Kurt Waldheim
ADEHIKNORSSW whiskerandos
ADEHILLOORWY woolly-haired
ADEHILLSSTTY lady's-thistle
ADEHILMNNOOP monodelphian
ADEHILMNOPSU sulphonamide
ADEHILMNORSU malnourished
ADEHILMNSWWY Wyndham Lewis
ADEHILNOPRRT Harold Pinter
ADEHILOPRRTY pyritohedral
ADEHILOPRSTU triadelphous
ADEHIMMNNNOS Hammond Innes
ADEHIMMNNOST admonishment
ADEHIMNRTTWW withdrawment
ADEHIMRSTTUW white mustard
ADEHINNOOPTY phytonadione
ADEHINNORTTY one-and-thirty
ADEHINNQSUUV unvanquished
ADEHINOOORTZ antherozooid
ADEHINOORSSS hors de saison
ADEHINOPPRST sharp-pointed
ADEHINORSTUU unauthorised
ADEHINORTUUZ unauthorized

ADEHINQRRSTU hindquarters
ADEHIOOPRSTT orthopaedist
ADEHIOPPRTTY Pteridophyta
ADEHKLMORRSU shoulder mark
ADEHKNNOORTV overhand knot
ADEHLLNOOSTW Shetland wool
ADEHLLOSUUXY Aldous Huxley
ADEHLMMNOTYY Tommy Handley
ADEHLMNNOSUY unhandsomely
ADEHLMNOOPSU monadelphous
ADEHLMOPSTUY splay-mouthed
ADEHLMORRSSU shoulder arms
ADEHLNNOPSTY Shetland pony
ADEHLOORSVWY hold sway over
ADEHMORRRTTU Morte d'Arthur
ADEHNNNORSTU turn one's hand
ADEHNNOPPTUU on the up and up
ADEHNOPRSTUY sound therapy
ADEHOOPSTTTT Photostatted
ADEHOORRRTVW Trevor Howard
ADEIIILLMNNT Indian millet
ADEIIILMNOTT delimitation
time dilation
ADEIIILORSTT editorialist
ADEIIIMNOPTT monti di pietà
ADEIIIMNORST dimerisation
ADEIIIMNORTZ dimerization
ADEIIIMNOSTV deviationism
ADEIIINNOOST de-ionisation
ADEIIINNOOTZ de-ionization
ADEIIINNORRV vin ordinaire
ADEIIINOSTTV deviationist
ADEIIINSTTTU attitudinise
ADEIIINTTTUZ attitudinize
ADEIIKKLNTTY take it kindly
ADEIILLMNORY meridionally
ADEIILLNPRUV Liverpudlian
ADEIILLPRRSW Prader-Willi's
ADEIILLSTUVV vaudevillist
ADEIILMNORTU Idiom Neutral
ADEIILMNOSVY Emily Davison
ADEIILMNSTTT dilettantism
ADEIILNNOPUV unpavilioned
ADEIILNNORTY inordinately
ADEIILNOOPPT deoppilation
ADEIILNOOPST depositional
despoliation
ADEIILNOOTTV dovetail into
ADEIILNOPRTV providential
ADEIILNORSST dilatoriness
ADEIILQSSSTU liquid assets
ADEIILSSSUVY dissuasively
ADEIIMMNNRSU Indian summer
ADEIIMMNOORT immoderation
ADEIIMNNNOOT denomination
ADEIIMNNOPRT Piet Mondrian
ADEIIMNNORSW Neo-Darwinism
ADEIIMNNOSTU mountainside
ADEIIMNNQRUU quadriennium
ADEIIMNNRSTT distrainment
ADEIIMNOOTTV demotivation
ADEIIMNOPRST postmeridian
ADEIIMNORSST disseminator
ADEIIMORSTTU audiometrist
ADEIINNNNRRU Indian runner
ADEIINNNQQUU quinquenniad
ADEIINNOORRT reordination
ADEIINNOPSST dispensation
ADEIINNORRSS ordinariness
ADEIINNORSTW Neo-Darwinist
ADEIINOOPRST disoperation
ADEIINOOPRTX peroxidation
ADEIINOOPSTT depositation
ADEIINORRSVY diversionary
ADEIINORSSTT dissertation
ADEIINOSTTUV adventitious
ADEIIOOOPRST radioisotope
ADEIIOPPRRST dispropriate
ADEIKLLOPSTU leukoplastid
ADEIKLNNNTTY kindly tenant
ADEIKNOOPTTY kidney-potato
ADEIKNOPRRTU turnpike road
ADEILLLNOOSY solenoidally
ADEILLLNRTUY ill-naturedly
ADEILLLORRSV silver dollar
ADEILLNOOTVY devotionally
ADEILLNPRTUY prudentially
ADEILLPPRSSY lady's-slipper
ADEILMNNNSTU disannulment
ADEILMNNOORY Leonard Nimoy
ADEILMNQTUUY quantum yield
ADEILMNSTTUU unstimulated
ADEILMRRRTUU ritual murder
ADEILNOOPPTU depopulation
ADEILNOPRRSU superordinal
ADEILNORRSTT dentirostral
ADEILNORRSTV dorsiventral
ADEILNORSSTW towardliness
ADEILNSSSTUY unassistedly
ADEILOOSTTTV devil's tattoo
ADEIMMOPRSUY praseodymium
ADEIMMOQRTUU medium quarto
ADEIMNNOORTW Andrew Motion
ADEIMNORRSUY in your dreams
ADEIMOOPRSTZ spermatozoid
ADEIMOPPRSTT stripped atom
ADEINNOOOPPT open adoption
ADEINNOORSSZ senza sordino
ADEINNOPRSSU underpassion
ADEINNOPRSTU unpatronised
ADEINNOPRTUZ unpatronized
ADEINNSSSTTW witness stand
ADEINOPRSSTY dispensatory
ADEINOPRTTVZ privat-dozent
ADEINORSSTUV disaventrous
ADEJLOOPRSUY jeopardously
ADEJLORSSSTU loss adjuster
ADEKLLNNPRSU knur and spell
ADEKLNNOORRZ Konrad Lorenz
ADEKMNNOORUY monkey around
ADEKMNNORRUW under-workman
ADELLLNRTUWY well and truly

ADELLMMORSTY troll-my-dames
ADELLMOOSSWY Oswald Mosley
ADELLNNORSSU all-roundness
ADELLNORSSUY slanderously
ADELLOOPRRST petrodollars
ADELLORSTUUY adulterously
ADELNOORRSTV dorsoventral
ADELNORRSUVY land-surveyor
ADELORRSSTUU dorsal suture
ADEMNNRSTTUU untransmuted
ADEMNOORRSTT demonstrator
ADEMNRRSTTUU understratum
ADEMOPRRSSTU superstardom
ADEMOPRRSTUY pseudomartyr
ADENNORSSTUW untowardness
ADENNORSTUUV unadventrous
ADENOOPRSSSW pass one's word
ADENOPQRRTUU quarter-pound
ADENOQRRRTUU quarter-round
ADEOORRRSUVY road surveyor
ADFFGIILNNTU fault-finding
ADFGGGINOORT foot-dragging
ADFGGILNNORY flying dragon
ADFGHIINRSTV driving shaft
ADFGHOOPRRTU draught-proof
ADFGIILLNRYZ flying lizard
ADFGIILNNOPR DNA profiling
ADFGILNNOORT front-loading
ADFGINOORTUW out of drawing
ADFHIMNOOORU maid of honour
ADFHINOORRRS Harrison Ford
ADFHMNOOOTTU foot-and-mouth
ADFIIILNNOST disinflation
ADFIIILNOSTU fluidisation
ADFIIILNOTUZ fluidization
ADFIIIOOPRRZ Porfirio Díaz
ADFIILNOORTU fluoridation
ADFIILOSSTUY fastidiously
ADFIINOSSTUU unfastidious
ADFILMOOSSTW salt of wisdom
ADGGGILNNORU grand guignol✧
ADGGHIILNOOT in a good light
ADGGHIKLNSTY Gladys Knight
ADGGIIIINNNV Indian giving
ADGGIILNNNST sting and ling
ADGGIIMNNORS gormandising
ADGGIIMNNORZ gormandizing
ADGGIINNNOOS a good innings
ADGGIINNORRS Grand Signior
ADGGILNNNOST long-standing
ADGGINNNORSU sound ranging
ADGGINNORRTU grand touring
ADGGINOPRRTU group trading
ADGHHHIILOSY High Holidays
ADGHHHILOSYY High Holy Days
ADGHHKOORSTU draught-hooks
ADGHIIMMNSST Midnight Mass
ADGHIKLNORSW world-shaking
ADGHILLLMNOS smallholding
ADGHIMRRRSYY hydrargyrism
ADGHINOORTTW tooth-drawing
ADGHLMNOOPUY Plough Monday
ADGHNOOOPRTY odontography
ADGHOOOPRSTT dogtooth-spar
ADGIIIIMNNTT intimidating
ADGIIIINOSTT digitisation
ADGIIIINOTTZ digitization
ADGIIIMNOSSS misdiagnosis
ADGIIINNRSTW winding stair
ADGIIKLMNNOT Latin Kingdom
ADGIILLNNNSU disannulling
ADGIILLNNOTU longitudinal
ADGIILNNPRST landing strip
ADGIINNOPRTW word-painting
ADGIINOPPRSV disapproving
ADGIKNNORRRU roaring drunk
ADGIKNOOOPRS Goodison Park
ADGILLNNTUUY undulatingly
ADGILMOOPRYY pyramidology
ADGILNNOSTUY astoundingly
ADGIMNNOOOST Santo Domingo
ADGIMNNOORST standing-room
ADGINNNNPRUU up and running
ADGINNOOOPRT gonadotropin
ADGINOPPRRWW word wrapping
ADGINORRSTUY agroindustry
ADGLLLNOSUUY glandulously
ADGLNNOORTUW long-drawn-out
ADGMNOOORSTW go down a storm
ADGOOOPRSSTU gastropodous
ADGOOPRRSTUV provost guard
ADHHIOPRSTTY hydropathist
ADHHLORSTUYY Holy Thursday
ADHHNOOPRSUY hydrophanous
ADHIIILLNTVY divinity hall
ADHIIIMMRSTT mithridatism
ADHIILMNOPRU dolphinarium
ADHIILNOPSTT Dantophilist
ADHIIMOORRTU radio-thorium
ADHIIMOPRSST diastrophism
ADHIINOOPRST radiophonist
ADHIKLNSSUUY Kyushu Island
ADHILLNOORSW Harold Wilson
ADHILLNOSTUY outlandishly
ADHILMNNSTUW Wild Huntsman
ADHILOPRSUYY your ladyship
ADHINNNOOPSY sindonophany
ADHIOORSTTYY History Today
ADHJNNOORSTW Dr John Watson
ADHLLOPSSUYY dasyphyllous
ADHLMNOOORST hold to ransom
ADHLNOOOOPRT odontophoral
ADHLNOOPRSTW Randolph Stow
ADHNNOOOOPRT odontophoran
ADHNOORRTUWY unroadworthy
ADIIIIMNNOTT intimidation
ADIIILLLMSWW wild Williams
ADIIILLMRSSY dissimilarly
ADIIILLNOSTT distillation
ADIIIMNORTTY intimidatory
ADIIINNNOORT inordination
ADIIINNNPRTU Indian turnip

ADIIINOPRTTU tripudiation
ADIIINORRTTV vitro-di-trina
ADIIINORSTTT traditionist
ADIIKLLNRSSU Kuril Islands
ADIILLMOPRRY primordially
ADIILLNOSSUY sinusoidally
ADIILLNRSTUY industrially
ADIILLOPSTUV post-diluvial
ADIILLORSTTY distillatory
ADIILMMNRUUU duraluminium
ADIILMNNQUUU unnilquadium
ADIILMNOPRST palindromist
ADIILMORSSTU dissimulator
ADIILNOORSTT distortional
ADIILNOPSTUV post-diluvian
ADIILNORSTTU stridulation
ADIILNOSTTUU altitudinous
latitudinous
ADIILOQRSTUX liquid storax
ADIIMNNNOOSS non-admission
ADIIOPSSTTUU disputatious
ADILLLLOOPPY lollipop lady
ADILLMNOOOPY monopodially
ADILLMOORTTY Old Mortality
ADILLNNOSSUZ Luzon Islands
ADILLNRSTTUY stridulantly
ADILLOORSTUY idolatrously
ADILORRSTTUY stridulatory
ADILORSSSTUY disastrously
ADIMMNNOORSW Norman Wisdom
ADIMNNOOOTUW mountain wood
ADIMNORRRSUY Sunday Mirror
ADINOOPRRUVY Yuri Andropov
ADIOOPRRSSUU sudoriparous
ADLLNOOORTUY Royal Doulton
ADMNOOOOSTTU odontomatous
ADNOOOOPPRST stoop and roop
ADNOOPPRSTUU stoup and roup
AEEEEELMNSSV levée en masse
AEEEEFHNORTV tree of heaven
AEEEEGGMNNRT re-engagement
AEEEEGHHITVV give the heave
AEEEEGHLPRST telegraphese
AEEEEGINRRTV regenerative
AEEEEGKNORRV evergreen oak
AEEEEGMPRRSV game preserve
AEEEEGNNRRSW Arsène Wenger
AEEEEGNNRRTU unregenerate
AEEEEHHKLTTW take the wheel
AEEEEHHPRRSS sheepshearer
AEEEEHLPRSST sheep-stealer
AEEEEHNOSTYY easy on the eye
AEEEEHNSSSTV the Seven Seas
AEEEEHRSSTTT three estates
AEEEEIIPRSTT tapsieteerie
AEEEEJNRSTWY New Jersey tea
AEEEEKLNNNOV on an even keel
AEEEEKLRSSVW weaker vessel
AEEEELPRRSSS press release
AEEEENPRRSTT serpent-eater
AEEEENRRRTTV ventre à terre
AEEEFFHPRRST Peter Shaffer
AEEEFFILMNTY effeminately
AEEEFFKOSSTW Feast of Weeks
AEEEFGIINNRT retaining fee
AEEEFGIKMNRT feeing-market
AEEEFGIOSSTT state of siege
AEEEFGLNNORS range oneself
AEEEFHHIRTTW white feather
AEEEFHIKLNRT leather-knife
AEEEFHILOTTY tail of the eye
AEEEFHILRSTV live-feathers
AEEEFHINRRTT thereinafter
AEEEFHINRSST featheriness
AEEEFHLMOPRT Temple of Hera
AEEEFHLOSSTT see the last of
AEEEFHPRRTVY fever therapy
AEEEFIKLNPTT palette knife
AEEEFILLMRTV famille verte
AEEEFILNNSTT festina lente
AEEEFILNPRRT preferential
AEEEFIMNRTTV fermentative
AEEEFKOPRSST for pete's sake
AEEEFLMNSSSS self-sameness
AEEEFLNOOSST feel one's oats
AEEEFLNRSSSS fearlessness
AEEEFLORSTTW telesoftware
AEEEGGHLNSTT snaggleteeth
AEEEGGIIMNTV give a meeting
AEEEGGIMSSTU Gamgee tissue®
gamgee tissue
AEEEGGINRRST steering gear
AEEEGGNRSTUY get a guernsey
AEEEGHIILMRW whigmaleerie
AEEEGHINOSST aesthesiogen
AEEEGHIRSTTZ gazetteerish
AEEEGHNRRSVY Henry Segrave
AEEEGIIMNNNR marine engine
AEEEGIIMORST troisième âge
AEEEGIJMNNRT ramjet engine
AEEEGIKLNNNW Wankel engine
AEEEGILNNPSS palingeneses
AEEEGILNNRRV line-engraver
AEEEGILNOPTV negative pole
AEEEGILNPRRU Paule Régnier
AEEEGILNRRSV River Selenga
River Sénégal
AEEEGILNRSST single-seater
AEEEGILNRSSU general issue
AEEEGILTTVVY vegetatively
AEEEGIMNNORT me generation
AEEEGIMNNSTV envisagement
AEEEGIMNRRTT René Magritte
AEEEGINNORRT regeneration
AEEEGINNSSTV negativeness
AEEEGINOPRTT prenegotiate
AEEEGINORRTT interrogatee
AEEEGINORSTV seronegative
AEEEGINORTTV revegetation
AEEEGIRRSTTV tergiversate
AEEEGKMNORSY grease monkey
AEEEGKNPRRTT Greek pattern

AEEEGLLNSSTT tassel-gentle
AEEEGLMNNNTT entanglement
AEEEGLMSSUUU amuse-gueules
AEEEGLNNRTTT tangle-netter
AEEEGLNOPSTT espagnolette
AEEEGMMNORTT magnetometer
AEEEGMMNOSSS gamesomeness
AEEEGMNNRRSS messenger RNA
AEEEGMNNRSTT estrangement
AEEEGMNOPRSU pergameneous
AEEEGMOPRSTT postage meter
AEEEGMORRRSS error message
AEEEGNNNQRTU queen regnant
queen-regnant
AEEEGNORRRTY regeneratory
AEEEGNORRSTY great oneyers
AEEEGNRRSTTW Great Western
AEEEGOPRRSTU supererogate
AEEEHHILRTTW white leather
AEEEHHLNPSST Stephen Hales
AEEEHHMNNRSS Hermann Hesse
AEEEHHMNNSTT ensheathment
AEEEHHNOTTXY ethoxyethane
AEEEHHORSTUW weather house
AEEEHHORSTVW have the worse
AEEEHIKLRTVY Harvey Keitel
AEEEHIKNRSTT take the reins
AEEEHILLORST ethereal oils
AEEEHILMPRTY ephemerality
AEEEHILNNSSV heavenliness
AEEEHILNPRSW Persian wheel
AEEEHIMNNOPP epiphenomena
AEEEHIMORTTV movie theatre
AEEEHIMSSTTT the estimates
AEEEHINPPRSV apprehensive
AEEEHINPRSST parenthesise
AEEEHINPRSTZ parenthesize
AEEEHINRRTTW interwreathe
AEEEHIRSSTUX heterauxesis
AEEEHKLPRRSS sleeper shark
AEEEHKNOPPRS speakerphone
AEEEHLLLPRRS pearl-sheller
AEEEHLLNNRTW lantern wheel
AEEEHLMNSTTY the last enemy
AEEEHLMOORTV leave the room
AEEEHLNPRTTW pattern-wheel
AEEEHLNSSSST hatelessness
AEEEHLORSTUX heterosexual
AEEEHLRRSTTY Harley Street
AEEEHMMNORTT methanometer
AEEEHMNNSTTW enswathement
AEEEHMNRTTTT the treatment
AEEEHMORRSTT Mother Teresa
AEEEHMORTTTX methotrexate
AEEEHNOPRRTT heteropteran
AEEEHNORSSTT Eratosthenes
AEEEHNQRSTUV harvest queen
AEEEHNRTTWWY three-went way
AEEEHQRRRTTU three-quarter
AEEEHRSTTTTW test the water
AEEEIIKLLMNN Melanie Klein
AEEEIILMNRRS remineralise
AEEEIILMNRRZ remineralize
AEEEIILMPRTT temperalitie
AEEEIILMRSTT semiliterate
AEEEIILNPRTX experiential
AEEEIKMNOSTT take one's time
AEEEIKNPRSVW sneak preview
AEEEILLMMNST elementalism
AEEEILLMNRTY elementarily
AEEEILLNPRTT interpellate
AEEEILMNPRTX experimental
AEEEILMNRTTY intemerately
AEEEILNRRSVW River Salween
AEEEILNRSSST easterliness
AEEEILNRSSTV relativeness
AEEEILNRTTVY inveterately
AEEEILOPRSTZ Zola Pieterse
AEEEIMNNNRTT entraînement
AEEEIMNPPSTT appetisement
AEEEIMNRRTUV remunerative
AEEEIMOPRRTV evaporimeter
AEEEIMORSTTV overestimate
AEEEIMPRSTTV septemvirate
AEEEINNORTTX exenteration
AEEEINPRRTTT interpretate
AEEEINPRSTTV presentative
AEEEINPRTTVV preventative
AEEEINRRSTTT interest rate
AEEEINRRTTUX extra-uterine
AEEEIOPPRRTV preoperative
AEEEIORRRSTV reserve ratio
AEEEIPRRRRTW Perrier water
AEEEIPRRSTVV preservative
AEEEIRRSTVVX extraversive
AEEEJLMNRSUW New Jerusalem
AEEEKLNOOPRS saloon-keeper
AEEEKLRRSTTW streetwalker
AEEEKLRSSTTW welter stakes
AEEEKMOPRRRT pro-marketeer
AEEELLLLNOTW let well alone
AEEELLLMRSUW Samuel Weller
AEEELLORRRSV role reversal
AEEELLPRSSSU pleasureless
AEEELLRRSTTW Wall-Streeter
AEEELMMNPRTT tramp element
AEEELMNNSSSS namelessness
AEEELMNORSYY eleemosynary
AEEELMNSSSST tamelessness
AEEELMOPPRRT temporal peer
AEEELNOOSSST lose one's seat
AEEELNPRSTUV present value
AEEEMNNORSTY earnest-money
AEEEMNNPRSTT permanent set
AEEEMNNSTTTW New Testament
AEEEMNORSSTT eat one's terms
AEEEMNRSSSST reassessment
AEEEMOOPRRTV evaporometer
AEEENNNPRSTY earnest-penny
AEEENNPRRSTT representant
AEEEOPRRRSTV perseverator
AEEFFGHIRRTU father figure

AEEFFGILNORT free-floating
AEEFFGIMNORT meat-offering
AEEFFGINORVW wave offering
AEEFFHHIKTTT take the Fifth
AEEFFHORRSTT foster-father
AEEFFIJNNORS Jeffersonian
AEEFFILMNNRU fenfluramine
AEEFFKOOPRTW power take-off
AEEFFLLRSTTY self-flattery
AEEFFLNNSSTU affluentness
AEEFGGHHNOTT get the hang of
AEEFGHINRSST sergeant fish
AEEFGHLLORTW lower the flag
AEEFGIILNNRV never-failing
AEEFGIKRRSTU figure skater
AEEFGILLNNOP longleaf pine
AEEFGILLNPSS self-pleasing
AEEFGILLNRTW Newgate frill
AEEFGILORSTV gate of silver
AEEFGINRRRSU sugar-refiner
AEEFGIORRRRT refrigerator
AEEFGLNOORRW orange-flower
AEEFGLNORSUX Alex Ferguson
AEEFGLNRSSTU gratefulness
AEEFHHILRSWY whale-fishery
AEEFHIKNRSSS freakishness
AEEFHILLNOSV have one's fill
AEEFHILLQRTU quill-feather
AEEFHILNNPRS Ralph Fiennes
AEEFHILNRSST fatherliness
AEEFHILPRRSY pearl-fishery
AEEFHIOORRST raise the roof
AEEFHIPRSSTT spit feathers
AEEFHKLOORTT take the floor
AEEFHLLMOPRT platform heel
AEEFHLLOOSTW follow the sea
AEEFHLLRRSTU fuller's earth✧
AEEFHLMNSSSU shamefulness
AEEFHLMOPRSS Marsh of Sleep
AEEFHLMORRTW flame-thrower
AEEFHLOOSTTT athlete's foot
AEEFHNOORSUV have no use for
AEEFHOOPRRTW weatherproof
AEEFHOORSSSW Sea of Showers
AEEFHORSTTTU fourth estate
AEEFIILLMNOR famille noire
AEEFIILMPPRR preamplifier
AEEFIILNORTT interfoliate
AEEFIILRRSTU filius terrae
terrae filius
AEEFIINQRRTU inquire after
AEEFIJLLMSWY family jewels
AEEFIKLLNNOR Keiren Fallon
AEEFIKLNNSTY Stanley knife®
AEEFIKMMORTT take it from me
AEEFIKNNNRST Frankenstein
AEEFILMNORRT interfemoral
AEEFILNRSTVV snifter-valve
AEEFILOPRSTU petaliferous
AEEFILPRRSST filter-passer
AEEFIMNNORTT fermentation
AEEFIMNNSSST manifestness
AEEFIMNORSTT Fortean Times
AEEFIMNORSTU amentiferous
AEEFIMOPRRTV performative
preformative
AEEFINNORSTT fenestration
AEEFJLLLRRWY Jerry Falwell
AEEFKLNORRSS Frank Loesser
AEEFKNNORSSS forsakenness
AEEFLLNOPPRR propeller fan
AEEFLLOPRTTU Letter of Paul
AEEFLMNOOPTT footplatemen
AEEFLMNORSTT forestalment
man of letters
AEEFLMOPRRUV marvel of Peru
AEEFLNNOPSTU en pantoufles
AEEFLNOORSSY Alfonso Reyes
AEEFLNOPRSST Fleet parsons
AEEFLNSSSTTU tastefulness
AEEFLNSSSTUW wastefulness
AEEFLOPQRSUW pasqueflower
AEEFLORRRSUY Earl of Surrey
AEEFLORRSTWW water flowers
AEEFMOORRTTY Treaty of Rome
AEEFNNORTTUV enfant trouvé
AEEFNOPRRSTT foster-parent
AEEFOOPRRSST professorate
AEEFOQRRRSTU forequarters
AEEFOSSTTUUZ Statue of Zeus
AEEGGGGHHILL higgle-haggle
AEEGGGGILLWW wiggle-waggle
AEEGGGHLMOPU phlegmagogue
AEEGGGILNOTW get a wiggle on
AEEGGGIMNNRV gem-engraving
AEEGGGINNNSS engagingness
AEEGGGLLOPRU George Gallup
AEEGGGLOORSY grey-lag goose
AEEGGHHNORTT hang together
AEEGGHMOORST George Thomas
AEEGGHNORTTU gang-there-out
AEEGGIINNOSS angiogenesis
AEEGGIINNSTV negative sign
AEEGGIJJLLNN jingle-jangle
AEEGGIKKLNSS keeking-glass
AEEGGILLMMNN mingle-mangle
AEEGGILNNORS sloganeering
AEEGGILRSSVY aggressively
AEEGGIMMNOST geomagnetism
AEEGGIMNOSTT geomagnetist
AEEGGINNTTTW wetting agent
AEEGGINORSST Saint George's
AEEGGINRSSTT resting stage
AEEGGIQRRRSU square-rigger
AEEGGMNRRTTU nutmeg grater
AEEGGNOOPRTT George Patton
AEEGHHIINSTV heave in sight
AEEGHHIKNTTW wake the night
AEEGHHILNRTT the real thing
AEEGHHILOPRR heliographer
AEEGHHIMNRTT The Nightmare
AEEGHHINRRUV Huang He River

AEEGHHINRSTT there's a thing
AEEGHHIOPRRR hierographer
AEEGHHLNOPST Loghtan sheep
AEEGHHNOPRRT ethnographer
AEEGHIINNRRV Rhinegravine
AEEGHILLMMRT hellgrammite
AEEGHILLNRSY Early English
Early-English
AEEGHILMNOPR Germanophile
AEEGHILNOPSU leaping-house
AEEGHILNORTW watering hole
AEEGHILNSSTW English sweat
AEEGHILORRUV heliogravure
AEEGHILPRSTT telegraphist
AEEGHINOPSST pathogenesis
AEEGHINPRSST sergeantship
AEEGHINPTTVY heavy petting
AEEGHINRRSTT straightener
AEEGHIPRSSTW stage whisper
AEEGHLLORRTT toll-gatherer
AEEGHLNOPRSY selenography
AEEGHLOORSTT theologaster
AEEGHMNOPRRS phrasemonger
AEEGHMOOPRRT meteorograph
AEEGHMOORSTU heterogamous
AEEGHNOPRRST stenographer
AEEGHNOPSSTT step on the gas
AEEGHNORRSTW snow-gatherer
AEEGHNORSSTU anotherguess
AEEGHOORSSTV harvest-goose
AEEGHOPPRRRR reprographer
AEEGHOPPRRRT petrographer
AEEGHOPRRSTY stereography
AEEGHORSSTTU argue the toss
AEEGIIILLMTT illegitimate
AEEGIIILNRRV Virginia reel
AEEGIIKLNNPW Lake Winnipeg
AEEGIIKLNPSV evil-speaking
AEEGIIKNNOSS kainogenesis
AEEGIILLMTTY legitimately
AEEGIILMNORS mineralogise
AEEGIILMNORZ mineralogize
AEEGIILNNORS legionnaires'
legionnaire's
AEEGIILNNPSS palingenesis
AEEGIIMNPRRT image printer
AEEGIINNNRTT entertaining
AEEGIINORRTV reinvigorate
AEEGIINPRRTV privateering
AEEGIJLMRSTU Jules Maigret
AEEGIJLNNTUY Jean Tinguely
AEEGIJLNSSVW Jews' leavings
AEEGIJMMRSVY Jimmy Greaves
AEEGIKLLNPSW sleepwalking
AEEGIKLMNRST single market
AEEGIKLNSTTT giant's-kettle
AEEGIKMNPRRT parking meter
AEEGIKNOORTW Rogation Week
AEEGIKNRRSTT street-raking
AEEGIKNRSTUY key signature
AEEGILLLMNNS Nigel Mansell
AEEGILLLNPST selling plate
AEEGILLLNPSW well-pleasing
AEEGILLMNRTU great mullein
AEEGILLMNRTY regimentally
AEEGILLRSSST legislatress
AEEGILLRTUVY regulatively
AEEGILMNNTTU integumental
AEEGILMNRRSV German silver
AEEGILMNRUVX grex venalium
AEEGILNNNOPR open learning
AEEGILNNNOPT longipennate
AEEGILNNPRST single parent
AEEGILNNPSSS pleasingness
AEEGILNNRTTY entreatingly
AEEGILNNSSSS gainlessness
AEEGILNORRTU reregulation
AEEGIMNNOSTT segmentation
AEEGIMNNRSST reassignment
AEEGIMNNSTTT statementing
AEEGIMNORRSU rose geranium
AEEGIMNPRTTX exempt rating
AEEGIMNRRRTU Martin Guerre
AEEGIMNRRSST mastersinger
AEEGIMOPPSTT stoppage time
AEEGIMORRTTV gravitometer
AEEGIMPRSSST Mistress Page
AEEGINNNOTUV agentive noun
AEEGINNNSSSU sanguineness
AEEGINNORRRV River Garonne
AEEGINNORRTY rotary engine
AEEGINNRSSST transgenesis
AEEGINNRSSVW waveringness
AEEGINNRTUVV Ivan Turgenev
AEEGINOPRRRT peregrinator
AEEGINOPRSTT poetastering
AEEGINORSSTT negotiatress
AEEGINRRTVYZ Yangtze River
AEEGKNOORSTU keratogenous
AEEGKNRTWYYZ Wayne Gretzky
AEEGLLMNOPSY splenomegaly
AEEGLLMNRUWZ mangel-wurzel
AEEGLLORRTUY lager loutery
AEEGLLPRRSSY press gallery
AEEGLLPRRSUU spurge laurel
AEEGLMNNORTV governmental
AEEGLMNNRSTT stranglement
AEEGMMNORTTU great omentum
AEEGMMNORTTY magnetometry
AEEGMNOPRRRY prayer-monger
AEEGMNOPRSTY spermatogeny
AEEGNOPRRSTU supererogant
AEEHHHILNSTY heathenishly
AEEHHHINOPTV have on the hip
AEEHHHOPRRTT threeha'porth
AEEHHILMMNTU Helianthemum
AEEHHILMNORT thermohaline
AEEHHILOPRTY heliotherapy
AEEHHIMNPRSW New Hampshire
AEEHHIMPRRTY hyperthermia
AEEHHINPPSSS Spanish sheep
AEEHHINPRSTY hypersthenia

AEEHHLLORTTY heterothally
AEEHHLMMOORT homeothermal
AEEHHLMPRRTY hyperthermal
AEEHHLNOSTVY heavenly host
AEEHHLORRSTT health resort
AEEHHLOSSTTW steal the show
AEEHHMNOTTUV have the mount
AEEHHNNOPSVY shove ha'penny
AEEHHNOOPRTT theatrophone
AEEHHNOORSSW snowshoe hare
AEEHHNOPPRTY phanerophyte
AEEHHNORRTTW hawthorn tree
AEEHHOPPRTTY phreatophyte
AEEHIIKNPRSY hyperkinesia
AEEHIIKNSSST kinaesthesis
AEEHIILMOPST epitheliomas
AEEHIILMPPRY hyperlipemia
AEEHIILNSTTV thieves' Latin
AEEHIIMNPRSX examinership
AEEHIIMNRSST Henri Matisse
AEEHIIMOOPSS haemopoiesis
AEEHIINORSTT etherisation
AEEHIINORTTZ etherization
AEEHIINPRRST retainership
AEEHIINSTUVX inexhaustive
AEEHIJKRRTTT Keith Jarrett
AEEHIJNPRSST serjeantship
AEEHIKLLMNRU humane killer
AEEHIKLRSTVY The Valkyries
AEEHIKMQRRSU requiem shark
AEEHIKNNSSSS sneakishness
AEEHIKNPPPRT The Pink Paper
AEEHILLMNNPS Panhellenism
AEEHILLMNNPU panhellenium
AEEHILLNNNOP panhellenion
AEEHILLNNOTY lay on the line
AEEHILLNNPST Panhellenist
AEEHILLNOSVW have one's will
AEEHILLPRRST Sir Peter Hall
AEEHILLPRSTT split leather
AEEHILMMNRST Simmenthaler
AEEHILMMOOST mesothelioma
AEEHILMNORST thermal noise
AEEHILMNSTUY lese-humanity
AEEHILMORSSV slasher movie
AEEHILMSSTTW steam whistle
AEEHILNNPSTU the Peninsula
AEEHILNOORSS lose one's hair
AEEHILNOPRRS prehensorial
AEEHILNOPUVY lie heavy upon
AEEHILNRSSSS hairlessness
AEEHILNSSSTT stealthiness
AEEHILOPRTTV private hotel
AEEHILPRRSUV River Alpheus
AEEHILPRSSTT spear thistle
AEEHILRSTVWY white slavery
AEEHILSTUVXY exhaustively
AEEHIMMORRTT arithmometer
AEEHIMNNOPPS psi phenomena
AEEHIMNNORTT nitromethane
AEEHIMNOPRTZ promethazine
AEEHIMOPRSSV overemphasis
AEEHIMORSTTT theorematist
AEEHINNOPPRS apprehension
AEEHINNRRSVY Sir Henry Vane
AEEHINOORSTU heteroousian✧
AEEHINOPRRTY erythropenia
AEEHINOPSSTT sheep station
AEEHINOPSSTV top-heaviness
AEEHINORRRST horse-trainer
AEEHINPRSTVY Pythian verse
AEEHINRRSTTY Sir Henry Tate
AEEHINRSSSTW waterishness
AEEHIOPPSTTV stovepipe hat
AEEHIOPRSTUV private house
AEEHIORRRRST hair restorer
AEEHIPPRRXYY hyperpyrexia
AEEHIPRRSTTW weather strip
AEEHIPRSSTTX sex therapist
AEEHIPRSTTTU therapeutist
AEEHJLNNOTTZ Johann Tetzel
AEEHJNRSTUUY René Just Haüy
AEEHKKLOORWY Hookey Walker
AEEHKKNOOOST take one's hook
AEEHKMMMNORY monkey hammer
AEEHKMNOPTTU put the make on
AEEHKMOORSVW makeover show
AEEHKNNOORTT heterokontan
AEEHKOORRRST arrester hook
AEEHLLMMORWY yellowhammer
AEEHLLMNNOPY phenomenally
AEEHLLMNNOTT Lotte Lehmann
AEEHLLMNNRTT enthrallment
AEEHLLMNOOPT metallophone
AEEHLLMORTXY exothermally
AEEHLLMPPSSU Samuel Phelps
AEEHLMNORSTT stenothermal
AEEHLMNRSSSS harmlessness
AEEHLMORSTTW Tower Hamlets
AEEHLMPRRSUU superhumeral
AEEHLNOPRTTU upon the alert
AEEHLNOPRTUY polyurethane
AEEHLNPRSSUY hypersensual
AEEHLOPRSTTY heteroplasty
AEEHLORRSTTU rule the roast
AEEHLORSSTUV harvest louse
AEEHMMNOORRT harmonometer
AEEHMMOOPRST metamorphose
AEEHMNNOPRTY hymenopteran
AEEHMNOOPRRT Enteromorpha
AEEHMOPRSTTU The Mousetrap
AEEHMORRSSTU short measure
AEEHMORSSTUV harvest mouse
AEEHMORSTTUY erythematous
AEEHMPRRSTUY serum therapy
AEEHNNORRSTT north-eastern
AEEHNOOPRSST epanorthoses
AEEHNORRSSSV overrashness
AEEHNORRSTWY Wayne Shorter
AEEHNORSSTTU south-eastern
AEEHNRRSTTUU treasure hunt
AEEHOPRRRSTW spear-thrower

 Words marked ✧ can also be spelled with one or more capital letters

AEEHOPRRSSTT	stratosphere
AEEHOQRRRSTU	quarter-horse
AEEIIILRSTTV	relativities
AEEIIIMMTTXX	mixtie-maxtie
AEEIIJNOQSSU	je ne sais quoi
AEEIIKLLLRRS	serial killer
AEEIIKLLMNSS	Milanese silk
AEEIIKLMNPRS	marline-spike
AEEIIKMNNSSY	Keynesianism
AEEIILLLRTTY	illiterately
AEEIILLMRSTU	mitrailleuse
AEEIILLMSTWW	sweet william
AEEIILLNOSTV	televisional
AEEIILLNPPSU	uillean pipes
AEEIILLNPSTT	pestilential
AEEIILLRRTVY	irrelatively
AEEIILMNOOST	emotionalise
AEEIILMNOOTZ	emotionalize
AEEIILMNSSST	essentialism
AEEIILMPRTVY	imperatively
AEEIILMRSTTU	multiseriate
AEEIILNNOPRS	isoprenaline
AEEIILNNPRTY	perenniality
AEEIILNNPSTT	penitentials
AEEIILNOPRTT	repetitional
AEEIILNOPSTT	potentialise
AEEIILNOPTTZ	potentialize
AEEIILNRRSST	literariness
AEEIILNRSSTU	Arne Tiselius
AEEIILNRSSUV	universalise
AEEIILNRSTUY	uniseriately
AEEIILNRSUVZ	universalize
AEEIILNSSSTT	essentialist
AEEIILNSSTTY	essentiality
AEEIILOPTTVX	exploitative
AEEIILPRRSTU	pluriseriate
AEEIILPRSTVV	Private Lives
AEEIIMNOQRTU	moire antique
AEEIIMNSSSTW	Siamese twins
AEEIINNNORTT	inteneration
AEEIINNORSTT	eternisation
AEEIINNORTTZ	eternization
AEEIINNPRTTY	penitentiary
AEEIINNQRTUW	quinine water
AEEIINNRRTTU	intrauterine
AEEIINORRSTV	inverse ratio
AEEIINRRSTVW	strain viewer
AEEIINSSTTVV	vitativeness
AEEIIPRTTUVV	vituperative
AEEIIQRSSTTU	sesquitertia
AEEIJLLLMNRY	mineral jelly
AEEIJLLRSTUW	Julie Walters
AEEIJLNNOPRT	jointer plane
AEEIJLOPRTVY	pejoratively
AEEIJMMOPRRS	major premise
AEEIJNNORTUV	rejuvenation
AEEIKLLLSTTY	skittle-alley
AEEIKLOPRRSU	Lake Superior
AEEIKMNNSSST	mistakenness
AEEIKMNOQSTU	make question
AEEIKNNOSSSV	save one's skin
AEEIKNOPRRST	take prisoner
AEEILLLLTVYY	tilley-valley
AEEILLLSTUVY	televisually
AEEILLMNRTTT	ill-treatment
AEEILLMRSSTU	Samuel Lister
AEEILLNNPRTT	interpellant
AEEILLNNPSTY	septennially
AEEILLNNSTTY	sententially
AEEILLNORSST	relationless
AEEILLNOSSTT	tessellation
AEEILLNOSSTV	volatileness
AEEILLNPRRTU	interpleural
AEEILLNPRSTY	presentially
AEEILLNQSTUY	sequentially
AEEILLNQTUVY	equivalently
AEEILLNRRSTT	interstellar
AEEILLNRRTVY	irrelevantly
AEEILLNRSSTY	lesser litany
AEEILLNSSSUV	allusiveness
AEEILLOPPRRR	air-propeller
AEEILLORTTTU	retail outlet
AEEILLTTTTTT	tittle-tattle
AEEILMNNNRSS	mannerliness
AEEILMNNRSTT	reinstalment
AEEILMNORRTU	euroterminal
AEEILMNRSSST	masterliness
AEEILMOPRTTU	Mitteleuropa Mittel-Europa
AEEILMPPRSTU	perpetualism
AEEILMPRRSSU	superrealism
AEEILMPSTTTU	multiseptate
AEEILMQRRRTU	quarter-miler
AEEILNNNNPTY	tenpenny nail
AEEILNNNOSST	non-essential
AEEILNNOPRUX	E Annie Proulx
AEEILNNPRSUV	rien ne va plus
AEEILNNPSSSS	painlessness
AEEILNNRTTUY	lieutenantry
AEEILNNSSSUU	unsensualise
AEEILNNSSUUZ	unsensualize
AEEILNOPRRTT	interpolater
AEEILNOPRSSX	expressional
AEEILNPRRRST	laser printer
AEEILNPRRSST	interspersal
AEEILNPRSSST	plasteriness
AEEILNRSSTUV	universal set
AEEILNRTTTUX	intertextual
AEEILPPRRSTU	pleasure trip
AEEILPPRRSTY	parsley piert
AEEILPPRSTTU	perpetualist
AEEILPPRTTUY	perpetuality
AEEILPRRSSTU	superrealist
AEEILPRSSUVY	persuasively
AEEILPRTTUVY	reputatively
AEEIMMNORSTT	amortisement
AEEIMMNORTTZ	amortizement
AEEIMMNRSSTU	immatureness
AEEIMMNRSTTT	mistreatment
AEEIMMNSSTTT	misstatement
AEEIMMRRTTXX	mixter-maxter
AEEIMNNNOOTV	envenomation

AEEIMNNNORTT intermontane
AEEIMNNOOPRT porte-monnaie
AEEIMNNOORSY raise money on
AEEIMNNORRTU remuneration
AEEIMNOPRRTT moiré pattern
AEEIMNORRSST marine stores
AEEIMNORRTTX exterminator
AEEIMNPPRSSW newspaperism
AEEIMNPRRRST printer's ream
AEEIMNRSTTVY vestimentary
AEEIMOQRSTUU mousquetaire
AEEIMPRSSSUV supermassive
AEEIMRSSSTTY systematiser
AEEIMRSSTTYZ systematizer
AEEINNOPRSTT presentation
AEEINNPRRRTU intrapreneur
AEEINOORRSSU aeroneurosis
AEEINOORTTTX extortionate
AEEINOPPRRTT perpetration
AEEINOPPRTTU perpetuation
AEEINOPPSSST appositeness
AEEINOPRRSTV preservation
AEEINORRRSVY reversionary
AEEINORRSTVX extraversion
AEEINPRRSSTX express train
AEEINPRSSUUV unpersuasive
AEEINPRSTUXY Saint-Exupéry
AEEINRSSTTTV transvestite
AEEINRSTTTUV sternutative
AEEINSSTTTUV sustentative
AEEIPPRRSSTV private press
AEEIPPRRSSTY spear pyrites
AEEIPPRRTTTT pitter-patter
AEEIPQSTUUUV sauve qui peut
AEEKKLOOOPTU keep a lookout
AEEKLLORRRST roller-skater
AEEKLLORSTWY yellow streak
AEEKLMNOSWWY Woman's Weekly
AEEKLMNRSSUW lukewarmness
AEEKLMOPSSUV speak volumes
AEEKMOPRRSTU posture-maker
AEEKMORRSSTT masterstroke
AEEKNNORSTTU take one's turn
AEELLLMNOTVY malevolently
AEELLLMRSSTT small letters
AEELLLNOPSWY Naples yellow
AEELLLORTTWY yellow rattle
AEELLMNOQRUW woman-queller
AEELLMNPPSTU supplemental
AEELLPRRSSYY prayerlessly
AEELMMNORTUY emolumentary
AEELMMORRSTV removal terms
AEELMNOPRSST temporalness
AEELMNPRRSTU premenstrual
AEELMOOPRSTU somatopleure
AEELMSSSTUWY sweet alyssum
AEELMSSSTUXY sexual system
AEELNOPRSSTT plasterstone
AEELNOPRSSTY stone parsley
AEELNORRRSTU sale or return
AEELNORSTUXY extraneously
AEELNPRRTTYY pretty nearly
AEELNPRSSSUU supersensual
AEELNRRSSTVY transversely
AEELOOPPRTUV overpopulate
AEELOPPPRSTY People's Party
AEELOPPRRRTY real property
AEELOPRSTUUV superovulate
AEELORRSTTVY travesty role
AEELQSSTTUUY statuesquely
AEEMMNNOOSTU momentaneous
AEEMMNORSSSU summer season
AEEMMRRSSTTU muster-master
AEEMNOOPRSTU temporaneous
AEEMNOORTUUV outmanoeuvre
AEEMNORRRTUY remuneratory
AEEMORRSSTWY Rosemary West
AEEMRRSSSTTT street smarts
AEENNNNOPSTT pennant stone
AEENNOOORSTU out on one's ear
AEENNOPRRSTU neuropterans
AEENNORSSSUV ravenousness
AEENNOSSSSUU nauseousness
AEENNPPRTTYY a pretty penny
AEENOORSSTTT Rosetta stone
AEENOPRRSTTU Streptoneura
AEENOPRSSSTT statesperson
AEENOPRSTTTY petty treason
AEENORRSSTXY extrasensory
AEENORRSTTUY treasury note
AEEOOPRRSTTT state trooper
AEEOOPRSTUUX autoexposure
AEEOPPRRTVWY wave property
AEEOPRRRSTVY preservatory
AEEOPRRSTTTU tetrapterous
AEEOQRRSSTTU sequestrator
AEEORRRTTTUW water torture
AEFFFGILNORY Fear of Flying
AEFFFIMORRRT Tariff Reform
AEFFFLOOOSST Feast of Fools
AEFFGGHIINNY hang in effigy
AEFFGHIMNRTT affrightment
AEFFGHINOTTU outfangthief
AEFFGIINORTU effiguration
AEFFGILLLMOR flagelliform
AEFFGNORSSTU staff surgeon
AEFFHILNSSTU faithfulness
AEFFIILMNRST fireman's lift
AEFFILLOORSW safflower oil
AEFFILMMORSU flammiferous
AEFFILNOSTUX exsufflation
AEFFILRRSSTU first refusal
AEFFINNORSTY fry in one's fat
AEFFIOPRRSTT tear-off strip
AEFFLNOORSTW flowers of tan
AEFGGGILNOPR leapfrogging
AEFGGIILMNNS singing flame
AEFGGILMNRST gangster film
AEFGHHIILNSW whale-fishing
AEFGHHOORRTU thoroughfare
AEFGHHOORTTU aforethought
AEFGHHORTTTU afterthought

AEFGHIILNPRS pearl-fishing
AEFGHIINRRTT freight-train
AEFGHIKLOTTT take to flight
AEFGHIKNORST for the asking
AEFGHIKNORTT for the taking
AEFGHILNRSST farthingless
AEFGHNNORRST staghorn fern
AEFGIILLLORU Liguliflorae
AEFGIILRTUVY figuratively
AEFGIIMNRSTU misfeaturing
AEFGIIMORRRS Mare Frigoris
AEFGIINNPRUY fairy penguin
AEFGIINPPSWW wife-swapping
AEFGIKLMNOST king of metals
AEFGILLMNNUY meaningfully
AEFGILLNNOST falling stone
AEFGILLNORST forestalling
AEFGILLNRTTY flatteringly
AEFGILLNSSUW wineglassful
AEFGILLOPRTY profligately
AEFGILMNOPSU go up in flames
AEFGILNNRTTU unflattering
AEFGILNOOTTV floating vote
AEFGILNORTWW water-flowing
AEFGIMNORRRT terraforming
AEFGINNNNOTT non-fattening
AEFGINNOPRTU put a finger on
AEFGINNRRRST transferring
AEFGINOOPRTT potato finger
AEFGINORSSUU sanguiferous
AEFGLLNRTUUY ungratefully
AEFGOORRRSTY agroforestry
AEFHHIINNOST in the fashion
AEFHHIMNPRSS freshmanship
AEFHHINOOSSU fashion house
AEFHIILPRTWY play with fire
AEFHIINNSSST faintishness
AEFHIINRRSST fish-strainer
AEFHIKLNRTTW Frank Whittle
AEFHILMNORSS salmon-fisher
AEFHINOSSSSU fashiousness
AEFHIOORTTUV hot favourite
AEFHKKOOOSST Sea of Okhotsk
AEFHKLMORSST Thermos® flask
AEFHKLNNSSTU thankfulness
AEFHLLLNOTWY fly-on-the-wall
AEFHLLNOSSTU loathfulness
AEFHLNOOSTTU Nat Lofthouse
AEFHLNRSSTUW wrathfulness
AEFHNOOORRSS rose of Sharon
AEFHNOPRRSTU turn of phrase
AEFHOOPRRSTT shatterproof
AEFIIILMNSST semifinalist
AEFIIILNQTUY equifinality
AEFIIILNRTTV infiltrative
AEFIIIMNNOST feminisation
AEFIIIMNNOTZ feminization
AEFIIKNNOPTT at knife-point
AEFIILLLNNOT fall into line
AEFIILLMORTW water milfoil
AEFIILLMOTTU multifoliate
AEFIILLNOOTU unifoliolate
AEFIILLNRTUV interfluvial
AEFIILNOOPRT perfoliation
prefoliation
AEFIIMNNNOTT infotainment
AEFIINOPRSTT fortepianist
AEFIINORSTTU titaniferous
AEFIJNNOSTTU Just Fontaine
AEFIKLNNPPRT flint-knapper
AEFILLMPRSTT splatter film
AEFILMMNNOOT monofilament
AEFILNNORRTT interfrontal
AEFILNNOSSTU fountainless
AEFILNNPPSST flippantness
AEFILNOOOSTT neat's-foot oil
AEFILNOOPRRT prefloration
AEFILNOOPRSS professional
AEFILNOOPRTV flavoprotein
AEFILNOOPSTU puftaloonies
AEFILNRRSSTT transfer list
AEFILOOPRRSS professorial
AEFILOPPRSUU papuliferous
AEFILOPRRSTT self-portrait
AEFILORSSTUU salutiferous
AEFIMNNORRST frontiersman
AEFIMNNORTTU frumentation
AEFIMNOOPRRT preformation
AEFINNOOPRSS for one's pains
AEFINNORSSTU stanniferous
AEFINNRRTUUV furniture van
AEFIOPPPRRST paper profits
AEFLLMOOPRST platform sole
AEFLLNNSSUUW unlawfulness
AEFLLOOPRSSY fool's parsley
AEFLLOORRSST salt of sorrel
AEFLLORSTTUY flatterously
AEFLMNNOORRW Norman Fowler
AEFLNOOPSSTU teaspoonfuls
AEFLNOPRRSTU superfrontal
AEFLNPRSTUVY Venus flytrap
AEFMNNOORRST Norman Foster
AEFOQRRSTTUU Four Quartets
AEGGGIINORRW Gregorian wig
AEGGGILNNOTU agglutinogen
AEGGGILNRSTY staggeringly
AEGGGILNRSWY swaggeringly
AEGGGIMNOTTU Montague Tigg
AEGGHINNOSTY anything goes✧
AEGGHIOORSTU South Georgia
AEGGHIPPRRTY trigger-happy
AEGGHLNOOSTT snaggletooth
AEGGHNOORRUY orange roughy
AEGGHOOOPRYZ zoogeography
AEGGIIILNNRV Virginia Leng
AEGGIILMNNST Angling Times
AEGGIJMNRSUU measuring jug
AEGGILMNNOTU Muggletonian
AEGGILNRSTTW tag wrestling
AEGGILORRSUY gregariously
AEGGIMNNORRW warmongering
AEGGINNPRSSS graspingness

AEGGLNORTUUV vulgar tongue
AEGGLOOORSTY astrogeology
AEGGMNNOORRT röntgenogram
AEGGNNOORSST gross tonnage
AEGHHHMOSSTU Thomas Hughes
AEGHHIILLLNS shealing-hill
AEGHHILOPRRT lithographer
AEGHHILPRTTY light therapy
AEGHHIMORSTT home straight
AEGHHINORRUV Huang Ho River
AEGHHINOSSUW washing-house
AEGHHIPRSUWY superhighway
AEGHHMNOPRRY hymnographer
AEGHHMOOSSTW game-show host
AEGHHMOPRRTY mythographer
thermography
AEGHHNOOPPRR phonographer
AEGHHNORSTTU through-stane
AEGHHOOPPRRT photographer
AEGHHOOPRRRT orthographer
AEGHHOPPRRTY phytographer
AEGHIIKLNNTY like anything
AEGHIIKLRSTT strike a light!
AEGHIIKNPPST take shipping
AEGHIILLTUWW williewaught
AEGHIILNRSTT straight line
AEGHIILNSTTY hesitatingly
AEGHIIMOPRSW image-worship
AEGHIINNORST training shoe
AEGHIINNSTTU unhesitating
AEGHIINOPRTU go up in the air
AEGHIINPPRSW sapphire-wing
AEGHIKLORRSY Arshile Gorky
AEGHIKLORSWY Whisky Galore!
AEGHIKNNRRTT knight errant
AEGHILLOPPRS ellipsograph
AEGHILLPRSTU sugar the pill
AEGHILMNNOSW Englishwoman
AEGHILMNNSTU languishment
AEGHILNNRTTU turning lathe
AEGHILNORSTT starting hole
AEGHILNPRRSW wranglership
AEGHILNRSTTY shatteringly
AEGHILNSTUXY exhaustingly
AEGHILOOPSTT hepatologist
AEGHILQRRTTU quarterlight
AEGHIMMNNRTU tuning hammer
AEGHIMMNOPRY hemp agrimony
AEGHIMNORSUW house-warming
AEGHIMNORTTV Gherman Titov
AEGHIMOPRSSY seismography
AEGHINOPRRSW power-sharing
AEGHINPRRSSU purse-sharing
AEGHINRRSSTT heart-strings
AEGHINRSSSTT straightness
AEGHINSSSSTY synthesis gas
AEGHIORSTTTV vote straight
AEGHKMORRTTW growth market
AEGHKMORRTUY yoghurt maker
AEGHLLMOPRRS shell program
AEGHLLOOSTTW go to the walls
AEGHLMMNOOOU homologumena
AEGHLMNNOORS longshoreman
AEGHLMOORTUY rheumatology
AEGHLOPPRRTT graph plotter
AEGHLORSSTUU slaughterous
AEGHMNOOOPTT photomontage
AEGHNNOOPRTY anthropogeny
AEGHNOOPPRRR pornographer
AEGHOOPRRSST gastrosopher
AEGHOOPRRTUV photogravure
AEGHOOQRSSUW how squares go
AEGHOPPRRTUY group therapy
AEGHOPPSSYYZ zygapophyses
AEGIIIILTTTV vitilitigate
AEGIIIKLNNPS Alpine skiing
AEGIIILMNOTT legitimation
AEGIIIMNNNOT ingemination
AEGIIINNPRSW awe-inspiring
AEGIIINRSTVW West Virginia
AEGIIKLMNSSY Kingsley Amis
AEGIIKLNNRSW walking reins
AEGIIKMMNRTX marketing mix
AEGIILLMRRTY Terry Gilliam
AEGIILLNNOTW wellingtonia✧
AEGIILLNNRTU interlingual
AEGIILLNPRVY prevailingly
AEGIILMMNNST misalignment
AEGIILMNOPRT primogenital
AEGIILMNORST mineralogist
AEGIILMOOPRS oligospermia
AEGIILNNNSSU ungainliness
AEGIILNNORTU urinogenital
AEGIILNNPRUV unprevailing
AEGIILNORSTY seigniorally
AEGIILNPPSTY appetisingly
AEGIILNPPTYZ appetizingly
AEGIILNPRSTT ear-splitting
AEGIILNRSTTW slate-writing
AEGIILNRSTVV vestal virgin
AEGIILRRRTUY irregularity
AEGIIMNNOPRT impregnation
AEGIIMNNOPTT pigmentation
AEGIIMNNRSTT tin-streaming
AEGIIMNOORRT morigeration
AEGIIMOPRSTV Gram-positive
AEGIINNNOPST nose-painting
AEGIINNNORST Ignorantines
AEGIINNNRSTT intransigent
AEGIINNPPSTU unappetising
AEGIINNPPTUZ unappetizing
AEGIINNPRSSS aspiringness
AEGIINNSTUXY exsanguinity
AEGIINORRSTT registration
AEGIINORSTTV investigator
AEGIINPPRRTW writing paper
AEGIIOPRRSTT prestigiator
AEGIJLPSUWZZ jigsaw puzzle
AEGIKLMNORTW metalworking
AEGIKLMNOSSS smoke signals
AEGIKLNNOPRW panel working
AEGIKNOPPRRW working paper

AEGILLMMORUY Molly Maguire
AEGILLMPRSSU aspergillums
AEGILLMRSTTU metallurgist
AEGILLNNOSTW stonewalling
AEGILLNNPSUY unpleasingly
AEGILLNPRSTY party selling
AEGILLPRSSTX Triplex® glass
AEGILLQRSSUU liqueur glass
AEGILMMNRSTY stammeringly
AEGILMNNNNOT non-alignment
AEGILMNNOQTU magniloquent
AEGILMNOOSTT nematologist
AEGILMNRRSTW arm wrestling
AEGILMNRSTTY smatteringly
AEGILMOOOPRY paroemiology
AEGILNNNOSTU sanguinolent
AEGILNNRSTTY astringently
AEGILNNRSTUY saunteringly
AEGILNNRUVWY unwaveringly
AEGILNNRUWYY unwearyingly
AEGILNOOPRSS sporangioles
AEGILNOOPRST antigropelos
AEGILNOOPRTY perinatology
AEGILNRRSSUY reassuringly
AEGILOORSTTT teratologist
AEGILORRSSTU grossularite
AEGIMMNOOSTZ zoomagnetism
AEGIMMORSSTU mesogastrium
AEGIMNNRTUUU unguentarium
AEGIMPPRRRST strippergram
AEGINNNPRRSU spear-running
AEGINNNRRTUW running water
AEGINNORSSTU nugatoriness
AEGINNOSSUUX exsanguinous
AEGINOORRRTT interrogator
AEGINOOSSTTV not give a toss
AEGINOPRRTVW private wrong
AEGINOPRSTTU pregustation
AEGINOPRSTWY staying power
AEGINPPRTTTY petting party
AEGIPRRSTUVY supergravity
AEGIRRRUUUVY River Uruguay
AEGLLLLNNSUY Sally Gunnell
AEGLLMNTTUUU multungulate
AEGLLMOSSSTY all systems go
AEGLMNNPSTTU tungsten lamp
AEGLMNOOPTUY pneumatology
AEGLNNOOTTUU notoungulate
AEGLNOOSTUUY autogenously
AEGLNOPRRTWY Pyotr Wrangel
AEGLOORSTUUY outrageously
AEGNNOOOSWWY go one's own way
AEGNORRRSSST transgressor
AEGOOPSSTTUY steatopygous
AEHHIIILMSST Ishmaelitish
AEHHIILNOPPS Hispanophile
AEHHIINPSSTW Spanish white
AEHHILLMSSTT Stahlhelmist
AEHHILLNORTY roll in the hay
AEHHILNOORRR rhinorrhoeal
AEHHILNOPPRT philanthrope
AEHHILOPSTTU thiosulphate
AEHHIMNNOOPR harmoniphone
AEHHIMNOPRSS horsemanship
AEHHIMOOPRRT Theriomorpha
AEHHIMOOPRST Thesmophoria
AEHHIMOOPRTY rhythmopoeia
AEHHIMOOPSTT homeopathist
AEHHINNOSTWY Antony Hewish
AEHHLMOOPSTX exophthalmos
AEHHLMOPSTUX exophthalmus
AEHHLOOOPPRT lophophorate
AEHHLOPPSTUY hyposulphate
AEHHNOPPRTYY hypnotherapy
AEHHOOPPRTTY phototherapy
AEHHOOPRRSST sharpshooter
AEHHOPRSSTTU Theophrastus
AEHIIIKPRSST sphairistike
AEHIIILNOOPS eosinophilia
AEHIIILNOPSS hispaniolise✧
AEHIIILNOPSZ hispaniolize✧
AEHIIIMNPRTY pyrithiamine
AEHIIKLNOSST Thessaloníki
AEHIILLNPTTY paint the lily
AEHIILLOOPRU ailourophile
AEHIILNNORUV in an evil hour
AEHIILNOPRST relationship
AEHIILPRRSTT hair-splitter
AEHIIMNNRRTY Martini-Henry
AEHIIMNRTTUU Uintatherium
AEHIINNOPRTT trephination
AEHIINNORSTW within reason
AEHIINNSSSSW swainishness
AEHIINOORSTT theorisation
AEHIINOORTTZ theorization
AEHIINOPRRST prehistorian
AEHIINORSSTU isosthenuria
AEHIINORSTVY The Visionary
AEHIINRSSTUW White Russian
AEHIINSSTTWW with a witness
AEHIIPPRRSST parish priest
AEHIIRRSSTTW shirtwaister
AEHIJKLSTTTU just like that
AEHIJLLNUUXY Julian Huxley
AEHIJLNOPSST Joseph Stalin
AEHIJLNORTVW javelin throw
AEHIJNNOORSS Sir John Soane
AEHIKKMNRRSS skrimshanker
AEHILLMORSTY isothermally
AEHILLMRRRTU Arthur Miller
AEHILLOORSTU heliolatrous
AEHILLPRSTTT lath-splitter
AEHILMMPRTWY triple whammy
AEHILMNOOPSU anemophilous
AEHILMNORSTW mothers-in-law
AEHILMNQSSSU qualmishness
AEHILMNRRTTU Martin Luther
AEHILMOOPRST photorealism
AEHILNNOPTUV upon the anvil
AEHILOOPRSTT strophiolate
AEHIMMMOPRST metamorphism
AEHIMMNNNOOT man in the moon

AEHIMMOPRSTT metamorphist
AEHIMMOPSTTU imposthumate
AEHIMNNOOPRT enantiomorph
AEHIMNNOOSSU mansion-house
AEHIMNNOPPSU one-upmanship
AEHIMNNOSSSW womanishness
AEHIMNNOSSTT astonishment
AEHIMNNPRSTT transhipment
AEHIMNNQSTUV vanquishment
AEHIMNOPRSTW with open arms
AEHIMOOOSSST homoeostasis
AEHIMOPPRRST primrose path
AEHIMOPRRTTW Matthew Prior
AEHINNNORRSV River Shannon
AEHINNNOSTTT on the instant
AEHINNOPRTTX xanthopterin
AEHINNPPSSSS snappishness
AEHINNQSSSTU squash tennis
AEHINOOPRRTT prototherian
AEHINOOPRSST epanorthosis
AEHINOOSSTTU station house
AEHINOPRSTTU neuropathist
AEHINOPRSTTY attorneyship
AEHINPPRRSST transshipper
AEHINPPSSSST Spanish Steps
AEHINPRRSTTW partner whist
AEHIOOPPRSST apostrophise
AEHIOOPPRSTZ apostrophize
AEHIOOPSSTTT osteopathist
AEHIOPQRSSTU quaestorship
AEHIOPRRSTWY praiseworthy
AEHIOPRSSSSS assessorship
AEHIORSTTTUW without tears
AEHJMMNOOSST James Thomson
AEHJNOOPPSTX Joseph Paxton
AEHKLMOORSTT smooth-talker
AEHLLMNORSTT stellar month
AEHLMMOORSTY Thomas Morley
AEHLMNPRSUUY superhumanly
AEHLMOOSSTWY Thomas Wolsey
AEHLMPRSTTTU the last trump
AEHLNOPRSSTU Southern Alps
AEHLNOPSSTUY polyanthuses
AEHLOPPRSTUY pyrosulphate
AEHMMMNOOPST Emma Thompson
AEHMMNORRSTU Thomas Murner
AEHMNOOPRTUX pneumothorax
AEHMNOPRTUUU Mount Ruapehu
AEHMOOOPRTTT Room at the Top
AEHMOPRSTTTY tapestry moth
AEHNNORSSTUY synantherous
AEHNOOPRRSSU sarrusophone
AEHNORRSSSTY synarthroses
AEHOOPRRSSUW house sparrow
AEHOPRRRRTTU Arthur Porter
AEIIILLLMNNZ Liza Minnelli
AEIIILLMNTUV illuminative
AEIIILNNNORT nitroaniline
AEIIILNPSTTU nuptialities
AEIIILNRSTTT interstitial
AEIIILPRSSTU spiritualise
AEIIILPRSTUZ spiritualize
AEIIILRSTTTV relativitist
AEIIIMMNORST immiseration
AEIIIMMNSSTT anti-Semitism
AEIIIMNNNOST insemination
AEIIIMNORSSS missionarise
AEIIIMNORSSZ missionarize
AEIIIMNOSSTT Semitisation
AEIIIMNOSTTZ Semitization
AEIIIMNRSTTV ministrative
AEIIINNOOPTV opinionative
AEIIINNRSTTV intransitive
AEIIINORSTTV revisitation
AEIIIOPPRTTV propitiative
AEIIKKNORSSY karyokinesis
AEIIKLNNPRVW Rip Van Winkle
AEIIKLNRSTTU unartistlike
AEIILLLLMMSY millesimally
AEIILLLMORSW William Osler
AEIILLLMRWWY William Wyler
AEIILLLNTUUX luxullianite
AEIILLLOOSTV volatile oils
AEIILLLPRRTU pluriliteral
AEIILLMMMORY immemorially
AEIILLMPRRWY William Perry
AEIILLNQRSTU tranquillise
AEIILLNQRTUZ tranquillize
AEIILLOORSTV alto-rilievos
AEIILLPRRSTT rail-splitter
AEIILLQRRSTU squirrel-tail
AEIILLRSTTUV illustrative
AEIILMMNOOST emotionalism
AEIILMMRSSST smart missile
AEIILMNNOPRT ion implanter
AEIILMNNOTVY nominatively
AEIILMNNRTTU terminal unit
AEIILMNOOSTT emotionalist
AEIILMNOOTTY emotionality
AEIILMNOPRSS impressional
AEIILMNRSSUV Universalism
AEIILMNRTUVY ruminatively
AEIILMNSTTUY simultaneity
AEIILMOPRSTV à l'improviste
AEIILMORSSTT Aristotelism
AEIILMPRTTTU multipartite
AEIILMPTTUVY imputatively
AEIILNNNQQUU quinquennial
AEIILNNOOPTY opinionately
AEIILNNOORTT intoleration
AEIILNNOOSTV novelisation
AEIILNNOOTVZ novelization
AEIILNNOPSST splenisation
AEIILNNOPSTZ splenization
AEIILNOOPSTX expositional
AEIILNOOPTTX exploitation
AEIILNOPPSTY inappositely
AEIILNOPTTTY potentiality
AEIILNORSSST solitariness
AEIILNPPRSST slipper satin
AEIILNQRRTUZ tranquilizer
AEIILNQTTUVY quantitively

AEIILNRSSSTW sisters-in-law
AEIILNRSSTUV Universalist
AEIILNRSTTVY transitively
AEIILNRSTUVY universality
AEIILNSTUUXY unisexuality
AEIILPRRTTTY tripartitely
AEIILRRSTUVV River Vistula
AEIIMMNNNOOS neonomianism
AEIIMMNNOTTU Mountain Time
AEIIMMNOORST memorisation
AEIIMMNOORTZ memorization
AEIIMNNOOSTT monetisation
AEIIMNNOOTTZ monetization
AEIIMNNOPSSX expansionism
AEIIMNNORRTU Mount Rainier
AEIIMNNORSST Nestorianism
AEIIMNNOSSST sensationism
AEIIMNNRRSTV vernis martin✧
AEIIMNOOPRST operationism
AEIIMNRSSSTV transmissive
AEIIMPRRSSTT spirit master
AEIINNNORTTU antineutrino
AEIINNOOPTTT potentiation
AEIINNOPRSTU resupination
AEIINNOPSSTX expansionist
AEIINNORSTTT strontianite
AEIINNOSSSTT sensationist
AEIINOOPRSTT operationist
AEIINOPPRRST perspiration
AEIINOPRSTTT strepitation
AEIINOPRTTUV vituperation
AEIINPRRSSSU Prussianiser
AEIINPRRSSUZ Prussianizer
AEIIOPRSSTVY positive rays
AEIIPPPRRRST spirit rapper
AEIJLLNORTVY Jayne Torvill
AEIJLMORRTUY majority rule
AEIKKKLLSSUY Lake Issyk Kul
AEIKLLNOSTTW sallow kitten
AEIKMNNRSTTU Turkmenistan
AEIKMNOPRRTW port-wine mark
AEIKMNOQRSTU question mark
AEIKMNPRRRST printer's mark
AEIKMRSSSSTT taskmistress
AEILLLLPRRRT pralltriller
AEILLMMMSSTY symmetallism
AEILLMMNOSTT misallotment
AEILLMNOPRSY impersonally
AEILLMNORSSV silver salmon
AEILLMNPRSUU superluminal
AEILLMPRSTTU multiple star
AEILLNNORTTY intolerantly
AEILLNNOSTTT to all intents
AEILLNOOPSXY polysiloxane
AEILLNOORTUV revolutional
AEILLNOOSTTW wollastonite
AEILLNOQRTUV ventriloqual
AEILLNORRTTY torrentially
AEILLNRRSTUU terra nullius
AEILLPPRSUUV visual purple
AEILMNNOOPRT melanotropin
AEILMNNOOPST Neoplatonism
AEILMNNOPRST minor planets
AEILMNNOSSTW Winston-Salem
AEILMNNRSTTU instrumental
AEILMNOOPRTT metropolitan
AEILMNOPPRSW Piers Plowman
AEILMNOQSUUY equanimously
AEILMNOSSTUU simultaneous
AEILMOORSTTT stromatolite
AEILNNOOPSTT Neoplatonist
AEILNNOSTTYY enantiostyly
AEILNNQRSSTU tranquilness
AEILNOOOPRRT poor relation
AEILNOOPRRSS responsorial
AEILNOOPRRTT interpolator
AEILNOOPSSSS possessional
AEILNOORSTTT isolator tent
AEILNOORTUVY evolutionary
AEILNOPRRTUU Paul Tournier
AEILNOPRSSSU suspensorial
AEILNOPSSSWY slip one's ways
AEILNORRSTTU tenuirostral
AEILNORRSUVY revulsionary
AEILNPPRRTUY Tyrian purple
AEILNPPRSTUU pursuit plane
AEILNPRRSSUU Sir Paul Nurse
AEILNRRRSTWY Larry Winters
AEILOOOPPPRS prosopopeial
AEILOOPRSTTY epistolatory
AEILOPRSSTUU Louis Pasteur
AEIMMNNOOTTU mutato nomine
AEIMMOPSSTTY symptomatise
AEIMMOPSTTYZ symptomatize
AEIMNNOORSST Montessorian
AEIMNNOPPSTT appointments
AEIMNNORSTTU menstruation
AEIMNNORTTUY monetary unit
AEIMNOOPPTTT tappet-motion
AEIMNOOPRRST impersonator
AEIMNOORRRWY one-way mirror
AEIMNOPRSSTU reassumption
AEIMNOQRSTUU terminus a quo
AEIMNPRSTTUV transumptive
AEIMNRSSSTTV transvestism
AEIMNSSSTUUU Sinus Aestuum
AEIMOPPRRSSU appressorium
AEINNNNOOTTT non-attention
AEINNNOOSWWY in one's own way
AEINNNOPRSTT transpontine
AEINNNORSSTT non-resistant
AEINNOOPRSTU put one's oar in
AEINNOOPRTTY enantiotropy
AEINNORRSSTV transversion
AEINNORSTTTU sternutation
AEINNOSSTTTU sustentation
AEINOOPRSTTT protestation
AEINOOPRSTTW power station
AEINOORRTTXY extortionary
AEINOOSSTTTU ostentatious
AEINOPPRSSTT poster paints
AEINOPRRSTTT trainspotter

AEINOPRRSTTV transportive
AEINRSSSTTTV transvestist
AEIOOOOPPPRS prosopopoeia
AEIOOPPRRRTX expropriator
AEIOPPRRRSTY perspiratory
AEIOPPRRSTTU superpatriot
AEIOPRRSTTTY Post-Tertiary
AEIOPRRTTUVY vituperatory
AEJJLOORRUUU au jour le jour
AEJMMOPRRTTU trumpet major
AEKLLPPSSTUU pull up stakes
AEKLNPPRSTTU splatterpunk
AEKLNRRRSTUY slurry tanker
AEKLOOPRRSTW postal worker
AEKNOOOPRSST sport one's oak
AELLLMORSUVY marvellously
AELLLOOPPRWY yellow poplar
AELLMMNNOTUY monumentally
AELLMMOORSST smallest room
AELLMNOOOSSS Solomon's seal
AELLMOPRSTUV Paul Elvström
AELLOOPPSSUY polysepalous
AELLOOPPSTUY polypetalous
AELMNNORRSTT storm lantern
AELMNNOSTTUY Mount Stanley
AELMNOOOPSSU monosepalous
AELMNOOOPSTU monopetalous
AELMOPRSSTTY portal system
AELMOPSSSTTY postal system
AELNNOOPRSTT entoplastron
AELOOORRTTVY levorotatory
AELOOPRSTTUX expostulator
AEMMNNORTUUV verumontanum
AEMMORRSSUVY summer savory
AEMNNNOOOSWW one's own woman
AEMNNOORSSTY stonemasonry
AEMNNOPRRSTT Premonstrant
AEMNOOOPRSTZ spermatozoon
AEMNOOOPRSZZ mezzo-soprano
AEMNOOORSTXY serotaxonomy
AEMNOORRRSTT remonstrator
AEMOOPPRSTUU opus operatum
AEMOOPRSSTUW water opossum
AEMOORRRSTTT starter motor
AEMPRRSSTTUU superstratum
AENOOPRSSSUV vaporousness
AENORRSTTTUY sternutatory
AEOOOPRRRTTU tour operator
AEOOPPRRSSTU Europassport
AEOOPRRSSTTU tetrasporous
AFFGILNNORTY affrontingly
AFFHILLNTUUY unfaithfully
AFFHINOOOSTU out of fashion
AFFIILNNOSTU insufflation
AFGGGILLNNUY unflaggingly
AFGGHHIILNTU highfaluting
AFGGHIIKLNTT fighting talk
AFGGHIINPRTW whip-grafting
AFGGIILNRTYY gratifyingly
AFGHIIRSSTTT at first sight
AFGHILMNNORU half-mourning
AFGHLOOPRRUY fluorography
AFGIIILLNSSU fissilingual
AFGIIKNOPRTT profit-taking
AFGIILLLLORU liguliforal
AFGIILLMNORU anguilliform
AFGIILLOSTUY flagitiously
AFGIILNSSTYY satisfyingly
AFGIIMNOPRRT profit margin
AFGIINNNNOWW winnowing-fan
AFGIINNSSTUY unsatisfying
AFGIKNOORSTT toasting fork
AFGILLMNOORT malting floor
AFGIMNNORRST transforming
AFGIMNORRSTY transmogrify
AFHIINOORTTU out of thin air
AFHIJKLNNNOR John Franklin
AFHIMMORSSST Marsh of Mists
AFHKLLNNTUUY unthankfully
AFHLNOOORSUW laws of honour
AFHNOOORRSUW honours of war
AFHOOOPRRSTU author's proof
AFIIILLNRSTU fustillirian
AFIIILMNNOST inflationism
AFIIILNNORTT infiltration
AFIIILNNOSTT inflationist
AFIILMORSTUU multifarious
AFIILNNOORTU fluorination
AFIILNOOOPRV pavilion-roof
AFIILOPRSSTT spirit of salt
AFIILORRSSST fissirostral
AFIIMMNNORST misinformant
AFIIMMNOORST misformation
AFIIMNNOSSSV Vinson Massif
AFIINOPRSSTU passion fruit
AFILLMNOPSTU slumpflation
AFILMNOOOSTW laws of motion
AFIMMNORRSST transformism
AFIMNORRSSTT transformist
AFIOOPRRSSTT artist's proof
AFLNOOPPRRTU popular front
AGGGHINORRUZ rough grazing
AGGGILLNRSTY stragglingly
AGGHHIIKNSWY king's highway✧
AGGHHILMOTUW Gough Whitlam
AGGHHLMTUUUZ Ulugh Muztagh
AGGHHLOPPRYY glyphography
AGGHHMOPPRSY sphygmograph
AGGHIIKLNPRT parking-light
AGGHIIKNNSTV thanksgiving✧
AGGHIILNPSTY sight-playing
AGGHILMNNRSY rhyming slang
AGGHILOOPRST graphologist
AGGHLNOOPRYY pharyngology
AGGHLOOPRSSY glossography
AGGHLOPPRTYY glyptography
AGGIIIKLLNNT giant-killing
AGGIIINNORTV invigorating
AGGIIKLLNOOO Nikolai Gogol
AGGIINNOPRSW growing pains
AGGIKLLNOOSS looking-glass
AGGIKLNNOSUW waulking-song

AGGIKLNPPRSU sparking-plug
AGGIKMNOORST Magnitogorsk
AGGIMMMNNOOR monogramming
AGHHHIOTTTUW with a thought
AGHHIIMNNOTU mountain-high
AGHHIIOPPPST hippophagist
AGHHILNNOOTT nothing loath
AGHHILNOPRTT triphthongal
AGHHILOOPSTU lithophagous
AGHHIMNOPSTY hypognathism
AGHHINOPPRYY hypophrygian
AGHHINORRTTU through train
AGHHIOOOPPSU ophiophagous
AGHHIOOPPPSU hippophagous
AGHHIOOPPRST opisthograph
AGHHIOOPRSUZ rhizophagous
AGHHIOPPRSYY physiography
AGHHLMOPPRYY lymphography
AGHHMOOPPRRY morphography
AGHHNOOPSTUY hypognathous
AGHHNOOPTTUU upon a thought
AGHHOOPPSTUY phytophagous
AGHIIINNPRST training ship
AGHIIKLLMNRS shilling mark
AGHIILMNPSTY lymphangitis
AGHIINNPPRST transhipping
AGHIINOPPRTU upright piano
AGHIKLNOOPRS sharp-looking
AGHIKNOORSTW Hawk Roosting
AGHILLMNOPPS shopping mall
AGHILLNNOORT All or Nothing
all-or-nothing
AGHILMNOOOOT homologation
AGHILMNOORTU ornithogalum
AGHILORSSTWW whitlow grass
AGHIMNOOPRST gramophonist
monographist
AGHIMOPRSTUY hypogastrium
AGHIMORSSTTY timothy grass
AGHINNOOPSST snapshooting
AGHINNOOPSWW whooping swan
AGHINNOOSTTY nothing to say
AGHINNOPSTTY St Anthony pig
AGHINOOPPQTU quota-hopping
AGHINOOPRSTT trapshooting
AGHINOORSSTT shooting star
AGHIOPPRSTTY typographist
AGHIOPPSSYYZ zygapophysis
AGHJNOSSTUUU Augustus John
AGHLLMOOPSUY gamophyllous
AGHLLNOOORTY orthogonally
AGHLMOOOPRSU lagomorphous
AGHLNNOOPRYY laryngophony
AGHLNOOOPRTY anthropology
AGHLOOOOPTYZ zoopathology
AGHMNOOPRTYY pharyngotomy
AGHMNOORSSST staghorn moss
AGHNNOOOPRTY anthropogony
AGIIIILNNOTV invigilation
AGIIILLMNNTU illuminating
AGIIILMNNSWZ Zwinglianism
AGIIILNNSTWZ Zwinglianist
AGIIILNRRTTY irritatingly
AGIIIMNORSTT migrationist
AGIIINNNORST Tironian sign
AGIIINNOORTV invigoration
AGIIJNNSSSUU jus sanguinis
AGIIKLMNSTTU multitasking
AGIIKLNNOPTT talking point
AGIILLLMNTUU multilingual
AGIILLMMNPST stamping mill
AGIILLNNPSUU Linus Pauling
AGIILLOPSSSS salpiglossis
AGIILMNNOPRT trampolining
AGIILMNNORSU unmoralising
AGIILMNNORUZ unmoralizing
AGIILMNNRTUY ruminatingly
AGIILMNOOPRS slip a mooring
AGIILNNNORRS snarling-iron
AGIILNNNPTTW twining plant
AGIILNNPRSUY unaspiringly
AGIILNOORSUV vainglorious
AGIILNOPRRRY rip-roaringly
AGIILNOSSTUU ustilaginous
AGIIMNNRSTTT transmitting
AGIIMNOORTTU outmigration
AGIINNNSSTUU unsustaining
AGIINNOORSTT toasting iron
AGIKMNNOORWW working woman
AGIKNOPRRTWY working party
AGILLNNOORST snarling-tool
AGILLNOOPPTW pot-walloping
AGILLNOOPSTY palynologist
AGILMNNSSUUY unassumingly
AGILMNOOOOSY onomasiology
AGILMNOOPRSU sporangiolum
AGILMNOOPRTU promulgation
AGILMOOOPSTT potamologist
AGILNNNNOPTW town planning
AGILNNOOOPRT prolongation
AGILNPRSSSUY surpassingly
AGILOOPPRSTY papyrologist
AGILORSTTUUY gratuitously
AGIMMNOPRSUY progymnasium
AGIMNNORRSTW storm warning
AGIMNOOOSSTU angiostomous
AGIMNOORSSTT gastronomist
AGIMNOPPRRTU input program
AGINNOOPPRTU propugnation
AGINNOORRSTW garrison town
AGINNOPRRSTT transporting
AGINOOPRSSTT protagonists
AGINOORSSUUV sanguivorous
AGINOPRSSTTT starting post
AGLLMOOPSUYY polygamously
AGLLNOORSUUY languorously
AGLMMNOOOSUY monogamously
AGMMNNOORUUV Novum Organum
AHHIILLPPPRS Phillip Sharp
AHHIILMOPSTT ophthalmitis
AHHIILOPPSST hospital ship
AHHIINOSTTUW in with a shout

AHHILLLLSSYY shilly-shally
AHHILLMMOOST homothallism
AHHILNOOPSTU anthophilous
AHHILNOPPRTY philanthropy
AHHIMNNPSSTU huntsmanship
AHHINNOPRSTT strophanthin
AHHIOSTTUWWY what's with you?
AHHNOPRSSTTU strophanthus
AHIIIKLLNPPR Philip Larkin
AHIIIKMMOSUY Yukio Mishima
AHIIILLMMSTW William Smith
AHIIILORSSTU urolithiasis
AHIIJLLMNOSW John Williams
AHIIKLLMPPRS Mark Phillips
AHIIKNOSTTWW know what it is
AHIILLMOSSTW Thomas Willis
AHIILMMPRSTU triumphalism
AHIILMPRSTTU triumphalist
AHIIMMNORSTU harmoniumist
AHIIMMNPRSST mantis shrimp
AHIIMNNOORSU inharmonious
AHIINNNOOPSS Spanish onion
AHIKLOORTTUW kilowatt hour
AHIKMOOQSTUW mosquito hawk
AHIKOOPSSTTW skip-tooth saw
AHILLMOPSTTY Timothy Spall
AHILLNOORTYZ horizontally
AHILLOORSTTU litholatrous
AHILMNOORSUY harmoniously
AHILMNPRTTUY triumphantly
AHILMOOOPRTY homopolarity
AHILNNOOPSTU sulphonation
AHILNOPPRSTY psilanthropy
AHILNOPRSTUU sulphuration
AHILOOOPRSTU ophiolatrous
AHIMMOOPRSTU automorphism
AHIMMOOPSSTU amphistomous
AHIMNNOORSUU unharmonious
AHIMNOOPRSST misanthropos
AHIMOOPPPSTU hippopotamus
AHIMOOPPRSTT haptotropism
AHIMOOPPRSTU amphitropous
AHIMOOPRSTTU autotrophism
AHIMOPPRSSTY saprophytism
AHINNNNOQTUY Anthony Quinn
AHINNOOPRSTT antistrophon
AHINNOPRSSTU Sinanthropus
AHINOOPSSTUY autohypnosis
AHINORRSSSTY synarthrosis
AHJKLOOSSSTU Lajos Kossuth
AHKLLNNOOOPT holoplankton
AHLNOOPPRSTY hypoplastron
AHMNOOOPRTTY anthropotomy
AHNOOOPRRTTY prothonotary
AIIIILLMNOTT illimitation
AIIIILNORSTV virilisation
AIIIILNORTVZ virilization
AIIIIMMNNOST minimisation
AIIIIMMNNOTZ minimization
AIIILLLNPSTU Lilliputians
AIIILLMNNOTU illumination
AIIILLNNOSTT instillation
AIIILMMNORST trinomialism
AIIILMMNTTUV multivitamin
AIIILMNOOSST isolationism
AIIILMNORSTT trinomialist
AIIILMPRSSTU spiritualism
AIIILNOORTTV vitriolation
AIIILNOOSSTT isolationist
AIIILNRSSTTY sinistrality
AIIILPRSSTTU spiritualist✧
AIIILPRSTTUY spirituality
AIIIMMNNORSS Rosminianism
AIIIMMNNOSTU immunisation
AIIIMMNNOTUZ immunization
AIIIMNNORSTT ministration
AIIIMNOOPSTT optimisation
AIIIMNOOPTTZ optimization
AIIIMNOSSTTU situationism
AIIINNNOOSTU unionisation
AIIINNNOOTUZ unionization
AIIINNOPSSST inspissation
AIIINOOPPRTT propitiation
AIIINOPRRTTT tripartition
AIIINOPRSTTT partitionist
AIIINOSSTTTU situationist
AIIINRSTTTVY transitivity
AIIKMMNNOTTU mutation mink
AIIKMNNOPRSS Parkinsonism
AIILLLNOOTVY volitionally
AIILLLNOSUVY villainously
AIILLLOSSTTY solstitially
AIILLMMNNOTU mill-mountain
multinominal
AIILLMNOORTY monitorially
AIILLMOPRTUW William Prout
AIILLNNOOTUV involutional
AIILLNOOPRTU air pollution
AIILLNOOPSTT postillation
AIILLNORSTTU illustration
AIILLNQRTTUY tranquillity
AIILMNNNOOTU mountain lion
AIILMNNORTTU malnutrition
AIILMNOPRSTT trampolinist
AIILMNOPRSTY postliminary
AIILMORSTUUV multivarious
AIILNNOOOPST Polonisation
AIILNNOOOPTZ Polonization
AIILNNOOOSST solonisation
AIILNNOOOSTZ solonization
AIILNNOTTUUV invultuation
AIILNOOOPPST oppositional
AIILNORRSSST sinistrorsal
AIILNORRSTTY transitorily
AIILOPRSUVVY viviparously
AIIMMMNOSSTU missummation
AIIMMNNORSTU instar omnium
AIIMMNOORTWY mini-motorway
AIIMMNOTTUUY auto-immunity
AIIMNNORSSST transmission
AIIMNOOORSTT motorisation
AIIMNOOORTTZ motorization

AIIMNOOPRSSU parsimonious
AIIMNOOQSTTU misquotation
AIIMNORRRTVY vanity mirror
AIIMOOORSTTV ovariotomist
AIIMOOPPRRRT impropriator
AIIMOOPRRSTV improvisator
AIINNORTTUVY vanitory unit✧
AIINOOPRRSVY provisionary
AIIOOPPRRTTY propitiatory
AIIOOPPRSTTT potato spirit
AIJMNRRSTTUY Justin Martyr
AIKLLLMMOPRS Plimsoll mark
AIKMOPPRRUWY Yom Kippur War
AILLMNNOOPRY pronominally
AILLNOOOPSST saloon pistol
AILLNOOPTTYY polytonality
AILLORRSTTUY illustratory
AILMNOOSSTUX oxonium salts
AILMNOPRRSTU splint armour
AILMNORSTUVY voluntaryism
AILMNOTTTUUU tumultuation
AILMORRSSTTY storm trysail
AILNOOOPPRRT proportional
AILNOPPRTUUY unpopularity
AILNORSTTUVY voluntaryist
AILOOPRRSUUY uproariously
AILOORRSTTUY traitorously
AIMNNOOPRSSU pons asinorum
AIMNNOPRSTTU transumption
AIMNOOOPRSTT somatotropin
AIMNOOPSTTTU mutation stop
AIMOORRRTWWY two-way mirror
AINOOORRSTTT rotor-station
AINOOPRRTTWY Watton Priory
AINPPRRRSSTTU stirrup pants
AIPPRRRSSTTU stirrup strap
AKMOOORSSUUY Yamoussoukro
ALLOOOPRSSUY porous alloys
ALMNOOOSTUUY autonomously
ALMOOPPRRSTU moral support
AMOOPRRSTTUY stump oratory

B

BBBBBEEHLLUU hubble-bubble
BBBBDDGILRUU Glubbdubdrib
BBBBDEELLOUU double-bubble
BBBCEFHIORSY Bobby Fischer
BBBDEEEIIRYY Bye Bye Birdie
BBBEELLRRTUU rubber bullet
BBBEELMMORUY bubble memory
BBCCEEHLOPST Scotch pebble
BBCCEEILLORY Colley Cibber
BBCCEKLOPRUY Percy Lubbock
BBCDEINRSSUU unsubscribed
BBCEEEHORSUY breeches-buoy
BBCEEEHQRRUU rubber cheque
BBCEEEKLORSZ breezeblocks
BBCEEEMNRRTU rubber cement
BBCEEGLOPRSS cobbler's pegs
BBCEEHKOORRS Becher's Brook
BBCEEILMNRST scribblement
BBCEEKORRRUY roebuck-berry
BBCEGHILNRTU nightclubber
BBCEHILORSTY Sir Toby Belch
BBCEJKOORSTY stockjobbery
BBCEKLLMOPRU plumber-block
BBCELLLOOSWY collywobbles
BBCENOORRSTU broncobuster
BBCGIILLNRSY scribblingly
BBCGIILMNOOT climbing boot
BBCGIJKNOOST stockjobbing
BBCGIKLNOSTU blockbusting
BBCIIKLORRST Bristol-brick
BBDDEEILLORU double bridle
BBDDGIILNOUY body-building
BBDEEEELORTW beetle-browed
BBDEEEHLNOTW bend the elbow
BBDEEELOPPRW pebble-powder
BBDEEEMNNSSU benumbedness
BBDEEFILLSTU stubble field
BBDEEGGKLOOO gobbledegook
BBDEEGGLORRU Rube Goldberg
BBDEEGIILNOS Gideon Bibles
BBDEEILLOORU double boiler
BBDEEILNOPRU Bible-pounder
BBDEELLMOOTT bell-bottomed
BBDEELLNOOTT bottle-blonde
BBDEELLOOSUU double obelus
BBDEEMNNORUY beyond number
BBDEGGKLOOOY gobbledygook
BBDEGHMNOORY hydrogen bomb
BBDEGIILNOTU double-biting
BBDEHLOOORRT blood brother
BBDEIIILSSUV subdivisible
BBDEILLOORST blood blister
BBDEILNOORTW born to be wild
BBDELMOOOTTU double-bottom
BBDGIILNOOVY voiding-lobby
BBDGIINNRSTU burst binding
BBEEEEEHIJSY heeby-jeebies
BBEEEHORRRTY Herbert Boyer
BBEEFORRSTUV Berufsverbot
BBEEGGORSSTU George Stubbs
BBEEGILLORRT Robbe-Grillet
BBEEGLLNORTU Günter Blobel
BBEEGLOOSSTU stubble goose
BBEEGMNORRUY money-grubber
BBEEGNOPRRSU sponge rubber
BBEEHHIMTTTU bite the thumb
BBEEHILMPRTU Bible-thumper
BBEEILLMNRRY Billy Bremner
BBEEILMMRSTU Mister Bumble
BBEEILMNORSW women's libber
BBEEILNORSTT brittle bones
BBEEKNRRSTUU bunker buster
BBEELLMMRTUU rumble-tumble
BBEENNNRRSUU bunsen burner✧
BBEENOOOSSTT bet one's boots
BBEENOORRRTW Robert Browne
BBEFGHLLOOTU bull-of-the-bog
BBEFHILRRSTU filbert brush
BBEFLORTTUWY butterfly-bow

BBEGIIILOPST bibliopegist
BBEGILLNRSUY slubberingly
BBEGINNORSTU rubbing stone
BBEHILNOSSSS slobbishness
BBEHINNOSSSS snobbishness
BBEIINNOPSTU put one's bib in
BBEILLNOORWY yellow ribbon
BBEILNOSSSUU bibulousness
BBENNORSSSTU stubbornness
BBENOSSTTTUU bust one's butt
BBGHIILMNOOS hobgoblinism
BBGHIMMNOTUY thingummybob
BBGIIILLOOST bibliologist
BBGINNOPSSTU snubbing post
BBHJNNOOOOSS Hobson-Jobson
BBHMOOOOPRSU ombrophobous
BBIIILLOOPST bibliopolist
BBINNOOSTTUY boy in buttons
BCCCEIIMRRSU circumscribe
BCCDEEHKLOPR perched block
BCCDEEIJORTT direct object
BCCDEGHIKNOY body-checking
BCCDIIIOSSTU disco biscuit
BCCDNOORSTUU bus conductor
BCCEEEHKRRRY checkerberry
BCCEEEILLRTU electric blue
BCCEEEILNNOS noble science
BCCEEELNOOSS obsolescence
BCCEEEMNOSTU obmutescence
BCCEEEMRRTUU cucumber tree
BCCEEHIKLNOS Chinese block
BCCEEHLLRSUU Hercules' club
BCCEEHNORRSS crossbencher
BCCEEHNORRUY cherry bounce
BCCEEIILNOSV obliviscence
BCCEEIKLLNOS license block
BCCEEINOORRT cerebrotonic
BCCEHHINOOPT technophobic
BCCEHNNOOORT corn on the cob
BCCEHNNOOSTT Scotch bonnet
BCCEHNOOOPRS bronchoscope
BCCEHOOPRSSS Bosch process
BCCEHORSTTTU butterscotch
BCCEIKKLLNOR clinker-block
BCCEILMOORTY motorbicycle
motor-bicycle
BCCEILOPRSTU public sector
BCCEKLOOPRSS process block
BCCGIIKLMNOR rock climbing
BCCHIIMOPRSU Orphic Cubism
BCCHILLOOPSU public school
public-school
BCCHNOOOPRSY bronchoscopy
BCCIIOOPRTTY cryptobiotic
BCCINOOSSSUU subconscious
BCCIOOOPRSST stroboscopic
BCCKOORSSTTU cross-buttock
BCDDDEEEKLOU double-decked
BCDDEEEIINOS disobedience
BCDDEEEKLORU double-decker
BCDDEEKLLOOU double-locked
BCDDEGINORSS cross bedding
BCDDEIIILTUY deducibility
BCDDEILLORSS scold's bridle
BCDEEEEINSST bene decessit
BCDEEEEKNSTW between-decks
BCDEEEEMNRSZ Mercedes-Benz®
BCDEEEFFORRT border effect
BCDEEEFIILNT indefectible
BCDEEEGGINST eggs Benedict
BCDEEEHINSTY Sidney Bechet
BCDEEEIILNTT indetectible
BCDEEEIINNST Benedictines
BCDEEEILNRSS credibleness
BCDEEEKORRST stockbreeder
BCDEEEMNNRUU unencumbered
BCDEEFHIILNT child benefit
BCDEEFHIMNOR Chief Bromden
BCDEEFIIKLRR brickfielder
BCDEEFIJNORT object finder
BCDEEFIJOSTU bed of justice
BCDEEGIIINPR birding-piece
BCDEEIILPRST discerptible
BCDEEIIOPPRR bodice-ripper
BCDEEILLOORR Border collie
BCDEEILOPRRU reproducible
BCDEEILRSTTU destructible
BCDEEIMNNRUU unincumbered
BCDEEINORRSS incrossbreed
BCDEEINPRRSU unprescribed
BCDEEKLLOSTY blocked style
BCDEELORSTUU tuberculosed
BCDEEMOOPRSS obcompressed
BCDEGIINOPRY body piercing
BCDEGMNORRUU cumber-ground
BCDEHHILNTUW The Wild Bunch
BCDEHILLMOPR problem child
BCDEHKNOOOST the boondocks
BCDEIIILRTUY reducibility
BCDEIIILSSUV subcivilised
BCDEIIILSUVZ subcivilized
BCDEIILNOORR incorrodible
BCDEIILNORTU introducible
BCDEIIMORTTU obiter dictum
BCDEIKLNNORT Lord Bentinck
BCDEIMOSSUUV Deus vobiscum
BCDEINORSTUU subintroduce
BCDEIORRSTUY subdirectory
BCDELOORRUUY ruby-coloured
BCDEMMNOOORT common debtor
BCDENORSTTUU unobstructed
BCDGIKLNOOSU bloodsucking
BCDGIKNOOSTY body stocking
BCDHINOOSTUW cut boon whids
BCDIKLNOSTUU bulk discount
BCEEEEEHKNRS knee-breeches
BCEEEEFNRRSU subreference
BCEEEEGHRRSU cheeseburger
BCEEEEGILLNR belligerence
BCEEEEGKLLLO Keble College
BCEEEEHLORRS breeches role
BCEEEEIIKRSX exercise bike

BCEEEFILNNTY beneficently
BCEEEGHILNSY beseechingly
BCEEEGILLNRY belligerency
BCEEEHINOSSX Chinese boxes
BCEEEIIILMMS semi-imbecile
BCEEEIKOORSX exercise book
BCEEEINRSSUV subservience
BCEEEIRRRSVY serviceberry
BCEEELNORTTU electron tube
BCEEEMMNNRTU encumberment
BCEEENPPRSTU prepubescent
BCEEFGIILMNR free climbing
BCEEFHILLLRU Hell-fire Club
BCEEFHIORRST before Christ
BCEEFHNNORRT front-bencher
BCEEFILNORSS forcibleness
BCEEGGHNORRU Georg Büchner
BCEEGHIINPRW weeping birch
BCEEGHLORTTU club together
BCEEGILLMNOW well-becoming
BCEEGILNOORT orogenic belt
BCEEGIMNNOSS becomingness
BCEEHIIKLRST lick the birse
BCEEHILLNRSU Brunelleschi
BCEEHJMNNOOW John Newcombe
BCEEHLLNOSST Stellenbosch
BCEEIIJSSTUV subjectivise
BCEEIIJSTUVZ subjectivize
BCEEIILLMOOP mobile police
BCEEIILLRSTT belletristic
BCEEIJLSTUVY subjectively
BCEEIJNNOOTV non-objective
BCEEIKPRRSTU Sir Peter Buck
BCEEILLOOPSU ebullioscope
BCEEILMNOPTT contemptible
BCEEILMOPRSS compressible
BCEEILOPRRTY pro-celebrity
BCEEIMMOSTTU subcommittee
BCEEIMNOPRRY pre-embryonic
BCEEIMORRRWY microbrewery
BCEEINORRRTU Robert Runcie
BCEEINRSSUVY subserviency
BCEEJLNOOSST object lesson
BCEEKKLNNOSU knuckle-bones
BCEEKNOPRSTU Purbeck stone
BCEELMMOORTU coulombmeter
BCEELMMORTTU commuter belt
BCEELMNOPRUU Melbourne Cup
BCEELNOORTVY conveyor belt
BCEELNORTUVY Coventry blue
BCEELOORRTTU butter-cooler
root tubercle
BCEELRRRTTUU butter curler
BCEFFHINOSUV bunch of fives
BCEFFLNORTUU counterbluff
BCEGHIILNTWY bewitchingly
BCEGHIMNNOOY honeycombing
BCEGHLOOORSU close borough
BCEGIIILNORR incorrigible
BCEGIIMNNNOU unbecoming in
BCEGIKKLNOOR booking clerk
BCEGIKLNOSTU bluestocking
BCEGILMNNOUY unbecomingly
BCEGILNOOOOY biocoenology
BCEGLMOORRSY symbol grocer
BCEHHIILLNOR Heinrich Böll
BCEHHKOORSTU butcher's hook
BCEHHLORSSTU clothes-brush
BCEHIIILOSTY cohesibility
BCEHIIKLLNSY kill by inches
BCEHIIMORSTY biochemistry
BCEHIINOPPRS prince-bishop
BCEHIINOSTTY biosynthetic
BCEHIKLNRSTU slink butcher
BCEHIKNSSSSU bush sickness
BCEHILNNNOOS Ben Nicholson
BCEHIMOORSTW witches' broom
BCEHIMORSTUY heir-by-custom
BCEHIMORSTWW West Bromwich
BCEHJORSSTTU short subject
BCEHKKOOOOST cook the books
BCEIIIILLRTVY civil liberty
BCEIIINOSSTT bioscientist
BCEIIJMSSTUV subjectivism
BCEIIJNNOSTU insubjection
BCEIIJSSTTUV subjectivist
BCEIIJSTTUVY subjectivity
BCEIIKLLNRTU clinker-built
BCEIILLLLMNY Billy McNeill
BCEIILMMSSTY limbic system
BCEIILNOORRS incorrosible
BCEIILNRSTTU instructible
BCEIINORTTUV contributive
BCEIIPRSSTUV subscriptive
BCEIKLORRSTW writer's block
BCEIKNNRSUWW New Brunswick
BCEIKNRTTTUY Tyburn-ticket
BCEILLLMNOOP Colonel Blimp
BCEILLOOPSUY ebullioscopy
BCEILLORTTUY butty-collier
BCEILMNOPTTY contemptibly
BCEILOOPRTUU probouleutic
BCEILORSSTUU tuberculosis
BCEILRRTTUUY trituberculy
BCEINNNOSTTU subcontinent
BCEINOPRSSTU subinspector
BCEIOOORSTTY Rosie Boycott
BCEIOPRSSSUY presbycousis
BCEKLLMMOPRU plummer-block
BCEKMOOSTTUU mouse-buttock
BCELMOPRSUUU suboperculum
BCEMMMNNOOUU commune bonum
BCEMNORSSSUU cumbrousness
BCEMOOOPPRTT copper-bottom
BCERRSSTTUUU substructure
BCFIILMMORRU lumbriciform
BCGGGIIKNNOR brick-nogging
BCGHHILNOTTU bolting-hutch
BCGHIKNOORRT Brighton Rock
BCGHILLNOOTT bolting cloth
BCGHOOORRTUU borough court
BCGIIILMNNOR climbing iron

BCGIIILNORRY incorrigibly
BCGIIKLLNNOO lino blocking
BCGIILMOOORY microbiology
BCGIILOOOOSY sociobiology
BCGIIMNNNNOO non-combining
BCGIINOOOSTT gnotobiotics
BCGIKKNOORST stockbroking
BCGILLNOORUY cryoglobulin
BCHHIIMORSTY biorhythmics
BCHHILOOOSSY schoolboyish
BCHHIMOOORRT orthorhombic
BCHIIIOPSSTY biophysicist
BCHIIIPSSSTU ship's biscuit
BCHIIOOOPRTT trophobiotic
BCHILMOORTTY thrombolytic
BCHILNOORRTT birth control
BCHIOOPRSSTU bishop's court
BCIILLMOOOTY locomobility
BCIILLORSUUY lubriciously
BCIINNOORSSU Robin Cousins
BCIINNOORTTU contribution
BCIINOPRSSTU subscription
BCIIOOPRSSTY cryptobiosis
BCIKNOOOOPRS book-scorpion
BCILMMNOSUUU cumulonimbus
BCIMMNOSTUUY subcommunity
BCINOORRTTUY contributory
BCINORSSTTUU substruction
BCNORSTTUUVY button scurvy
BDDDEEFIILNR Blind Freddie
BDDDEEFIILUZ fluidized bed
BDDDEEILMNOU double-minded
BDDDEGILNOOW Blood Wedding
BDDDEILMNOOY bloody-minded
BDDDGILNOOPU blood pudding
BDDEEEEFILMN feeble-minded
BDDEEEEFNNRR fender bender
BDDEEEEGGILN bleeding edge
bleeding-edge
BDDEEEEGNNRR gender bender
BDDEEEEKNNNO on bended knee
BDDEEEFINNRU unbefriended
BDDEEEINNSST indebtedness
BDDEEFHIORRS Bedfordshire
BDDEEFLMOORU double-formed
BDDEEGGIIRRR girder bridge
BDDEEGGINOOR good breeding
BDDEEGIINNRT interbedding
BDDEEGLOOUWW Wedgwood blue
BDDEEHNNORTU round the bend
BDDEEIKNNORW broken-winded
BDDEEILMNSSU undissembled
BDDEEILMOSUX mixed doubles
BDDEEILNRRUU underbuilder
BDDEEILOOPTT pottle-bodied
BDDEEILORWWW World Wide Web
BDDEFINOORRW bird of wonder
BDDEGHNNOORY hydrogen bond
BDDEGILLORSY Lloyd Bridges
BDDEIINSSSUU unsubsidised
BDDEIINSSUUZ unsubsidized
BDDEILMNORUU Mound Builder
mound-builder
BDDENNOOTTUW buttoned-down
BDDFGIILNORY forbiddingly
BDDGIILNORUW word-building
BDEEEEILPRST spider beetle
BDEEEEMMNRRU unremembered
BDEEEFIILNNS indefensible
BDEEEFILOOSU oeils-de-boeuf
BDEEEFMNOORT forebodement
BDEEEFMOORTT bottom feeder
BDEEEGGRSTTU buttered eggs
BDEEEGIILNNR line breeding
BDEEEGIILNTV diving beetle
BDEEEGILNNOS nosebleeding
BDEEEGINOSUU Eugène Dubois
BDEEEGLNORTU ground-beetle
BDEEEHIILLTW white-bellied
BDEEEHINRTTT the bitter end
BDEEEHMORRTU mouthbreeder
BDEEEIIMNOST bide one's time
BDEEEIIRSVWY bird's-eye view
BDEEEILLMRTW well-timbered
BDEEEILMNRTW bewilderment
BDEEEILNNSSV vendibleness
BDEEEILRTUVY delivery-tube
BDEEEIMMNORT re-embodiment
BDEEEIMNRTTU unembittered
BDEEEJORTTUV objet de vertu
BDEEELLOSUUY blue-eyed soul
BDEEELMNORTU redoublement
BDEEENOSSSTT besottedness
BDEEFGILORUU double-figure
BDEEFHINORTY The Boy Friend
BDEEFIIKLLSX flexible disk
BDEEFIILNNSY indefensibly
BDEEFILMNOOT nimble-footed
BDEEFLNNOTTY Floyd Bennett
BDEEGGNOORRZ Georg Bednorz
BDEEGHHIINRS Denbighshire
BDEEGIIILNST indigestible
BDEEGIILRRTY Bridget Riley
BDEEGIINORUW Brownie Guide
BDEEGIJNORST Bridget Jones
BDEEGKLNOOWX knowledge box
BDEEGLLNOORW golden bowler
BDEEGLMNNORU golden number
BDEEGLNOOTUU double-tongue
BDEEHIILLMSS disembellish
BDEEHIINOSTT bit on the side
BDEEHILNRSTU The Dubliners
BDEEHINOSTUU hebetudinous
BDEEHLLOORTT bottle-holder
BDEEHLLORSTU shoulder belt
BDEEHLNOORSU shoulder bone
BDEEHNNOORTU on the rebound
BDEEIIILNRTV indivertible
BDEEIILMNTTW nimble-witted
BDEEIILNNOTY inobediently
BDEEIILNORZZ Lizzie Borden
BDEEIILOORSV Oliver de Bois

BDEEIIMRRTTU turbidimeter
BDEEIINNRSST bend-sinister
BDEEIIRRSTTU redistribute
BDEEIJLRRRUY jerry-builder
BDEEILLORSTT bottle-slider
BDEEILMRRRTU tumbler-drier
BDEEILNNSTUU Blut und Eisen
Eisen und Blut
BDEEIMNRSSTU disbursement
BDEEIMOORRTW borrowed time
BDEEINNORSTV inverted snob
BDEEINOORRRT Robert De Niro
BDEEINORTTTW twitter-boned
BDEELMMNNOOT blonde moment
BDEELMRRRTUY tumbler-dryer
BDEELNORSUVY unobservedly
BDEELOORSTUY double-storey
BDEEOOPRRRSW brewer's droop
BDEFFGJLLMOU Jeff Goldblum
BDEFGGIILNRY flying bridge
BDEFGILNOORY forebodingly
BDEFGINNOORU unforeboding
BDEFGJKOOOSU Book of Judges
BDEFHNOOORTU debt of honour
BDEFHOOOTTUY out-of-the-body
BDEFIIINNOTY by definition
BDEFIILNORSW Lewis Binford
BDEFILLNOORU double florin
BDEFILNNOOST festoon blind
BDEFKOOOOSUX Book of Exodus
BDEFLLMOOTTU full-bottomed
BDEFLNOSSTUU doubtfulness
BDEGGGILNRUY begrudgingly
BDEGHHINOOOR neighborhood
BDEGHHOORRTU thoroughbred✧
BDEGHIILMNTU midnight blue
BDEGHILORRTU guild-brother
BDEGHJNNOOOY Johnny B Goode
BDEGIIILLNNU building line
BDEGIIILNSTY indigestibly
BDEGIILLNNPS spellbinding
BDEGIILLNOSW disbowelling
BDEGIILMNOTU doubling time
BDEGIINNRSST bird's-nesting
BDEGILLNNRUY blunderingly
BDEGILLNOOTT bloodletting
BDEGILNOOOPS pigeon's-blood
BDEGINOPRTUW powdering-tub
BDEHHIJLNNOT John the Blind
BDEHHLORSSTU subthreshold
BDEHHMNOOORR rhombohedron
BDEHIINOPRTU unprohibited
BDEHLORRSSUU rub shoulders
BDEHMOOORRTU mouthbrooder
BDEHMOOORSTW smooth-browed
BDEHMOORSTTU rush-bottomed
BDEHNOOORSSY Rhodes Boyson
BDEIIIILLNTY indelibility
BDEIIILLNOSV division bell
BDEIIILNNOSV non-divisible
BDEIIIORSTVY biodiversity
BDEIIIRSTTUV distributive
BDEIIKNRSTTU Denis Burkitt
BDEIILLNOSSU indissoluble
BDEIILNOOSUV double vision
BDEIILORSSUU subdelirious
BDEIKLLOOOST like old boots
BDEILMNNOOSW blow one's mind
BDEILMNOOSSY molybdenosis
BDEILNNPRSSU purblindness
BDEIMNNOOSTY endosymbiont
BDEIMNNOOTTU unbottomed in
BDELLLMOOOOP Leopold Bloom
BDELLNORTUUY untroubledly
BDELLOORRTUW trouble-world
BDELNORRSTUY Burt Reynolds
BDEOOPRTUWYY woodburytype
BDFGHILLOOSW goldfish bowl
BDFGIINORTUY fruiting body
BDFHIJKOOOTU Book of Judith
BDFIILMNNUUU infundibulum
BDGGGIILMNNO mind-boggling
BDGHHIOORRTU thirdborough
BDGHIIILNPSU shipbuilding
BDGHIIORRUVY hybrid vigour
BDGHILOOORYY hydrobiology
BDGIIKNNORTU drinking bout
BDGIILLNNOOT blind tooling
BDGIINNRSTUU undisturbing
BDGILLMNOOUW blow-moulding
BDGILNNOTUUY undoubtingly
BDGINOOORSUV Boris Godunov
BDHHOOOPRSUY hydrophobous
BDHIIMOORRSS bromhidrosis
BDHILOORSTTY bloodthirsty
BDHIOOTTTUUW without doubt
BDHJOOOPRSTU jodhpur boots
BDIIIIILSTVY divisibility
BDIIIILNOSTY libidinosity
BDIIILLNOSUY libidinously
BDIIILNNOSUU unlibidinous
BDIIINORSTTU distribution
BDIILLNOSSUY indissolubly
BEEEEEFLMNNT enfeeblement
BEEEEEGLNRTZ gentle breeze
BEEEEEHKNSST the bee's knees
BEEEEFHINORR hereinbefore
BEEEEGHNOTTW The Go-Between
BEEEEGNORRRT Robert Greene
BEEEEHNNPSTT Stephen Benét
BEEEEHNORTVW hover between
BEEEEHNPRRST Peter Behrens
BEEEEILPPRTU blue pipe-tree
BEEEEIMNSTTW between times
betweentimes
BEEEEKLMNRRT knee-trembler
BEEEELMMNTZZ embezzlement
BEEEELMMSTUU museum beetle
BEEEELNOSTTX sexton beetle
BEEEFGLNOSTT self-begotten
BEEEFHORRTTT for the better
BEEEFILLNSSX flexibleness

BEEEFLLMMORW	fellow member
BEEEGGGIRRUV	veggie-burger
BEEEGGIORSTZ	Georges Bizet
BEEEGHILOTVW	give the elbow
BEEEGHOORRUV	borough-reeve
BEEEGIILLMNS	ill-beseeming
BEEEGILNPRST	spring beetle
BEEEGILRSSTU	Geissler tube
BEEEGIMNPRSU	Supreme Being
BEEEGIMOORSU	embourgeoise
BEEEGLNORTTY	only begetter
BEEEGMMNRSTU	submergement
BEEEGNORRSTZ	strong breeze
BEEEHIINNRTT	terebinthine
BEEEHILLNOTW	below the line
	below-the-line
BEEEHILOPSSV	bishop sleeve
BEEEHIMPRSST	Septemberish
BEEEHLNOOPTX	telephone box
BEEEHNNOPRRT	Open Brethren
BEEEHQRRSTUU	Thurberesque
BEEEIILNNSTX	inextensible
BEEEIILRRRSV	irreversible
BEEEIIRRTTVZ	Zeitvertreib
BEEEILLMNTTT	belittlement
BEEEILLRSSTT	blister-steel
BEEEILNNOSST	sensible note
BEEEILNNSSSS	sensibleness
BEEEILNRRSST	terribleness
BEEEILOPPRST	tribespeople
BEEEILOPRRUZ	Pierre Boulez
BEEEILRSSTTU	tubeless tire
BEEEIMMNRTTT	embitterment
BEEEIMNORRSS	Bessemer iron
BEEEIMPRRSST	Septembriser
BEEEIMPRRSTZ	Septembrizer
BEEEINNNORTZ	nitrobenzene
BEEEIRRSSSSW	Besserwisser
BEEEKNORRSTU	bunko-steerer
BEEELLNNOTVY	benevolently
BEEELMNOSTTU	tout ensemble
BEEELNOOPRTT	bottle-opener
BEEELNOOSSST	obsoleteness
BEEELRSSTTUY	tubeless tyre
BEEENOSTTUWW	between us two
BEEFFFGINRTU	finger buffet
BEEFFGHILNUW	buffing-wheel
BEEFGGLOORTT	Gottlob Frege
BEEFGIINNRRT	birefringent
BEEFHILLOTTW	lift the elbow
BEEFHIOSSTTX	six of the best
BEEFHKOOORST	Book of Esther
BEEFHLOOTTUU	out of the blue
BEEFIILRRSTU	filibusterer
BEEFILMNNOOT	Bloemfontein
BEEFIORRSTUU	tuberiferous
BEEFLLOOTTUW	Woulfe bottle
BEEFLNRTTTUY	butterfly net
BEEGGHIINNNT	benightening
BEEGGIIOOOOW	boogie-woogie
BEEGGILNNORW	bowling green
BEEGHHILLRST	she'll be right
BEEGHIILRTTW	Gilbert White
BEEGHILLOSTT	globe thistle
BEEGHILNORSS	neighborless
BEEGHINNRTTU	hunger-bitten
BEEGHNOOOPRT	gerontophobe
BEEGHOOPRRTU	Peterborough
BEEGHOORSTWY	go by the worse
BEEGIIILLLNT	intelligible
BEEGIIILMNSV	misbelieving
BEEGIILNNPUX	inexpungible
BEEGIILNPSST	beesting lips
BEEGILMNOPPR	bog pimpernel
BEEGILMORSTY	boy-meets-girl
BEEGILNORTTX	letterboxing
BEEGILNPSSTU	beestung lips
BEEGKNOOOSST	get one's books
BEEGLMORRUUX	Luxembourger
BEEGLOORRTTT	globetrotter
BEEGPRRSSTTU	St Petersburg
BEEHHILOTTTT	hit the bottle
BEEHHLMPTUUY	hump the bluey
BEEHIIILTVXY	exhibitively
BEEHIIINORTX	exhibitioner
BEEHIILLNNTU	thin blue line
BEEHILLLRSVY	Beverly Hills
BEEHILLMOSTY	blithesomely
BEEHILMOOPST	phlebotomise
BEEHILMOOPTZ	phlebotomize
BEEHILNORRSS	horribleness
BEEHILOORRSU	broiler house
BEEHILORRSTY	liberty horse
BEEHINOPTTTU	put the bite on
BEEHJLOPRSTU	Joseph Butler
BEEHJMMOPSTU	jump the besom
BEEHKNNNORTW	Kenneth Brown
BEEHKNOORRST	honest broker
BEEHLMMNNOTU	hummel bonnet
	hummle bonnet
BEEHLOORSTUU	trouble-house
BEEHLORRRTWY	whortleberry
BEEHMNORRTUY	number theory
BEEHMOPRSTYY	embryophytes
BEEHNOOPRRTU	porte-bonheur
BEEIIILMRRSS	irremissible
BEEIIILRRSST	irresistible
BEEIIKLNSSSU	businesslike
BEEIILNRSSTU	unresistible
BEEIILRRRSVY	irreversibly
BEEIILRRSSTV	verslibriste
BEEIJLLMOOST	mosbolletjie
BEEIJOORSSST	Sir Jesse Boot
BEEILLLORSUY	rebelliously
BEEILMPRSUUY	impulse buyer
BEEILNNOPRST	splinter bone
BEEILPPRSSSU	suppressible
BEEILPRSSTUU	supersubtile
BEEIMNORTTUY	tribute money
BEEINNNOOQUZ	benzoquinone
BEEINNNOORRW	Ronnie Browne
BEEINNOOORTT	toorie bonnet

BEEINNORRTUW winterbourne
BEEKMNNNOOTY bonnet monkey
BEEKNNNORSSU unbrokenness
BEEKNNORRSTY Kenny Roberts
BEEKOOPRRRTU Rupert Brooke
BEELLLLOORTY loblolly tree
BEELLLOORRTW Robert Lowell
BEELLMNOOPRV problem novel
BEELLMNRSSUY numberlessly
BEELMNNOPRTU lepton number
BEELNNOSSSUU nebulousness
BEELNOOSSSST bootlessness
BEELNQSSTUUY subsequently
BEELORSTTUVY oversubtlety
BEEMMNRSSTUY number system
BEENNOQSTUUY queen's bounty
BEEOOPRRSSTU obstreperous
BEFFGHILOOOT go off the boil
BEFFGIINNRUY burn in effigy
BEFFHIOOTUWY be off with you
BEFGHIINNORT Bonfire night
BEFGIILNORTU foreign-built
BEFGIIOORSUY bourgeoisify
BEFHIJLLOSXY box jellyfish
BEFHIMOORSTT bottom fisher
BEFHINNOOORS one for his nob
BEFIILRSTTUY subfertility
BEFILLMNRSSU brimfullness
BEFILLNSSSSU blissfulness
BEFILMOPRSUU plumbiferous
BEFILOOORSSU soboliferous
BEFLMMNRTUUU brutum fulmen
BEFLNOORRTTU Robert Fulton
BEFLNRTTTUUY butterfly nut
BEGGHIINNORU neighbouring
BEGGHIINNOTY in the by-going
BEGGIILNNOSS obligingness
BEGHINNORSUU burning-house
BEGHJNNOORUY John Burgoyne
BEGHORSSSTTU Ghostbusters
BEGIIIILLLTY illegibility
BEGIIILLLNTY intelligibly
BEGIIILNNRRV Irving Berlin
BEGIILLMMNSW swimming-bell
BEGIILNNOOST stone boiling
BEGIILOOOSTX exobiologist
BEGIILRRSSTW Sir W S Gilbert
BEGIINNRSSUU burning issue
BEGIINORRSVW virgin's-bower
BEGIKLLNOOPS spelling book
BEGILLMNRSUY slumberingly
BEGILLNRSTUY blusteringly
BEGILMNNRSUU unslumbering
BEGILMOORSTY embryologist
BEGILNOOORUY neurobiology
BEGIMNORRSTT bring to terms
BEGINOPRRTUU Tribune Group
BEHHNOOPSTTY phytobenthos
BEHIIILPRSTT Blithe Spirit
BEHIILMNORSU nielsbohrium
BEHIILMNPSSS blimpishness
BEHIINOSSSTY biosynthesis
BEHIJLLNNORU John Lilburne
BEHILLMMRSTU miller's thumb
BEHILMOOPSTT phlebotomist
BEHILMORRTTU trouble-mirth
BEHINNORTTWW Whitten Brown
BEHINOOPTTTU put in the boot
put the boot in
BEHINOSSSSUW show business
BEHKORRSSSTU brush strokes
BEHLMMPRSTUU rumblethumps
BEHLNOORSTTU Southern blot
BEHLOOORSTTU troubleshoot
BEHNNORTTUUY bounty hunter
BEHNOOOPRTTW on the port bow
BEIIIIILSSTV visibilities
BEIIIIKLNNSV invisible ink
BEIIILLMMNNU bimillennium
BEIIILLNOSSU insolubilise
BEIIILLNOSUZ insolubilize
BEIIILMRRSSY irremissibly
BEIIILRRSSTY irresistibly
BEIIILSSTTUV vestibulitis
BEIILLLLLORU Lillibullero
BEIILLLLORRU Lilliburlero
BEIILLOORSTU Louis Blériot
BEIILLORSTUY resolubility
re-solubility
BEIILMMMOPRU primum mobile
BEIILMSSSUVY submissively
BEIILNORSSTY Boris Yeltsin
BEIIMNSSSUUV unsubmissive
BEIIMOORRRST bioterrorism
BEIINNOOPRTW brownie point
BEIINOOSSSST obsessionist
BEIINSSSSTUU business suit
BEIIOOPRSTTU obreptitious
BEIIOORRRSTT bioterrorist
BEIISSTTTUUV substitutive
BEIKNOOOSSTU suit one's book
BEILLLLNOOPY loblolly pine
BEILLOORSSTT stilboestrol
BEILMNRSTTUU butter muslin
BEILNOORRSTW Robert Wilson
BEILNOPRSSTY spiny lobster
BEILOOQSSUUY obsequiously
BEILOORSSTUY boisterously
BEILOPPRSTUU purpose-built
BEINPPRTTTUY Tyburn-tippet
BELLMORSSUUY slumberously
BELMNOOPRYYY polyembryony
BENNOOOSTTUZ snooze button
BEOOORRSTTUU tuberous root
BEOORRSSTTTU buttress-root
BFGGHIILLNTU bullfighting
BFGHIILLORST bill of rights✧
BFGIKKNOOOSS Books of Kings
BFIIIILNSTUY infusibility
BFIIILNNORSY fibrinolysin
BFIIILNORSSY fibrinolysis
BFIILLMMOORR morbilliform

BFIILMOORRST strobiliform
BGGGHIILNNTU lightning bug
BGGHHLOOORUU Loughborough
BGGHIILNORTT bring to light
BGGIIMNNOOSW swinging-boom
BGGILNOOOOTY gnotobiology
BGGINNRSSTUU Buggins's turn
BGHHHMORTTUU thumb through
BGHHINOORRTU honour bright
BGHIILNOOPRT birthing pool
BGHIILRRTUWW Wilbur Wright
BGHILLNNSUUY unblushingly
BGHILLNOOOPT polling booth
BGHILOOOOPTY photobiology
BGHINOPRRSTU bring up short
BGIIIIILNTTY ignitibility
BGIIIKNOOSTV visiting-book
BGIIILNNOOPT boiling point
BGIIJLMMNOOY jimmy-o'goblin✧
BGIIKLLNNNUY unblinkingly
BGIILMMNNOOU immunoglobin
BGIILMOORSTT timbrologist
BGIIMNNSTTUU unsubmitting
BGIINNNOPRTU burning-point
BGILLORSUUUY lugubriously
BGILNOORRUWW burrowing-owl
BHIINNOSSTTU in his buttons
BHIIOOOPRSST trophobiosis
BHIIORTTTTWY thirty-two-bit
BHIJNNOOORSS Boris Johnson
BHILMOOOPRSU ombrophilous
BHIOOPRSSSTU Russophobist
BIIIIILNSTVY invisibility
BIIILLNOSTUY insolubility
BIIKOOORSSTV visitors' book
BIILOQSTUUUY ubiquitously
BIINOSSTTTUU substitution
BILLORSSTUUY subsultorily
BILOORSSTUUY robustiously
BLOOOPRSSTUU obstropulous

C

CCCCEEENNORS concrescence
CCCCEHINOOSU echinococcus
CCCDEEILNOPY encyclopedic
CCCDEHNORTTU Dutch concert
CCCDHIIOOPRS dichroscopic
CCCEEGIIKNOP cocking piece
CCCEEHILORTY heterocyclic
CCCEEHKNORTU countercheck
CCCEEIINRTTY eccentricity
CCCEEILMNOTY Metonic cycle
CCCEEILNNOTU noctilucence
CCCEEIMNNOSY my conscience
CCCEEIMNRRTU circumcentre
CCCEENOORSTU enterococcus
CCCEFHIOPRSY psychic force
CCCEGIIMNNOO meningococci
CCCEHINOPRTT concert pitch
CCCEIINNOOST conic section
CCCEILMORTUU circumlocute
CCCEILOOTTUY leucocytotic
CCCEINNOPSTU concupiscent
CCCEINNSSSTU succinctness
CCCEIOOPRSTT streptococci
CCCEMNOOPSUU pneumococcus
CCCGIIILORTU logic circuit
CCCHHHIRRSTU Christ Church
Christchurch
CCCHHHLOORSU church school
CCCIIIMNORSU circumcision✧
CCCIIIMORRTU microcircuit
CCCIIKLRSTTY trick cyclist
CCDDEEEEHLLU dulce de leche
CCDDEEENNOPY co-dependency
CCDDEEENORSS decrescendos
CCDDEEHIILNR cliché-ridden
CCDDEEIIILPU pediculicide
CCDDEEINNOST disconnected
CCDDEFHILOST Scotch fiddle
CCDEEEEHINPR crepe-de-chine
crêpe-de-chine
CCDEEEEILNST delitescence
CCDEEEEMNSTU detumescence
CCDEEEFIILNV civil defence
CCDEEEFNNORS frondescence
CCDEEEHIINNS indehiscence
CCDEEEHIPRST direct speech
CCDEEEHNOSTU escutcheoned
CCDEEEIINRSV viridescence
CCDEEENRRSTU recrudescent
CCDEEFFIOORR Record Office
CCDEEFIINNNO in confidence
CCDEEFILOPSU self-occupied
CCDEEHIILMOY helicoid cyme
CCDEEHORSTUV overscutched
CCDEEIILNORR irreconciled
CCDEEIKNQSTU quick-scented
CCDEEILMORRS sclerodermic
CCDEEILNNORU unreconciled
CCDEEIMOSSTY Discomycetes
CCDEEIORRTTU correctitude
CCDEELLOOPSU close-coupled
CCDEELOOPPRS close-cropped
CCDEELOPRRSU red corpuscle
CCDEEMOOPRTU computer code
CCDEGIIILNRR circle-riding
CCDEGIIJRTUU circuit judge
CCDEGIILLNOU cloud ceiling
CCDEGIMNNOOS Second Coming
CCDEHHIKNTTU kitchen Dutch
CCDEHIILNSTY schindyletic
CCDEHIKLNRTU Dutch clinker
CCDEHILNNORU unchronicled
CCDEHIMNOSSY synecdochism
CCDEHIMOORTY orchidectomy
CCDEHIOOOPRS dichrooscope
CCDEIIIIRSTV recidivistic
CCDEIIIRRRTU circuit rider
CCDEIILLMOSU molluscicide
CCDEIILNNOTY coincidently
CCDEIKLLNORY cylinder lock

CCDEILNOORWY Colin Cowdrey
CCDEILNORTXY cyclodextrin
CCDEILNOTUVY conductively
CCDEINNOOSSU second cousin
CCDEIORRSTTU director's cut
CCDENOPRSTUU superconduct
CCDFHMOORTTU Dutch comfort
CCDGHIILNORW childcrowing
CCDGKNOOOORU drongo-cuckoo
CCDGKNOOORUU ground-cuckoo
CCDHHIILMORS chrisom child
CCDHHILOORRY hydrochloric
CCDHHINOOOPR chordophonic
CCDHLOOOORST school doctor
CCDIIILNRTYY cylindricity
CCDIINOTTUVY conductivity
CCDIKLOOPRTU Diplock court
CCDIOOPRRSTT script doctor
CCDNNNOOORTU non-conductor
CCEEEEHILRSS cheese slicer
CCEEEEHRSTTU cheesecutter
CCEEEEIIKKLO cockieleekie
CCEEEEINRSVV revivescence
CCEEEEJNNSUV juvenescence
CCEEEELLMNOS emollescence
CCEEEELLRRVV clever-clever
CCEEEFIILNSS life sciences
CCEEEFIILRRT electric fire
CCEEEFINNNOR in conference
CCEEEFINNORR conférencier
CCEEEFLNORSU fluorescence
CCEEEGHHIKRW checkweigher
CCEEEGILNORT electrogenic
CCEEEHIIMNPY chimney piece
CCEEEHINNOST ethnoscience
CCEEEHKLLPRS spellchecker
CCEEEHOOPRRT porte-cochère
CCEEEIILNRSV virilescence
CCEEEIIMNNRS reminiscence
CCEEEIINNRST inter-science
CCEEEIINPRSS resipiscence
CCEEEIINRSVV reviviscence
CCEEEILLORTV recollective
CCEEEILMNNRT encirclement
CCEEEILMNNSU luminescence
CCEEEILMORRT electromeric
CCEEEILOPRST secret police
CCEEEIMNNOPT incompetence
CCEEEIMNNSTU intumescence
CCEEEIMOPSTU costume piece
CCEEEINNNOST consentience
CCEEEINNORSU neuroscience
CCEEEINOOPSS coenospecies
CCEEEINORSSV coerciveness
CCEEEINRSVVY revivescency
CCEEELOOPRST electroscope
CCEEEMMMNNOT commencement
CCEEEMNOPPRT cement-copper
CCEEENNOQSSU consequences
CCEEENNORSST concreteness
CCEEFFIIINNY inefficiency
CCEEFFIIKOTT ticket office
CCEEFFIILOOP police office
CCEEFGIILNRT Celtic fringe
CCEEFGINNNOR conferencing
CCEEFHHILRRU Relief Church
CCEEFHIIJSTU chief justice
CCEEFHIPPRTT perfect pitch
CCEEFINNOORT confectioner
CCEEFNOORRTU counter-force
CCEEGGILNOTY glycogenetic
CCEEGGOORSTT George C Scott
CCEEGILLOOSY ecclesiology
CCEEGINNNORT concentering
CCEEGINNNORU incongruence
CCEEGINOOSTT geotectonics
CCEEGINOSTTY cytogenetics
CCEEHHIKNNTW kitchen-wench
CCEEHHLOPPRU churchpeople
CCEEHIILNORT heliocentric
CCEEHIILORTT heteroclitic
CCEEHIKLNPST pencil-sketch
CCEEHIKLNRRT lick-trencher
CCEEHIKLOSST socket chisel
CCEEHIKNOSTU chuckie-stone
CCEEHIKPRRRY cherry picker
CCEEHIMMNNOT mnemotechnic
CCEEHIMOSTYZ schizomycete
CCEEHINNORTT ethnocentric
CCEEHINNOSTU inescutcheon
CCEEHIOPTTUY hypoeutectic
CCEEHKLOORST electroshock
CCEEHKNORSTW socket wrench
CCEEHLMOORSU colour scheme
CCEEHMOPSTYY Phycomycetes
CCEEHOPRRRTY hypercorrect
CCEEIIIIKKKW kickie-wickie
CCEEIIILRSVV civil service
CCEEIIIPRRSS rice crispies
CCEEIIKOPPST pick to pieces
CCEEIILLOSTV collectivise
CCEEIILLOTVZ collectivize
CCEEIILMNSTU multiscience
CCEEIIMNORSV misconceiver
CCEEIINNNNOT incontinence
CCEEIINNOSST conscientise
CCEEIINNOSTZ conscientize
CCEEIINNPRTV Vincent Price
CCEEIINPRSSY resipiscency
CCEEIINRSVVY reviviscency
CCEEIKLNOPPR copper-nickel
CCEEIKOORTTU cookie-cutter
CCEEILLLOTVY collectively
CCEEILLNOORT recollection
CCEEILLORTTY electrolytic
CCEEILMORRST sclerometric
CCEEILNNORTV conventicler
CCEEILNNOTVY connectively
CCEEILNOORTT electrotonic
CCEEILOOPRTT electro-optic
CCEEILOPRRTY pyro-electric
CCEEILOPRTTY electrotypic

CCEEILORRTVY correctively
CCEEILORTTUY reticulocyte
CCEEILSSSUVY successively
CCEEIMMNOSTY meniscectomy
CCEEIMNNNOTV convincement
CCEEIMNNOOOZ economic zone
CCEEIMNNOORT economic rent
CCEEIMNNOPTY incompetency
CCEEIMNOORST econometrics
CCEEINNNOORT reconnection
CCEEINNNORTT interconnect
CCEEINOORRRT correctioner
CCEEINPRRRTU price current
CCEEINSSSUUV unsuccessive
CCEEIOOPRSST stereoscopic
CCEEIORRSTUV service court
CCEEKNORSSSU cocksureness
CCEELMNNOTUY locum tenency
CCEELNOORRSU colour screen
CCEEMRRSTUVY Steve McCurry
CCEENNORRTUY currency note
CCEENORRRUUY Eurocurrency
CCEEOOPPRSST spectroscope
CCEFHINOORSU conchiferous
CCEFIIIMNORT crime fiction
CCEFIIINNSTU unscientific
CCEFIILMRSUU circumfusile
CCEFILMNRTUU circumfluent
CCEFKLOOORUW cuckoo flower
CCEFLLSSSUUY successfully
CCEFLNSSSUUU unsuccessful
CCEFNORRSTUY soft currency
CCEFOOOPRRRT proof-correct
CCEGGINNNOOR going concern
CCEGHIIKQRTU get-rich-quick
CCEGHIINORTT ricochetting
CCEGHIKMNOOR checking-room
CCEGHILMOPYY hypoglycemic
CCEGIIIMNNOR criminogenic
CCEGIILNOPRS closing price
CCEGIINNOOTY oncogenicity
CCEGIINPRTTU price-cutting
CCEGILMMOORY myrmecologic
CCEGINNNNORU unconcerning
CCEHHHMORRTU mother church
CCEHHIILMOOR heliochromic
CCEHHIILNOPT technophilic
CCEHHLNORUUV lunch voucher
CCEHHORSTTUV overschutcht
CCEHIIKMOSSS seismic shock
CCEHIILLNOPU nucleophilic
CCEHIILMORRT chlorimetric
CCEHIIMORSTT stichometric
CCEHIINOORRT rhinocerotic
CCEHIKKOORSU cuckoo shrike
CCEHIKLNORRW clincher-work
CCEHIKORRSTW rocker switch
CCEHILLOQRUU Quiller-Couch
CCEHILMOORRT chlorometric
CCEHILNOORTU technicolour
CCEHILNOOSUU council house
CCEHIMNOORRT chronometric
CCEHIMNOSTYZ zymotechnics
CCEHIMOOPRST thermoscopic
CCEHIMOPRSTY psychometric
CCEHINOPRSTY pyrotechnics
CCEHIOOPSSTT stethoscopic
CCEHIORRTTYY erythrocytic
CCEHKLOORSTT throstle-cock
CCEHKLORSTUU culture shock
CCEHLOOORSUU ochroleucous
CCEHLOOSTTUY hectocotylus
CCEHMOOPRRTY cryptochrome
CCEHNNOPRTUU counter-punch
CCEHNOOPRSSY synchroscope
CCEHNOOSTTTU count the cost
CCEIIIMMORSS microseismic
CCEIIIMNRSTW new criticism
CCEIIINOORRT oneirocritic
CCEIIKKSTTWY sticky wicket
CCEIILLMOSTV collectivism
CCEIILLOSTTV collectivist
CCEIILLOTTVY collectivity
CCEIILMNRTTU multicentric
CCEIILMOORRT colorimetric
CCEIILNNOSUV inconclusive
CCEIILOOPRST poliorcetics
CCEIILPRSTUU pisciculture
CCEIILRRTTUU citriculture
CCEIIMMNOORY iconic memory
CCEIIMOOPSSS seismoscopic
CCEIINNNNOTY incontinency
CCEIINNOSSSU in succession
CCEIINNOTTVY connectivity
CCEIINOORSTV viscerotonic
CCEIINORSTTV constrictive
CCEIINRSSTTY syncretistic
CCEIKLNOOPTU cuckoo pintle
CCEIKLOOTTUY leukocytotic
CCEIKNOSSTTU cut one's stick
CCEILLNOSUVY conclusively
CCEILLOOOPSS oscilloscope
CCEILNNOSUUV unconclusive
CCEILNOOPRRT price control
CCEILNOPRSSU press council
CCEILOOORSTT otosclerotic
CCEILOOPRSUY precociously
CCEILOOSSTUY leucocytosis
CCEIMNOPRSTY cryptomnesic
CCEIMOOOPPST metoposcopic
CCEIMOOORRST microscooter
CCEINNOSTTUY constituency
CCEINOOPRSSU preconscious
CCEINOORSSST cross-section
CCEINOPSTTUY conspectuity
CCEINORRSSTU Russocentric
CCEINORSTTUV constructive
CCEKLLOOORRU cuckoo-roller
CCEKLNOSTUUY cut one's lucky
CCELNNORRTUY concurrently
CCELOPRSSUUU crepusculous
CCEMMNOOORST common scoter

CCENOPRRSTTU preconstruct
CCENORRRSSTU cross-current
CCENORRSTTUU constructure
CCEOOPPRSSTY spectroscopy
CCEORSSSSTUY success story
CCFGGHIIKNOT cockfighting
fighting cock
CCFIIMNORSUU circumfusion
CCFILMORSUUU circumfluous
CCFILOOOPRSU fluoroscopic
CCGHHIILOOTY ichthyologic
CCGHHIKLORTU click-through
CCGHIKNNORSU corn-shucking
CCGHIKNOORTW cockthrowing
CCGHILNOOOST conchologist
CCGIILNNNOVY convincingly
CCGIIMNOOPRY microcopying
CCGIIMNORSST cosmic string
CCGIINNNNOUV unconvincing
CCGIKKNNOOPY knocking copy
CCGIKLNOOSTU cucking stool
CCGILMNOORTY motorcycling
CCGINORSSTTU crosscutting
CCHHHHIIISWW which is which?
CCHHIIIIQQUU chiquichiqui
CCHHIIILOTTY ichthyolitic
CCHHIILMOOPR chromophilic
CCHHIIMOSTTY stichomythic
CCHHIIMOSTYZ schizothymic
CCHHIIOPSTYZ schizophytic
CCHHILMOORST chrisom-cloth
CCHHILMORSUW Low-Churchism
CCHHIMOOOPRR chromophoric
CCHHIMOOOPRT photochromic
CCHHNNOORSUY Oncorhynchus
CCHIIMOPRSSY microphysics
CCHIIMOPSSTY psychoticism
CCHIIOOPRSTY hypocoristic
CCHIIOORSSTT historic cost
CCHIIORRSTTU short circuit
short-circuit
CCHILMOOPRTY Olympic torch
CCHIMMNNOOPS pinchcommons
CCHIMNOOPSSY psychonomics
CCHIMOORSTUY cymotrichous
CCHIOOOSSTTU octostichous
CCHIOOPPRSTY psychotropic
CCHIORSSSTUU hortus siccus
CCHLMMNOOOOS common school
CCHLNOOOSTUY County school
CCHNOOORRSSU hors concours
CCIIILLOOSSU silicicolous
CCIIINNNNOTY inconcinnity
CCIIKKORSSSS scissors kick
CCIILMOOOPST cosmopolitic
CCIILNNNOOSU in conclusion
inconclusion
CCIILNOPRUVY privy council✧
CCIILORSTUUY circuitously
CCIIMMOOPRSU Microscopium
CCIIMOOPRSST microscopist
CCIINNNNOOSU inconcinnous
CCIINNOOPRST conscription
CCIINNOORSTT constriction
CCIIOOTTTXYY cytotoxicity
CCIKLNOORSTT control stick
CCIKLNOORSUW works council
CCIKNOOOPRRS rock scorpion
CCILLMOPRUUU plum curculio
CCILMOORSTTY motorcyclist
CCILMORRSUUU cirro-cumulus
cumulocirrus
CCIMMNNOOPUU communion cup
CCIMNOOPSTUU compunctious
CCIMNORSSTTU misconstruct
CCIMNORSTUUY country music
CCINNOORSTTU construction
CCLMOOOSSTUY cyclostomous
CCNOORRSSTUY cross-country
CDDDEEFIIOST eisteddfodic
CDDDEEFILNOS second fiddle
CDDEEEEFILSV self-deceived
CDDEEEEGNORS second degree
CDDEEEEINNNP independence
CDDEEEEJNSST dejectedness
CDDEEEFILRST self-directed
CDDEEEGIMOOS geodesic dome
CDDEEEIIRRVV device driver
CDDEEEILLRTW well-directed
CDDEEEINNNPY independency✧
CDDEEFLOPRSU self-produced
CDDEEFOOPRUU coup de foudre
CDDEEGILNOSU cloud-seeding
CDDEEHIMORTT direct method
CDDEEHIORRST Desert Orchid
CDDEEHLNNOSU non-scheduled
CDDEEHLNORTU underclothed
CDDEEHMOOPRU home-produced
CDDEEIIKLNSS slickensided
CDDEEIILMMNO middle-income
CDDEEIILORSU Red Delicious
CDDEEIJNPRUU unprejudiced
CDDEEINNORSU unconsidered
CDDEEINNOSTT discontented
CDDEEINOPSTU deep-discount
CDDEEINORSUV undiscovered
CDDEEMNNOTUU undocumented
CDDEEMNOOPSU undecomposed
CDDEEMNOOTUY duodenectomy
CDDEENOOPPRS dropped scone
CDDEENOPRRUU underproduce
CDDEFFGINOOR coffin-dodger
CDDEFIIKLSST fiddlesticks
CDDEFLNNOOUY confoundedly
CDDEGHILNOOR Gordon Childe
CDDEHILLMOOS middle school
CDDEHILNOSSS cloddishness
CDDEHLLOORSU cold shoulder
cold-shoulder
CDDEHLNORTUU thundercloud
CDDEHMOOORST odd-come-short
CDDEIIIKPRST script kiddie

CDDEIIINOPRW	periodic wind
CDDEIIINSTTY	identity disc
CDDEIINNNTVY	Vincent D'Indy
CDDEILNOOPRS	scolopendrid
CDDEIMNQSUUU	secundum quid
CDDEINNORTUU	unintroduced
CDDEMNNOOPUU	uncompounded
CDDGIINNORSU	undiscording
CDDGILLMNOOU	cold moulding
CDDHILLOOORY	hydrocolloid
CDDIIMMOOSTY	discommodity
CDDLNNOORTUW	turn down cold
CDEEEEEGHPRR	hedge-creeper
CDEEEEFGLLNO	golden fleece
CDEEEEFILNSV	self-evidence
CDEEEEFILRSV	self-deceiver
CDEEEEHNRRTT	three-centred
CDEEEEIILMNT	telemedicine
CDEEEEIINNPX	inexpedience
CDEEEEIIRRVW	wide receiver
CDEEEEIKLPRW	pickerel-weed
CDEEEEILRRST	Red Leicester
CDEEEELNNPRS	resplendence
CDEEEELORRSV	record sleeve
CDEEEEMRRSUY	rescue remedy
CDEEEENPRSSU	supersedence
CDEEEENSSTTW	sweet-scented
CDEEEFFGINOR	force-feeding
CDEEEFFIINNR	indifference
CDEEEFGIMNNN	fence-mending
CDEEEFHILRST	chesterfield
CDEEEFHORSUV	chefs d'oeuvre
CDEEEFIJLNTU	fuel-injected
CDEEEFILLORW	flower delice
	flower-delice
CDEEEFINRRSS	crise de nerfs
CDEEEFLLORUW	flower deluce
	flower-deluce
	flower-de-luce
CDEEEFLMNRTU	Clement Freud
CDEEEFLORRTT	retroflected
CDEEEGIILNOS	geodesic line
CDEEEGIILNOT	geodetic line
CDEEEGIKLNRS	single-decker
CDEEEGINOSTV	decongestive
CDEEEHIKNOTW	the wicked one
CDEEEHILNNOT	on the decline
CDEEEHILRRSV	River Schelde
CDEEEHIMNPRT	decipherment
CDEEEHIMORRY	heroic remedy
CDEEEHIOPRRT	tripe de roche
CDEEEHIRSSSS	des richesses
CDEEEHIRSTTW	white-crested
CDEEEHLMRTTU	Dutch elm tree
CDEEEHNOOPTT	detectophone
CDEEEHNOSSTX	The Second Sex
CDEEEHNRSSTW	wretchedness
CDEEEIIINSTZ	decitizenise
CDEEEIIINTZZ	decitizenize
CDEEEIINNPXY	inexpediency
CDEEEIINSSSV	decisiveness
CDEEEILMNORS	microneedles
CDEEEILMNORT	declinometer
CDEEEILNQSTU	deliquescent
CDEEEIMNORTT	mine detector
CDEEEINNNORS	non-residence
CDEEEINORSSV	coversed sine
CDEEEINPRSST	decrepitness
CDEEEINRSSST	discreetness
	discreteness
CDEEEIORRRSV	rediscoverer
CDEEEKLNPSSS	speckledness
CDEEEKLNRTTU	turtle-necked
CDEEELNNPRSY	resplendency
CDEEELNOORST	electrosonde
CDEEELNPTUXY	unexpectedly
CDEEELNRSSSW	endless screw
CDEEEMNNNOTU	denouncement
CDEEEMNNOORS	encomenderos
CDEEENPRSTUU	unpersecuted
CDEEFFFIILOR	field officer
CDEEFFGNORTU	ground effect
CDEEFFHILOOR	office-holder
CDEEFFHOORRT	off the record
	off-the-record
CDEEFFIINNRY	indifferency
CDEEFFILPRTU	perfect fluid
CDEEFFIMNOOT	domino effect
CDEEFFNOSSTU	sound effects
CDEEFGIINRTT	genetic drift
CDEEFGIOOOPS	piece of goods
CDEEFHIIKLNT	field kitchen
CDEEFHLLOOSS	self-schooled
CDEEFHLNOOOV	cloven-hoofed
CDEEFHOORRRT	for the record
CDEEFIILNORT	line of credit
CDEEFIINOSTT	defectionist
CDEEFIIORRST	corrie-fisted
CDEEFILNNNUU	uninfluenced
CDEEFILORRST	self-director
CDEEFLLOORSU	self-coloured
CDEEFLMNOSSU	self-consumed
CDEEFLNOOOTV	cloven-footed
CDEEFLRSSTTU	self-destruct
CDEEFNNOSSSU	confusedness
CDEEFOORRSTU	tours de force
CDEEFOORSSTT	soft-sectored
CDEEGHILNRSU	rescheduling
CDEEGIILLPRV	pelvic girdle
CDEEGIILNPRS	single-priced
CDEEGIILRRTY	triglyceride
CDEEGIKNOPRR	pecking order
CDEEGINNOOST	decongestion
CDEEGINNORSU	unrecognised
CDEEGINNORUZ	unrecognized
CDEEGLNOOSTU	close-tongued
CDEEGMMMNOUU	come ungummed
CDEEGMMNNOOR	common gender
CDEEHHILORRS	Lord Cheshire
CDEEHHKLLOSS	shellshocked
CDEEHIIINNOR	encheiridion
CDEEHIIRSTTW	wire-stitched

CDEEHIKLORTT ticket-holder
CDEEHILLNORY cylinder hole
CDEEHINNRSTU unchristened
CDEEHINORSST Édith Cresson
CDEEHINORTWW white-crowned
CDEEHINPRRSW spider wrench
CDEEHIOPRRRS recordership
CDEEHLMOOSTU close-mouthed
CDEEHLNORSTU underclothes
CDEEHLNPRSUU unsepulchred
CDEEHLOOORST close the door
CDEEHMOOPSUU pouched mouse
CDEEHNOORSTU Côtes du Rhône
CDEEHORSTTTU outstretched
CDEEIIILNSVY indecisively
CDEEIIILOPST depoliticise
CDEEIIILOPTZ depoliticize
CDEEIIINNSTV disincentive
CDEEIIINRTTV interdictive
CDEEIIJLSTTU lit de justice
CDEEIILLMPSU semipellucid
CDEEIILMNRSY semicylinder
CDEEIILMNRUV demi-culverin
CDEEIILNNORV overinclined
CDEEIILNOPRT predilection
CDEEIILNRSTY indiscreetly
indiscretely
iridescently
CDEEIILOPSTV velocipedist
CDEEIILORSVV silver-voiced
CDEEIILPRTVY predictively
CDEEIILRSTTT credit titles
CDEEIILRSTVY discretively
CDEEIIMNOPRV improvidence
CDEEIINNRSST indirectness
CDEEIIORSSTU discourteise
CDEEIKNORSST second strike
second-strike
CDEEILLNPSSU pellucidness
CDEEILMNOOPX complexioned
CDEEILNOORUW wine-coloured
CDEEILNORSTU uncloistered
CDEEILNPRTYY type cylinder
CDEEILRRSTTY restrictedly
CDEEIMMNOOXY mixed economy
CDEEIMNNOSTT miscontented
CDEEIMNOORTU Deuteronomic
CDEEIMOOSSTX sextodecimos
CDEEIMPRSTUW wide-spectrum
CDEEINNOPRRT drop-in centre
CDEEINNOPSSU second supine
CDEEINNORSWW window screen
CDEEINOPPRRT intercropped
CDEEINOPRSTW insect powder
CDEEINRRSTTU unrestricted
CDEEIOPRRRRT trip recorder
CDEEIOPRRTUV reproductive
CDEEIOPSSSUY pseudocyesis
CDEEIORRSTUV discoverture
CDEEKKLNNRUU knuckle under
CDEELLNNOSUU uncounselled
CDEELOOORRSU rose-coloured
CDEELOOPRSTW powder closet
CDEEMNOOPSSS composedness
CDEEMOOPRRSS decompressor
CDEENNNOOOST second-to-none
CDEENNOOPRSS second person
CDEENNOOPRST corespondent
CDEENNRRRTUU undercurrent
CDEENOORSSSU decorousness
CDEENOORSSTY second storey
CDEENRRSTTUU enstructured
CDEEOOPRSTUY deuteroscopy
CDEEORRRSSSS cross-dresser
CDEEORRRSSTU court-dresser
CDEFFHOOPSTU depth of focus
CDEFFIIILSTU difficulties
CDEFGHIOOTTY The City of God
CDEFHILNOORS school-friend
CDEFHINNORWW French window
CDEFIIINNOST disinfection
CDEFIIMORSTU discomfiture
CDEFIINOSTTU unscottified
CDEFILLOORSU field colours
CDEFILNNNOUY unconfinedly
CDEFLNNOSUUY unconfusedly
CDEGHHIIKSTT thick-sighted
CDEGHHILOORU high-coloured
CDEGHIIKQSTU quick-sighted
CDEGHILORSST cross-lighted
CDEGHINNOOSU echo-sounding
CDEGHIOOPSTU pseudo-Gothic
CDEGHNOORSTW second growth
CDEGHNORRRUY ground cherry
CDEGIIMNOOSY gynodioecism
CDEGIINNNRSU undiscerning
CDEGIKLLOORS slockdoliger
CDEGIKLMNNOU neck-moulding
CDEGIKNNOSTU unstockinged
CDEGINNORSST second string
CDEGINOORRVW overcrowding
CDEGKLLOOORS slockdologer
CDEGLMNORUUY curmudgeonly
CDEHHIIIPRTT diphtheritic
CDEHHIILNSSS childishness
CDEHHIMNOOPT phonic method
CDEHIIILOPRS siderophilic
CDEHIIILPPSS discipleship
CDEHIIKKNNST thick-skinned
CDEHIIKNORTY hydrokinetic
CDEHIILLOPRW chilli powder
CDEHIILLORSV shrill-voiced
CDEHIILNOOSV school-divine
CDEHIILNSSSY schindylesis
CDEHIIMMRSTW dimmer switch
CDEHIIMNOSUU eunuchoidism
CDEHIIMPSSTY dysphemistic
CDEHIINNRSTT herd instinct
CDEHIINOOOPR conidiophore
CDEHIINORTYZ hydrozincite
CDEHIIOOPRST Sothic period
CDEHIIOPRRST directorship

CDEHIIPRSSTT	spider stitch
CDEHIKKLLSTU	thick-skulled
CDEHILLOOOST	old school tie
CDEHILLOOPRY	policyholder
CDEHIMNNORRY	Chernomyrdin
CDEHIMNOOORS	chondriosome
CDEHIMNOOTWW	come down with
CDEHIMORTTYY	rhytidectomy
CDEHIORRTTWY	creditworthy
CDEIIIILNNPS	indiscipline
CDEIIIJRSTUV	jurisdictive
CDEIIILLNOSV	cell division
CDEIIILNNPSU	undiscipline
CDEIIILNTVVY	vindictively
CDEIIIMNORST	misdirection
CDEIIIMNOTTX	mitotic index
CDEIIINNORST	indiscretion
CDEIIINNORTT	interdiction
CDEIIKNOTTWW	ticket window
CDEIILMMNOOR	melodic minor
CDEIILMRTUUV	diverticulum
CDEIILNNPPRU	unprincipled
CDEIILOOPRTU	loop diuretic
CDEIILRSSUVY	discursively
CDEIIMMNOOSS	commissioned
	decommission
CDEIIMMRSSTY	dissymmetric
CDEIIMNNOORT	incident room
CDEIIMNOORTT	direct motion
CDEIIMNOPRRT	microprinted
CDEIIMNORSTU	reductionism
CDEIINNNOOSX	disconnexion
CDEIINNOOPRT	precondition
CDEIINNSSSTT	distinctness
CDEIINOOOPRS	conidiospore
CDEIINOOPRST	periodontics
CDEIINORRTTY	interdictory
CDEIINORSTTU	reductionist
CDEIINORTTUV	introductive
CDEIKNRSTTUY	sky-tinctured
CDEILMNOORUX	index locorum
CDEILMNORSSU	scoundrelism
CDEILNOORSUY	indecorously
CDEILOPRTUVY	productively
CDEIMMNOOPTU	compound time
CDEIMNNOOPST	Denis Compton
CDEIMOOPRSSU	discomposure
CDEINNRSTTUU	uninstructed
CDEINOOPRRTU	reproduction
CDEINOPRTUUV	unproductive
CDEIOORSSTUU	discourteous
CDEJKLLOORTY	Doctor Jekyll
CDEKNORRSTUW	wonder-struck
CDELLNNOORTU	uncontrolled
CDELLNOOTUVY	convolutedly
CDELNNOOPRUY	pronouncedly
CDELNOOOSTUY	cotyledonous
CDELNPRSTUUU	unsculptured
CDELOOORRSUY	rosy-coloured
CDELOORRSTUU	rust-coloured
CDENNNOOPRUU	unpronounced
CDENNOORRTUU	counter-round
CDENRRSTTUUU	unstructured
CDFFOORSSTTU	doctor's stuff
CDFGIIIMNOST	discomfiting
CDFGILNOORTY	flying doctor
CDFHILOORRUY	hydrofluoric
CDFIILMNORRY	cylindriform
CDFINNOORTUW	function word
CDGGGIIIKNST	digging stick
CDGGIKLLNUUY	ugly duckling
CDGHIIILPRTY	ditriglyphic
CDGHIILLOOTY	thiodiglycol
CDGHIILNOORS	riding school
CDGIIIKNNORS	Nordic skiing
CDGIIINNNOOT	conditioning
CDGIIKLNOSSU	cloud-kissing
CDGIILMNOOOS	sigmoid colon
CDGIIMMNNOOR	common-riding
CDGIKLNOOSTU	ducking-stool
CDGIMNNOOPRU	ring-compound
CDGMMNNOOORU	common ground
CDHHIIIMORTY	idiorhythmic
CDHHIJMNNOOR	John Richmond
CDHHIOOOPRTY	hypotrochoid
CDHIIIMOOPRS	isodimorphic
CDHIIMMNOORS	monorchidism
CDHILLOOSSST	List D schools
CDHILOORSSSS	scissors hold
CDHILOPPRSTU	child support
CDHIMNNOOSTY	synodic month
CDHIMOOORRST	orthodromics
CDHINOOORSTT	orthodontics
CDHINOOOSTUV	Viscount Hood
CDHIOOOPRSSU	discophorous
CDHIOOOPSSUZ	schizopodous
CDHOOSTTUUYY	youth custody
CDIIIJNORSTU	jurisdiction
CDIIILNNSTTY	indistinctly
CDIIIMNNSTTU	nunc dimittis✧
CDIILLORSUUY	ridiculously
CDIIMMNOOOSU	incommodious
CDIIMMNOSTUY	discommunity
CDIINNOORTTU	introduction
CDIINOOOOPSS	podoconiosis
CDIIOPRTTUVY	productivity
CDIKLNOOOPSS	spondoolicks
CDIKOOORRRRW	corridor work
CDILLNOOOSTW	Cotswold lion
CDILMMOOOSUY	commodiously
CDINNOOOPTUW	two pound coin
CDINOORRTTUY	introductory
CDMMNNOOOOPU	mono-compound
CEEEEEHNNRST	cheese-rennet
CEEEEELNPRST	telepresence
CEEEEFFIKORS	office-seeker
CEEEEFFNRSTV	effervescent
CEEEEFHNOSST	of the essence
CEEEEFHORTTV	cover the feet
CEEEEFHPSSSU	sheep's fescue
CEEEEFHRRSTZ	chest freezer
CEEEEFILLSTV	self-elective

CEEEEFILNNST life sentence
CEEEEFINNRRT interference
CEEEEFINRRTV enteric fever
CEEEEFLLNOSX excel oneself
CEEEEFLORRST free-selector
CEEEEFNPRSTT perfect tense
CEEEEGGLLNOR Green College
CEEEEGHMNORS cheesemonger
CEEEEGIMNNRY grey eminence
CEEEEGLLNRTT tercel-gentle
CEEEEHHOPPRS cheesehopper
CEEEEHIMNNPR preheminence
CEEEEHINRRSV His Reverence
CEEEEHKOORRS Cherokee rose
CEEEEHNOPRRY honey creeper
CEEEEHNORSVW whencesoever
CEEEEHNPQSSU Queen's Speech
CEEEEIILMPTT etepimeletic
CEEEEIINNPRX inexperience
CEEEEIKKPRTW wicketkeeper
CEEEEILLLSTV Celesteville
CEEEEILMNNOO Come on Eileen
CEEEEILRSSTV teleservices
CEEEEIMRRSTV service metre
CEEEEINPRSTX pre-existence
CEEEEINRRRSV sir-reverence
CEEEEIPRRRSV reserve price
CEEEELMORRTT electrometer
CEEEELNPRSST pretenceless
CEEEELORRSTT steel erector
CEEEEMNQSTUV Steve McQueen
CEEEENNNOPST open sentence
CEEEEPRSTTUZ crêpe suzette
CEEEFFFGINRT fringe effect
CEEEFFFILORT filter coffee
CEEEFFHLNNNR French fennel
CEEEFFIKLNTV Kelvin effect
CEEEFFILPPRT ripple effect
CEEEFFINNOTV non-effective
CEEEFFLNORST efflorescent
CEEEFFLNORTT left-of-centre
CEEEFGHHIMRT Fehmgerichte
CEEEFGHIIOPT piece of eight
CEEEFGHITTTY get itchy feet
CEEEFGILLNST self-electing
CEEEFHHILNPT feel the pinch
CEEEFHHNOSTW the chosen few
CEEEFHINRSST scene-shifter
CEEEFHLNRRTT French letter
CEEEFHLNRSSU cheerfulness
CEEEFIILRRTV irreflective
CEEEFIIMPRTV imperfective
CEEEFIKPRRRT Peter Fricker
CEEEFILLLMNU mellifluence
CEEEFILLNOST self-election
CEEEFILLNOSV self-violence
CEEEFILLRTVY reflectively
CEEEFILNNRTU interfluence
CEEEFILNPRSV splenic fever
CEEEFILNRTUV unreflective
CEEEFILPRTVY perfectively
CEEEFKLNSSSS fecklessness
CEEEFKLOPRRW flowerpecker
CEEEGGNORRRY greengrocery
CEEEGHHIMRTV Vehmgerichte
CEEEGHINOOSS Chinese goose
CEEEGIILLNNT intelligence
CEEEGIINRSTV receiving-set
CEEEGIKNNORT rocket engine
CEEEGILLLOOR Oriel College
CEEEGIMNOOSY siege economy
CEEEGINOOSTT osteogenetic
CEEEGINOPRTT petrogenetic
CEEEGJLLOSSU Jesus College
CEEEGLMNORRS Roger Clemens
CEEEHHIINSTW Chinese white
CEEEHHILMPSU helium speech
CEEEHHINRSSS cheerishness
CEEEHHIRSTTW Three Witches
CEEEHIIMRSTU euhemeristic
CEEEHIIPRRSV receivership
CEEEHIKPRRRT three-pricker
CEEEHILLOPRT electrophile
CEEEHILNOSUX Hélène Cixous
CEEEHIMNNPRT encipherment
CEEEHIMNPSWY chimney-sweep
CEEEHIMNRSTU hermeneutics
CEEEHINOSSSV cohesiveness
CEEEHIOORSTU heteroecious
CEEEHIPRRSTW speechwriter
CEEEHKORSTTY street hockey
CEEEHLLPSSSY speechlessly
CEEEHLNNOTTU luncheonette
CEEEHLNORTUW counter-wheel
CEEEHLNOSSST clothes-sense
CEEEHLOQQSUU quelque chose
CEEEHMNNNRTT entrenchment
CEEEHMNNRRTT retrenchment
CEEEHMOORRST stereochrome
CEEEHNOPRRST centrosphere
CEEEHNOSTTTU cut one's teeth
CEEEHNRSTTTU chestnut tree
CEEEHOORRSTV over the score
CEEEHPPPRRRY cherry-pepper
CEEEIILLNTTV intellective
CEEEIIMNNPRT impertinence
CEEEIIMPPRTV imperceptive
CEEEIINPRTTV interceptive
CEEEIINRRSTV interservice
CEEEIIPRRSTV irrespective
CEEEIJKLNRRT tercel-jerkin
CEEEIKNOPRSS specksioneer
CEEEIKNOPRST specktioneer
CEEEILLLMNSU selenium cell
CEEEILLNOPQU equipollence
CEEEILNNOPPT plenipotence
CEEEILNOPRST preselection
CEEEILNRRSSV silver screen
CEEEILNRRSTV client-server
CEEEILOPRRST Pierre Lescot
CEEEILPRSTVY respectively
CEEEIMNNOOSU cue someone in

CEEEIMNNOPRS omnipresence
CEEEIMNPPSTY type specimen
CEEEIMORRSTT stereometric
CEEEIMORRTVY recovery time
CEEEINNNOSTX non-existence
CEEEINNORSSV overniceness
CEEEINNOTUVX non-executive
CEEEINNQSSTU quintessence
CEEEINOPRSTU counterpeise
CEEEINOSSTVV covetiveness
CEEEINPPRTUV unperceptive
CEEEINPRSTUV unrespective
CEEEINRRRSTW screenwriter
CEEEIORRSSTV retrocessive
CEEEIOTTUVXY executive toy
CEEEIPPRSSSU superspecies
CEEEIPRRSSUV repercussive
CEEEIQSSTUUU cestui que use
CEEEIRRRSTUV resurrective
CEEEJOPRRTTX export reject
CEEEKLNOOOPS keep one's cool
CEEEKLNRSSSS recklessness
CEEELLNNORST electron lens
CEEELLNPRUUV pulverulence
CEEELLORRSTY electrolyser
CEEELMMORTTU telecommuter
CEEELMNOPSST completeness
CEEELMOORUWY you're welcome
CEEELMORRTTY electrometry
CEEELMPRRSTU spectre lemur
CEEELNOPRSTU Pleuronectes
CEEELNOPRSTW steeple-crown
CEEELNRRSTTU screen turtle
CEEELOPRRTTY electrotyper
CEEELORRSSSU resourceless
CEEELORSTTVV velvet-scoter
CEEELRSSTTVY select vestry
CEEEMNNNORTU renouncement
CEEEMOPRRSTT spectrometer
CEEENNORSSTU counter-sense
CEEENNPRTUUV venepuncture
CEEENOOPRRSV Provence-rose
CEEEOOPRRTTX exteroceptor
CEEEOPRRRSVY cryopreserve
CEEFFFHIPRTT perfect fifth
CEEFFGIORTUY city of refuge
CEEFFHIKLRRS sheriff clerk
CEEFFHINORTU office-hunter
CEEFFHIOORSU house officer
CEEFFHORRSTT stretcher off
CEEFFIILLOTT little office
CEEFFIINNNOT non-efficient
CEEFFIOPRRSS press officer
CEEFFIOPRTTY petty officer
CEEFFLNORSSU forcefulness
CEEFFNOORRTU counteroffer
CEEFGHOPRRTU rough-perfect
CEEFGIILNOPW fowling-piece
CEEFGIILNRTY electrifying
CEEFGIILNSTX self-exciting
CEEFGILLNRTY reflectingly
CEEFGILNNOTU genuflection
CEEFGILNNRTU unreflecting
CEEFGLLLNTUY neglectfully
CEEFGLORSTTU frog's lettuce
CEEFHHJLNORT John Fletcher
CEEFHIIKLMNO Michel Fokine
CEEFHIILMRRS firmer chisel
CEEFHLLNRUUY uncheerfully
CEEFHLNORRRS French sorrel
CEEFIIKLNORS flicker noise
CEEFIILNORRT irreflection
CEEFIILRTTVY reflectivity
CEEFIIMNOPRT imperfection
CEEFIINOPRST frontispiece
CEEFIJLNORTU fuel injector
CEEFIKKLNPRU kupfernickel
CEEFILMNRSSU mercifulness
CEEFILNNOORT on reflection
CEEFILNNORRW Colin Renfrew
CEEFILNOSSUV voicefulness
CEEFILNOSUVY veneficously
CEEFIMNOOPRY price of money
CEEFINNOPRTU unperfection
CEEFINOOPRTT to perfection
CEEFINOPRRTT profit centre
CEEFIOORSTUV out of service
CEEFLLPRSTUY respectfully
CEEFLMNOPSTT self-contempt
CEEFLNOORRTZ Lorentz force
CEEFLNOQRUWY low frequency
CEEFMOORRRTU recomforture
CEEFNOORSSSS confessoress
CEEGGHLNOOUZ cough lozenge
CEEGGIILNNPS gene splicing
CEEGGIKLLNOS King's College
CEEGGILLNNTY neglectingly
CEEGGILNOSSY glycogenesis
CEEGHIINORTZ rhizogenetic
CEEGHIINOSTT histogenetic
CEEGHILNOPTY phylogenetic
CEEGHILOOPRT herpetologic
CEEGHIMORSTY geochemistry
CEEGHINNOPTY hypnogenetic
CEEGHINOORTT orthogenetic
CEEGHINOPRSS sheep-scoring
CEEGHINOPTTY phytogenetic
CEEGHINORSTY hysterogenic
CEEGHINORTUW counter-weigh
CEEGHINPRSTU Peter Cushing
CEEGHKNORSTT G K Chesterton
CEEGHKOOPPRT pocket gopher
CEEGHMNNOOSU hoc genus omne
CEEGIIKLNSTW single-wicket
CEEGIILLNPRS selling-price
CEEGIINNORTT reciting-note
CEEGIINNPRSS piercingness
CEEGIINNSSTX excitingness
CEEGIINOPRTV precognitive
CEEGIKKNNOOR knee-crooking
CEEGIKLLNOPS glockenspiel
CEEGIKLNPTTU putting-cleek

CEEGILLNNNOR Lincoln green
CEEGILMOOORT meteorologic
CEEGILNNOORS corno inglese
CEEGINNOOSTT ontogenetics
CEEGINOORRVV vice-governor
CEEGINOPRRSS reprocessing
CEEGINOPRSSW Weeping Cross
weeping-cross
CEEGMNOORRST costermonger
CEEHHHJLNORS John Herschel
CEEHHIILLLNP philhellenic
CEEHHIILOPRS heliospheric
CEEHHIINOSTT henotheistic
CEEHHIMMOORT homeothermic
CEEHHINOPRST christophene
CEEHHINOPRSZ schizophrene
CEEHHINPRSTY hypersthenic
CEEHHLOORSST clothes-horse
CEEHHMNNORTY nychthemeron
CEEHHMOOPRRS chromosphere
CEEHHNOORRTY heterochrony
CEEHHOOPPRSS phosphoresce
CEEHHOOPRRST trochosphere
CEEHIIILLNOR Lionel Richie
CEEHIIKNPRTY hyperkinetic
CEEHIILLNPRS spine-chiller
CEEHIILNNSTT Lichtenstein
CEEHIINOOTVW with one voice
CEEHIINPPRST prenticeship
'prenticeship
CEEHIINPRTTU in the picture
CEEHIIOPRRSS perichoresis
CEEHIIPPRRST peristrephic
CEEHIJKNNOTU technojunkie
CEEHIKKLNTUW white-knuckle
CEEHIKLSTTTT kettlestitch
CEEHIKMNOSSS homesickness
CEEHIKOOPRSU cookie-pusher
CEEHILLOPRTV trophic level
CEEHILMMOPRY myrmecophile
CEEHILMNOOTT monotheletic✧
CEEHILMNOPRS chrome spinel
CEEHILMOSSTT Themistocles
CEEHILNNORTY incoherently
CEEHILNPPRSU pencil-pusher
CEEHIMMORRTT thermometric
CEEHIMMPRSST sprechstimme
CEEHIMNNNRTT intrenchment
CEEHIMNOOSTT The Economist
CEEHIMNOOSTU home counties
CEEHIMNOOSTY homocysteine
CEEHIMNPRRTY cypermethrin
CEEHINOOPRST stereophonic
CEEHINOORRSS rhinoceroses
CEEHINOORRST rhinocerotes
CEEHINOPPRTU Picturephone®
CEEHINOPSTTU theopneustic
CEEHINORSTTZ zenith sector
CEEHINRRRTWY winter cherry
CEEHIOOPRSTU Oreopithecus
CEEHIOPRSTUU picture house
CEEHIOPRSTUX executorship
CEEHIPPRRTYY hyperpyretic
CEEHKKNNOORT on the knocker
CEEHKLLOORRY roller hockey
CEEHKMNNORWY monkey wrench
CEEHKNOORSTW know the score
CEEHLLMOORWY chrome yellow
CEEHLLNPRRUY Henry Purcell
CEEHLLNQSSUY quenchlessly
CEEHLMOOPRTU thermocouple
CEEHLMOPSTUY The Lucy Poems
CEEHLOPRSSST clothes-press
CEEHMOORRSTY stereochromy
CEEHMOPRRSTY psychrometer
CEEHMORSTTYY hysterectomy
CEEHNOOQRRTU the Conqueror
CEEHNOQRRTUW torque wrench
CEEHNORSSSTT technostress
CEEHNRRSTTUW turn the screw
CEEHOOPRRSTU urethroscope
CEEHOORRRSSU horse-courser
CEEIIIKPRRSS Rice Krispies®
CEEIIIMNPPRT impercipient
CEEIIINNPRTT intercipient
CEEIIINNSSSV incisiveness
CEEIIIOPPSST episcopise it
CEEIIIOPPSTZ episcopize it
CEEIIJNNORTT interjection
CEEIIJNORSTT rejectionist
CEEIIKKLLRST stickler-like
CEEIIKLLNRSV nickel silver
CEEIIKLORRTU courtierlike
CEEIIKRRTTTW ticket writer
CEEIILLMNOTT monticellite
CEEIILLMNPSX mill-sixpence
CEEIILLNNORT intercolline
CEEIILLNNOTT intellection
CEEIILLNORVV live in clover
CEEIILLRRUUW curliewurlie
CEEIILMNNORT inclinometer
CEEIILMPRSST plessimetric
CEEIILNNPRSS princeliness
princess line
CEEIILNOSSTT selectionist
CEEIILNPSSTX explicitness
CEEIILOOPSSU leucopoiesis
CEEIIMMORSST seismometric
CEEIIMNNPRTY impertinency
CEEIIMNOORRT meteoric iron
CEEIIMNOPRSS mission creep
CEEIIMNOSSSS secessionism
CEEIIMNOSTTU cementitious
CEEIIMOPPRTT micropipette
CEEIIMOPRSSU semi-precious
CEEIIMORRSTU meretricious
CEEIIMORSSTV viscosimeter
CEEIINNNNOTV inconvenient
CEEIINNOPRST reinspection
CEEIINNOPRTT interception
CEEIINNORSST intercession
CEEIINNORSTT intersection

CEEIINNSSTTW New Scientist
CEEIINOPRRST peristeronic
CEEIINOPRSTT receptionist
CEEIINORSSUX excursionise
CEEIINORSUXZ excursionize
CEEIINOSSSST secessionist
CEEIINPSSTUV insusceptive
CEEIIPPRRSTV prescriptive
CEEIIPPRTTVY perceptivity
CEEIJKLLNPRU Purkinje cell
CEEIJNOORRTT retrojection
CEEIJNORRTTY interjectory
CEEIKLMNPPRU pumpernickel
CEEIKLNORSSS session-clerk
CEEIKLNORSTV love-stricken
CEEIKLNOSSSV lovesickness
CEEIKMNOORYY Mickey Rooney
CEEIKNNOOPST in one's pocket
CEEIKNNORSTV Kevin Costner
CEEIKNRRTTTU return ticket
CEEIKOPRRTTT ticket porter
CEEILLLORSST Sertoli cells
CEEILLMNOPTY incompletely
CEEILLNOPQUY equipollency
CEEILLOOPRSV pollice verso
CEEILLOPPSTU pull to pieces
CEEILLORSSTY electrolysis
CEEILLPRSUVY preclusively
CEEILMMNOPRT complimenter
CEEILMNNNOOS insomnolence
CEEILMNNOSSU uncomeliness
CEEILMOOPRSY co-polymerise
CEEILMOOPRYZ co-polymerize
CEEILMOOSTTU cole titmouse
CEEILMRRTUUV vermiculture
CEEILNNNOTVY conveniently
CEEILNNOPPTY plenipotency
CEEILNNPSSTU spinulescent
CEEILNOOPRSS necropolises
CEEILNORRTVW winter clover
CEEILOOPRSTT coleopterist
CEEILOPRTTVY protectively
CEEILPRSSUVY percussively
CEEIMMMNORTT recommitment
CEEIMMNNORTU intercommune
CEEIMMNOORST commorientes
CEEIMMRSSTTY metric system
CEEIMNNORTTV contrivement
CEEIMNOOPRST contemporise
CEEIMNOOPRTY Rome, Open City
CEEIMNOOPRTZ contemporize
CEEIMNOORSTT econometrist
CEEIMNORRSTU Eurocentrism
CEEIMNORSUZZ mizzencourse
CEEIMOORRRST ecoterrorism
CEEINNNOORTV conventioner
CEEINNNOQSTU inconsequent
CEEINNOORRRT reconnoitrer
CEEINNOORRSV reconversion
CEEINNOPRTUY Courtney Pine
CEEINNORRTTV interconvert
CEEINNORSSTT contriteness
CEEINNPRTUUV venipuncture
CEEINNRRRTTU intercurrent
CEEINOOPRRSS processioner
CEEINOOPRRSV province rose
CEEINOOPRRTT interoceptor
CEEINOOPRSTT stereopticon
CEEINOOPRSTU counterpoise
CEEINOORRSST retrocession
CEEINOORRSVV cover version
CEEINOPRRSSU repercussion
CEEINOPRSSSU preciousness
CEEINOPSSSSU speciousness
CEEINORRRSTU resurrection✧
CEEINORRSSTY intercessory
CEEINORSTTTU reconstitute
CEEINPPRRRTU Prince Rupert
CEEIOOPRRSTT stereotropic
CEEIOORRRSTT ecoterrorist
CEEIOPRRTTTW write protect
write-protect
CEEKLLNSSSSU lucklessness
CEEKLLOORTWY yellow rocket
CEEKLNOOSTTY cytoskeleton
CEEKNNOOPSTU up to one's neck
CEEKNORRSUVW nervous wreck
CEEKOOPRRSSU pressure-cook
CEEKORSSTTTU trustee stock
CEELLNOOOOSS lose one's cool
CEELLNOORRTV control lever
CEELLNOORTTV electronvolt
CEELLORRSSUW Russell Crowe
CEELMMNOOOPP Common People
CEELMNNOOSST somnolescent
CEELMNOPRSUZ crumple zones
CEELMOOORRTT electromotor
CEELNNOORTTV control event
CEELNNOQSTUY consequently
CEELNOOPPTUY county-people
CEELNOORSTTU electrotonus
CEELNORSSSUU ulcerousness
CEELOOOPRSTU coleopterous
CEELOOPPRSTU plecopterous
CEELPPSSSUXY excess supply
CEELPRRSSTUU supercluster
CEEMMORRRSUU Correr Museum
CEEMOPRRSTTY spectrometry
CEEMOPRRSTUU Supreme Court
CEENNOOQRSTU queen consort
CEENNOORRTTU counter-tenor
CEENNORRTUVY never country✧
CEENOOOPPRSS snooperscope
CEENOOSSSTUV covetousness
CEENORSTTUUV Venture Scout
CEEOOPRRSTTU Puerto Cortes
CEEOPPRSSSTU prospectuses
CEFFGIKNNOOR off-reckoning
CEFFGILNOSSU self-focusing
CEFFHIJLNOWY John Wycliffe
CEFFHIKNSTTU kitchen-stuff
CEFFHIORRSTU sheriff court

CEFFHMNOOPSU off one's chump
CEFFIIINNSTU insufficient
CEFFIIJNOORU office junior
CEFFIILNSTUY sufficiently
CEFFIILOOPRT pilot officer
CEFFIINNSTUU unsufficient
CEFFIORRSTUU fructiferous
CEFFIORSSTUU suffruticose
CEFFMOOORSTW come off worst
CEFFNOOOORTT foot-ton force
CEFGHIMNOORT home-crofting
CEFGHINOORSU forcing-house
CEFGIIIKLNNR fingerlickin'
CEFGIIKLLNRY flickeringly
CEFGIILNOSTT close-fitting
CEFHHIIKNOTT in the thick of
CEFHHILNOPRS French polish
French-polish
CEFHIIMNSTWY chimney swift
CEFHILMNNOUY ichneumon fly
CEFHILOOSSTV chest of viols
CEFHIMOORSSU moschiferous
CEFHKLNNOORU fork luncheon
CEFHLLLOOOSW schoolfellow
CEFHLMOOORRR chloroformer
CEFHLMOOORRS reform school
CEFHLMOOORRU fluorochrome
CEFIIILNNSTT life instinct
CEFIIILNOSTU infelicitous
CEFIIILORSSU siliciferous
CEFIIIORRSTU Fourieristic
CEFIILLOSTUY felicitously
CEFIILMNNTUY munificently
CEFIILMORRTU fluorimetric
CEFIILNOPRSS prolificness
CEFIILNOPRTY proficiently
CEFIILNORSST frictionless
CEFIILNOSTUY infectiously
CEFIIMNOOTUZ Zeno of Citium
CEFIIOORSTVY vociferosity
CEFILLMNRUUY unmercifully
CEFILLMOORSY frolicsomely
CEFILLOORRTU colour filter
CEFILLORRTUU floriculture
CEFILMOORRTU fluorometric
CEFILNNOSSTU functionless
CEFILOORSUVY vociferously
CEFILOPRSUUU cupuliferous
CEFINNOPSTTU step function
CEFKKLOORRSW clerk of works
CEFKKLOORSTU stroke of luck
CEFLMORRSWWY screw-worm fly
CEFLNNORSSSU scornfulness
CEFLNOORRTUY counter-flory
CEFMNNNOORTT confrontment
CEFNOOOPRRTU counterproof
CEFNOOOTTTUX out of context
CEGGGHMOORRU Roger McGough
CEGGHILOSTTW toggle switch
CEGGHINNRTUW gut-wrenching
CEGGIIINNRSY icing syringe
CEGGIIMNOTVY gingivectomy
CEGHHIILOPRY hieroglyphic
CEGHHIILOTVY high-velocity
CEGHHILNOSTT nightclothes
CEGHHINOOPTT photo-etching
CEGHHLNOPRTU trench plough
CEGHHOORRSTU score through
CEGHIILNRSTT chitterlings
CEGHIIOPSSTY geophysicist
CEGHIJORSTUU rough justice
CEGHIKNNOSSS shockingness
CEGHIKNOORRS rocking horse
CEGHILNOOORS chronologise
CEGHILNOOORZ chronologize
CEGHILNOOSTT technologist
CEGHILNORRUY chirurgeonly
CEGHILNORTTU counterlight
CEGHILOOORST choreologist
CEGHILOOOSTY stoechiology
CEGHILOOPSSY psychologise
CEGHILOOPSYZ psychologize
CEGHILOPPRTY petroglyphic
CEGHIMORTUUX cough mixture
CEGHINNOORSU corning house
CEGHINNOSSTU touchingness
CEGHINORRTWY cringeworthy
CEGHMOOPPSSY sphygmoscope
CEGIIILLNPST still-piecing
CEGIIILNNORS corni inglesi
CEGIIKLLMNRY mercy killing
CEGIIKLLNQSU quick-selling
CEGIIKLNNORT interlocking
CEGIIKMNNORS misreckoning
CEGIIKNRRSTT trickstering
CEGIILLOOSTX lexicologist
CEGIILNNPSTY inspectingly
CEGIIMNNOOST monogenistic
CEGIINNOOPRT precognition
CEGIINOPTTYY genotypicity
CEGIJKNOSSTT jesting-stock
CEGIKLNNOSSU King's Counsel
CEGIKLNOOSST stocking-sole
CEGIKLNOSSST stockingless
CEGIKLNOSSUU sucking louse
CEGIKNNOORST rocking stone
CEGIKNOSTTTU get stuck into
CEGILLLMNOPY compellingly
CEGILLMOPTUX guilt complex
CEGILLNORSSS cross-selling
CEGILMMOOTUY etymologicum
CEGILMNOOOTY etymologicon
CEGILNNNOSTY consentingly
CEGILNNNOTTY contingently
CEGILNNOQRUY conqueringly
CEGILNNORSTU curling-stone
CEGILNNOSTTY contestingly
CEGILNOOORTW cooling tower
CEGILNOOPRTU glucoprotein
CEGILNOOPRTY glycoprotein
CEGILNOOSSTY synecologist
CEGILNOPRTTY protectingly

CEGILOPRSSSU pusser's logic
CEGIMNOOPRSY myringoscope
CEGIMNOORRSU microsurgeon
CEGIMNOORSTT come it strong
CEGIMORRRSUY microsurgery
CEGINNNNOSTU unconsenting
CEGINNNOORTW conning-tower
CEGINNNORSTT constringent
CEGINNOSTTTU stonecutting
CEGINNPSSTUU unsuspecting
CEGINOORRSSV crossing over
CEGINOPPRSSY copying press
CEGINORRSSTU string course
CEGINORRTTUY tiger country
CEGINPRSSTTU press cutting
CEGLMORSTUUY ugly customer
CEGLNOOOPPSS pop one's clogs
CEGMNNOOORST come on strong
CEGMOOSTUYYZ zygomycetous
CEHHIIJNORST John Christie
CEHHIILLOSTV Cheviot Hills
CEHHIILMOPRT thermophilic
CEHHIILOPRST lithospheric
CEHHIIMORRTU Chirotherium
CEHHIIMOSSTT histochemist
CEHHIINOPRST christophine
CEHHIIRSTTTW switch hitter
CEHHILNRSSSU churlishness
CEHHILOOPRTY hypochlorite
CEHHILORSTTT torch-thistle
CEHHIMMOOOPR homeomorphic
CEHHIMOOPSTT photochemist
CEHHIMOORRTY hormic theory
CEHHIOOPPRST photospheric
CEHHIOPPRRTY hypertrophic
CEHHLOORSSTT short clothes
CEHHOOORSTTW shoot the crow
CEHIIIKLSTTT Sittlichkeit
CEHIIIKRRSTT strike it rich
CEHIIILNOOPS eosinophilic
CEHIIJLLMNOT Joni Mitchell
CEHIIKLNSSST ticklishness
CEHIIKNRSSST trickishness
CEHIILLNNORS Lincolnshire
CEHIILLNNOTT centillionth
CEHIILMNOPRS necrophilism
CEHIILNOPRTU neutrophilic
CEHIILNQSSSU cliquishness
CEHIILNRSSST Christliness
CEHIILOORSTU leiotrichous
CEHIILOPSTTY polytheistic
CEHIIMNOOSTT monotheistic
CEHIIMNOPRUY perionychium
CEHIIMNSSTTY syntheticism
CEHIIMOORSTT trichotomise
CEHIIMOORTTZ trichotomize
CEHIIMOPPRST propheticism
CEHIINNOPRTY pericynthion
CEHIIOPRRSTU peritrichous
CEHIIOPRTTUW without price
CEHIJNNOORSS John Ericsson
CEHIKMOOPRSU skeuomorphic
CEHILLNNOPSU Punchinellos
CEHILLNNORSU unicorn-shell
CEHILLOPPTYY polyphyletic
CEHILMMNOSTT Mont-St-Michel
CEHILMMOPRYY myrmecophily
CEHILMNOOPTY monophyletic
CEHILMNOPPTY nympholeptic
CEHILNNOSSSW clownishness
CEHILNOOPRSU necrophilous
CEHILNOPSSST splotchiness
CEHILOQSTTUY coquettishly
CEHILORRTTUU horticulture
CEHIMMOOPRST chemotropism
CEHIMNORRTYY erythromycin
CEHIMOOPRRTT thermotropic
CEHIMOORSTYZ zoochemistry
CEHIMOPPRSTY spermophytic
CEHINNORRSSY synchroniser
CEHINNORRSYZ synchronizer
CEHINOOPRRTU neurotrophic
CEHINOPRSTTY pyrotechnist
CEHINOQSTTUU uncoquettish
CEHINOSSSSTT Scottishness
CEHIOOPPRRST tropospheric
CEHIOOPRRSTU chiropterous
CEHIOOPRRTTT tithe-proctor
CEHIOPPRSSTY petrophysics
CEHJMNNNOOSU John Comnenus
CEHJNOOPRSTT John Prescott
CEHKKLOSUVYY Klyuchevskoy
CEHKLNOPSSUU push one's luck
CEHLLLOPRSYY sclerophylly
CEHLMMOORSSU summer school
CEHLMMOOSSTU smooth muscle
CEHLMNOORSSY Myron Scholes
CEHLOOOOPPST scoop the pool
CEHMOOOOPRTY oophorectomy
CEHMOOPRSTTU host computer
CEHMOOSSSTUU customs house
CEHMOPRRSTYY psychrometry
CEHNOOOPRRSU necrophorous
CEHNOOPRRTTU photocurrent
CEHNOORSTUUY country house
CEHOOOPPRSST photo-process
CEHOOPRRSTUY urethroscopy
CEIIIIILNSTV incivilities
CEIIILLMRTUV verticillium
CEIIILLNPTXY inexplicitly
CEIIILMNPSST implicitness
CEIIINNORSTU reunionistic
CEIIINOPRSST precisionist
CEIIINORTTWZ zwitterionic
CEIIJLNNTUVY injunctively
CEIIJNNOORTT introjection
CEIIJOPRTTVY projectivity
CEIIKKLMNSSS milk sickness
CEIIKLLNOPSS lick one's lips
CEIIKLLPSTTY lickety-split
CEIIKLQRSUVY quicksilvery
CEIIKLSSTWZZ swizzle-stick

CEIIKRRSSTUY security risk
CEIILLNOSTUY licentiously
CEIILLRSTUUV silviculture
CEIILMNNOOPT incompletion
CEIILMNNOSTY omnisciently
CEIILMNOSSUX exclusionism
CEIILMOPRTUV pluviometric
CEIILNNORSTU interclusion
CEIILNOOSTTU elocutionist
CEIILNOPRSUY perniciously
CEIILNOSSSTU seclusionist
CEIILNOSSTUX exclusionist
CEIILOPRSSUU supercilious
CEIIMMNOORSS commissioner
recommission
CEIIMMNOPRTU minicomputer
CEIIMNNNOTTZ zinc ointment
CEIIMOORSSTT sociometrist
CEIIMORSSTVY viscosimetry
CEIINNNORSTU internuncios
CEIINNNOSSTT inconsistent
CEIINNORRSTU insurrection
CEIINOOORRRV River Orinoco
CEIINOOPRRTY incorporeity
CEIINOPPRRST prescription
CEIINOPRRSTT prestriction
CEIINOPRRTUV incorruptive
CEIINORSSTUX excursionist
CEIINOSTTTUV constitutive
CEIIOPPRRSTV proscriptive
CEIIPRRRSTTW scriptwriter
CEIIPSSTTUVY susceptivity
CEIJKKLNNOTU knuckle joint
CEIJLOOPPRTT pilot project
CEIKKMNORSTY monkey tricks
CEIKLLORSTUY kill-courtesy
CEIKLOOPPSTT pocket-pistol
CEIKLOOSSTUY leukocytosis
CEIKLOPPRSSS slipper socks
CEIKMNNOORST moon-stricken
CEILLLNOOOSV violoncellos
CEILLMMMNOOT common millet
CEILLMOPSUVY compulsively
CEILLMOSTUUY meticulously
CEILLNOPRSSU curl one's lips
CEILLNOSUVVY convulsively
CEILLRSTUUVY sylviculture
CEILMNOOSTTY tonsilectomy
CEILMNOOSTUU contumelious
CEILNNOOORST noise control
CEILNNOSSTTY consistently
CEILNOORRTTU interlocutor
CEILNOORSSUY censoriously
CEILNOSSSSUU lusciousness
CEILNOSSTUUY incestuously
CEILOOORSSST otosclerosis
CEILOOPQRTUY pectoriloquy
CEILOOSSSSUW colossus-wise
CEIMMNOOPSST compos mentis
CEIMNNOOPRSU mispronounce
CEIMNNOORSTU conterminous
CEIMNOPRSTTY streptomycin
CEIMNOPSSTUY pneumocystis
CEIMOOPRRSTU micropterous
CEINNOOORRSV non-corrosive
CEINNOOPRTTU counterpoint
CEINNOORSSUU uncensorious
CEINNORSSTWW crown witness
CEINORRSSTUU run its course
CEINPSSSTTUU intussuscept
CEINRRSSSTTU instructress
CEIOOOPRSTT osteoporotic
CEIOPPPRRSTU price support
CEIOPRRSSTUU Sciuropterus
CEKORRRRSTTU terror-struck
CELLLOORSSUY colourlessly
CELMMNOOORRS common sorrel
CELMNOPRTUUU mucopurulent
CELMOPRSTUUU corpus luteum
CELNOOORRSTV servocontrol
CELNOOORRTTW control tower
CELOPRRSSTYY cross-ply tyre
CEMMNNNOOSSU uncommonness
CEMMNOORSTVY common vestry
CEMMOPPRSTUU come up trumps
CEMNOOORRVWY worm conveyor
CEMNOOPSTTUU contemptuous
CEMOOOORRSTT motor scooter
CENNOSSSTUUU unctuousness
CEOOPPRRSSSU cross-purpose
CFFGIIIOORRS frigorificos
CFFGINOORSSU offscourings
CFFHKLNOPSUU Suffolk punch
CFGHHIKLORTU flick through
CFGIILNOOSTV cost of living
CFGIKNOOOSTT stocking-foot
CFGILLMNNOUY flying column
CFGILMNOORTY comfortingly
CFGIMNNNOORU unconforming
CFHHHHLOORTU Rolf Hochhuth
CFHIINOOPRSS scorpion fish
CFIIILOSTTUY fictitiously
CFIILLNOOSTU solifluction
CFIIMMNOORST Cominformist
CFIIRRSSTTUU citrus fruits
CFIKNNOORTUW work function
CFILNORSSUUU furunculosis
CFIMNNOORTUY unconformity
CFIOORRSTUUV fructivorous
CGGHHIIIKNST high-sticking
CGGHHINOOOPU hooping cough
hooping-cough
CGGIINNOPRSW springing cow
CGGILNNORSTU curling tongs
CGHHIILLNORT rolling hitch
CGHHIINOPSTT hitching post
CGHHIINORTUW witching hour
CGHHILOOPPTY photoglyphic
CGHIIKKNNOPS shocking pink
CGHIIKNNOSSU king's-cushion
CGHIILNOOPTT pitching tool
CGHIILOOOPRT oligotrophic

CGHIILOOOSTY stoichiology
CGHIILOORSTT trichologist
CGHIIMNOOPSY physiognomic
CGHIIMOOPRTT thigmotropic
CGHIJKLNNOSU John Suckling
CGHIKKNNOOPS knocking shop
knocking-shop
CGHIKLNNORUW working lunch
CGHILLNOOPST slop-clothing
CGHILMOOPSSY psychologism
CGHILNOOORST chronologist
CGHILOOPSSTY psychologist
CGHINNOPSSTY post-synching
CGHINOOOPPTY photocopying
CGHINOOOSSUZ schizogonous
CGHINORRSSUU scouring rush
scouring-rush
CGIIIILNNOOT ignition coil
CGIIIMNNOPRR crimping-iron
CGIIIMNOSSTY misogynistic
CGIIINNRSSTU scrutinising
CGIIINNRSTUZ scrutinizing
CGIIKLNNORSS cross-linking
CGIIKNRSSSTU kissing-crust
CGIILMOOSSTU musicologist
CGIILNNOPRSY conspiringly
CGIILNNORRSU curling irons
CGIILOOOSTTX toxicologist
CGIINNOOSTUU incontiguous
CGIKLLNOORST rolling stock
CGIKNOOPRRST king's proctor✧
CGILLNOOOPRT protocolling
CGILMNNNOOPY non-complying
CGILMNOOPSSU gossip column
CGILNOOOPSSU spongicolous
CGILNOOSTUUY contiguously
CGILOOOPRSTT proctologist
CGILOOPRSTTY cryptologist
CGIMNNOOORTU counting room
CGINNNORSSTU running costs
CGINOOPRRTUX Prix Goncourt
CGINOOPRSSTY pyrognostics
CGLNOOOPRRTU control group
CHHIIMOOOPPR ophiomorphic
CHHILMOPRTYY polyrhythmic
CHHIMOOOPRRT orthomorphic
CHHINOOPRTTY trichophyton
CHHINORRSSTT Christ's-thorn
CHHIOOOPPRTT phototrophic
CHHMMOOOORSU homochromous
CHIIILMNOOPS iconophilism
CHIIILNOOPST iconophilist
CHIIILOOPTTX toxophilitic
CHIIILOPRTTT lithotriptic
CHIIKLNNOSSU insulin shock
CHIILMOPRSTU Turcophilism
CHIILNOOPRTY Trichinopoly
CHIILOOPRSTY polyhistoric
CHIIMNNRSSTY strychninism
CHIIMNOOPSTY monophysitic✧
CHIINOOOPSTT opisthotonic
CHIINOOPPRSW whip scorpion
CHIINOORSTTZ chorizontist
CHIINOPSSTUV viscountship
CHIJLNOOORSU junior school
CHIKNOPSSTTU stockpunisht
CHILOOOPPRSU coprophilous
CHIMMMNOOPRS common shrimp
CHIMMNOOORST monochromist
CHIMNOOOPRST monostrophic
CHIMNOOOSSTU monostichous
CHIMNOPRSTYY chymotrypsin
CHIMOOOPPRRT morphotropic
protomorphic
CHIMOOORSTTU trichotomous
CHINOOOPRSTY ornithoscopy
CHINOOPPSTTY post-hypnotic
CHIOOOPPRRTT prototrophic
trophotropic
CHIOOORSSSTT scissor-tooth
CHKLMOOPRTUY Plymouth Rock
CHKMNORSSTUU custom-shrunk
CHKOORRRRSTU horror-struck
CHMMNOOORSST short commons
CHNNOORRTTUY north-country
CIIIIIMNOSTU inimicitious
CIIIIOPSSTTV positivistic
CIIILLMPTTUY multiplicity
CIIIMMNNOOSS in commission
CIIINOOPPSST isotopic spin
CIIJLLNNOOTW conjoint will
CIIKLRTTTUUY utility truck
CIILLOOSSTUY solicitously
CIILMNNORSUY synclinorium
CIILMNOOOPST monopolistic
CIILMOOOTTVY locomotivity
CIILNOOSSTUU unsolicitous
CIILOORSTUVY victoriously
CIILOPSSSUUY suspiciously
CIIMNOPRSTTY nyctitropism
CIINNOOPRRTU incorruption
CIINNOOSTTTU constitution
CIINNORSSTTU instructions
CIINOOPPRRST proscription
CIINOPSSSUUU unsuspicious
CIJLNORSSTUU jurisconsult
CIJMMNNOORSY Jimmy Connors
CIKLOPPPPRYY prickly poppy
CILLMOOPRSUY compulsorily
CILLORRSSUUY scurrilously
CILNNOOSTUUY continuously
CILNORSSTUUY scrutinously
CILOPRSSTUUY scrupulosity
CIMMNNNNOOOU non-communion
CIMNNOOSSTUU customs union
CLLOPRSSUUUY scrupulously
CLNOOOSTTTUY Count Tolstoy
CLNOPRSSUUUU unscrupulous
CMNOOPRSTUYY cryptonymous

D

DDDDEEILLNNO niddle-noddle

Words marked ✧ can also be spelled with one or more capital letters

DDDEEEEFNNOS se defendendo
DDDEEENRRSSU underdressed
DDDEEFHILRSU Huddersfield
DDDEEGINORWW wedding dower
DDDEEGINRSSW wedding dress
DDDEEIIIMPSY epididymides
DDDEEIINORST Denis Diderot
DDDEEINORRSU undisordered
DDDEEINOSTTW sodden-witted
DDDEELMMTTUY muddy-mettled
DDDEGGHINOPU hodge-pudding
DDDEGHINOOSW woodshedding
DDDEGILMNORU middle ground
DDDEHHLNORTU Old Hundredth
DDDEHNNOOORR rhododendron
DDDEIIIKRSTV divided skirt
DDDEIIKLNTWY tiddledywink
DDDGILMNOPUU pudding mould
DDEEEEFHNRTT tender-hefted
DDEEEELLRSVW well-deserved
DDEEEEMNNSST dementedness
DDEEEENRSSSV deservedness
DDEEEFGNORRU ground-feeder
DDEEEFILOOTU folie de doute
DDEEEFMMMNOU femme du monde
DDEEEFMNORSS deformedness
DDEEEGGILPRS spider-legged
DDEEEGGILRST stridelegged
DDEEEGGLLNNO Golden Legend
DDEEEGGNORSS Green Goddess
DDEEEGMOOPRT good-tempered
DDEEEGNRSSTU get undressed
DDEEEHIILLNS shielded line
DDEEEIIMNNRT indetermined
DDEEEIKNRTWY dirty weekend
DDEEEILLMMPT Middle Temple
DDEEEILMNRRT intermeddler
DDEEEILMNRTY determinedly
DDEEEIMNNRTU undetermined
DDEEEINNOSSS one-sidedness
DDEEEINPSSSS despisedness
DDEEELLMMOSY meddlesomely
DDEEELNOPPRU underpeopled
DDEEELNOPRRT Old Pretender
DDEEELNOPRUV underdevelop
DDEEELNRSUVY undeservedly
DDEEENOPRRUW underpowered
DDEEENORSUVZ rendezvoused
DDEEEOPRRSSW power-dressed
DDEEEORRRSVW reserved word
DDEEFFGLLLUY fully-fledged
DDEEFFHILOPT depth of field
DDEEFFIIILNU unified field
DDEEFFINSSSU diffusedness
DDEEFGLORRRU flour dredger
DDEEFHHILLOT hold the field
DDEEFHIIIMRU dehumidifier
DDEEFIIINNTU unidentified
DDEEFIIKLLMO Mike Oldfield
DDEEFIIKLLSS self-disliked
DDEEFILLORSU Rudolf Diesel
DDEEGGHHOOOW wood hedgehog
DDEEGGINRRSU designer drug
DDEEGHIILMTW middleweight
DDEEGIILMNNS single-minded
DDEEGILMNOST dislodgement
DDEEGILNNSUY undesignedly
DDEEGINNNPWY penny-wedding
DDEEGINORSST droit des gens
DDEEGLLNORUW well-grounded
DDEEGNOORRTX Dexter Gordon
DDEEHHOPRRSS shepherd's rod
DDEEHILLOSTV The Old Devils
DDEEHIMNOSTU unmethodised
DDEEHIMNOTUZ unmethodized
DDEEHINRRTUV thunder-drive
DDEEHLNORSTW the world's end
DDEEHMMMNOOU homme du monde
DDEEHNOPRSTU depth sounder
DDEEIIIIKKNW kiddiewinkie
DDEEIIILORSV silver iodide
DDEEIILLMNVY evil-mindedly
DDEEIILMMNPS simple-minded
DDEEIIMNNOSU diminuendoes
DDEEIINPRRST priest-ridden
DDEEIKNNRRUW wunderkinder
DDEEILLOPSSW well-disposed
DDEEILMMNOTY motley-minded
DDEEILMNNOPY open-mindedly
DDEEILNNPSSS splendidness
DDEEILNOPSSS lopsidedness
DDEEILNSTUVY undivestedly
DDEEIMNNORSU unmodernised
DDEEIMNNORUZ unmodernized
DDEEIMNNOSTW disendowment
DDEEINNRRSUU underinsured
DDEEINOSSSTW two-sidedness
DDEEIOPSSSSS dispossessed
DDEELNNOPSTY despondently
DDEEMNOOSSTU outmodedness
DDEEOOPRRSVW Dover's powder
DDEFGHILLOOT floodlighted
DDEFGHOOORTW the Word of God
DDEFGIILNRST fiddle-string
DDEFGIMNRSUU Sigmund Freud
DDEFGINNNRUU underfunding
DDEFINOOPSSU undisposed-of
DDEGHIINPTUW white pudding
DDEGHILNRSUY shudderingly
DDEGHMOOORUU good-humoured
DDEGIINRSSTU Sigrid Undset
DDEGIKLLOSTU like gold dust
DDEGIKMNNORU underkingdom
DDEGILLNNOWY long-windedly
DDEGILNNOPSY despondingly
DDEGILNOORST dendrologist
DDEGIMNNORST strong-minded
DDEGINNNORUU ungrounded in
DDEGINNOPSTU pudding-stone
DDEGINNORSSW dressing-down
DDEGLNNORUUY ungroundedly
DDEGLNOOORSU dendrologous

DDEHHMORTTTY dotted rhythm
DDEHHOOSSTTU shout the odds
DDEHIIIMNNSU undiminished
DDEHILNNOOPR philodendron✧
DDEHILORRRTW Third-Worlder
DDEHINOORSTU ride to hounds
DDEHMMNOOTUV venom'd-mouth'd
DDEHMNOORTUU round-mouthed
DDEIIILPRSTY dispiritedly
DDEIIJLNOSTY disjointedly
DDEIILNNOORR liriodendron
DDEIILNOORRS Lord Ironside
DDEIILNOPSSU splendidious
DDEIIMNOSUVV modus vivendi
DDEILLMNOOWY woolly-minded
DDEILMNNOSUW Edmund Wilson
DDEILNOPRUVY unprovidedly
DDEILNPSTUUY undisputedly
DDEIMNOORRWW dormer window
DDEIMOOPPSUU pseudopodium
DDEINNORSTUW sit down under
DDEINOPPRSTW stripped-down
DDFGGGIINPUY figgy pudding
DDGHILMNOOOU hood-moulding
DDGHILMOOTWY Dwight L Moody
DDGIIIKNNRRV drink-driving
DDGIIKNNRRUV drunk-driving
DDIIIMPRTTUY rumpti-iddity
DDILMNOOUUWY would you mind?
DEEEEEGHLNTT get the needle
DEEEEEMNPRTV even-tempered
DEEEEFFILRRT filter-feeder
DEEEEFHIKLPT keep the field
DEEEEGGINORV George Devine
DEEEEGGNRRSU gens de guerre
DEEEEGIILNNS diesel engine
DEEEEGIKLNRV degree Kelvin
DEEEEGMNNNRT engenderment
DEEEEGRRRSUU ruse de guerre
DEEEEHHLNRTU under the heel
DEEEEHIKLNTT kitten-heeled
DEEEEHIMNOTV eventide home
DEEEEHLNNORT Heldentenöre
DEEEEHLNSSSS heedlessness
DEEEEILMPRTV evil-tempered
DEEEEILNNPTT lite pendente
pendente lite
DEEEEIMNPRRT predetermine
DEEEEIMNPRTX experimented
DEEEELLMPRTW well-tempered
DEEEELNNSSSS needlessness
DEEEENRRRVVY Very Reverend
DEEEENRRSSSV reservedness
DEEEFFINNOST find one's feet
DEEEFGIILMNT field meeting
DEEEFGIINSSU feigned issue
DEEEFGINRRYZ freeze-drying
DEEEFHILNNOT end of the line
DEEEFIINNSST definiteness
DEEEFILNOPRS pride oneself
DEEEFINPRRSU superrefined
DEEEFINRRTTT interfretted
DEEEFJLORTTU Letter of Jude
DEEEFLLMOPSY self-employed
DEEEFLMRRRSU self-murderer
DEEEFNNQRTUU unfrequented
DEEEFOPRSTTV spotted fever
DEEEGHILNPRS spring-heeled
DEEEGHIMMRRT hedge trimmer
DEEEGHIORTVW over-weighted
DEEEGHKLNOTW the knowledge
DEEEGIINNRRV engine-driver
DEEEGIKLNNNY Nigel Kennedy
DEEEGIKMOOPT keep good time
DEEEGIKNNNOY donkey-engine
DEEEGIMNNRTU unregimented
DEEEGINNNRTU engine-turned
DEEEGINNOOTV Ode to Evening
DEEEGINNRSSS resignedness
DEEEGINNRSSV evening dress
DEEEGINRRSTU unregistered
DEEEGJMNPRTU prejudgement
DEEEGLLMNOPT Golden Temple
DEEEGNNOPRRS gender person
DEEEGOOPPSST goose-stepped
DEEEHHILRTTY diethyl ether
DEEEHHIORSTT the other side
DEEEHHIPPRSS shepherd's pie
DEEEHHLPRSSS shepherdless
DEEEHHNRSTTU thunder sheet
DEEEHIIKLLTV like the devil
DEEEHIILRTVW white-livered
DEEEHILLLOTV hôtel de ville
DEEEHILMNSTV dishevelment
DEEEHILNSSTW swindle-sheet
DEEEHILPRTTT Pitt the Elder
DEEEHILRSSTV shirtsleeved
DEEEHINRRTUW under the wire
DEEEHINRSSTW witheredness
DEEEHISSTUWY Eyes Wide Shut
DEEEHKLLORTT kettle-holder
DEEEHLNNORST Heldentenors
DEEEHLOPRTUX heteroduplex
DEEEHLORSTTY heterostyled
DEEEHLRRSSSW Welsh dresser
DEEEHMNNORTT dethronement
DEEEHMOPPPRT peppered moth
DEEEHNOPRRTU three-pounder
DEEEHNORRSTU under the rose
DEEEHOOSTTTW sweet-toothed
DEEEIILLLNNS Dennis Lillee
DEEEIILPPRVY delivery-pipe
DEEEIINPRRRV River Dnieper
DEEEIINRSSST desensitiser
DEEEIINRSSSV derisiveness
DEEEIINRSSTZ desensitizer
DEEEILLMRSSY remedilessly
DEEEILLNRUVY unrelievedly
DEEEILMOPRSY depolymerise
DEEEILMOPRYZ depolymerize
DEEEILMPRTVY redemptively
DEEEILNORTVY delivery note

DEEEILNRSTTY interestedly
DEEEILNSSSUV delusiveness
DEEEILRRSSTV reserved list
DEEEIMNNOPST semideponent
DEEEIMNOORRV domineer over
DEEEIMNOPRRT redemptioner
DEEEIMNOPSTT monts-de-piété
DEEEIMNORRSS reindeer moss
DEEEIMNORSTT densitometer
DEEEIMNRRSTW Midwesterner
DEEEIMNRSSTV disseverment
DEEEIMPRRTTT pretermitted
DEEEINNOPRST pre-tensioned
DEEEINNRSTTU uninterested
DEEEINOPPRTU neuropeptide
DEEEINOPRRSS derepression
DEEEINORSTVW Stevie Wonder
DEEEINPRSSST presidentess
DEEEINPRSTUV superevident
DEEEINRSSTTU entertissued
DEEEIPRRSSSU depressurise
DEEEIPRRSSUZ depressurize
DEEEJLLOPPRT jet-propelled
DEEEKLNNOOST endoskeleton
DEEEKNOOPRSW keep one's word
DEEELLOPSUUX poules de luxe
DEEELMNOPRTY redeployment
DEEELNORSSSV resolvedness
DEEELNRRSUVY unreservedly
DEEEMMNOORST endosmometer
DEEEMNORRSTV Most Reverend
DEEENNORRTTW Donnerwetter
DEEENOPRRTUW reputed owner
DEEENORRSSST stone dresser
DEEENORSSUVZ rendezvouses
DEEEOPPRSSSS prepossessed
DEEFFGORRSUU ruffed grouse
DEEFFHINRRSU undersheriff
under-sheriff
DEEFFHIORSUY four-eyed fish
DEEFFHOOORRT of the order of
DEEFFIILNRRY friendly fire
DEEFFJLORRSY Lord Jeffreys
DEEFGGILLOOY field geology
DEEFGHINNRTU unfrightened
DEEFGIIKNNRR knife-grinder
DEEFGIILNNOS dig oneself in
DEEFGIINNOPT feeding point
DEEFGIKORTTY Kitty Godfree
DEEFGILNNOSS find one's legs
DEEFGINNORWZ freezing-down
DEEFGINORRSY rosy-fingered
DEEFGJMNORTU forejudgment
DEEFHIIIMNSS semi-finished
DEEFHIINNSSS fiendishness
DEEFHIINORSV overfinished
DEEFHILORRSY Sir Fred Hoyle
DEEFHINORTTW white-fronted
DEEFHIOPRTVY typhoid fever
DEEFHJKNNNOY John F Kennedy
DEEFHJLNNOOY John of Leyden
DEEFIIIKLLRW like wildfire
DEEFIIILNNTY indefinitely
DEEFIIILNTVY definitively
DEEFIIINNORT redefinition
DEEFIILNNRSS friendliness
DEEFIILNOORR indoor relief
DEEFIILNRSTU unfertilised
DEEFIILNRTUZ unfertilized
DEEFIILNSTTY self-identity
DEEFIILPPRTT filter-tipped
DEEFIIOPRSST dies profesti
DEEFIIPRRTVY perfervidity
DEEFILLMNORW well-informed
DEEFILLNOSSU self-delusion
DEEFILLNOSVV self-involved
DEEFILLPSTUY despitefully
DEEFILNOOSTV self-devotion
DEEFILNPRSSU pridefulness
DEEFILNRRSUY user-friendly
DEEFILOPRRSW spider flower
DEEFILOPRSTT potter's field
DEEFIMOORRRT order of merit✧
DEEFINNSSTTU unfittedness
DEEFINORRSTW Edwin Forrest
DEEFLOORSTUY surefootedly
DEEFMNOPRRRU underperform
DEEFNNOORSSV overfondness
DEEGGIKRRSSU Greg Rusedski
DEEGGIMNORST disgorgement
DEEGGINNORTU teeing ground
DEEGGINNOSTW weeding-tongs
DEEGGLMOORRS Lord Rees-Mogg
DEEGHHIKNRTT The Red Knight
DEEGHHILNPRS shepherdling
DEEGHHINNOTT the done thing
DEEGHHLOORTT hold together
DEEGHIILLNSV dishevelling
DEEGHIILNRVW driving wheel
DEEGHIINNSTW winding sheet
DEEGHILLLPTW well-plighted
DEEGHILMOSTU douse the glim
DEEGHILOOTTV go to the devil
DEEGHINOORTT go into the red
DEEGHINPTTUW get the wind up
DEEGHNNOOTUY honey-tongued
DEEGIIILPRSV disprivilege
DEEGIIINRSVW ringside view
DEEGIILLLNPW pile-dwelling
DEEGIILMOOPY epidemiology
DEEGIILNNSSY yieldingness
DEEGIILNOPSS diplogenesis
DEEGIILNPRTV diving petrel
DEEGIILNPRUV unprivileged
DEEGIILOOPPT oligopeptide
DEEGIILRSSVY digressively
DEEGIILSSSSU disguiseless
DEEGIIMNSSTU disguisement
DEEGIINOPRST predigestion
DEEGIINPRSTW Speedwriting®
DEEGIINRRSTW wire-stringed
DEEGIJMMNSTU misjudgement

DEEGIKLMNOSW misknowledge
DEEGILLLMNOR Golden Miller
DEEGILLLNORV levelling-rod
DEEGILLNOOOR golden oriole
DEEGILLNRSSW well dressing
DEEGILMNNNOY moneylending
DEEGILMNOOOY Mongoloid eye
DEEGILNNPRTY pretendingly
DEEGILNNRSTU Guildenstern
DEEGILNNRTTU underletting
DEEGILNOPRRV ringed plover
DEEGILNORRTT ring dotterel
DEEGILNPRSSY depressingly
DEEGILNRSSTW West End Girls
DEEGILNRSSUV Venus's girdle
DEEGINNNNSSU unendingness
DEEGINNNPRTU unpretending
DEEGINNNRSTU nurse-tending
DEEGINNRSTTT trendsetting
DEEGINOORSVW give one's word
DEEGLLNOOPRV golden plover
DEEGLLOOSTYY dysteleology
DEEGLNNOOSUY endogenously
DEEGLOOPRRST porter's lodge
DEEGMNNOORRW wondermonger
DEEGNNOOORRW Ron Greenwood
DEEGNNOOOTUW wooden tongue
DEEGNOORRSTT Gordon setter
DEEHHHLOOSTU the Household
DEEHHIIMOPRS hemispheroid
DEEHHINORTVW The Windhover
DEEHHMNOOTUY honey-mouthed
DEEHHOORSSTU Theodor Heuss
DEEHIIKRSSSW side whiskers
DEEHIILLNPPS nipple-shield
DEEHIILLSTTW Edith Sitwell
DEEHIILNSSSV devilishness
DEEHIIMNORTU deinotherium
DEEHIINPRSST residentship
DEEHIINPSSTW dispense with
DEEHIINRSSST dissenterish
DEEHIKLNNOSW whole-skinned
DEEHILLLNPSS spindle shell
DEEHILLPSSSY Les Sylphides
DEEHILMOSTTY dyotheletism✧
DEEHILNOOTWY dye in the wool
DEEHILOORRSS horse soldier
DEEHILPRSSUU desulphurise
DEEHILPRSUUZ desulphurize
DEEHIMMOPRST homme d'esprit
DEEHIMMRRSUY medium sherry
DEEHIMNOORTU time-honoured
DEEHINNOPPRS Dennis Hopper
DEEHIOPPRTTY pteridophyte
DEEHLLMMSTUY sell the dummy
DEEHLNOORSTU shoulder note
DEEHLOORRTVW the world over
DEEHLPRSTTUU sulphuretted
DEEHNNORSTTU thunderstone
DEEHOORRSSUV hors d'oeuvres
DEEIIIMNRTTV divertimenti
DEEIIINSSSVV divisiveness
DEEIILLPPRTT Little Dipper
DEEIILNNNNSS Dennis Nilsen
DEEIILNNSSUW unwieldiness
DEEIILNRSSTU unsterilised
DEEIILNRSTUU underutilise
DEEIILNRSTUZ unsterilized
DEEIILNRTUUZ underutilize
DEEIIMMOPRST post meridiem
DEEIIMNNNOSW new dimension
DEEIIMNNRSTT disinterment
DEEIIMNORSTT endometritis
DEEIIMNORTTV divertimento
DEEIIMNRSSST dissenterism
DEEIIMORRTTU dumortierite
DEEIINNSSSTU unsensitised
DEEIINNSSTUZ unsensitized
DEEIINPRSSST spiritedness
DEEIINQSSSTU disquietness
DEEIINRSSTTU intertissued
DEEIJLNOOOST loose-jointed
DEEIJNORRRSU surrejoinder
DEEIKKNNRRSU underskinker
DEEIKMNOPRSY spider monkey
DEEIKNNORSSV overkindness
DEEIKRSTTTUU skutterudite
DEEILLNNQTUY delinquently
DEEILLNORTTW little wonder
DEEILMMNOOPT dipole moment
DEEILMNNSSSS mindlessness
DEEILMNRTTUY unremittedly
DEEILNNOOPRS prednisolone
DEEILNNOSTTU unlistened-to
DEEILNNSTUWY Edwin Lutyens
DEEILNOOSTUV outside novel
DEEILNPRRTTU triple-turned
DEEILNQRTUUY unrequitedly
DEEIMMMMNRSU midsummer-men
DEEIMNNRSTTU instrumented
DEEIMNOOPRSS monodisperse
DEEIMNOOPSTY deposit money
DEEIMNORSTTY densitometry
DEEIMNORUUYY mud in your eye
DEEIMOPPRRST pteridosperm
DEEIMOPPRSSU superimposed
DEEIMOPRRSTT Redemptorist
DEEINNOOPSTU put on one side
DEEINNOQSTUU unquestioned
DEEINNRRTTUV inverted turn
DEEINOOPSSSS possessioned
DEEINOOPSTTU put to one side
DEEINOPPRRTU unpropertied
DEEINORSSSSU desirousness
DEEINOSSTTUU testudineous
DEEINPRSSUUV unsupervised
DEEIOORRTVWY ivory-towered
DEEKMNOOPRWY powder monkey
DEEKNNRRTUUY under-turnkey
DEEKNOORRRWW wonder-worker
DEELLNOPSSTU pollutedness
DEELMNOORRTW lower mordent

DEELMNORSTUY tremendously
DEELNOOSSSSW woodlessness
DEELNORSSSSW wordlessness
DEELNOSSSSUU sedulousness
DEELPPRSSSUY suppressedly
DEEMNNORSTUU untremendous
DEEMNOPPRRTU upper mordent
DEEMOOORSSTU osteodermous
DEENNNOORSSW nonsense word
DEENNNOSSTUW unwontedness
DEENOOPRRSTW snowdrop tree
DEENOOPRSSST dessertspoon
DEENOPRRSTTU under protest
DEENORSSSTUX dextrousness
DEENPPRSSSUU unsuppressed
DEEOOOOPPRTZ pteropod ooze
DEERRSSTTTUU Ust'-Urt Desert
DEFFGHNOORTU off the ground
DEFFGINOOORW wood-offering
DEFFHIRSSTTU stuffed shirt
DEFFHLNOOPSU pound of flesh
DEFFINOORRSU frondiferous
DEFFLNOORSSU fourfoldness
DEFFMNNOOORR from fordonne
DEFGGNOOORTT god-forgotten✧
DEFGHHIIILTY high fidelity
high-fidelity
DEFGHIILNNTU hunting-field
DEFGHILLLTUY delightfully
DEFGHILLNTUU undelightful
DEFGHINRRSUY rushy-fringed
DEFGIIIKLLLN killing field
DEFGIIIMNNNY indemnifying
DEFGIIINRSVY diversifying
DEFGIINOPPRR dropping fire
DEFGILMNNOOY folding money
DEFGINNOPTUY type founding
DEFHHINRTTUY unthriftyhed
DEFHHLLOOORT hold the floor
DEFHIINNPRSU unfriendship
DEFHILOPPRST Doppler shift
DEFHIMNOORST hindforemost
DEFHLOOORSSU House of Lords
DEFHOOOOTTUW out of the wood
DEFIILLNNRUY unfriendlily
DEFIILNOORSX dorsiflexion
DEFIILNOSSSU unfossilised
DEFIILNOSSUZ unfossilized
DEFIILOPRSUY perfidiously
DEFIKMMNOOUU Duke of Omnium
DEFILOOORRSU doloriferous
DEFILOORSTUY do-it-yourself
DEFILRSSSTTU self-distrust
DEFIMNORRSSU dress uniform
DEFIMORRSSST Mistress Ford
DEFINOOOPRRT point of order
DEFIOORRSSUU sudoriferous
DEFIOPRSTUUZ Dufourspitze
DEFMNOORRTUU out from under
DEFNNOOPRSSU profoundness
DEGGGLMRRSUU drug smuggler
DEGGHILLORRS shrill-gorged
DEGGHILNNOTU hunting-lodge
DEGGHILNOOSU lodging house
DEGGHLOOORYY hydrogeology
DEGGINNOOPRU ground-pigeon
DEGGINNORSSW dressing-gown
DEGGKLLRSUUY skullduggery
DEGHHHILORSU shoulder-high
DEGHHIIIPRST high-spirited
DEGHHIINOPST diphthongise
DEGHHIINOPTZ diphthongize
DEGHHIORRTUV drivethrough
DEGHHIORSSTT short-sighted
DEGHHJNNOOSY Johnny Hodges
DEGHHLOOTTUW low-thoughted
DEGHIIILNRSS disrelishing
DEGHIIORSTTU outside right
DEGHIKNOORRS drongo-shrike
DEGHILMORSTY goldsmithery
DEGHILNNRTUY thunderingly
DEGHINOORSTV overdo things
DEGHINORSSTU droughtiness
DEGHIOORTUWY Woody Guthrie
DEGHLOOORTTW go to the world
DEGHNNOOSTUU hound's-tongue
DEGHNOOOTTTT Hottentot god
DEGHNOOPPRRU groundhopper
DEGHNORRTUUW underwrought
DEGIIIKLNNNX index-linking
DEGIIILLNPPR drilling pipe
DEGIIINNRRST disinterring
DEGIIINNSTUY disingenuity
DEGIIKLMOPRR milk porridge
DEGIIKNOPRSW powder-skiing
DEGIILLNNUYY unyieldingly
DEGIILLNOPRR rope-drilling
DEGIILLOOSTT deltiologist
DEGIILNNNOSU sounding line
DEGIILNNOSUY indigenously
DEGIILNNSSTY dissentingly
DEGIILNOPRSU ligniperdous
DEGIILNORSSS Doris Lessing
DEGIINNNNPRU underpinning
DEGIINNOSSUU disingenuous
DEGIINNRRTUW underwriting
DEGIINOPPRSS predisposing
DEGIKLMNOORW working model
DEGILLNOPPRW dropping-well
DEGILMNOOOST demonologist
DEGILMNRSTUW mud wrestling
DEGILMOPPRRU plum-porridge
DEGILNNOPSTT settling pond
DEGILNNORSUY resoundingly
DEGILNOOOSTT deontologist
DEGILOOPRSTT proglottides
DEGIMNNOORUV mourning dove
DEGIMNNORRSS morning dress
DEGIMNOORRSS dressing-room
DEGINNNNRRUU underrunning
DEGINNORRTUW winter-ground
DEGINOOPPRST doorstepping

DEGINOORSTUW wrong side out
DEGKNOORRSTU ground stroke
DEGLLNORSSUY groundlessly
DEGMNOORRRUY merry-go-round
DEGNOORRSTUY ground storey
DEHHHMMORTTY rhythm method
DEHHIIIPRSTT diphtheritis
DEHHIILOPRTY hydrophilite
DEHHILMNOTTW withholdment
DEHHILNNOTUW unwithholden
DEHHILOSSSTU South Shields
DEHHIOPRRTYY hyperthyroid
DEHHNOOORSTU do the honours
DEHIIILLMQUU liquid helium
DEHIIILNPPSY Philip Sidney
DEHIIIMMNNST diminishment
DEHIIINNORSS disinherison
DEHIIKLLNOOU unlikelihood
DEHIILNOPRRV river dolphin
DEHIILOPRSVW devil-worship
DEHIIMOORSTU idiothermous
DEHIIOPRRSSY hyperidrosis
DEHIKLNRSTUW whistle-drunk
DEHILLLNORSW Lord Shinwell
DEHILLNOPRSW spindle whorl
DEHILLOOOSWY Hollywoodise
DEHILLOOOWYZ Hollywoodize
DEHILLOPPSUY polysulphide
DEHILLOPRSSU shoulder slip
DEHILOOPRRSV overlordship
DEHILOSSTWWW Wild-West Show
DEHIMNOOORTY domino theory
DEHIMORRSTWY wordsmithery
DEHINNOOQRUY hydroquinone
DEHINOOPRRTY pyritohedron
DEHINOOPRSST spinsterhood
DEHINOORRRST in short order
DEHINOORRSTW in other words
DEHINOORRSWY Sir Henry Wood
DEHINOOTTUWW out the window
DEHINOPPRSUW unworshipped
DEHINPPTTUUW put the wind up
DEHIOOOPRRTT orthopteroid
DEHKLNOORSTU shoulder knot
DEHLLNOOPSUY endophyllous
DEHLLOORRTWY otherworldly
DEHLLOORSTTW The Lost World
DEHLMNOOOPSU monodelphous
DEHLMNPPRTUU thunder-plump
DEHLNOORRSUY horrendously
DEHLNOORTTTW throttle down
DEHLNORSTUUY thunderously
DEHLOOOSTTTW two-toed sloth
DEHMNOORRSWY Mrs Henry Wood
DEHMNORRSTTU thunderstorm
DEHNOOORSTUW southernwood
DEIIIIQSSTUV disquisitive
DEIIILLNOPRR pillion-rider
DEIIILMNTUVY diminutively
DEIIILNOPRSV violin spider
DEIIIMNPRSTT dispiritment
DEIIINORSSTV diversionist
DEIIKLNNNSSU unkindliness
DEIIKNNPPRSY skinny-dipper
DEIILLORRTTT Little Dorrit
DEIILOPSSTUY dispiteously
DEIILPRSTUVY disruptively
DEIIMNNNOTUU unmunitioned
DEIIMNNOPRSU unimprisoned
DEIINOOPRSTT periodontist
DEIINOORSTUX nitrous oxide
DEIIOOPPRRST poor-spirited
DEIJMMOORSWY Jimmy Woodser
DEIJNPRRSTUU jurisprudent
DEIKLNNOOOTU unlooked into
DEIKMNNOOOOW wooden kimono
DEILLMORTUXY dolly mixture
DEILMMNOOPSY polydemonism
DEILNOORUVWW louver-window
louvre-window
DEILNOQSSUUU usus loquendi
DEILOOPRRRSU lord-superior
DEILRSSSSTTU distrustless
DEIMNNOPRTUU unimportuned
DEIMNOPSTUYY pseudonymity
DEINOOOPPRRT proportioned
DEINOOORTTTX tetrodotoxin
DEINOSSSSTUU studiousness
DEIOOPRSSSSS dispossessor
DEIOPRSTTUVY topside-turvy
DEKLNOOPRUVY unprovokedly
DELLLLOORTYY trolley dolly
DELMMNNOOSUU London Museum
DELNNNOORSTY Lord Tennyson
DELNNOOPSTYY polysyndeton
DELNOOORSSSU dolorousness
DELNOPSSTUUY stupendously
DEMNOOPSSUUY pseudonymous
DENNOORSSSUW wondrousness
DEOPPRRRSSTU Rupert's drops
DFFGIINNPPSU snuff-dipping
DFFIIIMNOSSU diffusionism
DFFIIINOSSTU diffusionist
DFGGIIIINNNY indignifying
DFGGILLNNOPU plunging fold
DFGHIINNOSTW downshifting
DFGIIKKLNOUY kilfud-yoking
DFGILLSSTUUY disgustfully
DFGIMNNOORRU on firm ground
DFGOOOPRRSUX Oxford groups
DFHIILMOOORU oil of rhodium
DFHILNOOOPSU pound foolish
pound-foolish
DFHNOOOORRUW word of honour
DGGGHIIILNTU guiding light
DGGGILNNRUUY ungrudgingly
DGGHHIINNOSU high-sounding
DGGHIIINNOOT go into hiding
DGGHIILNNORT lightning rod
DGGHIINNNOOT nothing doing
DGGHINNOTTUU doughnutting
DGGIILNSSTUY disgustingly

DGGIINNOPPRR	ring-dropping
DGHIIKNNNORR	drinking-horn
DGHIIMNNOOST	do-nothingism
DGHIINNNSTUW	shunt-winding
DGHINNORSTUW	hunting-sword
DGHLLNOOORUW	hollow-ground
DGIIILLNQRUV	quill-driving
DGIIILNNOOSV	long division
DGIIIOOPRSTY	prodigiosity
DGIILNNOSSUV	undissolving
DGIILOOPRSUY	prodigiously
DGIIMMNNOPSW	swimming-pond
DGILMOORSTTY	troglodytism
DGILNOOOOSTT	odontologist
DGINNORRSSUU	surroundings
DGLMNOOSUUUY	Young modulus
DGNOOPRRSSTU	sports ground
DHHIILOOPPPS	phospholipid
DHHILOOPRSUY	hydrophilous
DHHOOPRSTUYY	hydrophytous
DHIIMNNOORUY	hydronium ion
DHIKOOORTVVZ	Todor Zhivkov
DHILOOPRRSUY	your lordship
DHILOORRSUWY	I should worry!
DHIMOOOOPSST	opisthodomos
DHIMOOPRRSTY	hydrotropism
DHINOOORRTUZ	tour d'horizon
DHINOOORSTTT	orthodontist
DHIOOORSTTUW	without doors
DHKLNOOORSWW	Lord knows who
DHLNOOOPPTYY	polyphyodont
DHLNOOORTUXY	unorthodoxly
DHMMOOOORSUW	wood mushroom
DHMMPPTTUUYY	humpty-dumpty✧
DHMNNOOOOPTY	monophyodont
DHNOOOOPRSTU	Odontophorus
DIIIINOQSSTU	disquisition
DIIIOQRSSTUY	disquisitory
DIILNOOSSTUU	solitudinous
DIIOOOPRRSTU	proditorious
DIKLNNOOTUWW	I wouldn't know
DILMNOOORRRS	Lord Morrison
DINOOORRTTUY	ororotundity
DMNNNOOOSTUW	Mount Snowdon
DNOOOPRSTTUW	put down roots

E

EEEEEFFLNOST	feel one's feet
EEEEEFGINRRS	Friese-Greene
EEEEEHHLRRTW	three-wheeler
EEEEEKPRRSTT	streetkeeper
EEEEFGHILNRW	freewheeling
EEEEFGLLNOSS	feel one's legs
EEEEFINRRSTT	interest-free
EEEEFLNRRSTV	self-reverent
EEEEGGINNNOU	Eugene Onegin
EEEEGHHILNOT	eighteen-hole
EEEEGIILNPSS	spiegeleisen
EEEEGILLNNOU	Eugene O'Neill
EEEEGILLNRSW	Green Wellies
EEEEGINNOSTY	get one's eye in
EEEEGINNPRTT	Petter engine
EEEEHHKOPSTU	keep the house
EEEEHILPQRTU	téléphérique
EEEEHIMNRTTX	in the extreme
EEEEHINPRRSV	reprehensive
EEEEHLMNOPRT	nephelometer
EEEEHLNRRSTW	stern-wheeler
EEEEHLNRSSTV	nevertheless
EEEEHLOPSSTU	steeple house
EEEEHMNORRTV	neverthemore
EEEEHNOSSTTT	set one's teeth
EEEEIJMNPRRU	jeune premier
EEEEILLMRSUV	merveilleuse
EEEEILPPRSST	spire-steeple
EEEEIMNPRRTX	experimenter
EEEEIMNPRSST	presenteeism
EEEEIMNRRTTV	retrievement
EEEEIMNRSTTX	extensimeter
EEEEINNQRSTU	equestrienne
EEEEKNNRTTVY	Kenny Everett
EEEELLPRRSST	Peter Sellers
EEEELMNORTTY	Merlene Ottey
EEEELMNRSTTT	resettlement
EEEELNOPSSUV	up one's sleeve
EEEELNPRSSSS	peerlessness
EEEELNRSSSST	treelessness
EEEEMMNPRSST	empressement
EEEEMNNRRSTV	renversement
EEEEMNOPRRTT	penetrometer
EEEEMNORSTTX	extensometer
EEEENNPRRRTU	entrepreneur
EEEENNSSTWYY	teensy-weensy
EEEENPRRSSSV	perverseness
EEEEORRTTTTT	teeter-totter
EEEEPPRRRSSU	peer pressure
EEEFFGHOORWY	Geoffrey Howe
EEEFFIMORSTU	effusiometer
EEEFFINOSTTV	Tet Offensive
EEEFFINSSSUV	effusiveness
EEEFFLLNNORW	fennel-flower
EEEFGGHINRTT	get the finger
EEEFGGINNRRS	green fingers
EEEFGIINNRTT	engine-fitter
EEEFGILMNPRT	Peter Fleming
EEEFGILNORSY	foreseeingly
EEEFGINNORSU	unforeseeing
EEEFGLLNOOST	let oneself go
EEEFGLLNRUVY	revengefully
EEEFGLNNRUUV	unrevengeful
EEEFGLNNSSUV	vengefulness
EEEFGNNOORSS	foregoneness
EEEFHINRRRSW	Renfrewshire
EEEFHINRSSSV	feverishness
EEEFHLLMORTW	helmet flower
EEEFHMNRRSST	refreshments
EEEFHOOPRSSU	House of Peers
EEEFIIKLLNSS	lifelikeness
EEEFIILLLLMU	millefeuille
EEEFIILNRRTT	interfertile
EEEFIILNRSTT	life-interest
EEEFIIMNNNSS	feminineness

EEEFIKLLNRST Klinefelter's
EEEFILLNSSSS lifelessness
EEEFILNORSTX self-exertion
EEEFILNRSSTT self-interest
EEEFILNSSTTX self-existent
EEEFILORRSTV tree of silver
EEEFILPRRSSX express rifle
EEEFINNORSSV overfineness
EEEFJLNNOOSY enjoy oneself
EEEFLLNSSSSS selflessness
EEEFLLOOPPRW flower people✧
EEEFLLORRSST forset-seller
EEEFLLORSSST fosset-seller
EEEFLNNORSSZ Fresnel zones
EEEFLNNSSTUV eventfulness
EEEFLNOOPRSV prove oneself
EEEFNNQRSSTU frequentness
EEEFNOORSTVY every so often
EEEFOSSSTTTV Steve Fossett
EEEGGGILLNPV level pegging
EEEGGKOORSST George Stokes
EEEGGLLOORRW George Orwell
EEEGGNNOORRY orgone energy
EEEGHHILNTTY eighteenthly
EEEGHIKNOPSU housekeeping
EEEGHILORTTV live together
EEEGHILRTTTW letter-weight
EEEGHILRTTWW welterweight
EEEGHIMNOSTU meeting-house
EEEGHIMNSTUW W Eugene Smith
EEEGHIMNTTTT get the mitten
EEEGHINNRSSS greenishness
EEEGHINSTTVY seventy-eight
EEEGHNNRRSTT strengthener
EEEGHNORRRWZ Werner Herzog
EEEGHNORSSTT togetherness
EEEGHOORTTYZ heterozygote
EEEGIIILLTVW give it wellie
EEEGIIKNNPSW swine-keeping
EEEGIILMNNTV inveiglement
EEEGIIMNNPSW minesweeping
EEEGIINNORRT orienteering
EEEGIKMNNNOY monkey engine
EEEGIKNOPRST storekeeping
EEEGIKNPPRRS springkeeper
EEEGILNNOPRT petrol engine
EEEGILOQRRSU Grolieresque
EEEGILRRSSVY regressively
EEEGIMNRSSSU Messeigneurs
EEEGINNORSSU neurogenesis
EEEGINNPSSSW sweepingness
EEEGINOOSSST osteogenesis
EEEGINOPRSST petrogenesis
EEEGINPPPRRS spring peeper
EEEGINRRSSVW reverse swing
EEEGIOQRRSTU grotesquerie
EEEGLNNNSSTU ungentleness
EEEGMNORSSSU gruesomeness
EEEGMOORSTTX go to extremes
EEEGNNORSSSU generousness
EEEGNOOPRRRS Roger Penrose
EEEGNOOPRRST progesterone
EEEHHHIMMPRT hephthemimer
EEEHHILLOSTW oil the wheels
EEEHHINPSSSS sheepishness
EEEHHIRRTVWY everywhither
EEEHHJLLOPRS Joseph Heller
EEEHHLNORTUV eleventh hour
eleventh-hour
EEEHHMOPRRST thermosphere
EEEHHNRRSTUY heresy-hunter
EEEHIKPPPRRS pepper-shrike
EEEHILLMNNOS Neohellenism
EEEHILLOSTTT stiletto heel
EEEHILMNNORY Leonine rhyme
EEEHILMNRTTY trimethylene
EEEHILMOPRTX extremophile
EEEHILNNNTTY nineteenthly
EEEHILRRRSTW Welsh terrier
EEEHILRSTTTW white settler
EEEHIMMORSUX homme sérieux
EEEHIMNNNRST enshrinement
EEEHIMNOOSTT etheostomine
EEEHIMNRSTTU hermeneutist
EEEHIMORSSTX heterosexism
EEEHINNOPRRS reprehension
EEEHINNORSTW none the wiser
EEEHINOPRRSU superheroine
EEEHINPRSTVY hypertensive
EEEHINSSSSTW sweetishness
EEEHIORSSTTX heterosexist
EEEHJMOPRRTY Jeremy Thorpe
EEEHJMPQTUUU jump the queue
EEEHLLLORTWY trolley wheel
EEEHLLNOPTYY polyethylene
EEEHLLNPSSSS helplessness
EEEHLMNOPRTY nephelometry
EEEHLMNOSSSS homelessness
EEEHLNOPSSSS hopelessness
EEEHLOPRRSSS sheep's sorrel
EEEHLOPRSTTW potter's wheel
EEEHMNNNORTT enthronement
EEEHMOORRSTU heteromerous
EEEHMOORRSTW meteor shower
EEEHNNOORSTW none the worse
EEEHNOPRRRSY reprehensory
EEEHNORSSTTT on the streets
EEEHNOSSSTUY shut one's eyes
EEEHNRRSTTUV serve the turn
EEEHOPRRSSTZ herpes zoster
EEEIIINRRSVY River Yenisei
EEEIIKLNORSY Kyrie eleison
EEEIILMNOTTV line-item veto
EEEIILMNPRSU periselenium
EEEIILPRTTVY repetitively
EEEIIMNPSTTV intempestive
EEEIIMOPRRST isoperimeter
EEEIINNNRTTV intervenient
EEEIINNPRSST serpentinise
EEEIINNPRSTT serpentinite
EEEIINNPRSTZ serpentinize
EEEIINPRRTTV interpretive

EEEIINPRSSVX inexpressive
EEEIIPQRRSTU prerequisite
EEEIJLNNSSUV juvenileness
EEEIKLMNOOSV kimono sleeve
EEEILLLOPPTT little people
EEEILLPRSSVY Elvis Presley
EEEILMNNPRTY pre-eminently
EEEILMNNRSTT re-enlistment
EEEILMNNSSSU unseemliness
EEEILMNNTTUY unity element
EEEILMNORSTU son et lumière
EEEILMNPRSUV nerve impulse
EEEILMNSSSST timelessness
EEEILMOORVZZ mezzo-relievo
EEEILNNPRSTY serpentinely
EEEILNPRTVVY preventively
EEEILNRRRTVY irreverently
EEEILNRSSSST tirelessness
EEEILNRSSSTW westerliness
Western Isles
EEEILPRRSSVY repressively
EEEILPRSSVXY expressively
EEEILRRRTTTW letter-writer
EEEIMNNPRSTT presentiment
EEEIMNNPRSTU supereminent
EEEIMNNRSTTV reinvestment
EEEIMNOPRSST response time
EEEIMNORSSST tiresomeness
EEEIMNORSSTT sensitometer
EEEIMNPRRSST misrepresent
EEEIMOORRSST stereoisomer
EEEIMOPRRRST respirometer
EEEIMOPRSTUX time exposure
EEEIMORSVWWY worm's eye view
EEEINNNORRTU interneurone
EEEINNNOSSSS in one's senses
EEEINNOPRRST pretensioner
pre-tensioner
EEEINNPRSSTX inexpertness
EEEINNPRSTUV supervenient
EEEINOORRTVX overexertion
EEEINOPRRSSV overripeness
EEEINPRRSSTT interpretess
EEEINPRSSTUV eruptiveness
EEEINPRSSUVX unexpressive
EEEINRRTTTUX intertexture
EEEIOPRRTVWY Poetry Review
EEEIORRSTVVX extroversive
EEEJLLORSWYY yellow jersey
EEEKLOOPPPSS spokespeople
EEEKMNORTVVY vervet monkey
EEEKNNOOOPSS poke one's nose
EEELLLNRSSTY relentlessly
EEELLMORRTTU tellurometer
EEELLNOQSUWY queen's yellow
EEELLNOSSSSV lovelessness
EEELLOPPPRWY yellow pepper
EEELMNNOOSSS lonesomeness
EEELMNNSTTTU unsettlement
EEELMNOSSSSV movelessness
EEELMNPPRSTU supplementer
EEELMOPPRRTT Teleprompter®
EEELNNOSSSST tonelessness
EEELNNSSSSTU tunelessness
EEELNOOPPPRS people person
EEELNOPRSSSS responseless
EEELNORSSSTU resoluteness
EEELNRSSSSST restlessness
EEELOOPRSTTU teleutospore
EEEMMMNNOSTV men's movement
EEEMNORSTTUV Mount Everest
EEEMOPRRSTTX extreme sport
EEEMPRSSTTXY expert system
EEENNOPPRSSS propenseness
EEENNOPRSSTT serpent-stone
EEENNOPRSTTU enteropneust
EEENOORSSTTT testosterone
EEENOPRSSTTU up one's street
EEENPRRSSSSU pusser's sneer
EEEOOPRRSUVX overexposure
EEEOPRRRSSSU pressure sore
EEEOPRRRSSUV overpressure
EEEOPRRRSTTT Street-Porter
EEEORRSTTTVX vortex street
EEFFGHHINOST off the hinges
EEFFGHILLORY Geoffrey Hill
EEFFGHILLSTU gefüllte fish
EEFFHIORTTVY the Forty-five
EEFFHLLRRSUY refreshfully
EEFFIIILLORX elixir of life
EEFFJLOOORVW flower of Jove
EEFFLLORSSTY effortlessly
EEFGGIILNRSU single-figure
EEFGGINNOPRS sponge finger
EEFGGIOPRTTY pettifoggery
EEFGHIIINNSS seine fishing
EEFGHIIKNNRT freethinking
EEFGHIILNRRT Freightliner®
EEFGHIILNRTT Ferlinghetti
EEFGHIILRTTW weightlifter
EEFGHIIPRRTZ prizefighter
EEFGHILLNSTU English flute
EEFGHILNRRSY refreshingly
EEFGHIMORRTU mother figure
EEFGHINNRRSU unrefreshing
EEFGHINOPRSS sponge fisher
EEFGHLMOPTUU go up the flume
EEFGIILLNRTT little finger
EEFGIILMNPXY exemplifying
EEFGIIMMNRSW free-swimming
EEFGIIMNNNRT infringement
EEFGIINNNORZ zone refining
EEFGIINOPRRT profiteering
EEFGIINSSTUV fugitiveness
EEFGIKNNOORT foretokening
EEFGILLNSSUU guilefulness
EEFGINNORSUY fusion energy
EEFGINORRSUU ferrugineous
EEFGNOOPRSUV Group of Seven
EEFHHMMMOOOR home from home
EEFHIIILNPVW five-line whip
EEFHIILNNORT eflornithine

EEFHILNOPPST slip of the pen
EEFHIPRSSSTT St Peter's fish
EEFHLNORTTUY fourteenthly
EEFHLOPRSTTY flesh-pottery
EEFHMOOORTTY Otto Meyerhof
EEFHMOORRSTT foster-mother
EEFHNNNORRRT northern fern
EEFHNOOORTUW out of nowhere
EEFIIINNNSST infiniteness
EEFIIKLNORSS Leif Eriksson
EEFIIMNOPRST mifepristone
EEFIIMNORSSU seminiferous
EEFIIMOQRSTU equisetiform
EEFIINORRSSU resiniferous
EEFILLOPRSTT esprit follet
EEFILLORSSTU stelliferous
EEFILMORSTTU flitter-mouse
EEFILNNQRTUY infrequently
EEFILNOORRTX retroflexion
EEFILNPSSSTU spitefulness
EEFILOOPRRST profiteroles
EEFILRRRSSUV silver surfer
EEFIMNNOPRTT penitent form
EEFIMNNORTTZ frozen mitten
EEFIMNOPRRST serpentiform
EEFIMNOPRSST mesne profits
EEFIORRSSSTT foster-sister
EEFKLMNOORWY monkey flower
EEFLLMORRSUY remorsefully
EEFLLNNOOTUV tunnel of love
EEFLLNNTUUVY uneventfully
EEFLLNORSSUV overfullness
EEFLMNORRSUU unremorseful
EEFLMNORSSSS formlessness
EEFLNNQRTUUY unfrequently
EEFLNNSSSUUU unusefulness
EEFLNOOPPRST people's front
EEFLNOORSSSS rooflessness
EEFLNOPRSSUW powerfulness
EEFNNNOOPRUY fourpenny one
EEFNNORRSTTW Western Front
EEFNNORSTTUV turn of events
EEFNOPRTTTUY true-type font
EEFOOPPRSSTU of set purpose
EEFOOPRRSSSS professoress
EEGGGGHMRRUU hugger-mugger
EEGGGINORRRS Ginger Rogers
EEGGHIILNNNT enlightening
EEGGHIINNRTT teething ring
EEGGHOORRTTW grow together
EEGGILSSTUVY suggestively
EEGGINNPRTTU putting green
EEGGNOORSSSU gorgeousness
EEGHHHILMRTT right the helm
EEGHHHORRTTU therethrough
EEGHHHORRTUW wherethrough
EEGHHIILLLNS sheeling-hill
EEGHHIINRRTW white herring
EEGHHINOORSS horseshoeing
EEGHHINRTTVY the very thing
EEGHHIPRRSSU high-pressure
EEGHHLNOPSTY Loghtyn sheep
EEGHHNOSTTUU The Huguenots
EEGHIIMSTTX six-eight time
EEGHIINOSSST histogenesis
EEGHIINRSSST tigerishness
EEGHIINRSTUX extinguisher
EEGHIINRTTWW winter-weight
EEGHIKNNORST north-seeking
EEGHIKNOSSTU south-seeking
EEGHIKNRRSTU hunger strike
hunger-strike
EEGHILLSSTWY weightlessly
EEGHILMNORVW overwhelming
EEGHILNOOPRS phrenologise
EEGHILNOOPRT gerontophile
EEGHILNOOPRZ phrenologize
EEGHILNOPPST teleshopping
EEGHILNOPSSY phylogenesis
EEGHILNPSSUY upsey English
EEGHIMMRSTUW summer-weight
EEGHIMNOSSTY mythogenesis
EEGHINNOPSSY hypnogenesis
EEGHINOORSST orthogenesis
EEGHINOPSSTY phytogenesis
EEGHLLOOPRST hot gospeller
EEGHLLOPRTTU pull together
EEGHLNRSSSTT strengthless
EEGHLOOORSTU heterologous
EEGHMMOPRSTY sphygmometer
EEGHMNOORTTU mother tongue
EEGHMORSSTUW sweet sorghum
EEGHNOOORSTU heterogonous
EEGHNOORSSUU house surgeon
EEGHOOOPRTTV go over the top
EEGHOORSSTTY the story goes
EEGHOORSTUYZ heterozygous
EEGHOPPPRSST Pepper's ghost
EEGIIKLMNOUY Kylie Minogue
EEGIILLLNPPS sleeping pill
EEGIILLNNNST sentinelling
EEGIILLNORSS religionless
EEGIILLNPRST still-peering
EEGIILNORRTV green vitriol
EEGIILNPSSTU sleeping-suit
EEGIINNNPRST serpentining
EEGIINNPRRST enterprising
EEGIINNRRSST retiringness
EEGIINNRRTTY eternity ring
EEGIINNSTTTW Wittgenstein
EEGIIRRSSTVY regressivity
EEGIJMNPQUUU queue-jumping
EEGIKLNORSTW steelworking
EEGILLNNPSUX sun-expelling
EEGILLNOOSST selenologist
EEGILLNPPRXY perplexingly
EEGILLNRSUYY Guernsey lily
EEGILLOOPSST speleologist
EEGILLORRRSU guerrilleros
EEGILMMNORRV River Glommen
EEGILMNOOOST entomologise
EEGILMNOOOTZ entomologize

Words marked ✧ can also be spelled with one or more capital letters

EEGILMOOPPSS goose-pimples
EEGILMOOPSTY epistemology
EEGILMPPRSSU Geissler pump
EEGILNOORRSW lower regions
EEGILNOPRTTU triple-tongue
EEGILNORRSTU Eurosterling
EEGILORRSTUY elytrigerous
EEGILQRRRSUY grey squirrel
EEGIMNNORRTT retromingent
EEGIMNNPSSTT temptingness
EEGIMNNRRSTU interregnums
EEGIMNOORRTT trigonometer
EEGINNNRRSSU unerringness
EEGINNOSSSUY syngenesious
EEGINNPRRSTU turnip greens
EEGINNRSSTWW western swing
EEGINOOPRRVW overpowering
EEGINOOPRSSS sporogenesis
EEGINOPPRRSU upper regions
EEGINOPRRSST progenitress
resting spore
EEGINOPRSTTY stereotyping
EEGINORSSSUV grievousness
EEGINOSSSUUX exiguousness
EEGINRRSTTTY trysting-tree
EEGLMNNOOOPR prolegomenon
EEGLMNOPSSTU get one's lumps
EEGLNNOOOSSS Léon Goossens
EEGLNNOOPSSU upon one's legs
EEGLNNORSUUY ungenerously
EEGMMNORSSTY system-monger
EEGNNOORRSUU neurosurgeon
EEGNORRRSUUY neurosurgery
EEHHIIMMOPRT hemimorphite
EEHHIINSSSTV thievishness
EEHHIKLLMNUW Wilhelm Kühne
EEHHILLNOPTY theophylline
EEHHILNRTTTY thirteenthly
EEHHINRSSSSW shrewishness
EEHHLLOPRTYY heterophylly
EEHHLLRTTTTU tell the truth
EEHHLMNORTTY three-monthly
EEHHLNOOPTUW upon the whole
EEHHMMORRTTY rhythmometer
EEHHMOOPRRTY heteromorphy
EEHHNOORRTTW whether or not
EEHHOOOSSTUU house-to-house
EEHHOOPRRTTY heterotrophy
EEHHOOSSUUYY housey-housey
EEHIIIRRRRST Irish terrier
EEHIIKLNNTTW in the twinkle
EEHIIKNPRSSY hyperkinesis
EEHIILLLRTTT little Hitler
EEHIILNPRSST listenership
EEHIILNPRSTY prehensility
EEHIILNRSSSV liverishness
EEHIIMNPPRRU perinephrium
EEHIINOPRRVX River Phoenix
EEHIINOQTUVV on the qui vive
EEHIIPRSTTWY white pyrites
EEHIJLOPRSST Joseph Lister
EEHIKLLNRRTU hunter-killer
EEHILLMNNSSU sneeshin-mull
EEHILLMOTTVY methyl violet
EEHILLPRSTUW pull the wires
EEHILMNORSST motherliness
EEHILNNOPTTU put on the line
EEHILNNPSTWY penny whistle
EEHILNOOPSST siphonostele
EEHILNOPRSTT Peter Shilton
EEHILOPPRTTT throttle pipe
EEHILOPSSTTU spittle-house
EEHILOPSTTTV split the vote
EEHIMNOOPRTV on the improve
EEHIMNORSSST smotheriness
EEHINNOORTVZ event horizon
EEHINNOPRSTY hypertension
EEHINOOSSSSU session-house
EEHIQRSSTTTU the squitters
EEHKLMNOORWY howler monkey
EEHKMNORSSUY rhesus monkey
EEHKNOOPRSTW know the ropes
EEHLLLOOPSWY sleepy hollow✧
EEHLLMPRSTTU trumpet shell
EEHLMNNOTTUW Helmut Newton
EEHLMOPRSTTY stepmotherly
EEHLNRSSSSTU hurtlessness
ruthlessness
EEHLOORRSTTU rule the roost
EEHMMOOOORSU homoeomerous
EEHMNNOOORRU neurohormone
EEHMNNOOOSTT The Moonstone
EEHMNOOORSTU heteronomous
EEHMNRRRSUYY nursery rhyme
EEHMOPRRSSTU sumpter horse
EEHMORRSTUUY eurythermous
EEHNNORRSTTW north-western
EEHNORSSTTUW south-western
EEHOOPPRSTTU to the purpose
EEHOORRTTVXY vortex theory
EEIIIILLRRTW tirlie-wirlie
EEIIIJLNSTUV juvenilities
EEIIIKLNNNPW pinniewinkle
EEIIIKNNRSST interkinesis
EEIIILLMRSTV millisievert
EEIIIMNRSSTV intermissive
EEIIINPRRSTU perineuritis
EEIIINRSSSTW sinisterwise
EEIIJLLMMORS Joe Millerism
EEIIKLLMNRRV vermin-killer
EEIIKLLNNSSU unlikeliness
EEIIKLOOPSSU leukopoiesis
EEIILLMPQTUU equimultiple
EEIILLNNSSUV unliveliness
EEIILLNSSSUV illusiveness
EEIILMNNPTTY impenitently
EEIILMNNSSTU untimeliness
EEIILMNOPSST impoliteness
EEIILMOORVZZ mezzo-rilievo
EEIILMPRSSVY impressively
permissively
EEIILNPPRSSS slipperiness

EEIILNPRSSST priestliness
EEIILNPSSSST pitilessness
EEIILNRSSSST sisterliness
EEIILOOPPSTV positive pole
EEIILOPSTVXY expositively
EEIILOSSTTTU toilet tissue
EEIIMMNOPRRS minor premise
EEIIMNNOTTTU munitionette
EEIIMNNRTTTT intermittent
EEIIMNOOPRST senior optime
EEIIMNOPRRSS reimpression
EEIIMNOQSTTU question time
EEIIMNOSSSSV omissiveness
EEIIMNPRRSTT misinterpret
EEIIMNPRSSTT impersistent
EEIIMNPRSSUV unimpressive
EEIIMNPRSTTY sempiternity
EEIIMNRRTTUX intermixture
EEIIMOPRRSTY isoperimetry
EEIIMSSSSTUU tussie mussie
EEIINNNORTTV intervention
EEIINNOPQTTU inequipotent
EEIINNORSTTT retentionist
EEIINNOSSTTX extensionist
EEIINNPPSSST snippetiness
EEIINNRSSSST sinisterness
EEIINOPRRSSV irresponsive
EEIINOPSSSTV positiveness
EEIINORRSTVV introversive
EEIINORRTTVV introvertive
EEIINPRRTTUV interruptive
EEIIOOPRSSTV seropositive
EEIIPPRRRSTW wirestripper
EEIIPRSSTVXY expressivity
EEIJLMPPRRTU triple-jumper
EEIJNNNNPRSY jenny-spinner
EEIJNNORTTUV joint venture
EEIKLMNNOSTY Milton Keynes
EEIKLNOSSTTU skeleton suit
EEIKOPRRRSTW worker priest
EEILLLNSSSSW will-lessness
EEILLMOOPRST trompe l'oeils
EEILLMOSSTVY motivelessly
EEILLNNOQTUY ineloquently
EEILLNNOSSSV slovenliness
EEILLNNOSSUV unloveliness
EEILLNSSSSST listlessness
EEILLORRSTUY irresolutely
EEILLRSSSSTY resistlessly
EEILMNOOSSST toilsomeness
EEILMNORSTUV volunteerism
EEILMNPRSTTU multipresent
EEILMOOPRSST metropolises
EEILMOPPRRTY peremptorily
EEILMOPRSSTW Mister Wopsle
EEILMORSSSTU moistureless
EEILMPRSTUVY resumptively
EEILMRSSSSST mistressless
EEILNNOORTTU nitrotoluene
EEILNNOPQSTU Nelson Piquet
EEILNNOPSSTU unpoliteness
EEILNOOORSSU oleoresinous
EEILNOOPPRSY polyisoprene
EEILNOORRSTU resolutioner✧
EEILNOORRTUV revolutioner
EEILNOPRSSSU perilousness
EEILNOPRSSVY responsively
EEILNOQSSSTU questionless
EEILNORTUUVV vulvo-uterine
EEILNPRSSTTY persistently
EEILNPSSSUVY suspensively
EEILNRSSSTVY Sylvestrines
EEILOPPRSSVY oppressively
EEILOPRRSSTY proselytiser
EEILOPRRSTUV retropulsive
EEILOPRRSTYZ proselytizer
EEILOPSSSSVY possessively
EEIMMMNSSTUY immune system
EEIMMNNOOPST empoisonment
EEIMMNNOORST senior moment
EEIMNNNOPRSY money-spinner
EEIMNNOOPPRS perispomenon
EEIMNNOORSTV normotensive
EEIMNOORRSTT torsion meter
EEIMNORRRRTU run-time error
EEIMOOPPRTTU moto perpetui
EEINNOOPQSTU open question
EEINNOOPRSTU out-pensioner
EEINNOPRSSTT septentrions
EEINNOPRSSTU serpentinous
EEINNOPRSSUV unresponsive
EEINNOPRSTUV supervention
EEINNOPRTTTV ventripotent
EEINNORRSSTV Steven Norris
EEINNPRSSTTU unprettiness
EEINOOPPSSST oppositeness
EEINOOPRSSSS repossession
EEINOOPRSSTT enteroptosis
EEINOORRRSTV retroversion
EEINOORRSTVX extroversion
EEINOORSSSTU interosseous
EEINOPPRSSUV unoppressive
EEINOPRRSSTU pressure into
EEINOPRRSTTU neuropterist
EEINOPRSSSST Peter Sissons
EEINOPRSSSSU supersession
EEINOPRSSSTV sportiveness
EEINOPRSSSUV perviousness
previousness
EEINOPRSTTUV Peter Ustinov
EEINOQRSTUWY owner's equity
EEINORSSSTUV vitreousness
EEIOPPRRRSST proprietress
EEIPRRSSSTUU pressure suit
EEKLMNOPUYZZ monkey puzzle
puzzle-monkey
EEKLNOORTTUV true-love knot
EEKNNOORSTTT Stoke-on-Trent
EEKNNOORUVWY you never know
EEKNOOPPRSSS spokesperson
EEKNOPPRSTTY pretty-spoken
EELLLOOWWYYY yellow-yowley

Words marked ✧ can also be spelled with one or more capital letters

EELLNNNOOSSV nolens volens
EELLNNOORSSV lovelornness
EELLNNOPTTUW well putten on
EELLNOSSSSSU soullessness
EELLOPPRSTUV support level
EELMMNNOPTUY unemployment
EELMMNPSSTUY plenum system
EELMOOOSSTTU teleostomous
EELMOOPRSTTY Ptolemy Soter
EELMOPPRRSUY superpolymer
EELMOPRRSTTY stormy petrel
EELNNPPSSSUU unsuppleness
EELNOOPRSSTT streptosolen
EELNOORSSSST rootlessness
EELNOPRRSTUU seropurulent
EELNOPSSSSST spotlessness
EEMNNOOORRTU motor neurone
EEMNNOOPPSTT postponement
EEMNNOORSSSU enormousness
EEMNNOOSSSUV venomousness
EEMNNORSSSUU numerousness
EEMOOOPPRTTU moto perpetuo
EENNNOOOPRSS on one's person
EENNOOPPRSSU on one's uppers
EENNOOPRSTTY none-so-pretty
EENNOSSSSSUU sensuousness
EENNRRRSSUUY nursery nurse
EENNTTTTWWYY twenty-twenty
EENOOPRRSTUU neuropterous
EENOOPRRSTUV punto reverso
EENOPRRSSSUY supersensory
EEOOPPRRSSTU preposterous
EEOOPRRRSSTU root pressure
EEOPRRSSTTTW St Peter's wort
EEPPRRTTTTYY pretty-pretty
EFFGGHIIINRT firefighting
EFFGGIILNNSU glue-sniffing
EFFGHILORSTU foresightful
EFFGIINOOPRR fireproofing
EFFHIOPRSSST sheriff's post
EFFHNOOORSTU front of house
front-of-house
EFFILNRSSTUU fruitfulness
EFFIMOORRTUU four-four time
EFFINNNOOOOS off one's onion
EFGGGIINOPTT pettifogging
EFGGHHIIINSV high-five-sign
EFGGHHIINRTT night fighter
EFGGHIILLNST self-lighting
EFGGHIILNRST self-righting
EFGGHIOOPRTU Group of Eight
EFGGIILNNOPY pigeon-flying
EFGGIINRRSTU string figure
EFGGILNORTTY forgettingly
EFGHHIINRSTY night-fishery
EFGHHIKNORTU knife through
EFGHHILNTTTW Twelfth Night
EFGHIIKLNNST self-thinking
EFGHIIKNNNTU hunting-knife
EFGHIILORRTT right-to-lifer
EFGHIINRRSTT first-nighter
EFGHIKOORRSY Yorkshire fog
EFGHILNRSSTU rightfulness
EFGHINOOPRTW Night of Power
EFGHINOOTTTT Hottentot fig
EFGHINORRTTY right of entry
EFGHLLLNOOWW H W Longfellow
EFGIIILLMNST self-limiting
EFGIIINNNSTY intensifying
EFGIIKNNNPRU pruning knife
EFGIIILNNRSST triflingness
EFGIIILNOPRTW powerlifting
EFGIIILNORSUV griseofulvin
EFGIIILNRRTYY terrifyingly
EFGIIMORRSST Strigiformes
EFGIINNNOPRU infringe upon
EFGIINNOPRSY personifying
EFGIINNRRTUY unterrifying
EFGIINORRTTT retrofitting
EFGILLOORSSU self-glorious
EFGILNNNOORW non-flowering
EFGILOORRSSU self-rigorous
EFGIMNNOPRRU unperforming
EFGLNNORSSUW wrongfulness
EFHHILLOOOSY holy of holies
EFHHINORSSTU Southern Fish
EFHIILQRRSSU squirrel fish
EFHILLMNORTU run-of-the-mill
EFHILLRSSTTY thriftlessly
EFHILMNRSSTU mirthfulness
EFHILNOOPTTU put on the foil
EFHILNOPSSSY self-hypnosis
EFHILOORRSUV overflourish
EFHINNOORSSU sunshine roof
EFHJNOOOPRST not for Joseph
EFHLLMNOTTUY the full monty
EFHLLNOSSSTU slothfulness
EFHLNNOOPRTY horn of plenty
EFHLNOSSTUUY youthfulness
EFHLNRSSTTUU truthfulness
EFHLOOOOPTTU out of the loop
EFHNOOPRRRTY Northrop Frye
EFHOOOPPPSTT top of the pops
EFIIIILNNTVY infinitively
EFIIILNNOOPT infinite loop
EFIIILNNOOSV line of vision
EFIIINOPRSTW spirit of wine
EFIIILMNORSUU luminiferous
EFIIILMOPRSVY oversimplify
EFIIMMNOPSST postfeminism
EFIIMNOPSSTT postfeminist
EFIINOPRSSTU perfusionist
EFIIOPRRSTUY pyritiferous
EFIKLLLNSSSU skillfulness
EFILLMNOSSUU self-luminous
EFILLOPRSSTY profitlessly
EFILNOOPSSTT toploftiness
EFILORSSTUUY suit yourself
EFIOOOPRRSSU soporiferous
EFLLOPPRSUUY purposefully
EFLMNNORSSUU mournfulness
EFLMNORSSSTU stormfulness

EFLNOPRSSSTU	sportfulness
EFLNRSSSTTUU	trustfulness
EFMNNOOSTUUV	mount of Venus
EFMNOORTTUWY	twenty-fourmo
EFMOOOPRTTT	from top to toe
EFNNOORRSSSW	forswornness
EFNOOPRRSTTU	return of post
EGGGHJLOOPRU	plough-jogger
EGGGIILNNRSY	sniggeringly
EGGGIILORTYY	György Ligeti
EGGGILNNOOST	logging-stone
EGGHHIINPPST	high-stepping
EGGHHIINSSSW	Whiggishness
EGGHIIKLNNSS	king's English
EGGHIILNNNOT	neon lighting
EGGHIILNOSTU	soughing-tile
EGGHIINNNOPT	opening night
EGGHIINPRSSS	priggishness
EGGHILNSSSSU	sluggishness
EGGHLOOOOPTY	photogeology
EGGIILLMMNRY	glimmeringly
EGGIILLNRSTY	glisteringly
EGGIILLNRTTY	glitteringly
EGGIIMORSSTY	Giorgi system
EGGIINOPRRTT	trigger point
EGGILOOPSTTY	Egyptologist
EGGIMNOOPRSS	gossip-monger
EGGINORSTYYZ	Szent-Györgyi
EGGLNNOOORTY	röntgenology
EGHHHOORRTTU	through-other
EGHHIILPRSTY	high-priestly
EGHHIJOPRSTW	Joseph Wright
EGHHILNOSSSU	ghoulishness
EGHHIMNOOPPS	home shopping
EGHHINNOSTUU	house-hunting
EGHHMNOOPPSY	sphygmophone
EGHHMORRTTUY	merrythought
EGHHNOOOSTTU	go on the shout
EGHHNOOPRSTW	the wrong shop
EGHHNOORSSTU	thoroughness
EGHHNOORSTTU	through-stone
EGHIIIMNRSTV	shriving-time
EGHIIINOPRSS	seigniorship
EGHIIKLNNSST	knightliness
EGHIILLLNSSS	shillingless
EGHIILLNORSW	willing horse
EGHIILMMNRSY	shimmeringly
EGHIILMNOPRS	negrophilism
EGHIILMNPRWY	whimperingly
EGHIILNOPRST	negrophilist
EGHIILNOTTWZ	twilight zone
EGHIILNPRSWY	whisperingly
EGHIILOPSSTT	stegophilist
EGHIINNNNRTU	in the running
EGHIINNOSSTW	wishing stone
EGHIINNRSSTV	thrivingness
EGHIINOSSSUU	issuing house
EGHIINOSSTTU	house-sitting
EGHIKLNORSTY	Kentish glory
EGHIKNOORSUW	working house
EGHIKNOPPSST	pope's knights
EGHILLNORSST	short selling
EGHILLNRTTTU	truth-telling
EGHILMNORSTY	smotheringly
EGHILMOORSTY	mythologiser
EGHILMOORTYZ	mythologizer
EGHILNNNORTU	in the long run
EGHILNOOOSSU	loose housing
EGHILNOOPRST	nephrologist
	phrenologist
EGHILNPRSTUU	sulphureting
EGHILOOORSTT	heortologist
EGHILOOPPSST	psephologist
EGHIMNOOORSU	rooming house
EGHIMNORSSTW	women's rights
EGHINNORTTTU	otter-hunting
EGHINOOPRRSV	governorship
EGHINOOPSTTT	photosetting
EGHINORRRSTT	night terrors
EGHINORRSTTY	string theory
EGHINORRTTUW	interwrought
EGIIIILMPRST	pilgrimise it
EGIIIILMPRTZ	pilgrimize it
EGIIILLLNNPS	spilling line
EGIIILLNNRSV	silver lining
EGIIILNOSTTU	gentilitious
EGIIIMNNRTTT	intermitting
EGIIIMNOPSTU	impetiginous
EGIIINNNPRWZ	prize-winning
EGIIINNNRTTW	intertwining
EGIIINNNSSTV	invitingness
EGIIINOPSSTV	positive sign
EGIIINPPPPRS	pipers piping
EGIIJLNNORTU	jointing-rule
EGIIKKLNRRSS	Kriss Kringle
EGIIKLLNNORR	inking-roller
EGIIKLMMNOSU	mouse-milking
EGIIKLNPPRRS	klipspringer
EGIIKNNRSSST	strikingness
EGIIKNOPPPRS	skipping-rope
EGIILLMNOTUY	I'm telling you
EGIILLMNPTUY	timing pulley
EGIILMMNORVY	living memory
EGIILMNNNPSU	spinning mule
EGIILMNNOPTT	melting-point
EGIILMOOSSST	seismologist
EGIILNNNPRUY	unrepiningly
EGIILNNNRTTU	running title
EGIILNNPRSST	Silent Spring
EGIILNPRSSTY	persistingly
EGIILNRTTTWY	twitteringly
EGIIMMNNSSSW	swimmingness
EGIIMNNOPSSS	imposingness
EGIIMNOOPRRT	primogenitor
EGIIMNOORRST	risorgimento✧
EGIIMRSSSTTU	Trismegistus
EGIINNNORSST	non-resisting
EGIINOOPSTTV	give points to
EGIINPSSTTUY	tissue-typing
EGIIOPRRSSTW	gossip-writer
EGIJMMNOPSUU	jumping mouse
EGIKKNNOPRTY	pony-trekking

Words marked ✧ can also be spelled with one or more capital letters

EGIKLLMNOORY	Kremlinology
EGILLNNOORST	rolling stone
EGILLNORSTTY	storytelling
EGILLOORSUWW	willow grouse
EGILMNNORTTY	tormentingly
EGILMNOOOSTT	entomologist
EGILMNOORSTU	numerologist
EGILMNOOSTYZ	enzymologist
EGILNNNOSSUV	unlovingness
EGILNNRSUVWY	unswervingly
EGILNOOPRSUY	pyroligneous
EGILNOORSSSU	gloriousness
EGILNOPRSTTY	protestingly
EGILNPRSTTUY	sputteringly
EGILNRSTTTUY	stutteringly
EGIMMNOOPRSU	spermogonium
EGIMNOORRTTY	trigonometry
EGINNNORSSTW	Newton's rings
EGINNOPRSTTU	unprotesting
EGINNOPSSSSU	unpossessing
EGINNOPSTTTU	putting-stone
EGINNRSSSTTU	trustingness
EGINOORRSSSU	rigorousness
EGINOORSSSUV	vigorousness
EGINPRRSSSTU	purse strings
EGKNNOORSSTU	surgeon's knot
EGKNNORTTUUV	Kurt Vonnegut
EGLNNOOPRUYY	neurypnology
EHHHIMRRSTTU	hermit thrush
EHHIILLOOPSU	heliophilous
EHHIILOOPPSS	philosophise
EHHIILOOPPSZ	philosophize
EHHIIMMMOPRS	hemimorphism
EHHILMNOOSTU	Elihu Thomson
EHHILMRSSSTU	missel-thrush
EHHILMRSSTTU	mistle-thrush
EHHILOOPPSSS	philosophess
EHHILOPPSTUY	hyposulphite
EHHIMMOOPRST	theomorphism
EHHIMNOOPRST	thermosiphon
EHHIMNPSSSSU	sumphishness
EHHINNOOORTZ	on the horizon
EHHINOOOPPRS	siphonophore
EHHIOOPPRSTT	The Troop Ship
EHHMMOOOOPRY	homoeomorphy
EHHMMOOORSTU	homothermous
EHHMNOOOPRTY	phytohormone
EHHNOOPRTTTU	put to the horn
EHIIIILNPSST	Philistinise
EHIIIILNPSTZ	Philistinize
EHIIILORSTTT	lithotritise
EHIIILORTTTZ	lithotritize
EHIIILORTTVW	white vitriol
EHIIIMNPRSST	ministership
EHIIIOPTTTUY	it pitieth you
EHIIKLMOOPRT	poikilotherm
EHIIKNOOPSST	photokinesis
EHIIKNSSSSTT	skittishness
EHIILLMNPSTU	phillumenist
EHIILLNOPSTT	septillionth
EHIILLNOSTTX	sextillionth
EHIILLOPSTWW	will-o'-the-wisp
EHIILMOOPRST	heliotropism
EHIILOPRRTTT	lithotripter
EHIIMNPRSTUX	xiphisternum
EHIIMPRSSSST	mistress-ship
EHIINOOOPRSS	ionophoresis
EHIINORSTTUY	Trinity House
EHIINPPRSSST	spinstership
EHIIOPPRRSSU	superiorship
EHIIOPRRSSTV	servitorship
EHIJLNNOORST	Sir Elton John
EHIJMMNOORRT	John Mortimer
EHIJNNOOSSSS	John Sessions
EHIJORSTTUUY	the jury is out
EHIKLORSTTUW	Turkish towel
EHILLMOPPSTU	multiple shop
EHILLOPPRTYY	pyrophyllite
EHILLPPPSTUU	sulphite pulp
EHILMMOOPPRS	pleomorphism
EHILMMOPRSTU	lithospermum
EHILMMPRSSSU	mussel shrimp
EHILMNOORSWW	Winslow Homer
EHILMOOQRRTU	mother liquor
EHILNNOSSTYZ	Solzhenitsyn
EHILNOOPSUUY	euphoniously
EHILNOORTTWY	noteworthily
EHILNSSSSTTU	sluttishness
EHILOPPPRSYY	Shirley poppy
EHILOPRSSUWY	whisperously
EHIMMOOOORSU	homoiomerous
EHIMMOPSSTUY	The Symposium
EHIMMORRSSTT	short-termism
EHIMNPRSTUUY	murine typhus
EHIMOOPPRRSU	perimorphous
EHIMOOPPRRTY	pyromorphite
EHIMORRSSTTT	short-termist
EHINNOOPRRTU	neurotrophin
EHINNORSSTUW	unworthiness
EHINOOORSSTT	orthotonesis
EHINOOPPRSST	nephroptosis
EHINOPRRSTTY	phrontistery
EHINOPRTTTUZ	put on the ritz✧
EHIOOPRRSTTT	orthopterist
EHIOPRRSSUVY	surveyorship
EHKLNOOOOTTU	on the lookout
EHKMNOOOPSST	smooth-spoken
EHLMNNORSTUY	monthly nurse
EHLMOOOPPRSU	pleomorphous
EHLMOOOPPRTY	photopolymer
EHMMNNOORRST	the morn's morn
EHMMOOOPRSSU	mesomorphous
EHMNNOORRSTT	northernmost
EHMNOORSSSUU	humorousness
EHMNOORSSTTU	southernmost
EHMNOORSSTUY	honour system
EHMOOOPRRSUX	xeromorphous
EHMORRSSTTTU	storm shutter
EHNNOORRTUVW	unoverthrown
EHOOOPRRSTTU	orthopterous
EIIIILMRSTVY	verisimility
EIIILLMNOPST	pointillisme

EIIILLNOPSTT pointilliste
EIIILMMNOORS oil immersion
EIIILMORSSUV verisimilous
EIIIMMMNORSS immersionism
EIIIMMNORSST immersionist
EIIIMNNORSST intermission
EIIIMNOOPRST reimposition
EIIIMNORSSTV intromissive
EIIIMPRTTTVY permittivity
EIIINNOORSTT isotretinoin
EIIINOPQRSTU perquisition
EIIINQRSSSTU inquisitress
EIIJLLNNOOPS Lionel Jospin
EIIJMNOOPRTU junior optime
EIILLLLMNOPS Plimsoll line
EIILLMNOTTUV multivoltine
EIILLNOOSSTV volitionless
EIILLNORSSSU illusoriness
EIILLOOQRSSU soliloquiser
EIILLOOQRSUZ soliloquizer
EIILLPRSSSTY spiritlessly
EIILMNNNPTUU unnilpentium
EIILMNNPSTUU unnilseptium
EIILMNOOQSSU somniloquise
EIILMNOOQSUZ somniloquize
EIILMNOOSTUV evolutionism
EIILMOOPPRRV River Limpopo
EIILMOOPPRST pleiotropism
EIILMOPRSUVY imperviously
EIILMRSTTUVY multiversity
EIILNNNOSTUV tunnel vision
EIILNOOOPPST pole position
EIILNOORRSTU irresolution
EIILNOOSTTUV evolutionist
EIILNOPRSTUY polyneuritis
EIIMMNNOPRST imprisonment
EIIMNNNQQUUU quinquennium
EIIMNNORTTTT intromittent
EIIMNOOPRSSX expromission
EIIMNOOQRSUU querimonious
EIIMOPRSSSST prestissimos
EIIMORRRRRTW mirror writer
EIINNOORRSTV introversion
EIINNOPRRTTU interruption
EIINNOPRSSTU interspinous
EIINNOPRTTUU input routine
EIINOORSTTTX extortionist
EIINOPRRSSTU surprise into
EIINOPRSSTTU superstition
EIIOOPPSSTTV postpositive
EIIOOPRRSTTY posteriority
EIKLLNOORSWW work one's will
EIKMNNOSSTUZ Simon Kuznets
EIKMORRSSSTW workmistress
EILLLLRSSUWY Willy Russell
EILLMNOOSSTY motionlessly
EILLMNOQTTUU multiloquent
EILLMOPRTUVY overmultiply
EILLNOPPSTUV pulp novelist
EILMNNOOPTTY omnipotently
EILMNNOSSSUU luminousness
EILMNOORSTTV violent storm
EILMOPPRSTUU multipurpose
EILMOPSSSSTY spoils system
EILMORSSTUYY mysteriously
EILMRSSSSTTU mistrustless
EILNOOPRRSTU retropulsion
EILOOPRRSTUY pleurisy-root
EILOORRSSTUY roisterously
EILOPRRSTUVY protrusively
EIMMNNORSSUW snow-in-summer
EIMNNNOOOTTT not to mention
EIMNNNOSSSUU numinousness
EIMNNOOPTTUY put money into
EIMNNOSSSTUU mutinousness
EIMNOOOPPRRT proper motion
EIMNOOORRSST sensorimotor
EIMNOOOSSSTU isostemonous
EIMNOORSSSTU timorousness
EIMNOPRSSSUU suspensorium
EIMNORSSTUUV misventurous
EIMOPRSSSSTT postmistress
EINNOPRSSSUW win one's spurs
EINNRSSSTTUU untrustiness
EINOOPRRSTUV punto riverso
EINOORSSSUUX uxoriousness
EINOPRRSSTTW winter sports
EINOPRSSSSUU spuriousness
EINOQRTTTTUU Trout Quintet
EINORSSSSUUU usuriousness
EINORSSSTUUV virtuousness
EIOOOOPRSSST osteoporosis
EIOORRSTTTUU tourist route
EIOPRRRSSTTW sportswriter
EKLOOOORTTUW lookout tower
EKNOOORSTTYZ Otto Skorzeny
ELLNOORSTUUY ultroneously
ELLOOOPRRSTU porteous roll
ELNOOPPSSSUU populousness
ELNOOPRSTTUY portentously
ELNORSSSSTUU lustrousness
ELOOPPRRSSUY prosperously
ELOORRSSTTUY stertorously
EMOOOPPRRRTY property room
EMOOOPRRRSTT storm trooper
EMOPPRSSTUUU presumptuous
ENNOOORSSSSU sonorousness
ENOOPPRRSSST sportsperson
ENOOPPRRSSUU unprosperous
ENOORSSSTTUU tortuousness

F

FFFFGIIOTTYY go fifty-fifty
FFGGHHIIINST fighting fish
FFGIINOORSTT first-footing
FFGILNOPTTUY off-puttingly
FFHJLOORTUUY Fourth of July
FFIILOOPQRTU tip off liquor
FFILLNRTUUUY unfruitfully
FFLLOOSSTTYY softly-softly
FGGGILNOOOST footslogging
FGGHIILMPSTY pigs might fly

FGGHIINNNRTU running fight
FGGHINNOOORT go for nothing
FGGHINOOSUYY young fogyish
FGHHIIJNOTTW John Whitgift
FGHHILORRTTY forthrightly
FGHHLLOTTUUY thoughtfully
FGHHLNOTTUUU unthoughtful
FGHIIKNORSTW shift working
FGHIILLMNOTU mouth-filling
FGHIILNORRYY horrifyingly
FGHIINNNOOTT nothing if not
FGHILLNRTUUY unrightfully
FGHILLPRSTUY sprightfully
FGHINOPRTTTU forth-putting
FGIIILLNOSSV living fossil
FGIIILNOSTUY fuliginosity
FGIILLNOSUUY fuliginously
FGIILMNORTYY mortifyingly
FGIILMNSTYYY mystifyingly
FGILOORSTTUU futurologist
FGINNNNORRTU front-running
FGINOOPRRSTU rustproofing
FHIIIMNORRRS mirror finish
FHIIKKRSSWYY whisky-frisky
FHIILOOSTTWY foolish-witty
FHIIMOOQSSTU mosquito fish
FHIINOOOPSST photofission
FHILLOPRSUWY worshipfully
FHILNOPRSUUW unworshipful
FHLLNRTTUUUY untruthfully
FIIILLOOORTV oil of vitriol
FIIILLOPPSUU filius populi
FIIKLLNOOORS skillion roof
FIILLLMOPRUV pulvilliform
FIILMMORTTUY multiformity
FIIOOPRSSTTU out of spirits
FILLMNOSUUUX luminous flux
FILLMOORSTUU multiflorous
FILOORSTTUUY fortuitously
FMNNOORSSTUU from sun to sun

G

GGGHHINOORTU through-going
GGGHIIINNSST sight-singing
GGGILLNRSTUY strugglingly
GGHHHIITTTYY highty-tighty
GGHHILNRSTUY highly-strung
GGHHILOPRTUW ploughwright
GGHHOORRTUUW rough-wrought
GGHIIINNNNSY singing hinny
GGHIIJMMNTUY thingummyjig
GGHIILMNNOOT moonlighting
GGHIINNOOSTW wing shooting
GGHIINORSTTV voting rights
GGIIILLNNOTU guillotining
GGIIILMNPRSS pilgrim's sign
GGIIILNNRTUY intriguingly
GGIILLOORTUY liturgiology
GGIIMNNNORRU mourning ring
GGIINNOOPRTW growing-point
GGIINNOPSSTW swinging-post
GGILLOOOSSST glossologist
GGILMNNOORRY morning glory
GGILNOOOPSST spongologist
GHHHIKNORTTU think through
GHHHOOORSTTU shoot through
GHHILNOORTTW throw light on
GHHILOOPRSUY hygrophilous
GHHIMNORRSUU Sir Hugh Munro
GHHINOPRRTTU print-through
GHHMNPRRSTUY sprung rhythm
GHIIJNNOOSTU housing joint
GHIIKLNNNTUY unthinkingly
GHIILLNNSTTU still hunting
GHIILNNORSUY nourishingly
GHIILNOPPSST shopping list
GHIILOOORSTY historiology
GHIILOOPSSTY physiologist
GHIINNNORSUU unnourishing
GHIINNOOORST shooting iron
GHIINOPPPSTW whipping-post
GHIKNOORRSUW working hours
GHILMOOOPRST morphologist
GHILMOOOPSSU Ophioglossum
GHILNOOPPRRY lorry-hopping
GHIMMOOPRSYZ zygomorphism
GHIMNOOPSSTY gymnosophist
GHINOOPPSSTW show-stopping
GHLMOOOPPSUY pompholygous
GHLOOOOPTYYZ zoophytology
GHMOOOPRSUYZ zygomorphous
GIIILLMNNNPS spinning-mill
GIIIMNNORTTT intromitting
GIIKKOORRSSY Igor Sikorsky
GIIKLLMNOOST milking stool
GIILLNOORSUY ingloriously
GIILMMNOOPSW swimming-pool
GIILMMNOOSTU immunologist
GIILMNNOOSTU monolinguist
GIILMNORSSST Stirling Moss
GIILNORRSSTU soul-stirring
GIILNPRRSSUY surprisingly
GIILOOORSSTT storiologist
GIINNNOPRTTU turning point
GIINNPRRSSUU unsurprising
GILLMOOPRSSY prosyllogism
GILNOORSSSTY strongylosis
GILOOOPRSTTY protistology
GIMNOOOPRSST mosstrooping
GINOOOPRRSTU nitroso-group
GINOORRRSSTY Sir Roy Strong
GLLNOOSTTUUY gluttonously
GLLOOOPSTTUY polyglottous
GLOOOOOPRTYZ protozoology
GOOPPPRRSTUU support group

H

HHHJMNOPRSUY John Humphrys
HHIIILOOPPST ophiophilist
HHIILLOOPSTU lithophilous
HHIILMOOPPSS philosophism
HHIILNOOPRTY ornithophily

HHIILOOPPSST philosophist
HHIILOOPRSUZ rhizophilous
HHIIOOPRSSTU Histiophorus
HHIKLMOORSTY Miklós Horthy
HHILMMOOPRSY hylomorphism
HHILOOOPPSTU photophilous
HHIMMMOOOPRS homomorphism
HHIMNOOOPRRT ornithomorph
HHINOOPRRTTY thyrotrophin
HHIOOTTTUUWW tu-whit tu-whoo
HHMMOOOOPRSU homomorphous
HHMMOOOTTTUU mouth-to-mouth
HHMNOOOPPRTY pythonomorph
HIIIILMNPSST philistinism✧
HIIIILMNSTTW within limits
HIIILORSTTTT lithotritist
HIIJLLMNORSS Sir John Mills
HIILLMNOOPSU limnophilous
HIILLOOPPRWW whippoorwill
HIILMOPRSSSU Russophilism
HIILNOOPRSTU nitrophilous
HIILOOPRRTTT lithotriptor
HIILOPRSSSTU Russophilist
HIIMMNOORSTU Ornithomimus
HIIMNNOSSTTW Winston Smith
HIINOOPRRSZZ Prizzi's Honor
HIINOPRSTTUU in hot pursuit
HIIOOPRSSTUV virtuosoship
HIIOPRRSSUVV survivorship
HIJJMNOORSST Sir J J Thomson
HIJJNNOORRSU Sir John Junor
HIKMMNOOPRSU mushroom pink
HIKMNNOOOPST Tom Hopkinson
HILMMOOPPRSY polymorphism
HILMNNOPSYYZ Linz Symphony
HILOOOPPRSTU tropophilous
HIMMMNOOOPRS monomorphism
HIMOOOPPRSTT phototropism
HIMOOOPRRSTT orthotropism
HIMOORSTTTWY thirty-twomos
HINOOOOPSSTT opisthotonos
HIOOOPRRSTTY proto-history
HLLLOOPPSUYY polyphyllous
HLMMNOOOSUYY homonymously
HLMOOOPPRSUY polymorphous
HLMOOPSSTUUY posthumously
HMMNOOOOPRSU monomorphous
HMNNOOOPRUUY upon my honour
HOOOOPPRRSSU sporophorous
HOOOOPRRSTTU orthotropous

I

IIIIMMMNNPYY miminy-piminy
IIIIMMNNNPYY niminy-piminy
IIIIMNNOSTTU intuitionism
IIIINNOSTTTU intuitionist
IIILNOQSTUUY iniquitously
IIIMNNOORSST intromission
IIIMNOORTTUV vomiturition
IIINNOOOPPSU pious opinion
IIINNORSSTTU intrusionist
IIINNORSTTTU nutritionist
IIINNORSTTUU innutritious
IIIOPRSSTTUY spirituosity
IILLMNOPTTUY multiply into
IILMMNOOQSSU somniloquism
IILMNOOPSSTU postliminous
IILMNOOQSSTU somniloquist
IILMNOOSTUVY voluminosity
IILMOOPRRSSY promissorily
IILMOOPSSTYY polymyositis
IILNORSSSTUY sinistrously
IILNORSTTUUY nutritiously
IILOOPPRSTUY propitiously
IIMNNOOORRST Toni Morrison
IINNNNOORSTU non-intrusion
IINNOOOPPRRT in proportion
IINNOOOPPTTT point-to-point
IINOOOPPSSTT postposition
IINOOPPRSTUU unpropitious
IINOOPRSTTTU prostitution
IIOOPPSSSTUU suppositious
IJNOPRRSSTUY sports injury
IKNOOORSSSVY Novorossiysk
ILLMNOOOSTTY tonsillotomy
ILLMNOOSUUVY voluminously
ILLMOOQSTUUU multiloquous
ILLNNNOORSSY Sonny Rollins
ILMNOOORSUVY omnivorously
ILNORSTUUUVY unvirtuously
ILOOPSTTUUVY voluptuosity
ILOPRSTTUVYY topsy-turvily
IMNOORSSTTUY monstruosity
IMOOPPRRSTUY pityrosporum
INNNOOOOPSSU non-poisonous
INNOOOPRRRTY Norton Priory

L

LLMOSTTUUUUY tumultuously
LLOOPSTUUUVY voluptuously
LMMNOOPSTUUY Mount Olympus
LMNNOOOOSTUY monotonously
LMNNOOSSUYYY synonymously
LMNOSTTUUUUU untumultuous

M

MNPPRRSTTUUU turn up trumps

O

OOOOSSTTTWYY tootsy-wootsy

13 letters

A

AAAAAACCGMRRS cascara amarga
AAAAABHLNNNSS Hassan al-Banna
AAAAABHMNRTTY Bharata Natyam
AAAAACCDEEINR Anacardiaceae
AAAAACEEHMNRT Amaranthaceae
AAAAACEHIMSTT acatamathesia
AAAAADGGIINNN again and again
AAAAAHKMNNOTV Anna Akhmatova
AAAABBCELRRST Barbara Castle
AAAABBDEGGGGN bag and baggage
AAAABCCEELRTU baccalaureate
AAAABCCILNNOT tobaccanalian
AAAABCDIILLTY adiabatically
AAAABCEEILMNS Balsaminaceae
AAAABCEEKKSTT take a back seat
AAAABCEFHLLSS false calabash
AAAABCEIKLMOR Lake Maracaibo
AAAABCIMNNRRU Carmina Burana
AAAABCLOPPRSS pocas palabras
AAAABDDEENRRS Andreas Baader
AAAABDEEGLNTV advantageable
AAAABDEELLLNS Alan Bleasdale
AAAABDILMORSS ambassadorial
AAAABEGGGILMN baggage-animal
AAAABEGNPRSSU asparagus bean
AAAABEHILNPRT alphabetarian
AAAABELOPRSST Pablo Sarasate
AAAABHHINNNRR Brian Hanrahan
AAAABILMNRRTT Tartarian lamb
AAAACCCEEORRY Caryocaraceae
AAAACCDEEIPPR Capparidaceae
AAAACCDEINNNO Canadian canoe
AAAACCDIIKLLS lackadaisical
AAAACCEEINRSU Casuarinaceae
AAAACCEELMNPU Campanulaceae
AAAACCEELNPRV Cape Canaveral
AAAACCEELPRSS Caesar's Palace
AAAACCHILLNRT charlatanical
AAAACCILLLPRT parallactical
AAAACCLMNORST malacostracan
AAAACDEEMRSTT Atacama Desert
AAAACDGHINORS Garda Siochana
AAAACDIILLNRT cardinalatial
AAAACEEEILNRV Valerianaceae
AAAACEEFGIRSX Saxifragaceae
AAAACEGIKLNRU Lake Nicaragua
AAAACEGILMOST galactosaemia
AAAACEHILMNTT anathematical
AAAACEIMMNORS American Samoa
AAAACEKLRSSVV Vera Cáslavská
AAAACEMNORSTU amarantaceous
AAAACFHLMMNNO Man of La Mancha
AAAACGHHMMNPR Graham Chapman
AAAACGHILPPRR paragraphical
AAAACIIKLMORV Alicia Markova
AAAACIOPSSSTT apocatastasis
AAAACLNNORSST Carlos Santana
AAAADEEFGMNST damage feasant
AAAADEEFNRRRR Andrea Ferrara
AAAADEGHLMNOP alpha and omega
AAAADFFLNNORU fauna and flora
flora and fauna
AAAADILLLOPSV viola da spalla
AAAADILLLPRXY daily parallax
AAAADILLNNPSW Palawan Island
AAAADILMNOPTT maladaptation
AAAAEEGHJMMPT The Pajama Game
AAAAEEHILMRRT Amelia Earhart
AAAAEEJLMSSST laesa majestas
AAAAEGIMMNRST anagrammatise
AAAAEGIMMNRTZ anagrammatize
AAAAEHILNPPRR paraphernalia
AAAAEIILLRRWY aerial railway
AAAAEIKLLMMSU salaam aleikum
AAAAEJLMNPRTU Jean Paul Marat
AAAAELNNSTTVW savanna-wattle
AAAAGHIMNNRRT grain amaranth
AAAAGHKMPPRRR paragraph mark
AAAAGILLNNOUV Galina Ulanova
AAAAGIMMMNRST anagrammatism
AAAAGIMMNRSTT anagrammatist
AAAAGPRRSSTTW grasp at a straw
AAAAHILMNNPST phantasmalian
AAAAIKKORRSUW Akira Kurosawa
AAABBCCIILLST cabbalistical
AAABBCDDILOOU Claudio Abbado
AAABBCEEGIPST pe-tsai cabbage
AAABBCEFINORR Afro-Caribbean
AAABBCILMMNPY namby-pambical
AAABBDDEELLNT Debatable Land
AAABBDEHORRST Barbados earth
AAABBEIIMNRRS semi-barbarian
AAABBELNPRSTY Barnstaple Bay
AAABBHMMOORSS Abraham's bosom
AAABBIINORRST barbarisation
AAABBIINORRTZ barbarization
AAABCCCEKLLTU back-calculate
AAABCCEEHNOOR Orobanchaceae
AAABCCEILMNRT Bactrian camel
AAABCCELNNORR acorn-barnacle
AAABCCEMORRSU camera obscura
AAABCCENNRSSU bancassurance
AAABCCHILOPRR parabolic arch
AAABCCILLORTY acrobatically
AAABCDDELMSSU Damascus blade
AAABCDEEGIRSU bigarade sauce
AAABCDEELNRRS scandal-bearer
AAABCDEGHIRTW with a bad grace
AAABCDEHINRTU chateaubriand✧
AAABCDELMRTTU Dame Clara Butt
AAABCDIKNORTW backwardation
AAABCEEEHKPSY Chesapeake Bay

AAABCEEILNRST	ascertainable
AAABCEEIMNPRZ	carbamazepine
AAABCEENPPRSU	subappearance
AAABCEFHKNRRU	Frank Auerbach
AAABCEFILNOTT	labefactation
AAABCEFKKMSTU	make a fast buck
AAABCEGILLLRY	algebraically
AAABCEGILNORS	close a bargain
AAABCEHINRRTT	Tetrabranchia
AAABCEHJMNNSU	James Buchanan
AAABCEHMNRRTY	Carmarthen Bay
AAABCEIILNRTT	antibacterial
AAABCEILLLORV	local variable
AAABCEILLNORY	anaerobically
AAABCEILLNTTU	nautical table
AAABCEILNOOPT	palaeobotanic
AAABCEILORRST	Alberto Ascari
AAABCEKQRRRSU	barrack square
AAABCHHINOOPR	arachnophobia
AAABCIINNSSTY	Abyssinian cat
AAABCILLLOPRY	parabolically
AAABCILNORSTT	abstractional
AAABCIMNNNNOR	Briançon manna
AAABCKLNNORUY	Alan Ayckbourn
AAABDDDENRRST	standard bread
AAABDDDLMNNOR	Donald Bradman
AAABDDELNTTUW	wattle and daub
AAABDEEFLLRTW	draw-leaf table
AAABDEEINRRST	Arabian Desert
AAABDEEINRRTV	ardentia verba
AAABDEELNPSST	adaptableness
AAABDEGHHNRTY	hang by a thread
AAABDEGIILMTY	damageability
AAABDEGIINNRS	drainage basin
AAABDEGMNNNOR	rag-and-bone-man
AAABDELLNPSTU	Spandau Ballet
AAABDGHINNSST	Hastings Banda
AAABDHHINNSSW	washhand basin
AAABDHILMMMQU	Muhammad Iqbal
AAABDHMMOORTY	rhabdomyomata
AAABEEEGKLRRT	Great Bear Lake
AAABEEEKPRRTZ	zebra parakeet
AAABEEELLRTUV	rateable value
AAABEEGHKRRTT	Akbar the Great
AAABEEGIMRRRT	Greater Bairam
AAABEEGLLNSUV	unsalvageable
AAABEEGLNSSUU	unassuageable
AAABEEHLLRSTV	ballast-heaver
AAABEEILLNSSV	availableness
AAABEEILMMNRU	balneum Mariae
AAABEELLNPSST	palatableness
AAABEFHILNSUV	have a basinful
AAABEFILOPTTV	Battle of Pavia
AAABEFLNORTTV	Battle of Varna
AAABEGIILMNTY	manageability
AAABEGILNNSUY	ungainsayable
AAABEGILNSTTT	battle against
AAABEHIMSTTTY	be that as it may
AAABEHLMNOPRT	Roman alphabet
AAABEIINNRSST	artesian basin
AAABEILLMNPTU	manipulatable
AAABEILMMNPST	baptismal name
AAABEILNTTUVV	tableau vivant
AAABELNNRRTUW	unwarrantable
AAABGHIINNRST	Arabian Nights
AAABGIINNORTV	navigation bar
AAABGPRRRSSST	part brass rags
AAABHHINOOPTT	thanatophobia
AAABHIOOPPRST	astrapophobia
AAABIIILLNOST	labialisation
AAABIIILLNOTZ	labialization
AAABIIILMQRSU	aqua mirabilis
AAABIIILNTTTY	attainability
AAABIIKLNNOST	Balkanisation
AAABIIKLNNOTZ	Balkanization
AAABILNNRSSUY	Alan Sainsbury
AAABLNNRRTUWY	unwarrantably
AAACCCCDHIIRS	saccharic acid
AAACCCEEHLNTY	Cyclanthaceae
AAACCCEMMOPRT	compact camera
AAACCCGHILOPR	cacographical
AAACCCHKLOPRR	chaparral cock
AAACCDEEGLLNP	plagal cadence
AAACCDEGLORTU	card catalogue
AAACCDEHLLNPS	paschal candle
AAACCDEIILMMS	academicalism
AAACCDEIIMNNO	Nadia Comaneci
AAACCDEIIPSTT	discapacitate
AAACCDEILLNTU	canaliculated
AAACCDEIPRTTY	rated capacity
AAACCDEIRRRST	cardiac arrest
AAACCDHIILNOR	archidiaconal
AAACCDILNRSUY	canicular days
AAACCEEEILORU	Eriocaulaceae
AAACCEEELLNRS	clearance sale
AAACCEEFHLOTT	at the coalface
AAACCEEGINNTY	Nyctaginaceae
AAACCEEHILNRT	technical area
AAACCEEHMNRTT	catchment area
AAACCEEILLNRT	cancellariate
AAACCEELMMRRU	Marcel Marceau
AAACCEELNNRUU	Ranunculaceae
AAACCEELOPRTU	Portulacaceae
AAACCEGHMNOST	stagecoachman
AAACCEGILLNPT	galactic plane
AAACCEGILLPTY	legal capacity
AAACCEGILRTTX	extragalactic
AAACCEHILMOPY	hypocalcaemia
AAACCEHKLMRSY	Charles Mackay
AAACCEHPRRRTT	character part
AAACCEILLMORS	scleromalacia
AAACCEILNNOTT	Atlantic Ocean
AAACCEILNRRUY	canicular year
AAACCELLPRSTY	Crystal Palace
AAACCELNORTYY	cyanoacrylate
AAACCENNORTTV	vena contracta
AAACCGHLORRSU	sugar charcoal
AAACCGILLLMOO	malacological
AAACCGILLOOST	astacological
AAACCGIMMNNOR	Norman MacCaig
AAACCHIINPRST	captain's chair
AAACCHILLRTTY	cathartically

Words marked ✧ can also be spelled with one or more capital letters

AAACCHILPPRSY parapsychical
AAACCHLORSSTY thalassocracy
AAACCHLORTTTY thalattocracy
AAACCHRSSTTTW catch at straws
AAACCIILLSTTT stalactitical
AAACCIILMNOTT acclimatation
AAACCIILMSSTT salami tactics
AAACCIILPTTVY vital capacity
AAACCILLLNOTU calculational
AAACCILLLTTYY catalytically
AAACCILLMNORY macaronically
AAACCILLOPPTY apocalyptical
AAACCILLRSSTY sarcastically
AAACCILOTTTUY autocatalytic
AAACCILPRRSTT practical arts
AAACCMNORSTTU acta sanctorum
AAACDDDEGNRUV advanced guard
AAACDDEGHHILT Gaidhealtachd
AAACDDEIMMNSU unmacadamised
AAACDDEIMMNUZ unmacadamized
AAACDDELLMNNO Donald Maclean
AAACDDINNORSU Isadora Duncan
AAACDEEEGHNRY Hydrangeaceae
AAACDEEEJNPRS Japanese cedar
AAACDEEFLLLRW Alfred Wallace
AAACDEEGHISSS Chagas' disease
AAACDEEGIRRRT carriage trade
AAACDEEGJKNRT Jack Teagarden
AAACDEEHNRRST sandarach tree
AAACDEEIIMMRT materia medica
AAACDEEILLNTV dataveillance
AAACDEEINPPRS disappearance
AAACDEELLMORT moderate a call
AAACDEENNRTTT care attendant
AAACDEGHPRRTU drag-parachute
AAACDEGIILMRT digital camera
AAACDEGILLNOS diagonal scale
AAACDEGINRRSS airs and graces
AAACDEGKMNNRR rack and manger
AAACDEGLMMNUU magna cum laude
AAACDEGLMOSUY amygdalaceous
AAACDEGLNOOPS da capo al segno
AAACDEHILNSTT Canada thistle
AAACDEHIMNRTY adiathermancy
AAACDEHNNPSTY cheap and nasty
AAACDEIIILRUV Aviculariidae
AAACDEIIINPRT paediatrician
AAACDEIILMOPS Lasiocampidae
AAACDEIILMPRT pre-adamitical
AAACDEIINNRRV Canadian River
AAACDEILMNNOP pandemoniacal✧
AAACDEILMNORY aerodynamical
AAACDEIMNQRTU quadratic mean
AAACDEIMSTTUZ Azteca Stadium
AAACDEINNRRSS sandarac resin
AAACDELLNPSTT scale and platt
AAACDELNPPRRT part and parcel
AAACDESTTUUUX audax et cautus
AAACDGHIIMPRT diaphragmatic
AAACDGHLLLNOR Lord Callaghan
AAACDGILMNOOR macrodiagonal
AAACDGILMRRTU dramaturgical
AAACDHHINNRRY Richard Hannay
AAACDHIILOPRS aphrodisiacal
AAACDHIINOPRS anaphrodisiac
AAACDHILMRRTY Admiralty Arch
AAACDHILNOPTY anaphylactoid
AAACDIIILLNRT cardinalitial
AAACDIIMMORTU acaridomatium
AAACDILLOPRXY paradoxically
AAACDILNNRSSY Canary Islands
AAACDILNOORST Isla Contadora
AAACDILNORTUY auditory canal
AAACDIMMOORTU acarodomatium
AAACEEEEHLMTY Thymelaeaceae
AAACEEEFFILRS Rafflesiaceae
AAACEEEFIKNNR Frankeniaceae
AAACEEEGILMNR American eagle
AAACEEEHLPRTT Palace Theatre
AAACEEELMMOST Melastomaceae
AAACEEELOOPRT Tropaeolaceae
AAACEEFIILOQU Aquifoliaceae
AAACEEFLNNORT Anatole France
AAACEEGHIILMP Malpighiaceae
AAACEEGHINORT Archegoniatae
AAACEEGIRRRTW water-carriage
AAACEEGLLNORS on a large scale
AAACEEGLLOSTU sale-catalogue
AAACEEGLLSTVY slaty cleavage
AAACEEHINPSUU euphausiacean
AAACEEHKLMRTY the real Mackay
AAACEEIILNOPP Papilionaceae
AAACEEIJMPPPR Jamaica pepper
AAACEEILLMOPT palaeoclimate
AAACEEILMORRT araeometrical
AAACEEILMRSTU material cause
AAACEEILQSSTU aqua caelestis
AAACEEINNPPRT appertainance
AAACEEKKMNPPU pancake make-up
AAACEELLMNOSW seam allowance
AAACEELNRSTTY scaly anteater
AAACEENNNOPPR non-appearance
AAACEEOPPRSUV papaveraceous
AAACEFFILNPRS paraffin-scale
AAACEFGKLNOTT angle of attack
AAACEFIILNNRY financial year
AAACEFIMORRTW atomic warfare
AAACEFMORRRTT cream of tartar
AAACEGHILMNPS Agnes MacPhail
AAACEGHILOPPR palaeographic
AAACEGHLOORRT galactorrhoea
AAACEGILMNNOR Anglo-American
AAACEGILMTTUY Guatemala City
AAACEGIMMNPRS smear campaign
AAACEGIMNNORR American organ
AAACEGIMNOSTY gynaecomastia
AAACEGIMQRRUZ García Márquez
AAACEGLORSTTU star catalogue
AAACEHIILLMNV Machiavellian
AAACEHIIMMNNS Manichaeanism
AAACEHIIMMNTT mathematician
AAACEHILLMRRS Earl Marischal

AAACEHILLMTTY athematically
AAACEHILLPPRT alpha particle
AAACEHILLPTTY apathetically
AAACEHILMMRSY Michael Ramsay
AAACEHILNPRRT Central Pahari
AAACEHILNPRTU Alpha Centauri
AAACEHIMOOPPR pharmacopoeia
AAACEHLLMRSVY lachrymal vase
AAACEHLMNORST steal a march on
AAACEHLORRSTT Scarlett O'Hara
AAACEHNRRRSTW search warrant
AAACEIILLMRSU Maurice Allais
AAACEIILMNNRT Latin American
AAACEIJNOPRRT terra-japonica
AAACEIKLMNNOR Neo-Lamarckian
AAACEILLMNOTX exclamational
AAACEILLMOOST osteomalacial
AAACEILNNSSST satanicalness
AAACEILPSSSTT capital assets
AAACEIMNNRSTT instant camera
AAACEIMOPPRSS caesaropapism✧
AAACEINRSSSTT care assistant
AAACEKNOOPPTT potato pancake
AAACELLLMNOSS on a small scale
AAACELLMNRSTY sacramentally
AAACELLNORRTT contralateral
AAACELNRSSTUU natural causes
AAACELRRSTUVW water-vascular
AAACELRRSTUVX extravascular
AAACENRRRSTTU restaurant car
AAACFGIILMNPP facial mapping
AAACFGILNNRSU lingua francas
AAACFHILNOPPR final approach
AAACFHLNORSTY Choral Fantasy
AAACFIILLLMOX maxillofacial
AAACFIIMNNPRS Pan-Africanism
AAACFILLNSTTY fantastically
AAACFIMNORRTW aircraftwoman
AAACGGHIIMNOT gigantomachia
AAACGGHMNRTTU gum tragacanth
AAACGHIILPPRS pasigraphical
AAACGIILLMSTT stalagmitical
AAACGILLMMRTY grammatically
AAACGILLMNSTY synallagmatic
AAACGILLMPRTY pragmatically
AAACGILMMNRTU ungrammatical
AAACGILNNOTTU anticoagulant
AAACGLLSSSUWY Gay-Lussac's law
AAACHHINNNTTX canthaxanthin
AAACHHKMRRRTU Arthur Rackham
AAACHIILLPRSY pharisaically
AAACHIIMNSTTT antiasthmatic
AAACHILLMSTTY asthmatically
AAACHILLNOPRY anaphorically
AAACHILNRSSSU Halicarnassus
AAACHIMOOPRST achromatopsia
AAACHLORRTYYZ Zachary Taylor
AAACIIKLMMNRS Lamarckianism
AAACIILLMNOST anomalistical
AAACIILLMOTXY axiomatically
AAACIILLPRSTY parasitically
AAACIILLSTTVY atavistically
AAACIILNNNOTT incantational
AAACIILNOOSST associational
AAACIILNORSST sacralisation
AAACIILNORSTZ sacralization
AAACIILNOSSTU casualisation
AAACIILNOSTTU actualisation
AAACIILNOSTUZ casualization
AAACIILNOTTUZ actualization
AAACIIMNRRSTT Tractarianism
AAACIINRRTTVY intracavitary
AAACIINSTTTVY cast a nativity
AAACIIORSSTTU Austroasiatic
AAACIKOPRRSST sick as a parrot
AAACILLLMPSST small capitals
AAACILLMOTTUY automatically
AAACILLMRTTUY traumatically
AAACILNNORSSY narcoanalysis
AAACILNNORSTT transactional
AAACILNNRSTTT transatlantic
AAACILNORSTTU astronautical
AAACILNPRRSTU intracapsular
AAACILNRRSTUV intravascular
AAACILOSSTTUY autocatalysis
AAACINNNOOOTV Antonio Canova
AAACMOORSTTTY astrocytomata
AAADDDEEGILRZ Grazia Deledda
AAADDDEEINNOS Dido and Aeneas
AAADDDEELMNPS dead man's pedal
AAADDDEELTUVX value-added tax
AAADDDEGINSTV disadvantaged
AAADDDEGNRRST Standard grade
AAADDEEELMMST Madame de Staël
AAADDEGGIIMNR Dame Diana Rigg
AAADDEGGNRSTU standard gauge
AAADDEGIMNOOR Diego Maradona
AAADDEGLLNNRS adrenal glands
AAADDEGLLNORS Donald A Glaser
AAADDEHHISTVY have had its day
AAADDEHHMPRSY Madhya Pradesh
AAADDEHHNPRRS Andhra Pradesh
AAADDGLLRSWYY Gladys Aylward
AAADDHHNNSSTW washhand stand
AAADDHIINORRT hard radiation
AAADDILNPPSYY pay and display
pay-and-display
AAADDLNORRSTY royal standard
AAADEEEGLMNRR la Grande Armée
AAADEEEINNNRS Seanad Eireann
AAADEEELLNRRX Earl Alexander
AAADEEELMMRRT marmalade tree
AAADEEELMNORV Éamon de Valera
AAADEEEMRRSTU tread a measure
AAADEEERRSTTW aerated waters
AAADEEFHNRRTT tar and feather
AAADEEFLLLMNU Manuel de Falla
AAADEEFNRRRRW Andrew Ferrara
AAADEEGHHORTT gather to a head
AAADEEGHILNRX Alexander Haig
AAADEEGHKRTWW The Awkward Age
AAADEEGILNNSS Aegean Islands

 Words marked ✧ can also be spelled with one or more capital letters

AAADEEGKLMMOO make a good meal
AAADEEGLLNOPR Edgar Allan Poe
AAADEEGLMMNRY Magdalene Mary
Mary Magdalene
AAADEEGLNRTUV advantage rule
AAADEEHHLNRTY hale and hearty
AAADEEHLNRSST Alashan Desert
AAADEEHORSTUW data warehouse
AAADEEILQRTUU audita querela
AAADEELMNPRSW Pamela Andrews
AAADEEMNNNOST a means to an end
AAADEFFIMORRU affaire d'amour
AAADEFGHHILNT Eight and a Half
AAADEFGJNNORR Jean Fragonard
AAADEFGKLMNRU Gerald Kaufman
AAADEFHHILMNV have half a mind
AAADEFHIRSSSY fresh as a daisy
AAADEFINQRRSU fair-and-square
AAADEGGILNNRU guardian angel✧
AAADEGGINRSST gas and gaiters
AAADEGIILNNRT Italian garden
AAADEGILMQRSU quadragesimal
AAADEGINRSTTV avant-gardiste
AAADEHHIMNNRT Rhadamanthine
AAADEHHNPRSSZ haphazardness
AAADEHILMOPPR lampadephoria
AAADEHILNNNST Daniel Nathans
AAADEHMMNNRST Arms and the Man
AAADEIILMNOPR Daniel arap Moi
AAADEILLQRRTU quadrilateral
AAADEILMORRST air loadmaster
AAADEIMNNQRSU squandermania
AAADEINOPPRTT preadaptation
AAADELLLMNRSY small-and-early
AAADELLMMMPRU marmalade plum
AAADELMMOPSST plasmodesmata
AAADELRSSTUUV a vuestra salud
AAADEMNNOORSS Moses and Aaron
AAADFGILLMORR floral diagram
AAADFIIKLNOSU Island of Kauai
AAADFNNOOPTUY Antony of Padua
AAADGGILNOSUW Gawain Douglas
AAADGHILMNRTU draught animal
AAADGILLNORTY gradationally
AAADGILLNRSVY salivary gland
AAADGILNNNORT Grand National
AAADGILNNORTU National Guard
AAADGIMNOORST good Samaritan
AAADHLLLLOSWY All Hallows Day
AAADIIILNORST radialisation
AAADIIILNORTZ radialization
AAADIILNNSSVY Visayan Island
AAADIIMNORSTT dramatisation
AAADIIMNORTTZ dramatization
AAADILLORRSUV Salvador Luria
AAADILNNSTUUV Vanuatu Island
AAADINNNORTTU Antonin Artaud
AAADNNNORSSSU Susan Sarandon
AAAEEEGKNRTWY Kate Greenaway
AAAEEEHKNPRSS Shakespearean
AAAEEEJLMNPPS Japanese maple
AAAEEEJNPPPRS Japanese paper
AAAEEELLNPRTV parental leave
AAAEEFGILLRSS as large as life
AAAEEFGLORSVW law of averages
AAAEEFILORSTV Teresa of Avila
AAAEEFQRRRTTU a quarter after
AAAEEGGGHILOR George Alagiah
AAAEEGHLOPPRR palaeographer
AAAEEGKLLRSTT Great Salt Lake
AAAEEGLNPRRTY planetary gear
AAAEEGMMMNNNT man-management
AAAEEGMNNPRSS manganese spar
AAAEEGOPRTTTX toga praetexta
AAAEEHIKLLNRT alkaline earth
AAAEEHIKNPRSS Shakespearian
AAAEEHILMRRST raise the alarm
AAAEEHILNNPST Asian elephant
AAAEEHILTTTTV leave it at that
AAAEEHINPRRST Eastern Pahari
AAAEEHKLMRSWZ shalwar-kameez
AAAEEHLLRSSVW walls have ears
AAAEEHNRRSSTW Western Sahara
AAAEEIIKNOSST Setonaikai Sea
AAAEEIIMMNNRS miner's anaemia
AAAEEIKLLMPST Kailasa Temple
AAAEEILMNOPPR paraleipomena
AAAEEILMNPRTZ mazarine plate
AAAEEILNNPRTT plantain-eater
AAAEEILOPRRWY aerial ropeway
AAAEEJLLNNRRY Alan Jay Lerner
AAAEEJLNRSTTW serjeant-at-law
AAAEELNRRTTTY Lateran Treaty
AAAEENORSSUVY save as you earn
AAAEFFHILLORX Earl of Halifax
AAAEFFHINORST after a fashion
AAAEFGILLLMNO flagellomania
AAAEFGILLNRSV Gavarnie Falls
AAAEFGIORSSST as far as it goes
AAAEFGMOPRSSS passage of arms
AAAEFGNPRRSSU asparagus fern
AAAEFHILLMORT Thalamiflorae
AAAEFIILMMRST materfamilias
AAAEFIILMPRST paterfamilias
AAAEFINPRRSTT aspirant after
AAAEFLNNORSVW savanna flower
AAAEFNNORSSTV savanna-forest
AAAEGGILLNNPU plain language
AAAEGGIMNOPRS megasporangia
AAAEGHIINOOSW Hawaiian goose
AAAEGHNPRSSTU argus pheasant
AAAEGIIILNNRT inegalitarian
AAAEGIILMMNRS managerialism
AAAEGIILMNRST managerialist
AAAEGIILMRRRT trial marriage
AAAEGILLOPRRT alligator pear
AAAEGILMNORSU megalosaurian
AAAEGILMORRRY royal marriage
AAAEGILNNPRTU Pantagruelian
AAAEGILOPRSTU à la Portugaise
AAAEGIMMNNORR neogrammarian
AAAEGIMMNPRST paramagnetism

AAAEGINNRSTTU against nature
AAAEGINORTTVX extravagation
AAAEGIPRRRUVY River Paraguay
AAAEGKLNOOPPR kangaroo-apple
AAAEGLLLMOPRR parallelogram
AAAEGLMNNRTTU natural magnet
AAAEGLNRTTVXY extravagantly
AAAEHHILMPRTT amphitheatral
AAAEHHIMNRRRT Harriet Harman
AAAEHILNNPRST phalansterian
AAAEHJKLORSSV Jaroslav Hasek
AAAEHJMNRSTTY James Hanratty
AAAEHLMNOPRRT the paranormal
AAAEHLMRTTTUW Walter Matthau
AAAEIIKLLLMNR mineral alkali
AAAEIILLMRRSW Maria Walliser
AAAEIILMNNOTX examinational
AAAEIILNPRRTT intraparietal
AAAEIILNRRRTT intra-arterial
AAAEIKNRRRSSV Arkansas River
AAAEILLLNOPPT appellational
AAAEILLRRTXXY extra-axillary
AAAEILMMMNPRT in malam partem
AAAEILMMNNPRT parliament-man
AAAEILMNPRRTY parliamentary
AAAEILNNOPTTT tea plantation
AAAEILNNPRTTW water plantain
AAAEILNNRSTUW new Australian
AAAEILPPPRSTT papaprelatist
AAAEIMMMNRRTU armamentarium
AAAEINORSTTVX extravasation
AAAEKLMMNNSSW Selman Waksman
AAAELNORTTTWY attorney at law
AAAELOPPRRTVY lavatory paper
AAAELPRSSTTWY play at wasters
AAAEMMRRSSSTT masters-at-arms
AAAFFHIMORSTX Thomas Fairfax
AAAFFLOPRSSTT pastoral staff
AAAFGIILLNSTT Itatinga Falls
AAAFHILLLMORT thalamifloral
AAAFILLMORTWY away from it all
AAAFILMNNOSTW Tasmanian wolf
AAAGGGILNRTVY aggravatingly
AAAGGHLOPRSSY shaggy parasol
AAAGGIOPPRSTU appoggiaturas
AAAGGKNOORRSS kangaroo grass
AAAGHHNOPRTTY thanatography
AAAGHIINNNRTY anythingarian
AAAGIILNNOSTV galvanisation
AAAGIILNNOTVZ galvanization
AAAGIILNORTTV gravitational
AAAGIILNSSTVW waiting-vassal
AAAGIIMMNSSTT anastigmatism
AAAGIKLNRSSUV Sunil Gavaskar
AAAGILMOOPSTT Plagiostomata
AAAGIMMNPRSTT pangrammatist
AAAGIMMNRRTUY Mt Nyamuragira
AAAGKNORRSTTU Saratoga trunk
AAAGKOPRRRSVY Garry Kasparov
AAAGLLNOPSTVY galvanoplasty
AAAGPRRSSSTTW grasp at straws
AAAHHIILMSTTW what ails him at?
AAAHHILMNOPPT panophthalmia
AAAHIILLMMRWW William Warham
AAAHIINORRTTU authoritarian
AAAHILMNPSTTY phantasmality
AAAHILOPPPRSY parapophysial
AAAHIMNOQSSTU Aquinas Thomas
AAAHINRRSTTUZ Zarathustrian
AAAHKMMORSSTY Thomás Masaryk
AAAHLLLLMOSSW All-hallowmass
AAAHLMORTTTUY thaumatolatry
AAAIIILMNNOST animalisation
AAAIIILMNNOTZ animalization
AAAIIIMNNRSST sanitarianism
AAAIIINNQRTTU antiquitarian
AAAIILLMMRSWY William Ramsay
AAAIILMNRSSTU Australianism
AAAIILMRRSTTT martial artist
AAAIILNNNORTT intranational
AAAIILNNOSTTT tantalisation
AAAIILNNOTTTZ tantalization
AAAIIMNNPRSSS Parnassianism
AAAIIMNOORSTT aromatisation
AAAIIMNOORTTZ aromatization
AAAIINNORSTTV intravasation
AAAIINNOSSSST assassination
AAAIINORRSTTT tartarisation
AAAIINORRTTTZ tartarization
AAAIKLNOOPRTV Anatoli Karpov
AAAILLNNORSTT translational
AAAILLNORRSTT translatorial
AAAILLPRRSUXY supra-axillary
AAAILMNORSTVY Salvation Army
AAAILNNNORSTT transnational
AAAILNNOPRSTU supranational
AAAILNNQSSTUY quant analysis
AAAILOPPRRSUU aura popularis
AAAKKMNOORTTU Mount Krakatoa
AAAKLNOOPRTVY Anatoly Karpov
AAALNORSSTTUU Atlantosaurus
AAAMNORSTTTUY traumatonasty
AABBBCDEGIORR cribbage-board
AABBBCEFKSTUY Buckfast Abbey
AABBBEGINRTTY baby-battering
AABBBEILMSTTT Babbitt's metal
AABBBGHINRRTY Barnaby Bright
AABBBIILORSTY absorbability
AABBCCEEERSUU barbecue sauce
AABBCDEEEEIRR Berberidaceae
AABBCDEEEKLNY black-eyed bean
AABBCDEELNRST belt-and-braces
AABBCDEINORTU ab urbe condita
AABBCDELNORWY Crowland Abbey
AABBCEEHILNOS Belisha beacon
AABBCEELNNRRT brent barnacle
AABBCEELOPRSU probable cause
AABBCEGGINNRR grabbing crane
AABBCEGINPRTU turnip cabbage
AABBCEHIKNSTT stab in the back
AABBCEHJJLNOO John Jacob Abel
AABBCEILNRRST transcribable

AABBCEJKORRTU Barbour® jacket
AABBCELORRRTY Robert Barclay
AABBCGHINNSTY baby-snatching
AABBCHHLOOSST Sabbath school
AABBCHIILLOOP bacillophobia
AABBCIINRRSUU suburbicarian
AABBCILLMOSTY bombastically
AABBCIMNOORTU bamboo curtain
AABBDDDINRRSS dribs and drabs
AABBDDEEGILOR biodegradable
AABBDDEIOPRRS Barbados pride
AABBDEEEHLLMN Ahmed Ben Bella
AABBDEEENSTWY Newstead Abbey
AABBDEEHNOTTT to beat the band
AABBDEEINRTUV unabbreviated
AABBDEGGIINRT badger-baiting
AABBDEGIRRTWY Bridgwater Bay
AABBDEHMNORTY Mother and Baby
AABBDEIILLLRT billiard table
AABBDFHIKOOOO Book of Obadiah
AABBDIILORSTY adsorbability
AABBDIINORSTW boatswain-bird
AABBDILMNRSUU submandibular
AABBEEEKLNRSS breakableness
AABBEEELLMNSS blameableness
AABBEEFNNOTYY Fontenay Abbey
AABBEEGIMRTWZ Great Zimbabwe
AABBEEHILNSST habitableness
AABBEEHKLLRST break the balls
AABBEEIILMNRZ Mazarine Bible
AABBEEIJKMNNR Benjamin Baker
AABBEEILLMOST metabolisable
AABBEEILLMOTZ metabolizable
AABBEEILRUVXY Rievaulx Abbey
AABBEFLLLOOTT table football
AABBEGHINTTUY bathing beauty
AABBEGIKNNRRS barnsbreaking
AABBEHIILNNTU uninhabitable
AABBEHILNOPRT phenobarbital
AABBEIILLOSSU bouillabaisse
AABBEIIMMRRSS semi-barbarism
AABBEILNOPRTT pentobarbital
AABBEKKLLNNTY blankety-blank
AABBENORRSSSU barbarousness
AABBFINOORSWY Bay of Rainbows
AABBHIMMNPSYY namby-pambyish
AABBIIILNOTTY obtainability
AABBIILNRRUYZ Brazilian ruby
AABBIMMMNPSYY namby-pambyism
AABCCCEEIRTUU Cucurbitaceae
AABCCCEHKRRST backscratcher
AABCCDDEENOTU dead-cat bounce
AABCCDDIORRTY cardboard city
AABCCDEEILNRT credit balance
AABCCDEHLLORU Claude Chabrol
AABCCDELLNORT ballad concert
AABCCDHLRTYYY brachydactyly
AABCCDIINNOOT Indian tobacco
AABCCEEEEILLR Illecebraceae
AABCCEEEEKRRU rebecca-eureka
AABCCEEEHLMSU béchamel sauce
AABCCEEFNNRRT Cabernet Franc
AABCCEEHILMSU chemical abuse
AABCCEEHLMRRT charm bracelet
AABCCEEHLNTTT Cate Blanchett
AABCCEEKLRRRR cracker-barrel
AABCCEELLNNOU unconcealable
AABCCEFIIIIPT beati pacifici
AABCCEGIMMRSU circumambages
AABCCEHHLPRYY brachycephaly
AABCCEHILNPRS Special Branch
AABCCEHINOOPR cancerophobia
AABCCEHKNOSTW watch one's back
AABCCEIILMPRT impracticable
AABCCEIILPTTY acceptability
AABCCEILLMOSV clavicembalos
AABCCEILMNRSV canvas-climber
AABCCEILMOTUU bioaccumulate
AABCCEILNPRTU unpracticable
AABCCELMOPRTY campylobacter
AABCCELNNOTUU unaccountable
AABCCHHINOOPR arachnophobic
AABCCIIILLNOT actinobacilli
AABCCIIILNNST cannibalistic
AABCCIIJLLNOY Jacobinically
AABCCIILMPRTY impracticably
AABCCIJKKKLPS black skipjack
AABCCILLLOSTU lactobacillus
AABCCILLMMOSU comma bacillus
AABCCILLRSUUV subclavicular
AABCCLLNOSTUY by all accounts
AABCCLNNOTUUY unaccountably
AABCDDEEEORRR barcode reader
AABCDDEELNRRU Claude Bernard
AABCDDIKLMNOS black diamonds
AABCDEEEFNRSS barefacedness
AABCDEEEHLRRT cerebral death
AABCDEEFFHIIN dieffenbachia
AABCDEEFFLORT feel-bad factor
AABCDEEFIPRRT prefabricated
AABCDEEGHILRS dischargeable
AABCDEEHHKLTT the black death✧
AABCDEEHKLOOR backhoe loader
AABCDEEIIMRSZ semicarbazide
AABCDEEIOTTUW Watteau bodice
AABCDEELORSXY decarboxylase
AABCDEELRRSTT battle-scarred
AABCDEEMORRST Comte de Barras
AABCDEENNORUV overabundance
AABCDEFILMNNO balance of mind
AABCDEFLNORRT bareland croft
AABCDEGIKLLNP back-pedalling
AABCDEGILLNNT ballet-dancing
AABCDEGILLRRT ball cartridge
AABCDEGIMNORT magnetic board
AABCDEGINNORT botanic garden
AABCDEHIILTTY detachability
AABCDEHIIMORT thiocarbamide
AABCDEHIKLNTW black and white
AABCDEHINOSTW shadow cabinet
AABCDEHIRRRTX Richard Baxter
AABCDEIILNSTU East India Club

AABCDEIILNTTU cabin altitude
AABCDEIILTTUY educatability
AABCDEIIMPRST side-impact bar
AABCDEIKOPPRY payback period
AABCDEINNOORT decarbonation
AABCDEKLLPRSW spell backward
AABCDELLMNOOR ballroom dance
AABCDELLMOORR Carole Lombard
AABCDELOPPRRS clapperboards
AABCDENNNOORT non-carbonated
AABCDFHIOPRTU cupboard faith
AABCDGHIMNORT matchboarding
AABCDGIILMOPT diplomatic bag
AABCDGIKLMRSU blackguardism
AABCDGILMNSSY scambling-days
AABCDHIINSTTW bait and switch
AABCDHIMNORRS Chris Boardman
AABCDHIRRRRSY Barry Richards
AABCDHNNOORRT root-and-branch
AABCDIMNNORST contrabandism
AABCDINNORSTT contrabandist
AABCDNOORSTUY bad scran to you
AABCEEEELNPSS peaceableness
AABCEEEGGGSSX excess baggage
AABCEEEGHLLLN challengeable
AABCEEEGIINRZ Zingiberaceae
AABCEEEHIOPRU Euphorbiaceae
AABCEEEHLNSST teachableness
AABCEEEILLPRR irreplaceable
AABCEEEILRSTU Eubacteriales
AABCEEELLNPRU unreplaceable
AABCEEELLNSSV cleavableness
AABCEEELNRSST traceableness
AABCEEFHOSSST beasts of chase
AABCEEFLORSTU Beaufort scale
AABCEEGGLNRRW Lawrence Bragg
AABCEEGHIOPRT bacteriophage
AABCEEGINPRTT carpet beating
AABCEEGLNOORS barnacle-goose
goose-barnacle
AABCEEHHMMOST Thomas Beecham
AABCEEHILMNPU unimpeachable
AABCEEHILNPTT tip the balance
AABCEEHKMOSTT Thomas à Becket
AABCEEHLMNORT thermo-balance
AABCEEHLMNTUU Athenaeum Club
AABCEEHOOPRRV above reproach
AABCEEIILLMRR irreclaimable
AABCEEIILNPPR inappreciable
AABCEEIJMRRTU Maurice Béjart
AABCEEILLMNRU unreclaimable
AABCEEILLPRRY irreplaceably
AABCEEILMNRSV vraisemblance
AABCEEILMORVW microwaveable
AABCEEILNPRRU Republican era
AABCEEILPRSTT beta particles
AABCEEIRRSTUU bureaucratise
AABCEEIRRTUUZ bureaucratize
AABCEEKQRRSTU square bracket
AABCEELLNOSTU sublanceolate
AABCEELLPRRSY cerebral palsy
AABCEELMMORSU commeasurable
AABCEELMRSSTX Texas scramble
AABCEELNRSSTT tractableness
AABCEEMMNORSU membranaceous
AABCEENNOOSSV save one's bacon
AABCEERRSSTTV abstract verse
AABCEFGILLNNS self-balancing
AABCEFGIMOTTU combat fatigue
AABCEFIIINOTT beatification
AABCEFIINORTT abortifacient
AABCEFIOPRRRT prefabricator
AABCEGHIIINRV Virginia Beach
AABCEGHIILNTY changeability
AABCEGHILMMNO Michael Gambon
AABCEGHORRSTU Roger Staubach
AABCEGIIKMNNT cabinetmaking
AABCEGILNNPRS spring balance
AABCEGILOPSSY abyssopelagic
AABCEGINOORSU boraginaceous
AABCEGLLNORTU congratulable
AABCEHHIMPTTT champ at the bit
AABCEHHKLMPUW humpback whale
AABCEHHLLLORS bachelor's hall
AABCEHILLLMNR lamellibranch
AABCEHILLPSTY heptasyllabic
AABCEHILMRTTY bathymetrical
AABCEHILNPRTU runic alphabet
AABCEHILNSSTU unchastisable
AABCEHILNSTUZ unchastizable
AABCEHINORRSW rainbow-chaser
AABCEHINORSSW chase rainbows
AABCEHINRSTTT in the abstract
AABCEHKLNOPST slap on the back
AABCEHKMNPRRT parchment bark
AABCEHLNNSTUU unstaunchable
AABCEHLNPRSUU unpurchasable
AABCEHLOPRRTY bachelor party
AABCEIILLMRRY irreclaimably
AABCEIILNPPRY inappreciably
AABCEIIMNNORR American robin
AABCEIIMNNORS American bison
AABCEIINNNRSS cannabis resin
AABCEIINORRTT nitrobacteria
AABCEIIRSTTTY tetrabasicity
AABCEILLLMOTY metabolically
AABCEILLMNRUY unreclaimably
AABCEILLMOPRT problematical
AABCEILLNPSTY pentasyllabic
AABCEILLOORTV collaborative
AABCEILLPRTUY capillary tube
AABCEILLRSTTY tetrasyllabic
AABCEILMNNOOP companionable
AABCEILMNOORW elbow macaroni
AABCEILMNORSW American bowls
AABCEILNNNOTU uncontainable
AABCEILNNORST constrainable
AABCEILNNORUV navicular bone
AABCEILORSSTV variable costs
AABCEILRSTTVY abstractively
AABCEIMORSSUU simarubaceous
AABCEINOORRST Serbo-Croatian

AABCEIRRSTTUU bureaucratist
AABCEKNOORSSV book-canvasser
AABCELMMNNOSU somnambulance
AABCELNOOPRTY polycarbonate
AABCELNRRSTTU Burt Lancaster
AABCFHIKLMOOO Book of Malachi
AABCFIILORTTY factorability
AABCFIKMNOORT back-formation
AABCFILNNOOTU confabulation
AABCFILORRSUV fibrovascular
AABCFLNOORTUY confabulatory
AABCGGIMNRRUY Barry McGuigan
AABCGIILLOTUY coagulability
AABCHIIILMNTY machinability
AABCHIILLNRTY labyrinthical
AABCHIKKLPRST blacktip shark
AABCHIMNOPRRS marsipobranch
AABCHINOPRSUZ Baruch Spinoza
AABCHIORRSSUU brachiosaurus✧
AABCIIILLMPTY implacability
AABCIIILLNSTT antiballistic
AABCIIILLPPTY applicability
AABCIIILMNORT antimicrobial
AABCIIILOSSTY associability
AABCIIILQRTUY acquirability
AABCIILLLRSTY trisyllabical
AABCIILLNOSTY syllabication
AABCIILMNNOOT combinational
AABCIILMNOORT combinatorial
AABCIILMOPRTY comparability
AABCIILMRRUUV vibracularium
AABCIINNOORST carbonisation
AABCIINNOORTZ carbonization
AABCIINORRSTU carburisation
AABCIINORRTUZ carburization
AABCIKLLMNPTU platinum black
AABCILLNOOORT collaboration
AABCILLNOOSTU suballocation
AABCILLNOOSTV Balto-slavonic
AABCILMNNOOPY companionably
AABCILNNOORTY carbonylation
AABCNNOOORSST contrabassoon
AABDDDEEGNORR bearded dragon
AABDDDEEILRRZ bearded lizard
AABDDDELNOOST boot and saddle
AABDDDGILNNSW swaddling-band
AABDDEEELLRRV ravelled bread
AABDDEEHLLMRU armed bullhead
AABDDEEILLLOR radiolabelled
AABDDEEKLLNST saddle blanket
AABDDEGGINRRW badger-drawing
AABDDEGHORRTU daughter board
AABDDEIILNSSU indissuadable
AABDDELNORSTU Dunstable road
AABDDELRSSTWY Lady's bedstraw
AABDDGHILORTY broad daylight
AABDDGIINNORR draining board
AABDDIILNSSUY indissuadably
AABDDILLNOPRR bord and pillar
AABDEEEGILRSS disagreeables
AABDEEEGNNRSU Aberdeen Angus
AABDEEEHLMRRT marble-hearted
AABDEEEHLOORT Dorothea Beale
AABDEEEHNOOSV above one's head
AABDEEEMORSTU mouse-eared bat
AABDEEFGIILNT indefatigable
AABDEEFLNOSTT Battle of Sedan
AABDEEGGIPRSS bridge passage
AABDEEGIRSSTU sugar diabetes
AABDEEGLLNORR roller bandage
AABDEEGLNRRRW garden warbler
AABDEEIKKLOOR read like a book
AABDEEILMNRSS admirableness
AABDEEILNRRTT rattle-brained
AABDEEILNSSSV advisableness
AABDEEIMOTTTU meditate about
AABDEEIPPRTVY private pay bed
AABDEEKLLNORX Alexander Blok
AABDEEKMRSTTY masked battery
AABDEELLRRTUV barrel-vaulted
AABDEELMRRSSY embarrassedly
AABDEELNPRSUU unpersuadable
AABDEELORSTUW sweated labour
AABDEEMNRRSSU unembarrassed
AABDEERRSTTTU statute-barred
AABDEFGIILNTY indefatigably
AABDEFGIOPRSS bird of passage
AABDEFGKORSST dog's breakfast
AABDEGGKNNORW breakdown gang
AABDEGIILRRWY railway bridge
AABDEGIINNRRT grin and bear it
AABDEGIKNORST skateboarding
AABDEGINRRRTT barter trading
AABDEGLLNRTUY Argyll and Bute
AABDEHIIILSTT dishabilitate
AABDEHIINOSSV Siobhan Davies
AABDEHILMOTTU habitat module
AABDEHKNNRRTU handbrake turn
AABDEHLNORRST Roland Barthes
AABDEHMNORSTY Arms and the Boy
AABDEIILMNRST administrable
AABDEIILNPTXY expandability
AABDEIKLLORRY Royal Birkdale
AABDEILMNPRRU premandibular
AABDEILMRTUVY adumbratively
AABDEILORSSST tabes dorsalis
AABDELLMNRSTU umbrella stand
AABDELNORRUYY boundary layer
AABDELOOPRRSX Olbers' paradox
AABDENNPRSTUU superabundant
AABDFFIILNNOU Indian buffalo
AABDFFIILORTY affordability
AABDFIORRTTUW drawbar outfit
AABDGGINNOORR groaning board
AABDGIILPRTUY upgradability
AABDGINOPRRTY boarding party
AABDHIMNORSTT rhabdomantist
AABDHIMRRRTUU Arthur Rimbaud
AABDHIPRRTTYY birthday party
AABDHMMMOSTU Muhammad's Tomb
AABDIIJLSTTUY adjustability
AABDIILLMNRUW William Dunbar

AABDIILLNPRWZ Pinball Wizard
AABDIILNNRSTU Austrian blind
AABDIMMNOORTY morbid anatomy
AABEEEEGLNRSS agreeableness
AABEEEEHNRTTW weather-beaten
AABEEEFLMNSST self-abasement
AABEEEGHKLPRT Greek alphabet
AABEEEGILLNRS generalisable
AABEEEGILLNRZ generalizable
AABEEEGKNRRST Sergeant Baker
AABEEEHHRRTVY heavy breather
AABEEEHILRSTY breathe easily
AABEEEHLNNORU à la bonne heure
AABEEEHPRSTTT breast the tape
AABEEEHRRRTTW water-breather
AABEEEILPRSVW variable-sweep
AABEEELLLMNSS malleableness
AABEEELLNOPST sable antelope
AABEEELLNORTU Nobel laureate
AABEEELNNSSTU uneatableness
AABEEELNORSST elaborateness
AABEEELNPRSSS separableness
AABEEELOORRTV overelaborate
AABEEFGILNSST fatigableness
AABEEFGILTTTU battle fatigue
AABEEFGLORTTW wager of battle
AABEEFHHLLTTT half the battle
AABEEFIKMRSST make first base
AABEEFILNNOTU Fontainebleau
AABEEFLLMOTTY Battle of Mylae
AABEEFLNORSSV favorableness
AABEEFLNRRRST transferrable
AABEEFMNORRTV Batman Forever
AABEEGHIKNRRT heartbreaking
AABEEGHILMRSY Bashir Gemayel
AABEEGHILNNST absent healing
AABEEGHILRSTT Basil the Great
AABEEGHLLNSSU laughableness
AABEEGHLLRSTU slaughterable
AABEEGHLORTTW Walter Bagehot
AABEEGILMORST metagrabolise
AABEEGILMORTZ metagrabolize
AABEEGILNNSSV navigableness
AABEEHHLLLRTT The Albert Hall
AABEEHILLRTTZ blaze the trail
AABEEHILNRTYZ Elizabeth Ryan
AABEEHIMNOSTT in the same boat
AABEEHINSSTTW Bassenthwaite
AABEEHLLNOTTY lay on the table
AABEEHLNOPRTY balneotherapy
AABEEHLNRRRTV Arval Brethren
AABEEHPRTTUYY beauty therapy
AABEEIILLNNPX inexplainable
AABEEIILMNPRR Pierre Balmain
AABEEIILPRTTY repeatability
AABEEIKLMNSTU unmistakeable
AABEEIKMNORRT re-embarkation
AABEEILLNNPUX unexplainable
AABEEILLNORTY inelaborately
AABEEILMNNSSU unamiableness
AABEEILMNRSUV universal beam
AABEEILNOPRST parietal bones
AABEEINPPRSTW wastepaper bin
AABEEKMNNSTTT bank statement
AABEELLLNNSTV Van Allen belts
AABEELLLNOSSW allowableness
AABEELLLRSTTY tetrasyllable
AABEELLNPRSUU unpleasurable
AABEELLORRSUY rosebay laurel
AABEELLOSTUUV absolute value
AABEELMNNSSTU untamableness
AABEELMRRTTUX Albert Métraux
AABEELNNPRSUU superannuable
AABEELNOOPRTU elaborate upon
AABEELNRRSTUV untraversable
AABEEMMNRRSST embarrassment
AABEEMNNNRTTW Barnett Newman
AABEENOORSSTU about one's ears
AABEENRSTTTTY test-ban treaty
AABEFHILMOPRT alphabetiform
AABEFHILNNOSU unfashionable
AABEFIILLNQUU unqualifiable
AABEFIILNSSTU unsatisfiable
AABEFIINORRSZ Zoë Fairbairns
AABEFILLMMNNU uninflammable
AABEFILMOOPTT Battle of Maipó
AABEFILMOPTTU Battle of Maipú
AABEFILMORSSU balsamiferous
AABEFILNOOTTZ Battle of Anzio
AABEFILNRSTUU Laurent Fabius
AABEFKMOORRST breakfast-room
AABEFLLMOTTVY Battle of Valmy
AABEFLMNORRST transformable
AABEGGHILPRSS A Bigger Splash
AABEGGILLLLOV global village
AABEGGIMMNNRR Ingmar Bergman
AABEGHHIMOTUV have a big mouth
AABEGHHLLNTWY hang by the wall
AABEGHINNRRTU bargain-hunter
AABEGHINQRSSU square-bashing
AABEGHLMNRRUU ghubar numeral
AABEGIILLNOUV bougainvillea
AABEGIILNORTY gay liberation
AABEGIJKLNRWY jaw-breakingly
AABEGILLOOOPY palaeobiology
AABEGILNORRTU gubernatorial
AABEGILNRRSTT sabre-rattling
AABEGLLOPPRSS palpable-gross
AABEGLNORSTUU obtuse-angular
AABEHHIILPPRT Philip the Arab
AABEHIILORRTT rehabilitator
AABEHILLORUVY behaviourally
AABEHIMNOOPTZ Bohemian topaz
AABEHIMNRRTTU Harriet Tubman
AABEHLMOPPRSS blepharospasm
AABEHMORRRSTU harbour master
AABEIIILLRSTY realisability
AABEIIILLRTYZ realizability
AABEIIILMNTXY examinability
AABEIIKLMRTTY marketability
AABEIILLLOSTV volatilisable
AABEIILLLOTVZ volatilizable

AABEIILLMNRSW William Barnes
AABEIILLMNSSU unassimilable
AABEIILLNSTUY unsaleability
AABEIILMRSTUY measurability
AABEIILMSTTTY metastability
AABEIILNORSTV verbalisation
AABEIILNORTVZ verbalization
AABEIILNOSSTY seasonability
AABEIILNRSTWY answerability
AABEIILOPRTVY evaporability
AABEIILRRUVXY auxiliary verb
AABEIIMNNRSTU antisubmarine
AABEIIMNRRRTU ram-air turbine
AABEIINRRRSST arbitrariness
AABEIJLNOOTUV job evaluation
AABEIKKKLLOOT talk like a book
AABEIKLMNSTUY unmistakeably
AABEIKNNOORRT Anita Brookner
AABEILLNOPRSU unpolarisable
AABEILLNOPRUZ unpolarizable
AABEILLNRRRTY rental library
AABEILMNNOTTU Table Mountain
AABEILMNOPRTU perambulation
AABEILMNRSTTT transmittable
AABEILMOPRTUU aurum potabile
AABEILNNSSTUU unsustainable
AABEILNOOPPRT apportionable
AABEILNOORSTV observational
AABEILOQRSTUU subequatorial
AABELLLMNPRTU umbrella plant
AABELLNPRSUUY unpleasurably
AABELMMNOSSWY assemblywoman
AABELMNNRRTUU natural number
AABELMNOORSTU neuroblastoma
AABELMOPRRTUY perambulatory
preambulatory
AABELMOPRSSTT spermatoblast
AABELNOPRRSTT transportable
AABELNPRSSSUU unsurpassable
AABELNRRSTTUU subternatural
AABELOPRRTUUY beauty parlour
AABELORSTTTUU statute labour
AABEMNNNOSTYY not by any means
AABEMNNRRSTTU Batman Returns
AABFFIIILLMNW William Baffin
AABFGHIMNOUUZ Naguib Mahfouz
AABFGHINRRSST brass farthing
AABFHILNNOSUY unfashionably
AABFHLORRRTUU Arthur Balfour
AABFILMNNOTUU funambulation
AABFLLLOOOTTT total football
AABFLMNORTUUY funambulatory
AABGGILLMMNOU gamma globulin
AABGGILLMNORW global warming
AABGHIOOPRTUY autobiography
AABGHKNOORRSU brush kangaroo
AABGHKOOOPRTU autograph book
AABGIIILMNORS aboriginalism
AABGIIILNORTY aboriginality✧
AABGIILLNOOST globalisation
AABGIILLNOOTZ globalization
AABGIILLNOTTU tubal ligation
AABGILNRRSTUU subtriangular
AABGLLNOOSSSU Balanoglossus
AABGLMNNOORRU Norman Borlaug
AABHHIIMOOPRT arithmophobia
AABHIIILNPRRS librarianship
AABHIILOOOPRU ailourophobia
AABHILLNOOORT hot-air balloon
AABHILNOORRTZ horizontal bar
AABHNNNOSSTUY Susan B Anthony
AABIIIILNRTVY invariability
AABIIIILNSTTY insatiability
AABIIILLMPPTY impalpability
AABIIILMPSSTY impassability
AABIIILNOSSTT stabilisation
AABIIILNOSTTZ stabilization
AABIILNNNRTTU tintinnabular
AABIILNNSSTTU insubstantial
AABIILNORSTTU brutalisation
AABIILNORTTUZ brutalization
AABIKLMNNOTUU Mount Kinabalu
AABILLNSSTTUY substantially
AABILMNOOPRST malabsorption
AABILMOPSSTVW baptismal vows
AABILNNSSTTUU unsubstantial
AABIMMNNNORRT Martin Bormann
AABINNOOOPPRT on approbation
AABLMMNOORSTU somnambulator
AABLNPRSSSUUY unsurpassably
AACCCDEEHORRT character code
AACCCDEIIIMTV cevitamic acid
AACCCDEILMRSU cardiac muscle
AACCCDIIILLSY salicylic acid
AACCCDIIINOSY isocyanic acid
AACCCDILMORTY macrodactylic
AACCCEEHKLOOT chocolate cake
AACCCEEILNRRT recalcitrance
AACCCEENNNOPT non-acceptance
AACCCEGHNORTU charge account
AACCCEGIKLORR carriage clock
AACCCEGINORTY gynaecocratic
AACCCEHIILSTT catechistical
AACCCEHIJQRSU Jacques Chirac
AACCCEHILMOPR macrocephalic
AACCCEHKNOPST Scotch pancake
AACCCEHMORSSY Saccharomyces
AACCCEIILLMRT climacterical
AACCCFIIILNOT calcification
AACCCGHHILOPR chalcographic
AACCCHILLOORT ochlocratical
AACCCIIILMNTT anticlimactic
AACCCIILLLMTY climactically
AACCCILMOOPST social compact
AACCCLLNOOTTU call to account
AACCCNNOORTTU contra account
AACCDDEGILORU clouded agaric
AACCDDEHINORR Richard Deacon
AACCDDEIORRTX dextrocardiac
AACCDDHIIORYZ hydrazoic acid
AACCDDIIIILNX nalidixic acid
AACCDEEEHILTY Lecythidaceae

AACCDEEEIMRRT demi-caractère
AACCDEEEIOORS Dioscoreaceae
AACCDEEENRRTY day care centre
AACCDEEGIRRTT cigarette card
AACCDEEIIINOV Vaccinioideae
AACCDEEIILNRU clairaudience
AACCDEEILLMPS decimal places
AACCDEEILNOPY encyclopaedia✧
AACCDEEILOOPY Lycopodiaceae
AACCDEENNTTUU unaccentuated
AACCDEFHIOPRT edaphic factor
AACCDEFHNRRTY fetch and carry
AACCDEFIILPTY field capacity
AACCDEFILLNNO Iceland falcon
AACCDEFILNOST focal distance
AACCDEGHHNNOP chop and change
AACCDEHHIKNRZ chicken-hazard
AACCDEHIILLNT clinical death
AACCDEHIILMOR radiochemical
AACCDEHIIMNOT methanoic acid
AACCDEHIIRRST trisaccharide
AACCDEHIJKMSW James Chadwick
AACCDEHIOPRSU pseudo-archaic
AACCDEHLMMPRU Marcel Duchamp
AACCDEHMOOPWY campeachy wood
AACCDEIILLLTY dialectically
AACCDEIILMNST accidentalism
AACCDEIILNTTY accidentality
AACCDEIINNOPT pentanoic acid
AACCDEIINNSTT antidesiccant
AACCDEIINORTT accreditation
AACCDEILNNNOT non-accidental
AACCDEILNOOTU coeducational
AACCDEILNPTTY pentadactylic
AACCDEIMMOOTV accommodative
AACCDEIMNNOPU unaccompanied
AACCDEINOPRTT pedantocratic
AACCDERSSTUUX crux decussata
AACCDFIIIINOT acidification
AACCDGIILLOOR cardiological
AACCDGIMMNOOT accommodating
AACCDHIILNOOT diacatholicon
AACCDHIIMNOOR orchidomaniac
AACCDHIJKLRUY hydraulic jack
AACCDHILORSTY cold as charity
AACCDHIMRRSST Christmas card
AACCDHLLMRTUY lachrymal duct
AACCDIILLOPTY apodictically
AACCDIILNOSSS Caicos Islands
AACCDIINOOPPR propanoic acid
AACCDILMNOTYY dactyliomancy
AACCDIMMNOOOT accommodation
AACCDLOPRRSTU scalar product
AACCEEEGIRSTT cigarette case
AACCEEEHHNRST the chances are
AACCEEEHMNTTU catechumenate
AACCEEEILMMNO Commelinaceae
AACCEEENPRRRY canary-creeper
AACCEEFIIINRU in facie curiae
AACCEEFIRSTUV surface-active
AACCEEGHHIMNR charge machine
AACCEEGHIRRRR charge carrier
AACCEEGHLNRRU nuclear charge
AACCEEGIMORTT categorematic
AACCEEHHIMNNT the main chance
AACCEEHHLLRST Harlech Castle
AACCEEHIKLLMR Michael Clarke
AACCEEHILMNOT catecholamine
AACCEEHILMPRY hypercalcemia
AACCEEHIMNSVW wave mechanics
AACCEEHIMORRT archaeometric
AACCEEHIMRRST saccharimeter
AACCEEHIOSSUZ schizaeaceous
AACCEEHLLOPRR local preacher
AACCEEHLRRRST clear-starcher
AACCEEHLRRSST characterless
AACCEEHMNNORS chance one's arm
AACCEEHMORRST saccharometer
AACCEEIILMRST reacclimatise
AACCEEIILMRTZ reacclimatize
AACCEEIIMRSTY Myristicaceae
AACCEEIINNSTV Canes Venatici
AACCEEILLLMRS Mercalli scale
AACCEEILMRRSV cervical smear
AACCEEILPPRTU picture palace
AACCEEILRSSTT Caister Castle
AACCEEJOPQSUU Jacques Copeau
AACCEEKLNNOST Lake Constance
AACCEELLPPRRW clapperclawer
AACCEELMNRUUV vacuum cleaner
AACCEFHHIOTTT To Catch a Thief
AACCEFHMOPSST fetch a compass
AACCEFHMORSTV camshaft cover
AACCEFIIINOTT acetification
AACCEFILORRSU calcariferous
AACCEFINOOSTU cause of action
AACCEGGHINOST stagecoaching
AACCEGGHINPPR charge-capping
AACCEGHHLOPRR chalcographer
AACCEGHIJKKNT hacking jacket
AACCEGHILOPRR cerographical
AACCEGHINOOPR oceanographic
AACCEGIILLNRT critical angle
AACCEGIILNRTT intergalactic
AACCEGILLNOOO oceanological
AACCEGILLNORR Coralline Crag
AACCEGILLOOTU autecological
AACCEGILLORTY categorically
AACCEGILLOTTY geotactically
AACCEHHLOPPSY scaphocephaly
AACCEHIILMORT iatrochemical
AACCEHIILRSTU Eucharistical
AACCEHIINNORT chain reaction
AACCEHIKMRSST Christmas cake
AACCEHILLLNTY Chantilly lace
AACCEHILLMRSV clishmaclaver
AACCEHILLMSTY schematically
AACCEHILLPPTY platycephalic
AACCEHILLPRTY phylacterical
AACCEHILMNORT American cloth
AACCEHILMORTT tachometrical
AACCEHILMPSTY metapsychical

 Words marked ✧ can also be spelled with one or more capital letters

AACCEHILMRTTY tachymetrical
AACCEHILNOSSV volcanic ashes
AACCEHILOPRST Alcaic strophe
Social Chapter
AACCEHILORRST social charter
AACCEHILRRTTU architectural
AACCEHIMMORTT metachromatic
AACCEHIMPRSTU pharmaceutics
AACCEHIMRRSTY saccharimetry
AACCEHIPPRRST sharp practice
AACCEHKLRRRTU Arthur C Clarke
AACCEHLLMMNSS Schlemm's canal
AACCEHLLOSSTU casual clothes
AACCEHMNPRRST scrap merchant
AACCEHMOOPRSU camphoraceous
AACCEIILLMNTY cinematically
AACCEIILMNOST encomiastical
AACCEIILNOPTT acceptilation
AACCEIILNRSWY scenic railway
AACCEIILRSTTT critical state
AACCEIINNORRT incarceration
AACCEIINNORTV revaccination
AACCEIIOPRSTT ectoparasitic
AACCEIJKLOPRT practical joke
AACCEIJKMPRTY pyjama cricket
AACCEIKLLNSTW Alnwick Castle
AACCEIKLRSTWW Warwick Castle
AACCEIKNOOPRT Captain Cooker
AACCEILLMRTUV circumvallate
AACCEILLNOPRY porcelain clay
AACCEILLNSSSS classicalness
AACCEILMMORRT commercial art
AACCEILMNNORT necromantical
AACCEILNPRSST practicalness
AACCEILNRTTUU nutraceutical
AACCEILOPRSTY palaeocrystic
AACCEIMMNNOPT accompaniment
AACCEIMNORSTW water moccasin
AACCEINNNOOTT concatenation
AACCEINOPPPRT copper-captain
AACCEINOPSSSU capaciousness
AACCEKMNNRRTU nutcracker man
AACCEKNORTTTU counter-attack
AACCELLNOOPRR lance corporal
AACCELLPRSTUY spectacularly
AACCELMNPRTUY Paul McCartney
AACCELNOPRTTU conceptual art✧
AACCELNPRSTUU unspectacular
AACCELORSSSUU crassulaceous
AACCFFILNOPRY cycloparaffin
AACCFIIILLRSY sacrificially
AACCFIIILNORT clarification
AACCFIIINNORT carnification
AACCFIIINOPRT caprification
AACCFIIINORST scarification
AACCFIILLLORY calorifically
AACCFIILNOSTU fasciculation
AACCGGIILLLOO glaciological
AACCGHHIMNOST hatch coamings
AACCGHILLNOOT Anglo-Catholic
AACCGHIMORTYZ zygomatic arch
AACCGIILLNOOR craniological
AACCGILLLNTUY calculatingly
AACCGILLNNTUU uncalculating
AACCGILLNOSSV volcanic glass
AACCGILNORRST slot-car racing
AACCHIILMNOOT machicolation
AACCHIILMNORT chiromantical
AACCHIILMRSSU musical chairs
AACCHIILPRSTY psychiatrical
AACCHIILQRRSU squirarchical
AACCHIIMORTTY achromaticity
AACCHIIMPRSSU suprachiasmic
AACCHIINNORST anachronistic
AACCHIINORSTW wainscot chair
AACCHILLMNORY monarchically
AACCHILLMORTY chromatically
AACCHILLOPRTT trophallactic
AACCHILMNOORT Roman Catholic
AACCHILNOOSST Satanic school
AACCHILNOPSTY sycophantical
AACCHIOPSSTTU caustic potash
AACCIIILLLNRT clinical trial
AACCIIILLNSTV Calvinistical
AACCIIINNOOST cocainisation
AACCIIINNOOTZ cocainization
AACCIIINORSTT cicatrisation
AACCIIINORTTZ cicatrization
AACCIILLMOPTY apomictically
AACCIILLMPRTY impractically
AACCIILLNOOPP plica Polonica
AACCIILLSSTUY casuistically
AACCIILMNOOSS occasionalism
AACCIILMNPSTU scapulimantic
AACCIILNOOSST occasionalist
AACCIILNOOSTY occasionality
AACCIIMMNNOTU in contumaciam
AACCIIMOSSSTT staccatissimo
AACCIINOPRSTT pantisocratic
AACCIKKNNORTY nick-nackatory
AACCIKLNOPRTW prawn cocktail
AACCIKLOPRTTY cocktail party
AACCIKMNOORRY Rocky Marciano
AACCILLNPRTUY unpractically
AACCILLNSTTYY syntactically
AACCILLOPSSST postclassical
AACCILMNOPSTU scapulomantic
AACCILNNOOOTV convocational
AACCILNNOORTT contractional
AACCILNORTTUU acculturation
AACCILNPRTTYY cryptanalytic
AACCIMNOORSTU carcinomatous
AACCINOQRSTTU quasi-contract
AACCINORSSTTY sacrosanctity
AACCLLNORTTUY contractually
AACDDDENNRSUW Duncan Edwards
AACDDDLLMNOOR Lord Macdonald
AACDDEEEFFINT decaffeinated
AACDDEEEHLLRY clear-headedly
AACDDEEELLNVV advanced level✧
AACDDEEGIMRST direct damages
AACDDEEGJOTUV judge advocate

AACDDEEHHILRR Richard Hadlee
AACDDEEHLLRYY acrylaldehyde
AACDDEEIILMMR Middle America
AACDDEEILNOTY delayed action
AACDDEEIMOSSW mad cow disease
AACDDEFIKLNRT track and field
track-and-field
AACDDEGHHILNN Highland dance
AACDDEGHIIMNN adding machine
AACDDEGIILNNS ladies dancing
AACDDEGILLNRS scaling ladder
AACDDEGJLNORU Jean-Luc Godard
AACDDEHIINPST candidateship
AACDDEHINORRV Richard Avedon
AACDDEINOORTY Decoration Day
AACDDELMNORSU Dendrocalamus
AACDDEMNNORTU ordnance datum
AACDDFHIKNNNO finnan haddock
AACDDHKNOORWY Norway haddock
AACDDIIJLRSUY juridical days
AACDDKLNOORSW cloak-and-sword
AACDEEEFIMNRR Marie de France
AACDEEEFIPPRR acid-free paper
AACDEEEHLNPSS Passchendaele
AACDEEEIILLPR pedicellariae
AACDEEEMOOPST Podostemaceae
AACDEEFGKLNOO angel-food-cake
AACDEEFILMORR Air Force Medal
AACDEEFILMSTU sulfacetamide
AACDEEFLNOPRR façon de parler
AACDEEGHINNRS case-hardening
AACDEEGHKMNNR heck and manger
AACDEEGHLLMOW Wadham College
AACDEEGIIMMNT magnetic media
AACDEEGIIRRRV carriage-drive
AACDEEGINORRS coarse-grained
AACDEEGINRRRU undercarriage
AACDEEGNNNORR non-regardance
AACDEEHIILTTV ethical dative
AACDEEHIKLRRY Richard Leakey
AACDEEHIMNORT Echinodermata
AACDEEHIMNSUX deus ex machina
AACDEEHIOSTUZ autoschediaze
AACDEEHLMMPST matched sample
AACDEEHLMOORZ Mazo De La Roche
AACDEEHNRRSTY secretary hand
AACDEEHNRSSVZ ranz-des-vaches
AACDEEIILNOSS salade niçoise
AACDEEIILOSSS social disease
AACDEEIIMOSSS mosaic disease
AACDEEILLRTVY declaratively
AACDEEILMNPRT predicamental
AACDEEILNPPTU appendiculate
AACDEEILNQRUV quadrivalence
AACDEEILOOPPY Polypodiaceae
AACDEEILORSST sacerdotalise
AACDEEILORSTZ sacerdotalize
AACDEEILPSSST assisted place
AACDEEIMMNRTY medicamentary
AACDEEIMNNOTT decontaminate
AACDEEINNRSTU unascertained
AACDEEINPPRTU unappreciated
AACDEEINPRSSV Space Invaders®
AACDEEIOSSTTU audio cassette
AACDEEIQRSTTU acquired taste
AACDEELLNRSTU Arundel Castle
AACDEELMSSSTU Damascus steel
AACDEELNORRTX adrenal cortex
AACDEENNNNOTT non-attendance
AACDEFFIIMNRS disaffirmance
AACDEFFINRRTW traffic warden
AACDEFFLNOTUY Dean of Faculty
AACDEFGHIRSTT straight-faced
AACDEFHILMNNO Adolf Eichmann
AACDEFLLNNOOR once and for all
AACDEGGILLOPY pedagogically
AACDEGHIILOPR ideographical
AACDEGHILMPRS discharge lamp
AACDEGHINRRRT Richard E Grant
AACDEGHINRRRW Richard Wagner
AACDEGHIOPRRR cardiographer
AACDEGIILLOPR Glacial Period
AACDEGIILNRTT ringtailed cat
AACDEGIINRTTU Educating Rita
AACDEGILMNOPR old campaigner
AACDEGIMNNRST dancing-master
AACDEGINNQRSU square-dancing
AACDEGJKLNNOS Glenda Jackson
AACDEGJLNOSUU juglandaceous
AACDEGLMNNORS scandalmonger
AACDEGLMNOORT damage control
AACDEGMNOORTW democrat wagon
AACDEHHILMNOO Michael Doohan
AACDEHHILMORW Michael Howard
AACDEHHLLLMRS hardshell clam
AACDEHIIMNRRT archimandrite
AACDEHIJLMNOR Michael Jordan
AACDEHILNRRSW Charles Darwin
AACDEHILOOPRT orthopaedical
AACDEHIMOSSTU autoschediasm
AACDEHIORRSTT trisoctahedra
AACDEHLMNNORT calendar month
AACDEHLOSTUXY hexadactylous
AACDEHMNNOORT enchondromata
AACDEHNOPRSST stop-and-search
AACDEIIJLRTUX extrajudicial
AACDEIILLMRTY diametrically
AACDEIILMRTVY vice-admiralty
AACDEIILNORTV valedictorian
AACDEIILORTVY radioactively
AACDEIILRSTTU disarticulate
AACDEIINNOPST encapsidation
AACDEIINNPTTU unanticipated
AACDEIINNRSTT transactinide
AACDEIINOPRST endoparasitic
AACDEIJLLMNOR Camille Jordan
AACDEIKLLNPST slap and tickle
AACDEILLLORRU cellular radio
AACDEILLMORTY declamatorily
AACDEILLNOPUZ zona pellucida
AACDEILLNOTUY educationally
AACDEILLORRTY declaratorily

AACDEILMMORST melodramatics
AACDEILMORSST sacerdotalism
AACDEILMPRRTU capital murder
AACDEILNOPRST polar distance
AACDEILNRSTTU ultra-distance
AACDEILNRTTUU unarticulated
AACDEILOORTUW caliature-wood
AACDEILORSSTT sacerdotalist
AACDEILPQRTUU quadruplicate
AACDEIMMNORRS comrade-in-arms
AACDEIMNNNOTT decontaminant
AACDEIMNOQRTU quartodeciman
AACDEINNOPRSX expansion card
AACDEINNORSUU arundinaceous
AACDEINOSSSUU audaciousness
AACDEIORRRTTY carotid artery
AACDEJKNNORSW Andrew Jackson
AACDEKLLNORVY Vandyke collar
AACDEKLNORSVY sandy-laverock
AACDELMMMSUUU summa cum laude
AACDELMNNRSSU underclassman
AACDEMMNNOOST at one's command
AACDEMNORRRVY Raymond Carver
AACDFFIILNRST traffic island
AACDFFILNOPUW a capful of wind
AACDFFLNNORUY Carol Ann Duffy
AACDFHNOSSTTW downcast-shaft
AACDFIIIMNNOT damnification
AACDFIILLOPRS spadicifloral
AACDGHHOOPRTY cathodography
AACDGHIILLOTZ zodiacal light
AACDGHILNOSSS Chagos Islands
AACDGHINOSSTW shadowcasting
AACDGHLOPRTYY dactylography
AACDGIIILLOST dialogistical
AACDGIIINNOST diagnostician
AACDGIILLNNOO clinodiagonal
AACDGILMRRSTU garlic mustard
AACDGIMMOOORS dramma giocoso
AACDHHIIRRRRS Richard Harris
AACDHHILOPRTY hydropathical
AACDHHIPPPSTY happy dispatch
AACDHIIINORST arachnoiditis
AACDHIIIOPRST adiaphoristic
AACDHIILOORSU Dolichosauria
AACDHIIMNORRT harmonic triad
AACDHIIMNRRRT Richard Martin
AACDHILLLNOSU Nicholas Udall
AACDHILLLRUYY hydraulically
AACDHILLOPRSY rhapsodically
AACDHILORSTTY hydrostatical
AACDHIMMOOSSS sadomasochism
AACDHIMOOSSST sadomasochist
AACDHINOPQRSU quadraphonics
AACDHLLMNORRU Harold Clurman
AACDHLMMNOOSY chlamydomonas
AACDHOOOPRRTT Protochordata
AACDIIILLMOTY idiomatically
AACDIIILPQRTU quadricipital
AACDIIIMNORTU radio-actinium
AACDIIINNNORT incardination
AACDIIIORTTVY radioactivity
AACDIIJLLSTUY Judaistically
AACDIIJORSSTU Judas Iscariot
AACDIIKMNOOPR macropinakoid
AACDIIKNNNOPR rack and pinion
AACDIILLLSTUY dualistically
AACDIILLMNOPR palindromical
AACDIILLMPRYY pyramidically
AACDIILLORTTY dictatorially
AACDIILNNOPRT cardinal point
AACDIILNNOPTU pandiculation
AACDIILNOOORT radiolocation
AACDIILNOOOTU audio-location
AACDIIMNOPSST antispasmodic
AACDIIMNORRTY dramatic irony
AACDIKPRSSTTY St Patrick's Day
AACDILLMOPSSY spasmodically
AACDILLOQRRUU quadrilocular
AACDIMNORSSTY astrodynamics
AACEEEEHPRSTW swear the peace
AACEEEGGLLNRY general legacy
AACEEEGHHNRTX heat exchanger
AACEEEGHILRRW wheel carriage
AACEEEGHLRTTT rattle the cage
AACEEEGLNNRST lance sergeant
AACEEEHINOSST coenaesthesia
AACEEEHINPRRT Catherine pear
AACEEEHJKLRTT leatherjacket
AACEEEHKLLNTU Lake Neuchâtel
AACEEEIJKMNTT matinée jacket
AACEEEIKMMMNT make mincemeat
AACEEEIKNRRSW Wernicke's area
AACEEEILLPPRR Pierre Laplace
AACEEEILMNOOP Polemoniaceae
AACEEEILSSSSS classes aisées
AACEEEKLNOPST take one's place
AACEEELNORSTW Lawrence Oates
AACEEFFHORTTT theatre of fact
AACEEFGHHNORT change of heart
AACEEFGHIMNNP fine Champagne
AACEEFGHNOPRX par of exchange
AACEEFGHNOSTT change of state
AACEEFHHIJSTZ Jascha Heifetz
AACEEFHHLRSTT Charles the Fat
AACEEFHILNPST slap in the face
AACEEFHNRRRTW trench warfare
AACEEFIINOPTT capitation fee
AACEEFILNRRRU Friar Laurence
AACEEFILNRSSU life assurance
AACEEFLNRSSSU self-assurance
AACEEGGHMNOPR George Chapman
AACEEGGLMNORT Comte Lagrange
AACEEGHILOPRS archipelagoes
AACEEGHILOPST Stegocephalia
AACEEGHIORRRS carriage horse
AACEEGHLMNOPR encephalogram
AACEEGHLMNRST segmental arch
AACEEGHLMOPSU megacephalous
AACEEGHNOOPRR oceanographer
AACEEGIIMNRRT American tiger
AACEEGIINNRSV Gianni Versace

AACEEGILLLNVY evangelically
AACEEGILLNNUV unevangelical
AACEEGILMMRTT telegrammatic
AACEEGILNPRTW watering place
AACEEGILRSTTT strategetical
AACEEGINNOSTU gentianaceous
AACEEGLLOOOPY palaeoecology
AACEEGLLORSSV Vassar College
AACEEGLMNRSST scalar segment
AACEEHHLMMRTY chammy leather
AACEEHHNORRTW weather anchor
AACEEHIILRSTT theatricalise
AACEEHIILRTTZ theatricalize
AACEEHIIMMSTT mathematicise
AACEEHIIMMTTZ mathematicize
AACEEHIIMNPRT ramapithecine
AACEEHIJQSTTU Hattie Jacques
AACEEHIKLPRRR Charlie Parker
AACEEHIKMNPRT Patrick Meehan
AACEEHILLMMNY Michael Manley
AACEEHILLSTTY aesthetically
AACEEHILMNOPR pinhole camera
AACEEHILMORTT theorematical
AACEEHILMPSTY mesaticephaly
AACEEHILNPRTT parenthetical
AACEEHILPRTVY heavy particle
AACEEHIMNNOPT acetaminophen
AACEEHINNRSTU neurastheniac
AACEEHINPRRRT Catherine Parr
AACEEHKKLMRRS mackerel shark
AACEEHLLMRSTV velt-mareschal
AACEEHLNNOPPR parencephalon
AACEEHLNOPRST Encephalartos
AACEEHLPPRSST pass the parcel
AACEEHMNOORRT Rhaeto-Romance
AACEEHMNOPSUY nymphaeaceous
AACEEHMOPRSTT spermatotheca
AACEEHOPRRTXY archaeopteryx
AACEEIILNNOPT Neapolitan ice
AACEEIILNRTTV intercalative
AACEEIILPPRTT peripatetical
AACEEIIMNNRSU un-Americanise
AACEEIIMNNRUZ un-Americanize
AACEEIIMPPRST misappreciate
AACEEIINNRSST necessitarian
AACEEIJKRSTTW Jackie Stewart
AACEEIJLNRTTU interjaculate
AACEEILLLPRST parietal cells
AACEEILLMMRTY metamerically
AACEEILLMNRSS Leslie Scarman
AACEEILLMNRTW mercantile law
AACEEILMMNORT anemometrical
AACEEILMMRTTU multicamerate
AACEEILMRRTTX extrametrical
AACEEILNNOPPU panleucopenia
AACEEILNNPSTT Septennial Act
AACEEILNNQTUV quantivalence
AACEEILNNSUUV nuisance value
AACEEILNORRST race relations
AACEEILNQRSUV carnivalesque
AACEEILNRRSUV vernacularise
AACEEILNRRUVZ vernacularize
AACEEILRSTUUV avis au lecteur
AACEEIMMNNRTT remittance man
AACEEIMNNRSTT ascertainment
AACEEIMRRRSTW master aircrew
AACEEINPPRRST Persian carpet
AACEELLLRRTUX extracellular
AACEELLMNORSY Sorley MacLean
AACEELNNOPRUW nuclear weapon
AACEELNOPPRSS personal space
AACEELNOPRRTU palaeocurrent
AACEEMNORSSTU sarmentaceous
AACEEMNRRSSTU term assurance
AACEENNORSSST Saracen's-stone
AACEFFGHINRRW Erwin Chargaff
AACEFFGLLMORR fall from grace
AACEFFIIILLRT artifical life
AACEFGILNNORT floating crane
AACEFGLLLNOPU pull a long face
AACEFHHMMNOTT man of the match
AACEFHILLRSTV have first call
AACEFHLLOPRSW paschal flower
AACEFIIIILRST artificialise
AACEFIIIILRTZ artificialize
AACEFIIILMORR microfilariae
AACEFIIILQTUV qualificative
AACEFIILMNOTT metafictional
AACEFIILNORST fractionalise
AACEFIILNORTV african violet✧
AACEFIILNORTZ fractionalize
AACEFIINRRSVX Xavier Francis
AACEFIKLORRWW Earl of Warwick
AACEFIKPRRRTT Patrick Rafter
AACEFILLLNOPT fall into place
AACEFILLMNRUY nuclear family
AACEFILLTTUVY facultatively
AACEFILOORRRY Royal Air Force
AACEFILORRSTW articles of war
AACEFINNOORRT confarreation
AACEFINRSTTUY safety curtain
AACEFLLMMORRS Malcolm Fraser
AACEFLLNNQSUU Cuquenán Falls
AACEFLLOORRUY for all you care
AACEFLMOPPRST space platform
AACEFLOOPPRTU Court of Appeal
AACEFMNNOOSTW Scent of a Woman
AACEFNOPRRSTT transport café
AACEFNOPRSSSV press of canvas
AACEGGHILNORT gathering-coal
AACEGGHJKNNNU Kangchenjunga
AACEGGILNOPSU Paul Gascoigne
AACEGGLOPRTTY Clara Peggotty
AACEGHHIIKKNS Chiang Kai-Shek
AACEGHHIMNPST camp-sheathing
AACEGHHINOPRT ethnographica
AACEGHHINPRTY grape hyacinth
AACEGHIILLPRX lexigraphical
AACEGHILLLRTY lethargically
AACEGHILLMPRY graphemically
AACEGHILLOPPY plagiocephaly
AACEGHILMOPPT apophlegmatic

AACEGHILMOPYY hypoglycaemia
AACEGHILNOPRV venographical
AACEGHILOOPRR oreographical
AACEGHILOORST archaeologist
AACEGHIMNNORR harmonic range
AACEGHIMNOPRT cinematograph
AACEGHINNRRSS harness racing
AACEGHLMNORRS Charles Morgan
AACEGHLORRTTY Charlotte Gray
AACEGHMMRRSTT Master McGrath
AACEGHOPRSSSU sarcophaguses
AACEGIIILMRRV civil marriage
AACEGIILLMNOR mineralogical
AACEGIILLMNTY enigmatically
AACEGIILLNNTY antigenically
AACEGIILMRRTV gravimetrical
AACEGIKNNNRRY Nancy Kerrigan
AACEGILLLLORY allegorically
AACEGILLLMRTU metallurgical
AACEGILLNPRYY panegyrically
AACEGILLOORTT teratological
AACEGILLRSTTY strategically
AACEGILMNNNOW cleaning woman
AACEGILMNOOSU magnoliaceous
AACEGILMNORTV galvanometric
AACEGILNRRUVY carrying value
AACEGIMNOPSTU come up against
AACEGIMPRRTTU trumpet agaric
AACEGINOSSSSU sagaciousness
AACEGLLNRRTUY rectangularly
AACEGLLOOPSUY polygalaceous
AACEGLMNORRSS marrons glacés
AACEGMORRRTTU Margaret Court
AACEHHIIMPRTT amphitheatric
AACEHHINOSSTU South China Sea
AACEHHINPSSTY psychasthenia
AACEHHINRTTWY water hyacinth
AACEHHLMNOPSU Alphonse Mucha
AACEHHLOOPRTX cephalothorax
AACEHHMMOPSTU Thomas Peachum
AACEHIIIMNRTT arithmetician
AACEHIIIMPRST hemiparasitic
AACEHIILLMMSV Machiavellism
AACEHIILLNTUV hallucinative
AACEHIILLSTTY atheistically
AACEHIILMRSTT theatricalism
AACEHIILNOPST cephalisation
AACEHIILNOPTZ cephalization
AACEHIILNPSTT pantheistical
AACEHIILRTTTY theatricality
AACEHIIMMMSTT mathematicism
AACEHIIMMNNWZ Chaim Weizmann
AACEHIIMNNOST mechanisation
AACEHIIMNNOTZ mechanization
AACEHIIMNNRST Christian name
AACEHIIMNPSTY metaphysician
AACEHIIOPSSST associateship
AACEHILLMRTUY rheumatically
AACEHILLNRTTY intrathecally
AACEHILLNTTUY authentically
AACEHILMNORST Thomas Linacre
AACEHILMNPRRU hurricane lamp
AACEHILMOPRST atmospherical
AACEHILMOPTYY polycythaemia
AACEHILMPSTTY sympathetical
AACEHILNOPRRS personal chair
AACEHILNOPRTU neuropathical
AACEHILPRSTXY extra-physical
AACEHIMNOORRT Rhaeto-Romanic
AACEHIMPRSTTU pharmaceutist
AACEHINOPRTTY actinotherapy
AACEHINORTTTU authenticator
AACEHINPRSTTY parasynthetic
AACEHKQRSSSTU squash rackets
AACEHLLMORSTY Thomas Carlyle
AACEHLNOPSSYY psychoanalyse
AACEHLNOPSYYZ psychoanalyze
AACEHLOOPSTUU autocephalous
AACEHMMNORRST Thomas Cranmer
AACEHMSSSSTTU Massachusetts
AACEHNOPPRRTY parthenocarpy
AACEHNOPPTTUU put a cheat upon
AACEIIILMRSTT materialistic
AACEIIIMPRSST semiparasitic
AACEIIINORTTV ratiocinative
AACEIIIPPRTTV participative
AACEIIKLLMNTY kinematically
AACEIIKLOORST Alistair Cooke
AACEIIKORSTUY yakitori sauce
AACEIILLLMNOR Lamellicornia
AACEIILLLPRST parallelistic
AACEIILLLRSTY realistically
AACEIILLMNPRT planimetrical
AACEIILLMORSS social realism
AACEIILLNPSTY epinastically
AACEIILLNRRTY interracially
AACEIILLPRSTY peirastically
AACEIILMMNRSU unicameralism
AACEIILMNRSTT maternalistic
AACEIILMNRSTU unicameralist
AACEIILMNSSST ismaticalness
AACEIILMNTTUV licentia vatum
AACEIILMPTTTU multicapitate
AACEIILNNORTT interactional
intercalation
AACEIILNNOSTT cat-o'-nine-tails
AACEIILNOPPRT reapplication
AACEIILNORSTT cartelisation
AACEIILNORTTZ cartelization
AACEIILNOSSUV salviniaceous
AACEIILNPRSTT paternalistic
AACEIILNRSSST satiricalness
AACEIILPRRSTU particularise
AACEIILPRRTUZ particularize
AACEIIMMOSTTU semi-automatic
AACEIIMNNOTTV contaminative
AACEIIMNORRST reactionarism
AACEIIMNSSTTY systematician
AACEIINNNORRT reincarnation
AACEIINNORSST scenarisation
AACEIINNORSTZ scenarization
AACEIINOPRRTV prevarication

AACEIINORRSTT reactionarist
AACEIINORSTTU cauterisation
AACEIINORTTUZ cauterization
AACEIINRRRSTU curtain-raiser
AACEIKLMMNORS Neo-Lamarckism
AACEIKPRSTWYZ Patrick Swayze
AACEILLLNRRTU intracellular
AACEILLLORTTY collaterality
AACEILLMNNSUU sun animalcule
AACEILLMNPTUY pneumatically
AACEILLNNOTTT call attention
AACEILLNOORRT correlational
AACEILLNRSSTV class interval
AACEILLOPRRUY Royal Peculiar
AACEILLPRRRTY tricarpellary
AACEILMNRRSUV vernacularism
AACEILMOPRTVY comparatively
AACEILMORRSTT astrometrical
AACEILMORTTTU tautometrical
AACEILNNOPSTU encapsulation
AACEILNNOPTTU count palatine
AACEILNNORSTU connaturalise
AACEILNNORTUZ connaturalize
AACEILNOOPRRT procreational
AACEILNOORSTT trail one's coat
AACEILNOPRSSS prosaicalness
AACEILNOSSSSU salaciousness
AACEILNPRRSTU interscapular
AACEILNRRSTUV vernacularist
AACEILNRRTUVY vernacularity
AACEILOPRRTTX extratropical
AACEILRSSTTTU Trucial States
AACEIMMNORTUU communautaire
AACEIMNNOPRRT non-parametric
AACEIMNNRSTTT transmittance
AACEIMNOOPSST compassionate
AACEIMNOPSSTY synaposematic
AACEINNORRTUV averruncation
AACEINOPRRSTT procrastinate
AACEINOPRRTUY precautionary
AACEINOPRSSSU rapaciousness
AACEINORRSTUV avant-couriers
AACEINPRRSSTT transcriptase
AACEJOPRRRSTT Jasper Carrott
AACELLMNNORTU nomenclatural
AACELLMPRSUUU aural speculum
AACELMMNOPRTT compartmental
AACELNOOPPSWY Apocalypse Now
AACELNORRSUUV neurovascular
AACELNRSSTTUU sustentacular
AACELORSSSTUU assault course
AACEMNNOORSTT entomostracan
AACEMNNOPPRTY parent company
AACENNOPRRSTT transportance
AACFFIIILNOST falsification
AACFFIIINORTT tariffication
AACFGIIIMNNOT magnification
AACFGIIINORTT gratification
AACFGIILLLOUV fluvioglacial
AACFGIKLNPPRT flapping track
AACFGILNNOORT conflagration
AACFGILNNORST Francis Galton
AACFGIMNNRTUU manufacturing
AACFGNOOORTTT contrafagotto
AACFHIMNPRSST craftsmanship
AACFIIIILRTTY artificiality
AACFIIILMNOPT amplification
palmification
AACFIIILNOQTU qualification
AACFIIIMNNORT informatician
AACFIILLORSTV Victoria Falls
AACFIILMNORST fractionalism
AACFIILMORTTY matrifocality
AACFIILNORSTT fractionalist
AACFIILOPRTTY patrifocality
AACFIILOQRTUY qualificatory
AACFIINNOORTT fractionation
AACFIINOORSTT factorisation
AACFIINOORTTZ factorization
AACFILOQRTTUY quality factor
AACFILPRTTTUU catapult fruit
AACFINORSTTUY anfractuosity
AACFORRSSTTTU fractostratus
AACGGHIKLMPSY shaggy milk cap
AACGGHILLOOPR graphological
logographical
AACGGHILMNNST slanging match
AACGGIIKNNPTU unit-packaging
AACGGILLLLOOY algologically
AACGGILLOORST gastrological
AACGGILNRSTYZ crystal-gazing
AACGHHIINRSTT straight chain
AACGHHIMNNTTW night-watchman
AACGHHIPRSTTY tachygraphist
AACGHHMOOPRRT chromatograph
AACGHIILLMORT logarithmical
AACGHIILLPRST calligraphist
AACGHIINOPRRT Changi Airport
AACGHIIPRRSTT graphic artist
stratigraphic
AACGHILLNNOTY gnathonically
AACGHILLOPRXY xylographical
AACGHILMNOOPR monographical
nomographical
AACGHILMOPRTY climatography
AACGHILNNSUWY launching-ways
AACGHILNOORST arachnologist
AACGHILOOPPRR polarographic
AACGHILOOPPRT topographical
AACGHILOPPRTY typographical
AACGHIMRSTTUU thaumaturgics
AACGHLMMOORRS grammar school
AACGHLNOORRST staghorn coral
AACGHMNOOPRSY pharmacognosy
AACGIIILNNOST anglicisation
AACGIIILNNOTZ anglicization
AACGIIINPPRTT participating
AACGIILLLNTVY vacillatingly
AACGIILLLOOXY axiologically
AACGIILLLOPRT alligator clip
AACGIILLMSTTY stigmatically
AACGIILLNNORY inorganically

AACGIILLNOSTY agonistically
AACGIILLORSTY orgiastically
AACGIILMMOPRT lipogrammatic
AACGIILNORSTU cartilaginous
AACGIILNORTTU graticulation
AACGIILNPTTVY captivatingly
AACGIIMNNOOPT compagination
AACGIINNOOTTV noctivagation
AACGIJLNNOOTU conjugational
AACGILLLNOOPY palynological
AACGILLLNOSTY nostalgically
AACGILLMNSTYY gymnastically
AACGILLMOOOPT potamological
AACGILLMOOOST somatological
AACGILMNOOPST campanologist
AACGILMNOORST gastronomical
AACGILMNOPSSS compass signal
AACGILMNORSSU cum grano salis
AACGIMMMNOORT monogrammatic
AACGINNORRSTW narrowcasting
AACGKNOOORRTU kangaroo court
AACGLNOORRTTU congratulator
AACHHIILLMOPT philomathical
AACHHIIORSTUY Ichthyosauria
AACHHILLMRTYY arhythmically
AACHHILMPRRTU triumphal arch
AACHHILNNOPTY phthalocyanin
AACHHILPSTXYY tachyphylaxis
AACHHIMNOORTX xanthochromia
AACHHIMNOPRSY physharmonica
AACHHIMNPSSTY yachtsmanship
AACHIIIMNNOST Antiochianism
AACHIIINNRSTT antichristian
AACHIIINRRTTT antiarthritic
AACHIILLNNOTU hallucination
AACHIILRSTTWY railway-stitch
AACHIIMMNNORS Monarchianism
AACHIIMNNNOTU mountain chain
AACHIINOORSTT rhotacisation
AACHIINOORTTZ rhotacization
AACHIINOPRSTU haruspication
AACHILLLMPTYY lymphatically
AACHILLMOOPSU malacophilous
AACHILLNORRTU Carrantuohill
AACHILLNORSTY thrasonically
AACHILLNORTUY hallucinatory
AACHILMOPSTTU optic thalamus
AACHILMRSSSTT Last Christmas
AACHILNNOORRT North Carolina
AACHILNNORTTT North Atlantic
AACHILNOOPTTU tautophonical
AACHILNOORSTU South Carolina
AACHILNOSTTTU South Atlantic
AACHILOPRSSTY astrophysical
AACHIMMNOOPST Thomas Campion
AACHIMMNOPRST panchromatism
AACHIMMOOPRST apochromatism
AACHIMNNNOOPR panharmonicon
AACHIMOPRSSTT catastrophism
AACHIOPPRSSSY parapsychosis
AACHIOPRSSTTT catastrophist
AACHLLLLOORUY lauryl alcohol
AACHLLLOOPRST chloroplastal
AACHLNNOORSUY anachronously
AACHLNOPRRTTU portulan chart
AACHLNOPSSTYY psychoanalyst
AACHLOOPRSTTY thoracoplasty
AACHNNNOOORRY honorary canon
AACIIIILNOSTT italicisation
AACIIIILNOTTZ italicization
AACIIIILNOTVV civil aviation
AACIIILLMNOPT implicational
AACIIILLNNNOT inclinational
AACIIILLNPSTY pianistically
AACIIILLOPTTY apoliticality
AACIIILLPPRTY participially
AACIIILMNOSST antisocialism
AACIIILNNOSTT nationalistic
AACIIILNOOSST socialisation
AACIIILNOOSTZ socialization
AACIIILNORSTT rationalistic
AACIIILNOSSTT antisocialist
AACIIILNOSTTY antisociality
AACIIILNPPRSX principal axis
AACIIINNOORTT ratiocination
AACIIINNOTTVX X-inactivation
AACIIINOPPRTT participation
AACIIIOSSTTVY associativity
AACIIJMNRSUYZ janizary music
AACIILLLMRTUY multiracially
AACIILLMORTTY matrilocality
triatomically
AACIILLMOSTTY atomistically
AACIILLMPRSTY prismatically
AACIILLNPRTUY puritanically
AACIILLOPRTTY patriotically
AACIILLOSSTTY isostatically
AACIILLSSTTTY statistically
AACIILMNOOSTV vocationalism
AACIILMNORSSY microanalysis
AACIILMNORTTU matriculation
AACIILMNORTTY romanticality
AACIILMPRRSTU particularism
AACIILNNOOSTV volcanisation
AACIILNNOOTVZ volcanization
AACIILNNOSTUV vulcanisation
AACIILNNOTUVZ vulcanization
AACIILNOOSTUV vacuolisation
AACIILNOOTUVZ vacuolization
AACIILNPPRTTY participantly
AACIILOSSTTTU stalactitious
AACIILPRRSTTU particularist
AACIILPRRTTUY particularity
AACIIMMNNORTU communitarian
AACIIMNNNOOTT contamination
AACIIMORRSSTT aristocratism
AACIINNNNOSTT Constantinian
AACIINNNOOSTT cantonisation
AACIINNNOOTTZ cantonization
AACIINNOORSTT narcotisation
AACIINNOORTTZ narcotization
AACIINNOPSSTT panic stations

AACIINOORRTTY ratiocinatory
AACIIOPPRRTTY participatory
AACIKMNNOPRST Patrick Manson
AACILLLOOPSTY apostolically
AACILLMNOOSTY onomastically
AACILLMNOOTUY autonomically
AACILLMNOOTXY taxonomically
AACILLMNOPSTY complaisantly
AACILLMNSTUUY lunatic asylum
AACILLNOOPSTU unapostolical
AACILLNORTVYY clairvoyantly
AACILLOPRRTTU ultra-tropical
AACILMMOPSTTY symptomatical
AACILMNNOPSTU uncomplaisant
AACILMNOOPTTU computational
AACILMNRRSTUU intramuscular
AACILMORRSTTU court martials
courts martial
AACILMORRTTUY matriculatory
AACILNNOORSTT translocation
AACILNPRSSTYY cryptanalysis
AACILOOPRRRTU procuratorial
AACIMMPRSSTUU Campus Martius
AACIMNNOOPRST companion star
AACIMOPRSTTTU post-traumatic
AACINNOOOQRUZ Corazon Aquino
AACJLMNNORSTU Trajan's Column
AACLNNOORSSTT solar constant
AACLNOOORSTTV stratovolcano
AACLQRRSTTUYZ quartz crystal
AACORRSSSTUUY Styracosaurus
AADDDEEILNNOR Daniel Deronda
AADDDEHIPPRSV David Sheppard
AADDDELNOORSW red sandalwood
AADDDENOOPRTU unadopted road
AADDDGHINRRST granddad shirt
AADDEEEEFHHRT feather-headed
AADDEEEEHHRTW weather-headed
AADDEEEEPRRSS depressed area
AADDEEEFHLRST saddle feather
AADDEEEHIRRTW read-write head
AADDEEEHQRRTU headquartered
AADDEEELMNPTX expanded metal
AADDEEELMPRST paddle steamer
AADDEEGGILLRT draggle-tailed
AADDEEGHILLNR dihedral angle
AADDEEGHRRSTW Gareth Edwards
AADDEEGIINPRR paired reading
AADDEEGILMPSS middle passage
AADDEEGIMNNRT in great demand
AADDEEGNRRTUU undergraduate
AADDEEGORSTYY ready, steady, go
AADDEEHHIPSSW waspish-headed
AADDEEHHLRRTY hard-heartedly
AADDEEHIMNOSS Homes and Ideas
AADDEEHINORTY Die Another Day
AADDEEILRTTTU rated altitude
AADDEEIMQRSSU Marquis de Sade
AADDEELNRTTUU unadulterated
AADDEELORRTTU Edouard Lartet
AADDEFHHOOSTW shadow of death
AADDEGGHHIRRR H Rider Haggard
AADDEGGHKMORR Gerhard Domagk
AADDEGGHNRRTU granddaughter
AADDEGHIMNOOV have a good mind
AADDEGHNORRUY rough-and-ready
AADDEGHOPRRSS Addressograph®
AADDEGIILNRTW detail drawing
AADDEGILNRSSS salad dressing
AADDEGINORRRY Ordinary grade
AADDEHHIMORRT Dame Thora Hird
AADDEHHNNORSU hare and hounds
AADDEHILPPSUY head-up display
AADDEHIMNSSSU Saddam Hussein
AADDEHLMNNOSY Handsel Monday
AADDEHNNNOSST stand one's hand
AADDEIKNNORRW Andrea Dworkin
AADDEILNRSSST dastardliness
AADDEJLLOOOSS Ojos del Salado
AADDELMNNORSU Roald Amundsen
AADDELNNPRSTY Paddy's lantern
AADDENORRRRST standard error
AADDFFNNNOOST stand off and on
AADDFGLLNOOOR for good and all
AADDHIILMRSUU Darius Milhaud
AADDHIMNOOSST Thomas Addison
AADDHLLOOORRW Harold Larwood
AADDIIILNOPST dilapidations
AADDIIILNOTTY additionality
AADDIIKKLNOSS Kodiak Islands
AADEEEFIMMNTX dexamfetamine
AADEEEFNORRVY for ever and aye
AADEEEGGHIMRR hedge-marriage
AADEEEGGLRTXY exaggeratedly
AADEEEGGNRTUX unexaggerated
AADEEEGIPRSST rite de passage
AADEEEGIPSSST Paget's disease
AADEEEGIRSSSV Graves' disease
AADEEEGLLNNRS Greenland seal
AADEEEGMNRTUV adventure game
AADEEEHHKNOSS shake one's head
AADEEEHLNNRRT neanderthaler✧
AADEEEHMNOSTX dexamethasone
AADEEEIILMRST dematerialise
AADEEEIILMRTZ dematerialize
AADEEEIKMRSSS Marek's disease
AADEEEIKNSSWW wide-awakeness
AADEEEILRRRVW Delaware River
AADEEEIMNNRRT mediterranean✧
AADEEELNOPPRX Alexander Pope
AADEEELNRRTVW lavender water
AADEEELPRSTXY exasperatedly
AADEEEMMNRSTU admeasurement
AADEEEMMORSTU made to measure
AADEEEMNRRTUV Dame Eva Turner
AADEEENPRRTUW a new departure
AADEEFGKLLLRR Karl Lagerfeld
AADEEFHHLLRTY half-heartedly
AADEEFIKNORWY a week on Friday
AADEEFLNOPRTW dwarf antelope
AADEEFNSSSSTT steadfastness
AADEEGGGILNNS engaged signal

AADEEGGHLORST at loggerheads
AADEEGGILLNRV garden village
AADEEGGILMNUX mixed language
AADEEGHIMOOTV have a good time
AADEEGHLNOORT Dorothea Lange
AADEEGIIMMRRX mixed marriage
AADEEGILLLRSY ladies' gallery
AADEEGILLORRV alveolar ridge
AADEEGILMORRT radiotelegram
AADEEGILNTTTU attitude angle
AADEEGIMNPRST disparagement
AADEEGIMNRRTT reading matter
AADEEGINNNSTU ensanguinated
AADEEGINNRRTY radiant energy
AADEEGINORSSV Andrés Segovia
AADEEGINRSTTT trading estate
AADEEHHILPTUW Paul Whitehead
AADEEHHNPRSTT at the sharp end
AADEEHIKLNPRT leap in the dark
AADEEHIKMRRTT raid the market
AADEEHIMNOPRT diaphanometer
AADEEHINNORSS raise one's hand
AADEEHINRRSTT head restraint
AADEEHKKNNNTU Kenneth Kaunda
AADEEHKOORTTT take to the road
AADEEHLLRRTTY tetrahedrally
AADEEHLMRRTWY warm-heartedly
AADEEHLOPRRTZ trapezohedral
AADEEHLORRTTT tetartohedral
AADEEIILLMNTV Medieval Latin
AADEEIILLNTUU Daniel Auteuil
AADEEIILNNOST denationalise
AADEEIILNNOTZ denationalize
AADEEIIMNNRSU neuraminidase
AADEEIJMRRSSW Sir James Dewar
AADEEIKLMNRST tradesmanlike
AADEEILLNNRVY lay in lavender
AADEEILLRSUUV residual value
AADEEILMMORST melodramatise
AADEEILMMORTZ melodramatize
AADEEILMNOSSS salmon disease
AADEEILNNNORR noradrenaline
AADEEILNOPPSS epanadiploses
AADEEILNRSTTV travel-stained
AADEEILNRTTTV travel-tainted
AADEEILORRVVW draw a veil over
AADEEIMNNOSUV Madison Avenue
AADEEIMORRSTV overdramatise
AADEEIMORRTVZ overdramatize
AADEEINOPPPRR prepared piano
AADEEINPRSSST disparateness
AADEEIOOPSSTT potato disease
AADEEIOPRRSST parrot disease
AADEEKKMRRSTU Kara Kum Desert
AADEEKMNRSSTU keen as mustard
AADEELLMNNNOS Nelson Mandela
AADEELLMNORTW Walter Mondale
AADEELLMNRRVW Andrew Marvell
AADEELLNRRTWW well-warranted
AADEELMNOORRS Roman de la Rose
AADEELNNRRSTU sale and return
AADEELNPPPRST pepper-and-salt
AADEEMNPRRTTW War Department
AADEENNPRSTUU superannuated
AADEFFHJMRRUY Madhur Jaffrey
AADEFFIINORRT diffarreation
AADEFFMNOORSW meadow saffron
AADEFGHHINORR hard of hearing
AADEFGHHIOORT a hair of the dog
AADEFGHLNRRTY grandfatherly
AADEFGIKMOOST make a good fist
AADEFIILLMNSU sulfanilamide
AADEFIILNOSTU feudalisation
AADEFIILNOTUZ feudalization
AADEFIILOQRTU quadrifoliate
AADEFIKLMNPRS Mansfield Park
AADEFILMNOPPR manifold-paper
AADEFILMOOTWX meadow foxtail
AADEFILMORSSV devisal of arms
AADEFILOOPRSS fool's paradise
AADEFKLNOORRT foot-land-raker
AADEFKMORRRTW forward market
AADEFLLMNNTUY fundamentally
AADEFLLMNORTU dental formula
AADEFLNSSTTUY unsteadfastly
AADEGGGHINNNR hanging garden
AADEGGHHILMNS Highland Games
AADEGGHINPRSS Spanish dagger
AADEGGLLNORUW world language
AADEGGLNRTTUU gauntlet-guard
AADEGGNNORTUV vantage ground
AADEGHILNRTUW daughter-in-law
AADEGHLOPRTTY play hard to get
AADEGHMOPRRTY dermatography
AADEGIIIMPRRV primigravidae
AADEGIILMNQRU quadrigeminal
AADEGIILMRTUV multigravidae
AADEGILLMNORT road-metalling
AADEGILLNNRSW Wrangel Island
AADEGILLNOPRS lords a-leaping
AADEGILMNNRSU land-measuring
AADEGILNSTTVY devastatingly
AADEGIMNRRSTW drawing-master
AADEGINNOPRSS grande passion
AADEGINNQRRUY quadringenary
AADEGINNRSTTW water-standing
AADEGINNRTUUU uninaugurated
AADEGINNSSTVW standing waves
AADEGLNOPRSTT prostate gland
AADEGLOORRSUV Avogadro's rule
AADEGMOPRRRRT program trader
AADEGMORRRTTU Margaret Tudor
AADEHHIILLNPP Philadelphian
AADEHHILMOORR haemorrhoidal
AADEHHNNOSSSW wash one's hands
AADEHHOOORRTW a hard row to hoe
AADEHIILMOSSY haemodialysis
AADEHIILNPSUZ sulphadiazine
AADEHIIMRRSSY Sir Hardy Amies
AADEHILLLLOTW All-hallowtide
AADEHILMNRSSU Salman Rushdie
AADEHILNOOSSY holiday season

AADEHILNOPRRY hydro-airplane
AADEHIMNORSTU diathermanous
AADEHINORRSSV Sharron Davies
AADEHLLNOTWWY lay down the law
AADEHLMNORSTU sound the alarm
Thomas Arundel
AADEHLMNORTTW Matthew Arnold
AADEHLMNRSUYY Henry Maudslay
AADEHNORRSTTW north-eastward
AADEHNORSSSUZ hazardousness
AADEHORSSTTUW south-eastward
AADEIIILMSSST disassimilate
AADEIIIMNOSTT mediatisation
AADEIIIMNOTTZ mediatization
AADEIILLMMRTY military medal
AADEIILLMORTY mediatorially
AADEIILLNRRTY interradially
AADEIILLQRRTU quadriliteral
AADEIILMMNRST maladminister
AADEIILMNSSTU unassimilated
AADEIILNOPPSS epanadiplosis
AADEIILNRSSTU disnaturalise
AADEIILNRSTUZ disnaturalize
AADEIIMNNOORT enantiodromia
AADEIIMNNORSV animadversion
AADEIIMNORRTT Mario Andretti
AADEIINNRSTTY treaty Indians
AADEIINOPSSST dispassionate
AADEIIPQRRTTU quadripartite
AADEIKKMNPSSU kiss and make up
kiss-and-make-up
AADEIKLLNOSTU Tokelau Island
AADEIKNPPRRSU drunk as a piper
AADEILLLOSTWW swallowtailed
AADEILLNNQRUY quadrennially
AADEILLOPSTUY dialypetalous
AADEILLPRRTYY radial-ply tyre
AADEILMMORSTT melodramatist
AADEILMNORSST maladroitness
AADEILMNOSTTY Mayotte Island
AADEILNNRSTUU unnaturalised
AADEILNNRTUUZ unnaturalized
AADEILNORRSST rational dress
AADEILNRSSTTW Stewart Island
AADEIMQRRTUUV quadrumvirate
AADEINNORTTTW draw attention
AADEINORRRTXY extraordinary
AADEJLMMNSTTU maladjustment
AADELLOQRRRTU quarter dollar
AADELMOOORRST mater dolorosa
AADELMOPRSTTY dermatoplasty
AADELNNRRTUWY unwarrantedly
AADELNRRSSSUU Ursula Andress
AADEMNORSTTUY tetradynamous
AADENNNOPTTTU attendant upon
AADENNOORSSTT stand to reason
AADENOOPRRSTT toreador pants
AADFGHIIMPRST paradigm shift
AADFGNOOORRTW of good warrant
AADFHHIMNNOSS man of his hands
AADFHIMNPRSST draftsmanship
AADFHLLOOSTTY Lady of Shalott
AADFIINOORSTT soft radiation
AADFIIOQRRSUU quadrifarious
AADFIKLLMOORW maid of all work
maid-of-all-work
AADFILLOOPRSY April Fools' Day
AADFINRSSSTTT fits and starts
AADFJJMNNORTU Franjo Tudjman
AADGGIILNPRSY disparagingly
AADGGILORSSST dog's-tail grass
AADGHIIIMPRRS iris diaphragm
AADGHIILOPRST gladiatorship
AADGHIINNNRWZ winning hazard
AADGHIINNRSVY varnishing-day
AADGHILMMORRS marsh marigold
AADGHILNOOORT orthodiagonal
AADGHIMMPPPRU diaphragm pump
AADGHMNORSTUW draughtswoman
AADGIIIKLMMNS maids a-milking
AADGIIILNNTWY lady-in-waiting
AADGIIIMPRRSV primigravidas
AADGIIKLMMNNO animal kingdom
AADGIILLNQRUU quadrilingual
AADGIILMRSTUV multigravidas
AADGIILNNSSTT distant-signal
AADGILLNOPSTW pit and gallows
AADGILNNOPRST prostaglandin
AADGLMNNOOOSX Anglo-Saxondom
AADGLMNNOORSU Norman Douglas
AADHHILMNOPRS Harold Shipman
AADHIILLNNRST Rathlin Island
AADHILNNNOSTY Anthony Island
AADHILNORRSTY synarthrodial
AADHLNOPRSTTY short-day plant
AADHMNNOORTTW not worth a damn
AADIIIINNNOST Indianisation
AADIIIINNNOTZ Indianization
AADIIILLLRSUV Livia Drusilla
AADIIILNNNOSS Ionian Islands
AADIIJLLMNOSV Milovan Djilas
AADIILLLNTTUY latitudinally
AADIILLNNPRSS Praslin Island
AADIILLNOORST dollarisation
AADIILLNOORTZ dollarization
AADIILLNORTTY traditionally
AADIILLOSUUVY audiovisually
AADIILNNOPSTT displantation
AADIIMNNOORST randomisation
AADIIMNNOORTZ randomization
AADIIMNORRSTT administrator
AADIJMMNRSSVY Sammy Davis, Jnr
AADIKNNNOORTV Antonín Dvorák
AADILLLMOPPSU sapodilla plum
AADILLMNNOORR Romain Rolland
AADINNOPSSSUY Passion Sunday
AAEEEEKLNOSTV take one's leave
AAEEEFFNPRSST per fas et nefas
AAEEEFGLMNRRR farmer general
AAEEEFGLNSSTT Fêtes Galantes
AAEEEFLNRSSSW self-awareness
AAEEEFNPPRRST paper fastener

AAEEEGGHINORW here we go again
AAEEEGGHMORST George Eastham
AAEEEGGILNNTV negative angle
AAEEEGGLNNRST agents-general
AAEEEGGMNORST George Eastman
AAEEEGHORRSTT storage heater
AAEEEGIIKKNRV Nikkei average
AAEEEGIKLNRRV Greek valerian
AAEEEGJLMRSSU Jerusalem sage
AAEEEGLMMNRSS German measles
AAEEEGLNRSSTT States General
AAEEEGMNNRRRT rearrangement
AAEEEGNOORRRT aerogenerator
AAEEEGNRSTTUX États-Généraux
AAEEEHHISTTVY the ayes have it
AAEEEHIILLSSS Haile Selassie
AAEEEHILPPRRT Pre-Raphaelite
AAEEEHILRSTTT at the earliest
AAEEEHIMMSTTT at the same time
AAEEEHLLSTTUX sexual athlete
AAEEEHLNPRSST elephant's-ears
AAEEEHLNPRTTT patent leather
AAEEEHMNRTTTT heat treatment
AAEEEIKMNRRTT anti-marketeer
AAEEEIKNPRSTV native speaker
AAEEEILMNNNOS Neo-Melanesian
AAEEEILMNORRT Mare Orientale
AAEEEILNNORRS Sierra Leonean
AAEEEILNNRTTV anal retentive
AAEEEKLLMNRSU Emanuel Lasker
AAEEEKLMNORSV leave one's mark
AAEEELLPPPPUU appel au peuple
AAEEELMMNOPSU male menopause
AAEEELMMNPRTT temperamental
AAEEELMPQRRUY marquee player
AAEEELNSSTTUV net asset value
AAEEEMNNPRTVW permanent wave
AAEEEMQRRSSUU square measure
AAEEEMRRRSTUW water measurer
AAEEENNNQRSUW Queen Anne's War
AAEEENRRSSVWY Seven Years' War
AAEEFFGNRSSTT staff sergeant
AAEEFGIILMNRZ magazine-rifle
AAEEFGIKNNNSW Finnegans Wake
AAEEFGILLNNNS self-annealing
AAEEFGINRRTWY wayfaring tree
AAEEFGIOPRSST rite of passage
AAEEFGLLLMORS Selma Lagerlöf
AAEEFGLORSSSV Leaves of Grass
AAEEFGLRSTXYY Seyfert galaxy
AAEEFGMMNNORR Morgan Freeman
AAEEFHHLORSTT hear the last of
AAEEFHHORRSTT heart of hearts
AAEEFHIIMOTTV have a time of it
AAEEFHILNNSTT in the fast lane
AAEEFHJLMOTTW The Jew of Malta
AAEEFHMNSSSST shamefastness
AAEEFHNOOSTTY A Taste of Honey
AAEEFHORSTTTT state of the art
state-of-the-art
AAEEFIIMNSTTV manifestative
AAEEFIKLLRSTU Kaieteur Falls
AAEEFIKMNOSSU make an issue of
AAEEFILLNNORT à la Florentine
AAEEFILLNORST false relation
AAEEFIOPRRSTT state of repair
AAEEFKKMMNOOY make a monkey of
AAEEFKLMORTUW make foul water
AAEEFLMORRRTY femoral artery
AAEEFNPPRRRST transfer paper
AAEEGGHINPRTT gathering-peat
AAEEGGILMORTV agglomerative
AAEEGGILNNRSV seal-engraving
AAEEGGILNNRTU interlanguage
AAEEGGILNORST segregational
AAEEGGIMNORVV moving average
AAEEGGINNOPRT generation gap
AAEEGGLNQRUUY query language
AAEEGHHLNOPST Loaghtan sheep
AAEEGHHLPTTUW what the plague
AAEEGHIJMNSTU James Naughtie
AAEEGHILLRRTW Walter Raleigh
AAEEGHIMMORRT hierogrammate
AAEEGHIMOPSTT apothegmatise
AAEEGHIMOPTTZ apothegmatize
AAEEGHIRTTWWY Great White Way
AAEEGHKMRSTTT stag the market
AAEEGHKNORSST no great shakes
AAEEGHLNPRSST elephant grass
AAEEGHMNOOSTU haematogenous
AAEEGIIJLLNNO Angelina Jolie
AAEEGIILMNRRS marriage-lines
AAEEGIILMNRUV evangeliarium
AAEEGIILMPRTX exempli gratia
AAEEGIILNNORV evangeliarion
AAEEGIIMMPRST epigrammatise
AAEEGIIMMPRTZ epigrammatize
AAEEGIIMNRRRT intermarriage
AAEEGIIMNRSTV vegetarianism
AAEEGIIMSSTTT semi-sagittate
AAEEGIJMPRSST Sir James Paget
AAEEGIKKORSSV Sergei Aksakov
AAEEGIKMNRSTT make it strange
AAEEGILLMSSXY sexagesimally
AAEEGILMNOORR oleomargarine
AAEEGILNNPPSS appealingness
AAEEGILNNSSTV Venetian glass
AAEEGILNRRTTY literary agent
AAEEGILNRSTVY evangelistary
AAEEGIMMMNNST mismanagement
AAEEGIMNPRSTU measuring-tape
AAEEGIMNRTTUV argumentative
AAEEGINNOQTUU Equatoguinean
AAEEGINOPRSTU eusporangiate
AAEEGJLNPTTUY Jean Paul Getty
AAEEGJMNORRST sergeant-major
AAEEGKLMNNOOS make a long nose
AAEEGLLLMNSUY Samuel Langley
AAEEGLMMORSTT stalagmometer
AAEEGLMNNORUU Emanuel Ungaro
AAEEGLNNOPRTT General Patton
AAEEGLOOPSSUY go-as-you-please

AAEEGMMMNORRY memory manager
AAEEGMNRRSTTT strange matter
AAEEGMOOSTTTW set a game to two
AAEEHHILNRTTW White Hart lane
AAEEHHLMMRSTY shammy leather
AAEEHHMOPPSTT metaphosphate
AAEEHIILMNRST Isenheim Altar
AAEEHIILMNSSS leishmaniases
AAEEHIILMOPTT epitheliomata
AAEEHIILMPPRY hyperlipaemia
AAEEHIILNPSST elephantiasis
AAEEHIKLMMRRV Hammerklavier
AAEEHIKRRSSTW the Kaiser's war
AAEEHILLNNNPY phenylalanine
AAEEHILMNNOST ethanolamines
AAEEHILMOPRTU Palaeotherium
AAEEHILMPPRRS Pre-Raphaelism
AAEEHILPRRTTY retail therapy
AAEEHILRRSSTU russia leather✧
AAEEHIMNOSTUV mauvaise honte
AAEEHIMNPSSTT panaesthetism
AAEEHINNRRSTY Tyrrhenian Sea
AAEEHINOPRTTW weather a point
AAEEHINOSTVWY have it one's way
AAEEHINPRRSTW Western Pahari
AAEEHINRSSTTT heat-resistant
AAEEHINRSTVWZ Hertzian waves
AAEEHIPPRRSTW water sapphire
AAEEHIPPRRSTY hyperparasite
AAEEHJMNOPSST James Stanhope
AAEEHKMPRRTTW Matthew Parker
AAEEHKORRTTTT Tarka the Otter
AAEEHLLOOPRTT Apollo Theatre
AAEEHLNORSTTT alternate host
AAEEHLOSSTTTY to say the least
AAEEHLPRSTUXY sexual therapy
AAEEHMNOSTTUX exanthematous
AAEEHMOPRRRST spermatorrhea
AAEEHNORSSTTT east-north-east
AAEEHOSSSTTTU east-south-east
AAEEIIILMMRST immaterialise
AAEEIIILMMRTZ immaterialize
AAEEIILLMNSST Milesian tales
AAEEIILMNNRTT interlaminate
AAEEIILMRSSTU material issue
AAEEIILNNRTTU air lieutenant
AAEEIILNPRRTT interparietal
AAEEIIMNNNSST inanimateness
AAEEIIMNNORTX re-examination
AAEEIINNSSSTT insatiateness
AAEEIJJMNRSSS Sir James Jeans
AAEEIKLLNOSTX axial skeleton
AAEEIKLMNSSTT statesmanlike
AAEEIKLNSSTTV talkativeness
AAEEIKMNNNTTY Matti Nykaenen
AAEEILLLLNPRS parallel lines
AAEEILLLPPTVY appellatively
AAEEILLNRTTVY alternatively
AAEEILMMNORST mean solar time
AAEEILMNNPTTT mental patient
AAEEILNRRSTTT transliterate
AAEEILOPRTTVX extrapolative
AAEEILPPRRTVY preparatively
AAEEILPRSSSSZ laissez-passer
AAEEIMMNRRRST master-mariner
AAEEIMNNPPRTT appertainment
AAEEIMNPRRSTV privateersman
AAEEINNPRSTTY spiny anteater
AAEEINORRTUYY year in, year out
AAEEIOPPPRRRT reappropriate
AAEEIPRRSTTTZ trapeze artist
AAEEIPRRTTTVY private treaty
AAEEKMMNPRSTU amusement park
AAEELLLLPRRRU parallel ruler
AAEELLNOPPRTY Appleton layer
AAEELMNPRSSSU supersalesman
AAEELNPRRRTTU preternatural
AAEELNPRRSTUW water purslane
AAEEMNRRRTUUX ex natura rerum
AAEEMPPRRSSTU semper paratus
AAEEMQRRRSTTU quartermaster
AAEEPRRSSTTUU supersaturate
AAEFFGMNORSUW woman-suffrage
AAEFFHINORTUZ Haroun Tazieff
AAEFFHLMOORSU farmhouse loaf
AAEFFIILMNORR foraminiferal
AAEFFIILMRTVY affirmatively
AAEFFIIMNORRT reaffirmation
AAEFFINOORSTT afforestation
AAEFFIOPRRSTT tear a strip off
tear off a strip
AAEFFLOPRSTYY play for safety
AAEFFMMOORRTT a matter of form
AAEFGIKNNORRV King of Navarre
AAEFGILLLMNST flagellantism
AAEFGILMMNPRS sampling frame
AAEFGILMNRRTY fragmentarily
AAEFGIMNNORSU manganiferous
AAEFGIMNNORTT fragmentation
AAEFGMMMNNORU foramen magnum
AAEFHHILNNPST flash in the pan
AAEFHIILMPPSY happy families
AAEFHILLOSTUZ sulfathiazole
AAEFHILMPRTYY family therapy
AAEFHILOQRSTU Earl of Asquith
AAEFHLLLNOTWY a fly on the wall
AAEFHLMORSTTW Waltham Forest
AAEFHMORRTTTT for that matter
AAEFIIIILMRST familiarities
AAEFIILLNNRSS in all fairness
AAEFIILNNORRU Alain-Fournier
AAEFIIMNNOSTT manifestation
AAEFIJNORRSST Jean Froissart
AAEFILLNORRRW Fallen Warrior
AAEFILLOPRRTY prefatorially
AAEFILLRRTTTU ultrafiltrate
AAEFILMMMORSU mammaliferous
AAEFILMNOORRT reformational
AAEFILNNRRRST friar's lantern
AAEFILNOOPSTT at point of sale
AAEFILNQSTTUY false quantity
AAEFKKLMPRSSY make sparks fly

AAEFLLMNORSTU	a small fortune
AAEFLORRSTTWY	Wolf-Rayet star
AAEGGGRRSSSST	grass staggers
AAEGGHHILNNUY	laughing hyena
AAEGGHILLNNVY	hanging valley
AAEGGHILNRSTT	at right angles
	straight angle
AAEGGHIMNNRTT	hanging matter
AAEGGHINNPPRS	paperhangings
AAEGGHNOPRSTY	steganography
AAEGGIIKLMNNS	leasing-making
AAEGGIILLRTUV	villeggiatura
AAEGGIILNTTUV	agglutinative
AAEGGILMNOORT	agglomeration
AAEGGILNNNOUU	union language
AAEGGILORSTUV	Getúlio Vargas
AAEGGIMNNOORT	aggiornamento
AAEGGIMOPRRRU	group marriage
AAEGGLNNRSSSY	granny glasses
AAEGGLNOOPRTU	protolanguage
AAEGHHIKMRRTW	high-water mark
	high-watermark
AAEGHHILNRSST	The Shangri-las
AAEGHHNNOPSTU	hang up one's hat
AAEGHIILMNOPR	Germanophilia
AAEGHIIMMNSST	Isthmian Games
AAEGHIKMNOPRT	kinematograph
AAEGHILMNOTVW	Man with a Glove
AAEGHILMNRSTW	whaling-master
AAEGHILMOOSTT	haematologist
AAEGHIMOPSTTT	apothegmatist
AAEGHINNPPSWW	wappenshawing
AAEGHIOPRRRTY	arteriography
AAEGHIPRRRSTT	stratigrapher
AAEGHLLMOPRTY	metallography
AAEGHLMNNOORS	alongshoreman
AAEGHLOPPSYYZ	zygapophyseal
AAEGHLOPRTTUY	telautography
AAEGHMNOOPRSU	phanerogamous
AAEGHMORRTTUY	Great Yarmouth
AAEGHNOOPRRTY	organotherapy
AAEGIIILMNTVY	imaginatively
AAEGIIIMNNRSS	imaginariness
AAEGIIIMNNTUV	unimaginative
AAEGIIINNNPTV	naive painting
AAEGIIKLNNPPS	plain speaking
AAEGIIKNNSSWY	easy as winking
AAEGIILLLORST	legislatorial
AAEGIILLMRSTY	magisterially
AAEGIILLNNRTW	retaining wall
AAEGIILLNRRST	still air range
AAEGIILLNSSTU	Ustilaginales
AAEGIILMNNPRT	parliamenting
AAEGIILMNRSST	sailing master
AAEGIILNNTTTY	tangentiality
AAEGIIMMNNRST	mainstreaming
AAEGIIMMPRSTT	epigrammatist
AAEGIIMNNORST	Germanisation
AAEGIIMNNORTZ	Germanization
AAEGIIMNNOSTT	magnetisation
AAEGIIMNNOTTZ	magnetization
AAEGIIMNQQSUU	Quinquagesima
AAEGIINNNRSTT	intransigeant
AAEGIIRSSSTTU	Sagittariuses
AAEGIKLLMMNOR	mallemaroking
AAEGIKLNPPRSW	walking papers
AAEGIKLPRRSTV	Pär Lagerkvist
AAEGIKMMNRSST	mass-marketing
AAEGIKNOORRVV	River Okavángo
AAEGILLLNNOSW	Nigella Lawson
AAEGILLMNOOPT	megalopolitan
AAEGILLNPSSUU	lapsus linguae
AAEGILLNRTTUY	triangulately
AAEGILMMNRSUY	real gymnasium
AAEGILMNNOPST	Leamington Spa
AAEGILMNPRSTU	Pantagruelism
AAEGILNNOPRTU	Pantagruelion
AAEGILNPRSTTU	Pantagruelist
AAEGILOPRRTUX	expurgatorial
AAEGIMNNNORTU	mountain range
AAEGIMNNORTTU	argumentation
AAEGINNQQRUUY	quinquagenary
AAEGINOORSTTY	geostationary
AAEGINPPPPRRW	wrapping paper
AAEGIOPRRSTUY	Sauropterygia
AAEGKMNOOORSU	kangaroo mouse
AAEGLLNOOOPTY	palaeontology
AAEGLLOOOOPYZ	palaeozoology
AAEGLMMORSTTY	stalagmometry
AAEGLNNOOSSSU	analogousness
AAEHHIIKNNSTV	have a thin skin
AAEHHILMNNPTY	naphthylamine
AAEHHILMOPRTX	xerophthalmia
AAEHHIMMPRRSS	marsh-samphire
AAEHHIMNORSTT	a shot in the arm
AAEHHLLOPRSWY	Harlow Shapley
AAEHIIILMNSSS	leishmaniasis
AAEHIIIMNNSTT	antihistamine
AAEHIILLMRVWY	William Harvey
AAEHIILMMPSTU	epithalamiums
AAEHIIORTTTUV	authoritative
AAEHIIRRSSTWY	with a siserary
AAEHIKLMNPRTZ	Itzhak Perlman
AAEHIKMMOPSST	Thomas à Kempis
AAEHILMNPRSST	phalansterism
AAEHILMPPRRTY	primal therapy
AAEHILNNORSSS	Sir Hans Sloane
AAEHILNPRSSTT	phalansterist
AAEHIMNPSSSTT	statesmanship
AAEHINNNOQRTU	anthraquinone
AAEHINNOPPRST	siphonapteran
AAEHINNRSSSSU	Nasser Hussain
AAEHINOPPRSTU	aphanipterous
AAEHINPRSSSTY	parasynthesis
AAEHKMMNNNOUY	hanuman monkey
AAEHKMMORTUWY	make a wry mouth
AAEHKMNNORSSS	on Shanks's mare
AAEHKMNNRRSSS	shark's manners
AAEHLMNNSSTTY	Lytham St Anne's
AAEHLNNOPTTWY	play the wanton
AAEHLNNOQTUYY	Anthony Quayle
AAEHMNORRRSTU	Arthur Ransome

AAEHMOPPRSTTY Spermatophyta
AAEHNNOPRSTTY parasyntheton
AAEIIIKNNNSSX Iannis Xenakis
AAEIIILLLMNTT Italian millet
AAEIIILMMMRST immaterialism
AAEIIILMMRSTT immaterialist
AAEIIILMMRTTY immateriality
AAEIIILNNORST linearisation
AAEIIILNNORTZ linearization
AAEIIILNORRST irrationalise
AAEIIILNORRTZ irrationalize
AAEIIILNORSST serialisation
AAEIIILNORSTZ serialization
AAEIIIMNNPPRT imparipinnate
AAEIIKLMNPSST Semipalatinsk
AAEIIKMNNNOST Neo-Kantianism
AAEIIKMNORSTT marketisation
AAEIIKMNORTTZ marketization
AAEIILLLMNRTY matrilineally
AAEIILLLNPRTY patrilineally
AAEIILLMMMNPU animal implume
AAEIILLMNOSTT metallisation
AAEIILLMNOTTZ metallization
AAEIILLMNRSTU unilateralism
AAEIILLMRRSTT trilateralism
AAEIILLNOPSTT palletisation
AAEIILLNOPTTZ palletization
AAEIILLNRSTTU unilateralist
AAEIILLNRTTUY unilaterality
AAEIILLQTTUVY qualitatively
AAEIILLRRSTTT trilateralist
AAEIILMMNOPST semipalmation
AAEIILMMNOSTT lemmatisation
AAEIILMMNOTTZ lemmatization
AAEIILMNNORTT terminational
AAEIILMNORSTV Voltaireanism
AAEIILMNPRSST impartialness
AAEIILMPRSSTY paralysis time
AAEIILMRRTTXY extralimitary
AAEIILNNNORTT international✧
AAEIILNNNOSTT Italian sonnet
AAEIILNNOORTT orientational
AAEIILNNORSTV vernalisation
AAEIILNNORTVZ vernalization
AAEIILNOPRRTT intrapetiolar
AAEIILNOPRSSU plesiosaurian
AAEIILNORRTTT trilateration
AAEIILNOSSTUX sexualisation
AAEIILNOSTUXZ sexualization
AAEIILNPRRSST interrail pass
AAEIILNQRRTTU quartier latin
AAEIILORSTUUV suovetaurilia
AAEIIMNNNOSSZ zenana mission
AAEIIMNOPRSST separationism
AAEIIMOPPRTVX approximative
AAEIINNNOSTTX annexationist
AAEIINNNSTTTY instantaneity
AAEIINNOOPSTW weaponisation
AAEIINNOOPTWZ weaponization
AAEIINOPPPRRT inappropriate
AAEIINOPPRSTU pauperisation
AAEIINOPPRTUZ pauperization
AAEIINOPRSSTT separationist
AAEIIOPPPRRTV appropriative
AAEIJLMNORRTV major interval
AAEIKLLNOSSTY as likely as not
AAEIKLMMSTTUU mutual mistake
AAEILLLMNORTW mineral tallow
AAEILLMMNPTTU platinum metal
AAEILLMMOPRSU marsupial mole
AAEILLNNOSSTY sensationally
AAEILLNOOPRTX explorational
AAEILLNOOPRTY operationally
AAEILLNOPRTXY explanatorily
AAEILLNORRSUY lunisolar year
AAEILMMNNORST ornamentalism
AAEILMNNOOPPR paralipomenon
AAEILMNNORSTT ornamentalist
AAEILMNOPRTTU permutational
AAEILMNORRSTY Rila Monastery
AAEILMNPPRRTY primary planet
AAEILMNRSSTUX transexualism
AAEILMOPPRTXY approximately
AAEILNNNNPSVY Pennsylvanian
AAEILNNNOSSTU unsensational
AAEILNNOPRSTU supernational
AAEILNNORRSTT retranslation
AAEILNNORSTTT translate into
AAEILNNPRRSUW Peninsular War
AAEILNNPRSTTY instant replay
AAEILNNRRSSTU natural resins
AAEILNOOORTTV laevorotation
AAEILNOOPQRTU polar equation
AAEILNOOPRTTX extrapolation
AAEILNOOPRTTZ oriental topaz
AAEILNOORTUVV overvaluation
AAEILNORSTTWY sanitary towel
AAEILNPPRSTUU paper nautilus
AAEILNRSTTUXY transexuality
AAEILOOPPRRRT propraetorial
AAEILOPPPRRTY appropriately
AAEILOPPRRRTY preparatorily
AAEIMMMNOSTUV mauvais moment
AAEIMMNPPRSST panspermatism
AAEIMNNNOORTT ornamentation
AAEIMNNNOSTUV mountain avens
AAEIMNNOSTTUY ayuntamientos
AAEIMNNRRRTUU in rerum natura
AAEIMNOPRSSST master-passion
AAEIMNORSSTTT stationmaster
AAEIMNPPRSSTT panspermatist
AAEIMNRSTTTUV transmutative
AAEINNNOPSTTT attention span
AAEINNNOSSTTU instantaneous
AAEINOOPPRRRT propraetorian
AAEINOPPPQRTU appropinquate
AAEINOPPPRRTU unappropriate
AAEIOOPPRRSTT protospataire
AAELLMOOPSSTT small potatoes
AAELLNRRSSTVY transversally
AAELMMNNORRSU Roman numerals
AAELMMNRTTTUU alterum tantum

AAELMNNOOSSSU anomalousness
AAELMNRSSTTUY natural system
AAELMOPPRRSTU supratemporal
AAELNNNRSSTUU unnaturalness
AAELNNOPRRSST transpersonal
AAELNNOPRRSTU natural person
AAELNNPRRSTTY transparently
AAELOOORRTTVY laevorotatory
AAELOOPRRTTXY extrapolatory
AAEMMNPRRSTUU paramenstruum
AAENNNPRRSTTU untransparent
AAENOPPRRSTTT tape transport
AAENOQSSTTTUU status quo ante
AAEOPRRSTTTUY statutory rape
AAEORRRSTTTWW water starwort
AAFFGHINPRSSU suffraganship
AAFFIINNOPRRT nitroparaffin
AAFFINNOOSTTT staff notation
AAFGGILLNOPUW Wolfgang Pauli
AAFGGILNORSST floating grass
AAFGHIKLMNOTT Knight of Malta
AAFGIMNNOPRST Naming of Parts
AAFHIJNNOSTTW Jonathan Swift
AAFHINOOPRRST parrot-fashion
AAFHMOORSTUWY out of harm's way
AAFIIILMNRTUY unfamiliarity
AAFIIKLLMNRSW Frank Williams
AAFIILMNNOORT informational
AAFIILMNOORST formalisation
AAFIILMNOORTZ formalization
AAFIKLNNOOTTT flotation tank
AAFILNNNOORTT National Front
AAGGHHIIOPRST hagiographist
AAGGHIINNSSTV Gavin Hastings
AAGGIIIMNOORR Giorgio Armani
AAGGIIIOORRSV Giorgio Vasari
AAGGIILNNOTTU agglutination
AAGGIILNNPSST glass-painting
AAGGILLLNNOYY ylang-ylang oil
AAGGMNNNORUYY angry young man
AAGHHIKLMNRST knight marshal
AAGHHILOPRTWY highway patrol
AAGHHINOOPPRT anthropophagi
AAGHHNOOPPRTU phonautograph
AAGHHNOOPPRTY anthropophagy
AAGHHOPPRRRYY rhyparography
AAGHIIIKKLLMN Mikhail Glinka
AAGHIIIMNNRST Martina Hingis
AAGHIILMNORTT antilogarithm
AAGHIIMMPRSTU amphigastrium
AAGHIINOORRST honoris gratia
AAGHIINPRSSTU Spanish guitar
AAGHILOPPSYYZ zygapophysial
AAGHIMMRSTTUU thaumaturgism
AAGHIMNNORSTW Winston Graham
AAGHIMNOOPRST mastigophoran
AAGHIMRSTTTUU thaumaturgist
AAGHINOPRRSTU uranographist
AAGHIORRRSTTW straight arrow
AAGHIORRRSTTZ straight razor
AAGHKNNOOORRT kangaroo-thorn
AAGHNOORSSTUU saurognathous
AAGIIIKMRRSUU maurikigusari
AAGIIILLNOSTV villagisation
AAGIIILLNOTVZ villagization
AAGIIILMNNNOV Olivia Manning
AAGIIINNORSTT granitisation
AAGIIINNORTTZ granitization
AAGIIJNNOORST jargonisation
AAGIIJNNOORTZ jargonization
AAGIILLMOORST malariologist
AAGIILLNNSTTY tantalisingly
AAGIILLNNTTYZ tantalizingly
AAGIILMNNPRTU mural painting
AAGIILMNOORST glamorisation
AAGIILMNOORTZ glamorization
AAGIILNNORTTU triangulation
AAGIILNORSTUV vulgarisation
AAGIILNORTUVZ vulgarization
AAGIILNRRTTUY triangularity
AAGIIMNNPRSTY praying mantis
AAGIINNNPRSTT training pants
AAGIINNPPRSTY spray-painting
AAGIKLMNOVWWY moving walkway
AAGIKNNSSUUUY Aung San Suu Kyi
AAGILMMNNOSUY magnanimously
AAGILMNNOORTU angular motion
AAGILMNOPQSTU quota sampling
AAGILMNOPRRTU armour-plating
AAGILMNORRSTT mortal-staring
AAGILNNNPRSTT transplanting
AAGILNNOORSSW Gloria Swanson
AAGILNNORSTTU strangulation
AAGILNPRSSTTU pulsating star
AAGIMNORRRSTT transmigrator
AAGINOOOPPRSS prosopagnosia
AAGLLLLLNOSTY Long Tall Sally
AAGLMNOORSTUU granulomatous
AAHHIIKMRSTYZ Yitzhak Shamir
AAHHKNOSTTWWW know what's what
AAHHNOOPPRTTY anthropopathy
AAHIIILLOOPRU ailourophilia
AAHIIILNNOSTY hyalinisation
AAHIIILNNOTYZ hyalinization
AAHIILLPPRSTX xiphiplastral
AAHIILMMNSSTU Malthusianism
AAHIILMNOPRSW animal-worship
AAHIILNNPRRTY platyrrhinian
AAHIIMMNNOOPR morphinomania
AAHIIMNNOORST harmonisation
AAHIIMNNOORTZ harmonization
AAHIIMNNRSSTT transisthmian
AAHIIMNOOPPPT hippopotamian
AAHIINOORSTTU authorisation
AAHIINOORTTUZ authorization
AAHIINPSSSSTT assistantship
AAHIJMMOOOTYY Yohji Yamamoto
AAHILMNNORRSS ramshorn snail
AAHILNNOPSSYY hypno-analysis
AAHIMRRSSTTUZ Zarathustrism
AAHINOPSSSSTT shop assistant
AAHJNNORSSSTU Johann Strauss

AAHLLMOOPSTUY polythalamous
AAHLMMNOOOSTU monothalamous
AAHLNOOPRRTTY anthropolatry
AAIIILMNORRST irrationalism
AAIIILMNORSTV Voltairianism
AAIIILMNPRSST animal spirits
AAIIILNNOPRST inspirational
AAIIILNORRSTT irrationalist
AAIIILNORRTTY irrationality
AAIIILNORSTTU ritualisation
uralitisation
AAIIILNORTTUZ ritualization
uralitization
AAIIILNOSSTUV visualisation
AAIIILNOSTUVZ visualization
AAIIIMMNNNOST antinomianism
AAIIIMNNNOSST Saint-Simonian
AAIIINNNOSTTT instantiation
AAIIINNOSSTTT sanitationist
AAIIINOPRSTTV privatisation
AAIIINOPRTTVZ privatization
AAIIJKLMMNORT Mt Kilimanjaro
AAIILLLMNOTWW William Walton
AAIILLMMNORTY matrimonially
AAIILLMNNOTTU multinational
AAIILLMNNOTVY nominatively
AAIILLMNOPRTY patrimonially
AAIILLMNORSWW Rowan Williams
AAIILLNOOPRVY Royal Pavilion
AAIILLNOPRSTU pluralisation
AAIILLNOPRTTW partition wall
AAIILLNOPRTUZ pluralization
AAIILLNOSTTUY situationally
AAIILMNNOORST normalisation
AAIILMNNOORTZ normalization
AAIILMNNORSTU Rila Mountains
AAIILMNOOPTTT totipalmation
AAIILMNOSTTUU mutualisation
AAIILMNOTTUUZ mutualization
AAIILMOPPRSTU mariposa tulip
AAIILNSSSSTUY analysis situs
AAIILPRRSSSTT astral spirits
AAIIMNOOPPRTX approximation
AAIIMNOORRRST roman à tiroirs
AAIIMNORRSTTY martyrisation
AAIIMNORRTTYZ martyrization
AAIIMNRSSTTTV Vansittartism
AAIINNOPRRSTT transpiration
AAIINNORRSTTY transitionary
AAIINOOPPPRRT appropriation
AAIJLMMOORRTY moral majority
AAIKLMNNOOPRS Roman Polanski
AAIKLNNOPRSSW Parkinson's law
AAIKMNOOQRTTU quotation mark
AAIKNNNOORSTW Rowan Atkinson
AAILLLNOORTUV valuation roll
AAILLMOOPPSTU papillomatous
AAILLNOOPSTTU postulational
AAILMNNORSTUU Ural Mountains
AAILNNOPPSTTU supplantation
AAILNNORSTTTU National Trust
AAILNOOOPRRTT protonotarial
AAIMMNNNNOOST Anton Mosimann
AAIMNNORSTTTU transmutation
AAIMOPRRSUVXY paramyxovirus
AAINOOOPRRTTT protonotariat
AAINOPRRRSTTY transpiratory
AAJLMNNOORSUW Woman's Journal
AAKLNNNNNOOPT nannoplankton
AALMNOOOPRSTU protanomalous
AALMOOPSSTTTY stomatoplasty
AAMNOORRSTXYY X-ray astronomy
AANNORRSSTUUY tyrannosaurus
AAOOOQRSSTTTU Torquato Tasso
ABBBBCEEHLMRU bubble chamber
ABBBBGIKLNOOR babbling brook
ABBBCHLNOORTY Bobby Charlton
ABBBDEEGHJRUY Jedburgh Abbey
ABBCDDEEIKLNW black bindweed
ABBCDEEEHMORR robe-de-chambre
ABBCDEEGILMRU Cambridge blue
ABBCDEEGILRSU bascule bridge
ABBCDEEIILNRS indescribable
ABBCDEEILNRSU undescribable
ABBCDEHILNOSU Blanche Du Bois
ABBCDEIILNRSY indescribably
ABBCDGIILNPRS scribbling-pad
ABBCEEEFKLSTU Beefsteak Club
ABBCEEEIMORRS Ambrose Bierce
ABBCEEHJKORTW The Jabberwock
ABBCEEHKNOOTT to the backbone
ABBCEEIJLNOOT objectionable
ABBCEEKLMPRRU Purbeck marble
ABBCEEKLORRRY roe-blackberry
ABBCEEORRSTTY Robert Catesby
ABBCEGIKLNRRY blackberrying
ABBCEGILNOPUU bubonic plague
ABBCEGIMNOPRT carpet-bombing
ABBCEHIILORTY bibliothecary
ABBCEHILNORTU bronchial tube
ABBCEHKOORRSS shock absorber
ABBCEHNRRRSUY cranberry bush
ABBCEIILMOOPT biocompatible
ABBCEIJLNOOTY objectionably
ABBCEILNORTTU contributable
ABBCEINOORSTY obsecration by
ABBCGHIIILOPR bibliographic
ABBCGIIILLLOO bibliological
ABBCHHILOORSY hobby-horsical
ABBCIIILLLOOP bibliopolical
ABBCIIILMNOTY combinability
ABBCIIILOPRST probabilistic
ABBDDDEIILMVY David Dimbleby
ABBDDGIILNORU building-board
ABBDEEEEELNRV Venerable Bede
ABBDEEEEILNRT beetlebrained
ABBDEEFNORSTU beast of burden
ABBDEEHHLMOOT Theobald Boehm
ABBDEEHNOSTTU beat the bounds
ABBDEEILLNORU double bar line
ABBDEFGIOORST bridge of boats
ABBDEGIKLNNOU double-banking

ABBDEHHMORRTU	Mother Hubbard
ABBDEHINPRSTU	put behind bars
ABBDEHLOOORYY	Holyrood Abbey
ABBDEIILRSTTU	distributable
ABBDEILLNORTU	bulletin board
ABBDELNOOOSSU	double bassoon
ABBDFFILMNNSU	blindman's buff
ABBDFIILLLRWY	Willard F Libby
ABBDGINNORSSY	Song by Isbrand
ABBDHILNOORRS	Harold Robbins
ABBDHINOOORSY	Robin Hood's Bay
ABBEEEEFHMORT	before the beam
ABBEEEGHLNSTY	shabby-genteel
ABBEEEGLLPSSS	pebble-glasses
ABBEEEKLMOPRT	pembroke table
ABBEEGNORRRSU	barber-surgeon
ABBEEHINRRSSU	Henri Barbusse
ABBEEHLMORSTT	stealth bomber
ABBEEIIILLLOS	Isobel Baillie
ABBEEILMPRRTU	imperturbable
ABBEELMMNOOTZ	bamboozlement
ABBEELOOPRRRR	probable error
ABBEFHILLNOTY	Fonthill Abbey
ABBEGGHINORTY	Big Bang theory
ABBEGGIOOORRT	Roberto Baggio
ABBEGHIILOPRR	bibliographer
ABBEGILLNOSST	Stella Gibbons
ABBEGILNORRSU	rabble-rousing
ABBEHINORTTUZ	Benazir Bhutto
ABBEHKLNRRTUU	Luther Burbank
ABBEHPRRRSSUY	raspberry bush
ABBEIIILOPRST	probabilities
ABBEIILLMORRY	mobile library
ABBEILMPRRTUY	imperturbably
ABBEILSSTTTUU	substitutable
ABBENNOORSSTU	burn one's boats
ABBFGHNOORRUY	burgh of barony
ABBGHIIILOPST	bibliophagist
ABBIIILLORSTT	bibliolatrist
ABBIIILMOPRTY	improbability
ABBIILLOORSTU	bibliolatrous
ABBILMOOPRRSU	labor improbus
ABCCCDEEINNOS	bad conscience
ABCCCEEENNOST	contabescence
ABCCCIIINORUZ	cubic zirconia
ABCCCILLMOOXY	coxcombically
ABCCDDEHINORR	Richard Cobden
ABCCDEEEELNRT	credence table
ABCCDEEHMNORS	second chamber
ABCCDEEIKLNOR	cockle-brained
ABCCDEELNOOUV	double-concave
ABCCDEGNOTTUU	budget account
ABCCDEILORSTU	scrobiculated
ABCCDGHIILNOU	coachbuilding
ABCCDHHIIOPRW	coachwhip-bird
ABCCDIILLMORU	umbilical cord
ABCCDOOPRRTUU	court cupboard
ABCCEEEFFLOPT	placebo effect
ABCCEEEIMMORR	Eric Morecambe
ABCCEEEIMNORS	Coma Berenices
ABCCEEFFIINRY	efficiency bar
ABCCEEFILSTYY	safety bicycle
ABCCEEFLORTTY	Battle of Crécy
ABCCEEGJNOOTT	cognate object
ABCCEEHHIKNOR	Herbie Hancock
ABCCEEHHKRTTY	Becky Thatcher
ABCCEEHIKLRTU	Charlie Bucket
ABCCEEHIKNRST	chicken breast
ABCCEEIILMMRS	immarcescible
ABCCEEIILNNOV	inconceivable
ABCCEEILNNOSS	non-accessible
ABCCEEILNNOUV	unconceivable
ABCCEEJLNORTU	conjecturable
ABCCEEKNOORSV	cover one's back
ABCCEEOSSSTUY	sebaceous cyst
ABCCEFFHINORR	branch officer
ABCCEGIKLNRSY	cyberslacking
ABCCEHIILLMOY	biochemically
ABCCEHILORTTT	brattice-cloth
ABCCEHKLORRST	starch blocker
ABCCEIIILMPTY	impeccability
ABCCEIIILSSTY	accessibility
ABCCEIILLMORS	social climber
ABCCEIILLOOPT	occipital lobe
ABCCEIILNNOVY	inconceivably
ABCCEIILNOOPT	occipital bone
ABCCEIILORTTY	bacteriolytic
ABCCEIIMMNRTU	circumambient
ABCCEIKLNOSTW	constablewick
ABCCEILLLMNOP	Colin Campbell
ABCCEILNNOUVY	unconceivably
ABCCEIMMORTUY	mycobacterium
ABCCEINNOOPTY	Conception Bay
ABCCELNORSTTU	constructable
ABCCENOOPRRSS	carbon process
ABCCHHIIOPRRS	archbishopric
ABCCHKOQTTTUU	quatch-buttock
ABCCIIINNSSTT	Basic Instinct
ABCCIILORRTXY	tricarboxylic
ABCCIIMNOORST	combinatorics
ABCCIINORSTTU	antiscorbutic
ABCCILLLNOOSU	colon bacillus
ABCCILLORSTUY	scorbutically
ABCCILMNOPPUY	public company
ABCCNOORRSTTU	subcontractor
ABCDDEEEHNSSU	debauchedness
ABCDDEEEILLOR	bearded collie
ABCDDEEELNNSU	undescendable
ABCDDEEGHILMR	Gilded Chamber
ABCDDEEGINPRT	carpet-bedding
ABCDDEEHILRTT	battered child
ABCDDEEHLRRRY	bladder cherry
ABCDDEEHNRRUU	Eduard Buchner
ABCDDEEIILRST	discreditable
ABCDDEEIKLMRT	middle-bracket
ABCDDEEIKPRRS	redback spider
ABCDDEEILTTUX	tax-deductible
ABCDDEEIMNNOW	Ann Widdecombe
ABCDDEELSSUUY	Claude Debussy
ABCDDEIILRSTY	discreditably
ABCDDEIINOORX	carbon dioxide
ABCDDEIIRRSUV	Sir David Bruce

ABCDDHIOOOPRW woodchip board
ABCDEEEHLRRST barrel-chested
ABCDEEEHORRTT beat the record
ABCDEEEILMNRT clean-timbered
ABCDEEEINORRT decerebration
ABCDEEELMMNOR recommendable
ABCDEEFIMNNOS absence of mind
ABCDEEFLMRRUY mulberry-faced
ABCDEEGGLMRSS scrambled eggs
ABCDEEGGORRUY George Cadbury
ABCDEEGHILNOR breech-loading
ABCDEEGHIRSTU discharge tube
ABCDEEGIILRTT lattice-bridge
ABCDEEGILPPRR clapper bridge
ABCDEEGILRRTT cartridge-belt
ABCDEEHILPTTT pitched battle
ABCDEEHLRRRTU Albrecht Dürer
ABCDEEIIILTVY deceivability
ABCDEEIILLTTY delectability
ABCDEEIILMNNU unmedicinable
ABCDEEIILNNOT benedictional
ABCDEEIILNOST decision table
ABCDEEIILOPRT periodic table
ABCDEEIINPSST bits and pieces
ABCDEEILNNNOS incondensable
ABCDEEILNPRTU unpredictable
ABCDEEILOORTW eat boiled crow
ABCDEEINOPRVY Providence Bay
ABCDEEIRRRSTY secretary bird
ABCDEEKKNORSU break one's duck
ABCDEEKLMORSU measured block
ABCDEELLOORSU sable-coloured
ABCDEELLOPRST corps de ballet
ABCDEELLRSSUY Darcey Bussell
ABCDEELMMNNOU uncommendable
ABCDEELMMNORY recommendably
ABCDEELMOPPRW wamble-cropped
ABCDEEMNOOPRY beyond compare
ABCDEEMNORRTT Comte Bertrand
ABCDEGGIIMNRR Cambridge ring
ABCDEGHLMOTUY Clyde Tombaugh
ABCDEGIILLLNR cable-drilling
ABCDEGIINORTU auction bridge
ABCDEGILLMNOU cable-moulding
ABCDEGILNNPUW Wig and Pen Club
ABCDEGILNOPSU double spacing
ABCDEGINOPRTY body carpeting
ABCDEHIILNNRR brainchildren
ABCDEHILLRTUY hydraulic belt
ABCDEHILORRRT Robert Aldrich
ABCDEHILRRRTU Richard Butler
ABCDEHIMORSWW widow's chamber
ABCDEHINOPSSU subdeaconship
ABCDEIIILLNPS disciplinable
ABCDEIIILMNRS discriminable
ABCDEIIILMRTU mirabile dictu
ABCDEIIILNORT bidirectional
ABCDEIIILNOSS indissociable
ABCDEIIILNTUY ineducability
ABCDEIIILPRTY predicability
ABCDEIIILPSTY despicability
ABCDEIIILRTTY creditability
ABCDEIIINSTUV subindicative
ABCDEIILLOQTU quodlibetical
ABCDEIILMNORV Vince Lombardi
ABCDEIILMORTU Trombiculidae
ABCDEIILPSUVV bicuspid valve
ABCDEILNPRTUY unpredictably
ABCDEILNSSSUU undiscussable
ABCDEILORRRTY trial by record
ABCDEKKORRUUY break your duck
ABCDEKNORRSTU round brackets
ABCDELLNNOSUW Lansdowne Club
ABCDELMMNNOUY uncommendably
ABCDEMOOOQRSU Cordoba Mosque
ABCDEMOPRRSTU broad-spectrum
ABCDENOOOPRRT corporate bond
ABCDEOOOPRRTY body corporate
ABCDGHHIIRRRT Richard Bright
ABCDGHINOOPPR chopping-board
ABCDHIILLLORT billiard cloth
ABCDHIILLOPUY public holiday
ABCDHINORRRTU Richard Burton
ABCDIIIILNTVY vindicability
ABCDIIINNOSTU subindication
ABCDIINRRSTTU urban district
ABCEEEEGHILNU Eugène Labiche
ABCEEEELNRSSX execrableness
ABCEEEFFHORTT before the fact
ABCEEEFIILLRT electrifiable
ABCEEEFIILNNT beneficential
ABCEEEFILLNNU influenceable
ABCEEEFLNNORU unenforceable
ABCEEEGGHMORT George Macbeth
ABCEEEGHIMMNN Menachem Begin
ABCEEEHIINRRS Berenice's Hair
ABCEEEHMMRRRT charter member
ABCEEEILNOPTX exceptionable
ABCEEEILNORRT carrion beetle
ABCEEEILNPRUV unperceivable
ABCEEEILNRSUV unserviceable
ABCEEEILNSSTX excitableness
ABCEEEILORRRV irrecoverable
ABCEEEILORTVX overexcitable
ABCEEEKLMSTTU Samuel Beckett
ABCEEELMNOPRS recompensable
ABCEEELNORRUV unrecoverable
ABCEEELNORSSV revocableness
ABCEEELNSSSUX excusableness
ABCEEENRRRRTY cranberry tree
ABCEEFHILORSW bachelor's wife
ABCEEFIIINNOT beneficiation
ABCEEFILNNORU uninforceable
ABCEEGHILMNRS single-chamber
ABCEEGHILNOPT benthopelagic
ABCEEGHLMRRSU schlumbergera
ABCEEGHLNOSWX exchange blows
ABCEEGIILNOTW biogenetic law
ABCEEGILNORSW bowling crease
ABCEEGIMNNRSS embracingness
ABCEEGIRTTTTU cigarette butt
ABCEEGJNOPRRS Jacob Sprenger

ABCEEHHOORRSS horseshoe crab
ABCEEHIILLLOR Hilaire Belloc
ABCEEHIILMMOT hemimetabolic
ABCEEHILLPTUW the public weal
ABCEEHILNSSSU blanchisseuse
ABCEEHILORSTT heteroblastic
ABCEEHIMNRSTY chimneybreast
ABCEEHIMOPRRS promise-breach
ABCEEHINNNPRR perennibranch
ABCEEHKLOSSTT clothes-basket
ABCEEHLMMNPRU plenum chamber
ABCEEHLNOSSTU touchableness
ABCEEHLORSUUW warehouse club
ABCEEHNRRSTUY Treasury bench
ABCEEIIILRTVY receivability
ABCEEIILNPRSU republicanise
ABCEEIILNPRUZ republicanize
ABCEEILLMRSTY syllabic metre
ABCEEILLRSSVY syllabic verse
ABCEEILMOORSU bromeliaceous
ABCEEILMOOSSU Coomassie Blue®
ABCEEILNNORSV inconversable
ABCEEILNNOSTT incontestable
ABCEEILNNRRST Carl Bernstein
ABCEEILNNRSSU incurableness
ABCEEILNOPRRS cerebrospinal
ABCEEILNOPTXY exceptionably
ABCEEILNPRUVY unperceivably
ABCEEILORRRVY irrecoverably
ABCEEILPRSTTU piecrust table
ABCEEILRRSTTU battle-cruiser
ABCEEILRRSTTW Cetti's warbler
ABCEEIMNORSSV misobservance
ABCEEIMNOSSTV combativeness
ABCEEINNOPRRS Pierce Brosnan
ABCEEINORSSTX resistance box
ABCEEINPRRSSU pressure cabin
ABCEEJMRSTTTU subject matter
ABCEEKKLLLNRU knuckleballer
ABCEEKMNRRSTU numbers racket
ABCEEKNOOSTTY bayonet socket
ABCEEKNOPSSTU set one's back up
ABCEELMMNORSU commensurable
ABCEELNNOOPRU pronounceable
ABCEELNNOQRUU unconquerable
ABCEELNNORSUV unconversable
ABCEELNNOSTTU uncontestable
ABCEELNORRUVY unrecoverably
ABCEELOORSTTT bottle-coaster
ABCEENNNOORSV non-observance
ABCEENOSTTTUY beauty contest
ABCEEOPRRSUVX procès-verbaux
ABCEEQRRSTTUY cybersquatter
ABCEFFILNRRUY Barry Cunliffe
ABCEFGHIINRTW watching brief
ABCEFGHKNOOOS Book of Changes
ABCEFGIIILNNT filing cabinet
ABCEFGIILMMNR climbing-frame
ABCEFGKNRSTUU bracket fungus
ABCEFHIILLMRU Liebfraumilch
ABCEFHILMRTUY family butcher
ABCEFHILNORSY noble crayfish
ABCEFHNRRSTUZ Franz Schubert
ABCEFHORRSTTU breach of trust
ABCEFIIILNOPT plebification
ABCEFIIINORTV verbification
ABCEFILOORSTU cobaltiferous
ABCEFINOORRSU carboniferous✧
ABCEFLMNNOORU unconformable
ABCEFLMNOORTU uncomfortable
ABCEGHHILNOST High Constable
ABCEGHHOORRTU thoroughbrace
ABCEGHIKLNOSS slingback shoe
ABCEGHILOPRTY copyrightable
ABCEGHIMNNSUU submachine-gun
ABCEGIILLOOOX exobiological
ABCEGIINNOOSU bignoniaceous
ABCEGIKLNRSTY cyberstalking
ABCEGILLMOORY embryological
ABCEGILNNNOOZ non-cognizable
ABCEGIMNOOTYZ zygomatic bone
ABCEGINORRSSZ zebra crossing
ABCEGJMOOPRRT object program
ABCEHHHIINRRT Heinrich Barth
ABCEHHIILMOPS Michael Bishop
ABCEHIIIKLMNS mashie-niblick
ABCEHIIKLSTTY sketchability
ABCEHIKLNSTTT blanket stitch
ABCEHILLMOOOT holometabolic
ABCEHILNOPSST constableship
ABCEHILOOOPPT photocopiable
ABCEHILOPSTTU absolute pitch
ABCEHILORSTVY Vitaly Scherbo
ABCEHJLNNOOST John Constable
ABCEHKLLORSTU bullock's-heart
ABCEHKLNOPTTU put the black on
ABCEHLOOPRSTU claustrophobe
ABCEHMOOPSSTX box the compass
ABCEHOPRRSTUY brachypterous
ABCEIIJNOOTTV objectivation
ABCEIIKNNRSSS brainsickness
ABCEIILLLMPTU multiplicable
ABCEIILMNOPST incompatibles
ABCEIILMNPRSU republicanism
ABCEIILMORRUV Columbia River
ABCEIILNOPRTU republication
ABCEIILNORSTY bacteriolysin
ABCEIILORSSTY bacteriolysis
ABCEIILORSTUY burial society
ABCEIILPRSTTU subtriplicate
ABCEIILPSSTUY subspeciality
ABCEIIMMNOSTY meibomian cyst
ABCEIIMNNOORT recombination
ABCEIIMOORRST isobarometric
ABCEIIMOSSTTY biosystematic
ABCEIKNOPRSST Brass in Pocket
ABCEILLLPSTTU plastic bullet
ABCEILLMNORYY embryonically
ABCEILLMORTYY embryotically
ABCEILLORSTTY obstetrically
ABCEILMNOSSUU omnibus clause
ABCEILMOSSTUU absolute music

ABCEILNNORSTU	inconstruable
ABCEILNNOSTTY	incontestably
ABCEILNORTTUU	tuberculation
ABCEILNPRSTUV	public servant
ABCEILNSSSSSU	business class
ABCEILOORSSTU	strobilaceous
ABCEILORRRTUU	arboriculture
ABCEILRRRTTUU	tritubercular
ABCEIMMOPRSST	compass timber
ABCEIMOOPRRUV	copia verborum
ABCEIOOORRRTV	corroborative
ABCEIOPRSSSUY	presbyacousis
ABCEKLNOOSSTW	blow one's stack
ABCEKLNOPSTTU	buttock planes
ABCEKNNNORRTU	Anton Bruckner
ABCELMMNORSUY	commensurably
ABCELMNOSSTTU	mescal buttons
ABCELMORSSSTU	stumble across
ABCELNNOQRUUY	unconquerably
ABCFHLLOOOTTU	touch football
ABCFIILNOOOTV	act of oblivion
ABCFIILNOSTUY	confusability
ABCFILMMORRUU	umbraculiform
ABCFLMNNOORUY	unconformably
ABCFLMNOORTUY	uncomfortably
ABCGGHINORRTU	turbocharging
ABCGHHNOOPRRY	bronchography
ABCGHIIKNNSTW	bank switching
ABCGHIKLNSSUW	swashbuckling
ABCGIILLNNOOO	non-biological
ABCGIKLNORSTT	starting block
ABCGILLLNOOTU	lactoglobulin
ABCGILLMNOORU	macroglobulin
ABCHHILNOPSTU	tulchan bishop
ABCHHINOOPRST	opisthobranch
ABCHIILLRSTUY	hubristically
ABCHIILOOOPRU	ailourophobic
ABCHIKNOORRRS	Brian Horrocks
ABCHILOOPRSTT	trophoblastic
ABCIIIILNOSTY	insociability
ABCIIILLNOTUY	inoculability
ABCIIILMOPTTY	compatibility
ABCIIILNOSTUY	unsociability
ABCIILLMOSSTY	symbolistical
ABCIILLMOSTYY	symbiotically
ABCIILLMRSTUU	biculturalism
ABCIILLOPRSTT	triploblastic
ABCIILMMOTTUY	commutability
ABCIILMOPTTUY	computability
ABCILLOPRSTUY	subtropically
ABCILMNNOOSSU	no-claims bonus
ABCILNOORSTTU	obstructional
ABCINOOOORRRT	corroboration
ABCLRRSSTTUUU	substructural
ABCOOOORRRRTY	corroboratory
ABDDDEEILMNRU	muddle-brained
ABDDDEILMNORY	broadmindedly
ABDDEEEGILNRW	large bindweed
ABDDEEEHLORTU	double-hearted
ABDDEEEIKLMRR	middlebreaker
ABDDEEEIKNNRY	red kidney bean
ABDDEEEILMNOT	diamond-beetle
ABDDEEEIMNNRS	bedside manner
ABDDEEELLMNSS	dead-men's bells
ABDDEEELORTTX	dead-letter box
ABDDEEFGIINNR	Bendigeidfran
ABDDEEGGIMRRU	Bermuda rigged
ABDDEEGILLNOU	double-dealing
ABDDEEHLLORSU	shoulder blade
ABDDEEIILNPTY	dependability
ABDDEEILLMNSW	small bindweed
ABDDEELNORTUU	double-natured
ABDDEELNOTTUY	doubly dentate
ABDDEFHLLNOOS	flesh and blood
ABDDEGIINPRRY	bidding-prayer
ABDDEGNORRSST	St Bernard's dog
ABDDEHIILMNRS	Hildebrandism
ABDDEHLNOORRS	no holds barred
	no-holds-barred
ABDDEHMNOORUW	homeward-bound
ABDDEIKLNTTUV	David Blunkett
ABDDEIMNOSSXY	body mass index
ABDDEINORRRUY	boundary rider
ABDDGILMNOORU	moulding board
ABDDGINNOORSU	sound boarding
	sounding board
ABDDHJNOOOORW	John Broadwood
ABDDILNNOOOOT	blood donation
ABDEEEEGHLMRT	Lambeth degree
ABDEEEEHINRRS	Aberdeenshire
ABDEEEEILMRRS	irredeemables
ABDEEEFGINRST	breastfeeding
ABDEEEFLORTUU	double feature
ABDEEEGGHRRRR	Gerhard Berger
ABDEEEGHILNRT	bleeding heart
ABDEEEGIIKLLP	bleed like a pig
ABDEEEGILLNRS	designer label
ABDEEEGILNOST	désobligeante
ABDEEEGKLLNOW	knowledgeable
ABDEEEGKLNOSW	knowledge base
ABDEEEGLRSSUY	blue-eyed grass
ABDEEEHIKMRST	beside the mark
ABDEEEHIRSTTW	white-breasted
ABDEEEHKNORRT	broken-hearted
ABDEEEHLNOPTY	beyond the pale
ABDEEEHLNOSTY	lead by the nose
ABDEEEHLNRTTU	under the table
ABDEEEHMNNORS	on her beam-ends
ABDEEEHNRRRTU	thunder-bearer
ABDEEEHOPRSTW	sweep the board
ABDEEEIILMRTY	redeemability
ABDEEEIINNORT	Tenebrionidae
ABDEEEILLNRUV	undeliverable
ABDEEEILLNSSY	yieldableness
ABDEEEILMPRSY	bird's-eye maple
ABDEEEILNRSSS	desirableness
ABDEEEKNOOSTT	take to one's bed
ABDEEELLNOSST	tell one's beads
ABDEEELNNRSSU	endurableness
ABDEEELOSTTTT	estate-bottled
ABDEEEMNORSUY	beyond measure
ABDEEENORSSWW	brown seaweeds

ABDEEFFILLNRS snaffle-bridle
ABDEEFGHINRRT finger-breadth
ABDEEFIIILRSV diversifiable
ABDEEFIIILSTY defeasibility
ABDEEFIIMRRSU uberrima fides
ABDEEFLOORRTT order of battle
ABDEEGGNRSTTU butter-and-eggs
ABDEEGIILNRST disintegrable
ABDEEGILMNNOU double-meaning
ABDEEGILNRSST dressing-table
ABDEEGINNORSW Swedenborgian
ABDEEGINPRSTT spread betting
ABDEEGKLLNOWY knowledgeably
ABDEEHIINOSTT a bit on the side
ABDEEHILNSSTU unestablished
ABDEEHIMORRRT barrier method
ABDEEHMRSSTTU The Dam Busters
ABDEEHNPRRUUY Audrey Hepburn
ABDEEIILNNNTV Venetian blind
ABDEEIILNNPSS indispensable
ABDEEIILNNSSU inaudibleness
ABDEEIILNOPRT perditionable
ABDEEIILNPTXY expendability
ABDEEIILNTTXY extendability
ABDEEIILSTTTY detestability
ABDEEIIMRTTXY ambidexterity
ABDEEIJLMNRSY James Brindley
ABDEEIJPRRSTU Jupiter's beard
ABDEEIKLNNRSS drinkableness
ABDEEIKMMNRST disembarkment
ABDEEIKMNNORS break one's mind
ABDEEILLNORRS banderilleros
ABDEEILLOORTV blood relative
ABDEEILMNOPRS imponderables
ABDEEILMRRSTU master-builder
ABDEEILNNRTUY turn a blind eye
ABDEEIMORSTUX ambidexterous
ABDEEINNOPRRR Pierre Bonnard
ABDEEINNSSSSU unbiassedness
ABDEEKNOORRSW break one's word
ABDEELLLNORRV Bernard Lovell
ABDEELMNORSTT Mandelbrot set
ABDEELMORRSTT Lombard Street
ABDEELNNNORTT Arnold Bennett
ABDEELNNOORTY Arnold Toynbee
ABDEELNORRVWW brave new world✧
ABDEEMORRRRWY Drew Barrymore
ABDEFHILNORSW shield of brawn
ABDEFIIINNORT defibrination
ABDEFIILLORRT defibrillator
ABDEFIILMORTY deformability
ABDEFIILNNTUU infundibulate
ABDEFIJLMMNOS James Bond film
ABDEFKOOORSSS Books of Esdras
ABDEGGHNORSUY horse-and-buggy
ABDEGGIIMNNRR Ingrid Bergman
ABDEGGILLNOUZ double-glazing
ABDEGHILNORSU Gabriel hounds
ABDEGHINOORSU boarding house
ABDEGIILNPPRU building paper
ABDEGIILNSSUU undisguisable
ABDEGIILOOSTT diabetologist
ABDEGILLLNORR rollerblading
ABDEGILMOOSVY viol-de-gamboys
ABDEGINNOORUV overabounding
ABDEGNOSSSUYY anybody's guess
ABDEHHILMOSTT Theobald Smith
ABDEHIIILLLOY Billie Holiday
ABDEHIJLLLNOO John de Balliol
ABDEHILMNNSST blandishments
ABDEHILNOORSU dishonourable
ABDEHKLOOPPRT Prokop the Bald
ABDEHMORRSSTU Bermuda shorts
ABDEIIIILQRSU disequilibria
ABDEIILLNOSSV indissolvable
ABDEIILLOPRTY deplorability
ABDEIILNNPRSS Persian blinds
ABDEIILNNPSSY indispensably
ABDEIILNOPRTY ponderability
ABDEIILNRSSTU Siberut Island
ABDEIILOORSVY olivary bodies
ABDEIILPRRTUY perdurability
ABDEIINNORSTU insubordinate
ABDEIINNORTTW rainbow-tinted
ABDEIINORSTUV subordinative
ABDEIKLNOOSUZ Zuleika Dobson
ABDEILLNOOORT blood relation
ABDEILMNNORRU ordinal number
ABDEILMNNRRTU Martin Brundle
ABDEILNORSTUY subordinately
ABDEKNORRRTUW wardrobe trunk
ABDEKRRTUUYZZ turkey buzzard
ABDELNNOPTUUW unputdownable
ABDFFNOOOSTUU sound off about
ABDFGINNORSSU brassfounding
ABDFIIILMORTY formidability
ABDFILLNOTUUY lady bountiful✧
ABDFNOOOOPRSS basso profondo
ABDFNOOOPRSSU basso profundo
ABDGGIIOOORRR Rodrigo Borgia
ABDGHINOOORST shooting board
ABDGHNNOQRSUU brush quandong
ABDGIIILNNPRS spiral binding
ABDGIIILNOOST disobligation
ABDGIIKNORRST skirting-board
ABDGIILMNNPST blind stamping
ABDGIILOORSTY disobligatory
ABDGILMNNORSU Bildungsroman
ABDGINNOOORRU Giordano Bruno
ABDGINOORRSWY borrowing days
ABDHIIINORSTY hybridisation
ABDHIIINORTYZ hybridization
ABDHILNOORSUY dishonourably
ABDHIOOTTTUUW without a doubt
ABDIIIILMSSTY admissibility
ABDIIILNOSSUV subdivisional
ABDIIILOPSSTY disposability
ABDIIILPSTTUY disputability
ABDIINNOORSTU subordination
ABDIINNOORTTU dinoturbation
ABDIIOPRTTUYY pituitary body
ABDILLMNNOPTU platinum-blond

ABDILNORRSSUY Lord Sainsbury
ABDLLMMNOOOSS almond-blossom
ABDLLOOOOSSWW wood-wool slabs
ABDMMNOOOPRSS mops and brooms
ABEEEEEHLLLLN La Belle Hélène
ABEEEEFHLRRTY breathe freely
ABEEEEFLNORSU unforeseeable
ABEEEEGLMNRTU beleaguerment
ABEEEEILMMPRS semipermeable
ABEEEEIRRRTVV reverberative
ABEEEELLLOPQU la Belle Époque
ABEEEELNNRSSV venerableness
ABEEEELNPRRST representable
ABEEEEMNPSTTT tempest-beaten
ABEEEENPRRRST Serpent Bearer
ABEEEFFILNNSS ineffableness
ABEEEFGILLOTT Battle of Liège
ABEEEFHMORSTT before the mast
ABEEEFHNNORTT feather-bonnet
ABEEEFIILLMPX exemplifiable
ABEEEGGHMNORT George Bentham
ABEEEGGOQRRSU Georges Braque
ABEEEGHHIMNTV might-have-been
ABEEEGHILLOTT goliath beetle
ABEEEGHIMORRV megaherbivore
ABEEEGHKORRTZ Zorba the Greek
ABEEEGILNSTVW batwing sleeve
ABEEEGLMMNNRT embranglement
ABEEEGLOORTTV root vegetable
ABEEEGOORRSSY sea gooseberry
ABEEEHHLLSTYY lay by the heels
ABEEEHIILNTTV the inevitable
ABEEEHIKMRSTT strike the beam
ABEEEHILLRTTT the Little Bear
ABEEEHILNPPRS apprehensible
ABEEEHINRTTTW weather-bitten
ABEEEHJMMNRTY Jeremy Bentham
ABEEEHKNOTTTT take to the bent
ABEEEIIKLMNRS Berkeleianism
ABEEEIIKLRSTT take liberties
ABEEEIILLPRRV irrepleviable
ABEEEIILRRRTV irretrievable
ABEEEIKKRRRST strikebreaker
ABEEEILLMRSSS Les Miserables
Les Misérables
ABEEEILMNRSSS miserableness
ABEEEILNNRRSS inerrableness
ABEEEILNOPRRT interoperable
ABEEEILNPRRTT interpretable
ABEEEILNPRRUV unreprievable
ABEEEILNQSSTU equitableness
ABEEEILNRSSTV veritableness
ABEEEINORRRTV reverberation
ABEEEJLNNOSSY enjoyableness
ABEEELLMNSSSS blamelessness
ABEEELLNORSST tolerableness
ABEEELMMNORSS memorableness
ABEEELMNPSSTT temptableness
ABEEELNNNSSTU untenableness
ABEEELNNPRSTU unpresentable
ABEEELNNPRTUV unpreventable
ABEEELNRRRTVY reverberantly
ABEEELNRSSTTU utterableness
ABEEENOSSSTUU beauteousness
ABEEEORRRRTVY reverberatory
ABEEFFHHIOTTW The Wife of Bath
ABEEFGIILNRRR irrefrangible
ABEEFGILNRSTZ blast-freezing
ABEEFGLNORTTU unforgettable
ABEEFHLLORSTT all for the best
ABEEFHNORRTUY Henry Beaufort
ABEEFIILPRRTY preferability
ABEEFILNRRRST transferrible
ABEEFKMNNOOOS make no bones of
ABEEFLOPRSTTY Battle of Ypres
ABEEGGHIOOPRR biogeographer
ABEEGGIIKNNNN banking engine
ABEEGGILLNNRS Allen Ginsberg
ABEEGHHILNORT breathing hole
ABEEGHHLPRSTU bush telegraph
ABEEGHIIMNRTT breathing-time
ABEEGHIKNORSU housebreaking
ABEEGHILMNTTT batement light
ABEEGHILNRRRT Albert Herring
ABEEGHINORRTV over-breathing
ABEEGHLORSTTT ghetto-blaster
ABEEGHMNORRRT brother-german
ABEEGIILNNORT orbital engine
ABEEGIINORRTV verbigeration
ABEEGIKNRRTUY Yekaterinburg
ABEEGILLNORRR roller bearing
ABEEGILLRRTTW Walter Gilbert
ABEEGILMOORST metagrobolise
ABEEGILMOORTZ metagrobolize
ABEEGILNNNOOT non-negotiable
ABEEGILNORRVY overbearingly
ABEEGILNOSSST blastogenesis
ABEEGIORTTTTU Ettore Bugatti
ABEEHHIOOPPRT herpetophobia
ABEEHHMORRTTU mouthbreather
ABEEHIILNSTUX inexhaustible
ABEEHIIORSTTT rise to the bait
ABEEHILLNPSST spill the beans
ABEEHILLNSTUW unwhistleable
ABEEHILMNSSTT establishment✧
ABEEHILOPRTTZ Port Elizabeth
ABEEHILRSSSYY Shirley Bassey
ABEEHIMOPRSTT Hemerobaptist
ABEEHKNOPRTTU put the brake on
ABEEHLLMSSSWY Welsh Assembly
ABEEHLMNORSTU unsmotherable
ABEEHLMORSTWY weather symbol
ABEEHLNRSTTTU turn the tables
ABEEHLOOTTTUW out at the elbow
ABEEHMNOOPRTT on the port beam
ABEEIIJNQRTUY jequirity bean
ABEEIILLMNORS neoliberalism
ABEEIILLNNNRW Willie Brennan
ABEEIILLRRRTW braille-writer
ABEEIILMPRTTY temperability
ABEEIILNPRTTY penetrability
ABEEIILNRRSST irritableness

ABEEIILOPRRSV proverbialise
ABEEIILOPRRVZ proverbialize
ABEEIILQSTUYZ squeezability
ABEEIILRRRTVY irretrievably
ABEEIKLLSSTTT table skittles
ABEEIKNOPRRRS prison-breaker
ABEEILLMOTTTU tell me about it!
ABEEILLNPSSSU plausibleness
ABEEILMMNOSSV immovableness
ABEEILMMNSSTU immutableness
ABEEILMNNNOTU unmentionable
ABEEILMNPSSTU imputableness
ABEEILNNRSSSS brainlessness
ABEEILNNSTTUU sublieutenant
ABEEILNPRSSSU suprasensible
ABEEILNQSSTUU subsequential
ABEEILOOPSSTT stable isotope
ABEEINNOOPRSU European bison
ABEEINNOSSSTT obstinateness
ABEEINOPRRSSS prisoners' base
prisoner's base
ABEEKLMNPRSSU plumber's snake
ABEEKMNNORTUY mountebankery
ABEELLMORRTWX Robert Maxwell
ABEELLOOPRRTW Robert Walpole
ABEELLORRSTUU absolute ruler
ABEELMOOORRST morale-booster
ABEELMPPRRRUY paper mulberry
ABEELNNNORRTU non-returnable
ABEELNNNSSTUU untunableness
ABEENNORSTTUV St Bonaventure
ABEENORRSSTUU subterraneous
ABEFFIIMOPRST baptism of fire
ABEFFNNOOOSTW off one's own bat
ABEFGIILNRRRY irrefrangibly
ABEFGIMNOORTY Moreton Bay fig
ABEFGLNORTTUY unforgettably
ABEFHIIKLNNST blanket finish
ABEFIIIILNSTY infeasibility
ABEFIIIILRTVY verifiability
ABEFIIILLRTTY filterability
ABEFIIILNRTUV unvitrifiable
ABEFIIJLNSTUU unjustifiable
ABEFIILMORRTY reformability
ABEFILLOOPRSW pair of bellows
ABEFILOSSSTTU Battle of Issus
ABEFIMNNOSSSU man of business
ABEFIMNOORRSU neurofibromas
ABEFKLMOOOSSU Books of Samuel
ABEFKLOORRSTU ask for trouble
ABEFLLNOOPSTU tablespoonful
ABEFLLOSSTTUY Battle of Sluys
ABEGGHILMNOSU gambling house
ABEGGIIMNNOPT opening gambit
ABEGGLNORSTUW blow great guns
ABEGHIIIMMNRS Birminghamise
ABEGHIIIMMNRZ Birminghamize
ABEGHIILLNRTW whirling-table
ABEGHIIMNNOOT The Mabinogion
ABEGHIKNOORST shooting brake
ABEGHILNORTTW throwing table
ABEGHILNOSTTW washing-bottle
ABEGHINOOOPRT gerontophobia
ABEGHINRRSTTU thrust bearing
ABEGIIILLMRTW Wiliam Gilbert
ABEGIIILNOTTY negotiability
ABEGIIILNRTTY integrability
ABEGIIKNNOPRT breaking point
ABEGIILMNOPST imposing table
ABEGIILNORRSS Basil Ringrose
ABEGIILNORTVY governability
ABEGIILOOORST aerobiologist
ABEGIKMNNNOTU mountebanking
ABEGIKNNNORRT Ken Barrington
ABEGILMNNORTU Grumbletonian
ABEGILNNNRTTU running battle
ABEGILNOPPRTT blotting-paper
ABEGIMNOSSSUU ambiguousness
ABEGLLMOPRRUU umbrella group
ABEGLMNOOORSS orange blossom
ABEGLMORRSUUX Rosa Luxemburg
ABEHHINNOORST Heath-Robinson
ABEHHIOOPRRTY erythrophobia
ABEHIIILPRSTY perishability
ABEHIIINNORST hibernisation
ABEHIIINNORTZ hibernization
ABEHIILNSTUXY inexhaustibly
ABEHIINOORRST herborisation
ABEHIINOORRTZ herborization
ABEHIIPRRRSST barristership
ABEHIJNNOORSS John Bessarion
ABEHIKMNOORST thrombokinase
ABEHILNORRSTW brothers-in-law
ABEHINNOOSSTT The Bostonians
ABEHINNOOSTTT ethnobotanist
ABEHINORSSSTT basset-hornist
ABEHJLOOPRSTT Joseph Rotblat
ABEHLLMOPSSUY blasphemously
ABEIIIILMNNSZ Leibnizianism
ABEIIIILNTTVY inevitability
ABEIIILLNORSS billionairess
ABEIIILLNRTUY unreliability
ABEIIILLNSTTY listenability
ABEIIILMNORST liberationism
ABEIIILMNRTTY terminability
ABEIIILNOPRTY inoperability
ABEIIILNOQRTU equilibration
ABEIIILNORSTT liberationist
ABEIIILNORTXY inexorability
ABEIIILNPSTXY expansibility
ABEIIIMMNNRSU mini-submarine
ABEIIKMNNORTU mountain biker
ABEIILLMOPTYY employability
ABEIILLNNRSST brilliantness
ABEIILLNRTUVY vulnerability
ABEIILLORSTVY resolvability
ABEIILMNRSSST transmissible
ABEIILMNRSTTT transmittible
ABEIILMNRSTUY mensurability
ABEIILMOPRRSV proverbialism
ABEIILMPRTTUY permutability
ABEIILNORSSTV vibrationless

ABEIILNSSSTTU subsistential
ABEIILOPRRSTV proverbialist
ABEIILOPRTTXY exportability
ABEIILRTTTUVY attributively
ABEIIMNNOSSTT abstentionism
ABEIIMNOSSSTU ambitiousness
ABEIIMOORSTUV overambitious
ABEIINNOORSTV inobservation
ABEIINNORSSTT baton-sinister
ABEIINNOSSTTT abstentionist
ABEIINORRTTTU reattribution
ABEIINRRSSTTU tributariness
ABEIINSSSTTUV substantivise
ABEIINSSTTUVZ substantivize
ABEIKMMNNOSTU mountebankism
ABEIKNNNOOOSY in anyone's book
ABEILLLMOTTUU multilobulate
ABEILLLORRWWW willow warbler
ABEILLNOOSSSY obsessionally
ABEILMNNORRUY Brian Mulroney
ABEILMNNOSTUU Blue Mountains
ABEILNNOOPSTX expansion bolt
ABEILNOORSSSU laboriousness
ABEILNOPPRSTU insupportable
ABEILNOSSTTUU absolute units
ABEILNSSTTUVY substantively
ABEIMNNOPPTTY by appointment
ABEIMNNOSSSUW businesswoman
ABEIMORRRRSTU orbis terrarum
ABEIMORRSSTUV satis verborum
ABEINNORSTUVY subventionary
ABEINOOPRRTTU protuberation
ABEINORRSSUVY subversionary
ABEKNOQRSTTUU Quaker-buttons
ABELLNOOSTTUY absolutely not
ABELLOPRTTTUW two-ball putter
ABELMNNORSTTU Burnett salmon
ABELNOORRSTWY Norway lobster
ABELNOPPRSTUU unsupportable
ABELNOPRRTTUY protuberantly
ABELNPRRSTTUY butler's pantry
ABEMMNNQRTUUU quantum number
ABEMOPRSSSTTU sub-postmaster
ABFGHHIIMOSTT that's big of him
ABFGIJLMNPRUY barfly jumping
ABFHHIILNRSTY labyrinth fish
ABFIIIILLLMNS infallibilism
ABFIIIILLLNST infallibilist
ABFIIIILLLNTY infallibility
ABFIIILOPRTTY profitability
ABFIIINNORSSY binary fission
ABFIIJLNSTUUY unjustifiably
ABGGGIILLNORT ballot-rigging
ABGGHIILLLNNT ball lightning
ABGGHIILNNRTW night-warbling
ABGGHINNORTTU bring to naught
ABGGIILOOORST agrobiologist
ABGHIIMMNSSTW swimming-baths
ABGHLMOOPRSYY symbolography
ABGIIIILNNTTY intangibility
ABGIIINORRSTU subirrigation
ABGIIJNNNOORT on-job training
ABGIIILNNOPRTY bring into play
ABGIIMNNORRST brainstorming
ABGILLORRSUUY burglariously
ABGILMNNOOPTT planing bottom
ABGILMNOSUUUY unambiguously
ABHHIILMOOPRT thrombophilia
ABHHIILOOPPSY syphilophobia
ABHHIINOOOPRT ornithophobia
ABHHILLOOPRTW whirlpool bath
ABHIIILNPSTUY punishability
ABHIIILNRSTTY labyrinthitis
ABHIIKMNNPRSS brinksmanship
ABHIILOPRSTTU titular bishop
ABHILMNOORTTW browntail moth
ABHNOPRSTTUUW push-button war
ABIIIIILMNTTY inimitability
ABIIIILLNOTVY inviolability
ABIIIILMPRTTY impartibility
ABIIIILMPSSTY impassibility
ABIIILLMNORSW Robin Williams
ABIIILLNOSTVY insolvability
ABIIILMOPRTVY improvability
ABIIILNOSSTTU subtilisation
ABIIILNOSTTUZ subtilization
ABIIILNSTTUUY unsuitability
ABIIILRSTUVVY survivability
ABIIINOORSSTT sorbitisation
ABIIINOORSTTZ sorbitization
ABIILMNNNTTUU tintinnabulum
ABIILMNOOSSTY symbolisation
ABIILMNOOSTYZ symbolization
ABIILMNOSTUUY unambitiously
ABIILMOOPRTTY promotability
ABIILMORRTTUV multivibrator
ABIINSSTTTUVY substantivity
ABILLMOPSSYYY polysyllabism
ABILLMMNOOSSY monosyllabism
ABILNOOPPSTUU subpopulation
ABILNOPPRSTUY insupportably
ABIMNNOOPTTUU Mount Pinatubo
ACCCCEIJMNRUY circumjacency
ACCCCEIKKLLTY clickety-clack
ACCCCILLLNOYY concyclically
ACCCDDHIIIMOR dichromic acid
ACCCDEEEINNNS incandescence
ACCCDEHILNOSY synecdochical
ACCCDEINORTTU credit account
ACCCDGIILLOOO codicological
ACCCDIIIINNOT nicotinic acid
ACCCEEEHLLLLN Leclanché cell
ACCCEEEINSSTX exact sciences
ACCCEEELNNOSV convalescence
ACCCEEGIILPRY epicyclic gear
ACCCEEGILNOSY Gascoyne-Cecil
ACCCEEHIILRRT electric chair
ACCCEEHNOQTUU cheque account
ACCCEEIILNOSS social science
ACCCEEILLNRTY eccentrically
ACCCEEILMOSTU cosmeceutical
ACCCEEKOOPPPR peacock copper

ACCCEELNNOSVY	convalescency
ACCCEFFIILRRT	traffic circle
ACCCEFHIIRTTU	fetch a circuit
ACCCEGHIKMNTU	magnetic chuck
ACCCEGILMNNOO	meningococcal
ACCCEGKLLNOOS	longcase clock
ACCCEHHKLOTTW	watch the clock
ACCCEHIILMOPR	microcephalic
ACCCEHIINORTT	architectonic
ACCCEHILMMOOS	cosmochemical
ACCCEHINNOOSU	cinchonaceous
ACCCEIINOPSUU	pucciniaceous
ACCCEILNOOPRS	necroscopical
ACCCEILOORSTT	sclerotic coat
ACCCEIMMNOOOR	macroeconomic
ACCCEIMNRSSTU	circumstances
ACCCELOOOPRST	Protococcales
ACCCELOOPRSTT	streptococcal
ACCCEMMNPTUUU	punctum caecum
ACCCENNOOOVVX	concavo-convex
ACCCGHIKLNOTW	clock-watching
ACCCGHILLNOOO	conchological
ACCCGIIKMNORR	microcracking
ACCCHILOOPSTY	staphylococci
ACCCHINOPRSSU	capuchin cross
ACCCHJKMMNOOR	John McCormack
ACCCIIILMMORT	microclimatic
ACCCIIKKLOSTT	cocktail stick
ACCCIILMMOORS	microcosmical
ACCCIILMOOPRS	microscopical
ACCCIKLNOORSV	volcanic rocks
ACCCILLOOOPPS	colposcopical
ACCCILORRRTUU	court circular
ACCCIMMNOOSTU	common caustic
ACCDDEEEHHKLU	chuckle-headed
ACCDDEEHRRSTU	starch-reduced
ACCDDEGHIILNU	child guidance
ACCDDEHKOOOSW	woodcock's-head
ACCDDHIIIINOT	dithionic acid
ACCDEEEEMNSUX	excuse-me dance
ACCDEEEGHNORT	hedge-accentor
ACCDEEEGLLORS	Sacred College
ACCDEEEHKLRST	clear the decks
ACCDEEEHKQRSU	checked square
ACCDEEEIIMNPS	space medicine
ACCDEEEIMRSSS	crème de cassis
ACCDEEEINORTT	enteric-coated
ACCDEEELPPRRY	recycled paper
ACCDEEENNNRST	transcendence
ACCDEEENORRRT	catercornered
ACCDEEGNOORTT	grande cocotte
ACCDEEHHIKLPT	thick-pleached
ACCDEEHIILNPX	cephalic index
ACCDEEHIKNRRU	hurricane deck
ACCDEEHINOSTU	outside chance
ACCDEEHLOOPRU	peach-coloured
ACCDEEHORRRRS	crash recorder
ACCDEEIILLSWY	Cecil Day-Lewis
ACCDEEIILNOST	occidentalise
ACCDEEIILNOTZ	occidentalize
ACCDEEILNNOPY	encyclopedian
ACCDEEINNOPRT	accident-prone
ACCDEEINORTUU	outrecuidance
ACCDEELLNORSY	secondary cell
ACCDEELMOORRU	cream-coloured
ACCDEEMNOPSST	compactedness
ACCDEENNNRSTY	transcendency
ACCDEENNORSTU	unconsecrated
ACCDEENORRTTY	catty-cornered
ACCDEGIILMNRY	magic cylinder
ACCDEGIILPRRT	cartridge clip
ACCDEGILNOORT	Angelic Doctor
ACCDEHHIKLLTY	latchkey child
ACCDEHHILLOOP	dolichocephal
ACCDEHHILOPRY	hydrocephalic
ACCDEHIKNOOPS	pick and choose
ACCDEHINOORTW	with one accord
ACCDEHKLOPPRT	cock-thrappled
ACCDEHLNNORRY	corn-chandlery
ACCDEIIILLNNO	linolenic acid
ACCDEIIINNOTT	identic action
ACCDEIIKLOOPS	kaleidoscopic
ACCDEIILMNOST	Occidentalism
ACCDEIILNNOOT	codeclination
ACCDEIILNORUU	Curculionidae
ACCDEIILNOSTT	Occidentalist
ACCDEIINOOPPR	propenoic acid
ACCDEIINOORTT	decortication
ACCDEIINORTTV	contradictive
ACCDEIJNOSTTU	jointed cactus
ACCDEIKLORSST	cocktail dress
ACCDEILLMOPTY	complicatedly
ACCDEILMMOSUY	musical comedy
ACCDEILMNOPTU	uncomplicated
ACCDEILNOORSY	secondary coil
ACCDEILNORSUY	cylindraceous
ACCDEIMNNOORT	non-democratic
ACCDEIMOPRRST	spermatic cord
ACCDEINOORSSV	vers d'occasion
ACCDEIOORSSTY	Dorcas society
ACCDEMOOPPRTW	powder compact
ACCDFFINORSTU	custard coffin
ACCDFIIILNOTU	dulcification
ACCDGHIKNORRY	hydrocracking
ACCDHHINOOPRY	hypochondriac
ACCDHIIINORST	diachronistic
ACCDHIILNOPSU	sulphonic acid
ACCDHIILPRSUU	sulphuric acid
ACCDHILLOOPYY	hypocycloidal
ACCDHIMNOPSYY	psychodynamic
ACCDHLNOOOTTU	hold to account
ACCDIIILNNOOP	clinopinacoid
ACCDIIILNSSTY	syndicalistic
ACCDIIINOOPPR	propionic acid
ACCDIIINORSTY	idiosyncratic
ACCDIIKLNNOPT	point-and-click
ACCDIILLLMOSU	molluscicidal
ACCDIILLLNRYY	cylindrically
ACCDIILLOSSYY	cyclodialysis
ACCDIIMMNNOOU	incommunicado
ACCDIINNOORTT	contradiction
ACCDILNOORRTU	conductor rail

ACCDIMMNNOORU communion card
ACCDIMMNORTUY community card
ACCDINOOPRRTU production car
ACCDINOORRTTY contradictory
ACCDMNOOOPRTY company doctor
ACCDMNOORRTTU tram conductor
ACCEEEEGHOSTT cottage cheese
ACCEEEEHLLNOP encephalocele
ACCEEEEILNRTV Venice treacle
ACCEEEELLNPRX par excellence
ACCEEEELMORRT accelerometer
ACCEEEFINOPPR Prince of Peace
ACCEEEGHIRRSV service charge
ACCEEEGILMNOU leucaemogenic
ACCEEEGINNRSV ingravescence
ACCEEEHILLNPT telencephalic
ACCEEEHILMNPS mesencephalic
ACCEEEIIRSTVV active service
ACCEEEILLORST ecclesiolater
ACCEEEILMMORS commercialese
ACCEEEILNRSTX excrescential
ACCEEEJKNQRSU Jacques Necker
ACCEEENNNORRT Terence Conran
ACCEEFFHKLOST coffee klatsch
ACCEEFFIILRSS self-sacrifice
ACCEEFHIILMNS fine chemicals
ACCEEFIORRTTV tractive force
ACCEEFKLOOPRW peacock-flower
ACCEEGGHIINNP changing-piece
ACCEEGHHIKMNW checkweigh man
ACCEEGHIKLRRT trickle-charge
ACCEEGHILLMOY geochemically
ACCEEGHILNOPS sleeping coach
ACCEEGHILNTYY eye-catchingly
ACCEEGHKNOSTX stock exchange✧
ACCEEGHMNORTV Congreve-match
ACCEEGHNNORTU counterchange
ACCEEGHNORRTU countercharge
ACCEEGILNORRT electric organ
ACCEEGILNORTT electronic tag
ACCEEGINPRRSS Princess Grace
ACCEEHHILLNUV launch vehicle
ACCEEHHIOPSYZ Schizophyceae
ACCEEHHJKRTUW three-jaw chuck
ACCEEHHLOOPRY Chlorophyceae
ACCEEHHLOORST schoolteacher
ACCEEHHLRUVYZ Vézelay Church
ACCEEHHNRRSTU Eastern Church
ACCEEHHOSTTTU cut to the chase
ACCEEHIILMMOS semiochemical
ACCEEHIINNORT coinheritance
ACCEEHIIRSSUW Eric Wieschaus
ACCEEHIKLNSST kitchen scales
ACCEEHIKNSSTU chuckie-stanes
ACCEEHIKORTTW weathercock it
ACCEEHILLNOTY acetylcholine
ACCEEHILLOPPT leptocephalic
ACCEEHILMOPRT petrochemical
ACCEEHILNNSST technicalness
ACCEEHIMMNSTU catechumenism
ACCEEHIMNRRST screech-martin
ACCEEHINPRSTU curtain speech
ACCEEHKNOOPRT Peacock Throne
ACCEEHKNRRTTU The Nutcracker
ACCEEHLLNNOPS splanchnocele
ACCEEHLMNOSTT casement cloth
ACCEEHOORSSSY accessory shoe
ACCEEHORRSTTY oyster-catcher
ACCEEIILLPPST elliptic space
ACCEEIILMMNSU ecumenicalism
ACCEEIILMMORS commercialise
ACCEEIILMMORZ commercialize
ACCEEIILMNOSU Louis MacNeice
ACCEEIILNOPRT electric piano
ACCEEIILNSTTU encaustic tile
ACCEEIILORSSV social service
ACCEEIIMNPRRU Prince Maurice
ACCEEIIOPRRTV reciprocative
ACCEEIKLNOPRS cocker spaniel
ACCEEIKORRRRT carrier rocket
ACCEEILLOPSUX coeliac plexus
ACCEEILLORSTY ecclesiolatry
ACCEEILMNOORT econometrical
ACCEEILNNRSST centricalness
ACCEEILNOPRTT optical centre
ACCEEILNOPSTU conceptualise
ACCEEILNOPTTT tectonic plate
ACCEEILNOPTUZ conceptualize
ACCEEILNOSTTU council estate
ACCEEILNOSTUV vice-consulate
ACCEEILNQSTUY acquiescently
ACCEEILORRSUV varicose ulcer
ACCEEILORSTTT electrostatic
ACCEEILPQRRTU parquet circle
ACCEEIMMNOTUX excommunicate
ACCEEIMORSSTT microcassette
ACCEEINNNNOTU in countenance
ACCEEINNORTTV concentrative
ACCEEINOPRTTV contraceptive
ACCEEINORTTUV counteractive
ACCEEIORRRRST escort carrier
ACCEEJKORRSST jack-crosstree
ACCEELLMMOORU macromolecule
ACCEELNNOSSTT contact lenses
ACCEELNOSSTTY Scotney Castle
ACCEELOOPRTUV octave coupler
ACCEEMNORRSTT concertmaster
ACCEEMNORSTTU accoustrement
accouterments
accoutrements
ACCEENNOORTTY octocentenary
ACCEENNOOSSTU consectaneous
ACCEENORRSTTU counter-caster
ACCEEOORRSSTU stercoraceous
ACCEEORRSSTXY carry to excess
ACCEFFFHIINOO chain of office
ACCEFFIIINOSU inefficacious
ACCEFFIIINPRS infraspecific
ACCEFFIILOPRT traffic police
ACCEFFIILOSUY efficaciously
ACCEFGIJNOOTU conjugate foci
ACCEFGIKRRRSU Carrickfergus

ACCEFHILLNOTU technical foul
ACCEFHILMOORR cochleariform
ACCEFHILOPRSY physical force
ACCEFHKKLOOTW cock of the walk
ACCEFHNOORTTU for the account
ACCEFHOORRSTU Court of Arches
ACCEFIIINOPST specification
ACCEFIIINORTT certification
rectification
ACCEFIIINPRST intraspecific
ACCEFIIKLNSTT in a cleft stick
ACCEFIILMOORS Scoleciformia
ACCEFIIORRTTY certificatory
ACCEFINNOORTY confectionary
ACCEFIOORRRSS Air Force Cross
ACCEGHHIOOPRR choreographic
ACCEGHIILOPRX lexicographic
ACCEGHILLNOOT technological
ACCEGHILMOPYY hypoglycaemic
ACCEGHILNNORY encroachingly
ACCEGHILNOPTT plectognathic
ACCEGHIOPRRVY cervicography
ACCEGIIKLNPST sticking-place
ACCEGIILLLOOX lexicological
ACCEGIILNQSUY acquiescingly
ACCEGIINNNORT concertinaing
ACCEGIKKLNOPS speaking clock
ACCEGILLNOOSY synecological
ACCEGILMNOORT conglomeratic
ACCEGIMNORSST cross-magnetic
ACCEGINOORRTT gerontocratic
ACCEGINOORTTV covert coating
ACCEGIOPPRRTU group practice
ACCEHHHINOPTT catch on the hip
ACCEHHIILMOST histochemical
ACCEHHIIOPSTT Theopaschitic
ACCEHHILMOOPT photochemical
ACCEHHILMOPTY phytochemical
ACCEHHILNRSUW Church in Wales
ACCEHHILOSSTZ eschscholtzia
ACCEHHIMORSTT chrestomathic
ACCEHHIMRRSSW schwärmerisch
ACCEHHINOPRST Ctesiphon arch
ACCEHHORRRTTY carry the torch
ACCEHHORRSSTT Rorschach test
ACCEHIILLNSST callisthenics
ACCEHIILMNOSS soil mechanics
ACCEHIILMOSTT Catholic Times
ACCEHIILPRRTY hypercritical
ACCEHIIMRSSTT chrematistics
ACCEHIINNOOST chose in action
ACCEHIINNOPTT nicotine patch
ACCEHIKLLMOOT milk chocolate
ACCEHILLNOPRT phallocentric
ACCEHILLNOPRY chronicle play
ACCEHILLNOPTY polytechnical
ACCEHILLOOPSS special school
ACCEHILMNOTYZ zymotechnical
ACCEHILMOOSTT cosmothetical
ACCEHILNOPRTY pyrotechnical
ACCEHILOOPPRS chorepiscopal
ACCEHILOORRTY caloric theory
ACCEHILOORSTY choral society
ACCEHIOOPSSTT tachistoscope
ACCEHKLOPSTUV Svatopluk Cech
ACCEHLLNOOPRR pro-chancellor
ACCEHORRSSSTT stretch across
ACCEIIILLNRSV Clive Sinclair
ACCEIIILMNORT cliometrician
ACCEIIILNPPRV vice-principal
ACCEIIIMNNORS Ciceronianism
ACCEIIKLMORTX cocktail mixer
ACCEIIKLNOSTW anticlockwise
ACCEIIKNNPRST panic-stricken
ACCEIILLQRTUY quality circle
ACCEIILMMMORS commercialism
ACCEIILMMORRT micrometrical
ACCEIILMMORST commercialist
ACCEIILMMORTY commerciality
ACCEIILMNOSSS neoclassicism✧
ACCEIILMORSTV viscometrical
ACCEIILNOPRST painter's colic
ACCEIILNOSSST neoclassicist
ACCEIILNRRSSY acrylic resins
ACCEIILNRRSTT transit circle
ACCEIILOPRRTY reciprocality
ACCEIILPRRSTU supercritical
ACCEIIMMNOTUV communicative
ACCEIINNNRSST scintiscanner
ACCEIINOOPRRT reciprocation
ACCEIINOORTTX excortication
ACCEIIOPPRSSU perspicacious
ACCEIKKKKNNRY knick-knackery
ACCEIKLORSSST lacrosse stick
ACCEILMMNNOOR non-commercial
ACCEILMNNNOOP non-compliance
ACCEILMNOPPSS pencil-compass
ACCEILMNOPSTU conceptualism
ACCEILNOPSTTU conceptualist
ACCEILOOPRSTT proteoclastic
ACCEIMMNNOTUX excommunicant
ACCEIMMNOORRR common carrier
ACCEIMMNORTUY community care
ACCEINNNOORTT concentration
ACCEINNOOPRTT contraception
ACCEINNOORRTY concretionary
ACCEINNOORSSY concessionary
ACCEINNOORTTU counteraction
ACCEINOOPPRTU preoccupation
ACCEINOPPRSSU percussion cap
ACCEJLLNORTUY conjecturally
ACCELLOORSSUU sclerocaulous
ACCELMNOOORTV Levant morocco
ACCELOOPRRSST pectoral cross
ACCENNOPRSSTY Constance Spry
ACCFGHHIKNRTU chuck-farthing
ACCFGHILNOTTT contact flight
ACCFHIIILNOTY chylification
ACCFHIIIMNOTY chymification
ACCFHIIORRSTV Vicar of Christ
ACCFIIIINNOTZ zincification
ACCFIIINNOORT cornification

ACCFIIINOORST scorification
ACCFIIINOOSTT Scotification
ACCFIIKLORTTU fruit cocktail
ACCFIILLLNOOT floccillation
ACCFIILNOOPRX ciprofloxacin
ACCFINNOOTTUU unit of account
ACCFLMORSTUUU fractocumulus
ACCGHHHHIMNRU High-Churchman
ACCGHHIKKMMUU high-muck-a-muck
ACCGHHINORSST cross-hatching
ACCGHHIOPPRSY psychographic
ACCGHIIINPRST scintigraphic
ACCGHIILLOORT trichological
ACCGHIKLORSSU surgical shock
ACCGHILLNOOOR chronological
ACCGHILLOOPSY psychological
ACCGHILOOPRSY hygroscopical
ACCGHIMNNOORU mourning coach
ACCGHIMNORSST cross-matching
ACCGHIOPPRRTY cryptographic
ACCGIIIMNORRT microgranitic
ACCGIILLMOOSU musicological
ACCGIILLOOOTX toxicological
ACCGIILMORRSU microsurgical
ACCGIILNOORST carcinologist
ACCGIILNOOSTV vaccinologist
ACCGILLLOOTYY cytologically
ACCGILLOOPRTY cryptological
ACCGILNOOPRSY laryngoscopic
ACCGKOPRRSSSU cockspur grass
ACCHHHIMNPRSU churchmanship
ACCHHILOORSTY charity-school
ACCHHIMMOOORT homochromatic
ACCHIILLMORRT chloritic marl
ACCHIILMOPRSY microphysical
ACCHIILMOSSST scholasticism
ACCHIILNOPRSU parish council
ACCHIIMNOOPRT actinomorphic
ACCHIINOPSTTY antipsychotic
ACCHIINPPSSTY panpsychistic
ACCHIJKLNNOOS Jack Nicholson
ACCHIJKLNOORS Sir John Alcock
ACCHILMOOPRTY polychromatic
ACCHILNOOSSTT Nicholas Scott
ACCHIMMNOOORT monochromatic
ACCHIMNOOPPST phonocamptics
ACCHIMOOPSSTY psychosomatic
ACCHIOOPRSSUZ schizocarpous
ACCHKLLORSTUU cultural shock
ACCIIILLNNSST scintilliscan
ACCIIILNNORTU in circulation
ACCIIILNOPRTT critical point
ACCIIIMMNOOST iconomaticism
ACCIILLNNQUUY quincuncially
ACCIILLNRRTUU crinicultural
ACCIILLPRSTUU piscicultural
ACCIILMMNOSTU communalistic
ACCIILMNOOPRV comprovincial
ACCIILMNOOPST complications
ACCIILMNORRTU criminal court
ACCIILNORTTTY contractility
ACCIIMMNNOOTU communication
ACCIIMNOOSSTY actinomycosis
ACCIINOOPRSST cranioscopist
ACCIINOORRSTY Socratic irony
ACCIIOORRSSTV Victoria Cross
ACCIJLNNNOOTU conjunctional
ACCILMNNOOTTY concomitantly
ACCIMMNOORTUY communicatory
ACCIMNOOPRSTU pococurantism
ACCINNOOOPSTT contact poison
ACCINNOOPRSTU conspurcation
ACCINOOPRSTTU pococurantist
ACCINPRSTTUUU acupuncturist
ACCLLORRSSTUU cross-cultural
ACCNNOORTTTUU turn to account
ACDDDEEEIINPV peace dividend
ACDDDEEHIJMNU Dame Judi Dench
ACDDDEHINORRS Richard Seddon
ACDDDENNNOOPR pro'd and conned
ACDDDFHIKNNOO findon haddock
ACDDEEEFHNRSU schadenfreude
ACDDEEEHKKLNU knuckle-headed
ACDDEEEIIIMMR Marie de Médici
ACDDEEEINORRS coriander seed
ACDDEEEINPRTU undepreciated
ACDDEEEKMNOPR promenade deck
ACDDEEENOPRTT top dead centre
ACDDEEFFIIITU fide et fiducia
ACDDEEFFILSTY disaffectedly
ACDDEEGIIMNOR mid-ocean ridge
ACDDEEGIKNNOR dead-reckoning
ACDDEEGINNORS second reading
ACDDEEHHIITTW dice with death
ACDDEEHLLORTY cold-heartedly
ACDDEEHOOPPRU drophead coupé
ACDDEEIIKLMNN nickel-and-dime
ACDDEEIILLMRT middle article
ACDDEEIKORRSW Sir Edward Coke
ACDDEEILNORRU Claude Dornier
ACDDEEIMNOOTY adenoidectomy
ACDDEFFHINNOR Ferdinand Foch
ACDDEFGILNNOR forced landing
ACDDEFHINNNOR Ferdinand Cohn
ACDDEGIILNNPP candle-dipping
ACDDEGILLNOOR dendrological
ACDDEGILNOORU dead-colouring
ACDDEGINORSUU undiscouraged
ACDDEHIIPRRST dispatch rider
ACDDEHILMOSUY dichlamydeous
ACDDEHIMNOOPS dodecaphonism
ACDDEHINOOPST dodecaphonist
ACDDEHINOORSU deoch-an-doruis
ACDDEIIMNOORS androdioecism
ACDDEIINOSSTU undissociated
ACDDEILNNOOOR Enrico Dandolo
ACDDEIMMNNOPU Campion Edmund
ACDDEINNOORTU uncoordinated
unco-ordinated
ACDDEINORSTTU trade discount
ACDDEJLOORSUU Judas-coloured
ACDDELMMMNOOU command module

ACDDEOPRRSTUW custard powder
ACDDHIMNORSYY hydrodynamics
ACDDIIKNQRTUY quick and dirty
ACDDILLMNOSSU Diamond Sculls
ACDDIOPRRSTUY dairy products
ACDEEEEFFIOSS coffee disease
ACDEEEEILNRRV redeliverance
ACDEEEEILRUVV value received
ACDEEEELORSSU eau des creoles
ACDEEEENRRSST René Descartes
ACDEEEFFOPPRR force de frappe
ACDEEEFGHLQRU chequered flag
ACDEEEFHIKRST sick-feathered
ACDEEEFHILPRR field preacher
ACDEEEFHILRSV cheval-de-frise
ACDEEEFIJKNRR Frederick Jane
ACDEEEFINORTV confederative
ACDEEEGGLORSU Georges Claude
ACDEEEGHINPRS speech reading
ACDEEEGIKLMMR mackerel midge
ACDEEEGIKLMRU mackerel guide
ACDEEEGIKLNNP packing-needle
ACDEEEGILLNRS le Grand Siècle
ACDEEEGIORSTV storage device
ACDEEEGKNPRSS deck passenger
ACDEEEGNNRSUV unscavengered
ACDEEEHHKNNRT harden the neck
ACDEEEHIINNTV Death in Venice
ACDEEEHILRRST Richard Steele
ACDEEEHINRRUV underachiever
ACDEEEHLNOOPS hold one's peace
ACDEEEHMNPRST speed merchant
ACDEEEHOPRTTU coup de théâtre
ACDEEEHORRSTU terraced house
ACDEEEIIRSTTV carte-de-visite
ACDEEEIMNRSTV misadvertence
ACDEEEIMRRSSV armed services
ACDEEEIOSSTTV video cassette
ACDEEEIPQRRSU square-pierced
ACDEEEKNORRRY ready reckoner
ACDEEEKQRRRTU quarterdecker
ACDEEELLOPRTT electroplated
ACDEEELMOPPRR emerald-copper
ACDEEELMORTTT metal detector
ACDEEELNOORST tolerance dose
ACDEEELNOPRST preadolescent
ACDEEELNPRRSU supercalender
ACDEEELOPRSST Apostles' Creed
ACDEEENNOPPRR preponderance
ACDEEENNRSSTU uncreatedness
ACDEEFFIIRTUX feux d'artifice
ACDEEFFLNNRSU candle-snuffer
ACDEEFGHILRSS self-discharge
ACDEEFGIILMNT magnetic field
ACDEEFGILMNRU reducing flame
ACDEEFGIOOPRR period of grace
ACDEEFHHIKNRS handkerchiefs
ACDEEFHILOTWW field cow-wheat
ACDEEFHNORRTW thenceforward
ACDEEFIIILNRT delirifacient
ACDEEFIIINORT re-edification
ACDEEFILNNOST self-contained
ACDEEFILNOSTU self-education
ACDEEFINNOORT confederation
ACDEEFIORSSSU casus foederis
ACDEEFLLMOORU flame-coloured
ACDEEFNORRRTW centre-forward
ACDEEGGINNRTU reducing agent
ACDEEGGINRRST greetings card
ACDEEGHIKNNRT kitchen garden
ACDEEGHIKNOTW giant hockweed
ACDEEGHILLMRT Edgar Mitchell
ACDEEGHILLNRT candle-lighter
ACDEEGHIMNNNU machinegunned
ACDEEGHINOSTT go the distance
ACDEEGHINRSTY charge density
ACDEEGHNORRUY greyhound race
ACDEEGHNORSWX exchange words
ACDEEGHNRRSTU draught-screen
ACDEEGIILRRTT lattice-girder
ACDEEGIILRRTV live cartridge
ACDEEGIIPRRRT Eric Partridge
ACDEEGILLLNPW dwelling-place
ACDEEGILLNORW Darwin College
ACDEEGILMNRSU muscle-reading
ACDEEGILNPRTY deprecatingly
ACDEEGINOPRRT tape recording
tape-recording
ACDEEGORRRSST cross-gartered
ACDEEHHIINRSS Chinese radish
ACDEEHHKLNNTU The Naked Lunch
ACDEEHIIKMNNY kidney machine
ACDEEHIILLNTX hexactinellid
ACDEEHIILLOTT diotheletical✧
ACDEEHIILMNNR André Michelin
ACDEEHIKLOTTT tickle to death
ACDEEHILLOTTY dyotheletical✧
ACDEEHILMNOOT machine-tooled
ACDEEHILORRTT tetrachloride
ACDEEHILORTTV Old Vic Theatre
ACDEEHIMOPRRT Arc de Triomphe
ACDEEHINORSSS Crohn's disease
ACDEEHINPRSSS cash dispenser
ACDEEHIOPRRRS Seraphic Order
ACDEEHKNPQRSU quenched spark
ACDEEHLLOPRRU choral prelude
ACDEEHLNNOORR hole-and-corner
ACDEEHLNNOORS scalenohedron
ACDEEHLNOOORS Roedean School
ACDEEHOORSSTV overhead costs
ACDEEIIILMNRS decriminalise
ACDEEIIILMNRZ decriminalize
ACDEEIIJPRTUV prejudicative
ACDEEIILLNNNP inclined plane
ACDEEIILLRTTV verticillated
ACDEEIILMORTU eudiometrical
ACDEEIILNNSST identicalness
ACDEEIILNOSSU selenious acid
ACDEEIILNPSSU unspecialised
ACDEEIILNPSUZ unspecialized
ACDEEIILPRTUV reduplicative
ACDEEIILPRTVY predicatively

ACDEEIILRTTUV	diverticulate
ACDEEIIMMNNOW	medicine woman
ACDEEIIMNNRTY	indeterminacy
ACDEEIIMNOPRT	premedication
ACDEEIIMNOSTU	eudaemonistic
ACDEEIINNORST	inconsiderate
ACDEEIINNORTV	revendication
ACDEEIINNOSST	Ascensiontide
ACDEEIINOPRTT	decrepitation
ACDEEIINORSTV	considerative
ACDEEIINRSSTT	Testicardines
ACDEEIIORRSTV	radii vectores
ACDEEIKMNPRUY	numeric keypad
ACDEEIKNQRSUW	quick-answered
ACDEEILLMORRT	all-time record
ACDEEILLNNSTY	clandestinely
ACDEEILMMSSTY	decimal system
ACDEEILNNPTUV	Vincent de Paul
ACDEEILNOORST	reconsolidate
ACDEEILNORSTY	considerately
ACDEEILNPPRRU	perpendicular
ACDEEILNRSSSU	Anders Celsius
ACDEEILOPRRTY	deprecatorily
ACDEEIMNNRTUY	maiden century
ACDEEIMNORSTU	documentarise
ACDEEIMNORTUZ	documentarize
ACDEEIMNOSTTU	undomesticate
ACDEEIMOPRRSS	compressed air
ACDEEINNORSSS	secondariness
ACDEEINOPPRTU	predicate upon
ACDEEINPRSUVY	dispurveyance
ACDEEIOPPRSTU	propaedeutics
ACDEELLOORSTU	slate-coloured
ACDEELLPRRTUU	cultured pearl
ACDEELNNORSTW	Newton's cradle
ACDEELNRSSTTU	Dunster Castle
ACDEEMMNRSTUU	secundum artem
ACDEEMNNOPSTU	uncompensated
ACDEENNOPPRRY	preponderancy
ACDEENORRSTTU	unstercorated
ACDEFGHINNOSW	winds of change
ACDEFGIILMNTU	magnetic fluid
ACDEFGILLRSUY	disgracefully
ACDEFHILLLOTW	Call of the Wild
ACDEFHMNRRSTU	French mustard
ACDEFIIILNOST	fictionalised
ACDEFIIILNOTZ	fictionalized
ACDEFIIIMNTUV	mundificative
ACDEFIILNNOSS	non-classified
ACDEFIIMNORTX	mixed fraction
ACDEFILMORRTV	formal verdict
ACDEFIORRSTVY	first-day cover
ACDEFMOPRRTUU	computer fraud
ACDEGGHIINPRS	graphic design
ACDEGGHILORSW	glow discharge
ACDEGGHIOORTW	with good grace
ACDEGGIILNORR	ginger cordial
ACDEGGINORRSS	grade crossing
ACDEGHHHIMOST	high-stomached
ACDEGHHOOPRTU	thorough-paced
ACDEGHIIMNNRS	merchandising
ACDEGHIIMNNRZ	merchandizing
ACDEGHIMNORTY	hydromagnetic
ACDEGHIORRRRS	Richard Rogers
ACDEGHLNOORSU	Charles Gounod
ACDEGIIIMNNOR	indigo carmine
ACDEGIIKNNRTX	index-tracking
ACDEGIILLLOOY	ideologically
ACDEGIILLMRUY	demiurgically
ACDEGIILNNPRW	drawing-pencil
ACDEGIKMNPRSU	muckspreading
ACDEGILLMNOOO	demonological
ACDEGILLNOOOT	deontological
ACDEGILNOPPTY	peptidoglycan
ACDEGIMMNNORW	wing commander
ACDEGINPSTUUU	C Auguste Dupin
ACDEGIRRSTUUY	security guard
ACDEGLNOPRSSW	Cowper's glands
ACDEGMNOORRST	costardmonger
ACDEHHIKOORRR	Richard Hooker
ACDEHHILNPRSS	ship's chandler
ACDEHHILNPRSY	ship chandlery
ACDEHHLOPRSUY	hydrocephalus
ACDEHIILLOTTY	dyothelitical✧
ACDEHIILLRRTT	Little Richard
ACDEHIILMOSTT	Methodistical
ACDEHIILNOPRR	perichondrial
ACDEHIIMRSSTT	Christmas-tide
ACDEHIIOPSSTT	sophisticated
ACDEHIJKMNORR	Major Dick Hern
ACDEHIKLNQRUU	harlequin duck
ACDEHIKLNRRSS	Schindler's Ark
ACDEHIKMOOOSU	cook-housemaid
ACDEHILLNOOSV	shield volcano
ACDEHILMORRTY	hydrometrical
ACDEHILNOORST	school-trained
ACDEHIMMNOPRS	commandership
ACDEHIMMNORTY	thermodynamic
ACDEHIMNPPSTU	Dutchman's pipe
ACDEHIMOOPTTT	impacted tooth
ACDEHIMOPRTTY	dermatophytic
ACDEHIOOPPPRW	woodchip paper
ACDEHLLMNOOST	old-clothesman
ACDEHLMOOPRSY	chlamydospore
ACDEHMRSTTTUU	cut the mustard
ACDEHNOORSSSW	show one's cards
ACDEHOOOPRRTT	protochordate
ACDEIIILOPRST	periodicalist
ACDEIIINNORTV	revindication
ACDEIIINOQSTU	deacquisition
ACDEIIJLLPRUY	prejudicially
ACDEIIJNOPRTU	prejudication
ACDEIIKLNPRTV	Patrick Devlin
ACDEIIKMNPRTY	prick-me-dainty
ACDEIIKNNORWW	Dionne Warwick
ACDEIILNNOTTU	denticulation
ACDEIILNNSTTY	clandestinity
ACDEIILNOOSTV	consolidative
ACDEIILNOPRTU	reduplication
ACDEIILNOTTWW	lattice window
ACDEIILOSSSTU	social studies
ACDEIILRSTTVY	distractively

Words marked ✧ can also be spelled with one or more capital letters

ACDEIIMNNOORT	enantiodromic
ACDEIIMNOOSTT	domestication
ACDEIINNOORST	consideration
ACDEIINOQRSTU	quadrisection
ACDEIINORRSTY	discretionary
ACDEIINRRSTTY	Yaren District
ACDEIINRSTTUV	adventuristic
ACDEIIOPSSTTU	disceptatious
ACDEIKKNOSSWY	knock sideways
ACDEIKNNNORTT	Dark Continent
ACDEILLMMOUWY	cadmium yellow
ACDEILLORSTUU	tellurous acid
ACDEILLPPSTYY	dyspeptically
ACDEILMNOPSTY	listed company
ACDEILMNORTUY	documentarily
ACDEILMNOSTTU	documentalist
ACDEILNNORSTY	constrainedly
ACDEILNOORRSW	Sir Noël Coward
ACDEILNOOSTTW	Clint Eastwood
ACDEILNORSSTW	Windsor Castle
ACDEILNORSTTU	destructional
ACDEILOOORRRV	Colorado River
ACDEILOOPRRTU	parti-coloured
ACDEILOPRSSTY	perissodactyl
ACDEIMMMNORYY	dynamic memory
ACDEIMNNNOOPU	uncompanioned
ACDEIMNNOOTTU	documentation
ACDEIMNORSTTU	documentarist
ACDEIMNORTUUX	index auctorum
ACDEIMOPRRSTU	radio spectrum
ACDEINNNORSTU	unconstrained
ACDEINSSSTTUV	St Vitus's dance
ACDEIOOPRRRTT	tricorporated
ACDEIOPRRSTTW	post-war credit
ACDEKLLNOORRR	rock and roller
ACDEKLLNOPSYY	Sydney Pollack
ACDEKLMNORRUZ	Lord Zuckerman
ACDELNOOOSTUY	acotyledonous
ACDELOOPRRTUY	party-coloured
ACDELOORRRSSY	Royal Red Cross
ACDELOORRSTUW	straw-coloured
ACDEMMNNOSTUU	unconsummated
ACDEMNOOPQTUY	quoted company
ACDFGIIIINNOT	dignification
ACDFGMNOOORST	goodman's croft
ACDFIIILMNOTU	amniotic fluid
ACDFIIIMNNOTU	mundification
ACDFILNNOSTUY	dysfunctional
ACDFOORSSTTUU	Doctor Faustus
ACDGHHIIRRRTW	Richard Wright
ACDGHIIKLNNST	stickhandling
ACDGHIIKLNRUY	hydraulicking
ACDGHIILMNNOU	chain moulding
ACDGHINOOOPRT	gonadotrophic
ACDGHIOOORTVZ	Doctor Zhivago
ACDGIILMNOPSU	social dumping
ACDGIILNRSTTY	distractingly
ACDGIIMNNORRS	morris dancing
ACDGIINNRSTTU	undistracting
ACDGIINOOSSTY	cytodiagnosis
ACDGILLNOOOOT	odontological
ACDGILLOORTTY	troglodytical
ACDGILMOSTYYZ	zygodactylism
ACDGIMNOPRSUY	group dynamics
ACDGINNNNOOPR	pro-and-conning
ACDGLOOSTUYYZ	zygodactylous
ACDHHIINOOORS	Soichiro Honda
ACDHHIINOPSTY	ichthyopsidan
ACDHHILNOOORS	Rhodian school
ACDHHLOPRRTUW	Ralph Cudworth
ACDHIIINORRST	Christian Dior
ACDHIIKKNPSUY	kick up a shindy
ACDHIILMNOORT	mitochondrial
ACDHIIMNNORRX	Richard M Nixon
ACDHIINOPSSTU	custodianship
ACDHIJOOPRSTU	coadjutorship
ACDHILOORSSUU	Dolichosaurus
ACDHIMNNOOOOP	companionhood
ACDHINOOPQRSU	quadrophonics
ACDHKLORRSTUY	hard-luck story
ACDIIIILMNOOT	domiciliation
ACDIIIKLNNOOP	clinopinakoid
ACDIIILLORSTY	dioristically
ACDIIILNNOPTU	induplication
ACDIIILNORSSV	Sir Colin Davis
ACDIIILNORTVY	vindicatorily
ACDIIIMNORRST	discriminator
	doctrinairism
ACDIIIOOOPRST	radioisotopic
ACDIILLMOOSTY	sodomitically
ACDIILLNNOOTY	conditionally
ACDIILLNOOPST	Platonic solid
ACDIILLQRSTUY	liquid crystal
ACDIILNNNOOTU	unconditional
ACDIILNNNOSUY	syndical union
ACDIILNNOOOST	consolidation
ACDIILNOOORST	discoloration
ACDIILNRSTTUY	translucidity
ACDIILPQRTUUY	quadruplicity
ACDIINNOORRTT	indoctrinator
ACDIINNORTUWW	window curtain
ACDIINOORRRRT	corridor-train
ACDIINPRSSSTY	St Crispin's Day
ACDILLMOPSTYY	polydactylism
ACDIMNOOOPRTU	compound ratio
ACDIMNOOPSSWW	compass window
ACDINOOQRSSTU	conquistadors
ACDLLOOPSTUYY	polydactylous
ACDLMNOOOSTUY	condylomatous
	monodactylous
ACEEEEENRRSVV	save reverence
ACEEEEFFFLNOS	efface oneself
ACEEEEFFGLNRT	general effect
ACEEEEFFIRTTV	effective rate
ACEEEEFHMPRTT	fête champêtre
ACEEEEFKMNRRR	reference-mark
ACEEEEFLOPRTT	letter of peace
ACEEEEGIMNRRU	Maurice Greene
ACEEEEHILNSSV	Chinese leaves
ACEEEEHLPRSST	steeplechaser
ACEEEELLMNTTT	Clement Attlee
ACEEEELMNRRTT	tracer element

ACEEEELNPSSSS peacelessness
ACEEEENNPPPRY cayenne pepper
ACEEEEPPRRSTW carpet-sweeper
ACEEEFFGINOPR peace offering
ACEEEFFHJRRRY Jeffrey Archer
ACEEEFFLNSSTU effectualness
ACEEEFGHLNNOS change oneself
ACEEEFGHNNOUV change of venue
ACEEEFGHPRRRS prefer charges
ACEEEFGIJKNRT reefing-jacket
ACEEEFHHITTVY have itchy feet
ACEEEFHIKLRST sickle feather
ACEEEFHILLRRV lever arch file
ACEEEFIILLMST telefacsimile
ACEEEFIKLOTTV ticket of leave
ACEEEFILNORRT coreferential
ACEEEFINOPRTT perfectionate
ACEEEFINRRSTU user interface
ACEEEFKMPRRTT perfect market
ACEEEFLMPRSTT perfect metals
ACEEEFLOPRRTT polecat-ferret
ACEEEFLRSSSUV surface-vessel
ACEEEFMORRRTT refractometer
ACEEEFPQRRSTU perfect square
ACEEEGGGLSSUX excess luggage
ACEEEGGHILMOR George Michael
ACEEEGHIKNPST the king's peace
ACEEEGHIMORTT heterogametic
ACEEEGIKLMNOU leukaemogenic
ACEEEGILLNRTY energetically
ACEEEGILNRTTY lattice energy
ACEEEGIMMNORT geometric mean
ACEEEGINRTTUV give utterance
ACEEEGLMNORTT electromagnet
ACEEEGLMNORTY laryngectomee
ACEEEGLNNRRUY nuclear energy
ACEEEGLNORRTU Auger electron
ACEEEGLNRSSSS gracelessness
ACEEEGMNNORTU encouragement
ACEEEGNPRSSXY express agency
ACEEEGOPSSSTX excess postage
ACEEEHHILRSTV health service
ACEEEHHLMORRT chrome leather
ACEEEHHLOPRTT The Other Place
ACEEEHHNOPRST Hester Chapone
ACEEEHHOORTTT toothache tree
ACEEEHHOPRRST the Reproaches
ACEEEHHPPRSTY speech therapy
ACEEEHIKKMTTY take the mickey
ACEEEHIKLLMNO chameleon-like
ACEEEHIKLNRRT Earl Kitchener
ACEEEHIKLRSTT tickle a th' sere
ACEEEHILMNRTU hermeneutical
ACEEEHINNORST on the increase
ACEEEHINOSSST coenaesthesis
ACEEEHINRSTVY seven-year itch
ACEEEHKKLNNRT Kenneth Clarke
ACEEEHKLMORRS horse mackerel
ACEEEHLLNNOPT telencephalon
ACEEEHLMNNOPS mesencephalon
ACEEEHLMPSSSY Champs Elysées
ACEEEHLMRTTUY Lyceum Theatre
ACEEEHLNORTTW contrate-wheel
ACEEEHMORRSTY Home Secretary
ACEEEHMORSTVY Thomas Creevey
ACEEEHRRSSTTU treasure-chest
ACEEEIINNRSTV intensive care
ACEEEIINSSSTV case-sensitive
ACEEEIKNOPTTX take exception
ACEEEILLMPRST capellmeister
ACEEEILLNPRST Leicester plan
ACEEEILLPRSTV Peveril Castle
ACEEEILMNNRTT interlacement
ACEEEILNNNRTT tercentennial
ACEEEILOPPRRR people carrier
ACEEEILPSSTTX sextile aspect
ACEEEILRRRRTT letter-carrier
ACEEEIMNNORSS sans cérémonie
ACEEEIMNNOSST amniocenteses
ACEEEIMNNRRSS mercenariness
ACEEEIMNORRSY Oscar Niemeyer
ACEEEIMNORSVY yeoman service
ACEEEINNOPRVX Aix-en-Provence
ACEEEINNRSSSS necessariness
ACEEEINOSSTVV evocativeness
ACEEEIOPRTTVX expectorative
ACEEEIOQSSTUU equisetaceous
ACEEEKPPRSSTX express packet
ACEEELLNOOPSS lose one's place
ACEEELLNORTTV electrovalent
ACEEELLOORTTV electoral vote
ACEEELLOPRRTT electroplater
ACEEELLRRSTTT scarlet letter
ACEEELNOORRTZ zero tolerance
ACEEELNSSSSSU causelessness
ACEEELOPRSTXY X-ray telescope
ACEEELPPRRSSX express parcel
ACEEENNORRRTT contraterrene
ACEEEPRRSTTYY secretary type
ACEEFFFIORSTY safety officer
ACEEFFHINNPRS affenpinscher
ACEEFFHINOOTT on the face of it
ACEEFFIKNPRST packet sniffer
ACEEFFILLNTUY ineffectually
ACEEFFINOORTU auctioneer off
ACEEFFKKOORTT take-off rocket
ACEEFFKLLNORS Florence flask
ACEEFGGINRSTU gas centrifuge
ACEEFGHILMTTU The Magic Flute
ACEEFGHILNNRU lingue franche
ACEEFGHLNNSSU changefulness
ACEEFGHLOPRRT reflectograph
ACEEFGIIMNRRT ferrimagnetic
ACEEFGIINNOPR pigeon-fancier
ACEEFGIJOSTTU gate of justice
ACEEFGIMNNRST fencing-master
ACEEFGIMNORRT ferromagnetic
ACEEFGINNORRY ferricyanogen
ACEEFGJLNOSTU self-conjugate
ACEEFGLLMOORS College of Arms
ACEEFGNNOORRY ferrocyanogen
ACEEFHHIRSTTT feather stitch

ACEEFHIIKMMRS	mischief-maker
ACEEFHIINNNTT	tenant-in-chief
ACEEFHIKLMNOT	Michael of Kent
ACEEFHIKLNOOT	look in the face
ACEEFHIMNNRST	franchisement
ACEEFHJOPRSSU	Joseph Surface
ACEEFHLNNRRSU	channel-surfer
ACEEFHLNSSSTU	scathefulness
ACEEFHMNOSTUV	vouchsafement
ACEEFIIIMNPSS	infima species
ACEEFIILNNRSU	life insurance
ACEEFIINNQTUY	equity finance
ACEEFIINNRRSU	fire insurance
ACEEFILLNOPRW	pelican-flower
ACEEFILNNRSSU	self-insurance
ACEEFILNOPRSW	Prince of Wales
ACEEFIMNNOOPR	free companion
ACEEFINORRSTU	nectariferous
ACEEFINORRSUX	excursion fare
ACEEFINOSSSTU	facetiousness
ACEEFKMORRSSY	for mercy's sake
ACEEFKORRRSUW	surface worker
ACEEFLLOORSSS	collar of esses
ACEEFLOOPSSTV	Aspects of Love
ACEEFMNORSTUU	frumentaceous
ACEEFMORRRTTY	refractometry
ACEEFNNOOPSTU	put one's face on
ACEEFOOPRSSVY	a copy of verses
ACEEGGGINNNOR	George Canning
ACEEGGHIILMPS	Gilgamesh Epic
ACEEGGHIKMORW	George Wickham
ACEEGGHIMNRTY	The Crying Game
ACEEGGIJKNORS	Reggie Jackson
ACEEGGILNOTTT	telecottaging
ACEEGGINPRRRY	Percy Grainger
ACEEGHHIRTTWW	weight-watcher
ACEEGHHMNRRRU	hunger-marcher
ACEEGHHOOPRRR	choreographer
ACEEGHHOPRTTT	patch together
ACEEGHIILLNOS	collieshangie
ACEEGHIILNRRV	relieving arch
ACEEGHIIMNNSW	sewing machine
ACEEGHIINORRT	tragic heroine
ACEEGHILLOPSU	colleagueship
ACEEGHILMNOOT	homogenetical
ACEEGHILMPRYY	hyperglycemia
ACEEGHILNOPRS	selenographic
ACEEGHILNORSU	clearing house
ACEEGHILOPRRX	lexicographer
ACEEGHILOPSTU	Galeopithecus
ACEEGHIMNNNRU	machine-gunner
ACEEGHIMORRUZ	Maurice Herzog
ACEEGHINNOTTT	get in on the act
ACEEGHINNPRTT	tent-preaching
ACEEGHINNRSSS	searchingness
ACEEGHINORSTV	overnight case
ACEEGHINOTTTT	get into the act
ACEEGHIOPRRST	stereographic
ACEEGHLOPRRTY	electrography
ACEEGHMNRRSTU	surchargement
ACEEGHNNRSTUV	scavenger hunt

ACEEGIIKNOPSV	speaking-voice
ACEEGIILMMNRS	scrimmage line
ACEEGIILNOPRT	repeating coil
ACEEGIILNPRST	genetic spiral
ACEEGIILSTTUV	gesticulative
ACEEGIIMNNOST	miscegenation
ACEEGIIMNOPTZ	piezomagnetic
ACEEGIINNNRST	intransigence
ACEEGIINOPRRR	carrier pigeon
ACEEGIKNNRRVW	nerve-wracking
ACEEGILLLNOOS	selenological
ACEEGILLLOOPS	speleological
ACEEGILLMORTY	geometrically
ACEEGILLNNOOT	non-collegiate
ACEEGILMMNORR	miracle-monger
ACEEGILMNNOQU	magniloquence
ACEEGILMNOPST	magnetic poles
ACEEGILMNPSSS	specimen glass
ACEEGILNNPRRS	spring-cleaner
ACEEGILNNRRUV	learning curve
ACEEGILNNRSUX	nuclear sexing
ACEEGILNSSTTU	testing clause
ACEEGIMNOPRST	spermatogenic
ACEEGINOPPPRS	popping crease
	popping-crease
ACEEGINORRSTT	gastroenteric
ACEEGINORRSUW	wearing course
ACEEGINORSTTV	contragestive
ACEEGKLLMOOPR	Graeme Pollock
ACEEGLLNNORSU	consul general
ACEEGMOORSSTY	agroecosystem
ACEEGMRRSTTUU	megastructure
ACEEGNORRSSTV	governess cart
ACEEHHHOORRSS	horseshoe arch
ACEEHHIILLPRS	helispherical
ACEEHHIILMPRS	hemispherical
ACEEHHILLORTT	heterothallic
ACEEHHILNPSSS	seneschalship
ACEEHHIRVWWYY	every which way
ACEEHHLNNOPPR	channel-hopper
ACEEHHNRSTTTU	earth-chestnut
ACEEHHORTTTWW	The Watchtower
ACEEHIIJMRSST	James Christie
ACEEHIIKKLNOT	khaki election
ACEEHIIKNNNPT	pain in the neck
ACEEHIILLLNST	Hellenistical
ACEEHIILLMORT	heliometrical
ACEEHIILLPTTY	epithetically
ACEEHIILNOPRT	epitrachelion
ACEEHIILNPSST	Sistine Chapel
ACEEHIINNRSTV	even-Christian
ACEEHIJKPPRRT	Jack the Ripper
ACEEHIKNPSTUY	Kenyapithecus
ACEEHIKNRRSTT	heart-stricken
ACEEHIKNRSSST	heartsickness
ACEEHILLLMOPW	Michael Powell
ACEEHILLNPRTY	phrenetically
ACEEHILLORTTY	theoretically
ACEEHILMMOPSS	mesocephalism
ACEEHILMPRRTY	hypermetrical
ACEEHILNORRTW	chlorine water

ACEEHILNPPRWY Hawley Crippen
ACEEHILNPRSSS sphericalness
ACEEHILOPRRST terpsichoreal
ACEEHILOPRSTT heteroplastic
ACEEHILORRSUV River Achelous
ACEEHIMNOSTUY humane society
ACEEHIMRRSSTT Christmas tree
ACEEHINOPRRST terpsichorean
ACEEHINORSSTT thoracentesis
ACEEHINPPRRST ship carpenter
ACEEHIPRRSSTY secretaryship
ACEEHIPRSSTTY cryptesthesia
ACEEHKLOORRTW work the oracle
ACEEHLLMOOORT alcoholometer
ACEEHLLOPPSTU leptocephalus
ACEEHLMMNOOTW the common weal
ACEEHLMNOOPTY encephalotomy
ACEEHLMNORRTU thermonuclear
ACEEHLMNSSSST matchlessness
ACEEHLMOOPSSU mesocephalous
ACEEHLORRSTUY treacherously
ACEEHMMNORTTV movement chart
ACEEHMNOPPRRT rapprochement
ACEEHMNOPRSUY purchase money
ACEEHNNOORSTU Southern Ocean
ACEEHNOOPSSSW show one's paces
ACEEHNOPSSTTW watch one's step
ACEEHNPRRSSTU purse-snatcher
ACEEHNRSTTTUW water chestnut
ACEEHOOPRRSTU heterocarpous
ACEEHORSSTTUY stay the course
ACEEIIIKKLLNR Killiecrankie
ACEEIIILLNNPS penicillinase
ACEEIIIMNRRTV recriminative
ACEEIIINPSSTT antisepticise
ACEEIIINPSTTZ antisepticize
ACEEIIIPPRTTV precipitative
ACEEIIKLLNRRT Eric Linklater
ACEEIIKLRSSTT Rickettsiales
ACEEIILLLNRTY rectilineally
ACEEIILLMNRTT intermetallic
ACEEIILLMOSTY semeiotically
ACEEIILLMPSTY epistemically
ACEEIILLNRRTY rectilinearly
ACEEIILMMNORS ceremonialism
ACEEIILMNOPRS semiporcelain
ACEEIILMNORST ceremonialist
ACEEIILMNRSST Cesar Milstein
ACEEIILMPRRTV prime vertical
ACEEIILNORSTT electrisation
ACEEIILNORTTZ electrization
ACEEIILNPRTUV plantie-cruive
ACEEIILNRTTVY interactively
ACEEIILPPRTTY precipitately
ACEEIILPQSSTU sesquiplicate
ACEEIILPRTTTY rectipetality
ACEEIILSSSTTU elastic tissue
ACEEIIMMORSTV commiserative
ACEEIIMNNOSST amniocentesis
ACEEIIMNNPRSS Spencerianism
ACEEIIMNOPRTV private income
ACEEIIMNORRST mercerisation
ACEEIIMNORRTZ mercerization
ACEEIINNOPTTX inexpectation
ACEEIINNORTTW winter aconite
ACEEIINNOSSTT necessitation
ACEEIINNRSSTT intricateness
ACEEIIRSSTTUV resuscitative
ACEEIJLNOPRSU Jules Poincaré
ACEEIJLNRRTTU interjectural
ACEEIKLLSSTVW Sackville-West
ACEEIKLRRSTTW Walter Sickert
ACEEIKORSSTTU take its course
ACEEILLLNOTUV involucellate
ACEEILLLNPSTY splenetically
ACEEILLLNRRTU intercellular
ACEEILLLNSTTU intellectuals
ACEEILLMNNRTY incrementally
ACEEILLMNOSSU miscellaneous
ACEEILLMNPRSY simple larceny
ACEEILLMNTTUU multinucleate
ACEEILLNNNSSU uncleanliness
ACEEILLNOPTXY exceptionally
ACEEILLNPRTTY centripetally
ACEEILLORRTVY correlatively
ACEEILLPSTUVY speculatively
ACEEILLRRSSTY recrystallise
ACEEILLRRSTYZ recrystallize
ACEEILMNNSSSU masculineness
ACEEILMNOPTTV contemplative
ACEEILMNRRSSU mercurialness
ACEEILNNOPRTV convertiplane
ACEEILNNOPTUX unexceptional
ACEEILNNOQSTU consequential
ACEEILNNRRTUW nuclear winter
ACEEILNNRSSUY unnecessarily
ACEEILNOOPRSU porcelaineous
ACEEILNOQSSUV equivocalness
ACEEILNORSTTU interosculate
ACEEILNOSTTUX contextualise
ACEEILNOTTUXZ contextualize
ACEEILNPSTUUV unspeculative
ACEEILNRSSTUV lucrativeness
ACEEILOOPRTVY co-operatively
ACEEILOPRSSTV postal service
ACEEILOPRSTTY stereotypical
ACEEILORRTTVY retroactively
ACEEILPPPRRST carpet-slipper
ACEEIMMMOORTV commemorative
ACEEIMNNOOPTU once upon a time
ACEEIMNOORVVW microwave oven
ACEEIMNORRRST semantic error
ACEEIMNORRSSX cross-examiner
ACEEIMNPRTTUY pneumatic tyre
ACEEIMPPRRRTU turmeric paper
ACEEINNNORSST non-resistance
ACEEINNNOSTTY consentaneity
ACEEINNNQRTUY quincentenary
ACEEINNNRSSTU uncertainness
ACEEINNNSSSST incessantness
ACEEINNOORSVZ conversazione
ACEEINNORRSUV overinsurance

ACEEINNOSSSTU tenaciousness
ACEEINOOPRSTU proteinaceous
ACEEINOOPRTTX expectoration
ACEEINOOPRTUV uncooperative
unco-operative
ACEEINOORRSTV conservatoire
ACEEINRRRSSST Ernst Cassirer
ACEEIOPRRSTTV private sector
ACEEIORRSTUVY at your service
ACEEKKLMNOSUY make one's lucky
ACEEKLMNOOSSY sockeye salmon
ACEEKLNNOOPSW know one's place
ACEEKLNRSSSST tracklessness
ACEEKMMNOORTY market economy
ACEEKNNOPRSST socket spanner
ACEELLLLOORRT electoral roll
ACEELLLNORSUW enclosure wall
ACEELLMMPSTUU speculum metal
ACEELLMNRTTUY mental cruelty
ACEELLMOPRSUU supramolecule
ACEELLNOOPRSU porcellaneous
ACEELLNSSSSSS classlessness
ACEELLOORRRST rollercoaster
ACEELLOPRSSTU suspercollate
ACEELMMNOPRTY complementary
ACEELMNRSSSUU muscular sense
ACEELNNOPRRTY penalty corner
ACEELNNRRRSTU scarlet runner
ACEELNOOPRRTU counter-parole
ACEELNOOPRSTT creosote plant
ACEELNOPRRSTW Central Powers
ACEELNOPRSSTU specular stone
ACEELOQRRSSTU close quarters
ACEEMMMNOORSU common measure
ACEEMMNNOPSST encompassment
ACEENNNOORTVY novocentenary
ACEENNNOOSSTU consentaneous
ACEENOOPRRSST corporateness
Oscar Peterson
ACEENRRSSSTTU current assets
ACEFFFIMOORRS officer of arms✧
ACEFFGIILNNNS self-financing
ACEFFHIIKKNRT kitchen Kaffir
ACEFFHLSSTTUZ Schutzstaffel
ACEFGGHOPRSTY Peggy Ashcroft
ACEFGGIINRSTU figure-casting
ACEFGHHIORRST right of search
ACEFGHIIIILMN Michela Figini
ACEFGHIIKLNST fishing-tackle
ACEFGHIILMNNY flying machine
ACEFGHIINORSS coarse fishing
ACEFGHIINOSTW witch of Agnesi
ACEFGHINNOSTT Night of Ascent
ACEFGIIIINSTV significative
ACEFGIIKLNNPS scalping-knife
ACEFGIILLNTTT cattle-lifting
ACEFGIILMNNTY magnificently
ACEFGIILNNRTU lunatic fringe
ACEFGIKMNORST stocking frame
ACEFGILLNRTUY centrifugally
ACEFGIMNNORTU counting frame
ACEFGINOSSSUU fugaciousness
ACEFHHIIINPST chieftainship
ACEFHHILRSSTW flasher switch
ACEFHHLMNOOTT man of the cloth
ACEFHIJNOPRSS Francis Joseph
ACEFHINNORRRS Francis Horner
ACEFHLLLOORTW latch follower
ACEFHLLOPRRUY reproachfully
ACEFHLNOPRRUU unreproachful
ACEFHOORSSTWY Way of the Cross
ACEFIIIJLLNOT jellification
ACEFIIIJSTTUV justificative
ACEFIIILLMNOT mellification
ACEFIIILNOSTT felicitations
ACEFIIIMMNNTU immunifacient
ACEFIIIMNORTT metrification
ACEFIIINNNNOT infinite canon
ACEFIIINNORTU reunification
ACEFIIINOPRTT petrification
ACEFIIINORSTV versification
ACEFIIINOSTTT testification
ACEFIILLNOORT refocillation
ACEFIILLPRSUY superficially
ACEFIILMMNORT microfilament
ACEFIILNOPRRT frit porcelain
ACEFIILNORSTY forensicality
ACEFIINNNOORT fonctionnaire
ACEFIIORSTTTY testificatory
ACEFIJKNNORRS Nick Farr-Jones
ACEFILLLMOPRS scalpelliform
ACEFILLLOOORR Corolliflorae
ACEFILLOORRSU coralliferous
ACEFILMMNOOWW common-law wife
ACEFILNNORSUU nuclear fusion
ACEFILNNPRUUY funny peculiar
ACEFILNOORRRW carrion-flower
ACEFINNOORSSY confessionary
ACEFINNORRTTY confraternity
ACEFINOORRSTU fusion reactor
ACEFINORSSSTU fractiousness
ACEFINORSSSUU furaciousness
ACEFJKKLNOORT Norfolk jacket
ACEFLNOOORRSU fear no colours
ACEFMNOOORSST Ocean of Storms
ACEFMOOORSTUV favours to come
ACEFOPRRSTTTU Pott's fracture
ACEGGGHIINNNR change-ringing
ACEGGHHLNORTU glance through
ACEGGHIINSTTW casting-weight
ACEGGHILLLNNY challengingly
ACEGGHILLNNNU unchallenging
ACEGGHIOOOPRZ zoogeographic
ACEGGILLOOPTY Egyptological
ACEGGILNNORUY encouragingly
ACEGGILNOOSTY gynaecologist
ACEGGLLRSSSTU class struggle
ACEGHHHINTTTW The Night Watch
ACEGHHIMOPRRT thermographic
ACEGHHINRSUVY Harvey Cushing
ACEGHHNOOPRRR chronographer
ACEGHHOOPRRSY orchesography

ACEGHHOPRRSTU scrape through
ACEGHIILNNSTT ancient lights
ACEGHIILOPSTT phlogisticate
ACEGHIILORTVV Gothic Revival
ACEGHIIMMNNOW mowing machine
ACEGHIIMNNORW rowing machine
ACEGHIIMNNOTV voting machine
ACEGHIIMNNRTU Turing machine
ACEGHIIMNOORT image orthicon
ACEGHIIMNPPRW whipping cream
ACEGHIIMOPRSS seismographic
ACEGHIINOPTTY pathogenicity
ACEGHIINRTTWW water witching
ACEGHILLLOOTY ethologically
theologically
ACEGHILLNOOPR nephrological
phrenological
ACEGHILLNOOSV school-leaving
ACEGHILLNOOTU untheological
ACEGHILLOOORT heortological
ACEGHILLOOPPS psephological
ACEGHILMNOPRT chrome plating
ACEGHILMNRSSU Charles Mingus
ACEGHILMORRTY hygrometrical
ACEGHILNOORRU colour hearing
ACEGHILNORSSU soul-searching
ACEGHILOOSSTT eschatologist
ACEGHILORRRTY chlorargyrite
ACEGHILORRSTT cloister-garth
ACEGHIMNNNORT chrome tanning
ACEGHIMNNORRT North Germanic
ACEGHIMNNORTT magnetic north
ACEGHIMOOPRRT ergatomorphic
ACEGHINNNOOPT non-pathogenic
ACEGHINNOOPRT anthropogenic
ACEGHINNOOPRW whooping crane
ACEGHINNOPRRU unreproaching
ACEGHNOOPPRSY pharyngoscope
ACEGHOPPRRRTY cryptographer
ACEGHOPPRRSTY spectrography
ACEGIIILNOOPT geopolitician
ACEGIIILNOSSS Alec Issigonis
ACEGIIINORTTY iatrogenicity
ACEGIIKKLNTTW walking-ticket
ACEGIIKKNPRTT parking ticket
ACEGIIKLLNNPT nickel-plating
ACEGIILLLNOSS illogicalness
ACEGIILLMOOSS seismological
ACEGIILLNOOST neologistical
ACEGIILLOSTTY egotistically
ACEGIILMNOORT goniometrical
ACEGIILNOSTTU gesticulation
ACEGIIMNNOOTT metacognition
ACEGIINNNRSTY intransigency
ACEGIINNPRSTY praying insect
ACEGIINPRRSTT starting price
ACEGIJKKMNOST smoking jacket
ACEGIKKLLNPSU skulking-place
ACEGIKNRSSSSS grass sickness
ACEGILLLOORSY serologically
ACEGILLMNOOOT entomological
ACEGILLMNOORU numerological
ACEGILLMNOORY ergonomically
ACEGILLMNOOYZ enzymological
ACEGILLNNOOTY ontogenically
ACEGILLNOOOOS colonial goose
ACEGILLNOORSU coralligenous
ACEGILLNOOSTU glucosinolate
ACEGILLNOPTYY genotypically
ACEGILLOOPRTY geotropically
ACEGILMNOPSTY salpingectomy
ACEGILMOOSSTU cleistogamous
ACEGILNNOORSS congressional
ACEGILNNORSTU counter-signal
ACEGILNOPPPST stopping-place
ACEGILNORRSUU neurosurgical
ACEGILNPRSTTY trysting-place
ACEGILORSTTUY gesticulatory
ACEGIMMNORSTT magnetic storm
ACEGIMNNORSSU cousins-german
ACEGIMNOOPSTT magneto-optics
ACEGIMNOPRSTU pneumogastric
ACEGIMNORSSTU gastrocnemius
ACEGINNOORSTT contragestion
ACEGINOOPRSTT prognosticate
ACEGLNOOOPSUY polygonaceous
ACEGLOPPRSSST prospect-glass
ACEGMNNOORSSW Congresswoman
ACEHHIIJKNOPS Joseph Chaikin
ACEHHIILMNNTT anthelminthic
ACEHHIINOPRSZ schizophrenia
ACEHHIJKOPTTT hit the jackpot
ACEHHILPPRSYY hyperphysical
ACEHHIMNOPTTY chimney-pot hat
ACEHHINOOPTTY hypothecation
ACEHHIOPPRTTY phreatophytic
ACEHHLLLMOOTY methyl alcohol
ACEHHLMOOPPRT choropleth map
ACEHHLNNOPSUY play one's hunch
ACEHHMMNRSTUY chrysanthemum
ACEHHMOOOPRRT chromatophore
ACEHHMOOPRRTY chromotherapy
ACEHHOPPRSTYY psychotherapy
ACEHIIIKLNRST Christianlike
ACEHIIILRSTTT tritheistical
ACEHIIIMNSTTT a stitch in time
ACEHIIINNORST corinthianise
ACEHIIINNORTZ corinthianize
ACEHIIINNPRTT antinephritic
ACEHIIINRRSST Christianiser
ACEHIIINRRSTZ Christianizer
ACEHIIKLNOPST lick into shape
ACEHIILLLMOTY homiletically
ACEHIILLOOPRT heliotropical
ACEHIILLRSTUY heuristically
ACEHIILMNOPST machine-pistol
ACEHIILMNSSSW whimsicalness
ACEHIILOOPPRT apheliotropic
ACEHIILOORSTT orthosilicate
ACEHIILOPRRST prehistorical
ACEHIIMMNORRR mirror machine
ACEHIIMMRSSTT Christmas-time

ACEHIINNOPRST	container ship
ACEHIINNRRSST	Sir Ernst Chain
ACEHIINNRSSST	Christianness
ACEHIINOOPRSY	Syrophoenicia
ACEHIIPRTTVYY	hyperactivity
ACEHIJKLOORSU	Jailhouse Rock
ACEHIJKLPRSSY	physical jerks
ACEHIJLLMMORT	Major Mitchell
ACEHIKLLNORSU	unscholarlike
ACEHIKPRRSTTU	Turkish carpet
ACEHILLLMOOPR	allelomorphic
ACEHILLLOPPST	phelloplastic
ACEHILLLOPRTY	plethorically
ACEHILLMMOPRY	morphemically
ACEHILLMNOOSU	melancholious
ACEHILLNORSSS	scholarliness
ACEHILLNSTTYY	synthetically
ACEHILLOPPRTY	prophetically
ACEHILMNOORRS	rhinoscleroma
ACEHILMOPRSTT	thermoplastic
ACEHILNNOOPTT	technopolitan
ACEHILNOOPPRS	cephalosporin
ACEHILNOPPRTU	unprophetical
ACEHILOOPRSTV	private school
ACEHILOPPRSTY	petrophysical
ACEHILORRSSTT	orchestralist
ACEHILPPRSSUY	superphysical
ACEHILRSTTTWW	wristlet watch
ACEHIMNPSTTUY	unsympathetic
ACEHIMOPRSTUY	musicotherapy
ACEHIMORRSSST	Christmas rose
ACEHINOORRSTT	orchestration
ACEHINOORSTTT	at short notice
ACEHINOPPRRST	copartnership
ACEHINOPRSTTT	stretch a point
ACEHINOPSSTTU	pentastichous
ACEHINORRSTUW	shower curtain
ACEHIOPPRSSTT	spectatorship
ACEHIOPRRSSSY	hypersarcosis
ACEHIOPRRSSTT	stratospheric
ACEHIORSSTTTU	tetrastichous
ACEHLLMOOORTY	alcoholometry
ACEHLMNOOORSU	melanochroous
ACEHLNNPPRSTU	planter's punch
ACEHLNOORTTTW	Charlottetown
ACEHLNOOSTTTY	The Last Tycoon
ACEHLNORSTUWY	Courtney Walsh
ACEHLOOOPRRSU	rhopalocerous
ACEHLOOPRRTUY	colour therapy
ACEHMMOPSTTYY	sympathectomy
ACEHNNOORRTTY	on the contrary
ACEHNOORRTTTY	to the contrary
ACEHNOORSTTTU	cut one's throat
ACEIIIILMPRST	imperialistic
ACEIIIILLMPTVY	implicatively
ACEIIILLNRSSW	Sinclair Lewis
ACEIIILMPSSST	pessimistical
ACEIIILNOPRSV	provincialise
ACEIIILNOPRVZ	provincialize
ACEIIILNORSTV	Italic version
ACEIIILNOSTVV	vivisectional
ACEIIILQSTUVY	acquisitively
ACEIIIMNNORRT	recrimination
ACEIIIMNPSSTT	antisepticism
ACEIIINOORSTT	eroticisation
ACEIIINOORTTZ	eroticization
ACEIIINOPPRTT	precipitation
ACEIIINORSTTT	recitationist
ACEIIINRTTTVY	interactivity
ACEIILLLNOORT	citronella oil
ACEIILLLNOSVY	silicon valley
ACEIILLLNRUVY	curvilineally
ACEIILLMNOSTV	Volcán El Misti
ACEIILLMOPRWW	William Cowper
ACEIILLMORSTY	isometrically
ACEIILLNNOORT	intercolonial
ACEIILLNOQTUY	equinoctially
ACEIILLNORRTY	acrylonitrile
ACEIILLNRSTXY	extrinsically
ACEIILMNOPRRW	crown imperial
ACEIILMNOPSST	Neo-Plasticism
	neoplasticism
ACEIILMNORTUV	vermiculation
ACEIILMNOSSSU	maliciousness
ACEIILMNPRRSU	supercriminal
ACEIILNNOORTT	interlocation
ACEIILNNOPSST	non-specialist
ACEIILNNPPRSS	principalness
ACEIILNOOPSTT	police station
ACEIILNOPRRTT	intertropical
ACEIILNOPRSST	personalistic
ACEIILNPPRTTY	precipitantly
ACEIILNPQTTUU	quintuplicate
ACEIILORRTTVY	correlativity
ACEIIMMNOORST	commiseration
ACEIIMNNOOOST	economisation
ACEIIMNNOOOTZ	economization
ACEIIMNORRRTY	recriminatory
ACEIIMNPPRRTT	impact printer
ACEIIMOORSTTU	autoeroticism
ACEIIMOPSSSTU	spacious times
ACEIINNOOPRST	preconisation
ACEIINNOOPRTT	enantiotropic
ACEIINNOOPRTZ	preconization
ACEIINNOORSVZ	conversazioni
ACEIINOOPRRTV	incorporative
ACEIINOORRSTV	anticorrosive
ACEIINOORSSTT	sectorisation
ACEIINOORSTTV	vectorisation
ACEIINOORSTTZ	sectorization
ACEIINOORTTVZ	vectorization
ACEIINOPRRSTW	Erwin Piscator
ACEIINORSSSUV	vicariousness
ACEIINORSSTTU	resuscitation
ACEIINOSSSUVV	vivaciousness
ACEIINPRRSTTV	transcriptive
ACEIIORRTTTVY	retroactivity
ACEIJMNOOPPRT	map projection
ACEIKLMNOPSSS	smack one's lips
ACEIKMMMNOPSU	Communism Peak
ACEIKMMNNOOTU	take communion
ACEILLLLMRTUU	multicellular

ACEILLLLPSTYY syllepticallyACEILLLMOTTUU multiloculate
ACEILLLOPPRTY proleptically
ACEILLMMNOTYY metonymically
ACEILLMMRSTYY symmetrically
ACEILLMNOPRSU ceruloplasmin
ACEILLMOSSWZZ Czeslaw Milosz
ACEILLNNNOSSY nonsensically
ACEILLNNOOSTT constellation
ACEILLNOOPRRY incorporeally
ACEILLNOQUUVY unequivocally
ACEILLNORSTTY intercostally
ACEILLOPRSTUY plural society
ACEILLORSTTVY crystal violet
ACEILMMNNORTU intercommunal
ACEILMMNOPRTY complimentary
ACEILMMNRSTUY unsymmetrical
ACEILMMOTTUVY commutatively
ACEILMNNOOPSS companionless
ACEILMNNOOPTT contemplation
ACEILMNNOOPTU Montepulciano
ACEILMNNORRTU intercolumnar
ACEILMNOOPRSS compressional
ACEILMNOPRVYY livery company
ACEILMNOPSTTT contemplatist
ACEILMNOPTTUY pneumatolytic
ACEILMOOORTXZ co-trimoxazole
ACEILNNOOPRSU nuclear poison
ACEILNNOORSTY clay-ironstone
ACEILNNOOSSTU Nicolaus Steno
ACEILNNOPRSTX lex non scripta
ACEILNNORSTTU interosculant
ACEILNOORRSTV controversial
ACEILNOPRRSSY princess royal
ACEILOOPRRSTU prosecutorial
ACEILOOPRTVVY provocatively
ACEILOORRSTTW watercolorist
ACEILOPPRRSTU tropical sprue
ACEILRRSUUVVV survival curve
ACEIMMMNOOORT commemoration
ACEIMNNNNOOST cinnamon stone
ACEIMNNNOORTU connumeration
ACEIMNNORRTTU macronutrient
ACEIMNOOOPTT onomatopoetic
ACEIMNORSSSTU customariness
ACEIMOOPRRRSS air-compressor
ACEINNNOORSTT consternation
ACEINNNOORTTV contravention
ACEINNNOORTVY conventionary
ACEINNOOORTTT contortionate
ACEINNOOPRRTT container port
ACEINNOOPRSTT cornet-à-piston
ACEINNOORSTTT cotton stainer
ACEINNOORSTTW Coniston Water
ACEINNOPRRSTY RSA encryption
ACEINOOPRRSSY processionary
ACEINOOPRRSTW water scorpion
ACEINOOPRTUVV unprovocative
ACEINOORSSSTU atrociousness
ACEINOORSSSUV voraciousness
ACEINOPRRSSST conspiratress
ACEINOPRRSTTU perscrutation
ACEIOORRRSSTU stercorarious
ACEIOPRSSTUUU supercautious
ACEIORRRSSTTU stratocruiser
ACEKLMNNOORRY Norman Lockyer
ACELLLMMMOORY Malcolm Morley
ACELLMMNOOORU monomolecular
ACELLMNOORSTY Stan Collymore
ACELLNNRSTTUY translucently
ACELLNOORSTTY constellatory
ACELMNOORSSSU clamorousness
ACELMNOPRRSUU supercolumnar
ACELMNORRSUUU neuromuscular
ACELMNSSTTUUU sustentaculum
ACELNOORRSTUU coronal suture
ACELNOORSSSUU oraculousness
ACELOOPPRRTUY precopulatory
ACELOOPRSSSVY Solvay process
ACEMMMOOORRTY commemoratory
ACEMMNNOOORTU Mount Cameroon
ACEMOOPRSTTTY prostatectomy
ACENNNNORRSUY nursery cannon
ACENNOORRTTWY Crown attorney
ACEOPPRRSSTTU streptocarpus
ACEOQRRRSSSTU cross-quarters
ACFFFGHILNOTY flight of fancy
ACFFGHIILRSTT traffic lights
ACFFGILNOSTUY suffocatingly
ACFFIIILNOPST spifflication
ACFFIIINOORTT fortification
ACFFIINNOOPTT in point of fact
ACFGHHIINPRTT pitch-farthing
ACFGIIIILNNOT lignification
ACFGIIIINNNST insignificant
ACFGIIIINNOST signification
ACFGIIILNNSTY significantly
ACFGIIILNOORT glorification
ACFGIIINORSTY significatory
ACFGIILNNSTYY sanctifyingly
ACFGIINNOORTU configuration
ACFGILLOOOSTT olfactologist
ACFGILLOORTUU futurological
ACFGIMMNORUUV vacuum forming
ACFHIIIILNOTT lithification
ACFHIIIMNOSTV fashion victim
ACFHIIINOORRT horrification
ACFHIIINORTTU thurification
ACFHIILLNOORY honorifically
ACFHIKLNORRSV Karl von Frisch
ACFIIIIKNNOTZ zinkification
ACFIIIINNORTT nitrification
ACFIIIINORTTV vitrification
ACFIIIJLLNOOT jollification
ACFIIIJNOSTTU justification
ACFIIILLMNOOT mollification
ACFIIILLNNOTU nullification
ACFIIILMOPRST simplificator
ACFIIILNOOPRT prolification
ACFIIILNOPTTY pontificality
ACFIIIMMMNOTU mummification
ACFIIIMNOORTT mortification

ACFIIIMNOSTTY mystification
ACFIIINOPPTUY yuppification
ACFIIINORSSTU Russification
ACFIIJORSTTUY justificatory
ACFIILLLORSTY floristically
ACFIILMNNOSTU functionalism
ACFIILMORRSTU formularistic
ACFIILNNOSTTU functionalist
ACFIILNNOTTUY functionality
ACFILLLLOOORR corollifloral
ACFILLLORRTUU floricultural
ACFILNNNNOOTU non-functional
ACFILOOOPRRSU pair of colours
ACFINNNOOORTT confrontation
ACFLLMOPRRSTU call for trumps
ACFLMOOPRRSST cross-platform
ACGGHHILOPPRY glyphographic
ACGGHHKNNUUWY Kyung-Wha Chung
ACGGHIIJLMNNT jingling match
ACGGHIKLNOSTU laughing stock
ACGGHILOPPRTY glyptographic
ACGGILLLOOOSS glossological
ACGHHIIOPPRSY physiographic
ACGHHIIOPRRST chirographist
ACGHHIMNOSTTU shouting match
ACGHHINOOPSTY onychophagist
ACGHHINORSSSU Sir Hugh Casson
ACGHIIKNSSTTW task switching
ACGHIILLOOPSY physiological
ACGHIIMOOPRST mastigophoric
ACGHIINSSTTTY stay stitching
ACGHIJKNNOOOR Chinook Jargon
ACGHILLLMOOOY homologically
ACGHILLLNNORU rolling launch
ACGHILLMOOOPR morphological
ACGHILLOOPRSY oscillography
ACGHILNOOPSSU sphagnicolous
ACGHIMMMOORSU magic mushroom
ACGHIMNNOOOPT pathognomonic
ACGHIOOOPSTUX toxicophagous
ACGHKLLNNOORU Chulalongkorn
ACGHLLNNOOPSY splanchnology
ACGHLOOOPTTYY cytopathology
ACGHMNOOPSSTU Compsognathus
ACGHNOOPPRSYY pharyngoscopy
ACGIIIILNNSTU linguistician
ACGIIIIMNNNRT incriminating
ACGIIIIMNNRVY virginiamycin
ACGIIIKNORSTV Virginia stock
ACGIIILLNNSTT scintillating
ACGIIILLSSUUU Gaius Lucilius
ACGIIILMNPSTU linguistic map
ACGIILLLOSSTY syllogistical
ACGIILLMMNOOU immunological
ACGIILLMNNOPY complainingly
ACGIILLMOOSTT climatologist
ACGIILLNORSST glans clitoris
ACGIILMNNNOPU uncomplaining
ACGIILRRSTTUU agriculturist
ACGIIMMNOORRS micro-organism
ACGIIMNNNOOOT cognomination
ACGIINNNOSTUY consanguinity
ACGIINNOOPRRT incorporating
ACGIINNORRSST cross-training
ACGIKLMNNOORU mourning cloak
ACGIKLMNOORSU colour masking
ACGILLLNOOOTY ontologically
ACGILLLOOOPTY topologically
ACGILLNOOOSTV volcanologist
ACGILLNOOSTUV vulcanologist
ACGILLNOOSTYY glycosylation
ACGILNNOORTTU conglutinator
ACGILNORSSTUV cross-vaulting
ACGINNNOOOSTU non-contagious
ACGINOOPRRSSS scorpion grass
ACGINOPPRSTTU supporting act
ACHHIIINNORST ornithischian
ACHHIIINPPSSY physicianship
ACHHIILLOOPPS philosophical
ACHHIILNOPPRT philanthropic
ACHHIINNNOSTU Hutchinsonian
ACHHIJKLMNOOV John Malkovich
ACHHILMMOORSS schoolmarmish
ACHHIMNOORSTX xanthochroism
ACHHIMNOOSTTU autochthonism
ACHHIOPPSSTTY psychopathist
ACHHIORSSTUUY ichthyosaurus
ACHHLLMOPTUYY Cyathophyllum
ACHHLLNOOOSTU allochthonous
ACHHMNNOOPSTY Thomas Pynchon
ACHHNOOORSTUX xanthochroous
ACHHNOOOSTTUU autochthonous
ACHIIILLOOPRU ailourophilic
ACHIIILNPPPRS principalship
ACHIIIMNNORTY inharmonicity
ACHIIILLOPSSTY sophistically
ACHIILNNRSTUY unchristianly
ACHIILNOPPRST psilanthropic
ACHIIMMNNOORR harmonic minor
ACHIIMMORRSTT trichromatism
ACHIIMNNOOPPS companionship
ACHIIMNNOORTT ornithomantic
ACHIIOOPRSSTT sophisticator
ACHIKLMNNOOOS Chinook salmon
ACHILLORRTTUU horticultural
ACHILMNOOPRTT tropical month
ACHILMOOPRRSY primary school
ACHILMOPSTTYY sympatholytic
ACHILNOPRSTTY lycanthropist
ACHILOOOPSTTV photovoltaics
ACHIMNOORSTTU tautochronism
ACHIMOOOPRSTT somatotrophic
ACHINNOOPRSSY narcohypnosis
ACHLLLOOOPPRY propyl alcohol
ACHLLOOPSSSTU St Paul's School
ACHMMNOOOORRT monochromator
ACHNOOORSTTUU tautochronous
ACHOORRSSTUUY Corythosaurus
ACIIIIMNNNORT incrimination
ACIIIIMNOSTTV victimisation
ACIIIIMNOTTVZ victimization
ACIIILLLMOPTY impolitically

ACIIILLNNOSTT scintillation
ACIIILLNNRSTY intrinsically
ACIIILLNOOPTT pollicitation
ACIIILMNNORTU anticlinorium
inclinatorium
ACIIILMNOPRSV provincialism
ACIIILMNORSTY consimilarity
ACIIILNNOPRST inscriptional
ACIIILNOPRSTV provincialist
ACIIILNOPRTVY provinciality
ACIIIMNNORRTY incriminatory
ACIILLLMOOQSU colloquialism
ACIILLLOOQSTU colloquialist
ACIILLLSSTTYY stylistically
ACIILLMOPRTTU multiplicator
ACIILLNNSTTUY instinctually
ACIILLNOORTUY illocutionary
ACIILLNPSSTVY vinyl plastics
ACIILLNRSTTYY crystallinity
ACIILLORSTTUY touristically
ACIILMMNNOORU communion rail
ACIILMMNOOSSW Law Commission
ACIILMNOOOPST compositional
ACIILMNOORSUY acrimoniously
ACIILMNOORTTY microtonality
ACIILMORRSSTY military cross
ACIILMPRRSSTU scripturalism
ACIILNNOPRSTU Upton Sinclair
ACIILNNORSTTU instructional
ACIILNOOORSTU colourisation
ACIILNOOORTUZ colourization
ACIILNORSTTUV voluntaristic
ACIILOPPRSTTY party politics
ACIILPRRSSTTU scripturalist
ACIIMMOOPRSTT compatriotism
ACIIMNNNOTTUY continuity man
ACIIMNNOOSSTU sanctimonious
ACIIMNOOPRTTU protoactinium
ACIIMNOOSSTTU customisation
ACIIMNOOSTTUZ customization
ACIIMOOPRRSTV corporativism
ACIINNNOOPRTU pronunciation
ACIINNOOOPRRT incorporation
ACIINNOORSTTT contristation
ACIINNOPRRSTT transcription
ACIIOOPRRSTTV corporativist
ACIKLLLMOOPWY woolly milk cap
ACIKLOPRRRSTU parlour tricks
ACILLLMRTTUUU multicultural
ACILLLRSTUUVY sylvicultural
ACILLNNOOOTUV convolutional
ACILMNOSSSTTU sansculottism
ACILMRRSSTTUU structuralism
ACILNNNNOOSTY inconsonantly
ACILNNOORSUVY convulsionary
ACILNNPTTUUUY unpunctuality
ACILNOOPSSTTU suctional stop
ACILNOORRSTUY contrariously
ACILNOORRSUVY carnivorously
ACILNOSSSTTTU sansculottist
ACILRRSSTTTUU structuralist
ACIMNOOOPTTUX Mount Cotopaxi
ACIMNOOORRTTT motor-traction
ACIMNOQRRSUUZ Marquis Curzon
ACIMOOORRSTUU amour courtois
ACINNOOPRSTTU constupration
ACINNOPRSTTTU contrapuntist
ACINNOQRSTUWY squinancy wort
ACINOORSSTTUV Viscount Astor
ACINORRSTTTUU structuration
ACKKMNNOOPSST postman's knock
ACLMOOOOPPSTY omoplatoscopy
ACLMORSSTTUUU cumulostratus
stratocumulus
ACNNNOOOPSSTT stop-consonant
ACNOOOPPRSSTT contrappostos
ADDDDEEEIMNRV derived demand
ADDDDEEFFILLR fiddle-faddler
ADDDDEEGHINPU pudding-headed
ADDDEEEEHLLSW swelled-headed
ADDDEEEFGIMNN demand feeding
ADDDEEEFLRSSS self-addressed
ADDDEEEKNNRWY Edward Kennedy
ADDDEEGILLMNN Middle England
ADDDEEHIMNRSU dunderheadism
ADDDEEHLNNRUY underhandedly
ADDDEEIIMNOWW maiden-widowed
ADDDEEIMNNOOV video-on-demand
ADDDEEIMNOPST demand deposit
ADDDEGGLLNOSY daddy-long-legs
ADDDEHIIKRRSV hard disk drive
ADDDEIIMNNNOT Dandie Dinmont
ADDDEIMNOOPRW diamond-powder
ADDDEMNNOORST Edmond Rostand
ADDDFFMOOORRX Ford Madox Ford
ADDDINNNOPUWW wind up and down
ADDEEEEEGHILT Eddie the Eagle
ADDEEEEGNRTTV grande vedette
ADDEEEEHNRRTT tender-hearted
ADDEEEEILRRUV lever de rideau
ADDEEEFILMRSU Die Fledermaus
ADDEEEGHIKNOS hide-and-go-seek
ADDEEEGHINPSS pigheadedness
ADDEEEGHIRTTW trade-weighted
ADDEEEGHNORSY dehydrogenase
ADDEEEGHNORTY dehydrogenate
ADDEEEGILNNNR darning-needle
ADDEEEGIRRSST Reader's Digest
ADDEEEGNNRRST transgendered
ADDEEEHLLNOSW swollen-headed
ADDEEEHMNOSSS dead men's shoes
ADDEEEHNNORRY here and yonder
ADDEEEHNNPPRU unapprehended
ADDEEEIILLNTV Live and Let Die
ADDEEEIIMPSST sedes impedita
ADDEEEILLRSSW Leslie Edwards
ADDEEEILMMOSV medieval modes
ADDEEEILMNRST Middle-Eastern
ADDEEEILNNRSW Edwin Landseer
ADDEEELNRSSSS dreadlessness
ADDEEELNRSSTW western saddle✧
ADDEEENPPRRRU underprepared

 Words marked ✧ can also be spelled with one or more capital letters

ADDEEFFHNNOSS offhandedness
ADDEEFFLRRSUY Alfred Dreyfus
ADDEEFHILNRTV left-hand drive
ADDEEFHOORRTY order of the day
ADDEEFIKKNNRW Frank Wedekind
ADDEEFILNPRTT fiddle pattern
fiddle-pattern
ADDEEFLNNPRUY penny dreadful
ADDEEGHHILLTY light-headedly
ADDEEGHLNORWY wrong-headedly
ADDEEGIILLNPS speed dialling
ADDEEGIILMNPU mealie pudding
ADDEEGIMNNOTU maiden-tongued
ADDEEGIORSUUV Dieu vous garde
ADDEEGLLLRRRU Gerald Durrell
ADDEEGMNOORRW wood germander
ADDEEGNNRSSUU unguardedness
ADDEEGOPRRSUW powdered sugar
ADDEEHHILPPRS shepherd plaid
ADDEEHIKLNRTY kind-heartedly
ADDEEHIKNORSW whiskerandoed
ADDEEHILMNRTY earthly-minded
ADDEEHILNPPSS spindle-shaped
ADDEEHJKLLNYY Jekyll and Hyde
ADDEEHMNNOSSY Desmond Haynes
ADDEEHMPRRWWY Edward Whymper
ADDEEHNNNORSU under one's hand
ADDEEHNRRRTTU thunder-darter
ADDEEIILLLLWW Willie Waddell
ADDEEILLMNNRU Lemnian ruddle
ADDEEILMOPPRR pompier-ladder
ADDEEILNORUVZ Nevado del Ruiz
ADDEEIMNNPRRU unreprimanded
ADDEEIMNNSSSY many-sidedness
ADDEEIMNRSTUV misadventured
ADDEEINNSSSUV unadvisedness
ADDEELLNORVWY drowned valley
ADDEEMNOOPSSU pseudomonades
ADDEENNNSSTUU undauntedness
ADDEFFORSTTUY trade-off study
ADDEFGINORUVW wedding favour
ADDEFIILLLRRZ frilled lizard
ADDEFNOORRSTY Dornford Yates
ADDEGGIIILNST digital design
ADDEGGNORRSUU dangerous drug
ADDEGHHILNRSS Highland dress
ADDEGHHILNRTY right-handedly
ADDEGIIKNRRST redding-straik
ADDEGIIMMNNOT Maginot-minded
ADDEGIIMNNNPX mind-expanding
ADDEGINNNRSTU understanding
ADDEGINNORRST standing order
ADDEGIOOPRRTW partridge-wood
ADDEGLNOORTUY good-naturedly
ADDEHHINNORTY hither and yond
ADDEHHNNOORSU Horse and Hound
ADDEHIJNOOPSS Joseph Addison
ADDEHILLMNRUY Edmund Hillary
ADDEHNOOOORRT Theodor Adorno
ADDEIIIILNSUV individualise
ADDEIIIILNUVZ individualize
ADDEIIINOOSTX deoxidisation
ADDEIIINOOTXZ deoxidization
ADDEIILNORSTY disordinately
ADDEIILNPRSSW wind dispersal
ADDEIIMNNQRUU ad inquirendum
ADDEIINOOORST deodorisation
ADDEIINOOORTZ deodorization
ADDEIINOPRSTU superaddition
ADDEIKLNNRTUY kindly-natured
ADDEILLLMMNSY small-mindedly
ADDEILNNPRRST Per Lindstrand
ADDEIMMMRSSUY Midsummer's Day
ADDEIMNNRSSTU misunderstand
ADDEIMNOOPRSU modus operandi
ADDEINOOPPRSW wood sandpiper
ADDEMORRRRUWW Edward R Murrow
ADDFIIORRSSTV Sir David Frost
ADDGGIIIINPTZ digitizing pad
ADDGGILNNNORU landing-ground
ADDGGLNOOORSU Douglas Gordon
ADDGHHIKNOORW Howard Hodgkin
ADDGIILLLOSUW wild gladiolus
ADDGMNNRRSTUU Sturm und Drang
ADDHIMNNOOPTY diamond python
ADDHJNOOORRTY Dorothy Jordan
ADDHNNOOPSTUU thousand-pound
ADDIIIILMNSUV individualism
ADDIIIILNSTUV individualist
ADDIIIILNTUVY individuality
ADDIIIINNOTUV individuation
ADDIILMNNOORS Mindoro Island
ADDIINOOOPRTT Diprotodontia
ADDILLLNOOWWY wild and woolly
ADDILNOORRRSY Lords Ordinary
ADEEEEEGGLNRR general degree
ADEEEEEGNRSSW green seaweeds
ADEEEEEHLLRRW wheeler-dealer
ADEEEEGGLLNRR general ledger
ADEEEEGHKLPTT take the pledge
ADEEEEGHLNRTT gentle-hearted
ADEEEEGNNNRTU en grande tenue
ADEEEEGNNRRTU unregenerated
ADEEEEGRRSTVV Steve Redgrave
ADEEEEHHLORSV head over heels
heels over head
ADEEEEHKLNNNY Helena Kennedy
ADEEEEHNRTTVY three-day event
ADEEEEILNPPPW pineapple weed
ADEEEEILOTTTU eau de toilette
ADEEEENPRSSST desperateness
ADEEEFFGILNST self-defeating
ADEEEFFGIORRT agree to differ
ADEEEFFHNNORV heaven forfend
ADEEEFFIINRTT differentiate
ADEEEFGGHILLT eagle-flighted
ADEEEFHILOSST The Odessa File
ADEEEFHINOSST on the safe side
ADEEEFHRRSTTU feather duster
ADEEEFILLNRTY deferentially
ADEEEFILNNORS read oneself in
ADEEEFILNRSST slide fastener

ADEEEGGIMNNST	disengagement
ADEEEGGINORST	desegregation
ADEEEGHHORRTT	Herod the Great
ADEEEGHILNNTY	dental hygiene
ADEEEGHILNRST	single-hearted
ADEEEGHILNRTT	letter-heading
ADEEEGHILNRTW	leather-winged
ADEEEGHINOPRT	pigeon-hearted
ADEEEGHLLNRTU	leather-lunged
ADEEEGHLNOPSZ	lozenge-shaped
ADEEEGHLNORSS	drag one's heels
ADEEEGIILNOPS	ailes de pigeon
ADEEEGIINNORU	audio-engineer
ADEEEGINNNRSS	endearingness
ADEEEGINRRSTX	sex intergrade
ADEEEGIOPPRRS	pease-porridge
ADEEEGIORSSSU	grouse-disease
ADEEEGJMNSTTU	judgement-seat
ADEEEGLLLRTUW	well-regulated
ADEEEGLNORRSY	Roy Greenslade
ADEEEGMNRRRRY	gerrymanderer
ADEEEGNNRSSST	estrangedness
ADEEEGOPRRTUY	daguerreotype
ADEEEHHLNPSST	Shetland sheep
ADEEEHHLORSUV	heave-shoulder
ADEEEHHNNORTW	the here and now
ADEEEHIILRSTV	raise the devil
ADEEEHIJNOSSS	Johne's disease
ADEEEHILMPRST	simple-hearted
ADEEEHINRRTVW	weather-driven
ADEEEHIPPRSSS	disperse phase
ADEEEHKMNORSS	shoemaker's end
ADEEEHLLNORRU	Leonhard Euler
ADEEEHLLOPPRR	propeller-head
ADEEEHLNOPRTY	open-heartedly
ADEEEHLNSSSST	deathlessness
ADEEEHMMORSTT	smothered mate
ADEEEIILNRRST	intersidereal
ADEEEIIMMNSST	immediateness
ADEEEIIMNNRTT	indeterminate
ADEEEIIMNRTTV	determinative
ADEEEIIMPRTTV	premeditative
ADEEEIINPRSST	pedestrianise
ADEEEIINPRSTZ	pedestrianize
ADEEEIIORRTTV	deteriorative
ADEEEIKLNNORR	Kornelia Ender
ADEEEIKLNPRSV	spike lavender
ADEEEILMNRTTY	determinately
ADEEEILNNNRUV	inland revenue✧
ADEEEILNNOSTX	extension lead
ADEEEILNOPRSS	depersonalise
ADEEEILNOPRSZ	depersonalize
ADEEEILNPRTTV	inverted pleat
ADEEEILOPPPRR	apple-pie order
ADEEEILOPRTTY	radioteletype
ADEEEILRSSSST	ladies' tresses
ADEEEIMNNRTTU	undeterminate
ADEEEIMNPRTTV	tamper-evident
ADEEEIMNRSTTU	underestimate
ADEEEIMNRSTTV	advertisement
ADEEEIMNRTTVZ	advertizement
ADEEEINNNRTTU	unentertained
ADEEEINNRSSST	sedentariness
ADEEEINOPQRTU	equiponderate
ADEEEIPRRRTUU	Pierre Trudeau
ADEEEJMNOSTWW	Jamestown weed
ADEEELLMNOPSW	Epsom and Ewell
ADEEELLMNOPTV	developmental
ADEEELMNRSSSS	dreamlessness
ADEEELNNNRSSU	unlearnedness
ADEEEMNNORTUV	endeavourment
ADEEEMNORSTUV	adventuresome
ADEEENPPRRTTU	unperpetrated
ADEEEORSSTUVW	sweet-savoured
ADEEFFHHILPTT	plead the Fifth
ADEEFFHIKLOTT	take the lid off
ADEEFFIILSSST	self-satisfied
ADEEFGGILNRRS	self-regarding
ADEEFGHILOSTT	lag of the tides
ADEEFGIILNRSS	ladies' fingers
ADEEFGINRRRTY	tarry-fingered
ADEEFGLNRRSSU	regardfulness
ADEEFHIJLMNOS	John Masefield
ADEEFHIKMORTW	wide of the mark
ADEEFHIKNORRW	Frankie Howerd
ADEEFHIKNRRSV	Frederikshavn
ADEEFHILNNSST	left-handiness
ADEEFHIMMNOST	of the same mind
ADEEFHIORTUVW	white-favoured
ADEEFHJLMNOST	John Flamsteed
ADEEFHLOORRTU	rule of the road
ADEEFHNOOORRT	one for the road
ADEEFHNOOOSTU	out of one's head
ADEEFIILLNSSY	Elysian fields
ADEEFIILOQRUV	overqualified
ADEEFIILPRSSS	self-dispraise
ADEEFILLNOORV	oil of lavender
ADEEFILMNRTUV	adventure film
ADEEFILMOSTTV	self-motivated
ADEEFILNOPPST	self-appointed
ADEEFILNSSSTU	self-sustained
ADEEFIMOQRSSU	squire of dames
ADEEFINNOORRV	node of Ranvier
ADEEFINOORSTT	deforestation
ADEEFINOPRRSS	pinafore dress
ADEEFIOPSSTTY	safety-deposit
ADEEFLLRSSSUY	self-assuredly
ADEEFLNNRTUUV	undulant fever
ADEEFNNPRSSTU	enfants perdus
ADEEFOORRTTVY	Treaty of Dover
ADEEGGGILNOUY	Ogygian deluge
ADEEGGHINNNSX	Hang Seng index
ADEEGGHINNRTU	draught-engine
ADEEGGINNRRSU	grand seigneur
ADEEGGNNOORST	Georges Danton
ADEEGGPRRSSSU	pusser's dagger
ADEEGHHNORVYY	heavy hydrogen
ADEEGHHORRTTU	thought-reader
ADEEGHIIKLMRT	like grim death
ADEEGHIIMNNRR	maiden herring
ADEEGHIINNRST	disheartening
ADEEGHIINRRTT	ride at the ring

Words marked ✧ can also be spelled with one or more capital letters

ADEEGHILMNOPT dephlegmation
ADEEGHILNRSTY near-sightedly
ADEEGHINNNOST get one's hand in
ADEEGHJLLMNTU judgement-hall
ADEEGHKNNORTT The Knot Garden
ADEEGHLMNNOOT gentlemanhood
ADEEGHNORSTTT stand together
ADEEGIIINRTTT interdigitate
ADEEGIILNNNRX index learning
ADEEGIILNPPST signal peptide
ADEEGIILNPSSY Paisley design
ADEEGIKNNRRRT kindergärtner
ADEEGILLMNNOT Gideon Mantell
ADEEGILLNRRST drill-sergeant
ADEEGILMMORSV mermaid's glove
ADEEGILNNNNOO Lonnie Donegan
ADEEGILNNOOPS old age pension
old-age pension
ADEEGILORRSUU Louis Daguerre
ADEEGIMNNOSSY dynamogenesis
ADEEGIMNNPRTU unimpregnated
ADEEGIMORSTTU deuterogamist
ADEEGINNRRSTW winter gardens✧
ADEEGINOPPRSV eavesdropping
ADEEGINORSTTU deuteragonist
ADEEGIRSTTTUU tertius gaudet
ADEEGJLLMNTUY judgementally
ADEEGJMNPSSTU pass judgement
ADEEGLNNORSTU dental surgeon
ADEEGLNNRSUUW gunwales under
ADEEGLOOORTUV lead-out groove
ADEEGMMOPPRRR preprogrammed
ADEEGMOPPRSTU pumped storage
ADEEGNNORSSSU dangerousness
ADEEGOPRRTUYY daguerreotypy
ADEEHHHLORRTY Thor Heyerdahl
ADEEHHILNNRST Netherlandish
ADEEHHILNOOTT toad in the hole
toad-in-the-hole
ADEEHHILOPRST Adolphe Thiers
ADEEHHIMOPRRT hermaphrodite
ADEEHHINPSTTU put in the shade
ADEEHHINPTUVW have the wind up
ADEEHHLLOORTW hollow-hearted
ADEEHIILLSSTT satellite dish
ADEEHIILMMNTY dimethylamine
ADEEHIILMNNPY diphenylamine
ADEEHIIRSSSTT radiesthesist
ADEEHIKLMOOWZ Mike Hazelwood
ADEEHILMNORST sidereal month
ADEEHILMSSTUY Heysel Stadium
ADEEHILOPTTVY the devil to pay
ADEEHIMMOPRTX mixed metaphor
ADEEHIMNOORRU Honoré Daumier
ADEEHINOPPRST spider phaeton
ADEEHINORTWWW weather window
ADEEHINRRSSTV desert varnish
ADEEHIPRRSSTV harvest spider
ADEEHJNOPRSSW Joseph Andrews
ADEEHKMNORSTU make the rounds
ADEEHKOPRTTUW take up the word
ADEEHLLNOPRSU shoulder plane
ADEEHLMNORRSY dysmenorrheal
ADEEHLNOPPRST Portland sheep
ADEEHLNOPPSTU pentadelphous
ADEEHLOOOPPRS loosehead prop
ADEEHLORSTTTW the latest word
ADEEHMMOOOSUW Emma Woodhouse
ADEEHMNOORRSY dysmenorrhoea
ADEEHMNRRSTTU thunder-master
ADEEHMPPRSTTU trumpet-shaped
ADEEHNNOOSSTU Southend-on-Sea
ADEEHNOOPRRTZ trapezohedron
ADEEHNORSSTTW short and sweet
ADEEHNPSSSTTY St Stephen's Day
ADEEHORSSTUVY Shrove Tuesday
ADEEIIILNOSST dieselisation
ADEEIIILNOSTZ dieselization
ADEEIIILNTTVY evidentiality
ADEEIIIMMNPRR prime meridian
ADEEIIIMNSSTV disseminative
ADEEIIKLLLORV live like a lord
ADEEIILLMNOSV maison de ville
ADEEIILLNRSTY residentially
ADEEIILLSSSST Still's disease
ADEEIILMNNOTY demyelination
ADEEIILMNNSTT disentailment
ADEEIILMNPSST dissepimental
ADEEIILMNSTTT dilettanteism
ADEEIILNNOPPW People in a Wind
ADEEIIMMNNNOT eminent domain
ADEEIIMNNORTT determination
ADEEIIMNNOSTT sedimentation
ADEEIIMNOPRTT premeditation
ADEEIIMNORRTT intermediator
ADEEIIMNPRSST pedestrianism
ADEEIIMOPRSST Maori side-step
ADEEIIMORSSTV disaster movie
ADEEIINOORRTT deterioration
ADEEIINOPRTXY expeditionary
ADEEIINORSSTT desertisation
ADEEIINORSSTV disseveration
ADEEIINORSTTZ desertization
ADEEIINRRRSUV River Eridanus
ADEEIIOPSSSTU adipose tissue
ADEEIKMNNOPSS speak one's mind
ADEEILLMNRTTY detrimentally
ADEEILLNNRTTY interdentally
ADEEILLNOPPTW well-appointed
ADEEILLNORRVY Ordinary level
ADEEILMMNNSTT dismantlement
ADEEILMNNOSTW enlisted woman
ADEEILMNOORTZ metronidazole
ADEEILMPQRTUU quadruple time
ADEEILNNRTTVY inadvertently
ADEEILNOPRTUV Andrei Tupolev
ADEEILNORSSTY sedentary soil
ADEEILNPRRSTZ serpent-lizard
ADEEIMMNNOSSU one's name is mud
ADEEIMMPRRSSU mermaid's purse
ADEEIMNNOPRRT preordainment
ADEEIMNORSTTV demonstrative

ADEEIMNRRSTUV misadventurer
ADEEINNNSSTTU untaintedness
ADEEINNOPQRTU equiponderant
ADEEINNOSSTTW at one's wits' end
at one's wit's end
ADEEINNPPRRSS spider spanner
ADEEINOOPPRRS à propos de rien
ADEEINOPPRRSW Persian powder
ADEEINOPRRSST predatoriness
ADEEINOPRRSTT predestinator
ADEEINOPRRSTU superordinate
ADEEINOPSTTTU patent outside
ADEEINORRTUVY auditory nerve
ADEEINPRSSTUU unpasteurised
ADEEINPRSTUUZ unpasteurized
ADEEIOPRSSSTW power-assisted
ADEEJMMORRTTU drum majorette
ADEEKLLNOSTWY Daltons Weekly
ADEELLMMNOPTY maldeployment
ADEELLMMNOSWX Maxwell's demon
ADEELLNOOPRRW woollen-draper
ADEELMNOORSST star-nosed mole
ADEELNNNQSTUU Queensland nut
ADEELNNSSSSTU dauntlessness
ADEEMMOOSTUXY myxoedematous
ADEEMNNOORSTT ondes Martenot✧
ADEEMNRSTTTUU mature student
ADEEMOORRSTUX xerodermatous
ADEEMORRSSSUW measure swords
ADEENNOORRSST Sonoran Desert
ADEENOOPRRSTU autoresponder
ADEENPPRRRSTU understrapper
ADEENPRSSSUXY Sunday Express
ADEFFGKNOORTU Duke of Grafton
ADEFFHILLNOSU full-fashioned
ADEFFHIORRSST Staffordshire
ADEFGHHILNOST sleight of hand
sleight-of-hand
ADEFGHIIINRRT riding the fair
ADEFGHIIMNSTT midnight feast
ADEFGHINOORSW foreshadowing
ADEFGIJLNSSTU self-adjusting
ADEFGILNOORTW waterflooding
ADEFGILNRRSSS Flinders grass
ADEFGNNOOOORT good afternoon
ADEFHHINRTTUY unthriftyhead
ADEFHIILLOPST field hospital
ADEFHILNOORSS foolhardiness
ADEFHLMNOORTW man of the world
ADEFHLMOORSTT Thomas Telford
ADEFIIILMMRTU multiramified
ADEFIIIMNRRST first meridian
ADEFIILLMNNOT inlet manifold
ADEFIILLNQUUY unqualifiedly
ADEFIILNOTTWY law of identity
ADEFIINSSSTUU dies infaustus
ADEFIJMMORRSU Reform Judaism
ADEFILLLORUVY ill-favouredly
ADEFILLSSTTUY distastefully
ADEFINNNOOTTU foundation-net
ADEFLNNOOORSW Earl of Snowdon
ADEFLNOPPPRSY Flanders poppy
ADEFMNNORRSTU untransformed
ADEFMNOOORRST Stanford Moore
ADEFNOOOORSTU out of one's road
ADEGGIILNNRSS niggardliness
ADEGGIINNORRS Grand Seignior
ADEGGIINORSTU ruggedisation
ADEGGIINORTUZ ruggedization
ADEGGILNORRTU regulating rod
ADEGGIMNRSSTY grading system
ADEGGINNOORVW wood engraving
ADEGHHHORTTUY through the day
ADEGHHIINNNTW hang in the wind
ADEGHHIOPPRTT tight-head prop
ADEGHIILLLNRT drilling lathe
ADEGHIKLLNNSY Kenny Dalglish
ADEGHIKNNORRW work-hardening
ADEGHINNNOSTT one-night stand
ADEGHINNOORTY hydrogenation
ADEGHINNOPPRS pendragonship
ADEGHINOPRSWW washing powder
ADEGHKNNOOSST thank goodness
ADEGHLMNORRTY grandmotherly
ADEGHMNPRRRUY Gardner Murphy
ADEGIIILMTTTU multidigitate
ADEGIIINORSTV disinvigorate
ADEGIILLLNPSU pulse dialling
ADEGIILLMNOOT all in good time
ADEGIILLNPSSY displeasingly
ADEGIILMNTTUY unmitigatedly
ADEGIILNNOOPS lead poisoning
ADEGIILNNOTTU deglutination
ADEGIILNNTUVY undeviatingly
ADEGIILNORRSS sailing orders
ADEGIIMNSSTTU unstigmatised
ADEGIIMNSTTUZ unstigmatized
ADEGIIMOOPRST diageotropism
ADEGIINNNPRTU underpainting
ADEGIINOOSTTU auto-digestion
ADEGIINORRSTT disintegrator
ADEGIKLNNOTWY take lying down
ADEGIKLNORRSW walking-orders
ADEGIKMNOORRY Andrei Gromyko
ADEGILLMNOUZZ muzzle-loading
ADEGILLMNPPPU apple dumpling
ADEGILLNOSTUU solidungulate
ADEGILMOORSTT dermatologist
ADEGILNNOQRTU grandiloquent
ADEGILNNQRSUY squanderingly
ADEGILNNRSSSV les grands vins
ADEGILNNRSSTU standing rules
ADEGILNNRSUVY land-surveying
ADEGILNOPRSTX exploding star
ADEGIMNNOORRU ground moraine
ADEGINNNOSSTT standing stone
ADEGINNOSSTTU standing to sue
ADEGJLMNNNOTU non-judgmental
ADEGLLMNORUWZ mangold-wurzel
ADEGLLMNOSUWY Samuel Goldwyn
ADEGMOOPRRRST stored program
ADEGNOOOPSSTU steganopodous

ADEGOOOPRSSTU	gasteropodous
ADEHHIILMNPTU	Paul Hindemith
ADEHHILLLOSST	old as the hills
ADEHHILOOORTU	Holothuroidea
ADEHHOPRRSSTW	sharp's the word
ADEHIILMNPSTY	lymphadenitis
ADEHIILNRRTTV	third interval
ADEHIKLNNPSSS	spindle-shanks
ADEHILLLLORSW	heads will roll
ADEHILMMORSUY	Summer Holiday
ADEHILMNORXYY	hydroxylamine
ADEHILMNSSSTY	Myles Standish
ADEHILMOPPRST	tadpole shrimp
ADEHILMORTTUU	multi-authored
ADEHILNNOPRSW	land-ownership
ADEHILOOPRSTT	strophiolated
ADEHILPRSTTWY	sharp-wittedly
ADEHIMMOOPPRS	paedomorphism
ADEHIMNNOOTTW	The Tin Woodman
ADEHIMOOPRRST	moderatorship
ADEHINOQRSTUW	White Squadron
ADEHINRSTUVYY	heavy industry
ADEHIOPRSSTUY	disuse atrophy
ADEHJNNNOORSW	Andrew Johnson
ADEHLLNNOOTWY	Anthony Dowell
ADEHLLOOPPSUY	polyadelphous
ADEHLMNOOPSTY	Daley Thompson
ADEHLOPRRSSTU	shoulder strap
ADEHMNOORRSSW	horseman's word
ADEHNORRSTTWW	north-westward
ADEHORSSTTUWW	south-westward
ADEIIIILNOSSV	divisionalise
ADEIIIILNOSVZ	divisionalize
ADEIIILLMNSTU	disilluminate
ADEIIILMNORTY	meridionality
ADEIIILMSSTUV	dissimulative
ADEIIILNPSTTU	platitudinise
ADEIIILNPTTUZ	platitudinize
ADEIIILNRSSTU	industrialise
ADEIIILNRSTUZ	industrialize
ADEIIIMNNOSST	dissemination
ADEIIIMNOSSTT	disestimation
ADEIIINOOPRST	periodisation
ADEIIINOOPRTZ	periodization
ADEIIINOOPSTT	epidotisation
ADEIIINOOPTTZ	epidotization
ADEIIINORSTTV	derivationist
ADEIIINRSTTTU	attitudiniser
ADEIIINRTTTUZ	attitudinizer
ADEIILLLORSTZ	stellio lizard
ADEIILLMNNTUU	unilluminated
ADEIILMNNOTUV	mountain devil
ADEIILMNOPPRU	imperial pound
ADEIILMNOPSSY	impassionedly
ADEIILMNPRSTU	prudentialism
ADEIILMNRRTUY	rudimentarily
ADEIILNNNORSU	Réunion Island
ADEIILNNOOPTY	opinionatedly
ADEIILNOOSTTV	devotionalist
ADEIILNOOTTVY	devotionality
ADEIILNORSSTT	traditionless
ADEIILNPRRSTU	pre-industrial
ADEIILNPRSTTU	prudentialist
ADEIILNPRTTUY	prudentiality
ADEIILNQSTTUY	equidistantly
ADEIILPSTTUVY	disputatively
ADEIIMNNOOPRT	preadmonition
	predomination
ADEIIMNNOORST	modernisation
ADEIIMNNOORTZ	modernization
ADEIIMNNOPSSU	unimpassioned
ADEIIMNNORSTT	anti-modernist
ADEIIMNNORSTU	trade unionism
ADEIIMNORSTTU	sodium nitrate
ADEIINNNOSTTU	United Nations
ADEIINNOOPRRT	preordination
ADEIINNORSTTU	trade unionist
ADEIINOPRSTTU	disreputation
ADEIINPRRSSTT	ardent spirits
ADEIIPPRRSTTY	party-spirited
ADEIJLLORSUUX	Julius Axelrod
ADEIKLNNORSSY	Orkney Islands
ADEILLNRSTTUU	unillustrated
ADEILLOPRRSVY	Lord Privy Seal
ADEILMMNOOPSY	polydaemonism
ADEILMNNOPRTY	predominantly
ADEILNOORTUVY	devolutionary
ADEILNRSSSTUY	Surtsey Island
ADEIMNNOORSTT	demonstration
ADEIMNNOPRSTU	superdominant
ADEIMNNRSTTTU	untransmitted
ADEIMOOPRSSTZ	spermatozoids
ADEINOPRRRSUY	superordinary
ADEINOPRSTUVY	vapour density
ADEINOSSSSSUU	assiduousness
ADEKLNOOPRSSW	sponsored walk
ADEKMNNRSSSUU	Knud Rasmussen
ADELLMOOPRRST	Lords Temporal
ADELNNOOPRSTT	Portland stone
ADELNNOORSSSV	Sons and Lovers
ADELNOPRRSTTY	transportedly
ADELNORSTUUVY	adventurously
ADEMNNOOTTUWY	Don't You Want Me
ADEMNOORRSTTY	demonstratory
ADEMNOORSSTUU	Edmontosaurus
ADENNORSTUUUV	unadventurous
ADENOOPRRRSTU	proterandrous
ADEOOPRRRTTWW	water dropwort
ADFFGGINORSTU	Gustaf Fröding
ADFFGHILLNOOS	flash flooding
ADFFHIMNNOSTU	Dustin Hoffman
ADFGGHHIILLNN	Highland fling
ADFGHIIILRRSY	His Girl Friday
ADFGHNOOORRUU	guard of honour
ADFGIIILNQSUY	disqualifying
ADFGIIINORSTU	disfiguration
ADFGIIKLNNOOV	A Kind of Loving
ADFHHKLLNOOOO	Hook of Holland
ADFIIIILMNOSS	solifidianism
ADFIKLLNNOORS	Norfolk Island
ADFIKNNORRSSY	Sir Frank Dyson
ADGGGIILNNRSS	glass-grinding

ADGGGILNNNORU ground-angling
ADGGHHHIIMNTY high and mighty
ADGGIMNNNPRUY granny dumping
ADGHHILLNOPTY diphthongally
ADGHIIILNQSUW washing liquid
ADGHIILNNOPPS island-hopping
ADGHIILNNORTU hound-trailing
ADGHIINNNNOTU Huntingdonian
ADGHIINNRTUWW unwithdrawing
ADGHIINOPRTTV providing that
ADGHIKNOORSWW work shadowing
ADGHINNOOOPRT gonadotrophin
ADGHKNNOORSUY on shaky ground
ADGHMNNOOPRRY gynandromorph
ADGIIIINNOPST pidginisation
ADGIIIINNOPTZ pidginization
ADGIIILLMNOWW William Godwin
ADGIIILNNRSSV Virgin Islands
ADGIIILNPRSSY dispraisingly
ADGIIINNOPPST disappointing
ADGIIKLLNNRTU trunk dialling
ADGIINOPPRRST dripping roast
ADGIJLNOPPRWY jaw-droppingly
ADGILLMOOOPTY diplomatology
ADGILNNOSTTUY outstandingly
ADGILNOOOOSTT odonatologist
ADGILNOOQRSUU grandiloquous
ADGNNOORRUWWY wrong way round
ADHHIORRRSSTY hydrarthrosis
ADHHJKNNOORTW John Dankworth
ADHHNNOORSTTU North and South
ADHIIKNOOOPRT orthopinakoid
ADHIILLMNOSUW William Hudson
ADHIILLNOQRTU quadrillionth
ADHIILMNOPRSU dolphinariums
ADHIILNOPPSST spit and polish
ADHIIMNOORSSU disharmonious
ADHIINSSSTTWY St Swithin's Day
ADHIMNOPRSSSW swordsmanship
ADHINNOOOPSTT point-and-shoot
ADHINOOOPRSTT prosthodontia
ADHINOORRSTWW Wordsworthian
ADHIOOOPPRTTY diaphototropy
ADHJNOOOPSSSS John Dos Passos
ADHKLNOORSTWW Lord knows what
ADHKNOOOTUWWY what do you know?
ADHMOOORSSTUY hydrosomatous
ADIIIILMNOSST dissimilation
ADIIIILMRSSTY dissimilarity
ADIIIIMNNNOSS Mission Indian
ADIIILLMORRTW William Dorrit
ADIIILMMOPRRS primordialism
ADIIILMNOSSTU dissimulation
ADIIILMNPRTUV Vladimir Putin
ADIIILMNRSSTU industrialism
ADIIILMOPRRTY primordiality
ADIIILNOOPSST dispositional
ADIIILNRSSTTU industrialist
ADIILLMMOORST stillroom-maid
ADIILMNOORRTZ monitor lizard
ADIILMNRTTUUY multitudinary
ADIILNNOSTTUU undulationist
ADIILNOOOPSST podsolisation
ADIILNOOOPSTZ podsolization
podzolisation
ADIILNOOOPTZZ podzolization
ADIILNOOPRSSV poisson d'avril
ADIILNOPSTTUU platitudinous
ADIINNRSTTUYY Trinity Sunday
ADIKLNNOOPRRS Lord Parkinson
ADILNOORRRSSS Sir Ronald Ross
ADIMNNOORSSWY in so many words
ADIMNNOORSTWW transom window
AEEEEEFKMRRRT free-marketeer
AEEEEEINPRRRS arrière-pensée
AEEEEEMNPPTTZ appeteezement
AEEEEFGGIKOOR Georgia O'Keefe
AEEEEFGHLNRRV half-evergreen
AEEEEFHLOPPTY apple of the eye
AEEEEFHNNOQUV Queen of Heaven
AEEEEFLNOPRST repeat oneself
AEEEEGGHHORTV heave the gorge
AEEEEGGHMSSTT get the message
AEEEEGGIMNRRR Germaine Greer
AEEEEGGMNNPRT pre-engagement
AEEEEGHHHOTTV get the heave-ho
AEEEEGILNNRSS sales engineer
AEEEEGMPRRRSV game preserver
AEEEEHHNNSTVV seventh heaven
AEEEEHLMNPRSS ephemeralness
AEEEEHMOPPRRT Ephemeroptera
AEEEEHMORRTTW weatherometer
AEEEEHNNOOSVY have one's eye on
AEEEEHRRSTTTT street theatre
AEEEEILNRRSST rensselaerite
AEEEEILNRRTUV relieve nature
AEEEEIMNPRSST passementerie
AEEEEKMMNORST meet one's maker
AEEEEKOPPSSTY popeseye steak
AEEEEMMNRRSTU remeasurement
AEEEEMNNPRRST representamen
AEEEEMNPRSSTT temperateness
AEEEENRRRSTUV nature reserve
AEEEFFGHINORV heave-offering
AEEEFFGILSTUV Gustave Eiffel
AEEEFFINRRTUV revenue tariff
AEEEFFLMMNRRW Flammenwerfer
AEEEFGGINNRTW Newgate fringe
AEEEFGGMNOORR George Foreman
AEEEFGHHIRTTW featherweight
AEEEFGHINRRTT fringe theatre
AEEEFGHKRRRSY grey reef shark
AEEEFGHLNRTTU feature-length
AEEEFGIIRRRTV refrigerative
AEEEFGILLNRSV self-revealing
AEEEFGILMNNNT fine gentleman
AEEEFGILNPRST self-repeating
AEEEFGINOSSSU Sea of Geniuses
AEEEFGLNNNSSW newfangleness
AEEEFGNOOSUVY Eugene of Savoy
AEEEFHHORRSST horsefeathers
AEEEFHINQRTUY The Fairy Queen

AEEEFHLLLOTWY	the yellow leaf
AEEEFHMNOQTUY	Queen of the May
AEEEFHNPRRSST	Stephen Frears
AEEEFIIMMRTTT	time after time
AEEEFILLNRRTY	referentially
AEEEFILLQRTUU	quatrefeuille
AEEEFILRSSSTV	self-assertive
AEEEFINORSSTY	Sea of Serenity
AEEEFINQRTTUV	frequentative
AEEEFJLMORSTT	Letter of James
AEEEFKLMRRSWY	Farmers Weekly
AEEEFKLORRRWW	welfare worker
AEEEFKMNNNRTT	frank-tenement
AEEEFLMNRSTTT	self-treatment
AEEEFLNORSSST	assert oneself
AEEEFNORRSTTW	water softener
AEEEFNOSSTTTV	state of events
AEEEFNPRRSSST	press fastener
AEEEGGHNORSSU	greenhouse gas
AEEEGGIMNOSST	gametogenesis
AEEEGGORRSSTU	Georges Seurat
AEEEGHHINPRSS	sheepshearing
AEEEGHHIRRTTT	tithe-gatherer
AEEEGHHLORTTT	the altogether
AEEEGHILNPSST	sheep-stealing
AEEEGHILPRRTW	telegraph wire
AEEEGHIMNNRST	garnisheement
AEEEGHIMPRRRT	the grim reaper
AEEEGHINORSST	atherogenesis
AEEEGHINPRSTT	gene therapist
AEEEGHKLNPTTU	take the plunge
AEEEGHLLOPPRT	telegraph pole
AEEEGHLNOPRRS	selenographer
AEEEGHMNOPRST	magnetosphere
AEEEGIKLLLOPS	sleep like a log
AEEEGIKLLMNNT	gentlemanlike
AEEEGIKLMNRTT	telemarketing
AEEEGILLMNSTV	televangelism
AEEEGILLNNPRS	sleep learning
AEEEGILLNORSV	Seville orange
AEEEGILLNSTTV	televangelist
AEEEGILMNNORT	noli me tangere
	noli-me-tangere
AEEEGILMNPRSS	passenger-mile
AEEEGILNORRTX	exterior angle
AEEEGILPRRSTT	register-plate
AEEEGIMMNQRRU	German Requiem
AEEEGIMNPRRTY	prayer meeting
AEEEGINNORRTX	Generation Xer
AEEEGINOPPPSU	Giuseppe Peano
AEEEGINORRRTT	reinterrogate
AEEEGINORSSTT	teratogenesis
AEEEGLLNOUUVV	Nouvelle Vague
AEEEGLNORRTTY	Terry Eagleton
AEEEGMNORSSSU	Graeme Souness
AEEEGNNRSSTTY	Tyssetrengane
AEEEHHHLRRSTW	thresher whale
AEEEHHILNPTTW	white elephant
AEEEHHINOSTTV	the noes have it
AEEEHHIPRSSTY	hyperesthesia
AEEEHHLMORRTT	heterothermal
AEEEHHLNPRSTW	elephant shrew
AEEEHHNOPRSST	asthenosphere
AEEEHHOPPRSTU	paper the house
AEEEHIKNRSTVY	sneak-thievery
AEEEHILLRTTTT	little theatre
AEEEHILMMNPRT	penthemimeral
AEEEHILMNNOPP	epiphenomenal
AEEEHILMNNOPS	phenomenalise
AEEEHILMNNOPZ	phenomenalize
AEEEHILNRSSTW	the Lesser Wain
	weatherliness
AEEEHILNSSTWW	swanee whistle✧
AEEEHIMNNNNTT	nineteenth man
AEEEHIMOPRSSV	overemphasise
AEEEHIMOPRSVZ	overemphasize
AEEEHINNOSSSV	nose heaviness
AEEEHINQRRSTU	Thérèse Raquin
AEEEHIRRSSTTT	theatre sister
AEEEHIRSTTVWY	sweetheart ivy
AEEEHLLMNORTT	tell me another
AEEEHLLMNOSSW	meals on wheels
AEEEHLMNSSSSS	shamelessness
AEEEHLNPSSSSS	shapelessness
AEEEHLNRSSSST	heartlessness
AEEEHLOPRSSUU	pleasure house
AEEEHMMNORTTV	earth-movement
AEEEHMNNOPTTV	on the pavement
AEEEHOPRRRTTW	weather report
AEEEHORRSSTUU	treasure-house
AEEEHPPPRTTTU	puppet theatre
AEEEHQRRRSTTU	three quarters
AEEEHRSSTTTTW	test the waters
AEEEIILNRRRTV	irreverential
AEEEIIMNRTTVX	exterminative
AEEEIJLLLMMSV	James Melville
AEEEIJLMMRRSS	James Mirrlees
AEEEIKLLMPRST	kapellmeister
AEEEIKLLNOOSV	Aleksei Leonov
AEEEIKLLOPPST	sleep like a top
AEEEIKLMMNRRS	kermes mineral
AEEEILLNRRTVY	reverentially
AEEEILMNPRSSX	exemplariness
AEEEILMNPRTTY	intemperately
AEEEILNNSSSST	essentialness
AEEEILNORSSTU	at one's leisure
AEEEILNPRTTVY	penetratively
AEEEILNRSSSTV	versatileness
AEEEIMMNNPRST	semi-permanent
AEEEIMMNORSSU	in some measure
AEEEIMMPRSTUY	empyreumatise
AEEEIMMPRTUYZ	empyreumatize
AEEEIMNNNRTTT	entertainment
AEEEIMNNRSTTT	reinstatement
AEEEIMNORSSSW	wearisomeness
AEEEIMNPPPRTT	peppermint tea
AEEEIMNPRRSTV	imperseverant
AEEEINNNSSSST	insensateness
AEEEINNPSSSVX	expansiveness
AEEEINNSSSSTV	assentiveness
AEEEINNSSTTTV	attentiveness
	tentativeness

AEEEINOPRRSTV	perseveration
AEEEINOPRSSTV	operativeness
AEEEINPRSSSVV	pervasiveness
AEEEINRSSSSTV	assertiveness
AEEEIPPRRRSST	Sir Peter Pears
AEEEIRRSSTUUX	très au sérieux
AEEEJLMNSSSTU	Jules Massenet
AEEEKLLLNNRYY	Kennelly layer
AEEEKLLMRRSST	sellers' market
	seller's market
AEEEKMMORRRVY	make merry over
AEEELLLOSTVWW	low level waste
AEEELNNOOSSST	set one's seal on
AEEELNOOOPRSV	Paolo Veronese
AEEELNORRSTTX	external store
AEEELNPRSTTTT	letters patent
AEEELNSSSSSTT	statelessness
	tastelessness
AEEEMMNOPRTTU	pneumatometer
AEEEMMORRSSTT	meteor streams
AEEEMNORSTTTV	overstatement
AEEEMNPRRSSTU	prematureness
AEEENNOPRSTTU	Enteropneusta
AEEENOPRRSTTT	enter a protest
AEEENOPRSSTTT	poste restante
AEEEORRRSTTUV	treasure-trove
AEEFFGHHILRTT	flight-feather
AEEFFGHIMNRTT	affreightment
AEEFFGHORTTUU	The Art of Fugue
AEEFFGRRRRTYY	Gerry Rafferty
AEEFFHIKLOSTT	a kettle of fish
AEEFFHILLNRTU	in full feather
AEEFFLLLNNORW	flannel-flower
AEEFGGIINRUVW	figure-weaving
AEEFGHHINRRTT	three-farthing
AEEFGHIKLRSTT	strike the flag
AEEFGHILMOTTW	weight of metal
AEEFGHILNORSV	half-sovereign
AEEFGHLLRSSTU	self-slaughter
AEEFGHLOORRTT	for altogether
AEEFGHNORTTTY	Treaty of Ghent
AEEFGIIKLLOTV	fit like a glove
AEEFGIINORRRT	refrigeration
AEEFGIIPRRTUV	prefigurative
AEEFGILNOPRST	self-operating
AEEFGILNRSSST	self-asserting
AEEFGIMNORRRT	interferogram
AEEFGINORRSTU	argentiferous
	garnetiferous
AEEFGINRRRSUY	sugar-refinery
AEEFGIORRRRTY	refrigeratory
AEEFGJLLORSUU	Jules Laforgue
AEEFGLNNPRSTU	self-repugnant
AEEFGMOOPSSTT	mess of pottage
AEEFGNOOPRSST	foot passenger
AEEFHHLLNSSTU	healthfulness
AEEFHHLNOORST	one's other half
AEEFHIILMNNRS	line-fisherman
AEEFHIIMNPRSS	fisherman's pie
AEEFHIKNORTTW	war to the knife
AEEFHILLNOOPT	elephant folio
AEEFHILNSSSST	faithlessness
AEEFHIMNNORST	refashionment
AEEFHIMNOORTV	have no time for
AEEFHIMNOSSTT	F O Matthiessen
AEEFHINNORTTU	in the nature of
AEEFHLMOOPRRT	mother-of-pearl
AEEFHLMORRSTT	throstle frame
AEEFHLNOOPSTT	elephant's-foot
AEEFHMNNOOSST	son of the manse
AEEFHNORRTTUY	turn of the year
AEEFHOOPRRSUY	house of prayer
AEEFHOORSSTUW	software house
AEEFHOOSSSTTU	House of States
AEEFIILLNNRTY	inferentially
AEEFIILOPRRTV	proliferative
AEEFIINRRSSTT	fire-resistant
AEEFIJOSSTUVX	faites vos jeux
AEEFIKLMOPRRT	market profile
AEEFIKLNRSSTW	fitness walker
AEEFILLLNRSTY	self-reliantly
AEEFILLMORSTU	metalliferous
AEEFILLMOSSTY	Yosemite Falls
AEEFILMORRRTT	air letter form
AEEFILNORSSST	self-assertion
AEEFILNRRSSTT	self-restraint
AEEFIMOORSSTU	Sea of Moisture
AEEFIMOPRRSSS	Passeriformes
AEEFINNNORSTU	antenniferous
AEEFINNOQRTTU	frequentation
AEEFINNORSSSU	nefariousness
AEEFINOORRSTT	reforestation
AEEFINOPRSTTU	superfetation
AEEFIOOPRRSST	professoriate
AEEFLLNORSTVW	fellow servant
AEEFLLNSSSSTU	faultlessness
AEEFLMNRSSSTU	masterfulness
AEEFLNNOORSTY	treason felony
AEEFLNPRRSSUY	prayerfulness
AEEFLNRSSSTUW	wasterfulness
AEEFNNORSSTTU	fortunateness
AEEGGHILLNOTY	genethlialogy
AEEGGHIORRSTW	George Wishart
AEEGGHOOOPRRZ	zoogeographer
AEEGGIILNNNRV	line-engraving
AEEGGIINNNPRT	genre painting
AEEGGIIORRRSY	Sir George Airy
AEEGGIJMRRSST	Mister Jaggers
AEEGGIMNNNRRU	green manuring
AEEGGIMNSSTTX	text messaging
AEEGGINNOORSS	organogenesis
AEEGGINNRRSST	Singer Sargent
AEEGGLLMOORRY	George Mallory
AEEGGLLORRSUY	rogues' gallery
AEEGGNOOPRSTT	George S Patton
AEEGGOOTTTTUU	goutte à goutte
AEEGHHINQSUWY	Queen's highway
AEEGHHIOPPRTT	height to paper
AEEGHHIOPRRSY	heresiography
AEEGHHLOOTWWY	go the whole way
AEEGHHMOPRRRT	thermographer
AEEGHIIKNNSSV	heaven-kissing

AEEGHIIMNSSST Missing the Sea
AEEGHIINNSSTT satin sheeting
AEEGHIJNRSTZZ The Jazz Singer
AEEGHILLLNPRS pearl-shelling
AEEGHILMNNPST gentlemanship
AEEGHILMNPTTV pavement light
AEEGHILMOORST isogeothermal
AEEGHILNNRTTY threateningly
AEEGHILNPRTUV virulent phage
AEEGHIMOPRRSS seismographer
AEEGHINNPRSTZ Sherpa Tenzing
AEEGHINOOPTTV photonegative
AEEGHINOPRSST taphrogenesis
AEEGHINORSTUW watering-house
AEEGHINOSSTTU housing estate
AEEGHINRRSTTY earthing tyres
AEEGHLMNOOOTU theologoumena
AEEGHLNORRRSW horse-wrangler
AEEGHLNRRSSTT The Stranglers
AEEGIIINSTTVV investigative
AEEGIIKLNOSXY Alexei Kosygin
AEEGIILLLSTVY legislatively
AEEGIILMNORSS generalissimo
AEEGIILMNORST Gloria Steinem
AEEGIILNNORRT interior angle
AEEGIILNNOTTV gentian violet
AEEGIILNNPSST palingenesist
AEEGIILNNSSTY easy listening
easy-listening
AEEGIILNOPSTV positive angle
AEEGIILNORSTT state religion
AEEGIILNPRSTY Israel in Egypt
AEEGIIMNNORST generationism
AEEGIIMNNORTT regimentation
AEEGIIMNNRSTT mainstreeting
AEEGIIMNRSTTU time signature
AEEGIINNOORTT renegotiation
AEEGIINNOPRRT peregrination
AEEGIINNORRTT reintegration
AEEGIINORRRTT interior grate
AEEGIINORRTTV interrogative
AEEGIIOPRRRSU prairie grouse
AEEGIKLNRSTTW streetwalking
AEEGILLLNPRST selling-plater
AEEGILLLOTTUV outlet village
AEEGILLMNNSSY meaninglessly
AEEGILLMNRSTV serving mallet
AEEGILLNRSSTT signal letters
AEEGILLNRSTVY everlastingly
AEEGILLOOPSST spelaeologist
AEEGILMMNNORU lemon geranium
AEEGILNNOOPRY Alpine orogeny
AEEGILNNPRTTY penetratingly
AEEGILNNTTUXY extenuatingly
AEEGILNOOPRST antigropeloes
AEEGILNOPPRSS pipeless organ
AEEGILNRSTTTW Watling Street
AEEGILOPRRTVY prerogatively
AEEGIMMNOOTTV magnetomotive
AEEGIMNNNNSSU unmeaningness
AEEGIMNNRTTUY integumentary
AEEGINNNOORVW Norwegian oven
AEEGINNNORSTW Norwegian nest
AEEGINNNQRTUY quingentenary
AEEGINNOSSUUX exsanguineous
AEEGINNPPRRSV preserving-pan
AEEGINNPPRSTT step-parenting
AEEGINNRSTTUU signature tune
AEEGINOPPPPRR poppering pear
AEEGINOPRRRTY peregrinatory
AEEGINRRSSSTV transgressive
AEEGIORRRSTTV tergiversator
AEEGLLMNNNTUY ungentlemanly
AEEGLLMNNOTWY gentlewomanly
AEEGLMNNPSSTU puss-gentleman
AEEGLMNOOPRRY prolegomenary
AEEGLORRSSTUV true-love grass
AEEGMNOOOSSWY go someone's way
AEEGMNOORRSTV steam governor
AEEGMNORRSTTU outer garments
AEEGNNOOSTWWY get one's own way
AEEGNNQRRRTUU quarter-gunner
AEEHHHKRRRSST thresher-shark
AEEHHIINNOPTZ phenothiazine
AEEHHIIPPRSTW white sapphire
AEEHHIKMMORRX Max Horkheimer
AEEHHIKMNORTW Mike Hawthorne
AEEHHILLLNOTW hole in the wall
hole-in-the-wall
AEEHHILMMNNTT nemathelminth
AEEHHILNNSSTU unhealthiness
AEEHHIMNNRTTW with the manner
AEEHHJMNOPTUV have the jump on
AEEHHLMMOOORT homoeothermal
AEEHHLMORRTTY earth-motherly
AEEHHMNOOPRRY hypomenorrhea
AEEHHMNOORTTW the other woman
AEEHHMOPRRTTY thermotherapy
AEEHHNNORTTTU turn on the heat
AEEHIIILNPPPS Philippine Sea
AEEHIIIPPRSTT perihepatitis
AEEHIIKNPRSTY kinesitherapy
AEEHIILLLPPPS Philippe Sella
AEEHIILLNRSWW Willie Renshaw
AEEHIILMNNNSZ Heinz Sielmann
AEEHIILMNOSSS leishmanioses
AEEHIILMNRTTY triethylamine
AEEHIILPPRRTY peripherality
AEEHIIMMNPRTY pyrimethamine
AEEHIIMNRSTUW within measure
AEEHIINNORSTX hair extension
AEEHIKLNNPPST pink elephants
AEEHIKMOTTUWY take me with you
AEEHILLMNSSTT in the smallest
AEEHILLOPPPRS apple polisher
AEEHILMMNNOPS phenomenalism
AEEHILMNNOPST phenomenalist
AEEHILMNNOPTY phenomenality
AEEHILMNNRRTY internal rhyme
AEEHILMNOPRST Le Misanthrope
AEEHILMRSSTUU ultimus haeres
AEEHILNNRSSTU unearthliness

AEEHIMNNOPSTU mountain sheep
AEEHIMNNPSSSS misshapenness
AEEHIMNNRSTTU human interest
AEEHIMNORRTTT The Terminator
AEEHIMNPRSSUU superhumanise
AEEHIMNPRSUUZ superhumanize
AEEHIMNQSSSSU squeamishness
AEEHIMOPPRRTY hypermetropia
AEEHINNOPRTTX xanthopterine
AEEHINNRSTWYY Henry Steinway
AEEHINOPSSTTY enhypostatise
AEEHINOPSTTYZ enhypostatize
AEEHINORRSSUU Henri Rousseau
AEEHINORSSSTV overhastiness
AEEHINORSSSTW seaworthiness
AEEHIPRRRSSTU treasurership
AEEHKLNNSSSST thanklessness
AEEHLLMNNORST shell ornament
AEEHLLORTTTVV throttle valve
AEEHLMNOOSSST loathsomeness
AEEHLMORRSTWY whoremasterly
AEEHLNNOOPPSU open-plan house
AEEHLNNRRSTTW Walther Nernst
AEEHLNORRSTTY north-easterly
AEEHLNOSSTUWW New South Wales
AEEHLORRSTTYY Roy Hattersley
AEEHLORSSTTUY south-easterly
AEEHLPPRSSTTU the Last Supper✧
AEEHMMOOPRSST metamorphoses✧
AEEHMMOPSSTUY emphysematous
AEEHMNOOPPRTU pneumatophore
AEEHMNOORRRSY rhyme or reason
AEEHMOOPPRRST spermatophore
AEEHMOPPRSTTY spermatophyte
AEEHNOPPRSSST Stanhope press
AEEHOOQRRSSTU square shooter
AEEHOPPRRTTYY pyretotherapy
AEEHOPRRSTTVY the party's over
AEEHPPRRSSTUV harvest supper
AEEIIILMNPRRS preliminaries
AEEIIIMNSSTTV imitativeness
AEEIIJMNNRSTW winter jasmine
AEEIIKLLOPRRT realpolitiker
AEEIILLLMMPTW William Temple
AEEIILLLMNNPR premillennial
AEEIILLNNPPSU uilleann pipes
AEEIILLNNPTTY penitentially
AEEIILLNOPSTT pelletisation
AEEIILLNOPTTZ pelletization
AEEIILLNOSSST essential oils
AEEIILLNSTTXY existentially
AEEIILMNOPRSS impersonalise
AEEIILMNOPRSZ impersonalize
AEEIILMNRSTUV universal time
AEEIILMNRTTVY terminatively
AEEIILMOPRSTT temporalities
AEEIILNNNOTTT attention line
AEEIILNNORRTT interrelation
AEEIILNNOSSTV inviolateness
AEEIILNNPSSTV plaintiveness
AEEIILNNTTTVY inattentively
AEEIILNOPQTTU equipotential
AEEIILNOPRRTT interpetiolar
AEEIILNOPRTTV interpolative
AEEIILNOPSTVY pay television
AEEIILNORSTTV revelationist
AEEIILNORSTVY televisionary
AEEIILNPRRSTT interpilaster
AEEIILNPRSTTY presentiality
AEEIILNQSTTUY sequentiality
AEEIILNRRSTTV silver nitrate
AEEIILORRRTTX exterritorial
AEEIILPPRRSTU spiritual peer
AEEIIMMNORSST mesmerisation
AEEIIMMNORSTZ mesmerization
AEEIIMNNOPRTT impenetration
AEEIIMNNORTTX extermination
AEEIIMNPSSSSV impassiveness
AEEIIMNQRSSTU equestrianism
AEEIIMNRRRSST Sir Martin Rees
AEEIINNOORRTT reorientation
AEEIINNOQRSTU questionnaire
AEEIINOOPRRTT Pietro Aretino
AEEIINOPRRTTY repetitionary
AEEIIOPRRRSTY prairie oyster
AEEIJLMNNOTUW Jewel Mountain
AEEIKLLLMNOPR palm-kernel oil
AEEIKLNPRRSTW water-sprinkle
AEEIKLNPRTTTU perttaunt like
AEEIKNOPRSSTT streptokinase
AEEILLLNOPPPP Pineapple Poll
AEEILLLNOPTTW potential well
AEEILLMNNSTTY sentimentally
AEEILLMNORSST salmon leister
AEEILLMNPRSTY sempiternally
AEEILLMRSSTTT little masters
AEEILLNNOPTXY exponentially
AEEILLNNOSTXY extensionally
AEEILLNOPRRTT interpellator
AEEILLNORRSVY reversionally
AEEILLNOSTTTW satellite town
AEEILLNRRSTTY interstellary
AEEILLOPRRTTU Paul Tortelier
AEEILLPRSTUVY superlatively
AEEILLQRTTTUY letter quality
letter-quality
AEEILLRRRSTTY terrestrially
AEEILLRTTTTTT tittle-tattler
AEEILMMNNPRTY impermanently
AEEILMMNRSSTU semimenstrual
AEEILMNNNNPRY ninepenny marl
AEEILMNNNORTV environmental
AEEILMNNNSTTU unsentimental
AEEILMNOOORTV over-emotional
AEEILMOPRRTXY extemporarily
AEEILMOPRSTTV splatter movie
AEEILMORRSTUY temerariously
AEEILMORRTTVX Oliver Martext
AEEILNNNOOPPS Peloponnesian
AEEILNNNOPRST anti-personnel
AEEILNNOOORSS lie on one's oars
AEEILNNOPRRST interpersonal

 Words marked ✧ can also be spelled with one or more capital letters

AEEILNNOPRSTT septentrional
AEEILNNOQRUVX vernal equinox
AEEILNNPRRSTT silent partner
AEEILNNQQTUUV quinquevalent
AEEILNNRSSSUV universalness
AEEILNNSSSSST stainlessness
AEEILNOOPRTTT teleportation
AEEILNOPPRSYZ play one's prize
AEEILNOPPSSTU Palestine soup
AEEILNPSSSSUX Sussex spaniel
AEEILNRRRSTTU unterrestrial
AEEILNRRSTVVY livery-servant
AEEILOPRSSTUY erysipelatous
AEEILOPSTTUVX expostulative
AEEILORRSTTVY restoratively
AEEIMMNNORSST momentariness
AEEIMMNPRRTTU marine trumpet
trumpet marine
AEEIMNNOPPRTT reappointment
AEEIMNNORSSTV normativeness
AEEIMNOPRRSST temporariness
AEEIMNORRSTTV remonstrative
AEEIMNORRTTXY exterminatory
AEEINNNOOPRUU European Union
AEEINNNRSSSTT transientness
AEEINOOPRRTTX re-exportation
AEEINOOPSSSST possessionate
AEEINOORRSTUV arteriovenous
AEEINOPRRSSTT state prisoner
AEEINOPRRSSTY arsenopyrites
AEEINOPRSSTTT Protestantise
AEEINOPRSTTTZ Protestantize
AEEINOQRSSTTU sequestration
AEEINOSSSTUVX vexatiousness
AEEINPRSTTTTY paternity test
AEEIOOPPRSTTV post-operative
AEEIOORRSTTTW water tortoise
AEEIPPRRSSSTT asset-stripper
AEEJLLORRSTVY traveller's joy
AEEJLMNOPRSUY Jerusalem pony
AEEKLLMMSSUUY Samuel Slumkey
AEEKLMNOPSSTU take one's lumps
AEEKLNNORRTUW neural network
AEEKNRRSSSTUY nursery stakes
AEELLMOORRTTW martello tower
AEELLMOQRRSUY quarrelsomely
AEELMNPPRSTUY supplementary
AEELNOOORRRST sooner or later
AEELNOPPRRSWY plenary powers
AEELNOPPRRTUV apple turnover
AEELNOPRSTTTT talent spotter
AEELNRSSTTUVY Yves St Laurent
AEEMNPRRRSUUY supernumerary
AEEMNPRRSTTUW trumpeter swan
AEEMOPRRSSTTU posture-master
AEENNOPQRRSTU torque spanner
AEFFGHIKNNORT thank-offering
AEFFGHILOORST go off the rails
AEFFGIILLRUYZ Uffizi Gallery
AEFFGIMRSSTTU suffragettism
AEFFHHSSTTTTU that's the stuff!
AEFFHIILNRTTV fifth interval
AEFFIIKNNSTTU take it in snuff
AEFFIILLOQTUY quality of life
AEFFLNOORRSWW fowls of warren
AEFGGIIKNRSTU figure skating
AEFGGIINNRRSU sugar-refining
AEFGGMMORSTUU Fogg Art Museum
AEFGHILNORTTU light of nature
AEFGHINNNPRTY penny-farthing
AEFGHINNRRSTU nursing-father
AEFGHOOOTTUWY go out of the way
AEFGIIILNTTTT tattie-lifting
AEFGIILMNQRTU quilting-frame
AEFGIILNNSTVV snifting-valve
AEFGIINNORTUV non-figurative
AEFGIINOPRRTU prefiguration
AEFGILLNNNOTU outing flannel
AEFGILLNNRTUY unfalteringly
AEFGILNOORTTV floating voter
AEFGILNOPPRSV self-approving
AEFGILNORRSUU granuliferous
AEFGINOOPRRTW waterproofing
AEFGKLMNOORTV Graf von Moltke
AEFGMNNOORTTY Margot Fonteyn
AEFHHLLLNTUUY unhealthfully
AEFHILMNORSSY salmon fishery
AEFHILOPRTTXY trial of the pyx
AEFHIMNNOOSTT Timon of Athens
AEFHINNORSSUY ray of sunshine
AEFHLNNOOOSST Solon of Athens
AEFHNOOSSSSTT soothfastness
AEFHOORRSTTTY The Story of Art
AEFIIIILMNNST infinitesimal
AEFIIILNORSTT fertilisation
AEFIIILNORTTZ fertilization
AEFIIKNOPRRST pinafore skirt
AEFIILLLMOTTX foxtail millet
AEFIILLLNNOXY inflexionally
AEFIILLLNNTUY influentially
AEFIILLMMNTTU multifilament
AEFIILLMORTWY William of Tyre
AEFIILLNNNTUU uninfluential
AEFIILLOPPRSU papilliferous
AEFIILLPRSTTU fruit pastille
AEFIILMNNOOTT fail to mention
AEFIILMNORSUU aluminiferous
AEFIILMNORTVY informatively
AEFIILNOOPRRT proliferation
AEFIILNOPRSTU platiniferous
AEFIIMNNORTUV uninformative
AEFIIMNOOPRRT imperforation
AEFIIMNORSSTU staminiferous
AEFIINNORTTUV Trevi Fountain
AEFIINRRSTTTY interstratify
AEFIKNNOPRSWY Erwin Panofsky
AEFIKOPRRRTWY firework party
AEFILMNOPRSTT self-important
AEFILMOPPRRSV slipform paver
AEFILNOOPRSSW passion flower
AEFILNOOQSTUW question of law
AEFILNRSSTUVY transfusively

AEFIMNORRSTUU frumentarious
AEFINOOPRRRSW prisoner of war
AEFIOQRRSTUUZ quartziferous
AEFLLOORRSSST salts of sorrel
AEFLNNORTTUUY unfortunately
AEFLNPRSSTUVY Venus's flytrap
AEFMNOORSTTUU run out of steam
AEGGHHIKLLSTU Hugh Gaitskell
AEGGHHLOPPRRY glyphographer
AEGGHIILNRRTT right triangle
AEGGHIINNPPST shipping agent
AEGGHILNNOSTU tongue-lashing
AEGGHILNOORTW wool-gathering
AEGGHINNOORST shooting range
AEGGHLNNOOTTY go to any length
AEGGHLOOPRRSS glossographer
AEGGIIILNOPRY Ilya Prigogine
AEGGIIIMNNPRT image printing
AEGGIIIMNPSTT spitting image
AEGGIILLNPRTZ triple glazing
AEGGIILNNRRST Stirling Range
AEGGIIMNNRSST singing master
AEGGIINORRTTU regurgitation
AEGGIINRSTTTT sitting target
AEGGIKLNNOPRT plonking great
AEGGILLMNRRUY Gerry Mulligan
AEGGILLNRRTUV travelling rug
AEGGIMMNORSTY gyromagnetism
AEGGIMNOOOSTU geitonogamous
AEGGINNNOORSS non-aggression
AEGGINNNORTYZ Tenzing Norgay
AEGGINNORRSSS gross earnings
AEGHHIKMMNSTU make things hum
AEGHHILMNORST light horseman
AEGHHILMNOSTU lighthouseman
AEGHHINPPRRYY hyperphrygian
AEGHHIOPPRRSY physiographer
AEGHHKLOSSTTW the ghost walks
AEGHHKOQRSTUU squeak through
AEGHHMOOPPRRR morphographer
AEGHIIINNRSTV The Virginians
AEGHIIKLLOTTU out like a light
AEGHIIKNNPRSS pinking shears
AEGHIIKNOTTTW tattie-howking
AEGHIILNOOPRT gerontophilia
AEGHIILNORSTY oral hygienist
AEGHIILNRTTTT tilt at the ring
AEGHIINNSTTUX extinguishant
AEGHIINRRRSTT heart-stirring
AEGHIIPRRRSST registrarship
AEGHIJNNNOSUZ Jan Ingen-Housz
AEGHIKLNORSST stalking-horse
AEGHIKNNRRSTT knights errant
AEGHILLOOORTY aerolithology
AEGHILNOOPSTT pantheologist
AEGHILNORSTUV vaulting-horse
AEGHILNOSTUUV vaulting-house
AEGHILOOPRSST phraseologist
AEGHIMNOOPSTT entomophagist
AEGHIMNORTTUW mouthwatering
AEGHIMNPRSTTU presuming that
AEGHINNNOPTTT nothing patent
AEGHINNOORSST on a shoestring
AEGHINNPRRSSU pruning shears
AEGHINOORRTTY Grotian theory
AEGHINOPRSSTT stenographist
AEGHINORSTTTU straighten out
AEGHIOPRRSSTU surrogateship
AEGHLLMOOORTY moral theology
AEGHLMMNOOOOU homologoumena
AEGHLMMOORTTY thremmatology
AEGHLNNOORSTX Texas longhorn
AEGHLOPPRRTYY pterylography
AEGHMNOOOPSTU entomophagous
AEGHOOOPRSSTU ostreophagous
AEGIIIKLLMNPS Spike Milligan
AEGIIIKLNNNST in-line skating
AEGIIILLMNRTT time-trialling
AEGIIILNORRST solitaire ring
AEGIIIMMNNNNO moaning minnie
AEGIIIMNORSTT emigrationist
AEGIIINNOSTTV investigation
tenovaginitis
AEGIIINNRSSUU iure sanguinis
AEGIIIPRRSSTT perigastritis
AEGIIJLMNRSST James Stirling
AEGIIJLNNNOPT jointing plane
AEGIIKLNNPRSW sparkling wine
AEGIILLLLNRTY Lillie Langtry
AEGIILLMMNSST slamming stile
AEGIILLMORRSW Roger Williams
AEGIILLNOPRSS spoiler signal
AEGIILLOPRSSS aspergillosis
AEGIILMNNPRRS mineral spring
AEGIILMNORSYY syringomyelia
AEGIILMOOSSST semasiologist
AEGIILNNPPRRU purple-in-grain
AEGIILNNPPRTT plate-printing
AEGIILNOOPRRT progenitorial
AEGIILNOSSTUU ustilagineous
AEGIILNRRTTVW travel writing
AEGIIMNOPRRTY primogenitary
AEGIIMNRRSTTW writing-master
AEGIINNNORSST Raining Stones
AEGIINNNSTTTT sitting tenant
AEGIINNOORRTT interrogation
AEGIINNORRTUY genito-urinary
AEGIINNPPPRRT printing paper
AEGIINOOPRSTV positive organ
AEGIINOORSTTT giant tortoise
AEGIINORSTTVY investigatory
AEGIJLNRRRSWY Jerry Rawlings
AEGIKLLNORRST roller-skating
AEGIKMNORRRTW migrant worker
AEGIKNRRSTUUV River Tunguska
AEGILLLMNSSST smelling salts
AEGILLNOOPSTT planetologist
AEGILLNOSSSTT on its last legs
AEGILLNPRSSTY glyptal resins
AEGILMNNORRST Neil Armstrong
AEGILMNOPRRRS sampling error
AEGILMNOSTUWZ waltzing mouse

AEGILNNNORSUY	unreasoningly
AEGILNNORSTTU	transit lounge
AEGILNOOPRRSS	progressional
AEGILNOPPPRTT	plotting-paper
AEGILNORRTTTW	otter-trawling
AEGILOPRRSTUW	Walter Gropius
AEGILPRSTTUYZ	glaziers' putty
AEGIMMMNOPPRY	memory mapping
AEGIMMNORRSUW	measuring-worm
AEGIMNNOPRRRY	morning prayer
AEGIMNOOOPRRT	operating room
AEGIMNOOPRSSU	angiospermous
AEGIMNOPRRSSU	superorganism
AEGIMOOOPPRST	apogeotropism
AEGINNNPRSSSU	unsparingness
AEGINNORRSSST	transgression
AEGINNPRSSSTU	untrespassing
AEGINOORRRTTY	interrogatory
AEGINQRRSTTTU	string quartet
AEGLMNNOORTYY	Antony Gormley
AEGLMOOSSTTYY	systematology
AEGLNORRSSSUU	garrulousness
AEGLNRSSSSTUY	Ulysses S Grant
AEGMOOPPRRRRT	report program
AEHHHINOPRRRY	herniorrhaphy
AEHHIIILMNSST	helminthiasis
AEHHIIKPRSTTW	whitetip shark
AEHHIILORSTTV	health visitor
AEHHIINNOPSTY	hyphenisation
AEHHIINNOPTYZ	hyphenization
AEHHIINOPPSTW	whip into shape
AEHHILLMNPTTY	platyhelminth
AEHHILLNOPTTY	anthophyllite
AEHHILMMOOORT	homoiothermal
AEHHILOOPPPSS	phospholipase
AEHHIMNOPRSTT	theanthropism
AEHHIMOOOPSTT	homoeopathist
AEHHIMOORRRSW	horsehair worm
AEHHINOPRSTTT	theanthropist
AEHHINORRRSTY	North Ayrshire
AEHHIOPPRSTYY	physiotherapy
AEHHIORRSSTUY	South Ayrshire
AEHHLLOPSTTUW	push to the wall
AEHHLOOPPRSSY	phosphorylase
AEHHLOOPPRSTY	phosphorylate
AEHHNOOPPRTTY	anthropophyte
AEHHNORSSTTUY	hysteranthous
AEHHOOPPPRSTY	pyrophosphate
AEHIIIKNPSSTT	kinesipathist
AEHIIILMNOSSS	leishmaniosis
AEHIIIMNTTTUW	titanium white
AEHIIJMNORTTY	in the majority
AEHIIKLLNOSUV	Sihanoukville
AEHIIKLNNPRST	skirl-in-the-pan
AEHIILLMOPPRW	Philip Marlowe
AEHIILNRSTTVX	sixth interval
AEHIIMMPRSTUU	Mauritius hemp
AEHIIMNORTTTU	Titanotherium
AEHIIMNRSSTTU	Austin hermits
AEHIINNOOPSTT	phonetisation
AEHIINNOOPTTZ	phonetization
AEHIINORRSSTW	airworthiness
AEHILLMNNNORS	Shannon Miller
AEHILLMNNNSWY	Manny Shinwell
AEHILLMNNOOPT	Lionel Hampton
AEHILLOPPSSTY	Psilophytales
AEHILMMOOSSUX	homosexualism
AEHILMOOSSTUX	homosexualist
AEHILMOOSTUXY	homosexuality
AEHILMOPPRSTY	amphiprostyle
AEHILNNOOORST	Horatio Nelson
AEHIMMNOPRTUY	immunotherapy
AEHIMMOOPRSST	metamorphosis✧
AEHIMMOORRSST	Sir Thomas More
AEHIMNNOOPRTY	enantiomorphy
AEHIMNNPRSSTT	transshipment
AEHIMNPRSTUUY	superhumanity
AEHINNORRSSTY	Sir Antony Sher
AEHINOPPRSTUU	put up one's hair
AEHINOPRRSTUW	nature-worship
AEHINOPRSSSUV	vapourishness
AEHJLMNNOOSSU	Samuel Johnson
AEHJMOOPPRRST	major prophets
AEHLLNNOOPTWY	Anthony Powell
AEHLLNOPRSUUY	sulphonylurea
AEHLMNNOOPRST	plant hormones
AEHLMNOOPRTVW	Wolverhampton
AEHLNOORSSTTW	worth one's salt
AEHLOQRRRTUUY	quarter-hourly
AEHMMNORSTTUZ	Thomas Müntzer
AEHMNNOOORTTT	tooth-ornament
AEHMNOOPRRTTY	anthropometry
AEHMNOOPRSSSU	amorphousness
AEHMNOOPRTTWY	Oh, Pretty Woman
AEHMNOQRTTUUY	quantum theory
AEHMOOQRSUUUU	aqueous humour
AEIIILLLMNNST	millennialist
AEIIILLMMNNNS	millennianism
AEIIILLMMNNRS	millenniarism
AEIIILLMNNNOO	one in a million
AEIIILLMNORSS	millionairess
AEIIILLMNPRRY	preliminarily
AEIIILLMNRSTY	ministerially
AEIIILLMRRSTT	triliteralism
AEIIILLMRRSVY	verisimilarly
AEIIILMNNRSTU	unministerial
AEIIILNNOSTTU	luteinisation
AEIIILNNOTTUZ	luteinization
AEIIILNORSSTT	sterilisation
AEIIILNORSTTZ	sterilization
AEIIILPRRSSTU	spiritualiser
AEIIILPRRSTUZ	spiritualizer
AEIIIMMNNORST	Simone Martini
AEIIIMNOOPSTT	epitomisation
AEIIIMNOOPTTZ	epitomization
AEIIIMNOORSST	isomerisation
AEIIIMNOORSTZ	isomerization
AEIIINNNOSTTU	insinuate into
AEIIINNORSSSV	visionariness
AEIIINNORSTTW	winterisation
AEIIINNORSTVV	in vino veritas
AEIIINNORTTWZ	winterization

AEIIINNOSSSTT	sensitisation
AEIIINNOSSTTZ	sensitization
AEIIINPPRRRTU	prairie turnip
AEIIJLMNNORTU	journal intime
AEIIJLNSSUUVV	Juan Luis Vivés
AEIIKNPRRSTTU	turnpike stair
AEIILLLMMNSWY	Emlyn Williams
AEIILLMMNOPSW	William Empson
AEIILLMNSSUVW	Venus Williams
AEIILLNNNOSTY	intensionally
AEIILLNNNOTTY	intentionally
AEIILLNNORTVY	inventorially
AEIILLNOQRTUV	ventriloquial
AEIILLNQRRSTU	tranquilliser
AEIILLNQRRTUZ	tranquillizer
AEIILLNRSSTTU	Little Russian
AEIILLORRRTTY	territorially
AEIILLPRTTUYY	utility player
AEIILMMNOSSSS	missa solemnis✧
AEIILMNNOOSST	solemnisation
AEIILMNNOOSTZ	solemnization
AEIILMNNOPSTU	emulsion paint
AEIILMNNORRTV	minor interval
AEIILMNOORSTT	tolerationism
AEIILMNOPRRTX	interproximal
AEIILMNOPRSTY	impersonality
AEIILMNORSSST	trim one's sails
AEIILMNPRTTYY	amitryptyline
AEIILMNRRRSTY	Sir Martin Ryle
AEIILMNRSSTTV	St Martin's evil
AEIILNNNNOPRT	lantern pinion
AEIILNNNNOTTU	unintentional
AEIILNNNORTTU	interlunation
AEIILNNNSSSTU	unsaintliness
AEIILNNOOPRTT	interpolation
AEIILNNPRSTUY	peninsularity
AEIILNNQQTUUV	quinquivalent
AEIILNOOPPRST	prepositional
AEIILNOOPSTTX	sexploitation
AEIILNOORSTTT	tolerationist
AEIILNOPPSTTU	Pontius Pilate
AEIILNOPRSTUV	pulverisation
AEIILNOPRTUVZ	pulverization
AEIILNORRTTTY	torrentiality
AEIILNPRSSSTU	spiritualness
AEIILOOPPRRRT	proprietorial
AEIIMNNOOPRST	impersonation
AEIIMNNOPRTTT	partitionment
AEIIMNOOPRRTT	reimportation
AEIIMNOOPRSTT	temporisation
AEIIMNOOPRTTZ	temporization
AEIIMNOPRSSSU	mispersuasion
AEIIMNOSSSTTY	systemisation
AEIIMNOSSTTYZ	systemization
AEIIMNPRRRTTX	matrix printer
AEIIMOOPRSSUV	semioviparous
AEIINNNOORSTT	Tironian notes
AEIINNOOPPSTT	peptonisation
AEIINNOOPPTTZ	peptonization
AEIINNOOSTTTU	Teutonisation
AEIINNOOTTTUZ	Teutonization
AEIINNOPRSTTW	port-wine stain
AEIINNOQRSTTU	quaternionist
AEIINOOPPPRST	position paper
AEIINOOPPRRTX	expropriation
AEIINOOPRSSTT	posterisation
AEIINOOPRSTTX	extraposition
AEIINOOPRSTTZ	posterization
AEIINOORRRSTT	terrorisation
AEIINOORRRTTZ	terrorization
AEIINOPRSSTTV	transpositive
AEIINORRRSTTT	antiterrorist
AEIINORRSSSTT	transistorise
AEIINORRSSTTZ	transistorize
AEIINPRSTTTUY	paternity suit
AEIIPPRRSSSTU	spiritus asper
AEIKKLMNNORUW	unworkmanlike
AEIKLLNNPRRSW	lawn-sprinkler
AEIKLLNOOSTTT	take its toll on
AEIKLMNOPRSST	sportsmanlike
AEIKLOPPPRRRS	Sir Karl Popper
AEILLLMNOOSSS	salmonellosis
AEILLLNOOTUVY	evolutionally
AEILLMMMNOOST	monometallism
AEILLMMNOOSTT	monometallist
AEILLMNNOOTUY	unemotionally
AEILLNNOSSSUV	villanousness
AEILLNOPRTTWW	willow pattern
AEILLOOPRRRTY	reportorially
AEILMMMNNNRTU	Immelmann turn
AEILMMNNOORRY	Marilyn Monroe
AEILMMNNORSTU	neutral monism
AEILMMNNOTTUY	monumentality
AEILMMORRTUVY	virtual memory
AEILMNNNOSSUW	unwomanliness
AEILMNOOTTUVW	vowel mutation
AEILMNOPRTTUY	importunately
AEILMNOPSSTUY	pneumatolysis
AEILMNPRRSSUU	Sir Paul M Nurse
AEILNNNPRRTTU	turnip lantern
AEILNNOOPSSTX	expansion slot
AEILNNORSSTUV	voluntariness
AEILNNORSTUVY	intravenously
AEILNOOPRSTTT	petrol station
	tortoise plant
AEILNOOPSTTUX	expostulation
AEILNOORRTUVY	revolutionary
AEILNOORSUVXY	over-anxiously
AEILNOPRRSTTU	perlustration
AEILNPPRRSTTY	splinter party
AEILOOOOPPPRS	prosopopoeial
AEILOOQRSTUUZ	Louis-Quatorze
AEIMMNOPPRTUU	put a premium on
AEIMMNQRTTUUU	quantum meruit
AEIMMNRSSSUUU	Russian Museum
AEIMNNOOPPRTT	apportionment
AEIMNNOORRSTT	ariston metron
	remonstration
AEIMNNQSSSTUY	Quentin Massys
AEIMNOOOOPSST	onomatopoesis
AEIMNOPRSSTTT	Protestantism
AEIMORSSSSTTT	toastmistress

AEIMPRRRSSSTY	primary stress
AEINNORSSSUUV	unsavouriness
AEINOOOPPRRTT	proportionate
AEINOOPPRSSTU	opus operantis
AEINOOPRSSSSY	possessionary
AEINPPRSTTTUY	painters' putty
AEINRRSSSTTTU	rust-resistant
AEJKKLMNOOPSX	James Knox Polk
AEJLNOOPPRRRU	journal proper
AEKKKLLNNRUUX	Ku Klux Klanner
AELLMNOPRRSUY	supernormally
AELMNNORRSTTY	remonstrantly
AELMNOORRTTUY	Mary Lou Retton
AELMNOPRSSTTU	postmenstrual
AELNNOOPSSTUY	spontaneously
AELNOOOPPSSST	apostle spoons
AELOOPPRRSSTU	porous plaster
AELOOPRSTTUXY	expostulatory
AELPRRRRSSUYY	slurry sprayer
AEMMNNORSTUUV	verumontanums
AEMMNOOORSTTU	monotrematous
AEMNNNOOSSSUY	anonymousness
AEMNOOOPRSSZZ	mezzo-sopranos
AEMNOOORSSSTY	somatosensory
AEMNOORRRSTTY	remonstratory
AENOOOPPRRTXY	proparoxytone
AENOPRRSSSTUU	rapturousness
AFFGIIMNOSTUU	suffumigation
AFFGIINOPRTUY	affinity group
AFFMOOOOPRRRU	armour of proof
AFGGGINNOOORS	going for a song
AFGGHHIIRSTTT	straight fight
AFGGHIILLNOTT	floating light
AFGHHILRSSTTU	straight flush
AFGHHIORRSTTT	straightforth
AFGHIILMNNOSS	salmon-fishing
AFGHIILNNRTTY	light infantry
AFGHIINOPRRST	profit-sharing
AFGIIILNNRTUY	infuriatingly
AFGIIILNOORVW	Virginia Woolf
AFGIIKLNNNPPT	flint-knapping
AFGIINNOORTTU	out of training
AFGILNRRSTTUY	frustratingly
AFGNOOOPRTTUW	put a foot wrong
AFHHIIMOSSTUV	moshav shitufi
AFHMNOPSSTUYY	Faust Symphony
AFIIIILLNNTVY	infinitivally
AFIIILNOOSSST	fossilisation
AFIIILNOOSSTZ	fossilization
AFIIINNNOOTTX	infix notation
AFIIINNOOPRST	infraposition
AFIILLOORSTTV	salt of vitriol
AFIILLORSTTUY	flirtatiously
AFIILMNOORSUY	omnifariously
AFIILOPRSSSTT	spirits of salt
AFIILOPRSSSUY	fissiparously
AFIKLMNOOTWWZ	Wolf Mankowitz
AFJMNOORRSTUY	jury of matrons
AFKLNOORTTTUU	talk out of turn
AGGHHIIPRSTTT	straight-pight
AGGHHMOPPRSYY	sphygmography
AGGHIILLNNSUY	languishingly
AGGHIKLNOOPPR	grappling-hook
AGGHILNOOPSST	sphagnologist
AGGIIILNNOSTU	isoagglutinin
AGGIIILNNSTTY	instigatingly
AGGIIINNORTTU	ingurgitation
AGGIIKLMORRSS	kissogram girl
AGGIILLNOPRVY	payroll giving
AGGIILNNOPPRR	grappling-iron
AGGIILNQSSUZZ	quizzing-glass
AGGILLNOORSTY	laryngologist
AGGILOOORSSTT	agrostologist
AGGINPSSTUUUU	Augustus Pugin
AGHHIILLMNRST	thrashing-mill
AGHHIILMNRSTY	nightmarishly
AGHHIIMNNOSTU	mountains-high
AGHHIINPRSTTU	run a tight ship
AGHHIMNOORSTT	orthognathism
AGHHINOOPPRST	phonographist
AGHHINOOPRSST	sharpshooting
AGHHIOOPPRSTT	photographist
AGHHIOOPPRSTY	opisthography
AGHHIOOPRRSTT	orthographist
AGHHLLMOOOPTY	ophthalmology
AGHHLLOOPPSUY	phyllophagous
AGHHLMNNOOOPT	monophthongal
AGHHNOOORSTTU	orthognathous
AGHIIILNPRSTT	hair-splitting
AGHIIKOORSUUZ	Kazuo Ishiguro
AGHIILNNOSSTY	astonishingly
AGHIILNNSSTWW	whistling swan
AGHIINNPPRSST	transshipping
AGHIKLMNOOSTT	smooth-talking
AGHILNOOORTTY	orthogonality
AGHIMSSSTTUUU	tsutsugamushi
AGHINNOOPSTTT	stop at nothing
AGHINOOPSTTTT	Photostatting
AGHLLMOORSUUW	gallows humour
AGHOOOPPPRRSY	prosopography
AGIIILLLNTTTY	titillatingly
AGIIILLMNRSTU	trilingualism
AGIIILLNNRSST	straining sill
AGIIILNNNOOPT	no oil painting
AGIIILNNNSTUY	insinuatingly
AGIIILNNORTUY	unoriginality
AGIIIMNNOOPRT	impignoration
AGIIINPPPRRST	spirit-rapping
AGIILLNNOPRTY	rallying-point
AGIILLNOOSSTY	syllogisation
AGIILLNOOSTYZ	syllogization
AGIILMOOPPRST	plagiotropism
AGIILMOOPRSTT	primatologist
AGIILNNOPRSTY	patronisingly
AGIILNNOPRTYZ	patronizingly
AGIILNPQRTTUY	quilting party
AGIILOORSSSTY	Assyriologist
AGIIMNOORRSUV	graminivorous
AGIINNOOOPPRT	oppignoration
AGIINNOPRSTTT	starting point
	trainspotting✧
AGIINNOPRSTTY	star-ypointing

AGIINNOPRTTTY potty-training
AGILLPRSSUUUV lupus vulgaris
AGILMMNOOSTUY numismatology
AGILMOOOPSSTU plagiostomous
AGILMOORRSTTY martyrologist
AGILNNOPPRUVY unapprovingly
AGILOOOPPRSTU plagiotropous
AGIMNOOOPRSUZ zoosporangium
AGLLOOOSTTUUY tautologously
AGOOPRSSTTTUU put out to grass
AHHIILMMNOSTT Hamilton Smith
AHHIKLNORTTWY thankworthily
AHHILLMPPSTUY spathiphyllum
AHHIMOOPSSTTW Thomas Sopwith
AHHLLOPPRSYYY hypsophyllary
AHHMNOOOPPRRT anthropomorph
AHHMNOOOPPRTY Pythonomorpha
AHHNOOOPPRSTY anthroposophy
AHIIILNOOPRRT horripilation
AHIIILNOPSSTY syphilisation
AHIIILNOPSTTY inhospitality
AHIIILNOPSTYZ syphilization
AHIIINPRRSSTV spirit varnish
AHIIJMNNNOOSS Johnsonianism
AHIIKLLMOSSUV Mikhail Suslov
AHIILNOOPRSTY polyhistorian
AHIILNOORTTYZ horizontality
AHIILNOPPRSTX xiphiplastron
AHIIMNOPRSSTT misanthropist
AHIINNOOPSTTY hypnotisation
AHIINNOOPTTYZ hypnotization
AHIJNNOPRSTUZ Zinjanthropus
AHILLNOOPSSUY anisophyllous
AHILLNPPRSTUU push-pull train
AHILMMOOPPSSU psammophilous
AHILOPRSSTTTU hospital trust
trust hospital
AHIMNOOOPRSTT somatotrophin
AHIMNOPPRSSST sportsmanship
AHINOPPRRSSTT transport ship
AHKLNNOOPPTTY phytoplankton
AHKNNNOOPSSSY on Shanks's pony
AHLLMOPRTUUWY pull a wry mouth
AHMOOOPRRSTUU tauromorphous
AHNNNOSSTTTUY St Anthony's nut
AHOOOPPPRSSTT passport photo
AHOORRSSTTTUY that's your sort
AIIIILNNOQSTU inquisitional
AIIIILNOQRSTU inquisitorial
AIIIIMNOPSSSS pianississimo
AIIIIMNPPSSSS Mississippian
AIIILLMMORRSW William Morris
AIIILLMNNOSTU illuminations
AIIILLMNPSTUY pusillanimity
AIIILMMNOORST similar motion
AIIILMNOPRSTY postliminiary
AIIILNNOSTTTU institutional
AIIIMMNNOORSS Morisonianism
AIIIMMNNOSSST Saint-Simonism
AIIIMNNOSSSTT Saint-Simonist
AIIIMNOOPPRRT impropriation
AIIIMNOOPRSTV improvisation
AIIIMOPRRSTVX improvisatrix
AIIINNNOOSTTV innovationist
AIIINNOORSTTU routinisation
AIIINNOORTTUZ routinization
AIIINOOOPRSTT position ratio
AIIIOOPRTVVVY ovoviviparity
AIIJNOOPSTTUX juxtaposition
AIILLLNOSSUUV Louis Sullivan
AIILLMMNOOPSY polynomialism
AIILLMNOORSWY Roy Williamson
AIILLMNOPSSUU pusillanimous
AIILLMOPRTTUY multipolarity
AIILLNNORTUVY involuntarily
AIILLNOOPRSVY provisionally
AIILLNPRSTUUY unspiritually
AIILMMPRSTTUY multipartyism
AIILMNNOPSTUU luminous paint
AIILNOOOPPRST propositional
AIILNOOPPSSTU suppositional
AIIMMNOOPSTTU impostumation
AIIMNNOOPRSSU Surinam poison
AIIMNNOOPTTTU point mutation
AIIMNOPSSSTTU Assumptionist
AIIMOOPRRSTVY improvisatory
AIINNNOPSSTUU Antoninus Pius
AIINNOOPRSSTT transposition
AIINOOOPRSSST Poisson's ratio
AIINOPPPQRTUY appropinquity
AIIOOOPRSUVVV ovoviviparous
AILLLMNOOOPPW lollipop woman
AILLMOSSSVVYY Vasily Smyslov
AILMMNOPRTUUV multum in parvo
AILMOOOPSSSTX toxoplasmosis
AILNNOSSTTUUU It's Not Unusual
AILORRSTTUUUV ultra-virtuous

B

BBBCEEEEHILRS Breeches Bible
BBBEEEKLRSUYY Busby Berkeley
BBCCEEJJOSTTU subject-object
BBCCEHLNOPRSU cobbler's punch
BBCCEILNOORRU Robber Council
BBCDEEIILORTY liberty bodice
BBCDGIIKLLNOU building block
BBCEEHKOSSTYZ Sketches By Boz
BBCEEHLORRRSY sherry-cobbler
BBCEEHLORRTTT Bertolt Brecht
BBCEEIORRSSUV oversubscribe
BBCEEIRRSSSTU subscriber set
BBCEHMOORRSTU butcher's broom
BBCEIILMNOSTU incombustible
BBCEIIRSTTTUU butter-biscuit
BBCELNOORSUUY bob's your uncle
BBCGGHIILNNTU nightclubbing
BBCIILMNOSTUY incombustibly
BBDDEEGIILRRU bridge-builder
BBDDEELLOOORT blood-boltered
BBDEEGHHRRTUU Hubert de Burgh
BBDEEGIORRRST Robert Bridges
BBDEEIKLLOOSU double obelisk

BBDEGIILNNOPU Bible-pounding
BBDEHLOOORRST Blood Brothers
BBDIIILNOOSVY division lobby
BBEEEEEEHIIJS heebie-jeebies
BBEEEEILLRSTT blister beetle
BBEEEGILNRTUY burying beetle
BBEEEHILLTTTU bite the bullet
BBEEGGILNORSU robin's-egg blue
BBEEHILLLRRUY Blueberry Hill
BBEEHILNOSTUY the boys in blue
BBEEHIMNOSTTU bite one's thumb
BBEEIIKNNOOPS poke one's bib in
BBEEILLMNNRRU Brinell number
BBEEILMNOORTU Umberto Nobile
BBEFHLRSTTUUY butterfly bush
BBEFKMNOOORSU Book of Numbers
BBEGGIMNNORUY money-grubbing
BBEGHIILMNPTU Bible-thumping
BBEGHIIMORRST Big Brotherism
BBEHNNRSTTUUY Burnt by the Sun
BBEIILLNNOORS Lionel Robbins
BBEILMOORSTUY Bloomsburyite
BBEINNOOPRRTV Von Ribbentrop
BBELLLNRSTUUU Turnbull's blue
BBELOOORRRTUW borrow trouble
BBGIILNNOPRTU burbling point
BBHIIIILLMOPS bibliophilism
BBHIIIILLOPST bibliophilist
BCCCEEHILPRUZ Czech Republic
BCCCEIILNOPSU concupiscible
BCCCEIIMRRRSU circumscriber
BCCCHINOOOPRS bronchoscopic
BCCDDEIILOORR crocodile bird
BCCDEEEIILLLM Cecil B De Mille
BCCDEHKRSTTUU Cuthbert's duck
BCCDEIKLLNORY cylinder block
BCCDEILOPRRSU public records
BCCDELNOOOTUU double coconut
BCCDKMMNOOORU common burdock
BCCEEHIKKKTTU kick the bucket
BCCEEIILORRTT triboelectric
BCCEEIINRSTTY cyberneticist
BCCEEIKKKNORR knickerbocker✧
BCCEEILLPRTUU public lecture
BCCEEILNSSSUY business cycle
BCCEEILORRTTU turbo-electric
BCCEENNOOORTY Ebony Concerto
BCCEFIIIINOST bioscientific
BCCEGHIILMNPR climbing perch
BCCEGILLNOOTX collecting box
BCCEHHIILRSUV Visible Church
BCCEHHINOOOSS Hobson's choice
BCCEHIILLNRTU clincher-built
BCCEIIIJOSTTV objectivistic
BCCEIIILMMNOS incommiscible
BCCEIIILNNNOV inconvincible
BCCEIILLOOPSU ebullioscopic
BCCEILNORSTTU constructible
BCCENOORTTTUU coconut butter
BCCGHIKLNOOPP chopping-block
BCCGIILLMOOSY symbolic logic
BCDDDELLLOOOY cold-bloodedly
BCDDEEEFHILRV childbed fever
BCDDEEEILNNSU undescendible
BCDDEEEILNSSU deducibleness
BCDDEEFILLORU Bruce Oldfield
BCDDEEHILNNOU double-chinned
BCDDEEINORRTU counterbidder
BCDDEIIILTTUY deductibility
BCDDGILLNOORU bloodcurdling
BCDDHIORSSSTU Buddhist cross
BCDEEEGLMNOUU become unglued
BCDEEEILNRSSU reducibleness
BCDEEFFMNOOTU Comte de Buffon
BCDEEFIIILTTY defectibility
BCDEEFLMNORTU recumbent fold
BCDEEGIKNORST stockbreeding
BCDEEGINORRSS crossbreeding
BCDEEHHLPRSSU shepherd's club
BCDEEHNOOPRUU coup de bonheur
BCDEEHNORRSTT stretcher-bond
BCDEEIIILNNRS indiscernible
BCDEEIIILPTTY deceptibility
BCDEEIILNNRSU undiscernible
BCDEEIKLNRSTY tickly-benders
BCDEEINOPRSST bits per second
BCDEEIOORRSUU coureur de bois
BCDEEKKNRTUYY Kentucky Derby
BCDEELMRRRUUY cry blue murder
BCDEELOORRSSU double-crosser
BCDEGHIINPRRS perching birds
BCDEGHIKNORRU Edinburgh rock
BCDEHILMOOORR chlorobromide
BCDEIIIILNRTY incredibility
BCDEIIILNNRSY indiscernibly
BCDEIILNNRSUY undiscernibly
BCDEIILNSSSUU undiscussible
BCDEIIMNOOSTY endosymbiotic
BCDEIKLNNOORW born in wedlock
BCDELMMNOOPUU compound umbel
BCDEMOPRRSUUW spruce budworm
BCDGHIIKKRRTU Kirkcudbright
BCDGHINPRTUUY Burgundy pitch
BCDIIILOPRTUY producibility
BCEEEEEKNOORZ Ebenezer Cooke
BCEEEEFFILRSV effervescible
BCEEEEFKNOORR reference book
BCEEEEHLRRSTU beetle-crusher
BCEEEFGIINNRR birefringence
BCEEEFIILMPRT imperfectible
BCEEEFMNPRRTU perfect number
BCEEEFPRRSTUU subprefecture
BCEEEGHIKTTUV give the bucket
BCEEEGIINORST bioenergetics
BCEEEGILLNORT cobelligerent
BCEEEGILNOORS bernicle-goose
BCEEEHIILPSSV visible speech
BCEEEHILLQRUX exchequer bill
BCEEEHILOPQSU oblique speech
BCEEEHKNRRSTU trunk breeches
BCEEEHLNORRST Close Brethren
BCEEEIILMPPRT imperceptible

BCEEEIJNOSSTV objectiveness
BCEEEIJOSTTTV objective test
BCEEEINNNRRSU incense-burner
BCEEELNOOPRRT electron probe
BCEEFGHHIIITW big White Chief
BCEEFILNORRTY forcible entry
BCEEGIKLNNRSU beginner's luck
BCEEGIKLNRSUW swinge-buckler
BCEEGLMNOORRU Green Room Club
BCEEHIJKNNOST John Steinbeck
BCEEHIKMOORST hermetic books
BCEEHIKORRRRT Robert Herrick
BCEEHILMOOOTT come to the boil
BCEEHILOORRTZ Hector Berlioz
BCEEHIRSTTTUW witches' butter
BCEEHKLOOORTW crook the elbow
BCEEIIILPRTTY receptibility
BCEEIILMPPRTY imperceptibly
BCEEIILNNORTV inconvertible
BCEEIILNPSSTU insusceptible
BCEEIILPPRRST prescriptible
BCEEIINNNORTV Vincent O'Brien
BCEEIKMPRRSTU bumper sticker
BCEEILNNORTUV unconvertible
BCEEILNPSSTUU unsusceptible
BCEEILOPPRRST blister copper
BCEEILPRSTTUU public trustee✧
BCEEINNOORRTT Ronnie Corbett
BCEELMMNOPRUX complex number
BCEELMNNNORUU nucleon number
BCEFFGIIKNOOO booking office
BCEFFIOOOPSTX post-office box
BCEFFIOOPSSTU sub-postoffice
BCEFHIMNOOOTT fine-tooth comb
BCEFHINOOSSST sons of bitches
BCEFIILLPSSTU self-publicist
BCEFIILLPSTUY self-publicity
BCEFIJOORTTUV object of virtu
BCEFILLPRTTUY butterfly clip
BCEFJMOOORRST Job's comforter
BCEGHILNOOOTY biotechnology
BCEGHIRTTTUWY witchetty grub
BCEGHKOOOPRTU pocket borough
BCEGIKLNOSTTU sucking bottle
BCEGIMNORTUYZ zygotic number
BCEHHMMNOOOTY honeycomb-moth
BCEHIIJLLLRUU Julie Burchill
BCEHILMRSTTUW tumbler-switch
BCEHILNRSSTTU Ernst Lubitsch
BCEHIMMORRTTU Robert Mitchum
BCEHINORRRTTU Burton Richter
BCEIILMNOOPSS incompossible
BCEIILNNORTVY inconvertibly
BCEIILNOPRRTU incorruptible
BCEIILNPSSTUY insusceptibly
BCEIINNOOORSV bioconversion
BCEIJLNSTUUVY subjunctively
BCEILMNOOPRYY polyembryonic
BCEILORSTTUVY obstructively
BCEIMNOOORSSU cessio bonorum
BCEINORSTTUUV unobstructive
BCEIOOPRRSSSS probe scissors
BCEKLMNOOOSUY colobus monkey
BCELMMNOOORST common lobster
BCFGIIMMNNOOR combining form
BCFIIILNOSTUY confusibility
BCFIILOORSTTY City of Bristol
BCGGIIKLNNOSW swinging-block
BCGHHILNOTTUU boulting-hutch
BCGHILLNOOTTU boulting cloth
BCGHILNOOOORY chronobiology
BCGHILOOOPSYY biopsychology
psychobiology
BCGHNOOORTUUY county borough
BCGIIIILORRTY corrigibility
BCGIIKLNNOPRT block printing
BCGIILOOORSTY cryobiologist
BCGIKLMNNOOTU mounting block
BCGINOOSSTUUU subcontiguous
BCHIIILNOORST bronchiolitis
BCHIILLOOPPSY polyphloisbic
BCHIKMOOORTTT hit rock bottom
BCIIIIILMMSTY immiscibility
BCIIIIILNNTVY invincibility
BCIIILLPTTUUY public utility
BCIIILNNOOPPU public opinion
BCIIILNPQRUUY public inquiry
BCIIILOORRSTY corrosibility
BCIILNOPRRTUY incorruptibly
BCIIMMNOOSSSU subcommission
BCILLLLNNOOYY Billy Connolly
BCILLNOOORTUU court-bouillon
BCINNOOSSTUUU subcontinuous
BDDDEEFFKOORU Duke of Bedford
BDDDEEGILNOUW double wedding
BDDEEEGGINNNR gender-bending
BDDEEEGILORRV Lord Beveridge
BDDEEEGJMNTTU judgement-debt
BDDEEFLNOORTU double-fronted
BDDEEFLNOOTUU double-founted
BDDEEFOORRRRT Robert Redford
BDDEEGGLNOOOY golden goodbye
BDDEEGLNOOTUU double-tongued
BDDEEHLMOOTUU double-mouthed
BDDEEHLOOSTTU double-shotted
BDDEEIILNOSTY disobediently
BDDEEIIMMNOST disembodiment
BDDEEIJLNOOTU double-jointed
BDDEEILNNRSSU unbridledness
BDDEEILNOSTUY double-density
BDDEEINOPSTUY beyond dispute
BDDEENNNOSSUU unboundedness
BDDEGGGIILNOU double digging
BDDEGHILMORSU Middlesbrough
BDDEIINRSTTUU undistributed
BDDEILNNORSSW word blindness
BDDEILNRSTUUY undisturbedly
BDEEEEFILNOSS beside oneself
BDEEEEHLNRRRT Elder brethren
BDEEEFGILNOTT bottle-feeding
feeding bottle
BDEEEFHINORTW before the wind

BDEEEFIILLRVX flexible drive
BDEEEFLRTTUWY butterfly weed
BDEEEFMMNORRU founder member
BDEEEGIINNRRT interbreeding
BDEEEGIJLLNOU golden jubilee
BDEEEGILRRSTT trestle bridge
BDEEEGIMOORSU embourgeoised
BDEEEHHIILNNT Behind the Line
BDEEEHIINNRRS Inner Hebrides
BDEEEHILLMNSU unembellished
BDEEEHIORRSTU Outer Hebrides
BDEEEIILLNNSS indelibleness
BDEEEIILMPRRU empire-builder
BDEEEIIMPPRTV pre-emptive bid
BDEEEILLLLOWY yellow-bellied
BDEEEIMMMNRST dismemberment
BDEEEIORRRRRT Border terrier
BDEEEJORSTTUV objets de vertu
BDEEEKNNNOOSY beyond one's ken
BDEEELLMORSST bestsellerdom
BDEEELNNORSTU under one's belt
BDEEELNNSSSSU unblessedness
BDEEELNPRSSTU suspender-belt
BDEEENNNRRSYY Sydney Brenner
BDEEENOPSSSTT bespottedness
BDEEFFHLLOSUU double-shuffle
BDEEFGILORSUU double figures
BDEEFIIILNSTY defensibility
BDEEGGHIILMRT thimblerigged
BDEEGGIINNNRY binding energy
BDEEGHINNORUU unneighboured
BDEEGHLLNOOTW The Golden Bowl
BDEEGHNOOTTUW go down the tube
BDEEGIILLNRWY bewilderingly
BDEEGIILLOPPT potbellied pig
BDEEGIILMNOST disobligement
BDEEGIILMNSSX mixed blessing
BDEEGIILNRSSV Blessed Virgin
BDEEGIINORRUW Brownie Guider
BDEEGINNNNSSU unbendingness
BDEEGINOOPRTY pterygoid bone
BDEEGINOOTTUU tongue-doubtie
BDEEGLLOORSTU double Gloster
BDEEGNNNOORTT Gordon Bennett
BDEEHHLMMOTUU humble-mouthed
BDEEHINOSSSTU do the business
BDEEHIOOORRTV Theodor Boveri
BDEEHKMOOTTUY Buteyko method
BDEEHLMMPRTUU rumbledethump
BDEEHLMOOSTUY The Moody Blues
BDEEIIILNSSSV divisibleness
BDEEIIILNTTXY extendibility
BDEEIIMORSTTV totidem verbis
BDEEIKLNRSTTY kittly-benders
BDEEILLOSSTUV devil's boletus
BDEEILMNOORST slide trombone
BDEEIMNORRUVX index verborum
BDEELLMNOOSTW bellows to mend
BDEELLNOOSSSS bloodlessness
BDEELNNOSSSSU boundlessness
BDEELOOPRRSSU blood pressure
BDEFFHILLOOTW blow the lid off
BDEFFIINOSTUU diffusion-tube
BDEFFNOOOPRRU burden of proof
BDEFGGIIILNRT lifting-bridge
BDEFHILOORSTW Bosworth Field
BDEGGHHIORRTU through bridge
BDEGGINNOORVY governing body
BDEGHHINOOORU neighbourhood
BDEGIIIILSTTY digestibility
BDEGIIJLNRRUY jerry-building
BDEGIILLMNSSY dissemblingly
BDEGIIMNNORRU mourning-bride
BDEGIINNNNSUW unsewn binding
BDEGINNOOOPRT pontoon bridge
BDEHHMNOOORRS rhombohedrons
BDEHIIOPRSSTU subeditorship
BDEHILNNOORTU run in the blood
BDEHJKOOPRSSY Joseph Brodsky
BDEHJNOORRUUU bonheur-du-jour
BDEHNOOOPRSTU boustrophedon
BDEIIIILLNTUY ineludibility
BDEIIIILNNTVY invendibility
BDEIIIILRTTVY divertibility
BDEIIMNOOSSSY endosymbiosis
BDEILMNNNOOSS moon blindness
BDEILNNNOSSSW snow blindness
BDEILOOPRSSTU Lepidostrobus
BDEILOOQRSTUU double or quits
double-or-quits
BDEINOPRSSSTU bird's-nest soup
BDEKLNOOORTWY old boy network✧
BDELMNOOORRTU Robert Muldoon
BDELNOOORRRST Lord Robertson
BDFFIIIILSTUY diffusibility
BDFHMOOORTUWY by word of mouth
BDFILLLMOOOWY Bollywood film
BDGGIIIILLNOSY disobligingly
BDGGIIINNNOTU indigo bunting
BDGGINNORRUUY burying ground
BDGIILLMNNOWY mind-blowingly
BDHIIIIINNOST disinhibition
BDHIIIINORSTY disinhibitory
BDHINNNOOORUU in honour bound
BDIIILLOSSTUY dissolubility
BEEEEFHINORRT thereinbefore
BEEEEFLNORSTT better oneself
BEEEEGGHORRRT George Herbert
BEEEEGGLNOTTW toggle between
BEEEEGILLMNSW well-beseeming
BEEEEGIMNNSSS beseemingness
BEEEEHHILLSTY lie by the heels
BEEEEHHLSSTTY set by the heels
BEEEEHILNPRRS reprehensible
BEEEEHILNSTWW betweenwhiles
BEEEEHLLMNTUY methylene blue
BEEEEHLNNNPYZ phenylbenzene
BEEEEHMNRRSSY Henry Bessemer
BEEEEILLNPRTU belle peinture
BEEEEILMNRRST Tim Berners-Lee
BEEEELLLRSSTT belles-lettres
BEEEELOQSTTUZ squeeze bottle

BEEEFFGIINNRT fringe benefit
BEEEFGHNORRTU rub of the green
BEEEFIKKLOOOZ Book of Ezekiel
BEEEFIMNOORTT not before time
BEEEFLMORSSTY Froebel system
BEEEGGGILNRTT begging letter
BEEEGHHORRTUZ breeze through
BEEEGHILNPRST sleeping berth
BEEEGHNNORRTU rub on the green
BEEEGIILLLNSS illegibleness
BEEEGIIMNRTTT time-bettering
BEEEGIINNNRTU turbine engine
BEEEGIKNNOOST get on one's bike
BEEEGILLLNRTY belligerently
BEEEGILMNNSUY unbeseemingly
BEEEGIMMNNRRU unremembering
BEEEGIMNORSSY embryogenesis
BEEEGMNOPRSST September Song
BEEEGNRRSTTUW New Grub Street
BEEEHHOORRRTV Herbert Hoover
BEEEHIKMOPRRS Pembrokeshire
BEEEHIKRRSSTW West Berkshire
BEEEHILLMMNST embellishment
BEEEHILNPRRSY reprehensibly
BEEEHINNPRTTY threepenny bit
BEEEHKLLOORST The Bookseller
BEEEHKLNOOOPT telephone book
BEEEIIJLLRSUV silver jubilee
BEEEIILNPRSSX inexpressible
BEEEIILPRRRSS irrepressible
BEEEILLORRSWY yellow berries
BEEEILMMNRTTT embrittlement
BEEEILNPRSSSU supersensible
BEEEILNPRSSUX unexpressible
BEEEILOPRRRST Sir Robert Peel
BEEEIMMNRRSTU reimbursement
BEEEINNORRRTW Norbert Wiener
BEEEINNOSTTUX extension tube
BEEEINOSSSSSV obsessiveness
BEEEIOORRSTTW Bertie Wooster
BEEELLNORSSSU resolubleness
re-solubleness
BEEELMMNOOTVW bowel movement
BEEELOQSTTUYZ squeezy bottle
BEEFGIKNOOOSS Book of Genesis
BEEFGIKOORSTU Siege of Tobruk
BEEFGINORSTTT first-begotten
BEEFGINRRSTTU butterfingers
BEEFHHKLOOOTT The Book of Thel
BEEFHIMNRRSTU refurbishment
BEEFHOORRRSTT foster-brother
BEEFIIILLRTXY reflexibility
BEEFIIJNNRTUY injury benefit
BEEFILLMORSUU umbelliferous
BEEGGHIILMRRT thimblerigger
BEEGGIIILMNTU time-beguiling
BEEGGIILNNNSS beginningless
BEEGGIJMNNPUU bungee jumping
BEEGHHIIIMTTT hit the big time
BEEGHILNORSSU neighbourless
BEEGHJKLNOOTU The Jungle Book
BEEGIIIILLRTY re-eligibility
BEEGIILLNNUVY unbelievingly
BEEGMNORRSSTU Sune Bergström
BEEHHLOPSTTTU push the bottle
BEEHIKLNORRTU unbrotherlike
BEEHILLORSTWW whistle-blower
BEEHILNOPSTTT spin the bottle
spin-the-bottle
BEEHILNORRSST brotherliness
BEEHILOOQTTUU boutique hotel
BEEHIMNPRRSUU her number is up
BEEHIMOORRSTT Berthe Morisot
BEEHIPPRRSSTY presbytership
BEEHLOOPSTTUW up to the elbows
BEEHMNNOOSSTU thumb one's nose
BEEHOORRSTTUY Robert Southey
BEEIIIILNSSST sensibilities
BEEIIILMMPRSS impermissible
BEEIIILNNSSSV invisibleness
BEEIIILNSTTXY extensibility
BEEIIILRRSTVY reversibility
BEEIILMMMRRUV membrum virile
BEEIILMNPRSSU unimpressible
BEEIILNOPRRSS irresponsible
BEEIILNORRSTV introversible
BEEIILNPRRTTU interruptible
BEEIILNPRSSXY inexpressibly
BEEIILPRRRSSY irrepressibly
BEEIILRRTTUVY retributively
BEEILLNNOSSSU insolubleness
BEEILLOOPSTVX explosive bolt
BEEILLORSSTTW Osbert Sitwell
BEEILNPRSSSUY supersensibly
BEEILNRSSTUVY subserviently
BEEILOQRSTUUU turquoise-blue
BEEILORRRSUVY ruby silver ore
BEEINOOQRSTUU bone turquoise
bone-turquoise
BEEINOORRRSTT Boston terrier
BEEINORSSSTUV obtrusiveness
BEEJOORSSTTUV objets trouvés
BEELLMOORSTUY troublesomely
BEELLOPPRSTUU purple boletus
BEELPRSSTTUUY supersubtlety
BEEMNNNORRTUU neutron number
BEENNOOSSSTUU bounteousness
BEENOOPSTTTUY peyote buttons
BEFFGINNNRTUU running buffet
BEFFGINNORRTU burnt-offering
BEFFHILRSTTUY butterfly fish
BEFGGINOORSUY Guy of Gisborne
BEFGIIILNRSTU filibustering
BEFGILLOORSUU globuliferous
BEFIIIILLNTXY inflexibility
BEFIIILMRSSTU filibusterism
BEFIILORSSTUU filibusterous
BEFIKLRSSTTUY butterfly kiss
BEFILNNOSSTUU bountifulness
BEFINNNSSSUUY funny business
BEFLLNORTTUUW turbulent flow
BEGGHIILNNTTU lightning-tube

BEGGHMNOOORRU borough-monger
BEGGIIIILLNTY negligibility
BEGGILNOORTTT globetrotting
BEGHIIILNORST British Legion
BEGHIILLNORTT Little Bighorn
BEGHILNNORUUY unneighbourly
BEGHIMNOPRSTW bowstring-hemp
BEGHINNOORTWX in the wrong box
BEGHNOOORRTTU rotten borough
BEGIIIIILLNTY ineligibility
BEGIIILNNNORT bring into line
BEGIILLMMNNUU millennium bug
BEGIILLMOPRTT pilgrim-bottle
BEGIILMNPSUUY impulse buying
BEGIILNNNOPTW tenpin bowling
BEGILLMNNRTUY untremblingly
BEGILLMNORSUU serum globulin
BEGILLNNOTUWY yellow bunting
BEGILOPRSSSUV viper's bugloss
BEHHLOPSTTTUU put to the blush
BEHIIIIMNOSTX exhibitionism
BEHIIIINOSTTX exhibitionist
BEHIIILOPRTVY prohibitively
BEHIIMMRSSTUU British Museum
BEHIIMNPRSSUU his number is up
BEHIKLLOORSST shoebill stork
BEHILLLMRSTUU bulrush millet
BEHILNOOSTWWY The Winslow Boy
BEHIMNOOSSSTY tomboyishness
BEHIMNORTTUUW without number
BEHINORSSSSUU business hours
BEHMNOOORRSTT Robert Thomson
BEIIIILMRSSTY remissibility
BEIIIILNNSSTY insensibility
BEIIIILNRTTVY invertibility
BEIIIILOPSSST possibilities
BEIIIILRSSTTY resistibility
BEIIILLMMNNSU bimillenniums
BEIIILMMPRSSY impermissibly
BEIIILNOSSTTY ostensibility
BEIILMNOOOQTU oblique motion
BEIILNOOSSSUV obliviousness
BEIILNOPRRSSY irresponsibly
BEIILNORSTUVY inobtrusively
BEIINNOOPRSTW brownie points
BEIIOPRSSTTUU subreptitious
BEILLMNOPSTUV plumbisolvent
BEILMNPRSUUUU e pluribus unum
BEILMOOPSSTTT bottomless pit
BEILNORSTUUVY unobtrusively
BEIMNOOPRRSST Robert Simpson
BEIMNOPSSSTUU bumptiousness
BEINNOOOSSSUX obnoxiousness
BEINNOORRSTTW Robert Winston
BELLMNOOPSTUV plumbosolvent
BELNOORSSSTUU troublousness
BFILLOORSTUUU tubuliflorous
BFILMMOORRSTU strombuliform
BGHHNOORTTTUU button-through
BGIIILNNORSST Birgit Nilsson
BGIILMOQSSTTV Stig Blomqvist
BGIIMNNORRRRU burning-mirror
BHHMOOPPRRRYY rhombporphyry
BHIIILMOPRSTT timbrophilist
BHLMOOPRSTTUU sulphur-bottom
BIIIILMMOPSSS impossibilism
BIIIILMOPSSST impossibilist
BIIIILMOPSSTY impossibility
BIIILLMORRSUV morbillivirus
BIIINNOPPPRST Ribston pippin
BIIJOOOPRSTTZ Josip Broz Tito
BIILNNOOSTUUV subinvolution
BILMORSSTUUUY rumbustiously
BILNOOPRTTUUY button your lip
BILOOOPPRRSUY opprobriously

C

CCCCEEINNOPSU concupiscence
CCCCEGIIMNNOO meningococcic
CCCCEIIKKLLTY clickety-click
CCCCEIOOPRSTT streptococcic
CCCDDEFNOOOTU code of conduct
CCCDEEEENRRSU recrudescence
CCCDEEENRRSUY recrudescency
CCCDEEHIIOPRT cercopithecid
CCCDEHIORSTTV Scotch verdict
CCCDEIILLOOPR crocodile clip
CCCDEIILORSTU closed circuit
CCCDEIIMNRSUU uncircumcised
CCCDHIIOOOPRS dichrooscopic
CCCDIIMNORTUU circumduction
CCCDIMORRTUUY circumductory
CCCEEEEFILNRT electric fence
CCCEEEENNNOSS consenescence
CCCEEEFIMNRRU circumference
CCCEEEFIOORRV coercive force
CCCEEEHILMORT electrochemic
CCCEEEIILNOPT poetic licence
CCCEEEIKNORST rocket science
CCCEEENNNOSSY consenescency
CCCEEFHIKNRRT French cricket
CCCEEFILMNRUU circumfluence
CCCEEHHIRRSUV church service
CCCEEHIKLORST electric shock
CCCEEILOOPRST electroscopic
CCCEEIMNNOOSY o' my conscience
CCCEEIMNORSTU concrete music
CCCEFFHHIORRU church officer
CCCEFHKKOOORT cock-of-the-rock
CCCEFHMNOOORR French morocco
CCCEGIMNNOOSU meningococcus
CCCEHIIMOSTYZ schizomycetic
CCCEHILORSSTU Scotch curlies
CCCEIIILORSUV vicious circle
CCCEIIMMNOOOR microeconomic
CCCEIINNORTTY concentricity
CCCEIIORSSSTY cysticercosis
CCCEIKNORTTUY county cricket
CCCEILMPRSTUY circumspectly
CCCEIOOPPRSST spectroscopic
CCCEOOPRSSTTU streptococcus✧
CCCFHHIIKLMOT Hitchcock film

CCCHILLNOOOSU council school
CCCHLLOOOPSST Scotch collops
CCCIILLOOOPSS oscilloscopic
CCCIIMNORSTUU succinctorium
CCCILNNOOTUUY county council
CCDDEEGINNNOS condescending
CCDDEELLNOTUW well-conducted
CCDDEFLNOORTU occluded front
CCDDEIINNOOOT condition code
CCDDENOORTTUU conducted tour
CCDEEEEEFNRSV defervescence
CCDEEEEFHLNRS credence shelf
CCDEEEEFNRSVY defervescency
CCDEEEEILNQSU deliquescence
CCDEEEFHIINSU chef de cuisine
CCDEEEFIILLRT electric field
CCDEEEFILNOST self-conceited
CCDEEEFLLLOST self-collected
CCDEEEHHHKPRS shepherd check
CCDEEEHIIMNST medicine chest
CCDEEEHOQRSSU crossed cheque
CCDEEEHORSSUV duchesse cover
CCDEEEIMSSSTU succès d'estime
CCDEEEINNOSST conceitedness
CCDEEELLLORTY recollectedly
CCDEEELLNNOTW well-connected
CCDEEELLNORTU unrecollected
CCDEEELLNOSST collectedness
CCDEEENNNORSS concernedness
CCDEEFFINOORS second officer
CCDEEFILNOSTV self-convicted
CCDEEGHIIMNOU cough medicine
CCDEEHIILNNPY phencyclidine
CCDEEHILORRTY hydroelectric
CCDEEILMNOPSY encyclopedism
CCDEEILNOPSTY encyclopedist
CCDEEIMOORRTT microdetector
CCDEEINNNOOSS condescension
CCDEEINOOPRUW owner-occupied
CCDEEINOORSST cordocentesis
CCDEEINOPPRUU unpreoccupied
CCDEEINRRRTTU direct current
CCDEEIOOPRSTU deuteroscopic
CCDEEJNNORTUU unconjectured
CCDEELLOOPSTU closed couplet
CCDEELNNNORUY unconcernedly
CCDEELNOOPPRW copple-crowned
CCDEFOOORRRTU court of record
CCDEGIINNORST disconcerting
CCDEGIINORRST credit scoring
CCDEGINNNOORT connecting rod
CCDEHKLNOORTU round the clock
round-the-clock
CCDEHKLOOPPRT cock-throppled
CCDEIIIMMOSTU commit suicide
CCDEIILOPRSTU corpus delicti
CCDEIINNNOOST disconnection
CCDEIINNOORST disconcertion
CCDEILLMNOOPS minced collops
CCDEIMMORRUUX crux medicorum
CCDEIMNOORSTU semiconductor
CCDEIMOOSSTUY discomycetous
CCDEINOOPPRRT Doctor Crippen
CCDELMNOOOPUU leuco-compound
CCDEOOPRRTTUV vector product
CCDGINNNNOOTU non-conducting
CCDHHILLLORRU Lord Churchill
CCDHINOOPRSTU conductorship
CCDIIILNNOOTU induction coil
CCDIIMNNOOPUY pycnoconidium
CCDIIORRSTTTU district court
CCEEEEEFFNOSS coffee essence
CCEEEEEFFNRSV effervescence
CCEEEEEINNPPT tenpence piece
CCEEEEFFIORSV coffee service
CCEEEEFFLNORS efflorescence
CCEEEEFFNRSVY effervescency
CCEEEEIIPRRSX exercise price
CCEEEEINOPPTW two pence piece
CCEEEEINRRSSV scenic reserve
CCEEEEIRRSSTV secret service✧
CCEEEELMNORTT electrocement
CCEEEELNORSTT concrete steel
CCEEEFFIOSTTV cost-effective
CCEEEFGINNRTU centrifugence
CCEEEFILNNORS inflorescence
CCEEEFILORRRT ferroelectric
CCEEEFINPRSTT perfect insect
CCEEEFNOORRRT ferroconcrete
CCEEEHHIIKNNR chinkerinchee
CCEEEHHIKNORR Erich Honecker
CCEEEHIPRTTUY hypereutectic
CCEEEHLNORSST clothes-screen
CCEEEHMOOPRRT chemoreceptor
CCEEEIIIMNPPR impercipience
CCEEEIILOPRTZ piezoelectric
CCEEEIINNNNOV inconvenience
CCEEEILMNNORT reconcilement
CCEEEILMORRTT electrometric
CCEEEIMMNSSUU Science Museum
CCEEEIMNORRTX concrete mixer
CCEEEINNNOQSU in consequence
inconsequence
CCEEEINNOPSTT topic sentence
CCEEEINNRRRTU intercurrence
CCEEEINPRSSTT spectre insect
CCEEEIORSSTTY secret society
CCEEELNNOORST centre console
CCEEENOPRRSSS screen process
CCEEFFIIINNSU insufficience
CCEEFFIILOOPR police officer
CCEEFFIINOSTT cost-efficient
CCEEFFKKNNOOT knock-on effect
CCEEFGIIINOST geoscientific
CCEEFIIINPRST interspecific
prescientific
CCEEFINNOORTY confectionery
CCEEGGILNNOOU gluconeogenic
CCEEGHIINOSTZ schizogenetic
CCEEGHINOPSTY psychogenetic
CCEEGIIMNORST geocentricism
CCEEGIINORTTY egocentricity

CCEEGILNNORTY nitrogen cycle
CCEEHHHRRSSTU screech-thrush
CCEEHHINOORRT heterochronic
CCEEHHNRRSTUW Western Church
CCEEHIIKLNOPT kitchen police
CCEEHIILLOPRT electrophilic
CCEEHILOOPRTT photoelectric
CCEEHILOOPRTU heroic couplet
CCEEHIMMNNOST mnemotechnics
CCEEHIMMNOOOS home economics
CCEEHIMNNORRY chimney-corner
CCEEHIMOSSTYZ Schizomycetes
CCEEHINORSSTT crotchetiness
CCEEHIORRRSTT Scotch terrier
CCEEHKLMOPRSU hemlock spruce
CCEEHMMOORRRU Mercurochrome®
CCEEIIJOPSTTU poetic justice
CCEEIIKLLLNOT Licence to Kill
CCEEIILMNOPRT import licence
CCEEIILNOORST isoelectronic
CCEEIILRRSTUU sericiculture
CCEEIIMNRTUVV circumventive
CCEEIINNNOSST inconsistence
CCEEIINNOSTUV inconsecutive
CCEEIINOPTTTU eutectic point
CCEEIJMNORSTU misconjecture
CCEEIJNOOPRRT cine projector
ciné projector
CCEEILLNORSUU recoil nucleus
CCEEILMOORRTT electric motor
CCEEILMORRSTT electric storm
CCEEILNOORTTU electrocution
CCEEILNOSTUVY consecutively
CCEEILOOPRSTT electro-optics
CCEEIMMOPRRTU computer crime
CCEEIMOPRRSTT spectrometric
CCEEINNOOPPRT preconception
CCEEINNORRSST incorrectness
CCEEINOOPRRTU Europocentric
CCEEINOOPRRUW owner-occupier
CCEEINORSTTTU section-cutter
CCEEINPRRRSTU prices current
CCEEIOPRRSSTU prosecutrices
CCEEKLLORSSTT settler's clock
CCEEKOORRSTVY recovery stock
CCEELLNOORRTT rent-collector
CCEELLSSSSSUY successlessly
CCEELOORSSTUY oestrous cycle
CCEEMNNNNORTU unconcernment
CCEENNOOOVVXX convexo-convex
CCEENOPRRRTUY petrocurrency
CCEFFHKLOOOTT cock of the loft
CCEFFIIINNSUY insufficiency
CCEFIIIINSTTY scientificity
CCEFIIILMORST microfelsitic
CCEFIIILMRSST self-criticism
CCEFIIINNNOST non-scientific
CCEFIILMNORUX circumflexion
CCEFILNOOSSSU self-conscious
CCEGHIIKNNPRS spring chicken
CCEGHIIKNPRRY cherry-picking
CCEGHINNORSSS scorchingness
CCEGIIKKNOPPT pocket-picking
CCEGIIKNNQSTU quick-scenting
CCEGIILNNOPPY copying pencil
CCEGIILNNRRTU turning circle
CCEGILLNNOOSU co-counselling
CCEGILOOOOTXY ecotoxicology
CCEGINNNORSTY constringency
CCEHHIIKNPSTY kitchen physic
CCEHHIINOPRSZ schizophrenic
CCEHHILOSSTTT Scotch thistle
CCEHHIMOOPRRS chromospheric
CCEHIIKNOPSTY psychokinetic
CCEHIILOSSTTY cholecystitis
CCEHIKLNOOPSS lick one's chops
CCEHIKOQTTTUU cut to the quick
CCEHILLOOPRST collectorship
CCEHILMNOORTY Chloromycetin®
CCEHILPRSSUVY Culver's physic
CCEHIMOPRRSTY psychrometric
CCEHIMOPRSSTY psychometrics
CCEHIMORSTTYY cytochemistry
CCEHIMRRSTUWY mercury switch
CCEHIOOPRRSTU urethroscopic
CCEHIOPRSSSSU successorship
CCEHLNNOOOSTV convent school
CCEIIIMORSSTV viscosimetric
CCEIIIOPRRRTY irreciprocity
CCEIILMNOOPSY incomes policy
CCEIILNNNOSTY inconsciently
CCEIILNPPSTTY styptic pencil
CCEIIMNNNOOST connectionism
CCEIIMNNOOPST misconception
CCEIIMNNOPSTY spectinomycin
CCEIIMNNORTUV circumvention
CCEIIMNOORRST miscorrection
CCEIIMNOOSSSU semiconscious
CCEIINNNOSSTY inconsistency
CCEIINNOOPSTT Conceptionist
CCEIINNOOSSST concessionist
CCEIINNOOSSTU conscientious
CCEIINOSSSSTU successionist
CCEIJLNNOTUVY conjunctively
CCEIJNNNOTUUV unconjunctive
CCEIKKKLLOORW like clockwork
CCEIKLOOPSTTU cuckoo-spittle
CCEILMOOPRRSS cross compiler
CCEILNNNOOSUV non-conclusive
CCEILNOORRSTU cruise control
CCEIMMOOPRRTU microcomputer
CCEINNOOPRRST prince consort
CCEINNOOSSSSU consciousness
CCEINNOPRRSSW crown princess
CCEINORSSSUWY swine's succory
CCELMOOPRSSUY cyclospermous
CCELOOOPRRSSU colour-process
CCELOORRSSSST cross-crosslet
CCENNNNOORRTU non-concurrent
CCENOOORRRSTU coroner's court
CCENOORRRSTTU reconstructor
CCFGHILNOOSTU focusing cloth

CCFIIIMMORRST form criticism
CCGHHHHIIMRSU High-Churchism
CCGHHHINOORSU Cornish chough
CCGIIILOOOSST sociologistic
CCGIIKNNOOPTT cotton-picking
CCGIIKNORSSTU scouring stick
CCHHHIIIMNOTY Ho Chi Minh City
CCHHHIJLLNORU John Churchill
CCHHIILOPPRSY psychrophilic
CCHHIMOOOPRST photochromics
CCHHIOPPSSSYY psychophysics
CCHIIKLMORSTZ Moritz Schlick
CCHIILNOOPRSU councilorship
CCHIINNORSSTY synchronistic
CCHIINNORSTYY synchronicity
CCHIIOPRRSSTU Corpus Christi
CCHIJLMOOORSW Jim Crow school
CCHILNOOORRRU chlorocruorin
CCIIJNNNNOOTU in conjunction
CCIILMOOOPSST cosmopolitics
CCIIMOOOSSTXY mycotoxicosis
CCIINNOOPSSUU inconspicuous
CCILNNOOSSUUY unconsciously
CCILNOOPSSUUY conspicuously
CCINNOORSTUUY country cousin
CCIOORRRSSSSW criss-cross-row
CCLLMNNOOORTU control column
CDDDEEEGLNNOS long-descended
CDDDEHKLRSUUY ruddy shelduck
CDDEEEENNPRTU unprecedented
CDDEEEFFINNRU undifferenced
CDDEEEFIKKRRU Duke Frederick
CDDEEEFLMNNOS self-condemned
CDDEEEGGLORRW red-legged crow
CDDEEEGLNORST golden-crested
CDDEEEHIORRTT other-directed
CDDEEEHIRSTTW wide-stretched
CDDEEEIILMPRR Mildred Pierce
CDDEEEIINNRRT inner-directed
CDDEEEIOORRRV video recorder
CDDEEELNOORRS enclosed order
CDDEEEMMNNORU unrecommended
CDDEEENNOPSTY condensed type
CDDEEFHIOOPRT pitched-roofed
CDDEEGHINOSST second-sighted
CDDEEHIIKMNNT kitchen midden
CDDEEHIMNNOOY hidden economy
CDDEEIILLNORS ill-considered
CDDEEIILLNOST teledildonics
CDDEEIILOOPPS dipleidoscope
CDDEEIKLMNNOS condensed milk
CDDEEILLMOSTU deltoid muscle
CDDEEILNNRSUY undiscernedly
CDDEEILNOOSTY Dicotyledones
CDDEEINOSSSUU deciduousness
CDDEELLLOOUWY clouded yellow
CDDEELNNOSSUU uncloudedness
CDDEFFILOORST Clifford Odets
CDDEFIIMNOSTU undiscomfited
CDDEGIIJRSTTU district judge
CDDEGOOOPRRSU producer goods
CDDEHHILOORRY hydrochloride
CDDEHMOOORSST odd-come-shorts
CDDEIIIILNNPS indisciplined
CDDEIIILNNPSU undisciplined
CDDEIINNNOOTU unconditioned
CDDEIINOOPRSY synodic period
CDDEIOOOPRRTU Doctor Proudie
CDDIIMMOOOSSU discommodious
CDEEEEEHMMNRT crème de menthe
CDEEEEELMORRT decelerometer
CDEEEEFGINRRR grid reference
CDEEEEFINSSTV defectiveness
CDEEEEFLLNSSY defencelessly
CDEEEEFLLORUW flower-de-leuce
CDEEEEGHILNNT etching needle
CDEEEEGILRSSU degree Celsius
CDEEEEGLNNSST neglectedness
CDEEEEHNORRRT three-cornered
CDEEEEIINNPRX inexperienced
CDEEEEINNPRUX unexperienced
CDEEEEINPSSTV deceptiveness
CDEEEEIORSSTV vers de société
CDEEEEIQRSTUZ credit squeeze
CDEEEELLPRSTW well-respected
CDEEEFFGINORR coffee grinder
CDEEEFFILLSTU self-deceitful
CDEEEFFLNOSSS self-confessed
CDEEEFFLOPPRT Doppler effect
CDEEEFHKLNRSW Schwenkfelder
CDEEEFIILNRTU unelectrified
CDEEEFIINNSST deficientness
CDEEEFIKRRSTW Frederick West
CDEEEFILNOPST self-deception
CDEEEFILNSSTU deceitfulness
CDEEEFLLNRSTY self-centredly
CDEEEGHIILNSW weeding-chisel
CDEEEGHINOPST pigeon-chested
CDEEEGIIKNNSV King's evidence
CDEEEGILNORRT telerecording
CDEEEGIORRRUX croix de guerre✧
CDEEEGKLNNOOW On Wenlock Edge
CDEEEHHIOOPRT Pieter de Hooch
CDEEEIIMNNOTT mine detection
CDEEEIINNRRSV dinner service
CDEEEIINPRSTV vice-president
CDEEEIKMPQRTU quick-tempered
CDEEEILMORRST sclerodermite
CDEEEILMORSUV service module
CDEEEILNPRUVY unperceivedly
CDEEEIMOPRSSV decompressive
CDEEEINNNRSSU underniceness
CDEEEINNORSST reconditeness
CDEEEINRSSTUV reductiveness
CDEEEINSSSTUV seductiveness
CDEEEKMOORSTT smoke detector
CDEEELMNOPSSX complexedness
CDEEELOORRSUU couleur de rose
CDEEEMNNOPRSU unrecompensed
CDEEENNNOSSTT contentedness
CDEEENOORRSTV seroconverted
CDEEENPSSSSTU suspectedness

CDEEEPRRSTTUU deep structure
CDEEFFGNOORSU coffee grounds
CDEEFFIILLNST self-inflicted
CDEEFFILNNOST self-confident
CDEEFFINOORRT rodent officer
CDEEFFMNOORTU offer document
CDEEFGILNORRS self-recording
CDEEFHIRRSTUZ Der Freischütz
CDEEFHKMOOORT Dome of the Rock
CDEEFHLLOORSU flesh-coloured
CDEEFIIIKLMRT certified milk
CDEEFIILNORST self-direction
CDEEFIILNSTUV self-inductive
CDEEFILPRSSTU disrespectful
CDEEFINNOORTV over-confident
CDEEFNOORRRRU unforced error
CDEEGGHIINPTW pitching wedge
CDEEGIILLNRST direct selling
CDEEGIINNOORT derecognition
CDEEGILNNOOST golden section
CDEEGINPSTTUY speedy cutting
CDEEHHIILNORX chlorhexidine
CDEEHHILLOORT Hollerith code
CDEEHIKLNORRT Lord Kitchener
CDEEHILLNSSSS childlessness
CDEEHILMNNORW women-children
CDEEHILNOORTU leucitohedron
CDEEHIMMNOPRS miscomprehend
CDEEHIMNORRSY dysmenorrheic
CDEEHLLOOORUW whole-coloured
CDEEHNNOOOPPS phonendoscope
CDEEIIILLMNRS Miller indices
CDEEIIIMNRSTT deterministic
CDEEIIIMOSSTT domesticities
CDEEIIKLQRSUV quicksilvered
CDEEIIKNNOTUV Duke Vincentio
CDEEIILNORSST directionless
CDEEIILNOSSSU deliciousness
CDEEIILPRSTVY descriptively
CDEEIIMNORSTT densitometric
CDEEIINNSSTUV inductiveness
CDEEIINOORRTV eviction order
CDEEIINORRSTT derestriction
CDEEIJNPRRSUU jurisprudence
CDEEIKNORRTTY kitty-cornered
CDEEILLOORRUV liver-coloured
CDEEILLOPRRSU supercollider
CDEEILLORSVWY discovery well
CDEEILMMRTUUU culture medium
CDEEILNNOOPRS scolopendrine
CDEEILNOPRRTW triple-crowned
CDEEILNPRRSSY cylinder press
CDEEILOORRSUV versicoloured
CDEEILORRTUVY overcredulity
CDEEILRSTTUVY destructively
CDEEIMMNOORST endosmometric
CDEEIMNOOPRSS decompression
CDEEINNNOSSTU continuedness
CDEEINOPQSTTU cinque-spotted
CDEEINPRRSSSS princess dress
CDEEIOPPRRSST esprit de corps
CDEEKKLNRSTUU knuckleduster
CDEEKLOPRSTTU speckled trout
CDEELLMNOOORU lemon-coloured
CDEELMOOORSUU mouse-coloured
CDEELMOORRSSU sclerodermous
CDEELNOOORSTU stone-coloured
CDEELNORSSSUU credulousness
CDEELNPSSTUUY unsuspectedly
CDEELOORRSUUV overcredulous
CDEEMNOPRSSTU comptes rendus
CDEENNOOPRRST correspondent
CDEFFGIILNNOS self-confiding
CDEFFGINOORRU ground-officer
CDEFFLNOORSUU snuff-coloured
CDEFGIINNNOSS confidingness
CDEFIIIILMRSS mid-life crisis
CDEFIILNNOSTU self-induction
CDEFILNNOSTTU discontentful
CDEFOOOOPRRSS food processor
CDEGGHINNORTU etching ground
CDEGHHIKOSTTU sick-thoughted
CDEGHIIKNRSWY Henry Sidgwick
CDEGHIILNORST riding clothes
CDEGHIINOPRTW itching powder
CDEGHILNNORTU underclothing
CDEGHINRSTTUY synthetic drug
CDEGHMMNOOOOT the common good
CDEGIIKOPRRST porridge-stick
CDEGIILNNORSY consideringly
CDEGIIMMOOSTY sigmoidectomy
CDEGIIMOOOPSS sigmoidoscope
CDEGIINNNORSU unconsidering
CDEGIINNNOSTT discontenting
CDEGIINOOOSUY gynodioecious
CDEGIKNNNORUW uncrowned king
CDEGILNNOOORY endocrinology
CDEGINNOOPRRS corresponding
CDEGINORRSSSS cross-dressing
CDEGMNOOORSSU consumer goods
CDEHHILMMSTTU Helmut Schmidt
CDEHHIMNNOOST smooth-chinned
CDEHHIOOORRST rhodochrosite
CDEHIIIOPRSTY spheroidicity
CDEHIIKLTTTWY thick-wittedly
CDEHIIKMNSTTU stick-in-the-mud
CDEHIIKNORSTY hydrokinetics
CDEHIILLNORVY vinyl chloride
CDEHIILOPPRRS slipper orchid
CDEHIIMNOOPRT periodic month
CDEHIIMNOPRRU perichondrium
CDEHIIOOOPPRT photoperiodic
CDEHILNOORSTW clothe in words
CDEHILOOPRSUX choroid plexus
CDEHIMOOPPRSU pseudomorphic
CDEHIMOORTTYY thyroidectomy
CDEHINNORSTUU urchin-snouted
CDEHINOOSSTUU discount house
CDEHKNRRSTTUU thunderstruck
CDEHMMOORTTYY Tommy Docherty
CDEHMNORRSSUY crush syndrome
CDEHMOPRRRTUU Rupert Murdoch

CDEHNNOORSSSY synchondroses
CDEIIIINNSTTV indistinctive
CDEIIILLOQRUW wild liquorice
CDEIIILMNOSTU consimilitude
CDEIIILNOPSST split decision
CDEIIILNOPSTY epicondylitis
CDEIIILNSTTVY distinctively
CDEIIIMOOOPRS Piero di Cosimo
CDEIIIMPRSSTV descriptivism
CDEIIINNSTTUV undistinctive
CDEIIJLNSTUVY disjunctively
CDEIIJNOSSSUU judiciousness
CDEIILQRSUUUV liquidus curve
CDEIIMNOOOPST decomposition
CDEIINNRSSTUU unscrutinised
CDEIINNRSTUUZ unscrutinized
CDEIINOOPPRSY pycnidiospore
CDEIINOPRTUWW picture window
CDEIINORSTTUU rectitudinous
CDEIINRRSSTTU district nurse
CDEIIRSSTTTUV destructivist
CDEIIRSTTTUVY destructivity
CDEILLMOORTUU multicoloured
CDEILLNNSSUUU nulli secundus
CDEILLNORSUUY incredulously
CDEILMNOOPRSU scolopendrium
CDEILMNOOPSUY compendiously
CDEILNNOPRSTY nondescriptly
CDEILNORSSSUU ludicrousness
CDEILOORTUUUX tic douloureux
CDEINNOOPRTUV non-productive
CDEINOOOPPRUW porcupine wood
CDEINOOPPRRTU preproduction
CDEINOORRRRTY entry corridor
CDEINOORSSTTU discount store
CDEINOOSTTUWZ cut down to size
CDEIOOORRRTTY root directory
CDEKLMNOOOPUU leuko-compound
CDELLNOOOPTYY polycotyledon
CDELMNNOOOOTY monocotyledon
CDELOOORRTTUU trout-coloured
CDELOOPRTTUUY putty-coloured
CDELOORRSTUUY rusty-coloured
CDEMNNNOOOPRU non-compounder
CDEOOOPRRRSSW word processor
CDFGILNNNOOUY confoundingly
CDFIIMNOORSTY disconformity
CDGHIIKNORSTW Dickson Wright
CDGHIILOOORST orchidologist
CDGHILNOPRTUY drying-up cloth
CDGIIILOOSSTU suicidologist
CDGIIINOSTTUY discontiguity
CDGIIMOOOPSSY sigmoidoscopy
CDGIINOOSSTUU discontiguous
CDGLNNOOORRTU ground control
CDHHIIIMORRTY idiorrhythmic
CDHHIMNOOPRUY hypochondrium
CDHIIMNNOOORT mitochondrion
CDHILMOOOSTUY dichotomously
CDHINNOORSSSY synchondrosis
CDHLMMOOORSUU mushroom cloud
CDHMNOOOOPRTU ortho-compound
CDIIIINNNOSTT indistinction
CDIIIJLNOSUUY injudiciously
CDIIIMMNOOSSS discommission
CDIIIMNNNOOTT mint condition
CDIIINNOSTTUY discontinuity
CDIIINOORSSSV cross-division
CDIINNNNOOOOT on no condition
CDIINNOOPRTTU induction port
CDIINNOOSSTUU discontinuous
CDILMOORRTUUV victor ludorum
CDIMNNOOOPRTU nitro-compound
CDINNNOOOPRTU non-production
CDKKNOOOPRSTU knockout drops
CEEEEEFLNRRSV self-reverence
CEEEEEGHINNPT eighteen-pence
CEEEEEGHLNRSS Scheele's green
CEEEEEGLLORTX Exeter College
CEEEEEILNORRT electioneerer
CEEEEFFILPRTT Peltier effect
CEEEEFFINSSTV effectiveness
CEEEEFGLLOSTT Fettes College
CEEEEFGNNQRUY gene frequency
CEEEEFILNORST free-selection
CEEEEFILNSSTX self-existence
CEEEEFLMORRTT reflectometer
CEEEEFLNORSSW flower essence
CEEEEFLNOSSUX excuse oneself
CEEEEFLPRRTTT letter-perfect
CEEEEFMNNORRT re-enforcement
CEEEEFPPRRRTT preterperfect
CEEEEGHINORTT heterogenetic
CEEEEGHIOPRTT piece together
CEEEEGIIMNNRS éminence grise
CEEEEGIINOPRT epeirogenetic
CEEEEGIMNRTXY emergency exit
CEEEEGINNOOSU Eugène Ionesco
CEEEEGLLNOQSU Queens' College
Queen's College
CEEEEHIKPPRSS cheese skipper
CEEEEHLNRSSSS cheerlessness
CEEEEHNPRRSTT three-per-cents
CEEEEILLNNORT Terence O'Neill
CEEEEILNRRSTU leisure centre
CEEEEILNSSSTV selectiveness
CEEEEIMNNPRSU supereminence
CEEEEINNNPPTY tenpenny piece
CEEEEINNPRSUV supervenience
CEEEEINPRSSTV receptiveness
CEEEEINRSSSSV recessiveness
CEEEEINRSSSTV secretiveness
CEEEEINSSSSVX excessiveness
CEEEEIOPRTTVX exteroceptive
CEEEEJNNRSTUV rejuvenescent
CEEEEKLNOPRSU counsel-keeper
CEEEELNOOSSSY close one's eyes
CEEEELNORRTTV teleconverter
CEEEENORRRUVY Your Reverence
CEEEENRRTTUUV revenue cutter
CEEEFFIILNTVY ineffectively
CEEEFFPRRTTUU future perfect

CEEEFGILNSTUX self-executing
CEEEFHINNOSTT sit on the fence
CEEEFHIORSSTU force the issue
CEEEFHLNPSSSU speechfulness
CEEEFIINNSSTV infectiveness
CEEEFILLNRTTV left ventricle
CEEEFILORRSVW flower-service
CEEEFIMNNORRT reinforcement
CEEEFIMNPRSST imperfectness
CEEEFINORRTTU counterfeiter
CEEEFLMNOOOST come to oneself
CEEEFNNPRSSTU unperfectness
CEEEGGINORRTU Geiger counter
CEEEGGLNOOORY George Clooney
CEEEGHIIMNRTW Greenwich Time
CEEEGHIKNNOTU tongue in cheek
tongue-in-cheek
CEEEGHILLNOPT phellogenetic
CEEEGHIMNORTT thermogenetic
CEEEGHIPRTTTU get the picture
CEEEGHIRRSSTT chest register
CEEEGIIILNNRV civil engineer
receiving line
CEEEGIIINPSTT epigeneticist
CEEEGIIKNNRTY kinetic energy
CEEEGIILLNNRT intelligencer
CEEEGIJNNNPRY creeping Jenny
CEEEGIJNPRSSU creeping Jesus
CEEEGIKNNRSSS green sickness
CEEEGINNRSSTT screening test
CEEEGLLLNOSWY Selwyn College
CEEEGLLMNOORT Merton College
CEEEGMMNOORRY emergency room
CEEEHHHIIINNR Heinrich Heine
CEEEHHIPQRTTU queer the pitch
CEEEHHIPRSTTY hyperesthetic
CEEEHHKLRSTTU kletterschuhe✧
CEEEHIILNNSTT Liechtenstein
CEEEHIJLLMSTU Jules Michelet
CEEEHIKKLNOSS kick one's heels
CEEEHIKORTTVW over the wicket
CEEEHILLLMOSU hemicellulose
CEEEHILMNOPRT nephelometric
CEEEHILNPSUZZ Chinese puzzle
CEEEHIMNOPRSV comprehensive
CEEEHINNORSTT in on the secret
CEEEHKLOPRSTW sprocket wheel
CEEEHLLLNORST electron shell
CEEEHLLNOOOSS cool one's heels
CEEEHLMORRTTY electrothermy
CEEEHLNORSSSU lecherousness
CEEEHMMNOSTYY Hymenomycetes
CEEEHNSSTTTUW sweet chestnut
CEEEIILORSTTV toilet service
CEEEIILRRSSVV silver service
CEEEIIMNNRTTT intermittence
CEEEIIMNPRSSS impreciseness
CEEEIINNPPSXY sixpenny piece
CEEEIINOPRTTV interoceptive
CEEEIINORRSSV senior service
CEEEIINPPRSTV in perspective
CEEEILMMORRST electromerism
CEEEILMNPRSTU multipresence
CEEEILMNRSSSS mercilessness
CEEEILMOORTTV electromotive
CEEEILNOSSSSV voicelessness
CEEEILNOSUVXZ exclusive zone
CEEEILNPPRRSU pluripresence
CEEEILNPRSSSS pricelessness
CEEEILNSSSUVX exclusiveness
CEEEILPPRSTVY perspectively
CEEEINNNOORTV conventioneer
CEEEINNOORRRT reconnoiterer
CEEEINNOPPTWY twopenny piece
CEEEINNOQSTUX ex consequenti
CEEEINOOPRSSV voice response
CEEEINOOPRTTX exteroception
CEEEINOPSSTTX post-existence
CEEEINRSSSUVX excursiveness
CEEEIOPRRSTTV retrospective
CEEEKLMOOPRTU petroleum coke
CEEELLMNNORST ensorcellment
CEEELMNNOSSUW unwelcomeness
CEEELMNNOSTTU locum tenentes
CEEELNNOQSSUU Queen's Counsel
CEEEMNOPRSTYY Pyrenomycetes
CEEEOPRRRSSSV process-server
CEEFFFGIINOOR Foreign Office
CEEFFGHINOOSU coffee-housing
CEEFFGIMNNOOR coffee morning
CEEFFHIKLRRSS sheriff clerks
CEEFFHIKNPSST Seth Pecksniff
CEEFFHIKORSTU Turkish coffee
CEEFFHMNOOSTT Thomson effect
CEEFFHOPRRTTU perfect fourth
CEEFFIIILNNTY inefficiently
CEEFFIILNNOST self-infection
CEEFFIJNORSTY Jefferson City
CEEFFINOPTTTU put into effect
CEEFFIOORRRRS ferrosoferric
CEEFFKNOOORRS off one's rocker
CEEFFNRSSTTUU suffrutescent
CEEFGHHINQRUY high frequency
CEEFGHIINNSST scene-shifting
CEEFGHINORRTT right-of-centre
CEEFGIIKNRRST grief-stricken
CEEFGIINNNOTU eigenfunction
CEEFHHLNOOOTV the cloven hoof
CEEFHIJOOORRS rose of Jericho
CEEFIIILNSSTT life scientist
CEEFIIJLNNOST self-injection
CEEFIIJLNNOTU fuel injection
CEEFIIKLNORSU nickeliferous
CEEFIILLNOTWZ fellow citizen
CEEFIILNOSUVY veneficiously
CEEFIIMNOPRST perfectionism
CEEFIINOPRSTT perfectionist✧
CEEFIKNOOORTU fortune cookie
CEEFILLLORSUU celluliferous
CEEFILMMNOOST commit oneself
CEEFILMOOPRST telescopiform
CEEFILNOORRTT retroflection

CEEFILNORTTUY counterfeitly
CEEFIMNNOOTTY confetti money
CEEFINOORSSSU ferociousness
CEEFLLORRSUUY resourcefully
CEEFLMOORRSST recomfortless
CEEFLNORRTUUY counter-fleury
CEEGGHLNOOOTY geotechnology
CEEGGILLNOORT Girton College
CEEGHHHHORTUW wheech through
CEEGHHIIILNTT hit the ceiling
CEEGHHIINPPRW whipping-cheer
CEEGHHILNOPTT Phlegethontic
CEEGHHIMMNOOT The Homecoming
CEEGHHIMNOSSU housing scheme
CEEGHIIINPRSV receiving-ship
CEEGHIIKLMTTU Gemütlichkeit
CEEGHIIKLNPRR pickle-herring
CEEGHIIKNRSTV knight service
CEEGHIILPRSST The Spice Girls
CEEGHIIMOORST isogeothermic
CEEGHIINOSSSZ schizogenesis
CEEGHIIRRSTUW cruiserweight
CEEGHIKORSTTT stick together
CEEGHILNOPSTY phylogenetics
CEEGHIMNOOPRT morphogenetic
CEEGHINOOPRTT genetotrophic
CEEGHINOPSSSY psychogenesis
CEEGHINORTTUW counter-weight
CEEGHKKNOORTT knock together
CEEGIIMNNOPRU mourning piece
CEEGIIMNOORRV receiving-room
CEEGIINNRRSTW screenwriting
CEEGIJLLNOORU junior college
CEEGILLNORSSV level crossing
CEEGILMMNOTTU telecommuting
CEEGIMNNORRTY retromingency
CEEGJMORSTTUY Jeremy Guscott
CEEHHHIINRRTZ Heinrich Hertz
CEEHHILLMMRTU Much the Miller
CEEHHIMMOOORT homoeothermic
CEEHHIMMORSTT thermochemist
CEEHHIMOOPRRT heteromorphic
CEEHHIMRSTTUY The Eurythmics
CEEHHIOOPRRTT heterotrophic
CEEHHJMNNORRY Johnny H Mercer
CEEHHLLOPRSUY Holy Sepulchre
CEEHHNORSSTTU horse chestnut
CEEHIIKLLMMRT Mick the Miller
CEEHIIKLNRSSS lickerishness
CEEHIIKNORTTY kinetic theory
CEEHIILNNOPRS phenolic resin
CEEHIIMMOPSTT committeeship
CEEHIIMNRSTTZ Chester Nimitz
CEEHIIMORTTXY exothermicity
CEEHIINPRRSSV scrivenership
CEEHIJMMRTTWY Jemmy Twitcher
CEEHIKLOPRSTU prick-the-louse
CEEHIKNORSSSS horse-sickness
CEEHILLNNOPSU Punchinelloes
CEEHILMMORSTU chromium steel
CEEHILOOPRRTU Hercule Poirot
CEEHILOORSTTU heteroclitous
CEEHILOPRTVYY hypervelocity
CEEHIMMNNOSTT mnemotechnist
CEEHIMMNOOOST home economist
CEEHIMMRSSSTT Messerschmitt
CEEHIMNNOOPRS comprehension
CEEHIMNNORSTT ethnocentrism
CEEHIMNOPSSTU Semnopithecus
CEEHIMNRSSSTW Western schism
CEEHIMOORSTTY stoechiometry
CEEHIMOPPRRTY hypermetropic
CEEHIMPPRRSST spectre shrimp
CEEHINNOPSSSY synecphonesis
CEEHINNORRSSY resynchronise
CEEHINNORRSYZ resynchronize
CEEHINOPPRRST precentorship
CEEHINORRRSYY Sir Henry Royce
CEEHIOPPPRRST preceptorship
CEEHIOPRSTTTW with respect to
CEEHKKMNOSTUY suck the monkey
CEEHKLMORTTTU The Mock Turtle
CEEHLLMOORRRY morello cherry
CEEHLNOOOPRTT photoelectron
CEEHLOOPRRSTU electrophorus
CEEHMMOOORSSX sex chromosome
CEEHNNORRRTTU turn the corner
CEEHNOOPRTTWW twopenceworth
CEEHNOORSSTTW stone the crows
stone the crows!
CEEHNOPRSTTUW put on the screw
CEEHOOOPPRRTT photoreceptor
CEEIIILMNORST isometric line
CEEIIILMRSSSU cruise missile
CEEIIILNOQRUV liquorice-vine
CEEIIIMMMPRST metempiricism
CEEIIIMMPRSTT metempiricist
CEEIIIMORSTTT meteoriticist
CEEIIINNORSTZ senior citizen
CEEIIJNORRSUV junior service
CEEIIKKLNPRSW winkle-pickers
CEEIIKMMMRSTW Mister Wemmick
CEEIILMNNRSTY reminiscently
CEEIILMNRSTTU lectisternium
CEEIILMOPTTVY competitively
CEEIILNNSSSUV inclusiveness
CEEIILNPSSTTT spittle insect
CEEIILRRSTTVY restrictively
CEEIIMNNRTTTY intermittency
CEEIIMNOPPRST misperception
CEEIIMNOPTTUV uncompetitive
CEEIIMOPPRSTT micropipettes
CEEIIMPPRSSTV perspectivism
CEEIINOPRSTTV introspective
CEEIIOPRTTUVV votive picture
CEEIIPPRSSTTV perspectivist
CEEIJLNORTUUV juvenile court
CEEIKMNRSSSSU serum sickness
CEEIKOORRRRSV reservoir rock
CEEILLLOOSSTV Elvis Costello
CEEILLMNOQTUU multiloquence
CEEILLNSUUVXY unexclusively

CEEILMNNOOQSU somniloquence
CEEILMNNOPTTY incompetently
CEEILMNOORSUY ceremoniously
CEEILNNOOPRTU nucleoprotein
CEEILNNOOPRXY clinopyroxene
CEEILNNOOSUXZ exclusion zone
CEEILNOOPRRST scleroprotein
CEEILNOSSSTUY necessitously
CEEILOPPRSTVY prospectively
CEEILOPRSTTTY electrotypist
CEEILORRSTTUU ostreiculture
CEEILORSTTTUY courtesy title
CEEILPQRSTUUY picturesquely
CEEILRSSTTUUU tissue culture
CEEIMMNNOOPTT omnicompetent
CEEIMNNOORSUU unceremonious
CEEIMNOOOPRRT reception room
CEEIMNOOPRRSS recompression
CEEIMNOOPSSST compositeness
CEEINNORSTTTU reconstituent
CEEINOOPRRSSV corresponsive
CEEINOOPRRSTT retrospection
CEEINOOPRSSTU precious stone
CEEINOORRSSSV corrosiveness
CEEIOOPRSSSTT stereoscopist
CEEIOPPPRRSTY copper pyrites
CEEIOPRRSSTTT Sir Peter Scott
CEEIOPRRSSTUX prosecutrixes
CEEJMNOPRRTUU counter-jumper
CEEKMMNOORSSU smoke-consumer
CEEKNOORRSTTU counterstroke
CEELMNOOORRTT remote control
CEELNOOSSSSTU cut one's losses
CEELOOPPRSTTU plectopterous
CEELOOPRRSSTT protectorless
CEELPQRSSTUUU sculpturesque
CEELRRSSSTTUU structureless
CEEMMNNOOPTUY pneumonectomy
CEEMMPRRSSSUY summer cypress
CEEMNNNOOPRTU pronouncement
CEEMNOOPRRTUU neurocomputer
CEEMOPPPRRTTU copper trumpet
CEEMOPPRRSTUU supercomputer
CEENNOORRSTUU neutron source
CEENOOPQRRSTU queen's proctor✧
CEENOORSSSTUU courteousness
CEEOOOOPPPRRS pooper-scooper
CEEOOORRSSTVV crossover vote
CEEOOPRRRRTTU court reporter
CEFFFGIILNORY flying officer
CEFFFGIILNSSU self-sufficing
CEFFFIKOOORSW Office of Works
CEFFGIINNSSSU sufficingness
CEFFGIINOORST sorting office
CEFFGIKNNOORS off-reckonings
CEFFIINOOPRRS prison officer
CEFFIINOOSSSU officiousness
CEFFILNOORSWZ flowers of zinc
CEFGHIIKNNOPP chopping-knife
CEFGHIIKNNRSS French kissing
CEFGIIKLNPSTY flying pickets
CEFGILMNNOSSU self-consuming
CEFGINOORSSTT soft-sectoring
CEFHHIILMSSTT Flemish stitch
CEFHHILLMOOSS Flemish school
CEFHHINNOORTV von Richthofen
CEFHIINOPPRSU porcupine fish
CEFHIMMOORRRU ferro-chromium
CEFHINOOPRSSS confessorship
CEFHLOOORRSST cross the floor
CEFHMNOOORRTY cry for the moon
CEFIIILLMNOPR penicilliform
CEFIIINORRTTW fiction writer
CEFIILLLOSSSY Isles of Scilly
CEFIILLRTTTUY fertility cult
CEFIINNNOOPRT non-proficient
CEFIINNNOOSTU non-infectious
CEFIIOOPRSTTU profectitious
CEFIJLMOOPRRT film projector
CEFILMMNNOOSU self-communion
CEFILNNOORTUY line of country
CEFILNOPRRTUY perfunctorily
CEFIOOPRRSTUU furor poeticus
CEFLLNOORSSUU colourfulness
CEFLMOORTTWYY flow cytometry
CEFLOPRSSTTUU soft sculpture
CEGGHLNOOOORY geochronology
CEGGIIIILNNPRS single pricing
CEGGIINNNORRT groin-centring
CEGGIINNNORSU unrecognising
CEGGIINNNORUZ unrecognizing
CEGGIMOOORSTU cogito, ergo sum
CEGHHIILOPRSY hieroglyphics
CEGHHIINNSUUW Chien-Shiung Wu
CEGHHIKORTTTU through ticket
CEGHIIILLNNPS spine-chilling
CEGHIIKLNPPRS shipping clerk
CEGHIILLNOOST lichenologist
CEGHIILLNSSTT Schilling test
CEGHIILLNSSTW switch selling
CEGHIILOOOSTY stoicheiology
CEGHIINNNNPPY penny-pinching
CEGHIKNNNOORT neck or nothing
CEGHILORSTTUY courtesy light
CEGHIMNNOOOTT come to nothing
CEGHINNOOSTUU counting house
CEGHINOORRSTV short covering
CEGHLLNOOOTWY low technology
low-technology
CEGHOPRRSSUYY psychosurgery
CEGIIIKNPRRST striking price
CEGIIIKNRTTTW ticket-writing
CEGIIILLNPRST still-piercing
CEGIIILMOPRUV cum privilegio
CEGIIILNOORST coreligionist
CEGIIINNOORRT irrecognition
CEGIILLMNRTTU milling cutter
CEGIILNOOSSTT insectologist
Scientologist
CEGIIMMNNOSTU time-consuming
CEGIIMMNNOTTU cummingtonite
CEGIIMNOORRTT trigonometric

CEGIIMNORTTUY tumorgenicity
CEGIINNOOPRSS processioning
CEGIINNOPPRRT intercropping
CEGILMMOORSTY myrmecologist
CEGILMOOOSSTT cosmetologist
CEGILNNNORTUY incongruently
CEGILOORSSTTU Etruscologist
CEGIMMNNOOOSY gynomonoecism
CEGINNNNNOOST non-consenting
CEGINNOPRSTUY counterspying
CEGINOPRRRSSS cross-springer
CEGINRRRSTTUU restructuring
CEGNNOOOPRSTY röntgenoscopy
CEGNNOORSSSUU congruousness
CEHHIIINNORTT ornithichnite
CEHHIIIPSSTTY physitheistic
CEHHIILLLNRST Chiltern Hills
CEHHIILOPRSTY chrysophilite
CEHHIIMOOPRRT theriomorphic
CEHHIMMOOOOPR homoeomorphic
CEHHIMNNORSTT the morn's nicht
CEHHIMNORSTTY rhythm section
CEHHINOPRRTYY phycoerythrin
CEHHOOPRTTTTU put to the torch
CEHIIIKLNOPTT pile it on thick
CEHIIKNOPSSSY psychokinesis
CEHIILLPPRSSW Phillips screw®
CEHIILLPPRSUV Phillips curve
CEHIILMNOOPPR lip microphone
CEHIILMOSSUVY mischievously
CEHIILNNOOSTT coin-in-the-slot
CEHIIMMOOORST homoeroticism
CEHIIMNOOPRST chemisorption
CEHIIMNRRSSTT Christminster
CEHIIMOORSTTY stoichiometry
CEHIINOOOPRTT iontophoretic
CEHIINOPPRSST inspectorship
CEHIIOPRRSTTT trichopterist
CEHIJNOORTTUW to conjure with
CEHIKNOOSSTTY Schottky noise
CEHILNNNOOSTY Holy Innocents
CEHILNOOPRSSU counselorship
CEHILNOOSTTTT cotton thistle
CEHILNOPSTTYY polysynthetic
CEHIMMMNOOTUY community home
CEHIMMNOOPPSY symphonic poem
CEHIMOPRSSTTY psychometrist
CEHIOOPPRRSST prosectorship
CEHIOOPPRRSTT protectorship
CEHIOOPRRSTTU trichopterous
CEHIOOPRSSSTY spherocytosis
CEHIOOPSSSTTT stethoscopist
CEHLNOORRSSUY nursery school
CEHMNOORRTTUY mother country
CEHNNNOORRRTW Northern Crown
CEHNNOORRSTUW Southern Crown
CEHNOORRSSSTU Southern Cross
CEIIIKLLLNOSW Wilkie Collins
CEIIILMNOPSST impoliticness
CEIIILNNSTTVY instinctively
CEIIILNPRSTVY inscriptively
CEIIIMNNOOPTT in competition
CEIIIMNOPSTUY impecuniosity
CEIIIMORSTUVV vivisectorium
CEIIJNOOPRSTT projectionist
CEIIKKLRSTTUY strike it lucky
CEIIKLNOPSTTW Wilson Pickett
CEIILLLNOOSTV violoncellist
CEIILMNOPSUUY impecuniously
CEIILNNNNOTTY incontinently
CEIILNNOORTTU interlocution
CEIILNOPSSSSU suspicionless
CEIILNORRTTUX interlocutrix
CEIILNRSTTUVY instructively
CEIILOOPPRSTW power politics
CEIILOPPRSTUY precipitously
CEIILPRRSTTUU stirpiculture
CEIILRRSSTTUU sericulturist
CEIIMMRSSSSTU music mistress
CEIIMNNORRTTU micronutrient
CEIIMNNORSSSU criminousness
CEIIMNOOOPRST recomposition
CEIIMNOOPRSTT protectionism
CEIIMNOOPRTTU motion picture
CEIINNNOOSTTV conventionist
CEIINNNOPRTTU interpunction
CEIINNOOPRSTT introspection
CEIINNORSSSUU incuriousness
CEIINNRSTTUUV uninstructive
CEIINOOOPRSST oneiroscopist
CEIINOOPRSSTT retinoscopist
CEIINOOPRSTTT protectionist
CEIINOORSSTUV insectivorous
CEIINOORTTUXY neurotoxicity
CEIINOPRSSSTU percussionist
CEIIOOPRSSSTV visceroptosis
CEIKLMMNNOTUY Mount McKinley
CEILLLNOOPSTU sul ponticello
CEILLMNOOSTTY tonsillectomy
CEILLOPPRSTUU liposculpture
CEILMNNOOOSSU mononucleosis
CEILMNOORSTUY coterminously
CEILMNOPSTUVY consumptively
CEILNNOOSTTUY contentiously
CEILNNORSSTUU uncourtliness
CEILNOORRTTUY interlocutory
CEILNORRRTUUY Cyril Tourneur
CEILOPPRSSUUY perspicuously
CEIMMMNOORSTY monosymmetric
CEIMMMNOORSUU Eurocommunism
CEIMMNOORSTUU Eurocommunist
CEIMNNOOORTTU countermotion
CEIMNOOPPRSTU income support
CEIMNORRSSSTU Russocentrism
CEIMOOOPPSSTT metoposcopist
CEIMOPRRSTUUV computer virus
CEINNNOOPRSTT cotton spinner
CEINNNOOSSSUU innocuousness
CEINNNOOSTTUU uncontentious
CEINNOOOPRSTU counter-poison
CEINNOPRRSSTU incorruptness
CEINOOQRSSSTU cross-question

CEINOORRSTTTV controvertist
CEINORRSSSTTU Russocentrist
CEIOOOPPPRRRT proprioceptor
CEIOOPRRRSTUU superior court
CELLMNNNOOSSU Nelson's Column
CELLNOOSSUUVV convolvuluses
CELOOOPRRSSTU poster colours
CEOOPPRRSSSSU cross-purposes
CFFIIILNOOSUY inofficiously
CFFIKKLORRTTU fork-lift truck
CFFKKNOOOPSST knock spots off
CFGHIILLNNNUY unflinchingly
CFGHIMMNOOORT right of common
CFGHIMNNOORTU unforthcoming
CFGIIIKMNOSST kissing-comfit
CFGIIKNNOOOSU fusion cooking
CFGIKLNOOSTTU floutingstock
CFGILLNOORSUY flying colours
CFGIMNNNNOOOR nonconforming
CFHILMOOORRST chloroformist
CFHINNORTTTUU truth function
CFHNNOOORRSTW crown of thorns
CFHNOOOORRTUU Court of Honour
CFIIINNNOOPTT conniption fit
CFILLNNOORTUX influx control
CFILNORSTUUUY infructuously
CFIMNNNOOORST nonconformist✧
CFIMNNNOOORTY nonconformity
CFOOOPRTTTUUU put out of court
CGGHHINOOOPUW whooping cough
CGGHIIILMNORT microlighting
CGHHIILLOORSS schoolgirlish
CGHHIILOOSTTY ichthyologist
CGHHIKMNORSTU mockingthrush
CGHIIIILLTTVW civil twilight
CGHIIJNNOTTTU tight junction
CGHIIKNOOSSTT shooting stick
CGHIIKNORSTTW throwing stick
CGHIILNOORSTW writing-school
CGHIILNORRSTY Christ in Glory
CGHIILOORSSTT Christologist
CGHIINNNRSTTU running stitch
CGHLNNOOORSYY synchronology
CGHLOOOOPSYYZ zoopsychology
CGIIIKNNOPSTT sticking-point
CGIIIKNNOSSSU kissing cousin
CGIIILLOOOPST oligopolistic
CGIIILMNOORST criminologist
CGIIILMOOSTTV victimologist
CGIIILNOOSSTU sociolinguist
CGIIIMNNOPRRT microprinting
CGIIINPRRSTTW scriptwriting
CGIIJNNOORSTU coursing-joint
CGIIKNNOOPSTT pointing-stock
CGIINOPPPRRST strip cropping
CGIJNNNOORTUW grown-junction
CGILNNOORSUUY incongruously
CGIMMNOOOOPRS composing room
CGLOOOOPRTYYZ cryptozoology
CHHIILNOOPPSU unphilosophic
CHHILMOOPPRTY lymphotrophic
CHHILOPPRSUUY hyposulphuric
CHHIMMOOOPRST photochromism
CHHIOOORSSTTU orthostichous
CHHIOOPRSSTYY psychohistory
CHIIIIMNORSST histrionicism
CHIIIKKLLNORT Kirkintilloch
CHIIILNOPRTTT lithontriptic
CHIIILOOPRSST solicitorship
CHIIILOPPRSST scripophilist
CHIILOORSSSTU lissotrichous
CHIIOOOPRRSTT proto-historic
CHIIOOPTTTXYY phytotoxicity
CHILLMOOPRSUY microphyllous
CHILMMNNOOOUY Holy Communion
CHILNOOORSSUY isochronously
CHILNOOPPRSSU proconsulship
CHILOPPRRSUUY pyrosulphuric
CHIMNOOOPRSST monostrophics
CHLNNOORSSUYY synchronously
CIIIILLNOSSTU illusionistic
CIIIINNSTTTVY instinctivity
CIIILNRSTTUUV viniculturist
CIIILRSTTTUUV viticulturist
CIILLNOPSTUUY punctiliously
CIILMMOOOPSST cosmopolitism
CIILMNOOPSSTU compulsionist
CIILNNOOSSTUV convulsionist
CIIMNNOOOPSST monopsonistic
CIIMNNOOORSTT contortionism
CIIMNOPSTTUVY consumptivity
CIIMOOOPRRSTY microporosity
CIINNOOORSTTT contortionist
CIINOOPPRSTTU opportunistic
CIINOOPRRSTTU corruptionist
CIKMMNOORTUWY community work
CILMOOPRSSUUY promiscuously
CILMOPRSSTUUY scrumptiously
CIMMNNOOOPSTU post-communion

D

DDDEEGGILNNOW golden wedding
DDDEEIINNSSUV undividedness
DDDEEILNNOOPR Lepidodendron
DDDEENNOORUWW wonder-wounded
DDDEGIIKLMMNO Middle Kingdom
DDDEGIKNNNOOY nodding donkey
DDDEHIMOORSUY hydromedusoid
DDDEHNNOOORRS rhododendrons
DDDEIIKLNSTWY tiddledywinks
DDDEILLMNORWY worldly-minded
DDDIINOOOPRTT diprotodontid
DDEEEEFLNNPST self-dependent
DDEEEEHIRSTTT desert the diet
DDEEEEILNNOPT needle-pointed
DDEEEEINORRSW dree one's weird
DDEEEELLLOPVW well-developed
DDEEEENNNOPSS open-endedness
DDEEEENNOPRTV overdependent
DDEEEFFIINORS fidei defensor
DDEEEFGILNRRS fiddler's green
DDEEEFILLRTVV velvet-fiddler

DDEEEGGILLNPS spindle-legged
DDEEEGHILNSST delightedness
DDEEEGIILNNPP dipping-needle
DDEEEGILNPSUV pudding-sleeve
DDEEEGILOPRRW powered glider
DDEEEHHNPRRSU under-shepherd
DDEEEIILNOTUX édition de luxe
DDEEEIIMPRRST red spider mite
DDEEEIINRSSTT disinterested
DDEEEILMNRSTW Middle Western
DDEEEILNNNPTY independently
DDEEEIMNPRSTU undistempered
DDEEEINPRSSSS dispersedness
DDEEELMNOPRUY underemployed
DDEEEMNNPRSSU Edmund Spenser
DDEEFGGIINNRW wedding finger
DDEEFHIINNRSU underfinished
DDEEFHILORRSW Wilfred Rhodes
DDEEFIIINRSUV undiversified
DDEEFILMNORSY fiddler's money
DDEEGGINNRRRU gerund-grinder
DDEEGHHINRTUW hundredweight
DDEEGHIILLMNS Middle English
DDEEGHNOOSSTT send to the dogs
DDEEGIIILMSSU guided missile
DDEEGIILNRSVW silver wedding
DDEEGIINSSSSU disguisedness
DDEEGINNPQSUU queen's pudding
DDEEGINOORRRV River Dordogne
DDEEGINSSSSTU disgustedness
DDEEHHLOORSST threshold dose
DDEEHILNOOTWY dyed-in-the-wool
DDEEHINORTTYZ The Dirty Dozen
DDEEHLMNRSSUU Edmund Husserl
DDEEHLNORRTUW The Underworld
DDEEIIKMNRRST Kidderminster
DDEEIILNRSTUU underutilised
DDEEIILNRTUUZ underutilized
DDEEIIMNSSTTW dim-wittedness
DDEEIKLLORSST dressed to kill
DDEEILMNNOSSW low-mindedness
DDEEILMOPRWWY powdery mildew
DDEEILNOPRRST Lord President
DDEEINORRSSWW window-dresser
DDEEINORSSSTT distortedness
DDEELNOORRRWW new world order
DDEFHILOORSUW field wood rush
DDEFINOOPRRUV unprovided-for
DDEGGINNOPPSU sponge pudding
DDEGGINOOSUUV Veduggio Sound
DDEGHHLMORTUU muddle through
DDEGHHLOOOSSU household gods
DDEGHIIINSSTU distinguished
DDEGHIILNNOPS shielding pond
DDEGIIILLNNTW twiddling-line
DDEGIIKMNNOTU United Kingdom
DDEGIILNSSUUY undisguisedly
DDEGIMMNPRSUU summer pudding
DDEGINOPRSTUW dusting powder
DDEHHILOPRSUY hydrosulphide
DDEHHLOOORSUW household word
DDEHIIMOOSTTT smooth-dittied
DDEHIKLNRSTUW whistled-drunk
DDEHINNOORSUU undishonoured
DDEIIIILMSSTU dissimilitude
DDEIIILLNOSSU disillusioned
DDEIIINOOPSST dispositioned
DDEIILNOOSWWW low side window
DDEIKLMNOORUW Under Milk Wood
DDEIMMNOORRSS Desmond Morris
DDEIMNOORSSTU misunderstood
DDELLMOOORRTV Lord Voldemort
DDEMNNOORSSWY Down's syndrome
DDENOOORRRUWY Rory Underwood
DDFIIMNNOOTUY if you don't mind
DDGGHILNNOORU holding ground
DDGHILMMNORTU Drummond light
DDHIILMORRSTW Third-Worldism
DDNNOORRSSUUU surround sound
DEEEEEGHILNTV give the needle
DEEEEEJNORSSU jeunesse dorée
DEEEEEMPRSTTW sweet-tempered
DEEEEFFGIRRRZ fridge-freezer
DEEEEFFILNSSV self-defensive
DEEEEFGGINNRR green-fingered
DEEEEFHHOTTTT fed to the teeth
DEEEEFHNORTUY under the eye of
DEEEEGGHOORTV go over the edge
DEEEEGILNNNTT netting-needle
DEEEEGLNRSSTT gens de lettres
DEEEEHHNRRTTU The Deer Hunter
DEEEEHNPRRSTT The Pretenders
DEEEEIJNPRTTU petit déjeuner
DEEEEIMNPRRRT predeterminer
DEEEEKNNOPPSU keep one's end up
DEEEELLPRRSVW well-preserved
DEEEELMNOPRTV redevelopment
DEEEELNOOPRTZ ozone-depleter
DEEEELNPPRSSX perplexedness
DEEEEMNNORRST re-endorsement
DEEEENNPRRSTU unrepresented
DEEEFFGIILNRT filter-feeding
DEEEFFGINNRYZ feeding frenzy
DEEEFFHIPRSTU sheriff depute
DEEEFFIINQRTU equidifferent
DEEEFFLOPRSSS self-professed
DEEEFGHILPSST selfe-despight
DEEEFGIILNNRR life-rendering
DEEEFGILLNRRW fringe-dweller
DEEEFGINNNSSU unfeignedness
DEEEFGJLMNSTU self-judgement
DEEEFGJMNORTU forejudgement
DEEEFGKLLNOSW self-knowledge
DEEEFGKLNOORW foreknowledge
DEEEFHHIORRRS Herefordshire
DEEEFHIKNNRTU under the knife
DEEEFHLNORSST threefoldness
DEEEFIILMNPUX unexemplified
DEEEFIILMPRSS semper fidelis
DEEEFIINRSTTX fixed-interest
DEEEFIJLNRRSY Jerry Seinfeld
DEEEFILLNNOSV find one's level

DEEEFILLNSTVY self-evidently
DEEEFILNOPPRS People's Friend
DEEEFILNPPPTT felt-tipped pen
DEEEFIMNNOORT forementioned
DEEEFINPRRSSV perfervidness
DEEEFLLLOPPRS self-propelled
DEEEFLLNNOOST lend oneself to
DEEEFLNORRTTU letter-founder
DEEEFLNRRRSSU self-surrender
DEEEFLOPSSSSS self-possessed
DEEEGGHILNPST sign the pledge
DEEEGHILNNNTU unenlightened
DEEEGHINRRRTV Right Reverend
DEEEGHLMOORST Gödel's theorem
DEEEGHLOORSWY heels o'er gowdy
DEEEGHNOOSTUV Steve Donoghue
DEEEGIIILNORS dereligionise
DEEEGIIILNORZ dereligionize
DEEEGIILNOPRV pigeon-livered
DEEEGIIPPRSUV Giuseppe Verdi
DEEEGILLNOOPP lodgepole pine
DEEEGIMNNOSTU et id genus omne
DEEEGINNNORSU sound engineer
DEEEGINNRSSSV deservingness
DEEEGIPRRRSSU pressure ridge
DEEEHHIILTTVW The White Devil
DEEEHHNNPRSTY Stephen Hendry
DEEEHIINNSTWY in the wind's eye
DEEEHILNNPRSU unreplenished
DEEEHILNOORTW lied ohne worte
DEEEHINOPRSST the Depression
DEEEHINPPRRST pretendership
DEEEHLMNNOOWY honeydew melon
DEEEHLMNOPTUY the unemployed
DEEEHLNOPRSTT the old serpent
DEEEHMOPRRSTT short-tempered
DEEEIILNNPTXY inexpediently
DEEEIILRRSSWW wired wireless
DEEEIIMNRSTTV divertisement
DEEEIINOPRSSX epoxide resins
DEEEIINRRRSTV River Dniester
DEEEILLLMPRTY ill-temperedly
DEEEILLORSTUY deleteriously
DEEEINOQSTUVX vexed question
DEEEKLMMRRTTU kettledrummer
DEEEKNOPPRUUY keep your end up
DEEELLNNPRSTY resplendently
DEEELNNSSSTTU unsettledness
DEEEMNORRSSYY Reye's syndrome
DEEEMOOPRRTTX dextro tempore
DEEEMOPSSSTTT tempest-tossed
DEEENNNOORSSU under one's nose
DEEENOPRRSUUX underexposure
DEEENORSSSTUX dexterousness
DEEENPRRRSSUU under pressure
DEEFFFINORRST first offender
DEEFFGIILNORS Design for Life
DEEFFGNNOORUY young offender
DEEFFIIINORTW fortified wine
DEEFFIILNNRTY indifferently
DEEFFIINSSSUV diffusiveness
DEEFFOORSTUWW sweet woodruff
DEEFGGHIILNRT light-fingered
DEEFGHIILLNSS self-shielding
DEEFGHIILNNRY Henry Fielding
DEEFGHILNOORS shingle-roofed
DEEFGHILNRSTT field strength
DEEFGIIMNRSTU disfigurement
DEEFGIINORSSW Wings of Desire
DEEFGILLNNSTU self-indulgent
DEEFGILLNNSYY self-denyingly
DEEFGILMNRRSU self-murdering
DEEFGILMOPSTU gumple-foisted
DEEFGILNORSUV girdle of Venus
DEEFHHIORRRST Hertfordshire
DEEFHIIJLNTUW June Whitfield
DEEFHILLMNRUW Wilhelm Freund
DEEFHILLNNORU fille d'honneur
DEEFIIILMNOSS field emission
DEEFIIINNOPRT predefinition
DEEFIILNNOOPS self-opinioned
DEEFIIMNNNOOS find someone in
DEEFIKNNNORSU unforeskinned
DEEFILNNOORYZ ozone-friendly
DEEFILNOPRSSU splendiferous
DEEFILNORRSTU Rudolf Steiner
DEEFILOOORRTU outdoor relief
DEEFIMMOORSUX mixed foursome
DEEFIRSSTTUUU future studies
DEEFLNNORSSUW wonderfulness
DEEFLNORRUUVY Rudolf Nureyev
DEEFLOPPRSSTU self-supported
DEEGGHIOOSTTV give to the dogs
DEEGGIIINNNNW winding engine
DEEGGIILNNRSV diverging lens
DEEGHHIKNPRSS Shepherd kings
DEEGHILLNOSUW dwelling-house
DEEGHILMNNORS Modern English
DEEGHILMOOSTY demythologise
DEEGHILMOOTYZ demythologize
DEEGHILNNOOST on the long side
DEEGHILNOORST The Gondoliers
DEEGHILNRSTTY yield strength
DEEGHKOOOPRSU keep good hours
DEEGIIINNRSSW series winding
DEEGIIKLNOPRW dog-periwinkle
DEEGIILLNORSS single soldier
DEEGIKLLNNOTU Duke Ellington
DEEGILLLNORRV Lord Grenville
DEEGILMNOOSTY sedimentology
DEEGILNNORTUV overindulgent
DEEGILNNRSUVY undeservingly
DEEGILNORSTUV silver-tongued
DEEGIMNNNOPSY spending money
DEEGINNORSTTW Downing Street
DEEGINOPRRSSW power dressing
DEEGIOORRRSSV Reservoir Dogs
DEEHHIIMNNUUY Yehudi Menuhin
DEEHHIOOPPRSS dephosphorise
DEEHHIOOPPRSZ dephosphorize
DEEHHIOPPRRTY hypertrophied
DEEHHLLOORTWW the whole world

DEEHHLOORRTTW	the other world
DEEHHNORRSTUW	thundershower
DEEHHOOPPRSTT	phosphoretted
DEEHHOPPRSTTU	phosphuretted
DEEHIINNPRSTU	indentureship
DEEHIINORSSTT	hit one's stride
DEEHIINPPRSST	presidentship
DEEHIKNRRSTTU	thunderstrike
DEEHILMMNOSST	demolishments
DEEHILPRRSSUU	desulphuriser
DEEHILPRRSUUZ	desulphurizer
DEEHINOORTTWW	down to the wire
DEEHJKLLNRRYY	Dr Henry Jekyll
DEEHKNORRSTTU	thunder-stroke
DEEHNNOPPRSTY	the penny drops
DEEIIIMMNNRST	indeterminism
DEEIIIMNNRSTT	indeterminist
DEEIIIMNOPQRU	Dominique Pire
DEEIIINOPRSTY	Sidney Poitier
DEEIIINOQRSTU	derequisition
DEEIIINPRSSTT	serendipitist
DEEIIKLLNORSU	unsoldierlike
DEEIIKNNNNRSS	Dennis Skinner
DEEIILLNORSSS	soldierliness
DEEIILMNNOSSS	dimensionless
DEEIILMNNSSTU	unlimitedness
DEEIILNORSSSU	deliriousness
DEEIILNPRRSTV	printer's devil
DEEIILOPPRSTT	lepidopterist
DEEIILOPSTUXY	expeditiously
DEEIIMNNRTTTU	unintermitted
DEEIIMNNSSTTV	disinvestment
DEEIIMNOORSST	endometriosis
DEEIIMNOPRSTT	Redemptionist
DEEIIMOORRSTU	demeritorious
DEEIINNSSTTTW	nitwittedness
DEEIINOOPRRSU	urediniospore
DEEIINOPRSSTU	serendipitous
DEEIINOSSSSTU	seditiousness
DEEILLNNOOORT	rolled into one
DEEILMMNOPSTY	disemployment
DEEILMNOOSSSU	melodiousness
DEEILMNORSTUV	silver-mounted
DEEILMORTTUUV	overmultitude
DEEILNNOSTTUY	tendentiously
DEEILNORSSSTU	desultoriness
DEEILNOSSSSTU	dissoluteness
DEEILNPRRTTUY	interruptedly
DEEILOOPPRSTU	lepidopterous
DEEIMMNRSSTUY	unsymmetrised
DEEIMMNRSTUYZ	unsymmetrized
DEEIMNNNOOSST	set one's mind on
DEEIMNOORSTTU	Deuteronomist
DEEIMNOPRSSST	Simpson Desert
DEEIMNOSSSTUW	women's studies
DEEIMOPRRRSSV	dress-improver
DEEINNOOPSSTT	post-tensioned
DEEINNORRTWWY	re-entry window
DEEINNPRRTTUU	uninterrupted
DEEIOPRSTTUVY	topside-turvey
DEEIORSSSTTWY	West Side Story
DEEKLLOORTUWW	well-worked-out
DEELNNOPSSSUU	pendulousness
DEEMMRRRSTUYY	murder mystery
DEEMNORRSSSUU	murderousness
DEEMNORRSSTTY	Rett's syndrome
DEENNOOPRSSSU	ponderousness
DEENNOPSSSTTU	unspottedness
DEENOOPRRRRTY	Rodney R Porter
DEFFFHIILLOTT	lift the lid off
DEFFGIIKNNORR	drink-offering
DEFFGINOOOSST	goodness of fit
DEFFHILNOOORU	field of honour
DEFFIIILNOOSV	field of vision
DEFFIIIORRTTV	vitrified fort
DEFGHILNOORSX	Oxford English
DEFGHMOOORRTW	from the word go
DEFGIILNNOSUW	fusion welding
DEFGIILRRTTUY	fertility drug
DEFGILNNORUVV	revolving fund
DEFHIILLOPSSW	disfellowship
DEFHILMMOORSU	field mushroom
DEFHILMRRTTYY	Merthyr Tydfil
DEFHIMORRRTUU	rutherfordium
DEFHMOOOOPPRT	prophet of doom
DEFHOOOOSTTUW	out of the woods
DEFIILLNOPSUU	filipendulous
DEFIILPRSTUUY	superfluidity
DEFIIMMNOOTTU	time out of mind
DEFILLMOORRSU	Lord of Misrule
DEFILLRSSSTUY	distressfully
DEFILMNNNSSUU	unmindfulness
DEFILNNSSTUUU	undutifulness
DEFILNOOORSSS	Lord of Session
DEFILNOOQRRUU	furor loquendi
DEFILOOORRSUY	odoriferously
DEFIMNNOOOSTU	out of one's mind
DEFLNNOOOORTW	Tower of London
DEGGHIIILNNPS	pidgin English
DEGGHIKNNOORY	good-King-Henry
DEGGHILLNOSTY	long-sightedly
DEGGHILNOOOST	shooting lodge
DEGGHNNOOOOTU	not good enough
DEGGIILLNOPSS	disgospelling
DEGGINNOOPRWW	powdering-gown
DEGHHILOPRTTT	trothplighted
DEGHIIILPRSTT	light-spirited
DEGHIIINRSSTU	distinguisher
DEGHIIJLLNNOR	John Dillinger
DEGHIINNPRSTU	hunting spider
DEGHILLNORSTU	shrill-tongued
DEGHILMOOOSTT	methodologist
DEGHINNNOOSST	do-nothingness
DEGHINNOORTTU	into the ground
DEGHINNORSSTW	downrightness
DEGHMNOOOSTTU	smooth-tongued
DEGHNOOOSTTTT	Hottentot's god
DEGIIILNPSSTT	side-splitting
DEGIIILNQSTUY	disquietingly
DEGIIJMNPPRSU	jumping spider
DEGIILNNOORRS	soldering iron
DEGIILNNORSTV	Dr Livingstone

DEGIILNRSSSTY distressingly
DEGIILOOPRSTT pteridologist
DEGIIMNOPPRRW priming-powder
DEGIINOPRSSTU true-disposing
DEGIKLNORSTTU skittle-ground
DEGIKNNOORRWW wonder-working
DEGILLMNORSUY smoulderingly
DEGILNOOORRVV revolving door
DEGIMNOOOPRRW powdering-room
DEGINNOORRRRU rounding error
DEGOOOOPPRSTU to good purpose
DEHHIIOPRRSSY hyperhidrosis
DEHHILOORRSTW otherworldish
DEHHILOPRSTUY hydrosulphite
DEHHIMOPRRSUY Doris Humphrey
DEHIILNOPTTTU put the lid on it
DEHIINOOPPSST deipnosophist
DEHIJLNOORSTU shoulder joint
DEHIKNOPSSTTU put the skids on
DEHILLLMORUUY ill-humouredly
DEHINNOOORSTT odontornithes
DEHINOOPPRSWW window-shopper
DEHINORSTTTUW round the twist
DEHOOPRSTTTUW put to the sword
DEIIIKLMNNOTT milk-dentition
DEIIIKNOOPPST piked position
DEIIILMNOOSTT demolitionist
DEIIILOPSSTVY dispositively
DEIIINNOSSSSU insidiousness
DEIIINNOSSSUV invidiousness
DEIIINOOPRSTT periodontitis
DEIIIOPSSSTTU uti possidetis
DEIIKMNNOORSW dimension work
DEIIKNNOOSTUW know inside out
DEIILLNORSTWW trellis window
DEIILMNOPRTVY improvidently
DEIILNNOPSTUU plenitudinous
DEIILNOOPRRSV lion's provider
DEIILNOORSSTU redissolution
DEIILNOOSTTUV devolutionist
DEIIMNNNOOTTT don't mention it
DEIINNOOPRSUV unprovisioned
DEIINOOPSSSSS dispossession
DEILLMORRTUUW murder will out
DEILLNNORSSUW unworldliness
DEILNOOPSSTUX dust explosion
DEIMMMMNOORSU midsummer moon
DEIMMMNOSTTUU mutton-dummies
DEIMMNOOPRSST post-modernism✧
DEIMNNOOPSTTU put one's mind to
DEIMNOOPRSSTT post-modernist
DEINNOOORSSSU inodorousness
DEIOOPRSTTTUY studio pottery
DELNOPPRSTUUY unsupportedly
DFGGHIIKNNRTU fighting drunk
DFGGHIILLNOOT floodlighting
DFGGHIINNORSU fishing ground
DFGGHIINORSTW fighting words
DFGIINNOOOOPS food poisoning
DFGINNOOOPRSU soundproofing
DFIINOORSTTUU fortitudinous
DFILLRSSTTUUY distrustfully
DGGGGILMNRSUU drug smuggling
DGGHINNNORTUU hunting-ground
DGGINNOOPRRUV proving ground
DGHHIILNNOTUW unwithholding
DGHIIIILMNNSY diminishingly
DGHIILNRSTTUY light industry
DGIIIILNPRSTY dispiritingly
DGIIIKNNNPPSY skinny-dipping
DGIIIMNORRRRV driving-mirror
DGIIINNPRSSTW winding-strips
DGIILNNOOOSST sindonologist
DGIILNOPRSTTW word-splitting
DGIINNOPPRRTU roundtripping
DGILLNOOSSUUU solidungulous
DGINNNORRRSUU run rings round
DGLMNOOOOSSTU odontoglossum
DGLMNOOSSUUUY Young's modulus
DHHIIIOOOPRST histiophoroid
DHIIIMMOOPRSS isodimorphism
DHIIINOORSSTV short division
DHIILNOOPRSSS Risso's dolphin
DHIIMOOOPRSSU isodimorphous
DHINOOORRSTUZ tours d'horizon
DHNOOOOOPRSTU odontophorous
DIIIINNOOPSST indisposition
DIILLNOOOSSTU solid solution
DIILMNOSTTUUU multitudinous
DIILNORSSTUUY industriously
DIINOOOPPRRST disproportion
DILLMOPRSTUWY multiply words
DILLNOOPSSSYY spondylolysis
DILNOOOORSWWW Woodrow Wilson
DIMNOOORRTTWY dormitory town
DLNOOOOPPRTTY polyprotodont
DMOOPRSTTUVYY topsy-turvydom

E

EEEEEFFNNRRTV efferent nerve
EEEEEGIMNRRSV semi-evergreen
EEEEEIJMNPRRU jeune première
EEEEEIKNNOPSY keep one's eye in
EEEEEKNNOOPSY keep one's eye on
EEEEELNPRSSSV Seven Sleepers
EEEEENNPRRSTU entrepreneuse
EEEEEPRRSSTTW street sweeper
EEEEFILNRSSVX reflexiveness
EEEEFILPRRRSV life-preserver
EEEEFKLNOOPST keep to oneself
EEEEFLNOOPSSX expose oneself
EEEEGGIINNNRR re-engineering
EEEEGGIJNNORS jee one's ginger
EEEEGHILMORST eightsome reel
EEEEGHILNRSTW steering wheel
EEEEGHINNNPTY eighteen-penny
EEEEGHINORSST heterogenesis
EEEEGHINORTTY heterogeneity
EEEEGHLOPRSTT sleep together
EEEEGHNOORSTU heterogeneous
EEEEGIINOPRSS epeirogenesis
EEEEGILLNNNVY Evelyn Glennie

EEEEGILNORSST	Ernesto Geisel
EEEEGIMNRRSSW	messenger-wire
EEEEGINNRSTVY	yesterevening
EEEEHHOQRSTUV	shove the queer
EEEEHIIMMPRST	ephemeris time
EEEEHIINRSTTT	the eternities
EEEEHIIPPRTTW	white pipe-tree
EEEEHINORRSVW	whereinsoever
EEEEHINRRSTVW	never the wiser
EEEEHKLLRRSTT	helter-skelter
EEEEHKNOOPPSU	keep open house
EEEEHLNNSTTVY	seventeenthly
EEEEHMNNOSTTU	tenement house
EEEEIIMMPRRST	semiperimeter
EEEEIINPRRRRV	Pierre Vernier
EEEEIJLLRRSWY	Jerry Lee Lewis
EEEEIKKNOTUWW	week in, week out
EEEEILMNNNOST	in one's element
EEEEILNNPRTTT	Triple Entente
EEEEIMNNOPRTY	pine-tree money
EEEEIMNORSSTV	serve one's time
EEEEIMNPRRSTW	Western Empire
EEEEINNPSSSVX	expensiveness
EEEEINNRSSTTV	retentiveness
EEEEINNSSSTVX	extensiveness
EEEEINPQRSSTU	sesquiterpene
EEEEINPRRSSTT	preteriteness
EEEEJJKMMOORR	Jerome K Jerome
EEEEJNNSSTTUV	Just Seventeen
EEEELLMOPRRST	Ellesmere Port
EEEELLNPSSSSS	sleeplessness
EEEELMNOQRSUZ	lemon squeezer
EEEELNNOORSSV	lose one's nerve
EEEELNNRSSSSV	nervelessness
EEEELNNSSSSSS	senselessness
EEEELNNSSSSTV	eventlessness
EEEELPRRSSTTX	express letter
EEEEMNNPRRSTT	representment
EEEEMOPRRSTUX	exposure meter
EEEENNNORSSSV	nonsense verse
EEEFFGHOORSUU	house of refuge
EEEFFGILLLNOW	fellow feeling
EEEFFGILLNORY	forefeelingly
EEEFFGILNRRRS	self-referring
EEEFFGLNOORST	forget oneself
EEEFFINNOSSSV	offensiveness
EEEFGILLLLNSV	self-levelling
EEEFGILNNNSSU	unfeelingness
EEEFGIMNPRRTU	prefigurement
EEEFHHLOORRSS	horseflesh ore
EEEFHHLPRSSST	press the flesh
EEEFHIIMMNNRY	feminine rhyme
EEEFHIKOPSSUW	housewifeskep
EEEFHIMORRTTU	three-four time
EEEFHKNORRSTU	seek-no-further
EEEFHNOPRRSTT	for the present
EEEFHORRSUVWY	every few hours
EEEFIILLLLMSU	millefeuilles
EEEFIILNNOSTX	file extension
EEEFIIORRRSSU	Fourier series
EEEFIJLNNOPRZ	Jennifer Lopez
EEEFINNPRSSSU	superfineness
EEEFJLMNNOSTY	self-enjoyment
EEEFKLLMOSSSU	smokeless fuel
EEEFLLNORRTTU	fortune-teller
EEEFLNNRSSSTU	resentfulness
EEEFNNOOOSTTU	out on one's feet
EEEFNOOORSTTU	out of one's tree
EEEFNOPPSTTUU	put one's feet up
EEEGGHHINRRSU	Sir Hugh Greene
EEEGGHIORTTTT	get it together
EEEGGINORSSSU	egregiousness
EEEGHHHIRSTTT	the high street✧
EEEGHILMNNNTT	enlightenment✧
EEEGHILMNOSST	something else
EEEGHILNNQSSU	queen's English
EEEGHIMNORSST	thermogenesis
EEEGHINNORRST	nether regions
EEEGHINNRTVWY	green with envy
EEEGHIORRSSTU	Register House
EEEGIIMNRRSST	Meistersinger
EEEGIKLOORRSV	Sergei Korolev
EEEGILLNNRVWY	Greville Wynne
EEEGILLNSSSSU	guilelessness
EEEGILNNORVWY	overweeningly
EEEGILNOORSTV	venereologist
EEEGILNPRRSVY	perseveringly
EEEGIMMMNRSSU	summer-seeming
EEEGIMNNORSST	remote sensing
EEEGINNNNSSUU	ungenuineness
EEEGINOORRSTV	go into reverse
EEEGINOPRRSTW	power steering
EEEGIORRRSSTV	retrogressive
EEEGKLNOOSSTU	skeletogenous
EEEGLNNSSTTTU	tungsten steel
EEEGNNOOORSUZ	erogenous zone
EEEGNOQRSSSTU	grotesqueness
EEEHHHLNOOSTT	hot on the heels
EEEHHIILNPRTW	three-line whip
EEEHHINPRSTTY	hypersthenite
EEEHHIORRSTVW	whithersoever
EEEHHJKLNOOOR	John Lee Hooker
EEEHHLNRTTTTU	hunt the letter
EEEHHNNOPRRTT	threepenn'orth
EEEHIIILNNPPT	in the pipeline
EEEHIIKLLLMTW	Wilhelm Keitel
EEEHIKLLMOPTY	keyhole limpet
EEEHILLMPRSTY	Shirley Temple
EEEHILMNNPRST	replenishment
EEEHILMNOSSST	lithesomeness
EEEHILMOPRRTY	pyrheliometer
EEEHILMPPRSSX	herpes simplex
EEEHILNRSSTTT	enter the lists
EEEHIMNNNOOPP	epiphenomenon
EEEHINNOSTTTX	sixteenth note
EEEHLLNOOPSTT	telephoto lens
EEEHLLORRTTTV	throttle lever
EEEHLMNNOOOPT	monotelephone
EEEHLMNOOOTTU	homeoteleuton
EEEHLMNOOSSSW	wholesomeness
EEEHOOPRRSTTU	heteropterous
EEEIIILLNPRTV	perivitelline

EEEIILLNRSSSU leisureliness
EEEIILMRSSTTV letter missive
EEEIILNNPSVXY inexpensively
EEEIILNOSSTTV television set
EEEIIMNPRSTTX experimentist
EEEIINNNSSSTV intensiveness
EEEIINNNSSTVV inventiveness
EEEIINNSSSSTV sensitiveness
EEEIINORSSTVV oversensitive
EEEIINQRSSSTU requisiteness
EEEIINQSSSTUX exquisiteness
EEEIIOQRSTUVX over-exquisite
EEEIJLNRRSUUY Julius Nyerere
EEEILLMOPPSSY Smiley's People
EEEILMNNRTTUU ten-minute rule
EEEILMOORSVZZ mezzo-relievos
EEEILNNNPSSSS pennilessness
EEEILNNOSSSSS noiselessness
EEEILNNPSSSSS spinelessness
EEEILNNPSUVXY unexpensively
EEEILNOPSSSVX explosiveness
EEEILNORSSUVY sue one's livery
EEEILNPRSSSUV repulsiveness
EEEIMMOPRSSTY sympiesometer
EEEIMNNORSSTV montes veneris
EEEIMNOOPRTTT potentiometer
EEEIMOPRSSTUV Supreme Soviet
EEEINNOPPSSTU tune one's pipes
EEEINNOPRSSTT septentriones
EEEINNOSSSSTV ostensiveness
EEEINNRRSSSTY styrene resins
EEEINPRRRSSTT interpretress
EEEJJKLLNRUWY junk jewellery
EEEKLMNOOSSSZ smokeless zone
EEEKLMNOSSSSS smokelessness
EEEKLMOOPRRTT Otto Klemperer
EEELLMORRSSSY remorselessly
EEELLNPSSSSSU pulselessness
EEELMMNOORTUV volumenometer
EEELMNORRSSSU unremorseless
EEELMNORSTUVY venturesomely
EEELMNOSTTTTU outsettlement
EEELMOPPPRRRU purple emperor
EEELNNOPSSSTU plenteousness
EEELNOORTTVWW twelve-note row
twelve-tone row
EEELNOPRSSSSW powerlessness
EEENNOORRSSSU erroneousness
EEENNORRSSTUV serve one's turn
EEENOPRSSSTTU set up one's rest
EEFFFGLLORSTU self-forgetful
EEFFFLLLNOOSU full of oneself
EEFFGGHIIORTU figure of eight
EEFFGIIMORRTU figure of merit
EEFFGIKNOOSTT get one's kit off
EEFFGLNORSSTU forgetfulness
EEFFIILLRSTTY self-fertility
EEFFIILNNOSVY inoffensively
EEFFKNOOORSST off one's stroke
EEFGGGIINRRRT trigger finger
EEFGGIILNNOOR foreign legion✧
EEFGGIILNRSSU single figures
EEFGGILNNORSV self-governing
EEFGHIIRRSSTT shift register
EEFGHILNPRSSS flesh-pressing
EEFGHILORSSST foresightless
EEFGHILORSSTU self-righteous
EEFGIIINRRSST fire-resisting
EEFGIILLOOTTW gillie-wetfoot
EEFGIILMNOORT Legion of Merit
EEFGIILNNRRTY interferingly
EEFGIINNOPRRT finger-pointer
EEFGIINNOPRTZ freezing point
EEFGILLOORSTX reflexologist
EEFGILNOPRRSV self-reproving
EEFGINNOORSST frontogenesis
EEFGINNORSSUV unforgiveness
EEFGINOORRRRT Reign of Terror
EEFGNNOORSSTT forgottenness
EEFHHIILNOPST ship of the line
EEFHHIIOPSSUW housewifeship
EEFHIIKNSTTTW twist the knife
EEFHIILLLNOTY lily of the Nile
EEFHILNNSSSSU unselfishness
EEFHILNSSSSST shiftlessness
EEFHIORRSSTYY oyster-fishery
EEFHJLNOORSTT Letters of John
EEFHNNORRTTUU fortune-hunter
EEFIIKLRRRSTZ Fritz Kreisler
EEFIILLMNNOOS fill someone in
EEFIILLMNOSTU feuilletonism
EEFIILLNNOSSX inflexionless
EEFIILLNOSTTU feuilletonist
EEFIILLRSSTTY self-sterility
EEFIILOPRRSTU reptiliferous
EEFIIMNORSTTU fermentitious
EEFILLLLMNTUY mellifluently
EEFILLNNPSSTU plentifulness
EEFILNNNOOOST not on one's life
EEFILNNOOSSSU feloniousness
EEFILNOOPSTTU step out of line
EEFILNRSSSSTU fruitlessness
EEFILOOPRRSTU petroliferous
EEFILOPRSSTUY pestiferously
EEFLMNOORRSTT self-tormentor
EEFLMOPRRTTUW trumpet flower
EEFLNNNSSTUUU untunefulness
EEFLNNRSSSTUU unrestfulness
EEFMNOORRSSTT stern-foremost
EEGGGGIINORSS George Gissing
EEGGGINOORSWY grey-goose wing
EEGGHHHLOOOTW go the whole hog
EEGGHINNNRSTT strengthening
EEGGHMNOOOPRY geomorphogeny
EEGGHMNOOORST George Thomson
EEGGIIILMNORS in gremio legis
EEGGIINNNNRTU engine-turning
EEGGIINNPPRSW weeping spring
EEGGIINOSSSTU suggestionise
EEGGIINOSSTUZ suggestionize
EEGGIJKOPRRYY jiggery-pokery
EEGGIJLNOPPRS jogger's nipple

EEGGIJNNOORSW jow one's ginger
EEGGILNPPSSYY Sleeping Gypsy
EEGGILOPRSTTT Lester Piggott
EEGGINOOPPSST goose-stepping
EEGGIORRRSSST gross register
EEGGJLLNNNOSY jenny-long-legs
EEGHHIILLNORZ Heinz Holliger
EEGHHIILOPSVX high explosive
high-explosive
EEGHHIIPRSSST high priestess
EEGHHNNORSTTT on the strength
EEGHHOORRTTTW throw together
EEGHIIKLMNOST something like
EEGHIILLPSTTW twilight sleep
EEGHIILNNNPSW spinning-wheel
EEGHIILOORSST heresiologist
EEGHIIMNNOOTY inhomogeneity
EEGHIINNOOSST seine-shooting
EEGHIIPRRSSST ship's register
EEGHIJNORTUWY journey-weight
EEGHIKNRRRSTU hunger-striker
EEGHILLOPRRTT petrol lighter
EEGHILMMNOSST gentilshommes
EEGHILMNOSSST lightsomeness
EEGHILMNOSSTU smelting-house
EEGHILNSSSSST sightlessness
EEGHILOOPRSTT herpetologist
EEGHIMNNOOOSU inhomogeneous
EEGHIMNOOPRSS morphogenesis
EEGHIMNORSTTT thermosetting
EEGHINNOSSTTW sweet nothings
EEGHINOOORTTV Into the Groove
EEGHINOORSSTT orthogenesist
EEGHINORRTTUY Tyrone Guthrie
EEGHINORSSSTU righteousness
EEGHIOPRTTTTU put it together
EEGHLMNNOOOPY phenomenology
EEGHLNOOORTUY neuroethology
EEGHNOOPRSTTY phytoestrogen
EEGIIIMNOPRTV primogenitive
EEGIILLLMSUVY Sylvie Guillem
EEGIILLLNNTTY intelligently
EEGIILLNNNTTU unintelligent
EEGIILLNNPTTU little penguin
EEGIILLNOPWWW weeping willow
EEGIILLNOSTUV vitelligenous
EEGIILNNRSTTY interestingly
EEGIILNORSSSU religiousness
EEGIIMMMNSTTU summit meeting
EEGIIMNOPRRTU primogeniture
EEGIIMNORSSTU tumorigenesis
EEGIIMNPRRTTT pretermitting
EEGIINNNOSSSU ingeniousness
EEGIINNNRSTTU uninteresting
EEGIINNORSSSS session singer
EEGILLNNNRTUY unrelentingly
EEGILLNSSSSTU guiltlessness
EEGILMOOORSTT meteorologist
EEGILNNNPRTUY unrepentingly
EEGILOPRRSSVY progressively
EEGIMMNNORSTV misgovernment
EEGIMNNORRSTY yestermorning
EEGIMNOOPRRTT Otto Preminger
EEGIMNPRSSSST sempstressing
EEGINNNOSSSUU ingenuousness
EEGINNNRSSSTT stringentness
EEGINNNRSSSTU unrestingness
EEGINNOPPSSTT stepping-stone
EEGINOORRRSST retrogression
EEGINOPPRSSSS prepossessing
EEGINOPRRSSUV unprogressive
EEGINOPRRSTTU interest group
EEGINORSTTTUW tongue-twister
EEGLMNOOOPRSU prolegomenous
EEGMMNORRSTYY mystery-monger
EEGOPPRRRSSUU pressure group
EEHHHLOOOSTTW the whole shoot
EEHHIIIMPTTTT it pitieth them
EEHHIILLLMNPS philhellenism
EEHHIILLLNPST philhellenist
EEHHIINNOOPTW Winnie-the-Pooh
EEHHINOPPRSTT Pepin the Short
EEHHMMNOOOPPR morphophoneme
EEHHMMOOORSTU homeothermous
EEHHOOPRRSTTY heterostrophy
EEHIIINPPRRST perinephritis
EEHIIKLMOOSTT Some Like It Hot
EEHIIKNNSSSTT kittenishness
EEHIILLMNORRS horse-milliner
EEHIINOOPRRRT heir-portioner
EEHIINOPRRSST spheristerion
EEHIJLMOPRTUY Horyuji Temple
EEHIKORRSSTWY West Yorkshire
EEHILLNOSSSWY yellowishness
EEHILLOORSSTT tortoiseshell
EEHILMMNOOSTT monotheletism✧
EEHILMNRSSSST mirthlessness
EEHILMORSSTTY heterostylism
EEHILNNORRSST northerliness
EEHILNOORSSST lose one's shirt
EEHILNOORSSTT Ornitholestes
EEHILNORSSSTU southerliness
EEHILOPSSSTTX The Sex Pistols
EEHILQRRRSSUW squirrel shrew
EEHIMMNNOPRST premonishment
EEHIMNOPTTTUU up to the minute
up-to-the-minute
EEHIMORRSSSTW whoremistress
EEHIMORSSSSTU housemistress
EEHKNNOOORSTT on tenterhooks
EEHLLLNNOOTYY Only the Lonely
EEHLLMNOOSUWY unwholesomely
EEHLMNNOSSTTU Mount St Helens
EEHLNORRSTTWY north-westerly
EEHLNORSSSSTW worthlessness
EEHLNRSSSSTTU truthlessness
EEHLOORSSTTUY heterostylous
EEHLORSSTTUWY south-westerly
EEHMMNOOPTTTU up to the moment
up-to-the-moment
EEHMNOOOSSSTT toothsomeness
EEHMNOOPRSTUY hymenopterous

EEHMNOOPSTTUV put the moves on
EEHMNOORRSSTT North Somerset
EEHNORSSTTTWW west-north-west
EEHOOOPRRSSTU heterosporous
EEHOOPRSTTTUW put to the worse
EEHOSSSTTTUWW west-south-west
EEIIILNNSSTVY insensitively
EEIIIMMNPRRST prime minister
EEIIIMNPRSSTV primitiveness
EEIIINNRSTTTY in its entirety
EEIIINNSSTTUV intuitiveness
EEIIJKNNPRRTT ink-jet printer
EEIILLMNSSSST limitlessness
EEIILLMPPPRST slipper limpet
EEIILLMPRTUVY impurity level
EEIILMMNNORSS immersion lens
EEIILMNNPRTTY impertinently
EEIILMNPSSSUV impulsiveness
EEIILMOORSVZZ mezzo-rilievos
EEIILMOOSSTTY osteomyelitis
EEIILNOORSTUV revolutionise
EEIILNOORTUVZ revolutionize
EEIILNOQRSTUV ventriloquise
EEIILNOQRTUVZ ventriloquize
EEIILNRSSTUVW West Nile virus
EEIILOPPRSTVY prepositively
EEIILOPRSTTUY repetitiously
EEIILPPRRTUZZ Pulitzer Prize
EEIILPRSTUUVV vivisepulture
EEIIMNNNOOSTW in one's own time
EEIIMNOPRRSST pretermission
EEIIMNOPRSSSU imperiousness
EEIIMNOPRSSSX expressionism✧
EEIINNOPRRSST interspersion
EEIINNRSSSTUV intrusiveness
EEIINOPRSSSTX expressionist✧
EEIINOQRRTUUU in utroque iure
EEIIOOQSSTTTU toties quoties
EEIKLLNOPRTUV Oliver Plunket
EEILLLMOORRSV Oliver Mellors
EEILLLNNORSSZ Zöllner's lines
EEILLMNOOSSTY emotionlessly
EEILLMOPRSTTU multiple store
EEILLNOOPQRSU nolle prosequi
EEILLNOOSSWYY linsey-woolsey
EEILMMMNOPSTY misemployment
EEILMNNRTTTUY unremittently
EEILMPPRSTUVY presumptively
EEILNNOPSSSST pointlessness
EEILNNOSSTTUY sententiously
EEILNOOPSSTTV split one's vote
EEILNOPRSSSTU sur les pointes
EEILNOPRSTTUY pretentiously
EEILNPRRSTUUV supervirulent
EEIMMNRSSTTUY run-time system
EEIMMPRSSSTTY imprest system
EEIMNOOPRTTTY potentiometry
EEIMNOPSSSTUU impetuousness
EEIMOOPRRSSTT stereotropism
EEINNNOPRSSTT non-persistent
EEINNOORRSTVW It's Now or Never
EEINNOPRSSSUU penuriousness
EEINNOPRSTTUU unpretentious
EEINOOPPRSSSS prepossession
EEINOOPRSSSST poster session
EEINOPPRRSSTU pressure point
EEINOPPRSSSUV purposiveness
EEINOPSSSSTTY Petty Sessions
EEIOOOPRSSSTT osteopetrosis
EEKLMMRSSSTUU St Luke's summer
EEKLRRTTUUUVY turkey vulture
EEKMNRSSTTUYY turnkey system
EEKNNOOPSSSTU outspokenness
EEKNOOPPRSSSS spokespersons
EELLNOOPPPRYY polypropylene
EELLOPPRSSSUY purposelessly
EELMNORSSSTUU tremulousness
EELMOPSSTTUUY tempestuously
EELNOPRRSSSUY nursery slopes
EELNOQRSSSUUU querulousness
EELNRSSSSSTTU trustlessness
EEMMNNOOSSSTU momentousness
EEMMPRRSSTUYY supersymmetry
EEMNORSSSTUVY nervous system
EEMOOOPPRSSTU to some purpose
EENNOOPPRSSTU opportuneness
EENNORSSSSTUU strenuousness
EENNORSSSTUUV venturousness
EFFGGILNNORSU long-suffering
EFFGGINOOSTTU gift of tongues
EFFGHHILORRTU riffle through
EFFGHHIRSTTTU The Right Stuff
EFFGHILNRSSTU frightfulness
EFFGIINNNOORT non-forfeiting
EFFIILOORSSSU fossiliferous
EFFILLMNNNOTU non-fulfilment
EFFKNNOOSSTUW know one's stuff
EFGGGGHIINRUU figure-hugging
EFGGHIIILNTTW weightlifting
EFGGHIIINPRTZ prizefighting
EFGGHIILNNRTY frighteningly
EFGGHIINNOPSS sponge fishing
EFGGHINOOSUYY young fogeyish
EFGHHILOOTTWW go with the flow
EFGHHLLOOTTUW well-thought-of
EFGHIIILMNTWY mini flyweight
EFGHIIILNNSTT thing-in-itself
EFGHIILMMORTY Tommy Hilfiger
EFGHILLNORSTU flugelhornist
flügelhornist
EFGHILNORRSUW flowering rush
EFGHNOOORSTUU guest of honour
EFGIIIILLLNTTT tilting fillet
EFGIILLNPSTYY self-pityingly
EFGIILNRSSUVV self-surviving
EFGIKLNNOORWY foreknowingly
EFGIKNOORRRST king of terrors✧
EFGILLNOORVWY overflowingly
EFGKLLMOOOTYY folk etymology
EFHIINNRSSTTU unthriftiness
EFHILMNOPSSTY self-hypnotism
EFHIOOPPRRSSS professorship

EFHLNNRSSTUUU	unhurtfulness
EFHMMNOORTTTU	moment of truth
EFIIIMNRRSSTT	First Minister
EFIIINOPRSSTW	spirits of wine
EFIILLMPRTTUU	multiple fruit
EFIILLNOOPRSU	polliniferous
EFIILNNPSSTUU	unpitifulness
EFIILNOPRSSUU	spinuliferous
EFIIMMNOOORST	immersion foot
EFIIMOPRSTUXY	proximity fuse
EFIINNRRTTUUU	unit furniture
EFIKLLMNORTUY	Mull of Kintyre
EFIKLLNNSSSUU	unskilfulness
EFIKLMNOORSTY	Trofim Lysenko
EFILLLLMOSUUY	mellifluously
EFILLLNOOPSTU	self-pollution
EFILLOOPRRSUY	proliferously
EFILNNOOORTUY	not on your life
EFILNOOORSSTU	stoloniferous
EFILNOOPPRRST	splinter-proof
EFILNOORSSSUV	frivolousness
EFINOOOQSTTUU	out of question
EFKKLNOORRTUY	Norfolk turkey
EFLLOPRSSUUUY	superfluously
EFLNOORRSSSUW	sorrowfulness
EFLNOPRSSUUUU	unsuperfluous
EGGHIINOOPRSS	Sophie Grigson
EGGHILLNOOPST	hot gospelling
EGGHIMMNOOORS	Georg Simon Ohm
EGGHINNOOPSSU	sponging-house
EGGHINNOPSSUU	spunging-house
EGGHLMOOOOPRY	geomorphology
EGGIIILNNNPST	spine-tingling
EGGIILOORRSST	Sir Georg Solti
EGGIIMNOSSSTU	suggestionism
EGGIINOSSSTTU	suggestionist
EGGILNOOORSTT	gerontologist
EGHHIILLMNRST	threshing mill
EGHHIILOPRSTY	hieroglyphist
EGHHIKORRSTTU	strike through
EGHHILLMNOOTY	helminthology
EGHHLLOSSTTUY	thoughtlessly
EGHHMNOOORRTW	growth hormone
EGHIIIIKNNRVY	King Henry VIII
EGHIIIKNNRSST	kiss-in-the-ring
EGHIIILMNOSST	light emission
EGHIIIMMMNTUW	minimum weight
EGHIIKORRRSTY	Yorkshire grit
EGHIILLLMPRSS	pilgrim's shell
EGHIILLNNRSST	thrillingness
EGHIILLORRTVW	Orville Wright
EGHIILMNNOPSY	sphingomyelin
EGHIILNNOSTTU	ethnolinguist
EGHIILNNSSSTU	unsightliness
EGHIILNOPPSTU	tippling-house
EGHIILNPRSSST	sprightliness
EGHIIMNOPSSTU	something is up
EGHIIMNOPSSTY	physostigmine
EGHIINNNOPSSU	spinning-house
EGHIINNOPRSTU	printing house
EGHIKLMNNOOWY	howling monkey

EGHIKLNNOOOSS	sling one's hook
EGHILNORSTUUY	unrighteously
EGHILNPRSTTUU	sulphuretting
EGHILOPRSTUUY	uprighteously
EGHINNNOOTTTX	next to nothing
EGHINNOPRTTUW	put in the wrong
EGHINOOPRSSTU	sporting house
EGHKMOPRSTUUW	gum up the works
EGHLLLNOPPTUU	pull the plug on
EGHLNOPPRSSUU	sulphur sponge
EGIIIILNORRST	irreligionist
EGIIIKLNOOSST	kinesiologist
EGIIILLORRSUY	irreligiously
EGIIILNOOPPTZ	Leipzig option
EGIIILNOSSSTU	litigiousness
EGIIILNPRRSTZ	Stirling Prize
EGIIIMNOPRRTX	primogenitrix
EGIIJNNNNNPSY	spinning jenny
EGIIKLLNORRST	rolling strike
EGIILLLOOSTVX	vexillologist
EGIILLMNORSTT	millstone grit✧
EGIILLNNNSSUW	unwillingness
EGIILMNNRTTUY	unremittingly
EGIILMNOORSTT	terminologist
EGIILMNOPRSTY	temporisingly
EGIILMNOPRTYZ	temporizingly
EGIILNNOOSTTT	setting lotion
EGIILNNOPSSTT	listening post
EGIILNNOQSTUY	questioningly
EGIILNNORSTUU	neurolinguist
EGIILNNRSSTUY	unresistingly
EGIILNOPSTTTV	vote-splitting
EGIILNORSTUVY	vertiginously
EGIILNRSSTTTY	trysting-stile
EGIILOOOSSTTV	sovietologist✧
EGIIMNNNNOPSY	money-spinning
EGIIMNNOOPSST	imposing stone
EGIIMNOORRSST	risorgimentos
EGIIMOPRRSSSV	progressivism
EGIINNNOQSTUU	unquestioning
EGIINNNORRTUV	virgin neutron
EGIINNNSSTTUW	unwittingness
EGIINNOORRSST	introgression
EGIINNOPQRSUX	spring equinox
EGIINNOPRRRRT	printing error
EGIINNPPRRSST	printing press
EGIINPRSTTTTY	sitting pretty
EGIIOPRRSSSTV	progressivist
EGIKLMNORSSTW	smelting-works
EGIKLOOPRSTWY	grow like Topsy
EGIKMMNOORRWY	working memory
EGIKNNNNOSSUW	unknowingness
EGILLLNOORWYY	yellow yorling
EGILLNNOORSST	Rolling Stones
EGILLNOPSSSTU	spill one's guts
EGILLNPRSTTUY	splutteringly
EGILMMNOPRTUU	rumelgumption
	rumlegumption
EGILNNNRRTUUY	unreturningly
EGILNNOSSSTUU	glutinousness
EGILNOPPRRSTU	splinter group

EGINOOPPPRSTW stopping power
EGMMNOOPRSSUY gymnospermous
EGNOOOPRRSTUY proterogynous
EHHHIOOPPPSTY hypophosphite
EHHIIKLNOSTWW with whole skin
EHHIILOOPPRSS philosophiser
EHHIILOOPPRSZ philosophizer
EHHILMOOPRSTU thermophilous
EHHIMMMOOOPRS homeomorphism
EHHIMMNOORSTU Monmouthshire
EHHIMNOOPRSTT Mother Shipton
EHHINNORRSTTU in the short run
EHHIOOOPPRSST photophoresis
EHHKOOORSSTTW shoot the works
EHHMMOOOPRSU homeomorphous
EHHMMOOORRSSU horse mushroom
EHHOOPPRRSTUY hypertrophous
EHIIILLOPPPSU Louis-Philippe
EHIIILPPRSTTY perityphlitis
EHIIKLMOOPRTY poikilothermy
EHIIKLOSSSTTW kist o' whistles
EHIILLOPSSTWW will-o'-the-wisps
wills-o'-the-wisp
EHIILMMNOOSTT monothelitism✧
EHIILNOOOPSSU eosinophilous
EHIILNOQRSSSU liquorishness
EHIIMNOOOPSST photo-emission
EHIINOOOPRSST iontophoresis
EHIIOOOPPSTTV photopositive
EHIKLMNNOOSTU Thelonius Monk
EHIKLORRSSTTW silk-throwster
EHIKMMNPSSUUU Pushkin Museum
EHIKMMOOPRSSU skeuomorphism
EHILLNNOOPQUY phylloquinone
EHILMNOOOPSTU entomophilous
EHILNOOOPSSTX explosion shot
EHILNOPSSSTYY polysynthesis
EHIMMOOPRRSTT thermotropism
EHIMNOOPPRRST minor prophets
EHIMOPRSSSTTU stir the possum
EHINOPPRRSSUW sun worshipper
sunworshipper
EHIOOPPRSSSSS possessorship
EHIOORRSTTTWY twistor theory
EHKNNNOOOOOSW on one's own hook
EHLLLOOPPSTUY leptophyllous
EHLLNOOPSSTUY stenophyllous
EHLLOPRSSUUUY sulphureously
EHMMNOORRSTUU Mount Rushmore
EHMMNOPRTTTUU mutton-thumper
EHMMOOPSSTYYY symphyseotomy
EHNNOOPRTTWWY two pennyworth
two-pennyworth
EIIIILNQSTUVY inquisitively
EIIIINNQSTUUV uninquisitive
EIIIINNSSTTVY insensitivity
EIIILLMOOPSTY poliomyelitis
EIIILNPRSSSTU spiritus lenis
EIIILNSTTTUVY institutively
EIIIMMNOPRSSS impressionism✧
EIIIMNOPRSSST impressionist✧
EIIIMORRRSSUV Missouri River
EIIINNOOPRSTT interposition
EIIJNNORSSSUU injuriousness
EIILMNOOPRRTY premonitorily
EIILMNOORSTUV revolutionism
EIILMNOQRSTUV ventriloquism
EIILMOORRSTUY meritoriously
EIILNOORSSTTU resolutionist
EIILNOORSTTUV revolutionist
EIILNOQRSTTUV ventriloquist
EIILNORRSSSTY sinistrorsely
EIILOOPPRSSST leptospirosis
EIIMNNOOOPSSS Siméon Poisson
EIIMNPPPRRSTU sturmer pippin✧
EIINNNOOSSSUX innoxiousness
EIINNNQSSTUUU Quintus Ennius
EIINNOOSSTTVY tenosynovitis
EIINOOPPRSSTU superposition
EIINOOPPRSTTU opportunities
EIINOPRSSSSTU spiritousness
EIIOPRRSSTTUU surreptitious
EIIOPRSSSTTUU superstitious
EIJLNOOPPRSTU jet propulsion
EIJOORSSSSTTU Just So Stories
EILMMNOPRSSTY Myrtle Simpson
EILMNNORTTUUW intown multure
EILNNOOPPRTUY inopportunely
EILNOOQRSTUUV ventriloquous
EILNORSSSUUUX luxuriousness
EILOQRRSTTUUY triquetrously
EIMNOSSTUUUVV Mount Vesuvius
EIMOOOPPRRTUX ex proprio motu
EINNNOOOPRSTU neutron poison
EINNOOOPSSSSU poisonousness
EINNOOORSSSTU notoriousness
EKOOPPRRRSTUW support worker
ELMMNNOOOOPYY Monopoly money
EMNNOOPPRRTTU prompt neutron
EMNNOORSSSSTU monstrousness
EMNOPSSSSTUUU sumptuousness
ENOOPRSTTTUUU put out to nurse

F

FFGIIILLMNORR fringilliform
FFGIINNOSSSUU fission fungus
FFGIMNNORSTUU mourning-stuff
FFLLLLNOOOORR roll-on roll-off
FGGHIILNOPRTV proving flight
FGHHLLOOORTUW follow through
follow-through
FGHIIILLNNOSU infill housing
FGHIIINNOPSST finishing post
FGHIILLMNOOTT moonlight flit
FGHIILLNORSUY flourishingly
FGHIOOPSTTTUU put out of sight
FGLMNNOOOOOSS Song of Solomon
FHIIJKNOSTTTU just think of it
FHIILLORSTTUW without frills
FHIKLLMOPRSUU milk of sulphur
FHINNOOOOPRTU point of honour
FIIILLLNSSUUU filius nullius

FIIIMOORSSSST fortississimo
FIIINOQRRTUWY writ of inquiry
FIINNOOOPPRTT point for point
FILLMRSSTTUUY mistrustfully
FILMNRSSTTUUU unmistrustful

G

GGGHHINOOORTU thoroughgoing
GGHHHLOOPRTUU plough through
GGHHIIIKNNRTT right-thinking
GGHHIIKLLMNSU Hugh Kingsmill
GGHHINOOORSTU rough shooting
GGHIIILNPRSTT strip lighting
GGHIIINNPPRTT night-tripping
GGHIIKOORUVYZ Giorgiy Zhukov
GGHIILNNNRSTU running lights
GGIILLNNPRSTU string-pulling
GHHHILLORRTTU thrill through
GHHHORRSTTTUU thrust through
GHHIILNOPSSTW whistling-shop
GHHINNOOOSTTT shot to nothing
GHIIINORSSTUV visiting hours
GHIIKLNNNRSUY unshrinkingly
GHIILLOOPSSTY syphilologist
GHIILNOOORSTT ornithologist
GHIIMMOOPRSTT thigmotropism
GHIIMNNOOORST smoothing iron
GHIIMNOOPSSTY physiognomist
GHILOOOOPSYYZ zoophysiology
GHIOPPRSSTTTU support tights
GHLMNNOOOOOSU non-homologous
GIIIILNNPRSTY inspiritingly
GIIIKLLLMNSTU multiskilling
GIIILLMNSTTUU multilinguist
GIIILMNNOOSUY ignominiously
GIIIMNORRRRTW mirror writing
GIILMNNOPRSUY unpromisingly
GIILMNRSSTTUY mistrustingly
GIILNNOPRRSTY ripsnortingly
GIIMNOOPRRTUY minority group
GIINNOOOPPRRT proportioning
GIINOPRRSSTTW sportswriting
GILLLMOOPSSYY polysyllogism
GILLNNOOOPRST trolling-spoon
GILMMNNRRUUUY unmurmuringly

H

HHHJNNOOOPRRT John H Northrop
HHILLOOPPSUXY xiphophyllous
HHIMMOOOOPRSS homomorphosis
HHIMOOOOPPRSU ophiomorphous
HHIMOOOPRRSUZ rhizomorphous
HIIILLNNOQTTU quintillionth
HIIILOPRSTTTT lithotriptist
HIILNOOPRRTTT lithontriptor
HIIMMNOOPSSTY monophysitism✧
HILNOPPRSSTUY in short supply
HILORRSTTTUWY trustworthily
HIMMOOPPRSSSU opossum shrimp
HIMMOOPSSTYYY symphysiotomy
HIMOOOPPRRSTT trophotropism
HIOOPRRSTTTUY Tourist Trophy
HNORRSTTTUUWY untrustworthy

I

IIILLMORSSSTU illustrissimo
IIILMNOOPSSTU postliminious
IIINOOOPPSSTT oppositionist
IIINOOPRRSSTV prison visitor
IIKLNNOOOOPTZ zoon politikon
IILLLORSSTUUY illustriously
IILNOOOPSSTTU lotus position
IIMNNORSTTTUU strontium unit
IIMNOOOPPRRST misproportion
IINNOOPPRTTUY inopportunity
INNOOPPPSTTUU put upon points

14 letters

A

AAAAAABHILMSSY Bahasa Malaysia
AAAAAACCDGRRSS cascara sagrada
AAAAABDHHMRRWY Abraham Hayward
AAAAACEEILOPRT alopecia areata
AAAAACGILMMNRT anagrammatical
AAAAADDEHNNTTU Tuatha dé Danaan
AAAAADFGIILMRS Sagrada Familia
AAAAAGGINNRRTT rangatiratanga
AAAAAHMNRSSTUY Mahayana Sutras
AAAAALLLNNPRUX annual parallax
AAAAANNRRTTTUU natura naturata
AAAABBCEHILPRT Arabic alphabet
AAAABBCEILRSTY sabbatical year
AAAABBCJKNORRS Barbara Jackson
AAAABBIIMNRSST Sabbatarianism
AAAABCCEEHIRRT Archaebacteria
AAAABCCEJLNOPS José Capablanca
AAAABCCIKLLRRS cascarilla bark
AAAABDDILLNRSS Aldabra Islands
AAAABDEGILNNRS bargain and sale
AAAABEHLLMNPTU manual alphabet
AAAABEIILRRRSW Arab-Israeli War
AAAACCCEEHLNTY Calycanthaceae
AAAACCDEEEILPS Asclepiadaceae
AAAACCDEGIMRSS cardiac massage
AAAACCDEINORSU anacardiaceous
AAAACCEEEINRRS Sarraceniaceae
AAAACCEEGIMRRV Marcgraviaceae
AAAACCEEHIMNRT Marchantiaceae
AAAACCEHHLNOPT Acanthocephala
AAAACCILLPRTTY paratactically
AAAACCINNRSSTU transcaucasian✧
AAAACDDILLNNOR Canadian dollar
AAAACDEEEHILMM Hamamelidaceae

Words marked ✧ can also be spelled with one or more capital letters

AAAACDEEGHILOR	Haloragidaceae
AAAACDEEILLMRY	Amaryllidaceae
AAAACDEFHILMRY	Michael Faraday
AAAACDEHKLNRTZ	Kazan Cathedral
AAAACDEIINNNTV	Native Canadian
	Native-Canadian
AAAACDGIILMPRT	paradigmatical
AAAACDIIMMNOST	macadamisation
AAAACDIIMMNOTZ	macadamization
AAAACEEFINRSSS	as far as I can see
AAAACEEGILNNPT	Plantaginaceae
AAAACEFIIMNNNO	Fanconi anaemia
AAAACEGHJLLMNS	James Callaghan
AAAACEGILLMMNO	megalomaniacal
AAAACEHLLOPRTV	Hoare-Laval Pact
AAAACEHMNORSTU	amaranthaceous
AAAACEIMNNRRST	sacramentarian
AAAACHILPPRRST	paraphrastical
AAAACHLMMOSTUY	Thomas Macaulay
AAAACIMNPRRTTY	Captain Marryat
AAAADDEILLNOPR	Andrea Palladio
AAAADDEJNPRRRS	Rajendra Prasad
AAAADDFGIMMMRU	Muammar Gaddafi
AAAADDIKNOPRTT	dark adaptation
AAAADEEGMNNNRT	Andrea Mantegna
AAAADEELMMRRTX	extra marmalade
AAAADEGINNQRRU	quadragenarian
AAAADEIMMNRSST	as near as dammit
AAAADELLLNORRV	Andorra la Vella
AAAADGHIMMNOPU	Mahamuni Pagoda
AAAADGIIMMNORT	gamma radiation
AAAADHHNNORSWW	Anna Howard Shaw
AAAADHIILNOPRT	alpha radiation
AAAADHJLLNTTZZ	and all that jazz
AAAADILNRSSTVY	Transvaal daisy
AAAADIPPRSSTUV	Davis apparatus
AAAAEEGILMRRST	steal a marriage
AAAAEEHIKNPRSS	Shakespeariana
AAAAEGHINNOPRT	Patagonian hare
AAAAEGIKKLNNTY	Lake Tanganyika
AAAAEGLNRSTTUW	natural wastage
AAAAEIILMNOPTZ	Emiliano Zapata
AAAAEIJMNORRSZ	José María Aznar
AAAAEKLMMNNSSW	Selman A Waksman
AAAAELLLOOPRTV	palato-alveolar
AAAAFIILNNPRRS	Infralapsarian
AAAAFIIMNRRSST	Rastafarianism
AAAAGHIIINRTUW	Hawaiian guitar
AAAAGHIMNOPRST	phantasmagoria
AAAAGIMMPRRSTT	paragrammatist
AAAAIILLNOPSTT	palatalisation
AAAAIILLNOPTTZ	palatalization
AAAAIKMNNOSSTY	Anastas Mikoyan
AAAAILLNPRSSTU	Australian Alps
AAAAILNPPRRSSU	Supralapsarian
AAAANNNRRSTTUU	natura naturans
AAAANNOPRRSSVW	savanna-sparrow
AAABBBCEEGHLRS	Charles Babbage
AAABBBEEHKRRST	Sabbath-breaker
AAABBCDIKNORRS	Barbara Dickson
AAABBCEEEGHRTT	cabbage-tree hat
AAABBCEILNNPRU	banana republic
AAABBCEILRUVXY	Clairvaux Abbey
AAABBCEINOSSTT	Sebastian Cabot
AAABBCFHLLSSTU	Staubbach Falls
AAABBCHHIOOPRT	batrachophobia
AAABBCHIJKMRRS	Sir Jack Brabham
AAABBCIIILLMNO	bibliomaniacal
AAABBDDEEELLNT	Debateable Land
AAABBDGILORRRT	Gibraltar board®
AAABBEEFKLRSTT	breakfast-table
AAABBEEGLLNOOR	Boolean algebra
AAABBEGILLLORV	global variable
AAABBEGLLNOORR	balloon barrage
	barrage-balloon
AAABCCDIILOORV	viola da braccio
AAABCCEHHKKLRT	black-hat hacker
AAABCCEIILLMST	acclimatisable
AAABCCEIILLMTZ	acclimatizable
AAABCCFIIINPRS	Francis Picabia
AAABCCIKKLNPPT	pickaback plant
AAABCCILMNNOOY	cyanocobalamin
AAABCDEEFLNORT	balance of trade
AAABCDEEGLMNRR	Le Grand Macabre
AAABCDEEKPPRRT	trade paperback
AAABCDEGINOSTU	Santiago de Cuba
AAABCDEILLMPRT	lambda particle
AAABCDEINNORTU	abundance ratio
AAABCDGHILNORY	brachydiagonal
AAABCDHIINNRTU	Nudibranchiata
AAABCDHILOOPRR	parochial board
AAABCDIINOPRTT	dicta probantia
AAABCDILLLLRSY	Lyrical Ballads
AAABCEEEHMSSTY	as the case may be
AAABCEEEINRSSU	béarnaise sauce✧
AAABCEEFLNNOTT	Battle of Cannae
AAABCEEGGGILMR	baggage reclaim
AAABCEEGILMNPU	Plumbaginaceae
AAABCEEGKPRSTT	carpetbag steak
AAABCEEHIILLNZ	Achille Bazaine
AAABCEEHKPRRTU	brake parachute
AAABCEEIKLNRST	strike a balance
AAABCEEILLMNRU	bear-animalcule
AAABCEEIMNRTUY	American Beauty
AAABCEFLMNRTUU	manufacturable
AAABCEGHLMNSTU	calabash nutmeg
AAABCEHILLLPTY	alphabetically
AAABCEHILNOPPR	inapproachable
AAABCEHILRRRTY	brachial artery
AAABCEHLNOPPRU	unapproachable
AAABCEIILRSTTV	Bravais lattice
AAABCEILMNRRSU	Arabic numerals
AAABCEILMNRRTU	interambulacra
AAABCELLLMORST	Balmoral Castle
AAABCELLORRSUU	casual labourer
AAABCELMMNNOUW	ambulancewoman
AAABCEMNNORSTV	Marco Van Basten
AAABCGHHILPRTY	bathygraphical
AAABCGHINORTYZ	Zygobranchiata
AAABCHILLMNNOR	Abraham Lincoln
AAABCHILNOPPRY	inapproachably
AAABCHLNOPPRUY	unapproachably

Words marked ✧ can also be spelled with one or more capital letters

AAABCIILLLMRWY William Barclay
AAABCILLNOSSTW boatswain's call
AAABDDEELLLLNN be-all and end-all
AAABDDEENRRRST standard-bearer
AAABDDELMMNRRU Bernard Malamud
AAABDDILLNRSSV Svalbard Island
AAABDEEEJKMNRT Dame Janet Baker
AAABDEEFGINNNR banana-fingered
AAABDEEIIJLLNS Isabelle Adjani
AAABDEELLNRSUX Alexander Balus
AAABDEENNRRSSW brand awareness
AAABDEFGILLMOS balsam of Gilead
AAABDEGILNNORU Nadia Boulanger
AAABDEGKORRRST garboard strake
AAABDEHHNRRRST Sarah Bernhardt
AAABDEHIKNRSTT a stab in the dark
AAABDEHMORSSST The Ambassadors
AAABDEILMNORRV random variable
AAABDELNNORRWW Andrew Bonar Law
AAABDEMNNOORTT Donato Bramante
AAABDFFNORRSST bastard saffron
AAABDHIMOPRSSS ambassadorship
AAABDIILMNNORT intra-abdominal
AAABDIINORSSTT bastardisation
AAABDIINORSTTZ bastardization
AAABEEEEIMMORT beatae memoriae
AAABEEEGLMNNSS manageableness
AAABEEELPRSSTT Separate Tables
AAABEEGILMNRRU unmarriageable
AAABEEGIMRRRUU marriage bureau
AAABEEIILNOPRS Palaeosiberian
AAABEEILNNSSTT attainableness
AAABEEINNNORTV Antoine Barnave
AAABEELMMMNPRS plasma membrane
AAABEFGLMORTTW Battle of Wagram
AAABEFHLLORTTW Battle of Harlaw
AAABEGGIILNNPR plea bargaining
AAABEGGLNOOSSU Bologna sausage
AAABEGIIKNRRST strike a bargain
AAABEGIILLNOUV bougainvillaea
AAABEGKMNOOSTU make a song about
AAABEGNOOSSSSU sausage bassoon
AAABEIIILMNRSS Rabelaisianism
AAABEIILLMNPRR prima ballerina
AAABEIILMNNNTU unmaintainable
AAABEIILMNNRTT Britannia metal
AAABEILMOORRTV Alberto Moravia
AAABEILNOOPSTT palaeobotanist
AAABEILNORSTTT total abstainer
AAABEILNRRSTTU Alastair Burnet
AAABEILOORRRSU Aurora Borealis✧
AAABEILRRRSTTW barrister-at-law
AAABEIMNOSSTTW boatswain's mate
AAABELLNNPRSTT transplantable
AAABELLNNRSTTU untranslatable
AAABGHLMOPRTUU autograph album
AAABGIMNNSSTUY Saint Magnus Bay
AAABHMNNNORSSU Baron Haussmann
AAABIIILLNTUVY unavailability
AAABIILLNRRSTV Brillat-Savarin
AAABIILNORSTTU tabularisation
AAABIILNORTTUZ tabularization
AAABILNNNOOSTU banana solution
AAABILNOQSTTUU absquatulation
AAABLLNNRSTTUY untranslatably
AAACCCEEHLOPTY Phytolaccaceae
AAACCCEEILNNRR clearance cairn
AAACCCEHILRSTT catachrestical
AAACCCEHORRRTT character actor
AAACCCEINNORTT Antarctic Ocean
AAACCCILNOPTTU capital account
AAACCDDEILNNOR cardinal-deacon
AAACCDEEIKLLRT care killed a cat
AAACCDEFHINNNR Canadian French
French-Canadian
AAACCDEFIILRRU cardiac failure
AAACCDEFNORTVY advance factory
AAACCDEIIILNRV valerianic acid
AAACCDEIMNNOOR adenocarcinoma
AAACCDEIOPPRSU capparidaceous
AAACCDELORRTTY declaratory act
AAACCDGIIIMRRT margaritic acid
AAACCDIILOPRTT catadioptrical
AAACCDILORRSUV cardiovascular
AAACCEEFIILOPR Caprifoliaceae
AAACCEEHIKKNRT take a raincheck
AAACCEEHILMPRY hypercalcaemia
AAACCEEHINNOOR horae canonicae
AAACCEEILRSSST scale staircase
AAACCEEINNQRTU reacquaintance
AAACCEFLORSTUU calcareous tufa
AAACCEGHILLOOR archaeological
AAACCEGHKMRRRS graham crackers
AAACCEHILMPRTU pharmaceutical
AAACCEHILNRTTV naval architect
AAACCEHLLMRSSV clash-ma-clavers
AAACCEHLMMORTW claw-hammer-coat
AAACCEIILLMOPT palaeoclimatic
AAACCEILNNORTX extracanonical
AAACCEINNNQTUU unacquaintance
AAACCELMNOPSUU campanulaceous
AAACCGHHILPRTY tachygraphical
AAACCGHIILLLPR calligraphical
AAACCGHILLNOOR arachnological
AAACCGHILOPRRT cartographical
AAACCGILLMNOOP campanological
AAACCGMNNOOTUU Mount Aconcagua
AAACCHIINORSST saccharisation
AAACCHIINORSTZ saccharization
AAACCHILLMORTY achromatically
AAACCHILLNNORY anachronically
AAACCHILLOPRTY cataphorically
AAACCHILNOOPTU pain au chocolat
AAACCHINORRSST narcocatharsis
AAACCIIIMORTTU comitia curiata
AAACCIIINNOPTT incapacitation
AAACCIILLLNSST classical Latin
AAACCIILORRSTT aristocratical
AAACCIIMMNOSTU caustic ammonia
AAACCILLORTTUY autocratically
AAACCLLOOOPRRS corpora callosa
AAACCLMOORSSTU malacostracous

AAACCLNNNOSTUU annual accounts
AAACDDDELNNRST standard candle
AAACDDDGLLNORR granddad collar
AAACDDEGGKLNOR cloak and dagger
AAACDDENORRRSY secondary radar
AAACDEEEIINRSS acarine disease
AAACDEEEKOSTTT toasted teacake
AAACDEEGILMPSS special damages
AAACDEEHHLNNSV have clean hands
AAACDEEINNTTTW wait attendance
AAACDEEKNPSTUY Pancake Tuesday
AAACDEFFILLPRU Paula Radcliffe
AAACDEFGILNORR Earl of Cardigan
AAACDEFGNORRUV grace-and-favour
AAACDEGHIKLOPY package holiday
AAACDEGHIPRRRU purdah carriage
AAACDEGIMRRSTT scatter diagram
AAACDEGINNORST ascending aorta
AAACDEGINNRSVY advancing years
AAACDEGNORTTUV advantage court
AAACDEIIIMNNNR American Indian
American-Indian
AAACDEIILNPPRU Appendicularia
AAACDEIIMNOPRS Cinema Paradiso
AAACDEIJLLNNRU Julian calendar
AAACDEILLMOPRS Camelopardalis
AAACDEILMMMUUX maxima cum laude
AAACDEILMNNNRW Cardinal Newman
AAACDELLMNORRU all-round camera
AAACDFHIMNNRST handicraftsman
AAACDGHLLLMNRY lachrymal gland
AAACDGMNORSSTU coastguardsman
AAACDHHILMNSST Chatham Islands
AAACDHIINOPRST antaphrodisiac
AAACDHILNOOPRS achondroplasia
AAACDHINNRSTTU Tristan da Cunha
AAACDIIILNORST radicalisation
AAACDIIILNORTZ radicalization
AAACDIILNNOSST scandalisation
AAACDIILNNOSTZ scandalization
AAACDIIMOORRTT atomic radiator
AAACDILLMNNORR mandarin collar
AAACEEEGHNNTVW what a vengeance
AAACEEEHLNPSTV Elephanta caves
AAACEEELNOPPRS aerospace-plane
AAACEEFILOPRSS Passifloraceae
AAACEEFLNRRRUW nuclear warfare
AAACEEGHIMNSSU sausage machine
AAACEEGIILNSTT telangiectasia
AAACEEGIILNSTU Ustilaginaceae
AAACEEGILNNPRT captain-general
AAACEEGILNSSTZ elegiac stanzas
AAACEEHIKKMNOR karaoke machine
AAACEEHKLMMNOR Karma Chameleon
AAACEEHLLNRRSV Charles Laveran
AAACEEIILLMPPR Imperial Palace
AAACEEIILLPRTV palliative care
AAACEEIILNORST aeroelastician
AAACEEIIMNNRTV Native American
Native-American
AAACEEIKLMNPRT parliament-cake
AAACEEILMNOOSY Cooley's anaemia
AAACEEILMNRSST sacramentalise
AAACEEILMNRSTZ sacramentalize
AAACEEILNORSUV valerianaceous
AAACEEIMMNNNNT maintenance-man
AAACEEIMNNNRSS Renaissance man
AAACEFFGIMNRRT traffic manager
AAACEFGILLLMNO flagellomaniac
AAACEFGINNORSS Françoise Sagan
AAACEFGIORSSUX saxifragaceous
AAACEGHHIIRSTT Agatha Christie
AAACEGHILMOPTT apothegmatical
AAACEGHLOPRRST pastoral charge
AAACEGIILLMMRS magical realism
AAACEGIILLMRST magical realist
AAACEGIILMMPRT epigrammatical
AAACEGILNOORRS saloon carriage
AAACEGIMMRRSTT grammaticaster
AAACEGIMNRSTUU argumenti causa
AAACEGINSSTUWY Giant's Causeway
AAACEGORRRTTTT Great Attractor
AAACEHHIKKLTWW watch like a hawk
AAACEHHINNNTTX canthaxanthine
AAACEHHMOORTTY Heathcoat-Amory
AAACEHIILMRRSV air vice-marshal
AAACEHIILNPTTT antipathetical
AAACEHILLLMPRY alphamerically
AAACEHILLMMTTY mathematically
AAACEHILLMNPRU alphanumerical
AAACEHILLPPRST alpha particles
AAACEHILMMNTTU unmathematical
AAACEHILMOOPPR pharmacopoeial
AAACEHILNOPPRT palaeanthropic
AAACEHILOPRRTX extra-parochial
AAACEHIMNOOPPR pharmacopoeian
AAACEHJMPSSTTY the cat's pyjamas
AAACEHOOPRRTTT Prototracheata
AAACEIILLLLMWW William Wallace
AAACEIILLMNNRS miscellanarian
AAACEIILMNORST caramelisation
AAACEIILMNORTZ caramelization
AAACEIILNNNORR Carolina Nairne
AAACEIIMMNNPRS Pan-Americanism
AAACEIJLNRTTUU tarantula juice
AAACEIKMOPRRST mark/space ratio
AAACEILLMNNSTY anamnestically
AAACEILLNORTUY aeronautically
AAACEILMMNRSST sacramentalism
AAACEILMNRSSTT sacramentalist
AAACEILMNRSTTY sacramentality
AAACEIMNORSTTT castrametation
AAACFIIINNORST Africanisation
AAACFIIINNORTZ Africanization
AAACFIILNSTTTY fantasticality
AAACFIINNOSTTT fantastication
AAACFILNORSSTY factor analysis
AAACFIMNORRSTW aircraftswoman
AAACGGHHIILOPR hagiographical
AAACGHIJLNNOOR Johann Agricola
AAACGHILMNORSS glass harmonica
AAACGHILMRTTUU thaumaturgical

AAACGHILNOPPRT	pantographical
AAACGHILNOPRRU	uranographical
AAACGHIMNOPRST	phantasmagoric
AAACGIILLMSTTY	astigmatically
AAACGIILMMRTTY	grammaticality
AAACGIILMPRTTY	pragmaticality
AAACGILLMNORTY	morganatically
AAACGILLNOPSTV	galvanoplastic
AAACGIMNOOPRRS	macrosporangia
AAACGIMNOPPRTT	pantopragmatic
AAACHIILMMRRST	matriarchalism
AAACHIILMPRRST	patriarchalism
AAACHIILNOPSTT	chaptalisation
AAACHIILNOPTTZ	chaptalization
AAACHIILNPRSTT	antiphrastical
AAACHILLLLOPTY	allopathically
AAACHILMMNNOPY	nymphomaniacal
AAACHILMOPRRSY	Cyril Ramaphosa
AAACHILOSSTTWW	shawl waistcoat
AAACIIILNOPSTT	capitalisation
AAACIIILNOPTTZ	capitalization
AAACIIILNPSTTT	anticapitalist
AAACIIIMNPRSST	Sir Isaac Pitman
AAACIILNRRRTTU	intra-articular
AAACIKMOOPRSSS	Kaposi's sarcoma
AAACILMNOOPRST	paronomastical
AAACIOOPRRRSTT	corpora striata
AAACLLNPRSSTUV	vascular plants
AAACNNOPPTTWYY	Can't Pay? Won't Pay!
AAADDDEEHLMNNS	dead man's handle
AAADDDGNNORRST	dragon-standard
AAADDEEEHLLLMS	dames de la halle
AAADDEEFHLMMOY	Mohamed al-Fayed
AAADDEEGHINRRS	dead as a herring
AAADDEEGINSSTT	dead set against
AAADDEEGMOOORV	Amedeo Avogadro
AAADDEEHHNOSVY	have had one's day
AAADDEEHLNNSTW	Leda and the Swan
AAADDEEKLNORRX	Alexander Korda
AAADDEEKNNORRU	Konrad Adenauer
AAADDEELMNRSUX	Alexandre Dumas
AAADDEELNORRST	Andrea del Sarto
AAADDEFFIILSST	as fit as a fiddle
AAADDEGGNRRSTW	at daggers drawn
AAADDEHHNRSSTW	heads and thraws
AAADDEHLLNRRUY	Laurel and Hardy
AAADDGHHIMNNOS	Mohandas Gandhi
AAADDGHHINRSTY	A Hard Day's Night
AAADDIILMNNNOS	Mindanao Island
AAADEEEFGHHMOT	ahead of the game
AAADEEEFINRSTV	vasa deferentia
AAADEEEGGLMNRS	general damages
AAADEEEGJNNPRS	Japanese garden
AAADEEEHILMRTT	Almeida Theatre
AAADEEEJLMNPRS	Japanese medlar
AAADEEELLMRRTW	Walter De La Mare
AAADEEFFLLNORS	fall on deaf ears
AAADEEFHLLMSTU	full steam ahead
AAADEEFILMNRRS	fire salamander
AAADEEFLLNNWXZ	New Zealand flax
AAADEEFLMNRRTT	flame-retardant
AAADEEGHHINSTT	against the head
AAADEEGHHMSTTW	what's the damage?
AAADEEGHIMNRTV	have a great mind
AAADEEGILLNRRT	granadilla tree
AAADEEGJNOPRSW	Japanese War God
AAADEEGNNNVYYY	Gennady Yanayev
AAADEEHIKLRRST	Kalahari Desert
AAADEEHLLORTTT	lead to the altar
AAADEEHLMNNNRT	neanderthal man✧
AAADEEIKLLMNRS	salamander-like
AAADEEILLMNRRU	Uralian emerald
AAADEEILMRRRTT	radar altimeter
AAADEELLMMNORS	mole salamander
AAADEELNPPPRSS	apples and pears
AAADEEMNQSSUUU	usque ad nauseam
AAADEERRSSTTUY	Easter Saturday
AAADEFFILNORST	fore-and-aft sail
AAADEFGHHLTUUV	have had a gutful
AAADEFGIMMNNRY	Feynman diagram
AAADEFHLLLMRRS	Alfred Marshall
AAADEFNRSTTTUU	unsaturated fat
AAADEGGILNNRSU	Guardian Angels
AAADEGHIIRSSTT	straight as a die
AAADEGHIMMNORS	Dame Ngaio Marsh
AAADEGHIMOPRRT	dermatographia
AAADEGILLMNSST	laminated glass
AAADEGIMNNNORR	mandarin orange
AAADEGLNOSTUVY	advantageously
AAADEGMOORRTTW	Margaret Atwood
AAADEHIIMMNSTU	Anaheim Stadium
AAADEHIKNORRSV	Andrei Sakharov
AAADEHIMNORSTU	adiathermanous
AAADEHKLNPRSTU	Adela Pankhurst
AAADEHMNPSTTYY	tea and sympathy
AAADEIILMNNSTV	Tasmanian devil
AAADEIILNNRTUV	valetudinarian
AAADEIINNRTUVV	Viviana Durante
AAADEIJLMNNORR	Jean Mari Roland
AAADEILNNNORTU	Antoine Arnauld
AAADEILNNOPRRX	Alexandr Oparin
AAADEILNRSTTTY	Latter-day Saint
AAADEIMNNORRSY	ordinary seaman
AAADEMMNNNPRSU	Man and Superman
AAADEMPRRSSTTU	Sarepta mustard
AAADFFFILNOSST	Island of Staffa
AAADFHNNOOPTUY	Anthony of Padua
AAADFILMNOPRRT	D F Malan Airport
AAADFINRSSSTWY	waifs and strays
AAADGHIOOPRRTU	autoradiograph
	radioautograph
AAADGIILNOOSST	São Tiago Island
AAADGLLNQRRUUY	quadrangularly
AAADHIIKLLNNSS	Sakhalin Island
AAADIIILNNRTTU	altitudinarian
	latitudinarian
AAADIIINNRTTTU	attitudinarian
AAADIIJMMNORSU	a majori ad minus
	a minori ad majus
AAADIILLMORUXY	modal auxiliary
AAADIILNOOSTTV	vasodilatation
AAADIILORRTTUV	droit au travail

AAADIINORRSTTY stray radiation
AAADIKLLNORSWY all in a day's work
AAADILOORSTTVY vasodilatatory
AAADMNOORRRSTY radar astronomy
AAAEEEFILNNORS a flea in one's ear
AAAEEEGKLLRSTV Great Slave Lake
AAAEEEGLNNRSTT Staten-Generaal
AAAEEEHILPPRRT Praeraphaelite
AAAEEEILNORTTZ azione teatrale
AAAEEGGGLNRTTU target language
AAAEEGGILNNTUV native language
AAAEEGGLMNSSTU satem languages
AAAEEGGMNRRRST Margaret Sanger
AAAEEGHIKMMNRT take a hammering
AAAEEGILNPPRRW wearing-apparel
AAAEEGINNPPUUW Papua New Guinea
AAAEEGINNPRSTU septuagenarian
AAAEEGINOPRRTT praetorian gate
AAAEEGMNRRSSTT sergeant-at-arms
AAAEEHHIINRRTV heavier-than-air
AAAEEHHNORRTTW wear another hat
AAAEEHIIMNRRTT Henrietta Maria
AAAEEHIMNPRRTY hypernatraemia
AAAEEHMNRRSTWX Manx shearwater
AAAEEILMNPPRRU puerperal mania
AAAEEINNOTTTUW Antoine Watteau
AAAEEIOQSTTUVX vexata quaestio
AAAEEJLNPRRSTU Jean-Paul Sartre
AAAEEJMNRRSSTT serjeant-at-arms
AAAEEKLPQRRTUU take up a quarrel
AAAEELLLLNPPRS parallel planes
AAAEELMNPRRSST armes parlantes
AAAEFFFIORSSTT state of affairs
AAAEFGILNNQRTU quarantine flag
AAAEFGIMNNOORT Fontana Magiore
AAAEFGIMORRRUV marriage-favour
AAAEFHIKLNNRRT Aretha Franklin
AAAEFIILMMRSST matresfamilias
AAAEFIILMPRSST patresfamilias
AAAEFKNOORSTTT at a rate of knots
AAAEFLLOOPPRSV seal of approval
AAAEGGILLNNOSU analogue signal
AAAEGHHIINRSTT against the hair
AAAEGHHMOOPSTU haematophagous
AAAEGHIKMNNRST man-eating shark
AAAEGHILOPPRST palaeographist
AAAEGIIILMNRST egalitarianism
AAAEGIILLRRSTT terra sigillata
AAAEGIIMNNRSTT Tasmanian tiger
AAAEGIKOSTUUWY Ieyasu Tokugawa
AAAEGILLLOPPRT alligator apple
AAAEGILMRSSTTY salami strategy
AAAEGIMNNORSTT station-manager
AAAEGLMOPRRSSU massage parlour
AAAEGMMNORRTTT tetragrammaton✧
AAAEGNOPRSSSTU asparagus-stone
AAAEHIKLMNOPRX alexipharmakon
AAAEHIKLNPPRSU Paul Henri Spaak
AAAEHILMNNNOTT national anthem
AAAEHIMOPRRSTT aromatherapist
AAAEHLNOPPRSTU Palaeanthropus
AAAEHLNPRRTTUY natural therapy
AAAEIIKLLLLOTV volatile alkali
AAAEIILLNORSTT lateralisation
AAAEIILLNORTTZ lateralization
AAAEIILMPPRTTT palmatipartite
AAAEIILNNOPRRS pararosaniline
AAAEIIMNNOSSTX Ioannis Metaxas
AAAEILLLPPRSSW appraisal wells
AAAEILLMRRTTXY extramaritally
AAAEILMOPPPRRT malappropriate
AAAEILNSSSSSTT sales assistant
AAAEIMMMNRRSTU armamentariums
AAAEINORSTTVWY stationary wave
AAAEIOPPRSSTTT patria potestas
AAAEKLPPPRSSTT Krapp's Last Tape
AAAEKOPRSSSTWY Spasskaya Tower
AAAELLLLLMOPRS parallel slalom
AAAELLQQRSUUVY quaquaversally
AAAELMNOORSTUW anomalous water
AAAFGHHINOOSTW Song of Hiawatha
AAAFGILNORSTTY stagflationary
AAAFIILLMNRRXY inframaxillary
AAAFIILLNNOPRT intrafallopian
AAAGGILOPPRSTU Golgi apparatus
AAAGHHLOPRSSTY thalassography
AAAGHHMOPRTTUY thaumatography
AAAGHLLMNNSSTU lanthanum glass
AAAGIILNNOORST organisational
AAAGIILNNOORTZ organizational
AAAGIIMNOPRSTT pragmatisation
AAAGIIMNOPRTTZ pragmatization
AAAGIINNNOOSTT antagonisation
AAAGIINNNOOTTZ antagonization
AAAHHLMORSTTTU Lothar Matthaus
AAAHILORSSTTUU South Australia
AAAHNPPQSSTTUY pattypan squash
AAAIIIILNNOSTT Italianisation
AAAIIIILNNOTTZ Italianization
AAAIIILNOPRSTT patrialisation
AAAIIILNOPRTTZ patrialization
AAAIIIMNNQRSTU antiquarianism
AAAIIKNNNPRSTY sanitary napkin
AAAIILMNNOSTTU Altai Mountains
AAAIILNNORSTTU naturalisation
AAAIILNNORTTUZ naturalization
AAAIIMNNNORSTT transamination
AAAIIMNORSTTTU traumatisation
AAAIIMNORTTTUZ traumatization
AAAIKPPPPRSSTU Kipp's apparatus
AAAILLMMNORSWX Sir Max Mallowan
AAAILMMNNOSTUU Musala Mountain
AAAILMNNOSSTTU Atlas Mountains
AAAILNNORSTTUV transvaluation
AAAIMMNNORSTTU Matra Mountains
AAAIMNNORSTTTU Tatra Mountains
AAAMNNNNOPRTUU Mount Annapurna
AABBCCDDHKLOOR Harold D Babcock
AABBCCDIIIRRTU barbituric acid
AABBCCEEEGHINS Chinese cabbage
AABBCCEEEGLTTU cabbage-lettuce
AABBCCEEINNRRT Barbican Centre

AABBCCHHIOOPRT batrachophobic
AABBCDEGHIRRRU Richard Burbage
AABBCDEHORRRSY Barbados cherry
AABBCEEEGKNRTT Battenberg cake
AABBCEEFINORST absorbefacient
AABBCEEGKNORTT Battonberg cake
AABBCEEGKNRTTU Battenburg cake
AABBCEEIIMNRST Caribbean Times
AABBCEEKLLOTTX battle-axe block
AABBCEENSSSTUU substance abuse
AABBCEFGLOORTY cabbage-root fly
AABBCEGHLMRSTU Bamburgh Castle
AABBCEHHISSTTW witches' Sabbath
AABBCEHIIOOPRT bacteriophobia
AABBCEKLLMNOSU blueback salmon
AABBCELMNRRTUY Canterbury lamb
AABBDDEEEILTUU beauté du diable
AABBDDEENNOOVY above and beyond
AABBDDEENRRTTU bread-and-butter
AABBDEEELMRRST marble-breasted
AABBDEEHIMNORT broad in the beam
AABBDEIINRSSTY Saint Bride's Bay
AABBDEILNNOSTY Babes in Toyland
AABBDEINORRSTY Barberton daisy
AABBDGGIINNNOR brobdingnagian✧
AABBDILNNPRUWY Dublin Bay prawn
AABBEEEHHLPRTW Hebrew alphabet
AABBEEEHIRSTTW The Water-Babies
AABBEEELNNRSSU unbearableness
AABBEEENORSSTT beat one's breast
AABBEEFLNOSTTY Battle of Naseby
AABBEEGHIMNRTY Nightmare Abbey
AABBEEGILNNPRT rabbeting-plane
AABBEEHLMMRTTW Matthew Bramble
AABBEEILMNNOSS abominableness
AABBEEINNORSST beat one's brains
AABBEFINNOSTUY Fountains Abbey
AABBEHIKORSUYZ Bashi-Bazoukery
AABBEIKKLLRSTY Kirkstall Abbey
AABBEIMMNNPSSY namby-pambiness
AABBEKKLLNNTYY blankety-blanky
AABBFHKKKKOOOU Book of Habakkuk
AABBFKKMNNOORT from bank to bank
AABBHIIIILNTTY inhabitability
AABBHIKKMNOORS Simon Bar Kokhba
AABCCCDEIILMRU calcium carbide
AABCCCDHILRTYY brachydactylic
AABCCCDIILORXY carboxylic acid
AABCCCEHHILPRY brachycephalic
AABCCCGHIKNRST backscratching
AABCCDDEILLOSY dodecasyllabic
AABCCDEEKNORSW answer back code
AABCCDEENNORRS barcode scanner
AABCCDEHMNORTT Catchment board
AABCCDEILLNNOU Caledonian Club
AABCCDEILNORTT contradictable
AABCCDEKKLLNOT block and tackle
AABCCDIIJLMOTU judicial combat
AABCCEEELNPSST acceptableness
AABCCEEFHIKLNT black in the face
AABCCEEHLNRSST cartes blanches
AABCCEELNNORTU counterbalance
AABCCEENRRRSUY cranberry sauce
AABCCEHIIORRTT trichobacteria
AABCCEHILLMOPS accomplishable
AABCCEHIMNNSTT catchment basin
AABCCEHLNORRRU charcoal burner
AABCCEHNOOORSU orobanchaceous
AABCCEIIORSTTT bacteriostatic
AABCCEIKLMMNOR commercial bank
AABCCEILMMRTUU circumambulate
AABCCEIMNORTUY cyanobacterium
AABCCELMORTTUU accumulator bet
AABCCIIILPRTTY practicability
AABCCIILLNOSTU actinobacillus
AABCCIILNOTTUY accountability
AABCCIORSSSTUU costus arabicus
AABCDDEEKNPSTU bucket and spade
AABCDDEELLLOSY dodecasyllable
AABCDDEILMNOPR bladder campion
AABCDDELLLMNOP Donald Campbell
AABCDDFIIIRSUV David Fabricius
AABCDDHINORSSW sandwich boards
AABCDEEEGHNRUU bureau de change
AABCDEEEHLMRTV valet de chambre
AABCDEEEILLNRT cardinal beetle
AABCDEEFHLORRT Brother Cadfael
AABCDEEFHMORRT chamber of trade✧
AABCDEEFILLMNU field ambulance
AABCDEEFLNNRST flatbed scanner
AABCDEEGLNOSSU sebaceous gland
AABCDEEGRRSTTU carburetted gas
AABCDEEHHLLRST Charles the Bald
AABCDEEHHOSSTT St Dabeoc's heath
AABCDEEHILMNRS merchandisable
AABCDEEHILMNRZ merchandizable
AABCDEEHIMNRST Bedrich Smetana
AABCDEEHKPRSTY speak by the card
AABCDEEHLLORTT called to the bar
AABCDEEHLNOORZ Honoré de Balzac
AABCDEEHLOTTTU château bottled
AABCDEEHNNRUZZ nebuchadnezzar✧
AABCDEEHORTTUY cathode-ray tube
AABCDEEIJMMRST disjecta membra
AABCDEEIKRRSTV back-seat driver
AABCDEEINRRSTT scatterbrained
AABCDEEKLNSSUY black-eyed Susan
AABCDEELLMRSTU De Clerambault's
AABCDEELNOPSUU double saucepan
AABCDEELNORRST labradorescent
AABCDEENNPRSUU superabundance
AABCDEENRSSSTT abstractedness
AABCDEFIIMORRS Birds of America
AABCDEFLLNRSSY fancy dress ball
AABCDEGIKLNRRT blank cartridge
AABCDEHIINNRTU nudibranchiate
AABCDEHIKLRRUY hydraulic brake
AABCDEHOORRSST across the board
across-the-board
AABCDEIILNPSTY display cabinet
AABCDEILMNNRRU cardinal number
AABCDEILOOSSTV avoidable costs

AABCDEIMNNNORT	recombinant DNA
AABCDELLNRSUUV	vascular bundle
AABCDGIINOPRRU	airing cupboard
AABCDHIIKNOPRY	brachypinakoid
AABCDHIILNOPRS	cardinal-bishop
AABCDHINNORRRS	Richard Branson
AABCDHLLNOORWY	woolly-hand crab
AABCDIILLQRSUY	quadrisyllabic
AABCDIILNNORSS	Nicobar Islands
AABCDJKNOOORTU	jackboot around
AABCEEEEFLNOSV	leave of absence
AABCEEEGHLLPRT	telegraph cable
AABCEEEGHLNNSS	changeableness
AABCEEEGHLNRSS	chargeableness
AABCEEEHILLMNP	Blenheim Palace
AABCEEEKKLMRRT	black-marketeer
AABCEEELLMRTTT	Albert Calmette
AABCEEFFILNRTU	binaural effect
AABCEEFLLMOTTY	Battle of Mycale
AABCEEFLNOOPRW	balance of power
AABCEEGGHLLNOX	global exchange
AABCEEGGHNNORU	George Buchanan
AABCEEGGJLNOTU	object language
AABCEEGHINPRST	breathing space
AABCEEGHLNORUX	Labour Exchange
AABCEEGINNPRSS	cabin passenger
AABCEEGINORRSS	Isaac Rosenberg
AABCEEHILNRSST	charitableness
AABCEEHILOPRRR	irreproachable
AABCEEHINSTTUU	Eustachian tube
AABCEEHLMNNRTU	unmerchantable
AABCEEHLNPRSUU	unpurchaseable
AABCEEHLORSSTT	across-the-table
AABCEEIILLNNNS	canellini beans
AABCEEILLLMMTY	emblematically
AABCEEILLMNPSS	implacableness
AABCEEIMNORSSZ	semicarbazones
AABCEEKLNORRTW	tabernacle-work
AABCEEKQRRSSTU	square brackets
AABCEELLNNNORT	cannonball-tree
AABCEELMNOPRSS	comparableness
AABCEELNPRRTUU	unrecapturable
AABCEFGHILLSSS	Giessbach Falls
AABCEFGHIORTTU	right about face
	right about face!
AABCEFGIILORRT	fibrocartilage
AABCEFGILLLOOT	Gaelic football
AABCEFGILNNOOT	floating beacon
AABCEFHLMOOSTT	Battle of Mohács
AABCEFHLOORRST	Bachelor of Arts
AABCEFIIINOTTU	beautification
AABCEFIILLNSSU	unclassifiable
AABCEFIINOPRRT	prefabrication
AABCEFILMOTTTU	Battle of Actium
AABCEGGIKNORST	backing storage
AABCEGHHIIMNNT	bathing machine
AABCEGHIILMNRT	American blight
AABCEGHILPRSTT	graphics tablet
AABCEGHINORTYZ	zygobranchiate
AABCEGHIOPRTUY	pageboy haircut
AABCEGHLLNOTUW	chalet bungalow
AABCEGIILLOOOP	palaeobiologic
AABCEGIILLOOOR	aerobiological
AABCEGILNNNNRU	running balance
AABCEGINNORRTU	bargain-counter
AABCEHIILLRSTY	Hebraistically
AABCEHIILMNORS	Elasmobranchii
AABCEHIIMMOSTT	biomathematics
AABCEHILLPRTYY	hyperbatically
AABCEHILNNOOTT	ethnobotanical
AABCEHILOPRRRY	irreproachably
AABCEIILLOORTY	aerobiotically
AABCEIILRTTTXY	extractability
AABCEIIORSSSTT	bacteriostasis
AABCEIKNNORRSS	rack one's brains
AABCEILLLRSSTY	crystallisable
AABCEILLLRSTYZ	crystallizable
AABCEILLMORRTY	barometrically
AABCEILLNTTUUV	uncultivatable
AABCEILMNOOPSS	compassionable
AABCEILNNOORST	torsion balance
AABCEILNOOORRS	Corona Borealis
AABCEIMMRRSSTY	asymmetric bars
AABCEIMNORSTTT	Combretastatin®
AABCEIMOORSSUU	simaroubaceous
AABCEINNORTTUU	uncertain about
AABCEINOORRSTV	observation car
AABCELMNNORSTT	marble-constant
AABCGGHIIINNPR	bargaining chip
AABCGGIILLOOOR	agrobiological
AABCGGIKLNPPTY	piggyback plant
AABCGHIILLMOOP	amphibiological
AABCGHIILLOPRY	biographically
AABCGHIIOOPRTU	autobiographic
AABCGHIMOOPRRR	microbarograph
AABCGILNNNOSUV	Sauvignon Blanc
AABCHILOOPRSTU	claustrophobia
AABCHJJNOOORST	John Jacob Astor
AABCHNOORRSSSW	Baron Shawcross
AABCIIIJMNNOST	anti-Jacobinism
AABCIIILLMPRSY	imparisyllabic
AABCIIILNRTTTY	intractability
AABCIIIMORTTTU	comitia tributa
AABCIILLLOPSTY	collapsability
AABCIIMNORSSTT	abstractionism
AABCIINOOSSSTU	subassociation
AABCIINORSSTTT	abstractionist
AABCILLLLOPSYY	polysyllabical
AABCILLORRRTUU	arboricultural
AABCILMNNOOTTU	noctambulation
AABCILNNOSSTTU	consubstantial
AABCJKNOOPRSTY	Port Jackson Bay
AABCNOOPRRSSYY	coronary bypass
AABDDDEEILLORW	Edward de Baliol
AABDDDELNORSTU	double standard
AABDDEEHIILTVZ	Elizabeth David
AABDDEEHORRSTT	tread the boards
AABDDEEIMNNORT	one-armed bandit
AABDDEELNNRSTU	understandable
AABDDEFIIOPRRS	bird of paradise
AABDDEFIKNNORR	Afrikander Bond
AABDDEFINNNRRU	Ferdinand Braun

AABDDEFLNNOTTU Adolf Butenandt
AABDDEGHILLNOT Gnathobdellida
AABDDEGIINOORT biodegradation
AABDDEGNNRRRST Grand St Bernard
AABDDEHLNOPRRS drop handlebars
AABDDEIIINRRST Aristide Briand
AABDDEIILMORTV David Baltimore
AABDDEIILRSSTY addressability
AABDDEKKOORRVY Dvorak keyboard
AABDEEEEFLNORR Earl of Aberdeen
AABDEEEEILRSSU blue ear disease
AABDEEEFHINRRT feather-brained
AABDEEEHILNNNR banner headline
AABDEEEHILNRTV live and breathe
AABDEEEHILNRTZ Elizabeth Arden
AABDEEEHLLMORW wholemeal bread
AABDEEEHLRSSTW beardless wheat
AABDEEEHNNORUV have been around
AABDEEEHNRRSST threadbareness
AABDEEEILLMRTT maître de ballet
AABDEEEINSSSTT Batten's disease
AABDEEELNNRSSU unreadableness
AABDEEELNRRSSW rewardableness
AABDEEENNRRSTT Anne Bradstreet
AABDEEFLNOORVY Adolf von Baeyer
AABDEEGGIMNNRR gingerbread man
AABDEEGHLNNRRR Bernhard Langer
AABDEEGHLOPRRT telegraph board
AABDEEGIMRRSSU Marburg disease
AABDEEGLLLOTWY Belted Galloway
AABDEEHHLLTTTY That'll Be the Day
AABDEEHINPRTTU habit and repute
AABDEEHINRRSTT shatter-brained
AABDEEILMNORTW liberated woman
AABDEEILMNOTTY motte and bailey
AABDEELLLNPRST prebendal stall
AABDEELNNOPRSS pardonableness
AABDEELNORRTUY Robert Delaunay
AABDEEMORRRSTW wardrobe master
AABDEFGIILLRTY deflagrability
AABDEFIIILLQSU disqualifiable
AABDEFILMOTTWY Battle of Midway
AABDEFILNPRSST band-pass filter
AABDEGHILNRRTY bright and early
AABDEGIILNNSSW law-abidingness
AABDEGIILPRTUY upgradeability
AABDEGILNRRRSU Alan Rusbridger
AABDEGIMNNNNRR Bernard Manning
AABDEHIIKNNRRT Bernard Haitink
AABDEHILNNRRTU Bernard Hinault
AABDEIIILLORSV Basil D'Oliveira
AABDEIIILMNOPR imponderabilia
AABDEIIKLLMRRR billiard-marker
AABDEIIKMNORST disembarkation
AABDEIILNOQRTU quodlibetarian
AABDEIILNORSTT radiation belts
AABDEIILOORRST solitaire board
AABDEIIOPPRSTV disapprobative
AABDEIKNRRRSTZ Sir Bernard Katz
AABDEILLLLNNOY belladonna lily
AABDEILLLQRSUY quadrisyllable

AABDEILLNNSTWY Stanley Baldwin
AABDEILMOORTUZ Bartolomeu Diaz
AABDEINNOOPRSX expansion board
AABDELOOPRRRRU parlour-boarder
AABDFFFFOOORWY off-off-Broadway
AABDFLLNNOORUV Rudolf von Laban
AABDGHHIKNNOOR H Gobind Khorana
AABDGIIILNOSTY diagnosability
AABDGIIIMNOSTU disambiguation
AABDHILMNOSSUY busman's holiday
AABDHILMNRSSTZ Brahms and Liszt
AABDIIIILNSTVY inadvisability
AABDIIILNOOSTT tabloidisation
AABDIIILNOOTTZ tabloidization
AABDIIILNOTUVY unavoidability
AABDIILNORRSTU Sir Adrian Boult
AABDIINOOPPRST disapprobation
AABDIOOPPRRSTY disapprobatory
AABDJLNOORRSVY Jaroslav Drobny
AABDLLMOOPPRRY Lombardy poplar
AABEEEEEJLNPST Japanese beetle
AABEEEEGGLLNRU blue-green algae
AABEEEEGMRRTTV megavertebrate
AABEEEEHHLRRTT heather-bleater
AABEEEEHRRTTTT beat the retreat
AABEEEEILLLLOT à la belle étoile
AABEEEFHIJNNRR Jean Henri Fabre
AABEEEGHLRRTTT Albert the Great
AABEEEGINNORTT beat generation
AABEEEHJLMRRTU abjure the realm
AABEEEHJRRRSWY Jerry Abershawe
AABEEEHKLNRSTT bletheranskate
AABEEEHKNORRST break one's heart
AABEEEHKNORSTT take one's breath
AABEEEHLLMMNPR ballpeen hammer
AABEEEHNORSSTV save one's breath
AABEEEINORRSWY raise an eyebrow
AABEEEKLMNRRSS remarkableness
AABEEEKLMNRSST marketableness
AABEEEKMMNOSTT smoke abatement
AABEEELMNNSSTU untameableness
AABEEELMNRSSSU measurableness
AABEEELNNORSSS reasonableness
AABEEELNNOSSSS seasonableness
AABEEEMORRRTTW water barometer
AABEEFGHILNPRT finger-alphabet
AABEEFGILNNOST self-abnegation
AABEEFGILNSSTU fatiguableness
AABEEFGLLLNORT flagrante bello
AABEEFHKMORSTT mark of the Beast
AABEEFHLMNORTT Battle of Arnhem
AABEEFILMNOSTT Battle of Amiens
AABEEFKOPRRSTW power breakfast
AABEEFLMNORTTY flamboyant-tree
AABEEFLNNRRSTU untransferable
AABEEFLNOPRSTT roast-beef plant
AABEEFLNORSSUV favourableness
AABEEFLRRRSTWY strawberry leaf
AABEEFNORRSSTW beasts of warren
AABEEGGHRSTTTY The Great Gatsby
AABEEGHHINRTVY heavy breathing

AABEEGHHKNNNRT Kenneth Branagh
AABEEGHILNRTTZ Elizabeth Grant
AABEEGHINRRTTW water-breathing
AABEEGHJMNRRSU Jürgen Habermas
AABEEGIILMNNSS imaginableness
AABEEGIILNORRV variable region
AABEEGIKMORRRR marriage-broker
AABEEGILNOPRTT operating table
AABEEGLMMOPRRR reprogrammable
AABEEGORRSTTTY storage battery
AABEEHIIILRTTV rehabilitative
AABEEHIILMNSTZ Elizabethanism
AABEEHILMRRRRT thermal barrier
AABEEHKOOSTTTT take to the boats
AABEEIIKLLNRRT all-terrain bike
AABEEIILMNOTTT antimetabolite
AABEEIILNNRSSV invariableness
AABEEIILNNSSST insatiableness
AABEEIILNOPRST Isabelita Perón
AABEEIILNRRRST irrestrainable
AABEEILLMMORRT Albert Memorial
AABEEILLNNSSUV invaluableness
AABEEILMNPSSSS impassableness
AABEEILNNRRSTU unrestrainable
AABEEIMNNORTUV mountain beaver
AABEEKNOQRRSSU break no squares
AABEELNNPSSSSU unpassableness
AABEFGIKLLPRRU ballpark figure
AABEFILLMMNNNO non-inflammable
AABEFILLNOPSTU Fallopian tubes
AABEFIMNOORRTU neurofibromata
AABEGGGINORSTU subaggregation
AABEGHIINNORTT into the bargain
AABEGHIKLNRTTY breathtakingly
AABEGHILLNNQTU banqueting-hall
AABEGHINNNOTVY not be having any
AABEGHIOOPRRTU autobiographer
AABEGIIILMNNSS Albigensianism
AABEGIILLOOPST palaebiologist
AABEGILLNRRRUU urban guerrilla
AABEGILMNRRSSY embarrassingly
AABEGILMNRSTTU bang-tail muster
AABEGILNQSTUUU Auguste Blanqui
AABEGLMNRSSTUU Magnus Albertus
AABEHHIOSTTVWY have it both ways
AABEHHJMNNORSS Johannes Brahms
AABEHIIILNORTT rehabilitation
AABEHIILLNNSST Nathaniel Bliss
AABEHIKMOORRST Arbroath smokie
AABEHILNNQSUUV unvanquishable
AABEHINNOPSSTY Spanish bayonet
AABEHINOPRRTWY rainbow therapy
AABEHLLOPPRSTY blepharoplasty
AABEHMMORRRTWY bertha army worm
AABEIIIILLMNRS animal risibile
AABEIIIILLNNTY inalienability
AABEIIILLNORST liberalisation
AABEIIILLNORTZ liberalization
AABEIIILLNRTTY inalterability
AABEIIILMNRRST libertarianism
AABEIIILNPRSTY inseparability
AABEIIILPRRRTY irreparability
AABEIIIMPRSSSV ipsissima verba
AABEIILLLMNTUY unmalleability
AABEIILLMNOSTW William Bateson
AABEIILLMNRTWZ William Barentz
AABEIILLNRTTUY unalterability
AABEIILMNORSUV bulimia nervosa
AABEIILMPTTTTY attemptability
AABEIILNNNTTTU tintinnabulate
AABEIILNSSSTTU substantialise
AABEIILNSSTTUZ substantialize
AABEIIMPPRSTTV private baptism
AABEIINOPPSSTW boatswain's pipe
AABEIKNOPRRSST Boris Pasternak
AABEILMNNOOPRU lobar pneumonia
AABEILMNNORRTU rational number
AABEILMNNRSTTU intransmutable
AABEILMNOORSTT retinoblastoma
AABEILNNORSTTU subalternation
AABEILNOPRRTTU perturbational
AABEIMNNNRRTUV Martin Van Buren
AABEIMPRRRTTYY primary battery
AABEKMRRRRSTWY strawberry mark
AABELLMNPRSUUU Palus Nebularum
AABELMNNRRSTUU natural numbers
AABELMNNRSTTUU untransmutable
AABELMNOORSSTU neuroblastomas
AABENORRRRSTWY strawberry roan
AABFFIIIILLSTY falsifiability
AABFGHIILLORTT a bit of all right
AABFHIIILNOSTY fashionability
AABFIIILLMMNTY inflammability
AABFIILLNPPTUY unflappability
AABGIIILNORSTY organisability
AABGIIILNORTYZ organizability
AABHHINOOOPPRT anthropophobia
AABHIIIKKLMNNU Mikhail Bakunin
AABHIIINPPRSST bipartisanship
AABHNNNOPPTUYY not a happy bunny
AABIIILLMNPTUY manipulability
AABIIILMNNRSSU annus mirabilis
AABIIILNSSTTUY sustainability
AABIILLNOOPTTX blaxploitation
AABIILMNSSSTTU substantialism
AABIILNNNNTTTU tintinnabulant
AABIILNNNRTTUY tintinnabulary
AABIILNSSSTTTU substantialist
AABIILNSSTTTUY substantiality
AABIINNNOORTTY binary notation
AABIINNOSSTTTU substantiation
AABILLNSSTTUVY substantivally
AABILMMNNOOSTU somnambulation
AACCCCEGLOORSY sacrococcygeal
AACCCCEILLNRUY canicular cycle
AACCCCENNOOOVV concavo-concave
AACCCCILLNORTY contracyclical
AACCCDDDEIINOO dodecanoic acid
AACCCDEIIOPRTY pyro-acetic acid
AACCCDHIIINOTY thiocyanic acid
AACCCDHIIOORRT cardiothoracic
AACCCEEHILLTTY catechetically

AACCCEEHILMNTU catechumenical
AACCCEEHIRRSST saccharic ester
AACCCEEIILLSST ecclesiastical
AACCCEEIPSSTXY excess capacity
AACCCEFIRSSTUU caustic surface
AACCCEHHILOPPS scaphocephalic
AACCCEHIIRRSTT characteristic
AACCCEHILMORST chromatic scale
AACCCEHLNOSTUY cyclanthaceous
AACCCEILLLLORR clerical collar
AACCCGIILLNOOR carcinological
AACCCGIKNORRST stock car racing
AACCCGINNORTTT contact tracing
AACCCHKLMNOSTW watchman's clock
AACCCHLLOOPSTY staphylococcal
AACCCIILLMSSSU classical music
AACCCIILNNOTUV Vatican Council
AACCCILNOORSTT social contract
AACCCNNOOSTTTU cost-accountant
AACCDDEEHKNNSS cack-handedness
AACCDDEIMMOOST disaccommodate
AACCDDEMMNOOTU unaccommodated
AACCDEEEFIMPST impacted faeces
AACCDEEEHINOOP Chenopodiaceae
AACCDEEEIILOSS coeliac disease
AACCDEEHHNOSTT catch one's death
AACCDEEHLNRRST cradle-snatcher
AACCDEEIINRRST disincarcerate
AACCDEELNORRRW Clarence Darrow
AACCDEGHIMOORR echocardiogram
AACCDEGIILNOPR pelargonic acid
AACCDEGIPRSTUU Auguste Piccard
AACCDEHHILLORT Catholic Herald
AACCDEHILLLNOW child allowance
AACCDEHILOPRSY polysaccharide
AACCDEHIMNOORS monosaccharide
AACCDEHINNRRWY ward in Chancery
AACCDEIIIMNNRU neuraminic acid
AACCDEIILLOPTY apodeictically
AACCDEIILNNOSS oceanic islands
AACCDEIINNORTT contraindicate
AACCDEIKLLRSTU calculated risk
AACCDEILLMORTY democratically
AACCDEILMOORST social democrat✧
AACCDEILNNOSSV Slavonic Dances
AACCDEIMNORTVY Cadmean victory
AACCDELLLNOTUU Launcelot du Lac
AACCDFHIMMNNOO chain of command
AACCDFIIJLORTU judicial factor
AACCDGIIILMNTU glutaminic acid
AACCDGIILLOPRY pyrogallic acid
AACCDHHJMNOOSU John Couch Adams
AACCDHIILLNORY diachronically
AACCDHIILNORUY hyaluronic acid
AACCDHIMOPRSTY psychodramatic
AACCDHLOPSTUYY pachydactylous
AACCDHNNNOORRW crown and anchor
AACCDIIINRSTTU Traducianistic
AACCDIINNNORTT contraindicant
AACCDIINNOOOPR piano accordion
AACCDIKNORRSTT carrot and stick
AACCDIKNORSSTU Turks and Caicos
AACCDINNORSSTT Dirac's constant
AACCDLMOORSTUY macrodactylous
AACCEEEHHILMMR Michael Meacher
AACCEEEHIMNORS macaroni cheese
AACCEEEHKNNOST take one's chance
AACCEEEIIKRSTT Rickettsiaceae
AACCEEELMNORRT electron camera
AACCEEELNNOTYY cyanoacetylene
AACCEEELNPRSSY necessary place
AACCEEFFILNOPT capital offence
AACCEEFGIMNRRS screaming farce
AACCEEFHLRRSSU Charles Surface
AACCEEFIIMOORV Voice of America
AACCEEFKNOPRTT Pontefract cake
AACCEEGHHILNRT archgenethliac
AACCEEGIILNTTT telangiectatic
AACCEEGILLOOOP palaeoecologic
AACCEEGILMNNRS cleansing-cream
AACCEEGIPRRTTT target practice
AACCEEHHILMSVY heavy chemicals
AACCEEHIILMPST mesaticephalic
AACCEEHILMNNSS mechanicalness
AACCEEHILMORTT tacheometrical
AACCEEHILMOTUY leucocythaemia
AACCEEHLLRSSUY Charles Causley
AACCEEIJLLMOOS Camilo José Cela
AACCEEILNNRSTU natural science
AACCEEILORSTTT stereotactical
AACCEEIMRRSTUY security camera
AACCEEINNNORRT container crane
AACCEEINNNORSS reconnaissance
AACCEEINNRSSTU inaccurateness
AACCEELLNOOUVV Convolvulaceae
AACCEELMNORRTU currente calamo
AACCEELNNOPSTU clean up one's act
AACCEELNORRRTU nuclear reactor
AACCEEMNNNOOPR non-compearance
AACCEEMNOPRTTY pancreatectomy
AACCEFHHLMRRSU Ralf Schumacher
AACCEFHIORRSSU sacchariferous
AACCEFHOORRTTU out of character
AACCEFIILLORUV calorific value
AACCEFIKNRSTTY fantasy cricket
AACCEFILNOSSTU self-accusation
AACCEFIMNNNOPY finance company
AACCEFIMNNORRU circumforanean
AACCEFLNORTTUU counterfactual
AACCEFLORSSTUY self-accusatory
AACCEGGILLNOOY gynaecological
AACCEGHILLNOPY coelanaglyphic
AACCEGHILLOOST eschatological
AACCEGHILNOPRS scenographical
AACCEGHILNRRST clear-starching
AACCEGHLOORRTY characterology
AACCEGIILOOPTT galactopoietic
AACCEGIIMNRTUV circumnavigate
AACCEGILMNNUUV vacuum cleaning
AACCEGINNOSTUY nyctaginaceous
AACCEHHIILLNPR Charlie Chaplin
AACCEHHIILLRRY hierarchically

AACCEHHLOPPSSU	scaphocephalus
AACCEHIILOPPRS	archiepiscopal
AACCEHIILQRRSU	squirearchical
AACCEHIINORRSU	Cerro Incahuasi
AACCEHIJKLMNOS	Michael Jackson
AACCEHIKKLORST	cocktail shaker
AACCEHILLNOOPT	plain chocolate
AACCEHILLORTTY	theocratically
AACCEHILLPRTYY	archetypically
AACCEHINOPPRRT	parthenocarpic
AACCEHLMOOPRSU	macrocephalous
AACCEHOOOPRSST	cast a horoscope
AACCEIILLNOPRT	Captain Corelli
AACCEIILMNOOSS	semi-occasional
AACCEIILNORRTT	recalcitration
AACCEIILRRTUUV	curricula vitae
AACCEIIMNOPSTT	misacceptation
AACCEIJKLOPRRT	practical joker
AACCEILLLOPPTY	apoplectically
AACCEILLMTUUVY	accumulatively
AACCEILPRSTTUY	spectacularity
AACCEINNOOSTUZ	anacoustic zone
AACCELLMMOORRU	macromolecular
AACCELNNORSUUU	ranunculaceous
AACCENNORSSSST	sacrosanctness
AACCFFGIILMNRT	traffic-calming
AACCFHIILMMNNU	Finn mac Cumhail
AACCFIIILNOORT	calorification
AACCFIIILNOSST	classification
AACCFIIINNOSTT	sanctification
AACCFIILORSSTY	classificatory
AACCFNNORTTTUU	turf accountant
AACCGGIMNNORTT	gaming contract
AACCGHHIILNOPR	ichnographical
AACCGHHIILOPRR	chirographical
AACCGHHILOOPRR	chorographical
AACCGHHILOPRST	chalcographist
AACCGHIILLLORY	oligarchically
AACCGHIILNOOPR	iconographical
AACCGHIILNOPRZ	zincographical
AACCGHIJKMNNNU	Jack Cunningham
AACCGHILMOOPRS	cosmographical
AACCGHNNOOSTUU	à chacun son goût
	chacun à son goût
AACCGIILLLMOOT	climatological
AACCGIILLMORTY	tragicomically
AACCGIILNOTTTV	tactical voting
AACCGIIORSTTUU	acoustic guitar
AACCGILLLNOOOV	volcanological
AACCGILLLNOOUV	vulcanological
AACCHHHINRSTTY	starch hyacinth
AACCHHILNNORTU	national church
AACCHHIMNNOOPT	companion hatch
AACCHIILLMSSTY	schismatically
AACCHIILMTTTUX	Mt Ixtaccihuatl
AACCHILLLOPTTY	phyllotactical
AACCHILLLOSSTY	scholastically
AACCHILNNOORSU	canonical hours
AACCHILNOPSTYY	psychoanalytic
AACCHILOOPTTTY	photocatalytic
AACCHINNOPSTTU	accountantship
AACCHLMNOORSTU	schola cantorum
AACCHLRSSTTTUW	clutch at straws
AACCIIILMPRTTY	impracticality
AACCIIIMNOTTVY	amniotic cavity
AACCIILLMNOSTU	miscalculation
AACCIILMNRSTTU	circumstantial
AACCIILNNOOOST	consociational
AACCIILNPRSTTU	practical units
AACCIILNPRTTUY	unpracticality
AACCIILOOPRSTV	apostolic vicar
	vicar-apostolic
AACCIILPRSSTTU	rustic capitals
AACCIIMMNPRSSU	musicians' cramp
AACCIIMNOORSST	carcinomatosis
AACCILLNOOPTUY	occupationally
AACCILMNNNOOTU	nominal account
AACCILNOPRRSUU	corpuscularian
AACCINNOORRTTY	contractionary
AACCLLMNORSTYY	crystallomancy
AACDDDHILORTUV	David Coulthard
AACDDEEEHINRTT	detached retina
AACDDEEEOPTTUV	advocate-depute
AACDDEEFILLLNN	Decline and Fall
AACDDEEGHHINRV	Advanced Higher
AACDDEEHINOOTT	Chaetodontidae
AACDDEEHIPRSTT	death-practised
AACDDEEIILMMNR	Middle-American
AACDDEEIJQRRSU	Jacques Derrida
AACDDEEILOSTVV	devil's advocate
AACDDEELLORSSS	Dead Sea Scrolls
AACDDEIIIMMNOV	Divina Commedia
AACDDEKLMORRTT	cold dark matter
AACDDGHHIIMMRU	Hugh MacDiarmid
AACDDHIIKNRRSW	Richard Dawkins
AACDDHIILNNSSW	Sandwich Island
AACDDHILMNORYY	hydrodynamical
AACDEEEEHJLNNU	Jean-Luc Dehaene
AACDEEEEINOPRT	Pontederiaceae
AACDEEEFFIORRU	affaire de coeur
AACDEEEFHMNSSS	shamefacedness
AACDEEEGINNRRW	Andrew Carnegie
AACDEEEGLMNNTT	gentleman-cadet
AACDEEEIRRRSSV	careers adviser
AACDEEEIRRRSTT	restricted area
AACDEEELMNRSTT	Cadmean letters
AACDEEFGILOORS	Coolgardie safe
AACDEEFILLLNOW	field allowance
AACDEEGHHNORST	chase the dragon
AACDEEGHIIMNNR	reading-machine
AACDEEGIILLNRT	leading article
AACDEEGIIMORRT	radiometric age
AACDEEGIINORSS	organic disease
AACDEEGINPRSWY	speedway racing
AACDEEGIPPRRRT	cartridge-paper
AACDEEGLNNSTUV	Dunvegan Castle
AACDEEHHLLLOST	hold all the aces
AACDEEHHLRTTWY	Aldwych Theatre
AACDEEHIILLNRT	tail-end Charlie
AACDEEHIILLNTX	Hexactinellida
AACDEEHIIMMSTT	mathematicised
AACDEEHIIMMTTZ	mathematicized

AACDEEHIIMPSTV impact adhesive
AACDEEHILMPSTU sulphacetamide
AACDEEHILMRRST Reims Cathedral
AACDEEHINNNSTT in the ascendant
AACDEEHIORRTTT read the riot act
AACDEEHIPRRTTY Trachypteridae
AACDEEHKNRSTTT stand the racket
AACDEEHLLLRSTW Wells Cathedral
AACDEEHLMMNOOY Monochlamydeae
AACDEEHLMOPPRX Phaedra complex
AACDEEHLNPPSSU pleased as Punch
AACDEEHLPRRSTY The Card Players
AACDEEIILNRSTV Cartesian devil
AACDEEIINOSSSS caisson disease
AACDEEIINRRSTV Cartesian diver
AACDEEILLMMNTY medicamentally
AACDEEILLNQTUW well-acquainted
AACDEEILMNOPRW calamine powder
AACDEEILMOPRRT career diplomat
AACDEEILOPPRTU propaedeutical
AACDEEILPRRTTU ultracrepidate
AACDEEINQRRTTU quart and tierce
AACDEEIORRSTTV decorative arts
AACDEELLNNSUVY Lucas van Leyden
AACDEELMNOORSU morceau de salon
AACDEELMRRSTTU treacle mustard
AACDEELNNNRSTT transcendental
AACDEENORSSSUV cadaverousness
AACDEFGNOOOPTU put a good face on
AACDEFHILNORSW Earl of Sandwich
AACDEFIIINNOTZ denazification
AACDEFIILLNNOT LA Confidential
AACDEFILLNORRW cardinal flower
AACDEFILMOPSST foamed plastics
AACDEFMNNRTUUU unmanufactured
AACDEGGHIOORTW with a good grace
AACDEGHHILLNTT Highland cattle
AACDEGHHOOPRRT cathodographer
AACDEGHILLMOSU Michael Douglas
AACDEGHIMOPRRT dermatographic
AACDEGHLOORSTU graduate school
AACDEGHNNNORST Drang nach Osten
AACDEGIILLMRRR Marc Girardelli
AACDEGILLMOORT dermatological
AACDEGINOPRSST data processing
AACDEHHLLORRTY chloral hydrate
AACDEHILLMNNRR Richard Ellmann
AACDEHILLNNNSS Channel Islands
AACDEHILLNORST The Coral Island
AACDEHILMOOPRT camphorated oil
AACDEHILNNNOUU Un Chien Andalou
AACDEHILNOPRRT Ripon Cathedral
AACDEHIMMNRSTT Maarten Schmidt
AACDEHIMOPRSSU pseudo-archaism
AACDEHINRRTTUW draw the curtain
AACDEHIOPRSTUY acid-house party
AACDEHLLLNORTW tallow chandler
AACDEHLLMOTUWY what-d'you-call-'em
AACDEHLNOOPRSU androcephalous
AACDEHMOPRSTUY pachydermatous
AACDEIIILLLSTY idealistically
AACDEIIILMNOST decimalisation
medicalisation
AACDEIIILMNOTZ decimalization
medicalization
AACDEIIILMORST isodiametrical
AACDEIIIMNORTU audiometrician
AACDEIILLORTVY radial velocity
AACDEIIILNOSTTU educationalist
AACDEIIILNPRRST cardinal-priest
AACDEIIILNRRTUV cardinal virtue
AACDEIIILOPRSTT disceptatorial
AACDEIIILOPRTTU duplicate ratio
AACDEIIMNORSTY aerodynamicist
AACDEIIMORTTUV automatic drive
AACDEIINNNQTUU unacquainted in
AACDEILLLNOPST antipodal cells
AACDEILLMOPRYY polyacrylamide
AACDEILLNNRSTU slantendicular
AACDEILMMNORTY dynamometrical
AACDEILMNPSTTY pentadactylism
AACDEILMNRTTUU unmatriculated
AACDEILMOPRSTT dermatoplastic
AACDEILNNNOTTY continental day
AACDEILNNRSSTU lunar distances
AACDEILOPRSSTY Perissodactyla
AACDEIMMNORRSS comrades-in-arms
AACDEIMNNNOTTU uncontaminated
AACDEIMNNOORTT decontaminator
AACDEINOOPRTTT data protection
AACDELNNOSSSSU scandalousness
AACDELNOPSTTUY pentadactylous
AACDELORSTTTUY tetradactylous
AACDFHHLORSTTY cloth-yard shaft
AACDFIIIILNOPT lapidification
AACDFLMMNOOOTX common toadflax
AACDGGHHIORRRT Richard Hoggart
AACDGHHILOPRRY hydrographical
AACDGHIIMNRRRS Richard Ingrams
AACDGHILOPRTYY dactyliography
AACDGIILLLOORY radiologically
AACDGIILNNOOTT antiodontalgic
AACDGIINOPPRST propagandistic
AACDGIKMNNPRRU cup-and-ring mark
AACDHHIKLRRTUY Richard Hakluyt
AACDHIIILLOPTY idiopathically
AACDHIIINRRSVV Vivian Richards
AACDHIIMRSSSTY Christmas daisy
AACDHIKLLOORSY Kailyard school
AACDHILLOTTUWY what-d'you-call-it
AACDHIMMNNOPST commandantship
AACDHIMOOPRTYY cardiomyopathy
myocardiopathy
AACDHIRRRSSSTU Richard Strauss
AACDHLLLNOOPTU put a call on hold
AACDIIIILNNPRS disciplinarian
AACDIIIILNNRVW Indian Civil War
AACDIIIILNOPPST disapplication
AACDIIIILNORSTV Victoria Island
AACDIIINOOSSST disassociation
AACDIILLLMOPTY diplomatically
AACDIILLNNRSTU slantindicular

AACDILNOOSSTUY anisodactylous
AACDILOPPRRTTU partial product
AACDINNOORRSTY sanitary cordon
AACEEEEGHIMNTV achievement age
AACEEEEGHPRSTT The Great Escape
AACEEEEHMNPRSS Parmesan cheese
AACEEEEIMMNPRS Menispermaceae
AACEEEELNNNQSU Queen Anne's lace
AACEEEFGHNORTX rate of exchange
AACEEEFGHORRTY the Year of Grace
AACEEEFHINRSTT stare in the face
AACEEEFORSSTTV East Coast fever
AACEEEGHINNTVW with a vengeance
AACEEEGIKMNNRZ Mackenzie Range
AACEEEGILLLNTV televangelical
AACEEEGIPPRRTT cigarette paper
AACEEEGKLRSTWY greywacke-slate
AACEEEGLNOPSSU espagnole sauce
sauce espagnole
AACEEEHHIKLMTT take the michael
AACEEEHHILNNOT an ace in the hole
AACEEEHIJKLMRR Jeremiah Clarke
AACEEEHIJMMNRS James A Michener
AACEEEHIMNNOST in the same canoe
AACEEEHIMNRRST Increase Mather
AACEEEHKMRRRST market research
AACEEEHLMOSTUY thymelaeaceous
AACEEEIINNPPTT canine appetite
AACEEEIJKMMNSZ James Mackenzie
AACEEEILMNRSUX manual exercise
AACEEELLNSSTVW Wallace Stevens
AACEEELLPRRSTV space traveller
AACEEELPRSSTTY cassette player
AACEEFFILNOTTY affectionately
AACEEFGHLLOSTU shelf-catalogue
AACEEFGILORRTT of great article
AACEEFGLNNPRSY false pregnancy
AACEEFHHIPRRST Seraphic Father
AACEEFIILNRRTV trifacial nerve
AACEEFILLORRUW cauliflower ear
AACEEFILNORSTV fovea centralis
AACEEFKLLORSTU oak-leaf cluster
AACEEFLLNORTTU fault tolerance
AACEEFMNOPRRRT performance art
AACEEGGGILRRRU luggage-carrier
AACEEGGHILNNTT chelating agent
AACEEGGHLOOORY geoarchaeology
AACEEGGILLLNOY genealogically
AACEEGGILORSTT geostrategical
AACEEGGINORSTV average costing
AACEEGGJLNNOTU conjugate angle
AACEEGHHHLRSUY Charles Haughey
AACEEGHHINRRST heart-searching
AACEEGHHLNOPPR encephalograph
AACEEGHHLNOSSX hexagonal chess
AACEEGHIIMNNPR reaping machine
AACEEGHIKRRRTT Garrick Theatre
AACEEGHILLLNTY genethliacally
AACEEGHILLNPRS spherical angle
AACEEGHILMNNNS channel seaming
AACEEGHILMPRYY hyperglycaemia
AACEEGHILNNRTT central heating
AACEEGHILNOPST stegocephalian
AACEEGHKLMOPSU keep a calm sough
AACEEGHLLOPYYZ Zygophyllaceae
AACEEGIIKLLLMP Gamaliel Pickle
AACEEGIILLMNNX lexical meaning
AACEEGIILLMNSV evangelicalism
AACEEGIILLNNPT palingenetical
AACEEGIILMNNOR American Legion
AACEEGIILNSSTT telangiectasis
AACEEGIINNNRST intransigeance
AACEEGILLLOOPS spelaeological
AACEEGILLNRSTV vertical angles
AACEEGILLNSTTT Tintagel Castle
AACEEGILMNOSTT magneto-elastic
AACEEGINRRRRTU carriage return
AACEEGJLMNORRY major-generalcy
AACEEGKKNPRTUY turnkey package
AACEEHHHIKRTTW white-hat hacker
AACEEHHHINTTTT The Cat in the Hat
AACEEHHILLMMOS shalom aleichem
AACEEHHILMORST chamois leather
AACEEHHINORRST Archaeornithes
AACEEHHIOOPRRZ Rhizophoraceae
AACEEHHIRSTTTW wheat-ear stitch
AACEEHHLNOPPTY encephalopathy
AACEEHIIMMNRTT arithmetic mean
AACEEHIIMOOPTT haematopoietic
AACEEHIINNRTTX inheritance tax
AACEEHIKLMOTUY leukocythaemia
AACEEHILLLPTTY telepathically
AACEEHILLMPTTY empathetically
AACEEHILMMMRST Michaelmas term
AACEEHILMMNTTY enthymematical
AACEEHILMNPSST emphaticalness
AACEEHILNNPSTU a place in the sun
AACEEHILNRSSTT theatricalness
AACEEHILPRSTXY hypercatalexis
AACEEHILRRTUVX extravehicular
AACEEHIMORRSTT archaeometrist
AACEEHIPRSSTTY cryptaesthesia
AACEEHLLOPPRTT apple charlotte
AACEEHLMOPRSTT spermatothecal
AACEEHLMORRRTT thermal reactor
AACEEHLNOOPTTT the clean potato
AACEEHLOOPRSST separate school
AACEEHMNORSSTU sacrament house
AACEEHMNORSTUY aerenchymatous
AACEEHMNPPPRRT parchment paper
AACEEHMOOSTTVY have come to stay
AACEEHNNRRSTTT tenants' charter
AACEEHNPPPPRTU paper tape punch
AACEEIIINPPRTV inappreciative
AACEEIIKLLNOTW A Town Like Alice
AACEEIILLLNPRT Triple Alliance
AACEEIILLMMNWW William MacEwen
AACEEIILMMPRST apical meristem
AACEEIILOPRSTV overcapitalise
AACEEIILOPRTVZ overcapitalize
AACEEIILORSTTY aeroelasticity
AACEEIILPPRTVY appreciatively

AACEEIILPRTTUV recapitulative
AACEEIIMNNNRST centenarianism
AACEEIIMNNOSTV Venetian mosaic
AACEEIIMNNRSSS necessarianism
AACEEIINPPRTUV unappreciative
AACEEIJLMNSSST majesticalness
AACEEILLLMSTTY telesmatically
AACEEILLNNPRSU annular eclipse
AACEEILMMNSSTU immaculateness
AACEEILMMPRTUY empyreumatical
AACEEILNPRTTUV venture capital
AACEEILNRSSTTU articulateness
AACEEILNRSSTUV anvil secateurs
AACEEIMNOPRRTW a warm reception
AACEEIMOPRSTUX proximate cause
AACEEINNOPRRST a certain person
AACEEINRSSTTTV attractiveness
AACEEKLOSSSTTY Stokesay Castle
AACEELLNOPPRRT Peter Pan collar
AACEELMMOOSSTU melastomaceous
AACEELNNOPSTUU pennatulaceous
AACEELOOPRRRTX extracorporeal
AACEEMNNNOOPRT contemporanean
AACEEMNORRSSTU stoma-care nurse
AACEEOOPRRSTTT corporate state
AACEFFILNORSSS Francis of Sales
AACEFFINORRRTW warrant officer
AACEFFINPRRTTT traffic pattern
AACEFFINRRRSTU current affairs
AACEFFLMORTTTY matter-of-factly
AACEFGGHILNORT floating charge
AACEFGGINNOOTV coign of vantage
AACEFGHIINPRRR preaching friar
AACEFHIMNOPRTU paramount chief
AACEFHMNNOOSST canon of the mass
AACEFIIILMNNST Financial Times
AACEFIIILNRSST artificialness
AACEFIILOOQSUU aquifoliaceous
AACEFILLNOSSSU fallaciousness
AACEFILNQRRSSU Francis Quarles
AACEFINNORTTTY attorney in fact
AACEFKLLLOPPRW flock wallpaper
AACEGGHIINPRRT graphic granite
AACEGGHILLOPRY geographically
AACEGGHINNORRT Gregorian chant
AACEGGHINOPRST steganographic
AACEGGIINNNRTY Training Agency
AACEGGIINPRRRS spring-carriage
AACEGGILNNOORT congregational✧
AACEGHHIILLOPR heliographical
AACEGHHIILOPRR hierographical
AACEGHHIIMNNSW washing machine
AACEGHHILNOPRT ethnographical
AACEGHHILOPRTY hyetographical
AACEGHHIMOPPTT apophthegmatic
AACEGHIIILLNRS heliacal rising
AACEGHIIILMMNN mailing machine
AACEGHIIKLMNNT talking machine
AACEGHIIKLOOPR Oki Archipelago
AACEGHIILLNRTW with an ill grace
AACEGHIILLPPRY epigraphically
AACEGHIILMNNNP planing-machine
AACEGHIILMOOTY oligocythaemia
AACEGHIIMMORRT hierogrammatic
AACEGHIIMNNRSV vanishing cream
AACEGHIJKRSTTT straightjacket
AACEGHILLLMPTY phlegmatically
AACEGHILLMOPRT metallographic
AACEGHILLNRSTY crystal healing
AACEGHILLOOPRS phraseological
AACEGHILMNNRTT alignment chart
AACEGHILOPPRRT petrographical
AACEGHILOPRTTU telautographic
AACEGHIMNOPRTY cinematography
AACEGHJKMNNNTU Mt Kanchenjunga
AACEGHLNNOOPSZ Pancho Gonzales
AACEGHLNNSTUUW Weltanschauung
AACEGHLOOOORYZ archaeozoology
AACEGIILLLLSTY legalistically
AACEGIILLLOOTY aetiologically
AACEGIILLMOOSS semasiological
AACEGIILMOPRTY Malacopterygii
AACEGIILMPRSST sigma particles
AACEGIIMNOPRST Pietro Mascagni
AACEGIINNNNSTV Vincent's angina
AACEGIINNNRSTY intransigeancy
AACEGIINNOPRST angina pectoris
AACEGIINNORRTT terra incognita
AACEGIINOORSTT categorisation
AACEGIINOORTTZ categorization
AACEGIKMMNORRT macro-marketing
AACEGILLLOOPTY apologetically
AACEGILLMNOORT organometallic
AACEGILLMSSSSU musical glasses
AACEGILMNOOPTT magneto-optical
AACEGILMNOORUZ colour magazine
AACEGILNNOOTUU union catalogue
AACEGILNOOPPRR organ-pipe coral
AACEGILNORTTUV congratulative
AACEGILNRRTTUY rectangularity
AACEGLLMMNORST Malcolm Sargent
AACEGLNNOOORSW score an own goal
AACEGMNNOPRTTT argent comptant
AACEHHHILLMTTT that'll teach him
AACEHHIIKKNSTV have a thick skin
AACEHHIIMMNNSS Hamish MacInnes
AACEHHILNNOPTY phthalocyanine
AACEHHLLOTTTUY that'll teach you
AACEHHLMMORSST Thomas Chalmers
AACEHIILLMRTTY arithmetically
AACEHIILLNTTTY antithetically
AACEHIILMMNRST Ismail Merchant
AACEHIILMMNSUV male chauvinism
AACEHIILMNSTUV male chauvinist
AACEHIILNSSTTU enthusiastical
AACEHIILPPRRST periphrastical
AACEHIIMNOSSTT schematisation
AACEHIIMNOSTTZ schematization
AACEHIIMNPRRST Petrarchianism
AACEHIINNOTTTU authentication
AACEHIINOOSTTY isothiocyanate
AACEHIINPRRSTT Petrarchianist

AACEHIJLNNOSTU Anjelica Huston
AACEHIJNNOPSTW Captain W E Johns
AACEHIKLMNNOSW Coleman Hawkins
AACEHILLMNNORY enharmonically
AACEHILLMNOPTY phonematically
AACEHILLMOPRSY semaphorically
AACEHILLMOPRTY metaphorically
AACEHILLMPSTYY metaphysically
AACEHILMNNOPRS anamorphic lens
AACEHILMNOPRTU unmetaphorical
AACEHILMNORRTT merchant tailor
AACEHILMNPSTUY unmetaphysical
AACEHIMMMORSTT metachromatism
AACEHKKLLNOSSW walk one's chalks
AACEHKOOPPRRST approach stroke
AACEHLLOPPSTUY platycephalous
AACEHLOPRRSSTY sphaerocrystal
AACEHLPRRSTTYY crystal therapy
AACEHLQRRSTTUU Urquhart Castle
AACEHMNOPRSTUY parenchymatous
AACEHQQRSSSTUU squash racquets
AACEIIILNOPSST specialisation
AACEIIILNOPSTZ specialization
AACEIIILNPTTVY anticipatively
AACEIIINNOPPRT inappreciation
AACEIILLLMRTTY altimetrically
AACEIILLMNNOOT calamine lotion
AACEIILLMNRRWY criminal lawyer
AACEIILLNORRST lateral incisor
AACEIILLNPSTTY antiseptically
AACEIILLNRTTUY inarticulately
AACEIILMNNNOOT national income
AACEIILMNRRRTU intramercurial
AACEIILMOOPRTV imperial octavo
AACEIILMOSSSTT state socialism
AACEIILNNORSTT centralisation
AACEIILNNORSTU nuclearisation
AACEIILNNORTTZ centralization
AACEIILNNORTUZ nuclearization
AACEIILNNPSSST castles in Spain
AACEIILNOOPPSU papilionaceous
AACEIILNOPRTTU recapitulation
AACEIILNORRTVY early-Victorian
AACEIILNORSSTU secularisation
AACEIILNORSTUZ secularization
AACEIILOPSTTTT petticoat-tails
AACEIILPPPRSTT past participle
AACEIIMNNRSSTU unsectarianism
AACEIINNNRTTUY certain annuity
AACEIINNORSSTW Sir Isaac Newton
AACEIINORSSSUV avariciousness
AACEILLLMORSUU columella auris
AACEILLLNOPRSU parallel cousin
AACEILLLNOPSTY pleonastically
AACEILLMMNNRSU Macmillan nurse
AACEILLMMRSTYY asymmetrically
AACEILLMNNOORT nomenclatorial
AACEILLMNORRTU intramolecular
AACEILLMRTTTUU multarticulate
AACEILLMSSTTYY systematically
AACEILMMNOORTT commentatorial
AACEILMNNOOPST compensational
AACEILMNORRTTY moral certainty
AACEILMNOSSSTU calamitousness
AACEILMNSSTTUY unsystematical
AACEILMORSSSSS claims assessor
AACEILMRRSSUUU Marcus Aurelius
AACEILNNNRSSTY tyrannicalness
AACEILNNOOPRSW Napoleonic Wars
AACEILNNOORSTV conservational
conversational
AACEILNNOPTTUY county palatine
AACEILNNORSTTT Central Station
AACEILNORSTTUX exclaustration
AACEILNPRRSSTU particularness
AACEILNRTTTUVY unattractively
AACEILOPRRTTUY recapitulatory
AACEILORRSTVVY Victor Vasarely
AACEILRSSSTUUV vascular tissue
AACEIMMNSSTUUV Vatican Museums
AACEIMNOPPRTVY private company
AACEIMNOPRSTTU storm in a teacup
AACEINNRTTTUUY curtate annuity
AACEINOORRRSTT rostrocarinate
AACEINOPRSSSST cast aspersions
AACEJKLLMNOSSU Samuel L Jackson
AACEJKLMORRSSS James Clark Ross
AACEKLNNORSTUY cantankerously
AACELLMNOOPRRY monocarpellary
AACELLMOPRRSUU supramolecular
AACELLNOPPSSTU cast a spell upon
AACELNNNOOPRST preconsonantal
AACELNNNORSSTU connaturalness
AACEMMNOPRSSTU Castanospermum
AACENNOPRSSTTU counter-passant
AACENNORSSTTUU transcutaneous
AACENOORRRRTYY coronary artery
AACFFFIIILLMOY official family
AACFFGIILNRSST traffic signals
AACFFGIMNORRTY factory farming
AACFFIKLMNOPRS saffron milk cap
AACFGHILMOPRRU graphic formula
AACFGIIINNOSTU sanguification
AACFGILNORRTUV vulgar fraction
AACFGIMOOSSTYZ zygomatic fossa
AACFGNOOORSTTT contrafagottos
AACFHILNOOPRST Chilon of Sparta
AACFIIIIKLLRST artificial silk
AACFIIIILLNRTY inartificially
AACFIIIKNORSTT karstification
AACFIIILLNRTUY unartificially
AACFIIINNOOPST saponification
AACFIIINNOQTTU quantification
AACFIIINORSTTT stratification
AACFIILLMORTTU multifactorial
AACFIILLMRSSST first-class mail
AACFIILMNOPSST pontifical mass
AACFIILMORSTTT stalactitiform
AACFIILORSSTTY satisfactorily
AACFIINNOSSTTU unsatisfaction
AACFILMNNOOORT conformational
AACFINORSSTTUY unsatisfactory

AACGGHHILOPRRY	hygrographical
AACGGIILLMOSST	Glagolitic Mass
AACGGILLLNOORY	laryngological
AACGGILLOOORST	agrostological
AACGHHIILLOPRT	lithographical
AACGHHILOOPPRT	photographical
AACGHHILOOPRRT	orthographical
AACGHHIOPPRRRY	rhyparographic
AACGHHMOOPRRTY	chromatography
AACGHIIJKLLMRT	I'm all right, Jack
AACGHIIMNOPRST	panoramic sight
AACGHILLLOOPTY	pathologically
AACGHILLMOOORU	chaulmoogra oil
AACGHILLOOPRRY	orographically
AACGHILMOOPRST	pharmacologist
AACGHLOOOPRSTU	galactophorous
AACGHLOOPPRSYY	parapsychology
AACGHMNOORSSTT	a strong stomach
AACGHOOOPPRTUY	autocoprophagy
AACGIIILNPRSTU	paralinguistic
AACGIIINNNOPTT	action painting
AACGIIKLNOPRTW	working capital
AACGIIKOPRRTTW	Gatwick Airport
AACGIILLMMOOST	logical atomism
AACGIILLMNORSY	organismically
AACGIILLNNRTUW	curtain walling
AACGIILNNOOSTT	coaling station
AACGIILNOOSTTV	Vaticanologist
AACGIIMNOOPRRS	microsporangia
AACGIKLLOOOPRZ	zoological park
AACGILLLOORSTY	astrologically
AACGILLLOOTTUY	tautologically
AACGILLLRRTUUY	agriculturally
AACGILLMOORRTY	martyrological
AACGILMOOPRRTU	compurgatorial
AACGILNNOORTTU	congratulation
AACGIMOORSSTTT	stomatogastric
AACGLNOORRTTUY	congratulatory
AACHHIIMNRRTTY	antiarrhythmic
AACHHIINORSTUY	ichthyosaurian
AACHHILLMRRTYY	arrhythmically
AACHHINOOPPRTT	anthropopathic
AACHIILLNNOPTY	antiphonically
AACHIILLNOOOST	alcoholisation
AACHIILLNOOOTZ	alcoholization
AACHIILLOPRSTY	aphoristically
AACHIILMNOPRST	misanthropical
AACHIIMMNNOOPR	morphinomaniac
AACHIIMNNORSTT	antimonarchist
AACHILLNNOOOST	national school
AACHILLOORTTUY	local authority
AACHILLOPSTTYY	hypostatically
AACHILMOOPPRST	pharmacopolist
AACHILNNORTUVY	voluntary chain
AACHILNOPSSSYY	psychoanalysis
AACHILOOPSSTTY	photocatalysis
AACHIMPRRSSTTY	Christmas party
AACHINNOORRSTY	Sir Anthony Caro
AACHKKKKOOORSS	Oskar Kokoschka
AACHLLOOOPPPRY	Polyplacophora
AACHLMNOOOOPPR	Monoplacophora
AACHLOOPRSSTTY	Arctostaphylos
AACHNOORRTTUVW	vouch to warrant
AACIIIILMNOSST	Islamicisation
AACIIIILMNOSTZ	Islamicization
AACIIILLLSTTVY	vitalistically
AACIIILLMMRSTU	multiracialism
AACIIILLNRSTTY	inartistically
AACIIILMNOPPST	misapplication
AACIIILNNORTTU	inarticulation
AACIIILNOPRTTY	anticipatorily
AACIIIMNOOSSST	associationism
AACIIJLLNOPRTY	capillary joint
AACIILLLMORSTY	moralistically
AACIILLLRSTTUY	altruistically
AACIILLMMNOPTY	pantomimically
AACIILLMMNSTUY	numismatically
AACIILLOPPRTTY	party-political
AACIILMOOPTTTU	automatic pilot
AACIILNOOPRRST	conspiratorial
AACIILNPPPRRST	principal parts
AACIILNPRRSTTU	antiscriptural
AACIIMMNOSSTTU	atomic mass unit
AACIINNOOSSTTT	action stations
AACIINNOOTTTUX	auto-intoxicant
AACILLLNORSTUY	ultrasonically
AACILLMNNORTUY	unromantically
AACILLMNOORSTY	astronomically
AACILLMOPSTTYY	asymptotically
AACILLNOOPRSTT	castor-oil plant
AACILMMNNNOOPT	common plantain
AACILMOOPPRSTT	protoplasmatic
AACILNNNOORSTT	triconsonantal
AACILNNNOSTTUV	anticonvulsant
AACIMNNORSSSTT	smart sanctions
AACIMNNORSSTUU	Marcus Antonius
AACINOOOPRRTTX	corporation tax
AACINOOPRRRSTT	procrastinator
AACLLNNOPRTTUY	contrapuntally
AACNNORRSSTTUY	Stannary Courts
AADDDDEOORRWWW	Edward Woodward
AADDDEEEHIMMMO	Mohammed Aideed
AADDDEEHIISSTY	hydatid disease
AADDDEILLNORSS	lords and ladies
AADDDFFILLNOWY	daffadowndilly
AADDEEEENNNQSU	Queen Anne's dead
AADDEEEGLLMMNR	Gerald M Edelman
AADDEEEHIMNSTV	Dame Edith Evans
AADDEEEHINRTTW	dead in the water
AADDEEEIRRSSST	distressed area
AADDEEFGHLOORS	flog a dead horse
AADDEEGGILMOOR	Diego de Almagro
AADDEEGGILNRRR	Gerald Gardiner
AADDEEGHLLRTUY	glutaraldehyde
AADDEEGHNNORSU	House and Garden
AADDEEGILRRRSW	Sir Edward Elgar
AADDEEGINNPSTW	Peasant Wedding
AADDEEHHHMOSTT	death's-head moth
AADDEEHHIRRSTW	Sir Edward Heath
AADDEEHILLLNTV	the devil and all
AADDEEHILNNORT	neanderthaloid✧
AADDEEIILLNSWY	Daniel Day-Lewis

AADDEEIINPRTTY identity parade
AADDEEILLNRSSW Leeward Islands
AADDEELNOQRRSU squadron leader
AADDEENPPRRTWY wet-and-dry paper
AADDEENRRSTTUU undersaturated
AADDEGIJLNORSU Douglas Jardine
AADDEHHMNRRTTU thread and thrum
AADDEHILNORSVY Harley Davidson®
AADDEIIRRRRVWY River Irrawaddy
AADDEILLNNORTV Torvill and Dean
AADDEILLOORSSV Osvaldo Ardiles
AADDEINORSTTUW outward-sainted
AADDELMOOOPRRV Pedro Almodovar
AADDFFHLNOSTUU A Handful of Dust
AADDFIIJKLMSTU Afsluitdijk Dam
AADDHJLNNNOOOS Donald Johanson
AADDHMNRSTUUYY Maundy Thursday
AADDINPSSSTTUW spit and sawdust
AADEEEEGHNORVV have an edge over
AADEEEFFHNOOST eat one's head off
AADEEEFGHRSTTY fray at the edges
AADEEEFGIOPRST pâté de foie gras
AADEEEGGILNNRV gardening leave
AADEEEGHLLNNRW Greenland whale
AADEEEGILLRRRU dérailleur gear
AADEEEGILMPRSS spread-eagleism
AADEEEGIPRSSST rites de passage
AADEEEGKMNRRRT market-gardener
AADEEEHHILPRTT Adelphi Theatre
AADEEEHIILRSVY Heaviside layer
AADEEEHIIMNRRT maidenhair-tree
AADEEEHILLLNPS lead apes in hell
AADEEEHILLPSTU lead up the aisle
AADEEEHIMMNPTX dexamphetamine
AADEEEHIMMRRTT Mermaid Theatre
AADEEEHINNSSSS Hansen's disease
AADEEEHIPSSSTU pseudaesthesia
AADEEEHLLMNOST mean lethal dose
AADEEEHLLRTTTY lead tetraethyl
tetraethyl lead
AADEEEHLRRRSSS dress-rehearsal
AADEEEILLLNPRV parallel-veined
AADEEEILLLPPPR parallelepiped
AADEEEINNQSSTU inadequateness
AADEEELMNRSSTT elder statesman
AADEEELNOPSSTT set on a pedestal
AADEEFFHIMMORS homme d'affaires
AADEEFGGIMNNOT defoaming agent
AADEEFGHLPRSTU flaughter-spade
AADEEFGILLLNOT dinoflagellate
AADEEFGILLLRTZ Ella Fitzgerald
AADEEFGKNORRTT take for granted
AADEEFGLLNRRUV glandular fever
AADEEFHILNNRSU Sheridan Le Fanu
AADEEFHILNRTTY faint-heartedly
AADEEFHLMNOOST old man of the sea
AADEEFIILMNRST anti-federalism
AADEEFIILNORST federalisation
AADEEFIILNORTZ federalization
AADEEFIILNRSTT anti-federalist
AADEEFIJLMNNSY Jayne Mansfield
AADEEFKNOSSUWY a week of Sundays
AADEEFMNNOOTTY Day of Atonement
AADEEFNSSSTTUY Fastens Tuesday
AADEEGGIMNNRST aggrandisement
AADEEGGIMNNRTZ aggrandizement
AADEEGHIIILNRT Dante Alighieri
AADEEGHILOPRRT radiotelegraph
AADEEGHIMORRTW Maria Edgeworth
AADEEGHIMSSSSW Swedish massage
AADEEGHINNSTTT stand in the gate
AADEEGHIPPPRSU pseudepigrapha
AADEEGHKMORSTV God save the mark
AADEEGHLNNOPST golden pheasant
AADEEGHNPRRTTY The Garden Party
AADEEGIIMNQRTU quadrigeminate
AADEEGILLLNRTT Little and Large
AADEEGILMNNPTX expanding metal
AADEEGIMNNRRST disarrangement
AADEEGIMNOPRWZ powder magazine
AADEEGINRRSUUX au grand sérieux
AADEEGJNNRRSTY grand serjeanty
AADEEGLLOOOPPY palaeopedology
AADEEHHIMPRSST headmastership
AADEEHHNPRRSTT shepherd tartan
AADEEHIILNNNPT Indian elephant
AADEEHIIMNRTTY diathermaneity
AADEEHKMNORRSV mover and shaker
AADEEHLNOOPRRY aerohydroplane
hydro-aeroplane
AADEEIILMNRSTU unmaterialised
AADEEIILMNRTUZ unmaterialized
AADEEIILMORRTT radio altimeter
AADEEIILNNSTTV Saint Valentide
AADEEIILNPQSSU sesquipedalian
AADEEIILPSSSTU palisade tissue
AADEEIINNPRRST predestinarian
AADEEIINORRRTX extraordinaire
AADEEIKLMOPRTV evaporated milk
AADEEILLLOPPPR parallelopiped
AADEEILLMPRSTU simulated pearl
AADEEILLMPRSTW Dilwara temples
AADEEILLNOPPRS plane-polarised
AADEEILLNOPPRZ plane-polarized
AADEEILLOPRSTY isolated replay
AADEEILMNORTTT tatterdemalion
AADEEILNNOSSTV Adlai Stevenson
AADEEILNNPRRSW plains wanderer
AADEEILNRRSSTU Treasure Island
AADEEINNPRSSTT antidepressant
AADEELLMNPRTTY departmentally
AADEELMNNOORRX Alexander Monro
AADEELNOPPSTTU put on a pedestal
AADEENNORSSSST Tessa Sanderson
AADEENNPPRSSTT Past and Present
AADEENOOPRSSXZ Zeno's paradoxes
AADEEPRRSSTTUU supersaturated
AADEFGHIRRSTVY graveyard shift
AADEFGILLMUUUY Guillaume Dufay
AADEFHHLOOORRT Harefoot Harold
AADEFHNNOOOSTU one of a thousand
AADEFHNNORSSST Fathers and Sons

AADEFIILMNORST self-admiration
AADEFIIMNORSTU diamantiferous
AADEFILMMNNSTU fundamentalism✧
AADEFILMNNSTTU fundamentalist
AADEFILMNNTTUY fundamentality
AADEFIORRSSSTW Disasters of War
AADEFLNNNOOORS Fernando Alonso
AADEGGGHINNNRS Hanging Gardens
AADEGGGIINORST disaggregation
AADEGGHINNRRRW Warren G Harding
AADEGGINORSSWY going-away dress
AADEGHIILNNSTT distant healing
AADEGHILNNRSTT starting handle
AADEGHILNRSTUW daughters-in-law
AADEGHMMNNORST hammer and tongs
AADEGIIIIMPRTT imparidigitate
AADEGIILNNORVZ galvanized iron
AADEGIILNNPTZZ dazzle-painting
AADEGIINNORRTT intergradation
AADEGILNNOPRRW polar wandering
AADEGILNOORTVW vowel gradation
AADEGINOORRRTT retrogradation
AADEGMNOPRRTTU Margaret DuPont
AADEHHIKNORSTT a shot in the dark
AADEHHILOPRRSS A Shropshire Lad
AADEHHLLMOSSTW Thomas Shadwell
AADEHHMMNOSSTY Thomas Sydenham
AADEHIILLMNPSU sulphanilamide
AADEHIIOPRRSTT radiotherapist
AADEHILNORSTWZ Alan Dershowitz
AADEHILRRRRSUY Sir Harry Lauder
AADEHINNNOOSTU one in a thousand
AADEHINNOPSSSU diaphanousness
AADEHINORRRSSY ordinary shares
AADEHIOPRTTXYY hydroxyapatite
AADEHJLNNORSTU Joan Sutherland
AADEHLLLNORSSX Halldór Laxness
AADEHNORRSSTTW north-eastwards
AADEHORRSTTTTW two-start thread
AADEHORSSSTTUW south-eastwards
AADEIIILLLMNRW William Ireland
AADEIIILLMMPRW William Dampier
AADEIIILNNOSST desalinisation
AADEIIILNNOSTZ desalinization
AADEIIILNOSTTV devitalisation
AADEIIILNOTTVZ devitalization
AADEIIIMNORSST nematodiriasis
AADEIIIMNRSTTV administrative
AADEIILLLMNTWY William Tyndale
AADEIILLLNTUVY antediluvially
AADEIILLNSSSUW Sulawesi Island
AADEIILMNNNOOT denominational
AADEIILMNOORST demoralisation
AADEIILMNOORTZ demoralization
AADEIILNNOPSST dispensational
AADEIILNOOPRST depolarisation
AADEIILNOOPRTZ depolarization
AADEIILNOORSTV devalorisation
AADEIILNOORTVZ devalorization
AADEIILNORSSTT dissertational
AADEIIMNNNOSST Sistine Madonna
AADEIINORRSSTT radioresistant
AADEIIOPPPRRST disappropriate
AADEILLMNRRTUY intramedullary
AADEILMMRRSTYY radial symmetry
AADEILMNNSSSTW Westman Islands
AADEILMNOORTYY early day motion
AADEILNNORTUUV undervaluation
AADEILNOOPSSST at one's disposal
AADEILOPRTTTVY total depravity
AADEIMNNOPRTUV animadvert upon
AADEINNPRSSTUY Sunday painters
AADEINOPPPRRTU unappropriated
AADELMPRRSSTTU mustard plaster
AADEMMMOQSUUYY Ummayyad Mosque
AADEMNNORSSTVY savant syndrome
AADFFIIIILNOST disaffiliation
AADFFIIILNPQRU liquid paraffin
AADFFIIIMNORST disaffirmation
AADFFINORSSTUU fast and furious
AADFGIILLNNOST floating island
AADFHILLNOORYY hooly and fairly
AADFIIILNNNOST Finlandisation
AADFIIILNNNOTZ Finlandization
AADFIIILNNRSSS Frisian Islands
AADGGHIILNSTVY daylight-saving
AADGGILLNOPRUY uropygial gland
AADGGIMNOPRRRT program trading
AADGGINNORRRWY Garry Winogrand
AADGIIIILNOSTT digitalisation
AADGIIIILNOTTZ digitalization
AADGIIIMNNNRRT manriding train
AADGIILNORRSTU agroindustrial
AADGIILNPRTTUY pituitary gland
AADGINNOORSTUY Rogation Sunday
AADHHLOOSSSUWY as who should say
AADHIILLMMNWWY William Wyndham
AADHILMNSSTWYY Wayland's Smithy
AADHIMNRRSSTTY Tristram Shandy
AADHKLLMOORSTY matryoshka doll
AADHLMNNNOOORT London Marathon
AADHOOOSTTUWYY what do you say to?
AADIIILMNORSTT traditionalism
AADIIILNNOOTVV Antonio Vivaldi
AADIIILNNORSTU solitudinarian
AADIIILNORRTTY traditionarily
AADIIILNORSTTT traditionalist
AADIIILNORTTTY traditionality
AADIIIMNNORSTT administration
AADIIIMNRRSTTX administratrix
AADIIKLNPRRSTU industrial park
AADIILMNOORSTU modularisation
AADIILMNOORTUZ modularization
AADIILMNOSSTUZ diazonium salts
AADILLLMORSSTW it's a small world
AADILLLNOSSTYY Loyalty Islands
AADIMNOOORRSTY radio astronomy
AAEEEEGGHMNRTU Hague Agreement
AAEEEEGHLLNRTW the general weal
AAEEEEGHMNTTTY enemy at the gate
AAEEEEGHMPPRTT temperate phage
AAEEEEGLMNNSST manganese steel

AAEEEEGLNRSSTT	Estates General
AAEEEEGNPRRTWY	Peter Greenaway
AAEEEEHKKNSTTW	weak at the knees
AAEEEELLLLNOVW	leave well alone
AAEEEELNPRSSTT	lares et penates
AAEEEFGGKLOORR	George A Akerlof
AAEEEFGHNOORST	The Age of Reason
AAEEEFGIMOSTTV	set a game to five
AAEEEFGLMMNNST	self-management
AAEEEFGMNNORRS	ferro-manganese
AAEEEFHKNORSSV	for heaven's sake
AAEEEFHLMNOPTT	Temple of Athena
AAEEEFKMOORSST	make so free as to
AAEEEFLLLPRRTX	patellar reflex
AAEEEGGGHINRTT	in the aggregate
AAEEEGHHKMNNRT	Kenneth Grahame
AAEEEGHIMNOSST	haematogenesis
AAEEEGHINORVVY	have a roving eye
AAEEEGHLMNRRSY	Hamersley Range
AAEEEGILMMNNNT	line management
AAEEEGILNPRRSS	general paresis
AAEEEGLNNRRSTV	general servant
AAEEEGMNNPRRRT	prearrangement
AAEEEGMNRRSSTT	master sergeant
AAEEEHHHKRRSTT	the Earthshaker
AAEEEHHINRSSTV	heart-heaviness
AAEEEHHIPRSSTY	hyperaesthesia
AAEEEHHLMNNPTT	The Elephant Man
AAEEEHIKMRRSTT	raise the market
AAEEEHILLMNPRT	parliament-heel
AAEEEHILLOOSTV	have a tile loose
AAEEEHILLRSTTT	earth satellite
AAEEEHILMNORTU	eleutheromania
AAEEEHKKKNRSTW	The Kraken Wakes
AAEEEHKLLPRRST	shell parrakeet
AAEEEHNOPRSTTW	theatre weapons
AAEEEILLSSTTTT	satellite state
AAEEEILMNRTTVY	maternity leave
AAEEEILNPRTTVY	paternity leave
AAEEEIMNPPRRST	reappraisement
AAEEEJLLMNPSUV	Japanese vellum
AAEEEJLNOPPPPR	jalapeño pepper
AAEEELLLRRSTTV	traveller's tale
AAEEELNOPRSSTT	personal estate
AAEEELPPPRRSTT	saltpetre-paper
AAEEENNPRRRSTU	superterranean
AAEEENRRSSTVVW	transverse wave
AAEEEPQRRTTUUX	ex utraque parte
AAEEFGHILLNRRT	larger than life
	larger-than-life
AAEEFGHILNORSV	half-a-sovereign
AAEEFGHORSSTTY	The Forsyte Saga
AAEEFGILLLMRUU	Guillaume Farel
AAEEFGILLNNTTU	flag-lieutenant
AAEEFGIMNNORRS	ferromagnesian
AAEEFGIOPRSSST	rites of passage
AAEEFGLLMRRRTU	Margaret Fuller
AAEEFHHLORSTTT	salt of the earth
AAEEFHHORRSTTT	star-of-the-earth
AAEEFHILMNRTTW	wreath filament
AAEEFHNOPSSTTT	seat-of-the-pants
AAEEFILNNRRSTT	transferential
AAEEFILNORSSTV	fenestra ovalis
AAEEFIMNORSTTY	Treaty of Amiens
AAEEFLMMNOOPRT	Temple of Amon-Ra
AAEEFMORSSTTTT	states of matter
AAEEFNOORRSTUX	extraforaneous
AAEEGGHIIMMNRV	give a hammering
AAEEGGHIMNORRT	the roaring game
AAEEGGHKLPTTTU	gleg at the uptak
AAEEGGHNOPRRST	steganographer
AAEEGGIIILLLLO	Galileo Galilei
AAEEGGILNNOPRT	Georgian planet
AAEEGGMNRRSSUV	Musgrave Ranges
AAEEGHHIOPSSTY	Gaea hypothesis
AAEEGHIRRSTWYY	Eighty Years' War
AAEEGHLLMOPRRT	metallographer
AAEEGHLLNPPRTT	telegraph plant
AAEEGHLMNNOOPX	hapax legomenon
AAEEGHLPRSTTTY	Gestalt therapy
AAEEGHNNOOPRTY	Neopythagorean
AAEEGIILLMNTTZ	little magazine
AAEEGIILNNORST	generalisation
AAEEGIILNNORTZ	generalization
AAEEGIILNNOSTV	evangelisation
AAEEGIILNNOTVZ	evangelization
AAEEGIILORSSTV	Évariste Galois
AAEEGILMNQRTUV	gram-equivalent
AAEEGILNORSSSS	raise one's glass
AAEEGILNPRSTXY	exasperatingly
AAEEGILNRSSTVY	asseveratingly
AAEEGIMMNNRRST	misarrangement
AAEEGJLLNNORRU	general journal
AAEEGKOPRRRSSS	A Rake's Progress
AAEEGLLQRRRTUY	quarter-gallery
AAEEGLMNPRSSTU	suprasegmental
AAEEGMNOPRSSSU	rampageousness
AAEEHHINOSTTUX	heat exhaustion
AAEEHHMNORRSTT	Thomas Traherne
AAEEHIIKMNSTWW	What Maisie Knew
AAEEHIILLMORSZ	Alois Alzheimer
AAEEHIIMNSSTTT	antimetathesis
AAEEHIIMOOPSST	haematopoiesis
AAEEHIKLMNOTTT	take it on the lam
AAEEHILLLNOQSU	Shaquille O'Neal
AAEEHILMPPRSSS	plasmapheresis
AAEEHILNPRSSTV	silver pheasant
AAEEHIMNRSSSTU	amateurishness
AAEEHINORSTTTW	weather station
AAEEHKLLMNOSTY	Thomas Keneally
AAEEHLLORSSTWY	roses all the way
AAEEHMNNOOOTVY	have one too many
AAEEHMNOPRSTTU	apartment house
AAEEHMOOPRRRST	spermatorrhoea
AAEEHNNOOSVWWY	have one's own way
AAEEHNPPRRTTTY	pattern therapy
AAEEHOPRRSTUWY	warehouse party
AAEEIILLLRTTVY	alliteratively
AAEEIILLMNNPRR	premillenarian
AAEEIILLMNRSSW	Serena Williams
AAEEIILNNNORTT	Internationale
AAEEIILNNOQRTU	linear equation

AAEEIILNNORSTT eternalisation
AAEEIILNNORTTZ eternalization
AAEEIILNNOSSST sensationalise
AAEEIILNNOSSTZ sensationalize
AAEEIILNOPRRST proletarianise
AAEEIILNOPRRTZ proletarianize
AAEEIIMNRRSTTY tertiary amines
AAEEIINNPRRSTT painter-stainer
AAEEIINPPRTTTV private patient
AAEEIJLMMNPRSS Miss Jane Marple
AAEEIKLMMNRRTT terminal market
AAEEIKLMNNRRTT internal market
AAEEIKMMNNOSST mistake one's man
AAEEIKMNOSSTWY mistake one's way
AAEEILMMOPRSSU lapsus memoriae
AAEEILMNNOOPPR paraleipomenon
AAEEILMNOPRRTU Euro-Parliament
AAEEILMNRSTTTY testamentarily
AAEEILMOPSTUYY may it please you
AAEEILNNOPRSTT presentational
AAEEILNNOTTTUV attention value
AAEEILNNPRRTTY interplanetary
AAEEILNOOPPRRT preoperational
AAEEILNOPRTTTW water potential
AAEEILNPPRSTTY Paisley pattern
AAEEIMNPRSTTTV pavement artist
AAEEINNOPSSSST passionateness
AAEEINRRSSTTTW water-resistant
AAEEKLLNOPRSTY take personally
AAEEKLMNOPRRRS personal remark
AAEELLLLPRRRSU parallel rulers
AAEELLOPRRSTTT pastoral letter
AAEELNNNPSSSTU unpleasantness
AAEELNOPRSSTTV Peasants' Revolt
AAEEMNNOPPRSWW newspaperwoman
AAEEMNOOQRRSTU root mean square
AAEFFGILNOPTTU palagonite-tuff
AAEFFIIILMORST forisfamiliate
AAEFFILNOSTTUX in a state of flux
AAEFGHHINNSSTT Sant Fateh Singh
AAEFGHIIKMNOTT make a night of it
AAEFGHILLRRRSY Greyfriars Hall
AAEFGIIKLMMNOS milk of magnesia
AAEFGIILNOSTTU angustifoliate
AAEFGLLNOOPRTT fore-topgallant
AAEFHHMMOOTTTU foam at the mouth
AAEFHIILMNTWYY in the family way
AAEFHIMNOOORSS Heraion of Samos
AAEFIINNORRSTT fraternisation
AAEFIINNORRTTZ fraternization
AAEFILOPPRRSST plaster of Paris
AAEFIMNORRSTTV transformative
AAEFKKNNNORRTT Frank Tarkenton
AAEFLLNOPRRRUU funeral parlour
AAEFLMNOOOPTTW footplatewoman
AAEGGGLNNORSTU strong language
AAEGGHIILMMNRT thermal imaging
AAEGGHIILMNNTU haemagglutinin
AAEGGHIIMNNPUU human guinea pig
AAEGGHIMNOPRTY enigmatography
AAEGGIIILLNNRW Gillian Wearing
AAEGGIILNNOOPS algae poisoning
AAEGGIINNORRST grangerisation
AAEGGIINNORRTZ grangerization
AAEGGILMNOSSYZ glossy magazine
AAEGGIMMNOPRSU megasporangium
AAEGHHIILNRRTT lighter-than-air
AAEGHHIIOPSSTY Gaia hypothesis
AAEGHHIKLNRSTY earthshakingly
AAEGHHLLMNORRT Martha Gellhorn
AAEGHHOPPRRRRY rhyparographer
AAEGHIILLNRTXY exhilaratingly
AAEGHIILNNSSST Selina Hastings
AAEGHIIRRSTTTV right as a trivet
AAEGHIKLOPRTTW walk a tightrope
AAEGHIKMMNNPPR knapping-hammer
AAEGHILNOOSTTW against the wool
AAEGHIMNOPRSTY Pythagoreanism
AAEGHIMOOPPRRY paroemiography
AAEGHINOSTTUWY what's eating you?
AAEGHIPPRSSTTT spaghetti strap
AAEGIIILNNOSTT gelatinisation
AAEGIIILNNOTTZ gelatinization
AAEGIIKLMNRRTV viral marketing
AAEGIILLLMNOPR imperial gallon
AAEGIILLNOORST allegorisation
AAEGIILLNOORTZ allegorization
AAEGIILMNQQSUU quinquagesimal
AAEGIILMRSSTUU Miguel Asturias
AAEGIILNNPSTTU insulating tape
AAEGIILNORRSTU regularisation
AAEGIILNORRTUZ regularization
AAEGIILNQRTUUY equiangularity
AAEGIIMMRRSTTU Artium Magister
Magister Artium
AAEGIIMNRRSTTV transmigrative
AAEGIINNNOSTUX exsanguination
AAEGIINNNRSSSU sanguinariness
AAEGIINNOORRST reorganisation
AAEGIINNOORRTZ reorganization
AAEGIKLNPRRSTW sparkling water
AAEGILLMNNOPRT Long Parliament
AAEGILMMNOORSY serial monogamy
AAEGILNOOPRRTT great prolation
AAEGILRSSTTTUU sagittal suture
AAEGIMNNSSTUUW August Weismann
AAEGINOPRRSTUY sauropterygian
AAEGLLMMNNRRUY Murray Gell-Mann
AAEGLLNOOPSTTU stoope-gallaunt
AAEGMNOSSTUUUW Susumu Tonegawa
AAEHHILLOPSTUZ sulphathiazole
AAEHIIILPRSTTV viral hepatitis
AAEHIILLMNRSTW William Shatner
AAEHIILMNORSTT thermalisation
AAEHIILMNORTTZ thermalization
AAEHIIMOORTVWW A Room with a View
AAEHILLMNOPSTT mental hospital
AAEHILLNORSSTT Stationers' Hall
AAEHILNOPPSSSY psephoanalysis
AAEHIMOPRSSTTT stoma therapist
AAEHINRRRSSTUV Sir Arthur Evans
AAEHIOOPPRRSTT protospathaire

AAEHIPPQRRSTUZ sapphire-quartz
AAEHIRRRSTTWYY Thirty Years' War
AAEHJMOOORRSST José Ramos-Horta
AAEHKLLMOPSSTY Lake Stymphalos
AAEHKMMOOOPRTU make a poor mouth
AAEHLLMNNNORRT Norman Hartnell
AAEHLMNNOOSTUX xanthomelanous
AAEHNNORRSSSTU anarthrousness
AAEIIIILNRSTTU utilitarianise
AAEIIIILNRTTUZ utilitarianize
AAEIIIKNNORSTT keratinisation
AAEIIIKNNORTTZ keratinization
AAEIIILLMMNNRS millenarianism
AAEIIILMNNORST mineralisation
AAEIIILMNNORTZ mineralization
AAEIIILMNOPRTT imitation pearl
AAEIIILNNOORST Antonio Salieri
AAEIIILNORSTTT retaliationist
AAEIIILNORSTTV relativisation
revitalisation
AAEIIILNORTTVZ relativization
revitalization
AAEIIINNNRSSST insanitariness
AAEIIINNPPRTTT pinnatipartite
AAEIIINNRRSTUV universitarian
AAEIIINPRSSSTT antiperistasis
AAEIILLMNPTUVY manipulatively
AAEIILLMNRRTXY intermaxillary
AAEIILLNPRSTTY interspatially
AAEIILLRRTTUVY virtual reality
AAEIILMNNOPRTT reimplantation
AAEIILMNNOSSST sensationalism
AAEIILMNOOPRST operationalism
AAEIILMNOORRST remoralisation
AAEIILMNOORRTZ remoralization
AAEIILMNOPRRST proletarianism
AAEIILNNORSTTU neutralisation
AAEIILNNORTTUZ neutralization
AAEIILNNOSSSTT sensationalist
AAEIILNNOSSSTU sensualisation
AAEIILNNOSSTUZ sensualization
AAEIILNOOPRSTT operationalist
AAEIILNOORRSTV revalorisation
AAEIILNOORRTVZ revalorization
AAEIILNQTTTUVY quantitatively
AAEIILNRRSUUXY auxiliary nurse
AAEIIMOPPPRRST misappropriate
AAEIINNORSSSTT stationariness
AAEIINNPPRRSTT antiperspirant
AAEIINOPRSSTTU pasteurisation
AAEIINOPRSTTUZ pasteurization
AAEIJKMNNOPRSS James Parkinson
AAEIKKLLLOSSTW Stella Kowalski
AAEILLLLMORRST lamellirostral
AAEILLLLMRTTUY multilaterally
AAEILLLMNOOPRT parallel motion
AAEILLLNNOPSSY pollen analysis
AAEILLLNPRRTTY artillery-plant
AAEILLMNNNPSTT instalment plan
AAEILLMNNORTUU mountain laurel
AAEILLMNNPPRTW Walter Lippmann
AAEILLNPRSTUUY pearly nautilus
AAEILMMNPPRRTU Rump Parliament
AAEILMMOPRSSUU marsupial mouse
AAEILMNRSSSTUX transsexualism
AAEILMOOPPRSTT spatiotemporal
AAEILNNNOOOPRT non-operational
AAEILNORRRSTTT transliterator
AAEILNORTTTTTY yttro-tantalite
AAEILNRRSSTTVY transversality
AAEILNRRSTTUUV natural virtues
AAEILNRSSTTUXY transsexuality
AAEILORRRRSSTT serratirostral
AAEIMMNNORSTTU mountain stream
AAEIMMNOPSSSTY synaposematism
AAEIMNNOORSTTU neuroanatomist
AAEIMNORRSSSTT mesa transistor
AAEINNNOPRSTUU superannuation
AAEJLLNNOOOPRT Joanna Trollope
AAEJMOPRRSSTUY pyjama trousers
AAELLMNOPRUVVY pulmonary valve
AAELLNPRRSTUUY supernaturally
AAELMNOOPPSSTU postmenopausal
AAELMNSSSSTTYY systems analyst
AAELNNNOPRSTTX xenotransplant
AAENNNOPPRSSST Nansen passport
AAEORRRRSSSTTU Sartor Resartus
AAFFFHINOOORRU affair of honour
AAFFGIIIRRSTTT graffiti artist
AAFGIILLMNNNPY family planning
AAFHLLLMMNOSTU Multnomah Falls
AAFIIIMNNORRTU uniformitarian
AAFIILLLMOPRSS Pillars of Islam
AAFIILMNNOOSTU foam insulation
AAFIINOORRTTTW war of attrition
AAFILMNNOOPRTT plant-formation
AAFILMNOOPRSWY law of parsimony
AAFIMNNOORRSTT transformation
AAGGHILMMNOPRY lymphangiogram
AAGGIIILNNRTTY ingratiatingly
AAGHHIILLMORTW William Hogarth
AAGHHNOOPPRRTY anthropography
AAGHIIILMOPSTT stigmatophilia
AAGHIIINOPRSTT graphitisation
AAGHIIINOPRTTZ graphitization
AAGHIIPRRSSTTT stratigraphist
AAGHIMMNNOORRU organ-harmonium
AAGHOOPPRTTUYY autotypography
AAGIIIMNNSSTUU Augustinianism
AAGIIIMNOSSTTT stigmatisation
AAGIIIMNOSTTTZ stigmatization
AAGIIINNNOOPSV Giovanni Pisano
AAGIIINNNOORST inorganisation
AAGIIINNNOORTZ inorganization
AAGIILMMMOPRST lipogrammatism
AAGIILMMOPRSTT lipogrammatist
AAGIILOOPRSSTT parasitologist
AAGIIMMNNSSSWW swans a-swimming
AAGIIMMNOQRTTU quota immigrant
AAGIIMNNORRSTT transmigration
AAGILLNRSSSTTT starting stalls
AAGILNNNOOPSTT plantation song

AAGIMNOOOSSTTU angiostomatous
AAGIMNORRRSTTY transmigratory
AAGIMNQRTTUUVY quantum gravity
AAHIIIIKKLLMNN Mikhail Kalinin
AAHIIILLLMTTWZ William Hazlitt
AAHILLNRRSTUUV Arthur Sullivan
AAHILNOOOPRRTT prothonotarial
AAHILNORRSTTUY natural history
AAHIMORSSTTTWY Sir Thomas Wyatt
AAHINOOOPRRTTT prothonotariat
AAHLLOPPSSTTYY staphyloplasty
AAHLMOOPRRSSTV provost marshal
AAIIIIILNNOSTT initialisation
AAIIIIILNNOTTZ initialization
AAIIIILMNORSTT militarisation
AAIIIILMNORTTZ militarization
AAIIIILMNRSTTU utilitarianism
AAIIIILNORSTTV trivialisation
AAIIIILNORTTVZ trivialization
AAIIIIMNNRRSTT Trinitarianism
AAIIIINOPRSTTV aviation spirit
AAIIIKLLNOOVVV Nikolai Vavilov
AAIIILLNOOSTTV volatilisation
AAIIILLNOOTTVZ volatilization
AAIIILMNNNOOST nominalisation
AAIIILMNNNOOTZ nominalization
AAIIILMNOOPSTT optimalisation
AAIIILMNOOPTTZ optimalization
AAIIINNORSSSTU Russianisation
AAIIINNORSSTUZ Russianization
AAIIJKLNNSSVVY Vaslav Nijinsky
AAIIJLNNOORSTU journalisation
AAIIJLNNOORTUZ journalization
AAIILLLNORSTTU illustrational
AAIILLMNOOTTVY motivationally
AAIILLNNOOSSUV Sonia O'Sullivan
AAIILLNNORSTTY transitionally
AAIILMNNORSSST transmissional
AAIILMNNORSSTT mistranslation
AAIILNOOPPRSTU popularisation
AAIILNOOPPRTUZ popularization
AAIIMNOORRSSTZ Zoroastrianism
AAIKMNNOORSTUZ Ozark Mountains
AAILLMNNOOTTUW mountain tallow
AAILMMNNORSTTU ultramontanism✧
AAILMNNORSSTWY Wynton Marsalis
AAILMNNORSTTTU ultramontanist
AAIMMNNOORRTUW mountain marrow
AAINNOOPRRSTTT transportation
AAKKKLLMNNSUUX Ku Klux Klansman
AALLNNNORTTUUY not unnaturally
ABBBBEEILLPPRR pribble-prabble
ABBBCDGINORRSU scrubbing-board
ABBBEEEHNORRSY Sherborne Abbey
ABBBEILMNORRUY Blue Ribbon Army
ABBBGGIINNPRUY Bringing Up Baby
ABBBGHHILNRSTU babbling thrush
ABBCCEILNOORTY cyclobarbitone
ABBCDEEEHMORRS robes-de-chambre
ABBCDEEEIORRSU berberidaceous
ABBCDEEHLLNORW Chandler wobble
ABBCDEEHRSSTTU Cuthbert's beads
ABBCDEEIILNRSS indescribables
ABBCDEEIMOORST discomboberate
ABBCDEGHIKMPRU humpback bridge
ABBCDEIIMNNORY incendiary bomb
ABBCDEILMOOSTU discombobulate
ABBCDIKKKLNRSU skunk-blackbird
ABBCEEEFLOQTTU Battle of Quebec
ABBCEEFFIIKNST Babinski effect
ABBCEEHMORRRST Robert Chambers
ABBCEEILNOORRT Robbie Coltrane
ABBCEELLNRRTUY Canterbury bell
ABBCEENORRSSTU subarborescent
ABBCEGLLNOOOTU Launcelot Gobbo
ABBCEHLNNOSTTU Hubble constant
ABBCEHLNOORRSU Charles Bourbon
ABBCEHLOORSSYY Holy Cross Abbey
ABBCEIILLMOTTW William Cobbett
ABBCGHILLNOORU rubbing alcohol
ABBCHILNOOORSZ Barbizon School
ABBCIJKNOOORSW Jacob Bronowski
ABBCIKLOOPRRTU Lubbock Airport
ABBDDEEELLORRU double-barreled
ABBDDEEELORSTU double-breasted
ABBDEEEEFORSTT best-before date
ABBDEEEHLNRSST Bran the Blessed
ABBDEEFIINRRRV brain-fever bird
ABBDEEINORRRST robin redbreast
ABBDEFHINNORST forbid the banns
ABBDEGIIORRTTT Brigitte Bardot
ABBDFILMOOOPST baptism of blood
ABBDGIIILNNRRY library binding
ABBDGILNNOOORS Orlando Gibbons
ABBDIIIILNTTUY indubitability
ABBEEEEELLLMSS belle assemblée
ABBEEEEFKNORRV breakbone fever
ABBEEEHILNOTWZ Elizabeth Bowen
ABBEEEKLLORRTW Robert Bakewell
ABBEEELNORSSSV observableness
ABBEEGIIJKLMNS King James Bible
ABBEEHHIIRTTTW The White Rabbit
ABBEEHIMMORRSX Sir Max Beerbohm
ABBEEHINNOOPRT phenobarbitone
ABBEEIKKLLMMSS skimble-skamble
ABBEEINNOOPRTT pentobarbitone
ABBEENOPRRSSTU superabsorbent
ABBEGILLMNRRTU tumbling barrel
ABBEHINOORSSTW snowshoe rabbit
ABBEIIILLMORSW Robbie Williams
ABBEIILQRRRSTU rabbit-squirrel
ABBHIIJLLNOORR John Barbirolli
ABBIIILMOOPRRS probabiliorism
ABBIIILOOPRRST probabiliorist
ABCCCEEEEENRSX exacerbescence
ABCCCEEHKLNSUY Buckley's chance
ABCCCEEHMNORRT chamber concert
ABCCCEEIIMMNRU circumambience
ABCCCEHIIKLRSY bicycle ricksha
ABCCCEHILMNORU chamber council
council chamber
ABCCCEIILNNOTU Cabinet Council

Words marked ✧ can also be spelled with one or more capital letters

ABCCCEIIMMNRUY circumambiency
ABCCCEIKLLMORU calcium blocker
ABCCCEIORSTUUU cucurbitaceous
ABCCCIILMOOTXY coxcombicality
ABCCDEEIMNNRSU disencumbrance
ABCCDEEIMOORSS Scombresocidae
ABCCDEFIILOORS blood-sacrifice
ABCCDEGINORRTT contract bridge
ABCCDEHILRRSTU scratchbuilder
ABCCDEIIILNORS silicon carbide
ABCCDGIINNOORT robotic dancing
ABCCEEEELRSSSU causes célèbres
ABCCEEELORRRTX cerebral cortex
ABCCEEFHILNOST Chief Constable
ABCCEEGHIILMOO biogeochemical
ABCCEEHIIKNNTT kitchen cabinet
ABCCEEHIKLNPRT the Black Prince
ABCCEEHLMNORSU chamber counsel
ABCCEEIIKRRRTU circuit breaker
ABCCEEIILLNORR irreconcilable
ABCCEEIILNORST Sir Cecil Beaton
ABCCEEIINPRTTU cabinet picture
ABCCEEILLNNORU unreconcilable
ABCCEEILMMNOUX excommunicable
ABCCEEILNNOORT concelebration
ABCCEEILPRSTTU cubic saltpetre
ABCCEFHHNRSSTU Burschenschaft
ABCCEHHLMRSSUY Church Assembly
ABCCEHIIILMRUV brachium civile
ABCCEHIIIRSTTU rich tea biscuit
ABCCEHIINORSST bronchiectasis
ABCCEHLLOOOSTU Bluecoat School
ABCCEIIILNOTVY conceivability
ABCCEIILLNORRY irreconcilably
ABCCEIILMMNNOU incommunicable
ABCCEIILMRRSUV cruciverbalism
ABCCEIILNNNOOS inconscionable
ABCCEIILNNPSUU public nuisance
ABCCEIILRRSTUV cruciverbalist
ABCCEIJKNOOPRT back-projection
ABCCEILLNNORUY unreconcilably
ABCCEILMMNNOUU uncommunicable
ABCCEILMNNOSTU Uncle Tom's Cabin
ABCCEILNNNOOSU unconscionable
ABCCEOOOPPRSTT tobacco-stopper
ABCCGIIILLMNOS social climbing
ABCCGIILLOOORY cryobiological
ABCCGINNOORTTU bring to account
ABCCGINNORSTTU subcontracting
ABCCHILOOPRSTU claustrophobic
ABCCHIORRSSSTW crossbar switch
ABCCIILMMNNOUY incommunicably
ABCCILNNNOOSUY unconscionably
ABCCINOOORRSTT boa constrictor
ABCDDEEILMMNOS discommendable
ABCDDEEILNNNOY Bonnie and Clyde
ABCDDEEILNNORT Benedict Arnold
ABCDDEELMNOOPU decompoundable
ABCDDEGIINNPTU cabinet pudding
ABCDDHLLNOOOTW blow hot and cold
ABCDEEEEFHMMMR femme de chambre
ABCDEEEEILNSSV deceivableness
ABCDEEEEILORRS escalier dérobé
ABCDEEEEKNRSTW neck-sweetbread
ABCDEEEELLNSST delectableness
ABCDEEEELORSTU decree absolute
ABCDEEEEORRRRT breeder reactor
ABCDEEEFHILLMR fille de chambre
ABCDEEEGHHJKTY jack-by-the-hedge✧
ABCDEEEHIILMNR herbal medicine
ABCDEEEHIILNPR indecipherable
ABCDEEEHILNPRU undecipherable
ABCDEEEHKORRRT break the record
ABCDEEEHLNNOPT cannot be helped
ABCDEEEIILRSSV disserviceable
ABCDEEEILNPSSS despicableness
ABCDEEEILNRSST creditableness
ABCDEEEILPRSST disrespectable
ABCDEEELLOOORT Colorado beetle
ABCDEEFIILLLLO oil-filled cable
ABCDEEGHIIMRRS Cambridgeshire
ABCDEEGHIJNSTU subject heading
ABCDEEGLLNORSU Claes Oldenburg
ABCDEEHHIIRTTW watch the birdie
ABCDEEHIILNPRY indecipherably
ABCDEEHNOOPRRY beyond reproach
ABCDEEIIINNOTT cabinet-edition
ABCDEEIIJKORRS Sir Derek Jacobi
ABCDEEIILNNORS inconsiderable
ABCDEEIILNORSV indiscoverable
ABCDEEIIMOSSTY Basidiomycetes
ABCDEEILMNOOPS indecomposable
ABCDEEILNORSUV undiscoverable
ABCDEEILORRRTU erratic boulder
ABCDEEKLNNORRU blockade-runner
ABCDEELLLLOSSY closed syllable
ABCDEELLLMMNOU null-modem cable
ABCDEELMNOOPSU undecomposable
ABCDEELNNORSTU under-constable
ABCDEFILMNOORS disconformable
ABCDEFILMOORST discomfortable
ABCDEFOOOORRTT barefoot doctor
ABCDEGHHIRRSSU brush discharge
ABCDEGHHOORRTU thoroughbraced
ABCDEGHLMOTUWY Clyde W Tombaugh
ABCDEGIIILPRTY credibility gap
ABCDEGIILLMPTU Public Image Ltd
ABCDEGIILLNSTU castle-building
ABCDEGILNOSTTU Doubting-Castle
ABCDEGIORRRSTU Robert Guiscard
ABCDEHHKLNOORU black horehound
ABCDEHIORRRRST Richard Roberts
ABCDEHKLNORRTU alder-buckthorn
ABCDEIIILPRTTY predictability
ABCDEIIKORSTTY Rickettsia body
ABCDEIILNNORSY inconsiderably
ABCDEIILNNOSTY condensability
ABCDEILNORSUVY undiscoverably
ABCDEILOPRRUVY livery cupboard
ABCDEIMNNOOORX carbon monoxide
ABCDEKKNORRTUW breakdown truck
ABCDENOOORRRTU uncorroborated

ABCDGHILNOOORS boarding school
ABCDHILNOOORRT bronchodilator
ABCDIIIILOSSTY dissociability
ABCEEEEEHKKLOO Lake Okeechobee
ABCEEEEEILNPRX experienceable
ABCEEEEEKLMRRZ mackerel breeze
ABCEEEEFHLNSTT fence the tables
ABCEEEEILNRSSV receivableness
ABCEEEFIILNNSS beneficialness
ABCEEEFLORRTTY refectory table
ABCEEEGGHILNNR bleaching green
ABCEEEGILLLOST celestial globe
ABCEEEGOOPRRSY Cape gooseberry
ABCEEEHHLLPSTY clap by the heels
ABCEEEHIILMNNT Michael Bentine
ABCEEEHMRRRSTU Herbert Marcuse
ABCEEEIIILLLRT Beatrice Lillie
ABCEEEIILPRSST respectabilise
ABCEEEIILPRSTZ respectabilize
ABCEEEIRRRSTUY bearer security
ABCEEEKMNOOSST at someone's beck
ABCEEELNNRSSSU censurableness
ABCEEEMNOSSSTT asbestos cement
ABCEEENNQSSTUU queen substance
ABCEEFFINORRST fabric softener
ABCEEFGHILLNOX bill of exchange
ABCEEFIIILNPRT perfectibilian
ABCEEFIILNORTY enforceability
ABCEEFILLMOPST self-compatible
ABCEEGHIKLOORT globe artichoke
ABCEEGIILNORRS irrecognisable
ABCEEGIILNORRZ irrecognizable
ABCEEGIINORSUZ zingiberaceous
ABCEEGILLLLLOO Balliol College
ABCEEGILLNRSUY subgenerically
ABCEEGILMNOTTT magnetic bottle
ABCEEGILNNORSU unrecognisable
ABCEEGILNNORUZ unrecognizable
ABCEEGIMNNNOOP bonne compagnie
ABCEEGKNNOOSTW get one's own back
ABCEEGORSTTUUV Gustave Courbet
ABCEEHHHRTTTUY bury the hatchet
ABCEEHHIOQRTUW white quebracho
ABCEEHIIKSTTTU take the biscuit
ABCEEHILLLRRSS Sir Charles Bell
ABCEEHIOOPRSUU euphorbiaceous
ABCEEHIOPSSSSU sheep's scabious
ABCEEHKLNNOSTU luncheon-basket
ABCEEHLLLOOORW low-alcohol beer
ABCEEIIILRSTVY serviceability
ABCEEIILLLRSTT belletristical
ABCEEIILLNNNSS inclinableness
ABCEEIILMMORSY embolismic year
ABCEEIILMPRRUW Weimar Republic
ABCEEIILNPRSSS Sir Basil Spence
ABCEEIILORRTVY recoverability
ABCEEIILPRSTTY respectability
ABCEEIILRRSSTU irresuscitable
ABCEEIINORSUZZ zinziberaceous
ABCEEIIPRRSSTU ceteris paribus
ABCEEIKLLMNOOR Colin Blakemore
ABCEEILLMNPRSU clumber spaniel
ABCEEILMNOPSST compatibleness
ABCEEILNNNORUY Laurence Binyon
ABCEEILNNOSSSU unsociableness
ABCEEILRRTTTUU trituberculate
ABCEEINORRRSST Cartier-Bresson
ABCEEIORRSSSTT cross batteries
ABCEELLLRRSTUV Travellers Club
ABCEELMORRSSSS cross assembler
ABCEELMORRSTUY Curtley Ambrose
ABCEELNOPSTTTY petty constable
ABCEELPRRSSSTU Brussels carpet
ABCEEMMMNORSUU mucous membrane
ABCEENORRTTTUY counter-battery
ABCEEOOPRRSSTU a sop to Cerberus
ABCEFFFHKOOOTT off the back foot
ABCEFGLNOOSTUU bootlace fungus
ABCEFIIIINOSTV beatific vision
ABCEFIIINNORTU eburnification
ABCEFLMMORTTUY comma butterfly
ABCEGGHIIMNNRR ringing chamber
ABCEGHHIKLNORT knight bachelor
knight-bachelor
ABCEGHIILMNNRU burling-machine
ABCEGHIMNOSTTU bathing costume
ABCEGHLORSTTUY Broughty Castle
ABCEGIIKLNPPSU public speaking
ABCEGIILMNORRY genomic library
ABCEGIILOORSTT bacteriologist
ABCEGIKLLLMOTU black guillemot
ABCEGILNNORSUY unrecognisably
ABCEGILNNORUYZ unrecognizably
ABCEGINQRSTTUY cybersquatting
ABCEHHIILMRTUU Baluchitherium
ABCEHHIILORRST British cholera
ABCEHIINNRRSST Sir Ernst B Chain
ABCEHILLLOPRYY hyperbolically
ABCEHILLRRTTUW Walter Ulbricht
ABCEHILMNNORSU Michael Brunson
ABCEHILORRSTTY erythroblastic
ABCEHIMOPRSSTU subatmospheric
ABCEHJLNNOORRY John Barleycorn
ABCEHLMNOOPRTU Roehampton Club
ABCEHLNNOORRSS Charles Bronson
ABCEHMNNORRSTU Robert Schumann
ABCEIIILLNTTUY ineluctability
ABCEIIILNSTUXY inexcusability
ABCEIIILORRTVY irrevocability
ABCEIIJKNNOORS Jackie Robinson
ABCEIILRRSSTUY irresuscitably
ABCEIIMOSSSTTY biosystematics
ABCEIINOOPSSUV above suspicion
ABCEIINOPRRRTT Robert Pitcairn
ABCEIKKLNRSTUY Stanley Kubrick
ABCEILLLNNOORT incontrollable
ABCEILLMNOSSSY symbolicalness
ABCEILMMNNOOTU communion table
ABCEILNNNOSTTU subcontinental
ABCEILNOPRTTUY public attorney
ABCEINORRSTTUY subcontrariety
ABCEKLLOOOPRTW Blackpool Tower

ABCEKNNNOORSTU turn one's back on
ABCELLLNNOORTU uncontrollable
ABCELMNPRRTUUU lumbar puncture
ABCELNOSSTUUUY subcutaneously
ABCEMOORRSSTTU combat trousers
ABCFFLLMMNOOPU common puffball
ABCFIIIMNOORST bioinformatics
ABCFIILMNOORTY conformability
ABCGHHILLMNRUU Hurlingham Club
ABCGIIIILNOTTY incogitability
ABCGIILLMOOOTY bioclimatology
ABCGIKLNORSSTT starting blocks
ABCGILLMORSSUU morbus gallicus
ABCGILLNNOOOTU conglobulation
ABCHHINOOOPPRT anthropophobic
ABCHHIOPRSTTUU Archbishop Tutu
ABCHLLMMOOOSTT small-tooth comb
ABCIIILLLOPSTY collapsibility
ABCIIILLMOOSTY social mobility
ABCIIILNRSTTUY inscrutability
ABCIILMMNOSSTU somnambulistic
ABCIILMNOOSTUU bituminous coal
ABCIILNORSTTUY construability
ABCIJKKNNOOSTT joint-stock bank
ABCILLLNNOORTY incontrollably
ABCILMNORSTUUY rambunctiously
ABCLLLNNOORTUY uncontrollably
ABDDDEEEENNORU Edouard Beneden
ABDDDEEMOORVYY over my dead body
ABDDEEEFGHINRT featherbedding
ABDDEEEGKLNOSW knowledge-based
ABDDEEEHHIOTWY white-headed boy
ABDDEEEHLLNSSU bull-headedness
ABDDEEEHNNOOST on one's deathbed
ABDDEEELRRTUUV bearded vulture
ABDDEEFFINOOOX of no fixed abode
ABDDEEFFIOPRRS bid/offer spread
ABDDEEFGILNSTY flying bedstead
ABDDEEFILLNORY Barney Oldfield
ABDDEEHHNOORTT hot and bothered
ABDDEEHILLOSST old-established
ABDDEEIIJLMNOU diamond jubilee
ABDDEEILMNNSTY absent-mindedly
ABDDEEJLOOPRUY double jeopardy
ABDDEFGIMORRST Stamford Bridge
ABDDEGIIKORRRS Sir Dirk Bogarde
ABDDEGIINNORUV David Ben-Gurion
ABDDEIIKORTVWZ David Berkowitz
ABDDELNOORTUUY roundaboutedly
ABDDFMNOOORRWX Ford Madox Brown
ABDDHILLNRRSUY drill-husbandry
ABDDIILMNOORST Bristol-diamond
ABDEEEEELMNRSS redeemableness
ABDEEEEEMORRTZ moderate breeze
ABDEEEEFILNSSS defeasibleness
ABDEEEEHNORRWZ Ebenezer Howard
ABDEEEEILNRSST deliberateness
ABDEEEEILRRRTU Der Blaue Reiter
ABDEEEEIMRUUUX Deuxième Bureau
ABDEEEELNSSSTT detestableness
ABDEEEFFIILNRT differentiable
ABDEEEGHNORTTY the Great Beyond
ABDEEEGIKLLNRT darkling beetle
ABDEEEGILNOTUV double negative
ABDEEEGILNRSST single-breasted
ABDEEEGINOPRST pigeon-breasted
ABDEEEGLLMOTUV vegetable mould
ABDEEEHILNNORT on the breadline
ABDEEEHILNOSVY heavenly bodies
ABDEEEHINNOOST on one's head be it
ABDEEEIILLRTVY deliberatively
ABDEEEIILMNNRT indeterminable
ABDEEEIINNOPZZ benzodiazepine
ABDEEEILMNNRTU undeterminable
ABDEEEILMNPRTU unpremeditable
ABDEEEILNNNSSU undeniableness
ABDEEEIMNNOOTV above-mentioned
ABDEEELLLOPPRR propeller-blade
ABDEEELLNNQSUU Queensland blue
ABDEEELLNOPRSS deplorableness
ABDEEELNOPRRSU under bare poles
ABDEEEMMNOPRSU pseudomembrane
ABDEEEMNNNOOSS on one's beam-ends
ABDEEEMNQRRSTU Rembrandtesque
ABDEEFGHINRRST fingers-breadth
ABDEEFGILORRSS Garfield Sobers
ABDEEFGLNOOORV avenger of blood
ABDEEFHHOORRTT Order of the Bath
ABDEEFIIILNNTU unidentifiable
ABDEEFILLLNORS bells of Ireland
ABDEEFILMNORSS formidableness
ABDEEFINOORRRU Baron de Fourier
ABDEEFLNORTTUV Battle of Verdun
ABDEEGHIIRSSST Bright's disease
ABDEEGHIMMMNOU Mohammed Neguib
ABDEEGIKMNNPRS Dennis Bergkamp
ABDEEGILNNOOTU double negation
ABDEEGIPRRRRTY partridgeberry
ABDEEGKNNORRUW break new ground
ABDEEHHLNOORST hold one's breath
ABDEEHIIILRTTY hereditability
ABDEEHIIIRSSST British disease
ABDEEHILOOPRST oblate spheroid
ABDEEHIPRRRSSY Derbyshire spar
ABDEEHKOOOORRT Dorothea Brooke
ABDEEHRRSSTTTU buttress-thread
ABDEEIIILLRTVY deliverability
ABDEEIIILQRSTU disequilibrate
ABDEEIIJMNORSS Miss Jean Brodie
ABDEEIILMNNRTY indeterminably
ABDEEIILMNSSSS admissibleness
ABDEEIKNORRRST Sir Derek Barton
ABDEEILMMSTUWY Wembley Stadium
ABDEEILMNNORST indemonstrable
ABDEEILNOPSSSS disposableness
ABDEEILNPSSSTU disputableness
ABDEEIMNOOSTUZ sodium benzoate
ABDEEINNORSSSS in sober sadness
ABDEEKOQRRTWYY qwerty keyboard
ABDEELLNORRSTY Albert Reynolds
ABDEELMNNORSTU undemonstrable
ABDEELNNORSSSU danseurs nobles

ABDEFGGIILNORT floating bridge
ABDEFGHLLNOSUU bundle of laughs
ABDEFHILLNNSSS flash blindness
ABDEFHLLLNORSS Blashford-Snell
ABDEFIIILLNORT defibrillation
ABDEFIINNOSTUU subinfeudation
ABDEFINORSTUUY subinfeudatory
ABDEFMOOORRSTW from bad to worse
ABDEGGIIKNNRST stinking badger
ABDEGGIKNNORRU groundbreaking
ABDEGHIIJLNOOR John Logie Baird
ABDEGHILNORSSU Gabriel's hounds
ABDEGHILNRRSTT birth-strangled
ABDEGHLMNORTUU rough-and-tumble
ABDEGHLNOORTWW draw the long bow
ABDEGIILLNNRRY lending library
ABDEGIILLNRSST Gilbert Islands
ABDEGIILOOOPRT Pietro Badoglio
ABDEGIINNQRRTU quarter-binding
ABDEGINOOPRRUY I beg your pardon?
ABDEHHLMNRSTUY rhythm and blues
ABDEHIIILMNNSU undiminishable
ABDEHILNOPRSUY Rhapsody in Blue
ABDEHINNORRSTU Dunbartonshire
ABDEHLMNNORRTU Northumberland
ABDEHOOORRRTVW throw overboard
ABDEIIILMNOOST demobilisation
ABDEIIILMNOOTZ demobilization
ABDEIIILNORRTY library edition
ABDEIIILNPSSTY dispensability
ABDEIIILNRSTUY undesirability
ABDEIILNOORSTW bowdlerisation
ABDEIILNOORTWZ bowdlerization
ABDEIJLMOORTUY double majority
ABDEILLMNNOPTU platinum blonde
ABDEILLMOPRUWY upwardly mobile
ABDEILMNNORSTY indemonstrably
ABDEILMORSTUXY ambidextrously
ABDEINNNOORSSY in one's born days
ABDEINNOSTTUYY buoyant density
ABDEKMMMNOOORU memorandum-book
ABDENNOORSSTUU roundaboutness
ABDFGHIINORSST shifting-boards
ABDFGHOORRRTUW brought forward
ABDFNOOOPRSSSU basso profundos
ABDGHIMNOOSTTU doubting Thomas
ABDGIIILOOORST radiobiologist
ABDGIINOOORSTV Good Vibrations
ABDHILNNOORTTY labyrinthodont
ABDIIIILMNOTTY indomitability
ABDIIILLOSSTVY dissolvability
ABDIIILNORSTTU distributional
ABDIIINORSTTTU disattribution
ABDIILMOPRTUWY upward mobility
ABEEEEEGHLPSTV vegetable sheep
ABEEEEHILNQTUZ Queen Elizabeth
ABEEEELNNPRSST penetrableness
ABEEEFFLNRSSSU sufferableness
ABEEEFGHNOORTZ The Age of Bronze
ABEEEFHLNORSTT one's better half
ABEEEFIILNNSSS infeasibleness
ABEEEFIILORSTY foreseeability
ABEEEFILNNRRTT enfant terrible
ABEEEFINNORRTT beta interferon
ABEEEFLOORRRSY Earl of Rosebery
ABEEEGGHIILNTU in the big league
ABEEEGGILLLNNR green labelling
ABEEEGHHIMOTTW weigh to the beam
ABEEEGILORTVVY vegetable ivory
ABEEEGIMNNRTUV negative number
ABEEEHHILRRTTU heather-bluiter
ABEEEHHLRRTTTU heather-blutter
ABEEEHIILLLSTV Elisabethville
ABEEEHIJKNOPRS Josephine Baker
ABEEEHIKLNNTYZ Elizabeth Kenny
ABEEEHIKLRTTTY take the liberty
ABEEEHILNPRSSS perishableness
ABEEEHKLORTTTU take the trouble
ABEEEHKMNOSTTY by the same token
ABEEEHLMNORTTT three-bottle man
ABEEEHLNRSSSST breathlessness
ABEEEIILLPRRSV irreplevisable
ABEEEIILNNPSSX inexpiableness
ABEEEIILNNRSTT Albert Einstein
ABEEEIILNNSSTV inevitableness
ABEEEIINRRRTTT Tibetan terrier
ABEEEIKMOPRRRS promise-breaker
ABEEEIKOPQTTUU keep quiet about
ABEEEILLNNRSSU unreliableness
ABEEEILMNNRSST terminableness
ABEEEILMNORTTU minotaur beetle
ABEEEILNNOPRSS inoperableness
ABEEEILNNORSSX inexorableness
ABEEEILNRRRTTV intervertebral
ABEEEIMNPTTTTT petit battement
ABEEEIMNRRSTTU turbine steamer
ABEEELLNNRSSUV vulnerableness
ABEEELMMNORSTY Belém Monastery
ABEEELNNOPRSSS personableness
ABEEELNORRSSST restorableness
ABEEEMMNORRSSU serous membrane
ABEEERRRRSTTWY strawberry tree
ABEEFFHIILNORT The Life of Brian
ABEEFGGNOPRRST Gräfenberg spot
ABEEFGINNNORTU turbofan engine
ABEEFGIORSSTTT get to first base
ABEEFHHIKMNOOO Book of Nehemiah
ABEEFHIIKLNRTZ Elizabeth Frink
ABEEFHIJKMOOOR Book of Jeremiah
ABEEFIIKLNOPTT Battle of Pinkie
ABEEFIILMNRTTY fermentability
ABEEFILNOPRSST profitableness
ABEEFKLNNOORUW unforeknowable
ABEEFLLNOTTTUZ Battle of Lützen
ABEEFLLRTTUVVY butterfly valve
ABEEFMNORRRSTY embryo transfer
ABEEFORSSTTTTY battery of tests
ABEEGGLNORRSUY George Lansbury
ABEEGHHIILNRTW breathing-while
ABEEGHIILNSTUX extinguishable
ABEEGHIJNNORRS Johannisberger
ABEEGHIKNNNRTT knight banneret

ABEEGHINPRRRTU bring up the rear
ABEEGIIIJKLLNN Billie Jean King
ABEEGIIKKNRRST strikebreaking
ABEEGIILNNNSST intangibleness
ABEEGIKNRRSSST breaking stress
ABEEGINNORRRST Roger Bannister
ABEEGLLMMORSUU Bargello Museum
ABEEGMNORSSSUU umbrageousness
ABEEGNOORRRTTU turbogenerator
ABEEHIIINNSSTV inhabitiveness
ABEEHIILLMPRSU imperial bushel
ABEEHILMMOOSTU hemimetabolous
ABEEHILNOPSSST hospitableness
ABEEHILNRRTTUU turn the air blue
ABEEHKNOPRSTTU put the brakes on
ABEEHLMNNOPRRT Robert Helpmann
ABEEHLNNOORSSU honourableness
ABEEHLNNOPTUYZ phenylbutazone
ABEEHLOORTTTTW hot-water bottle
ABEEIIILMMPRTY impermeability
ABEEIIILMNNSST inimitableness
ABEEIIILNNOTVZ Annie Leibovitz
ABEEIILLNNOSSV inviolableness
ABEEIILMNOPRSS impressionable
ABEEIILMNPSSSS impassibleness
ABEEIILNPRSTTY presentability
ABEEIILNPRTTVY preventability
ABEEIILPRRSTVY preservability
ABEEIIMNNNNOOT innominate bone
ABEEIJJMNNOTTW Benjamin Jowett
ABEEIKMNNNSTTV investment bank
ABEEIKMNOOPRRZ Man Booker Prize
ABEEIKPRRSSTUY take by surprise
ABEEILLMRSSSTT ballet-mistress
ABEEILLNNPRSTU unsplinterable
ABEEILLPRRSSTT blister-plaster
ABEEILLPRRSTYY presbyterially
ABEEILMNNNOSTU unmentionables
ABEEILMNOPRSSV improvableness
ABEEILNNOQSTUU unquestionable
ABEEILNNSSSTUU unsuitableness
ABEEILRRRSSTTU subterrestrial
ABEEIMMORRSSTT strabismometer
ABEEIMNOSSSSTU abstemiousness
ABEEIMOOPRRSTT absorptiometer
ABEEINOPRSSSTV absorptiveness
ABEEIRRRRSTTTU utter barrister
ABEEKLNNNOSSUW unknowableness
ABEELMNOOPRTYY polyembryonate
ABEENNNNOORTVW Anton von Webern
ABEFFGHHIORTTT right off the bat
ABEFGGNNOORSTU burn one's faggot
ABEFGHLOOSTTUU ghetto fabulous
ABEFGIIILNRRTY refrangibility
ABEFGIINNOTTTY bayonet fitting
ABEFGNNOOORRTU gone for a Burton
ABEFHHILLOOSTT Battle of Shiloh
ABEFIIILRRTTUY irrefutability
ABEFIILLNORRRU neurofibrillar
ABEFILNOOPRSST self-absorption
ABEFKLOOOOSTTV Battle of Kosovo
ABEFLLNOOPSSTU tablespoonfuls
ABEFLNOOOTTTTW Battle of Towton
ABEGGHHINORRTU rough breathing
ABEGGIIIILMNNO Beniamino Gigli
ABEGHHMOPRRTUY Humphrey Bogart
ABEGHIKNOPPSST shopping basket
ABEGHILMNOOOXY oxyhaemoglobin
ABEGHKNORRRRTU Arthur Kornberg
ABEGHLMNRRSSTU bremsstrahlung
ABEGHNNORSSTUY Anthony Burgess
ABEGHNORRTUWWY rub the wrong way
ABEGIIILLLMRTW William Gilbert
ABEGIIILMNPRTY impregnability
ABEGIIKNNOPRRS prison-breaking
ABEGIILNOORSST obligatoriness
ABEGIILORRSSTY gyrostabiliser
ABEGIILORRSTYZ gyrostabilizer
ABEGIINNRRRRSU barrier nursing
ABEGILMNRSTTUU Sturmabteilung
ABEGINNNNQRTUU running banquet
ABEHHHIKRSTTTU The Turkish Bath
ABEHHIJNOPSTTT John the Baptist
ABEHHKOOORTTTW throw the book at
ABEHHOOPSTTTUU push the boat out
ABEHIIIILNRTTY inheritability
ABEHIIILSTTUXY exhaustibility
ABEHIILLMNNOWY William H Bonney
ABEHIIMNOPSSSU amphibiousness
ABEHIJKNOPRSSS Sir Joseph Banks
ABEHILLMMOOOST holometabolism
ABEHIMMOOPRSTY symmetrophobia
ABEHIPRRRRSTUY Sir Hubert Parry
ABEHLLMOOOOSTU holometabolous
ABEHLMNOOTTTUW Matthew Boulton
ABEIIIILMNNSTZ Leibnitzianism
ABEIIIILMNSTTY inestimability
ABEIIIILMPRTVY imperviability
ABEIIIILLNORTTY intolerability
ABEIIIILMNNRTUY innumerability
ABEIIIILMORRTVY irremovability
ABEIIIILNPRSTUY insuperability
ABEIIIILPRSSTUY persuasibility
ABEIIIIMNRSSTUU subminiaturise
ABEIIIIMNRSTUUZ subminiaturize
ABEIIILNNORRSTT Sir Leon Brittan
ABEIIMNOPRRTTU imperturbation
ABEIIMOPRSSTUU superambitious
ABEILLMOOSSTTT Tobias Smollett
ABEILMNNORSTUU insurmountable
ABEILNNOQSTUUY unquestionably
ABEILNOOOPPRRT proportionable
ABEILNORSSSSUU salubriousness
ABEIMOOPRRSTTY absorptiometry
ABEINNORSSTUYZ Russo-Byzantine
ABEINOOOPRRSTV over-absorption
ABEIOOPRRRRSTT Roberts Airport
ABELMNNORSTUUU unsurmountable
ABFFGIIJNNOORT off-job training
ABFGHIKLNOORST Knights of Labor
ABFGIIIILNNRTY infrangibility
ABFHIILNOORSST Bristol fashion

ABFIIIIJLSTTUY justifiability
ABFIILMMNNSTUU Limbus infantum
ABFIILNOOORTTV vibroflotation
ABFLMMOOOSSTUU Tomb of Mausolus
ABGGHIILLNNNPT planning blight
ABGHIINOSTTUWY what's biting you
ABGHLNNOOOSTTY not by a long shot
ABGIIIIILMMTTY immitigability
ABGIIIKMNNNOTU mountain biking
ABGLNOORRSTTUY Glastonbury Tor
ABHIIIKLNNTTUY unthinkability
ABHIIINOOPRRTY prohibitionary
ABHIILLOPPPRTY Port Phillip Bay
ABHIILRRRSSSTU Sir Arthur Bliss
ABHILLMNOPSTTU put in mothballs
ABHILMNOOPRSTT thromboplastin
ABIIIIILLLMTTY illimitability
ABIIIILLMPSTUY implausibility
ABIIIILMMNOOST immobilisation
ABIIIILMMNOOTZ immobilization
ABIIIIMNNOSTTU bituminisation
ABIIIIMNNOTTUZ bituminization
ABIIIKMMNORSTU Mount Karisimbi
ABIIILLNOOSSTU solubilisation
ABIIILLNOOSTUZ solubilization
ABIIILNOORSSTT strobilisation
ABIIILNOORSTTZ strobilization
ABIIIMNNNORTUY binary munition
ABIIINNNOSSTUU subinsinuation
ABIILLNORSSUUY insalubriously
ABIILMNOOOOSTT lobotomisation
ABIILMNOOOOTTZ lobotomization
ABIILNNNOSTTUU tintinnabulous
ABIILNOSSTTTUU substitutional
ABIIMNNNOOORTW Brownian motion
ABIJOQSSTTUUUU jusqu'auboutist
ABILMNNORSTUUY insurmountably
ABILNOOOPPRRTY proportionably
ACCCCEEIMMMMOO comme çi, comme ça
ACCCDEEEEFNPRT perfect cadence
ACCCDEEFIOOPRT code of practice
ACCCDEEIINOOPS pièce d'occasion
ACCCDEEILLNOPY encyclopedical
ACCCDEGIIORSUU Giosuè Carducci
ACCCDEIIIILNOR ricinoleic acid
ACCCEEEFLLNNOR conference call
ACCCEEEHIKNRRS Chinese cracker
ACCCEEEIILLNPS special licence
ACCCEEFFHINORY Chancery Office
ACCCEEFGHIIPRS specific charge
ACCCEEFGIILPSY specific legacy
ACCCEEHIILLPRR parhelic circle
ACCCEEHILLMOST chemical closet
ACCCEEHILLNORV vice-chancellor
ACCCEEHKLNNOSU chance one's luck
ACCCEEIILLRRTV vertical circle
ACCCEEIILSSSTU Ecclesiasticus
ACCCEEILMOSSTU cosmeceuticals
ACCCEEMNORTUUV vacuum concrete
ACCCEENNOOOVVX convexo-concave
ACCCEFINOOPRRT tropic of Cancer✧
ACCCEHHHIILNTT technical hitch
ACCCEHHILMOPSY psychochemical
ACCCEHIILLNNOR chilli con carne
ACCCEHIINOORSS onchocerciasis
ACCCEHIINORSTT architectonics
ACCCEILLNNORTY concentrically
ACCCEIMMNOOORS macroeconomics
ACCCENNORRTTUU current account
ACCCENOOPRSSTT contact process
ACCCGIIILNRSTU scaling circuit
ACCCGIIIMNOOPU Giacomo Puccini
ACCCGINNOOSTTU cost-accounting
ACCCHHILNORSUV Church Slavonic
ACCCHIIOOPSSTT tachistoscopic
ACCCHLOOPSSTUY staphylococcus
ACCCILLOSSSSUU locus classicus
ACCCILNOOSSSSU class-conscious
ACCCIMNNOOSSTT cosmic constant
ACCCLNNOOORTTU control account
ACCDDDEEEPSSTU deducted spaces
ACCDDDEKLOOOOO cock-a-doodle-doo
ACCDDEEHIINOTV The Da Vinci Code
ACCDDEINNORTTU uncontradicted
ACCDEEEEEELMMRR crème de la crème
ACCDEEEEHLRTTT lettre de cachet
ACCDEEEELNOPRS preadolescence
ACCDEEEFMMNOOY comedy of menace
ACCDEEEHHIKNRT chicken-hearted
ACCDEEEHIILLMN medicinal leech
ACCDEEEINNPRSS ens per accidens
ACCDEEFFIILMOR medical officer
ACCDEEFIINRTTU uncertificated
ACCDEEFILNNSTU self-inductance
ACCDEEGHNNORTU counterchanged
ACCDEEHHIKNNNS hen-and-chickens
ACCDEEHIKLNRSS Charles Dickens
ACCDEEHIKRRRTT three-card trick
ACCDEEHILOSTUY lecythidaceous
ACCDEEIIILMNRR meridian circle
ACCDEEIILPRSTV special verdict
ACCDEEILMNORTY dynamo-electric
electrodynamic
ACCDEEILNNNSTY incandescently
ACCDEEILOORRST crocodile tears
ACCDEEIMNOPPTY appendicectomy
ACCDEEINNNOSTU discountenance
ACCDEEINNOORST deconsecration
ACCDEEINOPRRTU unreciprocated
ACCDEEIOOORSSU dioscoreaceous
ACCDEEMNOSSSTU accustomedness
ACCDEENNORSSTT contractedness
ACCDEFGGHILLOT Decca Flight Log
ACCDEFHIILMNSU fluid mechanics
ACCDEFHIORRRSU Crouched-friars
ACCDEFHIRRRSTU Crutched-friars
ACCDEFNNOORTUU unaccounted-for
ACCDEGIILLNOOV Calvin Coolidge
ACCDEHHILLOOPY dolichocephaly
ACCDEHHIMNORSY hydromechanics
ACCDEHIIORRRST director's chair
ACCDEHILMNOPSU unaccomplished

ACCDEHIMOORSTT	Socratic method
ACCDEHINORSSUW	sandwich course
ACCDEHIOOPRRST	Seraphic Doctor
ACCDEHLLLNOORR	Lord Chancellor
ACCDEIIILOPPPR	Calippic Period
ACCDEIILLNNOTY	coincidentally
ACCDEIILNRSSTY	crystal indices
ACCDEIINNNOSTU	discontinuance
ACCDEILLNOOPSY	endoscopically
ACCDEIMMNNOTUU	uncommunicated
ACCDEIMMNOORTY	romantic comedy
ACCDEINNOOORSS	concession road
ACCDEINOOPSTTU	deposit account
ACCDELMOOPRTUY	pluto-democracy
ACCDEMMMNNOOOY	command economy
ACCDGINNNORTUY	country dancing
ACCDHHIINOOPPS	phosphonic acid
ACCDHHIIOOPPRS	phosphoric acid
ACCDHIIIINORTT	trithionic acid
ACCDHIMNNOORRU	chondrocranium
ACCDHIMNOPSSYY	psychodynamics
ACCDIINOORSTTU	contradictious
ACCEEEEENPQSSU	escape sequence
ACCEEEEHILRRTT	electric heater
ACCEEEELLNORTV	electrovalence
ACCEEEFFIINSTU	efficient cause
ACCEEEFFILPSST	special effects
ACCEEEFFIORRRS	careers officer
ACCEEEFHOPRTTU	Peace of Utrecht
ACCEEEFILNPTXY	life expectancy
ACCEEEGILLLNOR	Linacre College
ACCEEEHIKNOOST	take one's choice
ACCEEEHKLPPRTU	perpetual check
ACCEEEILOPSTVY	escape velocity
ACCEEELLMOPRTX	Electra complex
ACCEEELLNORTVY	electrovalency
ACCEEELMNOORTT	electromotance
ACCEEELNNRTTUU	canteen culture
ACCEEENNOPSTUX	expense account
ACCEEEORRSSTUW	Worcester sauce
ACCEEFFHHNNOOT	on the off chance
	on the offchance
	on the off-chance
ACCEEFGILLOORR	ergocalciferol
ACCEEFHNORRRTU	four-centre arch
ACCEEFIILNPPRS	facile princeps
ACCEEFILLMORTV	collective farm
ACCEEFIMORRRTT	refractometric
ACCEEFLLMNOPST	self-complacent
ACCEEFLLORRSTU	Colles' fracture
ACCEEFLMNOOOSY	economy of scale
ACCEEGHIIKNNOT	icing on the cake
ACCEEGHIKLRRRT	trickle charger
ACCEEGHINNNPSS	scanning speech
ACCEEGHINOPSTU	accepting house
ACCEEGIILRRTTU	electric guitar
ACCEEGIINNORSS	carcinogenesis
ACCEEGILLNNORU	general council
ACCEEGILLNORTY	egocentrically
	geocentrically
ACCEEGIMNRSTUV	magnetic curves
ACCEEHHIILNNPR	rhinencephalic
ACCEEHHILMMORT	thermochemical
ACCEEHHILPRRTY	Charley-pitcher
ACCEEHHIMNPSTU	catechumenship
ACCEEHIIIKNPRR	prairie chicken
ACCEEHIILLMOTT	chemical toilet
ACCEEHILLLNORS	Charles Nicolle
ACCEEHILNOPPRS	prosencephalic
ACCEEHIMMOTTTW	Watch Committee
ACCEEHIMNNPRRT	merchant prince
ACCEEHINORRSTW	Worcester china
ACCEEHIORSSSSS	chassés-croisés
ACCEEHIPRSTTTY	cryptaesthetic
ACCEEHKLNORRTU	rocket launcher
ACCEEHLMOOORRT	morocco leather
ACCEEIIIKKNNNV	nievie-nick-nack
ACCEEIILLMNORT	electronic mail
ACCEEIILMMNOSU	oecumenicalism
ACCEEIILNORSST	resistance coil
ACCEEIILORSSSV	social services
ACCEEIIMNNOORT	econometrician
ACCEEIINNOORSS	concessionaire
ACCEEIJORRTTUX	juice extractor
ACCEEIKKLLNNRR	crinkle-crankle
ACCEEILLLNORTY	electronically
ACCEEILLLOPSTY	telescopically
ACCEEILLLORTTY	electrolytical
ACCEEILLOOPRTT	electro-optical
ACCEEILLRRRTTU	circular letter
ACCEEILLRRTTTT	clitter-clatter
ACCEEILMOPRSTU	proceleusmatic
ACCEEILNOOPTUY	leucocytopenia
ACCEEILNOORRTU	calorie counter✧
ACCEEILNOPRSST	reception class
ACCEEILNOPSTTT	plate tectonics
ACCEEILNRRTTUU	curtain lecture
ACCEEILOOPRSST	stereoscopical
ACCEEILORSSTTT	electrostatics
ACCEEINNOORRST	reconsecration
ACCEELLMNRSTUY	menstrual cycle
ACCEELLNOOPTTY	cyclopentolate
ACCEELOORRRSST	cross-correlate
ACCEEMMNNNOORT	Common Entrance
ACCEENORSTTTUU	trustee account
ACCEFFIILLNOOO	Colonial Office
ACCEFFIILNNOOT	focal infection
ACCEFGGHHIINNT	fighting chance
ACCEFGIIIINNNS	insignificance
ACCEFHHIJKORSS	Joschka Fischer
ACCEFHILLMOTUU	Michel Foucault
ACCEFHINNNORSY	Inns of Chancery
ACCEFIIILLNSTY	scientifically
ACCEFILMNOORSW	moccasin flower
ACCEFILNNOPRSU	Francis Poulenc
ACCEFILNOOSTTU	Council of State
ACCEFLNOORRSTU	control surface
ACCEFMNNNNOOOR	non-conformance
ACCEFMNNOOOTUY	money of account
ACCEGHHILNOOST	schoolteaching
ACCEGHIILLNNOU	hallucinogenic
ACCEGHIIMNNPRR	Prince Charming

ACCEGHINNOPRST sporting chance
ACCEGHINOPRRSS preaching-cross
ACCEGHIOPPRRST spectrographic
ACCEGHIOPRRSTV vectorgraphics
ACCEGIILNRTUXY excruciatingly
ACCEGIKLLNNORT central locking
ACCEGIKLLNOOTU cocktail lounge
ACCEGILLMMOORY myrmecological
ACCEGILLNRRTUU cultural cringe
ACCEGILLOOPRST spectrological
ACCEGKLOPPRUUU pluck up courage
ACCEHHILLNOPRS chancellorship
ACCEHIILLLMNOS Michael Collins
ACCEHIILMMMNOU immunochemical
ACCEHIILMNNOPR harmonic pencil
ACCEHIILMORSTT stichometrical
ACCEHIILMRTUVY clavicytherium
ACCEHIINNOPRTY pyrotechnician
ACCEHIKLLMOORY mock-heroically
ACCEHIKMNNOPUY capuchin monkey
ACCEHILMMNOPST accomplishment
ACCEHILMNOORRT chronometrical
ACCEHILMOOPRSU microcephalous
ACCEHILMOPRSTY psychometrical
ACCEHILMOPSUUY sceuophylacium
ACCEHILNPRSSUY nuclear physics
ACCEHIMNOPRRSU proscenium arch
ACCEHNOORSTTTY Scotch attorney
ACCEIIILMMORSS microseismical
ACCEIIILNNOORT reconciliation
ACCEIIILNOORRT oneirocritical
ACCEIIKKLMPSUW Samuel Pickwick
ACCEIIKLNNOPRS Cecil Parkinson
ACCEIIKORSSUVX coxsackie virus✧
ACCEIILLLOSSTY solecistically
ACCEIILLMOORSY seriocomically
ACCEIILLMRRSUY semicircularly
ACCEIILLMRSSTY semicrystallic
ACCEIILLNOPSST scintillascope
ACCEIILNNOPTTU centuplication
ACCEIILNNORRST central incisor
ACCEIILNOORRTY reconciliatory
ACCEIILORSSTUY social security
ACCEIINNOORSTT concretisation
ACCEIINNOORTTZ concretization
ACCEIINOPRSSSU capriciousness
ACCEILLLNNOOOT loan collection
ACCEILLMNOORTT climate control
ACCEILLNOSSSUY successionally
ACCEILMMMOORR commercial room
ACCEILMMNNOOSS commonsensical
ACCEILMOOOPPST metoposcopical
ACCEILMOOPSSST composite class
ACCEILNOORSSST cross-sectional
ACCEIMMNOORTUX excommunicator
ACCEIMNOOOPRRS Persian morocco
ACCEIMNOOPRSTU pococuranteism
ACCEIMNOPRSTTU action spectrum
ACCEINNNOORSTT star connection
ACCELLMOOPRSTT stamp collector
ACCENORSSTTTTU construct state
ACCFFIIINORTTU fructification
ACCFGIIIINNNSY insignificancy
ACCFGILNOORTTT clotting factor
ACCFHHIKLLNRRU Frank Churchill
ACCFHHILLLLRSU Churchill Falls
ACCFIIIIILNOST silicification
ACCFIIIIKNNOTZ zinckification
ACCFIIINOOSTTT Scottification
ACCFIILNOPPRSU principal focus
ACCFIMMNNOOORT common fraction
ACCGHHIILLOOTY ichthyological
ACCGHHINOOOPRR choronographic
ACCGHHIOPPRSSY psychographics
ACCGHIILLOOPRS oscillographic
ACCGHIILLOORST Christological
ACCGIIIILMNOOR criminological
ACCGIIILNNOPRT calico-printing
ACCGIILLLMOORY micrologically
ACCGIIMNORRTUY circumgyration
ACCGILLOOPRSYY gyroscopically
ACCGIMNNOOTTTU coconut matting
ACCGIMORRRTUYY circumgyratory
ACCGINNOORSSTU toucan crossing
ACCHHIILMNRTTU church militant
ACCHHIILMOORTT lithochromatic
ACCHHIIMNNOPTU Mount Pichincha
ACCHHILOPPSSYY psychophysical
ACCHHIMOOORRTT orthochromatic
ACCHIIINNNOOST cinchonisation
ACCHIIINNNOOTZ cinchonization
ACCHIILLOPRTYY hypocritically
ACCHIILOOPRSTY hypocoristical
ACCHIILOORSSTT historical cost
ACCHIIMNOPRTTU phantom circuit
ACCHILLNNORSYY synchronically
ACCHIMOOPSSSTY psychosomatics
ACCIIILLNOORTY conciliatorily
ACCIIIMNORRSSU Rosicrucianism
ACCIIIOORRTTVV Victor/Victoria
ACCIILLMOOOPST cosmopolitical
ACCIILLMORRTTU circumlittoral
ACCIILMNOPRTUU municipal court
ACCIILNNOOPRST conscriptional
ACCIILNNOORTUY unconciliatory
ACCIIMMNNOOSTU communications
ACCIIMNNORTTUU circumnutation
ACCIINNNOORSTT triconsonantic
ACCIINNOOOSTTV convocationist
ACCIKKLLMNOORW Kilmarnock cowl
ACCIKKMMNNRRUU crinkum-crankum
ACCILLOPPRRTYY procryptically
ACCILMNOOSTUUY contumaciously
ACCILNNOORSTTU constructional
ACCILOPRRSTUUY corpuscularity
ACCIMMNNNNOOTU non-communicant
ACCIMNORRTTUUY circumnutatory
ACCJKKLLNOOOPS Jackson Pollock
ACCLLMOOPRSSUU corpus callosum
ACCLNOOORRSTTU colour contrast
ACDDDEEIIINORT ratio decidendi
ACDDDEEIILMNST middle distance

middle-distance
ACDDDEELLOOPRU clouded leopard
ACDDEEEEHINRTV heaven-directed
ACDDEEEFNNOOTV deed of covenant
ACDDEEEFNNORTU unconfederated
ACDDEEEHINRSTW Edward Steichen
ACDDEEEIKNPRST pedestrian deck
ACDDEEELORSTTY Decorated style
ACDDEEEMNORRTU document reader
ACDDEEENNORSTX extra-condensed
ACDDEEENORSVYY every second day
ACDDEEFIKLOOSV devil's food cake
ACDDEEFNNOSSST stand confessed
ACDDEEGIKLNOSW disacknowledge
ACDDEEGKLNNOUW unacknowledged
ACDDEEHHLORRSU shouldered arch
ACDDEEHIINRRSY arsenic hydride
ACDDEEHMMOORRS chordamesoderm
ACDDEEIIIIMNNN Indian medicine
ACDDEEIILRTTUV diverticulated
ACDDEEIJJRSTTU Jeddart justice
ACDDEEIKNOPSUW upside-down cake
ACDDEEIMNOSTTU undomesticated
ACDDEEINRSSSTT distractedness
ACDDEFILOOPPRS apple of discord
ACDDEGHIORRRRS Richard Rodgers
ACDDEGIIKKLNUY like a dying duck
ACDDEGIINNRSTT credit standing
ACDDEGLLNSSSTU ductless glands
ACDDEHMOOPRSTU proud-stomached
ACDDEIIINNOORT air-conditioned
ACDDEIIJLMRRUU judicial murder
ACDDEIIKLNOSVZ David O Selznick
ACDDEIINOOORSU androdioecious
ACDDEIKMNOORRR Roderick Random
ACDDEILNNOOSTU unconsolidated
ACDDEILNRSTTUY undistractedly
ACDDEIMNNOORWW income drawdown
ACDDEIOOORRRST corrida de toros
ACDDELMNOOOORW Coromandel wood
ACDDELMNOORRTV Trevor McDonald
ACDDGHINOORRRS Gordon Richards
ACDDGIILMNOOOP Plácido Domingo
ACDEEEEEGHLNNX needle exchange
ACDEEEEGHLNRTT lettre de change
ACDEEEEGILMNNT magnetic needle
ACDEEEEGMNQRRU grecque meander
ACDEEEEHIMSSST set-aside scheme
ACDEEEELNNRSUU Laurence Eusden
ACDEEEFFGILNOR goal difference
ACDEEEFFNNSSTU unaffectedness
ACDEEEFHIRSUVX chevaux-de-frise
ACDEEEFILNNORT dolce far niente
ACDEEEFMNNOSTU come unfastened
ACDEEEGHLLLORS Herald's College
ACDEEEGHNNOSST chanson de geste
ACDEEEGNORRRSU André Courrèges
ACDEEEHHIKNRSV handkerchieves
ACDEEEHIIMMNOU Comédie humaine
ACDEEEHIIMNSTU Eudemian Ethics
ACDEEEHIKLRSTT tickled a th' sere
ACDEEEHILMNNSS Michael Denness
ACDEEEHKLNNRSY Charles Kennedy
ACDEEEHLLOPRRU chorale prelude
ACDEEEHMNORRTT three-card monte
ACDEEEHNPRSTTU Stephen Decatur
ACDEEEIIINRSST actinide series
ACDEEEIIMNNPTT patent medicine
ACDEEEIIRSSTTV cartes-de-visite
ACDEEEILNOPRTU Pleuronectidae
ACDEEEILNRSSST Secrets and Lies
ACDEEEILOOPRST radio telescope
ACDEEEIMNNNORU unearned income
ACDEEEIMNOPRTX dementia precox
ACDEEEINNOPQRU equiponderance
ACDEEEINORSSTV decorativeness
ACDEEELNOPRRUW nuclear-powered
ACDEEEMNORRTTY endarterectomy
ACDEEEMNSTTTUU decus et tutamen
ACDEEEMOPRRSTU Peter Scudamore
ACDEEENNORTTTV contrat de vente
ACDEEENRRRSTUY under-secretary
ACDEEEOPRSTTTT protected state
ACDEEFFGLOOORT feel-good factor
ACDEEFFIMORRTT diffractometer
ACDEEFGHIILNPR field preaching
ACDEEFGHOOOOPP Cape of Good Hope
ACDEEFHHMORSST Schafer's method
ACDEEFHIINNRSS disenfranchise
ACDEEFHIKLNNSW Schwenkfeldian
ACDEEFHORRSSTW chest of drawers
ACDEEFIILNNOOT conditional fee
ACDEEFILLMOPRS self-proclaimed
ACDEEFINOQRRUY radio frequency
ACDEEFINOQRUUY audio-frequency
ACDEEFINRRRSTT credit transfer
ACDEEFNORSSTTU Acts of Sederunt
ACDEEGGILNNORR recording angel
ACDEEGGMNOORST second mortgage
ACDEEGHIILOOPT galeopithecoid
ACDEEGHIIMNNNV vending machine
ACDEEGHILLRSTY clear-sightedly
ACDEEGHILOOSSW wild-goose chase
ACDEEGHIMNNNOS change one's mind
ACDEEGHNNOORUY ocean-greyhound
ACDEEGIILNPRTY depreciatingly
ACDEEGIIMNORRZ organized crime
ACDEEGIINORSTT stage direction
ACDEEGIIRSTTTV digestive tract
ACDEEGIJKNRSST dressing-jacket
ACDEEGILLNNOSU leading counsel
ACDEEGILLOPRRT pectoral girdle
ACDEEGILNNOQRU grandiloquence
ACDEEGIMNORSTU discouragement
ACDEEGINRRSSTU drug resistance
ACDEEGKLMNNOTW acknowledgment
ACDEEGLNNORRSW second wrangler
ACDEEGLNOOORRU orange-coloured
ACDEEHHIIKMNSZ mechanized Sikh
ACDEEHHIKNSTTW what the dickens
ACDEEHHILMNORR Michael Hordern
ACDEEHHILNOPST Daphnis et Chloé

ACDEEHHINNRSVY Henry Cavendish
ACDEEHHKKNNOOT knock on the head
ACDEEHHMMNOTUY The Human Comedy
ACDEEHIIINNRST disinheritance
ACDEEHIIINRSST dechristianise
ACDEEHIIINRSTZ dechristianize
ACDEEHIILMNRTY identical rhyme
ACDEEHIINNSTTZ zenith distance
ACDEEHIINOORRT Rhinocerotidae
ACDEEHIINRSTTW Christian de Wet
ACDEEHILLNNOST Achilles' tendon
ACDEEHILLNNPRS Children's Panel
ACDEEHILMNOSST methodicalness
ACDEEHILNORSVY cash on delivery
cash-on-delivery
ACDEEHIMNNNSTT disenchantment
ACDEEHINNRSSST disenchantress
ACDEEHINOOPPRT apprenticehood
ACDEEHINOPPRTY cyproheptadine
ACDEEHKMNORSST Random Sketches
ACDEEHMNNOOOST come to one's hand
ACDEEIIIJLRUVW judicial review
ACDEEIILNNNSST incidentalness
ACDEEIIMMOTTTU audit committee
ACDEEIINORRSSU Cuisenaire rods
ACDEEILLLNNOOT clonal deletion
ACDEEILLMNTTUU multinucleated
ACDEEILMNOORTU Deuteronomical
ACDEEILMNOSSSU ondes musicales
ACDEEILMOSTUUV cumulative dose
ACDEEILMRSSTTU striated muscle
ACDEEILNNORSTV second interval
ACDEEILNOPSSST despoticalness
ACDEEIMMMOPRRS promise-crammed
ACDEEIMMNNOORT recommendation
ACDEEIMMNORSTV inverted commas
ACDEEIMNNOOPST decompensation
ACDEEIMNNOSTWW casement window
ACDEEINNNOORST recondensation
ACDEEINNOORSST co-ordinateness
ACDEEINOPRSSSU predaciousness
ACDEELLMNNOTTY malcontentedly
ACDEELLNPRSSYY Leyland cypress
ACDEELMNNNOOPY planned economy
ACDEELMNNOPRTT Portland cement
ACDEELMNNOPTTU uncontemplated
ACDEELNNNRSTTY transcendently
ACDEELNNOORTTV lavender cotton
ACDEEMMNOORRTY recommendatory
ACDEENNORRSUVY Ordnance Survey
ACDEENOOOORTVW wooden overcoat
ACDEFGHIILMNNO folding-machine
ACDEFGHIILNRSU Chladni figures
ACDEFGHILMNORR French marigold
ACDEFHMNNOPRRY pardon my French
ACDEFIIIILMPST fides implicita
ACDEFIIIINNOTT identification
ACDEFIIINNOSTY Disneyfication
ACDEFIIINOOTTX detoxification
ACDEFIIINORRTT denitrificator
ACDEFIIIRSSUUY fiduciary issue
ACDEFIILLNNOTY confidentially
ACDEFIIMNNOTTY Act of Indemnity
ACDEGGILMNOOYY dynamic geology
ACDEGHHIIKOSSU his cake is dough
ACDEGHHIILLMNO Michael Holding
ACDEGHILLMOOOT methodological
ACDEGHIMNORRRS marching orders
ACDEGHIMNORSTY hydromagnetics
ACDEGHINNORSTU countershading
ACDEGIILLOOSTT dialectologist
ACDEGIMMNOTTUY gated community
ACDEGIMNOPRTTU computer dating
ACDEGINNORRSSW crossing-warden
ACDEGINNORRTTU counter-trading
ACDEGINOORRRTU corrugated iron
ACDEGMMNNOOORR common-or-garden
ACDEHHIILMOPRT edriophthalmic
ACDEHHIILOORTZ chlorothiazide
ACDEHHIIMOPRRT hermaphroditic
ACDEHHILLMOORY Michael Holroyd
ACDEHHLOOPRSUY hydrocephalous
ACDEHHNNOORSTW Theodor Schwann
ACDEHIIILOOPRT diaheliotropic
ACDEHIILLMMOTY immethodically
ACDEHIILLNORSY Nicholas Ridley
ACDEHIILMORSTT direct mailshot
ACDEHIILNRSSTT child-resistant
ACDEHIILPPPSSY applied physics
ACDEHIIMORRSTY radiochemistry
ACDEHIKKLNORUV Leonid Kravchuk
ACDEHIKNOQRTUW quick on the draw
ACDEHILLMOPRYY hypodermically
ACDEHILLNOORRY hydrocoralline
ACDEHILLOOPRTY orthopedically
ACDEHILLOORRWY Richard Woolley
ACDEHILMOORSTU sodium chlorate
ACDEHILPRRSSUY hydraulic press
ACDEHIMMNORSTY thermodynamics
ACDEHIMNOPRTUY hydropneumatic
ACDEHINOORRSTT trisoctahedron
ACDEHINOSSTTTW cast to the winds
ACDEHKOPRSSTUY Sudeck's atrophy
ACDEHLOOOPPRSV approved school
ACDEHMMOORRSSU sacred mushroom
ACDEHOORRRTTXY hydroextractor
ACDEIIIIMNNRST indiscriminate
ACDEIIIIMNRSTV discriminative
ACDEIIILMNRSTY discriminately
ACDEIIILNNORTU unidirectional
ACDEIIILNNSTTW identical twins
ACDEIIILNORTTY directionality
ACDEIIINNOORRT air-conditioner
ACDEIIIOORSTTV Vittorio De Sica
ACDEIILLNORSTY discretionally
ACDEIILLNRSTUV lucid intervals
ACDEIILMMNOPTY limited company
ACDEIILMMRSSTY dissymmetrical
ACDEIILMPSTTUU multicuspidate
ACDEIILNNOOOST decolonisation
ACDEIILNNOOOTZ decolonization
ACDEIILNNOTUVV induction valve

ACDEIILNOOORST decolorisation
ACDEIILNOOORTZ decolorization
ACDEIILNOSSSTY Society Islands
ACDEIILPRSTUVV tricuspid valve
ACDEIINOOPRRST disincorporate
ACDEIKMNORSTTU discount market
ACDEIKNOPRRTTV davenport-trick
ACDEILLMNOOSTY endosmotically
ACDEILLNOOSSTY disconsolately
ACDEILLNRSSTUY uncrystallised
ACDEILLNRSTUYZ uncrystallized
ACDEILNNRSTTWY twinned crystal
ACDEILNOSSSTTU sansculottides
ACDEIMMNNOOORS andromonoecism
ACDEIMMNNOPSUY pneumodynamics
ACDEIMMNORSTTU contrast medium
ACDEIMOOPRSSST mastoid process
ACDEINNOOPRRTU unincorporated
ACDEINNORSTUUY consuetudinary
ACDEINOOQRSSTU conquistadores
ACDEIOOPPRRSTU dipterocarpous
ACDEKLMNOOORRW Coromandel work
ACDELLMNOOORSU salmon-coloured
ACDELLOOPSTTUY leptodactylous
ACDENORRSSSSTW St Andrew's cross
ACDFFILNNOOOTU functional food
ACDFFIOPPRRSST Stafford Cripps
ACDFGHILMNNTUY Flying Dutchman
ACDFGIINOPRRRW forward pricing
ACDFHIIIIMNOTU humidification
ACDFHIINNRSTUZ Fritz Schaudinn
ACDFIIIILNOOST solidification
ACDFIIKLLMMNOR Malcolm Rifkind
ACDGGHINOOOTTW chittagong wood
ACDGGIILNORSUY discouragingly
ACDGHILLLOORYY hydrologically
ACDGHILMNNOOPY holding company
ACDGIIIIMNNRST discriminating
ACDGIIILLMOSSU Guild Socialism
ACDGIIMNNORTUY dynamic routing
ACDGIIMNOPSSUV viscous damping
ACDGILNNOORRRT Lord Carrington
ACDGINNORRSSTU strand-scouring
ACDHHIIOPRRSST harpsichordist
ACDHHIMNOOPRSY hypochondriasm
ACDHHINOOPRSTY hypochondriast
ACDHIIOOOPPRTT diaphototropic
ACDHIKMOORRRTY Tom, Dick, or Harry
ACDHILLNNOOORS Harold Nicolson
ACDHILLNOOPRYY hydroponically
ACDHILOOOPRSTT hospital doctor
ACDHILOPRSSUUU sulphurous acid
ACDHIMNOOORSST chondromatosis
ACDIIIILMNPRSU disciplinarium
ACDIIIILNNNOST disinclination
ACDIIIIMNNORST discrimination
ACDIIIJLNORSTU jurisdictional
ACDIIILNNOOTTY conditionality
ACDIIILOSSTTUY adscititiously
ACDIIIMNORRSTY discriminatory
ACDIIINNNOOORT incoordination
inco-ordination
ACDIIINNNOORTT indoctrination
ACDIIINNOOORTT initiator codon
ACDIILMNNOPSTU induction lamps
ACDIILNNOOOSST disconsolation
ACDIILNOOORSTU discolouration
ACDIIMMNOORTUY community radio
ACDIINOOPPRRTU pair production
ACDIIOOPPRRSTY cryptosporidia
ACDILMNORTTUUU mutual inductor
ACDIMNOOPRSSTU mass production
ACDMMNOOORSTUY yours to command
ACEEEEFFFLMNST self-effacement
ACEEEEFFLNOSTV leave no effects
ACEEEEFGHINNRT interchange fee
ACEEEEFHHLNPRT three-halfpence
ACEEEEFIIPSSVY Five Easy Pieces
ACEEEEFLNPRSST false pretences
ACEEEEFLOPRSTT Letters of peace
ACEEEEGHINRRTT heritage centre
ACEEEEGHNRSTTT The Secret Agent
ACEEEEGILLPTXY epexegetically
ACEEEEHHILNRTW Catherine-wheel
ACEEEEHINNRSWY Chinese New Year
ACEEEEILMNPPRS malice prepense
ACEEEEILSSTUVX sales executive
ACEEEELNNRRSTU Laurence Sterne
ACEEEELNOPRRSU reopener clause
ACEEEFFGILNORR general officer
ACEEEFFLNSSSST affectlessness
ACEEEFGHLNRTTT the gentle craft
ACEEEFGLNNPRSU self-repugnance
ACEEEFHHILLLOS heel of Achilles
ACEEEFHIIIMNNX examine-in-chief
ACEEEFHIMRRTUV rheumatic fever
ACEEEFHINPRRST prince's feather
ACEEEFIIIMNPSS infimae species
ACEEEFIINPRRST Cape Finisterre
ACEEEFLLORRTUW fellow creature
ACEEEFLNNSSSTU self-sustenance
ACEEEGGHNRRSWZ Schwarzenegger
ACEEEGGILLLLOV village college
ACEEEGHHINNTWX win the exchange
ACEEEGHIILNOPT galeopithecine
ACEEEGHIINNNRS engineer's chain
ACEEEGHIINOSST aesthesiogenic
ACEEEGHIJKNNRT Jack-in-the-green
ACEEEGHILNPSST steeplechasing
ACEEEGHLLMNNOW Newnham College
ACEEEGHLNNSSSS changelessness
ACEEEGHLNORRTT Charlotte Green
ACEEEGHNNNOSTU change one's tune
ACEEEGHOPRRSTT scrape together
ACEEEGIILLNPTY epigenetically
ACEEEGIILNNORS social engineer
ACEEEGILLMNOTT metallogenetic
ACEEEGILLMPPSU eclipse plumage
ACEEEGILLNOORV venereological
ACEEEGILNNQSSU signal sequence
ACEEEGILNSSSTT cassette single
ACEEEGIMMOSTTT committee stage

ACEEEGIMNORRTV image converter
ACEEEGINNPRSTT genetic parents
ACEEEGKLMNNRSY clergyman's knee
ACEEEGLLNNOSST St Anne's College
ACEEEGLMNORSTT Egremont Castle
ACEEEGMORSSTTY Gasteromycetes
ACEEEHHIIMMNTT The Time Machine
ACEEEHHIPRSSTY hyperaesthesic
ACEEEHHIPRSTTY hyperaesthetic
ACEEEHIKOPPRTW a prophetic week
ACEEEHILLPRSTT Chile saltpetre
ACEEEHILMNPPRT hip replacement
ACEEEHILNNNRST Chinese lantern
ACEEEHILNORSST cholinesterase
ACEEEHILNRTTTY the Eternal City
ACEEEHILPRRUVX preux chevalier
ACEEEHKKLNNRTU near the knuckle
ACEEEHKLNOPRVV Pavel Cherenkov
ACEEEHLLMORRTT electrothermal
ACEEEHLLNOOSTW whole-tone scale
ACEEEHLNORRRTV trochlear nerve
ACEEEHLOPRRTTY electrotherapy
ACEEEHMMOORTTY haemocytometer
ACEEEHNORSSSUY necessary house
ACEEEHNPRSSTUY hyperacuteness
ACEEEIIJLMRSTU Jamie Lee Curtis
ACEEEIIKMNRRVZ Mackenzie River
ACEEEIILMNNNST semi-centennial
ACEEEIILMNRRTT recrementitial
ACEEEIILMNRTTX excrementitial
ACEEEIILOPRSSV overspecialise
ACEEEIILOPRSVZ overspecialize
ACEEEIKLNNPRRT percentile rank
ACEEEILLLOPSST celestial poles
ACEEEILLMNOPRY Emile Clapeyron
ACEEEILLMORSUV molecular sieve
ACEEEILLNORSST Elsinore Castle
ACEEEILLOPPPRU Peculiar People
ACEEEILLPRSSTU supercelestial
ACEEEILMORRSTT stereometrical
ACEEEILNNQQUUV quinquevalence
ACEEEIMNNOOSTY société anonyme
ACEEEIMNNPPRTT apprenticement
ACEEEIMNORSSVY yeoman's service
ACEEEIMNORSVWX ex-servicewoman
ACEEELLORSSSTW Steller's sea-cow
ACEEELMNNOORTT Ornette Coleman
ACEEELNNPRSSTY Stanley Spencer
ACEEELPPRRSTUW perpetual screw
ACEEEMNOOPRSTV overcompensate
ACEEEMNOPRRTTU contemperature
ACEEEMNORRSTUU countermeasure
ACEEENNORSSSTU nectareousness
ACEEFFFGILLNSY self-effacingly
ACEEFFGHINRSST Schiff's reagent
ACEEFFHIMNORSV charm offensive
ACEEFFHKMNOOOS hack someone off
ACEEFFIILNTTUY ineffectuality
ACEEFFILNOOPRS on special offer
ACEEFFLLOORRUV four-leaf clover
ACEEFFMMNOOORT moment of a force
ACEEFFMMNORSUY summary offence
ACEEFGHILLNOTW teaching fellow
ACEEFGHLOPRRTY reflectography
ACEEFGIILNRSTU centrifugalise
ACEEFGIILNRTUZ centrifugalize
ACEEFGILLLOORX reflexological
ACEEFGINNOOPRR Prince of Orange
ACEEFGLNNRSSUU ungracefulness
ACEEFHHIORRSTT ostrich-feather
ACEEFHIIINORTT etherification
ACEEFHILORSSTW as the crow flies
ACEEFIIILPRSSU superficialise
ACEEFIIILPRSUZ superficialize
ACEEFIIINORSTT esterification
ACEEFIIKLNNPRR Franklin Pierce
ACEEFIKNRRSTTT transfer ticket
ACEEFILMNOPRST self-importance
ACEEFILMPRRSTU simple fracture
ACEEFINNORSSTU surface tension
ACEEFINOORSSSW War of Secession
ACEEFINORRRSST refractoriness
ACEEFMNNNOOPRR non-performance
ACEEFMNOOPRRTU outperformance
ACEEFRRRSSSTTU stress fracture
ACEEGGHHINNRST ring the changes
ACEEGGHIILLNOT genethlialogic
ACEEGGHLMNOOTY megatechnology
ACEEGGIILLMOOT geological time
ACEEGGIMNNORRS scaremongering
ACEEGHHINOPRSU preaching-house
ACEEGHHNNOPTTU put the change on
ACEEGHIIKMNNRT niche marketing
ACEEGHIINNPRST speech-training
ACEEGHIKKLOOST go like hot cakes
ACEEGHIKPRRRTT prick-the-garter
ACEEGHILLNOPRY hypoallergenic
ACEEGHILLOOPRT herpetological
ACEEGHILNOPTTY phytogenetical
ACEEGHILNOSSSU chaises-longues
ACEEGHIMNOPRST magnetospheric
ACEEGHLMNNRSTU McNaghten rules
ACEEGHLNOORTTY Charlotte Yonge
ACEEGHLOOPSSTU stegocephalous
ACEEGHMNRRTTTU gutter-merchant
ACEEGHOOOOPPSS oesophagoscope
ACEEGHOPRRRSSS progress chaser
ACEEGIIINNORST genericisation
ACEEGIIINNORTZ genericization
ACEEGIIMMOPRTT micropegmatite
ACEEGIIMNPRSTT magnetic stripe
ACEEGIINNNORTT traction engine
ACEEGIKLLORRTY category killer
ACEEGIKLNPRSTU plague-stricken
ACEEGILLLLOOTY teleologically
ACEEGILLMOOORT meteorological
ACEEGILLNOPRTT electroplating
ACEEGILLPRRTUY picture gallery
ACEEGIMMMNNOTT magnetic moment
ACEEGIMNNORSUV misgovernaunce
ACEEGIMOOPRRSS image processor
ACEEGINNNORTTY octingentenary

ACEEGLLNNORSSU consuls general
ACEEGLMMOORRTY electromyogram
ACEEGLNOORRSTU colour-sergeant
ACEEGLNRRSTTUU structural gene
ACEEGNOORSSSUU courageousness
ACEEHHIKSTTTTT that's the ticket
ACEEHHILNNNOPR rhinencephalon
ACEEHHIMOPRSTT chemotherapist
ACEEHHMOOPRRST chromatosphere
ACEEHIIILLMNPT Michele Platini
ACEEHIIILNPSTT licentiateship
ACEEHIIKNNOSTT skate on thin ice
ACEEHIILLNNPST Panhellenistic
ACEEHIILLNRSTT carline thistle
ACEEHIILMOOPRR microaerophile
ACEEHIILMPPTTT Michael Tippett
ACEEHIIMNNSSTZ Nietzscheanism
ACEEHIIMNORRSS harmonic series
ACEEHIINPPPRST apprenticeship
ACEEHILLLNOPTY telephonically
ACEEHILLMNOOTT monotheletical✧
ACEEHILLMNRRTW Warren Mitchell
ACEEHILLMORTXY exothermically
ACEEHILMMNRSUY masculine rhyme
ACEEHILMMORRTT thermometrical
ACEEHIMMNORSSV servomechanism
ACEEHIMPRSTUWY white supremacy
ACEEHINORSUUVX nouveaux riches
ACEEHINPPRRSST ship's carpenter
ACEEHKMNORSTTT shock treatment
ACEEHKMNRRTTUY Turkey merchant
ACEEHKMOPSSSTU mocks the pauses
ACEEHLLOOPPSTU leptocephalous
ACEEHLLOPPRRTV Trevor Chappell
ACEEHLMOOOPPRS Marco Polo sheep
ACEEHLNNOOPPRS prosencephalon
ACEEHLOPPPRSTU copper sulphate
ACEEHLORRSSTTU charlotte russe
ACEEHMMNNOOSTW Thomas Newcomen
ACEEHMNORRSSUU human resources
ACEEHMPRSSSTUY purchase system
ACEEHNOORRSSST cross one's heart
ACEEHPRRRTTTTY Terry Pratchett
ACEEIIILLLMPST semi-elliptical
ACEEIIILMNNRST reminiscential
ACEEIIILMNPPRR prince-imperial
ACEEIIILNRRTTY rectilinearity
ACEEIIIMPPRSTT peripateticism
ACEEIIINOPRRSX excision repair
ACEEIIJKPRRRVV river-jack viper
ACEEIIJLNNORTT interjectional
ACEEIIKLLMNNRS Sir Ian McKellen
ACEEIIKLLMNPSY Mickey Spillane
ACEEIILLMMNPTU multiple cinema
ACEEIILLOPRSTV political verse
ACEEIILLRRSTTV verticillaster
ACEEIILMMORSST seismometrical
ACEEIILMNOPSTX exceptionalism
ACEEIILMNPRSTT centripetalism
ACEEIILNNNNQTU quincentennial
ACEEIILNNNOPTT epicontinental
ACEEIILNNORSST intercessional
ACEEIILNNORSTT intersectional
ACEEIILNOPTTXY exceptionality
ACEEIILNORRSST intercessorial
ACEEIILNOSSTTY coessentiality
ACEEIINORSSTTV service station
ACEEIINRRSSTTZ citizen's arrest
ACEEIKLNNPRSTT planet-stricken
ACEEIKLNOOPTUY leukocytopenia
ACEEIKLNORRTTW Walter Cronkite
ACEEIKLNRSSSTV travel sickness
ACEEILLLLNTTUY intellectually
ACEEILLLNNTTUU unintellectual
ACEEILLMNORRTU intermolecular
ACEEILMMNORTUV Victor Emmanuel
ACEEILMMOOPSTT metal composite
ACEEILMNOOOPSU polemoniaceous
ACEEILMNOPSSTT Pentecostalism
ACEEILMNORSSTY moral necessity
ACEEILMNSSTUUV cumulativeness
ACEEILMOPRSSTU precious metals
ACEEILMOTTUUVV cumulative vote
ACEEILNNOPSSTU unpoeticalness
ACEEILNNORSTTU counter-salient
ACEEILNOPSSTTT Pentecostalist
ACEEILNORRRSTU resurrectional
ACEEILNORSSTTU sansculotterie
ACEEILNORSTVVY conservatively
ACEEILORRRSTUY literary source
ACEEIMMMNOOTTW committeewoman
ACEEIMMMNORSTY semantic memory
ACEEIMMNNORSTU incommensurate
ACEEIMNNOOPRTT contemperation
ACEEIMNOOORRRT recreation room
ACEEIMNORRSSST Martin Scorsese
ACEEINNNORRSSY Sir Sean Connery
ACEEINNOORSSTT contesseration
ACEEINNOORSSVZ conversaziones
ACEEINNPRTTTUU interpunctuate
ACEEINOPRRSSSU precariousness
ACEEINOQQSTTUU quinquecostate
ACEEINOQRRSTTU quarter section
ACEEINOQSSSSUU sequaciousness
ACEEIPRRSSSTTU static pressure
ACEEJLMORRSSSU Jerusalem cross
ACEEJMMNNOORST Common Serjeant
ACEELLNORTUWYY yellow centaury
ACEELLOORRRSUV colour reversal
ACEELMMNORSTUY commensurately
ACEELMNOPRRTUU neural computer
ACEELMOOPPPTTT Mt Popocatepetl
ACEELNOPRSTUUY percutaneously
ACEELOORRRSTWY Royal Worcester
ACEEMNOOOPRSTU cotemporaneous
ACEEMNOPPRSSXY express company
ACEEMOOPRRSTTW two-pot screamer
ACEENNNOPSSTTY pennystone-cast
ACEENOPRRSSSTU Paterson's curse
ACEFFHIIOORRST Chariots of Fire
ACEFFIIILLMOSY semi-officially
ACEFFIIILNOORS liaison officer

ACEFFIIOSSTTUY suffice it to say
ACEFFINOOQSTTU question of fact
ACEFFINRRRSTTU traffic returns
ACEFFJLLLOOSTY calf's-foot jelly
ACEFGGIINNNOPY pigeon-fancying
ACEFGHIIIKMMNS mischief-making
ACEFGHILNNNRSU channel-surfing
ACEFGIIINNORTT gentrification
ACEFGIILLNORSU fringillaceous
ACEFGIINNORTTU centrifugation
ACEFGNNOOSSSST Songs of ascents
ACEFHHNOOSTTUU a touch of the sun
ACEFHIKLMNRSSU fisherman's luck
ACEFHILOOPPRSW place of worship
ACEFHIMORRTTTX rich text format
ACEFHLMNOSSSTU stomachfulness
ACEFHLNNSSTUUW unwatchfulness
ACEFIIIILMPSTV simplificative
ACEFIIIINNORST resinification
ACEFIIIINORTVV revivification
ACEFIIILMNOSTU emulsification
ACEFIIILPRSTUY superficiality
ACEFIIINOPRTTT prettification
ACEFIIKLNRRSTV Francis Kilvert
ACEFIILLLNNOTY inflectionally
ACEFIILMNOPRST simple fraction
ACEFIILNNORSSU nuclear fission
ACEFIILORRTTUV article of virtu
ACEFIINOORRSST fission reactor
ACEFIINOSSSTTU factitiousness
ACEFIIOOPRRSST pro aris et focis
ACEFILLNOOOSSY Isle of Colonsay
ACEFILMNOOPRSS self-comparison
ACEFILNOOQSTUU Nicolas Fouquet
ACEFINNOORSSSU facinorousness
ACEFINOOPPRRRT proper fraction
ACEFINRRRSTTUU infrastructure
ACEFLLNOORSTTW Wollstonecraft
ACEFLNOORSSSTU colour fastness
ACEGGHHIINTTWW weight-watching
ACEGGHIIMNNNNU machinegunning
ACEGGHINNNOTVV Vincent Van Gogh
ACEGGIILNNNPRS spring-cleaning
ACEGGILLNOOORT gerontological
ACEGGILLNOOSTY geognostically
ACEGHHIILLOPRY hieroglyphical
ACEGHHIKNORTTT on the right tack
ACEGHHILNNNOPP channel-hopping
ACEGHIIIKLMMNN milking machine
ACEGHIIILLMMNN milling machine
ACEGHIIKLLNRSV Granville Hicks
ACEGHIIKRSTTTT straight ticket
ACEGHIILLNOSTY histogenically
ACEGHIILNNOPST nothing special
ACEGHIILOOPSTT hepaticologist
ACEGHIILOPRSTX lexicographist
ACEGHIINNORSST right ascension
ACEGHIJKNOOSTT shooting jacket
ACEGHILLLNOOTY ethnologically
ACEGHILNNPQSTU splat quenching
ACEGHILOPPRRTY pterylographic
ACEGHILPRRSTTU turtle graphics
ACEGHINNPRSSTU purse-snatching
ACEGHIOPPRRSSU supercargoship
ACEGHKLNOOPRTY technology park
ACEGHKNNOORTTW on the wrong tack
ACEGHLMOOPSTYY metapsychology
ACEGHLNNNOOOTY nanotechnology
ACEGHLNOOPSTTU plectognathous
ACEGHMMOOPRSUY myrmecophagous
ACEGIIIKLLNOOS kinesiological
ACEGIIILMNSTTU metalinguistic
ACEGIIKMMNORRT micromarketing
ACEGIILLLOOPTY geopolitically
ACEGIILLLOSTUY eulogistically
ACEGIILLMNOORT terminological
ACEGIILLNRSSTT Stirling Castle
ACEGIILLOOORST soteriological
ACEGIILLOOOSTV sovietological✧
ACEGIILLORSSUY sacrilegiously
ACEGIILNNNOTUY uncongeniality
ACEGIILNNOTTUV conglutinative
ACEGIIMMNORRRT magnetic mirror
ACEGIINOOPRSTV Victoria sponge
ACEGIKLNORSSSW working classes
ACEGIKMNORRSST cross-marketing
ACEGIKMNSSSTTY stacking system
ACEGIKNORRSSWW corkwing wrasse
ACEGILLLMOOTYY etymologically
ACEGILLLNOORUY neurologically
ACEGILLLOOOSTY osteologically
ACEGILLLOOPRTY petrologically
ACEGILMNNOOORT conglomeration
ACEGILNOPRSSTU plastic surgeon
ACEGILPRRSSTUY plastic surgery
ACEGIMMMOPRRSU programme music
ACEGIMNNOORRST cairngorm-stone
ACEGINNNOOSSUU consanguineous
ACEGINNOOSSSTU contagiousness
ACEGINNOPRRSUU group insurance
ACEGINNOPSSSUU pugnaciousness
ACEGINNORSSSUU ungraciousness
ACEGINOPPRRSSU porcupine grass
ACEHHIIILLOSST cholelithiasis
ACEHHIIMOPSSTT Theopaschitism
ACEHHIIMRSSTTW white Christmas✧
ACEHHIINOPRRTT therianthropic
ACEHHIINOPSSUY house physician
ACEHHIJLMNNOOS Michael Johnson
ACEHHILLOOPSTY theosophically
ACEHHILLOPTTYY hypothetically
ACEHHILMORTTYY mythical theory
ACEHHILOPPRRTY hypertrophical
ACEHHIMOOPPRST metaphosphoric
ACEHHLMOOOPPST ophthalmoscope
ACEHHLNNOORSTT Charlton Heston
ACEHHMMNRSSTUY chrysanthemums
ACEHHMNOOSTTUW watch one's mouth
ACEHHMNORSTTTU turn the stomach
ACEHHMOOOPRTTU chemoautotroph
ACEHIIINNRSSTU unchristianise
ACEHIIINNRSTUZ unchristianize

ACEHIIINNTTTUY inauthenticity
ACEHIIKKNNPSTT kick in the pants
ACEHIIKMNPSTTY sympathetic ink
ACEHIILLOPSTTY polytheistical
ACEHIILLPSTUUY euphuistically
ACEHIILMNOOSTT monotheistical
ACEHIILNOOOPST opisthocoelian
ACEHIILOOPRSTT photorealistic
ACEHIIMNNOOPRT enantiomorphic
ACEHIIMORRSTTY iatrochemistry
ACEHIIMPRSSTTU music therapist
ACEHIINNOOPRSY Syrophoenician
ACEHIINNORSTTY ancient history
ACEHIINNSSTTUU unenthusiastic
ACEHIINNTTTUUY unauthenticity
ACEHIINOOPRTTU eutrophication
ACEHIINOPPRSST spinthariscope
ACEHIINOPSSTTU unsophisticate
ACEHIIOOPRSSST spirochaetosis
ACEHIIOORRSTTT osteoarthritic
ACEHILLLOPPSST phelloplastics
ACEHILLMNOPRST phallocentrism
ACEHILLMNOSWWY chimney swallow
ACEHILMNOOPRRZ chlorpromazine
ACEHILNOOPRRST hospital corner
ACEHILNORSSSUV chivalrousness
ACEHIMNOOPRRTT anthropometric
ACEHIMNOOPRSYY Eroica Symphony
ACEHIMOOPRTTUW without compare
ACEHIMOPPRSTTY spermatophytic
ACEHIMORRSSTTY astrochemistry
ACEHINNORSSSTY narcosynthesis
ACEHLLMMOORSTW Thomas Cromwell
ACEHLLMOORSSTY schoolmasterly
ACEHLNORSTTTYY Lytton Strachey
ACEHLOORRTTUWY court holy water
ACEHMOOORSTTTU tetrachotomous
ACEHNOOPPRSTUW throw up one's cap
ACEIIIILNPPRST principalities
ACEIIIINORSSTT sericitisation
ACEIIIINORSTTZ sericitization
ACEIIIKLLMRVWY William Vickrey
ACEIIIKLMNRSUW Maurice Wilkins
ACEIIILLMOPRTY military police
ACEIIILLMPTTUV multiplicative
ACEIIILLNPPRTV vital principle
ACEIIILMNOOSTT emotionalistic
ACEIIILNRRTUVY curvilinearity
ACEIIILNRSSTUV universalistic
ACEIIILNRSTTXY extrinsicality
ACEIIIMMNOORSS commissionaire
ACEIIIMMNORRTU microminiature
ACEIIIMMNTTUVY active immunity
ACEIIIMNNORSTT interactionism
ACEIIINNOOSSTT sectionisation
ACEIIINNOOSTTZ sectionization
ACEIIINNOPSSTX expansionistic
ACEIIINNORSTTT interactionist
ACEIIINOOPSTTV positive action
ACEIIINORSSTTU securitisation
ACEIIINORSTTUZ securitization
ACEIIJNOOPRSTT projectisation
ACEIIJNOOPRTTZ projectization
ACEIIKNNOORSST stick one's oar in
ACEIILLLNPPRST calliper splint
ACEIILLMNNOOOS neocolonialism
ACEIILLMNOOSTV El Misti Volcano
ACEIILLMOOPRTT metropolitical
ACEIILLMOPRTUV pluviometrical
ACEIILLMORRTUU Maurice Utrillo
ACEIILLNNOOORT Antonio Corelli
ACEIILLNNOOOST neocolonialist
ACEIILLNNOQSTU call in question
ACEIILLPSSUUUU Lucius Apuleius
ACEIILMNNNOOOT notional income
ACEIILMNNNOSTT continentalism
ACEIILMNOOPRTU peculiar motion
ACEIILMOPRSTUU opus latericium
ACEIILNNNOSSTY nonsensicality
ACEIILNNNOSTTT continentalist
ACEIILNNOOORST recolonisation
ACEIILNNOOORTZ recolonization
ACEIILNNOOPRST in loco parentis
ACEIILNNORRSTU insurrectional
ACEIILNNOSTUVV anticonvulsive
ACEIILNOOOPPRS nolo episcopari
ACEIILNOOPRRSV provincial rose
ACEIILNOOPRRTY incorporeality
ACEIILNOOPRRVY ivory-porcelain
ACEIILNOORSSTT sclerotisation
ACEIILNOORSTTZ sclerotization
ACEIILNOPRSTUY pertinaciously
ACEIILNOSSSSUV lasciviousness
ACEIIMNOOORRTT recitation-room
ACEIIMOOQRSTUV vicesimo-quarto
ACEIINNNNORSTV inconversant in
ACEIINNORRSTUX excursion train
ACEIINNOSSSTUU incautiousness
ACEIINOOPRSTTV contrapositive
ACEIINOPSSSSUU auspiciousness
ACEIKLNNOPSTTU pocket an insult
ACEILLLMORTUVY volumetrically
ACEILLMNOOSSTY colonial system
ACEILLNNNOOTVY conventionally
ACEILLNOOPRSST cross-pollinate
ACEILLNOPRSSUY supersonically
ACEILMMNORSTUY seral community
ACEILMMOORRTTU ultramicrotome
ACEILMNOOORTUV macroevolution
ACEILMNOOPRRTY contemporarily
ACEILMNORSSSUU miraculousness
ACEILNNNNOOTUV unconventional
ACEILNNNOOPSTT Constantinople
ACEILNNOOOPRST spironolactone
ACEILNOOORTUVY coevolutionary
ACEILNOOPRRTUY perlocutionary
ACEILNOOQSSSUU loquaciousness
ACEILOORRSTTUW watercolourist
ACEILORRRRSTUV recurvirostral
ACEILORRSSTTTW Sir Walter Scott
ACEIMMNNOORSTU commensuration
ACEIMNNNOOPRTU pronunciamento

ACEIMNOORRRRST narcoterrorism
ACEIMNOORRSTUV conservatorium
ACEIMNOQRSTTTU quattrocentism
ACEIMOOPSSSTTU posse comitatus
ACEIMOPPRRRSSY primary process
ACEINNNOOOOPRT non-cooperation
non-co-operation
ACEINNOOPRRSTY carry one's point
ACEINNOOPRSSTT cornet-à-pistons
ACEINNOOSTUUVW continuous wave
ACEINNORRSTUYY Tyrian cynosure
ACEINOQRSTTTTU quattrocentist
ACEINORRSSTTUY strain courtesy
ACEKLLMNORSUYZ Solly Zuckerman
ACELLMNNOOPRSU personal column
ACELLOORRSSTTU startle colours
ACELMNRSSSUUUU numerus clausus
ACELNNOSSSTTUU senatus consult
ACELRRRSTTTUUU ultrastructure
ACEMNNNOOQRSTU Norman Conquest
ACEMNOOORSSTTU entomostracous
ACEOOPPRRSSTTT spectator sport
ACFFFHIILOORTU fourth official
ACFFGHHIORRTTU through traffic
ACFFIIINOORSTT fortifications
ACFGIILLNOOPTY floating policy
ACFGIILMNNNOTU malfunctioning
ACFGIINOORSTUZ François Guizot
ACFGIMNNOORRTU contour farming
ACFHHIIINNNOTW within an inch of
ACFIIIILMNOPST simplification
ACFIIIINOQTUZZ quizzification
ACFIIILNOSTTTU stultification
ACFIIINOOPRRTT airport fiction
ACFIIINOPRSSTU Prussification
ACFIILLNNOORSV François Villon
ACFIILNNOSTTUV vital functions
ACFIIMNORRSSTT transformistic
ACFILMNORRSSUU Romulus Francis
ACFILOPRSSSSTT first-class post
ACFIMNOOORSTTT comfort station
ACGGHHIIILNNNT chain lightning
ACGGHHIMOPPRSY sphygmographic
ACGGHIJLNORSTU conjugal rights
ACGGIIILNORSUV gracious living
ACGHHHIIOPSTTY ichthyophagist
ACGHHHIOOPSTUY ichthyophagous
ACGHHIIOOPPRST opisthographic
ACGHHIJLLMNNOU John McLaughlin
ACGHHINOOSSTUZ schizognathous
ACGHHLOOORSSTW Hogwarts School
ACGHIIILNOPSTT antiphlogistic
ACGHIIKNNOSTTT stick at nothing
ACGHIILLLLOOPY philologically
ACGHIILLLLOOTY lithologically
ACGHIILLLOOSTY histologically
ACGHIILLNOOORT ornithological
ACGHIILMNOOPSY physiognomical
ACGHILLLMOOTYY mythologically
ACGHIOPPRRSTTY cryptographist
ACGIIIJLLNOSTY jingoistically
ACGIIILLLNSTUY linguistically
ACGIIILLLPSTUY pugilistically
ACGIIILMNOSSTY misogynistical
ACGIIILNNOTTXY intoxicatingly
ACGIIILNOPPRRV Gavrilo Princip
ACGIIILPRRSSTU surgical spirit
ACGIIINNNOTTUX unintoxicating
ACGIILLNPPSTUY supplicatingly
ACGIILMNOPPPTU optical pumping
ACGIILNNNOOTTU conglutination
ACGILLLOOOPRTY tropologically
ACGILNOOPRSSTY laryngoscopist
ACGINOOOPRRSTT prognosticator
ACHHILLMNRTUYY unrhythmically
ACHHILNOPSSTYY sycophantishly
ACHHILOORSTTUY ichthyolatrous
ACHHLMNOOPRSYY Choral Symphony
ACHHLMOOOPPSTY ophthalmoscopy
ACHHMMNOOORRSU mushroom-anchor
ACHIIIILMNOOPR Mario Chipolini
ACHIIIINNORSTT trichinisation
ACHIIIINNORTTZ trichinization
ACHIIILLNORSTY histrionically
ACHIIILNOORSTT chloritisation
ACHIIILNOORTTZ chloritization
ACHIIILOSSSTTY cystolithiasis
ACHIIIMMNNOOST Naomi Mitchison
ACHIIIMNOORSST trichomoniasis
ACHIIINOOPSSTT sophistication
ACHIILLLNNORTY Hillary Clinton
ACHIILLLOSTTYY histolytically
ACHIIMMNNOOORT harmonic motion
ACHIIMMOPRSSSY commissaryship
ACHIIOPRSSSTTY astrophysicist
ACHIJLNOSSSUUV Julius von Sachs
ACHIKLOPQRTTUW patchwork quilt
ACHIKNPSSSTTUU Aussichtspunkt
ACHIMMMNOOORST monochromatism
ACHIMNNOOOTUUY Cho Oyu Mountain
ACHIMNOPSSSSTU Spanish customs
ACHIOOPPRRRSTU procuratorship
ACHLMMNNOOOORS non-chromosomal
ACHLNNOORSSUYY asynchronously
ACIIIILNNRSTTY intrinsicality
ACIIIILNOOPSTT politicisation
ACIIIILNOOPTTZ politicization
ACIIIILPRSSTTU spiritualistic
ACIIILLLMPSSTY simplistically
ACIIILLMMSSTUU cum multis aliis
ACIIILLMNOPTTU multiplication
ACIIILLMOPSTTY optimistically
ACIIILNOPSSUUY inauspiciously
ACIIINNORSSTTU scrutinisation
ACIIINNORSTTUZ scrutinization
ACIILLNNOOPRRT Lincoln Airport
ACIILNNOOPSSSU Nicolas Poussin
ACIILNNOOSTTTU constitutional
ACIIMMNOOPSTTU miscomputation
ACIIMNNOPRTTUU Mount Paricutin
ACIIMNNOPSTTUU mispunctuation
ACIINNOOOPRSTT contraposition

ACIINNOPSTTTUU punctuationist
ACIKMNNOORSTUY Rocky Mountains
ACILLMMNNOOTTY non-committally
ACILLNOOQRTTUY quality control
ACILLNPRRSTUUY unscripturally
ACILMMNOORSSUU Lacus Somniorum
ACILMMOORRTTUY ultramicrotomy
ACILMOOPRRRSUY primary colours
ACILNOPRSSTUUY transpicuously
ACIMNNOOORRTTY contrary motion
ACIMNOOOPQSTUY mosquito canopy
ACIMOPRRSSTTUU corpus striatum
ACLMOOOPPRSTUY campylotropous
ADDDDEEEHLLMUY muddle-headedly
ADDDDEFFGIILLN fiddle-faddling
ADDDDEGIIMNNOW diamond wedding
ADDDEEEEHLRRTW Edward the Elder
ADDDEEEEIPRRSV Père David's deer
ADDDEEEGGLLRST straddle-legged
ADDDEEEKMNNRWY Edward M Kennedy
ADDDEEELOPRRTT dead-letter drop
ADDDEEFLNNOORT front-end loaded
ADDDEEGIMNPSTU steamed pudding
ADDDEEHHNRSTUY the Hundred Days
ADDDEEHILNORRS Rhode Island red
ADDDEEHLOORTTW dead to the world
ADDDEEINNOOORS endoradiosonde
ADDDEGHHIIIVWY divided highway
ADDEEEEFHNNRSS free-handedness
ADDEEEEFHRRRSS deferred shares
ADDEEEEHNNNSSV even-handedness
ADDEEEFHLNNSST left-handedness
ADDEEEFILLPSSS self-displeased
ADDEEEFILMNTXY extended family
ADDEEEFLMRSSTU Alfred de Musset
ADDEEEGGINNSSS disengagedness
ADDEEEGHLNNOSS long-headedness
ADDEEEGINORRRY ordinary degree
ADDEEEGNRRTTUU undergraduette
ADDEEEHILMNNVY heavenly-minded
ADDEEEHINRRSTU hidden treasure
ADDEEEHIOPRRTY Hydropterideae
ADDEEEHJNORRWY Edward John Eyre
ADDEEEHLNPSSTU Stephen Dedalus
ADDEEEHNNNOPSS open-handedness
ADDEEEIIINNNZZ Zinedine Zidane
ADDEEEIILOPRRS sidereal period
ADDEEEIKMNNSSW weak-mindedness
ADDEEEILMNOPTV development aid
ADDEEEILMPRTTY premeditatedly
ADDEEEILNNNPSS pins and needles
ADDEEEILNNRSTT landed interest
ADDEEEILNPSSSS displeasedness
ADDEEEIMNPRTTU unpremeditated
ADDEEELNNORTUY delayed neutron
ADDEEFFHLRRUUY furfuraldehyde
ADDEEFGJMNOTUY Day of Judgement
ADDEEFNNOOORST Fernando de Soto
ADDEEGGIMNNRTW wedding garment
ADDEEGHHHINNSS high-handedness
ADDEEGHILLNNSY single-handedly
ADDEEGIIILNNRS insider dealing
ADDEEGIILORTVV voltage divider
ADDEEGIIMNNORR Nadine Gordimer
ADDEEHHILPPRSS shepherd's plaid
ADDEEHHLNOOPSU hold up one's head
ADDEEHIKLNNPSS spindle-shanked
ADDEEHLNOORSTW The Woodlanders
ADDEEHMRSTTUWY muddy the waters
ADDEEHNNOOORST Hernando de Soto
ADDEEIILLRSTTW distilled water
ADDEEIILNSSTUY sustained yield
ADDEEIIMNSSSSV misadvisedness
ADDEEILMNNPRSU nil desperandum
ADDEEILNOOQSTU loaded question
ADDEEINNNORSWY nine days' wonder
ADDEEJNOOPPRSW one's jaw dropped
ADDEELMNORUWXY Edward Molyneux
ADDEELNOPPRTUU underpopulated
ADDEFGILLRRSUY disregardfully
ADDEFIILNNSSSU disdainfulness
ADDEFIIMNOORSU diamondiferous
ADDEFILMMORRRU Dial M for Murder
ADDEFKLNOOPRTU Duke of Portland
ADDEGHHIINRRTV right-hand drive
ADDEGHHINOOSTW wood nightshade
ADDEGHINNOORTW go down the drain
ADDEGIIINNRRST insider trading
ADDEGIKLNNOUWW walking wounded
ADDEGINNNRSSTU understandings
ADDEGINNORRSST standing orders
ADDEHIIILMNPSU sulphadimidine
ADDEHIIIMNOTYZ azidothymidine
ADDEHILLNOORSW Lord Howe Island
ADDEHILNOOORSW Elinor Dashwood
ADDEIIIIKLRSVW Sir David Wilkie
ADDEIIIMNOPSSS disimpassioned
ADDEILMNNORRWY narrow-mindedly
ADDEILORRRSTWY Sir Edward Tylor
ADDEIMNNOOORTX andromedotoxin
ADDEINORSSTUUV disadventurous
ADDEIOOPPRRRST trapdoor spider
ADDEIOOPRSSSTW dispose towards
ADDFGIIILMNORT fair to middling
ADDGHLOOOTTTUW would to God that
ADDGIIKLNPRRUY Rudyard Kipling
ADEEEEEGHPRRST three-speed gear
ADEEEEEGLNRRTX external degree
ADEEEEEGNNRSST degenerateness
ADEEEEEILLLNST Danielle Steele
ADEEEEFFGHKOTT take the edge off
ADEEEEFHINRSUW auf Wiedersehen
ADEEEEFIMPRRRT Pierre de Fermat
ADEEEEFJLNORTT Jean de Florette
ADEEEEGHILLNRW wheeler-dealing
ADEEEEGIJLNRSV Reginald Jeeves
ADEEEEHHLMMPST Hemel Hempstead
ADEEEEHILRRRVW rear-wheel drive
ADEEEEIILMNNST senile dementia
ADEEEEIKLMNRRW Lake Windermere
ADEEEEILMORRTT radiotelemeter
ADEEEEIMNPRRTT predeterminate

ADEEEEIORSSSTT rosette disease
ADEEEELLMNRRTY Dame Ellen Terry
ADEEEELMNRSSTT elder statesmen✧
ADEEEELMQRRTTU lettre de marque
ADEEEELNNNRRVV never-never land✧
ADEEEEMNPRSTTV desert pavement
ADEEEFFHHLNOST The Feel of Hands
ADEEEFFHILLPST Sheffield plate
ADEEEFGHHLRTTU feel the draught
ADEEEFGILORRTU Tierra del Fuego
ADEEEFGLNNNSSW newfangledness
ADEEEFHINRSSTV fives-and-threes
ADEEEFHNOOSSTY one of these days
ADEEEFIILLSTTX fixed satellite
ADEEEFILNRRSST self-restrained
ADEEEFILRRSSTV self-advertiser
ADEEEFIMNNOORT aforementioned
ADEEEFIMNNORTT after-mentioned
ADEEEFIMNPRRTT fire department
ADEEEFINNORSTT defenestration
ADEEEGGHILRTTU Gielgud Theatre
ADEEEGGILNNRSS endless gearing
ADEEEGHHMNPRRS German shepherd
ADEEEGHIIIMNTV The Divine Image
ADEEEGHIILNSSS English disease
ADEEEGHINORRRS garnishee order
ADEEEGHKOOOPSU keep a good house
ADEEEGHNNORRTT Enter the Dragon
ADEEEGIINRRTTV redintegrative
ADEEEGIKNNRRRT kindergartener
ADEEEGILLNRVVY Grenville Davey
ADEEEGILNNPPST leaden-stepping
ADEEEGILNORTTT grande toilette
ADEEEGILOQUVZZ Diego Velázquez
ADEEEGINNNRRVW wandering nerve
ADEEEGJLMNTUUV value judgement
ADEEEGLNRRSSSS regardlessness
ADEEEGOPRRRTUY daguerreotyper
ADEEEHHIILNSTW Inside the Whale
ADEEEHHILNNOTT Death on the Nile
ADEEEHHLLORTWY wholeheartedly
ADEEEHHLMORTTU leather-mouthed
ADEEEHHLNNRSTT The Netherlands
ADEEEHHMMNRRTU under the hammer
ADEEEHIINRRSST hereditariness
ADEEEHIKMNOSSU housemaid's knee
ADEEEHIKNNNOPS keep one's hand in
ADEEEHIKNOSSSS shake one's sides
ADEEEHILNNPSSS Spanish needles
ADEEEHILNOOPRT radiotelephone
ADEEEHIMNORRSV Mies van der Rohe
ADEEEHIMNPRSSU underemphasise
ADEEEHIMNPRSUZ underemphasize
ADEEEHIORRSSTT Riders to the Sea
ADEEEHJLNORRTT Dear John letter
ADEEEHMMNOPRTT Home Department
ADEEEHMNOORTTY enemy at the door
ADEEEIILLLNTVV live and let live
ADEEEIILLNPTXY expedientially
ADEEEIILMNNOSS Léonide Massine
ADEEEIILMNRTTY intermediately
ADEEEIIMMQRSUV demisemiquaver
ADEEEIIMNSSTTV meditativeness
ADEEEIINPRSTTV predestinative
ADEEEIKNPPRRST Terek sandpiper
ADEEEILLNOPRTY depletion layer
ADEEEILLNPPRSW Willesden paper
ADEEEILNOQSTUV dose equivalent
ADEEEILNPRSTUV penal servitude
ADEEEIMMNORSST immoderateness
ADEEEIMNPRRRSU premier danseur
ADEEEIMPRRSTTU distemperature
ADEEEINNRRSSST restrainedness
ADEEEINOOPRRTU Neuropteroidea
ADEEEKNPPRRSUW keep under wraps
ADEEELMNNOPRST Peter Mandelson
ADEEELNRRRSUUV surrender value
ADEEEMNNRSTTTU understatement
ADEEENNPPRRSSU unpreparedness
ADEEENNSTTTWWY sweet-and-twenty
ADEEFFFGHILRST self-affrighted
ADEEFFHIMMNNTT Fifth Amendment
ADEEFFIILLNRTY differentially
ADEEFFIINORRTT differentiator
ADEEFFLNOOSSTT flat-footedness
ADEEFGHILNNORS no hard feelings
ADEEFGHINRSSST far-sightedness
ADEEFGHORRSTTU foster-daughter
ADEEFGILNNRRSS Flinders Ranges
ADEEFGLLOOPRSU gold-of-pleasure
ADEEFGMOOORRSU for good measure
ADEEFHHHIOPSTT The Ship of Death
ADEEFHIKLLOTTV talk of the devil
ADEEFHILLNOSTU the life and soul
ADEEFHLLNORTWY the flowery land
ADEEFHNORRSSSU founders' shares
ADEEFIIKNORRTT Frankie Dettori
ADEEFIILLLRRTY field artillery
ADEEFIILLNRTWW Winifred Atwell
ADEEFILLLNOPST self-pollinated
ADEEFIMNORRSST maiden fortress
ADEEFLLLMOORWY follow-my-leader
ADEEFLLLMRSSUU Les Fleurs du Mal
ADEEFLNNNORSTY Alfred Tennyson
ADEEFLNNOPRTUY under penalty of
ADEEGGHIMNNORT dog in the manger
ADEEGGHLNOOSTT snaggle-toothed
ADEEGGIMNOORRS Gregorian modes
ADEEGHHILLRTTY light-heartedly
ADEEGHHILNOSSY highly-seasoned
ADEEGHHINNORTW wrong in the head
ADEEGHHLPRSSSS shepherd's glass
ADEEGHHNOOOSTV have the goods on
ADEEGHIIKLMNNT naked-light mine
ADEEGHIILLNRTW willing-hearted
ADEEGHILNRSSTU daughterliness
ADEEGHINRRSTTW wreathed string
ADEEGHIPPPRSUY pseudepigraphy
ADEEGHNNOPRRTU Uther Pendragon
ADEEGIIIKNSSSS kissing disease
ADEEGIIINRSTTV disintegrative
ADEEGIIMNNOPTT depigmentation

Words marked ✧ can also be spelled with one or more capital letters

ADEEGIINNOPRST predesignation
ADEEGIINNORRTT redintegration
ADEEGIINNSTTUV uninvestigated
ADEEGIINORRSTT deregistration
ADEEGILNNNORSY Algernon Sidney
ADEEGILOOOSSST Osteoglossidae
ADEEGILOPPRTTY pterygoid plate
ADEEGINOORRSST derogatoriness
ADEEGINOPRRSTY predesignatory
ADEEGINRSSTTUU tertius gaudens
ADEEGJLMNNNOTU non-judgemental
ADEEGLLLMNNOTY old-gentlemanly
ADEEGLLNOPRSSW Oswald Spengler
ADEEGLNOPRRSUU pleasure ground
ADEEHHHNNOORTT on the other hand
ADEEHHIILMOPRS hemispheroidal
ADEEHHLNORRTTU Leonhard Hutter
ADEEHHNOORRTUW water horehound
ADEEHHOORTTWWY woe worth the day
ADEEHIIILMPPRY hyperlipidemia
ADEEHIIIPRSTTW tidewaitership
ADEEHIKKMMORUV Irek Mukhamedov
ADEEHIKLLLRSTY The Ladykillers
ADEEHILLORTTVW drive to the wall
ADEEHILMNNRSTT disenthralment
ADEEHILNNNOOSS lie on one's hands
ADEEHILNOOPRTY radiotelephony
ADEEHILORSSTTU horse latitudes
ADEEHILORSSTUV side horse vault
ADEEHIMNSSTTUY The Sunday Times
ADEEHINNNORSTY Sir Anthony Eden
ADEEHLLORRSTTY Lord Hattersley
ADEEHLMNOORRSY dysmenorrhoeal
ADEEHLMORRRTTU Le Morte d'Arthur
ADEEHLORSTTTUY stout-heartedly
ADEEHMNNNOSSSU unhandsomeness
ADEEHNOOPRRSTZ trapezohedrons
ADEEIIIMNNORTT intermediation
ADEEIIINORSSST radiosensitise
ADEEIIINORSSTV radiosensitive
ADEEIIINORSSTZ radiosensitize
ADEEIILLLOOTTZ Eliza Doolittle
ADEEIILMNNNOOS one-dimensional
ADEEIILMNNOTVY denominatively
ADEEIILMNRTTUU teleradium unit
ADEEIILNNNORST non-residential
ADEEIILNNRSSUV island universe
ADEEIILNOSSSSW Wilson's disease
ADEEIILNPSSTVY dispensatively
ADEEIILPQSSTUY sesquipedality
ADEEIIMMOOPRTV imperative mood
ADEEIIMNNNRSTT disentrainment
ADEEIIMNNOOSTT demonetisation
ADEEIIMNNOOTTZ demonetization
ADEEIIMNORRTTY intermediatory
ADEEIINNNORSST inordinateness
ADEEIINNOPRSTT predestination
ADEEIJLMNOORTU Romeo and Juliet
ADEEIKMMNNOPSU make up one's mind
ADEEILLNNORTTU Lord Lieutenant
ADEEILLNNRSSTU ill-naturedness
ADEEILNNOOSSTV devotionalness
ADEEILNNRRSTUY unrestrainedly
ADEEILNORRSSWW world-weariness
ADEEIMMNQRSTUU terminus ad quem
ADEEIMNNOPRRST Modern Painters
ADEEIMNNORRSST arrondissement
ADEEIMNSSSTTUY unsystematised
ADEEIMNSSTTUYZ unsystematized
ADEEIOOPRRSTVW operative words
ADEELLLNOOORWY Leonard Woolley
ADEELLNOOPRRWY woollen-drapery
ADEELMMNOORRYY read only memory
ADEELNNOOOPRTZ Lorenzo Da Ponte
ADEELNNOPPRRTY preponderantly
ADEELNNORSSSSU slanderousness
ADEEMNNNORRUWY Newry and Mourne
ADEEMNNPPSSTUY suspend payment
ADEEMNORRSSYYZ Sézary syndrome
ADEEMOOORSSTTU osteodermatous
ADEENOPQRRRTUU quarter-pounder
ADEFFGHINNORTU founding father
ADEFFGILORSSST flag of distress
ADEFFHILLNOSUY fully-fashioned
ADEFFIJNNNORST Fridtjof Nansen
ADEFGHHILNOTTY lady of the night
ADEFGHIMOORRTY fairy godmother
ADEFGIIKLNNOTY floating kidney
ADEFGIIMNORRST transmogrified
ADEFGILLNORSUU glanduliferous
ADEFGILMNNNRSU Alfred Munnings
ADEFHIIIKKLNRS drink like a fish
ADEFHIKLMNOOTU Duke of Hamilton
ADEFHINOOOORTT a foot in the door
ADEFHINOORRTTU for the duration
ADEFHLLLOORRTW for all the world
ADEFHMNOORSSTU master of hounds
ADEFHNNNOOORSW for one's own hand
ADEFHNOOORRSVW have no words for
ADEFIIINNOSSTT disinfestation
ADEFIILMMNNORT Milton Friedman
ADEFIILMNNNORW Wilfred Mannion
ADEFIILMNORRTW manifold-writer
ADEFIIMNNORRSS Sir Denis Forman
ADEFIINNOOORRT foreordination
ADEFIINOSSSSTU fastidiousness
ADEFILLNNOOSST Lofoten Islands
ADEGGGHHORTTUU grudge a thought
ADEGGHHINORTTU thought-reading
ADEGGHIINNRSTT riding the stang
ADEGGHIKNNORTU kneading-trough
ADEGGIILNNRSST leading strings
ADEGGILLNRSSSU sluggardliness
ADEGHHLLNNOOYY Lloyd Honeyghan
ADEGHHLLNOOSSW Sheldon Glashow
ADEGHHLNOPSSTU plough the sands
ADEGHIIJLMOPRS Joseph Grimaldi
ADEGHIILMNRTTU multithreading
ADEGHIINOOSTTW a wise thing to do
ADEGHILMNRSSTU English mustard
ADEGHILNNOPRTT holding pattern
ADEGHILNNOPRTU hunting leopard

	hunting-leopard
ADEGHILNOOPRST	The Prodigal Son
ADEGHIMMOPRRRT	third-programme
ADEGHINNOPPSSX	sex-and-shopping
ADEGHNOPRRSSTU	draughtsperson
ADEGIIIINNNOST	indigenisation
ADEGIIIINNNOTZ	indigenization
ADEGIIILMNNRUU	Miguel Indurain
ADEGIIILNNPRVW	prevailing wind
ADEGIIINNORSTT	disintegration
ADEGIIINNOSTTV	tendovaginitis
ADEGIIKLMMNNOR	mineral kingdom
ADEGIIILLMNPRSY	pyramid selling
ADEGIILLNNOOPV	Golden Pavilion
ADEGIILLOPRTTT	digital plotter
ADEGIILNNPRSUY	undespairingly
ADEGIILNOPSSSU	pulse diagnosis
ADEGIILNRSSSST	distress signal
ADEGIIMNOQRSUU	quadrigeminous
ADEGIJNPRRRUYZ	Grand Jury Prize
ADEGIKMNNORRSU	make rings round
ADEGILLNOPTTUY	plead not guilty
ADEGILNNOQRSUV	silver quandong
ADEGILNOOORRUY	neuroradiology
ADEGINNPPRRSTU	understrapping
ADEHHIILNOOPRT	Ornithodelphia
ADEHIILNNOPSSX	Phoenix Islands
ADEHIIMOPRRSST	Sir Thomas Pride
ADEHIINNRSTTWW	straw in the wind
ADEHILNNOORRTW	in another world
ADEHILNNOSSSTU	outlandishness
ADEHILNOPRSTUU	desulphuration
ADEHIMNNPRSSTU	huntsman spider
ADEHIMOOOPPRSS	paedomorphosis
ADEHIMOOORTTUW	without more ado
ADEHINNNOOSSST	sit on one's hands
ADEHINOORRSSTW	roadworthiness
ADEHJLNOORSSUY	Joshua Reynolds
ADEHJMNOPPPSTU	hop, step and jump
ADEHLNORRSSTUV	Luther Vandross
ADEHLOORRSSTYY	Dorothy L Sayers
ADEHMMMOOORSUW	meadow mushroom
ADEHNORRSSTTWW	north-westwards
ADEHORSSSTTUWW	south-westwards
ADEIIILLNORSTT	redistillation
ADEIIILLNSTUVV	Viti Levu Island
ADEIIILMNNORST	tridimensional
ADEIIINNOORSTT	disorientation
ADEIIINNOPRSVZ	panzer division
ADEIIINOPRSTTU	repudiationist
ADEIILLNOPRTVY	providentially
ADEIILMNNNOOSX	Mason-Dixon Line
ADEIILMNNOOSTW	two-dimensional
ADEIILNNNORSSY	Sir Sidney Nolan
ADEIILNOPRSSTY	dispensatorily
ADEIILNOSTTUVY	adventitiously
ADEIIMNNOPPSTT	disappointment
ADEIJLLNOOOTTW	Joan Littlewood
ADEILNNOORRSUV	universal donor
ADEILNNORSSTUW	untowardliness
ADEIMNORSSTUUV	misadventurous
ADEINOOORRTTTX	dextrorotation
ADEINOPRRRRSTT	transport rider
ADEKLMNOSSTTWY	talk-down system
ADELLOORRSSWWW	sword-swallower
ADELMNOOORSSSU	malodorousness
ADEMNNOPRSSTTU	stand upon terms
ADEOOORRRTTTXY	dextrorotatory
ADFFHNNOORRSUU	ruff and honours
ADFFIILNNOPSTU	diffusion plant
ADFGGIINNNOORT	toing and froing
ADFGIKLNOOORRW	forward-looking
ADFHLLMOOOOPPT	photoflood lamp
ADFIIIMNNOORST	disinformation
ADFILNOOOORRSU	Orlando Furioso
ADFINNOOOPSTTU	foundation-stop
ADFLMOOOORSTWW	salt of wormwood
ADGGGHOORSSTYY	shaggy-dog story
ADGGHOOORSSSTT	dog's-tooth grass
ADGGIIILLLMNOW	William Golding
ADGGIIKNNORRWW	working drawing
ADGGIMNNOPRSTU	stamping-ground
ADGGINNNOPRSUW	spawning-ground
ADGHHIILNOTTWX	withholding tax
ADGHLNNOORSSST	longs and shorts
ADGHMNNOOPRRYY	gynandromorphy
ADGIIIINNNPRSU	Indian Uprising
ADGIIIINNSTTTU	attitudinising
ADGIIIINNTTTUZ	attitudinizing
ADGIIIINOPRRRT	drip irrigation
ADGIIILNNORSTW	lords in waiting
ADGIILLLNNOTUY	longitudinally
ADGIILMOOPRSTY	pyramidologist
ADGIILNOPPRSVY	disapprovingly
ADGINNNORRRSUU	run rings around
ADHHIMPRRSUVYY	Sir Humphry Davy
ADHHLMOOOPPSTU	podophthalmous
ADHHNOORSTTTUU	stouth and routh
ADHIILMNOOPXYY	hypomixolydian
ADHIIMMMMNRTUU	Urim and Thummim
ADHIJKMNOPPPSU	hop, skip and jump
ADHIKLOOORRRST	Sir Harold Kroto
ADHMNOORRSTUWW	marsh woundwort
ADIIIILNOQSSTU	disquisitional
ADIIIILOQRTTUY	liquidity ratio
ADIIILLNORSSUY	disillusionary
ADIIILMNOOOSTT	dolomitisation
ADIIILMNOOOTTZ	dolomitization
ADIIIMNNNNOOOPR	monoprionidian
ADIIKLNNOOSSTU	Dakin's solution
ADIILLOPRRSSTU	Lords Spiritual
ADIILMOOPPRRSU	primordial soup
ADIILNOPRSSTTU	postindustrial
ADIILOPSSTTUUY	disputatiously
ADIIMNOORRSTTU	radio-strontium
ADILLMNNOOOSSS	Solomon Islands
ADIMOOPPRRSSTT	Sir Tom Stoppard
ADINNNSSTTUUWX	'twixt sun and sun
AEEEEEGLNRRRSV	general reserve
AEEEEEKLPRRSSU	pleasure-seeker
AEEEEEMNNRRSTV	en ventre sa mère
AEEEEFFIMNNSST	effeminateness

AEEEEFHLMNOPTV Temple of Heaven
AEEEEFHLMOPRRT peer of the realm
AEEEEFLNOORSTV overeat oneself
AEEEEFLPPRRRUV puerperal fever
AEEEEGGILMNNRT general meeting
AEEEEGHHHIOTVV give the heave-ho
AEEEEGILNRRTVY regeneratively
AEEEEGINSSTTVV vegetativeness
AEEEEGMMNNOTVV Geneva movement
AEEEEGNOQRRSUZ orange-squeezer
AEEEEHHLNSSTTV The Seventh Seal
AEEEEHKNNORTTW water on the knee
AEEEEHMNNPRTTT permanent teeth
AEEEEILMNNRSST elementariness
AEEEEINNPRRTTT interpenetrate
AEEEEINNRSSTTV inveterateness
AEEEEINPRRSTTV representative
AEEEELLNPRRTTW water-repellent
AEEEELLRRRSTTV traveller's tree
AEEEEMNOPRSTTZ temperate zones
AEEEFFGIMNORTY affine geometry
AEEEFFLLNNOOST fall on one's feet
AEEEFGGILNNRST self-generating
AEEEFGHHLLOSTT The Gates of Hell
AEEEFGHLOOPTTU top of the league
AEEEFGILLNOPZZ Felipe González
AEEEFGILLNOSSY Isle of Anglesey
AEEEFGILNPRRSV relapsing fever
AEEEFGINOPRSTW Siege of Antwerp
AEEEFHHLLLORRT hell for leather
AEEEFHHLLNOTWY a fly on the wheel
AEEEFHHLNNPRTY three-halfpenny
AEEEFHLNRSSSST fatherlessness
AEEEFIILMNSSTV sensitive flame
AEEEFIILNNRRTT interferential
AEEEFILLNORSTV self-revelation
AEEEFILLNPRRTY preferentially
AEEEFLLOPRSSUY please yourself
AEEEFLLORRSTVY self-revelatory
AEEEFLMMNPRTTU temperamentful
AEEEFLMNSSSSST self-assessment
AEEEFLMOQRRTTU letter-of-marque
AEEEGGGIMNNNRT engagement ring
AEEEGGIKMMNRRT emerging market
AEEEGGILNNRSTV steel engraving
AEEEGGIMNNRSTT Strange Meeting
AEEEGGINRSSSSV aggressiveness
AEEEGGLNNORRSU surgeon general
AEEEGGLNORRTUY regulatory gene
AEEEGGLPRSSSTY sleepy staggers
AEEEGHHILLSTVW high-level waste
AEEEGHHINRTVVY have everything
AEEEGHHIOPRRRS heresiographer
AEEEGHHIOPRTTW great white hope
AEEEGHHNRRRTTU hunter-gatherer
AEEEGHIIKNPRTT keep a tight rein
AEEEGHILMNPPRT pamphleteering
AEEEGHILMNRSUW measuring-wheel
AEEEGHILMORTTX go the extra mile
AEEEGHILNRSTTV the everlasting✧
AEEEGHLMNNRSTU gentleman usher
AEEEGHLNPRSTTT grasp the nettle
AEEEGIILLRRSTY siege-artillery
AEEEGIILMNSSTT legitimateness
AEEEGIILMNSTTY siege mentality
AEEEGIILNNRSTT large intestine
AEEEGIILPRRTVW water privilege
AEEEGIINQTTUVY negative equity
AEEEGILMNNOOTU Eugenio Montale
AEEEGILMOPRRSU Primrose League
AEEEGILMRSTUUU Auguste Lumière
AEEEGILNNNRRTY internal energy
AEEEGILNRRRSVY reversing layer
AEEEGILRRRTTUY grey literature
AEEEGIMNOOSTTT get someone at it
AEEEGIOPRRSTUV supererogative
AEEEGLLNNNNSUZ Suzanne Lenglen
AEEEGLNOPPRRSU general-purpose
AEEEHHHILMMPRT hephthemimeral
AEEEHHHILNORTT hole in the heart
AEEEHHHINNSSST heathenishness
AEEEHHIJRSTTTV have the jitters
AEEEHHIMRRTTUX heather mixture
AEEEHHINOPRTTX Phoenix Theatre
AEEEHHKNOPRSST Hesketh Pearson
AEEEHHLLNSSSST healthlessness
AEEEHHLMNNOSTY Henley-on-Thames
AEEEHHOPPRRTTW weather prophet
AEEEHIILORRTTV Olivier Theatre
AEEEHIINNPPRSV inapprehensive
AEEEHIKNNOOPRS keep one's hair on
AEEEHIKNPRSTTU take up the reins
AEEEHILLLMMNRV Herman Melville
AEEEHILNPPRSVY apprehensively
AEEEHILNPRTTVY hyperventilate
AEEEHILNRSTTTW The Winter's Tale
AEEEHIMNNRSTTT man in the street
AEEEHINNPPRSUV unapprehensive
AEEEHINSSSTUVX exhaustiveness
AEEEHIPRRRSTUV River Euphrates
AEEEHJKLNNOPRS Johannes Kepler
AEEEHKLLNPRRST shark repellent
AEEEHKLNNRRTTU Kathleen Turner
AEEEHKLOPRRSUY keep early hours
AEEEHKLRSSTTTW walk the streets
AEEEHLLRRTTTUY leathery turtle
AEEEHLMOPRRSTT The Last Emperor
AEEEHLORSSTTTU The Lotus-Eaters
AEEEHNNOORSSTT set one's heart on
AEEEIILLNPRTXY experientially
AEEEIILLNRSSTT illiterateness
AEEEIILMMNNRSS melamine resins
AEEEIILMNNSSTT sentimentalise
AEEEIILMNNSSTV alimentiveness
AEEEIILMNNSTTZ sentimentalize
AEEEIILNRRSSTV irrelativeness
AEEEIILRRRTVWY Literary Review
AEEEIIMNPRSSTV imperativeness
AEEEIINPRRTTTV interpretative
AEEEIKLLMNNSVY Nevil Maskelyne
AEEEILLMNPRTXY experimentally
AEEEILLNPRSTTU Pauline Letters

AEEEILLNSSSTT stainless steel
AEEEILLORSTTTT ottrelite-slate
AEEEILMNNPRSTT presentimental
AEEEILMNOPRTTU Mitteleuropean
Mittel-European
AEEEILMNORRTTV intervalometer
AEEEILMNORSTUV vitreous enamel
AEEEILMNPPRRTW water pimpernel
AEEEILNOPRSTUV superelevation
AEEEILNORRRSUZ La Resurrezione
AEEEILNPRSSSTU superessential
AEEEIMMMNRSSTU mismeasurement
AEEEIMNNRRTUUV unremunerative
AEEEIMNOPRTTXY extemporaneity
AEEEINNNOPRTTV non-penetrative
AEEEINNNPRRTTT interpenetrant
AEEEINNOPRRSTT representation
AEEEINPRSSSSUV persuasiveness
AEEEIOOPRRRTTV retro-operative
AEEEJNPRSTTTYY petty serjeanty
AEEEKNOOOSSTTT take to one's toes
AEEELLOPRSSSTU Pasteurelloses
AEEELNNOPRSTTU enteropneustal
AEEELNOOPRRSST personal stereo
AEEELNPRRSSSSY prayerlessness
AEEEMNNPPRRSST permanent press
AEEEMNOOPRSTUX extemporaneous
AEEENNORSSSTUX extraneousness
AEEENQSSSSTTUU statuesqueness
AEEFFFIMORRRRT tariff reformer
AEEFFGILLLNSTV levelling-staff
AEEFFGILLLORSU flagelliferous
AEEFFGILLNRSTT self-flattering
AEEFFGMNORSSUW women's suffrage
AEEFFHILLMOOSU house of ill fame
AEEFFIILORSTTY Sea of Fertility
AEEFFIIMNRSSTU rime suffisante
AEEFFLRRRSSTUY Rafferty's rules
AEEFGGHJNNORSU Johannes Fugger
AEEFGGHOORSSTY grey-goose shaft
AEEFGGIINNORST get one's fairing
AEEFGGILLNRSTU self-regulating
AEEFGHHILRSTTT stealth fighter
AEEFGHHINRRSTT three-farthings
AEEFGHJLLNOTUW law of the jungle
AEEFGHKNOORRTY Gareth of Orkney
AEEFGIILLNNPSX self-explaining
AEEFGIIMMNRRST ferrimagnetism
AEEFGIINRSSTUV figurativeness
AEEFGILLLORSWY sea gillyflower
AEEFGILLNORSTU self-regulation
AEEFGIMMNORRST ferromagnetism
AEEFGLLORRSTUY self-regulatory
AEEFGLNNRSSTUU ungratefulness
AEEFGLNORSSSTW St Agnes's flower
AEEFGLRRSSTTUY Fergus Slattery
AEEFHHLNNOPSVY shove-halfpenny
AEEFHILNNNPRSU Ranulph Fiennes
AEEFHILOORRSVZ Zhores I Alferov
AEEFHLLLMMOPST smell of the lamp
AEEFHLLOPPRRST propeller shaft
AEEFHMMMNNOOTT man of the moment
AEEFHNOORSSSTU The Four Seasons
AEEFHOORRSSSTW Wars of the Roses
AEEFIILMNPRRTU tuner amplifier
AEEFIILMOPPRRW power-amplifier
AEEFIILNNOPRRU infopreneurial
AEEFIILNOQQTUU quinquefoliate
AEEFIIMNOOQTTU equation of time
AEEFILMNNOORZZ mezzanine floor
AEEFIMNOOPRRRT pre-Reformation
AEEFINOOPRSTTU superfoetation
AEEFIOPRRRSSTU ferroprussiate
AEEFLLLMOOOPPT Temple of Apollo
AEEFLLNOOOPSTW at one fell swoop
AEEFLMNOOOPTTW footplatewomen
AEEFLMNOORSTTW woman of letters
AEEGGHHNORRRTU Arthur Honegger
AEEGGHIKLNPTTU gleg in the uptak
AEEGGHIMNNNORR Hermann Goering
AEEGGHINOORRRS George Harrison
AEEGGIILLMRTUV Maggie Tulliver
AEEGGIILNPRSUV pleasure-giving
AEEGGIINORSSTT segregationist
AEEGGILNNOOSSV Love Songs in Age
AEEGGILNORSTVV revolving stage
AEEGGINNOORRST Gregorian tones
AEEGGINORRSSSU gregariousness
AEEGGIOSSTTUUV auto-suggestive
AEEGHHIKNNPSTW Stephen Hawking
AEEGHHILNNORTW Nigel Hawthorne
AEEGHHLOOPPRTT phototelegraph
telephotograph
AEEGHHLORSSTUU slaughterhouse
AEEGHIIILMPRTW imperial weight
AEEGHIIKLMNOST something like a
AEEGHIILNNRSTW training wheels
AEEGHIIPRRRSST parish register
AEEGHIKMNNNRTU make the running
AEEGHILLNOPSSS pinhole glasses
AEEGHILNNOOPTY pile on the agony
AEEGHILNOOSSTY anesthesiology
AEEGHILNOPPTUY pile up the agony
AEEGHILNRSSTUY Estuary English
AEEGHINNORSSTY there's no saying
AEEGHINRSSTTTW watertightness
AEEGHLNNNOPSTT Stephen Langton
AEEGHLNNRTTTUU run the gauntlet
AEEGIIILLLMTTY illegitimately
AEEGIIILLLNNTT intelligential
AEEGIIILLNNRST inertia selling
AEEGIIILLNNSTT intelligentsia
AEEGIIILLNNTTZ intelligentzia
AEEGIIINNORSST greisenisation
AEEGIIINNORSTZ greisenization
AEEGIIKNNNRSTT Saint Kentigern
AEEGIILMNORSSS generalissimos
AEEGIILNNNRTTY entertainingly
AEEGIILNNOORRT Oriental Region
AEEGIILNORRSTV visitor general
AEEGIIMMNOPSTZ piezomagnetism
AEEGIIMNNNORTU mountaineering

AEEGIIMNOORSTT geometrisation
AEEGIIMNOORTTZ geometrization
AEEGIINNNNRTTU unentertaining
AEEGIINNOOPRTT prenegotiation
AEEGIINORRSTTV tergiversation
AEEGIINORSTTVY seronegativity
AEEGIKNNOPSSTU speak in tongues
AEEGILMNOPRTUV Protevangelium
AEEGILNNOORSTT lost generation
AEEGILNNOOSSSU oleaginousness
AEEGILNNORRRSW senior wrangler
AEEGILNNRRSSTT Ernest Starling
AEEGIMMNNOPTVV moving pavement
AEEGIMNRRRTUWZ Gewürztraminer
AEEGIMNSSSTTWY sweating system
AEEGINNOOPRTTV negative proton
AEEGINOOPRRSTU supererogation
AEEGINOORSTTTU uterogestation
AEEGINOPRRRSUZ organizer-purse
AEEGIORRRSTTVY tergiversatory
AEEGLLMNNORTVY governmentally
AEEGLLNNOOSSST on one's last legs
AEEGMMMMPRSUUU Pergamum Museum
AEEGMNOOORRRTT motor generator
AEEGMNOOPRSSSU grass someone up
AEEGMNOOPRSSTU spermatogenous
AEEGNOORSSSTUU outrageousness
AEEGOOPRRRSTUY supererogatory
AEEHHIIITTTTWW whittie-whattie
AEEHHILLMORSTT heterothallism
AEEHHILOPSTUUW Paul Whitehouse
AEEHHINNOORTTW one with another
AEEHHLLOOPRSTV all over the shop
AEEHHLMMOOPRTT ophthalmometer
AEEHHMNOOOPRRY hypomenorrhoea
AEEHHOPPPRSSTU superphosphate
AEEHIIILLLTWWW Willie Whitelaw
AEEHIIILNPPPPT Philippe Pétain
AEEHIIKMOOPRRT Emperor Akihito
AEEHIILLNNOTTY lay it on the line
AEEHIILMMNRTTY trimethylamine
AEEHIILMNNPRTY triphenylamine
AEEHIILNNPSTTU lieutenantship
AEEHIILNPPRRTU peripheral unit
AEEHIILOPQTTUU haute politique
AEEHIILPRRSSTU Ithuriel's spear
AEEHIIMPRSSTTU serum hepatitis
AEEHIINNNOPPRS inapprehension
AEEHIJNNOPRSST Saint-John Perse
AEEHIKOPRRSSTY hyperkeratosis
AEEHILLMNOTTTW the little woman
AEEHILLMRSSSTW Wilhelmstrasse
AEEHILLNORSSSV all-overishness
AEEHILLORRRSTY horse artillery
AEEHILMNOOSTTZ Simon the Zealot
AEEHILMNPRRRTT thermal printer
AEEHILMNPRRTTU turpeth mineral
AEEHILPRRRSTTU stirrup leather
AEEHIMMNOOPRST pantomime horse
AEEHIMNOPSTTTT The Temptations
AEEHIMORSTTUUW without measure
AEEHINNOPRRTVY Henry IV Part One
Henry VI Part One
AEEHINNORSTTWY not any the wiser
AEEHINPPPPRRSW whippersnapper
AEEHKLORRRSTTU Arthur Koestler
AEEHKMNOPRTTTU put on the market
AEEHLMNNORRTTU thermal neutron
AEEHLMNOORRTTT thermotolerant
AEEHLOPPPRSSUY pleurapophyses
AEEHLOPPRRSTTT latter prophets
AEEHMOOORSSTTU heterosomatous
AEEIIIKKLNSTTV at it like knives
AEEIIILLMMNSSW William Siemens
AEEIIILMMMMORT time immemorial
AEEIIILMNOSSTT testimonialise
AEEIIILMNOSTTZ testimonialize
AEEIIILMNRRSSW Sir Lewis Namier
AEEIIILMNSSTTX existentialism
AEEIIILNNNORTT interlineation
AEEIIILNSSTTTX existentialist
AEEIIILORRRSTT territorialise
AEEIIILORRRTTZ territorialize
AEEIIIMNNNNOTV innominate vein
AEEIILLLNPSTTY pestilentially
AEEIILLMNNSSTT small intestine
AEEIILLNNOPPTT plenipotential
AEEIILLNNOPRTT interpellation
AEEIILMMNNOPTT implementation
AEEIILMMNNSSTT sentimentalism
AEEIILMNNNPRSY penny-a-linerism
AEEIILMNNOSSTX extensionalism
AEEIILMNNSSTTT sentimentalist
AEEIILMNNSTTTY sentimentality
AEEIILNNNORTTV interventional
AEEIILNNORRSVY inversion layer
AEEIILNNOSTTXY extensionality
AEEIILNNPSSTTV sensitive plant
AEEIILNNQSSTTU quintessential
AEEIILNQRSSTUU Tequila Sunrise
AEEIILNRSTTUXY intersexuality
AEEIILNRSTUVYY Yale University
AEEIILPRTTUVVY vituperatively
AEEIIMNNOORSTT remonetisation
AEEIIMNNOORTTZ remonetization
AEEIIMNOORSTTV overestimation
AEEIIMORRRRRVW rear-view mirror
AEEIINNOPPSSST inappositeness
AEEIINNOPRRTTT interpretation
AEEIINNORSSTTW westernisation
AEEIINNORSTTWZ westernization
AEEIINNRSSSTTV transitiveness
AEEIJLLMNORSTU telejournalism
AEEIJLLNORSTTU telejournalist
AEEIKKLOOPSSTW swoopstake-like
swoop-stake-like
AEEIKMNOPRRSSX expression mark
AEEIKMNRSSSSST risk assessment
AEEILLLNOSTTTW tell its own tale
AEEILLMMNNOSUU Lenin Mausoleum
AEEILLMMOORTVY volatile memory
AEEILLMNOOPRTT metalloprotein

AEEILLNNRSSSTT slatternliness
AEEILLOPRSSSTU Pasteurellosis
AEEILLPPRRTTTT prittle-prattle
AEEILMMNNORRTY internal memory
AEEILMNNNNRSSU unmannerliness
AEEILMNNOOOSST on someone's tail
AEEILNNOORSSTT listen to reason
AEEILNOORTTTXY extortionately
AEEIMNOOPPPRRS properispomena
AEEIMNOQRSSTTU question master
AEEINNOOPRSSTU up to one's ears in
AEEINNPPPPRRSS snipper-snapper
AEEINQRRRSTTUW winter quarters
AEEJKKOPRRUWYY joukery-pawkery
AEEKKLOOPSTVVY Petko Slaveykov
AEELLLMNPPSTUY supplementally
AEELLMNORSSSUV marvellousness
AEELNOORSSTTUW Waterloo Sunset
AEEMOOPRRSSTTY system operator
AEEMOPPRRRSTTY property master
AEENNOOORRSSST rest on one's oars
AEEOORSSSSTTTT Ettore Sottsass
AEEOPPRRRSSUUV vapour pressure
AEFFFINOPRRSSU pair of snuffers
AEFFGIILNNORTT not lift a finger
AEFFGIILNSSSTY self-satisfying
AEFFHILNNSSTUU unfaithfulness
AEFFIILPPPRSTU a stiff upper lip
AEFFIIMNOORRSU foraminiferous
AEFGGIIINNNPRT finger-painting
AEFGGNOORRSSYY Gregory of Nyssa
AEFGHHILLNORRY harrying of hell
AEFGHHIMNORSTT The Rights of Man
AEFGHIILMPRRST Pilgrim Fathers
AEFGHIIMNNRRSS fisherman's ring
AEFGHILLLNNOTW half-wellington
AEFGIILMNOSTTV self-motivating
AEFGIILNNSSSTU self-sustaining
AEFGIILNOORRSW Wars of Religion
AEFGIILNOSSSTU flagitiousness
AEFGIIMORSSTTU stigmatiferous
AEFGIINOORRRST roaring forties
AEFGIKLLLNORTV travelling folk
AEFGILLNNRTTUY unflatteringly
AEFGILNOOORRTW Rogation flower
AEFGIMNOPRRRST performing arts
AEFHHIILMNOSST a host in himself
AEFHHLNNOPRTWY halfpennyworth
AEFHIILMNNRTUY run in the family
AEFHIILNNOPRTY hyperinflation
AEFHIIMNOORSTT hesitation form
AEFHIINNNOOPST pin one's faith on
AEFHILNORRTTUV fourth interval
AEFHINNORSSTTY St Anthony's fire
AEFHKLNNNSSTUU unthankfulness
AEFHKMOOORRSTZ The Mask of Zorro
AEFHLLLORTTTTU at full throttle
AEFHMNNOOOTTWW woman of the town
AEFHMOOPRRSTTT for the most part
AEFIIKMNRSSSWY Swiss army knife
AEFIILLLMOOTTU multifoliolate
AEFIILLMMNOOST self-immolation
AEFIILLMNOSTTU self-mutilation
AEFIIILMNOOSTTV self-motivation
AEFIIILNRSSSUVY Sylvian fissure
AEFIIMNOORRSTT reformationist
AEFIINOQQRSUUU quinquefarious
AEFILLMOORRSTU multiflora rose
AEFILLNNOOOSWW a will of one's own
AEFILLNOOPRSSY professionally
AEFILLOOPRRSSY professorially
AEFILMNOPSSSTU self-assumption
AEFILNNOOPRSSU unprofessional
AEFILNORRSTUUY it's your funeral
AEFIMMORSSTXYY axis of symmetry
AEFIMNNOORRSTW frontierswoman
AEFKNOOPRSTTUU speak out of turn
AEFLLMNNOOSTWW fellow townsman
AEFMNNOOOOORSW A Room of One's Own
AEFNNNNOORSTUY Sunny Afternoon
AEGGGIILLNNRSY singing-gallery
AEGGHHLNNOSSTU Langston Hughes
AEGGHHOOPPRTYY phytogeography
AEGGHIIINNRTTW weight-training
AEGGHIILMNSSTT steaming lights
AEGGHINNOOPRTV photo-engraving
AEGGHINORRTTUW watering-trough
AEGGHLLLNOOSTT go to all lengths
AEGGHNNOOPRRTY röntgenography
AEGGIIILMNPSTT splitting image
AEGGIILLNNNRWY winning-gallery
AEGGIILMNNPRST spring ligament
AEGGIILNNOPRSS Singapore Sling
AEGGILOOORSSTT astrogeologist
AEGGINOOSSTTUU auto-suggestion
AEGHHILLOPRSUW Sir Hugh Walpole
AEGHHILLORSSTW laser-light show
AEGHHLMOPPRSTY plethysmograph
AEGHIIILLNNNPS in plain English
AEGHIIILNNSTTT sting in the tail
AEGHIILLNOPSST polishing-slate
AEGHIILLOPRSST legislatorship
AEGHIILNNSTTUY unhesitatingly
AEGHIILNOPPSST polishing-paste
AEGHIIMNNOOOST homogenisation
AEGHIIMNNOOOTZ homogenization
AEGHIKLMNPRSTT Knights Templar
AEGHIKNNRRRTTY knight errantry
AEGHILMNNOOPST smoothing plane
AEGHILMNPRRSST thermal springs
AEGHILMOORSTTU rheumatologist
AEGHILNOPRRSST personal rights
AEGHILOOPPRSTY epistolography
AEGHIMMMNORTUU omnium-gatherum
AEGHIMNNORRRSY Sir Henry Morgan
AEGHINOOOPPRRS sporangiophore
AEGHINOOQRSSTU square shooting
AEGHLLMOOPPRSY megasporophyll
AEGHLLORSSTUUY slaughterously
AEGHLNOOOPRTUY neuropathology
AEGHLNOPRTTWWY Gwyneth Paltrow
AEGHMMOOPRRTTY photogrammetry

AEGHMNNORRRSTY Henry Armstrong
AEGHMNOPPRSUYY Prague Symphony
AEGIIIILLMNOTT illegitimation
AEGIIIILMNOSTT legitimisation
AEGIIIILMNOTTZ legitimization
AEGIIILNNORTTT toilet training
AEGIIIMNNORRTT intermigration
AEGIIINNNOOPRT Pietro Annigoni
AEGIIINNOORRTV reinvigoration
AEGIIINNORSTTT integrationist
AEGIIKLMNNRSTY Kingsley Martin
AEGIIKMNOPSSSV passive smoking
AEGIILLLMORSUV Guillermo Vilas
AEGIILLLNNRTUY interlingually
AEGIILLNTTTTTT tittle-tattling
AEGIILMNNOORST mongrelisation
AEGIILMNNOORTZ mongrelization
AEGIILNNNRSTTY intransigently
AEGIILNOPRRSTU Negro spiritual
AEGIILNORRTTVX trailing vortex
AEGIIMOOQRSTUV vigesimo-quarto
AEGIINNNPRRRSU running repairs
AEGIINNNPRRTTU nature printing
AEGIINNNPRSSSU unaspiringness
AEGIINPPRSSSTT asset-stripping
AEGILLMNNOQTUY magniloquently
AEGILMMSSTUUUX gluteus maximus
AEGILMNNOPPSTU platinum sponge
AEGILMNOOORSTU osmoregulation
AEGILMNOOPSTTU pneumatologist
AEGILNNNOOPSTU louping-on-stane
AEGILNNPPRSTTU snapping-turtle
AEGIMMNOOPRSTU spermatogonium
AEGIMNNNSSSSUU unassumingness
AEGIMNNOOPRSSU measuring spoon
AEGIMNNOPRRRSY morning prayers
AEGIMNPRRSSSTT spring mattress
AEGINNPRSSSSSU surpassingness
AEGINOOOPPRRSS sporangiospore
AEGINOOPRRRSSY progressionary
AEGINORSSSTTUU gratuitousness
AEGLLLMNOSSTWY longwall system
AEGLLMOPRRTUYY pyrometallurgy
AEGLMOOORRSTUY osmoregulatory
AEGLNNOORSSSUU languorousness
AEGMMOPRRSSSTY systems program
AEHHHILNOORTTU holier-than-thou
AEHHHOOOPPRSTT orthophosphate
AEHHIIILMPRSUX xiphihumeralis
AEHHIILLLLRSSY shilly-shallier
AEHHILMOPPRSTU Periophthalmus
AEHHILOOPPRSST philosophaster
AEHHINNOPTTTTU put the tin hat on
AEHHINOPPRSTTY hypnotherapist
AEHHIOOPRRSTTW poor white trash
AEHHLMMOOPRTTY ophthalmometry
AEHHMMNOPTTUWY put the whammy on
AEHHNNOORRSTTT north-north-east
AEHHOOSSSTTTUU south-south-east
AEHIIIMNPRRSST parish minister
AEHIIKLLMOOPRT poikilothermal
AEHIILLLNOOTTT Otto Lilienthal
AEHIILMNOORSTY Hierosolymitan
AEHIILMOOPPRST apheliotropism
AEHIILNOPSTTUW with one's tail up
AEHIILNRSSSTTU Russian thistle
AEHIILOPRRSTWY praiseworthily
AEHIINNNOORSTT enthronisation
AEHIINNNOORTTZ enthronization
AEHIINORRRRSSX Sir Rex Harrison
AEHIIOORRSSTTT osteoarthritis
AEHIKLLORSSSWW swallow-shrikes
AEHIKMPRSSTTYY sympathy strike
AEHIKNNNOPRSTY Anthony Perkins
AEHILLLMMOOPRS allelomorphism
AEHILLORSSSTUU Louis Althusser
AEHILMMNNORSTU malnourishment
AEHILMNNOOSTTU Lhotse Mountain
AEHILNOPRSSTTW slap on the wrist
AEHILOPPPRSSUY pleurapophysis
AEHIMNNOORSSSU harmoniousness
AEHIMOOPPPSSTU hippopotamuses
AEHIMOPPRSSSTT postmastership
AEHINOPRRSTUWY unpraiseworthy
AEHINOPRRTTVWY Henry IV Part Two
Henry VI Part Two
AEHINOQRTTTUYY quantity theory
AEHIOOORRSSSTT osteoarthrosis
AEHJMNNNNNOOUV John Von Neumann
AEHLMNOOOPSSTU haplostemonous
AEHMMNORRTTUWY the worm may turn
AEHNOOPRSSTTUY thysanopterous
AEIIIIINNORTTT initiation rite
AEIIIILMNRSSTT ministerialist
AEIIIIMMNORSST immiserisation
AEIIIIMMNORSTZ immiserization
AEIIIILLMNNOSVW William Nevison
AEIIIILLNRSTTTY interstitially
AEIIIILMNPRRSST mineral spirits
AEIIIILMORRRSTT territorialism
AEIIIILNNNOTTTY intentionality
AEIIIILNNOOPTVY opinionatively
AEIIIILNNRSTTVY intransitively
AEIIIILNPRSSTUU unspiritualise
AEIIIILNPRSTUUZ unspiritualize
AEIIIILORRRSTTT territorialist
AEIIIILORRRTTTY territoriality
AEIIIMNORRTTWY minority waiter
AEIIINOQRRSTUY requisitionary
AEIIJLMNORSTTY silent majority
AEIIJLNNORSTUV universal joint
AEIIJNNNOOPSTX expansion joint
AEIILLLLMRSSUW William Russell
AEIILLLMNNOPST post-millennial
AEIILLLRSTTUVY illustratively
AEIILLMMNSTTUU altum silentium
silentium altum
AEIILLNNNQQUUY quinquennially
AEIILLNNOSSSUV villainousness
AEIILLNOORTUVY evolutionarily
AEIILMNOOPRSTY polymerisation
AEIILMNOOPRTYZ polymerization

AEIILMNOPRRSST tripersonalism
AEIILMNRSSSTVY transmissively
AEIILNNNPRSTUU peninsular unit
AEIILNOOOPPPRT apolipoprotein
AEIILNOOPRSTTX explorationist
AEIILNOPRRSSTT tripersonalist
AEIILNOPRRSTTY tripersonality
AEIILNPRRSSTTU neutral spirits
AEIIMMNORSSTTY symmetrisation
AEIIMMNORSTTYZ symmetrization
AEIIMNNORRSSST retransmission
AEIIMNOOOPSST onomatopoiesis
AEIIMNOORRSSTT restorationism
AEIIMNRSSSTTTV transvestitism
AEIIMOOPRRSTVV improvvisatore
AEIINNORRSSSTT transitoriness
AEIINOORRSSTTT restorationist
AEIINOPRRSSSTU pressurisation
AEIINOPRRSSTUZ pressurization
AEIINOPRSSSUVV viviparousness
AEIJMOOOPPRRRS Marjorie Proops
AEILLMNNRSTTUY instrumentally
AEILLMNOSSTUUY simultaneously
AEILMNNOORRSTU mountain sorrel
AEILMNOPRRSTUY supernormality
AEILNNOOSSTTUY enantiostylous
AEILNOOOPPRTUV overpopulation
AEILNOOPRSTUUV superovulation
AEILNOOSSTTTUY ostentatiously
AEIMNOPPRRSTTU superimportant
AEINNOOSSTTTUU unostentatious
AEINOOPRRSSSUU uproariousness
AEINOORRSSSTTU traitorousness
AEKMNOOOORTVWW know a move or two
AELLMNNOOOPPRT monopropellant
AFFGHHIIRRRTTU Arthur Griffith
AFFHILNOOORTTT froth flotation
AFFIILNNOOOPRT inflation-proof
AFGGHIIMNNNOOS fashionmonging
AFGGIILMNOPRUY family grouping
AFGHHILNOORRST thrashing-floor
AFGHHINORRSTTW farthingsworth
AFGIIILLNNOSTT filling station
AFGIKLMNNOORSY Lyon King of arms
AFGILMNOORRRSY lyriform organs
AFGIMNNNNOORTU running footman
AFHILLOORRSTTW for all it's worth
AFHMNNOOOORRTU matron of honour
AFIIIMMNNOORST misinformation
AFIILLMORSTUUY multifariously
AFIINNORSSSTTU transfusionist
AGGGGHHINNORTU through-ganging
AGGHIIILLMNSUW William Huggins
AGGHIIILNNOSTT Sailing Tonight
AGGHIILNPRSTUW Walpurgis night
AGGHILMNORRTUU Langmuir trough
AGGHILNOOOTUWY go along with you
AGGIIILMNNRRUV Irving Langmuir
AGGIIILNNORTVY invigoratingly
AGGILLNORSSSTY glossy starling
AGGLLNOOOORTYY otolaryngology
AGHHIIOOPRRSTY historiography
AGHHILOOOPSTTY histopathology
AGHHJLNOORSTWY John Galsworthy
AGHHLOOOPPTTYY phytopathology
AGHHOOOPPPRRTY pyrophotograph
AGHIIIKLNPPRSW King Philip's War
AGHIIINNNOPSTV vanishing point
AGHIILPPSSTUUU Philip Augustus
AGHIIMNNPSSTUY unsympathising
AGHIIMNNPSTUYZ unsympathizing
AGHILLOOOPSSST opisthoglossal
AGHILNOOOPRSTT anthropologist
AGHIMOOOPRSSTU mastigophorous
AGHLOOPPRRXYYY xylopyrography
AGHLOOPPRTXYYY xylotypography
AGIIIIILNOTTTV vitilitigation
AGIIILLLMNNTUY illuminatingly
AGIIILLMNNNTUU unilluminating
AGIIKLLMNOPRRU milking parlour
AGIIKNORRSSTVY Igor Stravinsky
AGIILLMMNNOOSU monolingualism
AGIILLNNOOPSTT polling station
AGIILLNOORSUVY vaingloriously
AGIILMOPRRTTUY utility program
AGIILNNORSSSUW Sir Angus Wilson
AGIILNOPRSSTTT starting pistol
AGIINNOORSSUUV sanguinivorous
AGILMNNOPPSTUY spongy platinum
AGILMNOORRSSTU Louis Armstrong
AGILNNOPRRSTTY transportingly
AGIMNNOOORRTTU Mount Tongariro
AGLMMOOOPSTTYY symptomatology
AHHHIKORTTTWWY Kathy Whitworth
AHHIIJKNNORSSW Sir John Hawkins
AHHIIJLNPRSUWY whiplash injury
AHHIILNOPPRSTT philanthropist
AHHIJKNNORSSWY Sir John Hawkyns
AHHIKNNNOOPSTY Anthony Hopkins
AHHIMNOOPPRSTU anthropophuism
AHIIILLNOOPSTY lyophilisation
AHIIILLNOOPTYZ lyophilization
AHIILLMMNOOSTW William Thomson
AHIILMNNOORSUY inharmoniously
AHIILMNOPPRSST psilanthropism
AHIILMOOPSSSST histoplasmosis
AHIILNNOOOPSTT Polish notation
AHIILNOPPRSSTT psilanthropist
AHIILNOPRSSTUU sulphurisation
AHIILNOPRSTUUZ sulphurization
AHIIMMNOOPSTTU imposthumation
AHIJLLMNORSTTU John Stuart Mill
AHILLOOOOPRSST alloiostrophos
AHOPPQRRRTUYYZ quartz-porphyry
AIIIIIKKKKRTTV Rikki-Tikki-Tavi
AIIIILMNNOSTTU intuitionalism
AIIIILNNOSTTTU intuitionalist
AIIIILNOORSTTV vitriolisation
AIIIILNOORTTVZ vitriolization
AIIIIMNNOPRSST inspirationism
AIIIINNOPRSSTT inspirationist
AIIIINNRSTTTVY intransitivity

AIIIINOOPRRSTT prioritisation
AIIIINOOPRRTTZ prioritization
AIIILMNNOOSTTY mylonitisation
AIIILMNNOOTTYZ mylonitization
AIIILOOPPRRTTY propitiatorily
AIIILPRRSTTUUV Trivial Pursuit®
AIIIMNRSSSTTVY transmissivity
AIIINNORSTTTUY institutionary
AIIJNNNOOSTTTU just intonation
AIIKLMOPRSTTXY proximity talks
AIILLNORRSSSTY sinistrorsally
AIILMNNOOOOPST monopolisation
AIILMNNOOOOPTZ monopolization
AIILMNOOPRSSUY parsimoniously
AIILNOOOPPSSTT postpositional
AIINOOPPRSSTUY suppositionary
AIJMNRRSSTTTUY St Justin Martyr
AIKKKMOORRSSVY Rimsky-Korsakov
AIKKMMNNRRTTUU trinkum-trankum
AILLMNNOOORSTU normal solution
AILLNOOOPPRRTY proportionally
AIMNNNOPPRSSSU snip-snap-snorum
ALLMMMNNOTTUUU multum non multa

B

BBBBINOOORRSSY Sir Bobby Robson
BBBCDEEEEIIKRX Bix Beiderbecke
BBBCGHINRRSSUU scrubbing-brush
BBBCGIIKLNOORS scribbling-book
BBBCIINOORSTUU Bourbon biscuit
BBBDGIIILNNORU ribbon building
BBBEILLOOSSWYY boys will be boys
BBBGIILLNOORYZ Big Bill Broonzy
BBCCDEIIMNRSUU circumbendibus
BBCCEEHLLLOSTU Scotch bluebell
BBCEEEEFFILLOR forcible feeble
BBCEEEGHLOORTT cobble together
BBCEEEHORRRTTU Robert the Bruce
BBCEIIIKNNOSST stick one's bib in
BBCGIKLLMNOSTU stumbling-block
BBCHIJKLNOORSU Sir John Lubbock
BBCIIILMOSTTUY combustibility
BBCILNOOOOPPRU pro bono publico
BBDDEEFILLORSY Sybille Bedford
BBDDEEHHLMOOOY hobbledehoydom
BBDDEELOOOPSTT blood-bespotted
BBDDEGGIIILNRU bridge-building
BBDEEHHHILOOSY hobbledehoyish
BBDEEHHILMOOSY hobbledehoyism
BBDEHOOORTTTYY Betty Boothroyd
BBDGHIILLORSTU British bulldog
BBEEEEIMNNRSTU bene merentibus
BBEEEGHJLOOPSS Joseph Goebbels
BBEEEGILLNOOSS noblesse oblige
BBEEEILLNOORRX Boxer Rebellion
BBEEGHLNOOOSTT The Boston Globe
BBEEGHOORRSSUY gooseberry-bush
BBEEHHMMRRTTUU Humbert Humbert
BBEFHJOOORSSTY jobs for the boys
BBEFKOOOOPRRSV Book of Proverbs
BBEGGIILLORSSU big girl's blouse
BBEGIIILMRSTUY submergibility
BBEGINNOORRRTW Robert Browning
BBEIIILMRSSTUY submersibility
BBEIIKLLNOOSSY Sibylline Books
BBEILNOORRSTUU rubber solution
BBEINNOOORRRST Robert Robinson
BBFIIILLLNOOOV bill of oblivion
BBFIIMMNOOSSTZ Bob Fitzsimmons
BBIKNNOOOORRSS Brooks Robinson
BCCCDFKLOORRSU Crockford's Club
BCCCIIMOOPRSSU submicroscopic
BCCDDEEHLLOTUU double-declutch
BCCDEEEENOORTT Benedetto Croce
BCCDEEIIJNORTT indirect object
BCCDEEILRSTUUU decubitus ulcer
BCCDEELNOOORTU double concerto
BCCDEILMNOPTUU public document
BCCDELLOOOPRSU blood corpuscle
BCCDIIILNOTTUY conductibility
BCCEEEEENORRTZ breeze concrete
BCCEEEEGILRTTU iceberg lettuce
BCCEEEHKLORTUV cover the buckle
BCCEEEKNOPRRST Brocken spectre
BCCEEHMNNRRRUU number-cruncher
BCCEEIIILORTTY bioelectricity
BCCEEIKKKNORRS knickerbockers
BCCEEIKLNOOORT electronic book
BCCEEJNORSTTUU counter-subject
BCCEIIIJSSTTUV subjectivistic
BCCEIILLRTUVYY City Livery Club
BCCFIIIORSSSTY cystic fibrosis
BCCILNOOSSSUUY subconsciously
BCDDEEEFILNPRU public defender
BCDDEEEHHILNSU behind schedule
BCDDEEEIMNRRTU directed number
BCDDEEGINNRRTU current bedding
BCDDEFLLLOOSUW Oddfellows Club
BCDEEEEHILRRVY breech delivery
BCDEEEEILRRSTT street-credible
BCDEEEGHIINRRS riding breeches
BCDEEEHIKNRRSY Derbyshire neck
BCDEEEHILRSSTU schedule tribes
BCDEEEHJORSTUU Jude the Obscure
BCDEEEIILMNOTT medicine bottle
BCDEEEIILNNRSS incredibleness
BCDEEFGIINNPRT perfect binding
BCDEEFHIMMNOOR come from behind
BCDEEGIKLNRSUW swindge-buckler
BCDEEHHILLPRSY Cybill Shepherd
BCDEEHILLLOOTW white blood cell
BCDEEIIILNPRST indiscerptible
BCDEEIILNOORTU ribonucleotide
BCDEEIILNRSTTU indestructible
BCDEEIILOPRRRU irreproducible
BCDEEILNOPRRUU unreproducible
BCDEELNOOORSST stone-cold sober
BCDEEMOOOPPRTT copper-bottomed
BCDEENOOORTTUY cry out to be done
BCDEEOORSTTUUY cry out to be used
BCDEFIINORRRSU furor scribendi
BCDEGHINNORSTT stretching-bond

BCDEGIILNNPPSU	public spending
BCDEHIINOORRRS	rhinoceros bird
BCDEHIMOPRRTUY	hybrid computer
BCDEIIIILPRSTY	discerpibility
BCDEIIIILRRTUY	irreducibility
BCDEIIILPPRSTU	public-spirited
BCDEIIJNOOPRST	job description
BCDEIILLNORSTU	bill-discounter
BCDEIILNRSTTUY	indestructibly
BCDEIKNOORRSTU	discount-broker
BCDEINNOOSTUUZ	subduction zone
BCDEMMNNOOPRUU	compound number
BCDENNOOOOPRUZ	zero-coupon bond
BCDFIILNNOOTUY	bodily function
BCDGHIIMNOOTWY	Midnight Cowboy
BCDGILMNNOOOSU	blood-consuming
BCDHHIIOOPRTYY	hydrophobicity
BCDIIILOPRTTUY	productibility
BCDMOOORRSSUWW	Wormwood Scrubs
BCEEEEEHLLRSTU	Hercules beetle
BCEEEEFILMNRST	fermentescible
BCEEEEGHINNSSS	beseechingness
BCEEEEGHLRSTUZ	Lëtzebuergesch
BCEEEEHILNQRRU	Henri Becquerel
BCEEEEHLOPRRRT	brothel creeper
BCEEEEHLRRSSTU	beetle-crushers
BCEEEEHNPRRRST	Herbert Spencer
BCEEEELLNOORTV	lector benevole
BCEEEFHHIILTUZ	Chief Buthelezi
BCEEEFIINOSTTY	benefit society
BCEEEFINNORRTU	Brief Encounter
BCEEEHILMNOPRS	comprehensible
BCEEEHLNOOOSTT	close to the bone
BCEEEIJNSSSTUV	subjectiveness
BCEEEIKLNORTUV	Lee Buck Trevino
BCEEEORRRRSTWY	worcesterberry
BCEEFHILNOSTTU	cuttlefish bone
BCEEFIIILMPRST	perfectibilism
BCEEFIIILPRSTT	perfectibilist
BCEEFIIILPRTTY	perfectibility
BCEEFIMNNOORSU	cuneiform bones
BCEEFLRRSTTUWY	butterfly screw
BCEEGHIKLNRRUY	huckleberrying
BCEEGILLOOORTY	electrobiology
BCEEGIMNNNOSSU	unbecomingness
BCEEHHIILMSTTW	witches' thimble
BCEEHHIILNORRS	Heinrich Olbers
BCEEHIIMNORTTU	thermionic tube
BCEEHILMNOPRSY	comprehensibly
BCEEHIMNOOPRTY	honeycomb tripe
BCEEIIIILLRSTV	civil liberties
BCEEIIILNNNSSV	invincibleness
BCEEIIILPPRTTY	perceptibility
BCEEIILMNNOSTU	bioluminescent
BCEEIILMNOPRSS	incompressible
BCEEILMNNSTTUV	investment club
BCEEILNOORRTTV	controvertible
BCEEIMNNPRSTUU	superincumbent
BCEEIMORRRRSTY	cyberterrorism
BCEEINOPRRSSTU	Inspector Rebus
BCEEIORRRRSTTY	cyberterrorist
BCEFFHILLRSSUY	Flyfishers' Club
BCEFGLNNOOOORU	Bruno of Cologne
BCEGIIJNORSTTU	bring to justice
BCEIIIILRSTTVY	vitrescibility
BCEIIILNORTTVY	convertibility
BCEIIILPSSTTUY	susceptibility
BCEIILMRRSTTUU	tritubercularism
BCEIIMNOOPRSTU	isotopic number
BCEIINOPPRRSTY	by prescription
BCEILLMNOPSUVY	plumbisolvency
BCEILMOORTTTUY	yttro-columbite
BCEILNOORRTTVY	controvertibly
BCEIMNOOOPRSSU	supersonic boom
BCEINNOOORRSSU	Robinson Crusoe
BCELLMNOOPSUVY	plumbosolvency
BCEMNNOOPRTTTU	Compton-Burnett
BCGHIINNNOORST	Chris Bonington
BCGIIILMOOORST	microbiologist
BCGIIILOOOOSST	sociobiologist
BCGIIKLMNNOOOT	blocking motion
BCIIILMOOPSSTY	compossibility
BCIIILOPRRTTUY	corruptibility
BCIIMNOORSSTTU	obstructionism
BCIINOORSSTTTU	obstructionist
BCIKMNNOPRTUUY	country bumpkin
BDDDEEELNOORSS	red-bloodedness
BDDEEEEFILLMNY	feeble-mindedly
BDDEEEELNNORTU	double entendre
BDDEEEFLLOORUW	double-flowered
BDDEEEILMOORSU	edible dormouse
BDDEEGGINNORRU	breeding ground
BDDEEGHNORRUYY	Greyhound Derby
BDDEEIKMNNOOSS	book-mindedness
BDDEELNNOOPRSU	drop one's bundle
BDDEFFIINORRTU	forbidden fruit
BDDEFGIINNORSS	forbiddingness
BDDEGIIILLNSTU	listed building
BDDHJLNNOOOPUY	John Boyd Dunlop
BDEEEEHLOSSSUU	Blue Suede Shoes
BDEEEEILLRSSTT	blistered-steel
BDEEEEILNRRRWY	elderberry wine
BDEEEEORRRTUVX	Robert Devereux
BDEEEFGIILMNNR	nimble-fingered
BDEEEFGINRRTTU	butterfingered
BDEEEFKNNORRTY	Robert F Kennedy
BDEEEFLNNORSUV	bundle of nerves
BDEEEGIMMNOSTU	disemboguement
BDEEEHHIIMNSTT	behind the times
BDEEEHIINOPSTT	beside the point
BDEEEHILNNORVZ	Leonid Brezhnev
BDEEEHINNRRTTU	United Brethren
BDEEEIILNOOSTV	I don't believe so
BDEEEIINNNORTZ	dinitrobenzene
BDEEEILMMNOSTW	disembowelment
BDEEEIMNNOOSST	in someone's debt
BDEEEKLOORRTWY	Robert Koldewey
BDEEELOOPRSUUX	double exposure
BDEEEMNOORRSUV	overburdensome
BDEEFLLNORSTUY	soft underbelly
BDEEGGHHLNOOTU	The Golden Bough
BDEEGGHLNOOOTY	The Long Goodbye

BDEEGHILLNORST	Gilbert Sheldon
BDEEGHNOOSTTUW	go down the tubes
BDEEGIIILMNPRU	empire-building
BDEEGIIMNOOSTU	disembogue into
BDEEGILLNRSTUW	Tunbridge Wells
BDEEHIINOSTTUY	hebetudinosity
BDEEHLMMPRSTUU	rumbledethumps
BDEEHMNNORSTUU	under one's thumb
BDEEHNOOORTTXY	the boy next door
BDEEIIIRRSTTUV	redistributive
BDEEIILNNRRSSV	river blindness
BDEEIINNOOOSST	die in one's boots
BDEEILLNOSSSSU	dissolubleness
BDEEIMNNNOSTTV	investment bond
BDEEINNOOSSSSU	do one's business
BDEELLLOOORRUV	double rollover
BDEELMNNORRSUY	Reynolds number
BDEEOOORSTTTWY	Betsey Trotwood
BDEFFILNOSSUVX	devil's snuff-box
BDEFGIINNOORSW	birds of one wing
BDEFHIILNORTWY	Winifred Holtby
BDEGGHILOOOPRW	Whoopi Goldberg
BDEGGHINOOORSU	good neighbours
BDEGGILNNOOTUU	double-tonguing
BDEGGIMMNORRSU	Sigmund Romberg
BDEGHIILLMNOST	Billings method
BDEGHIILNNNSST	night-blindness
BDEGIIILLNRSUV	sliver building
BDEGIILMNSSTUY	system building
BDEGIIMNOORSTT	bedsitting-room
BDEGILNOOPPSTU	double-stopping
BDEGIMNNOORRRU	mourning border
BDEHIIKLNORSTY	Sybil Thorndike
BDEHIILLORSTTT	thrilled to bits
BDEIIIILMQRSUU	disequilibrium
BDEIIIILNSSTTY	distensibility
BDEIIILNNOSSSU	libidinousness
BDEIIILRSTTUVY	distributively
BDEIIIMNNOOSTU	omnibus edition
BDEIIINORRSTTU	redistribution
BDEIMNNNORRSUU	in round numbers
BDGGGIILLMNNOY	mind-bogglingly
BDGHIILOOORSTY	hydrobiologist
BDGIILLMMNNNUY	mind-numblingly
BDGIILNNOOOOPS	blood poisoning
BDHIILLOORSTTY	bloodthirstily
BDHJLNNNNOOOSY	Lyndon B Johnson
BDIIIIIILNSTVY	indivisibility
BEEEEEGGKLORRY	George Berkeley
BEEEEEGHPRTTUZ	get the breeze up
BEEEEFGHORTTTT	get the better of
BEEEEFIMNOORST	before one's time
BEEEEGHILPRRTU	Pieter Breughel
	Pieter Brueghel
BEEEEGHLNORRST	Ethel Rosenberg
BEEEEGINNRSTVW	Steven Weinberg
BEEEEHHOORSTTZ	shoot the breeze
BEEEEILOORSTTT	tortoise beetle
BEEEEKLLNNORXY	Lennox Berkeley
BEEEELMNORSTUV	bouleversement
BEEEFFGIKNOOST	get off one's bike
BEEEFGHIOSTTTT	get the best of it
BEEEFGILLNNOTW	beef Wellington
BEEEFIILLNNSSX	inflexibleness
BEEEGGIIINNNOR	bioengineering
BEEEGGIOORRRSY	Sir George Robey
BEEEGHINOQSTTU	beg the question
BEEEGHLLNNOORT	longhorn beetle
BEEEGHMMORSSUU	Borghese Museum
BEEEGILLNNNORT	non-belligerent
BEEEGINOORRSWY	gooseberry-wine
BEEEHHLNOOOPTT	telephone booth
BEEEHILMNOSSST	blithesomeness
BEEEHKNORSTUVY	The Rokeby Venus
BEEEHLLNOOSTVY	The Lovely Bones
BEEEHLORRRSTVY	Everly Brothers
BEEEIILNNNSSSS	insensibleness
BEEEIILNOSTTUV	television tube
BEEEIILNPRSSSX	inexpressibles
BEEEILLNORSSSU	rebelliousness
BEEEILMNNNOOTV	omnibenevolent
BEEEJMNOORRTTY	remote job entry
BEEEKMOOSSTUUZ	Mobutu Seze Seko
BEEELMMNORSSSU	lumbersomeness
BEEELMNNOOOSSY	by one's lonesome
BEEELMNNRSSSSU	numberlessness
BEEFFGLNOOORTY	Geoffrey Bolton
BEEFFIKLNRTTUY	butterfly knife
BEEFGINRRSTTUY	buttery fingers
BEEFGLOOOORRSY	gooseberry-fool
BEEFIIMNORSTTU	benefit tourism
BEEFIINORSTTTU	benefit tourist
BEEGGHIILNNTTT	belt-tightening
BEEGGHIILNOTTW	weighing-bottle
BEEGGIIMNOORSU	embourgeoising
BEEGHIILLLMNSY	embellishingly
BEEGHIILMNNORV	Emil von Behring
BEEGHIILNNORSS	neighborliness
BEEGHMOOORRSTY	gooseberry-moth
BEEGIIILLLNNTU	unintelligible
BEEGIIOOPRSTTU	petit bourgeois
BEEGILLLMNOSTT	smelling bottle
BEEGILMOOOORTY	biometeorology
BEEGIOOPRSTTUY	petty bourgeois
BEEHHILLOSTTWW	blow the whistle
BEEHHKLOOPRTYY	by the holy poker
BEEHJNOOPRSSTU	Bustopher Jones
BEEHLOOORRSTTU	troubleshooter
BEEHNNOORRRSTY	Robert Henryson
BEEHNOPRSSTTTU	press the button
BEEIIILMOPPRSS	per impossibile
BEEIIILNOOPRST	obiit sine prole
BEEIIKLNNSSSUU	unbusinesslike
BEEIILLLLTTTTY	little by little
BEEIILLPRRRTTU	pit bull terrier
BEEIILNOSSTVWY	live by one's wits
BEEIILNPPRSSSU	insuppressible
BEEIILOPRSSTVX	visible exports
BEEIIMNOPRSTUV	positive number
BEEIIMNSSSSSUV	submissiveness
BEEIKMNNOSSSUY	monkey business
BEEIMNNNNPRSUY	in penny numbers

BEEIMNOOPPRSTU	opposite number
BEEINNOPRSSSSU	businessperson
BEEINOOQSSSSUU	obsequiousness
BEEINOORRRRSST	Sir Robert Ensor
BEEINOORSSSSTU	boisterousness
BEELNNNOOOPRRY	polynorbornene
BEELOOPRRSSTUY	obstreperously
BEFFILNOORSTUU	buffer solution
BEFGILNRSSTTUY	flying buttress
BEFKLLOOOORRTU	look for trouble
BEGGGHIIILMNRT	thimblerigging
BEGGHHILNOORSU	borough-English
BEGGHIILNORSTT	strobe lighting
BEGGIIILSSTTUY	suggestibility
BEGHIILLNOSTWW	whistle-blowing
BEGHLLLNOOPTUW	pull the long bow
BEGIIILLLNNTUY	unintelligibly
BEGIILNOOORSTU	neurobiologist
BEGILLNNOOOTTW	wellington boot
BEGILMMNOPRTUU	rumblegumption
BEGILNORSSSUUU	lugubriousness
BEHHIKNOOPSTTU	put the kibosh on
BEHHMNOOPPRRRY	rhombenporphyr
BEHHNOOOPPRRSZ	phosphor bronze
BEHIIILNOORSVZ	visible horizon
BEIIIILMPRSSTY	impressibility
	permissibility
BEIIILLORRSTUY	irresolubility
BEIIILMOPRSSTV	visible imports
BEIIILNOPRSSTY	responsibility
BEIIILNPSSSTUY	suspensibility
BEIILNPPRSSSUY	insuppressibly
BEIILSSTTTUUVY	substitutively
BEIKMNNOOORSSY	Smokey Robinson
BEINOORSSSSTUU	robustiousness
BELOPRRSSSSTUU	brussels sprout✧
BFGGHIINNORRST	bringings forth
BFGILLNORSTTUU	full to bursting
BGGGIJMNOOOSTT	jogging bottoms
BGHIILOOOOPSTT	photobiologist
BGIILLMMNNOOUU	immunoglobulin
BHIIIIMNOOPRST	prohibitionism
BHIIIINOOPRSTT	prohibitionist
BHMMNOOORSTTUU	button mushroom
BIIISSTTTTUUVY	substitutivity
BIILMNNOOTTUUX	botulinum toxin
BILMMNOOORSTTU	Mount Stromboli

C

CCCCDHKOOOOSTW	Scotch woodcock
CCCCDILMNOOPUY	cyclic compound
CCCCEEILNOSSTU	occult sciences
CCCCIKMMORRSUY	Cyrus McCormick
CCCCIOOOPRSSTY	cryptococcosis
CCCDDEEEENNNOS	condescendence
CCCDEEEFHIIKRT	certified check
CCCDEEELNOPRSY	cycle per second
CCCDEEGINNOOOS	good conscience
CCCDEEHIIOOPRT	cercopithecoid
CCCDEEIILORRRT	director circle
CCCDEFINNOOSST	soft-conscienc'd
CCCDGIILOOORTU	glucocorticoid
CCCEEEHHHIINNR	chincherinchee
CCCEEEHHILORSU	Hercules' choice
CCCEEEHILNORTT	electrotechnic
CCCEEEILLNOQSU	colliquescence
CCCEEEILNNOSSS	conscienceless
CCCEEFFIINOSTY	cost efficiency
CCCEEFIIINNOST	science fiction
CCCEEFILLLMORU	come full circle
CCCEEIIMPRSTUV	circumspective
CCCEEILNOOPTUY	leucocytopenic
CCCEEINNNOOPSU	upon conscience
CCCEENNNNOORRU	non-concurrence
CCCEGHHIIKLNTV	chickling vetch
CCCEHHINOPSSTY	psychotechnics
CCCEHIINORRSTT	Christocentric
CCCEIIILLOSTTV	collectivistic
CCCEIIILMRSSSU	circumscissile
CCCEIIMMNOOORS	microeconomics
CCCEIIMNOPRSTU	circumspection
CCCEILMORRRUUU	core curriculum
CCCIIIMNNORSUU	uncircumcision
CCCIIIMORRRTUY	microcircuitry
CCCIILMNOORTUU	circumlocution
CCCIIMORRRTUUX	crux criticorum
CCCILMOORRTUUY	circumlocutory
CCDDEEEHIILRUU	Duc de Richelieu
CCDDEEGILOOWWY	Cicely Wedgwood
CCDDEEIIIMMOOS	Cosimo de' Medici
CCDDEEILNNOSTY	disconnectedly
CCDDEEINNRRTUU	induced current
CCDDEENNNOOPSU	condescend upon
CCDEEEEIILLRST	diesel-electric
CCDEEEEIIRSSTT	et sic de ceteris
CCDEEEFFILNNOS	self-confidence
CCDEEEFGIINPRS	gender-specific
CCDEEEFINNOORV	over-confidence
CCDEEEGNOORRSS	Green Cross Code
CCDEEEHHHKPRSS	shepherd's check
CCDEEEHIIKLNRV	chicken-livered
CCDEEEHIINPRST	indirect speech
CCDEEEHLOORRST	close the record
CCDEEEIINNNRTT	incident centre
CCDEEEIINPRSVY	vice-presidency
CCDEEEILNOPSTY	Encyclopédiste
CCDEEELNOPRRTY	preconcertedly
CCDEEENNOOPRRS	correspondence
CCDEEFFIIINNOT	incident office
CCDEEFHIINOPRR	Frédéric Chopin
CCDEEFHKOSTTTY	Schottky defect
CCDEEGIIILNNRV	driving licence
CCDEEGIMNNNOOO	non-comedogenic
CCDEEHILNOORTU	technicoloured
CCDEEIILNORTWW	electric window
CCDEEIIMNOORTT	microdetection
CCDEEILLNOOPRU	coloured pencil
CCDEEIMNNORSTT	disconcertment
CCDEENNOOPRRSY	correspondency
CCDEGIIMNNOSTU	semiconducting
CCDEHILNORRSTU	children's court
CCDEIIINORSTTU	reductionistic

CCDEIIINPRRTTU printed circuit
CCDEIILMOORTTY clitoridectomy
CCDEIILNNOORRU order in council
CCDEIIOOORRSTT corticosteroid
CCDEINNOORSTTU deconstruction
CCDEINOSSSTUUY succession duty
CCDENOOPRRSTUU superconductor
CCDGIIIMOOOPSS sigmoidoscopic
CCDHHHOOORRTUX Orthodox Church
CCDHHILLNORSUW Churchill Downs
CCDHIIMOPRRSTY cryptorchidism
CCDIIIMOOSSSUV mucoviscidosis
CCDMMNOOOORSST Doctors' Commons
CCEEEEEFIINPPV fivepence piece
CCEEEEEFLNNORT teleconference
CCEEEEEHHHIRSS Cheshire cheese
CCEEEEEJNNRSUV rejuvenescence
CCEEEEFHIITUVX chief executive
CCEEEEFNNNORSW news conference
CCEEEEFNORRRSS cross-reference
CCEEEEHHHOORTT cheer to the echo
CCEEEEHIMOPRTV chemoreceptive
CCEEEEHMNNOOST come on the scene
CCEEEEMMMNNORT recommencement
CCEEEFFIMNOOTT come into effect
CCEEEFHIIOPRST heterospecific
CCEEEFHMNRSUXY excuse my French
CCEEEFIIOPRSST stereospecific
CCEEEGIIILNRSV service ceiling
CCEEEGJLNNORTU concrete jungle
CCEEEHILMORRTT electrothermic
thermoelectric
CCEEEHILMORSTT electrochemist
CCEEEIIKLNORTT electrokinetic
CCEEEILLLORTVY recollectively
CCEEEIMMNNOOPT omnicompetence
CCEEEINSSSSSUV successiveness
CCEEELLORRTTUU electroculture
CCEEELNNOORSTU close encounter
CCEEENOOPRRTTY concrete poetry
CCEEFFHKOSTTTY Schottky effect
CCEEFFIILOORST Coriolis effect
CCEEFFMOOPPRRU force force pump
CCEEFGILNORRST self-correcting
CCEEFHIILLNNOO colonel-in-chief
CCEEFHIILRRSTT The First Circle
CCEEFHIKKNNRRS French knickers
CCEEFIMNORRRTU circumferentor
CCEEFLNSSSSSUU successfulness
CCEEGHILLORSST Christ's College
CCEEGHINOPSSTY psychogenetics
CCEEGIILLOOSST ecclesiologist
CCEEGIINNOOSTT oncogeneticist
CCEEGIINOSTTTY cytogeneticist
CCEEGILLLLNNOO Lincoln College
CCEEGILNNRRSUY single currency
CCEEGLLOORSSST St Cross College
CCEEHIIIPRRSTY hypercriticise
CCEEHIIIPRRTYZ hypercriticize
CCEEHIIKKPRRYY hickery-pickery
CCEEHIILLMOPTU multiple-choice
CCEEHIILOQRTUV liquorice-vetch
CCEEHIIMOORSTT stoechiometric
CCEEHILOPRSTUW white corpuscle
CCEEHOOPRRSTTT chest protector
CCEEIIIMNNRSUU cuisine minceur
CCEEIILNORRTTU interlocutrice
CCEEIIMOPRSSTU Euroscepticism
CCEEIINORRTTUY Eurocentricity
CCEEIKLNOOPTUY leukocytopenic
CCEEILLMOORSTT collector's item
CCEEILLNNOOTUV collective noun
CCEEILMOOORSTT electro-osmotic
CCEEILNNOSSSUV conclusiveness
CCEEILNOOOPRTT optoelectronic
CCEEILNOOPRSTT electron optics
CCEEILNOSSSSSU successionless
CCEEINNNOORRTT interconnector
CCEEINOOORRRTV overcorrection
CCEEINOOORRSTT corticosterone
CCEEINOOPRSSSU precociousness
CCEEINORRSTTUV reconstructive
CCEELNORRTTUUU counterculture
CCEEMMNOOORRVY common recovery
CCEENNORRRTTUU counter-current
CCEFFHIIOOSSTT Scottish Office
CCEFHIIINORTUX the Crucifixion
CCEFIILNNOOSTV self-conviction
CCEFIINNOORSST cross-infection
CCEFLLNSSSUUUY unsuccessfully
CCEGIIIKLNRRST striking circle
CCEGIINOORRSST concerti grossi
CCEGIKMNNOORST smoking concert
CCEGINOPRSSTUY synectics group
CCEGNOOOORRSST concerto grosso
CCEHHIILORSSTT chlorite-schist
CCEHHIOOPSSUYZ schizophyceous
CCEHHMMNOOOTTU the common touch
CCEHIIIMOORSTT stoichiometric
CCEHIIIMPRRSTY hypercriticism
CCEHIILLNOTUWY Whitley Council
CCEHIILNOPSSUV vice-consulship
CCEHIIMMORRSTY microchemistry
CCEHILPRSSSTUY cluster physics
CCEHIMMNOSTTUY community chest
CCEHIMMOORSSTY cosmochemistry
CCEHIMOOSSTUYZ schizomycetous
CCEHINNOOSSTUU the unconscious
CCEHINOOPRSSUY hyperconscious
CCEHINOOPRSTUY psychoneurotic
CCEHLMOOOSTTYY cholecystotomy
CCEIIIJMNNOORT microinjection
CCEIIILMORRSTW lower criticism
CCEIILLNNOSUVY inconclusively
CCEIILLNOOPSST scintilloscope
CCEIILORRSTUUV virtuous circle
CCEIIMNNOOOPTU pneumoconiotic
CCEIINORSSSTUU circuitousness
CCEIKLNOOPRSSU percussion-lock
CCEILLOOSSTUYY leucocytolysis
CCEILNORSTTUVY constructively
CCEIMMNNOOOPRT microcomponent

CCEIMOOOPRRRSS	microprocessor
CCEIMORRRSTTUU	microstructure
CCEINNOORRSTTU	reconstruction✧
CCEIOOPPRSSSTT	spectroscopist
CCELNOOOPRRSST	process control
CCFFFIINOOSTUU	functus officio
CCGHHIKLOPRSTU	Christoph Gluck
CCGHIIKNOSSTTT	stocking stitch
CCGHIIOOPRSTYY	hygroscopicity
CCGIIKMNOOPSST	composing stick
CCGIIMMNOOPRTU	microcomputing
CCHIILLNOOPRSU	councillorship
CCHIINOOOPRRTT	corticotrophin
CCHIIOPRRRTVYY	Pyrrhic victory
CCHILMMNNOOOTU	communion cloth
CCHIOORRRSSSTW	Christ-cross-row
CCIIIJNNOSTTUV	conjunctivitis
CCIIILMMNOOOTV	civil commotion
CCIIILPRSSTTUU	pisciculturist
CCIIIMNOOPRSTU	circumposition
CCIILMNOORTUUV	circumvolution
CCIIMNORSSTTUV	constructivism✧
CCIINORSSTTTUV	constructivist
CCILLNNOOORTUW	town councillor
CCILMNOOPSTUUY	compunctiously
CCILNNOORSSTUY	try conclusions
CDDDEEEEFIRRRT	deferred credit
CDDDEEEEINRTTX	extended credit
CDDDEEFIKORRSY	Frederick Soddy
CDDDEEIILMOORS	discodermolide
CDDEEEEEFLNNPS	self-dependence
CDDEEEEENNOPRV	overdependence
CDDEEEFIMRRRUY	Freddie Mercury
CDDEEEHMNNOPRU	uncomprehended
CDDEEEHNNPRRTU	hundred-per-cent
CDDEEEIIMORSVW	received wisdom
CDDEEGGILLNOPU	college pudding
CDDEEGHLMNOOTU	dodge the column
CDDEEHILMNNOTW	child endowment
CDDEEIKLNNOUVY	Ludovic Kennedy
CDDEEILNNOSTTY	discontentedly
CDDEGIIIILLNRRT	direct drilling
CDDEGLLNOORRTU	controlled drug
CDDEGOOOPRRSSU	producers' goods
CDDEHIILMOORSU	sodium chloride
CDDEHILOOOPRSV	provided school
CDDEHLMOOORSTY	odd-come-shortly
CDDEIIILLNNOOT	ill-conditioned
CDDEILNOOOSTUY	dicotyledonous
CDEEEEEINNQSUV	Queen's evidence
CDEEEEFFINNORT	difference tone
CDEEEEFIKLORRW	Frederick Loewe
CDEEEEFMNNNOSS	mend one's fences
CDEEEEFMNNORRR	norm-referenced
CDEEEEHOPPRRST	reported speech
CDEEEEIRRSSSTV	dessert-service
CDEEEELNOPRSTW	steeple-crowned
CDEEEENNPSSTUX	unexpectedness
CDEEEFGIIIMNNR	fringe medicine
CDEEEFGILLNNSU	self-indulgence
CDEEEFGINOPRSW	weeding-forceps
CDEEEFHINNRRRT	trencher-friend
CDEEEFIIKMNNRZ	McKenzie Friend
CDEEEFIIRSTUVV	defective virus
CDEEEFILNNNUUU	undue influence
CDEEEFILORRTTT	letter of credit
CDEEEFIMNNOPRS	presence of mind
CDEEEFINOQRUVY	video frequency
CDEEEGIIMNPRRU	murdering-piece
CDEEEGIINORRRV	receiving order
CDEEEGILNNORUV	overindulgence
CDEEEHHPRRSSSS	shepherd's cress
CDEEEHIINNRRSV	Vreni Schneider
CDEEEHIKLNNOTV	devil-on-the-neck
CDEEEHLLOOPRRW	Rochelle-powder
CDEEEHLOOOPRTT	photoelectrode
CDEEEIIINNSSSV	indecisiveness
CDEEEIILNRRSSV	driver's license
CDEEEIINNRSSST	indiscreetness
	indiscreteness
CDEEEIIOPPRSTT	deposit-receipt
CDEEEINNNOORRU	neuroendocrine
CDEEEINOOPRRRT	reception order
CDEEEINRRSSSTT	restrictedness
CDEEEIORSTTTVY	detective story
CDEEELNNNOOORT	nolo contendere
CDEEENNNOQRUUW	uncrowned queen
CDEEFFILOORRRY	orderly officer
CDEEFGHILORRRT	flight-recorder
CDEEFGHINNRRSS	French dressing
CDEEFGIIKNRSTY	sticky-fingered
CDEEFGILMNNNOS	self-condemning
CDEEFHIILLMOOR	chloride of lime
CDEEFHKNOOOSTW	neck of the woods
CDEEFIIILLNPSS	self-discipline
CDEEFIKORRRTTW	Frederick Twort
CDEEFINNOPRSTU	superconfident
CDEEFLLLNOORST	self-controlled
CDEEGGHINOORRS	schooner-rigged
CDEEGGIILLNORT	electrogilding
CDEEGGILLNNOOW	Downing College
CDEEGHIIKLNPRR	pickled herring
CDEEGHINNOORSS	chondrogenesis
CDEEGHNOORRTUV	cover the ground
CDEEGIIINNOPTV	pointing device
CDEEGILNNORXYY	oxygen cylinder
CDEEGIMNNNOOPU	compound engine
CDEEHHILLMORTY	methyl chloride
CDEEHHINORRTTU	Henri Dutrochet
CDEEHIIIORRSTW	Cider with Rosie
CDEEHIIKNRSSTW	Winchester disk
CDEEHIINOORSTY	decision theory
CDEEHIKLNPRRSU	under-clerkship
CDEEHIKNORTTUW	round the wicket
CDEEHILNNRRSSU	children's nurse
CDEEHIMNOORRSY	dysmenorrhoeic
CDEEHLLLOORSUY	hydrocellulose
CDEEHLMOOORTTW	the world to come
CDEEHNNOORRRTU	round the corner
CDEEIIINNNORRT	inner-direction
CDEEIIINNSSTVV	vindictiveness
CDEEIIINOPPRST	editio princeps

Words marked ✧ can also be spelled with one or more capital letters

CDEEIILNRSSTTU scrutin de liste
CDEEIIMMNOORSS decommissioner
CDEEIIMNOPRSST sports medicine
CDEEIIMOPRSSTY periodic system
CDEEIINRSSSSUV discursiveness
CDEEIJLOOPRRST slide projector
CDEEIKNNORRSTW wonder-stricken
CDEEIKOORRRRTW worker director
CDEEILLNNNNOOS Ninon de Lenclos
CDEEILLNOOPTUY polynucleotide
CDEEILMOOPPSUX Oedipus complex
CDEEILNOORRSUX exclusion order
CDEEILNRRSTTUY unrestrictedly
CDEEILOPRRTUVY reproductively
CDEEIMNNNOSTTT discontentment
CDEEIMNNOOORRT Monroe doctrine
CDEEINNOORSSSU indecorousness
CDEEINNORSTTUV non-destructive
CDEEINNRRSTTUY current density
CDEEINOPRSSTUV productiveness
CDEEINPSSSTTUU intussuscepted
CDEELLOOPPRRUU purple-coloured
CDEENNOORRTTUV uncontroverted
CDEENNOORSTTVY send to Coventry
CDEFFNOOOOPRTU foot-pound force
CDEFGHOOOORRTT go for the doctor
CDEFGLNOOOSSTU slug-foot-second
CDEFHIIKPPRRRU Friedrich Krupp
CDEFLLNOOOORRT food-controller
CDEGHHIIILNPPR high-principled
CDEGHHNOOSSTTU second thoughts
CDEGHIKNORRSST Redcross Knight
CDEGHMNRRSTUUU Durchmusterung
CDEGIKNNOORSTU sounding rocket
CDEGINOOPRRSSW word processing
CDEHHIILNOOPRT ornithodelphic
CDEHHINNOOOPRR chondrophorine
CDEHHINOOPRRTY hydronephrotic
CDEHIILLNRSSST Schindler's List
CDEHIIOOPPRSSX xiphoid process
CDEHILMNNOOPTT hold in contempt
CDEHINOOORRSTY hydrocortisone
CDEIIIILRSTTUV diverticulitis
CDEIIIINRSSTTY identity crisis
CDEIIIKLMNNOSY Emily Dickinson
CDEIIILORSSTUV diverticulosis
CDEIIIMNOPRSST misdescription
CDEIIINNNSSSTT indistinctness
CDEIIJNNNOOSTW conjoined twins
CDEIILLMNOOORX loxodromic line
CDEIILMNORRRSU mirror nuclides
CDEIILNNOOPRTU production line
CDEIILNORSSSUU ridiculousness
CDEIINNOORRTTU reintroduction
CDEIINNOPRSSUU under suspicion
CDEIINNOPRSTUU superinduction
CDEIINOOPPRRSS scorpion spider
CDEIINORSSTTTU destructionist
CDEIIOPRRTTUVY reproductivity
CDEIKLNNOOSSUW lick one's wounds
CDEIKNOORRSTUW reduction works
CDEILNOPRTUUVY unproductively
CDEILOORSSTUUY discourteously
CDEIMMNOOOSSSU commodiousness
CDEINOOOPPRSSU pseudoscorpion
CDEINOOOPRRTUV overproduction
CDEKLNNNOOOSUW down on one's luck
CDELLLNNOORTUY uncontrolledly
CDFGIIKNOOTTTU fitting-out dock
CDFHKOORSSTTUU futtock-shrouds
CDFIINNOOOOTTU out of condition
CDGIIINOSTTWYZ dizygotic twins
CDGNNOOORSTUWY God's own country
CDHHILOPRRSUUY hydrosulphuric
CDHIIILNOOSTVY school-divinity
CDHIINNOORTTTU truth condition
CDHIKMNOOPRRTU durchkomponirt
CDHINOOOPRSSTT prosthodontics
CDHJNNOOSSSTUU John Duns Scotus
CDIIJNNNNOOSTU nondisjunction
CDIILMMNOOOSUY incommodiously
CDIILNOORRTTUY introductorily
CDIIMNNOOORTTU induction motor
CDIINOPRTTUUVY unproductivity
CDINOOOPPRSTTU post-production
CEEEEEGIKLRSSX Kegel exercises
CEEEEEILNPRSSX experienceless
CEEEEFFIMNRSST Meissner effect
CEEEEFFKNOSTTY keystone effect
CEEEEFFLLNNNOR Florence fennel
CEEEEFGINNQRUY eigen-frequency
CEEEEFILNRSSTV reflectiveness
CEEEEGIILNNORT electioneering
CEEEEGILNORSST electrogenesis
CEEEEHIILRRSST Leicestershire
CEEEEHIMNPRSWY chimney-sweeper
CEEEEHLNPSSSSS speechlessness
CEEEEIINOPPRSS pioneer species
CEEEEIKNOPRRWX work experience
CEEEEILMNNPSST simple sentence
CEEEEINNORSSTT enterocentesis
CEEEEINPPRSSTV perceptiveness
CEEEEINPRSSSTV respectiveness
CEEEEJKPPRRRST J Presper Eckert
CEEEELLNPRSTUX superexcellent
CEEEENNNOQSSTU sonnet sequence
CEEEEPRSSSTTUZ crêpes suzettes
CEEEFFGHIOPRSU figure of speech
CEEEFFGIIORRST register office
CEEEFFGILNRSVY effervescingly
CEEEFFHIKPRRSU Kupferschiefer
CEEEFFILPRSTTU Peter Sutcliffe
CEEEFFLLPRSSTU self-respectful
CEEEFGILNPRSST self-respecting
CEEEFGLLNNSSTU neglectfulness
CEEEFHIKNNORST Knotenschiefer
CEEEFHILMNNRST self-enrichment
CEEEFHLNNRSSUU uncheerfulness
CEEEFHNNORSSSU rush one's fences
CEEEFIILMPRTVY imperfectively
CEEEFILLNORSST reflectionless
CEEEFILOORRSSX floor exercises

CEEEFILOPRSTTV	self-protective
CEEEFIMNNORRST	reinforcements
CEEEFIMNOOOPRR	Fenimore Cooper
CEEEFLNNOQSSTU	self-consequent
CEEEFLNPRSSSTU	respectfulness
CEEEFLOORRRRTT	retroreflector
CEEEGGGKLLLLOO	Kellogg College
CEEEGGHILMNRTY	emergency light
CEEEGHIIKNNTTT	get it in the neck
CEEEGHIINORSUV	receiving-house
CEEEGHLLLNOTYY	ethylene glycol
CEEEGHLORRSTTV	glove-stretcher
CEEEGHMNNOOSTU	et hoc genus omne
CEEEGIKLNNOPSU	counsel-keeping
CEEEGILLLNRSVW	levelling screw
CEEEGILNOPRSST	teleprocessing
CEEEGILNORRTTV	covering letter
CEEEHHIIKKNTTT	kick in the teeth
CEEEHHIIKNSTTV	thieves' kitchen
CEEEHHIIMNNOST	mose in the chine
CEEEHHILOPRRST	Christopher Lee
CEEEHIJNOPSTTU	step on the juice
CEEEHIKNNOPPSU	keep one's chin up
CEEEHILRSSTTUV	shuttle service
CEEEHIMOORRSTW	meteoric shower
CEEEHIMORSSTTY	hysterectomise
CEEEHIMORSTTYZ	hysterectomize
CEEEHIORRRSSTW	Worcestershire
CEEEHKLMNORSTW	western hemlock
CEEEHMMOPSSSTY	metempsychoses
CEEEHMNNOOORTU	roche moutonnée
CEEEHNOORRTTUV	over-the-counter
CEEEIIKNNPRSST	pernicketiness
CEEEIILMPPRTVY	imperceptively
CEEEIILNPPPRRT	Peter principle
CEEEIILPRRSTVY	irrespectively
CEEEIIMMOORRTT	micrometeorite
CEEEIIMOORRSST	stereoisomeric
CEEEIIMOPPRTTV	precompetitive
CEEEIJOPRSTTTV	projective test
CEEEIKLNNOOPST	line one's pocket
CEEEIKLNPSSSSY	sleepy sickness
CEEEILMNNOPSST	incompleteness
CEEEILOOPRSSTZ	zeolite process
CEEEIMMNNOPRTV	pincer movement
CEEEIMNNORRSVY	money-scrivener
CEEEIMNNORTTUX	extreme unction
CEEEIMNOORSSTT	meteoric stones
CEEEINNOOPRSSS	con espressione
CEEEINOORRRTUX	execution error
CEEEINOPRSSTTV	protectiveness
CEEEINPSSSSTUV	susceptiveness
CEEEIOOPRRTTVV	overprotective
CEEEKOOPRRRSSU	pressure cooker
CEEELLNNOORTTY	non-electrolyte
CEEELLOPPRRRSW	screw propeller
	screw-propeller
CEEENOORSSTUYY	cry one's eyes out
CEEENORRRSSTUU	ruse contre ruse
CEEEPRSSTTTUUX	textus receptus
CEEFFFFHIIORRS	sheriff officer
CEEFFFIILNSSTU	self-sufficient
CEEFFGIILNRSTY	self-rectifying
CEEFFGIIORRSTY	registry office
CEEFGHKLOORTTU	tug the forelock
CEEFGIILLNRTYY	electrifyingly
CEEFGIINNORTTU	counterfeiting
CEEFGILLNNRTUY	unreflectingly
CEEFGILMNOORRT	electroforming
CEEFGILNOPRSTT	self-protecting
CEEFGLLLNOOOSW	Wolfson College
CEEFHHILNOPRRS	French-polisher
CEEFHHMNORRTUV	French vermouth
CEEFHINORTTUWY	The Country Wife
CEEFHMNOOORTTT	come to the front
CEEFIILLNNOSST	inflectionless
CEEFIILNOSSSTU	felicitousness
CEEFIILORRSSST	cross-fertilise
CEEFIILORRSSTZ	cross-fertilize
CEEFIINNOPRSTU	superinfection
CEEFIINNOSSSTU	infectiousness
CEEFIJOOSSSTUY	Society of Jesus
CEEFILMMMNOSTT	self-commitment
CEEFILMNNRSSUU	unmercifulness
CEEFILMNOORSSS	frolicsomeness
CEEFILNNOSSSTT	self-consistent
CEEFILNOOPRSTT	self-protection
CEEFIMORRSSSTY	sisters of mercy
CEEFINOORSSSUV	vociferousness
CEEFINOPRSSSUU	percussion-fuse
CEEFLLMMNOOORW	fellow-commoner
CEEGGHHLLOSSTU	St Hugh's College
CEEGGHIMNOOOPR	geomorphogenic
CEEGGOORRSSSST	St George's cross
CEEGHHIKNNRRTT	trencher-knight
CEEGHIILNRRTTV	right ventricle
CEEGHINNOPPRST	shopping centre
CEEGHJLLNOOSST	St John's College
CEEGHLNOOORTTY	terotechnology
CEEGIIINNOPPRT	precipitinogen
CEEGIILLNORTTY	Trinity College
CEEGIILNNNORTW	electrowinning
CEEGIILNNORRTY	nitroglycerine
CEEGIIMMNNOSTU	immunogenetics
CEEGIINNNPRRST	screen printing
CEEGILLLLNOOSU	lignocellulose
CEEGILMNNORSTU	steering column
CEEGILNOOPRSTU	group selection
CEEGINNNOOPRTU	counter-opening
CEEGINOPRSSTTX	text processing
CEEGNNOOPRRSSS	Congressperson
CEEGNNOOPRRTUU	encounter group
CEEHHHIINORRRR	Heinrich Rohrer
CEEHHIILMOPPST	Mephistophelic
CEEHHIILOOPSTY	heliosciophyte
CEEHHILMNORSTT	Trochelminthes
CEEHHIMNOORRST	heterochronism
CEEHHIMNOSSSTY	chemosynthesis
CEEHHINOOOPSUW	whoopee cushion
CEEHHIOOPRRSTT	heterostrophic
CEEHHKLLMOORSS	Sherlock Holmes
CEEHHMOOORRSTU	heterochromous

Words marked ✧ can also be spelled with one or more capital letters

CEEHHNOOORRSTU heterochronous
CEEHHNOOPPRSST phosphorescent
CEEHIIILLTTUVY utility vehicle
CEEHIILMOPRRTY pyrheliometric
CEEHIILNNOPRSS phenolic resins
CEEHIILNOPPRTY pyelonephritic
CEEHIILNOPSSTT sit on the splice
CEEHIIMOORSTTY stoicheiometry
CEEHIIMOPRSTYZ piezochemistry
CEEHIINNRSSTTY synthetic resin
CEEHIINOSSSTVY voice synthesis
CEEHIINOSSTTUX the Six Counties
CEEHIIOOPRRTTY erythropoietic
CEEHILLOORSTUV Louis Chevrolet
CEEHILMNOOPSTU photoluminesce
CEEHILMORSSTUV The Music Lovers
CEEHIMMMNOSTTT The Commitments
CEEHIMMOPSSSTY metempsychosis
CEEHIMOOOOPRST oophorectomise
CEEHIMOOOOPRTZ oophorectomize
CEEHIMOPRRSTTY petrochemistry
CEEHINNNOOSTTW with one consent
CEEHINOQSSSTTU coquettishness
CEEHINORRRSTUU run their course
CEEHKKNOOPRTTU up to the knocker
CEEHMOOOPRTTTY cytophotometer
CEEHNOOPRSSSUY psychoneuroses
CEEHNOPRSSTTUW put the screws on
CEEIIILMNPPRTY impercipiently
CEEIIILNNPSSTX inexplicitness
CEEIILLMNORSTT scintillometer
CEEIILMORRSTUY meretriciously
CEEIILNNNNOTVY inconveniently
CEEIILNNOSSSTU licentiousness
CEEIILNORSSTTW winter solstice
CEEIILNPSSTUVY insusceptively
CEEIILPPRRSTVY prescriptively
CEEIIMNNOOPTTV non-competitive
CEEIIMNOOPRTTT potentiometric
CEEIINNNNOORTX interconnexion
CEEIINNOPRSSSU perniciousness
CEEIINNORRSTTV non-restrictive
CEEIINNORSSTTU neuroscientist
CEEIIOOPPPRRTV proprioceptive
CEEIKMMOORSTTW works committee
CEEIKNOPPRRSTU counter-skipper
CEEIKNORRRRSTT terror-stricken
CEEILLLMOORRVW Oliver Cromwell
CEEILLLNOORSTU nitrocellulose
CEEILLMNOOPSSX complexionless
CEEILLMOTUVYZZ muzzle velocity
CEEILMMORSSSTU summer solstice
CEEILMNOSSSTUU meticulousness
CEEILMOOORSSST electro-osmosis
CEEILNNNOQSTUY inconsequently
CEEILNNOOPRSSU Cornelius Nepos
CEEILNNOSSSUVV convulsiveness
CEEILNORRSSTTU interlocutress
CEEILNORRSSUYY yours sincerely
CEEIMMMNOORTTV overcommitment
CEEIMMNNNOSTTT miscontentment
CEEIMNOOPRRSST Inspector Morse
CEEIMNOOQRRSUU croque-monsieur
CEEINNNOPRSTTU supercontinent
CEEINNOOORRSSV seroconversion
CEEINNOORSSSSU censoriousness
CEEINNOSSSSTUU incestuousness
CEEINOOOPPRSTY peritoneoscopy
CEEINOOPRRSTTU counter-riposte
CEEIPRRSSTTUUV superstructive
CEEIQRSSTTTUUU cestui que trust
CEEKNNOOOSSTTT Stockton-on-Tees
CEELLOPPRRSSSU suppressor cell
CEELLRRTTUUUUV culture vulture
CEEMNOOPRSTUYY pyrenomycetous
CEEOOORRRSSTVV crossover voter
CEEOPRRRSTTUUW power structure
CEEPRRRSSTTUUU superstructure
CEFFGGHHIINNRT Fighting French
CEFFGIIINNOPRT printing office
CEFFGIINNORRSU nursing officer
CEFFIIIIORTTUV virtute officii
CEFFIIILNNSTUY insufficiently
CEFFINOOOPRSST score points off
CEFGGIINNORRSS cross-fingering
CEFGHIIKNORSST night-fossicker
CEFGHINOORSSST sign of the cross
CEFGIIKLLNORST stocking filler
CEFHHIOPRRRSTY Christopher Fry
CEFHHJNOOORSST John of the Cross
CEFHMMNOOOOSSU House of Commons
CEFHNOOORTTTUU out for the count
CEFIIIIILOPSTT filiopietistic
CEFIIILLNOSTUY infelicitously
CEFINOOORSSSTU Court of Session
CEFLLOPRRSSTUU full-court press
CEFLOOORRTTUUU rule out of court
CEGGHHHILNOOTY high technology
CEGGHHIILNNSST lightning chess
CEGGHIIMRRSTTT Schmitt trigger
CEGGHILMOOOOPR geomorphologic
CEGGIIILNOSSTU geolinguistics
CEGHHIILLMNOOT helminthologic
CEGHHLNOOPSTUY push technology
CEGHHOOPRSSTTU thought process
CEGHIIILNOPRSS rice polishings
CEGHIINNORRSTT stretching iron
CEGHLLLNOOPTUY pull technology
CEGHNNOOORSSUY geosynchronous
CEGHNOOORTTTUY go to the country
CEGHNOORRTTUUW counter-wrought
CEGIIIKLNQRSUV quicksilvering
CEGIIILNOORRST correligionist
CEGIIIMMNNOTUY immunogenicity
CEGIIIMNORTTUY tumorigenicity
CEGIIINPRRTTUW picture-writing
CEGIIMNOPRSTUV moving pictures
CEGIINNOOORRTT retrocognition
CEGIIOOPRRSSTY Crossopterygii
CEGILNNPSSTUUY unsuspectingly
CEGIMNNOOOOSUY gynomonoecious
CEGIMNNOOPRTUU neurocomputing

CEGINNNNOOPTTU contingent upon
CEGINNOOSSSTUU contiguousness
CEHHIIMORSSTTY histochemistry
CEHHIKLMNPRRUY Humphry Clinker
CEHHILOPRRSSTY Christopher Sly
CEHHIMMNOOOPPR morphophonemic
CEHHIMOOPRSTTY photochemistry
CEHHIMOPRSTTYY phytochemistry
CEHHINOOPSTTTY photosynthetic
CEHHMOOPPSTYYY hypophysectomy
CEHIIIKLMOOPRT poikilothermic
CEHIIIKLQRSSUV quicksilverish
CEHIIIMNNORTTY ethnic minority
CEHIIOPPRSSTTY petrophysicist
CEHIJLNOOORSTU join the colours
CEHIKNOORRRRST horror-stricken
CEHIKRRSSTTTUW Kurt Schwitters
CEHILLNNORSSTW Stillson wrench®
CEHILLNOOPRRST controllership
CEHILLNOOPRSSU counsellorship
CEHILMMOOPRSUY myrmecophilous
CEHILMOORSSSST schoolmistress
CEHILOOOOPSSTU opisthocoelous
CEHINNOORRSTTY Sir Henry Cotton
CEHINOOPRSSSUY psychoneurosis
CEHLLLOOPRSSUY sclerophyllous
CEHMOOOPRTTTYY cytophotometry
CEIIIINOSSTTVV vivisectionist
CEIIILNOOSTTUV evolutionistic
CEIIIMPPRRSSTV prescriptivism
CEIIINORRSSTTT restrictionist
CEIIIPPRRSSTTV prescriptivist
CEIIKMNNOOSSST motion sickness
CEIILLOPRSSUUY superciliously
CEIILMNNNOOSTT Miltonic sonnet
CEIILMNOOORTUV microevolution
CEIILMNOPRSTWY Winter Olympics
CEIILMORRSSSUU risorius muscle
CEIILNNNOSSTTY inconsistently
CEIILNOOSSSSTU solicitousness
CEIILNOSTTTUVY constitutively
CEIILOPPRRSTVY proscriptively
CEIIMMNNNOORTU intercommunion
CEIIMMNNORTTUY intercommunity
CEIIMNNOOOPSSU pneumoconiosis
CEIINNOOPPRRST on prescription
CEIINNOORSTTTU reconstitution
CEIINOORSSSTUV victoriousness
CEIINOPPRRSSTU superscription
CEIINOPSSSSSUU suspiciousness
CEIKLLOOSSTUYY leukocytolysis
CEIKNOOPRSSTTU up to one's tricks
CEILLMMMNOOPTU common multiple
CEILLMNOOSTUUY contumeliously
CEILMNNOORSTUY conterminously
CEILMNOOPRSSSU compulsoriness
CEILMOOPRRSSTU multiprocessor
CEILNNNOOSSTUV Viscount Nelson
CEILNOPRRSTUUV proventriculus
CEILNORRSSSSUU scurrilousness
CEIMMMMOOORTTY commit to memory
CEIMMNNORSTUUY community nurse
CEINNNNOOOSTTU non-contentious
CEINNNOOSSSTUU continuousness
CEINOPRRSSTTUU superstruction
CEKLMOOPRSTTUU mock turtle soup
CELMNOOPSTTUUY contemptuously
CELNOPRSSSSUUU scrupulousness
CELOOPRRSSUUUV overscrupulous
CFFGIINNOPRSSU puffin crossing
CFFHIILMNOSTTU fifth columnist
CFGHHIIINNOSTU finishing touch
CFGIILMNNOORSU soul-confirming
CFIILLORRSTTUU floriculturist
CFILLLOOOORRSU corolliflorous
CGGIIKLNNOSSTW swingling-stock
CGHHIIIMMNOOSS High Commission
CGHIILNOPSSTUY psycholinguist
CGHIINOOPRSSTT shooting script
CGIIILNNORTTUY continuity girl
CGIIILNNRSSTUY scrutinisingly
CGIIILNNRSTUYZ scrutinizingly
CGIIILNOOOPSST oligopsonistic
CGIILLNNOOORRT oil-control ring
CGIILNNOOQTTTU quilting-cotton
CGIILNNOOSTUUY incontiguously
CGIIMMNNOOPRSU uncompromising
CGILMNNOOORSTU consulting room
CGIMNOOOPPSTTT potting compost
CHHHNOOOPRRSUY rhynchophorous
CHHIIILOOPPSST philosophistic
CHHIILNOPRTTTY lithonthryptic
CHHIIMNOOOPRRT ornithomorphic
CHHIIOOPRSSTTY trichophytosis
CHHIOOOPPPRRSY pyrophosphoric
CHHJMNOOORSSTY Chrysostom John
CHHKNOORSSTTUW not worth shucks
CHHLLLOOOPRSUY chlorophyllous
CHIIKKNOOORRTV Viktor Korchnoi
CHIILORRSTTTUU horticulturist
CHIINOPRRSSTTU instructorship
CHIIOOOPRRSSST sporotrichosis
CHIIOOORSSTTXY thyrotoxicosis
CHILMOOORSTTUY trichotomously
CHILOOOPPRRSTU prolocutorship
CHLMNOOOPRSUYY Colour Symphony
CIIIMNNORSSTTU misinstruction
CIILNOPSSSUUUY unsuspiciously
CIKKMNOOOSSTUU Mount Kosciusko
CLLNOPRSSUUUUY unscrupulously

D

DDDDEEIILNOOPR lepidodendroid
DDDEEEELNOPRUV underdeveloped
DDDEEIIJKLNSUU Julius Dedekind
DDDEEIIMNNORSU Ironside Edmund
DDEEEEEGNRRSWY dyer's-greenweed
DDEEEEFHILNOPT dip of the needle
DDEEEEFILMNRST self-determined
DDEEEEHINNNPTT The Independent
DDEEEEIMNNRSST determinedness
DDEEEEIMNORRTV over-determined

DDEEEEINNNPRTT interdependent
DDEEEELMMNOSSS meddlesomeness
DDEEEEMMNORTXY extended memory
DDEEEENNRSSSUV undeservedness
DDEEEFINNNRSSU unfriendedness
DDEEEGINNNSSSU undesignedness
DDEEEGNOPRSSST serpent goddess
DDEEEHILNOSTTW let the side down
DDEEEIIKLMNNSS like-mindedness
DDEEEIILMNNSSV evil-mindedness
DDEEEIIMORTUUX deuterium oxide
DDEEEIMNNNOPSS open-mindedness
DDEEEIMNNNORTU undermentioned
DDEEFGHINNORTU night-foundered
DDEEFHHNORRTUU the four hundred
DDEEGGIIIINNNV dividing-engine
DDEEGHHIIMNNSS high-mindedness
DDEEGHIIILMNPT pig-in-the-middle
DDEEGHILLORRSU shoulder girdle
DDEEGIIIIORTVZ video digitizer
DDEEGIILLMNNSY single-mindedly
DDEEGIKMNNOSWY monkey's wedding
DDEEGILNNNOSSW long-windedness
DDEEGNNNORSSUU ungroundedness
DDEEHIINNOSTWY on the windy side
DDEEHINNORRSUU undernourished
DDEEIIIILMNOTT limited edition
DDEEIIINPRSSST dispiritedness
DDEEIIJNNOSSST disjointedness
DDEEIILLMMNPSY simple-mindedly
DDEEIILNORRSSS disorderliness
DDEEIILOPRSTWZ Seidlitz powder
DDEEIIMNOOPRSS mode dispersion
DDEEIIMNOORTTU Dieu et mon droit
DDEEIINNOPSSSS indisposedness
DDEEILLMNOPRSU spindle moulder
DDEELMNOOORTUY Old Deuteronomy
DDEEMNOOOOPRSU do someone proud
DDEFHLOORRRRTU Lord Rutherford
DDEGHIKLNNOPSU lokshen pudding
DDEGHLMOOORUUY good-humouredly
DDEGHLNNOOORSU hold one's ground
DDEGIINNORSSWW window-dressing
DDEHIIIMNNORST third dimension
DDEHIILOPRSUUX sulphur dioxide
DDEHIMNNOPSTUW down in the dumps
DDGHHIKNOOORTY Dorothy Hodgkin
DEEEEFHLNORSTY self-heterodyne
DEEEEFIKNPRRSS finders keepers
DEEEEFILNRSSTT self-interested
DEEEEGGHIMORRT George Meredith
DEEEEGGIINNNRS design engineer
DEEEEGHHILPSST high-speed steel
DEEEEHILLOSTTT stiletto-heeled
DEEEEHILNOOPTV videotelephone
DEEEEHKLNOSTTW The Lost Weekend
DEEEEHLMMORSTT homme de lettres
DEEEEHMNORRRTV Reverend Mother
DEEEEHNNPPRSST Stephen Spender
DEEEEILLMMOSSS Mesdemoiselles
DEEEEILMNRSSSS remedilessness
DEEEEINNRSSSTT interestedness
DEEEEINRSSTTTV vested interest
DEEEELMNOPPRTV predevelopment
DEEEENNRRSSSUV unreservedness
DEEEEOPRRRSSTV reported verses
DEEEFFGHIMORRT freedom fighter
DEEEFFHIPRSSTU sheriff deputes
DEEEFFIMNOOORS ride someone off
DEEEFGGNOORSSS Songs of degrees
DEEEFGIIIMNNNN feminine ending
DEEEFGILLNOPSV self-developing
DEEEFHILORRUVW four-wheel drive
four-wheel-drive
DEEEFIIINNNSST indefiniteness
DEEEFIIINNSSTV definitiveness
DEEEFIILNPRRST Flinders Petrie
DEEEFILNNRSSSS friendlessness
DEEEFILNPSSSTU despitefulness
DEEEFNOORSSSTU surefootedness
DEEEGHIILNNOSS dig in one's heels
dig one's heels in
DEEEGHNNNRSTTU unstrengthened
DEEEGIIKLNNNTT knitting needle
DEEEGIINRSSSSV digressiveness
DEEEGILNNOOPTZ ozone-depleting
DEEEGIOPRRSSTT registered post
DEEEGNNOPRRTUY Young Pretender
DEEEHHLOORSTTT three-toed sloth
DEEEHHPPRRSSSU shepherd's-purse
DEEEHIIKLNOOTT kinetheodolite
DEEEHIINNOOSSS die in one's shoes
DEEEHIINORRRRT inherited error
DEEEHJKNNOPPSY Joseph P Kennedy
DEEEHLLNOPRRST Stephen Dorrell
DEEEIILLNNOSSV love-in-idleness
DEEEIILMPRSSTX limited express
DEEEIIMMNPRRST predeterminism
DEEEIIMNNNOSSY in one's mind's eye
DEEEIIMNRSSTTV divertissement
DEEEIINORRSSVV Revised Version
DEEEIJMOPRRSSU permis de séjour
DEEEIKMNNNOOPS keep one's mind on
DEEEILNNOOOPTZ ozone depletion
DEEEILNNOOPVWW window envelope
DEEEILNNOPRSST enlisted person
DEEEIMMNORRSTY memory-resident
DEEEIMNNRRSTTU reed instrument
DEEEINNNPRSTTU superintendent
DEEEINORRRRSST dernier ressort
DEEELNNORSSSUV unresolvedness
DEEEMNNORSSSTU tremendousness
DEEENNOOOPRSSW powder one's nose
DEEENOPPRSSSSU unprepossessed
DEEFFHHLOORSTU off the shoulder
DEEFFHILLOORST Lord of the Flies
DEEFFIIIMNNRST indifferentism
DEEFFIIINNRSTT indifferentist
DEEFGHILLNSSTU delightfulness
DEEFGIILMORSUX sigmoid flexure
DEEFGIIMMNNOST meeting of minds
DEEFGILNORSSTY self-destroying

DEEFGLNNOOORSW do oneself wrong
DEEFHIIINOSTTV definitive host
DEEFHLNOORRSUZ frozen shoulder
DEEFHLNOORSTWW News of the World
DEEFHNOOOPSTTU out of one's depth
DEEFIILLLORRWY Wilfred O'Reilly
DEEFIILNNNRSSU unfriendliness
DEEFIINOPRSSSU perfidiousness
DEEFIKLLORRTWY flowery-kirtled
DEEFILOORRSTUY do-it-yourselfer
DEEFINNOOSSTTY Stone of Destiny
DEEFLOORRRTTUW four-letter word
DEEFMMNOOORTVX Oxford movement✧
DEEFMNNORSSTTY front-end system
DEEGGMNNOORTTW don't get me wrong
DEEGGOOPRRRSWY Gregory's powder
DEEGHHHILORSTU shoulder-height
DEEGHHMOOORRST horse-godmother
DEEGHIIMNOPRSW whispering dome
DEEGHIINNSTUUX unextinguished
DEEGHIMNOOORST do someone right
DEEGHIOOPRSSUW Sir P G Wodehouse
DEEGHLNNOOOSTU hold one's tongue
DEEGIIILLPSYZZ Dizzy Gillespie
DEEGIIILMOOPST epidemiologist
DEEGIIINNORRST interior design
DEEGIIINNRRSTT riding-interest
DEEGIIINNRSSTT disinteresting
DEEGIIJMNNSTTU sit in judgement
DEEGIILNNNSSUY unyieldingness
DEEGIINNNOSSSU indigenousness
DEEGIINNNPRSTU superintending
DEEGILLOOSSTTY dysteleologist
DEEGILMNNRSTTU disgruntlement
DEEGILNNNPRTUY unpretendingly
DEEGLNNORSSSSU groundlessness
DEEGMNNOOOORSW do someone wrong
DEEGMNOPRTTTUU trumpet-tongued
DEEHHHINOORTUW white horehound
DEEHHIILLLMTWY Wilhelm Dilthey
DEEHHIILNOSTWW how the wind lies
DEEHHINOORSSTT on the short side
DEEHIIIMNNRSTU United Irishmen
DEEHIILMNNPSST displenishment
DEEHIILPQSSSUU sesquisulphide
DEEHIJKNNORRSW Sir John Kendrew
DEEHIMNOOPPRTY Epidermophyton
DEEHKLNOORSSTT the Lord's tokens
DEEHKMNOOOORSW do one's homework
DEEHMMMNOOORST Theodor Mommsen
DEEHNNOORRSSSU horrendousness
DEEHNNORSSSTUU thunderousness
DEEIIIILMRSTUV verisimilitude
DEEIIILLNNNOTT ill-intentioned
DEEIIILNOPRSTV vespertilionid
DEEIIIMNNSSTUV diminutiveness
DEEIIINRSSTTUV disinvestiture
DEEIILLNPPRSST tinsel-slipper'd
DEEIILNOPSSSST split one's sides
DEEIIMNOPRSSTT Redemptionists
DEEIINOPSSSSTU dispiteousness
DEEIMNOPPPPRRT peppermint-drop
DEEJLLNNOORSWY Lord Elwyn-Jones
DEEKKLMRSTUYYZ Kyzyl Kum Desert
DEEKNOOPPRRSTV Dnepropetrovsk
DEEKNOPRRSTTUY knotted spurrey
DEEMMOPRSSTUYY pseudosymmetry
DEENNOOOOPRSST on one's doorstep
DEENNOPSSSSTUU stupendousness
DEENOOPRTTTTUU put out to tender
DEFGHILLOOOPSW good fellowship
goodfellowship
DEFGHILNOORRST longshore drift
Lord of the Rings
DEFGHOOOPRRTUX the Oxford group
DEFGIINNORRSUU in round figures
DEFGILNSSSSTUU disgustfulness
DEFGNOOOORSSUW goods for own use
DEFHHIJLNOORRS Lord John Fisher
DEFHHJNOORRRTU John Rutherford
DEFHIIMNNRSSTU disfurnishment
DEFHILLNOQTTUU not the full quid
DEFHINOOOTTUWW out of the window
DEFHLNOOORRTTW not for the world
DEFIIJKLOPSSUZ Józef Pilsudski
DEFIIKNOOORRRW indoor firework
DEGGHIIJLNORSU Sir John Gielgud
DEGGHILOOORSTY hydrogeologist
DEGGIIIMOORRTV Georgi Dimitrov
DEGGIINNSSSSTU disgustingness
DEGHHHIIOOPRST high-priesthood
DEGHHIIKLRSTTU Turkish delight
DEGHHILORSSTTY short-sightedly
DEGHHOOORSTTTW throw to the dogs
DEGHILNNOORSWY Horse Lying Down
DEGHILNOOPRTUW go up in the world
DEGHILOOOOTTTV dogtooth violet
DEGHINNNOOOSTW do one's own thing
DEGIIIKMNNPRTU drinking-up time
DEGIIKLNNNOSSV loving kindness
DEGIIKNNOORRRW in working order
DEGIILNNOSSUUY disingenuously
DEGIINOOPRSSSU prodigiousness
DEGILLLNOORWYY yellow yoldring
DEGILNOOOOPRTY periodontology
DEGILNOORSSTUY soul-destroying
DEGILNOQRRRSUU ground squirrel
DEGIOPPRRRSSSU suppressor grid
DEHHHILNOOSSTW hold one's whisht
DEHHIMNNOOTTUW down in the mouth
DEHHINOOPRRSSY hydronephrosis
DEHHLOOORRSSUY hold your horses
DEHIIIILMNNPSUU in usum Delphini
DEHIIILOPPRSTT pteridophilist
DEHIILMOPSSTUY lymphoid tissue
DEHIILNNOPTTTU put the tin lid on
DEHIIMOOOPPRST photoperiodism
DEHIIOPSTTTUUW without dispute
DEHILNNOORRTTW Thornton Wilder
DEHIMMOOPPRSSU pseudomorphism
DEHLLMMOPRSUUY Sully Prudhomme
DEHMOOOPPRSSUU pseudomorphous

DEIIIILLNOSSSU disillusionise
DEIIIILLNOSSUZ disillusionize
DEIIINOOPPRSST predisposition
DEIIMNNNRSTTUW wind instrument
DEILLLLOPSSWYY psyllid yellows
DEILMNOOOPSSTU diplostemonous
DEILNOOOPSSTUU pseudosolution
DEINNOOOPPRRTU unproportioned
DELMNOOPSSUUYY pseudonymously
DFGGHINNOOOORT good-for-nothing
DFGHIIILLMNSTW fight windmills
DFHHIILNOORSUW Irish wolfhound
DFHILOOORSTTUW out of this world
DGGHIIIINNSSTU distinguishing
DGHIINNOOPPSWW window-shopping
DGHINORRSTTUWY growth industry
DGIIIKLNNQSUUV Vidkun Quisling
DHHIIMOOPRSTYY hypothyroidism
DHINOOOPRSSTTT prosthodontist
DIIILMNOOSSSTU dissolutionism
DIIILNOOSSSTTU dissolutionist

E

EEEEEEGLLNRRWZ Renée Zellweger
EEEEEFINPRRRST free enterprise
EEEEEGGHORRTTY Georgette Heyer
EEEEEINNRRSSTV Tennessee River
EEEEEINPRRSTTT preterite tense
EEEEELPRSTTTTY Teletypesetter®
EEEEFGHHILNSST The Selfish Gene
EEEEFGLNNRSSUV revengefulness
EEEEFILPRSSSVX self-expressive
EEEEFIMNNORRTV over-refinement
EEEEFIMNORRRTT interferometer
EEEEFIMNRRTTTV remittent fever
EEEEFKNNOPRSSS free-spokenness
EEEEFLNOPRSSSX express oneself
EEEEFLOPRRSTTT Letters of Peter
EEEEGGHIIMNTTV give the meeting
EEEEGGNNOOSSSU Eugene Goossens
EEEEGHMMOORRTT geothermometer
EEEEGILLMNNRTT little green men
EEEEGINRRSSSSV regressiveness
EEEEGJLLORRSUW jeweller's rouge
EEEEHHIINNOTTY hit one in the eye
EEEEHHILNNNOTT nineteenth hole
EEEEHILNPRRSVY reprehensively
EEEEHIMMNORRTT retirement home
EEEEHLMOPRRTTU petroleum ether
EEEEHLMPRRSSTU pressure helmet
EEEEIINPRSSTTV repetitiveness
EEEEILLLNOPPVY Penelope Lively
EEEEILPRRTTTWY teletypewriter
EEEEIMMOPPRRRS Prosper Mérimée
EEEEINNOPRRSTZ enterprise zone
EEEEINNPRRTTTU turpentine tree
EEEEINNPRSSSTV presentiveness
EEEEINNPRSSTVV preventiveness
EEEEINPRRRRSTV reverse printer
EEEEINPRRSSSSV repressiveness
EEEEINPRSSSSVX expressiveness
EEEELLNNRSSSST relentlessness
EEEELMMNOSSSTT mettlesomeness
EEEELPRRSSSSUV pressure vessel
EEEFFFGHIORRSY Geoffrey Fisher
EEEFFFHILMOORT for the life of me
EEEFFFNNOORSTU run off one's feet
EEEFFHIILLORTY the life of Riley
EEEFFHIJLOSSTU The Life of Jesus
EEEFFHLNOORTUW wheel of fortune
EEEFFILMMORSST Mr Mistoffelees
EEEFFLNORSSSST effortlessness
EEEFGGHIILNNRT flight engineer
EEEFGHILLNOPTV flight envelope
EEEFGHILORTUWZ zero fuel weight
EEEFGILNPRRSSV self-preserving
EEEFGLMNNORSTV self-government
EEEFHHLNORRTWY Henry the Fowler
EEEFHKOOPRSTWY power of the keys
EEEFILLNNRSTWX twin-lens reflex
EEEFILNOPRRSSS self-repression
EEEFILNOPRSSSX self-expression
EEEFIMNORRRTTY interferometry
EEEFLLMMNOPSTY self-employment
EEEFLMNORRSSSU remorsefulness
EEEGGGHINORRSW George Gershwin
EEEGGGIOORRRSV Sir George Grove
EEEGGHHILOPPRW George H Whipple
EEEGGHINNORSTW wigs on the green
EEEGGIKMNNRSSS king's messenger
EEEGGIMNNOORSS Georges Simenon
EEEGGIMNNORRSV verse-mongering
EEEGGIMNOOPSVY give someone gyp
EEEGGINOORRSSS one's gorge rises
EEEGGINSSSSTUV suggestiveness
EEEGHIILNRRRST English terrier
EEEGHIINNQRTUV the Virgin Queen
EEEGHILNSSSSTW weightlessness
EEEGHIMMNORSTT mothers' meeting
EEEGHKLORRSUYY keyhole surgery
EEEGIIKMNOPPRS promise-keeping
EEEGIIMNOPRSSS spermiogenesis
EEEGIIMNRRSSST Meistersingers
EEEGIJLLNOOSST get one's jollies
EEEGILLLLMRUUV Lemuel Gulliver
EEEGILLMNORTUY you're telling me
EEEGIMNNOPPRRU emperor penguin
EEEGINOQRRSTUU turquoise-green
EEEGLNNOOOSSTU lose one's tongue
EEEHHILMOPPSST Mephistopheles
EEEHIIILLMMRTT three-mile limit
EEEHIINNNOPPRR norepinephrine
EEEHIINPRSSSTY hypersensitise
EEEHIINPRSSTVY hypersensitive
EEEHIINPRSSTYZ hypersensitize
EEEHIINRSSTTUV intrusive sheet
EEEHIKKLNOOPST telephone kiosk
EEEHILLLMNOSST shell-limestone
EEEHILNOSSTTWW wet one's whistle
EEEHIMNORSSTTW sweet horsemint
EEEHINNOORRSTT norethisterone
EEEHINNOPRSTXY hyperextension

EEEHIOPPRRRSTW	tree worshipper
EEEHIORRSTTUVW	without reserve
EEEHJNOOPRRSTW	Joseph Rowntree
EEEHLMNOOOOTTU	homoeoteleuton
EEEHLNNNOORSTU	turn on one's heel
EEEHMNOOOORRST	someone or other
EEEIILMNPRSSTT	simple interest
EEEIILMNPSTTVY	intempestively
EEEIILNPRRTTVY	interpretively
EEEIILNPRSSVXY	inexpressively
EEEIILOPRSTVVX	explosive rivet
EEEIIMNNNRTTTW	intertwinement
EEEIIMNORSUVWY	Yoweri Museveni
EEEIIMNPRRRSTT	misinterpreter
EEEIIMNPRSSSSV	impressiveness
	permissiveness
EEEIINPRSSSTUV	supersensitive
EEEILMNNPRSTUY	supereminently
EEEILMNOPPRTTZ	Templeton Prize
EEEILMNOSSSSTV	motivelessness
EEEILMPPPSSTUX	exempt supplies
EEEILNOPRSSSSX	expressionless
EEEILNORRSSSTU	irresoluteness
EEEILNRSSSSSST	resistlessness
EEEIMMNNOPRSSU	immune response
EEEIMNOOPSSTUW	put someone wise
EEEIMNOPPRRSST	peremptoriness
EEEIMOORRSSSSV	reverse osmosis
EEEINNOPRSSSSV	responsiveness
EEEINOPPRSSSSV	oppressiveness
EEEINOPSSSSSSV	possessiveness
EEEIPPRRSTTTTY	pretty-pretties
EEEJLLLMOPRTUY	petroleum jelly
EEEJLLPRSTTUWY	jewellers' putty
EEEKLMNNOOOSTW	let someone know
EEEKLNNOOOOPSW	keep one's wool on
EEELLNRSSSSSTU	resultlessness
EEELMNNNOOOOSS	on one's lonesome
EEELMOPRSSSUVX	express volumes
EEEMMMNNOOSTVW	women's movement✧
EEFFFILLLMNSTU	self-fulfilment
EEFFFILLNNOSSU	fluff one's lines
EEFFHHILLOORTT	for the hell of it
EEFFHILOOORTTV	for the love of it
EEFFILNNOORRSU	run for one's life
EEFFLLNOOORSTY	off one's trolley
EEFGGILNOSSSTU	self-suggestion
EEFGHHIINRRRSY	herring-fishery
EEFGHILPRSTUWY	super flyweight
EEFGHINNOORRST	foreshortening
EEFGHINNOPRTTU	put the finger on
EEFGIIILNNPRRT	relief printing
EEFGIKNOORSSTU	stroke of genius
EEFGILLLNOPPRS	self-propelling
EEFGILLNNORTTU	fortune-telling
EEFGILMNNORSTT	self-tormenting
EEFHHILOORSSTW	two for his heels
	two-for-his-heels
EEFHIIOPPRRRSW	fire-worshipper
EEFHILMNNPSSTU	self-punishment
EEFHILNRSSSSTT	thriftlessness
EEFHLLOOOSTTWW	lowest of the low
EEFHLNNOOORSTW	throw oneself on
EEFHMOOPPRRRST	former prophets
EEFIIILNNORRST	Florentine iris
EEFIIMMMOORTTT	from time to time
EEFILLNNOOOPSW	in one fell swoop
EEFILNOOPSSSSS	self-possession
EEFLLMNORRSUUY	unremorsefully
EEFLLNNOOOOSSW	follow one's nose
EEFLNOPPRSSSUU	purposefulness
EEGGGHIKLNORTY	George Knightly
EEGGHHIILNNSTT	sheet lightning
EEGGHHINNOOSUU	enough is enough
EEGGHHIOPSTTUV	give up the ghost
EEGGHIILNRRSTV	reversing light
EEGGIIILNNNRST	Stirling engine
EEGGIIIPPSSTUU	Giuseppe Giusti
EEGGIILNNNSTTT	stinging nettle
EEGGILLOOQRSUY	grey-goose quill
EEGGNOOOPRRTTW	Port Georgetown
EEGHHHINOOPRST	on the high ropes
EEGHHHNOORSTTU	through the nose
EEGHHIILNPSSTW	sheep-whistling
EEGHHIILNSSTTT	in the slightest
EEGHHIOORSTTWW	go with the worse
EEGHIIILNRSSUY	Sergei Ilyushin
EEGHIIKNNRRSSY	Henry Kissinger
EEGHIIMNNSTTUX	extinguishment
EEGHIIMNOQSTTU	quite something
EEGHILLMNORVWY	overwhelmingly
EEGHILLNOPSTUW	pull one's weight
EEGHINOOPPRRTY	porphyrogenite
EEGHINOPRTTTUY	Pitt the Younger
EEGHIOORSTTYYZ	heterozygosity
EEGHLMNNOOOOTU	theologoumenon
EEGIIIILNPRRUV	Pier Luigi Nervi
EEGIIKLNNNOSTV	Ken Livingstone
EEGIILMNORTTUU	ultimogeniture
EEGIILMOOPSSTT	epistemologist
EEGIILNNNPRSTY	serpentiningly
EEGIILNNPRRSTY	enterprisingly
EEGIIMNNOORSST	Simone Signoret
EEGIIMNNRSSTUY	men in grey suits
EEGIINNNPRRSTU	unenterprising
EEGIKLOOORRSVY	Sergei Korolyov
EEGILLNORRTTWY	terry towelling
EEGILMNNORSUUY	luminous energy
EEGILNOOPRRSVW	resolving power
EEGILNOOPRRVWY	overpoweringly
EEHHHIJNNNORYZ	Henry John Heinz
EEHHIIMNORRSSV	Rhemish version
EEHHILMMNOTTTU	melt in the mouth
EEHHILNOORSTWW	worth one's while
EEHHILNPPRSTTU	hunt-the-slipper
EEHHILOOPPRSSS	philosopheress
EEHHIMMOOPRRST	heteromorphism
EEHHIOPPPPTTYY	hippety-hoppety
EEHHLLOOPRSTUY	heterophyllous
EEHHLLOORSTTUY	youth hosteller
EEHHMMOOOORSTU	homoeothermous
EEHHMOOOPRRSTU	heteromorphous

Words marked ✧ can also be spelled with one or more capital letters

EEHIIJLNNNORST	Sir John Tenniel
EEHIILMNNQRSTU	relinquishment
EEHIILNOPPRSTY	pyelonephritis
EEHIILNOSSSTTW	hostile witness
EEHIIMMNOPRSTV	impoverishment
EEHIIMNOORSSTY	emission theory
EEHIIMNORSTTVY	Timothy Severin
EEHIINOOPRRTTY	erythropoietin
EEHIINOOPSSSTT	photosensitise
EEHIINOOPSSTTV	photosensitive
EEHIINOOPSSTTZ	photosensitize
EEHIIOOPRRSSTY	erythropoiesis
EEHIJLOPPRSTUZ	Joseph Pulitzer
EEHIKLMNOPRSST	skeleton shrimp
EEHILNNNOPSTTY	penny-in-the-slot
EEHIMOOPRRRSTU	mother superior
EEHIMPPRSSSSST	sempstress-ship
EEHINNNOOOPPSS	pin one's hopes on
EEHINNOORSSTTW	noteworthiness
EEHINNOPRRTTTU	three-point turn
EEHINNORSSSTWW	newsworthiness
EEHINOOPPQSTTU	pop the question
EEHINOORSTTUVW	View on the Stour
EEHINOPPRRSSTW	serpent-worship
EEHKNOOPRSTTWY	The New York Post
EEHLLOORSSSTTY	hostess trolley
EEHMMNOORSSSUU	humoursomeness
EEIIIIKLLLSTTT	tell it like it is
EEIIIMNPSTTTVY	intempestivity
EEIIKKLNOPRSTW	Wilson Kipketer
EEIILMNNRTTTTY	intermittently
EEIILNNRSSSSTU	unsisterliness
EEIILNOPRRSSVY	irresponsively
EEIILNPRRTTUVY	interruptively
EEIILNPRSSSSST	spiritlessness
EEIIMMMNOPRSTV	misimprovement
EEIIMMNNNORRSS	nine men's morris
EEIIMNNNOOOPST	pin it on someone
EEIIMNOPRSSSUV	imperviousness
EEIINNOPRSTUVY	open university✧
EEIINOPRRSSSTT	Pointer Sisters
EEIKLLNOPRTTUV	Oliver Plunkett
EEIKLMNOQRRSUY	squirrel monkey
EEILMNNNNOOTVV	non-involvement
EEILMNOPRSSUUV	nervous impulse
EEILNNOPRSSUVY	unresponsively
EEILNOOPSSSTTV	split one's votes
EEIMNORSSSSTUY	mysteriousness
EEINNNOORSSTUV	nervous tension
EEINNOOOPQSTTU	open to question
EEINOOOOPRRTZZ	zero-zero option
EEINOOPPRSSSTX	expression stop
EEINOPRRSSSTUV	protrusiveness
EEIOPPRRSSSTTU	strepsipterous
EEKLNOORRSTTUV	true-lover's knot
EELNNOORSSSTUU	ultroneousness
EELOOPPRRSSTUY	preposterously
EENNOOOPPRRSST	person-to-person
EENNOOPRSSSTTU	portentousness
EENNOOPRSSTTUU	turn up one's toes
EENOOPPRRSSSSU	prosperousness
EENOORRSSSSTTU	stertorousness
EFFFGIILLLLNSU	self-fulfilling
EFFGHHLOORTTUU	forethoughtful
EFFGHIIJNORRTY	Griffith Joyner
EFFGHIJNORRSSY	Griff Rhys Jones
EFFGIIJLNSSTUY	self-justifying
EFFGIINNOPRSTT	offset printing
EFFGILNORRTUUV	griffon vulture
EFFHIILLMNSTUW	wish fulfilment
EFFILNNRSSTUUU	unfruitfulness
EFFNORSSSTTTUU	strut one's stuff
EFGGHHIILLTTWY	light flyweight
EFGGHIILNNORTW	night-flowering
EFGGIIINNNOPRT	finger-pointing
EFGGIIINNNPRRT	fingerprinting
EFGGOOORRRSTUY	Gregory of Tours
EFGHHHIJMOPRTU	for the high jump
EFGHHIILNOPTTT	in the top flight
EFGHHILNOORRST	threshing floor
EFGHHIMNOSSTTU	the sum of things
EFGHHINORRSSTT	forthrightness
EFGHHLNOSSTTUU	thoughtfulness
EFGHIIKLLRSTTY	skylight filter
EFGHIILNOORRTW	withering-floor
EFGHILNNOOOORU	Legion of Honour
EFGHILNNRSSTUU	unrightfulness
EFGHILNPRSSSTU	sprightfulness
EFGHLNOOORSTWY	glory of the snow
EFGIILLNQRRSUY	flying squirrel
EFGILNOPPRSSTU	self-supporting
EFHHIMNOOOTTTU	foot-in-the-mouth
EFHHIOOOPRSSUW	house of worship
EFHHLNOOOOPRST	on the shop floor
EFHILMNOOOSSST	tomfoolishness
EFHILNOPRSSSUW	worshipfulness
EFHKLOOORRTTUU	further outlook
EFHLNNRSSTTUUU	untruthfulness
EFHNNOOOOPRRSU	person of honour
EFHNOORRTTUUWY	twenty-four-hour
EFIIKKLLOOPSST	Feliks Topolski
EFIILLMNORSTTV	Sir Nevill F Mott
EFILLNOOPPRSSU	self-propulsion
EFILOOOPRRSSUY	soporiferously
EFINOORSSSTTUU	fortuitousness
EFKLLNOOOSSTUU	out of one's skull
EGGGHIIIJTTTWY	get jiggy with it
EGGHIIILMNPTTU	lighting-up time
EGGIIKLMNRSTWY	Mrs Tiggy-Winkle
EGGIILNNOPRTTU	triple-tonguing
EGHHIILNOORSTU	high-resolution
EGHHILNNOOOTTT	long in the tooth
EGHHILNNORRSTT	northern lights
EGHHILNORSSTTU	southern lights
EGHHIMNNOOOPST	monophthongise
EGHHIMNNOOOPTZ	monophthongize
EGHHINOPSTTTTU	putting the shot
EGHHLLOOTTTUUW	well-thought-out
EGHIIILMNRSSTV	silversmithing
EGHIIILNNSTTTY	light intensity
EGHIIINNRRRSVY	Sir Henry Irving
EGHIIKLNNNSSTU	unknightliness

EGHIIKNNNNSSTU	unthinkingness
EGHIILLMORSTTT	grist to the mill
EGHIILMNNOOPRT	Philo Remington
EGHIINNNOORSTW	in one's own right
EGHIINOOPPRRST	progenitorship
EGHIJLLNNOORSV	Long John Silver
EGHILLNPRSSTTU	pull the strings
EGHLNNOOOPRUYY	neurohypnology
EGHLOOOOPRRTTY	orthopterology
EGHMOOOPRRRTTW	growth promoter
EGIIILLLLNNORT	Lionel Trilling
EGIIILMMNNORVY	in living memory
EGIIILNNNRTTWY	intertwiningly
EGIIIMNNNRTTTU	unintermitting
EGIIKLLMNOORST	Kremlinologist
EGIILLMOORSSSU	miles gloriosus
EGIILNNOORSSSU	ingloriousness
EGIIMNOOPRRSSS	progressionism
EGIINNOPRRRSTU	interior-sprung
EGIINNPRRSSSSU	surprisingness
EGIINOOPRRSSST	progressionist
EGIJKOORRSTWYZ	Jerzy Grotowski
EGILMMMNOPRTUU	rummelgumption
	rummlegumption
EHHIIILMOPPSST	Mephistophilis
EHHIIIMNPRSSST	miner's phthisis
EHHIIMMOOPRRST	theriomorphism
EHHIKNOORRRSTY	North Yorkshire
EHHIKOORRSSTUY	South Yorkshire
EHHILMOOPPSSTU	Mephostophilus
EHHIMMMOOOOPRS	homoeomorphism
EHHIMOOOPRRSTU	theriomorphous
EHHINNOOSTTUWY	Whitney Houston
EHHINOOOPPPRST	phosphoprotein
EHHINOOPSSSTTY	photosynthesis
EHHLLMOOPRSTUY	thermophyllous
EHHMMOOOOOPRSU	homoeomorphous
EHHNNOORRSTTTW	north-north-west
EHHOOSSSTTTUUW	south-south-west
EHIIIINNOQSTTU	the Inquisition
EHIILMNOPRSTUW	multi-ownership
EHIILNNOOPRRTT	trinitrophenol
EHIIMMNOOPRSSU	immunophoresis
EHIINNOOPRSSWW	win one's worship
EHIIOOPPPRRRST	proprietorship
EHIIOPPRRSSSUV	supervisorship
EHIJJMMNNOOSTY	Jimmy Johnstone
EHIJLNOOPRSSSY	Sir Joseph Lyons
EHILMNOPSSTTYY	polysynthetism
EHILNNOOORSTTW	throw in one's lot
EHILOPPRSSTTUY	polishers' putty
EHIMOORRSTUUUV	vitreous humour
EHINNOOPRSSTTU	put one's shirt on
EHINOOOPRRSSTU	trophoneurosis
EHMMOOORRSSTUY	oyster mushroom
EIIIINNQRSTTUU	inquisiturient
EIIIINOQRSSTTU	requisitionist
EIIIKLLMOPRTTU	like it or lump it
EIIIMNORSSTTTU	restitutionism
EIIINNOPPPPRST	Ripstone pippin
EIIINNOQSSSTUU	iniquitousness
EIIINORSSTTTTU	restitutionist
EIIIOOPRSSTTVY	seropositivity
EIIKMNNOOOPSSU	pneumokoniosis
EIIKMNNOORRTUW	munition-worker
EIILLNNOOOPSTU	noise pollution
EIILMNOOQRSUUY	querimoniously
EIILOOPPSSTTVY	postpositively
EIIMNNOOOPRTTY	poetry in motion
EIINNOOOPPRTTT	point-to-pointer
EIINNOORRRTTUY	union territory
EIINNORSSSTTUU	nutritiousness
EIINOOPPPRSSTU	presupposition
EIINOOPPRSSSTU	propitiousness
EIINOPRSSSSTUU	spirituousness
EIJLLNOORTUUVY	July Revolution
EIKNNNNOOOOSSW	know one's onions
EIKNOORRRTTUYY	Yukon Territory
EILMNNOOSSSUUV	voluminousness
EILMNOOPPSSUUV	vulpine opossum
EILNOOOPPRRSST	proportionless
EIMMMORRRRSTYY	mirror symmetry
EIMMNOPPRSSSUU	immunosuppress
EIMNNOOOPPRRTT	proportionment
EIMNNOOORSSSUV	omnivorousness
EIMNOOOPRRSSTY	promissory note
EIMNOPRSSSSTTU	stir one's stumps
EIMOOOPPPPRSTT	opposite prompt
EINOPRSSSTTUVY	topsy-turviness
EIORRRRSTTTTUY	trust territory
EKMMOOOORRSSTY	smoke-room story
ELMNOSSSTTUUUU	tumultuousness
ELMOPPRSSTUUUY	presumptuously
ELNOOPPRRSSUUY	unprosperously
ELNOOPSSSTUUUV	voluptuousness
EMNNNOOOOSSSTU	monotonousness
EMNNNOOSSSSUYY	synonymousness
EMNOPPRSSTUUUU	unpresumptuous

F

FGGHIIIILLNOPTW	pillow-fighting
FGHHIIKNNNOOTT	think nothing of
FGHHIJKNNOOSTT	Knight of St John
FGHHLLNOTTUUUY	unthoughtfully
FGIILMNOPPRSTU	film supporting
FIIIIILLNOPPPP	Filippino Lippi

G

GGGGIIINNNNRRU	running rigging
GGHHILLLLOOTYY	Holly Golightly
GGHIIJJLNNNNOY	jingling Johnny
GGIIIKNNRSSSST	kissing-strings
GGIIILLOORSTTU	liturgiologist
GHHIILLNORSSTW	shillingsworth
GHIIKMNNNOOSTW	know-nothingism
GHIILLLNOOPTTU	light pollution
GHILOOOOPSTTYZ	zoophytologist
GIIIINPRRRSSTT	spirit-stirring
GIIKMMNNRSSTUW	swimming trunks
GIILOOOPRSSTTT	protistologist
GILOOOOOPRSTTZ	protozoologist

H

HHIILNOOOPRSTU ornithophilous
HIIILNOPRSTTTT lithontriptist

I

IIIOOPPSSSTTUU supposititious
IILLNOOORRTTTU trinitrotoluol
IILNOOPPRSTUUY unpropitiously
IKKNOOOPPRRTTY Pyotr Kropotkin

15 letters

A

AAAAAADDDDDDYYY yadda yadda yadda
AAAAABBCDLNRRRT Barbara Cartland
AAAAABBDDEMRRRW Dame Barbara Ward
AAAAACCILLMNNTU Nautical Almanac
AAAAACDIMMNRSTU Maracana Stadium
AAAAACEEHKLLRRT Haleakala Crater
AAAAACEIILMNPST aplastic anaemia
AAAAADDEPRRRSTU per ardua ad astra
AAAAADDIILNRSVV Aravinda Da Silva
AAAAADEEGKNTTTV take at advantage
AAAAAEKLLMMNSTU Alaskan malamute
AAAAAGJNNNRRTUU Arjuna Ranatunga
AAAABBCKNRRSTWY Barbara Stanwyck
AAAABBDHMNOORSY hamadryas baboon
AAAABCCDEJMSSUU Judas Maccabaeus
AAAABCCHIILMNNS bacchanalianism
AAAABCEEEKKLMNR make a clean break
AAAABCEEHLLLMTV balaclava helmet✧
AAAABCEFLMNRSTU MacFarlane's buat
AAAABCEHINRRTTT Tetrabranchiata
AAAABCEILLNOOPT palaeobotanical
AAAABDEFLNNORRR Fernando Arrabal
AAAABDEHIINNOSS Bahasa Indonesia
AAAABEEIKLLMRTV available market
AAAABEHIKMNOOTY Yamabe no Akahito
AAAABEILMNNRRSU Arabian numerals
AAAACCCCCHHNSTT catch-as-catch-can
AAAACCCILLLLTTY catallactically
AAAACCDEEHHLNRT Aachen Cathedral
AAAACCDIIKLLLSY lackadaisically
AAAACCEEEIILNPS Caesalpiniaceae
AAAACCEFIIMNNRR African-American
AAAACCEHHIMNPTT Captain MacHeath
AAAACCEHHLNNOPT acanthocephalan
AAAACCEIMMNOPRR panoramic camera
AAAACDDIKNORRVZ Radovan Karadzic
AAAACDDIMMNNOSS Cosmas and Damian
AAAACDDLMMNORSY Ramsay MacDonald
AAAACDEGIINPRRR carriage and pair
AAAACDEGILRRUWY dual carriageway
AAAACDELLLMMOPR Palma de Mallorca
AAAACDHNOORSSSU as sound as a roach
AAAACDIILMNNRRZ Cardinal Mazarin
AAAACDIILNPQRSU Aquila and Prisca
AAAACEEENPPRSSV save appearances
AAAACEFFMORSTTT as a matter of fact
AAAACEFIIMNNNOS Fanconi's anaemia
AAAACEFILLLMRTY material fallacy
AAAACEGHILLOPPR palaeographical
AAAACEGIILRRRWY railway carriage
AAAACEHILNNRSSV Haversian canals
AAAACEIILLMNRST Alistair Maclean
AAAACEILLMNNRTY alimentary canal
AAAACEILNNRRSTU Australian crane
AAAACFGHIMNNORY African mahogany
AAAACFILNORTTTT Fatal Attraction
AAAACGGIIMNNPST campaign against
AAAACGHILLPPRRY paragraphically
AAAACGIILNPSTTX capital gains tax
AAAACHIKKLNPSST as thick as a plank
AAAADDDEILNOORS dead as a doornail
AAAADDEGLMNORXY Andromeda galaxy
AAAADEEFGKNOTTV take advantage of
AAAADEEGILMMORR Marriage à la Mode
AAAADEEIIKKSSSW Kawasaki disease
AAAADEEIIMMNSST Minamata disease
AAAADEFINNORSUX Ariadne auf Naxos
AAAADEGIINOPSST A Passage to India
AAAADEGJLMRRTYY Lady Margaret Jay
AAAADGIJMNNORRT Joan Armatrading
AAAADHIIILNNSSW Hawaiian Islands
AAAADHILMNNNSTT Manhattan Island
AAAADILLLNPRRUX diurnal parallax
AAAAEEGGNNORSTY George Santayana
AAAAEEHMNNPRTTZ Tarzan the Ape Man
AAAAEEIIKMNNNTV take a name in vain
AAAAEEKLLMMNSTU Alaskan malemute
AAAAEELLMNPPRRT parametral plane
AAAAEFHIOPRRRYZ Prayer of Azariah
AAAAEGGLLNNRTUU natural language
AAAAEGILMNRRTTX marginal tax rate
AAAAEHHJLLNRRUW Jawaharlal Nehru
AAAAEIILLMNNORT animal rationale
AAAAEIILMNNPRRT parliamentarian
AAAAEILLMNNQRTU Allan Quatermain
AAAAELMORRSSTTT tarsometatarsal
AAAAGHIIKLMNRST Marghanita Laski
AAAAGHILMNOPRST phantasmagorial
AAAAILOOPRRRRTU La Aurora Airport
AAAAILORRRSSTUU Aurora Australis✧
AAAAIMNOOOSSSTZ Anastasio Somoza
AAABBBEGHIKNRST Sabbath-breaking
AAABBCDDEEGHMRU drumhead cabbage
AAABBCDEGIMNRSS screaming abdabs
AAABBCDEILLLORU Luca della Robbia
AAABBCEEGLMOPTT cabbage palmetto
AAABBCEEHINRRTT Barbican Theatre
AAABBCEFILMORTT Battle of Cambrai
AAABBCERRRSSSST St Barbara's cress
AAABBDDEEFKNRST bed and breakfast

bed-and-breakfast
AAABBDEEGLMRRRT Margaret Drabble
AAABBDEIMNRSTUU Bernabau Stadium
AAABBDEINRRRSST Barbra Streisand
AAABBDHHIILLMRU Abdullah Ibrahim
AAABBDJLLMOPSYY baby-doll pyjamas
AAABBEEGIMNNRST bargain-basement
AAABBEHHOPRRRTW Barbara Hepworth
AAABBEILLMMOSST basal metabolism
AAABBIIIILLOTVY bioavailability
AAABCCCDGIINORS carbonic-acid gas
AAABCCCIKLLNOTU back-calculation
AAABCCEEHLMNRSU ambulance-chaser
AAABCCEHIINRTTT Tectibranchiata
AAABCCEILLNOOST occasional table
AAABCCFINNORSSY San Francisco Bay
AAABCDDGHILORRR Archibald Garrod
AAABCDDIILRRSVY Sir David Barclay
AAABCDEEEHILMNR machine-readable
AAABCDEELLMNPRS landscape-marble
AAABCDEGILNNORT botanical garden
AAABCDEHIKPRSTT strike a bad patch
AAABCDEIILLNRSS Balearic Islands
AAABCDFNNOORRTW contraband of war
AAABCDIIIIORRSS Isidor Isaac Rabi
AAABCDLMNNRUVYY Army and Navy Club
AAABCEEELRRRSTV sacral vertebrae
AAABCEEFLNNORTU balance of nature
AAABCEEFNOPRTUV put a brave face on
put on a brave face
AAABCEEHHILMNSW machine-washable
AAABCEEHINRRTTT tetrabranchiate
AAABCEEILMRSSTU Beaumaris Castle
AAABCEEILNNRSTU unascertainable
AAABCEFLMNNRSTU blast-furnaceman
AAABCEGIILMNRSV balsamic vinegar
AAABCEGILNRTTVY galvanic battery
AAABCEILLLRSTTY tetrasyllabical
AAABCEILLMNRRTU interambulacral
AAABCEILNOPSTTU Captain Absolute
AAABCEILNRSTTUU tableau curtains
AAABCFHIKLLLRRS Blackfriars Hall
AAABCHIILOPPRTY approachability
AAABCHIINORSSTW boatswain's chair
AAABCHILNOPRRST Caspar Bartholin
AAABCIIILNNNOST cannibalisation
AAABCIIILNNNOTZ cannibalization
AAABCIKLNNORSTT back translation
AAABDDEEEHMNSTY many-headed beast
AAABDDEELMNNORU Andromeda nebula
AAABDDEELNNRRXY brandy Alexander
AAABDEFHIIMRTTW Fatima Whitbread
AAABDEFLMMRTTUY Madama Butterfly
AAABDHILMNNRSUY animal husbandry
AAABDLLLLMMNSSY by small and small
AAABEEEIINRSSST East Siberian Sea
AAABEEELMSSTTTT metastable state
AAABEEGHLLMNRTU The Grauballe Man
AAABEEHKLLNSTVY Helena Blavatsky
AAABEEILLNNSSUV unavailableness
AAABEEKKLLRSTTU talk a blue streak
AAABEELLNNPRTUY planetary nebula
AAABEELNNRRSSTW warrantableness
AAABEFGHIKLORSS Kasbah of Algiers
AAABEFIKLNOOTTW Battle of Okinawa
AAABEFIKLNSSSTU Sebastian Faulks
AAABEFILLMOSSTT Battle of Salamis
AAABEGIIILMRRTY marriageability
AAABEGIILLMRRST Gabriela Mistral
AAABEHIILNOPSTT alphabetisation
AAABEHIILNOPTTZ alphabetization
AAABEHLLLLORRTY Royal Albert Hall
AAABEIILLMNPRRS prima ballerinas
AAABEILNSTTUVVX tableaux vivants
AAABELMNOORSTTU neuroblastomata
AAABFFLLNOOSTTY fantasy football
AAABIIIILMNNTTY maintainability
AAABIILLNRSTTTY translatability
AAABIILMNPRSSSU Sublapsarianism
AAABILNNRSSTTTU transubstantial
AAACCCDDHIIINOR arachidonic acid
AAACCCDEELORRRT accelerator card
AAACCCDEIIIMNOT amino-acetic acid
AAACCCEEEHPRRST escape character
AAACCCEEFILNPST self-capacitance
AAACCCEEHIILLRT Callitrichaceae
AAACCCEHHKMNNOY hackney-coachman
AAACCCEILNOOSSU occasional cause
AAACCCGHHILLOPR chalcographical
AAACCCILLLMSTYY cataclysmically
AAACCDDEEENNNTT dance attendance
AAACCDDEGNNNOST song-and-dance act
AAACCDEEHHILMRY Archichlamydeae
AAACCDEEILOPSSU asclepiadaceous
AAACCDEEIMMMSUU Accademia Museum
AAACCDEEMOPRRYY camera-ready copy
AAACCDEGIMNNOTU cut and come again
AAACCDEIMNNOORS adenocarcinomas
AAACCDHKNORRTTU a hard nut to crack
AAACCEEEHMNNRTV avec acharnement
AAACCEEEILNOORU Eriocaulonaceae
AAACCEEFHILMRRW chemical warfare
AAACCEEGHIKNRRY hackney carriage
AAACCEEHKNOPPST peacock-pheasant
AAACCEEHLLOPRYY Caryophyllaceae
AAACCEEINNPQRTU preacquaintance
AAACCEEINORRSSU sarraceniaceous
AAACCEELLORSSTU escalator clause
AAACCEFHILLPTTY pathetic fallacy
AAACCEFHIOPRTTY capacity for heat
AAACCEFIIRRRRRT aircraft-carrier
AAACCEGHHILMORY Hoagy Carmichael
AAACCEGHILNOOPR oceanographical
AAACCEGHRRRSSST grass characters
AAACCEGILLRSSST Classical Greats
AAACCEGIOPRSTTY storage capacity
AAACCEHILMPRTTY thermal capacity
AAACCEHILNRRTTT Atlantic Charter
AAACCEHMNORTTTT chemoattractant
AAACCEIILLNNNTT antenatal clinic
AAACCEIILLNPRTY Capernaitically
AAACCEILLNNORTY anacreontically

AAACCEILNOPRRST practical reason
AAACCEMOPPRRSTU carpometacarpus
AAACCFIIMNORRSU François Mauriac
AAACCGIILLLNOTY analytical logic
AAACCHIILLNRSTY anarchistically
AAACCHIILMNNORT antimonarchical
AAACCHILMORRSST A Christmas Carol
AAACCIIILMNOSTT acclimatisation
AAACCIIILMNOTTZ acclimatization
AAACCIILLLSTTTY stalactitically
AAACCIILLMNORTY microanalytical
AAACCIILLNOPRTY capillary action
AAACCILLLOPPTYY apocalyptically
AAACDDDHILMNNNO Madonna and Child
AAACDDEEELLNRRX Alexander Calder
AAACDDEHHLMRRTU Durham Cathedral
AAACDDEHILMPRTU Dutch admiral pea
AAACDDGINNORSST rain cats and dogs
AAACDEEEGLNNRTW Newgate Calendar
AAACDEEEHHILLPP Philadelphaceae
AAACDEEEMMNRSTU amusement arcade
AAACDEEFFGHIRRS chargé-d'affaires
AAACDEEGHMNNRTX Exchange and Mart
AAACDEEHIJLMNOT Michael Ondaatje
AAACDEEHILMNRST Amiens Cathedral
AAACDEEHISSSSTY Tay-Sachs disease
AAACDEEILLMNORT moderate in a call
AAACDEEILRSSSUV vascular disease
AAACDEFGIORRRRW carriage-forward
AAACDEFJKLLORST jack-of-all-trades✧
AAACDEGGIILNNRR landing-carriage
AAACDEGGLMMNNOU command language
AAACDEGIILLMNTY diamagnetically
AAACDEHHINNRTUV Chavín de Huantar
AAACDEHIILMMSSY Michaelmas-daisy
AAACDEIILMMRTYY military academy
AAACDEIILMNQRSU Macquarie Island
AAACDEIILNNORST calendarisation
AAACDEIILNNORTZ calendarization
AAACDEIILNNPPRU appendicularian
AAACDEIILNORSST desacralisation
AAACDEIILNORSTZ desacralization
AAACDEILLMNORYY aerodynamically
AAACDEILLMORSUY amaryllidaceous
AAACDEILLNORSSS Coral Sea Islands
AAACDEILNOPRSSX paradoxicalness
AAACDEIMMMPRRSU dramma per musica
AAACDEIMNNOORTT animated cartoon
AAACDEJKLMMORSY Lord James Mackay
AAACDEJKMNNOSSS Sam Jackson Snead
AAACDFFIKMPRRRS Cardiff Arms Park
AAACDFGIILMNORR African marigold
AAACDFJLNOORSTU Acts of Adjournal
AAACDGILMNOOORR Girolamo Cardano
AAACDHILLLMMNOR Harold Macmillan
AAACDHILMNORRTY admiralty anchor
AAACDIIINORTTVY cavity radiation
AAACDIINNNNOTUY Annunciation Day
AAACEEEEKLMNPSW make a clean sweep
AAACEEEGHILNSTU Hanseatic league
AAACEEEMNNOPPRY appearance money
AAACEEFGLLLOSUX La Cage aux Folles
AAACEEFHILNNPRT African elephant
AAACEEFMMOPRRST stop-frame camera
AAACEEGGHILMNNU machine language
AAACEEGILLLMNOW milage allowance
AAACEEGILNORTTV lactovegetarian
AAACEEHIIMOPRST spirochaetaemia
AAACEEHILLMORTT Charlotte Amalie
AAACEEHILLNSSTW clean as a whistle
AAACEEHILLNSTTY anaesthetically
AAACEEHILLQRRTU equilateral arch
AAACEEHILNSTUVV Eustachian valve
AAACEEHIMMMSTTT metamathematics
AAACEEHJKQSTTUW Jacquetta Hawkes
AAACEEIIMNNNPRS Riemannian space
AAACEEIMMPPRRTT impact parameter
AAACEFGILNPRRSV Francis Palgrave
AAACEFHHIILMRRS air-chief-marshal
AAACEFHKKLLNOOP knock all of a heap
AAACEFILLLMNOWY family allowance
AAACEFILMNOPRTT act of parliament
AAACEFILNNSSSTT fantasticalness
AAACEGIINNSTTTT antistatic agent
AAACEGILLNPRSST Pascal's triangle
AAACEGILMNOPRTY malacopterygian
AAACEGILMNPRSST pragmaticalness
AAACEGILNNOPSTU plantaginaceous
AAACEHHIILMPRTT amphitheatrical
AAACEHHLLLOOPRS alpha-chloralose
AAACEHHMNOOPRST Athena Promachos
AAACEHHMOPPRRTY pharmacotherapy
AAACEHIILNPRSSS pharisaicalness
AAACEHILLORRSSW Clarissa Harlowe
AAACEHILNOOPPRT palaeoanthropic
AAACEHIMPPRSTTY parasympathetic
AAACEIIILLMRSTT materialistical
AAACEIIIMNNORST Americanisation
AAACEIIIMNNORTZ Americanization
AAACEIILLLNSSXY lexical analysis
AAACEIILMNORSTY anomalistic year
AAACEIILMPSSTTT state capitalism
AAACEIILNPRSSST parasiticalness
AAACEIILPRRSSST spiral staircase
AAACEIKLMMNORTX exclamation mark
AAACEILMNNOORTU neuroanatomical
AAACEILNORSTTUY Cautionary Tales
AAACEILNPRRSTWY special warranty
AAACEIMNOPRSTTU a storm in a teacup
AAACEINNNOQSSUU causa sine qua non
AAACELLLNNOSTTT Tantallon Castle
AAACFGIILLNOPTT floating capital
AAACFIILNOPRRTT partial fraction
AAACFILMNOOSSTW law of mass action
AAACGGHIJKLNSSU laughing jackass
AAACGHHILOPRSST thalassographic
AAACGHIILPRRSTT stratigraphical
AAACGHILLOPRTUY autographically
AAACGIIILLMNNST anti-Gallicanism
AAACGIILLLMSTTY stalagmitically
AAACGIILLLNOSSY logical analysis
AAACGIINNOPRTTT capitation grant

AAACGILLMMNRTUY ungrammatically
AAACGILLMOORTTU traumatological
AAACGIMNOPPRSTT pantopragmatics
AAACHIIMNNOORRT anharmonic ratio
AAACHIIMNOORSTT achromatisation
AAACHIIMNOORTTZ achromatization
AAACHILNOORSSTT carnassial tooth
AAACIIILLLMNOPT political animal
AAACIILLLMNNOOS colonial animals
AAACIILLLMNOSTY anomalistically
AAACIILMMNOPRST mari complaisant
AAACIILNORSSTUV vascularisation
AAACIILNORSTUVZ vascularization
AAACIIORSSTTTTW straitwaistcoat
AAACILLMOOSTTUY Louisa May Alcott
AAACILLNNOORTTV contravallation
AAACILLNNORSTTY transactionally
AAACILLNORSTTUY astronautically
AAACILMOOOORTTX locomotor ataxia
AAACILNOORRSSTU Corona Australis
AAADDDDEEILORRU Edouard Daladier
Édouard Daladier
AAADDDEEIMNPRRV Père Armand David
AAADDDEELOOPRRV Pedro de Alvarado
AAADDDILLNNORSV Randall Davidson
AAADDEEEHNORRSV over head and ears
AAADDEEINRSSSUY Raynaud's disease
AAADDEELLLNORSV Salvador Allende
AAADDEELNOPPRTT Tadpole and Taper
AAADDEFHNNRSSST hard-and-fastness
AAADDEGGHNOOPSW Shwe Dagon Pagoda
AAADDEGHIINNSTY in this day and age
AAADDEGINOORRRT do a roaring trade
AAADDEGINOSSTUV disadvantageous
AAADDEHJMMMNNOO Dame Joan Hammond
AAADDEHJNNORSTW Jonathan Edwards
AAADDEHNNNOOSTU a thousand and one
AAADDELLNRSSWWY Wladyslaw Anders
AAADDELMNNOOPRT Madonna del Prato
AAADDELOPRRSSST pastoral address
AAADDFIKLLLNNSS Falkland Islands
AAADDGHJKLMMORS Dag Hammarskjöld
AAADDGHLLNNOUWY laugh and lay down
AAADDIIILOSSUUV audiovisual aids
AAADDIINNORSSTT standardisation
AAADDIINNORSTTZ standardization
AAADEEEEPPPRRRT paper tape reader
AAADEEEGJRRSTUV average adjuster
AAADEEEGNRRSSVV Vanessa Redgrave
AAADEEEHJLNNPRT japanned leather
AAADEEEHNNOSVWY have one's end away
AAADEEEIILNRRST residential area
AAADEEEILLLPPPR parallelepipeda
AAADEEFGILMPRRS Admiral Graf Spee
AAADEEFGIMORSWX meadow-saxifrage
AAADEEFHHMORTTT The Death of Marat
AAADEEFMNNSSTWY sweet Fanny Adams
AAADEEGIILMMRTT legitimate drama
AAADEEGIIMNPRSS meridian passage
AAADEEGINOPRRST grade separation
AAADEEGJLNNRTTU adjutant-general
AAADEEHHHKMMRRS hammerhead shark
AAADEEHILLMORTT à la maître d'hôtel
AAADEEILMNNPRTT mandarin palette
AAADEEILNRSSSUV Andreas Vesalius
AAADEEKNORSTUWY a week on Saturday
AAADEEMNOOPSTTT meat and potatoes
AAADEFHHOOPRTTT at the drop of a hat
AAADEGGLNRRSTUU granulated sugar
AAADEGHIIKLLNRU laugh like a drain
AAADEGHIKLMNRTU Dame Laura Knight
AAADEGIIINNOSTV saeva indignatio
AAADEGIIMNNNRTT grant-maintained
AAADEGINOPRRRTU praetorian guard
AAADEGLNORRRSUY Sugar Ray Leonard
AAADEGMNPSSTUUY Guy de Maupassant
AAADEHIMNRRSTVY Martha's Vineyard
AAADEIILLMNNTVW William Davenant
AAADEIILLNNSSTU Aleutian Islands
AAADEIILNOOORRZ radiolarian ooze
AAADEIIMMNNORTU radium emanation
AAADEIKLNORRSTV Aleksandr Tairov
AAADEILNNRSTTTU Alastair Dunnett
AAADEILNRRSSTUY Sir Austen Layard
AAADELLNNPRTTUY day-neutral plant
AAADELLNOORSSTV Alessandro Volta
AAADFILLNNSTUUW Wallis and Futuna
AAADFNNOOPSTTUY St Antony of Padua
AAADGGHHIILNNSU Guiana Highlands
AAADGHIIIMPRSTT diaphragmatitis
AAADGHILLMNRRSY marshalling yard
AAADGHIMOPRRSSY mass radiography
AAADGHIOOPRRTUY autoradiography
AAADGIIILLNRRST Alistair Darling
AAADGIILLLLMNNW William Langland
AAADHILLLMNRSSS Marshall Islands
AAADIIILNNPRTTU platitudinarian
AAADIIJLNORTTZZ traditional jazz
AAAEEEEGHLNNNRT Nathanael Greene
AAAEEEFHIKMRRTW make fair weather
AAAEEEGGHIMTVWY give the game away
AAAEEEHLRRSSTVW wear several hats
AAAEEEJLNNNPRST Japanese lantern
AAAEEFHNOPRSTTZ Tarzan of the Apes
AAAEEFIILMMRSST materfamiliases
AAAEEFIILMPRSST paterfamiliases
AAAEEFLLMORRSTW A Farewell to Arms
AAAEEGGHLOOPPRY palaeogeography
AAAEEGHHIKMNRRT Katherine Graham
AAAEEGHIMMNOPSY hypomagnesaemia
AAAEEGILLNOPRST legal separation
AAAEEGILMMNOPST palaeomagnetism
AAAEEGILNNPRRTT greater plantain
AAAEEGIMNPRRRRT marriage partner
AAAEEGIMNRSSTTV Magna est Veritas
AAAEEGINNNPPUUW Papua New Guinean
AAAEEGLMMNNRSTT Gentleman-at-arms
AAAEEGLNNRRRTWY general warranty
AAAEEHHIKSTTTVW have what it takes
AAAEEHHINOTVWWY have a way with one
AAAEEHHLMMNNNSU Samuel Hahnemann
AAAEEHHLNRRTTUW Walther Rathenau

AAAEEHHNRRRTTYY Hay-Herrán Treaty
AAAEEHILNNORTTT National Theatre
AAAEEHLNPPRRTTY prenatal therapy
AAAEEINNOORRSVX anorexia nervosa
AAAEEINNORRSSTT Saorstát Eireann
AAAEEJJLNOORRSU Juan José Arreola
AAAEELMMMNORRRT Moral Rearmament
AAAEEORRRSTTTTV à tort et à travers
AAAEFFGGNNOOTTT go off at a tangent
AAAEFGGLLMNOORV Vale of Glamorgan
AAAEFGJMNOORRTU Margaret of Anjou
AAAEFHHIMNORSTW what is he for a man?
AAAEGGHIINNRSTT against the grain
AAAEGGIILLMNNRT regaliamantling
AAAEGHHLOPRRSST thalassographer
AAAEGHLLOOOPPTY palaeopathology
AAAEGHLNOOPPRTY palaeontography
AAAEGIIKLMNSTTT talk against time
AAAEGIILMMMNNST animal magnetism
AAAEGIILNRRSSTY Italian ryegrass
AAAEGIINNNQQRUU quinquagenarian
AAAEGILLLNNORTY National Gallery
AAAEGLMNNOORSSS as long as one's arm
AAAEGNNNOOPRRST persona non grata
AAAEHHLOPRSSTTY thalassotherapy
AAAEHIIMMNOSTTT mathematisation
AAAEHIIMMNOTTTZ mathematization
AAAEHILMMNOPRTT phantom material
AAAEHLNOOPPRSTU Palaeoanthropus
AAAEIIILMNORSTT materialisation
AAAEIIILMNORTTZ materialization
AAAEIIILMNQRSTU equalitarianism
AAAEIIILNORRSTT arterialisation
AAAEIIILNORRTTZ arterialization
AAAEIILLLPRSUWZ lapis lazuli ware
AAAEIILLMNPRRTY parliamentarily
AAAEIILMMNPRRST parliamentarism
AAAEILLNRRSSTUU Australian rules
AAAEILMMNNRSTTY Tasmanian myrtle
AAAEILMNNPRRTUY unparliamentary
AAAEKLMMOOSSTYZ Kalamazoo® system
AAAEMORRSSSTTTU tarsometatarsus
AAAFFIKMMNNRRTU Frankfurt am Main
AAAFLMOOPPPRSTV stamp of approval
AAAGHIILLMNSUVW Vaughan Williams
AAAGHILMOOPRTXY axial tomography
AAAGIIILMNNORST marginalisation
AAAGIIILMNNORTZ marginalization
AAAGIILLNORTTVY gravitationally
AAAGIINNOORSTTV astronavigation
AAAHIIIMMNNRSTU humanitarianism
AAAHIILLLLMMRSW William Marshall
AAAHIMNOQSSSTTU St Thomas Aquinas
AAAHLOOPPRRSSUU Parasaurolophus
AAAIIIINNNRRTTT antitrinitarian
AAAIIILLMMNOSST malassimilation
AAAIIILLMNNOPRS Apollinarianism
AAAIIILMNORSTTT totalitarianism
AAAIIILNNNOOSTT nationalisation
AAAIIILNNNOOTTZ nationalization
AAAIIILNNOORSTT rationalisation
AAAIIILNNOORTTZ rationalization
AAAIIIMNPPRSSST Patripassianism
AAAIILMNNORTUWY mountain railway
AAAIINNORTTTUXY unitary taxation
AAAILLLNNORSTTY translationally
AAAILLNNNOORSTT loan translation
AAAILMNNORSTTTU transmutational
AAAILNNNOPRSTTT transplantation
AABBBDEEKLNQSUU bubble and squeak
AABBBEELMMRSUYY Malmesbury Abbey
AABBCDDEILORUVY Baby Doc Duvalier
AABBCDLLMMORRUY Malcolm Bradbury
AABBCEEILMMNRSU amicable numbers
AABBCEEKLMNORRU ambulance broker
AABBCEHIMNOORTT bathroom cabinet
AABBCEHINOPRRTU ribbon parachute
AABBCEHLMOPRRRY Ralph Abercromby
AABBCEILLMMNORY emblic myrobalan
AABBCGHIIILLOPR bibliographical
AABBDEEEHHSTTWY wet the baby's head
AABBDEEELRRSUYY Aubrey Beardsley
AABBDEEGGNNRRTU Brandenburg Gate
AABBDEEHHIRTTTW with bated breath
AABBDEEIILMNNOR Daniel Barenboim
AABBDEEILLMNRRY mirabelle brandy
AABBDEGILNNRSUY bring and buy sale
AABBDINNOOPRSST absorption bands
AABBEEEILMORSST ambrosia beetles
AABBEEGHNNORRTY Northanger Abbey
AABBEFIILNORTTT Battle of Britain
AABBEFNNOOORSTU abbot of unreason
AABBEHIIORRTTTU thiobarbiturate
AABBEILMMNNORTU mountain bramble
AABBEILNNORTTTU non-attributable
AABBGHIMNNOOSTT Thomas Babington
AABBGHINORSTTTU bright as a button
AABBIINNORSSTUU suburbanisation
AABBIINNORSTUUZ suburbanization
AABBILNNORTTTUY non-attributably
AABCCCDEIMNNOSU cosmic abundance
AABCCCEEHIMPRRT chamber practice
AABCCCEHHIILOPR brachiocephalic
AABCCCELMOORSUU cool as a cucumber
AABCCDDEIIINOTU butanedioic acid
AABCCDEEEEMRSTW Dame Rebecca West
AABCCDEEELNORRS labradorescence
AABCCDEEHILLNSY hendecasyllabic
AABCCDEHILMNRSY syndical chamber
AABCCDHLORSTUYY brachydactylous
AABCCEEFKKLORST Black Forest cake
AABCCEEHHHINNRS Hans Reichenbach
AABCCEEHHNORSTT catch one's breath
AABCCEEHIILMNRV vice-chamberlain
AABCCEEHIINRTTT tectibranchiate
AABCCEEHLLRSSTU Chelsea Arts Club
AABCCEEIKLMMORR commercial break
AABCCEEILNPRSST practicableness
AABCCEELNNOSSTU accountableness
AABCCEELORRRSUV cerebrovascular
AABCCEGIILLOORT bacteriological
AABCCEGIILMNRUV circumnavigable

AABCCEHHLOPRSUY brachycephalous
AABCCELLLLMMMOP Malcolm Campbell
AABCCGIIMMORSUU circumambagious
AABCCIIILLLNTUY incalculability
AABCCIIILLMNPST clinical baptism
AABCCIIINPSSTTU captain's biscuit
AABCCIILMNOOTUU bioaccumulation
AABCCIILNORTTTY contractability
AABCDDDEEKLOORV broad-leaved dock
AABCDDEEEIKLLRT black-tailed deer
AABCDDEEEKLNRUX Alexander Dubcek
AABCDDEEFIKLNRR Frederick Blanda
AABCDDEGHLNOTUW caught and bowled
AABCDDEHINNORRY carbon anhydride
AABCDDHIKMMNOOT diamondback moth
AABCDDIINNNOOWY cowboy and Indian
AABCDEEEGILNNRR Anne Bracegirdle
AABCDEEEGKLLNOW acknowledgeable
AABCDEEEHIILPRV Cepheid variable
AABCDEEEHLLLNSY hendecasyllable
AABCDEEEIMMORTU Comte de Mirabeau
AABCDEEELMNRRTU candelabrum tree
AABCDEEFIILMORT democratifiable
AABCDEEFKKOORST cooked breakfast
AABCDEEGHHIILNT the big enchilada
AABCDEEGKLLNOWY acknowledgeably
AABCDEEHHKLMPUW humpbacked whale
AABCDEEHLNORSTT cards on the table
AABCDEEILLMORRT Liberal Democrat
AABCDEEILRRTTUW lubricated water
AABCDEELMNNORTU countermandable
AABCDEFILNOORRS Arnold of Brescia
AABCDEGHHIKLNST black nightshade
AABCDEHIIKLNNTW in black and white
AABCDEHIINORRST dorsibranchiate
AABCDEHIJLLMOUY Joachim du Bellay
AABCDEHILLMNORR Lord Chamberlain
AABCDEIINNOORST decarbonisation
AABCDEIINNOORTZ decarbonization
AABCDEIINORRSTU decarburisation
AABCDEIINORRTUZ decarburization
AABCDEILNOORTXY decarboxylation
AABCDEIMNOORSTU sodium carbonate
AABCDEIMOORSSTU sodium ascorbate
AABCDEMNNSSSTUU sum and substance
AABCDGIKKLNOORW backward-looking
AABCDGILLMNNOOR ballroom dancing
AABCDGKKNORSSTU background tasks
AABCDHIILLMRTYY dithyrambically
AABCDIIOOQRRTTU biquadratic root
AABCDIKMNORRRST bricks-and-mortar
AABCEEEELNNPSSU unpeaceableness
AABCEEEFKLRRTVW blackwater fever
AABCEEEGHILNNRT interchangeable
AABCEEEGHLLLNNU unchallengeable
AABCEEEGKLNORTV blanket coverage
AABCEEEGKMRRTTT Margaret Beckett
AABCEEEGLLNNOSS congealableness
AABCEEEHILLRRTV Albert Chevalier
AABCEEEHLNNSSTU unteachableness
AABCEEEHLORRRWW wheelbarrow race
AABCEEEHLPRRRST scrape the barrel
AABCEEELMMNNRRU nuclear membrane
AABCEEFFIIILNTY ineffaceability
AABCEEFHIORRTTU creature of habit
AABCEEFIILNNORS Californian bees
AABCEEFLLORTTTU Battle of Leuctra
AABCEEGHIILNTXY exchangeability
AABCEEGHILNNRTY interchangeably
AABCEEGHLLLNNUY unchallengeably
AABCEEGIILLNOTY abiogenetically
AABCEEGIMNRTTTY magnetic battery
AABCEEHHIMMPRRS Ephraim Chambers
AABCEEHHJLLNNOP Johann Pachelbel
AABCEEHILMNNORW Owen Chamberlain
AABCEEHIMNORRRT anterior chamber
AABCEEHLLNOORTT balloon catheter
AABCEEHLRRSTTTU Arts Theatre Club
AABCEEIILLNNNNS cannellini beans
AABCEEIKKMNNORT Aaron Temkin Beck
AABCEEIKNNOPRSS pin back one's ears
AABCEEILLNORTUV countervailable
AABCEEILNNRSSTT intractableness
AABCEEILOPPRRRU Paul Pierre Broca
AABCEEINOQRSSTU sesquicarbonate
AABCEEKNOOQRSTU back to square one
AABCEELLLMNRRUU nuclear umbrella
AABCEELNNRSSTTU untractableness
AABCEELNORRSSTT Osbert Lancaster
AABCEELNRRSTTUY Canterbury Tales
AABCEFFINORRSTU Francis Beaufort
AABCEFHHIKOOORZ Book of Zechariah
AABCEFILNOOSSTT Battle of Cassino
AABCEFILORSTTTT abstract of title
AABCEFIMNNORSTU Francis Beaumont
AABCEFLNNOORTTU Battle of Corunna
AABCEGGHIILOOPR biogeographical
AABCEGHIILNNTUY unchangeability
AABCEGIKKLNNOOR Look Back in Anger
AABCEGILMNOPSUU plumbaginaceous
AABCEGINORSSTTU nasogastric tube
AABCEHHIILMNPRS chamberlainship
AABCEHHILNOOPRT lophobranchiate
AABCEHIIJKMNRTT Bankim Chatterji
AABCEHIILLMMRSW William Chambers
AABCEHIILLMNRTW Wilt Chamberlain
AABCEHILMNOPRTU pulmobranchiate
AABCEHILPRRSTUU sulphur bacteria
AABCEHILRRRRSSY Sir Charles Barry
AABCEHLLLOOOSTU absolute alcohol
AABCEIIIMMNRSTY Batesian mimicry
AABCEIIILNOPQSTU qualis ab incepto
AABCEIIILNORSSSY abscission layer
AABCEIINORRSTTU nitrous bacteria
AABCEIIRRRSSTUU arrectis auribus
AABCEILLLMOPRTY problematically
AABCEILLLMORSTY meroblastically
AABCEILLLOORTVY collaboratively
AABCEILMMNRRTUU interambulacrum
AABCEILMNNNOOPU uncompanionable
AABCEILMNNOOPST stable companion
AABCEILMOPRSSTT spermatoblastic

AABCEILNNNORSTU unconstrainable
AABCEIMNNNORSUY submarine canyon
AABCEINNOSSTTTU consubstantiate
AABCELMNNORSTTT Constant Lambert
AABCFIIILLNOSTY syllabification
AABCHHIINOOPRST Opisthobranchia
AABCHIIIMNOPRRS Marsipobranchii
AABCHIINNORRSST Corinthian brass
AABCIIIILLNPPTY inapplicability
AABCIIILMNOPRTY incomparability
AABCIIINOPRSTTW parabiotic twins
AABCIIJMNORSSUU Jacobus Arminius
AABCIILLLLRSTYY trisyllabically
AABCIINOORSSTTU bioastronautics
AABDDDELNOOSSST boots and saddles
AABDDDELNORSSTU double standards
AABDDEEEELNNRUV unleavened bread
AABDDEEGHLNNORT Bel and the Dragon
AABDDEEGHLOOPRT photodegradable
AABDDEELLNRRTTU turntable ladder
AABDDEELORSSSTU absolute address
AABDDEGILORRSSU Sir Douglas Bader
AABDDENOORRSTWW bear down towards
AABDEEEEILLLMMN Dame Nellie Melba
AABDEEEHHLNORRT on the barrelhead
AABDEEEHLMNNOOR amende honorable
AABDEEFFHIORRST birds of a feather
AABDEEFGHINORRT feather-boarding
AABDEEFLMMRTTUY Madame Butterfly
AABDEEFLMNNNOST self-abandonment
AABDEEGHHIISTTW what's the big idea?
AABDEEGHINORRTW weatherboarding
AABDEEGIIILRSTY disagreeability
AABDEEGILMNRRTU Bermuda Triangle
AABDEEGILNNORSX Alexander Gibson
AABDEEGIMMRRSST gris-amber-steam'd
AABDEEHILMMNORY hyaloid membrane
AABDEEHILOOPRSV Rev Obadiah Slope
AABDEEHIMNNNRRR Bernhard Riemann
AABDEEIILNNSSSV inadvisableness
AABDEEILMNOORVW bowl a maiden over
AABDEEILNNOSSUV unavoidableness
AABDEEILNNSSSUV unadvisableness
AABDEELMMOPQRSU Marquês de Pombal
AABDEFGHILLNOOY Bay of Heligoland
AABDEFJLLNOTTTU Battle of Jutland
AABDEFLMNOOORRS Dame Flora Robson
AABDEHHINORSTWY win by a short head
AABDEHLMNNOORST Nathan Söderblom
AABDEIIILNORSTT detribalisation
AABDEIIILNORTTZ detribalization
AABDEIIILNOSTTZ destabilization
AABDEILNORRRRTY by trial and error
AABDEINNSSTTTUU unsubstantiated
AABDELNNPRSTUUY superabundantly
AABDGGHILNOPPSY shopping-bag lady
AABDGIILNNORSTU insulating board
AABDHIIIILNOSTT dishabilitation
AABDIIIIKLNRSST Kiribati Islands
AABDIIKLMNOORVV Vladimir Nabokov
AABDILNNORSTUUW rub salt in a wound
AABDINNOOORTTUU roundaboutation
AABEEEEHHORTTVW above the weather
AABEEEFHLNOTTTV Battle of the Neva
AABEEEFLMNORTTY flamboyante-tree
AABEEEGGHOPRRST The Beggar's Opera
AABEEEGGLLNNORR General Belgrano
AABEEEGIKLRRTTT Great Bitter Lake
AABEEEGIKMNOSTT take some beating
AABEEEGLLMNRSSY General Assembly
AABEEEGLMORRTVW vegetable marrow
AABEEEGMNNNORSZ manganese bronze
AABEEEHHIMNRSTT in the same breath
AABEEEHILLNNPST nepheline-basalt
AABEEEHIMNNORTT Three Men in a Boat
AABEEEHLMNORSSV have one's marbles
AABEEEHLNNOORRT Eleanor Rathbone
AABEEEHLNORSSTT breathe one's last
AABEEEHNORSSTTW waste one's breath
AABEEEILLNNRSST inalterableness
AABEEEILNNPRSSS inseparableness
AABEEEILNPRRRSS irreparableness
AABEEEJMNOOPRRT Jérôme Bonaparte
AABEEEKLNNPSSSU unspeakableness
AABEEELLNNRSSTU unalterableness
AABEEELLNPRSSSU pleasurableness
AABEEELNNORSSST treasonableness
AABEEFGINRRSTUX burnet saxifrage
AABEEFGLMNOORTT Battle of Marengo
AABEEFGLRSTTUUV Gustave Flaubert
AABEEFHILNNOSSS fashionableness
AABEEFILLMMNNSS inflammableness
AABEEFLLNOOPTTT Battle of Lepanto
AABEEFLLNOORSTT Battle of Salerno
AABEEFLLOPSSTTY Battle of Plassey
AABEEFLNNRRRSTU untransferrable
AABEEGGINORSSTY Saint George's Bay
AABEEGIMMNNNTUY management buy-in
AABEEGLORRSTTYY lay great store by
AABEEHHHORTTTVY have by the throat
AABEEHILLORTTYZ Elizabeth Taylor
AABEEHILNOPRUVY bear heavily upon
AABEEHINNORRTTW water on the brain
AABEEHNORSSTTTY north-east-by-east
AABEEHOSSSTTTUY south-east-by-east
AABEEIIILLPRRTY irrepealability
AABEEIILMNRTUVY maneuverability
AABEEILMMNRSTUU Albertina Museum
AABEEINNPPRRSTY Pan-Presbyterian
AABEELMNNORTTTU Earl Mountbatten
AABEELNNNOOPSST on one's pantables
AABEFGIIILRRRTY irrefragability
AABEFGILNORTTTY floating battery
AABEFHHIKNOOOPZ Book of Zephaniah
AABEFHILMOORRTW Bartholomew Fair
AABEFHLOPSSTTTU Battle of Thapsus
AABEFIIJLMOOTTW Battle of Iwo Jima
AABEFIILNRRSTTY transferability
AABEFILLNSSSTTU self-substantial
AABEFILNOOPPRST self-approbation
AABEFLNORRTTUZZ burnt to a frazzle
AABEFLOPRRRSTTU Flaubert's Parrot

AABEGHIILMNOORU haemoglobinuria
AABEGIILLOOOPST palaeobiologist
AABEGIIMMNNRRUY imaginary number
AABEGIINNSSSTTU St Ignatius's bean
AABEHHILMOORSTW Sheila Rowbotham
AABEHIIIILNRRSS Sir Isaiah Berlin
AABEHLNOOPRTTTT Neath Port Talbot
AABEIIJLLMNNNRW William J Brennan
AABEIIKLLMNORRT Robert A Millikan
AABEIILLLLPSUUZ lapis lazuli blue
AABEIILLMMNOTUW William Beaumont
AABEIILLNRRSSSW Sir Barnes Wallis
AABEIILMNORTUVY manoeuvrability
AABEIILNORSSSTU atrabiliousness
AABEILLNOORSTVY observationally
AABEILMMPRRSSYY primary assembly
AABEILNNPPRTTUY abruptly pinnate
AABEILNNSSSSTTU substantialness
AABEIMMMNNORRTU Mr Tambourine Man
AABEIMNOORSSSTV mass observation
AABELLNOSSTTTTU last but not least
AABFGIMNOQRRSUY Marquis of Granby
AABFIKNOORSTTWY a nasty bit of work
AABGGIIILLMRRSW Sir William Bragg
AABGHIIKKLLMOUV Mikhail Bulgakov
AABGHIIOPRRSTTY biostratigraphy
AABGHIJNNNOORRT Jonah Barrington
AABGIIIKLLNNNOU Nikolai Bulganin
AABGIILMMOPRRTY programmability
AABGIILNRRSTTUU trailing arbutus
AABHHHILMOOOPPT ophthalmophobia
AABHIIIKKMRSSUU Shikibu Murasaki
AABHIIKKLNNORUY Nikolay Bukharin
AABIILLNNSSTTUY insubstantially
AABIILMNRSTTTUY transmutability
AABIILNNOPRRTTW ribwort plantain
AABIILNOPRSSTTY transposability
AABILMOOORRTTWY orbital motorway
AACCCCEIILNRRTT Antarctic Circle
AACCCDDHIINORYY hydrocyanic acid
AACCCDEFIIILNOT decalcification
AACCCDEIIIILMST metasilicic acid
AACCCDEILMOORSY social democracy
AACCCEEHHKRRSTT character sketch
AACCCEEHILLOORT chocolate éclair
AACCCEEHILPRTTY hypercatalectic
AACCCEEIIJNPRTU pancreatic juice
AACCCEFHIIOPPRT Hippocratic face
AACCCEHIIOPPRSY archiepiscopacy
AACCCFFINNOORRS Francisco Franco
AACCCHIIMNOOORR choriocarcinoma
AACCCHILLLOORTY ochlocratically
AACCCHIMRSSSTTU Christmas cactus
AACCCILLMMOORSY macrocosmically
AACCCILLMOOPRSY macroscopically
AACCDDEEEILLNNR Cinderella dance
AACCDDIIIMOSTTU autodidacticism
AACCDEEEENORRTT aerated concrete
AACCDEEGHHOTTTT thatched cottage
AACCDEEGHILPRRT charged particle
AACCDEEGMNNRRUY managed currency
AACCDEEHHLOOPRT cephalochordate
AACCDEEHILLORRV Richard Lovelace
AACCDEEIMNOPRTU re-education camp
AACCDEEIOPRSSSU peasecod-cuirass
AACCDEENORSSSUY secondary causes
AACCDEFGINOORSY Francisco de Goya
AACCDEFIILMNORT decimal fraction
AACCDEGHHIOOPRR echocardiograph
AACCDEGHHNNOPSS chops and changes
AACCDEGHIILOORS oligosaccharide
AACCDEGHILNNRST cradle-snatching
AACCDEGIILLLOOT dialectological
AACCDEHIIOSSTTU autoschediastic
AACCDEHLOORRTTY Charlotte Corday
AACCDEIILNNPPRR principal dancer
AACCDEIILNOPRRU canicular period
AACCDEILLMNOSSS second-class mail
AACCDEILLNOOTUY coeducationally
AACCDEILNOOPRST accordion pleats
AACCDEILNOOPTTZ occidental topaz
AACCDEIMNNNOSTU Deccan Mountains
AACCDEINNOORSTY secondary action
AACCDFIIMMOORRR micromicrofarad
AACCDFNOORRRTTW forward contract
AACCDGGHHIINRRS discharging arch
AACCDGIIILMNPRT critical damping
AACCDGILMMNOOTY accommodatingly
AACCDGIMMNNOOTU unaccommodating
AACCDHHILNOOPRY hypochondriacal
AACCDHIIMOOSSST sadomasochistic
AACCDHILNOOPRST achondroplastic
AACCDHIMNORRRSS Richard Crossman
AACCDIIILNORSTY idiosyncratical
AACCDIIIMNOORST cosmic radiation
AACCDIILLOOPRSY radioscopically
AACCDIKLMNORRST clicks and mortar
AACCEEEEGHHNRTX exchange teacher
AACCEEEGIILMNRR marriage-licence
AACCEEEGILNPRRT general practice
AACCEEEGLMNORSS Glencoe Massacre
AACCEEEGNRRSTYY agency secretary
AACCEEEHIMMNPSS escape mechanism
AACCEEFGNNOORTV covenant of grace
AACCEEFLLOPRTUU palace of culture
AACCEEGHHIIMNNT teaching machine
AACCEEGILNORSST categoricalness
AACCEEHHILPRTTW Whitechapel cart
AACCEEHIIILMNRS Sir Michael Caine
AACCEEHIIMMNORT memoria technica
AACCEEHIIOPPRST archiepiscopate
AACCEEHIJLMPRSS Cecil James Sharp
AACCEEHILMNORSV servomechanical
AACCEEHILORSSTT the coast is clear
AACCEEHIMMNORRS Marchese Marconi
AACCEEHKLLRSTTT Tattersall check
AACCEEHNRRSSTTV canvas-stretcher
AACCEEIIPPRRTTV private practice
AACCEEILMMOPPRR commercial paper
AACCEEILMRRRSUU circular measure
AACCEEILNNORRTU nuclear reaction
AACCEEILORRSSTY social secretary

AACCEEIMNNRSTTU casement curtain
AACCEEJOQSSTUUU Jacques Cousteau
AACCEEKLOORRRTW Waterloo cracker
AACCEEKMMMNOOSU make common cause
AACCEELLMNRSTTY Stella McCartney
AACCEELOOORRSTT coal-tar creosote
AACCEFFHIIOPRTW War of the Pacific
AACCEFIILNRRSTU interfascicular
AACCEFIILOOPRSU caprifoliaceous
AACCEFIINRSSTUV Franciscus Vieta
AACCEFIIRSTTUVY surface activity
AACCEFILLNRTUVY natural cycle IVF
AACCEGHIILLOOPT hepaticological
AACCEGHIILLOPRX lexicographical
AACCEGHIIMNOPRT cinematographic
AACCEGHIKLNOSTT against the clock
AACCEGHILMNORST German Catholics
AACCEGIILLNNOSS social cleansing
AACCEGIINNRRTTY racing certainty
AACCEGIMMNOPSST magnetic compass
AACCEHHHILNOPRY Rhynchocephalia
AACCEHHILMNOOPT photomechanical
AACCEHHILMORSTT chrestomathical
AACCEHHLOOPPSSU scaphocephalous
AACCEHIIKMNOPRT pharmacokinetic
AACCEHIILLMNSTY mechanistically
AACCEHIKLNOOSVZ Czechoslovakian
AACCEHILLLLMNOY melancholically
AACCEHILLMPSTUU calcium sulphate
AACCEHILLRRTTUY architecturally
AACCEHINNNNOPTV pantechnicon-van
AACCEHKORRSSSTT across the tracks
AACCEHMNORSSTUY sarcenchymatous
AACCEHNOOPPRRTU counter-approach
AACCEIIILLMNRST anticlericalism
AACCEIILLMNOSTY encomiastically
AACCEIILLNPPRSU principal clause
AACCEIILMNPRSST impracticalness
AACCEIILNNOORTT Italian Concerto
AACCEIILNNORSSU social insurance
AACCEIIMNRSTTTU circumstantiate
AACCEIINNOPSSSU incapaciousness
AACCEIKLLMNOPRT Parliament clock
AACCEIKNNOOTTTU take into account
AACCEILLMNNORTY necromantically
AACCEILLNNORSTU Lateran Councils
AACCEILNNNNOSSU uncanonicalness
AACCEILNNOOORST consolation race
AACCEILRRRRTUUX extra-curricular
AACCFFFGHKLOOOT go off at half cock
AACCGHHILOPPRSY psychographical
AACCGHHIMOOPRRT chromatographic
AACCGHIMNOOPRST pharmacognostic
AACCGIIILNNNOOP Niccolò Paganini
AACCGIIMNORRTUV circumnavigator
AACCHHIILMRRSTY lachryma Christi
AACCHHIIOOPPRTT Hippocratic oath
AACCHIIILNOOSTT catholicisation✧
AACCHIIILNOOTTZ catholicization✧
AACCHIIIMNNORST Monarchianistic
AACCHIILLMOSSTY masochistically
AACCHILLNOPSTYY sycophantically
AACCIIILLLOSSTY socialistically
AACCIIILNORRSTU circularisation
AACCIIILNORRTUZ circularization
AACCIIILOPTTTVY optical activity
AACCIIILPRRSTTU particularistic
AACCIILLMNORTUV circumvallation
AACCIILMNRSSTTU circumstantials
AACCIINOOOPSSTY association copy
AACCIKKKKNNORTY knick-knackatory
AACCKLNNNOPSSTT Planck's constant
AACDDDEEFHINSTT catted and fished
AACDDEEEFHHNOTT The Dance of Death
AACDDEEEGIILPRS Alcide de Gasperi
AACDDEEELLNNOPS Donald Pleasence
AACDDEEFGHNORSS change of address
AACDDEEGIIMNRST indirect damages
AACDDEEHIILMRYZ maleic hydrazide
AACDDEEILNRRSTU ideal transducer
AACDDEEILRRRRST straddle carrier
AACDDEFIMNNORRS Ferdinand Marcos
AACDDEGGHILNRRT great-grandchild
AACDDEGGHIOTTTY act the giddy goat
AACDDEHHILNNOPS Daphnis and Chloe
AACDDEHHLLLORST hold all the cards
AACDDEHLMNNORRY Raymond Chandler
AACDDEIIIMMORRS ad misericordiam
AACDDEIILNNOORV Leonardo da Vinci
AACDDEILMNNOOPR companion ladder
AACDDELLOOPRRRS saddler-corporal
AACDDELNNORSTWY New Scotland Yard
AACDDEMNRRSSSTU mustard and cress
AACDDHIKMNORRTY Tom, Dick, and Harry
AACDDILLLMOOPRY dollar diplomacy
AACDEEEEFFIKMNR make a difference
AACDEEEEGHKNRUW Andrew Aguecheek
AACDEEEEHLLNPRT chapelle ardente
AACDEEEEHLRRTTX Exeter Cathedral
AACDEEEFHILPRRR Frederic Raphael
AACDEEEFLMNNSTV self-advancement
AACDEEEGGLLLMNO Magdalen College
AACDEEEGHHORRSV overhead charges
AACDEEEGHILMRRV Michael Redgrave
AACDEEEGHIRSSSU Gaucher's disease
AACDEEEGHLLLRSU Charles de Gaulle
AACDEEEHHILRRTW Rachel Whiteread
AACDEEEHLLNRTTY centrally-heated
AACDEEEHLPRRSTY Speyer Cathedral
AACDEEEHNNOOSTW see what one can do
AACDEEEHNPRRSTV chapter and verse
AACDEEEIMNOPRTX dementia praecox
AACDEEEMNNNOPRT permanent deacon
AACDEEFFIINOSTT disaffectionate
AACDEEFHHMNORTT merchant of death
AACDEEFHILSSTTY child-safety seat
AACDEEGGNNOOPRS egg-and-spoon race
AACDEEGHLLMOOSU Alec Douglas-Home
AACDEEGHLNOPRTU golden parachute
AACDEEGHLOORRSY Charles Goodyear
AACDEEGHOPRRTUU drogue parachute
AACDEEGIILLNPPS special pleading

AACDEEGKLLNNORW carnal knowledge
AACDEEGOPPRRRTU corrugated paper
AACDEEHHINORRTW Catherine Howard
AACDEEHHMNORSSY Sydenham's chorea
AACDEEHIIORRSTT icositetrahedra
AACDEEHIKLMMNRS hammer and sickle✧
AACDEEHINNOOPRT a drop in the ocean
AACDEEHINNTTTUU unauthenticated
AACDEEHMNORRTTT attachment order
AACDEEIILLNRTTT Tetractinellida
AACDEEIIMNNOTTV decontaminative
AACDEEIJKLLLNUY Jean Claude Killy
AACDEEILLPRRSSY laser disc player
AACDEEILMOPPRRT madreporic plate
AACDEEILNNNSSTU Dunsinane Castle
AACDEEILNNSSTTU indecent assault
AACDEEIOOPRRRRT corporate raider
AACDEFFGINRSSTU facts and figures
AACDEFFIMNNOSTX Mexican standoff
AACDEFHIMNNPRRY Richard P Feynman
AACDEFIIKNRRRSS Sir Francis Drake
AACDEFNPRRSSTYY fancy dress party
AACDEGGIIINRRRV carriage driving
AACDEGGIIIRRRSV verdigris agaric
AACDEGHIILLOPRY ideographically
AACDEGHIMORSTWY say the magic word
AACDEGIIIKKLNNV alive and kicking
AACDEGIILLOPSST glacial deposits
AACDEGIILMOOOPR Giacomo Leopardi
AACDEGIKNNORSVW advance workings
AACDEHHIILNPRST Christadelphian
AACDEHHKNOORSTT horse and hattock
AACDEHILLNOORRY Hydrocorallinae
AACDEHILLOOPRTY orthopaedically
AACDEHILMMNORTY thermodynamical
AACDEHILNNOSTUV Viscount Haldane
AACDEHLMMNOOTWY Commonwealth Day
AACDEIIJLLRTUXY extrajudicially
AACDEIILLMORRTY radiometrically
AACDEIILLMORTUY audiometrically
AACDEIILMNNOOPS ladies' companion
AACDEIILMNNOOTT decimal notation
AACDEIILNNNOSSS Ascension Island
AACDEIIMNNNOOTT decontamination
AACDEIIMNOORSTT democratisation
AACDEIIMNOORTTZ democratization
AACDEIINNOORRST cordon sanitaire
AACDEIKLNNNSTTU Nantucket Island
AACDEIKNNNPPSSW spick and span new
AACDEILLMORRTTU court-martialled
AACDEILMNRRSSUU Sir Samuel Cunard
AACDEIMNNOOPRRY Raymond Poincaré
AACDEIMNOOPRSST data compression
AACDEMMNNRSTUUU secundum naturam
AACDFFIINORRTXY X-ray diffraction
AACDFHIILNOOPRY Fyodor Chaliapin
AACDFHLLOOORTTW hard act to follow
AACDFIIILNSTTTU antistatic fluid
AACDFIIINOSSSTT dissatisfaction
AACDFIIORSSSTTY dissatisfactory
AACDGGHILLNNORW all-changing-word
AACDGHIMNOOOPRR phonocardiogram
AACDGIILLNRTUVY victualling-yard
AACDGIKNNOORRTU go to rack and ruin
AACDHHIILMNORRT Richard Hamilton
AACDHHILLOPRTYY hydropathically
AACDHHILNOPRRRS Ralph Richardson
AACDHIIILOTTVYY activity holiday
AACDHIILMNRSSST Christmas Island
AACDHIILSSTTYYZ lazy daisy stitch
AACDHIJMNNOQSUY John Quincy Adams
AACDHILLORSTTYY hydrostatically
AACDIIILLMNOTUY unidiomatically
AACDIIILNNPRSST Pitcairn Islands
AACDIIILNORSTTU disarticulation
AACDIIIMNNORRST doctrinarianism
AACDIILNOPQRTUU quadruplication
AACDIIMNORSSTTY astrodynamicist
AACDIINNNOOTTUY continuation-day
AACDIINOOORSSTW word association
AACDILMMNNOOPSU compound animals
AACDILMNOOPRRUY cardiopulmonary
AACEEEEFHKLNRTV take French leave
AACEEEEINNNNPRS near as ninepence
AACEEEFHINNQRTU The African Queen
AACEEEFHORRSTTW weather forecast
AACEEEFIIMNNRSU feminine caesura
AACEEEGHILNNUVX value in exchange
AACEEEGHIMMNNSV Geneva mechanism
AACEEEGHIMOPRRT Megacheiroptera
AACEEEGHLMNPUVY Emelyan Pugachev
AACEEEGILLNNRST scalene triangle
AACEEEGILLNNSSV evangelicalness
AACEEEGILMMNORT geometrical mean
AACEEEGILMNRSSU single use camera
AACEEEGINNRRTTT Terence Rattigan
AACEEEGMNOPRSTU pergamentaceous
AACEEEGNORRRTUU guerre à outrance
AACEEEHIJJLMNRR Jean-Michel Jarre
AACEEEHILLLMNUW wheel animalcule
AACEEEHIMPPRRRY periphery camera
AACEEEHIPRRTTVY creative therapy
AACEEEHLLLOPRTV all over the place
AACEEEHLOORSSVW have a screw loose
AACEEEIILNORSTV variae lectiones
AACEEEIILNPRRST special retainer
AACEEEILNRSSSST sales resistance
AACEEEILOSSTTVW sleeve waistcoat
AACEEEINRRSSSTT crease-resistant
AACEEEKMNOOSSTU make out one's case
AACEEELPPRRTTUU perpetual curate
AACEEENNQRRTTUY quatercentenary
AACEEFFHIMNNRST affranchisement
AACEEFFIKLORTTV vertical take-off
AACEEFFIKLRRSTV slave-trafficker
AACEEFGHLLLRSTV Cleve-Garth Falls
AACEEFHIILMNNNR infernal machine
AACEEFHILNPRRSY franchise player
AACEEFHIMNNRRST transfer machine
AACEEFHIPRRRRSS Friars Preachers
AACEEFHJLMORSSX Charles James Fox
AACEEFHLNNORRUV flavour enhancer

AACEEFHNOOPRTTU another cup of tea
AACEEFIINOORSST free association
AACEEFIMMNRSTUU semimanufacture
AACEEFJKLLLMTTU Full Metal Jacket
AACEEFMOORRSTTU a matter of course
AACEEGGHIILNNPT Cape nightingale
AACEEGGHLMORTTT chattel mortgage
AACEEGGJLNNOSTU conjugate angles
AACEEGGLMNNSTUU centum languages
AACEEGHHIIMNNNT high-maintenance
AACEEGHHIINRSTV have itching ears
AACEEGHHLLOSTTW cheat the gallows
AACEEGHHLNOPPRY encephalography
AACEEGHIILLNSTT heliacal setting
AACEEGHILLLPRTY telegraphically
AACEEGHILLNOPRS selenographical
AACEEGHILOOOPSS Ophioglossaceae
AACEEGHIMNOPRRT cinematographer
AACEEGHIMNPRTTY magnetic therapy
AACEEGHIOPRRRTT graphite reactor
AACEEGHLLLNORWY yellow archangel
AACEEGIIMMRSSTU gamma securities
AACEEGIKMORSTTY category mistake
AACEEGILLNPRSTV space travelling
AACEEGILLOOOPST palaeoecologist
AACEEGILLRSTTYZ Ziegler catalyst
AACEEGILMNRRSTU scarlet geranium
AACEEGILMRSSTTT strategic metals
AACEEGIMMMNNORT micromanagement
AACEEGIMNOQRTTU magnetic equator
AACEEHHHLNOOPRX hexachlorophane
AACEEHHIINPRRTY reichian therapy✧
AACEEHHILLLRRSS Sir Charles Hallé
AACEEHHILMNORTT Michael Atherton
AACEEHHIMNRRRST Carmarthenshire
AACEEHHJKNNORST Johannes Eckhart
AACEEHIILLMNRSY Shirley MacLaine
AACEEHIILMNQSTU salami technique
AACEEHIILNNOPST encephalisation
AACEEHIILNNOPTZ encephalization
AACEEHIILNRSSTT castles in the air
AACEEHIILPPRRST Pre-Raphaelistic
AACEEHIINORSTTT catheterisation
AACEEHIINORTTTZ catheterization
AACEEHIKLMNPRSS Spanish mackerel
AACEEHILLMORTTY theorematically
AACEEHILLNPRTTY parenthetically
AACEEHILLPRTTUY therapeutically
AACEEHILMOPSSTU mesaticephalous
AACEEHILNNOOOST a hole in one's coat
AACEEHIMMPRSTTU pure mathematics
AACEEHIMMRSTTUU acute rheumatism
AACEEHIMNNNOPRS Annie Macpherson
AACEEHLLLPRRTUY cellular therapy
AACEEHLNOORRSTT clear one's throat
AACEEHMNOPRRTWW come the raw prawn
AACEEHORRSSTUXX Artaxerxes Ochus
AACEEIIIMPPRSTV misappreciative
AACEEIIJMRRSSSY Sir Jeremy Isaacs
AACEEIIKNNORTTW weak interaction
AACEEIILNNORSTV national service
AACEEIILNOQRTUY equinoctial year
AACEEIIMNNNRRSU marine insurance
AACEEILLLMPSSTY esemplastically
AACEEILLMORTTTU automatic teller
AACEEILLNORSSTY electroanalysis
AACEEILLNPRRTTT tent caterpillar
AACEEILNNRRTTTU intertentacular
AACEEIMNNOPRSST castanospermine
AACEEIMNORRRSTV Sacramento River
AACEEIMPRRRSTTY spermatic artery
AACEELLLLRRTUXY extracellularly
AACEELOQRRSSTTU at close quarters
AACEFFHIILORSTT articles of faith
AACEFFKNNOOPRTT pocket an affront
AACEFGGIOPRRTUU paragogic future
AACEFGHIIKMNNNR franking-machine
AACEFGLMOPSSTUX flux-gate compass
AACEFHHIMRRSSTT Father Christmas
AACEFHIILLNOORT Hotel California
AACEFHILLLMOOST coat-of-mail shell
AACEFHIMOPRRSTU Triumph of Caesar
AACEFHKLNORSSYY Charles Yanofsky
AACEFIIOQRSTTUU autrefois acquit
AACEFIMOOPPRSSS pair of compasses
AACEGGGHIIMNOPY hypnagogic image
AACEGGGLLNOOOWY Goolagong Cawley
AACEGGHIINNOPRY cineangiography
AACEGGHILOOOPRZ zoogeographical
AACEGGHJKMNNNTU Mt Kangchenjunga
AACEGGHMORSSSTT stomach staggers
AACEGGIIKMNORRS smoking carriage
AACEGHHLLNORSTU Charles Laughton
AACEGHIILMNNPST stapling machine
AACEGHIILMOPRSS seismographical
AACEGHIILNRSTTW antiglare switch
AACEGHIIMMNNPST stamping machine
AACEGHILLMOORTU rheumatological
AACEGHILLOOPRRY oreographically
AACEGHILMNNNRRT Ringelmann chart
AACEGHILOOPSTTT cottage hospital
AACEGIIKLLMOORR kilogram-calorie
AACEGIILLLMNORY mineralogically
AACEGIILLMNNNSU luminance signal
AACEGIIMNORSSTV moving staircase
AACEGIJKNOORSTU kangaroo justice
AACEGILLLLMRTUY metallurgically
AACEGILLMNOOPTU pneumatological
AACEGILLNORRSST citronella grass
AACEGILLNORTUVY angular velocity
AACEGKLNOOORRSU kangaroo closure
AACEHHIIMNRRSTW within arm's reach
AACEHHILLMOOPTY homeopathically
AACEHHILOOPRSTT Charlotte Sophia
AACEHIIIKLMMRSV Kasimir Malevich
AACEHIILLNNTTUY inauthentically
AACEHIILLOPPSST special hospital
AACEHIILMNNOSSW Nicholas Wiseman
AACEHIILNRRSSTT Christian Slater
AACEHIILOOPPRRT paraheliotropic
AACEHIINNNNOTTU The Annunciation
AACEHILLMOPRSTY atmospherically

AACEHILLMPSTTYY sympathetically
AACEHILLOOPSTTY osteopathically
AACEHILMOOORRTV Violeta Chamorro
AACEHLLORRSSSTT orchestra stalls
AACEHLMORSSTUUW walrus moustache
AACEHOOPPRRSTTU parachute troops
AACEIIILMNOPPSS episcopalianism
AACEIIILNPRSTTT antiperistaltic
AACEIIIMNNOPSTT emancipationist
AACEIIIMNOPPRST misappreciation
AACEIIINNORSSTT canisterisation
AACEIIINNORSTTZ canisterization
AACEIIJMORRRRTY majority carrier
AACEIILLLPRSTTY peristaltically
AACEIILLMNNRSTY manneristically
AACEIILLMOPRRSS Camille Pissarro
AACEIILLMRTTTUU multiarticulate
AACEIILMNOPRRTT malpractitioner
AACEIILMNOPRTTT matric potential
AACEIILMNORRTVV Romantic Revival
AACEIILNNOOPTTT action potential
AACEIILNNOOSTTY National Society
AACEIILNOPRRTVX extra-provincial
AACEIIMNNNOOPTV native companion
AACEIIMNOPRRTUX Proxima Centauri
AACEIINNNOSTTTY coinstantaneity
AACEIINOPRRSTTV procrastinative
AACEIJLNORRTTUY interjaculatory
AACEILLLMPPRSUY papillary muscle
AACEILLNNORSSUU Carolus Linnaeus
AACEILLORRSSTTY cross-laterality
AACEILMNOOPSSTY compassionately
AACEILNNOORSTVW conservation law
AACEILNOOORRTTU autocorrelation
AACEIMMNOPRRSSS Mariner's Compass
AACEIMNNOOPSSTU uncompassionate
AACEINNNOOSSTTU coinstantaneous
AACEINOORRTTTUU tout au contraire
AACELLLMNOORRTY Monte Carlo rally
AACELLMMNOPRTTY compartmentally
AACFFIIINORSSSS Francis of Assisi
AACFGIIIINNORTT granitification
AACFGIILLNSTTUY fungistatically
AACFGIILNNOORTU configurational
AACFHIIKLLMMOOW William of Ockham
AACFHIJJKLMNPSU Jumpin' Jack Flash
AACFHLLLMNOOPSU paschal full moon
AACFIIINNOORSTT fractionisation
AACFIIINNOORTTZ fractionization
AACFIILNOOPPPRY California poppy
AACFILMMNNOOORT malconformation
AACFILNNNOOORTT confrontational
AACFILNRRRSTTUU infrastructural
AACGGHHILNOOPRY cholangiography
AACGGHILLLOOPRY logographically
AACGGHILLOOPRSS glossographical
AACGGHLNNOOPSSU lapsang souchong✧
AACGGIIIMNOOOST Giacomo Agostini
AACGHHIILOPPRSY physiographical
AACGHHILMRTUUUV ultra-high vacuum
AACGHHINOOPPRTU phonautographic
AACGHHMOOOPPRRT photomacrograph
AACGHIILLLMORTY algorithmically
logarithmically
AACGHILLMNOOPRY gramophonically
nomographically
AACGHILLNOOOPRT anthropological
AACGHILLOOPPRTY topographically
AACGHILLOPPRTYY typographically
AACGHIMNNNOOOTT thanatognomonic
AACGHIMNOOPRSST pharmacognosist
AACGHIMOPRRRXYY X-ray micrography
AACGHLLNOPRSSTT grasscloth plant
AACGHLLOPRRSTYY crystallography
AACGIIIINNNOSSV Giovanni Cassini
AACGIIILLNSSTTU linguistic atlas
AACGIIILNPRSSTU paralinguistics
AACGIIKNNORSTTT tracking station
AACGIILLMNOOOOS onomasiological
AACGIILLRRSTTUU agriculturalist
AACGIILNORRSSWY railway crossing
AACGIIMNOOPRRRT G Marconi Airport
AACGIINNOPRRSTT procrastinating
AACGILNNOORSTTU Congratulations
AACGILNOORSSTUY agranulocytosis
AACGIMMNOOPRRSU macrosporangium
AACGIMNOOORSTTW room to swing a cat
AACHHIILLNOPPRT philanthropical
AACHIIILNNRSTTY antichristianly
AACHIIILNPRSSVW Spanish Civil War
AACHIIKLLMOSTVY Michail Saltykov
AACHILLMOOPRTUY automorphically
AACHILLOPPRSTYY saprophytically
AACHNOORRTTUVWY vouch to warranty
AACIIIILMNNORST criminalisation
AACIIIILMNNORTZ criminalization
AACIIIILNORRSTT irrationalistic
AACIIILLLRSTTUY ritualistically
AACIIILMNNOSSTU masculinisation
AACIIILMNNOSTUZ masculinization
AACIIILNRRSSUVW Russian Civil War
AACIIILSSSTTTTV vital statistics
AACIIIMNNOORSTT romanticisation
AACIIIMNNOORTTZ romanticization
AACIIIMNOOPPRRT Ciampino Airport
AACIIKLNNNORSTT nick translation
AACIILLLMNOOTTU multilocational
AACIILLLMOPSTUY political asylum
AACIILLNOOPRSTY anisotropically
AACIILLNOPRTTUY unpatriotically
AACIILLNORSSTTY crystallisation
AACIILLNORSTTYZ crystallization
AACIILLOPSSTTTU political status
AACIILMMNNOOSTU communalisation
AACIILMMNNOOTUZ communalization
AACIILNNOPRRSTT transcriptional
AACIIMMNNNOOPRS companion-in-arms
AACIIMMNOOSTTTU somatic mutation
AACIINNOOPRRSTT procrastination
AACIINNOORRSTTU Arturo Toscanini
AACIKMNNOPRTTUU punctuation mark
AACILLLNOOPSTUY unapostolically

Words marked ✧ can also be spelled with one or more capital letters

AACILLMMOPSTTYY symptomatically
AACILLMNNOPSTUY uncomplaisantly
AACILLMNRRSTUUY intramuscularly
AACINOOPRRRSTTY procrastinatory
AACLNNNOOOPSSTT postconsonantal
AADDDEEEGILMPRS middle-age spread
AADDDEEEGIPRRRU Gérard Depardieu
AADDDEEIILOPRVV Pedro de Valdivia
AADDDEEIINOSSSS Addison's disease
AADDDEEILNNRSTV stand and deliver!
AADDDEHILNOPSWY head-down display
AADDDEIINNRRTVW dividend warrant
AADDDEIMNNNOORS Adrian Edmondson
AADDDGIIMNNNNOR nodding mandarin
AADDDIILNNRSSWW Windward Islands
AADDEEEFHHILRTW Alfred Whitehead
AADDEEEGLNRRSST saddler-sergeant
AADDEEEHHNRRSST hard-heartedness
AADDEEEILRRSSTV relative address
AADDEEEINNORRSS raise one's dander
AADDEEFGILNORST self-degradation
AADDEEGHHKLNNOS golden handshake
AADDEEGHMNNORSS Homes and Gardens
AADDEEGIKMNNOOR make a good dinner
AADDEEGIMNRRRSW Sir Edward German
AADDEEGINNNRSTV Evening Standard
AADDEEGINRRSTUZ Dzungaria Desert
AADDEEHIMNPRRUU Daphne Du Maurier
AADDEEHMRRRTTWY Edward the Martyr
AADDEEHNRRRSUWY Hundred Years' War
AADDEELNOPPRTVW Edward V Appleton
AADDEFGNNOOORTY Dog Day Afternoon
AADDEGHIJNNORRT Django Reinhardt
AADDEGHILLNNOUW laugh and lie down
AADDEGHILNNRSST standard English
AADDEHILLNNSSST Shetland Islands
AADDEHILNOOSTWW white sandalwood
AADDEHKNORRRTWW drawn-thread work
AADDEIILNOPRSTU superadditional
AADDEILOOOPRUZZ Eduardo Paolozzi
AADDGGHIMNORRST Thomas Gradgrind
AADDGHHIILLMORR Lord High Admiral
AADDIIKMNNOSTUW Skiddaw Mountain
AADDILLLMNNOOPU London Palladium
AADEEEEEGHLRRSW Where Eagles Dare
AADEEEEEILNRSSV venereal disease
AADEEEEGGHIRTVW weighted average
AADEEEEGILPRSSW spread-eaglewise
AADEEEEHHKRRTWW Hereward the Wake
AADEEEEIILRRRRT Airedale terrier
AADEEEELMNOPRTV development area
AADEEEFHHLNRSST half-heartedness
AADEEEFHIMNOOST ahead of one's time
AADEEEGHLLNNRST Hansel and Gretel
AADEEEGJNOORSVW Dow-Jones average
AADEEEGLMNNNOSU manganese nodule
AADEEEGLNNNRSTW New England aster
AADEEEGMNORRSUU grande amoureuse
AADEEEHLLORSVWY Lee Harvey Oswald
AADEEEHMNRRSSTW warm-heartedness
AADEEEHNNPQRRSU Harpers and Queen
AADEEEHNOORRSTT dear to one's heart
AADEEEIILNNRRVX Alexander Irvine
AADEEEIKLNNRSVX Alexander Nevski
AADEEEIKNORRTWW wide area network
AADEEEILLMNORRT oriental emerald
AADEEEILMNPRSTT departmentalise
AADEEEILMNPRTTZ departmentalize
AADEEEIMNSTTTTV testament-dative
AADEEEIMPRRRSTW Sir Peter Medawar
AADEEEKLNNRSVXY Nevsky Alexander
AADEEEKMMNOOSSY make someone's day
AADEEEMNPRSTTTT State Department
AADEEFFHINNORRU affaire d'honneur
AADEEFFHMORSTTU The Raft of Medusa
AADEEFFIKOSSSTT assisted take-off
AADEEFGGILNORSX golden saxifrage
AADEEFHILNOSSSV loaves and fishes
AADEEFKKLOORSSS for old sake's sake
AADEEFNNORRSTTU fenestra rotunda
AADEEFNNSSSSTTU unsteadfastness
AADEEGGHIIMMMST Dame Maggie Smith
AADEEGGIKMNNRRT market-gardening
AADEEGHIIIMNPRR hearing-impaired
AADEEGHILOPRRTY radiotelegraphy
AADEEGHILRRSTUY rear its ugly head
AADEEGHKLMMNOTU don't make me laugh
AADEEGHLMMNNORY Gene Myron Amdahl
AADEEGHLNPRSTUY Sunday Telegraph
AADEEGIILNPRSTT Patient Griselda
AADEEGIIMNNOSTT demagnetisation
AADEEGIIMNNOTTZ demagnetization
AADEEGIIMNPSTUV punitive damages
AADEEGMMMNRRTUU argumentum ad rem
AADEEGMMOPRRRRT programme trader
AADEEHHILLMMSTT Dashiell Hammett
AADEEHHILNSSTVY the lady vanishes
AADEEHHINNORRSV River Shenandoah
AADEEHHLLLLNRTW Leland H Hartwell
AADEEHHLLMRSTUY medullary sheath
AADEEHHNPRRSSTT shepherd's tartan
AADEEHIIILMPPRY hyperlipidaemia
AADEEHIIIMNRRST hereditarianism
AADEEHIIINRRSTT hereditarianist
AADEEHIILNNRSTW sail near the wind
AADEEHILLMNOSTU Thelma and Louise
AADEEHILMNPRRSY hyperadrenalism
AADEEHMNOORRSUW Donmar Warehouse
AADEEIILNOOPSST aeolian deposits
AADEEIILNOSSTUX desexualisation
AADEEIILNOSTUXZ desexualization
AADEEIINORRRSTX extraordinaries
AADEEIKLLPRRSSY laser disk player
AADEEIKLMMPRRSU Dame Muriel Spark
AADEEILLMNORTTT tatterdemallion
AADEEILMMNPRSTT departmentalism
AADEEILNNSSTTVY St Valentine's Day
AADEEIMQRRRRSTU married quarters
AADEELMNOPRRSTT mortar and pestle
AADEELMNPPRTTUX duplex apartment
AADEFFFLOORRRST Earl of Strafford
AADEFFGHMNOORSU manhood suffrage

AADEFGHILNNTTTT flight attendant
AADEFGIIIMNNRTT infra dignitatem
AADEFGIKLNRSSTT Kirsten Flagstad
AADEFHILMMNOORS horns of a dilemma
AADEFHILMNOSTUX exhaust manifold
AADEFHLLLNRSSTU Sutherland Falls
AADEFIILLNRSTTU field naturalist
AADEFILMNNNTTUU fundamental unit
AADEGGHINOOPSWZ Shwezigon Pagoda
AADEGGIIKLLNNRW walking dragline
AADEGGIIMRSTUUU gaudeamus igitur
AADEGHHIILLNPRS Gillian Shephard
AADEGHIINNNRRST strain hardening
AADEGHIMNOOOPRR radio-gramophone
AADEGHIOOPRRRXY xeroradiography
AADEGHMNOOPRRRT ergatandromorph
AADEGIILNNORRSW wandering sailor
AADEGIILNNPSSTU sustaining pedal
AADEGIMNNRRSTTU untransmigrated
AADEGINNNOPRRSY Grand Pensionary
AADEHHIIJNNNORY Johnny-head-in-air
AADEHHIILMNOPRT edriophthalmian
AADEHHLMNOPPTYY lymphadenopathy
AADEHHNOPRSSTTU pass round the hat
AADEHIIJKKLNNPV Nikhanj Kapil Dev
AADEHILMNOOPSTU phase modulation
AADEHILNOSSSSTU South Seas Island
AADEHIMMNOOPSTW shadow pantomime
AADEHIMMOOPRRTV Mohamed V Airport
AADEHLMMNNNOORS Rosamond Lehmann
AADEHLNORRSTTWY north-eastwardly
AADEHLORSSTTUWY south-eastwardly
AADEIIIILMSSSTV disassimilative
AADEIIILNNOSSTT de-Stalinisation
AADEIIILNNOSTTZ de-Stalinization
AADEIIILNOORTTV Adriano Olivetti
AADEIIKMNNOORST make inroads into
AADEIILMNOSTTUU demutualisation
AADEIILMNOTTUUZ demutualization
AADEIILNOPSSSTY dispassionately
AADEIILNORRRTXY extraordinarily
AADEILLLNOORSUV Love is all Around
AADEILLNOPRSTUY dual personality
AADEINPRRSSSSTT Stars and Stripes
AADELMNNOORSSWY lay down one's arms
AADELNOPRSTTUUY polyunsaturated
AADEMMNOORSSTWY motorway madness
AADEMNNOORSTTUU monounsaturated
AADEMNOOPRRTTUW portmanteau word
AADFGHILNNNOOSY laying-on of hands
AADFGHIORRRSTTW straightforward
AADFHMNNOOSSTUY a month of Sundays
AADFIIILNNORSTY disinflationary
AADFIIKLLMNOOOS Island of Molokai
AADFLOOORRSSSTW at a loss for words
AADGGHIIKNNSTVY Thanksgiving Day
AADGHHIKLNOOPPT Papal knighthood
AADGHHIMNPRSSTU draughtsmanship
AADGHIIKLLNNORS Sir Alan L Hodgkin
AADGIIINNOORSST disorganisation
AADGIIINNOORSTZ disorganization
AADGIINNNOOSTTV standing ovation
AADGLNOOOOPPRSV goods on approval
AADHIIILNNOTWWW with a wild wanion
AADHIILNNPSSSSW Spanish windlass
AADHILLNORRSTYY synarthrodially
AADIIIILMNOSSST disassimilation
AADIIINOPQRRTTU quadripartition
AADIIKKLNNSSWYY Wasily Kandinsky
AADIILLMMNORSWY Raymond Williams
AADIIMMNSSTTTUU mutatis mutandis
AADIINOORRRSSTT transistor radio
AAEEEEFFILLNOSW a new lease of life
AAEEEEFHHNNOSVV heaven of heavens
AAEEEEGHMORSTTT set a game to three
AAEEEEGILNNRRRT general retainer
AAEEEEGLLNRRTVW New-Age Traveller
AAEEEEGLNNRRTTY alternate energy
AAEEEEHMNOORSSV have someone's ear
AAEEEFGHINOTTXY The Age of Anxiety
AAEEEFGILNOSVWY give oneself away
AAEEEFGLMMNNRRT gentleman farmer
AAEEEFHIIKLORSU like a house afire
AAEEEFHILOSSSTY The Essays of Elia
AAEEEFHILRSTTTV Festival Theatre
AAEEEFHOOPPRRTU The Rape of Europa
AAEEEFIILLMRRTT fertile material
AAEEEFILLNRTTUV alternative fuel
AAEEEGGIILLNRRT General Galtieri
AAEEEGILLNNRRTT eternal triangle
AAEEEGILMNNRRUV marginal revenue
AAEEEGIMRSTTTUU Auguste Mariette
AAEEEGKNNOORSST senega snakeroot
AAEEEGLNNORRTTY Attorney-General
AAEEEGLNORRSTTX external storage
AAEEEGMMNNNPRTT permanent magnet
AAEEEGMMNRRSSST messenger-at-arms
AAEEEHHIMMMNPTT methamphetamine
AAEEEHHINNOSTTV one's native heath
AAEEEHHKOPRSTTT speak to the heart
AAEEEHIILNORSTT etherealisation
AAEEEHIILNORTTZ etherealization
AAEEEHIKMRRSSST Sir Seretse Khama
AAEEEHILMRRRSTY sealyham terrier✧
AAEEEHKMMORRTTT katathermometer
AAEEEHKNOORSTTT take to one's heart
AAEEEHNNOORRSTT near to one's heart
AAEEEHNOORSTTTU eat one's heart out
AAEEEHOOPRSTTTT The Potato Eaters
AAEEEIIKLORTTTV take it or leave it
AAEEEIILMMPRRSU imperial measure
AAEEEIIMNNORTTT Marie Antoinette
AAEEEIIMNRRSSTT Mare Serenitatis
AAEEEIJKNNNNRTT Jeannette Rankin
AAEEEILMNNPTTTU antepenultimate
AAEEEILNORTTTVV alternative vote
AAEEEILNQRTTUVW water equivalent
AAEEEKMMNNNORSS make one's manners
AAEEELLMMNPRTTY temperamentally
AAEEEMNPRRRTTUU run a temperature
AAEEFFFILMRSTTY staff-tree family
AAEEFFHKOPRSTTW take the wraps off

AAEEFFINOORRSTT reafforestation
AAEEFGHILLLNOTT The Flagellation
AAEEFGILNNOOSTU League of Nations
AAEEFGIMNNRRSST fragmentariness
AAEEFGMORRRRSTT Margaret Forster
AAEEFHILLNOOSTV The Isle of Avalon
AAEEFHILNRRSSTW freshwater snail
AAEEFHILRSSSTTT the fatal sisters
AAEEFHILRSSTTVV harvest festival
AAEEFHJNORSSTUZ Jesus of Nazareth
AAEEFIIILMRSSSZ laissez-faireism
AAEEFIILLNORSST self-realisation
AAEEFIILLNORSTZ self-realization
AAEEFIILMNNOSTX self-examination
AAEEFIIOPRRSSTT Treaties of Paris
AAEEFIJKNNORRSW War of Jenkins' Ear
AAEEFIJLORRSSTV Jaroslav Seifert
AAEEFILLNNRSTTV Lantern Festival
AAEEFILMNNOPRTY one-parent family
AAEEFILNOPPRRST self-preparation
AAEEFLLMOORSTUU out of all measure
AAEEFLLNOPRSTXY self-explanatory
AAEEFMNNPRRSTTY transfer payment
AAEEFNOOPRSTTUV put a fast one over
AAEEGGIJLMNPSTT Ggantija temples
AAEEGHHIKRRSTTW great white shark
AAEEGHHIMOPPTTZ apophthegmatize
AAEEGHHINOOPPST hope against hope
AAEEGHHINRRSTTT earthshattering
AAEEGHHIOSTVWWY give the show away
AAEEGHIILMNNPRT parliament-hinge
AAEEGHIKNNRSSST snake in the grass
AAEEGHILLLLNNOT all along the line
AAEEGHILNOOSSTY anaesthesiology
AAEEGHIMOOPPRRR paroemiographer
AAEEGHLLNOOOPTY palaeoethnology
AAEEGHLMNOSSTXY hexagonal system
AAEEGHMMMORSSTU Somerset Maugham
AAEEGIIILMMNPSS Semi-Pelagianism
AAEEGIIIMNNSSTV imaginativeness
AAEEGIILMNRSSST magisterialness
AAEEGIILNNORSTV evangelistarion
AAEEGIILNRRSUVY aerial surveying
AAEEGIINNRRSSTV Sir Geraint Evans
AAEEGIJLMNNNRSU Jungermanniales
AAEEGIKKLLNNPTU talk like a pen-gun
AAEEGIKMMNNRRST Ingemar Stenmark
AAEEGILMNRTTUVY argumentatively
AAEEGILNNORSSST essential organs
AAEEGKNOOPRSSSW work one's passage
AAEEHHIILPPRRST Pre-Raphaelitish
AAEEHHIMRSTVVWY Harvey Smith wave
AAEEHHNOPPRRSST Pharaoh's serpent
AAEEHIIJLLMNOTW Joe Willie Namath
AAEEHIILMPPRRST Pre-Raphaelitism
AAEEHILLMPRRRSY armillary sphere
AAEEHILLNOPRTTW wallop in a tether
AAEEHILMNNORTTU mountain leather
AAEEHILMNOPRSTU parliament-house
AAEEHILMNPRRRSW Sir Pelham Warner
AAEEHILNORSTTTV alternative host
AAEEHILPRSSTTUX sexual therapist
AAEEHINNOORTTTW weather notation
AAEEHINNRRSSTUV Svante Arrhenius
AAEEHINOORRSTTU tear one's hair out
AAEEHINOPRRSTVY aversion therapy
AAEEHLMMMNOSSUU Ashmolean Museum
AAEEHLMNSSTTTWY Stanley Matthews
AAEEHLNNNOOPRTT on another planet
AAEEIIILMMRSSTU immaterial issue
AAEEIILNNORSTTX externalisation
AAEEIILNNORTTXZ externalization
AAEEIILNNPRRRTU intrapreneurial
AAEEIIMNPPRRRST prima inter pares
AAEEIINNOOPRSTU Europeanisation
AAEEIINNOOPRTUZ Europeanization
AAEEIINNOOPSTTV open aestivation
AAEEIKLMNNSSTTU unstatesmanlike
AAEEILLLMORRSTT lamellirostrate
AAEEILLMNRSSUVV semilunar valves
AAEEILLRRSTTTUX extra-illustrate
AAEEILMNNOPRSTT malpresentation
AAEEILMNOOPRTTT metropolitanate
AAEEILNNOPRRRST personal trainer
AAEEILNOPRSTTUX superexaltation
AAEEILNPRRSSTUU supernaturalise
AAEEILNPRRSTUUZ supernaturalize
AAEEILPPRRRSSTU partial pressure
AAEEIMNNPRRSSTT semitransparent
AAEEIMNPRRSSTTT tamper-resistant
AAEEIMOPPRRTVXY very approximate
AAEEINOOPPRRRTV overpreparation
AAEEINOPPPRRSST appropriateness
AAEEINOPRRTTTVY private attorney
AAEELLNPRRRTTUY preternaturally
AAEELLOPRRSSTTT Pastoral Letters
AAEELMNRRRSTTWY Ernst Walter Mayr
AAEELNOPRRSTTWY Norway saltpetre
AAEENNNPRRSSSTT transparentness
AAEFFFIILMNORST self-affirmation
AAEFFHIMNOOORTT heat of formation
AAEFFHIOORSTTUW a fish out of water
AAEFGGHILLNNPRY flying phalanger
AAEFGGILNOPPRST self-propagating
AAEFGIIMORRRSTU margaritiferous
AAEFGILNOOPPRST self-propagation
AAEFHHIILLRRTTY heath fritillary
AAEFHHLNOORRSTT horns of the altar
AAEFHIILNORRSTU infusorial earth
AAEFIIILMORRTVY overfamiliarity
AAEFIIKLLLMNRUW William Faulkner
AAEFIILLNNORSTT intestinal flora
AAEFIILNORRSSUY Fourier analysis
AAEFIIMNOPPRRSU in forma pauperis
AAEFMNOORRRSTTU autotransformer
AAEGGHINOPRSSTT steganographist
AAEGGIIILLNNNOV Giovanni Agnelli
AAEGGIILNNNRRTW warning triangle
AAEGHHILLMOOPPT ophthalmoplegia
AAEGHHIMOPPSTTT apophthegmatist
AAEGHHINOOPPRTT anthropophagite
AAEGHHNOOOPPRST organophosphate

AAEGHHNOOOSTTTV not to have a ghost
AAEGHIIKLLNNRTT lateral thinking
AAEGHIIMMORRSTT hierogrammatist
AAEGHILLLNOTTTU let it all hang out
AAEGHIMNORRRSTU Montagu's harrier
AAEGHJKKLNRSTUY Karl Guthe Jansky
AAEGHLLNOORTTUY natural theology
AAEGHLLOOOPPTYY palaeophytology
AAEGIIILMNNTUVY unimaginatively
AAEGIIILNNOORST regionalisation
AAEGIIILNNOORTZ regionalization
AAEGIIILNNOSTTV investigational
AAEGIIINNOPSTTY Egyptianisation
AAEGIIINNOPTTYZ Egyptianization
AAEGIILLNNORRTU natural religion
AAEGIILNNOORRTT interrogational
AAEGIIMNOOPRRRT marriage-portion
AAEGIINNOPRRSTT Tigran Petrosian
AAEGILLLMNOOOPY palaeolimnology
AAEGILLNOOOPSTT palaeontologist
AAEGILLOOOOPSTZ palaeozoologist
AAEGILLOPRRRTTY portrait-gallery
AAEGILNNORRSSST transgressional
AAEGIMNOPRRSTTU tetrasporangium
AAEGINNPPRRRRST sparring partner
AAEGINOPRRRSSTT Sangster Airport
AAEGINORRSSTTTU angustirostrate
AAEGLMMMNNORTUU angular momentum
AAEHHIOOPRRRTTW Heathrow Airport
AAEHIIILLLMTWWW William Whitelaw
AAEHIILMNORTTUV Italian vermouth
AAEHIILNNOPSTTX Neapolitan sixth
AAEHIILNOSTTTWZ hesitation waltz
AAEHIILORTTTUVY authoritatively
AAEHIINNORRSTTW Sir Ian Trethowan
AAEHIINORTTTUUV unauthoritative
AAEHILNOPRSSTTW a slap on the wrist
AAEHILOPPRRTTYY polarity therapy
AAEHINNOOPPRRTZ apparent horizon
AAEHKMNNOORRTWY New York Marathon
AAEHLLLMMNORSUW al-hallown summer
AAEHMMNNOSTTTTU Thatta monuments
AAEIIILMNNNORTT interlamination
AAEIIILMNORSSTT Aristotelianism
AAEIIILNNNORSTT internalisation
AAEIIILNNNORTTZ internalization
AAEIIILNPRSSSTT antiperistalsis
AAEIIINOPRRSTTV reprivatisation
AAEIIINOPRRTTVZ reprivatization
AAEIIJNNOQRRSUV San Joaquin River
AAEIILLLMMRSTTU multilateralism
AAEIILLLMRSTTTU multilateralist
AAEIILLMNNOPRST post-millenarian
AAEIILLMNNRSTTU transilluminate
AAEIILLNNNORTTY internationally
AAEIILMNNOORRST renormalisation
AAEIILMNNOORRTZ renormalization
AAEIILMNNORSTTT transition metal
AAEIILMORRRRTTY Territorial Army
AAEIILNNOOPRSST personalisation
AAEIILNNOOPRSTZ personalization
AAEIILNNORRSTTT transliteration
AAEIILNOPPPRRTY inappropriately
AAEIIMMMNNORTTU ammonium nitrate
AAEIIMNOSSSTTTY systematisation
AAEIIMNOSSTTTYZ systematization
AAEIINOOPPPRRRT reappropriation
AAEIINOPPRRRTTT portrait-painter
AAEIKKLLNOSSTWY Stanley Kowalski
AAEILLLMNNNPSTT installment plan
AAEILLLMOPPRRST parallel imports
AAEILLNNOORTTTY National Lottery
AAEILLORRSTTTUV ultraviolet star
AAEILMNNOQTUUUX autumnal equinox
AAEILMNPRRSSTUU supernaturalism
AAEILMNSSSSSTYY systems analysis
AAEILNNNOSSTTUY instantaneously
AAEILNPRRSSTTUU supernaturalist
AAEINOPRRSSTTUU supersaturation
AAELMNOOORRRSTY Astronomer Royal
AAFFFHIJLNORSST Sir John Falstaff
AAFGGGIILMNNSSY magnifying glass
AAFGGIINOOTTUWY going-away outfit
AAFGIIILNOPRRSV pair of virginals
AAFGIINNORRSTTU transfiguration✧
AAFGILMOPRRTTVY gravity platform
AAFHILNORRTTTUV Valiant-for-Truth
AAFIIIMMNOOPRST spirit of ammonia
AAFIILLNORRTTTU ultrafiltration
AAFIILMNNORTTTY infant mortality
AAFIILMNOORRSTU formularisation
AAFIILMNOORRTUZ formularization
AAFIIOOPRRSSTTW two-pair-of-stairs
AAFILLMNOPRSTUY slumpflationary
AAGGHIIILNNOTTV navigation light
AAGGHIIKLNRSTTT straight talking
straight-talking
AAGGHIMNNOORSTU Hoggar Mountains
AAGGMMNNNOSSSUU Magnus Magnusson
AAGHHNOOOPPRSTU anthropophagous
AAGHIIIMNNNORST nothingarianism
AAGHIINNORSTTTV night starvation
AAGHLNOOPRRSTUY ultrasonography
AAGHMNNORTTUUUU Mount Tungurahua
AAGIIIKLLMNRSWW King William's War
AAGIIILNNORSSTU singularisation
AAGIIILNNORSTTU granulitisation
AAGIIILNNORSTUZ singularization
AAGIIILNNORTTUZ granulitization
AAGIIKLNNOPRSST stinking parasol
AAGIILMNPRRRSTU triangular prism
AAGIINNNOOPSTTT stagnation point
AAGILMOOOPSSTTU plagiostomatous
AAGIMNNOORSSTUZ Zagros Mountains
AAHHHLOPPRRSTYY staphylorrhaphy
AAHHIILMNOPPSTT panophthalmitis
AAHHIIRRRRRSSTU Sir Arthur Harris
AAHHIJLLMNORRSS Sir John Marshall
AAHHIMNOOPPRSTT anthropopathism
AAHIIIILMNNNOST annihilationism
AAHIIILLLMMNOTW William Hamilton
AAHIIILLMNORRSW William Harrison

AAHIIILNOOPSSTT hospitalisation
AAHIIILNOOPSTTZ hospitalization
AAHIIILNNOOORRTZ rational horizon
AAHIKLNPRSSTUVY Sylvia Pankhurst
AAHIOOPPRRSSTTU protospatharius
AAHLMMOOOPRRSSU parasol mushroom
AAIIIILMNOSSSTT assimilationist
AAIIIIMNNORSTTU miniaturisation
AAIIIIMNNORTTUZ miniaturization
AAIIILLNNOPRSTY inspirationally
AAIIILMMNOORSTT immortalisation
AAIIILMMNOORTTZ immortalization
AAIIILMNNNOOPTT ion implantation
AAIIILMNOOPRSTV improvisational
AAIIILMOOPRRSTV improvisatorial
AAIIILNNOQRTTUZ tranquilization
AAIIJLNOOPSTTUX juxtapositional
AAIIKLMNOOSSSTY ankylostomiasis
AAIILMMNNRTTUUY natural immunity
AAIILNNOOPRSSTT transpositional
AAIIMNOOPRSSSTY trypanosomiasis
AAIINNOOPPPQRTU appropinquation
AAIINNOOPRSTTTU saturation point
AAIJMNOPRRSSTTU Jan Smuts Airport
AAILLLNOOPSTTUY postulationally
AAIMNNORSSTTUUU Taurus Mountains
ABBBCEHIMMOORRT thermobaric bomb
ABBBDEEGIILNRRY Beryl Bainbridge
ABBBEFGIORRRSYY Greyfriars Bobby
ABBCCCEIILMRRSU circumscribable
ABBCCDEEGIIILLR gibberellic acid
ABBCDDEHIILMRRY Richard Dimbleby
ABBCDEEFHKNOOTY the back of beyond
ABBCDEEHLLNORSW Chandler's wobble
ABBCEEEFFKLOOOT coffee-table book
ABBCEEEGNORRTUU Centre Beaubourg
ABBCEEHKNNORRTU on the back burner
ABBCEEIJLNNOOTU unobjectionable
ABBCEEILMMOORRT bomb calorimeter
ABBCEGIILNPPRRS scribbling-paper
ABBCEHLNNOSSTTU Hubble's constant
ABBCEIJLNNOOTUY unobjectionably
ABBCENNOOORSTTT absorbent cotton
ABBCHIIILMORSTU British Columbia
ABBDDEEELLLORRU double-barrelled
ABBDDEELLMORSUU Albus Dumbledore
ABBDDELNOORTTUY total body burden
ABBDEEEHIMMNORT Meindert Hobbema
ABBDEEEIINRRRTU India rubber tree
ABBDEEIILNNSSTU indubitableness
ABBDEEIIMPRSSTY baptism by desire
ABBDEEKLOOORRRV Lord Beaverbrook
ABBDEGHILORRTYY daylight robbery
ABBDEHIJNOORSUY Josiah Bounderby
ABBDEIIILNRSTTU indistributable
ABBEEEEGLRTTTUV vegetable butter
ABBEEEEHILNNTTZ Elizabeth Bennet
ABBEEEFHLOORTTW The Tower of Babel
ABBEEEHLNOORSTW below one's breath
ABBEEEILORRTTUW water tube boiler
ABBEEEIMMNOORTY Baby One More Time
ABBEEHHIILOPSTZ Elizabeth Bishop
ABBEEIIJMNNNRTT Benjamin Britten
ABBEFLLLNORTTUU Battle of Bull Run
ABBEGHIILNSTTYY shabby-gentility
ABBEGINNORRRTTW Barrett Browning
ABBEHLMORRRRUUY Mulberry harbour
ABBEHRRRRSSTUWY strawberry shrub
ABBEIIILOPQRTUY equiprobability
ABCCCDEIIILNORU ribonucleic acid
ABCCCEHIIKLRSWY bicycle rickshaw
ABCCCEHKKLOPTTU put back the clock
put the clock back
ABCCCGIIKLLLOOO biological clock
ABCCCHILNOOOPRS bronchoscopical
ABCCDEEEEINRRTW Rebecca de Winter
ABCCDEEEIIIMNNT medicine cabinet
ABCCDEELLMORSWY screwball comedy
ABCCDEEMNNORTUU numbered account
ABCCDGHIILNRSTU scratchbuilding
ABCCDHINOOPRTTU batch production
ABCCDIILMOPRRST Lombardic script
ABCCDINNOOORTTU button accordion
ABCCEEEEHMNPRRS presence chamber
ABCCEEEHILRRTTU Crucible Theatre
ABCCEEEIKLLNRTT electric blanket
ABCCEEEILNNOSSV conceivableness
ABCCEEEILRRTTTY electric battery
ABCCEEFIIINORSS Fibonacci series
ABCCEEIILLNNORU unreconciliable
ABCCEEIILNNORRT electronic brain
ABCCEEILLNOOPST police constable
ABCCEEIMNORRTUY Corynebacterium
ABCCEELNORRSTTU reconstructable
ABCCEFHINOORRSU François Boucher
ABCCEFIIIJNOOTT objectification
ABCCEFIILLPSSUY subspecifically
ABCCEGHINOPRSST batch processing
ABCCEHHINNRTUYZ Byzantine Church
ABCCEHHINOORRST brachistochrone
ABCCEHIKLNOORRS black rhinoceros
ABCCEHNNOOOSTTU cannot choose but
ABCCEIIIILNSSTY inaccessibility
ABCCEIIILLNORTY reconcilability
ABCCEIILLLOOPSU ebullioscopical
ABCCEIILMNNOTUY mountain bicycle
ABCCEIINORSSSSU scribaciousness
ABCCEILLLMMRSUU lumbrical muscle
ABCCEKLMMNOOOOP commonplace book
ABCCGIIILLMOOOR microbiological
ABCCGIIILLOOOOS sociobiological
ABCCHIILOOOPSSY biopsychosocial
ABCCIIILMMNOTUY communicability
ABCCIIILNORTTTY contractibility
ABCCIIKLMNNOOOT combination lock
ABCDDEEEEILLOPS peasecod-bellied
ABCDDEEEFLNOSSU double-facedness
ABCDDEEGIILPRTU duplicate bridge
ABCDDEEGINNORRV David Cronenberg
ABCDDEEHIIOTWWW a widow bewitched
ABCDDEHHILLNORY Rhynchobdellida
ABCDDEHILLNOORT cloth-lined board

ABCDDEIINNOORTU induced abortion
ABCDDEINNOOORST co-ordinate bonds
ABCDDEKLNORRSUW sword-and-buckler
ABCDEEEGIJNORTV objective danger
ABCDEEEHLLLNSTY sell by the candle
ABCDEEEILLLRRUV Alec D'Urberville
ABCDEEEILNPRSST predictableness
ABCDEEELMMNNORU unrecommendable
ABCDEEELMMNNOSS commendableness
ABCDEEFGHILRUUW Ludwig Feuerbach
ABCDEEFIILNRUVZ vulcanized fibre
ABCDEEGHILNOPRW bleaching powder
ABCDEEGHILNRSTU Edinburgh Castle
ABCDEEGHLNOORTY Henry Cabot Lodge
ABCDEEGIILNSSTT dissecting table
ABCDEEGILLMORRR Cambridge roller
ABCDEEGINNRSTTU tungsten carbide
ABCDEEGKNOQRUUU background queue
ABCDEEHIIILPRTY decipherability
ABCDEEIILNOSSSS dissociableness
ABCDEELMNNOOORY coromandel ebony
ABCDEIIIILLNNPS indisciplinable
ABCDEIIILLNNPSU undisciplinable
ABCDEIILMOOPSTY decomposability
ABCDEIIMOOSSTUY basidiomycetous
ABCDEIKLLOORRWY yellow brick road
ABCDEILNOOORRUW rainbow-coloured
ABCDEINOOORSSTT corno di bassetto
ABCDEKNOPRRRTUY bankruptcy order
ABCDGHIILLOOORY hydrobiological
ABCDHIILNOOORRT bronchiodilator
ABCDIIIILRSTTTY distractibility
ABCEEEEEHHRRSTW wear the breeches
ABCEEEEFLLMNRSS self-resemblance
ABCEEEEHRRRRSTT stretcher-bearer
ABCEEEEILNRSSSV serviceableness
ABCEEEELNORRSSV recoverableness
ABCEEEELNPRSSST respectableness
ABCEEEFFIMNRSTU submarine effect
ABCEEEFFMORSSTU Mössbauer effect
ABCEEEGINNRRSST breast screening
ABCEEEGINSSSTUW subsistence wage
ABCEEEHHINORSTT raise to the bench
ABCEEEHILMRSSTT Christmas beetle
ABCEEEHKLNNOOSS back on one's heels
ABCEEEHMNNOPTTT beneath contempt
ABCEEEIILLNOSTV cable television
ABCEEEILNNOPTUX unexceptionable
ABCEEEILNNSSSUX inexcusableness
ABCEEEILNORRSSV irrevocableness
ABCEEELMNNNORST Clemens Brentano
ABCEEELNNOQRSSU conquerableness
ABCEEFFHLLORRTY carry off the bell
ABCEEFHILOORRSW a bowl of cherries
ABCEEFHIMOOPRRS breach of promise
ABCEEFHKORTTTUU Back to the Future
ABCEEFILNOPSSSU place of business
ABCEEFKLLNORRST Bracknell Forest
ABCEEFLLNOOOSTT Battle of Colenso
ABCEEFLMNOORSST comfortableness
ABCEEFLNOOPSTTW Battle of Cowpens
ABCEEGHINORSSTT tossing the caber
ABCEEGIILLNOSTU absolute ceiling
ABCEEHHLMNNOOPR rhombencephalon
ABCEEHKNNORSTTU South Bank Centre
ABCEEHLNOORRTTT Charlotte Brontë
ABCEEIIIMNNRSTT cabinet minister
ABCEEIIJNOPRSST Sir Jacob Epstein
ABCEEIINNORRTTU reaction turbine
ABCEEIJMOOPRTTX proximate object
ABCEEIKLNRSTTUY security blanket
ABCEEILMMNNORSU incommensurable
ABCEEILMNNNOOOU once in a blue moon
ABCEEILNNOPTUXY unexceptionably
ABCEEILNNRSSSTU inscrutableness
ABCEEILNORSTTTU reconstitutable
ABCEELLMNORRTUV vertebral column
ABCEELNNNOOPRUU unpronounceable
ABCEFFGIIJLNNRU luffing-jib crane
ABCEFLNOOOPRRRU perfluorocarbon
ABCEGHHIIKMNRSU Buckinghamshire
ABCEGHHIKLNORST knights bachelor
ABCEGHNORSSTTUW growth substance
ABCEGIIILNORSTY recognisability
ABCEGIIILNORTYZ recognizability
ABCEGIILLNOOORU neurobiological
ABCEGILLLMOORYY embryologically
ABCEGLLLORRSTUU globular cluster
ABCEHHIKLMNSTTU thumbnail sketch
ABCEHIIKNOTTTUW think twice about
ABCEIIIILLNPTXY inexplicability
ABCEIIIILNRTTXY inextricability
ABCEIIIJNOOSTTV objectivisation
ABCEIIIJNOOTTVZ objectivization
ABCEIIIKLLNPSST lipstick lesbian
ABCEIIIKLMNRSWW Wilkins Micawber
ABCEIIILLMNOPPR principal mobile
ABCEIIILLMPRSTT bimetallic strip
ABCEIIILNRSSTUV alternis vicibus
ABCEIILLNOPRSTU public relations
public-relations
ABCEIILLOPRSSSY perissosyllabic
ABCEIILMMNOPTVX vitamin B complex
ABCEIILNORSTTUU tuberculisation
ABCEIILNORTTUUZ tuberculization
ABCEIIMNNNOOOTV combination oven
ABCEIIMOOPRRSTT absorptiometric
ABCEIKNNOOPSTTU put one's back into
ABCEILLNNOSTUVY Viscount Allenby
ABCEILMMNNORSUY incommensurably
ABCGGIILLNOOOOT gnotobiological
ABCGHHIOOPPRSYY psychobiography
ABCGIIILLLLNTUV victualling-bill
ABCGIILLNOOOTTY gnotobiotically
ABCGIILNOORSTTU osculating orbit
ABCHILNOORRSTUZ horizontal scrub
ABCHIMMNOOORTUZ Mount Chimborazo
ABCIIIILMNOPTTY incompatibility
ABCIIIILNOSSTUV subcivilisation
ABCIIIILNOSTUVZ subcivilization
ABCIIILLNNOOSTY inconsolability
ABCIIILMMNOTTUY incommutability

ABCIIILNNOORSUV binocular vision
ABCIILLLMOPSSYY polysyllabicism
ABCIILLLNOORTTY controllability
ABCIILORRRSTTUU arboriculturist
ABCIIMMNNNOSSUU communibus annis
ABCIIMMNNOOORT combination room
ABCIKMNOOORSTTV Otto von Bismarck
ABCILLNOORSTTUY obstructionally
ABCILNOPPRRSTTU public transport
ABDDDEEIMNNORSS broadmindedness
ABDDDEHLNNOORTU blood-and-thunder
ABDDEEEFLLRSSTU full-dress debate
ABDDEEEFLNORSTT Battle of Dresden
ABDDEEEHNOORSUW bonded warehouse
ABDDEEFFLLNOOTT Battle of Flodden
ABDDEEFILNNOPRT forbidden planet
ABDDEEGHIIINNSV adhesive binding
ABDDEEGIKLLNPUW Bakewell pudding
ABDDEEHLLNOOPRR Bernhard Leopold
ABDDEELLLNOOPRW Lord Baden-Powell
ABDDEELMNOORSSW warm-bloodedness
ABDDEGINNOORRSW Edward G Robinson
ABDDEIKLLLORSST saddle-bill stork
ABDDGGIIIINORTZ digitizing board
ABDEEEEEGPRRSTT Debrett's Peerage
ABDEEEEEINRRRRT Aberdeen terrier
ABDEEEEILMNPRRT predeterminable
ABDEEEEMNNOTUWY between you and me
ABDEEEFIILNNNSS indefinableness
ABDEEEGHJLORRSU Joshua Lederberg
ABDEEEHKLNORRTY broken-heartedly
ABDEEEHNNOPRSST spend one's breath
ABDEEEHNNORRSTU under one's breath
ABDEEEIIILMRRTY irredeemability
ABDEEEIKLNRSSTT beer and skittles
ABDEEEILNNPSSSS dispensableness
ABDEEEILNNRSSSU undesirableness
ABDEEEKNNNORSSY Baroness Kennedy
ABDEEFIIIILNSTY indefeasibility
ABDEEFILLNORTUV bill of adventure
ABDEEGHKLMORSST God bless the mark
ABDEEGIILLMORTT Gottlieb Daimler
ABDEEGIILNNSSSU leading business
ABDEEGIKLNORSST gold-beater's skin
ABDEEHHILLOORRS Lord Hore-Belisha
ABDEEHHLNOOORSU Leonard Hobhouse
ABDEEHHLNOORSTT The Boston Herald
ABDEEHILLNNRRSS Brinell hardness
ABDEEHILMNOORSS Bornholm disease
ABDEEHILMOORTTW Bartholomew-tide
ABDEEHIMNNRSTUW white man's burden
ABDEEHNOORSTTTT Hottentot's bread
ABDEEIIILMNRTTY determinability
ABDEEIILLLNNORU Daniel Bernoulli
ABDEEIILMNNOSST indomitableness
ABDEEILLNOSSSSV dissolvableness
ABDEEILMNNOOPUU double pneumonia
ABDEEIMORRTUUXX Bordeaux mixture
ABDEEINNORSSSTU subordinateness
ABDEEINOPRRSSUU Pierre d'Aubusson
ABDEEKNNORSTTWY known better days
ABDEELLNRRRSSTU Bertrand Russell
ABDEELNORSSTUUV Sunset Boulevard
ABDEEOOOPPRSSTT à propos de bottes
ABDEFIKKLNORTTU Battle of Dunkirk
ABDEGGHHIILLNRV high-gravel-blind
ABDEGGIIIILNTTZ digitizing table
ABDEGHHINNOORTV Brighton and Hove
ABDEGHHNNORSTTY by the strong hand
ABDEGHIIILNSSTU distinguishable
ABDEGIIKLLNOTWY knowledgability
ABDEGIINNORRSSW rainbow dressing
ABDEHIIMNNNORRS Sir Hermann Bondi
ABDEIIILMNOPRTY imponderability
ABDEIIILPRSTTUY disreputability
ABDEIILMNORSTTY demonstrability
ABDEIILNNORSTUY insubordinately
ABDEIILOORRRRSU Dolores Ibárruri
ABDEIMNNORRSTTU instrument board
ABDFFGIIIILNRTY diffrangibility
ABDGHIIILNSSTUY distinguishably
ABDGHLOOOOSSTTU tough as old boots
ABDGILLMNNOTUWZ Ludwig Boltzmann
ABDHHIMOOOPPRSY dysmorphophobia
ABDHHINOORRSTUY birthday honours
ABDIIIIILMNSSTY inadmissibility
ABDIIIILNPSTTUY indisputability
ABDIIILMNORSTTU maldistribution
ABDIIINNNOORSTU insubordination
ABDIILNOORTTUUY roundaboutility
ABEEEEEGLNNRRWY renewable energy
ABEEEEGLORSTTVY vegetable oyster
ABEEEEILLNORRST Easter Rebellion
ABEEEEILMMNPRSS impermeableness
ABEEEEILNNPRRTT interpenetrable
ABEEEEILNRRSSTV retrievableness
ABEEEEKLNNOPRSV banker's envelope
ABEEEELNNPRSSST presentableness
ABEEEFFGKNSSTUU beefsteak fungus
ABEEEFGILNNRRSS refrangibleness
ABEEEFHHIOSTTTV have the best of it
ABEEEFHHLMORSTT star of Bethlehem
ABEEEFHILLNOTTT Battle of the Nile
ABEEEFHLLNORRSU Earl of Shelburne
ABEEEFILNRRSSTU irrefutableness
ABEEEGGILNNPRRT ginger beer plant
ABEEEGGINNORSST get one's bearings
ABEEEGINNORRSSV overbearingness
ABEEEGORRSSTTTY set great store by
ABEEEHHILOOPRTU eleutherophobia
ABEEEHHOPRSTTTW the powers that be
ABEEEHIIKLLNNRS Niels Henrik Abel
ABEEEHIILLMNNPS Blenheim spaniel
ABEEEHIILNNPPRS inapprehensible
ABEEEHIILNRRTTV Ivan the Terrible
ABEEEHILLPPRSTU Isabelle Huppert
ABEEEHILMNRSSTT re-establishment
ABEEEHILNNPPRSU unapprehensible
ABEEEHJLNNNOSTW John Bennet Lawes
ABEEEHKOOPRRRSW brake horsepower
ABEEEHLLOPSTTUY up to the eyeballs
ABEEEIILLNRRRTV Albert Nile River

ABEEEIILMNNSSST inestimableness
ABEEEIILMNPRSSV imperviableness
ABEEEIILNNQSSTU inequitableness
ABEEEIIMNNPRTYZ Byzantine Empire
ABEEEIINPRRSSTY presbyterianise✧
ABEEEIINPRRSTYZ presbyterianize✧
ABEEEILLNNORSST intolerableness
ABEEEILMNNNRSSU innumerableness
ABEEEILMNORRSSV irremovableness
ABEEEILNNPRRTTU uninterpretable
ABEEEILNNPRSSSU insuperableness
ABEEEILNRRSTUVV vestibular nerve
ABEEEIMNOOOSTTT beat someone to it
ABEEELLMNOORSSS lose one's marbles
ABEEELLMOPPSSSY People's Assembly
ABEEELNPPRRSTUU Peter Paul Rubens
ABEEFFGGHHIOTTT the gift of the gab
ABEEFFGHOORRRUU harbour of refuge
ABEEFFHNOOPRSTT bore the pants off
ABEEFFIIILLSTUU Life is Beautiful
ABEEFFMNOOORSSS brass someone off
ABEEFGIILLOPTTZ Battle of Leipzig
ABEEFGIILNNNRSS infrangibleness
ABEEFGIMNRRSTUU figurate numbers
ABEEFGNOORRRSTU Berengar of Tours
ABEEFHLMOOSSSUY House of Assembly
ABEEFIIJLNSSSTU justifiableness
ABEEFIILLRRSTUV filterable virus
ABEEFILNOORSSTV self-observation
ABEEFILORSTTTUY Statue of Liberty
ABEEGGIILNOOORZ globigerina ooze
ABEEGGIKLNRSSTU like gangbusters
ABEEGHHLNOOPRSU ploughshare bone
ABEEGHILNPRTTTY penlight battery
ABEEGHINNOQSTUU banqueting-house
ABEEHHMORRRSTTX The Marx Brothers
ABEEHIIILMNNSTV The Invisible Man
ABEEHIILMMNOORT binomial theorem
ABEEHIJJMNNORST Sir John Betjeman
ABEEHILMNORSSTW blameworthiness
ABEEHINNRRRRSUY Sir Henry Raeburn
ABEEHLLNOOOPPSY polyphloesboean
ABEEHMNNNOORRTT to the manner born
ABEEHNNNORRRUVW Wernher von Braun
ABEEHOPRRSSSTTU substratosphere
ABEEIIILLLMNSST illimitableness
ABEEIIILLRSTTTY reliability test
ABEEIIILMNPRTTY impenetrability
ABEEIILLMNPSSSU implausibleness
ABEEIILLMOOORRT Baltimore oriole
ABEEIILNNORSTUV labour-intensive
ABEEIIMNPRRSSTY presbyterianism✧
ABEEIINRSSTTTUV attributiveness
ABEEIKLMNNRTTUY bunker mentality
ABEEILLMNOORRRY Lionel Barrymore
ABEEILLMNORSUWY Yellow Submarine
ABEEILMNNOOPSUU pneumonia blouse
ABEEINNSSSSTTUV substantiveness
ABEELNOPPRSSSTU supportableness
ABEELNORRSSTUUY subterraneously
ABEENNOOOPRSSTU about one's person
ABEFGGHILORRTUY burgh of regality
ABEFHHILRSSTTTU at the first blush
ABEFHIIMNORRRST Martin Frobisher
ABEFIIIILNRTUVY unverifiability
ABEFIIJLMOORRTU Alberto Fujimori
ABEFIILLNORRRUY neurofibrillary
ABEFINNORRRSSUW Barrow-in-Furness
ABEFLLLNOORRWWW wallflower brown
ABEGGHINNRSSTTU hanging buttress
ABEGHHILNOORRTU Right Honourable
ABEGIIIILLNNNOV Giovanni Bellini
ABEGIIILNNPTUXY inexpugnability
ABEGILLMNOPPRRT trembling poplar
ABEHHHIORRSSTTY by the short hairs
ABEHHINORRRTTTU burr in the throat
ABEHIIIILMPRSTY imperishability
ABEHIINOOPPRRST probationership
ABEHIKLLLRSTTUW hawksbill turtle
ABEHILMOOPRSSTY strephosymbolia
ABEHIMNOORRSSTW Sir Thomas Browne
ABEHIOOOPPRRRSU harbour porpoise
ABEIIILLNNRTUVY invulnerability
ABEIIILLORRSTVY irresolvability
ABEIIILMMNRSTUY immensurability
ABEIIILMNNRSSST intransmissible
ABEIIILNOQSTTUY questionability
ABEIILMMNNORUUZ aluminium bronze
ABEIILMNNRSSSTU untransmissible
ABEIILNNOOPRSST absorption lines
ABEIINNNNORSTTU Anton Rubinstein
ABEIINNRRRSTTUU Artur Rubinstein
ABEIJMOQSSTUUUU jusqu'auboutisme
ABEIJOQSSTTUUUU jusqu'auboutiste
ABEIKLMOOORRTTY Tim Brooke-Taylor
ABEIKMNNOOOPPTT appointment book
ABEIMMNNNNOSTUU Nubian monuments
ABEINOOOPRSSTTV observation post
ABFGIIINNOSTTTU fitting-out basin
ABFIIILNOPRTTUY unprofitability
ABFIILLLMOORTTY bill of mortality
ABGHHIJNNORRSUV Sir John Vanbrugh
ABGHILNOOOOPRTY anthropobiology
ABGIIMNNNNORTUU burning mountain
ABHHIJJNOORSTTU Thojib N J Suharto
ABHIIILNNORRSSU annus horribilis
ABHIIILNOPSTTYY hypnotisability
ABHIIILNOPTTYYZ hypnotizability
ABHIKLMMOPRTTUY Burkitt lymphoma
ABHILMOPRSSSTUU brushtail possum
ABIINORSSTTTUUY substitutionary
ACCCCCDEIIILRTY citric acid cycle
ACCCCEGHIKNNOTU checking account
ACCCDDEIIILLRRU druidical circle
ACCCDDKLLNOOOUU Cloudcuckooland
cloud-cuckoo-land
ACCCDEEILMNRRUY decimal currency
ACCCDEFHHIKLORT Alfred Hitchcock
ACCCDEHHIILLOOP dolichocephalic
ACCCDEHIILLMORU calcium chloride
ACCCDEHILLNOSYY synecdochically
ACCCDEIOOOPRRSS coracoid process

ACCCEEEELNNORSV reconvalescence
ACCCEEEFILNRRTU electric furnace
ACCCEEEFLLMNOPS self-complacence
ACCCEEEHILLMORT electrochemical
ACCCEEEIINNORST creation science
ACCCEEFHHIIINNT chief technician
ACCCEEFHILLLOOR cholecalciferol
ACCCEEGHIILLNOO ecological niche
ACCCEEGIILLLOOS ecclesiological
ACCCEEHHIIILORS Escherichia coli
ACCCEEHIILNNOST cochineal insect
ACCCEEHLLNOORRT cache controller
ACCCEEIIILMSSST ecclesiasticism
ACCCEEIILLLNRTU clinical lecture
ACCCEEIILLNNNOS in all conscience
ACCCEEILNOOPSTT ice contact slope
ACCCEEILOORSTTU acousto-electric
electroacoustic
ACCCEEINORRSTTV service contract
ACCCEFIIKNNOOTY cockneyfication
ACCCEGHHILLLORU collegial church
ACCCEGIIINNORTY carcinogenicity
ACCCEHHIILMOPSY physicochemical
ACCCEHMOOPRSTTU come up to scratch
ACCCEIILLNNORTV clinical convert
ACCCEIILNOPSTTU conceptualistic
ACCCEILMMOORRTU Commercial Court
ACCCEILOOPPRSST spectroscopical
ACCCEILOOPRRRSS reciprocal cross
ACCCEILOOPRSTUU acoustic coupler
ACCCELLMNORRSSU Carson McCullers
ACCCIILLMOOPRSY microscopically
ACCCIILMMOORSST microcosmic salt
ACCCIINNOORRTVY carry conviction
ACCCILLLOOOPPSY colposcopically
ACCCILORRRRSSUU cross-curricular
ACCDDEEEFINOOSS deed of accession
ACCDDEEEHLSSSTU scheduled castes
ACCDDEEFILNNORU road fund licence
ACCDDEEINORRSTT I stand corrected
ACCDDEIIKNNOOST cask-conditioned
ACCDDEIMMNNNOOS second-in-command
ACCDEEEEMRRRSST crested screamer
ACCDEEEHIOOSSSU douche écossaise
ACCDEEEHKORSSTW socket head screw
ACCDEEEIILMNNRU nuclear medicine
ACCDEEENNORSSST consecratedness
ACCDEEFGIILORTT gold certificate
ACCDEEFIIINNOSX axis of incidence
ACCDEEHIILMORRR Mordecai Richler
ACCDEEHIILNOOPS poisoned chalice
ACCDEEHILMNRTUY hydraulic cement
ACCDEEHINOOOPSU chenopodiaceous
ACCDEEIINNRRSTU credit insurance
ACCDEEIKNOPRSTY secondary picket
ACCDEEILMNORSTY electrodynamics
ACCDEELLNORSSTU couldn't care less
ACCDEFGHHLNNORU Church of England
ACCDEFINNNOOSTU find one's account
ACCDEFLNOORSSTU curse of Scotland
ACCDEFNNOOOORSW of one's own accord
ACCDEGIINORRSTT casting director
ACCDEHIKKLNNSUW knuckle sandwich
ACCDEHLNOOORSSY secondary school
ACCDEIIILLMNRSY semicylindrical
ACCDEIIILLOPPPR Callippic Period
ACCDEIIILMNNSTU incidental music
ACCDEIILLMOOPSX acid soil complex
ACCDEIILMORRSTU musical director
ACCDEIILNORTTVY contradictively
ACCDEIILOPRSSTY perissodactylic
ACCDEIKLMOPSSTY slapstick comedy
ACCDEIOPPRRSTTU picture postcard
picture-postcard
ACCDELMNNOOPRUY compound larceny
ACCDELNOOORRSUY secondary colour
ACCDELNOOPSSSST second-class post
ACCDFFHIIILRRRS Sir Cliff Richard
ACCDFFLMMOOORRT Cold Comfort Farm
ACCDFHIIINNOORT chondrification
ACCDFHIILLNORTW wind-chill factor
ACCDFIIIMMNOOOT commodification
ACCDHIILMOOPPTU diplomatic pouch
ACCDHIIORRRSSTT Sir Richard Scott
ACCDHILMOOOPSSS Spasmodic School
ACCDIILMOOPPRST diplomatic corps
ACCDIILNOORRTTY contradictorily
ACCEEEEHILLMMNT chemical element
ACCEEEELNPPRRSV Spencer Perceval
ACCEEEFFGHORRUY Geoffrey Chaucer
ACCEEEFFIILRSTT self-certificate
ACCEEEFFILNOSTT coastline effect
ACCEEEFINNORSTU counterfeisance
ACCEEEFNNORSTUU counterfesaunce
ACCEEEGILLOPSTU elegiac couplets
ACCEEEGILMNORTT electromagnetic
magneto-electric
ACCEEEHHIMMNOTT The Iceman Cometh
ACCEEEHILORRTTY heterocercality
ACCEEEHIMNRRSTV merchant service
ACCEEEHMNOOPRRT mechanoreceptor
ACCEEEIILMNRSST éclaircissement
ACCEEEILLMORRTT electrometrical
ACCEEEILMNNOPRT porcelain cement
ACCEEELNOPRRTTU electron capture
ACCEEENNOPSSTUX expenses account
ACCEEFFHIIOSTVZ schizo-affective
ACCEEFFIINOSSSU efficaciousness
ACCEEFFINORRTTY carry into effect
ACCEEFHIIINOPST speechification
ACCEEFHILLNORST electronic flash
ACCEEFHILOPSSTT telescopic shaft
ACCEEFIIILNORTT electrification
ACCEEFIILMNRRTU circumferential
ACCEEFILNNOOPST false conception
ACCEEGGINNNORTU green accounting
ACCEEGHIILNNNST ethnic cleansing
ACCEEGHIIMNNRSW screwing machine
ACCEEGHILNOPSTY psychogenetical
ACCEEGHIMMNNNRU Merce Cunningham
ACCEEGHLNNOORTX exchange control
ACCEEGIIMOPRSUV Amerigo Vespucci

ACCEEGILLNOTTYY cytogenetically
ACCEEGILNNOORRT electronic organ
ACCEEHHIMOORRTT heterochromatic
ACCEEHIILNRRTTW technical writer
ACCEEHIINRRSTTZ Citizen's Charter
ACCEEHILMNOPSTU pencil moustache
ACCEEHILNNORRRY cornelian cherry
ACCEEHILOORRSTT atherosclerotic
ACCEEHINOORSSTT thoracocentesis
ACCEEIIKLLLRSTT sickle-cell trait
ACCEEIILNNOOPRT electronic piano
ACCEEIIMMNOOTTT action committee
ACCEEIIMMNOTUVX excommunicative
ACCEEIIMOPRSSTX proxime accessit
ACCEEIINNNOORSS concessionnaire
ACCEEIIOPPRRTTY cryoprecipitate
ACCEEILLLNNOOST clonal selection
ACCEEILLMORRSTT electrical storm
ACCEEILLNOOPTUV occupation level
ACCEEILLNOSSUUX exclusion clause
ACCEEILNNOOPRUU European Council
ACCEEILNORSSTUU Seleucus Nicator
ACCEEILNORTTUVY counteractively
ACCEEILNORTTXYY oxytetracycline
ACCEEKNOORRSSTV cover one's tracks
ACCEELMMNNOOPSS commonplaceness
ACCEENNOPSSSTUU suspense account
ACCEFFGIIILNRSS self-sacrificing
ACCEFFHIIINNORT Frenchification
ACCEFFIIILNOSUY inefficaciously
ACCEFGIIIINOSTV cosignificative
ACCEFGIIIPRSTVY specific gravity
ACCEFHHMMNOSSUU much of a muchness
ACCEFHHOOPRSSST Pasch of the Cross
ACCEFILNOOSSTTU Council of States
ACCEFIMNOORRSUU circumforaneous
ACCEFLNORRTTUUU Foucault current
ACCEGGHHILLNSTU Gleichschaltung
ACCEGHIIILNNORT anticholinergic
ACCEGHIIIMMNNPR crimping-machine
ACCEGHIIKNPSTTW packet switching
ACCEGHIILLOOOST stoechiological
ACCEGHIIMNOPRRY cinemicrography
ACCEGHIIOPRRSTY psychogeriatric
ACCEGHIKMNOPRTU computer hacking
ACCEGHILLLNOOTY technologically
ACCEGHIMMNORTUY community charge
ACCEGIIIMMOPRTT micropegmatitic
ACCEGIILLLLOOXY lexicologically
ACCEGIILLNNOORU regional council
ACCEGIILLNRRSUY clinical surgery
ACCEGIILNNOPRSS pelican crossing
ACCEGIIMMNNOORT economic migrant
ACCEGILLLNOOSYY synecologically
ACCEGILLMNOPSTT stamp collecting
ACCEGNNOOOOSTTU go to one's account
ACCEHHIINNOPSSS cash in one's chips
ACCEHHILLMNOOPR chloramphenicol
ACCEHHILNOOSSTU health-conscious
ACCEHHIMOPRSTYY chemopsychiatry
ACCEHIIILMOOPRR microaerophilic
ACCEHIILLPRRTYY hypercritically
ACCEHIILNORSSTT interscholastic
ACCEHIILPPRSSTY particle physics
ACCEHIIMNOPRSTY psychometrician
ACCEHIIMOOPRRRT Microchiroptera
ACCEHILLNOPRTYY pyrotechnically
ACCEHILMOPRRSTY psychrometrical
ACCEHILMORRSSTU orchestral music
ACCEHINNOOPRRTT anthropocentric
ACCEHINORSSSTTU scatter cushions
ACCEHLLMNOOSTUY collenchymatous
ACCEIIILMORSSTV viscosimetrical
ACCEIIILOSSTTVY viscoelasticity
ACCEIIIMMNNOTUV incommunicative
ACCEIIKNNORSSTW stick in one's craw
ACCEIILLLMNNOWW well-woman clinic
ACCEIILLNOOSSUX social exclusion
ACCEIILMMNOTUVY communicatively
ACCEIILMRRTUUUV curriculum vitae
ACCEIILOPPRSSUY perspicaciously
ACCEIIMMNNOOTUX excommunication
ACCEIIMMNNOTUUV uncommunicative
ACCEIIMNNORSTTU interim accounts
ACCEIINOPPRTTTU put into practice
ACCEILMOOOPRRSS solar microscope
ACCEILMOOPRRSTU ultramicroscope
ACCEILMOPPRSTTU optical spectrum
ACCEILNNOPSSSTU plant succession
ACCEIMMNOORTUXY excommunicatory
ACCEIMNOOOPRRSS acromion process
ACCEIMNOORSSTUV Viscount Camrose
ACCEIMORRSTTTUU atomic structure
ACCEINNOOOPRTUW owner-occupation
ACCELLNOOOSUUVV convolvulaceous
ACCFIIINNORRSTT intrinsic factor
ACCFIIINOOOPRRT corporification
ACCFIINNOOORTTT act of contrition
ACCGHIIILLOOOST stoichiological
ACCGHIILLMOTUXY oxy-calcium light
ACCGHIKNOPRRSST pork scratchings
ACCGHILLLNOOORY chronologically
ACCGHILLLOOPSYY psychologically
ACCGHILOOPRSSTY hygroscopic salt
ACCGIIIINNRRTTU circuit training
ACCGIIILNOPSSTT spoiling tactics
ACCGIILLLOOOTXY toxicologically
ACCHHIILMOORSTT lithochromatics
ACCHHILMOOOPPST ophthalmoscopic
ACCHHINOOPPRSTY anthropopsychic
ACCHIIKLOOOPPRT Hippocratic look
ACCHIILNNORSSTY synchronistical
ACCHIINOPRRSTTY crypto-Christian
ACCHILMMNOOPRRT Richmal Crompton
ACCHKKLNOOOSTWW know what's o'clock
ACCIIIILLMMPTTUU pactum illicitum
ACCIILMMMNOTUXY climax community
ACCIJLLNNNOOTUY conjunctionally
ACCIKKNNOOOTTUU knockout auction
ACCIKLLMOOOOTTV Molotov cocktail
ACCIKOPRRSSSSTT St Patrick's cross
ACCILMOOPRRSTUY ultramicroscopy

ACCIMMOORRSSTUY commissary court
ACCINOOORRSSTTV vasoconstrictor
ACDDDEEEEINNNPY Independence Day
ACDDDEEIINRRSST indirect address
ACDDDHINOORRUWY Richard Dunwoody
ACDDDIINOOPRTTU addition product
ACDDEEEEINNNRRT inner dead centre
ACDDEEEELNNPSTU dependent clause
ACDDEEEELNPRRSU supercalendered
ACDDEEEENORRTTU outer dead centre
ACDDEEEFFINSSST disaffectedness
ACDDEEEHHIKNSST thickheadedness
ACDDEEEHILMSSTU Dutch elm disease
ACDDEEEHLNORSST cold-heartedness
ACDDEEEHNNOPSSW sweep second hand
ACDDEEFHILLLNOU Holden Caulfield
ACDDEEGHHORRRRS Gerhard Schröder
ACDDEEGHINNORYY hydrogen cyanide
ACDDEEHIILLRSUY diesel-hydraulic
ACDDEEHIILNNNTW Candle in the Wind
ACDDEEHIINRSTUV Christian de Duve
ACDDEEHILMNNOUY Unchained Melody
ACDDEEILNOPPRSS displaced person
ACDDEEINNOSSTTV second-adventist
ACDDEEKKLNNORUY under lock and key
ACDDEEMNNOORRSY secondary modern
ACDDEFFGHLNNOSU golden handcuffs
ACDDEFGILNORSUU Figure and Clouds
ACDDEFHIRRRSSUY Richard Dreyfuss
ACDDEHIIINNRRTY nitric anhydride
ACDDEHIIMMORRSU Dame Iris Murdoch
ACDDEHLLMNOORST Arnold Dolmetsch
ACDDEIILNORRSUU Claudius Dornier
ACDDEIIMMNNOOST discommendation
ACDDENOORRRSSWY sword-and-sorcery
ACDDHIIMNORSTYY hydrodynamicist
ACDDIIIIILNSTUV individualistic
ACDEEEEEGGHLRRT three-legged race
ACDEEEEGHKLNRST the Greek calends
ACDEEEEGHNRRSTT The Secret Garden
ACDEEEEGILNORUX Eugène Delacroix
ACDEEEEILLNNRSS lesser celandine
ACDEEEEILNNORTT entente cordiale
ACDEEEELMORRSTW treacle wormseed
ACDEEEFFGIORTTZ gazetted officer
ACDEEEFFHIINRTW with a difference
ACDEEEFGIKNRRRS Frederick Sanger
ACDEEEFGILNPRST self-deprecating
ACDEEEFHIINTTTV antitheft device
ACDEEEFHILLNORS hall of residence
ACDEEEFIINRRTVX refractive index
ACDEEEFKLNOSTUW Duke of Newcastle
ACDEEEGGLLNNORT golden rectangle
ACDEEEGHIKNNRRT kitchen gardener
ACDEEEGHILORRTT cigarette holder
ACDEEEGHNNSTTUX exchange student
ACDEEEGILNORRRT director-general
ACDEEEGKLMNNOTW acknowledgement
ACDEEEGLLNORRVV Grover Cleveland
ACDEEEHHILNORRS Leonard Cheshire
ACDEEEHHNNORSTT ascend the throne
ACDEEEHIILMNRRT Marlene Dietrich
ACDEEEHIILPPRRS price leadership
ACDEEEHIMNORRSV Devonshire cream
ACDEEEHLLORTTUY eleutherodactyl
ACDEEEIILLPRSVY special delivery
ACDEEEIIMNNPRST canine distemper
ACDEEEIIMNPRSSV manic-depressive
ACDEEEIJLNPQRUU Jacqueline du Pré
ACDEEEIKLLLNRSW Erskine Caldwell
ACDEEEILNNNSSST clandestineness
ACDEEEILNOSTTUX decontextualise
ACDEEEILNOTTUXZ decontextualize
ACDEEEIMNNNRSTT disentrancement
ACDEEEINNORSSST considerateness
ACDEEEIPRRRRSTU scripture-reader
ACDEEELLLNRRRUW Lawrence Durrell
ACDEEEMNOOORSST cost someone dear
ACDEEFFFHIOORTY officer of the day
ACDEEFFGHINORST grind the faces of
ACDEEFFHIILLLOR Earl of Lichfield
ACDEEFGIINOORST age of discretion
ACDEEFGILNRSSSU disgracefulness
ACDEEFHIKNORRST Frederick Ashton
ACDEEFIIINORSTT desertification
ACDEEFIILMMORRR microfilm reader
ACDEEFIILMRRRST Frédéric Mistral
ACDEEFILNORRRTU funeral director
ACDEEFINNORSTUY Refection Sunday
ACDEEFKOQRRSSUW Wackford Squeers
ACDEEFLMNNORRRT Clermont-Ferrand
ACDEEFLOOPRSSUW due process of law
ACDEEFMMNNOORSY comedy of manners
ACDEEGGHIINPRRS graphic designer
ACDEEGGHIMOOPRS geodemographics
ACDEEGGIILLNORS logical designer
ACDEEGGILMNOOPR German police dog
ACDEEGHHIINORTU higher education
ACDEEGHIILOPSTT dephlogisticate
ACDEEGHIINSSSSU Cushing's disease
ACDEEGHIIPPPRSU pseudepigraphic
ACDEEGHILLLOSST St Hilda's College
ACDEEGIIILLMOOP epidemiological
ACDEEGIIKMNRRTT direct marketing
ACDEEGIILMNNNSU masculine ending
ACDEEGIKOOPRRST posigrade rocket
ACDEEGILLLOOSTY dysteleological
ACDEEGIMMNOOORR coram domino rege
ACDEEGLMMNRSUUU secundum regulam
ACDEEGNNOPPRSUY pseudopregnancy
ACDEEHHINOPRRST Christopher Dean
ACDEEHILNPPRRWY Dr Hawley Crippen
ACDEEHIMNOORSTU echinodermatous
ACDEEHIMNOQSTUY Thomas De Quincey
ACDEEHINOOPRSST drop one's aitches
ACDEEHLLMNNOOOY Ode on Melancholy
ACDEEHLLOPPRRSU shoulder-clapper
ACDEEHLNNOORTUV Under the Volcano
ACDEEHLOORSTTUY heterodactylous
ACDEEIIINNSSTVV vindicativeness
ACDEEIIJLRSTTUU judicial trustee
ACDEEIILLMNORTT dominical letter

ACDEEIILNNORSTY inconsiderately
ACDEEIILNORSTVY consideratively
ACDEEIIMNNOORTT co-determination
ACDEEIINNOORRST reconsideration
ACDEEILLNPPRRUY perpendicularly
ACDEEILMNNOPSTT displacement ton
ACDEEILNNOPRRUV under plain cover
ACDEEIMMNORSTUY semidocumentary
ACDEEIMNOPRRSST President Marcos
ACDEEINNPRSSSTU unpractisedness
ACDEELMOORRSSTU sclerodermatous
ACDEEMMMNNNOSTT Ten Commandments
ACDEEMNNNOORSTY stand on ceremony
ACDEEMNNOORSSSU Manon des Sources
ACDEENNNOORRSST stand one's corner
ACDEFFLOOOPRSSY pay off old scores
ACDEFGILORSTTTZ Scott Fitzgerald
ACDEFHIILMOORTU A Child of our Time
ACDEFHIMOOPPRSY Pyramid of Cheops
ACDEFIIIIMNNNOT indemnification
ACDEFIIIINNORTT denitrification
ACDEFIIIINORSTV diversification
ACDEFIIIINORTTV devitrification
ACDEFIIILMNOSTU demulsification
ACDEFIIILNNOSTV self-vindication
ACDEFIIILNNOTTY confidentiality
ACDEFIIIMNOSTTY demystification
ACDEFMMNOOOOPST common spadefoot
ACDEFMOOOPPRRSU damp-proof course
ACDEGGHINNORRUY greyhound-racing
ACDEGGHKLOOORRY hard-rock geology
ACDEGHHIKLNOORT chalking the door
ACDEGHHILMNOSTU Highland costume
ACDEGHIIILLMNNR drilling machine
ACDEGHIIINRSTTT district heating
ACDEGHILMOPRSTY dermatoglyphics
ACDEGIILMOPRTTU digital computer
ACDEGILNNNOSTTU consenting adult
ACDEGINORSTTTUY cottage industry
ACDEHHINORRSTTW throw in the cards
ACDEHHLMMOOOSUY homochlamydeous
ACDEHHOPRRSTTUW throw up the cards
ACDEHIILLMOSTTY Methodistically
ACDEHIILMMNORTY limited monarchy
ACDEHIIMNOOOPRR radio microphone
ACDEHIINOPSSTTU unsophisticated
ACDEHIINORRRSST Sir Richard Stone
ACDEHILLNOOPRTY polychlorinated
ACDEHILLNOORTWY The Cowardly Lion
ACDEHINOORRSSTT trisoctahedrons
ACDEHLMMNOOOSUY monochlamydeous
ACDEHLOOOPPRSSV approved schools
ACDEIIIILNNOQRU Indian liquorice
ACDEIIIKNNOPRRT Indian rope-trick
ACDEIIILMNNOORT omnidirectional
ACDEIIILNORRSTY discretionarily
ACDEIIINNNOORST inconsideration
ACDEIIJMORRTTVY majority verdict
ACDEIILNNOOORST reconsolidation
ACDEIILNOOORSTU decolourisation
ACDEIILNOOORTUZ decolourization
ACDEIIMNOOSTTUY situation comedy
ACDEIIMOPPRRSTW prismatic powder
ACDEIINOORRSTUV Victorien Sardou
ACDEIKMMMOORTTY commodity market
ACDEILLLMOOSSTY colloidal system
ACDEILNNNORSTUY unconstrainedly
ACDEIMNNOOOORSU andromonoecious
ACDEKNNOOSSSSTT stocks and stones
ACDELNOOOPRRTUW pour cold water on
ACDFIIIMNNOORST disconfirmation
ACDGHIIILMNNRUY hydraulic mining
ACDGHIMNNOOPRRY gynandromorphic
ACDGIIIINNNOORT air-conditioning
ACDGIILLLOSSTYY dyslogistically
ACDGILNOOOPRRSS Colorado Springs
ACDHHIINOOPRSSY hypochondriasis
ACDHHIOOOPPRSSU phosphorous acid
ACDHIIJLLLOORSU Juilliard School
ACDHIINOOPRSTUY hyponitrous acid
ACDHILLNOOORTTY orthodontically
ACDIIILNNNOPRSY non-disciplinary
ACDIIILNOORSTUV Divisional Court
ACDIIIMMNOOSSTU Audit Commission
ACDIIINNNOOSTTU discontinuation
ACDIILLNNNOOTUY unconditionally
ACDIILOOOORSTUV Ludovico Ariosto
ACDIINNORSSTTUU Titus Andronicus
ACDIINORRSSSSUU risus sardonicus
ACEEEEEEGILNRRRV receiver general
ACEEEEEHINRSSVV have seen service
ACEEEEFHHLMNTUU The Female Eunuch
ACEEEEFLNNORRUZ nuclear-free zone
ACEEEEGHHLNOSTX lose the exchange
ACEEEEGIIMMMNRS screaming meemie
ACEEEEGILLNNORT general election
ACEEEEGILMNOSSU leucaemogenesis
ACEEEEGILNORTTV electronegative
ACEEEEGINNRRSVV saving reverence
ACEEEEGLLLMMNOU Emmanuel College
ACEEEEHILLPRSST celestial sphere
ACEEEEHIMNORTVV overachievement
ACEEEEHLMNOPRTT temperance hotel
ACEEEEHLPRRSSTU Easter sepulchre
ACEEEEIILLMPRST Celestial Empire
ACEEEEIKNOPTTWX Expectation Week
ACEEEEKMNOSSSUX make one's excuses
ACEEEEMOPRRRTTU core temperature
ACEEEFFHHNORTTW Hawthorne effect
ACEEEFFHHOTTTTT to the effect that
ACEEEFFILNNSSTU ineffectualness
ACEEEFFLNOPRSST personal effects
ACEEEFGGHINNORX foreign exchange
ACEEEFGILNNOPRR peregrine falcon
ACEEEFHILMNNORT flehmen reaction
ACEEEFHIMNNNRST enfranchisement
ACEEEFHLOORRRST Earl of Rochester
ACEEEFIIILMPTVX exemplificative
ACEEEFIINNORRTT centre of inertia
ACEEEFILNPRRTTV perfect interval
ACEEEFKMNOORSTU take one's cue from
ACEEEFMNOOPPRRT performance poet

ACEEEFMNOPRRSTT performance test
ACEEEGGILORRSYY Sir George Cayley
ACEEEGGIMMORRTU micrometer gauge
ACEEEGGNOORRUVV George Vancouver
ACEEEGHIIILNTTV ethical genitive
ACEEEGHIILNNRSY Chinese layering
ACEEEGHILNNOPRT General Pinochet
ACEEEGHIMMNNRTU Munich Agreement
ACEEEGHIMNNNRTT interchangement
ACEEEGHINNOPRTT parthenogenetic
ACEEEGHNOORRRTV teacher-governor
ACEEEGIIINPRRRV Virginia creeper
ACEEEGIILLNORTT intercollegiate
ACEEEGIILMNSTTV selective mating
ACEEEGIINRRSSST crease-resisting
ACEEEGILLLMNOST logical elements
ACEEEGILLORRTTY tertiary college
ACEEEGILNNOPRSU reopening clause
ACEEEGIMNOPRSTT spermatogenetic
ACEEEHHHHLOPTTY the hale hypothec
ACEEEHHHLNOOPRX hexachlorophene
ACEEEHHHLNORSTU The Charnel House
ACEEEHHINORTTTT trine to the cheat
ACEEEHHIPPRSSTT speech therapist
ACEEEHIILLRRSST Leslie Charteris
ACEEEHIILNQRSTU serial technique
ACEEEHIKLLPPRST like the clappers
ACEEEHIKORRSTTU take their course
ACEEEHILLLPRTVY live cell therapy
ACEEEHILLMNRTUY hermeneutically
ACEEEHILLMOORST cholesterolemia
ACEEEHILNNPPRRS pencil-sharpener
ACEEEHILPRRSSSW Careless Whisper
ACEEEHNOOPRSSSU shape one's course
ACEEEHNORRSSSTU treacherousness
ACEEEIIINNSSSTV case-insensitive
ACEEEIIKKLMNNVZ Kelvin Mackenzie
ACEEEIILLLNSTTU intellectualise
ACEEEIILLLNTTUZ intellectualize
ACEEEIILLNORRUV Laurence Olivier
ACEEEIILMMORRSV memorial service
ACEEEIILNNPRTTV centinel private
ACEEEIJLMPRSTTU palm-tree justice
ACEEEIKKMMNOOST make someone tick
ACEEEILLNOSSTUX sexual selection
ACEEEILLORRSTWY Aleister Crowley
ACEEEILMNOPSTUX exemption clause
ACEEEILMNOSSSUU mousseline sauce
ACEEEILNOPQRSUV picaresque novel
ACEEEILNOPRRSSV personal service
ACEEEILNORRSSTV correlativeness
ACEEEILNPSSSTUV speculativeness
ACEEEILNRRRSTVW St Lawrence River
ACEEEIMMNOORSSV Mare Moscoviense
ACEEEIMMNOPRSSU menispermaceous
ACEEEIMMNPPPRRT peppermint cream
ACEEEINNNRSSSSU unnecessariness
ACEEEINNOORSTVV neoconservative
ACEEEINNQRSSTUY sesquicentenary
ACEEEINOOPRSSTV co-operativeness
ACEEEINOPRRSSTV procreativeness
ACEEEKLMMNOOSSW Mason Locke Weems
ACEEEMMNOOOSSWY come someone's way
ACEEENORSSTTUUV Venture Sea Scout
ACEEFFHHIKLLOTT take the chill off
ACEEFFHLLOPRRSU self-reproachful
ACEEFFILNNNOORS François Fénelon
ACEEFFILNOSTTUY affluent society
ACEEFGHIILLMNNU fuelling machine
ACEEFGHIKLNOSTT king of the castle
ACEEFGHIMNRRSTT stretching frame
ACEEFGIILMMNORS line of scrimmage
ACEEFGILMNNRSTU smelting-furnace
ACEEFGILNRRTTUU ultracentrifuge
ACEEFGINORRTTVY centre of gravity
ACEEFHIILNPRSTT in the first place
ACEEFHILNNOPRSY French Polynesia
ACEEFHIOOPRRTTV photorefractive
ACEEFHLNOPRRSSU reproachfulness
ACEEFHNOORRSTTU contour feathers
ACEEFHOOPRRRSTU par for the course
ACEEFIIILMNOPTX exemplification
ACEEFIIINNOSTTX extensification
ACEEFIILLNOPSTX self-explication
ACEEFIILNPRSSSU superficialness
ACEEFILNOPRSSSW Princess of Wales
ACEEFILNORSTTUU tentaculiferous
ACEEFINORRSTTUY it's a free country
ACEEFJLLLOOSTVY calves'-foot jelly
ACEEGGHHIIIMNNW weighing-machine
ACEEGGIILLNNORT training college
ACEEGGIIMNOPRSS image processing
ACEEGGINNOPPRRV copper engraving
ACEEGHHILMORRTU Homeric laughter
ACEEGHHLOOPPSTY speech pathology
ACEEGHIKLLNRSSY Charles Kingsley
ACEEGHILLMORTUW molecular weight
ACEEGHIMMNPPYYZ pygmy chimpanzee
ACEEGHINORTTUVY Young Vic Theatre
ACEEGHLMOOPRRTY electromyograph
ACEEGIIILMNNOST isomagnetic line
ACEEGIILLMNORVW William Congreve
ACEEGIILLMOOPST epistemological
ACEEGIILNNRSSSU Sir Alec Guinness
ACEEGIIMNPRSTTY magnetic pyrites
ACEEGILLNNOOTTY ontogenetically
ACEEGLLLLLOOSSU All Souls College
ACEEGLLMNNOORTV local government
ACEEGLMORRRSTUU regular customer
ACEEHHIIKNNOTTT take it on the chin
ACEEHHIILLLMRSW William Herschel
ACEEHHIILMMNNTT nemathelminthic
ACEEHHIKRSSSTTW the cat's whiskers
ACEEHHILNOORRTT trichloroethane
ACEEHHIMNOORRTT heterochromatin
ACEEHHINOOPPRST phosphocreatine
ACEEHHMMNORRRTY the merry monarch
ACEEHIIILNNOPSV Chinese pavilion
ACEEHIIJLLNNOTT lethal injection
ACEEHIILLLLNSTY Hellenistically
ACEEHIILLMNOORS Leonor Michaelis
ACEEHIILLMNRSTY hemicrystalline

ACEEHIILLMPSTUY euphemistically
ACEEHIILMNNOPST phenomenalistic
ACEEHIILMNORTVV thermionic valve
ACEEHIIMNNOORRS come rain or shine
ACEEHIINOOPRRRS prairie schooner
ACEEHIKNOOPPSST phenakistoscope
ACEEHILLLORSTTV Charlottesville
ACEEHILLNOPSSSU lissencephalous
ACEEHILOORRSSST atherosclerosis
ACEEHIMMNOPRSTU the Paris Commune
ACEEHLMMNNOOTWW new-Commonwealth
ACEEHNOORRSTTUY cry one's heart out
ACEEHNRRSSSTTUY necessary truths
ACEEIIILLNNOQTU equinoctial line
ACEEIIILMOPRRST isoperimetrical
ACEEIIILNPRSSSV Sicilian Vespers
ACEEIIINQSSSTUV acquisitiveness
ACEEIIJNNORRTTY interjectionary
ACEEIILLLMNSTTU intellectualism
ACEEIILLLNOOORT Coralline Oolite
ACEEIILLLNSTTTU intellectualist
ACEEIILLLNTTTUY intellectuality
ACEEIILLMNRSSTY semicrystalline
ACEEIILMNNOPRSS crime passionnel
ACEEIILMNOPRRTY primary election
ACEEIILNNNOOSTV conventionalise
ACEEIILNNNOOTVZ conventionalize
ACEEIILNNNOQSTU inconsequential
ACEEIJLNNNORSSU Cornelius Jansen
ACEEIKNOPPRRSSU prick up one's ears
ACEEILLLMNOSSUY miscellaneously
ACEEILLLMNOTTUU multinucleolate
ACEEILLLNNRSSTY crystalline lens
ACEEILLMMNOPRTY complementarily
ACEEILLMNOPTTVY contemplatively
ACEEILLNNOPTUXY unexceptionally
ACEEILLNNOQSTUY consequentially
ACEEILMMNNOOPTT complementation
ACEEILMMNOPRTTY complementarity
ACEEILMMNRSSSTY symmetricalness
ACEEILMMOOOSTTV steam locomotive
ACEEILMMOPSSTTY Ptolemaic system
ACEEILMMRSSTTUU semi-latus rectum
ACEEILMNNOOPRRS solar prominence
ACEEILMNNOPTTUY complete annuity
ACEEILMNNOSSUUX Alexius Comnenus
ACEEILMPRSSTUUZ trapezius muscle
ACEEILNNNNOSSSS nonsensicalness
ACEEILNOOPRTUVY uncooperatively
unco-operatively
ACEEILNPRRSSSVY scrivener's palsy
ACEEILOOPRRSSTY Sir Astley Cooper
ACEEIMMNNNNOTTU ancient monument
ACEEIMNNOOPRTTY contemporaneity
ACEEIMNNOORSSTV neoconservatism
ACEEIMNNORRRSTU resurrection man
ACEEIMNOORSSSTU music to one's ears
ACEEINOOPRSSTVV provocativeness
ACEEINORRRRSTUY resurrectionary
ACEEINORRSTTUUV Venture Air Scout
ACEEKLLLMOSSTUU musculoskeletal
ACEELLMNNNOORUY Maureen Connolly
ACEELLNOOPPRRRT contrapropeller
ACEELLOORSTTUUU Toulouse-Lautrec
ACEELLRRSSTTTUU structural steel
ACEELMOOPPRTTTU computer-to-plate
ACEELNNNOOSSTUY consentaneously
ACEELNNOORRSSTV transverse colon
ACEEMNNOOOPRSTU contemporaneous
ACEEMNOOPRRTTVY Coventry Patmore
ACEENNNNOOSSTUU unconsentaneous
ACEFFGIJLMNOPPU jumping-off place
ACEFFHIKKMOQRTU quick off the mark
ACEFFHIMOSSSTUU isthmus of fauces
ACEFFHOOOPPRRSU proof of purchase
ACEFFIIINOORRTT refortification
ACEFGGIIMMNNORT magnetic forming
ACEFGIIIIINNSTV insignificative
ACEFGIIIILNSTVY significatively
ACEFGIIKLLNNSSS falling sickness
ACEFGILMNPPRTUU centrifugal pump
ACEFHIILMNOQRSU marsh-cinquefoil
ACEFHILMORRSSTW Christmas flower
ACEFIIIINNNOSTT intensification
ACEFIIINNOOPRST personification
ACEFIIKLNOOPRRT replication fork
ACEFIILMNNOOSSS confessionalism
ACEFIILNNOOSSST confessionalist
ACEFILOPPRSSSUU purple of Cassius
purple of Cassuis
ACEFKNNOOORSTVW covenant of works
ACEFMMNOOOPRSTU common of pasture
ACEGGGHIIMNOOPY hypnogogic image
ACEGGHHIOOPPRTY phytogeographic
ACEGGHIIIMNNNRW wringing-machine
ACEGHHIIILMNNRW whirling-machine
ACEGHHIIOPRTTYY Ichthyopterygia
ACEGHHIKNORRTTT on the right track
ACEGHHILLMOOPPT ophthalmoplegic
ACEGHHILNOSSTTW swathing-clothes
ACEGHIIIKMNNNTT knitting machine
ACEGHIIILLNRSVW English Civil War
ACEGHIIILMMORST semi-logarithmic
ACEGHIIILMNORST logarithmic sine
ACEGHIIIMNNNPRT printing machine
ACEGHIILMNNOSTT slotting-machine
ACEGHIILNNOPSTT Giant Clothespin
ACEGHIIMNNPRRTV virgin parchment
ACEGHILLLNOOPRY phrenologically
ACEGHILMNOORSST schoolmastering
ACEGHILOPPRRSTT graphics plotter
ACEGHIMMOOPRRTT photogrammetric
ACEGHIMNOPRTTUU pneumatic trough
ACEGHINOOPSTTUU Augusto Pinochet
ACEGHINORRRSSTT string orchestra
ACEGHKNNOORRTTW on the wrong track
ACEGHLLOOPSUYYZ zygophyllaceous
ACEGIIILMNSSTTU metalinguistics
ACEGIIKLNPRSSTT sticking-plaster
ACEGIILLLMOOSSY seismologically
ACEGIILLMNOORTY goniometrically
ACEGIILLNRSSTYY synergistically

ACEGIILMNOORRTT trigonometrical
ACEGIIMMNNOOSST commission agent
ACEGIINOOPRSTTV prognosticative
ACEGILLLMNOOOTY entomologically
ACEGILMNNOPRTUU neural computing
ACEGILMOORSTUVY cytomegalovirus
ACEGIMNNOOSSUUU mucosanguineous
ACEGINOOPRRSSTY crossopterygian
ACEHHIILOOPSSTT theosophistical
ACEHHIJLNNORRSY Sir John Charnley
ACEHHILMMNOTTUY community health
ACEHHILMOORSSST schoolmasterish
ACEHHIMMMNOOPRS mechanomorphism
ACEHHINNPSSSTTU Spanish chestnut
ACEHHINOPPRSTTU Pithecanthropus
ACEHHINORRSSSTW crashworthiness
ACEHHIOPPRSSTTY psychotherapist
ACEHIIIILLMRSTW William Christie
ACEHIIIKLNNRSTU unchristianlike
ACEHIIILLNORSST schillerisation
ACEHIIILLNORSTZ schillerization
ACEHIIILNPPRTTY the Principality
ACEHIIIMNNOOPST phonemicisation
ACEHIIIMNNOOPTZ phonemicization
ACEHIIINNOOPSTT phoneticisation
ACEHIIINNOOPTTZ phoneticization
ACEHIIINNORSTTY Neo-Christianity
ACEHIIINOSSTTTU situation ethics
ACEHIIJKLNPPTTU Jack-in-the-pulpit
ACEHIIJMNRSSTTY Christ in Majesty
ACEHIILLLMOOPRT Michael Portillo
ACEHIILLLOOPRTY heliotropically
ACEHIILLNOORSTV historical novel
ACEHIILLOPRRSTY prehistorically
ACEHIILNOOPRSSW social ownership
ACEHIILOOPSTTTY photoelasticity
ACEHIIMMMOPSTTY sympathomimetic
ACEHIJMNNOORSTU Maurice Johnston
ACEHIKMNORSSTTW smack on the wrist
ACEHIKNPSSSTTUU Aussichtspunkte
ACEHILLLNOORSTY holocrystalline
ACEHILLNOPSTTYY polysynthetical
ACEHILMMPSSTTYY lymphatic system
ACEHINOOPRRSSTV conservatorship
ACEHINOOPRRSSTW ancestor-worship
ACEHINOPRRSTUYY neuropsychiatry
ACEHKLOOPSSSTTU Koch's postulates
ACEHLMMOOSSTUUU Holocaust Museum
ACEHMNNOORSSTTU turn one's stomach
ACEHMNOOPRSSTUY prosenchymatous
ACEIIIINNNOSTTV incentivisation
ACEIIIINNNOTTVZ incentivization
ACEIIIINNOSTTVV antivivisection
ACEIIIKLLLMMNWY William McKinley
ACEIIILLMPSSSTY pessimistically
ACEIIILNNNORSTU insulin reaction
ACEIIILNNNRSSST intrinsicalness
ACEIIILNNOPRRTV interprovincial
ACEIIIMNNOSSSSU session musician
ACEIIIMNORRRRTY minority carrier
ACEIIIMOPRRSTVV improvvisatrice
ACEIIJMNOPRSSTU jus primae noctis
ACEIIKMOOPRRRST Sir Patrick Moore
ACEIILLLMMNNOOR Lincoln Memorial
ACEIILLLNNOORTY intercolonially
ACEIILLOPPRSTTT optical splitter
ACEIILMNNNOOSTV conventionalism
ACEIILNNNOOSTTV conventionalist
ACEIILNNNOOTTVY conventionality
ACEIILNNOORSTTU interosculation
ACEIILNOOPRSSST processionalist
ACEIILNPRRSTTVY transcriptively
ACEIILPPRSSTTUY superplasticity
ACEIIMNNOORSSSU acrimoniousness
ACEIIMNNOORSSTV conversationism
ACEIIMNOOPRSTTU computerisation
ACEIIMNOOPRTTUZ computerization
ACEIINNOORSSTTV conservationist
conversationist
ACEIINNORRRSTUY insurrectionary
ACEIINNORRRTTTU counter-irritant
ACEIKLNNOOOORST a crook in one's lot
ACEILLLNOPRSTYY polycrystalline
ACEILLMMNRSTUYY unsymmetrically
ACEILLMNNOORSTY monocrystalline
ACEILLNOORRSTVY controversially
ACEILLNOPRSTTUY personality cult
ACEILMMMNOORSTY monosymmetrical
ACEILMMNNOPRTUY uncomplimentary
ACEILMOPRSTTUUU opus reticulatum
ACEILNNNNNOOOTV non-conventional
ACEILNNOORRSTUV uncontroversial
ACEILNOOOOPRRST corporation sole
ACEILOORRRSTTUY tertiary colours
ACEIMMNOSSSSUUU Sans Souci Museum
ACEIMNNNOOPRSTU pronunciamentos
ACEINNOORRRRTTU truncation error
ACEINNOORRSSSUV carnivorousness
ACEINOORRSSSTUU conus arteriosus
ACELLMNORSTUUVY voluntary muscle
ACELNOOOPPRRSTU counter-proposal
ACELPRRRSSTTUUU superstructural
ACEMMNOOOPPRRTY company promoter
ACEOOPPRRSSSSTU at cross purposes
ACFFHHIIMMNORST Fifth-monarchism
ACFFHHIIMNORSTT Fifth-monarchist
ACFFIIMNQSTTUUU quantum sufficit
ACFGIIIILNNNSTY insignificantly
ACFGILNNOOPRTUU functional group
ACFHIIJLNNOORUW Julian of Norwich
ACFIIMNNOOOSTTY comity of nations
ACGGIIILLLOORTU liturgiological
ACGHHIIIOOPRRST historiographic
ACGHHIMOOOPPRRT microphotograph
photomicrograph
ACGHHINOOOPPRTZ photozincograph
ACGHHLLMNNOPSUU ploughman's lunch
ACGHHLMOOOPRRXY chromoxylograph
ACGHHLOOOPPSTYY psychopathology
ACGHIIILLNPSTUV victualling-ship
ACGHIILLLOOPSYY physiologically
ACGHIINOPPPRRSW chipping sparrow

ACGHILLLMOOOPRY morphologically
ACGHILLNOSSTTUW swathling-clouts
ACGHILLOOOOPTYZ zoophytological
ACGHILMMMNOOORT common logarithm
ACGHILOOPPRTXYY xylotypographic
ACGIIILLLNNSTTY scintillatingly
ACGIILLLLOSSTYY syllogistically
ACGIILLMMNOOUY immunologically
ACGIILLMNNNOPUY uncomplainingly
ACGIIMMNOOPRRSU microsporangium
ACGIINNOOOPRSTT prognostication
ACGILLMMOOOPSTY symptomological
ACGILLOOOOOPRTZ protozoological
ACHHHHMNOPRRSUY Rhamphorhynchus
ACHHHKOOPRRSSST short sharp shock
ACHHIILLLOOPPSY philosophically
ACHHIILLNOOPPSU unphilosophical
ACHHIILOOPPRRST Schiphol Airport
ACHHIINOOPRSSTY psychohistorian
ACHHIMNOOOPPRRT anthropomorphic
ACHHIOOPRRSTTYY orthopsychiatry
ACHIIIMOOSSSSST schistosomiasis
ACHIILLMOOOPRRT allotriomorphic
ACHIIMNOOOPPSTT compotationship
ACHIINNNOORSSTY synchronisation
ACHIINNNOORSTYZ synchronization
ACHKLMNOOOOTTTU not much to look at
ACHLLNOOORSTUVY voluntary school
ACHMNNNOORRTTUY north-countryman
ACHNNOORSSSSTTY St Anthony's cross
ACIIIILLLNOSTVY violinistically
ACIIILLLNOOPSTU optical illusion
ACIIILLLOPSSSTY solipsistically
ACIIILNNOPQTTUU quintuplication
ACIIINPRSSSSTUU Piscis Austrinus
ACIILMMNOOOPSST cosmopolitanism
ACIILMMNOOORSSY royal commission✧
ACIILMNNOOSSTUY sanctimoniously
ACIIMNOOQRSTTUU mosquito curtain
ACILLLLMRTTUUUY multiculturally
ADDDEEEEHKNNSTY The Dead Kennedys
ADDDEEEEIINORTT dead tree edition
ADDDEEEGILLMNNR Middle Englander
ADDDEEEHNNNRSSU underhandedness
ADDDEEEILMNNPSX splendide mendax
ADDDEEEMNNOOSST do one's damnedest
ADDDEEFHILMOORT middle-of-the-road
ADDDEELNNOORSST Old Red Sandstone
ADDDEIILNNNORSS Sir Donald Sinden
ADDDEIINOOOPRTT Diprotodontidae
ADDEEEEFFHINRRT feathered friend
ADDEEEEFGHNNORT The Garden of Eden
ADDEEEEFMNPRRTY deferred payment
ADDEEEEHILNNRVV Henri van de Velde
ADDEEEEHLNRRTTY tender-heartedly
ADDEEEEILMNRRST Middle-Easterner
ADDEEEFGILNORRU folie de grandeur
ADDEEEFGIMNNRSS dead men's fingers
ADDEEEFHHNOORTT the end of the road
ADDEEEFIIKLRRRS Sir Freddie Laker
ADDEEEFINNRRTUY deferred annuity
ADDEEEGGINNORSS engrossing a deed
ADDEEEGHHILNSST light-headedness
ADDEEEGHNNORSSW wrong-headedness
ADDEEEGNNOPRSTU get one's dander up
ADDEEEHIKNNRSST kind-heartedness
ADDEEEHLNOPRTUX heteroduplex DNA
ADDEEEILMNPRTUU depleted uranium
ADDEEEILNNSSSVY seven deadly sins
ADDEEEINOPRRRRS Pierre de Ronsard
ADDEEELNPRSUVWY Pulver Wednesday
ADDEEENNNORSSTW New Red Sandstone
ADDEEENNOOORSUV do one's endeavour
ADDEEFGHLORRTTU The Artful Dodger
ADDEEFILORRRVWY forward delivery
ADDEEGHHINNRSST right-handedness
ADDEEGHIIKNOSSS Hodgkin's disease
ADDEEGIIKLNNORS like a dog's dinner
ADDEEGNNOORSSTU good-naturedness
ADDEEHHINNORRTY hither and yonder
ADDEEHHNNORSTTU send round the hat
ADDEEIIILNRSSTU deindustrialise
ADDEEIIILNRSTUZ deindustrialize
ADDEEILLMMNNSSS small-mindedness
ADDEEINOORRSTTW oriented towards
ADDEFFGINNOOSST standing-off dose
ADDEFFIILLPRSTY play first fiddle
ADDEFGILNNNOORT front-end loading
ADDEFILMNNOOSTU folded mountains
ADDEGGIINNNORWW window gardening
ADDEGHHILORRSTW Lord High Steward
ADDEGHHINOOSTWY woody nightshade
ADDEGHINNORRTTU Arthur Eddington
ADDEGIILNORRSSU Rodrigues Island
ADDEGILNNNRSTUY understandingly
ADDEGNNNOORSSTU stand one's ground
ADDEHILMMNOOSTT Thomas Middleton
ADDEHILNORRSTUW Sir Edward Hulton
ADDEIIIIMNOTTUX titanium dioxide
ADDEIIIMOOPSSTU potassium iodide
ADDEIMNNNOPQSSS mind one's p's and q's
ADDFFGGHIINNNOR offhand grinding
ADDFIILLNOORSTW Sir Donald Wolfit
ADDGHLNOORSTWYY Andy Goldsworthy
ADDIIILLNORSTTY dry distillation
ADEEEEEFHNRRSST free-heartedness
ADEEEEEGHHORTVV have the edge over
ADEEEEEHNRRTTVY three-day eventer
ADEEEEEIIMNRSSS Ménière's disease
ADEEEEFHNORSTVW Wars of the Vendée
ADEEEEFHPRRRRSS preferred shares
ADEEEEFLLNORSSY Aloys Senefelder
ADEEEEGHNOQSTUV God Save the Queen
ADEEEEGILLNRRVY general delivery
ADEEEEGILPRRSVY reverse yield gap
ADEEEEHHMORTTTT armed to the teeth
ADEEEEHHNRRTTUW under the weather
ADEEEEHIMMSTTTU meditate the muse
ADEEEEHNNOPRSST open-heartedness
ADEEEEHNRRSSTTU true-heartedness
ADEEEEIIMNOSSTZ time-zone disease
ADEEEEILLLMNRSS Ellesmere Island

Words marked ✧ can also be spelled with one or more capital letters

ADEEEEIMNNRSSTT determinateness
ADEEEEIMNRRSTTV readvertisement
ADEEEFGHLLOORTY federal theology
ADEEEFGHLLRSSTU self-slaughtered
ADEEEFGHLNOORTV The Garden of Love
ADEEEFHLMSSTTUY the feudal system
ADEEEFHLNOPRTTW Peter and the Wolf
ADEEEFIILLNQSTU field-sequential
ADEEEGGHIIILRSV Sergei Diaghilev
ADEEEGGHIIMNRRT Martin Heidegger
ADEEEGGIMORRRUU George Du Maurier
ADEEEGGINNNRRSU en grand seigneur
ADEEEGHILLNRSTY single-heartedly
ADEEEGHINNRSSST near-sightedness
ADEEEGIINNORSTT degenerationist
ADEEEGILLLNNRTT little Englander
ADEEEGILMNNNSTT disentanglement
ADEEEGILNNOOPRS old-age pensioner
ADEEEGKLNNORTUW nature knowledge
ADEEEGKOOPQRRTU keep good quarter
ADEEEGLLORSSWYY yellow-eyed grass
ADEEEGLNOORRTWW Walter Greenwood
ADEEEGLNOPRRTUU departure lounge
ADEEEGMMNRRRSTU sergeant-drummer
ADEEEHHHIILNSTT hit the headlines
ADEEEHHHNOSSTUW haud one's wheesht
ADEEEHHHORSSTTW sheathe the sword
ADEEEHHIINNSTTW a sheet in the wind
ADEEEHHILMNPTTY methylphenidate
ADEEEHHILMOSTTV hot-melt adhesive
ADEEEHHINOSTTTW a sheet to the wind
ADEEEHHIORRRSST horseradish tree
ADEEEHIIILORSVV Oliver Heaviside
ADEEEHIIOPRRSST sphaerosiderite
ADEEEHILLOSTTVW The Old Wives' Tale
ADEEEHIMNNOOSST tan someone's hide
ADEEEHLNNORRSST Anderson shelter
ADEEEHNNNORTVWY every now and then
ADEEEIILMMRSSSS slimmers' disease
ADEEEIILMNNRTTY indeterminately
ADEEEIILNNOSTTV Ninette de Valois
ADEEEIILNRSTTVY relative density
ADEEEIIMNNORRTT redetermination
ADEEEIIMOORRSST diastereoisomer
ADEEEILLMMNRSUY Süleyman Demirel
ADEEEIMMORRRTWY read-write memory
ADEEEIMNNOPRRTZ Martínez de Perón
ADEEEIMNNORRRTY oyer and terminer
ADEEELLLMNNSTWY Wendell M Stanley
ADEEELLLMNOPTVY developmentally
ADEEELNNRSTTTUX external student
ADEEEMNNOOOORSS do someone reason
ADEEEMNOPRRSTTT department store
ADEEEPRRSSSTTTU Sturt's desert pea
ADEEFFFHHLLNOTY fly off the handle
ADEEFFIIINNORTT differentiation
ADEEFFIMNORSSTT disafforestment
ADEEFGHNORSTUWY wages-fund theory
ADEEFGIILLRSTTZ Alfred Stieglitz
ADEEFGIILNOORZZ Le Nozze di Figaro
ADEEFGKNOOORSSS for goodness sake
ADEEFHIIIKNSSSS fish skin disease
fishskin disease
ADEEFHILMNRSTTW Matthew Flinders
ADEEFIIIJSSTTTU fides et justitia
ADEEFIIINRRSTTT interstratified
ADEEFIILNNOOPST self-opinionated
ADEEFIILNNQSSUU unqualifiedness
ADEEFIINNSSSSTU unsatisfiedness
ADEEFIKLMOORSST for old time's sake
ADEEFILLNORSSUV ill-favouredness
ADEEFILLOOORSTT slotted aerofoil
ADEEFILNSSSSTTU distastefulness
ADEEFNOORRRSSVW overforwardness
ADEEGGHILNPRSTU sleeping draught
ADEEGGHINOPSSSU pedagoguishness
ADEEGGILNNORSTY destroying angel
ADEEGGINNOORSVW dig one's own grave
ADEEGGMMNORRTTU Götterdämmerung
ADEEGGNNOOORTUV tongue-and-groove
ADEEGHHILNNOORT hen on a hot girdle
ADEEGHIILNNNNRU running headline
ADEEGHIILNNRSTY dishearteningly
ADEEGHIILNNSTTY dental hygienist
ADEEGHIINNORRTT third-generation
ADEEGHILNNORSTT on the danger list
ADEEGHJLMNSTTTU the Last Judgment
ADEEGHJLNOPSTUY Stephen Jay Gould
ADEEGHLNORRSSTY Gladstone sherry
ADEEGIILLMNRRTU ring-tailed lemur
ADEEGIILNNOQSTU leading question
ADEEGIILNNPSSSS displeasingness
ADEEGIIMNOOORRT radiogoniometer
ADEEGINNOPRSSSW spread one's wings
ADEEGIOPRRSTTUY daguerreotypist
ADEEGKLNNORRUVW Völkerwanderung
ADEEHHHHNOTTWWY the how and the why
ADEEHHHIMNNORSS Hamish Henderson
ADEEHHINOPRRSSW shared ownership
ADEEHHNOOPPSSYY adenohypophyses
ADEEHIIIJNOPSST hip joint disease
ADEEHIIILLMNNTY dimethylaniline
ADEEHIIMNNOORTT Dominion Theatre
ADEEHILLMNNRSTT disenthrallment
ADEEHILNNOORSTW let one's hair down
ADEEHILOOPPRRST prolate spheroid
ADEEHILOOSTTTTV the devil's tattoo
ADEEHIMNNOOOSTT hand it to someone
ADEEHINNNPRRSTU Arthur Pendennis
ADEEHINNOPRTTTW paint the town red
ADEEHINPRSSSTTW sharp-wittedness
ADEEHIOPPPPSTTT pipped at the post
ADEEHLMOORSSTTY the same old story
ADEEIIILNORSSTV desilverisation
ADEEIIILNORSTVZ desilverization
ADEEIIILNRRSSTU reindustrialise
ADEEIIILNRRSTUZ reindustrialize
ADEEIIIMNNNORTT indetermination
ADEEIIIMOPRRRTV airtime provider
ADEEIIINNOSSSTT desensitisation
ADEEIIINNOSSTTZ desensitization
ADEEIIINORRTTVV nitro-derivative

ADEEIIMMMNOOSSS Moses Maimonides
ADEEIIMNNNORTTU undetermination
ADEEIIMNNNOWWZZ mezzanine window
ADEEIIMNNOPRTTU unpremeditation
ADEEIIMNNOPSSSS impassionedness
ADEEIIMNNORSTTU underestimation
ADEEIIMNNRRSSTU rudimentariness
ADEEIIMNOPRRSSU Monsieur de Paris
ADEEIINNNOOPSST opinionatedness
ADEEIINPSSSTTUV disputativeness
ADEEIIORSSSTTVX oxidative stress
ADEEILLMOPRSSUU pullorum disease
ADEEILLNNORSTTU Lord Lieutenants
Lords Lieutenant
ADEEILMNORSTTVY demonstratively
ADEEILNNNRSTTTU internal student
ADEEIMNNORSTTUV undemonstrative
ADEEINQRRSSTUWY stewards' enquiry
ADEEKLLNNOOOPRV Leopold von Ranke
ADEENNOPRRSSSTT transportedness
ADEENNORSSSTUUV adventurousness
ADEFFHINNOSSSST standoffishness
ADEFGHHIKNOORTT knight of the road
ADEFGHILLNOOOPR Earl of Godolphin
ADEFGHILMNOSSUW Flushing Meadows
ADEFGHLLNOORTTU fall to the ground
ADEFGIIILLNQSTU self-liquidating
ADEFGIMOPPRSTYY Pyramids of Egypt
ADEFGLMNORRSUWY Gulf War syndrome
ADEFHIILNORRRSS Sir Ronald Fisher
ADEFHIILNORSTWW whistle for a wind
ADEFHIMNOPRSTUY Pyramid of the Sun
ADEFHLMNOOORTWW woman of the world
ADEFHMMNNOPRSYY Manfred Symphony
ADEFIIIIKLLMNRW William Friedkin
ADEFIILLLLMMORR Millard Fillmore
ADEFIILMNNOORSU four-dimensional
ADEFIKMMMNNOSUU Museum of Mankind
ADEFILMNORRTUUU Our Mutual Friend
ADEFILNOOORTUVW War of Devolution
ADEFINNNOOOSTTU foundation-stone
ADEGGGHINNORRTU gathering-ground
ADEGHIILLOSSTTT solid-state light
ADEGHIILNPSSSTW pigs and whistles
ADEGHILNORRSTTW world-shattering
ADEGHIMNNORSTUY Mothering Sunday
ADEGHIMNOPPRRSS grasshopper mind
ADEGHLLMORRTUYY hydrometallurgy
ADEGIIIINNORTTT interdigitation
ADEGIIILLLNOPRU Luigi Pirandello
ADEGIIILNNNRSTW Indian wrestling
ADEGIIILNOORTTU Giulio Andreotti
ADEGIIIOPRRSTTT prestidigitator
ADEGIIKLNNOTTWY take it lying down
ADEGIINNORSSSTT dressing station
ADEGIINNRRSSSSU Russian dressing
ADEGIINOPRSSTTV spot advertising
ADEGILLNNOQRTUY grandiloquently
ADEGIMNNORRSTTU nitrogen mustard
ADEGJLLMNNNOTUY non-judgmentally
ADEGNNNOOSSSTTU stand to one's guns
ADEHHIILNNOOPRT ornithodelphian
ADEHHIIMMOPRRST hermaphroditism
ADEHHILMOOPRSTU edriophthalmous
ADEHHINNNOORSTW throw in one's hand
ADEHHINOOPPSSYY adenohypophysis
ADEHIIILMOOPRST diaheliotropism
ADEHIIINOOPRSST spheroidisation
ADEHIIINOOPRSTZ spheroidization
ADEHIIKNNRSSVYY Andrei Vyshinsky
ADEHIILMRRSSTTY third-rail system
ADEHIINNOOPSTTY dehypnotisation
ADEHIINNOOPTTYZ dehypnotization
ADEHIKLLMSSSTVY Mstislav Keldysh
ADEHIKNNOPRRSST Perth and Kinross
ADEHILMNOOPSTTU Pentothal sodium
ADEHINNNOORRSSW draw in one's horns
ADEHLNORRSTTWWY north-westwardly
ADEHLORSSTTUWWY south-westwardly
ADEIIILMNOPTTUU Utopia Unlimited
ADEIIJLNPRRSTUU jurisprudential
ADEIIKNNSSSTTTV St Kitts and Nevis
ADEIILMNNOORTTU intermodulation
ADEIILNOPPRRSSS dispersal prison
ADEIILNORRSSTTX sinistrodextral
ADEIILNORRSTTVY dorsiventrality
ADEIILNPPRSSTUU Palus Putredinis
ADEIIMMMOOOOPTX Deo Optimo Maximo
ADEIIMMOORSSTTY dermatomyositis
ADEIINNOOPRRSTU superordination
ADEIKMMNOORRRSS smoke and mirrors
ADEILLLNOOPPRST solid propellant
ADEILLMNOOPSTUU pulse modulation
ADEILLMOORSSSWY Sir Oswald Mosley
ADEILNOOOSSSTWW sow one's wild oats
ADEIMNNPPRRSSSU prunes and prisms
ADELNNOORRRSTUY Norroy and Ulster
ADFFIILLNOPRSTW windfall profits
ADFGGHINNOOORTY good for anything
ADFGGHINOOPRRTU draught-proofing
ADFGGIILLMNNOTU fulminating gold
ADFGGIINOOORTTW Waiting for Godot
ADFGIILNNOQRUUY qualifying round
ADFIINORRRSSTTT drift transistor
ADGGGGIIINNNRST standing rigging
ADGHIIMNOORRTWW withdrawing-room
ADGHIINNNOSTTTW notwithstanding
ADGHILMOOPRSTWY sympodial growth
ADGHIMMNNOORRSU darning mushroom
ADGIIILNNOPPSTY disappointingly
ADGIIINNNOPPSTU undisappointing
ADGIIINNOQRRSTU Grand Inquisitor
ADHIILMNOORSSUY disharmoniously
ADHIILNOSSSTTUU South Uist Island
ADHIIMOOOPPRSTT diaphototropism
ADHIJLNNNOOSSST Johnston Islands
ADHIKMNNOOOORSU Norodom Sihanouk
ADIIIINOQRSSTUY disquisitionary
ADIIILLLMNSTTTW tilt at windmills
ADIILNOOOPPRRST disproportional
ADIIMNNNOPSSTUU Pindus Mountains
ADILNOOOOPPRTTY Polyprotodontia

ADINNNOOPPSSTTU stand upon points
ADMNOOOOOSSTTTU odontostomatous
AEEEEEEFHINQRTU The Faerie Queene
AEEEEEGHHLRSSTW grease the wheels
AEEEEEHKLRSSTVW the weaker vessel
AEEEEEKORRRSTVV reverse takeover
AEEEEFFHLOTTTVW have two left feet
AEEEEFFILLNRRST self-referential
AEEEEFGHNOSSTTV The Eve of St Agnes
AEEEEFHIKLNRRRT Kathleen Ferrier
AEEEEFHNNORSSTT feather one's nest
AEEEEFKLLMNRRSY Erlenmeyer flask
AEEEEFLLNOOPRSV overleap oneself
AEEEEGGILMORRST Georges Lemaître
AEEEEGIKLMNOSSU leukaemogenesis
AEEEEGIKLNPRSSU pleasure-seeking
AEEEEGILLNPRSST general epistles
AEEEEGLLNRRRYYY greenery-yallery
AEEEEHHINNNSTVV in seventh heaven
AEEEEHKLLPRSSTW The Sleepwalkers
AEEEEHKLNOOSSTT take to one's heels
AEEEEIILMNPRSTX experimentalise
AEEEEIILMNPRTXZ experimentalize
AEEEEIIMNPRTTVX experimentative
AEEEEILLNNNPRTT perennial nettle
AEEEEILNNPRRRTU entrepreneurial
AEEEEIMNNPRSSTT intemperateness
AEEEEINNPRSSTTV penetrativeness
AEEEELLMNNPSTTT penal settlement
AEEEFFGHLOORSTV the gloves are off
AEEEFFGINORRSST Easter offerings
AEEEFFHHIKNOSTT take the shine off
AEEEFFHKLOORTVW flavor of the week
AEEEFFILLRRTVVY Rift Valley fever
AEEEFFLLLNOORSV fall over oneself
AEEEFFLNOORRSSW forswear oneself
AEEEFGHIIINNPRT a finger in the pie
AEEEFGIILNORSSV give oneself airs
AEEEFGIIMNOTTUZ time-zone fatigue
AEEEFHHILPRRSST The Pearl Fishers
AEEEFHHORSTTTTU the fourth estate
AEEEFHIIKNNNOSV have one's knife in
AEEEFHIILLNNRST Leni Riefenstahl
AEEEFHIKMORRTTT take it from there
AEEEFHOORRRSTWW the worse for wear
AEEEFHORRSSSTTW stress of weather
AEEEFIILMNPRRST preferentialism
AEEEFIILNPRRSTT preferentialist
AEEEFIKLLOOPPRW keep a low profile
AEEEFILMMOPRSTT Temple of Artemis
AEEEFKLNNOOPSTU take upon oneself
AEEEFLLLLORRTVW fellow traveller
AEEEFLMOQRRSTTU letters-of-marque
AEEEFLNRRSSTTUV transverse flute
AEEEGGGHORRRTTY Gregory the Great
AEEEGGHIMNNORRR Hermione Granger
AEEEGGHLNNOOTVY Genevan theology
AEEEGGINNOPPRSS passenger-pigeon
AEEEGGLNNOORRRV governor-general
AEEEGGMNOOOSSTT get someone's goat
AEEEGHHMNOORSST horse-shoe magnet
AEEEGHILMNPRRTY germ-line therapy
AEEEGHIMMMRSTUU Hermitage Museum
AEEEGHIMNNRSTWY Ernest Hemingway
AEEEGHINNOPRSST parthenogenesis
AEEEGHINRRRSSVY Sir Henry Segrave
AEEEGHMNOPRSTTY gemstone therapy
AEEEGHMNRRSSTTU measure strength
AEEEGIIIKMNPTVW peak viewing time
AEEEGIILMNNRRTV trigeminal nerve
AEEEGIKLLMNNNTU ungentlemanlike
AEEEGILLMNNNSST gentlemanliness
AEEEGILMNNNRTTT intertanglement
AEEEGILMNNNSSSS meaninglessness
AEEEGILMPQRRSUU square leg umpire
AEEEGILNNOPRTTY potential energy
AEEEGILNNPPRRST sleeping partner
AEEEGILNNRSSSTV everlastingness
AEEEGIMNOPRSSST spermatogenesis
AEEEGINORRSUVWY Sigourney Weaver
AEEEGKNNOOSSSTT get one's skates on
AEEEGMMNORSTTTT tong-test ammeter
AEEEGMNNOPPRRTV government paper
AEEEHHIKORSTTUW Keith Waterhouse
AEEEHHILMMNNSTT Nemathelminthes
AEEEHHILMNOPPST Mephistophelean
AEEEHHMORRSTTTW weather the storm
AEEEHIIKLLMORSW Willie Shoemaker
AEEEHIIMMNORRST immersion heater
AEEEHIIMNPPRSSV misapprehensive
AEEEHIINOPPPPRT Ethiopian pepper
AEEEHILMNOPSSTT Spanish omelette
AEEEHILNNRSTTVV seventh interval
AEEEHILORSTTUXY heterosexuality
AEEEHJJNNNNOSSV Johannes V Jensen
AEEEHLLLRRSTUWY Arthur Wellesley
AEEEHLMMNOSSTTW Matthew Meselson
AEEEHMMNOPRTTVY movement therapy
AEEEHMOPPPRRSTU upper atmosphere
AEEEHORRRSSTTUW wear the trousers
AEEEHPPRRRSSTUY pressure therapy
AEEEIIILMNORSSV Olivier Messiaen
AEEEIIILMNPRSTX experientialism
AEEEIIILNPRSTTX experientialist
AEEEIILLMPRRTVY relatively prime
AEEEIILMMNPRSTX experimentalism
AEEEIILMNPRSTTX experimentalist
AEEEIILNRSTTTUX intertextualise
AEEEIILNRTTTUXZ intertextualize
AEEEIIMNNOPRTTX experimentation
AEEEIIMNORSSSTT semesterisation
AEEEIIMNORSSTTZ semesterization
AEEEIINNNSSTTTV inattentiveness
AEEEIINNOPRSSTV inoperativeness
AEEEIIPRRSSSSTV passive resister
AEEEIKLMOQRRSTU square kilometre
AEEEIKLNOOPRSZZ aerospike nozzle
AEEEILNPRSSSTUV superlativeness
AEEEILNQRRSTUWY Squire Trelawney
AEEEIMNOPRRSSTX extemporariness
AEEEKMNNOOOPSTU take someone up on
AEEELLLNNOOSTTW tell one's own tale

AEEELMNOQRRSSSU quarrelsomeness
AEEELMOPRRSSTUU poulters' measure
AEEELOPRRRSSSTW lesser spearwort
AEEEMMOOPRRRTTU room temperature
AEEEMNOPRRSSTUW Weston-super-Mare
AEEFFGHIIILMNRT Melanie Griffith
AEEFFGHIINNORTT fifth generation
fifth-generation
AEEFFHILNNORRSU Fraunhofer lines
AEEFFHIORRSTTTW of the first water
AEEFFHJMNOORSST Thomas Jefferson
AEEFFIILMRRTTUY family fruit tree
AEEFFMOPRSSTTTU feast of trumpets
AEEFGHILLMMNRTW Walther Flemming
AEEFGHILLNNOOST along the lines of
AEEFGHIMNNORRTT the morning after
AEEFGHIMNOORRTV mother of vinegar
AEEFGIINNORRSTT first generation
AEEFGILNNNOORSY lay one's finger on
AEEFGILNNOPPRVZ Graf von Zeppelin
AEEFGILNORRSSUX Sir Alex Ferguson
AEEFGIMNNRRSTTU transfigurement
AEEFGINNNOPRSSS snap one's fingers
AEEFGIOPRRSSSTT go-faster stripes
AEEFGNOOOSTTUWY get out of one's way
AEEFHHLLNNSSTUU unhealthfulness
AEEFHHLMOOOPRTT Temple of Hathoor
AEEFHIILLLNNOVW When I Fall In Love
AEEFHILLLLOTVYY lily of the valley
AEEFHILLMOSSTTU Thales of Miletus
AEEFHINORRSTTUY fraternity house
AEEFHLMMNOOPSTT Temple of Somnath
AEEFHLOPRRSSTUU ferrous sulphate
AEEFHNNOORRTTTW On the Waterfront
AEEFIILLNOSSTWY Wassily Leontief
AEEFIILNNOPRRST inferior planets
AEEFIILNNRSTTTU first lieutenant
AEEFIILNOOPRSSS professionalise
AEEFIILNOOPRSSZ professionalize
AEEFIIMMNNOORTT moment of inertia
AEEFIIMNNORSSTV informativeness
AEEFIIMNORSSTTT Minister of State
AEEFILLLOOOPRRV Earl of Liverpool
AEEFILMNNSSSTTU self-sustainment
AEEFILOPRRRSTTU self-portraiture
AEEFMORSSSSTTWY systems software
AEEFNNNORSSTTUU unfortunateness
AEEFNOOOPRRTTWY power of attorney
AEEGGGIILMNNRST singing telegram
AEEGGGLNNNOOOOV Evonne Goolagong
AEEGGHHOOPPRRTY phytogeographer
AEEGGHIKLNOOPRV Georgi Plekhanov
AEEGGHILNRRSSSY English ryegrass
AEEGGHIMOORRSST Sir George Thomas
AEEGGHKLLLNOSSW walk on eggshells
AEEGGIIILNNNOTV Giovanni Gentile
AEEGGIILLMMORSW William Rees-Mogg
AEEGGINNNORTUUY Annie Get Your Gun
AEEGGINNOTTTTUW wetting-out agent
AEEGHHIIKLLNSTT take the shilling
AEEGHHINNORSTTW now there's a thing
AEEGHHLOOPPRTTY phototelegraphy
telephotography
AEEGHHMOOPRRTTY hyetometrograph
AEEGHIIINNOOPRT Ethiopian region
AEEGHIILLRRTTTU light literature
AEEGHIIMNNRRRTU Mathurin Régnier
AEEGHIINNNSTTUY naughty nineties
AEEGHIINORSSSST raise one's sights
AEEGHIKLOPRRTTW tightrope walker
AEEGHIKNNORSSTT Kentish ragstone
AEEGHILNORSSTUY Henry Louis Gates
AEEGHIMNNORRSUZ Erziehungsroman
AEEGHINNNORSTTU sing another tune
AEEGHINNOOPRSST anthropogenesis
AEEGHKOPRRSSTUU Portuguese shark
AEEGHLLMNOOSSTZ Thomson's gazelle
AEEGHMOORRRSTTU surrogate mother
AEEGHNNOOPRRTTY röntgenotherapy
AEEGHORRSSSTTUU Roget's Thesaurus
AEEGIIKLLRRRSTU guerrilla strike
AEEGIILNNPPRRSS springer spaniel
AEEGIILNORRTTVY interrogatively
AEEGIINNOORRRTT reinterrogation
AEEGIINOPRRRSTT preregistration
AEEGIINORRSSTTT gastroenteritis
AEEGIKMNNOPRSST on speaking terms
AEEGILLLLNPPRUU purple gallinule
AEEGILNOORRRSST retrogressional
AEEGILNRRSSSTVY transgressively
AEEGIMNNNOORSST sensation-monger
AEEGIMNOPRSSTTY operating system
AEEGIMNRRRTTUWZ Gewürztraminer
AEEGINNNORRSTUV turn in one's grave
AEEGLMNNNNOORTV non-governmental
AEEGLOORRRSTTTY letters rogatory
AEEGMNNOPRRTTVY party-government
AEEGNOOPRRSSTTV provost-sergeant
AEEHHHIINRTTTWW whiter than white
AEEHHHILLMNORRT Herman Hollerith
AEEHHHILLNNOPPT phenolphthalein
AEEHHIILMNOPPST Mephistophelian
AEEHHIIMNNOTTWW The Woman in White
AEEHHILLMNPSTTY Platyhelminthes
AEEHHIMNNOOSSTU the Mansion House
AEEHHJNNOORSVY John Harvey-Jones
AEEHHJMNNNNORWY John Henry Newman
AEEHHKLOOORTTWY look the other way
AEEHIIIKNPRSSTT kinesitherapist
AEEHIIKLLMNNSTW Kenneth Williams
AEEHIIKLMORSTTT that's more like it
AEEHIILMOOPSTTU epitheliomatous
AEEHIILNNOORSTT lie in one's throat
AEEHIIMNNOPPRSS misapprehension
AEEHIKLNNOPRTUY phenylketonuria
AEEHILLLNOORTWW leather on willow
AEEHILMMNOOPRRY Holy Roman Empire
AEEHILMNOOSSTTT Toots Thielemans
AEEHILNORRSSTTT in the last resort
AEEHINNORSSSTUW unseaworthiness
AEEHLNOOPPPRRSS personal shopper
AEEIIIKMPRRSTTV primitive streak

AEEIIINNOSTTVXZ extensivization
AEEIIINOORRSTTX exteriorisation
AEEIIINOORRTTXZ exteriorization
AEEIILLLMNNRSST terminal illness
AEEIILLMMNNORRT Martin Niemöller
AEEIILMNOOPRSTT metropolitanise
AEEIILMNOOPRTTZ metropolitanize
AEEIILNNOPPRTTY plenipotentiary
AEEIILNORSSSTTW wireless station
AEEIILNRTTTTUXY intertextuality
AEEIIMMMPRRRSTY primary meristem
AEEIIMNNOPRSSTT presentationism
AEEIIMNOOPRSTTX extemporisation
AEEIIMNOOPRTTXZ extemporization
AEEIINNOPRSSTTT presentationist
AEEIINOPRRSSTTV preservationist
AEEIJLLOQRTTUUZ Quatorze Juillet
AEEIKLNNOPRSSUV Nikolaus Pevsner
AEEIKNNOOPRRSST take no prisoners
AEEILLMMNOOOPSS oil someone's palm
AEEILLMNNNORTVY environmentally
AEEILLMNPPRSTUY supplementarily
AEEILLNNOPRRSTY interpersonally
AEEILLNNOPRSTTY septentrionally
AEEILLNOOPRRSST lesser prolation
AEEILLNOOPRSTVY epistolary novel
AEEILMNNNPRSTTU instrument panel
AEEILMNNOOPPRUU pleuropneumonia
AEEILMNNOPPSTTU supplementation
AEEILMNOOPPRTTU perpetual motion
AEEILMNOPPRRSUU main purpose rule
AEEILNOPPRRSSTU superior planets
AEEILNORRSSTTUU Russian roulette
AEEIMNNOOPPRRTT reapportionment
AEEIMNNOPRSSTTU importunateness
AEEIMQRRRSSSTTU quartermistress
AEEINNOPRSSTTTU unprotestantise
AEEINNOPRSTTTUZ unprotestantize
AEEINOQRRSSSSTU quarter-sessions
AEELLNNOPRRSTTZ Zöllner's pattern
AEELPPRRSSTTTUY plasterers' putty
AEENNNOOPSSSSTU spontaneousness
AEFFHHMNNOPRSYY Haffner Symphony
AEFFIILLNNOOOTT line of flotation
AEFGGHJLOORRTUU go for the jugular
AEFGHHILLNOORRW harrowing of hell
AEFGHIINNNPRSST shifting spanner
AEFGHILNORRSTTT trial of strength
AEFGIIIIMNNRSTV visiting fireman
AEFGIIILLLMORSS millefiori glass
AEFGIIJLORSSSUU Lissajous figure
AEFGIKMNNNOOOSW of one's own making
AEFGILLLLLORWWY wall gillyflower
AEFGILLNOPPRSVY self-approvingly
AEFHHIINORSSTTW faithworthiness
AEFHIIILLMNOSTU self-humiliation
AEFHIIKLNRRSTTW Sir Frank Whittle
AEFHIJLOPSSSUUV Flavius Josephus
AEFHKKMOOORRSTW make short work of
AEFHLORRSTTTUUV overthrust fault
AEFIIIILLMNNSTY infinitesimally
AEFIIKLLPRSSTTU strike-slip fault
AEFIIILLLNNOOPST self-pollination
AEFIIILMMNNORSUU Arnolfini Museum
AEFIILMNOOPRSSS professionalism
AEFIIMMNOOPRRST preformationism
AEFIIMNNOORSSSU omnifariousness
AEFIIMNOOPRRSTT preformationist
AEFIINOPRSSSSSU fissiparousness
AEFIKNNSSSTWYYZ Stefan Wyszynski
AEFILLMNOPRSTTY self-importantly
AEFILMNNOORRRSW Sir Norman Fowler
AEFILNNNOOOPRSS non-professional
AEFIMNNOORRRSST Sir Norman Foster
AEFIMNOOOPRRSTT post-Reformation
AEFLOOPPRSTTUUU paulo-post-future
AEGGHIIILNNNRST insight learning
AEGGHIIKLLOOTTU go out like a light
AEGGHILLNOORSTY shooting gallery
AEGGHINNNOORSST sing another song
AEGGIIKLMNOORVY Giorgiy Malenkov
AEGHHIIMNNORSTT Nottinghamshire
AEGHHIIMNNRSSST nightmarishness
AEGHHIIOOPRRRST historiographer
AEGHHILNNNOSSTT nothing less than
AEGHHIOORRSSTTT straight shooter
AEGHIIIINNNNRST Singin' in the Rain
AEGHIIMNRRSTTTY maternity rights
AEGHIKLMNPRSSTT Knights Templars
AEGHINNNOOPRRST harp on one string
AEGHKLOOOORRTTY orthokeratology
AEGIIILNNOOOPTV Giovanni Tiepolo
AEGIIIMNNNRSSTT intransigentism
AEGIIINNNOORSTT nitrogenisation
AEGIIINNNOORTTZ nitrogenization
AEGIIINNNRSSTTT intransigentist
AEGIILMNNNORTTU mountain ringlet
AEGIJKLMNNNNRSU Jurgen Klinsmann
AEGIJMNNOOPPRRT J Pierpont Morgan
AEGIKLNNOORTUWY now you're talking
AEGILLLNOPRRSTY strolling player
AEGILLNNORSTUUV volutin granules
AEGILMNNORRSTTY remonstratingly
AEGILNNOPPRRSTU learning support
AEGIMNNNNNORRTU running ornament
AEGIMNNOOSSSTUV Vosges Mountains
AEHHIIMNOPRRSTT therianthropism
AEHHIIOPPRSSTTY physiotherapist
AEHHIKNNORSSTTW thankworthiness
AEHHLLORSTTTTUW thrust to the wall
AEHIIILLLMRSSWY Shirley Williams
AEHIIJJMNOORTTY join the majority
AEHIIJLLNRSUUXY Sir Julian Huxley
AEHIIKNNRRSSSTT shrink-resistant
AEHIILNNOOPTTVY hypoventilation
AEHIIMMNNOOPRST enantiomorphism
AEHIJNOOPPRSSTX Sir Joseph Paxton
AEHILNNOPPRSUYZ sulphinpyrazone
AEHIMNNOOOPRSTU enantiomorphous
AEHLLNNOOOPRTTY Anthony Trollope
AEHLNOOOPSTTTUY penalty shoot-out
AEIIILLLMORRSSW Sir William Osler

AEIIILMMMNNRSSX Marxism-Leninism
AEIIIMMNPSSTUVY passive immunity
AEIIKLLLMNRSTUW William Kunstler
AEIILLLNOQRTUVY ventriloquially
AEIILLNNNNOTTUY unintentionally
AEIILLNOOPPRSTY prepositionally
AEIILLOOPPRRRTY proprietorially
AEIILMMNNRSSTTU instrumentalism
AEIILMMNOOPRSTT metropolitanism
AEIILMNNRSSTTTU instrumentalist
AEIILMNNRSTTTUY instrumentality
AEIILMOPRSTTTWY military two-step
AEIILNNNORSSTUV involuntariness
AEIILOPQRRSSTUU res ipsa loquitur
AEIIMNNNORSTTTU instrumentation
AEIIMOPPRRSSTTU superpatriotism
AEIKLMNNOPRSSTU unsportsmanlike
AEILNOOOPPRRTTY proportionately
AEIMMMNRRSSSTTU St Martin's summer
AEIMMNNNOORSTUU Mourne Mountains
AEINNOOOPPRRTTU unproportionate
AELNNNOOOPPRRSU personal pronoun
AENNOOOPRRRSSTT retrotransposon
AEOOPPRSTTTTUUU put out to pasture
AFFGHOPPRRSTUUY rough puff-pastry
AFFHILLORSTUUYY yours faithfully
AFFIIIILLOPPPPR Fra Filippo Lippi
AFGGIIMNNORRSTY transmogrifying
AFGHIILMNOOPSTT hot foil stamping
AFGIIKMNNNOOPRT non-profit-making
AFGINOOOOPRRRSW arrow-poison frog
AFHHILLOOPSSSTY flash photolysis
AFHIIJKLNNNORRS Sir John Franklin
AFHIINNORRSSSUW Russo-Finnish War
AFIINNOOOPSTTTX postfix notation
AFMMNNOOOOPRTTU poor man of mutton
AGGHIINOOSTTUWY go without saying
AGGIIIILMMNNSSZ minimizing glass
AGGIKLLLNNOORWW longwall working
AGHHHILOOOPPRTT photolithograph
AGHHIILLLLNSSYY shilly-shallying
AGHHILLMOOOPSTT ophthalmologist
AGHHILOOOPPSTYY pathophysiology
AGHHINOOOPSSTTU opisthognathous
AGHHLOOOPPRTXYY photoxylography
AGHHOOOPPPRRTYY pyrophotography
AGHIIILLNNOPSTY lying-in hospital
AGHIIILMOPSSTTT stigmatophilist
AGHIILMNOOOSTTY mythologisation
AGHIILMNOOOTTYZ mythologization
AGHIKKLLNOOOSTW look who's talking
AGHIKNNOOORTTWW know a thing or two
AGHILMMNOOOPTUY immunopathology
AGIIILLLMMNSTUU multilingualism
AGIIILLNNQRTUYZ tranquilizingly
AGIIJKMNOORRTWY working majority
AGIILMMNOOSSTTU numismatologist
AHHIIJLNOOPPSSU John Philip Sousa
AHHILLMOOOPPRSY moral philosophy
AHHILNOOOPPRSTY phosphorylation
AHHINOOOPPRSSTT anthroposophist
AHIIIMOPPRSTTUY hypopituitarism
AHIIINNOOOOPTTZ photoionization
AHIILMMMNORTUUY humoral immunity
AHIILMNOORRSTUY military honours
AHIJLMNOOOPRSTU photojournalism
AHIJLNOOOPRSTTU photojournalist
AHINOOOPRRSSTTT phototransistor
AHINOOOPRSSTUWY what's your poison?
AHLLMNOOOPRRSTW Worrall Thompson
AIIIILLNOQRSTUY inquisitorially
AIIIIMMNNOOSSTU isoimmunisation
AIIIIMMNNOOSTUZ isoimmunization
AIIILLNNOSTTTUY institutionally
AIIILNOOPPRSTTY propylitisation
AIIILNOOPPRTTYZ propylitization
AIIINNNOOPRSTTT transition point
AIILLLMNOPSSUUY pusillanimously
AIILLNOOPPSSTUY suppositionally
AIILNNNOOPRRSST rosin rosin plant
AIILNOOOPPRRTTY proportionality
AIKNNNNOQTTUUWY unknown quantity

B

BBBBEEFGIIILRTT flibbertigibbet
BBBDEEFLOOOOTUY blue-footed booby
BBBDEEHLLLMNOOS blonde bombshell
BBCCEIIMNOOORTU Umberto Boccioni
BBCDDEEINRRSSUU undersubscribed
BBCDEEEILLNORRS Cornelis Drebbel
BBCDEEGHIIINRRY bigeneric hybrid
BBCDEEIILORSTTU biodestructible
BBCEEILMNOSSSTU combustibleness
BBCEEKKLOORRSTT stockbroker belt
BBCHKKOOOOORRYY by hook or by crook
BBDDEEHHHLOOOOY hobbledehoyhood
BBDEEEHIILNORTT bite on the bridle
BBDEEGINNORRSSU burn one's bridges
BBDEELLMMNOSSUY Summoned by Bells
BBDEGIILLNNOOWY bodyline bowling
body-line bowling
BBDEINNOOSSSSUY nobody's business
BBDIMOORRRSTUUY dormitory suburb
BBEEEEGGHIINNTU Begin the Beguine
BBEEEFHIILLORTY Lob-lie-by-the-fire
BBEEEGHIILLNNSW New English Bible
BBEEEHHILLOTTTW hit below the belt
BBEEEHILLNOTTTU bite on the bullet
BBEEEIILMMRSSSU semisubmersible
BBEEEKKNOORRRST kerbstone-broker
BBEGILLNNORTTUY belly-button ring
BBEHILMMMOOORST thromboembolism
BBGLMOOOPRRSUUY Bloomsbury Group
BCCCDEIIMNRRSUU uncircumscribed
BCCCEEEEIILRSXY exercise bicycle
BCCCEEEIIMNRTTU cubic centimetre
BCCDEHKRSSTTTUU St Cuthbert's duck
BCCEEEEHILNNOST the noble science
BCCEEEFHHIILTTY The Bicycle Thief
BCCEEEIILMNNOSU bioluminescence
BCCEEEIMNNPRSUU superincumbence
BCCEEILNORRSTTU reconstructible

BCCEEIMNNPRSUUY superincumbency
BCCEFIINOORRSUU Ferruccio Busoni
BCCEGHIMNNNRRUU number-crunching
BCCEHHIMNOOSTTY honeycomb stitch
BCCEHINOORRSSTU cross the Rubicon
BCCFHIOOOPPSTUU hoppus cubic foot
BCCGHIIIIKLNNPT pitching niblick
BCDDDEELLNOOOSS cold-bloodedness
BCDDEEGHHIOSSTT the bitch goddess
BCDDGILLLNOORUY bloodcurdlingly
BCDEEEEHHINNSST behind the scenes
BCDEEEEILORRRST Border Leicester
BCDEEEFHIILRRSS Friedrich Bessel
BCDEEEGIILNNORS Liebig condenser
BCDEEEHHJOPRRSU jodhpur breeches
BCDEEEIILMNNUYZ inducible enzyme
BCDEEEIILNRRSSU irreducibleness
BCDEEFHIMNOOOTT fine-toothed comb
BCDEEHIKNORRRTY Robert Henry Dick
BCDEFGHIINORTUY City of Edinburgh
BCDEFHILORRTTUY butterfly orchid
BCDEGIIILNOSTUY building society
BCDEHIOORRSSSTT Scottish Borders
BCDEIIIILRRTTUY irreductibility
BCDEIIILNNOOSSU inclusion bodies
BCDEIIILRSTTTUY destructibility
BCDEIINNOOPSSUY beyond suspicion
BCDEILLNNOORSSU colour blindness
BCEEEEEGNOORRSZ Ebenezer Scrooge
BCEEEEFGIKLORTW leg before wicket
BCEEEEGHILMRRSU Limburger cheese
BCEEEEGIMNORRSS corbie messenger
BCEEEEGKLLMOOPR Pembroke College
BCEEEEHLOPRRRST brothel-creepers
BCEEEEIILLMRRSV vermis cerebelli
BCEEEEILMNNNOOV omnibenevolence
BCEEEELMNOORRTT Roberto Clemente
BCEEEEMOPRRSSSS Bessemer process
BCEEEFFFLRTTTUY butterfly effect
BCEEEFFGILNORTY benefit of clergy
BCEEEFGHIIOPRTT tip of the iceberg
BCEEEFGIMNRRTUU Recumbent Figure
BCEEEFIIKNNSSST sickness benefit
BCEEEFLNORSTTUU fluorescent tube
BCEEEGIILLNNSTU subintelligence
BCEEEGILLNNNORY non-belligerency
BCEEEHHILOOPRTU eleutherophobic
BCEEEHHMORSTTTU so much the better
BCEEEHIIJLNOTTU Juliette Binoche
BCEEEHIILRRRSTV silver birch tree
BCEEEIIJNRSTTUV intersubjective
BCEEEIILNNOPRST bristlecone pine
BCEEEILLOPPPRSU People's Republic
BCEEEILNPSSSSTU susceptibleness
BCEEEJLMMORRTUY jerry-come-tumble
BCEEFFGOOORTTYY Geoffrey Boycott
BCEEFHIKLNNRRUY Huckleberry Finn
BCEEGHIIMOORSTY biogeochemistry
BCEEGIIMMNNOSSS misbecomingness
BCEEGILLNNOOORS Robinson College
BCEEHHHIOPRRRST herb Christopher
BCEEHLNOSSTTTUU chestnut boletus
BCEEIIILLNNNOVZ Vincenzo Bellini
BCEEIIILMPPRRST imprescriptible
BCEEIILLNNOSTTU subintellection
BCEEIILMPRSSTUV visible spectrum
BCEEIJOPRRSSTUU subject-superior
BCEEILNOPRRSSTU corruptibleness
BCEEINORSSSTTUV obstructiveness
BCEFHILORRSTTUY butterfly orchis
BCEFIIKLOOOSTUV Book of Leviticus
BCEGHIILNOOOSTT biotechnologist
BCEHHIMNOORSSUY Hieronymus Bosch
BCEHIIIIINOSTTX exhibitionistic
BCEHIILNOPPRSUW public ownership
BCEIIIILLPSTTUU public utilities
BCEIIILMNOPTTTY contemptibility
BCEIIILMOPRSSTY compressibility
BCEIIMMNOORSSSU subcommissioner
BCEIKMNOOOPRSSY proboscis monkey
BCGHIILOOOPSSTY psychobiologist
BCGIIIIILNORRTY incorrigibility
BCILLNOOORSSTUU courts-bouillons
BCINNNOOORRTTUY non-contributory
BDDDEFGINNOORRU forbidden ground
BDDEEEFILRSSTUY Tess Durbeyfield
BDDEEEGHINRRRTU third degree burn
BDDEEEGHOORRSTV Theodor Svedberg
BDDEEEILMNNNOSS noble-mindedness
BDDEEEIMNNORSSS sober-mindedness
BDDEEFGOOOORRSV over God's forbode
BDDEEIILMNNOTUY double indemnity
BDDEEIILMNOORTY demolition derby
BDDEEIKLOORSTUW work double tides
BDEEEEELMMRSUUV Belvedere Museum
BDEEEEFIMNNOORT before-mentioned
BDEEEELLNOOSSTV do one's level best
BDEEEFGINRRRSTU first degree burn
BDEEEFGINRRTTUY buttery-fingered
BDEEEFILNNPRSUW funnel-web spider
BDEEEGHILLMOSTT goldsmith beetle
BDEEEIILMOPRSSS permissible dose
BDEEEILLOOPSTTV pot-bellied stove
BDEEFIIIILNNSTY indefensibility
BDEEFILMNNRRSUY friendly numbers
BDEEFLMMNOORRUY ferro-molybdenum
BDEEGGLNOOORRRW Lord George-Brown
BDEEGOOOOORTTTU too good to be true
BDEEHLMORRSTUUU shout blue murder
BDEEHMNOOPRSTUU Prometheus Bound
BDEEIIIILNNSSSV indivisibleness
BDEEIIIMNORSTTV in totidem verbis
BDEELNNOOORRSSY Osborne Reynolds
BDEFGILLMOOTTUW full-bottomed wig
BDEFGILLNOOOORW Robin Goodfellow
BDEGGIIILNNOSSS disobligingness
BDEGIIIIILNSTTY indigestibility
BDEGIILLNOOSSTU blood-guiltiness
BDEGIMNRRTUUUXY Burgundy mixture
BDEHHILLOOORRTT Theodor Billroth
BDEHHILNOOSTWWW how the wind blows
BDEHIIILNNNOTWW Blowin' in the Wind

BDEHINOOORRSSSY Sir Rhodes Boyson
BDFFIIILMNNORUU infundibuliform
BDIIIILLNOSSTUY indissolubility
BEEEEELMOPPPRST September people
BEEEEFILNNNOOSS feel in one's bones
BEEEEFILNRRTTUU furniture beetle
BEEEEFINORSTTWW between two fires
BEEEEGHIMNPRSTU the Supreme Being
BEEEEGILNNSSSTU genteel business
BEEEEGILNPRSSTV Steven Spielberg
BEEEEGIMNOOSSTV give someone best
BEEEEHIILNNSTWW in between whiles
BEEEEHIILNPRRRS irreprehensible
BEEEEHLMNNOPRTU telephone number
BEEEFGHIIMNORTT for the time being
BEEEFIILLNNORSY fire in one's belly
BEEEGGHIIILLRTW whirligig beetle
BEEEGHILNNOSTTT tighten one's belt
BEEEGNOOORRSSTY gooseberry-stone
BEEEHIILNPRRRSY irreprehensibly
BEEEHKMNNOOPSTU keep one's thumb on
BEEEHOOPRSTTUWY up to the eyebrows
BEEEIINNNORRTTZ trinitrobenzene
BEEEIIPRRSSSSVX expressis verbis
BEEEILMMOPPRTUU perpetuum mobile
BEEEILNNOPRSSSS responsibleness
BEEELMNOORSSSTU troublesomeness
BEEFFLLORRTTUWY butterfly flower
BEEFGINNNORRSSU burn one's fingers
BEEFHHINORSTTUV The Birth of Venus
BEEFKLORRSTTTUY butterfly stroke
BEEGGGIINNOQSTU question-begging
BEEGGIJLOORRSSU Jorge Luis Borges
BEEGHIILNNORSSU neighbourliness
BEEGHIILNOORRTZ Lorenzo Ghiberti
BEEGIILOOORSSUU Louise Bourgeois
BEEGIJLNORRSSUU Julius Rosenberg
BEEGILNNORSTTTW western blotting
BEEHHILLOOSTTTT The Littlest Hobo
BEEHIIINOPRSSTV prohibitiveness
BEEHIILNNOORSSZ sensible horizon
BEEHIIMMRRSSTVY shiver my timbers
BEEHIINNRRRTTTY Trinity Brethren
BEEHILNNOPPRRTU born in the purple
BEEHLLOORRSTTUW Robert Southwell
BEEHNORSSTTTWWY north-west-by-west
BEEHOSSSTTTUWWY south-west-by-west
BEEIIIILNNSTTXY inextensibility
BEEIIIILRRRSTVY irreversibility
BEEIINNORSSSTUV inobtrusiveness
BEEIJKNNNOORRST Robert Jenkinson
BEEIKLLMNORRSTU Robert S Mulliken
BEEIKLOOPPRUZZZ puzzle-prize book
BEEINNORSSSTUUV unobtrusiveness
BEFFGILNORRSSSU Brussels griffon
BEFGINOOOSSSTUU go out of business
BEFILMOORRSSTUU strombuliferous
BEGGHHHIILRSTTT the bright lights
BEGHILNOOORSTTU troubleshooting
BEGIIIIILLLNTTY intelligibility
BEGIIILLNRSTTUU subintelligitur
BEGIIJLNOSSTUUV Justus von Liebig
BEGIINNNOQRSTUU burning question
BEGILNNOOORSSTT Toronto blessing
BEHHIJKLNOOOSTW John Wilkes Booth
BEHHLMOOPRRTTUY Plymouth Brother
BEHHMNOOPPRRRYY rhombenporphyry
BEHILMNORSSTTUW twirl one's thumbs
BEIIIIILMRRSSTY irremissibility
BEIIIIILRRSSTTY irresistibility
BEIIILMNNOOSSTU Benito Mussolini
BEIINNORRSTUVWY Brown University
BEILLLOOORTTUUY I'll trouble you to
BEILMNNNRSTTTUU blunt instrument
BEIMNORSSSSTUUU rumbustiousness
BEIMOPRSSSSSTTU sub-postmistress
BEINOOOPPRRSSSU opprobriousness
BENNNOOPRRTTTUU Burton-upon-Trent
BFGHIINNOORTTTU nothing for it but

C

CCCCDIIIMOOOSSY coccidiomycosis
CCCCDIILNOSSUUU cocculus indicus
CCCDDEEEHIKORSV discovered check
CCCDEEEIIMNOSST domestic science
CCCDEEFIIKNNORT confidence trick
CCCDEEHIKMMNOOW common chickweed
CCCDEHLLOOOPSST scotched collops
CCCDIIILNORSTTU district council
CCCEEEEHHIKNRSS Chinese checkers
CCCEEEFIINNORSS forensic science
CCCEEEHILNORSTT electrotechnics
CCCEEEHLOORSTUU eleutherococcus
CCCEEEILLOOPRST collector's piece
CCCEEEILNRRRTTU electric current
CCCEEEIMNNNOOSY conscience money
CCCEEEIMNOPRSTU computer science
CCCEEFINNOOOPRS conscience-proof
CCCEEHHIIKKLRST Schrecklichkeit
CCCEEHHINORSSSU Secession Church
CCCEEHLMOOSTTYY cholecystectomy
CCCEEHLNOSSTUUU succculent-house
CCCEEIILMNOORRT microelectronic
CCCEEIILMNORSTU electronic music
CCCEEIKLLOORTTT ticket collector
CCCEEIMNPRSSSTU circumspectness
CCCEFIIKLLNOORT Frick Collection
CCCEGIIIKNNOQUV quick-conceiving
CCCEHIILLNNOSUY succinylcholine
CCCEIIIMMOORRRU micromicrocurie
CCCEIIIMNNORSSU circumincession
CCCEIIIMPRRSTUV circumscriptive
CCCEIIJNNOOOPRT conic projection
CCCEIILNORSTUUY Security Council
CCCEINNOOOSSSSU coconsciousness
CCCIIIMNOPRRSTU circumscription
CCDDDEEEILNOORU Crocodile Dundee
CCDDDEHHILNOOOS second childhood
CCDDDEINOORRSTU conduct disorder
CCDDEEGILNNNOSY condescendingly
CCDDEEIIORRSSTU direct discourse
CCDEEEEFINNOORV videoconference

CCDEEEEINNORTUV counter-evidence
CCDEEEELLNORSST recollectedness
CCDEEEFINNNOOOV convenience food
CCDEEEFINNOPRSU superconfidence
CCDEEENNNNORSSU unconcernedness
CCDEEGHIMNNOOST The Second Coming
CCDEEHILNNORRRS Children's Corner
CCDEEHIMNOPRSTU mesonephric duct
CCDEEIIIIMNNOPS psionic medicine
CCDEEIIIJNNORTT direct injection
CCDEEIMMNOOOSTY domestic economy
CCDEEINNOORRRTU under correction
CCDEEINOPRSTUUV superconductive
CCDEELLMNORSTUU clustered column
CCDEENNORRSTTUU unreconstructed
CCDEFGIILNORRTU correcting fluid
CCDEFIILNOORRTU correction fluid
CCDEGILLLMNOOPU cloud-compelling
CCDEHINOOOPTTUV photoconductive
CCDEIIIMNOORSST microdissection
CCDEIINNOORSTUU induction course
CCDEIJMNNOOOTUV conjunctive mood
CCDEILMMNOOSTUY closed community
CCDEILMOOORRUVX loxodromic curve
CCDGHINNOOOPTTU photoconducting
CCDHIIKLLOSUWWW chuck-will's-widow
CCDINNOORRSTTUY dry construction
CCEEEEEHHILRSST Ilchester cheese
CCEEEEELLNPRSUX superexcellence
CCEEEEFFIINPPTY fifty pence piece
CCEEEEFGIMNOORU economic refugee
CCEEEEFILNRRSTT Fertile Crescent
CCEEEEFLNNOQSSU self-consequence
CCEEEEFNNOPRRSS press conference
CCEEEEGNNNOORVZ convergence zone
CCEEEEHHINQRSSU Chinese chequers
CCEEEEILMMOSTTT select committee
CCEEEEINNOPRRTT reception centre
CCEEEELMNNOPSTX complex sentence
CCEEEENRRRRSUVY reserve currency
CCEEEFFGIIINORV receiving-office
CCEEEFFILOOPPRT prefect of police
CCEEEFNNNOOOQSU of no consequence
CCEEEHHLOOSSTTT close to the chest
CCEEEHHNOOPPRSS phosphorescence
CCEEEHIIKPPPSTU pick up the pieces
CCEEEHILMORRSTT electrothermics
CCEEEHILOOPRRTT electrophoretic
CCEEEHMNNOORSTT the crescent moon
CCEEEIIKLNORSTT electrokinetics
CCEEEIILMNNORRT irreconcilement
CCEEEILLMNOORST mole-electronics
CCEEEIMNOQRSTUU musique concrète
CCEEEINNOSSSTUV consecutiveness
CCEEELNSSSSSSSU successlessness
CCEEEMNOOOPRRRT Emperor Concerto
CCEEENOORRRTTUV concert overture
CCEEFFFIILNSSUY self-sufficiency
CCEEFHIILLNNOOS colonels-in-chief
CCEEFHKLOORRTTU clerk of the court
CCEEFIIILMPPSSU specific impulse
CCEEFIIINOPRSTT perfectionistic
CCEEFIILLORTTUV collective fruit
CCEEFILNNOSSSTY self-consistency
CCEEFILNOOOPRUU Council of Europe
CCEEFKLOORRSTUY four-stroke cycle
CCEEGHIILOPSSTT telescopic sight
CCEEGHIINRRRSTU three-ring circus
CCEEGIMORRSSTUY cosmetic surgery
CCEEHHIINOPRSTZ schizophrenetic
CCEEHHLNNOORUUV luncheon voucher
CCEEHIIIMOORSTT stoicheiometric
CCEEHIINNORTTTY ethnocentricity
CCEEHIMMNOPSTUY speech community
CCEEHINOOPRRRTY hypercorrection
CCEEHINOOSSSSUU succession house
CCEEHKLLOORTUVW twelve-hour clock
CCEEHNORRSTTTUU technostructure
CCEEIIJJSSSTTUU justices' justice
CCEEIIKNORSSTTT rocket scientist
CCEEIIKNORSTTUX excursion ticket
CCEEIILNNOSTUVY inconsecutively
CCEEIILNOOPPRST police inspector
CCEEIILOPRRRTUY reciprocity rule
CCEEIILOPRRTTYY pyro-electricity
CCEEIINNNNOORTT interconnection
CCEEIJNNNOSSTUV conjunctiveness
CCEEILNOOOPRSTT optoelectronics
CCEEIMMNNORTTUY community centre
CCEEIMNOOPRRSTY pyrometric cones
CCEEIMNOORSSTUY consumer society
CCEEINORRSTTUUY counter-security
CCEFGINOOOPRRRT proof-correcting
CCEFHIILOOOPRST spoilt for choice
CCEFILLNOOSSSUY self-consciously
CCEFILNNOOSSSUU unselfconscious
CCEFINOOOOPRRRT proof correction
CCEFMNOOOPRTTTU contempt of court
CCEGHHIIIIMRRST higher criticism
CCEGHIIKNNNOPRS no spring chicken
CCEGHILMNOOORTY microtechnology
CCEGIILOOOOSTTX ecotoxicologist
CCEGIIMNOOPRRSS microprocessing
CCEHHIMOPRSSTYY psychochemistry
CCEHIIKLNNOOSTY cholecystokinin
CCEHIIMMOOPSSTY psychosomimetic
CCEHIIMMOOPSTTY psychotomimetic
CCEHILMOOOOPSST composite school
CCEHILNOOOPRSST school inspector
CCEHIMOOOOPPRST photomicroscope
CCEHLMOOOSSTTYY cholecystostomy
CCEIIIIMNOORRST oneirocriticism
CCEIIIILRRSSTTUU sericiculturist
CCEIIIMMNOOPRSS Price Commission
CCEIIIMNNORSSSU circuminsession
CCEIILLNOOORSSU collision course
CCEIILNNOOSSTUY conscientiously
CCEIINNNOOSSTUU unconscientious
CCEIMMNNNOOSSUU communi consensu
CCEINNNOOSSSSUU unconsciousness
CCEINNOOPRRSTTU preconstruction
CCEINNOOPSSSSUU conspicuousness

CCENOOOPRRRSTUW Crown prosecutor
CCGHIIIINOPRRST historic pricing
CCGIIIILNOOSSTU sociolinguistic
CCHHIIOPPSSSTYY psychophysicist
CCHIIILNNOOSTUV Luchino Visconti
CCHILMMNOOOSTUY community school
CCHINOOOPRSSTYY onychocryptosis
CCIIINNOOPRSSTT conscriptionist
CCIILLNOOPRRUVY privy councillor✧
CCIILNNOOPSSUUY inconspicuously
CCIIMNNOORSSTTU constructionism
misconstruction
CCIINNOORSSTTTU constructionist
CCIMMNOOPRSTTUY crypto-communist
CDDDEGIINNOOOOT good-conditioned
CDDEEEEEINNNPRT interdependence
CDDEEEEFIIOORRU Orfeo ed Euridice
CDDEEEEINNNPRTY interdependency
CDDEEEELNNPRTUY unprecedentedly
CDDEEEFIIKLRRSU Frederick Delius
CDDEEEHIIMNOTVY The Divine Comedy
CDDEEEIIMNOPPRR medicine-dropper
CDDEEFGIIINNPST deficit spending
CDDEEFIIILLNPSS self-disciplined
CDDEEFIIINNORRT direction-finder
CDDEEGIILLNOOSU Golden Delicious
CDDEEGIINNNOOST gens de condition
CDDEEIILLNNOOTW well-conditioned
CDDEEIMMNNORSUU secundum ordinem
CDDEELMNNOPSSUU seconds pendulum
CDDEFIIIILPRSTU dulcified spirit
CDDEFILLNOOSTTU Sutton Coldfield
CDDEFINOOSSUUUX Eudoxus of Cnidus
CDDEFNNOOOOPSTU foot-pound-second
CDDEGHIIILMNSTT middle-stitching
CDDEHILOOORSSTW with closed doors
CDDEINNOOPRRTUU underproduction
CDDEINOOOOPRSST odontoid process
CDDGILLLNOOOORW Lord Collingwood
CDDIILMMOOOSSUY discommodiously
CDDIILOORSSSUUU Diodorus Siculus
CDEEEEEFLNNSSSS defencelessness
CDEEEEEKNORSVWY every second week
CDEEEEFIKLMPRRT Frederick Temple
CDEEEEFIKRRRSTV Frederick Treves
CDEEEEFINRRRSTW fire-crested wren
CDEEEEFLNNRSSST self-centredness
CDEEEEGHIILNRSV Received English
CDEEEEGKNOOPRRW green woodpecker
CDEEEEGLOORRRVY Roger de Coverley
CDEEEEHILPRSTTW wield the sceptre
CDEEEEHIMNOPRSS ephemeris second
CDEEEEINNNORTTT detention centre
CDEEEEINNNPRSTU superintendence
CDEEEEMMOORRRVY recovered memory
CDEEEFFGILLLNOU Nuffield College
CDEEEFFIIILLNOR Federico Fellini
CDEEEFFIKNNSSST stiff-neckedness
CDEEEFGHIILNRRS Friedrich Engels
CDEEEFGHLLOORRT Hertford College
CDEEEFIIMNNOOPS piece of one's mind
CDEEEFILLNORTUY decree of nullity
CDEEEFILMNRRSTU Sir Clement Freud
CDEEEFILRSSTTUV self-destructive
CDEEEFIMMNQRUUY medium frequency
CDEEEFLNOORRTUW counter-flowered
CDEEEGINNORSTUU secundogeniture
CDEEEHHILPRSTUW whited sepulchre
CDEEEHIIKLNRRSS Erskine Childers
CDEEEHMMSSSTUUU Deutsches Museum
CDEEEHMNNOOORTU roche moutonnéed
CDEEEHNNORRTTUU under-the-counter
CDEEEIINNPRRSWW windscreen-wiper
CDEEEIINPRSSSTV descriptiveness
CDEEEIIOPRRRSVV service provider
CDEEEIKNOOPPRST pocket one's pride
CDEEEIMNNPRSTUU superinducement
CDEEEIMNOPPRTTV tempt providence
CDEEEINNNPRSTUY superintendency
CDEEEINRSSSTTUV destructiveness
CDEEEKLMMOOOPPR Commodore Keppel
CDEEELLOORSSSTT settle old scores
CDEEENNOPRSSTTU unprotectedness
CDEEENNPSSSSTUU unsuspectedness
CDEEFFILLNNOSTY self-confidently
CDEEFGIILNNORSS self-considering
CDEEFGILMNNOSTU self-documenting
CDEEFIILNORSTYY friendly society
CDEEFILLPRSSTUY disrespectfully
CDEEFILNORSSTTU self-destruction
CDEEFILNOSSTTTU self-constituted
CDEEFINNNOOPRST confident person
CDEEGHIMNNNOPRU uncomprehending
CDEEGIIIMMNORTT riding committee
CDEEGIILLNOOOTU oligonucleotide
CDEEGIILNORRTVV revolving credit
CDEEGILNOOPRSTW powdering-closet
CDEEGKLMMNNOOOW common knowledge
CDEEHIIKNSSTTTW thick-wittedness
CDEEHIKNNRRSTTU thunderstricken
CDEEHMNNNOOOOSY second honeymoon
CDEEHNOOOORSSST osteochondroses
CDEEIIIIMNNRSTT indeterministic
CDEEIIINNSSSTTV distinctiveness
CDEEIIKNQSSTTUW quick-wittedness
CDEEIINNOPRSTUV United Provinces
CDEEIINRRSSTUVY service industry
CDEEILNNORSSSUU incredulousness
CDEEIMNNOOPSSSU compendiousness
CDEEINNNOPRSSST nondescriptness
CDEEINOORRRRRTY re-entry corridor
CDEELMNNOOOOSTY Monocotyledones
CDEELNNOOPRRSTY correspondently
CDEFGIIILNNORTW friction welding
CDEFGIKNORRSUUU ferruginous duck
CDEFHIIILNORRST Linford Christie
CDEFHIMNOOSSTUU The Sound of Music
CDEFHMMOOORSUUY comedy of humours
CDEFIIMMOOOSSTT soft commodities
CDEFILMNOOOPRRS scolopendriform
CDEGHHLOOPPSTYY depth psychology
CDEGHHMOOOPRSTU through-composed

CDEGHIKLLNOOUVW Ludwig von Köchel
CDEGIIIMMNNOOSS decommissioning
CDEGIILLMNOOPTU clootie dumpling
CDEGIILMNOPRTUU picture moulding
CDEGIILNNOOORST endocrinologist
CDEGILNNOOPRRSY correspondingly
CDEHHIILOORTTUY ichthyodorulite
CDEHHIILOORTTYY ichthyodorylite
CDEHHLLOOORRSTU colour threshold
CDEHIKMNOOPRRTU durchkomponiert
CDEHINOOOORSSST osteochondrosis
CDEIIIILNNSTTVY indistinctively
CDEIIIJNNOSSSUU injudiciousness
CDEIIMMNNNOOOSS non-commissioned
CDELOOPRRSSUWZZ crossword puzzle
CDGIINOOPRSSSUU group discussion
CDGIMNNOOOOPRTU rooting compound
CDHIILNOPRSTUUU pulchritudinous
CDIIIINOSSSTUUV vicissitudinous
CDIIIIORRSSTTTV district visitor
CDIILNNOOSSTUUY discontinuously
CDIIMOOPPRRSTUY cryptosporidium
CDINOOOPSSSSTYY pycnodysostosis
CDLNNOOORSTUWWW clown's woundwort
CEEEEEEJPPRRRSS jeepers creepers
CEEEEEGINRRSSTV reverse genetics
CEEEEEHINNPPRTY threepenny piece
CEEEEEHLRRSSTTT Chester-le-Street
CEEEEEHNOSTTTUY cut one's eye teeth
CEEEEELOOPRSSTT telestereoscope
CEEEEFFIINNRRTT interference fit
CEEEEFFIINNSSTV ineffectiveness
CEEEEFILORRRTTV retroreflective
CEEEEFIORRRTTTT fortiter et recte
CEEEEGIIKLNPPRR Peregrine Pickle
CEEEEGLLOPRSSTT St Peter's College
CEEEEHHHIRSTTTW The Three Witches
CEEEEHHLNOOPPST the chosen people
CEEEEHHNOPRRTTW threepenceworth
CEEEEHIILNNRSTT Liechtensteiner
CEEEEHILNRRSSTV the silver screen
CEEEEHLMOOPRSTT telethermoscope
CEEEEIILLNOPRRR Pierre Corneille
CEEEEILLNNPRSTT insect repellent
CEEEEINNOPPRSST sense perception
CEEEFFGHNOOSSTT get off one's chest
CEEEFFHIIKLMNOT Elie Metchnikoff
CEEEFFILMOPRRTW imperfect flower
CEEEFGIMNNNORRR norm-referencing
CEEEFHIILNRRSTW Winchester rifle®
CEEEFIIMMMNOPRS femme incomprise
CEEEFIIMNORRRTT interferometric
CEEEFKMNNOORRTW enforcement work
CEEEFLLMNOSSSUX flex one's muscles
CEEEFLNORRSSSUU resourcefulness
CEEEGGILNNOOSSU gluconeogenesis
CEEEGHHINRSTTTW tighten the screw
CEEEGHIILNPRSTT creeping thistle
CEEEGHILORRSSTU Gloucestershire
CEEEGHIMMNNOOQU homecoming queen
CEEEGHIQRRRSUUU churrigueresque
CEEEGHLLMNOOORT Homerton College
CEEEGHLNORSSSTT stretch one's legs
CEEEGIIILLMNNST misintelligence
CEEEGINOPRRSSSW crossing-sweeper
CEEEGLNOOPPRSSS People's Congress
CEEEHHIINPRSSSW Chinese whispers
CEEEHHINPSSSSTY speech synthesis
CEEEHIILLNPRTTT The Little Prince
CEEEHIILNNRSTWZ Wiener schnitzel
CEEEHIIMNNOPRSV incomprehensive
CEEEHIIMNOPRSSV comprehensivise
CEEEHIIMNOPRSVZ comprehensivize
CEEEHIJLNNORTWW jewel in the crown
CEEEHIKKLNOPSSU kick up one's heels
CEEEHILMNOPRSVY comprehensively
CEEEHILOOPRRSST electrophoresis
CEEEHIMNNOPRSUV uncomprehensive
CEEEHIMORRSSTTY stereochemistry
CEEEHINOOPRRTTY reception theory
CEEEHLMMNOOOPPT the common people
CEEEHMNNOOORTUU rouche moutonnée
CEEEIIKMPQQRTUU emperick qutique
CEEEIILLNNOSUUV nouvelle cuisine
CEEEIILOOPRSTTV electropositive
CEEEIIMNNOPRRTV crime prevention
CEEEIIMNOPSSTTV competitiveness
CEEEIIMNORRSTTU recrementitious
CEEEIIMNORSTTUX excrementitious
CEEEIINOPRRRSTU resurrection pie
CEEEIINORRRSSTU resurrectionise
CEEEIINORRRSTUZ resurrectionize
CEEEIINRRSSSTTV restrictiveness
CEEEIIOPRTTTVXY exteroceptivity
CEEEIKLNNOOPSST line one's pockets
CEEEILMMRRSTTUU meristem culture
CEEEILOPRRSTTVY retrospectively
CEEEIMNNOORSSSU ceremoniousness
CEEEINNOSSSSSTU necessitousness
CEEEINOPPRSSSTV prospectiveness
CEEEINPQRSSSTUU picturesqueness
CEEEIOPRRRRSTTU picture restorer
CEEELLLOOPRTTYY polyelectrolyte
CEEELMNNOOORSSU run someone close
CEEEMMNNOORTTUV countermovement
CEEENOOQRRRTTUV torque converter
CEEENOPRRRSSTUU counter-pressure
CEEFFGIMNPRSTUU imperfect fungus
CEEFFGKNOOORSST get one's rocks off
CEEFFLMOOORRTTT letter of comfort
CEEFGGOOORRSSST Cross of St George
CEEFGHINNOORRST fight one's corner
CEEFGIIMNNRSSST fencing mistress
CEEFHIIIKMNNOTT in the nick of time
CEEFHIIMNOPRSSS Sphenisciformes
CEEFHKKLOORRSTW clerk of the works
CEEFHKLLLOOPRTU pull the forelock
CEEFIINOORTTUWX writ of execution
CEEFINNOPRRSSTU perfunctoriness
CEEFLMNOORSSSST comfortlessness
CEEFOOQRRSSTTUU Court of Requests
CEEGHHIJLNNORSS John Schlesinger

CEEGHIIKLNNSSSS English sickness
CEEGHINOOPRSTTY phytoestrogenic
CEEGIILLOSSSSTV logistics vessel
CEEGIILMNNRSUUV cingulum Veneris
CEEGIILOPRSSTTU gesture politics
CEEGIIMMNOOOTTT go into committee
CEEGIKOOPRRRSSV progressive rock
CEEGILNOORRRSTT control register
CEEGKMNNOORSTTV government stock
CEEGLLLNOOPPRYY propylene glycol
CEEHHHIJLNORRSS Sir John Herschel
CEEHHIINOORRSTW white rhinoceros
CEEHHIKLNOPSTTT the plot thickens
CEEHHIMMORRSTTY thermochemistry
CEEHHIMNORSTTUW not much the wiser
CEEHHINOPRRRSTW Christopher Wren
CEEHIIJLRRSSTUU Julius Streicher
CEEHIILNNORSTTY Roy Lichtenstein
CEEHIIMNNNOOPRS incomprehension
CEEHIIMNOOQRSTU Homeric question
CEEHIIMNOSSSSUV mischievousness
CEEHIINNRSSSTTY synthetic resins
CEEHIINPPRTTTUU put in the picture
CEEHIIORRRSSTTT Scottish terrier
CEEHIKLNNOPRTUY phenylketonuric
CEEHILNNOSSSTUY nucleosynthesis
CEEHILNOORSTTUW the Low Countries
CEEHIMMOPSSSTTY metempsychosist
CEEHIMNOORTTUWY without ceremony
CEEHINNOPRRSSTU puss in the corner
CEEHIOORRSTTUUW without recourse
CEEHKMNOOPRSTTU put the mockers on
CEEHLLNNOPPSSUU pull one's punches
CEEHLLNOOOPPRRY polychloroprene
CEEHLMNNOORSSST Loch Ness monster
CEEHMMOOOOORSTT come home to roost
CEEIIILLMMMORRT micromillimetre
CEEIIINOPRSSSTX expressionistic
CEEIILNOPRSTTVY introspectively
CEEIIMNNOPSSSUU impecuniousness
CEEIIMNNORRSSTU emission current
CEEIIMNORRRSSTU resurrectionism
CEEIINNNOORRSTV interconversion
CEEIINNORRRSTTT rent restriction
CEEIINNRSSSTTUV instructiveness
CEEIINOPPRSSSTU precipitousness
CEEIINORRRSSTTU resurrectionist
CEEIINPSSSTTUUV intussusceptive
CEEIKNOPRRSTTVY poverty-stricken
CEEILMMORSSSTUU Cloisters Museum
CEEILMNNOORSUUY unceremoniously
CEEIMMMNNOOPTTU immunocompetent
CEEIMNNNOOOOSTW come into one's own
CEEIMNNOOOPRTTY protection money
CEEIMNNOPSSSTUV consumptiveness
CEEIMOOPRRSSSTU osmotic pressure
CEEINNNOOSSSTTU contentiousness
CEEINOPPRSSSSUU perspicuousness
CEEKMNOOPRRTTUW network computer
CEELLOPPRRSSSTU suppressor T-cell
CEELNOOORRSSTUU one's true colours
CEFFGIILLLNNORU full-line forcing
CEFFGIKNORSSTTU stocking stuffer
CEFFIIINNOOSSSU inofficiousness
CEFGGKLOOOORSTY soft-rock geology
CEFGHHIILNNOPRS French-polishing
CEFGILMMNOORTTY Montgomery Clift
CEFHHLLOOOOTTUW out of whole cloth
CEFHMNOOORRSTTU Southern Comfort®
CEFIIILNPPRRSST first principles
CEFIILNNNNOOOTV non-fiction novel
CEFIIMNOPRSSSTU fission spectrum
CEGGHILNOOOORST geochronologist
CEGHHIIKLLNORSS shilling shocker
CEGHIIILNNOSTTU ethnolinguistic
CEGHIIILNOSSTTU theolinguistics
CEGHIIKNNOSTTTU Teutonic Knights
CEGHILMNOOOSTUY ethnomusicology
CEGHLNOOOPRSUYY neuropsychology
CEGIIIINNOORRST iris recognition
CEGIIIJNNNORSTT injection string
CEGIIILNNORSTUU neurolinguistic
CEGIIKMNNNORSSS morning sickness
CEGIILLMNNNORTU microtunnelling
CEGIILMNOPRSSTU multiprocessing
CEGIIMMMNOSSTUW swimming costume
CEGIKNNOOSSSTTU stick to one's guns
CEGILNOOPPSSSTY Synoptic Gospels
CEGINNNOORSSSUU incongruousness
CEHHIMMNOOOPPRS morphophonemics
CEHHINOPSSSSTYY psychosynthesis
CEHIILMMNNOOOST common in the soil
CEHIILMMNOPSTTW with compliments
CEHIILMNRRSSTTY Christy minstrel
CEHIIMMMNORSTUY immunochemistry
CEHIINNOOPRSSSU connoisseurship
CEHILMOORSSSSTY schoolmistressy
CEHILOOPRSTTTUU shoot tip culture
CEHINNOOPRSSSTY post-synchronise
CEHINNOOPRSSTYZ post-synchronize
CEHNNNOORSSSSUY synchronousness
CEIIIIKMNRSSTTT stickit minister
CEIIIIMNOPRSSST impressionistic
CEIIILNOQRSTTUV ventriloquistic
CEIIIMNNORRSSTU insurrectionism
CEIIINNORRSSTTU insurrectionist
CEIIKLMQRSSSTUY Mistress Quickly
CEIILNNOPSSSTUU punctiliousness
CEIILORRSSTTTUU ostreiculturist
CEIINNNOOPPRRST non-prescription
CEIINNOOPRSSTTU introsusception
CEIINNOPSSSTTUU intussusception
CEIKMMNOORRTUWY community worker
CEILLNOOPRRSUVY privy counsellor✧
CEILLOPRRSTTUUW pillow-structure
CEIMMNNNOOOPSST non compos mentis
CEIMNOPRSSSSTUU scrumptiousness
CEKLLNOOPPSSSUU pull up one's socks
CELLNOOOOSTTTUY Count Leo Tolstoy
CEMNNOSSSSTUUUU mutuus consensus
CFGHHIIILNNOOSS finishing school
CFGHIIIKNNRSSTY cry stinking fish

CFIIILNNOTTTUUY utility function
CFIIMMNOOOOSSTU out of commission
CGHIIJKLNNORSSU Sir John Suckling
CGHIIMMNNORSSWY synchro swimming
CGHILLNOOSSTTUW swothling-clouts
CGHMNOOOOOTTUUY too much too young
CGIILMNOOPSSSTU gossip columnist
CHHHINNOORRSTUY ornithorhynchus
CHHHIOOOOPPRRST orthophosphoric
CHIKMMNNNOOORST common stinkhorn
CHILLMOOOPPRRSY microsporophyll
CIIIMMNOPRSTTUY community spirit
CIIIMOORRSSTUVY myristicivorous
CIIINNOOSSTTTTU constitutionist
CINOOOPPRSTTTUY opportunity cost
CLMOOORRSSTTUUU custos rotulorum

D

DDDEEHLNOORRSUU round-shouldered
DDDEEIIIIMNNRTV interim dividend
DDDEHIIMOORSUXY sodium hydroxide
DDEEEEEEGHHLOSW wedge-heeled shoe
DDEEEEEFFGMOORR degree of freedom
DDEEEEEHHLNPRSS shepherd's needle
DDEEEEFFGHNOOPT go off the deep end
DDEEEEHINOPPRSU pseudoephedrine
DDEEEEIIMNNNPST semi-independent
DDEEEEILMNRRSTW Middle Westerner
DDEEEELLORSWWYY dyer's-yellowweed
DDEEEGGGINNOORR Gordon Greenidge
DDEEEGHHHOOPRST the Good Shepherd
DDEEEGHILOORSTV deliver the goods
DDEEEGIILNPRRUV underprivileged
DDEEEHIKNORRRVW Hendrik Verwoerd
DDEEEIILMNOPRTY redemption yield
DDEEEIILNRSSTTY disinterestedly
DDEEEIMNNORRTTV inverted mordent
DDEEFGINNOPQSUU queen of puddings
DDEEGHIILMNNSST light-mindedness
DDEEGHIIMNNRSST right-mindedness
DDEEGHIMNNOSSTU tough-mindedness
DDEEGIIINNOORTX nitrogen dioxide
DDEEGIINORRSTUU droit du seigneur
DDEEHHNNOORRSUU one hundred hours
DDEEHILLOPPRSSU shoulder-slipped
DDEEHILOORRSSUY disorderly house
DDEGHHIOORRSTTU thought disorder
DDEGHIIINNSSTUU undistinguished
DDEGHNNOOORTTUW down to the ground
DDEHHNOORRSTUUW two hundred hours
DDEHILNOORTTUWW world without end
world-without-end
DDGILLNOOPPRUYY roly-poly pudding
DEEEEEHNNNRSTUV seventeen-hunder
DEEEEFHHILNNOTT the end of the line
DEEEEFLLMNOPSTV self-development
DEEEEGILNORRRTV golden retriever
DEEEEHHKOOORRTT Theodore Roethke
DEEEEHNOPRRSTUY superheterodyne
DEEEEIILMNNTTTY identity element
DEEEEIIMNPQRSTU equine distemper
DEEEEILNORSSSTU deleteriousness
DEEEEILPRRSSVXY express delivery
DEEEEINRSSSTTTV vested interests
DEEEELMNOOPRTVV overdevelopment
DEEEFFHMOORRSTU the Four Freedoms
DEEEFGHIIILRRSTW Wilfred Thesiger
DEEEFGIILMNNRST self-determining
DEEEFGIKLLORRTT Gottfried Keller
DEEEFGIMOPRRSTT Gottfried Semper
DEEEFHHIOPRSSTT ship of the desert
DEEEFHIJNORRTTU Return of the Jedi
DEEEFHILNORRTVW front-wheel drive
DEEEGHNNOOOPRTT get the drop on one
DEEEGKLNNOOOSTW to one's knowledge
DEEEHHIMNNOPSST Stephen Sondheim
DEEEHHLMPRRSSTY shepherd's myrtle
DEEEHIIRRSSSTTW the Weird Sisters
DEEEHLLLOPRSTUW well-upholstered
DEEEIILLNNNOTTW well-intentioned
DEEEIILMMNRRSTU delirium tremens
DEEEIINOPSSSTUX expeditiousness
DEEEIJNOOOQRRSU José Enrique Rodó
DEEEILMOPRRSTWY Lord Peter Wimsey
DEEEINNNOSSSTTU tendentiousness
DEEELMMNNOPRTUY underemployment
DEEEMNOORRSSUVY overuse syndrome
DEEFGILLLNNSTUY self-indulgently
DEEFHHLMOORRSTU from the shoulder
DEEFHLMNOOSSTUU foul-mouthedness
DEEFILMNORRSTUW Mister Wonderful
DEEFILNRSSSSSTU distressfulness
DEEFINOOORRSSSU odoriferousness
DEEFLMNOOOOPRRY money for old rope
DEEFLNOOPRSSSTU dessertspoonful
DEEGGHILNNOSSST long-sightedness
DEEGGIMNNNOORRW wondermongering
DEEGGIMOOOPPRSU Georges Pompidou
DEEGHHIINNOTTWW Gone with the Wind
DEEGHHILOPSTTUY yield up the ghost
DEEGHIMNOORSSTW Weedon Grossmith
DEEGIIKLLMNNOOW Willem De Kooning
DEEGIILMNOOSSTT sedimentologist
DEEGILLNOOPRSST doorstep selling
DEEGILLOOOPPRTY lepidopterology
DEEHHLNOORSSTTU shoulder-shotten
DEEHIIKNNNNSSST thin-skinnedness
DEEHIILOPPRRSVW devil-worshipper
DEEHIINNRSSTWYZ wind synthesizer
DEEHILLLMNOOSWY Helen Wills Moody
DEEIIIILNOPRSSTT stilpnosiderite
DEEIILMNNRTTTUY unintermittedly
DEEIILNNRSSTUWY Sir Edwin Lutyens
DEEIILNOPRSSSTW low-spiritedness
DEEIILNOPRSSTUY serendipitously
DEEILNNPRRTTUUY uninterruptedly
DEEINOOOPRRSSSS possession order
DEEMNNOOOORSTUW drown someone out
DEFFIINOOOPRTTY proof of identity
DEFGGHIIKLNNORT forked lightning
DEFGHIILNNOSTTW fling to the winds
DEFGHILOPRSSTTY softly-sprighted

DEFGHINNOORSSTU shift one's ground
DEFHHIINOOOPRTZ dip of the horizon
DEFHIIMNNOORSTU fourth dimension
DEFHINOOORRTTTW not the word for it
DEFHLNOOOOPRTTW on top of the world
DEFIILLMNOOOTUV full motion video
full-motion video
DEFILNRSSSSTTUU distrustfulness
DEFIMMNNOOORSTT Simon de Montfort
DEFNNOOOOPSTTUW put one's foot down
DEGGHHHIINORTTT Do the Right Thing
DEGHHHILLORSSTT threshold lights
DEGHHIIILNRRSVW whirling dervish
DEGHHINNNOORTTU thin on the ground
DEGHHNOORSSTTTU God's honest truth
DEGHIIIMNNNORST in one's right mind
DEGHIIIMNNSSTTU distinguishment
DEGHIILLMOORSTV Oliver Goldsmith
DEGHIILNOOPPRSW polishing-powder
DEGHILOOOOSTTTV dog's-tooth violet
DEGIIILNOSSSVVW dissolving views
DEGIILNNOOPRSSU gird up one's loins
DEGILNOOOPPRTTX gold export point
DEGNNNNOOOORSUW on one's own ground
DEHHIIMOPRRSTYY hyperthyroidism
DEHHILNOOOPRSTU ornithodelphous
DEHHINOORSTTTWW throw to the winds
DEHHLOOOOPRSSTU household troops
DEHIIIILNPPRSSY Sir Philip Sidney
DEHIILOPRRSTUUX sulphur trioxide
DEIIILLMNNOSSTU disillusionment
DEIIIMMNNOPRSST disimprisonment
DEIILOOOPPUVVXX vox populi vox Dei
DEIIMMNOOOOPPTV doppio movimento
DEIIMNOOOPPRRST misproportioned
DEIINNORSSSSTUU industriousness
DEIINNRRSSSTUUY sunrise industry
DEIKMNNNNOOOSWW know one's own mind
DFGIKLLMNNOOPRU Norfolk dumpling
DFILMMNOOOOOSSW Wisdom of Solomon
DGHIINNNOOORVYZ Nizhniy Novgorod
DGIILMNOOOPPRTT gold import point
DIILLMNOSTTUUUY multitudinously
DIKNOOOPSSSSTYY pyknodysostosis

E

EEEEEGMNNQRSSSU queen's messenger
EEEEEHHIMNRSTTW the Three Wise Men
EEEEEHHIMRRSTTT three times three
EEEEEHNNNORRTVV on the never-never
EEEEEINNPRRSSTV serpentine verse
EEEEFFLNOPRSTUV envelope stuffer
EEEEFGIIMNOOSVV give someone five
EEEEGGGIIMNNRTT greeting meeting
EEEEGGGILLNORRV George Grenville
EEEEGGHNOORSVVY George von Hevesy
EEEEGHHINOORTTV one over the eight
EEEEGHHMNOOSTWY how goes the enemy?
EEEEGHILLMNOOSV give someone hell
EEEEGHIMNOORSST see someone right
EEEEGHLMNNRSSTU gentlemen ushers
EEEEGHLNOORSTUY heterogeneously
EEEEGHMOORTTUVY you've got me there
EEEEGILLNOORRTU Le Rouge et le Noir
EEEEGIMNOOOPRSV give someone rope
EEEEGINNNORSSVW overweeningness
EEEEGNNNOORSSTV get on one's nerves
EEEEHHIRRSSSTTT The Three Sisters
EEEEHHLNOPPSTUV push the envelope
EEEEHIILMRRSTWW Meriwether Lewis
EEEEHILMMORRRTW Mortimer Wheeler
EEEEHILNNOPSSST Elsie Stephenson
EEEEHIMNNOOSSTT in someone's teeth
EEEEHMNOOOSSTTT to someone's teeth
EEEEHNOPQSTTUUZ put the squeeze on
EEEEIINNNPSSSVX inexpensiveness
EEEEIINNRRSSTTV irretentiveness
EEEEILNNNOOPSSV pin on one's sleeve
EEEEIMNNPRRRSTU entrepreneurism
EEEELMNORRSSSSS remorselessness
EEEEMNNORSSSTUV venturesomeness
EEEENNOORRSSUVY run one's eyes over
EEEFFFHHILOORRT for the life of her
EEEFFGHHILORRTT right off the reel
EEEFFIINNNOSSSV inoffensiveness
EEEFGGHIIMNRTTX extreme fighting
EEEFGGHINORTTTU get the finger out
EEEFGGIILNRRSST self-registering
EEEFGIIKOOPRRSV Sergei Prokofiev
EEEFGIIMNRRTUXZ freezing mixture
EEEFGILMNOORTVW overflow meeting
EEEFGILNORSSTVY self-sovereignty
EEEFHIKNNNOOSTT think on one's feet
EEEFHILOOPSSTTV Lives of the Poets
EEEFHMMNOORRRST refreshment-room
EEEFILMMNOPRSTV self-improvement
EEEFINRRRSTTTUU street furniture
EEEFLNOOPRSSTTW power-on self-test
EEEFNNOOOSSSSTU out of one's senses
EEEFNNORSTTUVWY twenty-four-seven
EEEGGIKOORRSSST Sir George Stokes
EEEGHILLNNORSTT there's no telling
EEEGHILNNRSSTTT tensile strength
EEEGHMNNOOOSSSU homogeneousness
EEEGIILLMOSTVWY give it some welly
EEEGIIMNNOPRRSV evening primrose
EEEGIIMNOOOSTTV give it to someone
EEEGIINNNRSSSTT interestingness
EEEGILNNNNRSSTU unrelentingness
EEEGILNNOORRTUV green revolution
EEEGILORRRSSTVY retrogressively
EEEGINNOOPRRTYZ zero-point energy
EEEGINOPRRSSSSV progressiveness
EEEGKMNNOOPSTUY get one's monkey up
EEEGLLLMNOOPSSU pull someone's leg
EEEHHIINNORSTTW the nine worthies
EEEHHNNOPRRTTWY threepennyworth
EEEHHNOPSSSSTTU St Stephen's House
EEEHIILLMNNOTVW Willem Einthoven
EEEHIIMPPRRSTUV heir presumptive
EEEHIINPPRRRSTT interpretership
EEEHIJLMNNOORUV juvenile hormone

EEEHIJLOPPRSSTY Joseph Priestley
EEEHIKMNORSTTWY The New York Times
EEEHIKNNOOPRSST keep one's shirt on
EEEHILLLOPSSTUV split-level house
EEEHILLMNOOSSWW wish someone well
EEEHILLMSSSSTTT stemless thistle
EEEHJKLLNNOOPSS Joseph Nollekens
EEEHLMNNOOSSSUW unwholesomeness
EEEHMNOORRSSTVY every mother's son
EEEHOOPPRSTTTTY phototypesetter
EEEIIINNNSSSSTV insensitiveness
EEEIILMMNOSSTTU Meet Me in St Louis
EEEIIMMOORRSSST stereoisomerism
EEEIIMNNPRSSTUU neptunium series
EEEIINOPRSSSTTU repetitiousness
EEEILLLLNNRTTTT Little Nell Trent
EEEILLLMNOPPRWY yellow pimpernel
EEEILLNNNNOOOST not on one's nellie
EEEIMNNOOOPRSSW in someone's power
EEEINNNOSSSSTTU sententiousness
EEEINNOPRSSSTTU pretentiousness
EEELNOPPRSSSSSU purposelessness
EEEMNOPSSSSTTUU tempestuousness
EEFFFGLLLORSTUY self-forgetfully
EEFFFHHIILMOORT for the life of him
EEFFFHILNOORSST shift for oneself
EEFFGHIKNOORSTT king of the forest
EEFFGIIILLNRSTZ self-fertilizing
EEFFHHHIIORSSTT I Shot the Sheriff
EEFFHHIMOORSTTT fits of the mother
EEFFHHNOOORSTTU front of the house
EEFGGIIIMRSTWZZ Mister Fezziwigg
EEFGHHIOOPRSTTT fight to the ropes
EEFGHIIILLOOTTW gillie-white-foot
EEFGHIINOPRRSTT The Rite of Spring
EEFGHILLORSSTUY self-righteously
EEFGHILNOOPSTTU slip of the tongue
EEFGHIOORSTTTTW get the worst of it
EEFGHNOORRSTTTW tower of strength
EEFGIIILOPRRTVW writ of privilege
EEFGIILNNOQSSTU self-questioning
EEFGILLMNOORSSS smelling of roses
EEFGINNNOOPRSTU put one's finger on
EEFGIOOPRRRSSSU regius professor
EEFHHHILNNORSTT thorn in the flesh
EEFHLOOOORRSTVW The Sorrow of Love
EEFHMMNOOPRSTTU spur of the moment
EEFHNNOOPRSSTUU push one's fortune
EEFIILNNOOPRTTU oil of turpentine
EEFIIMNNOPRRSVY fivepenny morris
EEFILLLMNOSSSUU mellifluousness
EEFILNNNNOORSTU turn in on oneself
EEFIMNOORRSSSTU mortiferousness
EEFLLMMNOOOOPST Temple of Solomon
EEFLNOOORRSUYYY For Your Eyes Only
EEFLNOPRSSSSUUU superfluousness
EEFMMNOORRSSTTT from stem to stern
EEGGGHIMOORRSST George Grossmith
EEGGHIIMNNNOOSS eggs in moonshine
EEGGHIMNOOOPRST geomorphogenist
EEGGIMORRRSTUXY Gregory's mixture
EEGHHHILOOSTTTU To the Lighthouse
EEGHHHINNOOORSS on one's high horse
EEGHHHLMORSUUXY Hugh Esmor Huxley
EEGHHLNOSSSSTTU thoughtlessness
EEGHHOOPRRRRTUV Hugh Trevor-Roper
EEGHIIKLLNSTTTW whistling kettle
EEGHIILMNNOPTTT in the melting-pot
EEGHIIMNOPPRRTT pre-emption right
EEGHILMNNOOOPST phenomenologist
EEGHILNOORSSSTW lower one's sights
EEGHIMNOORSSTYZ Moog synthesizer®
EEGHINNOOSSSSTT set one's sights on
EEGHINNOPSTTTTU putting the stone
EEGHINNORSSSTUU unrighteousness
EEGHINOORSSTTTU get one's shirt out
EEGIIILNORRSSSU irreligiousness
EEGIIINOPSTTTVV positive vetting
EEGIILNNNRSTTUY uninterestingly
EEGIIMNNNRSSTTU unremittingness
EEGIINNORSSSTUV vertiginousness
EEGILNOPPRSSSSY prepossessingly
EEGILNOPRRSSUVY unprogressively
EEGIMNNORSSSTTV gross investment
EEGINNOPPRSSSSU unprepossessing
EEHHHILORSTTTWW worth the whistle
EEHHIIKLMSSTTTY the sky's the limit
EEHHILNOORTTTWW throw in the towel
EEHHILOOOPTTUVW Love without Hope
EEHHINOOPSSTTYZ photosynthesize
EEHHNOOPPRSSUYY neurohypophyses
EEHIIILLMNSTTWZ Wilhelm Steinitz
EEHIIKOPPRRRRSY Yorkshire Ripper
EEHIINOOORSSSVW show one's ivories
EEHIINOOPRSSSTT photosensitiser
EEHIINOOPRSSTTZ photosensitizer
EEHIINORRRSSTVW riverworthiness
EEHILMNOORRRSST Morrison shelter
EEHKOORRSSTTUUV Kossuth Overture
EEHLNOPRSSSSUUU sulphureousness
EEHMMMOORRRSTTY short-term memory
EEIIIINNQSSSTUV inquisitiveness
EEIIIMNNNORSTTV interventionism
EEIIINNNORSTTTV interventionist
EEIILNNOORRTTTU trinitrotoluene
EEIIMNNNNOPRRSY ninepenny morris
EEIIMNNNOORRTTT intention tremor
EEIIMNNOSSTTTUW Women's Institute
EEIIMNOORRSSSTU meritoriousness
EEIINNNNNOORTTV non-intervention
EEIINOPRRSSTTUV Sir Peter Ustinov
EEIKLMNPRRSSSTY sprinkler system
EEILLLPRSSTTTUV split-level trust
EEIMNNOOOPPPRRS properispomenon
EEIMNNRSSTTTTUV investment trust
EEINNNOOPPRSSTU inopportuneness
EFFGGILLNNORSUY long-sufferingly
EFFHHIILNRSSTTU in the first flush
EFFIILNOORSSSUU unfossiliferous
EFGGHIILNOPTTTY Flight into Egypt
EFGGHIIMNOPRRRT performing right
EFGGIINNNORSSUV unforgivingness

EFGGILNNORTTTUU flutter-tonguing
EFGHHHIIKNOPTTW knight of the whip
EFGHIIIKNNORSST finishing stroke
EFGHIIINOOPRTTT Petition of Right
EFGHIIJLNORTUWY junior flyweight
EFGHILLOORSTTUW Glorious Twelfth
EFGHINNNOORTTUU out of the running
EFGIIKLLLMNOSTY Killing Me Softly
EFGINOOORRSSSUU sonorous figures
EFHHHIMOOOPRSTT shoot from the hip
EFHINOORSTTTUXY sixty-fourth note
EFIIIIILNNPSTTV split infinitive
EFIIIILLOORRTVX elixir of vitriol
EFIILOOQRSSSTUU fossil turquoise
EFIINNOOOPSTTTU put one's foot in it
EFILMNRSSSSTTUU mistrustfulness
EFINNNOOOPRRTTU point of no return
EGGHHHHINORTTTU through the night
EGGHIIIKLNNRSTT lightning strike
EGGHIKNOPRRSSST knight's progress
EGGHILMOOOOPRST geomorphologist
EGGLNOOOSSSTTUU slog one's guts out
EGHHHHIIOPSSTTT hit the high spots
EGHHIILLMNOOSTT helminthologist
EGHHIIMNORSTTTY thirtysomething
EGHHILNOOPRSTTT plight one's troth
EGHIIIKLNNORSTV shrinking violet
EGHIIJLLNOOPSTU Joseph Guillotin
EGHILLNOORRSSTT Rollright Stones
EGHILNOOOPRSUYY neurophysiology
EGHIMMNNNOORRST the morn's morning
EGIIIILLMOORSST milites gloriosi
EGIIILNNRSTTTWY intertwistingly
EGIIIMNNNOOSSSU ignominiousness
EGIIILNNOORRSSTU Ringer's solution
EGJKNNNORRTTUUV Kurt Vonnegut, Jnr
EGKNOOORSSTTUUW work one's guts out
EHHHIJOOPRSTTWW Joseph Whitworth
EHHIIMOOOPRRSST theriomorphosis
EHHINOOPPRSSUYY neurohypophysis
EHHMNNOOPRSSTTU Hunter S Thompson
EHIIJMMNOORRRST Sir John Mortimer
EHIILLMOOPPRTTU photomultiplier
EHIILMPQSSSSTUY squish lip system
EHIIOPRRRSTTTUY shutter priority
EHIJMNOPPRSTUYY Jupiter Symphony
EHILLNNNOOPRSSU pull in one's horns
EHILOOPRSSTTTUW whistle-stop tour
EHINORRSSSTTTUW trustworthiness
EIIIMNOOPPRSSTU superimposition
EIIJLNNOOORSTTU joint resolution
EIILLMMNNOOORTT montmorillonite
EIILLNORSSSSTUU illustriousness
EIILOPRRSSTTUUY surreptitiously
EIILOPRSSSTTUUY superstitiously
EJLLLLMNOOORRTY Jelly Roll Morton

F

FFGHIINNORSSSTU soft furnishings
FFIIINORRSSTTTU first in, first out
FGHHIIIKLNNSTUW wishful thinking
FIIKMNOORRSSTWY Ministry of Works
FINOOOOOPPRRTTU out of proportion

G

GGGHHILNOOORTUY thoroughgoingly
GHIILOOOOPSSTYZ zoophysiologist

H

HIIKMNNOOOPRSST Sir Tom Hopkinson
HILNORRSTTTUUWY untrustworthily
HINOOOPPPRSTTUY opportunity shop

I

IIINNNNOORSSTTU non-intrusionist